THE NEW
Sunset
WESTERN
GARDEN
BOOK

The Ultimate Gardening Guide

Edited by Kathleen Norris Brenzel

Hardcover edition: ISBN-13: 978-0-376-03921-7
ISBN-10: 0-376-03921-3
Softcover edition: ISBN-13: 978-0-376-03920-0
ISBN-10: 0-376-03920-5
Library of Congress Control Number: 2011936541
First printing 2012
Printed in the United States of America

OXMOOR HOUSE

VP, Publishing Director: Jim Childs
Editorial Director: Susan Payne Dobbs
Creative Director: Felicity Keane
Brand Manager: Fonda Hitchcock
Managing Editor: Laurie S. Herr

SUNSET PUBLISHING

President: Barb Newton
VP, Editor-in-Chief: Katie Tamony
Creative Director: Mia Daminato
Art Director: Jim McCann
Photography Director: Yvonne Stender
Editorial Services Manager: Lorraine Reno

STAFF FOR THE NEW SUNSET WESTERN GARDEN BOOK

Editor: Kathleen Norris Brenzel
Senior Editors: Jim McCausland, Lance Walheim, Tom Wilhite
Managing Editor: Linda M. Bouchard
Art Director: Catherine Jacobes
Photo Editor: Linda Lamb Peters
Copy Editor: Elissa Rabellino
Assistant Photo Editor: Stephanie Rubin
Production Assistants: Danielle Johnson, Margaret Sloan
Proofreaders: Clare Chatfield, Denise Griffiths
Senior Imaging Specialist: Kimberley Navabpour
Project Editor: Sarah H. Doss
Assistant Editor: Elizabeth Jardina
Indexer: Mary Pelletier-Hunyadi

To order additional publications, call 1-800-765-6400
For more books to enrich your life, visit **oxmoorhouse.com**
Visit Sunset online at **sunset.com**
For the most comprehensive selection of Sunset books, visit
sunsetbooks.com
For more exciting home and garden ideas, visit **myhomeideas.com**

SPECIAL THANKS

Debra Lee Baldwin, Julie Chai, Sharon Cohoon, Jeffery Cross,
Owen Dell, Erika Ehmsen, Kate Frey, Flora Grubb, Mark Hawkins,
Brian Hjelmstad, Rick LaFrentz, Dennis Leong, Laura Martin,
Haley Minick, Marie Pence, Alan Phinney, Amy Quach, David Sauter,
Johanna Silver, Jeffrey Gordon Smith, Susan B. Smith, Vanessa
Speckman, Andreas Stavropoulos, Judith Stilgenbauer, E. Spencer Toy,
Susan Van Atta, Susan Wright

SPECIAL CONSULTANTS

Paul Bosland, New Mexico State University
Tom Carruth, Weeks Roses
Sandy Dittmar, Iseli Nursery
John R. Dunmire
John Greenlee, Greenlee & Associates
Gary Ibsen, TomatoFest.com
Ed Laivo, Devil Mountain Wholesale Nursery
Dan Meier, Briggs Plant Propagators
Jo O'Connell, Australian Native Plants Nursery
Ellie Sather, Whitney Gardens
Tom Spellman, Dave Wilson Nursery
Nicholas Staddon, Monrovia Nursery
Robin Stockwell, Succulent Gardens
Bernadine Strik, Oregon State University
Paul Vossen, University of California
Keith Warren, J. Frank Schmidt Jr. Nursery

ADVISORS

Janice Alexander, University of California
Allan Armitage, University of Georgia
Sharon Asakawa, GardenLife
John Bagnasco, GardenLife
James H. Baird, University of California
Randy Baldwin, San Marcos Growers
Sam Benowitz, Raintree Nursery
Susan Bergeron, American Hemerocallis Society
Phil Bergman, Jungle Music Palms & Cycads
VJ Billings, Mountain Valley Growers
Jim Borer, Certified Arborist
Charles Brun, Washington State University
Nancy Buley, J. Frank Schmidt Jr. Nursery
Whitney Cranshaw, Colorado State University
David Cristiani, The Quercus Group
Joseph Ditomaso, University of California
John Dixon, Skagit Gardens
Michael Dolan, Burnt Ridge Nursery
James Downer, University of California
Alice Doyle, Log House Plants
Steve H. Dreistadt, University of California
Janet Egger, Terra Nova Nurseries
Danielle Ernest, Proven Winners
David Fross, Cal Poly, San Luis Obispo
Ron Gass, Mountain States Wholesale Nursery
Pam Geisel, University of California
Bob and Diana Gibson, B&D Lilies
Steve Goto, Tomatomania
Beth Grafton-Cardwell, University of California
Harold Greer, Greer Gardens
Ali Harivandi, University of California
Kevin Hauser, Kuffel Creek Apple Nursery
Annie Hayes, Annie's Annuals & Perennials
Brent and Becky Heath, Brent and Becky's Bulbs
Dan Heims, Terra Nova Nurseries
Debbie Hewlett, Skagit Gardens
Mark S. Hoddle, University of California
Steve Hootman, Rhododendron Species Foundation
Robert Jamgochian, Mendocino Maples
Panayoti Kelaidis, Denver Botanic Gardens
Karen Kemp-Docksteader, Briggs Plant Propagators
Michael Marriott, David Austin Roses
Jeff Mason, Briggs Plant Propagators
Ken McCausland, Valley Crest Landscape Companies
Dick Mombell, Fall Creek Farm
Jesus Mora, West County Oasis Bamboo
Gary Moulton, Washington State University
Rose Marie Nichols McGee, Nichols Garden Nursery
Jay W. Pscheidt, Oregon State University
Janet Rademacher, Mountain States Nursery
Lon Rombough, bunchgrapes.com
Rick Schoellhorn, Proven Winners
Tom Shea, University of California
Alex Silber, Papaya Tree Nursery
Jeanine Standard, Sakata Ornamentals
Jimmy Turner, Dallas Arboretum and Botanical Garden
Richard J. Turner, Pacific Horticulture
Dan West, Oak Hills Nursery

Contents

Colorful even in dawn's early light, beautiful drought-tolerant flowers mingle in this hillside garden near Portland. Yellow yarrow, purple Russian sage, purple coneflower, grasses, and sunflowers frame the view of the garden's yoga pavilion.

Tomorrow's Garden

THERE'S NEVER BEEN A BETTER TIME THAN NOW to start a garden. Heirloom catalogs tout tempting novelties such as spotted watermelons and striped tomatoes. Nurseries sell surprising new plants. Fresh planting ideas fill the blogosphere daily, and the latest technologies help us to manage watering. While it's difficult to predict what tomorrow's garden will look like, the six words below—which describe today's Western gardens—offer clues.

Smart

We continue to explore sustainability—gardening in harmony with nature—by choosing plants that are appropriate for the region and site; by using recycled materials where possible; by planting rain gardens (depressions that channel rainwater into the soil); and by avoiding the use of chemicals. We try to rely on compost to feed the soil, plants to attract pollinators, and beneficial insects to help control pests.

Savvy

Gardeners who love plants are learning to combine them in communities of different species whose colors, textures, and shapes play off one another but go together. These plants take the same conditions and reflect a sense of place.

Surprising

Innovation is pushing aside the old rules of garden design. No soil to plant? No problem. We're growing plants everywhere now—on walls, rooftops, tabletops; in strips between driveways; in front yards and urban canyons; even along busy city streets.

Small

As homes grow larger or crowd closer together, gardens get smaller. But that isn't stopping us from getting inventive with the space we have, by playing with illusion.

Edible

In most areas, we can eat out of the garden 12 months of the year. So we find room to plant our own crops, even if that means tucking them between ornamentals in the front yard. We want to taste the full essence of a sun-warmed tomato harvested at its peak. We love unusual varieties like speckled lettuce, 'Cherokee Purple' tomatoes, and alpine strawberries—all hard to find in grocery stores because they don't ship well. We swap ideas and crops with friends.

A sculptural *Doryanthes palmeri* grows in this planter, rising from a lap pool in Pasadena, California. Globe lights on the wall behind it suggest bubbles rising from the water. Design: Anthony Exter Landscape Design.

Regional

Gardens in greater numbers are embracing the West's natural landscapes, especially those on the edge of wildland. Among the plantings that celebrate the West's true beauty: Vine maples and sword ferns beneath shapely conifers. Meadow grasses flecked with wildflowers in the Rocky Mountains. Sages and ceanothus cloaking sunny California hillsides. Bold cactus, bristly yuccas, and spatter-paint blooms in the desert.

Smart

Smart gardeners reuse and rethink everything—repurposed wood to make benches, broken concrete to build walls or steps, boulders found on-site. Smart plants are those that can (almost) fend for themselves.

⌃ Eco Chic

Sustainability is fun in this Santa Barbara backyard, which has a hot tub and rock-lined firepit behind the grassy meadow but uses 95 percent locally sourced or salvaged materials. The once-flat property was contoured to create rooms and to direct storm water into low spots. Mexican feather grass, feather reed grass, and sedges mingle among the sandstone boulders. Permeable decomposed granite covers the paths. Design: Margie Grace (garden); Michelle Kaufmann (Custom Prefab house).

⌃ Restyled

A raised bed filled with smoke tree, blue *Senecio mandraliscae*, and other easy-care plants is just the ticket outside this micro-house created from a retired shipping container. Dry-stacked New England wall stone edges the bed, while succulents and phormium fill pots in foreground. Pavers are made from recycled rubber tires; gravel between adds permeability. Design: DIG Gardens (planting); HyBrid Architecture, Seattle (Cargotecture house).

« Recycled

Steel plow discs welded to reclaimed pipe provide shallow bowls for a range of succulents, including chartreuse 'Angelina' sedum, *Senecio crassissimus*, echeverias, and *Euphorbia tirucalli* 'Sticks on Fire'. Design: DIG Gardens, Santa Cruz, California.

Savvy

All plants have their own unique presence. But magic happens when you blend them with others to reflect a sense of place.

⩓ Hawaiian Heat

Tillandsias, including red *Tillandsia rothii* and silvery *T. xerographica*, nest in bowls to brighten this sunny patio on Hawaii's Big Island. The lush edging behind them skillfully blends tropicals with various leaf shapes and colors, including apple green elephant's ear (*Colocasia esculenta*), coffee- and apricot-hued ti plants (*Cordyline fruticosa*), and a blue fan palm (*Bismarkia nobilis*). A feathery queen palm and an African tulip tree with orange blooms grow in back. Design: Davis Dalbok, Living Green.

California Gold »

Orange *Euphorbia tirucalli* 'Sticks on Fire' echoes the hues of the vibrant patina of the reclaimed-steel art piece (by 5 Feet from the Moon) on the fence. Its companions include chartreuse *Cotinus coggygria* 'Golden Spirit', silver tree (*Leucadendron argenteum*), 'Big Red' kangaroo paw, and purple smoke tree (clustered, center); and silvery Albany woollybush (*Adenanthos* × *cunninghamii*), *Agave attenuata* 'Nova', and *Senecio mandraliscae* (front). Design: DIG Gardens.

« Desert Dream

Crowned with ripening red fruits, a sculptural prickly pear cactus presides over this shapely planting in Ojai, California, along with columnar *Cereus peruvianus* and bristly *Yucca whipplei*. A tiny water feature adds a cooling touch. Design: Paul Hendershot.

Surprising

⌃ Jungle on a Wall

Ferns, bromeliads, grasses, elephant's ear, and spider plant create this leafy tapestry in San Diego. The plants' moss-wrapped rootballs are secured in synthetic felt and attached to a 7-foot frame that faces the 40-foot wall. Design: Amelia Lima.

Living Roof »

"Stuff falls from the trees, then moss grows over it," says the owner of the spongy mat of ferns, lichens, and moss that thrives atop his house in Sequim, Washington. The owner, architect Roy Hellwig, gathered moss from around his property and spread the "starter kit" on the flat roof's rubberized asphalt surface. Then lichens and more moss arrived.

Innovative gardeners grow plants everywhere—on walls and rooftops, along curb strips and driveways, even across sturdy dining tables.

Tabletop Garden

Basils, lettuce, and other edibles, along with grasses, edge a rill in this tabletop garden called "Future Feast in the Garden of Flow/Accumulation." Framed with rusted metal, the garden reflects out-of-the-box thinking at Cornerstone Sonoma's Late Show Gardens. Design: Suzanne Biaggi and Patrick Picard.

Small

Illusion makes small gardens appear larger. Use green walls as room dividers. Change levels. Set patios on the diagonal. Scatter polished globes to reflect views and light.

City Rooftop »

Prunus caroliniana hedges outlined with steel divide this San Francisco roof garden into three rooms, with surprises at every turn. A curved bronze fountain wall adds bold geometry and soothing sound in foreground. Just beyond, a Meyer lemon is espaliered against the wall, while an open window frames the city view. Design: Ron Lutsko.

« Urban Patio

The tiny garden pictured at left appears larger than its 1,000 square feet. Alternating bands of stone paving and pebbles give the ground rhythm and movement, while steel globes reflect light and clouds. The patio is set on the diagonal, which makes it look larger. Design: Vera Gates, Arterra Landscapes.

Edible

We want our own crops to determine what we're having for dinner. We know that fresh really is best.

Cool Crops

Lush but compact cool-season garden blends arugula, bronze 'Marvel of Four Seasons' lettuce, savoy cabbage, curly-leafed kale, tall Lacinato kale, deep red Swiss chard, green onions, and cauliflower.

Regional

Gardens that mimic their region's natural habitats celebrate the true beauty of the West.

⌃ Mountains

This rustic garden grows near Aspen, Colorado, against a backdrop of tall cottonwoods and conifers. Native grass meadows surround groves of aspen trees, while sprays of wildflowers—including blue lupines and white Shasta daisies— evoke true Rocky Mountain meadows. Design: Richard Shaw, Design Workshop.

Coast »

Rugged and windswept, a shapely Monterey cypress (*Cupressus macrocarpa*) accents this planting on a beach near Carmel, California. In foreground, *Calamagrostis nutkaensis*, California field sedge (*Carex praegracilis*), and *Leymus* 'Canyon Prince' catch the late-afternoon sunlight in their leaves. Fleshy, mounding aeoniums grow nearby. Design: Bernard Trainor.

⌄ Northwest

Native Douglas firs inspired the design of this meadow garden on Puget Sound. Gold-tinged bigleaf maples, tawny plumed Japanese silver grass, and mounds of cinnamon brown New Zealand hair sedge give the garden its billowy feel. Scotch moss and a mountain hemlock grow in foreground. Design: Susan Calhoun, Bainbridge Island, Washington.

⌄ Desert

A rich mix of desert plants fringe this patio in Tucson. Feathery cassia (*Senna artemisioides*), red lantana, and blue Cleveland sage create a sense of enclosure; golden barrel cactus cluster at the base of the boulder at left. Indian blanket flower (*Gaillardia*) fills a large container behind. Design: Elizabeth Przygoda, Tucson.

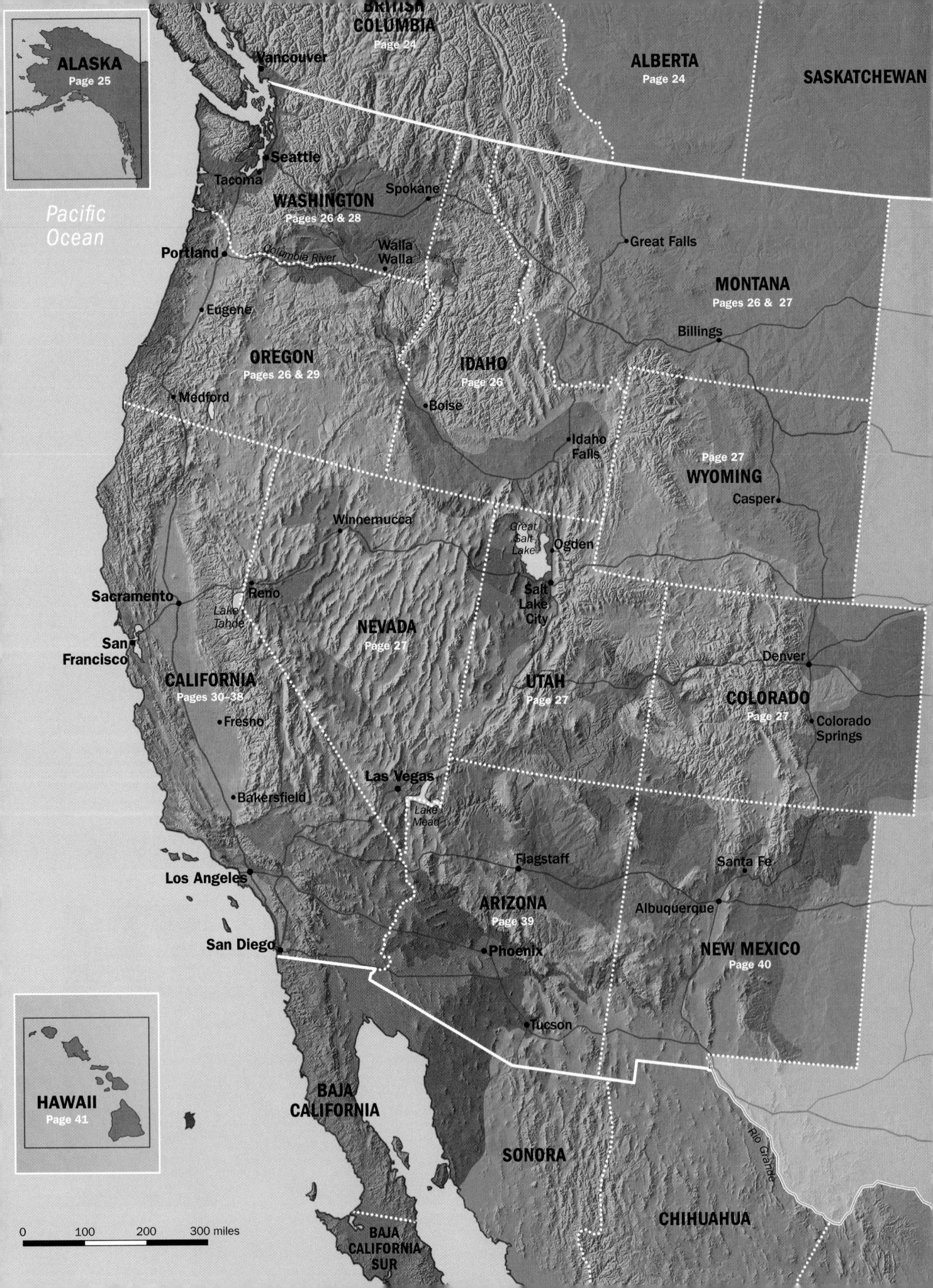

ALASKA
Page 25

Pacific
Ocean

HAWAII
Page 41

0   100   200   300 miles

BRITISH
COLUMBIA
Page 24

ALBERTA
Page 24

SASKATCHEWAN

Vancouver

Seattle
Tacoma

WASHINGTON
Pages 26 & 28

Spokane

Great Falls

Portland

Columbia River

Walla
Walla

MONTANA
Pages 26 & 27

Billings

Eugene

OREGON
Pages 26 & 29

IDAHO
Page 26

Medford

Boise

Idaho
Falls

Page 27

WYOMING

Casper

Winnemucca

Great
Salt
Lake

Ogden

Sacramento

Reno

Lake
Tahoe

Salt
Lake
City

San
Francisco

CALIFORNIA
Pages 30-38

NEVADA
Page 27

UTAH
Page 27

Denver

COLORADO
Page 27

Colorado
Springs

Fresno

Bakersfield

Las Vegas

Lake
Mead

Los Angeles

Flagstaff

Santa Fe

Albuquerque

San Diego

ARIZONA
Page 39

Phoenix

NEW MEXICO
Page 40

Tucson

BAJA
CALIFORNIA

SONORA

Rio Grande

BAJA
CALIFORNIA
SUR

CHIHUAHUA

The West's Climate Zones

IN THIS BOOK, CLIMATE ZONES ARE LISTED FOR EVERY PLANT. To identify the *Sunset* climate zone where you live, check the map at left, then turn to the page(s) listed there for your state to locate your specific climate zone. Find a description of your zone on pages 18–21; if you live close to a zone line, also read about the neighboring zone, which might be a better fit for your microclimate. The following factors make each zone unique.

Temperature Every plant has a minimum temperature that it can survive, so zone designations start there. Summer highs are also important, especially in the desert, where gardening mostly shuts down in summer.

Latitude Generally, the farther an area is from the equator, the longer and colder its winters. High latitudes also increase the number of daylight hours in summer and the length of night in winter.

Elevation Gardens high above sea level get longer and colder winters, often with intense sunlight, and lower night temperatures all year.

Ocean influence Weather usually moves from the ocean onto the continent, bringing mild, moist air with it, especially in the cool season.

Continental air influence The North American continent generates its own weather. Compared with coastal climates, it is colder in winter and hotter in summer, and is more likely to get precipitation any time of year. The farther inland you live, the stronger this continental influence. Incessant wind also becomes a major factor in open interior climates.

Mountains, hills, and valleys These determine whether areas beyond them will be influenced most by marine air or by continental air. The Coast Ranges take some marine influence out of the air that passes eastward over them. The Sierra-Cascades and Southern California's interior mountains further weaken marine influence. East of the Rocky Mountains, continental and arctic air dominate. In the opposite direction, first the Rockies, then the interior ranges, and finally the Coast Ranges reduce the westward influence of continental air.

Microclimates Local terrain can sharply modify the climate within any zone. South-facing slopes get more solar heat than flat land and north-facing slopes. Slope also affects airflow: warm air rises, cold air sinks. Because hillsides are never as cold in winter as the hilltops above them or the ground below them, they're called thermal belts. Lowland areas into which cold air flows are called cold-air basins. Microclimates exist within every garden (see page 22).

Growing season The average number of days between the last frost in spring and the first frost in fall is the growing season. Growing seasons, however, don't tell the whole story. For example, Zone 5 has a much longer average growing season than Zone 3a, but Zone 3a's extra heat makes it a much more favorable climate for heat-loving fruits and vegetables.

Soil Although soil is not a climate condition, it is closely related to climate. Abundant rain usually drives soil to the acid side of the spectrum, while scant rain drives it to the alkaline side. Further, soil's ability to drain when it's raining and to hold moisture when it's not is critical to plant health.

WHY DON'T WE USE OTHER CLIMATE ZONES?

The U.S. Department of Agriculture (USDA) calculates climate zones based on winter minimum temperatures. It provides a useful index for plant hardiness—the ability to withstand frost and low temperatures—but it has some drawbacks. This focus on cold-tolerance alone places the Olympic rain forest and parts of the dry Sonoran Desert in the same zone; and maritime Kodiak, Alaska, with continental Albuquerque, New Mexico.

Similarly, the American Horticultural Society (AHS) heat zone system is based on the average number of days above 86°F (30°C)—the temperature at which cellular protein is damaged in many plants. This system can help gardeners choose plants that won't cook in hot-summer climates, but it ignores other factors, like winter cold, growing season, and humidity.

The *Sunset* system bases each of its climate zones on a broad range of factors, such as cold, heat, humidity, wind, proximity to the Pacific Ocean, snow cover, and length of the growing season. In the end, it gives Western gardeners a more accurate picture of which plants will thrive where they live. Our thanks to the many experts who continue to help us refine the *Sunset* climate zones.

ZONES AND GROWING SEASONS

Every region has its own unique combination of heat and cold, rainy and dry periods, wind, humidity, and growing season. Each combination defines a climate zone that is hospitable to some plants but unfriendly to others. Find your own zone on the maps beginning on page 24, and read about what makes it unique in these zone listings. Before you buy a plant, check its zones in our encyclopedia to make sure it will grow in your area.

The growing season for each zone is shown as a green band in a bar indicating months from January to December. The yellow areas at the ends of the band represent shoulder seasons, when light frosts are possible but not likely to bother cool-season crops. Blue represents winter, when frosts can take out tender plants; and the orange band in Zone 13 (low desert) shows when summer heat shuts down most gardening.

■ **Growing Season**   ■ **Shoulder Seasons**   ■ **Summer Heat**   □ **Winter**

ZONE A1 — See map on page 25

ALASKA'S INTERIOR During summer, plants benefit from long days (19 hours) in the 70s, with rare spikes to 90°F (32°C). As rising temperatures warm raised beds and drive permafrost below root level, gardeners further boost soil temperature with mulch such as IRT plastic sheeting. In winter, snow cover usually insulates plants from winter minimums of –10°F to –20°F (–23°C to –29°C), with occasional dips to –60°F (–51°C).

ZONE A2 — See map on page 25

ANCHORAGE AND COOK INLET Though mountains and ocean moderate this region's weather, cloudy summer days are usually around 64°F (18°C), with occasional jumps to around 77°F (25°C). With permafrost hiding on north-facing slopes and in sheltered hollows, microclimates determine what you can grow (see Anchorage detail map on page 25). Winter lows average 6°F to 0°F (–14°C to –18°C), with drops to –20°F or –30°F (–29°C or –34°C).

ZONE A3 — See map on page 25

ALASKA'S MILD MARITIME CLIMATE After spring's repeated freeze-thaw cycles play havoc with cold-hardy plants like hybrid tea roses, summers bring cool, cloudy weather. Temperatures hover around 63°F (17°C), with a few days at 80°F (27°C)—perfect for cool-season flowers and vegetables. Blustery winters shut the garden down with 30°F to 20°F (–1°C to –7°C) minimums and periodic, ground-freezing drops to –5°F (–21°C).

ZONE 1A — See maps on pages 24, 26–29

COLDEST ZONE WEST OF THE ROCKIES High and bright, this zone has a short growing season, with summer days between 75°F and 86°F (24°C and 30°C), and chilly nights that favor summer perennials. Winter snow usually insulates plants against lows that average 11°F to 0°F (–12°C to –18°C); extremes reach –25°F to –50°F (–32°C to –46°C). But if snow comes late or leaves early, plant roots need the protection of 5 or 6 in. of organic mulch.

ZONE 1B — See maps on pages 26, 27

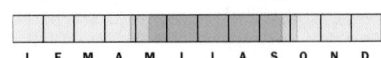

COLDEST ZONE EAST OF THE ROCKIES This zone sees January temperatures from 12°F to 0°F (–11°C to –18°C), with extremes between –30°F and –50°F (–34°C to –46°C). Arctic cold fronts sweep through 6 to 12 times a year, sometimes dropping temperatures by 35°F in 24 hours. The growing season tends to be long and warm, but relentlessly windy. Rain concentrates in late spring and summer, and hailstorms can decimate broad-leafed plants.

ZONE 2A — See maps on pages 26, 40

COLD MOUNTAIN AND INTERMOUNTAIN REGIONS This is the coldest zone in which sweet cherries and many apples grow, but it has enough summer heat to put sweetness into the fruit. Precipitation averages just 16 in. per year, much of it snow, so summer irrigation is essential. Winter nights usually hover between 20°F and 10°F (–7°C and –12°C), with killing freezes between –20°F and –30°F (–29°C and –34°C) every few years.

ZONE 2B — See maps on pages 26, 27, 39

WARMER-SUMMER INTERMOUNTAIN CLIMATE Fruit growers love this zone's perfect balance of long, warm summers and snowy winters. Annual precipitation averages 16 in., but it's much higher in the west and north ends of the zone. Winter minimums are 22°F to 12°F (–6°C to –11°C), with extremes from –10°F to –20°F (–23°C to –29°C). The growing season runs from 115 days in higher elevations and northerly areas to 160 days in southeastern Colorado.

ZONE 3A — See maps on pages 26, 27, 40

MILD MOUNTAIN AND INTERMOUNTAIN CLIMATES A long growing season and summer days around 90°F (32°C) give this zone some of the best melons, gourds, and corn in the West, plus excellent deciduous fruits and vigorous ornamentals. Just keep everything watered, since precipitation here averages only 14 in. per year. This is a lower-elevation zone in the northern states, but it moves higher farther south. Winter minimum temperatures average 25°F to 15°F (–4°C to –9°C), with extremes down to –18°F (–28°C).

ZONE 3B — See map on page 26

MILDEST MOUNTAIN AND INTERMOUNTAIN CLIMATES With its extra-long, warm growing season, this is the zone for anything that takes extra time to mature. Summer averages are around 93°F (34°C)—just a few degrees higher than in Zone 3a—and winters are milder, too, with average lows of 29°F to 19°F (–2°C to –7°C). Extreme cold usually bottoms out between –2°F and –15°F (–19°C and –26°C). Gardeners count on 180 to 210 frost-free days in this small zone.

ZONE 4 — See maps on pages 25, 28–30

COOL MARITIME AREAS ALONG THE NORTH COAST This zone runs from low-elevation southeastern Alaska through high elevations in Northern California's coastal mountains. Wet winters and dry summers prevail here, but Zone 4 is slightly warmer in summer and colder in winter than neighboring Zone 5. No zone grows better perennials, bulbs, and woodland perennials. Winter vegetables do well in the southern part of Zone 4 but not in the light-starved north. Average winter lows range from 34°F to 28°F (1°C to –2°C), with extreme lows reaching 8°F to 0°F (–13°C to –18°C).

ZONE 5 — See maps on pages 28, 29

NORTHWEST COAST AND PUGET SOUND This region's wet, breezy winters and mild summers favor leaf vegetables, root crops, and berries over fruits and warm-season vegetables that ripen in

fall (but if you choose early-maturing varieties, even these succeed). This zone also grows unsurpassed rhododendrons, Japanese maples, ferns, begonias, and woodland plants. January minimums average 41°F to 33°F (5°C to 1°C), with occasional drops to below 20°F (–7°C) and 10-year lows to 6°F (–14°C).

ZONE 6 — See map on page 29

WILLAMETTE AND LOWER COLUMBIA RIVER VALLEYS With summer days averaging 80°F (27°C), a long growing season, and cool, wet winters, this maritime zone's rich fields are quilted with grapes, berries, hazelnuts, irises, peonies, roses, and shade trees. Though winter minimums usually hover just above freezing, chilly interior air occasionally pushes west through the Columbia Gorge, layering everything with ice. Snow rarely stays long, but winter lows may reach 0°F (–18°C).

ZONE 7 — See maps on pages 29–31, 35, 36, 38

OREGON'S ROGUE RIVER VALLEY, THE CALIFORNIA GRAY PINE BELT, AND SOUTHERN CALIFORNIA MOUNTAINS Hot summers and mild, pronounced winters give Zone 7 sharply defined seasons without severe winter cold or enervating humidity. Gray pines define this zone around California's Central Valley, but more adaptable incense cedars replace them farther north and south. Typical winter lows range from 35°F to 26°F (2°C to –3°C), with record lows down to 0°F (–18°C). Rainfall averages 34 in. per year.

ZONES 8 & 9 — See maps on pages 30, 31

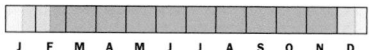

CALIFORNIA'S CENTRAL VALLEY Zone 9 is the thermal belt that edges California's Central Valley, while Zone 8 is the colder valley floor. The difference—just 2°F or 3°F (1°C or 2°C)—is crucial: citrus that flourishes in Zone 9 cannot be grown

commercially in Zone 8. The valley is hot and dry in summer, and occasionally filled with a deep, thick radiation fog in winter; this tule fog can last for days or weeks. Lows in both zones are 38°F to 34°F (3°C to 1°C), with extremes as low as 16°F (–9°C). Zone 9 averages 20 in. of rain per year, 5 in. more than Zone 8.

ZONE 10 — See maps on pages 39, 40

ARIZONA–NEW MEXICO HIGH DESERT This zone lies mostly in the 3,300- to 5,000-ft. elevations of the Southwest, and mostly in the Chihuahuan Desert. It is distinctly cooler in its northern and higher-elevation parts, including all of Zone 10 in the northern half of Arizona and most of the zone that falls north of Alamogordo. You can get away with growing such borderline plants as Mexican blue palm, blue palo verde, century plant, oleander, and fishhook barrel cactus in the warmer part, but not always in the cooler part. Summer highs throughout the zone are around 95°F (35°C), and average winter minimums range from 33°F to 22°F (1°C to –6°C), with drops to around 0°F (–18°C) every few years. More rain falls in the east than in the west, and the Chihuahuan Desert parts of the zone get more precipitation in summer than in winter.

ZONE 11 — See maps on pages 36–38

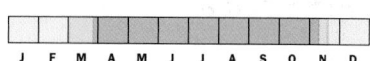

CALIFORNIA–SOUTHERN NEVADA MEDIUM TO HIGH DESERT Zone 11 has mild winter days, nights that hover around freezing, and occasional drops to 15°F to 5°F (–9°C to –15°C). In summer, many days cross 100°F (38°C), with highest temperatures recorded between 111°F and 117°F (44°C and 47°C). Zone 11 has less rain (about 7 in.) and more wind than adjacent parts of Zone 10. Las Vegas is in the warmest part of the zone at all seasons and has an uncharacteristically long growing season (267 days).

ZONE 12 — See map on page 39

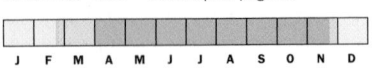

J F M A M J J A S O N D

ARIZONA'S INTERMEDIATE DESERT
Zone 12 has harder frosts spread over a longer season than Zone 13, with average minimums around freezing and extreme lows of 17°F to 10°F (–8°C to –12°C). That's enough to take out tropical plants, but not enough chill for some deciduous fruits. As in Zone 13, cool-season planting starts in early fall, and warm-season crops go in during late winter. Protect them against winds, which blow briskly from March to May.

ZONE 13 — See maps on pages 36–39

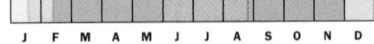

J F M A M J J A S O N D

LOW OR SUBTROPICAL DESERT
Gardening below sea level in the Imperial Valley or at 1,100 ft. in Phoenix, Zone 13 gardeners plant most vegetables in fall, and heat lovers like corn and melons in late winter, to avoid average summer highs of 107°F (42°C) with spikes to 120°F (49°C). Palms, citrus, and tropicals do well here if they get enough water. Winter lows average 40°F (4°C), with up to 15 frosty nights per year, and rare drops to 27°F to 15°F (–3°C to –9°C).

ZONE 14 — See maps on pages 30–33

J F M A M J J A S O N D

NORTHERN CALIFORNIA AREAS WITH SOME OCEAN INFLUENCE
Zone 14 lies mostly over the cold-winter valley floors that drain through the Coast Ranges from Santa Barbara County to Humboldt County. Marine air that moderates Zone 14 pushes clear to Sacramento and Modesto, and even down the Salinas Valley, which helps fruits that need summer heat and winter chill. Winter minimums average 40°F to 35°F (4°C to 2°C), with extreme lows from 27°F to 17°F (–3°C to –8°C). Precipitation averages 25 in. over most of the zone.

ZONES 15 & 16 — See maps on pages 30–33

J F M A M J J A S O N D

CHILLY WINTERS AND THERMAL BELTS ALONG THE COAST RANGE
These Central and Northern California zones are influenced by marine air about 85 percent of the time and by inland air 15 percent of the time. Zone 15 gets the most winter chill; it lies in cold-air basins and on exposed hills. Zone 16 is a prized thermal belt—the slopes from which cold air drains—between Zone 15's ridgetops and valley floors. North of Santa Rosa, Zone 15 stands alone, due to cooler winter temperatures here. Over a 20-year period, Zone 15 lows ranged from 28°F to 21°F (–2°C to –6°C), with record lows from 26°F to 16°F (–3°C to –9°C). Typical lows in Zone 16 range from 32°F to 19°F (0°C to –7°C), with record lows from 25°F to 18°F (–4°C to –8°C). In summer, both zones get more heat than coastal Zone 17, and both experience a nagging afternoon wind.

ZONE 17 — See maps on pages 30–33

J F M A M J J A S O N D

SOUTHERN OREGON AND NORTHERN CALIFORNIA COASTAL STRIP
Mild, wet, almost frostless winters and cool summers mark this climate. Summer fog usually comes in high and fast, cooling, shading, and humidifying the land. Cool-season vegetables, artichokes, flowers, and wind-tolerant ornamentals thrive here, but citrus, hibiscus, and gardenias don't get enough heat. Winter minimums are around 43°F (6°C), with rare extreme lows in the mid twenties (–4°C). Precipitation averages 38 in. but is lower in the south and much higher in the north.

ZONE 18 — See maps on pages 34–38

J F M A M J J A S O N D

SOUTHERN CALIFORNIA INTERIOR VALLEY COLD ZONE
An interior climate, this zone is influenced by ocean air only about 15 percent of the time. Many of Zone 18's chilly valley floors held commercial apricot, peach, apple, and walnut orchards before homes were built there. Average winter lows are 40°F to 34°F (4°C to 1°C). Over a 20-year period, winter lows bottomed out at 17°F (–8°C).

ZONE 19 — See maps on pages 34–38

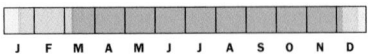

J F M A M J J A S O N D

SOUTHERN CALIFORNIA INTERIOR VALLEY THERMAL BELTS
Interior air dominates the climate of this mostly sloping land 85 percent of the time, keeping it warmer than adjacent Zone 18's valleys and hilltops. Navel oranges, macadamias, and most avocados thrive here. Average January minimums are 43°F to 37°F (6°C to 3°C), with drops every few years to 25°F (–4°C).

ZONES 20 & 21 — See maps on pages 34–37

J F M A M J J A S O N D

WARM AND COLD SPOTS IN SOUTHERN CALIFORNIA'S AREAS OF OCCASIONAL OCEAN INFLUENCE
In Zones 20 and 21, the same relative pattern prevails as in Zones 18 and 19: Zone 20 is made up of cold-air basins and hilltops, while Zone 21 comprises thermal belts. The difference is that Zones 20 and 21 get weather influenced by both maritime air and interior air. In winter, Zone 20's chilly hilltops and cold-air basins average 43°F to 37°F (6°C to 3°C), with summer highs around 90°F (32°C); 20-year lows average 25°F to 22°F (–4°C to –6°C). Slightly warmer Zone 21 has average winter lows around 40°F (4°C) and summer highs of 90°F to 94°F (32°C to 34°C). Ten-year lows are 28°F to 25°F (–2°C to –4°C).

ZONE 22 — See maps on pages 34–37

J F M A M J J A S O N D

COLD ZONES ALONG THE SOUTHERN CALIFORNIA COAST
Zone 22 consists of cold-air basins and hilltops influenced by the ocean approximately 85 percent of the time and inland air 15 percent. They get more winter chill than the slopes of neighboring Zone 23. Winter lows average 45°F to 40°F (7°C to 4°C), with 10-year drops to 25°F (–4°C).

ZONE 23 — See maps on pages 31, 34–37

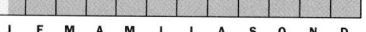

J F M A M J J A S O N D

THERMAL BELTS ALONG THE SOUTH-ERN CALIFORNIA COAST The best zone for avocados; good for cherimoyas, 'Valencia' oranges, guavas, mangoes, and papayas. But mild winters allow only low-chill pears, apples, and peaches. Winter lows average about 45°F/7°C, and summer highs reach 78°F to 89°F (26°C to 32°C). Frosts are rare, but Santa Ana winds dry plants every fall.

ZONE 24 — See maps on pages 31, 34–37

J F M A M J J A S O N D

SOUTHERN CALIFORNIA COASTAL STRIP Dominated by marine air but occasionally ripped by Santa Ana winds, winters here rarely dip below 45°F (7°C), and frosts are rare. In late spring, morning overcast rules. July highs hover around 75°F (24°C). Where the beach parallels high cliffs, Zone 24 extends to that barrier; where hills are low or absent, it runs inland several miles.

ZONE H1 — See map on page 41

J F M A M J J A S O N D

HAWAII'S MILD VOLCANIC SLOPES Cooler air makes higher volcanic slopes better for growing everything from sweet bulbing onions (Maui onions) to low-chill varieties of apples and even Mediterranean herbs. Warm-season highs range from 65°F to 80°F (19°C to 27°C); cool-season lows can dip to around 45°F (7°C), with extreme lows of 35°F (2°C).

ZONE H2 — See map on page 41

J F M A M J J A S O N D

HAWAII'S COCONUT PALM BELT Most lowland lees here get their heaviest rains from November through March, while May through September is relatively dry. On the wet windward sides, rain comes from passing storms and year-round trade-wind showers. The Kona Coast, however, gets most of its rain in the warm season. Highs hover around 86°F (30°C); lows can dip to around 64°F (18°C).

CLIMATE CHANGE AND GARDENING

"Climate is what you expect," wrote Robert Heinlein, science-fiction author, "and weather is what you get." Even so, climate is constantly changing. In the past 30 years, average temperatures in the western United States have risen by a degree or two. While that isn't enough to affect *Sunset* climate zones, it does have a practical effect on gardening.

"We've been seeing more warming in the spring months than in the fall months," says Kelly Redmond, regional climatologist for the western United States. "Latest spring frosts might be coming 2 to 3 weeks earlier than before." For gardeners, that's good news: you can probably get away with planting a few days earlier in spring. "Fall frost dates, to my knowledge, haven't changed," adds Redmond.

But is climate change to blame for the West's headline-stealing bad news: extreme heat, rain, drought, deep freezes, and mudslides? "Extreme events have happened forever," says Tye W. Parzybok, author of *Weather Extremes of the West.* The apparent increase in extreme weather events, he says, is largely the result of better monitoring and higher social costs than ever—there are simply more people and property affected by bad weather.

One downside to plan for: if continued warming reduces the snowpack as anticipated by the California Department of Water Resources, it will team up with increasing population to put significant pressure on water supplies all over the West. Water will get more expensive, less available, or both—and this will change the way we garden.

Protect Your Plants

- As a hedge against water shortages, install drip irrigation and skew your plant choices to less thirsty kinds, including dry-climate natives.

- Open up big trees by selective pruning so that strong storm winds pass through them instead of blowing them over.

- Where snow cover is unreliable, mulch every fall to protect shallow roots against hard frost.

Storm clouds darken the skies above agaves in Anza-Borrego Desert State Park, California.

KNOW YOUR MICROCLIMATES

How can one gardener grow perfect plumerias year after year, while a close neighbor fails? Or why does one vegetable plot produce tomatoes in October, while another just down the street nearly always freezes out two weeks earlier? You may not have the answer. But if you spend many evenings walking through your neighborhood, you've *felt* it. Maybe your route passes the cool mouth of a ravine, the south side of a stone wall that radiates heat for hours after sunset, or a usually breezy corner. Each of these is a microclimate that favors some plants and checks the growth of others.

Most gardens have microclimates—small pockets that are seasonally colder, warmer, shadier, or windier than the rest of the garden or neighborhood. Used thoughtfully, they can help you to locate your plants in the best possible spot. If you garden in a mild-winter climate, you might put deciduous fruit trees in a cold pocket to help them set buds; or in a cool-summer climate, use reflected heat from a wall to give tomatoes a boost. And if you don't like your garden's microclimates, you can always modify them—add hedges for windbreaks or trees for shade, for example. If all else fails, just move struggling plants from an unfavorable area to a more suitable one.

The following section describes common microclimates. To understand how they work in your own garden, make notes about midday sun angle (which varies remarkably by season in northern latitudes), wind direction, and daily minimum and maximum temperatures. And keep track of rainfall where you live: it can vary significantly from rainfall recorded at nearby weather stations, especially in mountainous areas.

NINE COMMON MICROCLIMATES

Exposure to wind Whether it barrels up a canyon to your property or flows off the ocean, wind can be hard on plants. Where it persists, choose wind-resistant trees, shrubs, and perennials. Or block it: a hedge or a windbreak of closely spaced trees planted on the windward side can create a sheltered area extending 10 to 20 times its height (a 10-ft.-tall hedge will shelter 100 to 200 ft. of ground behind it). If your property has a breezeway—a narrow passage between a house and a detached garage or other structure that funnels wind—you can buffer the upwind side with a hedge, or line the passage with conifers or other wind-tolerant plants.

South and west walls Masonry and stucco walls soak up solar energy and release it back at night. In cool-summer areas, the extra heat can help ripen summer vegetables such as tomatoes, eggplant, and peppers. In hot-summer areas, plant trees to shade walls, or screen them with heat-loving vines like trumpet creeper (*Campsis*).

North wall With little direct sun, it's ideal for woodland plants like ferns. In warm climates, the north side of the house is the place for temperate plants such as hydrangea and viburnum that would burn up with too much sun exposure.

Sloping ground As cold air flows downhill, it mixes with the warm air just above it, making the moving air a bit warmer than the still air on the hilltops above or in the valleys below. That's why sloping ground is favored for growing oranges. Grapes planted on south- or west-facing slopes pick up extra heat that helps sweeten the fruit.

Cold-air pockets Because cold air is heavier than warm air, low-lying fields and hollows allow cold air to pool. Chilly air also dams up behind structures, walls, and hedges that run across a slope. Frost-tender plants that need heat, like plumeria and citrus, don't belong in cold pockets, although they might succeed in one of your garden's warmer microclimates. But cold spots can be used to advantage in mild climates, where the extra chill encourages tulips to bloom and apples, pears, cherries, apricots, and peaches to set fruit.

East wall Although an east wall can get up to a half-day of sunshine, the sun is less intense here than on a west-facing wall. That makes it perfect for plants that want plenty of light but not much heat, such as azaleas and fuchsias.

Eaves They protect delicate flowers like camellias from shattering or turning mushy in the rain. Eaves also provide a couple of degrees of frost protection to tender plants underneath. Remember to irrigate under overhangs.

Shade trees and overhanging structures A canopy of leaves or the latticework of an arbor casts shade preferred by hostas, impatiens, and many other plants. On frosty nights, the air beneath stays a few degrees warmer than the air over open ground.

Dry banks They have fast-draining soil that's prone to erosion. Cover these banks with heat- and drought-tolerant groundcovers such as ice plant, trailing lantana, or rosemary; mediterranean plants like rockrose (*cistus*) or santolina; or western natives like manzanita (*arctostaphylos*), wild lilac (*ceanothus*), penstemon, or salvia.

FINDING COLD POCKETS

Cold air settles in low parts of the garden where the air is still, and where the sky above is unblocked by tree canopies or arbors. Following are two ways to find them, so you can choose appropriate plants:

- Put one thermometer in a fixed location and move a second one to a different location every evening. Compare them every morning around sunrise (that's usually when it's coldest).

- Walk your garden at dawn on a frosty morning: frost is thickest where the air is coldest.

If you don't like your garden's microclimates, you can always modify them—add hedges for windbreaks or trees for shade. If all else fails, just move struggling plants from an unfavorable area to a more suitable one.

Shade Trees

Eaves

Sloping Ground

Cold-Air Pockets

ZONING IN ON CLIMATE

Sunset's climate zones range from the coldest (Alaska's Zone A1) to the mildest (Hawaii's Zone H2). Here's a closer look at these extremes.

ALASKA (map, page 25)

Although many might try to compare Alaska with cold-winter parts of the Lower 48, this really can't be done. Unmatched seasonal differences in day length, wild swings in temperature, permafrost, Arctic desert, rain forests, warm-summer interior, and wind-scoured coasts make Alaska a land apart. Alaska's Zone A1, encompassing the interior climate centered in Fairbanks, is the coldest; Zone 4, the southernmost part of Alaska, is the mildest.

Garden successes here are striking, from the whopping vegetables in the Matanuska Valley to the intimate flower gardens that border southeastern Alaska's rain forests. Summer days are long in this northern latitude (with 22 hours of daily summer sun in Fairbanks); they stimulate unusually large growth in some plants (notably, delphiniums, which can reach 14 ft. tall).

To grow anything in the face of permanently low soil temperatures, gardeners here cover annual vegetable and flower beds with infrared-transmitting (IRT) plastic sheeting at planting time to raise soil temperatures, and grow varieties made for short seasons, such as subarctic apples and Siberian tomatoes.

HAWAII (map, page 41)

The West's southernmost state has the only true tropical zones in the Western states. Its two broad climate zones include the higher-elevation H1, which is cool enough for many temperate-zone plants, and the lower-elevation H2, which is evenly warm and frost-free. Moderated by the Pacific Ocean and persistent northeasterly trade winds, Hawaii is mild year-round with two seasons: the cool season (Ho'oilo, October through April) and the warm season (Kau, May through September). But the same sheer cliffs, deep valleys, broad slopes, ridges, high volcanic peaks, and windy points that give the Islands their awesome beauty also create a vast array of microclimates.

Rainfall can vary immensely within a short distance. The upper Manoa Valley on Oahu, for example, can receive 160 in. of rain per year, while Waikiki, 4 miles away, gets 20 in. per year. Below about 6,000-ft. elevation, it's difficult to grow

TOP: Fireweed near Mt. McKinley, Alaska.
BOTTOM: Cocoa palms edge Kaneohe Bay, Oahu.

plants that need winter chill to thrive. Such plants grow better at higher elevations on Maui and the Big Island, where air temperatures are cooler.

Throughout the Islands, the same benign climates that nurture lush plant growth also cause many introduced species to spread. Species that are well mannered on the mainland are crowding out native plants on the Islands. Among these are banana passion vine, kahili ginger, *Lantana camara*, princess flower, strawberry guava, and Queensland umbrella tree. Avoid importing any plants (or pieces of plants) without proper permits or inspections.

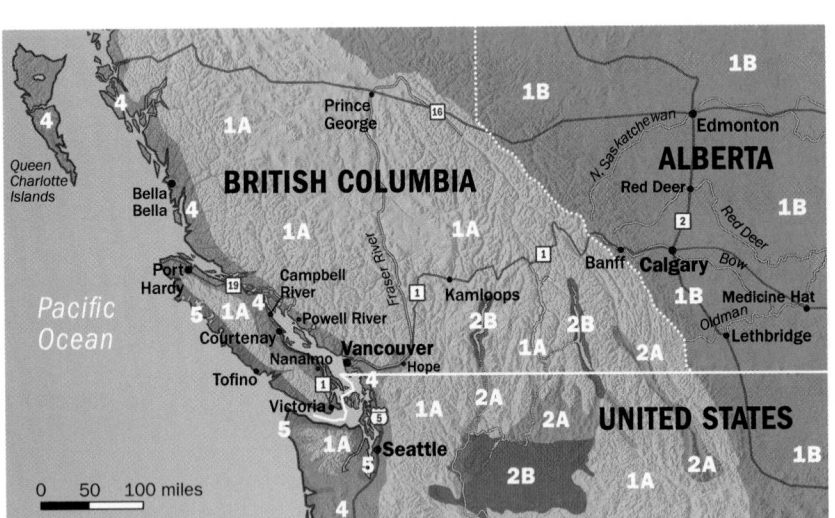

BRITISH COLUMBIA AND ALBERTA: Oceans, mountains, and latitude make all the difference in southwestern Canada. The Pacific Ocean keeps coastal Zones 4 and 5 mild and moist as storms move onshore almost every month of the year. The mountains (Zone 1a) check the ocean's influence, creating warmer summers in the valleys (Zone 2a), colder winters everywhere, and a shorter growing season. The Canadian prairies (Zone 1b) have more wind all year, very cold winters, mild summers.

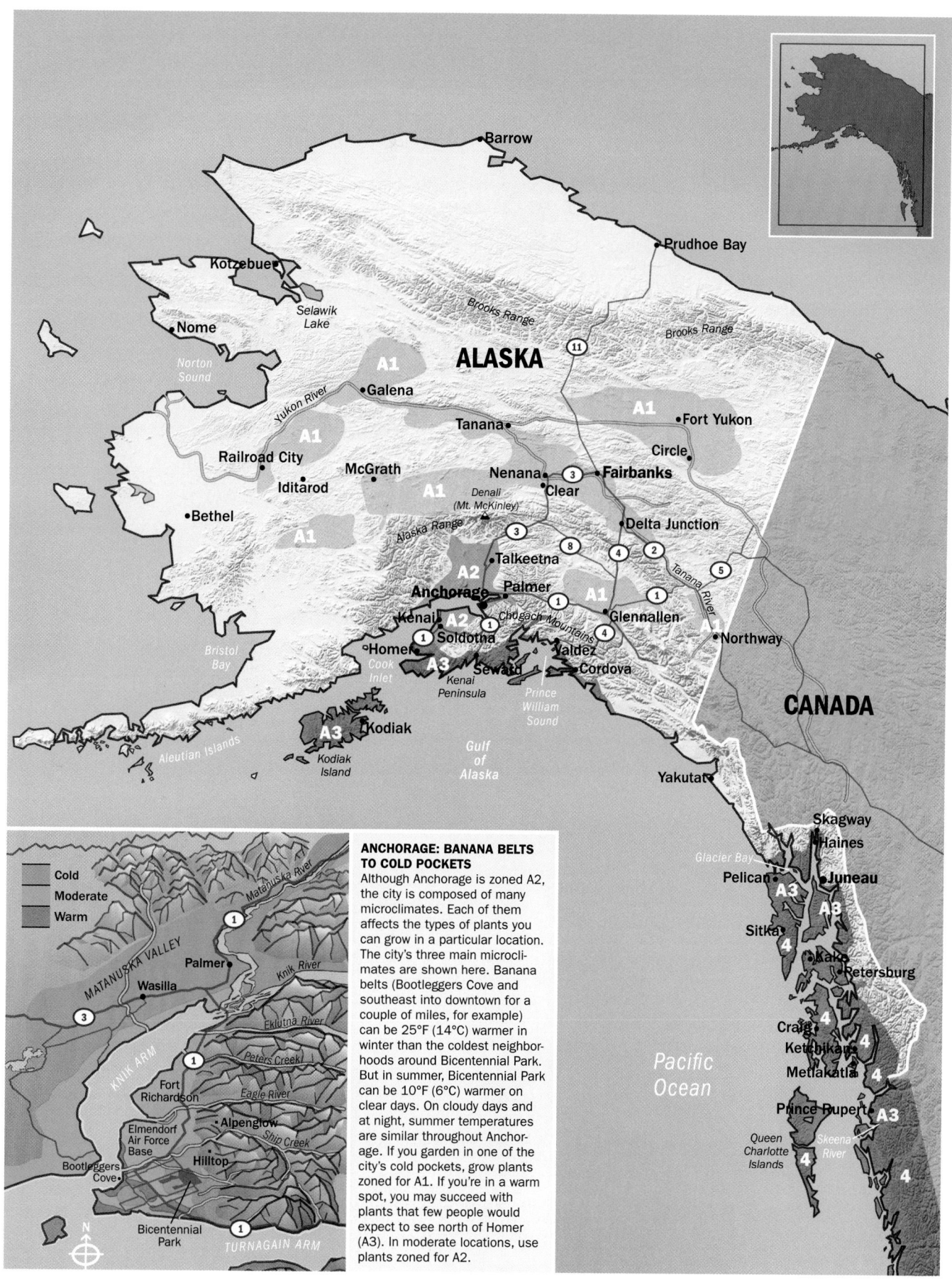

Barrow

Prudhoe Bay

Kotzebue
Selawik Lake
Nome
Norton Sound

Brooks Range

(11)

A1

ALASKA

A1
Fort Yukon

Yukon River
Galena

Tanana
Circle

A1

Railroad City

McGrath
Nenana
Fairbanks

Iditarod
(3)
Clear

Denali
(Mt. McKinley)
Delta Junction

Bethel
A1
Alaska Range
(3)
(8)
(2)

A1
(4)
(5)

A1
Talkeetna
(1)

Tanana River

A2
Palmer

Anchorage
A1

Kenai
Chugach Mountains
(1)
Glennallen

A2
(1)
Soldotna
A1

(1)
Homer
(1)
Northway

Cook Inlet
Kenai Peninsula
Valdez
(4)

A3
Seward

Bristol Bay
Cordova

Prince William Sound

CANADA

A3
Kodiak

Kodiak Island

Gulf of Alaska

Aleutian Islands

Yakutat

Skagway
Haines

Glacier Bay
Pelican
A3
Juneau

A3
Sitka

4

Kake
Petersburg

Pacific Ocean

4
Craig
Ketchikan
4
Metlakatla
4

Prince Rupert
A3

Queen Charlotte Islands
Skeena River
4

4

ANCHORAGE: BANANA BELTS TO COLD POCKETS

Although Anchorage is zoned A2, the city is composed of many microclimates. Each of them affects the types of plants you can grow in a particular location. The city's three main microclimates are shown here. Banana belts (Bootleggers Cove and southeast into downtown for a couple of miles, for example) can be 25°F (14°C) warmer in winter than the coldest neighborhoods around Bicentennial Park. But in summer, Bicentennial Park can be 10°F (6°C) warmer on clear days. On cloudy days and at night, summer temperatures are similar throughout Anchorage. If you garden in one of the city's cold pockets, grow plants zoned for A1. If you're in a warm spot, you may succeed with plants that few people would expect to see north of Homer (A3). In moderate locations, use plants zoned for A2.

Cold
Moderate
Warm

Matanuska River

MATANUSKA VALLEY

(1)
Palmer

Knik River

Wasilla

(3)

Eklutna River

KNIK ARM
(1)
Peters Creek

Fort Richardson
Eagle River

Elmendorf Air Force Base
Ship Creek
Alpenglow

Bootleggers Cove
Hilltop

Bicentennial Park
(1)

N

TURNAGAIN ARM

0   50   100   150   200 miles

Alaska

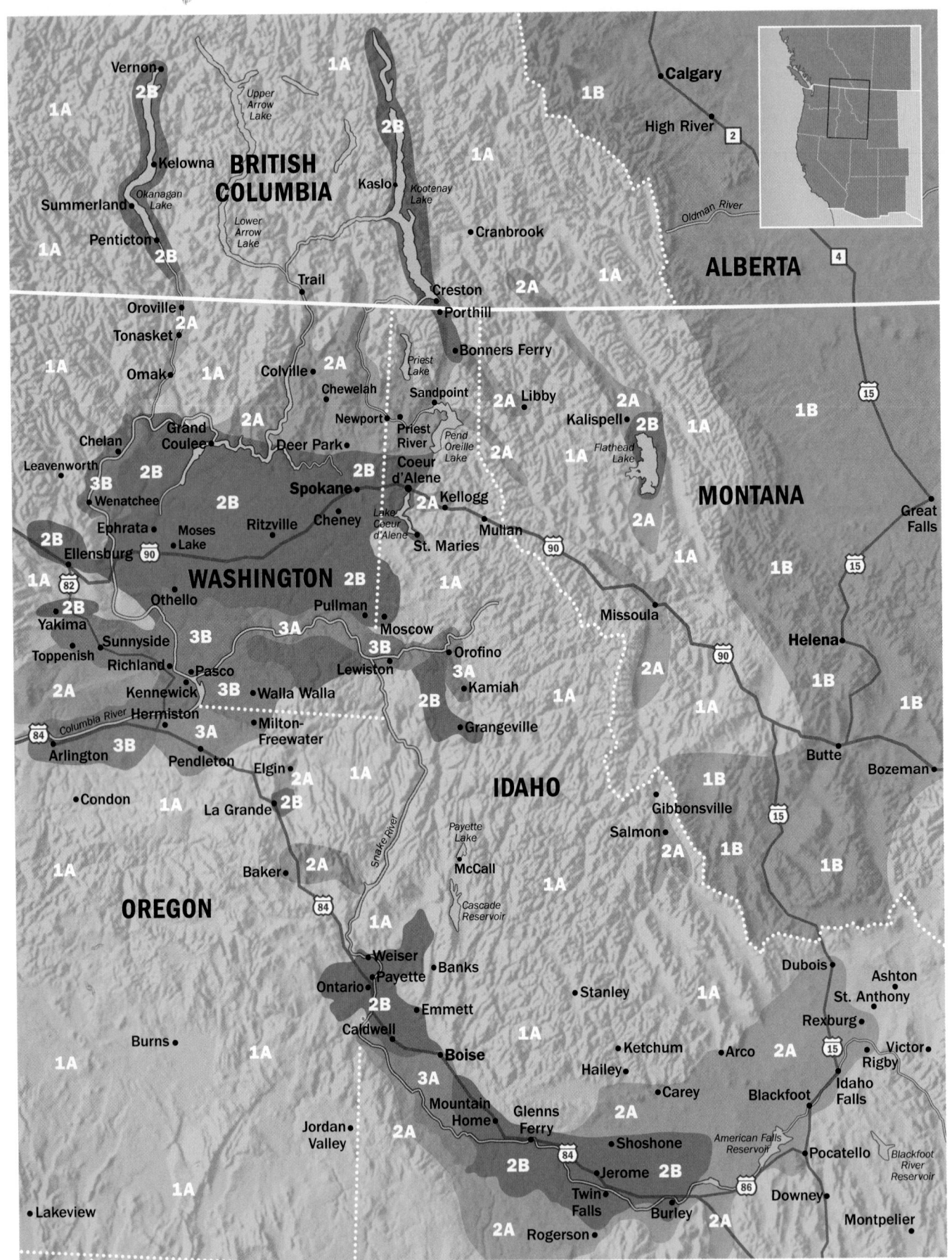

Eastern Washington, Eastern Oregon, Idaho

0   50   100   150 miles

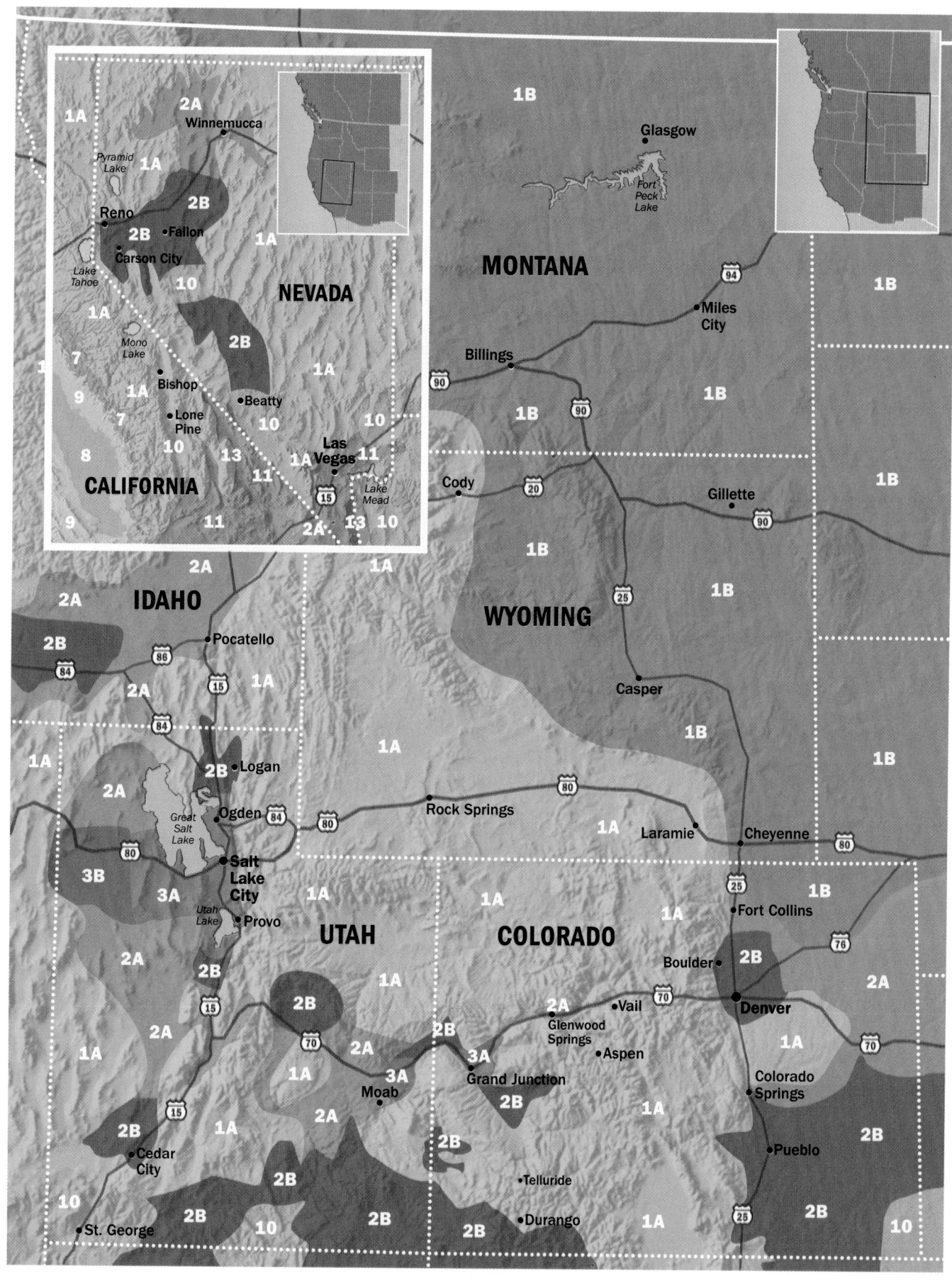

Glasgow

Fort
Peck
Lake

1A

2A
Winnemucca

Pyramid
Lake   1A

Reno
2B
2B   Fallon
Carson City

Lake
Tahoe   10

1A

Mono
Lake

7   1A
Bishop
1A   Beatty
9
7   Lone
Pine
10
8

9

10

2B

1A

10

Las
Vegas   13   11
10
1A
11
13   Lake
Mead

11   11
10

2A

1A
2A

13   10

NEVADA

2B

CALIFORNIA

MONTANA

94
1B

Miles
City

Billings
90   1B

90

Cody   20

Gillette
1B
90

1B

WYOMING

25

Casper

1B

1B

1B

1B

2A
IDAHO
2A

2B
84

2A
15

Pocatello
86

15   1A

84

1A   2B   Logan

2A   Ogden   84
Great
Salt
Lake

80

3B   3A   Salt
Lake
City
Utah
Lake   Provo

2A

2B
15

2A

1A

2B
70

2A

1A
1A

3A
Moab

2B
15   1A

2B
Cedar
City

10

St. George   2B   10

80
Rock Springs

1A   Laramie
Cheyenne   80

1A

UTAH

1A   COLORADO

1A

2B

2A   Vail
Glenwood
Springs
Aspen

3A
Grand Junction

2B

2B   Telluride

2B   Durango   1A

25   1B
Fort Collins
2B
76

Boulder   2B
70   2A

Denver

1A
70

Colorado
Springs

2B

Pueblo

2B

25   10

0   50   100   150 miles

Nevada, Montana, Wyoming, Utah, Colorado

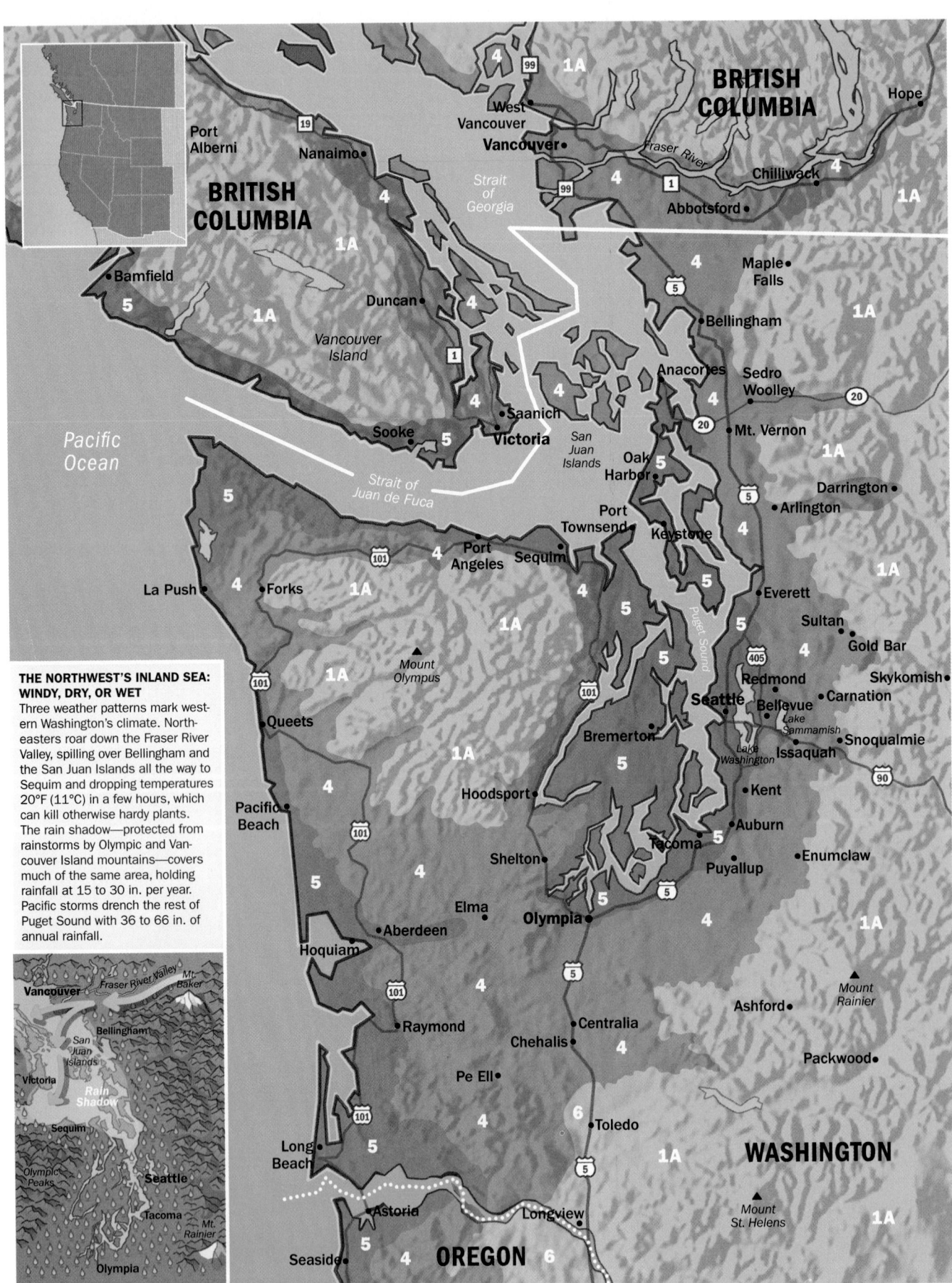

BRITISH COLUMBIA

Port Alberni

Nanaimo•

BRITISH COLUMBIA

Bamfield•

Duncan•

Vancouver Island

West Vancouver

Vancouver

Fraser River

Hope•

Chilliwack

Abbotsford•

Maple Falls•

•Bellingham

Anacortes

Sedro Woolley

•Mt. Vernon

Darrington•

•Arlington

Pacific Ocean

Sooke

Victoria

Saanich•

San Juan Islands

Oak Harbor•

Port Townsend

Keystone•

Everett•

Sultan•

Gold Bar•

Skykomish•

La Push•

•Forks

Port Angeles   Sequim

Mount Olympus

Redmond

Seattle   Bellevue•

Lake Sammamish

•Carnation

•Snoqualmie

Issaquah•

Lake Washington

Queets•

Bremerton•

•Kent

•Auburn

**THE NORTHWEST'S INLAND SEA:
WINDY, DRY, OR WET**
Three weather patterns mark western Washington's climate. Northeasters roar down the Fraser River Valley, spilling over Bellingham and the San Juan Islands all the way to Sequim and dropping temperatures 20°F (11°C) in a few hours, which can kill otherwise hardy plants. The rain shadow—protected from rainstorms by Olympic and Vancouver Island mountains—covers much of the same area, holding rainfall at 15 to 30 in. per year. Pacific storms drench the rest of Puget Sound with 36 to 66 in. of annual rainfall.

Pacific Beach

Hoodsport•

Shelton•

Elma•

•Aberdeen

Olympia

Tacoma•

Puyallup

•Enumclaw

Hoquiam•

Mount Rainier

Ashford•

•Raymond

Centralia•

Chehalis•

Packwood•

Pe Ell•

•Toledo

Long Beach•

Mount St. Helens

•Astoria   Longview

WASHINGTON

Seaside•   **OREGON**

Strait of Juan de Fuca

Strait of Georgia

Puget Sound

Vancouver

Fraser River Valley

Mt. Baker

San Juan Islands

Bellingham

Victoria

Rain Shadow

Sequim

Olympic Peaks

Seattle

Tacoma

Mt. Rainier

Olympia

Western Washington

0   20   40   60 miles

PORTLAND: MILD TO WILD

Portland usually has mild winters and warm summers. But when winter cold builds east of the Cascades and low pressure blankets the coast, winds can blast through the Columbia River Gorge at tree-ripping speed. They hit east Portland hard and usually curve south, sometimes icing up trees clear to Milwaukie. If you live east of Interstate 205, plant trees whose limbs bear up well in ice storms—for example, black walnut, ginkgo, linden, and sweet gum.

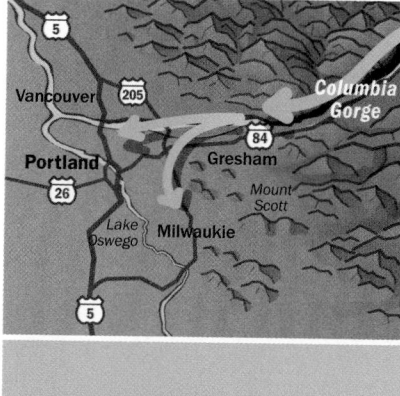

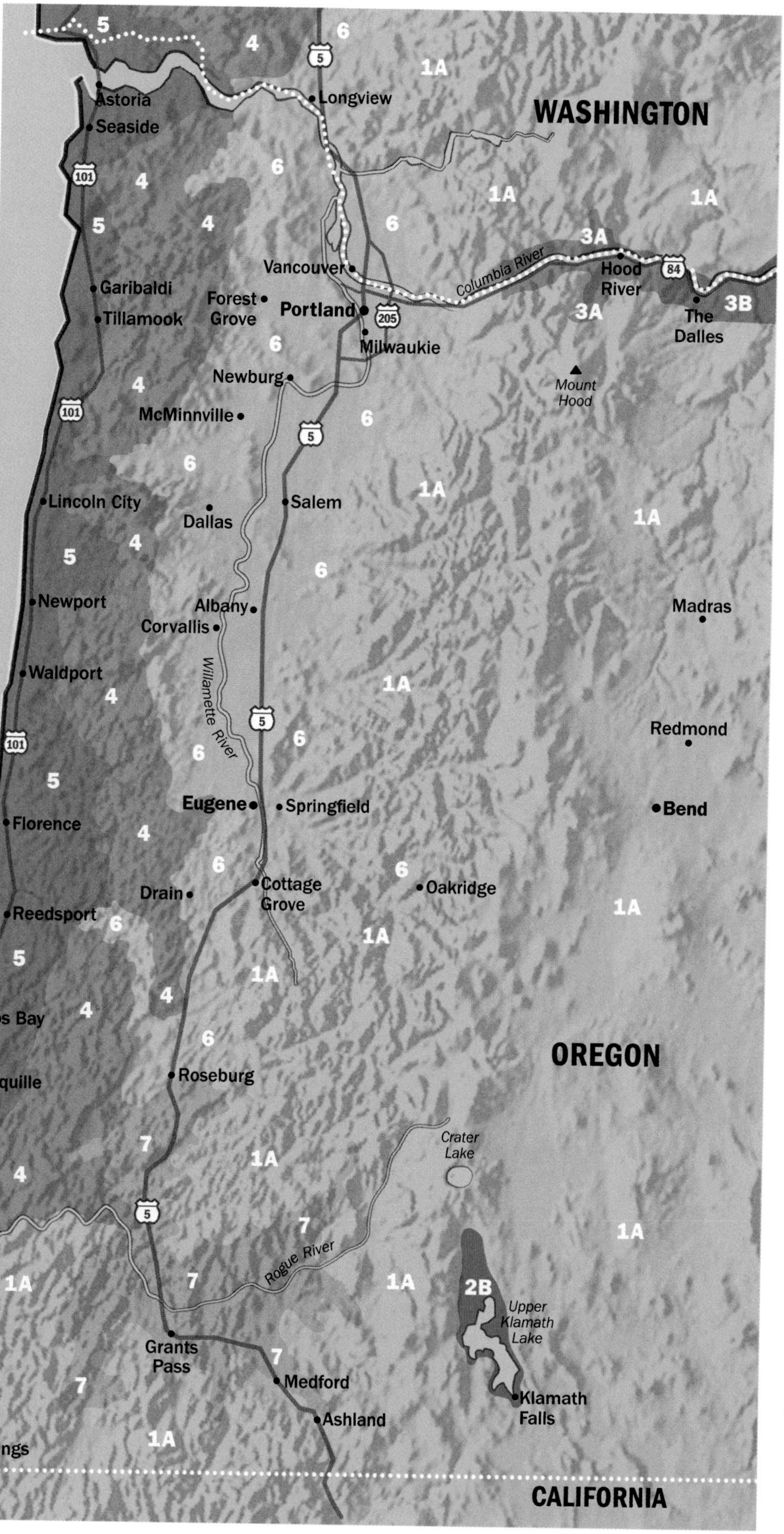

WASHINGTON

1A

1A

1A

Astoria
Seaside
Longview

5

4

6

101

4

6

6

3A

Hood River

84

3B

The Dalles

3A

5

4

Vancouver

Columbia River

Garibaldi
Tillamook

Forest Grove

Portland

205

Milwaukie

Newburg

McMinnville

4

6

Mount Hood

6

Lincoln City

Dallas

Salem

1A

5

4

6

5

Newport

Albany
Corvallis

Madras

Waldport

4

Willamette River

5

Redmond

101

Bend

Pacific Ocean

5

Florence

4

1A

4

6

6

Springfield

Eugene

Drain

Cottage Grove

Oakridge

Reedsport

6

1A

5

4

Coos Bay

6

1A

Coquille
Bandon

Roseburg

OREGON

7

Crater Lake

1A

Port Orford

101

5

4

5

Rogue River

7

7

1A

1A

Gold Beach

1A

7

Grants Pass

2B

Upper Klamath Lake

1A

5

7

7

Medford

Klamath Falls

17

Ashland

Brookings

1A

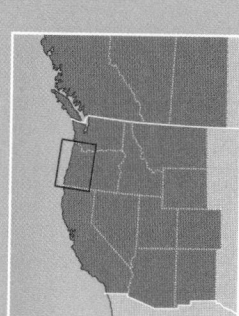

CALIFORNIA

0   10   20   30 miles

Western Oregon

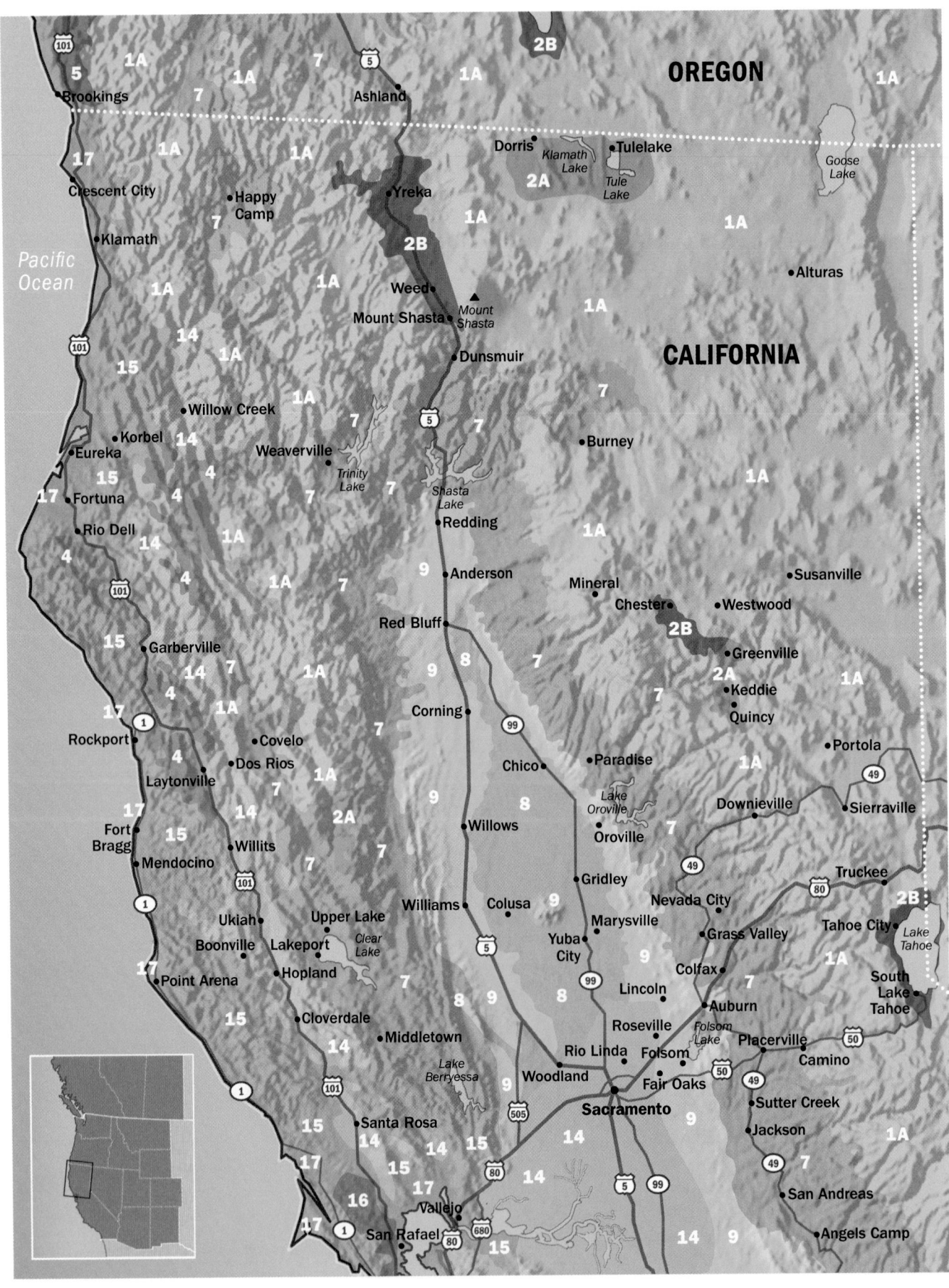

Northern California

0   20   40   60 miles

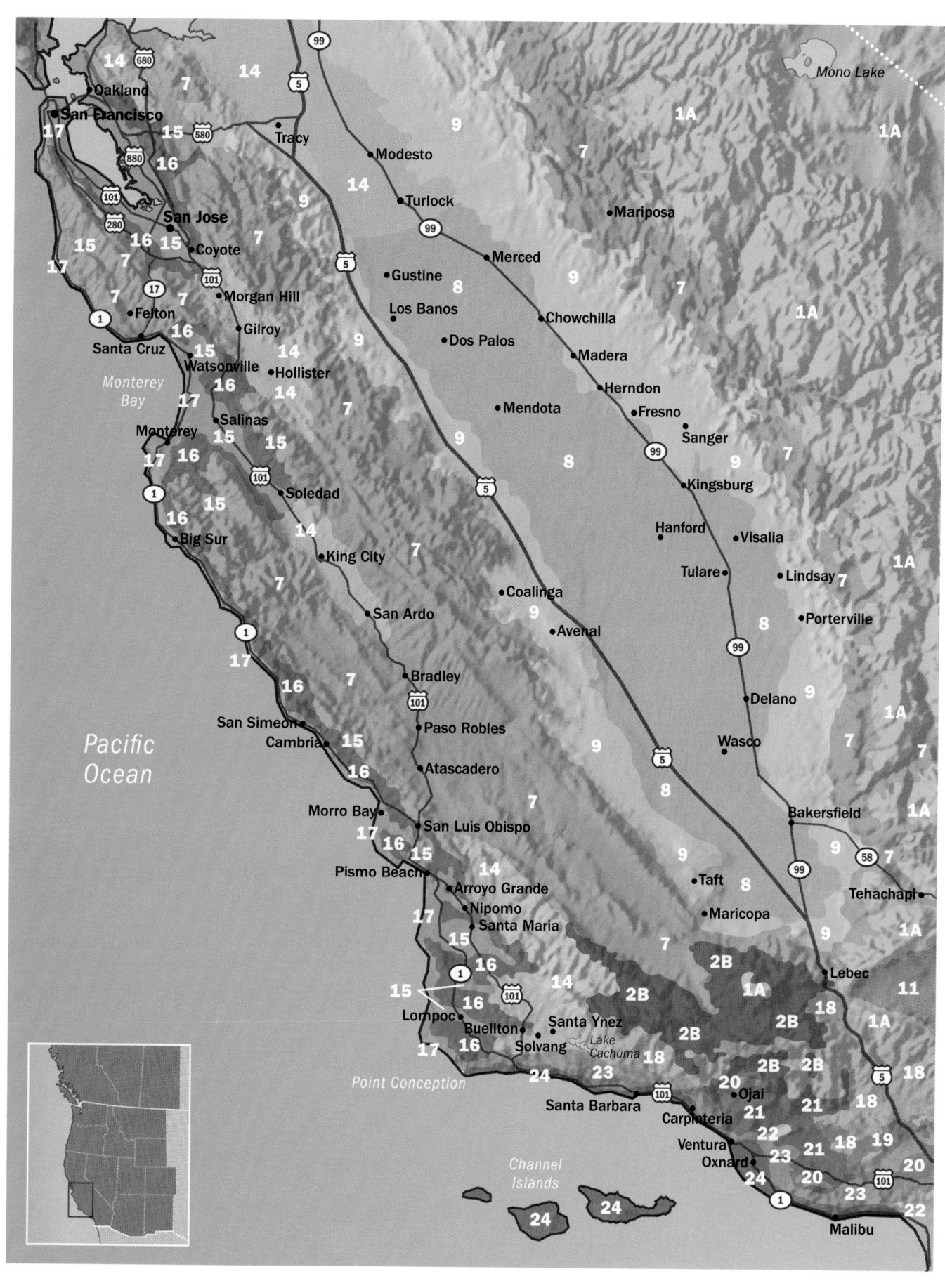

Mono Lake

Oakland

San Francisco

Tracy

Modesto

Turlock

Merced

Mariposa

1A

1A

Gustine

Los Banos

Dos Palos

Chowchilla

Madera

Herndon

Fresno

Sanger

Kingsburg

Hanford

Visalia

Tulare

Lindsay

Porterville

1A

San Jose

Coyote

Morgan Hill

Gilroy

Felton

Santa Cruz

Watsonville

Hollister

Salinas

Monterey

Monterey Bay

Soledad

Big Sur

King City

San Ardo

Bradley

Coalinga

Avenal

Mendota

Wasco

Delano

1A

1A

San Simeon

Cambria

Paso Robles

Atascadero

Morro Bay

San Luis Obispo

Pismo Beach

Arroyo Grande

Nipomo

Santa Maria

Taft

Maricopa

Bakersfield

Tehachapi

1A

Pacific Ocean

Lompoc

Buellton

Santa Ynez

Solvang

Lake Cachuma

Lebec

11

18

1A

Point Conception

Santa Barbara

Carpinteria

Ventura

Oxnard

Ojai

2B

2B

2B

2B

20

21

22

23

24

20

21

18

19

20

23

22

Channel Islands

24

24

24

Malibu

0 10 20 30 miles

Central California

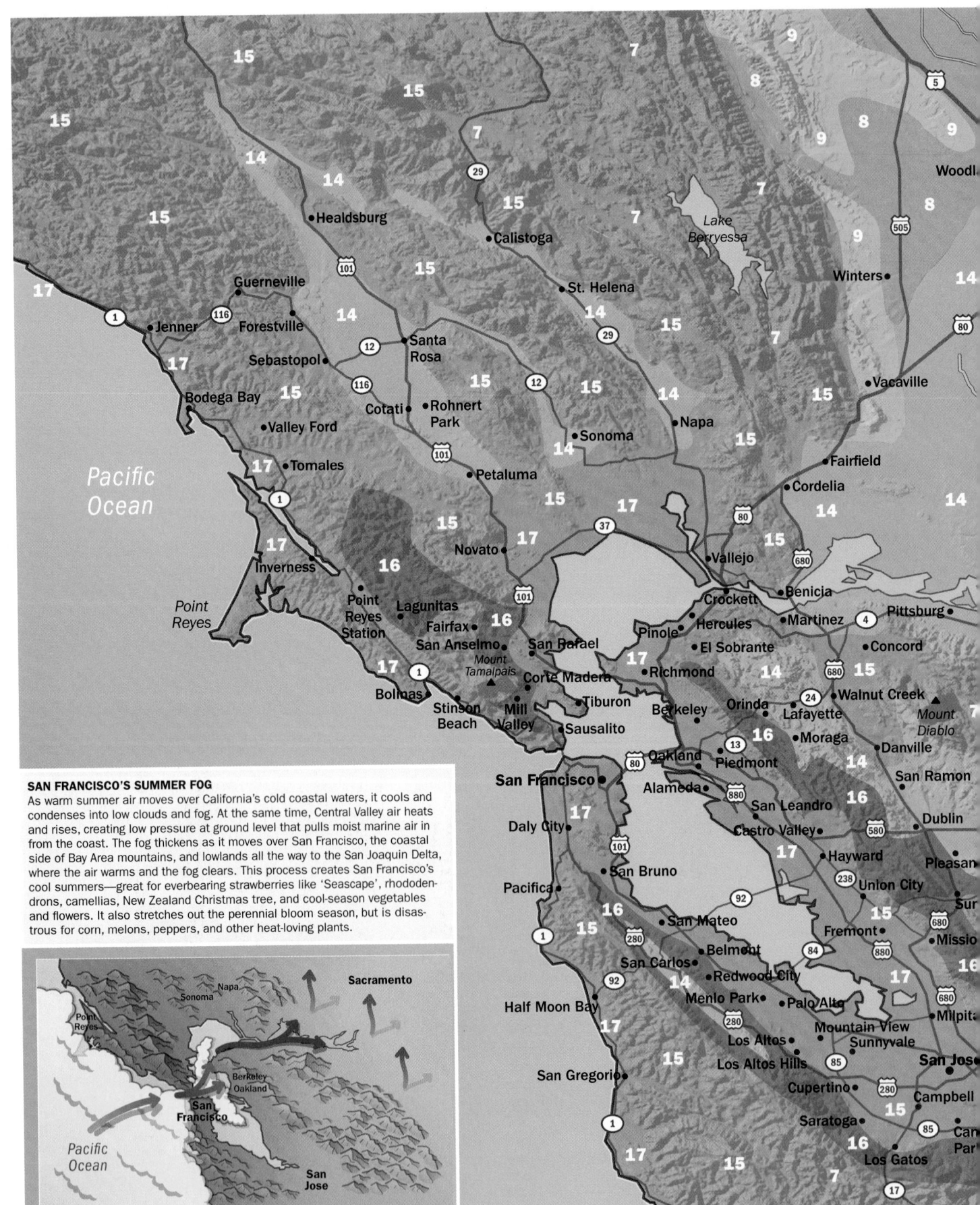

SAN FRANCISCO'S SUMMER FOG

As warm summer air moves over California's cold coastal waters, it cools and condenses into low clouds and fog. At the same time, Central Valley air heats and rises, creating low pressure at ground level that pulls moist marine air in from the coast. The fog thickens as it moves over San Francisco, the coastal side of Bay Area mountains, and lowlands all the way to the San Joaquin Delta, where the air warms and the fog clears. This process creates San Francisco's cool summers—great for everbearing strawberries like 'Seascape', rhododendrons, camellias, New Zealand Christmas tree, and cool-season vegetables and flowers. It also stretches out the perennial bloom season, but is disastrous for corn, melons, peppers, and other heat-loving plants.

San Francisco Bay Area and Inland

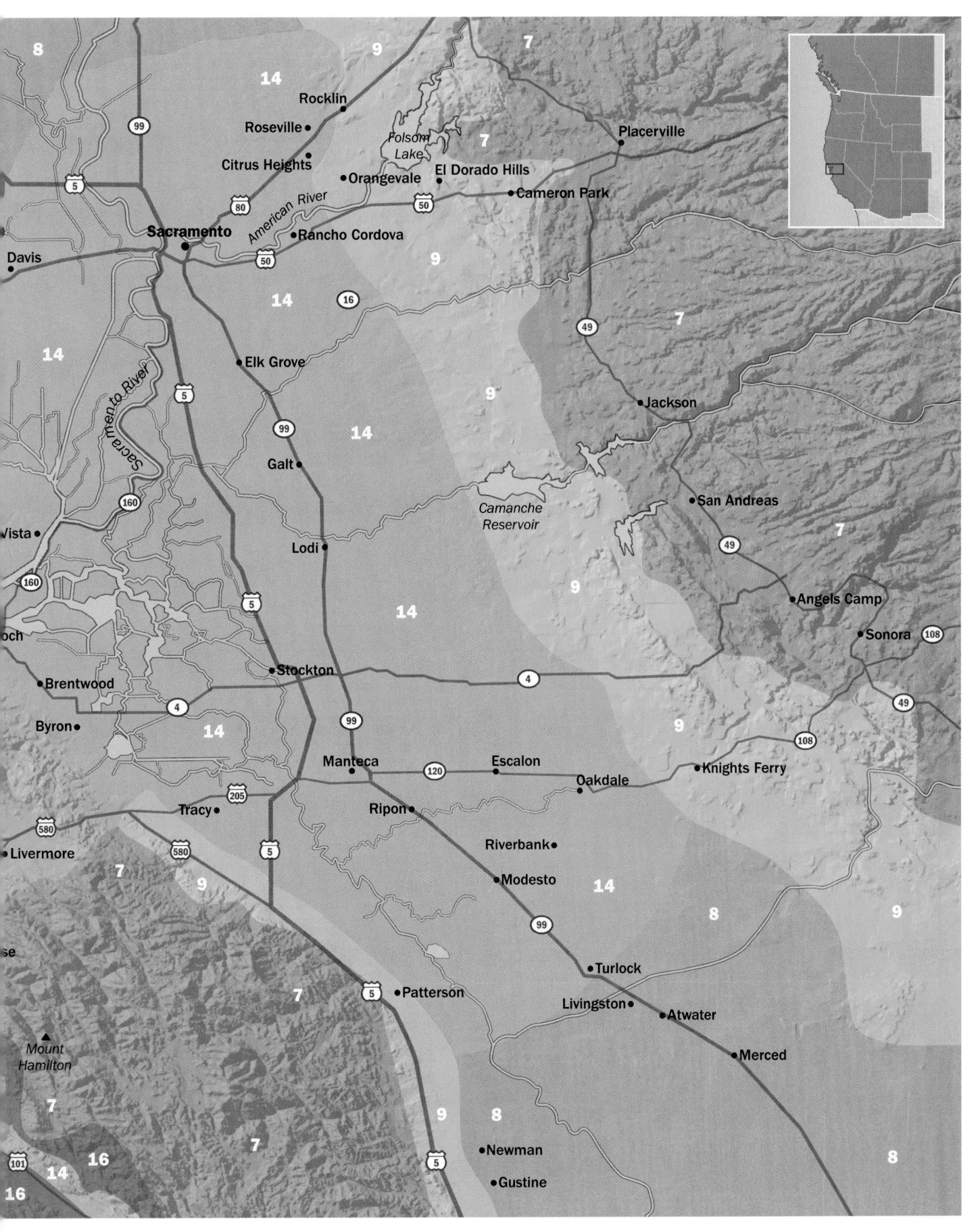

8

14

Rocklin

Roseville

Citrus Heights

Folsom Lake

9

7

7

Placerville

Orangevale

El Dorado Hills

Cameron Park

99

80

American River

5

Davis

Sacramento

50

Rancho Cordova

50

9

14

16

7

Elk Grove

49

14

9

Jackson

Galt

99

14

Camanche Reservoir

San Andreas

Lodi

49

7

Sacramento River

160

Vista

9

Angels Camp

160

14

Sonora

108

och

Stockton

4

9

49

Brentwood

Knights Ferry

Byron

14

99

108

Manteca

Escalon

120

Tracy

205

Oakdale

Ripon

5

Riverbank

580

Modesto

Livermore

580

9

14

7

99

8

9

Turlock

7

Patterson

5

Livingston

Atwater

se

Mount Hamilton

Merced

7

9

8

7

16

Newman

5

101

14

Gustine

16

8

0   5   10   15 miles

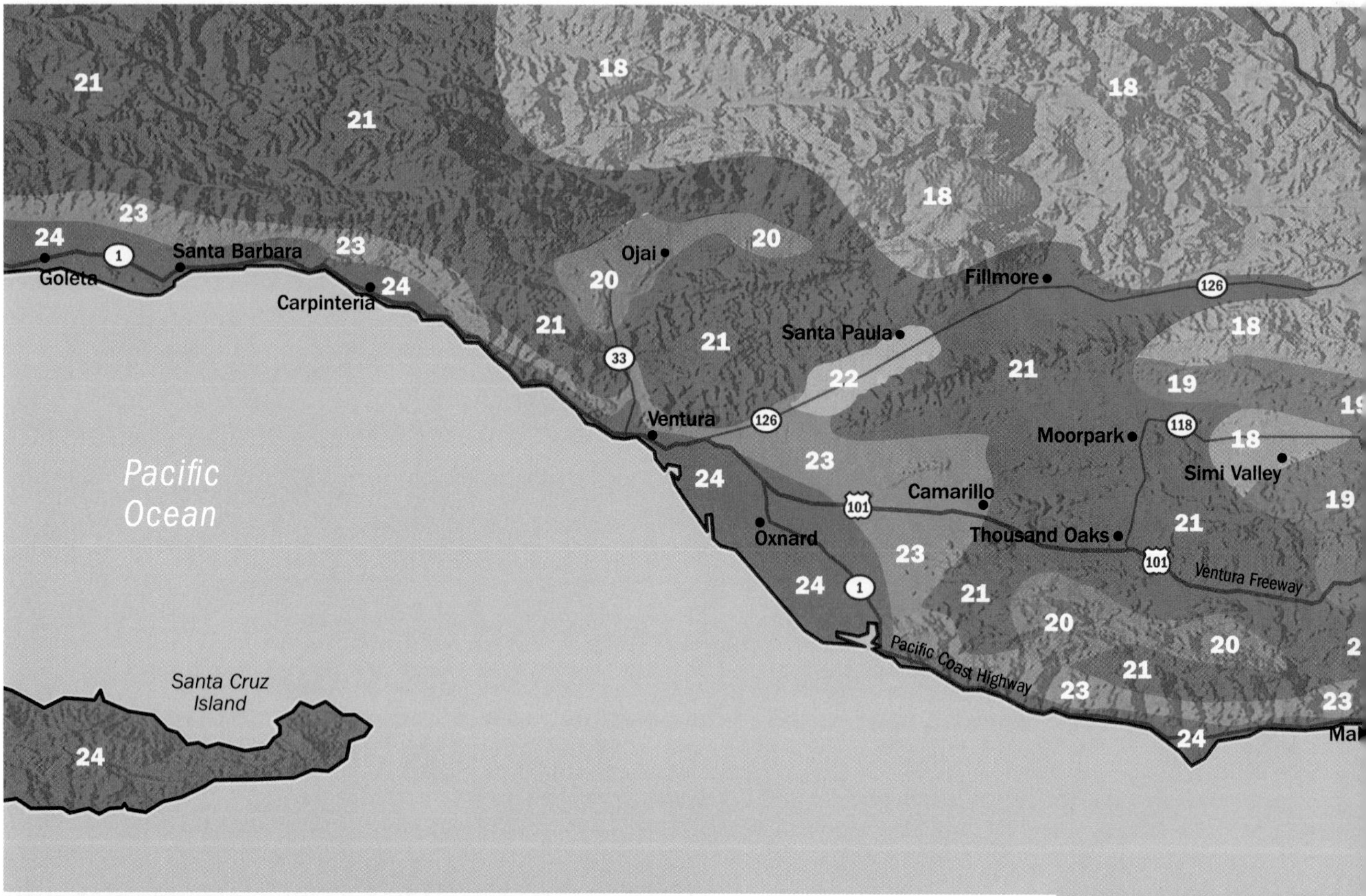

21

18

18

21

23

24   23

Goleta • Santa Barbara   23

24

Carpinteria

21

20

Ojai •

20

Fillmore •   126

Pacific Ocean

21

33

Santa Paula •

18

22

21

19

Ventura   126

Moorpark •   118

18

24

23

Camarillo   19

101

Oxnard •

Thousand Oaks •

21

24   1

23

101   *Ventura Freeway*

Santa Cruz Island

24

20

21

20   2

23

21

24   Ma

Pacific Coast Highway

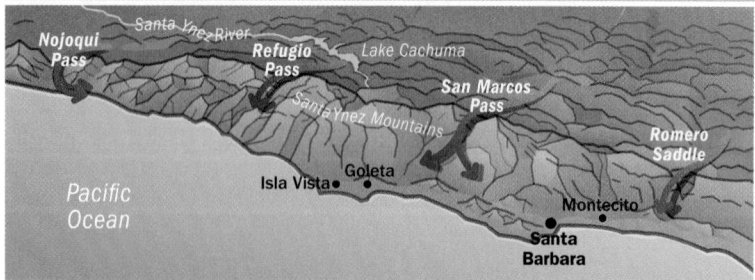

Santa Ynez River

Nojoqui Pass

Refugio Pass

Lake Cachuma

San Marcos Pass

Santa Ynez Mountains

Romero Saddle

Pacific Ocean

Isla Vista •   **Goleta** •

Montecito •

•
Santa Barbara

NATURE'S DESICCANTS: THE SUNDOWNERS…

In Santa Barbara, hot winds called Sundowners (which usually peak late in the day) blow south through passes in the Santa Ynez Mountains. Most common in late spring and summer, they only come three or four times per year, but they have driven some of Santa Barbara's most destructive fires.

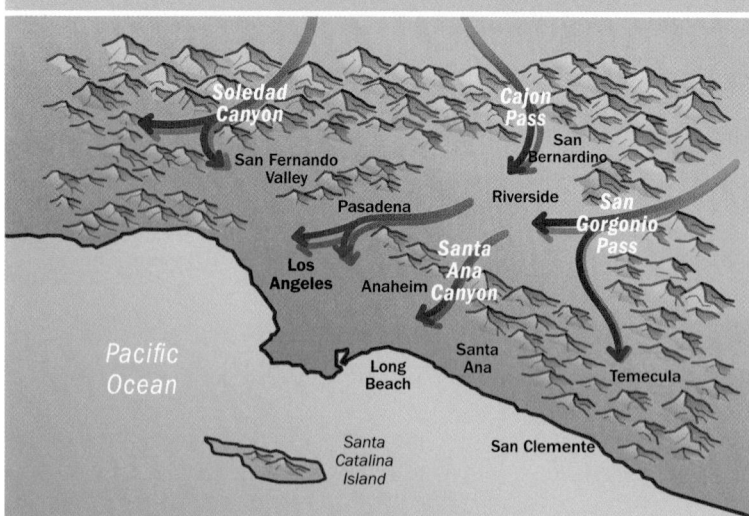

Soledad Canyon

Cajon Pass

San Fernando Valley

San Bernardino

Pasadena

Riverside

San Gorgonio Pass

Los Angeles

Anaheim

Santa Ana Canyon

Pacific Ocean

Long Beach

Santa Ana

Temecula

San Clemente

Santa Catalina Island

…AND THE SANTA ANAS

Every fall and winter, the Santa Ana winds rev up as the interior's cold, heavy air flows downhill toward low-pressure systems off the Southern California coast. As this air loses elevation, it compresses, heats up, dries out, and roars through the passes behind Los Angeles and San Bernardino. Cajon Pass and Soledad Canyon are two main routes, although the wind is named for Santa Ana Canyon. When the Santa Ana winds hit Los Angeles, they're so hot and dry that they can dehydrate plants to a crisp in a few hours. Santa Anas usually play out near the coast, though sometimes they blow all the way to Santa Catalina Island.

If you're in the path of the Sundowners or the Santa Anas, use sprinklers, windbreaks, and row covers to help keep garden plants hydrated.

Los Angeles and Inland

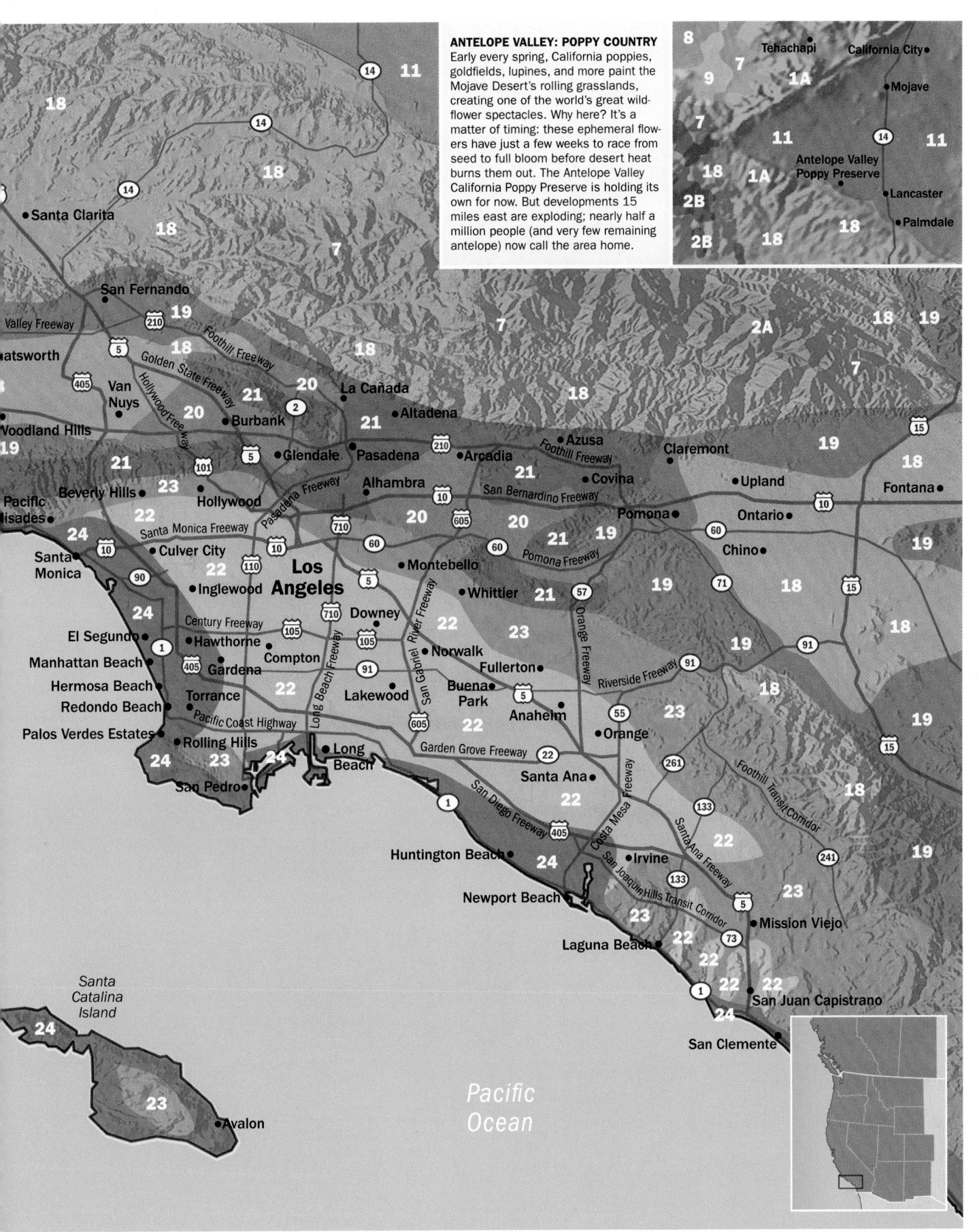

ANTELOPE VALLEY: POPPY COUNTRY
Early every spring, California poppies, goldfields, lupines, and more paint the Mojave Desert's rolling grasslands, creating one of the world's great wildflower spectacles. Why here? It's a matter of timing: these ephemeral flowers have just a few weeks to race from seed to full bloom before desert heat burns them out. The Antelope Valley California Poppy Preserve is holding its own for now. But developments 15 miles east are exploding; nearly half a million people (and very few remaining antelope) now call the area home.

Tehachapi
California City
8
7
9
1A
Mojave
7
11
11
18
1A
Antelope Valley
Poppy Preserve
14
2B
Lancaster
2B
18
18
Palmdale

14   11

18   18

Santa Clarita
San Fernando
19
210
18   2A   18   19
Valley Freeway
5
Foothill Freeway
7   7
atsworth
Golden State Freeway
405
Van Nuys
20   21   20   18
La Cañada
15
Woodland Hills
Hollywood Freeway
2
Altadena   18   19   18
19
21   5   Burbank   21
Pacific
isades
Beverly Hills   23   Glendale   Pasadena   210   Arcadia   Claremont   Fontana
22   Hollywood   Alhambra   Azusa   Foothill Freeway   Upland
24   Santa Monica Freeway   Pasadena Freeway   21   Covina   Pomona   Ontario
Santa Monica   10   710   20   605   20   San Bernardino Freeway   60   19
90   Culver City   60   60   21   19   Chino   18
24   22   110   Los Angeles   5   Montebello   Pomona Freeway   71   15
El Segundo   Century Freeway   Inglewood   Downey   Whittier   21   57   19   18
Manhattan Beach   1   710   Hawthorne   105   Norwalk   Orange Freeway   91   19   91
Hermosa Beach   405   Compton   105   22   Fullerton   Riverside Freeway   18
Redondo Beach   Gardena   91   Lakewood   Buena Park   5   91   18
Palos Verdes Estates   Torrance   22   605   Anaheim   55   23   19
24   Rolling Hills   22   Garden Grove Freeway   Orange   261   15
23   Pacific Coast Highway   Long Beach   22   Santa Ana   22   Foothill Transit Corridor   18
San Pedro   24   1   Huntington Beach   San Diego Freeway   133   22   19
405   24   Irvine   241   23
Newport Beach   133   5
San Joaquin Hills Transit Corridor   73   Mission Viejo
Laguna Beach   22   22
Santa Catalina Island   1   22   22   San Juan Capistrano
24   24
23   San Clemente
Avalon

Pacific Ocean

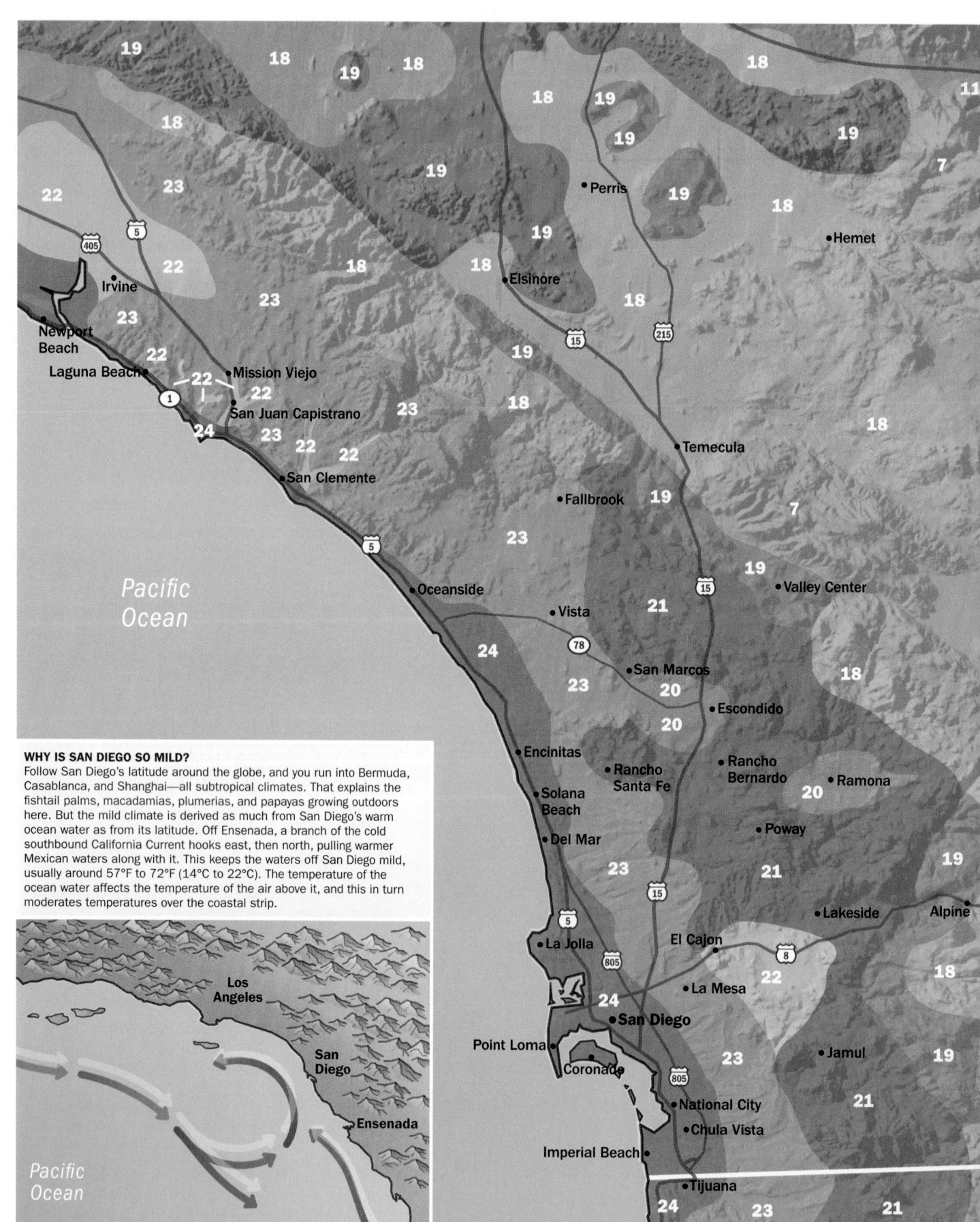

WHY IS SAN DIEGO SO MILD?
Follow San Diego's latitude around the globe, and you run into Bermuda, Casablanca, and Shanghai—all subtropical climates. That explains the fishtail palms, macadamias, plumerias, and papayas growing outdoors here. But the mild climate is derived as much from San Diego's warm ocean water as from its latitude. Off Ensenada, a branch of the cold southbound California Current hooks east, then north, pulling warmer Mexican waters along with it. This keeps the waters off San Diego mild, usually around 57°F to 72°F (14°C to 22°C). The temperature of the ocean water affects the temperature of the air above it, and this in turn moderates temperatures over the coastal strip.

San Diego and Environs

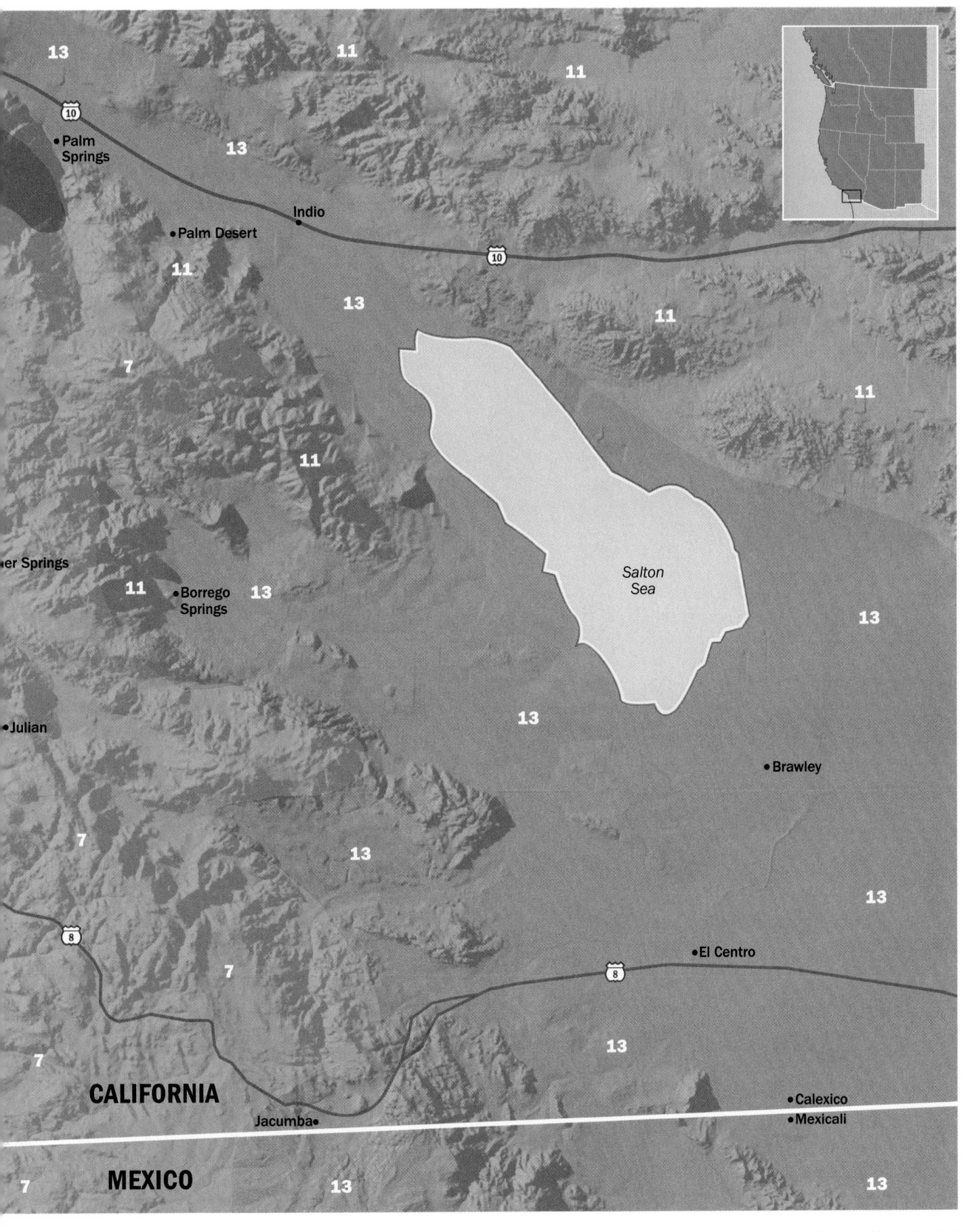

13

11

11

10

● Palm
Springs

13

11

Indio

● Palm Desert

10

11

13

11

7

11

Salton
Sea

11

er Springs

11   ● Borrego
Springs

13

13

● Julian

● Brawley

13

7

13

13

8

7

● El Centro

8

CALIFORNIA

13

● Calexico

Jacumba ●

● Mexicali

7

MEXICO

13

13

0   5   10   15 miles

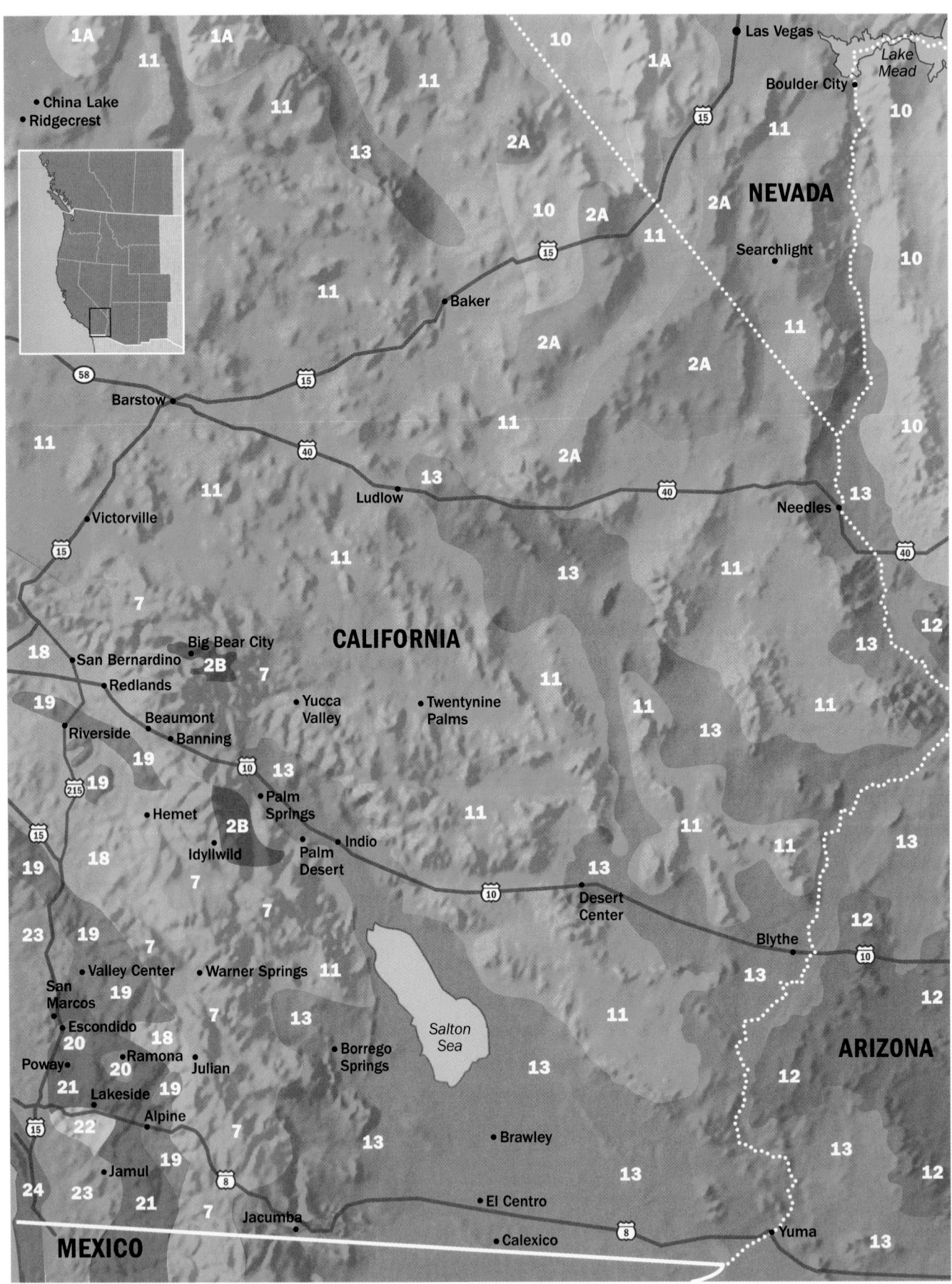

Southwest Deserts: Southern California

0   10   20   30 miles

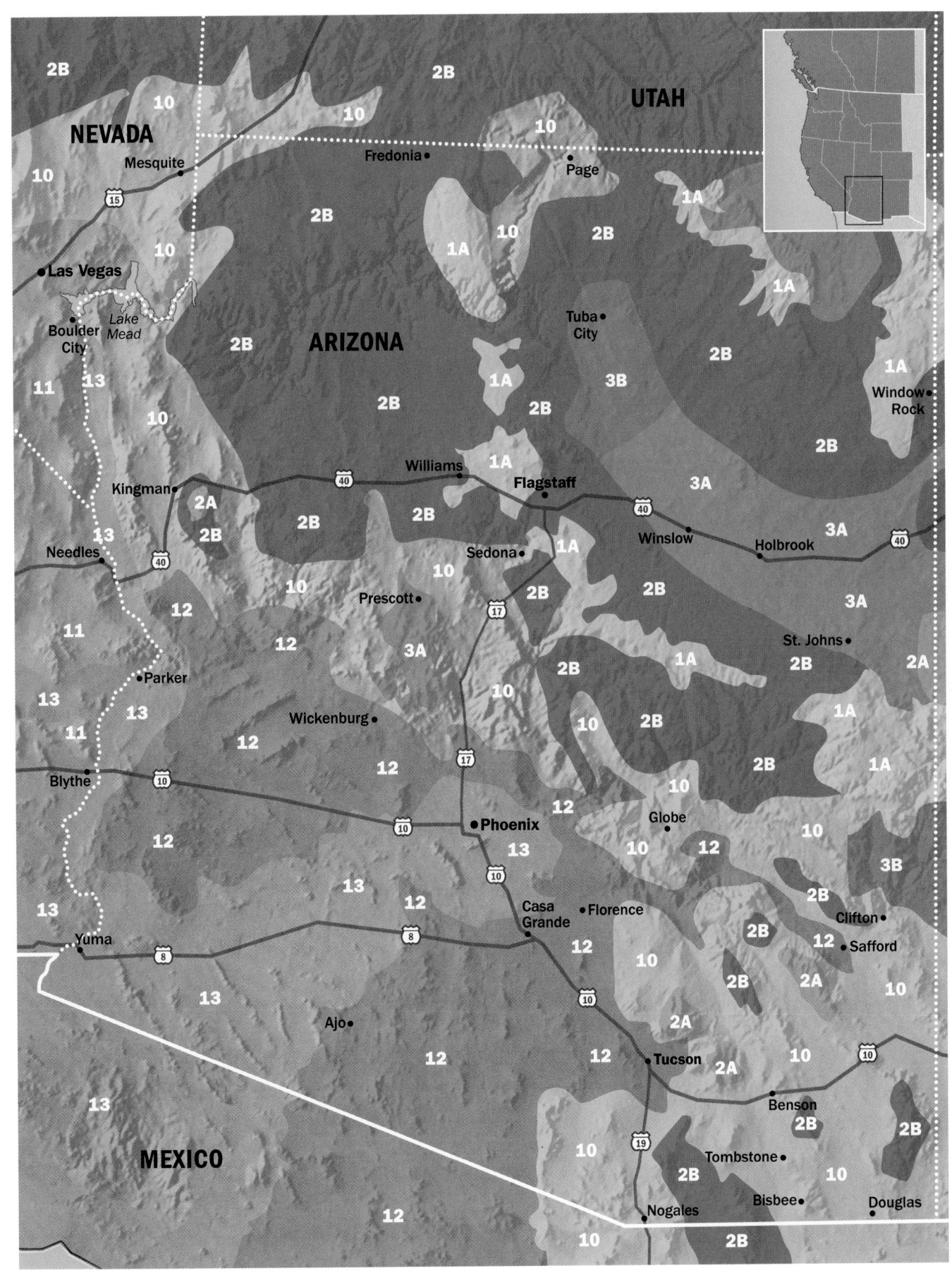

Southwest Deserts: Arizona

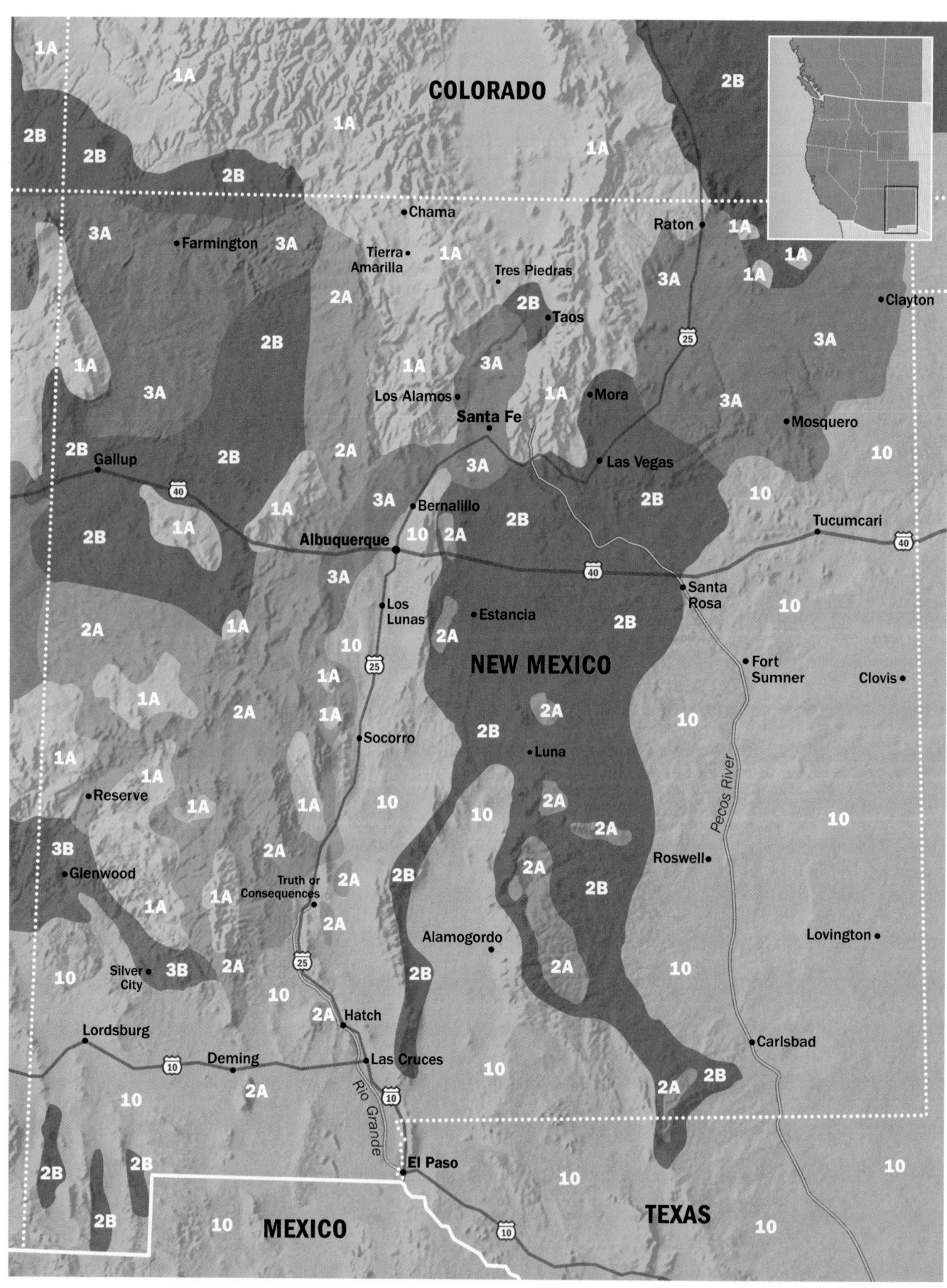

Southwest Deserts: New Mexico

0   25   50   75 miles

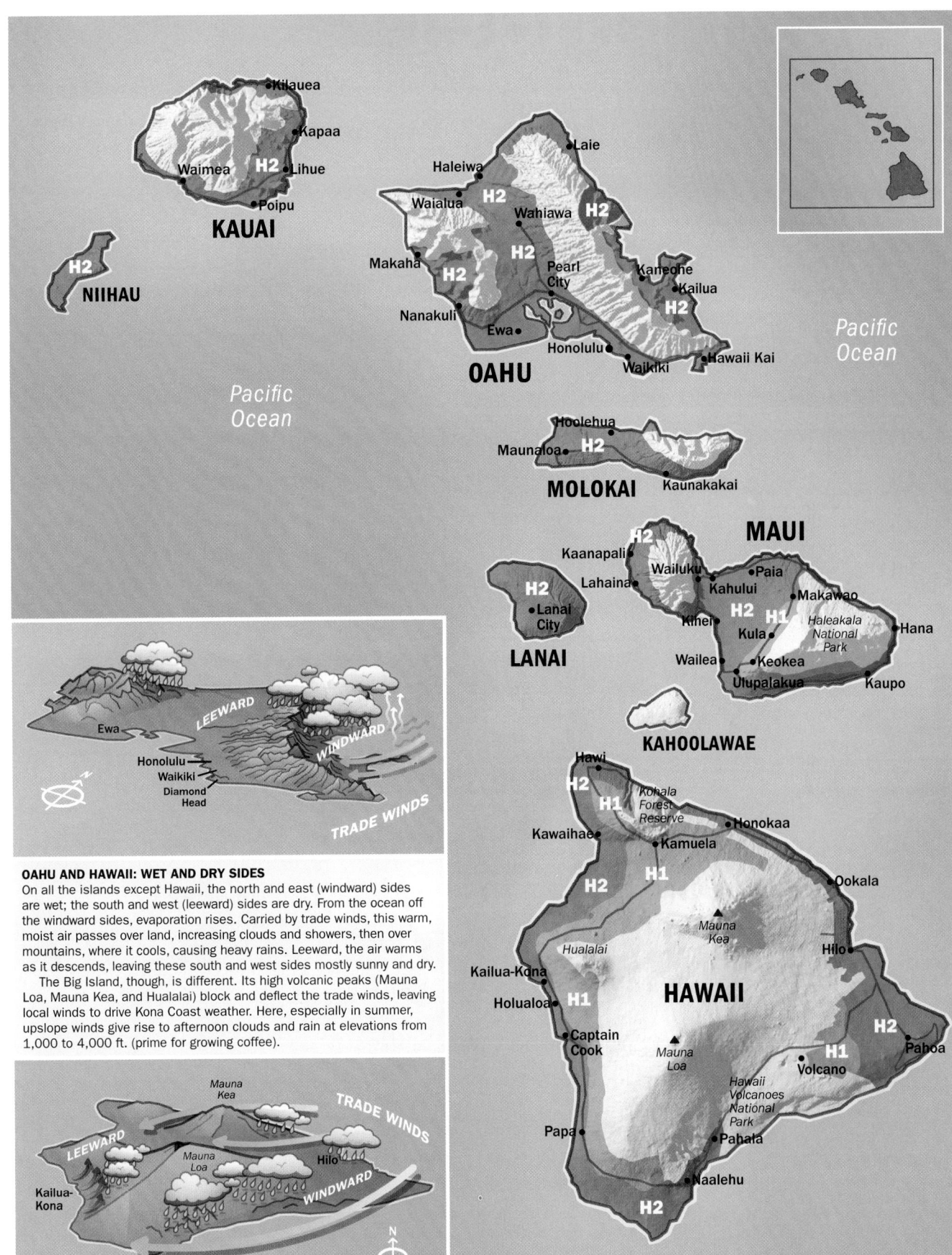

KAUAI

Kilauea
Kapaa
Waimea
Lihue
Poipu
H2

NIIHAU
H2

OAHU

Laie
Haleiwa
Waialua
Wahiawa
Makaha
Pearl City
Kaneohe
Kailua
Nanakuli
Ewa
Honolulu
Waikiki
Hawaii Kai
H2 H2 H2 H2 H2

Pacific Ocean

Pacific Ocean

MOLOKAI

Hoolehua
Maunaloa
Kaunakakai
H2

LANAI

Lanai City
H2

MAUI

Kaanapali
Lahaina
Wailuku
Paia
Kahului
Makawao
Kihei
Kula
Haleakala National Park
Hana
Wailea
Keokea
Utupalakua
Kaupo
H2 H2 H1

KAHOOLAWAE

HAWAII

Hawi
Kohala Forest Reserve
Kawaihae
Honokaa
Kamuela
Ookala
Mauna Kea
Hualalai
Hilo
Kailua-Kona
Holualoa
Captain Cook
Mauna Loa
Hawaii Volcanoes National Park
Volcano
Pahoa
Papa
Pahala
Naalehu
H2 H1 H1 H2 H1 H1 H2 H1 H2

OAHU AND HAWAII: WET AND DRY SIDES

On all the islands except Hawaii, the north and east (windward) sides are wet; the south and west (leeward) sides are dry. From the ocean off the windward sides, evaporation rises. Carried by trade winds, this warm, moist air passes over land, increasing clouds and showers, then over mountains, where it cools, causing heavy rains. Leeward, the air warms as it descends, leaving these south and west sides mostly sunny and dry.

The Big Island, though, is different. Its high volcanic peaks (Mauna Loa, Mauna Kea, and Hualalai) block and deflect the trade winds, leaving local winds to drive Kona Coast weather. Here, especially in summer, upslope winds give rise to afternoon clouds and rain at elevations from 1,000 to 4,000 ft. (prime for growing coffee).

LEEWARD
WINDWARD
TRADE WINDS
Ewa
Honolulu
Waikiki
Diamond Head
N

Mauna Kea
Mauna Loa
TRADE WINDS
LEEWARD
WINDWARD
Hilo
Kailua-Kona
N

0   20   40   60 miles

Hawaii

CHOOSING THE RIGHT PLANTS FOR YOUR GARDEN, from
the thousands of plants available, can be challenging.
But by using the lists in this chapter, you can head to the
nursery with confidence and a sense of adventure, and
choose just the right plants for the spot you have in mind.
Start with a single plant, then add others that take its same
conditions, mixing and matching them on your nursery
cart to get the look you want.

HOW TO USE THIS PLANT FINDER

This chapter lists plants by the roles that they can play in your garden. The lists are grouped into three categories, which are explained below. To find the types of plants you're looking for, check the table of contents at right.

Problem-solver plants Many gardens have at least one challenging area. Maybe it's a dark spot beneath a tree that needs a hit of shade-loving color. Maybe it's a planting bed on the edge of a cliff that's continually buffeted by wind, or a tiny corner with poor soil where only potted plants could thrive. Whatever the problem—whether a side yard that needs a privacy hedge, a patio that could use a litter-free tree nearby, or a tired-looking lawn that you want to replace with a groundcover—the plants on these lists offer solutions.

Earth-friendly plants The right plants can help you garden more sustainably. Waterwise plants can cut down your water usage. Plants that thrive in winter-damp basins can populate rain gardens, helping to filter runoff as it percolates into the soil. Plants native to your area —because they're so well adapted to your climate and conditions— need little in the way of care or resources such as fertilizer once established. And plants whose fruits, nectar, or seeds attract birds, pollinators, or beneficial insects can help keep your garden naturally healthier, while providing a much-needed habitat for wildlife.

Plants for special effects Maybe you want to re-create the look of the tropical garden you saw in Hawaii, but you need tropical look-alikes that can take your temperate climate. Maybe you entertain outdoors a lot on balmy summer evenings and want border plants that show up well in moonlight, or flowers that fill the air with heady perfumes. Perhaps you prefer plants whose stout trunks and bristly canopies fit best with your garden's bold geometric lines. These lists can help.

MOBILE AND ONLINE PLANT FINDER

Now you can take the best of the *Sunset Western Garden Book* with you to the garden center, nursery, and your yard. Get the free mobile edition of the *Western Garden Book's* Plant Finder on your smartphone. With it, you can access more than 2,000 plants and search by plant, zip code, climate zone, sun and water requirements, and type.

Surfing the Web? The online Plant Finder, updated with the new edition of this book, lets you browse by color, height, spread, and special needs too.

Visit *sunset.com/plantfinder* to find the perfect plants for your yard.

Sunset thanks Save Our Water, a California water-conservation public education program, for sponsoring the update of the online tool and the launch of the mobile Plant Finder.

PLANTS FOR HEDGES

Whether sheared for a formal look or allowed to grow naturally, a hedge is one of your garden's hardest-working elements. A tall hedge can create a privacy screen or form a green wall that divides your garden into separate rooms. A low one can frame a patio or garden bench, edge walks or paths, or even outline kitchen gardens or over-the-top mazes and parterres.

Plants with densely packed foliage from top to bottom make ideal living fences. Large shrubs are good candidates for screens; if grouped close together, they can block an objectionable view or direct attention to a garden focal point. Informal hedges need little pruning, but formal hedges need pruning at least once during the growing season, in midsummer.

Young sweet bay (*Laurus nobilis*) trees; Newport Beach, California

Deciduous

Acer campestre p. 128
Hedge maple
☼ ☽ ✿ 2–9, 14–17

Berberis (some) p. 193
Barberry
☼ ☽ ✿ ZONES VARY

Carpinus betulus p. 223
European hornbeam
☼ ☽ ✿ 2–9, 14–17

Chaenomeles p. 234
Flowering quince
☼ ✿ 2–23

Crataegus monogyna p. 269
☼ ✿ 2–12, 14–17

Elaeagnus angustifolia p. 299
Russian olive
☼ ☽ ✿ A2, A3; 1–3, 7–14, 18, 19

**Frangula alnus
'Columnaris'** p. 326
Alder buckthorn
☼ ☽ ✿ 1–7, 10, 11

Ligustrum (some) p. 411
☼ ☽ ✿ ZONES VARY

Salix purpurea 'Gracilis' p. 583
Dwarf purple osier
☼ ✿ A2, A3; 1–11

**Viburnum opulus
'Nanum'** p. 649
European cranberry bush
☼ ☽ ✿ A2, A3; 1–9, 14–24

Evergreen

Abelia × grandiflora p. 124
Glossy abelia
☼ ☽ ✿ 4–24; H1, H2

Arbutus unedo p. 164
Strawberry tree
☼ ☽ ✿ 4–24

Bamboo (many) p. 182
☼ ☽ ✿ ZONES VARY

Berberis (some) p. 193
Barberry
☼ ☽ ✿ ZONES VARY

Buxus p. 208
Boxwood
☼ ☽ ● ✿ ZONES VARY

Callistemon (some) p. 212
Bottlebrush
☼ ✿ ZONES VARY

Calocedrus decurrens p. 214
Incense cedar
☼ ☽ ✿ 2–12, 14–24

**Chamaecyparis
lawsoniana** p. 234
Port Orford cedar
☼ ☽ ✿ A3; 3–6, 15–17

Choisya ternata p. 241
Mexican orange
☼ ☽ ✿ 4–9, 14–24

**× Cuprocyparis
leylandii** p. 274
☼ ✿ 3B–24

Berberis thunbergii atropurpurea

Carpinus betulus 'Fastigiata'

Crataegus monogyna

Abelia × grandiflora 'Aurea'

Cupressus (most) p. 273
Cypress
☼ ◐ Z ZONES VARY

Dodonaea viscosa p. 291
Hop bush
☼ ◐ Z 7–24; H1, H2

Elaeagnus (some) p. 298
☼ ◐ Z ZONES VARY

Escallonia p. 309
☼ ◐ Z 4–9, 14–24

Euonymus (most) p. 313
NEEDS, ZONES VARY

Feijoa sellowiana p. 319
Pineapple guava
☼ Z 6–9, 12–24; H1, H2

Frangula alnus p. 326
Alder buckthorn
☼ ◐ Z 1–7, 10, 11

Garrya elliptica p. 333
Coast silktassel
☼ ◐ Z 4–9, 14–24

Grevillea (many) p. 347
NEEDS, ZONES VARY

Griselinia p. 348
☼ ◐ Z 9, 14–17, 20–24

**Heteromeles
arbutifolia** p. 360
Toyon
☼ ◐ Z 5–9, 14–24

Hibiscus rosa-sinensis p. 363
Chinese hibiscus
☼ Z 9, 12–16, 19–24; H1, H2

Ilex (some) p. 371
Holly
☼ ◐ Z ZONES VARY

**Juniperus
(shrub, columnar)** p. 386
Juniper
☼ ◐ Z ZONES VARY

Laurus nobilis p. 401
Sweet bay
☼ ◐ Z 5–9, 12–24; H1, H2

Leptospermum (most) p. 405
Tea tree
☼ Z 14–24; H1, H2

Ligustrum (some) p. 411
Privet
☼ ◐ Z ZONES VARY

Mahonia (tall) p. 431
NEEDS, ZONES VARY

Myrica californica p. 449
Pacific wax myrtle
☼ Z 4–9, 14–24

Myrsine africana p. 449
African boxwood
☼ ◐ Z 8, 9, 14–24

Myrtus communis p. 450
Myrtle
☼ ◐ Z 8–24; H1, H2

Nandina domestica p. 450
Heavenly bamboo
☼ ◐ ● Z 3–24; H1, H2

Osmanthus (several) p. 466
☼ ◐ Z ZONES VARY

Photinia p. 502
☼ Z ZONES VARY

Pittosporum (several) p. 512
☼ ◐ Z ZONES VARY

Prunus (evergreen) p. 531
NEEDS, ZONES VARY

Pyracantha p. 542
Firethorn
☼ Z ZONES VARY

Rhaphiolepis p. 554
☼ ◐ Z 4–10, 12–24; H1, H2

Taxus p. 625
Yew
☼ ◐ ● Z ZONES VARY

Teucrium fruticans p. 626
Bush germander
☼ Z 4–24

Thuja p. 627
Arborvitae
☼ ◐ Z ZONES VARY

Vaccinium ovatum p. 644
Evergreen huckleberry
☼ ◐ ● Z 4–7, 14–17, 22–24

Viburnum (several) p. 648
NEEDS, ZONES VARY

Xylosma congestum p. 657
☼ ◐ Z 8–24

TOP ROW: *Buxus sempervirens* 'Suffruticosa'; *Cupressus sempervirens* 'Glauca'.
SECOND ROW: *Grevillea.* THIRD ROW: *Ligustrum japonicum; Nandina domestica.*
BOTTOM ROW: *Rhaphiolepis indica* 'Pink Lady'; *Thuja occidentalis* 'Smaragd'

PLANTS FOR SLOPES

Steep hillsides can be more challenging for plants than level gardens. Soil may be shallow, poor, or—where the back is the result of a grading cut—virtually nonexistent. Slopes are more difficult to irrigate, unless you build watering basins around each new plant or set up a drip-irrigation system that will apply water more slowly. If not planted or stabilized properly, they can present hazards in wet weather. Yet in many areas, a slope may be the only available space for a garden.

The plants listed here will cope successfully with less than ideal conditions and provide good-looking cover for gentle or steep slopes; many have strong roots that will help prevent soil erosion, or thrive with minimal care. Arrange the plants in staggered rows on slopes where erosion may occur, and install drip-irrigation emitters on the uphill side of the plants.

Artemisia, kangaroo paw, junipers with cordyline, euphorbia, grasses, lavender

Shrubs

Anigozanthos　p. 153
Kangaroo paw
☼ ✂ 15–24

Arctostaphylos　p. 164
Manzanita
☼ ◐ ✂ ZONES VARY

Artemisia (several)　p. 169
☼ ✂ ZONES VARY

Ceanothus　p. 226
California wild lilac
☼ ✂ 1–3, 5–9, 14–24

Echium candicans　p. 298
Pride of Madeira
☼ ✂ 14–24

Eriogonum　p. 306
Wild buckwheat
☼ ✂ ZONES VARY

Grevillea rosmarinifolia　p. 348
Rosemary grevillea
☼ ◐ ✂ 8, 9, 12–24

Juniperus (low)　p. 386
Juniper
☼ ◐ ✂ ZONES VARY

Rosa rugosa　p. 577
Ramanas rose
☼ ◐ ✂ A1–A3; 1–24

Symphoricarpos　p. 620
Snowberry
NEEDS, ZONES VARY

Groundcovers, Perennials, and Vines

Achillea millefolium　p. 132
Common yarrow
☼ ✂ A1–A3; 1–24

Carex　p. 221
Sedge
☼ ◐ ✂ ZONES VARY

Lonicera japonica　p. 421
Japanese honeysuckle
☼ ◐ ✂ 1–24; H1, H2

Mahonia repens　p. 432
Creeping mahonia
☼ ◐ ✂ 2B–9, 14–24

Malephora　p. 432
Ice plant
☼ ✂ ZONES VARY

Polystichum munitum　p. 524
Western sword fern
◐ ● ✂ A3; 2–9, 14–24

Romneya coulteri　p. 567
Matilija poppy
☼ ✂ 4–12, 14–24; H1

Trachelospermum　p. 635
Star jasmine
☼ ◐ ✂ ZONES VARY

Vinca minor　p. 650
Dwarf periwinkle
☼ ◐ ● ✂ 1–24

Echium candicans

Grevillea rosmarinifolia

Achillea millefolium

Vinca minor 'Bowles'

WIND-RESISTANT PLANTS

Frequent strong winds can wreak havoc on plants. Water stress is one common problem; constant winds pull moisture from foliage faster than roots can draw it from the soil. And really powerful winds can virtually destroy many plants—defoliate them, uproot them, wrench off branches with such force that trunks may split. Fortunately, if you live in one of the West's windiest spots, you can protect your garden and its plants.

Start by choosing plants, such as the ones listed below, that will endure high winds without much damage to health or appearance. (For plants unfazed by ocean winds, see "Plants for Seacoast Gardens" on page 50.) Make sure young plants are properly staked and tied. For more ways to protect plants, see "Gardening, Start to Finish," pages 724–725.

Monterey cypress (*Cupressus macrocarpa*) with phormiums, kangaroo paw

Trees

Acacia (some)   p. 125
☼ ✿ ZONES VARY

Acer campestre   p. 128
Hedge maple
☼ ◑ ✿ 2–9, 14–17

Broussonetia papyrifera   p. 204
Paper mulberry
☼ ✿ 3B–24; H1, H2

Calocedrus decurrens   p. 214
Incense cedar
☼ ◑ ✿ 2–12, 14–24

Casuarina   p. 225
Beefwood
☼ ✿ 8, 9, 12–24; H1, H2

Chamaecyparis lawsoniana   p. 234
Port Orford cedar
☼ ◑ ✿ A3; 3–6, 15–17

Chilopsis linearis   p. 239
Desert willow
☼ ✿ 3B, 7–14, 18–23

Cupressus (most)   p. 273
Cypress
☼ ✿ ZONES VARY

Elaeagnus angustifolia   p. 299
Russian olive
☼ ◑ ✿ A2, A3; 1–3, 7–14, 18, 19

Eucalyptus (most)   p. 311
☼ ✿ ZONES VARY

Fraxinus 'Fan West'   p. 327
Ash
☼ ✿ 2–14

Fraxinus velutina 'Rio Grande'   p. 328
Fan-tex ash
☼ ✿ 8–24

Lagunaria patersonii   p. 397
Primrose tree
☼ ✿ 13, 15–24; H1, H2

Ligustrum lucidum   p. 411
Glossy privet
☼ ◑ ✿ 5–24; H1, H2

Lyonothamnus floribundus   p. 424
Catalina ironwood
☼ ✿ 14–17, 19–24

Melaleuca nesophila   p. 439
Pink melaleuca
☼ ✿ 13, 16–24; H1

Melaleuca quinquenervia   p. 439
Cajeput tree
☼ ✿ 9, 12, 13, 15–17, 20–24; H1, H2

Olea europaea   p. 460
Olive
☼ ✿ 8, 9, 11–24; H1, H2

Palms   p. 471
NEEDS, ZONES VARY

Parkinsonia aculeata   p. 475
Jerusalem thorn
☼ ✿ 8–24; H1, H2

Lagunaria patersonii

Picea abies

Pittosporum tenuifolium 'Golf Ball'

Quercus virginiana

TOP ROW: *Arbutus unedo; Berberis thunbergii atropurpurea* 'Rose Glow'.
SECOND ROW: *Buxus sempervirens; Cotoneaster apiculatus.* THIRD ROW:
Ceanothus 'Concha'. BOTTOM ROW: *Griselinia littoralis; Lavatera thuringiaca*

Picea abies p. 504
Norway spruce
☼ ◑ ✿ A2, A3; 1–6, 14–17

Pinus (many) p. 507
Pine
☼ ✿ ZONES VARY

**Pittosporum (except
P. phillyreoides)** p. 512
☼ ◑ ✿ ZONES VARY

Populus (several) p. 525
Poplar
☼ ✿ ZONES VARY

Prosopis glandulosa p. 530
Honey mesquite
☼ ✿ 10–13, 18–24

Pseudotsuga menziesii p. 537
Douglas fir
☼ ◑ ✿ A2, A3; 1–10, 14–17

Quercus ilex p. 547
Holly oak
☼ ✿ 4–24

Quercus virginiana p. 550
Southern live oak
☼ ✿ 4–24

Sequoia sempervirens p. 601
Redwood
☼ ◑ ✿ 4–9, 14–24

Tamarix p. 623
Tamarisk
☼ ✿ ZONES VARY

Thuja occidentalis p. 627
American arborvitae
☼ ◑ ✿ A2, A3; 1–9, 15–17, 21–24;
H1, H2

Thuja plicata p. 628
Western red cedar
☼ ◑ ✿ A3; 1–9, 14–24

Shrubs

Arbutus unedo p. 164
Strawberry tree
☼ ◑ ✿ 4–24

Arctostaphylos p. 164
Manzanita
☼ ◑ ✿ ZONES VARY

Artemisia p. 169
☼ ✿ ZONES VARY

Baccharis pilularis p. 182
Dwarf coyote brush
☼ ✿ 5–11, 14–24

Berberis p. 193
Barberry
☼ ◑ ✿ ZONES VARY

Buxus p. 208
Boxwood
☼ ◑ ● ✿ ZONES VARY

Callistemon p. 212
Bottlebrush
☼ ✿ ZONES VARY

Caragana arborescens p. 220
Siberian peashrub
☼ ✿ A1–A3; 1–12

Ceanothus p. 226
California wild lilac
☼ ✿ 1–3, 5–9, 14–24

Chamaecyparis p. 234
False cypress
☼ ◑ ✿ ZONES VARY

Cistus p. 244
Rockrose
☼ ✿ 4–9, 14–24

Correa p. 264
Australian fuchsia
☼ ◑ ✿ 14–24

Cotoneaster p. 267
☼ ✿ ZONES VARY

Dodonaea viscosa p. 291
Hop bush
☼ ◑ ✿ 7–24; H1, H2

Elaeagnus p. 298
☼ ◑ ✿ ZONES VARY

Escallonia p. 309
☼ ◑ ✿ 4–9, 14–24

Euonymus japonicus p. 314
Evergreen euonymus
☼ ✿ 4–20; H1

Frangula alnus p. 326
Alder buckthorn
☼ ◑ ✿ 1–7, 10, 11

Griselinia littoralis p. 348
☼ ◑ ✿ 9, 14–17, 20–24

Hakea p. 350
☼ ✿ 9, 12–17, 19–24

Bougainvillea 'Scarlett O'Hara'

Eriogonum umbellatum

Euphorbia characias wulfenii

Sidalcea 'Elsie Heugh'

PLANTS FOR SEACOAST GARDENS

Whipping winds and salt spray are as much a part of the Pacific Coast's marine climates as the mild winters and cool summers. Although gardeners living along the shoreline or on coastal bluffs in the Northwest's Zone 5 or California's Zones 17 and 24 have it easy in most respects, wind, ocean spray, and fog present challenges of their own.

Plants have no escape: they have to tough it out. Even on the breeziest coastlines, though, the plants listed below look fresh and healthy whatever the weather. Large perennials and grasses can sway and shiver in sea breezes, or glow in the setting sun. Shorter plants can be spotted among boulders. To help plants adjust to wind, buy the smallest sizes you can find. Younger plants are better able to bend, rather than break, in the wind.

Agave, Bougainvillea, and *Euryops pectinatus;* Laguna Beach, California

Trees

Casuarina stricta   p. 225
Mountain she-oak
☼ ✿ 8, 9, 12–24; H1, H2

✕ Cuprocyparis   p. 274
☼ ✿ 3B–24

Eucalyptus (some)   p. 311
☼ ✿ ZONES VARY

Juniperus virginiana   p. 389
Eastern red cedar
☼ ◑ ✿ A3; 1–24

Melaleuca quinquenervia   p. 439
Cajeput tree
☼ ✿ 9, 12, 13, 15–17, 20–24; H1, H2

Metrosideros   p. 442
☼ ◑ ✿ ZONES VARY

Myoporum laetum   p. 448
☼ ✿ 8, 9, 14–17, 19–24

Palms   p. 471
NEEDS, ZONES VARY

Pinus (some)   p. 507
Pine
☼ ✿ ZONES VARY

Quercus ilex   p. 547
Holly oak
☼ ✿ 4–24

Shrubs

Arbutus unedo   p. 164
Strawberry tree
☼ ◑ ✿ 4–24

Carissa macrocarpa   p. 222
Natal plum
☼ ◑ ✿ 22–24; H2

Cistus   p. 244
Rockrose
☼ ✿ 4–9, 14–24

Coprosma   p. 258
☼ ◑ ✿ ZONES VARY

Corokia cotoneaster   p. 264
☼ ◑ ✿ 4–24

Correa   p. 264
Australian fuchsia
☼ ◑ ✿ 14–24

Cotoneaster (many)   p. 267
☼ ✿ ZONES VARY

Cytisus   p. 278
Broom
☼ ✿ ZONES VARY

Dodonaea viscosa   p. 291
Hop bush
☼ ◑ ✿ 7–24; H1, H2

Elaeagnus   p. 298
☼ ◑ ✿ ZONES VARY

Escallonia   p. 309
☼ ◑ ✿ 4–9, 14–24

Metrosideros polymorpha

Phoenix canariensis

Cistus ✕ *pulverulentus* 'Sunset'

Coprosma 'Fire Burst'

Perennials

TOP ROW: *Correa pulchella; Cytisus battandieri.* SECOND ROW: *Hebe* 'Red Edge'. THIRD ROW: *Kalanchoe thyrsiflora; Leptospermum scoparium.* BOTTOM ROW: *Protea compacta; Viburnum plicatum tomentosum*

TOP ROW: *Achillea* 'Walther Funcke'; *Aloe arborescens*; *Armeria*. SECOND ROW: *Artemisia schmidtiana* 'Silver Mound'; *Centranthus ruber*. THIRD ROW: *Echeveria* 'Domingo'; *Echium candicans*; *Felicia amelloides*. BOTTOM ROW: *Gazania* hybrid; *Phormium* 'Sunset'

DEER-RESISTANT PLANTS

How mad can you get at a deer—this pretty-eyed creature that represents all the gentle qualities of primeval wilderness? The answer, if you don't know already, is that when you grow a garden and a deer comes in and eats a treasured plant, you can get very angry at him—or most often—her. But, browsing deer don't dine indiscriminately. Some plants, such as roses, are particular favorites, and others, such as grapes, plums, peas, and strawberries, are delicacies. But there are plants that deer leave more or less alone. If you live in deer country, you'll find it far simpler to build your garden around plants less-favored by them than to protect the choicer morsels.

Deer usually ignore the plants listed below, although few are totally deer-proof: deer in different areas may have different tastes, and tastes may vary from year to year.

Young deer grazing on grasses

Trees

Abies p. 124
Fir
☼ ◑ ⚡ ZONES VARY

Acacia p. 125
☼ ⚡ ZONES VARY

Acer p. 128
Maple
☼ ◑ ⚡ ZONES VARY

Agonis flexuosa p. 140
Peppermint tree
☼ ◑ ⚡ 15–17, 20–24

Albizia julibrissin p. 142
Mimosa
☼ ◑ ⚡ 4–23

Callistemon p. 212
Bottlebrush
☼ ⚡ ZONES VARY

Cedrus p. 228
Cedar
☼ ⚡ ZONES VARY

Celtis p. 230
Hackberry
☼ ◑ ⚡ ZONES VARY

Ceratonia siliqua p. 232
Carob
☼ ⚡ 9, 13–16, 18–24; H1

Cercis occidentalis p. 233
Western redbud
☼ ◑ ⚡ 2–24

Chamaecyparis p. 234
False cypress
☼ ◑ ⚡ ZONES VARY

Chilopsis linearis p. 239
Desert willow
☼ ⚡ 3B, 7–14, 18–23

Crataegus p. 269
Hawthorn
☼ ⚡ 2–12, 14–17

Cupressus p. 273
Cypress
☼ ⚡ ZONES VARY

Eucalyptus (some) p. 311
☼ ⚡ ZONES VARY

Fig p. 323
☼ ⚡ 4–9, 11–24; H1, H2

Fraxinus p. 327
Ash
☼ ⚡ ZONES VARY

Ginkgo biloba p. 339
Maidenhair tree
☼ ⚡ A3; 1–10, 12, 14–24

Magnolia p. 427
☼ ◑ ⚡ ZONES VARY

Maytenus boaria p. 437
Mayten
☼ ⚡ 8, 9, 14–24

Melaleuca p. 438
☼ ⚡ ZONES VARY

Olea europaea p. 460
Olive
☼ ⚡ 8, 9, 11–24; H1, H2

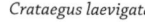

Acacia pravissima

Crataegus laevigata

Quercus palustris

Arctostaphylos uva-ursi

Berberis linearifolia 'Orange King'

Buddleja globosa

Callistemon citrinus

Ceanothus 'Dark Star'

TOP ROW: *Cistus × hybridus*. SECOND ROW: *Correa pulchella; Dodonaea viscosa.*
THIRD ROW: *Hypericum calycinum*. BOTTOM ROW: *Lantana* 'Lucky Pure Gold';
Lavandula angustifolia

Spiraea p. 610
Spirea
☼ ◐ ✎ ZONES VARY

Symphoricarpos p. 620
Snowberry
NEEDS, ZONES VARY

Syringa p. 620
Lilac
☼ ◐ ✎ ZONES VARY

Teucrium p. 626
Germander
☼ ✎ ZONES VARY

Tibouchina urvilleana p. 630
Princess flower
☼ ◐ ✎ 16, 17, 21–24; H1, H2

Trichostema lanatum p. 637
Woolly blue curls
☼ ✎ 14–24

Vaccinium ovatum p. 644
Evergreen huckleberry
☼ ◐ ● ✎ 4–7, 14–17, 22–24

Viburnum p. 648
NEEDS, ZONES VARY

Weigela p. 654
☼ ◐ ✎ 1–11, 14–21

Westringia fruticosa p. 654
Coast rosemary
☼ ✎ 8, 9, 14–24

Groundcovers and Vines

Ajuga p. 141
Carpet bugle
☼ ◐ ✎ A2, A3; 1–24

Arabis p. 162
Rockcress
☼ ✎ ZONES VARY

Bougainvillea p. 200
☼ ✎ 12–17, 19–24; H1, H2

Ceratostigma plumbaginoides p. 232
Dwarf plumbago
☼ ◐ ✎ 2B–10, 14–24

Epimedium p. 302
◐ ✎ 2–9, 14–17

Galium odoratum p. 331
Sweet woodruff
◐ ● ✎ A2, A3; 2–6, 15–17

Gazania p. 334
NEEDS, ZONES VARY

Gelsemium sempervirens p. 335
Carolina jessamine
☼ ◐ ✎ 4–24

Hedera helix p. 354
English ivy
☼ ◐ ✎ 3–24; H1

Hibbertia scandens p. 362
Guinea gold vine
☼ ◐ ✎ 16, 17, 21–24

Jasminum p. 383
Jasmine
☼ ◐ ✎ ZONES VARY

Osteospermum fruticosum p. 467
Trailing African daisy
☼ ✎ 8, 9, 12–24; H1, H2

Pachysandra terminalis p. 469
Japanese spurge
◐ ● ✎ 2–10, 14–21

Scaevola p. 593
☼ ✎ 8, 9, 14–24; H1, H2

Solanum laxum p. 605
Potato vine
☼ ◐ ✎ 8, 9, 12–24; H1, H2

Tecoma capensis p. 625
Cape honeysuckle
☼ ◐ ✎ 12, 13, 20–24; H1, H2

Vinca p. 650
Periwinkle
☼ ◐ ● ✎ ZONES VARY

Wisteria p. 655
NEEDS, ZONES VARY

Perennials and Bulbs

Acanthus mollis p. 128
Bear's breech
☼ ◐ ● ✎ 5–24

Achillea p. 132
Yarrow
☼ ✎ A1–A3; 1–24

TOP ROW: *Leptospermum scoparium; Nandina domestica* 'Fire Power'. SECOND ROW: *Plumbago auriculata; Bougainvillea* 'Barbara Karst'. THIRD ROW: *Galium odoratum.* BOTTOM ROW: *Hedera helix; Scaevola aemula* 'Top Pot Pink'

Aconitum carmichaelii

Aquilegia formosa

Tuberous begonia

Campanula poscharskyana

Aconitum   p. 133
Monkshood
☼ ◑ ✿ A1–A3; 1–9, 14–21

Acorus gramineus   p. 133
Japanese sweet flag
☼ ◑ ✿ 3B–10, 14–24

Agastache   p. 137
☼ ◑ ✿ ZONES VARY

Agave   p. 138
☼ ◑ ✿ ZONES VARY

Alchemilla   p. 142
Lady's-mantle
☼ ◑ ✿ ZONES VARY

Aloe   p. 145
☼ ◑ ✿ 8, 9, 12–24

Anemone   p. 151
Windflower
NEEDS, ZONES VARY

Aquilegia   p. 161
Columbine
☼ ◑ ✿ ZONES VARY

Argyranthemum frutescens   p. 167
Marguerite
☼ ✿ 14–24; H1

Armeria   p. 169
Thrift
☼ ✿ ZONES VARY

Artemisia   p. 169
☼ ✿ ZONES VARY

Asclepias   p. 172
☼ ✿ ZONES VARY

Aster   p. 176
☼ ✿ ZONES VARY

Astilbe   p. 177
False spirea
◐ ● ✿ A2, A3; 1–9, 14–24

Athyrium   p. 178
◐ ● ✿ ZONES VARY

Baptisia   p. 188
False indigo
☼ ✿ 1–24

Begonia, tuberous   p. 192
◐ ✿ 4–9, 14–24; H1

Brachyscome   p. 203
Swan River daisy
☼ ✿ ZONES VARY

Brunnera macrophylla   p. 206
Bugloss
☼ ◑ ✿ 1–24

Calamintha   p. 210
Calamint
☼ ◑ ✿ 1–9, 14–24

Campanula poscharskyana   p. 219
Serbian bellflower
☼ ◑ ✿ 1–12, 14–24

Carex   p. 221
Sedge
☼ ◑ ✿ ZONES VARY

Centaurea   p. 230
☼ ✿ ZONES VARY

Centranthus ruber   p. 231
Jupiter's beard
☼ ◑ ✿ 2–9, 12–24; H1

Cerastium tomentosum   p. 232
Snow-in-summer
☼ ◑ ✿ A1, A2; 1–24

Colchicum   p. 256
Autumn crocus
☼ ✿ 2–10, 14–24

Coreopsis   p. 260
☼ ✿ ZONES VARY

Crocosmia   p. 270
☼ ◑ ✿ ZONES VARY

Crocus   p. 271
☼ ◑ ✿ 1–24

Dahlia   p. 278
☼ ◑ ✿ 1–24

Dicentra   p. 287
Bleeding heart
◐ ● ✿ 1–9, 14–24

Dietes   p. 289
Fortnight lily
☼ ◑ ✿ 8, 9, 12–24; H1, H2

Digitalis   p. 289
Foxglove
NEEDS, ZONES VARY

Dryopteris   p. 293
Wood fern
◐ ● ✿ ZONES VARY

Echinacea purpurea   p. 296
Purple coneflower
☼ ✿ A2, A3; 1–24

Echium candicans   p. 298
Pride of Madeira
☼ ✿ 14–24

Erigeron   p. 305
Fleabane
☼ ◑ ✿ ZONES VARY

Erodium reichardii   p. 307
Cranesbill
☼ ◑ ✿ 7–9, 14–24

Erysimum   p. 308
Wallflower
☼ ◑ ✿ ZONES VARY

Eschscholzia californica   p. 310
California poppy
☼ ✿ 1–24; H1

Euphorbia   p. 315
NEEDS, ZONES VARY

Euryops   p. 317
☼ ✿ ZONES VARY

Felicia amelloides   p. 319
Blue marguerite
☼ ✿ 8, 9, 14–24

Festuca glauca   p. 321
Common blue fescue
☼ ◑ ✿ 1–24

Foeniculum vulgare   p. 324
Common fennel
☼ ✿ ZONES VARY

Freesia   p. 328
☼ ◑ ✿ 8, 9, 12–24

Gaillardia × grandiflora   p. 331
Blanket flower
☼ ✿ 1–24; H1, H2

Galanthus nivalis   p. 331
Common snowdrop
☼ ◑ ✿ 1–9, 14–17

Geranium   p. 336
Cranesbill
☼ ◑ ✿ ZONES VARY

TOP ROW: *Centaurea cyanus*; *Coreopsis rosea* 'Heaven's Gate'. SECOND ROW: *Echinacea* 'Secret Desire'. THIRD ROW: *Dahlia* 'Blown Dry'; *Geranium renardii*. BOTTOM ROW: *Hakonechloa macra* 'Albovariegata'; *Lupinus* Russell hybrid

Phlomis p. 499
☼ ✎ ZONES VARY

Phlox subulata p. 500
Moss pink
☼ ◐ ✎ 1–17

Phormium p. 500
☼ ◐ ✎ 5–9, 14–24; H1, H2

Polypodium p. 523
◐ ● ✎ ZONES VARY

Polystichum p. 524
◐ ● ✎ ZONES VARY

Pulmonaria p. 540
Lungwort
◐ ● ✎ 1–9, 14–17

Rodgersia p. 567
☼ ◐ ✎ 2–9, 14–17

Romneya coulteri p. 567
Matilija poppy
☼ ✎ 4–12, 14–24; H1

Rudbeckia hirta p. 580
Gloriosa daisy
☼ ✎ 1–24

Salvia p. 583
Sage
NEEDS, ZONES VARY

Santolina p. 591
☼ ✎ ZONES VARY

Saxifraga p. 592
Saxifrage
NEEDS, ZONES VARY

Scabiosa (some) p. 592
Pincushion flower
NEEDS, ZONES VARY

Scilla p. 596
Squill
☼ ◐ ✎ ZONES VARY

Sisyrinchium p. 604
☼ ◐ ✎ 4–9, 14–24

Stachys byzantina p. 612
Lamb's ears
☼ ◐ ✎ 1–24

Stipa p. 614
Feather grass
☼ ✎ ZONES VARY

Tagetes lemmonii p. 622
Copper Canyon daisy
☼ ✎ 8–10, 12–24; H1

Thymus p. 629
Thyme
☼ ◐ ✎ ZONES VARY

Tulbaghia violacea p. 640
Society garlic
☼ ✎ 13–24; H1, H2

Verbena p. 646
☼ ✎ ZONES VARY

Veronica p. 647
Speedwell
☼ ✎ ZONES VARY

Viola odorata p. 652
Sweet violet
☼ ◐ ● ✎ 1–24

Zantedeschia p. 658
Calla
☼ ◐ ✎ 5, 6, 8, 9, 12–24; H1, H2

Zauschneria p. 659
California fuchsia
NEEDS, ZONES VARY

Annuals

Catharanthus roseus p. 225
Madagascar periwinkle
☼ ◐ ✎ 1–24; H1, H2

Impatiens p. 373
Balsam
NEEDS, ZONES VARY

Ocimum basilicum p. 458
Basil
☼ ✎ ALL ZONES

TOP ROW: *Monarda didyma* 'Cambridge Scarlet'; *Penstemon* 'Apple Blossom'. SECOND ROW: *Sisyrinchium idahoense bellum*; *Viola odorata*. THIRD ROW: *Tulbaghia violacea* 'Variegata'. BOTTOM ROW: *Zantedeschia*; *Zauschneria californica*; *Ocimum basilicum* 'Purple Ruffles'

GROUNDCOVERS

Lawn is the best-known groundcover, unsurpassed as a surface to walk and play on. But where foot traffic is infrequent, many other plants offer much of a lawn's neatness with far less maintenance. These plants run the gamut of foliage textures and colors, and many are noted for their flowers. You can combine different plants to form a lovely tapestry on a low slope.

Groundcover heights vary from flat to knee-high. Some spread widely by rooting stems or underground runners; others form clumps and require close spacing to achieve a solid cover. Shrubby and vining types spread from individual root systems; space them according to their expected width at maturity. Planted between pavers in a path or patio, groundcovers make a garden appear more lush; they are especially valuable in small gardens, where the proportion of paving to planted areas is often greater.

FROM LEFT: *Dymondia margaretae*, prostrate juniper, *Senecio mandraliscae*, thyme

Walk-on Lawn Substitutes

Achillea millefolium   p. 132
Common yarrow
☼ ✁ A1–A3; 1–24

Ajuga reptans   p. 141
Carpet bugle
☼ ◑ ✁ A2, A3; 1–24

Carex pansa   p. 221
California meadow sedge
☼ ◑ ✁ 7–9, 11–24

Carex texensis   p. 222
Catlin sedge
☼ ◑ ✁ 7–9, 11–24

Chamaemelum nobile   p. 235
Roman chamomile
☼ ◑ ✁ 2–24

Dichondra micrantha   p. 288
☼ ◑ ✁ 8–10, 12–24; H1, H2

Mazus reptans   p. 438
☼ ◑ ✁ 1–9, 14–24

Phyla nodiflora   p. 503
Lippia
☼ ✁ 8–24; H1, H2

Zoysia tenuifolia   p. 661
Korean grass
☼ ◑ ✁ 8, 9, 12–24; H1, H2

For Between Pavers

Ajuga reptans   p. 141
Carpet bugle
☼ ◑ ✁ A2, A3; 1–24

Armeria maritima   p. 169
Sea thrift
☼ ✁ A2, A3; 1–9, 14–24

Bellis perennis   p. 192
English daisy
☼ ◑ ✁ 1–9, 14–24

Campanula portenschlagiana   p. 219
Dalmatian bellflower
☼ ◑ ✁ 2–9, 14–24

Cerastium tomentosum   p. 232
Snow-in-summer
☼ ◑ ✁ A1, A2; 1–24

Chamaemelum nobile   p. 235
Roman chamomile
☼ ◑ ✁ 2–24

Dymondia margaretae   p. 294
☼ ◑ ✁ 15–24

Erodium reichardii   p. 307
Cranesbill
☼ ◑ ✁ 7–9, 14–24

Pratia pedunculata   p. 527
Blue star creeper
☼ ◑ ✁ 4–9, 14–24

Ajuga reptans 'Atropurpurea'

Carex pansa

Chamaemelum nobile

Cerastium tomentosum

Annuals and Perennials

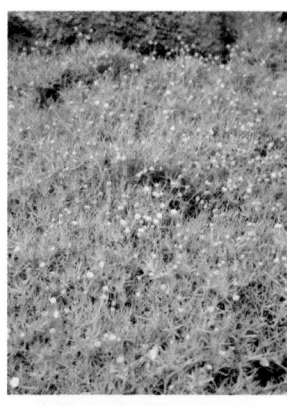

TOP ROW: *Dymondia margaretae*; *Sagina subulata glabrata* 'Aurea'. SECOND ROW: *Soleirolia soleirolii*; *Thymus serpyllum*. THIRD ROW: *Arctotheca calendula*. BOTTOM ROW: *Cephalophyllum* 'Red Spike'; *Diascia integerrima* 'Hardy Twinspur'

TOP ROW: *Convallaria majalis; Galium odoratum.* SECOND ROW: *Epimedium ×
youngianum* 'Niveum'. THIRD ROW: *Geranium dalmaticum; Houttuynia cordata*
'Flore Pleno'. BOTTOM ROW: *Liriope spicata; Osteospermum fruticosum*

TOP ROW: *Persicaria amplexicaulis* 'Inverleith'; *Phlox subulata*. SECOND ROW: *Saxifraga × urbium*. THIRD ROW: *Vinca minor*; *Arctostaphylos uva-ursi*. BOTTOM ROW: *Ceanothus griseus horizontalis* 'Diamond Heights'; *Lonicera japonica* 'Halliana'

PLANTS FOR NEAR POOLS

When you're selecting plants to enhance a swimming pool or spa area, keep several requirements in mind. First, look for ones with smooth branches, foliage, and flowers; avoid anything bristly, prickly, sharp, or thorny, which can injure pool users. Second, choose plants that are litter-free; any leaves or spent flowers they do shed should be too large to pass into the pool's filter (which rules out many conifers). Finally, of course, aim for good-looking plants that will fit into the poolside garden.

For striking effects, add a few plants whose silhouettes can reflect in the pool's still water. Palms are especially good for this, as are many ferns. Closest to the decking around the pool, use low grasses or groundcovers that are soft underfoot (and can take foot traffic).

Tree fern, variegated ginger (*Alpinia*), sago palm, *Ensete ventricosum*

Trees and Shrubs

Aucuba japonica p. 179
Japanese aucuba
◐ ● ✿ 4–24

Bauhinia × blakeana p. 188
Hong Kong orchid tree
☼ ✿ 13, 19, 21, 23, 24; H1, H2

Cordyline p. 259
NEEDS, ZONES VARY

Cycas revoluta p. 275
Sago palm
◐ ✿ 8–24; H1, H2

Ensete ventricosum p. 301
Abyssinian banana
☼ ◐ ✿ 13, 15–24; H1, H2

Eriobotrya deflexa p. 306
Bronze loquat
☼ ◐ ✿ 8–24

Fatsia japonica p. 319
Japanese aralia
◐ ● ✿ 4–9, 14–24; H1, H2

Ferns (tree types) p. 320
NEEDS, ZONES VARY

Fig, edible p. 323
☼ ✿ 4–9, 11–24; H1, H2

Geijera parviflora p. 334
Australian willow
☼ ✿ 8, 9, 12–24

Griselinia p. 348
☼ ◐ ✿ 9, 14–17, 20–24

Hibiscus rosa-sinensis p. 363
Chinese hibiscus
☼ ✿ 9, 12–16, 19–24; H1, H2

Hydrangea macrophylla p. 368
Bigleaf hydrangea
☼ ◐ ✿ 3B–9, 14–24; H1

Lantana p. 398
☼ ✿ 8–10, 12–24; H1, H2

Lavandula p. 401
Lavender
☼ ✿ ZONES VARY

Melianthus major p. 440
Honey bush
☼ ◐ ✿ 8, 9, 12–24; H1, H2

Musa p. 447
Banana
☼ ◐ ✿ ZONES VARY

Palms (some) p. 471
NEEDS, ZONES VARY

Pittosporum tobira 'Wheeler's Dwarf' p. 512
☼ ◐ ✿ 4–24; H1, H2

Plumeria p. 519
Frangipani
☼ ✿ ZONES VARY

Ternstroemia gymnanthera p. 626
◐ ● ✿ 4–9, 12–24

Viburnum davidii p. 648
◐ ✿ 4–9, 14–24

Aucuba japonica 'Picturata'

Cordyline australis 'Torbay Dazzler'

Lantana camara

Mandevilla laxa 'Chilean Jasmine'

TOP ROW: *Aeonium arboreum* 'Zwartkop'; *Alpinia zerumbet* 'Variegata'. SECOND ROW: *Anigozanthos* 'Yellow Gem'; *Limonium perezii*. BOTTOM ROW: *Miscanthus sinensis*; *Scaevola aemula*

PATIO TREES

A good patio tree is well mannered. It doesn't constantly drop leaves, flowers, seedpods, or messy fruit that stains hardscape and furnishings. It doesn't have roots that pry up paving, form sprouts, invade nearby planting beds, or out-compete other plants. And it casts pleasant shade. Patio trees are generally small, as trees go, but their canopies are tall enough to walk under and wide enough to sit under. They reward close viewing of details: flowers, fruit, fall foliage, decorative bark. Patio trees are also fine for garden planting.

While no tree is perfect in every way, the ones listed below come close. Fall is the best time to plant most ornamental trees; cool temperatures and rains are on the way—ideal conditions for getting a new tree established. Wait until spring before planting any tree that is just barely hardy in your area.

Acer palmatum

Deciduous

Acer buergerianum p. 128
Trident maple
☀ ◐ ☘ 2–9, 14–17, 20, 21

Acer circinatum p. 128
Vine maple
☀ ◐ ☘ A3; 2B–6, 14–17

Acer davidii p. 129
David's maple
☀ ◐ ☘ 2–6, 15–17, 20, 21

Acer palmatum p. 129
Japanese maple
☀ ◐ ☘ A3; 2B–10, 12, 14–24

Acer tataricum ginnala p. 132
Amur maple
☀ ◐ ☘ A1–A3; 1–9, 14–16

Amelanchier p. 149
Juneberry
☀ ◐ ☘ ZONES VARY

Bauhinia p. 188
Orchid tree
☀ ☘ ZONES VARY

Cercis p. 233
Redbud
☀ ◐ ☘ ZONES VARY

Chilopsis linearis p. 239
Desert willow
☀ ☘ 3B, 7–14, 18–23

Chionanthus p. 240
Fringe tree
☀ ☘ ZONES VARY

Chorisia speciosa p. 241
Floss silk tree
☀ ☘ 12–24; H1, H2

Cladrastis kentukea p. 251
Yellow wood
☀ ☘ 2–9, 14–16

Cornus florida p. 262
Flowering dogwood
☀ ◐ ☘ 2B–9, 14–16

Cornus kousa p. 263
Kousa dogwood
☀ ◐ ☘ 2–9, 14–17

Corylus (most) p. 265
Filbert, hazelnut
☀ ◐ ☘ 2–9, 14–20

Cotinus coggygria p. 267
Smoke tree
☀ ☘ 2–24

Crataegus p. 269
Hawthorn
☀ ☘ 2–12, 14–17

Erythrina (most) p. 308
Coral tree
☀ ☘ ZONES VARY

Franklinia alatamaha p. 326
☀ ◐ ☘ 3B–6, 14–17

Halesia carolina p. 350
Snowdrop tree
◐ ☘ 2B–9, 14–21

Koelreuteria p. 394
☀ ☘ ZONES VARY

Chilopsis linearis

Erythrina × bidwillii

Halesia carolina

Lagerstroemia indica

Prunus serrulata 'Pink Cloud'

Melaleuca quinquenervia

Podocarpus macrophyllus maki

Schefflera taiwaniana

PLANTS FOR SHADE

Shady spots, whether created by tree canopies, sun-blocking walls, or an overhead structure, are too dark and cool for some garden favorites. But many colorful plants will thrive with less light. They pump out showy flowers or berries; flaunt big, glossy leaves that nearly reflect light; or have foliage of rich plum, golden yellow, or chartreuse that creates sun-splashed effects. Below are stellar shrubs, vines, perennials, bulbs, and annuals for those shady spots.

Keep in mind that there are various kinds of shade. Partial shade may be dappled sunlight filtering through a tree canopy or overhead lath, or it may be cast in an area that gets morning sun but afternoon shade. Full or deep shade is found in parts of the garden that receive little or indirect sunlight, such as beneath tall, dense trees or on the north side of walls.

Brunnera macrophylla 'Jack Frost'

Foliage

Acanthus mollis p. 128
Bear's breech
☼ ◐ ● ✿ 5–24

Acer circinatum p. 128
Vine maple
☼ ◐ ✿ A3; 2B–6, 14–17

Acer palmatum p. 129
Japanese maple
☼ ◐ ✿ A3; 2B–10, 12, 14–24

Alchemilla p. 142
Lady's-mantle
☼ ◐ ✿ ZONES VARY

Aucuba japonica p. 179
Japanese aucuba
◐ ● ✿ 4–24

Caladium bicolor p. 210
Fancy-leafed caladium
◐ ● ✿ H2

Cercis canadensis p. 233
Eastern redbud
◐ ✿ 1–24

Colocasia esculenta p. 257
Taro
◐ ✿ 12, 16–24; H1, H2

Coprosma repens p. 258
Mirror plant
☼ ◐ ✿ 14–24; H1

Euonymus fortunei p. 314
☼ ◐ ● ✿ 2B–17

Fatsia japonica p. 319
Japanese aralia
◐ ● ✿ 4–9, 14–24; H1, H2

Hebe × andersonii 'Variegata' p. 353
☼ ◐ ✿ 14–24

Heuchera (many) p. 361
Coral bells
☼ ◐ ✿ ZONES VARY

× Heucherella (many) p. 362
◐ ✿ 1–10, 14–24

Hosta p. 365
Plantain lily
◐ ● ✿ ZONES VARY

Ilex p. 371
Holly
☼ ◐ ✿ ZONES VARY

Lamium p. 398
Dead nettle
◐ ● ✿ ZONES VARY

Loropetalum chinense p. 422
☼ ◐ ✿ 4–9, 14–24

Pittosporum tobira 'Cream de Mint' p. 512
Tobira
☼ ◐ ✿ 4–24; H1, H2

Plectranthus (some) p. 514
◐ ✿ 22–24; H2

Heuchera 'Georgia Peach'

× Heucherella 'Golden Zebra'

Hosta hybrid

Lamium maculatum

Solenostemon scutellarioides p. 606
Coleus
☼ ◑ ◪ ALL ZONES

Flowers or Berries

Abutilon p. 125
Flowering maple
☼ ◑ ◪ 8, 9, 12–24; H1, H2

Aquilegia p. 161
Columbine
☼ ◑ ◪ ZONES VARY

Arbutus unedo p. 164
Strawberry tree
☼ ◑ ◪ 4–24

Aruncus p. 172
Goat's beard
☼ ◑ ◪ ZONES VARY

Astilbe p. 177
False spirea
☼ ◑ ◪ A2, A3; 1–9, 14–24

Begonia p. 190
◑ ◪ 14–24; H1, H2

Bergenia p. 194
◑ ● ◪ A1–A3; 1–9, 12–24

Brunfelsia pauciflora p. 205
◑ ◪ 12–17, 20–24; H1, H2

Brunnera macrophylla p. 206
Bugloss
◑ ◪ 1–24

Camellia p. 215
◑ ◪ 4–9, 12, 14–24

Cornus p. 262
Dogwood
☼ ◑ ◪ ZONES VARY

Corydalis p. 265
◑ ◪ 2–9, 14–24

Cyclamen p. 275
☼ ◑ ◪ ZONES VARY

Dicentra (most) p. 287
Bleeding heart
◑ ● ◪ 1–9, 14–24

Fuchsia p. 329
☼ ◑ ◪ ZONES VARY

Gardenia jasminoides p. 332
☼ ◑ ◪ 7–9, 12–16, 18–24; H1, H2

Geranium p. 336
Cranesbill
☼ ◑ ◪ ZONES VARY

Helleborus p. 357
Hellebore
◑ ● ◪ ZONES VARY

Hydrangea p. 367
☼ ◑ ◪ ZONES VARY

Impatiens (most) p. 373
Balsam
NEEDS, ZONES VARY

Kalmia latifolia p. 391
Mountain laurel
◑ ◪ 2–7, 16, 17

Mahonia (some) p. 431
NEEDS, ZONES VARY

Myosotis p. 449
Forget-me-not
◑ ◪ A1–A3; 1–24

Pieris p. 505
◑ ◪ ZONES VARY

Primula p. 528
Primrose
☼ ◑ ● ◪ ZONES VARY

Rhododendron p. 556
Rhododendron, azalea
◑ ◪ ZONES VARY

Thalictrum p. 627
Meadow rue
◑ ◪ 2–10, 14–17

Tiarella p. 630
Foamflower
◑ ● ◪ ZONES VARY

Trillium p. 637
Wake robin
◑ ● ◪ ZONES VARY

Viburnum (evergreen) p. 648
☼ ◑ ◪ ZONES VARY

Vinca p. 650
Periwinkle
☼ ◑ ● ◪ ZONES VARY

Viola p. 651
Violet, pansy
☼ ◑ ● ◪ ZONES VARY

TOP ROW: *Bergenia* 'Lunar Glow'; *Cyclamen*. SECOND ROW: *Fuchsia* hybrid; *Hydrangea macrophylla*. THIRD ROW: *Kalmia latifolia* 'Olympic Fire'. BOTTOM ROW: *Rhododendron* 'Klondyke'; Semperflorens begonia

TREES AND SHRUBS FOR CONTAINERS

Annuals, perennials, herbs, and even vegetables are standard choices for container gardening. But larger, woody plants can create real drama in containers. Perhaps you want a tall, striking accent for the patio; a weeping atlas cedar or willowy, dark-leafed peppermint tree in a soft brown pot might be just the ticket. Maybe you long to grow a favorite camellia but have no available ground for planting; a container provides that ground. Perhaps you have your mind set on harvesting fresh lemons from your own tree, but the climate is too chilly in winter to permit its survival outdoors. Grow it anyway, in a large pot that you move to a protected spot in winter. If you consider yourself an artist at heart, with plants as your medium, large containers offer the chance to mix tall shrubs and trailers for color and texture.

Agonis flexuosa 'Jervis Bay Afterdark' (rear), *Heuchera, Grevillea*

Trees

Acer japonicum p. 129
Fullmoon maple
☼ ◑ ⚡ 2–6, 14–16

Acer palmatum p. 129
Japanese maple
☼ ◑ ⚡ A3; 2B–10, 12, 14–24

Agonis flexuosa p. 140
Peppermint tree
☼ ◑ ⚡ 15–17, 20–24

Apple (dwarf) p. 160
☼ ⚡ ZONES VARY

Cedrus atlantica 'Pendula' p. 228
Weeping atlas cedar
☼ ⚡ 3B–10, 14–24

Citrus p. 245
☼ ⚡ 8, 9, 12–24; H1, H2

Fig, edible p. 323
☼ ⚡ 4–9, 11–24; H1, H2

Pinus (several) p. 507
Pine
☼ ⚡ ZONES VARY

Wisteria (trained as tree) p. 655
☼ ◑ ⚡ ZONES VARY

Shrubs

Abutilon p. 125
Flowering maple
☼ ◑ ⚡ 8, 9, 12–24; H1, H2

Arbutus unedo (small) p. 164
Strawberry tree
☼ ◑ ⚡ 4–24

Berberis thunbergii p. 193
Japanese barberry
☼ ◑ ⚡ A3; 2B–24

Bougainvillea (shrubby types) p. 200
☼ ⚡ 12–17, 19–24; H1, H2

Brugmansia p. 205
Angel's trumpet
☼ ◑ ● ⚡ 12, 13, 16–24; H1, H2

Brunfelsia pauciflora p. 205
◑ ⚡ 12–17, 20–24; H1, H2

Buxus p. 208
Boxwood
☼ ◑ ● ⚡ ZONES VARY

Camellia p. 215
◑ ⚡ 4–9, 12, 14–24

Choisya ternata p. 241
Mexican orange
☼ ◑ ⚡ 4–9, 14–24

Corokia cotoneaster p. 264
☼ ◑ ⚡ 4–24

Correa p. 264
Australian fuchsia
☼ ◑ ⚡ 14–24

Acer palmatum

Citrus, 'Dancy' tangerines

Correa alba

Corylus avellana 'Contorta'

TOP ROW: *Enkianthus campanulatus*; *Fuchsia* hybrid. SECOND ROW: *Hydrangea macrophylla*; *Justicia brandegeeana*. THIRD ROW: *Picea glauca*. BOTTOM ROW: *Melianthus major*; *Sollya heterophylla*

PLANTS FOR BENEATH OAKS

The West is home to many centuries-old native oaks that are valued for their majestic beauty. Unfortunately, these same oaks have suffered the consequences of development and inappropriate watering and landscaping around them. The following list will help you select plants that don't demand lots of water, so are suitable for planting beneath these grand trees. Some are sun lovers that will tolerate filtered light around the canopy edges.

A few cautions: Do not plant, irrigate, or disturb the soil within 10 feet of the trunk, and avoid injuring the roots. Plant sparingly; use drip irrigation or soaker hoses, not sprinklers. Avoid areas under declining oaks, and allow trees that have suffered construction damage several years to recover before planting under them. Leave fallen foliage as mulch. Keep lawn outside the drip line.

Quercus agrifolia with *Geranium* × *cantabrigiense* and grasses

Shrubs

Arctostaphylos   p. 165
Manzanita
☼ ◐ ✿ ZONES VARY

Carpenteria californica   p. 222
Bush anemone
☼ ◐ ✿ 5–9, 14–24

Ceanothus   p. 226
California wild lilac
☼ ✿ 1–3, 5–9, 14–24

Cistus   p. 244
Rockrose
☼ ✿ 4–9, 14–24

Eriogonum   p. 306
Wild buckwheat
☼ ✿ ZONES VARY

Frangula californica   p. 326
Coffeeberry
◐ ◑ ✿ 3A–10, 14–24; H1, H2

Galvezia speciosa   p. 332
Island snapdragon
☼ ◐ ✿ 14–24

Geranium   p. 336
Cranesbill
☼ ◐ ✿ ZONES VARY

Grevillea rosmarinifolia   p. 348
Rosemary grevillea
☼ ◐ ✿ 8, 9, 12–24

Heteromeles arbutifolia   p. 360
Toyon
☼ ◐ ✿ 5–9, 14–24

Holodiscus discolor   p. 364
Ocean spray
◐ ✿ 1–9, 14–19

Mahonia   p. 431
NEEDS, ZONES VARY

Myrtus communis   p. 450
Myrtle
☼ ◐ ✿ 8–24; H1, H2

Plumbago auriculata   p. 519
Cape plumbago
☼ ◐ ✿ 8, 9, 12–24; H1, H2

Rhus integrifolia   p. 565
Lemonade berry
☼ ✿ 8, 9, 14–17, 19–24

Rhus ovata   p. 565
☼ ✿ 9–12, 14–24

Ribes   p. 566
Currant, gooseberry
☼ ◐ ✿ ZONES VARY

Symphoricarpos albus   p. 620
Common snowberry
☼ ◐ ✿ A3; 1–11, 14–21

Teucrium   p. 626
Germander
☼ ✿ ZONES VARY

Viburnum tinus   p. 650
Laurustinus
☼ ◐ ✿ 4–10, 12–24

Arctostaphylos edmundsii

Carpenteria californica 'Elizabeth'

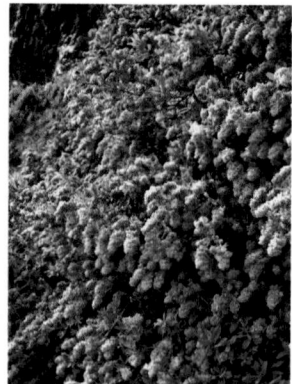

Ceanothus thyrsiflorus

Ribes sanguineum

Groundcovers

Perennials

TOP ROW: *Viburnum tinus* 'Spring Bouquet'. SECOND ROW: *Juniperus sabina* 'Tamariscifolia'; *Mahonia repens*. THIRD ROW: *Erigeron karvinskianus*; *Origanum dictamnus*. BOTTOM ROW: *Polystichum munitum*; *Zauschneria californica*

PLANTS FOR WATERWISE GARDENS

In most parts of the West, where a short rainy season is followed by many months during which there is no rainfall at all, gardeners recognize that they must carefully manage their use of supplemental water for their plants. Some municipalities place limits on supplemental watering, especially during drought years. Fortunately, many fine plants are both good-looking and well suited to the West's dry summers. Some have naturally deep roots that can reach water reserves far down. Others have hairy leaves that help reduce water loss. Although their moisture needs vary slightly—depending on climate, exposure, and soil type—most thrive with little or no irrigation once established. If you're planning a new garden, consider landscaping entirely with unthirsty plants. If you're renovating an old one, modify it in stages.

Artemisia, kangaroo paw (*Anigozanthos*), lavender, *Euphorbia characias*

Trees

Acacia (many)　p. 125
☼ ⚡ ZONES VARY

Arbutus　p. 163
☼ ⚡ ZONES VARY

Brachychiton　p. 202
☼ ⚡ ZONES VARY

Calocedrus decurrens　p. 214
Incense cedar
☼ ◐ ⚡ 2–12, 14–24

Casuarina　p. 225
Beefwood
☼ ⚡ 8, 9, 12–24; H1, H2

Cedrus　p. 228
Cedar
☼ ⚡ ZONES VARY

Celtis　p. 230
Hackberry
☼ ◐ ⚡ ZONES VARY

Ceratonia siliqua　p. 232
Carob
☼ ⚡ 9, 13–16, 18–24; H1

Chilopsis linearis　p. 239
Desert willow
☼ ⚡ 3B, 7–14, 18–23

× Chitalpa tashkentensis　p. 240
☼ ⚡ 3–24

Cupressus　p. 273
Cypress
☼ ⚡ ZONES VARY

Elaeagnus angustifolia　p. 299
Russian olive
☼ ◐ ⚡ A2, A3; 1–3, 7–14, 18, 19

Eucalyptus (most)　p. 311
☼ ⚡ 5, 6, 8–24; H1, H2

Geijera parviflora　p. 334
Australian willow
☼ ⚡ 8, 9, 12–24

Grevillea　p. 347
☼ ◐ ⚡ ZONES VARY

Lagerstroemia indica　p. 396
Crape myrtle
☼ ⚡ 2–10, 12–24; H1, H2

Laurus nobilis　p. 401
Sweet bay
☼ ◐ ⚡ 5–9, 12–24; H1, H2

Lophostemon confertus　p. 422
Brisbane box
☼ ⚡ 15–17, 19–24; H1, H2

Olea europaea　p. 460
Olive
☼ ⚡ 8, 9, 11–24; H1, H2

Olneya tesota　p. 460
Desert ironwood
☼ ⚡ 8, 9, 11–14, 18–23

Parkinsonia aculeata　p. 475
Jerusalem thorn
☼ ⚡ 8–24; H1, H2

Acacia cultriformis

Arbutus unedo

Chilopsis linearis

Grevillea 'Superb'

TOP ROW: *Lagerstroemia indica*; *Olea europaea*. SECOND ROW: *Styphnolobium japonicum*; *Anisodontea* × *hypomadara*. THIRD ROW: *Calliandra californica*. BOTTOM ROW: *Coprosma* 'Marble Queen'; *Euryops acraeus*

TOP ROW: *Fallugia paradoxa*; *Feijoa sellowiana*. SECOND ROW: *Leonotis leonurus*.
THIRD ROW: *Plumbago auriculata*; *Rosmarinus officinalis* 'Majorca Pink'. BOTTOM
ROW: *Salvia leucantha*; *Arctotheca calendula*

Thymus serpyllum

Wisteria

Agave 'Blue Flame'

Dasylirion wheeleri

Groundcovers and Vines

Euphorbia characias wulfenii

Linum grandiflorum

Narcissus 'Mount Hood'

Stachys byzantina

Annuals, Bulbs, and Perennials

PLANTS FOR DAMP AREAS

Whether you're gardening around a pond or stream, or just deciding how best to deal with a patch of perpetually boggy ground, making the best plant choices can be challenging. Constantly saturated soils lack the air that most plants need for good growth—the reason why not just any plant will grow in a swamp. Rain gardens, on the other hand, alternate between wet and dry. Rainwater is channeled from downspouts to these depressions in the ground, where it can percolate into the soil (which cleanses it of pollutants) instead of running off into streets and streams.

These two pages list the best choices for plants that take soggy soil, those that need the constant moisture found in nature beside a pool or brook, and those for rainscaping. (For more on rain gardens, see page 718.)

Scotch moss, *Acorus gramineus*, *Canna*, *Iris ensata*, *Cyperus alternifolius*, water hyacinth

Damp Soil or Shallow Water

Acorus   p. 133
Sweet flag
☼ ◑ ✿ ZONES VARY

Carex elata 'Aurea'   p. 221
Sedge
☼ ◑ ✿ 2–9, 14–19, 22

Chondropetalum elephantinum   p. 241
Cape rush
☼ ◑ ✿ 8, 9, 14–24

Colocasia esculenta   p. 257
Taro
✿ 12, 16–24; H1, H2

Cyperus   p. 277
☼ ◑ ● ✿ ZONES VARY

Equisetum hyemale   p. 302
Horsetail
☼ ◑ ✿ 1–24

Iris, Japanese   p. 379
☼ ✿ 1–10, 14–24

Iris laevigata   p. 380
☼ ✿ 1–10, 14–24

Iris, Louisiana   p. 379
☼ ◑ ✿ 3–24; H1, H2

Iris pseudacorus   p. 381
Yellow flag
☼ ◑ ✿ A2, A3; 1–24

Juncus   p. 386
Rush
☼ ◑ ✿ ZONES VARY

Osmunda regalis   p. 466
Royal fern
☼ ◑ ✿ 1–9, 14–17

Primula florindae   p. 528
☼ ◑ ● ✿ A2, A3; 3–6, 15–17

Primula japonica   p. 528
☼ ◑ ● ✿ A3; 2–6, 15–17

Schoenoplectus lacustris tabernaemontani 'Zebrinus'   p. 596
Zebra rush
☼ ◑ ✿ 5–24

Damp Soil Only

Aconitum   p. 133
Aconite
☼ ◑ ✿ A1–A3; 1–9, 14–21

Alocasia   p. 145
Elephant's ear
◑ ✿ 22–24; H1, H2

Athyrium   p. 178
◑ ● ✿ ZONES VARY

Darmera peltata   p. 281
Umbrella plant
◑ ✿ 2–7, 14–20

Farfugium japonicum   p. 318
◑ ● ✿ 4–10, 14–24; H1, H2

Colocasia esculenta 'Black Magic'

Cyperus papyrus

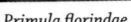

Primula florindae

Iris ensata

TOP ROW: *Filipendula rubra; Gunnera.* SECOND ROW: *Ligularia przewalskii;*
Dicentra formosa. THIRD ROW: *Iris versicolor; Matteuccia struthiopteris.*
BOTTOM ROW: *Mimulus cardinalis*

Filipendula (most) p. 323
Meadowsweet
☀ ◑ ● ⚡ ZONES VARY

Gunnera p. 349
◑ ⚡ 4–6, 14–17, 20–24

Hosta p. 365
Plantain lily
◑ ● ⚡ ZONES VARY

Houttuynia cordata p. 366
☀ ◑ ● ⚡ 2–9, 14–24

Iris setosa p. 381
☀ ⚡ A1–A3; 1–6

Iris, Siberian p. 380
☀ ◑ ⚡ A2, A3; 1–10, 14–23

Isolepis cernua p. 382
Fiber optics plant
◑ ⚡ 7–24

Ligularia p. 411
◑ ⚡ 1–9, 14–17

Lysimachia p. 425
☀ ◑ ⚡ ZONES VARY

**Milium effusum
'Aureum'** p. 443
Bowles' golden grass
◑ ⚡ 3B–9, 14–17

Molinia caerulea p. 444
Moor grass
☀ ◑ ⚡ 1–9, 14–17

Myosotis p. 449
Forget-me-not
◑ ⚡ A1–A3; 1–24

**Phalaris arundinacea
picta** p. 497
Ribbon grass
☀ ◑ ⚡ A1–A3; 1–10, 14–24

Rheum p. 556
Ornamental rhubarb
☀ ◑ ⚡ 2B–7, 14–17

Rodgersia p. 567
☀ ◑ ⚡ 2–9, 14–17

Trollius p. 639
Globeflower
☀ ◑ ⚡ A2, A3; 1–6

Woodwardia fimbriata p. 656
Giant chain fern
◑ ● ⚡ 2B, 4–9, 14–24

**Zantedeschia
aethiopica** p. 658
Common calla
☀ ◑ ⚡ 5, 6, 8, 9, 12–24; H1, H2

Plants Suitable
for Rain
Gardens

Achillea millefolium p. 132
Common yarrow
☀ ⚡ A1–A3; 1–24

Adiantum pedatum p. 134
American maidenhair fern
◑ ● ⚡ A3; 1–7, 14–17

Aquilegia formosa p. 162
Western columbine
☀ ◑ ⚡ A1–A3; 1–11, 14–24

Carex (many) p. 221
Sedge
☀ ◑ ⚡ ZONES VARY

**Deschampsia
cespitosa** p. 284
Tufted hair grass
☀ ◑ ⚡ ZONES VARY

Dicentra formosa p. 287
Western bleeding heart
◑ ● ⚡ 1–9, 14–24

Gaultheria shallon p. 333
Salal
◑ ⚡ 4–7, 14–17

Geranium (several) p. 336
NEEDS, ZONES VARY

Iris versicolor p. 381
Blue flag
☀ ◑ ⚡ 1–9, 14–17

Lobelia (some) p. 419
NEEDS, ZONES VARY

**Matteuccia
struthiopteris** p. 437
Ostrich fern
☀ ◑ ● ⚡ A1–A3; 1–10, 14–17

Mimulus cardinalis p. 443
Scarlet monkey flower
☀ ◑ ● ⚡ 2–24

Panicum virgatum p. 472
Switch grass
☀ ◑ ⚡ 1–11, 14–23

WESTERN NATIVES

Regional natives are wise additions to the garden. Naturally suited to the climate where you live, they typically need little or no irrigation, fertilizer, or pruning. Most have developed resistance to pests and diseases; many also attract birds and butterflies. On these pages, we list native plants for six Western regions: Alaska, the Pacific Northwest, the Rocky Mountain areas, California, the Southwest, and the Hawaiian Islands. For more on native plant gardens, see pages 684–685.

Garden centers sell many popular native plants, such as California lilacs and manzanitas. Native plant specialty nurseries offer even better selections, as do plant sales put on by botanical gardens and local native plant societies. If you start with nursery-raised plants, remember that even drought-tolerant natives need dry-season watering for a year or two. Plant in fall, when temperatures are cooling and rains are soon to come.

Lupines near Jackson, Wyoming

Alaska, Trees and Shrubs

Abies lasiocarpa p. 125
Alpine fir
☼ ◑ ✿ A2, A3; 1–9, 14–17

Amelanchier alnifolia p. 149
Saskatoon
☼ ◑ ✿ A1–A3; 1–6

Cornus sericea p. 263
Redtwig dogwood
☼ ◑ ✿ A1–A3; 1–9, 14–21

Elaeagnus commutata p. 299
Silverberry
☼ ◑ ✿ A1–A3; 1–3

Picea glauca p. 504
White spruce
☼ ◑ ✿ A1–A3; 1–7, 14–17

Populus tremuloides p. 525
Quaking aspen
☼ ✿ A1–A3; 1–7, 14–19

Rosa nutkana p. 577
Nootka rose
☼ ◑ ✿ A1–A3; 1–11, 14–21

Tsuga heterophylla p. 639
Western hemlock
☼ ◑ ✿ A2, A3; 2–7, 14–17

Viburnum edule p. 648
Highbush cranberry
☼ ◑ ✿ A1–A3; 1–11

Alaska, Groundcovers and Perennials

Aquilegia formosa p. 162
Western columbine
☼ ◑ ✿ A1–A3; 1–11, 14–24

Arctanthemum arcticum p. 164
Arctic daisy
☼ ✿ A1–A3; 1–10, 14–21

Arctostaphylos uva-ursi p. 166
Kinnikinnick
☼ ◑ ✿ A1–A3; 1–9, 14–24

Aruncus dioicus p. 172
☼ ◑ ✿ A2, A3; 1–9, 14–17

Chamerion angustifolium p. 236
Fireweed
☼ ✿ A1–A3; 1–7, 14–21

Cornus canadensis p. 262
Bunchberry
◑ ● ✿ A1–A3; 1–9, 14–16

Galium boreale p. 331
Northern bedstraw
◑ ● ✿ A1–A3; 1–6, 15–17

Iris setosa p. 381
☼ ✿ A1–A3; 1–6

Juniperus communis 'Alpine Carpet' p. 387
☼ ◑ ✿ A2–A3; 1–24

Amelanchier alnifolia

Populus tremuloides

Aruncus dioicus 'Kneiffii'

Cornus canadensis

Matteuccia struthiopteris   p. 437
Ostrich fern
☼ ◑ ● ✂ A1–A3; 1–10, 14–17

Polemonium pulcherrimum   p. 522
◑ ● ✂ A1–A3; 1–11, 14–17; H1

Rubus arcticus 'Kenai Carpet'   p. 579
Nagoonberry
☼ ◑ ✂ A1–A3; 1–3

Pacific Northwest, Trees

Abies (several)   p. 124
Fir
☼ ◑ ✂ ZONES VARY

Acer circinatum   p. 128
Vine maple
☼ ◑ ✂ A3; 2B–6, 14–17

Acer macrophyllum   p. 129
Bigleaf maple
☼ ◑ ✂ 2–9, 14–24

Alnus rhombifolia   p. 145
White alder
☼ ◑ ● ✂ 1B–10, 14–21

Alnus rubra   p. 145
Red alder
☼ ◑ ● ✂ 3–7, 14–17

Arbutus menziesii   p. 163
Madrone
☼ ✂ 4–7, 14–19

Cornus nuttallii   p. 263
Pacific dogwood
☼ ◑ ✂ 3B–9, 14–20

Larix occidentalis   p. 399
Western larch
☼ ✂ A3; 1–7

Pinus contorta   p. 507
Shore pine
☼ ✂ A3; 4–9, 14–24; H1

Pinus ponderosa   p. 510
Ponderosa pine
☼ ✂ 1–10, 14–21; H1

Pseudotsuga menziesii   p. 537
Douglas fir
☼ ◑ ✂ A2, A3; 1–10, 14–17

Quercus garryana   p. 547
Oregon white oak
☼ ✂ 2A–11, 14–23

Thuja plicata   p. 628
Western red cedar
☼ ◑ ✂ A3; 1–9, 14–24

Tsuga heterophylla   p. 639
Western hemlock
☼ ◑ ✂ A2, A3; 2–7, 14–17

Tsuga mertensiana   p. 639
Mountain hemlock
☼ ◑ ✂ A1–A3; 1–7, 14–17

Xanthocyparis nootkatensis   p. 656
Alaska cedar
☼ ◑ ✂ A2, A3; 2–6, 15–17

Pacific Northwest, Shrubs

Acer glabrum   p. 129
Rocky Mountain maple
☼ ◑ ✂ A2, A3; 1–7, 10

Amelanchier alnifolia   p. 149
Saskatoon
☼ ◑ ✂ A1–A3; 1–6

Arctostaphylos columbiana   p. 165
Hairy manzanita
☼ ◑ ✂ 4–6, 15–17

Cornus sericea   p. 263
Redtwig dogwood
☼ ◑ ✂ A1–A3; 1–9, 14–21

Corylus cornuta californica   p. 266
Western hazelnut
☼ ◑ ✂ 2–9, 14–20

Gaultheria shallon   p. 333
Salal
◑ ✂ 4–7, 14–17

Holodiscus discolor   p. 364
Cream bush
◑ ✂ 1–9, 14–19

Kalmia polifolia microphylla   p. 391
Western laurel
☼ ◑ ✂ A2, A3; 1–7, 16, 17

TOP ROW: *Alnus rhombifolia; Alnus rubra.* SECOND ROW: *Larix occidentalis; Gaultheria shallon.* THIRD ROW: *Kalmia polifolia microphylla; Oemleria cerasiformis.* BOTTOM ROW: *Physocarpus capitatus; Potentilla fruticosa* 'Coronation Triumph'

Adiantum aleuticum

Fragaria chiloensis

Fritillaria camschatcensis

Lilium columbianum

Abies concolor 'Candicans'

Picea pungens 'Hoopsii'

Cercocarpus ledifolius

Rhus glabra

TOP ROW: *Callirhoe involucrata*; *Geum triflorum*. SECOND ROW: *Iris missouriensis*; *Sphaeralcea munroana*. THIRD ROW: *Acer circinatum*. BOTTOM ROW: *Chamaecyparis lawsoniana* 'Nana Lutea'; *Washingtonia filifera*

TOP ROW: *Carpenteria californica*; *Baccharis pilularis*. SECOND ROW: *Galvezia speciosa*. THIRD ROW: *Eriogonum umbellatum* 'Shasta Sulfur'; *Myrica californica*. BOTTOM ROW: *Rhododendron occidentale*; *Ribes sanguineum*

Lithocarpus densiflorus p. 418
Tanbark oak
☼ ◗ ✀ 4–7, 14–24

Lyonothamnus floribundus p. 424
Catalina ironwood
☼ ✀ 14–17, 19–24

Picea breweriana p. 504
Brewer's weeping spruce
☼ ◗ ✀ 2B–7, 14–17

Pinus (several) p. 507
Pine
☼ ✀ ZONES VARY

Platanus racemosa p. 513
California sycamore
☼ ✀ 4–24

Populus (several) p. 525
Poplar
☼ ✀ ZONES VARY

Quercus (many) p. 544
Oak
☼ ✀ ZONES VARY

Sequoia sempervirens p. 601
Redwood
☼ ◗ ✀ 4–9, 14–24

Umbellularia californica p. 643
California laurel
☼ ◗ ● ✀ 4–9, 14–24

Washingtonia filifera p. 653
California fan palm
☼ ✀ 8–24; H1, H2

California, Shrubs

Arctostaphylos (many) p. 164
Manzanita
☼ ◗ ✀ ZONES VARY

Baccharis pilularis p. 182
Dwarf coyote brush
☼ ✀ 5–11, 14–24

Calycanthus occidentalis p. 214
Spice bush
☼ ◗ ● ✀ 4–9, 14–24

Carpenteria californica p. 222
Bush anemone
☼ ◗ ✀ 5–9, 14–24

Ceanothus (many) p. 226
California wild lilac
☼ ✀ 1–3, 5–9, 14–24

Cercis occidentalis p. 233
Western redbud
☼ ◗ ✀ 2–24

Cercocarpus betuloides p. 233
Hardtack
☼ ✀ 3, 5, 7–10, 13–24

Comarostaphylis diversifolia p. 257
Summer holly
☼ ◗ ✀ 7–9, 14–24

Dendromecon p. 284
Bush poppy
☼ ✀ ZONES VARY

Encelia californica p. 300
☼ ✀ 7–16, 18–24

Eriogonum (many) p. 306
Wild buckwheat
☼ ✀ ZONES VARY

Eriophyllum nevinii 'Canyon Silver' p. 307
Woolly sunflower
☼ ✀ 15–17, 19–24

Frangula californica p. 326
Coffeeberry
☼ ◗ ✀ 3A–10, 14–24; H1, H2

Fremontodendron californicum p. 328
Common flannel bush
☼ ✀ 4–24

Galvezia speciosa p. 332
Island snapdragon
☼ ◗ ✀ 14–24

Garrya p. 333
Silktassel
☼ ◗ ✀ ZONES VARY

Heteromeles arbutifolia p. 360
Toyon
☼ ◗ ✀ 5–9, 14–24

Lavatera assurgentiflora p. 404
Tree mallow
☼ ✀ 14–24

Lepechinia (some) p. 405
Pitcher sage
☼ ✀ 7–9, 14–24

Eschscholzia californica

Maianthemum bifolium kamtschaticum

Mimulus aurantiacus

Oxalis oregana 'Rosea'

Lupinus arboreus p. 423
Lupine
☼ ✂ 4, 5, 14–17, 22–24

Mahonia (several) p. 431
NEEDS, ZONES VARY

Myrica californica p. 449
Pacific wax myrtle
☼ ✂ 4–9, 14–24

Philadelphus lewisii p. 498
Wild mock orange
☼ ◑ ✂ 1–10, 14–24

Physocarpus capitatus p. 503
Pacific ninebark
☼ ◑ ● ✂ 2B–9, 14–19

Prunus ilicifolia p. 531
☼ ✂ 5–9, 12–24

Quercus vacciniifolia p. 550
Huckleberry oak
☼ ✂ 1–7, 14–23

Rhododendron occidentale p. 563
Western azalea
◑ ✂ 4–7, 14–17, 19–24

Rhus integrifolia p. 565
Lemonade berry
☼ ✂ 8, 9, 14–17, 19–24

Rhus ovata p. 565
☼ ✂ 9–12, 14–24

Ribes (several) p. 566
Currant
☼ ◑ ✂ ZONES VARY

Salvia (several) p. 583
Sage
NEEDS, ZONES VARY

Sambucus nigra caerulea p. 590
Blue elderberry
☼ ◑ ✂ 2–24; H1

Symphoricarpos albus p. 620
Common snowberry
☼ ◑ ✂ A3; 1–11, 14–21

Symphoricarpos mollis p. 620
Creeping snowberry
◑ ✂ 2–10, 14–24

Trichostema lanatum p. 637
Woolly blue curls
☼ ✂ 14–24

Vaccinium ovatum p. 644
Evergreen huckleberry
☼ ◑ ● ✂ 4–7, 14–17, 22–24

Vaccinium parvifolium p. 644
Red huckleberry
◑ ● ✂ A3; 2–7, 14–17

California, Groundcovers, Vines, and Perennials

Aquilegia formosa p. 162
Western columbine
☼ ◑ ✂ A1–A3; 1–11, 14–24

Aralia californica p. 163
Elk clover
◑ ● ✂ 4–10, 14–24

Arctostaphylos (several) p. 164
Manzanita
☼ ◑ ✂ ZONES VARY

Aristolochia californica p. 168
California Dutchman's pipe
☼ ◑ ✂ 5–10, 14–24

Artemisia californica p. 170
California sagebrush
☼ ✂ 7–9, 14–24

Artemisia pycnocephala p. 170
Sandhill sage
☼ ✂ 4, 5, 7–9, 14–17, 19–24

Asarum caudatum p. 172
◑ ● ✂ 4–6, 14–24

Atriplex lentiformis breweri p. 179
☼ ✂ 8, 9, 12–24

Carex barbarae p. 221
Santa Barbara sedge
☼ ◑ ✂ 4–9, 14–24

Carex pansa p. 221
California meadow sedge
☼ ◑ ✂ 7–9, 11–24

Ceanothus (many) p. 226
California wild lilac
☼ ✂ 1–3, 5–9, 14–24

Dicentra chrysantha p. 287
Golden eardrops
◑ ● ✂ 1–9, 14–24

Dicentra formosa p. 287
Western bleeding heart
◑ ● ✂ 1–9, 14–24

Dudleya p. 294
☼ ✂ ZONES VARY

Erigeron glaucus p. 305
Beach aster
☼ ◑ ✂ 4–6, 15–17, 22–24

Erythronium (several) p. 309
◑ ✂ ZONES VARY

Eschscholzia californica p. 310
California poppy
☼ ✂ 1–24; H1

Festuca californica p. 321
California fescue
☼ ◑ ✂ 4–9, 14–24

Fragaria chiloensis p. 325
Beach strawberry
☼ ◑ ✂ 4–24; H1

Heuchera maxima p. 362
Island alum root
☼ ◑ ✂ 15–24

Heuchera micrantha p. 362
☼ ◑ ✂ 1–10, 14–24

Iris, Pacific Coast p. 379
☼ ◑ ✂ 4–9, 14–24

Juncus patens p. 386
California gray rush
☼ ◑ ✂ 4–9, 14–24

Lewisia cotyledon p. 409
Cliff maids
☼ ◑ ✂ 1–7, 14–17

Leymus condensatus p. 410
Lyme grass
☼ ◑ ✂ 7–12, 14–24

Lilium humboldtii p. 413
Humboldt lily
☼ ◑ ✂ 3, 7, 14–24

Lilium pardalinum p. 414
Leopard lily
☼ ◑ ✂ 2–7, 14–17

Penstemon heterophyllus

Tellima grandiflora

Platanus wrightii

Calliandra californica

Southwest, Groundcovers and Perennials

TOP ROW: *Chrysothamnus nauseosus.* SECOND ROW: *Simmondsia chinensis; Sophora secundiflora.* THIRD ROW: *Calylophus hartwegii fendleri.* BOTTOM ROW: *Ratibida columnifera; Verbena bipinnatifida*

TOP ROW: *Muhlenbergia rigens; Opuntia ficus-indica.* SECOND ROW: *Cibotium glaucum; Gossypium tomentosum.* THIRD ROW: *Metrosideros polymorpha; Pritchardia hillebrandii.* BOTTOM ROW: *Sida fallax*

SHADE TREES

The perfect shade tree has a canopy that's dense enough to block out some or all sunlight during the hottest part of the day, spreading enough to shade outdoor living spaces, whole yards, or—when grouped—parks and city streets. Tall enough to sit or stand under, it can be evergreen or deciduous. But the best trees for saving energy are deciduous; plant these near your home's south- or west-facing windows and they'll cool the house in summer, then lose their leaves in winter to allow warming sun through your windows. For details on placing these trees for energy savings, see pages 696–697.

When you shop for a tree, consider how well it will suit its intended location. Because garden size is a crucial determinant, the trees in the list below are grouped in two size categories: Small to Medium, and Large.

Grand old sycamores cool a Sacramento home.

Small to Medium Trees
(UP TO 35 FT.)

Acacia smallii   p. 127
☼ ✿ 8, 9, 12–24

Acer circinatum   p. 128
Vine maple
☼ ◑ ✿ A3; 2B–6, 14–17

Acer griseum   p. 129
Paperbark maple
☼ ◑ ✿ 2–9, 14–21

Acer palmatum   p. 129
Japanese maple
☼ ◑ ✿ A3; 2B–10, 12, 14–24

Carpinus caroliniana   p. 223
American hornbeam
☼ ◑ ● ✿ 1–9, 14–17

Celtis reticulata   p. 230
Western hackberry
☼ ◑ ✿ 2, 3, 7–13, 18–21

Chilopsis linearis   p. 239
Desert willow
☼ ✿ 3B, 7–14, 18–23

Elaeagnus angustifolia   p. 299
Russian olive
☼ ◑ ✿ A2, A3; 1–3, 7–14, 18, 19

Erythrina (some)   p. 308
Coral tree
☼ ✿ ZONES VARY

Fraxinus (several)   p. 327
Ash
☼ ✿ ZONES VARY

Gleditsia triacanthos   p. 340
Honey locust
☼ ✿ 1–16, 18–20

Laburnum   p. 395
Goldenchain tree
☼ ◑ ✿ 1–10, 14–17

Lagerstroemia indica   p. 396
Crape myrtle
☼ ✿ 4, 5, 7–10, 12–14, 18–21;
    H1, H2

Lindera obtusiloba   p. 416
Japanese spicebush
☼ ◑ ✿ 3B–6, 14–17

Magnolia (many)   p. 427
☼ ◑ ✿ ZONES VARY

Malus   p. 433
Flowering crabapple
☼ ✿ 1–11, 14–21

Parkinsonia aculeata   p. 475
Jerusalem thorn
☼ ✿ 8–24; H1, H2

Persimmon   p. 495
☼ ✿ ZONES VARY

Prosopis   p. 529
Mesquite
☼ ✿ 10–13, 18–24

Acer palmatum

Carpinus caroliniana

Laburnum

Lindera obtusiloba

Prunus p. 531
Flowering cherry, peach, plum
☼ ☽ ☂ ZONES VARY

Sorbus aucuparia p. 608
European mountain ash
☼ ☽ ☂ A1–A3; 1–10, 14–17

Styrax p. 617
☼ ☽ ☂ 4–9, 14–21

Tipuana tipu p. 631
Tipu tree
☼ ☂ 12–16, 18–24; H1, H2

Vitex agnus-castus p. 652
Chaste tree
☼ ☂ 4–24; H1, H2

Large Deciduous Trees (OVER 35 FT.)

Acer (several) p. 128
Maple
☼ ☽ ☂ ZONES VARY

Albizia julibrissin p. 142
Mimosa
☼ ☽ ☂ 4–23

Betula (many) p. 195
Birch
☼ ☂ ZONES VARY

Carpinus betulus p. 223
European hornbeam
☼ ☽ ☂ 2–9, 14–17

Celtis occidentalis p. 230
Common hackberry
☼ ☽ ☂ 1–24

Celtis sinensis p. 230
Chinese hackberry
☼ ☽ ☂ 8–16, 18–20

Cercidiphyllum japonicum p. 232
Katsura tree
☼ ☽ ☂ 2B–6, 14–16, 18–20

Fraxinus americana p. 327
White ash
☼ ☂ 1–11, 14–17

Ginkgo biloba p. 339
Maidenhair tree
☼ ☂ A3; 1–10, 12, 14–24

Jacaranda mimosifolia p. 383
☼ ☂ 12, 13, 15–24; H1, H2

Liquidambar p. 416
Sweet gum
☼ ☂ ZONES VARY

Morus alba p. 445
White mulberry
☼ ☂ 2–24; H1, H2

Nyssa sylvatica p. 458
Sour gum
☼ ☽ ☂ 2–10, 14–21

Pistacia chinensis p. 511
Chinese pistache
☼ ☂ 4–23

Platanus p. 512
Plane tree
☼ ☂ ZONES VARY

Populus tremuloides p. 525
Quaking aspen
☼ ☂ A1–A3; 1–7, 14–19

Pyrus calleryana p. 543
Callery pear
☼ ☂ 2B–9, 14–21

Quercus (many) p. 544
Oak
☼ ☂ ZONES VARY

Robinia 'Purple Robe' p. 567
Locust
☼ ☂ 2–24

Styphnolobium japonicum p. 617
Japanese pagoda tree
☼ ☽ ☂ 2–24

Tilia (most) p. 631
Linden
☼ ☂ ZONES VARY

Ulmus parvifolia p. 642
Chinese elm
☼ ☂ 3–24

Ulmus pumila p. 643
Siberian elm
☼ ☂ A1, A3, 1–11, 14–21

Zelkova serrata p. 659
Sawleaf zelkova
☼ ☂ 3–21

TOP ROW: *Carpinus betulus.* SECOND ROW: *Cercidiphyllum japonicum* 'Rotfuchs'; *Ginkgo biloba* 'Fairmont'. THIRD ROW: *Nyssa sylvatica; Populus tremuloides.* BOTTOM ROW: *Styphnolobium japonicum* 'Regent'; *Tilia cordata*

ORNAMENTAL EDIBLES

Herbs, vegetables, and fruit trees have come out of hiding. No longer relegated to a concealed patch outside the kitchen door or in the back 40, most are now valued landscape plants for the long term, as with citrus and many fruit trees; or even for a season, as with basil or parsley. You can train apple or fig trees as espaliers, grow persimmon trees as hedges, or give citrus a place of honor over an arching trellis. Use parsley, sage, or thyme to edge beds. Or fill a gap in a perennial border with an artichoke plant, a trio of blueberries, or a clump of fragrant scented lemongrass. Strawberries make a fine fruiting groundcover; eggplant, lettuce, mint, peppers, Swiss chard, and kale rosettes are showstoppers in containers.

Here we list crops by some possible ways to use them. For more ideas on using herbs, see page 682; for vegetables, turn to page 698.

Citrus trained over an arbor

Trees and Shrubs

Apple p. 156
☼ ✿ ZONES VARY

Avocado p. 180
☼ ✿ ZONES VARY

Blueberry p. 198
☼ ✿ ZONES VARY

Citrus p. 245
☼ ✿ 8, 9, 12–24; H1, H2

Crabapple p. 268
☼ ✿ A1–A3; 1–9, 11–21

Currant p. 274
☼ ◑ ● ✿ A1–A3; 1–6, 15–17

Fig p. 323
☼ ✿ 4–9, 11–24; H1, H2

Laurus nobilis p. 401
Sweet bay
☼ ◑ ✿ 5–9, 12–24; H1, H2

Mango p. 436
☼ ✿ 23, 24; H1, H2

Papaya p. 474
☼ ✿ ZONES VARY

Persimmon p. 495
☼ ✿ ZONES VARY

Pomegranate p. 524
☼ ✿ 5–24; H1, H2

Borders and Edging Plants

Allium schoenoprasum p. 144
Chives
☼ ◑ ✿ ALL ZONES

Asian greens p. 173
☼ ◑ ✿ ALL ZONES

Lavandula angustifolia p. 401
English lavender
☼ ✿ 2–24

Lettuce p. 406
☼ ◑ ✿ ALL ZONES

Matricaria recutita p. 437
Chamomile
☼ ✿ 1–24

Origanum p. 463
Oregano, marjoram
☼ ✿ ZONES VARY

Petroselinum crispum p. 496
Parsley
☼ ◑ ✿ A1–A3; 1–24

Rosmarinus officinalis p. 578
Rosemary
☼ ✿ 4–24; H1, H2

Salvia officinalis p. 587
Garden sage
☼ ◑ ✿ 2–24; H1, H2

Thymus p. 629
Thyme
☼ ◑ ✿ 1–24

'Winter Banana' apples

Pomegranate

Lavandula angustifolia 'Vera'

Rosmarinus officinalis

TOP ROW: Scarlet runner beans; 'Himrod' grapes. SECOND ROW: Artichokes; kale. THIRD ROW: *Coriandrum sativum*; 'Hansel' eggplant. BOTTOM ROW: Banana peppers; strawberries

Vines

Bean, pole and scarlet runner   p. 189
☼ ✎ ALL ZONES

Grape   p. 342
☼ ✎ ZONES VARY

Kiwi   p. 392
☼ ◐ ✎ ZONES VARY

Passion fruit   p. 477
☼ ✎ 15–17, 21–24; H1, H2

Pea   p. 478
☼ ✎ ALL ZONES

Raspberry   p. 551
☼ ✎ A1–A3; 1–24

Spinach, Malabar   p. 610
☼ ✎ 3–24; H1, H2

Sweet potato   p. 619
☼ ✎ 8–10, 12–15, 18–24; H1, H2

Striking Accents

Artichoke   p. 171
☼ ◐ ✎ 3A–24

Banana   p. 187
☼ ✎ 15, 16, 19–24; H2

Bean, scarlet runner   p. 189
☼ ✎ ALL ZONES

Beet   p. 190
☼ ✎ ALL ZONES

Corn   p. 261
☼ ✎ 1B, 2B–24; H1, H2

Cymbopogon citratus   p. 276
Lemon grass
☼ ✎ 12, 13, 16, 17, 23, 24; H1, H2

Foeniculum vulgare   p. 324
Common fennel
☼ ✎ ZONES VARY

Helianthus   p. 355
Sunflower
☼ ✎ ZONES VARY

Kale   p. 391
☼ ◐ ✎ ALL ZONES

Opuntia (prickly pear)   p. 462
☼ ✎ ZONES VARY

Radicchio   p. 239
☼ ✎ ALL ZONES

Rhubarb   p. 564
☼ ◐ ✎ A1–A3; 1–11, 14–24

Swiss chard   p. 619
☼ ✎ ALL ZONES

Tomatillo   p. 632
☼ ✎ ALL ZONES

Good in Containers

Allium schoenoprasum   p. 144
Chives
☼ ◐ ✎ ALL ZONES

Arugula   p. 171
☼ ✎ ALL ZONES

Carrot   p. 223
☼ ✎ ALL ZONES

Coriandrum sativum   p. 261
Cilantro
☼ ◐ ✎ ALL ZONES

Eggplant   p. 298
☼ ✎ 1–24; H1, H2

Lettuce   p. 406
☼ ◐ ✎ ALL ZONES

Mentha   p. 441
Mint
☼ ◐ ✎ ZONES VARY

Ocimum basilicum   p. 458
Basil
☼ ✎ ALL ZONES

Pepper   p. 493
☼ ✎ ALL ZONES

Squash (compact varieties)   p. 611
☼ ✎ ALL ZONES

Strawberry   p. 615
☼ ✎ ALL ZONES

Swiss chard   p. 619
☼ ✎ ALL ZONES

Tomato   p. 632
☼ ✎ ALL ZONES

PLANTS THAT ATTRACT BIRDS

There are good reasons to invite birds into your garden besides the most obvious one—helping them along as their natural habitats continue to shrink. While they go about their daily lives among your trees and flowers, they dine on all kinds of insects, helping to control pests naturally. Hummingbirds pollinate plants as they forage for nectar.

To keep birds coming to your garden, you need to create a living smorgasbord that includes plants with berries, foliage, fruit, and nectar. Mix up natives and non-natives, and include plants that bloom at different times of the year. If your garden lacks food during certain months, put up bird feeders. Birds also need leafy or twiggy shrubbery to protect them from predators and to provide nesting places.

Bluebird house in *Quercus agrifolia*

Nectar Plants, Annuals and Perennials

Agastache p. 137
☼ ◐ ✎ ZONES VARY

Alcea rosea p. 142
Hollyhock
☼ ◐ ✎ 1–24

Aloe p. 145
☼ ◐ ✎ 8, 9, 12–24

Alstroemeria p. 147
Peruvian lily
☼ ◐ ✎ 5–9, 14–24; H1

Anigozanthos p. 153
Kangaroo paw
☼ ✎ 15–24

Aquilegia p. 161
Columbine
☼ ◐ ✎ ZONES VARY

Asclepias tuberosa p. 173
Butterfly weed
☼ ✎ 1–24

Centaurea p. 230
☼ ✎ ZONES VARY

Chamerion angustifolium p. 236
Fireweed
☼ ✎ A1–A3; 1–7, 14–21

Chasmanthe p. 236
☼ ◐ ✎ 13, 15–24

Clarkia p. 251
☼ ◐ ✎ A2, A3; 1–24

Cleome hasslerana p. 253
Spider flower
☼ ✎ 1–24

Crocosmia p. 270
☼ ◐ ✎ ZONES VARY

Delphinium p. 283
☼ ✎ ZONES VARY

Dicentra p. 287
Bleeding heart
◐ ● ✎ ZONES VARY

Dicliptera sericea p. 288
Hummingbird bush
☼ ◐ ✎ 12, 13, 15–17, 19, 21–24

Digitalis p. 289
Foxglove
NEEDS, ZONES VARY

Gladiolus p. 339
☼ ✎ 4–9, 12–24; H1

Hesperaloe parviflora p. 360
Red yucca
☼ ◐ ✎ 2B, 3, 7–16, 18–24

Heuchera p. 361
Coral bells
☼ ◐ ✎ ZONES VARY

Alstroemeria aurantiaca

Aquilegia chrysantha

Cleome hasslerana

Leonotis leonurus

Lupinus polyphyllus

Penstemon heterophyllus

Lonicera japonica 'Halliana'

Tecoma capensis

Kniphofia p. 393
Red-hot poker
☼ ◑ ✹ ZONES VARY

Leonotis leonurus p. 405
Lion's tail
☼ ✹ 8–24; H1, H2

Lobelia (red-flowered) p. 419
☼ ◑ ✹ ZONES VARY

Lobularia p. 419
Sweet alyssum
☼ ◑ ✹ ALL ZONES

Lupinus p. 423
Lupine
☼ ✹ ZONES VARY

Mimulus p. 443
Monkey flower
NEEDS, ZONES VARY

Monarda p. 445
Bee balm
☼ ◑ ✹ ZONES VARY

Pelargonium p. 487
Geranium
☼ ◑ ✹ A2, A3; 1–24

Penstemon (many) p. 490
Beard tongue
☼ ◑ ✹ ZONES VARY

Phygelius p. 502
Cape fuchsia
☼ ◑ ✹ 4–9, 14–24; H1, H2

Salvia (many) p. 583
Sage
NEEDS, ZONES VARY

Veronica p. 647
Speedwell
☼ ✹ ZONES VARY

Zauschneria p. 659
California fuchsia
NEEDS, ZONES VARY

Zinnia p. 660
☼ ✹ ZONES VARY

Nectar Plants, Vines

Campsis p. 218
Trumpet creeper
☼ ◑ ✹ ZONES VARY

Ipomoea quamoclit p. 376
Cypress vine
☼ ✹ ALL ZONES

Lonicera p. 420
Honeysuckle
☼ ◑ ✹ ZONES VARY

Pyrostegia venusta p. 543
Flame vine
☼ ✹ 13, 16, 21–24; H1, H2

Tecoma capensis p. 625
Cape honeysuckle
☼ ◑ ✹ 12, 13, 20–24; H1, H2

Nectar Plants, Shrubs

Abelia p. 124
☼ ◑ ✹ ZONES VARY

Abutilon p. 125
Flowering maple
☼ ◑ ✹ 8, 9, 12–24; H1, H2

Acacia p. 125
☼ ✹ ZONES VARY

Aesculus p. 136
Horsechestnut
☼ ✹ ZONES VARY

Arbutus unedo p. 164
Strawberry tree
☼ ◑ ✹ 4–24

Arctostaphylos p. 164
Manzanita
☼ ◑ ✹ ZONES VARY

**Bouvardia
(red-flowered)** p. 202
◑ ✹ 8–10, 12, 14–24

Buddleja p. 206
Butterfly bush
☼ ◑ ✹ ZONES VARY

Caesalpinia p. 209
☼ ✹ ZONES VARY

Calliandra p. 211
☼ ✹ ZONES VARY

Callistemon p. 212
Bottlebrush
☼ ✹ ZONES VARY

Ceanothus p. 226
California wild lilac
☼ ✹ 1–3, 5–9, 14–24

Cercis occidentalis p. 233
Western redbud
☼ ◑ ✹ 2–24

Cestrum p. 234
◑ ✹ ZONES VARY

Chaenomeles p. 234
Flowering quince
☼ ✹ 2–23

Correa p. 264
Australian fuchsia
☼ ◑ ✹ 14–24

Feijoa sellowiana p. 319
Pineapple guava
☼ ✹ 6–9, 12–24; H1, H2

Fuchsia p. 329
☼ ◑ ✹ ZONES VARY

Grevillea (red-flowered) p. 347
NEEDS, ZONES VARY

Heteromeles arbutifolia p. 360
Toyon
☼ ◑ ✹ 5–9, 14–24

Heuchera p. 361
Coral bells
☼ ◑ ✹ ZONES VARY

Hibiscus p. 363
☼ ✹ ZONES VARY

Hosta p. 365
Plantain lily
◑ ● ✹ ZONES VARY

Justicia (several) p. 390
NEEDS, ZONES VARY

Lantana p. 398
☼ ✹ 8–10, 12–24; H1, H2

Lavandula p. 401
Lavender
☼ ✹ ZONES VARY

Leucophyllum p. 408
Texas ranger
☼ ✹ 7–24

Lonicera p. 420
Honeysuckle
☼ ◑ ✹ ZONES VARY

Nectar Plants, Trees

Seed and Berry Plants, Evergreen Trees

Seed and Berry Plants, Deciduous Trees

TOP ROW: *Abutilon; Arbutus unedo rubra.* SECOND ROW: *Feijoa sellowiana; Justicia carnea.* THIRD ROW: *Albizia julibrissin rosea; Juniperus communis.* BOTTOM ROW: *Quercus robur*

Crataegus	p. 269
Hawthorn	
☼ ✄ 2–12, 14–17	

Fraxinus velutina	p. 327
Arizona ash	
☼ ✄ 3B–24	

Liquidambar	p. 416
Sweet gum	
☼ ✄ ZONES VARY	

Malus (most)	p. 433
Flowering crabapple	
☼ ✄ 1–11, 14–21	

Morus (fruiting kinds)	p. 445
Mulberry	
☼ ✄ ZONES VARY	

Sorbus	p. 607
Mountain ash	
☼ ◑ ✄ ZONES VARY	

Seed and Berry Plants, Evergreen Shrubs

Arctostaphylos	p. 164
Manzanita	
☼ ◑ ✄ ZONES VARY	

Atriplex	p. 178
Saltbush	
☼ ✄ ZONES VARY	

Berberis	p. 193
Barberry	
☼ ◑ ✄ ZONES VARY	

Cotoneaster	p. 267
☼ ✄ ZONES VARY	

Eremophila	p. 303
Emu bush	
☼ ✄ 8, 9, 13–24	

Garrya	p. 333
Silktassel	
☼ ◑ ✄ ZONES VARY	

Heteromeles arbutifolia	p. 360
Toyon	
☼ ◑ ✄ 5–9, 14–24	

Ilex	p. 371
Holly	
☼ ◑ ✄ ZONES VARY	

Ligustrum	p. 411
Privet	
☼ ◑ ✄ ZONES VARY	

Mahonia	p. 431
☼ ◑ ● ✄ ZONES VARY	

Pyracantha	p. 542
Firethorn	
☼ ✄ ZONES VARY	

Rhamnus	p. 554
☼ ◑ ● ✄ ZONES VARY	

Rhus	p. 564
Sumac	
☼ ✄ ZONES VARY	

Viburnum	p. 648
☼ ◑ ✄ ZONES VARY	

Seed and Berry Plants, Deciduous Shrubs

Amelanchier	p. 149
Juneberry	
☼ ◑ ✄ ZONES VARY	

Atriplex	p. 178
Saltbush	
☼ ✄ ZONES VARY	

Berberis	p. 193
Barberry	
☼ ◑ ✄ ZONES VARY	

Callicarpa	p. 212
Beautyberry	
☼ ◑ ✄ ZONES VARY	

Cercis	p. 233
Redbud	
☼ ◑ ✄ ZONES VARY	

Cornus	p. 262
Dogwood	
☼ ◑ ✄ ZONES VARY	

Cotoneaster	p. 267
☼ ✄ ZONES VARY	

Elaeagnus	p. 298
☼ ◑ ✄ ZONES VARY	

Euonymus	p. 313
NEEDS, ZONES VARY	

TOP ROW: *Betula pendula*; *Cornus sericea*. SECOND ROW: *Arctostaphylos densiflora* 'Howard McMinn'. THIRD ROW: *Cotoneaster apiculatus*; *Mahonia aquifolium*. BOTTOM ROW: *Pyracantha*; *Viburnum opulus*

Seed and Berry Plants, Annuals and Perennials

TOP ROW: *Amelanchier laevis; Ligustrum vulgare* 'Lodense'. SECOND ROW: *Symphoricarpos × doorenbosii; Cosmos sulphureus.* THIRD ROW: *Eriogonum umbellatum* 'Sulphur Flower'; *Rudbeckia hirta.* BOTTOM ROW: *Nigella damascena*

PLANTS THAT ATTRACT BUTTERFLIES

Butterflies are welcome visitors to most gardens, bringing beauty and motion as well as pollinating plants. Choose plants from this list and you can encourage these winged visitors to stay awhile. Butterfly larvae (caterpillars) need food plants; adult butterflies need nectar plants. Sunny areas that are sheltered from the wind and contain amenities such as leaf litter, rock crevices, brush piles, damp places, and even weeds are the most welcoming of gardens for butterflies, as are sun-warmed boulders with shallow, water-filled basins in the top. When you choose plants, keep in mind that not every plant will attract butterflies in every region. And avoid using pesticides, even organic formulations.

Western tiger swallowtail on a leopard lily (*Lilium pardalinum*)

Butterfly Larvae, Perennials and Annuals

Achillea millefolium p. 132
Common yarrow
☼ ⚡ A1–A3; 1–24

Alcea rosea p. 142
Hollyhock
☼ ◑ ⚡ 1–24

Ammi majus p. 150
Bishop's lace
☼ ◑ ⚡ ALL ZONES

Antirrhinum majus p. 155
Snapdragon
☼ ⚡ A1–A3; 1–24

Asclepias p. 172
☼ ⚡ ZONES VARY

Aster p. 176
☼ ⚡ ZONES VARY

Dicentra p. 287
Bleeding heart
◑ ● ⚡ 1–9, 14–24

Digitalis p. 289
Foxglove
NEEDS, ZONES VARY

Eriogonum p. 306
Wild buckwheat
☼ ⚡ ZONES VARY

Foeniculum vulgare p. 324
Common fennel
☼ ⚡ ZONES VARY

Helianthus p. 355
Sunflower
☼ ⚡ ZONES VARY

Linaria p. 415
Toadflax
☼ ◑ ⚡ 1–24

Lupinus p. 423
Lupine
☼ ⚡ ZONES VARY

Malva p. 433
Mallow
☼ ⚡ 1–9, 14–24

Mimulus aurantiacus p. 443
Sticky monkey flower
☼ ◑ ⚡ 5–9, 14–24

Penstemon p. 490
Beard tongue
☼ ◑ ⚡ ZONES VARY

Ruta graveolens p. 581
Rue
☼ ⚡ 2–24

Sidalcea malviflora p. 603
Checkerbloom
☼ ⚡ 2–9, 14–24

Sorghastrum nutans p. 608
Indiangrass
☼ ⚡ 1–24

Veronica p. 647
Speedwell
☼ ⚡ ZONES VARY

Ammi majus

Asclepias tuberosa

Helianthus

Lupinus latifolius

Passiflora 'Incense'

Holodiscus discolor

Spiraea japonica 'Magic Carpet'

Crataegus laevigata

TOP ROW: *Coreopsis tinctoria*; *Cosmos bipinnatus*. SECOND ROW: *Eryngium amethystinum*; *Gaillardia × grandiflora* 'Frenzy'. THIRD ROW: *Iberis sempervirens*. BOTTOM ROW: *Perovskia atriplicifolia*; *Salvia microphylla*

Buddleja davidii

Clematis 'Comtesse de Bouchard'

Lonicera × *heckrottii*

Metrosideros polymorpha

Rudbeckia p. 579
☼ ✂ 1–24

Salvia p. 583
Sage
NEEDS, ZONES VARY

Scabiosa p. 592
Pincushion flower
☼ ✂ ZONES VARY

Sedum (most) p. 597
Stonecrop
NEEDS, ZONES VARY

Silene p. 604
☼ ◐ ✂ ZONES VARY

Solidago p. 606
Goldenrod
☼ ◐ ✂ 1–11, 14–23

Tithonia rotundifolia p. 632
Mexican sunflower
☼ ✂ ALL ZONES

Trachelium caeruleum p. 635
☼ ✂ 1–24

Verbena p. 646
☼ ✂ ZONES VARY

Veronica p. 647
Speedwell
☼ ✂ ZONES VARY

Zauschneria p. 659
California fuchsia
NEEDS, ZONES VARY

Zinnia p. 660
☼ ✂ 1–24; H1, H2

PLANTS THAT ATTRACT BEES

Successful organic gardeners know that bees are among their best helpers, pollinating fruit trees and other crops. Their gardens teem with honeybees (from Europe) because there's a steady supply of nectar and pollen. But native bees can be good pollinators too. The West has thousands of species of bees, from fat yellow-and-black bumblebees to slim ant look-alikes. Encourage all bees. Listed below are plants that attract them. Keep in mind that bees will go for whatever's blooming, even if it's not their favorite. But they are especially attracted to blue, white, and yellow flowers.

Plant a bee garden like the one pictured on page 712, and hang up a bee box with a grid of small holes in front where solitary bees can nest. A healthy garden is buzzing with life.

Borage (*Borago officinalis*) with European honeybee

Agastache p. 137
☼ ◑ ✿ ZONES VARY

Aster × frikartii p. 176
☼ ✿ 2B–24

Asteriscus maritimus p. 177
Gold coin
☼ ✿ 9, 15–24

Bidens ferulifolia p. 196
☼ ✿ ALL ZONES

Borago officinalis p. 200
Borage
☼ ◑ ✿ A2, A3; 1–24; H1

Caryopteris × clandonensis p. 224
Blue mist
☼ ✿ 2B–9, 14–24

Ceanothus p. 226
California wild lilac
☼ ✿ 1–3, 5–9, 14–24

Centaurea p. 230
☼ ✿ ZONES VARY

Cephalophyllum 'Red Spike' p. 231
Red spike ice plant
☼ ◑ ✿ 8, 9, 11–24

Cerinthe major 'Purpurascens' p. 233
Honeywort
☼ ◑ ✿ 1–24

Chamaebatiaria millefolium p. 234
Fernbush
☼ ✿ 1–3, 7, 14–21

Choisya ternata p. 241
Mexican orange
☼ ◑ ✿ 4–9, 14–24

Citrus p. 245
☼ ✿ 8, 9, 12–24; H1, H2

Clarkia unguiculata p. 251
Mountain garland
☼ ◑ ✿ A2, A3; 1–24

Coreopsis grandiflora p. 260
☼ ✿ 2–24; H1, H2

Cosmos bipinnatus p. 266
☼ ✿ 1–24

Echinacea p. 296
Coneflower
☼ ✿ A2, A3; 1–24

Echium candicans p. 298
Pride of Madeira
☼ ✿ 14–24

Eriogonum p. 306
Wild buckwheat
☼ ✿ ZONES VARY

Eryngium p. 307
Sea holly
☼ ✿ 2–24

Eschscholzia californica p. 310
California poppy
☼ ✿ 1–24; H1

Frangula californica p. 326
Coffeeberry
☼ ◑ ✿ 3A–10, 14–24; H1, H2

Agastache foeniculum

Ceanothus 'Cynthia Postan'

Cerinthe major 'Purpurascens'

Choisya ternata

TOP ROW: *Coreopsis grandiflora*; *Cosmos bipinnatus*. SECOND ROW: *Echinacea purpurea* 'Doubledecker'; *Echium candicans*. THIRD ROW: *Gaillardia* × *grandiflora* 'Fanfare'; *Lobularia maritima*. BOTTOM ROW: *Nepeta* 'Walker's Low'; *Rosmarinus officinalis* 'Prostratus'; *Rudbeckia hirta* 'Denver Daisy'

PLANTS THAT ATTRACT BENEFICIAL INSECTS

Before insect pests get the chance to invade your garden, take time to recruit an opposing army of beneficial insects, poised for counterattack. Just one lacewing larva can devour hundreds of aphids, mites, thrips, leafhoppers, and other troublemakers. An adult ladybird beetle (ladybug) can eat about 50 aphids a day, while her larva can consume up to 25. Listed below are plants that attract these garden contributors. (For details on beneficial insects, see page 727.)

Don't trim blooms or uproot spent plants too quickly; the flowers of plants such as parsley, sage, dill, and fennel feed populations of beneficial insects.

Ladybird beetle

Achillea filipendulina p. 132
Fernleaf yarrow
☼ ✂ A1–A3; 1–24

Achillea millefolium p. 132
Common yarrow
☼ ✂ A1–A3; 1–24

Anethum graveolens p. 152
Dill
☼ ✂ 1–24

Asclepias tuberosa p. 173
Butterfly weed
☼ ✂ 1–24

Aurinia saxatilis p. 179
Basket-of-gold
☼ ◑ ✂ 1–24

Callirhoe involucrata p. 212
Poppy mallow
☼ ◑ ✂ 1–3, 7–14, 18–24

Carum carvi p. 224
Caraway
☼ ✂ 1–24

Chamerion angustifolium p. 236
Fireweed
☼ ✂ A1–A3; 1–7, 14–21

Coriandrum sativum p. 261
Cilantro
☼ ◑ ✂ ALL ZONES

Cosmos bipinnatus p. 266
☼ ✂ 1–24

Feijoa sellowiana p. 319
Pineapple guava
☼ ✂ 6–9, 12–24; H1, H2

Foeniculum vulgare p. 324
Common fennel
☼ ✂ ZONES VARY

Mentha spicata p. 442
Spearmint
☼ ◑ ✂ A2, A3; 1–24

Monarda fistulosa p. 445
Bee balm
☼ ◑ ✂ A2, A3; 1–10, 14–17

Penstemon strictus p. 492
Rocky Mountain penstemon
☼ ◑ ✂ 1–3, 10–13

Petroselinum crispum p. 496
Parsley
☼ ◑ ✂ A1–A3; 1–24

Rudbeckia p. 579
☼ ✂ 1–24

Tagetes tenuifolia p. 623
Signet marigold
☼ ✂ ALL ZONES

Tanacetum parthenium p. 624
Feverfew
☼ ✂ 2–24

Thymus serpyllum p. 629
Woolly thyme
☼ ◑ ✂ A2, A3; 1–24

Achillea millefolium 'Paprika'

Coriandrum sativum

Foeniculum vulgare

Tanacetum parthenium

FLOWERING TREES AND SHRUBS

Trees and shrubs are the backbone of the garden. But that doesn't mean they need to take a back seat to showy annuals and perennials. Many put on a striking show of bloom in winter, spring, summer, or even fall. If you mix several bloomers from each season, you can enjoy an explosion of color that comes and goes nearly all year long, much like fireworks. The plants listed are arranged by the time of year at which they flower. In Winter or Spring lists, ❄ indicates largely winter bloomers. Others flower in spring, or from winter into spring.

To use these plants effectively, stick to a color theme, and use other blooming plants nearby that play off the colors of the trees' or shrubs' flowers.

Flowering crabapple (*Malus*)

Trees, Winter or Spring

Acacia (most)   p. 125
☼ ✿ ZONES VARY   ❄

Bauhinia (some)   p. 188
Orchid tree
NEEDS, ZONES VARY

Cercis   p. 233
Redbud
☼ ◑ ✿ ZONES VARY

Chionanthus   p. 240
Fringe tree
☼ ✿ ZONES VARY

Cornus   p. 262
Dogwood
☼ ◑ ✿ ZONES VARY

Davidia involucrata   p. 282
Dove tree
☼ ◑ ✿ 4–9, 14–21

Erythrina (some)   p. 308
Coral tree
☼ ✿ ZONES VARY   ❄

Laburnum   p. 395
Goldenchain tree
☼ ◑ ✿ 1–10, 14–17

Magnolia (most deciduous)   p. 427
☼ ◑ ✿ ZONES VARY

Malus   p. 433
Flowering crabapple
☼ ✿ 1–11, 14–21

Metrosideros excelsa   p. 442
New Zealand Christmas tree
☼ ◑ ✿ 16, 17, 23, 24; H1, H2

Prunus (many)   p. 531
☼ ✿ ZONES VARY

Shrubs, Winter or Spring

Abutilon (most)   p. 125
Flowering maple
☼ ◑ ✿ 8, 9, 12–24; H1, H2

Alyogyne huegelii   p. 148
Blue hibiscus
☼ ✿ 13–17, 20–24; H1, H2

Brunfelsia pauciflora   p. 205
◑ ✿ 12–17, 20–24; H1, H2

Camellia (many)   p. 215
◑ ✿ 4–9, 12, 14–24

Ceanothus   p. 226
California wild lilac
☼ ✿ 1–3, 5–9, 14–24

Chaenomeles   p. 234
Flowering quince
☼ ✿ 2–23

Choisya ternata   p. 241
Mexican orange
☼ ◑ ✿ 4–9, 14–24

Davidia involucrata

Erythrina caffra

Abutilon

Cistus purpureus

Paeonia suffruticosa

Jacaranda mimosifolia

Fuchsia hybrid

Hibiscus rosa-sinensis

Cistus p. 244
Rockrose
☀ ✿ 4–9, 14–24

Cornus kousa p. 263
Kousa dogwood
☀ ◑ ✿ 2–9, 14–17

Corylopsis p. 265
Winter hazel
☀ ◑ ✿ ZONES VARY ❄

Echium candicans p. 298
Pride of Madeira
☀ ✿ 14–24

Forsythia p. 324
☀ ✿ ZONES VARY ❄

Fothergilla p. 325
☀ ◑ ✿ 2B–9, 14–17 ❄

Grevillea (some) p. 347
NEEDS, ZONES VARY

Hamamelis p. 351
Witch hazel
☀ ◑ ✿ ZONES VARY ❄

Jasminum (some) p. 383
Jasmine
☀ ◑ ✿ ZONES VARY

Kalmia latifolia p. 391
Mountain laurel
◑ ✿ 2–7, 16, 17

Leptospermum p. 405
Tea tree
☀ ✿ 14–24

Loropetalum chinense p. 422
☀ ◑ ✿ 4–9, 14–24

Mahonia (some) p. 431
NEEDS, ZONES VARY

Melaleuca (some) p. 438
☀ ✿ ZONES VARY

Paeonia (tree) p. 470
Tree peony
☀ ◑ ✿ 2–12, 14–23

Rhaphiolepis indica p. 555
Indian hawthorn
☀ ◑ ✿ 4–10, 12–24; H1, H2

Rhododendron p. 556
Azalea and rhododendron
◑ ✿ ZONES VARY

Rosmarinus officinalis p. 578
Rosemary
☀ ✿ 4–24; H1, H2

Spiraea (some) p. 610
Spirea
☀ ◑ ✿ ZONES VARY

Syringa p. 620
Lilac
☀ ◑ ✿ ZONES VARY

Viburnum (some) p. 648
NEEDS, ZONES VARY

Trees, Summer

Albizia julibrissin p. 142
Mimosa
☀ ◑ ✿ 4–23

Chilopsis linearis p. 239
Desert willow
☀ ✿ 3B, 7–14, 18–23

Delonix regia p. 282
Royal poinciana
☀ ✿ 22, 23; H2

Erythrina (some) p. 308
Coral tree
☀ ✿ ZONES VARY

Jacaranda mimosifolia p. 383
☀ ✿ 12, 13, 15–24; H1, H2

Lagerstroemia indica p. 396
Crape myrtle
☀ ✿ 7–10, 12–14, 18–21; H1, H2

**Robinia × ambigua
'Idahoensis'** p. 567
Idaho locust
☀ ✿ 2–24

Stewartia p. 614
☀ ◑ ✿ 4–6, 14–17, 20, 21

Vitex agnus-castus p. 652
Chaste tree
☀ ✿ 4–24; H1, H2

Shrubs, Summer

Abutilon p. 125
Flowering maple
☀ ◑ ✿ 8, 9, 12–24; H1, H2

Alyogyne huegelii p. 148
Blue hibiscus
☀ ✿ 13–17, 20–24; H1, H2

**Anisodontea ×
hypomadara** p. 154
Cape mallow
☀ ◑ ✿ 14–24

Buddleja (some) p. 206
Butterfly bush
☀ ◑ ✿ ZONES VARY

Caesalpinia (some) p. 209
☀ ✿ ZONES VARY

Callistemon p. 212
Bottlebrush
☀ ✿ ZONES VARY

Caryopteris p. 224
Bluebeard
☀ ✿ ZONES VARY

Fuchsia p. 329
☀ ◑ ✿ ZONES VARY

Gardenia jasminoides p. 332
☀ ◑ ✿ 7–9, 12–16, 18–24; H1, H2

Hibiscus p. 363
☀ ✿ ZONES VARY

Justicia (some) p. 390
NEEDS, ZONES VARY

Lantana p. 398
☀ ✿ 8–10, 12–24; H1, H2

Lavandula p. 401
Lavender
☀ ✿ ZONES VARY

Lavatera p. 404
Tree mallow
☀ ✿ ZONES VARY

Leucophyllum p. 408
Texas ranger
☀ ✿ 7–24

Philadelphus (some) p. 498
Mock orange
☀ ◑ ✿ ZONES VARY

Plumbago auriculata p. 519
Cape plumbago
☀ ◑ ✿ 8, 9, 12–24; H1, H2

Tecoma stans p. 625
Yellow bells
☀ ◑ ✿ 12, 13, 21–24; H1, H2

FALL FOLIAGE

Framed against autumn skies, fall foliage can stage a spectacular show in many parts of the West. The fiery reds, vivid oranges, rich burgundies, and vibrant yellows of Chinese pistache, crape myrtle, ginkgo, Japanese maple, liquidambar, and other deciduous trees can transform a garden or street into a blaze of color.

Although large trees provide the most dramatic displays, you don't have to wait years to enjoy the brilliant fall color. Even young trees can create an autumn show. And blazing shrubs can enhance the effect. Shop in fall while colors are changing to get exactly what you want, or buy varieties with known, reliable fall color. Keep in mind that climate can affect color change; where killing frosts and rains come late—if at all—many trees hold their color over a longer period of time. In Southern California, it's not unusual to find trees changing color from September to January.

Acer palmatum

Trees

Acer (many)   p. 128
Maple
☼ ◑ ✎ ZONES VARY

Betula   p. 195
Birch
☼ ✎ ZONES VARY

Cercidiphyllum japonicum   p. 232
Katsura tree
☼ ◑ ✎ 2B–6, 14–16, 18–20

Cercis canadensis   p. 233
Eastern redbud
☼ ◑ ✎ 1–24

Cladrastis kentukea   p. 251
Yellow wood
☼ ✎ 2–9, 14–16

Cornus (many)   p. 262
Dogwood
☼ ◑ ✎ ZONES VARY

Crataegus (some)   p. 269
Hawthorn
☼ ✎ 2–12, 14–17

Fraxinus (deciduous)   p. 327
Ash
☼ ✎ ZONES VARY

Ginkgo biloba   p. 339
Maidenhair tree
☼ ✎ A3; 1–10, 12, 14–24

Gleditsia triacanthos   p. 340
Honey locust
☼ ✎ 1–16, 18–20

Halesia   p. 350
◑ ✎ 2B–9, 14–21

Koelreuteria bipinnata   p. 394
Chinese flame tree
☼ ✎ 8–24; H1

Lagerstroemia indica   p. 396
Crape myrtle
☼ ✎ 7–10, 12–14, 18–21; H1, H2

Liquidambar   p. 416
Sweet gum
☼ ✎ ZONES VARY

Liriodendron tulipifera   p. 417
Tulip tree
☼ ✎ 2–12, 14–24

Malus   p. 433
Flowering crabapple
☼ ✎ 1–11, 14–21

Nyssa sylvatica   p. 458
Sour gum
☼ ◑ ✎ 2–10, 14–21

Oxydendrum arboreum   p. 468
Sourwood
☼ ✎ 2B–9, 14–17

Parrotia persica   p. 475
Persian parrotia
☼ ◑ ✎ 2B–7, 14–17

Acer palmatum 'Dissectum'

Cladrastis kentukea

Cornus florida

Fraxinus americana 'Autumn Purple'

TOP ROW: *Ginkgo biloba*; *Gleditsia triacanthos inermis*; *Liriodendron tulipifera*; *Nyssa sylvatica*. SECOND ROW: *Zelkova serrata*. THIRD ROW: *Pyrus*; *Cotinus coggygria*. BOTTOM ROW: *Rhus typhina*; *Parthenocissus tricuspidata* 'Veitchii'

PLANTS FOR FRAGRANCE

A garden's fragrance can bring back sweet memories. Perhaps a gardenia, plumeria, or Japanese honeysuckle reminds you of the heady perfumes that float in the air on balmy evenings in Hawaii. Maybe the aromas of agastache and lavender recall the scents of sun-warmed chaparral wafting through your car window on a California backroad in summer. But whatever your favorite scents, there's likely a plant to match. Dianthus blooms are scented like cloves or cinnamon red-hots. Chocolate cosmos smells as delicious as its namesake.

Some plants are so fragrant that a single one can scent a whole garden. Others are more subtle, best when sniffed up close. Listed below are our favorites in both categories. Locate fragrant plants near a path or patio.

Plumeria 'Intense Rainbow'

Trees

Citrus p. 245
☼ ❉ 8, 9, 12–24; H1, H2

Clethra arborea p. 254
Lily-of-the-valley tree
◐ ❉ 15–17, 21–24

Elaeagnus angustifolia p. 299
Russian olive
☼ ◐ ❉ A2, A3; 1–3, 7–14, 18, 19

Hymenosporum flavum p. 369
Sweetshade
☼ ◐ ❉ 8, 9, 14–24

Magnolia (many) p. 427
☼ ◐ ❉ ZONES VARY

Malus (some) p. 433
Flowering crabapple
☼ ❉ 1–11, 14–21

Styrax obassia p. 617
Fragrant snowbell
☼ ◐ ❉ 4–9, 14–21

Shrubs

Aloysia citrodora p. 147
Lemon verbena
☼ ❉ 9, 10, 12–21

Brugmansia (several) p. 205
Angel's trumpet
☼ ◐ ● ❉ 12, 13, 16–24; H1, H2

Cestrum nocturnum p. 234
Night jessamine
◐ ❉ 13, 16–24; H1, H2

Chimonanthus praecox p. 239
Wintersweet
☼ ◐ ❉ 4–9, 14–21

Choisya ternata p. 241
Mexican orange
☼ ◐ ❉ 4–9, 14–24

Clethra alnifolia p. 254
Summersweet
◐ ❉ A2, A3; 1–6

Daphne p. 280
NEEDS, ZONES VARY

Gardenia p. 332
☼ ◐ ❉ ZONES VARY

Jasminum (some) p. 383
Jasmine
☼ ◐ ❉ ZONES VARY

Lavandula (most) p. 401
Lavender
☼ ❉ ZONES VARY

Lonicera (some) p. 420
Honeysuckle
☼ ◐ ❉ ZONES VARY

Murraya paniculata p. 447
Orange jessamine
◐ ❉ 21–24; H1, H2

Osmanthus fragrans p. 466
Sweet olive
☼ ◐ ❉ 5–9, 12–24; H1

Philadelphus p. 498
Mock orange
☼ ◐ ❉ ZONES VARY

Citrus, Calamondin orange

Brugmansia sanguinea

Gardenia jasminoides 'White Gem'

Philadelphus 'Natchez'

Perennials, Annuals, and Bulbs

Vines

TOP ROW: *Syringa* × *hyacinthiflora*; *Heliotropium arborescens*. SECOND ROW: *Lathyrus odorata*; *Nicotiana*. THIRD ROW: *Polianthes tuberosa*; *Jasminum officinale*. BOTTOM ROW: *Lonicera japonica* 'Halliana'

SCULPTURAL PLANTS

Plants noted for their bold leaves, twisted trunks, muscular weeping branches, or tall columnar shapes make striking centerpieces in the garden. Like living sculptures, the tallest kinds, such as tree aloes, create drama whether you grow them as focal points in a corner of the garden, or beside a patio where—when lit from below at night—their shadows create patterns on nearby walls. Show off low growers such as barrel cactus in front of shapely boulders.

Perennials with big, glossy, deeply serrated leaves— such as *Acanthus mollis* and *Gunnera*—add drama to partly shaded borders. Groundcover types such as Japanese forest grass (*Hakonechloa macra*) and black mondo grass (*Ophiopogon planiscapus* 'Nigrescens') create striking patterns when clustered on gentle slopes where their textural mounds of foliage show up best.

Tree aloes (*Aloe thraskii*), phormium, grasses

Cactus and Succulents

Agave p. 138
☼ ◐ ✂ ZONES VARY

Aloe (many) p. 145
☼ ◐ ✂ 8, 9, 12–24

Carnegiea gigantea p. 222
Saguaro
☼ ✂ 12, 13, 18–21

Cephalocereus senilis p. 231
Old man cactus
☼ ✂ 12, 21–24; H1

Dudleya brittonii p. 294
☼ ✂ 16, 17, 21–24

Ferocactus p. 320
Barrel cactus
☼ ✂ 8–24

Fouquieria splendens p. 325
Ocotillo
☼ ✂ 10–13, 18–20

Furcraea p. 330
☼ ◐ ✂ 13, 16–17, 19–24; H1, H2

Opuntia ficus-indica p. 462
☼ ✂ 8, 9, 12–24; H1, H2

Stenocereus thurberi p. 613
Organpipe cactus
☼ ✂ 12–24

Trees and Shrubs

Acer palmatum (some) p. 129
Japanese maple
☼ ◐ ✂ A3; 2B–10, 12, 14–24

Aloe barberae p. 145
Tree aloe
☼ ◐ ✂ 8, 9, 12–24

Arbutus 'Marina' p. 163
☼ ✂ 8, 9, 14–24

Arctostaphylos (taller kinds) p. 164
Manzanita
☼ ◐ ✂ ZONES VARY

Cedrus atlantica 'Pendula' p. 228
Weeping atlas cedar
☼ ✂ 3B–10, 14–24

Cordyline australis p. 259
☼ ◐ ✂ 5, 8–11, 14–24; H1, H2

Cordyline fruticosa p. 259
Ti plant
☼ ◐ ✂ 21–24; H1, H2

Corylus avellana 'Contorta' p. 265
Harry Lauder's walking stick
☼ ◐ ✂ 2–9, 14–20

Dasylirion (many) p. 281
☼ ◐ ✂ ZONES VARY

Agave potatorum

Aloe polyphylla

Ferocactus wislizenii

Cedrus atlantica 'Glauca Pendula'

Leptospermum laevigatum p. 405
Australian tea tree
☼ ✀ 14–24; H1, H2

Olea europaea p. 460
Olive
☼ ✀ 8, 9, 11–24; H1, H2

Palms p. 471
NEEDS, ZONES VARY

Parkinsonia p. 475
Palo verde
☼ ✀ ZONES VARY

Pinus contorta p. 507
Shore pine
☼ ✀ A3; 4–9, 14–24; H1

Tsuga canadensis 'Pendula' p. 639
Sargent weeping hemlock
☼ ◑ ✀ A3; 2–7, 17

Yucca p. 657
☼ ✀ ZONES VARY

Perennials

Acanthus mollis p. 128
Bear's breech
☼ ◑ ● ✀ 5–24

Artichoke p. 171
☼ ◑ ✀ ZONES VARY

Astelia p. 175
☼ ◑ ✀ 5, 6, 14–17, 19–24

Beschorneria yuccoides p. 195
Mexican lily
☼ ◑ ✀ 13, 16–17, 19–24

Cyperus papyrus p. 277
Papyrus
☼ ◑ ● ✀ 16, 17, 23, 24; H1, H2

Ensete ventricosum p. 301
Abyssinian banana
☼ ◑ ✀ 13, 15–24; H1, H2

Etlingera elatior p. 310
Torch ginger
☼ ◑ ✀ H2

Gunnera p. 349
◑ ✀ 4–6, 14–17, 20–24

Hakonechloa macra p. 350
Japanese forest grass
☼ ◑ ● ✀ 2B–9, 14–24

Hedychium p. 354
Ginger lily
◑ ✀ 8, 9, 14–17, 19–24; H1, H2

Helictotrichon sempervirens p. 357
Blue oat grass
☼ ✀ 1–12, 14–24

Kniphofia p. 393
Red-hot poker
☼ ◑ ✀ ZONES VARY

Miscanthus sinensis p. 444
Eulalia
☼ ◑ ✀ 2–24

Ophiopogon planiscapus 'Nigrescens' p. 462
Black mondo grass
☼ ◑ ● ✀ 5–9, 14–24; H1, H2

Phormium (many) p. 500
☼ ◑ ✀ 5–9, 14–24; H1, H2

TOP ROW: *Cordyline fruticosa; Olea europaea.* SECOND ROW: *Corylus avellana* 'Contorta'. THIRD ROW: *Yucca schidigera; Astelia banksii; Gunnera tinctoria.* BOTTOM ROW: *Helictotrichon sempervirens; Kniphofia; Phormium*

PLANTS FOR MOON GARDENS

When long summer days fade into evening, most garden plants disappear into darkness. Not so the white flowers and silvery foliage whose shapes stand out from the shadows, especially when touched by moonlight. The plants listed below are excellent choices for night garden luminescence. Although most of the white-flowering types listed bloom in summer, consider adding a few plants that flower in spring and fall to prolong the effect.

Locate your moon garden around a patio or garden bench, where you can relax and savor the magic. Add a plant or two for fragrance; angel's trumpet (*Brugmansia*) and angelwing jasmine have perfumed white or light-colored flowers (for other choices, see page 111). Tuck in a trickling fountain nearby to add soothing sound, and solar lights to supplement the moonlight.

CLOCKWISE FROM BOTTOM: Nemesia, guava, cosmos, artemisia

White Flowers

Achillea millefolium p. 132
Common yarrow
☀ ✿ A1–A3; 1–24

Agapanthus (some) p. 137
Lily-of-the-Nile
☀ ◑ ✿ 4–9, 12–24; H1, H2

**Anemone × hybrida
(some)** p. 151
Japanese anemone
◑ ✿ 2B–24

Brugmansia (some) p. 205
Angel's trumpet
☀ ◑ ● ✿ 12, 13, 16–24; H1, H2

Buddleja davidii (some) p. 207
Butterfly bush
☀ ◑ ✿ 2–24; H1

**Cosmos bipinnatus
'Sonata White'** p. 266
Cosmos
☀ ✿ 1–24

Dahlia (some) p. 278
☀ ◑ ✿ 1–24

Gardenia jasminoides p. 332
Gardenia
☀ ◑ ✿ 7–9, 12–16, 18–24; H1, H2

Gaura lindheimeri p. 334
☀ ✿ 2B–24

**Hydrangea
(white forms)** p. 367
☀ ◑ ✿ ZONES VARY

Ipomoea alba p. 376
Moonflower
☀ ✿ 15–17, 23, 24; H1, H2

**Leucanthemum
× superbum** p. 407
Shasta daisy
☀ ✿ A1–A3; 1–24; H1

Lilium 'Casablanca' p. 412
Oriental hybrid lily
☀ ◑ ✿ 1–9, 14–22

Nicotiana sylvestris p. 456
Flowering tobacco
☀ ◑ ✿ ALL ZONES

Osteospermum (some) p. 467
African daisy
☀ ✿ ALL ZONES

Philadelphus p. 498
Mock orange
☀ ◑ ✿ ZONES VARY

**Phlox paniculata
(some)** p. 500
Summer phlox
☀ ◑ ✿ 1–14, 18–21

Romneya coulteri p. 567
Matilija poppy
☀ ✿ 4–12, 14–24; H1

Rosa (white varieties) p. 572
Floribunda rose
☀ ◑ ✿ ALL ZONES

Achillea millefolium

Anemone × hybrida 'Honorine Jobert'

Gardenia jasminoides

Hydrangea macrophylla

Silvery Foliage

Artemisia (several) p. 169
☼ ⚡ ZONES VARY

**Cedrus atlantica
'Glauca'** p. 228
Atlas cedar
☼ ⚡ 3B–10, 14–24

Centaurea cineraria p. 230
Dusty miller
☼ ⚡ 8–24; H1, H2

**Cerastium
tomentosum** p. 232
Snow-in-summer
☼ ◑ ⚡ A1, A2; 1–24

Dudleya brittonii p. 294
☼ ⚡ 16, 17, 21–24

Echeveria (many) p. 295
☼ ◑ ⚡ ZONES VARY

**Elaeagnus
'Coral Silver'** p. 299
☼ ◑ ⚡ 2B–24

Juniperus (some) p. 386
Juniper
☼ ◑ ⚡ ZONES VARY

Kalanchoe beharensis p. 390
Felt plant
☼ ◑ ⚡ 13, 21–24; H1, H2

Lavandula (some) p. 401
Lavender
☼ ⚡ ZONES VARY

**Leucophyllum
frutescens** p. 408
Texas ranger
☼ ⚡ 7–24; H1, H2

Lychnis coronaria p. 424
Crown-pink
☼ ◑ ⚡ 1–9, 14–24

Perovskia atriplicifolia p. 494
Russian sage
☼ ⚡ 2–24

Phlomis purpurea p. 499
☼ ⚡ 7–24

**Pittosporum tenuifolium
'Marjorie Channon'** p. 512
☼ ◑ ⚡ 9, 14–17, 19–24

Salvia (some) p. 583
Sage
☼ ⚡ ZONES VARY

**Santolina
chamaecyparissus** p. 591
Lavender cotton
☼ ⚡ 22–24; H1, H2

Senecio cineraria p. 600
Dusty miller
☼ ◑ ⚡ 4–24; H1, H2

Stachys byzantina p. 612
Lamb's ears
☼ ◑ ⚡ 1–24

Teucrium fruticans p. 626
Bush germander
☼ ⚡ 4–24

Zauschneria p. 659
California fuchsia
☼ ⚡ 2–11, 14–24

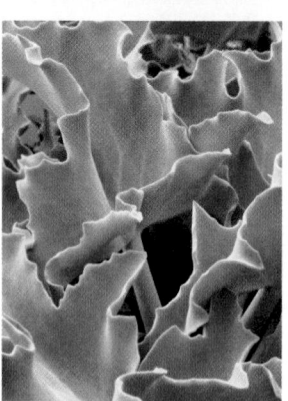

TOP ROW: *Philadelphus mexicanus; Phlox paniculata.* SECOND ROW: *Rosa* 'Iceberg'. THIRD ROW: *Artemisia schmidtiana* 'Silver Mound'; *Centaurea cineraria; Dudleya brittonii.* BOTTOM ROW: *Kalanchoe beharensis; Stachys byzantina* 'Silver Carpet'

PERENNIALS FOR POTS

These garden mainstays flower reliably, year after year. Unlike annuals, which live for only a year, perennials are semipermanent plants that need occasional cutting back and periodic division and replanting to keep up a spectacular display. Some are evergreen; others die to the ground at the end of the growing season, then reappear from their roots the following year.

The easiest way to ensure a steady stream of container displays during all seasons is to pot up perennials singly, grow them in a side yard that gets good light, then move them to center stage when they are in bloom or otherwise peaking. Some reliable choices for late-spring bloom into summer include astilbe and geum; for summer, cannas, heliotrope, lavender; for fall, asters or chrysanthemums; and for winter, English primroses, euryops, and hellebores. Heucheras, grown primarily for their foliage, make striking singular shows most of the year.

Helleborus 'Party Dress'

Achillea   p. 132
Yarrow
☼ ✿ A1–A3; 1–24

**Agapanthus
(dwarf forms)**   p. 137
☼ ◐ ✿ ZONES VARY

Alstroemeria   p. 147
☼ ◐ ✿ 5–9, 14–24; H1

Aquilegia   p. 161
Columbine
☼ ◐ ✿ ZONES VARY

Aster   p. 176
☼ ✿ ZONES VARY

Astilbe   p. 177
False spirea
☼ ◐ ✿ A2, A3; 1–7, 14–17

Canna   p. 220
☼ ✿ 6–9, 12–24; H1, H2

Coreopsis (some)   p. 260
☼ ✿ ZONES VARY

Dianthus   p. 285
Pink
☼ ◐ ✿ A2, A3; 1–24

Echinacea purpurea   p. 296
Purple coneflower
☼ ✿ A2, A3; 1–24

Erigeron   p. 305
Fleabane
☼ ◐ ✿ ZONES VARY

Felicia amelloides   p. 319
Blue marguerite
☼ ✿ 8, 9, 14–24

Gaillardia × grandiflora   p. 331
☼ ✿ 1–24; H1, H2

Gaura lindheimeri   p. 334
☼ ✿ 2B–24

Gerbera jamesonii   p. 338
Transvaal daisy
☼ ◐ ✿ 8, 9, 12–24; H1, H2

Geum   p. 338
☼ ◐ ✿ 2–24

**Heliotropium
arborescens**   p. 357
Common heliotrope
☼ ◐ ✿ 15–17, 23, 24; H1, H2

Helleborus   p. 357
Hellebore
◐ ● ✿ ZONES VARY

Hemerocallis (most)   p. 358
Daylily
☼ ◐ ✿ 1–24; H1, H2

Heuchera (most)   p. 361
Coral bells
☼ ◐ ✿ ZONES VARY

Hosta (smaller types)   p. 365
Plantain lily
◐ ● ✿ ZONES VARY

Kniphofia uvaria   p. 394
Red-hot poker
☼ ◐ ✿ 2–9, 14–24

Lavandula   p. 401
Lavender
☼ ✿ ZONES VARY

Achillea millefolium 'Apfelblüte'

Aster novae-angliae

Coreopsis verticillata

Dianthus

Leucanthemum × superbum   p. 407
Shasta daisy
☼ ✄ A1–A3; 1–24; H1

Ligularia   p. 411
◑ ✄ 1–9, 14–17

Lilium   p. 412
Lily
☼ ◑ ✄ ZONES VARY

Limonium (some)   p. 415
Statice
☼ ✄ ZONES VARY

Paeonia (herbaceous)   p. 469
Peony
☼ ◑ ✄ A1–A3; 1–11, 14–20

Pelargonium   p. 487
Geranium
☼ ◑ ✄ 8, 9, 12–24

Penstemon (many)   p. 490
Beard tongue
☼ ◑ ✄ ZONES VARY

Primula (many)   p. 528
Primrose
☼ ◑ ● ✄ ZONES VARY

Rudbeckia   p. 579
☼ ✄ 1–24

Salvia chiapensis   p. 584
Chiapas sage
☼ ◑ ✄ 15, 17, 23, 24

Salvia (many)   p. 584
Sage
☼ ◑ ✄ ZONES VARY

Sedum (many)   p. 597
Stonecrop
☼ ◑ ✄ ZONES VARY

Stokesia laevis   p. 614
Stokes' aster
☼ ✄ 2–10, 12–24

Thalictrum (some)   p. 627
Meadow rue
◑ ✄ 2–10, 14–17

Tiarella cordifolia   p. 630
Foamflower
◑ ● ✄ A3; 1–9, 14–24

TOP ROW: *Echinacea purpurea* 'Powwow Wild Berry'; *Gaillardia* 'Oranges and Lemons'; *Heuchera*. SECOND ROW: *Geum chiloense*; *Leucanthemum* × *superbum* 'Old Court'. THIRD ROW: *Limonium sinuatum*; *Pelargonium* × *hortorum*; *Rudbeckia hirta* 'Denver Daisy'. BOTTOM ROW: *Salvia* 'Wendy's Wish'; *Thalictrum rochebrunianum* 'Lavender Mist'

PLANTS FOR TROPICAL EFFECTS

Some like it hot. Or, more precisely, the look of warm, island-style gardens filled with palms, lush foliage, and vibrant flowers. Tropical plants may seem most at home in Hawaii's lower elevations, where the sunny-showery days that Islanders call "liquid sunshine" are abundant. But a surprising number of tropicals are succeeding in such decidedly nontropical climates as Seattle, Vancouver, and San Francisco.

   If Hawaii and Tahiti are among your favorite vacation spots, you can re-create the look using some of the plants listed here—trees, shrubs, perennials, and vines—whose big, luxuriant leaves, flashy flowers, or overall lushness define tropical destinations worldwide. In cool-winter climates such as the Pacific Northwest, some gardeners lift and store smaller kinds in a protected spot for winter.

A tropical garden in Kailua, Hawaii

Trees

Aralia p. 163
☼ ◑ ✄ ZONES VARY

Bauhinia p. 188
Orchid tree
☼ ✄ ZONES VARY

Catalpa p. 225
☼ ◑ ✄ 3–10, 14–24

Chorisia p. 241
Floss silk tree
☼ ✄ ZONES VARY

Delonix regia p. 282
Royal poinciana
☼ ✄ 22, 23; H2

Erythrina p. 308
Coral tree
☼ ✄ ZONES VARY

Ficus lyrata p. 322
Fiddleleaf fig
☼ ◑ ✄ 22–24; H1, H2

Musa p. 447
Banana
☼ ◑ ✄ ZONES VARY

Palms p. 471
NEEDS, ZONES VARY

Paulownia tomentosa p. 477
Empress tree
☼ ✄ 4–9, 11–24

Tabebuia p. 622
Trumpet tree
☼ ✄ 15, 16, 20–24; H1, H2

Shrubs

Abutilon p. 125
Flowering maple
☼ ◑ ✄ 8, 9, 12–24; H1, H2

Brugmansia p. 205
Angel's trumpet
☼ ◑ ● ✄ 12, 13, 16–24; H1, H2

Cordyline fruticosa p. 259
Ti plant
☼ ◑ ✄ 21–24; H1, H2

Fatsia japonica p. 319
Japanese aralia
◑ ● ✄ 4–9, 14–24; H1, H2

Hibiscus (many) p. 363
Hibiscus
☼ ✄ ZONES VARY

Melianthus major p. 440
Honey bush
☼ ◑ ✄ 8, 9, 12–24; H1, H2

Plumeria p. 519
Frangipani
☼ ✄ ZONES VARY

Schefflera p. 593
☼ ◑ ✄ ZONES VARY

Delonix regia

Livistona australis

Brugmansia

Cordyline fruticosa

Strelitzia p. 616
Bird of paradise
☼ ◑ ✄ ZONES VARY

Tecoma stans p. 625
Yellow bells
☼ ◑ ✄ 12, 13, 21–24; H1, H2

Tibouchina urvilleana p. 630
Princess flower
☼ ◑ ✄ 16, 17, 21–24; H1, H2

Perennials

Alocasia p. 145
Elephant's ear
◑ ✄ 22–24; H1, H2

Alpinia p. 147
Ginger lily
◑ ✄ 14–24; H1, H2

Aspidistra elatior p. 175
Cast-iron plant
◑ ● ✄ 4–10, 12–24; H1, H2

Bamboo p. 182
☼ ◑ ✄ ZONES VARY

Caladium bicolor p. 210
Fancy-leafed caladium
◑ ● ✄ H2

Canna p. 220
☼ ✄ 6–9, 12–24; H1, H2

Crinum p. 270
☼ ◑ ✄ 8, 9, 12–24; H1, H2

Ensete ventricosum p. 301
Abyssinian banana
☼ ◑ ✄ 13, 15–24; H1, H2

Epiphyllum p. 302
Orchid cactus
◑ ✄ 8, 9, 14–24; H1, H2

Gunnera p. 349
◑ ✄ 4–6, 14–17, 20–24

Hedychium p. 354
Ginger lily
◑ ✄ 8, 9, 14–17, 19–24; H1, H2

Platycerium p. 513
Staghorn fern
◑ ✄ ZONES VARY

Zantedeschia aethiopica p. 658
Common calla
☼ ◑ ✄ 5, 6, 8, 9, 12–24; H1, H2

Zingiber officinale p. 660
True ginger
◑ ✄ 9, 14–24; H1, H2

Vines

Beaumontia grandiflora p. 190
Herald's trumpet
☼ ◑ ✄ 12, 13, 16, 17, 21–24;
H1, H2

Bougainvillea p. 200
☼ ✄ 12–17, 19–24; H1, H2

Mandevilla p. 436
☼ ◑ ✄ ZONES VARY

Pandorea p. 472
☼ ◑ ✄ 16–24; H1, H2

Passiflora p. 476
Passion vine
☼ ◑ ✄ ZONES VARY

Solandra maxima p. 605
Cup-of-gold vine
☼ ✄ 15–24; H2

TOP ROW: *Fatsia japonica*; *Hibiscus rosa-sinensis* 'Jewel of India'. SECOND ROW: *Plumeria obtusa*. THIRD ROW: *Tibouchina urvilleana*; *Alpinia purpurata*; *Caladium bicolor*. BOTTOM ROW: *Canna* 'Tropicanna'; *Ensete ventricosum*; *Mandevilla sanderi*

The West's Best Plants, A to Z

THE PLANTS WE GROW IN THE WEST come from all parts of the world. Rhododendrons from China. Grevilleas from Australia. Proteas from South Africa. Palms and plumerias from the tropics. Native plants from our deserts, mountains, and coast. Because of their varied backgrounds, they respond differently to our 32 climate zones. On the following pages are 9,000 plants that thrive somewhere in the West.

HOW PLANTS ARE RELATED

In this encyclopedia, all plants except edibles are listed by their current scientific names, which break down as shown in the example below. Common names, where they exist, are also shown.

Family A group whose members share certain broad characteristics that set them apart from other plant families. Family names are in Latin, and typically end with "-aceae."

Genus (plural: genera) Groups of more closely related plants. The first word in a plant's botanical name is the genus. Some families contain only one genus; others contain hundreds of genera. The genus name is in italics, with the first letter capitalized.

Species Each genus is divided into individual species. Although distinctly different from one another, they may closely resemble other species in the genus, and they are capable of breeding together to produce similar offspring. The species name is the second word in a plant's botanical name; it is in italics and all lowercase.

Subspecies A major division within a species, it's a natural variant of the species. Where it's called for, it appears as the third word in a botanical name—always in italics and lowercase.

Variety A variant of a species. Like a subspecies name, it is written in italics as the third word in a plant's botanical name; it may be preceded by the abbreviation "var." (as in *Ilex pernyi veitchii* or *Ilex pernyi* var. *veitchii*). The word "variety" is also used to include cultivated varieties (called cultivars). Cultivars are genetically distinct plants, maintained in cultivation by human effort. They may be of hybrid origin or selected varieties of plants that occur in the wild. Cultivars are propagated by divisions, cuttings, or seed. Cultivar names are enclosed in single quotation marks and are not italicized—*Lobelia erinus* 'Crystal Palace', for example.

In general usage and throughout this book, the term "variety" refers to both cultivars and varieties found in nature.

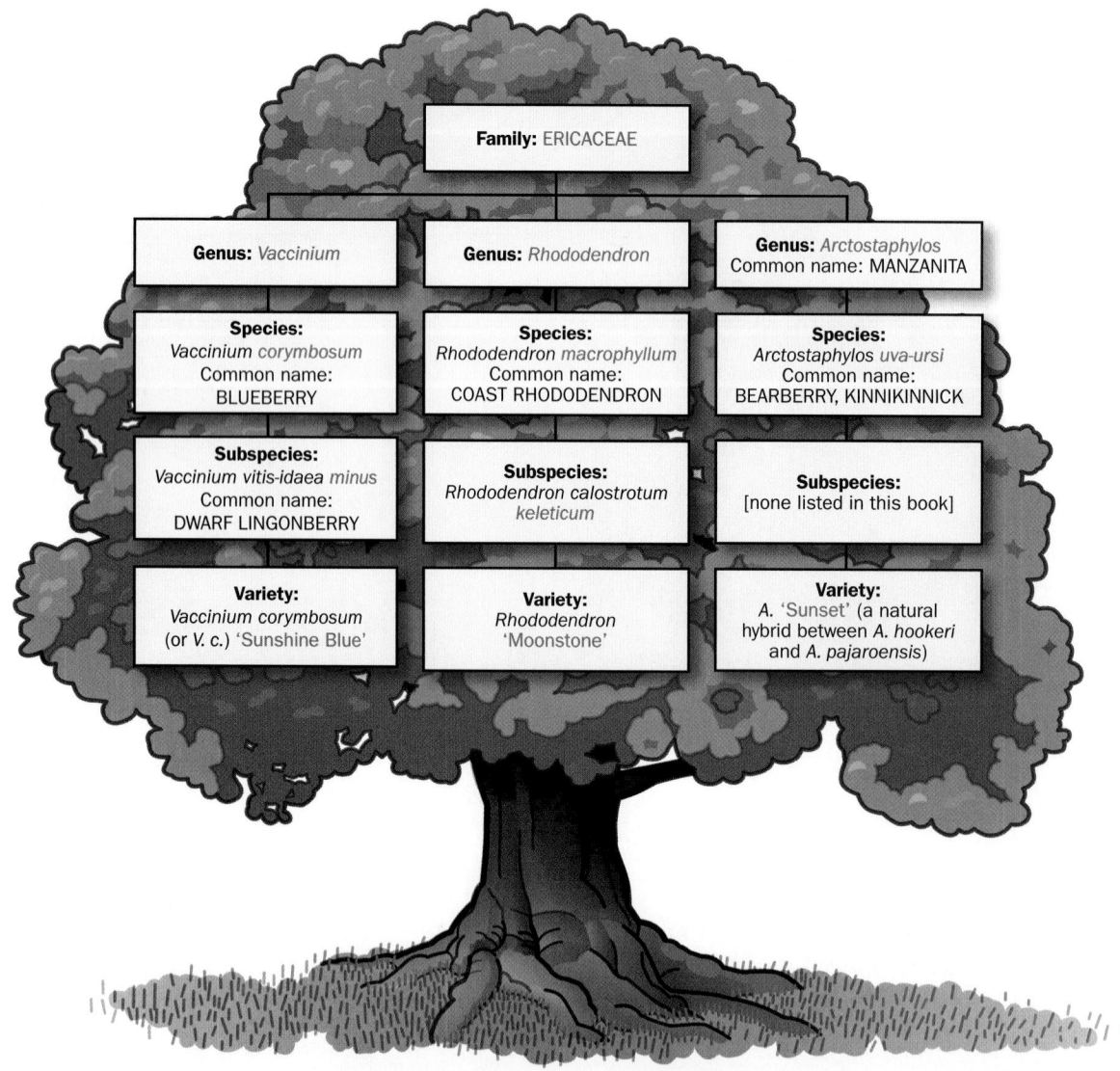

HOW TO USE THIS ENCYCLOPEDIA

The encyclopedia entries on pages 124–661 contain all the information you need to choose and grow plants successfully. Each entry begins with the information shown in the example below. Introductory text describes the plant and lists recommended varieties, some in chart form. Finally, many entries include a section titled "How to Grow," which gives guidelines on everything from soil and fertilizer requirements to dealing with common pests and diseases.

Genus

COMMON NAME
Family
PLANT TYPE

Schinus

PEPPER TREE
Anacardiaceae
EVERGREEN TREES

⚡ **ZONES VARY BY SPECIES**

☼ **FULL SUN**

◐◑● **WATER NEEDS VARY BY SPECIES**

🐦 **BIRDS EAT THE FRUITS**

◊ **FOLIAGE CAN CAUSE DERMATITIS; BERRIES OF S. TEREBINTHIFOLIUS CAN CAUSE GASTRIC DISTRESS**

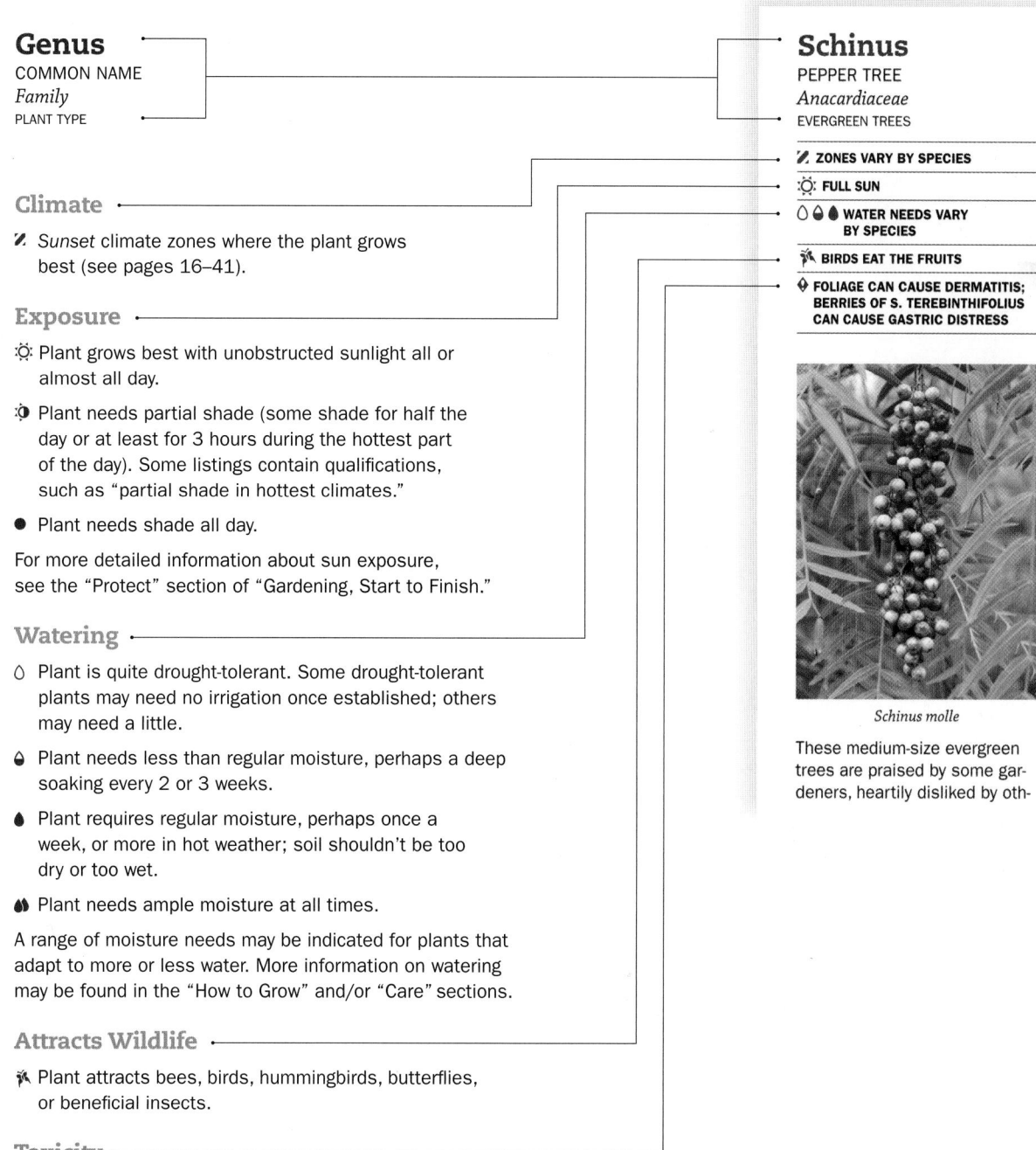

Schinus molle

These medium-size evergreen trees are praised by some gardeners, heartily disliked by oth-

Climate

⚡ *Sunset* climate zones where the plant grows best (see pages 16–41).

Exposure

☼ Plant grows best with unobstructed sunlight all or almost all day.

◑ Plant needs partial shade (some shade for half the day or at least for 3 hours during the hottest part of the day). Some listings contain qualifications, such as "partial shade in hottest climates."

● Plant needs shade all day.

For more detailed information about sun exposure, see the "Protect" section of "Gardening, Start to Finish."

Watering

◊ Plant is quite drought-tolerant. Some drought-tolerant plants may need no irrigation once established; others may need a little.

◑ Plant needs less than regular moisture, perhaps a deep soaking every 2 or 3 weeks.

● Plant requires regular moisture, perhaps once a week, or more in hot weather; soil shouldn't be too dry or too wet.

◖● Plant needs ample moisture at all times.

A range of moisture needs may be indicated for plants that adapt to more or less water. More information on watering may be found in the "How to Grow" and/or "Care" sections.

Attracts Wildlife

🐦 Plant attracts bees, birds, hummingbirds, butterflies, or beneficial insects.

Toxicity

◊ Some part of the plant is known to have toxic or irritant properties.

A

Abelia

Caprifoliaceae
EVERGREEN, SEMIEVERGREEN,
DECIDUOUS SHRUBS

🌿 **ZONES VARY BY SPECIES**

☼ ◑ **BEST IN SUN, TOLERATE SOME SHADE, EXCEPT AS NOTED**

💧 **REGULAR WATER**

🦋 **ATTRACT BIRDS, BUTTERFLIES**

Abelia × grandiflora
'Mardi Gras'

Graceful, arching branches are densely clothed with oval, usually glossy leaves; new growth is bronze. Tubular or bell-shaped flowers cluster at branch ends or among leaves, mostly summer and early fall. When blooms drop, purplish or copper-colored sepals usually follow, lasting into fall. Leaves also may take on bronzy tints in autumn.

A. chinensis. Deciduous. Zones 4–24. Chinese native to 4–5 ft. tall and wide, with fragrant, pink-tinted white flowers.

A. 'Edward Goucher'. Zones 5–24. Lacier, more compact (to 3–5 ft. tall and wide), and less cold-hardy than *A. × grandiflora*. Small lilac-pink flowers have orange throats.

A. floribunda. MEXICAN ABELIA. Evergreen. Zones 9, 12–24; some winter damage in Zones 7, 8. Severely damaged at 20°F (–7°C). Native to Mexico. Usually grows 3–6 ft. tall and wide but can reach 10 ft. tall and 12 ft. wide. Arching,

reddish, downy or hairy stems. Bright reddish purple flowers hang singly or in clusters. Heaviest bloom is in summer; sporadic bloom the rest of the year. Needs partial shade in hot climates.

A. × grandiflora. GLOSSY ABELIA. Evergreen to semievergreen. Zones 4–24; H1, H2. The best known and most popular of the abelias. To 8 ft. or taller, spreading to at least 5 ft. wide. Loses most of its leaves at 15°F (–9°C). Freezes to the ground at 0°F (–18°C) but usually recovers to bloom the same year, making a graceful border plant 10–15 in. high. Among the most popular varieties:

'Bronze Anniversary'. Grows 3–4 ft. high and wide, with new growth bronzy orange, maturing to lime green. White flowers.

'Confetti'. Dense grower to 2–3 ft. high, 4–5 ft. wide. Leaves variegated white, turning maroon in cold weather. White flowers.

'Francis Mason'. Compact (to 3–4 ft. high and wide) and densely branched. Pink flowers, yellow variegated leaves.

'Golden Anniversary'. Low grower to about 2 ft. tall and twice as wide. Green leaves are heavily edged and splashed with creamy yellow. Stems are red, flowers white.

'Kaleidoscope'. Compact (2–3 ft. tall, 3–4 ft. wide) with bright red stems. Yellow variegated leaves pick up orange and red tones in fall. White flowers.

'Little Richard'. Dense and compact growth 2–3 ft. high and wide. Shiny dark green leaves that hold on for a long time even in cold winters. White flowers.

'Mardi Gras'. Grows 2–3 ft. high and 4–5 ft. wide, with leaves edged and splashed with pink and creamy white. Pale pink to white flowers.

'Prostrate White' ('Prostrata'). Low grower (1½–2 ft. tall, spreading 4–5 ft. wide) useful as groundcover, bank planting. White flowers.

'Sherwoodii'. Dense, compact, refined growth to 3–4 ft. tall, 5 ft. wide. Pale lavender-pink flowers.

'Silver Anniversary'. Grows 2–2½ ft. high, spreading 3–4 ft. Leaves have silvery cream edges. White flowers.

'Sunrise'. To 3–5 ft. tall and a little wider. Densely branched, with glossy green leaves edged in yellow; foliage turns orange to red in fall. White flowers.

'White Marvel'. Dense (5 ft. high and wide), with white to yellow new growth. Mature leaves green with cream to golden yellow edges. White flowers.

CARE

To keep the shrub's graceful form, prune selectively; don't shear. The more stems you cut to the ground in winter or early spring, the more open and arching next year's growth will be.

Abies

FIR
Pinaceae
EVERGREEN TREES

🌿 **ZONES VARY BY SPECIES**

☼ ◑ **FULL SUN OR LIGHT SHADE, EXCEPT AS NOTED**

💧 **MODERATE TO REGULAR WATER, EXCEPT AS NOTED**

🦋 **SEEDS ATTRACT BIRDS**

Abies koreana

Firs are tall, erect, symmetrical trees with uniformly spaced branch whorls. Though sometimes confused with spruces (*Picea*), they have softer needles that fall directly from the stems (spruces leave short pegs behind), and their large cones grow up rather than down. Fir cones shatter after ripening, leaving a spiky stalk. Most firs are native to North America and are high-mountain plants that do best in or near their natural habitats. They grow slowly, if at all, in hot, dry, windy areas at low elevations; choose other conifers in such areas.

A. amabilis. PACIFIC SILVER FIR, CASCADE FIR. Zones 2b–7, 15–17. Native to southern Alaska south through the Coast Ranges and Cascades of Washington and Oregon. Grows 20–50 ft. tall and 12–15 ft. wide in gardens, much larger in the wild. Dark green needles, silvery beneath, curve upward along the branches. 'Spreading Star', a prostrate form, creates a thick, lush mat to 3 ft. high, 6 ft. wide, with minimal pruning.

A. balsamea. BALSAM FIR. Zones A3; 1–7, 15–17. Native to eastern North American mountains. Dwarf 'Nana' is the form most commonly sold in the West. Perfect for rock gardens; very slowly forms a dense, dark green cushion 2–3 ft. high and wide. Needs partial shade, regular water.

A. bracteata (A. venusta). SANTA LUCIA FIR, BRISTLECONE FIR. Zones 6–9, 14–21. From steep, rocky slopes on the seaward side of California's Santa Lucia Mountains. Grows to 70 ft. in 50 years, with spreading lower branches (to 15–20 ft. wide) and slender steeplelike crown. Sharp, stiff needles are dark green above with white lines beneath; roundish 4-in. cones have slender, pointed scales. Tolerates heat and aridity.

A. concolor. WHITE FIR. Zones A2, A3; 1–9, 14–24. Native to the mountains of southern Oregon, California, southern Rocky Mountains, Baja California. A popular Christmas tree and one of the most commonly grown native firs in Western gardens. Large, symmetrical tree reaches 80–120 ft. tall and 15–20 ft. wide in its native range and in the Northwest. Slower growing in California gardens, where it has reached 30 ft. in as many years in lowland areas. Best as a container plant in Southern California. Bluish green needles. Needs no irrigation where native; some elsewhere. Some consider 'Candicans', with bluish white foliage, the "bluest" of all conifers.

A. grandis. LOWLAND FIR, GRAND FIR. Zones 1–9, 14–17. Native from British Columbia inland to Montana and southward to coastal Northern California. Many Northwest gardeners live and garden successfully under this fast-growing tree; they just prune it high. One of the largest firs, it grows to 300 ft. tall in the wild (in gardens, it reaches 80–200 ft. tall, 15–25 ft. wide). Fragrant, deep green needles are glossy above, with white lines beneath; they grow in two rows along branches. 'Johnsonii' is suited to urban gardens, growing to 65 ft. tall and 10 ft. wide.

A. koreana. KOREAN FIR. Zones 3b–9, 14–24. Native to Korea. Slow-growing, compact, pyramidal tree seldom grows over 30 ft. tall and 20 ft. wide; its shiny, short green needles and blue to purple cones appear even on young, small trees. 'Aurea', with gold-green foliage, is even smaller and slower growing. 'Silberlocke' has needles that turn upward, showing silvery white undersides; use it to add a silver accent in wide foliage borders.

A. lasiocarpa. ALPINE FIR, ROCKY MOUNTAIN FIR. Zones A2, A3; 1–9, 14–17. Native to Alaska, south through the high Cascades of Washington and Oregon; nearly throughout the Rocky Mountains. In the wild in good, moist soil, it grows into a narrow, steeple-shaped tree, 60–90 ft. tall and 10 ft. wide. In gardens, it is usually much shorter and loses its narrow shape; allow for 15–20-ft. spread in Northwest. Extremely slow growing in California gardens. Bluish green needles.

A. l. arizonica. Zones 2–9. Native to San Francisco Peaks, Arizona, at 8,500-ft. elevation. Thick, corky, creamy white bark gives the tree its common name, "corkbark fir." Blue or silvery needles have a waxy coating. An excellent substitute for blue spruce (*Picea pungens*) in small spaces; more disease free.

A. nordmanniana. CAUCASIAN FIR, NORDMANN FIR. Zones 1–11, 14–24. Native to the Caucasus, Asia Minor, Greece. A vigorous, densely foliaged fir; grows 30–50 ft. tall and 20 ft. wide in cultivation. Shiny, dark green needles have whitish bands beneath. More adaptable to California gardens than native firs, it becomes a symmetrical, densely branched, cone-shaped tree. Needs regular water; will adapt to long-term container growing. 'Golden

Spreader' grows slowly to about 3 ft. tall and 5 ft. wide, with bright golden yellow leaves; does best in partial shade.

A. procera (A. nobilis). NOBLE FIR. Zones 2–6, 15–17. Native to the Siskiyou Mountains in California, northern mountains of Oregon and Washington. Sold in Northwest nurseries as a living Christmas tree. In the wild, it grows 90–200 ft. tall and 20–30 ft. wide; in Northwest gardens, it's almost as tall. Short, stiff branches hold blue-green needles. Cones are up to 10 in. long.

CARE

Give firs well-drained, slightly acid soil. Allow ample growing room at planting; if you later try to restrict a fir tree's size by pruning, you'll ruin its natural shape. Pruning is rarely necessary; plants are more attractive with branches all the way to the ground. New growth is susceptible to aphid damage. Firs struggle in polluted city air.

Abutilon
FLOWERING MAPLE
Malvaceae
EVERGREEN AND DECIDUOUS SHRUBS

⚡ **ZONES 8, 9, 12–24; H1, H2; EXCEPT AS NOTED**

☀ ◐ **PARTIAL SHADE IN HOTTEST CLIMATES**

◖ ◕ **MODERATE TO REGULAR WATER, EXCEPT AS NOTED**

🐦 **ATTRACT HUMMINGBIRDS AND BUTTERFLIES**

Abutilon

Showy members of the mallow family have thin stems, broad leaves, and colorful, out-facing or dangling blooms, many in the shape of bells or lanterns. They

come from warm regions of the world, particularly South America.

A. hybrids. Grown in zones listed and also as annuals in colder climates. Evergreen. These are the best-known flowering maples, with upright, arching growth to 8–10 ft. tall, equal spread. Their broad maplelike leaves are sometimes variegated white; drooping bell-like flowers are white, yellow, pink, or red. The main bloom season is spring, but white and yellow forms flower almost continually. Hybrids include dwarf varieties and ones with more spreading habits. Some of the best:

'Bartley Schwartz'. Arching branches, with a nearly constant show of drooping, salmon-orange flowers.

'Boule de Neige'. Upright, spreading plant; white blooms.

'Cascade Dawn'. Reddish orange flowers on an upright, spreading plant. Cold hardy.

'Kentish Belle'. Arching branches; striking yellow flowers with dark red calyxes.

'Moonchimes'. Compact grower; pale yellow flowers.

'Nabob'. Large, open-growing plant; crimson blooms.

'Souvenir de Bonn'. Erect plant with soft orange, red-veined flowers; leaves edged and splashed with creamy white.

A. megapotamicum. Evergreen vine-shrub from Brazil. Vigorous growth to 10 ft. and as wide, with arrowlike leaves up to 3 in. long. Flowers resembling red-and-yellow lanterns hang from long, rangy branches in spring and summer. Pinch branch tips to make the plant bushier and control its size. It usually looks best as a loose, informal espalier; also makes a good hanging-basket plant. 'Marianne' has more intense flower color; 'Variegatum' has leaves mottled with yellow; 'Victory' is compact and floriferous, with small, deep yellow blooms.

A. palmeri. INDIAN MALLOW. Zones 8, 9, 11–13. A sprawling evergreen shrub from the low deserts of western North America, it grows 3–5 ft. tall and wide. Clustered spring flowers are orange-yellow. Attractive gray-green leaves are soft, velvety, heart-shaped to roundish, 6 in. wide and 8 in. long. Needs little water.

A. pictum 'Thompsonii'. Similar in form to hybrids, but the foliage is strikingly variegated with creamy yellow. The plant blooms almost continually, bearing pale orange bells veined with red.

CARE

Good drainage is essential. Control whitefly and scale insects. In cold-winter climates, abutilon can be grown in pots; keep indoors in winter, put out on terrace or patio in summer. Tip-pinch to shape and control size, and prune back hard in spring for bushier plants.

Acacia
Mimosaceae
EVERGREEN AND DECIDUOUS SHRUBS AND TREES

⚡ **ZONES VARY BY SPECIES**

☀ **FULL SUN**

◊ **LITTLE OR NO WATER**

Acacia cultriformis

Native to tropics or warm regions of the world, notably Australia, Mexico, and the southwestern U.S. Many are relatively short-lived—20 to 30 years—but if a plant reaches 20 ft. high in 3 years, the short life can be accepted. Among the most popular acacias are those with clear yellow flowers in early or midwinter; some fragrant. Grow acacias on hillsides and banks; some species thrive in beach plantings. Those listed here are evergreen except where noted.

A. aneura. MULGA. Zones 8, 9, 12–24. This Australian native grows to about 15–20 ft. tall and nearly as wide, with thornless branches clothed in narrow, leathery, gray-green to silver leaves. Yellow, rodlike

A

flowers appear in winter and spring. Popular choice for desert landscapes.

A. baileyana. BAILEY ACACIA. Zones 8, 9, 13–24. From Australia. The most commonly planted acacia and one of the hardiest, this spreading tree reaches 20–30 ft. tall and 20–40 ft. wide. Leaves are feathery, finely cut, and blue-gray; bright yellow flowers in early to midwinter. Wonderful on banks when grown as multi-trunked shrub-tree. 'Purpurea', purple-leaf acacia, is as tall but not quite as wide; its new growth is lavender to purple. Cut it back to encourage new growth and prolong foliage color.

A. berlandieri. GUAJILLO. Zones 10–24. Extremely heat-tolerant species from southern Texas and northeastern Mexico. Shrubby growth to 5–12 ft. high and 5–20 ft. wide, with feathery, finely divided, light green leaves on thornless branches. Fragrant, white, spherical flowers appear in clusters in early spring. Can be trained into a tree but is especially useful for screening.

A. boormanii. SNOWY RIVER WATTLE. Zones 8, 9, 12–24. Native to eastern Australia. Grows 10–15 ft. tall and 6–15 ft. wide. Gray-green leaves are narrow and up to 3 in. long. Fragrant, bright yellow flower puffs at branch ends in winter to early spring. This shrubby plant can sucker to form thickets; excellent for screen or windbreak. Tolerates winter wet.

A. chinchillensis. CHINCHILLA WATTLE. Zones 8, 9, 13–17, 19–24. From eastern Australia. Quick, shrubby growth to 3–6 ft. tall and slightly wider. Feathery, gray-green leaves, and bright yellow, ball-shaped flowers in late winter or early spring. Good choice for a large container.

A. cognata (A. subporosa linearis). BOWER WATTLE, RIVER WATTLE, EMERALD CASCADE ACACIA. Zones 16–24. Grows quickly into a graceful weeping tree 15–25 ft. tall and wide, with narrow, drooping, bright green leaves up to 4 in. long. Springtime flowers are creamy yellow puffs. Damaged at 20°F (−7°C). Popular compact varieties (dense growers to just 3 ft. tall and wide) are 'Limelight', with lime green

leaves, and 'Mini Cog' ('Cousin Itt'); both are useful in containers and borders.

A. constricta. WHITE-THORN, MESCAT ACACIA. Zones 8–24. Native from Texas to Arizona and Mexico. Open grower to 10–20 ft. tall and wide, with tiny feathery leaves that drop with extreme drought or cold. Fragrant yellow flowers appear in late spring or early summer and are followed by slender reddish, 5-in.-long seedpods. Valuable in desert for texture; white thorns on branches make it a good barrier plant.

A. covenyi. BLUE BUSH. Zones 8, 9, 12–24. From eastern Australia. A fast-growing shrub or small tree (12–20 ft. tall and 10–15 ft. wide) with chocolate brown branches and narrow, blue-gray leaves. Bright yellow, fragrant flowers are profuse in late winter to early spring. Excellent colorful windbreak or screen.

A. craspedocarpa. LEATHERLEAF ACACIA. Zones 8, 9, 12–24. Native to Australia. Dense, round to upright shrub grows slowly to 5–10 ft. tall and 3–8 ft. wide; can be trained as a small tree. Leaves are round, thick, and leathery, emerging coppery and aging to gray-green. Bright yellow flowers resembling bottlebrushes dot the plant in spring, sometimes repeating in summer; flat seedpods follow. Very drought-tolerant; can take regular irrigation if drainage is excellent.

A. cultriformis. KNIFELEAF ACACIA. Zones 12–24. From eastern Australia. Multistemmed small tree to 10–15 ft. tall and wide, with silvery gray leaves shaped like paring knife blades. Clusters of fragrant yellow flowers in early spring. Useful as a barrier or screen, and on banks and slopes. Cut branches are attractive in arrangements.

A. dealbata (A. decurrens dealbata). SILVER WATTLE. Zones 8, 9, 14–24; borderline in 6. Native to southeastern Australia. Grows rapidly to 40–50 ft. tall and nearly as wide, with an open, rounded shape. Feathery, silvery gray leaves contrast with the bright yellow, ball-shaped flowers that appear on branch tips in late winter or early spring. Twigs and young branches are silvery gray.

Pick Your Foliage

Most nurseries sell only a few of the many acacia species, but you can easily grow acacias from seed you collect yourself, or order from a specialist.

Acacias differ widely in foliage and growth habit. Some have feathery, much-divided leaves; others have flattened leafstalks that function as leaves. Many start life with feathery leaves and later develop leathery ones.

Acacia baileyana 'Purpurea'   *A. longifolia*

Useful as a fast-growing windbreak or for erosion control.

A. fimbriata. BRISBANE GOLDEN WATTLE. Zones 8, 9, 12–24; H1. From eastern Australia. Grows quickly to 15–20 ft. high and 8–15 ft. wide, with dark green, lance-shaped leaves. Showy in spring, with many bright yellow flowers. Good screen or windbreak. Tolerates frost and wet winters well.

A. greggii. CATCLAW ACACIA. Zones 10–24. Deciduous shrub or small tree native from California to Texas and northern Mexico. Grows to 15–25 ft. high and 15 ft. wide. Finely divided, dark green leaves grow on branches armed with hooked thorns. Creamy yellow flowers are borne in spring and intermittently through fall. Plants are shrubby in drought, treelike with more water. Good barrier plant.

A. iteaphylla. WILLOW WATTLE. Zones 8, 9, 12–24. Native to southern Australia. A beautiful, slightly weeping, spreading shrub that grows to 8–12 ft. high and 10–15 ft. wide; narrow, gray-green leaves are reddish pink when young. Pale yellow flowers bloom late winter to early spring. Makes

a good screen or low windbreak, especially near the coast.

A. koa. KOA. Zones H1, H2. Native to Hawaii. Grows quickly to 60 ft. high and wide, possibly larger with great age. Young trees have feathery foliage; older ones develop leathery, curved leaves up to 6 in. long and ½ in. wide. Springtime flowers are pale yellow spheres. This highly prized Hawaiian tree produces a strong, beautiful hardwood that is used to make canoes, furniture, surfboards, and string instruments.

A. longifolia. SYDNEY GOLDEN WATTLE. Zones 8, 9, 14–24. Eastern Australian native sometimes sold as *A. latifolia*. Reaches 10–25 ft. high and 9–15 ft. wide. Bright green, lance-shaped leaves reach 3–6 in. long. Scented, golden yellow flower spikes appear along branches in late winter and early spring. Usually seen as a big, rounded, billowy shrub. Very fast growing and tolerant of various soils. Good as a soil binder near the beach (winds make it prostrate). Resists oak root fungus.

A. merinthophora. ZIGZAG WATTLE. Zones 13–17, 19–24.

From western Australia. Open-growing, weeping shrub to 8–12 ft. high and nearly as wide. Threadlike, gray-green leaves up to a foot long are held on zig-zagging branches. Bright yellow flowers in winter or spring are followed by slender, curving seedpods.

A. minuta. See *A. smallii*.

A. pendula. WEEPING ACACIA, WEEPING MYALL. Zones 13–24. From eastern Australia. Slow grower to 25 ft. high and about 15 ft. wide. Blue-gray leaves to 4 in. long hang from weeping branches. Blooms erratically in late winter or early spring, with small, pale yellow flowers in pairs or clusters. Prized for its beautiful form and dramatic foliage color. Let it cascade from behind a wall or trim into a graceful espalier.

A. podalyriifolia. PEARL ACACIA. Zones 8, 9, 13–24. Native to eastern Australia. Reaches 10–20 ft. high and about as wide. Roundish leaves, 1½ in. long, are silvery gray and satiny to the touch. Light yellow, fluffy, scented blooms cover the plant in late winter or early spring. Excellent patio tree with good winter color. Prune heavily after flowering to keep it compact. Will not tolerate summer water.

A. pravissima. OVENS WATTLE. Zones 12–24. From eastern Australia. Grows to 12–20 ft. high and wide, with short, triangular, gray-green leaves packed tightly along the branches. Profuse winter or spring show of cream to bright yellow, scented flowers. Endures frost, heat, wind, pollution, and marine exposure.

A. redolens. Zones 8, 9, 12–24. Native to western Australia. Variable grower to 1–6 ft. high and up to 15 ft. wide, with narrow, leathery, gray-green leaves. Puffy, yellow, ball-shaped flowers appear in spring. Useful groundcover for banks, large areas of poor soil. Tolerates drought and heat. 'Desert Carpet' and 'Low Boy' are prostrate forms to just 1–2 ft. high, spreading 12–15 ft. across.

A. rigens. NEALIE. Zones 5, 7–9, 11–24. Native to much of Australia. Reaches 6–9 ft. high and wide. Leaves are silvery gray, threadlike. In late winter or early spring, branches are

loaded with small, bright yellow, spherical flowers. Easy to grow in almost any soil. Interesting specimen planted in front of a wall or fence.

A. rigidula. BLACKBRUSH ACACIA. Zones 10–13. Semi-evergreen shrub or small tree native from Texas through central Mexico. Grows slowly to 10–15 ft. high and wide. Leaves are small, deep green, and rounded; branches are light gray and very thorny. Fragrant, pale yellow, springtime flowers in 2–3-in. spikes. Plant is multi-trunked; train to single trunk by pulling off suckers at base.

A. schaffneri. TWISTED ACACIA. Zones 8, 9, 12–24. From Mexico and southern Texas. This deciduous shrub or small tree grows to 18 ft. high and 20 ft. wide, with nearly black twisting or curving branches. Close-set, ferny leaves have short thorns concealed at their base. Spring brings yellow, ball-shaped flowers with a light fragrance. Prune to form trunk and shape branches.

A. smallii (A. minuta). Zones 8, 9, 12–24. From Mexico and the southwestern U.S. This variable plant grows to 10–35 ft. high and 15–25 ft. wide. The deciduous, finely divided leaves are held on thorny branches, with yellow, fragrant, puffy ball flowers appearing in spring. Often sold as *A. farnesiana*, which is cold-tender; plant *A. smallii* where frost occurs.

A. spectabilis. MUDGEE WATTLE. Zones 8, 9, 13–24. Native to eastern Australia. Grows quickly to 12–15 ft. tall and wide, with silvery white bark and gray-green, ferny leaves. Bright yellow flower clusters cover the branches in late winter or early spring, followed by long, slender, purplish seedpods. Tolerates frost but not poor drainage. Good choice for small gardens.

A. stenophylla. SHOE-STRING ACACIA. Zones 8, 9, 12–24. From Australia comes this fast-growing, open, weeping tree to 30–40 ft. high and 20–30 ft. wide. Common name refers to long (up to 18 in.), narrow, drooping, pale green leaves. New bark is maroon, and creamy yellow flowers like

½-in. balls appear in late winter and early spring. Attractive in groves; provides lightest shade for underplantings.

A. verticillata. PRICKLY MOSES. Zones 14–24. Native to southeastern Australia. Grows 6–15 ft. high and nearly as wide. Leaves are dark green, needlelike, and just ¾ in. long. Looks like an airy, shrubby conifer until spring, when pale yellow flowers appear in 1-in.-long spikes. Makes a good low hedge in windy areas and at the beach. Unpruned, it develops an open form with many spreading, twisting trunks; sheared, it grows dense and full. Resists oak root fungus.

A. vestita. HAIRY WATTLE. Zones 13, 15–17, 19–24. From southeastern Australia. Grows 12–20 ft. high and almost as wide, with long weeping branches and narrow, gray-green leaves that are soft and downy. Beautiful in spring, when plant is covered with brilliant yellow, ball-shaped flowers. This attractive weeping shrub can be used as a focal point, low screen, or windbreak. Tolerates drought as well as brief periods of flooding.

A. willardiana. PALO BLANCO. Zones 12–24. From Mexico. This airy, graceful deciduous tree grows 20 ft. high and about 10 ft. wide. The fernlike leaves fall early, leaving narrow leaflike stalks 3–12 in. long. Flowers are pale yellow and appear in early spring. The most striking feature is the beautiful white or cream-colored papery, peeling bark.

CARE

All acacias grow best in well-drained soil. Where water is bad and salts accumulate in the soil, many become chlorotic. Poor drainage and lack of trace elements—especially iron—in the soil are other causes. You can prune acacias or leave them to their own devices. Larger-growing species may end up as shrubs or trees, depending on how they are treated in youth. Remove the lead shoot, and the plant grows as a shrub; remove the lower branches for a tree-like effect. Prune trees to open up their interiors, which helps prevent wind damage. Thin by removing a few branches all the way to the trunk.

Acalypha
Euphorbiaceae
EVERGREEN SHRUBS AND DECIDUOUS PERENNIALS

🌡 **ZONES 24; H2; OR INDOORS**

☀ ◑ **FULL SUN OR PARTIAL SHADE; BRIGHT INDIRECT LIGHT**

💧 **REGULAR WATER, EXCEPT AS NOTED**

Acalypha wilkesiana

This large and varied genus includes many colorful plants—some with bright, fuzzy flowers, others with multihued foliage. All bloom intermittently during the warmest months, and all require good drainage. Pinch young plants regularly to encourage bushy growth.

A. hispida. CHENILLE PLANT. Evergreen shrub from Malaysia and New Guinea. Upright grower can reach 10 ft. tall and 6 ft. wide, with heavy, rich green leaves up to 10 in. long. Flowers come in hanging, 1½-ft.-long clusters that resemble tassels of crimson chenille. Heaviest bloom is in early summer, but scattered bloom may occur all year. Thrives in tropical climates and does well in a greenhouse or enclosed patio.

A. monostachya. ROUND COPPERLEAF, RASPBERRY FUZZIES. Deciduous perennial native to west-central Texas and northern Mexico. Plants form a low mound 6–18 in. high and 3–4 ft. wide. Fuzzy, oval to round leaves have deeply scalloped edges. Fuzzy, deep pink flowers cover the plant from spring to fall. Adaptable and heat-tolerant; needs little water once established. Leaves drop after first frost; cut back to ground for a neater winter appearance.

»

A. reptans (A. pendula).
FIRETAIL, CAT TAIL, DWARF CHE-
NILLE. Native to Florida and the
Caribbean, this plant is grown
as an annual in Zones 22 and
23. It resembles *A. hispida* in
flower form and color but is
much smaller (about 1 ft. high
and wide), with shorter tassels
that droop from trailing branches.
Good choice for growing in a
hanging basket.

A. wilkesiana. COPPER-
LEAF. Native to the Pacific
Islands. Foliage is more colorful
than many flowers. Often used
as an annual, substituting for
flowers from late summer to
frost. In a warm, sheltered spot,
copperleaf can grow as a shrub
to 6 ft. or taller, nearly as wide.
Leaves come in various blends
of bronzy green, red and purple,
or red. Hybrid 'Sizzle Scissors'
has finely dissected leaves
strongly edged in pink. Outdoor
potted plants should be kept
slightly dry through winter.

Acanthopanax sieboldianus.
See *Eleutherococcus
sieboldianus*

Acanthus
BEAR'S BREECH
Acanthaceae
PERENNIALS

🌡 **ZONES VARY BY SPECIES**

☼ ◐ ● **SUN OR SHADE**

◐ ● **MODERATE TO REGULAR WATER**

Acanthus mollis

Native to southern Europe and
the Mediterranean. Architectural
plants with large, deeply lobed,
sometimes spiny leaves form
clumps to about 3 ft. wide. They
bloom in late spring or summer,
sending up tall spikes of hooded

whitish, rose, or purple flowers
beneath spiny green or purplish
bracts. Effective in shade with
bamboo and large-leafed ferns
but will survive in dry, sunny
spots.

**A. hungaricus (A. balca-
nicus).** Zones 2–24. Smaller
than *A. mollis,* with more finely
cut and toothed leaves.

A. mollis. Zones 5–24. This
is the most commonly grown
species. In bloom, it reaches
4–5 ft. high. The spineless
leaves to 2 ft. long are deeply
lobed and cut. Plants in the Latifolius group have larger leaves
and are generally hardier. The
foliage of 'Hollard's Gold' is
yellow in spring and throughout
summer. 'Summer Beauty',
probably a hybrid with *A. spinosus,* is more heat-tolerant.

A. spinosus. Zones 4–24.
Similar to *A. mollis* in size, but
its leaves are more finely cut
and armed with long spines.
Foliage is silvery on the true
species. Hybrids have bright
green leaves and are known as
the Spinosissimus group.

CARE
Spreading roots can become
invasive, so give the plants
plenty of room or confine their
root zones with an 8-in.-deep
barrier. In dry-summer regions,
they lose their leaves if deprived
of moisture in summer, then
leaf out again with winter rains;
occasional soakings keep leaves
green during hot weather. Lop
off the prickly spikes after flowers fade. To propagate, dig and
divide between midfall and early
spring. Control snails and slugs.

*Acanthus mollis is
one of the boldest
plants you can grow;
its large, glossy
leaves spread out
like frilly skirts
beneath tall candles
of bloom. Cluster
several plants at the
back of a border.*

Acca sellowiana.
See *Feijoa sellowiana*

Acer
MAPLE
Sapindaceae
DECIDUOUS TREES AND SHRUBS

🌡 **ZONES VARY BY SPECIES**

☼ ◐ **FULL SUN OR PARTIAL SHADE**

◐ ● **MODERATE TO REGULAR WATER**

Acer tataricum ginnala

Admired for their graceful form
and brilliant autumn color,
maples range in size from the
tall eastern American natives to
the garden-scale eastern Asian
species that work so well in
landscapes and in containers.
Though leaves of many species
somewhat resemble the classic
maple leaf that adorns the
Canadian flag, they can also
be oval or finely dissected. All
maples produce pairs of winged,
nutlike samaras (they hold the
seeds); they're the little "heli-
copters" that delight children.
Some maples are also prized
for their bark—especially snakebark maples (vertically striped
bark) and paperbark maple
(brown, peeling, papery bark).

Maples do best in the Pacific
Northwest, in the intermountain
areas, and, to a lesser extent,
in Northern California. With the
few exceptions noted here, they
don't do well in Southern California or Southwest deserts.
Practically all maples in Southern California show marginal
leaf burn after mid-June and lack
the fall color of maples in colder
areas. For best fall color (which
can be extremely variable), shop
for maples while autumn leaves
are changing hues.

A. buergerianum. TRIDENT
MAPLE. Tree. Zones 2–9, 14–17,
20, 21. Native to China, Japan.
Grows 20–25 ft. high and wide.
Roundish crown of glossy green,
three-lobed leaves that are
paler beneath. Fall color is usually red, sometimes orange or
yellow, and older wood has
attractive, flaking bark. Growth
is naturally low and spreading;
stake and prune to make it
branch high. A favorite bonsai
subject.

A. campestre. HEDGE
MAPLE. Tree. Zones 2–9, 14–
17. Native to Europe, western
Asia. Slow growing to 70 ft., but
seldom over 30 ft. tall and wide
in cultivation. Forms a very
dense, compact, rounded head
in the Northwest; thinner in California. Leaves with three to five
lobes are dull green above,
downy beneath; turn yellow in
fall. 'Carnival' grows slowly to
about 10 ft. high and wide; new
growth is pink, gradually turning
green with white margins.
'Metro Gold' grows 35 ft. tall
and 20 ft. wide, with low seed
set (so it doesn't produce as
many seedlings) and good fall
color. 'Postelense' has a
spreading habit, reaches about
10 ft. tall, produces golden new
leaves that turn lime green in
summer. 'Pulverulentum' has
variegated leaves, grows 12 ft.
tall in 10 years.

A. capillipes. Tree. Zones
2–9, 12, 14–24. Native to
Japan, this snakebark maple
grows to 30 ft. tall and wide.
Red young branches gradually
turn brown with white stripes.
Shallowly three-lobed leaves are
red when new; they retain red
leafstalks and midribs at maturity, then turn scarlet in fall.
Give part shade in warmer
climates.

A. circinatum. VINE MAPLE.
Shrub or tree. Zones A3; 2b–6,
14–17. Native to moist woods
and stream banks from coastal
mountains of British Columbia
south to Northern California. In
forest shade, its multiple trunks
are sinuous and sprawling,
almost vinelike. In the open, it
becomes a nearly symmetrical
small tree 5–35 ft. high, with
one or several trunks. Leaves
are nearly circular, to 6 in.
across, with 5–11 lobes. Red-
tinted when new, they become
green as they mature, then

develop a red cast in mid- to late summer before turning orange, scarlet, or yellow in fall. Tiny reddish purple spring flowers are followed by winged red seeds.

'Monroe' has deeply cut foliage. 'Pacific Fire' has waxy, fiery red bark in winter and yellow autumn leaves tinted with orange; it grows more slowly than the species, reaching about 12 ft. 'Pacific Purple' leaves emerge as bronzy green, then go purple in summer, reddish in fall. 'Sunglow' grows slowly 6–10 ft. high and wide, with orange-pink new growth.

A. × conspicuum 'Phoenix'. Tree. Zones 2–6, 15–17, 20, 21. A garden hybrid between *A. davidii* and *A. pensylvanicum*, this shrubby tree grows to about 20 ft. tall, with 6-in., three-lobed green leaves that turn yellow in fall. Branches are yellowish in summer, turning a vivid coral red with white stripes in winter.

A. davidii. DAVID'S MAPLE. Tree. Zones 2–6, 15–17, 20, 21. Native to central China, this snakebark maple grows to 20–35 ft. high and wide. Its distinctive bark is shiny green striped with silvery white—particularly striking in winter. Leaves are glossy green, oval or lobed, and deeply veined. New foliage is bronze tinted; autumn color combines bright yellow, red-orange, and purple. Showy clusters of greenish yellow flowers appear in spring. Give part shade in warmer areas.

A. × freemanii. See *A. rubrum*.

A. ginnala. See *A. tataricum ginnala*.

A. glabrum. ROCKY MOUNTAIN MAPLE. Shrub or tree. Zones 1–7. Multitrunked clumps can be shrubby and under 10 ft., or eventually reach 30 ft. and more than half as wide in good conditions. Leaves 2–5 in. wide, three to five lobed or divided into three leaflets, borne on dark red twigs. Fruit tinged red. Fall foliage yellow. Needs well-drained soil and regular moisture. *A. g. douglasii* (*A. douglasii*) grows along shores of southeastern Alaska, south into Canada and parts of the Pacific Northwest and mountain states (Zones A2, A3; 1–7, 10). It reaches 20 ft. tall, 15 ft. wide; usually has shallowly three-lobed leaves.

A. griseum. PAPERBARK MAPLE. Tree. Zones 2–9, 14–21. Native to China. Grows to 25 ft. or higher; may be half as wide to equally as wide as tall. Is striking in winter with bare branches angling out and up from main trunk, and reddish bark peeling away in paper-thin sheets. Late to leaf out in spring. Leaves are divided into three coarsely toothed leaflets, dark green above, silvery below. Inconspicuous red flowers in spring develop into showy winged seeds. Brilliant red foliage in fall.

A. japonicum. FULLMOON MAPLE. Shrub or tree. Zones 2–6, 14–16. Native to Japan. Grows 20–30 ft. high, with equal or greater spread. Nearly round leaves are cut into 7 to 11 lobes. Good fall color in red, orange, and golden tones. Give regular moisture, part shade in warm regions.

'Aconitifolium'. FERNLEAF FULLMOON MAPLE. Grows fairly quickly to about 15 ft. tall and 20 ft. wide. Leaves are deeply cut, almost to leafstalk; each lobe is also cut and toothed.

'Aureum'. GOLDEN FULLMOON MAPLE. See *A. shirasawanum* 'Aureum'.

'Ed Wood'. Like 'Aconitifolium', but more vigorous.

A. macrophyllum. BIGLEAF MAPLE. Tree. Zones 2–9, 14–24. Native to stream banks and moist canyons, southern Alaska to Southern California. Dense shade tree grows 30–75 ft. tall, 30–50 ft. wide—too big for a small garden or a street tree. Large three- to five-lobed leaves are 6–15 in. wide, sometimes bigger on young sapling growth; leaves turn from medium green to yellow in fall. Impressive tassels of greenish yellow spring flowers are followed by tawny winged seeds hanging in long, chainlike clusters. Yellow fall color spectacular in cool areas. Resistant to oak root fungus.

A. negundo. BOX ELDER. Tree. Zones A2, A3; 1–10, 12–24. Native to most of U.S. The plain species is a weed tree of many faults—it seeds readily, hosts box elder bugs, suckers badly, and is subject to breakage. Fast growing to 60 ft. (usually less) and as wide or wider. Leaves divided into three to nine oval, 2–5-in.-long leaflets with toothed margins; yellow in fall. The following varieties improve on the species.

CLOCKWISE FROM TOP LEFT: *Acer palmatum* 'Dissectum'; *A. circinatum*; *A. pseudosieboldianum*

'Sensation'. Male form (no seeds to attract box elder bugs). Slower growth (to 40 ft. tall, 30 ft. wide) and better branch structure than the species. Doesn't sucker. Bronze new growth and pinkish red fall color.

'Variegatum'. VARIEGATED BOX ELDER. Not as large or weedy as the species. Combination of green and creamy white leaves is a standout. Large, pendent clusters of sterile white samaras are spectacular.

A. nigrum. BLACK MAPLE. Zones 1–10, 14–20. Similar to *A. saccharum* but more resistant to heat and drought. Light green leaves turn yellow in fall. 'Greencolumn' can reach 65 ft. tall, 25 ft. wide.

A. palmatum. JAPANESE MAPLE. Shrub or tree. Zones A3; 2b–10, 12, 14–24. Native to Japan and Korea. Slow growing to 20 ft. with equal or greater spread; normally many-stemmed. This is the most airy and delicate of all

A

maples. Leaves are deeply cut into five- to nine-toothed lobes.

Young spring growth is glowing red; summer leaves are soft green; fall foliage is scarlet, orange, or yellow. These common seedlings have uncommon grace and usefulness: they are usually more rugged, faster growing, and more drought-tolerant, and they stand more sun and wind than named forms do.

Grafted named varieties have the same seasonal patterns, but shape, size, and colors of the foliage, twigs, and bark vary to an amazing degree. They are usually smaller than seedlings, more weeping and spreading, brighter in foliage color, and more finely cut in leaf.

Japanese maple varieties are typically sorted into several groups based on the way their leaves are divided. But for practical purposes, there are two main divisions: the dissectums and all the rest.

Dissectum types (often listed as varieties of *A. p. dissectum*) are sometimes called laceleaf maples for their deeply divided and dissected leaves. Most grow slowly to 6–8 ft. high and 8–12 ft. wide, even bigger in the Northwest. Almost all take on a weeping umbrella form, with remarkably sinuous trunks and branches.

'Contorta'. Grows to 8 ft. tall, 12 ft. wide, with finely divided leaves and a weeping growth pattern. Yellow-orange fall color.

'Crimson Queen'. Small, shrubby, 9-ft. mound, with finely cut leaves that hold color all summer, turn scarlet before dropping off in fall.

'Dissectum' ('Dissectum Viridis'). LACELEAF JAPANESE MAPLE. Small shrub to 6 ft. high, 12 ft. wide, with drooping branches, green bark; pale green leaves turn gold in fall.

'Emerald Lace'. This small, cascading maple grows 8 ft. tall and 10 ft. wide, has very finely divided dark green foliage that turns bright red in autumn.

'Ever Red' ('Dissectum Nigrum'). A 7-ft. mound with weeping branches. Finely divided, purple-tinged, lacy foliage turns crimson in fall.

'Orangeola'. Compact, weeping form to about 6 ft. high, not quite as wide. Finely dissected leaves are orange as they emerge, then gradually turn green. Fall color is fiery orange-red.

'Seiryu'. THREADLEAF JAPANESE MAPLE. Upright grower to 10–12 ft. high and wide. Lacy, finely divided leaves, reddish in spring, green in summer, then golden yellow touched with crimson in fall.

'Viridis'. Develops a mounded form 6 ft. tall and 8 ft. wide, with lacy green leaves that turn golden orange in autumn.

'Waterfall'. Similar to 'Dissectum' but a little smaller, forming a weeping mound 4–6 ft. high and twice as wide. Green leaves finely cut, fernlike, flowing, and elegant. Brilliant yellow and gold fall color.

Nondissectum types are generally more upright and larger than dissectum types, and they don't have lacy leaves.

'Atropurpureum'. RED JAPANESE MAPLE. Grows 25–30 ft. tall; has dark wine red summer foliage, red leaves in fall. Many variable clones and seedlings sold under this name; buy in leaf so that you know what you're getting.

'Bloodgood'. Vigorous, upright growth to 18 ft. Deep red spring and summer foliage, scarlet in fall. Blackish red bark.

'Burgundy Lace'. Grows to 12 ft. high and 15 ft. wide. Leaves more deeply cut than those of 'Atropurpureum'; branchlets are bright green.

'Butterfly'. Grows to 10 ft. tall and 5 ft. wide. Light green leaves emerge with pink margins, mature with creamy white variegation, and develop a magenta flush in fall.

'Crimson Prince'. Grows to 20 ft. tall and 22 ft. wide, with purple-red foliage turning red in autumn. Tolerates heat and humidity.

'Emperor I' ('Wolff'). Vigorous, upright growth to 20–25 ft. high, eventually wider than tall. Red leaves, slightly darker than those of 'Bloodgood'. They hold color well into summer, turn deep crimson in fall.

'Fireglow'. Grows to 15–20 ft. tall, with red leaves that don't fade in summer heat.

'Osakazuki'. Upright grower, becoming wider with age; eventually to 20–25 ft. tall. Large leaves (to 5 in. wide) turn from rich green in summer to brilliant crimson in fall. Tolerates sun and heat.

'Sango Kaku' ('Senkaki'). CORAL BARK MAPLE. Vigorous, upright, treelike growth to 20–25 ft. tall and 18–20 ft. wide. Green summer leaves have a slight golden cast; yellow fall foliage. Twigs, branches striking coral red in winter.

'Shaina'. A dwarf selection of 'Bloodgood', this grows compactly to 5 ft. tall. Dark wine red summer leaves, red fall color.

'Shishigashira'. LION'S HEAD MAPLE. Upright form grows to 12–20 ft. tall, with a broad crown and deeply cut leaves growing densely along the stems. Slow growing but choice; often used in bonsai.

A. pensylvanicum. STRIPED MAPLE. Tree. Zones 3–6, 15–17, 20, 21. The only snakebark maple native to North America, this grows to 25 ft. tall by 20 ft. wide with vertically striped green and white bark. Yellow fall color.

A. platanoides. NORWAY MAPLE. Tree. Zones A2, A3; 1–9, 14–17. Native to Europe, western Asia. Broad-crowned, densely foliaged tree to 50–60 ft. tall, from two-thirds as wide to equally as wide as high. Leaves are five lobed, deep green above, paler beneath; yellow in fall. Showy clusters of small, greenish yellow flowers in early spring. Very adaptable, but its reputation has been tarnished by voracious roots, self-sown seedlings, and sooty mold from aphid honeydew. Here are some of the best varieties (purple-leafed forms perform poorly in alkaline soils unless soil is conditioned):

'Columnare'. Slower grower, narrower form than the species (about 20 ft. wide).

'Crimson King'. Holds purple foliage color until leaves drop. Slower growing than the species. Fine in Northwest and California foothills.

'Crimson Sentry'. Compact growth to 25 ft. tall. Dense foliage, brighter red in spring than 'Crimson King'.

'Deborah'. Grows to 45 ft. tall and 40 ft. wide. Purplish red leaves in spring turn dark bronzy green in summer, bronze in autumn.

'Drummondii'. Leaves are edged with silvery white; unusual and striking. Needs some shade in warm climates.

'Easy Street'. Similar to 'Columnare' but slightly wider, more pyramidal, to 40 ft. high. Dark green foliage turns yellow in fall.

'Emerald Queen'. Fast-growing oval, to at least 40–50 ft. high and 25–30 ft. wide.

Where to Grow Japanese Maples

All kinds of Japanese maples thrive everywhere in the Northwest. In colder zones (like Denver), plant them in a warm part of the garden sheltered from wind. They can also be grown with success in California if protected from hot, dry, or constant winds—and if local soil and water will allow it. Salt buildup in soil makes Japanese maples burn on leaf edges. To counteract it, flood occasionally to leach out salts. Filtered shade is best, but full sun can be satisfactory. Japanese maples resist oak root fungus.

Grow these maples near north and east walls, in patios and entryways, or as modest-size lawn trees. All are attractive in groves (like birches) as woodland plantings, and they're invaluable in tubs and for bonsai. In California, the more finely cut the leaf, the more likely that leaf burn will occur; in any warm-summer climate, thick organic mulch over the roots helps keep the tree hydrated and healthy.

Reddish new growth matures to glossy green, then turns yellow in autumn.

'Fairview'. Grows to 45 ft. tall and 35 ft. wide, with reddish purple new growth that matures to bronzy green.

'Globosum'. Slow growing with dense, round crown; eventually reaches 20–25 ft. high.

'Parkway'. A broader tree than 'Columnare' (about 25 ft. wide), with a dense canopy.

'Princeton Gold'. Oval shape to 35 ft. high. Golden yellow leaves hold their color all season, then turn bright gold in fall.

A. pseudoplatanus. SYCAMORE MAPLE. Tree. Zones 1–9, 14–20. Native to Europe, western Asia. Moderate growth to 40 ft. high or more, and two-thirds as wide to equally as wide as tall. Leaves 3–5 in. wide, five lobed, thick, prominently veined, dark green above, pale below. No particular fall color. 'Atropurpureum' ('Spaethii') has leaves that are rich purple underneath. 'Esk Sunset' ('Eskimo Sunset') leaves are blotched and spattered with salmon, green, and light yellow on top, purple-red beneath. Slow growing to 10 ft. in 12 years. 'Leopoldii' grows 50 ft. tall, has creamy yellow and green variegation in stained-glass pattern. 'Prinz Handjéry' leaves emerge pink, mature with purple undersides. Grows about 10 ft. in 10 years.

A. pseudosieboldianum. Tree. Zones 2–10, 14–18. Native to Korea, Manchuria. Rounded tree to 20 ft. tall and wide. Resembles *A. palmatum* in size, form, leaf shape, and fall color, but is hardier to cold. 'Northern Glow', a hybrid with *A. palmatum,* is a graceful, upright, spreading tree to 20 ft. tall and 24 ft. wide; its green leaves turn brilliant orange to red in autumn.

A. rubrum. RED MAPLE, SCARLET MAPLE. Tree. Zones A2, A3; 1–9, 14–17. Native to low, wet areas of eastern North America. Fairly fast growth to 60 ft. tall and 40 ft. wide (or even larger). Faster growing than *A. platanoides* or *A. pseudoplatanus.* Red twigs, branchlets, and buds; quite showy flowers. Leaves have three to five lobes, shiny green above, pale beneath; brilliant scarlet fall color in

frosty areas. Tolerates most soils. Not at its best in urban pollution. Some of the trees listed below, although sold as *A. rubrum,* are actually *A.* × *freemanii*—hybrids between it and *A. saccharinum.*

'Armstrong' (*A.* × *freemanii*). Very narrow (15 ft. wide) tree. Fall color (often poor) is orange to red.

'Autumn Blaze' (*A.* × *freemanii*). Dense oval, upright crown; excellent orange-red fall color.

'Autumn Fantasy' (*A.* × *freemanii*). Dense oval, with beautiful red fall color.

'Karpick'. Narrow grower (20 ft. wide) with red twigs, yellow to red fall color.

'New World'. Narrow (to 15 ft.), upright (to 30 ft.), with bright reddish orange fall color.

'October Glory'. Tall, round-headed tree; last to turn color in fall.

'Redpointe'. Grows quickly into a 45-ft.-tall, 30-ft.-wide pyramid with green leaves that turn bright red in autumn.

'Red Sunset'. Upright, vigorous branching pattern.

'Scarlet Sentinel'. Columnar form, to about 25 ft. wide. Fast growing.

'Somerset'. Narrow oval with brilliant, long-lasting, red fall color. 'Sun Valley' is similar.

A. saccharinum. SILVER MAPLE. Tree. Zones A2, A3; 1–9, 12, 14–24. Native to eastern North America. Grows fast to 40–100 ft. tall and wide. Open form, with semipendulous branches; casts fairly open shade. Silvery gray bark peels in long strips on old trees. Leaves are five lobed, light green above, silvery beneath. In colder part of range, fall color is a mixture of scarlet, orange, and yellow—often in same leaf. Aggressive roots are hard on sidewalks, sewers. 'Silver Queen' is more upright form than the species, seedless, with bright gold fall color. 'Skinner's Cutleaf' has finely divided leaves.

You pay a penalty for the advantage of fast growth: weak wood and narrow crotch angles make this tree break easily. Also, it's unusually susceptible to aphids and cottony scale. Suffers from chlorosis in alkaline soils.

A. saccharum. SUGAR MAPLE. Tree. Zones 1–10, 14–20. Native to eastern North

CLOCKWISE FROM TOP LEFT: *Acer palmatum* 'Bloodgood'; *A. p.* 'Sango Kaku'; *A. japonicum*

America, with a Rocky Mountain subspecies. The source of maple sugar. Moderate growth to 60 ft. or taller. Stout branches with upward sweep usually form fairly compact canopy to about 40 ft. wide. Leaves have three to five lobes, green above, pale below. In cold-winter climates, spectacular fall color ranging from yellow and orange to deep red and scarlet.

'Apollo'. Small for a sugar maple, this becomes a 25-by-10-ft. column. Yellow-orange to red fall color.

'Autumn Fest'. Grows as a 50-by-35-ft. upright oval. Early orange-red to red fall color.

'Autumn Splendor'. Grows to 45 ft. tall and 40 ft. wide. Heat- and drought-tolerant; best choice for the Southwest. Orange-red fall color.

'Bonfire'. Very fast growing to 50 ft. tall and 40 ft. wide. Orange to red fall foliage.

'Fall Fiesta'. Grows to 50 ft. tall and 40 ft. wide, with orange, red, and yellow fall color.

»

'Flashfire'. Grows to 45 ft. tall and 40 ft. wide, with bright red fall color.

'Green Mountain'. Tolerant of heat and drought; fall leaves vary from yellow to orange to reddish orange.

'Legacy'. Fast growing, drought-resistant. Fall color is red, sometimes yellow-orange.

A. shirasawanum 'Aureum'. GOLDEN FULLMOON MAPLE. Shrub or tree. Zones 3b–6, 14–16. Grows to 20 ft. tall and wide. Leaves open pale gold in spring and remain pale chartreuse all summer. Plant in partial shade. *A. s.* 'Autumn Moon' has burnt orange new growth, orange and red fall color.

A. tataricum. TATARIAN MAPLE. Shrub or tree. Zones A2, A3; 1–6, 14–16. Native to southeastern Europe, western Asia. Reaches 20–25 ft. high and wide. Tooth-edged leaves are lobed on young plants. Showy red-winged seeds appear in summer. Yellow to reddish brown fall color. 'Hot Wings' is broader than tall, has bright red samaras. 'Rugged Charm' has a symmetrical, upright, narrow oval form.

A. t. ginnala. AMUR MAPLE. Zones A1–A3; 1–9, 14–16. Native to Manchuria, northern China, Japan, and Korea. Amur maple grows to 15–20 ft. tall and wide in gardens, possibly eventually 25 ft. Toothed leaves are three lobed, even on mature plants. Clusters of small, fragrant yellowish flowers bloom in early spring; these are followed by handsome bright red, winged seeds. Striking red fall color, especially in selections like 'Flame', 'Red

In fall, leaf colors are most intense after weeks of sunny days and cold, frost-free nights. Even so, some maples are naturally brighter than others: paperbark, red, and vine maples nearly glow.

November', and 'Red Rhapsody'. Needs regular water during hot spells.

A. truncatum. Tree. Zones A2, A3; 1–9, 14–23. Native to China. Grows fairly rapidly to 25 ft., with equal or slightly smaller spread. Like a small *A. platanoides* with more deeply lobed leaves. Emerging leaves purplish red, summer leaves green, autumn leaves yellow-red-orange. A fine lawn or patio tree; tolerates heat and drought.

Several hybrids between this species and *A. platanoides* thrive in Zones A2, A3, 1–9, and 14–17. They grow to 30–35 ft. tall, with dark green, glossy leaves that turn yellow-orange to red in fall. 'Crimson Sunset' has heat-tolerant deep purple foliage that turns maroon to bronze in autumn; shape is an upright oval. 'Norwegian Sunset' has an oval shape, and branch structure similar to Norway maple. 'Pacific Sunset' is upright and spreading, with a rounded crown.

A. 'White Tigress'. WHITE TIGRESS MAPLE. Shrub or tree. Zones 2b–7, 14–17. Hybrid involving *A. tegmentosum*. This multitrunked snakebark maple grows to 30 ft. high and nearly as wide. Green bark striped with gray and bright white. Large, lobed leaves turn bright yellow in fall.

CARE

The larger maples have extensive fibrous root systems that take water and nutrients from the topsoil. The great canopy of leaves calls for a steady supply of water—not necessarily frequent watering but constantly available water throughout the root zone. Occasional deep watering and periodic feeding help keep roots deep.

Medium to large maple species need little pruning. Prune smaller types to accentuate their natural shapes. To minimize sap bleed, make any cuts in summer or early fall in mild-winter areas, or from summer to the end of January where temperatures remain below freezing.

Aceriphyllum rossii. See *Mukdenia rossii* 'Crimson Fans'

Achillea

YARROW
Asteraceae
PERENNIALS

- ⚡ **ZONES A1–A3; 1–24**
- ☀ **FULL SUN**
- ○◐ **LITTLE TO MODERATE WATER**
- 🦋 **ATTRACT BUTTERFLIES**

Achillea millefolium

Among the most carefree and generously blooming perennials for summer and early fall; useful in the garden and as cut flowers (taller kinds may be cut and dried for winter bouquets). The aromatic leaves are gray or green and usually finely divided (some with toothed edges). Tiny individual flowers are held in flattish clusters.

A. filipendulina. FERNLEAF YARROW. From the Caucasus. Erect plants that grow 4–5 ft. high and up to 3 ft. wide, with deep green, fernlike leaves. Bright yellow flower heads in flat-topped clusters. Dried or fresh, they're good for flower arrangements. Attract beneficial insects. Several horticultural varieties are available. 'Cloth of Gold' and 'Gold Plate' have bright golden flower clusters up to 6 in. wide. 'Parker's Variety' is a strong, erect grower to 4 ft. high, with golden yellow blooms. Hybrid 'Coronation Gold', to about 3 ft. high and half as wide, has silvery gray leaves and large clusters of golden yellow flowers.

A. × kellereri. Forms an attractive clump of gray-green ferny leaves. Clusters of flowers resembling small white daisies with yellow centers top stems 6–8 in. tall.

A. millefolium. COMMON YARROW, MILFOIL. Variable

species, native to much of the Northern Hemisphere. An erect grower with narrow green or grayish green leaves and flat-topped white flower clusters on stems up to 3 ft. tall. Attracts beneficial insects. Spreads by underground runners. Can be invasive, but garden varieties and hybrids are better behaved, shorter, and available in a range of colors. Look for pale yellow 'Hoffnung' ('Great Expectations'), bright rose-pink 'Fanal' ('The Beacon'), deep pink 'Cerise Queen', lavender-pink 'Lilac Beauty' and 'Apfelblüte' ('Appleblossom'), salmon-pink 'Lachsschönheit' ('Salmon Beauty'), and bright red 'Fire King', 'Fireland', and 'Paprika'. Blooms of 'Terracotta' open salmon-pink and age to russet and coppery orange tones.

Varieties developed from California's native yarrow include 'Calistoga', with silver foliage and white flowers on foot-high stems, and 'Island Pink' ('Pink Island Form'), with bright green leaves and rose-pink blossoms to 2 ft. high.

A. 'Moonshine'. This popular hybrid forms a 2-ft.-wide clump of gray-green leaves topped by 2-ft.-tall stems bearing long-lasting yellow flowers.

A. ptarmica. SNEEZEWORT. From Europe and Asia comes this erect plant to 2 ft. high and wide. Its narrow leaves have finely toothed edges, and its white flower heads are held in rather open, flattish clusters. 'The Pearl' has double flowers.

A. tomentosa. WOOLLY YARROW. This native of Europe and western Asia makes a flat, spreading mat (to about 1½ ft. wide) of fernlike, gray-green, hairy leaves. Golden flower heads in flat clusters top 6–10-in. stems. Makes a tidy edging or neat groundcover for small areas; useful in rock gardens. Shear off dead flowers to leave an attractive gray-green mat. 'Aurea' ('Maynard's Gold') is vigorous, with large heads of lemon yellow flowers. 'King George' is lower growing than the species, with grayer foliage and creamy yellow blooms.

CARE

Yarrows do best in well-drained soil. Water established plants occasionally (they tolerate considerable drought once established). Cut back after bloom to encourage rebloom. Divide when clumps get crowded.

Achnatherum hymenoides.
See *Oryzopsis hymenoides*

Acidanthera bicolor.
See *Gladiolus murielae*

Aconitum
ACONITE, MONKSHOOD
Ranunculaceae
PERENNIALS

✀ **ZONES A1–A3; 1–9, 14–21**

☼ ◑ **FULL SUN OR PARTIAL SHADE**

💧 **REGULAR WATER**

⬥ **ALL PARTS ARE HIGHLY POISONOUS IF INGESTED**

Aconitum carmichaelii

Most members of this genus grow in mountain meadows, where they receive regular moisture and winter chill. They don't thrive in warm, dry climates, but their distinctive, richly hued flowers make them worth trying. Grow them under trees, at the back of flower beds, or at the edge of a shaded bog garden. Attractive substitutes for delphinium in lightly shaded spots, they combine well with hosta, ferns, meadow rue (*Thalictrum*), and astilbe. Rich green leaves, usually lobed, emerge in clusters at the plant's base. Stunning flowers, shaped like hoods or helmets, are held on tall spikes above the leaves. The flowers are good for cutting, but gloves are recommended when handling, as foliage may irritate skin.

A. carmichaelii (A. fischeri). Native to eastern Asia. This densely foliaged plant grows to 2–4 ft. high and nearly as wide. Leathery, dark green leaves are lobed and coarsely toothed. Deep purple-blue flowers in dense, branching clusters bloom from late summer into fall. Plants in the Arendsii group have particularly strong stems; those in the Wilsonii group grow to 6–8 ft. high and 1–2 ft. wide, with more open flower clusters.

A. napellus. GARDEN MONKSHOOD. Native to Europe, this upright, leafy plant grows to 2–5 ft. high and 1 ft. wide. Leaves are divided into narrow lobes. The late-summer flowers, usually blue or violet, are held in dense spikelike clusters.

CARE

Sow seeds in spring, or in late summer or early fall for bloom the next year. Plant in moist, rich soil for best growth and bloom. Divide in early spring or late autumn, or leave undivided for years. Aconites die back completely in winter, so mark the site.

Acorus
SWEET FLAG
Acoraceae
PERENNIALS

✀ **ZONES VARY BY SPECIES**

☼ ◑ **LIGHT SHADE IN HOTTEST CLIMATES**

💧 **AMPLE WATER**

Acorus gramineus 'Ogon'

Found throughout the Northern Hemisphere, these bog or aquatic plants grow in water or in rich, well-irrigated soil. They look like clumps or tufts of iris but are related to calla (*Zantedeschia*). Flowers are inconspicuous. Use plants in damp borders, at pool edges, in shallow water, or in containers that are not allowed to dry out.

A. calamus. SWEET FLAG. Zones 2–10, 14–24. Sword-shaped leaves in an upright clump about 2 ft. wide. Foliage is delightfully fragrant when bruised, as are the thick rhizomes. Plants die back in winter but return in spring. The popular variety 'Variegatus' has showy white-bordered leaves.

A. gramineus. JAPANESE SWEET FLAG. Zones 3b–10, 14–24. From Japan and China. This trouble-free plant develops fans of semievergreen leaves that rise from the ends of slowly creeping rhizomes; these eventually form large, circular clumps. The leaves of 'Licorice' have a licorice scent and flavor; 'Ogon' has narrow, arching leaves of golden yellow. 'Variegatus' has leaves striped with white. Dwarf 'Pusillus', 3–5 in. high, spreads very slowly and is useful between steppingstones.

Actaea
(including Cimicifuga)
Ranunculaceae
PERENNIALS

✀ **ZONES 1–7, 17**

◑ **PARTIAL SHADE**

💧 **REGULAR WATER**

⬥ **BERRIES OF SOME TYPES ARE POISONOUS**

Actaea simplex

Botanists combined this genus with *Cimicifuga,* and in doing so, they lumped together plants of markedly different sizes and garden uses. Baneberries (*Actaea*) are small (under 2½ ft. tall), with short clusters of flowers that turn into attractive but poisonous berries. Bugbanes (*Cimicifuga*) are considerably taller (up to 7 ft. in bloom), with long, spikelike flower clusters that ripen into long-lasting and decorative seed capsules. Baneberries associate nicely with smaller woodland plants, while bugbanes are stately back-of-the-border plants, looking most at home with a forest background. Both have shiny, much-divided leaves that give an overall airy effect. All grow best in rich, moist, well-drained soil and at least partial shade (can take more sun in cool-summer zones, provided they don't dry out).

A. japonica (Cimicifuga japonica). Native to Japan. White autumn flowers on purplish black, leafless stalks. In bloom, plant is 3–4 ft. tall, 2 ft. wide.

A. pachypoda (A. alba). WHITE BANEBERRY, DOLL'S EYES. From eastern North America. Plants reach 2½–3 ft. tall and 1½–2 ft. wide. Small white flowers appear in spring on a stalk that swells and turns bright red after flowers fade. The highly toxic 1½-in.-wide berries that follow are white with a dark spot at the tip.

A. racemosa (Cimicifuga racemosa). BLACK SNAKE-ROOT, BLACK COHOSH. From eastern North America. Plant forms a leafy clump 3–4 ft. tall, 3 ft. wide. Typically branched stalks carry dense spikes of white flowers in midsummer or early autumn, increasing plant height to 7 ft.

A. rubra. RED BANEBERRY. Native to central and eastern North America. Similar to *A. pachypoda,* but with poisonous berries that are scarlet, somewhat larger, and borne on very slender stems.

A. simplex (Cimicifuga simplex). KAMCHATKA BUGBANE. Native to Siberia, China, Korea, and Japan. Foliage clumps to 2 ft. tall and wide, with 3–4-ft. flower stalks in fall. 'Atropurpurea' has purplish leaves and pink-tinted flower buds on 5-ft. stems. 'Brunette', 'Hillside Black Beauty', and 'Pink Spike' have even darker foliage and pinkish flowers.

FOR MORE ON PERENNIALS, SEE "GROW: PERENNIALS," PAGES 686–687.

A

A

Actinidia
Actinidiaceae
DECIDUOUS VINE

> ☀️ ◑ **FULL SUN OR PARTIAL SHADE**
> ◌ ◐ **MODERATE TO REGULAR WATER**
> ✎ **ZONES A1–A3; 1–9, 14–17**

Actinidia kolomikta

Most kiwi vines are grown for delicious fruit (see the entry on Kiwi), but the following two species are prized for their flamboyant foliage. Clusters of small, fragrant, white flowers appear in early summer. Female varieties produce a bonus crop of small, tasty fruits, but male plants (which are nonfruiting) typically have better leaf color.

A. kolomikta. This native of eastern Asia grows rapidly to 15 ft. or more, producing a marvelous foliage mass of 3–5-in.-long leaves with an elongated heart shape: some in solid green, others white-splashed green, and others green that is heavily variegated in pink to red. Colors are best in cool weather or in partial shade in warmer zones.

A. polygama. SILVER VINE. This flashy vine hails from Japan. Leaves are dark green, but the tip ends of many young leaves are silvery white, giving a sparkling effect. Cats find this plant intoxicating; they chew and roll around on the foliage, which can do serious damage to young plants.

CARE

Kiwis grow best in fertile, well-drained soil. They climb by twining, so provide a sturdy support and train new stems into place as they lengthen. Thin out growth in late dormant season, and trim stems to fit support.

Adenanthos
Proteaceae
EVERGREEN SHRUBS

> ✎ **ZONES 8, 9, 14–24**
> ☀️ ◑ **PARTIAL SHADE IN HOTTEST CLIMATES**
> ◌ ◐ **LITTLE TO MODERATE WATER**

Adenanthos cuneatus 'Coral Drift'

Australian natives valued for their unusual foliage and flowers. Kinds with furry, silvery, finely divided leaves are called woollybushes, and the rest are called jugflowers (their colorful, winter-to-spring blossoms are shaped like long-necked urns). Stems and blooms are long-lasting in arrangements.

A. cuneatus. COASTAL JUGFLOWER. This erect, spreading shrub grows to 3–5 ft. high and a bit wider. Silvery leaves are wedge-shaped, with prominently scalloped tips. New growth is red and somewhat translucent, giving it an appealing glow. Flowers are dark pink to dull red. 'Coral Drift' is compact, with bright pink new foliage.

A. × cunninghamii. ALBANY WOOLLYBUSH. This naturally occurring hybrid between *A. sericeus* and *A. cuneatus* grows 3–4 ft. high and 5–6 ft. wide. Scarlet flowers are mostly concealed by fine-textured, silver-gray foliage, which is particularly nice in fresh and dried arrangements.

A. detmoldii. YELLOW JUGFLOWER. To 8–10 ft. tall and not quite as wide. Graceful, upright shrub with narrow leaves and showy yellow to orange flowers topping slender stems. Tolerates winter wet.

A. sericeus. COASTAL WOOLLYBUSH. To 6–20 ft. tall and wide. Exceptionally silky, silvery, soft foliage. Red flowers appear scantily throughout the year. Can be grown as a screen or pruned into a small tree.

CARE

Like other members of the protea clan, these plants grow best with excellent drainage, good air circulation, and light feeding with nitrogen (fertilizers containing phosphorus will kill them).

Adiantum
MAIDENHAIR FERN
Pteridaceae
FERNS

> ✎ **ZONES VARY BY SPECIES**
> ◑ ● **PARTIAL OR FULL SHADE**
> ◐ **AMPLE WATER**

Adiantum aleuticum

Most members of this large genus come from moist tropical areas, where they grow on forest floors, along streams and waterfalls, and in damp crevices among stones. All form spreading clumps over time, with thin, wiry, dark stems and fronds that are finely divided. Leaflets are mostly fan-shaped, bright green, and thin textured; new growth is often dusky pink. Northwest woods offer great design lessons. Use these ferns as accents among swaths of lower-growing shade plants such as sweet woodruff or white foamflowers, or as an edging near a garden pool. Mossy rocks, especially when wet, make beautiful foils for these plants.

A. aleuticum. WESTERN FIVE-FINGER FERN, WESTERN MAIDENHAIR. Zones 1–7, 14–21. Native to western North America. Forked fronds make a fingerlike pattern atop slender stems reaching 1–2½ ft. tall. Excellent choice for containers or shaded beds; can take some sun if moisture is abundant.

A. capillus-veneris. SOUTHERN MAIDENHAIR. Zones 5–9, 14–24; H1, H2. Native to tropical and warm temperate regions worldwide. Plants grow to 1½ ft. tall and about as wide. Fronds are twice divided but not forked; leaflets are small and fan-shaped. This dainty-looking fern is actually quite durable and easy to grow.

A. hispidulum. ROSY MAIDENHAIR, ROUGH MAIDENHAIR. Native to tropics of Asia, Africa. Indoor or greenhouse plant. To 1 ft. tall. Young fronds rosy brown, turning medium green, shaped somewhat like those of *A. aleuticum.*

A. pedatum. AMERICAN MAIDENHAIR, FIVE-FINGER FERN. Zones A3; 1–7, 14–17. From eastern North America. Resembles *A. aleuticum*, with similar fronds and shiny black stems. It is very cold-hardy and spreads nicely beneath deciduous trees.

A. raddianum (A. cuneatum). Native to Brazil. Indoor or greenhouse plant. Fronds cut three or four times, 15–18 in. long. Many named sorts differing in texture and compactness. Grow in pots; move outdoors to a sheltered, shaded patio for summer. Commonly sold are 'Fritz Luth', 'Gracillimum' (very finely cut), and 'Pacific Maid'.

A. venustum. HIMALAYAN MAIDENHAIR. Zones 3–7, 14–17. This Chinese native grows 6–8 in. high and spreads slowly to form a lush-looking colony 5 ft. or wider. Young fronds are bright bronzy pink, maturing to medium green. Shear in late winter to encourage new growth; cut fronds last well in arrangements. Easy to propagate: use a sharp spade to divide plants in early spring.

CARE

These ferns need steady moisture and soil rich in organic matter. They also need protection from snails and slugs. Many maidenhair ferns die back to some extent in winter. Kinds listed as indoor or greenhouse plants may succeed in sheltered outdoor spots in mild-winter areas.

Aechmea
Bromeliaceae
EVERGREEN PERENNIALS

- ✎ ZONES 22–24; H1, H2; OR INDOORS
- ☼ PARTIAL SHADE; SUNNY WINDOW
- 💧 KEEP CUP WITHIN LEAF ROSETTE FILLED WITH WATER

Aechmea fasciata 'Variegata'

This genus is composed almost entirely of epiphytic plants that grow on the trunks and branches of trees. All have rigid, strap-shaped leaves (often with spiny margins) that form a funnel of foliage around a central tube. In summer, a plumelike flower rises from the center and provides a colorful accent for several months.

A. chantinii. Leaves are 1–3 ft. long, green to gray-green, banded with silver or darker green. Tall flower clusters have orange, pink, or red bracts holding yellow-and-red flowers. Fruit is white or blue.

A. fasciata. Gray-green leaves crossbanded with silvery white grow to 2 ft. long. From the center grows a cluster of rosy pink bracts in which nestle pale blue flowers that change to deep rose. Look for named varieties with intensely silvery foliage or leaves edged with creamy white bands.

A. fulgens. Leaves, 12–16 in. long, are green dusted with gray. Clusters of flowers in red, blue, and blue-violet rise above them; berries are pinkish red. *A. f. discolor* has brownish red or violet-red leaves, usually faintly striped.

A. hybrids. Dozens of hybrids have been developed from the various species. Among the most commonly grown are those in the Foster's Favorite group; they have bright wine red, lacquered, 1-ft.-long leaves and drooping, spikelike flower clusters in coral red and blue. Another favorite is 'Royal Wine', which forms an open rosette of somewhat leathery, glossy light green leaves with burgundy red undersides; it has drooping clusters of orange-and-blue flowers.

A. pectinata. Forms a stiff rosette of leaves to 1½ ft. long, strongly marked pink or red at bloom time. Flowers are whitish and green.

A. weilbachii. Leaves are shiny, to 2 ft. long, and green or suffused with red at the base. Flowers appear on a 1½-ft.-long stalk and develop into orange-red berries tipped with lilac.

CARE
In frost-free areas, grow outdoors in pots or hanging baskets filled with gritty soil (commercial orchid mixes work well) or in moss fastened in crotches of trees—always in shaded places with high humidity and good air circulation. Indoors, they need lots of light (such as from an east- or west-facing window) to bloom. Indoors or outdoors, give them fast-draining but moisture-retentive soil. Keep central tube or cup within leaves filled with water (distilled water or rainwater is best); water soil (or moss) when it's dry. Fertilize monthly with a low-nitrogen plant food; withhold fertilizer for 1 to 2 months during winter.

For a striking accent on a patio in summer, grow a bromeliad in a pot filled with loose, fast-draining, highly organic growing mix. Give it a lightly shaded location, and keep center cups filled with water. For a breezy "island" vignette, display it with other potted tropicals.

Aegopodium podagraria
BISHOP'S WEED, GOUT WEED
Apiaceae
PERENNIAL

- ✎ ZONES A1–A3; 1–9, 12, 14–24
- ☼ SUN OR SHADE
- 💧 MODERATE WATER

Aegopodium podagraria

Native from Europe to western Asia, this rampant groundcover has naturalized in North America. Many light green, three-leafleted leaves make a dense, spreading mass to 6–12 in. high. Flat-topped clusters of white flowers rise above the leaves in summer. The plants are deciduous even in mild-winter areas.

'Variegatum' is the most widely planted form; it has leaflets edged in white, for a luminous look in shade. Set plants 1 ft. apart for quick cover, and pull any that revert to solid green. In warm climates, locate where it will receive some shade during the hottest part of the day.

CARE
This extremely invasive plant spreads by creeping underground rootstocks; it's almost impossible to eradicate once established. Contain it with an underground barrier of wood, concrete, or metal extending 8–12 in. into the soil—or grow it in poor soil or shade where nothing else will thrive. To neaten plants, mow two or three times yearly. Shear off flowering stems before they set seed to limit volunteer seedlings.

Aeonium
Crassulaceae
SUCCULENT PERENNIALS

- ✎ ZONES 15–17, 20–24
- ☼ FULL SUN IN COOLER CLIMATES ONLY
- 💧 MODERATE WATER

Aeonium 'Sunburst'

Most aeoniums are native to the Canary Islands. Their fleshy leaves are held in rosettes at branch tips. After several years, rosettes may produce a single large flower stalk in spring or summer; branches that have flowered die. These cool-season growers go dormant in summer to save water. During dormancy, they may appear sick and lose leaves—but when the weather cools and the plants get a little water, they perk up and regrow leaves.

A. arboreum. Grows 3 ft. tall and wide. Each branch tip carries a 6–8-in.-wide rosette of bright green, fleshy leaves. The yellow flowers appear in long clusters. 'Atropurpureum', with magenta-and-green rosettes, is more striking and more widely grown than the species. Hybrid 'Zwartkop', sometimes called black rose, has very dark purple (nearly black) rosettes up to 10 in. across; it can reach 5 ft. tall.

A. 'Blushing Beauty'. Forms a full, tight mound of 8-in.-wide rosettes; the plant reaches 2 ft. tall and wide. Leaves are green with a pronounced red edge. Flowers are yellow.

A. canariense. Forms a low mound of large rosettes (to 18 in. wide) of light green leaves that are fuzzy in some forms, smooth in others. The

A

tips of mature leaves take on salmon tones. Pale green to white flowers.

A. 'Cyclops'. Resembles *A. arboreum* 'Zwartkop', but leaves are deep red rather than black, and each rosette has a green center, or eye. Plants grow 4–5 ft. tall and 3–4 ft. wide, with an open, branching habit.

A. decorum. Bushy, rounded, many-branched plant to 1 ft. high and at least as wide. Each branch ends in a 2-in. rosette. Fleshy, pale green, reddish-tinted leaves have red edges. A neat, compact grower with pink flowers.

A. haworthii. Free branching and shrubby, plants reach 2 ft. tall and 4 ft. wide. Rosettes of blue-green, red-edged leaves are 2–3 in. wide. Cream-colored flowers. Very tough, long-lasting plant that can take more cold than most.

A. 'Kiwi' (A. decorum 'Kiwi'). This popular, colorful plant forms a low, tight mound to about 1½–2½ ft. tall and 2 ft. wide. Leaves are tricolored: light green with pale yellow variegation and bright red edges. Pale yellow flowers.

A. nobile. To 2 ft. tall and nearly as wide. An unbranched stem holds a rosette of thick, fleshy green leaves, often tinted reddish with maturity. After several years, rosettes produce a large (to 1 ft. high and wide), flat-topped cluster of red flowers on a thick red stem. The plant dies after bloom but produces many seedlings.

A. 'Sunburst'. Showy plant with 12-in.-wide rosettes of green leaves variegated in light yellow or creamy white and edged with red. Usually grows 1½–2 ft. high and wide but can mound up to 4 ft. high. Flowers are cream-colored. Does not respond well to pruning. 'Starburst' is similar, but with less yellow in the leaves.

A. tabuliforme. Unusual species with unbranched stems holds single, nearly flat rosettes just 2–6 in. high and 10–18 in. across; sometimes called dinner plate. Light green, hairy-edged leaves radiate from the center in perfect symmetry. After several years, a single, 1–2-ft.-tall stalk of yellow flowers rises from the center. Plants die after flowering.

A. undulatum. Bright apple green leaves are wavy, forming unusual-looking rosettes 10–15 in. wide. Stalks are thick and up to 3–4 ft. tall; makes offsets freely. Yellow flowers.

A. urbicum. "Dinner plate" rosettes reach 8–15 in. wide. Long, narrow, gray-green leaves, loosely arranged, have reddish edges. Forms stems several feet tall, unbranched except for offsets at the base. Does not respond well to pruning. White or pinkish flowers.

CARE

Plant in well-drained soil; cut back on irrigation in summer. With age, most aeoniums grow leggy. To encourage branching, cut back branches several inches below rosettes anytime except during summer dormancy. Rosettes tend to be smaller after growing out from pruning. Cuttings are easily rooted: let dry for a few days, then plant in sandy soil kept barely moist until new growth appears.

Aesculus

HORSECHESTNUT, BUCKEYE
Sapindaceae
DECIDUOUS TREES OR SHRUBS

🌡 **ZONES VARY BY SPECIES**

☼ **FULL SUN**

💧 **REGULAR WATER, EXCEPT AS NOTED**

◊ **SEEDS OF ALL ARE SLIGHTLY TOXIC IF INGESTED**

🦋 **ATTRACT HUMMINGBIRDS, BUTTERFLIES**

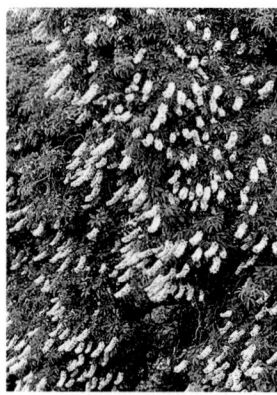

Aesculus californica

These big, bold plants have an almost tropical look. The leaves are divided like fans into large, toothed leaflets. Showy spring

flowers appear at branch ends in long, dense clusters. In fall, leathery fruit capsules enclose glossy seeds. Prune established horsechestnuts only to eliminate dead or damaged wood and any awkward-looking branches.

A. × arnoldiana 'Autumn Splendor'. Tree. Zones A2, A3; 1–9, 14–16. This attractive, cold-hardy hybrid grows to 35–40 ft. tall and nearly as wide. Glossy, dark green leaves with five (rarely seven) leaflets turn brilliant maroon in autumn and are resistant to leaf scorch. Yellow flowers, each with an orange-red blotch, are borne in clusters to 8 in. long. Best with some shade.

A. californica. CALIFORNIA BUCKEYE. Shrub or tree. Zones 3–10, 14–24. Native to dry slopes and canyons below 4,000-ft. elevation in Coast Ranges and Sierra Nevada foothills. This graceful plant grows 10–20 ft. or taller and spreads 30 ft. or wider, often with multiple trunks. The new foliage is pale apple green; mature leaves have five to seven rich green leaflets. California buckeye is striking in spring, when fragrant, cream-colored flower plumes make it look like a giant candelabra. (Unfortunately, the pollen and nectar of this species are poisonous to honeybees.) Big pear-shaped fruits split to reveal shiny brown seeds favored for dried flower arrangements. Seeds sprout freely; seedlings make unusual bonsai subjects.

In the wild, this plant drops its leaves by July, but if given moderate water, it will hold them until fall. After leaf drop, the silvery trunk, branches, and branchlets create an interesting silhouette.

A. × carnea. RED HORSECHESTNUT. Tree. Zones 1–10, 12, 14–17. Hybrid between *A. hippocastanum* and *A. pavia*. Grows to 40 ft. high and 30 ft. wide—smaller than *A. hippocastanum* and a better fit for small gardens. The tree is round headed, with large dark green leaves, each divided into five leaflets; a mature tree casts dense shade. Flowers with a profusion of 8-in.-long plumes of soft pink to red flowers. 'Briotii' has rosy crimson blossoms, 'Fort McNair' has pink

flowers with yellow throats, and 'O'Neill Red' has single flowers of bright red.

A. hippocastanum. COMMON HORSECHESTNUT. Tree. Zones 1–10, 12, 14–17. This European native grows to 60 ft. high with a 40-ft. spread—a bulky, densely foliaged plant that casts heavy shade. Its invasive roots can break up paved surfaces. Leaves are divided into five to seven toothed leaflets. The flower show is spectacular: ivory blooms with pink markings are borne in 1-ft.-tall plumes. 'Baumannii' has double flowers and sets no seed.

A. pavia. RED BUCKEYE. Shrub or tree. Zones 2–9, 14–24. Native to eastern U.S. This bulky tree grows 12–20 ft. tall, with an irregular rounded crown that is nearly as wide. Glossy deep green leaves with five to seven leaflets. Flowers in narrow, erect clusters are bright red or orange-red (rarely yellow). The best buckeye for humid climates.

Aethionema

STONECRESS
Brassicaceae
PERENNIALS

🌡 **ZONES 1–9, 14–21**

☼ **FULL SUN**

◊💧 **LITTLE TO MODERATE WATER**

Aethionema

Native to the Mediterranean region and Asia Minor. These shrublets, attractive in or out of bloom, are best adapted to colder climates and are favorites among rock gardeners. They grow best in a light, porous soil with considerable lime. Bloom comes in late spring to summer. Clip spent flowers to extend bloom season.

A. schistosum. To 5–10 in. high and 1 ft. wide. Its erect, unbranched stems are densely clothed with narrow, slate blue leaves. Fragrant flowers are rose-colored.

A. 'Warley Rose' (A. × _warleyense_). This neat, compact plant grows to 8 in. high and wide. Blue-green leaves and dense clusters of pink flowers have made it an old favorite. The most commonly planted stonecress in warmer climates.

Afrocarpus. See _Podocarpus_

Agapanthus

LILY-OF-THE-NILE
Agapanthaceae
PERENNIALS FROM FLESHY RHIZOMES

- ZONES 6–9, 12–24, H1, H2 FOR EVERGREEN KINDS; ZONES 4–9, 12–21 FOR DECIDUOUS KINDS
- FULL SUN OR PARTIAL SHADE
- LITTLE TO REGULAR WATER
- ATTRACT BUTTERFLIES

Agapanthus

South African natives that form fountainlike clumps of strap-shaped leaves. Plants are evergreen in some species and varieties, deciduous in others. Spherical clusters of blue or white funnel-shaped flowers appear in summer. Species names have been confused over the years, largely because the plants hybridize so easily.

Agapanthus combine well in garden beds with other easy-care performers, including pink-flowered _Amaryllis belladonna_ and _Phlox paniculata_, and orange-flowered poker plant (_Kniphofia uvaria_). In bouquets, display cut agapanthus flowers

with purple blooms of sea lavender (_Limonium perezii_).

For mass plantings, space plants from 1–1½ ft. apart (use the tighter spacing for smaller varieties). Divide infrequently; every 6 years or so. Superb in containers.

A. africanus. Evergreen. Leaves shorter, narrower than those of _A. praecox orientalis_; flower stalks shorter (to 1½ ft. high) with fewer flowers (20 to 50 per cluster). Blossoms are deep blue. Often sold as _A. umbellatus_.

A. campanulatus. Deciduous. To 3 ft. high, with drooping dark blue flowers. _A. c. albidus_ is white-flowered.

A. inapertus pendulus 'Graskop'. Deciduous. A neat clump of light green leaves grows to 2 ft. high, followed by flowering stems that rise another foot above the foliage. The compact, dark violet-blue blossoms droop gracefully.

A. praecox orientalis (_A. orientalis_). Evergreen. The most commonly planted agapanthus, it forms big clumps of broad, arching leaves, with stems to 4–5 ft. tall bearing up to 100 blue flowers. Varieties come in white ('Albus'), double ('Flore Pleno'), and light to fairly dark blue. Others have striped leaves. Often sold as _A. africanus_, _A. umbellatus_.

A. selections and hybrids. Types sold include the following. All are evergreen, except as noted.

'Baby Pete'. Dwarf, compact grower to just 6–9 in. tall, with light blue flowers held just above foliage mass. Blooms for a long period; does not set seed. Ideal for containers.

'Black Pantha'. Deep violet-blue flowers open from nearly black buds. The sturdy stems rise 2–3 ft. above gray-green leaves. One of the most cold-tolerant varieties.

'Blue Storm'. Abundant, deep purple-blue flowers rise on sturdy 2½-ft. stalks above foot-tall foliage clumps.

'Elaine'. Large clusters of nodding dark bluish purple blossoms borne on 3–4-ft.-tall stems.

'Ellamae'. Large dark blue flowers on stems to 5 ft. tall.

Headbourne hybrids. Deciduous. Flowers come in a range of

blues and in white on 2½-ft.-tall stems above fairly narrow, rather upright foliage. Some are quite cold-hardy.

'Henryi'. Resembles 'Peter Pan' but has white flowers.

'Midknight Blue'. To 3–4 ft. tall, with deepest blue flowers.

'Mood Indigo'. Deciduous. Hybrid involving _A. inapertus_, with deep violet blooms on stems that grow to 3–4 ft. tall.

'Peter Pan'. Outstanding free-blooming dwarf variety. Foot-high foliage mass and blue flowers on 1½-ft. stems.

'Queen Anne'. Foliage clump to 1½ ft. high; blue blossoms on stems to 2 ft. tall.

'Rancho White'. Foliage grows to 1–1½ ft. high; flower stalks to 1½–2 ft. tall carry heavy clusters of white flowers. Also known as 'Dwarf White' and 'Rancho'. 'Peter Pan White' is similar or identical.

'Snow Storm'. Abundant, snow-white blooms on stems 2½ ft. tall. Foliage clump is 1–1½ ft. high.

'Storm Cloud'. Evergreen in warmer part of range. Developed from deciduous 'Mood Indigo' and an evergreen agapanthus. Deep blue-violet blossoms on 4-ft. stems.

'Streamline'. Dwarf form to just 1½ ft. high, with grassy leaves and grayish blue flowers. Blooms over a long period.

'Summer Gold'. Compact grower to about 1 ft. tall, with medium blue flowers held 6–10 in. higher. Its most striking feature is the variegated foliage: gray-green leaves are edged in bright yellow.

'Tinkerbell'. Just 1–1½ ft. tall, with light blue flowers and narrow, gray-green leaves edged in white.

CARE

Plants thrive in full sun or light shade where summers are mild, but they need some afternoon shade in hottest areas. Evergreen kinds need protective winter mulch in Zone 6. All are best in loamy soil but will grow in heavy soils. They flourish with regular water, but established plants in the ground can grow and bloom without irrigation during prolonged dry periods in most areas; need supplemental water in the low desert. Protect from snails and slugs.

Agastache

Lamiaceae
PERENNIALS

- ZONES VARY BY SPECIES
- FULL SUN OR PARTIAL SHADE
- MODERATE WATER
- ATTRACT HUMMINGBIRDS, BUTTERFLIES, BEES

Agastache rupestris

Dependable, summer-blooming perennials with fragrant foliage. Upright stems packed with whorls of pink, purple, blue, red, or orange flowers make colorful additions to herb gardens and flower borders. Plants rebloom if deadheaded. Species from Mexico and the Southwest need excellent drainage, especially in wet-winter areas.

A. aurantiaca. ORANGE HUMMINGBIRD MINT. Zones 3–24. Native of northern Mexico; can be grown as an annual in cold or wet regions. Reaches 2½ ft. tall, 2 ft. wide, with pink flowers that fade to orange. 'Coronado' has yellow blooms suffused with orange.

A. barberi. Zones 2–24. From Arizona, New Mexico. To 2 ft. tall and 1½ ft. wide, with reddish purple flowers.

A. breviflora. Zones 6–24. From Arizona, New Mexico, northern Mexico. Grows to 2 ft. tall, 1½ ft. wide, with spikes of purplish red blossoms.

A. cana. TEXAS HUMMINGBIRD MINT. Zones 2–24. Native to Texas, New Mexico. To 2–3 ft. tall, 1½ ft. across. Blooms heavily, bearing reddish pink flowers that smell like bubble gum. A seed-grown selection, 'Heather Queen', blooms the first year from seed sown early in the season. 'Purple Pygmy' is compact, at just 16 in. tall.

»

A. foeniculum. ANISE HYSSOP. Zones A3; 1–24. From north-central North America. This erect, narrow plant reaches 3–4 ft. tall and 2 ft. wide, with dense clusters of lilac-blue flowers. Its anise- or licorice-scented leaves make a tasty tea. Useful in perennial borders and herb gardens. Tolerates more winter cold and wet than other species.

A. hybrids. Zones 4–24, except as noted. The following are among the many fine hybrids sold.

'Apricot Sunrise'. Zones 2b–24. Grows to 2½–3 ft. tall, 2–3 ft. wide. Deep orange flowers fade to apricot on opening.

'Blue Fortune'. To 3 ft. tall, 1½ ft. wide, with powder blue flower spikes. Long-blooming.

'Cotton Candy'. Grows 2 ft. tall and wide, with densely clad spikes of light pink flowers.

'Firebird'. To 2–3 ft. tall, 2 ft. wide. Blooms are coppery orange, coral pink, and red.

'Raspberry Summer'. Grows to 2½ ft. tall and 1½–2 ft. wide, with large spikes of dark pink flowers.

'Summer Breeze'. Zones 6–24. To 3 ft. tall, 2 ft. wide. Large lavender-pink flowers; dark gray-green leaves.

'Summer Glow'. Grows to 2–2½ ft. tall and 1½ ft. wide, with pale yellow flowers.

'Summer Love'. Grows to 3 ft. tall and 2 ft. wide, with large rose-purple flowers.

'Summer Sky'. Compact grower to 2 ft. tall and wide. Blooms are deep violet-blue.

'Tangerine Dreams'. Zones 6–24. Forms a 1½–2-ft.-wide clump. The orange flowers, larger and deeper in color than those of 'Apricot Sunrise', top 2–3-ft. stems.

'Tutti Frutti'. Zones 2b–24. To 3–4 ft. tall, 1–2 ft. wide, with purplish red blooms set off by gray-green foliage.

A. mexicana. GIANT MEXICAN LEMON HYSSOP. Zones 3–24. This somewhat rangy Mexican native grows 2–3 ft. (possibly to 5 ft.) tall and 1 ft. wide. Bears masses of pink flowers from spring to late fall. Lemon-scented leaves can be used in tea and as flavoring. Plants in the Acapulco series bear flowers in salmon-pink, rose-pink, and orange. 'Red Fortune' has red flowers; those of 'Sangria' are reddish purple.

A. rugosa. KOREAN HUMMINGBIRD MINT. Zones 4–24. Native to Korea. Grows to 5 ft. tall and 2 ft. wide. Licorice-scented foliage is glossy green with a purple tinge; flowers are purplish blue. Like *A. foeniculum*, it tolerates wet winters well. 'Golden Jubilee' (often sold as *A. foeniculum* 'Golden Jubilee') grows 2–3 ft. high and 2 ft. wide, with yellow-green new growth that's brightest in full sun. 'Honey Bee Blue' and 'Honey Bee White' grow to 2–2½ ft. high. The species and its varieties will bloom the first year from seed sown early.

A. rupestris. LICORICE MINT, SUNSET HYSSOP. Zones 1–24. From southern Arizona, northern Mexico. To 1½–2½ ft. tall and 1½ ft. wide, with narrow, fragrant gray-green leaves and spikes of orange flowers with lavender calyxes. Outstanding garden performance.

Agathaea coelestis.
See *Felicia amelloides*

Agave

Asparagaceae
SUCCULENT PERENNIALS

✎ **ZONES VARY BY SPECIES**

☼ ☽ **FULL SUN OR PARTIAL SHADE, EXCEPT AS NOTED**

◐ ● **LITTLE TO MODERATE WATER, EXCEPT AS NOTED**

❂ **SAP CAUSES SEVERE SKIN IRRITATION**

Agave 'Blue Glow'

Architectural succulents grown mainly for their attractive rosettes of fleshy leaves; many have toothed margins and a sharp terminal spine. Some grow as a single rosette; others produce numerous offsets to form a clump or spreading colony. Plants may not flower for many years; the flower stalk that eventually emerges from the rosette's center resembles a giant asparagus. Flowers are held in clusters on side branches or packed along the stalk, depending on the species. After flowering, the rosette dies, usually leaving behind suckers that make new plants.

Agaves shrivel from serious drought but plump up again with watering or rainfall. Provide good drainage. Species listed here are native to Mexico, except as noted.

A. americana. CENTURY PLANT. Zones 10, 12–24; H1, H2. This popular plant has blue-green leaves that grow to 6 ft. long, with hooked spines along the margins and a wicked spine at the tip. The species is variable but usually makes many offsets. Be sure you really want one before planting it: its bulk (to 8 ft. tall and 12 ft. wide) and spines make it formidable to remove. After 10 years or more, a branched, 15–40-ft. flower stalk bearing yellowish green flowers appears. Several varieties are available with yellow- or white-striped leaves; variegated types are about half the size of the species. Among them is the lovely 'Mediopicta Alba', with a broad central stripe of creamy white.

A. attenuata. FOX TAIL AGAVE. Zones 13, 20–24; H1, H2. Spineless, fleshy, somewhat translucent leaves are soft green or gray-green and up to 2½ ft. long. Clumps grow to 6–8 ft. across, and older plants develop a stout trunk to 5 ft. tall. Arching spikes to 12 ft. long are densely set with greenish yellow flowers. This species makes a statuesque container plant and looks good near water. Variegated forms are sometimes available. 'Nova' ('Boutin Blue') has broader and bluer leaves than the species, with a straight rather than arching flower spike. Grows best in fairly rich soil with regular water. Protect from frost and—except for along the coast—provide shade from hottest sun.

A. 'Blue Flame'. Zones 13, 19–24; H1, H2. An elegant, clump-forming hybrid with rosettes of spine-tipped, blue-green leaves to 2½ ft. high and 2 ft. wide. Looks like parent *A. attenuata* but has upward-curving leaf tips that suggest flames, and is hardier (to 25°F/–4°C).

A. 'Blue Glow'. Zones 9, 13–24; H1. This compact, colorful cross between *A. attenuata* and *A. ocahui* grows 1–2 ft. tall and 2–3 ft. wide. It forms a solitary rosette of blue-green leaves edged in red and yellow and tipped with a short red spine; leaves seem to glow when backlit. Hardy to at least 28°F (–2°C). In low desert, plants grow best with some shade.

A. bovicornuta. COW HORN AGAVE. Zones 19–24. This striking, medium-size species forms a solitary rosette 3 ft. tall and 4–5 ft. wide. Leaves are green to yellow-green, satiny, and up to 2½ ft. long and 6 in. wide. Prominent

---

Landscaping with Agaves

Agaves make dramatic accents, especially in water-wise gardens and beside pools, where their bold shapes reflect in still waters. But watch those spines. Locate sharp-tipped species away from paths or children's play areas, or grow them singly, in large containers, to display as sculpture atop low stone walls. Use caution when working around the plants. Or choose spineless kinds such as fox tail agave (*A. attenuata*) or spider agave (*A. bracteosa*). Wear long leather gloves when pruning or removing agaves, as the sap of most causes a severe and long-lasting rash.

hooked teeth and terminal spine are an attractive reddish brown. Flower spike grows to 23 ft. tall; plants may bloom after only 5 years in the ground. Damaged at temperatures below 25°F (–4°C). Needs light shade where summer sun is intense.

A. bracteosa. SPIDER or SQUID AGAVE. Zones 7–9, 12–24. A small, open grower (to 12 in. high and 18–24 in. wide), it spreads slowly to form a large, mounding colony. Arching, twisting pale green leaves have neither teeth nor terminal spines. Creamy white flowers appear on a short spike; this is one of the few agaves that do not die after flowering. Ideal for pots.

A. celsii. Zones 8, 9, 13–24. Forms a spreading clump of lovely rosettes, each about 2 ft. tall and wide. Leaves may be bright apple green or blue-gray; they're softly toothed and end in a weak terminal spine. Variegated forms are available. Needs shade in the desert and protection from frost wherever it is grown. Give it room to spread.

A. desmettiana. Zones 13, 20–24. Graceful and upright, it grows 2–3 ft. tall and wide. Arching blue-green to yellow-green leaves are tipped with a dark brown terminal spine; few if any teeth. When young, the plant forms offsets that grow nearly as large as the original rosette by the time it blooms. Some forms have leaves edged in yellow. Takes full sun or partial shade on the coast; sun or shade in low desert.

A. filifera. Zones 12–24. Hardy to 17°F (–8°C). Spreads fairly quickly to form a 2–3-ft.-wide clump of tight rosettes. Each narrow, dark green leaf is lined with white and edged with long white threads; terminal spine is dark brown. Adapted to very hot, dry conditions.

A. geminiflora. TWIN-FLOWERED AGAVE. Zones 13, 20–24; H1. This typically solitary species grows to 3 ft. high and wide, with many narrow, dark green, pencil-thin leaves. Yellow flowers, touched with red, are held in pairs along a spike to 12 ft. tall. Best in full sun along the coast; needs some shade in desert.

A. gentryi 'Jaws'. Zones 8, 9, 14–24. This selection from a high-mountain species grows as a solitary rosette to about 4 ft. tall and 6 ft. wide. Its light gray-green, glossy leaves are armed with large, curved, extremely sharp teeth and a terminal spine. As leaves age, they fold in on themselves, giving the impression of a mouth full of teeth. Very cold-hardy. Plant in light shade; can take sun along the coast.

A. havardiana. Zones 7–24. From southeastern New Mexico, western Texas, and adjacent areas of Mexico. Usually forms a single, compact, symmetrical rosette to 2 ft. tall and 2½–3 ft. wide, though it may develop a few offsets with age. Leaves are blue-gray to dull green, very thick at the base, and up to 2 ft. long; the margins are toothed and the terminal spine is sharp and stout. Flower spike can reach 15 ft. tall, with greenish yellow blooms. Hardy to at least 0°F (–18°C). Good choice for dry, cold gardens.

A. multifilifera. CHAHUIQUI. Zones 9, 13–24; H1. This slow grower eventually reaches 3 ft. tall and 4–5 wide, forming a solitary, round-topped rosette of 200 or more leaves; with age, plants form a short trunk. The gray-green leaves, each up to 2½ ft. long and only about 1 in. wide, are decorated with white filaments and tipped with a flexible green spine. Flower stalk rises to 16 ft. Good container plant or focal point.

A. murpheyi. Zones 8, 9, 12–24. Usually forms a solitary upright rosette to 3 ft. tall and nearly as wide, with leaves to about 2 ft. long and 3 in. wide. Leaf color varies among individual plants from dark green to blue-green or yellow-green; teeth are small and terminal spine is short. Flower stalks to 13 ft. tall bear waxy flowers and tiny plantlets (bulbils) that can be used for propagation. Very tolerant of heat and drought. 'Engard' is a heavily variegated selection with wide stripes of creamy white.

A. ocahui. Zones 8, 9, 12–24. This adaptable species forms a solitary, symmetrical rosette about 2 ft. tall and 3 ft. wide. The straight, narrow dark

CLOCKWISE FROM TOP: *Agave potatorum; A. geminiflora; A. 'Little Shark'*

green leaves have smooth edges and a sharp but flexible terminal spine. Leaf margins have a thin, dark red, fibrous border that detaches from mature leaves. Yellow flowers decorate a delicate bloom spike to 10 ft. tall. Plants thrive in sun or shade in any well-drained soil and are very cold-tolerant (to at least 15°F/–9°C). Good in pots or to bring a lush-looking accent to a desert garden.

A. ovatifolia. WHALE'S TONGUE AGAVE. Zones 8, 9, 12–24. Forms a solitary rosette (2–5 ft. tall and 3–6 ft. wide) of short, wide gray-green leaves that are cupped lengthwise. Small teeth line the leaf margins, and a sharp, dark gray spine arms the tip. Greenish yellow flowers appear on a spike up to 14 ft. tall. Takes full sun along the coast but needs some afternoon shade in the desert. Plants stay compact in hot, dry situations and grow larger with extra water.

A. parryi. Zones 2b, 3, 6–24. An attractive, compact, cold-hardy species native to Arizona and northern Mexico. Thick, blue-green or gray-green leaves are tipped with sharp

black spines. Mature size is about 2–3 ft. high and wide; spreads by offsets to form colonies. Sometimes called artichoke agave because the rosettes on some forms resemble giant artichokes. When about 20 years old, plants push up a stout stalk with clusters of yellow flowers. Thrives in partial shade. Several popular varieties are larger and have a less artichoke-like appearance. *A. p. truncata* has a distinct artichoke look.

A. potatorum. BUTTERFLY AGAVE. Zones 12–24. Grows 1–2 ft. high and 2–3 ft. wide, usually as a solitary rosette. Its short, broad, toothed, blue-gray leaves flare outward, giving a ruffled appearance. Each leaf is tipped with a distinctive, often twisted, reddish spine. Best in full sun. Needs regular water in desert, little to moderate water along coast. Fine choice for a large container.

A. schidigera. Zones 9, 13–24. Grows to a little over

A

2 ft. tall and wide. Forms a single rosette of many dark green, shiny, sword-shaped leaves with a sharp terminal spine. Instead of teeth, the leaf margins are set with thick, curly, white strings. Flower stalks to about 10 ft. tall bear purplish blooms. Needs regular water and protection from hot sun when grown in desert gardens. Excellent in containers. 'Durango Delight' is compact and symmetrical.

A. 'Sharkskin'. Zones 8, 9, 13–17, 19–24. This hybrid grows 2–3 ft. high and 3–4 ft. wide, with a stout habit. Gray-green leaves are toothless, tipped with sharp spines. The plant suckers freely to produce spreading colonies. Best in full sun; needs little water.

A. victoriae-reginae. Zones 10, 12, 13, 15–17, 21–24. Forms a distinctive, solitary rosette just 12–15 in. across, though occasionally a plant will form a few offsets. The many stiff, thick leaves are 6 in. long, and 2 in. wide; they are dark green with narrow white lines and sharp black tips. Plant is slow growing and may not flower for 20 years. Good in containers.

A. vilmoriniana. OCTOPUS AGAVE. Zones 12–24. Usually grows in a solitary rosette up to 3 ft. tall and 5–6 ft. wide. Leaves are pale green or yellow-ish green, 3–4 in. wide, fleshy, and deeply channeled above, with a single long spine at the end. Arching, twisted leaves give plant the look of an octopus or a huge spider.

A. weberi. WEBER AGAVE. Zones 8, 9, 12–24. Big, dramatic plant, to 5 ft. high and 10 ft. wide, with wide, fleshy, gray-green leaves that are finely toothed. Plants may make a few offsets. A branched stalk produces yellow flowers.

FOR MORE ON SUCCULENTS, SEE "MEET THE SUCCULENTS," PAGE 618.

Ageratina altissima.
See *Eupatorium rugosum*

Ageratum houstonianum
FLOSS FLOWER
Asteraceae
ANNUAL

☀ ◐ **FULL SUN IN COOLER CLIMATES ONLY**

💧 **REGULAR WATER**

Ageratum houstonianum

Native to Central America, West Indies. Easy-to-grow, dependable plants that bloom in summer and fall; they can be grown as winter annuals in mild-winter climates. Hairy, soft green leaves are roundish, usually heart-shaped at the base. Dense clusters of tiny blue flowers resemble powder puffs. Most floss flowers form foot-wide clumps. Low growers make excellent edgings or pattern plantings with other annuals of similar size. Taller types provide good cut flowers. All grow best in rich, moist soil.

Dwarf kinds (4–6 in. high) include 'Blue Blazer', 'Blue Danube', 'Blue Surf', and 'Royal Delft'. Somewhat taller (9–12 in.) types include 'Blue Mink' and 'North Sea'. 'Capri' and 'Southern Cross', to 1 ft. high, have clusters of blue flowers with white centers. 'Blue Horizon', to 2½ ft. tall, is good as a midborder plant and for cutting. Good varieties in other colors are bright pink 'Swing Pink' (6–8 in.), deep pink 'Red Top' (2–2½ ft.), and white-blooming 'Summer Snow' (9 in.). Plants in the Artist series are compact, strong growers to 8–18 in. high; they bloom profusely in shades of blue, violet, purple, or rose.

Agonis
Myrtaceae
EVERGREEN TREES OR SHRUBS

☘ **ZONES 15–17, 20–24**

☀ ◐ **FULL SUN OR PARTIAL SHADE**

◌ ◐ 💧 **LITTLE TO REGULAR WATER**

Agonis flexuosa 'Jervis Bay Afterdark'

These handsome Australian natives, relatives of *Leptospermum* and *Melaleuca*, are very tolerant of different soil types and watering practices.

A. flexuosa. PEPPERMINT TREE, AUSTRALIAN WILLOW MYRTLE. One of the best small trees for California gardens where temperatures stay above 27°F (–3°C). Will freeze to the ground at 25°F (–4°C) but may come back from a stump if not severely frozen. This spreading, medium-fast grower reaches 25–35 ft. tall and 15–25 ft. wide; narrow, willowlike leaves to 6 in. long densely clothe the weeping branches. Leaves smell like peppermint when crushed. In late spring, small white flowers bloom profusely. Use it in a lawn, train it as an espalier, or plant it in a large container. 'Jervis Bay Afterdark' grows slowly to about 18 ft. tall and 10–15 ft. wide and has beautiful burgundy foliage. 'Jedda's Dream' has the same colorful foliage but is dwarf and bushy, to just 9 ft. tall and 6 ft. wide. 'Nana' is like the species, but grows just 3–4 ft. tall and twice as wide; its new leaves are bright red.

A. juniperina. JUNIPER MYRTLE. More open and finely textured than *A. flexuosa* but about the same size. Its soft green leaves are narrow and ¼–½ in. long. Fluffy white flower clusters decorate the branches from summer into fall.

Agropyron magellanicus.
See *Elymus magellanicus*

Agrostemma coeli-rosa.
See *Silene coeli-rosa*

Agrostemma githago
CORN COCKLE
Caryophyllaceae
ANNUAL

☘ **ZONES 1–24**

☀ **FULL SUN**

💧 **MODERATE WATER**

⬥ **ALL PARTS ARE POISONOUS IF INGESTED**

Agrostemma githago

An attractive weed of roadsides and grain fields, this Mediterranean species has naturalized in North America. Several varieties are superior plants; they grow to 2–3 ft. tall and 1 ft. wide and are wispy but sturdy. (Like the species, they will self-sow.) Blooms are 2–3 in. wide, on 6–12-in. stems; they make good cut flowers. 'Milas' has deep purplish pink blossoms lined and spotted in deep purple; centered with a white eye; 'Purple Queen' bears deeper purple-pink blooms. 'Ocean Pearl' has white flowers with black flecks.

CARE

Sow seeds in spring or early summer for summer and fall bloom (or in fall for bloom from winter to spring in mild-winter climates). Mass at rear of border or in front of fence in fast-draining soil. Provide regular light waterings until established, then taper off irrigation. Then water only when the plants appear drought stressed. They will reseed year after year in the same spot. Over time, self-sown seedlings of varieties tend to revert to dark pink–flowered, plain species.

Agrostis
BENT, BENT GRASS
Poaceae
PERENNIAL GRASSES

🌡 ZONES 1–10, 14–24; BEST WHERE SUMMERS ARE COOL TO MILD

☀ FULL SUN

💧💧 REGULAR TO AMPLE WATER

Agrostis

All except *A. gigantea* make beautiful velvety lawns under proper conditions and with constant care. These cool-season grasses need frequent close mowing and feeding, occasional topdressing, and much water. In hot weather, they succumb to fungal diseases. In the San Francisco Bay Area and western Oregon and Washington, bent grasses (planted intentionally or distributed by birds) tend to dominate bluegrasses and fescues.

A. gigantea. REDTOP. Coarser than other bents; not generally used in lawns. Has been used as quick-sprouting nurse grass in mixtures or for winter overseeding of Bermuda and other winter-dormant grasses.

A. pallens. SAN DIEGO BENT GRASS, SEASHORE BENT. Fine-textured native of western U.S. Good for meadow plantings. Fairly fast, even growth with good tolerance for shade.

A. stolonifera (A. palustris). CREEPING BENT. Premium lawn but requires the most care, including frequent mowing to ½ in. tall with special mower.

Seed-grown strains include Emerald, Penncross, and Seaside. In some areas, you can buy sprigs or sod of the choice strains Congressional, Old Orchard.

A. tenuis. COLONIAL BENT. More erect than *A. stolonifera*; somewhat easier to care for but still fussy. Astoria and Highland are best-known strains; the latter is tougher, hardier, more disease-resistant. Mow to ¾ in.

Ajania pacifica
(Chrysanthemum pacificum)
GOLD AND SILVER CHRYSANTHEMUM
Asteraceae
PERENNIAL

🌡 ZONES 3–24

☀ FULL SUN

💧 REGULAR WATER

Ajania pacifica

This species from central and eastern Asia has been known by various botanical names over the years, including the two shown above. The plant is prized for its handsome foliage, bright fall flowers, and overall toughness. But it's prohibited in some areas as a host to white rust of chrysanthemum.

Forms a semitrailing, woody-based mound to 1 ft. tall and 3 ft. wide. Stems are densely clad in lobed, dark green leaves that look rimmed with white, actually the woolly white leaf undersides showing at edges. Broad clusters of small yellow flowers resembling brass buttons appear in autumn. Use as bank planting or groundcover or at the front of a perennial border. Lower leaves will die off without regular summer water.

To maintain compactness, cut back after bloom in mild-winter regions; in colder climates, cut back partway after plants put on strong new growth in spring. 'Pink Ice' has pale pink flowers.

Ajuga
CARPET BUGLE
Lamiaceae
PERENNIALS

🌡 ZONES A2, A3; 1–24

☀◐ FULL SUN IN COOLER CLIMATES ONLY

💧 REGULAR WATER

Ajuga reptans 'Black Scallop'

These low growers from Europe are useful, adaptable plants that form a solid foliage carpet and bloom from spring to early summer. Plant in well-drained soils. The highly variable *A. reptans* is better known and more tolerant of poor soils; it will escape into lawns unless contained.

A. pyramidalis. This upright, mounding plant grows to 2–10 in. high and 1½–2 ft. wide; it does not spread by runners. Stems have long, grayish hairs and are set with many roundish leaves. The violet-blue flowers are not obvious among the large leaves. 'Metallica Crispa' has crinkled, reddish brown leaves with a metallic glint.

A. reptans. The popular groundcover carpet bugle spreads quickly by runners, making a mat of dark green leaves in the basic species. Each oval to tongue-shaped leaf is 2–3 in. wide in full sun, to 4 in. wide in part shade; entire foliage mass tops out at around 4 in. high. Blue flowers in 6-in. spikes appear in spring and

early summer. Plant 1 ft. apart in spring or early fall. Mow or trim off old flower spikes. Subject to root rots and fungal diseases where drainage or air circulation is poor.

Many varieties of this species are available, some sold under several names. The following are among the best choices; all have blue flowers unless otherwise noted. Varieties with bronzy or metallic-looking leaves keep their color best in sun.

'**Alba**'. White-blooming form.

'**Atropurpurea**' ('Purpurea'). Bronze-tinted green leaves.

'**Black Scallop**'. Blackish purple foliage with scalloped edges.

'**Burgundy Glow**' ('Burgundy Lace'). Reddish purple foliage variegated with white and pink.

'**Catlin's Giant**'. Large, bronzy green leaves and flower spikes to 8 in. tall.

'**Chocolate Chip**' ('Valfredda'). Narrow, chocolate brown leaves on a slow-growing dwarf plant.

'**Giant Bronze**'. Deep metallic bronze leaves are larger, more vigorous, and crisper than in basic species. To 6 in. high in sun, 9 in. high in part shade.

'**Giant Green**'. Like 'Giant Bronze' but with bright green leaves.

'**Jungle Beauty**'. Clumps of large, rounded, wavy-edged, bronze-toned leaves; flower spikes to 10 in. high.

'**Multicolor**' ('Rainbow'). Leaves are green blended with white and pinkish purple.

'**Rosea**'. Pink blossoms.

'**Variegata**'. Dense, slow grower with gray-green leaves edged and splashed with creamy yellow.

Ajuga reptans makes a fine groundcover for small areas that are too shady for lawn, and it fits nicely between steppingstones and boulders. Or grow it in a pot with other spring-blooming annuals and perennials.

A

Akebia quinata

FIVELEAF AKEBIA

Lardizabalaceae

DECIDUOUS VINE, SEMIEVERGREEN
IN MILD WINTERS

☀ **ZONES 2–24**

☀ ◐ ● **SUN OR SHADE**

💧 **REGULAR WATER**

Akebia quinata

This native of Japan, China, and
Korea twines to 15–30 ft., growing quickly in mild regions, more
slowly where winters are cold.
Valued chiefly for its dainty
leaves on 3–5-in. stalks, each
divided into five deep green
leaflets, notched at tips. Dangling clusters of dull purple,
vanilla-scented flowers in spring
are more a surprise than a
show. Edible fruit, if produced,
looks like a thick, purplish sausage. 'Shirobana' ('Alba') bears
white flowers.

Provide support for climbing.
Can be invasive in moist areas.
Prune each winter. Recovers
quickly when cut to the ground.
For a tracery effect on a post or
column, prune out all but two
or three basal stems. Can also
be used as groundcover in large
spaces; plant 6 ft. apart.

A. trifoliata, threeleaf akebia,
has three instead of five leaflets per leaf.

One way to grow
this rambunctious
vine: train it up a
wrought-iron fence
and let it spill over
the top, forming
a lacy curtain.

Albizia julibrissin

MIMOSA

Mimosaceae

DECIDUOUS TREE

☀ **ZONES 4–23**

☀ ◐ **FULL SUN OR PARTIAL SHADE**

💧 **REGULAR WATER**

🦋 **ATTRACTS BIRDS, BUTTERFLIES**

Albizia julibrissin rosea

Native to Asia, ranging from Iran
to Japan. This open grower,
sometimes called silk tree, rapidly reaches 40 ft. tall, with a
canopy spreading to as much
as twice the tree's height. Ferny,
pale yellowish green leaves are
light sensitive and fold at night.
The fluffy pink, summertime
flowers look like pincushions or
powder-puffs and appear even
on young plants. *A. j. rosea*
has richer pink flowers and is
considered hardier. 'Boubri'
('Ombrella') bears hot pink
blooms. 'Summer Chocolate'
has rich burgundy foliage.

Mimosa does best with high
summer heat; it's a best seller
in Southern California's inland
valleys. In Zones 4 and 5,
choose the warmest locations
possible. With regular water, it
grows fast; given skimpy moisture, it usually survives but
grows slowly, looks yellowish.
Flat-topped, spreading canopy
makes this a good patio tree,
despite fallen leaves, flowers,
and pods. Beautiful when viewed
from above. Most attractive as a
multistemmed tree. Tough to get
started as a high-headed tree:
it must be staked and trained
(rub out any buds too low on the
trunk with your thumb). Start
with trees planted from containers established at least 1 year.

Alcea rosea

(Althaea rosea)

HOLLYHOCK

Malvaceae

BIENNIAL OR SHORT-LIVED PERENNIAL

☀ **ZONES 1–24**

☀ ◐ **PARTIAL SHADE IN
HOTTEST CLIMATES**

💧 **REGULAR WATER**

🦋 **ATTRACTS BIRDS, BUTTERFLIES**

Alcea rosea

This old-fashioned charmer from
the Mediterranean region is
best against a fence or wall or
at the back of a border. Old single varieties can reach 9 ft. tall;
newer strains and selections
are shorter. Big, rough, roundish
leaves, slightly lobed, form a
clump to about 3 ft. wide. Summer flowers are 3–6 in. wide
along upright stems; they may
be single, semidouble, or double and come in colors including white, pink, rose, purple,
red, creamy yellow, and apricot.
Chater's Double is a fine perennial strain; 6-ft. spires have
5–6-in.-wide flowers. Biennials
treated as annuals that bloom
the first year from seed include
5–6-ft.-tall Summer Carnival,
with double flowers, and 2½-ft.-
tall Majorette.

CARE

Sow seeds in ground in late
summer for next season's
bloom; seed annual strains
in early spring for bloom that
summer. After flowers fade,
cut stalks just above the
ground; continue to feed and
water plants to encourage late
summer or early fall rebloom.
Plants often self-sow. Destroy
any rust-infected leaves as
soon as disease appears.
Watch for slugs and snails.

Alchemilla

LADY'S-MANTLE

Rosaceae

PERENNIALS

☀ **ZONES VARY BY SPECIES**

☀ ◐ **FULL SUN IN COOLER
CLIMATES ONLY**

💧 **REGULAR WATER**

Alchemilla mollis

These soft-looking perennials
are useful for edgings in lightly
shaded areas, as groundcover,
and as a contrast to brightly
colored flowers. Rounded, pale
green, lobed leaves have a
silvery look. Summer flowers
are yellowish green, in large
branched clusters, attractive
as a frothy mass.

A. alpina. Zones 1–9,
14–17. Native to northern
Europe and Greenland. This
mat-forming plant creeps by runners, with flowering stems to
6–8 in. tall. Leaves are divided
into five to seven leaflets.

A. ellenbeckii. Zones 14–
24. From the mountains of East
Africa. Attractive small-scale
groundcover to about 2 in. high,
with creeping, rooting stems
and leaves less than 1 in. wide.

A. mollis. Zones A2, A3;
1–9, 14–24. This native of Asia
Minor is the most commonly
planted lady's-mantle. It forms
a clump to 2 ft. or taller and
about 2½ ft. wide, with nearly
circular, scallop-edged leaves.
To prevent self-sowing, deadhead plants soon after flowering. 'Auslese' bears bright lime
green flowers. 'Thriller' has
large, shiny, gray-green leaves
and golden yellow blooms.

A. pectinata. Zones 14–
24. Native to Mexico. Tiny
creeper with inch-wide leaves.

Aleurites moluccana

KUKUI, CANDLENUT TREE
Euphorbiaceae
EVERGREEN TREE

✓ ZONES 23, 24; H2

☼ FULL SUN

💧 REGULAR WATER

Aleurites moluccana

Native to Polynesia and southern Asia; has naturalized in Hawaii, where it has been designated the state tree. Grows rapidly to 35–60 ft. high and as wide, with an upright to spreading habit. The leaves are often lobed, and covered with short hairs that give them a frosted appearance. Tiny white flowers, produced in branched clusters, are followed by green, 2-in. fruits. These are rich in oil used by Polynesians for fuel and cooking; the polished kernels are used in leis. Best where litter won't present a problem. Needs well-drained soil. Tolerates wind, salt.

Hawaii's state tree is also a lush shade-maker for very large gardens, with a thick canopy of silvery green leaves that spread out like an umbrella. Pick up its fallen seeds or they'll germinate.

Allamanda

Apocynaceae
EVERGREEN VINES OR SHRUBS

✓ ZONES 23, 24; H1, H2; ANYWHERE AS INDOOR/OUTDOOR PLANTS

☼ FULL SUN

💧 REGULAR WATER

⚠ ALL PARTS ARE POISONOUS IF INGESTED

Allamanda blanchetii
'Cherries Jubliee'

From tropical South and Central America. These plants have striking foliage and trumpet-shaped flowers (borne nearly year-round). Grow them as permanent outdoor plants only in the mildest climates; elsewhere, grow as summer-blooming potted plants and move indoors in cold weather. They tolerate very little frost and need heat for proper growth and bloom; warm nights and warm days seem necessary. Remove spent flowers for increased bloom.

A. blanchetii (A. viola-cea). PURPLE ALLAMANDA. Shrubby grower to 6–10 ft. tall and wide, often with a few vining stems. Leaves are somewhat downy. Rose-purple flowers are 3½ in. across. 'Cherries Jubilee' (A. 'Cherries Jubilee') has brilliant burgundy red blooms.

A. cathartica. ALLAMANDA, GOLDEN TRUMPET. Can grow to great heights (over 50 ft.) as a vine; it can clamber through trees but must be tied to other supports. Often pinched back to grow as a large freestanding shrub. The leaves are glossy and leathery. Yellow trumpets are 5 in. wide and 3 in. long. 'Chocolate Swirl' has pinkish purple flowers with purple-brown throats. 'Flore Pleno' has double

yellow flowers. 'Hendersonii' bears exceptionally attractive orange-yellow blooms.

A. schottii (A. neriifolia). BUSH ALLAMANDA. A shrubby grower to 4–6 ft. high and wide; occasionally produces climbing stems. Flowers are bright yellow, sometimes with throats tinted orange or red.

Allium

Alliaceae
PERENNIALS FROM BULBS

✓ ZONES VARY BY SPECIES; OR DIG AND STORE

☼ ◐ FULL SUN OR PARTIAL SHADE

💧 REGULAR WATER DURING GROWTH AND BLOOM

Allium schoenoprasum

This genus includes at least 500 species, all from the Northern Hemisphere, many from the West's mountains. Relatives of the edible onion, they are peerless as cut flowers and useful in borders; smaller kinds are effective in rock gardens. Plants bear small flowers in clusters (umbels) atop leafless stems that range from 6 in. to 5 ft. tall or more. Umbels may be tightly or loosely arranged; some look like spheres, others like exploding fireworks. Many are delightfully fragrant. Bloom comes in spring or summer, with flowers in white and shades of pink, rose, violet, red, blue, and yellow.

A. aflatunense. Zones 2–24. Clusters of lilac flowers on stems 2½–5 ft. tall. Resembles A. giganteum but with smaller flower clusters; blooms in spring.

A. albopilosum. See A. cristophii.

A. atropurpureum. Zones 1–24. Stems to 2½ ft. tall carry

2-in. clusters of dark purple to nearly black flowers in summer.

A. caeruleum (A. azureum). BLUE ALLIUM. Zones 1–24. Cornflower blue flowers in dense clusters to 2 in. across on 1–2-ft.-tall stems. Late spring bloom.

A. carinatum pulchellum (A. pulchellum). Zones 3–24. Dainty clusters of reddish purple flowers on 2-ft. stems in summer. A white-flowered form is available.

A. cepa. See Onion.

A. cristophii (A. albopilosum). STAR OF PERSIA. Zones 1–24. A most distinctive flower. Late spring brings very large, round clusters (6–12 in. across) of lavender to deep lilac, star-like flowers with a metallic sheen; stems grow 12–15 in. tall. Leaves are long, white and hairy beneath. Dried flower cluster looks like an elegant ornament.

A. giganteum. GIANT ALLIUM. Zones 2–24. Summer bloomer bearing softball-size clusters of bright lilac flowers on stems to 5 ft. or taller.

A. 'Globemaster'. Zones 2–24. Popular variety bearing round clusters, 6–8 in. across, of deep violet flowers in summer. Stems rise to 2½ ft. or a little taller.

A. karataviense. TURKESTAN ALLIUM. Zones 1–24. Bears large, dense flower clusters in midspring, varying in color from pinkish to beige to reddish lilac. Broad, recurved leaves are 2–5 in. across.

A. moly. GOLDEN GARLIC. Zones 1–24. Bright, shining yellow flowers in open, 2-in.-wide clusters on stems 6–10 in. tall. Blooms in late spring. Flat leaves, to 2 in. wide, are almost as long as flower stems. 'Jeannine' blooms a bit earlier, with flower clusters to 3 in. across.

A. narcissiflorum. Zones 3–24. Foot-tall stems are topped in summer by loose clusters of ½-in., bell-shaped, bright rose flowers.

A. neapolitanum. Zones 4–24. Spreading clusters of large white flowers on 1-ft. stems bloom in midspring. 'Grandiflorum' is larger and blooms earlier. Plants in the Cowanii group are considered superior. Grown commercially as cut flowers.

»

A

A. oreophilum (A. ostrowskianum). Zones 1–24. Large, loose clusters of rose-colored flowers on 8–12-in. stems appear in late spring. Plants produce just two to three narrow, gray-green leaves. 'Zwanenburg' has deep carmine-red flowers on 6-in. stems. Good for cutting.

A. porrum. See Leek.

A. pulchellum. See *A. carinatum pulchellum*.

A. rosenbachianum. Zones 2–24. Similar to *A. giganteum* but slightly shorter (2 to 3 ft.) and earlier blooming (late spring). 'Album' has greenish white flowers.

A. sativum. See Garlic.

A. schoenoprasum. CHIVES. All zones. Plant forms clumps to 2 ft. high (usually shorter) of dark green leaves that look grasslike but are round and hollow. Clusters of rose-purple flowers (like clover blossoms) appear atop thin stems in spring. Use as edging in flower border or herb garden. Chop or snip leaves; use as garnish for a delicate onionlike flavor.

A. scorodoprasum. See Garlic.

A. siculum. See *Nectaroscordum siculum*.

A. sphaerocephalon. DRUMSTICKS, ROUND-HEADED GARLIC. Zones 1–24. Tight, dense, spherical red-purple flower clusters top 2-ft. stems in summer. Spreads freely.

A. tuberosum. CHINESE CHIVES, GARLIC CHIVES, ORIENTAL GARLIC. All zones. Forms clumps of gray-green, flat leaves to ¼ in. wide and up to 1 ft. long. In summer, bears an abundance of 1–1½-ft.-tall stalks bearing clusters of white flowers. The flowers smell like violets. Leaves have a mild garlic flavor.

A. unifolium. Zones 3–9, 14–24. California native. Satiny, lavender-pink flowers on 1–2-ft. stems in late spring. Spreads freely but is not a pest.

CARE

All alliums do best in well-drained soil (preferably on the sandy side), enriched before planting with organic matter. In fall or spring, plant bulbs as deep as their height or width, whichever is greater. Space smaller species 4–6 in. apart,

larger ones 8–12 in. apart. After flowering, when foliage begins to yellow, cut back on watering or let soil go dry; foliage dies to the ground, even in mild-winter areas. Lift and divide only after clumps become crowded. In areas colder than stated hardiness, dig and store bulbs for winter; or grow plants in pots and keep them in a protected spot during winter.

Almond
Rosaceae
DECIDUOUS TREES

| 🗡 ZONES 2B, 3B, 8–10, 12–16, 19–21 |
| ☀ FULL SUN |
| 💧 MODERATE WATER |

Almonds

Known botanically as *Prunus dulcis,* the almond is native to Asia Minor and North Africa. As a tree, it is nearly as hardy as the peach (its close relative), but as a nut producer, it's more exacting in climate adaptation. Trees bear best where summers are long, hot, and dry; nuts will not develop properly in areas with cool summers or high humidity. They need some winter chill yet must be spared from frosts at the wrong time. Trees bloom early (winter or early spring), but late frosts destroy small nuts that are forming. To experiment in areas where frost is a hazard, choose late-blooming varieties.

Unless you choose a self-fruitful type, two varieties that bloom at the same time are needed for pollination (they can be planted in the same hole if space is tight).

Trees reach 20–30 ft. high, erect when young, spreading and dome-shaped in age.

Leaves are 3–5 in. long, pale green with gray tinge; flowers are palest pink or white. Fruit looks like leathery, flattened, undersize green peach; in late summer or fall, the hull splits to reveal the pit, which is the almond. The following are the main varieties sold for nuts. (For flowering almonds grown as ornamentals, see *Prunus triloba*.)

'All-in-One'. Semidwarf tree with medium to large sweet, soft-shelled nuts. Self-fruitful. Best variety for home gardens.

'Butte'. Very productive tree with semihard-shelled nuts, slightly smaller than 'Mission'. Late bloomer, flowering just before 'Mission'. Pollinate with 'All-in-One', 'Mission', or 'Nonpareil'.

'Garden Prince'. Genetic dwarf with showy pink blooms and medium-size soft-shelled nuts. Self-fruitful.

'Hall' ('Hall's Hardy'). This tree may actually be a peach-almond hybrid. It bears a hard-shelled, bitter, small nut of low quality. Pink bloom comes late, an advantage in late-frost regions. Partially self-fruitful but better with 'Mission' as pollenizer.

'Mission' ('Texas'). Regular, heavy producer of small, semi-hard-shelled nuts. Late bloomer, one of the safest varieties for cold-winter, late-frost areas. Pollinate with 'Hall'.

'Ne Plus Ultra'. Bears large kernels in attractive soft shells. Pollinate with 'Nonpareil'.

'Nonpareil'. Excellent all-around variety with paper-thin, soft shells that are easily removed by hand. Midseason bloomer; some bud failure where summers are very hot. Pollinate with 'All-in-One', 'Mission', or 'Ne Plus Ultra'.

CARE

Almonds adapt to all soils except heavy, slow-draining ones, but the soil needs to be deep (at least 6 ft.). Space trees 20–30 ft. apart. Nuts are borne on spurs that are productive for about 5 years; each dormant season, remove about a fifth of the oldest fruiting wood to encourage development of new spurs. Harvest nuts after hulls have cracked open and are partially dry. You can knock

or shake them from the tree. Peel off hulls and spread nuts in the sun for a day or two to dry. To test for adequate dryness, shake nuts—kernels should rattle. Freeze almonds for 48 hours to kill any insects hiding inside the shells, then seal the nuts in an airtight container. Subject to attack by brown rot (causes fruit rot, twig dieback, cankers on trunk and branches) and mites (cause premature yellowing and falling of leaves).

Alnus
ALDER
Betulaceae
DECIDUOUS TREES

| 🗡 ZONES VARY BY SPECIES |
| ☀ ◐ ● SUN OR SHADE |
| 💧 💧 REGULAR TO AMPLE WATER |
| 🐦 ATTRACT BIRDS |

Alnus

These moisture-loving trees thrive in moist or wet soils and can tolerate periodic flooding, making them a good choice for planting near creeks. They are very fast growing. Clusters of tassel-like, greenish yellow male flower catkins give interesting display before leaf-out. Female flowers develop into small woody cones that decorate bare branches in winter. Alders need little pruning except to remove suckers, crossing branches, and dead wood.

A. cordata. ITALIAN ALDER. Zones 2b–9, 14–24. Native to Italy, Corsica. Young trees grow upright; older ones, to 40 ft. tall, spread to 25 ft. across. Heart-shaped leaves are glossy rich green above, paler beneath. Trees are leafless for only a

A

short period. More restrained than *A. rhombifolia*. Favored in Southwest, except high desert.

A. glutinosa. BLACK ALDER. Zones 1–10, 14–24. Native to Europe, North Africa, Asia. Not as fast growing as *A. rhombifolia*; eventually reaches 70 ft. tall and 30 ft. wide, forming a dense mass from the ground up. Roundish, coarsely toothed leaves are lustrous dark green. Good screening plant. 'Imperialis' has lighter green leaves that are deeply cut and fernlike.

A. rhombifolia. WHITE ALDER. Zones 1b–10, 14–21. Native along streams throughout most of California's foothills except along coast; mountains of Oregon, Washington, British Columbia, and Idaho. This fast grower reaches 50–90 ft. tall and 40–60 ft. wide. Branches spread out, then droop at the tips. Coarsely toothed leaves are dark green above, paler green beneath. Tolerates heat and wind. Susceptible to tent caterpillars, borers, and mistletoe in its native range.

A. rubra (A. oregona). RED ALDER. Zones 3–7, 14–17. Native to stream banks and marshy places from Alaska south to Northern California; usually found in areas with maritime influence. This is the most common alder of lowlands in the Pacific Northwest. It can grow to 90 ft. high but is usually seen at 45–50 ft. tall and 20–30 ft. wide. Attractive bark is light gray and smooth. Dark green leaves are rust-colored and hairy beneath; coarsely toothed margins are rolled under. Red alder can take brackish water and is useful wherever underground water is somewhat saline. It's generally disliked in the Pacific Northwest because it is a favorite of tent caterpillars.

A. tenuifolia (A. incana tenuifolia). MOUNTAIN ALDER, THINLEAF ALDER. Zones A1–A3; 2, 3, 7, 10. Shrub or small tree to 20–25 ft. tall, 15–20 ft. wide. Extremely cold-hardy. A popular tree in the Rocky Mountain region.

FOR OTHER PLANTS THAT THRIVE IN DAMP AREAS, SEE PAGE 79.

Alocasia
ELEPHANT'S EAR
Araceae
PERENNIALS

- 🗡 **ZONES 22–24, H1, H2, EXCEPT AS NOTED; OR INDOORS**
- ◐ **PARTIAL SHADE; BRIGHT INDIRECT LIGHT**
- 💧 💧💧 **REGULAR TO AMPLE WATER**
- ❂ **SAP IS POISONOUS IF INGESTED**

Alocasia

These big-leafed plants from the streamsides and marshes of tropical Asia are excellent for bringing a lush look to gardens. The flowers are like those of calla (*Zantedeschia*): a spikelike structure (spadix) surrounded by a fleshy, hoodlike bract (spathe). Flowers followed by reddish fruit that looks something like corn on the cob. Tropical plant specialists sell many kinds with leaves in coppery and purplish tones, often with striking white veins. Provide rich soil, frequent light feedings, and protection from wind.

A. × amazonica. AFRICAN MASK. Leathery, deep bronzy green leaves to 16 in. long have wavy edges and heavy white main veins. Plants may grow as tall as 4 ft. and about half as wide. This species is the one most commonly available as a houseplant.

A. cucullata. CHINESE TARO, CHINESE APE. Zones H1, H2. Slow-growing, clumping evergreen plant to 2 ft. high. Grown for shiny, deep green, pointed leaves to 15 in. long and 1 ft. wide. Usually massed as a groundcover (plant 1½–2 ft. apart), it also makes an excellent container plant. Requires well-drained soil.

A. gageana. DWARF ELEPHANT'S EAR. Looks like a smaller version of *A. macrorrhiza*, reaching only 3–4 ft. high and wide. Bright green leaves, to 2 ft. across, are prominently veined.

A. macrorrhiza. Evergreen at 29°F (–2°C); loses leaves at lower temperatures but comes back in spring if frosts are not too severe. Forms a dome-shaped plant 5 ft. tall and 4 ft. across, with arrow-shaped leaves that reach 2 ft. or longer.

A. sanderiana. Grows to 6 ft. tall and wide. Arrow-shaped, deeply lobed leaves grow 12–16 in. long. They are metallic dark purplish green with silver veining on the surface.

Aloe
Asphodelaceae
SUCCULENT TREES, SHRUBS, AND PERENNIALS

- 🗡 **ZONES 8, 9, 12–24, EXCEPT AS NOTED**
- ☀ ◐ **FULL SUN OR LIGHT SHADE, EXCEPT AS NOTED**
- ◑ 💧 **LITTLE TO MODERATE WATER, EXCEPT AS NOTED**
- 🦜 **ATTRACTS BIRDS**
- ❂ **LATEX BENEATH THE SKIN IS AN IRRITANT**

Aloe arborescens

Mostly from South Africa, aloes range from 6-in. miniatures to trees; all form clumps of fleshy, pointed leaves and bear clusters of orange, yellow, cream, or red flowers. Different species bloom every month, but the biggest show comes from midwinter through summer. Aloe leaves may be green or gray-green, often strikingly banded or streaked with contrasting

colors. Plants are showy and easy to grow in well-drained soil in reasonably frost-free areas; most need little water to survive but can take more. Except as noted, they need full sun in cooler climates, light shade in hotter regions. Where winters are too cold for all-year outdoor culture, grow in pots and shelter from frosts; most kinds make outstanding container plants. The species and varieties listed here are only a few of the many kinds available.

A. arborescens. TORCH ALOE, CANDELABRA PLANT. Zones 8, 9, 13–24; H1, H2. Forms a large, rounded shrub, to 10 ft. high and wide. Branching stems carry big clumps of gray-green, sword-shaped, spiny-edged leaves. Vermilion winter flowers are held above the foliage in spiky clusters. Withstands salt spray and tolerates shade. Foliage is damaged at 27°F (–3°C), but plants have survived 17°F (–8°C). Yellow-flowered and variegated forms are available.

A. aristata. Cold-hardy (to around 15°F/–9°C) dwarf for pots, edging, or groundcover. Forms spreading clumps of rosettes, each just 8–10 in. tall and wide and packed with 4-in.-long leaves ending in whiplike threads. Pink to red summer flowers in clusters.

A. barbadensis. See *A. vera*.

A. barberae (A. bainesii). TREE ALOE. Slow-growing tree to 20–30 ft. or taller, 10–20 ft. wide, with heavy, forking trunk and branches. Rosettes of 2–3-ft. leaves give rise in late winter to spikes of rose-pink flowers on 1½–2-ft. stalks. Sometimes called Dr. Seuss Tree, this aloe is valued for its stately, sculptural pattern in the landscape. Hardy to 28°F (–2°C).

A. 'Blue Elf'. This dwarf hybrid has 6-in. rosettes of upright, tooth-edged, blue-green leaves. It eventually forms a dense mound 1½ ft. high and 2 ft. wide. Orange flowers appear winter to spring.

A. brevifolia. SHORT-LEAF ALOE. This low grower forms spreading clumps of blunt, thick, blue-green, spiny-edged leaves just 3 in. long. Clusters of orange flowers on 20-in. stalks appear intermittently all year but most heavily in spring. Good for small areas.

A. ciliaris. CLIMBING ALOE. Zones 8, 9, 12–24; H1, H2. Climbing, sprawling plant with pencil-thin stems to 10 ft. long. Its small leaves of soft green are edged with white "eyelashes" where the leaf clasps the stem. Long-stalked, 3–6-in. flower clusters with 20 to 30 green- or yellow-tipped scarlet flowers appear intermittently year-round. This one takes a bit more shade than the other species but tolerates little frost.

A. dawei. DAWE'S ALOE. Zones 12–24. Rosettes of erect, narrow, bright green leaves with toothed margins form a clump 3–4 ft. tall and wide. In late winter or early spring, branched spikes hold bright orange-red flowers. Hardy to 25°F (−4°C). Best with light shade in hottest areas; can burn in reflected heat.

A. dichotoma. KOKERBOOM, QUIVER TREE. This impressive aloe forms a stocky, compact tree with gray-green, fingerlike leaves; short clusters of bright yellow flowers appear in winter. Grows very slowly to an eventual 12 ft. high or more, with a massive, sculptural trunk. Hardy to about 27°F (−3°C).

A. distans. JEWEL ALOE. Running, rooting, branching stems make clumps of 6-in., fleshy green leaves with yellow teeth along the edges (white in shade). In summer, forked flower stems, 1½–2 ft. tall, carry rounded clusters of red flowers.

A. ferox. CAPE ALOE. A single large trunk rises 6–10 ft. high (after 10 years), topped by a single crown of gray-green, spiny, red-toothed leaves 3–4 ft. long and 6–8 in. wide. Each branched inflorescence holds hundreds of bright scarlet or orange blossoms in late fall or early winter.

A. 'Hercules'. This treelike hybrid between *A. dichotoma* and *A. barberae* grows quickly to at least 25 ft. tall and 15 ft. wide, with broad, triangular, dark green leaves 2–3 ft. long. Orange blooms with green tips appear intermittently from spring to fall. Hardy to about 23°F (−5°C).

A. 'Johnson's Hybrid'. Compact grower to 1 ft. high and 2 ft. wide, with thin, bright green leaves that have faint

white spots and small teeth. Bright orange flowers on foot-high stalks bloom nearly year-round. Lovely in pots or as a small-scale groundcover. Hardy to 20°F (−7°C).

A. maculata (A. saponaria). SOAP ALOE. Short-stemmed rosettes a foot or more wide feature broad, white-spotted green leaves to 8 in. long. Multibranched, 1½–2½-ft. flower stalks rise in spring, topped with tight heads of nodding blossoms in salmon-orange or yellow. May grow as a solitary plant or send out suckers to form dense, expanding colonies. Dig and separate if plants become too crowded. 'Yellow Form' is dense, with lemon yellow flowers that bloom earlier.

A. × nobilis. GOLD-TOOTH ALOE. Dark green leaves edged with small hooked teeth grow in rosettes to 1 ft. wide and high; suckers freely, forming a spreading, mounded clump. Clustered orange-red flowers on 2-ft. stalks appear in early summer. Good in pots; takes limited root space.

A. polyphylla. SPIRAL ALOE. Zones 5, 6, 15–17. This unusual plant forms a single, stemless rosette 1 ft. tall and 1–2 ft. wide, with overlapping rows of leaves that all spiral in the same direction to produce a pinwheel-like or "spinning" effect when viewed from above. Mature plants generate a branching, 2-ft.-tall stalk of nodding light red to salmon-pink blossoms in late spring (may fail to bloom some years). Prefers moist, slightly acidic soil and needs partial shade in hot areas. Withhold fertilizer in summer. Hardy to 10°F (−12°C).

A. speciosa. TILT-HEAD ALOE. Zones 15–24. This tree-like aloe grows 12–15 ft. tall, with a trunk topped by a single rosette of sword-shaped, blue-green leaves, each up to 3 ft. long. The trunk stands straight, but the rosette tilts toward the brightest available sunlight; hence the common name. In fall, flower spikes about 1½ ft. long are densely set with tricolored flowers that age from white to dark pink. Hardy to 25°F (−4°C).

A. striata. CORAL ALOE. This tailored plant forms a single 2-ft.-wide rosette with broad, thick leaves to 20 in. long.

Leaves are spineless, pale gray-green, often spotted and striped, with a narrow pinkish red edge. Large, branched clusters of brilliant coral pink to orange flowers appear in midwinter into spring.

A. striatula. Scrambling, hardy shrub (to 15°F/−9°C) with dark green, sword-shaped leaves; distinctly striped leaf bases surround the stem. Multiple stems form a dense mound 5–6 ft. tall and to 15 ft. across, but plant may be kept much more compact with occasional hard pruning. Single spikes of yellow flowers, flushed with orange in bud, rise 6–18 in. above the foliage in summer.

A. thraskii. DUNE ALOE. Zones 8, 9, 12–24. Treelike succulent native to South Africa. Unbranched trunk is topped with graceful, arching, recurved leaves that give it a palm-like appearance. Leaves are fleshy, grayish green. Yellow-orange blooms appear in winter. Grows to 10 ft. tall or more and 4–5 ft. wide. Best near the coast; hardy to 32°F (0°C).

A. variegata. PARTRIDGE-BREAST ALOE, TIGER ALOE. Forms a foot-high, tight rosette of fleshy, triangular, dark green, 5-in.-long leaves strikingly banded and edged with white. Loose clusters of pink to dull red flowers appear in late winter to early spring. Best with some shade; can be grown as a houseplant.

A. vera (A. barbadensis). MEDICINAL ALOE, BARBADOS ALOE. Zones 8, 9, 12–24; H1, H2. Forms clustering rosettes of narrow, fleshy, stiffly upright leaves 1–2 ft. long. Yellow flowers appear in dense spike atop a 3-ft. stalk in spring and summer. This is a favorite folk medicine plant used to treat burns, bites, inflammation. Among the best aloes for Zones 12, 13. Survives without extra water but needs some to look good.

The best aloes for growing in low bowls are small clump-forming hybrids. They're perfect for tabletop displays.

Alopecurus pratensis 'Aureus'

YELLOW FOXTAIL GRASS
Poaceae
PERENNIAL GRASS

🌾 **ZONES 2–10, 14–17, 21–24**

☼ ◐ **PARTIAL SHADE IN HOTTEST CLIMATES**

💧 **REGULAR WATER**

Alopecurus pratensis 'Aureus'

This golden-variegated selection of a cool-season grass is native to Eurasia but has naturalized in North America (may be sold as 'Variegatus' or 'Aureovariegatus'). It's smaller and less vigorous than the plain (green-leafed) species, growing 2 ft. high and spreading slowly to form mats 1½ ft. wide or more. The translucent foliage ranges from green striped with gold to almost entirely yellow; in part shade, it is chartreuse. This grass dislikes drought, excessive moisture, and high heat, but it's a good filler or accent plant and makes an interesting, colorful groundcover. (For more on grasses, see "Meet the Grasses," page 346.)

When flower spikes form in midspring, shear them off (or, where summers are hot, cut plants back to about 5 in. high, as foliage can look ragged in summer's heat). Shearing prevents the appearance of volunteer seedlings, which would be green-leafed. Fresh foliage appears when temperatures fall, and growth continues until the first hard freeze. Nearly evergreen in climates with cool summers and mild winters. Divide clumps every 2 or 3 years in spring or fall.

Aloysia
Verbenaceae
DECIDUOUS OR SEMIEVERGREEN
SHRUBS

🗲 **ZONES VARY BY SPECIES**

☼ **FULL SUN, EXCEPT AS NOTED**

💧 **REGULAR WATER, EXCEPT AS NOTED**

Aloysia citrodora

These are highly aromatic shrubs with tiny flowers and a sparse growth habit; they are native to warmer parts of North and South America. All need good drainage.

A. citrodora (A. triphylla, Lippia citriodora). LEMON VERBENA. Zones 9, 10, 12–21; marginal in Zones 4–8. Native to Argentina, Chile. The fragrant verbena described in books about the antebellum South. It grows 6–8 ft. high and nearly as wide, with a somewhat sprawling, gangly form. Lemon verbena is cherished for the sweet, fresh, lemony scent of its foliage. The narrow, rough, bright green leaves can be used to flavor teas and iced drinks; when dried, they retain their scent for years. In summer, open clusters of very small lilac or whitish flowers appear.

Legginess is this shrub's natural state, so grow it among lower plants or locate it against a wall or fence and pinch-prune it to create an interesting tracery. Can also be trained into a standard and tolerates clipping into a hedge (do any major pruning in late winter or early spring). Borderline hardy as far north as Seattle if planted against a warm wall. In colder climates, grow it as a houseplant (pinch frequently), and let it spend the warm months outdoors.

A. virgata. SWEET ALMOND VERBENA. Zones 7–9, 11–24. From Argentina. Grows fairly quickly into a large, mostly evergreen shrub or small tree (to 15 ft. tall and 5 ft. wide) in warm regions; dies back where winters are cold. The leaves are medium green above, gray-green beneath, and up to 4 in. long. Tiny white flowers, which appear in large, spikelike clusters from early spring through summer, are very fragrant. Attracts butterflies, bees, and other beneficial insects. Shear lightly after bloom or prune up into a tree shape. Grows in full sun or partial shade with little to moderate water.

A. wrightii. OREGANILLO, WRIGHT'S BEEBRUSH. Zones 8–13, 19–24. Native to desert mountains from California to Texas and northern Mexico. This dense grower reaches 5 ft. high and wide, with numerous small stems and small (½ in.) leaves. From spring through fall, it produces sweet-scented white flowers that can be used as a flavoring or for tea. Performs best when it gets lots of heat. Good in natural landscape, in herb garden, as informal hedge.

Often confused with *A. lycioides,* a larger plant (to 8 ft. tall and 6 ft. wide) bearing blossoms that have a more vanillalike fragrance and are sometimes tinged with purple. Plants sold under either name may be one or the other—but both are outstanding ornamentals. Both make excellent honey. *A. lycioides* is the Mexican oregano of the spice trade.

Grow lemon verbena for its fragrance and flavor. Long, shiny leaves scent the area around them in the garden and add a lemony flavor to teas and iced drinks. Dry the leaves for potpourri.

Alpinia
GINGER LILY
Zingiberaceae
PERENNIALS

🗲 **ZONES 14–24; H1, H2**

◑ **LIGHT SHADE**

💧 **AMPLE WATER**

Alpinia zerumbet

These tropical beauties grow from rhizomes that produce leafy clumps. Plants are evergreen in Zones 22–24, H1, and H2; roots are hardy to about 15°F (–9°C). The tops die back in prolonged cool winter weather, but new shoots appear in spring. Ginger lilies need good soil and protection from wind. They must be established for at least 2 years before they will bloom. Each year, remove canes that have flowered.

A. purpurata. RED GINGER. Native to the Pacific Islands, it grows 9–12 ft. tall and 2–3 ft. wide, with 2½-ft.-long leaves. Blooms in late summer, producing brilliant inflorescence of red bracts and small white flowers. In California, will bloom only in a greenhouse.

A. vittata (A. sanderae). VARIEGATED GINGER. Native to Solomon Islands. Grows 3–4 ft. tall and 2 ft. wide, with 8-in.-long leaves striped with white. Good container plant, but rarely blooms.

A. zerumbet (A. nutans, A. speciosa). SHELL GINGER, SHELL FLOWER. From tropical Asia and Polynesia comes the grandest of gingers (to 8–9 ft. tall and 3–4 ft. wide) and the one with the best year-round appearance. The dark green leaves are shiny, 2 ft. long and 5 in. wide, with distinct parallel veins; leafstalks are maroon at maturity. Waxy white or pinkish, shell-like, fragrant flowers marked red, purple, or brown hang in clusters from arching stems in late summer. The leaves of 'Variegata' are heavily striped or banded with yellow.

Alsophila australis, A. cooperi. See *Cyathea cooperi*

Alstroemeria
PERUVIAN LILY
Alstroemeriaceae
PERENNIALS FROM TUBEROUS ROOTS

🗲 **ZONES 5–9, 14–24; H1**

☼◑ **AFTERNOON SHADE IN HOTTEST CLIMATES**

💧 **REGULAR WATER DURING GROWTH AND BLOOM**

🐦 **ATTRACT BIRDS**

◆ **CAN CAUSE DERMATITIS IN ALLERGIC PEOPLE**

Alstroemeria

These perennials fall into two horticultural classes, which might be called deciduous and evergreen. Both produce clustered flowers at the tops of leafy stems. The flowers are brightly hued and marked with contrasting blotches and flecks. Plants need good drainage. Mulch deeply where winters are severe.

DECIDUOUS TYPES
Seed-grown Ligtu hybrids and Dr. Salter's hybrids have azalealike flowers in beautiful, edible-sounding colors—orange, peach, shrimp, salmon—as well as red and near-white; all types are flecked and striped with deeper colors. They produce leafy shoots 2–5 ft. tall in late winter and into spring; as these shoots begin to brown, the flowering shoots appear, with blooms following in early to

A

midsummer. If allowed to set seed, they will self-sow. Plants go dormant after bloom and need no water unless winter rains fail. They naturalize where winters are not severe. Sow seeds in fall, winter, or earliest spring, either where plants are to grow or in pots for later planting out.

EVERGREEN TYPES

These include two species and a number of hybrids.

A. aurea (A. aurantiaca). From Chile. Plants grow 3–4 ft. tall, with numerous leafy flowering stems topped by yellow, orange, or orange-red flowers liberally sprinkled with dark stripes and flecks. Sometimes available in winter or spring as dormant roots; these are frail and easily broken. Plant them 8 in. deep and 1 ft. apart. Once established, the plant is vigorous, possibly even invasive.

A. hybrids. These include series such as Meyer, Premier, Inca, and Princess (which is particularly compact and free blooming). Hybrids vary in height and come in many colors, mostly in the purple-pink-red range with dark flecks. These plants are usually sold by color, so buy them in bloom to be sure of what you're getting. New hybrids show up constantly; check with local nurseries for availability. Some are root-hardy to 0°F (–18°C). Most hybrids will produce flowering shoots as long as the soil does not get too warm.

Repeat bloom can be stimulated by pulling up flowering shoots from the base rather than cutting them. The best way to do that: grasp each flower several inches above the soil and gently twist and pull upward to break the stem's base cleanly away from the rhizome. The best times to pick are in the cool months (spring and fall), when plants are growing best.

A. psittacina (A. pulchella). Oddly attractive native of Brazil. Flowering stems 2½–3 ft. tall are crowned by a few dark red flowers marked with green and blotched dark purple. Travels by rhizomes but is not usually a pest. It prefers partial to fairly deep shade. A variegated form has foliage marked in white.

Alternanthera ficoidea
(A. tenella)

JOSEPH'S COAT, PARROT LEAF
Amaranthaceae
PERENNIAL OFTEN TREATED AS ANNUAL

🌿 **ZONES H1, H2; ANYWHERE AS ANNUAL**

☼ **FULL SUN**

💧 **MODERATE WATER**

Alternanthera ficoidea

This unique foliage plant, native from Mexico to Argentina, grows 6–12 in. high and spreads variably. Its leaves often resemble artists' watercolors.

Among the many varieties are 'Bettzickiana' (*A. bettzickiana*), sometimes called calico plant, with spoon-shaped leaves blotched yellow and red; 'Green Machine', with dark green, quilted leaves; 'Red Threads', with narrow, burgundy leaves; 'Versicolor', with broad green leaves marked with yellow and pink veins; and 'White Carpet', with puckered green leaves boldly edged in white. A form from Thailand that is grown in Hawaii has larger green leaves with irregular white margins.

CARE

Plant 4–10 in. apart for best impact. *Alternanthera* is useful as an edging or groundcover and accepts most well-drained soils. It will take some shade but is not salt-tolerant. Striking in containers among other potted tropicals. Easy to grow from cuttings. Keep plants compact by shearing.

Althaea rosea.
See *Alcea rosea*

Alyogyne huegelii

BLUE HIBISCUS
Malvaceae
EVERGREEN SHRUB

🌿 **ZONES 13–17, 20–24; H1, H2**

☼ **FULL SUN**

💧 **LITTLE TO MODERATE WATER**

Alyogyne huegelii

Australian native hardy to about 23°F (–5°C). An upright grower, to 4–8 ft. tall and wide, with deeply cut, rough-textured dark green foliage. The glossy-petaled flowers resemble hibiscus blooms and can reach 4 in. across, in shades of lilac-blue to deep purple. Plant blooms off and on all year; individual flowers last 2 or 3 days. Pinch or prune as needed to keep it compact. Variable from seed. 'Santa Cruz' is a deep blue selection; 'Monterey Bay' and 'Mood Indigo' are deeper blue. Disease-resistant 'Leon's Purple Delight' has purple flowers. 'White Swan' has white blossoms.

Alyssum

Brassicaceae
PERENNIALS

🌿 **ZONES 1–24**

☼◐ **FULL SUN OR LIGHT SHADE**

💧 **MODERATE WATER**

Alyssum montanum

Mostly native to the Mediterranean region, these mounding plants brighten spring borders and rock gardens with their cheerful bloom. They thrive in poor, rocky soil as long as it is well drained.

A. montanum. Grows to 8 in. high and 1½ ft. wide, with gray leaves and dense, short clusters of fragrant yellow flowers. The compact and heavy-flowering 'Berggold' ('Mountain Gold') is the most commonly sold variety.

A. saxatile. See *Aurinia saxatilis*.

A. wulfenianum. Prostrate, trailing plant to about 1½ ft. wide, with fleshy, silvery leaves and sheets of yellow flowers.

Mediterraneans 101

Only 2 percent of the globe enjoys the same benign weather pattern of warm, dry summers followed by mild wet winters that's the norm in much of the West. The dry half of the year may not suit some thirsty plants here, but species from other Mediterranean climates can take summer-dry conditions. Blue hibiscus and alyssum are two.

Other stellar Mediterranean plants include grevillea and kangaroo paw from Australia; Cape plumbago, kniphofia, leucospermum, and lion's tail from South Africa; and, from the Mediterranean region, rockrose and herbs (rosemary, sage, and thyme).

Amaracus dictamnus.
See *Origanum dictamnus*

Amaranthus
AMARANTH
Amaranthaceae
ANNUALS

🌡 **ZONES 1–24; H1, H2**

☀ ☼ **FULL SUN OR PARTIAL SHADE**

💧 **REGULAR WATER**

Amaranthus caudatus

Coarse, sometimes weedy plants native to many regions of the world; ornamental kinds are grown for their brightly colored foliage or flowers. Sow seeds in place in early summer—soil temperature must be above 70°F (21°C) for germination. Or start indoors for planting out after frost danger is past in zones where the growing season is short.

If picked when young and tender, the leaves and stems of many species can be used like spinach, taking its place in hot weather. Some species have seeds that look like sesame seeds, have a high protein content, and can be used as grain.

A. caudatus. LOVE-LIES-BLEEDING, TASSEL FLOWER. A sturdy, branching plant 3–8 ft. high and 1½–3 ft. wide. The light green leaves can reach 10 in. long and 4 in. wide. Their color makes a nice contrast to the red flowers in drooping, tassel-like clusters to 2 ft. long. More of a curiosity than a pretty plant, but it does produce grain.

A. hypochondriacus. PRINCE'S FEATHER. To 5 ft. high, 2 ft. wide, usually with reddish leaves. Red or brownish red flowers in many-branched clusters. Some strains are grown as a spinach substitute or for grain.

A. tricolor. JOSEPH'S COAT. This branching plant grows to 1–4 ft. high and 1–1½ ft. wide, with leaves blotched in shades of red and green. 'Early Splendor', 'Flaming Fountain', and 'Molten Fire' bear masses of yellow to scarlet foliage at tops of main stems and principal branches. Green-leafed strains used as spinach substitute are sold under the name "tampala."

× **Amarcrinum memoriacorsii.** See *Crinum*

Amaryllis belladonna
NAKED LADY
Amaryllidaceae
PERENNIAL FROM BULB

🌡 **ZONES 4–24**

☀ **FULL SUN**

💧 **NO IRRIGATION NEEDED**

☠ **ALL PARTS ARE POISONOUS IF INGESTED**

Amaryllis belladonna

Not to be confused with its relative *Hippeastrum*, commonly called amaryllis—popular for indoor forcing during the winter holiday season. In fall or winter, this South African bulb puts out bold, straplike leaves that form a clump about 1 ft. high, 2 ft. wide; the foliage dies back completely by early summer. About 6 weeks later, stalks rise 2–3 ft. from bare earth, each topped by a cluster of 4–12 fragrant, trumpet-shaped, rosy pink flowers.

Best in areas with warm, dry summers; grows in well-drained soil and gets all the moisture it needs from winter rains. Plant bulbs 1 ft. apart right after bloom period ends. Where winter temperatures stay above 15°F (–9°C), keep bulb tops at or slightly above soil level. In colder-winter areas, choose a protected southern exposure and set bulbs slightly below ground level. Lift and divide clumps rarely; they may not bloom for several years if disturbed at the wrong time. Very long-lived.

A. hallii. See *Lycoris squamigera*.

Amelanchier
JUNEBERRY, SHADBLOW, SERVICEBERRY
Rosaceae
DECIDUOUS SHRUBS OR SMALL TREES

🌡 **ZONES VARY BY SPECIES**

☀ ☼ **FULL SUN OR PARTIAL SHADE**

💧 💧 **MODERATE TO REGULAR WATER**

Amelanchier alnifolia

These tall plants bloom in early spring, just before or during leaf-out. Drooping clusters of white or pinkish flowers are showy but short-lived. Fruits that follow in summer are similar to blueberries but have a musty flavor; use them in pies and preserves—if you can get to them before the birds do (in Alaska, birds have thus far seemed uninterested in fruit). Leaves are purplish in spring, turning deep green in summer and fiery hues in autumn.

Locate juneberries against a dark background—such as an evergreen hedge or the edge of a woodland—to show off their flowers, form, and fall color. Choose a site where litter from fruit and birds won't be a problem. Prune after bloom to remove crossing, crowded, diseased, or dead branches.

A. alnifolia. SASKATOON. Zones A1–A3; 1–6. Native to western Canada and mountainous parts of western U.S. Grows slowly to about 10–15 ft. tall and wide, spreading by suckers. Selections grown for larger, sweeter berries than the species include 'Martin', 'Northline', 'Smokey', 'Thiessen', and the heavy-fruiting dwarf 'Regent' (only 4–6 ft. tall).

A. canadensis. SHADBLOW. Zones A2, A3; 1–6. Plants offered under this name may actually belong to other species. Grows as a multistemmed shrub 10–20 ft. tall, about half as wide, with short, erect clusters of flowers.

A. × grandiflora. APPLE SERVICEBERRY. Zones 1–6. Hybrids between *A. arborea* (similar to *A. canadensis* but larger) and *A. laevis*. Most grow quickly to 20–25 ft. tall and nearly as wide, with drooping clusters of white flowers. Selected for disease resistance, strong stems, profuse bloom, and brilliant fall color, these are good choices for ornamental use. Among the best are 'Autumn Brilliance', with blue-green foliage that turns orange-red in fall; 'Cole's Select', with orange-red fall foliage; 'Princess Diana', with a long-lasting autumn show of pinkish red leaves; and 'Robin Hill', compact and upright, with light pink flowers.

A. laevis. ALLEGHENY SERVICEBERRY. Zones 2–6. Native to eastern North America. Grows to about 25 ft. tall and 15 ft. wide, with nodding or drooping clusters of flowers that are followed by sweet fruit. 'Snow Cloud' is vigorous and disease-resistant. 'Spring Flurry' forms an upright oval and turns orange in autumn. Hybrid 'Cumulus' has a narrower habit and yellow-orange to red fall color.

For glowing red-orange fall foliage, it's tough to beat *Amelanchier × grandiflora* 'Autumn Brilliance' and *A. × g.* 'Cole's Select'.

A

Ammi majus
BISHOP'S LACE
Apiaceae
ANNUAL

- ✎ **ALL ZONES**
- ☼ ◐ **FULL SUN OR PARTIAL SHADE**
- ◖ ◗ **MODERATE TO REGULAR WATER**
- ◈ **SAP MAY CAUSE A RASH**
- ✴ **ATTRACTS BUTTERFLIES AND BENEFICIAL INSECTS**

Ammi majus

Native to southern Europe, Turkey, and North Africa. A well-behaved relative of the roadside weed Queen Anne's lace (*Daucus carota*). Slender, branched stems grow quickly to 1–3 ft. tall, 1 ft. wide, with ferny light green leaves 6–8 in. long. In summer, each stem tip produces a 4–6-in.-wide, dome-shaped cluster of tiny white flowers. The lacy, delicate blooms are long lasting in vases; pair them with other wild-looking blossoms, such as deep blue larkspur and orange California poppies. They're also pretty in dried bouquets (hang upside down in a cool, dark place for 2 or 3 weeks to dry). Beautiful in meadow plantings; may self-sow, but not rampantly. In garden beds, plant them for a lacy effect among stout plants such as canna 'Tropicanna Black' and delphiniums.

Wash hands with soap and water after handling plants, as the sap can cause a rash. Plants are injurious to animals.

CARE

Tolerates many soils, but does best with moist, fertile, well-drained soil. Sow seeds in a sunny or lightly shaded spot. Cut blooms in the morning, when most are open.

Amsonia
BLUESTAR
Apocynaceae
PERENNIALS

- ✎ **ZONES 2–24**
- ☼ ◐ **FULL SUN OR LIGHT SHADE**
- ◖ ◗ **MODERATE TO REGULAR WATER**
- ✴ **ATTRACT BUTTERFLIES AND HUMMINGBIRDS**

Amsonia hubrichtii

From the southeastern U.S. Most of these elegant but tough plants, which resemble small shrubs, grow to 2–3 ft. high and wide. Narrow leaves and erect stems are topped by clusters of small, star-shaped blue flowers in late spring. The plants look good all summer; their bright yellow fall foliage is a bonus. Bluestars thrive in ordinary garden soil and tolerate heat and some occasional lapses in watering. They look especially lovely when massed.

A. ciliata. Crowded, needle-like (but soft) leaves are up to 2 in. long, with exceptional fall color. Pale blue flowers.

A. hubrichtii. HUBRICHT'S BLUESTAR, ARKANSAS BLUE-STAR. This award-winning plant is considered by many to be the finest of the bluestars. Its light green leaves are soft and very narrow, almost needlelike, and its fall color is an exceptionally bright, clear gold. Flowers are sky blue.

A. illustris. SHINING BLUE-STAR. Leathery, shiny green leaves are lance-shaped. Airy, open clusters of pale blue blossoms.

A. tabernaemontana. Leaves are willowlike and dull, dark green, making a nice backdrop for the dense clusters of slate blue flowers.

Anacyclus pyrethrum depressus
MOUNT ATLAS DAISY
Asteraceae
PERENNIAL

- ✎ **ZONES 2–24**
- ☼ **FULL SUN**
- ◖ ◗ **LITTLE TO MODERATE WATER**

Anacyclus pyrethrum depressus

Native to North Africa and Spain. This little charmer slowly forms a dense, spreading mat of finely divided, gray-green leaves; resembles chamomile (*Chamaemelum*). In summer, it bears many daisylike flowers to 2 in. across, with yellow center disks and white rays (red on reverse side).

Good in sunny, dry, hot rock gardens. May freeze in severe winters or rot in cold, wet, heavy soil. Dislikes humidity. Not long-lived, but reseeds.

To show off this tiny daisy, grow it in a stone trough with a small sand-colored rock as a foil and a mulch of decomposed granite. Display it on a sunny patio or atop a rock wall.

Anagallis
PIMPERNEL
Primulaceae
ANNUALS AND PERENNIALS

- ✎ **ZONES VARY BY SPECIES**
- ☼ **FULL SUN**
- ◊ ◖ ◗ **LITTLE TO REGULAR WATER**

Anagallis arvensis

Two colorful species are seen in the West, one an annual weed and the other an attractive perennial. Newer hybrids are becoming popular.

A. arvensis. SCARLET PIM-PERNEL. Annual. Zones 1–24. This low-growing, weedy plant from Europe has bright green leaves and ½-in., brick red flowers. Has naturalized in California. *A. a. caerulea* has deep blue, larger flowers; it tolerates most soils and heat, thrives in dry gardens, and grows well in containers.

A. hybrids. Summer annuals. 'Cinnamon' has medium pink blooms; those of 'Spice' are light pink. Both are low (3 in. high) and spreading, with small, spicily scented leaves. The Wildcat series is taller, 6–12 in. high, and comes in shades of blue, orange, and pink. All are good in pots and hanging baskets.

A. monelli. Perennial. Zones 4–9, 12–24. This Mediterranean native grows to 1–1½ ft. high and wide, with ¾-in. flowers of intense blue. 'Pacific Blue' and 'Skylover' are superior selections. 'Phillipsii' is compact at 1 ft. tall, and *A. m. linifolia* has narrower leaves than the species. All bloom from summer to frost.

Anchusa

ALKANET
Boraginaceae
ANNUALS, BIENNIALS, AND PERENNIALS

✀ **ZONES VARY BY SPECIES**

☼ **FULL SUN**

◑ ● **MODERATE TO REGULAR WATER**

Anchusa azurea

These strong growers are related to forget-me-not (*Myosotis*) but are larger and showier. Their vibrant blue flowers appear from late spring through summer. Alkanets—sometimes called buglosses—are also easy to grow: plant them in well-drained soil and cut back spent flowers for a second bloom. High humidity inhibits growth.

A. azurea (A. italica). Perennial. Zones 1–24. Native to the Mediterranean region. An open, spreading plant to 3–5 ft. tall and 2 ft. wide. Leaves grow 6 in. or longer and are covered with bristly hairs. Clusters of bright blue blossoms appear over a long period in summer, sometimes continuing into fall. Look for gentian blue 'Dropmore', sky blue 'Opal', and rich blue 'Loddon Royalist'.

A. capensis. SUMMER FORGET-ME-NOT. Biennial in Zones 6–24; annual anywhere. Native to South Africa, where it grows in disturbed areas such as along roads. Grows to 1½ ft. tall, about 8 in. wide with narrow leaves. Bright blue, ½-in.-wide flowers with white throats come in open clusters about 2 in. long. It prefers dry, sandy soils. Can be weedy, but sky blue blooms are welcome in many gardens. Bees love them. Plant in well-drained soil. Pretty with white or lavender African daisy (*Osteospermum*).

Andromeda floribunda.
See *Pieris floribunda*

Andropogon gerardii

BIG BLUESTEM, TURKEYFOOT
Poaceae
PERENNIAL GRASS

✀ **ZONES 1–9, 14–24**

☼ ◑ **FULL SUN OR LIGHT SHADE**

◐ ◑ ● **LITTLE TO REGULAR WATER**

Andropogon gerardii

This is the classic tall prairie grass of the Midwest, where it can reach 8 ft. high. In drier climates, it's more likely to grow 3–5 ft. tall. A clump former (to about 3 ft. wide), it does not ordinarily spread by rhizomes. Thin blades are blue-green in summer, turning bronzy red or coppery in fall. Flowers aren't exactly showy, but they are interesting: purplish spikes to 4 in. long, borne at stem ends in sets of three or more (arranged like a turkey's foot). The plant makes an effective screen when massed if given regular water. Or grow it singly in a mixed border.

Tolerates a range of soil and moisture conditions. Cut dried stems to their base yearly in late winter. Divide clump when center starts to die.

Anemanthele lessoniana
(Stipa arundinacea)

PHEASANT'S-TAIL GRASS
Poaceae
SEMIEVERGREEN GRASS

✀ **ZONES 14–24**

☼ ◑ **FULL SUN OR PARTIAL SHADE**

◑ ● **MODERATE TO REGULAR WATER**

Anemanthele lessoniana

From New Zealand. This fine-textured, colorful, cool-season grass grows quickly to form a dense tuft 2½–3 ft. tall and wide. Slender, arching leaves are olive green, streaked with orange in summer and completely suffused with coppery hues in fall and winter. In early summer, thin stems to 2½ ft. long arch outward to produce a purplish haze of feathery, dangling flowers. Excellent as a focal point or large-scale

---

Grasses, Three Ways

AS SCREENS Upright grasses like Big Bluestem make great screens; space plants 2–3 ft. apart.

IN MIXED BORDERS Grasses add textural interest to shrub borders where foliage is secondary to flowers. Grow pheasant's-tail with rounded apple green *Pittosporum crassifolium* 'Compactum', for example.

IN POTS For a fall look on the patio, try pheasant's-tail in a big, caramel-colored glazed container.

---

groundcover; grows well in a large container. Flowers pretty in fresh and dried arrangements.

Neaten its appearance by removing any dead leaves in early spring. Cut back to 6–10 in. tall in late winter every few years to rejuvenate the foliage.

Anemone

WINDFLOWER
Ranunculaceae
PERENNIALS

✀ **ZONES VARY BY SPECIES**

☼ ◑ ● **EXPOSURE NEEDS VARY BY SPECIES**

● **REGULAR WATER, EXCEPT AS NOTED**

◆ **ALL PARTS ARE POISONOUS IF INGESTED; SAP CAN IRRITATE SKIN**

Anemone × *hybrida*

This popular genus from the buttercup family includes alpine rock garden miniatures and tall Japanese anemones. Bloom times extend from very early spring to fall, depending on species. Plants typically produce a basal clump of roundish leaves, sometimes hairy and often lobed or divided into leaflets. Stems rise above the leafy mound to present open-faced blooms centered with a dense group of stamens.

Nontuberous anemones. The types described below grow from fibrous roots or creeping rhizomes or rootstocks, not tubers.

A. canadensis. MEADOW ANEMONE. Zones 1–4. A North American native that grows 1–2 ft. tall and spreads by creeping rhizomes. Its inch-wide, yellow-centered white flowers appear in twos and threes from the upper joints of divided leaves. Blooms profusely from

A

late spring to early summer. Spreads vigorously; too invasive for small gardens. Needs partial shade and more water than most windflowers.

A. × hybrida (A. japonica, A. hupehensis japonica). JAPANESE ANEMONE. Zones 2b–24. A long-lived, fibrous-rooted perennial—indispensable for fall flower color. Graceful, branching stems 2–4 ft. high rise from a clump of dark green, three- to five-lobed leaves covered with soft hairs. Many named varieties are available, with single or semidouble flowers in white, silvery pink, or rose. Effective in clumps in front of tall shrubbery or under high-branching trees. May be slow to establish, but it spreads widely and readily if roots are not disturbed. Space plants 2 ft. apart. Tallest varieties may need staking. Mulch in autumn where winters are severe. Increase by divisions in fall or early spring or by root cuttings in spring. Partial shade.

A. nemorosa. WOOD ANEMONE. Zones 1–9, 14–24. European native to 1 ft. high, with creeping rhizomes, deeply cut leaves, and inch-wide white (rarely pinkish or blue) spring flowers held above the foliage. Spreads slowly to make an attractive woodland ground-cover. Many named varieties are available, some with double flowers. Partial or full shade.

A. oregana. BLUE WIND-FLOWER. Zones 4–7, 15–17. Native to the Pacific Northwest and Northern California. This attractive woodland groundcover resembles *A. nemorosa*, with inch-wide white (sometimes blue or pink) spring flowers. Partial shade.

A. pulsatilla. See *Pulsatilla vulgaris*.

A. sylvestris. SNOWDROP ANEMONE. Zones 1–10, 14. European native growing from creeping rootstock to 1½ ft. tall. Fragrant, 1½–3-in., yellow-centered white flowers open in spring and are followed by cottony seed heads. Spreads readily in damp, wooded locations. 'Macrantha' has larger blossoms; 'Flore Pleno' is double-flowered. Partial or full shade.

A. tomentosa. Zones 2b–9, 14–21. Vigorous, fibrous-rooted Tibetan native often

sold as *A. vitifolia* 'Robustissima'. A spreading clump of foliage resembling grape leaves gives rise to branching, 3½-ft.-high stems bearing single pink flowers in late summer and early fall. Space plants 3 ft. apart. Partial shade.

Tuberous anemones. The types listed here are native to southern Europe and the Mediterranean; best treated as annuals in rainy-summer or warm-winter climates, where they tend to be short-lived. Tuberous anemones make great container plants.

A. blanda. GRECIAN WIND-FLOWER. Zones 2–9, 14–23. Tubers produce a spreading mat of finely divided, softly hairy leaves (clumps are wider spreading in colder climates). In spring, each 2–8-in.-tall stem bears a sky blue flower 1–1½ in. across. Selections with 2-in. flowers on 10–12-in. plants include 'Blue Star', 'Pink Star', 'White Splendor', and purplish red 'Radar'. All work well as underplantings for tulips, as groundcover drifts under deciduous shrubs and trees, and naturalized in short grass. Needs partial shade and distinct winter chill for best performance.

A. coronaria. POPPY-FLOWERED ANEMONE. Zones 4–24. The species is rarely seen in gardens; it has been replaced by showy large-flowered hybrids valued for cutting and for spectacular spring color. Blossoms are 1½–2½ in. across, borne singly on 6–18-in. stems above finely divided leaves; colors include red, blue, tones and mixtures of these colors, and white. Among the most popular strains are De Caen (single flowers) and St. Brigid (semidouble to double). Full sun or partial shade.

A. × fulgens. SCARLET WINDFLOWER. Zones 4–9, 14–24. Grows 1 ft. tall and 6 in. wide. Spring flowers, to 2½ in. across, are brilliant scarlet with black stamens. St. Bavo strain comes in an unusual color range, including pink and rusty coral. Same uses as for *A. coronaria*. Full sun or partial shade.

CARE

Nontuberous anemones. Plant in early spring in moist, rich, well-drained soil.

Tuberous anemones. These do best in light, sandy soil that is kept moist during growth and bloom but allowed to go dry after flowering. Set out *A. blanda* in fall; where winter temperatures drop below −10°F (−23°C), apply a thick mulch after first hard frost. Plant *A. coronaria* and *A. × fulgens* in fall where they are hardy in the ground; in cooler regions, plant in early spring. In warmer climates, soak tubers for a few hours before planting. Plant tubers scarred side up (look for depressed scar left by base of last year's stem), setting them 1–2 in. deep and 8–12 in. apart in rich, light, well-drained loam. Or start in flats of damp sand; set out in garden when stems are a few inches tall. Protect from birds until leaves toughen. In high-rainfall areas, excess moisture induces rot.

All anemones are susceptible to mildew and rust, and they need protection from slugs and snails.

Anemopsis californica

YERBA MANSA
Saururaceae
PERENNIAL

⬛ **ZONES 4–24; H1**

☼ ☀ **FULL SUN OR LIGHT SHADE**

💧💧 **REGULAR TO AMPLE WATER**

Anemopsis californica

Native to wetlands of the southwestern U.S. and adjacent areas of Mexico. This vigorously spreading, low-growing perennial is a good choice for planting alongside a stream or pond; beneath a moisture-loving tree; or in a low, wet part of the

garden. Tolerates alkaline and salty soils. Leaves and roots are used as a traditional medicine to treat a variety of ills.

Plants grow about 1 ft. tall and spread at least 2–3 ft. wide, eventually forming large, dense colonies. Upright stems hold thick, fleshy, deep green leaves 2–6 in. long; foliage has a strong, spicy, musty scent that is detectable from a distance on warm days. In late spring or summer, erect flower spikes rise just above the foliage mass, each topped with a conelike inflorescence dotted with tiny white flowers. Large, snowy white bracts at the base of each spike give the impression of a single flower. The whole plant takes on reddish hues as weather cools, turning brick red by winter. Cut back or mow to the ground each winter for fresh spring growth.

Anethum graveolens

DILL
Apiaceae
ANNUAL

⬛ **ZONES 1–24**

☼ **FULL SUN**

💧 **REGULAR WATER**

🐝 **ATTRACTS BENEFICIAL INSECTS**

Anethum graveolens

Native to southwestern Asia and naturalized in the northern U.S. It grows 3–4 ft. tall, with soft, feathery leaves and umbrella-shaped, 6-in.-wide clusters of small yellow flowers in summer (winter in the desert). The seeds and leaves have a pungent aroma, making this a popular culinary herb. Use

A

seeds in pickling and vinegar; use fresh or dried leaves in cooked dishes, salads, sauces. Makes an attractive potted plant; choose a container at least 1 ft. deep.

CARE

Sow seeds where plants are to grow; choose a sunny spot protected from wind. For a constant supply, sow several times in spring and summer (germinates and grows better in spring). In the desert, sow in later summer or fall. Thin seedlings to 1½ ft. apart (these can be chopped for use in cooking). Snip off leaves as needed through the growing season. To prevent reseeding, shear off flower heads when they begin to turn brown; in a casual garden, let one or two plants go to seed.

Angelica archangelica

ANGELICA
Apiaceae
BIENNIAL

🌿 **ZONES A2, A3; 1–10, 14–24**
☼ ☼ **FULL SUN IN COOLER CLIMATES ONLY**
💧 **REGULAR WATER**

Angelica archangelica

Native to northern Europe and western Asia. A tropical-looking plant with divided and toothed, yellow-green leaves 2–3 ft. long. When it blooms (in early summer), it sends up a thick, hollow stem to 6 ft. tall topped by a large (4 ft. wide), umbrella-shaped cluster of greenish yellow flowers. Angelica leaves are a nice addition to salads; the leafstalks can be cooked and eaten like asparagus. Both

leafstalks and hollow flower stems can be candied and used to decorate pastries. The seeds are used commercially to flavor wines, vermouth, and liqueurs.

Grow in moist, rich soil. Propagate from seeds as soon as they ripen in fall. Because angelica is taprooted and doesn't transplant well, sow seeds in place; space plants 4 ft. apart. To prolong plant's life for a few years, cut out flowering stem after it has formed.

Angelonia angustifolia

Plantaginaceae
PERENNIAL OFTEN TREATED AS ANNUAL

🌿 **ZONES 1–24; H1, H2**
☼ **FULL SUN**
💧 **REGULAR WATER**

Angelonia angustifolia

This native of Mexico and the West Indies is sometimes called summer snapdragon, though it more closely resembles a miniature delphinium. Showy 8-in.-tall spikes of small blue, purple, pink, or white blossoms appear in summer atop bushy plants that grow to 1–1½ ft. tall and about 1 ft. wide. Medium green leaves are narrow and pointed, up to 3 in. long. Excellent as a bedding plant and in containers. Hybrids in the Angelface series carry brightly colored blooms on well-branched plants; some have flowers marked with more than one color.

Angelonia is easy to grow in moist, well-drained soil. It is very tolerant of high heat and humidity and is rarely bothered by pests.

Anigozanthos

KANGAROO PAW
Haemodoraceae
PERENNIALS

🌿 **ZONES 15–24**
☼ **FULL SUN**
💧 **REGULAR WATER**
🐦 **FLOWERS ATTRACT HUMMINGBIRDS**

Anigozanthos hybrid

Evergreen from southwestern Australia. Thick rootstocks send up fans of dark green, swordlike leaves and spikes bearing fuzzy, tubular flowers in red, purple, green, or yellow. The striking blooms are curved at the tips like kangaroo paws (tips are split into six segments). Plants bloom from late spring to fall if spent flowering spikes are cut to the ground. Good cut flowers.

Grow in light sandy soil or heavier soil amended to improve drainage. Control snails and slugs.

A. flavidus. Branching stems to 5 ft. tall bear 1–1½-in.-long, yellow-green flowers tinged with red. Foliage clump is 2–3 ft. wide.

A. hybrids. Kangaroo paws hybridize freely in nature and in cultivation. The following are among the many superior garden plants that have been developed. Foliage clumps range from a foot across (for most dwarf varieties) to about 3 ft. wide; the smaller types make good container subjects.

'Big Red'. Extra-large bright red blossoms top 3–4-ft.-tall stems.

Bush Gems series. These were bred to resist the leaf and root diseases that afflict kangaroo paws. Two of the best are 2½–3-ft., easy-to-grow 'Bush Gold', which bears clear lemon yellow flowers above lime green leaves over a long bloom season, and 1½–2½-ft. 'Bush Ranger', a long-lived variety with clear red blooms. Other good varieties include 'Bush Baby', with flowers blending red, orange, and yellow on 1½-ft. stems; 'Bush Emerald', bearing surprising green flowers with contrasting yellow throats and brilliant orange anthers on 2–2½-ft. stems; 'Bush Lantern',

Paw Power

Strappy foliage and tall stems topped with vibrant, velvety blooms give kangaroo paws a striking presence in any garden—whether the plants are used singly or massed in borders. A few of the eye-catching displays we've spotted around the mild-climate West:

- A pair of orange-flowered varieties flanking an entry whose tangerine front door looked as if it had been dyed to match.

- A trio of patio pots (Tuscan terra-cotta), each containing a single plant—two orange-flowered varieties flanking a yellow-flowered one—huddled close on a patio. The effect: flaming.

- A row of rosy pink kangaroo paws behind mounding silvery gray artemisia.

- Orange paws mingling with 'Maori Sunrise' New Zealand flax.

A

a bright yellow dwarf 1–2 ft. tall; and 'Bush Pearl', with bubble-gum pink blossoms on 2-ft. stems.

'Harmony'. Yellow flowers on tall (4–6 ft.) stems clothed with bright red hairs.

'Pink Joey'. Silvery pink flowers on stems 1–3 ft. high.

A. manglesii. Unbranched green stems to 3 ft. high are thickly covered with red hairs; the peculiar 3-in. flowers are brilliant deep green, red at base. Foliage clump is 1½–2 ft. wide.

Anisacanthus
DESERT HONEYSUCKLE
Acanthaceae
EVERGREEN OR DECIDUOUS SHRUBS

ZONES 8–13, 18–23; H1, H2

EXPOSURE NEEDS VARY BY SPECIES

MODERATE WATER

ATTRACT BUTTERFLIES AND HUMMINGBIRDS

Anisacanthus quadrifidus wrightii

Heat-loving shrubs with nectar-filled tubular flowers resembling those of honeysuckle (*Lonicera*). Plants will survive with little water, but for best bloom, irrigate them deeply every 2 to 3 weeks in summer.

A. quadrifidus wrightii (A. wrightii). Deciduous. Native to southeastern Texas, northeastern Mexico. Grows to 3 ft. tall, 4 ft. wide, with dark green leaves 2 in. long and 1 in. wide. Spikes of 2-in.-long, brilliant red-orange flowers appear from early summer to autumn. Rabbits love the new shoots; protect with wire cage until a woody structure is established. For compact shape and prolific bloom, cut back by

one-half to two-thirds before new spring growth commences. 'Mexican Flame' is a superior selection grown from cuttings. Full sun or light shade.

A. thurberi. CHUPAROSA. Mostly evergreen. Native to northern Mexico and canyons and washes of the Sonoran Desert of southern Arizona and New Mexico. In mild-winter areas, grows to 4–8 ft. tall and as wide, with stout branches. Looks best when cut to the ground each year before spring growth begins. Valued for spikes of 1½-in.-long, yellow-orange flowers held above light green leaves 1½–2 in. long, ½ in. wide. Blooms most prolifically in spring, with occasional blossoms in summer and fall. Full sun. Plants with red or orange-red flowers sold under this name may be *Justicia spicigera*.

Anisodontea × hypomadara
(A. × hypomandarum)
CAPE MALLOW
Malvaceae
EVERGREEN SHRUB

ZONES 14–24

FULL SUN OR LIGHT SHADE

LITTLE TO MODERATE WATER

Anisodontea × hypomadara

This South African shrub grows quickly into a rounded shape about 4 ft. tall and wide, with small, lobed, bright green leaves. Profuse show of inch-wide, dark-veined, dark-eyed pink to purplish blooms resembling miniature hollyhocks; flowers come throughout warm weather, year-round in mildest

climates. Good for borders. Sometimes sold as single-trunk standard or "patio tree."

Hybrids include 'Slightly Strawberry', a compact grower (just 2–3 ft. tall and half as wide), with silvery green foliage and bright pink flowers; 'Tara's Wonder', an open grower to 6 ft. tall and wide, with narrowly lobed leaves and very large dark pink flowers; and 'Tara's Pink', a bushy plant with widely lobed leaves and light pink blossoms.

Give it well-drained soil. In an informal landscape, it complements plants with similar needs, such as Jerusalem sage, Mexican bush sage, sea lavender, westringia, and yarrow.

Antennaria dioica
PUSSY-TOES
Asteraceae
PERENNIAL

ZONES A1, A2; 1–3, 6, 7, 14–16

FULL SUN

MODERATE TO REGULAR WATER

Antennaria dioica 'Rosea'

Native to Europe, North America, and northern Asia. Forms inch-high mats of woolly foliage that slowly spread among rocks, between paving stones, or at the front of a border. Furry puffs of tiny flowers are pinkish white in the basic species, deep pink in 'Rubra', and rose-pink in 'Rosea'. Withstands some foot traffic and is extremely hardy to cold. 'Rubra' is especially pretty in alpine trough gardens or tucked between boulders in a summer rock garden.

Anthemis
Asteraceae
PERENNIALS

ZONES VARY BY SPECIES

FULL SUN

MODERATE TO REGULAR WATER

Anthemis tinctoria

Some species are weedy, but those listed here (from southern Europe and Turkey) are fine garden plants with long-lasting daisylike or buttonlike flowers. Their finely cut leaves are aromatic, especially when bruised. Provide good drainage.

A. carpatica. Zones 3b–10, 14–24. Forms low, 2-ft.-wide mounds of green to gray-green foliage. Stems about 6 in. high rise from foliage clumps in spring and summer, bearing 1½-in. white daisies with yellow centers.

A. marschalliana (A. biebersteiniana). Zones 1–9, 14–24. Rounded plant 1 ft. tall and wide, with finely cut, fernlike, silvery leaves and 1-in., brilliant yellow daisylike blooms in summer.

A. nobilis. See *Chamaemelum nobile*.

A. punctata cupaniana. Zones 4–9, 14–24. Forms a mound of silvery foliage 1 ft. tall and at least twice as wide, topped by 2½-in. long-lasting white daisies in summer.

A. tinctoria. GOLDEN MARGUERITE. Zones 1–11, 14–24. Erect, shrubby plant to 2–3 ft. tall and wide, with angular stems, light green leaves, and gold-yellow, 2-in. daisies in summer and early fall. Excellent cut flower. Cut back lightly after first flush of bloom to keep flowers coming. Plants are short-lived; root new ones from stem cuttings in spring or divide clumps in spring or fall. Varieties include 'Beauty of Grallagh', golden orange flowers; 'E. C. Buxton', white with yellow centers; 'Kelwayi', golden yellow; and 'Moonlight', pale yellow.

Anthriscus
Apiaceae
ANNUALS AND PERENNIALS OR BIENNIALS

- 🌿 **ZONES VARY BY SPECIES**
- ☀️◐ **EXPOSURE NEEDS VARY BY SPECIES**
- 💧 **REGULAR WATER**

Anthriscus cerefolium

Native to Europe, North Africa, and Asia. Though both of these plants produce many umbrella-shaped clusters of tiny flowers, they are valued for their fernlike foliage. In the first species, the leaves are used in cooking; in the second, the foliage brings deep, striking color to the perennial border.

A. cerefolium. CHERVIL. Annual. Zones 1–24. Forms low foliage mounds about a foot wide. In summer, flower stems 1–2 ft. tall are topped with white blossoms. The leaves taste like parsley with overtones of anise; use them like parsley, fresh or dried. Sow seeds in place in early spring (in cold-winter areas) or in autumn (where winters are mild). In the following years, volunteer seedlings will keep you supplied with new plants. Goes to seed quickly in hot weather; keep flower clusters cut to encourage leafy growth. Grow in partial shade.

A. sylvestris 'Ravenswing'. Perennial or biennial. Zones 1–9, 14–24. Forms a clump of very attractive purple-black foliage about 1½ ft. high and 2½ ft. wide. In late spring or early summer, flowering stems to 3 ft. tall bear white blossoms with purplish pink bracts. Deadhead for best appearance and to prevent self-sowing. Grow in full sun or light shade.

Anthurium
Araceae
PERENNIALS

- 🌿 **ZONE H2, EXCEPT AS NOTED; OR INDOORS**
- ◐ **PARTIAL SHADE; BRIGHT INDIRECT LIGHT**
- 💧 **REGULAR WATER**

Anthurium

Native to tropical American rain forests, these exotic-looking plants are prized for their large, often glossy leaves and distinctive "flowers" (a large, flattish bract surrounding a slender, fleshy spike). Among the species listed here, all but *A. hookeri* are usually grown as potted plants, even in tropical climates. Anthuriums, sometimes called flamingo flowers, make unusual houseplants in cooler climates.

A. andraeanum. Oblong leaves with a heart-shaped base grow 1 ft. long and 6 in. wide. Spreading, heart-shaped, puckered bracts to 6 in. long come in shades of red, rose, pink, and white, and shine as though lacquered. Spikes are yellow. Bloom is more or less continuous—plant may have four to six flowers during the year. Flowers last 6 weeks on plant, 4 weeks after cutting.

A. hookeri. Grown in the tropical landscape for its "nest" of large (to 3 ft. long) leaves. Erect flower spike is dark lilac. An excellent accent in a wind-sheltered garden or in large containers.

A. scherzerianum. Zones 23, 24; H2. Slow-growing, compact plant to 2 ft. tall and half as wide. Dark green leaves are lance-shaped. Flower bracts are broad, 3 in. long, deep red to rose, salmon, or white. The yellow flower spikes are spirally coiled. Easier to handle than *A. andraeanum*.

CARE

Bloom is best in moderate shade. The higher the humidity, the better: leaves lose shiny texture and may die if humidity drops below 50 percent for more than a few days. Indoors, keep pots on trays of moist gravel, or in a bathroom—or mist plant several times daily. Ideal temperature range is 80°F to 90°F (27°C to 32°C), but indoor plants get along at normal house temperature. Growth stops below 65°F (18°C), and plant is damaged below 50°F (10°C). Pot in coarse, porous mix of leaf mold, sandy soil, and shredded osmunda. Feed lightly every 4 weeks.

Antigonon leptopus
QUEEN'S WREATH
Polygonaceae
EVERGREEN OR DECIDUOUS VINE

- 🌿 **ZONES 12, 13, 18–24; H1, H2**
- ☀️ **FULL SUN**
- 💧💧 **MODERATE TO REGULAR WATER**

Antigonon leptopus

Native to Mexico. Where summers are long and hot, this tuberous-rooted perennial vine grows quickly, climbing by tendrils to 40 ft. to make an open, airy foliage cover. Leaves are bright green, and heart-shaped or arrow-shaped; small rose-pink flowers are carried in long, trailing sprays from midsummer to fall. A wonderful vine in the low deserts of California and Arizona, where it can grow without irrigation but may die back to the ground in summer. Elsewhere, give it the hottest place in garden; choose a warm, wind-sheltered spot in Southern California coastal gardens. Let it shade a patio or terrace, or drape its foliage and blossom sprays along eaves or fence. Varieties include rare white 'Album' and hot rose-pink (nearly red) 'Baja Red'.

Vine is evergreen in mild-winter areas; cut back vigorous growth in late winter or early spring. In frosty areas, the leaves drop in fall and most of the top dies, but recovery is quick when weather warms. Where winter temperatures dip below 25°F (−4°C), protect roots with mulch. Remove frost-killed stems from their support before new growth emerges in spring.

Antirrhinum majus
SNAPDRAGON
Plantaginaceae
PERENNIAL TREATED AS ANNUAL

- 🌿 **ZONES A1–A3; 1–24**
- ☀️ **FULL SUN**
- 💧 **REGULAR WATER**
- 🦋 **ATTRACTS BUTTERFLIES**

Antirrhinum majus

Snapdragons are among the best flowering plants for sunny borders and for cutting. Bushy and erect, they have glossy, lance-shaped, deep green leaves and flowers packed onto upright spikes. Snapdragon blooms have five lobes, divided into upper and lower "jaws"; by pinching sides of flower lightly, you can make jaws snap open. Plants are at their best in spring and early summer. In regions with mild winters and hot summers, they bloom in winter and spring.

Several variations on the basic snapdragon have been developed: the double flower; the bell-shaped kind, with round, open flowers; and the azalea-shaped bloom, which is a double bellflower. All are available in many colors. Plants range from about 6 in. across for smallest types to 2 ft. wide for tallest.

Tall and intermediate forms are superb vertical accents in borders. Tall kinds (to 2½–3 ft.) include Rocket and Topper strains (single flowers) and Double Supreme strain. Intermediate (to 1–2 ft.) are Cinderella, Coronette, Minaret, 'Princess White with Purple Eye', the Ribbon series, Sprite, and Tahiti. Dwarf kinds (just 6–8 in. high) are effective as edgings in rock gardens and raised beds, or in pots. Look for the following: Dwarf Bedding Floral Carpet, Kim, Kolibri, and Royal Carpet. Bell-flowered strains have round, open flowers and include Bright Butterflies and Wedding Bells (both 2½ ft.), La Bella (1½ ft.), and Little Darling and Liberty Bell (both 15 in.). Azalea-flowered strains include Madame Butterfly (2½ ft.) and Sweetheart (1 ft.). In a category of its own is the Chinese Lanterns strain: this bell-flowered snapdragon with trailing, cascading stems is ideal for hanging baskets.

CARE

Sow seeds in flats from late summer to early spring for later transplanting or buy plants at nursery. Set out plants in early fall in mild-winter areas, spring in colder climates. If snapdragons set out in early fall reach bud stage before night temperatures drop below 50°F (10°C), they will start blooming in winter and continue until weather gets hot.

Apple
Rosaceae
DECIDUOUS FRUIT TREES

✎ ZONES VARY BY VARIETY

☼ FULL SUN

💧 REGULAR WATER DURING FRUIT DEVELOPMENT

» See chart on pages 157–159.

CLOCKWISE FROM TOP LEFT: 'Jonagold', 'Granny Smith', 'Pink Lady', 'Gala', 'Braeburn'

Apples are the world's most widely adapted deciduous fruits. They are probably natural hybrids of *Malus sylvestris* and *M. pumila,* two species whose ranges overlap in southwestern Asia. Most apples ripen from July to early November, depending on variety and climate. Most need 500 to 1,000 hours of winter chill (temperatures at or below 45°F/7°C) to flower and fruit to their full potential, but low-chill varieties (noted in the chart) can bear apples in mild winters in the low desert and the marine and coastal climates of Southern California, where only 100 to 400 hours of winter chill can be expected. In the coldest climates, including Alaska, rootstock is as important as variety; apples in such areas are best grown on hardy crabapple rootstocks such as *Malus baccata, M. antonovka,* or *M. ranetka.* Or grow apple-crabapple hybrids in coldest-winter areas.

Many apples are self-fruitful to varying degrees ('Chehalis', 'Golden Delicious', and 'Mollie's Delicious' are closest to self-fruitful). But unless there are apples growing nearby in your neighborhood, plant two or more varieties for cross-pollination and good fruit set. If your tree is not bearing, graft a branch

of another variety onto it or place fresh bouquets of blossoms from another variety in a can of water at the base of the tree. Certain varieties (triploids) do not produce fertile pollen and cannot fertilize either their own flowers or those of other apples; they must be pollinated by a fertile apple to bear fruit. Pollen-sterile trees (including 'Gravenstein') are noted in the chart.

Every apple has different storage potential. But, generally, the later in the season an apple comes to harvest, the longer its storage life. In practice, early apples are best eaten immediately or made into sauce or cider (they quickly go bad). Late apples can often be stored for months.

For nearly perfect fruit, give apple trees much care in most regions. But even with less-than-perfect fruit, an apple tree is ornamental; it has more character, better form, and a longer life than most other deciduous fruit trees.

For ornamental relatives, see *Malus.*

Standard apples. A standard apple tree grows about to 20 ft. tall and 20–25 ft. wide, and takes several years to come to full harvest. If space is at a

premium, consider dwarf trees. For very small yards, multiple-variety trees provide an assortment of different apples as well as cross-pollination—all on a single tree. Available in standard and dwarf sizes, these "cocktail" trees have three to five varieties grafted onto a single trunk and rootstock.

Good apples are not necessarily red. Skin color is not an indicator of quality or taste. Make sure that name, eye appeal, or taste preference does not influence you to choose a difficult-to-grow variety. For example, if to your taste 'Golden Delicious' and 'Red Delicious' are nearly equal (and you live in an area where either can be grown), consider the differences in growing them. 'Golden Delicious' produces fruit without a pollenizer and comes into bearing at a younger age. It keeps well, while 'Red Delicious' fruit becomes mealy if not stored at temperatures of 35°F to 40°F (2°C to 4°C) or lower. And 'Golden Delicious' apples can be used for cooking, while 'Red Delicious' is principally a fresh eating apple.

In many apple-growing areas, the demand for popular varieties seen on fruit stands often causes nurseries to sell

Apples: Pushing the Chill Envelope

Most apples need 500 to 1,000 hours below 45°F (7°C) every year to produce healthy crops. With fewer chill hours, the fruit's skin may not color well. That's unacceptable for commercial growers, but not for home gardeners. In Southern California, gardeners usually grow low-chill varieties such as 'Anna', 'Beverly Hills', and 'Gordon'. But high-chill apples still may prosper there.

After testing more than 100 varieties in Riverside (Zone 19), grower Kevin Hauser hasn't found an apple that won't fruit there. Cold-climate apples like 'Honeycrisp' and 'Arkansas Black' are on his top-20 list. Not all of his high-chill fruits taste good. And low-chill varieties are still best in Zones 20–24. But Hauser's high success rate with out-of-zone apples shows the value of experimentation.

APPLE: TOP PICKS TO GROW

VARIETY	ZONES	HARVEST PERIOD	FRUIT	COMMENTS
'Akane'	1–7, 14–16	Early to midseason	Small to medium, round to flat; red. Crisp white flesh.	Scab- and mildew-resistant.
'Anna'	7–24; H1	Early; may bear light second and third crops	Large; pale green blushed red. Crisp, sweet with some acid.	Begins producing at a young age. Low-chill variety; useful in warmest-winter areas. Good annual bearer. Good pollenizer for 'Dorsett Golden' and 'Ein Shemer'.
'Arkansas Black'	1–3, 10, 11, 19	Late	Medium size; deep dark red. Hard, crisp, juicy, and aromatic. Flavor is best after storage for 2 months.	'Arkansas Black Spur' is a spurred variation.
'Ashmead's Kernel'	4–9, 14–17	Late	Medium size; red-orange blush over rough-textured yellow-green.	Good disease resistance.
'Beverly Hills'	12, 13, 18–24	Early	Small to medium; yellow skin splashed and striped red. Tender flesh is a bit tart. Fair quality. Somewhat resembles 'McIntosh'.	Definitely for cool areas; will not develop good quality in hot interiors. One of the best for Southern California coast.
'Braeburn'	1–4, 6, 14–16, 18, 22, 23	Late	Medium size; orange-red blush over yellow skin. Crisp, sweet-tart flesh. Stores well.	Fruit drops in hot climates. Alternate bearing. Very susceptible to mites.
'Chehalis'	4–6	Early	Large; yellow-green. Similar to 'Golden Delicious'. Mild flavor, melting flesh. Soft but bakes well. Also good in salads. Poor keeper.	Self-fruitful. Resists scab.
'Cox's Orange Pippin'	7, 14–16	Midseason	Medium size; dull orange-red skin. Yellow, firm, juicy flesh. Superb flavor. English dessert favorite.	Susceptible to scab and cracking. Dense growth; thin out branches. Worth trying for its unique flavor.
'Dorsett Golden'	12, 13, 18–24	Early	Medium to large; yellow or greenish yellow. Sweet flavor. Good for eating fresh or cooking. Keeps a few weeks.	Low-chill variety. Good pollenizer for 'Anna' and 'Ein Shemer'.
'Ein Shemer'	12, 13, 18–24	Early	Medium size; yellow to greenish yellow. Juicy, crisp, mildly acidic.	Low-chill variety. Good pollenizer for 'Anna' and 'Dorsett Golden'.
'Empire'	2–7, 14–16	Midseason	Cross between 'McIntosh' and 'Red Delicious'. Small to medium size, roundish; dark red skin. Creamy white flesh is juicy, crisp, mildly tart.	Semispur growth habit. Good tree structure. Susceptible to spring frost damage. Better adapted than 'McIntosh' to hot-summer areas.
'Fuji'	3b–9, 12–16, 18–22	Late	Medium to large; yellow-green skin with red stripes. Firm flesh with excellent, very sweet flavor. Stores exceptionally well.	Needs a long growing season (160 days) to ripen properly. Fairly low chill requirement. Tends to bear heavy crops in alternate years.
'Gala'	3b–9, 12–16	Early to midseason	Medium size; beautiful red-on-yellow color. Yellow flesh is highly aromatic, firm, crisp, juicy, sweet. Loses flavor in storage.	Vigorous, heavy bearer with long, supple branches that break easily; provide support if necessary. Very susceptible to fireblight.
'Garden Delicious'	1–3, 6–9, 14–20	Midseason	Medium to large; golden green with red blush. Crisp, sweet dessert apple also good for cooking.	Genetic dwarf 5–8 ft. tall and as wide.
'Golden Delicious' ('Yellow Delicious')	1–3, 6–11, 14–24	Late midseason	Medium to large; similar in shape to 'Red Delicious' with less prominent knobs. Clear yellow color, though it may develop russeting in some climates. Aromatic, crisp. Excellent for eating fresh and cooking.	Not related to 'Red Delicious'; different taste, habit. Long bloom season, heavy pollen production make it a good pollenizer. Self-fruitful. Spur types include 'Goldspur', 'Yellospur'.
'Golden Russet'	1–3, 6–9, 14–16, 18, 19	Early to midseason	Medium size; greenish yellow to golden brown skin with heavy russeting. Creamy yellow, sweet flesh. Good fresh or cooked.	Vigorous and productive. Partially self-fruitful but better crop with pollenizer.
'Gordon'	12, 13, 18–24; H1	Midseason	Large; greenish yellow blushed red. Sweet-tart flavor.	Vigorous, upright, semidwarf tree. Long blooming, bearing periods. Low-chill variety.
'Granny Smith'	3b, 7–11, 14–16, 19	Midseason (later in cool-summer areas)	Large; bright to yellowish green. Firm, tart flesh. Good quality. Stores well. Makes good pies, sauce.	Australian favorite before it came to U.S. Chancy in cold areas because of late ripening.

»

A

APPLE: TOP PICKS TO GROW

VARIETY	ZONES	HARVEST PERIOD	FRUIT	COMMENTS
'Gravenstein'	Widely sold in 4–11, 14–24; best in 15–17	Early to midseason	Large; deep yellow skin with brilliant red stripes. Crisp, aromatic, juicy. Excellent for fresh eating; makes applesauce with character.	Justly famous variety of California's North Coast apple district. Pollen-sterile; won't pollinate other varieties. Susceptible to mildew in Zones 4–6.
'Haralson'	1–3, 7, 14–16	Early to midseason	Medium size; greenish yellow ground with red stripes and spots. Crisp, juicy, mildly tart white flesh.	Hardy, vigorous, productive tree. Moderate resistance to fireblight.
'Honeycrisp'	1–7, 14–16	Midseason	Medium size; red. Firm, crisp flesh. Excellent sweet-tart flavor.	Hardy apple from Minnesota. Resistant to fireblight; somewhat resistant to scab.
'Hudson's Golden Gem'	2–7, 14–16	Early to midseason	Large, elongated; gold with light brown russeting. Crisp, nutty flesh. Good for desserts.	Productive. Fruit holds well on the tree. Resistant to scab, mildew, and fireblight.
'Jonagold'	2–9, 14–17	Late midseason	Large; yellow with heavy red striping. Firm, juicy flesh; fine mildly tart flavor. A frequent taste-test favorite.	Productive medium-size tree. Pollen-sterile; won't pollinate other varieties.
'Jonathan'	Sold everywhere; best in 2, 3, 7	Midseason	Small to medium, roundish oblong; bright red skin. Juicy, moderately tart, crackling crisp, sprightly. All-purpose apple. Good keeper.	Subject to mildew; somewhat resistant to scab.
'Liberty'	4–9, 14–16	Late midseason	Medium size; heavy red blush over greenish yellow. Crisp, with fine sweet-tart flavor. Dessert quality.	Productive tree. Immune to scab; can get mildew west of Cascades. Resists rust, fireblight.
'Lodi'	A2, A3; 1–3, 6–11, 14–16	Early	Medium size; greenish yellow. Tart flavor. Good for cooking. Keeps well.	Large, hardy tree. Tends to bear heavily in alternate years.
'McIntosh'	2, 3, 14–16	Midseason	Medium to large, nearly round; bright red. Snowy white, tender flesh. Excellent tart flavor.	Fine choice for cooler climates if given good care. Very susceptible to scab, preharvest fruit drop.
'Melrose'	1–7, 15, 16	Late	Medium to large, roundish; red skin striped deeper red. Flesh is white, mildly tart, aromatic. Stores very well. Good dessert apple.	Cross between 'Jonathan' and 'Red Delicious'. Somewhat mildew-resistant. Considered one of the best in Northwest.
'Mollie's Delicious'	8, 9, 14–20	Early	Large; light yellow blushed red. Light yellow, aromatic, juicy, sweet flesh. Stores well.	Self-fruitful; bears from an early age. Low-chill variety.
'Mutsu' ('Crispin')	4–9, 15, 16	Late	Very large; greenish yellow blushed red. Cream-colored, very crisp flesh. Excellent dessert and cooking apple with long storage life.	Exceptionally large and vigorous tree. Pollen-sterile; won't pollinate other varieties.
'Newtown Pippin' ('Yellow Newtown')	1–11, 14–22	Late	Large; green. Crisp and tart flesh. Fair for eating, excellent for cooking.	Large, vigorous tree. Excellent for California Central Coast. Gets mildew in Zones 4–6.
'Norland'	A1–A3; 1–3	Early	Medium size, oblong; yellow-green striped with red. Creamy white flesh is sweet-tart; good fresh or cooked. Stores well if picked just before fully ripe.	Hardy variety from Canada. Other Canadian introductions such as 'Noran', 'Norson', 'Parkland', and 'Westland' are also good in coldest-winter areas.
'Northern Spy'	1–3, 6, 7, 14–16	Late	Large; red. Tender, fine-grained flesh with sprightly flavor. Not attractive but excellent dessert and cooking apple. Keeps well.	Slow to reach bearing age.
'Pettingill'	23, 24	Midseason to late	Large, thick-skinned; red-blushed green to red. Firm, tasty, moderately acid white flesh.	Large, upright, productive tree; regular bearer. Very low chill requirement.
'Pink Lady'	6–15, 19	Late	Medium to large; pink blush over yellow skin. Firm, juicy flesh. Sweet-tart flavor; improves with storage. Good fresh or baked.	From Australia; does well in warm-summer areas. Very susceptible to fireblight. Moderately low chill requirement. Self-fruitful.
'Pink Pearl'	1–9, 14–16	Early	Medium size; pale green skin, sometimes blushed red. Sweet-tart pink flesh. Good keeper.	Very attractive in bloom; blossoms deeper pink than on most other varieties.

APPLE: TOP PICKS TO GROW

VARIETY	ZONES	HARVEST PERIOD	FRUIT	COMMENTS
'Red Delicious' ('Delicious')	Sold wherever apples will grow; best in 2, 3, 7	Midseason	Large; color varies with strain, climate (best with sunny, warm days, cool nights). Mildly sweet; good aftertaste. Older, striped kinds often taste better than highly colored commercial types.	Many strains that vary in ripening season, depth and uniformity of coloring. 'Crimson Spur' and 'Bisbee Spur' are popular varieties in home gardens. All types susceptible to scab.
'Rome Beauty' ('Red Rome')	3, 6, 7, 10, 11, 19	Late	Large, round, smooth; red. Greenish white flesh. Outstanding baking apple, only fair for eating fresh.	Bears at an early age.
'Shizuka'	1–9, 14–16	Late	Large, with full conical shape; gold with light red blush. High-quality fruit with good flavor. Stores well.	Productive tree.
'Sierra Beauty'	2, 3, 6–9, 14–16	Late	Large; exceptionally attractive yellow apple with red stripes. Firm, sweet-tart flesh. Keeps well.	Productive tree.
'Spartan'	3b–7, 15, 16	Midseason	Medium size; dark red with purplish bloom. Crisp flesh. Sweet-tart flavor.	Good tree habit. Heavy producer.
'Spitzenberg' ('Esopus Spitzenberg')	1–7, 14–16; best in 1–3	Late	Medium to large; red-dotted yellow. Crisp, fine-grained, tangy, spicy flesh.	Old favorite that still rates high. Subject to fireblight, mildew.
'Summerred'	A2, A3; 1–7, 15, 16	Early	Medium size; bright red. Tart flavor; good chiefly for cooking until fully ripe, then good dessert quality too.	Hardy. Consistent annual bearer for western Oregon and Washington.
'Tropical Beauty'	18–24; H1	Early	Medium to large; bright red. Juicy white flesh with mild, sweet flavor.	Partially self-fruitful; production enhanced if grown near 'Adina'.
'Winter Banana'	3b, 7–9, 14–24	Late midseason	Large; attractive, pale yellow blushed pink. Tender, tangy, aromatic flesh.	Low-chill variety. There is a 'Spur Winter Banana'.
'Winter Pearmain'	20–24	Midseason	Medium to large; pale greenish yellow skin with pink blush. Tender, fine-grained flesh; excellent flavor.	Low-chill variety. Performs better than standard cold-winter varieties in Southern California.
'Yellow Transparent'	A2, A3; 1–3, 7, 14–16	Early	Medium size; thin yellow skin. Tart white flesh. Good for cooking if harvested when greenish yellow.	Tall, vigorous tree with excellent hardiness.
'Zestar'	A2, A3; 1–7, 15, 16	Early midseason	Medium size; yellow with red stripes. Crisp white, juicy, sweet-tart flesh. Good for eating fresh and baking.	Bred in Minnesota; has excellent winter-hardiness.

'Winter Banana'

'Granny Smith'

'Fuji'

'Red Delicious'

»

A

How to Grow Apples

PLANTING Apple trees do best in deep, well-drained soil but get by in many imperfect conditions, including heavy soils. Choose a site in full sun, with protection from cold spring winds, which can interfere with pollination. Best time to plant bare-root stock is in winter or early spring, but containerized apples can be planted anytime where climates are mild and whenever the soil is workable in cold-winter climates.

PRUNING & TRAINING
For most home use, plant dwarf or semidwarf trees for ease in maintenance and harvest. Even commercial growers favor these smaller trees, since closer spacing permits more trees to the acre and a heavier crop. Preferred pruning style is pyramidal or modified leader, in which widely angled branches are encouraged to grow in spiral placement around the trunk.

Don't worry about fruit production the first 4 or 5 years—prune to develop strong, evenly spaced scaffold branches. Keep narrow-angled crotches from developing; don't let side branches outgrow the leader or secondary branches outgrow the primary branches.

To prune mature trees (do it late in the dormant season), remove weak, dead, or poorly placed branches and twigs, especially those growing toward the center of the tree (bearing is heaviest when some sun can reach the middle). Removing such growth will encourage development of strong new wood with new fruiting spurs (on apples, spurs may produce for up to 20 years, but they

tend to weaken after about 3 years) and discourage mildew. If you have inherited an old tree, selective thinning of branches will accomplish the same goal.

Dwarf trees can be grown as espaliers tied to wood or wire frames, fences, or other supports. The technique requires manipulating the branches to the desired pattern and pruning out excess growth. On columnar apples, just remove any wayward growth.

CHALLENGES Codling moth is the universal insect pest of apples. Pheromone traps, trichogramma wasps, or horticultural oil may be enough to thwart this pest in home gardens, but proper timing of controls is critical. Pesticides such as spinosad and carbaryl are also effective. Apple maggot is a problem in some areas (particularly western Washington); infested fruit is soft, rotten, and unusable. Various types of sticky traps may be of some help, but frequent insecticide sprays (such as spinosad) from midsummer to harvest are often needed for complete control. Apple scab causes hard, corky spots on the fruit, with subsequent defoliation and stunting of immature fruit. It is particularly severe in coastal areas of the Pacific Northwest. Planting disease-resistant varieties (see chart) is the best way to avoid the problem. Leaf rollers and aphids are potentially troublesome. Powdery mildew and fireblight can also infect apples in some regions. For timing of sprays and other control measures, consult your Cooperative Extension Office.

shallow roots and need the support of a post, fence, wall, or sturdy trellis to withstand wind and heavy rain. They are not reliable in the coldest regions. They also need good soil and extra care in fertilizing and watering. Genetic dwarf apples, such as 'Garden Delicious', are naturally small and stay that way; even grafting them onto a standard (nondwarfing) rootstock would not produce a standard-size tree.

Semidwarf apples. These are larger than dwarfs (and bear bigger crops) but smaller than standard trees. They bear bigger crops than dwarfs and take up less space than standards. Many commercial orchards get high yields by using semidwarf trees and planting them close together. Semidwarfing rootstocks MARK, M26, and M7 reduce normal tree height by about half; the trees may be espaliered or trellised if planted 12–16 ft. apart and allowed to grow 8–12 ft. tall. Semidwarfing rootstocks MM106 and MM111 reduce height by approximately 15 to 25 percent.

Spur apples. These apple trees bear flowers and fruit on spurs—short branches that grow from wood 2 years old or older. Spurs normally begin to appear only after a tree has grown in place 3 to 5 years, but on spur apples, they form earlier (within 2 years after planting) and grow closer together on shorter branches, giving more apples per foot of branch. Spur apples are natural or genetic semidwarfs about two-thirds the size of standard apple trees. They can be further dwarfed by grafting onto dwarfing rootstocks; EMLA27, M9, P22, and MARK give smallest trees.

Columnar apple trees. Zones 2a–9, 14–16. These develop a single spirelike trunk to 8–10 ft. tall, with fruiting spurs directly on the trunk or on very short branchlets. Total width does not exceed 2 ft. Varieties include 'Crimson Spire', (late midseason), which bears red fruit with tart-sweet white flesh; 'Emerald Spire' (midseason), mellow, sweet green fruit with gold blush; 'Golden Sentinel' (midseason), sweet, juicy yellow fruit; 'North-

pole' (early midseason), crisp, juicy McIntosh-type apple; 'Scarlet Sentinel' (midseason), large, sweet green-yellow fruit with red blush; 'Scarlet Spire' (midseason), juicy red-and-green eating fruit; and 'Ultra Spire' (midseason), tart, tangy red apple with yellowish blush. Two varieties are needed for pollination. Columnar trees are easy to maintain and attractive as accent, screen, or container plants. Plant 18 in. apart.

Apricot
Rosaceae
DECIDUOUS FRUIT TREES

🌢 **ZONES VARY BY VARIETY**

☼ **FULL SUN**

💧 **REGULAR WATER DURING FRUIT DEVELOPMENT**

Apricots

This stone fruit originated in China. It can be grown throughout much of the West, with some limitations. The ideal climate provides chilly winters and fairly warm, dry springs. Because apricot trees bloom early in the season, they will not fruit in regions with late frosts. In cool, humid coastal areas, tree and fruit are usually subject to brown rot and blight; in mild-winter areas of Southern California, only varieties with low requirements for winter chill do well.

Standard apricot trees reach 15–20 ft. high and wide and make good, easily maintained dual-purpose fruit and shade trees; they can also be espaliered. Thin, roundish leaves are reddish when new, maturing to bright green; flowers are pink or white. Apricot trees bear most of their fruit on short spurs that form on the previous year's

unsuitable selections. For example, many nurseries in mild-winter climates offer 'Red Delicious' because it is well known—but it won't fruit there. For this reason, the chart indicates where some standard varieties perform best, as well as where they are sold.

Dwarf and spur apples.
Dwarf apples (5–8 ft. tall and wide) are made by grafting wood from standard apple varieties onto dwarfing rootstocks such as M9, EMLA27, and P22. Dwarfs take up little room and bear at a younger age than standard apples, but they have

growth and remain fruitful for about 4 years. Most varieties ripen from late spring into summer.

The following nursery varieties are mostly available on dwarf and semidwarf rootstocks. Many are self-fruitful, but some need pollen from another apricot variety, as indicated. For ornamental relatives, see *Prunus*.

'August Glo'. Zones 8, 9, 12–16, 18–23. Medium-size fruit with exceptional sweet-tart flavor. Late.

'Autumn Royal'. Zones 2, 3, 6–9, 12–16, 18–24. Resembles 'Blenheim' but fruit ripens very late; only autumn-ripening apricot tree.

'Blenheim' ('Royal'). Zones 2, 3, 6–23. Standard variety in California's apricot regions. Good for canning or drying. Early to midseason.

'Chinese' ('Mormon'). Zones 1–3, 6. Late bloom, hardy tree; good production in late-frost and cold-winter regions. Mid- to late season.

'Floragold'. Zones 2, 3, 6–23. Full-size fruit grows on natural semidwarf tree (about two-thirds the size of standard apricot tree). Reliable producer. Early.

'Goldcot'. Zones 1–3. Developed for cold climates. Sweet flavor. Midseason.

'Golden Amber'. Zones 2, 3, 6–9, 12–16, 18–23. Like 'Blenheim' but blooms over month-long period; fruit ripens late.

'Gold Kist'. Zones 8, 9, 12–16, 18–23. Excellent sweet-tart flavor. Heavy bearing, even in mild-winter areas. Early.

'Harcot'. Zones 1–11, 14–16. Medium to large fruit is sweet, rich, and juicy. Frost hardy, blooms late. Early.

'Harglow'. Zones 1–11, 14–16. Medium-size orange fruit, sometimes blushed red. Firm, sweet, flavorful. Late blooming; disease-resistant. Early.

'Katy'. Zones 2, 3, 6–23. Large yellow fruit with red blush. Mild, sweet flavor. Favorite in mild-winter areas. Early.

Manchurian apricot (*Prunus armeniaca mandshurica*). Zones A2, A3; 1–3. Hardy shrub to small tree. Small, mild-flavored orange fruit, good for drying. Early.

'Montrose'. Zones 2–3, 6–12, 14–18. Yellow skin with a red blush; sweet and juicy, with excellent flavor. Large fruit and "sweet" edible kernel. A hardy, frost-resistant variety from Montrose, Colorado. Late.

'Moongold'. Zones 1–3. Plum-size, golden, sweet, and sprightly fruit. Developed for cold-winter climates. Late.

'Moorpark'. Zones 2, 3, 6–11, 14–16. Very large fruit, fine flavor. Color develops unevenly. Good home dessert or drying variety, poor canner. Midseason.

'Newcastle'. Zones 10–12, 20–23. Good Southern California variety; needs little winter chill. Midseason.

'Perfection' ('Goldbeck'). Zones 2–9, 12–16, 18–23. Fruit very large but flavor only mediocre. Low chill requirement; hardy tree. Needs pollenizer. Early.

'Puget Gold'. Zones 4–6. Medium-size fruit with good flavor; low in acid. Consistent bearer in Puget Sound area; fairly resistant to apricot diseases. Late.

'Riland'. Zones 2, 3, 6. Highly colored, roundish fruit. Needs pollenizer. Midseason.

'Rival'. Zones 2–6. Large, oval orange fruit blushed red. Needs early-flowering pollenizer, such as 'Perfection'. Early.

'Royalty'. Zones 2, 3, 6–9, 12–23. Extra-large fruit on heavy, wind-resistant spurs. Begins bearing at early age. Ripens early.

'Sun-Glow'. Zones 2–6. Highly colored, early fruit. Hardy tree with extra-hardy fruit buds. Midseason.

'Sungold'. Zones 1–3. Plum-size, slightly flattened, bright orange, sweet, mild fruit. Developed for cold-winter climates. Early.

'Tilton'. Zones 1–8, 10, 11, 18, 20. Higher chill requirement than 'Blenheim' but less subject to brown rot and sunburn. Midseason.

'Tomcot'. Zones 8, 9, 12–16. Large fruit with sweet orange flesh. Needs a pollenizer for best production. Early.

'Wenatchee' ('Wenatchee Moorpark'). Zones 2, 3, 6. Large fruit with excellent flavor. Difficult to pollinate; 'Perfection' does the best job. Midseason.

Plant trees in a sunny location with protection from cold spring winds. Light, loamy soil is best. Set out bare-root stock in late winter or early spring. Apply low-nitrogen complete fertilizer once in early spring.

To get a good crop of large fruit, thin excess fruit from branches in midspring, leaving 2–4 in. between fruits. Prune in summer (rather than in the dormant season, as is usually recommended) to avoid Eutypa dieback, a disease whose symptoms include sudden limb dieback and oozing cankers; spread by rain, it can infect trees through pruning wounds.

Apricots are subject to various other diseases and insect pests. To avert some problems, consult your Cooperative Extension Office for a local timetable and directions for preventive spraying. Essential treatment dates are during dormancy, before and after flowering, and at red-bud stage.

Aptenia cordifolia
(Mesembryanthemum cordifolium)
Aizoaceae
SUCCULENT PERENNIAL

▨ **ZONES 12, 13, 15–17, 21–24; H1, H2**

☼ ◑ ● **SOME SHADE IN HOTTEST CLIMATES**

◒ ◓ **LITTLE TO MODERATE WATER**

Aptenia cordifolia

This South African native, a relative of ice plant, produces trailing stems to 2 ft. long set with inch-wide, heart-shaped or oval, fleshy bright green leaves.

Purplish red, inch-wide flowers bloom in spring and summer. Use it as a low trailer in a rock garden or as a groundcover on a slope; plant 2 ft. apart for rapid coverage. Stems root wherever they touch moist soil, and plants can become invasive, overwhelming neighboring plants and escaping into wildlands. 'Variegata' has white-bordered leaves; hybrid 'Red Apple' has brighter red flowers.

Aquilegia
COLUMBINE
Ranunculaceae
PERENNIALS

▨ **ZONES VARY BY SPECIES**

☼ ◑ **FULL SUN OR LIGHT SHADE**

● **REGULAR WATER**

⚘ **ATTRACT BIRDS, BUTTERFLIES**

Aquilegia

Columbines are suited to woodland gardens, thanks to their lacy foliage and delicate flowers in pastels, deeper shades, and white. Erect plants range from 2 in. to 4 ft. high, depending on species or hybrid. The divided leaves are reminiscent of maidenhair fern (*Adiantum*) and may be fresh green, blue-green, or gray-green. Slender, branching stems carry erect or nodding flowers to 3 in. across, often with sepals and petals in contrasting colors; they usually have backward-projecting, nectar-bearing spurs. Some columbines have large flowers and very long spurs; these have an airier look than short-spurred and spurless kinds. Double-flowered types lack the delicacy of the single-flowered sort, but they make a bolder color mass. Bloom season comes in spring and early summer.

»

A

A. chrysantha. GOLDEN COLUMBINE, GOLDEN-SPURRED COLUMBINE. Zones 1–24. Native to Arizona, New Mexico, and adjacent Mexico. One of the showiest species, this large, many-branched plant grows 3–4 ft. tall and 1–2 ft. wide. Undersides of leaflets are densely covered with soft hairs. Upright, soft yellow, 1½–3-in. flowers have slender, hooked spurs 2–2½ in. long. 'Yellow Queen' has golden yellow blooms.

A. coerulea. ROCKY MOUNTAIN COLUMBINE. Zones A1–A3; 1–11, 14–24. Native to the Rockies, this is the state flower of Colorado. Grows 1½–3 ft. high, 2 ft. wide. Blue-and-white flowers are erect, 2 in. or more across, with straight or spreading spurs to 2 in. long. An important parent of many long-spurred hybrids. Often misspelled A. caerulea.

A. desertorum. ARIZONA COLUMBINE. Zones 2b, 3, 6–24. Native to northern Arizona, Utah, New Mexico. Grows 1½ ft. high, 15 in. wide, with rich bright orange to yellow, 1½-in. flowers. Spurs are held in the same plane as the rest of the blossom and extend beyond it, giving the bloom as a whole a distinct arrowhead shape.

A. flabellata. Zones A2, A3; 1–9, 14–24. Native to Japan. A stocky plant that grows 8 in.–1½ ft. high and about 1 ft. wide. Its nodding flowers are 1½ in. long, with hooked spurs to 1 in. long. The two-toned flowers are lilac-blue and creamy white. Differs from most other columbines in having thicker, darker leaves with often-overlapping segments. The Cameo series is dwarf (4–8 in. high) and comes with two-toned flowers of white and blue, pink, or rose.

A. formosa. WESTERN COLUMBINE. Zones A1–A3; 1–11, 14–24. Native from Alaska to Northern California, Montana, and Utah. Grows 1½–3 ft. tall, 1½ ft. wide. Nodding red-and-yellow flowers are 1½–2 in. across, with stout, straight red spurs. Good in a woodland garden. Allow it to set seeds, which are relished by song sparrows, juncos, and other small birds. A. f. truncata (sometimes sold as A. californica) bears yellow-and-orange blossoms that have red spurs.

A. hybrids. Zones A2, A3; 1–10, 14–24.These include graceful, long-spurred McKana hybrids and double-flowering Spring Song hybrids (both to 3 ft. tall, 2 ft. wide). Nora Barlow Mixed, reaching 2–2½ ft. tall and 2 ft. wide, has double flowers in a wide range of colors (the original 'Nora Barlow' has reddish pink blooms with white margins). About the same size is Vervaeneana Woodside Variegated Mixed, with variegated leaves and various flower colors. Lower-growing strains include Biedermeier and Dragonfly (1 ft. high and wide); early-blooming Spring Magic (14 in. tall and 12 in. wide); long-spurred Music (1½ ft. high and wide); long-blooming Origami (16–18 in. high); and single to double, upward-facing Fairyland (15 in. high and wide).

A. longissima. Zones 1–11, 14–24. Native to southwest Texas, southern Arizona, and northern Mexico. Grows 2½–3 ft. tall, 1½–2 ft. wide. Similar to A. chrysantha, with numerous erect, pale yellow blossoms with very narrow, drooping, 4–6-in.-long spurs.

A. sibirica. Zones A1–A3; 1–6. From Siberia and Mongolia. Grows 2 ft. tall and wide, with short-spurred, 1½-in., blue to dark purplish red flowers.

A. vulgaris. EUROPEAN COLUMBINE. Zones A2, A3; 1–10, 14–24. Naturalized in eastern U.S. Grows 1–2½ ft. tall, 1 ft. wide. The nodding blue or violet flowers are 2 in. across, with short, knobby spurs about ¾ in. long. Many selections and hybrids offer single to fully double blooms, either short spurred or spurless.

CARE

Plants are not fussy about soil as long as it is well drained. On all columbines, cut back old stems for second crop of flowers. Most are not long-lived and will need to be replaced every 3 or 4 years. Allow spent flowers to form seed capsules to ensure a crop of volunteer seedlings. If you're growing hybrids, the seedlings won't necessarily duplicate the parent plants, but seedlings from species (if grown isolated from other columbines) should closely resemble the originals.

Arabis
ROCKCRESS
Brassicaceae
PERENNIALS

🌡 **ZONES VARY BY SPECIES**

☀ **FULL SUN**

💧 **MODERATE WATER**

Arabis caucasica

These low-growing, spreading plants are ideal for edgings, rock gardens, and groundcovers. All have attractive year-round foliage and clusters of small white, pink, or rose-purple flowers in spring. Plant them in very well-drained soil.

A. alpina. MOUNTAIN ROCKCRESS. Zones 1–7. Native to high elevations of Europe. Low, tufted, rough-hairy plant 4–10 in. high and 2 ft. wide. White flowers in dense, short clusters. 'Rosea' bears pink flowers; 'Variegata' has yellow-edged green leaves. Plants sold as A. alpina are often really A. caucasica.

A. blepharophylla. CALIFORNIA ROCKCRESS, ROSE CRESS. Zones 5, 6, 15–17. Native to rocky hillsides and ridges along Northern California coast. A tufted plant to about 8 in. high and wide, with fragrant rose-purple flowers in short, dense clusters. Good in rock garden, containers. 'Spring Charm' ('Frühlingszauber') has brilliant magenta flowers in early spring.

A. caucasica (A. albida). WALL ROCKCRESS. Zones A1; 1–10, 14–24. This dependable old favorite is native from the Mediterranean region to Iran. It forms a mat of gray-green leaves to 6 in. high and 1½ ft. wide. White flowers almost cover plant during the bloom season. Excellent groundcover and base planting for spring-flowering bulbs such as daffodils and 'Paper White' narcissus. Provide some shade in hot climates. 'Variegata' has gray leaves with creamy white margins; 'Flore Plena' is double-flowered; 'Rosabella' and 'Pink Charm' bear pink blossoms.

A. ferdinandi-coburgi. Zones 2b–10, 14–24. Native to Bulgaria. Tight clumps to 4 in. high and 1 ft. wide, with white blossoms. 'Old Gold' has dark green leaves with margins widely outlined in gold.

A. procurrens. Zones 3–10, 14–24. Native to southeastern Europe. Creeping, wide-spreading plant with 1½-in. leaves and white flowers clustered on 4–12-in. stems. The most common form is 'Variegata', with leaves heavily edged and splashed with white.

A. × sturii. Zones 1–10, 14–24. Dense, fist-size cushions of small, bright green leaves eventually grow into small mats bearing clusters of white flowers on 2–3-in. stems. Some consider it among the finest rock garden plants.

Arachniodes simplicior
Dryopteridaceae
FERN

🌡 **ZONES 4–24**

🌓● **PARTIAL OR FULL SHADE**

💧💧 **REGULAR TO AMPLE WATER**

Arachniodes simplicior

This fern from Japan and China is usually seen in its variety 'Variegata', which grows 10–18 in. tall and nearly twice as wide. The fronds are broadly triangular and once-divided, the divisions deeply cut. Each division is marked by a yellow stripe along its full length. Evergreen where winters are warm; deciduous in frosty regions.

FOR MORE ON FERNS, SEE "MEET THE FERNS," PAGE 320.

Aralia
Araliaceae
DECIDUOUS SHRUB-TREES

🌡 **ZONES VARY BY SPECIES**

☀ ◑ **FULL SUN OR PARTIAL SHADE, EXCEPT AS NOTED**

◐ ● **MODERATE TO REGULAR WATER**

🦅 **ATTRACT BIRDS**

Aralia elata

Most aralias are striking bold-leafed plants that may eventually grow to 25–30 ft. tall under ideal conditions; they are not for small gardens. They're often shrublike and multistemmed (because of their suckering habit), especially in colder areas where they may grow to only 10 ft. tall. Clumps may be from one-half to almost as wide as they are tall. Branches are nearly vertical or slightly spreading, usually very spiny. Their leaves, clustered at ends of branches and divided into many leaflets, are huge. White flowers, small but in large, branched clusters in midsummer, are followed by purplish berrylike fruit enjoyed by birds.

Give them well-drained soil. Sharp spines make them poor choices to grow near swimming pools. Protect plants from wind to avoid burning foliage. Minimal pruning needed; just dig out suckers to limit spread.

A. californica. ELK CLOVER, CALIFORNIA SPIKENARD.

Zones 4–10, 14–24. Native to central and western California and Oregon. Reaches 4–10 ft. tall and wide, with 2–5-ft.-long leaves divided into oval, pointed leaflets. Leaves turn buttery yellow in fall. Grow in moist, rich soil in partial to full shade.

A. elata (A. chinensis). ANGELICA TREE. Zones 1–10, 14–24. Native to Asia. Only moderately spiny. Leaves are 2–3 ft. long, divided into toothed, stalkless, 2–6-in.-long leaflets. Leaflets of 'Aureovariegata' are bordered with gold; those of 'Variegata' with creamy white.

A. sieboldii. See *Fatsia japonica*.

A. spinosa. HERCULES' CLUB, DEVIL'S WALKING STICK. Zones 3–9, 14–24. Native to eastern U.S. Puts up several spiny, usually unbranched stems, each of them crowned by 2–6-ft.-long leaves. This is one of the most tropical-looking genuinely hardy plants. Has a coarse appearance in winter.

Araucaria
Araucariaceae
EVERGREEN TREES

🌡 **ZONES VARY BY SPECIES**

☀ **FULL SUN**

● **REGULAR WATER**

Araucaria heterophylla

These strange-looking conifers provide a distinctive silhouette with their evenly spread tiers of stiff branches. Most have stiff, closely overlapping, dark to bright green leaves. All do well in a wide range of soils with adequate drainage.

They make impressive skyline trees in parks and on old estates in California—but they

become so towering that they need lots of space. And they're not trees to sit under—with age they bear enormous, spiny, 10–15-lb. cones. They thrive in containers for several years, even in desert areas.

A. araucana (A. imbricata). MONKEY PUZZLE TREE. Zones 4–9, 14–24; H1, H2. Native to Chile. An arboreal oddity with heavy, spreading branches and ropelike branchlets closely set with sharp-pointed dark green leaves. Slow growing in youth, it eventually reaches 70–90 ft. tall and 30 ft. wide. Hardiest of araucarias.

A. bidwillii. BUNYA-BUNYA. Zones 7–9, 12–24; H1, H2. Native to Australia. Probably the most widely planted araucaria in both coastal and valley areas of California. Moderate growth to 80 ft. tall and 60 ft. wide, with a broadly rounded crown that supplies dense shade. Juvenile leaves are glossy, rather narrow, ¾–2 in. long, stiff, more or less spreading in two rows; mature leaves are oval, ½ in. long, rather woody, spirally arranged and overlapping along branches. Makes an unusual houseplant; very tough and tolerant of low light.

A. heterophylla (A. excelsa). NORFOLK ISLAND PINE. Zones 17, 21–24; H1, H2. Native to Norfolk Island, near Australia. Grows moderately fast to 100 ft. tall and 60 ft. wide, with a pyramidal shape. Juvenile leaves are rather narrow, ½ in. long, curved, sharp pointed; mature leaves are somewhat triangular, densely overlapping. Can be held in pots for years—outdoors in mild climates, indoors anywhere. Popular as a Christmas tree in Hawaii.

Don't sit under a big bunya-bunya tree. Its cones, borne high up in the tree, weigh 10 pounds (or more) each. When ripe in early fall, they crash to the ground, often taking small branches with them.

Arbutus
Ericaceae
EVERGREEN TREES OR SHRUBS

🌡 **ZONES VARY BY SPECIES**

☀ **FULL SUN, EXCEPT AS NOTED**

◐ ● **LITTLE TO REGULAR WATER, EXCEPT AS NOTED**

Arbutus unedo

These broad-leafed evergreens have ornamental bark, little urn-shaped flowers, decorative edible fruit, and foliage that looks good year-round. Provide well-drained soil, especially if plant receives regular water. Thin growth of all types as needed.

A. andrachne. Zones 8, 9, 14–24. Native to the eastern Mediterranean. Grows 20–40 ft. tall and wide. Resembles *A. menziesii* but is not as difficult to grow and has smaller, less shiny leaves. Peeling bark is especially beautiful.

A. arizonica. ARIZONA MADRONE. Zones 4–24. Native to Arizona, New Mexico, and northwestern Mexico. Grows to 30–45 ft. tall and wide, with attractively twisted trunk and branches, and lance-shaped leaves. Resembles *A.* 'Marina' but is more cold-hardy.

A. 'Marina'. Zones 8, 9, 14–24. Hybrid of uncertain parentage. This colorful tree grows to 25–40 ft. tall and almost as wide. Resembles *A. unedo* but has larger leaves and rosy pink fall flowers. Good garden substitute for *A. menziesii*.

A. menziesii. MADRONE, MADRONA. Zones 4–7, 14–19. Native from British Columbia to Southern California in Coast Ranges, occasionally in middle elevations of Sierra Nevada. Mature height ranges from 20 to 100 ft. Forms broad, round

A

A

head almost as wide as tall. Its smooth, reddish brown bark peels off in thin flakes. Leathery, 3–6-in.-long leaves are shiny dark green on top, dull gray-green beneath. In spring, large clusters of white to pinkish, bell-shaped flowers appear at branch ends. These are followed in early fall by clusters of brilliant orange to red, rough-coated berries that remain on the tree most of winter if birds don't get them. If you live in madrone country and have a tree in your garden, treasure it. Its requirements in gardens outside its native area are exacting: it must have fast drainage and nonalkaline water. Irrigate just enough to keep plants going until they are established, and then give only infrequent and deep watering. Look for new disease-resistant selections.

A. unedo. STRAWBERRY TREE. Zones 4–24; damaged in severe winters in Zones 4–7 but worth the risk. Native to southern Europe, Ireland. Thrives in a wide range of climates and soils, from desert to seashore; tolerates wind at the beach. In California, it is one of the best lawn trees. Attracts birds.

Trunk and branches have rich red-brown, shredding bark; tend to become twisted and gnarled in age. Dark green leaves are oblong. Clusters of small white or greenish white, urn-shaped flowers and yellow (young) or red (mature), round, ¾-in. fruit, like strawberries in texture, appear at the same time in fall and winter. Fruit is edible but usually mealy and bland in flavor.

Varieties include 'Elfin King', a dwarf form (not over 5 ft. tall at 10 years old) that flowers and fruits nearly continuously; 'Compacta', seldom exceeding 10 ft. tall; and 'Oktoberfest', a 6–8ft.-tall plant with deep pink flowers. *A. u. rubra* is like the species, but its flowers are deep pink.

CARE

Sun or part shade; needs some shade in the desert. Slow to moderate growth to 8–35 ft. with equal spread. Normally has basal suckers and stem sprouts. Thin its branches to make an open-crowned tree, or plant several and leave unpruned to make a big screen.

Archontophoenix

Arecaceae

PALMS

✂ **ZONES 21–24; OR INDOORS**

☀ ◑ **SUN OR PART SHADE; BRIGHT INDIRECT LIGHT**

💧💧 **MODERATE TO REGULAR WATER**

Archontophoenix alexandrae

Native to rain forests of eastern Australia; called bangalow or piccabeen palms in that country. They grow to 50 ft. or taller, with a 10–15-ft. spread. Mature specimens are handsome and stately but difficult to transplant. Where winds are strong, plant in lee of buildings to prevent foliage damage. Young trees can't take frost; mature plants may stand 28°F (–2°C). They tolerate shade and can grow for many years grouped under tall trees. Old leaves shed cleanly, leaving smooth green trunks. Feathery leaves on mature trees are 8–10 ft. long, green above, gray-green beneath. Good potted plants indoors or out. Both palms are stunning when lining a long driveway, or clustered at the end of a swimming pool, where their slender trunks and elegant canopies reflect in the still water.

A. alexandrae. ALEXANDRA PALM. Trunk enlarged toward base.

A. cunninghamiana (Seaforthia elegans). KING PALM. More common than *A. alexandrae*. Its trunk is not prominently enlarged at the base. Clustered amethyst flowers are handsome in summer. Highly recommended for nearly frost-free areas.

FOR MORE ON PALMS, SEE "MEET THE PALMS," PAGE 471.

Arctanthemum arcticum

(Chrysanthemum arcticum)

ARCTIC DAISY

Asteraceae

PERENNIAL

✂ **ZONES A1–A3; 1–10, 14–21**

☀ **FULL SUN**

💧 **REGULAR WATER**

Arctanthemum arcticum

This chrysanthemum relative from Alaska is extremely cold-hardy. It forms a foot-wide mound of dark green, leathery, usually three-lobed leaves. In fall, stems 6–12 in. high bear white or pinkish, 1–2-in. daisy-like flowers with yellow centers. 'Roseum' has pink flowers. Plant in well-drained soil and feed regularly from midsummer until flower buds begin to show color. Easy to propagate by division in spring.

Smothered in blooms in summer, Arctic daisies resemble snow. To play up that effect in the Far North, some gardeners grow them among low boulders toward the front of mounding borders, with small evergreens such as mugo pine behind.

Arctostaphylos

MANZANITA

Ericaceae

EVERGREEN SHRUBS

✂ **ZONES VARY BY SPECIES**

☀ ◑ **FULL SUN OR LIGHT SHADE**

💧 **LITTLE TO MODERATE WATER**

🦅 **ATTRACT BIRDS AND OTHER WILDLIFE**

Arctostaphylos uva-ursi 'Vancouver Jade'

Broad-leafed evergreens are native to the far West; the vast majority come from California. Plants vary from creeping groundcovers to treelike shrubs, but all have small, urn-shaped white or pink flowers, typically in late winter or early spring, followed by berrylike red or brown fruits that appeal to birds. The common name, "manzanita," is Spanish for little apple. Manzanitas have intricate branch patterns and smooth red to purple bark.

A. 'Austin Griffiths'. Zones 4–9, 14–24. Probable hybrid between *A. manzanita* 'Dr. Hurd' and *A. densiflora* 'Sentinel'. Grows 8 ft. tall and wide, with a treelike habit, gray-green leaves, white flowers, and burgundy-colored bark. Tolerates watering.

A. bakeri 'Louis Edmunds'. Zones 4–9, 14–17. Selection of a species native to Sonoma area, California. Elegant, upright shrub to 5–6 ft. tall and wide, with dark mahogany bark and small gray-green leaves. Showy pink flowers precede bright red berries. Tolerates heat and drought but will take some garden watering.

A. × coloradensis. Zones 1–3. Naturally occurring hybrid from cold, high-elevation regions of Colorado. Grows to 1–1½ ft.

How to Grow Arctostaphylos

PLANTING Manzanitas require excellent drainage, but they can tolerate poor soil and in fact prefer rocky or sandy, acid soils to rich, heavy ones. Choose a spot that has good air circulation and is not too close to established trees or shrubs. To get quick coverage from low groundcover types, plant 2–3 ft. apart, then mulch to suppress weeds and encourage rooting along stems.

WATERING The first summer after planting any manzanita, water every 4 to 7 days, depending on the weather. Once established, plants in warm-summer areas generally thrive on once-a-month watering in well-drained soil; in heavy soil and where summers are cool, they need less frequent irrigation. You may get away with watering just once or twice a summer.

PRUNING Regular pruning is not needed. To make plants denser and more uniformly compact, pinch new spring growth to force branching. On types with interesting branch structure, remove any limbs that detract from effect. Don't cut into bare wood; plants won't send out new growth.

A. densiflora. VINE HILL MANZANITA. Zones 7–9, 14–21. Native to a small area in Sonoma, California. Generally a low, spreading shrub, with outer branches taking root when they touch soil. Main stems are slender and crooked, with smooth, reddish black bark. Small, glossy leaves and dainty white or pale pink flowers give plants a refined look. The species is rarely sold, but several excellent selections have been developed. 'Howard McMinn' forms a mound 5–8 ft. tall and spreads to 7 ft. in 5 years (eventually to twice that wide). Its flowers are white. If you prune branch tips (but not those of prostrate branches) after flowering, the plant stays dense and tailored-looking. 'Harmony' is lower growing, about 4 ft. tall and 6 ft. wide, with a profuse show of pink flowers. 'Sentinel', with light green, downy leaves and pale pink flowers, is a good choice for warmer, inland gardens. It grows 6–8 ft. tall and spreads 4–10 ft. wide, with upright, open growth; easily trained into a small tree.

A. edmundsii. LITTLE SUR MANZANITA. Zones 6–9, 14–24. A low-growing species from California's coastal Monterey area. Several named selections are good groundcovers. 'Carmel Sur' grows quickly to 1–1½ ft. tall and 4–6 ft. wide, with neat gray-green foliage and soft pink flowers (though it rarely blooms). It has exceptionally good form and tolerates summer watering. Hybrid 'Greensphere' grows very slowly into a dense, nearly perfect 4-ft. sphere, with dark green leaves and a long bloom period; ideal for containers. Slow-growing 'Little Sur' has a dense, flat habit (10 in. high and 5 ft. wide), with pointed leaves edged in red (bronze when new) and soft pink flowers. *A. e. parvifolia* 'Bert Johnson' has shiny, dark green leaves (new growth is rich bronze) and pale pink flowers in late winter or early spring; plants grow 1–3 ft. high and 4–6 ft. wide; takes a wide range of garden conditions.

A. **'Emerald Carpet'.** Zones 6–9, 14–24. This natural hybrid between *A. uva-ursi* and *A. nummularia* is one of the greenest, most uniform groundcover manzanitas. Forms a

dense carpet 8–14 in. tall, mounding a bit higher after many years, and spreads about 5 ft. Roundish leaves remain bright green even in hot, dry weather. Tiny white flowers. Needs acidic soil and, especially in hot interior valleys, deep irrigation every 2 to 3 weeks.

A. glauca. Zones 4–9, 14–24. Native California to Baja California. Spreading shrub to 15 ft. tall, 20 ft. wide, with dark reddish brown bark and 3-in., blue-gray leaves. Clusters of pink to white flowers.

A. hookeri. MONTEREY MANZANITA. Zones 6–9, 14–24. Native to Monterey, California. Slowly forms a dense mound 1½–4 ft. high, spreading 6 ft. or more. Small, glossy green leaves; white to pinkish flowers; shiny, bright red fruit; smooth, red-brown bark. Good on hillsides. 'Monterey Carpet' grows to 1 ft. high, 12 ft. wide. 'Wayside' grows to 4 ft. tall, 8 ft. wide; may be slow to fill in but eventually forms a dense, attractive mound.

A. **'Indian Hill'.** Zones 6–9, 14–24. A groundcover that looks like a small-leafed *A. edmundsii.* New growth is bronzy, and winter

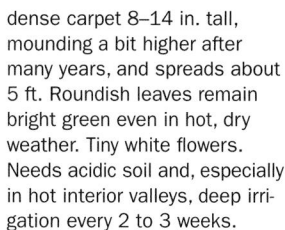

CLOCKWISE FROM TOP: *Arctostaphylos rudis; A. bakeri* 'Louis Edmunds'; *A. pungens*

flowers are palest pink to white. Very tolerant of garden watering.

A. insularis. ISLAND MANZANITA. From Channel Islands, California. Zones 16–24. Large, dense shrub to 10–12 ft. tall and not quite as wide, with bright green leaves and large, drooping clusters of white flowers in midwinter. 'Canyon Sparkles' is a compact selection (about 4 ft. tall, 6 ft. wide).

A. **'John Dourley'.** Zones 6–9, 14–24. A colorful, dependable low shrub or groundcover with gray-green foliage that is bright coppery pink when new; long-lasting show of abundant pink flowers is followed by purple-red fruits. It grows slowly into a mound 2–4 ft. tall and 4–8 ft. wide. Good tolerance for clay soil and garden watering.

A. manzanita. COMMON MANZANITA. Zones 4–9, 14–24. Native to inner Coast Ranges and Sierra Nevada foothills; widely adapted. In gardens, it grows into a tall shrub or shrub-tree 10–12 ft. high and wide

high and 4–6 ft. wide, a dense low grower that makes a good groundcover. Pink spring flowers are followed by red fruit; foliage takes on red tones in winter. Best in partial shade.

A. columbiana. HAIRY MANZANITA. Zones 4–6, 15–17. Native to low coastal mountains of central California to British Columbia. This treelike species grows to 10 ft. tall and wide, with reddish brown bark, gray-green leaves, white flowers, and red-cheeked brownish fruit. 'Oregon Hybrid', a compact form, grows to about 3 ft. high and 5–7 ft. wide, and is tough enough to be used along highways in western Oregon and Washington.

A

(possibly twice as large with great age), with a picturesque, crooked branching habit and purplish red bark. Leaves may be light blue-green, olive green, or dark green. Profuse show of white or pink flowers is followed by fruits that start out white and turn deep red. Excellent as a focal point or grouped as a large screen. 'Dr. Hurd' is an upright, treelike form with mahogany bark, large light green leaves, and white winter flowers. 'St. Helena' has gray-green leaves and a slightly more spreading shape. 'Hood Mountain' is similar, but with brighter purple trunks and narrower, grayer leaves.

A. nummularia. FORT BRAGG MANZANITA. Zones 14–24. Dense foliage, nearly dome-shaped, low shrub, usually under 2½ ft. high. Small, almost circular bright green leaves; little white flowers. Attractive but considered difficult to grow outside its native north coastal California forests. Needs good drainage, acid soil, and some shade except near coast. 'Small Change' is a compact selection with tiny, narrow, dark green leaves.

A. 'Pacific Mist'. Zones 7–9, 14–24. Grows 2–3 ft. tall, 6–15 ft. wide, with spreading, twisting stems that turn upward near ends. Deep reddish brown bark, narrow gray-green leaves, sparse white bloom. Needs pinching to force branching but eventually forms a good, dense groundcover that is also quite disease-resistant. Best away from the immediate coast; performs well even in dry shade.

A. pajaroensis. PAJARO MANZANITA. Zones 14–24. Native to central Monterey Bay area, California. Grows 3–8 ft. tall, 10–12 ft. wide. New growth is bronzy, maturing to bluish green; pink to white flowers bloom over a long period. 'Paradise' is a pink-flowered selection with long-lasting bronze foliage color. 'Warren Roberts' is similar, but with a tighter, more upright habit; mature leaves are bluer in color and new growth is darker bronze.

A. pumila. DUNE MANZANITA. Zones 16, 17. Native to dunes around Monterey Bay, California. Spreading, prostrate habit, to 1–2½ ft. high; branches

root freely where they touch ground. Plants are densely clothed in velvety, gray-green leaves, with short, dense clusters of small white to pink flowers. Near coast, plant 6 ft. apart as a groundcover in sandy soil.

A. 'Sunset'. Zones 6–9, 14–24. This natural hybrid between *A. hookeri* and *A. pajaroensis* was named in honor of the 75th anniversary of *Sunset* magazine. Dense, mounding, rapid growth to 5–8 ft. tall and at least as wide, with foliage that is coppery red when new and matures to bright green. Pinkish white flowers. Tolerates a wide range of soils and garden conditions.

A. uva-ursi. KINNIKINNICK, BEARBERRY. Zones A1–A3; 1–9, 14–24. Native from Northern California north to Alaska; also widespread in other northern latitudes. Long a popular ground- or bank cover in Pacific Northwest and intermountain areas. Plant is prostrate, spreading and rooting as it grows; eventually forms a mat 15 ft. wide. Small, glossy, leathery leaves are bright green, turning red or purplish in winter. White or pinkish flowers are followed by red fruits. Needs acidic soil. Slow to become established; mulch heavily between plants to suppress weeds until branches provide cover. The following varieties provide uniform appearance in large plantings.

'Massachusetts'. Small-leafed, flat growing. Abundant pinkish white flowers and plentiful fruit. Good resistance to leaf spot and leaf gall in Northwest.

'Point Reyes'. Dark green leaves are closely set along branches. More tolerant of heat and drought than 'Radiant'.

'Radiant'. Leaves brighter green and more widely spaced than those of 'Point Reyes'. Heavy crop of fruit in fall, lasting into winter (but sometimes fails to fruit if pollinating insects are not active at bloom time).

'Vancouver Jade'. Flat growing like 'Massachusetts' but not as wide spreading. Jade green leaves turn bronzy red in winter.

'Wood's Red'. A selection of a probable natural hybrid with *A. columbiana*. Compact grower, reaching about 1 ft. tall and 8 ft. wide. Small, leathery, dark green leaves redden in cold weather; bright red berries.

Arctotheca calendula
CAPE WEED
Asteraceae
PERENNIAL

🗡 **ZONES 8, 9, 13–24**
☼ **FULL SUN**
◌ **LITTLE OR NO WATER**

Arctotheca calendula

This South African native is a tough, easy-to-grow evergreen groundcover. Plants spread by runners to make a thick cover 6–12 in. high; space 1½ ft. apart for fast cover. Elongated gray-green leaves are deeply cleft. Yellow, 2-in. daisies bloom most of the year, peaking in spring. Not fussy about soil. Plant suffers some frost damage when temperature dips just below freezing, but recovers quickly.

Good for hillsides and large areas; plants can easily spread out of bounds (though they're easy to remove). Mow shaggy plantings to tidy them.

Cape weed is easily controlled in home gardens. But it has escaped and become invasive in parts of California. If you live near wildlands, choose a native groundcover, adapted to your region.

Arctotis
AFRICAN DAISY
Asteraceae
ANNUALS AND PERENNIALS

🗡 **ALL ZONES, EXCEPT AS NOTED**
☼ **FULL SUN**
◌ **MODERATE WATER**

Arctotis

The name "African daisy" can refer to any of several plants from southern Africa, and identities are often confused, even by many seed companies and nurseries. *Arctotis* species have lobed leaves that are rough, hairy, or woolly; their flower heads usually have a contrasting ring of color around the central eye. *Dimorphotheca* (commonly used for mass color in winter) have smooth green foliage, blooms that are white or in the yellow–orange–salmon range. Trailing groundcover African daisies and woody, shrubby white, yellow, or purple African daisies are *Osteospermum*.

In cold-winter areas, set out annuals (or perennials that are grown as annuals) in spring for summer bloom. Where winters are mild, plant in fall or winter for bloom from spring into early summer. Plants suffer in extreme heat and humidity.

A. acaulis. Perennial. Zones 5–9, 14–24. Spreading clumps of velvety gray leaves to 1 ft. high are topped by yellow, 3½-in.-wide flowers with purplish black centers. 'Big Magenta' has purplish red flowers.

A. breviscapa. Annual. Smaller than *A. acaulis* (to about 6 in. high), with brown-centered orange-yellow flowers.

A. fastuosa alba (Venidium fastuosum). Annual. Bushy growth to 2 ft. tall and

1½ ft. wide, with gray-green, slightly hairy leaves; white, 3-in.-wide daisies with a yellow ring surrounding a deep blue eye. In selection 'Zulu Prince', an inner ring of yellow and darkest purple encircles a black center.

A. hybrids. Most representatives of *Arctotis* sold in nurseries are hybrids that grow to 1–1½ ft. tall and wide. The 3-in.-wide flowers come in white, pink, red, purple, cream, yellow, and orange, often with a dark ring around a nearly black central eye. Will self-sow but tend to revert to orange; to perpetuate colors you like, take cuttings. Plants survive as perennials in Zones 7–9, 14–24, but even there they bloom best in their first year.

Ardisia

MARLBERRY
Primulaceae
EVERGREEN SHRUBS

🌡 **ZONES VARY BY SPECIES**

☼ ◑ ● **PARTIAL OR FULL SHADE**

💧 **REGULAR WATER**

Ardisia crenata

This genus includes 150 shrub species, but only the following two Asian natives are typically grown in Western gardens. Both are valued for their attractive foliage and ornamental, bead-like, bright red berries that persist during winter. Provide rich, moisture-retentive, well-drained soil. If necessary, prune lightly before bloom period.

A. crenata (A. crenulata, A. crispa). Zones 15–24; H1, H2; or indoors. In warmest frost-free climates, often grown in the ground or in patio planters. Most familiar as a 1½-ft., single-stemmed houseplant; in a large tub, though, it can reach 4 ft. tall and almost that wide. Spirelike clusters of tiny white or pinkish flowers bloom in spring, carried above the shiny, wavy-edged, 3-in.-long leaves. Houseplants require indirect light in summer, several hours of direct sun in winter.

A. japonica. Zones 6, 15–17. Low shrub that spreads by runners to produce a series of upright branches 6–18 in. high. A great groundcover in shade; set plants about 2 ft. apart. Leathery, 4-in.-long, bright green leaves are clustered at tops of branches. White, ½-in. flowers, two to six in a cluster, appear in fall. Forms with white or gold foliage variegation are sometimes sold.

Areca lutescens.
See *Dypsis lutescens*

Arecastrum romanzoffianum.
See *Syagrus romanzoffiana*

Argemone

PRICKLY POPPY
Papaveraceae
ANNUALS OR BIENNIALS

🌡 **ZONES VARY BY SPECIES**

☼ **FULL SUN**

💧 **LITTLE OR NO WATER**

Argemone polyanthemos

Prickly-leafed and prickly-stemmed plants to 3 ft. tall, 1½ ft. wide, with large, showy poppies that bloom mainly in summer. Easy to grow from seeds sown in place or in pots (transplant gently). Will reseed and colonize. Provide good drainage. Seed specialists may offer other species.

A. mexicana. MEXICAN POPPY. Annual. Zones 2, 3, 7–24; H1, H2. Native to West Indies and probably Central America and Florida; naturalized in the Southwest and Hawaii. Yellow to orange, 1½–2½-in. flowers. 'Yellow Lustre', to 1½–2 ft. tall, has lemony orange blooms and blue-green leaves veined in silver.

A. polyanthemos (A. intermedia). Annual or biennial. Zones 2, 3, 7–24. Western native with white, 2½–4-in. flowers.

Argyranthemum frutescens
(Chrysanthemum frutescens)

MARGUERITE, PARIS DAISY
Asteraceae
PERENNIAL SOMETIMES GROWN AS ANNUAL

🌡 **ZONES 14–24 AND H1 AS PERENNIAL; 3–13 AS ANNUAL**

☼ **FULL SUN**

💧 **REGULAR WATER**

Argyranthemum frutescens

This Canary Island native is grown as a short-lived perennial in Zones 14–24 and H1, as a summer annual in Zones 3–11, and as a winter annual in Zones 12, 13. Plant forms a neat mound of bright green, coarsely divided leaves on woody-based, 3-ft. stems bearing abundant 1½–2½-in. daisies in white or shades of yellow and pink. Splendid in containers and for quick effects in borders and mass displays. A small plant set out in spring can form a 4-by-4-ft. mound by summer. Blooms most of the year in mild climates. Thrives near coast; also inland if given sufficient water and good drainage, but may freeze in cold winters.

Dozens of fine selections and hybrids are available, and new ones come on the market each year. Flowers of many have classic daisy shape, with a single row of petals surrounding a large yellow center; double and anemone forms are delightful variations on the theme. Blooms come in white and every shade of yellow and pink; foliage color varies from blue through gray shades of green. Dwarf varieties are also available.

When buying plants, avoid large, vigorous-looking ones with big leaves—they will bloom sparsely. Also avoid plants showing signs of fasciation (flattening or widening of stems) near root crown (at plant's base).

CARE

Plant in well-drained soil. For best bloom, feed and prune lightly at frequent intervals. In mild-winter areas, do not prune severely, since plants seldom produce new growth from hardened wood; replace every 2 or 3 years. Subject to leaf miner and thrips (which reduce flower quality); old plants are susceptible to root galls and nematodes.

Arisaema

JACK-IN-THE-PULPIT
Araceae
PERENNIALS FROM TUBERS

🌡 **ZONES VARY BY SPECIES**

☼ ◑ ● **PARTIAL OR FULL SHADE**

💧 **REGULAR WATER DURING GROWTH AND BLOOM**

Arisaema

These curious relatives of calla (*Zantedeschia*) are attractive to children and to fanciers of the odd. Flowers are tiny, crowded on a club-shaped fleshy spike

A

(spadix) surrounded by an over-arching flower bract (spathe) that is usually green or dull purple and often striped in a contrasting color. In late spring, tubers send up one to three leaves, each divided into three or more leaflets. Inflorescences appear on a separate stalk in spring or early summer. As flowers fade, spathe withers and spadix forms striking orange to red berries. Species other than those listed below are usually available from specialists.

These woodland plants appreciate plenty of organic material in the soil. Plant in fall, setting tubers 1 ft. apart, 2 in. deep. Plants die to the ground in winter; don't let dormant tubers dry out completely.

A. sikokianum. Zones 3–6, 14–17. From Japan. Grows about 20 in. tall, with 6-in. leaflets and a 4–12-in. stalk supporting a 6-in. spathe that is erect rather than arching. Spathe is purplish brown on the outside, yellowish white within; spadix is pure white and expanded at the tip.

A. speciosum. Zones 4–6, 14–17. Himalayan native. A single leaf grows to 2 ft., with 8–16-in.-long leaflets on a stalk marbled with dark purple. Spathe is blackish purple outside, whitish within, and up to 8 in. long; spadix has a long, whiplike tip that can reach 2½ ft. long.

A. tortuosum. Zones 4–6, 14–17. This Himalayan native is one of the largest in the genus, reaching 4–6 ft. tall. Leaves have many narrow leaflets. Green or purple spathe to 6 in. long; spadix protrudes from spathe, then curves upward for several inches.

A. triphyllum. Zones 1–6. From eastern North America; the common Jack-in-the-pulpit familiar to Easterners. Grows to 2 ft. tall. Both spathe and spadix are green or purple; spathe is striped in white or green.

FOR COMMON NAME CROSS-REFERENCES, SEE THE PLANT INDEX.

Aristida purpurea
PURPLE THREE-AWN
Poaceae
PERENNIAL GRASS

✔ **ZONES 3B–24**
☼ **FULL SUN**
◐ **LITTLE OR NO WATER**

Aristida purpurea

Native to the western two-thirds of the U.S. and Canada and to northern Mexico. This warm-season bunchgrass grows 2–2½ ft. tall and wide, with fine-textured, green to blue-green leaves and purplish flower stalks. Silky, nodding, purplish flowers are produced over a long period in summer and deepen in color as the seed develops.

Mature flowers have thread-like awns that reflect light beautifully in late summer and fall. Attractive even in winter, when plant bleaches to a light straw color. Wonderful flowering accent among boulders or in a cactus garden.

CARE
Grows best in sandy or gravelly soils but will take most soils if drainage is good. Tolerates extreme heat. Controls erosion on slopes. Cut back to crown in late winter for fresh spring growth. Plants will reseed but usually not too aggressively; to control spread, remove flower stalks before seeds ripen. Seeds can be a nuisance, as they cling to clothing and pets.

FOR MORE ON ORNAMENTAL GRASSES, SEE "GROW: ORNAMENTAL GRASSES," PAGES 678–679.

Aristolochia
Aristolochiaceae
DECIDUOUS AND EVERGREEN VINES

✔ **ZONES VARY BY SPECIES**
☼ ◐ ● **EXPOSURE NEEDS VARY BY SPECIES**
◐ ◖ **REGULAR TO AMPLE WATER**

Aristolochia gigantea

These vigorous, twining vines are noted for their curiously shaped flowers in somber colors; they resemble curved pipes with flared bowls, or birds with bent necks. Thin out unwanted growth in late dormant season or wait until after bloom. If the plant is too thick and tangled for selective thinning, cut it to the ground before spring growth begins.

A. californica. CALIFORNIA DUTCHMAN'S PIPE. Deciduous. Zones 5–10, 14–24. Native to Coast Ranges and Sierra Nevada foothills of Northern California. Will cover an 8-by-12-ft. screen or fence with some training, or climb by long, thin shoots 10–15 ft. into any nearby shrub or tree without harming it; also makes an interesting small-scale groundcover. Flower display comes before leaf-out in winter or early spring; dangling, inch-long blooms are cream-colored with red-purple veins. The flowers have an unpleasant scent. Bright green, heart-shaped leaves grow up to 5 in. long. Accepts any soil; best in partial shade but will take full sun in coastal gardens.

A. gigantea. GIANT DUTCH-MAN'S PIPE. Evergreen. Zones H1, H2; 21–24. From Panama and Brazil. Stems grow 15–20 ft. long. Triangular to heart-shaped, dark green leaves can reach 4 in. across. In summer

to early winter, stems bear spectacular flowers to 1 ft. long and half as wide; blossoms are burgundy with white netting and a golden throat. They have an unusual fragrance reminiscent of lemony furniture polish. *A. g.* 'Brasiliensis' (*A. brasiliensis*) has flowers to 10 in. long and 7 in. wide with an intricate netting pattern of white and brown. Both grow best in frost-free areas. Sun or partial shade.

A. littoralis (A. elegans). CALICO FLOWER. Evergreen. Zones 23, 24; or indoors. Native to Brazil. Grows 15–25 ft. in its native habitat. Wiry, slender stems bear heart-shaped leaves. In summer, whitish buds shaped like little pelicans open to 3-in.-wide, heart-shaped flowers of deep purple veined in creamy white. Needs rich soil, partial shade.

A. macrophylla (A. durior). DUTCHMAN'S PIPE. Deciduous. Zones 2–24; short-lived in warm-winter areas. Native to eastern U.S. Easily grown from seed. Large, kidney-shaped deep green leaves are carried in a shinglelike pattern to form a dense cloak on a trellis; the vine will cover a 15-by-20-ft. area in a single season. Blooms in late spring, early summer. Flowers are almost hidden by leaves; each is a yellowish green, 3-in., curved tube flaring into three brownish purple lobes about 1 in. wide. Thrives in full sun to heavy shade. Average to good soil and ample water produce the fastest growth and the largest leaves. Needs protection from strong winds.

The blooms of *A. gigantea* look more like a well-marbled steak than a flower. Pollinated by flies, it tricks them into thinking it's meat. But its fragrance is pleasant, lemony.

Armeria

THRIFT, SEA PINK

Plumbaginaceae

PERENNIALS

- ⚡ **ZONES VARY BY SPECIES**
- ☼ **FULL SUN**
- ◊ ● **LITTLE TO MODERATE WATER**
- 🦋 **ATTRACT BUTTERFLIES**

Armeria

Plants form compact tufts or basal rosettes of narrow, stiff, evergreen leaves topped by dense globes of small flowers in white, pink, rose, or red. The main bloom period is spring to early summer, but shearing off faded flowers may prolong flowering. These are sturdy, dependable plants for edging walks or borders and for rock gardens.

Good drainage is essential and permits regular watering, but safest tactic is to water moderately in dry climates, sparingly in moister regions. Tolerate seaside conditions, infertile soil. Clumps spread slowly and need dividing only when bare centers show.

A. juniperifolia (A. caespitosa). Zones 2b–9, 14–24. Stiff, needle-shaped leaves just ½ in. long form low, compact rosettes about 6 in. across. Rose-pink or white flowers on 2-in. stems. This little mountain native is touchy about drainage; apply mulch of fine gravel around plants to prevent basal stem rot, especially in summer.

A. maritima (A. vulgaris). SEA THRIFT, COMMON THRIFT. Zones A2, A3; 1–9, 14–24. Native to Europe, North America. Tufted mounds spread to 1 ft.; white to rose-pink flowers are tight clusters atop 6–10-in. stalks. Bloom goes on almost all year in mildest climates.

'Bloodstone' has rose-red flowers, 'Cotton Tail' and 'Alba' have white blooms, and 'Splendens' has rose-pink blossoms. 'Rubrifolia', with purplish red foliage and rosy pink blossoms, brings color to a rock garden for much of the year.

Aronia

CHOKEBERRY

Rosaceae

DECIDUOUS SHRUBS

- ⚡ **ZONES VARY BY SPECIES**
- ☼ ◐ **FULL SUN OR LIGHT SHADE**
- ◊ ● ◗ **MODERATE TO AMPLE WATER**
- 🦋 **ATTRACT BIRDS**

Aronia arbutifolia 'Brilliantissima'

Native to southern Canada and the eastern U.S., chokeberries are tough, undemanding shrubs, useful as fillers or background plantings. Small white or pinkish flowers in clusters are pretty enough—but the fruits that follow are highly decorative and last well into winter. Fall foliage is brightly colored. All chokeberries tend to spread by suckering and are somewhat leggy (good for planting beneath). Tolerate many soils. Prune oldest stems to ground in late dormant season; restrict height and increase bushiness by heading back upright stems.

A. arbutifolia. RED CHOKEBERRY. Zones 1–7. Clumping shrub to 6–8 ft. tall, with many erect stems bearing shiny leaves that are rich green above, paler beneath. Clustered, long-lasting fruits are ½ in. wide and brilliant red. Fall foliage is likewise bright red, and plants tend to color early. 'Brilliantissima' (*A. × prunifolia* 'Brilliant') has fine fall color.

A. melanocarpa. BLACK CHOKEBERRY. Zones A2, A3; 1–7. Typically lower than *A. arbutifolia*—usually 3–5 ft. high, rarely to 10 ft. Fall foliage is purple-red. Shiny black fruits may be used for juice or preserves. Can handle soils in low, wet areas as well as dry, sandy sites. Suckers profusely; may get out of hand in small gardens. 'Autumn Magic' has fragrant flowers, reliable fall color, and large, long-lasting fruits.

Arrhenatherum elatius bulbosum 'Variegatum'

BULBOUS OAT GRASS

Poaceae

PERENNIAL GRASS

- ⚡ **ZONES 1–7, 15–17, 23, 24**
- ☼ ◐ **FULL SUN OR PARTIAL SHADE**
- ◊ **REGULAR WATER**

Arrhenatherum elatius bulbosum 'Variegatum'

This attractive variety of a European grass has narrow leaves boldly edged and striped in white. It looks great in a perennial border or large rock garden; also good for brightening dark places under trees or big shrubs. Makes a graceful clump about 1 ft. high and wide. Flowering stems in summer double the plant's height. Goes dormant in summer in hot climates; performs best in cool seasons and cool climates. If it flops over in heat, shear it for fresh growth in autumn. Bulbous structures at stem bases root on contact with soil to produce new plants; clumps may periodically need curtailing. Divide and replant as needed.

Artemisia

Asteraceae

PERENNIALS AND EVERGREEN SHRUBS

- ⚡ **ZONES VARY BY SPECIES**
- ☼ **FULL SUN, EXCEPT AS NOTED**
- ◊ ● **LITTLE TO MODERATE WATER, EXCEPT AS NOTED**

Artemisia 'Powis Castle'

Artemisias have been cultivated since the time of ancient Greece, and over the centuries many have been given colorful common names, such as mugwort, wormwood, and old man. Several species are valued for their silvery-gray or white aromatic foliage; the flowers are generally insignificant. Most kinds are excellent in mixed borders, where their white or silvery leaves soften harsh reds and oranges and blend beautifully with blues, lavenders, and pinks.

A. abrotanum. SOUTHERNWOOD, OLD MAN. Woody perennial. Zones 2b–24. Native to southern Europe. Grows 3 ft. tall and wide, with beautiful feathery, lemon-scented, gray-green foliage and yellowish white flower heads. Use for pleasantly scented leaves in shrub border. Hang dried sprigs in closet to discourage moths.

A. absinthium. COMMON WORMWOOD. Woody perennial. Zones 2–24. Native to Europe, temperate Asia. Reaches 2–4 ft. tall and 2 ft. wide. Silvery gray, finely divided leaves have a bitter taste and pungent odor. Tiny yellow flowers. Prune to shape. Divide every 3 years. Makes a fine background shrub; a good gray feature in a flower border beside delphiniums. 'Lambrook Silver' is 1½ ft. tall with silvery, finely cut leaves.

»

A. arborescens. Evergreen shrub or woody perennial. Zones 7–9, 14–24. This Mediterranean native grows 3 ft. (sometimes 5–6 ft.) tall and 4–5 ft. wide, with silvery white, very finely cut foliage. It is highly attractive but more tender than other artemisias; grow it against a warm wall in colder zones.

A. australis. AHINAHINA, HINAHINA KUAHIWI. Evergreen shrub or woody perennial. Zones H1, H2. Native to Hawaii. To 2–10 ft. tall and not quite as wide, with lacy, silvery leaves. Thrives in coastal gardens, on steep cliffs, and in containers.

A. californica. CALIFORNIA SAGEBRUSH. Evergreen shrub. Zones 7–9, 14–24. Native to coastal region from Northern California to Baja California. To 1½–5 ft. tall, 4–7 ft. wide, with finely divided, aromatic, grayish white leaves. Foliage is lush in winter and somewhat sparse in summer. Reseeds manageably. Superior selections include 'Canyon Gray', which grows 1–2 ft. tall (with occasional pruning of upright stems) and 6–10 ft. wide; and 'Montara', with a mounding habit to 2 ft. tall

and 3–5 ft. wide. Both make excellent groundcovers.

A. cana (Seriphidium canum). SILVER SAGEBRUSH. Evergreen shrub. Zones 2, 3, 7, 14–21. Native to region east of the Sierra-Cascade divide. To 3–5 ft. tall and wide, with narrow, fragrant, silvery green leaves. Very hardy to drought and cold.

A. caucasica. SILVER SPREADER. Evergreen shrublet. Zones 2–11, 14–24. This Caucasus native grows just 3–6 in. high and spreads to 2 ft. wide. Silky, silvery green foliage; small yellow flowers. Use as a ground- or bank cover in well-drained soil; plant 1–2 ft. apart. Takes extremes of heat and cold.

A. dracunculus. FRENCH TARRAGON, TRUE TARRAGON. Perennial. Zones A1–A3; 2b–10, 14–24. There are two common forms of this plant, which is native to central and eastern Europe and southern Russia. French tarragon, which may be labeled 'Sativa', is a sprawling, largely flowerless plant with shiny dark green, aromatic, flavorful leaves. It spreads slowly by creeping rhizomes, the stems becoming slightly woody and

the whole plant remaining less than 2 ft. tall. Russian tarragon, which may be labeled 'Inodorus', lacks the characteristic flavor and aroma of true tarragon; it has upright, branching growth to about 3 ft. and small white flowers. Any seeds you find for sale will be for this culinarily inferior Russian tarragon.

Cut sprigs in early summer for seasoning vinegar. Use fresh or dried leaves to season salads, cooked dishes. Plants in all zones die to the ground in winter but return in spring. Divide every 3 or 4 years to keep vigorous. Propagate by divisions or cuttings. Provide moderate to regular water, letting soil dry between waterings.

A. filifolia. SAND SAGEBRUSH. Woody perennial. Zones 2–11, 14–24. Native from South Dakota to Texas and as far west as Nevada. Airy, graceful plant to 3–4 ft. tall and wide, with upright, swirling stems. Feathery, fragrant, blue-green leaves are covered with a white-woolly coating that gives plants an overall silvery look. Flowers are insignificant. Tolerates clay soil; thrives in poor, sandy soil and helps prevent wind erosion.

A. frigida. FRINGED WORMWOOD. Perennial. Zones A1; 1–3, 7–10, 14, 18–21. Native to Southwest, interior Northwest, and Alaska. To 1–1½ ft. tall and wide, with finely cut, fragrant gray leaves and small yellow flowers. Plants are compact when young, becoming rangy as they grow; cut back after flowering.

A. 'Huntington'. Woody perennial. Zones 4–24. To 3 ft. tall and 4 ft. wide, with spreading stems covered by a thick dome of very silvery foliage. Similar to A. 'Powis Castle' but with bigger, softer leaves.

A. lactiflora. WHITE MUGWORT. Perennial. Zones 1–9, 14–21. This native of western China is one of the few artemisias with attractive flowers, bearing large, branched sprays of creamy white blooms in late summer. Plants grow into a straight column 4–5 ft. tall and

2 ft. wide. Dark green leaves have broad, tooth-edged lobes. Moderate to regular water. Members of the Guizhou group have purple stems and young leaves.

A. ludoviciana albula (A. albula). Perennial. Zones 1–24. Native to desert Southwest and mountains. Grows 4 ft. tall and half as wide, with slender, spreading branches and silvery white leaves. Lower leaves have three to five lobes; upper ones are narrow and unlobed. Spreads rapidly by rhizomes. Cut foliage is useful in arrangements. 'Silver King' is compact, to about 3 ft. 'Valerie Finnis' is even more compact, to 1½–2 ft. tall, with broader, nearly white leaves slightly lobed toward the tip.

A. 'Powis Castle'. Woody perennial. Zones 2–24. Most likely a hybrid of A. absinthium and A. arborescens. Grows into a silvery, lacy mound to 3 ft. tall, 6 ft. wide. Leaves have a wonderfully fruity fragrance. Makes a splendid background for bright flowers of other plants and is tough enough to use as a bank or berm cover. To keep compact, cut back moderately in early spring, and snip off flowers when they form in late summer.

A. pycnocephala. SANDHILL SAGE. Evergreen shrub or woody perennial. Zones 4, 5, 7–9, 14–17, 19–24. Native to beaches of Northern California. This is a rounded, somewhat spreading plant to 2½ ft. tall and 3 ft. wide. Erect stems are crowded with soft, silvery white or gray leaves divided into narrow lobes. When the spikes of very small yellow flowers open, remove them to keep plant compact. Replace every couple of years if plant becomes unkempt. 'David's Choice' is a lovely selection that grows just 6–12 in. high and 1½–2 ft. wide.

A. schmidtiana. ANGEL'S HAIR. Woody perennial. Zones A1–A3; 1–10, 14–24. Japanese native forms a 1–2-ft. dome of silky, silvery white, finely cut leaves. Dies back in winter. 'Silver Mound' is compact, usually under 1½ ft. high and wide.

A. 'Sea Foam' (A. versicolor 'Sea Foam'). Zones A3; 1–24. Perennial. Mounding growth to 6–12 in. high and 1½–3 ft. wide. Lacy, curly,

CLOCKWISE FROM TOP LEFT:
Artemisia ludoviciana albula;
A. dracunculus; A. absinthium

silvery blue foliage; flowers not showy. Useful as a groundcover in full sun or partial shade.

A. stelleriana. BEACH WORMWOOD, OLD WOMAN, DUSTY MILLER. Perennial. Zones A1–A3; 1–10, 14–24. Native to northeastern Asia; naturalized in eastern North America. Dense, silvery gray plant to 2½ ft. tall and 3 ft. wide, with lobed leaves. Hardier than *Senecio cineraria* (another dusty miller) and often used in its place in colder climates. Yellow flowers in spikelike clusters. 'Boughton Silver' ('Silver Brocade') is a superior, dense-growing selection, just 6 in. high and 1½ ft. wide.

A. tridentata (Seriphidium tridentatum). BIG SAGEBRUSH. Evergreen shrub. Zones 1–3, 6–11, 14–24. This native of the Great Basin region of the West is a many-branched, silvery-looking plant to 4–15 ft. tall and 3–10 ft. wide. Narrow, very aromatic, hairy gray leaves are usually tipped with three teeth. Flowers are insignificant. Emits the pungent fragrance for which Western deserts are known. Grows easily in any sunny, well-drained spot; does well with no irrigation.

A. vulgaris 'Oriental Limelight'. Zones A2, A3; 1–24. Perennial. Upright, mounding growth to 2–3 ft. high and wide. Finely cut, green leaves are variegated in yellow and gold. Clusters of small white flowers in summer. Spreads by rhizomes and can be invasive. Good choice for large container.

CARE

All artemisias need well-drained soil. Cut nonwoody-stemmed perennials to ground in fall to rejuvenate; prune back woody perennials and shrubs (into older wood if necessary) before first flush of spring growth. Divide perennials in spring or autumn.

For a striking, nonstop show of lush green-and-gold foliage on a patio in summer, grow *Artemisia vulgaris* 'Oriental Limelight' in a big (16- to 18-in. diameter) green glazed pot. The effect is as cooling as iced limeade. Pinch tips occasionally during the growing season to keep the plant bushy.

Artichoke
Asteraceae
PERENNIAL

🌡 **ZONES VARY; SEE BELOW**

☼ ◑ **FULL SUN OR LIGHT SHADE**

💧 **REGULAR WATER**

Artichokes

This attractive Mediterranean native is a big, coarse, ferny-looking plant with an irregular, somewhat fountainlike form to 4 ft. high and 6–8 ft. wide. Large, deeply lobed leaves are silvery green. Big flower buds form at tops of stalks: they are the artichokes you cook and eat. If not cut, the buds open into spectacular purple-blue, 6-in., thistlelike flowers that can be cut for arrangements (cut them just before blooms are fully open).

In Zones 8, 9, and 14–24, artichoke is a dependable perennial crop that grows luxuriantly at least from spring through fall, producing edible buds in early summer only. But in the mildest part of this region—central California coastal Zone 17, where it is grown commercially—artichoke can be both a handsome ornamental plant and a producer of tender artichokes from early fall to late spring.

In Zones 11–13, it is usually treated as an annual and planted in fall for spring harvest, but it may hang on to be a perennial. In Zones 3a–7 and 10, plant in spring and hope for the best—you will get foliage, maybe some flowers, and hopefully a crop if the season is long and mild enough.

How to Grow Artichokes

PLANTING Plant dormant roots or plants from containers in winter or early spring. Set root shanks vertically, with buds or shoots just above soil level; space 4–6 ft. apart in a full-sun location (light afternoon shade is best where summers are hot).

WATERING & FEEDING After growth starts, water plants once a week, wetting the entire root system. If grown only for ornamental value, artichokes can tolerate much drought, going dormant in summer heat. Give plants monthly doses of high-nitrogen fertilizer starting 4 weeks after transplanting.

PESTS Control aphids; after buds start to form, use strong jets of water to blast off aphids. Also keep snails, slugs, and earwigs away from plants. For gopher control, plant in raised beds lined with hardware cloth at the bottom.

HARVESTING Harvest buds (along with 1½ in. of stem) while they are still tight and plump. To encourage a second crop, cut off main stalk an inch above-ground after harvesting the last bud of the first crop; new sprouts at base will grow faster and produce sooner than an uncut plant would. In all recommended climate zones, cut off old stalks near ground level when leaves begin to yellow. In cold-winter regions, cut tops to 1 ft. in fall, tie them over root crown, and mulch heavily to protect from frost.

BEFORE COOKING Wash artichokes under running cold water, pull off small lower leaves, then cut off stems close to the base. Also cut off the top ¼ of the bud and the thorny petal tips (although these will soften with cooking).

Arugula
Brassicaceae
ANNUAL

🌡 **ALL ZONES**

☼ **FULL SUN**

💧 **REGULAR WATER**

Arugula

This weedy-looking Mediterranean native, sometimes called rocket, roquette, or rucola coltivata, is grown for its leaves, which resemble small mustard leaves and lend a nutty zing to green salads. Along with radishes, turnips, and the whole cabbage clan, it's a member of the cress family. Start from seed in winter or spring; grows best in cool weather. Thin to about 6 in. apart. Harvest tender young leaves; older, larger ones usually taste too sharp. Eventually, plants will shoot up to 3 ft. tall, then bloom; tender buds and flowers taste like the young leaves. Plants reseed. Easy to grow in containers; choose a wide bowl at least 6 in. deep.

Add arugula thinnings to salads, or pick individual leaves as plants get older and larger. Let a few plants bloom and set seed every year and you'll seldom be without arugula. Volunteers will provide all you want.

A

A

Arum
Araceae
PERENNIALS FROM TUBERS

- ◢ ZONES VARY BY SPECIES
- ☼ ◐ ● PARTIAL OR FULL SHADE
- ◗ REGULAR WATER DURING GROWTH AND BLOOM
- ◊ SAP IS AN IRRITANT IF INGESTED

Arum italicum

Attractively veined, arrow-shaped leaves grow from tubers in fall or winter. In spring, short stalks bear curious, often malodorous, callalike blooms featuring a bract (spathe) that half encloses a thick, fleshy spike (spadix) set with tiny flowers. These blossoms are followed by dense clusters of fruit, typically bright red, that look like little ears of corn and persist after leaves have died to the ground. Use this plant in shady flower borders or as a tropical-looking groundcover.

A. italicum. ITALIAN ARUM. Zones 2–24. Native to southern and western Europe. Foot-long leaves on leafstalks of equal length emerge in fall or early winter. Short stems carry white or greenish white (sometimes purple-spotted) flowers in spring and early summer, followed by orange-red fruits. The spathe stands erect, then folds over to conceal the short yellow spadix. Leaves die to ground after bloom. In favorable situations, plants naturalize by volunteer seedlings. 'Marmoratum' ('Pictum') has white-veined leaves.

A. palaestinum. BLACK CALLA. Zones 14–24. Native to Israel. In winter, leaves emerge on 1-ft. leafstalks. Spathe is green outside; it opens outward and curls back at tip to reveal purple interior and black spadix.

Blooms in spring and early summer; then leaves die back.

A. pictum. Zones 7–9, 14–24. Native to the western Mediterranean. May be called black calla; like *A. palaestinum*—but it has an 8-in. violet spathe with a white-base enclosing a dark purple spadix. Flowers appear in fall—sometimes with emerging foliage, sometimes before. Light green leaves with fine white veins reach 10 in. long and are borne on equally long leafstalks. Foliage dies to ground in hot weather.

CARE

Plant tubers in well-drained soil in late summer or early fall (toward the end of their dormancy), setting them 8–12 in. apart and 4–6 in. deep. Dormant plantings accept summer moisture but don't need it.

Aruncus
GOAT'S BEARD
Rosaceae
PERENNIALS

- ◢ ZONES VARY BY SPECIES
- ☼ ◑ FULL SUN IN COOLER CLIMATES ONLY
- ◗ REGULAR WATER
- 🦋 ATTRACT BUTTERFLIES

Aruncus dioicus

These soft-looking perennials resemble astilbe, with slowly spreading clumps of finely divided leaves topped in summer by plumy, branched clusters of tiny white or cream flowers. Good in perennial borders or at the edge of a woodland against a dark background.

A. aethusifolius. Zones 1–9, 14–17. Native to Korea. Deep green, finely divided leaves make a mound 1 ft. tall

and a little wider. White flower plumes can reach 16 in. high. Useful in rock garden, as edging, for small-scale groundcover.

A. dioicus (A. sylvester). Zones A2, A3; 1–9, 14–17. Native to Eurasia and to southeastern and south-central Alaska. Grows to 6 or 7 ft. tall, 4 ft. wide, with foamy plumes of white flowers in 20-in., branched clusters. Tolerates more sun than *A. aethusifolius*. 'Kneiffii' is half the size of the species, with more finely divided, near-ferny leaves. 'Child of Two Worlds' ('Zweiweltenkind') grows to 5 ft. tall, with gracefully drooping flower clusters.

Asarum
WILD GINGER
Aristolochiaceae
PERENNIALS

- ◢ ZONES VARY BY SPECIES
- ☼ ◐ ● PARTIAL OR FULL SHADE
- ◗ ◖◗ REGULAR TO AMPLE WATER

Asarum caudatum

The following wild gingers, mostly from North America and Europe, are handsome groundcovers for shady gardens, forming a low carpet of heart-shaped leaves. Their lustrous foliage contrasts well with lacy ferns. All have small, brownish or purplish red spring flowers, shaped like three-cornered bells or pitchers, with three tapering "tails." Roots and leaves have a spicy scent. The plants grow in average soil but will spread faster and look more luxuriant in rich, humusy soil. Start from divisions or container-grown plants; set about a foot apart. Watch for slugs and snails.

A. canadense. Zones 1–6. Native to eastern North America.

Deciduous, dark green, kidney-shaped leaves to 6 in. wide.

A. caudatum. Zones 4–6, 14–24. Native to the West Coast. Evergreen where winters are mild. Dark green, heart-shaped leaves are 2–7 in. wide. In the fog belt, it makes a choice groundcover and survives with just occasional water; with regular irrigation, it can take considerable sun there.

A. europaeum. Zones 2–6. Native to Europe. Evergreen, kidney-shaped, shiny dark green leaves are 2–3 in. wide. Slow spreader.

A. shuttleworthii. Zones 3b–6. Native to the Appalachians. Evergreen, shiny green leaves are heart-shaped or roundish and usually variegated with silvery markings. Slow growing.

A. splendens. Zones 3–6, 15–17. Native to China. Evergreen leaves are dark green, heavily mottled with silver, and heart-shaped with an elongated tip. Grows vigorously in rich, loose soil, forming large colonies.

Asclepias
Apocynaceae
PERENNIALS

- ◢ ZONES VARY BY SPECIES
- ☼ FULL SUN
- ◗ ◗ ◖◗ WATER NEEDS VARY BY SPECIES
- 🦋 ATTRACT BENEFICIAL INSECTS AND BUTTERFLIES
- ◊ ALL PARTS OF MANY SPECIES ARE POISONOUS IF INGESTED

Asclepias speciosa

Though some include the word "weed" in their common name, the plants listed here are anything but weeds—they're showy, easy-to-grow garden plants. All bloom in summer, typically bearing many small, starlike flowers in broad, flattened clusters at or near the tips of their branches. Their inflated seedpods split open to reveal silky seeds and milky sap. Their nectar attracts butterflies.

A. curassavica. BLOOD FLOWER. Zones 8, 9, 12–24; H1, H2; all zones as annual. Native to South America. This woody-based plant with stiff stems and narrow leaves grows 3 ft. tall and 2 ft. wide. Produces clusters of vivid red flowers. 'Silky Gold' is similar but bears bright yellow to yellow-orange blooms. Moderate water.

A. speciosa. SHOWY MILK-WEED. Zones 1–24. Native to western and central North America. This striking perennial grows 2–4 ft. tall and not quite as wide; may spread by underground stems to form colonies. Thick, upright stems hold big, softly hairy leaves of gray; summer flowers are 3-in.-wide balls of fragrant, purplish pink. Long winter dormancy; new shoots may not appear until midspring. Needs only occasional water once established.

A. subulata. DESERT MILK-WEED, RUSH MILKWEED. Zones 11–13. Native to the Southwest deserts. Forms a dense cluster (eventually about 4 ft. wide) of 4-ft.-tall, gray-green stems that are leafless most of the year; looks something like a rush (*Juncus*). Clusters of pale yellow flowers appear intermittently from spring to fall near stem tips; blooms are followed by horn-shaped seedpods. Tolerates drought and heat.

A. tuberosa. BUTTERFLY WEED. Zones 1–24. Native to eastern U.S. From a perennial root, many herbaceous stems rise every year to form a clump about 3 ft. tall and 1 ft. wide. Clusters of bright orange flowers attract butterflies. Also attract birds. Gay Butterflies strain features yellow, red, orange, pink, or bicolored blossoms; 'Hello Yellow' has bright yellow blooms. Provide good drainage, moderate water. *A. tuberosa* is especially popular for attracting Monarch butterflies. To lay their eggs, Monarchs go mostly to butterfly weed. Their eggs hatch into hungry caterpillars, which feed on the leaves.

Asian Greens
Brassicaceae
ANNUALS

🗷 **ALL ZONES**

☼ ◑ **FULL SUN IN COOLER CLIMATES ONLY**

💧 **REGULAR WATER**

Bok choy

The vegetables in this large group are mainstays of stir-fry dishes and salads. Primarily quick-maturing cool-season crops, they're planted in late winter to early spring for spring-to-summer harvest, and in late summer to early fall for harvest in fall and winter. In areas with short growing seasons and in mild-summer coastal regions, they can be grown all summer.

Many Asian greens, especially the mustards, have attractive foliage that's pretty in vegetable gardens and when mixed with flowering annuals or spring bulbs. Listed here are some of the most common Asian greens. For planting depth and row spacing, follow the instructions on the seed packet.

Bok choy (Chinese white cabbage, pak choi). One of the more familiar Asian greens,

> Asian greens take only minutes to prepare. Heat up some peanut oil, toss in some scallions, garlic, and ginger. After a few minutes, add the greens and cook them quickly.

bok choy has a mild flavor, with a hint of mustard. Tender, crisp, and sweet, it's especially good in soups and stir-fries. Many varieties are sold. 'Tatsoi' is similar but more compact. Thin or transplant seedlings to 6–12 in. apart. Harvest approximately 50 days after sowing seed, when plants are loose-headed and 10–12 in. tall.

Broadleaf mustard (dai gai choy). Large green leaves with a pungent, somewhat bitter, mustardlike flavor that gets stronger as the plant matures. Hot weather or inadequate moisture also increases pungency. Best used in soup to tone down the sharp flavor. Thin or transplant seedlings to 10 in. apart. Harvest plants when they are loose-headed and 10–14 in. high, about 65 days after sowing.

Chinese broccoli (gai lohn). Similar in flavor and texture to standard broccoli, but with a slight pungency like that of mustard. Thin or transplant seedlings to 10 in. apart. Harvest central stalk and side shoots when stalk is 8–10 in. tall or when flower buds just begin to form, usually about 70 days after sowing.

Chinese mustard greens (gai choy). Milder member of the mustard family. Thin or transplant seedlings to 10 in. apart. Harvest the first greens when the plants are 2 in. high; continue harvesting until leaves turn tough or bitter. It usually takes 45 days after sowing for plants to reach mature height of 6–8 in.

Flowering cabbage (yao choy, choy sum, ching sow sum). Tender, delicate, broccoli-type vegetable. Thin or transplant seedlings to about 6 in. apart. Harvest about 60 days after sowing, when 8–12 in. high.

Mizuna. Mild-flavored, leafy vegetable with finely cut, frilly, white-stemmed leaves. Great in salads. Thin or transplant seedlings to 8–10 in. apart. Start cutting leaves when plants are a few inches tall, or wait until mature at 8–10 in. high, about 40 days after sowing.

Asparagus
Asparagaceae
PERENNIAL

🗷 **ALL ZONES**

☼ **FULL SUN**

💧 **REGULAR WATER**

Asparagus

Native to the Mediterranean. Plants take 2 or 3 years to come into full production but then furnish delicious spears every spring for 10 to 15 years. They take up considerable space but the plants are tall, feathery, graceful, highly ornamental. Use along sunny fence.

Asparagus seeds and roots are sold as "traditional" ('Mary Washington' and others) and "all-male" ('UC 157', 'Jersey Giant', 'Jersey Knight', 'Jersey Supreme'). The latter kinds produce more and larger spears because they don't put energy into seed production. 'Millenium F1' is a cold-hardy all-male variety bred for the Far North.

Blanch It

Fresh white asparagus is a delicacy. It's not a special variety; blanching makes it white. In early spring before spears emerge, mound soil 8 in. high over a row of asparagus. When tips emerge from the mound, push a long-handled knife into the base of the mound to cut each spear well below the surface. Pull cut shoots out by the tips, then level the mounds.

»

A

How to Grow Asparagus

PLANTING Seeds grow into strong young plants in one season (sow in spring), but roots are far more widely used. Set out seedlings or roots (not wilted, no smaller than an adult's hand) in fall or winter in mild-winter climates, in early spring in cold-winter areas. Make trenches 1 ft. wide, 8–10 in. deep; space trenches 4–6 ft. apart. Heap loose, manure-enriched soil at bottom of trenches and soak. Space plants 1 ft. apart, setting them so that tops are 6–8 in. below surface; spread roots out evenly. Cover with 2 in. of soil and water again. (Where drainage is poor, plant in raised beds.) As plants grow, gradually fill in the trench; don't cover growing tips.

WATERING Soak deeply whenever the soil begins to dry out at root depth.

HARVESTING Don't harvest spears the first year; let plants build root mass. When plants turn brown in late fall or early winter, cut stems to the ground. In cold-winter areas, permit dead stalks to stand until spring; they will hold snow, which protect root crowns. The following spring, cut your first spears; cut only for 4 to 6 weeks or until appearance of thin spears indicates that roots are nearing exhaustion. Then permit plants to grow. Feed and irrigate heavily. The third year, you should be able to cut spears for 8 to 10 weeks. Spears are ready to cut when they are 5–8 in. long. Thrust knife down at 45° angle to soil; flat cutting may injure adjacent developing spears.

PESTS Clean up debris from asparagus beds in fall to help get rid of overwintering asparagus beetles. Use row covers over beds in spring.

Asparagus, Ornamental

Asparagaceae
PERENNIALS, SHRUBS, OR VINES

☑ **ZONES 12–24, EXCEPT AS NOTED**

☼ ◑ **SUN OR PART SHADE**

💧 **REGULAR WATER**

Asparagus densiflorus 'Myers'

There are about 150 kinds of asparagus besides the edible one. Those listed here are native to South Africa. Although valued mostly for textural foliage, some of the ornamental species have small but fragrant flowers and colorful berries. Green foliage sprays are made up of short branches called *cladodes*; these are needlelike in some types, broader in others. The true leaves are inconspicuous dry scales or prickles.

Most ornamental asparagus look greenest in partial shade but thrive in sun in cool-summer climates. Plants turn yellow in dense shade; will survive light frosts but may be killed to the ground by severe cold. After frost, plants often come back from roots.

A. asparagoides. SMILAX ASPARAGUS. Much-branched vine with spineless stems to 20 ft. or more. Broad, glossy, grass green "leaves" are sharp pointed and somewhat stiff; cut foliage sprays are prized for table decoration. Small, fragrant white flowers in spring are followed by blue berries. The roots are nearly immortal, surviving long drought and sprouting when rains come. If the plant gets little water, it dies back in summer, then revives with fall rains. Becomes a tangled mass unless trained. This asparagus may escape gardens and become an invasive pest, as birds feed on the berries and drop seeds later; plants also self-sow readily. 'Myrtifolius', commonly called baby smilax, is a more graceful form with smaller "leaves."

A. crispus. BASKET ASPARAGUS. Airy, graceful plant for hanging baskets. Drooping, zigzag stems have bright green, three-angled leaflike structures held in whorls of three. Often sold as *A. scandens* 'Deflexus'.

A. densiflorus. Zones 12–24; H1, H2; or indoors. The species is less commonly grown than its forms. The following are the two most popular:

'Myers'. MYERS ASPARAGUS. Several to many stiffly upright stems to 2 ft. or more, densely clothed with needlelike deep green "leaves"; sometimes called foxtail fern due to the appearance of these long, fluffy stems. Grows rather slowly to form a 3–4-ft.-wide clump. Performs well in containers. A little less hardy than 'Sprengeri'. Sometimes sold as *A. meyeri* or *A. myersii*.

'Sprengeri'. SPRENGER ASPARAGUS. Arching or drooping stems 3–6 ft. long are loosely clothed in shiny, bright green, needlelike "leaves." Berries are bright red. Popular for hanging baskets or containers. Train on a trellis; climbs by means of small hooked prickles. Grows in ordinary or even poor soil. Sometimes sold as *A. sprengeri*. A form sold as 'Sprengeri Compacta' or *A. sarmentosus* 'Compacta' is denser, with shorter stems.

A. falcatus. SICKLE-THORN ASPARAGUS. The cladodes are 2–3 in. long, in clusters of three to five at ends of branches. Tiny, fragrant white flowers in loose clusters; brown berries follow. Uses the curved thorns along its stems to clamber rapidly as high as 40 ft. in its native area (in gardens, it usually reaches about 10 ft.). Makes an excellent foliage mass to cover fence or wall, or to provide shade for pergola.

A. meyeri, A. myersii. See *A. densiflorus* 'Myers'.

A. officinalis. See Asparagus.

A. retrofractus (A. macowanii). This erect, shrubby, slightly climbing plant is very tender. Slender, silvery gray stems grow slowly to 8–10 ft. high. Cladodes are threadlike, in fluffy, rich green tufts. Clusters of small white flowers. Handsome in containers. Cut foliage lasts several weeks in water.

A. sarmentosus. See *A. densiflorus* 'Sprengeri'.

A. scandens. BASKET ASPARAGUS. Slender, branching vine climbing to 6 ft. Deep green, needlelike "leaves" on zigzag, drooping stems clothed in small greenish white flowers and scarlet berries.

A. scandens 'Deflexus'. See *A. crispus*.

A. setaceus (A. plumosus). ASPARAGUS FERN. Zones 12–24; H1, H2; or indoors. This branching woody vine climbs by wiry, spiny stems to 10–20 ft. Tiny threadlike cladodes form feathery dark green sprays that resemble fern fronds. Tiny white flowers; purple-black berries. Forms a

Asparagus for Pots

On sizzling days, the cool greens of simple foliage plants can be the most restful choice for containers on patios and decks. Here are two ways to go.

JUST THE GREENS For trailing, fernlike growth, put several potted Sprenger asparagus in a big raised planter. For fluffy upright plumes, choose *A. retrofractus*.

GREENS AND FLOWERS Plant an upright Myers asparagus in the center of a large (22 in.) container. Add a bright orange–flowered impatiens or snapdragon, and deep blue lobelia.

dense, fine-textured mass that is useful as a screen against walls and fences. Florists use foliage as filler in bouquets. Dwarf 'Nanus' is good in containers. 'Pyramidalis' has an upswept, windblown look and is less vigorous than the species.

A. sprengeri. See *A. densiflorus* 'Sprengeri'.

CARE

Plant in well-drained soil amended with peat moss or ground bark. Because of their fleshy roots, plants can go for some time without water, but they grow better when watered regularly. Feed in spring with a complete fertilizer. Trim out old shoots to make room for new growth.

Asperula odorata.
See *Galium odoratum*

Asphodeline lutea

YELLOW ASPHODEL, KING'S SPEAR
Asphodelaceae
PERENNIAL

🌿 **ZONES 3B–24**

☼ ◐ **FULL SUN OR PARTIAL SHADE**

● **REGULAR WATER**

Asphodeline lutea

This Mediterranean native forms a low clump (about 9 in. high and 1 ft. wide) of blue-green to dark green, grassy leaves. In spring, stiff, unbranched stems to 3 ft. high rise from the clump, topped by narrow clusters of fragrant yellow flowers that peer out from shaggy buff or reddish brown bracts. Needs well-drained soil.

Aspidistra elatior

CAST-IRON PLANT
Asparagaceae
PERENNIAL

🌿 **ZONES 4–10, 12–24; H1, H2; OR INDOORS**

◐ ● **PARTIAL OR FULL SHADE; BRIGHT TO DIM LIGHT**

◐ ● **MODERATE TO REGULAR WATER**

Aspidistra elatior 'Variegata'

This sturdy, long-lived evergreen foliage plant from China is best known as a houseplant, but it also makes striking accent clumps outdoors. Plants spread slowly by rhizomes. Tough, arching, glossy, dark green leaf blades with distinct parallel veins are 1–2½ ft. long, 3–4 in. wide; each is supported by a grooved, 6–8-in.-long leafstalk. Inconspicuous brownish flowers bloom near ground level in spring. 'Variegata' has white-striped leaves but loses its variegation if planted in too-rich soil. Other variegated and spotted forms are available.

True to its common name, this plant has a cast-iron constitution. Although extremely tolerant and requiring only minimal care, it grows best in porous, organically enriched soil and responds to spring and summer feeding. Will grow in dark, shaded areas (under decks or stairs) as well as in filtered sun—except in Zones 12 and 13, where it takes full shade only. To keep leaves dust-free and glossy, hose them off occasionally or clean with a soft brush or cloth.

Aspidium capense.
See *Rumohra adiantiformis*

Asplenium

Aspleniaceae
FERNS

🌿 **ZONES VARY BY SPECIES**

◐ ● **PARTIAL OR FULL SHADE**

● ●● **REGULAR TO AMPLE WATER**

Asplenium scolopendrium

This widespread and variable group of rhizomatous ferns was once called spleenwort for alleged medicinal value. The evergreen species listed below resemble one another only in botanical details and in their need for shade and liberal watering. Unlike many other ferns, they need a rest period from late fall to early spring when grown indoors; during that time, reduce watering and withhold fertilizer. Outdoors, they prefer gritty, well-drained soil.

A. bulbiferum. MOTHER FERN. Zones 14 (protected), 15–17, 20–24; or indoors. From Australia, New Zealand. Graceful, very finely cut light green fronds grow to 4 ft. tall; whole plant reaches about 4 ft. wide. Fronds produce plantlets that can be removed and planted. Hardy to 26°F (–3°C). Watch for snails and slugs.

A. nidus (A. nidus-avis). BIRD'S NEST FERN. Zones 23, 24; H2; or indoors. Tender fern native to many tropical regions. A striking foliage plant, with showy, undivided apple green fronds to 4 ft. long, 8 in. wide, growing upright in a cluster. Grow potted plants indoors in winter, move to shady patio in summer. One snail or slug can ruin an entire frond.

A. scolopendrium. HART'S TONGUE FERN. Zones 2b–9, 14–24. Native to Europe, eastern U.S. This odd-looking fern has undivided, strap-shaped leaves 9–18 in. long; forms a clump about 2 ft. wide. Fanciers collect various dwarf, crested, or forked varieties. Plants need humus; also add some limestone chips if soil is acidic. Difficult to grow where water quality is poor. Striking in woodland or rock gardens. Durable container plant; grows in a tight crown and can remain in the same pot for years.

A. trichomanes. MAIDENHAIR SPLEENWORT. Zones 2–9, 14–24; H1, H2. Native to much of the Northern Hemisphere, this delicate fern grows in a clump to 6 in. high, 8 in. wide. Narrow bright green fronds are 4–8 in. long; round (or nearly so) leaflets are only ½ in. long. Prefers alkaline conditions; add limestone chips if needed. Attractive in wall crevices where it can be seen close-up or in a shady rock garden.

FOR MORE ON FERNS, SEE "MEET THE FERNS," PAGE 320.

Astelia

Asteliaceae
PERENNIALS

🌿 **ZONES 5, 6, 14–17, 19–24**

☼ ◐ **FULL SUN OR LIGHT SHADE, EXCEPT AS NOTED**

● **MODERATE WATER**

Astelia chathamica

Grown for their silky, silvery, straplike foliage, these increasingly popular evergreen perennials offer a handsome contrast to low, mounding plants or billowing grasses. They make a striking centerpiece in a big container or a perennial border. Small spring flowers are borne in branched clusters on female plants but are not as showy as the berries that follow. Plants must have excellent drainage; they grow best in rich, acidic soil that is high in organic matter. The following are native to New Zealand.

A. banksii. SHORE ASTELIA. Grows 2–3 ft. high and 3–4 ft. wide, with arching, narrow, silvery green leaves. Greenish flowers are followed by berries that mature to purple-black. Best in light shade.

A. chathamica (A. nervosa chathamica). SILVER LEAF. Shiny, silvery swordlike leaves are 3–4 ft. long and 2–4 in. wide, forming a clump 4 ft. tall and 6 ft. wide. Small, cream-colored flowers are borne in clusters 20 in. tall; berries are orange.

A. nervosa. Variable in size and color, this plant typically grows 2–3 ft. high and up to twice as wide, with foliage that is silvery green above, green to bronzy beneath, with green midribs. Arching leaves may reach 7 ft. long. Greenish yellow to bronzy purple flowers appear on tall stalks; orange berries follow. 'Westland' is more compact, with a dusty red wash over silvery green foliage. Best in light shade.

A. nivicola 'Red Gem'. Clumps reach about 1½ ft. tall and 2 ft. wide. Narrow, arching leaves about a foot long have maroon stripes on a green background with typical silvery sheen. Excellent in containers.

For the look of a fountain without the water, plant a compact astelia— such as *A. nivicola* 'Red Gem'—in a shapely sand-colored (or light teal) container and let its graceful leaves arch out on all sides.

Aster
Asteraceae
PERENNIALS

✎ ZONES VARY BY SPECIES
☀ FULL SUN, EXCEPT AS NOTED
💧 REGULAR WATER
🦋 ATTRACT BUTTERFLIES

Aster × *frikartii*

There are more than 600 species of true asters, ranging from 6-in.-high, tightly clumping alpine natives to open-branching woodland plants to 6 ft. tall. Flowers come in white or shades of blue, red, pink, lavender, or purple, mostly with yellow centers.

Bloom time comes in late summer to early fall, except as noted. Taller asters are invaluable in large borders or among shrubs or ornamental grasses. Compact dwarf or cushion types make tidy edgings, mounds of color in rock gardens, good container plants. For the common annual or China aster sold at nurseries, see *Callistephus chinensis*. For Stokes' aster, see *Stokesia laevis*.

A. amelloides. See *Felicia amelloides*.

A. amellus. ITALIAN ASTER. Zones 2–24. Native to Europe, western Asia. A sturdy, hairy plant to 2 ft. tall and 1½ ft. wide. Branching stems bear yellow-centered violet flowers 2 in. across. Many named selections are available in the usual color range of asters. All thrive in alkaline soil.

A. dumosus 'Sapphire'. Zones 1–24. This selection of a species from the eastern U.S. grows 1–1½ ft. tall and 1½–2 ft. wide. A compact, dense plant that blooms profusely in late summer and fall; blooms are lilac-blue. Good in pots.

A. × frikartii. Zones 2b–24. This hybrid between *A. amellus*

and a Himalayan species is one of the most useful and widely adapted perennials. It forms loose mounds about 2 ft. tall and wide, with dark green, hairy leaves and abundant sprays of clear lavender to violet-blue single flowers that are 2½ in. across; excellent cut flowers. Blooms from early summer to fall—almost all year in mild-winter areas if spent flowers are removed regularly. May be short-lived. Attracts bees. 'Mönch' and 'Wunder von Stäfa' ('Wonder of Staffa') are favorites with blossoms in lavender-blue.

A. fruticosus. See *Felicia fruticosa*.

A. laevis. SMOOTH ASTER. Zones 1–10, 14–21. Native to central and eastern North America. Grows 3½ ft. tall, 1½ ft. wide, with smooth, mildew-free foliage and clustered deep purplish blue 1-in. flower heads.

A. lateriflorus. Zones 1–10, 14–21. This North American species grows to 4 ft. tall and 1 ft. wide. Most garden

CLOCKWISE FROM LEFT: *Aster novae-angliae* 'Alma Potschke'; *A. novae-angliae* 'Herbstschnee'; *A. oblongifolius*

selections are shorter (to 2 ft.), with profuse branching, tiny leaves, and a haze of small purplish pink flowers. Foliage turns a coppery purplish red in early fall. 'Lady in Black' and 'Prince' have blackish purple stems and leaves; their blooms are white with a red center. Partial shade.

A. novae-angliae. NEW ENGLAND ASTER. Zones 1–24. Native from Vermont to Alabama, west to North Dakota, Wyoming, and New Mexico. Stout-stemmed plant to 3–5 ft. tall and nearly as wide, with hairy leaves to 5 in. long. Flowers are 2 in. wide; they are violet-blue in the basic form, with selections in other blue shades, white, pink, nearly red, and deep purple. The following are among the best of the many selections offered: 'Alma Potschke' bears salmon-pink single blooms on 2–4-ft.-tall stems from late summer to early fall. 'Harrington's Pink' produces clear pink single flowers over a long fall season on 3–4-ft. stems. 'Purple Dome' is a mildew-resistant, compact grower to 1½ ft. tall, with brilliant purple blooms. All are tolerant of wet soils, where they may reseed. Full sun or partial shade.

A. novi-belgii. NEW YORK ASTER, MICHAELMAS DAISY. Zones 1–24. Native to eastern North America. Grows to 4 ft. tall and 3 ft. wide, with full clusters of bright blue-violet flowers. Similar to *A. novae-angliae* but with smooth leaves. Hundreds of selections are available, varying from less than a foot tall to over 4 ft.; flower colors include white, cream, blue, lavender, purple, rose, and pink. Among them are 'Alert' (ruby red, semidouble flowers), 'Jenny' (reddish purple, double), 'Little Pink Beauty' (soft pink, semidouble), 'Professor Anton Kippenberg' (lavender-blue, semidouble), and 'Snowsprite' (pink buds open to white flowers); all of these grow about 1 ft. high and 1½ ft. wide. 'Audrey', to 14 in. high and a bit wider, has lavender-blue flowers. 'Farmington' ('Baldco') reaches 1½ ft. tall and 2 ft. wide, with lilac blooms and good mildew resistance. 'Patricia Ballard' reaches 2½–3 ft. tall and 2 ft. wide, with dark pink flowers. In the 3-ft. range are 'Apple Blossom' (pink), 'Marie Ballard' (pale blue, double), and 'Winston S.

Churchill' (dark red, double). 'Climax' bears large sprays of single medium blue blossoms on stems to 6 ft. high. All grow well in full sun or partial shade.

A. tataricus. Zones 1–10, 14–21. Native to Siberia, China, and Japan. Not for small gardens, this giant (which can be invasive in moist soils) grows 5–7 ft. tall and 3 ft. wide, with inch-wide lavender-blue flowers in flat clusters in fall. 'Jindai' is compact, at just 3–4 ft. tall. Sun or partial shade.

CARE

Asters adapt to most soils, but growth is most luxuriant in fertile soil; add organic matter at planting time. Taller kinds may be cut back by half in late spring to encourage bushiness; very tall asters may need staking. Strong-growing hybrids and some species have invasive roots and can regrow from small fragments left in soil and spread to become nuisances. Divide yearly in late fall or early spring; replant vigorous young divisions from outside of clump and discard the old center. Divide smaller, tufted, less vigorous asters every 2 years.

Asteriscus
(Pallenis)
Asteraceae
PERENNIALS

🖊 **ZONES VARY BY SPECIES**
☼ **FULL SUN**
◯ ◗ **LITTLE TO MODERATE WATER**

Asteriscus sericeus

These leafy, evergreen, almost shrubby plants produce showy yellow, 1½–2-in. daisies throughout most of the year. Shear spent flowers to neaten appearance and prolong bloom.

A. maritimus (Pallenis maritima, Odontospermum maritimum). GOLD COIN. Zones 9, 15–24. Native to the Mediterranean region and the Canary Islands. Attractive, silvery green–foliaged groundcover to 1 ft. tall, 4 ft. wide. Tough, tolerant plant for most soils; takes seaside conditions. Attracts bees. 'Compact Gold Coin' is more mounding and a bit less sprawling; good in pots.

A. sericeus (Nauplius sericeus, Odontospermum sericeus). CANARY ISLAND DAISY. Zones 16, 17, 19–24. To 3 ft. tall and wide, shrubbier than *A. maritimus*. Silky, silvery leaves set off bright yellow flowers for a silver-and-gold effect. The foliage has an odd odor, and old leaves tend to blacken and adhere to the stems. If groomed, makes a striking container plant.

Astilbe
FALSE SPIREA
Saxifragaceae
PERENNIALS

🖊 **ZONES A2, A3; 1–7, 14–17; SHORT-LIVED IN ZONES 8, 9, 18–24**
☼ ◗ **FULL SUN IN COOLER CLIMATES ONLY**
◗ **REGULAR WATER**
🦋 **ATTRACT BUTTERFLIES**

Astilbe × arendsii

Astilbes are perfect for shady perennial borders, along woodland paths, and containers. Their flowers, which bloom from late spring through summer, are light and airy. The small white, pink, or red blooms are carried in graceful, branching, feathery clusters on slender, wiry stems ranging from 6 in. to 3 ft. or taller. Most plants grow 2–3 ft.

wide. Leaves are typically divided into several leaflets, for a soft, textural look.

In cool-summer climates, plants can withstand full sun if watered adequately. Survival in coldest areas (Zones 1a, 1b, 2a) depends on good snow cover. They need moist (but not boggy), rich soil with ample humus. Cut off faded flowering stems, and divide clumps every 4 or 5 years.

A. × arendsii. Most astilbes sold belong to this hybrid group or are sold as such. Parentage is complex, but plants often have *A. japonica*, *A. chinensis*, and/or *A. thunbergii* in their ancestry. The plants differ chiefly in technical details. The following are some of the best varieties:

'Amethyst'. Late. Lavender, 3–4 ft.

'Bridal Veil'. Midseason to late. Full white plumes, 3 ft.

Color Flash series. Midseason. Pink flowers and colorful foliage; about 2 ft. tall. Leaves of 'Color Flash' gradually turn from green to burgundy. 'Color Flash Lime' has light green foliage that picks up bright yellow tones.

'Deutschland'. Early. White, 1½ ft. Bright green leaves.

'Fanal'. Early. Blood red flowers, bronzy foliage, 1½–2½ ft.

'Ostrich Plume' ('Straussenfeder'). Midseason to late. Drooping pink clusters, 3–3½ ft. Often sold as a variety of *A. thunbergii*.

'Peach Blossom'. Midseason. Light salmon-pink, 2 ft.

'Rheinland'. Early. Deep pink, 2–2½ ft.

A. chinensis. Resembles *A. × arendsii* hybrids, but generally blooms in late summer, grows taller, and tolerates dryness a little better. Varieties and subspecies include the following:

'Diamonds and Pearls'. Pure white flowers on plumes 2–2½ ft. tall.

'Finale'. Pink blooms rise to 18–20 in. high.

'Purple Candles'. Deep purple plumes to about 3½ ft. tall.

'Visions'. Early. Upright grower to 15 in. tall, with raspberry pink plumes above bronzy green leaves.

A. c. davidii. Dense, narrow pink plumes to 3 ft. tall.

»

A. c. pumila. Low mats of leaves topped by lilac-pink flower clusters that rise 12–15 in. high.

A. c. taquetii 'Superba'. Bright pinkish purple flowers in spikelike clusters 4–5 ft. tall.

A. simplicifolia. Grows to about 1½ ft. high and wide. Leaves are merely cut or lobed, not divided into leaflets. Better known than the species are its garden varieties and hybrids. 'Pink Lightning' has delicate blooms that emerge purplish red and open to clear pink. 'Sprite' (the best known) is a low-growing, compact plant that blooms profusely in summer, bearing drooping pink, 1-ft. spires above bronze-tinted foliage. 'Hennie Graafland' is similar but grows a few inches taller and blooms a little earlier.

A. taquetii 'Superba'. See *A. chinensis taquetii* 'Superba'.

Astrantia
MASTERWORT
Apiaceae
PERENNIALS

🗡 **ZONES 1–9, 14–24**

☼ ◑ **FULL SUN OR PARTIAL SHADE**

⬤ **REGULAR WATER**

Astrantia major

Charming natives of meadows and alpine woods of Europe, the masterworts are especially at home in woodland and cottage gardens. Lush, leafy clumps give rise in summer to slender stems topped by dense, tight clusters of blooms. Each flower is surrounded by papery bracts, giving a pincushion look. Blossoms make attractive, long-lasting cut flowers that can also be dried for winter arrangements.

Plants spread slowly by underground runners. They die back in winter, even in mild climates. All need good drainage.

A. major. Reaches 3 ft. high and 1–2 ft. wide, with inch-wide clusters of blossoms that are white-green or white-pink. 'Abbey Road', 'Claret', 'Hadspen Blood', and 'Ruby Wedding' have deep pink to purplish red blooms. 'Sunningdale Variegated' has leaves heavily marked in shades of cream. *A. m. involucrata* 'Shaggy', 2½ ft. tall and 2 ft. wide, has long, soft-looking, silvery bracts with green tips.

A. maxima. Similar to *A. major* but grows 2 ft. high and half as wide. Pink bracts surround soft pink flowers.

Athyrium
Woodsiaceae
FERNS

🗡 **ZONES VARY BY SPECIES**

◐ ● **PARTIAL OR FULL SHADE**

⬤ ⬤ **REGULAR TO AMPLE WATER**

Athyrium niponicum pictum 'Silver Falls'

Graceful, fresh-looking ferns for shady areas and woodland gardens; their delicate fronds rise from erect or creeping rhizomes. Locate them away from high-traffic areas, as their fronds are quite fragile. Most types turn brown after repeated frosts. Leave the dead foliage on the plants through winter to provide mulch and to shelter emerging fronds in early spring; cut back after new fronds have appeared. The species described here prefer rich, damp soil and will tolerate considerable sun if grown in constantly moist soil. Propagate by dividing old clumps in spring.

A. filix-femina. LADY FERN. Zones A1–A3; 1–9, 14–24. Native to much of North America. This fern sometimes volunteers in mild-region gardens. Its vigorous root system can be invasive. Grows 4 ft. or taller, 2–3 ft. wide, with thin, finely divided fronds. The rootstock builds up on older plants to make a short trunk. Specialists stock many varieties with oddly cut and feathered fronds. In 'Frizelliae' (about 8 in. high, 1 ft. wide), the frond divisions are reduced to balls, giving each frond the look of a string of beads. 'Vernoniae Cristatum' (to 2½ ft. tall and wide) has crested and feathered fronds. 'Victoriae' has 2–3-ft.-long fronds with crisscrossing leaflets and crested tips.

A. 'Ghost'. Zones 1–9, 14–24. Popular hybrid between *A. niponicum pictum* and *A. filix-femina*. Grows upright to about 2½ tall and 2 ft. wide. Silvery gray fronds have dark purple midribs.

A. niponicum pictum. JAPANESE PAINTED FERN. Zones 1–9, 14–24. Fronds grow to 1–1½ ft. long, making a tight, slowly spreading, foot-high clump. Leaflets are purplish at the base, lavender midway up, then silvery greenish gray toward the tip.

A. otophorum. Zones 3–9, 14–24. Sometimes called English painted fern, this species is actually native to China, Japan, and Korea. It resembles Japanese painted fern, but its dark green fronds have reddish or purple midribs.

Japanese painted ferns color best in shady borders that get some morning sun. For striking combos, pair them with blue or green hostas, chocolate brown heucheras, × *Heucherella* 'Sweet Tea', or *Lamium maculatum* 'Orchid Frost'.

Atriplex
SALTBUSH
Amaranthaceae
EVERGREEN AND DECIDUOUS SHRUBS

🗡 **ZONES VARY BY SPECIES**

☼ **FULL SUN, EXCEPT AS NOTED**

◌ **LITTLE OR NO WATER**

🐦 **ATTRACT BIRDS**

Atriplex confertifolia

Prized for their gray or silvery foliage, saltbushes are also tough. They are unusually tolerant of direct seashore conditions, drought, and highly alkaline desert soils; they're also fire-resistant. Plants need good drainage. They often become straggly with age; to keep them compact, cut back previous year's growth by one-third each year before the first flush of spring growth. Flowers and seeds attract birds.

A. barklayana. Evergreen. Zones 16–24. This dwarf saltbush from Baja California forms a dense 1½-ft.-high mound to 4 ft. across. Inch-long leaves are covered with white powder.

A. canescens. FOUR-WING SALTBUSH. Evergreen. Zones 1–3, 7–24. Native throughout much of the arid West. Dense growth 3–6 ft. high, spreading to 4–8 ft. Narrow gray leaves are ½–2 in. long. Often sheared into a hedge.

A. confertifolia. SHADSCALE. Deciduous. Zones 1–3, 10. Native to high plains and mesas from eastern Oregon and California to North Dakota, and south to northern Arizona, western Texas, and Mexico. A mounded, woody, spiny subshrub, 1–3 ft. tall and wide, with rounded, whitish leaves and pinkish or yellowish flower spikes in early summer.

A. hymenelytra. DESERT HOLLY. Evergreen. Zones 3, 7–14, 18, 19. Native to deserts of Southern California, western Arizona, southern Nevada, and southwestern Utah. A compact shrub growing 1–3 ft. high and 3 ft. wide, with whitish branches and silvery, deeply toothed, roundish leaves to 1½ in. long. Looks something like a silvery white Christmas holly; much used for decorations. Outside its native range, needs very fast drainage. Can take heavy watering from midwinter into spring.

A. lentiformis. QUAIL BUSH. Deciduous. Zones 3, 7–14, 18, 19. Native to alkali wastes in California valleys and deserts and east to Nevada, Utah, Arizona, and New Mexico. Densely branched, sometimes spiny shrub, to 3–10 ft. high and 6–12 ft. wide. Oval, bluish gray leaves ½–2 in. long. Useful as salt-tolerant informal hedge or windbreak.

A. l. breweri. QUAIL BUSH, BREWER SALTBUSH. Nearly evergreen. Zones 8, 9, 12–24. Native to California coast south of San Francisco Bay and to Channel Islands. Resembles *A. lentiformis* but is not spiny. Grows 5–7 ft. high and 6–8 ft. wide. Useful gray plant on oceanfront; will grow in reclaimed marine soil. Sometimes sheared into a hedge.

A. nummularia. Evergreen. Zones 15–24. Native to Australia but naturalized in parts of Southern California. Dense, rounded, nearly white shrub to 6 ft. tall, 3 ft. wide. Tolerates summer drought, winter flooding. Will grow in full sun or light shade.

A. polycarpa. DESERT SALTBUSH, CATTLE SPINACH. Evergreen to deciduous. Zones 3, 7–13, 18, 19. Native to alkali flats and dry lakebeds from California's Owens Valley east to Utah and south to Baja California and Sonora, Mexico. Dense covering of grayish white scales gives the densely branched, symmetrical, 3–6-ft. mound a silvery glow. Needs no irrigation, but leaves will drop during periods of extreme drought and heat.

A. semibaccata. AUSTRALIAN SALTBUSH. Evergreen. Zones 8–10, 12–24. Native to Australia but naturalized in parts of the West and Southwest. Forms a dense, foot-high mat of gray-green leaves. Spreads from 1 ft. to 6 ft. or even wider. Excellent groundcover; plant 3 ft. apart.

Aubrieta deltoidea
COMMON AUBRIETA
Brassicaceae
PERENNIAL

✎ **ZONES 1–9, 14–21**

☀ ◐ **FULL SUN OR LIGHT SHADE**

💧 **REGULAR WATER**

Aubrieta deltoidea

Native from the eastern Mediterranean region to Iran. This mat-forming perennial is popular in Northwest and high-elevation rock gardens, where it blooms in early spring along with basket-of-gold, rockcress, perennial candytuft, and moss pink. Ideal for chinks in dry stone walls or between pavers. Plants grow 2–6 in. high and 1–1½ ft. across, with small gray-green leaves and tiny rose to deep red, pale to deep lilac, or purple flowers. Many varieties are available. 'Madly Blue Violet' and 'Madly Magenta' produce large flowers and may rebloom in late summer or fall. 'Novalis Blue' is a fine seed-grown variety with dark blue blossoms. 'Rokey's Purple' is a heavy producer of rich purple flowers. Selections with white- or yellow-variegated leaves are also available.

CARE
Provide good drainage. Needs regular moisture before and during bloom; takes some drought later on. After bloom, shear off flowers before they set seed.

Don't cut back by more than half—always keep some foliage. After trimming, top-dress with mixture of gritty soil and bonemeal. Sow seeds in late spring for blooms the following spring. Clumps are difficult to divide; make cuttings in late summer.

Aucuba japonica
JAPANESE AUCUBA
Garryaceae
EVERGREEN SHRUB

✎ **ZONES 4–24**

◐ ● **PARTIAL OR FULL SHADE**

💧💧 💧 **MODERATE TO REGULAR WATER**

Aucuba japonica 'Variegata'

Native from Japan and the Himalayas. Japanese aucubas are indispensable in dry, shady gardens, where they can be used in borders, as screens or hedges, or as accents. Or grow them in containers on shady patios, or beneath trees, where they compete successfully with tree roots. They need shade from hot sun but tolerate deep shade—and sea air. They'll grow in a wide range of soils but thrive and look better if poor or heavy soils are improved. Prune to control height or form by cutting back to a leaf joint. Watch for mealybugs and mites.

Standard green-leafed aucuba grows at a moderate rate up to 6–10 ft. (sometimes to 15 ft.) high and almost as wide, though it can easily be kept lower by pruning. Dark green leaves are toothed, polished. Minute dark maroon flowers in earliest spring are followed by clusters of bright red, ¾-in. berries in autumn and winter. Usually, both sexes must be planted to ensure a fruit crop. Green-leafed 'Rozannie' is self-fruitful,

producing a heavy crop of berries without a pollenizer. Other green-leafed types include 'Nana', a dwarf to about 3 ft. tall (female); 'Serratifolia', with long leaves that have coarsely toothed edges (female); and *A. j. longifolia* 'Salicifolia', with narrow willowlike leaves (female).

Variegated Japanese aucubas are usually slower growing and often smaller at maturity than the species; they're ideal for brightening shady areas and dark corners. Look for 'Crotonifolia', leaves heavily splashed with white and gold (male); 'Fructu Albo', leaves variegated with white, berries pale pinkish buff (female); 'Mr. Goldstrike', leaves heavily splashed with gold (male); 'Picturata', leaves centered with golden yellow, edged with dark green dotted yellow (female); 'Sulphur' ('Sulphurea Marginata'), green leaves with broad yellow edge (female). 'Variegata', often called gold dust plant, is the best-known aucuba. It has dark green leaves spotted with yellow; plants may be male or female.

Aurinia saxatilis
(Alyssum saxatile)
BASKET-OF-GOLD
Brassicaceae
PERENNIAL

✎ **ZONES 1–24**

☀ ◐ **FULL SUN OR LIGHT SHADE**

💧 **MODERATE WATER**

🐝 **ATTRACTS BENEFICIAL INSECTS**

Aurinia saxatilis

This mustard relative from the mountains of central and southern Europe and Turkey has gray leaves (sometimes variegated white) that form a spreading

A

evergreen mound 8–12 in. high; dwarf forms are half as tall. Dense clusters of single or double, tiny, yellow to apricot flowers cover the plant in spring and early summer. Use as foreground plant in borders or in rock gardens; plant about 1½ ft. apart. Poor soils or moderately fertile ones suit the plant perfectly—as long as drainage is good. Shear lightly (don't cut back stems by more than half) right after bloom. Generally hardy but may be killed in extremely cold winters. Self-sows.

Austrostipa ramosissima.
See *Stipa ramosissima*

Avocado
Lauraceae
EVERGREEN TREES

✎ **ZONES VARY BY VARIETY**

☼ **FULL SUN**

💧 **REGULAR WATER**

≫ See chart on facing page.

'Hass' avocado

In California, two races of avocados are grown: Guatemalan (*Persea americana guatemalensis*) and Mexican (*P. a. drymifolia*). Widely planted varieties 'Hass' and 'Fuerte' are hybrids. Ideal climates for Guatemalan varieties, which are generally hardy to 30°F (–1°C), are Zones 21, 23, and 24, but good results can be had in Zones 19, 20, and 22, and some success can be expected in Zones 9 and 15. Mexican varieties, which bear smaller, less attractive fruit, are hardy down to at least 24°F (–4°C); they grow in Zones 9, 15–24, and some warmer locations in Zones 8 and 14. (See the chart for cold-hardiness of hybrids.) Avocados bloom in late

How to Grow Avocados

WATERING Avocados need good drainage. Keep the soil evenly moist by using sprinkler irrigation when the soil near the surface begins to dry. Give plants an occasional deep soaking to wash accumulated salts from the soil around the roots. Let a mulch of fallen leaves build up under the tree to conserve soil moisture.

FERTILIZING Feed young trees lightly; mature trees need 1 lb. of nitrogen per year, split into two or more applications and applied in spring and summer.

CHALLENGES Avocado trees are very susceptible to *Phytophthora* root rot. Added mulch and gypsum can create soil conditions that suppress this fungus. After an avocado is planted, cover the soil around it with a 6–12-in.-deep layer of organic mulch or wood chips, but keep the mulching material at least 6 in. away from the trunk. Scatter a total of 25 lbs. of gypsum per year around the tree a little at a time. Control chlorosis with iron and zinc chelates. Persea mite is a problem in Southern California; it causes small yellow and black dead spots on the foliage and excessive leaf drop. It can be partially controlled by releasing one of several species of predatory mites.

winter to late spring, so even though older trees will survive these lows, temperatures much below freezing will damage flowers or fruit. In Hawaii, Guatemalan and hybrid varieties are best adapted to (and are grown throughout) Zone H2, but away from exposure to salt spray.

Avocado varieties have flowers categorized as either type A or type B, depending on the time of day they open and when pollen is released. Where avocados are common, isolated

trees may produce enough fruit for home use, but for best production, plant one of each type or graft a limb of one type into a bearing tree of the other type. The flower type for each variety is noted in the chart. Mexican avocados mature 6 to 8 months after flowering; Guatemalan avocados mature in 12 to 18 months. Most varieties grow to 30–40 ft. tall and spread wider (size can be controlled by pruning). They also produce dense shade and shed leaves throughout the year. Unless otherwise noted, the avocados listed in the chart have thin, smooth skin.

Azara
Salicaceae
EVERGREEN SHRUBS OR SMALL TREES

✎ **ZONES VARY BY SPECIES**

◐ **PARTIAL SHADE**

💧 **REGULAR WATER**

Azara dentata

These natives of lakesides and woodland edges in Chile and Argentina have attractive evergreen foliage and fluffy yellow flowers that smell like chocolate

What Causes Fingerling Avocados?

Often called cukes or cocktail avocados, small fingerling fruits form after the embryo of a pollinated flower dies. Drying winds or sudden heat can cause this to happen, especially on 'Fuerte' or Mexican-type avocado trees. Pick mature fingerling avocados and let them ripen. They're always seedless. Try peeling and cutting them in half, and serve them with a dip on top as an hors d'oeuvre.

to some, vanilla to others. Blooms are followed by small, shiny berries. Need fast drainage, regular fertilizer, and protection from hot afternoon sun and cold winds. Prune after bloom to remove crowded or wayward branches.

A. dentata. Zones 5 (with shelter), 6, 15–17. Grows to 15 ft. tall and 12 ft. wide, with toothed, rounded, shiny leaves. Rounded shape makes it useful for screen or informal hedge. Tolerates considerable shade. Blooms in spring.

A. lanceolata. LANCELEAF AZARA. Zones 5 (with shelter), 15–17. A large, arching plant to 20 ft. tall and 15 ft. wide. Equal to *A. microphylla* in pattern value, but its bright yellow-green, rather narrow leaves are much larger, producing a lusher effect. Blooms in spring.

A. microphylla. BOXLEAF AZARA. Zones 5–9, 14–24. Best-known species. Grows slowly in youth, faster once established. Typically reaches 12–18 ft. tall and 8–12 ft. wide, but may attain a treelike 30 ft. tall in great old age. Shiny, roundish, dark green leaves. Flat-branching habit and neatly arranged foliage make it natural for an espalier or freestanding wall plant. Blooms in late winter. 'Variegata' has leaves edged in creamy white.

A. petiolaris (A. gilliesii). Zones 15–17. Shrubby grower to 15–20 ft. tall and 12 ft. wide, but easily trained to form a single-stemmed tree. Oval to roundish, lustrous deep green leaves look somewhat like those of holly; they hang from branches like aspen leaves. Blooms in late winter.

AVOCADO: TOP PICKS TO GROW

VARIETY	ZONES	HARVEST PERIOD	FRUIT	COMMENTS
'Bacon'	9, 15–24	Midfall through winter	Medium size; green skin. Good quality.	Mexican. Upright grower. Bears heavier in alternate years. Type B flower. 'Jim Bacon' is a slightly hardier seedling selection.
'Fuerte'	9, 15, 19–24	Late fall through spring	Medium size; green skin. High quality.	Hybrid. Hardy to 27°F (–3°C). Well-known variety. Large tree. Early blooming. Tends to bear in alternate years. Type B flower.
'Gwen'	19–24	Spring into fall	Medium size; green skin. Good quality.	Guatemalan. Medium tree with narrow habit. Bears in alternate years. Type A flower.
'Hass'	16, 17, 19–24	Spring into fall	Medium to large; dark purple, pebbly, thick but pliable skin. Excellent flavor.	Hybrid. Hardy to 30°F (–1°C). Large, spreading tree. Bears heavier in alternate years. Type A flower. 'Lamb Hass' is more productive.
'Holiday'	19–24	Midfall through winter	Large; green skin. Very good flavor.	Guatemalan. Dwarf tree with weeping habit. Bears in alternate years. Often grown in large containers. Type A flower.
'Jim'	9, 15, 19–24	Late fall into winter	Medium size; with green skin and long neck.	Mexican. Type B flower.
'Kahaluu'	H2	Fall into winter	Medium to large; green skin. Superb flavor.	Hybrid. Hardy to 30°F (–1°C). Light producer. Type B flower.
'Mexicola'	9, 15–24	Late summer into fall	Small; with tender, dark purple skin. Outstanding, nutty flavor. Large seed.	Mexican. Very cold-hardy, to 20°F (–7°C). Heavy producer. Type A flower. 'Mexicola Grande' is larger and a bit hardier.
'Murashige'	H2	Spring to late summer	Medium to large; with green, pebbly skin. High quality.	Hybrid. Hardy to 30°F (–1°C). Heavy producer. Type B flower.
'Nabal'	19–24	Summer into fall	Medium to large; green skin. Excellent flavor.	Guatemalan. Tends to bear in alternate years. Type B flower.
'Pinkerton'	9, 15, 19–24	Winter through spring	Medium to large; green skin. Very good quality.	Guatemalan. Large tree. Consistent producer. Type A flower.
'Reed'	21–24	Summer into fall	Medium to large; with green, pebbly skin. Fine flavor.	Guatemalan. Slender, upright tree. Tends to bear well alone. Type A flower.
'Sharwil'	H2	Fall into spring	Medium size; with green, pebbly skin. Excellent flavor.	Hybrid. Hardy to 30°F (–1°C). Heavy producer. Type B flower.
'Sir Prize'	9, 16, 17, 19–24	Late fall into spring	Large size; with black, slightly pebbly skin with a distinct rib. Excellent, buttery flavor.	Hybrid descended from 'Hass'; probably hardier to cold. Upright grower. Type B flower.
'Stewart'	9, 15–24	Fall to winter	Small to medium size; with dark purple skin. Excellent flavor.	Mexican. Compact tree. Type B flower.
'Wertz' ('Wurtz')	19–24	Summer	Medium size; with green, pebbly skin. Rich flavor.	Guatemalan. Dwarf tree with weeping branches. Tends to bear in alternate years. Often sold as 'Littlecado' or 'Minicado'. Type A flower.
'Whitsell'	19–24	Midwinter into fall	Medium size; green skin. Very good quality.	Guatemalan. Medium tree. Tends to bear in alternate years. Type B flower.
'Yamagata'	H2	Late spring through summer	Medium to large; with green, pebbly skin. Rich flavor.	Hybrid. Hardy to 30°F (–1°C). Heavy producer. Type B flower.
'Zutano'	9, 16–24	Midfall to midwinter	Medium size; green skin. Average quality.	Hybrid. Hardy to 24°F (–4°C). Upright grower. Used to cross-pollinate 'Hass'. Type B flower.

B

Babiana
BABOON FLOWER
Iridaceae
PERENNIALS FROM CORMS

- ✂ **ZONES 4–24; OR DIG AND STORE**
- ☼ ◐ **FULL SUN OR LIGHT SHADE**
- ◗ **REGULAR WATER DURING GROWTH AND BLOOM**

Babiana stricta hybrid

These natives of sub-Saharan Africa are grown for their spikes of freesialike flowers. In mid- to late spring, each flowering stem produces six or more blooms, each to 2 in. across. Ribbed, usually hairy leaves typically grow in fans. Corms are reportedly tasty to baboons, hence the plant's common name.

B. rubrocyanea. Ruby-throated royal blue blossoms.

B. stricta. Royal blue bloomers.

CARE

Plant corms 4 in. deep and 4–6 in. apart; place them along the edge of a border or path. In Zones 8–24, plant in fall; in colder areas, plant in early spring, waiting until temperatures will remain above 20°F (−7°C). Cut back on water as leaves yellow. Trim off foliage after it dies back. Where corms can overwinter in ground, leave them in place for several years—they'll increase and bloom more profusely with each year. Beyond hardiness range, dig and store as for gladiolus.

Baccharis
Asteraceae
EVERGREEN SHRUBS

- ✂ **ZONES VARY BY SPECIES**
- ☼ **FULL SUN**
- ◍ ◗ **LITTLE TO MODERATE WATER**

Baccharis pilularis

These plants are tough and able to grow in difficult conditions: they withstand heat, wind, and poor soil. Most are densely foliaged. Male and female flowers, borne on separate plants, are inconspicuous. Female plants produce cottony seed clusters that can make a mess when blown about by wind; grow male varieties if they're available (or hoe out unwanted seedlings if they appear).

B. 'Centennial'. Zones 7–24; best in 10–13. Female hybrid between *B. pilularis* and *B. sarothroides*. Grows to 3 ft. tall and 4–5 ft. wide, with narrow leaves and tufted tan seed capsules in spring. Tolerates desert heat; resists root rot caused by water molds.

B. pilularis. DWARF COYOTE BRUSH. Zones 5–11, 14–24. Native to Northern California coast. This shrub adapts well to a wide range of climates and soils. Near the coast, it thrives with no water at all; inland, it looks better with monthly watering. In California's high desert, it's the most dependable of all groundcovers. It is a low-maintenance cover for sunny banks and flatlands everywhere. It makes a dense, billowy, bright green mat, 8–24 in. high and spreading to 6 ft. or more. Small, toothed leaves are closely set on branches.

The plants available in most nurseries are produced from cuttings of male plants. 'Twin Peaks' ('Twin Peaks #2') has small, dark green leaves and a moderate growth rate. 'Pigeon Point' has larger leaves in a lighter green and grows faster (9 ft. wide in 4 years); can make a 2–3-ft.-high hedge.

Needs shearing once a year in early spring before new growth starts. Cut out old arching branches and thin to rejuvenate. Feed with a nitrogen fertilizer after cutting back.

B. sarothroides. DESERT BROOM. Zones 7–24; most useful in 10–13. Native to the Southwest. Nearly leafless, but branches are bright green throughout year. Plant grows 5 ft. tall and wide; can be clipped to 2–3 ft. Drought-tolerant. Not fussy about drainage. Useful for erosion control, replanting disturbed land, or natural landscape in desert regions.

B. 'Starn' (B. 'Thompson'). Zones 7–24; best in 10–13. Has the same size and habit as 'Centennial' but offers an improvement, since it is a male plant and won't produce seed clusters.

Baileya multiradiata
DESERT MARIGOLD
Asteraceae
ANNUAL OR PERENNIAL

- ✂ **ZONES 1–3, 7–23**
- ☼ **FULL SUN**
- ◗ **MODERATE WATER**

Baileya multiradiata

This Western desert native grows 1–1½ ft. high, displaying bright yellow flowers above gray-green foliage. It blooms mostly in spring through fall, but year-round in low desert and other mild-winter areas if it gets periodic moisture. Sow seeds in autumn or spring, rake in, and water thoroughly. Keep moist until seeds sprout, then reduce watering to once or twice weekly. Thin to 1½ ft. apart. To prolong bloom, water every week or two. Self-sows.

Bamboo
Poaceae
GIANT GRASSES

- ✂ **SEE CHART FOR HARDINESS**
- ☼ ◐ **SUN OR PARTIAL SHADE, EXCEPT AS NOTED**
- ◍ ◗ ◗ **LITTLE TO REGULAR WATER**

» See chart on pages 184–186.

Himalayacalamus hookerianus

All bamboos, even tree-size ones, are actually grasses. They have woody stems (culms) that are divided into sections by obvious joints (nodes). Upper nodes grow buds that develop into branches and leaves. Bamboos spread by underground stems (rhizomes; like aboveground culms, they're jointed and carry buds). The way rhizomes grow differs for clumping and running bamboos.

In clumping bamboos, rhizomes grow a few inches from the edge of the clump, then send up shoots. Clumps expand continually but slowly. Most clumping bamboos are tropical or subtropical.

In running bamboos, rhizomes grow rapidly to various distances from the parent plant before sending up vertical shoots. These bamboos eventually form large patches or groves. They're generally hardy plants from temperate regions in China and Japan, and they'll

How to Grow Bamboo

PLANTING & PROPAGATING
Plant container-grown bamboos at any time of year. The more crowded a bamboo is in the container, the faster it will grow when planted. Do not cut or spread the rootball; this may kill some canes. Best time to propagate from existing clumps is just before growth begins; divide hardy kinds in late winter or early spring, tropical ones in mid- to late spring. Cut or saw out large divisions with roots and at least three connected culms. If divisions are tall, cut back tops to balance loss of roots and rhizomes. Foliage may wilt or wither, but culms will send out new leaves. Plant in rich soil mix with ample organic material added; keep moist.

WATERING For best growth, water bamboos frequently and deeply, soaking soil around the plant to at least 12 in. deep. Established plants tolerate considerable drought but look best with regular irrigation.

FERTILIZING Feed in-ground plants once a month, March to October, with a high-nitrogen fertilizer or a balanced controlled-release fertilizer. To restrict size and spread of an established bamboo, cut back on water and fertilizer.

GROOMING Even though individual culms won't grow taller after their first year, they become increasingly leafy. Plants are evergreen, but there is considerable dropping of older leaves; old plantings develop a nearly weedproof mulch of dead leaves. Individual canes live for several years but eventually die. Cut them out.

PESTS Scale, mealybugs, and aphids occasionally appear on bamboo but seldom do any harm; if they excrete honeydew in bothersome amounts, spray with insecticidal soap or summer oil. Mites can cause yellow streaking or disfigurement of leaves. To control them, use insecticidal soap.

CONTAINMENT
Running bamboos. Large expanses of concrete or asphalt won't prevent the spread of running bamboos, but it isn't difficult to contain them—provided you understand how they grow. Rhizomes are shallow and spread sideways, not down.

Block them. You can keep the runners from spreading by installing a 30–36-in.-deep, 40–60-mil-thick, continuous polypropylene plastic sheet around the perimeter of the planting. Leave a 2-in. lip aboveground to block runners. Never place plastic under roots, as they need excellent drainage. Continuously dry soil extending 10–20 ft. beyond the planting bed also stops runners. Or contain them by planting in aboveground pots.

Cut them. Equally effective but more labor-intensive is to periodically insert a spade down to its full length around the plant, severing the rhizomes and isolating the unwanted parts from the main plant. Break off any new shoots that rise from the isolated rhizomes; they are unlikely to resprout (if they do, follow instructions for removal in the text at right).

Surround with trenches. Another method is to dig a foot-deep, foot-wide trench around plants. Fill the trench with loose mulch or sand, then use a spading fork several times a year to search the trench for any roving rhizomes (they're easily severed).

Clumping bamboos. These types grow in an enlarging circle and do not gracefully adjust their shape, although a barrier on just one side is sometimes useful. Plant them well away from fences and sidewalks. Once a clump has expanded to the desired size, keep it in check by breaking off new shoots where you don't want them.

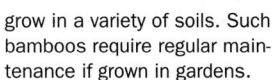

grow in a variety of soils. Such bamboos require regular maintenance if grown in gardens.

Mature bamboos grow very fast during their brief growth period—primarily March to July. The more tropical clumpers produce shoots in spring, summer, or fall and sometimes twice a year, again depending upon the species. Culms of all bamboos have already attained their maximum diameter when they emerge from the ground. In mature plants, new shoots usually reach their maximum height within 1 to 2 months. Culms of giant types may grow in length several feet a day. Don't expect such growth the first year after transplanting, though. Giant timber bamboo (*Phyllostachys bambusoides*), for instance, needs 3 to 5 years to build up a rhizome system capable of supporting its fast-growing culms; growth in early years will be less impressive.

Flowering of bamboos is a great mystery. Most species bloom periodically all over the world at the same time for a period of 2 to 7 years at intervals varying from 10 to 120 years, depending on the

CLOCKWISE FROM TOP: *Otatea acuminata aztecorum; Phyllostachys nigra; Bambusa vulgaris* 'Vittata'

species. Flowering generally weakens these plants, and although they may slowly recover, they often die. Very heavy feeding and watering may speed their recovery. Bamboo flowers resemble the seed heads of other grains. Most nurseries carry only a few types of bamboo. The American Bamboo Society has chapters in the Northwest, Northern California, and Southern California. Society members often propagate rare varieties for sale in connection with their meetings. Arboretum and botanical garden sales are other good sources. Plant names change so frequently that vendors cannot always keep up, so you may need to check for them under the principal names listed in the accompanying chart as well as under the synonyms.

The best way to eliminate unwanted bamboo is to dig it out with a mattock and spade. Rhizomes may be widespread, and if you don't remove them all,

BAMBOO: TOP PICKS TO GROW

NAME	ALSO SOLD AS	CONTROLLED (UNCONTROLLED) HEIGHT	GROWTH HABIT	STEM DIAMETER	HARDINESS	COMMENTS (FORM, CHARACTERISTICS, USES)
CLUMPING TYPES						
Bambusa chungii TROPICAL BLUE BAMBOO		25–28 ft. (30–33 ft.)	II	2½ in.	21°F (–6°C)	Graceful, upright culms are covered with white powder, for an overall soft blue effect. Branches high and clumps loosely, so colorful culms are easily seen.
B. c. barbelatta BABY BLUE BAMBOO		18–20 ft. (20–22 ft.)	II	1½ in.	21°F (–6°C)	Similar to species, but smaller, with thinner culms in tighter clumps. Good choice for smaller gardens or as an accent among other bamboos.
B. multiplex 'Alphonse Karr' ALPHONSE KARR BAMBOO		8–10 ft. (15–35 ft.)	II	½–1 in.	15°F (–9°C)	Branches from base to top. Dense growth. Culms brilliantly striped green on yellow. New culms pinkish and green.
B. m. 'Fernleaf' FERNLEAF BAMBOO	B. m. 'Floribunda'	6–10 ft. (10–20 ft.)	II	½ in.	15°F (–9°C)	Closely spaced leaves, 10–20 to twig, give ferny look. Loses this look, grows coarser with rich soil, ample water.
B. m. 'Golden Goddess' GOLDEN GODDESS BAMBOO		6–8 ft. (6–10 ft.)	II	½ in.	15°F (–9°C)	Golden-stemmed variety with graceful, dense, arching growth. Good container or screen plant. Give tops room to spread.
B. oldhamii OLDHAM BAMBOO, CLUMPING GIANT TIMBER BAMBOO	Sinocalamus oldhamii	15–25 ft. (20–55 ft.)	IV	4 in.	20°F (–7°C)	Densely foliaged, erect clumps; good for big, dense screens. Or use single plant as imposing vertical mass. Most common big bamboo in Southern California.
B. textilis WEAVER'S BAMBOO		16–20 ft. (30–50 ft.)	IV	2 in.	20°F (–7°C)	Stately, upright, forming a very tight column of blue-powdered canes that arch at the top. Grows taller where winters are warmer. Screen or specimen. A dwarf form, half the size of the species, is available.
B. vulgaris 'Vittata' PAINTED BAMBOO		15–25 ft. (to 50 ft.)	IV	4 in.	32°F (0°C)	Yellow culms have vertical green stripes. For Hawaii, mildest coastal climates, and well-lit interiors.
Borinda fungosa	Fargesia fungosa	10–12 ft. (15–20 ft.)	II	1 in.	10°F (–12°C)	Graceful, weeping, fountain-shaped. Culms on side facing sun turn rich chocolate brown. Best in light shade or morning sun. Screen or specimen.
Fargesia murielae UMBRELLA BAMBOO	Sinarundinaria murielae	6–8 ft. (to 15 ft.)	II	½ in.	–20°F (–29°C)	Light, airy, tight clump, arching and drooping at top. Best in shade. Select new-generation plants that will not bloom soon.
F. nitida FOUNTAIN BAMBOO	Sinarundinaria nitida	6–8 ft. (15–20 ft.)	II	½ in.	–20°F (–29°C)	Graceful, weeping, fountain-shaped with wide-spreading foliage. Greenish purple culms mature to deep purplish black. Needs shade to look its best. Rare. New culms of 'Jiuzhaigou' are bright red; grows best with morning sun.
F. robusta		12–15 ft. (18–20 ft.)	II	1 in.	–2°F (–19°C)	Lush, upright clumps. Persistent white sheaths create a checkerboard effect on growing culms. Needs some shade in hottest climates. 'Campbell' is compact, with smaller leaves. 'Green Screen' has broader leaves.

BAMBOO: TOP PICKS TO GROW

B

NAME	ALSO SOLD AS	CONTROLLED (UNCONTROLLED) HEIGHT	GROWTH HABIT	STEM DIAMETER	HARDINESS	COMMENTS (FORM, CHARACTERISTICS, USES)
F. rufa		6–8 ft. (12–15 ft.)	II	½ in.	−20°F (−29°C)	Culm sheaths orange-red. Resembles *F. nitida.* Good as specimen, hedge.
Himalayacalamus asper PRINCESS BAMBOO	*H. planatus, Neomicrocalamus microphyllus*	8–10 ft. (15–20 ft.)	II	1½ in.	15°F (−9°C)	Fountain-shaped, forming tight clump. Culms bright green in shade, shiny maroon in sun. Delicate, small leaves. Shade to half-day sun. Good screen or specimen.
H. hookerianus BLUE BAMBOO	*Drepanostachyum falcatum*	10–15 ft. (18–22 ft.)	II	1 in.	20°F (−7°C)	Culms are sky blue with white powder, sometimes developing a reddish blush. Medium-large blue-green leaves. Spectacular specimen plant for partial shade.
Otatea acuminata aztecorum MEXICAN WEEPING BAMBOO	*Yushania aztecorum*	8–10 ft. (15–20 ft.)	II	1½ in.	22°F (−6°C)	Long, narrow leaves give plants a lacy look. Foliage masses bend nearly to ground. Loose clumper; give it room to spread. Fairly drought-resistant when established. Needs some shade in hottest climates. A dwarf form reaches just 4 ft. high.

RUNNING TYPES

NAME	ALSO SOLD AS	CONTROLLED (UNCONTROLLED) HEIGHT	GROWTH HABIT	STEM DIAMETER	HARDINESS	COMMENTS (FORM, CHARACTERISTICS, USES)
Chimonobambusa quadrangularis SQUARE-STEM BAMBOO	*Bambusa quadrangularis*	10–15 ft. (20–25 ft.)	III	1½ in.	15°F (−9°C)	Squarish culms have prominent joints, carry heavy whorls of branches. Valued for vertical effect and cascading leaves. Culms grow in winter.
Indocalamus tessellatus BIG LEAF BAMBOO	*Sasa tessellata*	2–3 ft. (3–7 ft.)	I	½ in.	−17°F (−27°C)	Broad, handsome leaves are up to 2 ft. long, 3–4 ft. wide, and spread like fingers from stem and branch tips. Very shade-tolerant. Rapid spreader. Excellent in containers.
Phyllostachys aurea GOLDEN BAMBOO		6–10 ft. (10–27 ft.)	III	1¾ in.	0°F (−18°C)	Erect, stiff culms, usually with crowded joints at base (a good identifying mark). Dense foliage makes it a good screen or hedge. Can take much drought but looks better with regular water. Good choice for growing in tubs.
P. aureosulcata YELLOW GROOVE BAMBOO		12–15 ft. (15–25 ft.)	III	1½ in.	−10°F (−23°C)	Like more slender, more open *P. aurea.* Young culms green with pronounced yellowish groove. Several forms with different color patterns are available.
P. bambusoides GIANT TIMBER BAMBOO, JAPANESE TIMBER BAMBOO	*P. reticulata*	15–35 ft. (25–55 ft.)	IV	6 in.	−5°F (−21°C)	Once the most common of large, hardy timber bamboos. Many perished during blooming period in 1970s, but vigorous new plants from seed are now available. Makes beautiful groves. Dwarf and variegated forms are sold, some with colorfully striped culms.
P. edulis MOSO	*P. heterocycla pubescens*	40–50 ft. (50–80 ft.)	IV	4–7 in.	0°F (−18°C)	World's largest hardy bamboo, prized for its edible shoots and strong culms. Leaves are small, in contrast with the massive culms, giving a feathery look. Shoots early in spring. Slow to establish. Best in full sun.
P. nigra BLACK BAMBOO		4–8 ft. (10–30 ft.)	III	2 in.	0°F (−18°C)	New culms green, turning black in second year. Where summers are hot, does best in afternoon shade.

»

BAMBOO: TOP PICKS TO GROW

B

NAME	ALSO SOLD AS	CONTROLLED (UNCONTROLLED) HEIGHT	GROWTH HABIT	STEM DIAMETER	HARDINESS	COMMENTS (FORM, CHARACTERISTICS, USES)
P. n. 'Daikokuchiku' GIANT BLACK BAMBOO		25–30 ft. (45–57 ft.)	IV	3⅓ in.	0°F (−18°C)	Identical to *P. nigra* but grows twice as tall and wide. Does well in hot summers.
P. n. 'Hale'		10–15 ft. (15–20 ft.)	III	1½ in.	−5°F (−21°C)	Most culms turn jet black within 3–6 months of emerging, so the entire clump is solid black most of the year.
P. vivax		15–20 ft. (55–70 ft.)	IV	5 in.	−5°F (−21°C)	Hardiest giant bamboo and the quickest to attain large size. 'Aureocaulis' (*P. v. aureocaulis*) has golden yellow culms randomly striped with green. Other forms with multicolored culms are sold.
Pleioblastus chino 'Murakamiansus'		2–5 ft. (6–10 ft.)	I	¾ in.	10°F (−12°C)	Bright green leaves cleanly striped with white. Prune to 2 in. tall in late winter to refresh foliage. Excellent in containers. Looks best with half-day sun.
P. distichus DWARF FERNLEAF BAMBOO	*P. pygmaeus distichus*, *Sasa disticha*	1–2 ft. (2 ft.)	I	⅛ in.	5°F (−15°C)	Delicate in appearance. Tiny, two-ranked ferny leaves. Rampant; cut back to ground if rank or stemmy.
P. fortunei DWARF WHITE-STRIPE BAMBOO	*P. variegatus*	1–2 ft. (2–4 ft.)	I	¼ in.	10°F (−12°C)	Fast spreader; curb rhizomes. Use in tubs or as deep groundcover. Sun or light shade.
P. pygmaeus	*Sasa pygmaea*	2 ft. (2 ft.)	I	⅛ in.	0°F (−18°C)	Aggressive spreader; good bank holder, good for erosion control. Can be mowed every few years to keep it from growing stemmy and unattractive.
P. shibuyanus 'Tsuboi'	*P. variegatus* 'Tsuboi'	3–4 ft. (6–9 ft.)	I	½ in.	0°F (−18°C)	Green foliage striped with light yellow variegation; looks good all year. May be pruned into low groundcover or hedge. Good in pots.
P. viridistriatus DWARF GREEN-STRIPE BAMBOO	*Arundinaria auricoma*, *A. viridistriatus*	1–2 ft. (2–3 ft.)	I	¼ in.	0°F (−18°C)	Leaves 8 in. long, 1½ in. wide; strikingly variegated green and gold. Mow old culms in winter to make room for fresh spring growth. Partial to nearly full shade.
Pseudosasa japonica ARROW BAMBOO	*Arundinaria japonica*	6–10 ft. (10–18 ft.)	III	¾ in.	0°F (−18°C)	Stiffly erect culms with one branch at each joint. Large leaves with long, pointed tails. Rampant thick hedge in mild-winter climates; slow spreader where winters are cold, making dense, erect clumps. Needs partial shade in hottest climates.
Sasa palmata nebulosa		6–8 ft. (10–12 ft.)	I	½–1 in.	−10°F (−23°C)	Tropical appearance, with broad, handsome leaves. Culms green with black spots. Extremely vigorous; good choice for pots. Partial to nearly full shade.
S. veitchii		2–3 ft. (2–5 ft.)	I	¼ in.	−10°F (−23°C)	Rampant spreader with large (7 by 1 in.), dark green leaves that turn whitish buff all around the edges in autumn. Best in partial shade.
Semiarundinaria fastuosa NARIHIRA BAMBOO		8–10 ft. (25–30 ft.)	II or III	1½ in.	−5°F (−21°C)	Rigidly upright growth. Slow spreader easily kept to a clump. Plant close to make narrow, dense hedge or screen. Best in full sun.

regrowth will occur. Starve out any remaining root fragments by cutting off all shoots before they exceed 2 ft. in height; repeat as needed—probably several times over the course of a year. Without leaves to produce energy through photosynthesis, the rhizomes will soon be unable to send up new shoots. To be sure you're getting all of the remaining rhizomes, water and fertilize the area to encourage new shoots. Herbicides, such as glyphosate, have only a temporary effect on bamboo.

The chart lists two heights for each bamboo. Controlled height means average height under drier conditions with little feeding, or with rhizome spread controlled by barriers. Uncontrolled height refers to plants growing under best conditions without confinement. But even within these categories, climate and cultural practices affect eventual heights.

The chart lists hardiness for each type—the temperature at which leaf damage occurs. Stems and rhizomes may be considerably hardier. The chart also classifies each bamboo by the following growth habits, which determine its use.

Group I Dwarf types (5–10 ft. tall) and low-growing groundcover types (1–4 ft. tall) of running bamboos. These bamboos can be allowed to spread for erosion control or contained in small clumps in borders or rock gardens. Cut back in winter to maintain low stature and enhance new growth.

Group II Clumping bamboos with a fountainlike habit of growth and moderate height (10–30 ft. tall). They're noninvasive; useful for screens.

Group III Running types of moderate size (10–30 ft. tall), with more or less vertical growth; they should be contained. Useful for fast-growing screens and hedges.

Group IV Giant bamboos. Use running kinds for groves or for Asian effects on a grand scale. Clumping kinds have a tropical look, especially if they are used with broad-leafed tropical plants. All may be clipped to show off culms. Thin clumps or groves by cutting out old or dead culms at the base.

Banana
Musaceae
PERENNIAL

✏ **FOR ZONES, SEE TEXT**

☼ **FULL SUN**

💧 **AMPLE WATER**

Bananas

This fast-growing plant from Southeast Asia spreads by suckers and underground roots to form clumps 6–10 ft. wide or wider. The trunklike stem is soft and thick. The spectacular broad, long (5–9 ft.) leaves are easily tattered by wind, so plant in a protected spot. Orange-yellow spring flowers on long, drooping stalks are also striking. Attractive near pools.

Fruiting varieties are often grouped botanically under *Musa acuminata*. They are best adapted to Zone H2 in Hawaii and to Zones 21–24 in California, where planting near a warm, south-facing wall often results in sweet fruit. But even in warm microclimates of Zones 15, 16, 19, and 20, gardeners sometimes harvest edible bananas. In Zones 8, 9, 14, and 18, frost usually kills the tops of the plants each year, but the roots resprout in spring and plants are grown as ornamentals. Elsewhere, bananas can be grown in containers as ornamentals and brought indoors in winter. Plantains are bananas that require cooking before eating; most are tall and vigorous.

Dwarf banana varieties are the best bets for home gardens. They mature at about 7–15 ft. high and usually ripen fruit 70 to 100 days after blooming. Look for 'Apple' ('Manzano'), 'Dwarf Brazilian', 'Dwarf Cavendish' ('Chinese'), 'Enano Gigante' ('Dwarf Mexican'), 'Goldfinger', 'High Color Mini' (just 4 ft. high and wide), 'Ice Cream', and 'Williams'.

CARE

Bananas need ample moisture, rich soil, and heavy feeding with a balanced fertilizer like 10-10-10. To harvest quality fruit, let only one or two stalks per clump grow; prune out all others as they emerge. Allow replacement stalks (for next year's fruit) to develop after the fruiting stalks have bloomed. Remove stalks that have fruited. Harvest season is usually late summer into fall, or whenever the fruit at the top of the cluster starts to turn yellow. Cut the whole cluster and ripen at room temperature. If left on the plant, fruit will split and rot.

Banana sap will permanently stain fabric, so wear old clothes when harvesting or pruning. Control ants on banana trees to help prevent scale, aphids, and sooty mold. Plants are easily propagated by division.

For ornamental species, see *Ensete ventricosum* and *Musa*.

Banksia
Proteaceae
EVERGREEN SHRUBS AND TREES

✏ **ZONES 15–24; H1**

☼ **FULL SUN**

💧 **MODERATE WATER**

🦅 **ATTRACT BIRDS AND BENEFICIAL INSECTS**

Banksia spinulosa

Grow these Australian natives for their interesting leaves and showstopping flowers, much prized for arrangements. Leaves are usually long and narrow, sometimes with strikingly saw-toothed edges. The tiny flowers appear in dense round or cylindrical clusters and are followed by long-lasting woody seed cones. Blooms are rich in nectar.

B. ashbyi. ORANGE BANKSIA. Shrub. Grows quickly to 12 ft. tall and at least as wide. The gray-green leaves are 1 ft. long, just over 1 in. wide, with deeply serrated edges. Bright orange flower spikes to 6 in. long appear at branch tips in summer. Good choice for an informal screen or hedge; can take light shearing. Does well in coastal conditions. A dwarf form (to 6 ft. tall) is sometimes offered.

B. baxteri. BIRD'S NEST BANKSIA. Shrub. Erect and spreading growth to 6–10 ft. tall and nearly as wide. Leaves have large, distinctive, triangular lobes. Prolific summer bloomer, with up to 200 yellowish green, dome-shaped, 2–3-in.-wide flowers on a single plant. Grows on coast with protection from salt-laden winds.

B. ericifolia. HEATH BANKSIA. Shrub. A full, bushy plant to 10–20 ft. tall and 6–12 ft. wide, with short, needlelike leaves. In fall and winter, 6–8-in.-tall cylindrical clusters of orange to red flowers are produced. Tolerates coastal conditions. A 6-ft.-tall dwarf form is available.

B. grandis. BULL BANKSIA. Tree. Grows 15–25 ft. tall and 8–10 ft. wide, with deeply cut, dark green leaves and creamy flower spikes like 1-ft.-tall cylinders. Flowers appear in fall, winter, and spring and develop into hard, woody cones that are prized for carving. Dwarf forms to about 6 ft. tall are a better fit for small gardens.

B. integrifolia. COAST BANKSIA. Tree. Grows 30–60 ft. tall, 15–30 ft. wide, with smooth-edged or slightly toothed leaves to 6 in. long and 2 in. wide. Pale yellow flower clusters to 6 in. long appear in fall, winter, and spring. Highly tolerant of coastal conditions.

B. praemorsa. Shrub. Dense and upright plant, to 10–12 ft. tall and about 6 ft. wide, with toothed, blunt-tipped leaves. Cylindrical flower spikes of wine red, up to 1 ft. long, appear in winter, spring, or summer; a yellow-flowered form is sometimes offered. Prefers

B

well-drained soils. Takes windy and coastal conditions. Excellent flowering screen.

B. prionotes. ACORN BANKSIA. Large shrub or small tree. Grows 9–25 ft. tall and wide. Dark green leaves have deeply toothed margins. Cylindrical flower spikes up to 6 in. long at branch tips; orange flowers open from creamy buds.

B. speciosa. SHOWY BANKSIA. Shrub. Grows 12–20 ft. tall and 10–15 ft. wide. Leaves are 8–16 in. long, with strongly toothed edges. Flower cones are 6 in. tall, white opening to yellow in summer and fall.

B. spinulosa. HAIRPIN BANKSIA. Shrub. To 2–4 ft. tall, 4–5 ft. wide. Narrow, medium green leaves are serrated. Cylindrical blossoms, up to 5 in. across, are golden yellow to orange, sometimes with red; blooms fall through winter. One of the easier banksias to grow. 'Schnapper Point' has rich yellow-and-red flowers.

CARE

On level ground, amend heavy clay soil by adding perlite and shredded fir bark. Build a low mound of soil and plant on top. Add a gravel mulch to protect roots. To prevent disease, keep water away from the plant's crown. Plants are subject to root rot fungi and require perfect drainage. Water fairly regularly for the first year or two, then cut back to deep but infrequent irrigation; most banksias can withstand long dry periods. Treat chlorosis with iron chelates. Avoid fertilizers containing phosphorus, as they will kill the plants.

The tree species have no special pruning needs; on shrubs, shorten previous season's growth if needed to limit size, but don't cut into old wood. Banksias show varying tolerance to coastal conditions in California; in Hawaii, humidity is too high for them at sea level, and they are grown at higher elevations.

Banksias need excellent drainage and good air circulation. They grow best on slopes in very well-drained soil.

Baptisia
FALSE INDIGO, WILD INDIGO
Papilionaceae
PERENNIALS

✎ **ZONES 1–24**

☀ **FULL SUN**

💧 **MODERATE WATER**

Baptisia australis

These natives of the eastern and southern U.S., also called false lupine, have deep taproots that enable them to survive difficult conditions, including drought and poor, sandy soils. Their bluish green leaves are divided into three leaflets. Small, sweet pea–shaped blooms appear on tall, tapering spikes in late spring or early summer. Inflated seedpods follow.

Clumps gradually increase but don't need division; they also resent transplanting once established. Remove spent flowers to encourage repeat bloom.

The plant's spiky architectural shape makes it perfect for perennial borders; cluster several as a focal point behind *Artemisia* 'Powis Castle' (silvery gray foliage) and *Veronica repens* 'Sunshine' (golden yellow foliage). Also pretty with pink or yellow roses, or—for a meadow look—with ornamental grasses.

B. alba. WHITE FALSE INDIGO. Upright and bushy, to 3 ft. tall and wide, with white flowers on attractive, smoky gray stems.

B. australis. BLUE FALSE INDIGO. A slightly spreading plant to 3–5 ft. tall, 4 ft. wide, with deep blue flowers.

Bauhinia
ORCHID TREE
Caesalpiniaceae
EVERGREEN, SEMIEVERGREEN, DECIDUOUS TREES AND SHRUBS

✎ **ZONES VARY BY SPECIES**

☀ **FULL SUN, EXCEPT AS NOTED**

💧💧 **MODERATE TO REGULAR WATER**

Bauhinia × blakeana

These flamboyant flowering plants have a special place in Hawaii and mild-winter areas of California and Arizona. They vary greatly by species and climate. Common to all garden bauhinias are twin "leaves," actually twin lobes. Thin crowded growth after bloom.

Bauhinias flower best when grown in wind-sheltered spots in well-drained, semi-fertile soil. Though they thrive in heat, dry heat or drought may cause leaf edges to brown.

B. × blakeana. HONG KONG ORCHID TREE. Partly deciduous for short period. Zones 13, 19, 21, 23, 24; H1, H2. This tree grows into an umbrella shape and reaches 12–20 ft. high and 15–20 ft. wide. It blooms from late fall to spring, with flowers shaped like some orchids; they are much larger (up to 6 in. wide) than those of other bauhinias. Colors range from cranberry maroon through purple and rose to orchid pink, often in the same blossom. Gray-green leaves tend to drop off around bloom time, but the tree does not lose all of its foliage.

B. forficata (B. candicans, B. corniculata). BRAZILIAN BUTTERFLY TREE. Evergreen to deciduous shrub or tree. Zones 9, 12–23. Native to Brazil. Probably the hardiest

bauhinia. Grows to 20 ft. tall and broad, often with twisting, leaning trunk and picturesque angled branches; good canopy for patio. Short, sharp thorns at branch joints. Narrow-petaled, creamy white flowers to 3 in. wide appear from spring into summer. Deep green leaves have more pointed lobes than others. Give some afternoon shade in hot climates.

B. galpinii (B. punctata). RED BAUHINIA. Evergreen to semievergreen shrub. Zones 13, 15, 16, 18–24; H1, H2. Native to South Africa. Sprawling, half-climbing plant to about 10 ft. tall, spreading to 15 ft. Blooms from spring to fall, bearing 3-in.-wide, brick red to orange flowers as spectacular as those of bougainvillea. Best as espalier on warm wall. With hard pruning, it can make a splendid flowering bonsai in a large container.

B. lunarioides (B. congesta). ANACACHO ORCHID TREE. Evergreen to semievergreen shrub or tree. Zones 10–13, 18–23. Native from western Texas into northeastern Mexico. Grows 8–12 ft. high and 4–5 ft. wide, with rounded, very small leaves. White- and pink-flowering forms are available. Begins bloom in early spring and repeats many times over spring and summer. This is an open tree in afternoon shade; it grows bushier in full sun.

B. variegata (B. purpurea). PURPLE ORCHID TREE. Semievergreen to deciduous shrub or tree. Zones 13, 18–24; H1, H2. Hardy to 22°F (–6°C). Native to India, China. The most frequently planted bauhinia, it's inclined to grow as a many-stemmed shrub, but if staked and pruned, it becomes an attractive tree 20–35 ft. tall and wide. A wonderful show of light pink to orchid purple, 2–3-in.-wide flowers usually occurs in winter into spring. Light green, broad-lobed leaves generally drop in midwinter. After bloom, it produces a huge crop of messy-looking beans; trim them off if you wish (trimming brings new growth earlier). This is a spectacular street tree where spring is reliably and steadily warm. 'Candida' is white-blossomed but otherwise identical to the species.

Bean

Papilionaceae

ANNUALS AND PERENNIALS GROWN
AS ANNUALS

✎ **ALL ZONES**

☼ **FULL SUN**

🌢 **REGULAR WATER**

Purple snap beans

Gardeners can choose from many types of beans, the most common of which are described below. Except for the soybean (from eastern Asia) and the fava bean (from the Mediterranean region), beans are New World plants belonging to the genus *Phaseolus*. Most are frost-sensitive heat lovers and are easy to grow from seed. All are annuals except for scarlet runner bean, which is a perennial grown as an annual. Bean flowers are edible.

For more vigorous beans, buy seeds inoculated with *Rhizobium* bacteria, which helps the plants fix nitrogen from the air and store it in their roots. Or buy the inoculant from a nursery or mail-order seed supplier and treat the seeds yourself.

Dry bean. 'Pinto', 'Red Kidney', and 'White Marrowfat' belong to this group. Most are grown until pods turn dry or begin to shatter, but some varieties are best when harvested at the green shelling stage ("shelly beans") and cooked like green limas. These include the flageolet bean (a French favorite) and 'French Horticultural Bean', also known as 'October Bean'. Heirlooms such as 'Aztec Dwarf White', 'Mitla White', and 'New Mexico Appaloosa' were used by Native Americans of the Southwest and are very well adapted to that region. Dry

How to Grow Beans

PLANTING Sow seeds as soon as soil is warm. Plant in loose, open soil so that the heavy seed leaves can push their way through; soil needn't be particularly deep, since beans have shallow roots. Plant seeds 1 in. deep and 1–3 in. apart, allowing 2–3 ft. between rows of all kinds of bush beans. Pole beans need something to climb, and this can be provided in one of the following ways: (1) Set three or four 8-ft. poles in the ground and tie them together at the top in tepee fashion; plant four seeds around the base of each pole, thinning to two plants each. (2) Set single poles 3–4 ft. apart and sow six or eight beans around each, thinning to three or four strongest seedlings. (3) Insert poles 1–2 ft. apart in rows and sow seeds as you would bush beans. (4) Sow seeds along a sunny wall, fence, or trellis, and train vines on a web of light string supported by wire or heavy twine.

WATERING & FEEDING Moisten soil thoroughly before planting beans, then do not water again until seedlings have emerged. Once growth starts, keep soil moist. Fertilize soil after plants are in active growth and again when pods start to form.

PESTS Control aphids, cucumber beetles, spider mites, or whiteflies if they appear. Row covers help with insect control on bush beans; hosing down helps with aphids; use yellow sticky traps for whiteflies.

beans take 70 to 80 days to get to the shelly bean stage, then another 2 to 3 weeks to reach true dry bean stage. Let pods remain on the bush until they turn dry or begin to shatter; then remove beans from the pods, dry the beans, and

store them to soak and cook later as needed.

Fava bean (broad bean, horse bean). This is a cool-season bean (actually a giant vetch, *Vicia faba*), best known and grown in coastal climates. Cook and eat immature pods like edible-pod peas; prepare immature and mature seeds in same way as green or dry limas. Note that a very few people (mainly of Mediterranean ancestry) have an enzyme deficiency that can cause severe reactions to the beans and even the pollen.

Fava beans require different care than the other types described here. In cold-winter areas, plant them as early in spring as soil can be worked; in mild climates, plant in fall for harvest in late winter or early spring. Beans mature in 120 to 150 days. Space rows 1½–2½ ft. apart. Sow seeds 1 in. deep, 4–5 in. apart; thin to 8–10 in. apart. Plants produce bushy growth to 2–4 ft. high.

Lima bean. Like snap beans (which they resemble), lima beans come in either bush or vine (pole) form. They develop more slowly than snap beans—bush types need 65 to 75 days from planting to harvest, pole kinds 78 to 95 days—and do not produce as reliably in very hot weather. Before being cooked, they have to be shelled, a tedious chore but worth it if you like fresh limas.

Scarlet runner bean. Perennial twining vine grown as annual. Showy and ornamental, with slender clusters of vivid scarlet flowers and bright green leaves divided into three roundish leaflets. Use it to cover fences and arbors; it provides quick shade on porches. Pink-and white-flowered varieties exist. Flowers are followed by flattened, very dark green pods that are edible and tasty when young but toughen as they reach full size. Beans are ready in 50 to 80 days, depending on variety. Beans from older pods can be shelled and cooked like green limas.

Snap bean (string bean, green bean). The most widely planted bean type. Tender, fleshy pods, not stringy; may be

green, yellow (wax beans), or purple (these turn green when cooked). Plants grow as self-supporting bushes (bush beans) or as climbing vines (pole beans). Bush types bear earlier, but vines are more productive. Plants look like scarlet runner bean, but their white or purple flowers are not showy. Beans are ready in 50 to 80 days, depending on variety. Pick every 3 to 5 days; if pods mature, plants will stop bearing.

Soybean, edamame. Grown in Asia for millennia, *Glycine max* is a relatively recent arrival in American gardens. Plants grow like bush snap beans, producing short, fuzzy pods. The beans themselves are very high in protein. Plants thrive in warm, humid climates but struggle in dry ones. "Edamame" can refer to shelled green soybeans, to a dish made from cooked whole baby soybeans, or to soybeans generally (the Japanese word means "beans on a branch").

Beaucarnea recurvata

(Nolina recurvata)

BOTTLE PALM, PONYTAIL PALM

Asparagaceae

PERENNIAL

✎ **ZONES 13, 16–24; H1, H2; OR INDOORS**

☼ **FULL SUN, BRIGHT LIGHT**

🌢🌢 **LITTLE OR NO WATER TO MODERATE WATER**

Beaucarnea recurvata

Native to Mexico. To 12–15 ft. tall (possibly to 30 ft. in great age), 9–12 ft. wide. One or more trunks rise from a greatly swollen base. In young plants, the trunk base looks like a big onion

B

sitting on the soil; in old plants, it can measure several feet across. Clusters of bright green leaves arch and droop at ends of branches. Mature outdoor plants may bloom. Does exceptionally well indoors if given bright light and not overwatered.

FOR MORE ON PALMS, SEE "MEET THE PALMS," PAGE 471.

Beaumontia grandiflora

HERALD'S TRUMPET, EASTER LILY VINE
Apocynaceae
EVERGREEN VINE

- ZONES 12, 13, 16, 17, 21–24; H1, H2
- FULL SUN OR PARTIAL SHADE
- REGULAR WATER

Beaumontia grandiflora

This vigorous climber from the Himalayas uses arching, twining branches to reach as high as 30 ft., spreading about as wide. Its large, oval to roundish dark green leaves—smooth and shiny above, slightly downy beneath—give it a lush, tropical look. From spring through summer, it bears fragrant flowers that look like Easter lilies: trumpet-shaped, 5 in. long, green-veined white.

Grow as a big espalier on a warm, wind-sheltered wall or train it along the eaves of the house; sturdy supports are essential, since growth is heavy. Good choice for planting near swimming pools. Plant is hardy to 28°F (–2°C). Frost kills it to the ground, but it usually comes back from the roots.

Does best in well-drained soil enriched with organic matter; regular feeding produces most lavish display of foliage and flowers. Prune after bloom to shape or limit size; flowers are produced on wood 2 years or older, so keep a good proportion of old wood.

Beesia deltophylla

Ranunculaceae
PERENNIAL

- ZONES 4–9, 14–24
- PARTIAL TO FULL SHADE
- REGULAR WATER

Beesia deltophylla

Native to China. Lush-looking and easy to grow, this shade-loving evergreen groundcover reaches 1 ft. high and 1½– 2 ft. wide. Plant forms a dense, spreading rosette of glossy, quilted, heart-shaped leaves with finely toothed margins. Leaves emerge purplish green, age to deep emerald green, and finally take on an appealing metallic blue cast. Resembles wild ginger (*Asarum*) until it blooms in spring or early summer. Slender, erect stems rise 1½ ft. above the foliage to display airy clusters of star-shaped white flowers.

Plant in a woodland garden, along a shaded path, or as a carpet beneath trees.

Grow beesia in borders with other plants that take the same conditions. It contrasts beautifully with the foliage of ferns, hostas, and clivias. Also combines well with other small shade-loving bloomers, including corydalis and cyclamen. Needs rich, evenly moist soil and dappled to full shade. Direct sun will burn the leaves.

Beet

Amaranthaceae
BIENNIAL GROWN AS ANNUAL

- ALL ZONES
- FULL SUN
- REGULAR WATER

Beets

This European native, known botanically as *Beta vulgaris*, is best known for its edible roots, but its tender young leaves are delicious when steamed, sautéed, or chopped and added to salads. Types with round, red roots include old favorites like 'Detroit Dark Red' and newer varieties like 'Early Wonder' and 'Red Ace'. 'Bull's Blood' and 'Big Top' have particularly plentiful, tasty greens. Novelties include 'Cylindra' and 'Rodina' (with long, cylindrical roots) and 'Chioggia' (rings of red and white); there are also varieties with golden yellow or white roots.

CARE

Grow beets in fertile, well-drained soil without lumps or rocks. They grow best in relatively cool weather. In hot-summer climates, sow in early spring or late summer so that plants will mature before extreme heat sets in. In mild-winter areas, you can also plant in late summer for fall and winter harvest. To harvest beets over a long season, sow seeds at monthly intervals, spacing them 1 in. apart; cover them with ¼ in. of compost, sand, or vermiculite. Thin plants to 2 in. apart while small—the thinnings (both tops and roots) are edible. For tender roots, keep soil evenly moist. To thwart insect pests, grow beets under row covers.

Begin harvesting when roots are 1 in. wide, and complete it before they exceed 3 in.; they will be woody if allowed to grow bigger. In cold climates, harvest all beets before hard frosts in autumn.

Begonia

Begoniaceae
PERENNIALS, SHRUBS, TUBERS

- ZONES 14–24, H1, H2, EXCEPT AS NOTED; OR INDOORS; OR DIG AND STORE; OR TREAT AS ANNUALS
- FILTERED SUN; BRIGHT INDIRECT LIGHT
- REGULAR WATER

Begonia 'Richmondensis'

Native to many tropical and subtropical regions worldwide. Begonias are grown for their colorful blooms and textured, multicolored foliage. Outdoors, most grow best in containers in filtered shade. In the ground, they need rich, fast-draining soil, consistent but light feeding, and enough water to keep soil moist but not soggy. Most will also thrive as indoor plants, in a greenhouse, or under a lath. Almost all require at least moderate humidity. In areas with hot, dry summers or indoors in winter, set pots in pebble-lined saucers or trays kept filled with water to below pot level. Most begonias are easily propagated from leaf, stem, or rhizome cuttings.

Of the many hundreds of species and varieties, relatively few are sold widely. Begonia enthusiasts group or classify the different kinds generally by growth habit, which coincidentally groups them by their slightly differing care needs.

Cane-type begonias. They get their name from their stems, which grow tall and woody and have prominent bamboolike joints. The group includes so-called angel-wing begonias. These erect plants have multiple stems, some reaching 5 ft. or more under the right conditions. Most bloom profusely from early spring through autumn, bearing large clusters of white, pink, orange, or red flowers. Some are ever-blooming. Among the many available varieties are 'Bubbles', with spotted foliage and pink, apple blossom–scented flowers; 'Honeysuckle', with plain green foliage and fragrant pink flowers; 'Irene Nuss', with dark red-and-green leaves and huge drooping clusters of coral pink flowers; and 'Orange Rubra', with medium green leaves, sometimes spotted with silver, and bright orange flowers.

When roots fill 4-in. pots, plants can be placed in large containers or in the ground. Position plants where they will get plenty of light, some sun, and no wind. They may require staking. Protect from heavy frosts. Old canes that have grown barren should be pruned back to two leaf joints in early spring to stimulate new growth.

Hardy begonia. Zones 3–24. *B. grandis evansiana* grows from a tuber to 2–3 ft. tall and wide, with branching red stems carrying large, smooth, coppery green leaves with red undersides. Summer flowers are pink or white, carried in drooping clusters. Tops die down after frost. In colder regions, mulch to protect roots.

Hiemalis begonias. May be sold as Rieger begonias or Elatior hybrids. These profuse bloomers are outstanding outdoor or indoor plants. They form bushy, compact mounds to 1–1½ ft. tall and 1 ft. wide. Flowers appear over a long season that includes winter. The 2-in. blooms come in white, yellow, orange, many shades of pink, and red; available in single and double forms. Frinzie series has white or apricot blooms with fringed, red-edged petals. Plants in the Solenia series are vigorous growers with large, full flowers.

Give indoor plants plenty of light in winter. In summer, keep out of hot noonday sun. Water thoroughly when top inch of soil is dry, but don't sprinkle the leaves. Plants may get rangy, an indication of approaching dormancy; if they do, cut stems to 4-in. stubs.

Multiflora begonias. These are essentially small-flowered, profuse-blooming tuberous begonias. They are bushy and compact plants to 1–1½ ft. tall and wide, with profuse bloom in carmine, scarlet, orange, yellow, apricot, salmon, or pink. Includes the popular Nonstop and Pin Up strains. For instructions on care, see "Tuberous begonias" on next page.

Rex begonias. With their bold, multicolored leaves, these are probably the most striking of all foliage begonias. While many named varieties are grown by collectors, easier-to-find unnamed seedling plants are almost as decorative.

The leaves grow from a rhizome; see "Rhizomatous begonias" (below) for care. In addition, rex begonias need high humidity (at least 50 percent) to do their best. Provide it by misting with a spray bottle, placing pots on wet pebbles in a tray, or keeping plants in a greenhouse. When rhizome grows too far past edge of pot for your taste, either repot into slightly larger container or cut off rhizome end inside pot edge. Old rhizome will branch and grow new leaves. Make rhizome cuttings of the piece you remove and root in mixture of half peat moss, half perlite.

Rhizomatous begonias. Like rex begonias, these grow from a rhizome. Although some have handsome flowers, they are grown primarily for foliage, which varies widely in shape, color, and texture among species and varieties. Among the dozens of species and varieties in this group is the old favorite *B. masoniana*, called iron cross begonia; its large, puckered green leaves have a chocolate brown pattern resembling a Maltese cross.

Rhizomatous begonias perform well as houseplants: give them bright light and water only when the top inch or so of soil

is dry. Plant them in wide, shallow pots. They flower from winter through summer, the season varying among specific plants. White to pink flowers appear in clusters on erect stems above the foliage. Rhizomes will grow over edge of pot, eventually forming a ball-shaped plant; if you wish, cut rhizomes back to pot. The old rhizome will branch and grow new leaves. Root the pieces of rhizome in mixture of half peat moss, half perlite.

Semperflorens begonias. Sometimes called fibrous, bedding, or wax begonias, these are probably the most widely grown types. Dwarf (6–8 in.) and taller (10–12 in.) strains are grown in garden beds or containers like annuals, producing lots of small flowers in the white-through-red range. Plants bloom from spring through fall; they're used as a winter annual in hottest-summer climates. Foliage can be green, red, bronze, or variegated. In mild-winter climates, they can live for years (especially if divided each spring). They thrive in full sun in cool-summer regions and prefer broken shade in hotter climates

CLOCKWISE FROM TOP: Tuberous begonia; semperflorens begonia; rex begonia

(but dark-foliaged kinds will take sun there if well watered). The popular, bronze-leafed Cocktail series includes 'Brandy' (light pink blooms), 'Gin' (rose-pink), 'Rum' (pink-edged white), 'Vodka' (scarlet), and 'Whiskey' (white).

Shrublike begonias. This large class is marked by multiple stems that are soft and green rather than bamboolike. They are grown for both foliage and flowers. The leaves are very interesting—some are heavily textured; others grow white or red "hairs"; still others develop a soft, feltlike coating. Most grow upright and bushy, but others are less erect and are well suited to hanging baskets. Flowers in shades of pink, red, white, or peach can come at any time, depending on species or variety.

Outstanding examples include fern-leaf begonia (*B. foliosa*), with inch-long leaves packed tightly on a twiggy plant

B

for a fernlike look. Its long, drooping stems hold small white flowers nearly year-round in mild weather. Fuchsia begonia (sold as *B. fuchsioides* or *B. foliosa miniata*) has delicate stems to 2½ ft. tall, with dangling rose-pink to rose-red flowers that resemble fuchsias. The sturdy, sun- and wind-tolerant 'Richmondensis' can reach 2½ ft. tall and 3 ft. wide, with arching red stems and shiny, deep green leaves with red undersides. Its vivid pink to crimson or white flowers develop from darker buds nearly year-round.

Care consists of repotting into a larger container as the plant outgrows its pot. Water when soil begins to dry on surface. Prune to shape; pinch tips to encourage branching.

Trailing or climbing begonias. These have stems that trail or climb, depending on how you train them. They bloom sporadically during warm weather and are well suited to hanging basket culture or planting in the ground where well protected. They need conditions similar to those for tuberous begonias, though trailing types are not lifted for storage. Examples include hybrid 'Potpourri', with strongly scented deep pink flowers, and one of its parents, *B. solananthera*, with glossy light green leaves and fragrant white flowers with red centers. *B. glabra* has trailing stems to 3 ft. long, with heart-shaped, bright green leaves and profuse white flowers in winter and spring.

Tuberous begonias. Best in Zones 4–6, 15–17, 21–24, and H1; possible in 7–9, 14, 18–20 with attention to humidity. Among the best-known begonias in the West are these large-flowered hybrids that grow from tubers. They range from plants with saucer-size flowers and a few upright stems to multistemmed hanging-basket sorts covered in blossoms. Almost all bloom in summer or fall. Strains are sold as hanging or upright. The former bloom more profusely; the latter have larger flowers. Colors include almost everything but blue; shapes are frilly (carnation), formal double (camellia), and tight-centered (rose). Some have

petal edges in contrasting colors (picotee). Popular strains include Double Trumpet (improved rose form), Prima Donna (improved camellia), and Hanging Sensation. *B. boliviensis*, to 1 ft. tall and 2 ft. wide, with narrow, pointed leaves and orange flowers, is a parent of many hybrids in the tuberous group. Look for 'Bertini', with deep orange-red blooms; 'Bonfire', with bright orange-red blooms; and 'Bellfire', with dark purple leaves and coral blooms.

Most gardeners grow tuberous begonias in containers. You can buy small plants each year in early spring and plant them out in pots—but it's cheaper to buy dormant tubers (the bigger the better) in midwinter. Set them in pots filled with a rich, humusy soil mix, indented side up; cover them with no more than ¼ in. of mix. Place pots in a well-lit spot (but not in direct sun) where temperatures stay above 65°F (18°C); keep soil moist but not saturated during the rooting period. When the tubers have produced two leaves, move them outside, weather permitting (night temperature must remain above 50°F/10°C).

Locate young plants in filtered shade, such as under a lath, or in an open area that gets morning sun. Water enough to keep soil moist but not soggy. For best bloom, mist with water several times a day unless you live in a cool or foggy area. Begin feeding with liquid fertilizer a week or two after plants reach the two-leaf stage. For largest possible blooms, use a half-strength solution every other week, but monthly regular-strength feedings yield fine plants. Watch for fuzzy white spots on leaves; these signal powdery mildew.

When leaves begin to yellow and wilt in autumn, gradually reduce watering and stop fertilizing. When leaves fall off, lift tubers, shake off soil, and dry in a cool, dry spot for several days. Then store in a cool, dry place such as a shed or garage until spring; when small pink buds appear, plant the tubers once again.

Belamcanda chinensis
BLACKBERRY LILY
Iridaceae
PERENNIAL FROM RHIZOME

❀ **ZONES 1–24**

☀ ◐ **FULL SUN OR PARTIAL SHADE**

💧 **REGULAR WATER DURING GROWTH AND BLOOM**

Belamcanda chinensis

Native to East Asia; forms fans of sword-shaped leaves from slowly creeping rhizomes. The plants are pretty when clustered in the middle of a summer border; their zigzag, 3–4-ft. stems bear sprays of yellow-orange flowers dotted with red. Each flower has six equal petals and lasts only a day, but new blossoms keep coming.

After blooms fade, mature seed capsules split open to expose shiny black seeds that look like blackberries (hence the plant's common name); use stems in dried arrangements.

CARE

Set rhizomes 1 ft. apart, with tops just beneath the soil surface. Plant in fall everywhere except Zones 1–3, where bulbs should be planted in spring and dug up in fall for overwintering indoors. Divide infrequently for best show.

FOR MORE ON PERENNIALS, SEE "GROW: PERENNIALS," PAGES 686–687.

Bellis perennis
ENGLISH DAISY
Asteraceae
PERENNIAL OFTEN TREATED AS ANNUAL

❀ **ZONES 1–9, 14–24; ANYWHERE EXCEPT HAWAII AS ANNUAL**

☀ ◐ **LIGHT SHADE IN HOTTEST CLIMATES**

💧 **REGULAR WATER**

🐝 **FLOWERS ATTRACT BEES**

Bellis perennis

Native to Europe and Asia Minor, these tiny daisies grow so well in lawns that they've become a mainstay of flowering turf blends. Plump, double varieties sold as bedding plants are intended for edging or bedding out, either alone or with bulbs.

Dark green, 1–2-in.-long leaves form rosettes to 8 in. wide. Pink, rose, red, or white flowers rise on 3–6-in. stems in spring and summer; bloom is longest where weather is cool and flowers are deadheaded. Some can be grown from seed, but other sterile varieties only by division.

English daisies make beautiful underplantings for tulips: try light pink– and white-flowered kinds beneath pink tulips. Or, in low bowls, surround these daisies with Irish moss.

Beloperone guttata.
See *Justicia brandegeeana*

Berberis

BARBERRY
Berberidaceae
EVERGREEN, SEMIEVERGREEN,
AND DECIDUOUS SHRUBS

✎ ZONES VARY BY SPECIES

☼ ◑ FULL SUN OR LIGHT SHADE,
EXCEPT AS NOTED

◊ ◕ ● LITTLE TO REGULAR WATER

🐦 BERRIES ATTRACT WILDLIFE

Berberis thunbergii atropurpurea
'Rose Glow'

These dense, spiny-stemmed relatives of our Western native *Mahonia* are easy to grow, and thrive in climate and soil extremes (especially the deciduous kinds). But some have landed on invasive plant lists in parts of Canada and New England, and are on watch lists in the West. Choose sterile and low-fertility varieties, especially among Japanese barberries. Most make attractive hedges. Informal style is best for species grown for spring flowers (yellow, unless otherwise noted) and berries that follow—borne on previous year's growth.

B. darwinii. DARWIN BARBERRY. Evergreen. Zones 5–9, 14–24. Hardy to 10°F (–12°C). Very showy barberry from Chile. Fountainlike growth to 5–10 ft. tall, 4–7 ft. wide with dark green, hollylike leaves. Orange-yellow flowers are so thick that foliage is hard to see; profuse dark blue berries are popular with birds.

CLOCKWISE FROM LEFT: *Berberis thunbergii atropurpurea* 'Cherry Bomb'; *B. t. atropurpurea*; *B. t.* 'Limeglow'

Spreads by underground runners; may be invasive along coast.

B. × gladwynensis 'William Penn'. Evergreen, but drops some leaves below 10°F (–12°C). Zones 3b–24. Resembles *B. julianae* but has broader, glossier leaves and grows faster and more densely to 4 ft. tall and 4–6-ft. wide. Good display of spring flowers and bronzy fall color that shades to yellow and purple.

B. julianae. WINTERGREEN BARBERRY. Evergreen to semievergreen. Zones 4–24. Hardy to 0°F (–18°C), but foliage is damaged by cold. Chinese native. Can take full shade. Dense, upright, to 6–8 ft. tall and nearly as wide; angled branches. Spiny-toothed, dark green, leathery leaves to 3 in. long; red to burgundy fall color. Blue-black berries. Among the spiniest barberries, it makes an impenetrable hedge.

B. koreana. Deciduous. Zones 1–9, 14–17. Hardy to –35°F (–37°C). Korean native grows erect to 4–6 ft. and not quite as wide. Dense medium to dark green leaves that turn orangey purple in fall. Fragrant flowers in drooping, 3–4-in. clusters, bright red fruit.

B. linearifolia 'Orange King'. Evergreen. Zones 6–9, 14–24. Hardy to 0° to 10°F (–18° to –12°C). This variety of a Chilean species has an open growth habit to 5 ft. tall and wide, with narrow, glossy, 2-in. leaves. Short clusters of deep orange flowers; bluish black fruit.

B. × mentorensis. Evergreen or deciduous hybrid of *B. julianae* and *B. thunbergii*. Zones 2–24. Hardy to –20°F (–29°C) but loses some or all leaves below 0°F (–18°C). Compact growth to 7 ft. tall and wide. Dark green, 1-in.-long leaves turn a beautiful red in fall where winters are cold. Few or no berries. Easy to maintain as a hedge at any height. Tolerates hot, dry weather.

B. microphylla 'Pygmaea' (B. buxifolia 'Nana'). Evergreen. Zones 4–9, 14–24. Hardy to 0°F (–18°C). Grows 1½ ft. high, 2 ft. wide; makes a good hedge or rock garden plant. Purple fall berries follow spring flowers. Tolerates salt spray.

B. × stenophylla. ROSEMARY BARBERRY. Evergreen. Zones 4–9, 14–24. Hardy to 0°F (–18°C). Leaves narrow, ½–1 in. long, with rolled-in edges and spiny tip. Species

is 10 ft. tall, 15 ft. wide. 'Corallina Compacta', called "coral barberry," grows 1½ ft. high and wide and bears nodding clusters of bright orange flowers and bluish black fruit; effective as foreground plant. 'Irwinii', to 4–5 ft. tall and wide, resembles a compact-growing *B. darwinii*.

B. thunbergii. JAPANESE BARBERRY. Deciduous. Zones A3; 2b–24. Hardy to –20°F (–29°C), these widely sold barberries have a graceful habit with slender, arching, spiny branches; 4–6 ft. tall and wide. Roundish, ½–1½-in.-long leaves are deep green above, paler beneath; leaves turn yellow, orange, and red before they fall. Beadlike bright red berries stud branches in fall and winter. Use as hedge, barrier, or specimen. The following are among many grown for vivid foliage.

'Aurea'. Bright golden yellow foliage. Full sun where it's mild, part shade in hottest climates. Slow growing to 2½–3 ft. tall and wide. Sets few or no seeds.

'Golden Nugget'. Dwarf selection reaching 1½ ft. tall and wide, with golden leaves sometimes tinged orange. Good sun tolerance. Sets few or no seeds.

»

B

'Kobold'. Extra-dwarf green variety. Like 'Crimson Pygmy' in habit but fuller and rounder.

'Limeglow'. Grows 5 ft. tall, slightly less wide. New growth lime green against darker green mature foliage. Doesn't sunburn. Red-orange fall color.

'Sparkle'. Eventually to 5 ft. tall and 6 ft. wide, with rich green foliage that turns vivid yellow, orange, and red in fall.

'Sunsation'. Compact, upright to 3–4 ft. tall and wide. New growth is greenish gold, maturing to bright golden yellow. Sets few or no seeds.

B. t. atropurpurea. RED-LEAF JAPANESE BARBERRY. This group contains plants with leaves in the red to purple-red range. All develop most intense color in sun.

'Bagatelle'. Similar to 'Crimson Pygmy' but with smaller, glossier, deeper red-purple leaves and a narrower shape; 1½–2 ft. tall and wide. Sets few or no seeds.

'Cherry Bomb'. Like 'Crimson Pygmy', but 4 ft. tall, with larger leaves and more open growth. Regular water.

'Concorde'. Grows 18 in. tall and wide, produces maroon purple leaves that go red in fall; small flowers, red berries.

'Crimson Pygmy' ('Atropurpurea Nana'). The most widely sold Japanese barberry, this grows 1½–2 ft. high and 2½–3 ft. wide. New leaves are bright red, mature to bronzy blood red. Sets few or no seeds.

'Golden Ring'. Grows 3 ft. tall and wide. Reddish purple leaves with a thin green or golden green border.

'Golden Ruby'. Dwarf selection reaching 2 ft. high and wide. Leaves open coral, then turn purple-red with golden margins. Sets few or no seeds.

'Helmond Pillar'. Columnar form grows 6 ft. tall, 2 ft. wide, with reddish purple foliage. Sets few or no seeds.

'Pygmy Ruby'. Grows 1½ ft. high, 3 ft. wide, with deep red foliage. Sets few or no seeds.

'Rose Glow'. To 4–6 ft. tall and wide. New foliage marbled bronzy red and pinkish white, deepening to rose and bronze with age.

'Royal Cloak'. Compact, mounding to 4 ft. high and at least as wide. Large, dark purple-red leaves.

B. verruculosa. WARTY BARBERRY. Evergreen. Zones 4–9, 14–24. Hardy to 0°F (–18°C). Native to China. Tailored-looking. Will reach 5 ft. tall and wide but can be kept to 1½ ft. Perky 1-in.-long leaves glossy dark green above, whitish beneath. Black berries and occasional red leaves in fall, winter. Choice and effective on banks. Tolerates a wide range of poor soils.

B. wilsoniae. WILSON BARBERRY. Deciduous to semievergreen. Zones 6–9, 14–24. Hardy to 5°F (–15°C). Native to China. To 6 ft. tall and wide, but can be held to 3–4 ft. Light green, roundish, ½–1-in. leaves have a fine-textured look. Coral to salmon-red berries; a handsome barrier hedge. 'Ace' grows 2 ft. tall, 5 ft. wide; gray-blue leaves with blush.

CARE

Each year, thin out oldest wood and prune to shape—after bloom for evergreen and semievergreen types, late in the dormant season for deciduous kinds. Species grown for foliage can be sheared. To rejuvenate overgrown or neglected plants, cut to within a foot of the ground before spring growth begins.

Bergenia
Saxifragaceae
PERENNIALS

🌡 **ZONES A1–A3; 1–9, 12–24; EXCEPT AS NOTED**

◑ ● **PARTIAL OR FULL SHADE**

◊ **MODERATE WATER**

Bergenia 'Lunar Glow'

Native to Himalayas and mountains of China, bergenias are evergreen except in coldest areas. They are favored for rosettes of big green leaves,

hardiness, early bloom. Foliage clumps usually reach 12 to 18 in. high, with nodding clusters of pink, white, or red flowers on thick stalks that rise above the leaves. These plants lend a strong textural quality to borders and plantings under trees, make a bold groundcover. Effective with ferns, hellebores, or hostas and as foreground planting for Japanese aucuba, rhododendrons, Japanese aralia.

B. ciliata (B. ligulata). FRILLY BERGENIA. Zones 5–9, 14–24. Choice, but more tender than others: foliage and flowers damaged in hard frosts, but plant will survive 0°F (–18°C). Lustrous light green, nearly round leaves to 1 ft. across, smooth-edged but fringed with soft hairs; bronzy when new. White, rose, or purplish flowers.

B. cordifolia. HEARTLEAF BERGENIA. Glossy, roundish leaves are heart shaped at base, with wavy, toothed edges. Bears rose or lilac flowers in pendulous clusters. 'Autumn Glory' leaves go maroon in fall; flowers tend to rebloom. 'Morning Red' ('Morgenrote') has bronzy-toned leaves, dark red flowers. 'Tubby Andrews' has leaves splashed with golden yellow; flowers are pink. 'Winterglut' ('Winter Glow') has bright red flowers and leathery green leaves that turn reddish bronze in fall and winter.

B. crassifolia. WINTER-BLOOMING BERGENIA. Dark green leaves, to 8 in. or more across, have wavy, sparsely toothed edges. Rose, lilac, or purple flowers in dense clusters on erect stems that stand well above leaves. Blooms between midwinter and early spring, depending on climate.

B. hybrids. Some of the best are of English or German origin.

'Abendglut' ('Evening Glow'). Dark red flowers and dark reddish leaves with crimped edges.

'Bressingham Ruby'. Rose-red blooms rise over green leaves that turn bronzy purple in winter.

'Bressingham White'. White flowers.

'Dragonfly'. Small (10 in. tall), narrow-leafed plant with pink blooms, purple-tinged winter leaves.

'Herbstblute' ('Autumn Glory'). Leaves turn purplish in fall, when it also tends to rebloom.

'Silberlicht' ('Silver Light'). Large, slightly toothed leaves and white blossoms.

CARE

Bergenias tolerate neglect, poor soil, and some drought, but do better in good soil with regular watering, feeding, and grooming. Sun-tolerant where summers are cool. Plant 1½ ft. apart. Cut back yearly to prevent legginess. Divide crowded clumps in late winter or early spring. Control snails and slugs.

Berlandiera lyrata
CHOCOLATE FLOWER
Asteraceae
PERENNIAL

🌡 **ZONES 10–13, 18–23; ANYWHERE AS ANNUAL**

☼ **FULL SUN**

◊ ◐ **LITTLE TO MODERATE WATER**

Berlandiera lyrata

Native to the northern Chihuahuan Desert, this rounded, somewhat coarse-foliaged plant grows 1½–3 ft. high and wide. Yellow daisies with maroon-and-green centers appear in spring and summer, sometimes into fall. Blooms smell like chocolate; fragrance most intense in morning. Once seed heads form, shear lightly to encourage more blooms. Native Americans used the flower heads to flavor foods; they dry well for winter bouquets. Sow seeds in place at any time. Thrives in clay soil.

Beschorneria yuccoides

MEXICAN LILY, AMOLE
Asparagaceae
PERENNIAL

✂ ZONES 13, 16–17, 19–24

☀ ◑ PARTIAL SHADE IN HOTTEST CLIMATES

◊ ◉ LITTLE TO MODERATE WATER

🦅 ATTRACTS HUMMINGBIRDS

Beschorneria yuccoides

This Mexican native looks like a yucca, with rosettes of 2-ft.-long, 2-in.-wide gray-green leaves that are soft and spineless. Clumps increase slowly by offsets to eventually reach 3–4 ft. wide. In early summer, a thick coral pink stalk rises to 3–7 ft., its many pink branches hung with bell-shaped, yellow-tinted green flowers in yellow bracts. Thrives in well-drained garden soil or large container; suffers in cold, wet earth. 'Flamingo Glow' has yellow striped leaves, green flowers.

Mexican lily is especially striking when loosely clustered in a dry bed with a mulch of decomposed granite. The flowers may not bloom every year, but the plant is sculptural enough to carry the show. Remove spent leaves and flower stalks to keep it tidy.

Betula

BIRCH
Betulaceae
DECIDUOUS TREES

✂ ZONES VARY BY SPECIES

☀ FULL SUN

◉ REGULAR WATER

🦅 ATTRACTS BIRDS, BUTTERFLIES

Betula utilis jacquemontii

Ornamental birches have been dominated by European white birch, beloved for its tall, white-barked trunk, weeping side branches, and fine-toothed leaves. But other birches have recently gained popularity for superior bark color, heat tolerance, and resistance to birch borer. Most are shapely, with papery peeling bark and foliage that turns from green to yellow in fall; then delicate structure, handsome bark, and small conelike fruits carry them through winter.

B. albo-sinensis. Zones 3–11, 14–24. Native to western China. Large tree (to 100 ft. tall, 30 ft. wide) grown chiefly for pinkish brown to coppery bark that's covered with a powdery gray bloom. Oval leaves. *B. a. septentrionalis* has flaking, orange to orange-brown bark.

B. nigra. RIVER BIRCH, RED BIRCH. Zones 1–24. Native to stream banks and lowlands in eastern North America. Very fast growth in early years; eventually becomes a pyramidal tree 50–90 ft. tall, 40–60 ft. wide. Trunk often forks near ground, but the tree can be trained to a single stem. Young bark pinkish, smooth, shiny; on older trees, bark flakes and curls in cinnamon brown to blackish sheets. Diamond-shaped leaves are bright glossy green above

with silvery undersides. This is the most trouble-free birch. 'Dura-Heat' resists bronze birch borer and is more compact and heat-tolerant than the species. 'Heritage' is an excellent selection that has lighter-colored bark and resists bronze birch borer. 'Summer Cascade' is the first weeping birch that resists birch borer. Grows to 15 ft. tall and 20 ft. wide.

B. occidentalis (B. fontinalis). WATER BIRCH. Zones A3; 1–7. Native to stream banks from Alaska to Oregon, east to Colorado. Shrubby; usually grows 12–15 ft. tall and wide. Smooth, shiny, cinnamon brown bark. Ovate leaves.

B. papyrifera. CANOE BIRCH, PAPER BIRCH. Zones A1–A3; 1–6. The most widely distributed North American birch, this grows from New England to Washington State. Similar to *B. pendula* but larger (to 50–90 ft. tall and half as wide), with larger leaves (to 4 in. long) that are less densely borne; habit is more open, less weeping. More resistant to borer, leaf miners. Creamy white bark peels off in papery layers. 'Renaissance Reflection' has a more upright, oval shape.

B. pendula. EUROPEAN WHITE BIRCH. Zones A2, A3; 1–12, 14–24. Native from Europe to Asia Minor. Delicate, lacy appearance. Upright main branches, weeping side branches. This matures at 30–40 ft. tall and half as wide. Golden brown bark on twigs and young branches contrasts with mature white bark, which is marked with black clefts. Oldest bark (at base of tree) is blackish gray. Glossy, rich green leaves are diamond shaped, with a slender, tapered point. Often sold as weeping birch, although trees vary somewhat in habit, and young trees show little inclination to weep. Very susceptible to borer attack. Following are a few of the varieties offered.

'Crimson Frost'. This hybrid between *B. pendula* 'Purpurea' and an Asian birch has burgundy leaves whose color persists all season. Somewhat borer resistant.

'Laciniata' ('Dalecarlica'). CUTLEAF WEEPING BIRCH. Graceful, open tree with strongly

weeping branches, deeply cut leaves. Sunburns in hot, dry weather.

'Purple Rain'. This purple-leafed variety holds its color all summer.

'Trost's Dwarf'. To 3 ft. tall and wide. For bonsai, container, rock gardens. Needs excellent drainage.

'Youngii'. YOUNG'S WEEPING BIRCH. Decorative, dome-shaped tree with slender branches that hang straight down. Stake to desired height; branches then hang from that point. To 15 ft. tall, 20 ft. wide. Sunburns in hot, dry weather.

B. platyphylla japonica (B. mandshurica japonica). JAPANESE WHITE BIRCH. Zones 1–11, 14–24. Native to Japan. Fast growth to 40–50 ft. tall, about half as wide; open habit. White bark. Glossy green, diamond-shaped leaves to 3 in. long. 'Dakota Pinnacle' is narrower than the species, very upright.

B. populifolia 'Whitespire'. Grows 30–40 ft. tall and only 15 ft. wide; borer-resistant.

B. utilis jacquemontii (B. jacquemontii). HIMALAYAN BIRCH. Zones 3–11, 14–17. Native to northern India, this tall, narrow tree has the most brilliant white bark of any birch. Grows about 2 ft. a year to 40 ft., then more slowly to an eventual 60 ft. tall, 30 ft. wide. Some borer resistance.

CARE

All birches need regular moisture and nutrients. Don't plant them over a patio or parking area, since they are susceptible to aphids that drip sticky honeydew. Bronze birch borer can be a problem in the northern Rocky Mountain states; leaf miners in the Pacific Northwest. Prune established trees only to remove weak, damaged, or dead growth. To minimize sap bleed, prune in summer or early fall in mild-winter areas; where temperatures remain below freezing, wait until the end of January. To avoid providing entry points for pests and diseases, don't make unnecessary or large cuts. If birch borer is present locally, don't prune while it is active (check timing with your Cooperative Extension Office).

B

B

Bidens ferulifolia
Asteraceae
PERENNIAL

⚡ **ZONES 16–24; ANYWHERE AS ANNUAL**

☀ **FULL SUN**

◐ ◑ **LITTLE TO MODERATE WATER**

⚘ **ATTRACTS BEES, BUTTERFLIES**

Bidens ferulifolia
'Goldilocks Rocks'

Native to southern U.S., Mexico, and Guatemala; named varieties have more compact or relaxed habit and bigger flowers than the 3-by-3-ft. species. Effective as fillers and spillers in containers and borders. Bright green leaves are divided into thread-like segments. Flower heads are bright golden yellow, with a light honey fragrance. There are many named varieties, from 7 to 24 in. tall and wide, in mounded, spreading, and trailing versions. A representative sampling is listed here.

'Golden Eye'. Mounded, 10–12 in. tall and slightly wider.

'Goldilocks Rocks'. Mounded, to 14 in. tall and wide.

'Namid Compact Yellow'. Mounded, 7 in. tall, 16 in. wide.

CARE

Plants bloom almost continually during mild weather and tolerate heat. If they clamber or sprawl over their neighbors, just cut them back; they recover quickly.

FOR OTHER PLANTS THAT ATTRACT BUTTERFLIES AND BEES, SEE THE "PLANT FINDER," PAGES 100 AND 104.

Bignonia capreolata
CROSSVINE
Bignoniaceae
EVERGREEN OR SEMIEVERGREEN VINE

⚡ **ZONES 4–9, 14–24**

☀ ◑ **FULL SUN OR LIGHT SHADE**

◉ ◉ **MODERATE TO REGULAR WATER**

⚘ **ATTRACTS HUMMINGBIRDS**

Bignonia capreolata

Vigorous and showy, this woody Southern native can climb to 60 ft. by tendrils and holdfast disks, attaching itself to almost any surface. Each shiny, dark green leaf consists of two 2–6-in. leaflets and a branching tendril. Leaves turn purplish in cold weather, and some drop in coldest zones. Clustered, 2-in., trumpet-shaped reddish brown to orange or scarlet flowers appear in midspring, with intermittent summer bloom. 'Dragon Lady' has rich red blooms. 'Jekyll' has slightly smaller flowers that are yellow on the inside, orange on the outside. 'Tangerine Beauty' is a bright orange-red selection. The genus *Bignonia* once included many more vines with trumpet-shaped flowers, but taxonomists have moved them into *Campsis, Clytostoma, Distictis, Macfadyena,* and *Pyrostegia.*

CARE

Do any thinning or cutting back before spring growth begins. Crossvines can spread agressively by stolons. Crossvines are especially pretty when cloaking a sturdy trellis over an entry gate. Or train them over arbors.

Billbergia
Bromeliaceae
PERENNIALS

⚡ **ZONES 12, 13; 14 AND 15 WITH PROTECTION; 16–24; H1, H2; OR INDOORS**

◐ **FILTERED SUN; BRIGHT INDIRECT LIGHT**

◉ **REGULAR WATER**

Billbergia nutans

These exotic-looking South American pineapple relatives grow in rosettes of stiff, spiny-toothed evergreen leaves and produce drooping clusters of showy bracts and tubular flowers that are excellent for cutting. In the wild, they grow as epiphytes on trees, but wherever they're hardy, they're often planted under trees as an easy groundcover, or used in borders. Elsewhere, grow them in containers for display indoors or on patios. To grow them on limbs of trees or bark slabs, first wrap roots in sphagnum moss and leaf mold.

B. nutans. QUEEN'S TEARS. Common and easily grown. Narrow, spiny green leaves are 1½ ft. long. Spikes of rosy red bracts; drooping flowers with green petals edged deep blue. Vigorous. Easily propagated from offsets.

B. pyramidalis. Leaves to 3 ft. long, 2½ in. wide, with toothed margins. Flowers with red, violet-tipped petals and bright red bracts in dense spikes 4 in. long.

B. sanderana. Leaves are leathery, spiny-toothed, dotted with white, grow to 1 ft. long. Produces loose, nodding, 10-in.-long clusters of flowers with blue petals that are yellowish green at the base; blue-tipped sepals, rose-colored bracts.

CARE

Grow in well-drained soil; or pot in a light, porous mixture of sand, ground bark, and leaf mold. Need regular moisture during active growth in warm weather; reduce water as weather cools and growth slows. Plants usually hold water in the funnel-like center of the leaf rosette, which acts as a reservoir. Houseplants need warmth and lots of light. Increase by cutting suckers from base of plant. Bromeliad specialists list dozens of varieties.

Bismarckia nobilis
BISMARCK PALM
Arecaceae
PALM

⚡ **ZONES 19–24**

☀ **FULL SUN**

◐ ◑ **LITTLE TO MODERATE WATER**

Bismarckia nobilis

From Madagascar, these palms grow 30 to 40 ft. tall, come in blue and green forms. The fan-shaped fronds are each up to 10 ft. wide, making a round leaf crown about 25 ft. wide. The blue form is better inland because it's more tolerant of heat and cold, while the frost-intolerant green form excels along the coast.

Grow Bismarck palm where its low, stout trunk and shapely canopy can show off —in rows along a driveway, or as an accent in a lawn.

Blackberry

Rosaceae

BERRY-PRODUCING VINES OR CANES

🖊 **ZONES VARY BY VARIETY**

☼ **FULL SUN**

💧 **MODERATE TO REGULAR WATER**

'Black Satin' blackberries

Most blackberry varieties are derived from *Rubus* species native to North America. The West has its own, mostly trailing varieties of blackberries; these include 'Boysen', 'Logan', 'Marion', and 'Olallie', often simply called "boysenberry," "loganberry," and so on. Midwestern and Eastern blackberries are upright and stiff caned, generally hardier and easier to protect in winter (with a thick mulch) than trailing types. Crosses between trailing and erect blackberries are termed semierect. For ornamental relatives, see *Rubus*.

All kinds of blackberries bear fruit in summer, and a couple of everbearing varieties fruit in fall.

Some of the varieties available in Western nurseries are listed below. Combine early, midseason, and late varieties to get fresh fruit over the longest possible season.

'**Arapaho**'. Erect; midseason. Zones 1–24. Thornless, disease-resistant. Big crop of medium-size, firm, tasty berries. 'Apache', 'Navaho', and 'Oauchita' are similar thornless varieties; 'Chickasaw', 'Choctaw', 'Kiowa', and 'Shawnee' are also similar but have thorns. All thrive in hot-summer climates and are easy to grow without a trellis.

'**Black Satin**'. Erect; midseason. Zones 1–24. Thornless hybrid, possibly of *R. laciniatus*. Very large, juicy, and sweet.

Heavy producer; nonsuckering. Good disease resistance.

'**Boysen**' and '**Thornless Boysen**'. Trailing; midseason. Zones 2–24; not reliably hardy in Zone 1, but will survive winter if canes are left on ground and covered with snow or straw mulch. Popular for high yield and flavor. Propagated from a plant collected at the abandoned farm of Rudolph Boysen in 1923, this fruit put Knott's Berry Farm on the map. Very large berries are reddish, soft, and sweet-tart; have a delightful aroma; and can be used fresh, cooked, or frozen. Covered with a dusty bloom that slightly dulls color. 'Nectar' is identical.

'**Brazos**'. Erect; early. Zones 4–24. Disease-resistant Texas variety well adapted to hot-summer areas. Large, fairly firm, tart fruit.

'**Cherokee**'. Erect; early. Zones 1–24. Thorny. Medium-large, firm berries with excellent flavor. Resists anthracnose.

'**Chester**'. Semierect; late. Zones 2–9, 14–24. Thornless. Medium-size, firm berries with good flavor. Late ripening, greatly extending season. Very cold-tolerant.

'**Dirkson**'. Semierect; midseason. Zones 2–9, 14–24. Thornless. High yield of large, semitart berries. Resistant to anthracnose, leaf spot, and powdery mildew.

'**Evergreen**' and '**Thornless Evergreen**' (*R. laciniatus*). Trailing; late. Zones 4–6, 8, 9, 12, 13, 20–24. Strong canes bear heavy crop of large, exceptionally firm, black, sweet berries with large seeds. Leaves are divided into fives, then cut again into ferny subdivisions. Canes can last for years, thus "evergreen." Like Himalayan blackberry, 'Evergreen' is often seen along roadsides.

Himalayan blackberry (*R. armeniacus*). Trailing, midseason. Zones 1–6, 8–9, 12–24. Native to Armenia, this species grows anywhere moisture is available. An aggressive spreader, it is hard to control and should be kept out of gardens (it's illegal to grow in Oregon). Nevertheless, its fruit is so tasty that roadside colonies are often picked clean. Because road crews sometimes control weeds with toxic herbicides,

How to Grow Blackberries

PLANTING Blackberries need deep, well-drained soil and regular moisture throughout the growing season. Rows of all kinds should be 10 ft. apart. Plant trailing blackberries 5–8 ft. apart, erect blackberries 2–2½ ft. apart, and semierect blackberries 5–6 ft. apart. Container-grown blackberries can go in any time, but bare-root stock adapts to soil more quickly. Plant in winter or spring.

In cold-winter climates, cover crowns with 1 in. of soil. Some varieties can be grown in the desert—for best results, amend soil generously with organic matter. Water regularly, mulch heavily, and protect from wind and intense afternoon sun.

PRUNING & TRAINING Blackberry roots are perennial, but the canes are biennial: they develop and grow one year, bloom and fruit the next. Hence the need to distinguish first- and second-year canes. 'Prime Jan' and 'Prime Jim' are exceptions. They yield two crops per season and have their own pruning regime.

Trailing and semierect types should be allowed to grow unrestricted the first year. The second year, train year-old canes fanwise onto a trellis; after harvest, cut to the ground all canes that have fruited. Canes of the current season—those growing beneath the trellis—should now be trained onto it. By midsummer, thin trailing varieties to 12–16 canes, pruning each to 6–8 ft. long; thin semierect types to 4–8 canes, pruning each to 5–6 ft. long. These shortened canes will produce side branches during remainder of growing season; cut them back to 1 ft. in early spring. New spring growth will produce small fruiting branches from those side branches.

Erect types don't need support, but tying them to wire helps organize the canes. In midsummer of the

first year, cut the canes of all kinds (except 'Prime Jan' and 'Prime Jim') to 2½ ft. in midsummer to force side growth. Late in the dormant season, cut resulting side branches to 12–15 in. After canes bear fruit in the second year, cut them to ground. Start the process over with new canes growing from the ground.

'Prime Jan' and 'Prime Jim' produce their first berries in fall on the top third of each first-year cane, and the second crop the following summer on the bottom two-thirds of each second-year cane. Pruning is done in stages. After the fall harvest, cut off upper (just-harvested) portion of each cane; after the subsequent summer harvest, cut out the remainder of each cane that has fruited.

CHALLENGES Blackberries are subject to many pests and diseases, including scale, borers, anthracnose, leaf spot, and powdery mildew, so avoid the temptation to get starts from your neighbor and buy healthy plants from a reputable supplier. Also look for resistant varieties. Because they are susceptible to verticillium wilt, do not plant blackberries where potatoes, tomatoes, eggplant, or peppers have grown in prior 3 years. To control red-berry mite (mostly affecting 'Evergreen' and 'Thornless Evergreen'), spider mites, and whitefly, apply a dormant spray in winter and again as buds are about to break. A new pest, spotted-wing drosophila (a vinegar fly), makes tiny holes over sunken areas in ripe fruit. So far, the only control is to completely cover plants with fine netting.

Fertilize established plantings in the Pacific Northwest at blossom time. In California, split the yearly amount into three applications: before new growth starts, in mid-spring, and in midsummer. Elsewhere, fertilize just before new growth begins (rapidly swelling buds will tip you off).

B

pick fruit only from healthy canes well away from the road.

'Logan' and 'Thornless Logan'. Trailing; early. Same climate adaption as 'Boysen'. Probably a hybrid of Pacific dewberry (*R. ursinus*) and raspberry (*R. idaeus*). Large berries are light red, not darkening when ripe, with fine hairs that dull the fruit's color. More tart than 'Boysen'; excellent for canning and pies.

'Marion'. Trailing; midseason. Zones 4–9, 14–24. Rich, flavor-ful fruit sets the standard, but thorny canes can grow 10 ft. in a season. Control plants by pruning and trellising. 'Marion' types include 'Black Diamond', a thornless variety; late-ripening 'Waldo', with berries that main-tain their shape when cooked; and 'Black Butte', 'Silvan', and 'Siskiyou', all early ripeners with excellent flavor.

'Olallie'. Trailing; early. Zones 4–9, 14–24. About one-third raspberry, two-thirds blackberry, this variety's berries are medium to large, shiny black, and firm, with a sweet flavor that has some wild blackberry sprightliness.

'Prime Jan'. Erect; everbear-ing. Zones 4–6, 16, 17. Fruits on new canes in late summer and 2-year-old canes in spring. Very productive. Medium-size, sweet-tart berries. 'Prime Jim' is similar.

'Tay' or 'Tayberry'. Trailing; early. Zones 4–9, 14–24. Hybrid between blackberry and raspberry. Long, thorny canes. Heavy bearer of big, mild-flavored, dark red to purple-black fruit. Bears earlier than most other blackberries.

'Triple Crown'. Semierect; late. Zones 1–9, 14–24. An improved 'Chester' type with large, very flavorful berries. Vigorous canes. Hardy. 'Hull' is similar, not as tasty.

'Young' and 'Thornless Young'. Trailing; midseason. Climate adaptation same as for 'Boy-sen' but not as productive in all climates. Berries are same size and color as 'Boysen' but shiny and somewhat sweeter.

Blakella papuana.
See *Eucalyptus papuana*

Blechnum
Blechnaceae
FERNS

🌿 **ZONES VARY BY SPECIES**

◑ ● **PARTIAL OR FULL SHADE**

💧 **REGULAR WATER**

Blechnum spicant

This group includes tree ferns, a groundcover, and a rather for-mal Northwest native. All dislike overhead watering when air is humid or still.

B. brasiliense. Zones 19, 21–24. Native to Brazil, Peru. This dwarf tree fern reaches 4 ft. tall, 5 ft. wide. Its nearly erect fronds grow in compact clusters; reddish when young. 'Crispum' fronds are elegantly ruffled.

B. gibbum. Zones 19, 21–24; H1, H2. This dwarf tree fern from Fiji has a 3-ft.-wide crown of fronds atop a slender 3-ft. trunk. 'Moorei' has wider, more leathery leaflets and is more attractive in winter.

B. penna-marina. Zones 15–17, 20–24; with overhead protection (trees, for example) in Zones 4–6. Native to South America, New Zealand, Aus-tralia. Rhizomes spread slowly in cool, moist, sheltered places to make patches of refined-looking, 4–8-in. fronds. Sterile fronds have wider lobes than fertile ones.

B. spicant. DEER FERN. Zones 2b–7, 14–19, 24. Native primarily to coastal forests of Northern California and the Northwest. This glossy deep green fern grows 1–3 ft. tall, 3 ft. wide. It has two different kinds of fronds: spreading, sterile ones to 1¾ in. wide; and narrower, stiffly erect fertile ones, with slender, widely spaced leaflets.

Bletilla striata
(B. hyacinthina)
CHINESE GROUND ORCHID
Orchidaceae
TERRESTRIAL ORCHID

🌿 **ZONES 2B–9, 12–24**

◑ **PARTIAL SHADE**

💧 **REGULAR WATER DURING GROWTH AND BLOOM**

Bletilla striata

A natural companion to ferns and wildflowers, Chinese ground orchid is native to China, Japan, and Tibet. In spring, up to a dozen pinkish purple, 2-in.-wide, blossoms resembling those of *Cattleya* appear on each 1–1½-ft. stem. Bloom lasts about 6 weeks. Pale green leaves, three to six to a plant, remain attractive into early fall. 'Alba' is a white-flowered form. 'Mura-saki Shikibu' has bluish laven-der flowers. *B. s. albostriata* bears light pink blossoms above leaves striped in green and white.

CARE

Grow in containers or in moist (but not waterlogged), humus-rich woodland soil. Plant dor-mant pseudobulbs from late fall to early spring, positioning tops 1 in. below soil surface (2 in. below in colder regions) and 1 ft. apart. Mulch if tempera-tures will drop below 20°F (–7°C). Protect leaves from slugs and snails. Reduce water-ing when foliage begins to yellow in fall; discontinue when leaves die. Forms large clumps that can be divided in early spring, before growth starts. (However, blooms best when crowded.)

Blueberry
Ericaceae
DECIDUOUS SHRUBS

🌿 **ZONES VARY BY TYPE**

☀ **FULL SUN**

💧💧 **REGULAR TO AMPLE WATER**

Blueberries

Good fall color, tasty summer fruit, and manageable size are enough to earn blueberries a place in almost any garden. These eastern North America natives thrive under conditions that suit rhododendrons and azaleas, to which they are related; for ornamental species in the same genus, see *Vaccinium*.

Grow blueberries as individ-ual plants, in containers, or as hedges or shrub borders. Leaves, to 3 in. long, are bronze when new, maturing to dark green, turning scarlet or yellow in fall. Tiny, urn-shaped spring flowers are white or pinkish; blue fruit follows in summer. Most kinds need chilly winters and cool, moist, well-drained acid soil (pH 4.5–5.5), though some new hybrids, noted below, are adapted to milder climates.

Highbush blueberries. These are the blueberries found in grocery stores. Most varieties grow upright to 6 ft. or more; a few are rather sprawling and under 5 ft. The majority are Northern varieties (*Vaccinium corymbosum* selections; Zones 2–9, 14–17): they require defi-nite winter cold and ripen fruit from late spring to late summer. The Southern highbush hybrids (*V. darrowii* × *V. corymbosum*; Zones 8, 9, 14–24) are better adapted to mild-winter climates and are even finding success in Southern California; their fruit

How to Grow Blueberries

Blueberries are available bare-root or in containers. Plant at least two varieties for better pollination, choosing kinds that ripen at different times for a long harvest.

PLANTING For sufficient fruit throughout the season, allow two plants for each household member.

Set plants 4–5 ft. apart, or 3 ft. apart for an informal hedge. Blueberries also grow well in half wine barrels filled with acidic potting mix.

Plant in early spring in cold-winter regions, fall in mild climates. Position the crown so that it is no deeper than ½ in. below the ground. Blueberries have fine roots near the soil surface; keep them moist, but don't subject them to standing water.

A 3–4-in.-thick organic mulch will protect roots, help conserve soil moisture, and keep weeds down. Don't disturb roots by cultivating around plants.

FEEDING Use acid-forming fertilizers. California growers in particular may need to correct chlorosis in blueberries with iron sulfate or iron chelate.

PRUNING Pruning prevents overbearing. Plants shape themselves but often produce so many fruit buds that the berries are undersize and plant growth slows down. Keep first-year plants from bearing by stripping off flowers.

On older plants, cut back ends of twigs so that fruit buds are widely spaced. Or simply remove some of the oldest branches each year. Also remove weak shoots.

CHALLENGES Birds love blueberries; use netting to protect your ripening crop.

ripens in mid- to late spring, even before rabbiteye types. Except as noted, varieties below are Northern types.

'Berkeley'. Midseason. Open, spreading, tall. Large, light blue berries.

'Bluecrop'. Midseason. Erect, tall growth. Large berries. Excellent flavor. Attractive shrub.

'Blueray'. Midseason. Vigorous, tall. Large, highly flavored, crisp berries. Attractive shrub. Tolerates more heat than 'Bluecrop'.

'Bountiful Blue'. Midseason. Grows 3–4 ft. tall and wide with blue-green foliage. Low chill requirement makes it successful in Southern California.

'Chandler'. Midseason to late. Tall, upright. Very large, sweet berries produced over a long season.

'Darrow'. Late. Vigorous, upright. Very large fruit, up to the size of a quarter. Heavy producer.

'Earliblue'. Early. Tall, erect. Large, heavy leaves. Large berries of excellent flavor.

'Elliott'. Late. Tall, upright. Medium to large berries of excellent flavor.

'Emerald'. Southern highbush. Early. Upright, vigorous shrub with large, high-quality berries. Very low chilling requirement.

'Jubilee'. Southern highbush. Early. Tall, upright. Medium to large berries with excellent flavor.

'Legacy'. Late. Unusual shrub that doesn't lose its leaves in winter. Will color in cold winters, but stays mostly green in mild areas. Upright, arching. Medium-size berries with fine flavor.

'Misty'. Southern highbush. Very early. Large berries with excellent flavor. Bears heavily.

'Olympia'. Midseason. Medium-size fruit with exceptional, spicy flavor. Large, vigorous, arching bush with great autumn color.

'O'Neal'. Southern highbush. Very early. Large, flavorful fruit.

'Patriot'. Early. Extra-large, sweet fruit.

'Pink Champagne'. Blush pink fruit.

'Pink Lemonade'. Southern highbush. Midseason to late. Fruit ripens pink, has a mild, sweet-tart flavor. Grows 5 ft. high and wide.

'Rubel'. Early to late. Erect, tall growth. Small, firm, tart berries.

'Sharpblue'. Southern highbush. Early to midseason. Large, fast-growing shrub. Large, light blue berries with sweet-tart flavor.

'Southmoon'. Southern highbush. Midseason. Large, bright blue berries with excellent flavor.

'Spartan'. Early. Heavy bearer of large, flavorful fruit.

'Sunshine Blue'. Southern highbush. Midseason. Compact, evergreen, attractive; 3 ft. high. Large, light blue berries with tangy flavor. Self-fertile. Very low chilling requirement. Tolerates higher soil pH than most other blueberries.

'Toro'. Midseason. Compact plant with pinkish blooms. Large, firm berries with an excellent, sprightly flavor.

Rabbiteye blueberries.

Zones 8, 9, 14–24. These heat-tolerant selections of *Vaccinium virgatum* (*V. ashei*) are native to the southeastern U.S. and can be grown in Southern California and other mild-winter areas if given acid soil conditions. Often taller (4½ to 12 ft.) and rangier than highbush plants, they ripen large, light blue berries from May to July. Keep size in check with pruning. 'Bluebelle' and 'Southland' are best for eating; use 'Tifblue', whose quality is only fair, as a pollinator.

Hardy half-high varieties.

Zones A2, A3; 1–3. Highbush blueberries have been hybridized with the northeastern U.S. native lowbush blueberry (*Vaccinium angustifolium*) to create very hardy types called "half-high blueberries."

'Chippewa'. Midseason. Slightly larger plant than 'Northblue'. Large, light blue fruit with excellent sweet flavor.

'Northblue'. Midseason to late. To 3–4 ft. high. Large, firm, dark blue berries with trace of wild blueberry flavor.

'Northcountry'. Early midseason. Less than 3 ft. tall. Sweet, very light blue berries. Good choice for containers.

'Northsky'. Midseason to late. Densely branched, to 1–1½ ft. high. Light blue berries with hint of wild blueberry flavor. Good in containers.

'Polaris'. Early. To 4 ft. tall; upright, arching. Light blue fruit with delightful flavor.

'St. Cloud'. Early. To 3–4 ft. tall. Large, firm, flavorful berries.

'Tophat'. Midseason. Dwarf hybrid that stays under 1½ ft.; good for pots. Small fruit with mild flavor.

Boltonia asteroides
Asteraceae
PERENNIAL

✏ **ZONES 1–24**

☼ ◑ **FULL SUN OR LIGHT SHADE**

🌢 **REGULAR WATER**

Boltonia asteroides latisquama
'Jim Crockett'

These small daisies top tall plants that work well at the middle or back of the late-summer perennial border. Native to the eastern U.S., they bear yellow-centered white to blue flowers that resemble Michaelmas daisies (*Aster novi-belgii*). With regular moisture, they reach 6 ft. or taller, 3 ft. wide.

'Pink Beauty' has pink flowers. *B. a. latisquama* 'Snowbank' is more compact (to 5 ft. tall) and upright than the species, with larger, whiter flowers. 'Jim Crockett' grows 21 in. tall, 15 in. wide, with blue flowers. 'Nana', with lavender-pink blooms, reaches 2 ft. high.

Cluster several boltonias at the back of a border for a spatter-paint effect.

B

B

Borago officinalis
BORAGE
Boraginaceae
ANNUAL

🌿 **ZONES A2, A3; 1–24; H1**

☀️ ◐ **FULL SUN OR PARTIAL SHADE**

◐ 💧 **LITTLE TO MODERATE WATER**

🐝 **ATTRACTS BEES**

Borago officinalis

Delightful sky-blue, star-shaped flowers make this European native a kitchen-garden favorite. Plants grow 2–3 ft. high, 1½–2 ft. wide. Bristly gray-green leaves are edible, taste like cucumbers. Flowers appear in leafy clusters on branched stems in summer.

Tolerates poor soil. Seeds itself, but deep taproot prevents easy transplant. Sow seeds in place in spring after frost danger is past. Use small, tender leaves in salads; you can also pickle them or cook them as greens. Cut flowers for arrangements, in salads, or as a garnish. Borage has been used in herbal medicine for centuries.

Borage is one of our favorite summer blues. Its sky-colored, star-shaped blooms don't just look cool—they also taste cool, with a flavor similar to cucumbers. Drop the edible flowers into iced drinks, green salads, and fruit compotes.

Borinda. See Bamboo

Boronia
Rutaceae
EVERGREEN SHRUBS

🌿 **ZONES VARY BY SPECIES**

☀️ ◐ **FULL SUN OR LIGHT SHADE**

💧 **REGULAR WATER**

◊ **AT LEAST ONE CAN CAUSE DERMATITIS**

Boronia megastigma
'Jack Maguire's Red'

Clouds of small, fragrant flowers, mostly in the pink-white-mauve range, cover these relatively short-lived Australian shrubs in season. Finely divided leaves give the plant a wispy look.

B. 'Carousel'. Zones 15–17, 19–24. Upright growth, 4–6 ft. tall, with aromatic leaves. Covered with pink flowers that age to red in late spring.

B. clavata. HEATHER WAND. Zones 15–17, 19–24. Compact growth to 4–6 ft. tall and wide, with small, aromatic, light green leaves and lightly scented, greenish yellow flowers in spring. Best in partial shade. Useful, fragrant screen.

B. crenulata. Zones 16–24. To 2–3 ft. tall, 3–4 ft. wide, with tiny dark green leaves and small pink flowers in late winter and spring. 'Rosy Splendor' is more upright (3–4 ft. tall and 2–3 ft. wide), with flowers held on longer stems. 'Shark Bay' is a compact (to 3 ft. tall, 4 ft. wide) selection with licorice-scented leaves, pink flowers that appear all year, peaking from winter to early summer.

B. denticulata. Zones 15–17, 20–24. To 3–8 ft. tall, 1½–4 ft. wide, with strongly aromatic leaves that can cause

dermatitis. Flowers in mauve, pink shades, or more rarely white, in late winter and spring; sporadic bloom otherwise.

B. heterophylla. RED BORONIA. Zones 16–24. Dense grower to 6–8 ft. tall, 4–6 ft. wide, with finely cut foliage and profuse, intensely fragrant, deep pink flowers opening from red buds in late winter and spring.

B. megastigma. BROWN BORONIA. Zones 15–17, 20–24. Only 1–2 ft. tall and wide, with nodding, ½-in., bell-shaped brown to deep red flowers with yellow interior; winter bloom. Powerful, pleasant scent combines freesia, orange blossom, and other fragrances. Count on replacing plant every 2 or 3 years from seed or cuttings. Lasts longer grown in light potting mix in containers. 'Jack Maguire's Red' has deep orange-red blooms.

CARE

Plants need light, well-drained, slightly acid soil. Never let roots become completely dry or stay wet for long. Prune lightly after bloom to promote bushiness and rejuvenate plant.

Bougainvillea
Nyctaginaceae
EVERGREEN SHRUBBY VINES

🌿 **ZONES 12–17, 19–24; H1, H2**

☀️ **FULL SUN**

◐ 💧 **MODERATE TO REGULAR WATER**

Bougainvillea 'Thai Delight'

Bougainvilleas impress gardeners with brilliant colors, exuberant growth, and daunting thorns. But these tender South American natives also come in thornless versions and shrubby,

dwarf varieties that make perfect patio plants. All are reliably hardy in Zones 22–24, H1, H2, yet widely and satisfyingly grown in areas of minimum frost: Zones 12–17, 19, 21. In other zones, container-size types can be purchased in full bloom, displayed on patios and decks, and moved to a protected area over winter. Where frosts are routine (as in Zones 12, 14, 19–21), vines need a protected warm wall or warmest spot in garden. If vines get by first winter or two, they will be big enough to take most winter damage and recover. In any case, young plants bloom so readily that replacement is not a real deterrent.

Bougainvillea's vibrant colors come from the large, papery, petal-like bracts that surround the insignificant true flowers. Bloom reaches its peak in summer, but in mildest-winter regions, flowers may appear from spring through fall, and even into winter. Most flowers are singles; doubles are also available, but they can look messy when they don't drop faded blooms. White- and yellow-flowered varieties need light shade in hottest climates.

Vining bougainvilleas are fast, vigorous growers, reaching 15–30 ft., depending on variety. Long, needlelike thorns arm stiff stems that are moderately to densely clothed in medium green, 2½-in., heart-shaped leaves.

The following are tall-growing vines unless otherwise noted.

White 'Mary Palmer's Enchantment' is a vigorous, large-growing vine with pure white bracts. Thornless 'Singapore White' ('Miss Alice') is shrubby and compact, easily kept to 3–4 ft. high and wide. Bracts of 'White Madonna' are pure white.

Yellow to orange 'Bambino Baby Sophia' is orange, grows just 5 ft. tall. 'California Gold' ('Sunset') blooms young, with deep golden yellow bracts. 'Delta Dawn' has green-and-white variegated foliage, golden yellow flowers. 'Gold Rush' is fast growing, gold-colored. 'Orange King' is an open grower with bronzy orange bracts; it needs long summers to bloom well and cannot take frost.

TOP ROW: *Bougainvillea* 'Barbara Karst'. MIDDLE ROW: *B.* 'Bambino Baby Sophia'; *B.* 'Mary Palmer's Enchantment'. BOTTOM ROW: *B.* 'Rosenka'; *B.* 'Orange Ice'

Pink 'Camarillo Fiesta' has bracts in a blend of hot pink and gold. Double-flowered 'Cherry Blossom' sports rose-pink bracts with white to pale green centers. 'Rosenka' can be held to shrub proportions if occasional wayward shoots are pruned out; gold bracts age to pink. Thornless 'Singapore Pink' ('Silhouette') has bright pink bracts; shrubby and compact, it can easily be kept to 3–4 ft. high and wide. 'Tahitian Maid' ('Los Banos Beauty') offers extra rows of blush pink bracts that give a double effect. Choice, vigorous 'Texas Dawn' has large sprays of bracts in purplish pink. Unlike other bougainvilleas, 'Torch Glow' ('Bangkok Red') grows erect to form a multistemmed plant to 6 ft. tall that needs no support; its reddish pink flowers are held close to stems and are partially hidden by foliage.

Red Vigorous 'Barbara Karst' blooms young and for a long period, bearing bracts that are bright red in sun, bluish crimson in shade; it thrives in desert heat and comes back fast after frost. Vigorous, sprawling 'Crimson Jewel' is good in containers or as a shrubby bank cover, with lower growth and brighter crimson color than 'Temple Fire'; it blooms heavily over a long season. 'La Jolla,' with bright red bracts, has a compact, shrubby habit that makes it a good shrub or container plant. 'Manila Red' has many rows of magenta-red bracts for heavy clusters of double-looking blooms. 'Oo-La-La' is dwarf (1½ ft. tall, 6–8 ft. wide) with magenta-red bracts over a long season; it makes a good ground or bank cover or hanging basket plant. Hardy 'Raspberry Ice' ('Hawaii') is shrubby and mounding (good in hanging baskets), with red bracts and yellow-edged leaves that are tinged red when new. 'San Diego Red' is one of the best on all counts, with large, deep green leaves that hold on well in cold winters; deep red bracts that appear over a long season; and hardiness equal to that of old-fashioned purple bougainvilleas. Vigorous and high climbing, it can be trained to tree form by staking and pruning. 'Temple Fire' offers shrub-like growth to 4 ft. high, 6 ft.

wide on a partially deciduous plant; bracts are bronze-red.

Purple 'Don Mario' is a large, vigorous vine with huge clusters of deep purple-red bracts. Compact 'Purple Queen' sports deep purple bracts on vines that can reach 15 ft. with support; as a trailer, it grows 1½ ft. tall, 6–8 ft. wide. 'Tahitian Dawn' is a big vine with gold bracts that age to rosy purple. 'Vera Deep Purple' produces neon pink flowers on a thornless dwarf plant 2 ft. tall and wide; perfect for indoor containers. Hardy and vigorous *B. spectabilis* (*B. brasiliensis*) 'Lavender Queen' has big purple bracts and blooms heavily, even in cool summers (good choice for Zones 16, 17).

How to Grow Bougainvilleas

PLANTING In areas that typically have frosts, plant in early spring after danger of frost has passed. Vines are superb on walls and sturdy fences, trellises, arbors. Because they have no means of attachment (though the thorns help them scramble through shrubs and trees), you must tie stems to the support while basic structure is establishing.

PRUNING Do any major pruning after flowering has ceased (in frost-free regions) or as early as possible in spring after frost danger has passed (in other regions). During growing season, prune as needed to direct growth. Wear puncture-proof gloves, or pruning will be bloody work.

Heavily pruned vines and shrubby varieties make good self-supporting container plants for terrace or patio. Without support and with occasional corrective pruning, bougainvillea becomes a broad, sprawling shrub, bank or groundcover, or hanging-basket plant.

B

Bouteloua
GRAMA GRASS
Poaceae
PERENNIAL GRASSES

- ✂ **ZONES 1–3, 7–11, 14, 18–21**
- ☼ **FULL SUN**
- ◊ **LITTLE WATER**

Bouteloua gracilis

Once the food of buffalo on North America's short-grass prairies, these tough, heat- and drought-tolerant clumping grasses have narrow, gray-green leaves. Their oddly attractive flowering stems carry their summer flowers on one side only. One or a few plants are pretty in a border; en masse, they create natural meadows. Grow from seed or division.

B. curtipendula. SIDE-OATS GRAMA. Native from Canada to Argentina. To 1–2 ft. tall, 2 ft. wide. Flowering stems vary from arching to nearly horizontal, with purple-tinted green flowers dangling underneath. These, like the leaves, turn yellow in fall, then white in winter.

B. gracilis. BLUE GRAMA, MOSQUITO GRASS. To 1½–2 ft. high, 1 ft. wide. Inflorescences recalling hovering mosquitoes hang perpendicular to stems. Reddish in summer, they bleach to white. Tolerates sunny, arid, alkaline conditions in the High Plains and Rocky Mountains under 6,500-ft. elevation. 'Blond Ambition' has chartreuse flowers on 2½–3 ft. stems, fades to blond. Mow at 1½ in. high for a fair native lawn in low-traffic areas. Sow seed at 1–3 lb. per 1,000 sq. ft. in fall to take advantage of winter rain and snow. Irrigate to depth of 1 ft. until established; thereafter, it needs no irrigation.

Bouvardia
Rubiaceae
EVERGREEN SHRUBS

- ✂ **ZONES VARY BY SPECIES**
- ◑ **PARTIAL SHADE**
- ◊ ◕ **WATER NEEDS VARY BY SPECIES**
- 🐦 **ATTRACT HUMMINGBIRDS**

Bouvardia longiflora 'Albatross'

Pretty clusters of four-petaled tubular flowers appear on relaxed, 2–3-ft.-high plants. One type has fragrant blossoms, but it is also the most tender and looks poorest after flowers are gone. The unscented red-flowered species are hardier and easier to grow. All appreciate well-drained soil and midday shade. To encourage compact growth, prune hard annually after bloom period ends.

B. glaberrima. Zones 8–10, 12, 14–24. Native to mountain canyons in southern Arizona and New Mexico, this shrubby plant grows to 3 ft. tall and wide, with smooth, green, 1–3 in. leaves and clusters of 1-in., red (rarely pink or white), unscented flowers. Top growth dies back in cold weather. Needs little water.

B. longiflora 'Albatross' (B. humboldtii 'Albatross'). Zones 12, 16, 17, 19–24. These jasmine-scented, 3-in., snow-white flowers appear at almost any time; excellent in bouquets. This Mexican native is 2–3 ft. high and 2 ft. wide, with paired 2-in. leaves. Pinch out stem tips to make it bushier. If soil is poor, grow in large containers or raised beds in rich, fast-draining soil mix. 'Stephanie' is more compact and floriferous. Regular water.

B. ternifolia (B. jacquinii). Zones 8–10, 12, 14–24. Native to Texas, Mexico. To 3 ft. tall, 2½–3 ft. wide; 2-in. leaves in whorls of three or four. Unscented, inch-long red flowers in loose clusters at branch ends in summer and early fall. Forms have pink, rose, or coral blossoms. Little water.

Brachychiton
Malvaceae
EVERGREEN AND PARTLY OR WHOLLY DECIDUOUS TREES

- ✂ **ZONES VARY BY SPECIES**
- ☼ **FULL SUN**
- ◊ ◕ **LITTLE TO MODERATE WATER**

Brachychiton discolor

Depending upon variety, these Australian trees are grown for their spectacular flowers, swollen trunks, beautiful leaves, or the woody, canoe-shaped fruits that litter gardens and delight flower arrangers. Grow in well-drained soil. These form strong central leaders; require minimal pruning.

Blooming pattern and leaf drop in the two deciduous species listed here can be erratic. Young trees often bloom only in sectors rather than all over; those parts will drop their leaves while nonblooming areas retain their foliage. Older trees tend to be covered with bloom, dropping all their leaves before flowers appear. Bloom is best after a dry winter.

B. acerifolius (Sterculia acerifolia). FLAME TREE, AUSTRALIAN FLAME TREE. Briefly deciduous. Zones 15–24; H1, H2. Hardy to 25°F (–4°C). At its best, this spectacular red-flowering tree reaches 60 ft.

tall, 30 ft. wide, with a strong, smooth trunk, usually green. Glossy bright green leaves are maple-like, 10 in. wide, with long center lobes. Showiest bloom usually comes in late spring or early summer, when all or part of tree is covered with clusters of small, tubular red or orange-red bells.

B. discolor (Sterculia discolor). QUEENSLAND LACE-BARK, PINK FLAME TREE. Briefly deciduous. Zones 15–24. To 40–60 ft. tall; pyramidal in youth but more spreading (to about 30 ft.) in maturity. Ornamental bottle-shaped trunk. Leaves, only 6 in. wide, are narrower than those of *B. acerifolius* and are blue-green on top, whitish underneath. Leaves on young trees are deeply lobed; lobes become shallower as tree ages. Large, bell-like, deep rose-pink flowers appear in summer, then carpet the ground under the tree. Blossoms and subsequent fruit are densely covered with rusty wool on outside.

B. populneus (Sterculia diversifolia). BOTTLE TREE. Evergreen. Zones 12–24. Moderate growth to 30–50 ft. tall, 30 ft. wide. Common name refers to heavy trunk of mature trees, which is broad at base, tapering toward top. Fresh green leaves shimmer in the breeze like those of aspens. Clusters of small, bell-shaped white flowers in late spring only noticeable close up. Appreciated in low and intermediate deserts, where it is frequently used as a shade tree and as a screen or high, wide windbreak. Susceptible to Texas root rot.

B. rupestris (Sterculia rupestris). QUEENSLAND BOTTLE TREE. Evergreen. Zones 13, 21, 23, 24; hardy to 20°F (–7°C). To 25 ft. tall, 15 ft. wide, often much smaller. Leaves on young trees are deeply lobed (like fingers of a hand); on mature trees they are undivided. Though it has small, yellowish flowers, the tree is grown for its swollen, bottle-shaped trunk; it can eventually measure 5–6 ft. in diameter. Young plants confined to containers often produce grotesquely twisted trunks.

The Daisy Clan

Brachyglottis and *Brachyscome* are both members of Asteraceae—the largest family of flowering plants in the northern hemisphere. Among their thousands of "cousins" are asters, blue marguerite, euryops, gloriosa daisy, purple coneflower, sunflower, and creeping zinnia. Some daisies are low mounding annuals or perennials; others are woody shrubs. But what all these species have in common are the flowers: ray florets (petals) surrounding a tight disk-like cluster of smaller flower heads.

Brachyglottis 'Sunshine' is especially pretty beside purple-foliaged plants such as redleaf Japanese barberry (*Berberis thunbergii atropurpurea*) or smoke tree (*Cotinus coggygria* 'Royal Purple'). Grow Swan River daisies in pots and as border edgings.

Brachyglottis Dunedin Group 'Sunshine'
(B. greyi, Senecio greyi)
Asteraceae
EVERGREEN SHRUB

🗡 **ZONES 5–9, 14–24**

☼ **FULL SUN**

◊● **MODERATE TO REGULAR WATER**

Brachyglottis 'Sunshine'

So often called *Senecio greyi* that this has nearly become its common name. This classic gray-leafed plant grows 4–5 ft. high, 6 ft. or more wide. Stiff, slightly curving stems bear leathery gray-green leaves outlined in silvery white. In summer, it produces a profusion of inch-wide yellow daisies in flattish, 5-in.-wide clusters.

Prune out oldest growth yearly. Cut branches last long in arrangements.

Brachyscome
SWAN RIVER DAISY
Asteraceae
ANNUALS AND PERENNIALS

🗡 **ZONES VARY BY SPECIES**

☼ **FULL SUN**

◊● **MODERATE TO REGULAR WATER**

🦋 **ATTRACT BUTTERFLIES**

Brachyscome iberidifolia

These diminutive mounds of inch-wide Australian daisies make great fillers in mixed containers. Each plant grows up to 1 ft. tall, 1½ ft. across, with finely divided leaves and a profusion of inch-wide flowers in spring and summer.

B. hybrids. Perennials. Zones 14–24. Choices include 'City Lights', with light lavender-blue flowers; 'New Amethyst', dark purple; 'Toucan Tango', blue with green centers; and the Surdaisy series in mauve, pink, white, and yellow.

B. iberidifolia. Annual. Zones 1–24. Flowers are usually blue; white and pink also offered. In spring, sow seeds where plants are to grow.

B. multifida. Perennial. Zones 14–24. Very similar to *B. iberidifolia*. Blue flowers most common. Propagate by cuttings.

Brahea
Arecaceae
PALMS

🗡 **ZONES VARY BY SPECIES**

☼ **FULL SUN**

◊● **LITTLE OR NO WATER TO MODERATE WATER**

Brahea armata

These big Mexican fan palms are similar to *Washingtonias*. They need some summer water in desert regions.

B. armata. MEXICAN BLUE PALM. Zones 12–17, 19–24; H1; and warm parts of Zone 10. Hardy to 18°F (–8°C). Grows slowly to 20–40 ft. tall, top spreading 12–25 ft. Silvery blue, almost white leaves. Conspicuous creamy flowers. Takes heat and wind.

B. brandegeei. SAN JOSE HESPER PALM. Zones 13, 19, 21–24; H1, H2. Hardy to 26°F (–3°C). Slow grower to 40 ft. tall and 15 ft. wide, with slender, flexible trunk. Leaves are 3 ft. long, light gray-green, and drop from trunk with age.

B. edulis. GUADALUPE PALM. Zones 12–24. Hardy to below 20°F (–7°C). From Guadalupe Island off Baja California. Like *B. armata,* but leaves are light green, flowers less conspicuous. Slow grower, eventually reaching to 30 ft. tall and 15 ft. wide. Old leaves drop, leaving a naked, stout, elephant-hide trunk ringed with scars. Takes both beach and desert conditions.

B. elegans. FRANCESCHI PALM. Zones 13–17, 19–24. Hardy to 22°F (–6°C). Slowest of braheas, eventually reaching only 10–15 ft. tall; top spreads 6–8 ft. Gray-green leaves.

B. nitida. Grows 30 ft. tall, 10 ft. wide; hardy to 20°F (–7°C). Glossy green leaves are gray-green underneath.

Brassaia actinophylla. See *Schefflera actinophylla*

Briza maxima
RATTLESNAKE GRASS, QUAKING GRASS
Poaceae
ANNUAL GRASS

🗡 **ZONES 1–24**

☼ **FULL SUN**

◊ **NO IRRIGATION NEEDED**

Briza maxima

An ornamental grass of delicate, graceful form, this Mediterranean native is often planted for its seed heads. Grows 1–2 ft. high, with ¼-in.-wide, 6-in.-long leaves. Clusters of seed-bearing spikelets dangle from threadlike stems held above the plant. The dry, papery spikelets really do look like rattlesnake rattles.

Scatter seed where plants are to grow; thin to 1 ft. apart. Self-sows, often naturalizing along roadsides and in fields.

B. media is similar but is perennial.

FOR MORE ON GRASSES, SEE "MEET THE GRASSES," PAGE 346.

Broccoli

Brassicaceae
BIENNIAL GROWN AS ANNUAL

🌿 **ALL ZONES**

☀️ **FULL SUN**

💧 **REGULAR WATER**

Broccoli

Broccoli is the easiest of the cole crops (cabbage and its close relatives) for the home gardener. Probably a Mediterranean native, this cool-season crop has a long harvest period. The plant grows 2–3 ft. tall, its central stalk bearing a cluster (to 6 in. wide) of green or purple flower buds. When that cluster is removed, side branches lengthen and produce smaller clusters.

There are many excellent varieties to choose from. Sprouting broccoli forms many small florets that are harvested when the size of buttons. Broccoli raab (broccoli rabe), an Italian relative of broccoli, has slightly stronger flavor. 'Romanesco' broccoli produces striking light green heads that resemble sea coral and have the flavor and texture of cauliflower. For Chinese broccoli, see Asian Greens.

CARE

All types of broccoli are cool-season plants that tend to bolt into flower at high temperatures; plant them to mature during cool weather. In mild climates, plant in late summer, fall, or winter for crops in winter or early spring. In cold-winter areas, set out young plants 2 to 4 weeks before last frost (young plants resist frost, but not hard freezes).

Seedlings are ready to plant 4 to 6 weeks after sowing, and 2 to 4 weeks before average date of last spring frost; start harvesting 50 to 100 days later, but before clustered buds begin to open. Include 5–6 in. of edible stalk and leaves. A dozen plants will supply a family.

Space plants 1½–2 ft. apart in rows and leave 3 ft. between rows. Keep plants growing vigorously with regular deep irrigation during dry periods and one or two feedings of commercial fertilizer before heads start to form.

Brodiaea

Asparagaceae
PERENNIALS FROM CORMS

🌿 **ZONES VARY BY SPECIES**

☀️ **FULL SUN**

💧 **NO IRRIGATION NEEDED**

Brodiaea coronaria

Many are Pacific Coast natives that flower in sunny meadows during spring and early summer. Plants have a few grassy leaves. A cluster of funnel-shaped or tubular, ½–2-in.-long flowers tops the stem during bloom. After flowering, plants die to the ground.

Brodiaea once included many plants now listed under different names. For *B. grandiflora, B. hyacinthina, B. ixioides, B. laxa* 'Queen Fabiola', and *B. tubergenii,* see *Triteleia* with the same species names. *B. lactea* is now *T. hyacinthina, B. lutea* is now *T. ixioides,* and *B. uniflora* is *Ipheion uniflorum.*

B. coronaria (B. grandiflora). HARVEST BRODIAEA. Zones 4–9, 14–24. Clusters of dark blue, inch-long flowers on 6–10-in. stems.

B. elegans. HARVEST BRODIAEA. Zones 2–9, 14–24. Like *B. coronaria* but to 16 in. tall. Often sold as *B. grandiflora* or *B. coronaria.*

B. minor. Zones 7–9, 14–17, 19–24. Dark blue flowers on stems that may be 3–4 in., rarely 1 ft., long.

CARE

In nature, these plants are often found in adobe soil, in areas where rainfall is heavy in winter and early spring and corms dry out completely in summer. They appreciate similar conditions in gardens; if you can't keep corms dry in summer, plant in sandy or gritty soil. Set corms 2–3 in. deep and 2–4 in. apart. In cold-winter areas, grow in containers or mulch to protect from freezing and thawing.

Bromelia balansae

HEART OF FLAME
Bromeliaceae
PERENNIAL

🌿 **ZONES 13, 19–24; H1, H2**

☀️ **FULL SUN**

💧 **REGULAR WATER**

Bromeliad

This South American pineapple relative grows 4 ft. tall, 4–6 ft. across, with an impressive cluster of 30–50 arching, sawtoothed green leaves that are whitish below. The center leaves turn bright scarlet in spring or early summer, vividly contrasting with dark glossy green leaves below. This gives rise to a spike of white-edged, rose-colored flowers.

CARE

Needs warm nights and almost any soil with excellent drainage. Supply light shade in Zone 13. Feed lightly once or twice in summer.

Broussonetia papyrifera

(Morus papyrifera)
PAPER MULBERRY, WAUKE
Moraceae
DECIDUOUS TREE

🌿 **ZONES 3B–24; H1, H2**

☀️ **FULL SUN**

💧 **LITTLE TO REGULAR WATER**

Broussonetia papyrifera

This fast-growing tree can reach 50 ft. tall and 40 ft. wide, though it is often more shrublike in gardens. Native to China and Japan, the tree gets its common name from its fibrous inner bark, used for making paper and Polynesian tapa cloth. Smooth gray bark can become ridged and furrowed with age. Heart-shaped, 4–8-in. leaves are green and rough above, gray and velvety beneath; leaf edges are toothed, often lobed when young. Blooms in spring; pollen can trigger allergies. Male trees bear catkins; on female trees, rounded flower heads are followed by red fruits in early summer if a male tree is near.

Paper mulberry is most valuable where choices are otherwise limited by heat, pollution, and stony, sterile, or alkaline soils. Drought-tolerant except in Zones 11–13, where it is considered a high-water-use tree. Though suckering can be a problem in rainy climates, this tree works well in rough bank plantings.

Browallia

AMETHYST FLOWER

Solanaceae

ANNUALS AND PERENNIALS

- 🌿 **ZONES VARY BY SPECIES**
- ◑ ● **PARTIAL TO FULL SHADE**
- 💧 **REGULAR WATER**

Browallia

Choice South American natives come in brilliant blue, violet, or white; blue and violet flowers are more striking because of contrasting white eye or throat. Blooms are most profuse in warm shade or filtered sunlight, and make fine cut flowers.

B. americana (B. elata). Annual. All zones. Branching, 1–2 ft. high and wide; roundish leaves. Violet or blue flowers ½ in. long, ½ in. across, borne among leaves.

B. hybrids. These grow to about 1 ft. tall and wide. 'Endless Flirtation' is white; 'Endless Celebration' white with purple flush; 'Endless Illumination' purple; and 'Endless Sensation' lavender blue.

B. speciosa. Perennial in Zones 17, 23, 24; H1, H2; annual anywhere. Sprawling, to 1–2 ft. high, nearly a foot wide. Flowers dark purple above, pale lilac beneath. These grow to 12 in. tall, 14 in. wide: 'Bell Blue', lilac-blue; 'Bell Marine', magenta-purple; and 'Bell Silver', white flowers.

CARE

Sow seeds in early spring for summer bloom, in fall for winter color in warmest-winter areas or indoors. You can lift vigorous plants in fall, cut back, and pot; new growth will produce flowers through winter in warm spots. Usually sold as seeds.

Brugmansia

ANGEL'S TRUMPET

Solanaceae

EVERGREEN TO SEMIEVERGREEN SHRUBS

- 🌿 **ZONES 12, 13, 16–24; H1, H2**
- ☀ ◑ ● **SUN OR SHADE**
- 💧 **REGULAR WATER**
- ⬦ **ALL PARTS ARE POISONOUS IF INGESTED**

Brugmansia

These mound into big, tropical-looking shrubs covered with long trumpets of hanging flowers from summer through fall. In containers, these South American natives can make an astonishing focal point on any patio in the West. In their preferred zones, they can be trained into small trees. Blooms of all except *B. sanguinea* are fragrant, especially in the evening. Brugmansias are often confused with *Datura* species (low-growing, herbaceous plants with upward-pointing flowers and swollen, spiny seedpods).

B. × candida. Fast growing to 10–12 ft. tall and wide; dull green leaves to 1 ft. long. Sweet-scented, 8–12-in.-long cream to white trumpets hang straight down from the branches. 'Double White' has creamy white double blossoms, distinctly grayish green foliage. 'Variegata' ('Sunset') grows 5 ft. tall and wide, with light golden peach flowers and white-edged leaves.

B. 'Cherub'. This hybrid produces salmon-pink flowers early and profusely, grows to about 7 ft. tall and wide. Very fragrant.

B. × cubensis 'Charles Grimaldi'. Vigorous hybrid between *B. × insignis* 'Frosty Pink' and another variety. Fast

growing to 10–12 ft. tall and 10 ft. wide. Huge (15-in.), golden yellow to golden orange, powerfully fragrant trumpets cover the plant during bloom season.

B. × insignis. To 10–12 ft. tall and wide. Flowers are large, flaring trumpets that point outward at 45° angle from plant; they have a spicy-sweet fragrance and come in white, pink, yellow, and orange. 'Frosty Pink' has 8–10-in., salmon-pink blooms. 'Jamaica Yellow' has light yellow flowers. 'Betty Marshall' bears white blossoms on a compact plant 6–8 ft. high.

B. sanguinea. MOUNTAIN ANGEL'S TRUMPET. To 8–12 ft. tall, 6–8 ft. wide. Wavy-edged, narrow green or gray-green leaves; narrow trumpet-shaped blooms to 8 in. long. In typical form, flowers are orange-red with yellow veins; other varieties have orange to yellow or pink flowers. Doesn't bloom well in hot summers.

B. 'Snowbank'. Grown as much for the broad, cream white margins on its light-and-dark green leaves as for its apricot flowers; to 5 ft. high and wide. Tends to have big flushes of bloom in mid- and late summer.

B. versicolor. The most treelike species, to 15 ft. tall and wide. Huge (15-in.) flowers are a peachy apricot color; they hang straight down from the branches, covering the plant during bloom time. Blossoms are sweetly fragrant at night and in the morning. 'Ecuador Pink' is pink. 'Peaches and Cream' grows 5 ft. tall and wide, with peachy pink, 8-in. blossoms that open from buds striped white and green, keep coming spring to fall. Dark green leaves are splashed with light green and edged in white and pale yellow. White-flowered varieties are also available.

CARE

Provide shelter; wind tatters foliage. In colder part of range, expect frost damage and unattractive winter appearance. In desert, supply shade. Before spring growth, remove weak, dead, and crowded stems. Plants growing in containers can overwinter indoors even with low light and very little water.

Brunfelsia pauciflora

(B. calycina)

Solanaceae

EVERGREEN TO SEMIEVERGREEN SHRUB

- 🌿 **ZONES 12–17, 20–24; H1, H2; EXCEPT AS NOTED**
- ◑ **PARTIAL SHADE**
- 💧 **REGULAR WATER**
- ⬦ **ALL PARTS ARE POISONOUS IF INGESTED**

Brunfelsia pauciflora 'Floribunda'

Instantly recognizable by its range of blue to white flowers on the plant at the same time, this tropical American native flowers in spring and early summer. Showy clusters of rich purple, tubular flowers open to flat disks with white throats. In all but warmest locations, most of the foliage drops for a short period. Locate plants where you can admire the flower show. Good container subjects. The following forms are available.

'Floribunda'. YESTERDAY-TODAY-AND-TOMORROW. Common name comes from quick color change of blossoms: they turn from purple ("yesterday") to lavender ("today") to white ("tomorrow"). Flowers, several in a cluster and each opening to 2 in. wide, are borne profusely all over plant. Oval leaves, 3–4 in. long and 1½ in. wide, are dark green above, pale green below. Plant grows 10 ft., but it can be held to 3 ft. by pruning. Has a rather spreading habit, with width nearly equal to height.

'Macrantha' (B. magnifica). MAGNIFICENT BRUNFELSIA. Zones 12, 13, 16, 17, 20–24; H1, H2. Less cold-hardy than 'Floribunda' and has fewer, larger flowers (2–4 in. across)

B

B

and bigger leaves (to 8 in. long, 2½ in. wide), so it looks more tropical. Grows 4 ft. high and wide; must be kept well watered.

CARE

Give these rich, well-drained soil and regular feedings through the growing season. (Where soil tends to be alkaline, as in Zones 12 and 13, add iron to prevent chlorosis.) Prune in spring to remove straggly growth and to shape.

Brunnera macrophylla

BUGLOSS
Boraginaceae
PERENNIAL

⚘ ZONES 1–24
☼ ◐ FULL SUN IN COOLER CLIMATES ONLY
💧 REGULAR WATER

Brunnera macrophylla 'Jack Frost'

These big-leafed woodland plants thrive in the rich organic soil under tall trees and shrubs. They grow in clumps 1½ ft. tall and 2 ft. wide; leaves are heart shaped, dark green. Airy clusters of tiny, yellow-centered, clear blue flowers look like related forget-me-nots (*Myosotis*). In shade, spring blooms keep coming into summer. Besides the green species, look for 'Diane's Gold'; 'Langtrees', with a necklace of white marks penciled around the inside of each leaf; 'Jack Frost', with silvery leaves veined and bordered in green; and 'Looking Glass', whose leaves are nearly white.

Brunnera works well with heucheras, hostas, and similar woodland plants, freely self-sowing once established. To

increase germination, try freezing seeds before sowing. Needs well-drained, moisture-retentive soil. Increase by dividing clumps in fall.

Brussels Sprouts

Brassicaceae
BIENNIAL GROWN AS ANNUAL

⚘ ALL ZONES
☼ FULL SUN
💧 REGULAR WATER

Brussels sprouts

With a leafy crown supported by a stem covered with baby cabbage lookalikes, Brussels sprouts couldn't look stranger. But they're fairly easy to grow where summers are mild.

'Jade Cross Hybrid' is the most heat-tolerant; 'Diablo' produces heavy crops of uniform sprouts in most climates; 'Oliver' is the standard early variety for short-season climates; 'Rubine' is an heirloom variety with purple sprouts; and 'Prince Marvel' is the earliest to harvest in Alaska.

CARE

In cold-winter climates, set out seedlings (ones you started yourself) or nursery transplants in spring for summer-to-fall harvest; in mild-winter areas, plant in late summer and fall for winter-to-spring production.

When big leaves start to yellow, begin picking sprouts. Snap off sprouts from bottom first—they're best when slightly smaller than a golf ball. Leave little sprouts on upper stem to mature. After picking, remove only leaves below harvested sprouts. A single plant will yield from 50 to 100 sprouts. Same pests as cabbage.

Buchloe dactyloides

BUFFALO GRASS
Poaceae
PERENNIAL GRASS

⚘ ZONES 1–3, 7–12, 15, 16, 18–21
☼ FULL SUN
◔ LITTLE WATER

Buchloe dactyloides

This grass grows wild from central Montana to Arizona—and increasingly in lawns around the arid West. Slow to sprout and fill in, it spreads rapidly by surface runners once established (even into surrounding beds) and makes matted, reasonably dense turf that takes hard wear and looks fairly good with little summer water or fertilizer. Gray-green from late spring to hard frost, straw-colored through late fall and winter.

Male and female flowers appear on different plants. Males flower on top, look ragged. Females flower unobtrusively at the ground. Seed mixes always include both, but vegetative selections like 'Prestige' and 'Verde' are female, so they look more even.

CARE

Given minimal water, it grows to 4 in. tall and needs little or no mowing. More water means higher growth, some mowing. To start from seed, sow 2 lb. per 1,000 sq. ft. Soak occasionally to 1 ft. while grass is getting started. Or start from sod, planting 4-in.-wide plugs in prepared soil 3–4 ft. apart in spring; expect coverage in two seasons.

Buddleja

BUTTERFLY BUSH
Scrophulariaceae
EVERGREEN, SEMIEVERGREEN, OR DECIDUOUS SHRUBS

⚘ ZONES VARY BY SPECIES
☼ ◐ FULL SUN OR LIGHT SHADE
💧 MODERATE TO REGULAR WATER
🦋 IRRESISTIBLE NECTAR SOURCE FOR BUTTERFLIES; ATTRACT BIRDS

Buddleja davidii

Upright, fountain-shaped shrubs beloved for summer flowers. Of the many selections—all notable for flower color, fragrance, or both—these are among the most commonly available. Need well-drained soil.

B. alternifolia. FOUNTAIN BUTTERFLY BUSH. Deciduous. Zones 2b–24. This Chinese native grows to 12 ft. tall and wide. Arching, willowy branches have 1–4-in.-long leaves, dull green above, gray and hairy beneath. Small clusters of fragrant, lilac-purple flowers make sweeping wands of spring color. Tolerates many soils; thrives in poor, dry gravels. Prune after bloom, removing some of oldest wood just aboveground. Or train as a small tree. 'Argentea' has silvery leaves.

B. asiatica. Evergreen. Zones 8, 9, 14–24; H1, H2. From East Indies, this grows fast to 10–15 ft. tall and wide. Tiny flowers appear in narrow, erect, 10-in. spikes in winter and spring; powerful fragrance recalls freesia. Prune after bloom. Freezing weather kills it to the ground, but it can recover and flower the same year.

B. crispa. Deciduous. Zones 5–7, 14–17. Native to Himalayas. To 6–10 ft. tall and wide, with silvery gray foliage and 4-in. clusters of fragrant lilac flowers with orange or white throats. Blooms heaviest in late summer. For best blooms and to keep plant neat, cut nearly to ground in late winter. In cold-winter regions, grow in containers and protect over winter.

B. davidii. BUTTERFLY BUSH, SUMMER LILAC. Semievergreen to deciduous. Zones 2–24; H1. This East Asian native can put on several feet of rank growth in a season, maturing at 5–15 ft. high and wide. Tapering leaves are 4–12 in. long, dark green above, white and felted beneath. Lilaclike, 4-to-24-in. inflorescences of fragrant flowers (lilac with orange eye) appear in dense, arching clusters. Needs good drainage. Cut back heavily before spring growth begins. Top may die in freezing weather but will regrow from roots and bloom the same year.

There are many excellent varieties, including some variegated ('Harlequin') and dwarf; *B. d. nanhoensis* selections grow 5–8 ft. tall and 6 ft. wide and come in white, deep blue, or reddish purple flowers.

The species is invasive in mild parts of the Northwest. Its sale in Oregon is limited to sterile varieties like 'Asian Moon', 'Blue Chip', and 'Purple Haze' (all dwarfs), and sterile interspecific hybrids like 'Blue Cobbler', 'Peach Cobbler', 'Tangerine Dream', and 'Vanilla' (all in the Flutterby Grande series).

B. globosa. ORANGE BUTTERFLY BUSH. Evergreen or semievergreen. Zones 5–9, 14–24. From southern South America, this has an open habit 10–15 ft. tall and wide. Dark green leaves are downy beneath. Late-spring or early-summer flowers are tightly clustered into ¾-in. orange balls arranged in spikelike clusters that are 6–8 in. long. Prune as for *B. alternifolia*.

B. 'Lochinch'. Deciduous, but retains leaves in mildest climates. Zones 3b–9, 14–24. Grows 5–8 ft. (or taller) and as broad, with gray foliage and sweetly fragrant, light lavender-blue flowers over a long season in late summer and fall. Prune as for *B. davidii*.

B. marrubiifolia. WOOLLY BUTTERFLY BUSH. Zones 10–13, 18–24. This evergreen from southwest Texas and northern Mexico grows 5 ft. tall and broad. It is densely covered with soft, silvery, woolly foliage and small, ball-shaped, orange flower clusters in spring and summer. Prune after bloom.

B. × weyeriana. Zones 4–24. This hybrid resembles *B. globosa* but is deciduous (except in mildest-winter climates) and hardier, with more elongated orange-yellow flower clusters in late spring or early summer. Grows 6–10 ft. tall and wide. 'Bicolor' flowers are mauve-pink with peach-pink centers; 'Sungold' blooms are orange; 'Honeycomb', buttery yellow. Prune as for *B. alternifolia*.

Bulbine frutescens
(B. caulescens)
Asphodelaceae
SUCCULENT SHRUBBY PERENNIAL

✺ ZONES 8, 9, 12–24

☼ ◑ ● PARTIAL OR FULL SHADE IN HOTTEST CLIMATES

◌ ◓ ● LITTLE TO REGULAR WATER

Bulbine frutescens

Branching stems of this South African perennial make a sprawling clump 1 ft. high, 2–3 ft. wide. Leaves are fleshy, bright green, and shaped like slender, pointed pencils. Produces spikelike 6–12-in. clusters of tubular bright yellow flowers (reminiscent of red-hot poker, *Kniphofia*) most of the year. 'Hallmark' has gray-green leaves, orange flowers with fuzzy yellow stamens; plant is more compact, less

heat-tolerant than species. 'Tiny Tangerine' is another orange-flowered dwarf. Useful as ground or bank cover in dry, well-drained soil. Leaves are slippery when stepped on.

FOR MORE ON SUCCULENTS, SEE "MEET THE SUCCULENTS," PAGE 618.

Bulbinella floribunda
(B. robusta, B. setosa)
Asphodelaceae
PERENNIAL

✺ ZONES 14–24

☼ ◑ ● PARTIAL OR FULL SHADE IN HOTTEST CLIMATES

● REGULAR WATER DURING GROWTH AND BLOOM

Bulbinella floribunda

A large clump of narrow, 2-ft.-long floppy leaves emerges every fall, just as other plants are entering dormancy. Then in winter, this South African develops 4-in. spikes of yellow blooms that resemble red-hot poker (*Kniphofia*), but flower spikes are shorter and less pointed, and blossoms are bell shaped, not tubular. Good cut flowers.

CARE

Easy to grow from seed sown in well-drained soil in spring. Foliage dies to the ground after bloom; pull off old, dry leaves. Keep soil on dry side during spring and summer dormancy. Colonizes low-maintenance borders quickly. Divide crowded clumps in fall.

Butia capitata
PINDO PALM
Arecaceae
PALM

✺ ZONES 8, 9, 12–24; H1, H2

☼ ◑ FULL SUN OR LIGHT SHADE

● REGULAR WATER

Butia capitata

Crowned with 5–10-ft., green or blue-green leaves that curve in toward the trunk, this slow-growing South American native grows 10–20 ft., with a 10–15-ft. head and spikes of yellow flowers that develop into clusters of yellow to red, edible summer fruits (flavor is sweet-tart, like an apricot-banana-pineapple blend). It is among the hardiest feather palms, taking 15°F (–9°C). Its heavy trunk is patterned with stubs of old leaves; they look best if all are trimmed same length. (For more on palms, see "Meet the Palms," page 471.)

The pindo palm's spent fronds hang down over its stout trunk like a hula dancer's grass skirt. To show off the patterned trunk, keep spent fronds pruned off. Neaten the trunk's pattern by trimming the stubs of old leaves all the same length.

B

Buxus

BOXWOOD, BOX
Buxaceae
EVERGREEN SHRUBS

✂ **ZONES VARY BY SPECIES**

☼ ◐ ● **SUN OR SHADE**

💧 **REGULAR WATER**

Buxus sempervirens 'Suffruticosa'

Classic clipped hedges, these are soft and billowing when unsheared. Inconspicuous flowers. Easy to grow. Extra care with watering, feeding, and controlling mites and scale will pay off in better color and vigor.

B. Green series. Zones 2b–24. Group of Canadian hybrids derived from *B. microphylla koreana* and *B. sempervirens*. Hardy to between –20° and –30°F (–29° and –34°C). All have rich green foliage and a naturally attractive shape; they need very little pruning.

'Green Gem'. Slowly forms a 3–4 ft. mound, with some bronzing in winter cold.

'Green Mountain'. Becomes a dense cone 5 ft. high, 3 ft. wide; it was developed as an alternative to dwarf Alberta spruce (*Picea glauca albertiana* 'Conica').

'Green Velvet'. Rounded, 3–4 ft. tall and wide, stays green through winter.

B. microphylla. Zones 3b–24, except as noted. The species is rarely planted. Its widely used varieties include the following:

'Compacta'. Grows 1 ft. tall and wide; new leaves yellowish, greening with maturity.

'Faulkner'. Glossy, emerald green leaves all year on a dense, slow-growing, rounded plant. May reach 6 ft. high without shaping.

B. m. japonica. JAPANESE BOXWOOD. Hardy to –10°F (–23°C) but has poor winter appearance in cold-winter areas. Takes dry heat and alkaline soil but struggles in intense heat, saline soils of desert. Compact; round-tipped leaves are a lively bright green in summer, brown or bronze in winter in many areas. Grows slowly to 4–6 ft. high and wide if not pruned. Most often clipped as hedge or shaped into globes, tiers, pyramids in containers. Can keep to 6 in. tall as border edging. 'Green Beauty' holds its deep green color in coldest weather and is considerably greener than the species in summer heat. 'Winter Gem' retains its deep green foliage color through winter.

B. sempervirens. COMMON BOXWOOD, ENGLISH BOXWOOD. Zones 3b–6, 15–17, except as noted. Native to southern Europe, North Africa, western Asia. Dies out in alkaline soils, hot-summer areas.

Will grow 15–20 ft. high and wide. Densely foliaged with medium-size, lustrous dark green, oval leaves.

'Graham Blandy'. Narrow, columnar growth to 7–9 ft. tall, 1 ft. wide.

'Suffruticosa'. TRUE DWARF BOXWOOD. Slower growing than the species; to 4–5 ft. high but generally clipped lower. Small leaves, dense form and texture. A variegated form with silveredged foliage is available.

'Vardar Valley'. Zones 2b–6, 15–17. To 2–3 ft. tall, 6 ft. wide. Macedonian native; considered hardiest common boxwood.

'Variegata'. Leaves have creamy white edges.

B. sinica insularis (B. m. koreana). KOREAN BOXWOOD. Zones 2b–24. Hardy to –20°F (–29°C). Noted for its hardiness and ability to survive where others freeze. Slower growing and lower (to 2½ ft. high) than *B. m. japonica,* with smaller leaves (¼–½ in.).

🌿 3 Ways with Boxwood

These obliging plants with tailored glossy-green foliage have a mixed reputation in the gardening world. Some gardeners find them too formal, while others appreciate their toughness and versatility. Designers blend traditional uses with fresh new ones like the three below.

GLOBES For the look of green bubbles in a garden bed, plant three or five boxwoods, such as 'Green Gem' Japanese boxwoods (*Buxus microphylla japonica*), offsetting them slightly from one another. As the plants grow—gradually shape them into globes of various sizes. Plant low mounding grasses such as *Carex morrowii* around them.

INFORMAL HEDGE To edge a driveway, or to create a low privacy screen in the front or back yard, plant a row of true dwarf boxwoods such as *B. sempervirens* 'Suffruticosa'. Space plants far enough apart to show off their individual shapes, and leave them untrimmed.

CONTAINERS To dress a patio, plant a single boxwood in a large container. Choose a low-growing kind such as *B. microphylla* 'Compacta' or *B. m.* 'Golden Triumph', whose shiny green leaves have showy yellow margins.

Cabbage

Brassicaceae
BIENNIAL GROWN AS ANNUAL

✂ **ALL ZONES**

☼ ◐ **TOLERATES LIGHT SHADE IN HOT CLIMATES**

💧 **REGULAR WATER**

Savoy cabbage

Probably native to the Mediterranean coast of Europe, cabbage has green, red, or blue- or purple-tinted leaves that form tight round or pointed heads. Leaves can be smooth or, in savoy types, crinkly.

Early varieties mature 7–8 weeks after transplanting; late varieties take 3–4 months. 'Early Jersey Wakefield' and 'Charmont' are standard early varieties, while 'Danish Ballhead' and 'Kaitlin' are good late ones. Among savoys, try 'Samantha' and the red 'Deadon'. 'Gonzalez' is an excellent mini, and in Alaska, 'O.S. Cross' is the standard giant cabbage. Good reds include 'Red Express', 'Ruby Perfection', and the heat-resistant 'Ruby Ball'.

CARE

Time plantings so that heads form before or after summer heat. In low and intermediate desert, grow as a winter crop in full sun. Start seeds ½ in. deep in pots or flats; after six weeks, plant seedlings 2–2½ ft. apart in the garden. Soil should be moist, well drained. Apply frequent light doses of nitrogen fertilizer. A 10-ft. row yields 10–25 lbs. To avoid overproduction, set out a few plants every week or two, or plant both early and late kinds. Cut off firm, well-formed heads before they split or crack. Harvest and store before heavy freezes occur.

To prevent soil-borne pest buildup, plant in different site each year. Row covers will protect plants from aphids, cabbage loopers, imported cabbageworms, and root maggots. *Bacillus thuringiensis (Bt)* can control young larvae of cabbageworms and loopers. Handpick or bait for snails and slugs.

Cabbage and Kale, Flowering

Brassicaceae
BIENNIALS GROWN AS ANNUALS

🌿 **ALL ZONES**

☀️ ◐ **BEST IN SUN; TOLERATE SOME SHADE**

💧 **REGULAR WATER**

Kale

Flowering cabbage and flowering kale are grown for their leaf rosettes, which look like giant, deep blue-green peonies marbled and edged with white, cream, rose, or purple. Kale's head is slightly looser and its leaf edges are more heavily fringed than cabbage. Both are spectacular in the cool-season garden, and go well with pansies and violas.

CARE

Same as for cabbage. Plant 15–18 in. apart in beds, singly in 8-in. pots, or several in a large container. Colors are strongest after first frosts. A single rosette cut and placed on a spike holder in a decorative bowl makes a striking harvest arrangement. Foliage is edible, and quite striking as a salad garnish.

For the edible flowering cabbage typically used in Chinese cooking, see Asian Greens.

Caesalpinia
(Poinciana)

Caesalpiniaceae
EVERGREEN AND DECIDUOUS SHRUBS AND TREES

🌿 **ZONES VARY BY SPECIES**

☀️ **FULL SUN**

💧 **LITTLE TO MODERATE WATER**

🐦 **ATTRACT HUMMINGBIRDS**

❧ **PODS AND SEEDS ARE POISONOUS IF INGESTED**

Caesalpinia gilliesii

These garden-scale, ferny-leafed trees and shrubs are grown for branch-end clusters of colorful blossoms featuring (except *C. platyloba*) protruding stamens.

C. cacalaco. CASCALOTE. Evergreen tree. Zones 12, 13, 21–24. Mexican native grows slowly to 20 ft. tall and wide, with thorny branches and bright green foliage, coarser than that of *C. pulcherrima.* Very showy, large yellow flowers carried well above branches in winter.

C. gilliesii (Poinciana gilliesii). YELLOW BIRD OF PARADISE. Evergreen to deciduous South American shrub or tree; drops leaves in cold winters. Zones 8–16, 18–24; occasionally seen in Zones 6, 7. Tough, fast growing to 10 ft. tall, 8 ft. wide, with finely cut foliage and open, angular branch structure. Yellow summer flowers have bright red stamens.

MEET THE CACTUS CLAN

The cactus family contains a huge number of succulent plants (see also "Meet the Succulents," page 618). Generally leafless, cacti have stems modified into cylinders, pads, or joints that store water in times of drought. Thick skin reduces evaporation, and most species have spines for protection against browsing animals. Flowers are usually large and brightly colored; fruit may also be colorful and is sometimes edible. All are native to the Americas—from Canada to Argentina, from sea level into high mountains, from deserts to dripping tropical rain forests. Many are native to drier parts of the West. Cacti range in height from a few inches to 50 ft. tall.

Large Cacti

Use these striking, shapely plants to create desert landscapes. See *Carnegiea gigantea, Cephalocereus senilis, Echinocactus, Echinocereus, Ferocactus, Opuntia,* and *Stenocereus thurberi.*

Small Cacti

These usually have interesting forms and brightly colored flowers; grow them in pots or, if hardy, in rock gardens. See *Echinopsis.* Feed and water these plants well during warm weather for good display; taper off on fertilizer to encourage winter dormancy. Use fast-draining planting mix.

Tropical Cacti

Showiest in flower, these grow as epiphytes on trees or rocks. See *Epiphyllum* and *Schlumbergera.* They need rich soil with much humus, frequent feeding and watering, partial shade, and protection from frost. They grow outdoors all year in Hawaii; elsewhere, grow them in lathhouse or greenhouse, or treat them as outdoor/indoor plants.

HOW TO GROW

Water newly planted cacti very little; roots are subject to rot before they begin active growth. In 4 to 6 weeks, water thoroughly; then let soil dry before watering again. Reduce watering in fall to allow plants to go dormant. Feed monthly in spring and summer.

C. mexicana. MEXICAN BIRD OF PARADISE. Evergreen shrub or tree. Zones 12–16, 18–24. Moderately fast growth to 10–12 ft. tall and wide; keep to 6–8 ft. with pruning. Covered with 6-in. clusters of yellow flowers in all but coldest months.

C. platyloba. Evergreen tree. Zones 12, 13, 21–24. From Mexico. To 20 ft. tall and wide. Narrow, elongated clusters of tiny yellow flowers in spring lack the long, protruding stamens of other *Caesalpinias.* Open habit and few leaflets give it an attractively airy look. Leaves turn rust red in fall.

C. pulcherrima (Poinciana pulcherrima). RED BIRD OF PARADISE, DWARF POINCIANA. Deciduous shrub; evergreen in mildest winters. Zones 12–16, 18–23; H1, H2. Native to tropical America. Fast, dense growth to 10 ft. tall and wide. Dark green leaves with many ¾-in. leaflets.

In warm weather, this plant bears showy clusters of orange or red flowers with red stamens. 'Phoenix Bird' has bright yellow blooms. Various other salmon- and yellow-flowered forms are available in Hawaii. All make good quick screens.

Plants freeze to ground in the colder part of range but rebound in spring. In milder climates, you can cut them to ground in early spring to make more compact mound.

»

C

Plants grow quickly and easily in hot, sunny locations if given light, well-drained soil and infrequent, deep watering. Prune before first flush of spring growth to remove any dead or damaged wood and wayward branches; remove lower limbs for treelike shape in shrubby species.

Caladium bicolor
FANCY-LEAFED CALADIUM
Araceae
PERENNIAL FROM TUBER

- **ZONE H2; OR DIG AND STORE; OR GROW IN POTS**
- **SOME VARIETIES TOLERATE SOME SUN**
- **REGULAR TO AMPLE WATER**
- **SAP CAN CAUSE SWELLING IN MOUTH, THROAT**

Caladium bicolor

Tropical American natives grown for foliage: large, arrow-shaped, almost translucent leaves colored in bands and blotches of red, rose, pink, white, silver, bronze, and green. Usually 2 ft. (occasionally to 4 ft.) high and wide. Most require shade. Newer varieties tolerating some sun include 'Fire Chief', 'Rose Bud', 'Red Flash', and 'White Queen'.

Caladiums need rich soil, high humidity, and heat (above 70°F/21°C during days and rarely below 60°F/16°C at night). In Hawaii, tubers can remain in the ground all year. Elsewhere, dig and store after leaf dieback, or grow in pots and bring indoors during cold weather.

Calamagrostis
REED GRASS
Poaceae
PERENNIAL GRASSES

- **ZONES 2B–24**
- **FULL SUN OR PARTIAL SHADE**
- **REGULAR WATER**

Calamagrostis × *acutiflora* 'Karl Foerster'

These sturdy clumping grasses from Eurasia produce feathery flower plumes that persist into winter and can be used for fresh or dried arrangements. Cut back clumps low to the ground in late winter, before new growth begins.

C. × *acutiflora*. FEATHER REED GRASS. Known mainly through these evergreen to semievergreen selections. 'Avalanche' grows 4 ft. tall, with wide white band down each leaf center; 6-ft. flower plumes emerge reddish brown, turn golden. 'Karl Foerster' ('Stricta') forms an erect, somewhat arching clump of narrow, bright green leaves 2–3 ft. high, somewhat broader. Upright 6-ft. flower stems appear in late spring, early summer. 'Overdam' is similar, but its foliage is variegated with white; needs partial shade in hot-summer regions.

C. *brachytricha*. FALL-BLOOMING REED GRASS. Deciduous. Upright, arching clump to 1½–2½ ft.high, 2 ft. wide. In late summer or early fall, broad flower spikes bring plant height to 4 ft. One of the best grasses for partial shade. Great in containers.

FOR MORE ON GRASSES, SEE "MEET THE GRASSES," PAGE 346.

Calamintha
CALAMINT
Lamiaceae
PERENNIALS

- **ZONES 1–9, 14–24**
- **FULL SUN OR LIGHT SHADE**
- **MODERATE WATER**

Calamintha grandiflora 'Variegata'

Favored for minty foliage used to make tea, and for long-blooming clusters of two-lipped flowers. Plants need well-drained soil and, in coldest zones, winter protection. Can self-sow, but not aggressive like related mint.

C. *grandiflora*. Native from the Mediterranean region to Iran. Creeping rhizomes produce clump 2 ft. high and wide, with slender stems and 1½-in. pink summer flowers. 'Variegata' has variegated leaves. Better with some shade.

C. *nepeta* (*C. nepetoides*). Native from the Mediterranean region to Great Britain. To 1½ ft. high, 2½ ft. wide. Many tough, slender stems grow outward, then erect. Upper portion of the plant carries a profusion of ½-in. pale lilac to white flowers in late summer and fall.

Attractive in or out of bloom, calamint has leaves that give off a delicious scent—minty-lemon or juicy fruit with a dash of lime—when you brush against them. Plant near a garden path where you can savor it.

Calandrinia
Portulacaceae
PERENNIALS AND ANNUALS

- **ZONES VARY BY SPECIES**
- **PARTIAL SHADE IN HOTTEST CLIMATES**
- **MODERATE WATER, EXCEPT AS NOTED**

Calandrinia grandiflora

Native to the temperate Pacific coastal regions of North and South America, these clumping evergreen and annual perennials are grown for their satiny, cup-shaped flowers. All tolerate lean soil, but grow and flower best in humus-rich loam. Good drainage is essential.

C. *ciliata*. RED MAIDS. Annual. All zones. This common Western wildflower populates sunny meadows, growing 8–16 in. high and wide, with narrow, fleshy, gray-green leaves. From late winter into spring, dainty magenta flowers, about 1 in. wide, are produced on 8-in.-long stems. Grow from seed.

C. *grandiflora* (*Cistanthe grandiflora*). Perennial. Zones 15–17, 20–24. Native to Chile. Shrubby, clumping growth to 1–3 ft. high and 2–3 ft. wide. Thick, fleshy gray-green leaves are narrowly oval and pointed. From spring into fall, plants produce brilliant magenta blooms along tall (1½–3 ft.), slender stems. Lasting just one day each, flowers appear to float above the leaves. Most effective when massed. Easily propagated by cuttings taken in spring. Regular water.

C. *umbellata* (*Cistanthe umbellata, Calyptridium umbellatum*). ROCK PURSLANE. Perennial often grown as annual. Zones 15–17, 20–24. Native to Chile and Peru. Plants form 6-in.-high mounds of narrow, bluish to gray-green leaves. Crimson summertime flowers are held just above the foliage on branching stems.

Calceolaria

Calceolariaceae
PERENNIALS

🌡 **ZONES VARY BY TYPE**

☀ ☽ ● **EXPOSURE NEEDS VARY BY TYPE**

💧 **REGULAR WATER**

Calceolaria Herbeohybrida Group

Native from Mexico to Chile. Loose clusters of small pouchlike or slipperlike flowers, usually yellow but sometimes red-bronze or spotted with red or orange-brown. Bloom in spring and summer. Plants have dark green, crinkly leaves.

C. Herbeohybrida Group. Zones 14–24; anywhere as annuals or houseplants. This is the florists' calceolaria that produces masses of velvety, inch-long yellow or red flowers, often spotted and marbled. Plants are usually grown from seed sown in spring or summer in light, porous soil; they are ready for final potting or planting out in fall. Calceolaria can reach a height of 2½ ft., but some strains reach only 9–15 in. high, 6–12 in. wide. Even where plants winter over, they are usually discarded after flowering. Give bedding and outdoor potted plants partial or full shade.

C. integrifolia. Zones 14–24. Woody-based plant to 3 ft. high, 1 ft. wide. Leaves about 3 in. long, 1 in. wide. Clusters of yellow to red-brown, unspotted flowers ½ in. across. Good cut flower. 'Golden Nugget' has pure golden yellow flowers from spring to fall; 'Kentish Hero' has orange-red to brown blooms. Use in borders, pots, hanging baskets. Best bloom comes when rootbound. Full sun, but part shade in hottest climates.

Calendula officinalis

CALENDULA, POT MARIGOLD
Asteraceae
ANNUAL

🌡 **ZONES A2, A3; 1–24; H1**

☀ **FULL SUN**

💧 **MODERATE WATER**

🦋 **ATTRACTS BUTTERFLIES**

Calendula officinalis

This classic cool-season annual provides sure, easy color from late fall through spring in mild-winter areas, from spring to fall in colder climates. Besides familiar daisylike, orange or yellow double blooms 2½–4½ in. across, calendulas come in subtle shades of apricot, cream, and soft yellow, sometimes with contrasting tips or reverse sides of petals. Centers can be dark or light, and flowers come in singles and doubles. Plants somewhat branching, 1–2 ft. high, 1–1½ ft. wide. Leaves are long, narrow, round on ends, slightly sticky, and aromatic. Mass plants in borders, parking strips, or containers.

Dwarf strains (12–15 in. high) include Bon Bon (earliest) and Fiesta (Fiesta Gitana). Taller (1½–2 ft. high) are Flashback (orange, peach, apricot, or yellow with red or maroon reverse), Kablouna (pompon centers with looser edges), Pacific Beauty, and Radio (quilled, cactus-type blooms).

CARE

Sow seed in place or in flats in late summer or early fall in mild-winter climates, spring elsewhere. Or buy seedlings at nurseries. Will self-sow to some degree. Adapts to most fast-draining soils. Remove spent flowers to prolong bloom.

Calibrachoa

Solanaceae
PERENNIAL USUALLY GROWN AS ANNUAL

🌡 **ZONES 8, 9, 14–24 AS PERENNIAL; ZONES 2–7, 10–13 AS ANNUAL**

☀ ☽ **FULL SUN OR LIGHT SHADE**

💧 **MODERATE WATER**

Calibrachoa 'Cabaret Purple'

This cheery summer bloomer looks like a small petunia, to which it is related. It is native to Brazil and Peru, and its garden forms are hybrids. It was once called Million Bells—the name of an early and still-popular series—but now just *Calibrachoa*. Plants have tiny, closely set leaves and a profusion of small, single or double flowers that fall off as they fade; blooms keep coming all season long. Colors include solids, bicolors, and veined patterns in shades of white, yellow, orange, apricot, red, pink, blue, burgundy, lavender, and purple. For hybrids between *Calibrachoa* and *Petunia,* see × *Petchoa.*

There are many excellent *Calibrachoa* series with names like Callie, Colorburst, Can-Can, Million Bells, and MiniFamous. They sometimes differ by color range and pattern, but there is overlap. The heat- and disease-resistant Superbells series, for example, includes about 30 varieties in a wide range of colors and habits.

Trailing calibrachoas in all series grow lower (usually 3–7 in. high) and spill out to the sides, while mounding forms can be 8 to 15 in. high, and grow about as wide as high. Intermediates are just that.

A good rule of thumb is to put calibrachoas in pots and petunias in either the ground or pots—but never petunias and calibrachoas in the same pot, since the petunias will overwhelm the smaller plants. Calibrachoas struggle in garden beds that have anything less than perfect drainage. Consider them perennials only where frosts are nonexistent or light.

CARE

Calibrachoas are generally less hungry and thirsty than petunias grown in the same conditions, but because they are at their best in containers, regular watering and fertilizing are still the rule. (Avoid using water-retention gels.) The plants' wiry stems are less subject to breakage than are petunia stems, and tobacco budworms seem uninterested in foliage and flowers.

Calliandra

Mimosaceae
EVERGREEN AND DECIDUOUS SHRUBS

🌡 **ZONES VARY BY SPECIES**

☀ **FULL SUN, EXCEPT AS NOTED**

◌ ◐ ● **WATER NEEDS VARY BY SPECIES**

🦋 **ATTRACT HUMMINGBIRDS**

Calliandra californica

Group of about 200 species grown mainly for their flowers. Long, silky stamens make the blossoms look like feather dusters or powder puffs. They appear on medium to tall shrubs with ferny foliage. Prune out any dead or damaged wood after bloom.

C. californica. BAJA FAIRY DUSTER. Evergreen. Zones 10–24. Native to Baja California and Sonora, Mexico. To 5 ft. tall, 5–6 ft. wide. This species is sometimes likened to *C. eriophylla,* but it's bigger, with more luxuriant foliage and bright deep red stamens. Takes little to moderate water. With moderate water, blooms nearly year-round in Zone 13 (production drops off somewhat in midsummer and earliest winter), and close to that in Zone 12. Blooms throughout the warm parts of the year in other areas.

C. eriophylla. FAIRY DUSTER, FALSE MESQUITE. Deciduous. Zones 11–24; also warm parts of Zone 10. Native from Southern California east to Texas and south into Baja California. Open growth to 3 ft. high, 4–5 ft. wide. Leaves finely divided into tiny leaflets. Flower clusters show pink to white stamens in fluffy balls to 1½ in. across in late winter or early spring. No irrigation needed, but blooms and leaves (plant is summer deciduous) last longer with some summer water.

C. haematocephala. PINK POWDER PUFF. Evergreen. Best in Zones 22–24 and H2; but will grow in Zones 13, 16–21 if protected by overhang or trained to a warm, sunny wall. Native to Bolivia. Big puffs (2–3 in. across) of watermelon red stamens from fall to early spring. 'Alba' has white flowers. Leaflets are glossy copper when new, turning dark green; they're longer and broader than those of other species described here. Sprawler, growing quickly to 10 ft. high and wide—or more. Lax growth makes it very well suited to espaliering. Grow in light soil and provide regular water.

C. 'Sierra Star'. Evergreen to deciduous. Zones 10–24. Hybrid between *C. californica* and *C. eriophylla.* Produces red flowers sporadically all year on a shrub that is 4–5 ft. tall and wide. Densely branched.

C. tweedii. BRAZILIAN FLAME BUSH, TRINIDAD FLAME BUSH. Evergreen. Best in Zones 22–24; satisfactory in Zones 15–21; freezes back but recovers in Zones 7–9, 12–14. Native to Brazil and Uruguay. Graceful, picturesque growth to 6–8 ft. tall and wide. In mild-winter climates, can be pruned up to form a handsome small tree, to 15 ft. tall, with a wide, horizontal crown. Lacy, finely divided, fernlike leaves barely hide branching structure. Flower clusters, bright scarlet pompons at branch tips, are highly attractive to hummingbirds. Best flower show comes in early spring and fall, with occasional blossoms in between, but plant will bloom all winter if it gets enough heat. Little or no water.

Callicarpa

BEAUTYBERRY

Lamiaceae

DECIDUOUS SHRUBS

🌱 **ZONES VARY BY SPECIES**

☀️ 🌤 **FULL SUN OR LIGHT SHADE**

💧💧 **MODERATE TO REGULAR WATER**

🐦 **ATTRACT BIRDS**

Callicarpa bodinieri giraldii 'Profusion'

Graceful shrubs with arching branches. Small lilac or pink flowers in summer are followed by tight clusters of small, round, violet to purple fruits that persist well into winter. Effective in woodland gardens or massed in shrub borders. Bloom and fruit occur on current season's growth, so in late winter remove about a third of oldest stems or lop whole plant low to ground.

In the coldest regions, may freeze to ground but come back from roots.

C. bodinieri. BODINIER BEAUTYBERRY. Zones 3–9, 14–24. Native to China. Grows to 6 ft. or more and nearly as wide, with willowlike leaves that turn pink or orange to purple in fall. *C. b. giraldii* 'Profusion' is a heavy bearer.

C. dichotoma. PURPLE BEAUTYBERRY. Zones 2b–9, 14–24. Native to China, Korea, and Japan. About 4 ft. tall and slightly wider, with slender branches that sweep the ground. Resembles a smaller, finer-textured *C. bodinieri.* Fruits of *C. d. albifructus* are white. 'Early Amethyst' ripens its bright purple fruit earliest.

C. japonica. JAPANESE BEAUTYBERRY. Zones 2b–9, 14–24. Native to China, Taiwan, and Japan. To 5 ft. tall and wide, with deep reddish purple fall foliage. 'Leucocarpa' bears white fruit.

Callirhoe involucrata

POPPY MALLOW, WINE CUPS

Malvaceae

PERENNIAL

🌱 **ZONES 1–3, 7–14, 18–24**

☀️ 🌤 **PARTIAL SHADE IN HOTTEST CLIMATES**

💧💧 **LITTLE TO MODERATE WATER**

🐝 **ATTRACTS BENEFICIAL INSECTS**

Callirhoe involucrata

Native to prairies and plains from Wyoming to Missouri and Texas. Fleshy root produces a spreading plant 6 in. high and 2–3 ft. wide, with roundish, deeply cut leaves and a profusion of 2-in., purplish red, mallow-type flowers during hot weather. Needs good drainage but survives infertile soil and intense heat, except in desert, where it needs some shade and regular summer water.

Callistemon

BOTTLEBRUSH

Myrtaceae

EVERGREEN SHRUBS OR TREES

🌱 **ZONES VARY BY SPECIES**

☀️ **FULL SUN**

💧💧 **MODERATE TO REGULAR WATER**

🐦 **ATTRACT HUMMINGBIRDS**

Callistemon citrinus

The elongated flower spikes of these Australian natives are surrounded by long, bristlelike stamens that make blooms look almost exactly like bottlebrushes—hence the common name. Blooms are followed by woody capsules that can last for years.

Some bottlebrushes are dense and compact (making good informal hedges); others are sparse and open (can be pruned into small trees). Those with pliant branches can be espaliered. After bloom or before spring growth, remove weak or dead branches. Don't cut into bare wood beyond leaves—plant may not resprout. Endemic to moist sites, bottlebrushes can withstand waterlogged soil. Though tolerant of saline or alkaline soils, they sometimes suffer from chlorosis. Often severely damaged at 20°F (−7°C).

C. 'Canes Hybrid'. Zones 8, 9, 12–24. Grows 10 ft. tall and 15 ft. wide; prune to keep compact or shape into small tree. Slender, arching branches hold narrow leaves to 3 in. long; foliage is pink tinted when young, maturing to gray-green. Soft pink brushes appear in late spring and early summer.

C. citrinus. LEMON BOTTLE-BRUSH. Zones 8, 9, 12–24; H1, H2. Most commonly grown bottlebrush, and most tolerant of heat, cold, and poor soils. Naturally a shrub 10–15 ft. tall and wide, it is easily staked or pruned into a narrow, round-headed, 20–25-ft. tree. Nurseries sell it as shrub, espalier, or tree. Narrow leaves are coppery when new, maturing to vivid green. Bruised leaves smell lemony. Bright red, 6-in.-long brushes appear in waves throughout the year.

Variable plant when grown from seed. Among cutting-grown selections with good flower size and color: 'Violaceus' ('Jeffersii'), about 6 ft. tall and 4 ft. wide, has stiffer branching; narrower, shorter leaves; and reddish purple flowers fading to lavender. 'Mauve Mist' is the same but can reach 10 ft. 'Perth Pink', 10 ft. tall, has pink flower clusters.

C. rigidus. STIFF BOTTLE-BRUSH. Zones 8, 9, 12–24; H1, H2. Rigid, sparse shrub or small tree to 20 ft. with 10-ft. spread. Leaves sharp pointed, gray-green (sometimes purplish). Spring and summer red flower brushes are 2½–4½ in. long. Produces prominent seed capsules. Least graceful of the bottlebrushes.

C. salignus. WHITE BOTTLE-BRUSH. Zones 8, 9, 12–24. Shrub or tree to 20–25 ft. tall, 10–15 ft. wide. Dense crown of foliage. New growth bright pink to copper. Willowlike leaves 2–3 in. long. Pale yellow to cream-colored flowers appear in 1½–3-in. clusters in spring, early summer. Train as small shade tree or plant 4–5 ft. apart as hedge.

C. sieberi. ALPINE BOTTLE-BRUSH. Zones 5–9, 14–24. Shrub to 3–6 ft. tall and wide, with somewhat upright habit. Small, dark green leaves densely cover the pendulous branches. Cream to yellow flowers in 1½–6-in.-long brushes appear from late spring to midsummer. Good choice for colder areas.

C. viminalis. WEEPING BOT-TLEBRUSH. Zones 6–9, 12–24. Shrub or small tree with pendulous branches. Fast growing to 20–30 ft. tall, 15 ft. wide. Leaves narrow, light green. Bright red brushes appear late spring into summer, then sporadically. Not suitable for windy, dry areas. As a tree, needs staking; thin to prevent tangled,

top-heavy growth. Leaves tend to concentrate at branch ends.

'Little John' is a superior dwarf form to 3 ft. tall and wide, with dense growth pattern and blood red flowers in fall, winter, and spring. 'Captain Cook' is dense and rounded, to 6 ft. tall and wide, suitable for border, low hedge, or screen. 'Red Cascade' grows to a similar height with large, abundant, rosy red blooms. 'McCaskillii' is denser, with better flower color and form; to 20 ft. tall.

C. viridiflorus. GREEN BOT-TLEBRUSH. Zones 4–9, 14–24. Upright and open shrub to 6–8 ft. tall and wide. Golden, flaking bark. Dark green leaves are short and densely held along stems. Green to creamy yellow 3-in. brushes appear from spring to summer.

Callistephus chinensis

CHINA ASTER
Asteraceae
ANNUAL

📏 **ZONES 1–24**

☀️ **FULL SUN**

💧 **REGULAR WATER**

🦋 **ATTRACTS BUTTERFLIES**

Callistephus chinensis

This summer-flowering Chinese native makes a splendid cut flower and an effective bedding plant when well grown and disease free. Grows 8–36 in. high, 10–18 in. wide. Some types are branching; strong-stemmed types developed for florists have no side shoots. Leaves are deeply toothed or lobed.

Flower forms are classified as peony, pompon, anemone, and ostrich feather. Rays can

be quilled, curled, incurved, ribbonlike, or interlaced; some blooms have crested centers. Colors range from white to pastel pink, rose-pink, lavender, lavender-blue, violet, purple, crimson, wine, and scarlet.

CARE

Plant in rich, loamy or sandy soil. After danger of frost, sow seeds in place or set out plants started in flats. Keep growth steady; sudden checks in growth are harmful. Subject to aster yellows, a viral disease carried by leafhoppers. Discard infected plants; control leafhoppers. All but wilt-resistant types are subject to aster wilt or stem rot, caused by a soil-borne fungus. Overwatering encourages disease, especially in heavy or poorly drained soil. Never plant in the same location in successive years.

Calluna vulgaris

SCOTCH HEATHER
Ericaceae
EVERGREEN SHRUB

📏 **ZONES 1A, 2–6, 15–17**

☀️ **FULL SUN**

💧 **REGULAR WATER**

Calluna vulgaris

Scotch heather carpets the moors of Britain with finely textured foliage and pink summer flowers, and dots Europe clear to Asia Minor. It often keeps company with similar heaths (*Erica*) in the wild, as it does in Western gardens.

Horticultural varieties range from dwarf groundcovers only a couple of inches high to kinds reaching 3 ft. tall. Masses of tiny, urn-shaped flowers (actually

colored sepals) come in white, shades of pink, lavender, and purple. Most kinds flower in mid- to late summer, but a few bloom into late fall. All are good for cutting. Bud-blooming heathers produce flowers that don't open; the buds supply the color, which lasts much longer than buds that open. On all heathers, crowded, tiny, scalelike leaves come in paler and deeper greens, chartreuse, yellow, gray, or russet. As colors change or intensify in winter, they can deliver as much visual impact (especially when they contrast with each other) as the flowers they produce in summer.

Nurseries commonly carry several varieties of heather, while specialists stock scores of them. All begin blooming in summer, except as noted.

'Alicia'. Bud bloomer. Grows 12 in. high, 18 in. wide, with masses of white blooms from late summer through autumn.

'Anette'. Bud bloomer. Erect, to 1 ft. high, 16 in. wide. Medium green foliage; clear pink buds last well into fall.

'Aphrodite'. Bud bloomer. Grows 15 in. high, 24 in. wide, with red blooms in summer.

'Firefly'. Upright, to 1½ ft. high, 20 in. wide. Foliage is salmon-red in summer, turning bright red in winter. Deep mauve flowers.

'Kinlochruel'. Compact, to 10 in. high, 16 in. wide. Bright green foliage; spectacular white double flowers.

'Mrs. Ronald Grey'. Groundcover grows about 3 in. high, 18–21 in. wide. Purple flowers appear in mid- to late summer.

'Robert Chapman'. Spreading, to 10 in. high, 2 ft. wide. Greenish to reddish orange foliage; mauve flowers.

'Sandy'. Bud bloomer. Grows 15 in. high, 2 ft. wide, with white blooms in late summer through autumn.

'Silver Knight'. Upright, to 16 in. high, 20 in. wide. Downy gray foliage turns purple-gray in winter. Lavender flowers.

'Spring Torch'. Spreading, to 1 ft. high, 20 in. wide. Red-tipped green foliage and pink flowers.

'Tib'. Rounded, bushy, to 1 ft. high, 15 in. wide. Medium green foliage; deepest rosy purple double flowers.

»

Kramer's red Jan/april
Milky way July/Sept
Red Fred Aug/Sept

CARE

Heathers thrive in sandy, slightly acid, fast-draining soil. In the Northwest, they require little or no fertilizing. Where watering must be frequent, light feeding with acid plant food—once in late winter, again in early summer—will encourage good growth and bloom. To prune, shear off faded flowers and tip growth immediately after bloom; delay pruning on fall-flowering types until late winter.

C

Calocedrus decurrens

(Libocedrus decurrens)

INCENSE CEDAR

Cupressaceae

EVERGREEN TREE

ZONES 2–12, 14–24

FULL SUN OR LIGHT SHADE

NO IRRIGATION TO MODERATE WATER

Calocedrus decurrens

Native to the mountains from Oregon to northern Baja California, this beauty grows 75–90 ft. tall and 15 ft. wide with a dense, pyramidal crown. It adapts easily to many Western climates. Trunk bark is reddish brown. Rich green foliage is held in flat sprays, as though it had been ironed. Small, yellow-brown to reddish brown cones look like ducks' bills when opened. This tree produces a pungently sweet fragrance in warm weather. It was once a primary wood for pencils—thus the alternate common name, "pencil cedar."

Though slow at first, incense cedar may grow 2 ft. per year when established, tolerating blazing summer heat and poor soils. No supplemental water needed in Zones 2, 4–7, 15–17. This makes an excellent specimen, screen, or windbreak.

Calochortus

MARIPOSA LILY, SEGO LILY

Liliaceae

PERENNIALS FROM BULBS

ZONES VARY BY SPECIES

FULL SUN OR LIGHT SHADE

REGULAR WATER DURING GROWTH AND BLOOM

Calochortus superbus 'Fairy Lantern'

These beautiful, grassy Western natives come in three distinct flower forms. Globe tulips or fairy lanterns have nodding flowers, the petals turning inward to form a globe. Star tulips have upward-facing, cup-shaped flowers, with petal tips often rolled outward; those with long, straight hairs on the inner flower parts are called cat's ears or pussy ears. Mariposa lilies are generally the tallest, with striking cup- or bowl-shaped blossoms. Flower colors include yellow, purple, lavender, red, pink, and white. All demand the long, warm, dry summers of their native habitats. Bloom time for most is spring or early summer.

The most widely sold are the lavender hybrid 'Cupido'; yellow-cupped *C. luteus* 'Golden Orb'; *C. superbus,* in white, cream, or pale lilac with brown blotches; *C.*'Symphony', white with maroon throat; *C. venustus,* in white, yellow, purple, or red with dark red blotches; and wine red *C. v.* 'Burgundy'. One type, sego lily (*C. nuttallii*), is the state flower of Utah. Look for these at native plant nurseries and from mail-order bulb nurseries.

CARE

Plant in fall, setting bulbs 3–4 in. deep and about 6 in. apart in well-drained soil. Naturalize on sunny, grassy slopes that remain unwatered in summer, or grow in containers that you bury in the landscape, and then lift after bloom for storage.

Calonyction aculeatum. See *Ipomoea alba*

Calycanthus

Calycanthaceae

DECIDUOUS SHRUBS

ZONES VARY BY SPECIES

SUN OR SHADE

REGULAR WATER

SEEDS CAN PRODUCE CONVULSIONS

Calycanthus occidentalis

These bulky shrubs have lush foliage and flowers valued for their fragrance and form. Blooms appear at ends of current season's growth. Remove twiggy or crowded stems annually, but for best appearance don't prune further.

C. floridus. CAROLINA ALLSPICE. Zones 3–9, 14–17. Native from Virginia to Florida. Stiffly branched to 6–10 ft. tall and wide or wider; suckering, fast spreading. Oval leaves to 5 in. long are glossy dark green above, grayish green beneath. Flowers—2 in. wide, reddish brown, with heady, strawberry-like fragrance—come in late spring or early summer, and are followed by brownish, pear-shaped capsules, fragrant when crushed. Aroma varies, so buy plants in bloom. 'Athens' has yellow flowers.

C. occidentalis. SPICE BUSH. Zones 4–9, 14–24. Native along streams and moist slopes in California's Coast Ranges and Sierra Nevada foothills. To 4–12 ft. high and wide. Bright green leaves turn yellow in fall. Brownish red flowers to 2 in. across, resembling small water lilies, appear in mid-spring to summer, depending on climate. Both flowers and bruised leaves have the fragrance of an old wine barrel. Can be trained into a multistemmed small tree, but is most useful as a background shrub.

Calylophus

SUNDROPS

Onagraceae

PERENNIALS

ZONES 1–3, 6–16, 18–24

FULL SUN OR LIGHT SHADE

LITTLE TO MODERATE WATER

Calylophus hartwegii fendleri

These Western natives have bright yellow, four-petaled flowers that appear over a long summer bloom period. In Zone 13, flowering declines in summer heat, and plants flower in spring and from late summer to fall. Spread by rhizomes and are useful for summer color in difficult climates.

C. drummondianus. To 1½ ft. high, 2 ft. wide, with narrow, tooth-edged, somewhat drooping leaves and inch-wide flowers. This species blooms for a longer period than *C. hartwegii* in spring, but it does not rebloom as well in fall.

C. hartwegii fendleri. To 1 ft. high, 2 ft. across, with inch-wide flowers.

C. h. lavandulifolius. Narrow, gray leaves. Excellent in hot, dry locations and when mixed with desert perennials.

C. serrulatus. Prairie wildflower found from Saskatchewan to Texas. To 1½ ft. high and wide, with ¾-in. flowers.

CARE

Plant in well-drained soil. These tolerate regular water if drainage is superb. Shear just before spring growth begins.

Camassia

CAMASS
Asparagaceae
PERENNIALS FROM BULBS

☀ ZONES 1–9, 14–17, EXCEPT AS NOTED

☼ ☽ FULL SUN OR LIGHT SHADE

💧 💧💧 REGULAR TO AMPLE WATER DURING GROWTH AND BLOOM

Camassia quamash

Colonies of these grassy perennials paint moist meadows blue or white in their native Northern California and Pacific Northwest. Their slender spikes of loosely spaced, starlike blossoms appear in spring.

C. cusickii. Dense clusters of pale blue flowers on stems to 3 ft. high.

C. leichtlinii. Large, handsome clusters of creamy white flowers on 4-ft.-tall stems.
C. l. suksdorfii has blue to deep blue-violet flowers. This subspecies' variety 'Blue Danube' is deep blue. Varieties of the species include 'Alba' (*C. l. leichtlinii*), white with bluish tinge, and 'Semiplena', with creamy white semidouble blooms.

C. quamash. Zones 1–10, 14–17. Loose clusters of blue flowers on 1–2-ft. stems. Flowers of 'Blue Melody' are deeper blue, with variegated foliage.

CARE

Plant in fall after weather cools. Put bulbs 3–4 in. deep, 6 in. apart in moisture-retentive soil that can remain undisturbed for many years. Interplant with other grasses and perennials that will fill in when camass's leaves yellow and die. Bulbs need only rainfall during summer dormancy.

Camellia

Theaceae
EVERGREEN SHRUBS OR TREES

☀ ZONES 4–9, 12, 14–24, EXCEPT AS NOTED

☽ BEST OUT OF STRONG SUN

💧 💧 MODERATE TO REGULAR WATER

Camellia hiemalis 'Chansonette'

Camellias grow over a wider latitude range along the West Coast than anywhere else. Typically loaded with white, pink, red, or variegated blooms during the cool season, many of these robust shrubs flower heavily when other bloom is scarce. Native to southern and eastern Asia, they are unscented except as noted.

Big *C. japonica* varieties are the most popular, with fall- and winter-flowering *C. sasanqua* varieties coming in second. All are classic understory shrubs that thrive in filtered shade. They also grow well in pots.

Five camellia forms are shown on page 216. The sixth—rose-double form—is pictured above.

C. chrysantha (C. nitidissima nitidissima). GOLDEN CAMELLIA. Tall, vigorous, open grower to 6–16 ft. tall, 10–12 ft. wide, with glossy, net-veined leaves and 2–2½-in., golden yellow flowers. Hybridizers are using it to bring yellow into the camellia color palette.

C. granthamiana. Big shrub or small tree of open growth to 10 ft. tall, 6 ft. wide, with leathery, glossy, veined, and crinkled leaves. Autumn flowers are large white singles, often with fluted or folded ("rabbit ear") petals surrounding a heavy tuft of bright yellow stamens. A cross with *C. reticulata* produced 'China Lady', which looks like a big pink *C. granthamiana*. It has been the parent of several other remarkable seedling camellias. All need excellent drainage.

C. hiemalis. Includes a number of varieties often classed with sasanquas, but differing in their later, longer bloom; heavier-textured flowers; and usually smaller size.

'Chansonette'. Vigorous, spreading growth to 6 ft. tall, 8 ft. wide. Large, bright pink, formal double flowers.

'Shishi-Gashira'. One of the most useful and ornamental shrubs. Low growing (3 ft. high and 6 ft. wide), with arching branches that in time pile up tier on tier to make a compact, dark green, glossy-leafed plant. Medium-fine foliage texture. Flowers rose-red, semidouble to double, 2–2½ in. wide, heavily borne from fall through winter in a good year. Full sun or shade.

'Showa-No-Sakae'. To 3 ft. high, 6–8 ft. wide. Faster growing, more open than 'Shishi-Gashira'; willowy, arching branches. Semidouble to double soft pink flowers. Try this as an espalier.

C. japonica. Zones 4–9, 12, 14–24; H1. This is the plant most gardeners have in mind when they speak of camellias. Naturally a large shrub or small tree—expect 6–12 ft. tall and wide in the garden—but varieties vary considerably. Hundred-year-old plants in California reach 20 ft. tall and wide, and low forms exist.

The Higo japonicas are generally compact plants; they have dense, heavy foliage and thick-petaled single flowers with a broad, full brush of yellow stamens in the center; ideally, the stamens should cover at least half the flower's diameter. Colors include white, pink, and red—both solid and variegated, as with regular japonicas. Good examples include 'Hi-no-maru', a slow-growing, upright red with wavy petals and a good brush of stamens; and 'Ohkan', another slow grower whose white flowers have rose-colored edges.

The following japonica varieties are especially beautiful.

Bloom season is listed as early, midseason, or late. In California, early means October to January; midseason, January to March; late, March to May. In the Southwest, early means October to December; midseason, January and February; late, March and April. In the Northwest, early means December to February; midseason, March and April; late, May. In flower descriptions, very large blooms are over 5 in. wide; large are 4–5 in.; medium-large, 3½–4 in.; medium, 3–3½ in.; small, 2½–3 in.; miniature, 2½ in. or less.

'Alba Plena'. Early. Brought from China over two centuries ago and still a favorite. Large white formal double. Slow, bushy growth. Early bloom is a disadvantage in cold or rainy areas; protect blossoms from rain and wind.

'April Remembered'. Early to late. Cream-colored to blush, semidouble flowers. Fast growing and very hardy.

'Bob Hope'. Midseason. Large to very large deep red semidouble blooms have prominent golden stamens. Large, vigorous plant.

'Carter's Sunburst'. Early to late. Large to very large flowers, semidouble to peony form to formal double, in pale pink striped with deeper pink. Medium-size, compact plant.

'Debutante'. Early to midseason. Medium-large, light pink peony-form flowers. Profuse bloomer. Vigorous upright growth. Takes some sun.

'Elegans' (Chandler); also sold as 'Francine' ('Chandleri Elegans Pink'). Early to midseason. The founder of a large and growing family of sports. The original plant is slow growing and spreading, bearing large anemone-form blossoms in rose-pink; center petaloids are often marked with white. More frequently grown is 'Elegans Variegated', identical except for white variegation on all petals; it is often known simply as Chandleri Elegans.

»

C

CAMELLIA FLOWER FORMS

SINGLE:
C. japonica 'Spring's Promise'

SEMIDOUBLE:
C. hiemalis 'Shishi-Gashira'

PEONY: *C. japonica* 'Extravaganza'

ANEMONE:
C. japonica 'Elegans'

FORMAL DOUBLE:
C. japonica 'Pearl Maxwell'

'Glen 40' ('Coquettii'). Midseason to late. Large, deep red formal double. One of the best reds for corsages. Slow, compact, upright growth. Handsome even out of bloom. Hardy; good in containers.

'Guilio Nuccio'. Midseason. Considered by many to be the world's finest camellia. Coral rose, very large semidouble flowers of unusual depth and substance have inner petals fluted in "rabbit ear" effect. Vigorous upright growth. Forms with variegated, fringed blossoms are available.

'Herme' ('Jordan's Pride'). Midseason. Medium-large, pink semidouble flowers irregularly bordered in white and streaked with deeper pink. Sometimes bears solid pink blooms on certain branches. Free blooming and dependable.

'Korean Fire'. Early. Single red flowers with hardiness to −12°F (−24°C).

'Kramer's Supreme'. Midseason. Very large, full peony-form flowers in clear red. Some detect a faint fragrance. Compact, upright, unusually vigorous. Takes some sun.

'Kumasaka'. Midseason to late. Medium-large, rose-pink rose-form double to peony-form flowers. Vigorous, compact, upright growth and remarkably heavy flower production make it a choice landscape plant. Hardy. Takes morning sun.

'Magnoliiflora'. Midseason. Medium, pale pink semidouble flowers. Heavy bloomer; good cut flower. Medium-size plant with spreading form. Hardy.

'Mathotiana'. Midseason to late. Very large rose-form double to formal double blooms in deep crimson, sometimes with purplish cast. Vigorous, upright grower. Takes cold and stands up well in hot-summer areas.

'Nuccio's Bella Rossa'. Early through midseason. Bears large, crimson-red formal blossoms over a long period, even on young plants.

'Nuccio's Gem'. Midseason. Medium to large, white, perfectly formed formal double. Full, upright plant.

'Nuccio's Pearl'. Midseason. Medium, full formal double blossoms are white with a rim of deep pink outer petals.

'Pearl Maxwell'. Midseason to late. Large, soft, shell pink flowers with formal double form.

'Pink Parade'. Midseason. Large, clear pink semidouble to peony-form flowers. Erect and slow growing.

'Pink Perfection'. Early to late. Small, formal double shell-pink flowers.

'Purity'. Late. Medium white flowers, rose-form double to formal double, usually showing a few stamens. Vigorous, upright plant. Often escapes rain damage.

'Silver Waves'. Early to midseason. Large white semidouble blooms with wavy petal edges.

'Spring's Promise'. Early to midseason. Red single flowers bloom freely in winter.

'Swan Lake'. Midseason to late. Very large white flowers with formal double to peony form. Vigorous, upright growth.

'Tom Knudsen'. Early to midseason. Medium to large blooms in dark red with deeper red veining. Formal double to peony form to rose-form double.

C. j. rusticana. SNOW CAMELLIA. To 6–12 ft. tall, 3–10 ft. wide. A class of small-flowered camellias from a cold, extremely snowy part of Japan. Flowers may be white, pink, or red, and single to double in form. Plants tend to be spreading, and branches are remarkably supple. They are no hardier than *C. japonica* and are generally considered to be a subspecies. 'Botanyuki' is a good example, with miniature blush pink flowers, anemone form.

C. lutchuensis. Shrub to 10 ft. tall, 12 ft. wide, with tiny leaves and profusion of tiny white flowers with strong, pleasant fragrance. Used as parent to introduce fragrance to larger camellias. Long, pliant branches make it an easily trained espalier.

C. oleifera. Shrub or small tree 10–20 ft. tall, 6–12 ft. wide, with open growth habit and somewhat weeping branches. Leaves are glossy green. Flowers are small (1½ in.), white or cream, fragrant. Possibly the hardiest of all camellia species and a parent of hardy hybrids. The source of tea oil.

C. reticulata. Some of the biggest and most spectacular camellia flowers occur in this species, often on some of the lankiest and least graceful plants. Plants vary but generally start as gaunt, open shrubs that eventually attain considerable size—possibly 35–50 ft. tall. In gardens, consider them 10-ft.-tall shrubs, 8 ft. wide. Leaves are usually dull green, leathery, and strongly netted.

These are intolerant of heavy pruning. With their natural lankiness, this makes them difficult to place in garden. They are at their best in light shade of old oaks, where they should stand alone with plenty of room to develop. In Zones 4–6, grow them beneath an overhang or near wall.

All bloom January to May in California, January to April in the Southwest, March to May in the Northwest. 'Buddha' has a very large, rose-pink flower; inner petals unusually erect and wavy. Fast grower. True variety of 'Chang's Temple' is large, open-centered, deep rose flower, with notched and fluted center petals. 'Mandalay Queen' has very large semidouble pink flowers with fluted petals. 'Mouchang' has very large, single to semidouble salmon-pink flowers. Vigorous. 'William Hertrich' has very large, semidouble, deep red flowers with heavy petals.

C. saluenensis. Shrub of dense, leafy growth to 10–15 ft. tall and wide. Leaves elliptic, rather narrow, pointed, thick textured. Early-spring flowers are bell shaped and rather small, varying in color from white to fairly deep pink. Not of great value in itself, it has brought floriferousness, hardiness, and graceful appearance to a large group of its hybrids.

C. sasanqua. Useful broadleafed evergreens for espaliers, groundcovers, informal hedges, screening, and containers. Plants vary in form from spreading and vinelike to upright and densely bushy; sizes range from 1½ ft. high and 6 ft. wide to 12 ft. tall and wide. Leaves are dark green, shiny. Flowers, heavily produced in autumn and early winter, are short-lived, rather flimsy, but so numerous that plants make a show for months. Some are lightly (and pungently) fragrant.

Most sasanquas tolerate much sun, and in fact flower best in winter sun; some even thrive in full year-round sun with the right soil and regular water.

'Apple Blossom'. Single white flowers blushed with pink, from pink buds. Upright, somewhat leggy plant.

'Bonanza'. Early. Scarlet-red semidouble flowers. Low-growing, spreading plant.

'Cleopatra'. Rose-pink semidouble flowers with narrow, curving petals. Growth is erect and fairly compact. Takes clipping well.

'Jean May'. Double, shell pink flowers. Compact, upright grower with glossy foliage.

'Kanjiro'. Large semidouble flowers of rose-pink shading to rose-red at petal edges. Erect growth habit.

'Mine-No-Yuki' ('White Doves'). Large, full peony-form flower. Drops many buds. Spreading, willowy growth; effective espalier.

'Setsugekka'. Large, white semidouble flowers with fluted petals. Blossoms have substance; cut sprays hold well in water. Upright and rather bushy shrub.

'Yuletide'. The best of these, with its profusion of small, single, bright red flowers with yellow anthers on a dense, compact, upright plant. Bloom comes in late fall, early winter.

C. sinensis (Thea sinensis). TEA. In the West, the tea plant grows as a dense round shrub to 15 ft. tall and wide, with leathery, dull, dark green leaves to 5 in. long. White, 1½-in.-wide, fragrant flowers appear in fall. Takes well to pruning. Can be trimmed as hedge. Tea could be grown commercially in California, but the economics are against it. 'Sochi' also has fragrant white flowers.

C. × vernalis. These are likely natural hybrids between japonicas and sasanquas, with which they are often classed and sold. They tend to be denser in growth, shiny in leaf, and have firm-textured flowers. The following varieties grow 9 ft. tall and 6 ft. wide. 'Egao' is a large, vigorous, semidouble pink. 'Star Above Star' has white flowers that blush fuchsia at the edges.

How to Grow Camellias

EXPOSURE Camellias grow and bloom best when protected from strong sun, but tall old plants prove that some kinds of camellias can thrive in full sun when they are mature enough for their roots to be shaded by heavy leaf canopy. Young plants grow and bloom better in partial shade. A few camellias need shade at any age.

SOIL Moist, well-drained soil with high organic content. Avoid high pH. Because roots are not generally deep, plants benefit from thick organic mulch. To grow camellias in containers, plant gallon-size plants into 12–14-in.-wide pots, 5-gal. ones into 16–18-in. tubs. Fill with a planting mix containing 50 percent or more organic material.

WATERING & FERTILIZING Established plants (over 3 years old, vigorous, and shading their own roots) can get by with little supplemental water. Feed with a commercial acid plant food after bloom. Never feed sick plants.

PRUNING Prune away dead or weak wood, and thin when growth is too dense for flowers to open properly. Make cuts just above the scars that terminate the previous year's growth (often a slightly thickened, somewhat rough area where bark texture and color change slightly). This will usually force three or four dormant buds into growth. The best time for pruning is right after bloom.

CHALLENGES Poor drainage and salty soil or water are the main troublemakers for camellias. Best cure is to move plant into aboveground bed of pure ground bark or peat moss until it recovers. If you irrigate with water high in salts, leach accumulated salts out of the soil around camellia roots with deep soaking twice each summer.

Scorched or yellowed areas in center of leaves are from sunburn. Burned leaf edges, excessive leaf drop, or corky spots usually indicate overfertilizing. Yellow leaves with green veins are signs of chlorosis; treat with iron or iron chelates.

Camellia petal blight causes flowers to rapidly turn an ugly brown. (Browning at edges of petals—especially on whites and pale pinks—may be caused by sun or wind.) Sanitation is the best control. Pick up all fallen flowers and petals, pick off all infected flowers from plants, and dispose of them in covered trash bin; encourage neighbors to do the same. Remove any mulch, haul it away, and replace with fresh material; a 4–5-in.-deep mulch helps keep fungus spores from reaching the air and infecting flowers.

Some flower bud dropping is natural, some environmental. It can be caused by overwatering, but underwatering is more likely, especially during summer. It can also be caused by very low humidity. But some varieties just set more buds than they can open. To get nicest display from them, remove all but one or two round flower buds (leaf buds are more slender); along stems, remove enough to leave a single flower bud for each 2–4 in. of branch.

»

C

Hybrid camellias. These are crosses between two or more species. The following have medium-size flowers unless noted. See *C. japonica* for explanations of bloom season and flower-size terminology.

'Coral Delight'. Midseason. Coral pink semidouble flowers form garlands along the branches. Slow grower.

'Donation'. Midseason. Large semidouble flowers of orchid pink borne all along stems. Blooms young and heavily on vigorous, somewhat spreading, compact plant with slightly pendulous branches. Quite resistant to cold and sun. Appreciates a little shade in hot, dry areas. There is a form with variegated flowers.

'Dr. Clifford Parks'. Midseason. Very large blossoms in an orange-toned rich red. They are semidouble to loose peony form to anemone form. The plant is vigorous and upright.

'Fairy Blush'. Early to late. This *C. lutchuensis* hybrid has clusters of lightly fragrant single flowers colored like apple blossoms. Leaves are small and growth is fast.

'Frank Houser'. Midseason. This *C. reticulata* hybrid is vigorous, open, and upright, with very large, rose-colored flowers; semidouble to peony form with rabbit-eared petals.

'Freedom Bell'. Midseason. Small to medium semidouble, bell-shaped blooms of dark red open beneath branches.

'High Fragrance'. Mid- to late season. This *C. lutchuensis* hybrid has fragrant, ivory-pink, peony-form flowers with deeper pink edges. Vigorous growth, open habit.

'Taylor's Perfection'. Midseason. Profuse light pink semidouble flowers. Fast growing; ideal for trellis or espalier.

'Yume'. Mid- to late season. This medium, spreading grower produces a profusion of small single pink flowers blotched white, often with pink and white alternating petals.

Hardy hybrids. These camellias, bred from *C. oleifera,* are among the hardiest of all; they withstand temperatures to –10°F (–23°C) given an overhead tree canopy and protection from cold, drying winds.

Most produce semidouble flowers; bloom period is fall and winter. Pink varieties include 'Winter's Beauty', 'Winter's Joy', and 'Winter's Rose'; white ones include 'Lu Shan Snow', 'Winter's Snowman', and 'Winter's Waterlily'. 'Winter's Star' is purplish red.

Campanula
BELLFLOWER
Campanulaceae
MOSTLY PERENNIALS; SOME BIENNIALS OR ANNUALS

🗡 **ZONES 1–9, 14–24, EXCEPT AS NOTED**

☼ ◑ **FULL SUN IN COOLER CLIMATES ONLY**

◔ ◑ **MODERATE TO REGULAR WATER**

🐦 **ATTRACT HUMMINGBIRDS**

» See chart on facing page.

Campanula persicifolia 'Telham Beauty'

Campanulas are most often recognized by their blue or white flowers (they also come in pink, violet, and lavender). Usually, flower stalks rise above basal leaf rosettes. The perennial species tend to spread from the root; width depends mainly on vigor of their rootstocks and time they have been in one spot. Flowers are generally bell shaped, though some are star shaped, cupped, or round and flat. Bloom comes at some time from spring to fall, depending on species. Native throughout the Northern Hemisphere; those featured here come mostly from southern Europe, Turkey, the Caucasus, and northern Asia.

Uses are as varied as the plants. Gemlike miniatures deserve special settings—close-up situations in rock gardens, niches in dry walls, raised

beds, containers. Trailing kinds are ideal for hanging pots or baskets, wall crevices; vigorous, spreading growers serve well as ground covers. Upright growers are valuable in borders, for cutting, occasionally in containers.

CARE

Campanulas grow best in good, well-drained soil. Most species are easy to grow from seeds sown in spring or early summer. Set transplants out in fall for bloom the following year. Also may be increased by divisions or cuttings. Divide clumps in fall every 3 or 4 years; some may need yearly division. Some species seed freely, and a few have invasive tendencies; may be difficult to remove when entwined with roots of shrubs, trees, or other perennials. For these species, choose sites carefully. Some campanulas are attractive to slugs and snails. Watch for spider mites in hot, dry weather.

Campsis
TRUMPET CREEPER, TRUMPET VINE
Bignoniaceae
SEMIEVERGREEN TO DECIDUOUS VINES

🗡 **ZONES VARY BY SPECIES**

☼ ◑ **FULL SUN OR PARTIAL SHADE**

◔ ◑ **MODERATE TO REGULAR WATER**

🐦 **ATTRACT BIRDS**

Campsis radicans

With vigorous growth and hot-colored flowers, trumpet creepers give even cool-summer gardens a tropical look. All bear radiant blossoms shaped like flaring trumpets, in clusters at branch tips midsummer to fall. Glossy leaves are divided into leaflets. Stems have aerial

rootlets; they cling to wood, brick, stucco, and other surfaces. Unless pruned and tied to supporting surface, old plants can become top-heavy and pull away. Each dormant season, shorten some of the branches and thin others. Pinch back shoot tips in summer to keep plants bushy. Plants spread by suckering roots; pull any that appear. If older plants become unmanageable, cut to the ground before spring growth begins and train a few strong new stems.

C. grandiflora (Bignonia chinensis). CHINESE TRUMPET CREEPER. Zones 4–24. Not as vigorous, large, or hardy as the American native *C. radicans,* but flowers are slightly larger and redder. Each leaf has up to nine leaflets. Grows to 30 ft. under ideal conditions.

C. radicans (Bignonia radicans). COMMON TRUMPET CREEPER. Zones 1–21. Native to eastern U.S. Most widely used in cold-winter areas. Deep freeze will kill it to ground, but new stems grow quickly. Each leaf has up to 11 leaflets. Flowers are 3-in.-long orange tubes with scarlet lobes flaring to 2 in. wide. Grows fast to 40 ft. or more, bursting with health and vigor. 'Balboa Sunset' has darker red blooms. 'Flava' has yellow blossoms and somewhat lighter green leaves.

C. × tagliabuana. Zones 3b–24. Hybrid between above two species. 'Mme Galen', the best-known variety, has salmon-red flowers. 'Indian Summer' has salmon blooms with red-orange throat.

In lightly shaded beds, campanulas pair well with other plants that like the same conditions—ferns, hydrangeas, and meadow rue. For a cooling combo on a patio, plant white hydrangea with white-flowered campanula in a large container.

CAMPANULA: TOP PICKS TO GROW

NAME, TYPE	GROWTH HABIT, SIZE	FOLIAGE	FLOWERS	USES, COMMENTS
Campanula carpatica TUSSOCK BELLFLOWER Perennial	Compact, spreading, leafy tufts, to 6 in. high. Flower stems upright, branching; usually about 8 in. high but may rise 1–1½ ft.	Smooth, green, with wavy, toothed edges, 1–1½ in. long. Round basal leaves often dry up before bloom; stem leaves oval to triangular.	Profuse, upward facing, bell or cup shaped, 1–2 in.; light blue, violet, or white. Variable in flower size and color. 'Blue Clips' and 'White Clips' grow 9 in. tall, 11 in. wide; easy from seed. 'Pearl Deep Blue' and 'Pearl White' grow 7 in. high, 9 in. wide. Late spring.	Rock gardens, foreground in borders, edging. Excellent choice in damp sites.
C. cochleariifolia FAIRY THIMBLES Perennial	Dainty, ground-hugging mat of rosettes from spreading roots. Wiry, erect stems rise 3–6 in. high.	Shiny, ¾ in., heart-shaped or almost round with 3 large teeth on each side. Stem leaves narrow, lance-shaped.	Solitary, ½ in., nodding, thimble-shaped. 'Bavaria Blue', deep blue; 'Alba', pure white; 'Elizabeth Oliver', nested powder-blue bells; 'Advance Blue' and 'Advance White' are taller, more upright. All-summer bloom in cooler areas.	Rock crevices, troughs, between paving stones, edging. Easy to grow; spreads and seeds vigorously.
C. garganica Perennial Zones 1–9, 14–24	Tight mat, 3–6 in. high, with spreading or trailing flower stems to 6 in.	Small, gray or green, sharply toothed, kidney- or heart-shaped.	Upward-facing, flat, ½-in. stars in violet blue with white centers. One or several atop each stem. 'Baby Blue' is tiny, light blue. Late spring to fall.	Rock gardens, troughs, edging. Somewhat like miniature, prostrate *C. poscharskyana*. 'Dickson's Gold' has golden foliage given enough sun.
C. glomerata Perennial Zones A1, A2; 1–10, 14–24	Upright, with erect side branches to 1–2 ft.	Basal leaves broad, wavy edged. Stem leaves broad, toothed. Both somewhat hairy.	Narrow, 1-in. bells, flaring at the mouth, in violet, blue, white. Tightly clustered at tops of stems. Spring through summer. Plants have proportionately more foliage than flowers.	Shaded borders or large rock gardens. 'Alba' has white flowers; 'Acaulis' has 6-in. blue flower spikes; 'Joan Elliott' produces 2-ft. stems of purple flowers; 'Purple Pixie' has violet-purple flowers on 14-in. stems.
C. lactiflora Perennial Zones 1–9, 14–24	Erect, branching, leafy, 3½–5 ft. tall.	Oblong, pointed, finely toothed, 2–5 in. long.	Broadly bell- to star-shaped flower, 1 in.; violet to pale blue, white, pink. 'Avalanche' is white; 'Gloaming' is smoky lavender. Summer.	Back of border, sun or part shade. Endures even dry shade and is long-lived. 'Pouffe' (lavender) and 'White Pouffe' form 10-in., bloom-covered mound.
C. persicifolia PEACH-LEAFED BLUEBELL Perennial	Strong-growing, slender, erect stems 2–3 ft. high. Plants leafy at base.	Basal leaves smooth edged, green, 4–8 in. long. Stem leaves 2–4 in. long, shaped like leaves of peach tree.	Open, cup-shaped, about 1 in. across, held erect by short side shoots on sturdy stems. Blue, pink, or white. 'Telham Beauty', an old favorite, has 3-in. blue flowers. Summer.	Choice border plant. Easy from seed sown in late spring. 'Blue-Eyed Blond' has blue flowers over gold foliage, takes wet soil; 'Chettle Charm' has white flowers edged in lavender; 'Takion Blue' and 'Takion White' flower heavily on 18-by-16-in. plants.
C. portenschlagiana DALMATIAN BELLFLOWER Perennial Zones 2–9, 14–24	Low, leafy, mounding or trailing mats 4–6 in. high. Semi-erect, branching flower stems to 8 in. high.	Roundish, heart-shaped, deep green with deeply toothed, slightly wavy edges.	Flaring bell-shaped, violet-blue or grayish white to 1 in. long; several to each stem. Late spring into summer, sometimes blooming again in fall.	Fine plant for edging or as small-scale groundcover. Spreads moderately fast; is sturdy, permanent, and not invasive. Easily increased by dividing. 'Birch Hybrid' has cup-shaped, purple-blue flowers, spreads to 18 in.
C. poscharskyana SERBIAN BELLFLOWER Perennial Zones 1–12, 14–24	Spreading, mounding, leafy clump to 8 in. high. Branching, semiupright flower stems to 1 ft. or more.	Elongated heart shape, irregularly toothed, slightly hairy, 1–3½ in. long, ¾–3 in. wide.	Star-shaped, ½–1-in.-wide blooms in blue-lilac, lavender, or grayish white. Spring to early summer.	Vigorous. Place in a shaded border with fuchsias or begonias. Good small-scale, low-water groundcover. 'Alba' has white flowers; 'Blue Waterfall' has light blue flowers with white centers.
C. punctata Perennial	Flat basal rosette spreads rapidly by underground runners. Wiry 12–22-in. flower stems arch over at tip.	Dark green, toothed, 4–5 in., heart-shaped leaves narrower on upper stems.	Long (2–2½ in.), waxy, drooping bells; cream to deep maroon, inside paler and spotted crimson. 'Cherry Bells' is bright, deep rose. Late spring to early summer, then sporadic.	Forms dense, weed-suppressing mat among shrubs, but too invasive for mixed borders. Smaller forms such as 'Dwarf Pink' are available.
C. 'Samantha' Perennial Zones 2b–9, 14–24	Spreading mat 7 in. high, 18 in. wide, with flower stems rising 11 in.	Medium green leaves are elongated, heart-shaped, toothed.	Fragrant, cup-shaped, 1-in. flowers are violet-blue at edges, lighter toward the center, face upward.	Makes an excellent low edging for a border or a mixed container planting.

C

C

Candollea cuneiformis.
See *Hibbertia cuneiformis*

Canna
Cannaceae
PERENNIALS FROM RHIZOMES

🌡 ZONES 6–9, 12–24; H1, H2;
    OR DIG AND STORE

☀ FULL SUN

💧💧 REGULAR TO AMPLE WATER
     DURING GROWTH AND BLOOM

Canna 'Tropicanna'

Showy in leaf and flower, cannas are equally effective in containers and in the ground. Most are hybrids descended from species native to American tropics and subtropics. Large, lance-shaped leaves may be rich green, bronzy red, or variegated. Spikes of large, irregularly shaped flowers come in red, orange, yellow, pink, cream, white, or bicolors, flowering in summer and fall.

All show well in groups of single colors against plain backgrounds. Grow in borders, near poolside, in large pots or tubs on terrace or patio.

Many new varieties flaunt brightly colored leaves as well as showy flowers. Among those in the 4–6 ft. range, 'Bengal Tiger' ('Striata', 'Pretoria') has yellow-striped green leaves and orange blossoms; 'Tropicanna' ('Phasion') produces hot orange blooms over purple foliage that becomes striped with green, yellow, pink, and red; *C. indica* 'Tropicanna Gold' has yellow-orange flowers flecked with dark orange over leaves that are striped green and gold; 'Tropicanna Black' has deep bronzy chocolate leaves and red flowers that fade to orange; and 'Black Knight' has blackish bronze foliage and velvety, deep red flowers.

'Ermine' ('Ermine White') has white flowers on a 3–4-ft. plant; 'President' has scarlet blooms; 'Intrigue' has orange flowers on a 6–8-ft. plant.

For dwarf varieties that grow 24–30 in. high, try 'Red Futurity', with red flowers and dark-striped green leaves; and 'Yellow Futurity', with yellow flowers against green foliage.

Most cannas do well in wet soil, but water cannas (*C. glauca*) seem made for it. Try 'Erebus', salmon-pink, 4–6 ft. tall, with slender stems and small (for a canna) blue-green leaves.

CARE

Best adapted to warm- to hot-summer climates; in areas where soil freezes deeply, lift and store over winter. Plant in spring after danger of frost is past, setting rhizomes in rich, loose soil, 2–4 in. deep, 1½–2 ft. apart. For a good head start on bloom in colder regions, start rhizomes indoors 4 to 6 weeks before last frost date; then plant out. Cut each stem to ground after it finishes blooming; new stems will continue to grow into early fall. Divide clumps every 3 or 4 years.

Capparis spinosa
CAPER
Capparaceae
EVERGREEN OR DECIDUOUS SHRUB

🌡 ZONES 8, 9, 12–24

☀ FULL SUN

◐💧 LITTLE TO MODERATE WATER

Capparis spinosa

This Mediterranean native's habit varies: it can sprawl, or become a dense, rounded shrub 5 ft. tall and wide. Leaves deep green, nearly round, up to 2 in.

across on vinelike, sometimes spiny branches. In late spring through summer, white, 2–3-in. flowers with showy brushes of lavender stamens rise on long stalks from every leaf base. They open at dawn; close in late afternoon. The pickled unopened buds are commercial capers.

Propagate from cuttings or seed (seeds are slow to sprout and grow). Tolerates poor soil but needs good drainage.

Caragana
PEASHRUB
Papilionaceae
DECIDUOUS SHRUBS OR SMALL TREES

🌡 ZONES A1–A3; 1–12; EXCEPT
    AS NOTED

☀ FULL SUN

💧 MODERATE WATER

Caragana arborescens

Native to Russia, Manchuria, and Siberia, these thorny, spiny plants have ferny foliage and spring flowers shaped like bright yellow sweet peas. They are most useful where choice is limited by cold, heat, wind, and intense sunlight, making nearly indestructible mountain and desert windbreaks. Occasionally prune out old wood on the larger species to rejuvenate them; these can also be clipped as hedges.

C. arborescens. SIBERIAN PEASHRUB. Fast growing to 20 ft. tall and 15 ft. across; 'Pendula' is a weeping variety; 'Walkeri' is weeping dwarf to 6–8 ft. (may need staking). Leaves to 3 in. long, each with four to six pairs of leaflets.

C. frutex. RUSSIAN PEASHRUB. To 10 ft. tall, 8 ft. wide. Leaves have one or two pairs of 1-in. leaflets.

C. pygmaea. Zones A2, A3; 1–12. May form a 3-ft. mound or grow flat and sprawling to 3–4 ft. wide. Leaves have four ½–¾-in.-long leaflets. No pruning required.

Cardiocrinum giganteum
Liliaceae
PERENNIAL FROM BULB

🌡 ZONES 4–6, 14–17

◐ LIGHT SHADE

💧 REGULAR WATER

Cardiocrinum giganteum

This is a plant for the patient. Blossoms of this Himalayan native resemble oversize Easter lilies; glossy dark green leaves are broadly oval to heart-shaped, 1½ ft. long. In summer, the foliage rosette gives rise to a 6–12-ft. leafy stem. It remains flowerless at first, dying back to the ground each fall, but after 3 or 4 years bears up to 20 fragrant, 6–8-in., white trumpets with dark reddish throats. Flowers set seed; then the whole plant dies, leaving many small offset bulbs that flower within a few years.

CARE

Set out bulbs (or dig and separate offsets) in early spring or, in mild-winter regions, autumn. Space 2 ft. apart, planting so that tops are just beneath soil surface. You can also start new plants from seed, but seedlings may take up to 7 years to reach blooming size. In frost-prone areas, mulch in winter.

Cardoon

Asteraceae

PERENNIAL

- ☀ ZONES 4–9, 12–24
- ☼ FULL SUN
- 💧 REGULAR WATER

Cardoon

With the look of a giant arti-choke—they're related—this Mediterranean native (*Cynara cardunculus*) is grown for edible leafstalks rather than flower buds, or as an ornamental. It reaches 5–8 ft. tall and 4–6 ft. wide, attaining maximum size in the Pacific Northwest, with coarse, spiny, gray-green leaves up to 1½ ft. long. In summer, stems produce purple, thistle-like blossoms up to 3 in. across. They can be cut and dried for arrangements. Car-doon's perennial roots can handle 5°F (–15°C) if mulched. The plant can naturalize in mild-winter climates.

For climate, soil, and other requirements, see Artichoke.

CARE

To prepare leaves for harvest, blanch them by gathering them together, tying them up, and wrapping with paper to exclude light in late summer to early fall, 4 to 5 weeks before har-vesting. This removes bitter-ness and makes stems more tender.

To cook cardoon, cut heavy leaf midribs into 3–4-in. lengths, parboil until tender, then sauté; or serve boiled with butter or a sauce.

FOR MORE ON PERENNIALS, SEE "GROW: PERENNIALS," PAGES 686–687.

Carex

SEDGE

Cyperaceae

PERENNIALS

- ☀ ZONES VARY BY SPECIES
- ☼ ☽ FULL SUN OR PARTIAL SHADE, EXCEPT AS NOTED
- 💧💧💧 WATER NEEDS VARY BY SPECIES

Carex testacea

Large group of grasslike plants grown for foliage effect in bor-ders, rock gardens, containers, and water gardens. Some long-lived types are useful as lawn substitutes, as large-scale groundcovers, or for erosion con-trol. Plants are evergreen, except as noted; in cold climates, even evergreen types take on cop-pery, bronzy tones in winter.

Although characteristically found in damp soils, many sedges will grow under relatively dry conditions in cultivation. Many, particularly those from New Zealand, are short-lived in gardens, so they are used as annuals or rejuvenated by divi-sion every 2 or 3 years.

C. barbarae. SANTA BAR-BARA SEDGE. Zones 4–9, 14–24. A coastal species native from Southern California to Ore-gon. Rich green leaves form a slowly spreading clump to 1–3 ft. tall. Good for erosion control or for covering large damp areas. Moderate water. Spreads more aggressively with more water.

✓ **C. buchananii.** LEATHER LEAF SEDGE. Zones 2b–9, 14–24. From New Zealand. To 3 ft. tall, 2½ ft. wide. Curly-tipped, erect blades form clump of striking coppery brown. Good accent or container plant, espe-cially beside a caramel-colored heuchera such as 'Southern Comfort'. Moderate water.

' red rooster '

C. comans. NEW ZEALAND HAIR SEDGE. Zones 2b–9, 14–24. Native to New Zealand. Dense, fine-textured clumps reach about 1 ft. high. Leaves are narrow, silvery green. On flat ground, foliage mounds look 2½ ft. wide; where leaves are undisturbed on slopes or over ledges, they maintain their length and look like flowing water. Many named selections are offered; most resemble the species closely. 'Bronze' has coppery brown leaves. Moder-ate water. Occasionally invasive (by self-sowing) in moist areas.

C. divulsa. Zones 2b–9, 11–24. This popular sedge is from Europe, though it has been widely sold as the California native *C. tumulicola* (a shorter, brighter green plant). Dark, lus-trous green leaves form grace-ful clumps to 1½ ft. high and 2 ft. wide. Spikes of greenish flowers appear from winter to spring; shear flowers as soon as they begin to brown with age to prevent aggressive reseed-ing. Makes a fine groundcover; competes successfully with tree roots if well watered as it gets established. Thrives with mod-erate water in sun or shade but needs more irrigation in hot areas.

C. elata 'Aurea' ('Bowles Golden'). Zones 2–9, 14–19, 22. Clump to 2½ ft. high, 1½ ft. wide, with narrow leaves that emerge bright yellow in spring and hold some color until late summer. Dies back completely in winter. Needs ample mois-ture; will grow in standing water. Needs winter chill to grow well.

C. flacca (C. glauca). BLUE SEDGE. Zones 3–9, 14–24. From Europe. Many forms of this blue-gray creeper are in cultivation, ranging from 6 in. to 2 ft. high and wide. Evergreen except in coldest cli-mates. Not invasive but spreads slowly and can be clipped like a lawn or used as a filler between shrubs or along a path. Endures light foot traffic, moderate shade, competition from tree roots. Tolerates many soils and irrigation schemes; does best with moderate water.

C. flagellifera. Zones 4–9, 14–24. From New Zealand. Closely related to *C. buchananii* and distinguished from it only by small botanical details. It is

not as erect, and its 2-ft.-long leaves are redder and wider spreading. Often short-lived. Several named varieties are offered. Moderate water.

C. 'Ice Dance' (C. mor-rowii 'Ice Dance'). Zones 2b–9, 14–24. Grows 1–2 ft. high and spreads slowly. Dark green leaves edged in creamy white. Good edging or ground-cover. Regular water.

C. morrowii. JAPANESE SEDGE. Zones 3–9, 14–24. From Japan. To 1 ft. high, 1½ ft. wide, with shiny, drooping, medium green leaves. Good edging plant; individual plants attractive among stones. 'Gold-band' and 'Fisher's Form' have leaves with creamy yellow mar-gins. Various forms sold as 'Variegata' have leaves subtly edged in white. Regular water.

C. muskingumensis. PALM SEDGE. Zones 4–9, 14–24. From North America. This distinctive, underused sedge grows about 2 ft. high and spreads widely (but not aggressively) by rhizomes. Tapering green leaves radiate from lax stems to create the effect of small, feathery palms. Plant turns an attractive cop-pery color in fall before going winter dormant. 'Little Midge', to 10 in. high, is miniature in all its parts. Leaves of 'Oehme' are solid green when new but quickly develop golden margins. Regular water.

C. oshimensis 'Evergold' (C. morrowii 'Aurea-variegata'). Zones 3–9, 14–24. Stunning selection of a Jap-anese native. Clumping growth to 1–2 ft. high, 2–3 ft. wide. Dark green leaves have a broad central band of creamy white that matures to creamy yellow. Needs partial to full shade and regular water.

C. pansa. CALIFORNIA MEADOW SEDGE. Zones 7–9, 11–24. California native. Forms a 6–8-in.-high mat of narrow, dark green leaves that are mod-erately tolerant of foot traffic; excellent between pavers and steppingstones. Used as lawn alternative or in meadows. Needs less care than traditional lawn grasses, but occasional shearing and fertilization will keep it looking its best. Weed control is important during establishment, but it won't

C

tolerate herbicides typically used on lawns. Needs only moderate water once established; sensitive to overwatering. *C. praegracilis* (Western meadow sedge) and *C. subfusca* (rusty sedge) are closely related to *C. pansa* and can be used similarly, though they are more variable.

C. phyllocephala 'Sparkler'. SPARKLER PALM SEDGE. Zones 4–9, 14–19, 22. Selection of a Chinese species. Forms a slowly spreading clump of 1–2-ft.-high, narrow, red-purple stems topped with spirally arranged, dark green leaves edged and striped with creamy white. Candlelike fall blooms, 3–4 in. long, are creamy white, aging to brown. Winter dormant. Good-looking groundcover or container plant. Leafy stems are striking in cut-flower arrangements. Good for shady borders in areas with distinct winter chill. Regular water.

C. spissa. SAN DIEGO SEDGE. Zones 7–9, 14–17, 19–24. Native to boggy areas in Southern California. Forms slowly spreading, arching clumps. Coarse, upright silvery gray leaves to 3–4 ft. tall. Light golden brown clusters of dangling flowers appear in spring. Needs ample moisture and will grow in standing water.

C. testacea. Zones 4–9, 14–24. From New Zealand. To 2 ft. high, 3 ft. wide. Widely arching, fine-textured clumps of olive green and orange foliage; leaves turn greener in shade and deep orange in sun. Some tendency to self-seed and spread under moist conditions. Moderate water along the coast, regular water in hot inland gardens. Often short-lived.

C. texensis (C. retroflexa texensis). CATLIN SEDGE. Zones 7–9, 11–24. Southwestern native. Fine-textured, mat-forming sedge to 4–6 in. high. Medium green, drooping leaves form a wavy carpet dotted by lax flowering stems. Excellent small-scale lawn substitute or groundcover; often used in meadow mixes. Trim to remove seed heads. Needs partial to full shade and regular water.

C. tumulicola. See *C. divulsa.*

Carica. See Papaya

Carissa macrocarpa
NATAL PLUM
Apocynaceae
EVERGREEN SHRUB

⚟ **ZONES 22–24; H2; AND SEE BELOW**

☼ ☽ **BEST IN SUN; TOLERATES SOME SHADE**

◐ ◑ ● **LITTLE TO REGULAR WATER**

Carissa macrocarpa

Natal plum's best climates are Zones 22–24 and H2, but so many gardeners find this South African native appealing that it is also grown in Zones 12, 13, 16–21—far beyond safe limits. Fast-growing, strong, upright, rounded shrub of rather loose habit to 5–7 ft. tall and wide (occasionally much larger). Oval, leathery, 3-in. leaves are lustrous rich green. Spines along branches and at end of each twig discourage trespassers.

Blooms throughout the year, bearing white flowers almost as fragrant as those of star jasmine (*Trachelospermum jasminoides*) and with the same five-petaled star shape, but larger (to 2 in. across). Blossoms followed by oval, 1–1½-in., fleshy red or purple fruits. Flowers, green fruit, and ripe fruit often appear together. Fruit has cranberrylike flavor and can be eaten fresh or used in jelly, sauce, pie.

Natal plum is easy to grow and accepts a variety of soils. Excellent in ocean wind, salt spray. Prune to control erratic growth (milky sap oozes from cut stems). Tolerates clipping as formal hedge. In less favorable zones, treat it like bougainvillea: warm wall facing south or west, preferably with overhang to keep off frost. Too spiny to border walkways.

'Boxwood Beauty'. Exceptionally compact, thornless growth to 2 ft. high and wide. Deep green leaves like those of large-leafed boxwood (*Buxus*). Good for hedging and shaping.

'Fancy'. More upright growth than species, with unusually large fruit.

'Green Carpet'. Grows to 15 in. high, spreading to 4 ft. Smaller leaves than those of species. Excellent groundcover.

'Humphreyi Variegata'. Grows to 2½ ft. high, 3 ft. wide. Small (¾ in.) green leaves are striped and edged white.

'Tomlinson'. Thornless. Compact, slow growth to 2–2½ ft. high, 3 ft. wide. Good tub or foundation plant.

'Tuttle' ('Nana Compacta Tuttlei'). Compact, dense growth to 2–3 ft. high, 3–5 ft. wide. Heavy production of flowers and fruit. Effective as a groundcover.

Carnegiea gigantea
SAGUARO
Cactaceae
CACTUS

⚟ **ZONES 12, 13, 18–21**

☼ **FULL SUN**

◐ **NO IRRIGATION NEEDED**

Carnegiea gigantea

Archetypical cactus of the Sonoran desert, saguaro grows only 1 ft. every 10 years in the wild, ultimately to 50 ft. tall. It typically branches after attaining 12–15 ft. Light brown, ½–3-in.-long spines line fluted ribs. Mature plants produce 3–5-in.-long, single white blossoms (state flower of Arizona) on spring nights; they remain open until the next afternoon. Edible

oval fruits, sometimes mistaken for flowers, split open to show red pulp.

Saguaro is protected. When choosing a nursery-grown plant (the alternative to poached saguaros), look for one with a good root system. These are adapted to aridity, but regular water and fertilizer speeds growth. Provide good drainage.

Carpenteria californica
BUSH ANEMONE
Hydrangaceae
EVERGREEN SHRUB

⚟ **ZONES 5–9, 14–24**

☼ ☽ **PARTIAL SHADE IN HOTTEST CLIMATES**

◐ ● **LITTLE TO MODERATE WATER**

Carpenteria californica

This attractive, formal-looking California native grows slowly to 4–8 ft. tall and wide; many stems rise from base. Older bark light-colored and peeling; new shoots, purplish. Thick, narrow leaves are dark green above, whitish beneath. In late spring and summer, clusters of scented, 1½–3-in., yellow-centered, anemonelike white flowers appear at branch ends. Cutting-grown 'Elizabeth' is more compact, with many more, smaller flowers.

Accepts ordinary garden conditions. Inspect for aphid or mite infestation. Resistant to oak root fungus. If pruning is necessary to shape or restrain growth, do so after flowering. Left unpruned, bush anemones grow into rounded mounds.

Plants can take garden water, but are quite drought-tolerant once established.

C

Carpinus

HORNBEAM
Betulaceae
DECIDUOUS TREES

📏 ZONES VARY BY SPECIES

☼ ◐ ● EXPOSURE NEEDS VARY BY SPECIES

💧 REGULAR WATER

🐦 ATTRACT BIRDS

Carpinus betulus

These well-mannered, long-lived shade trees grow at a slow to moderate rate. Dark green, sawtooth-edged leaves color up in cold-winter climates, hang on late in season. Fruits (small, hard nutlets in leaflike bracts) hang in attractive drooping clusters to 5 in. long. Mature trees need little or no pruning—a good thing, since wood is tough and heavy.

C. betulus. EUROPEAN HORNBEAM. Zones 2–9, 14–17. Native from Europe to Iran. Dense, pyramidal tree to 40 ft. tall and wide, with drooping outer branches. Handsome, furrowed gray bark. Leaves turn yellow or dark red in fall. Best in full sun but tolerates light shade. Sometimes clipped into hedge or screen. Subject to scale infestation. Widely sold 'Fastigiata' develops an oval-vase shape with age. 'Frans Fontaine' is narrowest, to 35 ft. tall and 15 ft. wide, with inward-turning branches. 'Emerald Avenue' is upright, heat-resistant; a fine street tree.

C. caroliniana. AMERICAN HORNBEAM. Zones 1–9, 14–17. Native to eastern North America. Round headed, to 25–30 ft. tall and wide, sometimes larger; can be single- or multitrunked. Smooth blue-gray bark has undulations that look like mus-

cles flexing. Leaves turn mottled yellow and red (sometimes mostly yellow) in fall; 'Native Flame' leaves turn red. All drop ahead of *C. betulus.* Succeeds in full sun to heavy shade.

Carpobrotus

ICE PLANT
Aizoaceae
SUCCULENT WOODY-BASED PERENNIALS

📏 ZONES VARY BY SPECIES

☼ FULL SUN

◔ 💧 LITTLE TO MODERATE WATER

Carpobrotus chilensis

Both these trailing ice plants have coarse, succulent leaves and reddish summer blooms. Though gardeners use them to cover gently sloping banks (their weight can bring down steep ones), these have naturalized behind California beaches. They are not invasive inland, where they can be planted 18 in. apart. They rot in wet soil and die back if severely stressed by drought or nitrogen deficiency during the growing season. Susceptible to scale insects.

C. chilensis. Zones 12–24. Probably from South Africa. Straight, three-sided, fleshy leaves are 2 in. long; flowers lightly fragrant, rosy purple, about 2 in. across.

C. edulis. HOTTENTOT FIG. Zones 12–24; H1, H2. From South Africa. Curved, 4–5-in.-long leaves; pale yellow to rose, 4-in.-wide flowers. Figlike fruit is edible but not particularly tasty.

FOR MORE ON ICE PLANTS, SEE "MEET THE ICE PLANTS," PAGE 371.

Carrot

Apiaceae
BIENNIAL GROWN AS ANNUAL

📏 ALL ZONES

☼ FULL SUN

💧 REGULAR WATER

Carrots

Probably native to Afghanistan. Orange ones were selected from yellow ones in 17th-century Holland. Carrots reach smooth perfection only in light-textured soil that is free of stones and clods. Plant long market kinds such as the 12-in. 'Envy' only if you can give them a foot of such soil. If you can provide only a few inches, plant half-long Nantes types such as 'Bolero', 'Mokum', 'Nantes', 'Nelson', and 'Yaya'. For containers, try miniatures like 'Little Finger' and 'Short 'n Sweet', baby carrots like 'Baby Sweet' and 'Sweet Baby Jane', and round ones like 'Parmex' and 'Thumbelina'. For colors other than orange, try varieties like 'Purple Haze', 'Red Samurai', and 'White Satin'.

CARE

Sow lightly in rows 1 ft. apart. Too much nitrogen or manure promotes excessive top growth and makes roots fork. Maintain even soil moisture, also to prevent split roots. Sow each successive crop when previous planting is up and growing. Make last sowing 70 days before anticipated killing frost. When tops are 1–2 in. high, thin plants to 1½ in. apart; thin again if roots get crowded. Use thinnings steamed in butter or in salads. After first thinning, work in narrow band of commercial fertilizer 2 in. out from the

row. Begin harvest when carrots reach finger size, usually 30 to 40 days after sowing; most types mature in 60 to 70 days. In mild climates, carrots can be stored until needed in the ground.

Carthamus tinctorius

SAFFLOWER, FALSE SAFFRON
Asteraceae
ANNUAL

📏 ZONES 1–24; H1, H2

☼ FULL SUN

💧 MODERATE WATER

Carthamus tinctorius

This useful thistle relative (probably an Asian native) grows to 3 ft. tall, 1–1½ ft. wide, with erect, spiny-leafed stems. In summer, orange-yellow flower heads rise above leafy bracts; inner bracts are spiny. Durable cut flower. Fresh, it is used in Hawaiian leis. Dried, it is used as a substitute for saffron, which it resembles in color and flavor. Grown commercially for oil extracted from the seeds. Sow seeds in place in spring after frost danger is past. An ornamental spineless form is also available.

Safflower's orange-yellow blooms are used to make leis, and they yield yellow dyes used to color and flavor rice.

C

Carum carvi

CARAWAY
Apiaceae
BIENNIAL

▧ ZONES 1–24

☀ FULL SUN

💧 REGULAR WATER

🦋 ATTRACTS BENEFICIAL INSECTS

Carum carvi

Pungent seeds of this mounding, carrotlike plant flavor vegetables, pickles, baked goods. From meadows of Asia Minor, it grows 1–2 ft. in first year; in second spring, umbrellalike clusters of white flowers rise above foliage; they go to seed in summer, and the plant dies. Start seeds in place (taproot precludes transplant) in fall or early spring; thin seedlings to 18 in. apart. Demands well-drained soil.

Caraway seeds are used in rye breads. Leaves and shoots can flavor salads; roots can be shaved like carrots or parsnips and dropped into soups. But since the plant is a biennial (it flowers and produces seed in its second year), you'll need to dedicate a patch of ground to it, or plant it in a pot.

Caryopteris

BLUEBEARD
Lamiaceae
DECIDUOUS SHRUBS

▧ ZONES VARY BY SPECIES

☀ FULL SUN

💧 MODERATE WATER

Caryopteris × *clandonensis*
'First Choice'

Cool blue flowers top these upright Asian native shrubs from midsummer to frost. Bloom clusters spring from the current season's growth, so these are usually grown as woody-based perennials: cut them nearly to the ground before spring growth flush to ensure a good base for new growth. Trim after each wave of flowers to encourage rebloom. Good drainage is essential.

C. × clandonensis. BLUE MIST. Zones 2b–9, 14–24. Low-growing mound (2–3 ft. high and wide) of narrow, 3-in.-long leaves. Small blue flower clusters top upper parts of stems. Good varieties include 'Petit Bleu'; 'Blue Balloon', with round shape and lavender-scented leaves; 'Dark Knight' and 'Longwood Blue', with silvery foliage; and 'Summer Sorbet', with yellow-edged green leaves.

C. incana. COMMON BLUEBEARD, BLUE SPIRAEA. Zones 4–9, 14–24. Taller than *C. × clandonensis,* with looser, more open growth to 3–4 ft. tall, 5 ft. wide. Lavender-blue flowers in leaf joints. 'Jason' ('Sunshine Blue') has golden yellow leaves and medium blue flowers.

C. 'Lil Miss Sunshine'. This hybrid between *C. × clandonensis* and *C. incana* has bright yellow foliage and blue flowers; grows to 3 ft. high and wide.

Caryota

FISHTAIL PALM
Arecaceae
PALMS

▧ ZONES 23, 24; H2; OR INDOORS

☀ ◐ SUN OR PART SHADE; BRIGHT INDIRECT LIGHT

💧 REGULAR WATER

⬥ FRUIT CAN CAUSE CONTACT DERMATITIS

Caryota mitis

These Southeast Asian natives are feather palms with huge, finely divided leaves made up of leaflets flattened and split at the tips like fish tails. Plant in humus-rich soil that provides good drainage. Individual trunks die after flowering, which may not occur for 20 to 25 years.

C. gigas. GIANT FISHTAIL PALM. Grows 40–60 ft. tall with a single trunk, dark leaf bases, and beautifully ferny foliage.

C. mitis. CLUSTERED FISHTAIL PALM. Slow grower to 8–25 ft. tall, spreading 10–22 ft. Basal offshoots eventually form clustered trunks. Foliage light green. Very tender.

C. urens. FISHTAIL WINE PALM. Handsome single-stemmed palm grows fast to 40–80 ft. tall and 15 ft. wide in Southern California. This high-mountain selection is reported to withstand 20°F (−7°C) once established. Arching, dark green leaves.

FOR MORE ON PALMS, SEE "MEET THE PALMS," PAGE 471.

Casimiroa edulis. See White Sapote

Cassia leptophylla

GOLD MEDALLION TREE
Caesalpiniaceae
SEMIEVERGREEN TREE

▧ ZONES 15, 16, 20–24; H1, H2

☀ FULL SUN

◌💧 LITTLE TO MODERATE WATER

Cassia leptophylla

Nearly evergreen, this open-headed, fast-growing Brazilian tree grows 20–25 ft. tall, 30 ft. wide, and is spreading with a tendency to weep. Shapely and graceful when pruned to single trunk; otherwise, it becomes sprawling. Deep yellow flowers to 3 in. wide come in 6–8-in.-long spikes; main bloom in summer, sporadic bloom later. Blooms precede long, round seedpods that can present a litter problem. Plant in well-drained soil; prune when young to develop a strong framework, then as needed after flowering.

The genus *Cassia* once included many yellow-flowered trees and shrubs now reclassified as *Senna*. See that entry.

Gold medallion tree is shapely and graceful when pruned as a single-trunked tree. It blooms well near the ocean, but benefits from reflected heat of nearby pavement.

Castanea. See Chestnut

Casuarina

BEEFWOOD, SHE-OAK
Casuarinaceae
EVERGREEN TREES

⚡ **ZONES 8, 9, 12–24; H1, H2**

☼ **FULL SUN**

◐ ◑ ● **LITTLE TO REGULAR WATER**

Casuarina equisetifolia

At first glance, these Australian natives look something like pines; their thin, jointed, green branches look like long pine needles. True leaves are inconspicuous. These trees tolerate dry or wet soil, salinity, heat, and wind, and they're hardy to 15°F (–9°C). Especially useful in desert areas, where they are often confused with Athel tamarisk (*Tamarix aphylla*) because of similar foliage—but the casuarinas have conelike fruit. Cones range from ¼ to 1 in. long in species described here; those of *C. stricta* are largest. Little pruning required.

C. cunninghamiana. RIVER SHE-OAK. Tallest and largest species. To 70 ft. tall, 30 ft. wide. Finest texture, with dark green branches.

C. equisetifolia. HORSE-TAIL TREE. Fast grower to 40–60 ft. tall, 20 ft. wide. Has pendulous gray-green branches.

C. stricta (C. verticillata). MOUNTAIN or DROOPING SHE-OAK, COAST BEEFWOOD. Fast grower to 20–35 ft. tall and wide. Darkest green foliage and largest cones. Makes beautiful silhouette against sky. Attractive street tree. Good at seashore.

Catalpa

Bignoniaceae
DECIDUOUS TREES

⚡ **ZONES 3–10, 14–24, EXCEPT AS NOTED**

☼ ◐ **FULL SUN OR LIGHT SHADE**

◑ ● **MODERATE TO REGULAR WATER**

Catalpa bignonioides

Huge, heart-shaped leaves and large, upright clusters of trumpet-shaped, 2-in.-wide flowers give these trees a distinctly tropical look. White blooms marked with yellow and soft brown appear in late spring and summer, and are followed by long, bean-shaped seed capsules sometimes called Indian beans.

Takes a wide range of soils and temperatures, but plant where strong winds won't shred leaves. Dropped flowers and seed capsules can be messy. Shape young plants, shortening side branches as tree grows; when branching begins at the desired height, remove lower branches. On established trees, head back or thin out branches that look out of balance.

For the tree sometimes called desert catalpa, see *Chilopsis linearis*.

C. bignonioides. COMMON CATALPA, INDIAN BEAN. Native to southeastern U.S. Generally smaller than *C. speciosa*. Grows to 30–40 ft. tall, with equal spread. Leaves are often arranged in whorls, and give off an odd odor when crushed. Becomes chlorotic in alkaline soil. Resists oak root fungus. Yellow leaves of 'Aurea' are showier where summers are cool. 'Nana' (Umbrella catalpa) grows into a dense globe form usually grafted high on *C. bignonioides*. It never blooms.

Usually 6 ft. tall, 5 ft. wide; cut it back to keep it in scale. Sometimes confused with *C. bungei*.

C. bungei. Grows into a pyramid to 25 ft. tall, with white-spotted purple flowers. Like a smaller *C. bignonioides*.

C. × erubescens 'Purpurea'. Selection of a hybrid between *C. bignonioides* and a Chinese species; resembles *C. bignonioides*. Young leaves and branchlets are deep blackish purple, turning purplish green in summer.

C. speciosa. Zones 2–24. Native to central U.S. The most widely distributed catalpa in the West. Round-headed tree to 40–60 ft. tall, 20–40 ft. wide. Leaves 6–12 in. long, odorless when crushed. Fewer flowers per cluster than for *C. bignonioides*.

Catananche caerulea

CUPID'S DART
Asteraceae
PERENNIAL

⚡ **ZONES 1–10, 14–24**

☼ **FULL SUN**

● **MODERATE WATER**

Catananche caerulea

This wispy, free-flowering European native thrives in summer borders, where its cornflower-like blooms can be cut for fresh or dried arrangements. Gray-green, grassy leaves form a clump to 1 ft. high and wide. Lavender-blue, 2-in. flowers surrounded by strawlike, shining bracts appear atop leafless, 2-ft. stems. 'Alba' has white blossoms, 'Major' deep blue-violet blooms. Plants will flower

first year from seed sown in early spring; deadhead to prolong bloom. Short-lived, but volunteer seedlings provide replacements.

Catharanthus roseus

(Vinca rosea)
MADAGASCAR PERIWINKLE, VINCA
Apocynaceae
PERENNIAL USUALLY GROWN AS ANNUAL

⚡ **ZONES 1–24; H1, H2**

☼ ◐ **FULL SUN OR PARTIAL SHADE**

● **MODERATE WATER**

Catharanthus roseus

Madagascar periwinkle grows 1 to 2 ft. high, comes in mounding and trailing forms. It excels at producing summer-to-fall color in hot climates, and keeps flowering through Thanksgiving if weather stays mild. Glossy green, 1–3-in.-long leaves cover bushy plant 1–2 ft. high and wide; 1½-in. flowers come in white, white with rose or red eye, apricot, cherry, pink, and bright rose. Lives over, if a bit ragged, in frost-free areas. In desert regions, may also look poor in late summer. Self-sows. Provide good drainage and avoid overwatering.

The Cora series has mounding and trailing forms, many colors, extra-long bloom; grows 14–16 in. tall. Pacifica and Cooler series are compact 15-in. plants with 2-in. flowers.

The Mediterranean series, featuring apricot, pink, rose, lilac, or white blooms, grows 5–6 in. high and can spread 2½ ft. wide.

All types bloom first season from seed sown early indoors or

C

in a greenhouse or cold frame. Tropicana series blooms in only 60 days from seed, bears blooms in shades of pink and coral on 1-ft. plants.

Cattleya

Orchidaceae
EPIPHYTIC ORCHIDS

🗡 **ZONE H2; OR INDOORS**

☼ **LIGHT SHADE; BRIGHT INDIRECT LIGHT**

💧 **REGULAR WATER**

Cattleya skinneri

Bright, iconic, 2- to 6-in. flowers make even non-gardeners think "orchid" whenever they see these tropical American natives. Often used for corsages, cattleyas also make excellent garden subjects in warm, humid parts of the West.

Species, varieties, and hybrids are too numerous to list here. All have pseudobulbs 1–3 in. thick, bearing leathery leaves and a stem topped with one to several flowers. Plants range from a few inches tall to 2 ft. or more, with flowers in lavender and purple, white, and white with colored lip (semialba). Novelties—many of them hybrids between *Cattleya* and other genera—also come in yellow, orange, red, green, and bronze.

Cattleyas are year-round outdoor plants in Hawaii, both in containers and naturalized on trees. Elsewhere, they are indoor plants brought outdoors during warm weather. They grow best in a greenhouse where temperature, humidity, and light can be readily controlled. However, they make satisfactory houseplants with temperatures of 55–60°F (13–16°C) at night and 65–80°F (18–27°C) during the day, at least 50–60 percent humidity, and bright indirect light with protection from hot midday sun. Healthy foliage is light green and held erect; low light turns leaves dark green and makes new growth soft.

Cauliflower

Brassicaceae
ANNUAL OR BIENNIAL GROWN AS ANNUAL

🗡 **ALL ZONES**

☼ **FULL SUN**

💧 **REGULAR WATER**

Cauliflower

Like related broccoli and cabbage, cauliflower is a cool-season vegetable thought to have originated in the Mediterranean region, but cauliflower is more weather sensitive. It does best in cool, humid regions; where summers are hot, grow it to harvest well before or well after midsummer, and select heat-tolerant varieties. Home gardeners usually plant an early variety such as 'Snow Crown', or later-season self-blanching varieties such as 'Amazing' or 'Fremont'. There is also a passel of varieties with colored curds: 'Cheddar' (orange), 'Graffiti' (purple), and 'Panther' (green) are examples.

CARE

Start with small plants. Space them 1½–2 ft. apart in rows and leave 3 ft. between rows. Water and fertilize as for broccoli. Keep plants actively growing; any check in growth is likely to cause premature setting of undersize heads. When heads first appear, tie up the large leaves around them to keep them white. (Leaves of self-

blanching varieties curl over developing heads without assistance.) Harvest heads as soon as they reach full size. Most varieties are ready to cut 50 to 100 days after transplanting (6 months for overwintering types) but before clustered buds begin to open. Include 5–6 in. of edible stalk and leaves.

Ceanothus

CALIFORNIA WILD LILAC
Rhamnaceae
EVERGREEN SHRUBS AND GROUNDCOVERS

🗡 **ZONES 5–9, 14–24, EXCEPT AS NOTED**

☼ **FULL SUN**

○ **LITTLE OR NO WATER**

🦋 **ATTRACT BIRDS, BUTTERFLIES, BEES**

» See chart on pages 227–228.

Ceanothus 'Concha'

These beloved shrubs and groundcovers turn many Western hills blue in winter and spring. Most are native to California, but some come from the eastern U.S., Rocky Mountains, Northwest, and Mexico. Flowers range from white through all shades of blue, from pale powder blue to deep violet-blue. Most flower in spring; bloom time is not indicated in chart unless it is unusual. Generally evergreen, but some varieties can lose leaves in cold weather. Only types with small leaves tend to be deer-resistant. New varieties (most propagated from selected wild plants) appear frequently; at any given moment, there are upwards of 75 on the market. For the widest choice, buy plants from a specialist in Western natives. In Zones 1–3, 8, 9, stay with varieties tested and sold locally.

CARE

Plant in light, well-drained soil. Some kinds demand total dryness during summer, but others (particularly coastal groundcover types) need occasional summer water if grown away from the fog belt. A few tolerate more frequent summer moisture (see the chart). Wait to prune until blooms have faded, and avoid cutting off any branches more than an inch in diameter. Control plant growth by pinching back shoot tips during the growing season.

Ceanothus sometimes get aphids and whiteflies, but these are easy to control. As a group, plants don't live very long; 5 to 10 years is typical.

FOR OTHER PLANTS THAT ATTRACT BIRDS, BUTTERFLIES, AND BEES, SEE PAGES 95–105.

Cauliflower Secrets

If you've avoided planting cauliflower because you have heard it's difficult to grow, you've been misinformed. The truth is, cauliflower has gotten a bad rap. One reason: Gardeners often try to grow cauliflower at the wrong time of year. In the mild winter West, fall is prime planting time. Young plants can take advantage of balmy weather in early fall to get established and produce lush green growth.

To develop large, pearly white heads, cauliflower needs cool temperatures—our typical weather pattern—by the time heads start forming in late fall.

CEANOTHUS: TOP PICKS TO GROW

NAME	SIZE	FOLIAGE	FLOWERS	COMMENTS
GROUNDCOVERS				
Ceanothus 'Centennial'	2 ft. high, 10 ft. wide	Small, shiny dark green leaves.	Very dark blue, in short clusters.	More heat-resistant than *C. griseus horizontalis*.
C. gloriosus POINT REYES CEANOTHUS	1–1½ ft. high, 12–16 ft. wide	Dark green, oval, 1-in. leaves; tough and spiny.	Typically light blue, in 1-in. clusters.	Much used in Zones 4–6. Does not do well in summer heat of Zones 7, 14, 18–21.
C. g. 'Anchor Bay'	1–1½ ft. high, 6–8 ft. wide	Very dense.	Somewhat deeper blue than above.	Dense foliage holds down weeds.
C. g. 'Heart's Desire'	1 ft. high, 6–8 ft. wide	Very dense with smaller, shiny bronzy green leaves.	Pale blue.	Dense foliage holds down weeds. Does best along the coast.
C. griseus horizontalis CARMEL CREEPER Zones 5–9, 14–17, 19–24	1½–2½ ft. high, 5–15 ft. wide	Glossy, oval, 2-in., bright green leaves.	Light blue 1-in. clusters.	Sometimes suffers winter damage in Zones 5–7, 14.
C. g. h. 'Diamond Heights' VARIEGATED CARMEL CREEPER	1 ft. high, 6 ft. wide	1-in., rounded green leaves have greenish-white variegation.	Light blue flowers.	Less hardy than the species; trouble under 20°F (–6°C). Give afternoon shade inland.
C. g. h. 'Yankee Point'	2–3 ft. high, 8–10 ft. wide	Glossy, dark green 1½-in. leaves.	Medium blue 1-in. clusters.	One of best ground-covering kinds. Looks refined.
C. hearstiorum	6 in. high, 6–8 ft. wide	Puckered 1½-in. leaves.	Medium blue 1-in. clusters.	One of flattest, but lets in weeds. Spreads from center like a star. Variable performance; not dependable.
C. 'Joyce Coulter'	2–5 ft. high, 10–12 ft. wide	Medium green 1-in. leaves.	Medium blue, 3–5-in. spike-like clusters.	Tolerates heavy soil, some summer water, much pruning.
C. maritimus	1–3 ft. high, 3–8 ft. wide	Blue-green to grayish ½-in. leaves, typically gray or white beneath.	White to pale lavender ½-in. clusters.	Height and color vary greatly.
C. m. 'Frosty Dawn'	1–2 ft. high, 4–6 ft. wide	Gray-green leaves grow close against stems.	Dark lavender-blue flowers appear in winter.	Grows slowly, but lives longer than most *Ceanothus*.
C. m. 'Point Sierra'	2–3 ft. high, 4–6 ft. wide	Gray-green, ¼–½ in. leaves grow on arching branches, like cotoneaster.	Whitish buds produce blue-violet flowers in winter.	Tolerates interior heat.
C. m. 'Popcorn'	2–3 ft. high, 6–8 ft. wide	Gray-green leaves are larger than those of the species.	Clear white flowers come in spring.	Best along coast.
SHRUBS				
C. arboreus ISLAND CEANOTHUS	'Cliff Schmidt' (18 ft.), 'Powder Blue' (12 ft.), 'Trewithen Blue' (20–30 ft.)	Glossy dark green leaves, downy white beneath.	Blue, 5-in. sprays in spring and fall.	Excellent near the coast; needs some shade inland.
C. 'Blue Jeans'	7–9 ft. tall and wide	Small, dark green leathery leaves.	Profuse, pale powder blue clusters.	Tolerates heavy soil, drought, summer water. Shear after bloom for low-water-use hedge.
C. 'Concha' Zones 6–9, 14–24	6–7 ft. tall, 6–8 ft. wide	Densely clad in dark green, 1-in. leaves.	Dark blue 1-in. clusters.	One of the best for gardens. Tolerates summer water. Hardy to 15°F (–9°C).
C. 'Cynthia Postan'	6–8 ft. tall and wide	Crinkled, glossy dark green leaves, grayish beneath.	Violet-blue flowers, opening from bronzy red buds.	Tolerates heavy soils near coast.
C. 'Dark Star'	5–6 ft. tall, 8–10 ft. wide	Tiny (¼-in.), dark green leaves.	Dark cobalt blue 1½-in. clusters.	Similar to *C.* 'Julia Phelps', maybe better.

»

C

CEANOTHUS: TOP PICKS TO GROW

NAME	SIZE	FOLIAGE	FLOWERS	COMMENTS
C. 'Frosty Blue'	6–9 ft. tall, 8–10 ft. wide	Dark green, ½-in. leaves. Dense.	Deep blue, white-frosted, 2½–3-in. spikelike clusters.	White "frosting" makes flowers shimmer. Sturdy stems. Can be shaped as small tree.
C. griseus 'Louis Edmunds'	5–6 ft. tall, 9–20 ft. wide	Bright glossy green 1-in. leaves.	Medium sea blue 1-in. clusters.	Tolerates heavy soil, summer water. Can also be used as a large-scale groundcover.
C. impressus 'Vandenberg'	3–5 ft. tall, 4–6 ft. wide	Tiny, rough-textured, dark green leaves.	Cobalt blue flower clusters appear in spring.	There is a compact selection of this, 'Compact Vandenberg'.
C. i. 'Victoria'	6–9 ft. tall, 10–12 ft. wide	Leaves are shiny, medium green.	Deep blue flowers sometimes repeat bloom.	Takes well to shearing, tolerates ocean winds.
C. 'Julia Phelps'	4½–7 ft. tall, 7–9 ft. wide	Small (½ in.), dark green leaves.	Dark indigo 1-in. clusters.	One of best colors, best bloomers.
C. 'Ray Hartman'	12–20 ft. tall, 15–20 ft. wide	Big (2–3-in.), dark green leaves.	Medium blue, 3–5-in. spikelike clusters.	Can be trained as small tree.
C. 'Sierra Blue'	10–12 ft. tall, 8–10 ft. wide	Glossy, medium green 1½-in. leaves.	Bright medium blue, 6–8-in. spikelike clusters.	Very fast grower; weedy first few years.
C. thyrsiflorus 'El Dorado'	8 ft. tall and wide	Large, dark green leaves are variegated yellow.	Blue flowers.	There is another variegated form, C. t. 'Variegata'.
C. t. 'Skylark'	3–6 ft. tall, 5 ft. wide	Glossy, medium green, 2-in. leaves.	Dark blue clusters; profuse bloom over a long season.	Tolerates summer water.
C. t. 'Snow Flurry'	6–10 ft. tall, 8–12 ft. wide	Rich green 2-in. leaves.	Profuse pure white clusters.	Adaptable, dependable. Good choice for coastal gardens.
C. 'Wheeler Canyon'	To 6 ft. tall, 8 ft. wide	2-in. leaves are narrow and textured.	Bright blue flowers with red bracts appear in early spring.	Tolerates summer water better than many Ceanothus.

Cedrus

CEDAR

Pinaceae

EVERGREEN TREES

⚡ ZONES VARY BY SPECIES

☼ FULL SUN

💧 MODERATE WATER

Cedrus deodara

True cedars are among the most widely grown conifers in Western gardens. They bear needles in tufted clusters. Cone scales, like those of firs (*Abies*), fall from tree, leaving a spiky core behind. Male catkins produce prodigious amounts of pollen that may cover you with yellow dust on a windy day. Plant in deep, well-drained soil. All species are deep rooted and drought-tolerant once established.

C. atlantica (C. libani atlantica). ATLAS CEDAR. Zones 3b–10, 14–24. Native to North Africa. Slow to moderate growth to at least 60 ft. tall, 30 ft. wide. Growth is open and angular in youth, less open with age. Branches usually get too long and heavy on young trees unless tips are pinched out or cut back; branches of any age tend to break in heavy snow. Blue-green needles are less than 1 in. long. Color forms include 'Aurea' (golden), 'Glauca' (silvery blue), and 'Silberspitz' (creamy white new growth). 'Fastigiata' (columnar) also comes in silvery blue ('Glauca Pendula' and 'Glauca Fastigiata') forms. 'Horstman' is a compact form that grows 6–8 in. per year. Weeping atlas cedar (*C. atlantica* 'Pendula') has hanging branches; makes a striking specimen in a large container. (Set it against a blue-green wall, where its shape can stand out). Or grow it beside a garden pond and let it "weep" over a boulder.

C. brevifolia. CYPRUS (or CYPRIAN) CEDAR. Zones 5–10, 14–24. Native to Cyprus. Resembles *C. libani* but is smaller (to 50 ft. tall and 40 ft. wide), with shorter needles (¼–½ in.) and smaller cones. Slow growing.

C. deodara. DEODAR CEDAR. Zones 3b–10, 14–24. Native to the Himalayas. Fast growing to 80 ft., with 40-ft. spread at ground level. Lower branches sweep down to ground, then upward. Upper branches openly spaced, graceful. Nodding tip identifies it in skyline. Softer, lighter texture than in other cedars. Control spread of tree by cutting new growth of side branches halfway back in late spring. This kind of pruning also makes tree denser. Although deodars sold by nurseries are very similar in overall form, many variations occur within a group of seedlings—from scarecrowlike types to low, compact shrubs. Needles, to 2 in. long, may be green or have a blue, gray, or yellow cast. Dozens of varieties.

'Blue Snake'. Blue form crawls along ground or can be staked upright.

'Feelin' Blue'. Dwarf, spreading form, grows to 2 ft. high and 6 ft. wide.

'Gold Cone'. This full-size deodar's golden outer needles contrast with blue-green inner needles. Fast.

'Pendula' ('Prostrata'). Grows flat on ground or drapes attractively over rocks or wall.

'Prostrate Beauty'. To 1½–2 ft. high; may spread 7–8 ft. in 10 years.

'Snow Sprite'. To 12 ft. tall and broad in 10 years. Foliage is silvery green with cream-colored tips.

'White Imp'. Just 3 ft. high and wide. New growth is white.

C. libani. CEDAR OF LEBANON. Zones 3–10, 14–24. Native Lebanon to Turkey. To

80 ft., but grows just 1 ft. per year. Variable habit. Usually a dense, narrow pyramid in youth. In young trees, needles, less than 1 in. long, are brightest green of the cedars; in old ones, they are dark gray-green. Matures into a picturesque skyline tree with long horizontal limbs and an irregular shape that is ultimately about as broad as high. No pruning needed. 'Pendula' is a slow-growing, weeping form; 'Glauca Pendula', a weeping blue form.

Ceiba. See *Chorisia*

Celastrus

BITTERSWEET
Celastraceae
DECIDUOUS VINES

- ✂ **ZONES VARY BY SPECIES**
- ☼ **FULL SUN**
- ◑ ◑ **MODERATE TO REGULAR WATER**

Celastrus scandens

Vigorous, twining, ropelike vines are grown for clusters of yellow-and-orange fruit capsules that split open to display brilliant, red-coated seeds. They form in summer, last into winter. Fruit-bearing branches are prized for arrangements, but to get them you need both male and female plants. Unfortunately, nursery plants are not always labeled. Self-fruitful forms of all are available. Yellow fall foliage.

C. orbiculatus. CHINESE BITTERSWEET. Zones 2b–7, 10. Native to Asia. Aggressive grower to 30–40 ft. Leaves roundish, toothed. Fruit on short side shoots is partially obscured until leaves drop.

C. rosthornianus loeseneri (C. loeseneri). Zones 3b–7, 10. Chinese native. Grows to

20 ft., with oval leaves. Similar to *C. orbiculatus,* but not as rampant.

C. scandens. AMERICAN BITTERSWEET. Zones A3; 2–7, 10. Native to eastern North America. To 20 ft. or more. Oval, tooth-edged leaves. Fruit appears in scattered dense clusters that show well above leaves.

CARE

Plant where vines get support, but don't allow them to climb shrubs or small trees, which they can strangle. Prune to clear intertwined branches before new spring growth begins, then as needed during summer to manage growth. Lean soil helps control size.

Celeriac, Celery Root

Apiaceae
BIENNIAL GROWN AS ANNUAL

- ✂ **ALL ZONES**
- ☼ **FULL SUN**
- ◑ **REGULAR WATER**

Celeriac

This breed of celery has large, rounded, edible roots; it is the "celery root" sold in markets. Roots are peeled, then cooked or used raw in salads. 'Brilliant', 'Giant Prague', and 'Mentor' are among several improved varieties.

CARE

Needs a long, mild growing season; coastal gardens are optimal. Plant 6–8 in. apart in rows spaced 1½–2 ft. apart. Harvest when roots are 3 in. across or larger—about 100 to 120 days after transplanting.

Celery

Apiaceae
BIENNIAL GROWN AS ANNUAL

- ✂ **ALL ZONES**
- ☼ **FULL SUN**
- ◑ **REGULAR WATER**

Celery

Descended from wild plants native to Europe and Asia, this salad vegetable is grown for its thick, crunchy stalks. It performs best where it has a long, mild growing season. Optimal daytime temperatures should average below 75°F (24°C), and nights should be 50° to 60°F (10° to 15°C). Lower nighttime temperatures cause celery to bolt. In low and intermediate desert, it's a winter crop. In hot-summer climates, set out transplants a month before average date of last spring frost, mulching plants heavily, and keeping the soil evenly moist. Try 'Conquistador', which is very early and widely adapted; 'Golden Boy', whose short stalks are naturally lightly blanched; 'Monterey', an extra-early hybrid; or 'Tall Utah 52-70 Improved', with long, dark green stalks.

CARE

Plant seeds in flats in early spring; where winters are mild, start in summer for winter crop. (Celery plants started from seed are slow to reach planting size; to save time, you can purchase small nursery plants.) Plant seedlings in rich soil 6 in. apart in rows 2 ft. apart. Every 2 to 3 weeks, apply liquid fertilizer with irrigation water. To keep plants upright, work some soil up around them as they grow. For whitened stalks, set bottomless milk carton or

something similar over plants to exclude light from stalks (leaves must have sunlight). Or grow self-blanching varieties. Harvest 105 to 130 days after transplanting. Row covers will keep out many pests.

Celosia

COCKSCOMB, CHINESE WOOLFLOWER
Amaranthaceae
ANNUALS

- ✂ **ZONES 1–24; H1, H2; BEST IN ZONES 8–14, 18, 19; H1, H2**
- ☼ **FULL SUN**
- ◑ **MODERATE WATER**

Celosia

These flame-colored tropical plants, some with bizarre flower clusters, are effective as bedding plants or in containers. Cut blooms can be used fresh or dried for winter bouquets. Sow seed in place in late spring or early summer, or set out started plants.

There are two kinds of cockscombs, both derived from a silvery white–flowered species, *C. argentea,* which has narrow, 2-in. leaves.

Plume cockscombs (often sold as *C.* 'Plumosa') have plumy flower clusters. Some of these, like Chinese woolflower (sometimes sold as *C.* 'Childsii'), look like tangled masses of yarn. Flowers come in brilliant shades of pink, orange-red, gold, crimson. Some forms grow 2½–3 ft. high and 1½ ft. wide. Others grow 1 ft. high and half as wide, bearing heavily branched plumes.

Crested cockscombs (often sold as *C.* 'Cristata') have velvety, fan-shaped flower clusters, often much contorted and fluted. Flower colors include yellow, orange, purple, and red. Tall kinds grow to 3 ft. high, 1½ ft. wide; dwarf varieties grow to 10 in. high and 6 in. wide.

Celtis
HACKBERRY
Cannabaceae
DECIDUOUS TREES

* ZONES VARY BY SPECIES
* FULL SUN OR PARTIAL SHADE
* MODERATE WATER
* BERRYLIKE FRUITS ATTRACT BIRDS

Celtis reticulata

These big, tough, fast-growing shade trees are similar to elms, but smaller. Mature trees have picturesque bark with corky warts and ridges, and all species are deep rooting: old trees in narrow planting strips expand in trunk diameter to nearly fill strips without producing surface roots or heaving sidewalk or curb. Leaves turn yellow in fall.

Hackberry tolerates strong winds (stake young trees until well established); desert heat; and dry, alkaline soils. Leaf gall caused by psyllids may disfigure leaves in some regions (especially in the Rocky Mountain states and Pacific Northwest), but the trees are not harmed. Little pruning required. Bare-root plants, especially in larger sizes, sometimes fail to leaf out. Buy in containers or look for small bare-root trees with big root systems.

C. × magnifica. This fast-growing hybrid of *C. laevigata* and *C. occidentalis* has large, glossy, dark green leaves and good insect resistance.

C. occidentalis. COMMON HACKBERRY. Zones 1–24. Native to eastern North America. To 50 ft. or taller and nearly as wide, with rounded crown and spreading, sometimes pendulous branches. Bright green, finely toothed oval leaves, 2–5 in. long. Tree does not leaf out until midspring. Resistant to oak root fungus. In Zones 10–13, lives longer than and is superior to commonly planted Siberian elm (*Ulmus pumila*).

C. pallida. DESERT HACKBERRY, GRANJENO. Zones 10–13. Native to southwestern U.S. and northern Mexico. Small tree or shrub with dense, spiny growth to 18 ft. tall; variable in width, sometimes growing wider than tall. Small orange berries. Useful in desert as honey source or bird food, for screen or barrier planting, for erosion control.

C. reticulata (C. douglasii). WESTERN HACKBERRY. Zones 2–24; best in 2, 3, 7–13, 18–21. Native to Idaho, eastern Washington, northern Oregon, through intermountain area to Utah, and in the mountains of Arizona and Southern California. To 25–30 ft. tall and wide, with somewhat pendulous branches. Oval, tooth-edged leaves to 2½ in. long, pale beneath, strongly veined.

C. sinensis. CHINESE HACKBERRY, YUNNAN HACKBERRY. Zones 8–16, 18–20. From East Asia. Similar to *C. occidentalis,* but only 40 ft. tall and wide. Leaves to 4 in. long, smoother and glossier than those of other hackberries, with scalloped edges.

Centaurea
Asteraceae
ANNUALS, BIENNIALS, AND PERENNIALS

* ZONES VARY BY SPECIES
* FULL SUN
* MODERATE WATER, EXCEPT AS NOTED
* ATTRACT BEES, BUTTERFLIES, HUMMINGBIRDS

Centaurea

Annual forms of *Centaurea* are grown mainly for cut flowers, while perennial kinds are valued for soft, silvery foliage. All are relatively easy to grow. For best performance, add lime to acid soils. Sow seeds of annuals or set out plants of perennial kinds in spring or fall. In desert regions, plant all in autumn for winter and spring bloom.

C. americana. BASKET FLOWER. Annual. Zones 1–24; H1, H2. Native to central and southwestern U.S. To 5–6 ft. tall, 3 ft. wide. Rough leaves, oval, to 4 in. long. Summer flowers to 4 in. wide are rose-pink, paler toward center. Good in fresh or dried arrangements.

C. cineraria (C. gymnocarpa). DUSTY MILLER. Perennial in Zones 8–24, H1, H2; annual elsewhere. (This common name is used for many plants with whitish foliage; see the index.) Native to Italy. Compact growth to 1–3 ft. high, 1 ft. wide. Velvety white leaves are finely divided. Flowers usually purple; white forms available. Trim back after bloom. Very drought-tolerant but can take regular irrigation.

C. cyanus. CORNFLOWER, BACHELOR'S BUTTON. Annual. Zones 1–24; H1, H2. From northern temperate regions. Common in wildflower mixes, but a weed some places (like eastern Washington). To 1–1½ ft. high, less than a foot wide, branching if given enough space. Narrow gray-green leaves, 2–3 in. long. Spring to midsummer flowers are 1½ in. across, in blue, pink, rose, wine red, or white; blue varieties are traditional favorites for boutonnieres.

C. hypoleuca 'John Coutts'. Perennial. Zones 2–9, 14–24. Variety of species from Asia Minor. Resembles *C. montana* but has more deeply lobed leaves and deep rose flowers.

C. macrocephala. Perennial. Zones 2–9, 14–24. From the Caucasus. Attractive, coarse-foliaged, leafy plant 3–4 ft. tall, 2 ft. wide. Blooms in summer, bearing 2-in. clusters of yellow flowers tightly wrapped at the base with overlapping, shiny, papery brown bracts. Flower heads resemble thistles. Use in fresh or dried arrangements.

C. montana. Perennial. Zones 2–9, 14–24. Native to mountains of central Europe. It forms a clump 1½–2 ft. high and wide; grayish green leaves reach 7 in. long. Flowers resembling ragged 3-in. cornflowers top the stems in late spring to midsummer. 'Black Sprite' has spidery, almost black flowers. Protect from snails. Divide every other year. Regular water.

C. moschata (Amberboa moschata). SWEET SULTAN. Annual. Zones 1–24. From Asia Minor. Erect, branching at base, to 10 in. wide, 2–3 ft. high. Green, deeply toothed leaves. Fluffy, thistlelike, 1-in. flowers from spring to fall, mostly in shades of lilac through rose,

Smart Shade Trees

Can planting shade trees near your house save you money? Absolutely. How? Tree-shaded houses stay cooler in summer than do unshaded houses, resulting in lower energy bills. Plant large-growing deciduous trees on the east, west, and northwest sides of the house to provide shade from intense sun. In winter, the leafless branches will let in the sun's warming rays. Another tip: Plant a shade tree over your air-conditioning unit to help it run more efficiently. Hackberry is a prime shade tree in many parts of the West. Others to consider: Chinese pistache, flowering plum, and white ash.

sometimes white or yellow. Musky fragrance. Splendid cut flower. Needs lots of heat; don't give overhead water.

C. rothrockii. Annual or biennial. Zones 1–24. Southwest native to 3–6 ft. tall, 2 ft. wide, with 4-in.-long leaves. Big, exotic-looking flowers bloom from midsummer into fall; these are 5 in. wide, with pink outer rays and a creamy white to yellow center. Start seeds indoors in cold-winter areas and transplant after last frost. Good for arrangements if cut just before flowers open.

Centranthus ruber
(Valeriana rubra)
JUPITER'S BEARD, RED VALERIAN
Caprifoliaceae
PERENNIAL

⚡ **ZONES 2–9, 12–24; H1**

☀️ ☼ **FULL SUN OR PARTIAL SHADE**

◐ ◑ **LITTLE TO MODERATE WATER**

🦋 **ATTRACTS BIRDS AND BUTTERFLIES**

Centranthus ruber

With an apparent preference for untended rockeries and overgrown perennial gardens, this 3-ft., usually red-flowering Mediterranean native has a rustic charm. Put it in fringe areas of the garden where its dense terminal clusters of 1½-in. flowers bloom in late spring and early summer (sporadically into fall in cool-summer climates). Typical colors range from deep crimson to pale pink; 'Albus' has white blooms. Leaves are bluish green, 4 in. long. Cut off old flowering stems to shape plants and prevent self-seeding.

Cephalanthus occidentalis
BUTTONBUSH, BUTTON WILLOW
Rubiaceae
DECIDUOUS SHRUB OR TREE

⚡ **ZONES 2–10, 14–21**

☀️ ☼ **FULL SUN OR LIGHT SHADE**

◐ ◐◐ **REGULAR TO AMPLE WATER**

🦋 **ATTRACTS BUTTERFLIES**

Cephalanthus occidentalis

This rounded shrub grows 3–15 ft. tall and wide. Its bright green, paired or whorled leaves come out late in spring. Creamy white, slender-tubed flowers crowd into rounded, 1–1½-in.-wide heads in late summer; projecting stigmas give these heads a look one nurseryman described as "golf balls with antennae." Useful for naturalizing in wet areas. *C. o. californicus* is very similar.

Buttonbush blooms may resemble golf balls with antennae, but the round-headed shrub looks best when left to grow naturally in consistently moist areas. Plant it near a garden pond or in shallow depressions where rainwater pools—such as in a rain garden.

Living Sculptures

In nature's gallery, succulents and cacti keep company with unrelated but equally sculptural plants. Various agaves and aloes make bold accents. Hesperaloes have stiff, grasslike foliage and dramatic blossom spikes that shoot up like fireworks. Dasylirion's fountainlike clumps, yuccas' daggerlike leaves, and ocotillo's resemblance to a bunch of sticks when not in bloom—can all create garden drama. Use them singly—smaller kinds in containers—or in clusters of at least three. Ocotillo, planted in rows, makes a striking fence. Old man cactus looks good in a group of five or three, against a sand-colored boulder.

Cephalocereus senilis
OLD MAN CACTUS
Cactaceae
CACTUS

⚡ **ZONES 13, 21–24; H1; OR INDOORS**

☀️ **FULL SUN; BRIGHT LIGHT**

◐ **LITTLE OR NO WATER**

Cephalocereus senilis

A slender, columnar cactus from Mexico that is completely covered with long, grayish white hairs and yellow spines. Able to reach 45 ft. in great old age, but usually much smaller. Only old, large (over 15 ft. tall) plants bloom, with 2-in.-long, rose-colored flowers opening on spring nights.

Grow in rocky or loose soil. Supplemental water and fertilizer will speed growth of garden plants. Protect from hard frosts. In Zone 13, provide some shade. Indoors, give southern exposure.

Cephalophyllum 'Red Spike'
RED SPIKE ICE PLANT
Aizoaceae
SUCCULENT PERENNIAL

⚡ **ZONES 8, 9, 11–24**

☀️ ☼ **FULL SUN OR PARTIAL SHADE**

◐ ◐◐ **MODERATE TO REGULAR WATER**

🐝 **FLOWERS ATTRACT BEES**

Cephalophyllum 'Red Spike'

This South African native grows 3–5 in. high, slowly spreading to 15–18 in. wide. Spiky green to bronzy red leaves point up. Bright red, 2-in. flowers appear in winter or early spring; bloom is sporadic in other seasons. Sometimes sold as *Cylindrophyllum* 'Red Spike'.

CARE

To use as a groundcover, plant 6–12 in. apart in well-drained soil. Provide supplemental irrigation during active growth and bloom; cut back watering in summer. In the desert, needs afternoon shade.

C

Cerastium tomentosum

SNOW-IN-SUMMER
Caryophyllaceae
PERENNIAL

✂ ZONES A1, A2; 1–24

☼ ◗ LIGHT SHADE IN HOTTEST CLIMATES

◖◗ MODERATE TO REGULAR WATER

Cerastium tomentosum

Sheets of snow-white flowers smother this European ground-cover's mats of silvery gray leaves early every summer. Widely adapted, it grows 6–8 in. high, spreads 2–3 ft. in a year. Use as groundcover, bulb cover, in rock gardens, for edging along paths, or between steppingstones. Snow-in-summer is not long-lived, so avoid extensive planting in prominent situations. Conversely, in the Northwest it grows so enthusiastically that it can become a weed.

CARE

Takes any well-draining soil. Set divisions or plants 1–1½ ft. apart, or sow seeds. To speed growth, water regularly and feed two or three times a year. After bloom ends, shear off faded flower clusters or mow planting. May look shabby in winter but revives rapidly in spring. Repair bare patches in spring or early fall by digging clumps from healthy areas and replanting them in the bare areas.

FOR MORE ON PERENNIALS, SEE "GROW: PERENNIALS," PAGES 686–687.

Ceratonia siliqua

CAROB, ST. JOHN'S BREAD
Caesalpiniaceae
EVERGREEN SHRUB OR TREE

✂ ZONES 9, 13–16, 18–24; H1

☼ FULL SUN

◖◗◗ LITTLE TO REGULAR WATER

Ceratonia siliqua

Grown as a multistemmed shrub, this makes a big hedge; trained to a single trunk, it becomes a dense, round-headed tree. Reaches 20 ft. in 10 years, eventually 30–40 ft. tall and wide. As a street tree, carob needs extra ground space because its roots break side-walks. Foliage is glossy dark green, unusually dense. Leaves are divided into 4 to 10 round leaflets averaging 2 in. long. Small red flowers in spring.

Female trees produce (and drop) abundant 1-ft.-long, flattened, dark brown, leathery pods. Rich in sugar, the pods are milled to a fine powder and sold in health food stores as carob, a chocolate substitute.

Hardy to 18°F (–8°C); but in zones where frost is regular, give young trees winter protection first year or two. Resists oak root fungus. Overwatering in heavy or poorly drained soils can subject carob to root-crown rot. Very drought-tolerant. If raised for carob pods, needs regular moisture.

Rich in sugar, carob pods are milled to a fine powder and sold in health-food stores as a chocolate substitute.

Ceratostigma

PLUMBAGO
Plumbaginaceae
EVERGREEN AND DECIDUOUS SHRUBS AND PERENNIALS

✂ ZONES VARY BY SPECIES

☼ ◗ FULL SUN OR PARTIAL SHADE

◖◗ MODERATE TO REGULAR WATER

Ceratostigma plumbaginoides

These low-growing plants are valued for clusters of intense blue flowers that bloom summer to late fall. Tolerate inconsistent watering. In colder zones, cut back shrubby species after bloom and apply a thick mulch. For white- to light blue–flowered Cape plumbago, see *Plumbago auriculata.*

C. griffithii. BURMESE PLUMBAGO. Evergreen shrub. Zones 4–9, 14–24. This Himalayan native is similar to *C. willmottianum,* but with rounder leaves and slightly later bloom. Grows just 2½–3 ft. high and wide. Hardy, but evergreen leaves can be nipped back by frost.

C. plumbaginoides (Plumbago larpentae). DWARF PLUMBAGO. Perennial. Zones 2b–10, 14–24. Native to China. Wiry-stemmed ground-cover 8–16 in. high with bronzy to dark green leaves that turn reddish brown with frost. A long growing season encourages strong bloom and rapid spread by underground stems. Plant 1–1½ ft. apart for quick cover. Shear or mow annually before spring growth begins. When plants show signs of aging, dig up and replace with rooted stems in spring or summer.

C. willmottianum. CHINESE PLUMBAGO. Deciduous shrub. Zones 4–9, 14–24.

Grows as airy mass of wiry stems 2–4 ft. high and wide. Deep green leaves are somewhat diamond-shaped, with tapering tips; turn yellow or red and drop quickly after frost.

Cercidiphyllum japonicum

KATSURA TREE
Cercidiphyllaceae
DECIDUOUS TREE

✂ ZONES 2B–6, 14–16, 18–20

☼ ◗ FULL SUN OR LIGHT SHADE

◗ REGULAR WATER

Cercidiphyllum japonicum

In youth, this fine-textured native of China and Japan is upright and pyramidal, but it becomes more rounded with age. It tops out at around 40 ft. At all ages it has a light, dainty branch and leaf pattern. Brown bark is somewhat shaggy on old trees. Heart-shaped leaves emerge reddish purple, become bluish green in summer, then turn yellow to apricot in autumn. To enhance fall color, water less frequently in late summer. Foliage of some katsura trees smells like brown sugar on warm autumn days when leaves are falling—and when new growth opens in spring.

Some specimens have a single trunk, but multiple trunks are more usual. 'Heronswood Globe' grows 25 ft. tall. 'Rotfuchs' ('Red Fox') foliage opens dark purple. Weeping forms include 'Amazing Grace', 'Morioka Weeping', and *C. j. pendulum;* all grow quickly.

Katsura trees need regular moisture (especially during youth) and shelter from intense sun and drying wind. No serious pest or disease problems. Mature trees need little pruning.

Cercidium. See *Parkinsonia*

Cercis

REDBUD
Caesalpiniaceae
DECIDUOUS SHRUBS OR TREES

🌓 ZONES VARY BY SPECIES

☀️ ◐ FULL SUN OR LIGHT SHADE

◑ ◕ MODERATE TO REGULAR WATER, EXCEPT AS NOTED

🐦 ATTRACT BIRDS

Cercis canadensis 'Hearts of Gold'

Redbuds are beloved for brilliant buds that clothe bare branches and open into sweet pea–shaped, rosy to purplish pink blossoms in early spring. Flowers are followed by clusters of flat, beanlike pods that persist into winter. Attractive broad, rounded leaves have heart-shaped base. All provide fall color with first frost. Best in naturalized settings. Resents cold, wet soil; good drainage important. Prune in dormant season or after bloom.

C. canadensis. EASTERN REDBUD. Zones 1–24. Native to eastern U.S. Largest (to 25–35 ft. tall and wide) and fastest-growing redbud, and the most apt to take tree form. Round headed but with horizontally tiered branches in age. Green leaves have pointed tips. Needs some winter chill for profuse rosy pink flowers. Effective as specimen or understory tree.

'Ace of Hearts'. Grows 12 ft. tall, 15 ft. wide, with violet flowers.

'Forest Pansy'. A beautiful, graceful, purple-leafed form that

needs some shade in hot climates. Probably not long-lived.

'Hearts of Gold'. Lavender flowers precede foliage that opens pink, matures to lime and gold, then shades to green.

'Lavender Twist' ('Covey'). Pinkish purple flowers held on weeping, contorted branches; best with afternoon shade.

'Little Woody'. Vase-shaped, 8 ft. tall, 10 ft. wide, purple flowers and crinkled leaves.

'Merlot'. Has glossy purple leaves.

'Ruby Falls'. Weeping purple foliage.

'Silver Cloud'. Leaves marbled with white.

C. c. mexicana. Zones 4–24. Includes plants from many sources in Mexico. Most widely distributed is a single-trunked form to 15 ft. tall, with leathery blue-green leaves and pinkish purple flowers.

C. chinensis. CHINESE REDBUD. Zones 4–24. Native to China and Japan. Usually a light, open shrub to 10–12 ft. tall and 10 ft. wide. Flower clusters (3–5 in. long) are deep rose, almost rosy purple. Leaves are sometimes glossier and brighter green than those of *C. canadensis*, with transparent line around the edge. Spectacular in high deserts of Arizona. 'Avondale' is a superior form with deep purple flowers.

C. occidentalis. WESTERN REDBUD. Zones 2–24. Native to California foothills below 4,000 ft.; also in Arizona, Utah. Grows 10–18 ft. tall and wide; usually multitrunked. Magenta flowers bloom in spring (best where the winters are chilly); handsome blue-green leaves, notched or rounded at tip, and newly forming magenta seedpods adorn branches in summer. Foliage turns light yellow or red in fall. Resists oak root fungus. Excellent on seldom-watered banks. 'Alba' is 3–6 ft. tall and broader, with white flowers and leaves to 2½ in. wide.

C. reniformis (C. c. texensis). Zones 3–24. Native to north-central Texas into Oklahoma. Leathery blue-green leaves have rounded or notched tips. Flowers like those of *C. canadensis*; 'Oklahoma' has wine red flowers and thick, glossy, heat-resistant leaves. 'Texas White' has white blossoms.

C. siliquastrum. JUDAS TREE. Zones 3b–19. Native to Europe and western Asia, where it was said to be the tree on which Judas hanged himself. Generally shrubby, to 25 ft. tall and wide; occasionally a taller, slender, single-trunk tree. Purplish rose flowers that are pretty on the tree and good in salads. Large leaves, deeply heart-shaped at base, rounded or notched at tip. Best with some winter chill. Occasionally damaged by late frosts in Northwest. Resists oak root fungus.

Cercocarpus

MOUNTAIN MAHOGANY
Rosaceae
EVERGREEN AND DECIDUOUS SHRUBS AND TREES

🌓 ZONES VARY BY SPECIES

☀️ FULL SUN

◌ LITTLE OR NO WATER

Cercocarpus ledifolius

Several of these Western natives have a most attractive open structure and branching pattern. In fall, long-lasting small fruit appear, topped by a long, twisted, feathery, tail-like plume that sparkles in sunlight.

C. betuloides. HARDTACK, MOUNTAIN IRONWOOD, SWEET BRUSH. Evergreen shrub or tree. Zones 3, 5, 7–10, 13–24. Native to dry foothills below 6,000-ft. elevation in southwestern Oregon, California, and northern Baja California. Generally shrubby, 5–12 ft. high and wide. Can form a small tree with wide-spreading crown of arching branches to 20 ft. Wedge-shaped leaves cluster on short spurs; leaves are dark green above, pale beneath, with feathery veining, toothed edges.

C. intricatus (C. ledifolius intricatus). Evergreen shrub. Zones 2, 3, 7, 9–11, 14–16, 18–24. Native from eastern California to Utah, Arizona. Slow growth to 3–9 ft. tall and wide, with intricate branching and tiny inrolled leaves, green above, gray underneath.

C. ledifolius. CURL-LEAF MOUNTAIN MAHOGANY. Evergreen shrub or tree. Zones 1–3, 7–10, 14–21. Native from eastern slopes of Sierra Nevada–Cascade divide to the Rockies. In warmer western part of its range, can become a 20-ft. tree; in coldest part of range, it is an excellent slow-growing hedge or small tree. Leaves leathery, resinous, dark green above, white beneath, with inrolled edges.

C. montanus. Deciduous shrub. Zones 1–3, 7–10. Native to western U.S. mountains. Usually 4–6 ft. tall and as wide, rarely to 8–9 ft. Leaves white beneath.

Cerinthe major 'Purpurascens'

HONEYWORT
Boraginaceae
ANNUAL

🌓 ZONES 1–24

☀️ ◐ FULL SUN OR LIGHT SHADE

◕ REGULAR WATER

🐝 NECTAR ATTRACTS BEES

Cerinthe major 'Purpurascens'

Rising above clumps of fleshy, blue-green leaves, the purplish blue upper leaves and flower bracts of honeywort are what first attract gardeners to this Mediterranean native. They make the top of this 2-ft.-tall plant look as if it's been dipped

C

in blue dye. Bloom period runs from spring to fall. This is easy to grow from seed and even self-sows without being invasive. In mild-winter climates, seedlings may appear in late summer and bloom the following spring, behaving like biennials or short-lived perennials. (The plain species, whose flowers have a 1-in.-long purple tube opening to a yellow interior, is rarely seen.)

Cestrum
Solanaceae
EVERGREEN SHRUBS

🗡 **ZONES VARY BY SPECIES**

☼ **PARTIAL SHADE, EXCEPT AS NOTED**

💧 **REGULAR WATER**

🦋 **FLOWERS ATTRACT BUTTERFLIES AND HUMMINGBIRDS**

⚠ **FRUIT AND SAP ARE POISONOUS IF INGESTED**

Cestrum elegans

These brightly flowered shrubs grow fast in warm, sheltered spots, with an arching, lax growth habit that benefits from consistent pruning and pinching. May be cut back severely after flowering or fruiting. Plants respond well to feeding and organic soil amendments. Frost damage with quick recovery is possible in climates specified below.

C. aurantiacum. ORANGE CESTRUM. Zones 16, 17, 21–24; H1, H2. Native to Guatemala. To 8 ft. tall and wide (in frost-free areas, may become much larger). Brilliant show of orange flowers in late spring and summer, followed by white berries. Deep green, oval, 4-in. leaves. Good for espalier. May spread by suckers. Loses leaves with cold weather.

C. elegans. RED CESTRUM. Zones 13, 17, 19–24; H1, H2. Vining shrub from Mexico. To 10 ft. or greater in both height and width, with deep green leaves. Masses of purplish red blossoms in spring and summer are followed by red berries. 'Smithii' has pink flowers.

C. fasciculatum. Zones 13, 17, 19–24. Mexican native similar to *C. elegans* but larger.

C. 'Newellii'. Zones 13, 17, 19–24. Resembles *C. fasciculatum* but has crimson flowers.

C. nocturnum. NIGHT JESSAMINE. Zones 13, 16–24; H1, H2. Native to West Indies. To 12 ft. tall and wide, with creamy white summer blossoms. White berries. Powerfully fragrant at night—too fragrant for some. Give full sun for best bloom.

C. 'Orange Peel'. Light orange blossoms keep coming from spring through frost; scented only at night. Grows 6 ft. tall and wide.

Chaenomeles
FLOWERING QUINCE
Rosaceae
DECIDUOUS SHRUBS

🗡 **ZONES 2–23**

☼ **FULL SUN**

💧 **MODERATE TO REGULAR WATER**

🦋 **FLOWERS ATTRACT HUMMINGBIRDS**

Chaenomeles

Among the first shrubs to bloom each year. In the earliest days of spring, you can take a budded stem indoors, place it in water in a sunny window, and watch buds break into bloom. Blossoms are 1½–2½ in. across, single to semidouble or double, in white and soft to vibrant shades of pink, orange, and

red. Leaves are red-tinged when young, maturing to shiny green. Growth habit varies widely among the many selections: some grow to 10 ft. and spread wider, while others top out at 3 ft. Most are thorny, but a few are thornless or nearly so. Some bear small quincelike fruit. (To read about kinds grown for eating, see Quince, Fruiting.)

There are too many varieties to name: base your selection on flower color and shrub size and form. All are easy to grow, tolerating extremes of cold and heat, and light to heavy soil. May bloom sparsely in warm-winter areas. Prune to shape or to limit growth at bud and bloom season. New growth that follows bears next year's flowers.

Chamaebatiaria millefolium
FERNBUSH
Rosaceae
EVERGREEN TO DECIDUOUS SHRUB

🗡 **ZONES 1–3, 7, 14–21**

☼ **FULL SUN**

💧 **LITTLE TO MODERATE WATER**

🦋 **ATTRACTS BEES AND BUTTERFLIES**

Chamaebatiaria millefolium

This well-branched Rocky Mountains native grows 5–8 ft. tall and wide with finely divided, fernlike, aromatic foliage. Evergreen in warmer regions, semievergreen or deciduous elsewhere. Midsummer flowers are white, less than ½ in. wide, in many-blossomed upright clusters to 4 in. long. Cut off spent clusters after bloom. Needs good drainage.

Chamaecereus sylvestri. See *Echinopsis chamaecereus*

Chamaecyparis
FALSE CYPRESS
Cupressaceae
EVERGREEN SHRUBS AND TREES

🗡 **ZONES VARY BY SPECIES**

☼ ◑ **FULL SUN OR PARTIAL SHADE**

💧 **REGULAR WATER**

🦅 **EXCELLENT COVER FOR BIRDS**

Chamaecyparis lawsoniana

Intensive selection has brought these Japanese and American timber trees down in scale, so most varieties fit well into suburban gardens (some even work as container plants). Dense, richly textured foliage makes them easy to mistake for arborvitae (*Thuja*), but arborvitae's leaves are entirely green, while false cypresses have white lines on leaf undersides. Most have two distinct types of foliage: juvenile and mature. Juvenile leaves are short, needlelike, soft but often prickly; they appear on young plants and some new growth of larger trees. Mature foliage consists of tiny, scalelike, overlapping leaves. Cones are small and round.

New varieties appear each year—hundreds are on the market at any moment—and mislabeling is common, since many of these plants closely resemble one another. Numerous dwarf and variegated kinds are well suited for bonsai and rock gardens.

C. lawsoniana. PORT ORFORD CEDAR, LAWSON CEDAR. Zones A3; 3–6, 15–17. Narrow, graceful, 200-ft. Western timber tree (60 ft. in gardens) with lacy, drooping foliage. Its small selections once enjoyed popularity in landscape, but a fatal soil-borne disease, *Phytophthora lateralis,* quenched their popularity. A new phytophthora-resistant rootstock called the Guardian from Oregon State University has fueled a resurgence of interest in this beautiful native. The first varieties released on this rootstock are 'Blue Surprise' (6 ft. tall, 2 ft. wide, with silvery blue juvenile foliage), 'Golden King' (to 40 ft. tall and half as wide, with golden yellow foliage), 'Silberstar' (to 40 ft. tall and half as wide, with silver-blue foliage), and 'Yvonne' (to 20 ft. tall, 12 ft. wide, with golden-tipped green foliage). Many others will doubtless follow.

C. nootkatensis. See *Xanthocyparis nootkatensis.*

C. obtusa. HINOKI FALSE CYPRESS. Zones A3; 2b–6, 15–17. Native to Japan. There are dozens of golden, dwarf, and fern-leafed forms, but a few varieties are particularly important in landscaping. These include 'Filicoides', which grows 10 ft. or more with ferny foliage; 'Gracilis', a slender, upright tree to 20 ft. with nodding branch tips; 'Nana Gracilis', a miniature of the former, reaching 4 ft. in height; 'Nana Lutea', a 4-ft. dwarf with bright yellow foliage; and 'Pygmaea Aurescens', a slow grower to 2½ ft. high and 5 ft. wide, with fanlike foliage that runs from bronzy green in spring to coppery orange in fall.

C. pisifera. SAWARA FALSE CYPRESS. Zones A3; 2b–6, 15–17. Japanese native to 20–30 ft., rarely seen except in its garden varieties. Silvery blue-green 'Cyano-Viridis' ('Boulevard') is a dense, slow-growing bush to 6–8 ft. tall and wide. 'Filifera', a dense mound to 8 ft., has drooping, threadlike branchlets; 'Filifera Aurea' has similar branchlets in yellow. 'Mops' has threadlike branchlets, forms a 1–2-ft. mound.

C. thyoides. ATLANTIC WHITE CEDAR. Zones 1–6, 15–17. Eastern U.S. timber tree is represented in Western gardens by varieties 'Andelyensis', a dense, columnar, gray-green shrub to 10 ft., turning bronze in cold weather; and 'Heather Bun', broader than the former, with leaves that turn intense plum purple in winter.

CARE

All except *C. thyoides* are native to the Pacific Rim, so they prosper in humid environments. Pinch out or cut back tips of new growth to control size and shape; don't cut back into old, leafless wood. All types, including trees, can be sheared into hedges. All need good drainage and protection from wind.

Chamaedorea

Arecaceae
PALMS

🌿 **ZONES 16, 17, 22–24; H2; EXCEPT AS NOTED; OR INDOORS**

◐ ● **SOME SHADE; BRIGHT INDIRECT LIGHT**

💧 **REGULAR WATER**

Chamaedorea elegans

These small feather palms are easy to grow in compact landscapes, on shaded patio or lanai, in the ground on the north sides of buildings, and in containers. Native to Central and South America, some have single trunks, others clustered trunks. The following are among the most widely grown; other species are also sold.

C. cataractarum. CASCADE PALM, CAT PALM. Native to Mexico. Forms a dense clump to 6 ft. tall, 9 ft. wide. Does best in a moist, partially shaded location with protection from drying winds. Good as hedge, screen, border, or understory plant; fine tubbed specimen, indoors or out.

C. costaricana. If well fed and watered, develops fairly fast into bamboolike clump 8–10 ft. tall and wide. Lacy, feathery leaves 3–4 ft. long. Good potted palm; will eventually need good-size container.

C. elegans. Single-stemmed species. Outdoors, grows 6–10 ft. tall, 3–6 ft. wide. Often called parlor palm or *Neanthe bella,* this is the best indoor chamaedorea, growing very slowly to an eventual 3–4 ft. as a houseplant.

C. seifrizii. Zones 13, 16, 17, 22–24; H2. Forms clump to 8–10 ft. tall, 6–8 ft. wide. Stems may be somewhat vining on large, established plants. Narrow leaflets.

Chamaemelum nobile

(Anthemis nobilis)
ROMAN CHAMOMILE
Asteraceae
PERENNIAL

🌿 **ZONES 2–24**

◐ ◑ **FULL SUN OR PARTIAL SHADE**

💧 **MODERATE WATER**

Chamaemelum nobile

This soft-textured, spreading groundcover grows 3–12 in. high, with light green, finely cut, aromatic leaves. Blooms in summer most places, through fall in cool climates, and winter–spring in desert gardens. Blossoms can look like small yellow buttons or little daisies. To make a lawn substitute, plant 1 ft. apart, mow or shear occasionally. Or grow between steppingstones or as an edging. 'Treneague' is nonflowering, needs no mowing; 'Flore Pleno' has double daisylike flowers.

Though tea can be made from this plant, the familiar chamomile tea comes from the dried flowers of *Matricaria recutita.*

Chamaerops humilis

MEDITERRANEAN FAN PALM
Arecaceae
PALM

🌿 **ZONES 4–24; H1, H2**

☼ ◑ **FULL SUN OR PARTIAL SHADE**

💧 **MODERATE TO REGULAR WATER**

Chamaerops humilis

Europe's only native palm, this also grows on Mediterranean islands and in northwest Africa. Having survived brief temperature drops to 0°F (–18°C), it is among the hardiest palms. Curving offshoots develop clumps to 20 ft. tall and wide. Growth is slower in cooler parts of its range. Green to bluish green fans form on spiny leafstalks. Works in containers, massed under trees, or grown as an impenetrable hedge. Tolerates poor soil, strong winds. *C. h. argentea* (*C. h. cerifera*) has silvery blue foliage. (For more on palms, see "Meet the Palms," page 471.)

This palm forms multiple trunks, each covered with a dense mat of old leaf bases. Its blue-green leaves fan out at the top. Grow it beside a swimming pool, or as an accent among equally bold but lower plants such as *Agave attenuata.*

C

Chamelaucium

WAXFLOWER
Myrtaceae
EVERGREEN SHRUB

🌡 **ZONES 8, 9, 12–24**

☀ **FULL SUN**

◐ ◖ **LITTLE TO MODERATE WATER**

Chamelaucium uncinatum

These Australian natives' fragrant, bright green, needlelike leaves support showy sprays of white to reddish pink winter flowers cherished for arrangements. Most grow quickly to 3–8 ft. (perhaps taller when staked) with equal spread. Light and airy, loose and sprawling in appearance; looks somewhat like open-growing heather (*Calluna*). Can take ocean exposure. Very old plants have interesting twisted trunks and shaggy bark.

C. ciliatum. CAMEO PINK. Gray-green foliage with pink buds opening into white flowers on a 6-ft. shrub. 'Scaddan' grows to 3 ft. high and 4 ft. wide, with white flowers fading pink.

C. 'Lady Stephanie'. Light rose blossoms in spring and summer, lemon-scented foliage on 6-ft. plant.

C. 'Matilda'. White flowers age to purple, grows to about 4 ft. high and wide with citrus-scented foliage.

C. 'My Sweet Sixteen'. White flowers age to red on a shrub that grows to 6–8 ft. tall and almost as wide.

C. uncinatum. GERALDTON WAXFLOWER. Grows to 4–6 ft. tall. Seedling plants vary; select in bloom to get color you want. Named varieties include 'Dancing Queen' (double pink flowers, 6 ft. tall and wide); 'White' (white winter flowers); 'Escondido Rose' (also called 'M1'; magenta flowers); and 'Purple Pride' (6–7 ft., deep rosy purple).

CARE

Plant on dry, sunny bank or in fast-draining garden soil.

Chamerion angustifolium
(Epilobium angustifolium)

FIREWEED, WILLOW HERB
Onagraceae
PERENNIAL

🌡 **ZONES A1–A3; 1–7, 14–21**

☀ **FULL SUN**

◖ **MODERATE WATER**

🐝 **ATTRACTS BENEFICIAL INSECTS, HUMMINGBIRDS**

Chamerion angustifolium

This tall, pinkish purple wildflower forms colonies along northern roadsides and in burned-over areas, but is also effective in wild gardens. To 2–5 ft. tall and 1½–3 ft. wide; narrow leaves to 10 in. long. Loose clusters of four-petaled pink, rose-purple, or white ('Album') flowers appear in early summer. Native to North America and Eurasia.

Fireweed is Alaska's best known wildflower. It carpets glacier-backed meadows, hillsides outside Anchorage, and lends its name to everything from street signs to bicycle races. In gardens, its wispy flower stalks show up best in wild borders against a backdrop of greenery. Flowers open gradually toward the top of the stem; each one is short-lived. Long narrow seedpods follow; they explode in a web of silky white hairs. For low-growing, red-flowering relatives, see *Zauschneria.*

Chasmanthe

Iridaceae
PERENNIALS FROM CORMS

🌡 **ZONES 13, 15–24; OR DIG AND STORE**

☀ ◐ **FULL SUN OR PARTIAL SHADE**

◌ **NO IRRIGATION NEEDED**

🦜 **NECTAR FOR HUMMINGBIRDS**

Chasmanthe floribunda

These South African natives send up their 2-ft. irislike fans of bright green leaves shortly after the first rains of autumn. Narrow, 3–3½-ft.-high spikes of bright orange-red flowers follow in late winter or early spring, putting on a striking early show. Plants are fairly hardy, but late frosts may damage flower buds.

C. aethiopica. Unbranched flower spikes hold blossoms on just one side of spike.

C. floribunda. Unbranched and once-branched spikes bear blossoms along both sides; each spike carries 12–28 flowers. *C. f. duckittii* has yellow flowers.

CARE

In fall, plant corms 4 in. deep and 8–12 in. apart in well-drained soil. Corms multiply rapidly; dig and divide every 2 to 3 years. These plants spread easily; great for naturalizing. They are roadside weeds in some areas. During summer dormancy, plants don't need (but tolerate some) irrigation.

Chasmanthium latifolium
(Uniola latifolia)

SEA OATS, BAMBOO GRASS
Poaceae
PERENNIAL GRASS

🌡 **ZONES 2–10, 14–24**

☀ ◐ **PARTIAL SHADE IN HOTTEST CLIMATES**

◖ **REGULAR WATER**

Chasmanthium latifolium

Clumps of broad, bamboolike leaves support 2–5-ft. flowering stems in summer; they carry showers of silvery green spikelets that resemble flattened clusters of oats (or flattened armadillos). These turn copper in fall and look good through winter, drying to a greenish straw color that works well in dried arrangements. Cut them down before spring growth begins. Clumps widen slowly to 2 ft. and are not aggressive. Divide them every third spring. Stake if flowering stems sprawl. From eastern American woodlands. (For more on grasses, see "Meet the Grasses," page 346.)

Sea oats' large, graceful seed heads start out green in spring, then turn coppery in fall. In gardens, they sway in gentle breezes. In bouquets, they pair well with poppies and other wildflowers.

Chayote
Cucurbitaceae
PERENNIAL VINE OFTEN GROWN
AS ANNUAL

☀ **ZONES 14–16, 19–24; H1, H2;**
ANYWHERE AS ANNUAL

☀ **FULL SUN**

💧 **REGULAR WATER**

Chayote

Native to central Mexico, chayote (*Sechium edule*) plants look like related squashes, though their flowers are inconspicuous. Each vine can grow 20–30 ft. in the first year, 40–50 ft. in the second. Fruit is 3–8 in. long, green or yellow-green, irregularly oval, grooved, with a large edible seed surrounded by meaty flesh. Eat young fruit raw or cooked (tastes like summer squash); boil or bake mature fruit. Large, fleshy tuberous roots can also be eaten, but at the cost of the plant.

CARE

You can start plants from fruit sold in stores (check Latino markets). Buy in fall and let the fruit sprout in a cupboard; then plant in rich soil next to a fence or trellis, which it will climb by tendrils. Set fruit in the ground edgewise and slanted, with the sprouted end at the lowest point, narrow end exposed. If the shoot is long, cut it back to 1–2 in. In mild climates, plant in late winter; in areas where roots may freeze, pot in a 5-gal. container and store in a dark, cool spot until frost danger is past. Tops die down in frost. Bloom starts when day length shortens in fall; fruit is ripe within a month.

Cheiranthus. See *Erysimum*

Chenopodium
Amaranthaceae
ANNUALS AND PERENNIALS

☀ **ZONES VARY BY SPECIES**

☀ **FULL SUN**

💧 **REGULAR WATER**

Chenopodium quinoa

Most of these spinach relations are weeds, but some are eaten. Individual flowers are greenish, insignificant.

C. album. PIGWEED, LAMB'S QUARTERS. Annual. Zones 1–24. Leaves of this tall, common weed can reach 4 in. long; whitish underneath, smooth pale green above. They can be cooked like spinach.

C. ambrosioides. EPAZOTE, MEXICAN TEA. Perennial. Zones 8, 9, 14–24; H1, H2; Zones 1–7 as annual. Strongly scented leaves to 5 in. long, deeply toothed. Sometimes grown or collected roadside as seasoning for Mexican dishes.

C. quinoa. QUINOA. Annual. Zones 1–24, but see below. Pronounced KEEN-wa, quinoa grows to 5 ft. tall and produces dense flower and seed clusters. A traditional high-protein Andean grain; resembles sesame seed.

CARE

Plant in late spring and harvest in fall. Needs short days and mild weather to bloom and set seed; takes light frost. After harvest, seeds are rinsed to remove surface bitterness, then cooked like rice. (The saponins in unwashed quinoa trigger an allergic reaction in some people.) Excellent production in high Rocky Mountain valleys. Strains that yield at low elevation are also available.

Cherimoya, Custard Apple
Annonaceae
BRIEFLY DECIDUOUS SHRUB OR TREE

☀ **ZONES 21–24; H1, H2**

☀ **FULL SUN**

💧 **REGULAR WATER**

☠ **TOXIC SEEDS CAUSE GASTRIC UPSET**

Cherimoya

Native to the high-elevation American tropics, this small tree (*Annona cherimola*) yields yellow-green fruits whose custardy flesh tastes like pineapple crossed with banana. Hardy to about 25°F (–4°C). Grows fast the first 3 to 4 years, then slows, eventually forming a tree 12–15 ft. tall and wide, or 30 ft. unpruned. Leaves are 4–10 in. long, dull green above, velvety-hairy beneath; they drop in late spring, but tree quickly replaces them. Thick, fleshy, 1-in., hairy brownish or yellow flowers with a fruity fragrance open for 3 to 4 months beginning around leaf drop.

Large fruits weigh ½–1½ lb., and trees can bear 25 to 100 fruits per year. Harvest fruit in late fall or winter, when it turns yellowish green. Thin, tender skin of most varieties resembles short overlapping leaves of artichokes; can be warty. Let fruit mature indoors at room temperature; when ripe, it turns a dull brownish green (some varieties show tan freckles) and yields to gentle pressure like a ripe peach. Refrigerate ripe fruit, which tastes best cold. Creamy white flesh contains large black seeds and is almost custardlike; eat it with a spoon. Specialty nurseries offer several improved varieties, including

exceptionally flavorful 'El Bumpo', 'Honeyhart', 'Pierce', 'McPherson' (self-fruitful), and 'Sabor' (best flavor) in California. In Hawaii, where cherimoyas grow best above 1,000 ft., 'McPherson' (also sold as 'Spain') is the best choice.

Locate tree where you can enjoy fragrance. After 4 or 5 years, begin pruning yearly to produce fruiting wood.

To ensure fruit set, gather freshly opened flowers and place in a small jar. Keep in a cool place 12 to 24 hours, by which time the pollen will shed. Use a small paintbrush to pollinate freshly opened flowers.

Cherry
Rosaceae
DECIDUOUS FRUIT TREES

☀ **ZONES VARY BY TYPE**

☀ **FULL SUN**

💧 **REGULAR WATER THROUGH GROWING SEASON**

'Sweetheart' cherries

Both sweet and sour cherries perform well in gardens that have frosty winters and mild to moderate summer temperatures. For flowering cherry trees, see *Prunus*.

Sweet cherries. The most common market cherries, these are bred from *Prunus avium*, which is native to Europe, North Africa, and Southwest Asia, and naturalized in North America. They are at their best in Zones 2, 3, 6–9, 14, 15; and they are possible in adjacent zones (except desert). All need many winter hours below 45°F (7°C) to set fruit, so they don't do well in mild-winter areas of Southern California, the coastal strip, or low desert. Can't take

C

extreme summer heat or intense winter cold; frosts or rain in spring can damage crop.

In the past, many gardeners stayed away from sweet cherries because trees are naturally large (to 35 ft. high and wide), and most need cross-pollination, so you have to plant two. But breeding advances have produced many self-fruitful varieties (noted in descriptions) and much smaller sizes.

For varieties that need pollinators to produce fruit, the second tree must be chosen with care. No combination of these will produce fruit: 'Bing', 'Lambert', 'Royal Ann'. The following varieties will pollinate any other cherry: 'Angela', 'Black Tartarian', 'Republican', 'Sam', 'Stella' (though 'Stella' will not pollinate 'Bing' in mildwinter climates), and 'Van'. However, because 'Lambert' blooms late, it is pollinated best by 'Republican'.

Cherry trees are easier to grow and harvest when grown on a dwarfing rootstock, such as Colt, GM61/1, and the Giessen 148 series. Such trees can easily be maintained at less than half the size of those growing on standard rootstocks.

The following are among the best varieties.

'Angela'. Small, glossy black fruit with excellent flavor. Resists cracking. Midseason to late.

'Bing'. Top quality. Large, dark red, meaty fruit of fine flavor. Midseason.

'Black Tartarian'. Fruit smaller than that of 'Bing', purplish black, firm, sweet. Early.

'Craig's Crimson'. Medium to large, deep red to black; superb flavor. Naturally dwarf (about two-thirds normal size). Self-fruitful. Midseason.

'Early Burlat'. Like 'Bing'; ripens 2 weeks earlier.

'Early Ruby'. Dark red, purple-fleshed early cherry that performs well in all sweet cherry areas. 'Black Tartarian', 'Royal Ann', 'Van' are all good pollenizers. Early.

'Emperor Francis'. Medium-size, light red fruit with fine flavor. Favorite in the Northwest. Early.

'Hardy Giant'. Dark red fruit resembles that of 'Bing'. Good pollenizer, especially for 'Lambert'. Midseason.

'Hartland'. Good-flavored black cherry, softer fruit than 'Bing'. Early midseason.

'Kristin'. Large black fruit resists cracking. One of the hardiest sweet cherries; worth a try in Zones A2, A3; 1. Midseason.

'Lambert'. Very large, very firm black fruit. Flavor sprightlier than that of 'Bing'. Late.

'Lapins'. Resembles 'Bing' but is self-fruitful. Early to midseason.

'Mona'. Resembles 'Black Tartarian' but is larger. Very early.

'Rainier'. Has yellow skin with pink blush; fruit ripens a few days before that of 'Bing'.

'Republican' ('Black Republican', 'Black Oregon'). Large, spreading tree. Small, round, purplish black fruit with dark juice, tender yet crisp texture. Good flavor. Late.

'Royal Ann' ('Napoleon'). Large, spreading tree; very productive. Light yellow fruit with pink blush; tender, crisp. Sprightly flavor. Midseason.

'Sam'. Vigorous tree. Large, firm black fruit has excellent flavor. Midseason to late.

'Stella'. Dark fruit like that of 'Lambert'; ripens a few days later. Self-fruitful and a good pollenizer for other cherries. 'Compact Stella' is similar, but tree is half the size.

'Sweetheart'. Large, bright red; excellent flavor. Self-fruitful and heavy bearing. Late.

'Utah Giant'. Ripens with 'Bing' but is larger, sweeter; develops sweetness even before fully ripe. Holds color when processed. Pollinate with 'Van' or 'Stella'.

'Van'. Heavy-bearing tree. Shiny black fruit, firmer and slightly smaller than that of 'Bing'. Good flavor.

'Vandalay'. Large, black; excellent flavor. Self-fruitful; resists cracking. Midseason.

'White Gold'. Large, yellow with red blush; fine flavor. Self-fruitful and heavy bearing; resists cracking. Midseason.

Sour cherries. Also known as pie cherries. These are spreading trees to 20 ft. tall, best grown in well-drained soil in Zones A2, A3; 1–9, 14–17. They are self-fruitful but poor pollenizers for sweet cherries. There are far fewer types of sour cherries than sweet cherries; these are the most widely grown. The category name notwithstanding, a few varieties listed here are sweet enough to enjoy fresh.

'Early Richmond'. Small, bright red fruit is soft, juicy, and sweet-tart. Early.

'English Morello'. Darker, tarter fruit than that of 'Early Richmond'. Red juice. Late.

'Kansas Sweet' ('Hansen'). Large, red fruit is semisweet. Late.

'Meteor'. Fruit similar to that of 'Early Richmond', but tree is smaller. Late.

'Montmorency'. Like 'Early Richmond'. Midseason to late.

'North Star'. Red to dark red skin and sour yellow flesh. Small, very hardy tree. Midseason.

'Surefire'. Bright red skin and flesh; sweet flavor. Late.

CARE

Plant in deep, well-drained soil. Prune trees only to maintain good structure and shape; fruiting spurs are long-lived and need not be renewed by pruning. Fruit appears from late spring into midsummer, depending on variety and climate. Don't pick until the cherries are sweet; they don't ripen further after harvest. Use netting or reflective tape to discourage birds.

If the tree is putting out less than 6 in. of new growth per year, give mature trees 5 lbs. of 10-10-10 fertilizer in spring. Give young trees ½ lb. per year of age, and dwarf cherries ½ lb. of 10-10-10 fertilizer per inch of trunk diameter.

For control of brown rot and blossom blight, apply a copper spray just as leaves drop in autumn, then a fungicide when first blooms appear and weekly during bloom. Resume fungicide program about 2 weeks before harvest or if fruit rot begins to appear.

Good sanitation also helps limit disease—remove mummified fruit and prune out and discard diseased twigs as they appear. Spray horticultural oil during the dormant period to control many kinds of insects and diseases, including scale insects and mites.

To control the maggots of spotted-wing drosophila, spray with spinosad (a natural control) once when fruit turns pink, then again 7 to 10 days later.

Chestnut

Fagaceae
DECIDUOUS TREES

🌿 **ZONES 2–9, 14–17, EXCEPT AS NOTED**

☼ **FULL SUN**

💧 **MODERATE WATER**

Chestnuts

Where space allows, these dense, large shade trees bring lush beauty and delicious nuts into the landscape. They just need to be sited where their litter and rank-smelling pollen won't be too obtrusive. All have handsome green leaves, and small, 8–10-in., creamy white catkins that appear in summer. Prickly burs enclose large nuts that fall when ripe. Gather daily, remove from burs, and let dry in the sun (shade in hot climates). Plant two trees to ensure cross-pollination; unpollinated single trees bear little or nothing. Give occasional deep irrigation.

Chestnut blight has made American chestnut (*Castanea dentata*) nearly extinct, but other species and hybrids are available.

Chinese chestnut (*Castanea mollissima*). Native to China, Korea, and Taiwan. Grows to 35–40 ft. tall with rounded crown that may spread to 20–25 ft. Leaves 3–7 in. long, with coarsely toothed edges. Most nursery trees are grown from seed, not cuttings, so nuts are variable, but generally good. Resists chestnut blight. Intolerant of alkaline soil.

European chestnut

(C. sativa). Native to southern Europe, North Africa, western Asia. Can reach 100 ft. tall with greater spread, but typically 40–60 ft. tall in gardens. Leaves 4–9 in. long, with sharply toothed edges. These are the large, excellent nuts sold in markets. Resists oak root fungus but susceptible to chestnut blight.

Hybrid chestnuts. Zones 2–9, 14–24. Most are offspring of Japanese (*C. crenata*) or Chinese chestnuts crossed with American or European chestnuts. Trees usually grow 40–60 ft. tall and wide. They do not tolerate alkaline soils, but some resist chestnut blight. 'Colossal' sets the standard for nuts; 'Dunstan' is an American cross with high-quality, medium-size nuts, blight resistance; 'Nevada' is a small-nutted variety and proven pollenizer for 'Colossal'; 'Skioka' produces abundant small nuts but won't pollinate other trees; and 'Sleeping Giant' bears sweet, large nuts and is blight-resistant.

Chicory and Radicchio

Asteraceae
PERENNIAL

- 🌡 **ALL ZONES**
- ☀ **FULL SUN**
- 💧 **REGULAR WATER**

Radicchio

The wild form of this Mediterranean native is a perennial Western roadside weed with pretty, 2–4-ft.-tall, sky blue summer flowers. Different strains of it are grown for three purposes: for salad greens (small-rooted red- or green-leafed varieties);

for roots to make a coffee substitute (large-rooted varieties); and for Belgian or French endive ('Witloof' chicory). For the standard salad green called endive, see Endive.

"Radicchio" is the name given to red-leafed chicories grown for salads. 'Indigo', 'Palla Rossa', and 'Red Treviso' are good varieties. Radicchio makes lettucelike heads that color to a deep rosy red as weather grows cold in fall or winter; its slight bitterness lessens as color deepens. Harvest after heads form.

Among green-leafed varieties, try 'Catalogna' and 'Red Rib' for dandelion-leafed varieties, or the heirloom 'Crystal Hat', whose leaves grow like romaine lettuce. Pick tender young leaves as needed.

For roots to make a coffee substitute, 'Magdeburgh' ('Cicoria Siciliana') is a good choice.

To grow Belgian or French endive, try 'Witloof Bruxelles' or 'Totem'. Harvest after new growth appears.

CARE

Sow all types ¼–½ in. deep, 2 to 3 in. apart, in rows spaced 18 in. apart. Green-leafed types and root types: Sow starting in early spring (up to early summer where summers are not too hot). In areas with mild winters, you can also plant in mid- to late summer for fall and winter harvest (or, in the desert, in fall for winter harvest). Red-leafed types: Sow in mid- to late summer to mature in cool autumn months, though variety 'Giulio' can be sown in spring to harvest in summer. Belgian endive: Sow seeds in spring or early summer; plants will mature by fall. In winter, trim the greens to an inch of stem; then dig the roots, bury them diagonally in moist sand, and set in dark, cool room until pale, tender new growth has been forced.

"Radicchio" is the name given to red-leafed chicories grown for salads. Their leaves add color and bite.

Chilopsis linearis

DESERT WILLOW, DESERT CATALPA
Bignoniaceae
DECIDUOUS SHRUB OR TREE

- 🌡 **ZONES 3B, 7–14, 18–23**
- ☀ **FULL SUN**
- 💧 **LITTLE TO MODERATE WATER**
- 🐦 **ATTRACTS HUMMINGBIRDS**

Chilopsis linearis

Native to Southwest desert washes below 5,000 ft., desert willow grows 15–30 ft. tall, 10–20 ft. wide. At first it can grow 3 ft. per year, then slows, eventually developing shaggy bark and twisting trunks. Narrow, willowy leaves. From spring to fall, fragrant, trumpet-shaped blossoms with crimped lobes appear, similar to both catalpa and small cattleya orchids. Flower color varies among seedlings—may be reddish purple, lavender, rose, pink, or white, often marked with purple and gold. Nurseries select for good color, large size, ruffled form.

Gallon-size plants can bloom first year. Desert willow drops its leaves early but holds a heavy, messy-looking crop of seedpods through winter. Thin occasionally to enhance picturesque shape.

'**Art's Seedless**'. Sterile flowers produce no seedpods.

'**AZT Desert Amethyst**'. All-purple flowers; 15 to 30 ft. tall and wide.

'**Bubba**'. Lavender and purple summer–fall flowers; to 20 ft.

'**Burgundy**' ('**Burgundy Lace**'). Deep purplish red flowers.

'**Hope**'. White flowers with a pale yellow throat. Wispy, open growth.

'**Lois Adams**'. Profuse two-tone blooms in pale lavender and magenta; no seedpods. Compact, upright growth.

'**Lucretia Hamilton**'. Dark purple flowers in large clusters. To 15–18 ft. high and wide.

'**Regal**'. Combination of lavender and wine red; flat-faced, open-throated blooms make a great display.

'**Timeless Beauty**'. Long season of two-toned lavender and burgundy blooms; no seedpods. To 15–20 ft. high and wide.

'**Warren Jones**'. Large, ruffled blossoms in pure, unshaded pink with paler throat. Holds leaves long; evergreen in warm-winter climates.

Chimonanthus praecox

(C. fragrans)
WINTERSWEET
Calycanthaceae
DECIDUOUS SHRUB

- 🌡 **ZONES 4–9, 14–21**
- ☀ ◑ **AFTERNOON SHADE IN HOTTEST CLIMATES**
- 💧 **MODERATE WATER**

Chimonanthus praecox

Wintersweet's spicy-scented blossoms appear on leafless branches in winter or spring and may last for more than a month if not hit by hard frost. Native to China and Japan. Its open growth habit reaches 10–15 ft. high, 6–8 ft. wide, with many stems from base. Inch-wide, translucent pale yellow blossoms have darker centers marked with purple, chocolate, or maroon. Tapered, rough green leaves turn yellow-green in autumn.

C

C

CARE

In colder part of range, plant in sheltered site to prevent frost damage, but always put the plant where its winter fragrance can be enjoyed. Restrict size by pruning while in flower; shape as a small tree by removing excess basal stems. To rejuvenate a leggy plant, lop it to within a foot of the ground in late winter. Needs good drainage and some winter cold.

Chimonobambusa.
See Bamboo

Chinese Cabbage
Brassicaceae
BIENNIAL GROWN AS ANNUAL

🌿 **ALL ZONES**

☼ ◐ **PART SHADE IN HOT CLIMATES**

💧 **REGULAR WATER**

Chinese cabbage

With a looser head and more delicate flavor than ordinary cabbage (a close relative), Chinese cabbage falls into three categories: Michihli types (petsai), with tall, narrow heads; Napa types (wong bok), with short, broad heads; and loosehead varieties.

Favored Michihli varieties are hybrid 'Greenwich' and open-pollinated Michihli itself; among Napa varieties, try 'China Express' and the miniature 'Tenderheart'; and to sample loose head, start with 'Tokyo Bekana'.

For Chinese white cabbage (bok choy), see Asian Greens.

CARE

This cool-season crop bolts easily in hot weather. In Zones 1–6, 10, 11, plant seeds in midsummer; elsewhere, sow in late summer. Sow seeds thinly in rows spaced 2–2½ ft. apart, and thin plants to 1½–2 ft. apart. Heads should be ready in 70 to 80 days. Subject to same pests as cabbage.

Chionanthus
FRINGE TREE
Oleaceae
DECIDUOUS SHRUBS OR TREES

🌿 **ZONES VARY BY SPECIES**

☼ **FULL SUN**

💧 💧 **MODERATE TO REGULAR WATER**

🦅 **FRUIT ATTRACTS BIRDS**

Chionanthus retusus

These spectacular flowering plants are named for the narrow, fringelike white petals that are borne in a profusion of lacy flower clusters. Male and female plants are separate; males have larger flowers. If both plants are present, females produce clusters of small, dark, olivelike fruit favored by birds. Broad leaves turn bright to deep yellow in fall.

C. retusus. CHINESE FRINGE TREE. Zones 3–9, 14–24. Native to China and Taiwan. Grows to about 20 ft. tall, usually as a multistemmed shrub that can be trained as a small tree. Pure white, 4-in. blossom clusters open in late spring or early summer, 2–3 weeks before *C. virginicus* comes into flower. In bloom, looks something like a tremendous white lilac. Gray-brown bark (sometimes golden on young stems) provides winter interest.

C. virginicus. FRINGE TREE. Zones 2–6, 15–24. Native to southeastern U.S. Its leaves and flower clusters are often twice as big as those of

C. retusus. Lightly fragrant, greenish white flowers appear by the plant's third year. Can reach 30 ft. tall, but usually 12–20 ft. tall and wide in gardens. Can be shrubby and open, or a perfect small specimen tree. In Zones 2–6, where it is one of the last deciduous plants to leaf out in spring, it grows only 1 ft. per year and is best used as an airy shrub. Tolerates air pollution.

CARE

Give good drainage. Minimal pruning needed. Resist most pests and diseases, though fungal leaf spot and powdery mildew may occur.

Chionodoxa
GLORY-OF-THE-SNOW
Asparagaceae
PERENNIALS FROM BULBS

🌿 **ZONES A2, A3; 1–7, 14–20**

☼ ◐ **FULL SUN DURING BLOOM, LIGHT SHADE AFTER IN HOT CLIMATES**

💧 **REGULAR WATER DURING GROWTH AND BLOOM**

Chionodoxa nana 'Pink Giant'

Charming little spring-flowering bulbs native to alpine meadows of Crete, Cyprus, and Turkey are among the first spring bloomers. Six-pointed, starlike blossoms in blue, white, or pink rise above clumps of straight, narrow leaves. Species are similar; their names are often mixed up.

C. forbesii. Grows up to 1 ft. high. 'Blue Giant' has blue flowers. 'Violet Beauty' is more pink than violet.

C. luciliae. The most commonly grown chionodoxa, this one typically bears one to four 1½-in., violet-blue blooms.

'Alba' has white flowers larger than those of the species; 'Gigantea' has larger leaves and larger blooms of violet-blue.

C. nana. 'Pink Giant' has pink flowers; to 12 in. high.

C. sardensis. Inch-wide violet-blue flowers with small white eye; carried 4–12 to a stem.

CARE

In fall, plant bulbs in rich, well-drained soil, setting them 2–3 in. deep and 3 in. apart. In very hot, dry climates, supply some moisture during summer dormancy. When bloom quality declines, dig and divide clumps in early fall. Plantings may also self-seed.

× Chitalpa tashkentensis
Bignoniaceae
DECIDUOUS TREE

🌿 **ZONES 3–24**

☼ **FULL SUN**

◐ 💧 **LITTLE TO MODERATE WATER**

🦅 **ATTRACTS HUMMINGBIRDS**

× *Chitalpa tashkentensis* 'Pink Dawn'

Growing rapidly to 20–30 ft. tall and wide, this tree combines the larger flowers of its *Catalpa bignonioides* parent with the desert toughness and flower color of *Chilopsis linearis*, its other parent. Erect clusters of frilly, trumpet-shaped flowers in pink, white, or lavender appear from late spring to fall. 'Pink Dawn' has pink blooms, 'Morning Cloud' white ones.

Because it constantly drops spent blossoms and leaves in summer, don't plant over patios or walkways. It is susceptible to powdery mildew and anthracnose. Don't overwater.

Chlorophytum comosum

SPIDER PLANT
Asparagaceae
PERENNIAL

- **ZONES 15–17, 19–24; H1, H2**
- **PARTIAL SHADE; BRIGHT INDIRECT LIGHT**
- **REGULAR WATER**

Chlorophytum comosum 'Variegatum'

South African evergreen forms 1–3-ft.-high clumps of soft, curving leaves like long, broad grass blades with small white flowers in long clusters. Both 'Variegatum' and 'Vittatum' have white-striped leaves. Flowers are about ½ in. long, growing in loose, leafy-tipped spikes held above foliage. Greatest attraction: miniature duplicates of mother plant, complete with root, at ends of curved stems (as with offsets of strawberry plants). These can be cut off and potted individually.

Spider plant is a good choice for hanging baskets. To use as groundcover, set 2 ft. apart in diamond pattern; plants will fill in the same year. Often sold as *C. capense*.

If your spider plant refuses to sprout plantlets, reduce feeding and switch to a low-nitrogen fertilizer. An overabundance of nitrogen promotes vegetative growth at the expense of offspring.

Choisya ternata

MEXICAN ORANGE
Rutaceae
EVERGREEN SHRUB

- **ZONES 6–9, 14–24; BORDERLINE IN ZONES 4, 5**
- **FULL SUN IN COOLER CLIMATES ONLY**
- **MODERATE WATER**
- **ATTRACTS BEES**

Choisya ternata

This Mexican native grows quickly to 6–8 ft. tall and often slightly wider. Lustrous, rich green leaves held toward ends of branches are divided into fans of three leaflets. They give the shrub a textured, voluptuous look. Clusters of fragrant white flowers, somewhat like small orange blossoms, open in late winter or early spring, blooming continuously for at least two months and then intermittently through summer.

Attractive as an informal hedge or screen, this is sometimes called mock orange. Foliage of 'Sundance' is yellow when young, gradually turning green. 'Aztec Pearl' is a more compact hybrid with narrower leaves and white flowers opening from pink buds in spring and sometimes again in summer.

CARE

Plant in fertile soil with good drainage; suffers in alkaline soils or where water is high in salts. Under such conditions, amend the soil as for azaleas. During growing season, thin older branches in plant's center to force leafy new interior growth. Subject to damage from sucking insects.

Chondropetalum elephantinum

CAPE RUSH
Restionaceae
PERENNIAL

- **ZONES 8, 9, 14–24**
- **FULL SUN OR PARTIAL SHADE**
- **REGULAR TO AMPLE WATER**

Chondropetalum elephantinum

Forming a dense clump 3–5 ft. tall and 4–6 ft. wide, this rush-like South African marsh plant makes a striking, elegant accent in the ground or in a pot, particularly when a breeze produces a play of light and shadow on its stems. Papery bracts at each stem joint turn from tan to dark brown, then drop off. Narrow clusters of dark brown flower heads (male and female blossoms are on separate plants) top each shoot. Often sold as *C. tectorum*, a closely related but smaller plant (2–3 ft. high and 3–4 ft. wide).

CARE

Cape rush likes its feet in water but is also content with a regular watering regime; it will even tolerate considerable drought once new growth is complete. Does not do well with high fertility. Cut old growth to the ground just as new sprouts show in spring, or prune out old stems individually if new shoots are already established. Clump expands slowly by rhizomes. Propagate by seed, since roots do not like to be disturbed.

FOR MORE ON PERENNIALS, SEE "GROW: PERENNIALS," PAGES 686–687.

Chorisia (Ceiba)

FLOSS SILK TREE
Malvaceae
EVERGREEN TO BRIEFLY DECIDUOUS TREES

- **ZONES VARY BY SPECIES**
- **FULL SUN**
- **MODERATE WATER**

Chorisia speciosa

A heavy, spine-studded trunk and clouds of large, showy flowers have firmly embedded this South American native in Southern California horticulture. Its leaves are divided into leaflets like fingers of a hand, dropping during autumn flowering or whenever temperatures fall below 27°F (–3°C). Blooms resemble narrow-petaled hibiscus flowers.

C. insignis. WHITE FLOSS SILK TREE. Zones 12, 13, 15–24; H1, H2. To 50 ft. tall and wide. White to pale yellow, 5–6-in. flowers. Blooms from fall into winter; stopped by frost.

C. speciosa. Zones 12–24; H1, H2. Grows 3–5 ft. a year for first few years, then more slowly to an eventual 30–60 ft. tall and wide. Pink, purplish rose, or burgundy flowers are 4 in. or more across. Grafted varieties include 'Los Angeles Beautiful', with wine red flowers; and 'Pink Princess', a dwarf hybrid that grows 12 ft. high.

CARE

Fast drainage and controlled watering are keys to success. Irrigate established trees about once a month during growing season; ease off in late summer to encourage more flowers. Prune only to remove wayward or dead growth.

C

C

Chorizema
FLAME PEA
Papilionaceae
EVERGREEN SHRUBS

🌿 **ZONES 15–17, 19–24**

☀️ 🌓 **FLOWER COLOR MORE INTENSE IN PARTIAL SHADE**

🌢 🌢 **LITTLE TO MODERATE WATER**

Chorizema cordatum

These 2–5-ft.-tall Australian evergreens produce showy clusters of sweet pea–shaped flowers in a blend of orange and purplish red, late winter through spring. A lighter crop often blooms in fall. Fast growing, with slender, graceful branches. Let them spill over walls or banks, or out of containers. To keep them compact, pinch regularly and cut back after flowering. Hardy to 24°F (–4°C).

C. 'Bush Flame'. Grows 2–3 ft. high; more than 3 ft. wide. Sprays of orange and pink flowers in late winter, early spring.

C. cordatum. HEART-LEAF FLAME PEA. Grows 3–5 ft. tall and wide. Dark green leaves with small, prickly teeth along the edges; red, orange, and yellow flowers. Sometimes erroneously sold as *C. ilicifolium*.

Rock Garden Plants

Rock gardens are landscapes in miniature, simulations of boulder-strewn mountain slopes, rocky outcrops on coastal bluffs, and wind-swept high plains. The best plants for these gardens are usually groundhuggers that wander among boulders and reach out over a gravel mulch. But taller plants, such as flame pea (*Chorizema* 'Bush Flame') and damianita, pictured above, are excellent choices, too. Give them well-drained soil.

Chrysactinia mexicana
DAMIANITA
Asteraceae
EVERGREEN SHRUB

🌿 **ZONES 10–13, 18–24**

☀️ **FULL SUN**

🌢 🌢 **LITTLE TO MODERATE WATER**

Chrysactinia mexicana

A native of the high Chihuahuan Desert, this heavily branched shrub grows 2 ft. high and wide, with needlelike, strongly aromatic green leaves. Golden yellow, 1-in. daisies are borne singly at tips of 2–3-in.-long stems over a long period. Bloom peaks in spring and fall, easing off in high summer heat.

CARE

Damianita endures extreme heat as well as winter lows to 0°F (–18°C). It also tolerates a wide range of soils but does best with reasonably good drainage. Supplemental water in summer encourages more blooms. Shear annually in early spring; cut back more severely if plant becomes too woody.

Chrysalidocarpus lutescens.
See *Dypsis lutescens*

Chrysanthemum
Asteraceae
PERENNIALS

🌿 **ZONES VARY BY SPECIES**

☀️ **FULL SUN, EXCEPT AS NOTED**

🌢 **REGULAR WATER, EXCEPT AS NOTED**

🌢 **CAN CAUSE CONTACT DERMATITIS**

Chrysanthemum × grandiflorum

Beloved for late summer and fall bloom, *Chrysanthemum* once included around 160 species, but taxonomists have moved the vast majority to other genera. The cross-references below give new names of old favorites.

Chrysanthemums bred for the cut-flower industry, for forcing in pots (and sold in bloom every day of the year), and for exhibition are primarily florists' chrysanthemums. Some of these also make good garden subjects, as do all *C. weyrichii* and *C. zawadskii* selections. You may also find excellent hybrids between *C. zawadskii* and *C. × grandiflorum* called rubellums.

C. arcticum. See *Arctanthemum arcticum*.

C. balsamita. See *Tanacetum balsamita*.

C. carinatum. See *Glebionis carinatum*.

C. coccineum. See *Tanacetum coccineum*.

C. coronarium. See *Glebionis coronaria*.

C. frutescens. See *Argyranthemum frutescens*.

C. × grandiflorum (C. × morifolium). FLORISTS' CHRYSANTHEMUM. Perennial. Zones 2–24; H1. The most useful of all autumn-blooming perennials

How to Grow Chrysanthemums

How to Grow Chrysanthemums

It's easy to grow chrysanthemums, but not so easy to grow the prize-winning chrysanthemums that demand such meticulous attention to watering, feeding, pinching, pruning, grooming, and pest control.

PLANTING In early spring, plant in good loam that's free of competing roots. In hot climates, supply afternoon shade. Stake plants as needed.

WATERING Water deeply and frequently in porous soils, less often in heavy soils. Too little water causes woody stems and loss of lower leaves; overwatering makes leaves yellow, blacken, and drop. Water daily in warm weather, every other day in cool conditions.

FERTILIZING Feed with liquid fertilizer every 7 to 10 days until buds show color.

PINCHING To produce sturdy plants with big flowers, start pinching at planting time by removing plant tip. When lateral shoots form, select one to four for continued growth. Keep pinching all summer, nipping top pair of leaves on every shoot that reaches 5 in. long. Stop pinching earlier in coldest regions. For huge blooms on large-flowered sorts, remove all flower buds except one or two per cluster.

CUTTING BACK After bloom, cut back plants to within 8 in. of ground. Where soils are heavy and sodden in winter, dig clumps with soil intact and overwinter aboveground. Cover clumps with sand or sawdust in Zones 2, 3, and 10.

CHALLENGES Stems are attacked by borers in desert areas. Aphids cause trouble in all areas. To avoid them, feed plants with systemic insecticide/fertilizer combination.

for borders, containers, and cutting, and the most versatile and varied of all chrysanthemums, this hybrid group is available in many flower forms, colors, plant sizes (from under a foot to 6 ft. tall), flower sizes, and growth habits. Colors include white, yellow, red, pink, orange, bronze, purple, and lavender, as well as multicolors.

Florists and even grocery stores sell potted chrysanthemums in bloom every day of the year, though by nature a chrysanthemum blooms in late summer or fall. Growers force these plants to bloom out of season by subjecting them to artificial day lengths, using lights and dark cloths. You can plunge the potted flowering plants right into a garden bed or border for an immediate (but expensive) display, or enjoy them in the house while the flowers remain fresh and then plant them out. Either way, once plants are in the garden, they will revert to fall blooming.

CLOCKWISE FROM TOP LEFT: Flower forms quill, spider, pompon

C. hosmariense. See *Rhodanthemum hosmariense.*

C. leucanthemum. See *Leucanthemum vulgare.*

C. maximum. See *Leucanthemum × superbum.*

C. multicaule. See *Coleostephus myconis.*

C. pacificum. See *Ajania pacifica.*

C. paludosum. See *Leucanthemum paludosum.*

C. parthenium. See *Tanacetum parthenium.*

C. ptarmiciflorum. See *Tanacetum ptarmiciflorum.*

C. × superbum. See *Leucanthemum × superbum.*

C. weyrichii. Perennial. Zones 2–6. From Japan. Rock garden plant with finely cut leaves; forms a mat to 1–1½ ft. high and 1 ft. wide. Single, 2-in., white to pink daisies with yellow centers appear just above foliage in fall. 'Pink Bomb' has rosy pink rays, and 'White Bomb' has creamy white ones.

C. zawadskii (C. × rubellum). Perennial. Zones 1–24. From Russia, northern and eastern Asia. To 2 ft. high and wide, finely cut leaves, and 2–3-in. daisies over a long season beginning in late summer.

'Clara Curtis' has bright pink flowers; 'Mary Stoker' has blooms of soft yellow touched with apricot.

Chrysothamnus

RABBITBRUSH, CHAMISA
Asteraceae
DECIDUOUS SHRUBS

✎ **ZONES 1–3, 10, 11**

☼ ◑ **PART SHADE AT HOTTER, LOWER ELEVATIONS**

◐ **LITTLE OR NO WATER**

🦋 **ATTRACT BUTTERFLIES**

Chrysothamnus nauseosus

High-desert, Rocky Mountain natives. Erect, freely branching shrubs to 6 ft. tall, 3 ft. wide; branches are white, with greenish upper surfaces. Gray-green and narrow leaves often drop by bloom time in late summer or fall (especially at lower elevations), when abundant clusters of fluffy flowers appear at stem ends. Foliage aromatic. Useful for naturalistic plantings, lowcare borders. There are numerous subspecies.

C. nauseosus (Ericameria nauseosus). Yellow flowers.

C. viscidiflorus. Greenish yellow, somewhat sticky flowers on 3–4-ft. plants.

CARE

Plants are denser in full sun (but full sun at lower elevations can force summer leaf drop). Irrigation makes plants taller and lankier; prune in spring for compactness.

FOR OTHER PLANTS THAT ATTRACT BUTTERFLIES, SEE PAGE 100.

Cibotium glaucum

HAPUʻU, PULU, HAWAIIAN TREE FERN
Cibotiaceae
TREE FERN

✎ **ZONES 17, 23, 24; H2**

☼ ◑ **FULL SUN OR PARTIAL SHADE**

💧 **MODERATE WATER**

Cibotium glaucum

This is the most common tree fern found in its native Hawaii, growing slowly to 20 ft. tall, with crown spreading 15 ft. wide. Arching, intricately divided, 3–9-ft.-long fronds are medium green above, lighter beneath. Silky, fawn-colored wool (pulu) shrouds leaf bases and densely covers buds at the trunk tip.

CARE

Give plants well-drained, slightly acid soil. Needs protection from strong winds. Best with moderate water but tolerates dry or moist conditions. Give some shade in hot, dry areas. Prune to remove old or injured fronds. (For more on ferns, see "Meet the Ferns," page 320.)

These native tree ferns are most abundant in moist areas on the island of Hawaii. But numbers in the wild are shrinking. Purchase only plants propagated by nurseries.

Cimicifuga. See *Actaea*

Cinnamomum camphora

CAMPHOR TREE
Lauraceae
EVERGREEN TREE

- **ZONES 8, 9, 12–24; H1, H2**
- **FULL SUN OR LIGHT SHADE**
- **LITTLE TO REGULAR WATER**

Cinnamomum camphora

This big Asian native tree grows slowly to 50 or 60 ft. tall and wide. A heavy trunk and big, upright, spreading limbs give it powerful structure; it's especially beautiful in rain, when bark looks black. Aromatic leaves smell like camphor when crushed. New foliage in early spring is pink, red, or bronze; matures to shiny yellow green. Inconspicuous but fragrant yellow flowers bloom profusely in late spring, followed by small blackish fruits.

Though evergreen, camphor drops leaves heavily in early spring; flowers, fruits, and twigs drop later. Plant where litter will not be a problem. Competitive roots can invade garden beds, paved areas, and sewer lines. In the desert, it is sometimes affected by salt burn.

CARE

This tree is subject to verticillium wilt. Symptoms are wilting and death of twigs, branches, even the entire tree; diseased wood shows brownish discoloration. No cure is known, though trees often outgrow the problem. To treat, cut out diseased branches, apply nitrogen fertilizer, and water it in well.

Cissus

Vitaceae
EVERGREEN VINES

- **ZONES VARY BY SPECIES**
- **EXPOSURE NEEDS VARY BY SPECIES**
- **WATER NEEDS VARY BY SPECIES**
- **SOME KINDS CAUSE CONTACT DERMATITIS**

Cissus antarctica

These grape relatives are valued for their foliage; flowers are inconspicuous. Most climb by tendrils, and most will double as groundcovers in mild-winter climates. Easy to grow; not fussy about soil, water, or fertilizer. Prune anytime to remove tangled or weak stems or to restrict size.

C. antarctica. KANGAROO TREEBINE. Zones 16–24; or indoors. Native to Australia. Graceful, densely foliaged vine to 10 ft.; vigorous once established. Glossy leaves are spear-shaped; toothed edges and prominent veins are subtly decorative. In the ground, needs little or no irrigation. Good plant for climbing up or tumbling down—on trellis, wall, or hillside. Sun or shade.

C. hypoglauca. Zones 13–24. Native to Australia. Rapid growth to 15 ft. in one

> In warm climates, grape ivies are attractive concealers. Grow them up and over chain-link fences or against a wall-mounted trellis.

season; eventually reaches 30–50 ft. Climbs by means of flexible stems rather than tendrils. Highly polished, bronze-tinted leaves are divided into five rounded, leathery leaflets. New growth is covered with rust-colored fuzz. Use as climber or erosion-controlling bank cover. Sun or light shade. Little or no water.

C. rhombifolia. GRAPE IVY. Zones 13, 15, 16, 21–24; H1, H2; or indoors. Native to South America. Beautiful dark green leaves divided into diamond-shaped, toothed leaflets. Veins on leaf undersides have reddish hairs, giving foliage a bronzy overtone. Popular houseplant; tolerates low light. Outdoors, it grows to 20 ft. and can be trained on a support. Full sun to fairly deep shade; moderate water. 'Mandaiana' is more upright and compact than species, with larger, more substantial leaflets. 'Ellen Danica' is smaller than species, with lobed leaflets.

C. striata. MINIATURE GRAPE IVY. Zones 13–24; or indoors. Native to Chile. Handsome vine reaching 20 ft. Looks very similar to a miniature Virginia creeper (*Parthenocissus quinquefolia*), with small, leathery leaves divided into three to five leaflets. Foliage contrasts with reddish stems. Train it to make a tracery against a wall surface, let it spill over wall, or use as groundcover. Sun or shade. Moderate water.

C. trifoliata. GRAPE IVY. Zones 10–13; evergreen only in warmest locations. Native from the southern tier of the U.S. into Mexico. Climbs by simple or forked tendrils to 30 ft., or sprawls along the ground. Smooth dark green leaves are typically divided into three leaflets but are sometimes merely three lobed. Flowering stalks are reddish; inconspicuous flowers are followed in summer by black berries on bright red stalks. Useful for covering chain-link fences or trellises. Contact with plant may cause a skin rash. Full sun. Little to moderate water.

Cistanthe grandiflora. See *Calandrinia grandiflora*

Cistus

ROCKROSE
Cistaceae
EVERGREEN SHRUBS

- **ZONES 4–9, 14–24**
- **FULL SUN**
- **LITTLE OR NO WATER**
- **ATTRACT BUTTERFLIES**

Cistus × purpureus

In their favored dry-summer climate, these carefree Mediterranean natives are covered with flowers for a month or more from spring into early summer; may also bloom sporadically at other times. In some rockroses, leaves are coated with a perfumed resin; others have foliage covered with gray wool. Out of bloom, their soft green, silver, or grayish foliage and mounded form add subtle color and texture to the landscape.

Often planted in fire-hazard areas. Good erosion-control cover for dry banks. Useful in big rock gardens, in rough areas along drives, in wild plantings. Taller kinds make attractive informal hedges.

C. × aguilarii 'Maculatus'. To 6 ft. tall, 4–5 ft. wide. White, 3-in. flowers have wine-colored blotches at the base and yellow centers.

C. albidus. WHITE-LEAVED ROCKROSE. To 4 ft. tall, 8 ft. wide, with furry gray leaves. Bright purplish pink, 2-in. flowers. Repeat bloom in fall is common.

C. × argentius 'Silver Pink'. To 3 ft. high, 5 ft. wide, this bears masses of cupped, apricot-pink flowers.

C. 'Brilliancy'. See *C. × pulverulentus* 'Sunset'.

C. × corbariensis. See *C. × hybridus.*

C. × *crispatus* 'Warley Rose'. To 2 ft. high and 4 ft. wide, with pink flowers.

C. crispus. To 3 ft. high and 5 ft. wide, with furry, wavy-edged, gray-green leaves and 2–2½-in. purplish pink flowers. 'Descanso' grows 1 ft. high and 4 ft. wide, bears a profusion of 1½-in. cerise flowers with yellow centers.

C. × *fernandesiae* 'Anne Palmer'. Grows to 3 ft. high and 5 ft. wide; bears soft pink flowers. Leaves have wavy margins and purple tinge when new.

C. × *hybridus* (*C.* × *corbariensis*). WHITE ROCKROSE. Widely grown. To 3–4 ft. tall and 4–8 ft. wide. Gray-green, crinkly leaves are fragrant on warm days. White flowers 1½ in. across, yellow centers.

C. incanus (*C. villosus*). Bushy plant to 3–5 ft. tall and wide. Oval, 1–3-in. leaves are densely covered with down. Purplish pink flowers, 2–2½ in. wide. 'LASCA Select' grows to 3 ft. high and 5–8 ft. wide, with deep mauve blooms among soft grayish green leaves with white undersides. *C. i. creticus* (*C. creticus*) is similar but has wavy-edged leaves.

C. ladanifer. CRIMSON-SPOT ROCKROSE. Compact growth to 3–5 ft. tall with equal spread. Fragrant leaves are dark green above, lighter beneath; 3-in.-wide flowers are white with a dark crimson spot at each petal base. 'Blanche' grows to 8–12 ft. tall, 6–8 ft. wide, and bears 4-in. pure white blossoms. *C. l. petiolatus* 'Bennett's White' has 3–4-in. flowers resembling those of Matilija poppy (*Romneya coulteri*), with wavy, crepe paper–textured petals around a large cluster of yellow stamens. Good hedge or background shrub for dry areas.

C. laurifolius. Stiff, erect growth to 4–6 ft. tall and wide. Dark green, 5-in. leaves with pale undersides. White, 2–2½-in. flowers come in long-stalked clusters of three or more.

C. × *lenis* 'Grayswood Pink'. To 3 ft. high and 5 ft. wide, with gray-green leaves. Pink flowers have yellow centers.

C. 'Peggy Sammons'. To 3–6 ft. tall and wide, with gray-green leaves and 2½-in. pink flowers.

C. × *pulverulentus* 'Sunset' ('Brilliancy'). Dense, spreading growth to 2 ft. high, 6–8 ft. wide, with resinous gray-green leaves and 2-in.-wide flowers in dark magenta-pink.

C. × *purpureus.* ORCHID ROCKROSE. Zones 3b–9, 14–24. Compact grower to 4 ft. tall and wide, often shorter and wider when subjected to constant ocean winds. Leaves are dark green above, gray and hairy beneath. The 3-in., reddish purple flowers have a red spot at each petal base. Very fine where cool winds and salt spray limit choice of plants.

C. salviifolius 'Prostratus'. SAGELEAF ROCKROSE. Sometimes sold as *C. villosus* 'Prostratus'. Wide-spreading shrub to 2 ft. high, 6 ft. wide. Light gray-green leaves are crinkly, veined, crisp-looking. Profuse show of 1½-in.-wide flowers, white with yellow spot at petal base. Good bank or groundcover for rough situations.

C. 'Santa Cruz'. A compact, dense rockrose with fuzzy gray foliage and 3-in. blossoms in deep purplish rose.

C. × *skanbergii.* To 3 ft. high and 8 ft. wide. Gray-green leaves; great profusion of 1-in., pure pink flowers.

C. 'Snow Fire'. Produces white flower with a red blotch at the base of each petal, spring through summer. Grows to 2 ft. high and 4 ft. wide.

C. 'Victor Reiter'. Stiffly erect plant to 3–4 ft. high and wide. Gray-green leaves; 2½–3½-in.-wide blossoms in hot pink with paler pink center.

CARE

These fast-growing sun lovers tolerate aridity, poor soil, ocean winds, salt spray, and desert heat. Plants need well-drained soil if they will be watered. Don't plant root-bound stock, especially in unirrigated places; cut encircling roots and spread out the mass so roots can find moisture deeper in the soil.

Most rockroses resent hard pruning. To keep plants vigorous and neat, periodically cut out a few old stems. Tip-pinch young plants to thicken growth, or lightly shear new summer growth. When plants become woody and old, it is often easier to replace than rejuvenate them.

Citrus

Rutaceae

EVERGREEN TREES AND SHRUBS

| ZONES 8, 9, 12–24; H1, H2; OR INDOORS |
| FULL SUN; BRIGHT LIGHT |
| REGULAR WATER |
| ATTRACT BIRDS, BEES |

Sweet oranges

As landscaping plants, citrus offer year-round attractive form and glossy deep green foliage. They also bear fragrant flowers and decorative fruit in season.

CITRUS BASICS

If you want quality fruit, your choice of varieties will depend on the total amount of heat available through the fruit-developing period (need varies according to type) and on the winter cold in your zone.

Heat requirements. Generally, sweet-fruited varieties need moderate to high heat to form sugars, sour types less heat. Lemons and limes require the least warmth and will produce usable fruit in cool-summer areas (as long as winter temperatures are not too low). 'Valencia' orange has a lower heat requirement; it is adapted to areas near Southern California coast. Navel oranges demand more warmth and are better suited to inland regions; their fruit development period is shorter than that of 'Valencia', so trees will produce palatable fruit between winter frosts if summer heat is high. Mandarins (tangerines) require high heat for top flavor and are best adapted to inland areas. Grapefruit develops full flavor only where trees receive prolonged

high heat, as in the low desert. (In cooler areas, you're better off growing grapefruit-pummelo hybrids 'Oroblanco' and 'Melogold', which produce sweet fruit in more moderate temperatures.)

Hardiness. Citrus plants of one type or another are grown outdoors all year round in regions with warm to hot summers and mild winters. Lemons, limes, and citrons are most sensitive to freezes. Sweet oranges, 'Improved Meyer' lemon, grapefruit, and most mandarins and their hybrids are intermediate in cold resistance. Kumquats, satsuma mandarins, sour oranges, and calamondin are the most cold-resistant, with kumquats withstanding temperatures in the high teens.

Other factors affecting a tree's cold tolerance include preconditioning to cold (it has greater endurance if exposed to cold slowly and if first freeze comes late), type of rootstock, and location in garden. Prolonged exposure to freezing weather is more damaging than a brief plunge in temperature. All citrus fruit is damaged at several degrees below freezing—hence the importance of choosing early-ripening varieties in freeze-prone areas. For information on protecting plants from frost and cold, see "Gardening, Start to Finish."

Standard or dwarf. Practically all citrus plants sold have been budded or grafted on an understock. Grafted trees begin bearing fruit in just a few years, in contrast with 10 to 15 years for seedling trees. Standard trees (20–30 ft. tall and wide) are grown on a variety of understocks. Dwarf trees are grown on understocks of trifoliate orange (*Poncirus trifoliata*) or 'Flying Dragon'; the latter is a naturally dwarf, contorted, spiny form of trifoliate orange. Ordinary trifoliate orange understocks produce trees 8–10 ft. tall (some may reach to 15–20 ft.). 'Flying Dragon' produces even smaller trees (5–7 ft. at 13 years).

Harvest periods. Most citrus varieties ripen their fruit from late fall into winter, but some varieties, such as 'Valencia' orange and 'Gold Nugget' mandarin, ripen into spring and

Growing Citrus in Hawaii

Home gardeners in Hawaii can grow many of the varieties grown on the mainland, plus some specialty types adapted only to the Islands (these are included in the variety descriptions). Most citrus is best adapted to areas below 1,000 ft. in elevation. Above that, cooler temperatures often prevent many varieties from becoming sweet, so lemons and limes are often the best choice. Citrus grows differently in Hawaii, and the fruit often looks and tastes quite a bit different from the same variety grown in California or Arizona. The trees tend to bloom almost year-round, so harvest can be nearly continual but is often concentrated in fall to winter. The lack of cool nights results in a rind that's thinner and more greenish than the thicker, brightly colored skin of fruit grown in California. Lack of cool nights also reduces acid content, which is why Hawaiian citrus often tastes sweeter. The fruit is very juicy as well.

summer. In addition, many types can hold their fruit on the tree for long periods without loss of quality. By growing both 'Washington' navel and 'Valencia' oranges, for example, you can have fresh fruit almost 10 months of the year. Everbearing citrus like lemons and limes can produce throughout the year, but they fruit most heavily in winter and spring.

Citrus fruit ripens only on the tree. To judge its ripeness, pick a fruit and taste it; rind color is a poor indicator, since many varieties are fully colored before they are edible.

SWEET ORANGE

The commercial oranges of the West are typified by 'Washington' navel and 'Valencia'. In the list below, 'Washington' and other navel varieties are described first, then 'Valencia' and its counterparts, and finally the lesser-known sweet oranges.

Navel Varieties

'Washington'. Widely adapted except in desert regions; best in warm interiors. Standard tree is 20–25-ft. globe. On dwarf stock, it grows 8–12 ft. tall. Bears early to midwinter. 'Tabata' is identical (or nearly so) to 'Washington'; it is grown in Hawaii, as is the standard 'Washington'.

'Cara Cara'. First rosy-fleshed navel; bears the same time as 'Washington'. Rich flavor.

'Lane Late'. Late-ripening navel, extending the season well into summer.

'Summernavel' is also late ripening, but fruit flavor and quality is not as good.

'Robertson'. Variant of 'Washington'. Fruit identical but earlier by 2 to 3 weeks. Tends to carry fruit in clusters. Tree generally smaller than 'Washington'. Has same climate adaptation. Dwarf trees produce amazing amounts of fruit.

Valencia Types

'Valencia'. The juice orange of stores. Most widely planted orange in the world. Widely adapted in California but a poor risk in Arizona; if you plant it there, select a warm location or provide some protection to fruit, which must overwinter on tree. One of Arizona Sweets (see below) would be a safer bet. 'Valencia' oranges mature in summer and store on tree for months, improving in sweetness. Vigorous tree, fuller growing than 'Washington', both as standard and dwarf.

'Campbell', 'Delta', and 'Midknight' are early-ripening, nearly seedless selections of 'Valencia'.

Other Sweet Oranges

Arizona Sweets. A group of varieties grown in Arizona. They include 'Diller', which bears small to medium-size oranges with few seeds and high-quality juice in late fall (before heavy frost) on a vigorous, large, dense tree with large leaves; 'Hamlin', similar but not as hardy, producing medium-size fruit; 'Marrs', with tasty, low-acid, early-ripening fruit on a naturally semidwarf tree that bears young; and 'Pineapple', tending to bear rich-flavored, seedy fruit in alternate years.

Blood oranges. Characterized by red pigmentation in flesh, juice, and (to a lesser degree) rind. Flavor is excellent, with raspberry overtones. Generally, they thrive wherever sweet oranges produce good fruit. Pigmentation varies with local microclimates and weather. 'Moro' bears fruit with deep red flesh and variable amounts of red on the rind from early winter to early spring (no rind pigmentation on the coast); 'Sanguinelli' has red-skinned fruit and flesh streaked with red from late winter to midspring; and 'Tarocco' produces fruit with red or red-suffused pulp and pink to red juice from early to midwinter (color varies from year to year), with good quality in cooler areas. 'Tarocco' is very vigorous and open growing, with long, willowy, vinelike branches; dwarf makes ideal espalier.

'Shamouti' ('Palestine Jaffa'). Originated in Israel and considered there to be finest orange. Large, seedless, no navel. Not a commercial orange in California because not sufficiently superior to 'Washington' navel. Grown on dwarf rootstock for home gardens because of beauty in form and foliage. It is wider than tall. Larger leaves than those of navel oranges. Heavy crop of fruit in early spring. 'Pera' is a 'Shamouti' relative grown in Hawaii.

'Trovita'. Originated from seedling of 'Washington' navel. Thin skinned and about navel size, but without navel. Ripens in early spring. Apparently requires less heat than other sweet oranges and develops good-quality fruit near (though not on) coast. Nevertheless, it tolerates heat well enough to pass as one of the Arizona Sweets. Dwarf tree has 'Washington' navel look, with handsome dark green leaves.

SOUR ORANGE

Very ornamental trees with attractive leaves and big, perfumed, waxy white flowers. Clusters of usually deep red-orange, tart fruits ripen midfall to winter, hold for long periods. For all citrus-growing regions.

'Bouquet de Fleurs' ('Bouquet'). Big shrub or small tree to 8–10 ft. Graceful, dark green foliage. Use as hedge or windbreak. Flowers unusually large, very fragrant. Small, bitter fruit used only in marmalade.

'Chinotto' (myrtle-leaf orange). Dense, bushy, round headed, with closely set, small, almost myrtlelike leaves. Very slow grower to 7–20 ft. tall. Formal appearance; often rounded high on stem and clipped. Makes an ideal tub plant. Decorative small, round, bright orange fruit is used in Europe for candying.

'Seville'. Thorny, upright to 20–30 ft. tall. Used as a street tree in Arizona and Southern California. Good specimen plant or for hedge or tall screen. Fruit makes superior marmalade.

MANDARIN
(INCLUDES TANGERINES)

Varieties with orange-red peel are usually called tangerines. Many mandarins tend to bear heavily in alternate years. Some are always seedless, while others produce more seeds; the latter give seedier fruit if pollinated by another mandarin or mandarin hybrid or by 'Valencia' orange.

'Clementine' (Algerian tangerine). Fruit a little larger than 'Dancy', with fewer seeds. Ripens late fall into winter; remains on tree for months, staying juicy and sweet. Seems to develop full flavor in areas that are too cool for a 'Dancy'. Tree reaches 12 ft., semiopen with vertical, spreading, somewhat willowy branches. Usually bears lighter crops without another variety for pollination.

'Dancy'. Smaller and seedier than other mandarins. Best flavor in Zones 12 and 13 but good in Zones 8, 9, 14, 21–23.

C

Ripens late fall into winter; holds well on tree. Upright tree with erect branches. Dwarf tree handsome in container or as espalier.

'Encore'. Light orange, thin-skinned fruit ripens in summer (latest of all mandarin varieties), holds until fall. Good quality. Erect tree with slender branches and narrow leaves.

'Fairchild'. Hybrid between 'Clementine' mandarin and 'Orlando' tangelo. Medium-size, deep orange fruit peels easily, is seedy but juicy and tasty. Ripens late fall into winter. Small, compact tree bears every year. Needs another variety for pollination. Best in desert areas.

'Fremont'. Medium-size, seedy, bright orange fruit ripens late fall into winter. Good flavor. Tends to bear in alternate years; thin fruit when crop is unusually heavy. Best in desert areas.

'Gold Nugget'. Small to medium size, seedless, with rich, sweet flavor. Light yellow orange, often with rough rind (like 'Pixie'); easy to peel. Ripens late winter to spring.

'Honey'. Small, seedy fruit with rich, sweet flavor; matures winter into spring. Typically bears heavily in alternate years. Vigorous tree. Not the same as 'Murcott', a tangor often sold in markets as 'Honey'.

'Kara'. Large fruit (2½ in. wide) for mandarin. Tart-sweet, aromatic flavor when ripened in warm interior climates. Ripens winter to spring. From one season to another may be very seedy or nearly seedless. In form, tree resembles 'Owari' satsuma, one of its parents. Spreading, often drooping branches with large leaves. Grows to a rounded 15–20 ft., half that size as dwarf.

'Kinnow'. Medium-size fruit with rich flavor and fragrance. Stores well on tree. Ripens winter to early spring. Handsome tree—columnar, dense, very symmetrical to 20 ft. (dwarf will reach 10 ft.). Densely foliaged with slender leaves. Good in any citrus climate.

'Page'. Hybrid between 'Clementine' mandarin and 'Minneola' tangelo. Many small, juicy, sweet fruits autumn into winter. Few seeds, even with another variety for pollination.

'Pixie'. Easy-peeling, seedless fruit with excellent flavor,

usually with a bumpy rind. Ripens midseason to late. Upright tree. Tends to bear heavily in alternate years.

Satsuma. This group of mandarins is the source of imported canned "mandarin oranges." Sweet, delicate flavor; nearly seedless, medium to large fruit. Loose skin. Earliest mandarin to ripen—early fall to late December. Quickly overripens if left on tree but keeps well in cool storage. Standard trees are spreading, to 10–15 ft. tall. Dwarf trees can be used as 6-ft. shrubs. Open, angular growth when young, becoming more compact with age. Not suited to the desert. 'Owari' is the main satsuma grown in the West.

'Seedless Kishu'. Very small, loose skinned, easy to peel; exceptionally rich flavor. Ripens late fall to winter.

'Shasta Gold', 'Tahoe Gold', and 'Yosemite Gold'. Three recent introductions from the University of California. All produce large, seedless, deep orange fruit that is easy to peel and has a sweet, rich flavor. Ripen late winter to spring, 'Tahoe Gold' being the earliest of the three.

'W. Murcott' ('Afourer'). Mid- to late-season, medium-size fruit with excellent flavor. Often sold as Delite in supermarkets. Many seeds if cross-pollinated. A seedless form, called 'Tango', is also available.

SOUR ACID MANDARIN

These fairly compact plants produce usable fruit (and are ever-bearing in mild climates), but their best feature is good looks. They thrive outdoors in the ground or in pots.

Calamondin. Fruit looks like a tiny (¾–1½ in.) orange. Hundreds hang from tall, columnar plant (8–10 ft. tall and about half as wide, even as dwarf). Also available in a variegated form, with leaves marked with creamy yellow; developing fruit may be striped in yellow and green. Flesh is tender, juicy, sour, with a few small seeds. Skin and flesh good in marmalades.

'Rangpur'. Commonly called Rangpur lime, but probably not a lime at all: fruit looks and peels like a mandarin, does not have lime flavor. Less acid than lemon but with flavor overtones

CLOCKWISE FROM LEFT: 'Valencia' oranges; mandarins; 'Ruby' grapefruit

that make it a rich, interesting base for punches and mixed drinks. Good landscape tree: vigorous, sturdy, bushy, growing quickly to 15 ft. tall and wide (as dwarf to 8 ft.). Dense when pruned, open otherwise. Fruits are colorful and ornamental, hang on tree throughout year.

PUMMELO

Forerunner of the grapefruit, it bears clusters of enormous round to pear-shaped fruits with thick rind and pith. Once peeled, fruit is just slightly bigger than a grapefruit. Different varieties range in flavor from sweet to fairly acidic. They need a little less heat than grapefruit and ripen starting in winter in warmest areas. To eat, peel fruit; separate segments and remove membrane surrounding them. Because fruit is so heavy, prune pummelo trees to encourage strong branching.

'Chandler'. Most widely grown variety. Pink flesh; flavorful, moderately juicy, usually seedless.

»

C

How to Grow Citrus

SOIL Fast drainage is essential. If soil drains slowly, don't attempt to plant citrus in it regardless of how you condition it. Instead, plant above soil level in raised beds or on a soil mound.

WATERING Citrus trees need moist soil, but never standing water. They also need air in the soil. Danger from overwatering is greatest in clay soil where air spaces are minute. In soil with proper drainage, water newly planted trees almost as frequently as trees in containers—twice a week in normal summer weather, more frequently during hot spells. Water established trees at least every other week during summer. In clay soils, space watering intervals so that top 4–6 in. of soil dries between irrigations. Don't let tree reach wilting point. Be sure to water consistently. Fluctuating soil moisture can aggravate fruit splitting—a problem that can affect all citrus, but especially navel oranges (typically in autumn).

When you water, be sure to wet the entire root zone (soak the soil to a depth of 3–4 ft.).

MULCHING Since citrus roots grow near the surface as well as deeper, a mulch over the soil is beneficial. Use a 2–3-in. layer of compost or other organic matter to help maintain soil moisture. In mild-summer areas, large pebbles or gravel will increase reflected heat and hasten ripening. Don't allow grass to grow near the trunks of citrus trees.

FERTILIZING Nitrogen is the main nutrient that must be supplied in all regions. If you garden in sandy soil, choose a complete fertilizer containing a full range of nutrients. Apply 2 oz. of actual nitrogen the first year after a newly planted tree puts on new growth; then increase the amount by 4 oz. each year

for the next few years. After the fifth year, apply 1–1½ lb. yearly. (Depending on tree size, give plants growing in raised beds or with restricted root space, as well as trees grafted onto 'Flying Dragon' rootstock, about a third to half of the recommended amount after the fifth year.) To determine weight of actual nitrogen, multiply percentage of total nitrogen (as stated on fertilizer label) by total weight of fertilizer.

Divide total fertilizer into several feedings throughout the growing season. In freeze-prone areas, start feeding in late winter and stop in late summer.

Citrus may suffer from chlorosis due to iron, manganese, or zinc deficiency. In iron chlorosis, leaves turn yellow from edges inward; veins remain dark green. (Same symptom may be caused by overwatering, so check your irrigation practices.) Manganese deficiency shows up as fine mottling, usually on young leaves, and as pale or yellowish areas between dark green veins. Signs of zinc deficiency are yellowish blotching or mottling between leaf veins. Manganese and zinc deficiencies may occur together and be difficult to distinguish from each other. Commercial products containing chelates of all three nutrients are available as foliar sprays.

In Hawaii, some soils are strongly acidic and/or low in phosphorous, which can harm citrus trees. Have the soil tested to see if lime (to raise soil pH) or phosphate fertilizers should be added at planting.

PRUNING Commercial trees are allowed to carry branches right to the ground. Production is heaviest on lower branches. Growers prune only to remove twiggy growth and weak branches or, in young plants, to nip back wild growth and balance the

plant. Check citrus trees periodically for suckers (branches that arise below the graft line) and remove them before they compete with (or overwhelm) the desired variety.

You can prune garden trees to shape as desired; espaliering is traditional, though espaliered citrus is not very productive. Lemons and sour oranges are often planted close and pruned as hedges. 'Lisbon' and 'Eureka' lemons should be pruned to keep the trees within bounds and the fruit easily reachable. Many citrus are thorny, so wear gloves and a long-sleeved shirt when picking fruit or pruning. In freeze-prone areas, don't prune in fall or early winter. Wait until late spring or summer to prune frost-damaged trees—new growth will make it clear which wood is dead. If you're growing a multiple-variety citrus tree, you must continually cut back the vigorous growers (lemon, lime, pummelo, grapefruit) so that the weaker ones (sweet orange, mandarin) can survive. On all citrus, remove fruit from newly planted trees so that the trees' energy will be channeled into new growth rather than fruiting.

PESTS & DISEASES Citrus can get aphids, mites, scale insects, and mealybugs. If these pests' natural enemies fail to handle the infestations, and if jets of water fail to keep the pests in check, spray with appropriate chemicals. If scale remains troublesome, spray with horticultural oil in early spring. Reduce harmful insect populations by keeping ants out of trees with sticky bands on trunks. (Ants prey on natural insect predators of mites, scale, and aphids). Control snails and slugs whenever necessary, especially during warm-night spells in winter and spring. Copper bands, available in some areas, will keep

snails out of trees. Where it is legal to do so (in Southern California), colonize citrus groves with decollate snails, which prey on the garden snail.

The citrus bud mite causes weirdly deformed fruit (especially lemons). Control with horticultural oil spray in spring and in fall; spray only in fall in hot-summer areas.

Asian citrus psyllid has become the most serious insect pest of citrus (and citrus relatives) worldwide because of its potential to transmit the incurable and deadly bacterial disease Huanglongbing (HLB), also known as citrus greening. Discoveries of the insect in Western citrus states have triggered quarantines restricting movement of nursery plants and plant parts. For the latest information, contact your local cooperative extension office or visit the Citrus Pest & Disease Prevention Program website (www.californiacitrusthreat. org). If you think you have the pest, either will tell you whom to contact.

The few fungal ailments of citrus occur in poorly drained soil. Water molds, causing root rot, show up in yellowing and dropping foliage. Best control is to correct your watering schedule.

Brown rot gummosis usually occurs in older trees at base of trunk. Keep base of trunk dry; trim and clean the oozing wounds, removing decayed bark to a point where discolored wood does not show. Paint areas with Bordeaux paste mixture.

SUNBURN The bark of newly planted citrus trees is subject to sunburn in hot-sun areas. Trunks should be wrapped (paper trunk bands are available commercially). When heavy pruning exposes trunks or limbs, protect bark with whitewash or white latex paint diluted by half with water.

'Reinking'. White flesh; seedy. Not as sweet as 'Chandler'.

'Tahitian' ('Sarawak'). Greenish white flesh; moderately acidic flavor with lime overtones.

GRAPEFRUIT

Trees can reach 25–30 ft. tall (most are shorter), with large, dark green leaves. True grapefruit needs heat for sweet-tart fruit and is best grown in the desert, where fruit ripens in 9 months (can take a year or longer where there's less heat). Elsewhere, pummelo-grapefruit hybrids 'Oroblanco' and 'Melogold' are better; they will ripen in 9 to 12 months, depending on climate. At the end of the following list is a variety ('Cocktail') sold as a grapefruit, though it isn't really one.

'Flame'. Seedless red flesh similar to that of 'Rio Red'; slight rind blush.

'Marsh' ('Marsh Seedless'). Main white-fleshed commercial variety. Large, light yellow fruit.

'Melogold'. Grapefruit-pummelo hybrid developed by the University of California. Needs less heat than true grapefruit, but fruit doesn't hold as well on the tree. Fruit is bigger, heavier, and thinner skinned than that of 'Oroblanco', and its seedless white flesh has more of a sweet-tart flavor.

'Oroblanco'. Sister fruit to 'Melogold', with sweeter seedless white flesh. Has same low heat requirement but is smaller and thicker skinned.

'Redblush' ('Ruby', 'Ruby Red'). Seedless grapefruit with red-tinted flesh. Red internal color fades to pink, then buff.

'Rio Red'. Seedless grapefruit with good rind blush and flesh nearly as red as that of 'Star Ruby'. More dependable producer than 'Star Ruby'.

'Star Ruby'. Seedless grapefruit with reddest color. Prone to cold damage, erratic bearing, and other growing problems. Doesn't withstand desert heat.

'Cocktail'. Labeled a grapefruit, but actually a mandarin-pummelo hybrid. Large fruit with greenish orange (or mottled orange-and-green) skin and pale orange, very seedy flesh. Sweeter than grapefruit, with distinctive flavor. Best quality in warm-summer areas, but worth growing in cooler regions.

LEMON

Lemons' low heat requirement makes them widely adapted and especially appreciated in regions where sweet oranges and grapefruit won't ripen. They do best near the coast, where they usually bear year-round, though some varieties are very successful in the desert. Standard varieties like 'Eureka' and 'Lisbon' are best pruned every year or two to manage size.

'Eureka'. Standard lemon of markets. Bears all year. Not as vigorous as 'Lisbon'. To 20 ft. tall, with somewhat open growth; branches have few thorns. As a dwarf, it is a dense tree with large, dark leaves. New growth on both standard-size and dwarf plants is bronzy purple.

'Improved Meyer'. The word "improved" refers to the fact that it is a disease-free form, the only one that can be sold in California and Arizona. This is the best lemon for Hawaii. Fruit is quite different from commercial lemon—rounder, thinner skinned, orange-yellow in color. Tangy aroma but less acidic flavor than standard lemon; very juicy. Bears some fruit year-round, especially near the coast, and starts bearing at an early age. Tree is not a dwarf on its own roots, though it is sometimes sold as an own-root plant that can reach 12 ft. tall, 15 ft. wide. On a dwarf rootstock, it's half that size.

'Lisbon'. Vigorous, upright, thorny tree to 20–25 ft. tall; denser than 'Eureka'. Can be trimmed up into highly decorative small tree. Fruit practically identical to that of 'Eureka'. Ripens mostly in fall but has some ripe fruit all year. More resistant to cold than 'Eureka' and better adapted to high heat; best lemon for Arizona. There is also a seedless form.

'Ponderosa'. A novelty. Bears huge, rough lemons with thick, coarse skin; 2-lb. fruits are not unusual. Bears at early age, frequently at gallon-can size. Main crop in winter, with some fruit through year. Open, angular branching; large, widely spaced leaves. To 8–10 ft. tall; dwarf reaches 4–6 ft.

'Variegated Pink' ('Pink Lemonade'). Sport of 'Eureka' with green-and-white leaves and green stripes on immature fruit;

everbearing like 'Eureka'. Light pink flesh doesn't need heat to develop color. Handsome landscape tree.

'Villa Franca'. Generally similar to 'Eureka', but tree is larger and more vigorous, with denser foliage and thornier branches. Fruit is similar to that of 'Eureka'; comes mainly from fall through winter. Sold in Arizona to grow in Zones 12, 13; not common in California.

LIME

The various limes range from moderately to extremely cold sensitive; they are most reliable in areas where hard frosts are

CLOCKWISE FROM TOP: 'Eureka' lemons; 'Minneola' tangelos; kumquats

uncommon. They can succeed in colder areas if grown in pots and protected in winter. Depending on variety, fruit may be sour or nearly devoid of acid.

'Bearss'. Best lime for California and Hawaii gardens. It is a type of the "Persian" or "Tahitian" lime commonly grown in Florida. Tree is quite angular and open when young but forms a dense, round crown when mature; reaches 15–20 ft. (half that size on dwarf rootstock). It

C

Meet the New Citrus

Among all the new citrus coming onto market are five favorites of creative chefs.

AUSTRALIAN FINGER LIME This Australian native bears oblong fruits filled with tart, cavierlike juice capsules that burst out of the cut rind when fully ripe (in early fall). Fruit turns blackish and begins to drop as it matures. Wiry, small-leafed tree with nasty thorns (wear long leather gloves to pick). Use the capsules to flavor appetizers, drinks, salads, and grilled fish.

'BERGAMOT' SOUR ORANGE Thought to be a hybrid between sour orange and citron. A good-looking tree with large, light green leaves. Large, light green fruits have sour juice. Its highly aromatic rind is used in Earl Grey tea.

'INDIO' MANDARINQUAT Large, bright orange, bell-shaped fruit with sweet rind and sour juice. Easy to peel. Very ornamental, upright tree bears a heavy crop. Makes good marmalade.

'NORDMANN' KUMQUAT A seedless selection of 'Nagami' kumquat with teardrop-shaped fruit. Great in marmalade, preserves, sauces.

YUZU An acidic citrus with highly aromatic, bumpy rind. Both the juice and peel are prized in Asian recipes, especially for ponzu sauce. The fruit can be used from green to yellow color. The rangy tree has large thorns and is very hardy (at least into the high teens).

is thorny and inclined to drop many leaves in winter. Fruit is green when immature, light yellow when ripe, almost the size of a lemon; it is especially juicy when fully ripe. Seedless. Main crop is from winter to late spring, though some fruit ripens all year.

'Kieffer' ('Kaffir'). Leaves and bumpy, sour fall fruit are used in Thai and Cambodian cooking. Available mainly in California.

'Mexican'. Sometimes called key lime. Small, green to yellow-green fruit; standard bartender's lime. Main harvest fall to winter, though you will get some fruit all year. Very thorny tree to 12–15 ft., with upright, twiggy branches (there is also a thornless form). Very cold sensitive; best suited to Zones 21–23. Can be grown in Hawaii but is subject to viral diseases there.

'Palestine Sweet' (Indian lime). Shrubby plant with acidless fruit. Used in Mideastern, Indian, and Latin American cooking. Ripens fall or winter.

TANGELO

Early citrus-breeding experiments produced the tangelo, a cross between a mandarin and a grapefruit. A cross between a tangelo and a grapefruit ('Wekiwa') is sometimes called a tangelolo. All these hybrids produce their best fruit in warm-summer areas.

'Minneola'. Hybrid of 'Dancy' mandarin and a white-fleshed grapefruit. Large, smooth, bright orange-red fruit tastes much like a mandarin. Few seeds. Ripens mid- to late winter; stores on tree for 2 months. Tree not as large or dense as grapefruit.

'Orlando'. Same parents as 'Minneola'. Medium-large fruit looks like a flattened orange. Both rind and flesh are orange; rind adheres to flesh. Very juicy, mildly sweet; matures early in season. Tree is similar to 'Minneola' but has distinctly cupped leaves, is less vigorous, and is more resistant to cold.

'Wekiwa' (may be sold as pink tangelo or 'Lavender Gem'). A cross between a tangelo and a grapefruit; looks like a small grapefruit but is eaten like a mandarin. Juicy, mild flesh tastes like a mix of sweet orange, grapefruit, and mandarin; color is purplish rose in hot climates. Fruit ripens from late fall into winter.

TANGOR

Hybrid between mandarin and sweet orange; often labeled as an orange—or, in the case of 'Murcott', as a tangerine—when sold in grocery stores. These three tangors are thought to be naturally occurring hybrids rather than breeder-developed varieties. 'Temple' is widely grown in low desert; 'Murcott' and 'Ortanique' are sometimes grown in Hawaii.

'Murcott'. Bears more heavily in alternate years. Vigorous, upright tree bears very sweet, seedy, yellowish orange fruit from late winter into spring. Marketed in stores as 'Honey' tangerine (no relation to 'Honey' mandarin).

'Ortanique'. Sweet, juicy, variably seedy fruit ripening from spring to summer. Sometimes has a small navel. Large, spreading tree.

'Temple'. Flattened, deep bright orange fruit is loose skinned and easy to peel. Tender-textured, juicy pulp is flavorful but not too sweet. Fruit has best quality in Zone 13; it is too acidic in more temperate climates. Ripens in early spring. Bushy, thorny tree to 12 ft. tall with greater spread; 6–8 ft. wide on dwarf stock. More cold sensitive than other tangors.

KUMQUAT

Shrubby plants to 6–15 ft. or taller, with yellow to red-orange fruits that look like tiny oranges. Eat whole and unpeeled—spongy rind is sweet, pulp is tangy. Best in areas with warm to hot summers and chilly nights during fall or winter ripening. Hardy to at least 18°F (–8°C).

'Fukushu'. Large, oval fruit with a prominent neck. Skin and juice are sweet, but not as sweet as those of 'Meiwa'. Compact, thornless, very attractive tree.

'Marumi'. Slightly thorny plant with round fruit. Sweeter peel than that of 'Nagami', but the slightly seedy flesh is more acidic.

'Meiwa'. Round fruit is sweeter, juicier, and less seedy than that of other varieties. Performs better than other types in cool-summer areas. Considered the best kumquat for eating fresh. Nearly thornless.

'Nagami'. Main commercial variety. Oval, slightly seedy fruit is more abundant and sweeter in hot-summer climates. Plant is thornless.

KUMQUAT HYBRIDS

These were the results of early experiments by the citrus industry to produce cold-tolerant kinds of citrus. Fruit has never been a commercial success, but it's good for home gardens. Plants tend to be fairly small even as standards; on dwarfing rootstocks, they reach only 3–6 ft.

Limequat. These hybrids of 'Mexican' lime and kumquat are more cold-tolerant and need less heat than their lime parent. Good lime substitutes; edible rind like that of kumquat parent. Some fruit all year, but main crop comes from fall to spring. 'Eustis' bears fruit shaped like a big olive. 'Tavares' has elongated oval fruit on a more compact, better-looking plant than 'Eustis'.

Orangequat. 'Nippon', a cross between 'Meiwa' kumquat and satsuma mandarin, is most commonly grown. It is cold-tolerant and has a fairly low heat requirement. Small, round, deep orange fruit has sweet, spongy rind and slightly acidic flesh. Sweeter than kumquat when eaten whole. Ripens winter and spring but holds on the tree for months.

CITRON

Citron was the first type of citrus to be cultivated. Plant is small, thorny, irregular in shape; grown for big, fragrant, unusual fruit. Very sensitive to cold.

'Buddha's Hand'. Fruit is divided into "fingers" that contain all rind and no pulp. Bears some fruit all year round.

'Etrog'. Fruit resembles a big, warty-skinned lemon with dry pulp; the peel is sometimes candied.

Cladrastis kentukea
(C. lutea)
YELLOW WOOD
Papilionaceae
DECIDUOUS TREE

🌿 **ZONES 2–9, 14–16**
☼ **FULL SUN**
💧 **REGULAR WATER**

Cladrastis kentukea

Native to Kentucky, Tennessee, and North Carolina. Slow growing to 30–50 ft. tall, with a broad, rounded head half as wide as tree is high. Leaves are 8–12 in. long, divided into many (usually 7–11) oval leaflets resembling those of English walnut. Yellowish green when new, they turn bright green in summer and brilliant yellow in fall. Bark is gray in maturity; the common name "yellow wood" refers to the color of the freshly cut heartwood.

Yellow wood may not flower until 10 years old and may skip a bloom in some years, but the late-spring display is spectacular when it comes: dangling clusters of fragrant, wisterialike white flowers (those of 'Rosea' are pink) are up to 14 in. long. Blooms are followed by flat, 3–4-in.-long seedpods. An attractive terrace, patio, or lawn tree even if it never blooms. It is also deep rooted, so you can grow other plants beneath it. Tolerates alkaline soils; withstands some drought.

CARE

Prune when young to shorten side branches or correct narrow, weak branch crotches, which are susceptible to breakage in storms. Usually low branching; you can remove lower branches

entirely when tree reaches desired height. Prune in summer, since cuts made in winter or spring bleed profusely.

Clarkia
(includes Godetia)
Onagraceae
ANNUALS

🌿 **ZONES A2, A3; 1–24**
☼ ◑ **LIGHT SHADE IN HOTTEST CLIMATES**
💧 **REGULAR WATER**
🐦 **ATTRACT BIRDS**

Clarkia amoena

Native to western South and North America but especially numerous in California. Plants grow during cool times of year, bloom in spring and early summer; attractive in mixed borders.

C. amoena (Godetia amoena, G. grandiflora). FAREWELL-TO-SPRING, GODETIA. Native California to British Columbia. Two wild forms: one has coarse stems and sprawls 4–5 in. high; the other has more slender stems and grows 1½–2½ ft. high. Tapered leaves are ½–2 in. long. On both forms, upright buds open into cup-shaped, slightly flaring pink or lavender flowers, usually blotched in crimson. Although seeds of named varieties are rarely sold in the U.S., strains of mixed colors are easy to find. Dwarf Gem grows 10 in. tall; Tall Upright reaches 2–3 ft.

C. concinna. RED-RIBBONS. California native. To 1½ ft. tall. Deep pink to lavender flowers with three-lobed, fan-shaped petals. Rounded leaves are ½–2 in. long. May be found in wildflower seed mixes.

C. pulchella. Native to the Pacific Northwest. Slender,

upright, mostly unbranched, 1–1½ ft. high. Reddish stems; narrow, sparse leaves. Flowers are single; petals have a three-lobed tip and taper to a clawlike base. There are semidouble and dwarf forms.

C. unguiculata (C. elegans). CLARKIA, MOUNTAIN GARLAND. California native. Erect, to 1–4 ft. Reddish stems, and flowers in rose, purple, white. Some varieties have double flowers in white, orange, salmon, crimson, purple, rose, pink, or creamy yellow. Double-flowered kinds are the ones usually sold in seed packets. Attract bees.

CARE

Sow seeds in place in fall (in mild-winter areas) or spring. Seedlings are difficult to transplant, but volunteer seedlings grow well. Best in sandy soil without added fertilizer. Keep soil moist from seeding to flowering.

Clematis
Ranunculaceae
DECIDUOUS AND EVERGREEN VINES AND PERENNIALS

🌿 **ZONES VARY BY SPECIES**
☼ ◑ **FULL SUN OR PARTIAL SHADE, EXCEPT AS NOTED**
💧 **REGULAR WATER, EXCEPT AS NOTED**
🦋 **ATTRACT BUTTERFLIES, HUMMINGBIRDS**

Clematis viticella 'Wisley'

The most familiar clematis species are deciduous vines that clamber into trees and over fences and arbors. Some make their statement with impossibly big flowers, while others do it with profuse, colorful smaller

flowers. Evergreen clematis such as *C. armandii* are well loved for vanilla-scented spring bloom; upright herbaceous types are attractive, but still relatively little known. Unless otherwise specified, blooms are 4–6 in. across. The blossoms of the large-flowered hybrids and a few species are followed by fluffy clusters of seed heads. Leaves vary from pale to dark green, usually divided into leaflets. Leafstalks twist and curl to hold plant to its support.

C. alpina. Deciduous vine. Zones A2, A3; 1–11, 14–18. Native to Europe and Asia. To 6–8 ft., with lacy, soft green foliage. Early-spring blooms are nodding and bell-shaped, with four pointed sepals in white, pink, periwinkle blue, or purple, depending on the variety. An inner "skirt" of stamens is creamy white in most varieties. Blooms are followed by decorative seed heads. Plants are extremely cold-hardy. Varieties include 'Burford White' (white), 'Constance' (reddish pink), 'Pamela Jackman' (blue), 'Frances Rivis' (sky blue), 'Frankie' (soft blue), 'Ruby' (rosy pink).

C. armandii. EVERGREEN CLEMATIS. Zones 4–9, 12–24. From China. Fast-growing vine to 15–20 ft. Leathery leaves are divided into three glossy, dark green leaflets; they droop downward, creating a strongly textured look. Creamy white, vanilla-scented, saucer-shaped flowers, 1½–2 in. across, are borne in clusters in early to midspring. Leaves burn badly at the tips where the soil or water contains excess salts. Best in a sunny, sheltered spot (out of harsh winds) with adequate support, such as a sturdy fence. Slow to start but races once established. Makes a great privacy screen if not allowed to become bare at the base. Prune each year after bloom to avoid buildup of thatch on the inner part of the vine. Choice varieties include 'Apple Blossom' (pinkish white blooms), 'Snowdrift' (pure white flowers), 'Hendersonii Rubra' (soft pink flowers).

C. × cartmanii. Evergreen vine. Zones 4–9, 14–24. Grows quickly to 15 ft. long and is covered with white flowers in early

C

How to Grow Clematis

Most clematis need 5–6 hours of sunlight to produce the most blooms. Plant vining types next to an obelisk, trellis, fence, or arbor they can climb. Keep plants properly mulched and watered. Clematis don't like root competition.

PLANTING Dig a hole up to 2 ft. wide and deep, and plant in loose, fast-draining soil well amended with organic matter. Add lime only if soil tests indicate a calcium deficiency.

Large-flowered types: Includes hybrids and species such as *C. integrifolia, C. terniflora, C. texensis,* and *C. viticella.* Plant with the crown (the point where the stems emerge from the soil in the nursery container) 3–5 in. below ground level so that disease- or cold-damaged plants will resprout.

Other types: Plant with crowns at ground level. Stems are easily broken, so protect with wire netting if planting near a high-traffic part of the garden. Apply a 2–3-in.-thick layer of mulch around (but not touching) the stems to keep the roots cool.

PREPRUNING Before planting deciduous clematis, cut stems back to 6–12 in. from the ground or to two or three pairs of growth buds, whichever is lower. Late in the following dormant season, cut the plant back to two or three pairs of buds; train emerging shoots that second spring. Don't preprune evergreen vines; just start training shoots onto their support.

WATERING & FEEDING Don't let any kind of clematis dry out, and fertilize monthly during the growing season.

PRUNING Your goal is to get the most flowers on the shapeliest plant. Pruning method depends on bloom season; if you don't know when that is, watch plants for a year to find out (and know that dormant clematis stems can look dead).

Spring-blooming clematis: These may actually bloom in late fall or winter in mild-winter areas; flower on stems produced the previous year. After bloom has finished, thin out weak, tangled, dead, or injured growth, and cut stems back to the first (topmost) pair of healthy leaf buds.

Summer- and fall-blooming clematis: Bloom at the ends of new stems produced in spring of the same year. Prune when their leaf buds emerge—anytime from late fall to early spring, depending on whether your climate has mild or cold winters. Cut all the stems back to 12–18 in. above ground level, making each cut just above a pair of healthy leaf buds.

Twice-flowering clematis: Bloom on the previous year's stems in spring, then again on the current year's shoots in summer and fall. In late fall or early spring, prune lightly to thin out excess shoots or untangle stems. After the early blooms fade, prune more heavily so that new shoots will develop for the second round of flowers.

PEST CONTROL Aphids, mealybugs, scale, and whiteflies occasionally attack clematis. Snails, slugs, and earwigs may also require control. Powdery mildew can be a problem on some types. Stem rot is another potentially serious disease of clematis, causing browning and wilting of leaves along an entire stem (it is sometimes called wilt). Infection begins at the base of the stem, near the soil line. Small stems are more likely to become infected, so buy the biggest plant possible, and try not to break new shoots when planting. To treat infected plants, cut off diseased parts, then disinfect your shears with diluted bleach. Dispose of diseased stems in a sealed plastic bag to avoid spreading fungal spores. Infected plants will produce healthy new shoots.

to midspring. 'Avalanche' has white flowers; dwarf 'Pixie' has creamy lemon, fragrant flowers.

C. crispa. Deciduous vine. Zones A2, A3; 2–11, 14–24. From the southeastern U.S. To 5–8 ft. or more. Delicate leaves are divided into two to five leaflets. Fragrant flowers are dainty bells of pale lavender blue, 1–1½ in. across; sepal tips flare and curl back. Long bloom season in mild-winter climates, beginning in late spring and continuing into fall; blooms from summer to fall where winters are cold. Flowers are followed by interesting feathery seed heads. Train into a shrub to help protect delicate stems.

C. discoreifolia. See *C. terniflora.*

C. integrifolia. Herbaceous perennial. Zones A1–A3; 1–11, 14–24. Native to Europe and Asia. Nonclimbing growth to 2–3 ft. or taller and about 2 ft. wide, with dark green, undivided leaves. Nodding, sometimes fragrant, bell-shaped blue flowers, 1½–2 in. wide, appear in summer. Useful as a border plant because of its diminutive size. Varieties include white 'Alba', blue 'Caerulea', and bright pink 'Rosea', all 2–3 ft. tall. 'Rooguchi' ('Roguchi') grows to 5–8 ft. tall, with stunning deep purple blooms; and 'Sapphire Indigo' (Zones A3; 2b–11, 14–24) produces its indigo flowers on a 2½-ft. plant that can spill out of a container or hanging basket.

C. macropetala. DOWNY CLEMATIS. Deciduous vine. Zones A2, A3; 1–11, 14–18. Native to northern China and Siberia. To 6–10 ft., with feathery leaves. Nodding, bell-shaped, double flowers are 2½–3½ in. across and appear in early spring. Outer sepals come in light to periwinkle blue, purple, pink, mauve, or white. An inner skirt of cream-colored sepals looks like a ballerina's tutu. Handsome, long-lasting, silvery seed heads. Varieties include 'Blue Bird' (mauve-blue), 'Jan Lindmark' (purplish violet), 'Markham's Pink' (pink), 'Rosy O'Grady' (pinkish mauve), and 'White Swan' (creamy white).

C. montana. ANEMONE CLEMATIS. Deciduous vine. Zones 3b–9, 14–18. Native to the Himalayas. Vigorous grower to 20 ft. or more, with massive

display of 2–2½-in.-wide, anemone-like flowers from late spring to early summer; blooms in shades of pink. Give it plenty of room to roam; prune as for spring-blooming types. Varieties include 'Peveril' (white, early-summer bloom), 'Elizabeth' (soft pink flowers and bronzy foliage that matures to green), and 'Mayleen' (deep pink flowers and medium green to bronzy foliage); all have scented blossoms. *C. m. rubens* grows 20–25 ft., with pale pink flowers and rich bronze new foliage that matures to bronzy green. 'Pink-A-Boo' has plum-colored foliage, light pink bloom. 'Tetrarose' reaches 20 ft., with bronze foliage; its mauve-pink blooms have a spicy scent.

C. terniflora (C. discoreifolia, C. maximowicziana). SWEET AUTUMN CLEMATIS. Deciduous vine (semievergreen in milder areas). Zones 2–11, 14–24. Native to China, Korea, Japan. Very fast growing to 20 ft., with dark green leaves consisting of three to five oval leaflets. Produces masses of fragrant, creamy white flowers in late summer to fall. Can reseed. Plant in a warm, sunny location. Makes good privacy screen, arbor cover. Often confused with *C. paniculata,* a similar species from New Zealand.

C. texensis. SCARLET CLEMATIS. Deciduous vine. Zones 2b–11, 14–24. Native to Texas. Fast growth to 6–10 ft., with blue-green leaves divided into three to five heart-shaped leaflets. Tulip-shaped, 1–3-in. scarlet flowers are produced in abundance from early summer until late fall. Use on posts or tall trellis in a location with full sun and good air circulation to prevent powdery mildew. Crosses with large-flowered hybrids have produced eye-catching varieties such as the vivid pink 'Duchess of Albany', crimson 'Gravetye Beauty', and rich pink 'Princess Diana'.

C. viticella. Deciduous vine. Zones A2, A3; 2–11, 14–24. From southern Europe and western Asia. To 8–10 ft., with medium green leaves comprising five to seven small leaflets. Open, bell-shaped flowers are 1½–4 in. wide and come in a range of colors. Profuse bloom in summer and fall. One of the

Float the Flowers

Clematis flowers may resemble bells, stars, tulips, saucers, urns—even miniature lanterns. Each has a central brush of stamens surrounded by petal-like segments called sepals. Colors run from pastel pinks to crimson red; periwinkle blue through soft lavender, rich magenta, and dark purple; and pure white through cream to golden yellow. Floated in a bowl of water, cut flowers make a choice indoor display (sear cut stem ends with a flame to make flowers last longer).

easiest clematis to grow; very tolerant of heat and poor soil. Varieties include 'Abundance' (rosy pink), 'Alba Luxurians' (white with green tips), 'Betty Corning' (lavender-blue), 'Etoile Violette' (purple), 'Little Nell' (creamy white sepals edged with soft violet), 'Madame Julie Correvon' (red), 'Pagoda' (mauve-pink), 'Purpurea Plena Elegans' (double blooms in rosy purple), 'Royal Velours' (reddish purple), and 'Venosa Violacea' (white sepals edged with a wide band of deep purple).

Large-flowered hybrids.
Deciduous vines. Zones A2, A3; 2–11, 14–24. Grow 6–10 ft. Flowers of most are saucer-shaped and 4–8 in. across. Although there are hundreds of large-flowered hybrids in commerce, local nurseries usually offer only a limited selection; mail-order catalogs are the best source for collectors seeking the new and different. Following is a list of time-honored hybrids, along with some noteworthy newer varieties.

White 'Henryi' is the standard. 'Huldine', 'Hyde Hall', 'Jackmanii Alba', 'Marie Boisselot', and 'Snow Queen' are also excellent choices, as is longtime favorite C. lanuginosa 'Candida'.

Pink Look for 'Caroline' (pale pink sepals marked with dark pink), 'Comtesse de Bouchard' (bright mauve-pink), 'Hagley Hybrid' (mauve-pink), 'Kakio' (also known as 'Pink Champagne', with vivid pink sepals and a pale central band), and 'Proteus' (mauve-pink double flowers). Where summers are hot, plant in bright shade to pre-

vent the soft colors from fading.

Red Great choices include vivid magenta 'Ernest Markham', deep red 'Niobe', velvety crimson 'Rouge Cardinal', carmine-red 'Ville de Lyon', and deep maroon 'Warsaw Nike' ('Warszawska Nike').

Purple The classic 'Jackmanii', with velvety, dark purple sepals, remains the most popular; 'Jackmanii Superba' has larger flowers with wider petals. Other fine choices include rich dark purple 'Aotearoa'; deep blue-violet 'Daniel Deronda'; velvety, dark violet 'Gipsy Queen'; rosy purple 'Richard Pennell'; purple-blue 'The President'; and rosy mauve 'Viola'.

Blue Sky blue 'Ramona' is deservedly popular. Other varieties include 'H. F. Young' (periwinkle blue, tinged with mauve), 'Ken Donson' (deep lavender-blue), and 'William Kennett' (lilac-blue).

Bicolor Choices include 'Asao' (deep rosy pink sepals with a pale pink central bar), 'Barbara Jackman' (lavender with vivid magenta bar), 'Charissima' (cerise-pink with deep pink bar), 'Danielle' ('Vancouver Danielle', violet-blue with carmine bar), 'Kilian Donahue' (opens pink with red bar, then fades to lavender), the ever-popular 'Nelly Moser' (purplish pink with reddish bar), 'Piilu' ('Little Duckling', pastel pink with raspberry bar), and 'Starry Nights' ('Vancouver Starry Nights', 8-in. fuchsia flowers with reddish center bar). In hot-summer areas, plant these varieties in bright shade to prevent fading.

Double Fully double, roselike blooms in early summer on old

wood are usually followed later by single or semidouble flowers on new wood. Choice varieties include silvery blue 'Belle of Woking', lavender-blue 'Blue Light' ('Vanso Blue') and 'Multi Blue', and white 'Duchess of Edinburgh'. 'Josephine' has unusual flowers of mauve-pink with a dark blue central stripe.

Cleome hasslerana
(C. spinosa)
SPIDER FLOWER
Cleomaceae
ANNUAL

✿ **ZONES 1–24**

☀ **FULL SUN**

🌢🌢 **MODERATE TO REGULAR WATER**

🗶 **FLOWERS ATTRACT HUMMINGBIRDS**

Cleome hasslerana

Shrubby, branching South American native topped in summer and fall with many open, fluffy clusters of pink or white flowers that have extremely long, protruding stamens (hence the name "spider flower"). Slender seed capsules follow the blossoms. Stems have short, strong spines. The lower leaves are divided, upper ones undivided. Both the leaves and the stems are sticky and have a strong but not unpleasant smell.

Plant grows 4–6 ft. tall, 4–5 ft. wide; especially vigorous in warm, dry inland areas. Grow in background, as summer hedge, against walls or fences, in large containers; or—since plants self-sow to a fault—naturalize in fringe areas of garden. Flowers and dry seed capsules useful in arrangements.

CARE
Sow seeds in place in spring; they sprout rapidly in warm soil. A number of varieties can be grown from seed.

Clerodendrum
Lamiaceae
EVERGREEN AND DECIDUOUS SHRUBS AND VINES

✿ **ZONES VARY BY SPECIES**

☀ ☽ **EXPOSURE NEEDS VARY BY SPECIES**

🌢 **REGULAR WATER**

Clerodendrum bungei

Diverse group of plants grown for big clusters of showy, brightly colored flowers that are fragrant in some species. Bloom comes on the current season's growth.

C. bungei (C. foetidum). CASHMERE BOUQUET. Evergreen shrub. Zones 5–9, 12–24. Native to China. Plant grows rapidly to 6 ft. tall and wide; spreads rapidly by suckers, eventually forming a thicket if not restrained. Big (to 1 ft.), coarse, broadly oval leaves with toothed edges are dark green above, with a rust-colored fuzz beneath. Leaves smell unpleasant when bruised or crushed. Loose clusters of delightfully fragrant rosy red flowers in summer, sometimes into fall. Plant where its appearance (except during bloom time) is not important. Prune severely in spring and pinch back throughout the growing season to make a compact, 2–3-ft. shrub. Resists oak root fungus. Deer-resistant. Deep shade in desert regions, partial shade elsewhere.

C. chinense chinense (C. fragrans pleniflorum). Evergreen to semievergreen shrub.

C

Zones 8, 9, 12–24. Native to southern China. Coarse plant to 5–8 ft. tall, spreads freely by root suckers unless controlled or confined. Its 10-in. leaves resemble those of *C. bungei* but are not malodorous when bruised. (This species may also be called cashmere bouquet, a name more often applied to *C. bungei*.) Pale pink double flowers with a sweet, clean fragrance are carried in broad clusters resembling hydrangea. Partial shade.

C. myricoides 'Ugandense' (*C. ugandense*). Evergreen shrub. Zones 9, 14–24; H1, H2. Native to tropical Africa. Grows to 10 ft. tall and about half as wide, though often much smaller in California. Glossy dark green leaves. Each five-petaled blossom has one violet-blue petal and four pale blue ones; pistil and stamens arch outward and upward. Partial shade; can take full sun in Hawaii.

C. trichotomum. HARLE-QUIN GLORYBOWER. Deciduous shrub. Zones 15–17, 20–24. Plant can be grown in Zones 5 and 6 but may periodically freeze to the ground and come back from roots. Native to Japan. Shrub reaches 10–15 ft. tall and as wide, with many stems growing from base. Can be trained as a small tree. Soft, hairy, oval dark green leaves to 5 in. long. Fragrant blossoms—each a white tube almost twice as long as the prominent, fleshy, scarlet calyxes surrounding it—come in late summer. Calyxes hang on and contrast pleasingly with metallic-looking turquoise or blue-green fruit. Give this shrub plenty of room to spread at top; add plants underneath it to hide its legginess. *C. t. fargesii*, from China, is somewhat hardier and smaller; it has smooth leaves and green calyxes that turn pink. Partial shade.

Amenable to pruning. Provide support for climbing species. Grow in well-drained soil. Good greenhouse plants in areas beyond their hardiness limits.

Clethra
Clethraceae
DECIDUOUS SHRUBS AND EVERGREEN TREES

⚡ **ZONES VARY BY SPECIES**

☀ ◐ **BEST IN PARTIAL SHADE BUT ADAPTABLE**

💧 **REGULAR WATER**

🦋 **FLOWERS ATTRACT BUTTERFLIES, HUMMINGBIRDS**

Clethra alnifolia 'Hummingbird'

Grow these attractive plants for their small, five-lobed, sweet-scented white or pink flowers that cluster at branch tips in mid- to late summer.

C. alnifolia. SUMMER-SWEET, SWEET PEPPERBUSH. Deciduous shrub. Zones A2, A3; 1–6. Eastern U.S. native grows 4–10 ft. tall and wide; spreads slowly by suckers. Thin, strong branches form vertical pattern. Green, tooth-edged leaves appear late in spring, turn yellow to brownish in fall. During bloom season, each branch tip carries several 4–6-in.-long spires of tiny white flowers with a spicy perfume.

Selections include the following; most grow wider than tall and hold their flowers loosely upright. 'Crystalina' is a white-flowered, dwarf form (2–2½ ft.). 'Hummingbird' is also dwarf and white-flowered but grows a little taller (2½–3 ft.). 'Pink Spires' (to 4 ft.) has deep pink blooms. 'Rosea' (6–10 ft.) has pale pink flowers. 'Sixteen Candles' is similar to 'Hummingbird', but flower spikes are held straight up like candles on a birthday cake.

C. arborea. LILY-OF-THE-VALLEY TREE. Evergreen tree. Zones 15–17, 21–24. Native to Madeira. Stiff upright growth to 20 ft. tall and about half as wide.

Plant is densely clothed with 4-in. leaves in glossy, bronzy green. White flowers in upright, branched clusters are fragrant. Leaf tips burn with frost, but plant comes back from old wood or from roots when damaged. Control spider mites in summer. For lily-of-the-valley shrub, see *Pieris japonica*.

C. barbinervis. JAPANESE SWEET SHRUB. Deciduous shrub. Zones 5–9, 14–24. Slow growing to 15–18 ft. tall and about one-half to two-thirds as wide; attractive, peeling, glossy gray to brown bark when plant matures. Produces drooping, 4–6-in. clusters of fragrant, bell-shaped white flowers. Heavily veined, sharply toothed leaves turn bright yellow in fall.

Best in moist, organic, slightly acidic, well-drained soil. Plants prefer partial shade but can adapt to less light as well as to full sun; they need some shade where summers are very hot. On deciduous shrubs, remove some old wood from base annually before spring growth begins. *C. arborea* doesn't need routine pruning.

Cleyera japonica
(Eurya ochnacea)
Pentaphylaceae
EVERGREEN SHRUB

⚡ **ZONES 4–6, 8, 9, 14–24; H1**

◐ **PARTIAL SHADE**

💧 **MODERATE TO REGULAR WATER**

Cleyera japonica

Native to Japan and Southeast Asia; related to camellia. Grows at a moderate rate to 15 ft. tall and as wide, with graceful, spreading, arching branches.

New leaves are deep brownish red. Mature leaves are 3–6 in. long, glossy dark green with reddish midrib. The plant produces small clusters of fragrant creamy white flowers in early fall that are followed by small, dark red, puffy berries; fruit lasts through winter. Flowers and berries are attractive but not showy; they don't form on young plants. 'Tricolor' (*C. fortunei*) has yellow-and-rose variegation on its young leaves.

Clianthus puniceus
PARROT BEAK
Papilionaceae
EVERGREEN SHRUBBY VINE

⚡ **ZONES 8, 9, 14–24; H1**

☀ ◐ **FULL SUN ONLY IN COOLER CLIMATES**

💧 **REGULAR WATER**

Clianthus puniceus

This New Zealand native grows to 12 ft. high and nearly as wide. It produces sprays of 3–6-in., glistening dark green leaves divided into many narrow leaflets that hang gracefully from the branches, forming an open foliage pattern. In late spring or early summer, bright red, sweet pea–shaped flowers with 3-in. keels resembling parrot beaks swing downward between the leaves. The pods that follow are 3 in. long. Forms with pink or white flowers are also available.

To display beauty of leaves and flowers, train as espalier or on a support. Mix an organic soil amendment into heavy soil. Watch for slugs, snails, and spider mites.

Clivia miniata
Amaryllidaceae
PERENNIAL FROM TUBEROUS RHIZOMES

⚡ **ZONES 12–17, 19–24 (SEE BELOW); H1, H2; OR INDOORS**

☼ ◑ ● **PARTIAL TO FULL SHADE; BRIGHT INDIRECT LIGHT**

💧 **REGULAR WATER**

Clivia miniata

A showy and striking member of the amaryllis family from South Africa for garden borders, beds, or containers. It produces brilliant, large clusters of funnel-shaped orange flowers on 2-ft. stalks that appear above dense clumps of dark green, strap-shaped, 1½-ft.-long evergreen leaves. The flowering period ranges from early winter to midspring, but most are spring bloomers. Ornamental red berries follow flowers.

French and Belgian hybrids have very wide leaves and yellow to deep red-orange blooms on thick, rigid stalks. 'Flame' is an exceptionally hot orange-red. Solomone hybrids come in yellow, cream, red, and pastel shades. There are also varieties with variegated leaves. 'San Marcos Yellow' has clear yellow blooms.

Clivias are damaged by freezing temperatures lower than 30°F to 25°F (–1°C to –4°C) and are best in relatively frost-free areas or well-protected parts of garden; use them in borders with azaleas, ferns, other shade plants.

CARE

Set the rhizomes 1½–2 ft. apart, then let the clumps grow undisturbed for years. In areas too cold for year-round outdoor culture, grow in pots and move to shelter or bring indoors (and water sparingly) in winter. Container plants bloom best with regular fertilizing and crowded roots.

Clytostoma callistegioides
VIOLET TRUMPET VINE
Bignoniaceae
EVERGREEN VINE

⚡ **ZONES 8, 9, 12–24**

☼ ◑ **FULL SUN OR PARTIAL SHADE**

◐ 💧 **MODERATE TO REGULAR WATER**

Clytostoma callistegioides

Formerly classified as *Bignonia violacea* or *B. speciosa*. A strong-growing vine from Brazil and Argentina that will clamber over anything by tendrils but needs support on walls. Each leaf is divided into two glossy dark green leaflets with wavy margins. The extended terminal shoots hang down to give a curtainlike effect. Blooms from late spring to fall, when sprays of trumpet-shaped violet, lavender, or pale purple flowers, 3 in. long and nearly as wide at the flare, appear at ends of shoots. Top is hardy to 20°F (–7°C), roots to 10°F (–12°C).

CARE

Prune in late winter to discipline growth and prevent tangling. At other times of year, remove unwanted long runners and spent flower sprays.

FOR MORE ON VINES, SEE "GROW: VINES," PAGES 708–709.

Cobaea scandens
CUP-AND-SAUCER VINE
Polemoniaceae
PERENNIAL VINE USUALLY GROWN AS ANNUAL

⚡ **ZONES 24, H1, H2 AS PERENNIAL; ZONES 3–23 AS ANNUAL**

☼ **FULL SUN**

💧 **REGULAR WATER**

Cobaea scandens

An extremely vigorous Mexican native that can grow to 25 ft. tall in only one season. Its bell-shaped flowers are first greenish, then turn violet or rose-purple. There is also a white-flowered form. Called cup-and-saucer vine because a 2-in.-long cup of petals sits in a large, green, saucerlike calyx. Leaves divided into two or three pairs of oval, 4-in. leaflets. At ends of leaves are curling tendrils that enable vine to climb rough surfaces without support.

Blooms first year from seed. May not bloom until very late summer in coolest climates. In mildest-winter areas, lives from year to year, eventually reaching over 40 ft. long; blooms heavily in midsummer the first year, from spring to autumn in subsequent years.

CARE

The hard-coated seeds may rot if sown outdoors in cool weather. Start indoors in 4-in. pots; notch seeds with knife and press edgewise into moistened potting mix, barely covering seeds. Keep moist but not wet; transplant seedlings to warm, sunny location when weather warms. Protect from strong winds.

Cocculus laurifolius
Menispermaceae
EVERGREEN SHRUB OR TREE

⚡ **ZONES 8, 9, 12–24**

☼ ◑ ● **SUN OR SHADE**

💧 **REGULAR WATER**

☠ **BARK IS TOXIC IF INGESTED**

Cocculus laurifolius

Himalayan native useful as screen or background plant. Grows slowly at first, then moderately fast to 25 ft. tall or more. Usually multistemmed shrub with arching, spreading growth as wide as it is high, though plant can be kept smaller with pruning. Staked and trained as a tree, it takes on a low, sprawling umbrella shape. Shiny, leathery, oblong leaves to 6 in. long have three strongly marked veins running from base to tip.

CARE

Long, willowy branches are as easy to train as vines; fastened to a trellis, they make an effective screen. They can also be espaliered.

This glossy-leafed beauty is one of the few large shrubs that will thrive in full shade. Try pruning it into a screen in a narrow side yard.

C

Cocos nucifera

COCONUT PALM, NIU

Arecaceae

PALM

🌡 **ZONE H2**

☀ **FULL SUN**

💧 **MODERATE WATER**

Cocos nucifera

One of the world's best-known and most economically important palms. Its solitary trunk rises 60–100 ft. and is topped with a majestic crown of glossy, feathery fronds. Many varieties are known, with large edible fruit varying in size, shape, and color (green, yellow to orange). The plant tolerates many different soil conditions; it has excellent salt and drought tolerance and can also be found growing in brackish water. Superb for large gardens, parks, or avenues. Dwarf forms are available and more suitable for the medium-size garden; some of these reach to 10–15 ft. tall, with a feathery crown about equally wide. For queen palm, formerly called *C. plumosa*, see *Syagrus romanzoffiana*.

CARE

Requires pruning off old fronds and removing mature coconuts (which can become a hazard as they drop).

Dwarf forms of this graceful, tropic-island icon are best for medium-size gardens in Hawaii; they grow 10 to 15 feet tall.

Colchicum

MEADOW SAFFRON,
AUTUMN CROCUS

Colchicaceae

PERENNIALS FROM CORMS

🌡 **ZONES 2–10, 14–24; OR INDOORS**

☀ **FULL SUN; BRIGHT INDIRECT LIGHT**

💧 **REGULAR WATER DURING GROWTH AND BLOOM**

☠ **ALL PARTS ARE POISONOUS IF INGESTED**

Colchicum

This group of delightful Mediterranean natives includes many species. They are sometimes called autumn crocus but are not true crocuses. Shining, brown-skinned, thick-scaled corms send up clusters of long-tubed, flaring lavender-pink, rose-purple, or white flowers to 4 in. across in late summer or early autumn, whether corms are sitting in a dish on a windowsill or planted in soil. When corms are planted out, broad leaves 6–12 in. long emerge in spring, last for a few months, and then die long before flower cluster rises from ground.

Corms are available during a brief dormant period in the summer. Common varieties include 'The Giant', single lavender, and 'Waterlily', double violet.

CARE

Best planted where they need not be disturbed more often than every 3 years or so. Plant corms 3 in. deep and 6–8 in. apart. Cut back on watering during dormancy, but don't let the soil dry out. To plant in bowls, set upright on 1–2 in. of pebbles or in special fiber sold for this purpose, and fill with water to the base of the corms.

Coleonema

BREATH OF HEAVEN

Rutaceae

EVERGREEN SHRUBS

🌡 **ZONES 7–9, 14–24**

☀ ☀ **FULL SUN OR LIGHT SHADE**

💧 💧 **MODERATE TO REGULAR WATER**

Coleonema pulchellum

South African natives of filmy appearance and delicate character with slender branches and narrow, heathlike leaves that are fragrant when brushed or bruised. Tiny flowers are borne freely over long season in winter and spring. Plants can continue with scattered bloom at any other time.

You may find plants in nurseries under either *Coleonema* or their former name, *Diosma*. Actually, your choice amounts to a white- or a pink-flowering breath of heaven.

Good on banks or hillsides, along paths where you can break off and bruise a twig to enjoy the foliage's fragrance. Frequently used next to buildings, though a little wispy for such use.

C. album (Diosma alba). WHITE BREATH OF HEAVEN. To 5 ft. or taller and as wide, with white flowers. Often sold as *Diosma reevesii*; once known as *D. ericoides*.

C. pulchellum (C. pulchrum). PINK BREATH OF HEAVEN, PINK DIOSMA. Grows to 5 ft. tall and as wide, occasionally to 10 ft. Bears tiny pink flowers. Species often sold as *Diosma pulchra*. 'Sunset Gold' has yellow foliage, grows 1½ ft. tall and 4 ft. wide.

CARE

Plant in light soil; fast drainage is a must. Quite drought-tolerant once established but better with regular water. To control size and promote compactness, shear lightly after main bloom is over. For an even filmier look, thin out some interior stems.

Coleostephus myconis

(Chrysanthemum multicaule)

Asteraceae

ANNUAL

🌡 **ZONES A1–A3; 1–24**

☀ **FULL SUN**

💧 **REGULAR WATER**

Coleostephus myconis

This delightful native of southern Europe blooms in spring, when broad-rayed, buttery yellow daisies ¾ in. across rise above 6–8-in.-wide mats of bright green, fleshy foliage. Blooms best in cool weather; usually sold in fall, winter, or early spring in cell packs or pots. In Alaska, blooms all summer until frost. In cool-summer/mild-winter climates, plants may live over a second year. 'Moonlight' has lemon yellow flowers.

FOR MORE ON ANNUALS, SEE "GROW: ANNUALS, BULBS," PAGES 674–675.

Coleus × hybridus. See *Solenostemon scutellarioides*

Collinsia heterophylla
(C. bicolor)
CHINESE HOUSES
Scrophulariaceae
ANNUAL

🌡 **ZONES 1–24**

☼ ◑ **PART SHADE IN HOTTEST CLIMATES**

💧 **REGULAR WATER**

🦋 **ATTRACTS BUTTERFLIES**

Collinsia heterophylla

This California native is rather uncommon in nature. It blooms from spring to early summer, with 1-in.-long blossoms that resemble snapdragons (*Antirrhinum*). Flowers are held in tiers at top of 1–2-ft.-tall, somewhat hairy stems. The upper lip of the flower is white, the lower one rose or violet. Plant produces oblong leaves to 2 in. long. Gives light, dainty effect in front of borders, scattered under deciduous trees, or as bulb cover.

CARE

Sow seeds in place in fall or early spring in rich, moist soil. Can also be sown in late spring for early fall bloom. Self-sows under favorable conditions.

Plant this charming California native on lightly shaded slopes or under high tree canopies. It especially attracts checkerspot butterflies.

Colocasia esculenta
TARO, ELEPHANT'S EAR
Araceae
PERENNIAL FROM TUBER

🌡 **ZONES 12, 16–24; H1, H2; OR DIG AND STORE**

◑ **BEST IN WARM, FILTERED SHADE**

💧 **AMPLE WATER**

☠ **ALL PARTS MAY CAUSE INDIGESTION IF INGESTED RAW; CONTACT WITH SAP MAY IRRITATE SKIN**

Colocasia esculenta 'Black Magic'

An iconic foliage plant from tropical Asia and Polynesia. Leathery green to gray-green, heart-shaped leaves are big (to 2½ by 3 ft.), carried at ends of succulent stalks from spring through fall. Fast growing to 6 ft. tall. Sometimes available are varieties with foliage marked in various purple shades; two of the most striking are 'Black Magic', with solid purple leaves, and 'Illustris', with green-veined, charcoal black foliage. All create a lush effect in the course of a single season and are effective with tree ferns and other large-leafed tropical plants. Also handsome in large containers, in raised beds, near swimming pools. Flowers resembling greenish callas (*Zantedeschia*) appear only in the warmest climates. The starchy tubers are a staple food of Polynesians; in Hawaii, where nearly 300 forms of wetland and upland (dry) taro are recorded, the plant is still grown commercially for the edible roots.

CARE

Enrich soil with organic matter before planting. Set tubers 1–1½ ft. apart and about 2 in. deep. Tops die down at 30°F

(–1°C). In listed zones, tubers can be left in ground all year; in Zones 14 and 15, a thick mulch will allow in-ground survival over the average winter. Elsewhere, lift and store tubers after frost kills foliage; or grow in containers and shelter over winter. Protect plants from wind, which tears leaves. Feed lightly once a month during growing season. When clumps become overcrowded, divide them in early spring.

Comarostaphylis diversifolia
SUMMER HOLLY
Ericaceae
EVERGREEN SHRUB OR TREE

🌡 **ZONES 7–9, 14–24**

☼ ◑ **FULL SUN IN COOLER CLIMATES ONLY**

◯ 💧 **LITTLE TO MODERATE WATER**

Comarostaphylis diversifolia

Native to coastal Southern California and Baja California, this rather formal plant grows to 6–18 ft. high and 4–8 ft. wide. Its leathery, 1–3-in.-long leaves are shiny dark green above, white and hairy beneath, with inrolled margins. (Variety *C. d. planifolia* has flat leaves.) Small, white, bell-shaped flowers appear in spring, followed by clusters of red, warty berries similar to those of madrone (*Arbutus menziesii*).

CARE

Needs little pruning, but some thinning improves appearance. Water occasionally outside of its native coastal range.

Conoclinium dissectum.
See *Eupatorium greggii*

Consolida ajacis
(Delphinium ambiguum)
LARKSPUR
Ranunculaceae
ANNUAL

🌡 **ZONES 1–24**

☼ **FULL SUN**

💧 **REGULAR WATER**

☠ **ALL PARTS, ESPECIALLY SEEDS, ARE POISONOUS IF INGESTED**

🦋 **ATTRACTS BUTTERFLIES**

Consolida ajacis

The colorful spires of this southern Europe native are a welcome spring sight throughout the West. Upright plants grow to 1–5 ft. tall and 1 ft. wide, with deeply cut, almost ferny leaves. Blossom spikes are densely set with 1–1½-in.-wide flowers (most are double) in white or shades of blue, lilac, pink, rose, salmon, carmine; there are also blue-and-white bicolors. Best bloom in the cooler spring and early-summer months. Giant Imperial strain has many 4-ft., compactly placed vertical stalks. Regal strain has 4-ft. base-branching stems, thick spikes of large flowers similar to perennial delphiniums. Disease-resistant Cannes mix grows to over 5 ft. tall and comes in a wide range of single and bicolor shades. 'Frosted Skies' has lovely blue-and-white flowers.

CARE

Sow seeds and lightly rake in. Fall planting is best except in heavy, slow-draining soils. Thin plants to avoid crowding and to get the biggest flowers. Nursery transplants are also available for early-spring planting.

Constancea nevinii.
See *Eriophyllum nevinii*

C

C

Convallaria majalis
LILY-OF-THE-VALLEY

Asparagaceae

PERENNIAL FROM RHIZOME

ZONES A1–A3; 1–7, 14–20

PARTIAL SHADE

REGULAR WATER

ALL PARTS ARE POISONOUS IF INGESTED

Convallaria majalis

Lush, spreading, 6–8-in.-high groundcover that blooms for a short period in early spring, sending up arching stems that bear small, nodding, sweet-scented, waxy white bells along one side. Native to many northern regions of the Old World but has naturalized in U.S. and Canada. Broad, glossy green, deciduous leaves are attractive throughout growing season. Bright red berries (poisonous, like the rest of the plant) may appear in fall. Double- and pink-flowered forms are sold, as are types with variegated leaves. All are charming as carpet between camellias, rhododendrons, or pieris, under deciduous or high-branching evergreen trees. Can become invasive where well adapted.

CARE

Plant single rhizomes (called pips) or clumps in rich soil in fall before ground freezes. Set 1½ in. deep; space clumps 1–2 ft. apart, single pips 4–5 in. apart. Mulch planting each year before new growth emerges. Large, prechilled pips for forcing are available in winter (even in mild climates) and can be potted for bloom indoors. After bloom, plunge pots in ground in

a cool, shaded area. Once plants are dormant, remove them from pots and set out in garden; or wash soil off pips, enclose them in plastic bags, and refrigerate them (in vegetable bin) until time to repot in December or January.

Convolvulus
Convolvulaceae

ANNUALS, PERENNIALS, AND EVERGREEN SHRUBS

ZONES VARY BY SPECIES

BEST IN SUN, TOLERATE SOME SHADE

MODERATE WATER

Convolvulus sabatius

These Mediterranean natives have funnel-shaped morning glory flowers. Common vining morning glories (*Ipomoea*) are sometimes sold as *Convolvulus*.

C. althaeoides tenuissimus. Perennial. Zones 7–9, 14–24. To 6 in. high, 2–3 ft. wide. There are two kinds of foliage. The basal leaves are less than 1 in. long, oval to arrow-shaped, sometimes lobed; leaves on trailing or creeping flowering stems are divided into narrow segments. Summer flowers are pink, 1–1½ in. wide. Spreads by rhizomes and can be invasive. Good in rock gardens, hanging baskets.

C. cneorum. BUSH MORNING GLORY. Evergreen shrub. Best in Zones 7–9, 12–24; marginal in Zones 5, 6. Grows fast to 2–4 ft. tall and as wide. Silky smooth, silvery gray, lance-shaped leaves 1–2½ in. long. White or pink-tinted morning glories with yellow throats open from pink buds in late spring and summer. 'Snow Angel' is

compact, 1½–2 ft. tall, with pinkish white flowers. Give light soil and fast drainage. Prune severely to renew plant; can get leggy if left alone.

C. sabatius (C. mauritanicus). GROUND MORNING GLORY. Perennial. Zones 4–9, 12–24. Grows 1–2 ft. high with branches trailing to spread 3 ft. or more. Soft, hairy, gray-green, roundish, evergreen leaves ½–1½ in. long. Lavender-blue, 1–2-in.-wide flowers bloom from early summer into fall. Grows well in light, gravelly soil with good drainage but will take clay soil if not overwatered. Tends to become woody; prevent by trimming in late winter.

C. tricolor. DWARF MORNING GLORY. Annual. Zones 1–24. Bushy, branching, somewhat trailing plant to 1 ft. high and 2 ft. wide. Small, narrow leaves. Summer flowers, 1½ in. across, variable in color but usually blue with yellow throat. Nick tough seed coats with knife and plant in place when soil has warmed up. In mild-winter climates, can be planted in fall for spring bloom. Use as edging or at top of wall. 'Blue Flash' and Ensign series (red, blue, rose, white) grow 6 in. tall.

Coprosma
Rubiaceae

EVERGREEN SHRUBS

ZONES VARY BY SPECIES

FULL SUN OR PARTIAL SHADE

LITTLE TO REGULAR WATER

Coprosma 'Tequila Sunrise'

Where hardy, these New Zealand natives are valued for ease of maintenance in difficult situations and for their handsome, glossy foliage. Male and female

flowers are borne on separate plants; female plants bear attractive small fruits when a male is nearby for pollination.

C. hybrids. Zones 8, 9, 14–24. A dramatic group of colorful foliage plants, growing 4–5 ft. tall and nearly as wide. Bright accents for borders or in pots. Avoid pruning in hot summer months. 'Evening Glow' has glossy green leaves that are variegated gold during growing season and turn orange-red in fall and winter. 'Rainbow Surprise' bears leaves variegated with cream and pink, washed with red in fall and winter. 'Tequila Sunrise' produces shiny green new growth, edged with gold. As they mature, the leaves gradually pick up shades of gold and orange before turning bright red and orange in winter. More compact than others. 'Coppershine' can reach up to 6 ft. tall. Its leathery leaves are bright green heavily shaded with copper. New growth is even more heavily tinted; entire plant is bright copper in winter. Good hedge or screen.

C. × kirkii. Zones 14–24; H1, H2. To 1–3 ft. high or nearly prostrate; spreading 4–6 ft. wide. Long, straight stems slant outward from base. Small (½–2 in.), narrow yellow-green leaves are closely set on stems. White fruits speckled red. Tough groundcover or bank cover; prune regularly to keep dense. Grows in wide range of soils; tolerates coastal winds, salt spray. Give part shade inland. 'Variegata', 6–24 in. high and up to 5 ft. wide, has white-edged gray-green leaves and translucent white berries; good trailing plant for wall pot, hanging basket.

C. petriei (C. pumila). Zones 8, 9, 14–24. Spreading, mounding plant to 2–2½ ft. high, eventually 6–8 ft. wide. Small, roundish oval leaves are bright shiny green. Set 2–2½ ft. apart for groundcover in 3 years. Cut out upward-growing branches. Tolerates more cold, heat than C. × kirkii. Egg-shaped fruits are translucent purplish red or blue. 'Verde Vista' (C. 'Prostrata'), a natural hybrid, is an improvement on the parent.

C. repens (C. baueri). MIRROR PLANT. Zones 14–24;

H1. Rapid growth to 10 ft. tall, 6 ft. wide; much lower and more compact when subjected to seacoast conditions. Inland, an open, straggly shrub if neglected—but beautiful, dense form if pruned twice yearly (at any height desired). Oval or oblong leaves are 3 in. long, 1½ in. wide, dark to light green, almost unbelievably shiny and glossy. Yellow or orange fruits. Use as hedge, screen, informal espalier. Sometimes grown as a houseplant.

Variegated forms include 'Argentea', with green leaves flecked silvery white; 'Marble Queen', to 2–3 ft. tall, with creamy white leaves irregularly splashed and dotted with green; 'Marble King', slow grower with cream-colored leaves heavily speckled in lime green; 'Picturata', green leaves blotched creamy yellow in the middle; 'Exotica', female version of 'Picturata' with orange-yellow fruits; 'Marginata', with green leaves irregularly edged in creamy white; 'Pink Splendor', green leaves with yellow margin that takes on a pink edging with maturity.

Cordia
Boraginaceae
EVERGREEN SHRUBS AND TREES

⚡ **ZONES VARY BY SPECIES**

☼ **FULL SUN**

◊ ◓ ⬤ **WATER NEEDS VARY BY SPECIES**

Cordia boissieri

These members of the forget-me-not family are grown for their showy flowers. Some species are at home in the desert Southwest, others in more tropical climates.

C. boissieri. TEXAS OLIVE. Shrub or tree. Zones 8–24. Native to New Mexico, Texas, Mexico; adapted to low and intermediate deserts. To 12 ft. tall, 8–10 ft. wide. Oval, rough-surfaced, grayish green leaves to 5 in. long. Clustered, 2½-in. white flowers with yellow throats begin bloom in midspring and continue over a long season; repeat bloom is possible in fall. Can be kept pruned as a low (3–5 ft.) shrub or trained into a small tree. Moderate water.

C. parvifolia. LITTLE-LEAF CORDIA. Shrub. Zones 8–14, 18–24. Native to Baja California. Similar to *C. boissieri* but somewhat smaller, with smaller leaves (most are ½ in. or less), flowers (to 1½ in. wide). Plant 8–9 ft. apart for an informal hedge or a barrier. Little to moderate water.

Cordyline
Asparagaceae
EVERGREEN PALMLIKE SHRUBS OR TREES

⚡ **ZONES VARY BY SPECIES; OR INDOORS**

☼ ◑ **EXPOSURE NEEDS VARY BY SPECIES**

◓ ⬤ **WATER NEEDS VARY BY SPECIES**

Cordyline australis 'Royal Star'

Striking woody plants with swordlike, often brightly colored leaves. Related to yuccas and agaves but usually ranked with palms in nurseries and landscapes. Good next to swimming pools. Cordyline is often sold as *Dracaena*.

C. australis (Dracaena australis). Zones 5, 8–11, 14–24; H1, H2. From New Zealand. Hardiest of cordylines, surviving to at least 15°F (–9°C). In youth, forms a fountain of narrow, 3-ft.-long leaves. Upper leaves are erect; lower ones arch and droop. In maturity, a tree to 20–30 ft. tall, 6–12 ft. wide, branching high on trunk; rather stiff-looking (like Joshua tree, *Yucca brevifolia*). Fragrant, ¼-in. flowers in long, branching clusters in late spring. For more graceful plant, cut back when young to force multiple trunks. Grows fastest in soil deep enough for big, carrotlike root. Used for tropical effects, with boulders and gravel for desert look, near seashore. Full sun. Moderate to regular water.

Colorful varieties include 'Atropurpurea', known as bronze dracaena, with bronzy red leaves; 'Pink Champagne', a more compact plant with narrow leaves edged with white and pink at the base; 'Pink Stripe', bronze with pink margins; 'Red Star', purplish red; 'Sundance', green with a pink midrib; 'Sunrise', dark reddish pink leaves with bright pink margins; 'Southern Splendor', dark green with bright pink margins; and 'Torbay Dazzler', green leaves with cream margins.

C. baueri. Zones 8, 9, 14–24. From New Zealand. To 8–10 ft. high, 3 ft. wide, with 2-ft.-long leaves in deep purple-red. Fragrant white flowers in summer. Full sun, moderate water.

C. fruticosa (C. terminalis). TI PLANT. Zones 21–24; H1, H2. Frequently used as houseplant. From tropical Southeast Asia. Many named forms with black, red, yellow, or variegated leaves. White or red, footlong flower clusters in summer or sporadically throughout the year. Plants are usually started from "logs"—small sections of mature stems imported from Hawaii. Lay logs flat in mixture of peat moss and sand, covering them to about one-half their diameter. Keep moist. When shoots grow out and root, cut them off and plant them. In frost-free locations where it receives regular water and soil stays warm, reaches 6–15 ft. high, 3–8 ft. wide. Full sun or partial shade (types with colorful leaves show more intense hues in sun).

C. hybrids. Zones 8, 9, 14–24. Several cordyline hybrids (parentage not always certain) are extremely colorful plants. Most are shorter than *C. australis*; are clump forming; and have tall clusters of fragrant, white to pale lilac flowers in summer. All are great in pots or as an accent. 'Electric Pink' grows 4–5 ft. tall and wide. Narrow, dark maroon leaves are edged in bright pink. 'Festival Grass' forms a fountainlike clump 2–3 ft. high and wide. Glossy, brilliant burgundy leaves are ¾ in. wide and 2–3 ft. long. 'Renegade' forms a tight clump, 2 ft. high and wide with very dark purple, almost black, leaves.

C. indivisa. BLUE DRACAENA. Zones 16, 17, 20–24. Hardy to 26°F (–3°C). From New Zealand. Trunk grows to 25 ft. tall and is topped with 8–10-ft.-wide crown of huge (6 ft. long, 6 in. wide), rather stiff leaves. White summer flowers in 4-ft.-long clusters. Tolerates seaside conditions. Give full sun, moderate water.

C. stricta. Zones 13, 16, 17, 20–24; H1, H2. Hardy to 26°F (–3°C). From Australia. Slender, erect stems clustered at base or branching low. Leaves are 2 ft. long, dark green, with hints of purple. Very decorative during spring bloom, bearing fragrant lavender flowers in large, branched clusters. Reaches 15 ft. high and 6 ft. wide but can be kept lower by cutting tall canes to ground; new canes replace them. Long cuttings stuck in ground will root quickly. Fine container plant indoors or out; good for tropical-looking background in narrow areas, lanais, side gardens. Needs some shade except in cool-summer climates. Regular water.

C. terminalis. See *C. fruticosa*.

Two *Cordyline* hybrids are choice plants for pots. For a striking, fountain-like effect in a deep glazed container, choose C. 'Electric Pink' or C. 'Festival Grass'. Both practically sizzle in sunlight.

Coreopsis
Asteraceae
PERENNIALS AND ANNUALS

⚡ ZONES VARY BY SPECIES

☼ FULL SUN

◐ ◖ LITTLE TO MODERATE WATER, EXCEPT AS NOTED

🦋 ATTRACT BUTTERFLIES; SEED HEADS ATTRACT BIRDS

Coreopsis 'Jethro Tull'

These easy-to-grow members of the sunflower family yield a profusion of yellow, orange, maroon, or reddish flowers. The following are from the eastern and southern U.S. unless otherwise noted.

C. auriculata 'Nana'. Perennial. Zones 1–24. Makes a 5–6-in.-high mat of 2–5-in.-long leaves. Under ideal conditions, it will spread by underground runners to form a 2-ft.-wide clump in a year. Bright orange-yellow, 1–2½-in. flowers rise well above foliage; blooms profusely over a long season (from spring to fall) if you deadhead faithfully. Best used in front of taller plants, in borders, or as edging.

C. grandiflora. Perennial. Zones 2–24; H1, H2. To 1–2 ft. high, spreading to 3 ft. Narrow dark green leaves with three to five lobes. Bright yellow, 2½–3-in. single flowers bloom all summer, carried high above foliage on long, slender stems. Attracts bees. 'Flying Saucers' is a nearly sterile selection with single, flat, 2-in.-wide yellow flowers over a long period. 'Sunburst' has semidouble flowers; it will bloom the first year from seed sown early in spring, then spread by self-sowing. 'Early Sunrise' is similar and blooms even earlier. 'Sunray' is a dense, compact selection with

double and semidouble flowers. All are tough enough for use in roadside beautification.

C. hybrids. A beguiling array of hybrid coreopsis, both annuals and perennials, have stormed nurseries and garden centers. They offer a wide range of flower colors and varied habits. In general, perennial hybrid coreopsis can be grown in Zones 2a–24, but hardiness varies. They bloom from late spring through summer and into fall, and can also be treated as annuals. Most grow about 1½–2 ft. tall and 2½ ft. wide, and look best with moderate water. 'Autumn Blush' bears butter yellow flowers with red centers. As the weather cools, the flowers blush reddish pink. 'Limerock Ruby' has ruby red flowers to 1 in. wide. 'Limerock Passion' is similar, but with yellow-centered, lavender-pink flowers. 'Snowberry' has creamy white flowers with bright red centers. 'Sterntaler' has yellow flowers with a reddish brown circle in the center. 'Tequila Sunrise' is compact to 1½ ft. high and 1 ft. wide. Narrow, olive green leaves are irregularly variegated with cream and yellow, with touches of pinkish red in spring and deeper red in fall. Golden yellow flowers with deep orange-red centers. Members of the Jewel series are more compact perennials, including 'Citrine', bright yellow; 'Ruby Frost', deep red with white edges; and 'Garnet', garnet red.

Hybrid annual coreopsis include compact 'Little Penny', which grows less than a foot tall and twice as wide, and has small copper-red blooms; the mounding (under a foot high) Punch series in bright shades of red, yellow, orange, and red-and-white bicolors; and the Lemonade series, with feathery golden foliage and red, pink, or rose flowers. Many are perennials in mild-winter areas of Southern California.

C. lanceolata. Perennial. Zones 1–24; H1, H2. Grows to 1–2 ft. high, 1–1½ ft. wide. Narrow, somewhat hairy foliage,

mostly in tuft near plant's base; some leaves on lower part of flower stems have a few lobes. Yellow, 1½–2-in. blossoms on pale green stems bloom in late spring and summer, make excellent cut flowers. When well established, persists year after year. Has naturalized in Hawaii.

C. maritima. Perennial. Zones 14–24. Native to coast of Southern California. Sometimes called sea dahlia. Grows from a tuberous taproot to reach 1–3 ft. high, 1–2 ft. wide. Stems are hollow; leaves are somewhat succulent, divided into very narrow lobes. True yellow, 2½–4-in. blossoms on 9–12-in. stems in spring; make striking cut flowers. Use in borders, for naturalizing.

C. rosea. Perennial. Zones 2b–24. Fine-textured plant, 1½–2 ft. tall, 1 ft. wide, with pink, yellow-centered daisylike flowers from summer to fall. Unlike other species, prefers moist soil. 'American Dream' has rosy pink flowers with a yellow center. 'Heaven's Gate' flowers are pink with a dark crimson ring around the center. 'Sweet Dreams' has threadlike leaves

and masses of big white flowers with a raspberry ring surrounding a yellow eye.

C. tinctoria. ANNUAL COREOPSIS, CALLIOPSIS. Annual. Zones 1–24; H1, H2. Native to much of North America. Slender, upright, 1½–3 ft. tall, 1–1½ ft. wide, with wiry stems; much like cosmos in growth habit. Smooth leaves and stems. Summer-to-fall flowers in yellow, orange, maroon, bronze, and reddish, banded with contrasting colors; purple-brown centers. Dwarf and double varieties are available. Sow seeds in place in dryish soil.

C. verticillata. Perennial. Zones 1–24. To 2½–3 ft. tall, half as broad. Many erect or slightly leaning stems carry many whorls of finely divided, very narrow leaves. Bright yellow, 2-in. daisies are freely borne at stem tips over a long bloom season—from summer through autumn. One of the most tolerant of drought, neglect. 'Moonbeam', 1½–2 ft. tall, has pale yellow flowers; 'Zagreb', 1 ft. tall, has golden yellow flowers.

CLOCKWISE FROM TOP LEFT: *Coreopsis* 'Mambo'; *C.* 'Snowberry'; *C. tinctoria* 'Tiger Stripes'

CARE

Deadhead for longer bloom; use hedge shears to remove large numbers of spent blooms. Both annual and perennial kinds are easy to propagate—annuals from seed sown in place or in pots, perennials from seed or division. Plants tend to self-sow. Best in well-drained soil.

Coriandrum sativum

CILANTRO, CORIANDER, CHINESE PARSLEY
Apiaceae
ANNUAL

✎ **ALL ZONES**

☼ ◐ **LIGHT SHADE IN HOTTEST CLIMATES**

⬤ **REGULAR WATER**

🐝 **ATTRACTS BENEFICIAL INSECTS**

Coriandrum sativum

Western Mediterranean native. Grows 1–1½ ft. high, 9 in. wide. Its delicate fernlike foliage is topped by flat clusters of pinkish white flowers in summer.

Both fresh leaves (cilantro, sometimes called Chinese parsley) and seeds (coriander) are widely used as seasoning, and roots are used in Thai cooking. You can even eat the flowers. Leaves are popular in salads and many cooked dishes; crush the aromatic seeds for use in sausage, beans, stews.

CARE

Cilantro is taprooted and transplants poorly, so start from seed (including coriander seed sold in grocery stores). Grow in good, well-drained soil. In all but low-desert areas, sow in place in early spring after all danger of frost has passed. Cilantro

grows and flowers extremely quickly ('Delfino', with finely cut leaves, and 'Calypso' are slower to flower). Keep it coming by succession planting every couple of weeks and trim flower heads as soon as they appear. Or, sow densely in bands 8–12 in. wide and use scissors to shear off leaves (almost to the base of the plant). Plants will regrow. You can also sow in pots. In low-desert areas, plant in autumn; cilantro will go to seed and die in late-spring heat.

If you are growing cilantro for seeds only, two or three plants is all you need. To collect seeds, pull up whole plants when seed heads begin to turn gray-brown; then put the plants headfirst into bags and shake them, or hang them over paper and let the seeds drop.

Corn

Poaceae
ANNUAL

✎ **ZONES 1B, 2B–24; H1, H2**

☼ **FULL SUN**

⬤ **REGULAR WATER**

Corn

Sweet corn is the one cereal crop that home gardeners are likely to grow; the 5–10-ft.-tall plants require considerable space but are still well worth planting. Once standard sweet corn is picked, its sugar changes to starch very quickly; by rushing ears from garden directly to boiling water, you can capture full sweetness.

Sugar-enhanced (se) varieties like 'Kandy Korn', and supersweet (sh2) varieties like 'Supersweet Jubilee' and 'Xtra-Tender' are sweeter than standard sweet kinds such as 'Silver Queen' and

'Golden Bantam'. They also maintain their sweetness longer after harvest because of a gene that increases the quantity of sugar and slows its conversion to starch. An increasing number of synergistic (sy) varieties are also sold; they blend sugar-enhanced and supersweet genes. 'Honey Select' and the bicolored 'Frisky' and 'Montauk' varieties are examples.

Corn needs heat, but suitable early hybrid varieties will grow even in cool-summer areas. In northern climates and at high altitudes, grow short-season varieties such as 'Earlivee' or 'Fleet', which come to harvest in fewer than 70 days; plant seeds you have pregerminated and grow with black plastic or infrared transmitting (IRT) mulch and a row cover to hasten growth.

Sugar-enhanced varieties are more widely sold than any others and have become the new standards. In addition to yellow 'Kandy Korn', other good choices include yellow 'Miracle', white 'Whiteout', and bicolored 'Luscious'.

In Hawaii, try varieties developed especially for Island gardens, such as 'Hawaiian Supersweet #9' and 'Hawaiian Supersweet #10'. For traditional corn, try 'H68'.

Baby corn. Special varieties that are harvested very early, when the ears are only a few inches long. The tender ears are eaten whole, often pickled or used in salads or Asian cuisine. Plant seeds 1–2 in. apart; thin seedlings to 4 in. apart. Harvest shortly after the first silks appear, which may be only a few weeks after sowing.

Ornamental corn. Some kinds of corn are grown for the beauty of their shelled ears rather than for eating. Calico, Indian, Squaw, and Rainbow are some names given to strains with bright-colored kernels—red, brown, blue, gray, black, yellow, or mixed colors. 'Indian Summer' has brightly colored, edible kernels. Grow ornamental corn well away from sweet corn; mix of pollen can affect the latter's flavor. For ornamental display, grow like sweet corn, but let ears ripen fully; silks will be withered, husks will turn the

How to Grow Corn

Corn grows in various soils but does best in deep, rich ones; good drainage is important.

PLANTING Sow seeds 2 weeks after average last-frost date, then make three or four more plantings at 2-week intervals; or plant early, midseason, and late varieties. In Hawaii, you can plant corn year-round. Plant in blocks of four or more short rows rather than in single long row; pollination is by wind, and unless a good supply of pollen falls on silks, ears will be poorly filled. Don't plant popcorn near sweet corn; pollen of one kind can affect characteristics of another. For the same reason, some supersweet varieties must be grown at a distance from standard sweet kinds. Plant in rows 3 ft. apart and thin seedlings to 1 ft. apart. Or plant in "hills" (actually clumps) spaced 3 ft. apart on all sides. Plant six or seven seeds in each hill and thin to three strongest plants. Give plants plenty of water.

WATERING & FEEDING Feed with high-nitrogen fertilizer when stalks are 12–15 in. tall, again when they are 2–2½ ft. tall. Just as tassel emerges from stalk, give good deep watering that thoroughly wets entire root zone; repeat when silks form. Don't remove suckers that appear.

HARVESTING Check crop when ears are plump and silks have withered; corn is usually ready to eat 3 weeks after silks first appear. To check, pull back husks and try popping a kernel with your thumbnail. It should squirt milky juice; watery juice means that corn is immature, while doughy consistency indicates overmaturity.

C

color of straw, and kernels will be firm. Cut ear from plant, including 1½ in. of stalk below ear; pull back husks (leave attached to ears) and dry thoroughly.

Zea mays japonica includes several kinds of corn grown for ornamental foliage. One occasionally sold is 'Gracilis', a dwarf corn with bright green leaves striped white.

Popcorn. Grow and harvest just like ornamental corn. When ears are thoroughly dry, rub kernels off cobs and store in dry place. White, red, and yellow kinds of popcorn look like other types of corn. Strawberry popcorn, grown either for its ornamental value or for popping, has stubby, fat, strawberry-like ears packed with red kernels.

Cornus

DOGWOOD
Cornaceae
DECIDUOUS AND EVERGREEN SHRUBS AND TREES AND A PERENNIAL

✎ **ZONES VARY BY SPECIES**

☼ ◐ **FULL SUN OR LIGHT SHADE, EXCEPT AS NOTED**

💧 **REGULAR WATER, EXCEPT AS NOTED**

🐾 **BERRIES ATTRACT A VARIETY OF WILDLIFE**

Cornus florida 'Cherokee Chief'

All dogwoods offer attractive foliage and blossoms. Some have spectacular fruit or colorful winter bark. Leaves of many types turn brilliant colors in fall. What appear to be flower petals in many dogwoods are actually bracts—petal-like modified leaves. These surround the inconspicuous true flowers.

C. alba. TATARIAN DOGWOOD. Deciduous shrub. Zones

A2, A3; 1–9, 14–24. Native to Siberia, northern China, Korea. In cold-winter areas, its bare, blood red twigs are colorful against snow. Wide spreading, eventually producing thicket of many upright stems to 10 ft. tall. Branches densely foliaged with leaves to 2½–5 in. long, 2½ in. wide; leaves are deep rich green above and paler beneath, turn red in fall. Spring bloom; small, fragrant, creamy white flowers in 1–2-in., flattish clusters. Small bluish white to white fruits. In species and varieties below, new wood is brightest; cut back in late dormant season to force new growth.

'Elegantissima' ('Argenteomarginata'). Showy green-and-white leaves on red stems.

'Ivory Halo'. Compact, to 3–6 ft. tall and wide; red stems hold white-edged green leaves.

'Sibirica'. SIBERIAN DOGWOOD. Smaller and not as wide spreading as species; grows to about 7 ft. high and 5 ft. wide. Gleaming coral red branches. There is also a variegated form.

C. canadensis. BUNCHBERRY. Perennial. Zones A1–A3; 1–7; difficult but possible in Zones 8, 9, 14–16. Native from Northern California to Alaska and eastward. Groundcover 6–9 in. high, found in the wild under trees by lakes and streams. Creeping rootstocks send up stems topped by whorls of oval or roundish, 1–2-in.-long, deep green leaves that turn yellow in fall, die down in winter. In late spring or early summer, plants bear small, compact clusters of tiny flowers surrounded by (usually) four oval, ½–¾-in., pure white bracts. Clusters of small, shiny red fruits follow in late summer.

Best performance in part or full shade in cool, moist climates, in acid soil with generous amounts of organic matter. Set out small plants from pots about 1 ft. apart. Small rooted pieces gathered from the woods may not establish easily. Excellent with rhododendrons, ferns, trilliums, lilies.

C. controversa. GIANT DOGWOOD. Deciduous tree. Zones 4–9, 14, 18, 19. From Asia. Resembles typical big shrubby dogwoods in leaves, flowers, and fruit, but grows rapidly into a magnificent tree 40–60 ft.

tall and wide, with picturesque horizontal branches. Luxuriantly foliaged with oval, 3–6-in.-long leaves that are dark green above, silvery green beneath, glowing red in fall. Creamy white spring flowers in fluffy, flattish, 3–7-in. clusters are not spectacular but are so abundant that they give a good show. Blossoms are followed in late summer by ½-in., shiny blue-black fruit. Full sun for best bloom, brightest fall color. 'June Snow' bears abundant large flower clusters and has mottled orange-yellow, red, and purplish red fall leaf color. Foliage of 'Variegata' is edged white.

C. 'Eddie's White Wonder'. Deciduous tree. Zones 3–9, 14–20. Hybrid between *C. florida* and *C. nuttallii*. A little taller and more erect than *C. florida*, twiggier and easier to transplant than *C. nuttallii*. Midspring bloom. Clusters of tiny true flowers are surrounded by four to six white bracts.

C. florida. FLOWERING DOGWOOD, EASTERN DOGWOOD. Deciduous tree. Zones 2b–9, 14–16. Native to eastern U.S. May reach 40 ft. high and wide, but more commonly seen at 20–30 ft. Trees tend to branch low, the branches building up in horizontal layers (with

gray twigs pointing upward at branch ends). Mature trees—often wider than tall—have a gently rounded to flat crown. Small flower clusters are surrounded by four roundish, 2–4-in. bracts with notched tips. The species has white bracts, but selections offer bracts in pink shades to nearly red (as well as white). Bracts form in fall; tips may dry out in harsh, dry winters, preventing inflorescence from opening fully. Flowers almost cover the tree in midspring before leaves expand. Oval, 2–4-in.-long leaves are bright green above, lighter green beneath; turn glowing red in fall. Clusters of small, oval scarlet fruit last into winter or until birds eat them. Subject to anthracnose, a fungus that can cause leaf damage, stem cankers, and decline or death of the tree. Avoid injury to bark from mowers and string trimmers; try to keep the tree healthy with adequate feeding, watering, and air circulation. The following are among the varieties offered (*C. florida* has been bred with *C. kousa* to produce more disease-resistant hybrids; see *C.* Stellar series).

'Cherokee Brave'. Red bracts with white centers. Resists mildew.

Dogwoods for Every Season

When it comes to deciduous spring-flowering trees and shrubs, few areas in the world can match the rich diversity of the Pacific Northwest. There's a dogwood for every garden and for every season.

SPRING Pacific dogwoods (*Cornus nuttallii*) put on a spectacular show of gleaming white bracts on bare branches. Flowering dogwoods (*C. florida*) unfurl ice cream–hued bracts.

LATE SPRING, EARLY SUMMER Kousa dogwoods (*C. kousa*) show off white or pink bracts. Bunchberry (*C. canadensis*), a groundcover, is dotted with pure white bracts.

FALL Kousa dogwood leaves turn yellow or scarlet; red-purple leaves cloak *C. florida* 'Cherokee Sunset'.

WINTER Now-leafless stems of redtwig dogwood (*C. sericea* 'Isanti') are bright red. They banish the winter blues.

'Cherokee Chief'. Deep rosy red bracts, paler at base.

'Cherokee Daybreak' ('Daybreak'). Green leaves with white variegation turn pink and red in fall. White bracts.

'Cherokee Princess'. Very heavy display of white blooms.

'Cherokee Sunset' ('Sunset'). Yellow-variegated leaves turn red-purple in fall. Reddish bracts. Resistant to anthracnose.

'Cloud Nine'. White-bracted selection blooms young and very heavily. Gives better bloom in cold climates than other *C. florida* varieties; also tolerates heat and lack of winter chill better than other varieties.

'Prairie Pink'. Soft pink bracts. Well adapted to areas of the West, east of the Rocky Mountains.

'Rubra'. Longtime favorite for its pink or rose bracts.

'Welchii'. TRICOLOR DOGWOOD. Leaves about 4 in. long, variegated in creamy white, pink, deep rose, and green throughout spring and summer; turn solid deep rose to almost red in fall. Rather inconspicuous pinkish to white bracts are not profuse. Best with some shade.

C. kousa. KOUSA DOGWOOD. Deciduous shrub or tree. Zones 2–9, 14–17. Native to Japan and Korea. Can be a big multistemmed shrub or—with training—a small tree to 20 ft. tall and wide (or even larger). Dense, spreading, horizontal growth habit and delicate limb structure. Lustrous medium green leaves, 4 in. long, have rusty brown hairs at base of veins on undersurface. Flowers along tops of branches show above leaves in late spring or early summer (later than other flowering dogwoods). Creamy white, rather narrow, 2–3-in.-long bracts with slender, sharp-pointed tips turn pink along edges. In late summer and fall, inch-wide red fruits appear, resembling large raspberries hanging below branches. Yellow or scarlet autumn leaf color. Less susceptible to anthracnose than *C. florida* and *C. nuttallii*. Except as noted, the following selections bear white bracts.

'Autumn Rose'. To 20 ft. tall, 25 ft. wide. Leaves are light green when new, reddish in fall.

'Gold Star'. To 12 ft. tall; yellow-centered green leaves.

'Heart Throb'. Large, deep red to rose-pink flowers over a long period.

'Milky Way Select'. More floriferous than species.

'National'. To 25–30 ft. tall, 12–15 ft. wide, with earlier bloom than species and bright red fall color.

'Satomi' ('Satomi Red', 'Rosabella'). Reaches 20 ft. tall and wide. Rose-red bracts.

'Wolf Eyes'. Gray-green leaves edged with white. Pinkish red fall color. 'Samaritan' and 'Summer Fun' are other excellent forms of *C. kousa* with leaves variegated white.

C. k. chinensis. Larger leaves and bracts than species.

C. mas. CORNELIAN CHERRY. Deciduous shrub or tree. Zones 1–6. Native to southern Europe and Asia. Usually an airy, twiggy shrub but can be trained as small tree (15–20 ft. high and wide). One of earliest dogwoods to bloom, bearing clustered masses of small, soft yellow blossoms on bare twigs in mid- to late winter. Oval, 2–4-in.-long leaves turn from shiny green to yellow (or red, in some forms) in autumn. Fall color is enhanced by clusters of cherry-size, bright scarlet fruits that hang on until birds get them. Fruit can be used for preserves. In winter, flaking, mottled gray-and-tan bark provides interest. Tolerates alkaline soils. Leaves of 'Variegata' are marbled creamy white. 'Golden Glory' is slightly more upright; produces more bloom.

C. nuttallii. PACIFIC DOGWOOD, WESTERN DOGWOOD. Deciduous tree. Zones 3b–9, 14–20. Native to Pacific Northwest and Northern California. To 50 ft. tall, 20 ft. wide, with one trunk or several. Gray branches in pleasing horizontal pattern. Spectacular when it shows off its gleaming white bracts on bare branches in spring; there is often a second flowering in late summer, when tree is in full leaf. Flowers are ringed by four to eight large (to 3 in. long), rounded or pointed bracts; they may be white or pink-tinged white. Oval, 3–5-in. green leaves turn yellow, red, and pink in fall. Decorative red fruit in knoblike clusters in fall.

Dislikes routine garden watering, fertilizing, pruning; injury to tender bark provides entrance

CLOCKWISE FROM TOP: *Cornus nuttallii; C. kousa; C. k. chinensis* 'China Girl'

for insects and diseases. For better chance of success, give exceptionally good drainage and infrequent summer water, and plant under high-branching trees so that bark will not sunburn. In Northwest, however, planting under larger trees is not advisable. *C. nuttallii* is very susceptible to anthracnose in this region; a location under larger trees creates conditions that favor the disease—reduced air circulation and shadiness that extend time for wet foliage to dry.

'Colrigo Giant' is vigorous and heavy trunked, with low-branching but erect habit; bears profusion of 6-in. flower heads. 'Goldspot' has leaves splashed with creamy yellow; because it is grafted, it blooms from an early age (when only 2 ft. high). 'Starlight' is a hybrid between *C. nuttallii* and *C. kousa*, with an upright habit to 30 ft. tall and 20 ft. wide. Blooms are white; fall leaf color is red. Resists anthracnose and powdery mildew. 'Venus', another cross between these two species, grows 25 ft. tall and 20 ft. wide, with very large (6 in.) white blooms and few fruits.

C. sanguinea. BLOODTWIG DOGWOOD. Deciduous shrub. Zones 1–7. From Europe. Grows as large multistemmed shrub to 12 ft. high, about 8 ft. wide. Big show comes in fall, thanks to dark blood red foliage, and in winter, when bare, purplish to dark red twigs and branches are on display. Prune severely in late dormant season to produce new branches and twigs for winter color. Dark green, 1½–3-in.-long leaves; greenish white late-spring flowers in 2-in. clusters. Black fruit. 'Midwinter Fire' has brilliant orange-red fall color and red berries.

C. sericea (C. stolonifera). REDTWIG DOGWOOD, RED-OSIER DOGWOOD. Deciduous shrub. Zones A1–A3; 1–9, 14–21. Like *C. sanguinea*, this one is grown for brilliant red fall foliage and winter twigs, and it too should be cut back severely in late dormant season. Native to moist places, Northern

California to Alaska and eastward. Thrives not only in the coldest mountain areas of the West but also throughout California—even in intermediate valleys of Southern California if given frequent water. Grows rapidly to form a multistemmed shrub 7–9 ft. high; spreads to 12 ft. or wider by creeping underground stems and rooting branches. Oval fresh deep green leaves. Small, creamy white flowers in 2-in. clusters appear among leaves throughout summer; white or bluish fruits follow.

Use as a space filler on moist ground (good for holding banks) or plant along property line as a screen. Shade-tolerant. To control spread, use a spade to cut off roots; also trim branches that touch ground.

'Arctic Fire'. Dark red stems on a compact 3–4-ft.-tall plant.

'Arctic Sun'. Yellow stems tipped red; grows 3–4 ft. tall.

'Baileyi'. To 6–8 ft. tall; exceptionally bright red twigs.

'Flaviramea'. YELLOWTWIG DOGWOOD. Yellow twigs and branches.

'Hedgerow's Gold'. Foliage variegated green and gold. Red stems.

'Isanti'. Compact grower to 5 ft. tall, with bright red stems.

'Silver and Gold'. Yellow branches and cream-edged green leaves.

C. s. coloradensis. COLORADO REDTWIG. Native from Yukon to New Mexico and California. To 5–6 ft. high, with brownish red stems. Its selection 'Cheyenne' is redder.

**_C. Stellar series (C. ×
rutgersensis)._** STELLAR DOGWOODS. Deciduous trees. Zones 3–9, 14–17. These disease-resistant, single-trunked hybrids between _C. florida_ and _C. kousa_ grow to about 20 ft. tall and 25–30 ft. wide. Bloom comes between the midspring bloom of _C. florida_ and late-spring or early-summer bloom of _C. kousa._ Blossoms appear with the leaves. 'Celestial' has broad white bracts; 'Constellation' has narrow white ones, giving a starlike effect. 'Stellar Pink' produces pink bracts. All have brilliant autumn color.

Corokia
Argyrophyllaceae
EVERGREEN SHRUBS

✎ **ZONES 4–24**

☼ ◑ **FULL SUN OR PARTIAL SHADE**

💧 **MODERATE WATER**

Corokia × _virgata_ 'Sunsplash'

New Zealand natives grown for zigzag branching habit; small, starlike yellow flowers; and red, orange, or yellow fruits. Night lighting from below emphasizes bizarre branch pattern and casts interesting shadows.

C. cotoneaster. Slow growing to 8–10 ft. high and wide, but usually seen as a 2–4-ft. container plant. Slim, contorted, reddish to nearly black branches. Sparse, oval leaves to ¾ in. long, dark glossy green above, white beneath. Yellow, ½-in. flowers are followed on older plants by small orange or red fruit. 'Little Prince' grows 4 ft. high, has bright orange-red fruit.

C. × virgata. A series of hybrids with more erect growth habit than _C. cotoneaster_; eventually reach 10 ft. tall, 6 ft. wide. Most have spoon-shaped leaves up to 1½ in. long. Use in pots, as accent plants in garden, as hedge or screen. 'Red Wonder' and 'Yellow Wonder' are named for the color of their showy fruits. 'Bronze King' has tiny bronze-tinged leaves; 'Bronze Lady' has darker bronze foliage (of the usual size) and bright red fruit. 'Sunsplash' has bronzy stems and bright green leaves margined with creamy yellow.

CARE

Sculptural form is enhanced by selective removal of a third or more of the branches and by heading back strong new shoots to maintain a compact outline. If intertwining branches are left intact, plants make dense hedges. Need good drainage. Thrive in containers.

FOR OTHER PLANTS THAT THRIVE IN CONTAINERS, SEE "TREES AND SHRUBS FOR CONTAINERS," PAGES 70–71.

Correa
AUSTRALIAN FUCHSIA
Rutaceae
EVERGREEN SHRUBS

✎ **ZONES 14–24**

☼ ◑ **PARTIAL SHADE IN HOTTEST CLIMATES**

💧 **MODERATE WATER**

🐦 **FLOWERS ATTRACT HUMMINGBIRDS**

Correa backhouseana

These Australian natives may resemble fuchsia in their flower form, but in all other ways they are far from fuchsialike. Plants range from low growing to tall and are usually dense and spreading. The roundish, 1-in. leaves are densely felted underneath. Their gray or gray-green color contrasts subtly with other grays, distinctly with dark greens. All are valued for their long flowering season, usually late fall into spring (_C. alba_ is a summer bloomer). Small (½–¾ in.) flowers hang from branches like little bells; they are individually handsome but not showy. Use as groundcover on banks or slopes. Attractive in large pots placed where flowers can be enjoyed close-up.

C. alba. To 8 ft. high and wide, with rusty-haired stems and dark green leaves. Flowers are white, and more open and star-shaped than those of other correas. Withstands seashore conditions. Apparently not relished by deer. _C. a. pannosa_ 'Western Pink Star' grows 3–4 ft. tall and 4–6 ft. wide, with pale pink flowers.

C. backhouseana. Upright and rather sprawling growth to 4–5 ft. tall and wide. Pale cream or yellow to chartreuse flowers. More successful in Southern California than _C. pulchella_. Often sold as _C. magnifica_.

C. 'Dusky Bells' ('Carmine Bells'). Low growing (2–2½ ft.), spreading as wide as 8 ft. Deep red flowers.

C. 'Ivory Bells'. Resembles 'Dusky Bells' but has creamy white flowers.

C. pulchella. To 2–2½ ft. high, spreading as wide as 8 ft. Leaves green above, gray-green below; flower color ranges from light pink to reddish orange. Most widely grown correa in Northern California. 'Mission Bells' has deep pink to red flowers; 'Orange Flame' has somewhat smaller orange blossoms. 'Pink Eyre' is compact, 2–3 ft. high and wide, with showy rose-pink blooms nearly year-round. 'Pink Flamingo' is similar, with salmon-pink blooms.

C. 'Ray's Tangerine'. Grows to 2 ft. tall with orange blooms.

C. reflexa. Variable species, with many forms ranging from 1 to 9 ft. tall and 3 to 9 ft. wide. Flowers are 1–1½ in. long, tubular, with color that varies from yellow-green to red, with yellow to green tips. 'Cape Carpet' reaches 1 ft. high and 8–10 ft. wide; flowers are bright red with chartreuse tips. 'Carpenter Rocks' has similar flowers but grows to just 3–4 ft. high and wide. 'Yanakie' is 4 ft. tall and wide, with large red flowers tipped in cream or green.

C. 'Wyn's Wonder'. Leaves variegated white. Grows to 2–3 ft. tall.

CARE

Need fast drainage; do well in poor, rocky soil. Easy to kill with kindness (overwatering and overfertilizing). Should not get reflected heat from a wall or pavement.

Corydalis
Papaveraceae
PERENNIALS

- ZONES 2–9, 14–24
- PARTIAL SHADE
- REGULAR WATER

Corydalis lutea

These useful perennials produce handsome clumps of dainty divided leaves like those of bleeding heart (*Dicentra*, to which it is closely related) or maidenhair fern (*Adiantum*). Clusters of small, spurred flowers rise above the foliage.

C. 'Blackberry Wine'. Creeping habit, 10–16 in. high and wide. Small, fragrant purple flowers. Will spill over walls or sides of containers. 'Berry Exciting' is a yellow-foliaged variation.

C. 'Canary Feathers'. Bright yellow flowers. Grows 7–10 in. high by 10 in. wide.

C. cheilanthifolia. Chinese native, 8–10 in. high and wide, with fernlike green foliage. Clusters of yellow, ½-in.-long flowers in spring.

C. curviflora rosthornii 'Blue Heron'. Clumping growth to 10 in. high, 8 in. wide. Finely cut gray-green foliage. Large, very fragrant, sapphire blue flowers from spring into summer. Doesn't reseed.

C. flexuosa. From western China. Typically to 1 ft. high, 8 in. wide, but under favorable conditions it rapidly spreads wider from bulblets on the roots. Finely divided foliage and spikelike clusters of blue flowers in early spring, often continuing into summer. May go dormant in summer, especially in hot climates, but will reappear the following spring.

Selections include 'Blue Panda', with gentian blue flowers; 'China Blue', pure sky blue flowers; 'Nightshade', blue-and-lavender flowers; 'Père David', lavender to light blue flowers. 'Purple Leaf', the earliest bloomer, has purplish blue flowers and green leaves blotched purple.

C. lutea. Native to southern Europe. To 15 in. tall, 1 ft. wide. Masses of delicate foliage on many stems. Golden yellow, ¾-in.-long, short-spurred flowers throughout summer. Self-sows and can become somewhat weedy.

C. solida. From northern Europe, Asia. To 10 in. high, 8 in. wide. Blooms in spring, producing spikes containing up to 20 purplish red flowers. Grow from fall-planted tubers.

CARE
Plant in rich, moist soil. Effective in rock crevices, in open woodland, and near a pool or streamside. Divide clumps or sow seeds in spring or fall. Plants self-sow. Tend to be short-lived in mild-winter Southern California zones.

Corylopsis
WINTER HAZEL
Hamamelidaceae
DECIDUOUS SHRUBS

- ZONES VARY BY SPECIES
- FULL SUN OR PARTIAL SHADE
- REGULAR WATER

Corylopsis pauciflora

These Asian natives are valued for sweet-scented, bell-shaped, soft yellow flowers that hang in short, chainlike clusters on bare branches in early spring. The

new foliage that follows is often tinged pink then later turns bright green. Mature leaves are toothed, nearly round, and somewhat resemble those of hazelnut (*Corylus*). Fall color varies from none to poor to a good clear yellow. Plants have a rather open structure with attractive, delicate branching pattern.

C. glabrescens. FRAGRANT WINTER HAZEL. Zones 2–7, 14–17. Hardiest species. To 8–15 ft. high and wide. Can be trained as a small tree. Flower clusters are 1–1½ in. long.

C. pauciflora. BUTTERCUP WINTER HAZEL. Zones 4–7, 14–17. Dainty habit to 4–6 ft. high and wide. Blossom clusters are 1¾ in. long, each containing two or three blooms.

C. sinensis. Zones 4–7, 14–17. A variable species. The typical form is a spreading shrub to 15 ft. tall and wide, bearing crowded flower spikes to 2 in. long. *C. s. sinensis* (*C. willmottiae*) has velvety blue-green leaves, hairy leafstalks, and flower clusters to 3 in. long. Its selection 'Spring Purple' has purplish young stems that mature to green. *C. s. calvescens* (*C. platypetala*) has smooth leaf surfaces and largely hairless leafstalks.

C. spicata. SPIKE WINTER HAZEL. Zones 3b–7, 14–17. To 8 ft. high, 10 ft. wide. New growth is purple, maturing to bluish green; 6–12 blossoms in each 1½-in.-long flower cluster. 'Aurea' has yellow foliage.

CARE
Give same soil conditions as you would rhododendrons. Grow in a wind-sheltered location in a shrub border or at the edge of woodland.

Winter hazel is one of the best plants for Northwest gardens. Its cheerful yellow blooms emit a delicious perfume in winter when little else is blooming.

Corylus
FILBERT, HAZELNUT
Betulaceae
DECIDUOUS SHRUBS AND TREES

- ZONES 2–9, 14–20, EXCEPT AS NOTED
- FULL SUN OR PARTIAL SHADE
- REGULAR WATER, EXCEPT AS NOTED

Corylus avellana 'Contorta'

Although usually grown for their edible nuts (see Hazelnut), the following make very attractive ornamental shrubs or small trees. The plants have separate female and male flowers. Female blossoms are inconspicuous; male ones are showy, appearing in pendent catkins on bare branches in winter or early spring. Leaves are roundish to oval, with toothed margins.

C. avellana. EUROPEAN FILBERT. Shrub. To 10–15 ft. high and wide. One of the species grown commercially for nuts. The following are widely grown ornamental varieties.

'Contorta'. HARRY LAUDER'S WALKING STICK. Rounded to 8–10 ft. tall and wide. Grown for fantastically gnarled and twisted branches and twigs, revealed after its 2–2½-in. leaves turn yellow and drop in autumn. Branches are used in flower arrangements. Plants are almost always grafted, so suckers arising from the base below the graft should be removed; they won't have contorted form.

'Fuscorubra' ('Atropurpurea'). Grows to 10–15 ft. high and wide, with 3–4-in., reddish purple leaves.

'Red Dragon'. Red new growth is held long into the season but eventually fades to green.

»

Branches are contorted. Resistant to eastern filbert blight (see Hazelnut). 'Red Majestic' is similar but may not hold its red color as long and is not disease-resistant.

C. colurna. TURKISH HAZEL. Tree. Zones 2b–9, 14–20. From southeastern Europe into western Asia. Pyramidal in form; usually 40–50 ft. (possibly to 75 ft.) tall and about half as wide, with leaves to 6 in. long. Can be grown as a single- or multitrunked tree. Flaking, mottled bark provides winter interest. Produces small clusters of edible nuts. Flourishes in areas with hot summers and cold winters. Attractive tree in its own right, and a parent (with *C. avellana*) of hybrids called trazels. Quite drought-tolerant once established.

C. cornuta californica. WESTERN HAZELNUT. Shrub. Native to damp slopes below 7,000-ft. elevation, northern Coast Ranges and Sierra Nevada of California, north to British Columbia. Open, multi-stemmed, to 5–12 ft. high and wide. Roundish, somewhat hairy, coarsely toothed, 1½–3-in. leaves turn bright yellow in autumn. Small nuts with flavorful kernels are enveloped in a leafy husk with a long, attenuated beak.

C. maxima. Shrub or tree. Zones 2b–9, 14–17. Native to southeastern Europe. One of the species grown commercially for nuts. Suckering shrub to 12–15 ft. high and wide; can be trained as a small tree. Most widely grown ornamental form is 'Purpurea', with rich dark purple leaves to 6 in. long and heavily purple-tinted male catkins. Leaf color fades to green in hot climates.

CARE

Thin branches as needed in late winter; remove suckers when you see them.

FOR OTHER TREES THAT ARE GOOD FOR PATIOS, SEE "PATIO TREES," PAGES 66–67.

Corymbia. See *Eucalyptus*

Corynocarpus laevigatus
NEW ZEALAND LAUREL
Corynocarpaceae
EVERGREEN SHRUB OR TREE

- 🌡 **ZONES 16, 17, 20–24; H1, H2; BEST IN ZONES 17, 24; H1, H2**
- ☀ ◐ **FULL SUN OR PARTIAL SHADE**
- 💧 **REGULAR WATER**
- ☇ **FRUIT IS EXTREMELY POISONOUS IF INGESTED**

Corynocarpus laevigatus

A handsome, upright tree or shrub reaching 20–40 ft. high by 5–15 ft. wide. Its beautiful, dark green, very glossy, leathery leaves grow to 7 in. long by 2 in. wide. (Leaves of 'Variegatus' have a showy yellow border.) Flowers are noticeable but of no importance—tiny, whitish, in 3–8-in.-long upright clusters. Orange, oblong fruit to 1 in. long follows the blooms. Good in containers. Slow growing, keeping its attractive form for years. Needs only minimal pruning. Use as screen or large hedge, background. Good in sheltered areas, entryways, beneath overhangs. Has naturalized in Hawaii.

New Zealand laurel, called karaka in its homeland, makes an attractive tree with thick, glossy leaves.

Cosmos
Asteraceae
PERENNIALS AND ANNUALS

- 🌡 **ZONES 1–24, EXCEPT AS NOTED**
- ☀ **FULL SUN**
- 💧 **MODERATE WATER**
- 🐦 **ATTRACT BIRDS, BUTTERFLIES**

Cosmos sulphureus

Native to tropical America (mostly Mexico), these showy summer- and fall-blooming plants reliably produce daisylike flowers in many colors and forms (single, double, crested, and frilled). They are open and branching in habit, with bright green divided leaves. Heights vary from 2½ to 8 ft. Use for mass color in borders or background, or as filler among shrubs. Useful in arrangements if flowers are cut just after they open and placed immediately in deep, cool water.

C. atrosanguineus. CHOCOLATE COSMOS. Perennial from tuberous roots. Zones 4–9, 14–24. Where winters are colder, dig and store as for dahlias. Grows 2–2½ ft. tall, 1½ ft. wide, with coarsely cut foliage. Blooms in late summer and fall, with deep brownish red, nearly 2-in.-wide flowers with a strong perfume of chocolate (or vanilla). Attractive companion for silvery-foliaged plants. Provide well-drained soil. Winter mulch is prudent in all but mildest regions (where plant tends to be rather short-lived).

C. bipinnatus. Annual. Heights up to 8 ft., widths to 1½–2½ ft. Blossoms are 3–4 in. wide, with tufted yellow centers and rays in white and shades of pink, rose, lavender, purple, or crimson. Attract bees and beneficial insects. Among the many types are 3–4-ft.-tall

'Candystripe', with white-and-rose flowers; Doubleclick strain, to 4 ft. high with frilly, double flowers in a range of colors; 'Picotee', to 2½ ft. high, white flowers edged red; Sensation strain, 3–6 ft. tall, including 'Dazzler' (crimson) and 'Radiance' (rose with red center); and 'Sea Shells', to 3 ft. tall, grown for quilled ray flowers that look like long, slender cones. Sonata is a dwarf strain 1½–2 ft. high; 'Sweet Dreams' reaches 3 ft. tall and has pale pink to white blossoms with rose centers; Versailles strain, bred for cut flowers, reaches 3½ ft. and bears its blossoms on long, strong stems.

C. sulphureus. YELLOW COSMOS. Annual. To 7 ft. tall, 1½–2½ ft. wide, with yellow-centered, yellow or orange-yellow single flowers. Tends to become weedy-looking at end of season. Two 3–4-ft.-tall, semidouble-flowering strains are Bright Lights, with 3½-in. flowers in yellow, gold, orange, and orange-red; and Klondike, with 2-in. flowers ranging from scarlet-orange to yellow. Dwarf Klondike or Sunny strain is 1½ ft. tall, bears 1½-in. flowers. Foot-tall semidouble bloomers include Ladybird mix, with 2½-in. scarlet, yellow, and orange flowers; and 'Sunny Red', with orange-red blooms. 'Yellow Garden' grows 3 ft. tall and wide, bears light yellow blooms with white center and edge.

CARE

Sow seeds in open ground where plants are to grow, or set out transplants from spring to summer. Plant in not-too-rich soil. Plants self-sow freely.

Cosmos comes in many colors and flower forms. Cluster 'Sonata White' cosmos beside zucchini plants in a kitchen garden. Or plant a few of each color in a cutting or butterfly garden.

Cotinus

SMOKE TREE
Anacardiaceae
DECIDUOUS SHRUBS OR TREES

🗡 **ZONES 2–24**

☼ **FULL SUN**

💧 **MODERATE WATER**

Cotinus coggygria

Unusual and colorful shrub-trees create a broad, urn-shaped mass usually as wide as high. They are naturally multi-stemmed but can be trained to a single trunk. Common name derived from dramatic puffs of "smoke" from fading flowers: as the tiny greenish blooms wither, they send out elongated stalks clothed in a profusion of fuzzy lavender-pink hairs. For another plant with the common name smoke tree, see *Psorothamnus spinosus*.

C. coggygria. Native from southern Europe to central China. Typically 12–15 ft. high and wide, though it may eventually reach 25 ft. The roundish, 1½–3-in. leaves are bluish green in the species, but purple-leafed types are more commonly grown. Leaves of 'Purpureus' emerge purple, then gradually turn green; 'Royal Purple' and 'Velvet Cloak' hold their purple color through most of the summer. Those with purple foliage have richer purple "smoke puffs" than the species. 'Golden Spirit' reaches about 7 ft. high and 6 ft. wide, with leaves that are lime green in spring and turn golden yellow in summer. 'Pink Champagne' is a green-leafed selection with pinkish tan puffs. Leaves of all types change in fall, taking on colors from yellow to orange-red.

C. 'Grace'. Hybrid between *C. coggygria* and *C. obovatus*. To 15 ft. tall and wide, with blue-green foliage shaded purple, large deep pink puffs. Orange and purple-red fall foliage.

C. obovatus. From eastern U.S. Grows to 20–30 ft. tall and wide. Bluish to dark green leaves turn yellow, orange, and reddish purple in fall.

CARE

Plants are at their best under stress in poor or rocky soil. In cultivated gardens, give them fast drainage and avoid overly wet conditions. Resistant to oak root fungus.

Cotoneaster

Rosaceae
EVERGREEN, SEMIEVERGREEN, AND DECIDUOUS SHRUBS

🗡 **ZONES VARY BY SPECIES**

☼ **FULL SUN, EXCEPT AS NOTED**

◐ 💧 **LITTLE TO MODERATE WATER**

🦜 **ATTRACT BIRDS**

◆ **SOME TYPES INVASIVE**

Cotoneaster dammeri
'Coral Beauty'

Varied natives to China, Himalayas, and northern India. Plants range from low types used as groundcovers to small, stiffly upright shrubs to tall (25 ft.) shrubs of fountainlike growth with graceful, arching branches. White or pink springtime flowers resembling tiny single roses are pretty because of their abundance, though not especially showy. Berries (typically red or orange-red) follow the blossoms in fall and winter. Some species can be invasive, spreading by seeds into wild areas.

Cotoneasters are useful, if not striking, shrubs and can be good-looking in the proper setting. Some are especially attractive in form and branching pattern (*C. congestus, C. horizontalis*), while some others (*C. microphyllus*) are notable for colorful fruit that is long lasting if birds don't get it. Trailing varieties make excellent groundcovers. Low horizontal kinds die out in desert heat.

C. acutifolius. PEKING COTONEASTER. Deciduous. Zones A1–A3; 1–3. To 10 ft. tall and as wide, with glossy green foliage turning red in fall. Fruit is black. Useful as hedge or screen.

C. apiculatus. CRANBERRY COTONEASTER. Deciduous. Zones A3; 2–24. Best in cold-winter climates. Dense grower to 3 ft. tall, 6 ft. wide, with small, round leaves turning deep red in autumn. Clustered fruits about the size of large cranberries. Can take some shade. Use as bank cover, hedge, background planting. 'Tom Thumb' is a miniature mound 4–6 in. high, 10 in. wide. It may be the same as 'Little Gem'.

C. congestus. PYRENEES COTONEASTER. Evergreen. Zones 3b–24. Slow grower reaches to 3 ft. tall and as wide, with dense, downward-curving branches and tiny dark green leaves. Plant produces small, bright red fruit. Use in containers, rock gardens.

C. dammeri (C. humifusus). BEARBERRY COTONEASTER. Evergreen. Zones 2–24. Fast, prostrate growth to 8 in. high, 10 ft. wide. Branches root along ground. Leaves are bright glossy green, fruit bright red. 'Coral Beauty' (*C.* × *suecicus* 'Coral Beauty') is 6 in. high; 'Eichholz' grows 10–12 in. high, shows a scattering of red-orange leaves in fall; 'Lowfast' is 1 ft. high; 'Mooncreeper' grows 8–10 in. high and has large flowers; 'Skogsholmen' grows 1½ ft. high. 'Streib's Findling' (which may be a hybrid with *C. procumbens* or a selection of that species) grows 4–6 in. high, has dark bluish green foliage. All are good groundcovers in sun or partial shade and can drape over walls, cascade down slopes.

C. divaricatus. SPREADING COTONEASTER. Deciduous.

Zones 1–24. Stiff growth to 6 ft. tall and wide. Dark green leaves closely set on branches turn orange-red in fall. Egg-shaped, bright red fruits are ½ in. long. Informal hedge, screen, bank planting.

C. glaucophyllus. Evergreen. Zones 11–14, 18–20. To 6–8 ft. tall and broad, with gracefully arching branches clothed in gray-green foliage. Dense clusters of white flowers are followed by dark red berries. Attractive in shrub beds or as informal hedge.

C. horizontalis. ROCK COTONEASTER. Deciduous. Zones A3; 2b–11, 14–24. Can be 2–3 ft. tall, 15 ft. wide, with stiff horizontal branches and many branchlets set in herringbone pattern. Small, roundish, bright green leaves turn orange and red before falling. Leafless period may be brief. Showy red fruit. Effective when given enough room to spread; disfigured by cutting branches short to accommodate traffic. Fine bank cover or low traffic barrier. 'Hessei' grows 18 in. high and resists spider mites and fireblight. 'Variegatus' has leaves edged in white. *C. h. perpusillus* (*C. perpusillus*) is smaller, more compact.

C. microphyllus. ROCK-SPRAY COTONEASTER. Evergreen. Zones A3; 2–9, 14–24. Its horizontal branches trail and root, forming a mass 6 ft. across; secondary branches grow erect to 2–3 ft. Leaves are very small (⅓ in.), green, and gray beneath. Fruit is rosy red. Effective in rock gardens or on banks. 'Cooperi', a miniature mound-forming selection to 1 ft. across, is a good rock garden plant.

C. salicifolius. WILLOW-LEAF COTONEASTER. Evergreen or semievergreen. Zones 3b–24. Shrub to 15–18 ft. tall and wide, with narrow, dark green leaves 1–3½ in. long and bright red fruits. Graceful screening or background plant but can be invasive. Some shade in low desert. Better known are the trailing forms used as groundcover. 'Emerald Carpet' is 12–15 in. tall, to 8 ft. wide, with compact habit and small leaves. 'Herbstfeuer' ('Autumn Fire') grows 2–3 ft. high and up to 8 ft. wide. 'Repens' is similar in appearance; it is sometimes grafted to a tall stem of some other cotoneaster species and used as a weeping tree. 'Scarlet Leader' grows 1–2 ft. high and bears a heavy crop of red berries.

CARE

All cotoneasters thrive with little or no maintenance. In fact, they look better and produce better crops of berries if planted on dry slopes (where they can reduce erosion) or in poor soil rather than in rich, moist garden soil. While some medium and tall growers can be sheared, they look best when allowed to maintain natural fountain shapes. Prune only to enhance graceful arch of branches. Keep medium growers looking young by pruning out portion of oldest wood each year. Prune groundcovers to remove dead or awkward branches. Give flat growers room to spread. Don't plant near walk or drive where branch ends will need stubbing. Some cotoneasters are susceptible to fireblight.

Cotyledon
Crassulaceae
SUCCULENT SHRUBS

✎ **ZONES VARY BY SPECIES; OR INDOORS**

☼ ◑ **SUN OR LIGHT SHADE**

◐ ◖ **LITTLE TO MODERATE WATER**

Cotyledon orbiculata

South African natives that vary in size and appearance. Easily grown from cuttings, and handsome in containers, raised beds, or open ground beds. Aphids may attack during bloom season.

C. orbiculata. PIG'S EAR. Zones 12, 13, 16, 17, 21–24.

Grows quickly to 3 ft. tall, 2 ft. wide. Opposing pairs of fleshy leaves are 2–3 in. long, rounded, gray-green to nearly white, narrowly edged red. Green-leafed forms are available. Flower stems rise above plant and carry clusters of orange, bell-shaped, drooping flowers in summer. Good landscaping shrub in mild climates and well-drained soils. Splendid container plant. *C. o. oblonga* 'Macrantha' grows 2–3 ft. high and wide with pale green leaves and orange-red flowers.

C. undulata. SILVER CROWN. Zones 17, 23, 24. Striking 1½-ft. plant with broad, thick leaves dusted with white powder. Wavy leaf edges. Orange, clustered flowers in spring and early summer. Overhead watering washes off powder.

Crabapple
Rosaceae
DECIDUOUS FRUIT TREES

✎ **ZONES A1–A3; 1–9, 11–21**

☼ **FULL SUN**

◖ **REGULAR WATER DURING FRUIT DEVELOPMENT**

Crabapples

Crabapple is a small, usually tart apple, used alone for jelly and pickling, and with apples to give cider its tang. For those grown for their springtime flowers and small, typically inedible, colorful fruit, see flowering crabapple, described under *Malus*.

Of the crabapple varieties grown for fruit, one of the most popular is 'Transcendent', with 2-in., red-blushed yellow crabapples that ripen in summer. Others include 'Centennial' and 'Dolgo', both with 1½-in. fruit;

that of 'Centennial' is sweet. 'Evereste' bears red, round, tart 1-in. fruit.

To yield well, crabapple trees need about 600 hours of temperatures at 45°F (7°C) or lower. In coldest areas, crabapples should be grafted onto hardy rootstocks (for more information, see Apple).

Crambe
Brassicaceae
PERENNIALS

✎ **ZONES A2, A3; 2–9, 14–17**

☼ ◑ **FULL SUN OR LIGHT SHADE**

◖ **REGULAR WATER**

Crambe maritima

Two useful cabbage relatives in this genus; both are ornamental, one is edible. They produce large, smooth blue-green leaves like those of cabbage and large, loose heads of small, honey-scented, white flowers in summer. The leaves turn yellow and fade after bloom, leaving an empty space to plant with annuals. Watch out for cabbage worms on foliage.

C. cordifolia. From the Caucasus. Forms a 2–3-ft. mound of long-stalked, 1–3-ft.-long leaves. Intricately branched flowering stems bear huge, billowing cloud of blossoms. When in bloom, it may occupy a space 6 ft. high, 4–6 ft. wide.

C. maritima. SEA KALE. From coastal northern Europe; naturalized on the Oregon coast. To 2 ft. tall and wide; blue-green leaves a foot wide. In Europe (but apparently not in the U.S.), plants are blanched in late winter or early spring by covering with pots or a deep mulch; the pale sprouts are harvested like asparagus. Grow from seed.

Crassula
Crassulaceae
SUCCULENT PERENNIALS

✎ **ZONES 8, 9, 12–24, EXCEPT AS NOTED; OR INDOORS**

☼ **FULL SUN, EXCEPT AS NOTED; BRIGHT LIGHT**

◐ **LITTLE TO NO WATER**

Crassula ovata

These are mostly South Africa natives. All have succulent foliage; in many it creates strange geometric forms. Excellent in containers.

C. arborescens (C. atropurpurea arborescens). SILVER JADE PLANT, SILVER DOLLAR. A shrubby, heavy-branched plant much like jade plant (*C. ovata*), but with gray-green, red-edged, red-dotted leaves. Produces summer flowers (usually seen only on old plants) that are star-shaped, white aging to pink. Good change of pace from jade plant; smaller and slower growing.

C. argentea. See *C. ovata*.

C. capitella thyrsiflora (C. corymbulosa). To 6–30 in. high and a little wider than tall. Slightly branched, with rosettes of long, triangular, fleshy leaves; leaves are dark red when plant is grown in intense sunlight and poor soil. Tiny white flowers in summer. 'Campfire' (may also be sold as *C. coccinea* or *C. erusola*) has spreading growth, 6–12 in. high with bright green leaves edged with bright orange-red. It is frost sensitive.

C. lactea. Spreading, semi-shrubby plant grows 1–2 ft. tall and 3 ft. wide, with fleshy dark green leaves. Bears white flowers in 4–6-in. clusters during fall. Grows in shade, even dense shade.

C. 'Morgan's Pink' ('Morgan's Pride'). Fine miniature hybrid. Densely packed, fleshy leaves in tight cluster to 4 in. high and wide. Big, brushlike clusters of pink flowers are nearly as big as the plant; spring bloom.

C. mucosa (C. lycopodioides). WATCH CHAIN. Leafy, branching, erect stems to 1 ft. high and wide, closely packed with tiny green leaves in four rows; effect is that of braided chain or of some strange green coral. Very small, inconspicuous greenish flowers. Easy to grow and useful in dish gardens.

C. multicava. Zones 8, 9, 12–24; H1, H2. To 1–1½ ft. high, 3 ft. wide. Dark green, spreading groundcover or hanging plant. Loose clusters of light pink flowers that resemble mosquitoes bloom in late winter and spring. Rampant grower in sun or shade, in any soil.

C. nudicaulis platyphylla. To 8–12 in. high and wide with 1-in.-wide green new leaves that pick up deeper maroon tones as they age. Small yellow flower clusters in summer.

C. ovata (C. argentea). JADE PLANT. Zones 8, 9, 12–24; H1, H2. Sometimes sold as *C. portulacea*. Top-notch houseplant, large container plant, landscaping shrub in mildest climates. Use only as potted plant in hottest desert regions. Plant has a stout trunk and sturdy limbs; stays small in container. Can reach 9 ft. high, half as wide, but is usually smaller. Leaves are thick, oblong, fleshy pads 1–2 in. long, glossy green, sometimes with red-tinged edges. 'Crosby's Dwarf' is a low, compact grower; variegated kinds are 'Sunset' (yellow-tinged red) and 'Tricolor' (green, white, and pinkish). 'Gollum' and 'Hobbit' have reddish, concave leaf tips. Clusters of pink, star-shaped flowers bloom in profusion, from fall into spring. Good near swimming pools.

C. perfoliata falcata (C. falcata). Zones 8, 9, 12–24; H1, H2. Grows to 4 ft. high, 2½ ft. wide. Thick, fleshy, gray-green, sickle-shaped leaves are vertically arranged in two overlapping columns on erect stems. Dense clusters of scarlet flowers are held well above the leaves in late summer.

C. pyramidalis. Interesting oddity grows to 3–4 in. high and wide; flat, triangular leaves closely packed in four rows give plant a squarish cross section.

C. schmidtii. Mat-forming, spreading plant to 4 in. tall, 1 ft. wide, with long, slender, rich green leaves. Clusters of small dark rose or purplish flowers put on a show in winter and spring. Good choice for pots or rock gardens.

C. tetragona. Upright plants with treelike habit, 1–2 ft. high and a little narrower. Leaves are narrow, 1 in. long; cream-colored flowers are borne in clusters. Widely used in dish gardens to suggest miniature pine trees.

CARE

Need good drainage. May not survive winter without overhead protection in Zones 8, 9, 12–15, 18–21. To cope with extreme summer heat in Zones 12 and 13, grow in containers or coolest sites (such as a northern exposure).

Crataegus
HAWTHORN
Rosaceae
DECIDUOUS TREES

- ✏ **ZONES 2–12, 14–17, EXCEPT AS NOTED**
- ☀ **FULL SUN**
- 💧 **MODERATE WATER**
- 🦋 **ATTRACT BIRDS, BUTTERFLIES**

Crataegus phaenopyrum

These members of the rose family are known for their clusters of pretty, usually white flowers that appear after the plants leaf out in spring, and for their showy fruit resembling tiny apples in summer and fall (and often into winter). Typically multitrunked, with thorny branches. Attract bees, birds.

C. ambigua. RUSSIAN HAWTHORN. Zones 1–10, 14. Native to southeastern Russia, Turkey, and Iran. Extremely cold-hardy. To 15–25 ft. tall and as wide or wider. Vase-shaped form and twisting branches give attractive silhouette. Leaves to 2½ in. long, deeply cut. Profuse small red fruit.

C. crus-galli inermis. THORNLESS COCKSPUR THORN. Native to eastern U.S. and Canada. Zones 1–12, 14–17. To 20–30 ft. high, 20–35 ft. wide. Smooth-textured, tooth-edged leaves are glossy dark green, turning orange to red in fall. Dull orange-red fruit.

C. laevigata (C. oxyacantha). ENGLISH HAWTHORN. Zones A2, A3; 2–12, 14–17. Native to Europe and North Africa. To 18–25 ft. high and 15–20 ft. wide. Leaves have toothed lobes. Best known through its varieties, among them 'Paul's Scarlet', with clusters of double rose to red flowers; 'Double White' and 'Double Pink', double-flowered forms that set little fruit; and 'Crimson Cloud' ('Superba'), with white-centered, bright red single flowers and vivid red fruit. All have toothed, lobed, 2-in. leaves that lack good fall color. In Northwest, susceptible to a leaf spot fungus that can defoliate trees in late spring to early summer.

C. × lavallei (C. carrierei). CARRIERE HAWTHORN. Zones 3–12, 14–21. To 25 ft. with 15–20-ft. spread. More erect and open branching than other hawthorns, with less twiggy growth. Dark green, leathery, toothed leaves are 2–4 in. long, turn bronze-red after first sharp frost and hang on well into winter. Loose clusters of ¾-in., orange to red fruit last all winter. Fruit makes a mess on walks.

C. monogyna. Zones 1–12, 14–17. From Europe, North Africa, and western Asia. Classic hedge plant of English countryside. The popular upright variety 'Stricta' grows to 30 ft. tall and 8 ft. wide; plant 5 ft. apart for a dense, narrow screen.

C. oxyacantha. See *C. laevigata*.

C. phaenopyrum (C. cordata). WASHINGTON THORN. Native to southeastern U.S. Moderate growth to 25 ft. with 20-ft. spread. Graceful, open limb structure. Glossy, 2–3-in.-long leaves with three to five sharp-pointed lobes (like some maples); foliage turns beautiful orange, scarlet, or purplish in fall. Shiny red fruit hangs on well into winter. More graceful and delicate than other hawthorns; preferred street or lawn tree. One of the least prone to fireblight.

C. 'Toba'. Zones A3; 1–10. Canadian hybrid with great cold tolerance. To 20 ft. tall and a bit wider. Leaves are similar to those of *C. × lavallei*. Double white flowers age to pink. Sparse crop of large fruit. 'Snowbird' is similar but slightly more upright with double white flowers.

C. viridis. GREEN HAWTHORN. Native to eastern U.S. To 25–30 ft. high and wide, with broad, spreading crown. Fall color varies; it can be showy yellow to orange. Clustered white flowers are followed by red fruit. 'Winter King' is vase-shaped, with silvery stems and larger red fruit that lasts all winter; it's an attractive and trouble-free hawthorn.

CARE

Hawthorns will grow in any soil as long as it is well drained. It's best to grow them under somewhat austere conditions, since good soil, regular moisture, and fertilizer promote succulent new growth that is particularly susceptible to fireblight. The disease makes entire branches die back quickly. Aphids and scale are potential pests. The plants usually need some pruning to thin out excess twiggy growth. Many hawthorns produce water sprouts, which should also be pruned out.

Green hawthorn (*Crataegus viridis*) is especially beautiful in fall. That's when its leaves turn a vibrant bronze-orange, and its glossy red berries attract birds.

C

Cress, Garden
Brassicaceae
ANNUAL

- 🌿 **ALL ZONES**
- ☼ ◑ **FULL SUN OR PARTIAL SHADE**
- ● **REGULAR TO AMPLE WATER**

Garden cress

Garden cress is sometimes called pepper grass because of its peppery taste. It comes in broad- and curly-leafed forms. The broad-leafed form is used most often in soups; both kinds are used in sandwiches and salads. The curly-leafed form can also be used as a garnish.

CARE

Easy to grow as long as weather is cool. Sow seeds as early in spring as possible. Plant in rich, moist soil. Make rows 1 ft. apart; thin plants to 3 in. apart (eat thinnings). Cress matures fast; make successive sowings every 2 weeks up to middle of May. Where frosts are mild, sow through fall and winter. Try growing garden cress in shallow pots of soil or planting mix in a sunny kitchen window. It sprouts in a few days, can be harvested (with scissors) in 2 to 3 weeks. Or grow it by sprinkling seeds on pads of wet cheesecloth; keep damp until harvest in 2 weeks.

Both leaves and stems of garden cress have a delicate peppery taste, great for flavoring salads and sandwiches. Young shoots are especially spicy.

Crinum and × Amarcrinum
Amaryllidaceae
PERENNIALS FROM BULBS

- 🌿 **ZONES 8, 9, 12–24; H1, H2; EXCEPT AS NOTED; OR INDOORS**
- ☼ ◑ **SOME SHADE IN HOTTEST CLIMATES; BRIGHT FILTERED LIGHT**
- ● ●● **REGULAR TO AMPLE WATER**
- ◆ **ALL PARTS ARE POISONOUS IF INGESTED**

Crinum asiaticum procerum 'Splendens'

These tough perennial bulbs produce lush foliage and large, impressive lilylike flowers. They are native to many warm and tropical parts of the world. Each bulb tapers to an elongated, stemlike neck, from which radiate long, broad, strap-shaped leaves. They are evergreen in mild-winter climates if given year-round moisture. The thick stems to 4 ft. or taller rise from the foliage, each bearing a cluster of long-stalked flowers. Blossoms resemble those of naked lady (*Amaryllis belladonna*), but they're twice as big and open out a bit wider. Many are highly fragrant; colors include white and many shades of pink, from light to dark. Most bloom in spring or summer; flowering goes on all year in Hawaii.

C. asiaticum. SPIDER LILY, GRAND CRINUM, ST. JOHN'S LILY. Zones 20–24. From Southeast Asia. Can form a mass 4–6 ft. high, 7 ft. wide. Clusters of large, spidery-looking, fragrant white flowers, 6–8 in. across. Tolerant of poor soils, salt, drought, light shade. *C. a. procerum* is an even larger plant. Its variety 'Splendens',

with purple leaves and pink flowers, is called Queen Emma lily, as is the following species.

C. augustum. QUEEN EMMA LILY. Zones 20–24. From Mauritius and Seychelles. Similar to *C. asiaticum* but slightly larger, with wider white flower segments and dark red markings.

C. bulbispermum (C. longifolium). From South Africa. Long, narrow, twisting gray-green leaves tend to lie on the ground. Fragrant flowers are deep pink.

C. 'Ellen Bosanquet'. Broad bright green leaves. Flowers are deep rose, nearly red; fragrant.

C. moorei. From South Africa. Large (6–8 in. wide) bulbs with stemlike necks to 1 ft. or longer. Long, thin, wavy-edged bright green leaves. Fragrant, bell-shaped flowers typically are soft pink, though colors run from white to pinkish red.

C. × powellii. Resembles *C. moorei* (one of its parents) but has fragrant flowers on shorter (2 ft.) stems. Range of flower colors is similar to that of *C. moorei*. 'Album' is a pure white form, vigorous enough to serve as a tall groundcover in shade.

× Amarcrinum memoria-corsii (Crinodonna corsii). Hybrid between *Amaryllis belladonna* and *C. moorei*. Resembles *Crinum* in growth habit and foliage, but its soft pink, very fragrant flowers look more like those of *Amaryllis belladonna*, with narrower funnel shape than blooms of most crinums.

CARE

Bulbs generally are available year-round, but spring and fall are best times to plant. Amend soil with plenty of humus. Set bulbs 2–4 ft. apart, with tops of necks even with soil surface. Divide infrequently. Protect from snails and slugs. In colder part of range, mulch heavily in winter; move plants in containers to a frost-proof location. These plants (especially *C. × powellii* and × *Amarcrinum*) are grown as houseplants in most areas; don't let soil dry out.

Crocosmia
Iridaceae
PERENNIALS FROM CORMS

- 🌿 **ZONES VARY BY SPECIES; OR DIG AND STORE**
- ☼ ◑ **SOME SHADE IN HOTTEST CLIMATES**
- ● **REGULAR WATER DURING GROWTH AND BLOOM**
- 🦅 **ATTRACT BIRDS**

Crocosmia 'Lucifer'

These natives of tropical and southern Africa were formerly called tritonia and are related to freesia, ixia, and sparaxis. Like their brethren, they produce sword-shaped leaves in basal clumps. Small orange, red, or yellow flowers bloom in summer (spring in hottest areas) on branched stems.

C. × crocosmiiflora (Tritonia crocosmiiflora). MONTBRETIA. Zones 5–24; H1, H2. A favorite for generations, montbretias can still be seen in older gardens where they have spread freely, producing orange-crimson flowers 1½–2 in. across on 3–4-ft. stems. Sword-shaped leaves grow to 3 ft. tall, ½–1 in. wide. Many once-common named forms in yellow, orange, cream, and near-scarlet are making a comeback. Good for naturalizing on slopes or in fringe areas. Montbretia has established itself in wildlands throughout the Hawaiian Islands.

C. hybrids. Zones 4–24. Among 2-ft.-high choices are 'Citronella', light yellow flowers with dark eye; 'Emily McKenzie', orange with red eye; and 'Solfatare', bronze foliage and yellow flowers. In the 2–3-ft. range are 'Babylon' (orange flowers with scarlet throats), 'Emberglow' (scarlet), 'Jenny Bloom' (golden yellow), 'Voyager' (bright yellow), and 'Walberton Yellow'. 'Lucifer' grows 4 ft. tall; red blossoms.

C. masoniorum. Zones 5–24. Leaves 2½ ft. long, 2 in. wide. Bright orange to orange-scarlet flowers, 1½ in. across, borne in dense, one-sided clusters on 2½–3-ft. stems that arch over at the top. Buds open slowly from base to tip of clusters, and old flowers drop cleanly from stems. Flowers last about 2 weeks when cut.

Plant in well-drained, enriched soil; set corms 2 in. deep, 3 in. apart. Where winter temperatures remain above 10°F (–12°C), needs no winter protection. Where lows range from 10°F to –5°F (–12°C to –21°C), provide winter mulch. In colder areas, dig and store over winter. Divide clumps only when vigor, flower quality begin to decline.

Crocus
Iridaceae
PERENNIALS FROM CORMS

- ZONES 1–24; BEST IN COLD-WINTER AREAS
- FULL SUN DURING BLOOM, LIGHT SHADE AFTER IN HOT CLIMATES
- REGULAR WATER DURING GROWTH AND BLOOM

Crocus sativus

Crocus are low growers, mainly from the Mediterranean region and the Caucasus. All have grasslike leaves. The foliage comes before, with, or after flowers, depending on the species. Flowers in a wide range of colors are 1½–3 in. long, with long, stemlike tubes and flaring or cup-shaped petals.

The short (true) stems are hidden underground.

Most crocuses bloom in winter or earliest spring, but some bloom in fall, the flowers rising from bare earth weeks or days after planting. Mass them for best effect. Attractive in rock gardens, between stepping-stones, in containers.

C. ancyrensis. Small yellow flowers in early winter.

C. angustifolius. CLOTH OF GOLD CROCUS. Formerly *C. susianus*. Orange-gold, starlike flowers with dark brown center stripe. Early-winter blooming.

C. biflorus. SCOTTISH CROCUS. White flowers with yellow throat, striped purple on the outside. Late-winter bloom. Some forms are fall blooming.

C. chrysanthus. Orange-yellow, sweet-scented blooms. Hybrids and selections of the species range from white and cream through yellows and blues, often marked with deeper colors. Usually even more free-flowering than *C. vernus*, but with smaller flowers. Blooms in the spring. Popular varieties include 'Blue Pearl', palest blue; 'Cream Beauty', pale yellow; 'E. P. Bowles', yellow with purple featherings; 'Ladykiller', outside purple-edged white, inside white-feathered purple; 'Princess Beatrix', blue with yellow center; and 'Snow Bunting', pure white.

C. goulimyi. Plant produces deep lavender-blue flowers during fall. Needs warmth, excellent drainage; tolerates warm winters of Southern California.

C. imperati. Bright lilac inside, buff veined with purple outside. Early spring.

C. korolkowii. Bright yellow to bronze-yellow flowers in late winter. Very cold-tolerant.

C. kotschyanus (C. zonatus). Pinkish lavender or lilac flowers in early fall.

C. pulchellus. Pale lilac flowers with purple veins and yellow throat in fall.

C. sativus. SAFFRON CROCUS. Lilac flowers in fall. Orange-red stigma is true saffron of commerce. To harvest saffron, pluck stigmas as soon as flowers open, dry them, and store in glass or plastic vials. Stigmas from a dozen flowers will season a good-size paella or similar dish. For continued good yield of saffron, divide corms as soon

as leaves turn brown; replant in fresh or improved soil.

C. sieberi. Flowers of delicate lavender-blue with golden throat. One of the earliest to bloom in winter.

C. speciosus. Showy blue-violet flowers in early fall. Lavender and mauve varieties available. Fast increase by seed and division. Showiest autumn-flowering crocus.

C. tommasinianus. Slender buds; star-shaped, silvery lavender-blue flowers, sometimes with dark blotch at tips of segments. Blooms very early in the year.

C. vernus. DUTCH CROCUS. Familiar crocus in shades of white, yellow, lavender, and purple, often penciled and streaked. Late-winter or early-spring bloom. This is the most vigorous crocus (and the only one widely sold in all areas).

Set corms 2–3 in. deep, 3–4 in. apart, in light, porous soil. Protect from gophers. Divide every 3 or 4 years. Won't naturalize where winters are warm.

Cryptomeria japonica
JAPANESE CRYPTOMERIA
Cupressaceae
EVERGREEN TREE

- ZONES 4–9, 14–24
- FULL SUN
- REGULAR WATER

Cryptomeria japonica

This graceful conifer is fast growing (3–4 ft. a year) in its youth, eventually becoming a prominent skyline tree to 100 ft. tall and 30 ft. wide at base. Its

straight columnar trunk has thin red-brown bark that peels off in strips. The foliage is soft bright green to bluish green in growing season, turning brownish purple in cold weather. Slightly pendulous branches are clothed in ½–1-in.-long, needlelike leaves. The roundish, red-brown cones are ¾–1 in. wide. These trees are sometimes used in closely planted groves for a Japanese garden effect. Resistant to oak root fungus. Dwarf varieties are most popular.

'Black Dragon'. Vigorous growth to 4–6 ft. tall, then slows and fills in. Light green new growth darkens to deep green, almost black in winter.

'Cristata'. Unusual, twisted, cockscomb-like growth at branch ends. Grows into an upright cone 12–15 ft. tall, 6–7 ft. wide, after 10 years, eventually twice as large.

'Elegans'. PLUME CEDAR, PLUME CRYPTOMERIA. Quite unlike species. Feathery, grayish green foliage turns rich coppery red or purplish in winter. Grows slowly into a dense pyramid 20–60 ft. tall, about 20 ft. wide. Trunks may lean or curve. For effective display, give it room. 'Elegans Aurea' is similar but turns yellow in winter.

'Kitayama'. Narrow upright (to 15–18 ft. tall and 8–10 ft. wide), more compact form and better winter color make this an improvement over 'Yoshino'.

'Nana'. Upright dwarf grows very slowly to 4 ft. high and wide. Dark green foliage.

'Pygmaea' ('Nana'). DWARF CRYPTOMERIA. Bushy dwarf 1½–2 ft. high, 2½ ft. wide. Dark green, needlelike leaves; twisted branches.

'Sekkan-sugi'. Slow-growing, cone-shaped tree to 18–25 ft. high and 12–20 ft. wide. New growth is creamy yellow.

'Tansu'. An extreme dwarf, seldom exceeding 15 in. high and wide.

'Vilmoriniana'. Slow-growing dwarf to 1–2 ft. high and wide. Fluffy gray-green foliage turns bronze during late fall and winter. Rock garden or container plant.

'Yoshino'. Resembles the species but is smaller (to 30–40 ft. tall and 20 ft. wide), with bluish green foliage that takes on reddish tones in winter.

C

Cucumber
Cucurbitaceae
ANNUAL VINE

✎ ALL ZONES

☼ FULL SUN

💧 REGULAR WATER

Lemon cucumber

Most cucumbers are trailing vines that need at least 25 sq. ft. to sprawl, but you can run vines up a fence or trellis to conserve space. Seeds require warm soil to sprout, and flowers need heat for pollination.

There are long, smooth, green, slicing cucumbers like 'Marketmore 76'; numerous small pickling cucumbers like 'Alibi'; and roundish, yellow, mild-flavored lemon cucumbers. Novelty varieties include an Asian type called 'Suyo Long' (long, slim, and very mild), Armenian cucumber (actually a long, curving, pale green, ribbed melon with cucumber look and mild cucumber flavor), and English greenhouse cucumber. The last type must be grown in a greenhouse to avoid pollination by bees and subsequent loss of form and flavor; when well grown, it's the mildest of all cucumbers.

Bush cucumbers like 'Fanfare' and other varieties with compact vines take up little garden space. Burpless varieties resemble hothouse cucumbers in shape and mild flavor but can be grown out-of-doors. They are called burpless because the skin can be eaten without causing indigestion. Pickling cucumbers should be harvested as soon as they have reached the proper size—tiny for sweet pickles (gherkins), larger for dills or pickle slices.

How to Grow Cucumbers

SHOPPING Catalogs are specific about cucumber pollination requirements. Most cucumbers bear male and female flowers on the same plant, so bees cross-pollinate them easily. But some produce only female flowers; when you buy these, a few seeds in the packet will be marked to show that they will produce male plants. You must plant at least one of these for every six female plants. Some cucumbers produce seedless fruit without a pollinator, so they're popular both outdoors and in bee-free greenhouses. 'Diva' and 'Sweet Success' are mild-tasting and seedless.

PLANTING Plant seeds in a sunny spot 1 to 2 weeks after the average date of last frost. To grow cucumbers on trellis (the best way to keep them straight), plant seeds 1 in. deep and 1–3 ft. apart, and permit main stem to reach top of support. In containers, plant three bush cucumbers in a wide, 12-in.-deep pot with a tomato cage on it. Pick while young to ensure continued production.

WATERING & FEEDING Apply water in furrows or drip irrigation—never overhead (encourages downy mildew). Feed after plants start vigorous growth, then repeat a month later.

CHALLENGES Row covers will protect seedlings from slugs, snails, and insect pests, including cucumber beetles and flea beetles; remove covers when flowering begins so that pollination can occur.

Whiteflies are a potential pest late in season. Misshapen fruit is usually due to uneven watering or poor pollination; bitter fruit is usually a result of uneven irrigation.

Cunninghamia lanceolata
CHINA FIR
Cupressaceae
EVERGREEN TREE

✎ ZONES 4–6, 14–21

☼ FULL SUN

💧 MODERATE WATER

Cunninghamia lanceolata

This picturesque conifer from China has a heavy trunk; stout, whorled branches; and drooping branchlets. It grows at a moderate rate to 30 ft. tall with 20-ft. spread. Stiff, needlelike, sharp-pointed leaves are 1½–2½ in. long, green above and whitish beneath. Its brown, 1–2-in. cones are interesting but not profuse. Among palest of needled evergreens in spring and summer, China fir turns red-bronze in cold winters. 'Glauca', with striking gray-blue foliage, is more widely grown and hardier than the species. The dwarf 'Little Leo' slowly forms a flattened mound of bright green foliage that turns bronze to purple in winter.

CARE

Needs protection from hot, dry wind in summer and cold wind in winter. Becomes less attractive as it ages. Prune out dead branchlets.

China fir is a large tree, prized for timber in Asia. But for small gardens, dwarf forms are best; 'Little Leo' is lovely in a container.

Cupaniopsis anacardioides
CARROT WOOD
Sapindaceae
EVERGREEN TREE

✎ ZONES 16–24; H1, H2

☼ FULL SUN

💧 ANY AMOUNT OF WATER

Cupaniopsis anacardioides

This tough Australian native is loved by some, loathed by others. It has a slow to moderate growth rate to 40 ft. tall and 30 ft. wide. Its glossy dark green leaves are divided into 6 to 10 leathery, 4-in.-long leaflets.

Carrot wood tolerates seacoast conditions, heat, drought, and poor soils. It is generally neat in appearance, but as the trees approach maturity, they may produce marble-size, leathery yellow to orange fruit that splits but does not squash or stain. Some trees fruit heavily enough to be an annoyance, while others never fruit, for reasons not understood. One theory is that young trees selected for unusual vigor and broader-than-usual leaflets will produce less fruit than others. Another is that trees under stress tend to develop more female flowers, hence more fruit. It is also believed that thinning out the tree every 2 years or so will result in production of young, nonfruiting wood. In its younger years, it makes an attractive, well-behaved tree. Consider underplanting with a groundcover deep enough to swallow the fruit drop, but be prepared to pull volunteer seedlings when they appear. Many landscape architects feel that the tree's virtues outweigh its faults.

Cuphea
Lythraceae
EVERGREEN SHRUBS OR WOODY PERENNIALS

⚡ **ZONES 16–24; H1, H2; EXCEPT AS NOTED; ANNUALS ANYWHERE**

☀ ◑ **FULL SUN OR PARTIAL SHADE**

💧 **REGULAR WATER**

🦎 **FLOWERS ATTRACT HUMMINGBIRDS**

Cuphea llavea

These natives of Mexico and Central America provide color throughout warm months. Use them in small beds, as formal edging for borders, along paths, or in containers. Reliably perennial only in frost-free areas, though they may survive light frosts in Zones 16, 17, 21–23. *C. hyssopifolia* and *C. ignea* have both naturalized on Hawaii (Big Island).

C. hyssopifolia. FALSE HEATHER, HAWAIIAN HEATHER, MEXICAN HEATHER. Grows 1–2 ft. tall, to about 2½ ft. wide. Flexible, leafy branchlets clothed in very narrow, ½–¾-in.-long leaves. Tiny flowers (scarcely half as long as leaves) in pink, purple, or white. Plants in the Itsy Bitsy series grow 8 in. tall, 18 in. wide; they're excellent in rock gardens. 'Caribbean Sunset', to 2 ft. tall, has orange blooms. 'Riverdene Gold', 1 ft. tall and 2 ft. wide, has golden foliage and deep pink blooms.

C. ignea. CIGAR PLANT. Zones 11–13, 16–24; H1, H2. Leafy, compact plant to 1 ft. or taller, as wide as tall. Narrow dark green leaves, 1–1½ in. long. The appearance of the flowers explains the "cigar" of the common name: they're tubular, ¾ in. long, bright orange-red with white tip and dark ring at end. 'David Verity' has orange-red blooms. 'Starfire' has a pink flower tube and purple petals.

C. llavea. BAT-FACED CUPHEA. Zones 11–13, 21–24; H1, H2. To 2–3 ft. tall, 3 ft. wide. Leaves to 3 in. long. Red-and-purple, 1½-in.-long flowers are said to look like a bat's face. Occasionally spreads by seed in gardens. Though cultivated in the desert, it is not drought-tolerant—in nature, it grows along stream banks in Mexico. Compact varieties (12–16 in. high, 18 in. wide) include 'Flamenco Rumba', coral red flowers; 'Flamenco Tango', vibrant pink blooms; and 'Totally Tempted', bright red blooms.

C. micropetala. To 4 ft. tall, 3–4 ft. wide. Arching stems closely set with narrow, 5-in. leaves and topped by a slender, spikelike cluster of 1½-in., bright red flowers tipped with yellow. Deciduous in cold weather.

C. × purpurea. Zones 11–13, 21–24; H1, H2. Hybrid to 1–1½ ft. high and wide; excellent as a groundcover or spilling from a hanging basket. Red flowers to 1¼ in. long; dark green leaves. 'Firecracker' has dark purple flowers with two earlike bright red petals. 'Firefly' bears magenta petals with a white ring in the center.

CARE

Pinch tips of shoots for compact growth; severely cut back older plants in late fall or early spring. Easy to grow from cuttings.

In summer, Cuphea llavea covers itself with lipstick red blooms that resemble little bat faces. Pair compact varieties with lacy white 'Diamond Frost' euphorbia or a fringe of 'Angelina' sedum.

Cupressus
CYPRESS
Cupressaceae
EVERGREEN TREES

⚡ **ZONES VARY BY SPECIES**

☀ **FULL SUN**

◌ ◐ **LITTLE TO MODERATE WATER, EXCEPT AS NOTED**

Cupressus cashmeriana

These conifers have tiny scale-like leaves that are closely set on cordlike branches and bear interesting globular, golf ball–size cones made up of shield-shaped scales. They need little pruning.

C. arizonica. ARIZONA CYPRESS. Zones 7–24. Native to central Arizona. To 40 ft. tall, 20 ft. wide. Seedlings variable, with foliage from green to blue-gray or silvery. Rough, furrowed bark. *C. a. glabra* (often sold as *C. glabra*) is virtually identical to the species but has smooth cherry red bark. Other forms include 'Blue Pyramid' and 'Blue Ice', forming dense blue-gray pyramids to at least 20–25 ft. high; 'Carolina Sapphire', to 30 ft. with steely blue-green foliage and a broad, symmetrical form; 'Gareei', with silvery blue-green foliage; and compact, symmetrical 'Pyramidalis'. Mass for windbreak or screen.

C. cashmeriana. KASHMIR CYPRESS. Zones 8, 9, 14–24. Native to Kashmir and Tibet. Striking, narrowly pyramidal tree, 40–60 ft. tall and 15–20 ft. wide. Main branches are upright but produce beautiful long, pendulous, flattened branchlets of aromatic blue-green foliage. Best with regular water. Not tolerant of strong winds or extreme heat.

C. forbesii. TECATE CYPRESS. Zones 8–14, 18–20. Native to coastal mountains of Southern California. Low-branching tree to 10–25 ft. tall and 20 ft. wide, with cherry red bark and green foliage. Very fast growing. In fact, it may get too top-heavy for size of root system; keep on the dry side to slow growth, thus lessening likelihood that tree will topple in strong winds. Useful as hedge or screen.

C. macrocarpa. MONTEREY CYPRESS. Best in Zone 17. Native to California's Monterey Peninsula. Beautiful tree to 40 ft. or taller, with rich bright green foliage. Narrow and pyramidal in youth, spreading as wide as high as it grows older; picturesque in age, especially in windy coastal conditions. Away from cool coastal winds, it is very subject to coryneum canker fungus, for which there is no cure. Look for foliage that first turns yellow, then deep reddish brown, and falls off slowly. Destroy infected trees. A fast-growing windbreak tree in coastal conditions. 'Goldcrest' ('Lemon Yellow') has yellowish green, lemon-scented foliage, stays conical to 30 ft. tall, and reportedly is more tolerant to inland conditions. 'Wilma Goldcrest', similar to and often confused with 'Wilma', appears to be like 'Goldcrest' but more compact to 15 ft. tall.

C. sempervirens. ITALIAN CYPRESS. Zones 4–24; H1, H2; best in Zones 8–15, 18–21. Native to southern Europe and western Asia. Species has horizontal branches and dark green foliage, but variants such as 'Stricta' ('Fastigiata'), columnar Italian cypress, and 'Glauca', blue Italian cypress (blue-green in color), are more common and are classic Mediterranean landscaping plants; both are dense, narrow trees to 60 ft. high and 5–10 ft. wide at maturity. 'Swane's Golden' is a narrowly columnar form with golden yellow new growth. 'Tiny Tower' is a slow, dense grower that reaches only 8 ft. tall and 2 ft. wide after 10 years; foliage is deep blue-green.

C

× Cuprocyparis

Cupressaceae

EVERGREEN TREE

🌿 **ZONES 3B–24**

☼ **FULL SUN**

💧 **MODERATE TO REGULAR WATER**

× Cuprocyparis

A hybrid between *Chamaecyparis nootkatensis* and *Cupressus macrocarpa*, this conifer grows very fast—from cuttings to 15–20 ft. high in 5 years. It is most often planted as quick screen. In gardens, it usually reaches 60–70 ft. tall by 8–15 ft. wide and can be pruned into a tall (10–15 ft.) hedge but will quickly get away from you without regular maintenance. Long, slender, upright branches with flattened gray-green foliage sprays give youthful trees a narrow, pyramidal form, though they can become open and floppy. It produces small cones composed of scales.

'Naylor's Blue' has grayish blue foliage; 'Castlewellan' has golden new growth and narrow, erect habit; 'Golconda' has a more refined, formal pyramidal habit with bright lemon yellow new growth; 'Gold Rider' also has golden new growth and eventually forms a pyramid 35 ft. high by 15 ft. wide; and 'Emerald Isle' has bright green foliage on a plant 20–25 ft. tall, 6–8 ft. wide.

CARE

Will accept a wide variety of soils and climate conditions. It also takes strong wind. To maintain as a hedge, shear several times during the growing season, making sure not to cut into old wood. In warm-summer regions, loses stiff, upright habit and is subject to coryneum canker fungus, reaching only 30–40 ft. tall before dying from the disease (see *Cupressus macrocarpa* for information on this fungus).

Curcuma alismatifolia

SIAM TULIP

Zingiberaceae

PERENNIAL FROM RHIZOMES

🌿 **ZONES 14–24; H1, H2; OR DIG AND STORE**

☼ **FULL SUN OR LIGHT SHADE**

💧 **AMPLE WATER DURING GROWTH AND BLOOM**

Curcuma alismatifolia

This perennial from Thailand is not unlike a tulip in appearance (hence the common name), but it's actually a ginger rather than a tulip. It grows 2 ft. tall with foliage like small canna leaves. The flowering stem is topped by a cluster of pink, rose, or white bracts that hide tiny flowers. The inflorescence is shaped a bit like a flaring pinecone. Each blossom lasts for several weeks and is replaced by others as new plants arise from the rhizome. Plant goes dormant in winter.

CARE

Plant in the spring, setting rhizomes 1 in. deep and 6 in. apart. Blooms from early summer to early fall. Beyond its hardiness range, dig and store over winter, being careful not to damage the bulbous storage organs on the roots.

Currant

Grossulariaceae

DECIDUOUS SHRUB

🌿 **ZONES A1–A3; 1–6, 15–17**

☼ ◐ ● **SOME SHADE IN HOTTEST CLIMATES**

💧 **REGULAR WATER**

Currants

These many-stemmed, thornless shrubs grow to 3–5 ft. high and wide, depending on vigor and variety. They have attractive lobed, toothed leaves to 3 in. wide that drop early in fall, sometimes turning bright red, orange, or yellow first. Drooping clusters of white or yellowish flowers bloom in early spring, and are followed in summer by fruit used for jellies, jams, preserves. For ornamental relatives, see *Ribes*.

Like other members of *Ribes*, currant may be host to white pine blister rust and is still banned in some areas where white pines grow; check with your Cooperative Extension Office or a local nursery for regulations in your area.

Black currants, derived from *R. nigrum* or *R. aureum* (see descriptions under *Ribes*), have rich, pungent flavor and are good in jams and preserves. Since they are the most favored host of white pine blister rust, grow rust-immune hybrids such as 'Consort', 'Crandall', 'Mina Smyriou', and 'Titania'. 'Ben Sarek' has good-quality fruit on compact, mildew- and rust-resistant plants.

Red and white currants, derived from *R. sativum*, are less likely to be hosts to the rust. These tart fruits are used mainly for jelly. Red-fruited varieties include 'Cherry', 'Jonkheer Van Tets', 'Red Lake', and 'Wilder'; white types include 'Blanca' and 'Primus'.

CARE

Generally self-fruitful. Do not grow where water or soil is high in sodium. Mulch well. Prune during dormant season. On red and white currants, cut stems older than 3 years to the ground; on black currants, remove stems older than 2 years. Older canes are often darker and peeling. Currant worm can defoliate plants; control with *Bacillus thuringiensis* (Bt).

Cyathea cooperi

AUSTRALIAN TREE FERN

Cyatheaceae

TREE FERN

🌿 **ZONES 15–24; H1, H2**

☼ ◐ **PARTIAL SHADE IN HOTTEST CLIMATES**

💧 **REGULAR WATER**

Cyathea cooperi

This is the fastest growing of the fairly hardy tree ferns, able to withstand lows to 20°F (–7°C), but with some damage to the fronds. It will eventually reach 20 ft. tall and 12 ft. wide but starts out as a low, wide clump (can spread from 1 ft. to as much as 6 ft. in a year) before growing upward. It has broad, bright green, finely cut fronds. The brownish hairs on the leafstalks and leaf undersurfaces can irritate skin, so wear long sleeves, hat, and neckcloth when grooming plants. Reasonably certain to survive in sheltered places along coast and in warm coastal valleys of California.

Becoming a pest in Hawaiian rain forests. 'Brentwood' is a more robust form. Often sold as *Alsophila australis, A. cooperi,* or *Sphaeropteris cooperi.*

FOR MORE ON FERNS, SEE "MEET THE FERNS," PAGE 320.

Cycas
Cycadaceae
CYCADS

⚡ **ZONES VARY BY SPECIES**

◑ **PARTIAL SHADE**

💧 **REGULAR WATER**

Cycas revoluta

Neither ferns nor palms, these evergreen plants are primitive, cone-bearing relatives of conifers and are excellent for tropical effects. A rosette of dark green, feathery leaves grows from a central point at the top of a single trunk (sometimes several trunks). They are eventually as wide as tall. Female plants bear conspicuous, egg-shaped red to orange seeds.

C. circinalis. QUEEN SAGO. Zones 23, 24; H1, H2. Native to Old World tropics. Beautiful specimen plant to 20 ft. tall. Graceful, drooping leaves to 8 ft. long atop unbranched trunk. Protect from frost.

C. revoluta. SAGO PALM. Zones 8–24; H1, H2; hardy to 15°F (–9°C). Native to Japan. As a 2–3-ft.-tall youngster, has an airy, fernlike appearance; with age (grows very slowly to as high as 10 ft.), looks more like a palm. Leaves are 2–3 ft. long (larger on very old plants), divided into many narrow, leathery segments. Tough, tolerant patio or houseplant; also good subject for bonsai.

Cyclamen
Primulaceae
PERENNIALS FROM TUBERS

⚡ **ZONES VARY BY SPECIES**

☼ ◑ **FULL SUN OR PARTIAL SHADE**

💧 **REGULAR WATER**

💧 **TOXIC IF EATEN IN LARGE QUANTITIES**

Cyclamen persicum
'Winter Ice White'

Native to Europe, the Mediterranean region, and Asia, these lovely perennials are grown for their pretty flowers carried atop an attractive clump of basal leaves. The blossoms resemble shooting stars or butterflies, and typically come in white and shades of pink, rose, red. Most go through near-leafless or leafless dormant period at some time during summer.

Large-flowered florists' cyclamen (*C. persicum*) is most often seen as a container-grown gift plant, though it is increasingly being used as a bedding plant in favorable climates. The other species described here are smaller-flowered, hardier plants better adapted to outdoor culture. Use them in rock gardens, in naturalized clumps under trees, or as carpets under camellias, rhododendrons, and large noninvasive ferns. Hardy types also grow well under native oaks. All are good container plants if grown out of direct sun.

C. × atkinsii. Zones 4–9, 14–24. Crimson flowers on 4–6-in. stems in winter. Deep green, silver-mottled leaves. There are also varieties with pink or white blooms.

C. cilicium. Zones 3–9, 14–24. Fragrant pale pink flowers with purple blotches on 2–6-in.

stems, fall into winter. Leaves are mottled. 'Album' has white blossoms.

C. coum. Zones 2–9, 14–24. Deep crimson-rose flowers on 4–6-in. stems in winter and early spring. Round deep green leaves. Varieties with pink or white flowers are available.

C. europaeum. See *C. purpurascens.*

C. hederifolium (C. neapolitanum). Zones 2–9, 14–24. Large light green leaves marbled silver and white. Rose-pink flowers bloom on 3–4-in. stems in late summer, early fall. One of the most vigorous and easiest to grow; very reliable in cold-winter climates. Set tubers a foot apart. There is a white-flowered variety.

C. persicum. FLORISTS' CYCLAMEN. Zones 15–24. Original species has 2-in., fragrant, deep to pale pink or white blooms borne on 6-in. stems. Selective breeding has resulted in large-flowered florists' cyclamen (the old favorites) and newer, smaller strains; with rare exceptions, fragrance has disappeared. Plants typically have heart- or kidney-shaped dark green leaves, often with silvery mottling. They bear crimson, red, salmon, purple, pink, or white flowers on 6–8-in. stems from late fall to spring. Good choice for color in place to be occupied in summer by tuberous begonias. Shade is required where summers are hot. Plants lose leaves and go dormant in hot weather, but usually survive if drainage is good and soil not waterlogged. Protect from slugs and snails; plants are especially vulnerable because tops of tubers and growing points are exposed.

Dwarf or miniature florists' cyclamens are replicas of standards with half- or three-quarter-size leaves and blossoms. Can bloom in 7 to 8 months from seed. Miniature strains (profuse show of 1½-in. flowers on 6–8-in. plants) include Miracle and Laser, both with fragrant blossoms.

C. purpurascens (C. europaeum). Zones 4–9, 14–24. Distinctly fragrant crimson flowers on 5–6-in. stems, late summer or early fall. Bright green leaves mottled silvery white; almost evergreen.

CARE

All cyclamens grow best in fairly rich, porous soil with lots of humus. Plant tubers 6–10 in. apart, ½ in. deep. (Florists' cyclamen is an exception: upper half of tuber should protrude above soil level.) Best planting time for tubers is dormant period in summer—except for florists' cyclamen, which is always sold as a potted plant and can be planted out anytime. Top-dress annually with light application of potting soil with complete fertilizer added (being careful not to cover top of florists' cyclamen tubers). Do not cultivate around roots.

Plants grow readily from seed. Small-flowered hardy species take several years to bloom; older strains of florists' cyclamen need 15 to 18 months from seed, while newer strains can bloom 7 months after planting. Grown in open ground, plants often self-sow.

Cydonia. See Quince, Fruiting

Cylindrophyllum 'Red Spike'. See *Cephalophyllum* 'Red Spike'

Cymbidium
Orchidaceae
TERRESTRIAL ORCHIDS

⚡ **ALL ZONES—SUBJECT TO CONDITIONS BELOW**

◑ **PARTIAL SHADE**

💧 **REGULAR WATER**

Cymbidium

Native to high altitudes in Southeast Asia, these orchids are very popular because of their relatively easy culture. The long-lasting flowers grow on erect or arching spikes.

»

C

How to Grow Cymbidiums

TEMPERATURE To set buds, plants need 50°F to 55°F (10°C to 13°C) night temperatures. Daytime temperatures of 60°F to 75°F (16°C to 24°C) or even as high as 80°F to 90°F (27°C to 32°C) suit them. They will stand temperatures as low as 28°F (−2°C) for short time only. Where there's danger of harder frosts, cover plants with polyethylene film or move to a protected location.

LIGHT For best bloom, give as much light as possible without burning the foliage. During flowering period, give plants shade. Plants with yellow-green leaves generally flower best; dark green foliage means too much shade. In areas subject to frost, grow in pots in lathhouse, in greenhouse, or beneath overhang or high-branching tree.

SOIL Potting mix for cymbidiums should drain fast yet retain moisture. Many commercial orchid mixes are available. Keep the potting medium moist when new growth is developing and maturing—usually spring through summer.

WATERING & FEEDING In winter, water plants just enough to keep bulbs from shriveling. On hot summer days, mist foliage early in day. Watch for slugs and snails at all times. Feed with complete liquid fertilizer every 10 days to 2 weeks. Use a high-nitrogen formula in winter to early summer, a low-nitrogen product from late summer through fall. Transplant potted plants when the bulbs fill pots. When dividing plants, keep minimum of three healthy bulbs (with foliage) in each division. Dust cuts with sulfur or charcoal to discourage rot.

Standard types usually bloom from midwinter to midspring. Bloom season for miniatures starts in earliest fall, but is heaviest late fall into winter. All make excellent cut flowers. The long, narrow, grasslike foliage forms a sheath around the short, stout, oval pseudobulbs.

Most cymbidium growers list only hybrids—large-flowered varieties with white, pink, yellow, green, or bronze blooms. Most have yellow throat, dark red markings on lip. Large-flowered forms produce 12 or more 4½–5-in. flowers per stem. Miniature varieties, about a quarter the size of large-flowered forms, are popular for their size, free-blooming qualities, and flower colors. A growing class of intermediate-climate cymbidiums (the only types suited to Zone H2) will thrive alongside cattleyas in a greenhouse or in climates where night temperatures are too warm for standard cymbidiums. Many hybrid cymbidiums bloom in summer and fall, and some are fragrant.

Cymbopogon citratus

LEMON GRASS
Poaceae
PERENNIAL

✂ **ZONES 12, 13, 16, 17, 23, 24; H1, H2**

☼ **FULL SUN**

💧 **REGULAR WATER**

Cymbopogon citratus

All parts of this plant from India are strongly lemon scented and are widely used as an ingredient in Southeast Asian cooking. Clumps of inch-wide leaves grow 3–4 ft. tall (or more) and

3 ft. wide. The base of clump, composed of overlapping leaf bases, is nearly bulbous in appearance. Lemon grass can live over in the mildest-winter regions, but it's safer to pot up a division and keep it indoors or in a greenhouse over winter. Easily planted from divisions.

To harvest lemon grass, cut off the thick, bulbous stems just above the crown (ground level). Only the bottom third of each stalk is used; the bigger the better. Peel off the outer sheath and finely slice or pound the inner stem for salads or cooking. The sharp-edged blades (the upper part of the stems) are too tough to eat.

Cynodon dactylon

BERMUDA GRASS, BERMUDA
Poaceae
PERENNIAL GRASS

✂ **ZONES 5–10, 12–24; H1, H2**

☼ **FULL SUN**

💧 **MODERATE TO REGULAR WATER**

Cynodon dactylon

These subtropical fine-textured grasses spread rapidly by surface and underground runners (rhizomes and stolons). They tolerate heat and look good if well maintained. They turn brown in winter, although some varieties stay green longer than others, and most stay green longer if well fed.

Common Bermuda is a good minimum-maintenance lawn for large areas. Needs feeding, careful and frequent mowing to remove seed spikes. Runners invade shrubbery and flower beds if not carefully

confined. Can become very difficult to eradicate.

Hybrid Bermudas are finer in texture and better in color than the common kind. They're harder to overseed with rye, bluegrass, or red fescue. Help them stay green longer in winter by feeding in early fall and by removing thatch. Useful in areas with short dormant season.

There are many varieties of hybrid Bermuda and improved turf-type common Bermuda grass. Newer, improved seeded varieties of common Bermuda, which do produce pollen, include 'Blackjack' and 'Yukon'. 'GN-1', a recently developed hybrid Bermuda, is wear-resistant, deep green; it has a slightly wider blade than 'Tifway 419'.

Below are long-standing varieties of hybrid Bermuda.

'Santa Ana'. Deep green, coarse, smog-resistant. Takes hard wear; holds color late.

'Tifdwarf II'. Extremely low and dense; takes very close mowing. Slower to establish than others, but slower to spread where it's not wanted. Useful as small-scale ground-cover on banks, among rocks.

'Tifgreen 328'. Fine-textured, deep blue-green, dense. Few seed spikes, sterile seeds. Takes close mowing; preferred for putting greens.

'Tifway 419'. Low growth; dense, fine texture. Stiff dark green blades. Wear-resistant. Slow to start. Sterile (no seeds).

CARE

Common Bermuda is usually planted from seeds or sprigs (stolons). Hybrid Bermuda can be grown from sprigs, plugs, or sod. Both can be overseeded with cool-season grasses for winter color. Should be cut low; 1 in. is desirable for common Bermuda, ½–¾ in. for hybrid Bermuda. Contact your local water department for specific watering guidelines. Needs dethatching—removal of matted layer of old stems and stolons beneath the leaves—to look its best.

FOR MORE ON GRASSES, SEE "MEET THE GRASSES," PAGE 346.

Cynoglossum
Boraginaceae
PERENNIALS AND BIENNIALS GROWN
AS ANNUALS

🌿 **ZONES VARY BY SPECIES**

☼ ◐ ● **EXPOSURE NEEDS VARY
BY SPECIES**

◊ ● **WATER NEEDS VARY BY SPECIES**

⬥ **SOME PARTS TOXIC TO LIVESTOCK**

Cynoglossum amabile 'Azul'

These bedding, border, or wild
garden plants bear little blue,
white, or pink flowers like forget-
me-nots (*Myosotis*), to which
they are related.

C. amabile. CHINESE
FORGET-ME-NOT. Biennial grown
as annual. Zones A2, A3; 1–24;
H1, H2. East Asian native reaching 1½–2 ft. high, 1 ft. wide.
Lance-shaped leaves are soft,
hairy, grayish green. Loose sprays
of rich blue, pink, or white flowers (larger than forget-me-nots)
appear in spring, continue into
summer where weather is cool.
Widely available 'Firmament', the
most popular variety, has rich
blue blooms on compact plants
about 1½ ft. high. All varieties
bloom from seed sown in fall or
early spring, in a location where
plants are to grow. Hardy except
in most severe winters. Give full
sun, regular water.

C. grande. WESTERN
HOUND'S TONGUE. Perennial.
Zones 4–9, 14–24. Native to
Oregon and California coast
ranges and to Sierra Nevada
slopes below 4,000 ft. Hairy,
mostly basal leaves 6–12 in.
long. Blue spring flowers with
white centers. Plants reach
1–2½ ft. tall and 1 ft. wide; die
back in summer to a heavy
underground root. Choose a
shaded, woodsy site with cool
soil; provide little summer water.

Cyperus
Cyperaceae
PERENNIALS

🌿 **ZONES VARY BY SPECIES**

☼ ◐ ● **SUN OR SHADE**

● **AMPLE WATER**

Cyperus papyrus

These African natives are
sedges—grasslike plants distinguished from true grasses by
three-angled, solid stems and
very different flowering parts.
Valued for their striking form,
silhouette, and shadow pattern.
Most cyperus grow in rich,
moist soil or with roots submerged in water. Keep plants
groomed by removing dead or
broken stems. Divide and
replant vigorous plants when
the clump becomes too large,
saving smaller, outside divisions
and discarding the overgrown
centers. Beyond their hardiness
range, pot up divisions and overwinter as houseplants.

**C. albostriatus (C. diffu-
sus).** Zones 14–24. Resembles
C. alternifolius, but tends to be
less hardy, shorter (to 20 in.),
with broader leaves and lusher,
softer appearance. Vigorous,
invasive plant; best used in contained space.

C. alternifolius. UMBRELLA
PLANT. Zones 8, 9, 12–24; H1,
H2. Narrow, firm, spreading
leaves arranged like ribs of an
umbrella at tops of 2–4-ft.
stems. Flowers are held in dry,
greenish brown clusters. Grows
in water or moist soil. Effective
near pools, in pots or planters,
or in dry streambeds or small
rock gardens. Self-sows. Can
become weedy and take over a
small pool. Naturalized in parts
of Hawaii. 'Gracilis' ('Nanus')
is a dwarf form to 1½ ft. high.

C. papyrus. PAPYRUS.
Zones 16, 17, 23, 24; H1, H2.
Tall, graceful, dark green stems
6–10 ft. high, topped with clusters of green threadlike parts to
1½ ft. long (longer than small
leaves at base of cluster). Will
grow quickly in 2 in. of water in
shallow pool, or can be potted
and placed on bricks or inverted
pot in deeper water. Protect
from strong wind. Also grows
well in rich, moist soil out of
water. Naturalized on Kauai.
Used by flower arrangers.

C. prolifer (C. isocladus).
DWARF PAPYRUS. Zones 16,
17, 23, 24; H1, H2. Flowers
and long, thin leaves combine
to make filmy brown and green
clusters on slender stems
about 1½ ft. high. Use in Asian-
style gardens; sink in pots in
water gardens where delicate
design of slender, leafless
stems will not be lost among
larger and coarser plants.

Cyrtanthus
Amaryllidaceae
PERENNIALS FROM BULBS

🌿 **ZONES 16–24**

◐ **LIGHT SHADE**

● **REGULAR WATER**

Cyrtanthus elatus

South African natives with
glossy, strap-shaped, evergreen
leaves that remain attractive
all year. The flowers appear in
clusters at ends of stems that
rise just above the leaves. Good
potted plants.

**C. elatus (C. purpureus,
Vallota speciosa).** SCARBOR-
OUGH LILY. Looks like a more
delicate version of hybrid amaryllis (*Hippeastrum*). Leaves 1–
2 ft. long. In summer and early
fall, each thick flower stalk is

topped with up to ten 3–4-in.,
funnel-shaped orange-red
blooms. (White- and pink-
flowered forms are less common.) Succeeds in competition
with tree roots. Excellent
houseplant.

C. mackenii. Foot-long,
narrow leaves, somewhat wavy
edges. Each stem holds up to
five tubular, curved, 2-in.-long,
fragrant white blooms in spring.
There are also cream- and yellow-
flowered forms and hybrids in
coral, orange, and red shades.
If in pots, will need annual
repotting.

CARE

Plants are frost sensitive, so
give them a sheltered spot in
Zones 18–22. Plant in spring,
in well-drained, enriched soil.
Set the bulbs 1–1½ ft. apart,
with tips just beneath soil surface. Give less water during
semidormant period (winter and
spring for *C. elatus,* summer for
C. mackenii), but don't let plants
dry out. To increase plantings,
remove bulblets that form
around larger bulb and plant
separately.

Cyrtomium
Dryopteridaceae
FERNS

🌿 **ZONES VARY BY SPECIES**

◐ ● **PARTIAL OR FULL SHADE**

● **REGULAR WATER**

Cyrtomium falcatum

These are coarse-textured
but handsome ferns with firm-
textured, glossy fronds 2–
3 ft. long.

C. falcatum. JAPANESE
HOLLY FERN. Zones 5–9,
14–24; H1, H2; or indoors.
Native to Asia, South Africa,

Polynesia; naturalized in Hawaii. Fronds to 10 in. wide, with 3–11 pairs of divisions. Takes houseplant conditions well.

C. fortunei. Zones 4–9, 14–24. From China, Japan, and Korea. Fronds to 6 in. wide; more finely cut and with more divisions (12–26 pairs) than those of other species.

C. macrophyllum. Zones 7–9, 13–24. From China and the Himalayas. Fronds (to 10 in. wide) are the coarsest among the species listed here, with three to eight pairs of divisions.

CARE

Provide soil with high organic content. Do not plant these ferns too deeply.

Cytisus
BROOM
Papilionaceae
EVERGREEN, SEMIEVERGREEN, AND DECIDUOUS SHRUBS

- ✓ **ZONES VARY BY SPECIES**
- ☼ **FULL SUN**
- ◐ **LITTLE OR NO WATER**

Cytisus scoparius 'Pomona'

Most widely planted brooms belong to this genus, but look for other choice shrubs under *Genista*. The sweet pea–shaped flowers of *Cytisus* are often fragrant. Plants tolerate wind, seashore conditions.

C. battandieri. ATLAS BROOM. Semievergreen or deciduous. Zones 4–6, 14–17. Moroccan native puts on fast growth to 12–15 ft. high and as wide. Can be trained as small tree. Leaves divided into three roundish leaflets covered with silky hairs. Fragrant, pure yellow flowers in spikelike 5-in. clusters at branch ends in summer.

C. × kewensis. KEW BROOM. Evergreen. Best in Zones 2–6; less vigorous in Zones 16, 17. Low (less than 1 ft. high) and spreading, with cascading branches to 4 ft. or more. Creamy white, ½-in. flowers in spring. Tiny leaves.

C. lydia. See *Genista lydia*.

C. × praecox. WARMINSTER BROOM. Deciduous. Zones 2–9, 14–22. Compact growth to 3–5 ft. high and 4–6 ft. wide, with many slender stems. Mounding mass of pale yellow to creamy white flowers in spring. Small leaves fall early. Effective as informal screen or hedge, along drives, paths. 'Allgold', slightly taller, has bright yellow flowers; 'Hollandia' has pink ones.

C. purgans. PROVENCE BROOM. Deciduous. Zones 1–7. From Europe, North Africa. Dense, mounding growth to 3 ft. high and wide. Roundish, silky, hairy leaves are ¼–½ in. long. Fragrant chrome yellow flowers in late spring, early summer. 'Spanish Gold' grows 4 ft. tall, 6 ft. wide; hardy in the Colorado Rockies to 8,000-ft. elevation.

C. scoparius. SCOTCH BROOM. Evergreen. Zones 2–9, 14–22; H1. This aggressive European species has given all brooms a bad name. It forms an upright-growing mass of wandlike green stems (often leafless or nearly so) that may reach 10 ft. Golden yellow, ¾-in. flowers, spring and early summer. A tenacious weed from Seattle to San Diego and in Hawaii, especially on the Big Island. Much less aggressive are lower-growing, more colorful hybrid forms. Most of these grow 5–8 ft. tall and wide. 'Burkwoodii' has red blooms touched with yellow; 'Dorothy Walpole', rose-pink and crimson; 'Lena', red and lemon yellow; 'Lilac Time', lilac-pink blooms on a compact plant; 'Minstead', white-flushed lilac and deep purple; 'Moonlight', pale yellow blossoms, compact grower; 'Pomona', orange and apricot; and 'Stanford', red.

CARE

Where soil is highly alkaline, give them iron sulfate. Prune after bloom to keep to reasonable size and lessen the production of unsightly seedpods.

Daboecia cantabrica
IRISH HEATH
Ericaceae
EVERGREEN SHRUB

- ✓ **ZONES 3B–9, 14–24**
- ☼ ◐ **FULL SUN ONLY IN COOLER CLIMATES**
- ◐ **REGULAR WATER**

Daboecia cantabrica 'Cinderella'

This colorful shrub from western Europe forms a slightly spreading plant with erect stems to 1½–2 ft. high. Its narrow, dark green leaves are closely set. The pinkish purple, egg-shaped, 1½-in.-long flowers are produced in narrow clusters 3–5 in. long from late spring to early autumn. In warmer part of the range, bloom may begin in early spring.

Varieties include white-flowered *D. c. alba* and magenta-blooming 'Waley's Red' and 'Arielle'. 'Cinderella' has bicolored white-and-pink flowers and gray-green leaves. *D. c. scotica* 'William Buchanan' is a low grower (just 10 in. high) with reddish purple blossoms; 'William Buchanan Gold' is similar but shows some yellow variegation in the foliage.

CARE

Needs fast-draining, acidic soil. Most useful on hillsides and in rock gardens or natural landscapes.

Dahlia
Asteraceae
PERENNIALS FROM TUBEROUS ROOTS

- ✓ **ZONES 1–24, EXCEPT AS NOTED**
- ☼ ◐ **LIGHT SHADE IN HOTTEST AREAS**
- ◐ **REGULAR WATER**

Dahlia 'Blown Dry'

Through centuries of hybridizing and selection, dahlias, which originated from Mexico and Guatemala, have become tremendously diversified, available in numerous flower types and sizes (from 2 to 12 in. across) and all colors but true blue.

Bush and bedding dahlias range from 1 ft. to over 7 ft. tall. The tall bush forms are useful as summer hedges and screens; lower kinds give mass color in borders and containers.

Modern dahlias, with their strong stems, long-lasting blooms that face outward or upward, and substantial, attractive foliage, make striking cut flowers. Leaves are generally divided into many large, deep green leaflets. Some forms have brownish purple leaves; a well-known example is 'Bishop of Llandaff'.

Dahlia flower forms. The dahlia flowerhead contains many small individual structures called florets. Some dahlia flowers are made up of ray florets (which look like petals) surrounding a central cluster of disk florets. Others have ray florets only. Blooms may be single or double, with florets arranged to produce various forms, several of which are pictured at right. Flowers range in size from 2 to 10 in. To learn more, visit the website of the American Dahlia Society (*dahlia.org*).

»

DAHLIA FLOWER FORMS (SAMPLER)

Ball

Collarette

Pompon

Novelty

Orchid

Informal decorative

How to Grow Dahlias

PLANTING Most dahlias are started from tuberous roots planted in spring after frost is past and soil is warm. Several weeks before planting, dig the soil in the planting area to 1 ft. deep and work in plenty of organic matter, such as garden compost. At planting time, dig a foot-deep hole for each root; make holes 1½ ft. wide for dahlias that grow over 4 ft. tall, and 9–12 in. wide for smaller types. Space holes for larger varieties 4–5 ft. apart, for smaller ones 1–2 ft. apart. Mix about ¼ cup of granular low-nitrogen fertilizer into the soil at the bottom of each planting hole, then add 4 in. of soil before placing the root in the center of the hole, with its growth bud pointing up. Before planting a tall variety, drive a 5–6-ft. stake into the hole just off center, then place the root horizontally in the bottom of the hole, 2 in. from the stake and with the growth bud pointing toward it. Cover roots with 3 in. of soil, and water thoroughly.

As shoots grow, gradually fill hole with soil.

THINNING & PINCHING On tall-growing dahlias, thin out shoots when they're about 6 in. high, leaving only the strongest one or two. When remaining shoots have three sets of leaves, pinch off tops just above upper set; dahlias with smaller flowers, such as pompons, singles, and dwarfs, need only this first pinching. For best show of larger-flowered types, pinch again by removing all but terminal flower buds on side shoots.

PLANT CARE After shoots are aboveground, start watering regularly to a foot deep; continue throughout active growth. Dahlias planted in enriched soil shouldn't need additional food, but if your soil is light or if roots stayed in the ground the previous year, apply a granular low-nitrogen fertilizer when the first flower buds show. Mulch to discourage weeds and to eliminate cultivating, which may injure feeder roots.

CUTTING FLOWERS Pick nearly mature flowers in early morning or evening. Immediately place cut stems in 2–3 in. of hot water; let stand in gradually cooling water for several hours or overnight.

LIFTING & STORING In mild-winter regions, roots may remain in the ground as long as drainage is excellent and winter temperatures remain above 20°F (–7°C). In borderline climates, mulch with 4-in. layer of straw or similar material.

Gardeners in most areas, however, prefer to dig the roots annually. After tops turn yellow or are frosted, cut stalks to 4 in. aboveground. Dig a 2-ft.-wide circle around each plant; carefully pry up clump with spading fork, shake off loose soil, and let the clump dry in sun for several hours. Then, follow either of the following methods.

Method 1: Divide clumps immediately. Freshly dug roots are easy to cut, and eyes (growth buds) are easy to recognize at this time. To divide, cut the stalks with a sharp knife, leaving 1 in. of stalk attached to each section; make sure each division has an eye so that it will produce a new plant. Dust cut surfaces with sulfur to prevent rot; bury in dry sand, sawdust, peat moss, or perlite and store over winter in a cool 40°F to 45°F (4°C to 7°C), dark, dry place.

Method 2: Leave clumps intact. Cover them with dry sand, sawdust, or perlite and store in cool, dark, dry place as directed in method above. With Method 2, roots are less likely to shrivel.

About 2 to 4 weeks before planting in spring, separate intact clumps, cutting them apart as described under Method 1. Then place all roots—whether fall- or spring-divided—in moist sand to encourage sprouting.

D. imperialis. TREE DAHLIA. Zones 4–6, 8, 9, 14–24. Multistemmed tree grows each year from permanent roots to a possible 10–20 ft. tall, 4–6 ft. wide. Daisylike, 4–8-in.-wide lavender flowers with yellow centers bloom at branch ends in late fall. Leaves divided into many leaflets. Frost kills tops completely; cut back to ground afterward. If tree dahlia were longer blooming or evergreen, it would be a valued landscape plant, but annual dieback relegates it to tall novelty class. Available from specialists; seldom sold in nurseries. Grow from cuttings taken near stem tops (or from side shoots) in fall; root in pots of moist sand kept in a protected place over winter. Or dig root clump and divide in fall. Give full sun or partial shade. *D. excelsa, D. maxonii* are similar.

Dalea
Papilionaceae
EVERGREEN AND DECIDUOUS SHRUBS, PERENNIALS

✿ **ZONES VARY BY SPECIES**

☼ **FULL SUN**

◐ ◑ **LITTLE TO MODERATE WATER**

Dalea greggii

Extremely useful and attractive desert shrubs from the southwestern states and northern Mexico. All have finely divided foliage and clusters of small sweet pea–shaped flowers.

D. bicolor. INDIGO BUSH. Deciduous. Zones 10–13. To 6–8 ft. tall, 5–6 ft. wide. Silvery leaves; deep blue autumn flowers. Rapid regrowth from hard winter pruning brings a quick crop of fresh foliage. 'Monterrey Blue' has good flower color.

D. capitata. Evergreen. Zones 10–13. Groundcover to 8 in. high and 3 ft. wide. Finely divided light green foliage has a lemon scent. Bears yellow flowers during spring and autumn. Control whiteflies. Requires some water in summer and survives regular irrigation. 'Sierra Gold' is a cutting-grown variety.

D. frutescens. BLACK DALEA. Evergreen. Zones 10–13. Mounded growth to 3 ft. tall, 4 ft. across, with silvery green, lacy foliage. Purple flower clusters appear from fall to spring. A cutting-grown form is called 'Sierra Negra'.

D. greggii. TRAILING INDIGO BUSH. Evergreen. Zones 10 (warmer parts)–13. Has mounding habit to 1½ ft. high and spreading 6 ft. wide. Pearl gray foliage and clusters of lavender to purple flowers in spring and early summer. Good desert groundcover.

D. lutea. Evergreen. Zones 12, 13. To 6 ft. tall and wide, with deep green leaves and clustered yellow flowers in late fall. 'Sierra Moonrise' is a selected form.

D. pulchra. INDIGO BUSH. Evergreen. Zones 12, 13. To 8 ft. high and 5 ft. wide. Silvery foliage; purple flowers in spring.

D. purpurea (Petalostemon purpureum). PURPLE PRAIRIE CLOVER. Perennial. Zones 1–3, 10–12. An attractive perennial for the wild garden, native from Saskatchewan to Texas. Grows to 1½ ft. high and wide, with many rigid, outward-leaning stems covered with dark green leaves. In summer, stems are tipped with tight heads of small reddish purple flowers. Deep roots supply fertility to the soil through nitrogen-fixing bacteria. This tough plant is well suited to the extremes of its native prairies and plains. Tolerates any soil.

D. spinosa. See *Psorothamnus spinosus*.

CARE

The taller shrub types should be cut back by half during their first 3 or 4 years to encourage dense growth. Overwatering or summer drought can result in partial leaf drop.

Sweetly Scented Shrubs

Many daphnes are cherished for the powerful fragrance of their blooms. *D. odora* is perhaps the best known; its clusters of tiny flowers have an intense perfume, similar to that of jasmine or citrus blossom. Many other flowering shrubs offer their own special perfumes. Among those with the sweetest-smelling flowers are Mexican orange (*Choisya ternata*), winter hazel (*Corylopsis*), gardenia, witch hazel (*Hamamelis*), orange jessamine (*Murraya paniculata*), sweet olive (*Osmanthus fragrans*), mock orange (*Philadelphus*), tobira (*Pittosporum tobira*), lilac (*Syringa*), and several viburnums, including Viburnum × *burkwoodii*, fragrant snowball (*V. × carlcephalum*), Korean spice viburnum (*V. carlesii*), and *V. farreri*.

Dalechampia dioscoreifolia
COSTA RICAN BUTTERFLY VINE
Euphorbiaceae
EVERGREEN VINE

✿ **ZONES 17–24**

☼ ◑ **FULL SUN OR LIGHT SHADE**

💧 **REGULAR WATER**

Dalechampia dioscoreifolia

A twining vine from Central and South America. Grows 16–25 ft., with oval, pointed leaves that are dull dark green above and paler green and fuzzy beneath. The blossoms measure up to 6 in. across and resemble purple butterflies, with tiny yellow flowers appearing between two violet bracts. With adequate warmth and moisture, growth is rapid and blooms abundant. Heaviest bloom comes from early summer to late fall, but the vine can flower nearly year-round.

Daphne
Thymelaeaceae
EVERGREEN, SEMIEVERGREEN, AND DECIDUOUS SHRUBS

✿ **ZONES VARY BY SPECIES**

☼ ◑ **EXPOSURE NEEDS VARY BY SPECIES**

◑ **MODERATE WATER, EXCEPT AS NOTED**

⚠ **ALL PARTS, ESPECIALLY FRUITS, ARE POISONOUS IF INGESTED**

Daphne odora 'Aureomarginata'

Although some daphnes are easier to grow than others, all require fast-draining soil and careful summer watering. They are more temperamental in California than in the Northwest.

D. × burkwoodii. Evergreen or semievergreen to deciduous. Zones 2b–6, 14–17. Erect, compact growth to 3–4 ft. tall and wide, densely foliaged with narrow leaves. Abundant small clusters of fragrant flowers (white fading to pink) appear at branch ends in late spring and again in late summer. 'Briggs Moonlight' has pale yellow leaves with a narrow green border; 'Carol Mackie' has gold-edged green leaves. 'Somerset' is larger (to 4 ft. tall, 6 ft. wide) and bears pink flowers. Use all in shrub borders or at woodland edges. Full sun or light shade.

D. cneorum. GARLAND DAPHNE. Evergreen. Zones 2b–9, 14–17. From mountains of central and southern Europe. Forms mat less than 1 ft. high and 3 ft. wide. Good container plant. Trailing branches covered with narrow, 1-in.-long, dark green leaves. Clusters of fragrant rosy pink flowers appear in spring. Choice rock garden plant; give it light shade in warm areas, full sun in cool-summer areas. After bloom is through, top-dress with mix of peat moss and sand to keep roots cool and induce additional rooting of trailing stems.

Varieties include 'Eximia', lower than the species (to 8 in. high) and with larger flowers; 'Ruby Glow', with larger, more deeply colored flowers than the species and with late-summer rebloom; and 'Variegata', with gold-edged leaves.

D. odora. WINTER DAPHNE. Evergreen. Zones 4–10, 12, 14–24. From China and Japan. So prized for its pervasive floral perfume that it continues to be widely planted despite its unpredictable behavior—it can die despite the most attentive care, or flourish with little attention until you invite all your gardening friends over to admire it, at which point it promptly succumbs without warning just to show you who's in charge. Very neat, handsome plant, usually to about 4 ft. high (occasionally 8–10 ft. high) and 6 ft. wide. Glossy leaves. Nosegay clusters of charming, intensely fragrant flowers—pink to deep red on outside, with creamy pink throats —appear at branch ends in winter. 'Aureomarginata' ('Marginata'), more widely grown than species, has yellow-edged leaves. 'Mae-jima' has a compact habit with leaves edged cream and yellow and is an improvement over 'Aureomarginata'. *D. o. alba* has white flowers; terminal growth sometimes distorted by fasciation (growths resembling cockscombs).

This species needs much air around its roots, so plant in porous soil (as you would rhododendrons). Always set plant a bit high, so that the juncture of roots and stems is 1–2 in. above soil grade. Where soil is heavy and poorly drained, grow in porous, organic soil mixture in raised bed or container. In Zones 18–24, transplanting an existing *D. odora* often fails—digging cuts roots, the plant suffers, and water molds get at it. Transplanting has a somewhat better chance of success in Zones 4–9, 14–17.

Plant this daphne where it can get at least 3 hours of shade each day around midday. If possible, shade soil around roots with living groundcover. A soil pH of 7.0 is right for it (important in Zones 4–6). Feed right after bloom with complete fertilizer but not acid plant food. During dry season, water as infrequently as plant will allow. Little or no water in summer increases flowering next spring and helps prevent death from water molds.

D × susannae 'Lawrence Crocker'. Zones 4–9, 14–17. Forms a compact mound 12 in. high and wide with dark green leaves. Fragrant, deep pink to lavender blooms in late spring. Can be grown as a small hedge. Grow in partial shade.

D. × transatlantica. Semievergreen to deciduous. Zones 2b–9, 14–17. Mounded growth to 3–4 ft. tall and 5–6 ft. wide after 10 years. Small gray-green leaves. Very fragrant, pink-flushed white flowers bloom over long season, from spring to fall. Produces the most blooms in full sun but can take part shade. 'Eternal Fragrance' is an improved form more available than the species. 'Summer Ice' bears leaves that are edged with creamy white.

CARE

Plants respond to heavy pruning but rarely need more than the occasional snip to correct their shape. Cut back to lateral branches or to just above obvious growth buds. You can cut budded branches of deciduous types for forced bloom indoors. See above for specifics on caring for *D. odora*.

Darmera peltata
(Peltiphyllum peltatum)
UMBRELLA PLANT, INDIAN RHUBARB
Saxifragaceae
PERENNIAL

🖉 **ZONES 2–7, 14–20**

◐ **PARTIAL SHADE**

💧 **AMPLE WATER**

Darmera peltata

This lovely perennial is native to the mountains of Northern California and Oregon. Its large, round clusters of pink flowers appear on bare stalks to 6 ft. tall in spring. The shield-shaped leaves appear later on 2–6-ft. stalks. Each plant spreads up to 4–8 ft. wide. Stout rhizomes to 2 in. thick grow in damp ground or even into streams. A spectacular plant for stream, pond, or damp woodland site.

To create a bog garden in a partly shady, constantly damp area, group umbrella plant with other large-leafed perennials like *Farfugium japonicum*, hosta, or *Ligularia*. Add royal fern (*Osmunda regalis*) or giant chain fern (*Woodwardia fimbriata*) for striking textural contrast.

Dasylirion
Asparagaceae
EVERGREEN SHRUBS

🖉 **ZONES VARY BY SPECIES**

☼ ◐ **FULL SUN OR LIGHT SHADE**

💧 **LITTLE OR NO WATER TO MODERATE WATER**

Dasylirion longissimum

Grassy-looking shrubs, native to the deserts and mountains of the Southwest and Mexico. Their clumps of narrow leaves spring from a woody base that can, with age, grow into a tree-like trunk. The tiny flowers are tightly clustered on a tall, narrow spike.

D. berlandieri. ZARAGOSA BLUE TWISTER. Zones 10–24. Twisted, steel blue leaves have sharp barbs. Grows at least 4 ft. high and wide. White to cream flowers on tall spikes (up to 15 ft. tall) in summer.

D. longissimum (D. quadrangulatum). MEXICAN GRASS TREE. Zones 12–24. Smooth-edged green leaves in fountainlike clump to about 5 ft. high and wide. Trunk is slow to form but may reach 10 ft. tall. Eventually bears white to cream-colored flowers in early summer.

D. texanum. GREEN DESERT SPOON. Zones 10–24. Forms neat clump about 5 ft. high and wide. Narrow, leathery, dark green leaves have small teeth along the edges. In summer, plant produces an 8-ft.-tall spike of creamy white flowers.

D. wheeleri. DESERT SPOON, SOTOL. Zones 10–24; most widely used in 10–13. Forms a near-spherical clump 3–5 ft. high, 4–5 ft. wide. Spiky bluish gray leaves to 3 ft. long have teeth along the edges and are stiffer than those of

D

D

D. longissimum. Leaves slowly form a trunk to 3 ft. tall, covered with dried, drooping shag of old leaves. Base of each leaf broadens where it joins the trunk to form a long-handled "spoon" prized in dried arrangements. Eventually produces white flowers on 9–15-ft.-tall spike in early summer.

CARE

Provide good drainage. Very drought-tolerant, but some irrigation will speed growth. Definitely need summer water in Zone 13.

Datura. See *Brugmansia*

Davallia trichomanoides

SQUIRREL'S FOOT FERN
Davalliaceae
FERN

- ✿ ZONES 17, 23, 24; H1, H2; OR INDOORS
- ☼ PARTIAL SHADE; BRIGHT INDIRECT LIGHT
- ◗◖ MODERATE TO REGULAR WATER

Davallia trichomanoides

This Asian fern has very finely divided evergreen fronds to about 1 ft. long and 6 in. wide. They rise from light reddish brown, furry rhizomes (resembling squirrel's feet) that creep over the soil surface. Hardy to 30°F (–1°C). It can be used in mild-winter locations as small-scale groundcover in partly shaded areas. Best use in any climate is as a hanging-basket plant. Use light, fast-draining soil mix. Feed occasionally.

FOR MORE ON FERNS, SEE "MEET THE FERNS," PAGE 320.

Davidia involucrata

DOVE TREE
Nyssaceae
DECIDUOUS TREE

- ✿ ZONES 4–9, 14–21
- ☼◖ PARTIAL SHADE IN HOTTEST CLIMATES
- ◗ REGULAR WATER

Davidia involucrata 'Sonoma'

When this eye-catching tree from China comes into bloom in spring, the general effect is that of white doves resting among green leaves—or, as some say, like handkerchiefs drying on branches. Small, clustered, red-anthered flowers are carried between two large white or creamy white bracts that are unequal in size—one is 6 in. long, the other about 4 in. Because leaves are already present at bloom time, the large blossoms aren't as showy as smaller flowers of many deciduous fruit trees. Trees often take 10 years to come into flower, and then may bloom more heavily in alternate years. Dove tree grows to 35–65 ft. tall, with strong branching pattern and a rounded crown 15–40 ft. wide. It has a clean look both in and out of leaf. The roundish to heart-shaped leaves are 3–6-in. long and vivid green. The variety 'Sonoma' blooms as young as 2 years old. Brown fruits about the size of golf balls persist on tree well into winter, sometimes until spring. Plant this tree by itself; it should not compete with other flowering trees. Looks pleasing in front of dark conifers, where its vivid green and white stand out.

Delonix regia

ROYAL POINCIANA, FLAMBOYANT TREE
Caesalpiniaceae
PARTIALLY OR WHOLLY DECIDUOUS TREE

- ✿ ZONES 22, 23; H2
- ☼ FULL SUN
- ◌ LITTLE WATER

Delonix regia

This native of Madagascar, which Hawaiians call ohai'ula, is as flamboyant as it is shapely. Its large trusses of 4-in., orange to scarlet flowers with white or yellow markings put on a spectacular display in late spring or early summer. The blooms are followed by 2-ft.-long black seedpods that hang on the bare winter branches. Rapidly grows to 30–40 ft. tall and as wide, with umbrella-shaped silhouette. Fernlike leaves, finely cut into many tiny leaflets, give filtered shade. Good drought tolerance; moderate tolerance to wind and salt. A form with pure yellow flowers, called yellow royal poinciana, is also grown in Hawaii.

Royal poinciana is a stellar tree, especially in Hawaii. Its wide-spreading canopy of feathery foliage creates welcome shade, and its flame-colored blooms are spectacular.

Delosperma

ICE PLANT
Aizoaceae
SUCCULENT PERENNIALS

- ✿ ZONES 2–24, EXCEPT AS NOTED
- ☼◖ LIGHT AFTERNOON SHADE IN HOTTEST CLIMATES
- ◗◖ MODERATE TO REGULAR WATER

Delosperma cooperi

This large group of ice plants includes useful groundcovers and several unusually hardy South African rock garden plants. Except as noted, fleshy leaves are rich green and are often tinged red in cold weather.

D. 'Alba'. WHITE TRAILING ICE PLANT. Zones 12–24. Spreading dwarf plant, rooting freely from stems. Roundish leaves; small white summer flowers that attract bees. Good bank and groundcover; plant 1 ft. apart for quick cover.

D. basuticum. Zones 1–24. Grows ½ in. high, 9 in. wide, with roundish leaves and inch-wide, bright yellow flowers with white central zones. Spring to early-summer bloom.

D. cooperi. Reaches 3 in. high, 1½ ft. wide, with cylindrical leaves and a summer-long display of rich purple flowers.

D. dyeri 'Psdold'. RED MOUNTAIN ICE PLANT. Forms a neat carpet 2–4 in. high and 10–20 in. wide. Summer flowers are pinkish red fading to bronze with creamy white centers. Good groundcover.

D. floribundum 'Starburst'. Clumping to 2 in. high and 10–18 in. wide. Roundish leaves and 1-in., pink to magenta, daisylike flowers; blooms late spring to fall.

D. hybrids. 'Kelaidis', also called Mesa Verde ice plant, is a vigorous, cold-tolerant hybrid that grows 2 in. high and 1–2 ft. wide, with pale salmon-pink flowers (1½ in. across) from spring until fall. 'John Proffitt', Table Mountain ice plant, is similar but has fuchsia flowers. 'Psfave', lavender ice plant, is also similar but has pale lavender blooms. All make excellent groundcovers.

D. nubigenum 'Lesotho'. Only 1 in. high, spreading to 3 ft. The cylindrical leaves turn red in fall and winter, green up again in spring. Bright golden yellow, 1–1½-in. flowers cover the plant in late spring.

D. sphalmanthoides. Only ½ in. high and 8 in. wide, with tiny, plump gray-green leaves and an early-spring show of pinkish purple flowers.

CARE

Withhold water in fall to harden off plants for winter; they also appreciate a gravel mulch to keep crowns dry. All species do best with regular water in summer, but they will get by with just enough water to keep them looking bright and fresh.

Delphinium
Ranunculaceae
PERENNIALS, SOME TREATED
AS BIENNIALS OR ANNUALS

⚡ **ZONES VARY BY SPECIES**

☼ **FULL SUN, EXCEPT AS NOTED**

💧 **REGULAR WATER**

🐦 **ATTRACT BIRDS**

Delphinium elatum
Pacific strain 'Blue Jay'

Most people associate delphiniums with blue flowers, but colors also include white and shades of red, pink, lavender, and purple. Leaves are lobed or fanlike, variously cut and divided. Taller hybrids offer rich colors in elegant spires. All kinds are effective in borders and make good cut flowers; lower-growing kinds serve well as container plants. For an annual delphinium (larkspur), see *Consolida ajacis*.

D. ambiguum. See *Consolida ajacis*.

D. × belladonna. Zones 1–9, 14–24. Sturdy and bushy, to 3–4 ft. tall, 2 ft. wide. Deeply cut leaves and short-stemmed, airy flower clusters. Varieties, sometimes referred to as the Belladonna group, include light blue 'Belladonna', dark blue 'Bellamosum', white 'Casablanca', and deep turquoise-blue 'Cliveden Beauty'. All have flowers 1½–2 in. wide; longer-lived than tall hybrids listed under *D. elatum*.

D. cardinale. SCARLET LARKSPUR. Zones 7, 14–23. Native to California coastal mountains. Grows to 3–6 ft. tall and 2 ft. wide, with erect stems growing from deep, thick, woody roots. Leaves have deep, narrow lobes. Flowers are 1 in. across, with scarlet calyx and spur and scarlet-tipped yellow petals. Sow seeds early for first-year bloom.

D. elatum. CANDLE DELPHINIUM, CANDLE LARKSPUR. Zones A1–A3; 1–10, 14–24. Siberian native to 3–6 ft. tall, 2 ft. wide, with small flowers in dark or dull purple. This species is among the parents of modern delphinium strains, with flower colors including shades of lilac-pink to deep raspberry rose, clear lilac, lavender, royal purple, and darkest violet.

Pacific strain (also called Pacific Giants, Pacific Coast hybrids, and Pacific hybrids) grows to 5–8 ft. tall. Available as seed-raised mixed-color plants and in named series that produce specific colors, including light blue 'Summer Skies'; medium blue 'Blue Bird'; medium to dark blue 'Blue Jay'; and 'Galahad', clear white with white center. Additional purple, lavender, and pink selections are sold.

Blue Fountains, Blue Springs, and Magic Fountains strains are like Pacific strain but shorter (2–2½ ft. high). Stand Up strain is even shorter (15–20 in. high).

These lower-growing types seldom require staking.

Centurion is a long-stalked (4–5 ft. tall), large-flowered hybrid strain similar to the Pacific strain. It too will bloom the first year from seed, but it's more reliably perennial.

English Delphinium Mix grows 6–8 ft. tall, produces double flowers of blue, purple, mauve, pink, and white. The spikes are much denser-looking than those of Pacific strain. English types may be sold under other names, such as 'English Seedlings'.

D. grandiflorum (D. chinense). CHINESE or BOUQUET DELPHINIUM. Short-lived perennial treated as biennial or annual. Zones A1–A3; 1–10, 14–24. Bushy, branching, to 1 ft. high or less and about as wide. Varieties include 'Dwarf Blue Mirror', 1 ft. high, upward-facing flowers of deep blue; and 'Tom Thumb', 8 in. high, pure gentian blue flowers. Blue Butterfly strain grows 14 in. high, has deep blue blooms.

D. nudicaule. SCARLET LARKSPUR. Zones 5–7, 14–17. Native of Northern California and southwestern Oregon. Slender plant to 1–3 ft. tall and less than a foot wide. Long-stalked, mostly basal leaves are broadly divided. Sparse show of long-spurred red flowers. Sun or part shade; best in woodland situations.

CARE

All kinds of delphiniums are easy to grow from seed. In mild-winter areas, sow fresh seeds in flats or containers of light soil mix in summer; set out transplants in early fall for bloom in late spring and early summer. (In mild-winter climates, most perennial forms are short-lived, often treated as annuals.) In cold climates, refrigerate summer-harvested seeds in airtight containers until it is time to sow. Sow seeds in spring and set out transplants in early summer for first bloom by late summer; plants will live over and bloom again earlier in the following summer.

Delphiniums need rich, porous soil and regular fertilizing. Improve poor or heavy soils by blending in soil conditioners. Add lime to strongly acid soils.

Work small amount of superphosphate into soil around the rootball. Be careful not to cover the root crown with soil. Protect from snails, slugs. In Alaska, the delphinium defoliator eats the plants' leaves in its green caterpillar stage; handpick caterpillars or spray with *Bacillus thuringiensis* (Bt).

Dendrobium
Orchidaceae
EPIPHYTIC ORCHIDS

⚡ **ZONES VARY BY TYPE; OR INDOORS**

☼ **LIGHT SHADE; BRIGHT INDIRECT LIGHT**

💧 **REGULAR WATER**

Dendrobium anosmum

This huge genus (it may include as many as 1,400 species and even more hybrids) ranges from Japan and the Himalayas to Australia and the Pacific Islands. Many are grown by orchid fanciers in greenhouses (outdoors in the tropics or mildest subtropical and the Mediterranean climates). Many are also commercially grown for the cut flower trade. Some have thin, canelike pseudobulbs (see "Meet the Orchids," page 463), others short, fat ones. Only a few of the more widely grown are mentioned here.

D. bigibbum phalaenopsis (D. phalaenopsis). Intermediate grower. Zone H2. Native to Australia and New Guinea. Blooms throughout the year, with canes up to 3 ft. tall producing arching spikes that carry as many as ten 3-in. purple flowers. The parent of many hybrids.

D. hybrids. Zone H2. A bewildering number of hybrids have been produced in Hawaii and elsewhere, both for ornamental potted plants and for cut flowers and leis. Most are intermediate growers. Buy plants in bloom to get desired flower color and bloom season.

D. kingianum. Cool grower. Zones 16, 17, 22–24; H1. Native to Australia. Makes large clumps of 2–20-in. pseudobulbs topped by 4-in. leaves. In late winter or early spring, erect spikes to 8 in. long carry a few or up to as many as 20 fragrant, inch-wide flowers in pink, white, or red. Thrives outdoors along California coast if protected from frost.

D. nobile. Cool grower. Zone H1. Himalayan native. Canes 12–20 in. high carry two ranks of leaves, which last for about 2 years. Short inflorescences borne on leafy and leafless canes carry two to four fragrant, 1½-in., white to purplish pink flowers with a yellow or white zone surrounding a dark purple eye. Blooms almost anytime of year.

D. speciosum. Cool grower. Zones 16, 17, 22–24; H1. From Australia. Large masses of 4-in. to 3-ft. pseudobulbs topped with 1½–10-in.-long leaves. Blooms in late winter or early spring. Inflorescences are crowded spikes of fragrant, creamy to yellow flowers; they resemble bushy foxtails, can reach 2–2½ ft. long.

CARE

Culturally, dendrobiums fall into two classes. Intermediate-climate types are evergreen; they need water throughout the year (somewhat less in winter) and temperatures similar to those required by cattleyas. Cool growers drop some or all of their leaves during a period of winter dormancy, at which time they need very little water (only enough to keep pseudobulbs from shrinking) and temperatures suitable for green-leafed paphiopedilums.

Dendrobiums have large, tough, long-lasting blooms—great for cut flowers.

Dendromecon
BUSH POPPY
Papaveraceae
EVERGREEN SHRUBS

- ZONES VARY BY SPECIES
- FULL SUN
- NO IRRIGATION NEEDED

Dendromecon harfordii

Both species described below give showy display of bright yellow, 2-in.-wide, poppylike flowers. Use on banks and roadsides, with other native shrubs.

Both species can be propagated from cuttings taken in summer. And both get very few pests or diseases.

D. harfordii (D. rigida harfordii). ISLAND BUSH POPPY. Zones 7–9, 14–24. Native to Santa Cruz and Santa Rosa islands off coast of Southern California. Rounded or spreading large shrub or small tree 8–20 ft. tall and as wide, with deep green leaves. Free flowering from spring into early summer, with scattered bloom throughout year. Prune to thin or shape after bloom.

D. rigida. BUSH POPPY. Zones 4–12, 14–24. In Zones 4 and 5, grows best as a south-wall shrub. Native to dry chaparral in lower elevations in California. Untidy growing wild. Freely branched shrub 4–8 ft. tall and 4–6 ft. wide, with shredding yellowish gray or white bark. Thick, veiny, gray-green leaves. Flowers in spring. Prune back to about 2 ft. after bloom.

FOR MORE UNTHIRSTY PLANTS, SEE "PLANTS FOR WATERWISE GARDENS," PAGES 74–78.

Deschampsia ✓
HAIR GRASS
Poaceae
PERENNIAL GRASSES

- ZONES 2–24, EXCEPT AS NOTED
- FULL SUN OR PARTIAL SHADE
- WATER NEEDS VARY BY SPECIES

Deschampsia cespitosa

Hair grasses are grown for their graceful clumps of arching foliage and airy clouds of flowers. Although they grow over much of North America, most garden selections are imports from Europe. Use in mass plantings.

D. cespitosa. TUFTED HAIR GRASS. Clumps of narrow dark green leaves to 1–2 ft. high and 2 ft. wide, evergreen except in colder climates. Airy inflorescences in late spring or early summer can increase plant height to 4 ft. or taller; they are green to greenish gold, turning straw color in winter. Good subject for planting under native oaks. 'Bronzeschleier' ('Bronze Veil') has bronzy yellow inflorescences; 'Goldstaub' is golden yellow. The leaves of 'Northern Lights' are variegated creamy white and turn pink in winter. *D. c. vivipara*, also known as 'Fairy's Joke', produces plantlets instead of seeds; these droop to the ground and may take root. All of the above forms of *D. cespitosa* take regular water. *D. c. holciformis*, Pacific hair grass, grows in Zones 4–9, 14–24. It has darker green foliage than the species and dense, narrow, relatively coarse inflorescences. Takes marshy, even brackish conditions.

D. flexuosa. CRINKLED HAIR GRASS. Smaller than *D. cespitosa* (usually less than 2 ft. high and about a foot wide

in bloom), with more open, bronze to pale greenish yellow inflorescences in midsummer. Succeeds in dry woodland shade as well as in sunnier or moister situations.

Deutzia
Hydrangeaceae
DECIDUOUS SHRUBS

- ZONES 2–11, 14–17, EXCEPT AS NOTED
- FULL SUN OR LIGHT SHADE
- REGULAR WATER

Deutzia gracilis 'Nikko'

These shrubs are best used among evergreens, where they can make a show when in flower, then blend back in with other greenery later on. The sometimes fragrant blooms coincide with those of late-spring bulbs such as tulips.

D. crenata. Native to Japan. Similar to *D. scabra*, but with white flowers. Deep purple-red fall foliage. 'Pride of Rochester' (formerly *D. scabra*) has large clusters of small, frilly, double white flowers tinged pink. *D. c. nakaiana*, dwarf and spreading, has double flowers.

D. × elegantissima. Grows to 6 ft. tall and wide, with pink flowers. 'Rosealind', 4–5 ft. tall and wide, has deep rose flowers.

D. gracilis. SLENDER DEUTZIA. Native to Japan. To 2–4 ft. (possibly 6 ft.) tall, 3–4 ft. wide. Many slender stems arch gracefully, and carry bright green, 2½-in., sharply toothed leaves and clusters of snowy white, fragrant flowers. 'Chardonnay Pearls' has chartreuse foliage. 'Nikko' grows only 1–2 ft. by 5 ft. and can be used as a groundcover.

D. hybrids. Zones 2b–9, 14–23. These include 'Pink-a-Boo', an erect grower to 6–8 ft. tall and 6 ft. wide, with large clusters of pink flowers; and 'Magicien', similar but with dark red flowers.

D. × rosea. To 3–4 ft. tall and wide, with finely toothed leaves. Short clusters of pinkish flowers with white interiors.

D. scabra. Native to Japan, China. To 7–10 ft. by 6 ft. Oval, scallop-toothed, dull green leaves are somewhat rough to touch. White or pale pink flowers in narrow, upright clusters. 'Codsall' ('Codsall Pink') bears double pink blooms. Leaves of 'Variegata' are marked with white.

CARE

Prune shrubs after bloom. With low- or medium-growing kinds, cut some of oldest stems to ground every other year. Prune tall-growing kinds severely by cutting back wood that has flowered. Cut to outward-facing side branches.

Dianella

FLAX LILY
Hemerocallidaceae
PERENNIALS

📏 **ZONES 8, 9, 14–24**

☼ ◖ **FULL SUN IN COOLER CLIMATES ONLY**

💧 **REGULAR WATER**

Dianella tasmanica

These interesting plants are grown for their grassy, straplike foliage and small, star-shaped blue flowers followed by shiny berries. Provide rich, porous soil and routine fertilizing. Attractive near swimming pools.

D. caerulea. BLUE FLAX LILY. Native to eastern Australia. Tufted or mat-forming plants 1–2 ft. high and 2–3 ft. wide. Shiny, medium green leaves are lightly toothed, to 2½ ft. long. Light or dark blue flowers about ¾ in. across have prominent yellow stamens and are followed by translucent blue to purple berries. 'Casitas Springs' has grayish foliage. 'Cassa Blue' is compact to about 18 in. high and has soft blue foliage.

D. revoluta. BLACK ANTHER FLAX LILY. Native to eastern Australia and Tasmania. Tight, clumping perennial that spreads slowly by rhizomes. Two varieties are most common. 'Baby Bliss' has blue-green foliage, 12–18 in. high, and pale violet blooms followed by green berries. 'Little Rev' grows 2–3 ft. high with leaves that are yellowish green on the upper surface and blue-green on the more visible lower surface. Rarely blooms.

D. tasmanica. From southeastern Australia, including Tasmania. Grows 3–4 ft. tall; narrowly upright when young but spreading slowly by rhizomes with age. Sturdy, medium green leaves (striped white in 'Variegata' and yellow in 'Yellow Stripe'). Loose clusters of small, blue summer flowers on straight, slender stalks are followed by large (¾ in.), glistening blue berries that last 2 months or longer on the plant. 'Tasred' has green leaves that are red at the base. The red color intensifies in cold.

> Try *Dianella tasmanica* as a low edging along a garden path, where its striped yellow leaves can be enjoyed. *D. revoluta* 'Little Rev' makes a striking low accent in front of a boulder.

Dianthus

PINK
Caryophyllaceae
PERENNIALS, BIENNIALS, AND ANNUALS

📏 **ZONES A2, A3; 1–24, EXCEPT AS NOTED**

☼ ◖ **LIGHT SHADE IN HOTTEST CLIMATES**

💧 **REGULAR WATER**

🦋 **ATTRACT BUTTERFLIES**

Dianthus chinensis Telstar

This genus is made up of over 300 species and an extremely large number of hybrids. Most kinds form attractive evergreen mats or tufts of grasslike green, gray-green, blue-green, or gray-blue leaves. Single, semidouble, or double flowers in white and shades of pink, rose, red, yellow, and orange. Many have a rich, spicy fragrance. The main bloom period for most is spring into early summer, but some kinds rebloom later in the season or keep going into fall if faded flowers are removed. Among dianthus are favorites such as cottage pink and sweet William, highly prized cut flowers such as carnation (clove pink), and rock garden miniatures. There are hundreds of varieties and hybrids available, including some local favorites.

D. Allwoodii hybrids. Perennial. Group of pinks derived from crossing carnation (*D. caryophyllus*) and cottage pink (*D. plumarius*). Plants vary in size, but most are 12–15 in. high and 2 ft. wide, with gray-green foliage and two blossoms per stem. Pink, white, or red flowers are strongly clove scented. Long bloom period if deadheaded regularly. More compact and floriferous than their *D. plumarius* parent.

D. arenarius. Perennial. From Europe. Tufted plant to 1½ ft. high and wide, with narrow, grass green leaves and 1½-in.-wide, fringed white flowers sometimes marked with green or purple. Highly fragrant; can tolerate some shade.

D. barbatus. SWEET WILLIAM. Vigorous biennial often grown as annual. From southern Europe. To 20 in. high and 1 ft. wide, with sturdy stems. Leaves are flat, light to dark green. Dense clusters of white, pink, rose, red, purplish, or bicolored flowers, about ½ in. across, set among leafy bracts; not very fragrant. Sow seeds in late spring for bloom the following year. Double-flowered and dwarf strains are obtainable from seed. Indian Carpet is only 6 in. high. The Amazon series grows 18–36 in. high.

D. caryophyllus. CARNATION, CLOVE PINK. Perennial. Zones A2, A3; 1–24; H1. Highly bred Mediterranean species. Two distinct categories exist: florists' and border types. Both have double flowers, bluish green leaves, and branching, leafy stems that often become woody at base.

Border carnations are bushier and more compact (12–14 in. high and wide) than florists' type. Fragrant, 2–2½-in.-wide flowers are borne in profusion in a multitude of single and bicolored shades. Effective as shrub border edgings, in borders of mixed flowers, and also in containers. Hybrid carnations grown from seed are usually treated as annuals but often live over. Among the many fine varieties are bright red 'Cinnamon Red Hots' to 1 ft. high and the Super Trouper series, 8–10 in. high and available in a wide range of single and multicolored shades. There is also a strain called simply Trailing Carnation Mixed, with pink- or red-flowered plants that hang or sprawl from pot or window box.

Florists' carnations are grown commercially in greenhouses, outdoors in gardens in mild-winter areas, including higher-elevation gardens in Hawaii. Greenhouse-grown plants reach 4 ft., have fragrant flowers 3 in. wide in many colors—white, shades of pink and red, orange, purple, and yellow; some are

D

D

CLOCKWISE FROM TOP: *Dianthus plumarius; D. gratianopolitanus* 'Firewitch'; *D. caryophyllus*

variegated. For large flowers, leave only terminal bloom on each stem, pinching out all other buds down to fifth joint, below which new flowering stems will develop. Stake to prevent sprawling. Start with strong cuttings taken from the most vigorous plants of selected named varieties. Sturdy plants conceal supports, look quite tidy.

D. chinensis. CHINESE PINK, RAINBOW PINK. Biennial or short-lived perennial; most varieties grown as annuals. Erect plant to 6–30 in. high and 6–10 in. wide; stems branch only at top. Stem leaves narrow, 1–3 in. long, ½ in. wide, hairy on margins. Basal leaves are usually gone by flowering time. Flowers about 1 in. across, rose-lilac with deeper-colored eye; lack fragrance.

Modern strains are compact domes (1 ft. high or less) covered with bright flowers in white,

pink, red, and all variations and combinations of those colors. Petals are deeply fringed on some, smooth-edged on others. Some flowers have intricately marked eyes. 'Fire Carpet' is solid red; 'Snowfire', white with a red eye. Telstar is a bushy, extra-dwarf (6–8 in.) strain with dark green leaves. Sow directly in ground in spring, in full sun, for summer bloom. Pick off faded flowers with their bases to prolong bloom.

D. deltoides. MAIDEN PINK. Perennial (even though it blooms in just a few weeks from seed). From Europe and Asia. To 8–12 in. high, forming a loose mat to 1 ft. wide. Blossoms about ¾ in. wide, with sharp-toothed petals, are borne at ends of forked flowering stems with short leaves. Colors include white and light or dark rose to purple, spotted with lighter colors. Blooms in summer, sometimes again in fall. Useful, showy groundcover or bank cover. Can tolerate half-day shade.

Varieties include white 'Albus'; 'Arctic Fire', white with red

centers; 'Brilliant', reddish pink blooms; and 'Pixie Star', pink with dark pink centers.

D. gratianopolitanus (D. caesius). CHEDDAR PINK. Perennial. From Europe. Neat, ground-hugging, foot-wide mat of blue-gray foliage. Stems 6–10 in. high bear small, typically pink to rose, single blossoms (less than an inch across) that are very fragrant. Bloom season lasts from spring to fall if plants are deadheaded regularly. Effective as groundcover or edging or in rock garden. Varieties include 'Firewitch', with magenta-pink flowers; 'Baths' Pink', with soft pink fringed blooms on 12–15-in. stems; and 'Tiny Rubies', a dwarf selection with double, ruby red flowers on 4-in. stems.

D. plumarius. COTTAGE PINK. Perennial. Zones A1; 1–24. Charming, almost legendary European species, cultivated for hundreds of years and used in developing many hybrids. Typically has loosely matted gray-green foliage in clump to 2 ft. wide. Flowering stems 10–18 in. high; spicily fragrant, dark-centered flowers in rose, pink, or white, with more or less fringed petals. Highly prized are old laced pinks, with white flowers in which each petal is outlined in red or pink. Cottage pinks bloom from summer to fall if deadheaded. Indispensable edging for borders or for peony or rose beds. Perfect addition to small arrangements and old-fashioned bouquets. Choice selections include 'Essex Witch', with semidouble, rose-pink flowers on 5-in. stems; 'Sweetness', with a mix of darker-centered shades on 4-in. stems; and 'Musgrave's Pink', a foot-high classic that's at least 200 years old and bears intensely fragrant, single white blooms with a green eye.

CARE

All kinds of dianthus thrive in light, fast-draining soil. Carnations, sweet William, and cottage pinks need fairly rich soil. Rock garden or alpine types require a gritty growing medium, with added lime if soil is acid. Avoid overwatering. Sow seeds of annual kinds in flats or directly in garden. Propagate

perennial kinds by cuttings made from tips of growing shoots, by division or layering, or from seed. Carnation and sweet William are subject to rust and fusarium wilt.

Diascia
TWINSPUR
Scrophulariaceae
PERENNIALS AND ANNUALS

⚡ **ZONES VARY BY SPECIES**

☼ ◑ **PARTIAL SHADE IN HOTTEST CLIMATES**

◗ ◆ **MODERATE TO REGULAR WATER**

Diascia integerrima 'Diamonte Coral Rose'

These increasingly popular South African natives are related to snapdragon (*Antirrhinum*). The coral to purplish pink flowers each have two prominent spurs on the back that bear oils attractive to pollinating bees. Blooms are carried in spikelike clusters at stem ends from spring through early summer and often into fall. At their best used in rock gardens, borders, or containers.

D. barberae. Perennial often grown as a cool-season annual. Zones 5–10, 14–24; H1. Mat-forming plant to 10 in. high, 20 in. wide, with rose-pink blossoms. 'Blackthorn Apricot' bears apricot-colored flowers. 'Fisher's Flora' (Zones 7–9, 14–24) forms a low green mat to 6 in. high and 20 in. wide, with 10-in. sprays of salmon-pink blossoms. 'Ruby Field', to 10 in. high and 2 ft. wide, bears salmon-pink blossoms and has a long bloom season.

D. fetcaniensis. Zones 4–9, 14–24. To 10 in. high, 20 in. wide, with rose-pink blooms.

D. hybrids. Zones 4–9, 14–24; H1. These include 'Blue Bonnet', with unusual mauve-blue to lavender flowers to 12 in. high; 'Emma', an especially cold-hardy selection to 2 ft. high and 4 ft. wide, with raspberry-colored blossoms; 'Flirtation Orange', to 8–12 in. high with orange flowers; 'Ice Pole', to 10–14 in. high and 18 in. wide, with pure white flowers; 'Langthorn's Lavender', to 1 ft. high, with lavender blooms; and 'Red Start', to 8 in. high and 1 ft. wide, with watermelon red flowers. A group of hybrids from England (all 7–10 in. high and 1½ ft. wide) includes coral pink 'Coral Belle'; 'Little Charmer', pink with a dark red eye; rosy red 'Red Ace'; and deep pink 'Strawberry Sundae'. Plants in the Flying Colors series have large flowers in shades of red, pink, apricot, and coral; most grow to 6–12 in. high (some grow upright, others are more trailing).

D. integerrima. Zones 2–9, 14–24. To 1½ ft. high, creeping to 3–4 ft. wide. Leaves are small, linear. Loose spikes of rich purplish pink flowers. 'Coral Canyon' grows 12–15 in. high and 1½ ft. wide, bears salmon-pink flowers.

D. rigescens. Zones 7–9, 14–24. To 1 ft. high. Sprawling stems form clumps to 1 ft. high and 2 ft. wide, turn up at ends to display 6–8-in. spikes of rich pink flowers. Cut out old stems.

D. vigilis. Zones 4–9, 14–24. To 20 in. high and slightly wider, with fleshy green leaves and light pink flowers. 'Jack Elliott' has large blooms that are pink with yellow and maroon markings.

CARE

Treat as you would snapdragons or other cool-season annuals, planting in fall or spring. Plants may die in winter if planted in cool, wet soil. Shear back after bloom period.

For a cottage garden effect in a container, combine pale coral twinspur with coral Calibrachoa *and sky blue lobelia.*

Dicentra
BLEEDING HEART
Papaveraceae
PERENNIALS

- ✏ **ZONES 1–9, 14–24, EXCEPT AS NOTED**
- ◐ ● **PARTIAL OR FULL SHADE**
- 💧 **REGULAR WATER, EXCEPT AS NOTED**
- 🦋 **ATTRACT BIRDS, BUTTERFLIES**

Dicentra spectabilis

Bleeding hearts are delicate-looking plants with graceful, divided, fernlike foliage. Dainty pendent flowers are usually heart-shaped, in pink, rose, yellow, or white on leafless, horizontal to arching stems.

D. chrysantha. GOLDEN EARDROPS. Native to inner Coast Ranges and Sierra Nevada foothills of California. Erect plant with sparse, blue-gray, divided leaves on stout, hollow, 4–5-ft. stems. Golden yellow, short-spurred flowers, held upright in large clusters. Grows to 1½ ft. wide. Requires warmth. Unlike many dicentras, this species needs soil that is not too rich; make sure drainage is good. Plant has deep taproot and does not need irrigation during its flowering in spring and summer. Seed available from wildflower specialists.

D. eximia. FRINGED BLEEDING HEART. Native to northeastern U.S. Forms tidy clump 1–1½ ft. high and wide. Blue-gray basal leaves are more finely divided than those of *D. formosa*. Deep rose-pink flowers with short, rounded spurs bloom from midspring into summer. Cut back for second growth and occasional repeat bloom. Does not spread by rhizomes but may extend itself by self-sowing.

D. formosa. WESTERN BLEEDING HEART. Native to moist woods along Pacific Coast. To 1½ ft. high, 3 ft. or wider. Blue-green foliage. In spring, leafless flower stalks hold clusters of pendulous pale or deep rose flowers on reddish stems. Spreads freely by rhizomes and seeding, forming large colonies. 'Bacchanal' has finely cut, gray-green leaves and dark red flowers. 'Langtrees' has silvery green foliage and white flowers shaded pink. 'Zestful' is everblooming, with deep rose flowers. *D. f. oregana* grows to 1 ft. high, has silvery green leaves and cream-colored flowers that are tipped with purple.

D. hybrids. *D. eximia* and *D. formosa* cross freely to yield hybrids, many of which have been named. The following are among the most commonly cultivated; they grow 1–1½ ft. high and 1½–2 ft. across (eventually spreading more widely) and bloom from spring into summer.

'Bountiful'. Dark blue-green foliage and purplish pink to dusky red flowers.

'King of Hearts'. Finely cut blue-green leaves with rosy pink flowers produced over a long period. 'Candy Hearts' and 'Ivory Hearts' are similar but with dark pink and white flowers, respectively.

'Luxuriant'. Zones A1–A3; 1–9, 14–24. Medium to dark green leaves and red flowers.

D. spectabilis. COMMON BLEEDING HEART. Zones A1–A3; 1–9, 14–24. Native to Japan. Old garden favorite; showiest and largest-leafed of all bleeding hearts. To 2–3 ft. high, 3 ft. wide; stems are set with soft green leaves. Blooms in late spring, bearing flowers on one side of arching stems—rose-pink, pendulous, heart-shaped, with protruding white inner petals. 'Alba' ('Pantaloons') is a pure white form. 'Gold Heart' has bright yellow foliage.

Plants generally die down and become dormant by midsummer, but they'll keep going longer in cool-summer climates if given adequate moisture. Plant summer-maturing perennials nearby to fill the gap. Dormant roots—fleshy and

sometimes even woody—are available at nurseries from late fall to earliest spring; plant as soon as they become available in your area. In the Southwest, you can sometimes establish plants permanently in a cool, moist spot in foothill canyons, but the usual practice there is to plant new roots in the ground or a container each year and discard plants in early summer after blooming. In Southern California, plants usually last for only one season. Best in partial shade.

CARE

In general, dicentras need rich, light, moist, porous soil. Never let water stand around roots. Foliage dies down even in mild-winter climates; mark clumps to avoid digging into roots in dormant season. Short-lived in mild-winter areas.

Dichondra
Convolvulaceae
PERENNIALS

- ✏ **ZONES 8–10, 12–24; H1, H2**
- ☼ ◐ **FULL SUN OR PARTIAL SHADE**
- 💧 **REGULAR WATER**

Dichondra argentea 'Silver Falls'

These low-growing plants spread by rooting surface runners. One species is an often-seen small-scale groundcover; the other is an interesting foliage plant.

D. argentea 'Silver Falls'. Grows 2–3 in. high and spreads 4–6 ft. wide. Heart-shaped leaves are covered with silvery down, as are the stems. Eye-catching, shimmering container plant; cascades over the edge of pots or window boxes. Can also be used as a small-scale groundcover. Easy to grow from seed. Use as an annual in cold-winter areas.

D. micrantha. Small round leaves look like miniature water lily pads. In shade and with regular moisture and nutrients, it can grow to 6 in. high and require frequent mowing. Spreads widely; may become invasive. Once favored and commonly used as a lawn, but large plantings were so often devastated by flea beetles that it is now used mainly in limited spaces. Good in small areas that are subject to foot traffic—as between steppingstones—where it stays low and seldom (if ever) needs trimming or mowing. Often sold as *D. carolinensis* or *D. repens*.

Dicksonia

Dicksoniaceae
TREE FERNS

🌿 ZONES VARY BY SPECIES

☼ ◑ ● FULL SUN IN COOLER CLIMATES ONLY

💧 REGULAR WATER

Dicksonia antarctica

Hardy, slow-growing tree fern from Southern Hemisphere. Easy to transplant and establish. See "Meet the Ferns" on page 320 for culture.

D. antarctica. TASMANIAN TREE FERN. Zones 8, 9, 14–17, 19–24; H1. Native to southeastern Australia, Tasmania. Hardiest of tree ferns; well-established plants tolerate 20°F (−7°C). Thick, red-brown, fuzzy trunk grows slowly to 15 ft. Many arching, 3–6-ft. fronds grow from top of trunk; mature fronds are more finely cut than those of Australian tree fern (*Cyathea cooperi*).

D. squarrosa. Zones 17, 23, 24; H1. Native to New Zealand. Slender, dark trunk grows slowly to 20 ft. tall. Flat crown of 8-ft.-long, stiff, leathery fronds with whitish undersides. Much less frequently grown than *D. antarctica*.

Dicliptera

Acanthaceae
PERENNIALS

🌿 ZONES VARY BY SPECIES

☼ ◑ FULL SUN OR PARTIAL SHADE

💧 WATER NEEDS VARY BY SPECIES

🐦 ATTRACT BIRDS

Dicliptera sericea

Tender perennials with narrow, tubular, two-lipped blossoms. Where stems are not killed to ground by frost, shear to about 6 in. high in late winter.

D. resupinata. Zones 13, 18–23; root hardy to about 22°F (−6°C). Native to washes and rocky slopes from southeastern Arizona and southwestern New Mexico into Mexico. Open, sparse growth to 2 ft. high, 2–3 ft. wide. Elongated heart-shaped leaves are dark green, with an attractive purplish cast in cool weather. Slender, rosy purple, ¾-in.-long flowers from late spring to fall. Sometimes reseeds but is not invasive. Little or no water.

D. sericea (D. suberecta). HUMMINGBIRD BUSH. Zones 12, 13, 15–17, 19, 21–24. Native to Uruguay. Woody-based perennial 2 ft. high, 1½ ft. wide, with grayish green, softly downy leaves. Summertime clusters of bright orange-red, 1½-in.-long flowers attract hummingbirds. Moderate to regular water.

Dictamnus albus

GAS PLANT, FRAXINELLA
Rutaceae
PERENNIAL

🌿 ZONES 1–9

☼ ◑ FULL SUN OR LIGHT SHADE

💧 ● MODERATE TO REGULAR WATER

◊ OIL FROM IMMATURE SEED CAPSULES MAY CAUSE AN ALLERGIC SKIN REACTION

Dictamnus albus

A sturdy, long-lived perennial, native from Europe to northern China. It's extremely permanent in colder climates, needing little care once established. It forms clumps 2½–4 ft. high and 3 ft. wide. In early summer, it produces loose spires of blossoms at branch tips. Each flower resembles a wild azalea, with narrow petals and prominent greenish stamens. Pink is the basic color, but nurseries offer lilac-purple *D. a. purpureus* and white *D. a. albus*. Seedpods that follow can be left in place for fall interest. Glossy olive green leaves with 9 to 11 leaflets, each 1–3 in. long, are handsome throughout the growing season.

Plant emits strong lemony scent when rubbed or brushed against. In warm, humid weather, oils from immature seed capsules may briefly ignite if you hold a lighted match immediately beneath a flower cluster—hence the common name, "gas plant" (this "ignition test" does not harm plant). Effective in borders; good cut flower.

CARE

Divide infrequently, since divisions are difficult to establish and often take 2 or 3 years to bloom well. Propagate from seed sown in fall or spring; or take root cuttings in spring.

Dierama

FAIRY WAND
Iridaceae
PERENNIALS FROM CORMS

🌿 ZONES 4–24

☼ FULL SUN

💧 REGULAR WATER

Dierama pendulum 'Album'

Although these natives to South Africa are evergreen, they will die to the ground in extreme cold. Their swordlike leaves are 2 ft. long. In late spring or summer, slender, arching stems, 4–7 ft. tall, are topped with pendulous flowers that range in color from purplish pink to other pink shades to white. Blooms of *D. pendulum* are bell-shaped; those of *D. pulcherrimum* more funnel-shaped. Effective against background of dark green shrubs or at end of pool where graceful form can be displayed.

CARE

Plant in spring, setting corms 3–5 in. deep and about 2 ft. apart. When dividing clumps, include several corms in each division.

FOR MORE ON PERENNIALS, SEE "GROW: PERENNIALS," PAGES 686–687.

Dietes

FORTNIGHT LILY, AFRICAN IRIS

Iridaceae

PERENNIALS FROM RHIZOMES

⚡ **ZONES 8, 9, 12–24; H1, H2**

☼ ◑ **FULL SUN OR PARTIAL SHADE**

◗ ◗ **MODERATE TO REGULAR WATER**

Dietes grandiflora

These irislike plants with fans of stiff, narrow evergreen leaves form dense, long-lasting clumps. The flowers, resembling small Japanese irises, consist of three outer and three inner segments. They appear on branched stalks throughout spring, summer, and fall, sometimes well into winter in mild climates. Bloom bursts seem to occur at 2-week intervals, hence the common name "fortnight lily." The flowers come in solid colors—white, cream, yellow; each of the three outer segments features a small blotch of contrasting orange, yellow, or brown. Each flower lasts only a day (with one exception), but the supply of flowers on a stem is seemingly endless. Excellent in permanent landscape plantings with pebbles and rocks, shrubs, and other long-lived perennials.

D. bicolor. From South Africa. Stems 2–3 ft. tall. Flowers about 2 in. wide and circular in outline, light yellow with dark brown to maroon blotches. Flower stems last only one year.

D. grandiflora (D. iridioides 'Johnsonii'). From South Africa. This is a somewhat taller (up to 3 ft.), larger version of *D. iridioides* and is usually sold as a variety of that species. Other differences include brown markings at the bases of inner segments and, on outer segments, yellow blotches that are

actually bearded. Unlike all the others, this species has flowers that last for 3 days before folding; flower stems are perennial (see *D. iridioides*). 'Variegata' has dull green leaves with creamy yellow margins. 'Sunstripe' has yellow-striped leaves.

D. hybrids. 'Lemon Drops' and 'Orange Drops' are hybrids of *D. bicolor* and resemble it except for flower color. 'Lemon Drops' is ivory with yellow blotches, 'Orange Drops' ivory with orange blotches. As is true for their other parent, *D. iridioides*, these hybrids' flower stems last more than a year; see below for care. 'Jack Catlin', of uncertain parentage, grows to 1½–2 ft. high and 3–4 ft. wide, with wider, more arching, dark green leaves. White flowers are marked yellow.

D. iridioides (D. vegeta, Moraea iridioides). From East Africa. Stems to 3 ft. tall. Waxy white flowers to 3 in. across have yellow-orange blotches, a few orange marks at bases of inner three segments; three style arms—appendages radiating from flower's center—are usually pale violet. To prevent self-sowing and prolong bloom, break off blossoms individually. Don't cut flower stems (they last for more than a year) until they clearly have stopped producing blooms; then cut back to lower leaf joint near base of stem. 'John's Runner' is a dwarf form growing only 1–2 ft. high and 2–3 ft. wide with white flowers marked with yellow and purple. Spent flower stalks produce plantlets that root as the stalks fall over, allowing the plant to spread. For the plant sold as *D. iridioides* 'Johnsonii', see *D. grandiflora*.

CARE

Plant from containers (bare rhizomes are not sold) at any time of year, setting plants about 2 ft. apart. All types look best with good soil and regular watering; but once established, they will perform satisfactorily even in poor soil or with infrequent or erratic watering. Clumps can remain undisturbed for years; when you need to divide, do so in fall or winter.

Digitalis

FOXGLOVE

Plantaginaceae

PERENNIALS AND BIENNIALS

⚡ **ZONES VARY BY SPECIES**

☼ ◑ ● **EXPOSURE NEEDS VARY BY SPECIES**

◗ **REGULAR WATER, EXCEPT AS NOTED**

🦅 **ATTRACT BIRDS, BUTTERFLIES**

◊ **ALL PARTS ARE POISONOUS IF INGESTED**

Digitalis purpurea

Mainly from Europe and the Mediterranean region, these erect plants grow 2–8 ft. high, forming low clumps of hairy gray-green leaves topped by spikes of tubular flowers shaped like the fingertips of a glove. Flower colors include purple, yellow, white, and pastels. Common foxglove (*D. pupurea*) is widely grown for height and color display in shaded gardens, though it will thrive in full sun in cool-summer regions. In parts of California and the Pacific Northwest, it has escaped from gardens to decorate roadsides. Other, less well-known species are deserving subjects for borders, woodland edges, and larger rock gardens. Most tend to be biennials, but some can be coaxed into a second year of bloom if spent flowers are removed before they set seed.

D. ferruginea. RUSTY FOXGLOVE. Biennial or short-lived perennial. Zones 1–10, 14–24. To 4 ft. tall, 1½ ft. wide, with stems densely clothed in deeply veined leaves. Long, dense spikes of yellowish flowers netted with rusty red. Full sun or light shade. 'Gelber Herold' and 'Gigantea' are common varieties similar to the species.

D. grandiflora (D. ambigua). YELLOW FOXGLOVE. Biennial or short-lived perennial. Zones 1–10, 14–24. To 3 ft. tall, 1½ ft. wide. Toothed leaves wrap around stem. Flowers are 2–3 in. long, yellowish marked with brown. 'John Innes Tetra' is a choice hybrid to 20 in. high, with gray-green leaves and pale yellow flowers richly netted with gold and brown. 'Carillon', to 12–15 in. high, has light yellow flowers. Full sun or light shade.

D. laevigata. Perennial. Zones 3b–10, 14–24. To 3 ft. high, 1½ ft. wide, with smooth, narrow dark green leaves and inch-long, creamy yellow flowers speckled with purplish brown. Full sun; tolerates light shade.

D. lanata. GRECIAN FOXGLOVE. Biennial or short-lived perennial. Zones 2b–10, 14–24. To 2 ft. high and 1 ft. wide, with cream to light tan flowers netted with brown. Full sun or light shade.

D. lutea. Perennial. Zones 1–10, 14–24. Mediterranean native. To 2–2½ ft. high, 15 in. wide, with narrow, tightly packed spires of pale yellow flowers dotted with brown. 'Flashing Spires' has leaves splashed with creamy yellow. Partial or full shade; can take full sun in cool-summer climates.

D. × mertonensis. Perennial. Zones 1–10, 14–24. Spikes to 2–3 ft. high, bearing attractive coppery rose blooms above a foot-wide clump of furry leaves. Though a hybrid, it comes true from seed. Partial or full shade; can take full sun in cool-summer climates.

D. obscura. NARROW-LEAF FOXGLOVE. Woody-based perennial. Zones 2–10, 14–24. To 1½ ft. high, 1 ft. wide; lance-shaped leaves and spikes of drooping brown-and-yellow bells. 'Sunset' is a dwarf selection. Takes full sun or light shade, well-drained but not rich soil, and occasional deep watering.

D. purpurea. COMMON FOXGLOVE. Biennial or short-lived perennial. Zones A2, A3; 1–24. Variable, appearing in many garden forms. Bold, erect growth to 4 ft. or taller, with stems rising from clumps of large, rough, woolly light green leaves. Short-stalked stem leaves become smaller toward top of the plant; these are the

D

D

source of digitalis, a valued but highly poisonous medicinal drug. Pendulous flowers 2–3 in. long, borne in one-sided, 1–2-ft.-long spikes, purple with darker spots on lower, paler side. Partial or full shade; can take full sun in cool-summer climates.

Garden strains include Camelot, which reaches 3½–4 ft. tall in sun or shade and blooms consistently the first and second year in shades of rose, white, lavender, or cream with a speckled throat; 5-ft.-tall Excelsior, with fuller spikes than species and flowers held more horizontally to show off interior spotting; 3-ft. Foxy, which performs as an annual and blooms in 5 months from seed; 4-ft. Gloxiniiflora, bearing flowers that are larger and wider than those of species; 3-ft.-high Peloric Mixed, with topmost flower of each spike open or bowl-shaped and 3 in. wide; and Shirley, a tall (6 ft.), robust strain with a full range of colors.

D. thapsi. Perennial. Zones 2–10, 14–24. From Spain. To 1 ft. high and wide, with furry foliage and short spires of drooping purplish pink flowers. Thrives under the same conditions as *D. obscura*. 'Spanish Peaks' is a selection chosen as outstanding by the Denver Botanic Gardens.

CARE

Foxgloves need moist, well-drained soil and appreciate enrichment. Set out plants in fall for bloom the following spring and summer. Sow seeds in spring. Control snails and slugs. After first flowering, cut off main spike; side shoots will develop and bloom late in the season. In hottest climates, plants will usually die out in summer heat. Plants self-sow freely; blooms of volunteers are often white or light-colored.

Foxgloves love company. Plant them in clusters for the most striking effects—at the back of a border or centered in square beds with lower plants around them.

Dimorphotheca
AFRICAN DAISY,
CAPE MARIGOLD
Asteraceae
ANNUALS

✿ **ZONES 1–24; BETTER IN WARM–SUMMER CLIMATES**

☼ **FULL SUN**

💧 **MODERATE WATER**

Dimorphotheca sinuata
'Spring Flash Orange'

Free-blooming South African natives with daisy flowers that are unsurpassed for winter and spring color in dry-summer, warm-winter areas. In those regions, broadcast seeds in late summer or early fall where plants are to grow (preferably in light soil). In colder climates, sow in spring for summer bloom. Flowers close when shaded, on heavily overcast days, and at night. Use in broad masses as groundcover, in borders and parking strips, along rural roadsides, as filler among low shrubs. For other plants known as African daisy, see *Arctotis* and *Osteospermum fruticosum*.

D. barberae. See *Osteospermum jucundum*.

D. ecklonis. See *Osteospermum ecklonis*.

D. fruticosa. See *Osteospermum fruticosum*.

D. pluvialis (D. annua). Branched stems 4–16 in. high. Leaves are coarsely toothed. Yellow-centered, 1–2-in.-wide flower heads, with rays that are white above, violet or purple beneath. 'Glistening White', dwarf form with flower heads 4 in. across, is especially desirable.

D. sinuata (D. aurantiaca). Best known of annual African daisies. To 4–12 in.

high. Narrow leaves with a few teeth or shallow cuts. Flowers 1½ in. wide with yellow centers or dark centers with flecks of yellow, and orange-yellow rays sometimes deep violet at base. Hybrids between this species and *D. pluvialis* come in white and shades of yellow and light orange, often with contrasting dark centers. Widely used for winter-to-spring color in Zones 10–13, where plantings reseed yearly. Provide some supplemental water if winter rains don't come; leave dry over summer. Highly invasive in hot desert regions; should not be used near parks, preserves, or natural areas.

Diosma. See *Coleonema*

Diospyros. See Persimmon

Diplacus aurantiacus. See *Mimulus aurantiacus*

Dipogon lignosus. See *Dolichos lignosus*

Disanthus cercidifolius
Hamamelidaceae
DECIDUOUS SHRUB

✿ **ZONES 4–7, 14–17**

☼ ☽ **LIGHT SHADE IN HOTTEST CLIMATES**

💧 **REGULAR WATER**

Disanthus cercidifolius

This slender-branched shrub, native to Japan, is grown for its magnificent fall color. Leaves are nearly round and smooth, and turn from bluish green to shades of deep red with orange tints at the onset of colder weather. The tiny, purplish fall

flowers are mildly scented. The shrub grows to 10–12 ft. tall and wide. Provide rich soil and protection from wind. No special pruning needed.

Disporum cantoniense
CHINESE FAIRY BELLS
Colchicaceae
PERENNIAL

✿ **ZONES 4–9, 14–17**

☼ ☽ ● **PARTIAL OR FULL SHADE**

💧 **REGULAR WATER**

Disporum cantoniense

From China, Southeast Asia, and the Himalayas; worthy addition to woodland gardens. In spring, colorful, bamboolike shoots emerge from rhizomes in shades of white, pink, purple-pink, or green. Shiny, bright green leaves are lance-shaped. Fragrant, creamy white or reddish purple spring flowers are bell-shaped and dangle among the new growth. Flowers are followed by purplish black berries. The plant forms an upright clump 4–6 ft. tall and 3 ft. wide and dies to the ground in cold weather. 'Night Heron' has dark purple new growth that fades to blackish green. 'Green Giant' has new growth that emerges in shades of white, pink, and green. Plant in moist soil, rich in organic matter.

Chinese fairy bells are best in woodland gardens with other plants that like the same conditions, such as ferns.

Distictis

Bignoniaceae
EVERGREEN VINES

- ⚡ **ZONES VARY BY SPECIES**
- ☀️ ◐ **FULL SUN OR PARTIAL SHADE**
- 💧 **REGULAR WATER**

Distictis buccinatoria

These Mexican natives are spectacular vines for milder climates, reaching heights of 20–30 ft. Glossy leaves consist of two leaflets with a central, three-part tendril that plants use for climbing. All bear long-lasting, trumpet-shaped flowers.

D. buccinatoria (Bignonia cherere, Phaedranthus buccinatorius). BLOOD-RED TRUMPET VINE. Zones 8, 9, 14–24; H1. Oblong to oval leaflets 2–4 in. long. Clusters of 4-in.-long, yellow-throated flowers in orange-red fading to bluish red; blossoms stand out well from vine. Blooms in bursts throughout year when weather warms. Give protected site in interior valleys of California.

D. laxiflora (D. lactiflora, D. cinerea). VANILLA TRUMPET VINE. Zones 16, 22–24; H1, H2. More restrained than most trumpet vines and requires less pruning. Oblong leaflets. Vanilla-scented, 3½-in.-long trumpets appear in generous clusters throughout warmer months, sometimes giving 8 months of bloom; they are violet at first, fading to lavender and white.

D. 'Rivers'. ROYAL TRUMPET VINE. Zones 16, 22–24; H1, H2. Plants sold under this name are nearly a match for *D. buccinatoria* in vigor and foliage, and have flowers of about the same size that are mauve to purple with a yellow to orange throat. Sometimes labeled *D. riversii.*

CARE

Plant in good, well-drained soil; provide sturdy support, since growth is dense and heavy. Prune in winter to thin stems, control size.

Dizygotheca elegantissima. See *Schefflera elegantissima*

Dodecatheon

SHOOTING STAR
Primulaceae
PERENNIALS

- ⚡ **ZONES VARY BY SPECIES**
- ☀️ ◐ **FULL SUN OR PARTIAL SHADE**
- 💧 **REGULAR WATER DURING GROWTH AND BLOOM**

Dodecatheon clevelandii insulare

Mostly native to the West, these perennials form basal rosettes of pale green leaves in spring, which later dry up in summer heat. The spring flowers are somewhat like small cyclamen blooms. Few to many form in clusters on leafless stems ranging from a few inches to 2 ft. high. Rarely available in nurseries, but you can buy seeds for types native to your area (not all are hardy everywhere) from specialists in native plant seeds. Give porous, rich, well-drained soil. Let soil dry out after bloom.

Many species with flower colors ranging from white to pink, lavender to magenta. Western *D. hendersonii* (Zones 7–9, 14–24), for example, bears blossoms in white, pink shades, or magenta, carried 3 to 15 on each 1½-ft. stalk. Plant forms a clump just under a foot wide.

Dodonaea

HOP BUSH, HOPSEED BUSH
Sapindaceae
EVERGREEN SHRUBS

- ⚡ **ZONES VARY BY SPECIES**
- ☀️ ◐ **FULL SUN OR LIGHT SHADE**
- ◐ 💧 **LITTLE TO REGULAR WATER**

Dodonaea viscosa 'Purpurea'

These tough shrubs are mostly from Australia, although the most common species, *D. viscosa*, is native to the American Southwest and Hawaii, as well as to many other parts of the world. All tolerate wind, poor soil, heat. Foliage is finely divided and fernlike in some, undivided in others. Flowers are insignificant, but seedpods are often showy and long lasting.

D. microzyga. BRILLIANT HOP BUSH. Zones 8, 9, 12–24. Spreading shrub 3–10 ft. tall and somewhat wider, with finely cut leaves and very showy red fruits.

D. viscosa. Zones 7–24; H1, H2. Native to many warmer regions, such as Arizona and Hawaii (where it is called 'a'ali'i). Fast-growing shrub with many upright stems; reaches 10–15 ft. high and spreads almost as wide (can be trained to tree form by cutting out all but single stem). Willowlike green leaves to 4 in. long. Inconspicuous flowers followed in late spring or summer by ornamental, papery seed capsules that may be red, pink, tan, yellow, or green. In Hawaii, the capsules are used in leis.

'Purpurea', purple hop bush, is a selected form with strongly bronze-tinted foliage that darkens in winter; seedlings can vary greatly in color. Cutting-grown 'Saratoga' is uniformly deep purple. Seed capsules cream to pinkish in color. Plant purple-leafed kinds in full sun to retain rich foliage color; they will turn green in shade.

CARE

You can prune all members of this species into an espalier or hedge, or plant 6–8 ft. apart and leave unpruned for a big informal screen. Plants take any kind of soil, ocean winds, and dry desert heat. Quite tolerant of aridity when established but will also take regular water (grows well in flower beds).

Dolichos

Papilionaceae
PERENNIAL VINES

- ⚡ **ZONES VARY BY SPECIES**
- ☀️ **FULL SUN**
- 💧 **REGULAR WATER**
- ◆ **SEEDS TOXIC IN LARGE QUANTITIES**

Dolichos lablab

Twining vines produce dense cover of light green leaves divided into three leaflets.

D. lablab (Lablab purpureus). HYACINTH BEAN. Perennial vine usually grown as annual. All zones. Fast growing to 10 ft. Broad, oval, medium green leaflets to 3–6 in. long. Sweet pea–shaped purple or white flowers in loose clusters on long stems stand out from foliage. Flowers followed by velvety, beanlike magenta-purple pods to 2½ in. long. Grow like string beans for quick screening. Needs good drainage. Naturalized in Hawaii. 'Ruby Moon' has dark green leaves with purple undersides.

»

D. lignosus (Dipogon lignosus). AUSTRALIAN PEA VINE. Zones 16, 17, 21–24; H2. Somewhat woody vine to 10 ft. or more, with small, triangular leaflets and small rose-purple flowers clustered at ends of long stalks. Evergreen in mild winters. Grow from seed and train on trellis or frame for summer screen.

Dombeya

Malvaceae
EVERGREEN SHRUBS AND TREES

⚘ ZONES 21–24; H2

☼ ◐ FULL SUN OR PARTIAL SHADE

◐ ◆ WATER NEEDS VARY BY SPECIES

Dombeya

This genus includes around 225 species of trees and shrubs native to Africa, Madagascar, and nearby islands in the Indian Ocean. They are grown primarily for their big, dense flower clusters, which dangle from branches on long stems. Many also have attractive large leaves.

D. cacuminum. STRAWBERRY SNOWBALL TREE. Native to Madagascar. Tree to 40–50 ft. tall and 15–25 ft. wide. Very large, maplelike leaves are glossy green. In spring, coral red flowers in clusters to 1 ft. across hang from branches; these fall to the ground before drying to create a colorful carpet. Best in full sun with occasional deep irrigation.

D. wallichii. PINK BALL TREE. Zones 19–24. Native to East Africa and Madagascar. Shrub or small tree to 15–25 ft. tall and 15–30 ft. wide. Large heart-shaped, bright green leaves pick up brownish cast

with first frost. Fragrant pink flowers appear in 4–6-in.-wide clusters in fall to winter; these fade to light pink then brown as they dry on the plant. Best with regular water.

Doronicum

LEOPARD'S BANE
Asteraceae
PERENNIALS

⚘ ZONES A2, A3; 1–7, 14–17

◐ PARTIAL SHADE

◆ REGULAR WATER

Doronicum orientale
'Little Leo'

Summer is the season for most yellow daisies, but these European natives bear a profusion of showy daisylike flowers in early to midspring. The blossoms are carried on long, slender, branching stems that rise from low, spreading, dense clumps of tooth-edged dark green leaves that are rounded to heart-shaped at base. They are good cut flowers.

D. × excelsum (D. plantigenium). PLANTAIN LEOPARD'S BANE. Larger, coarser-leafed plant than *D. orientale*, suitable for a wild garden. Stout stems 2½–4 ft. tall rise above a 2-ft.-wide clump, each producing a few 2–4-in. flowers. Goes dormant in summer.

D. orientale. Flower heads to 2 in. wide, borne singly on 1–1½-ft. stems above a foot-wide foliage clump. Usually dies back in summer. 'Magnificum' and 'Finesse' are a little taller, with bigger blossoms. 'Little Leo' is compact, growing just 12–15 in. high and wide.

CARE

Mark location of plants before they die back, and provide some moisture during dormancy. Young plants bloom best. Divide clumps every 2 or 3 years in early autumn. Tolerate full sun in cool-summer climates; light, dappled, or partial shade otherwise.

Dorotheanthus bellidiformis

LIVINGSTONE DAISY
Aizoaceae
SUCCULENT ANNUAL

⚘ ZONES A2; 1–24

☼ FULL SUN

◆ MODERATE WATER

🐝 ATTRACTS BEES

Dorotheanthus bellidiformis

Unlike most others, this ice plant from South Africa is an annual. It is a pretty and useful temporary carpet. Trailing plant a few inches high, with fleshy, bright green leaves and daisy-like, 2-in. flowers in white, pink, orange, or red. Sow seeds in warm weather. Comes into bloom quickly. 'Mazoo Trailing Red' bears red flowers and has leaves edged with creamy white. Tolerates poor, dry soil.

Doxantha unguis-cati.
See *Macfadyena unguis-cati*

Dracaena australis.
See *Cordyline australis*

Drepanostachyum.
See Bamboo

Drimys winteri

WINTER'S BARK
Winteraceae
EVERGREEN TREE

⚘ ZONES 5–9, 14–24

☼ ◐ FULL SUN IN COOLER CLIMATES ONLY

◆ REGULAR WATER

Drimys winteri andina
'Andina Winter's Bark'

This slender tree from southern Chile and Argentina has attractive foliage and a dignified presence. It grows to 25 ft. tall and 20 ft. wide with stems and branches that tend to droop gracefully, and have aromatic, mahogany red bark. Leathery, fragrant, bright green leaves are elliptical. Small clusters of jasmine-scented, inch-wide, creamy white flowers appear in winter and spring. Tree is usually multistemmed but easily trained to a single trunk. It may require pruning from time to time to maintain a pleasingly symmetrical outline. Provide a frost-sheltered location in Zones 5–7. Needs good drainage.

D. winteri andina (D. andina) is dwarf, growing slowly to about 3 ft. tall and wide.

Winter's bark blooms over a long period in winter and spring. Its blossoms, which have a jasmine fragrance, appear in bouquet-like clusters at branch tips.

Drosanthemum

Aizoaceae
SUCCULENT PERENNIALS

ZONES 14–24; H1

FULL SUN

LITTLE TO MODERATE WATER

Drosanthemum floribundum

These South African ice plants are often confused with one another. Their leaves are covered by glistening dots that look like ice crystals. Their flowers, with many narrow petals, bloom in late spring and early summer. Plants endure poor soil.

D. floribundum. ROSEA ICE PLANT. Grows to 6 in. high, but stems trail to considerable length or drape over rocks, walls. Best ice plant for reducing erosion on steep slopes (plant 1½ ft. apart). Pale pink, ¾-in.-wide flowers form shimmering sheets of bloom, attract bees. Often sold as *D. hispidum*.

D. hispidum. Grows to 2 ft. high and 3 ft. wide, less inclined to stem-root than *D. floribundum*. Showy, 1-in. purple flowers.

D. speciosum. Grows to 2 ft. high and 3 ft. wide; bright orangish red flowers with yellow centers.

Rosea ice plant makes a fine groundcover for areas with no foot traffic. It fills in densely enough to discourage weeds and it looks great in or out of bloom.

Dryas

MOUNTAIN AVENS
Rosaceae
PERENNIALS

ZONES A1–A3; 1–6

FULL SUN

MODERATE WATER

Dryas octopetala

Hardy, choice plants for rock gardens. Evergreen or partially so and somewhat shrubby at the base, they form a carpet of leafy, creeping stems. The oblong leaves look like little oak leaves. Plants bloom from late spring into summer, bearing shiny white or yellow flowers that resemble strawberry blossoms. Ornamental seed capsules with silvery white tails follow the blooms.

D. drummondii. Grows to 4 in. high, spreading 3 ft. or wider. Leaves are long, white and woolly beneath. Nodding ¾-in. yellow flowers.

D. octopetala. Grows to 2–3 in. high and 3 ft. wide, with inch-long leaves and erect, ½-in. white flowers.

D. × suendermannii. Hybrid between the two species above. Grows to 4 in. high and 3 ft. wide. Nodding 1¼-in. flowers are yellowish in bud, white in full bloom.

FOR MORE ON PERENNIALS, SEE "GROW: PERENNIALS," PAGES 686–687.

FOR OTHER PLANTS THAT CAN BE USED AS GROUNDCOVERS, SEE "GROUNDCOVERS," PAGES 60–63.

Dryopteris

WOOD FERN
Dryopteridaceae
FERNS

ZONES VARY BY SPECIES

PARTIAL OR FULL SHADE

REGULAR WATER

Dryopteris erythrosora

This is one of the largest genera of ferns, with well over 100 species from many parts of the world. Use them in shade or woodland gardens, where their fronds contrast nicely with the foliage of other plants, especially large-leafed sorts such as hostas and hydrangeas.

D. affinis. GOLDEN MALE FERN. Semievergreen. Zones 3b–9, 14–24. Native to Europe and southwestern Asia. To 3–5 ft. tall and wide. Finely cut, arching fronds are chartreuse-green when they unfold, dark green later. 'Cristata' ('Cristata The King') is more compact, with 3-ft. arching fronds with crested tips. 'Crispa Gracilis' is an evergreen dwarf form to only 6–12 in. high and wide.

D. carthusiana (D. spinulosa). NARROW BUCKLER FERN, SHIELD FERN. Deciduous. Zones A2; 1–9, 14–17. A native of Europe, Asia, and North America. Clumps reach 2 ft. high, 1 ft. across. Coarsely cut, yellowish green fronds to 6–18 in. high and half as wide, have shaggy black scales on frond stem and lower part of midrib. Tolerates bog conditions.

D. × complexa 'Robust'. Semievergreen. Zones 3b–9, 14–17. Sometimes sold as *D. filix-mas* 'Undulata Robusta', this hybrid has 3–4-ft.-long, dark green fronds that are deeply divided, with undulating edges. Vigorous and easy to grow.

D. dilatata (D. austriaca). BROAD BUCKLER FERN. Usually deciduous. Zones 2–7, 14–17. From western and central Europe. Vigorous grower to 3–4 ft. high and wide, with rich green fronds that are broadly triangular. Stalks and midribs are covered in dark brown scales. Adaptable and easy to grow. 'Lepidota Cristata' is a 2-ft.-high form with narrower fronds. 'Crispa Whiteside' has wavy, golden green leaves.

D. erythrosora. AUTUMN FERN. Semievergreen. Zones 2–9, 14–24. Native to China and Japan. Erect growth to 2 ft. high, 1½ ft. wide. One of the few ferns with seasonal color variation. Expanding fronds in spring are a blend of copper, pink, and yellow; they turn green in summer, then rusty brown in fall. Bright red spores, produced on leaf undersides, are an attractive winter feature. 'Brilliance' has especially bright coppery red new growth.

D. filix-mas. MALE FERN. Usually evergreen, sometimes deciduous. Zones 2–9, 14–17. Native to much of the Northern Hemisphere. Grows 2–5 ft. tall and wide, with finely cut, medium green fronds to 1 ft. wide. 'Linearis Polydactyla', to 2½ ft. high, is easy to grow and has very narrow leaf divisions with spreading, fingerlike tips; fronds are favorites for cut arrangements. 'Crispa Cristata' has split fronds that twist and curl at the ends, giving a frillier look. All male ferns tolerate considerable drought when grown in full shade.

D. wallichiana. WALLICH'S WOOD FERN. Semievergreen. Zones 4–6, 14–17; H1. Native to India and China. Stately fern 3–5 ft. high, not quite as wide. Bright golden green fronds turn dark green as they mature; brown stems have shiny black scales. Slow growing.

CARE

Wood ferns grow best in rich soil with plenty of organic matter and regular moisture. They tolerate dry shade. As a rule, they are rather forgiving; a good choice for beginning gardeners. These plants are seldom bothered by deer or other pests.

D

Duchesnea indica

INDIAN MOCK STRAWBERRY

Rosaceae

PERENNIAL

- 🌿 **ZONES 1–24; H1, H2**
- ☀️🌤️⚫ **SUN OR SHADE**
- 💧 **MODERATE WATER**
- 🐦 **FRUIT ATTRACTS BIRDS**

Duchesnea indica

A native of Japan, eastern Asia, and India, this perennial grows like strawberry, with trailing stems that root firmly along ground. The bright green, long-stalked leaves have three leaflets. Yellow, ½-in. blossoms are followed by red, ½-in., nearly tasteless fruit that stands above foliage rather than under leaves as in true strawberry. Grows readily without much care. Best used as groundcover among open shrubs or small trees. Plant 1–1½ ft. apart. In a well-watered garden, it can become a rampant invader.

Indian mock strawberry tastes nothing like the real thing, but birds love it. This plant's tiny red berries follow yellow flowers. The plant spreads—too agressively in some areas—by stolons.

Dudleya

Crassulaceae

SUCCULENT PERENNIALS

- 🌿 **ZONES VARY BY SPECIES**
- ☀️ **FULL SUN**
- 💧 **MODERATE WATER**

Dudleya farinosa

These succulents are native to California, Arizona, coastal Oregon, and Baja California. About 40 species are known, some common on California's coastal cliffs or inland hills.

Best known species in cultivation is Baja California native *D. brittonii* (Zones 16, 17, 21–24), with 1½-ft.-wide leaf rosettes on stems that gradually lengthen into 1–2-ft. trunks; these lean or become prostrate as the plant ages. Fleshy leaves are covered with a heavy coat of chalky powder that can be rubbed off. When plants flourish, they produce reddish stalks with little yellow flowers in spring. Striking plant when well grown; needs bright light and shelter from rain, hail, and frost. Best under glass or plastic roof to keep powder from being washed off.

Others are valued for use in containers, rock gardens, and low borders. *D. caespitosa* (from Southern California; grows in Zones 9, 14–17, 19–24) and *D. farinosa* (Northern California and southern Oregon coast; succeeds in Zones 5, 7, 14–17, 19–24) are familiar sea-cliff plants; both are sometimes called cliff lettuce.

FOR MORE ON SUCCULENTS, SEE "MEET THE SUCCULENTS," PAGE 618.

Duranta

Verbenaceae

EVERGREEN SHRUBS

- 🌿 **ZONES VARY BY SPECIES**
- ☀️ **FULL SUN**
- 💧 **REGULAR WATER**
- ◈ **D. ERECTA BERRIES ARE POISONOUS IF INGESTED**

Duranta erecta

Durantas produce glossy green leaves arranged in pairs or whorls along the stems. The attractive blue flowers are borne in clusters and draw butterflies in summer. They are followed by bunches of berrylike yellow fruit. Plants sold as *D. stenostachya* are often actually *D. erecta*; distinguishing characteristics are described below. Use as quick, tall screen. Thrive in hot-summer areas. Need continual thinning and pruning to stay under control.

D. erecta (D. repens, D. plumieri). SKY FLOWER, GOLDEN DEWDROP, PIGEON BERRY. Zones 13, 16, 17–24; H1, H2. Native to southern Florida, West Indies, Mexico to Brazil. Fast growing to 10–25 ft. tall, 6–10 ft. wide. Tends to form multistemmed clumps; branches often drooping and vinelike. Stems may or may not have sharp spines. Oval to roundish leaves are rounded or pointed at tip. Tubular violet-blue flowers flare to less than ½ in. wide. Waxy yellow berries in clusters 1–6 in. long. 'Alba' has white flowers. 'Sweet Memory' is thornless, with flower petals edged in white. 'Geisha Girl' ('Sapphire Swirl') and 'Sapphire Showers' also have purple flowers edged with white. 'Gold Mound', only 1½ ft. high and wide, has brilliant gold leaves;

it rarely flowers but is excellent for adding color to container plantings.

D. stenostachya. BRAZILIAN SKY FLOWER. Zones 13, 16, 21–23; H2. Not as hardy as *D. erecta*; seems to require more heat. Makes neater, more compact shrub than *D. erecta*, growing to about 4–6 ft. tall, 3–5 ft. wide (under ideal conditions, 15 ft. high). Stems are spineless. Leaves are larger than those of *D. erecta* and taper to long, slender point. Lavender-blue flowers are also somewhat larger; fruit clusters grow to 1 ft. long.

Dymondia margaretae

Asteraceae

PERENNIAL

- 🌿 **ZONES 15–24**
- ☀️🌤️ **FULL SUN OR LIGHT SHADE**
- 💧💧 **MODERATE TO REGULAR WATER**

Dymondia margaretae

This groundcover from South Africa forms a tight mat 2–3 in. high and spreading slowly by offsets to 20 in. wide. Narrow evergreen leaves are deep grayish green above and rolled in at the edges to show cottony white undersides. Summer flowers are yellow, 1–1½-in.-wide daisies half-buried in the foliage. Deep roots give established plants considerable drought tolerance, but they'll spread faster if watered. Use between paving blocks and steppingstones and in rock gardens; can take light foot traffic.

Dypsis
(Neodypsis, Chrysalidocarpus)
Arecaceae
EVERGREEN TREES

⬛ ZONES VARY BY SPECIES; OR INDOORS

☀ ◐ EXPOSURE NEEDS VARY BY SPECIES

◔ ● WATER NEEDS VARY BY SPECIES

Dypsis lutescens

Madagascar natives better known by the alternative botanical names shown above. Both of these tropical species are rather tender, small to medium-size feather palms with graceful foliage and attractive trunks. Good container plants for patio or lanai.

D. decaryi (Neodypsis decaryi). TRIANGLE PALM. Zones 20–24; H2. Slow-growing, single-trunked palm reaches 18–20 ft. tall, 12–15 ft. wide. Trunk is triangular in cross section because heavily keeled leafstalks grow in three ranks about the stem. Gray-green fronds to 15 ft. long are strongly upright but arching at tips. Native to arid parts of Madagascar and requires little water. Full sun or light shade.

D. lutescens (Chrysalido-carpus lutescens, Areca lutescens). CANE PALM. Zones 23 (light shade), 24; H1, H2 (full sun). Clumping palm with slender yellowish trunks, yellow-green leaves, and clusters of golden yellow fruit. Slow growth to 28 ft. tall, 20 ft. wide; unlikely to reach that size in California. Protect from hot, dry wind. Drought-tolerant but does best with regular water. Moderate salt tolerance.

Dyssodia. See *Thymophylla*

E

Ebenopsis ebano
(Pithecellobium flexicaule)
TEXAS EBONY
Fabaceae
PARTIALLY DECIDUOUS TO EVERGREEN TREE OR SHRUB

⬛ ZONES 12, 13

☀ FULL SUN

◔ LITTLE WATER ONCE ESTABLISHED

Ebenopsis ebano

This tough tree, native to arid parts of Texas and northern Mexico, is well suited to desert areas. Plant grows slowly to 30–40 ft. tall and wide, with branches that grow in a zigzag pattern and are sharply thorned. Without pruning, it will branch to the ground and form a tall, dense shrub. The medium to dark green leaves are divided into 6–10 rounded leaflets and drop briefly in spring, but the trees will remain evergreen with supplemental water. Small creamy flowers with a musty fragrance are produced in short clusters in early summer and followed by 6–12-in.-long seedpods, which can be messy when they drop. The tree may bloom again after fall rains. The rich grained wood is prized by woodworkers.

CARE
Water occasionally until established; then it needs little water. Prune lower branches to create tree form (wear gloves to protect from thorns).

Echeveria
Crassulaceae
SUCCULENT PERENNIALS

⬛ ZONES VARY BY SPECIES

☀ ◐ FULL SUN OR PARTIAL SHADE, EXCEPT AS NOTED

● MODERATE WATER, EXCEPT AS NOTED

Echeveria nodulosa

These Mexican natives form rosettes of fleshy green or gray-green leaves, often marked with deeper colors. They bear long, slender, sometimes branched clusters of bell-shaped, nodding flowers, usually in shades of pink, red, orange, or yellow. Good in rock gardens and pots. Those that grow in Zone 12 need cool spot, partial shade there. Those suitable for Zone 13 need extra attention to grow outdoors in that area. Some types make good houseplants. There are approximately 180 species of *Echeveria* and many more hybrids.

E. agavoides. Zones 8, 9, 12–24. Rosettes 6–8 in. across. Firm, fleshy, sharp-pointed leaves are smooth and bright green, often marked deep reddish brown at tips and edges. Flower stalks to 1½ ft. bear small red-and-yellow blooms. 'Lipstick' has bright green leaves with a crisp red edge. 'Maria' grows up to 12 in. wide and has green leaves edged and tipped with red.

E. elegans. HEN AND CHICKS. Zones 8, 9, 12–24. Tight grayish white rosettes to 4 in. across, spreading freely by offsets. Pink flowers lined in yellow, in clusters to 8 in. long. Useful for pattern planting, edging, containers. Can burn in hot summer sun.

E. hybrids. Zones 8, 9, 12–24; or indoors. Generally have large, loose rosettes of big leaves on single or branched stems; plant size varies by hybrid. Leaves are crimped, waved, wattled, or heavily shaded with red, bronze, or purple. All are splendid potted plants; they do well in open ground in mild-summer areas. Among them are 'Afterglow', with powdery, pinkish lavender leaves edged with brighter pink edges; 'Arlie Wright', with large, open rosettes of wavy-edged, pinkish leaves; 'Big Red', with large triangular leaves that start light green, edged red, turning entirely rose-red; 'Black Prince', which grows only 3 in. wide and has dark reddish purple leaves; 'Blue Curls', with frilly-edged, blue-green leaves that pick up pink tones in cool weather; 'Domingo', with powder blue leaves; 'Lola', which has silvery pink to mauve leaves and is about 4 in. wide; and 'Perle von Nürnberg', with pearly lavender-blue foliage. 'Doris Taylor' is smaller, with short, close-set leaves densely covered with short hairs. Showy, nodding flowers are red and yellow. 'Pulv-oliver' ('Red Edge') has fuzzy, red-tipped leaves and grows to 12 in. high. 'Imbricata' (*E. × imbricata*) forms rosettes 4–6 in. across with saucer-shaped, gray-green leaves. Loose clusters of small, bell-shaped, orange-red flowers. Makes offsets very freely. Probably most common hen and chicks in California gardens.

E. nodulosa. PAINTED ECHEVERIA. Zones 8, 9, 13–24. A branching species that forms multiple rosettes 1–2 ft. high and 2–3 ft. wide. The pointed, concave leaves are ribbed on the underside and brightly marked with red on the margins and midleaf. Light yellow summer flowers are also marked with red. Best in partial shade in hot summer areas.

E. runyonii 'Topsy Turvy'. Zones 8, 9, 14–24. An unusual plant forming rosettes 1 ft. high and wide; silvery blue leaves, prominently keeled and pointing back toward the center of the plant. Orange and yellow flowers from late summer to fall.

E. secunda. HEN AND CHICKS. Zones 8, 9, 14–24.

»

E

Gray-green or blue-green rosettes to 4 in. across. Makes offsets freely. *E. s. glauca* (*E. glauca*) leaves are faintly edged purple-red, and the blue-green rosettes have a purplish tinge.

E. setosa. Zones 17, 23, 24. Dense rosettes to 4 in. across are dark green and densely covered with stiff white hairs. Red flowers are tipped with yellow. Good choice for rock gardens, shallow containers. Very tender.

E. subrigida 'Fire and Ice'. Zones 8, 9, 14–24. Large rosettes, 9–12 in. high, 1–2 ft. wide. Light blue-green leaves are edged with dark pink. Coral pink and orange flowers from late spring to summer.

Echinacea

CONEFLOWER

Asteraceae

PERENNIALS

⚗ **ZONES A2, A3; 1–24**

☀ **FULL SUN**

💧 **MODERATE TO REGULAR WATER**

🦋 **ATTRACT BUTTERFLIES, BEES**

Echinacea 'Sunrise'

Tough, colorful perennials from central and eastern North America. Daisylike flowers, usually with narrow, arching rays, have brownish orange, dome-shaped centers and are held on straight stems above clumps of bristly foliage. Flowers are often lightly fragrant. Generally bloom over a long period in summer (may start in spring in mild-winter climates). Flowering may continue until frost.

Use on the outskirts of gardens or in wide borders with other robust perennials. Excellent in pots. Good cut flowers.

CLOCKWISE FROM TOP: *Echinacea* 'Flame Thrower'; *E.* 'Quills and Thrills'; *E. purpurea* 'Pink Poodle'

E. hybrids. Complex crosses have produced hybrid coneflowers that are popular for their vigor and extended color range. 'Green Envy' has fragrant, lime green blooms that pick up magenta-purple near the cone as they age. The green cone also fades to purple. It grows 2–3 ft. high. 'Mango Meadowbrite' grows 2–3 ft. high and wide; orange-yellow petals surround orange-brown centers. 'Orange Meadowbrite' ('Art's Pride') grows about the same size, bears reddish orange flowers. 'Pixie Meadowbrite' grows only about 1½ ft. tall and a bit wider, with pink, nondrooping petals surrounding a yellow-brown center. 'Tomato Soup' has bright red flowers up to 6 in. wide on 2-ft.-high plants. 'Tiki Torch' has bright orange to rose blooms on a 2–2½-ft.-tall plant. Plants in the Big Sky series grow 2–3 ft. high and 2 ft. wide; choices include butter yellow 'Sunrise', bright orange 'Sunset', and reddish orange 'Sundown' ('Evan Saul').

E. purpurea. PURPLE CONE-FLOWER. Bristly, oblong, 3–4-in.-long leaves form a 2-ft.-wide, dense foliage clump from which rise sparsely leafed flowering stems 3–4 ft. tall. Showy, 4-in. flowers have drooping, rosy purple rays and a central orange-brown cone that resembles a beehive. If faded flowers are left in place, bristly seed heads hang on into winter; seeds are favored by finches.

Many fine varieties are available. 'Coconut Lime' is a double flower, with a single row of large white petals surrounding a tuft of smaller light green petals around the cone. Grows to 2–3 ft. high. 'Doubledecker' ('Doppelganger'), another 2-footer, has something extra: a second set of pink petals emerging from the top of the cone. 'Fragrant Angel' grows 2–2½ ft. high with sweetly scented white flowers. 'Kim's Knee High' grows 1½–2 ft. high and has clear pink flowers. 'Magnus' grows 3–4 ft. tall and has deep purplish pink, orange-centered flowers to 7 in. wide.

'Pink Poodle' produces fully double pink flowers that resemble zinnias. 'Rubinstern' ('Ruby Star') grows 2–3 ft. high with carmine-red, nondrooping rays. Both 'White Lustre' (2½ ft. high) and 'White Swan' (1½–2 ft. high) have white rays and orange-yellow cones.

E. tennesseensis 'Rocky Top'. Narrow, medium green leaves form a mound 1½–2 ft. high and nearly as wide. Flowers 2–3 in. across consist of narrow, rich pink rays that bend distinctively upward around a large, greenish black cone.

CARE

Coneflowers generally do not need staking. They perform well in summer heat (though not in the hottest desert areas, where they are mainly spring blooming). Clumps spread slowly, become crowded after 3 or 4 years. Fleshy rootstocks can be difficult to separate; divide carefully, making sure that each division has a shoot and roots. Plantings can also be increased by taking root cuttings, seeding, or transplanting self-sown seedlings.

Echinocactus

BARREL CACTUS

Cactaceae

CACTI

⚗ **ZONES 12–24**

☀◑ **PARTIAL SHADE IN HOTTEST CLIMATES**

💧 **MODERATE WATER**

Echinocactus grusonii

Large, cylindrical cacti with prominent ribs and stout thorns. Many are native to the Southwest. Best known in gardens is *E. grusonii*, golden barrel, a Mexican cactus of slow growth to 4 ft. tall, 2½ ft. in diameter. With age, often produces offsets to form clumps 6 ft. across. Showy, stiff, yellow, 3-in. spines; yellow, 1½–2-in. flowers at top of plant in summer. Protect from hard frosts. Water every couple of weeks in summer.

Echinocereus
HEDGEHOG CACTUS
Cactaceae
CACTI

🌿 **ZONES VARY BY SPECIES**

☼ **FULL SUN**

◐ ◓ **LITTLE TO MODERATE WATER**

Echinocereus engelmannii

Nearly 50 species of hedgehog cactus grow in the southwestern U.S. and northern Mexico, with some growing at fairly high elevations in Utah and Colorado, where they are subject to freezing temperatures. All have cylindrical, ribbed bodies in clumps; showy red, yellow, purple, or white flowers with many rows of petals; and fleshy fruit, which is edible in some species. Although cold-hardy in most zones, and often seen in collections, they are used in landscaping chiefly in desert or interior mountain gardens.

E. engelmannii. Zones 2, 3, 7, 10–24. Clumps 1–2 ft. tall and 3 ft. wide, with 3–4-in.-thick stems. Lavender to deep purplish red flowers 2–3 in. wide. Inch-long red fruits are edible.

E. triglochidiatus. CLARET CUP. Zones 2, 3, 10–14, 18–23. Dense clump, up to 3 ft. wide, sometimes with hundreds of 2–3-in.-diameter stems to a foot high. Flowers are 3½ in. wide, orange to red; inch-long fruits (not edible) are pink to red. Needs little water.

Echinops
GLOBE THISTLE
Asteraceae
PERENNIALS

🌿 **ZONES A2, A3; 1–24**

☼ **FULL SUN**

◐ **MODERATE WATER**

Echinops

These well-behaved, decorative thistle relatives are great for the perennial border. The rugged-looking plants are erect, rigidly branched to 2–4 ft. tall and 2 ft. wide, with coarse, prickly, deeply cut gray-green leaves to 1 ft. long. Their distinctive flower heads are spherical, about the size of golf balls, and they look like pincushions stuck full of tubular metallic blue pins. Globe thistles bloom from midsummer to late fall. Flowers are excellent for dried arrangements; cut them before they open and dry them upside down.

Plants may be offered as *E. bannaticus, E. exaltatus, E. ritro,* or possibly *E. sphaerocephalus.* Whatever name you encounter, you're likely to get a plant closely resembling the general description above. 'Arctic Glow' and 'Star Frost' have white flowers on 3–4-ft.-tall plants. 'Blue Globe' ('Blue Glow') has intense blue flowers on 4-ft.-tall plants. 'Taplow Blue' has bright blue blossoms on 3–4-ft. stems. 'Veitch's Blue' has darker blue flowers on a plant 2½–3 ft. high.

CARE

Grow from divisions planted in spring or fall, or sow seeds in flats or open ground in spring. Provide average, well-drained soil and moderate water. (With enriched soil and regular moisture, may grow too robustly and require staking.) Clump can be left in place, undivided, for years.

Echinopsis
Cactaceae
CACTI

🌿 **ZONES 8–10, 12–24, EXCEPT AS NOTED; OR INDOORS**

☼ **FULL SUN; BRIGHT SUNNY WINDOW**

◐ **REGULAR WATER DURING GROWTH**

Echinopsis hybrid

Small, spiny cacti from South America; generally grown in pots. There are many species, hybrids, and selections. The genus also includes plants formerly named *Lobivia* and *Lobivopsis* and still often sold under those names. All are showy and easy to grow, with many-petaled flowers in white and shades of yellow, pink, red, and orange. Blooms during warm months if given good light, regular moisture from spring to fall, and fast-draining soil. Give little or no water in winter.

E. ancistrophora (E. hamatacantha). Zones 16, 17, 21–24. Rounded, to 4 in. high and 2 in. thick, with red to yellow, 3-in. flowers.

E. bruchii (Lobivia bruchii). SOUTH AMERICAN GOLDEN BARREL. Single, nearly round stem is 1 ft. high and thick, with yellow spines and red, 3-in. flowers.

E. chamaecereus (Chamaecereus sylvestri). PEANUT CACTUS. To 4 in. high, 1–2 ft. wide. The cylindrical, ribbed, 2–3-in. joints fall off easily and root just as easily; even tiny ones produce flowers. Blooms are bright scarlet, nearly 3 in. long.

E. chrysantha (Lobivia chrysantha). Single stem is 2½ in. high, 3 in. wide. Orange-yellow, 2-in.-wide flowers with purple center.

E. eyriesii. Zones 16, 17, 21–24. Cylindrical, dark-spined cactus to 6–12 in. high and 2–4 ft. wide. Very large white flowers 8–10 in. long, 2–4 in. wide. Eventually forms clumps.

E. haageana (Lobivia haageana). Single stem grows 1 ft. high, 3 in. thick. Flowers are 3 in. long, yellow with red throat.

E. maximiliana caespitosa (E. caespitosa, Lobivia caespitosa). Clustered and cylindrical bodies, each 6 in. high and 2 in. thick, have dark, inch-long spines and orange, 3-in. flowers.

E. pentlandii (Lobivia boliviensis). Clustered round stems to 4 in. high and wide. Red, 2½-in.-long flowers.

Echium
Boraginaceae
BIENNIALS, PERENNIALS, AND SHRUBS

🌿 **ZONES VARY BY SPECIES**

☼ **FULL SUN**

◐ ◓ **LITTLE TO MODERATE WATER**

⬥ **E. VULGARE IS POISONOUS IF INGESTED**

Echium candicans

Echiums are grown for their striking form and flower clusters. All do well in dry, poor soil but need good drainage. All are excellent for seacoast gardens. Flowers attract bees.

»

**E. candicans (E. fastuo-
sum).** PRIDE OF MADEIRA.
Shrub. Zones 14–24. From
Madeira, as its common name
indicates. Large, picturesque
plant to 5–6 ft. tall, 6–10 ft.
wide, with many coarse, heavy
branches. Narrow, hairy, gray-
green leaves form roundish,
irregular mounds at ends of
stems. Great spikelike clusters
of ½-in., bluish purple flowers
stand out dramatically, well
above foliage, in spring. There
are selections with truer blue or
pink flowers. 'Star of Madeira'
has gray-green leaves striped
with creamy white. 'Starburst'
has light green on the leaves.
Branch tips and developing
flower spikes may be killed by
late frosts. Use for bold effects
against walls, at back of wide
flower borders, on slopes. Prune
lightly to keep bushy. Cut off
faded flower spikes to prevent
rampant reseeding. Attracts
bees.

E. pininana. Woody-based
perennial. Zones 16, 17, 22–
24. From the Canary Islands.
Sparsely branched, to 18 ft.
tall, 2–3 ft. wide. Stems packed
with long, narrow, bristly gray-
green leaves and topped with
long, spikelike clusters of blue
flowers. Typically short-lived
and rarely sold but occasionally
seen in old gardens near California coast.

E. vulgare. Biennial grown
as annual. Zones 4–9, 14–24.
European native blooms first
year if sown between early fall
and earliest spring. To 1–3 ft.
high, 1 ft. wide. Leaves covered
with stiff white bristles; blue,
white, or pink flowers in spikelike clusters. Endures aridity,
poor soil. Seeds freely and can
become a pest.

E. wildpretii. TOWER OF
JEWELS. Biennial. Zones 15–
17, 21–24. Striking oddity from
the Canary Islands spends its
first year as an attractive, roundish mass of long, narrow leaves
covered with silvery gray hairs.
It starts to grow the second year.
By mid- or late spring, it forms a
6–10-ft.-tall column 1 ft. or more
in diameter, made up of many
little rose to rose-red flowers.
When all flowers have faded, the
plant dies, leaving behind many
seeds. The resulting seedlings
may grow and bloom the next
year if they are not hoed out.

Give little or no water in mild-
summer climates, weekly
irrigation during summer in
hotter areas.

Edgeworthia chrysantha
(E. papyrifera)
PAPER BUSH
Thymelaeaceae
DECIDUOUS SHRUB

⚬ ZONES 5–9, 14–24
☼ ◑ FULL SUN OR LIGHT SHADE
💧 REGULAR WATER

Edgeworthia chrysantha

A daphne relative from China
grown in Asia for its bark, which
is used in the manufacture of
fancy paper. Grows to 6 ft. tall
and wide, with pliable stems
produced freely from the base
and 4-in. leaves that cluster
toward the branch tips. In winter
or earliest spring, many small,
fragrant pale yellow flowers in
tight clusters to 2 in. across
open from interesting-looking
silky whitish buds formed the
previous fall. 'Akebono' has
orange-red flowers. Protect blossoms from late-spring frosts.
Little pruning required.

> Paper bush has
> small, fragrant
> blooms that hang
> like little bouquets
> on the branches—
> a welcome sight in
> the winter garden.

Eggplant
Solanaceae
ANNUAL

⚬ ZONES 1–24; H1, H2
☼ FULL SUN
💧 REGULAR WATER

'Hansel' eggplants

Few vegetable plants are hand-
somer than eggplant, which
hails from Southeast Asia. It
resembles a little tree, 2–3 ft.
high and equally wide. Big
leaves (usually lobed) are purple tinged; drooping violet flowers are 1½ in. across. And, of
course, big purple fruits are
spectacular. A well-spaced row
of eggplant makes a distinguished border between vegetable and flower garden. Eggplant
are also effective in large containers or raised beds.

Large, roundish or oval varieties such as 'Black Beauty',
'Burpee Hybrid', 'Dusky', and
'Zebra' are often sold as Italian
types.

Long, slender Asian varieties
are sold under a number of
names, including 'Fairy Tale'
and 'Millionaire'.

Specialists in imported vegetable seeds offer numerous
colored varieties, including the
full-size 'Casper' and a host of
smaller varieties in a range of
sizes (down to ½ in.) and colors—for example, white, yellow,
red, green, and variegated
plum. Some of the smaller ones
genuinely resemble eggs. All
are edible as well as attractive.

Eggplant can be grown from
seed (sow indoors 8 to
10 weeks before date of last
expected frost), but starting
from nursery-grown plants is

much easier. To produce a crop,
eggplant needs 2 to 3 months
of warm days and nights (night
temperatures no lower than
65°F/18°C). Set plants out in
spring when danger of frost is
past and soil is warm. Space
3 ft. apart in loose, fertile soil.
Feed once every 6 weeks and
control weeds.

If you enjoy tiny whole eggplants, allow plants to produce
freely. If you prefer larger fruits,
keep too much fruit from setting
by pinching out some terminal
growth and some blossoms;
three to six large fruits per plant
will result. Harvest fruits after
they develop some color, but
don't wait until they lose their
glossy shine. A second crop for
late-summer and fall harvest
can be grown in warmest
climates.

Colorado potato beetle, cutworms, and flea beetles can
be a problem on young plants;
grow under row covers until big
enough to tolerate leaf damage.
Control aphids and whiteflies.

Elaeagnus
Elaeagnaceae
DECIDUOUS AND EVERGREEN SHRUBS
AND TREES

⚬ ZONES VARY BY SPECIES
☼ ◑ FULL SUN OR PARTIAL SHADE
○◐💧 LITTLE TO REGULAR WATER
🐦 ATTRACT BIRDS

Elaeagnus × ebbingei 'Gilt Edge'

All elaeagnus are splendid
screen plants. They grow fast
when young, becoming dense,
full, firm, and tough—and they
do it with little upkeep. All tolerate seashore conditions, heat,
and wind.

The foliage is distinguished
in evergreen forms by silvery

Russian Olive— One Tough Cookie

Elaeagnus angustifolia can take almost any kind of punishment, including hot summers, bitterly cold winters, drought, poor soil. It has naturalized in many areas east of the Cascades in the Pacific Northwest, although it doesn't do as well in mild-winter, cool-summer climates. Grow it as a backdrop plant for borders, or as a barrier plant. Resistant to oak root fungus.

(sometimes brown) dots that cover leaves, reflecting sunlight to give plants a special sparkle. Deciduous kinds have silvery gray leaves. Small, insignificant, but usually fragrant flowers are followed by decorative fruit, usually red with silvery flecks. Evergreen kinds bloom in fall; in addition to their prime role as screen plants, they are useful as natural espaliers, clipped hedges, or high bank covers.

E. angustifolia. RUSSIAN OLIVE. Deciduous tree. Zones A2, A3; 1–3, 7–14, 18, 19. Native from Europe to Asia. To 20 ft. tall and wide, but can be clipped to make a medium-height hedge. Angular trunk and branches (sometimes thorny) are covered with shredding dark brown bark that is picturesque in winter. Bark contrasts with narrow, willowlike, 2-in.-long silvery gray leaves. Small, very fragrant, greenish yellow flowers in early summer are followed by fruit that resembles miniature olives. 'Red King' ('King Red') has fruit in a bright rust red shade. May become invasive.

E. commutata. SILVER-BERRY. Deciduous shrub. Zones A1–A3; 1–3. Native to Alaska, the Rocky Mountains, and the northern plains of U.S. and Canada. Grows upright to 12 ft. tall and 6 ft. wide, with open form and slender, spineless, red-brown branches that become coated with silvery scales. Oval leaves are silvery gray on both surfaces. Tiny, fragrant spring flowers followed in early fall by dry, mealy, ⅓-in.-long, oval fruits, also silver-coated and a favorite of birds. Plant spreads by suckers to form colonies.

E. 'Coral Silver'. Shrub. Zones 2b–24. Evergreen in Zones 19–24, deciduous or partially deciduous elsewhere. Grows 5–10 ft. tall with yellow flowers. Has unusually bright gray foliage, coral red berries in autumn.

E. × ebbingei. Evergreen shrub. Zones 4–24. More upright (to 10–12 ft. high and wide) than *E. pungens*, with thornless branches. Leaves 2–4 in. long, silvery on both sides when young, later dark green above and silvery beneath. Tiny, fragrant silvery flowers. Red fruit makes good jelly. 'Gilt Edge' has striking yellow margins on its leaves.

E. multiflora. Deciduous shrub. Zones 2b–24. From China, Japan. To 6–10 ft. high and wide. Leaves silvery green above, silvery brown below. Small, fragrant spring flowers followed by attractive, ½-in.-long, bright orange-red berries on 1-in. stalks. Fruit is edible but tart, loved by birds.

E. pungens. SILVERBERRY. Evergreen shrub. Zones 4–24. Has rather rigid, sprawling, angular habit of growth to 10–15 ft. tall and wide; can be kept lower and denser by pruning. Even tolerates shearing into a hedge. Grayish green, 1–3-in.-long leaves have wavy edges and brown tinting from rusty dots. Branches are spiny, also covered with rusty dots. Overall color of shrub is olive drab. Oval fruit, ½ in. long, red with silver dust. Tough container plant in reflected heat, wind. The following forms are more commonly planted than the plain olive drab variety and have a brighter, lighter look in the landscape, but they are less hardy (grow in Zones 5–24). All make effective barriers, thanks to dense, twiggy, spiny growth.

'Fruitlandii'. Large silvery leaves.

'Maculata'. GOLDEN ELAEAG-NUS. Leaves have large gold blotch in center.

'Marginata'. SILVER-EDGE ELAEAGNUS. Silvery white leaf margins.

'Variegata'. YELLOW-EDGE ELAEAGNUS. Yellowish white leaf margins.

Elaeocarpus decipiens
(E. sylvestris ellipticus)
JAPANESE BLUEBERRY TREE
Elaeocarpaceae
EVERGREEN TREE

⟋ **ZONES 8, 9, 14–24; H1**

☼ **FULL SUN**

● **REGULAR WATER**

Elaeocarpus decipiens

This evergreen tree from Japan and China grows to 30–60 ft. tall and 20–30 ft. wide, with a densely branched upright habit. The new leaves are rusty and hairy, turning smooth and bright green. The oldest leaves eventually drop, turning red before they fall. Blooms in summer, producing tiny, scented white flowers in 1½–3-in.-long clusters; followed by blue-black fruits that look like small olives. Attractive street or lawn tree.

Grow in rich, well-drained soil. Needs little pruning. 'Little Emperor' is a slow, dense grower to 6–10 ft. tall and wide, with interesting twisted leaves; a good choice for hedge or screen.

Elegia capensis
FOUNTAIN RUSH
Restionaceae
EVERGREEN PERENNIAL

⟋ **ZONES 8, 9, 14–24**

☼ ◐ **FULL SUN OR LIGHT SHADE**

● ●● **REGULAR TO AMPLE WATER**

Elegia capensis

This unusual, grassy-looking perennial is native to stream-sides and other moist areas in South Africa. Its stately, 6–8-ft.-tall, reedlike stems are decorated at evenly spaced nodes with dense whorls of long, feathery branches and golden, papery leaf bracts. Plants spread by rhizomes to form dense clumps up to 7 ft. wide. Small, coppery brown flowers are borne in attractive clusters atop stems from fall into winter. Needs constant moisture and well-drained soil that is not too rich; avoid fertilizers high in phosphorus. Arching stems sway and rustle gently in the wind. Beautiful near swimming pools or ponds. Can also be grown in very large pots.

Fountain rush is just one of several members of the restio family gaining popularity in Western gardens. Attractive cousins include cape rush (*Chondropetalum*) and broom restio (*Ischyrolepis*).

E

Eleutherococcus sieboldianus
(Acanthopanax sieboldianus)
Araliaceae
DECIDUOUS SHRUB

🌿 ZONES 2B–10, 14–17

☀️ ☀️ ● SUN OR SHADE

◐ ◑ ● ANY AMOUNT OF WATER

Eleutherococcus sieboldianus
'Variegatus'

A native of China and Japan, this shrub grows 8–10 ft. tall and wide. Its erect, eventually arching stems have short thorns below each leaf. The bright green leaves have five to seven 1–2½-in.-long leaflets arranged like fingers on a hand. Small, inconspicuous white flowers are borne in clusters, which are rarely followed by clusters of small black berries. This plant's virtues are its somewhat tropical appearance, adaptability (takes rich or poor soil, any exposure, any amount of irrigation), and high tolerance for difficult conditions, including air pollution. 'Variegatus', a 6–8-ft. shrub with white-bordered leaflets, is more widely grown than the species.

Beautiful foliage makes this a choice shrub for tropical effects in the garden. 'Variegatus' adds a splash of leafy sunshine.

Bluegrass Sampler

The silvery blue leaves of Magellan wheatgrass—perhaps the bluest of all grasses—combine delightfully with many garden plants. They provide a soothing contrast to bright flower colors such as vivid red, and to plants with plum- or chocolate-colored foliage. And they add subtle color to gray- and white-themed borders. Other blue-leafed grasses include blue fescue (*Festuca*), blue oat grass (*Helictotrichon sempervirens*), and lyme grass (*Leymus arenarius*).

Elymus arenarius.
See *Leymus arenarius*

Elymus magellanicus
(Agropyron magellanicus)
MAGELLAN WHEATGRASS
Poaceae
PERENNIAL GRASS

🌿 ZONES 3–6, 14–17, 21–24

☀️ ☀️ PARTIAL SHADE IN HOTTEST CLIMATES

● REGULAR WATER

Elymus magellanicus

Botanists have moved some species formerly in this genus to *Leymus* (see that entry for other blue-leafed grasses). Of the species remaining in *Elymus*, this clump-forming native of South American mountains is the most ornamental. It grows 1½ ft. high and wide, with metallic blue leaves (probably the bluest of all grasses). Magellan wheatgrass is a cool-season grass and nearly evergreen in mild climates. It is grown for its foliage rather than the flower spikelets produced in summer. Likes humidity along the California coast and well-drained soil. To increase your planting, divide in spring. Good container plant.

Embothrium coccineum
CHILEAN FIRE BUSH
Proteaceae
EVERGREEN OR DECIDUOUS SHRUB OR TREE

🌿 ZONES 5, 6, 14–17, 21–24

☀️ ☀️ FULL SUN OR LIGHT SHADE

◐ ●● REGULAR TO AMPLE WATER

Embothrium coccineum

This variable plant is from the many altitudes and latitudes in Chile. It is sometimes a large, suckering shrub of variable habit. Sometimes it is a tree to 50 ft. tall and half as wide. It may be evergreen or deciduous. The deciduous forms are hardier. All have shiny green leaves that are oblong to narrow, up to 4½ in. long. They also put on a showy floral spectacle in late spring or early summer, bearing clusters of long, narrow, brilliant red flowers.

Lanceolatum forms are narrow-leafed and semievergreen. It needs good drainage, acid soil, nonalkaline water, and protection from cold wind.

Encelia
Asteraceae
DECIDUOUS SHRUBS

🌿 ZONES VARY BY SPECIES

☀️ FULL SUN

◐ LITTLE OR NO WATER

Encelia farinosa

These much-branched shrubs grow to 3 ft. high and 4 ft. wide, with typically sparse foliage that tends to drop in times of drought. Loose clusters of yellow daisies bloom in spring.

E. californica. Zones 7–16, 18–24. Native to Southern California. Bright green leaves to 2½ in. long; brown-centered flowers to nearly 3 in. across.

E. farinosa. BRITTLEBUSH, INCIENSO. Zones 8–16, 18–24; H1. Native to the Southwest. Rounded, stiff-branched, aromatic shrub (sap is fragrant) with silvery, woolly leaves to 3 in. long in dense clusters. Shrub bears a profusion of yellow- or brown-centered daisies that are somewhat smaller than those of *E. californica*.

CARE

After bloom, cut back by at least a third to encourage repeat flowering. Useful for out-of-the-way places out of reach of irrigation. Be especially careful not to overwater in summer in hot desert regions.

FOR OTHER UNTHIRSTY PLANTS, SEE "PLANTS FOR WATERWISE GARDENS," PAGES 74–78.

Endive

Asteraceae

BIENNIAL OR ANNUAL

- 🌿 **ALL ZONES**
- ☀️ **FULL SUN**
- 💧 **REGULAR WATER**

Curly endive

This Mediterranean native includes curly endive (also called frisée), as well as broad-leafed endive (escarole), both of which form a rosette of leaves. Tolerate more heat than lettuce does. Grow faster in cold weather, maturing in 90 to 95 days from seed. 'Green Curled', 'Keystone', 'Rhodos', and 'Salad King' are standard curly endives. 'Broad-Leaved Batavian', 'Full Heart Batavian', and 'Full Heart NR65' are good full-leafed varieties. Belgian and French endives are the blanched sprouts of a kind of chicory; see Chicory.

CARE

In cold-winter areas, sow from spring into summer. In mild-winter climates, sow so that plants mature after summer heat is past. Plant in rows 15–18 in. apart. Be sure to thin plants to 10–12 in. apart. When plants have reached full size (a foot across), pull outer leaves over center and tie them up at top (but not when they're wet, as that may cause decay). Covered center leaves will blanch to yellow or white. Endive can be used unblanched by cutting outer leaves, as for Swiss chard.

Plants may be bothered by aphids, armyworms, flea beetles, leafhoppers, snails and slugs, and downy mildew.

Enkianthus

Ericaceae

DECIDUOUS SHRUBS

- 🌿 **ZONES 3–9, 14–21, EXCEPT AS NOTED**
- ☀️ ◑ **FULL SUN ONLY IN COOLER CLIMATES**
- 💧💧 **REGULAR TO AMPLE WATER**

Enkianthus campanulatus

These shrubs from Japan produce upright stems with tiers of nearly horizontal branches. The plants are narrow in youth, broader in age, but always attractive. Their leaves are clustered or crowded near branch ends and turn orange or red in autumn. Clusters of nodding, bell-shaped flowers bloom in spring. Plant in location where silhouette, flowers, and fall color can be enjoyed close-up.

E. campanulatus. RED-VEIN ENKIANTHUS. Zones 2–9, 14–21. Slow-growing shrub to 10–20 ft. tall and half as wide. Bluish green, 1½–3-in.-long leaves turn brilliant red in fall. In late spring, pendulous clusters of yellow-green, red-veined, ½-in.-long bells hang below leaves. 'Red Bells' has red flowers and notably deep red fall color. 'Showy Lantern' produces an abundant display of cherry red blooms and has orange and red fall color. *E. c. albiflorus* bears white blooms; *E. c. palibinii* bears deep red blossoms. *E. c. sikokianus* has deep red flowers streaked with pink and yellow; autumn leaves are orange and red.

E. cernuus. Seldom over 10 ft. tall and wide, with 1–2-in.-long leaves. White flowers. Not as well known as *E. c. rubens*, which has translucent deep red flowers in late spring. Leaves turn yellow and red in autumn.

E. perulatus. WHITE ENKIANTHUS. To 6–8 ft. tall and wide. Roundish, 1–2-in.-long leaves; good scarlet fall color. Small white flowers open in early spring before leaves emerge.

CARE

Require moist, well-drained acid soil enriched with plenty of organic matter, such as peat moss or ground bark. Prune only to remove dead or broken branches.

Ensete ventricosum

(Musa ensete)

ABYSSINIAN BANANA

Musaceae

PERENNIAL

- 🌿 **ZONES 13, 15–24; H1, H2**
- ☀️ ◑ **FULL SUN OR PARTIAL SHADE**
- 💧 **REGULAR WATER**

Ensete ventricosum 'Maurelii'

African native is grown for its lush, attractive tropical-looking foliage. For fruit-bearing banana trees, see Banana. Fast growing to 15–20 ft. tall, 10–15 ft. wide. Dark green leaves with stout midribs grow out in arching form from a single vertical stem; each leaf is 10–20 ft. long, 2–4 ft. wide. 'Maurelii' has dark red leafstalks and leaves tinged with red on upper surface, especially along edges. Bloom typically occurs 2 to 5 years after planting, when inconspicuous flowers form within a cylinder of bronzy red bracts at end of stem. Plant dies to roots after flowering; it's possible then to grow new plants from shoots that sprout from the crown, but easier to simply discard the old plant and replace it with a new one from the nursery.

Leaves are easily shredded by wind, so plant in a wind-sheltered location. Evergreen in mildest climates. In Zones 13, 15, 16, 18, will die back in a cold winter, regrow in spring. Good container subject to grow outdoors in summer and then move indoors or into a greenhouse over winter.

Epidendrum

Orchidaceae

EPIPHYTIC OR TERRESTRIAL ORCHIDS

- 🌿 **ZONES VARY BY SPECIES**
- ☀️ ◑ **FULL SUN OR PARTIAL SHADE**
- 💧 **REGULAR WATER**

Epidendrum

All of these orchids are easy to grow and bear large clusters of blooms. The genus formerly included a number of plants with hard, round pseudobulbs and thick, leathery leaves, but most of those species have been reassigned to *Encyclia*. Described below are reed-stemmed epidendrums with thin, stemlike pseudobulbs.

E. ibaguense (E. radicans). Zones 17, 21–24; H1, H2; or indoors. Native to Colombia. Erect, leafy stems 2–4 ft. tall. Globular clusters of 1–1½-in., orange-yellow flowers with fringed lips held at tips of slender stems well above foliage. Blooms almost continuously in warm weather. Hybrids are available in shades of yellow, orange, pink, lavender, and white.

E. × obrienianum. Zones 17, 21–24; H1, H2; or indoors. Stems rise 1–2 ft. above foliage; clusters of vivid red flowers look like tiny cattleyas. Plants bloom nearly continuously during warm weather.

E

E

CARE

These cool growers need plenty of sun to flower, but also coolness and shade at roots. Mulch plants growing in the ground. If sun is too hot, foliage turns bright red and burns. Tip growth damaged at 28°F (−2°C), killed at about 22°F (−6°C). In cold-winter areas, grow plants in pots and move them indoors in winter. Both species listed grow well in ground bark or other orchid media. Feed with diluted high-nitrogen liquid fertilizer during the growing season. Feed plants grown in ground bark at every other watering, plants in other media monthly. When blooms fade, cut flower stems back to within one or two joints above soil. For more information, see "Meet the Orchids," page 463.

Epilobium angustifolium.
See *Chamerion angustifolium*

Epimedium
Berberidaceae
PERENNIALS

✂ **ZONES 2–9, 14–17, EXCEPT AS NOTED**

◐ **PARTIAL SHADE**

💧 **MODERATE WATER**

Epimedium pinnatum

These low growers spread with creeping underground stems. The thin, wiry leafstalks hold leathery leaves divided into heart-shaped leaflets 3–4 in. long. The foliage is bronzy pink in spring, green in summer, and bronze in fall. Even in deciduous species, the leaves last late into the year. In spring, the plants bear loose spikes of small, waxy flowers in pink, red, creamy yellow, or white. The

flowers have four petals, which may be spurred or hooded, and eight sepals—four inner ones resembling petals and four (usually small) outer ones.

Use as groundcover under trees or among rhododendrons, azaleas, and camellias. Good in large rock gardens, containers. Foliage and flowers are long lasting in arrangements. Keep an eye out for interesting new species coming in from China and Japan.

E. alpinum. Zones 1–9, 14–17. From southern Europe. Evergreen, 6–9 in. high. Small flowers have red inner sepals and yellow petals. Spreads faster than other epimediums.

E. × cantabrigiense. To 8–12 in. high, with olive-tinted semievergreen foliage and small red-and-yellow flowers.

E. grandiflorum. BISHOP'S HAT, LONGSPUR EPIMEDIUM. From China, Korea, Japan. Deciduous epimedium to about 1 ft. high. Relatively large blooms (to 2 in. across) are shaped like a bishop's mitre, with red outer sepals, pale violet inner sepals, and white petals with long spurs. There are varieties with white, pinkish, or violet flowers. 'Rose Queen' bears crimson flowers with white-tipped spurs; 'White Queen' has silvery white blooms.

E. × perralchicum. Evergreen hybrid between *E. perralderianum* and *E. pinnatum colchicum*. Grows 16 in. high; bears ¾-in. yellow flowers. Yellow blooms of 'Frohnleiten' and yellow-and-bronze ones of 'Wisley' are 1 in. across.

E. perralderianum. From North Africa. To 1 ft. tall, with shiny evergreen leaves and ¾-in., bright yellow flowers.

E. pinnatum. Zones A2; 2–9, 14–17. From northern Iran. To 8–12 in. high, with nearly evergreen foliage. Flowers have yellow sepals and very short reddish brown spurs. *E. p. colchicum* is taller (to 16 in.), with larger flowers; its selection 'Black Sea' (*E.* 'Black Sea') has foliage that turns inky purple-black in winter.

E. × rubrum. Semievergreen hybrid between *E. alpinum* and *E. grandiflorum* grows to 1 ft. high. Flowers, borne in showy clusters, have crimson inner sepals, pale yellow or

white petals, and upward-curving spurs. Selections include rosy pink 'Pink Queen', white 'Snow Queen', and red-and-white 'Sweetheart'.

E. × versicolor. Best known of several selections is 'Sulphureum', 12–20 in. tall, with light yellow flowers and semievergreen leaves marked with brownish red.

E. × warleyense. Evergreen hybrid to 1½ ft. high, with light green foliage and clusters of small, coppery orange-red flowers. 'Orangekönigin' has paler orange-red flowers.

E. × youngianum 'Niveum'. Deciduous; to 8–12 in. high. Bears pure white flowers.

CARE

Set out plants 1 ft. apart. They will tolerate heavy shade. Cut back in late winter before new growth resumes. Divide large clumps in spring or fall by cutting through tough roots with a sharp spade.

Epiphyllum
ORCHID CACTUS
Cactaceae
CACTI

✂ **ZONES 8, 9, 14–24; H1, H2; OR INDOORS**

◐ **PARTIAL SHADE; BRIGHT INDIRECT LIGHT**

💧 **REGULAR WATER**

Epiphyllum 'Space Rocket'

Growers use the name "epiphyllum" to refer to a wide range of plants—both the genus *Epiphyllum* itself and a number of crosses with related plants. All are tropical (not desert) cacti, and most grow on tree branches as epiphytes, like some orchids.

Most have arching (to 2 ft. high), trailing stems and look best in hanging pots, tubs, or baskets. Stems are long, flat, smooth, quite spineless, and usually notched or scalloped along the edges. Spring flowers vary in size from medium to very large (up to 10 in. across). The color range includes white, cream, yellow, pink, rose, lavender, scarlet, and orange. Many varieties have blends of two or more colors.

CARE

In the California zones listed, protect by growing under lath or trees. Plants need rich, quick-draining soil with plenty of sand and leaf mold, peat moss, or ground bark. Cuttings are easy to root in spring or summer. Let the base of the cutting dry for a day or two before potting it up. Overwatering and poor drainage cause bud drop. Feed with low-nitrogen fertilizer before and after bloom. In winter, epiphyllums need frost protection.

Equisetum hyemale
HORSETAIL
Equisetaceae
PERENNIAL

✂ **ZONES 1–24**

☀◐ **FULL SUN OR PARTIAL SHADE**

💧 **LOCATE IN MARSHY AREA OR POOL**

Equisetum hyemale

A rushlike survivor of Carboniferous Age in Europe and North America. The common name "horsetail" refers to the bushy look produced by the many whorls of slender, jointed green stems that radiate out from joints of main stems on some.

There are several species, but *E. hyemale* is most common. Its slender, hollow, 4-ft. stems are bright green, with a ring of black and ash gray at each joint. Spores are borne in conelike spikes at the stem ends. Miniature *E. scirpoides* is similar, but only 6–8 in. high.

CARE

Although horsetail is effective in some garden situations, especially near water, use it with caution: it is extremely invasive and difficult to get rid of. Best confined to containers. In open ground, root-prune or dig out unwanted shoots rigorously and constantly.

Eragrostis
LOVE GRASS
Poaceae
PERENNIAL GRASSES

- ZONES VARY BY SPECIES
- FULL SUN TO PARTIAL SHADE
- LITTLE TO MODERATE WATER
- CAN BE INVASIVE, SPREADING BY SEED

Eragrostis spectabilis

Of about 250 species native to many temperate and tropical regions of the world, only a few love grasses are cultivated in gardens. These form graceful clumps of fine-textured foliage, and airy floral plumes float like clouds above the leaves. They are useful as textural accents or as bank or groundcovers.

E. curvula. WEEPING LOVE GRASS. Zones 4–24. From southern Africa and India. Billowing mass of slender, dark green, hairlike leaves reaches 3 ft. high and wide. In summer, lavender-gray flower plumes

increase plant height to 4 ft. Foliage picks up yellow and bronzy hues in cold weather. Evergreen in mild-winter zones. Excellent for massing. Tolerates almost any soil and may be used to control erosion.

E. elliottii. ELLIOT'S LOVE GRASS. Zones 8, 9, 14–24. From Puerto Rico, the Virgin Islands, and southeastern U.S. Narrow leaves form a blue-gray clump 3 ft. high and wide; foliage turns plum purple in fall. Airy tan flower plumes are held above the leaves in spring and keep their good looks well into autumn. Dramatic as a specimen plant.

E. spectabilis. PURPLE LOVE GRASS. Zones 1–24. Native from Maine to Minnesota, south to Florida, Arizona, and Mexico. Light green leaves form a compact clump to about 1½ ft. high and wide. In late summer, plants are covered with wispy clouds of rosy purple plumes that increase the overall height to 2 ft. Leaves turn reddish purple in fall, when flowers have faded to soft cream. Good color combination with gray-leafed plants.

E. trichodes. SAND LOVE GRASS. Zones 1–24. Native from Illinois to Colorado and Texas. Narrow, bright green leaves grow in an upright clump to 1½–2 ft. high and wide; foliage turns bronze-red in autumn. Delicate bronze to purplish blooms appear on stout stems to 4 ft. tall in late summer and last well into winter.

CARE

All are drought-tolerant and need excellent drainage; they grow best in sandy soils. They reseed readily. Plants are tough and carefree; cut back to a few inches high in late fall or winter to make way for new spring growth.

The airy flower plumes that float like clouds above love grass leaves are highly reflective, so they shimmer and sparkle in the slightest breeze.

Eranthis hyemalis
WINTER ACONITE
Ranunculaceae
PERENNIAL FROM TUBER

- ZONES 1–9, 14–17
- FULL SUN DURING BLOOM, PART SHADE DURING REST OF YEAR
- REGULAR WATER DURING GROWTH AND BLOOM

Eranthis hyemalis

This charming plant from Europe and Asia reaches 2–8 in. high and blooms in late winter or early spring. The single yellow flowers resemble buttercups and are about 1½ in. wide, with five to nine petal-like sepals. Each bloom sits on a single, deeply lobed, bright green leaf that looks like a ruff. Round basal leaves are divided into narrow lobes and emerge immediately after the flowers bloom. All traces of the plant disappear by the time summer arrives. The species *E. cilicica* is similar but blooms later, bears slightly larger flowers, and has bronze-tinted new leaves.

CARE

Plant tubers in late summer. If they look dry or shriveled, plump them up in wet sand before planting. Plant 3 in. deep and 4 in. apart, in moist, porous soil. Reduce water in summer but don't let soil dry out completely. Divide clumps infrequently. When doing so, separate into small clumps rather than single tubers.

Eremophila
EMU BUSH
Scrophulariaceae
EVERGREEN SHRUBS

- ZONES 8, 9, 13–24, EXCEPT AS NOTED
- FULL SUN
- LITTLE TO MODERATE WATER, EXCEPT AS NOTED
- ATTRACT BIRDS, BUTTERFLIES

Eremophila decipiens

Of the more than 200 species of these Australian shrubs, just a few are grown in warmer parts of California and the Southwest. All tolerate aridity, heat, wind, and poor soil but like good drainage. All have slender stems that change direction abruptly and interlace to form dense growth. Some may become leggy, but all respond well to pruning. Common name comes from the flightless bird that eats the small fruits of some species. In North America, fruits are food for many birds and animals. Hummingbirds visit the flowers.

E. decipiens. Compact, spreading mound 3 ft. high and wide. Leaves are about 1 in. long and seem to clasp the stems. Brilliant scarlet, slender-tubed blossoms to 1 in. long provide winter color for 2 to 3 months. Thrives without irrigation.

E. glabra. COMMON EMU BUSH. Variable species with creeping or upright growth to 5 ft. tall, 3–10 ft. wide. Narrow leaves to 2 in. long; tubular, 1¼-in.-long flowers in red, orange, yellow, or green from early spring to autumn. 'Murchison River' grows 3 ft. high and wide, has silvery foliage and bright red flowers. 'Kalgoorlie'

E

E

grows to a similar height but has orange flowers.

E. hygrophana. Compact shrub, 2–3 ft. high, about 3 ft. wide, with silvery foliage. Tubular purplish blue flowers appear on and off year-round but mostly in spring and summer.

E. laanii. Spreading shrub 3–6 ft. tall and 4–10 ft. wide, with narrow, 2-in. gray-green leaves. White, pink, or light red flowers to 1 in. long. White-flowered form reputedly is more vigorous and may sucker. Very adaptable species. Tolerates dappled shade. A pink-flowering form is sold as 'Pink Beauty'.

E. maculata. SPOTTED EMU BUSH. Most widely grown type occurs naturally on flood plains and is more tolerant of moisture and humidity than other species. Variable in habit. Most forms grow 3 ft. tall and twice as wide, but some are much larger. Narrow leaves are often hairy when young. Heavy winter and spring crop of flowers, with a scattering at other times of year. Blossoms are 1–2 in. long and come in dark red, yellow, orange, or pink, often with dark spotting inside. 'Aurea' has lighter green leaves and bears 1-in.-long, unspotted yellow flowers; it grows 3–6 ft. tall and to 10 ft. wide with irrigation. 'Valentine' may freeze to the ground in Zones 11 and 12 but will recover. Upright growth 4–5 ft. tall and 5–6 ft. wide. Brilliant rose-red, 1-in.-long blossoms in late winter almost hide the foliage. Leaves have a purplish cast that makes this shrub particularly handsome even when out of bloom.

E. racemosa. EASTER EGG BUSH. Upright grower to 4–5 ft. tall and 3–4 ft. wide, with narrow, pale green leaves. Tubular flowers start as yellow buds that turn orange, then shades of pink and purple as they mature, looking like a collection of brightly colored Easter eggs. Blooms heavily in spring, then intermittently in summer. Blooms are followed by grape-like berries. Prune to encourage bushy growth. Good in pots.

E. × 'Summertime Blue'. Spreading, almost fountainlike habit to 6 ft. tall and at least 8 ft. wide. Produces lilac-blue flowers for a long period in summer.

Eremurus
FOXTAIL LILY, DESERT CANDLE
Asphodelaceae
PERENNIALS FROM TUBEROUS ROOTS

⚡ **ZONES 2–10, 14–16, 18–21**
☀ **FULL SUN**
💧 **REGULAR WATER DURING GROWTH AND BLOOM**

Eremurus × isabellinus
Shelford hybrid

These imposing lily relatives from western and central Asia are grown for their 3–9-ft.-tall spires of blooms. The bell-shaped, ¼–1-in.-wide white, pink, or yellow flowers are massed closely in graceful, pointed spikes on upper one-third to one-half of stem. The plants bloom in late spring, early summer and need winter cold to bloom well. Rosettes of strap-shaped basal leaves appear in early spring, then fade away after the bloom in summer. Foxtail lilies are magnificent in large borders against background of dark green foliage, wall, or solid fence. Dramatic in arrangements; cut when lowest flowers on spike open.

E. himalaicus. To 4–8 ft. tall, with white flowers. Leaves to 1½ ft. long.

E. × isabellinus. Probably best known in this group are the Shelford hybrids, to 4–5 ft. tall, with blossoms in mixed colors (white, yellow, pink, and orange). 'Cleopatra' is a 3–6-ft.-tall, orange-and-red selection of the Ruiter hybrids, a Dutch strain featuring bright, clear flower colors.

E. robustus. To 6–9 ft. tall, with pink flowers that are lightly veined with brown. Dense basal rosettes of leaves to 2 ft. long.

E. stenophyllus (E. bungei). To 3–5 ft. tall, with bright yellow flowers aging to orange-brown. Leaves to 1 ft. long.

CARE

Handle the thick, brittle roots carefully; they tend to rot when bruised or broken. Plant them in rich, fast-draining soil, setting crown just below surface in mild-winter climates, 4–6 in. deep in colder ones. Space roots 2–4 ft. apart. When leaves die down, mark spot; don't disturb roots. Don't let soil dry out completely during dormancy. Provide winter mulch in coldest areas.

Erica
HEATH
Ericaceae
EVERGREEN SHRUBS

⚡ **ZONES VARY BY SPECIES**
☀ ◐ **PARTIAL SHADE IN HOTTEST CLIMATES**
💧 **REGULAR WATER**

Erica cinerea
'Purple Beauty'

Heaths are grown for their small, needlelike leaves and abundant, usually small flowers that may be bell-shaped, urn-shaped, or tubular. By choosing varieties of both heaths and their close relative heather (*Calluna*) carefully, you can have color year-round.

The hardiest heaths, native to northern and western Europe, are widely used as shrubs or groundcover plants in the cool-summer, humid regions of California and the Pacific Northwest. Fanciers sometimes plant the shortest types in masses for a multicolored Persian-carpet effect. Good on slopes. South

African species are tender to frost and about as hardy as fuchsias; where temperatures dip below 28°F (–2°C), it is safest to grow them in containers and provide shelter.

A third group of heaths, native to the Mediterranean and southern Europe, is intermediate in hardiness. Taller heaths can be used as screens. All attract bees.

E. arborea alpina. TREE HEATH. Zones 15–17, 21–24. Southern Europe and North Africa. A dense, upright shrub to 6 ft. tall and 3–4 ft. wide. It is slow to reach blooming age, then is free blooming. It is also hardier than the species and a surer bet in Zones 4–6.

E. canaliculata (usually sold as *E. melanthera* and often called Scotch heather). Zones 15–17, 20–24. From South Africa. A bushy, spreading plant but with general spired effect. To 6 ft. tall and 4 ft. wide. Foliage is dark green above, white beneath. Flowers pink to rosy purple in fall and winter. Sometimes called Christmas heather because of winter bloom. Pink-flowered form is sold as 'Rosea', reddish purple form as 'Rubra'. One of the best for Southern California. Cut flowers last for weeks, whether or not stems are immersed in water.

E. carnea (E. herbacea). Zones A3; 2–10, 14–24. From European Alps. Dwarf to 6–16 in. high, 2 ft. wide. Upright branchlets rise from prostrate main branches. Medium green leaves. Rosy red flowers in winter to spring. Unsightly unless pruned every year. This species and its varieties tolerate neutral or slightly alkaline soil. Unless described otherwise, the following varieties grow about 6–8 in. high and 1½ ft. wide. 'December Red' has pink to reddish purple flowers in winter. Early blooming. 'Myretoun Ruby' has dark green leaves and very striking magenta to crimson blooms. 'Pink Spangles' has shell pink to deep pink flowers. 'Ruby Glow' has dark green leaves and among the richest, deep ruby red flowers. 'Springwood White' is a tough, fast-growing heath with a neat habit, 8 in. high and 14 in. wide. It bears white flowers opening from creamy buds among light green foliage. 'Springwood Pink' is similar but has pink flowers and deep green foliage. 'Vivellii' has dark green leaves that turn bronzy red in winter and carmine-red flowers. Interesting for seasonal change in foliage color as well as for bloom.

E. cinerea. TWISTED HEATH. Zones 4–6, 15–17. From the British Isles and northern Europe. To 1 ft. high, 2½ ft. wide. Forms a dainty low mat of dark green foliage. Purple flowers in summer. Good groundcover. 'Atrosanguinea' grows slowly to 9 in. high, 2½ ft. wide, with scarlet flowers in summer and early fall. 'C. D. Eason' reaches 10 in. high, 20 in. wide, and has an outstanding display of red flowers from late spring through summer. 'P. S. Patrick', to 15 in. high, 20 in. wide, produces long, sturdy spikes of large purple flowers in summer.

E. × darleyensis. Zones 2–10, 14–24. This hybrid is represented by several excellent varieties: 'Darley Dale' is a bushy grower to 1 ft. tall, 2 ft. wide, with medium green foliage. Shell pink to light rosy purple flowers; darken with age from fall to midspring. Tough, hardy plant that takes both heat and cold surprisingly well. Tolerates neutral soils. In Northern California, the most foolproof heath. 'Furzey' is bushy, 14–18 in. high, 2 ft. wide, and has deep rose-pink flowers among dark green leaves in winter and early spring; one of the best all-around heaths. 'Kramer's Rote' is a spreading, vigorous plant to 14 in. high, 2 ft. wide, with dark bronze-green leaves and magenta flowers in winter and early spring. 'Silberschmelze' grows vigorously to 1½–2 ft. high, 2½ ft. wide, with white, fragrant flowers from winter to spring. Easy to maintain.

E. melanthera. See E. canaliculata.

E. tetralix. CROSS-LEAFED HEATH. Zones 4–6, 15–17. From England and northern Europe. Upright, to 1 ft. tall, 2 ft. wide. Dark green leaves, silvery beneath. Rosy pink flowers from summer to early fall. Best with afternoon shade. 'Alba Mollis' is upright, slightly spreading, to 1 ft. high and wide. Its silvery gray foliage sheen is most pronounced in spring and summer. Pure white flowers from summer to early fall. 'Darleyensis' (do not confuse with E. × darleyensis, which blooms from fall to midspring, depending on variety) has spreading, open growth to 8 in. high, 1 ft. wide, and gray-green foliage. Rosy pink flowers in summer. E. t. aureifolia 'Swedish Yellow' is compact and spreading to 4–6 in. high, 12 in. wide. Greenish yellow foliage intensifies to yellow in cold weather. Pale rose-pink flowers in summer.

E. vagans. CORNISH HEATH. Zones 3b–6, 15–17, 20–24. From Cornwall, Ireland. Bushy, open, to 2–3 ft. high and wide with bright green leaves. Flowers white to shell pink or rose in summer. Robust and hardy. 'Lyonesse' is rounded, to 1½ ft. high and wide, with bright, glossy green foliage. White flowers from summer to early fall. It is the best white Cornish heath. 'Mrs. D. F. Maxwell' is similar in habit, with dark green leaves and cherry pink or red flowers. It is outstanding for color and heavy bloom. 'St. Keverne' has light green leaves and a profuse bloom of rose-pink flowers.

E. × watsonii 'Dawn'. Zones 4–9, 14–24. Spreading mound, 1 ft. tall, 2–3 ft. wide. New growth is golden, turning green. Deep pink flowers in summer and early fall. Excellent groundcover. Easy to grow. Hybrid between E. ciliaris and E. tetralix.

CARE
Heaths demand excellent drainage, and most need acid soil. Sandy soil amended with organic matter such as peat moss and compost is ideal; heavy clay is usually fatal. Feeding with an annual sifting of compost is usually sufficient, but if plants lose color, feed lightly with acid plant food in early spring. When it comes to watering, be careful and consistent. Heaths will not tolerate standing water or absolute dryness. To keep plants looking neat, shear or cut off faded flower spikes. Don't cut back into leafless wood; new growth may not resprout.

Ericameria nauseosus.
See Chrysothamnus nauseosus

Erigeron
FLEABANE
Asteraceae
PERENNIALS

🌿 **ZONES VARY BY SPECIES**
☼ ◖ **FULL SUN OR LIGHT SHADE**
💧 **MODERATE WATER**
🦋 **ATTRACT BUTTERFLIES**

Erigeron glaucus

Free-blooming plants with daisy-like flowers. They are similar to closely related Michaelmas daisy (*Aster novi-belgii*), except that erigeron's flower heads have threadlike rays in two or more rows rather than broader rays in a single row. White, pink, lavender, or violet flowers, usually with yellow centers.

E. glaucus. BEACH ASTER, SEASIDE DAISY. Zones 4–6, 15–17, 22–24. Native to California, Oregon coasts. Burns in hot sun inland. Forms a clump to 1 ft. high and 1½ ft. wide, with blue-green foliage and stems. Stout, hairy stems are topped by lavender, 1½–2-in.-wide flower heads in spring, summer. 'Cape Sebastian' grows to 6–8 in. high with lavender-pink flowers. 'Sea Breeze' has large pink flowers. 'Arthur Menzies' is a compact selection to 8 in. high with lavender-pink blooms. 'Wayne Roderick' ('W. R.') also grows to 8 in. high, bears large lavender blooms in summer; possibly a hybrid, it's similar to E. glaucus but has larger leaves and does better in warmer areas.

E. karvinskianus. MEXICAN DAISY, SANTA BARBARA DAISY. Zones 8, 9, 12–24; H1, H2. Native to Mexico. Graceful, trailing plant 10–20 in. high, 3 ft. wide. Leaves 1 in. long, often toothed at tips. Dainty flower heads ¾ in. across, with numerous white or pinkish rays. Rarely out of bloom. Use as groundcover in garden beds or large containers, in rock gardens, in hanging baskets, on dry walls. Drought-tolerant. Naturalizes easily (a pest in Hawaii); invasive unless controlled. 'Moerheimii' is more compact, with slightly larger leaves and lavender-tinted flower heads.

E. speciosus. Zones 1–9, 14–24. Native to Pacific Northwest. Erect, leafy stemmed, 2 ft. high and wide. Summer flowers are 1–1½ in. across, with dark violet or lavender rays. Widespread through Rocky Mountain area is *E. s. macranthus*, aspen daisy, which bears three to five flowers on each stalk; stalks nod near top. Hybrids between E. speciosus and other species are available; they have larger flowers and come in white and pink as well as blue shades. Some of the best are azure blue 'Blue Beauty', violet-blue 'Darkest of All', light violet 'Strahlenmeer', 'Pink Jewel' (with blooms in various pink shades), carmine-pink 'Förster's Liebling' ('Förster's Darling'), and white 'Schneewittchen' ('Snow White').

CARE
Cut back after flowering to prolong bloom. Grow best in sandy soil. Rock garden species need especially fast drainage.

Beach aster, native to California and Oregon coasts, forms clump of foliage just a foot tall. Play up its sea-breeze heritage by planting it in a beachy bowl or trough. Add a mulch of sand or fine gravel, and finish with a few shells or a piece of driftwood.

E

E

Eriobotrya
LOQUAT
Rosaceae
EVERGREEN TREES OR SHRUBS

- ⚡ **ZONES VARY BY SPECIES**
- ☼ ◐ **FULL SUN OR PARTIAL SHADE**
- ◐ ● **MODERATE TO REGULAR WATER**
- 🐦 **FRUIT ATTRACTS BIRDS**

Eriobotrya japonica

Both species described here (one of which bears edible fruit) are Chinese natives with large, prominently veined, sharply toothed leaves that can be cut and used for indoor decoration. Both can be espaliered on fence or trellis (but not in reflected heat) and make good container plants. Attractive to birds.

E. deflexa. BRONZE LOQUAT. Zones 8–24. Fast-growing, shrubby plant. Though easily trained into small tree similar in size to *E. japonica,* it is often espaliered. New leaves emerge bright copper and hold that color for a long time before turning green. The leaves are shinier, more pointed, less leathery, and less deeply veined than those of *E. japonica.* Garlands of creamy white flowers in spring. No edible fruit.

E. japonica. Zones 6–24; H1, H2. Though this loquat produces edible fruit, it's most often used as an ornamental. It grows 15–30 ft. tall and spreads as wide as it is high in sun but grows narrower in shade. Leathery, crisp, stoutly veined and netted leaves are 6–12 in. long, 2–4 in. wide, deep glossy green above, woolly and rust-colored beneath. New branches are woolly. Small, dull white flowers, fragrant but not showy, appear in woolly 3–6-in. clusters in fall.

Orange to yellow, 1–2-in.-long fruit with large seeds in the center ripens in winter or spring. Flesh may be sweet, sweet-tart, or tart, depending on tree and variety. Eat fresh or use in preserves, pies.

Most trees are sold as seedlings, good ornamental plants with unpredictable fruit quality. If you want to harvest a crop, look for a grafted variety such as 'Champagne' (best in warm areas), 'Gold Nugget' (best in cooler regions), or 'MacBeth' (exceptionally large fruit). For good fruit, thin the branches somewhat to let light into tree's interior. If the tree sets fruit heavily, remove some while it's small to increase size of the remaining fruit and to prevent limb breakage.

CARE

Plant in well-drained soil. Subject to fireblight. Moderate water for ornamental plants; regular moisture for a good fruit crop.

Eriogonum
WILD BUCKWHEAT
Polygonaceae
SHRUBBY PERENNIALS

- ⚡ **ZONES VARY BY SPECIES**
- ☼ **FULL SUN**
- ◐ ● **LITTLE TO MODERATE WATER**
- 🐦 **FLOWERS ATTRACT BUTTERFLIES, BEES; SEEDS ATTRACT BIRDS**

Eriogonum cinereum

Native to most areas of the West (the few sold at nurseries are mostly native to California coast). Individual blossoms are tiny but grow in long-stemmed or branched clusters—usually domed, flattish, or ball-like. Flowers age to an attractive tan

or reddish brown and persist for a long time; good in dried arrangements. Useful for covering dry banks, massing among rocks; smaller forms make good specimens in rock gardens.

E. arborescens. SANTA CRUZ ISLAND BUCKWHEAT. Zones 5, 7–9, 14–24. Native to Santa Cruz, Santa Rosa, and Anacapa islands, Southern California. Grows to 3–4 ft. (sometimes 8 ft.) tall, spreading to 4–5 ft. or more. Trunk and branches with shredding gray to reddish bark make attractive open pattern. Rather narrow, ½–1½-in.-long, gray-green leaves cluster at ends of branches. Long-stalked, flat clusters of pale pink to rose flowers, late spring through summer.

E. cinereum. ASHYLEAF BUCKWHEAT. Zones 5, 14–17, 19–24. Native to coastal bluffs and canyons of Southern California. Grows 2–5 ft. tall and 3 ft. wide, with ash-colored, 1-in. leaves and pale pink flowers in ball-shaped clusters in summer. Best planted in groups.

E. crocatum. SAFFRON BUCKWHEAT. Zones 14–24. Native to Southern California. Low, compact plant to 1½ ft. high, 2 ft. wide. Stems and roundish, 1-in.-long leaves are covered with white wool. Sulfur yellow flowers in broad, flattish clusters, early spring to late summer.

E. fasciculatum. CALIFORNIA BUCKWHEAT. Zones 7–9, 12–24. Native to foothills of California (from Santa Clara to San Diego) and to desert mountain slopes of Southern California. Forms a clump 1–3 ft. high, spreading to 4 ft. Leaves narrow, ½–¾ in. long; may be dark green above, white and woolly beneath, or gray and hairy. White or pinkish flowers in headlike clusters, late spring to early fall. Good for erosion control. 'Theodore Payne' is lower growing, makes an attractive green groundcover, as does 'Warriner Lytle'.

E. f. polifolium. ARIZONA BUCKWHEAT. Native to inland mountains and deserts of California into western Utah, Arizona, and northwest Mexico. Differs from the species only in minor botanical details.

E. giganteum. ST. CATHERINE'S LACE. Zones 5, 7–9, 14–24. Native to Santa Catalina and San Clemente islands, Southern California. Differs from *E. arborescens* in its more freely branching habit; grayish white, broadly oval, 1–2½-in.-long leaves; and longer period of bloom.

E. grande rubescens (E. rubescens, E. latifolium rubescens). RED BUCKWHEAT. Zones 5, 14–24. Native to San Miguel, Santa Rosa, and Santa Cruz islands, Southern California. Woody stems at the base; branches tend to lie on ground, spreading to 1–1½ ft., with upright tips about 10–12 in. high. Gray-green, oval leaves 1–3½ in. long. Branch tips and sturdy upright branchlets are topped by headlike clusters of rosy red flowers in summer.

E. umbellatum. SULFUR FLOWER. Zones 1–24. Plants grow to timberline and above. Low, broad mats of woody stems set with 1-in. leaves that are green above, white and felted beneath. In late spring or early summer, 4–12-in. stalks carry clusters of tiny yellow flowers that age to rust. 'Shasta Sulfur' makes a silvery green mound 1½ ft. high and 3 ft. wide, adorned in spring with sulfur yellow flowers. 'Sierra' (grown from seed and somewhat variable) forms a dome 1–2 ft. high and 3–4 ft. wide, above which rise golf ball–size clusters of bright yellow flowers. *E. u. aureum,* Kannah Creek sulphur buckwheat, is a seed-grown selection from Colorado, also with bright yellow flowers that age to orange and rusty red.

E. wrightii. WRIGHT'S BUCKWHEAT. Zones 7–11, 14–24. Widely distributed species native from eastern and Southern California to western Texas and northern Mexico. Selections from higher elevations and northern part of range take more cold. Wandlike stems form a mound 1½ ft. high by 2 ft. wide. Silvery green, felted leaves, ½ in. long and ¼ in. wide, narrow to a point. Tiny white or pinkish flowers appear in clusters along stalks from midsummer through fall.

CARE

Wild buckwheats grow best in well-drained, loose, gravelly soil. They may self-sow; transplant when they're small to extend planting or replace overgrown plants. Shrubby kinds get leggy after several years. You can do some pruning to shape if you start when plants are young, but if they have had no attention, it's better to replace them. Most buckwheats withstand wind and heat. In hottest climates, plants look best with deep watering twice monthly in summer.

Eriophyllum nevinii 'Canyon Silver'
(Constancea nevinii)
WOOLLY SUNFLOWER
Asteraceae
EVERGREEN SHRUB

ZONES 15–17, 19–24

FULL SUN

LITTLE TO MODERATE WATER

Eriophyllum nevinii
'Canyon Silver'

This California native from the Channel Islands has finely cut, silvery foliage similar to dusty miller. Clusters of small, yellow flowers bloom from spring into summer and turn chocolate brown as they age. The shrub grows to 4–6 ft. high and wide. It is ideally adapted to Southern California coastal gardens. Plant in full sun and well-drained soil. Can get by on little water near the coast. To maintain a compact habit, prune back in fall to winter.

Erodium reichardii
(E. chamaedryoides)
CRANESBILL
Geraniaceae
PERENNIAL

ZONES 7–9, 14–24

FULL SUN OR PARTIAL SHADE

REGULAR WATER

Erodium reichardii

This dainty-looking but tough plant from the Balearic Islands and Corsica forms a dense foliage tuft 3–6 in. high and 1 ft. across. The long-stalked, dark green, roundish, ⅓-in.-long leaves have scalloped edges. Profuse, cup-shaped, ½-in.-wide flowers with white or rose-pink, rosy-veined petals notched at tips appear from early spring into fall. Cranesbill makes a good small-scale groundcover or rock garden plant. A double-flowered pink form and a single-flowered white form exist. Plant in porous soil.

E. chrysanthum has silvery foliage and pale yellow flowers. *E. petraeum crispum* (*E. foetidum*) has white flowers with lavender veins and a conspicuous purple spot on one petal.

> Plant cranesbill in a rock garden with a small, shapely boulder as a foil. Or tuck it between steppingstones to show off its small flowers and pretty, roundish foliage.

Eryngium
SEA HOLLY, AMETHYST ERYNGIUM
Apiaceae
ANNUALS, BIENNIALS, AND PERENNIALS

ZONES 2–24, EXCEPT AS NOTED

FULL SUN

WATER NEEDS VARY BY SPECIES

ATTRACT BEES

Eryngium

These mostly spiny-leafed, rosette-forming plants produce erect, thistlelike, leafy stalks bearing tight, silvery or blue-tinted flower heads surrounded by showy bracts. They bloom in summer (sometimes into fall). Upper leaves, leafstalks, bracts, and flowers may all be frosted with silver or tinted in shades of blue or amethyst. Useful in rock gardens and for long displays in borders. Good choice for dried arrangements.

E. alpinum. ALPINE SEA HOLLY. Perennial. From southeastern Europe. To 2½ ft. high, 1½ ft. wide, with taproot. Spiny, heart-shaped basal leaves 3–6 in. long. Upper leaves and stems are tinged with soft blue to steel blue near top. The conical, 1½-in. flower heads are surrounded by purplish blue, intricately cut bracts. 'Blue Star' has prominent metallic blue flowers and foliage. Tolerates very light shade. Moderate water.

E. amethystinum. Perennial. Zones 1–24. From Italy and the Balkans. To 2½ ft. high, 1½ ft. wide, with taproot. Spiny, medium green leaves to 6 in. long. Silvery blue stems and conical, 1-in. amethyst flower heads surrounded by 2-in., silvery blue bracts. Attract butterflies. Moderate water.

E. foetidum. CULANTRO. Biennial grown as an annual where temperatures drop below 0°F (−18°C). Zones 4–9, 12–24; H1, H2. Native to American tropics. To 2 ft. tall and wide. Rosettes of green, spiny, lance-shaped leaves to 5 in. long; foliage has aroma similar to coriander or cilantro. Succulent new leaves can substitute for true coriander and are produced long after the latter has gone to seed. Flowering stems bear dark green, ¾-in., egg-shaped flower heads. Fertile soil, regular water.

E. giganteum. MISS WILL-MOTT'S GHOST. Biennial to short-lived perennial. From the Caucasus and Iran. To 3–4 ft. or taller, 2½ ft. wide. Oval or heart-shaped, medium green leaves to 6 in. long. Three-lobed stem leaves. In late summer, bears blue or pale green, conical flower heads surrounded by silvery, 2½–4-in. bracts; the plant dies after flowering ends. Reseeds well. Provide fertile soil, regular water.

E. planum. FALSE SEA HOLLY. Perennial. From southeast Europe to central Asia. To 3 ft. high, 1½ ft. wide, with taproot. Oblong to heart-shaped, deep green leaves to 4 in. long. Stem leaves are blue-tinted, with three to five lobes or sections. Rounded, ½–¾-in.-wide, light blue flower heads are surrounded by narrow blue-green bracts. Varieties, such as 'Blaukappe', with more intense blue color are available. 'Silver Salentino' has silvery white blooms. Moderate water.

E. variifolium. MOROCCAN SEA HOLLY. Perennial. Zones 4–9, 14–24. From Morocco. To 1½ ft. high, 10 in. wide, with taproot. Oval, tooth-edged, spiny, somewhat fleshy leaves are 2 in. long, heart-shaped at base, dark green marbled with white veins. Stiff, silvery blue, branching stems bear 1-in. blue-gray flower heads surrounded by silvery blue bracts to ½ in. Moderate to regular water.

E. yuccifolium. RATTLE-SNAKE MASTER, BUTTON SNAKEROOT. Perennial. From central and eastern U.S. To 4 ft. tall, 2 ft. wide. Sword-shaped, spiny-edged, blue-gray leaves to a little over 3 ft. long. Strong, branched stems. Cylindrical, whitish green to pale blue flower heads are 1½ in. across, lack showy bracts. Fertile soil, regular water.

CARE

Sea hollies from dry, rocky areas in Europe, North Africa, Turkey, central Asia, China, and Korea tend to be taprooted and prefer dry, well-drained, poor to moderately rich soils. They need protection from excessive winter water. Those from wet grasslands in Mexico, Brazil, and Argentina have fibrous root systems and prefer moist, well-drained soils. Taprooted forms are difficult to divide but may be propagated by root cuttings. If seeding, sow in place. Some species reseed vigorously. Watch out for snails and slugs.

Erysimum

WALLFLOWER
Brassicaceae
PERENNIALS, SOME GROWN
AS BIENNIALS OR ANNUALS

- ✿ ZONES VARY BY SPECIES
- ☼ ◐ FULL SUN OR LIGHT SHADE
- ◊ ◖ ● WATER NEEDS VARY BY SPECIES

Erysimum 'Pastel Patchwork'

This genus swallowed up *Cheiranthus*, which included the old-fashioned biennial bedding-plant wallflowers and several choice perennials. All have the typical clustered four-petaled flowers that give the crucifers their name, but their habits and uses differ widely.

E. × allionii. SIBERIAN WALLFLOWER. Perennial, often grown as biennial or annual. Zones A3; 1–9, 14–24. Branching plants 1–1½ ft. high and somewhat wider are covered in spring with fragrant flowers in rich orange or yellow. In mild-winter climates, sow seeds in fall; elsewhere, sow in spring for well-established plants by fall. Full sun, moderate water. Sometimes sold as *E. asperum* or *E. hieraciifolium*.

E. cheiri (Cheiranthus cheiri). ENGLISH WALLFLOWER. Perennial in Zones 4–6, 14–17, 22, 23, but usually grown as a biennial or annual. From southern Europe. Best in cool, moist regions. Branching, woody-based plants to 1–2½ ft. high, 1–1½ ft. wide, with narrow bright green leaves and broad clusters of showy, sweet-scented flowers in spring. Blossoms are yellow, cream, orange, red, brown, or burgundy, sometimes shaded or veined with contrasting color. Main bloom period falls between that of primroses and summer bedding plants. Under ideal conditions in coastal Pacific Northwest, it may bloom year-round. Sow seeds in spring for bloom the following year (some strains flower the first year if seeded early); or set out plants in fall or earliest spring. May self-sow. Regular water.

E. hybrids. Perennials. Zones 4–9, 14–24. Many excellent choices available. Most popular is 'Bowles Mauve', 3 ft. high and 4–6 ft. wide, with narrow gray-green leaves held on erect stems, each topped by a 1½-ft.-long, narrow, spikelike cluster of mauve flowers. Best in areas with cool summers and mild winters, where bloom is practically continual; elsewhere, plants bloom from winter through spring. Often short-lived. 'Compact Bowles Mauve' is about half the size. 'Lemon Zest' grows 8–12 in. high and wide, with pale to lemon yellow blooms in early spring. 'Sweet Sorbet' has lilac-pink flowers on a 14–18-in. plant. 'Wenlock Beauty' grows 2 ft. high and wide, with springtime flowers varying from buff to purple in a single spike. All these hybrids take moderate water.

E. insulare suffrutescens (E. suffrutescens). Perennial. Zones 14–17, 22–24. Native to central and Southern California coasts. Woody-based growth 6–24 in. high, 4–12 in. wide, with narrow leaves and fragrant orange-yellow flowers in spring. Little water.

E. kotschyanum. Perennial in Zones 3b–11, 14–21; often treated as a winter annual in hot-summer climates. Light green leaves form a mat 6 in. high and a foot wide; in spring, fragrant deep yellow flowers appear on 2-in. stems. Use in rock garden or with other small perennials between paving stones. If plants hump up, cut out central portion, transplant it, and press original plant flat again. Divide clumps in fall. Provide moderate water.

E. linifolium 'Variegatum'. Zones 4–6, 14–24. Shrubby growth to 2 ft. high, 2–3 ft. wide. Prized for its narrow, 3½-in.-long leaves, which are gray-green and edged in creamy white. Mauve flowers about ½ in. across appear from spring to fall. Moderate water.

Erythea. See *Brahea*

Erythrina

CORAL TREE
Papilionaceae
DECIDUOUS OR NEARLY EVERGREEN
TREES AND SHRUBS

- ✿ ZONES VARY BY SPECIES
- ☼ FULL SUN
- ◖ MODERATE WATER
- 🦜 ATTRACT BIRDS
- ◊ SEEDS ARE POISONOUS IF INGESTED

Erythrina crista-galli

There are many species of coral tree, known and used chiefly in Southern California. Some are also cultivated in Hawaii, and a few are grown in Arizona. They are valued for their brilliant flowers in colors ranging from greenish white through yellow to light or vivid shades of orange and red. The flat, bean-like pods following bloom contain poisonous seeds. Leaves are divided into three leaflets. These are typically thorny plants with strong structural value, both in and out of leaf.

E. × bidwillii. Deciduous shrub. Zones 8, 9, 12–24. To 8 ft. tall and as wide; sometimes treelike to 20 ft. or taller. Spectacular spring-to-winter display of 2-ft.-long clusters of pure red flowers on long, willowy stalks; main show in summer. Cut back flowering wood after blossoms fade. Very thorny; plant away from paths, and use long-handled pruners when trimming.

E. caffra (E. constantiana). CORAL TREE. Briefly deciduous tree. Zones 21–24; H2. Native to South Africa. To 24–40 ft. tall, 40–60 ft. wide. Drops leaves in early winter; then angular bare branches produce big clusters of deep red-orange, tubular flowers that drip nectar. In late winter or earlier, flowers give way to fresh, light green foliage.

E. coralloides. NAKED CORAL TREE. Deciduous tree. Zones 12, 13, 19–24. Native to Mexico. To 30 ft. tall and as wide or wider, but easily contained by pruning. Fiery red blossoms like fat candles or pinecones bloom at tips of naked, twisted, black-thorned branches in spring. At end of flowering season, 8–10-in. leaves develop; they give shade in summer, turn yellow in late fall, then drop—revealing a bizarre branching structure that's almost as valuable as spring flower display. 'Bicolor' has white flower clusters, red flower clusters, and ones that have both colors. Sometimes sold as *E. poianthes*.

E. crista-galli. COCKSPUR CORAL TREE, COMMON CORAL TREE. Nearly evergreen (in Hawaii) to deciduous tree. Zones 7–9, 12–17, 19–24; H1, H2. Shrub or tree to 15–20 ft. tall and as wide in nearly frost-less areas; perennial to half that size in colder part of range. Native to South America. Many-stemmed, rough-barked plant, with 6-in. leaves divided into 2–3-in.-long leaflets. First flowers form after leaves unfurl in spring, when each branch tip flaunts a big, loose, spikelike cluster of velvety, birdlike blossoms in warm pink to wine red (color varies with the plant). Depending on environment, there may be as many as three distinct flowering periods, spring through autumn. Cut back old flower stems after each wave of bloom.

E. falcata. Nearly evergreen tree. Zones 19–24; H1, H2. Native to Brazil and Peru. Upright habit reaching 30–40 ft. tall. Must be in ground several years before it flowers (may take 10 to 12 years). Dark red (occasionally orange-red), sickle-shaped flowers in hanging, spikelike clusters at branch ends in winter, early spring. Some leaves drop at bloom time.

E. humeana. NATAL CORAL TREE. Normally deciduous tree (sometimes almost evergreen). Zones 12, 13, 20–24; H1, H2. Native to South Africa. May grow to 30 ft. tall, but begins blooming when only 3 ft. high. Flowers continuously from late summer to late autumn, carrying bright orange-red blossoms in long-stalked clusters at branch ends well above the leaves (unlike many other types). Dark green foliage. 'Raja' is shrubbier and has leaflets with long, pointed "tails."

E. sandwicensis. WILIWILI, HAWAIIAN CORAL TREE. Deciduous tree. Zone H2. Hawaiian native to 20–45 ft. tall and as wide. Masses of white to chartreuse, coral, orange, red, or bicolored flowers bloom in late summer to winter, preceding the flush of new foliage. Extremely drought-tolerant; good selection for xeriscape gardens.

E. × sykesii. Deciduous tree. Zones 19–24. Hybrid from Australia. To 24–30 ft., with spreading habit. Showy red flowers appear in winter before leaves emerge. Unlike the other species, does not form pods.

CARE

To eliminate too rapid, succulent growth and limb breakage in larger species, give little or no irrigation during dry weather and prune after flowering.

FOR MORE PLANTS THAT ATTRACT BIRDS, SEE PAGES 95–99.

Erythronium
Liliaceae
PERENNIALS FROM BULBS

✎ **ZONES VARY BY SPECIES**

☀ **LIGHT SHADE**

💧 **REGULAR WATER DURING GROWTH AND BLOOM**

Erythronium revolutum

Spring-flowering plants with dainty, nodding, lily-shaped blooms 1–1½ in. across, on stems usually 1 ft. high or less. All have two (rarely three) broad, tongue-shaped basal leaves that are mottled in many species. Lovely in groups under deciduous trees, in rock gardens, beside pools or streams.

E. californicum. FAWN LILY. Zones 4–7, 14–17. Native to Northern California. Dark green leaves are mottled with brown. Creamy white flowers with a yellowish green central ring are held on 6–10-in. stems. 'White Beauty' is vigorous, spreading readily by offsets; its flowers are white, with rusty orange marks at the base of each petal.

E. dens-canis. DOG-TOOTH VIOLET. Zones 1–7, 15–17. From Europe. Medium green leaves are mottled brown and white. Deep pink to purple flowers on 6–12-in. stems. Specialists offer many named varieties with white, pink, rose, or violet blossoms, some marked in contrasting colors.

E. hendersonii. Zones 4–7, 15–17. Native to Northern California and southern Oregon. Foot-tall stems carry light to deep lavender flowers that are dark maroon at the base and rimmed with yellow or white; petals are deeply curled back at tips. Dark green leaves are

attractively mottled with brown. A choice plant for the front of the border.

E. 'Pagoda'. Zones 2–7, 14–17. Probable cross between *E. tuolumnense* and *E. californicum* 'White Beauty'. Vigorous grower, with deep green leaves heavily mottled in bronze. In spring, 6–14-in.-tall stems hold up to 10 bright yellow flowers with rusty central rings.

E. revolutum. Zones 1–7, 14–17. Western native quite similar to *E. californicum*, but with larger foliage and flowers. Flower stems up to 16 in. hold pink blossoms marked yellow in the center. 'Pink Beauty' has deep pink flowers without yellow center.

E. tuolumnense. Zones 2–7, 14–17. Native to California. Robust plant with solid green leaves and 12–15-in.-tall stems. Golden yellow flowers are greenish yellow at base. 'Kondo' is an extra-vigorous selection.

CARE

Plant bulbs in rich, porous soil in fall as soon as you receive them; don't let them dry out. Set them 2–3 in. deep and 4–5 in. apart. If gophers are a problem in your area, plant in buried cages. Western species need no water while dormant, but give *E. dens-canis* moisture year-round. Divide clumps infrequently—only when vigor and bloom quality decline.

Most of the *Erythronium* species listed here are native to Northern California or Oregon. In the wild, these pretty little plants grow in forests and meadows. Group them in lightly shaded beds beneath tall deciduous trees.

Escallonia
Escalloniaceae
EVERGREEN SHRUBS

✎ **ZONES 4–9, 14–24**

☀ ◐ **PARTIAL SHADE IN HOTTEST CLIMATES**

💧 **REGULAR WATER**

🦋 **ATTRACT BUTTERFLIES**

Escallonia rubra

Native to South America, principally Chile. These fast-growing plants look good year-round in a border or as a screen. They have handsome, glossy leaves; foliage of some exudes a resinous fragrance. Clusters of small (to 1 in.) flowers appear in summer and fall (nearly year-round in mild climates). Plants may freeze badly at 10°F to 15°F (−12°C to −9°C) but will recover quickly. They stand up to coastal conditions and high winds, and grow in most soils, except those that are highly alkaline. Prune taller types by removing one-third of old wood each year after bloom, cutting to the base; or shape into multitrunked trees. Tip-pinch smaller kinds to keep them compact. They can be sheared as formal hedges, but this may sacrifice some bloom.

E. 'Apple Blossom'. Dense grower to 5 ft. high and wide, sprawling unless pinched back. Large, pinkish white flowers open from pink buds.

E. bifida (E. montevidensis). WHITE ESCALLONIA. As a shrub, it can be kept to 8–10 ft. tall and wide; useful as a big screening plant. It can also grow as a multitrunked small tree to 25 ft. tall. Leaves are glossy, dark green; white flowers appear in large, rounded clusters at branch ends. Many

E

E

plants sold under this name are *E. illinita,* a plant to 10 ft. tall with smaller flower clusters and a pronounced resinous odor.

E. 'C. F. Ball'. Upright, open grower to 5–8 ft. tall and wide (pinch tips to keep to 3 ft.). Glossy dark green leaves make a nice backdrop for the rich red flowers.

E. × exoniensis. This cross between *E. rubra* and another Chilean species is a strong, erect grower to 12–20 ft. tall and nearly as wide. Leaves are deep green above, lighter beneath. Loose clusters of white or pale pink flowers appear at the branch tips. 'Frades' is more compact, with a prolific show of pure pink to rose flowers.

E. 'Jubilee'. Compact-growing, 6-ft. shrub that is densely leafy right to the ground. Clustered pinkish to rose flowers. Set 4 ft. apart for informal hedge or screen.

E. laevis (E. organensis). PINK ESCALLONIA. Leafy, dense-growing shrub to 12–15 ft. tall and wide, with bronzy green leaves. Pink to red buds open into white to pink flowers in short, broad clusters. Use as a large screen or train as a small tree. Leaves burn in seacoast wind and salt, as well as in high heat. Gold-leafed forms are sometimes offered.

E. 'Newport Dwarf' (E. 'Compakta'). Dense, uniform growth to 2–3 ft. high and twice as wide, with shiny, bright green leaves and rose-red flowers.

E. 'Pride of Donard'. Dense, mounding shrub to 5 ft. tall and 8 ft. wide, with glossy dark green leaves and large rose-pink flowers.

E. 'Red Elf'. Dense, spreading shrub to 8 ft. tall, 12 ft. wide, with inch-long, dark glossy green leaves and short clusters of deep red flowers.

E. rubra. Upright, variable, compact shrub grows to 6–15 ft. tall and wide. Leaves are smooth, very glossy dark green. Flowers are red or crimson, in 1–3-in. clusters. Much used as a screen or hedge, especially near the coast. 'Crimson Spire' is an upright grower with large, bright crimson flowers. *E. r. macrantha* is similar, but with rose-red flowers and a more sprawling shape.

E. virgata. Partially deciduous shrub grows to 6 ft. tall and 8 ft. wide; produces short clusters of pale rose or white flowers. This is the hardiest escallonia—it does well in the frostiest parts of these plants' hardiness range.

Eschscholzia
Papaveraceae
PERENNIALS AND ANNUALS

🖊 **ZONES 1–24; H1**

☀ **FULL SUN**

◔◍◐ **LITTLE TO REGULAR WATER**

🐦 **ATTRACT BIRDS, BEES**

Eschscholzia californica

These delightful poppy relatives form mounds of finely cut foliage topped by upward-facing, four-petaled, paper-thin blooms. Of the several species native to western North America and Mexico, *E. californica* is the most outstanding and the most widely used; it is the state flower of California. All are drought-tolerant, but giving them summer water will extend their flowering season.

E. caespitosa. Annual. Native to California and southwestern Oregon. Grows about 6 in. high and wide, with threadlike leaves and bright yellow flowers. Use for edging, in containers. 'Sundew' has densely tufted growth and lemon yellow flowers to 1 in. across.

E. californica. CALIFORNIA POPPY. Perennial often grown as annual. Native to California, Oregon. Free branching from base, with slender, 8–24-in.-long stems and blue-green, finely divided leaves. Individual plants grow about 1 ft. high and up to 1½ ft. wide. Single, satiny-petaled flowers are up to 3 in.

wide; color varies from pale yellow to deep orange. Flowers close at night and on overcast days. In mild climates, it blooms from spring to summer and reseeds freely. Naturalized in California and also in Washington and parts of Hawaii. In cold-winter areas, generally used as a summer annual.

There are dozens of garden forms of California poppy, and new ones appear on the market regularly. The flowers come in shades of yellow, pink, rose, flame orange, red, reddish purple, and creamy white; some have petals streaked or bordered in contrasting colors; they may be single, semidouble, double, fluted, or frilled. All tend to revert to the basic orange or yellow form when they reseed. Thai Silk strain has bronze-tinted foliage, with semidouble flowers in a wide color range. 'Golden Tears' bears single golden yellow blooms on trailing stems to 2 ft. long.

California poppy is not the best choice for important beds viewed close up—unless you trim off dead flowers regularly, plants go to seed and all parts turn straw color. It can't be surpassed, however, for naturalizing on sunny hillsides; along drives; or in dry fields, vacant lots, parking strips, or country gardens. Sow in fall in mild-winter areas, in spring in colder regions. Broadcast on cultivated, well-drained soil; if rain is absent, water to keep ground moist until seeds germinate. For large-scale sowing, use 3–4 lb. of seeds per acre. Birds are attracted to the seeds.

Etlingera elatior
TORCH GINGER
Zingiberaceae
PERENNIAL

🖊 **ZONE H2**

☀◐ **FULL SUN OR PARTIAL SHADE**

◐ **REGULAR WATER**

Etlingera elatior

From the jungles of Malaysia and Indonesia. An impressive, clump-forming plant to 20 ft. high and wide (spreading wider over time). Canelike stems are clothed with dark green, pointed leaves, each 12–28 in. long and 4–6 in. wide. The plant blooms most of the year, producing striking foot-long, bright red or pink, conelike inflorescences on 2–5-ft.-tall stalks that rise directly from the ground. Good candidate for tropical bouquets. Best in rich, organic soil with protection from wind. Sometimes sold as *Phaeomeria magnifica* or *Nicolaia elatior*.

Western Wildflowers

California poppies are the most commonly planted Western native wildflowers. They combine beautifully with other choice wildflowers: the sky-blue blooms of globe gilia (*Gilia capitata*) and baby blue eyes (*Nemophila menziesii*); the yellow-and-white daisies of tidy tips (*Layia platyglossa*), and the various colors of annual lupine (*Lupinus microcarpus densiflorus*).

Look for wildflower mixes sold by nurseries that contain some or all of these. Or purchase separate seed packets and sow in drifts to create your own annual compositions.

Eucalyptus

Myrtaceae

EVERGREEN TREES AND SHRUBS

✿ ZONES 5, 6, 8–24; H1, H2
(SEE HARDINESS IN ENTRIES)

☼ FULL SUN

◐ LITTLE OR NO WATER, EXCEPT
AS NOTED

Eucalyptus polyanthemos

Impressive plants native to Australia. They range from sprawling shrubs (many bearing the common name "mallee") to skyline trees. They are the most widely planted nonnative trees in California and Arizona, where they've been used for windbreaks, shade, firewood, and hardwood timber.

Eucalypts are appealing on several levels: Depending on the species, they may have attractive form, striking bark, good-looking foliage, or some combination of these features. Most have two conspicuously different kinds of foliage: soft, variously shaped juvenile leaves, found on seedlings, saplings, and new branches that grow from stumps; and (typically) tougher adult or mature leaves. Almost all leaves, juvenile and adult, have a distinctive pungent aroma, though some must be crushed to release it. Most eucalypts have small, inconspicuous white flowers followed by small, woody seed capsules; exceptions are noted in the text.

Although they were popular landscape trees through much of the latter part of the 20th century, serious pest problems and smaller lot sizes have lessened their popularity, especially in California. In addition, they contain highly combustible oil, and many drop considerable litter that is also quite flammable. Do not plant eucalypts near homes or other flammable structures.

Also pay attention to plant size; many species are best suited to larger properties. A few species grow as much as 10 ft. annually in their early years. Such a growth rate is typically associated with short-lived trees, but not in this case—fast-growing tree eucalypts can live for at least a century if given proper care from the start. Occasional deep or prolonged freezes may kill even large eucalyptus trees. Don't be too quick to remove them; they can sprout new growth from trunk or large branches, though heavy freeze damage may alter their appearance.

Some botanists now divide *Eucalyptus* into several genera, with many of the plants listed here assigned to *Symphyomyrtus*. Other new names are listed in parentheses.

E. cinerea. SILVER DOLLAR TREE. Hardy to 14°F to 17°F (−10°C to −8°C). Grows 20–50 ft. tall and 20–40 ft. wide. Juvenile leaves are gray-green, roundish to heart-shaped. Mature leaves are long, narrow, and mid-green. Cut back often for a supply of decorative juvenile foliage, which lasts well in cut or dried arrangements. Withstands wind; grows best in a dry site or one with fast drainage. Can be used as a perennial in borderline climates.

E. citriodora (Corymbia citriodora). LEMON-SCENTED GUM. Hardy to 24°F to 28°F (−4°C to −2°C). A stately tree to 45–90 ft. tall, 15–45 ft. wide, or considerably larger with great age. Mature leaves are golden green and powerfully lemon scented. Bark is smooth and powdery white, sometimes with a blush of pink or blue. An attractive, narrow tree that can be grown close to walls and walks, as the lower half to two-thirds of the tree is bare trunk. Stake young trees, as trunk is weak. Cut back and thin often to strengthen. Can take much or little water.

E. cladocalyx. SUGAR GUM. Hardy to 23°F to 28°F (−5°C to −2°C). Growing at least 45–90 ft. tall and 45–75 ft. wide, sugar gum is familiar as

How to Grow Eucalyptus

PLANTING Buy vigorous-looking plants; they are not necessarily the biggest. Avoid those with many leafless twigs or evidence of hard pruning. If possible, do not buy rootbound plants. If such plants are all you can get, loosen the rootball and cut off any kinked roots that cannot be straightened; then spread remaining roots out as straight as possible (in a fan shape) in premoistened planting hole, with stem's old soil line ½–1 in. below grade. Immediately fill in around the roots with moistened soil and irrigate heavily. If the plants are top-heavy, cut back and stake.

FEEDING & WATERING Complete fertilizer is seldom needed, although iron often is required for eucalypts whose leaves chronically turn yellow between veins (chlorosis). In the desert, plants are especially subject to chlorosis in dense or shallow soils. Iron chelate applied in spring and fall is helpful for young trees. Overwatering can cause chlorosis. Newly planted trees may need water every day for their first week if weather is hot and dry. Soak deeply once every week or 10 days for the rest of the first growing season. Once established, most eucalypts need no watering at all, except in the low desert.

PRUNING This is best done in early spring. Many eucalypts need selective pruning to improve their shape or to remove dead or dying growth. Some benefit from cutting back to make them bushier or stouter; wait until they have been in the ground for at least a year, then cut back to just above a side branch or bud. If there are no side branches or visible buds, cut back trunk to desired height—if the plant is established, new growth will break out beneath the cut. Later, remove all excess new branches that form; keep only those that are well placed.

PESTS The eucalyptus long-horned beetle—first observed in Southern California in 1984—has now been successfully controlled by natural predators introduced from Australia. But several other beetles, at least one gall wasp species, and as many as eight psyllid species have been introduced since then. Without natural predators to keep them in check, many have become serious pests, especially on stressed trees.

Beetles. Signs of long-horned beetle infestation include oval holes in the plant's wood, and individual branches or the whole plant dying with its leaves still attached. If you see tunnels under bark of firewood, immediately burn or bury the wood. Remove dead or dying trees; bury logs or cover tightly with tarpaulins for at least 6 months. Tightly cover eucalyptus firewood and do not transport it.

Psyllids. These tiny insects suck sap from leaves, excreting honeydew in the process; foliage may look black due to sooty mold growing on the honeydew. If present in high numbers, the pest can cause severe leaf drop. Infested plants are more susceptible to attack by other pests, including borers.

Minimize stress by irrigating deeply (but not near the trunk) during long dry spells; don't fertilize. Don't spray leaves with any kind of insecticide—parasitoid wasps have been released to control the psyllid. Soil drenches and trunk injections of the systemic insecticide imidacloprid protect healthy trees from psyllids.

For the most current information on pests of eucalyptus, including resistant species, contact your county's Cooperative Extension Office.

E

E

CLOCKWISE FROM TOP: *Eucalyptus macrocarpa*; *E. deglupta*; *E. ficifolia*

a skyline tree on the Southern California coast. It has a stout trunk and characteristic puffy clouds of foliage separated by open spaces. Shiny reddish leaves are oval or variably shaped. Smooth, pale gray bark peels to show creamy patches. Creamy yellow flowers are profuse in summer. 'Nana' is a small, bushy grower to 20–25 ft. tall and wide; good as a windbreak.

E. conferruminata. BUSHY YATE. Hardy to 25°F to 28°F (−4°C to −2°C). Usually sold as *E. lehmannii*. Grows to 12–27 ft. tall and 15–30 ft. wide, with elongated oval, light green leaves; some turn red in autumn. Green flowers in 4-in. clusters open from horn-shaped buds. Large woody capsules remain on the branches. Fast-growing, flat-topped, dense tree for windbreak or seashore. Left unpruned, its branches touch the ground.

E. dalrympleana. MOUNTAIN GUM. Hardy to 8°F to 12°F (−13°C to −11°C). Grows quickly to 70–120 ft. tall and 25–50 ft. wide. Bright green leaves are lance-shaped, up to 11 in. long. Bark is smooth and white. One of the best large eucalypts for cold areas. Tolerates alkaline soils.

E. erythrocorys. RED-CAP GUM. Hardy to 23°F to 26°F (−5°C to −3°C). To 12–30 ft. tall and 9–25 ft. wide, with a white trunk and thick, shiny, deep green, lance-shaped leaves to 7 in. long. Bright red caps tilt up and fall off to reveal yellow flowers in brushlike clusters. Blooms anytime of year, heaviest from fall to early spring. Best with multiple trunks; sprawling but attractive. To make dense, head back main shoots several times. Can take much water if drainage is good; can even be grown in a lawn. Attractive choice for desert gardens.

E. ficifolia (Corymbia ficifolia). RED-FLOWERING GUM. Hardy to 25°F to 30°F (−4°C to −1°C). Grows to 18–45 ft. tall,

15–60 ft. wide; usually single-trunked and round headed. Deep green, leathery, 3–7-in.-long leaves. Showy foot-long clusters of red flowers (sometimes white, cream, pink, or orange) all year, peaking in summer. Heavy 1-in. seed capsules resemble dice cups; prune these from young trees to avoid weighing down the branches and spoiling the form. Seldom thrives in lawns or hottest climates.

E. gunnii. CIDER GUM. Hardy to 5°F to 10°F (−15°C to −12°C). Grows 30–75 ft. tall, 18–45 ft. wide, with silvery blue-green young foliage and dark green, 3–5-in.-long mature leaves. Green-and-tan bark. One of the fastest-growing, hardiest eucalypts. Dense form makes it good for shade, windbreak, or screen.

E. lehmannii. See *E. conferruminata.*

E. leucoxylon. WHITE IRON-BARK. Hardy to 14°F to 18°F (−10°C to −8°C). Reaches 30–90 ft. tall, 18–60 ft. wide. Gray-green, sickle-shaped leaves are 3–6 in. long. Trunk brownish or bluish gray, shedding to reveal white new bark. Flower color may be white to cream, pink, or reddish; goblet-shaped capsules follow. Habit is somewhat variable; usually slender, upright, open, with pendulous branches. Tolerates adverse conditions, including heat, wind, and heavy soils or light, rocky ones.

E. microtheca. COOLIBAH. Hardy to 5°F to 10°F (−15°C to −12°C). A bushy, round-headed, single- or multitrunked tree to 30–60 ft. tall and 24–54 ft. wide. Blue-green, ribbonlike leaves to 8 in. long. Wind-resistant and creates hardly any litter. One of the best eucalypts for Arizona.

E. 'Moon Lagoon'. Hardy to 20°F to 25°F (−7°C to −4°C). This hybrid of uncertain parentage grows 4–10 ft. tall and about as wide, forming a dense, soft-looking mass. Delicate branches hold small, oval juvenile leaves of blue-gray. Red caps open to expose white flowers in spring or summer. Cut back hard in early spring to ensure a supply of fresh new foliage, which lasts a long time in arrangements.

E. neglecta. OMEO GUM. Hardy to 0°F (−18°C), making it one of the hardiest. To 40–60 ft. tall and wide, with large, round, very attractive juvenile leaves that persist even on older trees. Takes on rosy hues in cold weather. Fast-growing specimen tree in borderline climates; can also be grown as a perennial there. Tolerates wet soil.

E. nicholii. NICHOL'S WILLOW-LEAFED PEPPERMINT. Hardy to 12°F to 15°F (−11°C to −9°C). Grows 36–48 ft. tall, 15–36 ft. wide, with narrow, 3–5-in.-long, light green leaves and furrowed, rich reddish brown bark. Graceful, weeping garden or street tree. Crushed leaves smell like peppermint. Too much water can cause chlorosis.

E. papuana (Blakella papuana). GHOST GUM. Hardy to 20°F to 22°F (−7°C to −6°C). Upright, semiweeping tree to 30–50 ft. tall and 20–35 ft. wide. Lance-shaped, 2–5-in., light green leaves are tinted purplish by frost. Smooth white bark is its most striking feature. Produces only sparse litter. A tough, wind-tolerant tree that does well in desert soils.

E. parvula (E. parvifolia). SMALL-LEAVED GUM. Hardy to 0°F (−18°C); one of the two hardiest eucalypts listed here. Upright, spreading tree to 25–40 ft. tall and 15–30 ft. wide, with semiweeping branches. Dark to light blue-green, highly fragrant leaves are narrow and usually under 3 in. long. Smooth, tan to grayish bark. Tolerates poorly drained soils and more shade than most.

E. polyanthemos. SILVER DOLLAR GUM. Hardy to 14°F to 18°F (−10°C to −8°C). Grows 30–75 ft. tall, 15–45 ft. wide, with gray-green, nearly round, 2–3-in. juvenile leaves and dark green, lance-shaped mature leaves. Young leaves useful for fresh and dried arrangements. Select young trees carefully; some have leaves less round and gray than others. Good as specimen or street tree. Can be used as perennial in borderline climates.

E. pulverulenta. SILVER MOUNTAIN GUM. Hardy to 15°F to 21°F (−9°C to −6°C). Grows 18–30 ft. tall, 6–15 ft. wide, with silver-gray, shish kebab–style juvenile foliage (stems appear to pierce leaves). Bark peels off in ribbons. Small, fuzzy, creamy white flowers sandwiched between round leaves along waxy white stems from fall to spring. Branches popular for arrangements. Cut back often to encourage juvenile foliage. 'Baby Blue' is a superior selection.

E. salmonophloia. SALMON GUM. Hardy to 20°F to 25°F (–7°C to –4°C). Grows slowly to about 40 ft. tall and wide. Narrow bright green leaves shimmer in the sun. Prized for its salmon-colored bark. Tolerates drought, some salt in soil. Good choice for home landscape in desert.

E. salubris. GIMLET. Hardy to 20°F to 25°F (–7°C to –4°C). Grows 20–25 ft. tall and wide, with glossy, deep green, narrow leaves to 4 in. long. Bark is smooth, shiny, reddish brown. Flowers are creamy white and somewhat showy. Can be single- or multitrunked. Like a smaller *E. salmonophloia*. Withstands heavy soils. Good in desert landscapes.

E. sargentii. SALT RIVER MALLET. Hardy to 22°F (–6°C). Grows as a single- or multitrunked tree to 30–40 ft. tall and wide, with narrow green leaves to 4 in. long and dark gray, peeling bark. Cream-colored flowers open from slender buds with long horns. Stout, exceptionally tough tree that is very salt-tolerant.

E. sideroxylon. RED IRON-BARK. Hardy to 20°F to 25°F (–7°C to –4°C). Reaches 30–90 ft. tall and 30–60 ft. wide. Slim blue-green leaves turn bronze in winter. Trunk is heavily furrowed and nearly black. Fluffy light pink to crimson flowers in pendulous clusters appear mainly in fall to late spring. A variable grower that may be open or dense, slender or squat, weeping or upright. Use as specimen, screen, or street tree. Does not do well in wet, heavy soils.

E. torquata. CORAL GUM. Hardy to 17°F to 22°F (–8°C to –6°C). Grows 18–36 ft. tall, 15–30 ft. wide, with light green to yellow-green leaves. Flower buds are like tiny Japanese lanterns, opening to blooms of coral red and yellow, on and off all year. Grown for bloom (good cut flowers) and small tree size. Stake and prune or head back to make more graceful. Branches often droop from weight of flowers and seed capsules. Good accent in a desert garden.

Eucomis
PINEAPPLE FLOWER
Asparagaceae
PERENNIALS FROM BULBS

🌿 **ZONES 4–9, 14–24; H1, H2**

☼ ◐ **FULL SUN OR LIGHT SHADE**

💧 **REGULAR WATER DURING GROWTH AND BLOOM**

Eucomis bicolor

Bold, distinctive plants from tropical southern Africa. A rosette of large leaves gives rise to thick spikes closely set with ½-in.-long flowers that are topped with clusters of leaflike bracts resembling pineapple tops. Good cut flowers. Bloom in late summer or early fall; persistent purplish seed capsules carry on the show even longer.

E. autumnalis. Rosette of wavy-edged, light green leaves, each up to 18 in. long. Flower spikes to 1 ft. tall hold pale greenish white flowers above wavy-edged, light green, 18-in.-long leaves. Blooms in late summer or early fall.

E. bicolor. Spikes to 2 ft. tall hold green flowers with purple-edged petals in late summer. Wavy-edged leaves to 1 ft. long, 3–4 in. wide.

E. comosa (E. punctata). In late summer, thick spikes 2–3 ft. tall are set with greenish white flowers tinged pink or purple; stems are spotted purple at the base. Leaves to 2 ft. long

and are less wavy than those of *E. bicolor*. 'Sparkling Burgundy' has dark purple leaves.

CARE

Need rich soil with plenty of humus. Plant in ground in fall, setting bulbs 6–8 in. deep, 1 ft. apart. Fairly easy to grow from seed sown in spring. In areas where ground freezes, mulch to protect plantings. Divide every 5 or 6 years. Interesting potted plants; set bulbs with tips just beneath soil surface and repot yearly in fresh soil mix.

Eucryphia
Cunoniaceae
EVERGREEN OR SEMIEVERGREEN SHRUBS OR TREES

🌿 **ZONES 5, 6, 15–17**

☼ ◐ **BEST IN SUN, TOLERATE SOME SHADE**

💧 **REGULAR WATER**

Eucryphia × nymansensis 'Nymansay'

These slender, upright growers, usually multitrunked, offer handsome, generally evergreen leaves and pure white flowers with tufts of yellow stamens in the center. Good accent plants. Give them neutral or slightly acid soil and shelter from strong winds. In Zones 5 and 6, protect young plants from temperatures below 15°F (–9°C).

E. glutinosa. Native to central Chile. Upright growth to 10–25 ft. tall and 5–15 ft. wide. Shiny dark green leaves are divided into three to five leaflets with serrated edges; they turn yellow, orange, or red in fall. Fragrant flowers to 2½ in. across appear in late summer.

E. lucida. Native to Tasmania. To 20–30 ft. tall, half as wide. Smooth-edged, glossy leaves to 3 in. long. Fragrant 2-in.-wide blooms appear in early summer. 'Pink Cloud' has red-centered rosy pink blossoms. In Zones 5 and 6, plants may be damaged in coldest winters; those that are sheltered (growing at woodland edges, for example) fare better.

E. × nymansensis. Group of hybrids between two species from Chile. Among the best are 'Mount Usher', which grows about 20 ft. tall and 8 ft. wide, with (often double) flowers to 2 in. across; and 'Nymansay', to 15 ft. tall and 10 ft. wide, which is somewhat faster growing and produces honey-scented flowers to 2½ in. wide. Both bloom in late summer.

Eugenia myrtifolia (E. paniculata).
See *Syzygium paniculatum*

Euonymus
Celastraceae
EVERGREEN AND DECIDUOUS SHRUBS AND VINES

🌿 **ZONES VARY BY SPECIES**

☼ ◐ ● **EXPOSURE VARIES BY SPECIES**

💧 ● **MODERATE TO REGULAR WATER**

🐦 **ATTRACT BIRDS**

Euonymus japonicus

Deciduous and evergreen euonymus species differ; the characteristic squarish "hatbox" fruit common to both offers the only hint that they're related. Deciduous types are valued for fall leaf color or showy fruit. Evergreen kinds, used mainly for background plants and hedges, include some of the most cold-tolerant broad-leafed plants. Most species take a range of

E

Using Euonymus

No matter what role you'd like a shrub to play in your garden, there's probably a *Euonymus* that fits the bill. Need an evergreen groundcover? Choose one of the many prostrate varieties of *E. fortunei*. Looking for a colorful, easy-care hedge or screen? Try a variegated form of evergreen *E. japonicus* or the deciduous *E. alatus*. The latter also works well as an accent plant, and is especially lovely in fall.

exposures, from full sun to fairly deep shade; deciduous kinds with fall color give best display in a sunny location. Some species are very susceptible to mildew. Scale can be a problem on any euonymus.

E. alatus. WINGED EUONYMUS. Deciduous shrub. Zones A3; 2–10, 14–16. From China and Japan. Eventually reaches 15–20 ft. tall and wide; a dense, twiggy, flat-topped shrub with horizontal branching. Twigs have flat, corky wings that disappear on older growth. Though fruit is smaller and less profuse than that of *E. europaeus*, fall color is impressive: the dark green leaves turn flaming red. (On plants grown in shade, fall color is pink.)

The following are among the best varieties. Larger types make good screens. All make wonderful specimen plants; set them off against dark evergreens for greatest color impact. 'Compactus' grows 6–10 ft. tall and nearly as wide, and makes an excellent unclipped hedge. It isn't quite as hardy as the species (Zones A3; 2b–10, 14–16). 'Little Moses' is smaller still, just 2½–3 ft. high and slightly wider, with particularly long-lasting fall color. 'Rudy Haag' is a dense grower to just 4–5 ft. tall and wide, with rose to red fall color. 'Timber Creek' ('Chicago Fire'), to 8 ft. tall and wide, is an extra-hardy selection that succeeds in Zones A3, 1–10, 14–16.

E. americanus. STRAWBERRY BUSH. Deciduous shrub. Zones 3b–9, 14–17. From eastern U.S. To 4–6 ft. tall and wide, with tough, leathery dark green leaves that turn yellow in autumn. Plentiful fall crop of

scarlet fruits that open to show orange seeds. Tolerates much shade and is good in woodland plantings.

E. europaeus. SPINDLE TREE. Deciduous shrub or tree. Zones 1–9, 14–16. From Europe and western Asia. Can reach 20 ft. tall and 15 ft. wide but is usually smaller. Green branches bear shiny green leaves; fall color varies from yellowish green to yellow to red. Inconspicuous flowers mature into showy pink to red fruits that split to reveal white seeds with a fleshy bright orange appendage. 'Aldenham' ('Aldenhamensis') is a vigorous selection with bright pink-and-orange fruits and red fall foliage. 'Red Cascade' has deep purple-red fall foliage and profuse dark red fruit. Full sun or partial shade.

E. fortunei. Evergreen vine or shrub. Zones 2b–17. From China. One of the best broadleafed evergreens where temperatures drop below 0°F (−18°C). Trails or climbs by rootlets. If plant is used as a shrub, its branches will trail and sometimes root; if allowed to climb, it will form a spreading mass to 20 ft. or more. Prostrate forms can be used to control erosion. Rich deep green leaves are 1–2½ in. long, with scallop-toothed edges; flowers are inconspicuous. Mature growth (like that of ivy) is shrubby and bears fruit; cuttings taken from this shrubby wood produce upright plants. Grows in sun or shade. In desert, takes full sun better than ivy.

The varieties of *E. fortunei*, some of which are listed here, are better known than the species itself. Many nurseries still sell them as forms of *E. radicans*,

once thought to be the species but now considered another variety (see *E. f. radicans*).

'Blondy'. Neat, mounding growth to about 2 ft. high, 3 ft. wide; golden yellow leaves have irregular green edges.

'Canadale Gold'. Compact growth to 4 ft. tall, 3–3½ ft. wide, with light green leaves edged in yellow.

'Coloratus'. PURPLE-LEAF WINTER CREEPER. To 1½ ft. high, 6–8 ft. wide. Same sprawling growth habit as *E. f. radicans*, though it makes a more even groundcover. Dark green leaves turn dark purple in fall and winter.

'Emerald Gaiety'. To 2–4 ft. tall, 3 ft. wide. Dense-growing, erect shrub with deep green leaves edged in white; blushes pink in cold weather.

'Emerald 'n Gold'. Similar to above but with gold-edged leaves.

'Golden Prince'. To 4 ft. tall and wide. New growth tipped gold; older leaves turn solid green. Extremely hardy; good hedge plant.

'Green Lane'. To 3–4 ft. high and 4–5 ft. wide, with erect branches, deep green foliage, orange fall fruits.

'Harlequin'. Just 6–12 in. high and 12–18 in. wide. New growth is almost all white, becoming mottled green and white. Makes a nice edging or container plant.

'Ivory Jade'. To 3 ft. high, 6 ft. wide. Resembles 'Green Lane' but has creamy white leaf margins that show pink tints in cold weather.

'Moonshadow'. To 3 ft. high, 5 ft. wide. Bright yellow leaves with dark green margins.

'Sunspot'. To 3–6 ft. tall and wide. Dark green leaves have a central bright yellow spot.

'Wolong Ghost'. Just 8–10 in. high and 2 ft. wide. Very narrow, dark green leaves are prominently veined in white. Makes an interesting groundcover.

E. f. radicans. COMMON WINTER CREEPER. Zones 4–9, 14–17. Tough, hardy, trailing or vining shrub from Korea and Japan. Dark green, thick-textured, 1-in. leaves. Given no support, it's a sprawling, foot-high groundcover. Given a wall to cover, it does the job completely.

E. japonicus. EVERGREEN EUONYMUS. Evergreen shrub. Zones 4–20; H1. From China, Korea, and Japan. Upright grower to 8–12 ft. tall and 6–10 ft. wide; usually kept lower. Inconspicuous flowers. Can be grouped to form a hedge or screen. Older shrubs are attractive trained as trees, pruned and shaped to show their curving trunks and umbrella-shaped tops. Very glossy, leathery deep green leaves are 1–2½ in. long, oval to roundish.

Though the species and its varieties tolerate heat, unfavorable soil, and seacoast conditions, they are prone to scale, thrips, and spider mites, and they're notorious for susceptibility to powdery mildew; to lessen likelihood of mildew infection, give a full-sun location with good air circulation.

Variegated forms are the most popular and are among the few shrubs to maintain their variegation in full sun in hot-summer climates. (There may be some confusion in nursery labeling of these varieties.)

'Aureovariegatus'. GOLD SPOT EUONYMUS. To 6 ft. tall, 3 ft. wide. Green leaves with a brilliant yellow central blotch.

'Chollipo'. Narrow, erect plant to 12 ft. tall, half as wide. Green leaves bordered with white. Dense grower; good for topiary.

'Grandifolius'. To 6–8 ft. tall, 4–6 ft. wide, with shiny dark green leaves larger than those of species. Compact, well branched.

'Green Spire'. Columnar, to 6–8 ft. tall and only 1–2 ft. wide. Lustrous, dark green leaves. Excellent as a narrow hedge.

'Microphyllus'. BOX-LEAF EUONYMUS. Compact, small-leafed shrub to 1–2 ft. high and half as wide. Formal-looking; usually trimmed as low hedge. Similar in form are 'Microphyllus Butterscotch' ('Microphyllus Aureovariegatus'), with yellow-variegated leaves, and 'Microphyllus Variegatus' ('Microphyllus Albovariegatus') with leaves splashed in white.

'Ovatus Aureus'. Grows to 8 ft. tall, 6 ft. wide. Dark green leaves have irregular margins of bright yellow.

'Silver King'. To 6 ft. tall and about half as wide, with green leaves edged silvery white.

'Silver Princess'. Similar to above, but just 2–3 ft. high and wide.

Eupatorium

Asteraceae

PERENNIALS

⚡ **ZONES VARY BY SPECIES**

☀ ◐ **LIGHT SHADE IN HOTTEST CLIMATES**

💧 💧💧 **WATER NEEDS VARY BY SPECIES**

🦋 **BUTTERFLIES LOVE THEM**

Eupatorium purpureum
'Atropurpureum'

These large plants have impressive domes of small flowers that are rich in nectar and pollen. Most of the species (including two of the five described here) are wild plants of eastern U.S. meadows, popular in perennial borders and naturalistic meadow plantings. Tip-pinching in early summer produces bushier plants.

E. dubium 'Little Joe'. DWARF JOE PYE WEED. Zones 1–9, 14–17. From eastern U.S. To 4 ft. tall and about as wide. Large domes (to 10 in. across) of small lavender flowers are held above whorls of deep green foliage in late summer and fall. 'Baby Joe' is even smaller, at 2–2½ ft. high and wide. Moderate water.

E. greggii (Conoclinium dissectum). Zones 3, 10–13. Native to Arizona, Texas. Weak-stemmed plant to 1½–2½ ft. high, 2–3 ft. wide, with clusters of fluffy lavender flowers from spring to fall. Lacy, divided leaves are somewhat hairy and usually sparse. Best with

afternoon shade or light shade all day; good groundcover beneath desert trees. Drought-tolerant though it looks best with occasional water. 'Boothill', first found near Tombstone, Arizona, is a choice form.

E. maculatum (E. purpureum maculatum). SPOTTED JOE PYE WEED. From eastern U.S. Similar to *E. purpureum* but somewhat smaller (to 6 ft. tall and 3 ft. wide). Plants in the Atropurpureum group have darker flowers and purple-spotted stems. Commonly sold is 'Gateway', a compact and bushy plant to 5 ft. tall, with purplish stems topped by dusky purplish rose flowers. Plants need ample water. Add lime at planting time if soil is acidic.

E. purpureum. JOE PYE WEED. Zones 1–9, 14–17. From eastern U.S. To 3–9 ft. tall, 1–3 ft. wide. Forms a clump of hollow stems set with tiered whorls of strongly toothed leaves to a foot long. Leaves have a vanilla scent when bruised. Big domes of pale purple flowers in late summer or fall. 'Album' has creamy white blooms. Needs rich (preferably alkaline) soil and ample water.

E. rugosum (Ageratina altissima). WHITE SNAKE-ROOT. Zones 1–10, 14–17. From eastern U.S. To 4 ft. tall, 2 ft. wide. Stems and lance-shaped leaves to 5 in. long are heavily marked with deep brownish red; 'Chocolate' has especially deep color. Fluffy white flowers in late summer and early fall. Reseeds. Give rich, alkaline soil, ample water.

For a colorful border guaranteed to attract butterflies, plant joe pye weed with asters, gayfeather (*Liatris spicata*), lobelia, bee balm (*Monarda*), and elderberry (*Sambucus*). Add a shallow bowl of water and steer clear of pesticides.

Euphorbia

Euphorbiaceae

ANNUALS, BIENNIALS, PERENNIALS, AND EVERGREEN AND DECIDUOUS SHRUBS OR TREES

⚡ **ZONES VARY BY SPECIES**

☀ ◐ ● **EXPOSURE NEEDS VARY BY SPECIES**

💧 💧 **MODERATE TO REGULAR WATER, EXCEPT AS NOTED**

☘ **SAP IS IRRITATING OR POISONOUS IN MANY SPECIES**

Euphorbia amygdaloides
'Helena's Blush'

Diverse genus of about 2,000 species, ranging from small flowery annuals to sculptural trees. What looks like a flower is technically a cyathium, a structure (unique to this genus) that consists of fused bracts that form a cup around the very small true flowers. In some cases, as with poinsettia (*E. pulcherrima*), large bracts below provide most of the color. Many euphorbias are succulents; these often mimic cactus in appearance. Fruit is usually a dry capsule that releases seeds explosively, shooting them up to several feet away. Plant all in well-drained soil.

Euphorbias have milky white sap that is irritating on skin contact and/or toxic if ingested (degree of irritation or toxicity varies, depending on species). Wear gloves when pruning or working near these plants, and be careful not to get the sap in your eyes. Before using cut flowers in arrangements, dip stems in boiling water or hold in a flame for a few seconds to prevent sap bleed.

E. amygdaloides. Perennial. Zones 2b–24. From Europe and Turkey. To 3 ft. high, 1 ft. wide, with reddish green stems.

Evergreen dark green leaves have red undersides that turn darker red in winter. Greenish yellow flowers in 8-in. clusters appear at stem ends in mid-spring to early summer. Best in sun but tolerates some shade. Hybrid 'Efanthia' is compact at 1 ft. high, 2 ft. wide; 'Helena's Blush' is similar, but with leaves variegated in pink and cream. 'Purpurea' has foliage heavily tinted purple and bright green inflorescences. *E. a. robbiae* is shorter (to 1 ft. high) and more shade-tolerant than the species; also more likely to spread, sometimes becoming invasive. It has interbred with the plain species, and intermediates are often sold as this variety.

E. antisyphilitica. CANDELILLA. Succulent shrub. Zones 12, 13, 18–21. Native to southwestern U.S. and Mexico. Erect plant to 3 ft. high, spreading by underground stems. Cylindrical pale green stems are covered with wax used commercially in making candles. Inflorescence consists of red bracts and white petal-like appendages in a star shape. Good in containers. Withstands light frosts. Full sun, little water.

E. biglandulosa. See *E. rigida*.

E. 'Blue Haze'. Zones 7–9, 14–17. Hybrid between *E. seguieriana niciciana* and a species from Europe. Compact, bushy growth to 1½ ft. high and 2–3 ft. wide, with narrow, powder blue leaves held on reddish stems. Loaded with chartreuse inflorescences from late spring well into summer. Full sun to partial shade. Tolerates aridity.

E. 'Breathless Blush'. See *E. hypericifolia* 'Breathless Blush'.

E. characias. Perennial. Zones 4–24. Mediterranean native. Upright stems crowded with narrow blue-green leaves form a dome-shaped bush 4 ft. tall and wide. Chartreuse or lime-green flowers in dense, round to cylindrical clusters appear in late winter, early spring. Color holds with only slight fading until seeds ripen; then stalks turn yellow and should be cut out at base, since new shoots have already made growth for next year's flowers. All of the following are fairly drought-resistant and

E

CLOCKWISE FROM LEFT: *Euphorbia pulcherrima* 'Marblestar'; *E. tirucalli* 'Rosea'; *E. × martini*

perform best in full sun. 'Black Pearl' has large inflorescences; cyathia have darkest red, nearly black nectar glands. 'Humpty Dumpty' is a short (to 2½ ft. high), vigorous selection. 'Portuguese Velvet' has blue-gray, lightly hairy leaves and large bronzy golden inflorescences. 'Tasmanian Tiger' grows 3 ft. high and wide, with leaves and flower bracts edged in white.

E. c. wulfenii, the most commonly grown form, has broader clusters of yellow flowers. 'Lambrook Gold' is choice, with glowing yellow blooms.

E. cyathophora. See *E. heterophylla*.

E. 'Diamond Frost'. See *E. hypericifolia* 'Diamond Frost'.

E. dulcis 'Chameleon'. Perennial. Zones 2b–24. Forms a mound to 2 ft. high and wide. New spring growth is burgundy, maturing to dark bronzy green. Greenish yellow flower heads with a purplish tint appear at stem ends in early summer. Leaves and bracts turn rich

purple in fall. Spreads by self-sowing; comes true from seed. Full sun. Tolerates dry soil.

E. epithymoides. See *E. polychroma*.

E. griffithii. Perennial. Zones 2–10, 14–24. Erect-stemmed Himalayan native to 3 ft. high and wide; spreads by creeping roots but is not aggressive. Narrow green leaves are red tinged when new. Reddish orange to red bracts in early summer; those of 'Fireglow' are vivid orange-red. 'Dixter' has coppery, dark green leaves and orange-red inflorescences. Dies back in winter. Full sun or light shade.

E. heterophylla. FALSE POINSETTIA, MEXICAN FIRE PLANT, PAINTED SPURGE. Annual. Zones 1–24; H1, H2. Plants labeled as this species are almost always *E. cyathophora*, a native of eastern U.S. and Mexico. To 3 ft. high, 1 ft. wide. Bright green leaves of varying shapes, larger ones resembling those of poinsettia (*E. pulcherrima*). In summer, upper leaves are blotched bright red and white, giving the appearance of a second-rate poinsettia. Useful in hot, dry

borders in poor soil. Sow seeds in place after danger of frost is past. Heavy reseeder in desert gardens. Full sun.

E. hypericifolia (E. graminea). Perennial in Zones 13, 21–24; H1, H2. Annual anywhere. Delicate, airy mounds to 12–18 in. high and nearly as wide. Small white flowers look like snowflakes interspersed with the sparse, olive green foliage. Plant resembles baby's breath (*Gypsophila paniculata*). Blooms year-round in mild winter areas, spring to fall elsewhere. Excellent in pots and hanging baskets. 'Diamond Frost' is popular and dependable. 'Breathless Blush' has leaves and flowers flushed in deep pink. Full sun to partial shade.

E. 'Jessie'. Perennial. Zones 1–24. Hybrid between *E. griffithii* and *E. polychroma*. Grows 3–6 ft. tall and 3 ft. wide, with light yellow-green leaves and bright yellow bracts boldly edged in orange. Very showy in bloom and late in the season, when the whole plant takes on orange and yellow tones. Does not reseed.

E. marginata. SNOW-ON-THE-MOUNTAIN. Annual. Zones

1–24. From central North America. To 2–3 ft. high, 1 ft. wide. Oval light green leaves; upper ones are striped and margined white, sometimes even solid white. Summer flowers are variegated in green and white. Good for contrast with bright-colored bedding plants. 'Summer Icicle' has particularly bright white markings. Sow seeds in place in spring, in sun or partial shade. Thin to only a few inches apart, since plants are somewhat rangy.

E. × martini. Perennial. Zones 3–24. Hybrid between *E. amygdaloides* and *E. characias*. Usually misspelled as *E. × martinii*. Grows 2–3 ft. high and wide. Resembles a compact *E. characias*, with dense clusters of brown-centered chartreuse flowers in late winter, spring. Evergreen leaves are often tinged purple when young. Stems are red in winter. 'Red Martin' has leaves held nearly upright, showing off red color of stems and new foliage. Full sun or light shade. Fairly drought-resistant.

E. milii. CROWN OF THORNS. Woody shrub; evergreen but sparsely leafed. Zones 13, 21–24; H1, H2; or indoors. Some frost damage below 28°F (–2°C). From Madagascar. To 1–4 ft. tall, 1½ ft. wide. Stems armed with long, sharp thorns. Roundish, thin, light green leaves usually appear only near branch ends. Clustered pairs of red bracts put on a show nearly all year. Many varieties and hybrids available in various forms, sizes, and bract colors (yellow, orange, pink). *E. m. splendens* (*E. splendens*) is low growing and scrambling, forming a tangled mound.

In windy or frost-prone areas, grow against a sheltered wall; or grow in a container. Salt tolerance makes it an ideal choice for seaside plantings. Grow in porous but not rocky soil, in full sun or light shade (needs afternoon shade in Zone 13). Give bright light indoors.

E. palustris. Perennial. Zones 2b–9, 14–17. From Europe, western Asia. Forms robust clump to 2–3 ft. high and 3–4 ft. wide, with many medium green leaves that turn yellow and orange in fall. Wide-branching clusters of yellow flowers appear in spring, early summer. Dies back in winter. Self-sows. Full sun or partial shade. One of the few euphorbias that will grow in damp or boggy conditions; also does well in ordinary garden soil, whether dry or moist.

E. polychroma (E. epithymoides). Perennial. Zones A2; 1–24. From Europe. Neatly rounded hemisphere to 1½ ft. high, 2 ft. wide, with deep green leaves symmetrically arranged on closely set, hairy stems. From midspring to midsummer, plant is covered with rounded clusters of bright yellow flowers surrounded by whorls of yellow-green bracts. Effect is of a gold mound suffused with green. Displays good fall color (yellow to orange or red) before going dormant. 'Bonfire' has leaves that emerge green but mature to red and hold their color all summer. 'Candy' has purple-green stems and pale yellow bracts. 'Lacy' has white-variegated leaves. All need some shade in hottest climates.

E. pulcherrima. POINSETTIA. Evergreen, semievergreen, or deciduous shrub. Zones 13, 16–24; H1, H2; or indoors. From Mexico. Leggy plant to 10 ft. or taller, 6 ft. wide, with coarse leaves growing on stiffly upright canes. Showy part of plant consists of petal-like bracts; true flowers in center are yellowish, inconspicuous. Red single form is the most familiar; less well known are double-bracted red sorts and forms with white, yellowish, pink, or marbled bracts. Plants bloom in winter and into spring. Milky sap is not poisonous; most people find it either completely harmless or at most mildly irritating to skin or stomach.

Useful garden plant in well-drained soil and full sun (light shade in Zone 13). Where

For a striking composition, surround E. tirucalli 'Sticks on Fire' with blue Senecio mandraliscae or chartreuse Sedum rupestre 'Angelina'.

adapted outdoors, it needs no special care. Grow as informal hedge in frost-free areas; where winter weather is frosty (but not severely cold), plant against sunny wall, in sheltered corner, under south-facing eaves (east-facing ones in Zone 13). Thin branches in summer to produce larger bracts; or prune them back at 2-month intervals for bushy growth and smaller bracts. To improve red color, feed every 2 weeks with high-nitrogen fertilizer, starting when color begins to show.

E. rigida (E. biglandulosa). Perennial. Zones 4–24. Mediterranean native forms a 3–5-ft.-wide clump of stems that angle outward, then rise up to 2 ft. high. Fleshy gray-green leaves to 1½ in. long are narrow and pointed, their bases set tightly against stems. Broad, domed flower clusters in late winter or early spring are chartreuse-yellow fading to pinkish. After seeds ripen, stems die back and should be removed; new stems take their place. Reseeds in mildest-winter areas, but not enough to become a pest. Showy display plant in borders, rock gardens, containers. Full sun. Tolerates drought.

E. robbiae. See E. amygdaloides robbiae.

E. tirucalli. MILKBUSH, PENCILBUSH. Succulent tree or shrub. Zones 13, 23, 24; H1, H2; or indoors. From tropical eastern Africa. Fast growing to possible 30 ft. tall and 6 ft. wide, usually much smaller. Single or multiple trunks support tangle of light green, pencil-thick, succulent branches with tiny leaves present only on actively growing tips. Flowers are unimportant. 'Sticks on Fire' has pale pink to fiery salmon-pink stems; new growth has the most intense color in bright light. Very tolerant of seacoast conditions. Full sun. Be sure to keep milky sap away from eyes. As a houseplant, thrives in driest atmosphere; needs all the light you can give it, well-drained potting mix, routine watering and fertilizing.

E. veneta, E. wulfenii. See E. characias.

Eurya ochnacea. See *Cleyera japonica*

Euryops
Asteraceae
EVERGREEN SHRUBS

🌿 **ZONES VARY BY SPECIES**

☀ **FULL SUN**

◐ ◖ ● **LITTLE TO REGULAR WATER**

Euryops pectinatus 'Munchkin'

Native to South Africa. Grown for profuse show of cheerful yellow daisies over a long season. Plants need excellent drainage; take well to container culture. They thrive on buffeting ocean winds but are damaged by sharp frosts. Pick off old flower heads.

E. acraeus. Zones 5–9, 12–24. Mounded growth to 2 ft. high and wide, with silvery gray leaves. Inch-wide, bright yellow daisies cover plant in spring. Mountain native and thus hardier to frost than *E. pectinatus* and its varieties. Has been used as a rock garden plant in western Washington and Oregon. May not survive winters in colder zones unless protected from excess moisture.

E. pectinatus. Zones 8, 9, 12–24; H1, H2. To 3–6 ft. high and wide. Easy care and an extremely long flowering season make it a good filler, background plant, or low screen. Gray-green, deeply divided, 2-in.-long leaves. Bright yellow, 1½–2-in.-wide daisies on 6-in. stems bloom most of the year. Shear lightly in late spring or early summer to maintain compactness and limit size. 'Viridis' is like species in all but leaf color; its foliage is deep green. 'Munchkin', with gray-green foliage, grows to 3 ft. high and 4 ft. wide.

Eustoma grandiflorum
(Lisianthus russellianus)
LISIANTHUS, TULIP GENTIAN, TEXAS BLUEBELL
Gentianaceae
BIENNIAL OR SHORT-LIVED PERENNIAL GROWN AS ANNUAL

🌿 **ZONES 1–24**

☀ ◑ **FULL SUN OR LIGHT SHADE**

● **REGULAR WATER**

Eustoma grandiflorum 'Forever Blue'

Native to high plains of the West. Longtime favorite for pots, borders, and especially for cutting gardens. In summer, a foot-wide clump of gray-green foliage sends up 1–3-ft. stems topped by tulip-shaped, 2–3-in. flowers in purplish blue, pink, or white; these are excellent in bouquets. Bloom lasts all summer if old blossoms are cut off. Fully double flowers of Double Eagle and Echo series resemble roses. Color range of single-flowered Heidi series includes red and a so-called yellow (actually ivory). 'Forever White' and 'Forever Blue' are bushy and compact, to about 1 ft. high, with large single blooms. Mermaid and Lizzy are dwarf (8-in.) strains.

For a pretty patio display, grow several purplish-flowered lisianthus plants in a large brown stoneware pot with lower purple-flowered angelonias. Soften the pot's edges with a trailing chartreuse bacopa (*Sutera cordata* 'Gold 'n Pearls').

CARE

All need good garden soil, good drainage. Plants grow better and have longer stems where nights are warm. Best cut flowers are produced in greenhouses. Tallest types may need staking.

E

F

Fagus
BEECH
Fagaceae
DECIDUOUS TREES

⚡ **ZONES VARY BY SPECIES**

☀ ◐ **FULL SUN OR LIGHT SHADE**

◖ ● **MODERATE TO REGULAR WATER**

Fagus grandifolia

Handsome forest trees native to much of the Northern Hemisphere. Of the beeches described here, European beech (*F. sylvatica*) is the most widely grown. The species differ very little except in leaf details. Capable of growing 90 ft. tall and 60 ft. wide but usually much smaller, they typically have a broad cone shape, with wide, sweeping lower branches that can reach the ground unless pruned off. Smooth gray bark contrasts well with the glossy dark green foliage. New foliage has a silky sheen. In fall, leaves turn bronzy and then brown; many hang on the tree well into winter. Lacy branching pattern and pointed leaf buds provide an attractive winter silhouette. Little three-cornered nuts enclosed in spiny husks are edible but small.

All beeches cast heavy shade and have a dense network of fibrous roots near soil surface, inhibiting growth of lawn or other plants beneath.

F. crenata. JAPANESE BEECH. Zones 2b–6. From Japan. Scallop-edged leaves are somewhat smaller than those of other beeches. Golden brown fall color. Popular bonsai subject.

F. grandifolia. AMERICAN BEECH. Zones 1–6. From eastern North America. Leaves up to 5 in. long are glossy green, turning golden bronze in fall.

F. sylvatica. EUROPEAN BEECH. Zones A3; 2b–9, 14–21. Native from central Europe to the Caucasus. Glossy green leaves to 4 in. long, turning russet and bronzy in autumn.

'Aspleniifolia' (*F. s. heterophylla* 'Aspleniifolia'). FERNLEAF BEECH. Robust, spreading tree (50–80 ft. tall, 40–45 ft. wide), with delicate foliage: narrow leaves are deeply lobed or cut nearly to midrib.

'Dawyck' ('Fastigiata'). DAWYCK BEECH. Narrow, upright tree; just 8 ft. wide when 35 ft. tall. Broader in great age, but still narrower than the species.

'Dawyck Gold'. Columnar tree to 60 ft. tall, 20 ft. wide. New leaves emerge yellow, mature to light green, and turn yellow again in autumn.

'Dawyck Purple'. Columnar, to 70 ft. tall, 15 ft. wide, with purple foliage.

'Pendula'. WEEPING BEECH. Irregular, spreading form. Long, weeping branches reach to ground. Without staking to establish vertical trunk, it will grow wide rather than high. Glossy green leaves.

'Purple Fountain'. To 25 ft. tall and 12 ft. wide, with weeping branches from an upright trunk that needs staking only in youth. Purple to purple-red foliage.

'Purpurea Pendula'. WEEPING COPPER BEECH. Purple-leafed weeping form. Usually no larger than 10 ft. tall and wide; may need staking to maintain upright growth. Splendid container plant.

'Purpurea Tricolor' ('Roseo-marginata'). Upright, oval tree to 30 ft. tall and 20 ft. wide. Purple leaves edged and striped in rose-pink and white.

'Riversii'. COPPER BEECH, PURPLE BEECH. The most widely sold of the Atropurpurea group, all of which have purple leaves. Grows to 50–60 ft. tall and 35–45 ft. wide. Deep reddish or purple leaves. Good in containers. Seedlings of copper beech are usually bronzy purple, turning bronzy green in summer.

'Rohan Obelisk' ('Red Obelisk'). Columnar tree with dark purple-red foliage. Some leaves are deeply cut, others smooth edged.

'Rohanii'. Leaves with wavy scalloped edges are brownish purple maturing to dark green; unimpressive fall color (reddish or purplish brown).

'Zlatia'. GOLDEN BEECH. Young leaves yellow, aging to yellow green. Subject to sunburn. Slow grower; good container plant.

CARE

Grow in any good garden soil, though salts in soil or water will stunt growth and turn leaves brown. Woolly beech aphids cause little trouble except for dripping honeydew. Trees withstand heavy pruning; they can be planted close together and trimmed to form a dense, impassable hedge as low as 4 ft.

Fallugia paradoxa
APACHE PLUME
Rosaceae
SEMIEVERGREEN SHRUB

⚡ **ZONES 2–23**

☀ **FULL SUN**

◖ **LITTLE WATER**

Fallugia paradoxa

Native to mountains of medium and high deserts of California, southwestern U.S., northern Mexico. Grows 4–6 ft. tall and 5 ft. wide, with straw-colored branches and flaky bark. Small, lobed leaves are deep green on top, rusty beneath; carried in clusters. Flowers resembling single white roses just 1½ in. wide bloom in spring and summer. Large, showy clusters of feathery seed heads follow; greenish at first, later turning pink or taking on reddish tinges, they create a soft-colored, changing haze through which you can see the shrub's rigid branch pattern. Needs gritty, well-drained soil. Best with deep monthly soakings during summer; needs no water at other times of year. Pruning usually not needed.

Farfugium japonicum
(Ligularia tussilaginea)
Asteraceae
PERENNIAL

⚡ **ZONES 4–10, 14–24; H1, H2; OR INDOORS**

☀ ● **SOME SHADE; BRIGHT INDIRECT LIGHT**

◖◗ **AMPLE WATER**

Farfugium japonicum 'Aureomaculatum'

From China, Japan. Big-leafed, water-loving plant forms a clump about 2 ft. high and wide. Glossy bright green, kidney-shaped, scalloped, or shallowly lobed leaves up to 15 in. wide are carried on long (1–2 ft.) leafstalks. Flower stems to 2 ft. tall carry several 1½–2½-in. yellow daisy flowers. The species is not as popular or widely grown as its selections.

'Argenteum' has somewhat smaller deep green leaves marbled with gray-green and white. 'Aureomaculatum', also known as leopard plant, has thick, leathery leaves that are heavily, evenly speckled with yellow. 'Crispatum', sometimes called pie crust ligularia, has thick, ruffle-edged gray-green leaves.

All are choice container plants for shady beds, entryways; good groundcover in constantly moist but well-drained soil. Tops hardy to 20°F (−7°C). Plants die back to roots at 0°F (−18°C), put on new growth in spring. Control snails and slugs.

Fargesia. See Bamboo

× **Fatshedera lizei**
Araliaceae
EVERGREEN SHRUB OR VINE

🌿 **ZONES 4–10, 12–24; H1, H2**

◐ ● **PARTIAL OR FULL SHADE**

💧 **REGULAR WATER**

× Fatshedra lizei 'Lemon & Lime'

Hybrid between Japanese aralia (*Fatsia japonica*) and English ivy (*Hedera helix*), with characteristics of both parents. Highly polished, 4–10-in.-wide leaves with three to five pointed lobes look like giant ivy leaves; plant also sends out long, trailing or climbing stems like ivy, though without aerial holdfasts. It inherited shrubbiness from its Japanese aralia parent, though it is a bit more irregular and sprawling. Leaves of 'Lemon & Lime' ('Annemieke') are splashed with yellow; those of 'Variegata' are bordered with white.

Leaves are injured at 15°F (−9°C), tender new growth at 20°F to 25°F (−7°C to −4°C). Seems to suffer more from late frosts than from winter cold. Protect from hot, drying winds, and watch out for slugs and snails. The plant tends to grow in a straight line, but it can be shaped if you work at it. Pinch tip growth to force branching. Two or three times a year, guide and tie stems before they become brittle. If plant gets away from you, cut it back to ground; it will regrow quickly. If you use it as groundcover, cut back vertical growth every 2 or 3 weeks during growing season. Grown as vine or espalier, plants are heavy, so give them strong supports. Even a well-grown vine is leafless at base.

Fatsia japonica
(*Aralia sieboldii*, *A. japonica*)
JAPANESE ARALIA
Araliaceae
EVERGREEN SHRUB

🌿 **ZONES 4–9, 14–24; H1, H2**

◐ ● **PARTIAL OR FULL SHADE**

💧 **REGULAR WATER**

Fatsia japonica

From Korea and Japan. Dramatic, tropical-looking shrub with long-stalked, glossy dark green, deeply lobed leaves to 16 in. wide. Plant grows moderately fast to 5–8 ft. tall and wide (rarely more); sparsely branched. Many roundish clusters of small, creamy white flowers in fall and winter are followed by clusters of small, shiny black fruit. Most effective when thinned to show some branch structure. Provides year-round good looks for shaded entryway or patio; excellent in large containers. Useful near swimming pools. 'Moseri' has a compact habit. 'Spider's Web' has leaves heavily speckled and broadly edged in white. 'Variegata' has leaves edged golden yellow to creamy white.

CARE
Grows in nearly all soils except soggy ones. If leaves are chronically yellow, add iron to soil. During prolonged dry spells, spray leaves occasionally with hose to clean them and to lessen insect attack. Control slugs and snails. Established plants sucker freely; keep suckers or remove them with spade. Rejuvenate spindly plants by cutting back hard in early spring. Plants that set fruit often self-sow.

Feijoa sellowiana
(*Acca sellowiana*)
PINEAPPLE GUAVA
Myrtaceae
EVERGREEN SHRUB OR TREE

🌿 **ZONES 6 (MARGINAL), 7–9, 12–24; H1, H2**

☼ **FULL SUN**

💧 **REGULAR WATER**

🐦 **FLOWERS ATTRACT BIRDS AND BENEFICIAL INSECTS**

Feijoa sellowiana

This South American native is normally a large multistemmed plant reaching 18–25 ft. with equal spread if not pruned or killed back by frosts. Can take almost any amount of training or pruning (late spring is the best time) to shape as espalier, screen, hedge, or small tree. Oval, 2–3-in.-long leaves are glossy green above, silvery white beneath. Blooms in spring, bearing unusual inch-wide flowers with big central tufts of red stamens and four fleshy white petals tinged purplish on inside. Flower petals are delicious and can be added to fruit salads or used for jams and jellies. Oval, grayish green,

1–4-in.-long fruit has soft, sweet to bland pulp with flavor somewhat like pineapple.

If you're growing this plant for fruit, look for improved varieties 'Apollo', 'Coolidge', 'Mammoth', 'Nazemetz', and 'Trask'. These are self-fruitful, although cross-pollination will produce a better crop. Single plants of seedlings or other named varieties may require cross-pollination.

Plant is drought-tolerant but needs regular water for best fruiting. Fruit ripens 4 to 5½ months after flowering in warmest regions, 5 to 7 months after bloom in cooler areas. The best way to harvest is to wait until first fruit drops, then spread a tarp underneath and give the tree a shake. Repeat every few days.

Felicia
Asteraceae
SHRUBS, PERENNIALS, AND ANNUALS

🌿 **ZONES VARY BY SPECIES**

☼ **FULL SUN**

○ 💧 **WATER NEEDS VARY BY SPECIES**

Felicia amelloides

South African plants put on a profuse show of daisy-like flowers in shades of blue. Though more than 80 species are known, only a few are commonly cultivated in Western gardens.

F. amelloides (*Aster amelloides, Agathaea coelestis*). BLUE MARGUERITE. Woody perennial in Zones 8, 9, 14–24; treated as winter annual in Zone 13 and summer annual elsewhere. About 1½ ft. tall and spreading 4–5 ft. wide, with oval, aromatic green leaves about 1 in. long. Produces an abundance of 1¼-in., yellow-centered sky blue daisies.

»

F

A form with white-variegated leaves is available. As a perennial, blooms almost continually if dead flowers are picked off; prune back hard in late summer to encourage new blooming wood. Grow in pots or containers, let spill over wall or edge of raised bed, or plant in any sunny spot. Regular water.

F. bergeriana. KINGFISHER DAISY. Annual. Zones 1–24. Freely branching plant with grayish green, 1½-in. leaves. Forms a mat 4–6 in. high and up to a foot across. Bright blue, inch-wide flowers appear all summer long. Sow in early spring (in autumn where winters are warm). Excellent in pots, window boxes, borders, edgings. Regular water.

F. fruticosa (Aster fruticosus). SHRUB ASTER. Evergreen shrub. Zones 8, 9, 14–24. Bushy, densely branched growth to 2–4 ft. tall, 3 ft. wide, with narrow, dark green leaves. Profuse, inch-wide lavender flowers in spring. Prune after bloom. Needs little to moderate water.

Ferocactus

BARREL CACTUS

Cactaceae

CACTI

⚡ **ZONES 8–24**

☼ **FULL SUN**

◊ **NO IRRIGATION NEEDED**

Ferocactus cylindraceus

Medium to large cactus prized for their interesting shape and showy flowers. Ribbed and formidably spiny, they are globular when young, cylindrical with increasing age.

F. cylindraceus (F. acanthodes). COMPASS BARREL CACTUS. Native to Southern

MEET THE FERNS

Grow these flowerless perennials for the exquisite patterns of their fronds. Some ferns are evergreen and some are deciduous, losing their leaves in fall. But every spring, each sends out a fresh batch of fiddleheads, which unfurl from a tight coil of delicate foliage. Their colors include lime to emerald green, soft bluish gray, silver, burgundy, and even reddish orange. Ferns vary in height from a few inches to more than 50 ft. tall and are found in all parts of the world. They reproduce by spores that form directly on the fronds. Fertile fronds may have a different shape and color than sterile ones.

Accent Ferns

Evergreen ferns with shiny, waxy foliage are especially fine; see *Cyrtomium, Dryopteris, Polystichum,* and *Rumohra adiantiformis.* Ferns with burgundy, silver, or creamy foliage make especially colorful garden highlights; these include named varieties of Athyrium and Pteris. Newly emerging orange fronds of *Dryopteris erythrosora* are outstanding.

Container Ferns

Almost any fern can thrive in a container outdoors. For hanging baskets, plant *Davallia* or *Platycerium.*

Ferns for Mixed Plantings

Choose a fern with an upright habit or a single crown, such as *Blechnum, Dryopteris, Osmunda,* or *Polystichum.*

Groundcover Ferns

Choose spreading, colonizing ferns such as *Adiantum, Blechnum, Matteuccia, Nephrolepis,* and *Polypodium.* Types with horizontally arching fronds are also good groundcover candidates; see *Davallia, Polypodium,* and *Polystichum.*

Large Ferns

In frost-free areas, tree ferns are the obvious choice for use as garden focal points. See *Blechnum, Cibotium, Cyathea,* and *Dicksonia.* Frost-tolerant ferns of impressive size include larger types of *Dryopteris, Osmunda,* and *Woodwardia.*

Woodland Ferns

These ferns thrive in shaded gardens among trees. See *Adiantum, Asplenium, Athyrium, Blechnum, Dryopteris, Nephrolepis, Osmunda, Pellaea, Polypodium, Polystichum, Rumohra,* and *Woodwardia.*

HOW TO GROW

Most ferns tolerate a variety of soils, but all grow best in well-drained soil enriched with organic matter. After planting, put down a generous (2- to 3-in.) layer of mulch (such as fine bark or shredded fir bark) to keep the soil moist and roots cool.

WATERING Regular watering suits most ferns, but some grow in wet soil (see *Athyrium, Matteuccia, Osmunda,* and *Woodwardia*). Others do well in dry shade, such as under trees or next to house foundations (see *Dryopteris, Pellaea,* and *Polystichum*). Some ferns grow in considerable sun, provided they are regularly watered (see *Blechnum, Osmunda,* and *Pellaea rotundifolia*).

FEEDING Established ferns growing in reasonably fertile soil rarely need more than a yearly application of well-rotted manure or organic compost. If foliage yellows, apply a half-strength organic fertilizer such as blood meal or fish emulsion; concentrated fertilizers can burn surface roots. Fertilize potted ferns annually with a long-term (9 months or more) controlled-release fertilizer.

GROOMING Cut off broken or misshapen fronds anytime of year. In cold climates, leave spent foliage in place through the winter months to protect the plant's crown; remove old fronds when spring bulbs emerge. Prune the fronds of evergreen ferns when the stems become limp.

Few plants are as at home in shaded gardens as ferns. Most are forest plants, thriving in cool, moist locations, but some grow in deserts, in open fields, or near the timberline. Everywhere, their richly textured fronds bob gracefully in the gentlest breeze.

Nephrolepis exalta 'Bostoniensis'

California, Nevada, Arizona, and Baja California. Grows slowly to 8–9 ft. tall and 3 ft. wide. Yellow to orange, bell-shaped flowers, 3 in. across, bloom midspring into summer. Plant grows faster on its shady side than on sunny side, producing curve toward the south.

F. wislizenii. FISHHOOK BARREL CACTUS. Native to Arizona, Texas, Mexico. Similar to above, with yellow or yellow-edged red flowers in summer.

Festuca ✓

FESCUE
Poaceae
PERENNIAL GRASSES

🌿 **ZONES VARY BY SPECIES**

☀️ ◐ **BEST IN SUN; TOLERATE SOME SHADE**

💧 💧 **MODERATE TO REGULAR WATER**

Festuca glauca 'Elijah Blue'

Some of these popular grasses are quite ornamental, with colorful leaves and showy flowers; others are used for lawns, erosion control, or pasture. All can withstand dry conditions and severe frosts but require good drainage. Clumps can be divided in autumn.

F. amethystina. Zones 2–10, 14–24. From the Alps and southern Europe. To 1½ ft. high, 10 in. wide. Extremely fine-textured, threadlike leaves are blue-green to intensely blue-gray. Drooping, violet-tinged flower spikes are held above foliage in late spring, early summer. Use like *F. glauca*.

F. arundinacea. TALL FESCUE. Zones A1–A3; 1–10, 14–24. From Europe and northern Asia; naturalized in cooler parts of North America. Clumping, tall-growing pasture grass (to

4 ft.) also used for moderately low-water-use lawns. Forms no runners, so plants must be close together to make dense turf. Tough blades, tolerance of compacted soils make it a good turf for playing or sports; finer-textured strains are used alone or mixed with bluegrass. Mow to 2–3 in. Left unmowed, it makes an excellent deep-rooted erosion-control cover on slopes, banks. Check locally for best-adapted varieties. Invasive in some areas, notably California.

F. californica. CALIFORNIA FESCUE. Zones 4–9, 14–24. Native to the Coast Ranges from Northern California to Oregon. Grows as loose clump of blue-green or blue-gray leaves to 2–3 ft. high, 1–2 ft. wide. Airy flowers rise 1–3 ft. above the foliage in late spring, early summer. Flower spikes are green at first, later turning purple and finally maturing to yellow. Long-lived and does well in various soil types. Tolerates summer drought in its cooler climate zones. Use as specimen plant or massed as groundcover. 'Horse Mountain Green' is a strong grower with leaves that are dark green above, chalky blue beneath; flower spikes can reach 6 ft. tall. 'Scott Mountain' and 'Serpentine Blue' have intensely blue-gray foliage.

F. glauca (F. cinerea). COMMON BLUE FESCUE. Zones 1–24. From Europe. To 1 ft. high, 10 in. wide. Dense tuft of very narrow, fine leaves; color varies from blue-gray to silvery white. Showy spikes of summer flowers rise above the foliage mass. Use as edging or groundcover. Center of clump commonly dies out after several years. Sometimes sold as *F. ovina glauca*. 'Boulder Blue' has very narrow leaves of intense silver-blue. 'Elijah Blue' forms an 8–12-in.-high clump of intensely silver-blue leaves and is one of the tougher, longer-lived selections. 'Golden Toupee' grows about 8 in. high, with fine-textured chartreuse foliage; does best in light shade.

F. idahoensis. Zones 1–10, 14–24. Native from British Columbia to Alberta, south to central California and Colorado. Blue-green to silvery blue foliage in dense clump to 14 in. high, 10 in. wide. Longer-lived

than *F. glauca*, and clumps are less likely to die out in center. May also be more tolerant of wet winter soils. Good slope stabilizer. Hybrid 'Siskiyou Blue', to 2 ft. high and wide, has luminous blue leaves and tolerates considerable shade.

F. mairei. ATLAS FESCUE, MAIRE'S FESCUE. Zones 2–11, 14–24. Native to mountainous areas of Morocco. Grows 2–3 ft. high and wide, forming a neat, dense mound of fine-textured, pale yellowish to gray-green leaves. Very slender, gray-green flower spikes are held above foliage mass in early summer. Evergreen in mild-winter areas; groom by raking out dead leaves in spring. Heat-tolerant. Tolerates drought but looks better with moderate irrigation. Good for erosion control or as a large-scale groundcover; also makes an attractive specimen.

✓ **F. rubra.** RED FESCUE, CREEPING RED FESCUE. Zones A2, A3; 1–10, 14–24. From Europe and North America. Spreads by rhizomes. Narrow dark green blades are somewhat lax. Often used in blends with other lawn grasses but can be used alone; mow to 1½–2 in. high. Unmowed, red fescue makes an attractive meadow; useful for slopes too steep to mow. One of the most shade-tolerant of good lawn grasses. Not fussy about soil, but needs regular water for good growth. For drought-tolerant red fescues, look for California selections with blue-gray leaves such as 'Jughandle' (to 6 in. high) and 'Patrick's Point' (1 ft. high).

Threadlike leaves and delicate flowers give common blue fescue a cool, wispy look. But this plant is actually quite tough, tolerating poor soils and high temperatures. If plants look ratty after a couple of years, shear them nearly to the ground in late winter.

Ficus

Moraceae
EVERGREEN AND DECIDUOUS TREES, SHRUBS, AND VINES

🌿 **ZONES VARY BY SPECIES**

☀️ ◐ ● **EXPOSURE NEEDS VARY BY SPECIES**

💧 **REGULAR WATER**

Ficus benjamina 'Variegata'

The average gardener would never expect to find the commercial edible fig, small-leafed climbing fig, banyan tree, and potted rubber tree under one heading—but they are classed together because they bear small or large figs (inedible in most species). Ornamental types are discussed here; for sorts grown for tasty fruit, see Fig.

F. auriculata (F. roxburghii). Briefly deciduous shrub or small tree. Zones 20–24; H1, H2. Native to India. To 15–25 ft. tall and wide. Leaves have sandpapery texture and are unusually large—broadly oval to round, about 15 in. across. New growth is mahogany red, turning to rich green. Large figs (more ornamental than edible) are borne in clusters on trunk and framework branches. Can be shaped as small tree or espaliered. Beautiful in large container; good near swimming pools. Grow in wind-protected, sunny location.

F. benjamina. BENJAMIN TREE, BENJAMIN FIG, WEEPING FIG. Zones 13, 23, 24; H1, H2; or indoors. From India and Malaysia. In Hawaii, fast growing to 60 ft. tall with an even greater spread. Good shade or specimen tree for larger gardens or parks, since it requires space for its invasive surface

F

CLOCKWISE FROM TOP: *Ficus auriculata; F. pumila; F. elastica* 'Variegata'

root system. In Southern California and Arizona, the plant reaches about half the size it does in Hawaii and is often used as an entryway or patio tree; also good as a screen, espalier, or clipped hedge. Leathery, 5-in.-long, shiny green leaves densely clothe drooping branches. 'Exotica' has wavy-edged leaves with long, twisted tips; often sold simply as *F. benjamina*. New plants are easy to start from cuttings taken in late spring or early summer. Give a frost-free, wind-protected location in sun or shade. Very popular as a houseplant.

F. deltoidea diversifolia. MISTLETOE FIG. Evergreen shrub. Zones 19–24; H1, H2; or indoors. Native to Southeast Asia. Grows very slowly to 8–10 ft. tall, about half as wide. Interesting open, twisted branch pattern. Thick, dark green, roundish, 2-in. leaves are sparsely stippled with tan specks on upper surface and a few black

dots below. Attractive, small greenish to yellow fruit borne continuously. As outdoor plant, most often grown in container on patio. Partial shade.

F. elastica. RUBBER TREE. Evergreen shrub or tree. Zones 13, 16, 17, 19–24; H1, H2; or indoors. Native to India and Malaysia. In Hawaii, it is a wide-spreading tree 60–80 ft. tall (up to 100 ft. in damp, tropical forests). On the mainland, it can become a 40-ft. tree in frost-free zones; often seen as a small tree or shrub in shaded patios and garden entrances in cooler part of range. Narrow, leathery dark green leaves are 8–12 in. long. New leaves unfold from rosy pink sheaths that soon wither and drop. Comes back quickly if killed to ground by frost. Good in containers; if potted plant becomes too tall and leggy, you can cut off the top and select a side branch to form a new main shoot. One of the most foolproof indoor plants. Partial or full shade.

F. lyrata. FIDDLELEAF FIG. Evergreen tree or vining shrub.

Zones 22–24; H1, H2; or indoors. Native to tropical Africa. Dramatic structural form with prominently veined, fiddle-shaped, huge leaves (to 15 in. long, 10 in. wide) in glossy dark green. In Hawaii, forms a dense, round-headed tree to 35–50 ft. tall and about 35 ft. wide. In California, can grow to 20 ft. tall and as wide, with trunks 6 in. thick. Good near swimming pools. To increase branching, pinch back when plant is young. Full sun or light shade. Highly effective as a houseplant.

F. microcarpa (F. retusa). INDIAN LAUREL FIG, CHINESE BANYAN. Evergreen tree. Zones 9, 13, 16–24; H1, H2. Native from Malay peninsula to Borneo. One of the more common banyans in Hawaiian landscapes, where it grows quickly to 60 ft. tall, with a dense canopy spreading to about 75 ft. wide; produces multiple aerial roots in wet areas. In California and Arizona, it grows at a more moderate rate to 25–30 ft. tall, 35–40 ft. wide. Beautiful weeping form, with long, drooping branches thickly clothed with blunt-tipped leaves. Light rose to chartreuse new leaves, produced almost continuously, give pleasing two-tone effect. Prune at any time of year to shape as desired. Responds well to shearing into formal hedge as low as 5 ft. Makes a highly satisfactory tree or tub plant; very popular for bonsai. Unfortunately, subject to thrips damage in California. 'Green Gem' has thicker, darker green leaves and is apparently unaffected by thrips. Full sun.

F. m. crassifolia. WAX FIG, TAIWAN FIG. To 10–12 ft. tall and sprawling as wide. Tolerates salt, wind, drought, various soil types. In Hawaii, more likely to be used for hedges or containers than the species. Easily pruned to maintain size and shape. Full sun or partial shade.

F. pumila (F. repens). CREEPING FIG. Evergreen vine. Zones 8–24; H1, H2; or indoors. Native to China, Japan, Australia. Has a most unfiglike habit; it is one of the few plants that attach themselves securely to wood, masonry, or even metal in barnacle fashion. Because it is grown on walls and thus protected, it is found in colder

climates more often than any other evergreen fig. Grows in sun or shade but will burn on hot south or west wall. Looks innocent enough in youth, making a delicate tracery of tiny, heart-shaped leaves. Juvenile foliage ultimately develops into big (2–4-in.-long), leathery leaves borne on stubby branches that bear large oblong fruits. In time, stems will envelop a three- or four-story building so completely that it becomes necessary to keep them trimmed away from windows. It's safe to use on house walls if you cut it to the ground every few years; also control by removing fruiting stems from time to time as they form. Roots are invasive. 'Minima' has shorter, narrower leaves than species. 'Variegata' has standard-size leaves with creamy white markings. *F. p. quercifolia* (*F. p.* 'Oakleaf') has small, lobed leaves that resemble miniature oak leaves.

F. rubiginosa. RUSTYLEAF FIG. Evergreen tree. Zones 18–24; H1, H2. Native to Australia. Single- or multitrunked, densely foliaged tree to 20–50 ft. tall, with broad crown 30–50 ft. wide. Leaves about 5 in. long, deep green above, generally rust-colored and woolly beneath. May develop hanging aerial roots characteristic of many of the evergreen figs that grow in tropical environments. 'Variegata', with leaves mottled green and cream, is sometimes sold as a houseplant. *F. r. australis* is virtually identical to the species but may vary in having leaf undersides with a less pronounced rust color. Full sun.

Ficus pumila is beautiful as a youngster; it creates a delicate tracery of neat foliage against house walls. But with time, it develops the habits of a rambunctious teenager, galloping off in every direction. Cut it to the ground every few years; remove fruiting stems as they form.

Fig

Moraceae

DECIDUOUS FRUIT TREES

✎ **ZONES 4–9, 11–24; H1, H2; OR IN POTS**

☀ **FULL SUN**

◐◗ **MODERATE TO REGULAR WATER**

Fig

Native to western Asia, eastern Mediterranean, *Ficus carica* is grown for edible fruit; for ornamental relatives, see *Ficus*. Grows fairly fast to 15–30 ft. tall and wide and is generally low branched. Where temperatures regularly drop below 10°F to 15°F (–12°C to –9°C), fig wood freezes back severely and plants act like big shrubs. With pruning, figs can be held to 10 ft. in a large container or espaliered along a fence or wall.

Heavy, smooth, gray trunks are gnarled in really old trees, picturesque in silhouette. Rough, bright green leaves with three to five lobes are 4–9 in. long and nearly as wide, casting dense shade. The tree's strong trunk and branch pattern, which looks good by itself in winter and when it's clothed with tropical-looking leaves in summer, also makes fig a top-notch ornamental tree, especially where it can be illuminated from beneath. Choose a site where fallen fruit won't make a mess on a path or patio. Figs are not particular about soil, but good drainage is a plus. Avoid deep cultivation near trees, as this may damage surface roots.

Home-garden figs do not need pollinating, and most varieties bear two crops a year. The first comes in early summer on last year's wood; the second, more important one comes in late summer or early fall from the current year's growth. (In the Northwest, expect only the summer crop.) When figs are ripe, they detach easily when lifted and bent back toward the branch. Keep fruit picked as it ripens; protect from birds if you can. In late fall, pick off any remaining ripe figs and clean up fallen fruit.

Varieties differ in climate adaptability. Most need prolonged high temperatures to bear good fruit, while some thrive in cooler conditions. In colder part of range, trees planted near south walls or trained against them benefit from reflected heat. In-ground figs need no frost protection when temperatures remain above 20°F (–7°C). Protect container plants from light frost by covering them at night; protect pots from heavier freezes by bringing them into a cool frost-free place for winter. In hot-summer regions, paint trunks of newly planted figs with white-wash or white latex to prevent sunburn.

Dried figs from the market are usually 'Calimyrna' or imported Smyrna figs. These require special pollenizers (male trees called caprifigs) and a special pollinating insect, and are not recommended for home gardens. The following self-fruitful figs are superior choices.

'Black Jack'. Purple skin with sweet pink flesh. Similar to 'Mission'. Widely adapted to warm climates. Easily kept small by pruning.

'Celeste' ('Blue Celeste', 'Celestial'). Violet-tinged bronzy skin, rosy amber flesh. Good fresh; resists spoilage. Dries well on the tree in warm climates.

'Conadria'. Choice thin-skinned white fig blushed violet; white to red flesh with fine flavor. Best in hot areas; takes intense heat without splitting.

'Desert King'. Green-skinned, red-fleshed fruit. Adapted to all fig climates but better in cooler areas like the Northwest. Bears one late-summer crop.

'Genoa' ('White Genoa'). Greenish yellow skin and strawberry-colored to yellow flesh. Good in coastal valleys and along California coast.

'Improved Brown Turkey'. Brownish purple fruit. Adaptable to most fig-growing climates. Good, small garden tree.

'Italian Everbearing'. Resembles 'Improved Brown Turkey' but has somewhat larger fruit with reddish brown skin. Good fresh or dried.

'Kadota' ('White Kadota'). Tough-skinned greenish yellow fruit. One of the best figs for Hawaii; in California, grows best in hot interior valleys.

'Lattarula'. Also known as Italian honey fig. Green skin, amber flesh. Grown in Northwest, where it can ripen in summer and produce fall crops in good seasons.

'Mission' ('Black Mission'). Large tree. Purple-black figs with pink flesh. Good fresh or dried. Widely adapted; popular in California.

'Osborn Prolific' ('Neveralla'). Dark reddish brown skin; amber flesh, often tinged pink. Very sweet; best eaten fresh. Best in Northern California coastal areas and Pacific Northwest. Light bearing in warm climates.

'Panachée' ('Striped Tiger', 'Tiger'). Greenish yellow skin with dark green stripes. Strawberry-colored flesh is sweet but dry. Best eaten fresh. Requires long, warm growing season. One crop late in summer.

'Peter's Honey' ('Rutara'). Greenish yellow skin, amber flesh. Needs extra warmth in mild climates, so plant it in a warm spot in the garden, such as against a south-facing wall.

'Texas Everbearing'. Mahogany to purple skin, strawberry-colored flesh. Bears at a young age. Produces well in short-season areas of Southwest.

CARE

Set out nursery plants anytime except during the heat of summer. Plant bare-root trees in late winter or spring. Water regularly for the first 2 years, then deeply every 2 weeks during the growing season. Apply a balanced fertilizer once after growth starts in spring; avoid high-nitrogen fertilizers, which stimulate leafy growth at the expense of fruit. As tree grows, prune lightly each winter, cutting out dead wood, crossing branches, and low-hanging branches that interfere with traffic. Pinch back runaway shoots in any season. Gophers love fig roots; if they or other burrowing animals are a problem in your garden, plant fig trees in ample wire baskets. If necessary, use netting to protect ripe fruit from birds.

Filbert. See *Corylus*; Hazelnut (Filbert)

Filipendula

MEADOWSWEET

Rosaceae

PERENNIALS

✎ **ZONES VARY BY SPECIES**

☀◐● **FULL SUN IN COOLER CLIMATES ONLY**

◐◗ **REGULAR TO AMPLE WATER**

Filipendula rubra

These lush plants bear plumes of tiny flowers above large, coarsely divided leaves in summer. Plants go dormant in winter, even in mild-winter areas. Most species prefer moist to constantly damp but well-drained soil. Good in borders and beside ponds.

F. purpurea. Zones 3b–9, 14–17. Red, 3–4-ft. plumes rise above a 2-ft.-wide foliage clump. Leaves resemble large (to 7 in.) maple leaves. 'Elegans' is compact at 1½–2 ft. high, with white flowers and red stamens.

F. rubra. QUEEN OF THE PRAIRIE. Zones A1–A3; 1–9, 14–17. Given plenty of moisture and rich soil, can reach 8 ft. tall in bloom; bears pink plumes above 4-ft.-wide clump of jagged-edged leaves with big, lobed leaflet at tip. 'Venusta' has purplish pink flowers and is a little shorter (4–6 ft. tall).

F. vulgaris (F. hexapetala). DROPWORT. Zones A1–A3; 1–9, 14–17. White (sometimes pink-tinged) plumes on 2-ft. stems rise above a 1½-ft.-wide mound of ferny leaves divided into inch-long leaflets. Double-flowered 'Multiplex' ('Flore Pleno') has heavier-looking plumes. Needs less water than other species; also prefers full sun in all but the warmest regions.

Foeniculum vulgare

COMMON FENNEL

Apiaceae

PERENNIAL SOMETIMES TREATED AS ANNUAL

🗲 ZONES VARY BY FENNEL TYPE

☼ FULL SUN

⬥ MODERATE WATER

🦋 ATTRACTS BUTTERFLIES AND BENEFICIAL INSECTS

Foeniculum vulgare

Two forms of this Mediterranean native are commonly grown—one as a perennial for its flavorful seeds and young leaves, the other as an annual for its edible leaf bases.

The perennial species, which is cultivated for licorice-flavored seeds and young leaves, is grown as a perennial in Zones 2b–11, 14–24, H1, and H2; and as a winter annual in Zones 12 and 13. It is similar in appearance to dill (*Anethum graveolens*), growing 3–5 ft. tall and producing flat clusters of yellow flowers in summer. Use seeds to season baked goods; use young leaves as garnish for salads, fish, and other dishes. Fennel often grows as a roadside or garden weed in Hawaii and along the West Coast from California to Washington. It's attractive until tops turn brown, and even then birds like the seeds. New stems grow in spring from perennial root. Bronze fennel

('Purpurascens', 'Smokey') reaches 6 ft. tall, has bronzy purple foliage.

F. v. azoricum, Florence fennel or finocchio, is a summer annual in all zones except 12 and 13, where it is a winter annual. It grows about 2 ft. high, with large leafstalk bases that are used as a vegetable, cooked or raw. Its feathery leaves are used as a garnish and seasoning.

Start fennel plants from seed where they are to be grown. Sow in light, well-drained soil; thin seedlings to 1 ft. apart. Shear off flower heads before they go to seed if you don't want the plant to self-sow, which it does vigorously.

Forestiera neomexicana

NEW MEXICAN PRIVET, DESERT OLIVE

Oleaceae

DECIDUOUS SHRUB

🗲 ZONES 1–3, 7–24

☼ FULL SUN

⬥ MODERATE WATER

🦋 ATTRACTS BIRDS

Forestiera neomexicana

Native to New Mexico, Colorado, and Arizona west to California. Popular in arid regions but seldom grown elsewhere, this shrub or small tree grows to 12–18 ft. tall, about 12 ft. wide. Smooth, medium green leaves turn bright yellow in fall. Flowers are inconspicuous. Small (¼ in. long), egg-shaped, blue-black fruits are produced on female plants if male plants are growing nearby. Fairly fast growth makes it a good screen plant; can also be trained as a small multitrunked tree.

Forsythia

Oleaceae

DECIDUOUS SHRUBS

🗲 ZONES A2, A3; 2B–11, 14–16, 18, 19; EXCEPT AS NOTED

☼ FULL SUN

⬥⬥ MODERATE TO REGULAR WATER

Forsythia viridissima

Native to China and Korea. From late winter to early spring, leafless branches of these fountain-shaped shrubs are covered with yellow flowers up to 1½ in. across. Budded branches can be brought indoors to bloom in a vase. During the rest of the growing season, the medium green foliage blends well with other background shrubs. Use as screen, espalier, or bank cover; or plant in shrub border. Tolerate most soils. Prune after bloom by cutting to the ground a third of the branches that have flowered; also remove the oldest branches and weak or dead wood. In coldest-winter climates, flower buds may be destroyed by temperatures below −20°F (−29°C).

F. 'Arnold Dwarf'. Grows to about 1½–3 ft. high, 6 ft. wide. Flowers are sparse and not especially attractive, but the plant is a useful, fast-growing groundcover popular in cold climates.

F. hardy hybrids. Zones A2, A3; 1a, 2–11, 14–16, 18, 19. These cold-hardy introductions have extended the range of forsythia into regions formerly too cold for successful flowering—or even for the plant's survival.

'Meadowlark'. To 6–9 ft. tall, 10 ft. wide; semiarching habit. Bright yellow flowers open from buds hardy to −35°F (−37°C).

'New Hampshire Gold'. Mounding habit to 5 ft. tall and broad, with drooping yellow flowers. Buds are hardy to −35°F (−37°C).

'Northern Sun'. Erect grower to 8–10 ft. tall and slightly narrower; reliably bud-hardy to −30°F (−34°C).

F. × intermedia. This group of hybrids between *F. suspensa* and *F. viridissima* includes the following selections.

'Beatrix Farrand'. Upright to 10 ft. tall, 7 ft. wide. Branches thickly set with deep yellow flowers marked with orange.

'Fiesta'. To 3–4 ft. tall and somewhat broader, with deep yellow flowers and yellow-variegated leaves.

'Gold Tide'. Just 20 in. high and 4 ft. wide, with profuse yellow blooms.

'Goldzauber'. Erect growth to 6–8 ft. tall and slightly narrower. Deep yellow blooms.

'Karl Sax'. Resembles 'Beatrix Farrand' but is lower growing (to about 8 ft.), neater, and more graceful.

'Lynwood' ('Lynwood Gold'). Stiffly upright to 7 ft.; 4–6 ft. spread. Profuse tawny yellow blooms survive spring storms.

'Magical Gold'. Upright grower to 4–5 ft. tall and wide. Deep golden yellow blooms clothe stems densely from base to tip. Good cut flower.

'Show Off'. Upright, 5–6 ft. tall and wide, with bright yellow flowers and handsome, dark green foliage.

'Spectabilis'. Dense, upright, vigorous shrub to 10 ft. tall, 6 ft. wide. Deep yellow flowers.

'Spring Glory'. To about 6 ft. tall and wide, with heavy crop of pale yellow flowers.

F. mandshurica 'Vermont Sun'. Zones A2, A3; 1–11, 14–16. Erect, extremely bud-hardy shrub to 8 ft. tall, 6 ft. wide; lemon yellow flowers appear before those of other forsythias.

F. ovata. KOREAN FORSYTHIA. To 4–6 ft. tall, 10 ft. wide. Early bloomer (about a week after *F. mandshurica* 'Vermont Sun') bearing a profusion of bright yellow flowers. 'Tetragold' is lower growing (about 3 ft. high).

F. suspensa. WEEPING FORSYTHIA. Dense, upright shrub reaches 8–10 ft. tall, 6–8 ft.

wide, with golden yellow blossoms on drooping, vinelike branches that root where they touch damp soil. Useful as a large-scale bank cover. Plant can also be trained as a vine; if you support main branches, branchlets will cascade.

F. viridissima. GREENSTEM FORSYTHIA. Zones A2, A3; 2b–11, 14–16, 18, 19. Stiff-looking shrub 6–10 ft. tall and wide, with deep green foliage, olive green stems, and greenish yellow flowers. 'Bronxensis' is a slow-growing dwarf to 1 ft. high, 2–3 ft. wide; useful as a groundcover or in borders.

Fothergilla
Hamamelidaceae
DECIDUOUS SHRUBS

🌿 **ZONES 2B–9, 14–17**
☼ ◑ **PARTIAL SHADE IN HOTTEST CLIMATES**
💧 **REGULAR WATER**

Fothergilla gardenii

Native to southeastern U.S. Grown mainly for fall foliage color, but spring bloom is pretty too: small, honey-scented white flowers in 1–2-in., brushlike clusters on zigzagging stems. Blossoms may appear before or with leaves. Performs best in moist, well-drained, acid soil.

F. gardenii. DWARF FOTHERGILLA. Typically 2–3 ft. high (though it can grow considerably taller) and as wide or wider, with dark green leaves to 2½ in. long. Foliage turns intense yellow to orange to scarlet in fall, often with all three colors in same leaf. 'Blue Mist' has blue foliage that doesn't color up as well in fall.

F. major (F. monticola). Erect shrub to 9 ft. tall and 6 ft.

wide, with roundish leaves turning yellow to orange to purplish red in autumn. 'Mount Airy' (*F.* × *intermedia* 'Mount Airy') grows to 3–6 ft. tall and nearly as wide, with abundant bloom, dark green leaves, and superb autumn color in yellow, orange, and scarlet.

Fouquieria
Fouquieriaceae
DECIDUOUS SHRUBS OR TREES

🌿 **ZONES VARY BY SPECIES**
☼ **FULL SUN**
💧💧 **LITTLE TO MODERATE WATER**
🦋 **ATTRACT HUMMINGBIRDS**

Fouquieria splendens

These desert natives have grooved, spiny branches, making them formidable barrier plants. They drop their leaves during hot, dry periods, then resprout and bloom quickly after rains, bearing tubular flowers to 1 in. long. Will survive on rainfall alone but grow and bloom best if soaked deeply once a month. Need excellent drainage, intense summer heat. Easily propagated from softwood cuttings in warm weather; cut branches stuck in ground will root and grow.

F. diguetii. ADAM'S TREE. Zones 13, 18–20. Native to Sonoran deserts and northwest Mexico. Grows to 7 ft. tall and nearly as wide, with a very short trunk and upright, spiny branches clothed in oval, light green leaves. Wands of tubular red flowers are produced near the branch tips in summer.

F. macdougalii. MEXICAN TREE OCOTILLO. Zones 11–13. This native to Mexico has brown branches covered with gray spines that rise from a short,

smooth, yellowish green trunk. Usually grows 6–8 ft. tall and 4 ft. wide, though it may eventually reach 24 ft. tall, 18 ft. wide. Lance-shaped light gray leaves are 1½ in. long. Deep red flowers come in open sprays reminiscent of exploding skyrockets. In frost-prone areas, grow in pot and move indoors in winter.

F. splendens. OCOTILLO. Zones 10–13, 18–20. Native to Colorado and Sonoran deserts east to Texas and south into Mexico. Forms a 5–10-ft.-wide clump of stiff, whip-thin, gray stems 8–25 ft. tall, heavily furrowed and covered with stout thorns and small, fleshy, roundish leaves. Attractive foot-long clusters of flowers; color ranges from bright to deep red-orange (occasionally yellow). Use as screen, hedge, living fence for animal enclosures; or grow for silhouette against bare walls. Easily killed by overwatering.

Fragaria
ORNAMENTAL STRAWBERRY
Rosaceae
PERENNIALS

🌿 **ZONES VARY BY SPECIES**
☼ ◑ **AFTERNOON SHADE IN HOTTEST CLIMATES**
💧 **REGULAR WATER**
🦋 **ATTRACT BUTTERFLIES**

Fragaria vesca

For strawberries grown strictly for their edible fruit, see Strawberry; the plants described here are grown for their ornamental qualities, though *F. vesca* also produces delectable fruit. Grow in well-drained soil.

F. chiloensis. BEACH STRAWBERRY, SAND STRAWBERRY. Zones 4–24; H1. Native to Pacific Coast beaches and

bluffs of North and South America. A parent of the commercial strawberry; forms lush, compact mat 4–8 in. high. Glossy dark green leaves have three tooth-edged leaflets; take on red tones in winter. White, 1-in., springtime flowers are occasionally followed by a few bright red, seedy, ¾-in. fruits in fall. For groundcover, set out nursery-grown plants 1–1½ ft. apart. Mow or cut back annually in early spring to force new growth and prevent stem buildup.

F. 'Lipstick'. Zones 2b–24. Results from a cross between *Fragaria* and *Potentilla*. Similar to *F. chiloensis* in general appearance but bears rich rosy red flowers in spring and intermittently through summer. Use in borders, edgings, rock gardens. Produces very few fruits.

F. 'Pink Panda'. Zones 4–24. Resembles *F.* 'Lipstick' and is used in the same way, but it bears pink flowers from spring to autumn.

F. vesca. ALPINE STRAWBERRY, FRAISE DU BOIS, WOOD STRAWBERRY. Zones 2b–9, 14–24; H2. Bears a small crop of tiny but fragrant, delicious berries over a long summer season. Good choice as an edging for flower or herb beds (space plants 8–12 in. apart). Does not produce runners but may be grown from seed; bears the first year from seed sown early. Varieties include red-fruiting 'Alexandra', 'Baron Solemacher', 'Improved Rügen', 'Mignonette', and 'Semper-florens'; there are also yellow- and white-fruiting selections. 'Golden Alexandra' has lime green foliage. 'Variegata' has gray-green leaves heavily and irregularly edged in white.

For a surprising and satisfying dessert, serve tiny red alpine strawberries on a small plate with white alpine strawberries and golden raspberries.

F

F

Francoa ramosa

MAIDEN'S WREATH
Saxifragaceae
PERENNIAL

⚊ ZONES 4–9, 14–24

☽ PARTIAL SHADE

◐ ● MODERATE TO REGULAR WATER

Francoa ramosa

Native to Chile. This old-fashioned favorite is more often shared among gardeners than sold in nurseries. Large, wavy-edged leaves to 6 in. long grow in a rosette 1–2 ft. high and wide (and spreading wider by rhizomes). Graceful, slender stems rise 2–3 ft. above the foliage in midsummer, with upper portions carrying spikes of many small white blossoms, sometimes blushed pink or marked with deep pink.

A selection sold as 'Rogerson's Form' is compact, with dark pink blooms. *F. sonchifolia* is similar but bears light pink flowers, usually with deep pink markings. Some botanists believe that all maiden's wreaths belong to a single highly variable species. Excellent cut flowers.

CARE

In just a few years, one plant increases sufficiently in size to let you divide and replant fresh new segments from clump's outside edges. Needs rich, well-drained soil. Best with dappled shade all day or with sun for half the day.

FOR MORE ON PERENNIALS, SEE "GROW: PERENNIALS," PAGES 686–687.

Frangula

Rhamnaceae
EVERGREEN AND DECIDUOUS SHRUBS OR TREES

⚊ ZONES VARY BY SPECIES

☀ ☽ ● EXPOSURE NEEDS VARY BY SPECIES

◐ ● ◆ WATER NEEDS VARY BY SPECIES

🜨 BERRIES ATTRACT BIRDS

Frangula californica

The first two species below give mass and lovely texture to the garden, while the third makes a good garden-scale deciduous native tree.

F. alnus (Rhamnus frangula). ALDER BUCKTHORN. Deciduous shrub or tree. Zones 1–7, 10, 11. Native to Europe, western Asia, and North Africa. Grows 10–12 ft. (possibly 18 ft.) tall and wide. Oval to roundish, glossy dark green leaves turn yellow in autumn. Berries ripen from red to black. 'Asplenifolia' grows 10–12 ft. high, 6–10 ft. wide, with fernlike, medium to dark green, wavy-edged leaves. 'Columnaris' grows 12–15 ft. tall, 4 ft. wide; set plants 2½ ft. apart for a tight, narrow hedge that can be kept as low as 4 ft. 'Tallhedge' grows 14 ft. tall, 4 ft. wide. Full sun or partial shade. Moderate water.

F. californica (Rhamnus californica). COFFEEBERRY. Evergreen shrub. Zones 3a–10, 14–24; H1, H2. Native to California, southwest Oregon, and Arizona. To 3–15 ft. tall, 8 ft. wide. Grown near the ocean, this plant may have a low, spreading habit; in woodlands, it grows upright. Leaves are shiny or dull, dark green to yellowish green, usually paler on undersides (some forms are gray and hairy beneath). Berries ripen from green to red to black. Attracts bees. Tolerant of pruning and shaping. Not fussy about soil. Full sun or partial shade. Established plants need no irrigation, but the broader-leafed types look better with moderate water.

'Eve Case'. Dense grower 4–8 ft. tall and wide, with large berries and broader, flatter, brighter green leaves than the species.

'Leatherleaf'. Grows 5–6 ft. tall, with dark green, convex, 3-in. leaves along reddish stems; does best in sandy soil.

'Mound San Bruno'. To 4–6 ft. tall and wide, has narrower leaves than species. Especially tolerant of variable moisture.

'Seaview'. Grows 1½–2 ft. high, 6–8 ft. wide, with leaves like those of 'Eve Case'.

'Seaview Improved'. Like 'Seaview' but lies nearly flat on the ground.

F. purshiana (Rhamnus purshiana). CASCARA, CHITTAM BARK. Deciduous shrub or tree. Zones 1–9, 14–17. Native from Northern California to British Columbia and Montana. To 20–40 ft. tall, 10–30 ft. wide, with smooth gray or brownish bark that has medicinal value. Picturesque branching pattern. Dark green, prominently veined leaves are elliptical, 1½–8 in. long, usually borne somewhat more heavily (in tufts) at branch ends. Good yellow foliage color in fall. Black berries. Takes full sun to dense shade. Moderate to regular water.

Coffeeberry (*Frangula californica*) has a chameleon habit. Its overall shape changes in response to environmental conditions. Its leaves change too. Plants grown in hot, dry locations have smaller, thicker leaves than those grown in cooler conditions with more water.

Franklinia alatamaha

Theaceae
DECIDUOUS TREE

⚊ ZONES 3B–6, 14–17

☀ ☽ PARTIAL SHADE IN HOTTEST CLIMATES

● REGULAR WATER

Franklinia alatamaha

This graceful small tree is the only member of its genus, which was named in honor of Benjamin Franklin. Open and airy, it may grow 30 ft. tall but more typically reaches 10–20 ft. tall. When grown with single trunk, it tends to be fairly slender; grown with multiple trunks, it spreads wider than high. Attractive gray bark has faint white vertical striping. Glossy green 4–6-in.-long leaves turn orange and red in fall. In late summer, round white buds open to fragrant white blossoms resembling single camellias: 3 in. wide, five petaled, with central clusters of yellow stamens. Bloom may coincide with fall foliage color. Small, woody capsules follow the flowers. Tree blooms less during wet autumns in Northwest. Provide well-drained, rich, light, acid soil. Easy to grow from seed, flowering in 6 or 7 years. Makes an unusual lawn or patio tree; good for contrast in azalea and rhododendron plantings.

FOR MORE BLOOMING TREES, SEE PAGES 107–108.

Fraxinus

ASH
Oleaceae
DECIDUOUS AND EVERGREEN TREES

✎ ZONES VARY BY SPECIES

☼ FULL SUN

**◊ ◗ ● WATER NEEDS VARY BY
SPECIES**

Fraxinus americana
'Autumn Purple'

Ashes are fairly fast growing and useful as street, shade, lawn or patio trees. Most tolerate hot summers, cold winters, and many kinds of soil. Leaves are typically divided into leaflets. Male and female flowers (generally inconspicuous) grow on separate trees in some species, on the same tree in others. In the latter case, flowers are often followed by clusters of single-seeded, winged fruit in such abundance that they can be a litter problem. When flowers are on separate trees, you'll get fruit on female tree only if a male tree grows nearby.

Ashes are prone to borers. In some parts of California, ash whitefly is a problem; the chalky white, ⅛-in.-long insects colonize in patches on leaf undersides. Outbreaks are usually controlled by natural enemies; avoid spraying with broad-spectrum insecticides, which are likely to wipe out these beneficial predators.

F. americana. WHITE ASH. Deciduous. Zones 1–11, 14–17. Native to eastern U.S. Grows to 80 ft. or taller; straight trunk and oval-shaped crown to 50 ft. wide. Leaves up to 15 in. long have five to nine dark green, oval leaflets, paler beneath; turn purplish in fall. Leaf edges burn in hot, windy areas. Regular water.

Male and female flowers are on separate trees, but plants sold are generally seedlings, so you don't know what you're getting. If you end up with both male and female trees, you will get a heavy crop of seed; both litter and seedlings can be a problem. Seedless selections include 'Autumn Applause', 'Autumn Purple', and 'Royal Purple', all with exceptionally good, long-lasting purple fall color; 'Rosehill', with bronzy red fall color; and 'Skyline', an upright, somewhat narrow oval with brown and purple fall color.

**F. angustifolia 'Raywood'
(F. oxycarpa 'Raywood').** RAYWOOD ASH, CLARET ASH. Deciduous. Zones 2b–9, 12–24. Variety of a small-leafed, fine-textured ash from the Mediterranean. Grows quickly into a dense oval 45–60 ft. tall and 30–40 ft. wide, with dark green leaves that turn wine red in fall. Produces no seeds. Prone to branch dieback in parts of California—especially when trees are stressed by drought—but otherwise fairly disease-resistant. Moderate water.

F. 'Fan West'. Deciduous. Zones 2–14. Seedless hybrid between *F. pennsylvanica* and *F. velutina* 'Modesto'. Resembles the latter in size and habit. Light olive green leaves, good branch structure; tolerates cold, desert heat, and wind. Best with regular water but tolerates some aridity.

F. greggii. LITTLE LEAF ASH. Evergreen. Zones 10–13. Native from Arizona to Texas. Shrubby tree to 18–20 ft. tall and 10–15 ft. wide, with bright green leaves divided into three to seven leathery leaflets. Useful in desert; good patio tree. Survives on little water but grows faster with moderate irrigation.

F. mandshurica 'Mancana'. MANCHURIAN ASH. Deciduous. Zones A1–A3; 1–3. Very cold-hardy, seedless, cutting-grown variety to 35–45 ft. tall and 25–30 ft. wide, with a dense, oval crown. Foot-long, yellowish green leaves have coarsely toothed leaflets to 5 in. long; take on good yellow color in fall. Thrives on regular water but tolerates drought. Hybrid 'Northern Treasure' is vigorous and disease-resistant,

growing to 40 ft. tall and 30 ft. wide, with glossy green leaves that turn pale orange-yellow in autumn.

F. ornus. FLOWERING ASH. Deciduous. Zones 3–9, 14–17. Native to southern Europe and Asia Minor. Grows rapidly to 40–50 ft., with broad, rounded crown 20–30 ft. wide. Supplies luxuriant mass of foliage. Leaves 8–10 in. long, divided into medium green, 2-in.-long leaflets with toothed edges. Foliage turns to soft shades of lavender and yellow in fall. In spring, displays quantities of fluffy, branching clusters of fragrant white to greenish white blossoms followed by unsightly seed clusters that hang on until late winter unless removed. Moderate water. 'Urban Bouquet' is a heavy bloomer that sets no seed.

F. oxycarpa 'Raywood'. See *F. angustifolia* 'Raywood'.

F. pennsylvanica (F. lanceolata). GREEN ASH, RED ASH. Deciduous. Zones A2, A3; 1–6. Native to eastern U.S. To 30–50 ft. tall and wide, with compact, oval crown. Gray-brown bark; dense, twiggy structure. Leaves up to 12 in. long are divided into bright green, rather narrow leaflets. Male and female flowers on separate trees. Takes wet soil and severe cold, but foliage burns in hot, dry winds. Regular water. Seedless varieties include 'Marshall' ('Marshall's Seedless'), a fast-growing tree with tapered crown; 'Patmore', with handsome form and good resistance to pests and diseases; 'Summit', with uniformly upright habit and good golden yellow fall color; and 'Urbanite', with pyramidal form and bronze fall color.

F. uhdei. EVERGREEN ASH, SHAMEL ASH. Evergreen to semievergreen. Zones 9, 12–24. Native to Mexico and a favorite in Southern California and low-elevation deserts. Grows fast to 25–30 ft. tall and 15 ft. wide in 10 years; may eventually attain 70–80 ft. in height and 60 ft. in width. Leaves divided into glossy dark green leaflets about 4 in. long. Foliage may burn in hot winds. In mildest climates, leaves hold on through winter; in colder areas, tree loses most or all of its foliage, but leafless period is usually short. Sharp

frosts may kill branch tips; tree will suffer serious damage at 15°F (−9°C). Cut back any long, unsightly branches when tree is young. Texas root rot sometimes causes dieback and will kill young trees, but established ones usually survive. Resistant to oak root fungus. Tolerates aridity but does best with regular water and an occasional deep soaking.

'Majestic Beauty' has exceptionally large leaves and is more reliably evergreen than the species. 'Sexton' is very compact, with a rounded crown; it has larger, deeper green leaflets than those of species. 'Tomlinson' grows slowly (to just 10–15 ft. in 10 years) and is more upright and dense when young; leaflets are more leathery, with wavy-toothed margins.

F. velutina. ARIZONA ASH. Deciduous. Zones 3b–24. Native to southwestern U.S. and Mexico. Withstands hot, dry conditions; cold hardy to about −10°F (−23°C). Grows about 30 ft. (possibly to 50 ft.) tall. Pyramidal when young; spreading to 30–40 ft. wide when mature, more open form. Velvety, gray-green leaves are divided into three to five leaflets and turn bright yellow in fall. Male and female flowers on separate trees. Attracts birds. Regular water.

'Berrinda'. Zones 3–24. Very tough, cold-hardy selection from New Mexico, with a strongly upright form to 35 ft. tall and about as wide.

'Bonita'. Zones 8–24. Good substitute for 'Modesto', especially in the Southwest. Broadly oval to 30–35 ft. tall and slightly wider. Bright yellow fall color lasts longer than that of 'Modesto'.

'Modesto'. MODESTO ASH. Zones 3–24. Originated in Modesto, California. Vigorous form growing to about 50 ft. tall, with 30-ft. spread. Leaflets are medium green, glossier than those of species; bright yellow fall color. Resistant to oak root fungus but subject to so many other diseases that most communities have removed it from their lists of recommended trees. Good replacements include 'Bonita', 'Rio Grande', *F. angustifolia* 'Raywood', and *F. uhdei*.

F

»

'Rio Grande'. FAN-TEX ASH. Zones 8–24. Thrives in hot, dry climates and alkaline soils. Has larger, darker green, more succulent leaflets than 'Modesto'; they turn golden yellow in late autumn. Foliage resistant to windburn.

F. v. coriacea. MONTEBELLO ASH. Zones 8, 9, 12–24. Native mostly to Southern California. Broader, more leathery leaves than the species.

Freesia
Iridaceae
PERENNIALS FROM CORMS

🌱 **ZONES 8, 9, 12–24**

☀️ ◑ **FULL SUN OR PARTIAL SHADE**

💧 **REGULAR WATER DURING GROWTH AND BLOOM**

Freesia hybrid

South African natives prized for the rich perfume of their flowers. In spring, wiry, 1–1½-ft. stems bear spikes of tubular flowers that reach 2 in. long and flare to 2 in. wide. Each stem bends at nearly a right angle just beneath the lowest bud. Narrow, sword-shaped leaves to 1 ft. tall grow in iris-like fans.

The old-fashioned favorite *F. lactea* (*F. alba*) has white blooms with a powerfully sweet scent, but more commonly available today are hybrids (Dutch and Tecolote hybrids represent the majority of those sold) with single or double blossoms in yellow, orange, red, pink, lavender, purple, blue, and white. You can buy mixed-color assortments as well as named varieties in specific colors. Hardy to 20°F (–7°C).

Plant in fall, setting corms 2 in. deep and 2 in. apart in well-drained soil. Cut back on watering when leaves start to yellow in late spring; withhold moisture during summer dormancy. In dry-summer regions, corms can be left in ground; in rainy-summer climates, it's best to dig them when foliage yellows and store the corms until it's time to replant them in early fall. Plantings will increase rapidly; dig and divide when vigor and quality of bloom decline. Unless you remove faded flowers, freesias tend to set seed and provide you with volunteer seedlings; these will usually revert to creamy white, sometimes marked with purple and yellow.

Fremontodendron
FLANNEL BUSH, FREMONTIA
Malvaceae
EVERGREEN SHRUBS OR SMALL TREES

🌱 **ZONES 4–24**

☀️ **FULL SUN**

◌ **NO IRRIGATION NEEDED**

Fremontodendron
'California Glory'

Fast-growing, usually short-lived plants native to dry woodlands, canyons, and mountain slopes. They typically have a sprawling, irregular shape, reaching 20 ft. tall and 12 ft. wide, except as noted. Rounded, lobed, leathery leaves are dark green above and felted beneath. Spectacular in bloom, when large, saucer-shaped, yellow blossoms appear in profusion; plants bloom heavily even when young. Flowers are produced over a long period, typically in spring, and are followed by persistent

conical seed capsules. These and the leaf undersides are covered with bristly, rust-colored hairs that penetrate and irritate skin; wear gloves when pruning flannel bushes, and locate them away from paths and patios. Plant in front of a sunny wall in marginal climates; they are good as espalier, but frequent pruning is required to keep up with their fast growth. Excellent on dry hillsides or spilling over a stone wall.

F. californicum. COMMON FLANNEL BUSH. From California, Arizona, and Baja Mexico. Eye-catching show of lemon yellow flowers to 1½ in. across; tend to bloom all at once in mid- to late spring.

F. hybrids. Several oustanding plants in a range of sizes have been produced from crosses between the two species listed here.

'California Glory'. Rich yellow flowers to 3 in. across have red-tinged backs. Prolific bloom over long period. Can grow to 20 ft. tall and at least as wide.

'Dara's Gold'. Compact grower to just 3–4 ft. tall and 6–8 ft. wide, with glossy green leaves. Yellow flowers to 2 in. wide appear over a long period from late winter to late spring.

'Ken Taylor'. Cascading growth to 4–6 ft. tall and 8–12 ft. wide. Gray-green leaves. Cup-shaped, 3-in.-wide golden flowers with orange backs open from late winter through summer.

'Pacific Sunset'. Grows 12–15 ft. tall and wide. Deep orange-yellow flowers up to 4 in. wide. Bloom peaks in spring, is sporadic later. Good disease resistance.

'San Gabriel'. To 15–20 ft. tall and not quite as wide. Deeply lobed leaves resemble those of maple. Sunny, cup-shaped yellow blooms to 3 in. wide appear in spring.

F. mexicanum. SOUTHERN FLANNEL BUSH. Endangered species from Southern California and northern Mexico. Brilliant display of orange-tinted yellow blossoms to 2½ in. across. Blooms less profusely than *F. californicum,* but flowers appear over a longer period—from late spring well into fall. Leaves reach 3 in. long and have three to five distinct lobes.

Flannel bushes are completely drought-tolerant and are easily killed by overwatering. They will accept occasional light irrigation during summer only if drainage is excellent (hillside planting is recommended). Roots are shallow, so stake plants while young to prevent them from being blown over in windy areas. Pinch young growth to encourage branching; prune off overly long shoots. Upright growers can be shaped into small trees by removing lower branches.

Fritillaria
FRITILLARY
Liliaceae
PERENNIALS FROM BULBS

🌱 **ZONES VARY BY SPECIES**

◑ **LIGHT SHADE, EXCEPT AS NOTED**

💧 **REGULAR WATER DURING GROWTH AND BLOOM**

Fritillaria meleagris

Colorful, odd-looking flowers are common in this genus. Unbranched stems ranging from 6 in. to 3 ft. high are topped in spring by bell-shaped, nodding flowers, often unusually colored and mottled. Most have lance-shaped leaves.

F. biflora. MISSION BELLS. Zones 7, 14–21. California native grows 6–16 in. high, with one to six brownish, 1½-in. bells on each blossom stalk. 'Martha Roderick' has rusty orange flowers with a white center.

F. camschatcensis. BLACK LILY, CHOCOLATE LILY. Zones A1–A3; 1–7, 15–17. Native near Pacific Coast, Japan to northwestern U.S. Grows 9–18 in. high, with whorls of leaves around the stem. Flowering stem carries one to eight 1¼-in.-long, deep purple to nearly black bells.

F. imperialis. CROWN IMPERIAL. Zones 1–7, 14–17. Native to Europe. Stout stalk to 3 ft. high, clothed with broad, glossy leaves and crowned by a circle of large (2–3 in. long) bells in red, orange, or yellow; a tuft of leaves tops the flowers. Bulb and plant have musky odor that some people find offensive. Can take full sun in cooler climates.

F. meleagris. CHECKERED LILY, SNAKESHEAD. Zones 1–7, 15–17. Native to damp meadows in Europe and Asia; tolerates occasional flooding. One to three distinctive, 2-in. bells top each foot-high stem; purple, pinkish, or white blossoms are boldly checkered and veined with dark reddish purple. Excellent in a meadow planting.

F. michailovskyi. Zones 2–7, 14–17. From Turkey. Stems to 6 in. high bear one to six 1–1½-in. bells that are purplish brown at base, bright yellow toward tip.

F. pallidiflora. Zones A1–A3; 1–7. From northern China and Siberia. Each 2–3-ft. stem carries one to six 1¼-in. bells in pale yellow tinted with green.

F. persica 'Adiyaman'. Zones 2–7, 14–17. Choice variety of a species from western Asia. Stems 2–3 ft. high carry up to 30 deep plum purple, inch-long flowers on upper half. Plant is hardy and easy to grow, but emerging stems need protection from late frosts in colder regions. Can take full sun in cooler climates.

CARE

In fall, plant bulbs on their sides in porous soil with ample humus; handle carefully, as they are prone to injury and subsequent rot. Set smaller bulbs 3–4 in. deep and 6 in. apart; set largest ones (*F. imperialis*) 4–5 in. deep, 8–12 in. apart. Bulbs sometimes rest for a year after planting or after blooming, so put in enough for yearly display. All appreciate some winter chill and tend to perform poorly where summers are hot and dry. Reduce watering as foliage dies back in summer. Once the foliage is gone, withhold water from *F. biflora* until fall.

F. meleagris needs moderate to regular water during dormancy; the others require some summer moisture.

Fuchsia
Onagraceae
EVERGREEN AND DECIDUOUS SHRUBS

✎ **ZONES VARY BY SPECIES**

☼ ◑ **FULL SUN OR PARTIAL SHADE**

💧 **REGULAR WATER**

🐦 **ATTRACT HUMMINGBIRDS**

Fuchsia magellanica molinae

From wet, mountainous areas, mainly in tropical America. Most fuchsias bloom from late spring to first frost, bearing intricate, often multicolored flowers. They grow best in cool-summer areas with much moisture in atmosphere and soil. Plant in-ground fuchsias in full sun in the Northwest; give potted ones there and all fuchsias farther south either morning sun or all-day dappled shade. If you live where fog rolls in on summer afternoons, any place in your garden will supply ideal conditions. Where summers are warm, windy, or dry, seek or create favorable exposure protected from wind and hot afternoon sun. A heavy mulch (2–3 in. thick) helps keep soil moist in hot climates.

Fuchsia gall mite has caused serious problems for fuchsia growers primarily in California (see "How to Grow Fuchsias," page 330). Most hybrid fuchsias have susceptible parentage and are prone to infestation, but many species fuchsias are resistant.

F. boliviana. Evergreen. Zones 17, 22–24. From South America. Woody, erect growth to 12 ft. or taller and 8 ft. wide, with softly hairy pale green leaves to 7 in. long. Blooms throughout the year, producing large, dangling clusters of red flowers with slender tubes to 3 in. long. Pinkish red fruit. May spread by seed in moist gardens. Resistant to fuchsia gall mite. 'Alba' has two-tone flowers in white and pinkish red; its fruit is white.

F. campos-portoi. Deciduous. Zones 3b–9, 14–24. From Brazil. Similar to *F. magellanica* and bears very similar blossoms, but has a denser habit and smaller leaves. Inflated buds with rounded teardrop shape; profuse bloomer. Can be grown as a dense shrub or allowed to clamber up into trees. Resistant to fuchsia gall mite.

F. denticulata. Evergreen. Zones 17, 22–24. From Peru and Bolivia. Parent of many mite-resistant hybrids. Grows about 8 ft. tall, 3 ft. wide, with dark green, 2–7-in.-long leaves. Summer and fall flowers are up to 3 in. long; petals orange-red, sepals and slender floral tubes red. Good-size red fruits that follow are edible. Resistant to fuchsia gall mite. Best known hybrid is 'Fanfare', which produces strong canes to 10 ft. or longer; excellent trained on trellis or as espalier.

F. excorticata. NEW ZEALAND TREE FUCHSIA. Deciduous. Zones 7–9, 15–17, 22–24. Evergreen in frost-free areas. From New Zealand. Grows slowly to about 10 ft. tall and wide in gardens, larger in the wild, with a gnarled, twisted trunk and cinnamon-colored bark that peels attractively. Oval, pointed leaves are midgreen above and silvery beneath. Inch-long springtime flowers open green and gradually turn dark burgundy, with bright blue pollen. Small red or purple berries are edible. Resistant to fuchsia gall mite. 'Kiwi Sheen' has shiny, purple-red leaves with silvery pink undersides.

F. fulgens. Evergreen. Zones 15–17, 22–24. From Mexico. To 5 ft. tall and wide, with heart-shaped, light green leaves to about 8 in. long. Blooms from winter into spring, bearing pendent clusters of orange-red flowers to 3 in. long. Resistant to fuchsia gall mite.

F. × hybrida. HYBRID FUCHSIA. Zones 4–6 (with protection), 15–17, 22–24, H1; can also be grown with some difficulty in Zones 7–9, 14, 20, 21. Where frosts are light, plants lose their leaves, and tender growth may die. Where freezes are hard, most plants die back to hard wood, sometimes to the ground.

The vast majority of fuchsias with showy flowers fall into this hybrid group, and hundreds of selections are sold in the West. Plant form varies widely, from erect-growing shrubs 3–6 ft. tall and wide to trailing types grown in hanging baskets. Sepals (top parts that flare back) are white, red, or pink. Corolla (inside part of flower) may be almost any color in range of white, blue-violet, purple, pink, red, and shades approaching orange. Flowers range from pea-size to giants as big as a child's fist. Some flowers are single, with just one layer of closely set petals in corolla; some are very double, with many sets of ruffled petals in corolla.

Many hybrids are susceptible to mite damage in California. Mite-resistant selections include 'Arouet Fils', 'Campo Molina', 'Campo Thilco', 'First Success', 'Galfrey Blush', 'Grand Harfare', 'Hinnerike', 'Mendonoma Belle', 'Red Fanling', and 'Strybing's Peach'.

The main concern in the Northwest is winter protection. Most hybrid fuchsias there are grown in containers and brought into a garage or basement in winter. In-ground fuchsias will have a better chance of survival if planted deeper than normal. Dig hole deep enough that you can place juncture of roots and stems 4–5 in. below soil level; gradually fill in soil as plant grows. Most hybrids need the insulation of a thick mulch in winter; mounding a 5–6-in. layer of sawdust over roots is effective. Hardier selections will survive winters unmulched; these include 'Cardinal', 'Jingle Bells', 'June Bride', 'Mrs. Popple', 'Phyllis', 'Rufus', 'Santa Cruz', 'Speciosa', 'Surprise', 'Tessie', 'Voltaire', 'Whiteknights Amethyst', and 'Whiteknights Pearl'.

Hybrid fuchsias in all regions —whether in pots or beds— need porous, water-retentive

F

F

soil rich in organic matter. To keep blooms coming, apply light doses of complete fertilizer frequently. Prune potted plants severely before spring growth begins, cutting back each stem of last year's growth to one or two pairs of buds. Let about three pairs of leaves develop, then pinch off stem tips to stimulate branching. Continue pinching new growth for several weeks. Pick off old flowers as they start to fade. Prune in-ground hybrid fuchsias mainly to remove dead growth and to shape as desired; pinching is unnecessary.

F. magellanica. Zones 3b–9, 14–24; H1. Deciduous where frosts are light. Top dies back with first hard frost; protection of a mulch is needed in coldest-winter areas. Native to Chile, Argentina. In virtually frost-free areas, attains 10 ft. or taller and as wide or wider. In the Northwest, can reach 6½ ft. tall and wide if not frozen back. Profuse production of drooping, 1½-in.-long, red-and-violet flowers over a long period. Very vulnerable to fuchsia gall mite. Parent of most hybrid fuchsias, which have inherited its mite susceptibility. Vigorous, frost-hardy 'Hawkshead' has dainty white blooms; those of long-blooming 'Windcliff Fury' are purple-red.

F. paniculata. Evergreen. Zones 16, 17, 22–24. From Mexico and Central America. Woody, erect growth to 12–14 ft. tall and 8 ft. wide (or larger), with small-toothed, somewhat shiny leaves to 8 in. long. Each lavender-pink flower is tiny, but blooms are massed in clusters to 10 in. across. Resistant to fuchsia gall mite.

F. procumbens. Semievergreen or deciduous. Zones 4–6, 15–17, 21–24. From New Zealand. Prostrate, spreading growth to about 6 in. high and 3–4 ft. wide. Heart-shaped, half-inch-long leaves. Tiny, petal-less flowers in summer deserve close inspection: they have pale orange sepals with green markings and purple tips, and their anthers and pollen are bright blue. Showy, ¾-in. bright red berries follow. Good as groundcover and in containers. Resistant to fuchsia gall mite.

F. thymifolia. Evergreen. Zones 14–17, 20–24. From Mexico. Erect grower 3–9 ft. tall and wide, with glossy, inch-long leaves and profuse, dangling, tiny white to pink flowers that age to deeper pink. Attractive close up; good for bonsai. Resistant to fuchsia gall mite.

F. triphylla. Evergreen. Zones 16–17, 23, 24. From the West Indies. The species is seldom seen, but hybrid 'Gartenmeister Bonstedt' is well known. Somewhat more tender than most fuchsia hybrids but said to be more tolerant of heat. To 2 ft. tall and wide. Leaves are reddish bronze above, purplish beneath. Drooping clusters of intense orange-red, long-tubed flowers. Blooms all year in mildest climates. Protect from frost. Susceptible to fuchsia gall mite.

How to Grow Fuchsias

FEEDING Fuschias are heavy feeders; give monthly applications of a balanced liquid fertilizer during bloom period.

PRUNING Flowers appear on new wood, so do any pruning before spring growth begins. Remove broken or crossing branches, and prune as little or as much as desired to maintain size or to shape the plant. In colder areas, wait to cut out frost-damaged stems until all danger of frost is past.

CHALLENGES Fuchsia gall mites, visible only under magnification, cause large, unsightly masses of distorted leaves, usually covered with reddish hairs. Pinch or cut off and destroy any distorted tissue as soon as you see it; do not compost. Heavily infested plants are probably best replaced. In the Northwest, aphids are the main pest. Spider mites and whiteflies are other common pests of fuchsias, though in the Northwest they tend to cause trouble primarily on potted plants.

Furcraea
Agavaceae
SUCCULENT PERENNIALS

🌡 **ZONES 13, 16–17, 19–24; H1, H2**

☼ ◑ **LIGHT SHADE IN HOTTEST CLIMATES**

💧 **MODERATE WATER**

Furcraea foetida mediopicta

Agave relatives native to Mexico and South America. These bold specimen plants bring an exotic look to the garden. Large, fleshy, sword-shaped leaves are held in huge rosettes (up to 8 ft. across) that grow into attractive fountain shapes in some species and are held like a pinwheel atop a trunk in others. Mature plants (at least 10 years old) send up spectacular bloom spikes, to 25 ft. tall, lined with dangling, greenish white, bell-shaped flowers that are powerfully fragrant in some species. Plants die after bloom, but the small plantlets (bulbils) that develop from the flowers can be easily pulled off and planted to reproduce the parent. Provide rich, well-drained soil and allow it to dry between waterings. Plants need little water in winter but thrive with moderate summer irrigation. Protect from frost.

F. foetida. MAURITIUS HEMP. Forms a practically stemless clump to 5 ft. tall and 8 ft. wide. Glossy, deep green leaves up to 8 in. wide and 8 ft. long have slightly wavy margins, suggesting undulating ribbons. The species was once grown commercially for the strong, hemplike fibers in its leaves. Considered invasive in Hawaii. Leaves of popular *F. f. mediopicta* have a broad central stripe of creamy white.

F. macdougalii. Slender, rigid, gray-green leaves, to 7 ft. long and less than 3 in. wide, are held stiffly upright; plant grows about 8 ft. wide. Leaf margins are lined with small, widely spaced teeth. With age, forms a thick trunk that can grow to 20 ft. or taller.

F. selloa. Clumps grow to 6 ft. wide, eventually forming a 5-ft.-tall trunk. Dark green leaves, to 4 ft. long and 3 in. wide, are narrow at the base, wide in the middle, sharply pointed at the tip. Wavy leaf margins are lined with brown, hooked teeth. *F. s. marginata* is a popular variegated form with a thin strip of creamy yellow along the leaf edges.

Gaillardia
BLANKET FLOWER
Asteraceae
PERENNIALS AND ANNUALS

🌡 **ZONES 1–24; H1, H2**

☼ **FULL SUN**

💧 **MODERATE WATER**

Gaillardia × grandiflora 'Arizona Sun'

Native to central and western U.S. Low-growing summer bloomers with daisylike flowers in warm colors—yellow, bronze, scarlet. Plants thrive in heat, need good drainage and soil that is not too rich. Easy to grow from seed and fine for cutting and borders; often reseed.

G. aristata. Perennial. Parent of popular hybrid G. × grandiflora. Has been largely replaced in garden culture by its many offspring, but the wild form is still much used in revegetation and wildflower mixes. Grows 2–2½ ft. tall and 2 ft. across. Flower heads to 4 in. wide are yellow to red; the most common form has red rays with a jagged yellow border.

G. × grandiflora. Perennial. Hybrid between G. aristata and G. pulchella. Grows 2–4 ft. high, 1½ ft. wide, with gray-green foliage and single or double flowers 3–4 in. across. Flower color range includes various shades of red and yellow, with orange or maroon bands. Exceptionally long bloom period for perennial—early summer until frost. Plants flower first year from seed. Attracts butterflies.

'Arizona Sun', about 10 in. high, has orange-red petals with yellow tips. 'Goblin' grows 1 ft. high, with large deep red flowers bordered in yellow. 'Goblin Yellow' is similar but has yellow blooms. 'Mesa Yellow' is compact and uniform at 1½ ft. high, with solid yellow flowers that bloom 2–3 weeks earlier than the others listed here. Also about 1½ ft. high are 'Oranges and Lemons', with orange centers and yellow-tipped orange petals; and 'Fanfare', with a burgundy center and trumpet-shaped orange petals tipped in yellow. In the 2-ft.-high range are 'Dazzler', with bright red petals tipped in yellow; 'Frenzy', with rich red, tubular petals tipped in yellow; 'Mandarin', with mahogany centers and flame orange, yellow-tipped petals; and 'Tizzy', with trumpet-shaped petals of pinkish orange. Among 2½-ft.-high varieties are 'Amber Wheels', with frilled, golden yellow, red-centered flowers; deep red 'Burgunder'; and pure orange 'Tokajer'.

G. pulchella. Annual. To 1½– 2 ft. high, 1 ft. wide, with soft, hairy leaves and long, whiplike stems carrying 2-in. flowers in shades of red, yellow, gold. Easy to grow; sow seeds in warm soil after frost danger is past (in Zones 12 and 13, sow in fall). 'Red Plume' and 'Yellow Plume' are double-flowered, with 2-in. blossoms on uniform 12–14-in. plants. Attracts birds.

Galanthus
SNOWDROP
Amaryllidaceae
PERENNIALS FROM BULBS

⚡ **ZONES 1–9, 14–17, EXCEPT AS NOTED**

☼ ◑ **FULL SUN DURING BLOOM, LIGHT SHADE AFTER**

💧 **REGULAR WATER**

⚘ **BULBS ARE POISONOUS IF INGESTED**

Galanthus

These natives of Europe and Asia Minor perform best in cold-winter climates. They are among the first bulbs to bloom as winter ends, charming when peeking up through a blanket of snow. Nodding, bell-shaped white flowers are borne one per stalk; inner flower segments are infused or marked with green, while larger outer segments are pure white. Plants have two or three strap-shaped basal leaves. Closely related to and often confused with *Leucojum* (snowflake).

Use under flowering shrubs or trees, naturalize in woodland, or grow in pots. Plant in fall, setting bulbs 3–4 in. deep and 3 in. apart in moist soil with ample humus. Prefer year-round moisture. Do not divide often; when division is necessary, do the job right after bloom.

G. elwesii. GIANT SNOWDROP. Stems 6–9 in. high carry 1½-in. flowers; inner segments each have two green marks. Robust plant that is better adapted to mild-winter zones than G. nivalis.

G. ikariae. Zones 4–9, 14–24. Vigorous grower to 4–6 in. high. Glossy, rich green leaves are curved and slightly broader than those of other species listed here. Large green spot

marks inner petals of flowers, which appear a little later than blooms of other snowdrops.

G. nivalis. COMMON SNOWDROP. More delicate version of G. elwesii. Stems 4–8 in. high bear inch-long flowers, their inner segments marked at tips with a green crescent. 'Flore Pleno' has double blooms.

Galium
Rubiaceae
PERENNIALS

⚡ **ZONES 1–6, 15–17, EXCEPT AS NOTED**

◑ ● **PARTIAL OR FULL SHADE**

💧 💧 **REGULAR TO AMPLE WATER**

Galium odoratum

These woodland and meadow natives have whorls of narrow leaves spaced along thin, usually sprawling stems. Flowers are tiny, often profuse. All can become invasive.

G. boreale. NORTHERN BEDSTRAW. Zones A1–A3; 1–6, 15–17. From Alaska, Canada, northern Europe, and Asia. To 2½ ft. high and wide, with 2-in. leaves and clusters of tiny white summer flowers. Nice wildflower for shade.

G. odoratum (Asperula odorata). SWEET WOODRUFF. Zones A2, A3; 2–6, 15–17. Native to Europe, North Africa, Siberia. Attractive low spreader that brings to mind deep, shady woods. Slender, square stems are encircled every inch or so by six to eight aromatic, emerald green leaves; when dried, they have the scent of fresh hay. Clusters of tiny white fragrant flowers appear just above foliage in late spring and summer. Use as a groundcover or pathway edging. Spreads rapidly in

rich soil with abundant moisture and can become a pest.

G. verum. LADY'S BEDSTRAW. From Europe and Asia. Sprawling, weak-stemmed plant to 3½ ft. high and wide. Tiny leaves; loose, open clusters of tiny yellow flowers in summer and fall.

Galtonia candicans
SUMMER HYACINTH
Liliaceae
PERENNIAL FROM BULB

⚡ **ZONES 4–24; H1; OR DIG AND STORE**

☼ ◑ **LIGHT SHADE IN HOTTEST CLIMATES**

💧 **REGULAR WATER DURING GROWTH AND BLOOM**

Galtonia candicans

Native to South Africa. In late summer—when little else is blooming—stout 2–4-ft.-tall stems are topped with loose clusters of 1–1½-in.-long, sweet-scented white flowers. Blooms are drooping funnels up to 1½ in. long, with three outer segments often tipped in green. Bold, strap-shaped leaves can reach 3 ft. long.

CARE

Plant in fall where winter lows won't fall below 10°F (–12°C), in spring in colder regions; set bulbs 6 in. deep and 1 ft. apart, in organically enriched soil. Floral display is best if clump is not disturbed from one year to the next. Where winter lows reach 10°F (–12°C), mulch planting after foliage dies down. In colder regions, dig annually and store as for gladiolus. Control slugs and snails.

Galvezia speciosa

ISLAND SNAPDRAGON
Scrophulariaceae
EVERGREEN SHRUB

☀ ZONES 14–24

☀ ◑ LIGHT SHADE IN HOTTEST CLIMATES

◊ NO IRRIGATION NEEDED

🐦 ATTRACTS HUMMINGBIRDS

Galvezia speciosa

Native to Catalina, San Clemente, and Guadalupe islands (off the coasts of Southern California and Mexico). This spreading, open grower usually reaches 3–4 ft. tall and 5–7 ft. wide, but its stems can climb or lean on other shrubs and grow to 15 ft. long. Pinch regularly for a more bushy plant, or rejuvenate by cutting stems back to the ground in late winter. Small green or yellow-green leaves are about 1 in. long, half as wide. Scarlet, tubular, inch-long flowers appear at tips of branches, with heavy bloom in midspring and intermittent bloom throughout the year. Provide good drainage. 'Firecracker' is a compact form (2–3 ft. high and 3 ft. wide) with bright red flowers.

Island snapdragon responds well to frequent light shearing. It makes a good low, formal hedge that pumps out pretty red flowers most of the year.

Gardenia

Rubiaceae
EVERGREEN SHRUBS

☀ ZONES VARY BY SPECIES

☀ ◑ FULL SUN OR PARTIAL SHADE

● ◖ REGULAR TO AMPLE WATER

Gardenia jasminoides 'Veitchii'

Prized for their intensely fragrant white blossoms, which contrast beautifully with their shiny, leathery, dark green leaves. Double forms are a classic choice for corsages.

G. jasminoides (G. augusta). Zones 7–9, 12–16, 18–24; H1, H2, except as noted. Native to China, Taiwan, and Japan. Glossy bright green, lance-shaped leaves and very fragrant, single or double white flowers. Hardy to 20°F (–7°C) or even lower but must have summer heat to thrive and bloom well. Hard to grow in adobe or alkaline desert soils. Give northern or eastern exposure in desert. Useful in containers or raised beds, as hedges, espaliers, low screens, or specimens.

Some of the following varieties are available grafted onto *G. thunbergia* rootstock, which is said to improve their uptake of soil nutrients and result in bigger blooms.

'Aimee' ('First Love'). Upright grower to 4–6 ft. tall and wide, with very large (to 5 in.), very double, roselike blossoms with elegantly spiraled form. Blooms from spring well into summer.

'August Beauty'. Erect growth to 4–6 ft. tall, 3–4 ft. wide. Loosely double, 2–3-in.-wide flowers produced primarily in early summer.

'Belmont'. Vintage estate variety to 5 ft. tall (or taller) and 5 ft. wide, with large leaves and 4-in., roselike blossoms. Bulk of bloom comes from late spring to early summer.

'Chuck Hayes'. Zones 6–9, 12–16, 18–24; H1, H2. Extra-hardy variety; also very heat-tolerant. Grows 4 ft. tall and wide. Double, 3-in. flowers in summer, with heavy rebloom in autumn.

'Frostproof'. Upright grower to 5 ft. tall, 4 ft. wide, with profuse show of 3-in. flowers spring through summer. Buds are undamaged by late frosts.

'Kimura Shikazaki' ('Four Seasons'). Compact growth to 2–3 ft. high and wide. Flowers similar to those of 'Veitchii' but slightly less fragrant. Extremely long bloom season, from spring to fall.

'Kleim's Hardy'. Zones 6–9, 12–16, 18–24; H1, H2. Slowly grows into a mound 2–3 ft. high and wide. Intensely fragrant single, star-shaped flowers are 1–3 in. wide. Blooms profusely in early summer, sporadically through rest of growing season. Reportedly has survived to 0°F (–18°C).

'Miami Supreme'. To 6 ft. tall and wide, with large (4-in. or wider), very double flowers in spring; periodic rebloom through summer.

'Mystery'. Grows 6–8 ft. tall and wide, even larger in time. Pure white, formal, 4–5-in. blossoms are the standard variety for florists' corsages. Blooms from midsummer through early fall—longer if warm weather continues. Intense fragrance carries through the air, even in dry climates. Rangy growth needs pruning to keep it neat and within bounds.

'Radicans' ('Prostrata'). True miniature gardenia. Just 6–12 in. high and 2–3 ft. wide, with inch-long leaves and profuse inch-wide double flowers, mainly in early summer. Good small-scale edging, groundcover, or container plant. 'Radicans Variegata' ('Prostrata Variegata') is similar but somewhat less vigorous, and its leaves are irregularly edged or splashed with creamy yellow and white.

'Summer Snow'. Zones 4–9, 12–16, 18–24; H1, H2. Bushy, full-looking plant to 4–5 ft. tall and wide, with sweet-scented, fully double, 2-in.-wide flowers in profusion from late spring through summer. Very hardy, surviving –5°F (–21°C) and possibly colder.

'Veitchii'. Sometimes sold as "everblooming gardenia." Compact form 3–4½ ft. tall, to 6 ft. wide. The oldest variety, but still the most reliable bloomer. Roselike, pure white blossoms to 2 in. across open from late spring to fall; bloom may continue during a warm winter.

'White Gem'. Dense, compact dwarf to 1–2 ft. high and wide. Rounded, five- or six-petaled, 1½–2-in. single flowers bloom continuously from spring through summer. Sweet, carrying fragrance. Excellent in containers.

G. thunbergia. Zones 16, 17, 21–24; H1, H2. Native to South Africa. Winter-blooming shrub 6–12 ft. tall, 5–10 ft. wide, with angular branches and dark green leaves to 6 in. long. Single, 3–4-in. flowers have a long tube and overlapping, petal-like lobes. Somewhat more tolerant than *G. jasminoides* of cool conditions and less-than-perfect soil, but tender to frost. With age, becomes more vigorous and blooms more profusely. Rough, brownish gray, elliptical fruits to 5 in. long remain on plant for 2 or 3 years.

CARE

Provide fast-draining but moisture-retentive soil conditioned with plenty of organic matter such as peat moss or ground bark. Plant gardenias high (like azaleas and rhododendrons) and avoid crowding from other plants and competing roots. To suppress weeds, mulch plants instead of cultivating around them. Unless water is high in salts (residue from salt in water may burn leaves), mist plants in early morning except during bloom time. Where water contains dissolved salts, irrigate deeply once a month to leach salts from soil. Feed every 3 to 4 weeks during growing season with acid plant food, fish emulsion, or blood meal. Magnesium deficiency can result in yellow leaves with green veins; treat by dissolving one tablespoon of Epsom salts in a gallon of water and soaking the root zone (best done in early spring).

Prune to remove dead wood, straggling branches, and faded flowers.

To control aphids and brown scale, wash plants frequently with jet spray from hose or spray plants with light horticultural oil. In hot weather, spray in the evening—though not if temperatures exceed 90°F (32°C)—then wash off foliage next morning.

Garlic
Liliaceae
PERENNIAL

🌱 **ALL ZONES EXCEPT A1**

☼ **FULL SUN**

💧 **REGULAR WATER**

Garlic

This onion relative, known botanically as *Allium sativum,* is not known in the wild. Seed stores and some mail-order seed houses sell disease-free mother bulbs ("sets") for planting—and some gardeners have had good luck planting bulbs from grocery stores. Plant in fall for early summer harvest. Break up bulbs into individual segments ("cloves") and select largest ones. Plant in rich, well-drained soil, setting cloves pointed end up, 1 in. deep, 3–6 in. apart, in rows 15 in. apart. Harvest when leafy tops fall over; lift out with garden fork rather than pulling. Air-dry bulbs, cut off most of tops and roots, and store in cool, well-ventilated place out of sunlight.

Giant or elephant garlic (*A. ampeloprasum*) has unusually large (fist-size) bulbs and mild garlic flavor. Grow as for regular garlic, but space 8–12 in. apart.

For ornamental relatives, see *Allium*.

Garrya
SILKTASSEL
Garryaceae
EVERGREEN SHRUBS

🌱 **ZONES VARY BY SPECIES**

☼ ◐ **FULL SUN OR PARTIAL SHADE**

💧 **WATER NEEDS VARY BY SPECIES**

🐦 **ATTRACT BIRDS**

Garrya elliptica

West Coast natives prized for their handsome foliage and pendulous male and female catkins, which appear on separate plants in winter; male catkins are longer, more slender, and more decorative than female ones. Both sexes must be present for female plants to produce their grapelike clusters of fruit.

G. elliptica. COAST SILKTASSEL. Zones 4–9, 14–24. Native to Coast Ranges from southern Oregon to Southern California. Densely foliaged plant reaches 8–15 ft. tall and wide in gardens; can be trained as a small tree. Wavy-edged leaves to 3 in. long are dark green above, gray and woolly beneath. Male catkins are greenish yellow, 3–8 in. long; female ones are pale green, rather stubby, 2–4 in. long. Clustered purplish fruits on female plants hang on all summer—even longer if not eaten by birds. Excellent foliage plant; use as screen, informal hedge, or specimen. Needs well-drained soil. For unusually long catkins, plant male varieties 'Evie' (10 in.) or 'James Roof' (1 ft.). Moderate water.

G. fremontii. FREMONT SILKTASSEL. Zones 3–10, 12, 14–17. Native to mountains of Washington, Oregon, California, Arizona. To 9 ft. tall and wide. Leaves are glossy, smooth edged, and lively yellow-green on both upper and lower surfaces. Yellowish or purple catkins; purple or black fruit. Takes heat and cold better than *G. elliptica*. No irrigation needed.

FOR MORE UNTHIRSTY PLANTS, SEE "PLANTS FOR WATERWISE GARDENS," PAGES 74–78.

Gaultheria
Ericaceae
EVERGREEN SHRUBS

🌱 **ZONES VARY BY SPECIES**

◐ **PARTIAL SHADE, EXCEPT AS NOTED**

💧 **REGULAR WATER**

⚬ **FRUITS ARE EDIBLE; ALL OTHER PARTS CAUSE STOMACH UPSET IF INGESTED**

Gaultheria shallon

Grown for attractive foliage, urn-shaped flowers, and colorful, berrylike fruits. They need moist, acid soil rich in organic matter. Smaller kinds are favored for rock gardens and woodland plantings. Larger kinds are good companions for rhododendrons and azaleas.

G. miqueliana. Zones 3–7, 14–17. Native to Japan and the Aleutian Islands. Grows 8–12 in. high and 1½–3 ft. wide; stiff stems hold oval, pointed dark green leaves to 1½ in. long. Small white flowers appear in late spring, followed by white or pink-flushed ½-in. fruits that taste like wintergreen. Lovely alongside a path or in a container. Full sun or partial shade.

G. mucronata (Pernettya mucronata). Zones 4–7, 15–17. From Chile and Argentina. Grows 2–3 ft. high, spreading by underground runners to form a 4-ft.-wide clump. Small leaves are glossy dark green; some turn red or bronzy in winter. Tiny, bell-shaped, white to pink flowers appear in late spring, followed by colorful, long-lasting fruits in white, pink, red, rose, purple, or near black, all with a notable metallic sheen. To get more fruit, grow male and female plants together. Can be invasive; control by trimming roots with a spade. Thin regularly and shear lightly to keep plant compact and attractive. Interesting as an informal low hedge or border plant; also good in tubs or large window boxes. Grows well in partial shade; takes full sun in all but hottest climates.

G. procumbens. WINTERGREEN, CHECKERBERRY, TEABERRY. Zones 1–7, 14–17. Native to eastern North America. Creeping stems send up erect branches to 6 in. high, with oval, 2-in., glossy dark green leaves that turn reddish purple with winter cold. Foliage emits a strong wintergreen odor when bruised. Small pinkish white summer flowers are followed by scarlet berries that smell and taste like wintergreen. Use as groundcover; plant 1 ft. apart. 'Red Baron' has notably large fruits; 'Very Berry' is heavy fruiting.

G. shallon. SALAL. Zones 4–7, 14–17. Native from central California coast north to British Columbia. In good growing conditions, can reach 4–10 ft. tall and slightly wider; in poor, dry soil and full sun, it's a tufted plant only 1–2 ft. high (a good low bank cover). Glossy bright green leaves are nearly round, can reach 4 in. long. Loose, 6-in.-long clusters of white or pinkish flowers on reddish stalks bloom in spring. Edible black fruits resembling large huckleberries follow the blossoms; they're bland flavored, but birds like them. Only neglected plantings need pruning; cut back in spring, remove dead wood, and mulch with organic material such as leaf mold or peat moss.

Cut branches of salal are sold by florists as "lemon leaves." They last a long time in fresh arrangements.

G

Gaura lindheimeri

Onagraceae
PERENNIAL

🌿 **ZONES 2B–24**

☀ **FULL SUN**

💧 **MODERATE WATER**

🦋 **ATTRACTS BUTTERFLIES**

Gaura lindheimeri

Native to Texas and Louisiana. Tough but graceful plants produce airy, upright growth to 3–4 ft. high and wide. Narrow leaves to 3½ in. long are stalkless, growing directly from stems. Branching flower spikes bear many closely set, inch-long white blossoms that open from pink buds. Long bloom period (often from late spring into fall), with only a few flowers opening at a time. Blossoms age to a rosy shade, then drop off cleanly, but seed-bearing spikes should be sheared off occasionally to improve overall appearance, prolong bloom period, and prevent overly enthusiastic self-sowing. Whole plant can be cut nearly to ground in winter for fresh spring growth. Deep taproot makes it drought-tolerant but also difficult to transplant. Needs well-drained soil. Best with some shade in low desert.

'Corrie's Gold'. To 3 ft. high, 2 ft. wide, with leaves broadly edged in gold.

'Karalee Petite Pink'. Just 1–2 ft. high, 1 ft. wide, with pink blooms. Good choice for a deep container.

'Passionate Blush'. Upright and compact, to 1–2 ft. high and wide, with red stems and pink flowers.

'Passionate Rainbow'. Compact grower to 2–2½ ft. high,

half as wide. Leaves are thinly edged in white; flowers are rose-pink.

'Pink Cloud'. Upright growth to 2½–3 ft. tall, 2–3 ft. wide, with red-tinged foliage and plentiful deep pink flowers.

'Pink Fountain'. To 2–3 ft. high, with an especially dense mass of soft pink flowers.

'Siskiyou Pink'. Grows to 2–2½ ft. high and 2–3 ft. wide, with maroon-mottled leaves and deep maroon buds opening to rose-pink flowers. Choice.

'Whirling Butterflies'. Profuse, large white flowers on a 3-ft. plant.

Gazania

Asteraceae
PERENNIALS, SOME GROWN AS ANNUALS

🌿 **ZONES VARY BY SPECIES**

☀◑ **EXPOSURE NEEDS VARY BY SPECIES**

💧 **MODERATE TO REGULAR WATER**

Gazania 'Tiger Eye'

Native to South Africa. Low, clumping or spreading plants grown for colorful daisies over a long season. They tolerate heat as well as seacoast conditions and grow well in most soils.

G. hybrids. Zones 8–24, H1, H2 as perennials; in colder climates, carry plants through winter by taking cuttings in fall as you would for pelargoniums. Dazzling color display during peak bloom in late spring, early summer. In mild-winter climates, they continue to bloom intermittently through the rest of year. Grow in full sun. There are basically two types: clumping and trailing.

Clumping gazanias form a mound of evergreen, typically

lobed leaves that are dark green above with gray and woolly undersides. Flowering stems are 6–10 in. high, bearing 3–4-in.-wide blossoms in colors including yellow, orange, white, and rosy pink; undersides of rays are reddish purple. Blossoms often have dark centers; some have petals striped in contrasting colors. You can also get a mixture of hybrids (as plants or seeds) in different colors. Flowers open on sunny days and close at night and in cloudy weather. Use clumping gazanias in parking strips, as edging along sunny paths, in rock gardens. Good temporary fillers between young shrubs or as replaceable groundcover for relatively level areas not subject to severe erosion.

Named hybrids of special merit include 'Aztec Queen' (multicolored), 'Burgundy', 'Copper King', and 'Fiesta Red'; these are best used in small-scale plantings, though the last is sturdy enough for large expanses. 'Christopher Lloyd' has pink petals with yellow centers surrounded by a bright green band. 'Moonglow' is double-flowered bright yellow of unusual vigor; unlike most gazanias, it has blooms that stay open even on dull days.

Trailing gazanias grow about as tall as clumping types but spread rapidly by long, trailing stems. Foliage is a clean silvery gray; flowers are yellow, white, orange, or bronze. Trailing types are useful on banks as well as level ground. Or grow them at the top of a wall and let them drape over the edge. Attractive in hanging baskets.

G. krebsiana. Zones 3, 7–24. Grows about 6 in. high and 1 ft. wide, with deeply divided leaves that are dark green on top and silvery white beneath; foliage takes on purple hues in cold weather. Rich reddish orange flowers to 3 in. across have a central disk of orange or dark yellow; base of each petal is green and black, with a single white spot. Long bloom season, from spring to fall. May reseed a bit. Full sun.

G. linearis 'Colorado Gold'. Zones 2–9, 14–19. Unlike other gazanias, this is a hardy perennial in much of the

cold-winter West. Grows to 4 in. high, 15 in. wide. Strap-shaped leaves are dark green above, woolly white beneath. Bright yellow flowers to 3 in. wide bloom all summer. Self-sows. Full sun or partial shade.

Geijera parviflora

AUSTRALIAN WILLOW
Rutaceae
EVERGREEN TREE

🌿 **ZONES 8, 9, 12–24**

☀ **FULL SUN**

💧 **LITTLE TO MODERATE WATER**

Geijera parviflora

This fine-textured tree from Australia combines the grace of a willow with the toughness of a eucalyptus. Grows to 25–35 ft. tall and 20 ft. wide, with main branches sweeping up and out, smaller branches hanging down. Common name refers to the narrow, drooping leaves, which give a weeping willow effect. Leaves are olive green and pleasantly aromatic. With age, produces loose clusters of small, fragrant, creamy white flowers in early spring and sometimes in early fall. Trouble-free patio, street, or grove tree. Casts light shade. Grow in well-drained soil. Needs pruning only to correct form (much less pruning than true willow).

Deep, noninvasive roots and minimal litter make Australian willow a fine choice for planting near sidewalks and pathways.

Gelsemium

Gelsemiaceae

EVERGREEN VINES

🌿 **ZONES 4–24**

☀️ ◐ **FULL SUN OR PARTIAL SHADE**

💧💧 💧💧 **WATER NEEDS VARY BY SPECIES**

⚜️ **ALL PARTS ARE POISONOUS IF INGESTED**

Gelsemium sempervirens

Native to southeastern U.S. Shrubby, twining vines to about 20 ft., with pairs of shiny, light green leaves borne on long branches that look almost like streamers. Flowers are bright yellow trumpets. On a trellis or fence, these vines cascade and swing in the wind; trained against a house wall, they make a delicate green curtain of branches. Thin stems will not damage their support. If they become top-heavy, cut them back to stimulate fresh new growth. Also used as ground-covers, especially nice tumbling down banks; keep trimmed to 3 ft. high. In full sun, the plants are more shrubby and florifer-ous; in partial shade, they grow longer and bloom a bit less.

G. rankinii. SWAMP JESSA-MINE. Scentless, inch-wide flowers bloom in spring and fall. Needs regular to ample water; tolerates boggy soil.

G. sempervirens. CARO-LINA JESSAMINE. Fragrant, 1½-in.-long flowers appear in late winter, early spring, with occasional sporadic bloom in autumn. Needs regular water in youth but is fairly drought-tolerant once established. 'Pride of Augusta' ('Plena') is a double-flowered form.

Genista

BROOM

Papilionaceae

DECIDUOUS AND EVERGREEN SHRUBS

🌿 **ZONES VARY BY SPECIES**

☀️ **FULL SUN**

💧 💧 **LITTLE TO MODERATE WATER**

Genista

Grown for their profuse yellow sweet pea–shaped blooms. Leaves are often small and short-lived, but green branches give deciduous species an ever-green look. Smaller kinds are attractive on banks. Need good drainage; tolerate rocky or infer-tile soil. Less aggressive than other brooms (see *Cytisus*); the species listed here are not invasive.

G. aetnensis. MT. ETNA BROOM. Deciduous. Zones 5–9, 14–24. From Sardinia and Sic-ily. Large shrub or small tree to 18 ft. or more, with graceful arching, weeping green branch-lets, bare or with a very few tiny leaves during growing season. Branches are covered with fra-grant golden yellow blooms in summer. Hardy to 5°F (–15°C).

G. hispanica. SPANISH BROOM. Deciduous. Zones 4–22. Native to southwestern Europe. Mass of spiny stems to 1–2 ft. high, at least 5 ft. wide. Only the flowering stems are set with tiny leaves. Clus-ters of golden yellow blooms appear at stem tips in spring.

G. lydia. Nearly leafless. Zones 2b–6, 14–17. From the eastern Balkans and western Asia. Grows slowly to 1–2 ft. high and 3–4 ft. wide; slender, low-arching branches make it a good groundcover. Bears pro-fuse bright yellow blossoms at tips of shoots in spring.

G. pilosa. Deciduous. Zones 2b–22. From western and central Europe. Fairly fast-growing prostrate shrub, ulti-mately to 1–1½ ft. tall with 7-ft. spread. Intricately branched gray-green twigs bear small, roundish leaves and are cov-ered with bright yellow blooms in spring. 'Vancouver Gold' has golden yellow blooms. 'Gold Flash' is tough and compact, reaching just 6–12 in. high and 3 ft. wide.

G. sagittalis. Leafless. Zones 2–22. From southern and central Europe. Spreads quickly to 3 ft. wide and just 6 in. high. Upright, flattened bright green branchlets make the plant look evergreen. Stems are topped by golden blooms in late spring or early summer.

G. tinctoria. DYER'S GREENWEED. Deciduous. Zones 2–24. Variable, upright grower to 2–3 ft. high and wide, with narrow leaves to 2 in. long. Upright spikes of golden yellow flowers appear in late spring or early summer. 'Royal Gold' is a compact, heavy-blooming selection.

Gentiana

GENTIAN

Gentianaceae

PERENNIALS

🌿 **ZONES 2–6, 14–17, EXCEPT AS NOTED**

☀️ ◐ **FULL SUN IN COOLER CLIMATES ONLY**

💧 **REGULAR WATER**

Gentiana asclepiadea

Gentians are prized for their tubular flowers in intense blue shades. Many are considered difficult to grow, but the following need little more than consistent moisture and humus-rich soil with excellent drainage. Some require lime-free soil, as noted. Well worth extra care, as they produce some of the richest blues in the garden.

G. acaulis. From the moun-tains of central and southern Europe. Forms a mat 3–4 in. high, 1 ft. wide, of inch-long, glossy dark green leaves. In summer, trumpet-shaped flow-ers to 2 in. long are held aloft on short stems. Blooms are deep, rich blue, with green spots inside. Blooms better if divided every couple of years in spring.

G. asclepiadea. WILLOW GENTIAN. Native to Europe and western Asia. Arching, large-leafed stems form a clump 2–3 ft. high and 1½ ft. wide. In late summer and early fall, rich, deep blue, 1½-in., trumpet-shaped flowers open into stars atop the stems and among the upper leaves. Thrives in rich, neutral to acidic soil; makes a choice companion for ferns. Partial shade.

G. cruciata. CROSS GEN-TIAN. From Europe, Turkey, and Siberia. Forms a foot-wide rosette of thick, glossy, lance-shaped leaves up to 8 in. long. Leafy stalks rise 8–16 in. tall, with clusters of dark blue, inch-long flowers at stem tips and among upper leaves. Not picky about soil. Blooms in summer and early fall.

G. septemfida. Zones A1–A3; 1–6, 14–17. From Turkey, Iran to central Asia. Arching or sprawling stems 9–18 in. long form a spreading leafy mass about 8 in. high, 1 ft. wide. Clusters of 2-in., dark purplish blue flowers appear in late sum-mer. *G. s. lagodechiana*, the form commonly sold, is similar but has more widely spaced flowers.

G. sino-ornata. From China and Tibet. Bright green foliage rosette to 7 in. high and some-what wider sends out trailing stems that end in 2-in. flowers of brightest blue in early fall. Fairly easy to grow in acidic soil in half shade. Mulch with gravel.

FOR MORE ON PERENNIALS, SEE "GROW: PERENNIALS," PAGES 686–687.

G

Geranium

CRANESBILL

Geraniaceae

PERENNIALS

✂ ZONES VARY BY SPECIES

☀ ◐ AFTERNOON SHADE IN HOTTEST CLIMATES

💧 REGULAR WATER, EXCEPT AS NOTED

Geranium 'Rozanne'

The bright-flowered, fleshy-leafed plant often called geranium actually belongs to the genus *Pelargonium*. Considered here are true geraniums, sometimes called hardy geraniums, as most can take considerable cold. Many bloom over a long period, with flowers held singly or in few-flowered clusters. Colors include blue, purple, magenta, bluish rose, and pink, as well as white. Beaklike fruit that follows the flowers accounts for the common name "cranesbill." The leaves are roundish or kidney-shaped, lobed or deeply cut; plants may be upright and mounding or trailing and scrambling. Good along paths, in perennial borders, or in rock gardens; some are useful as groundcovers. A few shrubby species are good for holding slopes.

Best climates for most geraniums are cool- and mild-summer regions, where plants can grow in full sun or light shade. In hot-summer areas, provide afternoon shade. South African species are less cold-hardy but are more tolerant of heat and afternoon sun. All types appreciate moist, well-drained soil.

Some geraniums benefit from being cut back after flowering or in the fall; these are noted in text. Clumps of most types can be left in place for many years before they decline due to crowding; at that point, divide in early spring. Increase by transplanting rooted portions from a clump's edge; or take cuttings. Many produce lots of seedlings, and some can become naturalized pests.

G. 'Ann Folkard'. Zones 2b–9, 14–24. Mounding, billowing plant (1½ ft. high, to 5 ft. wide) with chartreuse leaves that age to light green. Saucer-shaped, 1½-in.-wide blossoms are rich magenta-purple suffused with pink and blue, centered and veined in black. Blooms from spring into fall. Effective planted at edge of patio and sprawling onto it.

G. 'Brookside'. Zones 2b–9, 14–24. Hybrid between *G. pratense* and a purple form of *G. clarkei*. To 2½ ft. high and as wide, with deeply serrated, 3-in.-wide leaves. Plant is covered from late spring into summer with bowl-shaped flowers to 2 in. across. Long-lasting blooms are rich, deep blue with pale centers and pink veins. Its seedling 'Orion' is similar, but with larger flowers (2½ in. across) of an even richer blue. Both can be cut back after flowering for repeat bloom.

G. × cantabrigiense. Zones 1–24. Excellent groundcover, 6–8 in. high, spreading slowly but widely. Pleasantly scented, dark green leaves up to 2½ in. wide are deeply cut with multiple lobes. Long-lasting flowers are about 1 in. across. Plants may be sheared in late fall for fresh spring growth. Moderate to regular water. Popular 'Biokovo' has white blooms with a pink blush. 'St. Ola' is similar but more vigorous, with creamy white blooms that age to light rusty pink. Blossoms of 'Cambridge' and 'Karmina' are bright bluish pink, and those of 'Westray' are dark pinkish red. All bloom from early spring well into summer.

G. cinereum. Zones 1–24, but very short-lived where summers are hot. From the Pyrenees. Forms wide, 8–12-in.-high mats composed of soft gray-green, deeply cut leaves. In early to midsummer, slender, trailing stems bear many cupped flowers to 1½ in. wide; blooms are pale pink with dark veins.

'Ballerina' is pinkish lilac with dark veins and a wine-colored center; continues blooming into fall. The slightly larger 'Laurence Flatman' has light lavender blossoms with reddish center blotches between red veins. 'Purple Pillow' has bright purple flowers with dark purple veins.

G. dalmaticum. Zones 1–24. From the Balkans. Low (4–5 in.) carpeting plant, creeping slowly by rhizomes to 2 ft. or wider. Glossy, deeply cut dark green leaves contrast beautifully with the soft pink, 1-in. flowers that appear in late spring. Leaves turn orange to red in fall. Good among pavers or spilling over a rock wall.

G. endressii. Zones 1–9, 14–24. From southern Europe to southwest Asia. Bushy, mounding plant to 1½ ft. high, spreading by rhizomes to 2 ft. or wider. Light green leaves are finely cut. Blossoms are rose-pink with a silvery sheen, about 1 in. across. Blooms late spring into fall in mild-summer areas; peters out in early summer where summers are hot. Evergreen in mild climates.

G. 'Frances Grate' ('Silver Sugar Plum'). Zones 14–24. Hybrid between *G. incanum* and *G. robustum*. Billowy, scrambling plant 1½ ft. high by 5 ft. or wider. Finely cut leaves are gray-green above, silvery beneath. Saucer-shaped lilac-mauve flowers to 1 in. across, early spring through fall. Takes hot afternoon sun. Seeds profusely and can be invasive; seedlings vary widely.

G. harveyi. Zones 5–9, 14–24. From South Africa. Woody-based mound to 8 in. high by 2 ft. or wider. Small, deeply lobed, silky leaves are gray-green above, silvery underneath. Magenta, 1¼-in.-wide flowers from late spring through fall. Tolerates hot sun. Good on slopes or trailing among rocks.

G. himalayense (G. grandiflorum). Zones 1–24. Himalayan native to 1½ ft. high, spreading by rhizomes to about 2 ft. wide. Leaves are roundish, with prominent veins and five broad, deeply divided lobes. Blooms from late spring into summer; foot-tall stems bear clusters of large (to 2½ in. wide) blue flowers with reddish veins and purple eye. Excellent

deciduous small-scale bulb cover; plant 1–1½ ft. apart. 'Gravetye' is a dependable selection typical of the species. 'Baby Blue' has larger light blue flowers. 'Plenum' ('Birch Double') is less vigorous, with double light lavender blossoms.

G. incanum. Zones 14–24. From South Africa. To 6–10 in. high, spreading fast to form a 2-ft.-wide cushion of finely cut leaves. Inch-wide light magenta flowers appear from spring to fall. Cut to ground every other year to keep neat. Endures heat and drought better than most geraniums, but needs some summer water. Self-seeds profusely and can be invasive.

G. 'Johnson's Blue'. Zones A2, A3; 2–9, 14–24. Hybrid resembling its *G. himalayense* parent, but leaf divisions are narrower. Mounds 1½–2 ft. wide and spreads by rhizomes; excellent summer groundcover. Abundant 2-in., blue-violet flowers in loose clusters from spring to fall.

G. macrorrhizum. Zones 1–24. From southern Europe. To 8–10 in. high, spreading fast by underground rootstocks and fleshy rhizomes that root on soil surface. Leaves have a strong, musky fragrance and attractive autumn coloring ranging from dull yellow to orange and scarlet. Inch-wide flowers in white, pink, or magenta appear late spring through early summer, with some repeat in fall. Good groundcover for small areas, though it can overwhelm smaller plants. Grows well in fairly dry shade. 'Album' is white with a blush of pale pink. 'Bevan's Variety' has vibrant combination of deep magenta petals and red sepals. 'Ingwersen's Variety' has soft bluish pink flowers, long blooming season.

G. maculatum. WILD CRANESBILL, SPOTTED CRANESBILL. Zones 1–24. Native to moist woodlands and meadows of eastern North America; the only commonly cultivated U.S. native cranesbill. To 1½ ft. high, 2 ft. wide, with deeply divided leaves. Profuse lilac-pink, 1–1½-in. flowers in spring to early summer. 'Album' has white blossoms. Leaves of 'Elizabeth Ann' and 'Espresso' are dark chocolate brown. All

G

may be cut back after bloom to encourage fresh foliage and flowers.

G. maderense. Zones 14–24. Dramatic native of Madeira likes moist conditions, shade. Largest of all geranium leaves (to 2 ft. long)—overlapping, glossy, deeply divided, shaped like giant snowflakes. Reddish brown leafstalks help buttress the 3–4-ft. "trunk" supporting hundreds of densely packed, fuzzy buds and magenta-eyed deep pink blossoms to 1½ in. wide. Blooms early spring through midsummer. Biennial or short-lived perennial; dies after blooming but spawns many seedlings.

G. × magnificum. Zones 1–9, 14–24. Vigorous sterile hybrid that spreads steadily, forming broad clumps 2–2½ ft. high and wide. Rounded, quilted, 3-in. leaves are divided into broad segments. Profuse 2-in. violet blossoms heavily veined in deep purple; blooms late spring, early summer.

G. × oxonianum. Zones 2–9, 14–24. Among the best selections of this hybrid group is 'Claridge Druce', which forms a vigorous clump 2–3 ft. high, 3 ft. wide. Rounded leaves are deeply cut. Funnel-shaped, broad-petaled, 1½-in., cool pink flowers with purplish veins bloom late spring to summer. Good large-scale groundcover but can overwhelm adjacent plants. Self-sows profusely; seedlings resemble parent, but blossoms often have narrower petals. Cut back hard after flowering to encourage fresh foliage and discourage reseeding. 'Wargrave Pink' is similar but a little less vigorous, with glossy warm pink blossoms that resemble those of *G. endressii* (one of the parents). 'Winscombe' has flowers that open pale pink and turn deep pink with age, giving an overall multicolored effect.

G. palmatum (G. anemonifolium). Zones 4–9, 14–24. From Madeira; similar to the other giant from that island, *G. maderense*. Plants reach 4 ft. tall and wide, with huge, ferny leaves (to 14 in. across) that are dark green, turning reddish in sun. Purplish pink 1½-in.-wide flowers with deep crimson centers appear in great numbers in late spring to

summer. Grows best in a sunny, sheltered spot. Will reseed.

G. 'Patricia'. Zones 2–9, 14–24. This hybrid between *G. endressii* and *G. psilostemon* is durable and easy to grow. Plants reach 2½ ft. high and 3 ft. wide, with deeply lobed and veined leaves. Eye-catching flowers, to 1½ in. wide, are a warm reddish magenta with deep burgundy veins and centers. Long bloom period, from spring to late summer. Cut back after first flush of bloom for fresh growth and flowers.

G. phaeum. MOURNING WIDOW, DUSKY CRANESBILL. Zones 2b–9, 14–24. Shade-loving native of southern and central European mountains. To 2 ft. high, 1½ ft. wide. Leaves are shallowly cut into tooth-edged lobes, often with dark markings. Clusters of dusky purple or maroon blossoms rise above foliage mound from spring to fall. Cut back flowering stems after bloom to neaten appearance and encourage rebloom. 'Album' has blooms of pure white. 'Lily Lovell' has purplish maroon blooms with a white eye. Leaves of 'Margaret Wilson' are heavily streaked

with creamy yellow; flowers are light purple. 'Samobor' has light maroon flowers and leaves with distinctive maroon markings.

G. 'Philippe Vapelle'. Zones 3–9, 14–24. Tight clump 1 ft. high and 1½ ft. wide. Medium green, rounded leaves are quilted, shallowly cut into scalloped lobes. Violet-blue flowers with darker veins have deeply notched petals. Blooms spring through midsummer.

G. 'Pink Spice'. Zones 3b–9, 14–24. Compact mound 8–10 in. high, to 1 ft. wide. Reddish bronze leaves form a dark background for 1-in.-wide pink blossoms on long, trailing stems. Blooms from late spring through fall. Foliage color is best with at least half-day direct sun.

G. pratense. MEADOW CRANESBILL. Zones 2–7, 14–24. Native from Ireland to Siberia and Japan. Forms a clump to 2 ft. high, 3 ft. wide. Hairy, deeply cut leaves to 6 in. wide are held on upright stalks. Flowers about 1 in. wide, typically blue with reddish veins; bloom from spring through summer. Self-seeds profusely; cut to ground when flowers fade to prevent seedlings and encourage

CLOCKWISE FROM TOP LEFT: *Geranium* 'Johnson's Blue'; *G. maderense*; *G. × cantabrigiense*

rebloom. 'Midnight Reiter' is dramatic, with dark purple leaves and rich blue blooms. 'Mrs. Kendall Clark' has pale blue flowers with lighter veins. 'Plenum Caeruleum' has double flowers of lavender-blue. 'Striatum' has white blossoms irregularly splashed, streaked, or spotted with violet-blue.

G. psilostemon (G. armenum). Zones 2b–9, 14–24. Native to Armenia and Turkey. Large clump—to 4 ft. tall and wide—with big, deeply cut leaves and an early summer show of 1–1½-in. magenta flowers with black centers and veins. Leaves turn brilliant flame color in fall.

G. renardii. Zones 2b–9, 14–24. From the Caucasus. Compact grower to 1 ft. high and wide, with velvety gray-green leaves. Early to midsummer flowers are white with violet veining; overall effect is pearly gray. May be cut back hard in fall. Blooms of 'Tcschelda' are pale violet with dark purple veins.

»

G. × riversleaianum.
Zones 2b–9, 14–24. Forms
foot-high, wide-spreading mat
of silky, silvery green leaves.
Continuous show of rounded,
¾-in. blossoms on long, trailing
stems from late spring through
fall. 'Mavis Simpson' has soft,
shell pink blossoms with dark
veins. 'Russell Prichard' is brilliant magenta-rose.

G. robustum. Zones 14–24.
Shrubby species from South
Africa grows 3 ft. high, 4 ft.
wide. Finely divided leaves are
silky gray-green above, silvery
below. Summer flowers 1 in.
across, light purple with a white
eye. Survives with little water.
Use on slopes with other drought-
tolerant plants like lavender
(*Lavandula*) and rockrose (*Cistus*). Self-sows profusely; cut
back fairly hard after bloom to
freshen plant and keep seedlings in check.

G. 'Rozanne'. Zones 2–11,
14–24. This naturally occurring
hybrid between *G. himalayense*
and *G. wallichianum* 'Buxton's
Variety' is very popular and
easy to grow. Plants reach 1½–
2 ft. high and spread a little
wider, forming a lush mound of
deeply lobed, dark green leaves;
foliage takes on attractive red
tones in the fall. Stunning flowers, to 2½ in. wide, are rich
violet-blue with a large white
eye. Blooms all summer and
into autumn, doing especially
well in warm, sunny spots. For
freshest spring growth, cut back
plants in late fall.

G. 'Salome'. Zones 4–6,
14–17. A cross between two
Himalayan species. This low,
trailing plant grows about 1 ft.
high and 3–4 ft. wide. Leaves
emerge golden green and age
to a fresh light green. Foliage is
a lovely foil for the 1¼-in. blossoms of pale violet-pink, centered and veined with deepest
violet. Blooms midsummer to
late fall; cut back after bloom
period to freshen plants. Good
choice for cooler parts of Pacific
Northwest; struggles in heat.

G. sanguineum. BLOODY
CRANESBILL. Zones A2, A3;
1–9, 14–24. Native from western Europe to the Caucasus
and Turkey. Forms dense clump
8–18 in. high, spreading by rhizomes to 2½ ft. or wider. Dark
green leaves are deeply divided;
turn blood red in fall. Typical

forms have deep purple to
almost crimson flowers 1½ in.
wide; bloom late spring well into
summer and will rebloom if cut
to ground. Good 1–1½-ft.-tall
selections include white 'Album';
'John Elsley', pink with deeper
pink veins; reddish purple 'Max
Frei'; and 'New Hampshire',
reddish magenta petals with
magenta veins. Vision, a variable seed-grown strain, has
magenta flowers with dark purple veins.

G. s. striatum is a compact
form only 5–6 in. high. It bears
light pink flowers heavily veined
with red (its seedlings may vary
somewhat) and makes an excellent rock-garden or foreground
plant.

G. wallichianum. Zones
2–9, 14–24. Himalayan native
of low, sprawling or trailing but
not rooting habit, 1 ft. high and
3 ft. wide. Blooms from early
summer until autumn, bearing
1–1½-in.-wide flowers in lilac or
purplish blue with a white eye.
'Buxton's Variety' has pure blue
flowers with large white eye and
striking black stamens.

G. wlassovianum. Zones
A2, A3; 1–7. Native to Siberia,
Mongolia, and northeastern
China. Clump-forming plant to
1½–2 ft. high and wide. Velvety,
2-in., divided leaves emerge
pinkish bronze, mature to dusky
green tinged with brown, and
then turn cinnamon brown in
fall. Reddish purple, 1¼-in.-wide
flowers with small white eye and
deep violet veins. Blooms midsummer to early fall.

Several geraniums
thrive in one of the
most challenging
garden conditions:
dryish shade. Try *G.
endressii, G. macror-
rhizum, G. phaeum,*
or (especially good
for a large area,
such as beneath
a tree, where little
else will grow)
G. × oxonianum
'Claridge Druce'.

Gerbera jamesonii

TRANSVAAL DAISY
Asteraceae
PERENNIAL OFTEN GROWN AS ANNUAL

✿ **ZONES 8, 9, 12–24; H1, H2; ANYWHERE AS ANNUAL**

☼ ◖ **PARTIAL SHADE IN HOTTEST CLIMATES**

💧 **REGULAR WATER**

Gerbera jamesonii
'Revolution Orange'

This South African native is
among the most elegant and
sophisticated of daisies. Clump
of tongue-shaped, lobed, 10-in.-
long leaves sends up slim yet
sturdy stems to 1½ ft. high,
each bearing one slender-
petaled, 4–5-in. daisy. Colors
are pure, unshaded, and glowing; include cream through yellow to coral, orange, flame, and
red. Basic flower has single ring
of rays surrounding prominent
central disk. Hybrid forms may
have two rows of long rays, or
an outer ring of long rays and a
central ring of short, tufted
ones; or they may be fully double, with a fluffy look. Many
strains are sold, including dwarf
types only 7 in. high. As perennial, can bloom anytime of year,
with peaks in early summer and
late fall. Beyond hardiness
range, treat as summer annual.
In Zones 12 and 13, best as
winter annual (may last longer
during a cool spring).

CARE

Needs organically enriched soil
with excellent drainage (if soil
drains poorly, grow in raised bed).
Plant 2 ft. apart; to avoid rot,
keep root crown slightly above
soil level. Protect from snails
and slugs. Water deeply and let

soil become nearly dry before
watering again. Fertilize monthly
for best flowering. Divide (in
late winter) only when clump is
crowded and flowering declines.
When cutting blooms for arrangements, slit the bottom inch of
stem before placing in water.

Geum

AVENS
Rosaceae
PERENNIALS

✿ **ZONES 2–24, EXCEPT AS NOTED**

☼ ◖ **PARTIAL SHADE IN HOTTEST CLIMATES**

💧 **REGULAR WATER**

🦋 **ATTRACT BUTTERFLIES**

Geum chiloense
'Lady Stratheden'

Lovely roselike flowers in bright
orange, yellow, or red keep coming from spring to late summer
if faded blooms are removed.
Foliage is handsome too, with
leaves divided into many leaflets; evergreen except in coldest winters. Good in borders
and for cut flowers. Provide
good drainage.

G. chiloense. Native to
Chile. Foliage mounds to 15 in.
high, 2 ft. wide. Leafy stems to
2 ft. high carry flowers about
1½ in. across. Among the many
varieties are double golden yellow 'Lady Stratheden'; semidouble scarlet 'Mrs. J. Bradshaw';
and single warm orange 'Totally
Tangerine'. Hybrids include
'Alabama Slammer', with semidouble, deep orange-red-tipped
blooms, and 'Georgenberg',
with light yellow-orange blooms.

G. coccineum. From the
Balkans, Asia Minor. To 12–20 in.
high and wide, with coarsely
divided foliage and brick red,
1½-in. flowers. 'Borisii' is

compact at 1 ft. high and wide, with bright orange-red flowers. 'Cooky' and 'Werner Arends' are also compact, both with blooms of bright orange. 'Red Wings', to 28 in. high and broad, has semidouble scarlet flowers.

G. 'Starker's Magnificum'. To 1½ ft. high and wide, with double flowers in tangerine orange over a long season.

G. triflorum. PRAIRIE SMOKE, OLD MAN'S WHISKERS. Zones 1–3. From North America. Foot-wide leafy mound produces stems to 20 in. high, each bearing clusters of nodding maroon flowers. Seeds have long, feathery gray "tails."

Gilia
Polemoniaceae
ANNUALS

🌡 **ZONES 1–24**

☀ **FULL SUN**

◐ ◑ **LITTLE TO MODERATE WATER**

🐝 **ATTRACT BUTTERFLIES, BEES**

Gilia capitata

Easy-to-grow Western natives with finely cut leaves and flowers in shades of blue from late spring to early fall. In fall or early spring, sow seeds in well-drained soil where plants are to grow. Thin seedlings to avoid crowding. Fine companions for California poppy (*Eschscholzia californica*). For plants formerly known as *G. aggregata* and *G. rubra*, see *Ipomopsis*.

G. capitata. BLUE THIMBLE FLOWER, GLOBE GILIA. Native from British Columbia to California. Grows 6–24 in. high, about 9 in. wide. Pale violet-blue to blue flowers with blue pollen are carried in dense clusters that look like pincushions.

G. tricolor. BIRD'S EYES. Native to California. Grows to 4–18 in. high, about 9 in. wide. Subtly beautiful flowers, carried singly or in clusters, are ½ in. wide or wider, with pale to deep violet with yellow throat spotted purple; blue pollen.

Ginkgo biloba
MAIDENHAIR TREE
Ginkgoaceae
DECIDUOUS TREE

🌡 **ZONES A3; 1–10, 12, 14–24**

☀ **FULL SUN**

◐ ◑ **MODERATE TO REGULAR WATER**

Ginkgo biloba

Ancient survivor from prehistoric times, when it grew worldwide; now believed to be native to only two small areas in China. Graceful tree, attractive in any season, especially in fall when leathery light green leaves of spring and summer suddenly turn golden yellow. Leaves hang on for a time, then drop quickly and cleanly to make a golden carpet where they fall. Related to conifers but differs in having broad (up to 4 in. wide), fan-shaped leaves rather than needlelike foliage. In shape and veining, leaves resemble leaflets of maidenhair fern, hence the tree's common name. Can grow to 70–100 ft. tall, but most mature trees top out at 35–50 ft.

Good tree for street or lawn. Extremely long-lived and not usually bothered by insects or diseases. Very tolerant of air pollution, heat, and acid or alkaline conditions. Resistant to oak root fungus. Plant male trees (grafted or grown from cuttings of male plants); female trees produce messy, fleshy,

ill-smelling fruit in quantity. The following recommended varieties are male. 'Autumn Gold' is an upright grower to 45 ft., eventually spreading to about 35 ft. 'Golden Colonnade' is rather narrow, at 45 ft. tall and 25 ft. wide. 'Presidential Gold' is broadly oval, reaching 50 ft. tall and 40 ft. wide. 'Princeton Sentry' forms a narrow pyramid 50 ft. tall and just 15–20 ft. wide. 'Saratoga' resembles 'Autumn Gold', with a distinct central leader.

CARE

Plant in deep, loose, well-drained soil. Be sure nursery plants are not rootbound. Water young trees regularly until they reach about 20 ft. tall, then cut back to occasional irrigation. On young trees, cut back any awkward branches and vertical shoots growing parallel to central leader. Older trees need minimal pruning; just remove weak, broken, or dead branches.

Gladiolus
Iridaceae
PERENNIALS FROM CORMS

🌡 **ZONES 4–9, 12–24; H1; EXCEPT AS NOTED; OR DIG AND STORE**

☀ **FULL SUN**

◑ **REGULAR WATER DURING GROWTH AND BLOOM**

🐦 **ATTRACT HUMMINGBIRDS**

Gladiolus × *hortulanus*
'Mon Amour'

Gladiolus is Latin for "small sword," a reference to the leaf shape of plants in this genus that are grown for their colorful blooms. Tubular, often flaring or ruffled flowers in an extremely wide color range line a slender

G

How to Grow Gladiolus

PLANTING TIME Plant corms of baby gladiolus in fall or early spring for flowers in late spring. Plant all others from mid-winter (in mildest regions) into spring, after soil has warmed. Grandiflora hybrids will flower about 100 days after planting; the smaller hybrids and species will bloom in about 80 days. Ideal planting times are from January through March in Zones 7–9, 14–24, H1; April through June in Zones 4–6; and November through January in Zones 12, 13.

PLANTING Shop for corms that are high crowned for their width; broad, flat ones are older and less vigorous. Plant in rich, sandy loam. Set corms about four times deeper than their height, somewhat more shallowly in heavier soils. Space big corms 6 in. apart, smaller ones 4 in. apart. You can cut flower spikes when lowest buds begin to open, but keep at least four leaves on plants to build up corms.

POST-BLOOM CARE After blossoms fade, trim off stems beneath lowest flower—uncut stems will set seeds, diverting energy from food storage. Corms can be left in the ground from year to year where plants are perennial (dig, divide, and replant when performance declines). Grandiflora hybrids are usually dug and stored yearly even in mild-winter regions. In colder areas, dig after foliage yellows completely (in rainy areas, dig while leaves are still green to avoid botrytis infection). Dry corms on a flat surface in a dark, dry area for 2 to 3 weeks; then store over winter in a single layer in flats or ventilated trays in a cool place (40°F to 50°F/4°C to 10°C).

G

spike, opening from the bottom to the top of the spike. Superb cut flowers. Good in borders or beds behind mounding plants that cover lower parts of stems, or in large containers with low annuals at base.

Baby gladiolus. Zones 4–9, 12–24, H1 for most; also Zones 2b and 3 for winter-hardy types. These hybrids sport flaring blooms to about 3 in. across in short, loose spikes on 1½-ft. stems. Blooms come in late spring and may be white, pink, red, or lilac, either solid or blotched with contrasting color. When left in the ground, these glads will form large clumps.

G. communis byzantinus (G. byzantinus). BYZANTINE GLADIOLUS. From southern Europe. Summer bloom of up to 12 mainly maroon, sometimes reddish or coppery, 1–3-in. flowers on stems to 3 ft. tall.

Grandiflora hybrids. GARDEN GLADIOLUS. The best-known glads, producing spikes that reach 3–6 ft. tall, depending on variety and growing conditions. Late spring and summer flowers (up to 30 per spike) are widely flaring, up to 8 in. across, available in a rainbow range of colors and white. Diminutive selections are often called miniature gladiolus; these grow 3–4 ft. tall, stand upright without staking, and bear up to 18 flowers per spike.

G. murielae (G. callianthus, Acidanthera bicolor). ABYSSINIAN SWORD LILY. Native to Africa. In late summer and fall, each 2–3-ft. stem bears up to ten 3-in.-wide, fragrant, creamy white flowers marked with chocolate brown.

Primulinus and butterfly hybrids. These summer bloomers derive in part from an African species with hooded (rather than funnel-shaped), primrose yellow flowers. Named varieties grow 3–4 ft. tall, each spike carrying up to 18 widely spaced blossoms in a wide range of colors. Group known as butterfly gladiolus has 2–3-ft. stems bearing more closely spaced blossoms; distinct throat markings or blotches of contrasting color give butterfly appearance.

G. tristis. Native to South Africa. Dainty species with 3-in. flowers on slender, 1½-ft.

stems in summer. Creamy to yellowish white blossoms are veined with purple, fragrant at night. *G. t. concolor* has soft yellow to nearly white flowers.

Glebionis

Asteraceae
ANNUALS

🗡 **ZONES 1–24; H1, H2**
☼ **FULL SUN**
💧 **MODERATE WATER**

Glebionis coronaria

Small genus of plants formerly included in *Chrysanthemum*. The fast-growing species listed here have ferny foliage and colorful daisy blooms. Sow seeds in spring, either in pots or in open ground. In mild-winter areas, *G. carinatum* can be sown in autumn for winter and spring bloom.

G. carinatum (Chrysanthemum carinatum). TRICOLOR DAISY, PAINTED DAISY. This Moroccan native grows wild in sand dunes along parts of the Southern California coast. Grows 1–3 ft. high and 3 ft. wide, with deeply cut, bright green leaves. Showy bloom in summer and fall: 2-in. single daisies in purple, orange, scarlet, salmon, rose, yellow, or white, with contrasting bands around a dark center. Long-lasting cut flowers. Foliage may cause skin irritation or allergic reaction.

Court Jesters is an excellent strain. In 'German Flag', scarlet rays and a golden yellow band surround the central disk. Merry mix has multicolored bull's-eye flowers on 2–3-ft.-high plants. Summer Festival mix includes the full color range; single, semi-double, and double blooms.

G. coronaria (Chrysanthemum coronarium). CROWN DAISY. Mediterranean native; sometimes seen naturalized on roadsides. To 2½ ft. high and 1½ ft. wide, with coarsely cut light green leaves and yellow daisies in spring and summer. The variety usually still listed as *C. c. spatiosum* is the vegetable known as shungiku, chop-suey greens, or edible chrysanthemum; young leaves can be lightly steamed or added to soups.

Glechoma hederacea 'Variegata'

VARIEGATED GROUND IVY
Lamiaceae
PERENNIAL

🗡 **ZONES A2, A3; 1–10, 14–24**
☼ ◐ ● **SUN OR SHADE**
💧 **REGULAR WATER**

Glechoma hederacea 'Variegata'

Variegated selection of a species from Europe that has naturalized in much of North America. Neat pairs of round, scallop-edged leaves to 1½ in. across are spaced along the trailing stems. Foliage is bright green and irregularly edged with white. Small, trumpet-shaped blue flowers in spring and summer are not showy. Plant grows to 3 in. high, with stems spreading quickly to at least 2½ ft., rooting at joints. Use as a small-scale groundcover (tolerates foot traffic) or in hanging baskets or window boxes. If plants become shabby, mow or cut back hard in early spring. Can become a serious pest in lawns.

Gleditsia triacanthos

HONEY LOCUST
Caesalpiniaceae
DECIDUOUS TREE

🗡 **ZONES 1–16, 18–20**
☼ **FULL SUN**
💧● **MODERATE TO REGULAR WATER**

Gleditsia triacanthos

Native to central and eastern North America, this tough but delicately foliaged tree is especially nice planted as specimen. Grows quickly to 35–70 ft. tall and 25–35 ft. wide, with upright trunk and spreading, arching branches. Bright green, fernlike leaves to 10 in. long are divided into many oval leaflets. Late to leaf out; leaves turn yellow before dropping early in fall. Inconspicuous flowers are followed by seedpods to 1½ ft. long.

Foliage casts filtered shade, allowing growth of lawn or other plants beneath canopy. Small leaflets dry up and filter into grass, decreasing raking chores. Roots of old plants will heave adjacent pavement. Tolerant of acid or alkaline conditions, salt, drought, cold, heat, wind, and pollution. Does best in areas with sharply defined winters, hot summers.

Trunks and branches of the species are formidably thorny, and its pods make a mess. These selections of its thornless form *G. t. inermis* are better choices for gardens, most having few or no pods.

'Halka'. Fast growing. Forms sturdy trunk early, has strong horizontal branching pattern. Can bear a heavy crop of seedpods.

'Imperial'. Tall, spreading, symmetrical tree to about 35 ft. More densely foliaged than other forms; gives heavier shade.

'Rubylace'. Deep red new growth turns bronzy green in summer and reddish in fall. Prune to correct irregular growth. Subject to wind breakage.

'Skyline'. Symmetrical and broadly pyramidal. Makes a good street tree.

'Street Keeper'. Narrow, dense, upright grower to just 20 ft. wide. Deep green leaves.

'Sunburst'. Golden yellow new foliage ages to yellow-green. Defoliates easily in response to temperature changes, drought. Subject to wind breakage.

'True Shade'. Rounded head of light green foliage. Strong, fast grower.

Godetia. See *Clarkia*

Gomphrena
GLOBE AMARANTH
Amaranthaceae
ANNUALS AND PERENNIALS GROWN AS ANNUALS

🌡 **ZONES 1–24; H1, H2**

☼ ◐ **FULL SUN OR PARTIAL SHADE**

💧 **MODERATE WATER**

Gomphrena haageana
'Strawberry Fields'

Stiffly branching plants to 2 ft. high, 1 ft. wide, covered in summer and fall with rounded, papery flower heads up to 2 in. long. These may be dried quickly and easily, retaining color and shape for winter arrangements. Very heat-tolerant.

G. globosa. Annual. From Central America. White, pink, lavender, or purple flower heads on 1–2-ft. stems. 'All Around Purple' is compact and bushy. Magenta-pink 'Fireworks' is open growing and soft-looking; good for a cottage garden or large border. Dwarf varieties for edging or bedding include 6-in. 'Buddy' (deep reddish purple) and 'Gnome Series' (mixed colors); these can be planted closely in large containers—six to a shallow 10-in. pot—for a long-lasting living bouquet.

G. haageana. Perennial treated as annual. From southern U.S. and Mexico. Tightly clustered heads of bright orange bracts resembling inch-wide pinecones are borne on 2-ft. stems. Peeping from the bracts are tiny yellow flowers. Dependable 'Strawberry Fields' has vibrant red bracts.

Goniolimon
Plumbaginaceae
PERENNIALS

🌡 **ZONES 2–21**

☼ **FULL SUN, EXCEPT AS NOTED**

💧 **MODERATE WATER**

🦋 **ATTRACT BUTTERFLIES**

Goniolimon tataricum

These rugged plants form dense, low rosettes of tough, leathery leaves growing from a woody rootstock. In mid- to late summer, sturdy but delicate-looking sprays of flowers are held above the foliage on leafless stems about 1½ ft. high. Excellent in fresh or dried arrangements. Bloom best where summers are hot and dry. Provide well-drained soil. Rarely bothered by pests or diseases.

G. collinum 'Sea Spray'. Zones 3–21. Aptly named variety of a species from the Balkan Peninsula and eastern Romania. Handsome, oval, blue-green leaves form a tidy rosette to 16 in. wide. In bloom, the plant is covered with a profusion of tiny white flowers.

G. tataricum (Limonium tataricum). GERMAN STATICE. Zones 1–21. From southern Russia and the Caucasus. Dense, 18-in.-wide clumps of dark green, narrowly oval leaves. Flowering stems fork repeatedly to form a broad, domed cluster. Tiny flowers are light purplish to white. Plant withstands both cold and heat. Needs partial shade in Zone 13.

Gooseberry
Grossulariaceae
DECIDUOUS SHRUB

🌡 **ZONES A1–A3; 1–6, 15–17; EXCEPT AS NOTED**

☼ ◐ **SOME SHADE IN HOTTEST CLIMATES**

💧 **REGULAR WATER**

Gooseberries

Grown for its pretty, edible fruits, which are often marked with longitudinal stripes and are delicious in pies and jams. Plants are upright and multistemmed, growing 3–5 ft. tall and wide; varieties range from thorny to nearly spineless. Lobed, somewhat maplelike leaves usually turn bright colors in fall. Fruit ripens from late spring to summer. Needs same growing conditions as currant; prune as for red and white currants. Generally self-fruitful. Like currant, prohibited in some areas where white pines grow; check with your Cooperative Extension Office. Gooseberries are derived from several *Ribes* species; for strictly ornamental relatives, see *Ribes*.

'Black Velvet'. Thorny, disease-resistant variety whose sweet, dark red fruit has a hint of blueberry.

'Captivator'. Large, teardrop-shaped, sweet pink fruit on an extra-hardy, mildew-resistant, nearly thornless plant.

'Friend'. Thornless Ukrainian variety with large, sweet pink fruit that can be eaten fresh.

'Invicta'. Large green fruit on a thorny bush that is resistant to mildew.

'Oregon Champion'. Bears a heavy crop of green fruit on a thorny plant.

'Pixwell'. Extremely hardy, nearly thornless variety with tart, pink fruit.

'Poorman'. Vigorous grower; not as thorny as most. Red fruit sweet enough to eat fresh, though skin is tart.

'Welcome'. Bears medium-large, dull red, tart fruit on a productive, disease-resistant plant.

Jostaberry. These are disease-resistant hybrids between gooseberry and black currant. Their black fruit tastes like currants but isn't as astringent; it makes great jams and jellies. Plants are less hardy than currants or gooseberries; they grow in Zones A3, 1–6, 15–17.

Use these pretty little berries to make desserts. For gooseberry fool, a popular English dessert, combine in a saucepan 1 pint fresh gooseberries with ½ cup sugar and 2 tablespoons water; cook until berries are soft, then cool and mash them. Gently fold into 1 cup sweetened whipped cream and serve chilled.

Gossypium
Malvaceae
EVERGREEN SHRUBS

- ✎ ZONES VARY BY SPECIES
- ☼ FULL SUN
- ◐ ● WATER NEEDS VARY BY SPECIES

Gossypium tomentosum

This genus includes the species used to make cotton fabric, but the two plants described here are better-looking and more suitable for use in gardens. Both are mounding, spreading, leafy shrubs with an almost tropical look. Adapted to hot, dry areas.

G. harknesii. SAN MARCOS HIBISCUS. Zones 12–24. From Baja California and Mexico. Grows to 3–5 ft. tall and 4–6 ft. wide, with reddish stems and thick, heart-shaped, shiny green leaves. From late spring to fall, bears 2-in.-wide, lemon yellow flowers with five maroon spots inside (one at the base of each petal). Small fruits split open to reveal seeds and dense white fibers. Thrives in poor, well-drained soil with moderate irrigation (deep infrequent soakings). Very salt-tolerant. Takes heat, but leaves may turn yellow in intense reflected heat. Hardy to 25°F (−4°C).

G. tomentosum. HAWAIIAN COTTON, MA'O. Zone H2. Native to Hawaii. Grows 3–6 ft. tall and wide. Pure yellow, 2–3-in.-wide flowers are produced much of the year and show off nicely against the silvery green, maple-like leaves. Seed capsules have brown fuzzy seeds with short cottony hairs. This plant has been used to breed disease- and insect-resistant commercial cotton plants. Good as specimen

shrub, informal hedge, or high groundcover. Performs best in well-drained soil with little water.

FOR MORE UNTHIRSTY PLANTS, SEE "PLANTS FOR WATERWISE GARDENS," PAGES 74–78.

Gourd
Cucurbitaceae
ANNUAL VINES

- ✎ ALL ZONES
- ☼ FULL SUN
- ● REGULAR WATER

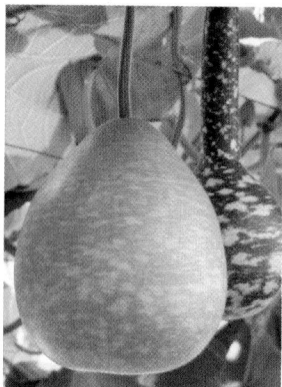

Gourds

Many plants bear the hard-shelled fruits we call gourds. One of the most commonly planted is *Cucurbita pepo ovifera,* a yellow-flowered vine that produces small ornamental gourds in various shapes and sizes, solid-colored or striped; many of the little gourds you see in stores likely come from this plant. *Luffa cylindrica* (*L. aegyptiaca*), called dishcloth gourd or vegetable sponge gourd, is another yellow-flowered plant; it bears cylindrical, 1–2-ft.-long fruits with a fibrous interior that when dried may be used in place of a sponge or cloth for scrubbing or bathing. *Lagenaria siceraria* (*L. vulgaris*), white-flowered gourd, produces fruits from 3 in. to 3 ft. long, in round, crooknecked, coiled, bottle, dumbbell, or spoon shapes.

CARE

Plant in fertile, well-drained soil. Gourds need a long growing season; sow seeds as soon as ground is warm, or start indoors if growing season is short. Set out transplants or thin seedlings to 2 ft. apart. Vines grow quickly to 10–15 ft., so grow on

a trellis, fence, or arbor to hold ripening fruits off ground. Leave fruits on the vine as long as possible (until they turn yellow or brown), but harvest before heavy frost, which can discolor them. Cut each gourd with some stem attached, so that you can hang it up to dry slowly in a cool, airy spot. When thoroughly dry, preserve them with a coating of paste wax, lacquer, or shellac.

Grape
Vitaceae
DECIDUOUS VINES

- ✎ ZONES VARY BY VARIETY
- ☼ FULL SUN
- ● MODERATE WATER

» See chart on pages 344–345.

Cabernet sauvignon grapes

Vigorous woody vines grown for fresh fruit, wine, shade, and fall color. (For strictly ornamental types, see *Vitis*.) Climbing by tendrils, a single grapevine can produce enough new growth every year to arch over a walk, roof an arbor, form a leafy wall, or provide an umbrella of shade over a deck or terrace. Grape is one of the few fruiting vines

that offer bold-textured foliage, colorful edible fruit, and a dominant trunk and branch pattern for winter interest. To produce good-quality fruit, you must choose a variety that suits your climate well, train it carefully, and prune it regularly.

European grapes (*Vitis vinifera*). These have tight skin, a generally high heat requirement, and cold tolerance to around 5°F (−15°C). They include the table grapes of the market, including 'Thompson Seedless'. The classic wine grapes, such as 'Cabernet', 'Chardonnay', and 'Pinot Noir', are also European in origin. Production of European wine grapes has greatly increased in the Northwest, but the bulk of the commercial crop is grown in California. For more information about growing wine grapes in your region, consult your local Cooperative Extension Office.

American grapes (*Vitis labrusca*). These include slipskin grapes (the skin slips off easily when the berry is squeezed). These 'Concord' types have a moderate summer heat requirement and tolerate temperatures as low as −20°F to −35°F (−29°C to −37°C). American grapes are used in jelly, in unfermented grape juice, and as a flavoring for soft drinks; some wine, usually sweet, is also made from these grapes.

American hybrid grapes. American varieties crossed with European grapes, with a mix of their parents' characteristics. In general, these vines are almost as disease-resistant and hardy as American species (most will need protection below −15°F/

A Basic Grape Trellis

To build a custom wire trellis large enough to accommodate two grapevines, set stout posts in the ground 15–20 ft. apart; posts should rise 5 ft. above the soil. Set two smaller posts (support stakes for the vines) 4–5 ft. from the end posts. String sturdy galvanized wire (10- or 11-gauge) across the four post tops. For a double-wire trellis, string a lower wire at the 2½-ft. level. Space multiple trellises 10–12 ft. apart.

How to Grow Grapes

PLANTING Provide deep, moderately fertile, well-drained soil. Purchase year-old bare-root vines, and plant during the dormant season. Trim roots to 6 in. just before planting in holes spaced 8–10 ft. apart. Cut back top growth to two or three buds.

WATERING, WEEDING & FEEDING Water plants regularly. Avoid splashing water on leaves; drip irrigation is ideal. Keep weeds in check. Fertilize each spring with a balanced fertilizer; for newly planted vines apply one-fourth the amount recommended on the bag, then gradually increase the amount each year until the fourth year, when you can start applying the full recommended dose each spring.

TRAINING The first summer after planting, let each vine grow unchecked. During the first winter, select the sturdiest shoot for the trunk and tie it to the support; shorten it to the three or four lowest buds and remove all other shoots. In the second spring, once the buds have grown out to 6–8-in.-long shoots, choose the strongest upright shoot for the continuation of the trunk and tie it to the post. (If you're training plants on a two-wire trellis or against a fence, also select two strong lower shoots for "arms" and tie them to the lower horizontal support.) Cut off all other shoots.

On wire trellises. When the trunk reaches the top wire, pinch it back to force branching. Train the two strongest resulting shoots along the top wire and remove any others. (For a two-wire trellis, also tie the lower arms' new growth along the lower wire; pinch back any lateral shoots developing from those arms to about 10 in. long.) In the second winter, cut back all growth on the trunk and arms and make sure that both sets of arms are loosely tied to the wire. During the third summer, allow the vine to grow but remove any shoots sprouting on the trunk. At this point,

you've established a permanent framework for your trellis-grown vine, and you can choose between cane pruning and spur pruning from the third winter on (see "Pruning," below).

On an arbor. The second summer is the time to direct its growth onto the roof of the structure. When the vine has grown just beyond the top of the vertical support, gently bend it over and secure it to the roof as it grows. Remove side shoots to encourage the tip to grow. During the second winter, cut back the main stem to a point just beyond where you want the last set of branches. Cut off all the side shoots. During the third spring, thin new shoots to 1 ft. apart. In the third winter, you're ready to create the final framework; its form depends on how you plan to prune your vines in subsequent years. If you're planning to do spur pruning, cut back each of the shoots you selected in the spring to two buds. If you will be cane pruning your vines, cut branches alternately to long canes (12 buds) and spurs (two buds).

PRUNING Grapes are produced on stems that develop from year-old wood—stems that formed in the previous season. These stems have smooth bark, whereas older stems have rough, shaggy bark. The purpose of yearly pruning is to limit the amount of potential fruiting wood to ensure that the plant doesn't produce too much fruit and that the fruit it does bear is of good quality. Pruning should be done in the dormant season.

The two most widely used methods for pruning grapevines are spur pruning and cane pruning; see the accompanying chart for recommended method for each variety. Begin using either method in the third winter, and repeat yearly thereafter.

Spur pruning. Start by removing weak side shoots from the arms. Leave the

strongest shoots (spurs) spaced 6–10 in. apart; cut each to two buds. Each spur will produce two fruit-bearing shoots during the next growing season. The next winter and every winter thereafter, remove the lower shoot on each spur and cut the upper stem to two buds. Those buds will develop into stems that bear fruit the following summer.

Cane pruning. Select one strong lateral shoot near the trunk on each arm, cut it back to 12 buds, and tie it to the support; these will produce fruiting shoots in the coming summer. Select another strong lateral shoot near the trunk on each arm, and cut it back to two buds; these will be the renewal spurs. Remove all other shoots. Each winter, remove the arms that have fruited, and choose as their replacements the two longest and strongest shoots that grew from the renewal spurs. Cut each to 12 buds and tie the two shoots to the support; select the two next-best shoots as renewal spurs, and cut each to two buds. Remove all other shoots.

CHALLENGES Pierce's disease, caused by a bacterium spread by the sharpshooter insect, is a serious threat to grapes in California. It causes afflicted vines to die in just a season or two. For more information, contact your Cooperative Extension Office. The grape leafhopper may cause leaf drop on grapevines in California. Get rid of nearby weeds, which may harbor the pest. Spraying with insecticidal soap is usually sufficient. Grape mealybug may infest vines in the Northwest and parts of California; control with horticultural oil spray in late winter. Powdery mildew is a serious disease of European grapes (most American varieties are immune). To control, dust vines with sulfur when shoots are 6 in. long, again at 12–15 in. long, then every 2 weeks until harvest.

–26°C), but the fruit is more like that of European grapes. Varieties called French hybrids—examples include 'Aurore', 'Baco Noir', 'Foch', and 'Seyval Blanc'—can be used for making wine in cold-winter climates. Consult your Cooperative Extension Office for varieties that will grow best locally.

Almost all grapes are self-fruitful and do not require pollination from another variety to bear fruit—but since they differ greatly in hardiness and heat requirements, choosing the right type and variety is important. Varieties listed in the chart are widely available and of high quality where adapted, but they represent only a small portion of what can be grown.

The Pacific Northwest is primarily American grape country, but European grapes grow well in the warmest parts of the Columbia River basin and the lower Willamette Valley. Regions of California and Arizona with a long warm season favor European varieties; California's coastal and inland valleys offer an ideal climate for most types. In short-season, high-elevation areas, choose either American or hardy European varieties, and plant in warm microclimates. If your climate is cooler or growing season shorter than is desirable for grape growing, look for early-ripening varieties.

Plant grapes in an open, sunny spot with plenty of room. Free air movement is important. If you garden on hilly terrain, it's better to plant grapes on a slope than in a low-lying basin, where trapped air increases danger from frost or mildew.

Once established, grapevines are rampant; they need support. For a leafy cover for an arbor or patio with some fruit as a bonus, simply train a strong vine up and over the structure, and thin out entangling growth each year. For good production, you'll need to provide a sturdy trellis, arbor, chain-link or rail fence, or wall strung with wire to support the big vines and their heavy bunches of fruit.

Cut bunches from vines in late summer or autumn, when grapes are sweet, never sooner, since they stop ripening at the moment of harvest.

G

»

GRAPE: TOP PICKS TO GROW

VARIETY	ZONES	SEASON	PRUNING METHODS	COMMENTS
AMERICAN AND AMERICAN HYBRID VARIETIES				
'Alden'	6–22	Early midseason	Spur	Large, firm, seeded reddish blue grape with light muscat flavor. Good for fresh eating, juice, wine. Very productive. Good fall leaf color.
'America'	7–22	Midseason	Cane or spur	Seeded blue grape with intense flavor. Good for juice, fresh eating, wine. Resistant to Pierce's disease.
'Black Spanish' ('Lenoir')	7–9, 11–24	Late midseason	Spur	Very old black grape. Small seeded fruit is fine for eating but best for wine and juice. Resistant to Pierce's disease.
'Bluebell'	2–7	Early	Cane or spur	Seeded blue grape with a flavor like that of 'Concord'. Excellent for juice, good for fresh eating. Very hardy (to –35°F/–37°C). Grows in warm-summer areas but may taste flat there.
'Buffalo'	2–7	Early	Cane or spur	Seeded black fruit with spicy flavor. Good for fresh eating or juice. Can produce secondary crop if subjected to early frost.
'Campbell Early'	5–22	Early midseason	Spur	Large, seeded black grape of 'Concord' type. Good for fresh eating, juice. Colors before achieving full flavor.
'Canadice'	2b–9, 11–21	Early	Spur	Seedless red fruit. Excellent for fresh eating or juice. Ripens in very cool areas, such as around Puget Sound. Overcrops easily; must be pruned hard or have crop thinned. Hardy to –20°F (–29°C) if well pruned.
'Champanel'	7 (warmer parts), 8, 9, 11–16, 18–24	Midseason	Cane	Seeded black grape. Good for juice, fresh eating. Tolerant of alkaline soil; resistant to Pierce's disease.
'Concord'	2b, 3, 6–9, 14–23	Midseason	Cane or spur	Seeded blue fruit. Standard American slipskin for cooking, juice, jelly.
'Edelweiss'	2–9, 14–21	Early	Cane or spur	Seeded white grape. Good for fresh eating or juice. Milder flavor than 'Niagara', but vine is more manageable. Flavor goes flat in hot-summer areas.
'Golden Muscat' AMERICAN HYBRID	3b, 6–24	Late	Spur	Very large, juicy, seeded green-yellow fruit. Flavor is citruslike, not true muscat; good for fresh eating. Cracks in wet weather.
'Himrod' AMERICAN HYBRID	3–9, 11–21	Very early	Cane	Seedless white fruit with spicy flavor. Good for fresh eating. Very vigorous, suited to arbors. Hardy to –15°F (–26°C).
'Interlaken' AMERICAN HYBRID	2–9, 14–21	Very early	Cane or spur	Firm, seedless green or yellow grape with fruity flavor. Excellent for fresh eating; only one for raisins in cool-summer areas. Ripens a week earlier than 'Himrod'. One of few that matures in the coolest areas of Pacific Northwest.
'Lakemont'	3, 6–22	Early	Cane or spur	Seedless white fruit with mild flavor; very productive. Fine table grape; keeps well in cold storage.
'Mars'	4–9, 14–21	Early midseason	Cane or spur	Blue fruit; large for a seedless grape. Fine for fresh eating, juice, wine, raisins. Flavor improves after harvest.
'New York Muscat'	2b–9, 14–21	Early	Cane or spur	Seeded blue grape with sweet muscat flavor. Excellent for fresh eating, juice, wine. Less vigorous than other varieties. Can be tried in hotter areas, but quality may suffer.
'Niabell'	7–9, 14–16, 18–22	Early	Cane or spur	Large, seeded black grape similar to 'Concord' at its best. Excellent for arbors. Vigorous and productive in wide range of climates. Succeeds in hot interiors where 'Concord' fails.
'Niagara'	2, 3, 6–10, 14–21	Midseason	Cane	Seedless green to pale yellow fruit. Good for fresh eating, juice, wine.
'Price'	2–9, 14–21	Very early	Spur	Seeded blue grape. Sweet and juicy, with refined 'Concord'-type flavor. Very good for fresh eating and fine for juice. Ripens in coolest areas of range, even around Puget Sound. May succeed in Zone 1 with cold protection.

GRAPE: TOP PICKS TO GROW

VARIETY	ZONES	SEASON	PRUNING METHODS	COMMENTS
'Reliance' AMERICAN HYBRID	2b–9, 14–21	Early midseason	Spur	Seedless red grape with mild, sweet flavor. Good for fresh eating or juice. Dependably productive.
'Swenson Red' AMERICAN HYBRID	2–9, 14–21	Early	Spur	Firm, meaty, seeded red or red-blue grape with unique fruity flavor. Excellent for fresh eating, juice, wine.
'Valiant'	A2, A3; 1–9	Early	Spur	Seeded blue fruit with 'Concord'-like flavor. Makes very good juice and jelly. Hardy to –50°F (–46°C).
'Vanessa'	2–9, 14–21	Early	Cane	Firm, seedless red grape with fruity flavor. Resists cracking. Good replacement for European variety 'Flame' in cool-summer areas. Use for fresh eating or raisins.
'Venus'	3–9, 14–21	Early midseason	Cane or spur	Seedless blue grape. Fruity, muscat-like flavor; fine choice for fresh eating or juice. Excellent fall color.

EUROPEAN VARIETIES

VARIETY	ZONES	SEASON	PRUNING METHODS	COMMENTS
'Autumn Royal'	6–9, 11–16, 18–21	Midseason to late	Cane or spur	Large, seedless purplish black grape. Good for fresh eating or raisins.
'Autumn Seedless'	6–9, 11–16, 18–21	Midseason	Cane or spur	Seedless pale green to golden grape. Good for fresh eating or raisins.
'Black Monukka'	3, 6–16, 17 (warmer parts), 18–24	Early midseason	Cane or spur	Seedless purplish black fruit in large, loose clusters. Popular home variety. One of hardiest European grapes.
'Crimson Seedless'	6–9, 12–16, 18–22	Late	Cane	Large, seedless red grape with excellent flavor. Good for fresh eating, raisins.
'Delight'	6–9, 12–16, 17 (warmer parts), 18–24	Early	Spur	Large, seedless, dark greenish yellow fruit. Good for fresh eating, raisins. Succeeds in mild-winter areas.
'Early Muscat'	6–9, 11–16, 18–24	Early midseason	Spur	Seeded green fruit in large clusters. Excellent muscat flavor. Used for muscat wine in Northwest.
'Fantasy'	6–9, 11–14, 18–21	Midseason	Cane	Large, seedless bluish black fruit with sweet, rich flavor. Good fresh or for wine. Vigorous; leave six to eight canes when pruning.
'Flame'	6–9, 11–16, 17 (warmer parts), 18–24	Early midseason	Cane or spur	Seedless red grape. Good for fresh eating, raisins. Very vigorous. Keep on dry side to reduce vigor, encourage ripening.
'Muscat' ('Muscat of Alexandria')	6–9, 11–16, 18–21	Late midseason	Spur	Large, rounded, seeded green to amber fruit. Renowned for sweet, musky, aged-in-the-vat flavor. Fine for fresh eating, juice, wine, raisins.
'Muscat Hamburg'	6–9, 11–16, 18–21	Late midseason	Spur	Seeded black grape. Intense, almost orangelike muscat flavor. Good fresh or for wine.
'Perlette'	6–9, 11–16, 17 (warmer parts), 18–24	Early	Spur	Seedless pale yellow fruit. Earlier, larger, less sweet than 'Thompson Seedless'. Excellent fresh. Needs less heat than most European varieties.
'Ribier'	7–9, 11–16, 18–21	Early midseason	Spur	Very large, seeded black grape with mild flavor. Good for fresh eating.
'Ruby Seedless' ('King's Ruby')	7–9, 12–16, 18–24	Late midseason	Cane or spur	Large clusters of seedless red to reddish black fruit. Sweet dessert grapes. Very susceptible to powdery mildew.
'Thompson Seedless'	7–14, 18, 19	Midseason	Cane	Big clusters of small, sweet, seedless greenish amber fruit. Good for fresh eating, raisins. Widely planted but does best in hot, dry areas.

G

G

Sizable Succulents

Although not as large as succulents like agave and aloe (some of which can reach shrub or even tree proportions), the two described below can mound up to respectable heights and spread indefinitely. Their plump, colorful leaves give them visual heft in borders and large containers, and they make excellent groundcovers on slopes, above retaining walls, and in parts of the garden where they won't be crushed by foot traffic.

Graptopetalum paraguayense
GHOST PLANT
Crassulaceae
SUCCULENT PERENNIAL

⚡ ZONES 17, 19–24; OR INDOORS
☼ ◑ FULL SUN OR PARTIAL SHADE
◊ LITTLE WATER

Graptopetalum paraguayense

Thick-leafed succulent native to Mexico. Forms mound 8 in. high and at least 1 ft. wide; can spread widely, if slowly. Stems branch as they creep along the ground or spill over walls or from containers. Suitable as a groundcover in areas where there is no foot traffic. Rosettes of fleshy, pointed leaves range in color from pale blue-gray (when grown in bright shade) to yellowish pink (in full, hot sun). Star-shaped flowers are white or yellow, on branching stems. Grow in coarse, well-drained soil that goes dry between waterings. Does not do well in desert heat, but will tolerate temperatures down to about 25°F (−4°C). Plants grow readily from cuttings; handle carefully, as leaves break off easily.

× Graptoveria 'Fred Ives'
Crassulaceae
SUCCULENT PERENNIAL

⚡ ZONES 17–24
☼ ◑ FULL SUN OR PARTIAL SHADE
◊ ◐ LITTLE TO MODERATE WATER

× *Graptoveria* 'Fred Ives'

A big, beautiful, fast-growing hybrid between *Graptopetalum paraguayense* and a large-growing *Echeveria* species. Forms spreading clumps of large rosettes, each about 8 in. high and nearly 1 ft. wide. The fleshy, oval, pointed leaves are bronzy pink. In summer, a slender, branched stem rises 1–2 ft. above the leaves to hold pale yellow flowers with orange centers and dotted petals. Durable, dependable, and very easy to grow. Great in containers. Plant in well-drained soil. Takes considerable shade, but color fades to blue-gray in low light. Easily propagated from stem cuttings.

FOR MORE ON SUCCULENTS, SEE "MEET THE SUCCULENTS," PAGE 618.

MEET THE GRASSES

The grasses in this book are lawn, meadow, or ornamental plants—except for corn, the only cereal commonly grown in home gardens. They perform various roles in the garden, from groundcovers to dramatic accents. Bamboos, which are grasses, are charted under Bamboo.

Lawn Grasses
The most common ones in the West are bent grass (*Agrostis*), buffalo grass (*Buchloe*), Bermuda grass (*Cynodon*), fescue (*Festuca*), ryegrass (*Lolium*), bluegrass (*Poa*), St. Augustine grass (*Stenotaphrum*), and zoysia grass (*Zoysia*). Specialty lawn grasses include grama grass (*Bouteloua*) and seashore paspalum (*Paspalum*).

Groundcover and Meadow Grasses
Ranging in height from 1 to 3 ft. tall and sometimes taller, these types make good meadows and natural lawns. Look for *Festuca mairei*; *Muhlenbergia capillaris*, *M. dubia*, and *M. rigens*; needle grass (*Nassella*), and moor grass (*Sesleria*).

Sedges for Color and Texture
Although not true grasses, sedges in the genus *Carex* are often grouped with ornamental grasses for their similar appearance and uses. Many varieties of *Carex* are now being used as lawn substitutes; see *C. divulsa*, *C. pansa*.

Small to Medium-Size Accent Grasses
These grasses and grasslike plants have beautiful foliage or flowers: yellow foxtail grass (*Alopecurus*), bulbous oat grass (*Arrhenatherum*), rattlesnake grass (*Briza*), Japanese blood grass (*Imperata*), lyme grass (*Leymus*), and fountain grass (*Pennisetum*).

Taller Grasses for Accents and Screens
These bring texture, color, and motion to the garden; they combine well with a variety of other plants in beds and borders. Many change dramatically from season to season, while others provide an evergreen backdrop. See big bluestem (*Andropogon gerardii*), reed grass (*Calamagrostis*), sea oats (*Chasmanthium*), hair grass (*Deschampsia*), Magellan wheatgrass (*Elymus magellanicus*), love grass (*Eragrostis*), Japanese forest grass (*Hakonechloa*), blue oat grass (*Helictotrichon*), lyme grass (*Leymus*), natal ruby grass (*Melinis*), Bowles' golden grass (*Milium*), silver grass (*Miscanthus*), moor grass (*Molinia*), bamboo muhly and deer grass (*Muhlenbergia*), Indian rice grass (*Oryzopsis hymenoides*), switch grass (*Panicum*); ribbon grass (*Phalaris*), little bluestem (*Schizachyrium*), dropseed (*Sporobolus*), and feather grass (*Stipa*).

Sesleria autumnalis among boulders

Grevillea

Proteaceae
EVERGREEN SHRUBS AND TREES

✎ **ZONES VARY BY SPECIES**

☼ ◑ **EXPOSURE NEEDS VARY BY SPECIES**

◐ **LITTLE OR NO WATER, EXCEPT AS NOTED**

◈ **LEAVES OF SOME CAN CAUSE SKIN RASH**

Grevillea 'Noelii'

Australia is home to a multitude of grevillea species and hybrids; many of these have great garden merit, including plants not described here. Watch for new introductions in nurseries. Though grevilleas vary in size and appearance, they generally have fine-textured foliage and long, slender, curved flowers, usually borne in dense clusters. Many cannot tolerate salt-laden soils, poor water quality, heavy summer irrigation, or heavy frost, but all are attractive enough to warrant some risk taking. Like other members of the protea family, they are sensitive to high phosphorus levels in the soil. Lightly fertilize; avoid high-phosphorus fertilizers.

G. alpina. MOUNTAIN GREVILLEA. Shrub. Zones 9, 15–24. Highly variable in size and form. Among the best is 'East Grampians', to 2½ ft. high and at least 5 ft. wide, with bright green leaves and masses of red-and-yellow flowers from fall to spring. Full sun or light shade.

G. asplenifolia. Shrub. Zones 15–24. To 9–15 ft. tall, 9–20 ft. wide, with foot-long leaves. Deep red, 2½-in.-long flower clusters appear in late winter and spring. Showy in bloom and excellent for screening. Takes sun but prefers partial shade.

G. 'Australflora Fanfare'. See G. 'Fanfare'.

G. australis. ALPINE GREVILLEA. Shrub. Zones 15, 16, 23, 24. Spreading or erect habit; can reach 7 ft. tall, 9 ft. wide. Small, narrow dark green to olive green leaves. Cream-colored flowers—not showy, but powerfully fragrant—bloom in winter and spring. Full sun or partial shade. Moderate water.

G. banksii. Shrub or tree. Zones 16–24; H1. Tall, open grower to 9–25 ft. tall and 6–12 ft. wide, with dark green, deeply cut leaves. Erect, 3–6-in.-long clusters of dark red flowers appear sporadically all year but are most profuse in late spring. Wind-resistant plant; parent of several popular hybrids. Hardy to 24°F (–4°C). Prostrate and white-flowered forms are sometimes offered. Full sun. Moderate water.

G. 'Bonfire'. Shrub. Zones 8, 9, 14–17, 21–24. Upright and rounded, to 4–6 ft. tall and 6–8 ft. wide, with feathery, finely divided, bright green leaves. Shiny, deep rose-red flowers appear mostly in spring, reblooming sporadically through fall. Full sun or partial shade.

G. 'Boongala Spinebill'. Shrub. Zones 15–24. Sprawling growth to 3–5 ft. tall and at least 15 ft. wide; good choice for erosion control on hillsides. Deeply cut leaves are coppery when new, later turn deep green. Toothbrushlike clusters of red flowers bloom nearly all year, most heavily in late winter. Full sun or partial shade.

G. 'Canberra Gem'. Shrub. Zones 8, 9, 12–24; worth trying in Zone 5. Open, graceful growth to about 8 ft. tall, 12 ft. wide. Bright green leaves are needlelike and prickly; makes a good barrier plant. Clusters of red flowers in winter and spring (and intermittently at other times). Often confused with G. 'Pink Pearl', which is somewhat smaller, with rose-pink flowers. Full sun or partial shade.

G. 'Fanfare' ('Australflora Fanfare'). Shrub. Zones 15–24. Low, spreading plant, to 1 ft. high and 10–15 ft. wide. Narrow, sawtoothed leaves are coppery red and covered with silky hairs when young, maturing to dark green. Toothbrushlike flowers in deep red appear

winter to spring. Tough, fast-growing, weed-suppressing groundcover; tip prune after flowering to keep dense. Best in acidic soils. Full sun or partial shade; takes more shade than most types listed here.

G. 'Firesprite'. Shrub. Zones 8–9, 14–17, 21–24. Grows 9–12 ft. tall, 6–8 ft. wide, with bright green, 10-in.-long leaves divided into very narrow leaflets. Spidery, shiny red-and-yellow flowers appear over most of the year, though heavier in spring and summer. Full sun.

G. 'Ivanhoe'. Shrub. Zones 14–24. Dense, spreading growth to 6–15 ft. tall, 9–15 ft. wide. Narrow, finely divided leaves. Pinkish red flowers in toothbrushlike clusters form at branch tips from late winter to summer. Full sun or light shade.

G. lanigera. WOOLLY GREVILLEA. Shrub. Zones 15–24. Spreading, mounding growth to 3–6 ft. tall, 6–10 ft. wide. Small, closely set leaves are covered with hairs that give foliage a grayish cast. Clusters of crimson-and-cream flowers are profuse in winter and spring. Good bank cover in hot, sunny area; good transition between garden and wild area.

Compact varieties are attractive as groundcovers or in rock gardens. These include 'Coastal Gem' (1–1½ ft. high, 4–5 ft. wide), which starts blooming in fall; 'Low Form' (2 ft. high, 4 ft. wide), which is very dense and looks good in containers; and 'Mount Tamboritha' (2 ft. high, 4–6 ft. wide), which blooms practically year-round. Full sun or partial shade. Plants tolerate extended wet periods.

G. lavandulacea. LAVENDER GREVILLEA. Shrub. Zones 15–24. Variable, but all forms are dense growers with half-inch-long gray leaves. 'Billywing', to 2½ ft. high and 6 ft. wide, has red-and-cream flowers in winter and spring; requires very well-drained soil. 'Penola', to 5 ft. tall and 12 ft. wide, bears deep rose-red blossoms fall through spring. 'Tanunda' is 1½–3 ft. high, 3–6 ft. wide, with profuse coral pink flowers; main show comes in winter, with occasional repeat bloom in mid-summer. Full sun or light shade.

G. 'Long John'. Shrub. Zones 15–24. To 8–10 ft. tall and 12–15 ft. wide, with foot-long leaves divided into many needlelike lobes. Early spring brings a heavy display of pink-and-red flowers; scattered bloom continues into fall. Easy to grow; useful for screening. Best in full sun.

G. 'Moonlight'. Shrub. Zones 15–17, 21–24. Big, soft-looking plant grows quickly to 8–12 ft. tall and 6–8 ft. wide. Ferny, dark gray-green leaves make a pretty backdrop for the many creamy to pale yellow, toothbrushlike blossoms produced in winter and spring, nearly year-round in ideal conditions. Good cut flowers. To keep plants compact and encourage fresh new growth and bloom, shear or cut back by about one-third after flowering. Full sun or partial shade.

G. 'Noelii'. Shrub. Zones 8, 9, 12–24. To 4–5 ft. tall, 5–8 ft. wide. Densely clad with needlelike, glossy green leaves. Clusters of pink-and-white spidery flowers bloom in spring. Easy to grow. Takes light shearing well; good formal or informal hedge. Full sun or partial shade. Moderate water.

G. 'Poorinda Signet'. Shrub. Zones 8, 9, 14–24. Dense, spreading plant to 4–9 ft. tall and wide, with inch-long, lance-shaped leaves that are dark green above, gray-green beneath. In winter and spring, clusters of pale pink flowers appear along the branches. Responds well to shearing. Full sun or partial shade.

G. 'Red Hooks'. Shrub or small tree. Zones 16–24. Robust, thick-trunked plant grows 12 ft. tall and up to 18 ft. across, with finely cut leaves. Coral red, toothbrushlike flower clusters from late winter to late spring, with a scattering at other times of year. Benefits from hard pruning when young to encourage bushiness. Full sun or light shade.

G. robusta. SILK OAK. Tree. Zones 8, 9, 12–24; H1, H2. Weedy in parts of Hawaii. Fast growing to 50–60 ft. (rarely 100 ft.) tall. Young trees are symmetrical and pyramidal. Old ones are broad topped (30–35 ft. wide), usually with a few heavy, horizontal limbs;

picturesque against skyline. Ferny leaves are golden green to deep green above and silvery beneath. Heavy leaf fall in the spring, sporadic leaf drop throughout the year. Large clusters of bright golden orange flowers in early spring.

Wood is brittle and easily damaged in high winds; for sturdier branches, cut central leader back hard at planting time and shorten branches to well-balanced framework. Useful as quick, tall screen; can be clipped as tall hedge. Thrives in heat; one of lushest greens for low desert. Young trees damaged at 24°F (–4°C); older ones hardy to 16°F (–9°C). Grows in poor, dense soils if not overwatered; can take regular water in fast-draining soils. Full sun.

G. 'Robyn Gordon'. Shrub. Zones 16–24. To 4–6 ft. tall and wide. Large (6–8 in.) light green leaves divided into many narrow segments. Dangling 6-in. clusters of bright red flowers are showy most of year. Full sun.

G. rosmarinifolia. ROSEMARY GREVILLEA. Shrub. Zones 8, 9, 12–24. To 6 ft. tall, nearly as broad. Narrow leaves are dark green on top, silvery beneath; look somewhat like those of rosemary. Red-and-cream flower clusters (rarely pink or white) in fall and winter; scattered bloom in other seasons. Use as clipped or informal hedge in dryish places. Impervious to heat and aridity. A popular dwarf form, just 3 ft. high and 6 ft. wide, bears pink-and-cream flowers in waves throughout the year, most heavily in spring and fall. Full sun or partial shade.

G. 'Ruby Clusters'. Shrub. Zones 9, 14–24. Dense growth to 6–10 ft. tall and 9–15 ft. wide, with lance-shaped, dark green leaves. Deep red flowers appear nearly nonstop throughout the year, with the heaviest show in early spring. Responds well to pruning. Full sun or partial shade.

G. 'Scarlet Sprite'. Zones 8, 9, 12–24. Grows to 3–5 ft. tall and wide, with bright green, needlelike leaves. Bright red, spidery flowers appear almost year round. Takes well to shearing; good low hedge. Full sun or partial shade.

G. sericea. Shrub. Zones 8, 9, 14–24; worth trying in 5. Grows 5–6 ft. tall and wide, with strap-shaped, inch-long leaves and a profusion of small, lavender-pink spidery flowers over a long period, with heaviest bloom in late winter and early spring. 'Collaroy Plateau' is a bit more compact, with deep rose-pink blooms. Easy to grow. Drought-tolerant but needs moderate water in hot areas. Full sun or partial shade.

G. 'Superb'. Shrub. Zones 16–24. Similar to 'Robyn Gordon', but grows just 3–4 ft. tall and 6 ft. wide, and has apricot-orange flowers. Full sun.

G. 'Sylvia'. Shrub. Zones 16–24. Upright grower to 8–12 ft. tall and 6–8 ft. wide. Finely cut leaves are dark green above, silvery beneath. Raspberry pink flowers are held upright. Strong stems make blooms good for cutting. Shear or cut back plant by one-third after bloom to keep compact. Disease-resistant and wind-tolerant; good hedge or screen. Full sun or light shade.

G. thelemanniana. HUMMINGBIRD BUSH, SPIDER-NET GREVILLEA. Shrub. Zones 9, 14–17, 19–24. Graceful, open, rounded habit 5–8 ft. tall and wide. Blue-green leaves are needlelike but soft to the touch. Clusters of bright red flowers tipped yellow can appear in any season. 'Baby' is a dwarf light-green-leafed selection 6–8 in. high and 3–4 ft. wide, useful for trailing over a wall or down a bank. 'Magic Lantern' ('Gilded Dragon') has feathery gray leaves, and grows to 2–3 ft. tall and 4–6 ft. wide. All forms can be temperamental in Northern California; prefer dry, warm winters of Southern California. Full sun or partial shade.

G. victoriae. Shrub. Zones 8, 9, 14–24; worth trying in 5. Variable in size; the form most commonly seen is 6 ft. or taller and as wide, with gray-green leaves and orange-red flowers in drooping clusters during late winter and spring. 'Murray Valley Queen' is an outstanding selection with profuse flowers; new growth is covered with attractive rust-colored hairs. Occasional summer water will prevent bud drop. Takes sun but prefers partial shade.

G. 'White Wings'. Shrub. Zones 15–24. To 6–9 ft. tall and spreading 10–15 ft. wide, with finely divided, bright green leaves. Masses of fragrant white flowers appear in spring, with a scattering at other times. Good for bank or slope planting. Full sun or partial shade.

Grewia occidentalis
LAVENDER STARFLOWER
Malvaceae
EVERGREEN SHRUB

🌿 **ZONES 8, 9, 12–24; H1, H2**

☼ **FULL SUN**

💧 **REGULAR WATER**

🦋 **FLOWERS ATTRACT BUTTERFLIES**

Grewia occidentalis

Fast-growing South African native with dark green, finely toothed leaves and star-shaped, inch-wide flowers of lavender-pink. Blooms in late spring and sporadically into fall, especially if cut back lightly after first heavy bloom. Can be used in various ways. Tends to branch freely in flat pattern, making it a natural for espalier. Unstaked, it grows 6–10 ft. tall (sometimes taller) with equal spread; can be planted 4 ft. apart and used as tall clipped hedge or screen. Becomes dense with pinching and pruning. If upright stems are removed, it can serve as a bank cover. Can be trained as a single-trunked tree or tied in place to cover arbor or trellis. Do any major pruning in fall after flowering is over. Tolerates wind.

FOR OTHER PLANTS THAT ATTRACT BUTTERFLIES, SEE PAGE 100.

Griselinia
Griseliniaceae
EVERGREEN SHRUBS

🌿 **ZONES 9, 14–17, 20–24**

☼ ◑ **FULL SUN OR PARTIAL SHADE**

💧💧 **MODERATE TO REGULAR WATER**

Griselinia littoralis 'Variegata'

These natives of New Zealand are neat, upright growers that always look well-groomed. Roundish leaves are thick, leathery, and lustrous green. Flowers and fruit are insignificant. Good plants for near swimming pools.

G. littoralis. A 50-ft. tree in New Zealand, but usually seen in Western gardens as 10-ft.-tall shrub of equal spread. Leaves roundish, to 4 in. long. With regular moisture, it can reach 8 ft. in 3 years. Dense, compact screen or windbreak. Fine beach plant, good espalier. 'Dixon's Cream' and 'Variegata' have leaves marked with cream.

G. lucida. Slower growing, a little smaller, more open and slender than *G. littoralis,* with larger (to 7-in.-long) leaves. Excellent foliage plant for partial shade. Thrives in containers. 'Variegata' has white markings on leaves.

Griselinias make excellent hedges, especially in coastal areas where they stand up well to wind and salt spray. Prune by snipping individual stems rather than shearing.

Guava

Myrtaceae
EVERGREEN SHRUBS OR TREES

🌱 **ZONES VARY BY SPECIES**

☼ ◐ **FULL SUN OR PARTIAL SHADE**

💧 **MODERATE WATER**

Guava

These tropical American natives, known botanically as *Psidium*, bear white, brushlike flowers that develop into round to pear-shaped fruits that mature from late summer into fall, though some may be produced year-round. Guavas are self-fruitful, but trees may yield a heavier crop with another variety of the same species to pollinate them. Grow best in rich soil. Plants thrive in full sun in mild coastal climates, partial shade in hot areas. Take pruning well; can be sheared into a hedge (but at expense of fruit).

Fruit is best picked when skin is fully colored. Good eaten fresh or used in jellies, purées, or juice drinks. Fresh guavas don't store well, so use them right away.

Common or tropical guava (*P. guajava*). Zones 23, 24, H1, H2 (a weed in Hawaii, where it is choking out native species). To 25 ft. tall and nearly as wide, with strongly veined leaves to 6 in. long. Yellow-skinned, 1–3-in.-wide fruit has white, pink, or yellow flesh and a musky, mildly acid flavor. 'Holmberg', 'Indonesian Seedless', and 'Ruby × Supreme' are sweet dessert varieties grown mostly in Hawaii. 'Beaumont', 'Ka Hua Kula', and 'Waiakea', tarter and used mainly for juice, are also grown primarily in Hawaii.

Strawberry guava (*P. cattleianum*). Zones 9 and 14 (sheltered locations), 15–24, H1, H2 (has naturalized throughout Hawaii but is less invasive than common guava). In Hawaii, it is usually grown as a single-trunked tree to 20 ft. tall and wide; in California, it is more often seen as a shrub to 8–10 ft. tall and wide. Especially beautiful reddish to golden brown bark. Leaves are bronze when new, maturing to glossy green. Fruit is dark red (nearly black when fully ripe), 1½ in. wide, with white flesh and a sweet-tart, slightly resinous flavor. Yellow strawberry guava or lemon guava (*P. cattleianum lucidum*) differs in its more open, taller growth habit (to 30 ft. tall by 15 ft. wide in Hawaii), greenish gray to golden bark, and larger, yellow-skinned fruit.

For the plant known as pineapple guava, see *Feijoa sellowiana*.

Gunnera

Gunneraceae
PERENNIALS

🌱 **ZONES 4–6, 14–17, 20–24**

◐ **PARTIAL SHADE**

💧💧 **AMPLE WATER**

Gunnera tinctoria

Big, bold, awe-inspiring South American plants grow 8 ft. tall and as wide or wider, with giant leaves (4–8 ft. across) on 4–6-ft.-long stalks covered in stiff hairs. Leaves are conspicuously veined, with lobed and cut edges. New sets of leaves grow each spring. In mild-winter areas, old leaves remain green for more than a year; elsewhere, leaves die back completely in

winter. Flower clusters to 1½ ft. long resemble corncobs clustered at the plant's base. Tiny fruits are red. Use plants where they can be focal point in summer—beside a pool or dominating a bed of low, fine-textured groundcover.

Soil must be rich in nutrients and organic material; feed three times a year, beginning when new growth starts, to keep leaves maximum size. Give overhead sprinkling when humidity is low or drying winds occur.

G. manicata. Native to Brazil and Colombia. Leaves carried fairly horizontally. Spinelike hairs on leafstalks and leaf ribs are red. Leaf lobes are flatter than those of *G. tinctoria* and do not have frilled margins.

G. tinctoria (G. chilensis). From Chile. Most common species. Leaf margins are lobed, toothed, somewhat frilled. Leaves are cupped and flaring, held more vertically than those of *G. manicata*.

Gymnocladus dioica

KENTUCKY COFFEE TREE
Caesalpiniaceae
DECIDUOUS TREE

🌱 **ZONES 1–3, 7–10, 12–16, 18–21**

☼ **FULL SUN**

💧 **REGULAR WATER**

Gymnocladus dioica

Native to eastern U.S. Grows very fast to 8–10 ft., then slowly to 60–100 ft. tall and 45–50 ft. wide. Provides year-round interest. Attractive leaves to 3 ft. long are divided into many small leaflets; pinkish when emerging late in spring, deep bluish green by summer.

In leaf, the tree casts light shade. The heavy, contorted branches and stout twigs make bare tree picturesque in winter. Narrow, creamy to greenish white flower panicles at ends of branches in spring are up to 1 ft. long (and fragrant) on female trees, to 4 in. long on males. Blossoms on female trees are followed by flat, 6–10-in.-long, reddish brown pods containing hard black seeds. Pods persist through winter. Early settlers roasted the seeds to make a coffee substitute, hence the tree's common name. Grows best in moist, rich, deep soil but adapts to poor soil, drought, city conditions. Can take much heat and cold. 'Espresso' is a good male (and therefore seedless) form.

Gypsophila

Caryophyllaceae
ANNUALS AND PERENNIALS

🌱 **ZONES VARY BY SPECIES**

☼ **FULL SUN**

💧 **MODERATE WATER**

Gypsophila paniculata

Grown for their profuse summer bloom, when plants are covered in clusters of tiny single or double flowers in white, pink, or rose. Slender-stemmed, much-branched plants are upright or spreading, ranging from 3 in. to 4 ft. tall. Leaves (sparse when plants are in bloom) are typically blue-green. Use for airy look in borders and bouquets, for contrast with large-flowered, coarse-textured plants. Dwarf kinds are ideal for rock gardens or spilling over stone walls.

If your soil is acidic, add lime before planting. Protect roots from gophers; protect tender

G

new growth from snails and slugs. To encourage repeat bloom on perennial sorts, cut back flowering stems before seed clusters form.

G. cerastioides. Perennial. Zones 2–10, 14–21. Native to the Himalayas. Gray foliage forms a mat to 3 in. high and twice as broad; clustered flowers vary from pink-veined white to pure pink. Use in rock garden, between steppingstones.

G. elegans. Annual. Zones 1–24. Native to Asia Minor, the Caucasus, and southern Ukraine. Upright grower to 1½ ft. high and wide. Lance-shaped, rather fleshy leaves. Profuse single white flowers to ½ in. wide or wider; pink and rose forms are also available. Plants live only 5 to 6 weeks; for continuous bloom, sow seeds in open ground every 3 to 4 weeks from late spring into summer. Excellent cut flower.

G. paniculata. BABY'S BREATH. Perennial. Zones A2, A3; 1–10, 14–16, 18–21; H1. Native to central Asia, central and eastern Europe. The classic filler in bouquets. Grows 3 ft. or taller and as broad, with slender, pointed leaves up to 4 in. long. Hundreds of tiny single white flowers are held in sprays. 'Bristol Fairy' is an improved, more billowy form to 4 ft. tall, covered with double blossoms ¼ in. wide. Florists' favorite is 'Perfekta', which bears even larger flowers (to about ½ in. wide). These dwarf varieties have double flowers: 'Compacta Plena' (1½ ft. high, with white flowers), 'Pink Fairy' (1½ ft. high, with pink blooms), and 'Viette's Dwarf' (12–15 in. high, with pink flowers).

G. repens. Perennial. Zones 1–11, 14–16, 18–21. Alpine native 6–9 in. high, with trailing stems to 1½ ft. long set with small, narrow leaves and clusters of small white or pink flowers. Varieties include 'Alba' (white) and 'Rosea' (pink).

FOR OTHER PLANTS THAT MAKE GOOD GROUNDCOVERS, SEE "GROUNDCOVERS," PAGE 60.

Haemanthus katherinae. See *Scadoxus multiflorus katherinae*

Hakea
Proteaceae
EVERGREEN SHRUBS

- ✿ **ZONES 9, 12–17, 19–24**
- ☀ **FULL SUN**
- ○ **NO IRRIGATION NEEDED**

Hakea laurina

Native to Australia. Remarkably diverse in foliage and flower, hakeas are high-quality shrubs for difficult sites; especially good for seacoast. Tougher than many other *Proteaceae* family members, they adapt to a variety of soils as long as they're well drained. Fertilizer is usually not needed; if you do apply it, make sure it is low in phosphorus. In addition to the species described below, other hakeas are offered from time to time in nurseries.

H. laurina. SEA URCHIN, PINCUSHION TREE. Dense, rounded habit to 10–15 ft. tall and 9–20 ft. wide; often trained as single-trunked tree. Narrow, gray-green leaves are often red margined. Showy flower clusters look like round crimson pincushions stuck with golden pins. Blooms in winter, sometimes in late fall. Good patio tree.

H. suaveolens. SWEET HAKEA. Dense, broad, upright plant to 10–20 ft. tall and wide. Stiff, dark green leaves, branched into stiff, needlelike segments. Small, fragrant white flowers in dense, fluffy clusters, fall and winter. Useful, fast-growing barrier plant, background, or screen. Good with conifers. Can be pruned into tree form.

H. victoria. ROYAL HAKEA. Erect, narrow plant to 6–15 ft. tall and 5–9 ft. wide. Leathery leaves, flat or slightly cupped, stemless, toothed, deep green beautifully netted with yellow and variegated with cream and orange. Flowers insignificant. Cut foliage dries well, lasts well in arrangements.

Hakonechloa macra
JAPANESE FOREST GRASS
Poaceae
PERENNIAL GRASS

- ✿ **ZONES 2B–9, 14–24**
- ☀ ◐ ● **FULL SUN IN COOLER CLIMATES ONLY**
- ● **REGULAR WATER**

Hakonechloa macra

Graceful mounds of arching leaves characterize this choice grass from Japan. Grows 1–3 ft. high, somewhat wider; spreads slowly by underground runners; never invasive. Leaves turn from green to coppery orange in fall. Prefers rich, moist, well-drained soil; excellent in containers.

Colored-leaf selections are more widely grown than the species. 'Albovariegata' ('Albostriata'), to 3 ft. high, has green leaves with longitudinal white stripes. 'Fubuki' is similar but grows only 14–18 in. high. The vigorous 'All Gold' is aptly named, with leaves of golden yellow; similar in size to 'Aureola' but more upright. 'Aureola',

the most widely grown variety, reaches 14 in. high and has green leaves with longitudinal yellow stripes that turn chartreuse in dense shade, pale creamy yellow in more sun; foliage is sometimes suffused with pink in fall. Leaves of 'Benikaze' are green in summer but turn various shades of red when weather cools.

Halesia
Styracaceae
DECIDUOUS TREES

- ✿ **ZONES 2B–9, 14–21**
- ◐ **PARTIAL SHADE**
- ● **REGULAR WATER**

Halesia diptera

Elegant flowering trees native to southeastern U.S.; put on best floral show in cold-winter areas. Bell-shaped, dangling white flowers bloom in spring, usually just as leaves begin to appear. Leaves turn yellow in fall. Brown, winged fruits hang on almost all winter—or even into spring or summer. Plants grow best in cool, deep, humus-rich soil. Attractive in woodland gardens, with rhododendrons and azaleas planted beneath.

H. carolina (H. tetraptera). SNOWDROP TREE, SILVER BELL. To 30–40 ft. tall, with 20–35-ft. spread. Clusters of ½–¾-in. bells. Oval, finely toothed leaves. Train plant to single trunk when young or it will grow as large shrub. 'Wedding Bells', to about 15 ft. tall and wide, has larger flowers.

H. diptera. To 20–30 ft. tall and as wide, often with multiple trunks. Deeply lobed bells, ½–¾ in. long, appear 2 to 3 weeks later than those of other species. Leaves and fruits are similar to those of *H. carolina*. Larger and more profuse blooms appear on *H. d. magniflora*.

H. monticola. MOUNTAIN SILVER BELL. Similar to *H. carolina* but taller (eventually to 60–80 ft.), with larger flowers (1 in.). 'Arnold Pink' and 'Rosy Ridge' have rosy pink blooms; those of 'Rosea' are pale pink.

× **Halimiocistus**
Cistaceae
EVERGREEN SHRUBS

⚡ **ZONES 4–24**

☼ **FULL SUN**

◐ 💧 **LITTLE OR NO WATER TO MODERATE WATER**

× *Halimiocistus wintonensis*
'Merrist Wood Cream'

These mound-forming hybrids between *Halimium* and *Cistus salviifolius* combine the good qualities of both parents, offering dense foliage, abundant bloom, and high tolerance for sun and heat. They need excellent drainage and cannot live in wet soil; water from lawn sprinklers can kill them. Use in rock gardens, on dry banks, spilling over a wall. Or plant on sunny side of the house under eaves where rains seldom reach.

H. sahucii. To 1–2 ft. high, 3–4 ft. wide, with narrow dark green leaves. Profuse, 1½-in. white flowers with central puff of yellow stamens in spring.

H. wintonensis. To 2 ft. high, 4–5 ft. wide, with furry gray-green leaves. Sheets of 2-in. white flowers with pronounced dark reddish purple central band in spring and early summer. Flowers of 'Merrist Wood Cream' have a red central band on creamy yellow petals.

Hamamelis
WITCH HAZEL
Hamamelidaceae
DECIDUOUS SHRUBS OR TREES

⚡ **ZONES VARY BY SPECIES**

☼ ◐ **FULL SUN OR PARTIAL SHADE**

💧 **REGULAR WATER**

Hamamelis mollis

Beloved for bright fall foliage and nodding clusters of odd-looking yellow to red blooms that typically appear in winter. Flowers consist of many narrow, crumpled petals and are said to resemble shredded coconut, mop heads, or spiders. Most witch hazels are fragrant and bloom over a long period. These are medium-size to large shrubs, sometimes treelike, usually with spreading habit and angular or zigzag branches. They appreciate rich, organic soil. Prune only to guide growth, remove poorly placed branches and suckers, or obtain flowering stems for scented winter bouquets.

H. × intermedia. Zones 3–7, 15–17. Group of winter-blooming hybrids between *H. mollis* and *H. japonica*. Big shrubs (12–15 ft. tall and wide). Often grafted; remove any growth originating from below graft. The following varieties are among the best.

'Arnold Promise'. Early show of bright yellow flowers. Yellow, orange, and red fall foliage.

'Carmine Red'. Light red flowers; red-orange fall foliage.

'Diane'. Dark red flowers aging to orange-red. Red-purple fall foliage.

'Feuerzauber' ('Magic Fire', 'Fire Charm'). Flowers in coppery orange blended with red. Fiery red fall foliage.

'Jelena' ('Copper Beauty'). Coppery orange flowers. Fall foliage in orange, red, scarlet.

'Moonlight'. Pale yellow blooms marked red at base; yellow fall foliage.

'Pallida'. Luminous light yellow blossoms; yellow fall foliage.

'Primavera'. Early, broad-petaled, light yellow flowers. Yellow-orange autumn foliage.

'Ruby Glow'. Coppery red flowers; bright red fall foliage.

'Sunburst'. Heavy clusters of radiant yellow, unscented flowers. Yellow fall foliage.

'Westerstede'. Unshaded yellow-orange flowers. Orange-red fall foliage.

H. japonica. JAPANESE WITCH HAZEL. Zones 2b–7, 15–17. From Japan. Much like *H. × intermedia*, though perhaps somewhat more erect and treelike (to 12–20 ft. tall and broad). Small, lightly scented yellow flowers in late winter or earliest spring. Chief draw is fall foliage in shades of red, purple, and yellow.

H. mollis. CHINESE WITCH HAZEL. Zones 2b–7, 15–17. From China. Moderately slow-growing shrub to 8–10 ft. tall and wide, or small tree that may reach 30 ft. Roundish leaves are dark green and rough above, gray and felted beneath, turning pure yellow in fall. Sweetly fragrant, 1½-in.-wide, rich golden yellow flowers with red-brown sepals bloom on bare stems in winter. Flowering branches are excellent for cutting. Selections include 'Coombe Wood', a very heavy bloomer with especially fine fragrance; 'Early Bright', earliest to bloom; 'Goldcrest', with larger flowers that appear later than those of others; and 'Wisley Supreme', a vigorous grower with perfumed flowers and disease-resistant blue-green foliage.

H. virginiana. COMMON WITCH HAZEL. Zones 1–9, 14–16, 18–21. Native to eastern North America. Sometimes reaches 25 ft. tall but usually grows slowly to 10–15 ft. high and wide. Open, spreading, rather straggling habit. Bark is the source of the liniment witch hazel. Roundish leaves turn yellow to orange in fall. Small, fragrant golden yellow blossoms appear in fall.

Hardenbergia
LILAC VINE
Papilionaceae
EVERGREEN SHRUBBY VINES

⚡ **ZONES VARY BY SPECIES**

☼ ◐ **PARTIAL SHADE IN HOTTEST CLIMATES**

💧 **MODERATE WATER**

Hardenbergia violacea
'Happy Wanderer'

Native to Australia. Grown for handsome evergreen foliage and clusters of sweet pea–shaped flowers that enliven the garden in late winter or early spring. Grow at moderate rate to 10 ft., climbing by twining stems. Need light, well-drained soil. Provide support for climbing; cut back to support and thin after bloom to prevent tangling. Subject to spider mites, nematodes; otherwise, fairly free of pests and diseases.

H. comptoniana. Zones 15–24. Light, delicate foliage pattern; leaves divided into three to five dark green, narrow leaflets. Flowers are violet-blue, ½ in. long, and held in long, narrow clusters. Where temperatures drop below 24°F (–4°C), plant beneath overhang.

H. violacea (H. monophylla). Zones 8–24. Coarser textured than *H. comptoniana*; leaves usually undivided, 2–4 in. long. Flowers are lilac or violet to rose or white. 'Happy Wanderer' is a tough, vigorous selection with pinkish purple blooms. 'Canoelands' is similar but with narrower leaves and a longer bloom period. 'Icicle' has pure white blossoms. 'Rosea' (*H. v. rosea*) has pink flowers. 'Mini-Ha-Ha' is a shrubby dwarf form growing just 3 ft. tall and wide.

H

H

Haworthia

Asphodelaceae

SUCCULENT PERENNIALS

⚟ ZONES 15–17, 20–24; OR INDOORS

◐ PARTIAL SHADE; BRIGHT INDIRECT
LIGHT

◯ ◌ LITTLE TO MODERATE WATER

Haworthia fasciata

Small, rosette-forming succulents from South Africa. Many types produce offsets to form dense, spreading colonies. Fleshy leaves may be slender and rough textured or pillowlike and smooth; some have small white bumps or ridges. Tiny flowers are held on long, whiplike stems from spring to fall; these may be clipped off as they fade to keep plants tidy.

Haworthias are well suited to containers, and their small size and tolerance of low humidity make them good houseplants. In pots or in the ground, provide sandy, fast-draining soil that is allowed to dry between waterings. Protect from frost and hot sun. Acclimate nursery plants to the garden gradually or leaves may sunburn. Numerous species and hybrids make these variable plants popular with collectors.

H. attenuata. Similar to *H. fasciata,* but inner leaf surface is dotted with white bumps.

H. cymbiformis. To 3 in. high, looking something like a small, chubby artichoke. Wedge-shaped leaves have light and dark green markings.

H. fasciata. ZEBRA PLANT. To 6 in. high. Rigid, dark green leaves up to 3 in. long are slender and triangular; each leaf is smooth on the inner surface and banded with raised white horizontal ridges on the

outside. Give just enough sun to make outer leaves blush red-orange.

FOR MORE ON SUCCULENTS, SEE "MEET THE SUCCULENTS," PAGE 618.

Hazelnut

(Filbert)

Betulaceae

DECIDUOUS NUT TREES

⚟ ZONES 2–7, EXCEPT AS NOTED

☀ ◑ AFTERNOON SHADE IN HOTTEST
CLIMATES

◯ ◌ LITTLE TO MODERATE WATER

Hazelnuts (filberts)

Hazelnuts, sometimes called filberts, are selections of the European species *Corylus avellana* that are grown for nut production. Growing just 10–18 ft. tall and wide, they are handsome and nicely structured trees, a good choice for garden or terrace. From spring to fall, the roundish, ruffle-edged leaves cast a pleasant spot of shade. Showy catkins (male flowers) hang long and full on bare branches in winter. Hazelnuts ripen in late summer and drop in early fall; the roundish or oblong nuts form inside frilled husks. A 10-year-old tree may yield up to 20 lb. of nuts per year. Best crops are produced in cold-winter areas.

Eastern filbert blight, a destructive bark disease, has devastated old standby varieties 'Butler', 'Daviana', 'Du Chilly', and 'Ennis'; they are no longer recommended in the prime hazelnut-growing areas of Oregon. The following varieties have partial to excellent blight resistance. Since cross-pollination is necessary, plant at least two varieties. For a

boundary hedgerow, plant mixed varieties 4 ft. apart and let suckers grow.

'Barcelona'. Fine flavor. Some resistance to blight. Good pollenizer for 'Santiam'.

'Delta'. Richly flavored nuts on a compact plant. High blight resistance. Pollinates 'Gamma', 'Jefferson', and 'Lewis'.

'Eta'. Large harvests of thin-shelled, small nuts with good flavor on a compact tree. Very high blight resistance. Pollinates nearly all other varieties.

'Gamma'. Sweet, good-quality nuts on a vigorous tree. High blight resistance. Good pollenizer for 'Barcelona', 'Delta', 'Hall's Giant', 'Lewis', 'Sacajawea', 'Santiam', 'Tonda di Giffoni', and 'Yamhill'.

'Hall's Giant'. Flavorful. Good resistance to blight. Pollinates 'Gamma', 'Jefferson', 'Lewis', and 'Sacajawea'.

'Jefferson'. Big yields of tasty, attractive nuts. High blight resistance. Pollinates 'Yamhill'.

'Lewis'. Good-quality nut. High blight resistance. Pollinates 'Gamma', 'Hall's Giant', and 'Sacajawea'.

'Santiam'. New blight-resistant variety that produces abundant, high-quality nuts on a smallish tree. Good pollenizer for 'Yamhill'.

'Theta'. Large harvests of thin-shelled, small nuts with good flavor on a vigorous, upright tree. Very high blight resistance. Pollinates nearly all hazelnuts except 'Delta' and 'Hall's Giant'.

'Tonda di Giffoni'. Excellent flavor. Highly resistant to blight. Pollinates all varieties except 'Barcelona'.

'Yamhill'. Good-quality nuts on a small tree. Highly resistant to blight. Good pollenizer for 'Delta', 'Gamma', 'Hall's Giant', and 'Santiam'.

Two types of hybrids, called filazels and trazels, can be grown in Zone 1a. Filazels—hardy, 10–15-ft. producers of good-quality nuts—are hybrids between *C. avellana* and the North American beaked hazelnut *(C. cornuta).* Trazels—upright, 20–30-ft. trees that produce sweet, fine-flavored nuts—are crosses between *C. avellana* and Turkish hazel *(C. colurna).* Plant two of the same type for cross-pollination.

How to Grow Hazelnuts

PLANTING Choose a site in full sun west of the Cascades but partial afternoon shade in hot areas east of the Sierra Nevada–Cascade Ranges. Plant in late winter or early spring in deep, well-drained soil.

PRUNING Trees tend to sucker; clear these out three or four times a year if you wish to maintain a clean trunk.

HARVESTING Harvest by picking up nuts from the ground, then dry them in the sun for a few days. Squirrels and jays are a nuisance, often picking the nuts before they fall. Hand-picking when the nuts are tree-ripe (when they separate easily from the hulls) will thwart animal thieves.

CHALLENGES Eastern filbert blight is evident as raised, oval black bumps in vertical lines on infected branches and twigs. Individual branches die out, and the entire plant can succumb. To protect existing plants, spray with copper and horticultural oil together at bud break (usually late March), again in mid-April, and a third time in early May. Remove dead branches, cutting 2 ft. back into healthy growth. Burn or bury prunings. Severely infected trees should be removed entirely.

Hazelnuts are considered a heart-healthy food/snack. They contain about 4 percent saturated fat. They're also a good source of vitamin E.

Hebe

Plantaginaceae
EVERGREEN SHRUBS

- ✿ **ZONES 14–24, EXCEPT AS NOTED**
- ☼ ◗ **PARTIAL SHADE IN HOTTEST CLIMATES**
- ◗ **REGULAR WATER**
- ❀ **ATTRACT BUTTERFLIES**

Hebe × andersonii 'Variegata'

New Zealand natives closely related to *Veronica* and occasionally still sold under that name. Most types are grown mainly for attractive form and foliage (neat pairs of opposite leaves); some give good flower display in summer, and a few produce a scattering of bloom throughout the year. Whipcord types have small, scalelike leaves pressed tightly against the stems.

Most hebes are fast growing. All do best in cool-summer, mild-winter climates—in the San Francisco area, for example. Dry summer heat and winter frosts shorten their lives. Larger-leafed types are more susceptible to winter damage. Very prone to root rot if drainage is anything less than excellent. Take seacoast conditions. Prune after bloom, shortening stems that have flowered by about half to keep plants compact and bushy. Rejuvenate ragged plants by cutting back severely; they'll resprout easily from old, leafless wood.

H. 'Amy'. Zones 5, 6, 14–24. To 5 ft. high and wide, with dark green leaves tinged purple on top, purplish red beneath. Short spikes of reddish purple flowers in summer.

H. × andersonii. Mounding, compact plant to 5–6 ft. tall and wide, with fleshy, deep green leaves. Flowers are white at base, violet at tip, carried in 2–4 in. spikes. 'Variegata' has white-bordered leaves.

H. 'Autumn Glory'. Zones 5, 6, 14–24. Upright, somewhat open grower to 2 ft. high and 3 ft. wide. Dark green leaves have red margins. Many 2-in., deep lavender-blue flower spikes in late summer, fall.

H. buxifolia. See *H. odora*.

H. 'Caledonia'. Zones 5–7, 14–24. Grows 1½–2 ft. high and wide, with reddish stems and lustrous green leaves. Spikes of violet flowers appear from late spring to autumn.

H. carnosula. To 1 ft. high and 2–3 ft. wide, thickly clothed in rounded, grayish green leaves. Small white flowers in dense spikes. Interesting edging or groundcover.

H. 'Coed'. Compact shrub to 2–3 ft. high and wide. Reddish stems densely set with dark green leaves. Spikes of small pinkish purple flowers.

H. cupressoides 'Boughton Dome'. Zones 4–7, 14–24. Forms a dense, symmetrical mound to 1½–2 ft. high and 2½–3 ft. wide. Gray-green leaves just ¼ in. long give it the look of a dwarf cypress. Not known to flower.

H. × franciscana 'Variegata'. See *H.* 'Silver Queen'.

H. glaucophylla. Zones 5–7, 14–24. Compact, rounded, about 2 ft. high and wide. Tiny, roundish, blue-green leaves. White flowers in short, dense clusters. Good low foundation plant or tidy divider between lawn and walkway.

H. 'Great Orme'. Zones 5–7, 14–24. Rounded form to 4 ft. tall and wide, with narrow leaves; deep pink, 3-in.-long flower spikes fade to white at base.

H. 'Hinerua'. Zones 4–7, 14–24. Whipcord type with attractive yellow-green foliage. Dense, upright growth to 2–3 ft. high and 4–5 ft. wide. Small white flowers are rarely seen.

H. imperialis. See *H. speciosa* 'Imperialis'.

H. ochracea 'James Stirling'. Zones 4–7, 14–24. Slow-growing whipcord type with ochre-yellow foliage. Upright then arching growth to 1½ ft. high and 2 ft. wide, with small white flowers in late spring and early summer.

H. odora (H. buxifolia). BOXLEAF HEBE. Zones 5–7, 14–24. Rounded and symmetrical, to an eventual 3 ft. high and 5 ft. wide; easily shaped into 3-ft. hedge. Small, deep green leaves densely cover branches, giving plant the look of a boxwood (*Buxus*). Small white flowers in dense clusters. 'Nana' grows just 8 in. high and a little wider. Leaves of 'New Zealand Gold' are glossy green and neatly edged in yellow.

H. pinguifolia. Zones 5–7, 14–17, 22–24. To 3 ft. high and wide. Blue-gray leaves (sometimes with a pinkish edge) are very closely set or even overlapping. White flowers are tiny but profuse. 'Pagei' is a prostrate form that can grow 9 in. high and 4 ft. across in 5 years. 'Sutherlandii' grows 1½ ft. tall and 3 ft. wide, with beautiful gray foliage.

H. 'Red Edge' (H. albicans 'Red Edge'). Zones 5–7, 14–24. Mounded growth to about 2 ft. high and wide. Blue-gray leaves have a distinctive red edge, especially on new growth or in cold weather. Pale lilac flowers are held in 2-in. spikes. Popular and dependable; good in containers.

H. 'Silver Queen' (H. × franciscana 'Variegata'). Dense, rounded growth to 2–4 ft. wide. Leaves up to 2½ in. long are dark green, widely and irregularly edged in creamy white, stunning in combination with the large pinkish purple flowers.

H. speciosa. SHOWY HEBE. Zones 14–24; H1. Dense shrub to 5 ft. tall, 4 ft. wide. Stout stems bear glossy dark green leaves and 3–4-in.-long spikes of reddish purple. 'Imperialis' has reddish foliage, magenta flowers.

H. topiaria. Zones 5–7, 14–24. Forms a dense, neat ("topiary") mound 3–4 ft. tall and 4–5 ft. wide, with gray-green, yellow-edged and (rarely) small white flowers. Good informal hedge or specimen plant.

H. 'Veronica Lake'. Dense growth to 3 ft. high and wide, with 1½-in. dark green leaves and abundant short spikes of lilac flowers.

H. 'Wiri Blush'. Zones 5–7, 14–24. Rounded form to 4 ft. tall and wide, with narrow, shiny dark green leaves. Rose-pink, 3-in.-long spikes of flowers.

H. 'Wiri Dawn'. Zones 5–7, 14–24. Compact growth to about 1½ ft. high and 1½–2 ft. wide, with narrow olive green leaves. Short spikes of pale pink flowers open from rosy pink buds.

Hedera

IVY
Araliaceae
EVERGREEN VINES

- ✿ **ZONES VARY BY SPECIES**
- ☼ ◗ **SOME SHADE IN HOTTEST CLIMATES**
- ◗ ◗ **MODERATE TO REGULAR WATER**

Hedera helix 'Glacier'

Ivy is appreciated by some gardeners for its ability to cover quickly, reviled by others for its invasive tendencies. Often used as a groundcover, it also climbs to cover walls, fences, and trellises, attaching itself firmly by aerial rootlets (a factor to consider when planting against surfaces that must be painted). This type of growth occurs during the juvenile stage, which can last up to 10 years; during this stage, the thick, leathery leaves are usually lobed. At maturity, ivies become shrubby, with stiff branches clothed in unlobed leaves, and they begin blooming: domelike clusters of greenish white flowers appear in late summer and are followed by black berries in autumn.

H. algeriensis (H. canariensis). ALGERIAN IVY. Zones 5–9, 12–24. Native to Canary Islands and the Mediterranean coast of North Africa. Shiny, rich green leaves 5–8 in. wide with 3 to 5 shallow lobes. Leaves

H

H

The Dark Side of English Ivy

English ivy (*H. helix*) and several of its varieties have been placed on noxious-weed lists in some parts of the West because of their ability to crowd out native plants and endanger trees upon which they grow. Whether they creep out of gardens over ground or spread into natural areas by birds that eat the berries, invasive ivies are destructive when left to grow unchecked. They can grow to 90 ft., with stems to 1 ft. in diameter, and can completely cover the trunks of large trees, promoting rot. Once they grow up into the canopy, these ivies can shade out the foliage of deciduous trees and make any type of tree top-heavy and thus more prone to breakage.

In areas where ivy is invasive, grow only named varieties and, if possible, confine the ivy to containers or well-defined garden areas. Ivy has been widely planted on hillsides in the belief that it will decrease erosion, but studies have shown that slopes covered in single species are actually more prone to slides. Many trees and shrubs can grow compatibly in ivy groundcover, but small, soft, or fragile plants will be smothered. Ivy groundcovers can be a haven for slugs and snails and can also harbor rodents, especially if the ivy is never cut back.

are more widely spaced along stems than those of *H. helix.* Coarse-looking plant; aggressive grower. 'Gloire de Marengo' ('Variegata') has dark leaves marbled with gray-green, irregularly margined in creamy white; does not take extreme heat.

H. colchica. PERSIAN IVY. Zones 3b–24. Native to Turkey and the Caucasus Mountains. Oval to heart-shaped leaves are largest among all ivies: 3–7 in. wide, to 10 in. long. 'Dentata' has slightly toothed leaves; 'Dentata Variegata' is marbled with deep green, gray-green, and creamy white. 'Sulphur Heart' ('Paddy's Pride') has central gold variegation.

H. helix. ENGLISH IVY. Zones 3–24, H1, except as noted. From Europe. Dull dark green, three- to five-lobed leaves with paler veins are 2–4 in. wide at base and as long. Hundreds of named varieties are available from specialty growers. Many are small- and miniature-leafed forms that are good for pots, hanging baskets, and topiary frames; for training into intricate patterns on walls; and for small-scale groundcovers. In general, their leaves are about half as large as those of the species, and some are even smaller. Leaf shapes vary widely: they may be deeply lobed and cleft, ruffle edged, arrow-shaped and narrow, or divided into distinct leaflets. Variegated types are popular. *H. h. baltica* ('Baltica'), with whitish-veined leaves, is often considered the hardiest variety of English ivy (Zones 2b–24); its leaves take on purplish tones in winter.

CARE

Plant ivy in spring; where winters are not excessively cold, you can also plant in fall. Standard spacing is 1½–2 ft. apart. Amend soil (to depth of 8–12 in. if possible) with organic matter such as ground bark or peat moss. Before planting, thoroughly moisten soil; also make sure that transplants' roots are moist and their leaves and stems are not wilted. Feed with high-nitrogen fertilizer after planting (for spring-planted ivy) or, for fall-planted ivy, in first spring after planting. Feed again in midsummer. For best growth, continue to feed every year in early spring and midsummer.

Most ivy groundcovers should be trimmed around edges two or three times a year (use hedge shears or a sharp spade). Fence and wall plantings also need trimming two or three times a year. When groundcover builds up higher than you want, mow it with a rugged rotary power mower or cut it back with hedge shears. Do this in spring so that ensuing growth will quickly cover bald look.

Hedychium
GINGER LILY
Zingiberaceae
PERENNIALS

☀ **ZONES 8, 9, 14–17, 19–24; H1, H2**
◐ **LIGHT SHADE**
💧 **AMPLE WATER**

Hedychium gardnerianum

Native to tropical Asia, India, and the Himalayas. Grown for their dramatic leaves and fragrant, colorful blooms. Foliage is especially handsome in tropical conditions, as in Hawaii. Dense spikes of richly perfumed flowers are produced in late summer or early autumn. Plants spread indefinitely by rhizomes. Frost can kill them to ground, but new stalks appear in early spring. Useful in large containers but will not grow as tall there as in open ground. Ginger lily does best in rich soil high in organic matter. To encourage fresh new growth, remove old stems after flowers fade.

H. coccineum. RED GINGER LILY, SCARLET GINGER LILY. To 6–9 ft. tall, with leaves to 20 in. long and just 2 in. wide. Particularly showy, bearing orange-scarlet flowers with prominent red stamens on blossom spikes to 10 in. long. Flowers of cold-hardy 'Tara' are tangerine.

H. coronarium. WHITE GINGER, BUTTERFLY LILY, GARLAND FLOWER. To 3–7 ft. tall, with narrow leaves to 2 ft. long. White flowers in 6–12-in.-long clusters are especially fragrant; good cut flowers. Naturalized in Hawaii, where the flowers are used in leis. In California, it looks best where humidity is moderate to high (in coastal areas, for example).

H. densiflorum. To 9 ft. or taller, with leaves to 14 in. long and 4 in. wide. Orange-yellow flowers are produced in dense spikes to 8 in. long.

H. flavescens. YELLOW GINGER. To 6 ft. or taller, with narrow, oblong leaves that can reach nearly 2 ft. long. Heavily perfumed creamy yellow flowers to 3 in. across are produced in oval heads with many broad, overlapping green bracts. Naturalized in Hawaii.

H. flavum. Like *H. flavescens* but a little shorter (to about 5 ft.) and with yellow or orange flowers in slightly smaller heads.

H. gardnerianum. KAHILI GINGER. Plant grows to 8 ft. tall, with narrow leaves to 1½ ft. long. Pure yellow flowers with red stamens are borne in 1½-ft.-long spikes. Naturalized in Hawaii and considered a pest on most of the Islands.

H. greenii. To 5 ft. tall. Slender leaves grow 8–10 in. long. Orange-red flowers are held in 5-in. spikes.

Kahili ginger produces showy flowers. For striking effects, grow it in large containers or cluster several in leafy tropical borders. Avoid planting it in the Hawaiian Islands, where it has become a serious pest.

Hedyscepe canterburyana

UMBRELLA PALM

Arecaceae

PALM

✀ **ZONES 17, 23, 24; H1, H2**

☼ ☼ **FULL SUN OR LIGHT SHADE**

💧 **REGULAR WATER**

Hedyscepe canterburyana

This striking palm—the only member of its genus—is native to Lord Howe Island in the South Pacific, where it grows in moist forests and on cliffs at least 900 ft. above sea level.

Once assigned to *Kentia*, it is closely related to *Archonto-phoenix*, but *Hedyscepe* grows smaller, broader, and lower, with wider leaf segments and more arching, lighter green feather-type leaves. The trunk is an attractive blue-green in young trees, turning green with age. It grows slowly to 30 ft. tall, with fronds spreading 15 ft. wide. Flowers are produced just below the leaves and are not showy, but they are followed by large, dull red fruits. Hardy to 28°F (−2°C).

Needs partial shade when young, especially in warmest zones. Since *Hedyscepe* is native to a cool, humid climate, it thrives in foggy or cloudy weather, taking well to the Southern California coast's persistent spring and early summer overcast. Protect it from hot, dry winds, which can burn leaves. Its down-curved leaves give it its common name.

FOR MORE ON PALMS, SEE "MEET THE PALMS," PAGE 471.

Helenium

SNEEZEWEED

Asteraceae

PERENNIALS

✀ **ZONES VARY BY SPECIES**

☼ **FULL SUN**

💧 **REGULAR WATER, EXCEPT AS NOTED**

🦋 **ATTRACT BUTTERFLIES**

Helenium 'Double Trouble'

Rather coarse-looking, but valuable for profuse bloom in late summer and autumn. Good companions for ornamental grasses. Numerous leafy stems hold daisylike, typically brown-centered blossoms with yellow, orange, red, or coppery rays; good cut flowers. Perform best in hot-summer areas. Provide well-drained soil; need little fertilizer. Trim off faded blossoms to encourage long bloom. Taller kinds require staking and are best in the back of borders. All need division and replanting every few years.

H. autumnale. Zones 1–24. Native to much of North America. To 5 ft. tall and 1½ ft. wide, with yellow, 2-in.-wide flowers. Most plants sold under this name are really hybrids; see *H.* hybrids.

H. bigelovii. Zones 1–10, 14–24. From California, Oregon. To 2–3 ft. high, 1 ft. wide. Yellow blossoms to 2½ in. across have reflexed rays. 'The Bishop' and 'Tip Top' are compact and free flowering.

H. hybrids. Zones 1–24. Flowers are 2–3 in. across, in shades of yellow, orange, red, rust, copper, and blends of these colors. Tall types (4–5 ft. tall, 2 ft. wide) include 'Baudirektor Linne', brownish red with a brown center; 'Butterpat', light yellow with a deeper yellow center; 'Mardi Gras', yellow splashed with red and orange, and a brown center; and 'Waldtraut', with coppery brown rays around a dark central disk. Compact varieties (about 3 ft. high, 1½ ft. wide) include 'Coppelia', copper orange with a brown disk; 'Crimson Beauty', dusky deep red with a brown disk; 'Double Trouble', fully double, bright yellow blooms. 'Moerheim Beauty', coppery red with a brown center; 'Rubinzwerg', rusty red with a yellow-and-brown center; and 'Wyndley', butter yellow with a yellow-brown central disk.

Helianthemum nummularium

SUNROSE

Cistaceae

EVERGREEN SHRUB

✀ **ZONES 2B–9, 14–24**

☼ **FULL SUN**

💧 **MODERATE WATER**

Helianthemum nummularium
'Henfield Brilliant'

The various commonly sold forms of this species and other sunroses used in hybridization are native to Europe and Asia Minor. All grow 6–8 in. high and spread to about 3 ft. Leaves may be gray on both surfaces, or glossy green above and fuzzy gray beneath. Midspring to early summer display of inch-wide, single or double flowers in bright or pastel colors—flame red, apricot, orange, yellow, pink, rose, peach, salmon, or white. Each blossom lasts only a day, but new buds continue to open. Let sunroses tumble over rocky slopes, set them in niches in dry rock walls, or grow them in planters on a sunny patio. Good at seashore. Specialists offer many named varieties.

Shear plants back after flowering to neaten appearance and encourage repeat bloom. If used as groundcover, set out 2–3 ft. apart. In cold-winter areas, lightly cover plants with evergreen boughs to keep foliage from dehydrating. Plants will be hardier if soil is not too rich and is kept on the dry side (good drainage is essential).

Helianthus

SUNFLOWER

Asteraceae

ANNUALS AND PERENNIALS

✀ **ZONES VARY BY SPECIES**

☼ **FULL SUN**

💧💧 **REGULAR TO AMPLE WATER, EXCEPT AS NOTED**

🦋 **SEEDS ATTRACT BIRDS, BUTTERFLIES**

Helianthus annuus

Sturdy plants grown for their familiar, colorful blooms in summer and fall; most make great cut flowers. Perennial kinds spread rapidly and may become invasive. Tall sunflowers may need staking.

H. annuus. COMMON SUNFLOWER. Annual. All zones. The wild ancestor of today's familiar sunflowers, native to much of the central U.S. and southward to Central America, is a coarse, hairy plant with 2–3-in.-wide flowers. It has been bred to produce giant plants as well as a host of smaller varieties for cut flowers. Blooms may be yellow, red, orange, or creamy white; some have several colors on each flower, others are frilled or doubled. Centers are brown, dark purple, or nearly black.

»

H

H

Giant forms grow 10–15 ft. tall and 2 ft. wide and typically produce a single huge head (sometimes more than a foot across) consisting of a circle of short rays with a brown central cushion of seeds. Sunflowers for cutting come on compact, branching plants and bear 4–8-in.-wide blooms in a wide variety of colors. They fall into two basic categories: pollen-bearing types and pollenless ones. Kinds without pollen have the advantage of not shedding on tabletops. Some annual sunflowers are bred to produce especially large seeds. New varieties and hybrids come on the market each year.

For children, annual sunflowers are fun and easy to grow. People eat the roasted seeds and birds enjoy raw ones in autumn and winter. Sow seeds in spring where plants are to grow. Large-flowered kinds need rich, moist soil. Attract bees.

H. 'Lemon Queen'. Perennial. Zones 2–24. Fast-growing hybrid to 6–8 ft. tall and 3–4 ft. wide, with long, narrow leaves. Produces many 2-in.-wide, semidouble, pale yellow flowers with a dark brown center. Use at back of casual border or in combination with large ornamental grasses. Takes moist or dry soil. Does not require staking, provided soil is not too rich and plants are not overfertilized.

H. maximilianii. Perennial. Zones 1–24. From central and southwestern U.S. Forms a clump 3 ft. wide, with 10-ft.-tall stems clothed in long, narrow leaves and topped by a spire of 3-in. yellow flowers.

H. × multiflorus. Perennial. Zones 1–24. To 5 ft. tall and 3 ft. wide, with thin, toothedged leaves and many yellow, 3-in., yellow-centered blossoms. Excellent for cutting. 'Loddon Gold' (H. 'Loddon Gold') is double-flowered. 'Capenoch Star' (H. 'Capenoch Star') is single, but disk flowers are quilled (rolled into long, slender tubes), giving a pincushion effect.

H. salicifolius (H. orgyalis). Perennial. Zones 1–24. Native to central U.S. To 6–8 ft. tall and 3 ft. wide, with narrow, gracefully drooping leaves to 8 in. long. Stems are topped by sheaves of 2-in. yellow flowers with purplish brown centers.

Helichrysum
Asteraceae
SHRUBS AND PERENNIALS

⚡ ZONES VARY BY SPECIES

☀ FULL SUN

💧 MODERATE WATER

Helichrysum petiolare

These denizens of sunny, dry sites are grown mainly for their handsome, woolly leaves, though *H. italicum* also has attractive blooms.

H. italicum (H. angustifolium). CURRY PLANT. Perennial. Zones 13–24. From southern Europe. To 2 ft. high and wide, with woody base and crowded, narrow, nearly white leaves. Leaves emit a strong fragrance of curry powder when bruised or pinched. Not used in curry, but a few can add a pleasant aroma to a salad or meat dish. Yellow flowers in 2-in.-wide clusters appear from midsummer to fall.

H. petiolare. LICORICE PLANT. Shrub in Zones 16, 17, 22–24; treated as annual elsewhere. From South Africa. To 3 ft. tall, with trailing stems to 4 ft. wide. White, woolly leaves; insignificant flowers. A licorice aroma is sometimes noticeable—in hot, still weather, for example, or when leaves are dry. 'Limelight' has luminous light chartreuse leaves; 'Licorice Splash' has variegated yellow-green foliage; 'Variegatum' has leaves with white markings. All are useful for their trailing branches, which thread through mixed plantings or mingle with other plants in large pots or hanging baskets.

In parts of coastal Northern California, licorice plant has

escaped cultivation to become an invasive pest; to reduce seed production, shear off blooms when they begin to fade.

Heliconia
LOBSTER-CLAW, FALSE BIRD-OF-PARADISE
Heliconiaceae
PERENNIALS

⚡ ZONES 24; H1, H2; EXCEPT AS NOTED; OR GROW IN POTS

☀ FULL SUN OR LIGHT SHADE

💧 AMPLE WATER

Heliconia angusta

More than 100 species of tropical plants from Central and South America and the southwest Pacific populate this genus. They are grown for their large, showy, waxy flower clusters made up of brightly colored bracts; the small true flowers peep out from the bracts. Clusters may be erect or drooping, from a few inches to several feet in length; spectacular in flower arrangements. In growth habit, plants resemble banana. Oblong to spoon-shaped evergreen leaves are large, and plants form sizable clumps that keep increasing with age.

H. angusta. To 4–10 ft. tall, with leaves to 3 ft. long. Erect flower clusters to 2½ ft. long. Yellow or orange to vermilion or scarlet bracts; white or pale yellow flowers.

H. caribaea. WILD PLANTAIN. To 6–15 ft. tall, with 5-ft.-long leaves and erect flower clusters to 1½ ft. Bracts are red or yellow, often marked with contrasting colors; flowers are white with green tips.

H. latispatha. Can reach 10 ft. tall, with leaves to 5 ft. long. Erect flower clusters to 1½ ft. high, with spirally set orange, red, or yellow bracts and green-tipped yellow flowers.

H. pendula (H. collinsiana). To 6 ft. tall, with leaves to 3 ft. long. Dangling, 2-ft.-long inflorescence has spirally arranged red bracts with yellow flowers.

H. psittacorum. PARROT HELICONIA. Highly variable species; more vigorous than other heliconias. Grows 4–8 ft. tall, with leaves to 20 in. long, blossom clusters to 7 in. long. Bracts spread upward at a 45° angle. They vary in color; may be red, sometimes shading to cream or orange, and are often multicolored. Flowers are yellow, orange, or red, usually tipped in dark green or white. Many named selections are available.

H. rostrata. To 4–6 ft. tall, with 2–4-ft.-long leaves. Hanging inflorescences to 1–2 ft. long contain red bracts shading to yellow at the tip; flowers are greenish yellow.

H. schiedeana. Zones 21–24; H1, H2. To 6–10 ft. tall, with leaves to 5 ft. long. Upright, 1½-ft.-long blossom clusters feature red or orange-red, spiraling bracts that enclose yellow-green flowers. 'Fire and Ice' has bright yellow flowers with deep red bracts.

H. wagneriana. To 6–12 ft. tall, with 4–6-ft.-long leaves. Erect flower clusters 6 in.–1½ ft. long. Heavy, overlapping, green-edged bracts are deep pink to pale crimson, shading to cream at base; flowers are white.

CARE

Heliconias grow best with rich soil, heavy feeding, and plenty of water—all of which will keep clump expanding. Cut away stems that have flowered to make room for new growth. In areas with frosts, grow plants in tubs and shelter from winter cold. Potted plants can bloom anytime; those in the ground flower in spring and summer.

FOR MORE ON PERENNIALS, SEE "GROW: PERENNIALS," PAGES 686–687.

Helictotrichon sempervirens

BLUE OAT GRASS
Poaceae
PERENNIAL GRASS

ZONES 1–12, 14–24

FULL SUN

REGULAR WATER

Helictotrichon sempervirens

Native to the western Mediterranean region. Bright blue-gray, narrow leaves form a symmetrical fountainlike mound 2–3 ft. high and wide; resembles a giant blue fescue (*Festuca glauca*) but is more graceful. In spring, stems to 2 ft. or higher rise above foliage, bearing wispy, straw-colored flower clusters. Attractive in borders or among boulders. Evergreen in mild-winter climates; semievergreen in colder areas. Pull out occasional withered leaves. Best in rich, well-drained soil.

The bright leaves of blue oat grass combine well with silver-leafed plants such as artemisia, snow-in-summer (Cerastium tomentosum), and lamb's ears (Stachys byzantina). They also contrast nicely with purple hop bush (Dodonaea viscosa 'Purpurea') or purple Heuchera varieties.

Heliopsis helianthoides

OX-EYE SUNFLOWER
Asteraceae
PERENNIAL

ZONES 1–11, 14–24

FULL SUN

MODERATE WATER

ATTRACTS BUTTERFLIES

Heliopsis helianthoides
'Loraine Sunshine'

Native to the eastern half of North America, extending southwest to Arizona. The species is rarely offered, but several varieties are available. Most grow 3–4 ft. tall and 3 ft. wide, topped by yellow blooms resembling 2–3-in.-wide sunflowers from late summer into fall. Plants may be staked or allowed to arch gracefully.

Outstanding 4-ft.-tall selections include 'Bressingham Doubloon', with semidouble golden yellow flowers, and 'Prairie Sunset', with golden yellow flowers sporting a dark red spot at the base of each petal. 'Summer Sun' ('Sommersonne'), to 2½ ft. high and 1½ ft. wide, has bright yellow flowers that may be single or semidouble. 'Loraine Sunshine' is about the same size, but its leaves are white with green veins, and its single yellow flowers begin blooming in midsummer. 'Tuscan Sun' is compact, just 1½–2 ft. tall and wide. All kinds are good in cutting gardens and in borders.

CARE

Plant in a sunny location with well-drained soil. Tolerate some light shade, but can get leggy in too much shade. To prolong bloom, pick off spent flowers.

Heliotropium arborescens

COMMON HELIOTROPE
Boraginaceae
PERENNIAL USUALLY TREATED AS ANNUAL

ZONES 15–17, 23, 24; H1, H2 AS PERENNIAL; ANNUAL ANYWHERE

FULL SUN IN COOLER CLIMATES ONLY

REGULAR WATER

ALL PARTS ARE POISONOUS IF INGESTED

Heliotropium arborescens

From Peru. This old-fashioned favorite delivers handsome foliage and clusters of tiny flowers with a sweet, delicate fragrance. Can reach 4 ft. tall, 2 ft. wide as a perennial, but it's typically treated in all regions as a summer bedding annual to 1½–2 ft. high, 1½ ft. wide. Tiny dark violet, purple, blue, or white blossoms are held in rounded, 3–4-in. clusters. Veined leaves have a dark purple cast. 'Black Beauty', 'Iowa', and 'Marine' are among varieties with deep purple flowers. Dwarf forms, under 1 ft. high, include 'Princess Marina' and 'White Lady'. Provide well-drained soil. Good in containers (in cold climates, overwinter in a frost-free spot).

A single heliotrope can live for years on a patio in a large (18-in. diameter) container. Prune the plant lightly each spring to keep it from looking rangy, then top the root zone with a layer of fresh potting soil and mix in a granular controlled-release fertilizer. During the growing season, water regularly, and clip off spent bloom clusters.

Helleborus

HELLEBORE
Ranunculaceae
PERENNIALS

ZONES VARY BY SPECIES

PARTIAL OR FULL SHADE

WATER NEEDS VARY BY SPECIES

ALL PARTS ARE POISONOUS IF INGESTED

Helleborus × *hybridus*
Party Dress group

Distinctive, long-lived plants that add color to the garden for several months in winter and spring; also appreciated for their attractive, leathery foliage.

Flowers are usually shaped like cups or bells, either outward facing or drooping; they consist of a ring of petal-like sepals ranging in color from white and green through pink and red to deep purple (rarely yellow). Flowers persist beyond the listed bloom periods, gradually turning green. Blossoms are attractive in arrangements: seal ends of cut stems by searing over a flame or immersing in boiling water for a few seconds. Then place in cold water. Or simply float flowers in a bowl of water.

Mass hellebores under high-branching trees, on north or east side of walls, or in beds. Not damaged by rodents or deer.

H. argutifolius (H. corsicus). CORSICAN HELLEBORE. Zones 3b–9, 14–24. From Corsica, Sardinia. Erect or sprawling, to 2–3 ft. high and wide. Substantial enough to use as a small shrub. Blue-green leaves are divided into three sharply toothed leaflets. Leafy stems carry clusters of 2-in., pale green flowers. This is the best hellebore for Southern California; more sun-tolerant than others.

H

H

CLOCKWISE FROM TOP: *Helleborus orientalis*; *H. × hybridus*; *H.* 'Ivory Prince'

Two compact varieties with white-marbled leaves are 'Janet Starnes' (with a touch of pink in new foliage) and 'Pacific Frost'. 'Silver Lace' has blue-gray foliage overlaid with a silver lace pattern. Moderate water.

H. × ballardiae. Zones 3–7, 14–24. This cross between *H. niger* and *H. lividus* grows to 1–1½ ft. high and 2 ft. wide, with 2½-in.-wide outward-facing blooms on deep red stems. 'Cinnamon Snow' has dark green leaves and white flowers with warm rose and cinnamon tones. 'Pink Frost' has gray-green leaves with silvery veins; its flowers combine pale pink and rose. Regular water.

H. × ericsmithii. Zones 2–9, 14–24. Hybrid of complex parentage. Grows 1–1½ ft. high and 1½ ft. wide, with dark green, pale-veined leaves and large sprays of pale pink or white flowers, each up to 4 in. across. Blooms face out, not down. Regular water.

H. foetidus. BEAR'S-FOOT HELLEBORE. Zones 2b–9, 14–24. From western and central Europe. To 2½ ft. high and wide, the stems clothed with dark green leaves divided into many narrow leaflets. Clusters of inch-wide flowers are light green with purplish red edges. 'Red Silver' has red stems, narrow leaflets with a silver sheen, and green flowers with a red edge. Plants in the Wester Flisk group have stems, flower stems, and leafstalks infused with purplish red, with the color extending into leaf bases. All tolerate considerable sun in cool, humid areas. Self-sow freely where adapted. Moderate water.

H. × hybridus. Zones 2b–10, 14–24. Leaves have no obvious stems. These hybrid plants generally resemble principal parent, *H. orientalis,* but flower color range has been extended and superior parents selected for seed production. Some are sold under the breeder's name, such as Ballard's Group, which has flowers in several colors. Others are sold as color strains, such as Sunshine selections (white, pink, yellow, or red flowers), Royal Heritage strain (pink, purple, maroon, or white blooms), and Winter Queen mix (white, pink, maroon, or spotted flowers). Others are grouped according to form, such as Party Dress group, which has double flowers. Moderate to regular water.

H. 'Ivory Prince'. Zones 2–9, 14–17. Hybrid of complex parentage, with foliage like that of *H. niger*. Grows 1 ft. high, 1½–2 ft. wide; red buds open into ivory white flowers that take on rose and chartreuse tones as they age. Regular water.

H. lividus. Zones 5 (with protection), 6–9, 14–24. From Majorca. To 1½ ft. high and twice as wide. Leaves resemble those of *H. argutifolius* but lack noticeable teeth and have purplish undersides and a network of pale veins above. Flowers are pale green washed with pinkish purple. Moderate water.

H. niger. CHRISTMAS ROSE. Zones 1–7, 14–17. From Europe. Leaves have no obvious stems. Elegant plant to 1 ft. high, 1½ ft. wide. Dark green leaves are divided into several lobes with a few large teeth. White, 2-in. flowers appear singly or in groups of two or three on a stout stem about the same height as the foliage clump. Blooms turn pinkish with age. 'White Magic' and 'Potter's Wheel' are large-flowered varieties. Needs more shade than other hellebores. Also needs alkaline soil; if your soil is acidic, mulch plants with ½-in.-deep layer of lime or granite chips. Regular water.

H. orientalis. LENTEN ROSE. Zones 2b–10, 14–24. Greece, Turkey, and the Caucasus. Leaves have no obvious stems. Basal leaves have sharply toothed leaflets; branched flowering stems to 1 ft. high. Flowers are 2–4 in. wide, in colors including white, pink, purplish, cream, and greenish, often spotted with deep purple. Easier to transplant than other hellebores. A widely variable plant, but all forms are attractive. Encourage self-sowing and keep the colors you like. Moderate to regular water.

H. × sternii. Zones 4–9, 14–24. Hybrid between *H. argutifolius* and *H. lividus*, with bluish green foliage netted with white or cream. Greenish flowers are suffused with pink. Grows 1–1½ ft. high and wide. Moderate water. 'Boughton Beauty' has silver-gray leaves with pink stems. Plants in Blackthorn Group have boldly veined leaves, purple stems, and purplish flowers.

CARE

Plant in well-drained soil amended with plenty of organic matter. Plants prefer soil that is somewhat alkaline but will also grow well in neutral to slightly acid conditions (*H. niger* is an exception; it must have alkaline soil). Feed once or twice a year. Don't disturb once planted; they resent moving and may take 2 or more years to reestablish (if they survive at all). If well sited, however, they may self-sow, and young seedlings can be transplanted in early spring. Offspring may not resemble the parent, but all are attractive.

Helxine soleirolii.
See *Soleirolia soleirolii*

Hemerocallis
DAYLILY
Hemerocallidaceae
PERENNIALS FROM TUBEROUS ROOTS

✿ **ZONES 1–24; H1, H2; EXCEPT AS NOTED**

☼ ◐ **PARTIAL SHADE IN HOTTEST CLIMATES**

◗ **REGULAR WATER**

Hemerocallis hybrid

Few plants offer flowers in so many colors with so little care. Tuberous, somewhat fleshy roots give rise to large clumps of arching, sword-shaped leaves—evergreen, semievergreen, or deciduous, depending on daylily type. Deciduous types go completely dormant in winter and are the hardiest, surviving without protection to about −35°F (−37°C); where winters are very mild, however, they may not get enough chill to perform well. Evergreen kinds succeed in mild-winter regions as well as in colder areas, but they need a protective mulch (such as a 4–6-in. layer of hay) where temperatures dip below −20°F (−29°C). Semievergreen sorts may or may not retain their leaves, depending on where they are grown.

Clusters of flowers resembling lilies appear at the ends of generally leafless stems that stand well above foliage. Each bloom lasts for only a day, but replacements are plentiful. Older yellow, orange, and rust red daylilies have for the most part been replaced by newer kinds in an expanded range of colors and patterns; both tall and dwarf varieties are available.

Use in borders, on banks under high-branching deciduous trees, along driveways, or among evergreen shrubs near pools, along streams. Plant dwarf daylilies in rock gardens or as edgings or low groundcovers. All are good cut flowers. Cut stems with well-developed buds; these open on successive days, though each flower is slightly smaller than the preceding one. Arrange individual blooms in low bowls. One caution: plants are reportedly toxic to cats.

H. hybrids. Deciduous, evergreen, and semievergreen. Standard-size hybrids generally grow 2½–4 ft. tall, 2–3 ft. wide; some selections reach 6 ft. tall. Dwarf types grow just 1–2 ft. high and wide. Flowers of standard kinds are 4–8 in. across, those of dwarfs 1½–3½ in. wide. Some have broad petals, others narrow, spidery ones; many have ruffled petal edges. Colors range far beyond the basic yellow, orange, and rusty red to pink, vermilion, buff, apricot, plum- or lilac-purple, cream, and near-white, often with contrasting eyes or midrib stripes that yield a bicolor effect. Many varieties are sprinkled with tiny iridescent dots known as diamond dust. Selections with

semidouble and double flowers exist. Tetraploid varieties have unusually heavily textured petals.

Bloom usually begins in mid- to late spring, but early and late bloomers are also sold. By planting all three types, you can extend bloom period. Scattered bloom may occur during summer, and reblooming types put on second display in late summer to midautumn. Some varieties bloom throughout warm weather. These include 3-ft.-high Starburst series, which comes in a variety of colors, as well as 2-ft.-high dwarf varieties 'Black-eyed Stella' (yellow with red eye), bright yellow 'Happy Returns' and 'Stella de Oro', and red 'Pardon Me'.

New hybrids appear in such numbers that no book can keep up. To get the ones you want, visit daylily specialists, buy plants in bloom at your local nursery, study catalogs, or visit the website of the American Hemerocallis Society (*daylilies.org*).

H. lilioasphodelus (H. flava). LEMON DAYLILY. Deciduous. From China. Reaches 3 ft. high and wide, with 2-ft.-long leaves; 4-in., fragrant, pure yellow flowers bloom in mid- to late spring. Newer hybrids may be showier, but this species is still cherished for its delightful perfume and early bloom time.

H. minor. GRASS-LEAF DAYLILY. Deciduous. Zones A1–A3; 1–9, 14–17. From eastern Asia. To 2 ft. high and wide, with slender leaves. Blooms for a relatively short time in late spring or early summer; when fragrant, bright golden yellow flowers are held just above the foliage. This is among the few daylilies hardy enough to succeed in Alaska's interior.

CARE

Daylilies adapt to almost any kind of soil. Set out bare-root plants at any time during the growing season; spring and summer are better in cold-winter zones, while fall and winter are preferred where winters are warm. Plant from containers at any time from early spring through midautumn (year-round in mild-winter areas). For best results, provide well-drained soil amended with organic matter;

give regular moisture from spring through autumn. When clumps become crowded (usually after 3 to 6 years), divide them in fall or early spring in hot-summer areas, during summer in cool-summer regions or where growing season is short.

Hepatica
LIVERLEAF
Ranunculaceae
PERENNIALS

⚟ **ZONES 1–6, 14–17**

☼ ◐ **PARTIAL OR FULL SHADE**

💧 **REGULAR WATER**

Hepatica nobilis japonica

Diminutive woodland plants (just 6–9 in. high and 6 in. wide) with evergreen or nearly evergreen leaves and charming blooms. Flowers resemble small anemones, with narrow, petal-like sepals arranged around a central mass of yellow stamens. Bloom comes in early spring, each flower rising on its own stalk above the clump of last year's leaves. A new crop of leaves follows bloom. Choice plants for woodland gardens and shaded rock gardens.

H. acutiloba. Native to eastern and central North America. Leathery leaves are divided into three sharp-pointed lobes. Flowers may be blue, pale rose-purple, or white, to 1 in. across, on stems to 9 in. high.

H. americana. Native to eastern and central North America. Leathery, 4-in. leaves with three rounded lobes. Flowering stems are usually just 6 in. high. Flowers are typically light blue, but sometimes pink or white, ½–1 in. wide.

H. nobilis (H. triloba). Native to Europe. Very similar to *H. americana*. Bears flowers that are usually bluish purple though sometimes are white or pink.

Heptacodium miconioides
SEVEN SONS FLOWER
Caprifoliaceae
DECIDUOUS SHRUB OR TREE

⚟ **ZONES 2B–6, 14–17**

☼ ◐ **FULL SUN OR LIGHT SHADE**

💧 **REGULAR WATER**

Heptacodium miconioides

From China. Handsome, fountain-shaped shrub to 15–20 ft. tall and 8–10 ft. wide; can be trained as a single- or multi-trunked tree. Large, narrowly heart-shaped leaves are shiny green and deeply veined. Fragrant, creamy white flowers in large clusters at branch ends open over a long bloom season in late summer and fall. Blooms are succeeded by even showier masses of small fruits that devlop inside rosy-purple calyxes. Picturesque even in winter, when strips of thin, pale bark peel away to reveal dark brown bark beneath.

The common name derives from the number of flowers in each of the clusters forming part of the larger inflorescence. Good substitute for crape myrtle (*Lagerstroemia*) in cooler zones, where that plant does not succeed. Not fussy about soil and not bothered by pests or diseases.

Heptapleurum arboricolum.
See *Schefflera arboricola*

H

Hesperaloe
Asparagaceae
PERENNIALS

- ✎ **ZONES VARY BY SPECIES**
- ☼ ◑ **FULL SUN OR LIGHT SHADE**
- ◐ ◗ **LITTLE TO MODERATE WATER**
- ✿ **FLOWERS ATTRACT HUMMINGBIRDS**

Hesperaloe parviflora

Rosettes of stiff, narrow, evergreen leaves give these plants the look of a coarse grass or yucca. Each leaf is edged with a threadlike fringe. Foliage clumps give rise to tall, branching inflorescences set with many tubular flowers. Established plants can get by with little summer water, but they look and bloom better with a deep soaking every 2 weeks or so during warm weather. Quite heat-tolerant. Remove spent flower clusters to neaten appearance.

H. funifera. Zones 12, 13. From northern Mexico. Clumps grow to 6 ft. tall and wide. Stems up to 15 ft. tall bear inch-wide, greenish white flowers in late spring or early summer.

H. nocturna. Zones 12, 13. From northern Mexico. Foliage clump 5 ft. tall, 6 ft. wide. Flowers in late spring and early summer, producing blossom spikes up to 12 ft. tall that bear many 1-in., night-blooming, slightly fragrant greenish lavender flowers.

H. parviflora. RED YUCCA. Zones 2b, 3, 7–16, 18–24. From Texas and New Mexico. Leaf clumps 3–4 ft. tall and at least as wide produce 5-ft. stalks carrying many rose-red to salmon-pink flowers from late spring through midsummer, sometimes into early fall. Good cut flowers. Especially heat-tolerant; can take reflected

heat. Excellent container plant. Long-blooming 'Brakelight' is compact at 2 ft. high and wide, with bright red blooms. There is a yellow-flowered form.

Hesperis matronalis
DAME'S ROCKET
Brassicaceae
PERENNIAL OR BIENNIAL

- ✎ **ZONES A2, A3; 1–24**
- ☼ ◑ **FULL SUN OR LIGHT SHADE**
- ◗ **REGULAR WATER**

Hesperis matronalis

Old-fashioned cottage garden plant from central and southern Europe; naturalized in North America. Free-branching growth to 3 ft. high and wide. From late spring into summer, bears rounded clusters of ½-in., four-petaled lilac to purple flowers similar to those of stock (*Matthiola*); blossoms are fragrant at night. Grows readily from seed and often self-sows. When plants get old and woody, replace them with young seedlings. White- and double-flowered forms exist.

Colorful Cottage Gardens

Among the most useful plants for casual, exuberant cottage gardens are medium-height, free-blooming perennials. These include dame's rocket (*Hesperis matronalis*), *Agastache*, butterfly weed (*Asclepias tuberosa*), chrysanthemum, daylily (*Hemerocallis*), iris, peony, and salvia. To keep color coming in the foreground and along path edges, plant Spanish shawl (*Heterocentron elegans*), woolly yarrow (*Achillea tomentosa*), sweet alyssum (*Lobularia maritima*), and violets.

Heterocentron elegans
SPANISH SHAWL
Melastomataceae
PERENNIAL

- ✎ **ZONES 15–24**
- ◑ **PARTIAL SHADE**
- ◐ ◗ **MODERATE TO REGULAR WATER**

Heterocentron elegans

Colorful Mexican and Guatemalan native formerly known as *Schizocentron elegans*. Grows just 2–4 in. high, 1½ ft. wide, with creeping, vinelike habit. Glossy, oval evergreen leaves may take on reddish tones as the season advances. In summer, inch-wide magenta flowers appear among the leaves; calyxes remain after blossoms have withered. When used as a groundcover, blooming plants look like a carpet of bright bougainvillea. Great in hanging baskets. Needs frost protection in Zones 15, 16, 18–20. Best in partial shade but tolerates full sun (in cooler climates) as well as full shade. Protect from snails and slugs.

Heteromeles arbutifolia
TOYON
Rosaceae
EVERGREEN SHRUB OR TREE

- ✎ **ZONES 5–9, 14–24**
- ☼ ◑ **FULL SUN OR PARTIAL SHADE**
- ◗ **MODERATE WATER**
- ✿ **ATTRACTS BIRDS, BUTTERFLIES**

Heteromeles arbutifolia

Native to the California Coast Ranges, Sierra Nevada foothills, and Baja California. Sometimes called Christmas berry or California holly, this handsome evergreen plant forms a dense shrub to 8–15 ft. tall and broad or a multitrunked small tree to 25 ft. tall and spreading almost as wide.

Leathery dark green leaves are variable in shape, usually 2–4 in. long and edged with bristly, pointed teeth. Profuse small white flowers in flattish clusters appear in summer; these are followed in fall to winter by pea-size bright red berries, much relished by birds. Disease-resistant 'Davis Gold' has golden yellow berries. *H. a. macrocarpa,* from Southern California's Channel Islands, has larger berries.

CARE

Toyon improves under cultivation. If trimmed to give abundance of year-old wood, it produces even more berries than in the wild. Valuable as a screen or bank planting. Subject to fireblight. Tolerates drought but looks better with moderate irrigation.

FOR MORE PLANTS THAT ATTRACT BUTTERFLIES, SEE PAGES 100–103.

Heuchera

CORAL BELLS, ALUM ROOT

Saxifragaceae

PERENNIALS

- 🌿 **ZONES VARY BY SPECIES**
- ☀️ ◑ **FULL SUN IN COOLER CLIMATES ONLY**
- 💧 ◐ **MODERATE TO REGULAR WATER**
- 🐦 **ATTRACT BIRDS**

Heuchera 'Green Spice'

Compact, mounding, evergreen plants prized for their handsome foliage, which comes in an incredible array of colors. Leaves are roundish, with lobed or scalloped edges. The dainty blossoms are attractive too: slender, wiry 1–3-ft. stems bear loose clusters of tiny, nodding, bell-shaped flowers that are long lasting in cut arrangements. Floral color range includes white, green, and shades of red to pink. Bloom time varies by type from early spring to late summer; some kinds continue into autumn.

All grow best in humus-rich soil; they require good drainage. Will take full sun in cool climates, but in warmer regions they do best with afternoon shade or a northern exposure with open sky above. Use among boulders, as groundcover, in front of shrubs, or as edging for beds of taller perennials. They make excellent "fillers" in container compositions.

H. × brizoides. Zones 1–10, 14–24. Diverse group of hybrids to 1–2½ ft. high, 1–1½ ft. wide, with spring or summer bloom. Seed-grown strain called Bressingham hybrids offers profuse flowers in white and shades of pink and red. Cutting-grown varieties include 'Firefly' ('Leucht-käfer'), with fragrant, fiery scarlet bells; and 'June Bride', with large pure white blossoms.

H. Canyon series. Zones 2–11, 14–24. Spring-blooming group of mat-forming hybrids. Foliage mounds are 3–6 in. high, 1–2 ft. or more wide, with small, rounded leaves. Two choices with sprays of ½-in. flowers on 8–16-in. stems are rose-red 'Canyon Delight' and medium pink 'Canyon Pink'. Growing to 12–18 in. high in bloom are dark pink 'Canyon Chimes', bicolored pink and white 'Canyon Duet', medium pink 'Canyon Melody', and rich red 'Canyon Belle'.

H. hybrids. Zones 1–9, 14–24; often short-lived in warm-summer areas. The following varieties have been selected for their marvelously colored and sometimes ruffled foliage. Some have as a parent *H. americana*, a species from the central U.S. with marbled and veined leaves up to 4½ in. across. Many newer hybrids involve *H. villosa*, native to the mid-southern U.S. and thus quite tolerant of heat and humidity. Both form mounds of foliage about 1½ ft. high and not quite as wide. Tiny summer flowers are held on thin stalks to 2–3 ft. high and are white to cream unless otherwise noted.

'Amethyst Myst'. Deep burgundy leaves age to silver with dark purple veins.

'Caramel'. Leaves emerge dusky red and mature through apricot tones to golden yellow.

'Chocolate Ruffles'. Leaves dark chocolate above, burgundy below; burgundy color also shows in ruffles on leaf edges. Purple blossom spikes and flowers.

'Chocolate Veil'. Chocolate-colored leaves with maroon undersides; top surfaces of leaves marbled with light purple and silver between veins. Purple flowers tinged lime green.

'Citronelle'. Leaves are chartreuse to bright lemon yellow.

'Crème Brûlée'. Peachy orange foliage and creamy yellow flowers.

'Crimson Curls'. Deep red, ruffled leaves, fading to gray-green in summer.

CLOCKWISE FROM TOP: *Heuchera* 'Midas Touch'; *H.* 'Electric Lime'; *H.* 'Midnight Rose'

'Georgia Peach'. Leaves emerge peachy orange and age through red tones to rosy purple; dark veins and a silvery sheen.

'Ginger Ale'. Ginger gold foliage with silvery markings. Flowers are soft yellow and pink.

'Green Spice'. Silver-gray leaves with dark green or purple veins.

'Lime Rickey'. Chartreuse leaves with ruffled edges.

'Mahogany'. Lightly ruffled leaves emerge purple and mature through mahogany tones to deep red.

'Marmalade'. Ruffled leaves emerge bright red and age to shades of orange and rich reddish brown; deep red flowers.

'Miracle'. Leaves emerge chartreuse with central splotches of burgundy and mature to brick red thinly edged in gold. Pale pink flowers.

'Moonlight'. Leaves are blackish purple with a silvery overlay. Pale green flowers are larger than those of other hybrids listed here.

'Obsidian'. Foliage deepest burgundy, nearly black, with glossy sheen.

'Peach Flambé'. Bright leaves of apricot to peach take on purple tones in winter.

'Persian Carpet'. Silver leaves with dark purple veins and leaf edges.

'Pewter Moon'. Silvery leaves with maroon undersides; pink blooms.

'Pewter Veil'. Shining silvery leaves with dark veins; small purple flowers.

'Plum Royale'. Shiny, plum-purple leaves with a silver coating and dark purple veins. Holds color well if given good light.

'Ruby Veil'. Large (8 in.) silvery leaves; veins red near leaf base.

'Shenandoah Mountain'. Purple and bronze leaves with a silver sheen.

'Silver Scrolls'. Silvery leaves with dark purple veins.

'Snow Angel'. Light green leaves splashed with cream; pinkish red flowers.

'Southern Comfort'. Very large (9 in.) leaves are peachy orange when new, taking on copper and amber tones as they age.

H

»

'Stormy Seas'. Leaves with tones of silver, lavender, and pewter, with red undersides that show on curly edges.

'Tiramisu'. Chartreuse foliage is centrally blushed with red when young; with age, leaves turn mostly red, with a bright golden edge.

'Velvet Night'. Deep bluish purple to blackish plum leaves with a silver sheen.

'Vesuvius'. Burgundy-purple foliage topped by profuse bright red flowers.

H. maxima. ISLAND ALUM ROOT. Zones 15–24. Native to the Channel Islands off coast of Southern California. Foliage clumps grow 1–2 ft. high, spreading 3–4 ft. or more in time. Lobed dark green leaves have a roundish heart shape. Hundreds of small whitish or pinkish blossoms appear on each narrowly branched 1½–2½-ft. stem in early spring. Good casual groundcover.

H. micrantha. Zones 1–10, 14–24. Native to California, Washington, Oregon, and Idaho. Plant in protected spot in coldest part of range; in desert, give full shade but good light. Long-stalked, roundish, gray-green leaves to 3 in. wide form attractive mounds. Late spring to early summer flowers are whitish or greenish, about ⅛ in. long, carried in loose clusters on leafy, 2–3-ft. stems. 'Martha Roderick' has bright green leaves and profuse rose-pink flowers. 'Painted Lady' has purple leaves marked with silvery gray. 'Palace Purple' has maplelike, rich brownish or purplish leaves that retain their color all year if given adequate sunlight. Leaves of 'Ruffles' are deeply lobed and ruffled around the edges.

A low, mounding habit makes coral bells a natural choice for the front of the border, along paths, or grouped at the base of upright, spiky plants. Planted en masse, they make exquisite groundcovers.

H. Rancho Santa Ana hybrids. Zones 14–24. These hybrids between *H. sanguinea* and *H. maxima* are vigorous and free flowering. Foliage clumps grow 1–2 ft. high and 2–4 ft. wide, with leaves up to 4 in. across. Stems 2–3 ft. high carry a profusion of small flowers. Long bloom season, from late spring through summer, nearly all year in mild-winter areas. 'Genevieve' has green leaves marbled with gray; deep pink, white-centered flowers. 'Opal' has medium green leaves and white flowers that open from pink buds. 'Santa Ana Cardinal' sports shiny dark green leaves and rose-pink flowers. Leaves of 'Wendy' are light green, pretty in combination with its medium pink flowers.

H. sanguinea. Zones A1–A3; 1–11, 14–24. Native to New Mexico and Arizona. Round, 1–2-in. leaves with scalloped edges form neat foot-wide foliage tufts. From spring into summer, slender, wiry, 1–2-ft. stems bear open clusters of nodding, bell-shaped flowers. 'Cherry Splash' has red flowers and white-and-gold variegation on the leaves. 'Frosty' has red flowers and silver-variegated foliage. Pink-flowered 'Geisha's Fan' has silver leaves with purple veins. 'Snow Storm' has green leaves heavily splashed with white and flowers that are cerise-red. 'White Cloud' has light green, silver-flecked foliage and profuse white blossoms.

CARE

Divide clumps every 3 or 4 years in spring (or in fall in mild-winter climates). Use young, vigorous rooted divisions, or cut old woody stems to within an inch of the ground and let them regrow. Easy to propagate from cuttings started in sand in the spring or from seed sown in the spring. Strawberry root weevils chew on foliage, but these can be shaken off lifted plants. Mealybugs can damage the base of plants; treat with insecticidal soap.

FOR MORE PLANTS THAT ATTRACT BIRDS, SEE PAGES 95–99.

× Heucherella
Saxifragaceae
PERENNIALS

- ZONES 1–10, 14–24
- LIGHT SHADE
- REGULAR WATER

× Heucherella 'Stoplight'

These hybrids combine the flowering habit of coral bells (*Heuchera*) with the heart-shaped leaves of foamflower (*Tiarella cordifolia*). Most produce foliage clumps 4–6 in. high and about 1 ft. wide; leaves are deeply lobed and up to 4 in. across. Late spring or summer blooms of pink or white are held on thin stalks 1–2 ft. high, creating a candlelike effect. Excellent choice for shaded rock gardens or as woodland groundcover. Require rich, well-drained soil.

× H. 'Alabama Sunrise'. Deeply lobed, bright golden yellow leaves with red veins; develops coral tones in fall. White flowers.

× H. alba 'Bridget Bloom'. Bright green leaves marked with reddish brown; pink flowers from spring to midsummer.

× H. 'Burnished Bronze'. Bronze-red leaves; pink flowers.

× H. 'Dayglow Pink'. Rich green, deeply cut leaves marked in chocolate brown; pink blooms.

× H. 'Kimono'. Deeply lobed leaves patterned green and silver with purple veins and a dark central stripe; flowers are tawny white and not showy. Clumps reach 1 ft. high and at least twice as wide.

× H. 'Stoplight'. Large chartreuse to lime green leaves are veined and centered with bright red; white blossoms.

× H. 'Sweet Tea'. Large, rich apricot orange leaves are veined and centered in burgundy; flowers are white. Foliage mound reaches 1½ ft. high and 2 ft. wide.

× H. tiarelloides. Light green leaves and sprays of pink flowers spring to midsummer, often with repeat bloom in autumn.

Hibbertia
Dilleniaceae
EVERGREEN SHRUBS AND VINES

- ZONES VARY BY SPECIES
- FULL SUN OR PARTIAL SHADE
- REGULAR WATER

Hibbertia scandens

These Australian natives are grown for their attractive foliage and bright yellow flowers resembling wild roses.

H. cuneiformis (Candollea cuneiformis). Shrub. Zones 12, 13, 15–24. Grows to 4 ft. tall and 6 ft. wide. Polished, bright green leaves are nice in contrast with the flowers, which are carried all along new growth in spring. Prune after flowering to control outline. Requires exceptionally fast drainage. Tolerates wind.

H. scandens (H. volubilis). GUINEA GOLD VINE. Zones 16, 17, 21–24. Fast-growing vine climbs by twining stems to 8–10 ft. In ideal climate, foliage is handsome all year—narrow, waxy dark green leaves to 3 in. long. Blooms from spring into early fall. Good for small garden areas if trained on trellis or against low fence; can be grown as groundcover. Do any significant thinning in late fall or winter; remove errant stems as needed during bloom time.

Hibiscus

Malvaceae

PERENNIALS, ANNUALS, AND
EVERGREEN AND DECIDUOUS SHRUBS
OR TREES

✿ **ZONES VARY BY SPECIES**

☀ **FULL SUN**

💧 **REGULAR WATER**

🦋 **ATTRACT HUMMINGBIRDS
AND BUTTERFLIES**

Hibiscus rosa-sinensis
'Largo Breeze'

Big, brilliant flowers on plump shrubs rank this among the showiest flowering shrubs in Western gardens. Some are very tender tropical species grown in Hawaii, others very hardy. Plants typically bear funnel-shaped blossoms, often with prominent stamens.

Giant whitefly is the most important pest of hibiscus in central and Southern California, coating the undersides of leaves with wax and eventually defoliating the plant. A parasitoid wasp has been released to control it, and research continues on its control.

H. arnottianus. HAWAIIAN WHITE HIBISCUS. Shrub or tree. Zones 23, 24; H1, H2. Native to Hawaii, island of Oahu. To 30 ft. tall and 25 ft. wide. Produces slightly fragrant white flowers with a central column of magenta stamens almost year-round. Beautiful small entryway tree or landscape accent.

H. brackenridgei. Shrub or tree. Zones 23, 24; H1, H2. Native to Hawaii, and the official state flower there. Plant grows to 8–15 ft. tall and about half as wide, with a profusion of large, pure yellow flowers borne in spring and early summer. Somewhat short-lived (4 to 6 years in the wild).

H. calyphyllus. Woody-based perennial or shrub. Zones 23, 24; H1, H2. Native to tropical Africa. Sprawling growth to 3–9 ft. tall and as wide. Flowers are 3–4 in. wide, sulfur yellow marked maroon at the base.

H. moscheutos. PERENNIAL HIBISCUS, ROSE-MALLOW. Perennial. Zones 2–24; H1. Native to eastern U.S. Produces the largest flowers of all hibiscus, some reaching 1 ft. across; grows 6–8 ft. tall and 3 ft. wide. Bloom runs from late spring or early summer until frost. Oval, toothed leaves are deep green above, whitish beneath. Plants die to the ground in winter, even in mild climates. For most spectacular bloom, feed at 6- to 8-week intervals during growing season and protect from wind.

Most varieties are probably hybrids. Southern Belle grows 4 ft. tall; Disco series reaches 2–2½ ft. high. All have 8–12-in.-wide flowers in red, pink, rose, or white, often with red eye. The Luna series grows to 3 ft. high, with 6–8-in. flowers in shades of red, rose, white, and pink. The many cutting-grown selections and hybrids include

these 4-footers: 'Blue River II', 10-in. pure white flowers; 'Lady Baltimore', 6–8-in. glowing pink flowers with a large red center; and 'The Clown', 6–8-in. light pink flowers with a red eye. Plants in the Cordials and Vintage Splash series—with names like 'Cherry Brandy' (red), 'Peppermint Schnapps' (pink), and 'Pinot Grigio' (white)—grow 3–4 ft. tall, have 8–10-in. blooms. 'Moy Grandé' produces record-size, 12-in. pink flowers on a 5-ft. plant. 'Crimson Wonder' can reach 5 ft. tall and wide, with slightly ruffled rose-red flowers 9–11 in. across.

H. mutabilis. CONFEDERATE ROSE. Deciduous shrub or tree. Zones 4–24; H1, H2. From China. In the warmest climates, shrubby or treelike to 15 ft. tall and 8 ft. wide. Behaves more like a perennial in colder part of range, growing flowering branches from woody base or short trunk. Broad, oval leaves with three to five lobes. Summer flowers are 4–6 in. wide, opening white or pink and changing to deep red by evening. 'Flore Pleno' has double, rosy pink flowers.

H. rockii. See *H. calyphyllus.*

H. rosa-sinensis. CHINESE HIBISCUS, TROPICAL HIBISCUS. Evergreen shrub. Zones 9, 12–16, 19–24; H1, H2. Probably from tropical Asia; in cultivation for centuries. One of the most flamboyant flowering shrubs, it reaches 30 ft. tall and 15–20 ft. wide in Hawaii, but typically 8–15 ft. tall, 5–8 ft. wide on the mainland. Glossy leaves vary in size and texture, depending on variety. Growth habit may be dense, or loose and open. Summer flowers are single or double, 4–8 in. wide. Colors range from white through pink to red, from yellow and apricot to orange. Individual flowers usually last only a day, but the plant blooms continuously.

There are many series with a full range of flower colors. The TradeWinds series puts full-size plants in the Winds group and 2–3-ft. dwarfs in the Breeze category. The Luau series includes selections in most colors on 2–3-ft. plants.

CLOCKWISE FROM TOP LEFT: *Hibiscus rosa-sinensis* 'Jewel of India'; *H. syriacus* 'Blue Bird'; *H. brackenridgei*

H

»

H

CARE

Use Chinese hibiscus as screen, espalier, or container plant (indoors or out). It needs excellent drainage. Provide overhead protection where winter lows hit freezing; where temperatures go lower, grow in containers and shelter indoors over winter; or treat as annual, setting out fresh plants each spring. To develop good branch structure, prune poorly shaped young plants when you set them out in spring. To keep a mature plant growing vigorously, prune out about a third of old wood in early spring. Tip-pinching in spring and summer increases flower production. All varieties susceptible to aphids.

H. syriacus. ROSE OF SHARON, SHRUB ALTHAEA. Deciduous shrub. Zones 2–24; H1. From eastern Asia. To 10–12 ft. tall and 6 ft. wide. Upright and compact when young, spreading and open with age. Easily trained to a single trunk with a treelike top, or as an espalier or hedge. Leaves, often three lobed, are coarsely toothed. Leafs out later in spring than most other deciduous shrubs; foliage drops in fall without coloring. Blooms from mid- or late summer until frost, resembling a bush covered with hollyhocks. Blossoms are single, semidouble, or double, 2½–3 in. across, some with contrasting red to purple throat. Single flowers are slightly more effective, opening somewhat wider, but they tend to produce many unattractive capsule-type fruits—which in turn produce many unwanted seedlings.

H. tiliaceus. TREE HIBIS-CUS, HAU, MAHOE. Evergreen tree. Zones 23, 24; H1, H2. Native to tropical Asia and Polynesia. Reaches 30 ft. tall and wide, with leathery green leaves to 6 in. long. The 4-in. flowers open yellow and deepen to orange by day's end. Excellent tolerance of salt, wind, drought, and heat. Tangled mess in the wild; requires heavy pruning to make it an attractive tree, regular pruning to maintain it.

Himalayacalamus.
See Bamboo

Hippeastrum
AMARYLLIS
Amaryllidaceae
PERENNIALS FROM BULBS

- ☀ ZONES VARY BY TYPE; OR INDOORS
- ☀ ◑ LIGHT SHADE IN HOTTEST CLIMATES; BRIGHT LIGHT
- ⬤ REGULAR WATER DURING GROWTH AND BLOOM
- ☠ BULB CAUSES GASTROINTESTINAL PROBLEMS IF INGESTED

Hippeastrum 'Venusto'

Known best as large-flowered Christmas gift plants, hybrid amaryllis can also be grown outdoors year-round in Zones 13, 15–17, 21–24, H1, H2; and with some shelter, in Zones 8, 9, 14, 18, 20. Available as singles and doubles in reds, pinks, salmon, near-orange, creamy yellow, and white; some are striped, picoteed, and variously marked; as miniatures with 3–5-in. flowers topping 12–15-in. stems; and as an unusual evergreen Brazilian species, *H. papilio* (Zones 8, 9, 13–24), with 5-in., greenish white flowers heavily patterned in pinkish purple or red. These blooms are 8–9 in. across, on a stout, 2-ft. stem. For the fall-blooming amaryllis commonly called naked lady, see *Amaryllis belladonna*.

Outdoors, amaryllis blooms in spring, appearing either before or with the broad, strap-shaped leaves. Indoors, they bloom just a few weeks after planting.

CARE

In fall, plant in large clumps or drifts by setting bulbs 1 ft. apart in organically enriched, well-drained soil; keep tops of bulb necks even with soil surface. Protect from slugs and snails. Water thoroughly, then keep soil barely moist until leaves emerge. Once plants have sprouted, increase watering, but don't let soil become soggy. Leaves will grow through summer and disappear in fall if plants are dried off; otherwise, some foliage will remain. Divide infrequently.

For container culture, indoors or out, plant in fall in a rich, sandy potting mix amended with bonemeal or superphosphate. Allow a 2-in. space between the bulb and the edge of the pot; set upper half of bulb above soil surface. Firm soil, water well, and then keep soil barely moist until plant growth begins. When flowers fade, cut off stem; keep up regular watering and feeding until late summer. Then cut back on watering. When leaves are completely yellow, withhold water and let plants dry out.

Holodiscus
Rosaceae
DECIDUOUS SHRUBS

- ☀ ZONES 1–9, 14–19, EXCEPT AS NOTED
- ◑ PARTIAL SHADE
- ◐ ◑ ⬤ LITTLE TO REGULAR WATER
- 🦋 ATTRACT BIRDS, BUTTERFLIES

Holodiscus discolor

From big shrubs with beautiful plumes of creamy white, early-summer flowers to a low groundcover, those listed here are Western natives. Nodding, branched clusters of many small, creamy white flowers at branch tips in late spring or early summer make quite a show. Blooms age to tannish gold. Thin plants after flowers have turned brown. Use shrubby kinds in native plantings or low-maintenance gardens where they can fend for themselves.

H. discolor. CREAM BUSH, OCEAN SPRAY. Native to Coast Ranges, Sierra Nevada; north to British Columbia, east to Rocky Mountains. May reach 20 ft. tall and 15 ft. wide in moist, rich soil. In dry, sunny situations east of Cascades, it may grow just 3 ft. high and 4 ft. wide. Triangular leaves to 3 in. long are deep green above, white and hairy beneath, toothed. Flower clusters reach 1 ft. long.

H. dumosus. MOUNTAIN SPRAY, ROCK SPIRAEA. Zones 1–3, 10. Native to the eastern slopes of the Cascades of Oregon and to shady canyons in the Rockies from Wyoming southward. Smaller than *H. discolor* (15 ft. tall in good conditions), with narrower flower clusters to 7 in. long. Coarsely toothed leaves are less than 1 in. long.

H. microphyllus. ROCK SPIRAEA, SMALL-LEAVED CREAM BUSH. Native to high Western mountains. Spreading to matting, with ¼–1-in. leaves, 3-in. flower clusters.

Homeria collina
(Moraea collina)
Iridaceae
PERENNIAL FROM CORM

- ☀ ZONES 4–24; OR DIG AND STORE
- ☀ FULL SUN
- ⬤ REGULAR WATER DURING GROWTH AND BLOOM

Homeria collina

Native to South Africa, where it is often found growing on slopes at all altitudes. One floppy, grasslike leaf is followed by branching or unbranched,

1½-ft. stems bearing 2½–3-in.-wide flowers in soft yellow or muted orange. Soon after bloom, the foliage yellows and dies down.

Plant fall through winter, setting corms 2 in. deep, 3 in. apart; corms will multiply freely. If they will receive moisture during their long summer dormancy, however, soil must be very well drained. If it isn't, dig after leaves have died down and store over summer; or grow in pots. In areas beyond hardiness range, plant as soon as soil can be worked in spring for summer flowers; lift corms in late summer or early fall and store over winter.

Horseradish

Brassicaceae
PERENNIAL

* **ALL ZONES**
* **FULL SUN**
* **REGULAR WATER**

Horseradish

Looking part dandelion and part carrot, this large (to 3 ft.), coarse, weedy-looking plant is grown for its big white roots, which are peeled, grated, and mixed with vinegar or cream to make a condiment. Does best in rich, moist soils in cool regions. From southeastern Europe.

In late winter or early spring, set root horizontally in a 3–4-in.-deep trench and cover with 2 in. of soil. One plant should provide enough horseradish for a family of four. For multiple plants, space 2½–3 ft. apart. Through fall, winter, and spring, harvest pieces of horseradish roots from the outside of the root clump as you need them.

Hosta

PLANTAIN LILY
Asparagaceae
PERENNIALS

* **ZONES VARY BY SPECIES**
* **PARTIAL OR FULL SHADE**
* **REGULAR WATER**
* **ATTRACT HUMMINGBIRDS**

Hosta 'Earth Angel'

Large clumps of big, fresh-looking spring leaves make these perfect understory plants; spikes of blue, lavender, or white trumpet-shaped flowers are a summer bonus. Leaves may be heart-shaped, lance-shaped, oval, or nearly round; they can be glossy or dull, smooth or textured, straight or wavy edged. Mounds range from 3–4 in. across to 5 ft. in diameter. Foliage runs from lime to dark green, greenish gold, gray, and blue, with many variegated forms whose colors vary with climate and soil type.

New varieties are legion. To get what you want, buy the plant in full leaf or from a reputable mail-order specialist. All are native to eastern Asia.

Though hostas are shade lovers, some tolerate sun, especially in cool-summer zones (those with white or yellow in leaves are least sun-tolerant). Plants grown in sun will be more compact and will produce more flowers. All go dormant in winter (even in mild climates), collapsing to almost nothing.

H. fortunei. Zones A1–A3; 1–10, 14–21. Variable plant known mainly for its many varieties, which offer a wide range of foliage colors. Two choices, both to 2 ft. high and 3 ft. wide, are *H. f. aureomarginata,* with distinctly veined, deep olive green leaves irregularly rimmed in yellow, and *H. f. hyacinthina,* which has slightly puckered gray-green leaves edged with a fine white line. Both bear lavender blooms in late spring.

H. hybrids. Zones 1–10, 14–21; some succeed in Zones A2, A3, and 22–24. The following list represents just a few of the many hundreds of possibilities. Size given at the start of each listing is for foliage clump. Performance in Zones 22–24 will vary, but all are worth a try in these areas.

'**Blue Angel**'. To 2½ ft. high, 6 ft. wide. Blue leaves; near-white flowers on 4-ft. stalks.

'**Christmas Tree**'. To 2 ft. high, 3 ft. wide. Large, deep green leaves have creamy white edges; light lavender flowers rise on 2-ft. stems.

'**Francee**'. To 15 in. high, 3 ft. wide. Dark green leaves with a sharply defined white border; light lavender flowers on 2½-ft. stalks.

'**Great Expectations**'. To 2 ft. high, 2½ ft. wide. Leaves are creamy yellow in center, surrounded by a wide blue-green edge. White flowers on 3-ft. stalks.

'**Guacamole**'. To 2 ft. high, 4 ft. wide. Green-edged, golden lime foliage gives rise to large, white, fragrant flowers.

'**June**'. To 14–16 in. high and 2½ ft. wide. Heart-shaped leaves are blue-gray at margins, irregularly variegated with greenish yellow and bright yellow. Lavender blooms on 1½-ft.-high stems.

'**Patriot**'. To 15 in. high, 3 ft. wide. Resembles 'Francee', but leaves have a wider white border. Lavender flowers on 2½-ft.-high stems.

'**Paul's Glory**'. Grows to 2 ft. high and 4 ft. wide. Greenish gold leaves with green edges, pale lavender flower spikes.

> Hostas are mainstays of the shaded summer garden: light up a corner with an electric chartreuse variety, or visually cool the garden with a deep blue-green one.

'**Sagae**'. To 2 ft. high, 3 ft. wide, with upswept foliage forming a vase shape. Blue-gray leaves with a wide creamy white border. Lavender flowers on 4½-ft. stalks.

'**Stained Glass**'. Grows 15 in. high, to 4 ft. wide. Deeply veined golden foliage has dark green brushstrokes around edges; fragrant lavender flowers.

'**Sum and Substance**'. To 3 ft. high, 6 ft. wide, with textured chartreuse leaves that turn golden with age. Pale lavender flowers.

H. plantaginea. FRAGRANT PLANTAIN LILY. Zones 1–10, 14–24. To 2 ft. high, 3 ft. wide. Glossy bright green leaves to 10 in. long, broadly oval with parallel veins and quilted surface. Large, noticeably fragrant white flowers on 2½-ft. stalks.

H. sieboldiana. Zones 1–10, 14–21. To 3 ft. high, 4 ft. wide. Blue-green, broadly heart-shaped leaves, 10–15 in. long, heavily veined and puckered. Many slender pale lilac flowers nestle close to leaves. Foliage of 'Elegans' is covered in a blue-gray bloom. 'Frances Williams' grows to 20 in. high, 3 ft. wide, with white flowers on 2-ft. stalks. Heavily corrugated blue leaves are bordered with yellow.

H. tokudama flavocircinalis. Zones 1–10, 14–21. To 2 ft. high, 4 ft. wide. Each blue-green, heavily textured leaf is surrounded by broad, creamy golden margin. Pale lavender flowers rise on 2-ft. stalks.

CARE

Plant in organically enriched soil, with regular feeding during the growing season. Clumps expand in size over the years and shade out weeds, remaining vigorous without division. But to increase a planting, carefully remove plantlets from a clump's perimeter. Or cut a wedge-shaped piece from a clump and transplant it; the clump will fill in quickly. Protect from slugs and snails. Hostas with heavily textured or waxy leaves are less attractive to these pests. Hostas are good in containers.

FOR MORE PLANTS THAT ATTRACT HUMMINGBIRDS AND OTHER BIRDS, SEE PAGES 95–99.

H

Runaway Groundcovers

Some low-growing groundcovers—like *Houttuynia cordata*—spread so quickly and fill in so completely that you may be tempted to plant them in large numbers. But their vigorous growth is a double-edged sword: you'll need to make sure there's a barrier to contain their relentless spread. Other examples are carpet bugle (*Ajuga*), Serbian bellflower (*Campanula poscharskyana*), dichondra, sweet woodruff (*Galium odoratum*), and baby's tears (*Soleirolia soleirolii*).

H

Houttuynia cordata

Saururaceae
PERENNIAL

🌿 ZONES 2–9, 14–24

☼ ◑ ● SUN OR SHADE

💧💧 REGULAR TO AMPLE WATER

Houttuynia cordata
'Chameleon'

Covered with heart-shaped leaves, this 9–12-in. spreading Asian groundcover grows rapidly in summer, vanishes in winter—even in mild climates. Crushed leaves emit a scent reminiscent of orange peel. Inconspicuous clusters of white-bracted flowers look like tiny dogwood (*Cornus*) blossoms. Most commonly grown is 'Chameleon' ('Tricolor', 'Variegata'), with showy splashes of cream, pink, yellow, and red on foliage; colors are most intense in sun.

Can spread aggressively in wet ground. Plant 1½–2 ft. apart; curb growth with wood, concrete, or metal barrier extending 8–12 in. into the soil. Attractive in containers.

Howea

KENTIA PALM
Arecaceae
PALMS

🌿 ZONES 17, 21–24; H1, H2; OR INDOORS

◑ PARTIAL SHADE; BRIGHT INDIRECT LIGHT

💧 REGULAR WATER

Howea forsteriana

These slow-growing feather palms, native to Australia's Lord Howe Island, are most familiar as houseplants. But outdoors, where they are typically planted under other trees for frost protection, they become statuesque beauties. With age, leaves drop to show clean, green trunk ringed with leaf scars. These are the kentia palms of florists' shops and make ideal potted plants.

H. belmoreana. SENTRY PALM. Less common than *H. forsteriana*, and tends to be smaller (grows to 25 ft. tall and 15 ft. wide), with 6–7-ft.-long leaves.

H. forsteriana. PARADISE PALM. To 60 ft. tall, 20 ft. wide, with leaves to 9 ft. long; leaflets are long and drooping.

Humulus

HOP VINE
Cannabaceae
PERENNIAL VINES

🌿 ZONES A2, A3; 1–10, 14–21

☼ FULL SUN

💧 REGULAR WATER

Humulus lupulus

Fast, twining growth from multiple leaders plus a dense covering of hand-size, lobed leaves make these effective seasonal coverings for arbors and deck rails. But they must be cut to the ground (and dead stems removed) every winter to make room for subsequent growth. Common hop is used in beer. Plants flower in late summer, with males producing flower panicles and females bearing spikes of greenish blossoms resembling tiny pinecones.

H. japonicus. JAPANESE HOP. From eastern Asia. Grows to 20–30 ft. Bears ¾-in. female flower spikes. Its dark green leaves have five to seven lobes; 'Variegatus' marked with white. Sow seeds in place in spring.

H. lupulus. COMMON HOP. From many northern temperate regions of the world. The hops, or female flowers, are soft, flaky, 1–2-in., light green cones of bracts and blossoms that emit a fresh, piney fragrance used as the traditional flavoring for beer. Bright green leaves have three to five lobes. Tender top shoots can be cooked as a vegetable. Attract butterflies. Plants sold in nurseries are typically female; no pollenizer needed. May be offered as potted plants or as dormant roots. Plant roots, thick end up, just below surface of rich soil in early spring. Most popular of many varieties is

'Aureus', which has attractive chartreuse foliage. *H. l. neomexicanus* (*H. americanus*), native to central and southern Rockies, differs from the plain species only in botanical details.

Hunnemannia fumariifolia

MEXICAN TULIP POPPY, GOLDEN CUP
Papaveraceae
PERENNIAL USUALLY TREATED AS ANNUAL

🌿 ZONES 1–24; H1, H2

☼ FULL SUN

◐💧 LITTLE OR NO WATER TO MODERATE WATER

Hunnemannia fumariifolia

This Mexican relation of California poppy (*Eschscholzia*) is a bushy, open grower to 2–3 ft. high, with finely divided blue-green leaves. Cup-shaped, pure yellow blooms, 3 in. across with crinkled petals, appear in summer, early fall. If cut in bud, blooms last for a week in water. Plant from pots or start from seed, sowing seeds in place in warm, sunny location and thinning seedlings to 1 ft. apart. Showy when massed. Reseeds. Needs excellent drainage.

For an unthirsty cutting garden, plant Mexican tulip poppy with yarrow (*Achillea*), coreopsis, globe thistle (*Echinops*), blanket flower (*Gaillardia*), lavender (*Lavandula*), and statice (*Limonium*).

Hyacinthella azurea.
See *Muscari azureum*

Hyacinthoides
BLUEBELL, WOOD HYACINTH
Hyacinthaceae
PERENNIALS FROM BULBS

- ✿ **ZONES VARY BY SPECIES**
- ◐ **FILTERED SUN OR LIGHT SHADE**
- ⬥ **REGULAR WATER DURING GROWTH AND BLOOM**
- ⬥ **BULBS MAY CAUSE AN ALLERGIC SKIN REACTION**

Hyacinthoides hispanica

In growth habit, bluebells are something like hyacinths, but taller, with looser flower clusters and fewer, narrower leaves. Classic spring-flowering woodland gems, these were long classed in the genus *Scilla* and are still called that by many; they were later reclassified as *Endymion*, and now *Hyacinthoides*.

Climate can help you choose the best species for your garden. Spanish bluebell (*H. hispanica*) is the only choice in most of lowland California, while English bluebell (*H. nonscripta*) definitely prefers colder winters and moderate to cool summers. Where their zones overlap, the two species sometimes hybridize when they're grown together. Plant bulbs in fall, setting them 6 in. apart and 3 in. deep in mild climates, or as deep as 6 in. where winters are severe. A propensity for reseeding makes these good subjects for naturalizing among tall shrubs and under deciduous trees. When division is needed (infrequently), do it in fall. Plants thrive in pots, and flowers are good for cutting.

H. hispanica (Scilla campanulata, S. hispanica). SPANISH BLUEBELL. Zones 1–11, 14–24. From Spain and North Africa. Prolific and vigorous, with strap-shaped leaves and sturdy, 20-in. stems bearing 12 or more nodding, unscented bells about ¾ in. long. Blue is the most popular color, 'Excelsior' (deep blue) the most popular variety. There are also white ('White City'), pink, lavender-pink ('Queen of Pinks'), and rose forms.

H. non-scripta (Scilla non-scripta). ENGLISH BLUEBELL, WOOD HYACINTH. Best in Zones 2b–6, 15. From western Europe. Fragrant blue flowers are narrower and smaller than those of *H. hispanica*, on 1-ft. stems that nod at the tip. Leaves are about ½ in. wide. 'Alba' is white-flowered; 'Rosea' is pink.

Hyacinthus orientalis
COMMON HYACINTH
Hyacinthaceae
PERENNIAL FROM BULBS

- ✿ **ZONES VARY BY TYPE**
- ☼ **FULL SUN**
- ⬥ **REGULAR WATER DURING GROWTH AND BLOOM**
- ⬥ **BULBS MAY CAUSE AN ALLERGIC SKIN REACTION**

Hyacinthus orientalis

Heady fragrance and bright colors make these compact, spring-flowering bulbs especially endearing. Fat spikes of bell-shaped flowers rise from basal bundle of narrow, bright green leaves. For *H. azureus*, see *Muscari azureum*.

Showy Dutch hybrids are derived from *H. orientalis*, a Mediterranean native. They reach 1 ft. high, with straplike erect or arching leaves. Large flower spikes are tightly packed with waxy blooms in white, cream, buff, yellow, pink, salmon, red, blue, or purple. Largest bulbs produce the largest spikes, and are the best choice for containers and forced flowers. The next-largest size is good for massing in beds. Smallest bulbs produce smaller, looser flower spikes—just like larger bulbs left in the ground from year to year. Dutch hybrids can be grown in all zones outside Hawaii, but bulbs left in the ground will persist only in regions with distinct winter cold. Treat as annuals in Zones 8, 9, 11–24.

Roman or French Roman hyacinths (*H. o. albulus*), native to south of France, grow smaller than the Dutch hybrids and bloom earlier. Each bulb usually produces several slender, foot-high stems, each with loose spikes of white, pale blue, or pink flowers. These are good for naturalizing and informal drifts. They thrive in regions with little or no winter chill; will persist year after year in Zones 4–24.

CARE

Plant early enough to establish roots before ground freezes. Where winter temperatures drop below 20°F (–7°C), set out bulbs in earliest fall; in warmer regions, delay until mid- to late fall (keep bulbs cool until then). Plant in organically enriched, sandy, well-drained soil. Set largest Dutch hybrid bulbs 4–5 in. deep, 5 in. apart; set smaller hybrid bulbs and Roman hyacinth bulbs 3 in. deep, 4–5 in. apart. (Hyacinth bulbs have invisible barbs on their surfaces that can cause some people's skin to itch; after handling, wash hands before touching face or eyes.) If the bulbs will remain in the ground, fertilize just as blossoms fade, remove spent spikes, and water regularly until foliage yellows.

In containers, plant in porous mix with tip of bulb near the surface. Cover potting mix with thick mulch of sawdust, wood shavings, or peat moss to keep bulbs cool, moist, and shaded until top growth shows; then remove mulch and place in full light.

Hydrangea
Hydrangeaceae
DECIDUOUS SHRUBS AND VINES, EXCEPT AS NOTED

- ✿ **ZONES VARY BY SPECIES**
- ☼ ◐ **PARTIAL SHADE IN HOTTEST CLIMATES**
- ⬥ **REGULAR WATER**

Hydrangea 'Shooting Star'

Big, bold leaves and large clusters of long-lasting flowers in white, pink, red, or blue. Summer and fall bloom. Flower clusters may contain sterile flowers (conspicuous, with large, petal-like sepals) or fertile flowers (small, starry petaled); or they may feature a cluster of small fertile flowers surrounded by ring of big sterile ones (these are called lacecap hydrangeas). Sterile flowers last for a long time (often holding up for months), gradually fading in color. Hydrangeas are good-looking as single plants, massed, or in tubs on the patio. Grow fast in rich, porous soil. For Japanese hydrangea vine, see *Schizophragma hydrangeoides*.

Prune as needed to control form—in late dormant season for those producing blooms on new growth, after bloom for those flowering on previous year's growth. For hydrangeas that bloom on both new and old wood, prune dead wood out when new growth starts in spring, then prune for shape after bloom. To get biggest flower clusters, reduce number of stems; for numerous medium-size clusters, keep more stems.

H. anomala petiolaris (H. petiolaris). CLIMBING HYDRANGEA. Vine. Zones A2, A3; 2–21. From Russia, Korea,

H

Blue or Pink Blooms

In some hydrangea varieties, blue or pink flower color is affected by soil pH—bluest color is produced in strongly acid soils (below pH 5.5), pink or red in neutral to alkaline soils (pH 7.0 and higher). Florists control flower color of potted hydrangeas by controlling the soil mix; blue-flowered florists' plants may show pink blossoms when planted out in less-acid soil, and pink-flowered types will turn blue in less-alkaline soil. In either case, the plants may go through a year or two of transition, showing murky purple flower colors. To make (or keep) flowers blue, apply aluminum sulfate to the soil. To keep them red (or pink), add lime to the soil or apply superphosphate (follow package directions). Flower-color treatment is not effective unless started well ahead of bloom. Varieties with white flowers stay white.

Hydrangea macrophylla

Hydrangea macrophylla

and Japan. Climbs high (as far as 60 ft.) with its clinging aerial rootlets; shrubby and sprawling without support. Green, 2–4-in.-long leaves have a rounded heart shape. Mature plants develop short, flowering branches with flat, white, 6–10-in.-wide lacecap flower clusters. Becomes woody with age. Prune out overly vigorous growth only after vine is well established and climbing. Can be rejuvenated by cutting back to framework in late dormant season. 'Mirranda' has leaves with irregular yellow margins; it is slower growing than the species.

H. arborescens. SMOOTH HYDRANGEA. Shrub. Zones A3; 1–21. Native from New York to Iowa, south to Florida and Louisiana. Upright, dense growth to 10 ft. tall and wide. Oval, grayish green, 4–8-in. leaves; white flowers. Prune in late dormant season. In basic species, most flowers in a cluster are fertile; the few sterile ones are not plentiful enough for full lacecap effect. Much showier is 'Annabelle', which produces enormous (to 1 ft.) globular clusters of sterile flowers over a long season on a plant about 4 ft. tall and wide. 'Incrediball' is similar, but stems are stronger, so flowers don't flop. 'Bella Anna' and 'Invincibelle Spirit' are pink-flowering versions of 'Annabelle'. 'White Dome' grows about 5 ft. tall and wide, with sturdy stems holding white, dome-shaped flower clusters to 10 in. across; a few sterile flowers surround the tightly packed fertile ones.

H. aspera. Shrub. Zones 4–9, 14–24. From eastern Asia. Imposing shrub to 10–12 ft. tall, spreading nearly as wide. Dark green, somewhat hairy leaves to 10 in. long, 4 in. wide.

Rather flat, 10-in. flower clusters contain purplish white to pink fertile flowers surrounded by 1-in. white, pink, or purple sterile blooms. Prune in late dormant season. To make a broad, many-stemmed plant, cut back hard for first 3 years; flowering will be delayed, but the plant's form will be improved.

H. macrophylla (H. hortensia, H. opuloides, H. otaksa). BIGLEAF HYDRANGEA, GARDEN HYDRANGEA. Shrub. Zones 3b–9, 14–24; H1. From Japan. Symmetrical, rounded habit; grows to 4–8 ft. tall (or more) and as wide. Thick, shiny, coarsely toothed leaves; flowers of white, pink, red, or blue (often depending upon soil pH; see sidebar at left) are held in big clusters.

Most garden hydrangeas bloom on old wood, but a few—mostly recent introductions—bloom on the current season's growth as well, significantly lengthening the bloom season. All kinds do well where winters are fairly mild. Those that bloom only on old wood are disappointing in cold-winter climates where plants freeze to ground every year. Those that bloom on new wood can freeze to the ground (or be pruned hard) every winter, and they'll still flower if the season is long enough.

The varieties that follow bloom only on old wood unless noted. Good ones with rounded flower clusters (mophead or hortensia types) include 'Glowing Embers', which grows 6 ft. tall, 8 ft. wide, with deep pink flowers; especially cold-hardy 'Madame Emile Mouillère', which grows 6 ft. tall, 6–8 ft. wide, producing white flowers with blue or pink eye, and fall foliage in the red and orange range; 'Nigra', with dark purple-black stems bearing light green leaves and flowers that vary from soft pink to blue; 'Nikko Blue', with large blue blossom clusters; and 'Pia' ('Pink Elf'), just 1½ ft. high and 2 ft. wide, with deep pink flowers. Those that produce pink or blue flowers on new wood include 'All Summer Beauty', 'Endless Summer', and 'Penny Mac'. 'Blushing Bride' has white flowers that age to pink.

Varieties with lacecap flowers include 'Blue Wave', with light

blue to pink sterile flowers and darker fertile flowers; 'Lanarth White', just 3–4 ft. tall and wide, with white sterile flowers and fertile flowers of blue or pink; 'Teller Red' ('Teller Rot'), with a double row of rose-red sterile flowers surrounding pink-and-blue fertile ones; and old favorites 'Mariesii Variegata' and 'Maculata' ('Variegata'), with dark green leaves marked with cream and light green. 'Twist-n-Shout' blooms blue or pink, depending on soil pH, on both new and old wood.

H. paniculata. Shrub. Zones A2, A3; 1–21. Native to Japan and China. Upright, spreading growth to 10–20 ft. tall and wide or larger. Medium to dark green leaves are oval and pointed, 3–6 in. long. Flowers begin as elongated clusters of greenish white buds in early summer, opening to 4–8-in.-long cones of white sterile flowers hiding tiny fertile flowers within. Blooms age to tawny pink, giving a show that lasts for months; flower spikes can be removed in late fall to neaten plant's appearance. Prune to shape in late dormant season.

'Grandiflora'. An old, well-known variety, with 1½-ft. flower clusters.

'Limelight'. Chartreuse blooms in summer, chartreuse and pink flowers in fall.

'Little Lime'. Has flowers like 'Limelight', but the whole plant is scaled down to 3–5 ft. tall.

'Quick Fire'. Deep pink flowers.

'Tardiva'. Similar to 'Grandiflora' but blooms later, in early and midautumn.

'Unique'. Big flower clusters, to 16 in. long and 10 in. wide.

H. petiolaris. See *H. anomala petiolaris*.

H. 'Preziosa' ('Pink Beauty'). Shrub. Zones 3b–9, 14–24. From Japan and Korea. Grows 4–5 ft. tall and wide, with medium green leaves that are oval, pointed. Round, 3–5-in.-wide clusters of white sterile flowers age to red, blue, or mauve, depending on soil acidity. Prune after bloom.

H. quercifolia. OAKLEAF HYDRANGEA. Shrub. Zones 2b–23. From southeastern U.S. Broad, rounded shrub to 6 ft. tall and 8 ft. wide, with handsome, deeply lobed leaves that

H

resemble those of oaks, turn bronze or crimson in autumn. Elongated clusters of white flowers (to 8 in. long) in late spring and early summer turn pinkish purple as they age; fertile flowers are usually concealed by larger sterile flowers. 'Alice' has foliage that turns rich red in fall, 'Snowflake' bears double flowers, and 'Snow Queen' has larger flower clusters.

Dwarf varieties include 'Little Honey', 4 ft. tall, with white flowers and good fall color; 'Pee Wee', 4 ft. tall and wide, with 5-in.-long flower clusters; 'Sike's Dwarf', to 3 ft. high and 4 ft. wide. 'Munchkin' grows to 3 ft. high, 5 ft. wide, with 6½-in. flower clusters that open white and age to red, with mahogany red fall foliage. 'Ruby Slippers' is similar, but with 9-in. flower clusters. Prune after bloom. Stems and flower buds may be damaged where temperatures go much below –10°F (–23°C); in these areas, oakleaf hydrangea is best grown for its foliage.

H. serrata. Shrub. Zones 3b–9, 14–24. From Korea and Japan. Resembles *H. macrophylla*. To 4–6 ft. tall and wide. The following selections have lacecap flowers. 'Beni Gaku' has pale blue fertile blooms surrounded by white, red-edged sterile flowers that age to rosy purple. 'Bluebird' has deep blue fertile flowers surrounded by pale blue sterile ones. 'Fuji Waterfall' is compact, just 3–4 ft. tall and a little wider, with double white sterile flowers on long stems that appear to dance above the flower heads. 'Woodlander' is compact, to 4 ft. tall and wide, with leaves that age to a dusky purple; nice contrast with the dainty white to shell pink sterile flowers. Prune all after bloom.

Truly a hydrangea for all seasons, oakleaf hydrangea (H. *quercifolia*) blooms white to pink in spring and summer and puts on a second show in fall with crimson leaves.

Hymenocallis
Amaryllidaceae
PERENNIALS FROM BULBS

🌡 **ZONES 5, 6, 8, 9, 14–24, EXCEPT AS NOTED; OR DIG AND STORE**

☀ ◑ **FULL SUN OR PARTIAL SHADE**

💧 **REGULAR WATER DURING GROWTH AND BLOOM, EXCEPT AS NOTED**

☣ **BULBS ARE POISONOUS IF INGESTED**

Hymenocallis narcissiflora

Imagine a cross between a naked lady (*Amaryllis belladonna*) and a daffodil. Like naked lady, most *Hymenocallis* have strap-shaped, 2-ft.-long leaves and thick flower stems carrying several large, fragrant blooms—though leaves and flowers appear together. Like daffodils, the flowers have two sets of segments: inner ones form a funnel, while outer ones are longer, spidery, and recurved. Native to the southern U.S. and South America.

H. × festalis. Each stem bears about four horizontally held flowers 3–5 in. across. Outer segments resemble curled white ribbons; these surround a broadly chalice-shaped cup with fringed lobes. 'Zwanenburg' has larger flowers.

H. harrisiana. Zones 13–17, 19–24; H1. From Mexico. Scented white flowers appear on 18–24-in. stalks. Gray-green leaves are 12–18 in. long. Little to moderate water during growth and bloom.

H. narcissiflora (Ismene calathina). BASKET FLOWER, PERUVIAN DAFFODIL. From Peruvian Andes. Most commonly grown hymenocallis, with green-striped white flowers about 4 in. wide and held in clusters of two to five. 'Advance' has pure white flowers faintly lined with green in throat.

H. 'Sulphur Queen'. Soft primrose yellow blossoms with green stripes in the throat; they reach 6 in. wide and have a more circular cup surrounded by broader, less spidery segments than the other hymenocallis described here.

CARE
Plant in rich, well-drained soil—in late fall or early winter in frostless areas, after frost danger is past in colder climates. Set bulbs with tips 1 in. below surface; space 1 ft. apart. The foliage keeps all summer if watered, dies in fall. Dig bulbs after leaves have yellowed (do not cut off fleshy roots), dry with roots facing up, and store in open trays in cool, dry, dark place.

Hymenocyclus. See *Malephora*

Hymenosporum flavum
SWEETSHADE
Pittosporaceae
EVERGREEN TREE OR SHRUB

🌡 **ZONES 8, 9, 14–24**

☀ ◑ **FULL SUN OR LIGHT SHADE**

💧 **MODERATE WATER**

Hymenosporum flavum

This graceful, upright Australian grows naturally as a 12–40-ft. tree with 9–20-ft. spread, but it can be maintained as a shrub with regular pruning. Narrow, glossy dark green leaves are 2–6 in. long. In early summer, creamy flowers with honeyed orange-blossom fragrance appear, aging to yellow. Early training is necessary to correct two problems. First, branches spread out in almost equal

threes, creating weak crotches that are likely to split. Second, leaves tend to cluster near ends of branches and twigs. Frequent pinching and shortening of growth in early years make plant stronger and denser. Locate away from strong winds. Grow in well-drained soil; tolerates alkalinity.

Hymenoxys. See *Tetraneuris*

Hypericum
ST. JOHNSWORT
Hypericaceae
EVERGREEN, SEMIEVERGREEN, AND DECIDUOUS SHRUBS OR PERENNIALS

🌡 **ZONES VARY BY SPECIES**

☀ ◑ **PARTIAL SHADE IN HOTTEST CLIMATES**

💧 **MODERATE TO REGULAR WATER**

Hypericum androsaemum

All forms bear shallowly cup-shaped, five-petaled yellow flowers with prominent sunbursts of stamens in center. Blooms may be solitary or clustered. Neat, fresh green foliage. Various species used for mass plantings, groundcovers, informal hedges, and borders. Mild, moist regions are optimal.

Pacific Northwest plantings (especially *H. calycinum*) often face difficult-to-control rust. Remove and destroy blighted leaves and any leaf litter; avoid overhead watering of plants in the evening.

H. androsaemum. Semievergreen shrub. Zones 3b–24. Shade-tolerant native of Europe, western Asia. To 3 ft. high and wide, with stems arching toward the top. Leaves are medium green above, paler beneath, to 4 in. long and 2 in. wide. Clusters of ¾-in., golden yellow

H

summer flowers are followed by inedible berrylike fruits that turn from red to purple to black as they age. Useful as a tall groundcover at edge of woods, on shaded slopes, or in a wild garden. 'Albury Purple', to 2 ft. high and wide, has new growth flushed dusky purple. Leaves of 'Glacier' are pink when new, then heavily splashed with white.

H. calycinum. AARON'S BEARD, CREEPING ST. JOHNSWORT. Evergreen to semievergreen shrub; tops often killed in cold winters but come back in spring. Zones 2b–24. From Bulgaria and Turkey. Grows to 1 ft. high, spreading fast by vigorous underground stems, even over tree roots and in poor soil; invades other plantings unless confined. Good hillside erosion control. Short-stalked leaves to 4 in. long are medium green in sun, yellow-green in shade. Bright yellow summer blossoms are 3 in. wide. Plant at 1½-ft. intervals. Clip or mow during dormant season.

H. frondosum. Deciduous shrub; evergreen in mildest climates. Zones 2b–24. From southeastern U.S. Grows 1–3 ft. high, mounding. Blue-green leaves set off clusters of 1½-in., bright yellow flowers from midsummer to early fall. 'Sunburst' forms a tight mound to 3 ft. high and wide.

H. 'Hidcote'. Can be an evergreen to semievergreen shrub, or even a perennial that dies to the ground in coldest part of range. Zones 3–9, 14–24. To 4 ft. tall and 5 ft. wide in mildest climates; in cold areas, freezes keep plant to half that size. Dark green leaves 2–3 in. long. Yellow, 3-in. flowers all summer.

H. kalmianum. KALM'S ST. JOHNSWORT. Deciduous shrub. Zones 2–7, 10. From Quebec and Ontario to Illinois. Grows 2–3 ft. high and wide, with blue-green, willowy foliage and yellow, 1–1½-in. flowers. 'Blue Velvet' grows to 3 ft. high, 4 ft. wide; 'Gemo' has narrow leaves, smaller but more profuse flowers; 'Sunny Boulevard' bears deep yellow flowers all summer on a compact shrub.

H. × moserianum. GOLD FLOWER. Evergreen shrub, but perennial whose top dies in winter in coldest climates. Zones 3–9, 14–24; H1. Mounding habit to 3 ft. high and wide, with arching, reddish stems. Leaves 2 in. long, medium green above, blue-green beneath. Golden yellow, 2½-in. blossoms are borne singly or in clusters of up to five. Blooms in summer, possibly into fall. Cut back in early spring. 'Tricolor' has gray-green leaves edged in white and tinged with pink.

H. patulum 'Hidcote'. See H. 'Hidcote'.

Hypoestes phyllostachya
FRECKLE FACE, PINK POLKA-DOT PLANT
Acanthaceae
PERENNIAL OFTEN GROWN AS ANNUAL

✂ **ZONES 23, 24; H1, H2; ANNUAL ANYWHERE; OR INDOORS**

☼ ◑ **FULL SUN OR LIGHT SHADE; BRIGHT LIGHT**

💧 **REGULAR WATER**

Hypoestes phyllostachya

Grown for its pink-and-white-spotted green leaves, this 1–2-ft. high and 1-ft.-wide foliage plant is grown as a perennial in Hawaii and its native South Africa, but as a summer annual or houseplant on the mainland. Plants bloom very rarely.

'Splash' has larger spots. 'Confetti' has more, smaller flecks. Pair it with green-leafed plants such as baby's tears or small ferns. Tip-pinch to make bushy. Growth can be cut to within an inch or so of the soil in early spring to renew; plants tend to become woody and need replacing every few years.

Hyptis emoryi
DESERT LAVENDER
Lamiaceae
EVERGREEN SHRUB

✂ **ZONES 8–14, 18–24**

☼ **FULL SUN**

○💧 **LITTLE TO MODERATE WATER**

🦋 **ATTRACTS BUTTERFLIES**

Hyptis emoryi

Covered with woolly gray leaves to conserve moisture in its native Southwest deserts, this erect or spreading shrub grows 6–10 ft. tall and wide. Its roundish leaves have scalloped and toothed edges. Numerous tiny blue-violet flowers crowd into short spikes near branch ends; they can appear anytime, but bloom is heaviest in spring. Plant gives off a pleasant lavender fragrance following rains or when brushed. May die back to roots at about 25°F (–4°C). Needs excellent drainage. Drought-tolerant but looks better with irrigation. Prune freely to control size and shape. 'Silver Lining' is slightly more narrow and upright, with silvery white leaves and purple-flushed stems.

Hyssopus officinalis
HYSSOP
Lamiaceae
PERENNIAL

✂ **ZONES 1–24**

☼ ◑ **FULL SUN OR LIGHT SHADE**

💧💧 **MODERATE TO REGULAR WATER**

🦋 **ATTRACTS BEES AND BUTTERFLIES**

Hyssopus officinalis

This compact southern European herb grows to 2 ft. high, 3 ft. wide. Narrow, glossy dark green leaves emerge from woody-based stems; foliage has pungent scent. Profusion of dark blue flower spikes appears in summer and autumn; not a dramatic show, but pleasing. 'Rosea' has pink blooms; selections with white and lavender blooms also exist.

Start from seed sown in early spring or from stem cuttings in late spring or early summer. Once established, it may self-sow. Needs good drainage. Tolerates trimming as a low hedge. Peppery-tasting leaves are sometimes used (sparingly) in cooking.

Fragrant Foliage

Desert lavender and hyssop both have scented leaves. Plant them near walkways, where you'll brush against them and release their fragrance. Among the many other scented-leaf favorites are lemon verbena (*Aloysia citrodora*), many artemisias, lavender (*Lavandula*), scented geraniums (*Pelargonium*), rosemary (*Rosmarinus*), and many sages (*Salvia*)—whose rugged herbal notes recall the scent of chaparral on a warm summer day.

I

Iberis
CANDYTUFT
Brassicaceae
PERENNIALS AND ANNUALS

- ✿ **ZONES 1–24, EXCEPT AS NOTED**
- ☼ ◑ **FULL SUN OR PARTIAL SHADE**
- ❍ **REGULAR WATER**
- ❀ **ATTRACT BUTTERFLIES**

Iberis sempervirens

Foot-high, free-blooming plants from southern and western Europe create sheets of white, lavender, lilac, pink, rose, purple, carmine, or crimson blossoms. Perennial candytufts flower from early spring to summer. Annual species bloom in spring and summer; they are most floriferous where summer nights are cool. Use all kinds in borders, containers, for cutting. Perennials are also good as edgings, in rock gardens, as small-scale groundcovers.

In spring or (in mild climates) fall, sow annuals in well-drained soil or flats for later transplant. Set out perennials in spring or fall. Shear lightly after bloom to stimulate new growth.

I. 'Absolutely Amethyst'. Perennial. This 1-ft.-high, spreading perennial grows like evergreen candytuft but is pinkish purple.

I. gibraltarica. Perennial. Zones 4–9, 14–24. Resembles *I. sempervirens* but bears flatter clusters of light pinkish or purplish flowers, which may be white near the center.

MEET THE ICE PLANTS

These low-growing, succulent perennials (and a few annuals) were once conveniently lumped together as *Mesembryanthemum*, but they are now classified under several genus names.

The various perennial genera included in this book are *Aptenia, Carpobrotus, Cephalophyllum, Delosperma, Drosanthemum, Malephora,* and *Oscularia. Dorotheanthus* (Livingstone daisy) is an annual genus. *Mesembryanthemum*—the original, all-encompassing genus—now contains annuals that have naturalized along the California coast but are rarely seen elsewhere.

HOW TO GROW

Where hardy, ice plants are among the most useful and colorful of flowering groundcovers. In colder climates, grow them as summer bloomers in window boxes or hanging baskets; or treat as houseplants. All grow best in well-drained soils; none will tolerate foot traffic. Feed lightly in fall, again after bloom.

I. 'Masterpiece'. Perennial. To 12 in. high and 24 in. wide; upright. Produces 3-in. white flowers with pink centers.

I. sempervirens. EVERGREEN CANDYTUFT. Perennial. To 12 in. (sometimes 18 in.) high, spreading about as wide. Narrow, shiny dark green leaves are attractive all year. Pure white flower clusters appear on stems long enough to cut for bouquets. Lower, more compact varieties include 'Alexander's White', a 6-in.-high plant with fine-textured foliage; 'Little Gem', 4–6 in. high; and 'Purity', 6–12 in. high and wide spreading. 'Snowflake', 4–12 in. high and 1½–3 ft. wide, has broader, more leathery leaves than the species; it also has larger flowers in larger clusters on shorter stems. It is extremely showy in spring, with sporadic bloom through summer and fall. 'Snow White' grows into 12- by 24-in. mound. Early-flowering 'Tahoe' is 10–12 in. high and wide and upright.

I. umbellata. GLOBE CANDYTUFT. Annual. Bushy plants 12–15 in. high, 9 in. wide. Lance-shaped leaves to 3½ in. long; flowers in pink, rose, red, salmon, purple, lilac, and white. 'Candy Cane' comes in rose, purple, lilac, and white. Lower-growing Dwarf Fairy series, available in the same colors, reaches 6 in. high.

FOR MORE PLANTS THAT ATTRACT BUTTERFLIES, SEE PAGES 100–104.

Ilex
HOLLY
Aquifoliaceae
EVERGREEN AND DECIDUOUS SHRUBS AND TREES

- ✿ **ZONES VARY BY SPECIES**
- ☼ ◑ **FULL SUN OR PARTIAL SHADE**
- ❍ **REGULAR WATER**
- ❀ **ATTRACT BIRDS**
- ◊ **BERRIES CAUSE GASTRIC UPSET**

Ilex cornuta 'Berries Jubilee'

An exceptionally diverse group, hollies range from foot-high dwarfs to trees 40–50 ft. tall, and include shrubby, treelike, weeping, and columnar forms. Smaller kinds are attractive as foundation plantings or low hedges; larger evergreen sorts make attractive and impenetrable tall hedges or screens.

Nearly all holly plants are either male or female, and as a rule both sexes must be present in order for female plants to set fruit. Plant a male of the same species as the fruiting female (if you use a different species, berries will form only if both plants flower at the same time); or plant a grafted male-female pair (these are becoming increasingly common). Varieties described below are female unless otherwise noted. Self-fruitful varieties are noted.

Most hollies are dense and symmetrical. Prune to remove poorly placed, broken, wiry, or dead branches. Winter holiday season is a good time to prune, because clipped branches can be used for indoor decoration. You can restore a holly that has become too open or ragged by severely shortening its branches and allowing new growth to fill in. Shear small-leafed hollies into formal hedges or topiary figures, or clip larger-leafed hollies into informal hedges (selectively clip with hand pruners to avoid the ragged leaves caused by shearing).

I. aquifolium. ENGLISH HOLLY. Evergreen shrub or tree. Zones 4–9, 14–17; H1 (above 4,000 ft.). Native to southern and central Europe and Great Britain. Slow growth to 40 ft. tall and 25 ft. wide, usually much less. Highly variable in leaf shape, color, and degree of spininess. Some varieties produce seedless berries without a pollenizer, but these berries are usually small, slow to develop, and quick to drop. In the Northwest, where this holly is invasive, we recommend only male or seedless female varieties. Give partial shade where hot. Resistant to oak root fungus.

'Big Bull'. Very ornamental male with large, nearly smooth-edged leaves.

'Ferox'. HEDGEHOG, PORCUPINE HOLLY. Male with sterile pollen. Twisted, fiercely spined leaves are what give it its common names.

'San Gabriel'. Bears seedless berries without pollination.

Variegated varieties are available with silver-edged leaves ('Argentea Marginata' and 'Ferox Argentea'), gold-edged leaves ('Aurea Marginata' and 'Gold Coast', a 6–8-ft.-tall male), and gold-centered leaves ('Britebush' and 'Pinto').

I. cornuta. CHINESE HOLLY. Evergreen shrub or tree. Zones

CLOCKWISE FROM TOP: *Ilex × meserveae* 'Goliath'; *I. × m.* 'Cousin'; *I. aquifolium* 'Silver Queen'

3–24, but needs long warm season to set fruit. In desert climates, give protection from hot sun; grow in eastern or northern exposure. From China, Korea. Dense or open growth to 10 ft. or taller, often wider in maturity. Leaves are typically glossy, leathery, nearly rectangular, with spines at the four corners and at tip. Exceptionally large, long-lasting bright red berries. Selections show great variation in fruit set, leaf form, spininess. In the following list, those setting fruit do so without a male variety.

'Burfordii'. BURFORD HOLLY. To 15 ft. tall, 10 ft. wide. Widely planted in low-elevation California. Leaves nearly spineless, cupped downward. Useful as espalier.

'Carissa'. Dwarf, dense grower to 3–4 ft. high and 4–6 ft. wide, with small leaves. Use for small containers, low hedge. Female, but no berries.

'Dwarf Burford' ('Burfordii Nana'). Resembles 'Burfordii' but is much smaller—to just

6 ft. tall and wide. Branches densely set with small, light green, spineless leaves.

'Needlepoint'. Grows 10 ft. tall, 12 ft. wide, with narrow, twisted leaves and bright red berries.

I. crenata. JAPANESE HOLLY. Evergreen shrub. Zones 3–9, 14–24. From Russia, Japan, and Korea. Looks more like boxwood (*Buxus*) than holly. Dense, erect, usually to 4–10 ft. tall and wide, sometimes much larger. Narrow, finely toothed, ½–1-in.-long leaves. Black berries. Extremely useful where winter cold limits choice of polished evergreens for hedges, edgings. Varieties include the following.

'Compacta'. Rounded shrub to 6 ft. tall and wide, with dense habit. Many different plants sold under this name.

'Convexa'. Compact, rounded shrub to 4–6 ft. tall and somewhat wider. Leaves are roundish, cupped downward at the edges. Use as clipped or unclipped hedge. Many different plants sold under this name.

'Drops of Gold'. Grows 3 ft. high, 6 ft. wide; yellow outer leaves and green inner leaves.

'Helleri'. Remains very small (about 1 ft. high, 2 ft. wide) for many years. May reach twice that size in 30 years.

'Sky Pencil'. Columnar plant to 6 ft. tall and only 10 in. wide.

I. glabra. INKBERRY. Evergreen shrub. Zones 2b–24. Native to eastern North America. To 10 ft. tall and wide, with thick, spineless dark green leaves and black berries. More widely available are the dwarf forms 'Compacta' (female) and 'Nordic' (male), which grow to 4 ft. tall and wide but can be sheared to make a 2-ft. hedge. 'Shamrock' grows 5 ft. tall and wide, with fine-textured, compact growth and black berries.

I. 'Little Rascal'. Evergreen shrub. Zones 2b–9, 14–22. Dense, rounded, compact growth to just 2 ft. high and 3 ft. wide. Medium green leaves turn deep purple in winter. Male.

I. × meserveae. Evergreen shrub. Zones 3–9, 14–17. Most plants in this category are hybrids between *I. aquifolium* and a cold-tolerant species from northern Japan. Dense, bushy plants; apparently the hardiest of hollies with the true holly look. To 10 ft. tall and wide, though more commonly seen 3–5 ft. tall and broad. Purple stems and spiny, glossy blue-green leaves. Red-fruiting female varieties include 'Blue Girl' and 'Blue Princess'; male pollenizers include 'Blue Boy' and 'Blue Prince'. 'Golden Girl' has yellow berries. 'Castle Wall' is a columnar variety that can reach 8 ft. tall, 4 ft. wide, with shiny dark green leaves and red berries. 'China Boy' and red-fruited 'China Girl' are crosses between *I. cornuta* and the northern Japanese species; slightly hardier and more tolerant of summer heat than the other hybrids.

I. 'Nellie R. Stevens'. Evergreen shrub or tree. Zones 4–9, 14–24. Hybrid between *I. cornuta* and *I. aquifolium*. Fast growing, densely conical to 15–20 ft. tall, 10 ft. wide. Glossy, leathery, sparsely toothed leaves. Self-fruitful, but forms a heavier crop if pollinated by male variety of *I. cornuta*.

I. 'Red Beauty'. Evergreen shrub. Zones 3b–9, 14–24. Grows 7–10 ft. tall, 4–5 ft.

wide. With a pollinator such as *I. × meserveae* 'Blue Prince', this produces abundant crops of red berries. Foliage is dense, dark green.

I. 'Sparkleberry'. Deciduous shrub or tree. Zones 1–7. Hybrid between *I. serrata* and *I. verticillata*. Upright growth to 12–15 ft. tall and wide. Tooth-edged dark green leaves to 4 in. long persist until early winter before dropping. Masses of bright red berries from fall into spring. 'Apollo' is a male pollenizer.

I. verticillata. WINTERBERRY, CHRISTMAS BERRY. Deciduous shrub. Zones A2, A3; 1–7. Native to eastern North America. Unlike most hollies, will thrive in boggy soils, although it also succeeds in any moist, organic soil. Grows 6–10 ft. tall and spreads wider by suckering. Oval leaves. Enormous crop of bright red berries ripens in early fall and lasts all winter (unless eaten by birds). 'Afterglow' has orange-red berries on a globe-shaped plant. 'Berry Heavy' and 'Berry Nice', both to 8 ft. tall and wide, are especially heavy producers of red berries. 'Winter Red' has dark red berries. 'Red Sprite' is a dwarf (to 3 ft. high and wide) with larger red fruit. Plant a male variety such as 'Jim Dandy' (to 4 ft.) or 'Southern Gentleman' (to 6 ft.) for pollination.

I. vomitoria. YAUPON. Evergreen shrub or tree. Zones 3–9, 11–24; H1, H2. Native to southeastern U.S. Takes extremely alkaline soils better than other hollies. To 15–20 ft. tall and 10–15 ft. wide, with narrow, inch-long, shallowly toothed dark green leaves. Often trained as standard or sheared into columnar form; good topiary plant. Pea-size scarlet berries borne in profusion.

'Nana'. DWARF YAUPON. To 3–5 ft. tall and slightly wider. Refined, attractive; formal appearance when sheared. Fruit often hidden among leaves.

'Pendula'. Weeping branches show to best effect when plant is trained as standard. Male and female forms available.

'Stokes' ('Stokes Dwarf', 'Schillings'). To 3–4 ft. tall and wide, with closely set dark green leaves. Male.

Illicium

ANISE TREE
Schisandraceae
EVERGREEN SHRUBS OR TREES

🌡 **ZONES 4–9, 14–24**

◑ ● **PARTIAL OR FULL SHADE**

💧 **AMPLE WATER**

⬥ **ALL PARTS OF I. ANISATUM ARE POISONOUS IF INGESTED**

Illicium mexicanum

Little-used but attractive clan of shrubs or small trees noted for thick, leathery, glossy leaves (anise scented when crushed) and spring flowers with many petal-like segments reminiscent of small magnolia blossoms. Fruits that follow are small, one-sided pods arranged in a ring. Though related to the star anise (*I. verum*) of Chinese cookery, these species are inedible. All like rich soil with abundant organic material. Big, bold foliage gives the impression of rhododendrons. Seldom need pruning.

I. anisatum. ANISE SHRUB, JAPANESE ANISE. Native to Japan, South Korea, and Taiwan. To 6–10 ft. (possibly 15 ft.) tall and 6–8 ft. wide; conical growth habit. Oval to lance-shaped, blunt-tipped, glossy leaves. Inch-wide, scentless flowers on short, nodding stalks cluster in leaf axils; they open yellowish green, then fade to creamy white. Much planted in Buddhist cemeteries; cut branches are used to decorate graves. Highly fragrant wood used for incense. Seeds, foliage, and wood are toxic if ingested.

I. mexicanum. MEXICAN ANISE. Shrub. Native to northern Mexico. To 4 ft. tall and wide. Narrowly oval, pointed leaves are medium green with red stems. Reddish pink flowers, to 2 in. across, are produced mainly in spring, with some repeat bloom through summer.

I. parviflorum. YELLOW ANISE. Native to Florida, Georgia. Grows slowly, 8–15 ft. tall, with olive green foliage and inconspicuous yellow summer flowers; a lovely small, fragrant (in leaf, not flower) evergreen tree.

Impatiens

BALSAM, TOUCH-ME-NOT
Balsaminaceae
PERENNIALS AND ANNUALS

🌡 **ZONES VARY BY SPECIES**

☀ ◑ ● **EXPOSURE NEEDS VARY BY SPECIES**

💧 **REGULAR WATER**

Impatiens 'Fusion Peach Frost'

Known best for their power to bloom in the garden's shady spots, garden impatiens are part of a clan that contains hundreds of species. Most of the ones listed here are annuals or tender perennials treated as annuals, and most bloom all summer. When lightly touched, ripe seed capsules burst open and scatter seeds.

I. auricoma 'Jungle Gold'. Perennial. Zones 24; H1, H2; grow as annual elsewhere. African. Dense, bushy plant to 1½ ft. high and wide, with glossy, bright green leaves that are oval, pointed, and up to 6 in. long; leaf margins are serrated and toothed. Intricate orchidlike blooms to 1 in. long are rich golden, throats marked in red. Give shade and regular applications of balanced fertilizer for profuse bloom over a long period in summer. Superb in containers.

I. balfourii. Annual. All zones. From the Himalayas. To 20 in. high and broad, with 4–5-in. leaves and loose clusters of inch-wide, pink-tinted white flowers. Seldom planted but often pops up unannounced. It can become a pest by reseeding, but it is attractive in shady, informal plantings.

I. balsamina. BALSAM. Annual. All zones. From Southeast Asia. Erect, branching plant reaches 8–30 in. high, 6–8 in. wide. Sharp-pointed, 1½–6-in.-long leaves with deeply toothed edges. Large, spurred flowers borne among leaves along main stem, branches. Solid-colored or variegated, in white or shades of pink, rose, lilac, or red. Compact, double camellia–flowered forms are most frequently grown. Sow seeds in flats or pots in early spring; after frost danger is past, set out young plants (or purchased transplants) in full sun (light shade in hottest climates).

I. namchabarwensis. BLUE DIAMOND IMPATIENS. Perennial. Zones 4–9, 14–24. Grows 16–20 in. high and wide, and bears pure, deep blue flowers. Partial to full shade.

I. New Guinea hybrids. Perennials in Zones 24, H1, H2; can be grown as annuals in all zones. A varied group of striking plants developed from a number of species native to New Guinea, especially *I. hawkeri* (*I. schlechteri*). Plants can be upright to spreading; most are 1–2 ft. high and as wide or wider (though some are much bigger or much smaller). Leaves are typically large, often variegated with cream or red. Flowers usually large (3 in. wide) though not profuse, held well above foliage; colors include lavender, purple, pink, red, orange, and white. Once considered primarily container plants, they may also be grown in the open ground; provide ample fertilizer and plenty of water, and give somewhat more sun than you would common impatiens (*I. walleriana*).

Popular strains include Celebration (with 3-in. flowers), ColorPower, and Infinity (which does well in sun or shade). The

CLOCKWISE FROM TOP: *Impatiens walleriana* 'Fiesta Olé Purple Stripe'; *I. auricoma* 'Jungle Gold'; *I. walleriana* 'Fiesta Salmon'

I

SunPatiens strain was bred to thrive in full sun, even in hot, humid climates. Plants grow 2–4 ft. tall and wide.

I. niamniamensis. Perennial. Zones 23, 24; H1, H2. From eastern tropical Africa. Grows 2 ft. high, with 1-in., cornucopia-shaped flowers under the leaves. 'African Princess' flowers are red and cream; 'Congo Cockatoo' flowers are orange-red and yellow. Needs shade.

I. sodenii (I. oliveri). POOR MAN'S RHODODENDRON. Perennial in Zones 15–17, 21–24; indoor/outdoor plant elsewhere. From eastern tropical Africa. To 4–8 ft. tall, 10 ft. wide, with woody-based stems clothed in whorls of 8-in.-long, glossy dark green leaves. Produces many 2½-in., slender-spurred flowers in lilac, pale lavender, or pinkish shades, and white. 'Madonna' ('Full Moon', 'Alba') has white flowers to 3 in. across; 'Flash' has 2½-in. white flowers with magenta streaks. Tolerates seacoast conditions. Frosts kill it to ground, but it regrows in spring. Blooms in partial or deep shade; takes sun in cool-summer areas.

I. walleriana. BUSY LIZZIE. Perennial in Zones 17, 24, H1, H2; can be grown as an annual in all zones. These are generally easier and more forgiving than New Guinea impatiens. Native to eastern Africa. Rapid, vigorous growth; tall types to about 2 ft. high, dwarf kinds 6–12 in. high. Narrow, glossy dark green leaves on juicy pale green stems. Flowers 1–2 in. wide, in all colors but yellow and true blue. All bear five-petaled blooms, and all are useful for many months of bright color in partial or full shade. Grow plants from seed or cuttings; or buy them in cell-packs or pots. Space taller types 1 ft. apart, dwarfs 6 in. apart. If plants overgrow, cut them back as low as 6 in. aboveground—it's a tonic. New growth emerges in a few days, and flowers cover it in 2 weeks. Plants in moist ground often reseed.

At any given moment, there are dozens of excellent strains on the market; many are just nuanced versions of the others. Following are some popular samples.

Accent. To 10 in. high. In numerous individual colors or a mix.

Blitz. To 16 in. high, with 2-in. flowers in mixed or single colors.

Dazzler. To 11 in. high, in all colors plus a star pattern.

Stardust. To 12–14 in. Central white star tapers off into a dusting of white.

Super Elfin. To 8–10 in. Comes in an exceptionally wide range of individual colors and blends of harmonizing hues. One example is 'Blue Pearl', with flowers in an unusual bluish lilac shade.

Swirl. To 10–12 in. Pastel shades with picotee edges of deeper color.

Among doubles, 'Victorian Rose', with its frilly, rose-pink, semidouble flowers, is a classic. The Fiesta, Rockapulco, and Tioga strains are also fine doubles. Any of these are best used in containers, located where double-flower detail can be observed close-up.

Imperata cylindrica 'Rubra' ('Red Baron')
JAPANESE BLOOD GRASS
Poaceae
PERENNIAL GRASS

🗡 **ZONES 2B–24**

☀ ◐ **FULL SUN OR PARTIAL SHADE**

💧 **REGULAR WATER**

Imperata cylindrica 'Rubra'

Elegant clumps of bright red, nearly vertical grass blades give Japanese blood grass both textural and visual punch. In spring, this Japanese grass's leaves emerge medium green at the base, red at the tip. The color extends along the leaf over summer; by autumn, the top half of each leaf may be brilliant red. Forms an upright clump 1–2 ft. high and 1 ft. wide, and spreads slowly by underground runners. Striking where sun can shine through blades. Rarely (if ever) flowers. Turns straw-colored in winter; best cut to the ground yearly.

Incarvillea
Bignoniaceae
PERENNIALS

🗡 **ZONES VARY BY SPECIES**

☀ ◐ **LIGHT SHADE IN HOTTEST CLIMATES**

💧 **REGULAR WATER**

Incarvillea delavayi

With trumpet-shaped flowers that seem large for the size of the plant, these trumpet-vine relatives are from the Himalayas and western China. Plants are deep rooted and need reasonably deep soil and excellent drainage (they can take a certain amount of cold, but not cold, soggy soil). Protect from slugs and snails.

I. arguta. Zones 4–6, 15–24; can be treated as annual elsewhere, since it will bloom first year from seed if started in earliest spring. Erect plant to 2–5 ft. tall and 3 ft. wide, sometimes sprawling to 5 ft. wide; somewhat shrubby at base. Leaves divided into 4–12 leaflets, each up to 2 in. long. Blooms in spring and summer; inflorescences have 5–20 pink or white, 1½-in.-long flowers. Effective leaning over walls or spilling down slopes. Self-sows but does not become a pest.

I. delavayi. HARDY GLOXINIA. Zones 2–24. Grows 2 ft. high, 1 ft. wide. Grows from a carrot-shaped perennial root and forms a rosette of foot-long leaves, each divided into many leaflets. The foot-long flower stalk is topped by 2–12 blossoms that are 3 in. long and wide, rosy purple outside, yellow and purple within. Blooms in late spring, early summer. 'Snowtop' has white flowers. In cold-winter regions, mulch plants after ground has frozen (to prevent ground from heaving).

Indigofera
INDIGO BUSH
Papilionaceae
DECIDUOUS SHRUBS

🗡 **ZONES 2B–9, 14–21**

☀ ◐ **EXPOSURE NEEDS VARY BY SPECIES**

💧 **REGULAR WATER**

Indigofera kirilowii

Called indigo bushes because some of their near relations are sources for indigo dye, these woody-stemmed plants have finely divided, almost ferny foliage. Dense clusters of tiny, sweet pea–shaped flowers appear in summer. Plants can be killed to the ground in a hard winter, but they recover quickly from the roots and bloom on new wood in spring and summer. Even in mild-winter areas, plants are more compact and attractive when cut back hard in late dormant season. Good drainage essential.

I. australis. AUSTRAL INDIGO. Zones 14–24. Native to temperate Australia. To 5 ft. tall and wide, with erect and arching shoots. Magenta flowers are clustered close to the stems. Partial shade. Tolerates salty soil.

I. decora (I. incarnata). From China and Japan. To 1–2½ ft. high and 3 ft. wide, with arching branches. Narrow, somewhat drooping blossom clusters to 8 in. long hold as many as 40 small white blooms suffused with pink. Full sun.

I. kirilowii. Native to northern China, Korea, and Japan. To 2½–3 ft. high, 3 ft. wide, with upright shoots and erect, 5-in. clusters of rose-pink flowers. Full sun.

Indocalamus. See Bamboo

Inula
ELECAMPANE
Asteraceae
PERENNIALS

✂ **ZONES VARY BY SPECIES**

☼ **FULL SUN**

◐ ◑ **LITTLE TO MODERATE WATER**

🦋 **ATTRACT BUTTERFLIES**

Inula magnifica

These big perennials cover themselves with narrow-rayed, yellow daisies in summer. Foliage is coarse, and most of the available species are large, back-of-the-border plants. Flowers can be cut for the vase. Given good drainage, these demand little attention. Of many species, the following two are most widely sold. Smaller ones such as *I. hookeri* (4 ft.) and *I. ensifolia* (2 ft.) are also sometimes offered.

I. magnifica. MAGNIFICENT ELECAMPANE. Zones 3b–9, 14–24. From Europe. To 7 ft. tall with 3–6-in. daisies on branching stems in late summer. Docklike leaves are larger at the base, smaller toward the top of the plant.

I. racemosa 'Sonnenspeer'. Zones 4–9, 14–24. China. To 7 ft. tall, with yellow daisies to 3-in. diameter, flowering from early summer to fall. Covered with hairy leaves up to 1 ft. long, stems are streaked with red.

Iochroma
Solanaceae
EVERGREEN VINING SHRUBS

✂ **ZONES 15–17, 19–24**

☼ ◐ **FULL SUN OR PARTIAL SHADE**

💧 **REGULAR WATER**

🦅 **ATTRACT HUMMINGBIRDS**

Iochroma cyaneum
'Royal Queen Purple'

These fast-growing, vining shrubs have drooping tubular or trumpet-shaped flowers in clusters of up to 20 near ends of branches. Blooms from early spring through fall—or year-round in frost-free areas. Leaves 5–8 in. long, 1½–3 in. wide. Fruits are pulpy berries. From the forests of Central and South America.

Lax growth is best staked up, espaliered, or draped over a fence or wall. Prune selectively to maintain size and shape— and to keep flowers coming. Avoid pruning in late fall or when cold weather approaches. Hard pruning delays bloom. Protect from hard frosts. Cucumber beetles love to eat the leaves.

In addition to the following, specialists have a number of other species and hybrids.

I. cyaneum. Grows to 8 ft. or more, with dull dark green leaves. Stems and new shoots covered with soft, grayish down. Narrow trumpets are 2–3 in. long. Blossom color of seed-lings varies from blues through violets and deep reds to purplish rose and pink. All have a metallic sheen. Buy plants in bloom to get the color you want, or select named varieties. 'Indigo' is glossy violet-blue; 'Royal Blue' is a lighter, more brilliant blue; and 'Sky King' is a pure light blue. 'Peachy Keen' has peachy red flowers; 'Royal Queen Purple' has bright purple flowers.

I. fuchsioides. To 10 ft. or more, with glossy bright green leaves. Brilliant orange-scarlet, tubular flowers with yellow throats look like fuchsia flowers.

Ipheion uniflorum
(Brodiaea uniflora)
SPRING STAR FLOWER
Alliaceae
PERENNIAL FROM BULB

✂ **ZONES 2B–24**

☼ ◐ **FULL SUN OR PARTIAL SHADE**

💧 **REGULAR WATER DURING GROWTH AND BLOOM**

Ipheion uniflorum

An excellent choice for naturalizing, this bulb produces several slender stems up to 1 ft. high, each bearing a single, ½-in., fragrant blossom with six overlapping petals. Usual color is white tinged with blue, but variants include white 'Album', pink 'Charlotte Bishop', deep violet 'Froyle Mill', bright blue 'Rolf Fiedler', and dark blue 'Wisley Blue'. All have narrow, nearly flat leaves that smell like onions when bruised. From Argentina. Use in borders, under deciduous shrubs, in woodland areas, or among low grasses.

CARE

In fall, set bulbs 2 in. deep and 2 in. apart. This plant prefers dry conditions during summer dormancy but will accept water if drainage is good.

Divide infrequently—plantings become more attractive over time as bulbs multiply. They'll grow, multiply, and live happily in a low container for several years or more.

Ipomoea
MORNING GLORY
Convolvulaceae
PERENNIAL AND ANNUAL VINES

✂ **ZONES VARY BY SPECIES**

☼ **FULL SUN**

◐ ● **MODERATE TO REGULAR WATER**

⬥ **SEEDS OF SOME KINDS ARE TOXIC**

Ipomoea tricolor 'Wedding Bells'

In this genus, ornamentals and edibles abound, from edible sweet potatoes (see Sweet Potato) to trellis-climbing morning glories and the sweet potato vines that fill out container plants so well.

Most have hard seeds; to encourage faster sprouting, nick the coating or soak overnight in water before planting. For annual display, sow seeds in place after frost danger is past; or, for an earlier start, sow seeds indoors, then set out plants 6–8 in. apart. Use morning glory vines on fence or trellis or as groundcover. Or grow in containers; provide stakes or a wire cylinder for support, or let plant cascade. For cut flowers, pick stems with buds in various stages of development and place in deep vase; buds will open on consecutive days. The morning glories in the list that follows do not include

How to Propagate Sweet Potato Vine

When plants die back in fall, dig the tubers, put them in a container full of dry peat moss or vermiculite, and overwinter them in a cool, dark place. In spring, pull them out and cut them into sections with at least one eye per piece. Let them dry (callus) for a couple of days, and then plant out after danger of frost is past.

the weedy plant known as wild morning glory or bindweed (*Convolvulus arvensis*). These are similar only in appearance.

I. alba (Calonyction aculeatum). MOONFLOWER. Perennial in Zones 15–17, 23, 24, H1, H2; annual elsewhere. Fast growing (20–30 ft. in a season), providing quick shade for arbor, trellis, or fence. Luxuriantly clothed in heart-shaped leaves to 8 in. long, closely spaced on stems. Blooms in the evening, showing off fragrant, 6-in., funnel-shaped white blossoms after sundown and into the night (flowers also open on cloudy or dark days). Needs heat to bloom.

I. batatas. SWEET POTATO VINE. Perennial from tuberous roots. Zones 13, 21–24; H1, H2; or indoor/outdoor plant. For the edible sort, see Sweet Potato; following are fancy-leafed forms grown for ornament. Trailing in habit, they have leaves that vary in size from 2 to 4 in. long and in shape from heart-shaped to deeply lobed. 'Ace of Spades' has heart-shaped, deep purple leaves. 'Blackie' is a fast grower with purple-black leaves. 'Marguerite' has golden green foliage. 'Tricolor' ('Pink Frost') has green leaves with white and pink variegation. 'Emerald Lace' (green) and 'Midnight Lace' (black) have deeply lobed leaves. The Sweet Caroline strain includes selections whose leaves are purple, bronze, red, and shades of green. All are attractive in hanging baskets but can overrun less vigorous companion plants.

I. indica (I. acuminata, I. learii). BLUE DAWN FLOWER. Perennial. Zones 8, 9, 12–24;

H1, H2. Vigorous, rapid growth to 15–30 ft. Dark green, heart-shaped or three-lobed leaves. Clusters of 3–4-in., funnel-shaped flowers from spring into fall; blooms open bright blue, then fade to pinkish purple by day's end. Use to cover large bank, wall, or unsightly fence or other structure. Blooms in 1 year from seed; can also be grown from cuttings, divisions, and layering of established plants.

I. nil. MORNING GLORY. Annual. All zones. Summer bloomer resembling *I. tricolor*. The large-flowered (to 6 in. wide) Imperial Japanese strain belongs to this species. Other available selections include rosy red 'Scarlett O'Hara', odd pinkish tan 'Chocolate', and the mixed-color Early Call strain, which is useful where summers are short.

I. purpurea. COMMON MORNING GLORY. Annual. All zones. Grows 6–9 ft. tall, usually with blue, purple, or white flowers 1½–2½ in. wide. 'Grandpa Otts' has deep purple flowers with a wine-shaped central star. The white flowers of the Carnival (or Carnival of Venice) strain are marked with pink or purple radial stripes.

I. quamoclit (Quamoclit pennata). CYPRESS VINE, CARDINAL CLIMBER. Annual. All zones. To 20 ft., with 2½–4-in.-long leaves finely divided into slender threads. Summer flowers are 1½-in.-long tubes that flare at mouth into a five-pointed star; they're usually scarlet, rarely white. Attract birds.

I. tricolor. MORNING GLORY. Annual. All zones. Vigorous growth to 10–15 ft., with large, heart-shaped leaves. Showy,

funnel-shaped to bell-like flowers are single or double, in solid colors of blue, lavender, pink, red, or white, often with throats in contrasting colors; some are bicolored or striped. Most types open only in morning, fade in afternoon. Bloom from summer until frost. Among the most popular selections is 'Heavenly Blue', to 15 ft., bearing 4–5-in., pure sky blue flowers with yellow throat. Seeds are toxic, with ingestion causing nausea and chronic psychosis.

Ipomopsis
Polemoniaceae
BIENNIALS OR PERENNIALS

🌡	**ZONES VARY BY SPECIES**
🔆	**FULL SUN**
💧	**NO IRRIGATION NEEDED**
🐦	**ATTRACT HUMMINGBIRDS**

Ipomopsis aggregata

These American natives have a definite wildflower look, with erect single stems, finely divided leaves, and tubular red (or yellow-and-red) flowers. Individual plants are narrow and somewhat startling in appearance; best massed. They survive on rainfall but can take irrigation if grown in a watered border. Sow seeds in spring or early summer for bloom the following summer.

I. aggregata (Gilia aggregata). Biennial. Zones 1–3, 6–14, 18–21. Native from California to British Columbia, east to Rocky Mountains. To 2½ ft. high and 1 ft. wide. Flowers are red marked yellow (sometimes pure yellow), about an inch long, borne in long, narrow clusters.

I. rubra (Gilia rubra). Biennial or perennial. Zones 2, 3,

7–9, 14–24. Native to southern U.S. To 6 ft. tall and 1 ft. wide. Flowers red outside, yellow marked red inside.

Iresine herbstii
BLOODLEAF
Amaranthaceae
PERENNIAL

🌡	**ZONES 22–24; H1, H2; OR INDOORS**
🔆	**FULL SUN; BRIGHT LIGHT**
💧	**REGULAR WATER**

Iresine herbstii 'Blazin' Rose'

This tender, upright plant is grown for its vibrant leaf colors; flowers are inconspicuous and may be pinched out. From Brazil. Grows 1–3 ft. high and wide, or larger under ideal conditions. Leaves are 1–3 in. long, oval to round, usually notched at the tip. Leaf colors run from purple to red, bronze, and green, with light or yellowish midrib and veins. Stems may be green, purple, or red. 'Blazin' Rose' and 'Brilliantissima' are red-leafed varieties; 'Purple Lady' is purple.

Performs best in rich, well-drained soil. Pinch tips of young plants to encourage bushiness. Good in containers. Beyond hardiness range, bring indoors for winter or treat as an annual. Easy to propagate from cuttings taken in fall and grown for spring and summer display.

Show off bloodleaf's smoldering red and brown foliage in a chocolate brown pot, with white 'Snowstorm' bacopa to soften the edges.

Iris

Iridaceae

PERENNIALS FROM BULBS AND
RHIZOMES

✔ **ZONES VARY ACCORDING
TO SPECIES OR TYPE**

☼ ☼ ● **EXPOSURE NEEDS VARY
BY SPECIES**

◐ ◐ ◑ **WATER NEEDS VARY BY
SPECIES**

✿ **TOXIC KINDS NOTED IN ENTRIES**

Siberian iris 'Caesar's Brother'

Named for the Greek rainbow
goddess and stylized as the
fleur-de-lis, irises typically have
grassy or swordlike foliage and
flower parts in threes. A remarkably diverse group of more than
250 species, these vary in
flower color and form, cultural
needs, and blooming periods
(although the majority flower in
spring or early summer). Flowers, often fragrant, are showy
and complex. The three inner
segments (the standards) are
petals; they are usually erect
or arching but, in some kinds,
may flare to horizontal. The
three outer segments (the falls)
are petal-like sepals; they are
held at various angles, from
nearly horizontal to drooping.

Irises grow from bulbs or rhizomes. Flowers are grouped
into three broad categories:
bearded (each of the falls bears
an adornment resembling a
fuzzy caterpillar); beardless
(falls are smooth); and crested
(falls have a comblike ridge
instead of a full beard).

Tall bearded irises (and other
bearded classes) are the most
widely sold; many new hybrids
are cataloged every year. A
smaller number of growers offer
various beardless classes and
some species. Retail nurseries
usually carry bulbous irises for
fall planting, plus a few containerized irises during bloom season, and often plants from the
Pacific Coast, Siberian, and Japanese iris groups.

BULBOUS IRISES

Irises that grow from bulbs
have beardless flowers. Bulbs
become dormant in summer
and can be lifted and stored
until planting time in fall.

Dutch and Spanish irises

Zones 2b–24. The parent species of this group come from
Spain, Portugal, Sicily, and
northern Africa. (Dutch irises
are named for the Dutch bulb
growers who hybridized them.
They are often sold as *I.* × *hol-
landica* varieties.) Flowers are
borne atop slender stems that
rise from rushlike foliage. Standards are narrow and upright;
oval to circular falls project
downward. Colors include white,
mauve, blue, purple, brown,
orange, yellow, and bicolor combinations—usually with a yellow
blotch on falls. Dutch iris flowers reach 3–4 in. across, on
stems 1½–2 ft. high; these are
the irises sold by florists. Bloom
period is early spring in warm-
winter climates, late spring in
colder areas. Spanish irises are
similar but have smaller flowers
that bloom about 2 weeks after
Dutch irises.

Plant bulbs in autumn, setting them 4 in. deep, 3–4 in.
apart; give full sun. Bulbs are
hardy to about –10°F (–23°C),
but in coldest adapted zones,
apply a mulch in winter. Give
regular water during growth.
Bulbs can be left in the ground
for several years where summers are dry; elsewhere, they
should be lifted. After bloom, let
foliage ripen before digging;
store bulbs in a cool, dry place
for no more than 2 months
before replanting. Dutch and
Spanish irises are good in containers; plant five bulbs in a
5–6-in. pot.

The widely sold 'Wedgwood'
is a Dutch hybrid hardy only in
Zones 4–24. Large flowers are
lavender-blue with yellow markings, blooming earlier than others (generally coinciding with
early midseason daffodils).
Bulbs are larger than those of
average Dutch hybrid. Vigorous
foliage dies down after bloom
and is best masked by bushy
annuals or perennials that
mature later in the season.

English irises

Zones 3–6, 15–17, 21–24. The
species (*I. latifolia*) from which
named selections were made is
native to the Pyrenees, where it
grows in moist meadows. Early
botanists first noticed the iris
growing in southern England,
where it had been brought by
traders. Flowers are similar in
structure to Dutch and Spanish
irises, but falls are broader and
decorated with a hairline stripe
of yellow. Colors include bluish
purple, wine red, maroon, blue,
mauve, white. Bloom comes in
early summer. Plant bulbs in
fall, 3–4 in. deep, 4 in. apart, in
cool, moist, acid soil. Choose a
partly shaded location in warm-
summer areas, full sun where
summers are cool. Because
English irises don't need complete dryness after flowering,
they can be left in the ground
in suitable climates. Bulbs are
hardy to about –10°F (–23°C).
Or the bulbs can be lifted and
replanted.

Reticulata irises

Zones 3–24; safer in containers
in colder zones. The netted
("reticulate") outer covering on
the bulbs gives the group its
name. These are classic rock
garden and container plants,
the flowers (like small Dutch
irises) appearing on 6–8-in.
stems in very early spring (midwinter in mild areas). Narrow
blue-green leaves appear after
bloom. The available species
include *I. reticulata*, with 2–3-in.
violet-scented flowers (purple,
in the usual forms), and bright
yellow–flowered *I. danfordiae*.
Large-flowered, blue-and-yellow
I. histrioides is carried by some
specialists. Far more common
are named hybrids such as
'Cantab' (pale blue with orange
markings), 'Harmony' (blue
marked in yellow), and 'J. S.
Dijt' (reddish purple).

Bulbs are hardy to about
–10°F (–23°C) and need some
subfreezing winter temperatures
to thrive. Plant in autumn, in
well-drained soil in a sunny location; set bulbs 3–4 in. deep and
3–4 in. apart. Need regular
moisture from autumn through
spring. Soil should be kept dry
during summer dormant period;
in rainy climates, lift bulbs in
summer or grow in pots so that
you can control moisture. Divide
only when vigor and flower quality deteriorate. Watch for slugs
and snails.

RHIZOMATOUS IRISES

Irises that grow from rhizomes
(thickened, modified stems with
fleshy roots) may have bearded,
beardless, or crested flowers;
among this group are the most
widely grown types. Leaves
are swordlike, overlapping one
another to form flat fans of
foliage.

Bearded irises

Zones 1–24. The most widely
grown irises fall into the
bearded group. More than a
century of breeding has produced a vast array of beautiful
hybrids. All have upright standards and flaring to pendent
falls that have characteristic
epaulettelike beards. Tall

Refresh Crowded Irises

When clumps of rhizomatous irises become overcrowded after 3 or 4 years, the quantity and quality
of blooms decrease. Lift and divide crowded clumps
at best planting time for your area. Save large rhizomes with healthy leaves; discard old and leafless
ones from clump's center. Break rhizomes apart or
use a sharp knife to separate. Trim leaves, roots to
about 6 in.; let cut ends heal for several hours before
replanting. If replanting in the same soil, amend it
with organic matter.

I

How to Grow Bearded Irises

July to October is best planting period; in regions with mild winters and cool to moderate summers, you can plant throughout this time. In cold-winter zones, plant during July or August; where summer temperatures are high, plant in September or October. Plant in full sun in cool climates; in hottest regions, they'll accept light shade during the afternoon.

SOIL Bearded irises need good drainage. They'll grow in soils from sandy to claylike; but if your soil is clay, plant in raised beds or on ridges to ensure drainage, avoid rhizome rot.

PLANTING Space rhizomes 1–2 ft. apart; set with tops barely beneath soil surface, spreading roots well. Growth proceeds from the leafy end of rhizome, so point that end in direction you want growth initially to occur. For quick show, plant three rhizomes 1 ft. apart—two with growing ends pointed outward, the third aimed to grow into the space between them. On slopes, set rhizomes with growing end facing uphill. If weather turns hot, shade newly planted rhizomes to prevent sunscald, possible rot. Where winters are severe, mulch new plantings to prevent heaving from alternate freezing, thawing.

CARE Water to settle soil and start growth. Thereafter, water judiciously until new growth shows that plants have rooted; then water regularly until fall rains or frosts arrive. From the time growth starts in late winter or early spring, water regularly until about 6 weeks after flowers fade; increases and buds for next year's flowers form during postbloom period. During summer, plants need less water. In heavy soil, it may be sufficient to water every other week in hot climates, monthly in cool ones. In lighter soils, try watering weekly in hot areas, every other week in cool ones.

For best performance, feed plants with moderate-nitrogen commercial fertilizer as growth begins in spring, then after bloom has finished. In cool, moist spring, leaf spot may disfigure foliage; use an appropriate fungicide at first sign of infection. Remove old and dry leaves in fall.

---

bearded irises are the most familiar of these, but they represent just one subdivision of the entire group. Eating any part of these causes gastric upset, and plants have poisoned livestock; in addition, some people get contact dermatitis from handling the rhizomes.

DWARF AND MEDIAN IRISES

These irises generally have flowers shaped like the familiar tall beardeds, but flower size, plant size, and stature are smaller. Median iris is a collective term for the categories of standard dwarf, intermediate and border bearded, and miniature tall bearded.

Miniature dwarf bearded irises. Grow to 8 in. tall; flowers large for size of plant. Earliest to bloom of bearded irises (about 6 weeks before main show of tall beardeds). Hardy, need winter chill. Plants multiply quickly. Shallow root systems need regular moisture and periodic feeding.

Standard dwarf bearded irises. Grow 8–15 in. high. Flowers and plants are larger than miniature dwarfs. Profuse bloom. Easier to grow than miniature dwarfs in Western gardens but perform best with some winter chill.

Intermediate bearded irises. Grow 15–28 in. high, bear flowers 3–5 in. across.

Flower later than dwarfs but 1 to 3 weeks before tall bearded irises. Most are hybrids of standard dwarfs and tall bearded varieties, and resemble larger standard dwarfs rather than border beardeds. Some give second bloom in fall.

Border bearded irises. Grow 15–28 in. high—proportionately smaller versions of tall beardeds in the same wide range of colors and patterns. Bloom period is same as for tall bearded.

Miniature tall bearded irises. Grow 15–28 in. high and flower with tall beardeds. Their small flowers (2–3 in. wide), narrower foliage, and pencil-thin stems give them appearance of tall bearded irises reduced in every proportion. Good for cutting and arrangements—hence their original name, "table irises."

TALL BEARDED IRISES

Among choicest perennials for borders, massing, cutting. Most are hybrids, but they are often incorrectly listed as *I. germanica* varieties. Easy to grow. Mid-spring flowers, on branching stems 2½–4 ft. tall. All colors but pure red and green; patterns of two colors or more, blends produce infinite variety. Countless named selections are available. Modern hybrids often have elaborately ruffled, fringed flowers. Available variegated foliage selections include 'Pallida Variegata' ('Zebra'), with green leaves striped with cream; and 'Argentea', producing green leaves with white stripes. Both bear smallish blue-lavender flowers on stems to 2 ft. high.

Remontant (repeat blooming or reblooming) tall bearded irises flower in spring, again in

Bearded iris blooms are gorgeous, but they don't last long. One solution: put them at the backs of borders, where they'll disappear among other plants after their flowers fade.

mid- to late summer, fall, or winter, depending on variety and climate. In mild climates, some are nearly everblooming. Plants need fertilizer, regular moisture for best performance. These now account for a large segment of the tall bearded irises sold.

ARIL AND ARILBRED IRISES

The aril species and interspecies hybrids (characterized by an aril, or collar, on their seeds) offer strange and often remarkably beautiful flowers on unattractive plants. Exacting cultural requirements. Most species come from semidesert areas of the Near East and central Asia; they need limy soil, perfect drainage, full sun, and no summer water (and thus do best in areas with scant or no summer rain). There are two main groups: Oncocyclus and Regelia. Oncocyclus group includes a number of species with huge, nearly globular flowers in lavender, gray, silver, maroon, and gold, often intricately veined and stippled with deeper hues. Regelia group has smaller, narrower-petaled flowers, veined or unmarked; they come in brighter shades than Oncocyclus, often with a lustrous sheen. Oncocyclus is more difficult to grow; somewhat easier are Regelia group and hybrids between the two (Oncogelia).

Arilbreds—hybrids between the arils and bearded irises—offer some of the arils' exotic beauty on plants nearly as easy to grow as tall beardeds, given well-drained, neutral to alkaline soil. Amount of aril ancestry can determine ease of culture: hybrids containing half aril ancestry or more usually are more demanding than those of one-quarter or three-eighths aril ancestry. Specialists' catalogs sometimes state hybrid ancestries for this reason.

Beardless irises

Flowers in this group all have smooth, beardless falls but otherwise differ considerably in appearance from one type or species to another. Rhizomes have fibrous roots (unlike fleshy roots of bearded types); most prefer or demand more moisture than bearded irises. Many can perform well from crowded clumps but will eventually need division. Timing varies; dig and replant quickly, keeping roots moist until planted.

The following five hybrid groups contain the most widely sold beardless irises. Also described are individual species (and their named selections) available from growers of specialty irises and perennials.

JAPANESE IRISES

Zones 1–10, 14–24. Derived solely from *I. ensata* (formerly *I. kaempferi*), these irises feature sumptuous blossoms 4–12 in. across on slender stems to 4 ft. tall. Flower shape is essentially flat. Single types have three broad falls and much-reduced standards, giving triangular flower outline; double blossoms have standards marked like the falls and about the same size and shape, resulting in circular flower outline. Colors are purple, violet, pink, rose, red, white—often veined or edged in contrasting shade. Plants have graceful narrow, upright leaves with distinct raised midribs. Of dozens of excellent named varieties on the market, purple-flowered 'Variegata', with white-margined leaves, is the most common.

Plants need much moisture during growing, flowering period. Acid to neutral soil and water are required. If soil or water is alkaline, apply aluminum sulfate or iron sulfate (1 oz. per 2 gal. water) several times during growing season. Plant rhizomes in fall or spring, 2 in. deep and 1½ ft. apart; or plant up to three per 12-in. container. Use in moist borders, at edge of pools or streams, or even in boxes or pots plunged halfway to rim in pond or pool during growing season. Full sun except in hottest areas.

LOUISIANA IRISES

Zones 3–24; H1, H2. Approximately four species from the lower Mississippi region and Gulf Coast compose this group of so-called swamp irises. Graceful, flattish blossoms on stems 2–5 ft. tall, carried above and among leaves that are long, narrow, and unribbed. The range of flower colors and patterns is extensive—nearly the equal of tall beardeds.

Specialists offer a vast array of named hybrids; some may carry the basic species as well. *I. brevicaulis* (*I. foliosa*) has blue flowers with flaring segments carried on zigzag stems among the foliage. *I. fulva* has coppery to rusty red (rarely yellow) blossoms with narrow, drooping segments. *I. giganticaerulea* is indeed a "giant blue" (sometimes white) with upright standards and flaring falls; stems may reach 4 ft. or more, with proportionally large leaves. *I. hexagona* also comes in blue shades with upright standards, flaring falls. *I. × nelsonii*, a natural hybrid population derived from *I. fulva* and *I. giganticaerulea*, resembles the *I. fulva* parent in flower shape and color, and approaches the *I. giganticaerulea* parent in size.

Plants thrive in well-watered, rich garden soil as well as at pond margins; soil and water should be neutral to acid. Locate in full sun where summer is cool to mild; choose light afternoon shade where summer heat is intense. Plant in late summer; set rhizomes 1 in. deep, 1½–2 ft. apart. Mulch for winter where ground freezes.

PACIFIC COAST IRISES

Best in Zones 4–9, 14–24; grown with mixed success in Zone 3. Eleven species native to Pacific Coast states constitute a homogeneous group within the genus Iris, from which breeders have developed hybrids in a broad range of colors and patterns; flowers may be white, blue shades, pink, copper, brown, maroon, violet—many with elaborate veining or patterning. Foliage is narrow; clumps are like coarse grass. Slender flower stems reach 8–24 in., depending on variety.

Best conditions are sun to light shade, well-drained soil, moderate to scant water in summer. Intense heat coupled with water and poor drainage can be fatal; in clay soil, grow in raised beds in organically amended soil. Plant from containers anytime; spring and fall are best. Dig, divide, and

> Pacific Coast irises are perfect for tucking into rock gardens, or use them to edge woodland borders.

CLOCKWISE FROM LEFT: *Iris douglasiana* 'On the Edge'; tall bearded iris 'Flammenschwert'; Spuria iris

replant when new roots are starting to form (scrape away soil at plant base to check); this ranges from early fall in colder regions to midwinter in mild-winter areas.

I. douglasiana is native to the California coast from Santa Barbara north and into Oregon. Evergreen leaves 1½–2 ft. long; stems 1–2 ft., sometimes branched, with flowers in purple and blue shades to white and cream. Tolerates less-than-perfect conditions. *I. innominata* comes from northwestern California and southwestern Oregon. Evergreen leaves; 8–12-in. stems bear flowers in yellow, orange, lavender, purple, brown, many attractively veined. Best in mild-summer regions, in woodland or rock garden. *I. tenax*, from Washington and Oregon, makes grassy clumps of foot-tall deciduous leaves. Flowers may be white, blue, purple, pink, cream, often veined in purple or brown. Best with mild summers, some winter chill.

»

CLOCKWISE FROM TOP: Tall bearded iris 'Edith Wolford'; Reticulata iris 'Harmony'; Spuria iris 'Betty Cooper'

SIBERIAN IRISES

Zones A2, A3; 1–10, 14–23. The most widely sold members of this group are named hybrids derived from *I. sibirica* and *I. sanguinea* (formerly *I. orientalis*)—species native to Europe, Asia. Clumps of narrow, almost grasslike leaves (deciduous in winter) produce slender stems to 4 ft. tall (depending on variety), each bearing two to five blossoms with upright standards and flaring to drooping falls. Colors include white and shades of blue, lavender, purple, wine, pink, and light yellow.

Give plants full sun (partial or dappled shade where summer is hot), neutral to acid soil. Set rhizomes 1–2 in. deep, 1–2 ft. apart. In cold-winter regions, plant in early spring or late summer; in fall in milder regions. Water liberally from onset of growth until several weeks after bloom. Divide infrequently—when clumps stop sending up leaves from centers—at best planting time for your region.

Specialists may offer various Sino-Siberian species. Most feature drooping falls and erect to flaring standards. Predominantly yellow colors are found in *I. forrestii* and *I. wilsonii*; predominantly purple to violet flowers occur in *I. chrysographes, I. clarkei, I. delavayi,* and *I. dykesii*. These species and their hybrids perform best in Zones 4–6, 15–17, where climate is moist and relatively mild. Give plants good, acid soil; regular moisture. Interesting hybrids between these species and Pacific Coast irises are called Cal-Sibes; flowers resemble the Siberian parents but have expanded color range. Garden needs are the same as for Sino-Siberian types.

SPURIA IRISES

Zones 2–24. In flower form, the spurias resemble Dutch irises. Older members of this group had primarily yellow or white-and-yellow blossoms; *I. orientalis* (*I. ochroleuca*) has naturalized in many parts of the West, its 3–5-ft. stems bearing white flowers with yellow blotches on the falls. Dwarf *I. graminea* bears narrow-petaled, fragrant blue-and-maroon blossoms on foot-high stems. Modern hybrids show a great color range: blue, lavender, gray, orchid, tan, bronze, brown, purple, earthy red, and near black—often with a prominent yellow spot on the falls. Flowers are held closely against 3–6-ft. stems, rising above handsome clumps of narrow dark green leaves. Flowering starts during latter part of tall bearded bloom and continues for several weeks beyond.

Plant rhizomes in late summer or early fall, in rich, neutral to slightly alkaline soil; set them 1 in. deep, 1½–2 ft. apart. Plants grow well in full sun but will also take light shade for part of the day. They need ample moisture from onset of growth through bloom period but little moisture during summer. Divide clumps (not an easy task) infrequently; mulch for winter where temperatures drop to –20°F (–29°C) or lower.

SPECIES IRISES

I. foetidissima. GLADWIN IRIS, ROAST BEEF PLANT. Zones 3–24. Native to Europe. Glossy evergreen leaves to 2 ft. make handsome foliage clumps. Stems 1½–2 ft. tall bear subtly attractive flowers in blue-gray and dull tan; specialists may offer color variants in soft yellow ('Aurea', 'Lutea') and lavender-blue, as well as a form with white-variegated leaves ('Variegata'). The large seed capsules that open in fall to show numerous round, orange-scarlet seeds are the real attraction; the cut stems with seed capsules are attractive in arrangements. Grow in sun to shade in cool-summer regions, light or partial shade to full shade elsewhere. Tolerates aridity. Bruised leaves have a meaty fragrance. Ingestion causes gastric upset.

I. germanica. Zones 1–24. Native to Europe. Mediterranean native; likely a natural hybrid between *I. pallida* and *I. variegata*. Gray-green leaves 12–16 in. long and 1–1¾ in. wide. Flowers are blue, violet, or white with yellow beards; they rise on 2–4-ft. stems. Because *I. germanica* is the type genus for bearded iris, those hybrids are often listed as *I. germanica* varieties. See "Tall bearded irises." Ingestion causes gastric upset.

I. laevigata. Zones 1–10, 14–24. Native to China, Korea, Japan. Smooth, glossy leaves reach 1½–2½ ft. high, to 1 in. wide. Flower stems grow to about the same height, bearing violet-blue blossoms with upright standards and drooping falls enlivened with yellow central stripes. Bloom period comes after that of tall bearded irises. Named color variants include kinds with white, magenta, and patterned purple-and-white blooms, as well as a purple-flowered selection with leaves striped in ivory white. There also are varieties whose standards mimic falls in shape, pattern, and carriage, producing the effect of a double blossom. This is a true bog plant, best in constantly moist, acid soil—even in shallow water. Full sun.

I. missouriensis. WESTERN BLUE FLAG, ROCKY MOUNTAIN IRIS. Zones 1–10, 14–24. Native to 2,000–12,000-ft. elevations from western Nebraska and the Dakotas into the Sierra Nevada/Cascade mountain ranges and mountains of Southern California, and from the Yukon into northern Mexico. In zones where plant is adapted, local forms are more likely to succeed. Narrow, flat, bluish green, winter-deciduous leaves range from 12 to 22 in. high. Blooms in late spring and summer; blossoms have narrow, upright standards and semiflaring to drooping falls, on stems a bit higher than the foliage. Colors range from lavender to white, with veins in darker lavender to purple; the darker colors are found in the more southerly and westerly forms. Give a sunny location and neutral to alkaline, water-retentive soil that is kept moist throughout growth and bloom, dry thereafter. Best time to plant or transplant is from early spring into the flowering period.

A similar species, *I. longipetala,* is considered by some botanists to be a form of *I. missouriensis*. It differs from *I. missouriensis* in its nativity (Northern and central California Coast Ranges, up to about 1,200 ft.) and in having evergreen foliage and an early-spring bloom period.

I. pseudacorus. YELLOW FLAG. Zones A2, A3; 1–24. Native to Europe but now found worldwide in temperate regions; seeds float, aiding plant's dispersal. Impressive foliage plant; under best conditions, upright leaves may reach 5 ft. tall. Flower stems grow 4–7 ft. (depending on culture), bear bright yellow flowers 3–4 in. across. Selected forms offer ivory and lighter yellow flowers, double flowers, variegated foliage, and plants with shorter and taller leaves. Plant in sun to light shade. Needs acid soil and plenty of moisture; thrives in shallow water, and can become invasive where running water spreads its seeds. Ingestion causes gastric upset. A noxious weed in Montana, Washington, and Oregon.

I. setosa. Zones A1–A3; 1–6. Native to Siberia, Alaska, eastern Canada, and New England. Leaves are a slightly grayed green, ½–1 in. wide; plants vary from less than 1 ft. to about 2 ft. high, with flower stems taller than leaves. Blooms in late spring and summer, bearing typically blue-purple to red-purple flowers with broadly rounded falls, standards reduced to mere bristles. Garden culture as for Siberian irises: moist, well-drained, neutral to acid soil, and full sun except in hottest areas. Will grow where buffeted by salt-laden ocean spray. Plant in late summer, early fall.

I. unguicularis (I. stylosa). WINTER IRIS. Zones 4–9, 14–24. Native to Greece, the Near East, and northern Africa. Dense clump of narrow dark green leaves. Depending on variety and mildness of winter, flowers appear from November to March. Typical form has violet-tinted blue blossoms elevated on 6–9-in. tubes that serve as stems. Named selections vary in flower color (lighter and darker lavender, orchid pink, white) and coarseness and length of foliage. Plants need neutral to acid soil, heat, and scant water during summer (but will take moderate water if soil is very well drained). In Zones 4 and 5, grow against sunny wall or house foundation to increase summer heat and to lessen winter cold. Divide

overcrowded clumps in early fall (mild regions) or in late winter after flowering (colder regions). Slugs and snails are attracted to the flowers.

I. versicolor. BLUE FLAG. Zones 1–9, 14–17. Widely distributed North American species, found in bogs and swamps from Mississippi Valley to eastern Canada. Grows 1½–4 ft. tall; narrow leaves are thicker in the center but not ribbed. Shorter-growing forms have upright leaves, but foliage of taller types may recurve gracefully. The typical wild flowers are a light violet-blue, but lighter and darker forms exist. 'Mysterious Monique' is deep violet, almost black; 'Raspberry Slurp' is white with raspberry veins. Like *I. pseudacorus*, *I. versicolor* thrives in sun to light shade, in moist, acid soil or shallow water. Ingestion causes gastric upset.

Specialty growers offer hybrids between *I. versicolor* and other species. Violet-flowered 'Gerald Darby', a hybrid with *I. virginica*, has striking wine red stems. Violet-flowered 'Black Gamecock', a hybrid with *I. × fulvala*, has dark purple blooms.

Crested irises. Though these are botanically placed with beardless irises, they represent a transition between beardless and bearded: each fall bears a narrow, comblike crest where a beard would be in bearded sorts. Slugs and snails dine on foliage and flowers.

I. cristata. Zones 2b–6. Leaves 4–6 in. long, ½ in. wide; slender greenish rhizomes spread freely. Flowers white, lavender, or light blue with golden crests. Give light shade, organically enriched soil, regular water. Divide just after bloom or in fall after leaves die down.

I. tectorum. ROOF IRIS. Zones 3–9, 14–24; H1, H2. Native to Japan, where it is planted on cottage roofs. Foliage fans to 1 ft. high look like those of bearded irises, but leaves are ribbed and glossy. Flowers suggest an informal bearded iris with fringed petals and crests in place of beards. Colors are violet-blue with white crests or white with yellow crests; standards are upright at first, opening to horizontal as flower matures. Provide organically enriched soil, light shade, regular water. Short-lived in

CLOCKWISE FROM LEFT: Tall bearded iris 'Nel Jape'; *I. tectorum*; standard dwarf bearded iris 'Baby Blessed'

regions where summers are hot and dry. 'Paltec', a hybrid of *I. tectorum* with a bearded iris, will grow with bearded irises; it reaches about 1 ft. high, with lavender flowers suggesting a bearded iris with beards superimposed on crests.

Tender crested irises. Several tender species and hybrids form bamboo-type stems carrying foliage fans aloft; flower stems to 2 ft. are widely branched, bearing orchidlike sprays of fringed flowers in lavender to white with orange crests. These include *I. confusa, I. japonica, I. wattii*, and hybrids such as 'Nada' (white with gold crests and lavender style arms). Grow in sun where summer is cool, light shade elsewhere; plant in organically enriched soil. Regular water during growth. Reliable outdoors in Zones 17, 23, 24, and H1; in other zones, grow in containers and move to shelter over winter.

I

Ischyrolepis subverticillata

BROOM RESTIO
Restionaceae
PERENNIAL

🌿 **ZONES 14–24**
☀ ◐ **FULL SUN OR PARTIAL SHADE**
💧 **MODERATE WATER**

Ischyrolepis subverticillata

Resembling a big, clumping horsetail (*Equisetum hyemale*), this reedlike South African plant can reach 8 ft. tall and 4 ft. wide. Erect or slightly arching, canelike stems hold whorls of long, thin leaves at evenly spaced nodes. Insignificant flowers appear at branch tips in late summer; small, silvery, showy seed heads follow on female plants. Remove outer stems every 2 or 3 years to rejuvenate plant. Good in large pots. Stems are excellent in cut-flower arrangements.

Ismene calathina.
See *Hymenocallis narcissiflora*

Contained Exuberance

Grasslike plants are especially striking in containers. Try big, upright growers such as broom restio in a large urn-shaped pot for an accent, or place two as sentinels beside a path or driveway. True grasses like *Calamagrostis* and *Panicum* give the same effect.

Fiber optics plant (as well as some fescues and *Carex* species) has a mounded shape that looks cooling—like a fountain of green—in a low bowl.

Isolepis cernua
(Scirpus cernuus)

FIBER OPTICS PLANT
Cyperaceae
PERENNIAL

🌿 **ZONES 7–24**
◐ **PARTIAL SHADE**
💧 **AMPLE WATER**

Isolepis cernua

A 6–10-in. bundle of tiny green fiber optic cables would make an uncanny likeness of this sedge. Native from the British Isles to North Africa, it eventually becomes about twice as wide as high. Small brown flower spikelets appear all year at the ends of the drooping, threadlike green stems. Occasional division will keep it small. An ideal plant for the edge of a shallow pond, it also makes a good container plant, especially when placed where you can see its blooms.

Isotoma fluviatilis.
See *Pratia pedunculata*

Itea

SWEETSPIRE
Iteaceae
EVERGREEN, SEMIEVERGREEN, AND DECIDUOUS SHRUBS

🌿 **ZONES VARY BY SPECIES**
☀ **FULL SUN, EXCEPT AS NOTED**
💧 **REGULAR WATER**

Itea virginica

Itea's Greek root means "willow," probably for the graceful catkin-like flower clusters that hang from some kinds. Individual blooms are small and fragrant. Little pruning required.

I. ilicifolia. HOLLYLEAF SWEETSPIRE. Evergreen. Zones 4–9, 14–24. Native to China. Shrub has graceful, arching, open habit to 15 ft. tall, 10 ft. wide. Leaves are oval, spiny-toothed, to 4 in. long; new foliage is bronzy red, matures to glossy dark green. Lightly fragrant, greenish white flowers hang in clusters to 14 in. long in autumn; blooms sparsely where winters are mild. Not striking, but a graceful plant of distinction. Needs partial shade in hottest climates.

***I. japonica* 'Beppu'.** Semievergreen. Zones 4–6. Collected in Japan, but possibly from an imported *I. virginica,* which it resembles in most respects—and may turn out to be. Grows 2½ ft. high and suckers widely. Reddish purple fall foliage is its best feature.

I. virginica. Deciduous. Zones 2b–6, 15–17. Native to eastern U.S. Grows 3–15 ft. tall, spreading by suckers to form large patches where well adapted. Narrow, oval, 4-in.-long, dark green leaves turn purplish or bright red in fall, hang on the plant well into

winter. Fragrant, creamy white summer flowers open in erect clusters to 6 in. long. Compact varieties include 'Henry's Garnet', 3–4 ft., a superior (maybe the best) selection with brilliant purplish red fall foliage; 'Merlot', 3 ft., with rich red fall foliage; 'Scarlet Beauty' ('Morton') grows 3–4 ft., with orange-red fall foliage; and the charming 2-ft.-high 'Little Henry'. All are good in woodland gardens.

Ixia

AFRICAN CORN LILY
Iridaceae
PERENNIALS FROM CORMS

🌿 **ZONES 7–9, 12–24; OR DIG AND STORE**
☀ **FULL SUN**
💧 **REGULAR WATER DURING GROWTH AND BLOOM**

Ixia

Spikes of up to 20 brightly colored flowers per stem rise above *Ixia's* grasslike leaves in late spring. Each six-petaled blossom opens nearly flat in full sun but remains cupped or closed on overcast days. Colors include cream, yellow, red, orange, and pink, typically with dark centers. Stems are 18–20 in. high. Most ixias sold are hybrids of the South African *I. maculata.*

CARE

Grow in well-drained soil. Where winter lows usually stay above 20°F (–7°C), plant corms in early fall, 2 in. deep and about 3 in. apart. Where temperatures may drop to 10°F (–12°C), plant in late fall, setting corms 4 in. deep; cover planting with mulch. In colder areas, plant in spring for early summer flowers. Let soil go dry when foliage yellows after bloom. Where corms won't be subject to rainfall or irrigation during dormant period, they can be left undisturbed until the planting becomes crowded or flowering declines. When this occurs, dig corms in summer and store as for gladiolus until recommended planting time in your area. Where corms will receive summer moisture, dig and store them after foliage dies back; or treat as annuals. Plant potted corms close together and 1 in. deep; after bloom, put the pots where they won't get summer water.

Ixiolirion tataricum
(I. pallasii)
Ixioliriaceae
PERENNIAL FROM BULB

- 🌱 **ZONES 2 AND 3 WITH SHELTER, 4–11, 14–21; OR DIG AND STORE**
- ☀️ **FULL SUN**
- 💧 **MODERATE WATER DURING GROWTH AND BLOOM**

Ixiolirion tataricum

Loose clusters of silver-dollar-size, violet-blue flowers rise above clumps of narrow, gray-green leaves in late spring. Each bloom has six narrow petals marked with a darker central line; stems are 12–16 in. long. Foliage dies down in summer, not to reappear until the following spring.

CARE

Plant in fall, setting bulbs 3 in. deep, 3 in. apart. Beyond hardiness range, however, plant in early spring; dig in fall and store until planting time the next year. Where bulbs are hardy in the ground, they can remain in

place for many years. Dig and divide clumps in fall when they become crowded. Bulbs accept moderate summer moisture but don't need any.

J

Jacaranda mimosifolia
Bignoniaceae
DECIDUOUS OR SEMIEVERGREEN TREE

- 🌱 **ZONES 12, 13, 15–24; H1, H2**
- ☀️ **FULL SUN**
- 💧 **MODERATE WATER**
- 🐦 **ATTRACTS HUMMINGBIRDS**

Jacaranda mimosifolia

Where climate and space permit, jacaranda's blue-flowered canopy makes it nearly irresistible. Native to Brazil (and pronounced with the hard J used by the indigenous people who named it), it grows 25–40 ft. tall and 15–30 ft. wide, with an open, oval shape; sometimes it can be multitrunked or even shrubby. Its finely cut, ferny leaves usually drop in late winter. New leaves may emerge quickly or wait until the tree flowers—typically in mid- to late spring, though blossoms may appear earlier or open at any time throughout summer. Flowers are lavender-blue, tubular, 2 in. long, carried in profuse 8-in.-long clusters. White-flowered 'Alba', with more lush foliage and sparser bloom over a

longer season, is sometimes sold. Flattened, clamlike seed capsules are decorative in arrangements.

The tree gains hardiness with maturity. Young trees are tender below 25°F (–4°C) but often rebound from freezes to make multistemmed, shrubby plants. Takes wide variety of soils but does best in sandy soil. Ocean winds or insufficient heat can prevent flowering. Resists oak root fungus. Established trees need little pruning; cut any awkward limbs back to strong laterals.

Jacobinia carnea, J. ovata.
See *Justicia candicans, J. carnea*

Jasminum
JASMINE
Oleaceae
EVERGREEN, SEMIEVERGREEN, AND DECIDUOUS SHRUBS AND VINES

- 🌱 **ZONES VARY BY SPECIES**
- ☀️🌤 **FULL SUN OR LIGHT SHADE**
- 💧 **MODERATE TO REGULAR WATER**

Jasminum polyanthum

When one thinks of jasmine, a fragrant vine probably comes to mind. Yet not all jasmines are fragrant or vining—or even members of the genus *Jasminum*: intensely sweet star jasmine is actually the unrelated *Trachelospermum jasminoides*. Jasmines can be vining, vining-shrubby, or decidedly shrubby. True vining types climb by twining stems. Vining shrubs do not twine, but rather put out long, slender, lax stems that must be tied into place if the plants are to function as vines. Otherwise, they'll flop over to make green haystacks of foliage. To grow

these plants as shrubs, shorten any shoots that become too long. *J. parkeri* is the only true shrub listed below.

Jasmines grow more rapidly in good soil and bloom more profusely in sunny sites, but all adapt well to less-than-perfect conditions. When plants become tangled or untidy, cut them back heavily just before spring growth begins. Pinch and prune as needed throughout the year to control growth.

J. angulare. SOUTH AFRICAN JASMINE. Evergreen vining shrub. Zones 16–24; H1. From South Africa. Vigorous grower with stems 10–20 ft. long. Rich green leaves are divided into three leaflets. White, 1-in. flowers are borne in groups of three, appear in summer; some gardeners detect a subtly sweet scent, others no fragrance.

J. azoricum. Evergreen vining shrub. Zones 17–24; H1, H2. From the Azores. To 10–15 ft. tall, with dark green leaves divided into three leaflets and clusters of fragrant white flowers in summer.

J. floridum. Evergreen or semievergreen vining shrub. Zones 4–9, 12–24; H1. From China. To 5 ft. tall. Dark green leaves divided into three (rarely five) small (½–1½ in. long) leaflets. Clusters of golden yellow, ½–¾-in., scentless flowers bloom primarily from spring into autumn.

J. humile. ITALIAN JASMINE. Evergreen vining shrub. Zones 5–10, 12–24; H1, H2. From the Middle East, Myanmar, and China. Erect, willowy shoots reach to 20 ft., arch to make 10-ft. mound. Light green leaves with three to seven 2-in.-long leaflets. Clusters of ½-in., fragrant bright yellow flowers all summer. Can be trained as a shrub or clipped into a hedge. 'Revolutum' has larger flowers (to 1 in. wide) and larger, darker green leaves than the species.

J. laurifolium nitidum (J. nitidum). SHINING JASMINE, ANGELWING JASMINE. Evergreen or semievergreen vine. Zones 12, 16, 19–24; H1, H2. From Admiralty Islands in the southwest Pacific. Requires long, warm growing season to bloom satisfactorily. Hardy to about 25°F (–4°C). Moderate growth to 10–20 ft. Undivided

glossy green leaves to 2 in. long. Fragrant flowers shaped like 1-in. pinwheels open from purplish buds in late spring and summer. Flowers are white above, purplish beneath, borne in clusters of three. Can be used as groundcover. Often sold as *J. magnificum*.

J. leratii. PRIVET-LEAFED JASMINE. Evergreen vine. Zones 22–24; H1, H2. Native to New Caledonia. To 15 ft., with glossy dark green leaves to 2 in. long that resemble those of privet (*Ligustrum*). Slightly fragrant white flowers in spring.

J. magnificum. See *J. laurifolium nitidum*.

J. mesnyi (J. primulinum). PRIMROSE JASMINE. Evergreen vining shrub. Zones 4–24; H1, H2. From China. Long, arching branches 6–10 ft. long. Dark green leaves with three lanceshaped, 2–3-in. leaflets. Lemon yellow, unscented flowers to 2 in. across are semidouble or double, produced singly rather than in clusters. Main bloom in winter or spring; may flower at other times. Needs space. Best tied up at desired height and permitted to spill over, waterfall fashion. Use to cover pergola,

CLOCKWISE FROM TOP: *Jasminum laurifolium nitidum; J. humile; J. azoricum*

bank, or large wall, or clip as a 3-ft.-high hedge. In any form, may need occasional severe pruning to avoid brush-pile look.

J. multiflorum. DOWNY JASMINE, PIKAKE-HOKU. Evergreen vining shrub. Zones 21–24; H1, H2. From India. Leaves (to 2 in. long) and stems have a downy coating, producing an overall gray-green effect. Clustered white flowers in early spring; not strongly scented. Often called star jasmine in Hawaii, where it is commonly used as a hedge. (For true star jasmine, see *Trachelospermum jasminoides*.)

J. nudiflorum. WINTER JASMINE. Deciduous vining shrub. Zones 2–21; best adapted to cooler climates. From China. If unsupported, reaches 4 ft. or higher and 7 ft. wide; if trained on a trellis or wall, can grow to 15 ft. Slender, willowy green stems stand out in winter landscape. Unscented, bright yellow, 1-in. flowers appear in winter or early spring, before handsome,

glossy green, three-leafleted leaves unfurl. Good bank cover; spreads by rooting where stems touch soil. Attractive planted at the top of retaining walls, with branches cascading over side. Can be trained like *J. mesnyi*. A variegated form is available.

J. officinale. COMMON WHITE JASMINE, POET'S JASMINE. Semievergreen or deciduous vine. Zones 5–9, 12–24; H1. From the Himalayas and the Caucasus. To 30 ft. Very fragrant white flowers to 1 in. across; blooms throughout summer and into fall. Rich green leaves have five to nine leaflets, each to 2½ in. long. 'Argenteovariegatum' has leaves edged in creamy white. 'Aureum' has striking golden yellow foliage. *J. o. affine* (*J. grandiflorum*), commonly known as Spanish jasmine, climbs only to 15 ft. but bears larger (1½ in.) blooms.

J. parkeri. DWARF JASMINE. Evergreen shrub. Zones 5–9, 12–24. From India. Dwarf, twiggy, tufted shrub to 1 ft. high and 1½–2 ft. wide. Bright green, ½–1-in.-long leaves with three to five tiny leaflets. Small, scentless yellow flowers borne profusely in spring. Good choice in rock garden or containers.

J. polyanthum. Evergreen vine. Zones 5–9, 12–24; H1. From China. Fast-climbing, strong-growing vine to 20 ft. Bright to dark green leaves are slightly paler on undersides, have five to seven leaflets with the terminal leaflet slightly longer than the rest. Highly fragrant blossoms are white inside, rose-colored outside, borne in dense clusters. Blooms in late winter and spring; sporadic flowers rest of year. Can be used as groundcover; sometimes grown in large containers or hanging baskets. 'Variegatum' has leaves with pale yellow margins.

J. primulinum. See *J. mesnyi*.

J. sambac. ARABIAN JASMINE, PIKAKE. Evergreen vining shrub. Zones 13–21, 23, 24; H1, H2. Thought to be native to tropical Asia. To 6–10 ft. Undivided glossy green leaves to 3 in. long. Blooms in summer, bearing clusters of powerfully fragrant, ¾–1-in. white flowers. 'Grand Duke' has double flowers. In Hawaii, blossoms of this

species are a favorite for leis and are used in making perfume. In Asia, they're used in jasmine tea.

J. × stephanense. Evergreen or deciduous vine. Zones 5–9, 14–24. To 15–20 ft., with dull green foliage that persists year-round in Southern California. Leaves may be undivided and about 2 in. long or divided into five 2-in.-long leaflets. Pale pink, ½-in., fragrant flowers in clusters of five or more appear in late spring and summer.

J. tortuosum. TWISTED JASMINE. Evergreen vine. Zones 17, 19–24. From South Africa. Grows about 25 ft., with clusters of 1-in. white flowers forming at branch ends. Fragrance is light, citrusy.

Jicama
Fabaceae
ANNUAL VINE

✎ **BEST IN ZONES H1, H2; MAINLY ORNAMENTAL IN ZONES 8, 9, 12–14, 18–24**

☼ **FULL SUN**

💧 **AMPLE WATER**

⬦ **SEEDS ARE POISONOUS IF INGESTED**

Jicamas

Aboveground, this luxuriant tropical American vine grows 14 ft. long, with deep green leaves and upright spikes of pretty, sweet pea–shaped purple or violet summer flowers. Underground, it grows an enlarged edible taproot that tastes something like a sweet water chestnut. Of the Western states where it grows, the edible root develops fully only in Hawaii; use it as an ornamental on the mainland. Leaves have three leaflets. Botanically, this is *Pachyrhizus erosus*.

CARE

Trellis jicama or grow it on the ground as a trailing mound. Plant in spring, after danger of frost is past. Sow seeds 2 in. deep and 4 in. apart; thin seedlings to 8–12 in. apart. Needs long, warm growing season and rich soil. Apply high-nitrogen fertilizer monthly. Flowers should be pinched off for maximum root production (each vine yields one edible root weighing 1–6 lbs.), but you can allow seed for next year's crop to form on one or two plants. Roots enlarge in fall as days begin to grow shorter, but weather must stay warm to produce a good crop; you can leave them in the ground until they're needed. Peel off the rough brown skin and eat the white flesh raw or cooked.

Jubaea chilensis

CHILEAN WINE PALM
Arecaceae
PALM

ZONES 12–24

FULL SUN

LITTLE OR NO WATER

Jubaea chilensis

This slow-growing, potentially big (to 80 ft. tall, 25 ft. wide) tree develops the biggest trunk of any palm. It can be over 3 ft. thick and is often swollen above its base. Flowers insignificant. From Chile, wine palms were traditionally cut down so that sap could be harvested and made into syrup or wine—hence the common name. Hardy to at least 10°F (–12°C), this is the most cold-tolerant feather palm. For more on palms, see "Meet the Palms," page 471.

Juglans

WALNUT
Juglandaceae
DECIDUOUS TREES

ZONES VARY BY SPECIES

FULL SUN

WATER NEEDS VARY BY SPECIES

Juglans nigra

Though most walnut species covered here are large and spreading, the Southern California native black walnut is a garden-scale tree. On all kinds, leaves are divided into many leaflets, and trees bear roundish nuts enclosed in a fleshy husk. For English walnut, see Walnut. American native walnuts are sometimes planted as shade trees (with a bonus of edible nuts) or used as an understock for grafting English walnut. Nuts of these species typically contain little meat, and the shells are very thick and hard to crack.

J. californica. CALIFORNIA BLACK WALNUT. Known chiefly through the following two geographic variants. Both produce roundish nuts with rich flavor; they are resistant to oak root fungus and require no irrigation.

J. c. californica. Zones 18–24. Native to Southern California. Grows 15–30 ft. tall and wide, usually with several stems from ground level. Leaves are 6–12 in. long, with 9 to 19 leaflets (each 2½ in. long). Tree is not grown commercially but is worth saving if it grows as a native.

J. c. hindsii. Zones 5–9, 14–20. Native to scattered localities in Northern California. To 30–60 ft. tall and wide, with a single trunk. Leaves have 15 to 19 leaflets, each 3–5 in. long. Widely used as a rootstock for English walnut in California.

J. major (J. rupestris major). NOGAL, ARIZONA WALNUT. Zones 10–13. Native to Arizona, New Mexico, northern Mexico. Broad-headed tree to 50 ft. tall and wide. Leaves have 9 to 13 leaflets. Small, round nuts are enclosed in husks that dry on the tree; nuts drop still in the husk. Rich flavor like that of *J. nigra*. Takes desert heat and wind. Needs deep soil, moderate water.

J. nigra. BLACK WALNUT. Zones 1–9, 14–21. Native to eastern North America. High-branched tree to about 100 ft. tall, 70 ft. wide, with round crown and furrowed blackish brown bark. Leaves have 11 to 23 leaflets, each 2½–5 in. long. Round, 1½-in.-diameter nuts have rich flavor. Big, hardy shade tree for large sites. Don't plant near flower or vegetable gardens, rhododendrons, or azaleas; black walnut curbs these plants either by secreting a growth-inhibiting substance or by root competition. Long dormant season. Moderate water.

J. regia. See Walnut.

Jujube

Rhamnaceae
DECIDUOUS TREE

ZONES 6–16, 18–24; H1

BEST IN SUN; TOLERATES SOME SHADE

LITTLE TO REGULAR WATER

Jujubes

Known botanically as *Ziziphus jujuba* and pronounced *joo-JOOB*, jujube has been cultivated for millennia in its native China. Its datelike fruit grows on a tree 15–20 ft. (possibly 30 ft.) tall and 10–15 ft. wide. Branches are spiny, gnarled, and somewhat pendulous. Glossy green, 1½-in. leaves have three prominent veins and turn yellow in fall. Clusters of small yellowish flowers appear in late spring or summer. Round to oval fruit with a central pit matures in fall; it can be eaten fresh or dried. Attractive silhouette, foliage, and fruit, as well as toughness, make this a good decorative tree, especially for high desert.

The dried fruits look and taste like dates—for that reason, the plant is sometimes called Chinese date. Fruit may not ripen fully on tree in cool-summer areas; pick at half-brown stage and ripen indoors. Fruit of seedling trees is ½–1 in. long.

The two most common cultivated varieties are 'Lang', with 1½–2-in., elongated fruit, and 'Li', bearing 2-in., round fruit with a very small pit. 'Lang' needs 'Li' as pollenizer; 'Li' is more productive with 'Lang' planted nearby, though it will produce some fruit if planted alone. 'Sherwood' does especially well in hot-summer climates, has fewer spines. There is also a contorted form.

CARE

Deep rooted and drought-tolerant, jujube takes well to desert conditions. It is also very cold-hardy but not productive in short-summer areas. Takes saline and alkaline soils but grows better in good garden soil and thrives in lawns if there is adequate drainage (though suckering from roots can be a problem, particularly in moist soil).

No serious pests, but subject to Texas root rot in deserts. Prune in winter to shape, encourage weeping habit, or reduce size. Harvest when fruit begins to turn from yellow-green to reddish brown; it has a crisp texture and tastes like a sweet apple. If allowed to turn completely brown and become mushy, fruit is better for drying.

FOR MORE UNTHIRSTY PLANTS, SEE "PLANTS FOR WATERWISE GARDENS," PAGES 74–78.

J

Juncus

RUSH

Juncaceae

PERENNIALS

🌿 **ZONES VARY BY SPECIES**

☀️ ◐ **FULL SUN OR LIGHT SHADE**

💧 **AMPLE WATER**

Juncus patens 'Carman's Gray'

Rushes resemble grasses, with leaflike, cylindrical stems and inconspicuous flowers near stem tips. Plant them with grasses or aquatic plants at water's edge or among pebbles. Prune dead or shabby foliage to the ground in late winter to make way for fresh spring growth.

J. decipiens. Zones 1–24; H1. Native to Asia. Similar to *J. effusus*, and usually sold as such; best-known variety is the twisty 'Curly Wurly' ('Spiralis').

J. effusus. SOFT RUSH. Zones 1–24; H1. Temperate zone native. To 2½ ft. high and wide. Green stems to ¼ in. thick arch somewhat toward tips, turn brown with frost. Fine-textured 'Carman's Japanese' can grow 2 ft. high; *J. e. spiralis* and its selections 'Twister' and 'Unicorn' have corkscrew foliage. 'Quartz Creek', to 3 ft., is a selection of West Coast native *J. e. pacificus*.

J. inflexus. BLUE MEDUSA RUSH. Zones 3–9, 14–24. Grows 18 in. high, 2 ft. wide. Like *J. effusus*, but with bluer, thicker stems, and more drought-tolerant. 'Blue Arrows' grows 3 ft. high, 1 ft. wide.

J. patens. CALIFORNIA GRAY RUSH. Zones 4–9, 14–24. Native to California and Oregon. To 2 ft. high and wide, with stiffly upright green or gray-green stems. Tolerates more

heat and drought than *J. effusus* but thrives in moist soil or shallow water. 'Carman's Gray' is a good gray-stemmed selection.

Juniperus

JUNIPER

Cupressaceae

EVERGREEN SHRUBS AND TREES

🌿 **ZONES VARY BY SPECIES**

☀️ ◐ **FULL SUN OR PARTIAL SHADE**

💧 💧 💧 **LITTLE OR NO WATER TO REGULAR WATER**

🐦 **ATTRACT BIRDS**

» See chart on pages 387–389.

Juniperus rigida conferta 'Blue Pacific'

Few plants come in as many forms, from groundcovers, weeping and upright shrubs, and pillars to trees. These are conifers, though they produce fleshy, berrylike fruits instead of woody cones. Foliage may consist of small, prickly needles (juvenile foliage) or tiny overlapping scales (mature foliage); or the same plant may show both types. Leaf colors include green shades as well as silvery blue, gray, and creamy yellow.

In the accompanying chart, junipers are grouped by form. But many shrub junipers can grow to the size of small trees.

Groundcovers. This group includes plants from a few inches to a few feet high. In the first few years after planting, mulch will help keep soil cool and suppress weeds as the junipers fill in. That's important, since weeding through prickly juniper foliage is very rough on your skin.

Shrub types. These range from low to quite tall. Shapes include mounding, gracefully spreading, irregularly twisted,

and spirelike. In the chart, the columnar shrubs are listed separately, since these narrow, upright plants perform a distinct function in the landscape. They are excellent accents.

Tree junipers. These are valued for picturesque habit. Their height and form depend on growing conditions; plants are lower in poor soil and arid climates, larger if given good soil and more moisture. Many larger junipers serve well as screens or windbreaks in cold-winter areas.

Junipers tolerate all soils, but constantly wet feet make plants turn yellow and collapse.

TOP ROW: *Juniperus sabina* 'Buffalo'; *J. horizontalis* 'Blue Chip'. MIDDLE: *J. squamata* 'Blue Star'. BOTTOM ROW: *J. procumbens* 'Nana'; *J. chinensis* 'Lemon Pfizz'

Deer don't usually browse junipers. But the plants are subject to spider mites (symptoms are gray or yellow, dry-looking plants with fine webbing on twigs); aphids (look for sticky deposits, falling needles, sooty mold); twig borers (browning and dying branch tips). Juniper blight causes twigs and branches to die back; control with copper sprays in summer.

JUNIPERUS: TOP PICKS TO GROW

NAME	ZONES	HEIGHT	WIDTH	COMMENTS
GROUNDCOVERS				
Juniperus chinensis 'Parsonsii' (J. squamata expansa 'Parsonii')	1–24	To 1½ ft.	8 ft. or more	Slow growing. Dense, short twigs on flat, rather heavy branches. Blue-green new leaves mature to dark green.
J. c. 'San Jose'	1–24	To 2 ft.	6 ft. or more	Slow growing and heavy trunked. Dark sage green, with both needle and scale foliage.
J. c. sargentii SARGENT JUNIPER	A2, A3; 1–24	To 2½ ft.	6–10 ft.	Feathery gray-green or green foliage. Classic bonsai plant.
J. c. s. 'Saybrook Gold'	1–24	2–3 ft.	To 6 ft.	Like *J. c. sargentii* but with rich yellow foliage.
J. c. s. 'Viridis'	1–24	1½–2 ft.	6–10 ft.	Bright green version of *J. c. sargentii.*
J. communis 'Alpine Carpet'	A2, A3; 1–24	8 in.	3–4 ft.	Slow growing. Deep blue-green, soft-looking foliage.
J. conferta. See *J. rigida conferta*				
J. horizontalis 'Blue Chip'	A1–A3; 1–24	To 1 ft.	6–8 ft.	Silvery blue foliage.
J. h. 'Blue Rug'. See *J. h.* 'Wiltonii'				
J. h. 'Hughes'	A1–A3; 1–24	To 1 ft.	6–8 ft.	Showy silvery blue foliage.
J. h. 'Icee Blue'	1–24	4 in.	8 ft.	Maintains dense crown of silvery blue foliage.
J. h. 'Mother Lode'	1–24	To 4 in.	8–10 ft.	Similar to *J. h.* 'Wiltonii' but with yellow foliage that turns bronze in winter.
J. h. 'Plumosa' ANDORRA JUNIPER	1–24	To 1½ ft.	To 10 ft.	Feathery foliage is gray-green in summer, turns plum color in winter. Flat branches with upright branchlets.
J. h. 'Prince of Wales'	A1–A3; 1–24	To 8 in.	8–10 ft.	Medium green foliage turns purplish in fall.
J. h. 'Wiltonii' ('Blue Rug') BLUE CARPET JUNIPER	A1–A3; 1–24	4–6 in.	6–8 ft.	Very flat juniper. Dense, short branchlets on long, trailing branches. Foliage is an intense silver-blue.
J. h. 'Youngstown'	1–24	To 1 ft.	To 6 ft.	Resembles *J. h.* 'Plumosa' but is flatter, more compact.
J. procumbens JAPANESE GARDEN JUNIPER	1–24	1–2½ ft.	To 12 ft.	Feathery yet substantial blue-green foliage on strong, spreading branches.
J. p. 'Green Mound'	1–24	To 8 in.	To 6 ft.	Mounding habit; will trail over walls. Light green foliage.
J. p. 'Nana'	1–24	To 1 ft.	To 6 ft.	Curved branches radiating in all directions. Shorter needles and slower growth than *J. procumbens.* Can be staked into upright, picturesque shrub. Give it some protection from sun in hot climates.
J. rigida conferta (J. conferta) SHORE JUNIPER	3–9, 14–24; H1, H2	To 1 ft.	6–8 ft.	Native to Japan. Prostrate and trailing, with soft bluish green needles. Excellent for seashore but will stand warmer climates if given moist, well-drained soil.
J. r. c. 'Blue Pacific'	3–9, 14–24	To 1 ft.	6–8 ft.	Denser, bluer, more heat-tolerant than *J. r. conferta.*
J. sabina 'Arcadia'	1–24	To 1 ft.	6–8 ft.	Lacy bright green foliage.
J. s. 'Broadmoor'	A2, A3; 1–24	2–3 ft.	To 10 ft.	Dense, mounding habit. Soft bright green leaves.

»

JUNIPERUS: TOP PICKS TO GROW

NAME	ZONES	HEIGHT	WIDTH	COMMENTS
J. s. 'Buffalo'	A2, A3; 1–24	8–12 in.	To 8 ft.	Soft, feathery bright green foliage.
J. s. 'Calgary Carpet'	A2, A3; 1–24	6–9 in.	10 ft.	Soft green foliage.
J. s. 'Moor-Dense'	1–24	To 1 ft.	To 8 ft.	Resembles J. s. 'Broadmoor' but is denser. Has layered look.
J. s. 'Skandia' (J. s. 'Scandia')	A2, A3; 1–24	To 1 ft.	6–8 ft.	Dense bright green foliage.
J. s. 'Tamariscifolia' (J. tamariscifolia) TAMARIX JUNIPER, TAM	A2, A3; 1–24	1½– 2½ ft.	10 ft. or more	Symmetrically spreading, with dense blue-green foliage. Widely used, probably overused. More pest problems than other junipers. J. s. 'Tamariscifolia New Blue' foliage is bluer.
J. scopulorum 'Blue Creeper'	A2, A3; 1–24	To 2 ft.	6–8 ft.	Spreading, mounding habit. Bright blue-green foliage.

SHRUBS

NAME	ZONES	HEIGHT	WIDTH	COMMENTS
J. chinensis 'Gold Lace'	1–24	4 ft.	6 ft.	Green foliage with gold tips; spreading.
J. c. 'Gold Star'	1–24	4 ft.	6 ft.	Blue-green foliage inside, outer foliage gold; compact.
J. c. 'Kaizuka' ('Torulosa') HOLLYWOOD JUNIPER	1–24; H1, H2	To 15 ft.	To 10 ft.	Irregular and upright, with twisted appearance. Rich green foliage.
J. c. 'Kaizuka Variegata' VARIEGATED HOLLYWOOD JUNIPER	1–24; H1, H2	8–10 ft.	To 6 ft.	Irregular cone, though growth is more regular than that of J. c. 'Kaizuka'. Green foliage variegated with creamy white.
J. c. 'Mint Julep'	1–24	4–6 ft.	6–8 ft.	Vase-shaped, with arching branches. Mint green foliage.
J. c. 'Sea Green'	1–24	4–5 ft.	4–5 ft.	Compact dark green selection with fountainlike, arching branches.
J. × pfitzeriana	A2, A3; 1–24; H1, H2	5–6 ft.	10– 12 ft.	Arching, with sharp-needled, feathery gray-green foliage.
J. × p. 'Armstrongii' ARMSTRONG JUNIPER	1–24	4–5 ft.	4–5 ft.	Upright, with medium green foliage. More compact than J. × pfitzeriana.
J. × p. 'Aurea' GOLDEN PFITZER JUNIPER	1–24; H1, H2	4–5 ft.	8–10 ft.	Blue-gray foliage; current season's growth is golden yellow. J. × p. 'Old Gold' is similar or identical.
J. × p. 'Daub's Frosted'	1–24	2–3 ft.	6 ft.	Yellow new growth matures to blue-green. Mounding habit.
J. × p. 'Glauca'	1–24; H1, H2	5–6 ft.	6–8 ft.	Arching branches; silvery blue foliage.
J. rigida 'Pendula'	3b–24	12–20 ft.	30 ft.	An upright main stem gives rise to horizontal secondary branches with weeping tips; green foliage, blue-black fruits. Fast growth.
J. sabina SAVIN JUNIPER	A2, A3; 1–24	4–6 ft.	5–10 ft.	Creeping or shrubby dark green plant. Exceedingly tough.
J. scopulorum 'Table Top Blue'	1–24	To 5 ft.	7–12 ft.	Flat-topped gray plant.
J. squamata 'Blue Star'	1–24	2–3 ft.	3–4 ft.	Uniform branching; silver-blue foliage.
J. s. 'Chinese Silver'	1–24	7 ft.	4 ft.	Silvery blue foliage covers branches cascading from a vertical leader.
J. s. 'Holger'	1–24	To 6 ft.	To 6 ft.	Dense, broad, flat topped. Yellow-tipped new growth.

J

JUNIPERUS: TOP PICKS TO GROW

NAME	ZONES	HEIGHT	WIDTH	COMMENTS
COLUMNAR TYPES				
J. chinensis 'Blue Point'	1–24	To 12 ft.	To 8 ft.	Densely branched blue-green cone.
J. c. 'Robusta Green'	1–24	12–16 ft.	3–5 ft.	Brilliant green, dense column.
J. c. 'Spartan'	1–24	To 15 ft.	3–5 ft.	Dense rich green column.
J. communis 'Compressa'	A1–A3; 1–24	To 2 ft.	To 6 in.	Dwarf column; for rock gardens.
J. c. 'Gold Cone'	A1–A3; 1–24	6 ft.	3 ft.	Green leaves have yellow tips. Since this variety is female, it produces juniper berries.
J. pingii wilsonii (J. squamata 'Loderi')	A3; 2a–24	6 ft.	2 ft.	Conical form with ascending branches; green foliage has silvery undertones.
J. scopulorum 'Cologreen'	1–24	To 15 ft.	5–7 ft.	Narrow bright green column.
J. s. 'Gray Gleam'	1–24	To 15 ft.	5–7 ft.	Slow growing, attaining full height in 30–40 years. Symmetrical blue-gray column.
J. s. 'Medora'	1–24	To 10 ft.	To 2½ ft.	Slow growing, narrow, dense, bluish green.
J. s. 'Moonglow'	1–24	9 ft.	4–5 ft.	Broadly pyramidal, dense growth.
J. s. 'Skyrocket'	A2, A3; 1–24	15–20 ft.	2–3 ft.	Very narrow blue-gray spire. Sometimes sold as J. virginiana 'Skyrocket'.
J. s. 'Wichita Blue'	A2, A3; 1–24	10–15 ft.	4–6 ft.	Broad silver-blue cone.
J. virginiana 'Blue Arrow'	A2, A3; 1–24	15 ft.	2 ft.	Blue-green foliage, pencil-like form.
J. v. 'Idyllwild'	A2, A3; 1–24	15 ft.	5 ft.	Dark green foliage, upright form. Good for hedges.
J. v. 'Prairie Pillar'	A2, A3; 1–24	15–20 ft.	2–3 ft.	Blue-green foliage, columnar form. Short branches hold up under heavy snow.
J. v. 'Taylor'	A3; 1–24	25–30 ft.	3 ft.	These columnar trees can be used as formal sentinel trees or planted shoulder to shoulder as screens. Gray-green foliage.
TREES				
J. californica CALIFORNIA JUNIPER	3, 6–12, 14–24	10–40 ft.	10–40 ft.	Native to desert regions of California and Southwest. Yellowish to rich green foliage.
J. cedrus CANARY ISLANDS JUNIPER	5, 8, 9, 11, 12, 14–22	30 ft.	18 ft.	Native to the Canary Islands. Soft-textured foliage; weeping branches.
J. deppeana pachyphlaea ALLIGATOR JUNIPER	1–3, 10–12	10–60 ft.	10–60 ft.	Native to Southwest and Mexico. Blue-gray foliage; striking checked bark (like alligator hide).
J. occidentalis WESTERN JUNIPER	1–10, 14, 18–21	50–60 ft.	30–50 ft.	Massive, long-lived native of Sierra Nevada and intermountain regions from central Washington to Southern California. Fragrant green foliage.
J. scopulorum 'Tolleson's Blue Weeping' ('Repandens')	1–24	To 20 ft.	To 10 ft.	Drooping branchlets clothed in blue-green foliage make a graceful, weeping tree.
J. virginiana EASTERN RED CEDAR	A3; 1–24	40–50 ft. or more	15–30 ft.	Native to eastern North America. Conical dark green tree; turns reddish in cold weather.

Justicia
Acanthaceae
EVERGREEN, SEMIEVERGREEN, AND DECIDUOUS SHRUBS

⚡ **ZONES VARY BY SPECIES**

☀ ◗ ● **EXPOSURE NEEDS VARY BY SPECIES**

◌ ◐ ● 💧 **WATER NEEDS VARY BY SPECIES**

🗲 **ATTRACT HUMMINGBIRDS**

Justicia spicigera

These New World natives are grown chiefly for tubular, tightly clustered flowers—or, in the case of *J. brandegeeana,* for showy spikes of flowerlike bracts. Leaves are paired.

J. brandegeeana (Beloperone guttata). SHRIMP PLANT. Evergreen. Zones 12, 13, 15–17, 21–24; H1, H2; elsewhere as annual or indoor/outdoor plant. From Mexico. To 3–4 ft. high and wide. Apple green, oval to elliptical leaves. Purple-spotted white flowers are enclosed in overlapping coppery bronze bracts to form compact, shrimplike, 3–7-in. spikes. Blooms produced mainly from spring to fall, sporadically rest of year. 'Pink' has pink bracts; 'Variegata' has green-and-white leaves.

Good in containers and for close-up planting near terraces, patios, entryways. To shape, pinch young plant continuously until it is a compact mound of foliage, then let it bloom. Give moderate water; leaves often drop in cold weather or if soil is too wet or dry. Bracts and foliage fade unless plant is grown in partial shade; needs at least a half-day in hottest climates.

J. californica. CHUPAROSA, CALIFORNIA BELOPERONE. Semievergreen or deciduous. Zones 10–14, 18–24. Native from edges of southeastern California's Colorado Desert to Arizona and northern Mexico. To 6 ft. tall and wide, with arching, grayish branches and sparse, ¼-in., roundish light green leaves. Clusters of tubular, bright red, 1½-in.-long flowers give a good show from fall through spring. ('Yellow' has yellow blossoms.) Can freeze to ground in winter but comes back in spring. Full sun or light shade. Little to moderate water. Summer-deciduous but will hold much of its foliage if irrigated.

J. candicans (Jacobinia ovata). Evergreen. Zones 12, 13, 21–24. Native to southern Arizona, Mexico. Erect growth to 3 ft. high and wide, with gray branchlets and dark green, heart-shaped leaves to 3 in. long. Clusters of 1-in., tubular, vivid red flowers from fall to early summer, with intermittent bloom later in summer. Full sun or light shade. Regular water.

J. carnea (Jacobinia carnea). BRAZILIAN PLUME FLOWER. Evergreen. Zones 8, 9, 13–24; H1, H2; elsewhere as annual or indoor/outdoor plant. From South America. Soft-wooded, erect shrub 4–6 ft. tall, 2½–3 ft. wide. Medium green, 10-in.-long, veined leaves. Dense clusters of pink to crimson, tubular flowers from mid-summer to fall. Cut back plants in early spring to encourage strong new growth. Upper portions of branches freeze at 29°F (–2°C). Give partial or full shade, rich soil, regular to ample water.

J. rizzinii. FIRECRACKER FLOWER. Evergreen. Zones 8, 9, 12–24; H1, H2. This Brazilian native grows 3–4 ft. tall and wide, bearing clusters of yellow-tipped red flowers in winter and spring. Sun along coast, shade inland. Moderate water.

J. spicigera. MEXICAN HONEYSUCKLE. Evergreen. Zones 12–24. From Mexico and Central America. To 3 ft. high, 4 ft. wide, with light green, smooth or velvety leaves. Few-flowered clusters of 1½-in. orange or orange-red flowers appear nearly year-round, peaking in spring and fall. Full sun or partial shade. Little to regular water.

J. suberecta. See *Dicliptera sericea.*

Kalanchoe
Crassulaceae
SUCCULENT PERENNIALS

⚡ **ZONES VARY BY SPECIES; OR INDOORS**

☀ ◗ **FULL SUN OR PARTIAL SHADE; BRIGHT LIGHT**

◐ ● **MODERATE TO REGULAR WATER**

Kalanchoe luciae

Succulent green leaves (often with scalloped edges or unusual shapes) and typically bell-shaped flowers mark these perennials. Some kinds are marketed as houseplants but can be planted outdoors where winters are mild. In Zone 13, grow in a shady spot. In borderline climates, give protection of lath, eaves, or other overhead structure.

K. beharensis. FELT PLANT. Zones 13, 21–24; H1, H2. Stems usually unbranched, to 4–5 ft. (sometimes 10 ft.) tall. Very narrow plant—just 1–2 ft. wide. Thick, triangular to lance-shaped leaves (usually six to eight pairs) at stem tips. Leaves are 4–8 in. or longer, half as wide as long, strikingly waved and crimped at edges, covered with dense, feltlike coating of white to brown hairs. Flowers not showy. Hybrids between this and other species differ in leaf size, color, and degree of felting and scalloping. Striking in big rock garden, raised bed.

K. blossfeldiana. Zones 17, 21–24; H1, H2. To 1½ ft. high and wide. Shiny, red-edged dark green leaves may be smooth edged or slightly lobed. Small flowers in big clusters held above leaves. Comes in various sizes and flower colors, including red, yellow, orange, and salmon; blooms in winter, early spring. Popular gift plant at Christmas.

K. fedtschenkoi. Zones 13, 17, 21–24; H1, H2. From Madagascar. Grows 18–24 in. high and wide, with gray-green scalloped leaves, and dusty reddish flowers in late spring. As its stems root, it spreads into colonies. Escaped in Hawaii. 'Variegata' has creamy-edged leaves.

K. luciae. PADDLE PLANT. Zones 13, 17, 21–24; H1, H2. From southeastern Africa. Colorful, sculptural plant grows 1–1½ ft. high and wide, spreading by offsets. Short, thick trunk holds fleshy, broadly oval leaves to 8 in. long and 6–8 in. wide. Leaves are gray-green, with margins that turn bright red in full sun. In winter or early spring, a single stem rises 2–3 ft. high and bears clusters of ½–¾-in.-long, tubular, dark yellow flowers with a pleasing fragrance. Provide protection from slugs and snails, which can permanently disfigure leaves. 'Fantastic' (also sold as *K. thyrsiflora* 'Fantastic') has gray-green leaves striped with cream variegation, and shading red at the margins.

K. pumila. Zones 13, 17, 21–24; H1, H2; or indoors. Native to Madagascar. Mounded, trailing plant to about 1 ft. high and 2 ft. wide. Gray-green leaves are covered with fine white powder, giving an overall frosted look; toothed leaf edges are lightly tinged with pink. Blooms in winter, with each leafy stem producing a cluster of ½-in. pink flowers with yellow anthers. Tolerates considerable shade and drought. Indoors, site in a sunny window, reducing water in winter and providing temperatures below 60°F (16°C) to promote flowering. Lovely in hanging baskets.

K. thyrsiflora. Zones 13, 17, 21–24; H1, H2. From southeast coast of South Africa. Grows 18 in. high with fragrant, dark yellow flowers; very similar to *K. luciae* (the two are often confused), but the leaves of *K. thyrsiflora* are chalky green with no red flush.

K. tomentosa. PANDA PLANT. Zones 13, 23, 24; H2. Branching plant eventually reaches 3 ft. high, 8 in. wide. Leaves have a dense, feltlike coating of white hairs. Leaf tips and shallow notches in leaves are strongly marked dark brown. Yellowish green flowers in spring.

Kale and Collards

Brassicaceae
BIENNIAL GROWN AS ANNUAL

- 🌡 **ALL ZONES**
- ☼ ◐ **FULL SUN OR LIGHT SHADE**
- 💧 **REGULAR WATER**

'Toscano' kale

These knee-high cool-season cabbage relatives are grown for their leaves, which can be steamed, stir-fried, sautéed, or added to soups. Both are high in vitamins A and C, and in calcium. Hardy to 5°F (–15°C), these vegetables are winter staples. Kale grows 14–30 in. high, and collards average 2–3 ft. high.

Curly-leafed kales (such as 'Redbor' and 'Winterbor') form compact clusters of tightly curled leaves. 'Toscano' ('Lacinato') is a noncurly green kale, 'Red Russian' a noncurly red kale whose leaves are gray-green with purple veins. Flowering kale is similar to flowering cabbage, with brightly colored, decorative foliage; it too is edible and is sometimes sold in markets under the name "salad savoy."

Collard greens come from large, smooth-leafed plants that do not form a head. Collard varieties include 'Champion', 'Flash', and 'Vates'.

CARE

Sow seeds in place and thin to 1½–3 ft. apart; or set out transplants at the same spacing. Plant kale in late summer for a fall crop; in cool-summer areas, it can also be planted in early spring for a summer crop (intense sun in hotter climates makes leaves turn bitter). Plant collards in summer for fall and winter harvest; or plant in early spring for a spring-into-summer crop (collards are heat-tolerant).

Harvest leaves by removing them from the outside of clusters, or harvest entire plant. Light frost sweetens flavor. Plants suffer far fewer pest and disease problems than most other crops in the cabbage family.

Kalmia

Ericaceae
EVERGREEN SHRUBS

- 🌡 **ZONES VARY BY SPECIES**
- ☼ ◐ **EXPOSURE NEEDS VARY BY SPECIES**
- 💧 **REGULAR WATER**
- ☙ **LEAVES AND FLOWER NECTAR ARE POISONOUS IF INGESTED**

Kalmia latifolia

Elegant rhododendron relative, with similar habit, generally narrower leaves, and big, showy flower clusters. Unique starburst buds open into chalice-shaped blooms with 10 starlike points. These plants share rhododendron's need for moist atmosphere and moist, acid, humus-rich soil.

K. latifolia. MOUNTAIN LAUREL. Zones 2–7, 16, 17. Native to eastern North America. Slow growing to 6–8 ft. or taller, with equal spread. Glossy, leathery, oval leaves are dark green on upper surface, yellowish green beneath. Blooms in late spring, bearing clusters to 5 in. across. Flowers are typically 1 in. wide, light pink or white opening from darker pink buds—but blossoms often have subtly different color in their throats and may have contrasting stamens. Hardy well below 0°F (–18°C). Partial shade. Has proved difficult to grow in the ground in Zones 16, 17; seems to do better in containers there. In Zones 2 and 3, give plants protection from winter sun and winds, which could cause dehydration.

Dozens of named varieties are available. Here are examples by color.

Those with flowers marked in contrasting colors include 'Freckles', white with spots and splashes of purplish red; and 'Bullseye', which has cream-colored blossoms with white and purple-red markings in throat, white edge, and broad, purple-red band around the inside—new foliage is reddish.

Red-budded selections include 'Firecracker', 'Nathan Hale', and 'Olympic Fire', which all have pink flowers, and 'Sarah', with reddish pink flowers.

'Pristine' is a white-flowered selection; 'Snowdrift' is white with faint red markings.

Dwarf varieties (to 3 ft. in 10 years) include 'Elf', with pink buds opening to white flowers; 'Minuet', light pink buds opening to white flowers with a maroon ring inside; and 'Tinkerbell', whose pink buds open to deep pink flowers.

K. polifolia microphylla (K. microphylla). WESTERN LAUREL, ALPINE LAUREL. Zones A2, A3; 1–7, 16, 17. Native from Alaska to Northern California. To 1 ft. high and 8 in. wide, with spreading branches and erect branchlets. Small leaves are dark green above, whitish beneath. Rounded clusters of ½-in., rose to purple flowers bloom in summer. Partial shade, or full sun where summers are cool.

Kalmiopsis leachiana

Ericaceae
EVERGREEN SHRUB

- 🌡 **ZONES 4–6, 14–17**
- ◐ **PARTIAL SHADE**
- 💧 **REGULAR WATER**

Kalmiopsis leachiana

Native to the mountains of southwest Oregon, this shrublet grows 1 ft. high, 2 ft. wide, and is covered with ½-in., rose-pink flowers in early spring; stamens are prominent. Branches are densely clothed with thick, dark green leaves. May rebloom. Roots need soil with perfect drainage, high organic content. 'Umpqua Form' is tidy, heavy-blooming.

Most plants in the heath family (*Ericaceae*) need fast-draining, acidic soil in order to thrive. If your garden's soil is alkaline or clay, plant *Kalmia*, *Kalmiopsis*, and their ericaceous cousins in raised beds or containers. Check your garden center for bagged potting soils specially formulated for rhododendrons and azaleas.

K

Keckiella

Scrophulariaceae

EVERGREEN OR DECIDUOUS SHRUBS

🗡 **ZONES 7–9, 12–24**

☼ ☽ **EXPOSURE NEEDS VARY BY SPECIES**

◊ ◊ ◔ **LITTLE TO REGULAR WATER**

🦅 **ATTRACT HUMMINGBIRDS**

Keckiella antirrhinoides

These woody-stemmed Southern California natives with tubular, lipped flowers were once listed as shrubby penstemons. Extremely drought-tolerant, they drop their leaves in summer unless watered. Need excellent drainage.

K. antirrhinoides. Erect to spreading habit to 4 ft. tall, 3 ft. or wider; leaves less than 1 in. long. Abundant show of fragrant yellow flowers in late spring and summer. Full sun.

K. cordifolia (Penstemon cordifolius). CLIMBING PENSTEMON. To about 5 ft. tall and wide, sprawling. Behaves almost like a vine when growing among taller shrubs. Dark green leaves. Red, 1–2-in.-long, unscented flowers appear from late spring into early summer. A yellow-flowered variety is available. Full sun or partial shade.

Keckiellas bloom heavily as temperatures rise. But then they're likely to drop their leaves, especially in hot inland areas. To neaten the dormant plants, cut them back to 6 inches tall.

Kerria japonica

Rosaceae

DECIDUOUS SHRUB

🗡 **ZONES 2–23**

☼ ☽ **FULL SUN IN COOLER CLIMATES ONLY**

◔ ◔ **MODERATE TO REGULAR WATER**

Kerria japonica

Open and graceful, this rounded shrub is appreciated for its bare green winter stems and yellow spring flowers. Native to China and Japan, it grows about 6 ft. tall and 8 ft. wide, with toothed, heavily veined bright green, somewhat triangular leaves. They unfold early in spring, turn yellow in fall. Small, buttercup-yellow flowers look like small (1¼–2 in.), single yellow roses and appear in spring. Plant continues sporadic bloom into early summer.

'Golden Guinea' has larger (to 2½ in.) flowers. 'Picta' ('Variegata') has white-edged leaves. 'Pleniflora', the most commonly grown kerria, is a vigorous grower to 8–10 ft. tall and wide, with double yellow, 1¼-in. blossoms that appear throughout the summer and sometimes into early fall. Flower color of all forms fades in strong sunlight.

Allow room for plant to display its arching form. Plants produce clumps of stems from roots; 'Pleniflora' in particular is likely to spread freely. Cut out unwanted shoots to keep clumps more compact. Prune heavily after bloom, cutting out branches that have flowered and all dead or weak wood. The green branches are a favorite subject in Japanese wintertime flower arrangements.

Kirengeshoma palmata

YELLOW WAXBELLS

Hydrangeaceae

PERENNIAL FROM RHIZOME

🗡 **ZONES 2–9, 14–24**

☽ **PARTIAL SHADE**

◔ **REGULAR WATER**

Kirengeshoma palmata

A perennial of great elegance, yellow waxbells grows 2–4 ft. tall, 2–2½ ft. wide, with dark purplish stems carrying deeply lobed and toothed leaves. Pale yellow flower clusters appear in joints of upper leaves and at tops of stalks in late summer and early autumn. Blossoms are drooping and narrowly bell-shaped, 1½ in. long. Lovely in partially shaded border or woodland garden. Needs ample organic matter in soil. Native to Japan and Korea.

Plant yellow waxbells as the centerpiece of a mostly green woodland garden where its pale yellow summer flowers and soft-looking foliage can really shine. Surround it with ferns for textural contrast. Or mass it beneath trees as a tall groundcover.

Kiwi

Actinidiaceae

DECIDUOUS VINES

🗡 **ZONES VARY BY SPECIES**

☼ ☽ **FULL SUN OR PARTIAL SHADE**

◔ **REGULAR WATER**

'Hayward' kiwis

These East Asian vines are remarkably vigorous and beautiful, producing fruit whose flavor is a combination of melon, strawberry, and banana. Fuzzy-skinned kiwifruit (the type sold in markets) has a delicious piquancy; other kinds taste sweeter. Unless you have a self-fruitful variety, you will need to grow a male plant nearby to pollenize the fruit-bearing female.

Supply sturdy support such as a pergola, fence, or wall; guide and tie vines to the structure as necessary.

Fuzzy-skinned kiwi (Actinidia deliciosa or A. chinensis). Zones 4–9, 12–24. Note that this vine can take 5 years from planting to flowering. Sometimes called Chinese gooseberry vine, it twines to 30 ft. if not curbed. Roundish leaves are rich dark green above, velvety white below. New growth often has rich red fuzz. Spring flowers are 1–1½ in. wide, opening cream-colored and fading to buff. Fuzzy, brown-skinned, green-fleshed fruit is the size and shape of an egg.

'Hayward' is the most common fruiting variety. 'Saanichton', a female type from Vancouver Island, Canada, is a good choice for cooler areas. Use 'Chico Male', 'Tomuri', or plants sold simply as "male" to pollenize 'Hayward' and 'Saanichton'. 'Vincent', in spite of its masculine name, is a female variety that needs little winter chill and grows well in warmest-winter climates; use 'Chico Male' as a pollenizer. Male hardy kiwi varieties can also supply pollen for female fuzzy-skinned kiwis.

Start harvesting when the first fruits just begin to soften or when fruits turn from greenish brown to fully brown. Let kiwis finish ripening off the tree; egg cartons make perfect ripening/storage containers.

Hardy kiwi (A. arguta). Zones A1–A3; 1–10, 12, 14–24. It is much like fuzzy-skinned kiwi vine in appearance but has smaller flowers, fruit, and leaves (which are smooth and fuzzless). The 1–1½-in.-long, fuzzless fruits are eaten skin and all. Green-fruited female varieties 'Ananasnaja', 'Jumbo', and 'Hood River' need a male variety (may be sold simply as "male") for pollen. 'Issai', also with green fruit, is a self-fruitful variety. *A. purpurea* and its hybrid 'Ken's Red' produce small red fruit with red flesh; each needs a pollenizer. Pick when grape-size fruit starts to soften slightly; taste is the best test of ripeness.

Arctic beauty kiwi (A. kolomikta). Zones A2, A3; 1–9, 14–17. Male plants are ornamental vines grown for their splashy, heart-shaped foliage (see description under *Actinidia kolomikta*). Female plants typically have somewhat less colorful leaves than males, but they produce small green fruit a little smaller than hardy kiwi; a male vine must be growing nearby to supply pollen (and *A. arguta* won't pollenize *A. kolomikta*). Plants typically grow to 15 ft. or more. Prefers partial shade, especially in hotter climates. 'September Sun' has sweet fruit and the best foliage variegation among female varieties. Harvest as for hardy kiwi.

Grow in well-drained soil with regular applications of nitrogen fertilizer. Plants burn in salty or alkaline soils. During dormancy, prune for best form and fruit production. Cut back to one or two main trunks and remove closely parallel or crossing branches. Fruit is borne on shoots from year-old or older wood; cut out shoots that have fruited for 3 years and shorten younger shoots, leaving three to seven buds beyond previous summer's fruit. In summer, shorten overlong shoots and unwind any shoots twining around main branches. Because male pollenizer's sole purpose is flower production, you can prune it back drastically after bloom.

Kleinia. See *Senecio*

Knautia
Caprifoliaceae
PERENNIALS

🌿 **ZONES 2–10, 14–24**
☼ **FULL SUN**
💧 **REGULAR WATER**

Knautia macedonica 'Mars Midget'

These mid-height perennials are covered with pincushion flowers in summer. Basal leaves are barely lobed, but those on upper stems are deeply divided. These undemanding meadow plants are at home in cottage gardens, wild gardens, perennial borders, and roadside plantings. Cut flowers are good for fresh or dried arrangements.

K. arvensis. BLUE BUTTONS. From Europe, the Caucasus, and the Mediterranean region. To 1–5 ft. tall, 1½ ft. wide. Blue, 1½-in. flower heads in summer.

K. macedonica. From central Europe. To 1½–3 ft. high and as wide. Deep purplish red flower heads bloom from early summer to fall. Reseeds manageably. 'Mars Midget', to 16 in. high, is more upright and has crimson flowers. Melton Pastels grow 1½–3 ft. or higher, 1½ ft. wide. Flower heads in tones of blue, mauve, pink, rose, salmon-pink, and crimson from late spring to fall.

Kniphofia
RED-HOT POKER, TORCH LILY
Asphodelaceae
PERENNIALS

🌿 **ZONES VARY BY SPECIES**
☼ **FULL SUN OR PARTIAL SHADE**
💧 **MODERATE TO REGULAR WATER**
🐦 **FLOWERS ATTRACT HUMMINGBIRDS**

Kniphofia

Flowering stems that look like glowing pokers or torches give this its common names. Each cylindrical or flame-shaped inflorescence is made up of tubular flowers packed into tight, overlapping, often nodding clusters. They rise above dense clumps of grasslike, finely toothed foliage. Blossoms open from bottom to top over the course of several days, changing color as they mature. Increasing numbers of species, mostly from South Africa, are now grown in gardens and hybridized. The old 3-ft.-high forms of *K. uvaria* in shades of coral orange and yellow have given way to kinds with blooms ranging from coral red through every conceivable shade of orange, peach, and yellow to near-white and light green, on plants varying in size from 1½-ft. dwarfs to 6-ft. giants.

K. galpinii. Zones 3–9, 14–24. Native to South Africa. Grows 2–3 ft. high and wide. Narrow, fibrous, grasslike leaves give rise to flowers that are red at the tip shading to orange; blooms not flared at the tip. Blooms early summer to early autumn. Often confused with *K. triangularis*, whose flowers are flared at the tip.

K. hybrids. Zones 2–9, 14–24, except as noted.

Although these hybrids involve several species, they generally share the narrow leaves and summer bloom season of *K. uvaria*. A distinct departure is 'Christmas Cheer', a hybrid of vigorous species *K. rooperi*.

'Alcazar'. Dark, bronzy stems to 3½ ft., with brick red flowers that age to pinkish orange.

'Border Ballet'. Buds are a soft, dusty coral pink opening to cream blooms. Stems reach 4–4½ ft.

'Bressingham Comet'. Stems to 2 ft. high; flower clusters are orange with a yellow base.

'Christmas Cheer'. Zones 19–24. Brilliant orange buds open to deep gold flowers on 4–5-ft. stems. Blooms fall through late spring in mild-winter areas, fall until frost elsewhere. Give it room; leaves (to 5 ft. long and 2 in. wide) become lax and collapse on the ground, smothering any plants in their way. Clump increases rapidly to 6–8 ft. or more across. Divide in early summer after flowering stops.

'Cobra'. Stems 3–4 ft. tall. Flower clusters are orange at the top, fading through peach to creamy white at the base.

Flamenco. Seed-grown strain that blooms first year in early autumn, in subsequent years in summer. Flower colors range from coral through orange and yellow to creamy white. Stems to 2½ ft. high.

'Little Maid'. Thin, grassy leaves and narrow flower stems to 2 ft. high. Creamy white blossoms open from buds in buff-tinted pale yellow.

'Nancy's Red'. Zones 4–9, 14–24. To 2 ft. high and wide, with semievergreen, grassy leaves that give rise to coral red flowers in early to midsummer.

'Percy's Pride'. To 4 ft. tall, with green-tinted yellow buds opening cream.

'Primrose Beauty'. To 3 ft. high, with blossoms in clear light yellow.

'Shining Scepter'. Plant sold in North America under this name is 3 ft. high, with tangerine orange flowers; the English original is 4 ft. tall, with pale yellow buds opening ivory.

'Toffee Nosed'. Stems to 2 ft., with flower spikes that are creamy white at the base and tawny orange at the top.

»

CLOCKWISE FROM TOP: *Kniphofia* 'Percy's Pride'; *K.* 'Bees' Lemon'; *K. rooperi*

K. northiae. Zones 4–9, 14–24. Very large, dramatic-looking species with solitary rosette of broad, bluish green leaves (up to 6 in. wide at base, 5 ft. long) on a woody, trunklike stem 1–3 ft. high. Does not form clumps. Thick blossom stalks rise 1–2 ft. above foliage in summer, bearing large, oblong heads of orange buds opening light yellow.

K. rooperi. Zones 4–9, 14–24. Native to South Africa's eastern Cape. To 4 ft. tall and wide, with keeled green leaves that remain evergreen only in mildest part of range. The inflorescence is more egg-shaped than spherical, yellow at the very bottom and orange above; blooms in winter.

K. thomsonii. Zones 6–9, 14–24. Alpine species from East Africa. Clumps grow 3–5 ft. tall and 2–4 ft. wide. Narrow blue-green leaves grow to about 3 ft. long. Individual blooms are orange, not as tightly packed onto the spike as those of other *Kniphofia* species and hybrids. 'Triploid Form' grows to 4 ft. tall and 2 ft. wide, with orange-red flowers.

K. triangularis. Zones 3–9, 14–24. Native to South Africa. Grows 2 ft. high, with grassy foliage and coral flowers that are flared at the tips. Blooms midsummer to midfall. Often confused with *K. galpinii.*

K. uvaria. Zones 2–9, 14–24. Leaves to 1 in. wide, 2 ft. long. Oblong flower heads on stems 3–3½ ft. high. Coral red buds open to orange or deep yellow blossoms in summer (in fall, in cold-winter climates). Most varieties sold under this name are hybrids (see *K.* hybrids).

CARE

Red-hot pokers require adequate moisture when blooms are forming and will fail to flower if conditions are too dry then. In summer, they'll tolerate even marshy conditions—but for winter survival, well-drained soil is essential. Most of these plants flower in summer, but some start in late spring and repeat throughout the growing season; others bloom all winter in mild climates. Where winter temperatures drop to 0°F (–18°C) or below, tie foliage over clumps in fall to protect growing points (or at least leave all foliage in place over winter).

In milder climates, remove ratty-looking leaves in fall; new leaves will replace them by spring. Crowns increase slowly, forming clumps 2–3 ft. or wider at base; you will get the best show if clumps are left in place for several years. Increase plantings by division in spring except for types still blooming then; for these, wait until summer to divide. Some strains are available as seed; individual plants vary in color and quality. Protect from slugs and snails.

Red-hot pokers are stunning in bloom, producing tall candles of yellow, red, or white. Cluster them in groups of three or five as seasonal accents in a border, with phormiums, billowy grasses, or mounding shrubs.

Koelreuteria
Sapindaceae
DECIDUOUS TREES

✿ ZONES VARY BY SPECIES

☼ FULL SUN

◐ ● MODERATE TO REGULAR WATER

Koelreuteria paniculata

Small trees native to eastern Asia, these are noted for large, loose clusters of yellow flowers followed by fat, papery fruit capsules resembling little Japanese lanterns. Capsules are used in fresh and dried arrangements. Good patio, lawn, or street trees. Soil adaptability is excellent when drainage is good. Control self-sown seedlings.

K. bipinnata. CHINESE FLAME TREE. Zones 8–24; H1. To 20–40 ft. tall and slightly less wide, eventually flat topped. Leaves are 1–2 ft. long, divided into 7 to 12 oval leaflets; they briefly turn yellow before dropping. Late-summer flower clusters resemble those of *K. paniculata*, but 2-in. capsules develop shades of orange, red, or salmon; they quickly follow flowers and persist into fall. Blooms very young. Prune tree to develop high branching. Brittle wood may break under heavy snow. Deep, noninvasive roots make this a good tree to plant under.

K. paniculata. GOLDEN-RAIN TREE. Zones A2; 2–24. To 20–35 ft. tall, 25–40 ft. wide. Open branching, giving slight shade. Leaves to 15 in. long with 7 to 15 oval, toothed or lobed leaflets, each 1–3 in. long. New leaves are purplish, maturing to bright green in summer; may (or may not) turn yellow-gold in fall. Very showy,

8–14-in.-long flower clusters in early to midsummer. Fruit capsules are red when young, maturing to buff and brown shades; last well into autumn. Tree takes cold, heat, drought, wind, and air pollution. Prune to prevent gawkiness. 'Coral Sun' is a nonflowering selection with coral new growth that matures to green, contrasting with coral stems. 'Fastigiata' is 25 ft. tall, 3 ft. wide. 'Golden Candle' grows 35 ft. tall, 3–4 ft. wide. 'Rose Lantern' has seedpods flushed with pink. 'September' blooms a month after the species.

Kohlrabi

Brassicaceae
BIENNIAL GROWN AS ANNUAL

🌿 **ALL ZONES**

☀ **FULL SUN**

💧 **REGULAR WATER**

Kohlrabi

Resembling a tennis ball sprouting kale leaves, kohlrabi looks odd, but tastes great. Leaves and leafstalks of this cabbage relative are edible, but most gardeners grow it for the enlarged, bulblike part that forms just above the soil surface. Probably native to Europe's west coast. Plants go from seed to harvest in 50 to 60 days; the quality declines if harvest is delayed.

Standard varieties are 'Early White Vienna' and 'Early Purple Vienna', which are similar in all but skin color. They're ready when globes are 2–3 in. in diameter. 'Kolibri' is a popular purple-skinned variety with 4–6-in. globes. 'Superschmelz', 'Kossack', and 'Gigante' all reach 8–10 in. in diameter.

CARE

Sow seeds ½ in. deep in rich soil about 2 weeks after average date of last frost; apply complete fertilizer a month after sowing. Follow first planting with successive sowings 2 weeks apart. In warm-winter areas, plant again in late fall and early winter.

Space rows 1½ ft. apart; thin seedlings to 4–6 in. apart. Plants are rarely troubled by pests or diseases.

Peel, slice, and serve bulbs raw; or steam or sauté slices or chunks. Steam young leaves and leafstalks.

Kolkwitzia amabilis

BEAUTY BUSH
Caprifoliaceae
DECIDUOUS SHRUB

🌿 **ZONES 2–11, 14–20**

☀ ◑ **FULL SUN OR PARTIAL SHADE**

💧 **REGULAR WATER**

Kolkwitzia amabilis

This fountainlike central Chinese native grows quickly to 10–12 ft. tall and wide. In partial shade, it has an arching form; in full sun, it's denser and shorter. Mid- to late spring is its best season, when beauty bush is covered with clusters of 1-in.-long, yellow-throated pink flowers. Gray-green leaves sometimes turn reddish in fall. Blossoms are followed by conspicuous pinkish brown, bristly fruits that prolong color display. Brown, flaky bark gradually peels from stems during winter. 'Pink Cloud' is a particularly floriferous selection with extra-large, light pink blooms.

Adapts to many soils and climates. Blooms on wood formed the previous year. Thin out oldest stems after blossoms have faded; or, to enjoy seeing the fruit, wait until early spring to prune, then do so lightly. Tends to get leggy with age; plant can be renewed by cutting to ground after bloom.

Lablab purpureus.
See *Dolichos lablab*

Laburnum

GOLDENCHAIN TREE
Papilionaceae
DECIDUOUS TREES OR SHRUBS

🌿 **ZONES 1–10, 14–17**

☀ ◑ **AFTERNOON SHADE IN HOTTEST CLIMATES**

💧 💧 **MODERATE TO REGULAR WATER**

☠ **ALL PARTS, ESPECIALLY SEEDPODS, ARE HIGHLY POISONOUS IF INGESTED**

Laburnum × watereri

Chains of hanging yellow flowers give these a distinctly weeping look, akin to wisteria. Upright growers, these are usually pruned into single-trunked trees but can be maintained as shrubs. Bark is green; bright green leaves are divided into three leaflets, reminiscent of clover. Clusters of sweet pea–shaped flowers appear in mid- to late spring. Use singly, in groups, or regularly spaced

in a long shrub or perennial border. Flexible branches are easy to espalier: Allées of laburnums are famously trained into yellow-flowered tunnels in North American and European show gardens.

Both species are native to central and southern Europe.

L. alpinum. SCOTCH LABURNUM. To 30–35 ft. tall and 20–25 ft. wide. Flower clusters 10–15 in. long. 'Pendulum' has weeping branches.

L. anagyroides. COMMON GOLDENCHAIN. To 20–30 ft. tall and 15–20 ft. wide. Flower clusters 6–10 in. long. It has a compact, upright variety, 'Columnaris'; and a weeping variety, 'Pendulum'.

L. × watereri. Hybrid between the above two species. To 15–30 ft. tall and 10–20 ft. wide, with 10–20-in.-long flower clusters. 'Sunspire' ('Columnaris') grows to 20 ft. tall and 10 ft. wide. 'Vossii' is the most widely grown, most graceful variety, with flower clusters near 20 in. long.

CARE

Provide well-drained soil. Prune regularly after bloom to keep tidy; remove dead or crowding branches in tree's center (avoid large cuts, because cut areas callus over slowly). Remove seedpods if possible—not only are they toxic, but a heavy crop drains the plant's strength.

Create your own golden tunnel of blooms. Place three or four arched steel trellises together and train the flexible branches of laburnum to grow over them. In midspring, the walk under the bright, weeping blossoms will be magical.

L

Lachenalia
CAPE COWSLIP
Asparagaceae
PERENNIALS FROM BULBS

- 🌡 **ZONES 16, 17, 23, 24; OR INDOORS**
- ☀◐ **LIGHT SHADE IN HOTTEST CLIMATES; BRIGHT LIGHT**
- 💧 **REGULAR WATER DURING GROWTH AND BLOOM**

Lachenalia aloides 'Aurea'

Grow these South African bulbs for spikes of tubular, hyacinth-like blossoms that appear at the tops of thick flowering stems in late winter or early spring. Each grows from two broad, succulent, strap-shaped leaves, often spotted with brown.

There are scores of species, a handful of which are on the market at any given time.

L. aloides. Stems 10–12 in. high, with yellow flowers tipped in red and green. Inch-wide leaves. 'Pearsonii' has yellow-orange flowers with red-orange bases; slightly taller than the species, with maroon-spotted leaves.

L. bulbifera. Stems to 15 in. high, with coral red and yellow flowers tipped in purple. Leaves are 2 in. wide and unspotted.

L. reflexa 'Romaud'. Grows 8–10 in. high, with dense spikes of yellow flowers.

L. rubida 'Rupert'. Grows 8–10 in. high, with dense spikes of violet flowers shading to magenta at the tips.

CARE

Planted in late summer or early fall, cape cowslip does best where winters are wet and mild, summers dry. Set bulbs in well-drained soil, 1–1½ in. deep, 3 in. apart. Water sparingly until growth starts, then give regular moisture until foliage yellows after bloom. Gradually let soil dry out and keep as dry as possible until fall. Bait for slugs and snails.

Laelia
Orchidaceae
EPIPHYTIC ORCHIDS

- 🌡 **ZONES VARY BY SPECIES; OR INDOORS**
- ◐ **LIGHT SHADE; BRIGHT LIGHT**
- 💧 **REGULAR WATER**

Laelia anceps

Closely related to (and resembling) *Cattleya,* these orchids are easy to grow but variable in appearance. Pseudobulbs can be plump and large flowered, like cattleya, or slender and canelike, with plants bearing clusters of smaller flowers. All have fleshy leaves. Laelias cross freely with cattleyas. A few are hardy enough to grow outdoors along the California coast as far north as San Francisco. Outdoor plants are usually grown on tree trunks or in pots on the patio; indoor plants can be brought outdoors at warm times of year. For cultural needs, see *Cattleya.*

L. anceps. Zones 16, 17, 21–24; H1, H2. From Mexico. Plump pseudobulbs carry thick 6-in. leaves. Flower spikes range from 6 in. to 3 ft. long, carry three to six fragrant, 4-in. pinkish lilac flowers in winter. Some varieties have pink, white, purple, or lavender-blue blossoms.

L. autumnalis. Zones 16, 17, 21–24; H1, H2. From Mexico. This species is similar to *L. anceps,* but its scented flowers bloom in autumn. Rosy purple flowers have a pinkish white lip with purple and yellow markings.

Lagenaria. See Gourd

Lagerstroemia
CRAPE MYRTLE
Lythraceae
DECIDUOUS SHRUBS AND TREES

- 🌡 **ZONES VARY BY SPECIES**
- ☀ **FULL SUN**
- 💧 **MODERATE WATER**

Lagerstroemia indica

The signature plant for many hot-summer regions, crape myrtle has showy summer flowers, good-looking bark, and (in many cases) brilliant fall color. Taken together, these features make crape myrtles attractive all year. Long, cool autumns yield the best leaf display; the first hard frost ends the show. (In cool-summer regions, these plants flower less, and mildew is a more serious problem among susceptible varieties.)

Most crape myrtles in gardens are varieties of *L. indica* or hybrids between it and *L. fauriei,* which is valued for its hardiness and exceptionally showy bark.

L. fauriei. JAPANESE CRAPE MYRTLE. Tree. Zones 7–10, 12–14, 18–21. Native to Japan. To 20–30 ft. tall and as wide, with upright habit and outward-arching branches. Leaves are light green, turning yellow in fall. Smooth gray bark flakes away to reveal shiny cinnamon bark beneath. White flowers are carried in 4-in. clusters. Highly mildew-resistant; the parent of many resistant hybrids, but itself not widely grown.

L. hybrids. Zones 7–10, 12–14, 18–21; H1, H2. The following hybrids between *L. indica* and *L. fauriei*—just a few of those introduced by the U.S. National Arboretum—have been selected for hardiness and mildew resistance. Grow as shrubs or train into small trees.

'Acoma'. To 10 ft. tall, 11 ft. wide, with pendulous branches. White flowers, dark red fall color.

'Arapaho'. To 20 ft. tall, 10 ft. wide. Cranberry red flowers. New growth is deep red, fades to green; red-purple fall color.

'Hopi'. To 8 ft. tall, 10 ft. wide. Medium pink flowers, orange-red autumn color.

'Miami'. To 16–20 ft. tall, 8–12 ft. wide. Dark pink flowers, orange fall color.

'Muskogee'. To 25 ft. tall, 12 ft. wide. Lavender flowers, red fall color.

'Natchez'. Reaches 25 ft. tall, 12 ft. wide. White flowers, orange-red autumn color.

'Pecos'. To 8 ft. tall, 6 ft. wide. Pink flowers, maroon fall color.

'Tonto'. To 15–20 ft. tall and wide. Large clusters of red flowers; red autumn color.

'Tuscarora'. To 22 ft. tall, 12 ft. wide. Pinkish red flowers. Orange-red autumn color.

'Zuni'. To 9 ft. tall, 8 ft. wide. Lavender flowers, orange-red fall color.

L. indica. CRAPE MYRTLE. Tree or shrub. Excellent performance in Zones 7–10, 12–14, 18–21; H1, H2. Mildew is a serious problem in Zones 15–17, 22–24. Hardy in Zones 4 and 5 but seldom flowers well there except in hottest summers. Thrives in Zone 6 but flowers late. Sometimes treated as perennial in Zones 2 and 3; will come back from roots if frozen to the ground.

Native to China. To 25 ft. tall and wide. Dark green leaves are often tinged red on opening and turn brilliant orange or red in the fall. Crinkly-petaled, crepe-like, 1–1½-in. flowers in dense clusters range from white to pink to red and purple. Trained as a tree, develops an attractive trunk and branch structure. Smooth gray or light brown bark peels off to reveal smooth, pinkish inner bark. Winter trunk and branches look polished.

L

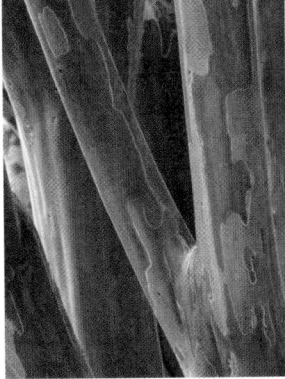

CLOCKWISE FROM TOP: *Lagerstroemia* 'Muskogee'; *Lagerstroemia* bark; *Lagerstroemia* fall color

The following are among the best selections, including trees, large shrubs, and dwarfs. Mildew can be a problem; plant mildew-resistant hybrids (see *L. hybrids*).

'Catawba'. Roundish, dense growth to 6–10 ft. tall and equally wide (can be trained as a 15-ft. tree). Dark purple flowers, orange-red fall color.

'Centennial Spirit'. Multistemmed large shrub or small tree to 20 ft. tall and as wide

or nearly so. Dark red flowers, orange-red fall color.

'Chica Red'. Compact, dense, 3–4 ft. tall and wide. Rosy red flowers; yellow fall color.

'Dynamite'. To 20 ft. tall, 15 ft. wide. Ruffled red flowers, and orange-red fall foliage.

'Glendora White'. As a shrub, grows erect to 9 ft. tall and 6–7 ft. wide. With training, makes a tree to 25 ft. tall and 20 ft. wide. Bears white flowers. Red fall foliage.

'Near East' ('Shell Pink'). Rounded growth to 15–20 ft. tall and wide, with soft pink flowers. Orange-red fall color.

'Peppermint Lace'. Erect shrub 6–7 ft. tall and wide, or tree to 15–20 ft. tall and wide. Deep pink flowers with a white picotee edge. Red fall color.

Petite series. To 5 ft. tall and 4 ft. wide, with names that describe their flower color: 'Petite Embers', 'Petite Orchid', 'Petite Pinkie', 'Petite Plum', 'Petite Red Imp', 'Petite Snow'. All have yellow fall foliage.

'Pink Velour'. Vase-shaped shrub or small tree to 10 ft. tall and wide. Neon pink flowers and yellow-orange fall color.

'Pocomoke'. To 5 ft. tall and wide. Dark rosy pink flowers, bronze-red fall foliage.

'Red Rocket'. To 20 ft. tall and wide. Deep red flowers cover this plant all summer. Bronze-red fall foliage.

'Seminole'. To 6–12 ft. tall and as wide. Bright pink flowers, red fall color.

'Watermelon Red'. Rounded habit to 20–25 ft. tall and as wide. Bright red flowers, yellow fall color.

'White Chocolate'. To 8–10 ft. tall and wide. Foliage emerges burgundy in spring, then matures to chocolate-tinged green. Pure white flowers. Bright orange-yellow fall color.

L. speciosa. GIANT CRAPE MYRTLE. Tree. Zones H1, H2. Native from India to Australia. To 80 ft. tall, 30 ft. wide, with leaves 8–12 in. long, 4 in. wide. White to purple flowers are borne in clusters to 16 in. long.

CARE

Because crape myrtles bloom on new wood, they should be pruned in winter or early spring. On large plants, remove basal suckers, twiggy growth, crossing branches, and branches growing toward the center of the plant. Also gradually remove side branches up to a height of 4–5 ft.; this exposes the handsome bark of the trunks. To reduce a large crape myrtle's height, shorten the topmost branches by 1–3 ft. in late winter, cutting back to a side branch or bud. For branches more than 2 in. thick, cut back to the crotch or trunk. Also prune dwarf forms periodically throughout the growing season, thinning out small, twiggy growth. Snip off spent flower clusters of all types to neaten appearance and promote a second, lighter bloom.

Heavy watering and any fertilizing in summer can significantly decrease hardiness in marginal climates. Give plants infrequent but deep watering.

Lagunaria patersonii
PRIMROSE TREE, COW ITCH TREE
Malvaceae
EVERGREEN TREE

🗡 **ZONES 13, 15–24; H1, H2**

☼ **FULL SUN**

💧 **MODERATE WATER**

⬥ **POD FIBERS CAN IRRITATE SKIN AND EYES**

Lagunaria patersonii

Native to the South Pacific and Australia. Grows fast to 30 ft. tall and wide. Young trees are narrow and erect; old ones are sometimes spreading, with a flat-topped look. Densely foliaged in thick, oval leaves that are olive green above, gray beneath. Pink to rose, 2-in.-wide summer blossoms look similar to hibiscus flowers, fade almost to white with age. 'Royal Purple' has purple blossoms. Brown seed capsules, popular with flower arrangers, hang on for a long time; they split into five sections, revealing bright brown seeds.

Tolerates wide variety of soils and growing conditions. Resists ocean wind, salt spray; tolerates intense heat. Foliage is damaged at 25°F (−4°C) but recovers quickly. Blooms best in coastal conditions. Use as specimen tree, or plant in groups as a showy windbreak or screen.

L

Lamium

DEAD NETTLE

Lamiaceae

PERENNIALS SOMETIMES GROWN AS ANNUALS

✎ ZONES VARY BY SPECIES

◐ ● PARTIAL OR FULL SHADE

● REGULAR WATER

Lamium maculatum 'Orchid Frost'

Native from Europe to western Asia, these vigorous, shade-tolerant, clumping or ground-covering perennials have opposite pairs of tooth-edged, typically heart-shaped leaves, often marked with silver or white. Clustered flowers come in pink, white, or yellow. Evergreen in mild-winter climates.

L. galeobdolon (Lamiastrum galeobdolon). DEAD NETTLE, YELLOW ARCHANGEL. Perennial in Zones 2–11, 14–24; winter annual in Zones 12, 13. Trailing plant with roundish or heart-shaped leaves. Blooms in late spring, bearing yellow flowers (not showy). 'Hermann's Pride' is a clump former to 2 ft. tall and wide, with sharply tapered leaves that are evenly and symmetrically marked with white spots and streaks. *L. g. montanum* 'Florentinum'

(*L. g.* 'Variegatum') has trailing stems that root as they spread. Dull medium to dark green leaves are edged in green and marbled with silvery gray in the center. Attractive plant in hanging baskets, where it will trail to 2–3 ft., or as groundcover (it can be invasive but is easily curbed). Considered a noxious weed in the Seattle area.

L. maculatum. DEAD NETTLE, SPOTTED NETTLE. Perennial in Zones A2, A3; 1–11, 14–24; winter annual in Zones 12, 13. To 8 in. high; spreads by rhizomes and stolons to 3 ft. wide. Leaves are 1–3 in. long, green with a central white stripe or zone. Pink or white flowers in late spring and early summer. All the following selections bloom from spring to midsummer and make excellent groundcovers for shady spots, nicely lighting up darker garden areas. They are also useful in hanging baskets. They need some grooming to remove old, shabby growth.

'Anne Greenaway'. Pink flowers and green leaves edged in yellow and striped with silver down the center.

'Aureum'. Golden foliage with silver center marks and pink flowers. 'Lemon Frost' has lime green leaves with a white center line.

'Beacon Silver'. Pink flowers and green-edged, silvery gray leaves; similar in leaf color are 'Orchid Frost' (orchid pink flowers), 'Purple Dragon' (purple blooms), 'Red Nancy' (deep rosy pink flowers), and 'White Nancy' (white blooms).

'Chequers'. Pink flowers and green leaves with a white center stripe.

'Pink Pewter'. Pink blooms and silvery leaves edged in greenish gray.

Lampranthus

ICE PLANT

Aizoaceae

SUCCULENT PERENNIALS

✎ ZONES 14–24, EXCEPT AS NOTED

☼ FULL SUN

◊ LITTLE OR NO WATER

Lampranthus blandus

From South Africa. Most of the ice plants with large, brilliant flowers belong to this genus, which includes many (but not all) plants formerly called *Oscularia*. Plants are fleshy, erect or trailing, woody at base. Select in bloom for the color you want. Cut back lightly after bloom to eliminate fruit capsules, encourage new leafy growth. Good at seashore. Flowers attract bees.

L. aurantiacus. To 10–15 in. tall. Gray-green, inch-long, three-sided leaves. Flowers 1½–2 in. across, orange; midwinter to spring bloom. 'Glaucus' has bright yellow flowers; those of 'Sunman' are golden yellow. Plant 15–18 in. apart for bedding, borders, low bank cover.

L. blandus. PINK VYGIE. Zones 13–17, 19–24. To 6 in. high. Leaves look like agglomerations of tiny green pyramids. Flowers are pale pink daisies.

L. deltoides. See *Oscularia deltoides*.

L. filicaulis. REDONDO CREEPER. Thin, creeping stems; fine-textured, glistening green foliage. Spreads slowly to form mats about 3 in. high. Small pink flowers bloom in early spring. Use for small-scale groundcover, mound, or low bank cover. Plant 3 ft. apart.

L. spectabilis. TRAILING ICE PLANT. Zones 12–24. Sprawling or trailing to 1 ft. high, 1½–2 ft. wide. Three-sided

gray-green leaves. Planting becomes a carpet of gleaming color from late winter to spring, when the 2–2½-in.-wide, pink, rose-pink, red, or purple flowers are in bloom.

Lantana

Verbenaceae

EVERGREEN SHRUBS, GROUNDCOVERS

✎ ZONES 8–10, 12–24; H1, H2; ANNUALS ELSEWHERE

☼ FULL SUN

◊ ● LITTLE TO MODERATE WATER

🦋 ATTRACT BIRDS, BUTTERFLIES

◊ FRUITS ARE POISONOUS IF INGESTED

Lantana 'Spreading Sunset'

Most often used as groundcovers, shrubs, or in containers, these fast-growing tropical American natives produce tiny flowers in tight clusters that look like miniature nosegays. Valued for profuse show of color over long season—every month of the year in frost-free areas. Light frosts merely keep plants in check. Freezes (possible in Zones 8–10, 14) may seriously damage or kill plants in some but not all winters. In colder zones, lantana is grown as a summer annual.

L. camara. One of the two species used in hybridizing. Coarse, upright grower to 6 ft. tall and wide. Rough dark green leaves; yellow, orange, or red flowers in 1–2-in. clusters. In lowland parts of Hawaii, this species is considered a noxious weed; various insects that attack it have been imported in attempts to control it.

L. montevidensis (L. sellowiana). The other species used in crossbreeding. This one is sold at nurseries.

A Colorful Cover-Up

Dead nettle is most widely used in containers and as a groundcover beneath shrubs. But it also makes a fine companion for spring-blooming bulbs that thrive in partial shade; its multihued leaves can conceal the declining foliage as the bulbs fade into dormancy. Try dead nettle with glory-of-the-snow (*Chionodoxa*), crocus, freesia, *Fritillaria*, and *Scilla*.

A little hardier than *L. camara*, it's a groundcover to 2 ft. high, with branches trailing to 3 or even 6 ft. Dark green, 1-in.-long, coarsely toothed leaves are sometimes tinged red or purplish, especially in cold weather. Rosy lilac flowers in 1–1½-in.-wide clusters. 'Alba' and 'White Lightnin' have white flowers. 'Lavender Swirl' has flower clusters in pure white, solid purple, and white-and-purple.

L. selections and hybrids. In the following list, some of the selections are forms of *L. camara* or hybrids between those forms; others are hybrids between *L. camara* and *L. montevidensis*.

'American Red'. To 4–6 ft. tall and wide. Bright red flower clusters with yellow florets in center.

Bandana series. Plants have compact growth to 2–2½ ft. high and wide. Large flowers open yellow and turn orange, pink, or cherry red.

'Confetti'. To 2–3 ft. by 6–8 ft. Blossoms mix yellow, pink, purple.

'Cream Carpet'. To 2–3 ft. by 6–8 ft. Cream with bright yellow throat.

'Dwarf Yellow'. To 2–4 ft. tall and wide.

'Gold Rush'. To 1½–2 ft. by 4–6 ft. Rich golden yellow.

'Irene'. To 3 ft. by 4 ft. Compact. Magenta and lemon yellow clusters.

'Lemon Swirl'. Slow growing to 2 ft. high, 3 ft. wide. Bright yellow band around each leaf; yellow flowers.

Luscious series. These mound to 2 ft. high and wide, come in shades of yellow, light purple, orange.

'Miss Huff'. To 3–5 ft. by 10 ft. Orange and pink. Hardier than other lantanas, surviving sharp frosts.

'New Gold'. To 2–3 ft. by 6–8 ft. Golden yellow.

Patriot series. Plants range from 12–15 in. high and wide to 4–5 ft. tall and wide, depending on variety. Flowers in different combinations of yellow, pink, purple, orange, and red.

'Radiation'. To 3–5 ft. tall and wide. Rich orange-red.

'Rainbow' ('Patriot Rainbow'). Compact plant to 1 ft. by 15 in. Flowers combine yellow, orange, and fuchsia pink.

'Spreading Sunset'. To 2–3 ft. high by 6–8 ft. wide. Vivid orange-red.

'Sunburst'. To 2–3 ft. high by 6–8 ft. wide. Bright golden yellow.

'Tangerine'. To 2–3 ft. high by 6–8 ft. wide. Burnt orange.

CARE

Prone to mildew in shade or during prolonged overcast weather. Prune hard in spring to remove dead wood and prevent woodiness. Too much water and fertilizer cuts down on bloom. Shrubby kinds are used as low hedges or as substitutes for annuals in beds or containers. Spreading kinds are excellent bank covers and will control erosion. Effective spilling from raised beds, planter boxes, or hanging baskets. Crushed foliage has a pungent odor that some people dislike. Blackberry-like fruits are attractive but highly toxic, especially before ripening. Remove spent flowers before berries form.

Larix

LARCH
Pinaceae
DECIDUOUS TREES

- **ZONES VARY BY SPECIES**
- **FULL SUN**
- **REGULAR WATER**
- **ATTRACT BIRDS**

Larix kaempferi

Most larches form slender pyramids with horizontal branches, drooping branchlets, and the habit of turning yellow and orange in fall before dropping all their foliage. Needles are ½–1½ in. long, in fluffy tufts; except as noted, those of the following species are soft to the touch. Woody, roundish, ½–1½-in.-long cones are scattered along branchlets. In spring, bright purple-red new cones stand out against pale green tufts of new needles. Best in regions with cool summers and cool to cold winters. Not particular about soils. Plant with dark evergreen conifers as background or near water for reflection.

L. decidua (L. europaea). EUROPEAN LARCH. Zones A1–A3; 1–9, 14–17. From the mountains of Europe. Moderate to fast growth to 30–60 ft. tall and 10–25 ft. wide. Grass green summer foliage. In 'Pendula', branches arch out and down, and branchlets hang nearly straight down.

L. gmelinii. DAHURIAN LARCH. Zones A1–A3. Native to eastern Siberia. Tall tree to 100 ft. tall and 30 ft. wide; shrubby in extremely cold or very windy regions. Summer leaves are light green. Cones are brown, oval, 1 in. long. 'Romberg Park' is a globe-shaped dwarf that grows about 1 in. per year.

L. kaempferi. JAPANESE LARCH. Zones 1–9, 14–19. Native to Japan. Most frequently planted larch in the West. Fast growing to 60 ft. or taller, 20–30 ft. wide, but can be dwarfed in containers. Summer foliage is bluish green. 'Diana' grows 45 ft. tall, 20 ft. wide, with twisted growth.

L. occidentalis. WESTERN LARCH, TAMARACK. Zones A3; 1–7. Native to the Cascades and northern Rocky Mountains. Grows 150–200 ft. tall as timber tree, but usually just 30–50 ft. tall, 10–15 ft. wide in gardens. Sharp, stiff needles are blue-green to gray-green in summer.

L. sibirica (L. russica). Zones A1–A3; 1, 2. Native from northeastern Europe to Siberia. Narrowly conical tree to 30–90 ft. tall and 15 ft. wide, with horizontal or upward-angled branches and yellow twigs. Needles are bright green in summer. Tolerates extreme cold but can be damaged by spells of early warming followed by hard freezes. 'Pendula' has weeping branches. 'Conica' makes a narrow, upright spire.

Larrea tridentata

CREOSOTE BUSH
Zygophyllaceae
EVERGREEN SHRUB

- **ZONES 7–14, 18–21**
- **FULL SUN**
- **LITTLE OR NO WATER TO MODERATE WATER**

Larrea tridentata

One of the most common native shrubs in Southwest deserts, creosote bush grows 4–8 ft. tall and wide, with many upright branches. Straggly and open in shallow, dry soil; attractive, dense, rounded but spreading where water accumulates. Leathery yellow-green to dark green leaves divided into two tiny, ⅜-in.-long crescents; gummy secretion makes them look varnished and yields distinctive creosote odor, especially after rain. Small yellow flowers appear off and on all year, followed by small roundish fruit covered with shiny white or rusty hairs. With water and fertilizer, grows taller and denser with larger, shiny dark green leaves. Use as wind or privacy screen, or trim into formal hedge.

Even in the hottest regions, creosote bush keeps its evergreen leaves, and it blooms faithfully each spring. It's a star among the few plants that thrive in both high- and low-desert conditions.

L

Lathyrus
SWEET PEA
Papilionaceae
ANNUALS AND PERENNIALS

- ✎ **ZONES VARY BY SPECIES**
- ☀ **FULL SUN**
- ◯◑⬤ **WATER NEEDS VARY BY SPECIES**
- ⬥ **SEEDS CONTAIN TOXIC AMINO ACIDS**

Lathyrus odoratus 'Senator'

Delicious scent, lovely flowers, and vining or bush habit earn these a place in gardens all over the West. Throughout this book, you will find flowers described as "sweet pea–shaped": each blossom has one large, upright, roundish petal (banner or standard); two narrow side petals (wings); and two lower petals that are somewhat united, forming a boat-shaped structure (keel).

L. latifolius. PERENNIAL SWEET PEA. Zones 1–24. Native to Europe. Strong-growing vine to 9 ft., with blue-green foliage. Flowers are usually mixes of reddish purple, white, and pink; single colors may be sold. Blooms all summer if not allowed to go to seed. Grows with little care, tolerates aridity (give moderate water). May escape and become naturalized, even weedy. Use as bank cover, as trailer over rocks, on trellis or fence.

L. odoratus. Annual. All zones. Native to the Mediterranean region. Blooms in winter, spring, or summer, bearing many spikelike clusters of crisp-looking flowers with a clean, sweet perfume. Blossoms come in single and mixed colors. Mixes include deep rose, blue, purple, scarlet, white, cream, salmon, and bicolors. Vining

types grow to 5 ft. or more, climbing with tendrils that coil around supporting strings or other supports; bush kinds grow 8 in. to 3 ft. high. Sweet peas make magnificent cut flowers in quantity.

Heirloom varieties. Not as large and showy as modern hybrids, these old spring-blooming varieties (some dating back hundreds of years) are notable for powerful fragrance.

'America'. Crimson to scarlet with white stripes.

'Blanche Ferry'. Carmine-rose standard, pink wings. Similar to 'Painted Lady' but with more intense color.

'Cupani'. Deep blue standard, purple wings. Very close to the original wild *L. odoratus*.

'Henry Ekford'. Red-orange; climbs 5–7 ft.

Old Spice Mix. A mixture of eight old-fashioned varieties with flowers in white and in shades of pink, red, and purple.

'Painted Lady'. Dates from the 18th century; bears small rose-and-white flowers.

Early flowering. Includes Early Spencer, Early Multiflora. The name "Spencer" once described a type of frilled flower (with wavy petals) that is now characteristic of almost all varieties. "Multiflora" indicates that plants carry more flowers per stem than the old Spencers did.

These bloom in midwinter when days are short. (Spring- and summer-flowering types will not bloom until days have lengthened to 15 hours or more.) Where winter temperatures are mild (Zones 12, 13, 17, 21–24; H1, H2), sow seeds in late summer for winter bloom. Use these varieties for forcing in greenhouse. They are not heat-resistant. Generally sold in mixed colors.

Spring flowering. Includes spring-flowering heat-resistant Cuthbertson type, Cuthbertson's Floribunda, Floribunda-Zvolanek strain. Both mixtures and single-color named varieties are available in seed packets. Flowers have a wide color range: pink, lavender, purple, white, cream, rose, salmon, cerise, carmine, red, and blue. Royal or Royal Family are somewhat larger-flowered, more heat-resistant than the others. In Zones 7–9,

12–24, plant between early fall and earliest winter. Elsewhere, plant just as soon as soil can be worked.

Summer flowering. Includes Galaxy, Plenti-flora. Available in named varieties and mixtures in wide color range. Bloom from early summer on. Large flowers, five to seven on each long stem. Heat-resistant, but not enough so for Zones 7–15, 18–21.

Bush type. These are strong vines with predetermined growth, heights. Unlike vining kinds, these stop their upward growth at 8 in. to 3 ft. high. Some are self-supporting; others need support of a few sticks or pieces of brush (similar to what you would provide for many perennials). Flowers come in all colors, grow in all regions. Most are early or spring blooming; follow planting dates given for early- or spring-flowering vining types.

Bijou. To 1 ft. Available in single or mixed colors. Each 5–7-in. stem produces four or five flowers. Self-supporting plants are spectacular in borders, beds, window boxes, or pots. Not as heat-resistant or as long stemmed as Knee-Hi; performs better in containers.

Cupid. To 4–6 in. by 1 ft. Trails on ground or hangs from containers.

Jet Set. Bushy plants grow 2–3 ft. high; need some support.

Knee-Hi. To 2½ ft.; need some support. Large, long-stemmed blooms are carried five or six to the stem. Has all the virtues and color range of Cuthbertson's Floribunda, but on bush-type plants. Good for mass display in beds, borders. Growth will exceed 2½ ft. where planting bed joins a fence or wall; keep in the open for uniform height.

Little Sweethearts. These are rounded bushes to about 8 in. high; they need no support, bloom over a long season.

Supersnoop. Grows to 2 ft. tall; needs no support.

L. splendens. PRIDE OF CALIFORNIA. Perennial. Zones 14–24. Native to chaparral in San Diego County and adjacent Baja California. Grows to 8–10 ft. Each stem bears clusters of 3 to 10 deep red blooms in

How to Grow Sweet Peas

To hasten germination, soak seeds for a few hours before planting. In less-than-perfect soil, prepare the ground by digging a 1–1½-ft.-deep trench.

SOIL Mix 1 part peat moss or other organic soil amendment to 2 parts soil, also adding a complete fertilizer according to label directions; backfill trench with mix.

SPACING Sow seeds 1 in. deep and 1–2 in. apart. When seedlings are 4–5 in. high, thin to at least 6 in. apart. Pinch out tops to encourage strong side branches. Where climate prevents early planting or soil is too wet to work, start three or four seeds in each small peat pot, indoors or in a protected place, and set out when weather has settled. Plant peat pots 1 ft. apart, thinning each to one strong plant. This method is ideal for bush types.

TENDING Protect young seedlings from birds and control slugs and snails. Never let vines dry out. To prolong bloom, cut flowers at least every other day and remove all seedpods. Regular monthly feeding will keep vines vigorous and productive.

TRAINING For vining sweet peas, provide trellis, strings, or wire before planting. Seedlings need support as soon as tendrils form. Free-standing trellis running north and south is best. When planting against fence or wall, keep supports away from structure to ensure good air circulation.

early spring. Start from seed in pots in autumn or spring; plant out in fall or winter. Long-lived in dry, well-drained soil.

Laurentia fluviatilis. See *Pratia pedunculata*

Laurus nobilis

SWEET BAY, GRECIAN LAUREL
Lauraceae
EVERGREEN SHRUB OR TREE

- **ZONES 5–9, 12–24; H1, H2; OR INDOOR/OUTDOOR PLANT**
- **FULL SUN OR PARTIAL SHADE**
- **MODERATE WATER**

Laurus nobilis

The leathery, aromatic leaves of this Mediterranean native are the traditional bay leaves used in cooking. The plant grows slowly to 12–40 ft. tall and wide, compact and multistemmed, with a broad base. Oval leaves are dark green. Clusters of small yellow spring flowers are followed by black or dark purple, ½–1-in. fruit. 'Saratoga' has broader leaves and a more treelike habit.

Dense habit makes it a good large background shrub, screen, or small tree (though trees eventually grow large). Tends to sucker heavily, but takes well to clipping into standards, hedges, or topiary. Not fussy about soil but needs good drainage. Subject to black scale and laurel psyllid ('Saratoga' is resistant to psyllid).

This is a classic formal container plant in all climates; where temperatures drop to 20°F (−7°C) or below, move to a greenhouse or cool, well-lighted room during the cold months.

Sweet bay is both beautiful and useful. Its leaves add flavor to everything from soups, sauces, and fish, to meats and pickles.

Lavandula

LAVENDER
Lamiaceae
EVERGREEN SHRUBS

- **ZONES VARY BY SPECIES**
- **FULL SUN**
- **MODERATE WATER**
- **ATTRACT BIRDS, BEES, BUTTERFLIES**

Lavandula angustifolia 'Vera'

Few plants are as strongly identified with fragrance and color as lavender. Blooming on plants that range from ankle to waist high, flowers can be lavender, purple, pink, or white—and are often set off by colorful bracts. Aromatic foliage is usually gray, gray-green, or yellowish green. The blossom spikes of some species are used for perfume, aromatic oil, soap, medicine, and sachets. Native to the Mediterranean region, Canary Islands, and Madeira.

Use as informal hedge or edging, in herb gardens, or in borders with plants that also thrive in full sun and no more than moderate water. Where winters are too cold for year-round growth outdoors, potted lavenders can grow in sunny windows. When they are grown outside in marginal climates, self-sown seedlings often show up in summer after parent plants die from winter cold.

Since lavenders have been in cultivation for centuries and some species cross easily, many varieties and hybrids have arisen. Names are often confused, so some of the variety names that follow may not agree with those on nursery labels. Only cutting-grown stock is truly uniform. Several varieties originally propagated by cuttings are now grown from seed (for example, plants labeled Hidcote strain and Munstead strain); seedlings vary in color and growth habit.

L. × allardii. Zones 8, 9, 12–24. A natural hybrid of *L. dentata* and *L. latifolia*—and the real identity of most lavenders sold in the U.S. as *L.* × *heterophylla*. Fairly open growth to 3–3½ ft. high, 3 ft. wide. Dull gray-green leaves vary from entirely smooth-edged to toothed near the tip, all on the same plant. Bright violet-blue flower spikes are slender; interrupted (that is, with blossom clusters separated on the stem rather than massed together); carried on long, wiry, sometimes branched stems. Blooms from mid- to late summer. Scent is more medicinal than sweet. More tolerant of heat and humidity than English lavenders and lavandins.

L. angustifolia (L. officinalis, L. vera). ENGLISH LAVENDER. Zones 2–24. This is the sweetly fragrant lavender used for perfume and sachets. Common name notwithstanding, it is native not to England but to mountains of southern Europe. It's the hardiest, most widely planted species. In Zones 2 and 3, it is shorter-lived, lasting only 3 to 5 years. Most varieties are fairly low growing, forming mounds of foliage from 8 in. to 2 ft. high and wide. Narrow, smooth-edged, gray-green or silvery gray leaves to 2 in. long. Unbranched flower stems rise 4–12 in. above foliage, and are topped with 1–4-in.-long flower spikes in white, pink, lavender-blue, or various shades of purple. Blooms mainly from early to mid-summer, but some varieties repeat in late summer or autumn.

The following is a sampling of many named selections.

'**Alba**'. To 1½–2 ft. high and wide. Pure white flowers, gray-green foliage.

'**Blue Cushion**'. To 1½ ft. high, 2 ft. wide. Profuse bright violet-blue flowers above medium green foliage.

'**Buena Vista**'. Repeat bloomer to 1½–2 ft. high and wide. Deep violet-blue flowers with superb fragrance.

CLOCKWISE FROM TOP: *Lavandula angustifolia* 'Thumbelina Leigh'; *L. stoechas* 'Hazel'; *L. stoechas* 'Bella White'

L

»

L

CLOCKWISE FROM LEFT: *Lavandula dentata candicans*; *L.* 'Goodwin Creek Grey'; *L. angustifolia* 'Martha Roderick'

'Compacta'. To 1½ ft. high and wide; good dwarf hedge plant. Light violet flowers; gray-green leaves.

'Hidcote'. The original had deep violet flowers and medium green foliage on a plant 1½–2 ft. tall. The plants sold under this name today are frequently grown from seed; they may bear gray foliage and/or vary in size from the original. 'Hidcote Blue' (with deep blue flowers) and 'Hidcote Superior' (compact, uniform, 16 in. high and 18 in. wide) are popular selections.

'Jean Davis'. To 1½–2 ft. high and wide. Flowers in pale lilac-pink; gray-green foliage.

Lady (Lavender Lady, Cambridge Lady). Seed-grown strain that blooms in 3 months from spring-sown seed. Gray-green foliage. Short spikes of lavender-blue flowers on a plant 1–1½ ft. high and wide; some variation in flower color and growth habit.

'Martha Roderick'. Compact growth to 1½–2 ft. high and wide. Dense gray foliage. Bright violet-blue blossoms in great abundance from late spring to early summer.

'Melissa'. Dense, compact grower to 1½ ft. high and wide. Good pink flower color, fading to white in hottest sun. Gray-green leaves.

'Munstead'. The original is 1½ ft. high, 2 ft. wide, with bright lavender-blue flowers and medium green foliage. Long bloomer; makes a good low hedge. Quite variable when grown from seed.

'Rosea'. To 1½–2 ft. high and wide. Light mauve-pink flowers; light green foliage.

'Thumbelina Leigh'. Very compact mound of medium green leaves to just 6 in. high and 12 in. wide. Bright violet-blue flowers rise 6 in. above foliage.

L. canariensis. CANARY ISLAND LAVENDER. Zones 16–24. Bushy, rounded habit to 3–4 ft. tall and wide. Divided, ferny-looking leaves are light green. Spikes of bright lavender-blue flowers are held on branched stems well above foliage. Blooms from early spring to late fall (all year in warm-

winter areas). Resents hard pruning; remove faded bloom stems to keep tidy.

L. dentata. FRENCH LAVEN-DER, TOOTHED LAVENDER. Zones 8, 9, 12–24. To 3–4 ft. tall and 4–6 ft. wide. Narrow green or gray-green leaves have square-toothed edges. Purple flowers in short, rounded spikes, each topped with a pair of flag-like bracts that look like rabbit ears. Long spring-into-summer flowering period, almost year-round in mild-winter areas. L. d. candicans ('French Gray') has grayer, somewhat larger leaves than the species, with dense grayish white down on young foliage.

L. 'Goodwin Creek Grey'. Zones 8, 9, 12–24. Most likely a hybrid between L. lanata and L. dentata. This densely foliaged plant grows to 2½–3 ft. high and 3–4 ft. wide, with silvery leaves that are toothed at tips. Deep violet-blue flowers from spring to late fall; virtually year-round in mild-winter climates. Similar to L. × allardii in scent and tolerance for heat and humidity.

L. × heterophylla. SWEET LAVENDER. Zones 8, 9, 12–24.

The original is probably a cross between L. dentata and L. angustifolia, occurring wild in southern France. Most plants labeled as this lavender are actually L. × allardii. Both hybrids have dull gray-green leaves, but the upper leaves of L. × heterophylla are mostly smooth-edged, while those near the plant's base are usually toothed in the middle and near the tip. L. × heterophylla is also shorter (1½–2 ft. high), with shorter, unbranched spikes of bright violet flowers—and the spikes are less interrupted, having one whorl of blossoms below the main flower spike. Bloom starts in midsummer; slightly hardier to cold.

L. × intermedia. LAVAN-DIN, HEDGE LAVENDER. Zones 4–24. This group of sterile hybrids between parents L. angustifolia and L. latifolia is distinguished from the English lavenders by larger growth and by branching stems topped with interrupted flower spikes; blooms from mid- to late summer. Long used in the perfume and soap industries, lavandins are vigorous, fragrant plants. Almost as hardy as English lavender parent and more tolerant of warm, humid summers. They include the following selections.

'Abrialii'. Once the mainstay of the French lavender oil industry. To 2½ ft. high, 3 ft. wide, with gray-green foliage. Dark violet-blue blossoms in narrow, conical, 3½–5-in.-long spikes are excellent for drying.

'Dutch' ('Hortensis'). To 3 ft. high and 2–2½ ft. wide, with gray foliage. Few-branched stems topped with narrow, conical, 2–3-in. spikes of flowers in deep violet-blue.

'Fred Boutin'. To 3–4 ft. tall and wide. Dense, silvery gray foliage topped in early to midsummer with 1½–3-in.-long spikes of violet-blue blossoms on unbranched stems.

'Grosso'. Widely planted commercial variety in France and Italy; possibly the most fragrant lavandin of all. Compact growth to 2½ ft. high and wide. Silvery foliage; large (2–3½ in. thick), conical spikes of violet-blue flowers with darker calyxes. Often gives repeat bloom in late summer. Excellent flower for drying.

'Provence'. Though it is often described as a traditional perfume lavandin, this selection does not produce the kind of oil that is used in perfumery. Grows to 2 ft. high and 3 ft. wide, with fragrant light violet flower spikes that dry well. Makes a good hedge plant.

'Silver Edge' ('Walberton's Silver Edge'). To 2½ ft. high and wide, with lavender-blue flowers held above broad, gray-green leaves uniformly edged in creamy white. Remove stems with foliage that reverts to green.

'White Spikes' ('Alba'). To 2½ ft. high and wide, with silvery leaves. Spikes of white blossoms and sage green calyxes are 1½–2 in. long, bloom from early summer through fall. Becomes woody with age.

L. lanata. WOOLLY LAVENDER. Zones 8, 9, 12–24. To 1½–2½ ft. high, 2–3 ft. wide. Thickly woolly, near-white leaves are broad (¼–⅜ in. wide), 1½–2 in. long. Widely branching stems that are 10–18 in. long support 1–4-in.-long, interrupted spikes of deep violet blossoms in late summer. Very slow growing; do not cut back hard. This shrub needs perfect drainage; more subject to root rot than English lavenders and lavandins. Difficult to propagate. Many plants sold under this name are varieties of L. × intermedia.

L. lanata hybrids. Zones 4–24. The following crosses of L. lanata with forms of L. angustifolia bloom in mid- to late summer.

'Lisa Marie'. Compact growth to 12–15 in. high and 18–24 in. wide, with silvery leaves that have the color but not the woolly texture of L. lanata. Short spikes of deep violet blossoms with distinct white base, giving bicolor effect. Has cold-hardiness and resistance to root disease of L. angustifolia.

'Richard Gray'. Dense growth to 15 in. high and wide. Silvery gray foliage. Flower stems 4–8 in. long carry short (1–1¼ in.) spikes of vivid violet blossoms; buds and calyxes are deep violet-blue, with a woolly coating.

L. latifolia (L. spica). SPIKE or BROADLEAF LAVENDER. Zones 4–24. Compact growth to 3 ft. high, 1½–2 ft. wide;

gray-green leaves; resembles L. angustifolia. Slender, widely branching flower stems support interrupted spikes 1½–4 in. long; blossoms range from soft mauve to bright violet-blue, with woolly gray calyxes tipped in violet. Blooms in late summer.

L. minutolii. GREEN FERNLEAF LAVENDER. Zones 8, 9, 14–24. Native to Canary Islands. To 2 ft. high and 3 ft. wide, with deeply divided green foliage. Tiny, bright blue flowers are held on stems up to 3 ft. high, summer through fall. Very tolerant of heat and humidity. Responds well to pruning.

L. multifida. FERNLEAF LAVENDER. Zones 16–24. Sprawling growth to 1½ ft. high and 2–3 ft. across. Gray-green to silvery foliage is finely divided into branched segments that are heavily felted with fine hairs. Wiry, branching flower stems rise 10–14 in. above the leaves, with deep blue-violet flowers arranged spirally around a 3–4-in. spike. Blooms spring to fall (all year in mild-winter areas). Remove faded bloom stalks and oldest stems to keep it neat. Has a strong, earthy, medicinal scent. Plants offered as L. pinnata are likely to be L. multifida.

L. officinalis. See L. angustifolia.

L. pinnata. See L. multifida.

L. stoechas. SPANISH LAVENDER. Zones 4–24. Includes several subspecies, all stocky plants 1½–3 ft. high and wide, with narrow gray or gray-green leaves. Small flowers are typically blackish maroon, borne on short, fat, 2-in. spikes topped by two to four flaglike bracts resembling rabbit ears; the bracts come in shades of pink and purple. Blossoms open first in four vertical rows around the spike; then rest of spike fills in with flowers. Blooms spring into summer; often repeats if sheared. Flower stem length varies from 1½ in. to 8 in. or more. Very drought-resistant. Seeds profusely; can be invasive. Named forms include the following.

'Hazel'. To 2½ ft. high, 2 ft. wide. Dense, sturdy mound of gray-green foliage is topped by darkest purple flowers and bright violet bracts. Heavy bloom in spring, modest autumn rebloom.

Lavenders for Fragrance, Flavoring

For sachets and potpourri, cut flower spikes or strip flowers from stems just as blossoms show color; dry in a cool, shady place. Dried spikes make fragrant wreaths, swags, wands. Dried flowers can be used to scent water or soap (the root word for lavender is the Latin for "wash"). To flavor ice cream, pastries, salads, you can use fresh flowers of L. angustifolia and L. × intermedia varieties; other species contain harmful chemicals that should not be ingested.

'Kew Red'. Grows 3–4 ft. tall and wide, with aromatic gray-green foliage. Reddish violet flowers have pink bracts, peak in spring and fall, but bloom nearly all year in mild climates.

'Otto Quast'. To 2 ft. high or a bit more, 2½–3½ ft. wide. Flower stems 2–3 in. long, with maroon blossoms and red-purple bracts. Medium green to gray-green leaves. Plants sold under this name are usually grown from seed and often are shorter than the plant just described, with shorter flower stalks.

Ruffles series. These grow 2 ft. high and wide, and flower about 2 weeks earlier than other Spanish lavenders. All the following are variations on the pink to lavender-pink theme: 'Blueberry Ruffles', 'Boysenberry Ruffles', 'Mulberry Ruffles', and 'Sugarberry Ruffles'.

'Willow Vale'. Vigorous, upright, to 1½ ft. high and wide. Wispy gray-green leaves; deep blue-violet flowers and bluish purple bracts. Short (1–2 in.) flower stems.

'Wings of Night'. Heavy bloomer that resembles 'Otto Quast' but has a broader habit.

'Winter Bee'. About 2 ft. high, with equal or greater spread. Gray-green foliage. Dark purple flowers and lavender bracts appear in early spring, about 3 weeks earlier than those of other Spanish lavenders. Blooms are long lasting.

L. s. pedunculata. Taller than other forms, with longer flower stems. Green or gray-green foliage. Its selection 'Atlas' grows 2½–3 ft. high, about as wide, with 7–14-in.

flower stalks and vibrant red-violet bracts.

L. vera. See L. angustifolia.

L. viridis. GREEN LAVENDER, YELLOW LAVENDER. Zones 8, 9, 12–24. To 2–3 ft. high and wide, with bright green, pine-scented foliage. Short, densely packed, cylindrical flower heads are carried on 1–2-in.-long stems in spring. White or creamy flowers; bracts vary in color from cream through light yellow to bright chartreuse or pale green. Closely related to L. stoechas, with which it crosses readily, producing hybrids with foliage in gray, gray-green, or yellow-green; flowers and bracts come in white, cream, yellow, shrimp pink, salmon, magenta, rose-pink, shades of red-violet and blue-violet, and various greens.

CARE

Lavenders need well-drained soil and little or no fertilizer. They will succeed in cool coastal or mountain climates or inland valleys and deserts but succumb to root rot in areas where heat is accompanied by humidity. Fernleaf sorts (L. canariensis, L. minutolii, L. multifida) as well as L. × allardii, L. 'Goodwin Creek Grey', and L. × heterophylla are tender, but they're more resistant to heat and humidity than English lavenders and lavandins (L. angustifolia, L. × intermedia). Give good air circulation. If mulching around lavenders, use pea gravel, decomposed granite, or sand rather than organic materials. To keep plants neat and compact, shear back by one-third to one-half (even by two-thirds)

L

every year immediately after bloom. If plants become woody and open in center, remove a few of the oldest branches; take out more when new growth comes. If this doesn't work, dig and replace.

Lavatera

TREE MALLOW
Malvaceae
ANNUALS AND EVERGREEN SHRUBS

- 🌡 **ZONES VARY BY SPECIES**
- ☼ **FULL SUN, EXCEPT AS NOTED**
- 💧 **REGULAR WATER, EXCEPT AS NOTED**
- 🦋 **ATTRACT BUTTERFLIES**

Lavatera

These easy-to-grow plants bear hollyhocklike summer flowers on 1½–6-ft. plants.

L. assurgentiflora. Evergreen shrub. Zones 14–24. Native to Southern California's Channel Islands but naturalized on the coastal mainland. Erect growth to 12 ft. tall and wide. Maplelike leaves are lobed and toothed. Rosy lavender, white-striped, 2–3-in.-wide flowers bloom almost throughout the year, heaviest from midspring to late summer. Resists wind, salt spray. Use as fast-growing windbreak hedge. Will reach 5–10 ft. and bloom first year from seed. Shear to keep dense. Little to moderate water.

L. × clementii. Evergreen shrub. Zones 2–9, 14–24. A hybrid between *L. olbia* and *L. thuringiaca*. 'Barnsley' grows 6–8 ft. tall and 6 ft. wide; its rose-centered flowers open white and fade to pink. 'Barnsley Baby' is similar, but grows just 32 in. high. 'Blushing Bride' grows about 5 ft. tall and wide; white flowers like 'Barnsley', but

they don't age to pink. 'Bredon Springs' is a strong grower to 6 ft. tall and wide, with rose-pink flowers and soft gray-green foliage. 'Burgundy Wine', to 4–5 ft. tall and wide, has reddish pink flowers. 'Kew Rose' sports large, mauve-pink flowers on an open-growing plant to 12 ft. tall. 'Rosea', to 6 ft. tall and 6 ft. wide, has pink blossoms.

L. maritima (L. bicolor). Evergreen shrub. Zones 6–9, 12–24. Native to the western Mediterranean. Grows quickly to 6–8 ft. tall and about as wide, with gray-green, maplelike leaves and a summer-long show of light pink, 2–3-in. flowers with dark rose veining and a deep purple center. Open grower; cut back hard to keep it compact. Needs partial to full shade in Zones 12 and 13.

L. thuringiaca. Evergreen shrub. Zones 2–9, 14–24. Native to central and southeastern Europe. Resembles *L. maritima* but has denser growth, greener leaves. Flowers are purplish pink, 3 in. across, nearly everblooming (except in colder-winter zones). 'Red Rum' grows about 4–5 ft. tall and 3–4 ft. wide, with deep pink flowers held on burgundy stems. Plants need winter protection in Zones 2 and 3.

L. trimestris. ANNUAL MALLOW. All zones. Mediterranean native reaches 3–6 ft. tall and wide from spring-sown seed. Satiny flowers up to 4 in. across. Species is seldom seen in gardens; more commonly grown are named varieties with blossoms in white, pink, and rosy carmine. Bloom extends from midsummer to frost if spent flowers are removed to halt seed production. Thin seedlings to allow each plant ample room to spread. Makes a colorful, fast-growing summer hedge or background planting. In mild-winter regions, can also be sown in autumn for winter-to-spring bloom.

Compact (2–3 ft.) varieties include 'Mont Blanc', white; and 'Silver Cup', bright pink. 'Loveliness' has 3½-in. flowers of deep rose veined in a deeper shade, grows up to 3–4 ft. tall and wide. Twins ('Cool White' and 'Hot Pink') grow to 16–20 in. high.

Layia platyglossa

TIDYTIPS
Asteraceae
ANNUAL

- 🌡 **ZONES 1–10, 14–24**
- ☼ **FULL SUN**
- 💧 **LITTLE OR NO WATER**

Layia platyglossa

A classic spring wildflower, this California native crops up in lowland meadows and grasslands, where it covers itself with 2-in. yellow daisies tipped in white. Clumps grow 5–16 in. high and wide. Narrow, hairy, gray-green leaves reach 1¼ in. long; lower leaves are toothed or lobed, upper ones smooth-edged. In cool-summer climates, flowering continues into early summer.

Takes poor and rather heavy soils (but not standing water). Prepare soil as for any garden bed; seeds are usually sown in fall but can also be planted in early spring. Self-sows and will naturalize on banks or in other well-drained sites as long as competition from grasses is minimal. Very drought-tolerant; give occasional water if winter rains fail.

For a classic wild-flower combination, plant tidytips in drifts along with baby blue eyes (*Nemophila menziesii*), sky lupine (*Lupinus nanus*), and globe gilia (*Gilia capitata*).

Leek

Alliaceae
BIENNIAL GROWN AS ANNUAL

- 🌡 **ZONES A3; 1–24; H1, H2**
- ☼ ◐ **PARTIAL SHADE IN HOTTEST CLIMATES**
- 💧 **REGULAR WATER**

Leek

Leeks are related to onions but don't form distinct bulbs. To 2–3 ft. high, with an edible, mild-flavored stem that resembles a long, fat green onion. Eaten by itself or in soups. Excellent varieties include 'Giant Musselburgh', 'Lancelot', 'Lincoln', and 'Shelton'.

Performs best in cool-summer climates, but does well in hotter areas if given some shade.

CARE

Give very rich soil. In cold-winter regions, set out transplants in early spring, or direct sow seeds in late summer for harvest the following year. In mild-winter areas, set out transplants in fall. Sow seeds indoors, ½ in. deep, 1 in. apart, 8 weeks prior to planting date. Space seedlings 2–4 in. apart in a 5-in.-deep furrow. As plants grow, mound soil around stalks to blanch them (this makes the stem bottoms white and mild), keeping mounded soil just below leaf joints.

Harvest when stems are ½–2 in. thick, usually about 4 to 7 months after setting out plants. In cold-winter climates, harvest before ground freezes. (Where ground doesn't freeze, you can leave leeks in place and harvest as needed.) Lift out with spading fork. Offsets may be detached and replanted. If leeks bloom, small bulbils may appear in

L

flower clusters; plant these for later harvest. To prepare leeks for cooking, slice off the roots and all but 2–3 in. of the green leaves; rinse thoroughly, separating layers. Leeks are not bothered by many of the pests and diseases that attack onions.

Lemaireocereus thurberi. See *Stenocereus thurberi*

Leonotis leonurus

LION'S TAIL
Lamiaceae
EVERGREEN SHRUB

🗡 **ZONES 8–24; H1, H2**

☀ **FULL SUN**

◐ **LITTLE OR NO WATER**

🐦 **ATTRACTS BIRDS**

Leonotis leonurus

An open-branching South African shrub that grows to 4–6 ft. tall and wide, lion's tail bears dense whorls of downy orange flowers from summer into fall. Individual blooms are tubular, 2-in. long; leaves are 2–5 in. long. A striking shrub if kept well groomed. Pretty combined in Mediterranean-style perennial beds with lavender and summer–fall blooming salvias.

Combine it with other plants that like the same conditions, such as agaves, aloe, matilija poppy (*Romneya coulteri*), and woolly blue curls (*Trichostema lanatum*). If burned by frost, cut plant back to live growth in spring. Naturalized in Hawaii. There is also a white-flowered form, *L. l. albiflora*.

FOR MORE UNTHIRSTY PLANTS, SEE "PLANTS FOR WATERWISE GARDENS," PAGES 74–78.

Leontopodium alpinum

EDELWEISS
Asteraceae
PERENNIAL

🗡 **ZONES 1–9, 14–17**

☀ **FULL SUN**

💧 **REGULAR WATER**

Leontopodium alpinum

Much loved and legally protected in many Eurasian countries, this small, short-lived alpine perennial is native to the mountains of Europe. To 1 ft. high and wide, it has woolly white stems, leaves, and bracts. Small white flower heads are crowded at stem tips; a collar of slender leaves radiates out from below each flower head—more like the arms of a starfish than like a member of the sunflower family. Tiny bracts of flower heads are tipped with black. Blooms in early summer. Needs excellent drainage.

The "wool" on edelweiss leaves and flowers is an adaptation to its high-elevation origins in the Alps. It helps the plant reflect too-intense ultraviolet light and prevents water loss from drying winds. As a nod to the plant's alpine heritage, plant it in a rough stone trough with rocks as foils.

Lepechinia

PITCHER SAGE
Lamiaceae
EVERGREEN SHRUBS

🗡 **ZONES 7–9, 14–24, EXCEPT AS NOTED**

☀◐ **PARTIAL SHADE IN HOTTEST CLIMATES**

◐ **LITTLE OR NO WATER TO MODERATE WATER**

Lepechinia fragrans 'El Tigre'

Like some sages, these reach 6 ft. tall and nearly as wide, with a rustic native look; once established, they can do without irrigation except in the hottest regions. All have opposite pairs of leaves and short, spike-like clusters of tubular, 1¼-in. flowers with a gaping mouth and prominent calyx. Except as noted, the species listed here are from California's Coast Ranges and bear white to pale pink or lavender blooms. Pitcher sage is almost never browsed by deer.

L. calycina. Lance-shaped to narrowly egg-shaped leaves. Blooms in late spring. 'Rocky Point' grows 2 ft. high, spreading, with lavender flowers in spring.

L. fragrans. Furry gray-green leaves, somewhat squared off at base. Blooms in spring and summer.

L. hastata. Zones 7–9, 14–24; H1. From Mexico; possibly native to Hawaii, where it is called pakaha. Spreads by rhizomes. Arrow-shaped leaves; reddish purple flowers. Main bloom comes in summer, with sporadic flowering during the rest of the year.

FOR OTHER PLANTS THAT DEER TEND TO IGNORE, SEE "DEER-RESISTANT PLANTS," PAGES 53–59.

Leptospermum

TEA TREE
Myrtaceae
EVERGREEN SHRUBS OR TREES

🗡 **ZONES 14–24, EXCEPT AS NOTED**

☀ **FULL SUN**

◐ **LITTLE OR NO WATER TO MODERATE WATER**

Leptospermum scoparium

Soft and casual shrubs or trees, most of these make a display of five-petaled single flowers (somewhat like tiny wild roses) along stems among the small leaves. Blooms are typically white, pink, or red. Petals surround a hard central cone or cup that matures to a woody seed capsule that hangs on for a long time after the petals drop. Native to Australia and New Zealand. Called tea tree because Captain Cook brewed a tea from the leaves and gave it to his crew as a scurvy preventive.

L. laevigatum. AUSTRALIAN TEA TREE. Zones 14–24; H1, H2. Large shrub or small tree 10–30 ft. tall and wide, with oval or teardrop-shaped, dull green to gray-green leaves. Bears ½-in. white flowers in spring. Solitary plants develop picturesque character in maturity, with shaggy, gray-brown, muscular-looking trunks that twist and curve gracefully, reach 2 ft. across at base. Handsome branches range out from trunk and carry canopies of finely textured foliage; some weeping branches hang down from the foliage canopies. To make a windbreak, screen, or clipped hedge, set the plants 3–6 ft. apart, depending on ultimate size of selection. 'Reevesii' grows only 4–5 ft. high and

L

CLOCKWISE FROM TOP: *Lepto-spermum rotundifolium* 'Manning's Choice'; *L. laevigatum*; *L. scoparium* 'Snow White'

wide; has rounder, slightly larger, more densely set leaves, but without the picturesque form of the species.

L. macrocarpum (*L. niti-dum* '**Macrocarpum**'). To 3–15 ft. tall and wide. Tiny, narrow leaves are reddish when new, then mature to purplish bronze. Spring flowers nearly 1 in. wide, chartreuse-yellow with dark green central disk. 'Dark Shadows' grows to 15 ft. tall, 20 ft. wide, with burgundy-flushed leaves.

L. petersonii. LEMON-SCENTED TEA TREE. To 9–20 ft. tall and 6–15 ft. wide. Erect, somewhat open growth with arching or weeping branchlets. Medium green leaves give off strong lemon scent when bruised; Australians occasionally use the dried leaves to make tea. Flowers are small, white, inconspicuous.

L. polygalifolium. Variable size and habit; ranges from 3 to 18 ft. tall, 1½ to 9 ft. wide, and can be upright or spreading.

Narrow leaves are deep green. Showy, very profuse bloom from late spring into summer, when stems are densely set with white, honey-scented, ¾-in.-wide flowers. Attractive cut flowers and foliage. 'Yarra River' has red leaves and grows to 12 ft. tall and wide.

L. rotundifolium '**Manning's Choice**'. Grows 6 ft. tall and slightly wider, with spreading, arching branches. Tiny roundish leaves. Spring flowers to 1 in. across are lavender-pink. Extremely showy in bloom but has a shorter flowering period than *L. scoparium*.

L. scoparium. NEW ZEALAND TEA TREE, MANUKA. Zones 14–24; H1, H2. Not as bold in form or as serviceable in hedges and screens as *L. laevigatum*, but its half-inch flowers are showier: single or double, in white, pink, or red, profuse in spring and summer. Branches densely set with needlelike green leaves. Good in containers.

'**Apple Blossom**'. Upright growth to 8 ft. tall and wide. Pale pink double flowers age to white. Leaves tinge pink in cold weather.

'**Burgundy Queen**'. Upright, dense grower to 12 ft. tall, 10 ft. wide. Double flowers are deep burgundy. Cold weather flushes foliage with burgundy tones.

'**Crimson Glory**'. Grows 6–7 ft. tall and wide. Crimson double flowers; bronzy foliage.

'**Gaiety Girl**'. Slow growing to 5 ft. tall, 4 ft. wide. Double flowers are pink with lilac tint. Reddish foliage.

'**Helene Strybing**'. To 6–10 ft. tall and wide with an open, picturesque habit. Rich, deep pink, single flowers are a bit larger than those of other varieties.

'**Horizontalis**'. Fast growing to 3–4 ft. tall, 12 ft. wide, with horizontal branches and drooping branchlets. Single white flowers. Good bank cover.

'**Pink Cascade**'. To 1 ft. high, 3–4 ft. wide. Single pink flowers on sprawling, weeping branches. Attractive trailing over walls, among rocks.

'**Pink Pearl**'. To 6–10 ft. tall, 5–8 ft. wide. Pale pink buds open into double blush pink to white flowers.

'**Ruby Glow**'. Compact, upright growth to 6–8 ft. tall, 4–5 ft. wide. Dark foliage and ¾-in. double blooms in oxblood red; entire shrub looks red.

'**Silver and Rose**'. Dense growth to 4–5 ft. tall and wide. Abundant rose-pink, green-centered flowers; bright gray-green foliage.

'**Snow White**'. Spreading, compact growth 2–4 ft. tall, 4–5 ft. wide. Double white flowers with green centers.

CARE

If planted in well-drained, slightly acid soil, tea trees are long-lived plants requiring little care. Where drainage is poor, they sometimes succumb quickly to root rot. Need minimal pruning, though you may want to thin growth to emphasize a picturesque habit. When clipping or shearing into hedges, don't cut into bare wood—new growth is unlikely to sprout. Old shrubs that become overgrown or bare at the base can be limbed up into small trees. Plants thrive in seacoast conditions.

FOR OTHER PLANTS THAT MAKE GOOD HEDGES, SEE PAGES 44–45.

Lettuce
Asteraceae
ANNUAL

⚊ ALL ZONES

☼ ◑ **PARTIAL SHADE IN HOTTEST CLIMATES**

💧 **REGULAR WATER**

Butterhead lettuce 'Marveille des Quatre Saisons'

Probably from Asia Minor, leaf lettuce has been popular for at least 2,000 years, and head lettuce for about 500. There are four principal types of lettuce: crisphead, butterhead or Boston, loose-leaf, and romaine.

Crisphead is the most exasperating for home gardeners to produce. Heads form best when monthly average temperatures are 55°F to 60°F (13°C to 16°C). In mild climates, this type of lettuce does well over a long season, but in hot-summer areas, the timing of planting becomes critical. Start with the Iceberg type 'Summertime', or try one of the easier Batavian varieties (also called Summer Crisp and French Crisp) such as 'Nevada' or 'Loma'. The Batavians have young leaves like leaf lettuce, and form small crisp heads.

Butterhead or Boston type has a loose head with green, smooth outer leaves and yellow inner leaves. Good varieties include 'Bibb' ('Limestone'), 'Buttercrunch', and 'Tom Thumb'.

Loose-leaf lettuce makes a rosette rather than a head. Because these are easy and stand heat well, this is the biggest category of lettuce. Choice selections include 'Blackseeded Simpson', 'Simpson Elite', and 'Oak Leaf' (all with green leaves); 'Salad Bowl' (with deeply cut green leaves); and 'New Red Fire' and 'Red Sails' (red-tinged leaves).

Romaine lettuce is also called Cos, for the Aegean island where it originated. It has an erect, cylindrical head of smooth leaves; outer leaves are green, inner ones whitish. Stands heat moderately well. Try 'Flashy Trout Back', 'Little Gem', or 'Winter Density'.

Lettuce leaves that are tinted or splashed with bronzy or reddish hues add color to a salad. 'Flashy Butter Oak', 'Marveille des Quatre Saisons', and 'Speckles' are butterheads; 'Dark Lollo Rossa', 'Merlot', 'Red Oak Leaf', and 'Red Deer Tongue' are loose-leaf varieties; 'Rouge d'Hiver' and 'Outredgeous' are romaines.

Various loose-leaf and romaine lettuce varieties are typically included in mesclun mixes—mixtures of fast-growing, tender salad greens (usually some mild and some tangy) that may include mustards, arugula, cress, chicory, radicchio, and/or mizuna.

Many lettuce varieties have been bred to resist bolting (going to seed) when it gets hot. If you live in a hot-summer climate or one where temperatures jump suddenly, look for these.

CARE

Lettuces need loose, well-drained soil. Sow in open ground, barely covering the seeds. Loose-leaf lettuce can be grown as close as 4 in. apart; thin all other types to 1 ft. apart.

For prolonged harvest, sow at 2-week intervals. In cold-winter regions, begin sowing seeds for all types after frost; where summers are very short, sow indoors, then transplant seedlings outdoors after last frost. In mild-winter, cool-summer regions, sow in early spring for spring and summer harvest, then make further sowings in late summer or early fall for winter harvest. In mild-winter, hot-summer areas, grow only as a winter and early-spring crop.

Feed plants lightly and frequently. Control snails, slugs, and earwigs. Harvest when heads or leaves are of good size; once lettuce reaches maturity, it rapidly goes to seed, becoming quite bitter. With loose-leaf lettuce, clip off just the outer leaves as you need them.

Leucadendron
Proteaceae
EVERGREEN TREES AND SHRUBS

⚟ **ZONES 16, 17, 20–24; H1**
☀ **FULL SUN**
💧 **MODERATE WATER**

Leucadendron 'Safari Sunset'

Some of these South African natives are trees, some shrubs; some are grown for their flowers, some for their foliage. All are related to *Protea*; see that entry for culture. Male and female flowers are borne on separate plants at stem tips. In some shrubby species, conelike male flower clusters sit above showy colored bracts and have the look of giant daisies. Female flower clusters are less showy and develop into conelike seed clusters.

L. argenteum. SILVER TREE. Tree. Young plants are narrow, stiffly upright, and, thanks to their more symmetrical form, more spectacular than older ones. Mature trees have twisted gray trunks and a spreading, irregular silhouette; can reach 40 ft. by 25–30 ft., though they are more typically half that size. Silky, silvery white leaves densely cover the branches. Leaves are good for arrangements; flowers and fruit are inconsequential.

Needs fast-draining soil; doesn't tolerate soil that is alkaline or amended with animal manure. Needs humid air; takes ocean winds but not dry winds. Small plants are picturesque container subjects for 3 or 4 years; larger ones are effective on slopes (good way to give them the excellent drainage they need) when combined with boulders, succulents, and pines in sheltered seaside gardens. Use singly or in groups.

L. discolor. Shrub. Upright, slightly spreading growth to 4–8 ft. tall and wide. Stems are densely set with gray-green leaves. Red-centered gold inflorescences appear in early fall or winter, and dry well for arrangements. 'Flame Tip' has yellow bracts that underlie orange and red blossoms. 'Pom Pom' is a showy male selection with white to pale yellow bracts surrounding orange-red cones.

L. galpinii. Shrub. Erect growth to 6–8 ft. tall and 4–6 ft. wide. Narrow, gray-green foliage. Male plants sport yellow pompon flowers; female plants produce soft gray, pink-tinged cones favored in arrangements.

L. hybrids. Shrubs. 'Pisa' is a fast, dense grower to 6 ft. tall, 3–5 ft. wide, with willowy, gray-green leaves; silver cones are surrounded by yellow-green bracts in spring. 'Jester' has cream-and-green-variegated leaves that flush deep pink at branch ends. 'Red Gem' is compact, 4 ft. tall, 5 ft. wide, with red bracts and yellow cones. 'Safari Sunset' is vigorous and upright, to 8–10 ft. tall and 6–8 ft. wide, with intensely red bracts in summer that fade to light yellow in the center by late winter; tolerant of frost and clay soils.

Leucadendron stems are great in fresh and dried arrangements. Snip branch tips when color is at its height, strip off any leaves that would be submerged in the vase, and change water frequently. To dry, hang stems upside down or stand them up in an empty bucket in a cool, dry spot for about three weeks.

Leucanthemum
Asteraceae
PERENNIALS AND ANNUAL

⚟ **ZONES VARY BY SPECIES**
☀ **FULL SUN**
💧 **MODERATE WATER**
🦋 **ATTRACT BUTTERFLIES**

Leucanthemum × superbum 'Old Court'

Until recently, the following three species—including Shasta daisy, which is arguably the most well-known chrysanthemum—were classed as *Chrysanthemum* species. All bear the beautiful white summer daisies that are cottage-garden essentials.

L. paludosum (Chrysanthemum paludosum). Annual. Zones A1–A3; 1–24. Western Mediterranean native forms about 8-in.-wide clumps of dark green, deeply toothed leaves. In summer, bears white flowers resembling miniature Shasta daisies on 8–10-in. stems. Sometimes lives over for a second bloom season. Popular annual in Alaska.

L. × superbum (Chrysanthemum maximum). SHASTA DAISY. Perennial. Zones A1–A3; 1–24; H1. To 2–4 ft. tall, 2 ft. wide. Luther Burbank's original hybrid, with coarse, leathery leaves and gold-centered, 2–4-in.-wide white flowers, has been largely superseded by longer-blooming varieties with larger, better-formed flowers. Available in single, double, quilled, and shaggy-flowered forms. Most are white. All bloom in summer; some start in late spring and continue into fall. All are splendid in borders and as cut flowers. Easy from seed. Catalogs

L

offer many strains, including some yellow forms and dwarfs that reach only 10–15 in. high.

Set out container-grown plants at any time, divisions in autumn or early spring (divide established clumps every 2 or 3 years). Give these moist, well-drained, fairly rich soil, fertilizing before and during bloom to encourage large flowers. Full sun is optimal, but partial shade is acceptable in hot-summer climates; double-flowered kinds hold up better in very light shade. In coldest regions, mulch around plants without smothering foliage. Shasta daisies are generally easy to grow but can be troubled by gall, a disease that causes the root crown to split into many weak, poorly rooted growing points that soon die. Dig out and discard affected plants, and do not replant Shasta daisies in the same spot. When buying plants, avoid those with signs of fasciation (flattening or widening of stems) near root crown. Control slugs and snails.

L. vulgare (Chrysanthemum leucanthemum). OX-EYE DAISY, COMMON DAISY. Perennial. Zones A2, A3; 1–24; H1. European native naturalized in many places; spreads by rhizomes and self-seeding. To 2 ft. high, 1 ft. wide, with bright green foliage and yellow-centered daisies from late spring to fall. 'May Queen' begins blooming in early spring.

Shasta daisy is a cutting-garden essential whose snowy white blooms last a long time in a vase. Grow it with other vigorous perennials good for cutting, like Peruvian lily (*Alstroemeria*), coreopsis, purple coneflower (*Echinacea purpurea*), and pincushion flower (*Scabiosa*).

Leucojum
SNOWFLAKE
Amaryllidaceae
PERENNIALS FROM BULBS

✎ **ZONES VARY BY SPECIES**

☼ ☽ **FULL SUN DURING BLOOM, LIGHT SHADE AFTER IN HOT CLIMATES**

💧 **REGULAR WATER DURING GROWTH AND BLOOM**

Leucojum aestivum

These lovely white, bell-shaped spring flowers are prettier the closer you look. Native to Europe, they are sometimes confused with closely related snowdrops (*Galanthus*) because of their similar common names and flowers (white marked with green). But *Leucojum* is generally bigger and, in cold-winter climates, later to bloom. Naturalize these under deciduous trees or in shrub borders.

L. aestivum. SUMMER SNOWFLAKE. Zones 1–10, 14–24. Leaves 1–1½ ft. long. Stems are 1½ ft. tall, each carrying three to five inch-long flowers. 'Gravetye Giant' is a bit taller and larger-flowered than the species and bears as many as nine flowers per stem. Common name "summer snowflake" is misleading—in mild-winter areas, plants can bloom during the period from late fall through winter; in colder regions, blossoms appear in midspring.

L. vernum. SPRING SNOWFLAKE. Zones 1–6. Flourishes in areas with definite winter cold; generally unsuccessful where temperatures remain above 20°F (–7°C). Leaves are 9 in. long. In earliest spring, each foot-long stem bears a single large white flower (occasionally two).

CARE

Plant in fall, setting bulbs 3–4 in. deep, 4 in. apart. Give some water during summer dormancy; *L. aestivum* can get by without any if soil is shaded. Don't disturb clumps until really crowded. When this occurs, dig clumps after foliage dies down, then divide and replant immediately.

Leucophyllum
TEXAS RANGER, SILVERLEAF
Scrophulariaceae
EVERGREEN SHRUBS

✎ **ZONES 7–24, EXCEPT AS NOTED**

☼ **FULL SUN**

◐ 💧 **LITTLE TO MODERATE WATER**

🐦 **ATTRACT BIRDS**

Leucophyllum langmaniae

Compact and slow growing, these shrubs have silvery or green foliage and a good show of ½–1-in.-wide flowers with an open bell shape. Bloom may come at varying times of the year, often after summer showers. Need very good drainage. Tolerate heat, wind, and alkaline soil. Use as informal or clipped hedges, massed as shrub cover, or in mixed dry-country gardens. Unless hedged, plants require little pruning. Rejuvenate old and straggling plants by cutting them close to the ground. Native to the Southwest and northern Mexico.

L. candidum. VIOLET SILVERLEAF. To 5 ft. tall and wide, with small, silvery leaves and deep purple flowers. 'Silver Cloud' is a heavy bloomer with very white foliage. 'Thunder Cloud' is smaller than the species (to 3–4 ft. tall and wide) and has deeper purple, more closely spaced blossoms.

L. frutescens. TEXAS RANGER, TEXAS SAGE, CENIZO. Zones 7–24; H1, H2. To 6–8 ft. tall and wide, with gray foliage and light purple flowers. 'Green Cloud' has bright green foliage and dark rose or magenta flowers; it may be deciduous in coldest winters. 'White Cloud' has gray foliage and white flowers. 'Compacta', with gray foliage and pink flowers, grows to 5 ft. tall and wide.

L. laevigatum. CHIHUAHUAN SAGE. Open, angular growth to 4 ft. tall, 5 ft. wide. Tiny dark green leaves; profuse lavender flowers.

L. langmaniae. Dense grower to 5 ft. tall and wide, with bright green leaves and lavender flowers. 'Lynn's Legacy' ('Lynn's Everblooming') flowers profusely over a long period in summer, even in coastal California. 'Rio Bravo' has rich green foliage and requires little pruning to maintain a tight, rounded form.

L. pruinosum. Open growth habit to 6 ft. tall and wide, with silvery foliage. Purple flowers have a strong fragrance of grape bubble gum. 'Sierra Bouquet' is exceptionally fragrant.

L. 'Rain Cloud'. Hybrid derived from *L. frutescens*. Erect growth to 6 ft. tall, 3–4 ft. wide. Small, silvery leaves; violet-blue flowers.

L. revolutum. Slow growth to about 4 ft. tall, 4–5 ft. wide, with light green, somewhat succulent foliage. Bears purple flowers that appear in fall, later than for other leucophyllums. 'Houdini' has larger, showier blossoms than the species.

L. zygophyllum. To 3 ft. high and wide, with gray-green, slightly cupped leaves and light blue flowers. 'Cimarron' is a dense grower with bluish purple flowers tightly packed along stems; leaves have a distinctly cupped shape.

Texas rangers can bloom in response to increased humidity. They flower a few days before a rainstorm, earning them the nickname "barometer bush."

Leucospermum

PINCUSHION
Proteaceae
EVERGREEN SHRUBS

✎ ZONES 15–17, 21–24; H1

☼ FULL SUN

💧 MODERATE WATER

Leucospermum

Like proteas, pincushions are difficult to grow, but extra effort is rewarded with spectacular clusters of many long, slender tubular flowers in a large, thistlelike head. These South African natives produce stunning cut flowers that last for a month in water. Leaves are narrow, stalkless ovals, crowded along stems. Bloom peaks in late winter and early spring, but can start earlier and last up to 6 months in mild winters. Well-established plants can take several degrees of frost; side buds will produce flowers even if main flower buds freeze. Prune only to shape or remove dead flowers. For cultural information, see *Protea*.

L. cordifolium. NODDING PINCUSHION. Compact habit to 4 ft. tall and wide. Medium green leaves. Best species for cut flowers: blossom clusters are 4 in. across, with individual tube-shaped, yellow-tipped coral flowers that curve gracefully outward, then inward again. 'Flame Giant' has orange inflorescences, while 'Yellow Bird' has yellow ones.

L. reflexum. ROCKET PINCUSHION. Sprawling growth to 12 ft. tall and wide, with attractive gray foliage. Orange-rose, 4-in. flower heads. As the flowers age, the "pins" curl downward, giving blossoms a shaggy look.

Leucothoe

Ericaceae
EVERGREEN SHRUBS

✎ ZONES VARY BY SPECIES

☼ ☽ FULL SUN IN COOLER CLIMATES ONLY

💧 💧 💧 WATER NEEDS VARY BY SPECIES

☘ LEAVES AND NECTAR ARE POISONOUS IF INGESTED

Leucothoe axillaris 'Curly Red'

Good filler plants that are best used in masses; smaller ones are even effective in mixed containers. They have leathery leaves and clusters of small, urn-shaped creamy white flowers. Need deep, acid, humus-rich soil; well suited to woodland gardens. Keep out of drying winds. For shape and neatness, prune oldest stems to the ground occasionally.

L. axillaris. COAST LEUCOTHOE. Zones 4–7, 15–17. Native to southeastern U.S. Spreading, arching plant 2–4 ft. tall, 3–6 ft. wide. Leaves are bronze when they emerge; they mature to dark green, then turn red in winter. Drooping, 1–3-in.-long flower clusters held along stems in midspring. Regular water. 'Curly Red' has red new growth that ages to apple green; leaves are tightly curled.

L. davisiae. SIERRA LAUREL. Zones 2, 4–7, 15–17. Native to bogs and wet places in Siskiyou and Sierra Nevada mountains. Upright shrub to 3 ft. high and 5 ft. wide. Glossy green leaves are bronze-tinted in winter. Flowers in erect, 2–4-in.-long clusters bloom in early summer. Ample water.

L. fontanesiana (L. catesbaei, L. walteri). DROOPING LEUCOTHOE. Zones 4–7, 15–17. Native to eastern U.S. Grows slowly to 3–6 ft. tall and wide, spreading by underground stems. Branches arch gracefully. Leaves turn bronzy purple in fall (remain greener in deep shade). Drooping, 1½–2½-in.-long clusters of flowers bloom in midspring. Moderate water.

'Nana'. To 2 ft. high, spreading to 6 ft. wide. Leaves turn bronzy red in winter.

'Rainbow'. To 5 ft. tall and 6 ft. wide, with green leaves marbled cream and pink.

'Rollissoni'. Grows 3 ft. high and 6 ft. wide, with shorter, narrower leaves that turn beet red in fall.

'Scarletta'. To 2 ft. high and 4 ft. wide. Leaves are bright red when new; they turn green by summer, then deep red in fall and winter.

Levisticum officinale

LOVAGE
Apiaceae
PERENNIAL

✎ ZONES 4–9, 12–24

☼ ☽ LIGHT AFTERNOON SHADE IN HOTTEST CLIMATES

💧 REGULAR WATER

Levisticum officinale

Used as an ornamental, an herb, and as an edible plant, lovage grows in clumps that can reach 6 ft. tall (but 3 ft. is typical). Divided, glossy deep green leaves rise from clumps in summer, hollow stems crowned by sprays of flat-topped greenish yellow flower clusters. It is similar to angelica. Seeds are valued for their celery flavor, leaves are added to salads and soups, and even the roots are eaten. Sow seeds in place in fall; or start in containers and transplant into the spring garden. You can also divide an established clump in early spring. From the eastern Mediterranean region.

Lewisia

Portulacaceae
PERENNIALS

✎ ZONES 1–7, 14–17, EXCEPT AS NOTED

☼ ☽ FULL SUN OR LIGHT SHADE

💧 💧 LITTLE TO MODERATE WATER

Lewisia cotyledon Sunset strain

Exquisite flowers in many colors cover low plants that rise from thick, drought-adapted roots. All need excellent drainage; plant with fine gravel around crowns. Of the many kinds offered by specialists, the following are outstanding.

L. columbiana. From Oregon and Washington. Pink and white flowers emerge in airy sprays from an 8-in. rosette of narrow leaves.

L. cotyledon. From Northern California, southern Oregon; widely known as 'Cliff Maids'. To about 1 ft. high, 10 in. wide. Rosettes of narrow, fleshy, evergreen leaves bear 10-in. stems topped by large, extremely showy clusters of 1-in., white or pink flowers often striped rose or red. Blooms from spring to early summer. Prune out side growth to maintain air circulation around root crown. Can be grown in pots of fast-draining sterilized soil or growing mixes. Several floriferous hybrids, such as the Sunset strain, are also available in many colors.

L. rediviva. BITTERROOT. Native to mountains of the West. To 2 in. high, 4 in. wide.

L

»

State flower of Montana. Fleshy roots; short stems with short, succulent, strap-shaped leaves that typically die back before flowers appear (seemingly from bare earth) in spring. Flowers, borne singly on short stems, look like 2-in.-wide water lilies in rosy pink or white. Not difficult if drainage is excellent.

L. tweedyi. Zones A2, A3; 1–7, 14–17. Native to mountains of south central Washington. To 8 in. high, 1 ft. wide. Stunning big, satiny, salmon-pink flowers, one to three to a stem, bloom above fleshy, evergreen, 4-in. leaves. Prune out side growth to keep root crown open to air. Winter moisture is a problem; grow plants in pots and turn them on their sides in wet weather.

Leycesteria formosa

HIMALAYAN HONEYSUCKLE, HIMALAYAN PHEASANTBERRY
Caprifoliaceae
DECIDUOUS SHRUB

| 🌡 **ZONES 4–6, 14–17, 20–24** |
| ☀ ◑ **FULL SUN OR LIGHT SHADE** |
| 💧 **REGULAR WATER** |
| 🐦 **BERRIES ATTRACT BIRDS** |

Leycesteria formosa

This shrub grows fast to 6 ft. tall and wide, producing impressive flowers and berries. Stems are a handsome gray-green when young, later turning bright green. Paired bright green leaves to 6 in. long.

From summer to early fall, inflorescences form at branch tips and in upper leaf joints; the small white flowers are less conspicuous than the purplish bracts that partially conceal them. Inflorescences are 1–2 in. long at first, then gradually lengthen to 6 in. Blossoms are followed by berries that start out green, rapidly turn deep red, then become purplish black (all three colors are present at once). In cold-winter areas, shoots may freeze back; cut to the ground in late winter or early spring, they quickly regrow.

Leymus

LYME GRASS, WILD RYE
Poaceae
PERENNIAL GRASSES

| 🌡 **ZONES VARY BY SPECIES** |
| ☀ ◑ **FULL SUN OR LIGHT SHADE** |
| 💧 **LITTLE TO MODERATE WATER** |

Leymus arenarius
'Blue Dune'

These sturdy grasses are grown principally for their blue-gray or silvery blue foliage. Very drought-tolerant; will remain evergreen with some summer water. These were formerly assigned to *Elymus* but are now known as *Leymus* (an anagram of "Elymus"). For other types of blue-leafed grasses, see *Elymus magellanicus, Festuca,* and *Helictotrichon sempervirens.*

L. arenarius (Elymus arenarius). BLUE LYME GRASS. Zones A2, A3; 1–9, 14–24. From coastal northern and western Europe. Low, vigorous clump of gray-blue leaves topped by clusters of inconspicuous flowers. To 3–4 ft. in bloom, spreading widely by thick rhizomes. Good soil binder; may need curbing. Flowers are not especially attractive, and plant looks best when cut back after bloom to stimulate fresh foliage. Does best in cool weather but withstands considerable heat.

Grows in sandy soils in the wild; tolerates clay soils. Often sold as 'Glaucus', which is identical to the species. 'Blue Dune' is especially silvery blue.

L. condensatus. Zones 7–12, 14–24. Native to coastal Southern California and Channel Islands. Species is usually green-leafed, reaching 9 ft. tall and 6 ft. wide in bloom. More commonly grown is 'Canyon Prince', to 4 ft. tall and 3 ft. wide; foliage is green when new, maturing to brilliant silvery blue. Spreads slowly by rhizomes.

Liatris spicata

GAYFEATHER, BLAZING STAR
Asteraceae
PERENNIAL FROM CORMS

| 🌡 **ZONES A2, A3; 1–10, 14–24** |
| ☀ **FULL SUN** |
| 💧 **REGULAR WATER** |
| 🦋 **ATTRACTS BUTTERFLIES** |

Liatris spicata

From eastern and central North America. Showy bloomer to 4 ft. tall, 1½ ft. wide. Basal tufts of grassy leaves grow from thick, often tuberous rootstocks. In summer, tufts lengthen into tall stems densely set with leaves and topped by "foxtails" of small light purple flowers with prominent stamens. Blossom spikes open from the top downward. Best-known selection is 'Kobold' (2 ft. tall), with bright rosy lilac flowers. The Blazing Stars series comes in purple and white. 'Floristan White' ('Floristan Alba' or 'Alba') has white flowers; 30 in. tall.

Endures heat, cold, aridity, poor soil. Needs moderately fertile, well-drained soil; sensitive to soggy soil during winter dormancy. In spring, start nursery transplants or set out rootstocks 2 in. deep, 6–8 in. apart. When performance declines, divide clumps in early spring.

Libertia

Iridaceae
PERENNIALS

| 🌡 **ZONES 8, 9, 14–24** |
| ☀ ◑ **LIGHT SHADE IN HOTTEST CLIMATES** |
| 💧 **REGULAR WATER** |

Libertia peregrinans

Iris relatives with swordlike leaves in fans and clusters of white flowers from late spring to midsummer. Blooms consist of three large petals and three much smaller ones, giving them a triangular look. Those listed here are New Zealand natives.

L. grandiflora. Relatively broad, bright green leaves make a clump 2 ft. high, 1½ ft. wide. Branching clusters of ¾-in. flowers on 2½-ft. stems.

L. ixioides. Like *L. grandiflora,* but leaves are narrower, each with a light green to orange-hued central stripe. 'Goldfinger' has a yellow-gold central leaf band. 'Taupo Blaze' leaves turn shades of pink, orange, and green in fall, with orange berries.

L. peregrinans. To 2 ft. high, 1 ft. wide; forms colonies by rhizomes. Narrow, stiffly erect olive green leaves have an orange to brownish orange center stripe; especially attractive when backlit. Branching clusters of inch-wide flowers on stems shorter than leaves. Good in containers. 'Bronze Sword' is more compact at 1–1½ ft. tall.

Libocedrus. See *Calocedrus*

Ligularia

Asteraceae
PERENNIALS

- ✿ **ZONES 1–9, 14–17, EXCEPT AS NOTED**
- ◑ **PARTIAL SHADE, EXCEPT AS NOTED**
- ◌ **AMPLE MOISTURE**

Ligularia dentata

These stately East Asian perennials form 3-ft.-wide clumps of large leaves topped by yellow to orange daisies. All need rich soil and plenty of moisture; they do not tolerate heat or low humidity. Best with morning or afternoon sun and midday shade; or with dappled shade all day. The more sun they get, the more water they need. Good around pools, along streambeds, in bog gardens. Control slugs and snails. Clumps can remain undisturbed for years, but divide them in early spring when you want more.

L. dentata. Grown primarily for big, attractive leaves (to more than 1 ft. across), roundish with heart-shaped base. In midsummer to early fall, sends up 3–5-ft. stems topped by large, branching heads of 4-in.-wide, orange-yellow daisies. 'Othello' (grows in Zones A2, A3; 1–9, 14–17) and 'Desdemona' have deep purple leafstalks, veins, and leaf undersides; upper surfaces of leaves are green.

L. 'Osiris Café Noir'. Grows 20 in. high and nearly as wide. Purple-black new growth progressively lightens through bronze to green. Leathery leaves have serrated margins. Yellow flowers appear on 20-in. stems in mid- to late summer.

L. przewalskii. Deeply lobed and cut leaves grow to 1 ft. wide. Dark purplish flower-

ing stalks rise to about 6 ft., topped with dense, narrow spires of ¾-in. yellow daisy flowers in summer. In the Pacific Northwest, can take full sun.

L. stenocephala. Zones A2, A3; 1–9, 14–17. Especially stunning flower spikes. Usually represented by variety 'The Rocket', which forms a large clump of foot-wide, irregularly toothed leaves topped by tall (up to 5 ft.), narrow, dark-stemmed spires bearing many 1½-in. yellow daisies in summer.

L. tussilaginea. See *Farfugium japonicum*.

Ligustrum

PRIVET
Oleaceae
EVERGREEN, SEMIEVERGREEN, AND DECIDUOUS SHRUBS AND TREES

- ✿ **ZONES VARY BY SPECIES**
- ☀ ◑ **FULL SUN OR PARTIAL SHADE**
- ◌ **REGULAR WATER**
- ◊ **LEAVES AND FRUITS CAUSE GASTRIC DISTRESS IF INGESTED**
- 🐝 **FLOWERS ATTRACT BEES, BERRIES ATTRACT BIRDS**

Ligustrum japonicum 'Texanum'

More useful than beautiful, these Old World natives are widely used as hedges, though one type is a street tree; can also be clipped into formal shapes and featured in tubs or large pots. All bear abundant, showy clusters of white to creamy white flowers in late spring or early summer (some people find the scent unpleasant). Clipped hedges bloom less heavily, since shearing removes most of the flower-bearing branches. Blossoms are followed by small berries that birds spread around.

Nurseries sometimes misidentify certain privets. The plant sold as *L. japonicum* very often turns out to be the tree species *L. lucidum*. The true *L. japonicum* is available in two or more forms. The tall, shrubby kind is the true species; the lower-growing and more densely foliaged form is often sold as *L. texanum* but probably should be called *L. japonicum* 'Texanum'.

Smaller-leafed hardy privets used for hedging are also often confused. *L. ovalifolium* and *L. vulgare* look much alike, and any of these are likely to be sold as "common privet"—a name that rightly belongs only to *L. vulgare*.

L. japonicum. JAPANESE PRIVET, WAX-LEAF PRIVET. Evergreen shrub. Zones 4–24; H1, H2; except as noted. From northern China, Korea, and Japan. To 10–12 ft. tall, 8 ft. wide, with dense, compact habit. Roundish oval leaves have a thick, slightly spongy feel; they are glossy medium to dark green above, distinctly paler beneath. Excellent for hedges, screens, and topiary. With lower limbs pruned off, also makes an attractive small standard tree. Sunburns in hot spells. In areas where there is hardpan or where Texas root rot prevails, grow it in containers.

'Nobilis'. Grows to 8 ft. tall and 3 ft. wide.

'Recurvifolium'. Leaves are wavy-edged, twisted at the tip, and slightly smaller than those of the species. Somewhat open grower.

'Rotundifolium'. To 5 ft. tall and 3 ft. wide, with nearly round leaves to 2½ in. long. Give partial shade in hottest climates.

'Texanum'. Zones 3a–24; H1, H2. Very similar to species but lower growing (to 8–10 ft. tall, 4–6 ft. wide), with somewhat denser, lusher foliage. Useful as a windbreak. This plant is often sold as the species.

'Variegatum'. Leaves have creamy white margins and blotches.

L. lucidum. GLOSSY PRIVET. Evergreen tree. Zones 5–24; H1, H2. Native to China, Korea, and Japan. Roundheaded tree to 20–40 ft. tall and wide, with one or several trunks. Glossy leaves are tapered and pointed, medium to dark green on both sides. They feel leathery but lack the slightly spongy feel of *L. japonicum* leaves. Flowers bloom in especially large, feathery clusters in late spring and early summer; they are followed by a profuse crop of fruit. Can be used as lawn tree or planted 10 ft. apart for tall privacy

L

screen or windbreak. Performs well in large pots.

Before planting this tree, carefully consider its disadvantages. Eventual fruit crop is immense; never plant where fruit will fall on cars, walks, or other paved areas (it stains). Fallen seeds (and those dropped by birds) sprout profusely in groundcovers and will need pulling. Many people dislike the flowers' odor, and fruiting clusters are bare and unattractive after fruit drop.

L. ovalifolium. CALIFORNIA PRIVET. Evergreen only in warmest winter climates. Zones 3b–24; H1, H2. Native to Japan. Dark green, oval, 2½-in. leaves. Grows rapidly to 8–15 ft. tall, 6–10 ft. wide, but can be kept sheared as a 4-ft. hedge. For hedging, set plants 9–12 in. apart. Clip early and frequently to encourage low, dense branching. Greedy roots. Well-fed, well-watered plants hold their foliage longest. Tolerates heat. 'Aureum', golden privet, has yellow-edged leaves; it is often sold as 'Variegatum'.

L. 'Suwannee River'. Evergreen shrub. Zones 4–24. Reported to be a hybrid between *L. japonicum* 'Rotundifolium' and *L. lucidum*. Slow-growing, compact plant grows 3–4 ft. tall and wide. Leathery, somewhat twisted dark green leaves; no fruit. Use as low hedge, foundation planting, or in containers.

L. 'Vicaryi'. VICARY GOLDEN PRIVET. Deciduous shrub. Zones 2–24. To 8–10 ft. tall and wide. Yellow leaves; color is most pronounced on plants in full sun. Best planted alone; color does not develop well under hedge shearing.

L. vulgare. COMMON PRIVET. Deciduous shrub. Zones 2–24; H1. From northern Europe, the Mediterranean, and Asia Minor. To 15 ft. tall, 12 ft. wide. Dark green leaves are less glossy than those of *L. ovalifolium*, and root system is not as greedy. Clusters of black fruit are conspicuous on unpruned or lightly pruned plants. 'Lodense' is a dense dwarf that reaches only 4 ft. tall and wide.

FOR OTHER PLANTS THAT ATTRACT BIRDS AND BEES, SEE PAGES 95–99 AND 104–105.

Lilium

LILY
Liliaceae
PERENNIALS FROM BULBS

- 🖊 ZONES VARY BY SPECIES OR TYPE
- ☼ ◑ ROOTS COOL, TOPS IN SUN OR FILTERED LIGHT
- 💧 REGULAR WATER, EXCEPT AS NOTED
- 🦋 ATTRACT BUTTERFLIES

Oriental lily 'Casablanca'

The most stately and varied of bulbous plants, these range in height from 1 to 9 ft., and have large, colorful, often fragrant flowers that are equally effective on the plant or in the vase. Most are easy to grow in the ground or in containers. Lilies range wild across Asia, Europe, and North America, and many of these species make excellent garden subjects. But most gardeners grow hybrid lilies optimized for fragrance, color, habit, and garden performance. Both species and hybrids are rewarding landscape subjects.

Although the official classification of lilies lists eight divisions of hybrids and a ninth division of species, the following describes only the lilies easily available to Western gardeners. Advances in breeding continue to produce new lilies faster than books can list them. Consult specialists' catalogs to learn about these wonders.

Asiatic hybrids. Zones A1–A3; 1–9, 14–24. Derived primarily from Chinese species. These are easy to grow and the most reliable for the average garden, so breeders produce them by the score. They are also the first to bloom (early summer). Flowers are usually unscented. Some of the hybrids have upward-facing flowers, while others have horizontal or drooping blooms. Stems are strong and erect, and range in height from short (1½ ft.) to moderate (4½ ft.). Flowers (mostly singles, but a few doubles as well) come in virtually every color but blue, many with dark spots or contrasting bands of color. Some noteworthy examples include 'Fata Morgana' (double yellow), 'Graffity' (greenish yellow petals with maroon speckles coalescing into a deep maroon center), 'Landini' (plum black), 'Orange Cocotte' (clear orange, upward facing, pollen free), and 'Red Velvet' (dark red, pendant flowers).

Aurelian hybrids (trumpet lily hybrids). Zones 3–9, 14–24. Derived from Asiatic species such as *L. henryi* and *L. regale* (but not *L. auratum* or *L. speciosum*). Midsummer bloomers with trumpet- or bowl-shaped flowers are usually scented. Blossoms range from white and cream through yellow and pink, many with green, brown, or purple shading on their outer surfaces. Plants are typically 3–6 ft. tall; each stem carries 6 to 15 flowers. Examples include the Golden Splendor strain, deep gold with maroon striping on petal backs; the Pink Perfection strain; and 'White Henryi', white with cinnamon speckles and a gold throat.

Martagon hybrids (Turk's cap lilies). Zones A1–A3; 1–9, 14–22. Most are bred from *L. martagon*, *L. hansonii*, and *L. tsingtauense*. The petals of these fragrant early-summer flowers curve back strongly (that's the Turk's cap look); colors are mostly in the wine red to orange to gold range. Blooms tend to be small but abundant. Plants do best in the filtered light of woodland settings but are slow to establish. Extremely virus-resistant. Best in cottage gardens and wild gardens. The classic hybrid in this series is 'Mrs. R. O. Backhouse', which grows 3–5 ft. tall, producing 1½–2-in., magenta-backed yellow flowers in late spring or early summer. Look also for 'Arabian Knight' (mauve flecked with yellow-orange), 'Claude Shride' (mahogany red with gold-orange center), and 'Sunny Morning' (mahogany red with gold overlay).

Oriental hybrids. Zones 1–9, 14–22. The most exotic of the hybrids, bred primarily from Japanese species. Bloom midsummer to early fall, with big (to 9 in.), fragrant flowers of white or pink, often banded with gold or red on the center of each petal, and spotted with red. Most are 3–5 ft. tall, with flowers that face upward or outward (a few have nodding blooms). If you live where summer temperatures routinely rise above 90°F (32°C), plant these in dappled afternoon shade. Examples are 'Casablanca', pure white; 'Mona Lisa', pink, intensifying toward the center, with darker pink center lines and freckles, 1½–2 ft. tall; 'Muscadet', white with pink freckles and pink center lines; 'Salmon Star', pink flushed with salmon toward the

Lilies in Pots

Lilies are fine container plants. Place one bulb in a deep 8-in. pot or five in a 16-in. pot. Plant at the same depth required for planting in the ground (see "How to Grow Lilies," page 414). Place bulbs with roots spread and pointing downward, fill the container with soil, and gently hand-pack it until the soil surface is firm. Leave an inch of space between surface of soil and rim of pot for watering. Water thoroughly and place in a cool room, a garage, or a greenhouse that is heated (in colder climates) just enough to keep out frost. During root-forming period, water whenever the top 2 in. of soil dries out. Move pots to a partially shaded area during blooming period if temperatures rise above 90°F (32°C).

LEFT COLUMN: *Lilium longiflorum;* LA hybrid 'Kentucky'. MIDDLE: *L. columbianum.* RIGHT COLUMN: Oriental lily; Aurelian hybrid lily Golden Splendor

center and base of each petal, 2–3 ft. high; and 'Stargazer' (rose-red with white margins). There are also double-flowered versions; all require dappled sun or afternoon shade because their petals are not as substantial as those of their single-flowered siblings.

Interdivisional hybrids. During the past few years, breeders have accomplished considerable hybridization between divisions, resulting in the two main groups described below. Work is also being done on other combinations. 'Triumphator', for example, is a cross between *L. longiflorum* and Oriental lilies. Its fragrant flower (white with a deep pink center) combines Easter lily's shape with Oriental lily's heavier texture; it grows about 4 ft. tall.

OT hybrids (also called Orienpets). Zones 1–9, 14–23. This breeding blends China's trumpet lilies with Japan's Oriental lilies to produce heavy-stemmed, 3–5-ft. plants. They tolerate a little more heat and demand less winter chill than their Oriental parents, and most have a light, sweet fragrance with lemony overtones. The color range is mostly in shades of yellow but also includes reds and pinks; "whites" are really cream-colored. Examples include 'Black Beauty', very deep wine color edged with a white line, strongly curled petals; 'Conca d'Or' (heady perfume), lemon yellow petals with pale edges; 'LaVern Freimann' ('Miss Freya'), maroon red, 6–7 ft. tall, late-summer bloom; and 'Scheherazade', a tetraploid (genetically very robust), rose-red with creamy yellow margins, light fragrance.

LA hybrids. Zones A2, A3; 1–9, 14–24. Hybrids between Easter lilies (*L. longiflorum*) and Asiatic hybrid lilies. These plants grow quickly to 3–4 ft., bloom early, and make great cut flowers. Blooms face up and are available in yellow, pink, red, white, and orange. Examples include 'Eyeliner', petals white with black edge, a few black freckles; 'Kentucky', whose fragrant, early-summer flowers have an orange-yellow base with paprika speckles, 3 ft. high; and 'Red Alert', deep, shiny red. Along with OT hybrids, LA hybrids are among the best-performing lilies for Southern California.

Species and variants. A number of excellent species lilies are listed below. Those described as having Turk's cap flowers bear blooms with strongly recurved petals.

L. auratum. GOLD-BAND LILY. Zones 1–7, 14–17. Native to Japan. To 4–6 ft. tall. Very fragrant white flowers with crimson spots and gold band are carried 6 to 30 per stem. Blooms in late summer.

L. cernuum. Zones 1–9, 14–24. Native to Korea, Manchuria, Siberia. Summer bloomer only 12–20 in. high, with fragrant lilac-colored flowers often dotted in darker purple. Usually bears up to six blossoms per stem. Needs sandy soil.

L. columbianum. COLUMBIA LILY, TIGER LILY. Zones 2–7, 14–19. Native from British Columbia to Northern California. To 5–6 ft. tall, with one to six small, golden orange, unscented lilies per stem in midsummer.

L. formosanum. FORMOSA LILY. Zones 2–9, 14–22. Native to Taiwan. Beautiful pure white trumpets with reddish purple shading on back midrib of each petal. Plants grow 5–9 ft. tall. Full sun or light shade. 'Little Snow' grows 3 ft. tall.

L. hansonii. Zones 1–9, 14–22. Native to Japan, Korea. Grows 2–4 ft. tall, producing fragrant, nodding, yellow-orange summer blooms. Leaves grow in whorls around stems. Prefers light shade and slightly moist soil with lots of organic content. Slow to establish. Extremely virus-resistant.

L. henryi. Zones 1–10, 14–21; H1. Native to China. Slender stems to 8–9 ft., each topped by 10 to 20 barely scented, bright orange Turk's cap flowers. Summer bloom. Does best in light shade in all regions.

L. humboldtii. HUMBOLDT LILY. Zones 3, 7, 14–24. Native to open woodlands of the Sierra Nevada. To 3–6 ft. tall. Unscented, nodding, Turk's cap blooms are bright orange with large maroon dots; early-summer bloom. *L. h. ocellatum* is similar, but its maroon dots are margined in red.

»

How to Grow Lilies

Plant bulbs in fall or spring as soon as possible after you get them. If you must wait, keep them in a cool place briefly until you plant. Don't buy bulbs with dry, withered scales; they won't rehydrate, and their appearance may indicate that the growing tip inside is dead. Before planting bulbs, remove any injured scales, then let the bulbs callus in a cool place for a few hours before planting.

PLANTING To plant in already cultivated, good garden soil, dig a planting hole the depth of your shovel blade. To plant in uncultivated ground, dig a hole 1 ft. deeper than height of bulb. In either situation, place enough soil at bottom of hole to bring it up to proper level for bulb. Set bulb with its roots spread; fill in hole with soil, firming it in around bulb to eliminate air pockets. If your garden has gophers, plant each bulb in a 6-in.-square wire basket made of ½-in. hardware cloth. (The depth of the basket will depend on the planting depth.)

Planting depth varies according to size and rooting habits of bulbs. General rule is to bury each bulb 2½ times as deep as its diameter, but exact depth can be quite flexible. It is better to plant lily bulbs too shallow than too deep; they have contractile roots that draw them down to proper depth if the soil has been deeply loosened before planting. Ideal spacing for lily bulbs is 1 ft. apart, but you can plant as close as 6 in. for a densely massed effect.

WATERING Flooding is preferable to overhead watering, which can spread disease spores and also topple tall lilies when they're in flower. If you use drip irrigation, keep the emitter 8 in. from the stem. Irrigate in the morning, so that leaves have time to dry before disease sets in.

Since most lilies never really enter a dormant period, they need moisture year-round; water when the top 2 in. of soil has dried out. Cut back on watering somewhat after tops turn yellow in fall, but never let roots go completely dry. Exceptions are species native to dry-summer areas with gravelly soils (*L. columbianum, L. humboldtii, L. pardalinum*). These are adapted to dry periods after bloom and will rot if they get too much water.

WEEDING Pull weeds by hand if possible; hoeing may injure roots. Avoid preemergent weed suppressants; they can also suppress lily root growth.

POST-BLOOM CARE Remove faded flowers to prevent seed formation. Wait until stems and leaves turn yellow before you cut plants back. If the clumps become too large and crowded, dig, divide, and transplant them in fall. If you're careful, you can lift lily clumps at any time, even when they are in bloom.

CHALLENGES When they occur, the following can spell trouble for lilies.

Incurable viral infection. To avoid the problem, buy healthy bulbs from reliable sources, or stick with virus-resistant species and hybrids (noted). Dig and destroy any lilies that display mottled leaves or seriously stunted growth (unless those problems are linked to hail or other severe weather). Control aphids, which spread the infection. Don't plant tiger lilies in your garden, since they can carry virus without showing it.

Botrytis. Reduce risk of botrytis blight (a fungal disease) by maintaining good air circulation around plants; don't let dense foliage surround lilies. Botrytis can be controlled with a fungicide and by keeping lily foliage dry; if you've struggled with botrytis in the past, spray the ground with fungicide as new lilies emerge in spring.

L. lancifolium (L. tigrinum). TIGER LILY. Zones 2–9, 14–21. Native to East Asia, naturalized in North America. Grows 6 ft. tall, producing about a dozen orange flowers with purple spots and recurved petals every summer. It also grows marble-size bulbils along the stem; they drop to the ground (or you plant them) for more tiger lilies. 'Pink Tiger' is a pink hybrid; 'Flore Pleno' is a double. This species carries virus without showing it; don't plant it if you have virus-susceptible lilies in the garden.

L. lankongense. Zones 2b–24. Alpine native of China. To 3–5 ft. tall, spreading by stoloniferous stems. Powerfully fragrant Turk's cap flowers in rose-red with purple spots, carried up to 15 per stem. Midsummer bloom. Tolerates alkaline soils. Many consider this the most beautiful lily.

L. leichtlinii. Zones 1–9, 14–24. Native to Japan. Grows 3–4 ft. tall, producing maroon-speckled yellow flowers in early summer. Good drainage essential.

L. leucanthum centifolium. Zones 2–9, 14–24. Native to China. To 7–8 ft. tall. Up to 18 fragrant, white, midsummer flowers with external purple-red streaks. Funnel-shaped blooms, slightly pendulous.

L. longiflorum. EASTER LILY. Zones 2–9, 14–24; H1. Native to Japan, Taiwan. Up to six trumpet-shaped, very fragrant white flowers on each short stem. Usually purchased in bloom at Easter. Stems will die down. Plant may rebloom in fall; in 1 or 2 years, will likely begin flowering in midsummer, its normal bloom season. Recent hybridization has yielded pink, red, and yellow types.

L. martagon. TURK'S CAP LILY. Zones 1–10, 14–17. Native from Europe to Mongolia. To 3–5 ft. tall. In midsummer, each stem bears up to 50 pendent flowers 1–2 in. wide with sharply recurved petals. Blossoms are typically purplish pink with darker spots, but darker-colored and pure white variants exist. Easy to grow but slow to establish; eventually forms big clumps. Extreme virus resistance.

L. pardalinum. LEOPARD LILY. Zones 2–7, 14–17. Native from southwestern Oregon to Southern California. To 4–8 ft. tall, with unscented Turk's cap flowers in orange or red-orange shading to yellow, with brown spotting in center. Up to 10 flowers per stem. Blooms in late spring or early summer.

L. pumilum. CORAL LILY. Zones 1–10, 14–24. Native to northern China, Mongolia, and Siberia. To 1–1½ ft. high, with up to 20 fragrant red Turk's cap flowers per stem. Blooms in early summer.

L. regale. REGAL LILY. Zones 1–9, 14–24. Native to western China. Popular and easy to grow. Stems to 6 ft. tall; in midsummer, each bears up to 25 fragrant, funnel-shaped white blossoms flushed purple outside, carried horizontally.

L. speciosum. Zones 1–7, 14–17. Native to China, Japan, Taiwan. To 3–5 ft. tall. Large, wide, fragrant Turk's cap flowers are white, heavily suffused with rose-pink and sprinkled with raised crimson dots. Usually up to 12 flowers per stem. Blooms in late summer. *L. s. album* has pure white blooms, *L. s. rubrum* red ones. 'Uchida' is the most popular selection; it has white-edged pink blooms with deep pink speckles and red anthers.

L. superbum. SWAMP LILY. Zones 3–9, 14–24. Native to the eastern U.S. Reaches 6–9 ft. tall, producing nodding orange, Turk's cap flowers whose petals turn red-orange at the tips with maturity. In the wild, it prefers moist meadows or woodlands but does fine in regularly watered gardens.

Lilium longiflorum is striking in garden borders where its fragrant white trumpets can really show off. Combine several plants with yellow Asiatic lilies and Shasta daisies. When not forced into bloom for Easter, these lilies flower naturally in midsummer.

Limnanthes douglasii

MEADOWFOAM, POACHED EGGS
Limnanthaceae
ANNUAL

🌿 **ZONES 1–9, 14–24**

☼ **FULL SUN**

💧 **REGULAR WATER**

Limnanthes douglasii sulphurea

This low annual produces a blanket of yellow-and-white flowers on wet meadows in California and southwestern Oregon in spring. Can be coaxed into a longer bloom with regular watering. Grows 6–12 in. high and broad, with yellowish green, finely divided leaves and clusters of inch-wide yellow flowers with white petal tips. *L. d. sulphurea*, sometimes called Point Reyes meadowfoam, is a coastal subspecies with pure yellow blooms. Flowers of *L. d. nivea* are almost entirely white. Sow seeds in fall or earliest spring. Plants self-sow where adapted.

Want to grow meadowfoam but don't have a meadow? Sow seeds along a sunny path for a cheerful springtime edging. Or create a miniature California native garden in a pot by planting bulbs like *Brodiaea*, Mariposa lily (*Calochortus*), or *Triteleia*, and sowing seeds of meadowfoam on top.

Limonium

STATICE, SEA LAVENDER
Plumbaginaceae
PERENNIALS AND ANNUALS

🌿 **ZONES VARY BY SPECIES**

☼ **FULL SUN**

💧 **MODERATE WATER**

Limonium sinuatum

Large, leathery, green basal leaves contrast with airy flower clusters on nearly leafless, many-branched stems. Mostly in the blue to white range, blooms consist of an outer, papery calyx and an inner corolla. The two often have different colors, which hold when dried. Plants tolerate heat, need good drainage. They self-sow.

L. gmelinii. Perennial. Zones 1–10, 14–24. From eastern Europe, Siberia. Much like a slightly smaller *L. platyphyllum*, with 5-in. basal leaves and widely branching clusters of blue flowers in mid- to late summer.

L. perezii. Perennial. Zones 13, 15–17, 20–24. Native to the Canary Islands. To 3 ft. high, with flower clusters spreading nearly as wide. Calyx is rich purple, corolla white. Long spring and summer bloom. Leaves up to 1 ft. long, including stalks. First-rate beach plant. Often naturalizes in coastal Southern California. Damaged at 25°F (−4°C). Needs afternoon shade in Zone 13.

L. platyphyllum (L. latifolium). Perennial. Zones 1–10, 14–24; H1. Native to central and southeastern Europe. Vigorous plant to 2½ ft. high, covered in a haze of flowers up to 3 ft. wide in summer. Calyx is white, corolla bluish; pure white and pink kinds exist. Smooth-edged leaves to 10 in. long.

L. sinuatum. Annual. All zones. Mediterranean native widely grown for use as a fresh or dried cut flower. To 1½ ft. high and 1 ft. wide, with basal leaves lobed nearly to midrib and winged flower stems. Calyx is blue, lavender, or rose; corolla is white. Improved garden strains come in yellow, apricot, orange, peach, rose, light blue, deep blue, purple, and white. For spring and summer bloom, sow indoors and move to garden when weather warms up; or sow outdoors in early spring for later bloom.

L. suworowii. See *Psylliostachys suworowii*.

L. tataricum. See *Goniolimon tataricum*.

L. vulgare. Perennial. Zones 4–9, 14–24. Native to British Isles and coastal western Europe, the Mediterranean, and North Africa. Grows 1–2 ft. high and wide. Dainty lavender blooms appear in summer on branched stems held above foliage. Leaves are narrowly oval, with pointed tips, reaching 6–8 in. long. Grow from seed or root cuttings.

Linanthus grandiflorus

MOUNTAIN PHLOX
Polemoniaceae
ANNUAL

🌿 **ZONES 1–9, 14–24**

☼ **FULL SUN**

💧 **LITTLE OR NO WATER TO MODERATE WATER**

Linanthus grandiflorus

This Northern Californian phlox relative resembles annual phlox (*Phlox drummondii*), bearing heads of inch-wide, pink-tinged white or lavender-pink blossoms with yellow throats. Good cut flower. Plant grows to 2 ft. high, 1 ft. wide. Sow in fall or earliest spring. In cooler areas, needs little or no water for spring bloom; in warmer regions, give occasional irrigation.

Linaria

TOADFLAX
Plantaginaceae
ANNUALS AND PERENNIALS

🌿 **ZONES 1–24**

☼ ◐ **FULL SUN OR LIGHT SHADE**

💧 **REGULAR WATER**

🦋 **ATTRACT BUTTERFLIES**

Linaria 'Enchantment'

Brightly colored blooms like small, spurred snapdragons (*Antirrhinum*). Medium green, very narrow leaves. Easy to grow. Best in masses; individual plants are rather wispy.

L. hybrids. Annuals. The Fantasy series produces compact plants to 1 ft. high, 6–8 in. wide, with very narrow bluish green leaves. Clusters of ½–1-in. flowers appear in spring and summer, come in blue with yellow throat, magenta, pink, yellow, and white. 'Enchantment' has very fragrant magenta-and-gold flowers on plants to 16 in. high.

L. maroccana. BABY SNAPDRAGON, TOADFLAX. Annual. From Morocco. Grows to 1½–2 ft. high, 6 in. wide. Summer flowers in red-and-gold, rose, pink, mauve, chamois, blue, violet, or purple, blotched with a different shade on the lip. Northern Lights strain offers shades of red, orange, and yellow as well as bicolors. Sow seeds in early spring after danger of frost is past. In Zones 10–13, sow in fall for winter bloom.

L

»

L. reticulata. Annual. From Portugal and North Africa. To 2–4 ft. tall, 10 in. wide, with very narrow bluish green leaves and showers of small purple-and-orange flowers in late spring and summer. 'Flamenco' (1–1½ ft. high) has yellow flowers with a conspicuous maroon blotch. 'Flaming Passion' (16 in. high, 8 in. wide) has red flowers with yellow centers.

Lindera
SPICEBUSH
Lauraceae
DECIDUOUS SHRUBS OR TREES

✿ ZONES VARY BY SPECIES

☼ ◑ FULL SUN OR PARTIAL SHADE

💧 REGULAR WATER

Lindera obtusiloba

Spicebushes are grown for the beauty of their yellow fall foliage and named for the spicy scent of crushed leaves. On female plants, fruits will follow the blossoms if a male plant is nearby. Best used at woodland edge or filling in a shrub border. Good drainage essential; some drought-tolerance.

L. benzoin. Zones 2–6. Native to eastern U.S. Reaches 6–12 ft. tall and broad. Light green leaves are 3–5 in. long, half as wide. Fall color is most yellow and plant form is most compact in full sun. Fruits (noticeable after leaf fall) are bright red, to ½ in. long.

L. obtusiloba. JAPANESE SPICEBUSH. Zones 3b–6, 14–17. Native to Japan, China, and Korea. To 10–20 ft. tall and a little narrower. Leaves are occasionally mitten-shaped. Fall color is an exceptionally brilliant yellow that develops even in

shade and holds for 2 weeks or more. Fruits are ¼ in. wide, mature from red to black.

Linnaea borealis
TWINFLOWER
Caprifoliaceae
PERENNIAL

✿ ZONES A1–A3; 1, 2, 4–6, 14–17

☼ ◑ PARTIAL OR FULL SHADE

💧 REGULAR WATER

Linnaea borealis

A delicate woodland ground-cover, twinflower forms ground-hugging mats of evergreen, glossy green leaves that spread 3–5 ft. by runners. In late spring or early summer, pairs of pale or rosy pink, fragrant, trumpet-shaped, ⅓-in.-long flowers appear on 3-in. stems. Mulch around plants with leaf mold to induce spreading. Tolerates sun in cool-summer climates. North American native; in the West, found from Northern California to Alaska and Idaho.

The genus *Linnaea* was named for—and by—Carl Linnaeus, the 18th-century physician and botanist who developed the system for naming, ranking, and classifying living organisms that is still in use today. His "binomial" system (naming plants by genus and species) was revolutionary.

Linum
FLAX
Linaceae
PERENNIALS AND ANNUAL

✿ ZONES VARY BY SPECIES

☼ FULL SUN

💧 MODERATE WATER

Linum perenne

These upright, narrow-leafed plants produce an abundance of open, five-petaled flowers over a long period. Each bloom lasts only a day, but others keep coming. The flax of commerce, *L. usitatissimum,* is grown for its fiber and seeds, which yield linseed oil.

L. flavum. GOLDEN FLAX. Perennial. Zones 2–24. From central and southern Europe. To 12–15 in. high, 1 ft. wide, with somewhat woody base. Grooved branches, green leaves. Spring and summer flowers are golden yellow, about 1 in. wide, carried in many-branched clusters. 'Compactum' is just 6 in. high and wide.

L. grandiflorum. FLOWERING FLAX. Annual. Zones 1–24. From North Africa. To 2½ ft. high and 12 in. wide, with gray-green leaves. Summer flowers are rose-pink, to 1½ in. wide. Sow seeds thickly in place in early spring or (in mild-winter climates) in fall. Self-sows without becoming a pest and is often included in wildflower mixes. 'Rubrum', scarlet flax, has bright red flowers.

L. lewisii. BLUE FLAX. Perennial. Zones A1–A3; 2–12, 14–18. Native to western North America. Upright, 3 ft. high, with abundant sky blue flowers. Does best at higher elevations in southern part of range.

L. narbonense. Perennial. Zones 3–24. Wiry-stemmed Mediterranean native to 2 ft. high, 1½ ft. wide. Open clusters of 1¾-in., azure blue flowers with white eye; blooms in late spring and early summer.

L. perenne. PERENNIAL BLUE FLAX. Perennial. Zones 2–24. Native Europe to central Asia. Most vigorous blue-flowered flax, to 2 ft. high, 1½ ft. wide. Profuse spring and summer bloomer, producing branching clusters of light blue flowers that close in shade or late in the day. Self-sows freely.

CARE
Use in borders of light, well-drained soil; some naturalize freely in uncultivated areas. Most perennial kinds live only 3 or 4 years and should be replaced regularly. Easy from seed; perennial kinds can also be propagated from cuttings.

Lippia citriodora.
See *Aloysia citrodora*

Lippia repens.
See *Phyla nodiflora*

Liquidambar
SWEET GUM
Altingiaceae
DECIDUOUS TREES

✿ ZONES VARY BY SPECIES

☼ FULL SUN

💧 MODERATE TO REGULAR WATER

🦋 ATTRACT BIRDS

Liquidambar styraciflua

Beautiful foliage and late, intense fall color make these valuable shade trees. Moderate growth rate. Young and middle-aged trees are generally upright and somewhat cone-shaped; older ones have a more spreading habit. Leaves are lobed, maple-like. Flowers are inconspicuous; fruits are spiny balls that ornament trees in winter but must be raked up throughout the year.

Good street trees only if given a wide parking strip in which to grow: their surface roots can crack sidewalks and create a nuisance in lawns. The spiny seedpods are hard enough to damage bicycle tires. Effective planted 6–10 ft. apart to form tall screens or groves. Brilliant fall foliage (color is less effective in mildest climates or in mild, late autumns).

L. formosana. CHINESE SWEET GUM. Zones 4–9, 14–24. Native to China. To 40–60 ft. tall, 25 ft. wide. Free-form outline; sometimes pyramidal, especially when young. Three- to five-lobed leaves are violet-red when expanding, maturing to deep green. Fall color ranges from red in northern part of range to yellow-beige in Southern California. Leaves drop late, usually in early winter.

L. styraciflua. AMERICAN SWEET GUM. Zones 3–9, 14–24. Native to eastern U.S. To 60 ft. in gardens; much taller in the wild. Narrow and erect in youth; lower limbs eventually spread to 20–25 ft. Tolerates damp soil; resists oak root fungus. Good-looking all year. Branching pattern, furrowed bark, and corky wings on twigs provide winter interest, as do hanging seedpods—1½-in., spiky spheres reminiscent of tiny medieval maces. On mature trees, seedpods are profuse enough to cause a litter problem.

Five- to seven-lobed leaves are deep green in spring and summer, turning to purple, yellow, or red in fall. ('Burgundy', 'Festival', and 'Palo Alto' were developed in California and color better there than in the Northwest.)

'**Burgundy**'. Deep purple-red fall color. Foliage hangs on late into winter—or even into early spring if storms are not heavy.

'**Cherokee**'. Produces very few seedpods. Fall color is burgundy red (yellow on trees grown in shade).

'**Emerald Sentinel**'. To 30 ft. tall by 12 ft. wide; pyramidal to columnar. Yellow-orange or orange fall color.

'**Festival**'. Narrow, columnar. Light green foliage turns a combination of yellow, peach, pink, orange, and red in fall.

'**Gold Dust**'. To 45 ft. tall, 30 ft. wide. Green foliage is heavily flecked with golden yellow. Pink, yellow, and burgundy fall color.

'**Golden Treasure**'. Deep green leaves bordered in gold. In fall, gold rim lightens to pale yellow, then white; green center turns burgundy.

'**Moraine**'. This is the most cold-tolerant *Liquidambar*. Grows 40 ft. tall, 25 ft. wide, with dark green foliage, a compact habit, and burgundy red fall foliage.

'**Palo Alto**'. Orange-red to bright red fall color.

'**Rotundiloba**'. Leaves have rounded rather than sharp-pointed lobes. Sets no seedpods. Fall colors are yellow, red, burgundy, and purple.

'**Slender Silhouette**'. Grows 60 ft. tall, 8 ft. wide; orange to burgundy fall color.

'**Variegata**'. Green leaves with yellow streaks and splotches. In autumn, the yellow variegation turns pink; green part of leaf becomes red.

'**Worplesdon**'. Narrow-lobed leaves turn orange-red in fall.

CARE

Give neutral or slightly acid, well-amended garden soil. Trees branch from the ground up and look most natural that way, but lower limbs can be removed to expose the trunk. To develop a strong central leader on young trees, pinch back side branches. Without proper training in youth, trees can develop weak branching pattern. Mature trees need little or no pruning.

Sweet gums are big, beautiful trees with great fall color. But beware of planting them too close to buildings, driveways, or walkways: their vigorous root system can heave the pavement and their large, spiny seedpods can puncture bicycle tires.

Liriodendron tulipifera

TULIP TREE
Magnoliaceae
DECIDUOUS TREE

ZONES 2–12, 14–24

FULL SUN

REGULAR WATER

Liriodendron tulipifera

Eastern U.S. native. Fast growth to 60–80 ft., 40 ft. wide; considerably larger in the wild. Straight, columnar trunk, with spreading, rising branches that form a tall, pyramidal crown. The leaves look like blunt-tipped maple leaves missing the end lobe. Foliage turns from bright yellow-green to bright yellow in fall, usually even in Southern California. Tulip-shaped, 2-in.-wide spring flowers are greenish yellow, orange at base—handsome at close range, but usually too high up to appreciate on the trees. First bloom usually comes on 12–15-year-old trees. Columnar 'Arnold' ('Fastigiata') grows 25–50 ft. tall and 10–15 ft. wide; blooms 2 to 3 years after planting. 'Aureomarginatum' ('Majestic Beauty') grows 40–60 ft. tall and 15–25 ft. wide, has yellow-edged leaves. 'Emerald City' grows 55 ft. tall and 25 ft. wide.

Thrives in deep, rich, well-drained, neutral to slightly acid soil. This tree makes a good large shade or lawn tree, but its wide-spreading network of shallow, fleshy roots makes it difficult to garden under. Control scale insects and aphids as necessary. Immune to oak root fungus.

Liriope

LILY TURF
Asparagaceae
PERENNIALS

ZONES VARY BY SPECIES

EXPOSURE VARIES BY SPECIES

REGULAR WATER

Liriope muscari 'Pee Dee Gold Ingot'

With grassy leaves and spikes of pretty violet, blue, or white flowers, these popular and durable Asian plants make attractive groundcovers, borders, and edgings along streams and garden pools. They compete well with roots of other plants; try them under bamboo or to cover bare soil at bases of trees or shrubs. Blooms last well in arrangements. For a closely related plant that is not quite as cold-hardy, see *Ophiopogon*.

Plants look best from spring until cold winter weather arrives. Extended freezes make leaves yellow; they take quite a while to recover.

Provide filtered sun—even full sun in cool-summer regions—to full shade. Plant in well-drained soil; tip burn appears on leaves if soil is waterlogged or contains excess salts. Though plants don't require heavy feeding, they do become ragged and brown with neglect; cut back shaggy old foliage after new leaves appear. To increase, divide in early spring before new growth starts. Protect from snails and slugs.

L. gigantea. GIANT LILY-TURF. Zones 4–10, 14–24. Grows into a grassy clump 3 ft. high and wide, with spikes of lavender-blue summer flowers. Metallic blue fruits follow. Takes full shade.

L

»

L. muscari. BIG BLUE LILY TURF. Zones 2b–10, 14–24; H1, H2. Forms large clumps 1–1½ ft. high and eventually a bit wider—but does not spread by underground stems. Loose habit, with arching, dark green leaves to 2 ft. or longer, ½–¾ in. wide. Dense, spikelike, 6–8-in. flower clusters appear on 5–12-in. stems. Flowers are held above the foliage on young plants, partly hidden by leaves on older ones. Round, shiny black fruits follow. Part shade in hot climates.

The following grow 12–15 in. high unless noted.

'Big Blue'. To 18 in. high. Stiffly arching, narrow leaves; dark violet flowers. Does well even in dry shade.

'Gold Band'. Broad green leaves are edged with bright gold. Lavender flower spikes are held well above foliage.

'Lilac Beauty'. Dark green leaves; pale violet flowers.

'Majestic'. To 1½ ft. high. Somewhat open-growing clumps. Blooms heavily, bearing large (up to 10 in. long) clusters of dark violet blossoms resembling cockscombs; flowers are held well above the leaves on young plants.

'Monroe's White'. Broad leaves. Large white flower spikes stand well above foliage. Fruit is purple. Prefers more shade than most types.

'Royal Purple'. Similar to 'Majestic' but with deeper purple flowers.

'Silvery Sunproof'. Strong, open, vertical growth. Medium green leaves have gold stripes that age to white; whole leaf is whiter in sun, more yellow or green in shade. Lilac flowers are held well above foliage. One of the best for full sun and for flowers.

'Variegata'. Forms loose, soft clumps. Leaves are green with yellow edges when new, then turn solid dark green in second season. Violet flowers are held well above the leaves. May be sold as *Ophiopogon jaburan* 'Variegatus'.

L. spicata. CREEPING LILY TURF. Zones 3–10, 14–24; H1, H2. Dense groundcover that grows 8–9 in. high and spreads widely by underground stems; can be invasive. Deep green, grasslike leaves are just ¼ in.

wide. Foliage is not as upright as that of *L. muscari*. Pale lilac to white flowers appear in spikelike clusters barely taller than the leaves. Set plants 1 ft. apart for quick cover. Mow early every spring before new growth emerges. In Northwest, suffers less winter damage than *L. muscari*. 'Silver Dragon' is slower growing and has a somewhat less dense habit; its leaves are striped silvery white, and its pale purple flowers are held on short spikes. Good fine-textured groundcover for shade.

Lisianthus russellianus.
See *Eustoma grandiflorum*

Litchi

LITCHI NUT, LYCHEE
Sapindaceae
EVERGREEN TREE

🌿 **ZONES 21–24; H1, H2**
☀️ **FULL SUN**
💧 **REGULAR WATER**

Litchi

Growing 20–40 ft. tall and wide, this round-topped Chinese evergreen can bear thousands of brittle, warty fruits at once. When the easy-to-peel rind turns from green to red, harvest by snipping off whole clusters. The smooth, white edible portion inside looks something like a grape with a pit in the middle. The most desirable varieties have a small or shriveled seed known as a chicken tongue. The tree's leathery leaves are coppery red when new, maturing to dark green; each has three to nine 3–6-in.-long leaflets. Tiny cream-colored flowers bloom in late spring. Trees are usually self-fruitful, but an individual tree may set more male flowers

than female ones, reducing fruit production. Botanically, this is *Litchi chinensis*.

Fruit is sweet—juicy when fresh, raisin-like when dried. Varieties include small-pitted 'Groff', 'Kaimana' (the best variety for Hawaii), and 'Kwai Mi' ('Mauritius'). 'Sweet Cliff' has a small to medium-size seed; the slightly more acidic 'Brewster' has a large one.

Litchi needs a frost-free site, acid soil, moist atmosphere, and light nitrogen fertilizer. It has fruited in a few coastal areas of Southern California; reliable in Hawaii.

Lithocarpus densiflorus

TANBARK OAK, TANOAK
Fagaceae
EVERGREEN TREES

🌿 **ZONES 4–7, 14–24**
☀️◐ **FULL SUN OR LIGHT SHADE**
💧 **MODERATE WATER**

Lithocarpus densiflorus

Grown primarily for its attractive foliage, tanbark oak provides a stately presence in the garden or open woodland. The tree can reach 80 ft. tall and 50 ft. wide under forest conditions, but where it doesn't have to compete with other trees, it is perhaps half as high and proportionally broader. Leathery, 1½–4-in.-long, toothed leaves are covered with whitish or yellowish wool when they expand, then mature to smooth green above, gray-green beneath. Tiny, whitish male flowers in large, branched clusters bloom in summer, giving off an odor that some people dislike. They are followed by acorns in burlike cups.

Native to the coast ranges from southern Oregon to Santa Barbara, California, its wild populations are being decimated by sudden oak death, caused by a fungus called *Phytophthora ramorum*. To learn more about this disease, see the *Quercus* entry.

L. d. echinoides is a shrub 3–10 ft. tall and wide; its bluish leaves are smaller than those of the species and bear few or no teeth.

Tanbark oaks do best in well-drained soil.

Lithodora diffusa

Boraginaceae
PERENNIAL

🌿 **ZONES 5–7, 14–17**
☀️◐ **LIGHT SHADE IN HOTTEST CLIMATES**
💧 **MODERATE WATER**

Lithodora diffusa 'Star'

Probably the most recognizable blue-flowered groundcover in its range, *Lithodora* forms a prostrate, somewhat woody, slightly mounded mass 6–12 in. high, 3–4 ft. wide. Narrow evergreen leaves are ¾–1 in. long; both foliage and stems are hairy. In late spring (and often later), plant is sprinkled with brilliant blue, tubular, ½-in.-long flowers. Native to southern and western Europe.

Give loose, well-drained, lime-free soil. Best suited to mild-summer climates. 'Heavenly Blue' and 'Grace Ward' are the forms most commonly seen. 'Star' ('Blue Star') has white-edged blue blossoms.

FOR MORE ON PERENNIALS, SEE "GROW: PERENNIALS," PAGES 686–687.

Livistona
Arecaceae
PALMS

- ☀ ZONES 9, 13–17, 19–24; H1, H2
- ☀ FULL SUN
- ● REGULAR WATER, EXCEPT AS NOTED

Livistona chinensis

These slow-growing fan palms somewhat resemble *Washingtonia* but generally have shorter, darker, shinier leaves. They are hardy to about 22°F (–6°C). All make good potted plants.

L. australis. From coastal forest of eastern Australia. To 40–50 ft. tall and 15 ft. wide. Has clean, slender trunk with interesting-looking leaf scars. Dark green leaves are 3–5 ft. wide.

L. chinensis. CHINESE FOUNTAIN PALM. From Japan, Taiwan. Very slow growing; eventually to 40 ft. tall, 15 ft. wide. Roundish, bright green, 3–6-ft.-wide leaves droop strongly at outer edges.

L. decipiens. RIBBON FAN PALM. From northeastern Australia. To 30–40 ft. tall and 15 ft. wide in 20 years. Stiff, open head of deeply divided leaves that are green on top, bluish beneath, 2–5 ft. across. Leaves are carried on long, spiny stems, and have wispy terminal leaflets that hang downward.

L. mariae. From hot, dry interior Australia. To 10–15 ft. tall after many years (ultimately to as high as 80 or even 100 ft.), 15 ft. wide. Leaves 3–4 ft. wide. Young plants and those grown in containers have attractive reddish leaves and leaf stems. Little to moderate water.

FOR MORE ON PALMS, SEE "MEET THE PALMS," PAGE 471.

Lobelia
Campanulaceae
PERENNIALS AND ANNUALS

- ☀ ZONES VARY BY SPECIES
- ☀ ☀ EXPOSURE NEEDS VARY BY SPECIES
- ◐ ● ● WATER NEEDS VARY BY SPECIES
- ✿ ATTRACT BUTTERFLIES, HUMMINGBIRDS
- ✿ LEAVES OF MOST CONTAIN POISONOUS ALKALOIDS

Lobelia × speciosa 'Monet Moment'

Annual kinds are low plants for edgings or hanging baskets; perennial sorts are larger, vertical-growing plants with flowering stalks that rise above the foliage. All are grown for their tubular, lipped flowers, which resemble those of honeysuckle or salvia.

L. cardinalis (L. fulgens). CARDINAL FLOWER. Perennial. Zones 1–7, 14–17. Native to eastern U.S., to a few sites in mountains of the Southwest, and to Mexico. Erect, single-stemmed plant to 2–4 ft. tall, 1 ft. wide. Sawtooth-edged leaves are set directly on the stems. Spikes of flame red, inch-long flowers in summer. A bog plant in nature, it needs rich soil and ample moisture throughout the growing season. Full sun or partial shade. 'Queen Victoria' grows 4–5 ft. tall, with purple-red foliage and scarlet flowers. 'St. Elmo's Fire' ('Elm Fire') grows 3 ft. tall, with bronze foliage, scarlet flower spikes.

L. erinus. Annual. All zones. From South Africa. Popular, dependable edging plant to 3–6 in. high. Compact forms reach 5–9 in. wide; trailing types spread to 1½ ft. Leafy, branching stems with green or bronzy green foliage. Blooms from early summer to frost, bearing ¾-in.-wide flowers in light blue to violet (sometimes pink, reddish purple, or white) with white or yellowish throats. Lives over winter in mild climates. In mild-winter, hot-summer regions, grow it as a winter-to-spring annual. If started from seed sown in pots, takes about 2 months to reach planting size. Give rich soil, regular water. Self-sows where adapted. Can take full sun in cooler climates; needs some shade in warmer regions.

There are dozens of varieties on the market, most grouped into series. For example, the heat-tolerant Magadi series comes in mounding (12 by 10 in.) and trailing (10 by 12 in.) forms, in several shades of purple, blue, and white. The Regatta series (8 by 12 in.) is bred to bloom a month ahead of other lobelias, comes in shades of blue, lilac, rose, and white. The Riviera series is extra compact (5 by 8 in.), comes in lilac, blue, rose, and white. Waterfall is a big (12 by 12 in.) mounding series in blue, lavender, and white.

L. laxiflora. Perennial. Zones 7–9, 12–24. Native to Arizona and Mexico. To 3 ft. high, 3–6 ft. wide. Erect stems set with narrow leaves grow from creeping underground rootstock, bear open clusters of tubular orange-red flowers over a long summer season. Withstands considerable aridity and neglect; often persists in abandoned gardens. Can be invasive. Little water. Full sun or partial shade.

L. siphilitica. Perennial. Zones 1–9, 14–17. Native to eastern U.S. Leafy plant to 2–3 ft. high and 1 ft. wide. Blue flowers in summer. Ample water, partial shade.

L. × speciosa (L. × gerardii). Perennial. Zones 2–9, 14–17. Group of hybrids of uncertain ancestry. Can reach 5 ft. tall, 1 ft. wide; many combine red leaves and red flowers. Compliment series, to 2½ ft. high, has dark green leaves; blossoms may be scarlet, deep red, or blue-purple. Fan series grows 2 ft. high, 16 in. wide; comes in blue, burgundy, red, rose, salmon, and scarlet. 'Grape Knee-Hi', 2 ft. high, is a sturdy plant with rich purple blooms. Provide rich soil, ample water, full sun or partial shade.

L. tupa. DEVIL'S TOBACCO. Perennial. Zones 4–9, 14–24. This impressive Chilean native has a distinctly tropical look. Plants form a 3–4-ft.-wide clump of upright, red stems holding felted, light green, lance-shaped leaves to 1 ft. long. Each stem is topped in mid- to late summer by a bloom spike that brings the overall height to 6 ft. Clusters of tubular, 2-in.-long flowers in a rich, warm red are held on reddish stems; blooms attract hummingbirds. Grow in a sunny, wind-sheltered position in fertile, well-drained soil. In cold-winter zones, mulch plants until well established. Does not require division, but if more plants are desired, divide clumps in spring. Regular water.

Lobivia, Lobivopsis.
See *Echinopsis*

Lobularia
SWEET ALYSSUM
Brassicaceae
ANNUAL

- ☀ ALL ZONES
- ☀ ☀ BEST IN SUN; TOLERATES LIGHT SHADE
- ● REGULAR WATER
- ✿ FLOWERS ATTRACT BEES, BUTTERFLIES, HUMMINGBIRDS

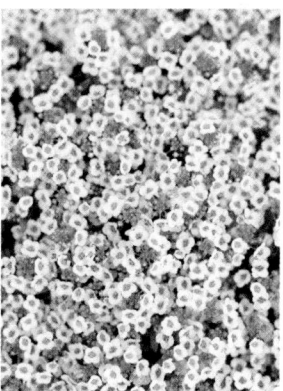

Lobularia maritima

These easy-to-grow mounds of white, pink, or purple, honey-scented flowers work well in containers or casual landscaping situations. Plants are low and branching, to 1 ft. high and wide, with narrow or lance-shaped leaves ½–2 in. long.

L

»

Crowded clusters of tiny, four-petaled flowers can bloom for months, and most self-seed. In cold-winter regions, flowers can keep coming from spring until frost; in mild climates, self-sown seedlings supply all-year bloom. Sweet alyssum seeds are sometimes included in wild-flower mixes.

L. hybrids. 'Snow Princess' is a trailing variety that grows 6 in. high. Because it's sterile, it keeps on blooming—and is vigorous enough to overrun adjacent plants.

L. maritima. Mediterranean native. Garden varieties are better known than the species, but when they self-sow, they tend to revert to taller, looser growth and bear smaller, paler blossoms than the parent. 'Carpet of Snow' (2–4 in. tall) is a good compact white. 'Rosie O'Day' (2–4 in.) has lavender-pink blooms. 'Snow Crystals' (10 in. high, trailing) and the Clear Crystal series (mounded 10 in. high, 14 in. wide; in white, rose, pink, lavender, peach, lemonade, and violet) are tetraploids whose genetics give them extra vigor and heat resistance. An increasing number of strains combine many colors in each seed packet.

CARE

Alyssum blooms from seed in 6 weeks; grows in almost any soil. If you shear plants halfway back 4 weeks after they come into bloom, new growth will make another crop of flowers, and plants won't become rangy.

The tiny white blooms of sweet alyssum resemble sea foam. Plant in a white ceramic container for a beachy look on a patio table. Or—for the look of a bubbling stream—tuck plants among small boulders in a narrow channel that meanders down a small sunny slope.

L

Lolium
RYEGRASS
Poaceae
ANNUAL AND PERENNIAL GRASSES

- ✂ **ZONES VARY BY SPECIES**
- ☼ **FULL SUN**
- ● **REGULAR WATER**

Lolium perenne

Because these European natives are clumping (not running) grasses, they must be sown heavily to make tight turf. Ryegrass is often mixed with other lawn grass species for low-cost, large-area coverage in cool-summer climates. In Bermuda grass country, it is often sown in fall on reconditioned Bermuda lawns to give winter green.

L. multiflorum. ANNUAL RYEGRASS, ITALIAN RYEGRASS. Annual. Zones 1–24. Larger, coarser than perennial ryegrass, but the seed is cheap, so it's used to overseed large areas. Some plants live for several seasons in mild climates. Fast growing, deep rooted.

L. perenne. PERENNIAL RYEGRASS. Perennial. Zones A2, A3; 1–6, 15–17. Finer in texture than *L. multiflorum*; deep green with high gloss. Sprouts quickly, grows fast, and has good wear resistance. Best in cool-summer climates and the best choice for overseeding Bermuda grass lawns in winter. Has become the most popular lawn grass in the Northwest, west of the Cascades. Mow at 2 in. high.

FOR MORE ON GRASSES, SEE "MEET THE GRASSES," PAGE 346.

Lonicera
HONEYSUCKLE
Caprifoliaceae
EVERGREEN, SEMIEVERGREEN, AND DECIDUOUS SHRUBS AND VINES

- ✂ **ZONES VARY BY SPECIES**
- ☼ ◑ **FULL SUN OR PARTIAL SHADE, EXCEPT AS NOTED**
- ◐ ● **MODERATE TO REGULAR WATER, EXCEPT AS NOTED**
- 🦋 **FLOWERS ATTRACT BUTTERFLIES AND HUMMINGBIRDS, BERRIES FEED OTHER BIRDS**

Lonicera sempervirens

Paired, often fragrant, tubular flowers are the main draw for many honeysuckles, but others are valued for foliage and even fruit. Blossoms typically deepen in color after opening, so clusters contain both pale and darker blooms. There are both vining and shrubby forms. Vining kinds climb by twining and need staking until they are tall enough to reach a trellis or other support. As they grow, they may need to be tied to the support here and there to distribute the branches well.

Provide good drainage. Honeysuckles typically need some thinning after bloom. Cut old, straggling honeysuckles to the ground before spring growth begins; they will regrow rapidly. Generally free of serious pests, though aphids sometimes infest them.

L. × americana 'Pam's Pink'. Evergreen to semievergreen shrub. Zones 4–12, 14–24. Fragrant pink-and-white blooms peak in spring, then come sporadically to fall. Grows 4–5 ft. tall and 6 ft. wide, with blue-green foliage. Favored in desert for tolerance to drought, heat, alkalinity, and salinity. Part shade in hot-summer climates.

L. × brownii. SCARLET TRUMPET HONEYSUCKLE. Deciduous vine. Zones A3; 1–7. Represented in nurseries by its superior selection 'Dropmore Scarlet', which climbs to 9–10 ft. Unscented, bright red flowers that look like trumpets bloom from late spring or early summer until frost. Pairs of triangular blue-green leaves appear to be joined at the bases.

L. caerulea edulis. SWEETBERRY HONEYSUCKLE. Deciduous shrub. Zones A1–A3; 1–3. Native to northern Europe and Asia. To 4–6 ft. tall and 4–5 ft. wide, with pointed bright green leaves. Small, unscented, pale yellow tubular flowers bloom in early spring. Edible, teardrop-shaped blue berries ripen in mid- to late spring, resemble highbush blueberries (but are not as sweet, though experimentation in Russia is producing improved varieties). Bears fruit even north of the Arctic Circle. Early warm spells sometimes induce flowers to open before the last frost; they then suffer cold damage. For best fruiting, set at least two plants in a sunny location and keep soil moist. For an ornamental hedge, space plants 3–4 ft. apart; for a living snow fence, space 1½–2 ft. apart.

L. × heckrottii. GOLD-FLAME HONEYSUCKLE, CORAL HONEYSUCKLE. Deciduous or semievergreen vining shrub. Zones 2–24; H1, H2. Vigorous. To 12–15 ft. tall, with 2½-in., oval, blue-green leaves. Free blooming spring to frost. Clusters of coral pink buds open to 1½-in., slightly fragrant, two-lipped flowers that are bright coral pink outside and rich yellow within. Train as espalier or on wire along eaves.

L. hildebrandiana. GIANT BURMESE HONEYSUCKLE. Evergreen vine. Zones 9, 14–17, 19–24; H1, H2. Native to China. Fast growing to 30 ft., with oval, glossy dark green leaves on ropelike stems. Bears fragrant, 6–7-in., two-lipped summer flowers that open white, then turn yellow to dull orange; blossoms slow to drop. May bear dark green berries. Thin out older stems occasionally and remove some of the growth that has bloomed.

CLOCKWISE FROM LEFT: *Lonicera × brownii* 'Dropmore Scarlet'; *L. periclymenum* 'Honeybush'; *L. japonica* 'Halliana'

Striking along eaves, on arbor or wall. Needs sturdy support.

L. japonica. JAPANESE HONEYSUCKLE. Vine. Evergreen in mild-winter climates, semievergreen or deciduous in colder areas. Zones 1–24; H1, H2. Native to eastern Asia. Can reach 30 ft. Rampant (even invasive) plant that can become a weed, since birds spread the seeds; consider planting the similar but less aggressive *L. periclymenum*. Basic species has oval deep green leaves and sweet-scented, two-lipped, purple-tinged white flowers from spring to fall. 'Aureo-reticulata', goldnet honeysuckle, with leaves veined in yellow, is better behaved than *L. japonica*; variegation is especially strong in full sun. 'Halliana', Hall's honeysuckle, is the most vigorous and widely grown variety, with pure white flowers that age to yellow and attract bees. 'Purpurea' (probably same as *L. j. chinensis*) has leaves with purple-tinged undersides and flowers that are purplish red outside, white inside.

Of those mentioned, 'Halliana' is the most commonly used as bank and groundcover and for erosion control in large areas; as groundcover, set plants 2–3 ft. apart. Unless curbed, it can smother less vigorous plants. Hard annual pruning keeps undergrowth from building up and becoming a fire hazard. Train as privacy or wind screen on chain-link or wire fence. Takes drought well when established; tolerates poor drainage.

L. 'Mandarin'. Deciduous vine. Zones 2b–9, 14–21. Hybrid between a Chinese species and *L. × brownii*. Grows as much as 6 ft. per year to 15–20 ft. at maturity. Foliage emerges coppery in spring, deepens to glossy green; accented by young stems of deep purplish brown. Appearing in late spring to midsummer (and sometimes again in fall) are deep red buds that open into 2–3-in.-long flowers that are orange-red outside, golden yellow within. Flowers are not particularly fragrant and not followed by fruit.

L. nitida. BOX HONEYSUCKLE. Evergreen shrub. Zones 4–9, 14–24; H1, H2. Native to southwestern China. To 11 ft. tall and 10 ft. wide. Branches densely clothed in tiny, egg-shaped, shiny dark green leaves that may turn an attractive bronze to plum color in winter. Late-spring or early-summer flowers are straight tubes—fragrant, creamy white, ½ in. long. Translucent blue-purple berries. Grows fast and tends toward untidiness but is easily pruned as specimen plant or hedge. Tolerates salt spray. 'Baggesen's Gold', to 4–6 ft. tall and wide, has foliage that is golden in sun (though very strong sun may burn leaves), chartreuse in shade. 'Lemon Beauty', to 4–6 ft. tall and wide, has dark green leaves edged in shades of lemon and chartreuse. 'Red Tips', to 4–6 ft. tall and wide, has deep raspberry red new growth that ages to dark green with red-tinted tips and edges. 'Silver Beauty', 3–4 ft. tall and wide (possibly up to 6 ft.), has bright silver leaf margins.

L. periclymenum. WOOD-BINE. Evergreen or deciduous vine. Zones 1–24. Native to Europe and the Mediterranean region. Grows 10–20 ft. tall. Resembles *L. japonica* but is less rampant. Whorls of 2-in.-long, fragrant, two-lipped flowers in summer and fall. Blooms of 'Serotina' (late Dutch honeysuckle) are purple outside, yellow inside. 'Berries Jubilee' has yellow flowers followed by a profusion of red berries. 'Belgica' (early Dutch honeysuckle) is less vining and more bushy than most, with abundant purple-flushed white flowers that fade to yellow and are followed by large red fruit. 'Winchester' has leaves that are purple tinged when young, pinkish red flowers with creamy throats, and bright reddish purple berries.

L. sempervirens. TRUMPET HONEYSUCKLE. Evergreen in mild-winter climates, semievergreen or deciduous in colder areas. Zones 2–24. Native to eastern and southern U.S. Can climb 10–20 ft. tall but shrubby if not given support. Showy, unscented, trumpet-shaped flowers are 1½–2 in. long, orange-yellow to scarlet, carried in whorls at branch ends from late spring into summer. Scarlet fruit. Oval, ½–3-in.-long leaves are medium green above, bluish green underneath. 'Blanche Sandman' has orange-red flowers. 'Leo' produces vivid coral red blooms with orange throats over a long period. Forms with larger flowers may be sold as 'Magnifica' or 'Superba'. For hybrid 'Dropmore Scarlet', see *L. × brownii*.

The blooms of many honeysuckles are so fragrant, you'll detect their presence before you actually see them. Grow them on an upwind fence to create a perfumed breeze, or over an arching trellis at the garden's entry.

L

L

Lophomyrtus × ralphii
Myrtaceae
EVERGREEN SHRUB

🌿 **ZONES 8–9, 14–24**

☀️ ◐ **FULL SUN OR PARTIAL SHADE**

💧💧 **MODERATE TO REGULAR WATER**

Lophomyrtus × ralphii
'Red Dragon'

The genus *Lophomyrtus* contains just two species, both native to New Zealand. This hybrid between the two grows 6–15 ft. tall and 5–8 ft. wide, with attractive, dark green leaves that are broadly oval, up to 1 in. long, and held in pairs along the stems. Small white summer flowers resemble those of closely related myrtle (*Myrtus communis*) and are followed by reddish black berries. Can be pruned into a hedge or trained as a small tree. Stems of many forms are popular in the cut-flower trade. Colored-leaf forms show more pronounced color in full sun.

Forms selected for their dense growth habit include 'Kathryn', to 6–8 ft. tall and wide, with glossy, puckered maroon leaves; 'Lilliput', just 2–3 ft. high and wide, with bronzy leaves; 'Red Dragon', 6 ft. high and 3 ft. wide, with reddish pink leaves that deepen to dark red in cool weather; and 'Sundae', to 8–12 ft. tall and 4–8 ft. wide, with glossy, puckered, burgundy-flushed green leaves edged in creamy yellow.

FOR OTHER PLANTS THAT MAKE GOOD HEDGES, SEE PAGES 44–45.

Lophostemon confertus
(Tristania conferta)
BRISBANE BOX
Myrtaceae
EVERGREEN TREE

🌿 **ZONES 15–17, 19–24; H1, H2**

☀️ **FULL SUN**

💧💧💧 **LITTLE TO REGULAR WATER**

Lophostemon confertus 'Variegatus'

This Australian native somewhat resembles eucalyptus. Erect, moderate to fast growth to 30–45 ft. tall and 25 ft. wide. Trunk and limbs resemble those of madrone (*Arbutus menziesii*), with reddish brown bark flaking off to reveal smooth, light-colored bark beneath. Oval, leathery bright green leaves tend to cluster at tips of branchlets; those of 'Variegatus' are marked with brilliant yellow. White to cream-colored, ¾-in. flowers in clusters of three to seven appear in summer, followed by woody capsules like those of eucalyptus. Good street or lawn tree.

CARE

Takes almost any soil, but young plants get a better start with good soil; chlorosis can be a problem in poor soils. Pinch and prune to get more twiggy growth.

Brisbane box hits all the high points for a shade tree: it's shapely, leafy, and long-lived. And its canopy can spread—to 50 feet across in some very old specimens.

Loropetalum chinense
Hamamelidaceae
EVERGREEN SHRUB

🌿 **ZONES 6–9, 14–24; BORDERLINE IN ZONES 4, 5**

☀️ ◐ **PARTIAL SHADE IN HOTTEST CLIMATES**

💧 **REGULAR WATER**

Loropetalum chinense
'Razzleberri'

Native to China and Japan, this evergreen shrub has a neat, compact habit, with tiers of arching or drooping branches. It grows to 6–10 ft. tall and wide. Roundish, light green, soft-textured leaves 1–2 in. long; throughout the year, the occasional leaf turns yellow or red, providing a nice touch of color. White to greenish flowers, each with four narrow, twisted, inch-long petals, appear in clusters of four to eight at branch tips. Flowering is heaviest in spring, but some bloom is likely at any time. Subtly beautiful plant; good in raised beds, woodland gardens. The following varieties have purple foliage and pink to purple flowers and look much alike: 'Blush', 'Burgundy', 'Fire Dance', 'Pippa's Red', 'Razzleberri', 'Ruby', 'Sizzlin' Pink', 'Suzanne'.

CARE

Young plants can be grown in hanging baskets. Provide rich, well-drained soil. Can take any amount of pruning. In the Pacific Northwest, needs protection against hard freezes.

FOR OTHER FLOWERING SHRUBS, SEE "FLOWERING TREES AND SHRUBS," PAGES 107–108.

Lotus
Papilionaceae
PERENNIALS

🌿 **ZONES VARY BY SPECIES**

☀️ ◐ **FULL SUN OR PARTIAL SHADE**

💧 **REGULAR WATER**

Lotus berthelotii

Trailing perennials that are often completely prostrate. Leaves are divided into leaflets. Flowers come in shades of red to yellow. (The pink-flowered water plants with the common name "lotus" are not in this genus.)

L. berthelotii. PARROT'S BEAK. Zones 9, 15–24; H1. Woody-based perennial native to the Canary Islands and Cape Verde Islands. To 8–12 in. high, with trailing, 2–3-ft.-long stems thickly covered with feathery, silvery gray leaves. Very narrow, 1-in., scarlet blossoms in summer. Very effective in hanging baskets or cascading over wall or rocks. Dies back in cold weather; suffers root rot where drainage is poor. Not a long-lived plant in Southern California.

L. maculatus. Zones 9, 15–24. Canary Island native resembling *L. berthelotii*. To 8–12 in. high, 2–3 ft. wide. Known mainly through its selections. 'Gold Flash' has bright yellow flowers with striking orange-red markings; needs cool nights to set flower buds. 'New Gold Flash' (blossom color similar to that of 'Gold Flash') and 'Amazon Sunset' (bright orange-red) are similar in plant and flower form to 'Gold Flash', but they bloom better where nights remain warm.

Lunaria annua

MONEY PLANT
Brassicaceae
BIENNIAL

✀ ZONES 2–10, 14–24

☼ ◑ AFTERNOON SHADE IN
HOTTEST CLIMATES

◐ ◐ ● LITTLE TO REGULAR WATER

Lunaria annua

This old-fashioned garden plant from Europe is grown for the translucent, 1¼-in.-wide papery circles that hang on to flower stalks; these "coins" are all that remain of the ripened seedpods after the outer coverings have dropped with seeds. Reaches 1½–3 ft. high, 1 ft. wide, with coarse, heart-shaped, tooth-edged leaves. Spring flowers resemble wild mustard blooms but are purple or white. Plant in an out-of-the-way spot in poor soil or in mixed flowerbed where shining pods can be admired before they are picked for dried arrangements. Tough and persistent; can reseed and become weedy.

With attractive round seedpods resembling translucent silver dollars, *Lunaria annua* is at its best after it has gone to seed. Use it in arrangements with or without seeds. Rub off husks and seeds to reveal the silvery circles.

Lupinus

LUPINE
Papilionaceae
ANNUALS, PERENNIALS, AND
EVERGREEN SHRUBS

✀ ZONES VARY BY SPECIES

☼ FULL SUN

◐ ◐ ● ◈ WATER NEEDS VARY
BY SPECIES

✁ FLOWERS ATTRACT BUTTERFLIES,
HUMMINGBIRDS

Lupinus

There are hundreds of species of lupines, many of them native to the western U.S. and found in a wide range of habitats. Leaves are divided into many leaflets. Sweet pea–like flowers are borne in dense spikes at ends of stems. Seeds of some species are toxic to livestock.

L. arboreus. Evergreen shrub. Zones 4, 5, 14–17, 22–24. Native to California coastal areas. To 5–8 ft. tall and wide. Spring flowers, in clusters 4–16 in. long, are usually yellow but may be lilac, bluish, white, or some mixture of those colors. Striking beach plant. Little or no water.

L. argenteus. SILVERSTEM LUPINE. Perennial. Zones 1–7. Native to the Southwest, Sierra Nevada, and the Rocky Mountains. To 2 ft. high, 1 ft. wide, with silvery-haired stems and (usually) smooth leaves. Flowers variable in color—usually blue, sometimes lilac or white. Moderate to regular water.

L. hartwegii. Annual. Zones 1–24. Native to Mexico. To 1½–3 ft. high, 1 ft. wide. Flowers in shades of blue, white, and pink. Sow seeds in place in spring for summer bloom. Moderate water.

L. hybrids. Perennials. Zones A1–A3; 1–7, 14–17. Grows to 4–5 ft. tall and 2 ft.

wide. These English-bred hybrid groups are descended from plants native to western America. Regular water.

Russell hybrids—the classic lupines—bloom during late spring or early summer, bearing tall flower spikes in white, cream, yellow, pink, red, orange, blue, purple, or bicolors. Little Lulu and Minarette are small strains—to 1½ ft. high and wide. All Russell hybrids tend to be short-lived. They are prone to powdery mildew; provide good air circulation. Grow from seed or buy nursery plants.

New Generation hybrids have all the merits of the Russell hybrids (from which they were developed) but are sturdier, needing no staking; longer-lived, requiring replacement only after 7 or 8 years; and mildew-resistant. They also come in a wider range of brighter, more intense colors. Bloom period is longer, too—from late spring to the end of summer, with possible autumn rebloom if plants are deadheaded regularly. Sold as seedling plants. The Band of Nobles is another series of improved Russell hybrids.

L. microcarpus densiflorus (L. densiflorus). Annual. Zones 3–24. California native to 1½–2 ft. high and wide, with white, yellow, pink, or lavender-tinged flowers in spikes to 1 ft. long. 'Ed Gedling', a selection of *L. m. d. aureus*, is a choice form with bright yellow flowers. Sow in fall for spring bloom. Little or no water to moderate water.

L. nanus. SKY LUPINE. Annual. Zones 3–24. Native from California to British Columbia. To 8–24 in. high, 9–12 in. wide. Spring flowers are rich blue marked with white. Sow seeds in fall or winter; combine California poppies (*Eschscholzia californica*) with the lupines for contrast. Self-sows readily where it gets little competition. Excellent for barren banks. No irrigation needed except in desert zones.

L. polyphyllus. Perennial. Zones 3–7, 14–21. Native to moist places from California to British Columbia. Grows 1½–4 ft. tall, 2–2½ ft. wide. Blooms in summer, bearing blue, purple, or reddish flowers in clusters 6–24 in. long. One important

ancestor of the Russell hybrids. Regular water.

L. succulentus. Annual. Zones 7–24. California native. To 3 ft. high, 2½ ft. wide; lush and leafy, with 6-in. spikes of blue flowers in spring. Normally found in damp places but adapts elsewhere; sometimes used for erosion control. Moderate to ample water.

CARE

Most lupines are not fussy about soil, though hybrids prefer rich, slightly acidic soil. All need good drainage. Except as noted, start plants from seed sown in fall, winter, or early spring. To hasten germination, soak seeds for a few hours before planting.

Lychnis

Caryophyllaceae
PERENNIALS, SOME TREATED
AS ANNUALS

✀ ZONES VARY BY SPECIES

☼ ◑ FULL SUN OR LIGHT SHADE

◐ ◐ ● WATER NEEDS VARY
BY SPECIES

Lychnis coronaria

Old-fashioned garden flowers, all tolerant of poor soils. The different kinds vary in appearance, but all come in eye-catching colors.

L. × arkwrightii. Short-lived perennial best treated as annual. Zones 3–9, 14–24. To 1½ ft. high, 1 ft. wide, with brown-tinted green leaves. Clusters of 1½-in. orange-scarlet flowers. 'Vesuvius' has brownish purple leaves. Regular water.

L. chalcedonica. MALTESE CROSS. Perennial. Zones A1–A3; 1–10, 14–24. Native to Russia. Loose, open form. Grows to

L

Some Like It Dry... In Summer

Spider lily (*Lycoris*) grows best with no water during dormancy. That's what makes it ideal for arid gardens. But it's not alone. Other bulbs that need a summer vacation from water are *Brodiaea*; *Calochortus*; Western native species of *Erythronium* and *Fritillaria*; freesia; aril, arilbred, and reticulata irises; *Ixia*; *Narcissus*, *Nerine* (some); *Sparaxis*; and *Tritonia*.

2–3 ft. high, 1 ft. wide. Leaves and stems are hairy; scarlet, ½-in. flowers with deeply cut petals are borne in dense terminal clusters. Particularly effective in large borders alongside white-flowered or gray-foliaged plants. 'Alba' has white blossoms. Regular water.

L. coeli-rosa. See *Silene coeli-rosa*.

L. coronaria. CROWN-PINK, DUSTY MILLER, MULLEIN PINK, ROSE CAMPION. Perennial. Zones 1–9, 14–24. From southeastern Europe. To 1½–2½ ft. high, 1½ ft. wide, with attractive, silky white foliage and magenta to crimson flowers a little less than an inch across. Effective massed. 'Alba' produces white flowers; 'Angel's Blush' bears white blooms with a cherry red eye. All self-sow freely if faded blossoms are not removed. Moderate water.

L. viscaria 'Splendens'. Perennial. Zones 1–10, 14–24. Selection of a Eurasian native to 1 ft. high and wide. Forms a low, compact, evergreen clump of grasslike leaves; stalks with clusters of ½-in.-wide, pink to rose blooms rise above the foliage clump. 'Splendens Plena' is a double-flowered selection. Good rock garden plant; flowers last well when cut. Regular water.

A perennial staple in carefree cottage gardens, rose campion (*Lychnis coronaria*) will decline after a few years. Allow seedpods to fully develop, and it will self-sow.

Lycianthes rantonnetii
(Solanum rantonnetii)
BLUE POTATO BUSH
Solanaceae
EVERGREEN SHRUB

☀ ZONES 12, 13, 15–24; H1, H2

☼◐ FULL SUN TO PARTIAL SHADE

💧💧 REGULAR TO AMPLE WATER

Lycianthes rantonnetii 'Variegatum'

From Paraguay and Argentina. As a shrub, it grows to 8–12 ft. tall and 6–10 ft. wide. But it can be staked into a tree form or, with support, grown as a vine to 12–15 ft. or more. Can also be allowed to sprawl as a groundcover. Leaves are bright green, oval; violet-blue, ½–1½-in. flowers throughout warm weather, often nearly year-round. Informal, fast growing, not easy to use in tailored landscapes; prune hard to keep it neat. In severe cold, leaf drop is heavy and branch tips may die back. 'Royal Robe' is more compact (to 6–8 ft. high and wide), bears darker purple flowers over a longer season. A variety with white-variegated leaves is sometimes offered.

Lycoris
SPIDER LILY
Amaryllidaceae
PERENNIALS FROM BULBS

☀ ZONES VARY BY SPECIES; OR GROW IN POTS

☼ FULL SUN

💧 REGULAR WATER DURING GROWTH AND BLOOM

Lycoris radiata

These natives to China and Japan produce narrow, strap-shaped leaves in fall (in mild-winter regions) or in spring; they remain green until some point in summer, then die down completely. Leafless flower stalks emerge after the foliage disappears. In late summer or early fall, each stalk bears a cluster of blooms with narrow, pointed petal-like segments and—in some species—projecting, spidery-looking stamens. Blossoms may be funnel-shaped or have segments splayed outward or reflexed.

L. aurea. GOLDEN SPIDER LILY. Zones 16, 17, 19–24; H1. Bright yellow, 3-in. flowers on 2-ft. stems. Slightly protruding stamens.

L. radiata. Zones 4–9, 12–24; H1. Best known and easiest to grow. Stems 1½ ft. high bear 1½–2-in., coral red flowers with a golden sheen; stamens are very prominent. 'Alba' has white flowers.

L. sanguinea. Zones 4–24. To 2 ft. high, with 2½-in., bright red to orange-red blooms. Stamens do not protrude.

L. sprengeri. Zones 4–24. Similar to *L. squamigera*, but with slightly smaller flowers in a more purplish pink.

L. squamigera (Amaryllis hallii). Zones 2–24. Fragrant, lilac-pink, 3-in. blossoms on

2-ft. stems resemble those of naked lady (*Amaryllis belladonna*). Stamens do not protrude.

CARE

Grow in a sunny site that stays dry during summer dormancy. (In areas with summer rainfall, grow in pots that can be protected from moisture.) Plant in late summer, setting bulbs in well-drained soil about 1 ft. apart. Keep tops of bulb necks at or just above soil surface—except in coldest part of range, where tops of necks should be just under surface. Water regularly while plants are growing and again when flower stalks emerge. It's best to withhold water and let soil go dry in summer when foliage begins to wither, though plants can take some summer water if drainage is excellent. Disturb clumps (after bloom) only when you want to move them or divide them to increase a planting. Beyond hardiness range, grow spider lilies in containers and overwinter them indoors.

Lyonothamnus floribundus
CATALINA IRONWOOD
Rosaceae
EVERGREEN TREE

☀ ZONES 14–17, 19–24

☼ FULL SUN

💧 MODERATE WATER

Lyonothamnus floribundus asplenifolius

Native to the Channel Islands off the coast of Southern California. The species has lobed or scallop-edged leaves; it is seldom seen in cultivation.

Much better known is *L. f. asple-nifolius*, fernleaf Catalina iron-wood. It grows at a moderate rate to 20–35 ft. tall, 15 ft. wide. Red-brown bark peels off in long, thin strips; young twigs are often reddish. Leaves are deep green above, gray and hairy beneath, divided into three to seven deeply notched or lobed leaflets. Blooms in late spring or early summer, bearing small white blossoms in flat, 8–18-in.-wide clusters that contrast well with the dark foliage. Old clusters turn brown; if it is practical to do so, cut them off.

Needs excellent drainage and should be pruned in winter to shape and control growth. Sometimes suffers from chlorosis in heavy soils. Easiest to grow near coast. Handsome in groves.

Lysiloma watsonii
(L. microphylla thornberi)
FEATHER BUSH,
FERN-OF-THE-DESERT
Fabaceae
EVERGREEN OR DECIDUOUS SHRUB
OR TREE

* ZONES 12–24; H1, H2
* FULL SUN
* NO IRRIGATION NEEDED

Lysiloma watsonii

Native to the foothills of Arizona's Rincon Mountains. Grows to 12–15 ft. tall and as wide, with multiple stems and a broad canopy of finely cut bright green leaves somewhat like those of acacia. Blooms in late spring or early summer, bearing masses of creamy white, clustered flowers like little puffballs emerging from round buds. These are followed by flat, ridged brown seedpods 4–8 in. long. Good informal background shrub, patio tree (can be trained to a single stem), or transition plant between garden and desert. To accentuate plant's filmy look, thin out crowded and weak branches in center. Evergreen in frost-free areas; deciduous elsewhere. May be killed to the ground by heavy frosts but usually comes back from the roots.

Lysimachia
Primulaceae
PERENNIALS

* ZONES VARY BY SPECIES
* FULL SUN OR PARTIAL SHADE
* MODERATE TO REGULAR WATER

Lysimachia nummularia

Most are vigorous perennials capable of spreading beyond their allotted space, especially if they receive plenty of water. Check them regularly to make sure they don't invade choicer plantings. Useful for naturalizing at woodland edges or in barely maintained areas. Blossoms are yellow or white; except as noted, they appear in summer.

L. ciliata. Zones 1–9, 14–21. Native to northeastern U.S. Erect clump to 4 ft. tall, 2 ft. wide, with narrow green leaves. Nodding, 1-in., yellow flowers with red-brown centers appear singly or in loose clusters in upper leaf joints. 'Firecracker' is similar but has reddish leaves.

L. clethroides. GOOSE-NECK LOOSESTRIFE. Zones A2, A3; 1–9, 14–24. Native to China, Korea, and Japan. To 3 ft. high, quickly spreading as wide or wider. Erect stems are clothed with pointed olive green leaves. Flower spikes densely packed with tiny white blooms are 6–8 in. long, arched like a goose's neck. Long lasting as a cut flower.

L. congestiflora. GOLDEN GLOBES. Zones 8, 9, 14–24; H1, H2. Native to China. Mat-forming plant grows to 4 in. high and 1 ft. or wider. Oval green leaves. Upturned yellow flowers, ½ in. across, grow in leafy terminal clusters from spring to summer. 'Outback Sunset' has red-tinged leaves with yellow variegation and yellow flowers with red centers.

L. ephemerum. Zones 2b–10, 14–24. Native to southwestern Europe. Leathery gray-green leaves form a neat clump to 3 ft. high and 1 ft. wide. Slender clusters of white, ½-in.-wide, long-lasting flowers. Not invasive.

L. nummularia. CREEPING JENNY, MONEYWORT. Zones 1–9, 14–24. Native to Europe; naturalized in eastern North America. To 4–8 in. high, spreading 2 ft. or more, rooting as it goes. Forms attractive mat of roundish, light green, 1-in. leaves. Yellow flowers about 1 in. across appear singly in leaf joints. Best use is in corners or containers where it need not be restrained. Will spill from wall, hanging basket. 'Aurea' has bright yellow leaves; needs shade. 'Goldilocks' has yellowish green foliage.

L. punctata. LOOSESTRIFE. Zones 1–9, 14–24. Native to central Europe and Asia Minor. To 3 ft. high, spreading to 2 ft. or more by underground stems. Narrow green leaves are borne in whorls on erect stems; inch-wide yellow flowers, also in whorls, appear on top third of stems. 'Alexander', to 2–3 ft. high and wide, has leaves edged with creamy white; 'Golden Alexander', to 2 ft. high and wide, has yellow-edged leaves. Divide clumps every 2 or 3 years in early spring.

For a drapelike effect around a tall, shapely urn, plant golden creeping jenny (*L. nummularia* 'Aurea') near the rim and let it trail.

Maackia
Papilionaceae
DECIDUOUS TREES

* ZONES 1–10, 14–17
* FULL SUN
* REGULAR WATER

Maackia chinensis

Related to locust (*Robinia*) and yellow wood (*Cladrastis kentukea*), these are small to medium-size trees with leaves divided like feathers into many small, narrow leaflets. They grow at a slow to moderate rate. Summer flowers resemble small sweet peas; creamy to yellowish white, crowded into erect, 4–6-in.-long, spikelike clusters. Flat, 2–3-in.-long seedpods follow the blossoms. Plants are not fussy about soil. Need minimal pruning.

M. amurensis. AMUR MAACKIA. Native to Manchuria and Siberia. Possibly to 60 ft. tall and wide but unlikely to exceed 30 ft. in gardens. Broad, rounded head; dark green leaves. Bark on trunk is an attractive bronze color and peels in curling flakes. 'Starburst' is more compact and vigorous.

M. chinensis. CHINESE MAACKIA. Chinese native reaches 20–30 ft. high and wide. Shrubbier than *M. amurensis*, with leaves divided into more and smaller leaflets. Foliage unfolds silvery grayish green, matures to dark green.

M

Macadamia

Proteaceae
EVERGREEN TREES

- ZONES 9, 16, 17, 19–24; H1, H2
- FULL SUN
- REGULAR WATER

Macadamias

Macadamias are clean, handsome ornamental trees where frosts are light. Where best adapted (Zones 23, 24, H1, H2), they produce clusters of delicious hard-shelled nuts, usually within 3 to 5 years after planting. Although most macadamias are sold under the name *M. ternifolia*, any tree you buy will likely be one of the two species (or their hybrids) described below.

Trees grow 30–40 ft. tall and almost as wide, with whorls of glossy, leathery, narrow leaves. Look for grafted, named varieties of proven nut-bearing ability. Seedlings take longer to bear nuts, and their quality is unpredictable. Macadamias are self-fruitful, but planting two different varieties often produces bigger harvests.

Trees bloom in winter and spring, bearing small, sometimes fragrant white to pink flowers in dense, pendent, 1-ft. clusters. Roundish fruit to 1½ in. wide consists of a leathery husk containing a hard-shelled nut. To harvest nuts, pick them up as they fall from tree (husks of ripe nuts split, making the nuts easy to remove). If nuts don't fall naturally, strip the tree when the birds and squirrels start to take them.

M. hybrids. Crosses between *M. integrifolia* and *M. tetraphylla*. 'Beaumont' is one of the best varieties for Southern California, bearing over a very long period. It produces medium to large nuts with moderately thick shells; new leaves are reddish. 'Cooper' has small nuts, also with moderately thick shells. 'Vista' produces small to medium-size, very thin-shelled nuts.

M. integrifolia. SMOOTH-SHELL MACADAMIA. Commercial species best adapted to Hawaii. Can be grown near the coast in Southern California. Leaves are smooth edged. Nuts ripen from late fall to late spring. Popular varieties include 'Kakea', 'Kau', 'Keaau', 'Mauka', and 'Purvis'.

M. tetraphylla. ROUGH-SHELL MACADAMIA. More widely grown than *M. integrifolia* in California, where it performs best slightly inland. Differs from *M. integrifolia* in having a more open growth habit, spiny leaves, and thinner-shelled nuts that ripen from fall to midwinter. Varieties include 'Burdick', 'Cate', and 'Fenton'.

CARE

Set out macadamias from containers anytime of year, but they'll suffer less stress from moisture loss and heat if planted in fall. Avoid planting in windy sites.

These trees perform best in deep, rich soil, with light applications of fertilizer at least twice a year. They are weak wooded, so prune young plants to encourage strong structure. New growth that emerges during winter is usually yellow; this is caused by cold, not health problems. Later growth will be green. Macadamias are resistant to oak root fungus.

Though mites, scale, and thrips sometimes appear, macadamias rarely have serious pest problems in California. In Hawaii, the tropical fruit borer pierces the shell and lays eggs in the nut; it is a serious and widespread pest. The best controls are to harvest frequently and pick up fallen fruit as soon as possible.

FOR MORE ON PEST MANAGEMENT, SEE PAGES 726–731.

Macfadyena unguis-cati

CAT'S CLAW, YELLOW TRUMPET VINE
Bignoniaceae
EVERGREEN OR DECIDUOUS VINE

- ZONES 8–24; H1, H2
- FULL SUN OR PARTIAL SHADE
- MODERATE WATER

Macfadyena unguis-cati

Vigorous vine native from Mexico and West Indies to Uruguay. It climbs high (to 25–40 ft.) and fast by hooked, clawlike, forked tendrils. Each leaf consists of two oval, glossy light green leaflets; a tendril is centered between them. Blooms in early spring, bearing lobed yellow trumpets to 2 in. long, 4 in. across.

Succeeds in cool-summer areas but is faster growing and stronger where summers are hot—even on south walls in Zones 12, 13. Can climb any surface that isn't slick, including stone, wood, chain-link fences, and tree trunks; vines are even seen clinging to undersides of freeway overpasses. Can be used as a groundcover; it puts down roots where stems touch the ground, making it a good choice for erosion control on slopes. Evergreen where frosts are light or absent; partially to almost completely deciduous in colder areas.

CARE

Tends to produce leaves and flowers at stem ends; after bloom, cut back some stems nearly to the ground to stimulate new growth lower down. During growing season, pinch back vigorous shoots as needed.

Mâche

Valerianaceae
ANNUAL

- ZONES A1–A3; 1–24; H1
- FULL SUN
- REGULAR WATER

Mâche

This cool-season crop, sometimes called corn salad or lamb's lettuce, is among the most cold-hardy of traditional salad and cooking greens. Plants form rather loose rosettes of spoon-shaped leaves to 6 in. long with a mild, nutty flavor.

CARE

Grow in well-drained soil. In warmer climates, sow seeds from fall through early spring for harvest in about 90 days. In cooler climates, sow seeds directly in the ground in summer, or in late winter as soon as soil is workable. Space rows 8 in. apart; sow seeds ½ in. deep and 1 in. apart. Thin to 6 in. apart. Start extra plants so a few can reseed. Plants overwinter in areas where the ground does not freeze. Harvest entire rosette at once. Mâche quickly bolts in warm weather, so be sure to harvest while temperatures are still cool.

Mâche's juicy leaves are perfect for simple salads. Toss them with olive oil, balsamic vinegar, minced shallots, and quartered strawberries for a taste of spring.

M

Macleaya

PLUME POPPY

Papaveraceae

PERENNIALS

⚡ **ZONES VARY BY SPECIES**

☼ ◑ **LIGHT SHADE IN HOTTEST CLIMATES**

● **REGULAR WATER**

Macleaya cordata

These tall perennials from China and Japan produce tall, branching stems that carry clouds of tiny flowers. The leaves are large and deeply lobed. Plants look tropical, and their garden value lies in size and structure rather than floral impact. Spread by creeping rhizomes and can be invasive if not controlled; plant them among sturdy shrubs rather than among delicate perennials.

M. cordata. Zones A2, A3; 1–24. To 7–8 ft. tall and 3 ft. wide, with grayish green, 10-in. leaves. White to beige flowers. Considered less invasive than *M. microcarpa*.

M. microcarpa. Zones 2b–24. Similar to *M. cordata* but has pinkish beige flowers. Blossoms of 'Coral Plume' are more decidedly pink.

Best at the back of a large summer border, plume poppy's blue- and purple-tinged leaves provide a dramatic backdrop for bright yellow rudbeckias or spikes of purple blazing star (*Liatris spicata*).

Magnolia

Magnoliaceae

DECIDUOUS AND EVERGREEN TREES AND SHRUBS

⚡ **ZONES VARY BY SPECIES**

☼ ◑ **FULL SUN OR PARTIAL SHADE**

● **REGULAR WATER**

Magnolia × *soulangeana* 'San Jose'

Magnificent flowering plants featuring blossoms in white, pink, red, purple, or—a more recent development—rich yellow. These plants show a remarkable variety of leaf shapes and plant forms. New varieties and hybrids appear every year, but distribution is spotty in local nurseries. Many more kinds are available from mail-order specialists.

EVERGREEN MAGNOLIAS

M. champaca (Michelia champaca). CHAMPACA. Shrub or tree. Zones 16–24; H1, H2. To 10–20 ft. tall and broad. Glossy bright green, 10-in. leaves. Orange-yellow, 3-in. flowers with up to 20 segments are borne intermittently throughout the year, most often in winter and summer; their perfume is legendary. 'Alba' (*M.* × *alba*) has white flowers.

M. doltsopa (Michelia doltsopa). Zones 14–24; H1, H2. To 90 ft. tall in its native Himalayas; in San Francisco, it has grown to 25 ft. in as many years. Varies from bushy (nearly as wide as high) to narrow and upright (about half as broad as tall); choose plants for desired form, then prune to shape. Thin-textured, leathery dark green leaves. In winter and spring, furry brown buds open to blos-

soms ranging from cream-colored to white, with a slight green tinge at the base; they are 5–7 in. across, with 12–16 segments, each 1 in. wide. 'Silver Cloud' presents an abundance of large, cream-colored blossoms in spring.

M. figo (Michelia figo). BANANA SHRUB. Zones 6 (borderline), 9, 14–24; H1, H2. Slow growing to 6–8 ft. tall (possibly to 15 ft.) and about two-thirds as wide. Densely clothed with glossy, leathery leaves. Plant blooms most heavily in spring but produces scattered flowers throughout summer. Blossoms are 1–1½ in. wide, creamy yellow with a thin brownish purple border on each segment. Notable feature is the powerful, fruity fragrance, like that of ripe bananas; the perfume is strongest in a warm, wind-free spot. Choice plant for entry or patio. 'Port Wine' has rose to maroon flowers.

M. × foggii (Michelia × foggi). Shrub. Zones 9, 14–24. Group of hybrids between *M. figo* and *M. doltsopa*. 'Allspice' grows 15–18 ft. tall, 6–8 ft. wide, with glossy dark green foliage; from spring to summer bears fruity-scented, 1½-in., light yellow flowers bordered in maroon. 'Jack Fogg', about 18 ft. tall and 6–8 ft. wide, has fragrant spring flowers of white, with each segment bordered in purplish pink.

M. grandiflora. SOUTHERN MAGNOLIA, BULL BAY. Zones 4–12, 14–24; H1, H2. Pure white blooms, aging to buff; large (8–10 in. across), powerfully fragrant. Species and its varieties bloom throughout summer and fall. Useful street or lawn tree, big container plant, or wall or espalier plant. Unpredictable in form and age of bloom. Grafted plants more predictable but may need pruning to become single-trunked trees. Grows to 80 ft. tall and 60 ft. wide. Can grow as a multitrunked tree. Glossy, leathery leaves. Attracts birds. Needs warmest location (or warm wall) in Zones 4, 5. Expect breakage, some yearly pruning in Zones 6, 7. Give wind-sheltered spot in the desert. In Hawaii, does best in Zone H1 and in the inland valleys of H2.

'Bracken's Brown Beauty'. Pyramidal to 35 ft. tall and

15 ft. wide. Hardier than most other varieties. Flowers and leaves smaller than species but still showy.

'D. D. Blanchard'. A handsome pyramidal selection to 50 ft. tall or more and 25–35 ft. wide. Lustrous dark green leaves are orange-toned brown on undersides.

'Edith Bogue'. A shapely, vigorous tree, 35 ft. tall and 20 ft. wide, and one of the hardiest selections of *M. grandiflora*; has withstood −24°F (−31°C). Keep it out of strong winds. Young plants are slower to come into heavy bloom than some other varieties.

'Little Gem'. Slow growing to 20–25 ft. tall and 10–15 ft. wide. Small (5–6-in.-wide) flowers from spring through late summer (fewer blooms form during midsummer heat). Narrow form makes it good in a container, as an espalier, or in a confined area. Branches to the ground. Half-size leaves are dark green above, rusty beneath. Reportedly less hardy than the species.

'Majestic Beauty'. Not as widely adapted (Zones 7–12, 14–24; H1, H2). It has very large flowers (to 1 ft. across). Vigorous, dense-branching street or shade tree of broadly pyramidal form grows to 35–50 ft. tall and 20 ft. wide. Leaves are exceptionally long, broad, and heavy.

'St. Mary'. Usually grows to 20 ft. tall; much larger in old age. A heavy producer of 8–10-in. flowers on small tree. Fine where standard-size magnolia would grow too large and too fast. Left alone, it will form a big, dense bush. Can be trained as a small tree. Good plant for containers and espalier.

'Victoria'. Reaches only 20 ft. tall and 15 ft. wide. Withstands −10°F (−23°C) with little damage but should be located out of wind. Leaves dark green, exceptionally broad and heavy.

M. 'Timeless Beauty'. Zones 4–9, 14–24. A natural hybrid between *M. grandiflora* and *M. virginiana*. Creamy white, fragrant flowers to 10 in. wide. Blooms in spring and summer. Extremely dense crown, to 15–20 ft. tall and 20–25 ft. wide, with spreading branches.

M

»

Magnolia Types

Magnolias include both evergreen and deciduous types. Most have large, striking blossoms, but a few are grown for use as foliage plants.

EVERGREEN MAGNOLIAS. In California and Arizona, "magnolia" usually means *M. grandiflora*, the classic Southern magnolia with glossy leaves and big, fragrant white blossoms. Loved for its foliage and flowers, it also offers the advantages of heat resistance and tolerance for damp soil. On the other hand, it requires a fair amount of maintenance and has limited uses. It's messy, shedding its big, hard leaves (they look almost like plastic) and other litter constantly from late spring into earliest autumn. And though it's generally considered a street or lawn tree, it tends to lift paved walks with its surface roots, and it casts dense, year-round shade that prevents the growth of a healthy lawn beneath. Furthermore, it is slow growing in heavy soil or where root area is restricted. Before planting this tree, carefully consider whether its advantages outweigh its drawbacks.

Also in this group are plants previously listed under the genus *Michelia*. These trees and shrubs are native to China and the Himalayas, generally less hardy than other evergreen magnolias. They are known for their profuse, wonderfully fragrant flowers, which are borne among their leaves as opposed to branch ends.

DECIDUOUS MAGNOLIAS WITH SAUCER FLOWERS. This group includes saucer magnolia (*M. × soulangeana*) and its many varieties, often called tulip trees because of the shape and bright colors of their flowers. Also included here are yulan magnolia (*M. denudata*) and lily magnolia (*M. liliiflora*). All are hardy to cold, thriving in various climates throughout the West—but early flowers are subject to frost damage, and all do poorly in hot, dry, windy areas.

DECIDUOUS MAGNOLIAS WITH STAR FLOWERS. Included in this group are *M. kobus* and *M. stellata* and its varieties (the star magnolias). All are hardy, slow-growing, early-blooming plants with wide climatic adaptability.

OTHER MAGNOLIAS. This group includes *M. macrophylla*, a medium-size tree with huge leaves and blooms, and *M. acuminata*, a big shade tree with inconspicuous greenish yellow flowers; the similar *M. a. subcordata* is a smaller tree with slightly showier blossoms. Hybrids of the last are grown for their flowers, which show better yellow color than their parent. Blossoms of some of these hybrids appear on bare branches; others bloom as leaves emerge. *M. sieboldii* and *M. wilsonii* constitute another flowering category; they bear drooping, cup-shaped, fragrant white blossoms after leafout.

M. virginiana. SWEET BAY. Zones 4–9, 14–24. Creamy white, fragrant, nearly globular blossoms are 2–3 in. wide. Late spring to late summer. Prefers moist, acid soil (native to swamps in eastern U.S.). Big evergreen or semievergreen tree in milder climates; deciduous shrub in colder areas. Can reach 50 ft. tall and 20 ft. wide. Leaves bright green above, nearly white beneath. Twigs and branches are bright green. 'Moonglow' ('Jim Wilson') is a bit hardier and more upright (35–40 ft. tall, 15–18 ft. wide) than the species, with glossy, dark green leaves. Grows fast and starts blooming young.

DECIDUOUS MAGNOLIAS

M. acuminata. CUCUMBER TREE. Zones 2–9, 14–21. Grows 60–80 ft. tall and 30 ft. wide. Greenish yellow flowers to 3½ in. wide; glossy, not conspicuous. Appear after leaves in late spring, summer. Handsome reddish seed capsules with red seeds. Dense shade or lawn tree. Dislikes hot, dry winds. 'Koban Dori' is a smaller selection, to 15–20 ft. tall, with canary yellow flowers. *M. a. subcordata* is shrubbier (25–35 ft. tall by 20–30 ft. wide) with larger, showier blooms.

M. 'Apollo'. Zones 4–9, 14–24. Abundant, fragrant, star-shaped flowers to 10 in. across. Blooms in early to midspring, before leafout. First blossoms to open are deep violet outside, paler inside; later ones are deep rose-pink. Smallish, round-headed tree to 35 ft. tall and 18–20 ft. wide.

M. 'Athene'. Zones 3b–9, 14–24. Large (8–10 in.) cup-and-saucer-shaped blooms; rosy purple at base shading to pale pink, with ivory white interior. Richly fragrant. Grows 18–25 ft. tall and wide. Moderate to fast growth. Flowers well when young.

M. 'Butterflies'. Zones 2b–9, 14–24. Produces many 4–5-in., light yellow flowers with red stamens. Blooms in midspring, before leaves emerge. Upright and pyramidal when young; later spreading. Grows 20 ft. tall and 15 ft. wide. Leaves 8 in. long, medium to dark green, sparsely hairy.

M. cordata. See *M. acuminata*.

M. 'Daybreak'. Zones 4–9, 14–24. Large (8–10 in.), very fragrant, bright rose-pink flowers. Blooms in late spring, escaping frost damage. Narrow form to 30 ft. tall and 10–15 ft. wide; useful in small lots, side yards.

M. denudata (M. heptapeta). YULAN MAGNOLIA. Zones 3b–9, 14–24. Fragrant white flowers, sometimes tinged purple at base. Blossoms are erect; somewhat tulip-shaped, 3–4 in. long, spreading to 6–7 in. Early bloom on base branches; often a few flowers appear in summer. Tends toward irregular form; good with dark background in informal garden or at woodland edge. Grows 35 ft. tall and 30 ft. wide. Does well in Southern California.

M. 'Elizabeth'. Zones 3b–9, 14–24. Fragrant soft yellow flowers, 6–7 in. wide. Color is paler in mild-winter areas. Blossoms appear before or with the leaves. Grows to at least 40 ft. tall and 20 ft. wide as single-trunked tree or multitrunked shrub-tree.

M. 'Galaxy'. Zones 3b–9, 14–24. Abundant bright red-purple, slightly fragrant, goblet-shaped blossoms to 5 in. across. Blooms in midspring, before leaves emerge but usually after last frost. Fast-growing, broadly conical tree to 40 ft. tall and 25 ft. wide.

M. kobus. KOBUS MAGNOLIA. Zones 2b–9, 14–24. White, slightly fragrant blossoms to 4 in. wide. Blooms in early to midspring, before leaves emerge. Grows 30 ft. tall and 20 ft. wide. Cold-hardy, sturdy tree for planting singly in a lawn or in informal groupings.

M. Kosar-De Vos hybrids ("Little Girl" series). Zones 2b–9, 14–24. Hybrids bred to bloom later than *M. stellata*, thus avoiding frost damage. Star-shaped flowers range from deep to pale purple (sometimes with pink or white interior), depending on variety. Trees bloom in spring before leafout; sporadic rebloom in summer. Erect, shrubby growers to 12 ft. tall and 15 ft. wide. Varieties bear girls' names such as 'Betty' (rose-pink) and 'Susan' (purplish red). Use in shrub border or singly in lawn.

M

M. liliiflora (M. quinque-peta). LILY MAGNOLIA. Zones 2b–9, 14–24. Tulip-shaped flowers are white on the inside, purplish outside. Blooms over long spring, summer season. Tends to have two distinct bloom periods in Northwest. Grows 12 ft. tall and 15 ft. wide. Good for shrub border; strong vertical effect in big flower border. Spreads slowly by suckering. Leaves 4–6 in. long. Blooms of 'Gracilis', 'Nigra', and 'O'Neill' are dark purplish red outside, pink inside.

M. × *loebneri*. Zones 2b–9, 14–24. Hybrids between *M. kobus* and *M. stellata* that grow slowly to 12–15 ft. tall (can reach 50 ft. tall) and wide. Narrow, strap-shaped flower segments similar to those of *M. stellata*, but generally fewer and somewhat longer and wider. Blooms appear before leaves in midspring. Some selections are fragrant. 'Ballerina', white with faint pink blush, and taller, pure white 'Spring Snow' are both fragrant. Very lightly scented are 'Leonard Messel', with pink blooms from darker buds, and 'Merrill' ('Dr. Merrill'), a vigorous, free-flowering white-blossomed form. Use in lawn, shrub border, at woodland edge.

M. macrophylla. BIGLEAF MAGNOLIA. Zones 4–9, 14–21. Fragrant white flowers to 16 in. across in late spring and early summer, after leafout. Showy tree with leaves 1–3 ft. long and 9–12 in. wide. Grows slowly to 30 ft. tall and 20 ft. wide. Needs to give it some shade in warm climates. Be sure to give it some shade in warm climates.

M. 'Pegasus'. Zones 4–9, 14–17. Grows 10 ft. tall and wide in 10 years, at least twice that with age. White flowers with a flush of pink at the base to 4 in. wide, borne on bare branches. They are followed by bright red seed capsules. Best in light shade.

M. 'Royal Crown'. Zones 2b–9, 14–24. Vigorous, densely branched, grows 20–25 ft. tall and wide. Candle-shaped pink buds open to upright, 10–12-in. blooms with narrow segments; blossoms dark red to violet outside, white inside. Blooms in early spring, before leafout.

M. salicifolia 'Wada's Memory'. Zones 2b–9, 14–24.

White, slightly fragrant blossoms over 4 in. across. Blooms in early to midspring, before leaves emerge. Grows 30 ft. tall and 20 ft. wide. Same uses as *M. kobus* but grows faster. Coppery red new leaves.

M. sargentiana robusta. Zones 5–9, 14–24. Among the most spectacular of flowering plants. Huge (8–12 in.), fragrant mauve-pink bowls open erect, then nod. Blooms in mid- to late spring, before leaves open. Not for hot, dry areas. Grows to 35 ft. tall and wide. Must have ample room. 'Blood Moon' is more upright and can reach 45 ft. tall.

M. sieboldii. OYAMA MAGNOLIA. Zones 4–9, 14–24. Grows 6–15 ft. tall and wide; good choice for small gardens. Leaves are 3–6 in. long. Blooms from late spring through late summer. Flower buds resembling white Japanese lanterns open into cup-shaped, fragrant, white blossoms centered with crimson stamens; bright pink seedpods follow. Nice planted on a hill, where you can look up into the nodding flowers. Best in partial shade.

M. × *soulangeana*. ✔ SAUCER MAGNOLIA (often called TULIP TREE). Zones 2b–10, 12–24. White to pink or purplish red, fragrant flowers variable in form and size (3–6 in. wide). Blooms from late winter into spring, both before leaves emerge and as they open. Grows to 25 ft. tall and wide. Good lawn plant; good anchor plant in big container plantings. Medium green, rather coarse-looking leaves 4–6 in. long or longer. Seedlings highly variable; look for named selections (especially later-blooming ones for frost-prone regions).

'Alba Superba' ('Alba'). Purple-suffused buds open to large, nearly pure white flowers. Early blooming. Rather more upright and slightly taller than most varieties.

'Black Tulip'. Bears large, goblet-shaped blooms of deep wine red. Slender, upright grower (30 ft. tall, 15 ft. wide). Excellent for small gardens. In mild climates, can be grown in containers when young. Can be pruned as a hedge.

'Brozzonii'. White blossoms very slightly flushed purplish rose at base; 8 in. across.

CLOCKWISE FROM TOP LEFT: *Magnolia stellata* 'Royal Star'; *M.* × *loebneri* 'Merrill'; *M.* 'Star Wars'

Late. One of the most handsome white-flowered magnolias. Vigorous tree.

'Lennei'. Bears very large, globe-shaped blossoms that are deep purple outside, white inside. Spreading, vigorous plant. Late bloom helps it escape frosts in cold areas. 'Lennei Alba' (*M. lennei* 'Alba') is similar but with earlier, pure white, slightly smaller blooms.

'Lilliputian'. Grows to just 18 ft. tall and 10–15 ft. wide. Good where a smaller magnolia is called for. Flowers are pink outside, white inside, somewhat smaller than those of other selections. Late blooming.

'Rustica Rubra'. Bears large, cup-shaped, deep reddish purple flowers. Blooms somewhat past midseason. Big (6 in.) dark rose seedpods. Vigorous grower for large areas. More treelike than many varieties.

'San Jose'. Large white flowers flushed with pink. Very early.

M. 'Star Wars'. Zones 3b–9, 14–24. Deciduous. Rich

How to Grow Magnolias

LOCATION For any magnolia, choose the planting site carefully—these trees are hard to move once established. Pick a location where the shallow, fleshy roots won't be damaged by digging or by soil compaction from constant foot traffic. Magnolias never look their best when crowded.

Larger deciduous types are most effective standing alone against a background that will display their flowers and, in winter, their strongly patterned, typically gray limbs and big, fuzzy flower buds.

Smaller deciduous magnolias show up well in large flower or shrub borders and make choice ornaments in Japanese gardens.

All magnolias may be used as lawn trees; try to provide a good-size grass-free area around the trunk, and don't plant under the tree. In frost-prone areas, plant early-flowering magnolias in a northern exposure to delay bloom as long as possible and lessen frost damage.

SOIL Magnolias appreciate fairly rich, neutral to fairly acid soil amended with plenty of organic matter at planting time. At least in the early years, keep a cooling mulch over the root area.

PLANTING Balled-and-burlapped plants are available in late winter and early spring; container plants are sold anytime. Do not set plants lower than their original soil level. In windy locations, stake single-trunked or very heavy plants to keep them from rocking to and fro—the movement would tear the thick, fleshy, sensitive roots. Soggy soil can topple newly planted large magnolias, so stake big specimens if you are planting them just before the rainy season; to avoid damaging roots, set stakes in the planting hole before placing the tree. Remove stakes as soon as the tree is firmly rooted.

WATERING Irrigate deeply and thoroughly, but don't waterlog the soil or the tree will drown. Only *M. virginiana* can take constantly wet soil.

FERTILIZING Magnolias are subject to problems caused by nutrient deficiencies. Chlorosis from lack of iron in alkaline soils shows up as yellowing between leaf veins; iron chelates will correct this condition. Fertilizer will remedy nitrogen deficiency. Feed trees if new growth is sparse and weak, or if the tree shows a fair amount of dieback despite adequate watering and drainage. Use a controlled-release product, since magnolias are very susceptible to salt damage from overfertilizing, which can cause burned leaf edges.

The same leaf damage can result from excess mineral salts in the soil or salts in irrigation water. The latter is a problem in Southern California and, typically, the factor limiting success of magnolias in desert regions. Frequent heavy waterings will help leach out salts and carry them to lower soil levels—as long as drainage is good. In the Northwest, late frosts may burn edges of new leaves.

PRUNING For deciduous magnolias, best time is after bloom; for evergreen kinds, do the job before the spring growth flush. Best method is to remove the entire twig or limb to the base. Cuts on deciduous kinds are often slow to callus over, so prune these only when necessary to correct shape, eliminate or cut back wayward branches, or remove lower branches from trunk as tree gains height.

CHALLENGES Watch for scale and aphids at any time and for spider mites in hot weather. Protect lower leaves of shrubby types from snails and slugs. Magnolias are not immune to oak root fungus, but they seem somewhat resistant.

bright pink blossoms (paler inside), 11 in. across. Blooms for 1–2 months, beginning in early spring (before leafout). Grows 30–35 ft. tall and 20 ft. wide. Especially good magnolia for Southern California and inland areas.

M. stellata. STAR MAGNOLIA. Zones 2b–9, 14–24. White flowers to 3 in. across, with 12–18 narrow, strap-shaped segments. Profuse bloom comes very early—late winter to early spring, before leafout. Some varieties are fragrant.

Slow growing, shrubby to 10 ft. tall and 20 ft. wide. Use for borders, entryway gardens, edge of woods. Plant this early bloomer where you can see flowers from indoors. Quite hardy, but flowers often nipped by frost in colder part of range. Fine texture in twig, leaf. Fair yellow-and-brown fall leaf color.

'Centennial' bears white blossoms faintly marked pink, 5 in. across, with 40–50 segments. It's like an improved 'Waterlily'. 'Dawn' has white flowers with 25 or more segments, each with a longitudinal pink stripe. 'Jane Platt' grows a little bigger than the species (12–15 ft. tall by 10–12 ft. wide) and has rich pink, 4–5-in. blossoms with 40–50 segments. 'Rosea', pink star magnolia, has pink buds; flowers open pink-flushed white, age to plain white. Various plants are sold under this name. 'Royal Star' grows quickly to 18–20 ft. tall and 15 ft. wide, with fragrant white blooms with 25–30 segments. It blooms 2 weeks later than species. 'Rubra' bears rosy pink blooms to 5 in. across and is more treelike in form than other varieties. 'Waterlily' has pink buds opening to very fragrant white blossoms to 5 in. across, with 40–50 segments. Blooms later and is faster growing than most star magnolias. Various plants are sold under this name.

M. 'Sundance'. Zones 3b–9, 14–24. Fragrant, pale golden yellow, saucer-shaped flowers to 8 in. across. Blooms in spring, before leafout. Fast-growing, pyramidal tree to 25–30 ft. tall and 20 ft. wide.

M. × veitchii. VEITCH MAGNOLIA. Zones 4–9, 14–24. Spectacular tree. Profuse show

of goblet-shaped, 8–10-in.-wide blooms in soft white flushed with pink. Blooms in midspring, before leafout. Fast growing and vigorous to 30–40 ft. tall and 30 ft. wide. Needs plenty of room. Protect from wind; branches are brittle. Good magnolia for Southern California. Give it afternoon shade in hottest areas. 'Columbus' bears 4–5-in.-wide, white flowers with purple highlight at base of each segment. Narrower than the species, growing 30–35 ft. tall and 15–20 ft. wide. Has a thicker trunk and stronger branching structure than other magnolias, making it a sturdy choice for urban plantings.

M. 'Vulcan'. Zones 4–9, 14–24. Showy, ruby red blossoms to 10–12 in. across. Flowers borne in tree's younger years may be smaller and paler than those on older trees. With good care, trees will produce mature flowers in 3 or 4 years. Blooms in spring, before leafout. Open form when young, becoming more rounded with age. Grows 25 ft. tall and wide.

M. wilsonii. WILSON MAGNOLIA. Zones 4–9, 14–24. Fragrant, pendulous, 3–4-in.-wide, white blossoms with red stamens in late spring. Spreading shrub or tree, to 25 ft. tall and wide, with rich purple-brown twigs. Plant high on bank where you can look up into flowers. Best in light shade.

M. 'Yellow Bird'. Zones 3b–9, 14–24. Deepest yellow color of the yellow hybrids. Slight green tinge at base of erect, 3-in.-long flower segments. Blooms for 2–3 weeks in early to midspring, as leaves emerge. Upright and pyramidal when young, broadly oval when mature. Grows 40 ft. tall and 20 ft. wide. Furrowed bark. Sometimes available as a multi-trunked form.

M. 'Yellow Lantern'. Zones 3b–9, 14–24. Clear yellow blossoms (darker than those of M. 'Elizabeth', paler than those of M. 'Yellow Bird') with upright or slightly spreading segments to 6 in. long. Open from large, furry buds. Midspring, before leafout. Upright, single-trunked tree to 50 ft. tall and 20–25 ft. wide.

M

Mahonia

Berberidaceae

EVERGREEN SHRUBS

- ZONES VARY BY SPECIES
- EXPOSURE NEEDS VARY BY SPECIES
- WATER NEEDS VARY BY SPECIES
- ATTRACT BIRDS, BUTTERFLIES

Mahonia aquifolium

Related to barberry (*Berberis*) and described under that name by some botanists, these evergreen shrubs are easy to grow and good-looking all year. Spiny-edged leaves are divided into leaflets; foliage can be prickly, so avoid setting mahonias too close to walkways or in other areas where they might snag passersby. Yellow flowers are borne in dense, rounded to spikelike clusters, followed by berrylike, typically blue or blue-black (sometimes red or brown) fruit with a powdery bloom.

M. aquifolium. OREGON GRAPE. Zones 2–12, 14–24. Native from British Columbia to Northern California, mostly west of the Cascades. State flower of Oregon. Dense, bushy plant grows erect to 6 ft. tall, spreading by underground stems to 5 ft. wide. Leaves are typically glossy green, with five to nine leaflets that resemble holly leaves. Ruddy or bronze new growth; scattered mature red leaves throughout the year (more pronounced in fall and winter). Leaves turn purplish or bronze in winter, especially in cold-winter areas or where plants are grown in full sun. Early-spring flowers appear in 2–3-in. clusters along stems. Edible blue-black fruit with gray bloom (makes good jelly).

'Compacta' grows to 2–3 ft. high. New foliage is a glossy light to coppery green; mature leaves are matte medium green. 'John Muir' is about the same size, with somewhat finer foliage and denser growth. 'Orange Flame', 2 ft. high and 3 ft. wide, has bronzy new growth, glossy green mature leaves that turn wine red in winter.

Mass as a low screen or garden barrier; plant in woodland or in tubs. Control height and form by pruning; if any woody stems jut out too far, cut them down to ground (new growth fills in quickly). Can be sheared as a formal hedge. Resistant to oak root fungus. Give wind protection in cold-winter areas. Can take any exposure but performs best with shade in hottest climates (northern exposure recommended in desert). Little to regular water.

M. fortunei. Zones 5–9, 14–24. Native to China. To 6 ft. tall and 3 ft. wide, with an unusual stiff charm. Erect stems bear 10-in.-long leaves with 7–13 leaflets; matte green above, yellowish green with heavily netted veins on undersides. Short clusters of flowers in late fall. Full sun or light shade. Regular water.

M. fremontii. DESERT MAHONIA. Zones 2b–24. Native to deserts of the Southwest. Upright, many-stemmed plant to 3–12 ft. tall, 6 ft. wide. Gray-green to yellowish green leaves, each with three to five thick leaflets that are edged with very sharp, tough spines. Flowers in 1–1½-in.-long clusters in late spring; dark blue to brown fruit. Full sun or light shade. Little or no water.

M. 'Golden Abundance'. Zones 2b–12, 14–24. Vigorous, densely foliaged plant reaches 6 ft. tall, spreading by underground stems to 5 ft. wide. Glossy green leaves with red midribs. Profuse bloom in early spring with clusters of yellow flowers; later produces an abundant crop of purplish blue berries with gray bloom. Full sun in cooler climates, some shade in hotter ones. Little to regular water.

M. japonica Bealei group. LEATHERLEAF MAHONIA. Zones 3b–12, 14–24. Native to China. To 10–12 ft. tall and 10 ft. wide,

CLOCKWISE FROM TOP: *M. japonica* Bealei group; *M. × media* 'Charity'; *M. aquifolium* 'Orange Flame'

with strong pattern of vertical stems and horizontal leaves. The leaves reach over a foot long, divided into 7–15 broad, thick, leathery leaflets to 5 in. long. Foliage is yellowish green above, gray-green below, with a small yellow patch at the base of each leaflet. Blooms in late winter, producing erect, 3–6-in.-long blossom spikes at ends of branches. Powdery blue berries. Striking against background of

stone, brick, wood, or glass. Plant in rich soil amended with ample organic matter. Takes sun in cool-summer areas; does best in partial shade elsewhere. Regular water.

M. lomariifolia. Zones 6 (borderline), 7–9, 14–24. Native to China. To 6–12 ft. tall and 6 ft. wide, with erect stems that branch only slightly. Young plants often have a single, vertical unbranched stem; older ones produce more branches (almost vertical growing) from near base. Clustered deep green leaves are held horizontally near ends of branches. Each leaf reaches 2 ft. long,

M

Mostly Mahonias

These broad-leafed evergreens take such a wide range of conditions, they could serve as the main theme for plantings along a woodland path that transitions from sun to shade. In mostly shade, surround a group of stately *M. lomariifolia* with wild ginger (*Asarum caudatum*). In half-shade, combine Oregon grape (*M. aquifolium*) with salal (*Gaultheria shallon*) and rhododendrons. And in mostly sun, surround *M. pinnata* 'Ken Hartman' with drifts of creeping mahonia (*M. repens*) and hummingbird sage (*Salvia spathacea*).

has 19–41 barbed leaflets arranged symmetrically along both sides of central leafstalk (with a single leaflet at the tip). Midwinter flowers grow in long, erect clusters at branch tips, just above topmost cluster of leaves. Blue berries. Strong-structured plant for dramatic effect. Partial shade, especially in afternoon. Regular water.

M. × media. Zones 6–9, 14–24. Hybrids between *M. lomariifolia* and a Japanese species. Plants bear upright clusters of fragrant flowers in late fall and winter; generally resemble *M. lomariifolia* and require the same conditions. 'Arthur Menzies' grows to 10–12 ft. tall, 8–10 ft. wide; 'Buckland' and 'Charity' grow to 15 ft. tall and 12 ft. wide; 'Faith' reaches 6–10 ft. tall and 6 ft. wide; 'Hope' and 'Lionel Fortescue' both grow to 6 ft. tall and wide; and 'Winter Sun' reaches 4–5 ft. tall and as wide.

M. pinnata. CALIFORNIA HOLLY GRAPE. Zones 4–9, 14–24. Native from southern Oregon to Southern California. To 4–5 ft. tall (often taller along the coast) and as wide. Similar to *M. aquifolium* but with spinier, more crinkly leaves; new growth

The tart blue-black berries that follow mahonia's billowy yellow flower clusters are as popular with jelly-makers as they are with birds.

often shows lots of red and orange. Spikelike springtime flower clusters; dark blue berries. 'Ken Hartman' has dense, uniform growth. Full sun in cooler areas, light shade in hottest climates. No irrigation needed (takes aridity better than *M. aquifolium*).

M. repens. CREEPING MAHONIA. Zones 2b–9, 14–24. Native from British Columbia to Northern California, eastward to Rocky Mountains. To 1 ft. high and 3 ft. wide, spreading by underground stems. One of the best mahonias for winter color: dull blue-green leaves turn bronzy or pinkish when cold weather arrives. Short clusters of flowers in mid- to late spring are followed by blue berries. Good groundcover. Full sun or partial shade. Little or no water.

M. 'Skylark'. Zones 4–9, 14–24. Grows to 5 ft. tall or higher, 5 ft. wide. Shiny leaves to 6 in. long are reddish when new; they mature to deep green, then take on purple tints in winter. Spring flowers in dense, 4–6-in. spikes. Dark blue berries. Full sun in cooler areas, partial shade in hotter ones. No irrigation needed.

CARE

Generally pest-resistant, though foliage is sometimes disfigured by a small looper caterpillar. In general, pruning is needed only to remove old, damaged stems or to correct rank growth; cut those stems all the way to the ground.

FOR OTHER PLANTS THAT ATTRACT BIRDS, SEE PAGES 95–99.

Maianthemum
Asparagaceae
PERENNIALS

- **ZONES VARY BY SPECIES**
- **PARTIAL SHADE**
- **REGULAR WATER**

Maianthemum bifolium kamtschaticum

Botanists have brought two Western natives together under this single genus name. Both are woodland plants that need loose, rich, slightly acidic soil to look their best.

M. bifolium kamtschaticum (M. dilatatum). FALSE LILY-OF-THE-VALLEY. Zones A2, A3; 2–9, 14–17. Native from Northern California to Alaska and Idaho. To 6–8 in. high; in good growing conditions, spreads rapidly by creeping rootstocks to form broad mats. Stems 2–6 in. high bear neat, roundish to heart-shaped, heavily veined leaves to 8 in. long and half as wide. Bears foamy clusters of white flowers in spring, followed by red berries in summer. Makes an attractive woodland groundcover but is capable of overwhelming more delicate plants growing nearby. Disappears in winter.

M. racemosum (Smilacina racemosa). FALSE SOLOMON'S SEAL. Zones 1–7, 14–17. Commonly seen in shaded woods from California to British Columbia, east to the Rockies. Grows 1–3 ft. high, spreading by creeping rhizomes to form dense colonies. Each single, arching stalk has several medium green, oval to lance-shaped, 3–10-in.-long leaves with hairy undersides; foliage turns golden yellow in fall. In spring, stalks are topped by

fluffy, conical clusters of small, fragrant, creamy white flowers. Red berries with purple spots ripen in autumn and are favored by wildlife. Good for naturalizing in wild gardens. Tolerates more sun in cool-summer climates. Resembles true Solomon's seal (*Polygonatum*).

Majorana hortensis. See *Origanum majorana*

Malephora
(Hymenocyclus)
ICE PLANT
Aizoaceae
SUCCULENT PERENNIALS

- **ZONES VARY BY SPECIES**
- **FULL SUN**
- **LITTLE OR NO WATER**
- **ATTRACT BEES**

Malephora

Groundcover plants from South Africa. Small, dense, smooth, fleshy leaves are highly resistant to heat, wind, exhaust fumes, and fire. Used for streetside and freeway plantings. Plants bloom over a long season, but their daisylike flowers are scattered rather than in sheets.

M. crocea. Zones 11–24. To 6 in.–1 ft. high and 6 ft. wide, with blue-green foliage. Sparse production of reddish yellow flowers nearly year-round, with heaviest bloom in spring. Good choice for moderately steep slopes. *M. c. purpureocrocea* has bluish green foliage, salmon-colored flowers.

M. lutea. ROCKY POINT ICE PLANT. Zones 12–24. To 1 ft. high and 6 ft. wide, with bright green foliage. Inch-wide yellow flowers bloom most of the year. More vigorous than *M. crocea*.

Malus

FLOWERING CRABAPPLE
Rosaceae
DECIDUOUS TREES

🌡 **ZONES 1–11, 14–21, EXCEPT AS NOTED IN CHART**

☀ **FULL SUN**

💧💧 **MODERATE TO REGULAR WATER, EXCEPT AS NOTED IN CHART**

» See chart on pages 434–435.

Malus 'Weeping Candied Apple'

More widely adapted than other flowering trees, flowering crabapple is valued for lavish clouds of white, pink, red, or purplish red flowers and for fruit that is showy, edible, or both. All are native to North America, Europe, or Asia. Hundreds of varieties are in cultivation, most about 20 ft. tall, though sizes range from 4 to 35 ft. Leaves are usually pointed ovals, often fuzzy, varying from light green to purple. Fall foliage is rarely noteworthy; exceptions noted.

Bloom comes in spring, usually before leaves unfurl, but it is as brief as it is spectacular: early varieties go from first flower to 50 percent petal drop in less than 10 days; later varieties are faster. Masses of single, semidouble, or double flowers sometimes have a musky, sweet scent. Small red, orange, or yellow apples, ranging from under ¾ in. to almost 2 in. wide, ripen from midsummer into autumn; in some varieties, the fruit makes a brilliant display that continues well after leaves drop. Some varieties flower and fruit more heavily in alternate years; some don't fruit at all.

Those listed in the chart are primarily ornamental. For crabapples used chiefly in cooking, see Crabapple.

How to Grow Malus

Plant bare-root trees in winter or early spring; set out container plants anytime. Although they take heat, they are not at their best in low desert. For optimal growth and productivity, plants need winter chill—about 600 hours at 45°F (7°C) or lower. These make fine lawn trees, but protect trunks from lawn mower injury, which creates an entry point for diseases, with a sod-free, mulched area around the trunk.

SOIL All are best in fertile, well-drained, deep, neutral soils but will grow in rocky, gravelly, acidic, or slightly alkaline ones.

PRUNING Prune to build a framework, remove suckers, and correct the shape. Crabapple trees can be trained as espaliers.

CHALLENGES Flowering crabapple varieties differ widely in disease resistance. Many old favorites are prone to diseases such as apple scab, cedar-apple rust, fireblight, and powdery mildew. But newer disease-resistant varieties are displacing them. The chart notes the degree of resistance or susceptibility for each variety. In the Pacific Northwest, choose trees that resist cedar-apple rust, scab, and powdery mildew. Fireblight may afflict susceptible trees anywhere when weather conditions are favorable for its development.

The same pests attack both flowering crabapples and apple trees. Scale, aphids, spider mites, and tent caterpillars may require control; codling moths and apple maggots should be controlled with a pesticide containing spinosad if you intend to harvest the fruit—or if you don't want the tree to incubate pests that will trouble nearby apples and pears.

Malva

MALLOW
Malvaceae
PERENNIALS OR BIENNIALS

🌡 **ZONES 1–9, 14–24, EXCEPT AS NOTED**

☀ **FULL SUN**

💧 **REGULAR WATER**

🦋 **FLOWERS ATTRACT BUTTERFLIES**

Malva moschata

These plants are related to and somewhat resemble hollyhock (*Alcea rosea*), but are bushier, with smaller, roundish to heart-shaped leaves. They are from Europe but have naturalized in the U.S. Mallows bloom from summer to fall and are easy to grow. They need good drainage, average soil. Grow from seed; usually bloom first year. Use in perennial borders or for a quick tall edging. Not long-lived.

M. alcea. Perennial. To 4 ft. tall, 2 ft. wide; upper leaves deeply divided. Saucer-shaped pink flowers to 2 in. wide. Most common form is 'Fastigiata'; it is narrower than the species and looks much like hollyhock.

M. moschata. MUSK MALLOW. Perennial. Zones A2, A3; 1–9, 14–24. Erect, branching plant to 3 ft. high, 2 ft. wide. Finely cut leaves; pink or white flowers to 1 in. wide or somewhat wider. Entire plant emits a mild, musky odor if brushed against or bruised. Named selections are more frequently grown than the species. *M. m.* 'Rosea' has pink blossoms; *M. m.* 'Alba' is 2 ft. high, bears white flowers.

M. sylvestris. Perennial or biennial. Erect, bushy growth to 2–4 ft. tall, 2 ft. wide. Can become invasive. Flowers 2 in. wide; often bloom until frost.

Common variety 'Zebrina' (often sold as *M. zebrina*) has blossoms in pale lavender-pink with pronounced deep purple veining. 'Mauritiana' has darker, often semidouble flowers.

Malvaviscus arboreus drummondii
(M. drummondii)

TURK'S CAP, SLEEPY HIBISCUS
Malvaceae
SHRUBBY PERENNIAL

🌡 **ZONES 4–9, 14–24**

☀◑ **FULL SUN TO PARTIAL SHADE**

💧 **REGULAR WATER**

🦋 **ATTRACTS BUTTERFLIES AND HUMMINGBIRDS**

Malvaviscus arboreus drummondii

This stiff perennial, native to the southeastern U.S. through Central America, grows 4–10 ft. tall and wide. In mild-winter areas, it can be grown as an evergreen shrub; elsewhere it freezes to the ground in summer. Small, vermilion-red blooms with overlapped petals resemble a turban and appear from summer to fall. Red stamens extend above the petals as in a hibiscus. Large, downy, heart-shaped leaves. 'Big Momma' has coral red blooms.

Sleepy hibiscus blooms always seem poised to open to sunlight. But they stay closed, hence the plant's common name.

M

MALUS: TOP PICKS TO GROW

NAME	HABIT, SIZE	FLOWERS	FRUIT	COMMENTS
Malus 'Adams' Zones A2, A3; 1–21	Dense, round headed, to 20 ft. tall and wide.	Red buds open to single pink flowers.	Dull red, small, long lasting.	Orange fall foliage. Good disease resistance.
M. 'Adirondack'	Columnar, to 12 by 6 ft.	Red buds; large, red-tinged, single, waxy white flowers.	Red to orange red.	Formal in appearance. High disease resistance.
M. 'Brandywine'	Vigorous, shapely, to 15–20 ft. tall and wide.	Double rose-pink. Fragrant.	Yellowish green.	Leaves have a reddish cast. Fair disease resistance.
M. 'Centurion'	Oval crowned, to 25 by 15–20 ft.	Red buds open to single red flowers.	Shiny deep red, profuse, long lasting.	Blooms young. High disease resistance.
M. 'Donald Wyman'	Broad, to 20 by 25 ft.	Pink to red buds open to single white flowers.	Heavy crops; shiny, bright red, small, long lasting.	Lustrous foliage. Good disease resistance.
M. floribunda JAPANESE FLOWER-ING CRABAPPLE	Broad, dense grower to 12 by 18 ft.	Deep pink buds open to single white flowers. Fragrant, incredibly profuse blooms.	Red-blushed yellow, small; does not last long.	Moderate disease resistance.
M. 'Harvest Gold'	Vigorous, narrow, to 30 by 15 ft.	Pink buds open to single white flowers. Late-blooming.	Yellow, showy; hangs on until spring.	High disease resistance.
M. 'Indian Magic'	Round headed, to 15–20 ft. tall and wide.	Red buds open to single deep pink flowers.	Very productive, shiny red to orange, small, long lasting.	Moderate susceptibility to disease.
M. ioensis 'Klehm's' KLEHM'S IMPROVED BECHTEL	Round headed, open, to 30 ft. tall and wide.	Double pink 2-in. flowers. Fragrant.	Dull yellow-green, large.	Good disease resistance, except to cedar apple rust.
M. 'Lollipop'	Round, compact growth 8–10 ft. tall and wide.	Profuse white, single flowers.	Yellow, small.	Green leaves. Good to excellent disease resistance.
M. 'Louisa'	Broad, weeping, to 15 ft. tall and wide.	Single rose-pink. Profuse bloomer.	Golden orange, small.	Excellent, graceful weeper. Glossy, dark green foliage. Good disease resistance.
M. 'Madonna'	Narrow, erect tree grows to 15–20 by 10–15 ft.	Pink buds open to double white flowers. Long bloom season.	Red-blushed yellow, small.	Bronzy new growth. Good disease resistance.
M. 'Marilee'	Narrow, upright, inverted cone to 24 ft. tall, 10 ft. wide.	Large double white flowers.	Fruitless.	Medium green leaves with good disease resistance.
M. 'Molten Lava'	Spreading, weeping tree to 12 by 15 ft.	Deep red buds open to single white flowers.	Red orange, small; lasts well on tree.	Attractive yellow winter bark. Good disease resistance.
M. 'Prairifire'	Round headed, to 20 ft. tall and wide.	Red buds open to single flowers in deep pinkish red.	Dark red, small; hangs on well.	Leaves emerge reddish maroon, turn dark green. High disease resistance.
M. 'Profusion'	Upright, spreading, to 20 ft. tall and wide.	Deep red buds, single deep purplish pink flowers.	Dark red, long lasting.	Foliage is purple when young, matures to bronzy green. Moderate disease resistance.
M. 'Purple Prince'	Rounded, 20 ft. tall and wide.	Rose-red.	Maroon, small.	Leaves open purple, become bronzy green. Good to excellent disease resistance.

MALUS: TOP PICKS TO GROW

NAME	HABIT, SIZE	FLOWERS	FRUIT	COMMENTS
M. 'Red Jade' Zones A2, A3; 1–21	Irregular, weeping form; to 15 ft. tall and wide.	Small, single white flowers.	Bright red, heavy crop; holds well into fall.	Moderate disease resistance.
M. 'Robinson'	Dense, upright, vase-shaped tree to 25 by 15 ft.	Deep red buds open to single deep pink flowers.	Dark red.	Copper-tinged foliage. Some scab susceptibility.
M. 'Royal Fountain'	Weeping form; to 15 ft. tall and wide.	Single rose red.	Deep red.	Leaves start purple, turn summer bronze. Susceptible to scab, some fireblight resistance.
M. 'Royal Raindrops'	Upright, spreading form to 20 ft. tall, 15 ft. wide.	Bright rose-colored flowers.	Red fruits hang from long stems on the tree.	Purple cutleaf foliage has excellent disease resistance.
M. 'Royalty' Zones A1–A3; 1–21	Upright, to 20 by 18 ft.	Single purplish crimson.	Dark red.	Foliage is dark purple in spring and fall, purplish green in summer. Susceptible to scab, fireblight.
M. sieboldii 'Calocarpa'. See *M. × zumi calocarpa*				
M. 'Snowdrift' Zones A1–A3; 1–21	Rounded, dense, to 20–25 ft. tall and wide.	Red buds open to single white flowers. Long bloom season.	Orange-red, small, long lasting.	Good disease resistance.
M. 'Spring Snow'	Upright, oval crown reaches 25 ft. by 22 ft.	Large, single, pure white flowers.	Fruitless, or nearly so.	Green foliage. Susceptible to scab; some resistance to rust, fireblight, mildew.
M. 'Sugar Tyme'	Upright, oval, to 18 by 15 ft.	Delicate light pink buds open to single white flowers. Fragrant.	Red, abundant, long lasting.	High disease resistance.
M. 'Thunderchild' Zones A2, A3; 1–21	Erect, oval, to 20 by 18 ft.	Single rose-pink.	Dark red.	Purple foliage. Scab susceptible.
M. toringo sargentii SARGENT CRABAPPLE	Broad, densely branched, to 10 by 20 ft.	Single white flowers. Blooms are small, fragrant, profuse.	Red, tiny, long lasting.	Good disease resistance. 'Candymint' has pink flowers outlined in red. 'Firebird' (5–8 ft. tall and wide) and 'Tina' (4–6 ft. tall and 8–10 ft. wide) are excellent dwarf forms.
M. transitoria 'Golden Raindrops' ('Schmidtcutleaf') Zones 3–11, 14–21	Upright, vase-shaped, to 20 ft. tall by 15 ft. wide.	Small, star-shaped white flowers from pink buds. Profuse blooms.	Golden yellow, abundant, long lasting.	Unique crabapple with deeply cut, dark green foliage. Excellent resistance to scab, cedar-apple rust, mildew; poor resistance to fireblight.
M. tschonoskii	Upright, narrowly oval; 28 ft. tall, half as wide.	White single flowers.	Sparse greenish fruit reaches 1 in. diameter.	Green leaves open silvery green, shift apricot-red in fall. Good disease resistance, except to fireblight.
M. 'Weeping Candied Apple'	Weeping form; to 10–15 by 20 ft.	Outer petals deep pink, inner petals whitish edged in pink, opening from reddish buds.	Bright red, small; persists all winter.	Moderate scab susceptibility.
M. 'Weeping Madonna'	Semiweeping habit, to 15 ft. by 12–15 ft.	Large, semidouble white flowers.	Cherry-size fruit is gold with a red blush.	Green foliage. Some disease resistance.
M. × zumi calocarpa (M. sieboldii 'Calocarpa')	Densely branched, rounded, to 15 ft. tall and wide.	Single flowers open pale pink, then fade to white. Fragrant.	Glossy, bright red, small; lasts well on tree.	Moderate susceptibility to fireblight.

Mandevilla
Apocynaceae
EVERGREEN AND DECIDUOUS VINES
OR VINING SHRUBS

☀ ◑ **ZONES VARY BY SPECIES**

☀ ◑ **FULL SUN OR PARTIAL SHADE**

💧 **REGULAR WATER**

Mandevilla laxa

Grown for their showy flowers, which feature five broad lobes that flare out from a tubular throat. Except as noted, they are unscented. Plants climb by twining.

M. hybrids. Evergreen. Zones 21–24; H1, H2. The hybrid mandevillas described here are sometimes sold as selections of *M.* × *amabilis* or *M.* × *amoena*. Plants grow to 15–20 ft., with glossy dark green, oval leaves. Most widely grown is 'Alice du Pont', with clusters of glowing pink, 2–4-in. flowers appearing among the leaves from spring to fall; even very small plants in 4-in. pots will bloom. Other varieties, including those in the Sun Parasol series that also bloom at a young age, are available in

In areas where mandevilla is borderline hardy, grow this tropical-looking vine in a large container (about 20 inches wide), with a shapely, freestanding trellis (obelisk) in the center for it to climb. Move the pot to a protected spot for winter.

shades of red, pink, and white. Some, such as 'Pink Parfait', have double flowers. Plant all hybrids in rich soil and provide a frame, trellis, or stake for support. Pinch tips of young plants to induce bushiness.

M. laxa. CHILEAN JASMINE. Deciduous; evergreen in frost-free areas. Zones 4–9, 14–24; H1. From Chile and Argentina. Grows to 15 ft. or more, with heart-shaped leaves. Blooms in summer. Clustered flowers are white, 1½–2 in. across, with a powerful perfume like that of gardenia. Requires less heat to bloom than other mandevillas. Provide rich soil. If plant becomes badly tangled, cut to ground in winter; it will resprout and bloom on new growth. Roots hardy to about 5°F (–15°C).

M. sanderi. Evergreen. Zones 21–24; H1, H2. Native to southeastern Brazil. Compact, shrubby plant to 2 ft. high, 3 ft. wide; eventually starts to twine (to 15–20 ft. tall with support), but you can keep it bushy by pinching climbing shoots. Deep green leaves are tinged with bronze when new. Flowers are 3–4 in. wide, rose-pink with yellow throats; color grows paler as blossoms age. Varieties that are lower growing and shrubbier than the species (to 6–8 ft.) are superb in hanging baskets; these include 'My Fair Lady' (white blooms), 'Red Riding Hood' (deep cherry red flowers), and 'Scarlet Pimpernel' (scarlet flowers). Similar in form is 'Strawberry Lemonade', with deep pink, yellow-throated flowers; its leaves are beautifully variegated in mint green, cream, and white, with pink flushes when young.

CARE

Mandevillas survive outdoors only in mildest regions. In colder areas, treat as annuals, or grow them in containers and move them indoors or to a greenhouse for the winter. Need heat to bloom; in coastal areas, train against a protected south- or west-facing wall, preferably with additional reflected heat from paving. Watch for spider mites. Growth may need thinning from time to time.

Mangifera indica. See Mango

Mango
Anacardiaceae
EVERGREEN TREE

☀ **ZONES 23, 24; H1, H2**

☀ **FULL SUN**

💧 **REGULAR WATER**

◈ **SAP AND JUICE FROM FRUIT CAUSE SKIN RASH IN SOME PEOPLE**

Mangoes

Tropical Asian native, known botanically as *Mangifera indica*. In Hawaii, mango trees reach upwards of 50 ft. tall and spread to 30 ft. or more. These trees are very long-lived and produce heavy crops of fruit. In mildest parts of Southern California, however, plants often remain shrubby (8–10 ft. tall and nearly as wide) and are likely to fruit only in the most favorable frost-free locations. Large leaves are often coppery red or purple when new; they later turn dark green.

Trees are self-fruitful. Long clusters of yellow to reddish flowers appear at branch ends from spring into summer; these are followed by oval fruits up to 9 in. long, weighing up to 2 lbs. in good growing conditions. Fruit has green to reddish or yellowish skin, a large seed, and very juicy pale yellow to deep orange flesh that tastes somewhat like that of a peach with flowery overtones. Poorer-quality fruit may be stringy and/or have a flavor reminiscent of varnish. In Southern California, skin may not color well, but fruit quality can still be excellent.

Mangoes are most flavorful if allowed to ripen on the tree; they are usually ready to harvest 4 to 5 months after bloom. Reliable varieties include the standard-size 'Ah Ping' and

'Pope', and the compact 'Carrie', 'Fairchild', 'Keitt', and 'Rapoza'. 'Manila' is a compact grower widely sold in California. Trees tend to bear more heavily in alternate years. They tolerate fairly poor, shallow soil as long as it is well drained. Fertilize as recommended for citrus. Anthracnose, scale, and powdery mildew can be serious problems. Little pruning is needed. Wear gloves when harvesting or pruning: sap can cause a rash.

Mascagnia
ORCHID VINE
Malpighiaceae
DECIDUOUS VINES

☀ **ZONES 12–24**

☀ **FULL SUN**

💧 **MODERATE WATER**

Mascagnia macroptera

Twining vines native to Mexico; useful in desert gardens where they bloom at the hottest time of year. Bright green leaves. Bears clusters of five-petaled blossoms (the petals are shaped like ping-pong paddles); each bloom is centered with 10 stamens. Oddly winged seedpods that look something like butterflies follow the flowers.

M. lilacina. LAVENDER ORCHID VINE. To 15–20 ft., with lilac flowers that are followed by inch-wide seedpods. Plant is hardy to 15°F to 18°F (–9°C to –8°C).

M. macroptera. YELLOW ORCHID VINE. Listed as a species of *Callaeum* by some botanists. To 15 ft., with abundant bright yellow flowers followed by conspicuous 2-in., yellow-green seedpods. Hardy to 22°F to 24°F (–6°C to –4°C).

M

Matricaria recutita
(M. chamomilla)

CHAMOMILE
Asteraceae
ANNUAL

- ZONES 1–24
- FULL SUN
- MODERATE WATER

Matricaria recutita

Native to Europe and western Asia, this aromatic plant has naturalized in North America. It grows to 2 ft. high and 1½ ft. wide, with finely cut, almost fernlike foliage. White-and-yellow daisy-type flowers to 1 in. wide bloom in summer. Grows easily in ordinary soil; sow seeds in late winter or spring. Valued for its herbal use: dried flowers are used in making the familiar, fragrant chamomile tea. (For more on herbs for tea, see page 682.)

Matricaria 'White Stars' is often sold as a variety of *Tanacetum parthenium*. It has white flowers with an extended row of outer petals and yellow centers. Chamomile sold as a walk-on groundcover is *Chamaemelum nobile* (*Anthemis nobilis*).

A Soothing Cup

Chamomile is well known as a tonic, general cure-all, and soothing tea. The foliage has a pleasant scent, but the flowers contain the ingredients for tea. Pick them when they are fully open, let them dry, then brew. Flowers of the "other chamomile" (*Chamaemelum nobile*) can also be used to make tea, but their flavor is not as sweet.

Matteuccia struthiopteris

OSTRICH FERN
Onocleaceae
FERN

- ZONES A1–A3; 1–10, 14–17
- FULL SUN IN COOLER CLIMATES ONLY
- REGULAR TO AMPLE WATER

Matteuccia struthiopteris

This extremely hardy fern is native to northern regions of North America, Europe, and Asia. It does not grow with full vigor in mild-winter areas. Clump is narrow at base, then spreads out at top like a shuttlecock. Plant can grow to 6 ft. tall and 3 ft. wide in moist, moderate climates, but it may reach only a quarter or a third of that size in mountain regions with a short growing season and low humidity. 'Jumbo' is a hefty-looking variety that can reach 7 ft. tall under ideal conditions; mature plants form a short trunk.

The plant spreads by underground rhizomes. Attractive in woodland or beside pond or stream. Needs rich soil. Unfolding young fronds (fiddleheads) are edible.

Matthiola

STOCK
Brassicaceae
BIENNIALS OR PERENNIALS GROWN AS ANNUALS

- ZONES 1–24
- FULL SUN OR LIGHT SHADE
- REGULAR WATER

Matthiola incana

Old-fashioned favorites from the Mediterranean region with narrow gray-green leaves and profuse, erect spikes of fragrant flowers. Best in cool weather.

M. incana. Valued for spicy-sweet perfume, cut flowers. Flowers are single or double, 1 in. wide, in colors including white, pink, red, purple, lavender, blue, yellow, and cream.

Many strains are available, ranging from under 1 ft. to as tall as 3 ft., from 10 to 16 in. wide. Taller varieties are best for cutting. Stock needs light, fertile soil and good drainage. In cold-winter areas, plant in earliest spring to get flowers before hot weather (choose early bloomers). In mild-winter regions, plants set out in early fall will bloom in winter or early spring. Take moderate frost but will not set flower buds if nights are too chilly; late planting means no flowers until spring. Where winter rainfall is heavy, plant in raised beds for good drainage.

M. longipetala (M. bicornis). EVENING SCENTED STOCK. To 1 ft. or a little taller, 9 in. wide, with lance-shaped leaves. Small purplish flowers are not showy, but they give off a powerful fragrance at night. In hot-summer, mild-winter climates, grow as a winter annual.

Maytenus

Celastraceae
EVERGREEN TREES AND SHRUBS

- ZONES VARY BY SPECIES
- FULL SUN
- WATER NEEDS VARY BY SPECIES

Maytenus boaria

Two species of this genus of primarily South American natives are grown in the West. Both have inconspicuous flowers and fruit, but they are otherwise remarkably dissimilar in appearance.

M. boaria. MAYTEN. Zones 8, 9, 14–24. From Chile. Graceful tree with narrow, light to medium green leaves. Resembles a small-scale weeping willow (*Salix babylonica*), with long, pendulous branchlets hanging down from branches. Slow to moderate growth to an eventual 30–50 ft. tall and wide; 20 ft. tall by 15 ft. wide is typical at 12 years of age. For uniformity, plant 'Green Showers'; its weeping branchlets are densely clad with deep green leaves that are a little broader than those of the species.

Give well-drained soil. Disturbing the roots by cultivating may cause suckers to appear. Tree produces much side growth; remove unwanted branches along trunk or keep some of them for multiple-trunk effect. May show partial defoliation after a cold snap, but recovery is rapid. Resistant to oak root fungus. Needs moderate to regular water; irrigate deeply to keep tree from rooting near the soil surface and invading planting beds.

M. phyllanthoides. MANGLE DULCE. Zones 12, 13, 23, 24. From Baja California,

M

M

Mexico, the Caribbean. Like mangroves, this plant grows in or near salt water and in brackish, swampy soils inland. Usually grows as a 6–12 ft. shrub but occasionally a small tree up to 24 ft.; usually as wide as it is tall. Smooth, light gray bark; fleshy dark green to gray-green leaves. Little to moderate water.

Mazus reptans
Phrymaceae
PERENNIAL

🌿 **ZONES 1–9, 14–24**

☼ ◐ **PARTIAL SHADE IN HOTTEST CLIMATES**

💧 **REGULAR WATER**

Mazus reptans

Himalayan native growing to 2 in. high, spreading 1 ft. or wider by slender stems that creep and root along the ground. Small, sparsely toothed, rather narrow leaves are bright green. Spring and early summer flowers are ¾ in. across, purplish blue with white and yellow markings; they appear in clusters of two to five. In shape, the blossoms resemble those of monkey flower

(*Mimulus*). Use in a rock garden, as a small-scale groundcover, or as a filler between pavers (it takes heavy foot traffic in this last role). Needs rich soil. Evergreen in mild-winter climates; in colder areas, freezes to ground but usually recovers quickly in spring if protected over winter by snow cover or light mulch.

Mecardonia 'Goldflake'
Plantaginaceae
ANNUAL

🌿 **ZONES 3–24**

☼ **FULL SUN**

💧 **REGULAR WATER**

Mecardonia 'Goldflake'

Low growing, spreading, to 2–5 in. high and 12–16 in. wide. Small yellow flowers resembling nemesia bloom from late spring through frost. Makes a nice edging; pretty when sprawling over the sides of containers. May overwinter where temperatures stay above 25°F (–4°C). Heat-tolerant. Also sold as 'Gold Dust'.

Colorful Carpets

Short plants located at path edges or between steppingstones need to be able to withstand occasional foot traffic. *Mazus reptans* is tough enough, and it offers bright purplish flowers. Among other rugged but colorful choices are English daisy (*Bellis perennis*), blue star creeper (*Pratia pedunculata*), and many violets, including *Viola labradorica*. And for the added bonus of pleasing fragrance, try chamomile (*Chamaemelum nobile*) and woolly thyme (*Thymus serpyllum*).

Meconopsis
Papaveraceae
PERENNIALS

🌿 **ZONES VARY BY SPECIES**

◐ ● **PARTIAL OR FULL SHADE**

💧 **REGULAR WATER**

Meconopsis betonicifolia

Ardent collectors and shade-garden enthusiasts sometimes attempt the many species offered by specialist seed firms. Most of these are difficult to grow outside their native climates, but the choices listed here are not too trying if given loose, acid soil and cool, humid, shady conditions. Protect seaside plantings from wind.

Plants consist of foliage rosettes with elongated leaves that vary in shape from undivided to lobed or cut; these foliage clumps send up flowering stems at bloom time. Blossoms are large and brilliantly colored. Plants self-sow without becoming invasive.

M. betonicifolia (M. baileyi). HIMALAYAN POPPY. Zones A1–A3; 1–6, 17. Native to the Himalayas. In the right climate, can reach 6 ft. tall and 2 ft. wide. Abundant hairy leaves with serrated edges; silky, 3–4-in., sky blue poppies with yellow stamens. In less favorable locales, it is a much squatter, shorter-lived plant with smaller flowers verging on mauve. Blooms in late spring or early summer.

M. cambrica. WELSH POPPY. Zones 1–9, 14–17. Native to western Europe. To 1–2 ft. high, 1 ft. wide, with divided leaves. Easier to grow than *M. betonicifolia*. Produces orange or yellow, 3-in. poppies from late spring to fall. In the

coolest-summer areas, it tolerates full sun and some drought. *M. c. aurantiaca* flore-pleno has semidouble flowers.

Melaleuca
Myrtaceae
EVERGREEN SHRUBS OR TREES

🌿 **ZONES VARY BY SPECIES**

☼ **FULL SUN**

🌢 **LITTLE WATER, EXCEPT AS NOTED**

🐦 **FLOWERS ATTRACT BIRDS**

Melaleuca nesophila

Australia is home to 140 or more species of melaleucas, and many of these show up in Western gardens. All have narrow, sometimes needlelike leaves and bear clustered flowers with prominent stamens; the blossoms attract birds. Since each flower cluster resembles a bottlebrush, some melaleucas are called bottlebrushes, though that name is more generally applied to members of the genus *Callistemon*. Tight clusters of woody seed capsules are attached directly to branches; these hang on for several years, forming odd, decorative cylinders around twigs and branches. Many melaleucas have interestingly contorted branches and bark that peels off in thick, papery layers.

Almost all melaleucas make good screens; some of the larger ones are useful as flowering or shade trees.

M. armillaris. DROOPING MELALEUCA. Shrub or tree. Zones 8, 9, 12–24; H1, H2. As sprawling shrub, grows 12–15 ft. tall, 15–30 ft. wide; trained as a tree, reaches 15–30 ft. tall and wide. Branches are drooping. Furrowed gray bark peels off in strips near base of trunk. Light green leaves; fluffy white flowers in 1–3½-in.-long spikes from spring to fall. Tough and adaptable; especially useful in sea winds. Use as a clipped hedge or an unclipped informal screen; prickly leaves make it a good barrier plant.

M. decussata. LILAC MELA-LEUCA. Shrub or tree. Zones 9, 12–24; H1. To 8–20 ft. tall and wide. Brown, shredding bark. Tiny bluish leaves closely set on arching, pendulous branches. Lilac to purple flowers in 1-in. spikes from late spring to summer. Withstands some neglect. Use it for big masses of fine-textured foliage in the landscape. Thin to improve appearance and show off trunk and branch character.

M. hypericifolia. DOTTED MELALEUCA. Shrub. Zones 9, 12–24; H1. To 6–12 ft. tall, 3–12 ft. wide, with thin, peeling pale gray bark and drooping branches. Coppery green to dull green, 1¼-in. leaves. Blooms from late spring through winter, producing bright orange-red flowers in dense 2-in. clusters (often hidden by foliage). Can be clipped into a hedge but blooms more profusely as an informal, unclipped screen. Not suitable for planting at beach, though it takes ocean wind.

M. incana. GRAY HONEY MYRTLE. Shrub or tree. Zones 8, 9, 12–24. Spreading, arching plant with semiweeping branch-lets. Gray, furry foliage gives the plant an overall pale, smoky look. Small clusters of yellowish white flowers in spring. Naturally grows as a broad shrub to 9 ft. tall and wide but can be shaped into a handsome small tree. There is also a prostrate form available, growing 1–2 ft. high and 4–6 ft. wide. It's a useful groundcover.

M. linariifolia. FLAXLEAF PAPERBARK. Tree. Zones 9, 13–24; H1. To 20–30 ft. tall, 20–25 ft. wide, with dense, umbrellalike crown. White bark sheds in papery flakes. Slender branchlets covered with stiff, bright green or bluish green leaves. In summer, numerous fluffy spikes of small white flowers give the effect of snow on branches. Young plants are willowy and need staking until the trunk firms up.

M. nesophila. PINK MELA-LEUCA. Tree or shrub. Zones 13, 16–24; H1. Fast growth to 15–20 ft. tall (possibly to 30 ft.) and about as wide. Grows naturally as a small tree. Develops gnarled, heavy branches that sprawl or ascend in picturesque patterns. Grayish cream to pale brown bark is thick and spongy; gray-green leaves are thick, roundish. Roundish bottlebrush flower clusters to 1 in. wide are produced at branch ends most of the year; they open mauve-pink, fade to white with yellow tips. Use as tree or big, infor-mal screen; or shear as hedge. Takes ocean winds and spray; poor, rocky soil; desert heat. Little to regular water.

M. quinquenervia. CAJE-PUT TREE, PAPERBARK TREE. Zones 9, 12, 13, 15–17, 20–24; H1, H2. Upright, open growth to 20–40 ft. tall, 15–25 ft. wide; can become twice as large in the tropics. Pendulous young branches. Thick, spongy, light brown to whitish bark peels off in sheets (you can use these sheets to line wire hang-ing baskets). Narrowly oval leaves are shiny pale green, covered with silky hairs when

young. The foliage turns purple with light frosts. Yellowish white (sometimes pink or purple) flow-ers bloom in 2–3-in. spikes in summer and fall. Good street tree. Trees planted 8–10 ft. apart and thinned occasionally make a pleasant grove. Little to regular water. In Hawaii, cajeput tree has escaped cultivation to become an invasive pest.

M. styphelioides. PRICKLY PAPERBARK. Tree. Zones 9, 13–24; H1. To 20–40 ft. tall, 10–20 ft. wide, with lacy, open growth and pendulous branch-lets. Thick, spongy bark turns from pale tan to charcoal-colored with age, peels off in papery layers. Light green, prickly leaves are sometimes twisted. Creamy white flowers in 1–2-in. brushes from summer through fall. Thrives in any soil. Resistant to oak root fungus. Good lawn tree. Best trained with multiple trunks.

M. thymifolia. THYMELEAF MELALEUCA. Shrub. Zones 8, 9, 12–24. Low, spreading bush 2–4 ft. tall, 4–8 ft. wide. Bark is corky, flaking, grayish brown. Narrow blue-green leaves are fragrant when crushed. Blooms spring through early summer,

CLOCKWISE FROM TOP LEFT: *Melaleuca quinquenervia; M. thymifolia; M. quinquenervia* bark

with 2–3-in.-wide flower clusters resembling bundles of tiny ostrich feathers in white, pink, deep mauve, or dusky purple. Prefers acid soil but tolerates soils that lack fertility, are somewhat alkaline, or have sluggish drainage. Prune after flowering to keep compact. Takes occasional drought; best with regular water.

M. viridiflora. BROAD-LEAFED PAPERBARK. Shrub or tree. Zones 13, 19–24. To 12–25 ft. tall, 6–18 ft. wide, with papery gray or light tan bark. Thick, leathery, dark green or gray-green leaves. Flowering comes sporadically throughout the year; blossoms are narrow brushes to 6 in. long in white, cream, or green. *M. v. rubriflora* has pink to red flowers.

M. wilsonii. VIOLET HONEY MYRTLE. Shrub. Zones 8, 9, 12–24. To 3–10 ft. tall, 5–12 ft. wide, with spreading or arching habit. Leaves very narrow, dark green. Clusters of two to five

M

pink or purplish pink, ½-in.-wide flowers line the branches to make spikes that may or may not be interrupted by leaves. Can be pruned as a hedge. A prostrate form just 2 ft. high and 8 ft. wide is available; it makes a good small-scale groundcover. Will tolerate hard frost and occasional flooding. Takes extended dry spells but looks best with regular water.

CARE

All melaleucas are easy to grow. Most withstand heat, wind, seacoast conditions, poor soil, and limited moisture. Most are vigorous and fast growing; for a natural appearance, control by cutting back selected branches to a well-placed side branch.

Melampodium leucanthum

BLACKFOOT DAISY
Asteraceae
PERENNIAL

⚡ **ZONES 2, 3, 10–13**
☼ **FULL SUN**
◐ **MODERATE WATER**

Melampodium leucanthum

Short-lived perennial from Arizona, New Mexico, Texas, and Mexico. Narrow gray leaves in clumps to 1 ft. high and wide are topped by clouds of inchwide, honey-scented white daisies with yellow centers. Showy when in bloom. In mild climates, it flowers off and on during the winter months and more heavily from midspring into early fall—if given some water. Where freezing temperatures are routine, expect bloom in spring and summer only. Grow in fast-draining soil; in nature, blackfoot

daisy grows principally in decomposed granite. If plant becomes straggly, cut it back in fall. For the annual daisy, sometimes sold as *M. paludosum*, see *Leucanthemum paludosum*.

Melianthus major

HONEY BUSH
Melianthaceae
EVERGREEN SHRUB

⚡ **ZONES 8, 9, 12–24; H1, H2**
☼ ◐ **PARTIAL SHADE IN HOTTEST CLIMATES**
◌◐◕ **LITTLE TO REGULAR WATER**

Melianthus major

This soft-wooded plant from South Africa grows rapidly to 6–12 ft. tall and 8–10 ft. wide but is easily kept much shorter. It has an irregular habit, with stems that may be semierect or sprawling and spreading. Bold-looking foliage—grayish green, foot-long leaves divided into strongly toothed leaflets. Foliage is malodorous when brushed against or bruised. Foot-tall spikes of reddish brown, 1-in. flowers bloom in late winter, early spring. Adapts to most soils. Use for tropical effects; good as accent plant. To get a tall shrub, stake a few stems; for a sprawling, bulkier plant, shorten some stems in early spring before new growth begins. Worth trying in Zone 5, where it has borderline hardiness.

M. minor has greener and shorter leaves than those of *M. major* (6–7 in. long), on a shorter (3-ft.-high) plant. Its flowers are hidden among the leaves.

Melinis nerviglumis

NATAL RUBY GRASS
Poaceae
PERENNIAL GRASSES

⚡ **ZONES 2B–24; H1, H2; ALL ZONES AS ANNUAL**
☼ **FULL SUN**
◕ **REGULAR WATER**

Melinis nerviglumis

This short-lived African native grass has narrow blue-green leaves that are first erect, then arching, forming clumps 1 ft. high and slightly wider. From these rise 2-ft. flower spikes that open deep pink to purplish red and gradually fade to light pinkish tan. It can reseed, and plants may live over from year to year. In cold regions, treat as an annual; or pot up divisions and protect them during winter. In the tropics, it becomes a harmless weed. But in parts of the Southwest deserts, it is invasive enough to avoid. Formerly known as *Rhynchelytrum nerviglume*. A strain of this species introduced by the Denver Botanic Gardens is sold as 'Pink Crystals'. It blooms in late summer and has survived winters in Pueblo, Colorado.

Melissa officinalis

LEMON BALM, SWEET BALM
Lamiaceae
PERENNIAL

⚡ **ZONES 1–24**
☼ ◐ **FULL SUN OR PARTIAL SHADE**
◕ **REGULAR WATER**
🐝 **ATTRACTS BEES**

Melissa officinalis

From southern Europe; somewhat resembles its cousins, the mints. A single plant grows to about 2 ft. high, 1½ ft. wide—but plants self-sow and spread rapidly, sometimes becoming pests. Lemon-scented, heavily veined foliage is light green in the species. 'Aurea' ('Variegata') has green foliage variegated in yellow. 'All Gold' has solid yellow leaves. In summer or early fall, small, two-lipped flowers appear in spikes; blooms are pale yellow or white, maturing to pale blue.

Leaves are used fresh in cold drinks, fruit cups, salads, fish dishes; dried leaves give lemon perfume to sachets, potpourris. Likes rich soil; grow it in large pots or raised beds to keep it somewhat contained. Shear occasionally to keep compact.

Tame the Spreaders

When you see phrases like "spreads rapidly" or "reseeds itself" used to describe a plant, take them as warnings, not stop signs. Wanderers like natal ruby grass and lemon balm can be useful in a casual corner of the garden. Just be sure to keep an eye out for escapees.

Melon

Cucurbitaceae
ANNUALS

✎ **ZONES 2–24**

☼ **FULL SUN**

💧 **REGULAR WATER**

Cantaloupe

Thought to have originated in Africa. The principal types cultivated in the West are muskmelons ("cantaloupes") and late melons. True cantaloupes are a type of hard-shelled melon rarely grown in North America. Also see Watermelon.

Muskmelons are ribbed, with netted skin and typically salmon-colored flesh; they are more widely adapted than late melons. Choice varieties include 'Ambrosia', 'Athena', 'Fastbreak' (very early), and a small personal-size cantaloupe called 'Lil' Loupe'. Hybrids are superior to others in disease resistance and uniformity of size and quality. (Growing melons resistant to mildew and other diseases is particularly important in humid, coastal regions.) Seed packets and catalogs will usually tell you if a variety is a hybrid. Other muskmelons include small, tasty, highly perfumed types from the Mediterranean such as Charentais types, like 'Edonis', and larger Galia varieties, such as 'Arava' and 'Passport'.

Late melons are a varied group, including Canary ('Amy'), honeydew ('Earlidew'), casaba ('Golden Beauty'), and Piel de Sapo ('Lambkin'). Though less widely cultivated than muskmelons, they are gaining in popularity as more garden-friendly varieties are developed. Most dislike high humidity and grow

---

How to Grow Melons

To ripen to full sweetness, melons need steady heat for 2½–4 months.

PLANTING Sow seeds in light, well-drained soil 2 weeks after average last-frost date; don't rush it, since melons are truly tropical plants and will perish in even a light frost. In regions where summers are cool or relatively short, start plants indoors in pots a few weeks before last-frost date, then plant outdoors in warmest southern exposure.

Row covers allow for earlier planting outdoors. Clear plastic mulch (in areas where summers are very short) or black plastic mulch under melons warms soil, speeds harvest, and helps keep fruit from rotting.

Though you can grow melons on sun-bathed trellises, the heavy fruit must be supported in individual cloth slings. These plants are best grown in hills or mounded rows a few inches high at center; you will need to provide considerable space. Make hills about 3 ft. in diameter and space them 3–4 ft. apart; encircle each with a furrow for irrigation. Make rows 3 ft. wide and as

long as desired, spacing them 3–4 ft. apart; make furrows for irrigation along both sides. Plant seeds 1 in. deep—four or five seeds per hill, two or three seeds every 1 ft. in rows. When plants are well established, thin each hill to the best two plants; thin rows to one strong plant per foot. Fill furrows with water from time to time (furrows let you water plants without wetting foliage), but do not keep soil soaked. Feed (again in furrows) every 6 weeks.

HARVESTING To determine if a cantaloupe is ready for harvest, lift the fruit and twist; it will easily slip off the stem if ripe. A pleasant, perfumy fragrance also indicates ripeness. Late melons do not slip from stems when ripe. Honeydews are ready to pick when the area where the melon rests on the ground turns from yellow to white. Harvest 'Crenshaw', casaba, and other late melons when the fruit begins to turn yellow and starts to soften at the blossom end. As 'Crenshaw' approaches maturity, protect fruits from sunburn by shading them on the southwest side with a wooden shingle.

---

best in areas with hot, relatively dry summers (Zones 8, 9, 12–14, 18, 19).

There are also crosses between muskmelons and late melons—'Crane', 'Crenshaw', and 'Twice as Nice', for example —and wild cards with unknown ancestry, like the heirloom ananas melons (also called pineapple melons)—'Creme de la Creme' and 'San Juan', for example. As breeding blurs traditional melon categories, many seed sellers are lumping together new hybrids as "specialty melons."

FOR MORE ON MELONS AND OTHER VEGETABLES, SEE "GROW: VEGGIES," PAGES 698–707.

Although they have a reputation as ramblers, melons can be compact. Try early cantaloupes such as 'Lil' Loupe' in a large container or half wine barrel, then let the vines spill over the sides. Or train melons to climb a trellis (provide support for ripening fruits).

Mentha

MINT
Lamiaceae
PERENNIALS

✎ **ZONES VARY BY SPECIES**

☼ ◗ **FULL SUN OR PARTIAL SHADE**

💧 **REGULAR WATER**

Mentha spicata
'Kentucky Colonel'

These Mediterranean natives spread rapidly by underground stems and can be quite invasive; to keep them in bounds, grow them in pots or boxes. Tough and unfussy, they grow almost anywhere but perform best with light, moist, medium-rich soil; regular water; and full sun or partial shade. Plants disappear in winter in colder part of range. Replant about every 3 years; propagate from runners.

M. × gracilis (M. × gentilis). GOLDEN APPLE MINT. Zones 3–24. To 2 ft. high. Smooth deep green leaves with yellow variegation have a spicy apple fragrance and flavor. Inconspicuous flowers. Use in flavoring foods. Foliage is excellent in mixed bouquets.

M. × piperita. PEPPERMINT. Zones A2, A3; 1–24. To 3 ft. high. Strongly scented, tooth-edged leaves to 3 in. long, dark green often tinged with purple. Small purplish flowers in 1–3-in. spikes. Leaves are good for flavoring tea. *M. × p. citrata*, known as orange mint (crushed leaves have slight orange flavor) or bergamot mint, grows to 2 ft. high and has small lavender flowers. It is used in potpourris and in flavoring foods. There are also "fruit-flavored" varieties. 'Chocolate' has the slightest hint of chocolate mint flavor.

M

»

M. pulegium. PENNYROYAL. Zones 4–24. Creeping plant 4–16 in. high with small, oval, bright green leaves. Small lavender flowers in tight, short whorls. Strong mint fragrance and flavor. Poisonous if consumed in large quantities but safe as a flavoring. Needs a cool, moist site.

M. requienii. JEWEL MINT OF CORSICA. Zones 5–9, 12–24. Creeping, mat-forming mint reaches only ½ in. high. Tiny, round, bright green leaves give this plant a mossy appearance; leaves release a delightful minty or sagelike fragrance when bruised. Can be used as an aromatic filler between steppingstones (won't take heavy foot traffic). Bears tiny, tubular light purple flowers in summer.

M. spicata. SPEARMINT. Zones A2, A3; 1–24. To 1–3 ft. high. Dark green, toothed leaves are slightly smaller than those of M. × piperita. Leafy spikes of pale blue flowers. Use leaves fresh from the garden or dried, as flavoring for foods, cold drinks, jelly. Attracts bees and other beneficial insects. Leaves of M. s. crispa have curly margins. 'Kentucky Colonel' has large, flavorful leaves.

M. suaveolens (M. rotundifolia). APPLE MINT. Zones 3–24. Stiff stems grow 1½–3 ft. high, bearing rounded, slightly hairy gray-green leaves. Purplish white flowers in 2–3-in. spikes. Foliage has scent combining fragrances of apple and mint. 'Variegata', pineapple mint, has leaves with white markings, faint scent of pineapple.

A low, wide bowl of scented mint is welcome in any garden. But don't underestimate this herb's tenacious root system. If you park the bowl atop bare soil, the roots can escape through the drain hole, anchor the bowl in place, and send up new shoots everywhere.

Mertensia
Boraginaceae
PERENNIALS

🗡 **ZONES VARY BY SPECIES**

☼ ● **PARTIAL OR FULL SHADE**

💧 **REGULAR WATER**

Mertensia virginica

Resemble giant-size forget-me-nots (*Myosotis*) and belong to the same family. Plants emerge and flower early, then go dormant soon after going to seed (usually before midsummer). Typically smooth, gray-green or blue-green leaves. Nodding, bell-shaped flowers are carried in gradually uncoiling clusters. Buds are pink or lavender, opening to blue flowers that sometimes have a pinkish cast. Good in woodland gardens.

M. ciliata. CHIMING BELLS, MOUNTAIN BLUEBELL. Zones 1–7, 14–17. Native to damp places in the Rocky Mountains and the Blue Mountains of Oregon. To 3 ft. high and 1 ft. wide, with ½–¾-in. flowers. Several other species, most of them lower growing than M. ciliata, also are native to mountainous areas of the West.

M. virginica (M. pulmonarioides). VIRGINIA BLUEBELLS. Zones 1–9, 14–21. From eastern U.S. Most widely planted species. To 1–2 ft. high and 1½ ft. wide, with 1-in. flowers.

CARE

Provide moist, rich soil. Use summer annuals to fill void after plants die back. Clumps can be left in place indefinitely; they will slowly spread. To increase a planting, transplant volunteer seedlings or dig and divide the clump in early fall.

Metasequoia glyptostroboides
DAWN REDWOOD
Cupressaceae
DECIDUOUS TREE

🗡 **ZONES A3; 3–10, 14–24**

☼ **FULL SUN**

💧 **REGULAR WATER**

Metasequoia glyptostroboides

Thought to have been extinct for millions of years, this plant was found growing in a few isolated sites in its native China during the 1940s. It is a pyramidal tree with small cones and soft, pale green needles that turn light bronze in autumn, then drop to reveal attractive winter silhouette. Branchlets tend to turn upward. Young trees have reddish bark; older ones have darker, fissured bark and rugged, fluted trunk bases. Grows very fast when young—sometimes as much as 4–6 ft. a year in California (less in colder areas). Reaches about 90 ft. tall and about 20 ft. wide at the age of 40 or so (trees haven't been in cultivation long enough to determine the maximum garden size). Looks somewhat like bald cypress (*Taxodium distichum*). While in leaf, it also bears superficial resemblance to coast redwood (*Sequoia sempervirens*). 'Ogon' and the very similar (if not identical) 'Gold Rush' have yellow foliage.

CARE

Grows best in good, well-drained soil with regular moisture. Good lawn tree, though in time, surface roots may interrupt smooth flow of turf. Not suited to arid regions or seacoast. Resistant to oak root fungus.

Metrosideros
Myrtaceae
EVERGREEN TREES OR SHRUBS

🗡 **ZONES VARY BY SPECIES**

☼ ☼ **BEST IN SUN; TOLERATE SOME SHADE**

💧 **MODERATE WATER**

🦋 **FLOWERS ATTRACT BUTTERFLIES AND BIRDS**

Metrosideros polymorpha

Grown for their attractive, leathery foliage and showy flowers with prominent stamens. Best near coast; tolerate wind and salt spray. Grow in well-drained soil. Sensitive to frost.

M. collina. Zones 16, 17, 23, 24. From Hawaii. Shrubby, upright species with a profusion of powder-puff blooms in late spring and early summer. Useful as a flowering hedge, specimen, or container plant. 'Springfire' is the best-known variety; it grows to 8–12 ft. tall and 4–6 ft. wide, with orange-red blooms and gray-green leaves. 'Fiji', just 2 ft. high and wide, has red flowers and coppery new growth.

M. excelsa. NEW ZEALAND CHRISTMAS TREE, POHUTUKAWA. Zones 16, 17, 23, 24; H1, H2. Native to New Zealand. To 30 ft. tall or more, spreading as wide as tall; prune lower branches to get tree form. On young plants, leaves are glossy green; on older ones, they are dark green above, white and woolly beneath. Big clusters of dark red flowers cover branch ends in late spring and early summer. Useful lawn or street tree (if given ample root space) in coastal gardens. 'Aurea' has yellow flowers. Leaves of 'Gala' are centered with bright yellow; its dark red flowers have stamens tipped with gold.

M

M. polymorpha (M. collina polymorpha). 'OHI'A LEHUA, LEHUA. Zones H1, H2. Native to Hawaii. Slow-growing, highly variable plant; may form a small, erect to prostrate shrub or grow as a tree up to 100 ft. tall. The foliage is also variable—as are the flowers, which are produced throughout the year. Blossoms are commonly red but are also seen in white and shades of orange, pink, and yellow; they are used in leis.

M. villosa 'Tahiti' (M. kermadecensis 'Tahiti'). DWARF POHUTUKAWA. Zones 16, 17, 23, 24; H1, H2. Native to New Zealand. Compact shrub to 3 ft. high and wide with thick, round, gray-green leaves. Clusters of orange-red flowers appear in early to late spring; sporadic rebloom. Good plant for small gardens, around pools and foundations. 'Tahitian Sunset' has cream-and-pink-variegated foliage. Prolific seed set; remove seed heads to encourage new growth and rebloom.

Michelia. See *Magnolia*

Microbiota decussata

SIBERIAN CARPET CYPRESS
Cupressaceae
EVERGREEN SHRUB

| 🗺 ZONES A3; 1–10, 14–17 |
| ☀ ◑ PARTIAL SHADE IN HOTTEST CLIMATES |
| 💧 MODERATE WATER |

Microbiota decussata

Native to Siberian mountains and hardy to any amount of cold, this neat, sprawling shrub resembles a trailing arborvitae (*Thuja*). Grows 1½ ft. high and 7–8 ft. wide, with many plumy, horizontal or trailing branches closely set with scalelike leaves. Foliage is green in summer, turning purplish or reddish brown in winter. More shade-tolerant than junipers. Needs excellent drainage. 'Fuzz Ball' has softer-textured new growth and more open habit to 3 ft. high and 4 ft. wide. Use as a bank cover.

Micromeria chamissonis. See *Satureja douglasii*

Milium effusum 'Aureum'

BOWLES' GOLDEN GRASS
Poaceae
PERENNIAL GRASS

| 🗺 ZONES 3B–9, 14–17 |
| ◑ LIGHT SHADE |
| 💧 💧 REGULAR TO AMPLE WATER |

Milium effusum 'Aureum'

This cool-season grass is native to eastern North America and Eurasia. Its colorful selection 'Aureum' forms a clump to 2 ft. high and wide. Bright greenish gold leaves first grow erect, then take on arching, weeping form. Foliage is brightest in spring, turns light green by summer. In spring or late summer, look for delicate sprays of tiny golden flowers.

Effective for a spot of color in a woodland garden or shaded rock garden. Does best where summers are cool or mild; in hotter regions, plant goes partially dormant in summer. Seedlings usually have yellow foliage, though color may vary.

FOR MORE ON GRASSES, SEE "MEET THE GRASSES," PAGE 346.

Mimulus

MONKEY FLOWER
Phrymaceae
PERENNIALS, ONE GROWN AS ANNUAL

| 🗺 ZONES VARY BY SPECIES |
| ☀ ◑ ● EXPOSURE NEEDS VARY BY SPECIES |
| ◌ 💧 💧 💧 WATER NEEDS VARY BY SPECIES |
| 🐦 FLOWERS ATTRACT HUMMINGBIRDS |

Mimulus hybrid

A wide-ranging group of plants with different needs. All have funnel-shaped, two-lipped flowers said to resemble a grinning monkey face—hence the common name.

M. aurantiacus (Diplacus aurantiacus). STICKY or SHRUBBY MONKEY FLOWER. Woody-based perennial. Zones 5 and 6 (with protection), 7–9, 14–24. Native to southern Oregon, California, and Baja California. To 4½ ft. tall and wide, with narrow, sticky dark green leaves. Buff-toned orange, 1¾-in. flowers bloom over a long spring-and-summer season. Attract butterflies.

Mix moisture-loving, shade-tolerant yellow and orange mimulus hybrids in a container with a blue- or purple-flowering companion, such as Lobelia erinus.

Several species were formerly considered subspecies of *M. aurantiacus*. These include *M. bifidus*, with large pale yellow to peach flowers; *M. longiflorus*, with cream to orange-yellow blooms; and *M. rutilus*, with deep red blossoms. All thrive in full sun or partial shade, with little water.

More important than the species or subspecies themselves are the showy hybrids derived from them (Verity, Georgie, and Jelly Bean hybrids). These plants grow 1–4 ft. tall and wide, with narrow, glossy dark green leaves that are sometimes sticky. Flowers are 1–3 in. long, in colors ranging from white and cream to yellow, orange, copper, salmon, red, and maroon. Plant in full sun or light shade; give good drainage. Prune in spring before growth starts. Pruned again after first flowering, they often rebloom in fall—and, if given moderate water with good drainage, they may flower repeatedly throughout the year. Because plants are not long-lived, take cuttings of your favorites; they root easily in moist sand.

M. cardinalis. SCARLET MONKEY FLOWER. Perennial. Zones 2–24. Native to damp or wet locales throughout much of the West. Grows to 2½ ft. high and wide, with upright or sprawling stems and bright green, sticky leaves. Tubular, scarlet, 1½–2-in.-long flowers bloom throughout summer. Give full shade in Zones 12 and 13, sun or shade elsewhere. Ample water.

M. × hybridus. Short-lived perennial grown as annual. Zones 1–24. To 1 ft. high and wide, with smooth, succulent leaves. Flowers are 2–2½ in. across, in colors including cream, rose, orange, yellow, scarlet, and brown, usually with heavy brownish maroon spotting or mottling. Mystic Mix and Bounty series have virtually unspotted flowers. Sow in spring for summer bloom, or set out plants for early-spring show. Provide rich soil with high organic content, regular water, partial or full shade.

FOR OTHER PLANTS THAT ATTRACT BIRDS, SEE PAGES 95–99.

M

Mirabilis

FOUR O'CLOCK

Nyctaginaceae

PERENNIALS, ONE OFTEN GROWN
AS ANNUAL

🌡 **ZONES VARY BY SPECIES**

☀ **FULL SUN**

◊ **LITTLE WATER**

⚠ **SEEDS AND ROOTS ARE POISONOUS
IF INGESTED**

Mirabilis multiflora

Strong-looking, mounding plants
with the substance and character of shrubs—albeit only seasonal or temporary ones. In
summer, branch ends bear clusters of trumpet-shaped, 2-in.-
long flowers that open late in
the afternoon. Plants are killed
to the ground by frost but
resprout from their large tuberous roots. Sow seeds in fall or
spring. Plants self-sow freely.

M. jalapa. FOUR O'CLOCK,
MARVEL OF PERU. Zones 4–24,
H1, H2 as perennial. In colder
climates, treat as annual; or dig
and store like dahlia. Native to
Peru. To 3–4 ft. tall and wide.
Flowers in white and shades of
red, pink, or yellow; several colors may appear on the same
plant or even the same flower.
Blossoms are fragrant at night.
Jingles strain is lower growing
than old-fashioned kinds, has
flowers splashed and stained
in two or three colors at once.

M. multiflora. DESERT
FOUR O'CLOCK. Zones 1–3,
7–16, 18–24. Native to much of
the Southwest. To 1–2 ft. high,
3–5 ft. wide, with magenta flowers and gray-green leaves to
3 in. long.

FOR MORE ON PERENNIALS, SEE
"GROW: PERENNIALS," PAGES
686–687.

Miscanthus

SILVER GRASS

Poaceae

PERENNIAL GRASSES

🌡 **ZONES VARY BY SPECIES**

☀ ◑ **FULL SUN OR PARTIAL SHADE**

◊ ◊ **MODERATE TO REGULAR WATER**

Miscanthus sinensis

Among the showiest and liveliest-
looking of ornamental grasses,
these are clump-forming plants
that range from very large kinds
to dwarf types good for small
gardens and containers. Attractive flower panicles appear atop
tall stalks; they open as tassels
and gradually expand into silvery
to pinkish or bronze plumes
that usually last well into winter.
Leaves are broad or narrow,
always graceful; they may be
solid-colored, striped lengthwise, or banded crosswise. In
fall and winter, foliage of most
species turns shades of yellow,
orange, or reddish brown; it
looks especially showy against
snow or a background of dark
evergreens. Stunning accent
plants in large pots or tubs.

M. × 'Giganteus'. GIANT
SILVER GRASS. Zones 1–24.
Impressive upright grass to 10–
14 ft. tall, 8–10 ft. wide; self-
supporting on stems to 2 in.
thick. Arching, drooping leaves
are dark green with white midrib. In cold-winter areas, plant
does not bloom. In other areas,
however, flower plumes to 1 ft.
long rise 1–2 ft. above foliage
in very late summer to fall; they
emerge tan, open silver. Leaves
turn purplish green in fall, then
drop to leave tall, bare stalks
over winter. Good summer
screen or hedge; provides tropical effect. Takes seacoast conditions. Give partial shade in

hottest climates. Often mislabeled as *M. floridulus.*

M. sinensis. EULALIA, JAPA-
NESE SILVER GRASS. Zones
2–24. Native to Japan, Korea,
and China. Variable in size and
foliage. Blooms in late summer
or fall. Flowers are usually held
well above foliage clumps; they
may be cut for fresh or dried
arrangements. Many varieties
are obtainable, and new ones
arrive on the market every year.
Some of the choicest include
dwarf 'Adagio', with silver-green
foliage and pink plumes; white-
striped 'Morning Light', 'Variegatus', and *M. s. condensatus*
'Cabaret' and 'Cosmopolitan';
and 'Gold Bar' and 'Strictus',
with horizontal yellow stripes.

M. transmorrisonensis.
EVERGREEN MISCANTHUS.
Zones 4–24. Native to Taiwan.
Forms a compact clump 2½–
3½ ft. high and 3–4 ft. wide,
with narrow leaves 2–3 ft. long,
½ in. wide. Foliage remains
green into early winter (and is
evergreen in mildest-winter
areas). Slender, silvery flower
plumes on stems 5–7 ft. tall.

Plant begins blooming in
spring in mild-winter climates;
cutting stems back to ground
when plumes begin to fade will
produce a second bloom
flush—sometimes even a third
one. Where winters are cold,
bloom time comes in mid- to
late summer. Plumes age to tan
and drop seed before winter,
leaving bare stems. Makes a
good large-scale groundcover
if given regular moisture and
yearly mowing.

CARE

Cut old foliage back to the
ground before new leaves
sprout in early spring; in climates with a long growing
season, cut back again in midsummer to keep compact and
to freshen foliage. Some varieties collapse at bloom time
unless given support of four or
five narrow stakes inserted
inconspicuously at edge of
clump, concealed by foliage;
wind twine or wire around
stakes and clump at two levels.
Divide every 2 or 3 years to
limit clump size and prevent
decline in vigor.

FOR MORE ON GRASSES, SEE "MEET
THE GRASSES," PAGE 346.

Molinia caerulea

MOOR GRASS

Poaceae

PERENNIAL GRASS

🌡 **ZONES 1–9, 14–17**

☀ ◑ **FULL SUN OR PARTIAL SHADE**

◊ ◊ **REGULAR TO AMPLE WATER**

Molinia caerulea

Native to moist places from the
British Isles to Siberia, south
to the Caucasus and Turkey,
this plant resents dry, alkaline
conditions. Long-lived but slow
growing, it takes several years
to reach full size. Erect, narrow,
light green leaves form a neat,
dense clump. In summer, spikelike clusters of yellowish to purplish flowers rise above clump;
they turn to tan and last well
into fall. Inflorescences are profuse but narrow, giving clump a
see-through quality. Good cut
flowers. In late fall, both leaves
and flower clusters detach from
bulbous crown, leaving nothing
visible aboveground. There are
two forms of moor grass, each
with numerous varieties.

The typical form, *M. c. caerulea*, often called purple moor
grass, produces a leafy clump
1–2 ft. high and wide; flower
stalks are 2–3 ft. high. 'Moor-
flamme' ('Moor Flame') has
airy flower heads held 2 ft.
above the foliage, good red-
orange autumn foliage color.
'Moorhexe', purple moor grass,
bears purple-green flower
spikes. 'Variegata' has leaves
broadly edged in creamy white;
yellowish flower stems arch out
in all directions, giving perfect
fountain effect. 'Heidebraut'
('Heather Bride') produces
stems to 5 ft. tall; leaves
become distinctly yellowish
in autumn.

M. c. arundinacea, known as tall moor grass, has broader gray-green leaves that form a clump 2–3 ft. high and wide. Flowering stems are 5–8 ft. tall; they arch to the ground when wet, then straighten up as they dry. Give this one space so that you can enjoy its form and motion in the wind. Among its forms are old favorite 'Karl Foerster', still one of the best; it has arching, 2½-ft.-long leaves and semierect flower stalks to 7 ft. tall. 'Skyracer' has erect, 3-ft.-high leaves and 7–8-ft. stems bearing yellow flowers that sparkle with morning dew. Arching, 6-ft. stems of 'Transparent' have a translucent section between highest leaf and beginning of flower spike; plant bears tiny, airy blossoms and has bright orange-yellow fall foliage. 'Windspiel' ('Windplay') has wiry vertical stems 7–8 ft. tall that sway with the slightest breeze.

Moluccella laevis
BELLS-OF-IRELAND, SHELL FLOWER
Lamiaceae
ANNUAL

🌿 **ZONES 1–24; H1, H2**

☀ **FULL SUN**

💧 **REGULAR WATER**

Moluccella laevis

Though its common name implies Irish origin, this plant is in fact native to the Mideast. It grows to 2–3 ft. high, 10 in. wide. Flowers are carried almost from base in whorls of six. Showy part of flower is large, apple green, shell- or bell-shaped calyx, very veiny and crisp textured; small white tube of united petals in center is inconspicuous. Calyx-blossom spikes are quite attractive and long lasting in either fresh or dried arrangements; be sure to remove the unattractive leaves. 'Pixie Bells' is shorter, to 20–24 in. high.

CARE
Needs loose, well-drained soil. Doesn't perform well in hot, humid climates. Sow seeds in the ground in early spring for summer bloom; in mildest climates, can be sown in fall for winter bloom. Usually grown as a winter annual in the desert. If weather is warm, refrigerate seeds for a week before planting. For long blossom spikes, fertilize regularly.

Monarda
BEE BALM, OSWEGO TEA, HORSEMINT
Lamiaceae
PERENNIALS

🌿 **ZONES VARY BY SPECIES**

☀☀ **LIGHT SHADE IN HOTTEST CLIMATES**

💧💧 **REGULAR TO AMPLE WATER**

🦋 **FLOWERS ATTRACT HUMMINGBIRDS AND BUTTERFLIES**

Monarda

Native to eastern North America. Bushy, leafy clumps to 2–4 ft. tall, initially about 1½ ft. wide; spread rapidly at edges but are not really invasive. Dark green leaves have a strong, pleasant odor like a blend of mint and basil. In summer, upright stems are topped by tight clusters of long-tubed flowers. Divide every 3 or 4 years. Not long-lived in areas with warm winters and long, hot summers.

M. didyma. Zones A2, A3; 1–11, 14–17. Basic species has scarlet flowers surrounded by reddish bracts. Garden selections include varieties with flowers in shades of red, pink, and lavender. Mildew-resistant varieties include lavender 'Violet Queen', pink 'Marshall's Delight', and rosy lavender 'Petite Delight' (just 1–1½ ft. high, 2 ft. wide). 'Claire Grace' (*M. fistulosa* 'Claire Grace') is an upright grower to 4–5 ft. tall, with lavender-rose flowers and good resistance to mildew; performs well in California gardens. All bloom over period of 2 months or more when spent flowers are removed. Don't let soil dry out.

M. fistulosa. Zones A2, A3; 1–10, 14–17. Bears lavender to light pink flowers encircled by whitish bracts; they are less showy than blossoms of *M. didyma.* Best suited to wild garden; attracts beneficial insects.

Monardella
Lamiaceae
PERENNIALS

🌿 **ZONES VARY BY SPECIES**

☀ **FULL SUN**

💧 **LITTLE WATER**

Monardella odoratissima

Aromatic mint-family perennials native to California and adjacent states. Typically sprawling, with two-lipped flowers in clusters at stem ends. All require excellent drainage. Use in wild gardens or rock gardens.

M. macrantha. Zones 7–9, 14–24. To 6 in. high, 1 ft. wide. Stems of shiny dark green leaves sprawl, turn up at ends to show tight, 1–1½-in. clusters of bright red, 1½-in.-long flowers in late spring and summer. 'Marian Sampson' is a vigorous, disease-resistant selection.

M. odoratissima. Zones 1–3, 7–10, 14–24. Bushy plant with a sprawling, woody base. Grows from 4 in. to 2 ft. high, spreading as wide as high. Hairy gray-green leaves; 1-in.-wide heads of small purplish flowers in summer and early fall. Has been used to make a fragrant tea.

M. villosa. COYOTE MINT. Zones 7–9, 14–24. Bushy grower 1–2 ft. high, 1–1½ ft. wide, with furry gray-green leaves and 1½-in. heads of small purplish, pink, or white flowers in late spring and summer. Attracts bees.

Moraea collina.
See *Homeria collina*

Moraea iridioides.
See *Dietes iridioides*

Morus
MULBERRY
Moraceae
DECIDUOUS TREES

🌿 **ZONES VARY BY SPECIES**

☀ **FULL SUN**

💧 **REGULAR WATER**

🦋 **FRUITING TYPES ATTRACT BIRDS**

Morus nigra

Deciduous trees with leaves of variable size and shape, often on the same plant. Yellow fall color ranges from subdued to bright. Fruits somewhat resemble miniature blackberries and are favored by birds. Fruitless forms of *M. alba* provide shade in home gardens.

M. alba. WHITE MULBERRY, SILKWORM MULBERRY. Zones 2–24; H1, H2. Native to China. Fast-growing tree can reach 30–50 ft. tall and wide, though it's often smaller. Leaves often lobed. Fruit-bearing (female) trees have inconspicuous flowers followed by white, pink, or purple fruit that is sweet but rather insipid; it stains paved surfaces (as well as clothing). 'Pendula' ('Teas' Weeping') is a low-growing, strongly weeping form—but a fruit producer. Fruitless (male) forms are better for home gardens, though they do produce pollen in prodigious amounts. Varieties include 'Chaparral' (weeping), 'Fan-San', 'Fruitless', 'Kingan', and 'Stribling' ('Mapleleaf').

Tolerates desert heat, alkaline soil, seacoast conditions. Resistant to Texas root rot. Subject to sooty canker disease. Stake new plants; they quickly develop large crowns, which may snap from slender trunks in high winds. For first few years, branches may grow so long that they droop from their own weight; shorten such branches to a well-placed upward-growing bud. Heavy surface roots make it difficult to garden under. Takes some aridity but does better with regular moisture.

M. australis 'Unryu' (M. bombycis 'Unryu', M. alba 'Unryu'). CONTORTED MULBERRY. Zones 3–24. Selection of an eastern Asian native. To 25 ft. tall and wide, with twisted, contorted branches useful in dried floral arrangements or for winter silhouette. Fast growth means that branches may be cut freely with no harm to the tree. Dark green, broadly oval leaves 6–7 in. long.

M. nigra. BLACK MULBERRY, PERSIAN MULBERRY. Zones 4–24; H1, H2. Likely a native of western Asia. To 30 ft. tall, 35 ft. wide, with short trunk and dense, spreading head. Heart-shaped leaves to 8 in. long. Large, juicy, dark red to black fruit. 'Oscar' and 'Wellington' are heavy bearers. 'Black Beauty' is smaller (15 ft. tall). Need regular water.

M. papyrifera. See *Broussonetia papyrifera*.

M. rubra. RED MULBERRY. Zones 2–7. Native to eastern and central U.S. Resembles *M. alba* but bears fruit that is somewhat larger and has a better flavor. Fruit is red when immature; it ripens to black. Does best in rich soil.

Muehlenbeckia
WIRE VINE
Polygonaceae
EVERGREEN SHRUBS AND VINES

✎	**ZONES VARY BY SPECIES**
☼ ◐	**FULL SUN OR PARTIAL SHADE**
💧	**REGULAR WATER**

Muehlenbeckia complexa

Unusual New Zealand natives with thin, wiry stems; small leaves; and insignificant flowers. Both of the species below spread by rhizomes, but one is a noninvasive creeper, the other a vigorous climber or sprawler that can overrun other plants.

M. axillaris (M. nana). CREEPING WIRE VINE. Shrub. Zones 3–9, 14–24; H1. Small, dense, creeping plant; can grow just a few inches tall or mound to 1 ft. high. Closely spaced leaves are oblong to nearly round, glossy dark green. Bears very small (⅛ in.), translucent white fruits with black seeds. Use in rock garden or plant 1½–2 ft. apart for a small-scale groundcover. Can be mowed yearly to keep flat. Deciduous where winter chill is pronounced.

M. complexa. MATTRESS VINE, WIRE VINE. Vine. Zones 8, 9, 14–24. Twining vine can climb to 20–30 ft. or more; sprawls in the absence of support. Used as a groundcover, it spreads over a 30-ft.-wide area. Forms a dense tangle of thin black or brown stems. Light green leaves are variable in shape—may be oval, rounded, or fiddle-shaped. Good for beach planting or screen. Curb growth by shearing or cutting back as much as desired; plant will regrow vigorously.

Muhlenbergia
Poaceae
PERENNIAL GRASSES

✎	**ZONES VARY BY SPECIES**
☼ ◐	**FULL SUN OR LIGHT SHADE**
◌ ◑	**LITTLE OR NO WATER TO MODERATE WATER**

Muhlenbergia rigens

Narrow-leafed grasses large and showy enough to stand out in the garden. Except as noted, evergreen in mild winters but turn tan or brown with hard freezes. They are very drought-tolerant plants but look better and grow larger if given some supplemental water.

M. capillaris. PINK MUHLY. Zones 4–24. From the eastern U.S. Dark green foliage forms a mound to 3 ft. high, 6 ft. wide; airy plumes of feathery reddish flowers rise an additional 2½ ft. in fall. Evergreen in the low desert. Cut plants back in late winter for fresh new growth in spring. 'Regal Mist' ('Lenca') has deep rosy pink flowers.

M. dubia. PINE MUHLY, MEXICAN DEER GRASS. Zones 3b, 7–24. Native to Arizona, western Texas, New Mexico, and northern Mexico. Densely tufted plant, similar to *M. rigens* but smaller (2–3 ft. high and wide). Fine-textured leaves and upright, creamy flower spikes in summer and fall. Plant in well-drained soil.

M. dumosa. BAMBOO MUHLY. Zones 8–24. Native to Arizona, Mexico. To 3–6 ft. tall and wide. Resembles bamboo, with slender, woody stems set with narrow bright green leaves to about 3 in. long. Branching flower clusters appear in spring; blossoms are barely distinguishable from foliage.

M. emersleyi. BULL GRASS. Zones 2–24. Native to Arizona, New Mexico, Texas. Glossy green leaves form a mound 1½ ft. high, 3–4 ft. wide, with flower spikes rising 2–3 ft. above the foliage from summer into fall. Spikes are purplish or reddish, fading to cream with age.

M. lindheimeri. Zones 6–24. From Texas, Mexico. Clump of soft, arching, blue-green leaves grows to 5 ft. tall and wide, with amber flower spikes arching 2 ft. above foliage in autumn. Blooms of the species fade to gray; flowers of 'Autumn Glow' are yellow in fall. Attractive in dried arrangements. Semievergreen in mild-winter areas; dies to the ground in colder climates.

M. porteri. BUSH MUHLY. Zones 3, 7–14, 18–24. Native to southwestern U.S., northern Mexico. To 3 ft. high and wide. Fine, short, blue-green stems and blades. Profuse small, pinkish purple seed heads form a gauzy mass from late summer through fall. Best in well-drained soils but will tolerate heavy soils.

M. pubescens. SOFT BLUE MEXICAN MUHLY. Zones 8–24. From central Mexico. Downy blue-green foliage forms a clump 1 ft. high, 2 ft. wide. In spring or early summer, soft flower spikes rise 1–1½ ft. above the clump; they are light blue, aging to amber. Light frosts turn foliage purplish red; harder freezes kill it to the ground.

M. rigens. DEER GRASS. Zones 4–24. Native from California to Texas and south into Mexico. Bright green leaves form a dense, tight clump to 4 ft. tall and wide. Slender yellow or purplish flower spikes in autumn are erect at first, then leaning; rise 2 ft. above the leaves.

M. rigida. PURPLE MUHLY. Zones 6–24. From Texas and New Mexico. Green clump to 2 ft. high and wide, producing 3-ft. spikes of brownish purple to deep purple flowers in late summer and fall. 'Nashville' flowers are an attractive true purple.

FOR MORE ON GRASSES, SEE "MEET THE GRASSES," PAGE 346.

Mukdenia rossii 'Crimson Fans'
(Aceriphyllum rossii)
RED-LEAFED MUKDENIA
Saxifragaceae
PERENNIAL

🌡 **ZONES 2A–9, 14–24**

☼ ☽ **FULL SUN TO PARTIAL SHADE**

💧 💧 **MODERATE TO REGULAR WATER**

Mukdenia rossii
'Crimson Fans'

Charming deciduous perennial from northeastern Asia. Maple-shaped leaves start out bright green, pick up a bronzy color in summer, and eventually become red streaked or flushed. Forms spreading clumps to 1 ft. high and 2 ft. wide. Small, white, bell-shaped flowers appear in clusters in early spring. Space 2–3 ft. apart as a groundcover. Good in woodland gardens. 'Karasuba' is similar if not identical.

For a better look at this distinctive plant's fan-shaped leaves, which evolve over the growing season from bright green to orange-tinged red, grow it in a container. Or plant a patch beside a green groundcover such as wild ginger (*Asarum*) in a partly shaded border.

Murraya paniculata
(M. exotica)
ORANGE JESSAMINE
Rutaceae
EVERGREEN SHRUB

🌡 **ZONES 21–24; H1, H2**

☽ **FILTERED SUNLIGHT**

💧 **REGULAR WATER**

🐝 **BLOOMS ATTRACT BEES**

Murraya paniculata

An open, fast-growing shrub from Southeast Asia related to citrus and subject to the same quarantines due to Asian citrus psyllid (see Citrus). Grows to 6–15 ft. tall and wide. Good as hedge, filler, or foundation plant. Sometimes grown as a small single- or multitrunked tree. Has graceful, pendulous branches with glossy dark green leaves divided into three to nine oval leaflets.

Blooms in late summer and fall (sometimes in spring); its white, bell-shaped blossoms have a wonderful jasmine fragrance. On mature plants, small red fruits follow flowers.

CARE

Needs rich soil, frequent feeding. Slowly recovers its beauty after cold winters. A dwarf variety is usually sold as *M. exotica*. It is slower growing, more upright, and more compact than the species, reaching 6 ft. tall, 4 ft. wide. Its leaves are a lighter shade of green and have smaller, stiffer leaflets; bloom is usually less profuse.

FOR OTHER PLANTS THAT ATTRACT BEES, SEE PAGES 104–105.

Musa
BANANA
Musaceae
PERENNIALS

🌡 **ZONES VARY BY SPECIES**

☼ ☽ **FULL SUN OR PARTIAL SHADE**

💧 **AMPLE WATER**

Musa velutina

For information on fruiting types, see Banana. The ornamental bananas described here include tall, medium-size, and dwarf plants; some of the tall sorts are the size of trees. All are fast growing; all have soft, thickish stems and spread by suckers or underground roots to form clumps that are often as wide as or wider than the plant is tall. Spectacular-looking long, typically broad leaves are easily tattered by strong winds, so choose protected planting sites. Will usually regrow from roots if cut down by frost; in frost-prone areas, locate plants where their absence won't be conspicuous. Attractive near swimming pools. Can be grown in tubs and wintered indoors (cut tops off tall plants). Give rich soil; feed heavily.

M. acuminata. Zones 8, 9, 14–24; H1, H2. From Southeast Asia. Many varieties available. Plants are grown for fruit in warmest gardens, but they also make handsome ornamentals in cooler areas. Some have especially attractive foliage. 'Enano Gigante' grows 6–8 ft. tall and wide, with large, dark green leaves that are marked with red when young; produces rich, creamy fruit. Leaves of 6–10-ft.-tall 'Zebrina' ('Roja', 'Rojo', 'Sumatra', 'Sumatrana') are green with maroon stripes; the plant produces tiny, inedible

dark maroon fruit. 'Siam Ruby' has dark red leaves and stalks marked with yellowish green.

M. basjoo. JAPANESE BANANA. Zones 2 and 3 (with protection), 4–9, 14–24; H1, H2. From Japan. The hardiest of the banana clan. To 15 ft. tall, with narrow green leaves about 8 ft. long. Terminal spikes of yellow flowers may be followed by small, unpalatable fruit. Where plants freeze to the ground, spring regrowth will be quicker if trunks are heavily mulched in winter.

M. ensete. See *Ensete ventricosum*.

M. lasiocarpa (Musella lasiocarpa). CHINESE YELLOW BANANA. Zones 5–9, 11–24; H1, H2. From mountains of China. To 5–6 ft. tall, with dark green, 3–4-ft.-long leaves. Grown for unusual inflorescence that looks like a giant (8 in. wide) yellow artichoke and can last all summer. Plant dies after flowering, but new growth sprouts from base. Not at its best in hot-summer regions.

M. × paradisiaca (M. sapientum). Zones 9, 12–16, 19–24; H1, H2. This is the most common form of the ornamental bananas. Makes a clump to 20 ft. tall and half as wide. Leaves to 9 ft. long. Flower stalks are pendent, bearing large, showy, powdery purple bracts; fruit (usually seedy and inedible) sometimes follows.

M. velutina. Zones 23, 24; H2. From India. To 5–7 ft. tall; 3-ft.-long leaves are green above, bronzy beneath. Upright pink bracts, orange flowers, and small, velvety pink bananas that are inedible but highly decorative.

Few plants evoke the feel of a tropical oasis better than an ornamental banana. But there is no need to move south to grow one. With winter protection, Japanese banana (*Musa basjoo*) can thrive in the Pacific Northwest and even in some colder climates.

M

Muscari
GRAPE HYACINTH
Asparagaceae
PERENNIALS FROM BULBS

✎ ZONES VARY BY SPECIES

☼ ◑ FULL SUN OR LIGHT SHADE

💧 REGULAR WATER DURING GROWTH AND BLOOM

Muscari armeniacum 'Valerie Finnis'

Native to the Mediterranean and southwestern Asia, these bulbs form clumps of grassy, fleshy leaves that appear in fall and live through cold and snow. Spikes of small, typically urn-shaped blue or white flowers (fragrant, in some species) bloom in early spring.

M. armeniacum. Zones A1–A3; 1–24. Bright blue flowers on 8-in. stems rise above a clump of floppy foliage. 'Blue Spike' has double blue flowers in a tight cluster at top of spike. 'Early Giant' blooms somewhat earlier than the species, has darker blue flowers edged in white. 'Cantab', with light blue blossoms, grows lower than the species and has neater foliage and a later bloom time. 'Pink Sunrise' has pale pink flowers and may be a hybrid.

M. aucheri (M. tubergenianum). Zones A1–A3; 1–24. Stems to 8 in. high. Flowers on lower part of spike are bright blue; those on upper part are paler blue.

M. azureum (Hyacinthella azurea, Hyacinthus azureus). Zones 2–24. Blossom spires are between those of hyacinth and grape hyacinth in appearance. Stalks to 8 in. high bear tight clusters of fragrant sky blue flowers that have a bell shape (rather than the usual urn shape).

M. botryoides. Zones A1–A3; 1–24. Medium blue flowers on stems to 1 ft. high. 'Album' has white flowers.

M. comosum. FRINGE HYACINTH, TASSEL HYACINTH. Zones 1–24. Bears rather loose clusters of unusual, tattered-looking flowers on 1–1½-ft. stems. In the species, blossoms are greenish brown on lower part of spike, bluish purple on upper part. 'Plumosum' ('Monstrosum'), feathered or plume hyacinth, bears violet-blue to reddish purple flowers that look like shredded coconut.

M. latifolium. Zones 1–24. Possibly the showiest of the grape hyacinths. Each bulb produces just one leaf and a flowering stem to 1 ft. high. Flowers on lower part of spike are deepest violet, those on upper part are vivid indigo-blue.

M. macrocarpum. Zones 5–9, 14–24. Curving, straplike, gray-green leaves to 1 ft. long. Stems to 6–8 in. high bear tubular flowers that are soft yellow on lower part of spike, brownish purple at its top, with a lovely, sweet perfume. 'Golden Fragrance' has golden yellow flowers below, rich purple ones above. Flowers best after a hot, dry summer dormancy.

M. neglectum. STARCH HYACINTH. Zones 1–24. Stems about 6 in. high. Lower part of bloom spike holds tightly crowded, dark blue blossoms edged in white, while upper part is set with pale blue blooms. Flowers are said to smell like laundry starch.

CARE

Plant in early fall, setting bulbs about 2 in. deep and 3 in. apart in well-drained soil. Plant in masses or drifts under flowering trees or shrubs; use in edgings and rock gardens; grow in containers. Very long-lived. Dig and divide when clumps become crowded. Plants self-sow under favorable conditions.

FOR MORE ON BULBS, SEE "GROW: ANNUALS, BULBS," PAGES 674–675.

Musella lasiocarpa.
See *Musa lasiocarpa*

Mustard
Brassicaceae
ANNUAL

✎ ALL ZONES

☼ FULL SUN

💧 REGULAR WATER

'Green Wave' mustard

Two kinds of mustard are popular in Western gardens, both derived from plants native to the Mediterranean eastward into Asia. Curly-leafed mustard looks similar to curly-leafed kale, with leaf margins that are frilled or curled, or leaves cut clear to the center vein. It is usually cooked like spinach or cabbage; young leaves are sometimes eaten raw in salads or used as garnishes. 'Golden Frill', 'Green Wave', 'Ruby Streaks', and 'Southern Giant Curled' are good examples.

Mustard spinach (also called tendergreen mustard) has smooth, dark green leaves with a spinachlike flavor. It matures earlier than curly-leafed mustard and is more tolerant of hot, dry weather. 'Komatsuna' and 'Tendergreen' are most common varieties. Use young mustard spinach as a salad green; older leaves can be cooked.

To learn about broadleaf or flatleaf mustard and Chinese mustard greens, see Asian Greens.

CARE

Mustard is easy to grow, and it grows fast—it's ready for the table 35–60 days after planting. Sow in rows in early spring; make successive sowings when young plants from each previous planting are established. Thrives in cool weather but quickly goes to seed in summer heat. For fall harvest, sow in late summer; in mild-winter areas, plant again in fall and winter. Thin seedlings to 6 in. apart. Harvest outer leaves as needed.

Myoporum
Scrophulariaceae
EVERGREEN SHRUBS OR TREES

✎ ZONES VARY BY SPECIES

☼ FULL SUN, EXCEPT AS NOTED

◐💧 LITTLE TO MODERATE WATER, EXCEPT AS NOTED

Myoporum laetum

Tough, fast-growing plants with bell-shaped flowers that are attractive at close range but not showy; fruit small but colorful. Shiny dark green leaves with translucent dots. Myoporum thrips, a relatively new pest in the West, can severely distort foliage of several species of *Myoporum*, notably *M. laetum*, *M.* 'Pacificum', and *M. sandwicense*. Drought-stressed plants are more severely infested. Control measures include spinosad and imidacloprid. Or plant resistant varieties.

M. floribundum. Shrub. Zones 15–17, 19–24. Native to Australia. Interesting sculptural form; graceful, open growth to 5–9 ft. tall, 6–12 ft. wide. Sticky, very narrow leaves droop from horizontally held branches. White to cream flowers are borne profusely along branches in spring; they are followed by tiny purplish fruits. Full sun or partial shade. Does best with regular water but takes wetter and drier conditions.

M. laetum. Shrub or tree. Zones 8, 9, 14–17, 19–24. Temperatures below 24°F (–4°C) can cause severe damage. Native to New Zealand. Exceptionally fast growth to 30 ft. tall, 20 ft. wide. Densely clothed in rather narrow leaves. If allowed to grow naturally, it forms a billowing mass, but it can be trained as an attractive multitrunked tree. To use it as a groundcover, peg down branches so they'll root and spread. Clusters of small white summer flowers with purple markings are followed by reddish purple fruits. Good seaside plant. Susceptible to myoporum thrips. 'Clean n Green' is a thrips-resistant variety similar to the species. 'Compactum' is a dense grower to 16 ft.; good choice for a tall hedge, with some resistance to thrips.

M. 'Pacificum'. Shrub. Zones 16–24. Extremely fast growing to 2 ft. high and 30 ft. wide. As groundcover, can cover 100 sq. ft. in a year. Medium green leaves have an elongated oval shape. Bears small white flowers in summer. Performs best in cooler regions. Prune as needed; regrowth is rapid. Susceptible to myoporum thrips.

M. parvifolium (M. p. 'Prostratum'). Shrub. Zones 8, 9, 12–24. Native to Australia. Groundcover to 3–6 in. high, 9 ft. wide, with dense covering of light green leaves. Tiny white summer flowers are followed by purple fruits. Plant 6–8 ft. apart; plants will fill in within 6 months, rooting where stems touch moist soil. Good on banks and slopes. Will not tolerate foot traffic. 'Burgundy Carpet' has red stems, purple new growth; 'Pink' bears pink flowers. 'Putah Creek' is taller than the species and not quite as wide spreading; it grows 1–2 ft. high, 8 ft. wide. 'Tucson' is more densely branched than the species and has smaller leaves. Resistant to myoporum thrips.

M. sandwicense. FALSE SANDALWOOD, NAIO. Shrub or tree. Zones H1, H2. Moderately slow-growing Hawaiian native to 30 ft. tall and wide; extremely variable in the wild, where it is seen both at tree size and as low as 3 ft. Fragrance of wood is similar to that of sandalwood. Pointed, glossy green leaves. Blooms come in both spring and summer, bearing small white or pink flowers clustered close to the stems; these are followed by small white fruits that shrivel and turn brown with age. Excellent windbreak, hedge, screen, or specimen plant. Good tolerance for wind, salt, and drought. Needs well-drained soil. Normally does not require pruning but can be shaped during growth. Susceptible to myoporum thrips (called naio thrips in Hawaii).

Myosotis
FORGET-ME-NOT
Boraginaceae
PERENNIALS, BIENNIALS, AND ANNUALS

- 🌱 **ZONES A1–A3; 1–24**
- ☼ **PARTIAL SHADE**
- 💧 **REGULAR WATER**

Myosotis sylvatica

Both of the forget-me-not species described here feature profuse, typically blue springtime flowers, tiny but exquisite. Grow easily and densely as groundcovers. Do best in cool, moist areas, as in woodland gardens, at pond edges, along stream banks. They have invaded damp woodlands in some areas. Not usually browsed by deer.

M. scorpioides. Perennial. Native to Europe, Asia, and North America. Also known as water forget-me-not because roots need nearly constant moisture, such as alongside a stream or pond. This species is similar in most respects to *M. sylvatica*, but it grows a little lower, blooms even longer, and has roots that live over from year to year. Flowers are about ¼ in. wide; they come in blue with a yellow eye, white, or pink. Plant spreads by creeping roots.

M. sylvatica. Annual or biennial. Native to Europe. State flower of Alaska. To 6–12 in. high, 2 ft. wide. Soft, hairy foliage. Pure blue flowers with a white eye are 1 in. wide, set loosely along top portions of stems. Blooms and seeds profusely for a long season, beginning in late winter or early spring. Self-sows and will persist for years unless weeded out. Often sold as *M. alpestris*. Improved varieties include 'Blue Ball', 'Royal Blue Improved' and 'Victoria Blue'. Forget-me-nots are attractive beneath pink, rose, and salmon-colored tulips.

Myrica
Myricaceae
EVERGREEN AND SEMIEVERGREEN OR DECIDUOUS SHRUBS OR TREES

- 🌱 **ZONES VARY BY SPECIES**
- ☼ **FULL SUN**
- 💧 **WATER NEEDS VARY BY SPECIES**
- 🐦 **SEEDS ATTRACT BIRDS**

Myrica californica

The two species described here are coastal natives: one comes from the Pacific coast; the other comes from the Atlantic. Both are cultivated for their attractive, pleasantly aromatic foliage. Flowers are inconspicuous, but the fruits that follow are effective in autumn and winter. Plants are useful as screens and as informal or clipped hedges.

M. californica. PACIFIC WAX MYRTLE. Evergreen shrub or tree. Zones 4–9, 14–24. Native to coast and coastal valleys from Southern California to Washington. In windy oceanfront conditions, it can be a low, flattened mass. Grown out of wind, it's a big shrub or tree to 10–30 ft. tall and wide, usually with many upright trunks. One of the best-looking native plants for gardens. Branches are densely clad with tooth-edged, narrow leaves that are glossy dark green above, paler beneath, and clean-looking throughout the year. Purplish, wax-coated nutlets are attractive to birds. Moderate water. A selection sold as 'Buxifolia' is more densely branched than the species, with smaller leaves.

M. pensylvanica (M. caroliniensis). BAYBERRY. Deciduous to semievergreen shrub. Zones 1–7. Native to coastal eastern North America. Dense, compact growth to 9 ft. tall, 5–12 ft. wide. Narrow, glossy green leaves to 4 in. long are dotted with resin glands. Rounded fruit is covered with white wax—the bayberry wax used for candles. Tolerates poor, sandy soil. Resistant to oak root fungus. Regular water.

Myrsine africana
AFRICAN BOXWOOD
Primulaceae
EVERGREEN SHRUB

- 🌱 **ZONES 8, 9, 14–24**
- ☼☽ **FULL SUN OR PARTIAL SHADE**
- 💧 **MODERATE WATER**
- ☠ **ALL PLANT PARTS ARE POISONOUS**

Myrsine africana

Native to the Azores, Africa, the Himalayas, and China, this shrub grows to 3–8 ft. tall and 2½–6 ft. wide. Form is slightly floppy when young, but plant stiffens as it matures into a dense, rounded bush that is easily kept to 3–4 ft. with pinching and pruning. Erect-growing dark red stems are closely set with very dark green, small, glossy, rounded, aromatic leaves. Insignificant flowers. 'Scarlett Marglin' has creamy-white-and-green-variegated leaves. Good choice for low hedges, narrow beds, and containers. Cut foliage is attractive in arrangements. Withstands air pollution.

Myrtus communis

MYRTLE
Myrtaceae
EVERGREEN SHRUB

🌿 **ZONES 8–24; H1, H2**

☼ ◑ **FULL SUN OR PARTIAL SHADE**

◌ ◒ **LITTLE TO MODERATE WATER**

Myrtus communis

This rounded plant from the Mediterranean is bulky and dense but has fine-textured foliage. Reaches 5–6 ft. tall and 4–5 ft. wide (as much as 15 ft. by 20 ft. in old age). Glossy bright green leaves are pointed, pleasantly aromatic when bruised or brushed against. White, sweet-scented, ¾-in. flowers with many stamens bloom in summer, followed by bluish black, ½-in. berries. Named selections vary in foliage character and overall size. 'Variegata' has white-edged leaves. 'Boetica' is especially upright, with thick, twisted branches and larger, darker leaves. 'Buxifolia' has small leaves like those of boxwood (*Buxus*). Dwarf forms include *M. c. tarentina* 'Compacta', a small-leafed variety popular for edgings and low formal hedges; *M. c. t.* 'Compacta Variegata', similar but with white-margined foliage; and *M. c. t.* 'Microphylla', with tiny, closely set leaves.

M. ugni. See *Ugni molinae.*

Takes any soil, but good drainage is essential. Makes a good informal hedge or screen, requiring little or no pruning; as a specimen shrub, it can be selectively pruned to reveal limb structure. Withstands shearing into formal hedges and topiary.

Nageia.
See *Podocarpus*

Nandina domestica

HEAVENLY BAMBOO, SACRED BAMBOO
Berberidaceae
EVERGREEN OR SEMIEVERGREEN SHRUB

🌿 **ZONES 3 (WITH SOME PROTECTION), 4–24; H1, H2**

☼ ◑ ● **SOME SHADE IN HOTTEST CLIMATES**

◌ ◒ ● **LITTLE TO REGULAR WATER**

◆ **BERRIES CAN BE TOXIC, ESPECIALLY TO LIVESTOCK**

Nandina domestica

This fine-textured shrub from China and Japan belongs to the barberry family but is reminiscent of bamboo in its lightly branched, canelike stems and delicate, lacy-looking foliage. Slow to moderate growth to 6–8 ft. tall, 3–4 ft. wide. Old clumps may be wider than tall because of slow, steady spread

by suckers. Leaves are divided into many leaflets shaped like pointed ovals. Foliage emerges pinkish and bronzy red, then turns to soft light green; takes on purple and bronze tints in fall and often turns fiery crimson in winter, especially in a sunny location and with some frost. A good filler in bouquets. Pinkish white or creamy white blossoms in loose, erect, 6–12-in. clusters bloom at branch ends in late spring or early summer. If plants are grouped, shiny red berries follow the flowers; isolated plants seldom fruit heavily. Makes a light, airy-looking hedge, screen, or tub plant. Good for bonsai and in narrow, restricted spaces. Dramatic with night lighting.

Many varieties are available, most with improved foliage color in spring and fall. Dwarf varieties include 'Fire Power' (2 ft.), 'Gulf Stream' (3–4 ft.), 'Harbor Dwarf' (2–3 ft.), and 'Sienna Sunrise' (3–4 ft.). Taller varieties include 'Moyers Red' (6–8 ft.), 'Plum Passion' (4–6 ft.), and 'Royal Princess' (6–8 ft.). 'Filamentosa' (1–3 ft.), also sold as 'San Gabriel', has very finely cut leaves.

In climates where summers are very hot, requires some shade; in milder climates, can take sun or shade. Does best in rich soil with regular water but can even compete with tree roots in dry shade. Subject to chlorosis in alkaline soil. Resistant to oak root fungus. In time, unpruned clumps become top-heavy and bare at the base; to encourage denser foliage lower down, cut oldest canes to the ground each year before new growth begins in spring. Loses leaves at 10°F (–12°C); stems are damaged at 5°F (–15°C), but the plant usually recovers quickly. Has withstood –12°F (–24°C) with some snow cover and little wind; severely damaged at 0°F (–18°C) if exposed to strong winds.

Though it tolerates shade, nandina develops best winter leaf color when it gets full sun.

Narcissus

DAFFODIL, NARCISSUS, JONQUIL
Amaryllidaceae
PERENNIALS FROM BULBS

🌿 **ZONES A2, A3, 1–24, EXCEPT AS NOTED**

☼ ◑ **FULL SUN DURING BLOOM, PARTIAL SHADE AFTER IN HOT CLIMATES**

● **REGULAR WATER DURING GROWTH AND BLOOM**

Jonquilla hybrid 'New Baby'

Beyond their fascinating variety in flower form and color, these natives of Europe and North Africa offer numerous appealing traits. They are permanent, increasing from year to year; they stand up to cold (most are hardy to –30°F/–34°C) and heat; and they are useful in many garden situations. Given minimum care at planting, they thrive with virtually no further attention. These plants do not require summer watering (but will take it if drainage is good), need only infrequent division (will survive without it), and are totally unappetizing to gophers and deer. They bloom in late winter or spring.

All plants known by the names "daffodil," "narcissus," and "jonquil" are properly *Narcissus*. In gardeners' terms, however, "daffodil" refers to large-flowered kinds, "narcissus" denotes small-flowered (usually early-blooming) types bearing blossoms in clusters, and "jonquil" refers to *N. jonquilla* and its hybrids.

All have the same basic flower structure. Each bloom has a perianth (six outer petal-like segments) held at right angles to the corona (also called trumpet or cup, depending on its

TOP ROW: Trumpet daffodil 'Bravoure'; double daffodil 'Tahiti'. MIDDLE: Poeticus daffodil 'Actaea'. BOTTOM ROW: Cyclamineus hybrid daffodil; Tazetta hybrid 'Falconet'

length) in the blossom's center. Flowers may be borne singly or in clusters. Colors are basically yellow and white, but there are many variations—shades of orange, red, apricot, pink, cream. Some are fragrant. Leaves may be straight and flat (strap-shaped) or narrow and rushlike.

Daffodils perform well in containers. They also make fine cut flowers, though freshly cut stems release a substance that causes other cut flowers to wilt. To prevent this, soak cut flowers in cool water overnight, rinse stem ends, and then combine with other flowers in fresh water.

Following are the 13 generally recognized divisions of daffodils and representative varieties in each division.

Trumpet daffodils. Trumpet is as long as or longer than surrounding perianth segments; one flower to each stem. Best known are yellow 'King Alfred' and 'Dutch Master', but newer yellow-flowered 'Marieke' and 'Primeur' are superior. Pure white varieties include 'Mount Hood'. Bicolors with white segments and yellow trumpet include 'Bravoure', 'Las Vegas', and 'Topolino'; among those with yellow segments and some white on the trumpet are 'Pistachio' and 'Pay Day'.

Large-cupped daffodils. Cup is shorter than perianth segments but always more than one-third their length; one flower per stem. Varieties include 'Stainless' (white); 'Carlton' and 'Saint Keverne' (both yellow). Varieties with white perianth segments and colored cup include 'Ice Follies' (yellow cup); 'Accent', 'Salome' (pink cup); 'Fragrant Rose' (reddish pink cup); 'Redhill' (reddish orange cup). 'Ambergate', 'Ceylon', and 'Fortissimo' all have yellow perianth segments and orange or red cup. Those with yellow segments and white cup include 'Fellows Favorite' and 'Altun Ha'.

Small-cupped daffodils. Cup no more than one-third the length of perianth segments; one flower per stem. Varieties include 'Audubon' (white segments, pale yellow cup banded pink) and 'Barrett Browning' (white segments, orange-red cup).

Double daffodils. Cup has segments that are separate rather than joined together. Flower looks like a peony rather than a typical daffodil. One flower or more per stem. Examples are 'Delnashaugh' and 'My Story' (white perianth segments, pink cup segments), 'Tahiti' (yellow segments, red cup), and 'Manly' (white segments, yellow cup).

Triandrus hybrids. Cup at least two-thirds the length of perianth segments; several flowers to each stem. White 'Thalia' is an old favorite. Others include 'Hawera' (yellow) and 'Kate Heath' (white segments, pink cup).

Cyclamineus hybrids. Early bloomers with one flower per stem. Perianth segments are strongly recurved. Yellow 'February Gold' is best known. Yellow 'Rapture' has an especially long trumpet. 'Jack Snipe' and 'Wisley' have white segments, yellow trumpets.

Jonquilla hybrids. Each stem bears two to four small, sweetly fragrant flowers; foliage is often rushlike. Choices include 'Sweet Smiles' (white segments, pink cup); 'Pipit' (yellow segments, white cup); 'Sun Disc' and 'Quail' (solid yellow).

Tazetta daffodils and Tazetta hybrids. Zones 5–24. Hardy to about 10°F (−12°C). Early-blooming, cluster-flowering types popularly known by the name "narcissus." Each stem bears four to eight or more very fragrant flowers with short cup. Many have white perianth segments and yellow cup, but there are other color combinations. *N. tazetta* 'Orientalis', Chinese sacred lily, has light yellow segments and darker yellow cup. 'Paper White' is pure white; 'Geranium' has white segments, orange cup; 'Grand Soleil d'Or' has yellow segments, orange cup. Newer varieties include 'Falconet' and 'Scarlet Gem' (yellow segments, orange cup). Tazettas are often grown indoors in bowls of pebbles and water (keep cool until growth is well along, then gradually bring into bright light).

Poeticus daffodils. Perianth segments are white; very short, broad cup is in a contrasting

N

How to Grow Daffodils

BUYING THE BULBS Look for those that are solid and heavy, with no injury to the basal plate. So-called double-nose bulbs will give you the most and largest flowers the first season after planting. In most climate zones, it's best to plant bulbs in mid- to late fall when soils have begun to cool.

SITE SELECTION Daffodils grow best in full sun. Plant among flowering shrubs and perennials in groundcover plantings, near water, in rock gardens, or in borders. Plant in sweeping drifts where space is available. In hot summer regions, daffodils are often planted beneath high-branching deciduous trees where they receive full sun while they are blooming; after bloom, dappled shade. This can be effective but often results in declining bloom if the shade is too dense. Flowers usually face the sun—another factor to keep in mind when selecting planting locations.

SOIL Daffodils are not fussy about soil as long as it is well drained. To improve drainage in heavy soils, dig in plenty of organic matter prior to planting. Or cover the planting area with several inches of compost, set bulbs on top, and cover with 6–8 in. of compost or amended soil.

PLANTING Set bulbs approximately twice or three times as deep as they are tall—typically 5–6 in. deep for large bulbs, 3–5 in. deep for smaller ones. Space bulbs at least 6–8 in. apart (or three times their width for smaller varieties). Water newly planted bulbs thoroughly.

WATERING In many regions, fall and winter are wet or snowy enough to provide all the moisture daffodils require. If precipitation fails before bloom period ends and leaves begin to yellow, keep plantings well watered. Summer watering is not needed.

DEADHEADING Faded blooms can be removed to neaten plants' appearance, but leave the foliage in place to mature naturally; as long as the leaves are green, they are using sunlight to rebuild the bulbs' energy for next year's growth. After foliage has turned yellow, remove it and lightly cultivate the soil so that insects will not have an easy way in.

DIVIDING Established clumps need dividing only when flower production and bloom quality decline. It's easiest to dig clumps just before foliage completely dies down, when you can still see where plants are. After digging bulbs, replant immediately or store them as you would gladiolus corms until planting time.

FORCING Fill a deep pot (8–12 in.) three-quarters full with potting soil. Set bulbs close together, tips level. Fill with soil to an inch from the top. Place pots in a well-drained trench, in a cold frame, or on a ground cloth in a uniformly cool area and cover with 6–8 in. of moist peat moss, wood shavings, mulch, leaves, sawdust, or sand. Look for roots in 8 to 12 weeks (tip pot carefully). Remove pots with well-started bulbs to a greenhouse, a cool room, or full sun to bloom. Keep well watered until foliage yellows; then plant out in the garden. You can sink containers of bulbs in borders when plants are almost ready to bloom, and then lift them when flowers fade.

PESTS The most serious pest is the narcissus bulb fly. An adult fly resembles a small bumblebee. The female lays eggs on leaves and on necks of bulbs; when eggs hatch, young grubs eat their way into the bulbs. Check bulbs before planting and discard any that are damaged, soft, or infested. Cultivate and mulch around bulbs after leaves die down.

color, usually with red edges. Very fragrant. 'Actaea' and 'Pheasant's Eye' are favorites.

Bulbocodium hybrids. Hoop petticoat flowers; small, mostly trumpet with almost threadlike perianth segments. 'Golden Bells' (yellow), 'Kenellis' (white segments with light yellow cup), and 'Spoirot' (white) are varieties.

Species, varieties, and hybrids. This category includes species, their naturally occurring forms, and wild hybrids. Included here are many miniature types popular with collectors and rock garden enthusiasts. Prominent among these are the following.

N. bulbocodium. HOOP PETTICOAT DAFFODIL. Zones 3–24. Plant is hardy to about −10°F (−23°C). Stems to 6 in. high bear small yellow flowers that are mostly trumpet, with almost threadlike perianth segments. Foliage is grassy.

N. jonquilla. JONQUIL. Very fragrant golden yellow flowers with short cups in clusters of two to six on 1-ft. stems. Rush-like foliage.

Split-corona hybrids. Cup is split for at least one-third its length into two or more segments. 'Tripartite' (all yellow); 'Cassata' and 'Smiling Twin' (white perianth segments, yellow cup) and 'Hungarian Rhapsody' (white segments, pink cup) are three of the more readily available varieties in this small but growing class.

Miscellaneous. This category contains all types that don't fit the other divisions. 'Tête-à-tête' and fragrant 'Tiny Bubbles' (both yellow) are rock garden dwarfs to about 6 in. high.

For a natural meadow effect, broadcast handfuls of narcissus bulbs across prepared ground. Adjust their pattern so the drift is denser at one end and toward the center, as if the bulbs gradually spread outward.

Nassella

NEEDLE GRASS
Poaceae
PERENNIAL GRASSES

✎ **ZONES VARY BY SPECIES**

☼ **FULL SUN**

◯ **LITTLE OR NO WATER, EXCEPT AS NOTED**

Nassella

These needle grasses were once included in *Stipa*. All are clump formers characterized by long awns—needlelike or threadlike appendages that give a feathery look to the inflorescence. They are California natives that look much alike; all are useful for revegetation of wild areas, for stabilizing soil, and for restoring natural meadows. They can be started from seed. Clear area of weeds and other grasses first; *Nassella* species can self-sow once established, but initially they cannot compete with other vegetation.

All these needle grasses are cool-season growers that go dormant during hot, dry summers, reviving with cooler autumn weather and rains.

N. cernua. NODDING NEEDLE GRASS. Zones 7–9, 11, 14–24. To 3 ft. high, 2 ft. wide, with deep green leaves. Purple-toned awns reach 4½ in. long, age to a silvery color. Blooms in late winter, early spring.

N. lepida. FOOTHILL NEEDLE GRASS. Zones 7–9, 11, 14–24. Similar to *N. cernua* in appearance and bloom season, but the awns are shorter (to 2 in. long).

N. pulchra. PURPLE NEEDLE GRASS. Zones 5–9, 11, 14–24. The classic native California bunch grass. Much like the two species listed above, but with 4-in. awns. Same early bloom period.

N. tenuissima. See *Stipa tenuissima*.

FOR MORE ON GRASSES, SEE "MEET THE GRASSES," PAGE 346.

Nectaroscordum siculum
(Allium siculum)
Alliaceae
PERENNIAL FROM BULB

〽 **ZONES 2B–9, 14–24**

☼ ◐ **FULL SUN OR LIGHT SHADE**

💧 **REGULAR WATER DURING GROWTH AND BLOOM**

Nectaroscordum siculum

Onion relative from the Mediterranean region and western Asia that creates an attractive silhouette. Strap-shaped, 12–16-in.-long leaves emerge in spring, give off garlic scent if crushed or bruised. Thick, fleshy stems to 4 ft. tall appear in summer, each carrying a baseball-size cluster of up to 30 nodding, 1-in., bell-shaped flowers. Blooms are white, suffused with pink or purple and tinged green at the base.

Leaves die back at or just after bloom. As blooms fade, flowers become upright and form decorative seed capsules that can be dried for winter arrangements.

In fall, plant bulbs 1½ ft. apart and 2 in. deep in well-drained soil, or start from seed in early spring. Attractive in a flower border or wild garden. May reseed in optimal conditions but does not become a pest.

Nemesia
Scrophulariaceae
ANNUALS AND PERENNIALS

〽 **ZONES VARY BY SPECIES**

☼ **FULL SUN**

💧 **REGULAR WATER**

Nemesia caerulea

Colorful South African natives, some with fragrant flowers. Not at their best in hot weather, though new *N. caerulea* hybrids are more heat-tolerant than other types. All need well-drained soil. Remove faded flowers to prolong bloom. Use as bedding or rock garden plants, in hanging baskets, or as bulb covers.

N. caerulea (N. foetens, N. fruticans). Perennial in Zones 14–24; annual anywhere. To 2 ft. high, 1 ft. wide, with small bright green leaves and upright stems carrying many intensely fragrant blossoms in blue, pink, or lavender. Flowers are narrower than those of *N. strumosa*. Often blooms for months without special attention (almost all year in

Everblooming, easygoing, and neat— nemesia makes a charming companion. Tuck plants, with their plentiful blooms, into large containers with roses.

cool-summer, mild-winter climates), but if flowers decline, cut plant back to stimulate new growth and more bloom. Tolerates light afternoon shade.

While the species prefers cool weather, the many hybrids withstand temperatures as high as 95°F (35°C). Growing about 1 ft. high and wide are 'Innocence Compact', with yellow-centered white flowers, and 'Innocence Compact Pink', with pink blooms. The Poetry (12–14 in. high), Aromatica (12–14 in. high), and Sunsatia (6–12 in. high) series all come in a range of colors. Particularly heat-tolerant 'Bluebird' has blue-violet blossoms centered with yellow. Well-established plantings of the species and hybrids are hardy to 15°F (–9°C).

N. strumosa. Annual. Zones 1–24. The true species grows to 1½ ft. high and 1 ft. wide, but plants sold under this name are usually more compact hybrids between *N. strumosa* and *N. versicolor*; they remain under a foot high, reach about 6 in. wide, and produce small, unscented flowers in clusters to about 4 in. across. Blossoms are chalice-shaped, flaring at the mouth into two unequal lips, the lower one larger than the upper. They come in every color but green. Several mixtures offer a wide range of bright solid colors and bicolors.

Buy started plants or sow seeds in place. Time plantings of this rapid grower to avoid frost but come into bloom during cool weather. In cold-winter climates, sow in early spring for late spring, early summer bloom; in mild-winter areas, sow in fall for bloom in winter and spring. Give rich soil and regular moisture. Pinch to induce bushiness. Good bulb cover or hanging basket plant.

N. versicolor. Annual. Zones 1–24. Grows to 8–10 in. high and as wide. Unscented flowers are similar to those of *N. strumosa*, but color range of *N. versicolor* contains more blue, yellow, and white. Time plantings as for *N. strumosa*.

FOR MORE ON ANNUALS AND PERENNIALS, SEE "GROW: ANNUALS, BULBS," PAGES 674–675, AND "GROW: PERENNIALS," PAGES 686–687.

Nemophila
Boraginaceae
ANNUALS

〽 **ZONES VARY BY SPECIES**

☼ ◐ **FULL SUN OR PARTIAL SHADE**

💧 **REGULAR WATER**

Nemophila menziesii

These lovely annuals grow 6–12 in. high and trailing to 1 ft. wide, with bell-shaped flowers to 1 in. across in spring. Pale green, hairy, ferny leaves give plants a delicate appearance. Often used as bulb cover. Broadcast seed in place. In cold-winter areas, sow as soon as the ground is workable in spring; in mild-winter regions, plant in fall. Plant is quickly killed by heat and humidity. Reseeds when grown under cool, moist conditions.

N. maculata. FIVE-SPOT NEMOPHILA. Zones 1–9, 12–24. Native to California. Flowers are white, marked with fine purple lines and dots; a large purple dot appears at the tip of each of the five lobes.

N. menziesii (N. insignis). BABY BLUE EYES. Zones 1–24. Native to California and southern Oregon. Blooms as freely in gardens as it does in the wild, bearing sky blue blossoms with a white or near-white center. 'Snow Storm' (*N. m. atomaria*), the baby blue eyes variety most commonly grown in Oregon, has white flowers dotted with black. 'Penny Black' (*N. m. discoidalis*) produces blooms that are blackish purple rimmed in white.

Neodypsis decaryi.
See *Dypsis decaryi*

N

Neomarica

Iridaceae
PERENNIALS

✀ ZONES 16, 17, 21–24; H2;
OR INDOORS

☀ ◑ FULL SUN OR LIGHT SHADE;
BRIGHT INDIRECT LIGHT

💧 REGULAR WATER

Neomarica caerulea

Like iris, these perennials produce fans of lance-shaped leaves. Foliage arises from short rhizomes; leaves and flowering stems grow to about the same height. Flowers are intricate, with three large, rounded outer segments surrounding three smaller, curled segments that are banded in contrasting colors. Individual flowers last only a day, but others follow over an extended period.

N. caerulea. From Brazil. To 5–5½ ft. tall, 2–3 ft. wide, with stiffly erect leaves. As plant grows, lower leaves fan out to the side. Branching flower stems carry a succession of 3–4-in. blue blossoms, their centers intricately banded in yellow, white, and brown. Blooms in early summer. Offsets are produced at flowering points on the stems; they detach for additional plants.

N. gracilis. WALKING IRIS. From Mexico to Brazil. To 2–2½ ft. high, 1–1½ ft. wide. Blooms in late spring and summer; flower stems resemble the leaves so closely that blossoms appear to emerge directly from the foliage. Flowers are 2½ in. wide. Outer segments are white; inner ones combine blue, brown, and yellow. As flowers fade, the blossom stalk bends downward and produces plantlets that take root—hence the common name.

Nepeta

Lamiaceae
PERENNIALS

✀ ZONES 1–24, EXCEPT AS NOTED

☀ ◑ FULL SUN OR PARTIAL SHADE

💧 MODERATE WATER

🐝 ATTRACT BEES

Nepeta racemosa

Vigorous, spreading members of the mint family with aromatic foliage. With the exception of catnip (*N. cataria*), these plants are valuable for their spikes of two-lipped blue or blue-violet (or sometimes pink, white, or yellow) flowers. Plants make attractive, informal low hedges or edgings.

N. cataria. CATNIP. From the Mediterranean and western Asia. To 2–3 ft. high and wide, with downy, heart-shaped, tooth-edged, gray-green leaves. Spikes of small (¼–½ in.) whitish or pinkish flowers in late spring, early summer. Not very ornamental but worthy of a place in the herb garden. Grows easily in light soil and self-sows readily. Common name refers to stimulant effect on cats, but their susceptibility to the herb varies: some felines fall into a rapturous frenzy, rolling wildly on the plant; others ignore it. If necessary, protect crown of plant with an inverted wire basket; stems will grow through. The same tactic also helps preserve potted plants grown outdoors and brought indoors occasionally for cats to enjoy. You can sprinkle dried leaves over your cat's food or use them to stuff cloth toys. Some people use catnip to flavor tea. 'Citriodora' has lemon-scented foliage.

N. clarkei. Zones 2b–9, 14–24. Himalayan native to 2½–4 ft. tall, 1½–3 ft. wide. Truest

blue flowers of all nepetas, with white patch on lower lip. Blooms in summer and early fall. Lance-shaped green leaves.

N. × faassenii. CATMINT. Sterile hybrid of *N. racemosa* and a European species; often sold as *N. mussinii*. Soft, silvery gray-green, spreading mound grows to 1 ft. high, 1½–2 ft. wide. Scallop-edged, heart-shaped, gray-green leaves. Attractive to some cats, who enjoy nibbling on and rolling in plantings; insert short sticks in the ground among the foliage to discourage cats and prevent destruction. Loose, lax spikes of ½-in. lavender-blue flowers in late spring, early summer. Set plants 1–1½ ft. apart for groundcover. 'Select Blue' has darker flowers than the species; 'Snowflake' has pure white blooms.

N. grandiflora. Native to Europe, Caucasus. Open clump to 2½ ft. high, 1½ ft. wide. Gray-green, hairless or sparsely hairy, scallop-edged, egg-shaped leaves. Violet-blue, ¾-in. flowers in late spring, early summer. 'Bramdean' has lavender-blue blossoms with purple calyxes; 'Dawn to Dusk' has lilac-pink flowers, smoky violet calyxes.

Calyxes of both these varieties persist after flowers have faded.

N. hederacea. See *Glechoma hederacea* 'Variegata'.

N. nervosa. Zones 3–10, 14–24. Native to Kashmir. Bushy habit to 1–2 ft. high, 1 ft. wide. Bright green, conspicuously veined, tooth-edged leaves are lance-shaped. Brilliant violet-blue (rarely yellow), ½-in. flowers bloom from midsummer to early fall. 'Pink Cat' has pink flowers.

N. racemosa (N. mussinii). Native to the Caucasus, Turkey, and Iran. Sprawling plant grows from 6 in. to 1 ft. high and about 2 ft. or more wide. Roundish, scallop-edged leaves can range in shades from medium green to gray-green; they are covered with fine hairs. The typical form produces ⅓-in.-long lavender flowers for a short period in midsummer; may rebloom if sheared. Reseeds prodigiously. Inferior to its hybrid *N. × faassenii*, but several worthwhile selections are more compact than the species

CLOCKWISE FROM TOP: *Nepeta reichenbachiana; N. × faassenii; N. cataria*

N

and bloom over a longer period. 'Blue Ice' has dense gray-green foliage and pale blue flowers that fade to near-white. 'Superba' has a dense, matlike habit and gray-green leaves that are smaller than those of the species; it bears lavender-blue blossoms from spring through fall. 'Walker's Low' grows 2– 3 ft. high and has vivid lavender-blue flowers (sometimes sold as *N. × faassenii*).

N. reichenbachiana. Native to Armenia and the Caucasus. May be a form of *N. racemosa*. Makes a thick, low mound to 1 ft. high, 2–4 ft. wide. Woolly, heart-shaped, deeply veined leaves have pointed tips and scalloped edges; they are pale green above, gray or white beneath, ¾–1¼ in. long. Blooms from late spring through fall, producing 6–8-in.-high spikes of deep blue flowers with just a hint of violet. Good groundcover; space plants 3 ft. apart.

N. sibirica (N. macrantha, Dracocephalum sibiricum). SIBERIAN CATNIP. Native to Siberia. Sturdy, upright habit to 2–3 ft. high, 1½–2 ft. wide. Dark green, oblong to lance-shaped leaves are softly hairy beneath. Spikes of large (1½ in.) violet-blue blossoms appear for about a month, beginning in early summer. 'Six Hills Giant' is possibly a hybrid of *N. × faassenii*—but grows taller (reaches 2½–3 ft. high and as wide), has greener foliage, and bears deeper blue flowers. More tolerant of damp climates than other nepetas. 'Souvenir d'André Chaudron' ('Blue Beauty') is similar but grows only 1½ ft. high and blooms for a longer period, with season extending into late summer.

CARE

As soon as blossoms fade, shear plants back by half or cut faded flower stems to the ground to encourage rebloom. (Most species seed freely and can become invasive if spent flowers are not removed.) When buying named varieties, be sure to obtain cutting-grown plants; seedlings vary in flower color and habit. In cold-winter climates, nepetas are occasionally used as a substitute for lavender (*Lavandula*) in borders and edgings. Most

species resent heat combined with high humidity. In Zones 12 and 13, most are best treated as winter annuals. Tolerate regular moisture if soil is well drained. In winter or early spring, cut out last year's growth to make way for new stems. At that time, you can also divide clumps for increase, though it's easy to start new plants from cuttings (take them before flower buds form).

Nephrolepis cordifolia

SOUTHERN SWORD FERN
Lomariopsidaceae
FERN

ZONES 8, 9, 12–24; H1, H2

SOME SHADE; BRIGHT INDIRECT LIGHT

REGULAR WATER

Nephrolepis cordifolia

Tough, easy-to-grow fern native to many tropical regions of the world (this genus also includes tender houseplant species, such as *N. exaltata* 'Bostoniensis', the Boston fern). It grows to 2–3 ft. high, 5 ft. wide. Tufts of bright green, narrow (2 in. wide), upright fronds with closely spaced, finely toothed leaflets. Roots often have small, roundish tubers. Plant spreads by thin, fuzzy runners and can be invasive. Will not take hard frosts but is otherwise adaptable, tolerating poor soil and erratic watering. Good in narrow, shaded beds. Effective groundcover; also good in pots and hanging baskets. 'Lemon Buttons' grows only 12 in. high with rounded leaflets. For native Western sword fern, see *Polystichum munitum*.

Nerine

Amaryllidaceae
PERENNIALS FROM BULBS

ZONES 5, 6, 8, 9, 13–24

PARTIAL SHADE IN HOTTEST CLIMATES

REGULAR WATER DURING GROWTH AND BLOOM

Nerine bowdenii

South African relatives of spider lily (*Lycoris*), which they closely resemble. Most have strap-shaped leaves to about 1 ft. long; these die back well before bloom time in late summer or early fall, then reappear later in the year (typically around bloom time or shortly afterward). Some types are essentially evergreen. All have broad, funnel-shaped flowers carried in clusters atop leafless stems; each blossom has six spreading segments that are recurved at their tips.

N. bowdenii. Lightly scented flowers to 3 in. long, soft pink marked with deeper pink, in clusters of 8–12 on 2-ft. stems. Forms with taller stems and larger flower clusters are available in deeper pink, crimson, and red.

N. filifolia. Essentially evergreen, since new leaves—narrow, grassy, 6–8 in. long—are produced as old ones fade. Inch-wide, rose-red flowers with narrow, crinkled segments are carried in clusters of 8–12 on 1-ft. stems. Spreads rapidly.

N. masoniorum. Virtually evergreen species like *N. filifolia*, but it bears its flowers in clusters of 4–12 on 9-in. stems.

N. sarniensis. GUERNSEY LILY. Large clusters of 1½-in., iridescent crimson flowers with prominent stamens are borne on stalks to 2 ft. high. Pink,

orange, scarlet, and pure white varieties. *N. s. curvifolia fothergillii* has scarlet flowers overlaid with shimmering gold.

CARE

Same planting instructions, cultural conditions as for *Lycoris*. Withhold summer water for species that experience summer dormancy, but keep watering the essentially evergreen kinds. As is true for *Lycoris*, these plants can be grown in pots in areas beyond their hardiness range or where soil cannot be kept dry for summer-dormant types.

Nerium oleander

OLEANDER
Apocynaceae
EVERGREEN SHRUB

ZONES 8–16, 18–24; H1, H2

FULL SUN

LITTLE TO MODERATE WATER

ALL PARTS ARE POISONOUS IF INGESTED. DON'T BURN PRUNINGS; SMOKE CAN CAUSE SEVERE IRRITATION.

Nerium oleander

Once indispensible Mediterranean native still widely seen and planted throughout much of the West. Moderate to fast growth to 3–20 ft. tall and 4– 12 ft. wide, depending on variety. Larger types can be easily trained into single or multitrunked trees. Narrow leaves are dark green, leathery, and semiglossy; attractive in all seasons. Blooms from late spring to fall, bearing 2–3-in.-wide, often fragrant flowers clustered at twig or branch ends. Forms with double and single flowers are sold, in colors ranging from white to shades of yellow, pink,

N

How to Grow Oleanders

Oleanders need little water once established, but they can take moderate amounts. They tolerate poorly drained and relatively salty soils. In shade or ocean fog, they produce weak or leggy growth and few flowers. Routine pruning isn't necessary, but you may need to prune to guide growth. To control size and form, cut oldest stems to the ground before spring growth begins; shorten remaining stems to restrict height. To prevent bushiness at base, pull (don't cut) any unwanted suckers. To renew an old, unattractive, leggy plant, lop it to the ground before new growth begins in spring.

CHALLENGES Oleander was once the basic landscaping shrub for regions with hot, dry summers and mild winters, but it is now facing a severe threat from leaf scorch, a bacterial disease spread by the glassy-winged sharpshooter (an insect pest). Leaves of infected plants turn brown and drop, and the plant quickly declines and dies. No cure is known, although the disease's progress may be slowed by pruning out affected parts (sterilize tools after each cut). The disease is already serious in Southern and central California, and in parts of Arizona and Texas. Efforts are being made to curb its spread by controlling the insect carrier. Previously, chief problems were scale, yellow oleander aphid, and bacterial gall disease (causing deformed flowers and warty growths).

salmon, and red. 'Mrs. Roeding', double salmon-pink, grows 6 ft. tall and has smaller leaves, finer-textured foliage than big oleanders. 'Petite Pink' and 'Petite Salmon' grow 3–6 ft. tall and nearly as wide; keep at lower end of range with

moderate pruning. They make excellent informal flowering hedges, though they are not as cold-hardy as standard-size oleanders.

All parts of this plant are highly toxic. Caution children against eating leaves or flowers; keep prunings and dead leaves away from hay or other animal feed; don't use wood for barbecue fires or skewers. Smoke from burning prunings can cause severe irritation to mucous membranes. Wash hands thoroughly after handling plants.

For a plant called yellow oleander, see *Thevetia neriifolia*.

Nicolaia elatior.
See *Etlingera elatior*

Nicotiana

FLOWERING TOBACCO
Solanaceae
PERENNIALS, MOST GROWN AS ANNUALS

✎ **ALL ZONES, EXCEPT AS NOTED**

☼ ◑ **FULL SUN OR PARTIAL SHADE**

⬤ **REGULAR WATER**

🦋 **ATTRACT HUMMINGBIRDS AND BUTTERFLIES**

◈ **ALL PARTS ARE EXTREMELY POISONOUS IF INGESTED**

Nicotiana 'Perfume Deep Purple'

Tender perennials from South America. All are grown as annuals, but they may live over in mild-winter areas. Upright-growing plants with large, soft, oval leaves; both foliage and stems are slightly sticky. Flowers—very fragrant, in some species—are tubular, typically flaring at the mouth into five pointed lobes; they appear near tops of branching stems in summer. They usually open at night

or on cloudy days, though some kinds open during the day. Some nicotianas reseed readily.

N. alata (N. affinis). Wild species (for which seed is available) grows 2–4 ft. tall (possibly to 6 ft. under ideal conditions), 1 ft. wide. Bears large, intensely fragrant white flowers that open toward evening. Selection and hybridization with other species have produced many garden strains that stay open day and night and come in colors including white, pink shades, red, and lime green, but their perfume is often not as strong as that of the "unimproved" common species. Many of the newer hybrids, such as the Perfume series (to 20 in. high), are sold as *N. × sanderae* and have nice fragrance. 'Avalon Pink' is very compact, rarely exceeding 12 in. high. Domino strain grows to 12–15 in. high and has upward-facing flowers that take heat and sun better than taller kinds. Nicki strain is taller, to 15–18 in. The older Sensation strain is taller still (to 4 ft.) and looks more at home in informal mixed borders than as a bedding plant. Fragrance in these strains is erratic. If scent (especially during evening) is important to you, plant 3-ft.-high 'Grandiflora'.

N. langsdorffii. To 5 ft. tall, 1½ ft. wide. Branching stems are hung with drooping sprays of bell-shaped, bright green flowers. Unusual blossom color blends well with blues, yellows in flower border. No noticeable scent.

N. sylvestris. To 5 ft. tall, 2 ft. wide. Intensely fragrant, long, tubular white flowers are borne in tiers atop a statuesque plant. Striking in a night garden.

Tubular flowers in rich colors make these fragrant garden favorites fine companion plants. Combine a cool *N. alata* such as 'Saratoga Lime' or 'Lime Green' in a container with purple heliotrope and electric green coleus.

Nierembergia

CUP FLOWER
Solanaceae
PERENNIALS

✎ **ZONES VARY BY SPECIES**

☼ ◑ **LIGHT SHADE IN HOTTEST CLIMATES**

⬤ **REGULAR WATER**

Nierembergia linariifolia
'Augusta Blue Skies'

Small genus of plants from sunny, moist areas in South America. The first species listed here grows as a spreading mound; the second is a ground-covering mat. Both are blanketed with broadly cup-shaped blooms in summer. Beyond hardiness range, treat as annuals.

N. linariifolia (N. caerulea, N. hippomanica). DWARF CUP FLOWER. Zones 8–24; H1, H2. To 6–12 in. high and wide. Much-branched, mounding plant, with very small, stiff leaves. Flowers are blue to violet. Trimming back plant after bloom to induce new growth seems to lengthen its life. 'Purple Robe' and the white 'Mont Blanc', usually sold as *N. hippomanica*, may be varieties of the similar *N. scoparia*. 'Augusta Blue Skies' is a compact hybrid with lavender-blue flowers and improved heat tolerance.

N. repens (N. rivularis). WHITE CUP. Zones 5–9, 14–24; H1. Mat to 4–6 in. high, 2 ft. wide, with bright green foliage and white blossoms. For best performance, don't crowd it with more aggressive plants. Not as heat-tolerant as *N. linariifolia*.

FOR MORE ON PERENNIALS, SEE "GROW: PERENNIALS," PAGES 686–687.

Nigella damascena

LOVE-IN-A-MIST
Ranunculaceae
ANNUAL

- 🌱 **ALL ZONES**
- ☀️ 🌤️ **FULL SUN OR PARTIAL SHADE**
- 💧 **REGULAR WATER**
- 🐦 **ATTRACTS BIRDS**

Nigella damascena

An old-fashioned Mediterranean favorite to 1–1½ ft. high, 10 in. wide. All leaves, even those that form under the collar beneath each flower, are finely cut into threadlike divisions. Blue, white, or rose-colored blooms, 1–1½ in. across, are borne singly at branch ends in spring. Curious papery-textured, horned seed capsules lend an airy effect to bouquets and mixed borders and look decorative in dried arrangements. 'Miss Jekyll', to 1½ ft. high, has semidouble cornflower blue blossoms. Persian Jewels, to 15 in. high, is a superior strain in a mix of colors. 'African Bride' is a variety of the similar *N. papillosa*. It has flat white petals with prominent blackish purple stamens. The black seedpods are useful in dried arrangements. Reaches 3 ft. high and about 1 ft. wide.

CARE

Love-in-a-mist comes into bloom quickly in spring, dries up in summer heat. Start from seed in spring, as soon as ground is workable and frost danger is past; can be sown in autumn in mild-winter areas. Sow seeds where plants are to grow, since the long taproot makes transplanting unsatisfactory. Self-sows freely.

Nolina

Agavaceae
SUCCULENT PERENNIALS

- 🌱 **ZONES VARY BY SPECIES**
- ☀️ **FULL SUN**
- 💧 **LITTLE OR NO WATER TO MODERATE WATER**

Nolina nelsonii

Accent plants with tough, grassy leaves usually about 3 ft. long, typically on a thick trunk. In spring or summer, 3–4-ft. stalks rise from the center of the foliage rosette, carrying tiny greenish or creamy white flowers. Plants are valued for their strong vertical silhouette rather than their blossoms. Good for desert or other dry landscapes.

N. bigelovii. Zones 7–16, 18–24. Native to California and Arizona. Stout stem to 3 ft. high is topped by a rosette of gray-green, 3–4-ft. leaves. Eventually reaches about 6 ft. wide.

N. longifolia. MEXICAN GRASS TREE. Zones 12–24. Native to central Mexico. In youth, forms a fountain of bright green, grasslike leaves. In time, leafy whorls top trunks 6–10 ft. tall, sometimes with a few branches. Plant can eventually spread to 9 ft. wide.

N. matapensis. TREE BEAR GRASS. Zones 10–13. From Mexico. To 10–25 ft. tall, 10 ft. wide, with a branching trunk that is slow to develop. Each branch ends in a shower of bright green, broad-based leaves with sharp edges; leaves may reach 9 ft. long.

N. microcarpa. Zones 3, 10–13. Native from Arizona to Texas and Mexico. Unlike others, doesn't form a noticeable trunk; instead, branching and slowly spreading underground stems give rise here and there to rosettes of narrow (less than ½ in. wide) olive green leaves with tips split into tufts. Each foliage clump can reach 3 ft. high and 6 ft. wide.

N. nelsonii. Zones 5, 8, 9, 11–24. NELSON'S BLUE BEAR GRASS. Native to Mexico. Long, narrow, gray-green to powdery blue leaves with toothed edges. Grows to 10 ft. tall and 4–5 ft. wide. Distinctive accent.

N. parryi. Zones 2, 3, 7–24. Native to deserts of Southern California. Resembles *N. bigelovii*, but leaf bases are expanded into a spoonlike shape. *N. p. wolfii* is taller with longer leaves and flower spikes.

N. recurvata. See *Beaucarnea recurvata*.

FOR MORE ON SUCCULENTS, SEE "MEET THE SUCCULENTS," PAGE 618.

Nymphaea

WATER LILY
Nymphaeaceae
AQUATIC PLANTS

- 🌱 **ZONES 1–24; H1, H2**
- ☀️ **FULL SUN**
- 💧 **LOCATE IN PONDS, WATER GARDENS**

Nymphaea alba

These aquatic perennials grow with their roots in submerged soil and their long-stalked leaves floating on the surface. Floating leaves are rounded, with a deep notch at one side where leafstalk is attached. Showy flowers either float on surface or stand above it on stiff stalks. There are hardy and tropical kinds. Hardy types come in white, yellow, copper, pink, and red. Tropical types add blue and purple to the color range; recent introductions include an unusual greenish blue. Some tropicals in the white-pink-red color range are night bloomers; all others close at night. Many are fragrant.

Hardy kinds. These are easiest for beginners. Plant them from February to October in mild-winter areas, from April to July in cold-winter regions. Set 6-in.-long pieces of rhizome on soil at pool bottom or in boxes (not redwood ones, since these can discolor the water), placing rhizome in a nearly horizontal position with its bud end up. In either case, top of soil should be 8–12 in. below surface of water. Feed at planting time and monthly thereafter, using a controlled-release product. Groom plants by removing spent leaves and blossoms. They usually bloom throughout warm weather and go dormant in fall, reappearing in spring. In very cold areas, protect plants by covering pond or by adding more water to it.

Tropical kinds. These begin to grow and bloom later in summer but last longer, often until the first frost. Buy started tropical plants and set them at the same depth as hardy rhizomes. Tropical types go dormant but do not survive really low winter temperatures. Their best chance of long-term survival is in regions where orange trees grow. Where winters are colder, store dormant tubers in damp sand over winter or buy new plants each year.

No pond? No problem. Grow a hardy water lily in a tall, glazed container without drain holes. Set the potted water lily inside the large container—atop an empty, upside-down pot to raise it. Fill the container with water, nearly to the rim. Then let the lily foliage fan out over the water's surface.

N

Nyssa sylvatica

SOUR GUM, TUPELO,
PEPPERIDGE
Nyssaceae
DECIDUOUS TREE

ZONES 2–10, 14–21

FULL SUN OR PARTIAL SHADE

MODERATE TO REGULAR WATER

Nyssa sylvatica

This native to the eastern U.S. grows at a slow to moderate rate to 30–50 ft. or taller, 15–25 ft. wide. Pyramidal when young; spreading, irregular, and rugged in age. Crooked branches and dark, red-tinged bark make dramatic picture against winter sky. Glossy dark green leaves emerge late in spring. Male and female flowers borne on separate plants. Both sexes bear inconspicuous flowers; females will bear fruit if a male is growing nearby (males may set some fruit as well). Fruits are bluish black, shaped like small olives, and can make a mess on decks and driveways; birds like them. In fall, even in mild-winter regions, leaves turn yellow and orange, then bright red before dropping. Excellent shade tree; very attractive in naturalized landscapes 'Autumn Cascades' has a strongly weeping form. 'Forum' has an upright, pyramidal shape, ideal for planting on streets. 'Wildfire' has red new growth.

CARE

Sour gum prefers moist, deep, acid, well-drained soil containing lots of organic matter, but tolerates poor drainage. Does not thrive in polluted air. Select a permanent location, since this tree's taproot makes it difficult to move later on.

Ochna serrulata
(O. multiflora)

BIRD'S-EYE BUSH,
MICKEY MOUSE PLANT
Ochnaceae
EVERGREEN SHRUB

ZONES 14–24; H1, H2

PARTIAL SHADE

MODERATE WATER

Ochna serrulata

This South African shrub grows slowly to 4–8 ft. high and wide. Oblong leaves are leathery, fine toothed, bronzy in spring, deep green later. Early summer flowers are the size of buttercups (*Ranunculus*). After the yellow petals fall, sepals turn vivid red; then five or more green, seedlike fruits protrude from red center. Fruits later turn glossy jet black, in strong contrast to red sepals; at this stage, the configuration can be said to resemble the eyes, ears, and nose of a mouse. Prefers slightly acid soil. Good in a tub or box or as a small espalier. Makes an interesting accent in a shrub border.

Ochna serrulata is like two plants in one: first enjoy bright yellow blooms, then cardinal red sepals with fruits that turn from green to black.

Ocimum basilicum

BASIL
Lamiaceae
ANNUAL OR TENDER PERENNIAL

ALL ZONES

FULL SUN

REGULAR WATER

Genovese basil

From tropical and subtropical Asia. Basil is a somewhat bushy plant to 2 ft. high and 1 ft. wide, with green, shiny, 1–2-in.-long leaves and spikes of white flowers. But there are endless variations on the theme, including forms with purple or variegated foliage, dwarf globe or columnar habits, giant or tiny leaves, and purple flowers. Flavors cover a wide range, including anise, cinnamon, clove, coriander, lemon, and lime.

As a culinary herb, basil is critical to everything from pesto to Indian and Southwestern cuisine. Used fresh or dry, its leaves lend a pleasant, mildly sweet flavor to sauces and cooked dishes of all sorts. The most flavorful leaves are from younger stems that have not yet borne flowers.

There are too many varieties to list here, but following is a sampling of what's available. All are annuals unless otherwise noted.

Big leaves. 'Napolitano', 'Large Green', and 'Mammoth Sweet' have especially big leaves; use them as wraps for appetizers.

Compact plants. Try 'Finissimo Verde a Palla'; 'Greek' ('Spicy Globe'), which makes a fine-leafed, 1-ft. globe; 'Magical Michael' or 'Marseillais Dwarf',

which is covered with extremely aromatic leaves.

Flavored leaves. Because basil comes in so many flavors, taste a leaf, if possible, before you buy. Most of the varieties that follow have names that describe their flavors: 'Cinnamon', 'Clove', 'Lemon', 'Lettuce Leaf' (licorice), 'Lime', 'Sweet Dani' (intense lemon).

Perennial types. Grow these outdoors in virtually frost-free climates or indoors: 'Magic Mountain' (3 ft.) or 'Pesto Perpetua' (to 4 ft., with light green leaves that have creamy variegation).

Bests for pesto. Start with Genovese type such as 'Aroma 1' or 'Aroma 2', 'Genova' or 'Nufar'; or use a standard variety such as 'Sweet Basil'.

Purple foliage. These *O. b. purpurascens* varieties can be touchy to grow, but they are beautiful and much used in Asian cooking: 'Purple Ruffles', 'Red Lettuce Leaved', 'Red Osmin' (an improved 'Dar Opal'), 'Red Rubin', and 'Rubra'.

CARE

Sow seeds of any basil in early spring, or set out nursery plants after all danger of frost is past. Space plants about 10–12 in. apart or thin to this distance. Fertilize once during the growing season with a complete fertilizer. To prolong leaf production—which will cease when plants come into bloom—pinch out flower spikes as they form.

Where the growing season is long, though, flowering always wins out and plants will mature and stop producing new growth. In these regions, make successive sowings about every 2 weeks to ensure a steady supply of leaves throughout the season.

Basil is susceptible to fusarium wilt, which causes plants to collapse in a day. Defeat it by growing tolerant varieties such as one of the 'Aroma' varieties, 'Magical Michael', or 'Nufar', and never plant basil in the same bed more than once every 4 years. Alternately, plant in containers.

Odontospermum maritimum.
See *Asteriscus maritimus*

N

Oemleria cerasiformis
(Osmaronia cerasiformis)
OSO BERRY, INDIAN PLUM
Rosaceae
DECIDUOUS SHRUB OR TREE

- ZONES 4–9, 14–24
- FULL SUN IN COOLER CLIMATES ONLY
- AMPLE WATER
- FRUIT ATTRACTS BIRDS

Oemleria cerasiformis

In damp woodlands and meadows in the Northwest and in parts of California, oso berry's tiny, almond-scented white flowers are among the first signs of spring. This is a fine-textured, suckering shrub that grows to 3–15 ft. tall, eventually spreading into thickets that become 12 ft. wide or more. Lance-shaped leaves are dark green on top, gray-green and slightly fuzzy beneath. Crushed leaves have a fresh scent like that of cucumbers. Bell-shaped, fragrant blooms in drooping clusters up to 4 in. long appear with the foliage, which emerges very early in the year. Male and female plants are separate; if a male is nearby, females will bear small (less than 1/2 in. long) blue-black fruits that are relished by birds and other wildlife. Nice addition to a shrub border or woodland planting.

To keep the plant looking its best, remove some of the oldest stems after bloom. Or revive an old, overgrown shrub by cutting it back almost to the ground.

FOR OTHER PLANTS THAT ATTRACT BIRDS, SEE PAGES 95–99.

Oenothera
EVENING PRIMROSE, SUNDROPS
Onagraceae
PERENNIALS OR BIENNIALS

- ZONES VARY BY SPECIES
- FULL SUN OR PARTIAL SHADE
- LITTLE TO MODERATE WATER, EXCEPT AS NOTED

Oenothera speciosa

Valued for showy, four-petaled, silky flowers in bright yellow, pink, or white. Some types display their blossoms during the day; others open in late afternoon and close the following morning. Flowers of some are fragrant. Plants succeed in tough, rough places.

O. berlandieri. See *O. speciosa* 'Rosea'.

O. caespitosa. TUFTED, FRAGRANT, or WHITE EVENING PRIMROSE. Perennial or biennial. Zones 1–3, 7–14, 18–21. Native to western U.S. Clump to 8–12 in. high, 2 ft. wide, with many rosettes of narrow, fuzzy gray-green leaves. Fragrant, 3–4-in. flowers fade from white to pink; they open in the evening. Blooms heavily in late spring, early summer.

O. drummondii. See *O. stubbei*.

O. fruticosa. SUNDROPS. Perennial or biennial. Zones 1–21. Native to eastern U.S. Erect growth to 2 ft. high and wide. Branching reddish stems are set with medium green leaves that turn dull red with frost. Clusters of 1–2-in.-wide, deep yellow flowers from late spring through summer; open in daytime. 'Fireworks' ('Fyrverkeri') has red flower buds and leaves tinted purplish brown. *O. f. glauca* (*O. tetragona*) has light yellow flowers and red stems;

its leaves are broader than those of species and red tinted when young. Foliage of 'Solstice' ('Sonnenwende') turns bright red in summer, darkens to burgundy in fall.

O. macrocarpa (O. missouriensis). OZARK SUNDROPS. Perennial. Zones 1–24. Native to south-central U.S. To 6 in. high and 2 ft. wide. Late spring to early fall, bears pure yellow, 4-in. flowers that remain open all day. Large winged seed-pods follow the flowers. Good in rock gardens. Give partial shade in hottest climates. *O. m. fremontii* 'Silver Blade' has silvery blue leaves.

O. speciosa. MEXICAN EVENING PRIMROSE. Perennial. Zones 2b–24; H1, H2. Native to southwestern U.S. and Mexico. To 1 ft. high and 3 ft. or more wide, spreading by rhizomes. Fragrant, 2-in. flowers are white to pinkish, aging to pink; despite the plant's common name, they open during the day. Blooms spring or early summer into fall, then stems die back. Good groundcover for dry slopes or parking strips, but can be aggressive and is potentially invasive. Varieties include pure white 'Alba', light pink 'Rosea' (*O. berlandieri, O. speciosa childsii*), pink 'Siskiyou', and 'Woodside White' (white blossoms with a chartreuse eye).

O. stubbei. SALTILLO EVENING PRIMROSE. Perennial. Zones 10–14, 18–24. Native to Mexico. Evening-blooming plant that forms a dark green mat 5 in. high and 4 ft. wide; prostrate stems root along the ground, forming offset plants. Yellow, 2 1/2-in. flowers rise on stems 6–8 in. above foliage. Blooms heavily in spring, sporadically the rest of the year. Endures heat and drought but does better with occasional water. Often sold as *O. drummondii*.

O. tetragona. See *O. fruticosa glauca*.

For a pretty wildflower effect in a contained space, plant Mexican evening primrose with pale yellow poppies and dwarf *Godetia*.

Okra
Malvaceae
ANNUAL

- ZONES 1B–3B, 6–16, 18–23
- FULL SUN
- REGULAR WATER

Okra

This heat-loving vegetable hails from tropical Asia. It is a large, erect, bushy plant to 6 ft. tall, with big, bold, deeply lobed leaves; the edible pods are produced in leaf joints.

'Clemson Spineless' and 'Cajun Delight' are early varieties that mature in areas with a short growing season. 'Burgundy' has red leaves and pods, looks attractive in containers. Grown in a large tub in a warm spot, a single okra plant can yield a crop large enough to make it worth growing. Okra is used to flavor and thicken soups and gumbos; it can also be sautéed, steamed, or batter-fried.

CARE

Grows well under same conditions as sweet corn. Plant when danger of frost is past and ground has warmed to 70°F (21°C). To speed germination, soak seeds for 24 hours before planting; use only seeds that are swollen. Leave 2 1/2–4 ft. between rows; thin plants to 1–1 1/2 ft. apart. Apply a complete fertilizer when the first pods set, again when plants are shoulder high. Begin picking when pods are 2–4 in. long (wear gloves; pods are prickly). Pick every 2 days or so; plants stop producing if pods are not harvested. Okra takes 55 to 60 days from planting to harvest.

O

Olea europaea

OLIVE

Oleaceae

EVERGREEN TREE

✎ **ZONES 8, 9, 11–24; H1, H2**

☼ **FULL SUN**

◐ **LITTLE TO MODERATE WATER**

Olives

Olives come from the Mediterranean region. They thrive in areas with hot, dry summers but also perform adequately in coastal areas. Along with palms, citrus, and eucalyptus, olives are practically trademarks along avenues and in gardens of California and southern Arizona. The trees' beauty has been appreciated in those areas since they were introduced to mission gardens for the oil their fruit produces. In recent years, growers have experimented with extra-hardy olives that fruit in Oregon.

Willowlike foliage is a soft gray-green that goes well with most colors. Smooth gray trunks and branches become gnarled and picturesque in age. Trees grow slowly, typically to 25–30 ft. tall and as wide; however, young ones put on height (if not substance) fairly fast. They tolerate temperatures down to 15°F (–9°C).

Fruiting varieties. 'Arbequina' is a Spanish variety grown for fruit, oil, and home gardens. Widely sold in the Pacific Northwest, where it is said to be hardy to 10°F (–12°C) but needs warm summers to bear fruit. Worth growing in the Willamette Valley. 'Ascolana' (large fruit, small pit), 'Manzanillo' (spreading tree, apple-shaped fruit), 'Mission' (taller tree), and 'Sevillano' are commercial

How to Grow Olives

Olive trees look best when grown in deep, rich soil, but they will also grow in shallow, alkaline, or stony soil and with little fertilizer. They can get by on little water but produce better crops with a deep soaking every 2 weeks during midsummer.

TRAINING & THINNING Begin training young trees early. For single trunk, prune out or shorten side branches below point where you want branching to begin; cut off basal suckers. For multiple trunks, stake lower branches or basal suckers to continue growth at desired angles. Large old trees can (with reasonable care) be boxed and transplanted with near certainty of survival. Mature olives withstand heavy pruning. Thinning each year shows off branch pattern and eliminates some flowering/fruiting wood, reducing the fruit crop—which can be a nuisance in gardens.

HARVESTING Olives ripen and drop late in the year. Without processing, the olives are inedible, and they can stain paving and harm lawns if not removed. In addition to pruning, reduce crop by spraying with fruit-control hormones when tiny white flowers appear. Or spread tarpaulin at dropping time, knock off all fruit, and dispose of it. "Fruitless" varieties are not always reliably barren.

PESTS The larvae (maggots) of olive fruit fly eat virtually all the fruit on infected trees; chemical sprays are available to fight them, but for homeowners, better choices may be a fruit fly bait containing spinosad, or a spray containing kaolin clay, which acts as a barrier. Picking up fallen olives as soon as they are noticed will also help.

varieties sold as specimen trees by landscaping firms.

Fruitless varieties. With exception of 'Swan Hill', most of these will occasionally bear fruit. 'Bonita' has tiny fruit resembling that of privet (*Ligustrum*). 'Little Ollie' is a big, dense shrub (to 6–8 ft. tall and wide), very dark green; excellent as hedge or screen. 'Majestic Beauty' is airy and fluffy looking; suitable as specimen or as hedge or screen. 'Skylark Dwarf' is typically a large, compact, multitrunked shrub to 16 ft. tall and wide. 'Swan Hill' has deep green leaves, bears no fruit, and has little or no pollen—a boon to allergy sufferers. 'Wilsonii' ('Wilson's Fruitless', 'Fruitless') occasionally bears small fruit crop.

Olneya tesota

DESERT IRONWOOD

Fabaceae

EVERGREEN TREE

✎ **ZONES 8, 9, 11–14, 18–23**

☼ **FULL SUN**

◐ **LITTLE OR NO WATER TO MODERATE WATER**

Olneya tesota

A thorny native of the Southwest's Sonoran Desert, also found in warm-winter areas of California. Grows slowly to 15–30 ft. tall, with equal spread; common name "ironwood" refers to its extremely hard, heavy heartwood. May be single- or multitrunked; prune to maintain desired form. Branches are erect in youth, later spreading. Gray-green leaves, each with two spines at base, are divided into many ¾-in. leaflets. In late spring, clusters of pinkish

lavender, ½-in., sweet pea–shaped flowers put on a good show. These are followed by dark brown, fuzzy, 2-in.-long pods. Tree drops leaves heavily around bloom time, but new foliage emerges quickly.

Plants thrive near washes, where some deep water is usually available. In the garden, it is extremely drought-tolerant but will grow faster with occasional summer water. Drops its leaves in hard frosts and cannot endure prolonged freezes.

Omphalodes

Boraginaceae

PERENNIALS

✎ **ZONES VARY BY SPECIES**

☼ **PARTIAL SHADE**

● **REGULAR WATER**

Omphalodes verna

These resemble forget-me-nots (*Myosotis*) but typically have deeper blue, somewhat larger (½-in.) flowers and more restrained behavior—these plants don't have the irritating habit of reseeding themselves all over the place.

Omphalodes thrive in woodland gardens or shaded rock gardens and look especially attractive on a wall or bank where their flowers may be viewed at eye level.

O. cappadocica. Zones 2b–9, 14–21. Native to Turkey. Slowly spreading clump of bright green foliage to 1½ ft. wide. Sends up 1–1½-ft.-high sprays of bright blue, white-eyed flowers in spring. 'Lilac Mist' is shorter (to 10 in.), with grayish lavender flowers. 'Starry Eyes', also to 10 in. high, has pale lilac flowers with dark blue spots at the base of each petal.

There also is a form with pure white flowers.

O. verna. BLUE-EYED MARY. Zones 2–9, 14–21. Native to mountains of Europe. Forms a foliage mat 3 in. high, 3 ft. or more wide, with dark green leaves. In spring, leafy stalks to 8 in. high bear clustered deep blue flowers with a white eye.

Oncidium
Orchidaceae
EPIPHYTIC ORCHIDS

- ✐ **ZONES 17, 20–24; H1, H2; OR INDOORS**
- ☼ **PARTIAL SHADE; BRIGHT INDIRECT LIGHT**
- ◗ **REGULAR WATER**

Oncidium ornithorhynchum

These orchids are native from Florida and Mexico through central and South America. Several hundred species and countless hybrids range from tiny plants just 1 in. high to giants with 6-ft. flower spikes bearing dozens of blooms. Most produce long spikes of yellow or brown-and-yellow flowers; a few come in white or rose. Some (including the plants described here) have compressed pseudobulbs with one or two large leaves; others are almost without pseudobulbs; still others have cylindrical, pencil-like leaves. Plants typically produce a few large blossoms or many small ones, but some have numerous large flowers and a few bear their blooms singly. In many, flowers have a large, flaring lip reminiscent of a flamenco dancer's skirt; these are sometimes called dancing ladies. Blossoms of some are scented. As outdoor plants, oncidiums are usually grown on tree trunks or in

pots on the patio; indoor plants can be brought outdoors during warm weather. Take the same houseplant culture as cattleyas. Also see "Meet the Orchids," page 463.

O. crispum. In fall, produces a branching, 3-ft.-high spike carrying many 4-in. flowers in chestnut brown spotted with yellow. Each bloom has a brown lip with a large bright yellow spot.

O. ornithorhynchum. In summer, many branching, 8–12-in.-high spikes carry a cloud of ½–1-in. pink or purplish pink, spice-scented flowers with yellow markings.

O. Sharry Baby 'Sweet Fragrance'. Powerfully fragrant hybrid selection. Bears 2–3-ft. spikes of reddish or purplish brown, inch-wide blossoms in summer and fall. Some liken the flowers' perfume to chocolate, others to vanilla.

Onion
Alliaceae
BIENNIAL GROWN AS ANNUAL

- ✐ **ALL ZONES**
- ☼ **FULL SUN**
- ◗ **REGULAR WATER**

Onions

Botanically, the onion is *Allium cepa*, and although it has been in cultivation since the time of ancient Egypt, the species is not known in the wild. Scallions, or green onions, are grown from bulbing onions that are harvested young or from bulbless bunching onions. More so than for other vegetables, growing onions successfully requires proper variety selection, appropriate planting methods, and good timing. Consult a local nursery or your

How to Grow Onions

Onions can be grown from seed, sets (small bulbs), or transplants. Sets and transplants are easiest for beginners, though starting from seed gives a larger crop for a smaller investment and offers a wider choice of varieties.

In mild-winter climates, onions grow well from seed planted in fall to early winter. Sets and transplants can be planted all winter long and through early spring, although sets are generally long-day varieties that will not bulb up well in southern regions. They can, however, be grown for scallions or green onions, which are standard onions harvested before they can form bulbs.

In Hawaii, short-day varieties are usually started from seed from the earliest part of the cool season; intermediate types are planted later in the cool season for warm-season harvest. Types called Maui onions are actually any sweet, bulbing onion grown in Hawaii. In cold-winter climates, planting can begin in early spring as soon as the soil is workable; or start seed indoors in late winter and transplant later.

PLANTING Soil should be loose, rich, and well drained. If planting sets, push them just under the soil surface so that the point of the bulb is visible. Space sets and transplants 4–5 in. apart (closer if you want to harvest some as green onions). Sow seeds ¼ in. deep, in rows 15–18 in. apart. Thin seedlings to separate them by 4–5 in.; they can be eaten or transplanted to extend planting. Trim back tops of transplants about halfway.

WATERING, FEEDING & WEEDING Onions are shallow rooted and need moisture fairly near the surface. Feed plants regularly, especially early in the season: the larger and stronger the plant, the bigger the bulb it forms. Carefully eliminate weeds.

HARVESTING When most of the tops have begun to yellow and fall over, dig bulbs and let them cure and dry on top of the ground for several days. Cover bulbs with tops to prevent sunburn. When the tops and necks are completely dry, pull off the tops and brush dirt from bulbs; then store bulbs in dark, cool, airy place.

Cooperative Extension Office for advice on varieties that grow well in your area.

Bulbing onions. Varieties differ in size, shape, color, flavor, and storage life. More important, many onions require specific amounts of daily sunlight in order to produce bulbs. Day length depends on latitude, and if you choose a type inappropriate for your area, it may bolt, form small premature bulbs, or not bulb up at all. Seed suppliers often list optimal latitude ranges for each variety or identify onions as long-, intermediate-, or short-day varieties.

Long-day varieties need 14 to 16 hours of daylight to form bulbs and are best adapted to northern latitudes, such as Alaska and the Pacific Northwest. They tend to be pungent, and they store well. Examples

include yellows like 'Copra' and 'Walla Walla Sweet'; reds such as 'Mars' and 'Redwing'; and whites like 'White Sweet Spanish'. Generally, long-day onions are planted in early spring and form bulbs as the days get longer in summer.

Intermediate-day onions, requiring 12 to 14 hours of daylight, are best suited to interior valleys of central California, the San Francisco Bay Area, and northern Nevada. They store moderately well. Examples are 'Red Torpedo' and 'Ruby Ring'. They are usually planted in early spring.

Short-day varieties need 10 to 12 hours of daylight and are best adapted to southern latitudes, such as Southern California, the Southwest, and Hawaii. They are typically planted in fall to early winter, grow vegetatively

O

through winter, then begin to bulb up in spring. These onions tend to be sweet and are poor keepers. Examples are yellow onions like 'Granex' and 'Texas Supersweet'; reds like 'Desert Sunrise', 'Red Burgundy' ('Bermuda'), and 'Southern Belle'.

Day-neutrals will bulb up anywhere. Plant these hybrids, such as yellow 'Candy' and white 'Super Star', in early spring.

Bunching onions (scallions). Grown for their tops, these have mixed heritage. Some are perennial, nonbulbing *A. fistulosum* varieties such as 'Evergreen Hardy White'. There are two types in this species: Welsh onions and (preferred) Japanese bunching onions. Others, such as 'Ishikura Improved' and 'White Lisbon', are bunching forms of *A. cepa*.

Cipollini onions. These very small bulbing onions are usually listed as their own class in catalogs. They are flattish, 2–3-in.-diameter, sweet, long-day onions that come in red, yellow, or white.

Ophiopogon

Asparagaceae

PERENNIALS

ZONES 5–9, 14–24; H1, H2

SOME SHADE IN HOTTEST CLIMATES

MODERATE TO REGULAR WATER

Ophiopogon planiscapus 'Nigrescens'

These grasslike Asian natives are slightly less cold-hardy than their close cousins *Liriope*. They are easy to grow, requiring little more than well-drained soil and protection from snails and slugs. Good as informal groundcover in small areas, along paths, or in rock gardens. Attractive when planted in large sweeps in areas where lawns don't succeed, such as under trees. They also do well in containers. Grow them for their lush, evergreen foliage; the summer flowers, borne on short spikes, are largely hidden by the leaves.

It's easy to obtain more plants by division. Use a sharp spade to divide clumps in early spring; or use a knife to divide clumps sold in flats or cell-packs at garden centers.

O. jaburan. GIANT LILY TURF. Sometimes sold as *Liriope gigantea*. Grows 2–3 ft. high, 1–1½ ft. wide, with dark green, slightly curved leaves. Forms clumps; does not spread by underground stems. Nodding clusters of small white flowers are followed by showy, ½-in.-long oval fruits in a metallic violet-blue (attractive in arrangements). 'Vittatus' (sometimes sold as *Liriope muscari* 'Variegata') has leaves edged in creamy white. Grows best in partial or full shade.

O. japonicus. MONDO GRASS. Forms a dense clump to 6–8 in. high; spreads wider by underground stems, many of which are tuberlike. Slow to establish as groundcover. Light lilac flowers in short spikes, usually hidden by dark green leaves 8–12 in. long and just ⅛ in. wide. Blue fruits are round, about ¼ in. across. If plants look shabby, mow or shear before spring growth begins. Set divisions 6–8 in. apart. 'Kyoto Dwarf' and 'Nana' are half the size of species, spread more slowly. 'Kigimafukiduma' ('Silver Mist') is a white-variegated form.

***O. planiscapus* 'Nigrescens' ('Arabicus', 'Ebony Knight').** BLACK MONDO GRASS. Tufts to 8 in. high, 1 ft. wide. Spreads slowly and does not make a solid cover. Leaves grow to 14 in. long, ⅛–¼ in. wide, emerging green but soon darkening to nearly black. Bell-shaped white or purple-flushed flowers are ¼ in. long. Dramatic in containers, especially when combined with yellow or chartreuse foliage, such as that of yellow creeping Jenny (*Lysimachia nummularia* 'Aurea').

Opuntia

Cactaceae

CACTI

ZONES VARY BY SPECIES

FULL SUN

LITTLE OR NO WATER, EXCEPT AS NOTED

Opuntia microdasys

The species described here originate in the desert Southwest and Mexico; other species are native to those areas and/or to other parts of the western U.S., the Great Plains, Canada, and Florida. Many kinds, with varied appearance. Most species fall into one of two sorts: those having flat, broad joints (pads) or those having cylindrical joints. Though the use of common names is somewhat inconsistent, members of the first group are often called prickly pear; those in the second group are frequently known as cholla. Flowers are generally large and showy. The fruit is a berry, often edible.

O. basilaris. BEAVERTAIL CACTUS. Zones 2, 3, 7–24. Low-branching plant to 1 ft. high, 4 ft. wide. Oval to roundish gray-green to purplish pads are 2–12 in. wide and ½ in. thick, set with spines up to 2 in. long. Rich rose-purple, 2–3-in. spring flowers.

O. ficus-indica. Zones 8, 9, 12–24; H1, H2. Big, shrubby or treelike cactus to 15 ft. tall, 10 ft. wide, with woody trunks and smooth, flat green pads. Few or no spines; has clusters of bristles. Bears 3–5-in.-wide, yellow to orange flowers in late spring and early summer. Blossoms are followed by roundish, 2–3½-in.-long fruits that ripen from yellow to red; these are the prickly pears found in grocery stores. Handle fruit carefully—bristles break off easily and irritate the skin. Use rubber gloves when peeling fruit, or impale it on a fork and strip skin carefully, avoiding bristly areas. This plant is very drought-tolerant, but in hottest regions it needs regular moisture for best fruit. 'Burbank Spineless' is a nearly spineless selection. 'Gray Form' has gray pads.

O. leptocaulis. DESERT CHRISTMAS CACTUS, CHRISTMAS CHOLLA, PENCIL CACTUS. Zones 3, 7–24. To 2–3 ft. (rarely to 6 ft.) high and equally wide. Joints are 1–12 in. long, ¾ in. thick, and have 1–2-in.-long spines. Spring flowers, to ¾ in. across, are green to yellow. Fleshy fruits about the size and shape of olives mature from green to red, usually around Christmastime; hang on all winter. Very striking cold-hardy species.

O. macrocentra (O. violacea). Zones 2, 3, 7–24. To 4 ft. tall and 6 ft. wide, with round, 8-in., purplish green pads that turn rich purple in cool weather. Yellow-and-red flowers in spring are 3–3½ in. wide. 'Tubac' (often sold as variety of *O. santa-rita*) is said to hold its purple pad color more consistently throughout the year.

O. microdasys. BUNNY EARS. Zones 12–24; or indoors. Fast growth to 2–3 ft. high, 4–5 ft. wide (much smaller in pots). Flat, thin, nearly round pads to 6 in. across, in a soft, velvety green; neatly spaced tufts of short golden bristles give a polka-dot effect. 'Albispina' has white bristles. New pads atop larger old ones give plant the shape of an animal's head.

With the spines removed (use a vegetable peeler), young pads of prickly pear cactus can be sliced, grilled, and served like a vegetable with meats, or in egg dishes such as *nopales con huevos.*

MEET THE ORCHIDS

The orchid family is probably the largest in the plant kingdom, with nearly 1,000 genera and more than 22,000 species. Best known in the West are *Bletilla, Cattleya, Cymbidium, Dendrobium, Epidendrum, Laelia, Oncidium, Paphiopedilum, Phalaenopsis,* and *Pleione.*

ORCHID TYPES

EPIPHYTIC In nature, epiphytic orchids cling to high branches of trees in tropical or subtropical jungles, deriving their nourishment from air, rain, and whatever decaying vegetable matter they can trap in their root systems. These include *Cattleya, Dendrobium, Laelia, Oncidium,* and *Phaelenopsis.*

TERRESTRIAL Some orchids (including most native North American orchids) are terrestrial and must grow in loose, moist, humus-rich soil. They often occur in wooded areas but sometimes grow in open meadows as well. These orchids require constant moisture and food. They include *Bletilla, Cymbidium,* and *Paphiopedilum.*

TEMPERATURE NEEDS

The various orchids of the world's tropical regions can be grown outdoors year-round in one or another part of Hawaii; some thrive outdoors in coastal Southern California. Elsewhere, you may be able to grow certain types outdoors all year or just during warm weather; others must be kept indoors.

The following list divides tropical orchids into three classes according to their temperature needs; lowland natives need the warmest conditions, higher-altitude natives the coolest ones. The terms "cool-growing," "intermediate," and "warm-growing" refer to the greenhouse temperatures that approximate ideal conditions for good growth and regular flowering in the plants' native environments. (Most of these orchids will get along fine in somewhat less than ideal situations, though.)

COOL-GROWING ORCHIDS These do best with temperatures of 50°F to 55°F (10°C to 13°C) at night, 60°F to 75°F (16°C to 24°C) during the day. This group includes *Cymbidium* (some), *Dendrobium* (some), *Epidendrum* (some), *Laelia* (some), *Paphiopedilum* (green-leafed forms), *Pleione.* Some cool growers are thoroughly hardy to many cold-winter zones of the West, and others can withstand winters outdoors in mildest parts of California.

INTERMEDIATE ORCHIDS These thrive at temperatures of 55°F to 60°F (13°C to 16°C) at night, 65°F to 80°F (18°C to 27°C) during the day. Members of this group include *Cattleya, Cymbidium* (some), *Dendrobium* (some), *Epidendrum* (some), *Laelia* (some), *Oncidium, Paphiopedilum* (the mottled-leafed forms). These can be grown in pots or on a windowsill with other houseplants but will perform best with additional humidity. An excellent method of supplying humidity is described in "Care" (below). Most can be moved outdoors in summer; place them in the shade of high-branching trees, on the patio, or in a lathhouse.

WARM-GROWING ORCHIDS *Phalaenopsis,* the warm-growing orchids described in this book, do best with temperatures of 60°F to 65°F (16°C to 18°C) at night, 70°F to 85°F (21°C to 29°C) during the day. These orchids can grow outdoors in warmest parts of Hawaii but need greenhouse conditions (uniform warm temperatures and high humidity) in colder climates.

CARE

Nearly all orchids, terrestrial or epiphytic, are grown in pots. A few are grown on "rafts" (slabs of bark or wood) or in baskets of wood slats; a few natives are grown in open ground. For most epiphytic orchids, the easiest potting materials to use are the ready-made mixes—typically ground bark—sold by orchid growers; these are blended for proper texture and acidity. Watering and fertilizing needs vary, depending on the orchid type. In general, though, water plants when the potting mix dries out and becomes lightweight (usually about once a week), and apply a water-soluble orchid fertilizer every 2 weeks during the growing season. To provide humidity for plants growing indoors, fill a plastic tray with gravel to within an inch of the top, then add just enough water to reach almost to top of gravel. Stretch hardware cloth over the tray. Set pots on top of hardware cloth; and add more water to tray as needed.

Bletilla striata

Origanum

OREGANO, MARJORAM
Lamiaceae
PERENNIALS

✿ **ZONES VARY BY SPECIES**
☼ **FULL SUN, EXCEPT AS NOTED**
◐ ◖ **LITTLE TO MODERATE WATER**
🦋 **ATTRACT BUTTERFLIES, BEES**

Origanum majorana

Mint relatives with tight clusters of small flowers. Each blossom has a collar of bracts—large, colorful, and quite decorative in some species—that can overlap to give the inflorescence the look of a small pinecone. Blossoms are especially attractive to bees, butterflies. Many species have aromatic foliage, and the leaves of several have culinary use. Some are good as groundcovers, as trailers to cascade over rocks or retaining walls, or in hanging baskets. Those with conspicuous bracts are attractive dried and used in wreaths and arrangements; cut and hang just as first flowers open.

O. 'Betty Rollins'. Zones 6–9, 12–24. Hybrid forms a dense, neat mat 3–6 in. high and 1–1½ ft. wide. Small, oval, dark green leaves are topped in summer by clusters of light pink flowers.

O. dictamnus (Amaracus dictamnus). DITTANY OF CRETE, HOP MARJORAM. Zones 8, 9, 12–24. Native to Crete. Aromatic herb to 8 in. high and 1½–2 ft. wide, with slender, arching stems to 1 ft. long. Small, thick, roundish, woolly white leaves. Pink to purplish flowers emerge from rose-tinted light green bracts; blooms summer to autumn. Shows up best when planted individually.

»

Culinary Oreganos and Marjorams

All types of *Origanum* look good in the garden. But for kitchen use, the following are best. Sweet marjoram (*O. majorana*) has a sweet, spicy flavor; it can even be used to make tea. Italian marjoram (*O. × majoricum*) has a more complex, slightly less sweet flavor, while pot marjoram (*O. onites*) has a savory, thymelike taste.

Flavor of the plain oregano (*O. vulgare*) is variable; choose a selected form with an aroma and flavor you like. Biblical hyssop (*O. syriacum*) and Greek oregano (*O. v. hirtum*) are pungent and spicy-hot.

O. laevigatum. Zones 2–24. Native to Turkey and Cyprus. Sprawling plant with grayish green leaves; reaches 2 ft. high in bloom. It spreads by rhizomes and arching stems that root at the joints to form a dense clump 2–3 ft. wide. Branching, airy clusters of ½-in., tubular pink or purple flowers and small purplish bracts appear from late spring to fall. Useful as bank or groundcover. 'Herrenhausen' has larger bracts and more compact heads of lilac-pink flowers. 'Hopley's' blooms from mid- to late summer, bearing denser heads of purplish pink flowers and purplish bracts. Both 'Herrenhausen' and 'Hopley's' have purple leaves in cool weather. 'Rosenkuppel' has large heads of deep purple blooms and may be a hybrid.

O. libanoticum. Zones 2b–24. Native to Lebanon. Attractive trailing plant to 2 ft. high and wide, with small, roundish, smooth green leaves. From midsummer to fall, produces cascades of pale green to pinkish bracts (similar to those of hop, *Humulus*) and small rose-pink flowers; heads elongate as the season progresses, ending up several inches long. For best effect, plant at top of a wall or in a hanging basket.

O. majorana (Majorana hortensis). SWEET MARJORAM, KNOTTED MARJORAM. Zones 8–24; summer annual anywhere. Native to the Mediterranean and Turkey. To 1–2 ft. high and wide. Oval gray-green leaves. Inconspicuous white flowers emerge from clusters of knotlike heads at top of plant. Keep blossoms cut off and plant trimmed to encourage fresh growth. Fresh or dried leaves are used for seasoning meats, scrambled eggs, salads, vinegars, casseroles, and tomato dishes. Often grown in pots indoors on a sunny windowsill in cold-winter areas.

O. × majoricum. ITALIAN MARJORAM, SICILIAN MARJORAM. Zones 4–24. Similar to *O. majorana* but with wider, greener leaves. Some gourmet cooks consider this the best marjoram for seasoning.

O. 'Marshall's Memory'. Zones 6–9, 12–24. Hybrid to 1–1½ ft. high, 2 ft. wide. Forms a dense mat of small, rounded leaves that are bright green when new, aging to a darker shade. Profuse lavender-pink flowers with rosy bracts in summer. Best with moderate water.

O. 'Norton Gold'. Zones 2b–24. Hybrid of *O. laevigatum* and *O. vulgare* 'Aureum'. To 1 ft. high and 1½–2 ft. or more wide, with open habit like that of *O. laevigatum*. Rounded leaves are brilliant gold with a bluish sheen. Foliage is aromatic, with a good flavor; for mealtime color, use sprays of leaves as garnish. Pink flowers bloom in midsummer. Protect from hottest sun.

O. onites. POT MARJORAM, RHIGANI. Zones 8–24. Eastern Mediterranean native. To 2 ft. high and wide, with bright green, aromatic, inch-long leaves and 2-in.-wide, flattish heads of white or purplish flowers in late summer. Sometimes called Cretan oregano.

O. rotundifolium. Zones 2b–24. Native to Turkey, Armenia, and Georgia. Dense, suckering plant grows to 8 in. high and 1 ft. wide, bearing numerous wiry stems set with pairs of virtually stemless, blue-green leaves that have a rounded heart shape. Blooms throughout summer, bearing spikes of small, pale pink blossoms and green, 2–3-in.-long bracts like those of hop (*Humulus*) at stem ends (bracts almost obscure the flowers). 'Kent Beauty' is a hybrid with *O. scabrum*; has a more compact habit (4 in. high, 8 in. wide) and bears conspicuous mauve-toned pink blossoms and deep rose bracts in the summer. 'Rose Beauty' has even darker reddish bracts. 'Barbara Tingey' is a hybrid with *O. calcaratum* and similar to 'Kent Beauty'; its rose-pink flowers peep out from under light green bracts that age to deep purplish pink.

O. sipyleum. SHOWY PINK OREGANO. Zones 4–9, 12–24. Native to Turkey. To 1–2 ft. high. Small, blue-green, oval to lance-shaped leaves. In summer, thin stems hold sprays of pale green bracts and pinkish violet flowers well above the foliage. Good cut flowers for dried arrangements.

O. syriacum (O. maru). BIBLICAL HYSSOP, SYRIAN MARJORAM. Zones 7–24. Native to Syria, Turkey, and Cyprus. With its strong, sweet, pungent flavor, this plant is a favorite herb for flavoring Middle Eastern dishes. Grows to 1½ ft. high and wide. Soft gray-green leaves. Blooms in late spring and early summer, with pale pink, ¼-in. flowers in branching, 2–3-in. clusters.

O. vulgare. OREGANO, WILD MARJORAM. Zones 1–24, except as noted. Native to most of Europe and temperate Asia. Upright growth to 2½ ft. high, 2–3 ft. wide. Oval dark green leaves; white or purplish pink blossoms from midsummer to early fall. Fresh or dried leaves are used in many dishes, especially Spanish and Italian ones.

Most wild forms have scentless leaves; be sure to choose a selected form with a good aroma and a flavor that you like. For best flavor, keep this plant trimmed to prevent flowering.

'Aureum' has white flowers, pink bracts, and bright golden foliage in spring (with morning sun), turning to green by late summer and fall; 'Thumble's Variety' is similar. 'Aureum Crispum' has curly golden leaves. 'Compactum' ('Humile') is a wide-spreading plant just a few inches high, suitable for a groundcover or between paving stones; it seldom flowers, but leaves turn purple in winter. 'Country Cream' (with white flowers) and lilac-pink-flowered 'Polyphant' ('White Anniversary') are compact growers to 4–6 in. and have leaves with a distinct creamy white edge; they are often confused in commerce (and both are sometimes sold as 'Variegatum'). 'Roseum' has rose-pink flowers, green leaves.

O. v. hirtum (O. heracleoticum). GREEK OREGANO. Zones 8, 9, 12–24. Native to Greece, Turkey, and the Aegean Islands. Like the species, but with broader, slightly fuzzy gray-green leaves. Has a spicy, pungent flavor.

CARE

Not fussy about soil type but need good drainage. In milder climates, many species can become woody with age, but wood of previous seasons is seldom as productive as new growth from the base. For best results, cut previous year's stems to ground in winter or early spring. Propagate by division or from cuttings taken before flower buds form. The various species hybridize freely, and seedlings may not resemble the parents. Colored-leaf varieties need a half-day of direct sun for best color but can burn in afternoon sun in hot-summer areas.

Your nose is your best guide to finding a delicious oregano to grow. Seeds are often mislabeled, and fragrance varies much from plant to plant within the species.

Ornithogalum

Asparagaceae
PERENNIALS FROM BULBS

- ⬗ **ZONES VARY BY SPECIES**
- ☼ ◐ **FULL SUN OR PARTIAL SHADE**
- ○ ◐ ● **WATER NEEDS VARY BY SPECIES**
- ✧ **ALL PARTS, ESPECIALLY BULBS, ARE POISONOUS IF INGESTED**

Ornithogalum thyrsoides 'Chesapeake Snowflake'

Clusters of typically star-shaped flowers appear in the spring; *O. dubium* may start blooming in late winter. Leaves vary from narrow to broad and tend to droop. In mild-winter areas, ornithogalums can fill many different roles. Set them in open woodlands, wild gardens, or rock gardens, where many kinds will naturalize; plant them in containers or mass them in borders. Where cold winters prevent growing ornithogalums outdoors, plant the bulbs in pots and force them to early flowering indoors or in a greenhouse.

O. arabicum. STAR OF BETHLEHEM. Zones 5–24. From the eastern Mediterranean. Stems to 2 ft. high carry clusters of 2-in., waxy-looking white flowers, each centered with a shiny, beadlike black eye. Bluish green, strap-shaped leaves may reach same length as stems, but they are usually floppy. Best where summers are warm and dry.

O. dubium. Zones 8, 9, 14–24. From South Africa. Stems 8–12 in. high bear blooms resembling those of *O. arabicum*, but petals surrounding the beady black eye come in shades of yellow and orange. Dark green to yellowish green, lance-shaped leaves nearly prostrate.

O. nutans. Zones 3–24. From the eastern Mediterranean. To 1½–2 ft. high. Starlike to nearly bell-shaped flowers are white striped with green on the outside; they have pronounced central clusters of stamens. Up to 15 blooms are spaced along upper part of each stalk. Narrow, floppy, bright green leaves. Spreads rapidly and may become weedy. Sometimes called silver bells.

O. thyrsoides. CHINCHE-RINCHEE. Zones 4–24. Native to South Africa. Flowering stems grow 1½–2 ft. tall and produce elongated clusters of 2-in. white flowers with centers often tinted green or cream. Upright, bright green leaves reach about 1 ft. tall and usually start to die back while the plants are in bloom. Excellent cut flowers. Hybrids 'Chesapeake Starlight' (pure white flowers) and 'Chesapeake Snowflake' (white flowers with a very dark center) have especially showy flowers and sturdy stems; they were developed for containers and for cutting.

O. umbellatum. STAR OF BETHLEHEM. Zones 1–24; H1. From the eastern Mediterranean. Stems to 1 ft. high bear clusters of inch-wide white flowers striped green on the outside. Semierect, grassy-looking leaves about as long as flower stems. Cut flowers last well but close at night. Once established, may naturalize and become weedy.

Ornithogalums tend to spread. Foil this habit by keeping the plant in a pot. Bulbs can live in the same container for several years, so be sure to choose a good-size pot—at least 8 inches across and 12 inches deep. Also make sure it has adequate holes in the bottom to provide the fast drainage these bulbs require.

CARE

Plant bulbs in early fall in well-drained soil amended with plenty of organic matter, setting them 3 in. deep and 3–4 in. apart. Provide regular moisture during growth and bloom. *O. arabicum, O. dubium,* and *O. thyrsoides* need a dry dormant period: after flowering has finished and leaves have died down, withhold water until new foliage begins to emerge. In areas with summer rainfall, grow them in pots to keep them dry. *O. nutans* and *O. umbellatum* can take moisture during dormancy. Dig and divide plantings of all species only when plant vigor and bloom quality decline.

Orthrosanthus

MORNING FLAG, MORNING IRIS
Iridaceae
EVERGREEN PERENNIALS FROM RHIZOMES

- ⬗ **ZONES 14–17, 19–24**
- ☼ ◐ **PARTIAL SHADE IN HOTTEST CLIMATES**
- ◐ **MODERATE WATER**

Orthrosanthus multiflorus

These *Sisyrinchium* relatives have dark green, grasslike leaves arising from short, woody rhizomes. Showy blooms of blue, lavender, or white open in succession on slim, erect stems in summer. Individual flowers look their best in the morning, then fade as the day progresses. Wonderful plants for sunny slopes, rock gardens, and containers. Tolerate poor, sandy soils but bloom better in fertile, well-drained soil.

O. chimboracensis. Forms clumps 1–1½ ft. high and wide, with rough-edged leaves. Pale to medium blue, 1½–1¾-in. flowers are held on stems to 2 ft. high.

O. multiflorus. Clumps reach 1–2 ft. high, 1 ft. wide. Smooth-edged leaves. Pale to bright blue flowers are about 1½ in. across. Grassier appearance than *O. chimboracensis*; also tolerates more drought. Effective foliage plant for commercial plantings or home gardens; pretty flowers are a bonus.

Oryzopsis hymenoides
(Achnatherum hymenoides)

INDIAN RICE GRASS
Poaceae
PERENNIAL GRASS

- ⬗ **ZONES 1–3, 10–13**
- ☼ **FULL SUN**
- ○ **LITTLE OR NO WATER**

Oryzopsis hymenoides

Native to the dry regions of the Southwest and northward to Canada. Forms a clump 1–2 ft. high and wide; tight at the base, spreading and open above. Very narrow, 6–8-in.-long leaves are bright green in cool weather, turning golden brown when summer heat comes. Open, airy flower clusters (attractive for cutting) produce seeds that were harvested by Native Americans for food. Useful plant in high elevation and desert landscapes.

FOR MORE ON GRASSES, SEE "MEET THE GRASSES," PAGE 346.

O

Oscularia deltoides
(Lampranthus deltoides)
ICE PLANT
Aizoaceae
SUCCULENT PERENNIAL

🌡 **ZONES 14–24**

☀ **FULL SUN**

◌ **LITTLE OR NO WATER**

🐝 **FLOWERS ATTRACT BEES**

Oscularia deltoides

South African native with brilliant flowers. Stems to 2 ft. long; they grow erect to 1 ft., then begin to lean and trail. Triangular blue-green leaves with a pink flush are short (less than 1 in. long), very thick and fleshy, closely set on stems. Fragrant, purplish rose, ½-in.-wide flowers in late spring, summer. Attractive trailing over walls or in hanging baskets. Cut back after bloom to eliminate fruit capsules. Good near the coast. (For more on ice plants, see "Meet the Ice Plants," page 371.)

Cascading over a wall or spreading between boulders, *Oscularia deltoides* is a fine choice for rock gardens. Succulent blue-green foliage is almost as interesting as the brilliant pink flowers.

Osmanthus
Oleaceae
EVERGREEN SHRUBS

🌡 **ZONES VARY BY SPECIES**

☀ ◐ **FULL SUN OR PARTIAL SHADE**

◌ ◔ ● **LITTLE TO REGULAR WATER**

Osmanthus heterophyllus
'Variegatus'

All have clean, leathery, attractive foliage and, typically, white flowers that are inconspicuous but fragrant. Fruits (on female plants) are rarely seen. Plants tolerate broad range of soils, including heavy clay. Most are dense shrubs that can eventually reach tree size. To grow them as background shrubs, pinch tips of new growth on young plants to encourage bushiness; on older, established plants, occasionally cut back any wayward branches. These shrubs also make good informal or lightly clipped tall hedges.

O. × burkwoodii (× Osmarea burkwoodii). Zones 4–9, 14–17. Slow growing to 6–10 ft. tall, 8–12 ft. wide. Densely clothed in glossy bright green, tooth-edged leaves. Spring bloom. Useful as a hedge.

O. delavayi. DELAVAY OSMANTHUS. Zones 4–9, 14–21. From China. Slow-growing, graceful plant with arching branches; reaches 4–6 ft. tall, 6–8 ft. wide. Dark green, oval, tooth-edged leaves. Blooms profusely in spring, bearing clusters of four to eight blossoms (largest flowers of any osmanthus). Attractive all year. Good choice for foundation plantings, massing. Handsome on retaining walls where branches can

hang down. Needs partial shade in hot-summer areas.

O. × fortunei. Zones 4–10, 14–24. Hybrid between *O. heterophyllus* and *O. fragrans*. Slow, dense growth to an eventual 15–20 ft. tall, 6–8 ft. wide; usually seen at about 6 ft. tall. Leaves resemble those of holly (*Ilex*). Spring and summer bloom. 'San Jose' blooms in fall, bears flowers ranging in color from cream to orange.

O. fragrans. SWEET OLIVE. Zones 5–7 (with shelter), 8, 9, 12–24; H1. Native to China, Japan, and the Himalayas. Broad, dense, compact. Grows at a moderate rate to 10 ft. tall and 6–8 ft. wide (though older plants may reach 30 ft. tall and 10–12 ft. wide). Oval, glossy, medium green leaves are toothed or smooth edged. Flowers are powerfully fragrant, with a sweet scent like that of ripe apricots. Bloom is heaviest in spring and early summer, but plants flower sporadically throughout the year. Sometimes trained as an espalier. Give afternoon shade in hottest climates.

O. heterophyllus (O. ilicifolius). HOLLY-LEAF OSMANTHUS. Zones 4–10, 14–24. From Japan. Grows to 10–20 ft. tall and slightly wider, with spiny-edged, glossy green leaves. Resembles English holly (*Ilex aquifolium*), but leaves are opposite one another on stems rather than alternate. Late-fall and winter bloom. Useful as a hedge.

'Goshiki' has erect growth to 3½ ft. high, 5 ft. wide. New leaves have pinkish orange markings; in mature foliage, the variegations are creamy yellow. 'Gulftide' is a dense grower to 8 ft. tall, 10 ft. wide. 'Purpureus' is similar to the species, but its leaves are dark purple when new, maturing to purple-toned deep green. 'Variegatus' is slow growing to about 8–10 ft. tall and wide, with densely set leaves edged in creamy white. Useful for lighting up shady areas. Foliage is somewhat more prone to freeze damage than that of other species.

Osmaronia cerasiformis. See *Oemleria cerasiformis*

Osmunda
Osmundaceae
FERNS

🌡 **ZONES VARY BY SPECIES**

☀ ◐ **FULL SUN OR LIGHT SHADE**

● **AMPLE WATER**

Osmunda regalis

Large deciduous ferns for damp (even wet) soils in regions with cold (or at least chilly) winters. Rather coarse-looking but handsome nonetheless. They produce large masses of matted roots; root masses of *O. regalis* provide the osmunda fiber used in potting mixes for orchids. Fronds are twice divided; they turn orange, brown, and yellow as they approach dormancy. Use at woodland edges or in cool, moist or wet areas. Both species described here are native to much of the Northern Hemisphere. *O. cinnamomea* has separate sterile and fertile fronds; in *O. regalis*, each frond has a fertile segment near the tip. (For more on ferns, see "Meet the Ferns," page 320.)

O. cinnamomea. CINNAMON FERN, FIDDLEHEADS. Zones 1–6. To 2–5 ft. tall and 2 ft. wide. This fern has two types of fronds. Sterile fronds are erect, up to 5 ft. tall, and divided in typical fern fashion. Fertile ones are shorter and consist of stalks topped by short, tightly clustered, brown spore-bearing bodies.

O. regalis. ROYAL FERN, FLOWERING FERN. Zones 1–9, 14–17. To 6 ft. tall, 3 ft. wide; each frond segment is quite large. Fertile segments are smaller, clustered near frond tips; they look something like flower buds. 'Cristata' has crested fronds; 'Purpurascens' has purplish red new growth and stems that remain purple throughout the season. The species and its varieties love moisture and can grow even in shallow water.

Osteospermum
AFRICAN DAISY
Asteraceae
PERENNIALS

⚡ **ZONES 8, 9, 12–24, EXCEPT AS NOTED; ANYWHERE AS ANNUALS**

☼ **FULL SUN**

◐ ● **MODERATE TO REGULAR WATER**

Osteospermum ecklonis

Woody-based perennials native to South Africa; closely related to *Dimorphotheca* and often sold as such. Mounded or trailing in habit, bearing a profusion of daisylike flowers over a long season; blossoms are more profuse during cooler parts of bloom period. Grow as summer annuals in areas beyond hardiness range, as winter annuals in hot desert areas. Oval leaves are smooth edged or with a few large teeth. Flowers of most kinds open only in sunlight, but many have a second color on the backs of rays that shows on half-open flowers during overcast weather. Flowers with spoon-shaped petals will often revert to normal petals in cool weather.

Tolerate drought and neglect but look better with good garden soil and irrigation. Tip-pinch young plants to induce bushiness. Deadheading produces more blooms. Cut back old, sprawling branches to young side growth in late summer to midautumn. Mass along driveways or paths, or use in borders, rock gardens, or containers.

Types that spread by rooting stems are good on slopes.

O. barberae. See *O. jucundum.*

O. ecklonis. To 2–5 ft. tall, 2–4 ft. wide. Long stems bear 3-in. flowers with dark blue centers and rays that are white above, lavender-blue on backs. Blooms in spring.

'Lavender Mist'. Zones 2b–24. To 1 ft. high, 15 in. wide; 3-in. flowers open white, age to soft pale purple. Blooms from midspring until fall.

'Passion Mix'. Compact growth to 1–1½ ft. high and about as wide, with 2–2½-in. flowers in a variety of colors (pink, rose, purple, white), all with sky blue centers. Blooms throughout the year, more heavily in spring and fall. Blossoms stay open in low light better than those of many nonhybrid varieties.

O. fruticosum. TRAILING AFRICAN DAISY, FREEWAY DAISY. Zones 8, 9, 12–24; H1, H2. To 6–12 in. high, spreading rapidly by trailing, rooting stems; will cover a 2–4-ft.-wide circle in a year. Deep lilac buds open to 2-in.-wide flowers with a dark purple center; rays are lilac above (fading nearly to white by second day), deeper lilac beneath. Blooms intermittently all year, more heavily in fall and winter. Needs well-drained soil. Does well near the ocean. Use as groundcover or bank cover; if it gets too tall or weedy, mow or cut back in midsummer. Also good planted at top of a wall.

O. hybrids. An everincreasing group of plants in an amazing array of colors (single and bicolor) and flower shapes, including some with spoonshaped petals. Plants in the Symphony series have mounding habits to 8–12 in. high, 3 ft. wide (1 ft. as annual). They are among the most heat-tolerant of osteospermums, flowering throughout moderately hot summers as well as during cool weather. Flowers are 2–2½ in. wide, with dark blue centers. The Sunny series has compact habits to about 12 in. high as annual bedding plants and are free blooming in a wide range of colors and flower shapes.

The following hybrids reach 18–20 in. high. 'Nairobi Purple' ('African Queen') and 'Burgundy' have purple blooms. Blooms of

Side series stay open on overcast days and at night; selections include 'Brightside' (white with a blue eye), 'Highside' (bicolor blooms in white and dark pink), 'Riverside' (yellow), 'Seaside' (bicolor in white and light pink), and 'Wildside' (dark purple).

O. jucundum (O. barberae). Grows to 4–20 in. high; spreads by rooting stems to 2–3 ft. across. Bears long-stalked, 2-in.-wide flowers with purple centers; rays vary in color from mauve-pink to magenta, with bronzy purple to purplish pink undersides. Blooms more heavily in spring and fall, generally less profusely in summer.

O. j. compactum 'Purple Mountain'. Zones 2b–24. Choice plant for colder climates. To 10 in. high, 1 ft. wide, with a profusion of bright purple, 2–3-in. flowers from spring to midsummer. If deadheaded, continues to bloom (albeit sparingly) until fall.

Otatea. See Bamboo

Oxalis
Oxalidaceae
PERENNIALS

⚡ **ZONES VARY BY SPECIES**

☼ ◐ **PARTIAL SHADE IN HOTTEST CLIMATES, EXCEPT AS NOTED**

● **REGULAR WATER**

Oxalis oregana

The leaves of oxalis are typically divided into three leaflets, giving them the look of clover leaves. Flowers may be pink, white, rose, or yellow. Most can be slightly to highly invasive in the open ground; see individual entries for specific cautions.

O. acetosella. WOOD SORREL, SHAMROCK. Zones 1–10, 14–24. From many northern temperate regions of the world. To 5 in. high, spreading widely by rhizomes. Clover-type leaves with three heart-shaped leaflets. Blooms in late spring, bearing ¾-in.-wide white flowers with purple to pink veins; blossoms rise just above foliage. Can be somewhat invasive in woodland conditions.

O. adenophylla. Zones 4–9, 12–24. Native to South America. Dense, compact, leafy tuft 4 in. high, 6 in. wide. Each leaf has 9–22 crinkly gray-green leaflets. In late spring, 4–6-in.-high stalks bear 1-in., bell-shaped flowers in lilac-pink with deeper veins. Good rock garden plant or companion to bulbs, in pots or in the ground. Needs good drainage. Plant tubers in fall, setting 1 in. deep, 3–5 in. apart.

O. hirta. Zones 8, 9, 14–24. Native to South Africa. To 1 ft. high, 1½ ft. wide, with upright, branching stems that gradually fall over with weight of leaves and flowers. Small pale green leaves are set directly on stems or very short stalks. General effect is feathery. Bright rosepink, 1-in. flowers in late fall or winter. Plant is dormant in summer. Grow from bulbs planted in fall; set them 1 in. deep, 3–5 in. apart. Good for rock gardens.

O. lasiandra. Zones 8, 9, 12–24; H1, H2. Native to Mexico. Taprooted plant forms a clump to 1 ft. high and wide, with reddish leafstalks and green, wheel-shaped leaves, each with as many as 10 narrow leaflets. Dark red, 1-in.-wide flowers through summer and autumn.

O. oregana. REDWOOD SORREL, OREGON OXALIS. Zones 4–9, 14–24. Native to coastal forests from Washington to California. Grows to 10 in. high, spreading indefinitely by creeping rhizomes. Medium green, velvety leaves. Blooms in spring, sometimes again in fall, bearing white or pink, 1-in.-wide flowers with lavender veining. Makes an attractive groundcover for partial to deep shade in areas with mild winters and cool summers. The plant may outcompete other groundcovers. Dies down in winter in colder part of the climate range;

elsewhere, mow to renovate. Tolerates wet conditions.

O. purpurea (O. variabilis). Zones 8, 9, 12–24. Native to South Africa. Grows to 4 in. high and 6 in. wide; dark green leaves have large (up to 1½-in. wide) leaflets. Bears 1–2-in. rose-red flowers over a long period in fall and winter. Spreads by bulbs and rhizomelike roots but is not aggressive or weedy. Plant bulbs in fall, setting them 1 in. deep, 3–5 in. apart. Improved kinds, sold under the name "Grand Duchess," have larger flowers in rose-pink, white, or lavender.

O. spiralis vulcanicola. Zones 8, 9, 12–24. Best known by its varieties. 'Zinfandel' has blackish purple, shamrock-like leaves that form a neat mound 6–10 in. high. Small yellow flowers from spring to fall do not produce seed, so plant is less invasive. Nice in pot or the edge of beds. 'Molten Lava' is similar but has light yellowish green to orange leaves.

O. tetraphylla (O. deppei). LUCKY CLOVER. Zones 7–9, 12–24. Native to Mexico. Forms a clump 6–10 in. high and wide, spreading slowly by tubers.

Medium green leaves have four leaflets, each one banded purple toward the base. Each leaf is held like a little umbrella atop a fleshy stem. Bright pink, 1-in. blooms late spring through summer. Needs well-drained soil. Good in containers. 'Iron Cross' has defined, dark leaf markings that form a cross shape; its flowers are a deep pink.

O. triangularis papilionacea 'Atropurpurea' (O. regnellii triangularis). PURPLE SHAMROCK. Zones 7–9, 12–24. Native to South America. Grows 12 in. high and 18–24 in. wide, forming a mound of deep burgundy, triangular leaves. Light pink flowers. Not invasive. Great in pots.

O. versicolor. CANDY CANE SORREL. Zones 6–9, 14–24. Native to South Africa. To 3–6 in. high and 8 in. wide. Medium green leaves with deeply notched leaflets less than ½ in. wide. Funnel-shaped white flowers over 1 in. wide, with a crimson margin on the petal backs; buds also show striping. Plant bulbs in fall for spring flowers (set them 1 in. deep, 3–5 in. apart); bloom lasts for months.

Shamrocks

The small potted shamrocks usually sold around St. Patrick's Day are *Medicago lupulina* (hop clover, yellow trefoil, black medick), an annual plant; *Oxalis acetosella* (wood sorrel), a perennial; or *Trifolium repens* (white clover), also a perennial. The last is the most common. All have leaves divided into three leaflets, symbolic of the Trinity. They can be kept on a sunny windowsill or planted out, but they have little ornamental value and are likely to become weeds.

Oxalis acetosella

Oxydendrum arboreum

SOURWOOD, SORREL TREE
Ericaceae
DECIDUOUS TREE

⚞ **ZONES 2B–9, 14–17**
☼ **FULL SUN**
💧 **REGULAR WATER**

Oxydendrum arboreum

Native to the eastern U.S., this beautiful flowering tree offers year-round interest. Slow growth to 15–30 ft. (eventually to 50 ft.) high, 20 ft. wide. Pyramidal shape with slender trunk, somewhat rounded crown, and slightly pendulous branches; creates a handsome winter silhouette. Narrow leaves look a bit like peach leaves; they are bronze tinted in early spring, rich green in summer. In fall, leaves turn orange, scarlet, or blackish purple; all colors may be present on the same tree. Vividly colored autumn leaves remain on the tree for a long time, dropping over an extended period much like the leaves of liquidambar. Tree blooms in the summer, bearing fragrant, bell-shaped, creamy white flowers in 10-in.-long, drooping clusters at branch tips. In autumn, branching clusters of seed capsules extend outward and downward from branches like fingers; capsules ripen from greenish to light silvery gray and hang on late into winter.

Best known in areas with cool summers, well-defined winters. Needs acid, well-drained soil. Not competitive; doesn't do well in lawns without careful attention (you must remove grass from beneath canopy, mulch well, and irrigate deeply).

Avoid underplanting with anything that may need cultivation.

Use as specimen in a woodland garden or as patio shade tree. Young plants make good container subjects.

Ozothamnus rosmarinifolius

Asteraceae
EVERGREEN SHRUB

⚞ **ZONES 14–24**
☼ **FULL SUN**
💧 **REGULAR WATER**

Ozothamnus rosmarinifolius 'Silver Jubilee'

Native to Australia. Dense, erect habit to 6–10 ft. tall, 3–5 ft. wide. Close-set, upright branches are thickly clothed with straight, narrow, 1½-in.-long, dark green leaves that resemble those of rosemary. In early summer, closely packed red buds appear at branch tips; these open into 1½-in. clusters of tiny white daisies. The entire plant has a pleasant aroma, especially in warm weather—variously described as herbal or clover. 'Silver Jubilee' has silvery foliage.

Silvery or gray-foliaged plants are soft, subtle, and sometimes dramatic, depending on how you use them. Plant them beside greens or flowers in shades of pink, coral, blue, and lavender.

P

Pachysandra
Buxaceae
PERENNIALS

✍ **ZONES VARY BY SPECIES**

◐ ● **PARTIAL OR FULL SHADE**

◐ ● **MODERATE TO REGULAR WATER**

Pachysandra terminalis

Spreading slowly but surely by underground runners, these are invaluable groundcovers for shady places. Compact growth and clean-looking, attractive foliage are their chief virtues. Spring flowers are not showy when viewed casually but are attractive at close range. Plants have somewhat woody growth, *P. terminalis* more so than *P. procumbens*. Give them moist, somewhat acid soil, well amended with organic material; for good coverage, plant both species 1 ft. apart. They can compete successfully with tree roots. Too much sun yellows the foliage and causes poor growth. Hardy to cold.

P. procumbens. ALLEGHENY SPURGE. Zones 2–6, 15–17. From the southeastern U.S. To 6–12 in. high. Grayish green, broadly oval to roundish leaves are 2–4 in. long, clustered near stem tips; they are often mottled with gray or brown. Small, fragrant white or pinkish flowers in 2–4-in. spikes. Spreads more slowly than *P. terminalis*. Deciduous in northern part of range, semievergreen to evergreen farther south.

P. terminalis. JAPANESE SPURGE. Zones 2–10, 14–21; performs better in northern part of range. From Japan and northern China. To 8–12 in. high. Evergreen leaves are shiny dark green, about same length as those of *P. procumbens* but somewhat narrower; upper half of each leaf is shallowly toothed. Small white flowers are borne in 1–2-in. spikes. Withstands heavy shade and is widely used under trees. 'Green Carpet' is shorter (to 4 in.) and denser than the species, with deeper green leaves. Leaves of 'Green Sheen' are especially glossy; those of 'Silver Edge' ('Variegata') have a creamy border.

Pachystima. See *Paxistima*

Paeonia
PEONY
Paeoniaceae
PERENNIALS AND DECIDUOUS SHRUBS

✍ **ZONES VARY BY TYPE**

☼ ◐ **AFTERNOON SHADE IN HOTTEST CLIMATES**

● **REGULAR WATER**

Paeonia 'Sea Shell'

Though a few species peonies may be found through seed exchanges and specialists' catalogs, most garden peonies are hybrids. The basic types are herbaceous and tree peonies, both descended from Chinese species. A new third category, intersectional hybrids, combines the best traits of herbaceous and tree types. All peonies are extremely long-lived plants of significant size; they provide choice cut flowers and are a mainstay of big perennial borders. They demand more than ordinary care in site prepara-

tion—but in return for the effort, they can produce flowers of outstanding beauty for a lifetime.

Herbaceous peonies, largely descendants of the perennial *P. lactiflora*, die to the ground in late fall. Intersectional hybrids leave woody stems standing when they die back after first frost, but since these stems rarely resprout, they're best cut to the ground. Both types are usually grown on their own roots (compact rhizomes with thick, tuberous roots and several growth buds called eyes).

Tree (actually shrub) peonies produce flowers on permanent woody branches and are chiefly descendants of *P. suffruticosa*, a 6-ft. shrub. Tree peonies usually start out as grafts on herbaceous peony roots, but in the long run they do best on their own roots. Shop for tree peonies that have already started to form their own substantial root systems.

Herbaceous peonies. Perennials. Zones A1–A3; 1–11, 14–20. Well-grown clumps reach

---

How to Grow Peonies

PLANTING All peonies are best set out in fall, either as bare-root plants or from nursery containers. Ideally, the planting site for peonies should be deeply dug at least several days before planting. Work in plenty of compost, especially in heavy soil, and incorporate a high-phosphorus fertilizer; then allow the soil to settle before planting. Plant herbaceous peony roots with eyes 2 in. deep in cold climates, 1 in. deep in warmer regions (planting too deeply prevents flowering). Intersectional hybrids should be planted 3 in. deep in cold climates, 2 in. deep in warmer areas. Set tree peonies with the graft line 6–8 in. below soil surface (the aim is to get the shrubby top graft to root on its own). In cold-winter areas, plant at least 6 weeks before the ground usually freezes; mulch only after the ground has frozen. Plants are unlikely to bloom the first spring after planting, but they should bloom every year after that.

WATERING All peonies need regular water and should not be allowed to dry out. Apply 2–3 in. of organic mulch.

FERTILIZING Feed with low-nitrogen fertilizer (such as 5-10-10) as the first leaves unfurl in spring, then again after the last flower fades. When leaves drop in autumn, apply 1 cup of a 50-50 mix of bonemeal and triple super-

phosphate to the soil around each plant.

GROWING IN POTS Peonies of all types can be grown in large (18–24 in.) containers. Herbaceous and intersectional hybrid peonies do best in pots that are wider than they are deep, while tree peonies prefer containers that are as deep as they are wide. Replant every third autumn in the same or a slightly larger pot, replacing most of the soil when you do.

CUTTING THE FLOWERS To gather peonies for bouquets, cut them just as flower buds begin to open. Leave at least three leaves on every cut stem, and do not remove more than half of the blooms from any clump. The object is to preserve leaf growth so that it nourishes the plant for the following year.

PESTS During cool, humid periods, the fungal disease botrytis is sometimes a problem, especially on herbaceous peonies. Young buds on infected plants blacken and wither, fuzzy brown spots develop on flowers and leaves, and stems wilt and collapse. To help prevent the problem, provide good air circulation around the plants, and keep the planting area free of fallen leaves. In autumn, cut herbaceous and intersectional peonies to the ground; as new growth emerges in spring, spray with copper fungicide.

P

CLOCKWISE FROM TOP: *Paeonia* 'Bartzella'; *P.* 'Festiva Maxima'; *P.* 'Raspberry Sundae'

2–4 ft. tall and wide. Large, glossy, deep green, attractively divided leaves are an effective background for the plants' spectacular spring or early-summer flowers and look good throughout summer. Flower colors range from pure white through cream to pink and red; some of the reds are very deep, with chocolate brown overtones. Depending on variety, blossoms range from 2 in. to as much as 10 in. across; many have a perfume similar to that of old-fashioned roses, though in some varieties the scent is either unimpressive or absent. In form, they fall into three basic categories: single or semidouble, with one or two rows of petals; Japanese, with a single row of petals and a large central mass of narrow petal-like segments called staminodes; and double, with full flowers composed of many petals. Varieties are too numerous to list.

Herbaceous peonies bloom well only where they get an extended period of pronounced winter chill. Summer heat is not a problem for the plants, but their flowers do not last as well where spring days are hot and dry. In such areas, choose singles, semidoubles, and Japanese varieties, as they bloom before the season heats up; also give plants some afternoon shade and be sure they have adequate water. (Japanese types in particular do well in the warmest zones.) In the mildest-summer parts of Zones 1–7, where these plants grow best, they thrive in full sun. Provide support for very large or double varieties, which can become so heavy with water during spring rains that they fall over.

Divide herbaceous peonies only to increase your stock. Dig clumps in early fall, hose off soil, and divide into sections, making sure that each has at least three eyes; these appear at the tops of root clusters, at or near the bases of the past season's stems. Plant immediately to allow plants time to put down roots before the onset of freezing weather. Transplants may take a year or two to establish before blooming.

Intersectional hybrids. Woody perennials. Zones A1–A3; 1–11, 14–20. Moderate growth rate to about 3 ft. high and wide. Attractive leaves resemble those of tree peonies. Compared with herbaceous and tree peonies, intersectional hybrids produce more flowers and bloom over a longer period, sport better-looking foliage throughout the growing season, and have superior resistance to botrytis. Flowers may be single, semidouble, or double in single and multicolored shades of lavender, pink, red, copper, yellow, or cream. There are many varieties to choose from, including the new Itoh hybrids, named for the first person to successfully cross a herbaceous peony with a tree peony. Intersectional hybrids require less winter chill than herbaceous peonies.

Tree peonies. Deciduous shrubs. Zones 2–12, 14–23. Slow growth to 2–6 ft. tall and eventually as wide, with handsomely divided blue-green to bronzy green leaves. Single to double flowers, typically very large (to 10–12 in. across), appear in spring. These peonies seldom show their full potential until they have spent several years in the garden, but the spectacular results are worth the wait.

Catalogs offer named varieties of Japanese origin in white and shades of pink, red, and purple. These are generally semidouble and display their flowers well. Some of the older European hybrids in pink and yellow are fully double, with flowers so heavy that they hang their heads. More recent hybrids come in yellow, copper, and a coral that approaches orange; all result from crosses of *P. suffruticosa* with *P. delavayi* and *P. d. lutea*. These bear semidouble blooms that face outward and upward.

Tree peonies require much less winter chill than herbaceous peonies. The large flowers are fragile and should be sheltered from strong winds. Snip off blooms when they fade. After leaf drop in fall, prune to remove dead wood and to control the height of mature plants; do this by removing about half the current season's growth on the tallest branches that have bloomed, always making your cuts just above an outward-facing side branch. In coldest climates, protect from winter sun and wind with a burlap curtain.

Peonies are worth growing for their richly colored flowers and luxuriant foliage alone. But many kinds are also richly perfumed, blending citrus, spice, and floral notes in their silky petals. Among these are P. 'Sarah Bernhardt' (pink) and P. 'Festiva Maxima' (white). P. 'Keiko' (pink) and P. 'Misaka' (peachy yellow) are subtly fragrant.

P

MEET THE PALMS

Most palms are tropical or subtropical; a few are surprisingly hardy in Portland, Seattle, and Denver. In nature, they grow in solid stands and also with other plants, notably broad-leafed evergreen trees and shrubs. They are especially effective near swimming pools, where mirror-smooth water reflects their graceful shapes. All tropical palms grow during warm times of year. Winter rains wash down the foliage and leach out salts from the soil.

For details on the palms listed below, turn to their individual entries elsewhere in this book's encyclopedia.

Large Palms

Archontophoenix, Brahea, Cocos, Jubaea, Livistona, Phoenix canariensis, P. dactylifera, P. rupicola, Pritchardia (some), *Rhopalostylis, Roystonea, Sabal* (tall species), *Syagrus, Washingtonia.*

Small to Medium Palms

FOR FROST-FREE GARDENS *Archontophoenix, Caryota, Chamaedorea, Dypsis lutescens, Hedyscepe, Howea, Ptychosperma.*

TOLERATE LIGHT, BRIEF FROSTS
Brahea, Butia, Chamaedorea cataractarum, C. elegans, Dypsis decaryi, Livistona, Phoenix roebelenii, Trachycarpus.

Hardiest Palms

Brahea armata, B. edulis, Butia capitata, Chamaerops, Jubaea, Phoenix canariensis, P. dactylifera, Rhapidophyllum, Rhapis, Sabal, Syagrus romanzoffiana, Trachycarpus, Washingtonia.

Salt-Tolerant Palms

These tolerate coastal conditions. *Brahea edulis, Butia, Chamaerops, Cocos, Phoenix canariensis, P. dactylifera, P. reclinata, Sabal palmetto, Washingtonia robusta.*

Hot-Climate Palms

These tolerate hot, dry conditions. *Brahea armata, Butia, Chamaerops, Livistona chinensis, L. mariae, Phoenix canariensis, P. dactylifera, P. sylvestris, Sabal mexicana, S. minor, Washingtonia.*

Palms for Shade

Grow these under a lath. *Caryota mitis, C. urens, Chamaedorea, Hedyscepe, Howea, Livistona* (young), *Phoenix reclinata* (young), *P. roebelenii, Rhapidophyllum, Rhapis, Rhopalostylis, Trachycarpus* (when young).

Understory Palms

Young palms, especially slow growers such as *Livistona chinensis* and *Chamaerops*, stay low for 5 to 10 years and can be used effectively under tall trees. They may have to be moved if they get too tall, a project you won't want to undertake yourself. Two shrubby palms that remain small are *Rhapidophyllum* (6–8 ft. tall) and *Sabal minor* (rarely exceeds 6 ft.).

Palms for Lighting

All palms are good subjects for creating nighttime drama. Light them from behind or below; or direct floodlights to silhouette them against light-colored walls.

Palms for Pots

Keeping plants in pots usually slows growth of faster-growing kinds. Some shade-tolerant palms such as *Chamaedorea, Howea*, and *Rhapis*, may spend decades in pots indoors. Others that later may reach great size—*Chamaerops, Phoenix, Washingtonia*—make charming temporary indoor plants but must eventually be moved outdoors.

HOW TO GROW

EXPOSURE Most young palms prefer shade. As they grow, they can be moved into full sun or partial shade, depending on species. Move indoor palms outdoors periodically into soft light.

SOIL Established palms thrive in fertile, well-drained soil.

PLANTING Make the planting holes generally the same depth as the rootball and 1–2 ft. wider. Backfill with unamended native soil unless your soil is very poor, alkaline, or clay. In that case, some experts suggest the following procedure. For a 5-gal.-size palm, dig a 3-ft.-wide hole that is 8 in. deeper than the rootball. Place 1–2 cu. ft. of well-rotted manure or other organic amendment in the hole, then mix in a handful or two of blood meal and top with a 6-in. layer of soil. Set in the palm and fill in around it with a mixture of half native soil and half nitrogen-fortified ground bark.

WATERING Irrigate newly planted palms faithfully until established. See individual entries for recommendations on long-term water needs.

FEEDING Feed established garden palms with a granular 8-4-12 fertilizer formulated for palms (the best ones include micronutrients such as calcium, iron, zinc, manganese, and magnesium). Feed two or three times during the warm growing season, following the package

Date palms (*Phoenix*)

directions; water the soil thoroughly beforehand.

Potted palms. If temperatures are 60°F (16°C) or higher, fertilize potted palms often.

CLEANING Hose off palms periodically to help control spider mites and sucking insects that find refuge in the long leaf stems—especially in dry or dusty areas. Beach plantings should also be washed off occasionally to keep salt from accumulating on the leaves. Additionally, frequent washing provides some humidity.

PRUNING Some palms shed the old leaf bases on their own. Others, including *Syagrus* and *Chamaedorea*, may hold old bases. You can remove them by slicing them off at the very bottom of base (be careful not to cut into trunk).

Feather palms and many fan palms. These look neater when old leaves are removed after they have turned brown. Make cuts close to the trunk, leaving the leaf bases.

Washingtonia. Admirers say that dead leaves should remain on the tree, the thatch being part of the palm's character. If you agree but prefer a neater look, you can cut lower fronds uniformly close to the trunk but leave the leaf bases, which present an attractive leaf surface.

TRANSPLANTING Most palms transplant easily in late spring or early summer. Since new roots form from the base of the trunk, the rootball need not be big; a new root system will form and produce lush new growth. When transplanting large palms, contractors usually tie leaves together over the center "bud" or heart to protect it.

P

Pandanus tectorius

SCREW PINE, HALA
Pandanaceae
EVERGREEN TREE

🌿 **ZONE H2**

☀️ **FULL SUN**

💧 **REGULAR WATER**

Pandanus tectorius

Native to many Pacific islands, including Hawaii. Striking palm-like tree sends down large aerial roots, or "stilt roots," near its base. Grows into a round-headed tree 20–30 ft. high and 20–40 ft. wide, with spirals of stiff, spiny, 3-ft.-long leaves at the ends of stubby branches. Female plants develop large, edible fruits resembling pineapples. Good wind and salt tolerance; thrives in any well-drained soil, even beach sand. Excellent shade or windbreak tree for the beach garden. Produces litter; needs maintenance to remove old leaves. Young plants can be grown in pots on the patio or indoors.

Pandanus leaves, called *lauhala* in Hawaii, are used to weave hats and mats. Female trees produce large, edible, segmented fruits that resemble pineapples; segments turn orange as they mature.

Pandorea

Bignoniaceae
EVERGREEN VINES

🌿 **ZONES 16–24; H1, H2**

☀️◐ **PARTIAL SHADE IN HOTTEST CLIMATES**

💧💧 **WATER NEEDS VARY BY SPECIES**

Pandorea jasminoides

Twining vines noted for clusters of trumpet-shaped flowers and for rich green, glossy, divided leaves; the foliage is so attractive that the plants look lovely even when out of bloom. Perform best in good, organically enriched soil. Blooms are borne on previous year's growth; prune to shape or thin vines after flowering.

P. jasminoides (Bignonia jasminoides). BOWER VINE. Native to Australia. Fast growth to 20–30 ft. Blooms from late spring to early fall, producing pink-throated white flowers 1½–2 in. long. 'Alba' has pure white flowers. Vigorous 'Lady Di' has white flowers with a creamy yellow throat. 'Rosea' produces soft pink blooms with a nearly red throat. 'Rosea Superba' is heavy blooming, and its pink, purple-throated flowers are fragrant. 'Charisma' has leaves edged in white; blooms are soft pink, with a darker throat. Plant in lee of prevailing wind. Prolonged freezes may kill the plant. Regular water.

P. pandorana (Bignonia australis). WONGA-WONGA VINE. Native to Australia, Pacific islands. More vigorous than *P. jasminoides*, covering twice the space; give it plenty of room. Small (to ¾ in. long), unscented spring flowers are typically creamy white, often spotted brownish purple in

the throat. 'Golden Showers' has golden yellow blossoms. Tougher, more wind-resistant, and less susceptible to freeze damage than *P. jasminoides*. Moderate water.

Panicum virgatum

SWITCH GRASS
Poaceae
PERENNIAL GRASS

🌿 **ZONES 1–11, 14–23**

☀️◐ **FULL SUN OR LIGHT SHADE**

💧💧💧💧 **ANY AMOUNT OF WATER**

Panicum virgatum 'Cloud Nine'

Native to much of the U.S. except the far West. This handsome, reliable grass forms an upright, 2–4-ft.-wide clump of narrow deep green or gray-green leaves. In midsummer, slender flower clusters rise above the foliage, increasing height of clump to 4–7 ft.; clusters open into loose, airy clouds of pinkish blossoms that fade to white, then brown. Foliage turns yellow in fall, gradually fades to beige. Both foliage and flowers persist all winter, providing interest in cold-weather gardens. Tolerates coastal winds. The following varieties reach 5 ft. tall in bloom unless otherwise noted.

'Cloud Nine'. Metallic blue foliage that turns gold in autumn; billowing clouds of reddish brown flowers bring height to 6 ft. tall.

'Dallas Blues'. Wide, powder blue leaves and reddish purple flowers; robust and dependable.

'Hänse Herms'. Open, fountainlike shape, with delicate, light green leaves that turn bright red in fall, then deepen to burgundy; reaches 4 ft. tall in bloom.

'Heavy Metal'. Silvery blue, sturdy leaves that turn bright yellow in fall.

'Northwind'. Strongly vertical form, with olive green foliage that turns yellow in autumn.

'Prairie Sky'. Grows quickly into an upright column of blue leaves that turn yellow in autumn.

'Rotstrahlbusch'. An upright grower, to about 4 ft. tall in flower, with green, red-tinged leaves that turn rich, deep red in fall and burgundy flowers.

'Shenandoah'. Cascading form, with red-tipped blue-green leaves that turn maroon in early fall and airy red flower clusters; reaches 4 ft. tall in bloom.

'Squaw'. Resembles 'Shenandoah', but its leaves are solid green until turning red in fall.

Papaver

POPPY
Papaveraceae
PERENNIALS AND ANNUALS

🌿 **ZONES VARY BY SPECIES**

☀️ **FULL SUN**

💧💧 **MODERATE TO REGULAR WATER**

Papaver rhoeas

Poppies provide bright spring and summer color for borders, containers, and bouquets. Plant in ordinary, well-drained soil; feed lightly until established. Perennial species tend to be short-lived. When using poppies as cut flowers, sear cut stem ends in a flame before placing them in water.

P. alpinum (P. burseri). ALPINE POPPY. Perennial. Zones 1–9, 14–17. In keeping with its origin in the Pyrenees, Alps, and Carpathians, this species is best adapted to colder climates and requires the exceptionally fast-draining soil of a rock garden. Produces 4-in.-wide basal rosette of divided, 2–6-in.-long leaves; foliage is blue green, nearly hairless. In spring or summer, leafless flower stems to 5–8 in. tall bear 1½–2-in. blossoms in white, orange, yellow, or salmon. Blooms first year from seed sown in fall or early spring. Where adapted, self-sows freely.

P. atlanticum. Perennial. Zones 2b–9, 14–24. Native to Morocco. To 2 ft. high, with downy gray-green leaves in basal rosette 6 in. across. Flowers are soft orange, 2–4 in. across, opening in late spring and early summer. 'Flore Pleno' has semidouble blooms. Sow seeds in fall. To prolong bloom period, remove spent flowers.

P. commutatum 'Lady Bird'. Annual. Zones 1–24. Selection of a species native to Greece, Turkey, the Caucasus, Iran. To 1½ ft. high and nearly as wide. Blooms profusely for several weeks in midsummer, producing 3-in., bright red flowers with a black blotch in the middle of each petal. Sow in late winter or early spring, or set out plants in midspring.

P. nudicaule. ICELAND POPPY. Short-lived perennial in Zones A2, A3, 1–6, 10; grown as annual in Zones 7–9, 12–24. Native to subarctic regions. Blue-green leaves make basal rosettes 6 in. wide; from these rise 1–2-ft. stalks bearing cup-shaped, slightly fragrant flowers to 3 in. across, in yellow, orange, salmon, rose, pink, cream, and white. In cold-winter areas, sow seeds in earliest spring for summer bloom; or set out plants in fall for bloom the following year. In mild-winter climates, set out plants in fall for winter and early-spring bloom. To prolong flowering, pick flowers freely.

P. orientale. ORIENTAL POPPY. Perennial. Zones A1–A3; 1–11, 14–21. Native to the Caucasus, northeastern Turkey, and northern Iran. Needs winter chill for best performance. In mild-winter areas, flowers tend to form without stalks, so they may be hidden among leaves. Height ranges from 16 in. to 4 ft. tall, depending on variety. Plants spread by offsets to 2 ft.

or more, forming leafy clumps. Blooms are 4–6 in. across; deeply crinkled petals often have a black blotch at the base. Many named varieties are sold, offering single or double flowers in orange, scarlet, red, pink, salmon, or white.

Plants bloom from late spring to early summer, then die back (sometimes not completely) later in summer. New leafy growth appears in fall, lasts over winter, and develops rapidly in spring. Set sprawling plants such as baby's breath (*Gypsophila*) nearby to cover the bare areas left after poppies die down. Plant dormant crowns in fall with tops 3 in. deep; or set out container-grown plants. Provide good drainage and room for air circulation. Divide every 3 to 5 years in mid- to late summer, after foliage has died back.

P. rhoeas. FLANDERS FIELD POPPY, SHIRLEY POPPY. Annual. Zones A1–A3; 1–24. Best in cool-summer areas. Native to Eurasia and North Africa. Slender, branching plant to 3 ft. high, 1 ft. wide. Single or double flowers are 2 in. or more wide, in white, pink, red, orange, salmon, scarlet, lilac, soft blue,

and bicolors. Mix seed with an equal amount of fine sand, and then broadcast it where plants are to grow. For bloom from spring through summer, make successive sowings starting in early spring. In low and intermediate desert, plant in fall for outstanding early-spring show. For cut flowers, pick when buds first show color. Remove seed capsules (old flower bases) weekly to prolong the bloom season. Notorious self-sower.

Selections bearing single scarlet flowers with a black base are sold as 'American Legion' or 'Flanders Field'. Angels' Choir group offers double flowers in a wide range of colors, including some with creamy picotee edges. Mother of Pearl group has single flowers, primarily soft pastels and white, with an occasional red; also includes some bicolors and picotees, as well as speckled blooms.

P. somniferum. OPIUM POPPY, BREADSEED POPPY. Annual; may self-sow or overwinter in mild-winter areas. All zones. Probably from southeastern Europe and western Asia. Reaches 4 ft. tall, with late-

CLOCKWISE FROM TOP LEFT:
Papaver orientale 'Lauren's Lilac';
P. somniferum 'Single Black';
P. nudicaule

spring flowers to 5 in. across, in white, pink, red, purple, and deep plum, sometimes single, usually double; some of the double forms have fringed petals. Blooms are followed by large seed capsules used in dried arrangements. Ripe pods include large quantities of the poppy seed used in baking. Shake pods over a tray to collect the seeds.

Opium is derived from the seedpods of *P. somniferum*, and it is technically illegal to grow the plant in the U.S. But this law is often ignored by growers and gardeners who appreciate the striking beauty of the flowers.

P

Papaya

Caricaceae

PERENNIAL

🌿 **ZONES 21–24; H2, EXCEPT AS NOTED**

☀ **FULL SUN**

💧 **REGULAR WATER**

Papayas

It may look like a tree or large shrub, but this tropical American native, known botanically as *Carica papaya*, is actually a big perennial with hollow stems. Upright, narrow plants grow to 20–25 ft. tall in Hawaii, perhaps half that in California, with a straight stem topped by a 3–6-ft.-wide crown of broad, fan-like leaves on 2-ft.-long stalks. Inconspicuous cream-colored flowers. Fruit—the papaya found in markets—takes 6 to 10 months to ripen, depending on climate; in Hawaii, it is borne throughout the year. Plants produce crops when young.

This heat-loving plant thrives in Hawaii. In California, the key to success is choosing the right location; root rot in cold, wet soil is the principal cause of failure, so locate on south slope or south side of house where winter sun can heat soil. Plant will also benefit from reflected heat in winter.

To get the most fruit, keep a few plants coming along each year and remove old ones. Grow three to five plants in a group; you ordinarily need both male and female plants for fruit production, though some types are self-fruitful, producing either bisexual flowers or both male and female flowers.

Varieties with yellow-orange flesh grown primarily in Hawaii include 'Kapoho', 'Solo', and dwarf 'Waimanalo'. Types with pinkish flesh grown in Hawaii and California include 'Sunrise', 'Sunset', and 'Thai Dwarf'. Varieties grown in Hawaii have pear-shaped fruit 6–9 in. long and weighing 1–2 lbs. Mexican varieties bear much bigger fruit (to more than 1 ft. long and up to 10 lbs.) with yellow, orange, or pink flesh and a less intense flavor. Harvest papayas of both types when skin begins to turn yellow; let ripen fully at room temperature. Papaya seeds are edible, with a somewhat peppery flavor.

Two other papayas, both from highland areas of South America, are less widely grown. Mountain papaya (*C. pubescens*), native to the Andes, can be grown in Zones 21–24, H1, H2. It reaches 10–12 ft. tall; foliage is borne in dense clusters at tops of its multiple trunks. Elaborately lobed, foot-wide leaves are fan-shaped, deeply veined, and sandpapery in texture; they are dark green above, lighter beneath. Small fruit is edible when cooked (it's unpalatable raw). Male and female plants are needed for fruit set. Babaco is the common name of Ecuadorean native *C. × heilbornii pentagona*, a self-fruitful, naturally occurring hybrid between *C. pubescens* and another Andean species. It can be grown in Zones 17, 19–24, H1. Plant resembles a dwarf (5–8-ft.-tall) *C. papaya*. Foot-long, seedless fruit has juicy flesh similar to that of 'Crenshaw' melon in color and texture; the unique sweet-tart flavor combines papaya, pineapple, and strawberry. Needs partial shade in hottest climates.

CARE

Plant in very well-drained soil. Give regular moisture and apply complete fertilizer every 2 months. Grow from seeds saved from fruit or start with purchased plants. Papayas grow quite well in large containers.

Powdery mildew is treatable with sulfur. Bait for slugs and snails, and fence young plants where deer are prevalent. In Hawaii, papaya is subject to mosaic virus carried by aphids; keep ants (which protect aphids) out of trees and spray for aphids as they appear.

Paphiopedilum

LADY'S SLIPPER

Orchidaceae

TERRESTRIAL ORCHIDS

🌿 **ZONES VARY BY TYPE; OR INDOORS**

◑ **PARTIAL SHADE; BRIGHT INDIRECT LIGHT**

💧 **REGULAR WATER**

Paphiopedilum 'Lord Derby'

Sometimes sold as *Cypripedium*, these terrestrial orchids are native to tropical and subtropical regions of Asia. They are usually grown in a greenhouse or as houseplants but can be brought outdoors in warm weather. Some green-leafed forms can stay outdoors all year in mildest parts of the West Coast (Zones 17, 20–24); more tender, mottled-leafed forms can be grown outdoors year-round in Zone H2.

Leaves are graceful and arching. Green-leafed types usually flower in winter, mottled-leafed kinds in summer. Most plants obtained from orchid dealers are hybrids. Blooms are perky, usually one to a stem, occasionally two or more; each has a distinctive pouch. Many of them shine as if lacquered. Flowers may be white, yellow, green with white stripes, or pure green; or they may show a combination of background colors and markings in tan, mahogany, brown, maroon, green, and white.

A noteworthy species is *P. insigne*. Among the cold-hardiest of the green-leafed types, it can withstand brief exposure to 28°F (–2°C). It blooms at any time from early fall through winter, bearing polished-looking flowers on stiff, hairy brown stems. Sepals and petals show a combination of green and white, with brown spots and stripes; pouch is reddish brown.

CARE

Lady's slippers lack pseudobulbs in which to store moisture, so their roots must never be allowed to go completely dry (water freely in spring and summer, less in fall and winter). Use same potting mix as for cymbidiums. Feed with a half-strength solution of liquid fertilizer every week during spring and summer, then taper down to every other week during winter months. Don't plant in oversize pot; plants thrive when crowded. They flourish with less light than most orchids require.

The least fussy types can be grown in pots in the house. For indoor culture, green-leafed forms generally require temperatures of 50°F to 55°F (10°C to 13°C) at night, 60°F to 75°F (16°C to 24°C) during the day. Mottled-leafed forms do best with temperatures of about 55°F to 60°F (13°C to 16°C) at night, 65°F to 80°F (18°C to 27°C) during the day. Heat requirements are best met in a greenhouse.

Parahebe

Plantaginaceae

SHRUBBY PERENNIALS

🌿 **ZONES 5, 6, 15–17, 20–24**

☀◑ **FULL SUN OR LIGHT SHADE**

💧 **REGULAR WATER**

Parahebe catarractae 'Alba'

These evergreen perennials were formerly classified as *Hebe*, and before that as *Veronica*. Regardless of their name, they are a fine choice for the front of borders, among stones, or trailing over walls. Plants form loosely sprawling, leafy mounds and bloom profusely in summer, bearing small (½ in.), saucer-shaped flowers. Cut back any frost-damaged stems to near base of plant.

P. catarractae. From New Zealand. To 1 ft. high, 2 ft. wide, with narrow dark green leaves. Flowers are white with blue or pink veining and a red eye, carried in clusters to 4 in. long. Stems root where they touch moist soil. If plants begin looking leggy, you can cut them back somewhat, but not as severely as *P. perfoliata*.

P. perfoliata. From Australia. To 1½–4 ft. tall, 6 ft. wide. The pairs of 2-in.-long, gray-green leaves clasp the stem completely, so that stem seems to be piercing the foliage. Clusters of deep blue flowers appear at branch ends and in upper leaf joints. To restore an old plant to beauty, cut it back nearly to the ground.

Parkinsonia
(Cercidium)
PALO VERDE
Caesalpiniaceae
DECIDUOUS TREES

🖋 **ZONES VARY BY SPECIES**
☼ **FULL SUN**
◊ ◗ **LITTLE TO MODERATE WATER**
🪶 **ATTRACT BIRDS**

Parkinsonia

Tough, trouble-free desert trees valued for floral display, shade, and colorful bark. Clusters of small, bright yellow flowers nearly hide the spiny branches. Lightly filtered shade is cast by intricate canopy of twigs rather than by the leaves, which are divided into tiny leaflets and quickly drop in drought or cold. Prune only to enhance form, removing crossing, wayward, or too-low branches; hold off on pruning when temperatures rise above 100°F (38°C). Flowering branches are attractive in arrangements.

P. aculeata. JERUSALEM THORN, MEXICAN PALO VERDE. Zones 8–24; H1, H2. Native to southwestern U.S. and Mexico. Grows 15–30 ft. tall and wide. Yellow-green bark, spiny twigs, picturesque form. Numerous yellow flowers in loose clusters to 7 in. long. Long bloom season in spring; intermittent bloom throughout year. Flowers are followed by 2–6-in.-long seedpods that mature in summer; litter drop is a problem. Thorns, sparse foliage rule it out of tailored gardens. Reseeds freely in the desert. Tolerates alkaline soil.

P. 'Desert Museum'. Zones 8–14, 18–20. This hybrid involving *P. aculeata*, *P. microphyllum*, and *P. floridum* combines the best traits of all three. It grows to 20 ft. tall and as wide in 3 to 5 years. Large (1 in.) blossoms appear over a long period; flowering is most profuse in spring, with rebloom possible in summer. Light green stems and leaves. A clean, thornless tree that produces few seedpods and scant litter.

P. floridum. BLUE PALO VERDE. Zones 8–14, 18–20. Native to the deserts of Southern California, Arizona, and Baja California. In gardens, it grows fast to 35 ft. tall and 30 ft. wide. Bluish green leaves and branches. Bright pure yellow flowers in 2–4½-in. clusters appear in spring.

P. microphyllum. LITTLE-LEAF PALO VERDE, FOOTHILLS PALO VERDE. Zones 8–14, 18–20. From Southern California, Arizona's Sonoran Desert, and Baja California. Slow growth to 20 ft. tall and wide. Leaves and bark are yellowish green. Pale

The delicate, often leafless branches of palo verde cast a light shade that's just right for many understory plants.

yellow springtime flowers in 1-in. clusters.

P. praecox. PALO BREA, SONORAN PALO VERDE. Zones 10–14, 18–20. Native from the Sonoran Desert to South America. Moderate growth to an umbrella shape 20 ft. tall and wide. Lime green bark and leaves. Bright yellow blooms appear in spring.

Parrotia persica
PERSIAN PARROTIA
Hamamelidaceae
DECIDUOUS TREE OR SHRUB

🖋 **ZONES 2B–7, 14–17**
☼ ◑ **FULL SUN OR LIGHT SHADE**
◗ ◗ **MODERATE TO REGULAR WATER**

Parrotia persica

Native to the Caucasus and northern Iran. A choice, colorful tree with good looks in all seasons. Grows slowly to 15–35 ft. tall and wide; naturally multistemmed but can be trained to a single trunk. Oval leaves to 6 in. long have noticeably wavy margins. Most dramatic display comes in autumn: leaves usually turn golden yellow, then orange or rosy pink, and finally scarlet. Smooth gray bark flakes off to reveal white patches; showy when on display in winter. Dense clusters of tiny flowers with red stamens appear in late winter or early spring before leaves open; they give the plant an overall reddish haze. New foliage unfurls reddish purple, matures to lustrous dark green. Prefers slightly acid soil but tolerates alkaline soil. 'Pendula' is a weeping form to just 5 ft. tall and 10 ft. wide. 'Vanessa' is dense and narrowly upright, to about 30 ft. tall and half as wide.

Parsnip
Apiaceae
BIENNIAL GROWN AS ANNUAL

🖋 **ALL ZONES**
☼ **FULL SUN**
◗ **REGULAR WATER**
◊ **LEAVES MAY CAUSE RASH**

Parsnips

This cold-hardy carrot relative from Siberia and Europe is grown for its delicately sweet, creamy white to yellowish roots (delicious roasted or in stews). To accommodate these long roots (up to 15 in. in some varieties), provide well-prepared, loose, deep soil.

In cold-winter areas, sow seeds in late spring, harvest in fall; leave surplus in the ground to be dug as needed in winter. Cold makes the roots sweeter. In mild-winter climates, sow in fall and harvest in spring. Soak fresh seeds in water for a day before planting to improve germination. Sow ¼–½ in. deep, in rows spaced 2 ft. apart; thin seedlings to 3 in. apart. Apply a complete fertilizer a month after seedlings emerge. Harvest before they flower; if parsnip goes to seed, it can become a noxious weed.

Some people develop a sunburn-like rash, and even blistering, after handling parsnip leaves in the sunlight (ultraviolet light triggers the reaction). Wear gloves as a precaution.

Parthenocissus
Vitaceae
DECIDUOUS VINES

- ✎ **ZONES VARY BY SPECIES**
- ☼ ◐ ● **SUN OR SHADE**
- 💧 **MODERATE WATER**
- 🦅 **FRUITS ATTRACT BIRDS**

Parthenocissus tricuspidata

Valued for handsome foliage, which reliably takes on superb orange or red shades in fall. Blossoms are insignificant; more noticeable are clusters of small blue-black fruits that form in late summer or fall and hang on into winter if not consumed by birds. Vines cling to walls by suction disks at ends of tendrils. All but the fairly restrained *P. henryana* are said to grow to 50–60 ft., but they are really limited only by the size of the support. Thrive in organically enriched soil.

Think twice before letting them attach to shingles, clapboard, or mortared brick or stone. Their clinging tendrils are hard to remove, and vines can creep under siding. They also hasten deterioration of wood and mortar. When vines reach desired size, prune them each dormant season to restrain their spread and—for those trained on buildings—to keep them away from doors, windows, and eaves. Cut out any wayward branches; cut out any that have pulled away from their support, since disks will not reattach. Trim as needed during the growing season.

P. henryana. SILVERVEIN CREEPER. Zones 4–9, 14–17. Native to China. Grows to 20 ft.; less aggressive growth than the other species listed. Leaves open purplish, then turn dark

---

Clinging Vines

Most vines climb using twining stems or coiling tendrils, but *Parthenocissus* species—along with crossvine (*Bignonia capreolata*)—attach directly to walls and other surfaces with disklike structures called holdfasts. A few other vines use aerial rootlets to cling directly to surfaces: trumpet creeper (*Campsis*), *Euonymus fortunei*, creeping fig (*Ficus pumila*), climbing hydrangea (*Hydrangea anomala petiolaris*), and Japanese hydrangea vine (*Schizophragma hydrangeoides*). For more on vines, see page 708.

---

bronzy green with pronounced silver veining and purple undersides. Color is best in partial or full shade; in strong light, leaves fade to plain green. Foliage turns rich red in autumn. This vine clings to walls, but it needs some support to get started. Also a good choice for spilling over walls or as a small-scale groundcover.

P. inserta. VIRGINIA CREEPER, WOODBINE. Zones 1–24. Native to Rocky Mountains and eastward; the Western form of *P. quinquefolia*. Scrambles; tendrils have few or no suction disks.

P. quinquefolia. VIRGINIA CREEPER. Zones A2, A3; 1–24. Native to the eastern U.S., this big, vigorous vine clings to or runs over ground, fences, trellises, arbors, and trees. Looser growth than *P. tricuspidata*; has a see-through quality. Five-lobed leaves are bronze tinted when new, matures to semiglossy dark green, turns crimson and burgundy in early fall. Good groundcover on slopes; can control erosion. Leaves of 'Star Showers' are splashed with white, take on pink tones in fall, then turn red. *P. q. engelmannii* is a denser grower than the species, with smaller leaves.

P. tricuspidata. BOSTON IVY. Zones 1–24. Native to China and Japan. Semievergreen in mild-winter areas. The most vigorous of species listed here. Foliage color is similar to that of *P. quinquefolia* in spring and summer but covers a broader spectrum in fall. Three-lobed leaves are glossy, to 8 in. wide, and variable in shape. Fall color varies from orange to wine red. Clings tightly, grows fast to

make a dense, uniform wall cover. This is the "ivy" of the Ivy League; covers brick or stone in areas where English ivy (*Hedera helix*) freezes. In intensely hot regions, plant only on walls with northern or eastern exposure. 'Green Showers' has large (10 in.) leaves that turn burgundy in fall. 'Lowii' and 'Veitchii' produce half-size leaves on less rampant vines.

Paspalum vaginatum
SEASHORE PASPALUM
Poaceae
PERENNIAL GRASS

- ✎ **ZONES 17, 24; H2**
- ☼ **FULL SUN**
- 💧 **MODERATE TO REGULAR WATER**

Paspalum vaginatum

Native to the southeastern U.S. Makes an attractive lawn near coast; tolerates salty soil, heat, wear. Color is close to that of bluegrass, and lawns are pest-free. In interior climates, it develops tough stems that turn

---

brown after cutting. Mow to ¾ in. with a reel mower and feed only between midautumn and late spring. Usually sold as sod under names like Adalayd and Excalibre.

Passiflora
PASSION VINE
Passifloraceae
EVERGREEN, SEMIEVERGREEN, AND DECIDUOUS VINES

- ✎ **ZONES VARY BY SPECIES**
- ☼ ◑ **FULL SUN OR PARTIAL SHADE**
- 💧 💧 **MODERATE TO REGULAR WATER**
- 🦋 **ATTRACT BUTTERFLIES**

Passiflora caerulea

These floriferous South American natives climb quickly by tendrils to 20–30 ft. Foliage is typically rich green and divided into several lobes. Plants bloom during warm weather. Flower parts can be seen to symbolize elements of the passion of Christ, hence the plant's common name: the crown represents a halo or crown of thorns; the 5 stamens, the 5 wounds; the 10 petal-like segments, the 10 faithful apostles. Many species produce edible fruit as a bonus; for the species cultivated specifically for its edible crop, see Passion Fruit.

Train passion vines on trellises or walls for their vigor and bright, showy flowers; or use as a soil-holding bank cover. Vigorous, likely to overgrow and tangle; require rigorous thinning and untangling. Winter and early spring are best times for major pruning, but you can thin excess new growth at any time in the growing season. Tolerate many soil types. These vines are the favorite food of caterpillars of the gulf fritillary butterfly.

P

P. × *belotii (P.* × *alato-caerulea, P. pfordtii).* Evergreen or semievergreen. Zones 5–9, 12–24; H1, H2. Dies to ground in colder part of range. Hybrid between *P. caerulea* and *P. alata,* a species not described here. Among the best-known, most widely planted passion vines, and probably least subject to damage from caterpillars. Fragrant, 4-in. flowers are white shaded with pink and lavender, with a deep blue or purple crown. Forms no fruit. In colder areas, give it a warm place out of wind, such as against a wall or beneath an overhang; mulch roots in winter.

P. caerulea. BLUE CROWN PASSION FLOWER. Evergreen or semievergreen. Zones 5–9, 12–24; H1, H2. Dies to the ground in colder part of range. Faintly fragrant flowers in greenish white with white-and-purple crown are also smaller. Egg-shaped, yellow to orange, 2½-in. fruit isn't very tasty. Can be invasive. Has naturalized in Hawaii. 'Constance Eliott' has pure white flowers with a purple crown.

P. edulis. See Passion Fruit.

P. × *exoniensis.* Evergreen. Zones 16, 17, 23, 24; H2. Drooping, 5-in., unscented flowers are dark green and brownish red outside, brilliant pink inside, with a touch of purple in the throat. Banana-shaped, yellow, 3-in.-long fruit.

P. incarnata. WILD PASSION VINE, MAYPOP. Deciduous. Zones 4–10, 12–24; H1, H2. Native to eastern U.S. Hardiest of the passion flowers, surviving to at least −10°F (−23°C). Dies to the ground in colder part of range. Freely produced fragrant, 3-in. flowers are white or pale lavender, with a showy crown of filaments banded in purple and pink. Egg-shaped, yellow, 2-in. fruit. Spreads vigorously from underground roots and can become an attractive pest. Seldom offered as plants; easy to grow from seed.

P. 'Incense'. Deciduous. Zones 5–24; H1, H2. Hardy to 0°F (−18°C); holds its leaves through short cold spells, dies to the ground when the weather turns colder. Hybrid between *P. incarnata* and an Argentinean species. Flowers are 5 in. wide, violet with lighter crown, with fragrance similar to that of

sweet peas (*Lathyrus*). Egg-shaped, 2-in., olive green to yellow-green fruit with fragrant, tasty pulp.

P. 'Lavender Lady'. Evergreen. Zones 16–24; H2. Profuse and long-lasting show of unscented, 4-in. lavender flowers with deep violet crown.

P. vitifolia. Evergreen. Zones 16, 17, 23, 24; H2. Large, deep green leaves shaped like grape leaves set off bright red, 3½-in., unscented flowers with red to yellow coronas. Egg-shaped, greenish yellow, 2-in. fruit. Does not attract caterpillars. Has naturalized in Hawaii.

Passion Fruit
Passifloraceae
EVERGREEN OR SEMIEVERGREEN VINE

🌢 **ZONES 15–17, 21–24; H1, H2**

☼ **FULL SUN**

💧 **REGULAR WATER DURING GROWTH AND BLOOM**

Passion fruit

Known botanically as *Passiflora edulis,* this vigorous South American native climbs by tendrils to 20–30 ft. Light yellow-green leaves are divided into three lobes. Blooms during warm weather, bearing white, 2–3-in.-wide flowers with white-and-purple crown (for more on flower form, see *Passiflora*). Fragrant, roundish fruit 1½–3 in. wide ripens mainly in summer and fall; at maturity, waxy rind turns from green to deep purple, and fruit falls from the vine. Pick the fruit when it turns color or gather it from the ground every few days. The orange pulp has an exotic, citruslike flavor; use it for juice or cut fruit in half and eat pulp, seeds and all, with

a spoon. There is a form with larger, more acidic, yellow-skinned fruit.

Sweet-fruited hybrids that have good-size fruit include red-skinned 'Red Rover' and 'Frederick', and purple-skinned 'Edgehill' (particularly good in Southern California) and 'Kahuna'. All are semievergreen in colder part of range. Plants are often short-lived. This plant has naturalized in Hawaii and become a serious pest there.

Grow in well-drained, well-amended soil; give wind protection. Train on trellis or wall to show off flowers. Withhold water during cold months. Prune yearly after harvest: thin out excess stems by cutting them to the ground, and cut back vigorous growth by a third.

Patrinia
Caprifoliaceae
PERENNIALS

🌢 **ZONES 2B–6, 15–17**

☼ **FULL SUN**

💧 **REGULAR WATER**

Patrinia scabiosifolia

Native to eastern Asia. Deeply cut or lobed leaves form attractive mounds, but the real show comes in summer, when tall, slender stems produce flat-topped clusters of tiny blossoms. Good in perennial borders. Long-lasting cut flowers. Appreciate rich, well-drained soil. Do not plant near daylilies (*Hemerocallis*), since *Patrinia* species serve as the alternate host for daylily rust.

P. scabiosifolia. To 4–6 ft. tall, 2 ft. wide. Flowering stems produce sprays of tiny yellow blossoms. Because stems have a see-through quality, plant can

be grown either at front or at rear of border. May need staking.

P. villosa. To 2–3 ft. high, 2 ft. wide, with leaves that may be divided or uncut. Showers of white blossoms.

Paulownia tomentosa
EMPRESS TREE
Paulowniaceae
DECIDUOUS TREE

🌢 **ZONES 4–9, 11–24**

☼ **FULL SUN**

💧 **REGULAR WATER**

Paulownia tomentosa

Native to China. Large leaves and exotic-looking flowers give a tropical effect. The tree grows quickly to 40–50 ft., with nearly equal spread. Heavy trunk; brittle, nearly horizontal branches. Light green, roughly heart-shaped leaves are up to 1 ft. long. Brown flower buds the size of small olives form in autumn and persist over winter, then open in early spring, before leafout. Fragrant, 2-in., trumpet-shaped flowers are lilac-blue, marked on the inside with darker spotting and yellow stripes; they appear in erect clusters up to 1 ft. high. Flowers are followed by seed capsules shaped like tops; these are persistent, remaining on the tree along with next season's flower buds. This tree does not bloom well where winters are very cold (buds freeze) or very mild (buds may drop off).

Grows best in deep, moist, well-drained soil. Tolerates air pollution. Protect from strong winds. Plant where falling flowers and leaves are not a problem. Not a tree to garden under due

P

to dense shade, surface roots. If cut back yearly or every other year from an early age, it will produce a mass of giant-size leaves to 2 ft. long but at the expense of flower production.

Paxistima
(Pachystima)
Celastraceae
EVERGREEN SHRUBS

☑ ZONES VARY BY SPECIES

☼ ◐ PARTIAL SHADE IN HOTTEST CLIMATES

◔ ◐ MODERATE TO REGULAR WATER

Paxistima myrtifolia

Low-growing shrubs prized for small, shiny, leathery leaves. Flowers are insignificant. Hardiness and compact habit make them useful as low hedges, edgings, and groundcovers in cold-winter areas. Lower stems root when they contact the soil. Best in well-drained soil.

P. canbyi. Zones 1–10, 14–21. Native to the mountains of the eastern U.S. Slowly makes a mat to 1 ft. high, 3–5 ft. wide. Narrow dark green leaves.

P. myrtifolia (P. myrsinites). OREGON BOXWOOD. Zones 2–7, 15, 16. Native to the mountains of the West. Dense plant of variable habit; may be nearly prostrate or as tall as 4 ft. Spreads about 4 ft. Growth is more compact in sun. Leaves are dark green above, paler beneath.

Paxistimas are native to high elevations and are sometimes known by the common name "mountain lover."

Pea
Papilionaceae
ANNUAL

☑ ALL ZONES

☼ FULL SUN

◉ REGULAR WATER

'Oregon Giant' snow pea

Peas are native to southern Europe. They come in two general types: shelling peas and edible-pod peas. The latter includes snow peas, which are eaten when pods are young, before the peas inside mature; and snap peas, which are eaten when pods are filled out.

All peas are easy to grow when conditions are right. They need coolness and humidity and must be planted at just the right time. For more vigorous peas, buy seeds inoculated with *Rhizobium* bacteria, which helps the plants to fix nitrogen from the air and store it in their roots. Or buy the inoculant from a nursery or mail-order seed supplier and treat the seeds yourself.

If you have space and don't mind the bother, grow tall (vining) peas on trellises; they climb by tendrils to 6 ft. or more and bear heavily. Bush types are more commonly grown in home gardens; no support is required, though they can be grown on short trellises for easy picking.

Shelling peas. Superior bush varieties include 'Alderman' ('Tall Telephone'), 'Mr. Big', 'Caseload', and 'Maestro'. In France, tiny peas called *petits pois* are considered a delicacy because of their tenderness and sweet flavor. These aren't just immature versions

How to Grow Peas

PLANTING Choose a site in full sun with good air circulation. Grow peas in organically enriched, well-drained soil. Where winters are cold, sow as early in spring as the ground can be worked; for a fall crop, sow about 12 weeks before the first frost date. Where winters are mild, plant at any time from fall to early spring—but don't sow after midwinter in areas where spring days quickly become too warm for peas. Successive plantings several days apart will lengthen the bearing season; most varieties are ready to pick 60–70 days from planting.

Soak seeds overnight in water before planting them. If planting in winter, sow ½–1 in. deep. At other times of year, sow 2 in. deep in light soil, ½–1 in. deep in heavy soil. Leave 2 ft. between rows for bush types, 5 ft. for tall vines; thin seedlings to 2–4 in. apart. (Thinnings can be steamed or stir-fried.)

TRAINING Have supports in place in advance for tendrils to grab (even bush peas benefit from trellising). You can use sticks, string, bamboo poles, or wide-mesh stock fencing—anything that tendrils can grab on to and that you can get your hand through when it comes time to harvest.

WATERING Moisten ground thoroughly before planting; then hold off on watering until

seedlings are up. If weather turns warm and dry, supply water in furrows; overhead watering encourages mildew.

FEEDING Plants need little fertilizer, but if soil is very light, give one application of complete fertilizer about 6 weeks after planting.

HARVESTING When peas reach harvesting size, pick all pods that are ready; if seeds are allowed to ripen, plant will stop producing. Vines are brittle; steady them with one hand while picking with the other.

Shelling peas. Begin harvesting shelling peas when the pods have swelled to almost a cylindrical shape but before they lose their bright green color.

Edible-pod peas. Harvest edible-pod peas when they are 2–3 in. long, before the seeds begin to swell.

Eat all kinds of peas immediately; like corn, they start converting their sugar to starch as soon as they're picked.

CHALLENGES Avoid powdery mildew by planting in an area with good air circulation. Blast off aphids with a jet of water. Row covers protect emerging plants from cucumber beetles, but covers should be removed once young plants are growing well. Peas are also subject to a number of viruses and wilts; look for resistant varieties.

of shelling peas; they are genetically smaller (2–3 in. long at maturity), with six to nine small peas per pod. Try 'Waverex'.

Edible-pod peas. An unusually good vegetable (and one popular in Asian cooking), usually called snow or sugar peas. The heirloom 'Mammoth Melting Sugar' is a 4-ft.-tall variety; 'Manoa Sugar' is another tall type, developed for Hawaiian gardens. 'Oregon Sugar Pod II' and 'Oregon Giant' are bush

varieties. 'Atitlan' has few leaves on its upper stems, putting all its energy into producing peas.

'Super Sugar Snap' (tall), 'Sugar Ann' (bush), and short-vine 'Sugar Sprint' (26 in.) combine the qualities of shelling peas and edible-pod peas. You can eat the immature pods, eat pods and peas together as you would string beans (the most popular way), or wait for the peas to mature and harvest them for shelling.

Peach and Nectarine

Rosaceae
DECIUOUS FRUIT TREES

🖊 ZONES VARY BY VARIETY

☼ FULL SUN

💧 REGULAR WATER DURING FRUIT DEVELOPMENT

» See chart on pages 480–482.

'Redhaven' peaches

Native to China. Peach (*Prunus persica*) and nectarine (*P. p. nucipersica*) trees look alike and have the same cultural needs. Where fruit is concerned, both peaches and nectarines may be clingstone (flesh adheres to the pit), freestone (flesh easily separates from pit), or semifreestone (between the two). But nectarines differ from peaches in several respects: they have smooth rather than fuzzy skin; in some varieties, flavor is slightly different; and many are more susceptible to brown rot of stone fruit. Discussed here are fruiting peaches and nectarines. For strictly flowering types, see *Prunus*.

In most regions, crops ripen between June and September, depending on variety. Early varieties grown in mild-winter climates may mature as early as April. For good harvests, most peaches and nectarines need 600 to 900 hours of winter temperatures below 45°F (7°C). Insufficient chilling results in delayed leafout, a scanty crop, and eventual death of the tree. In extremely mild-winter areas, only low-chill varieties do well (and very few of those are satisfactory in the low desert). A few low-chill peach varieties have been tried successfully at higher elevations in Hawaii; nectarines tend to split in Hawaii and so are not commonly grown there. In areas subject to late frosts, early-blooming varieties are risky. Where spring is particularly cold and rainy, plants set few flowers, pollinate poorly, and get peach leaf curl. They need clear, hot weather during the growing season.

A standard-size peach or nectarine tree grows rapidly to 25 ft. tall and wide, but properly pruned trees are usually kept to 10–12 ft. tall and a little wider. They start bearing large crops when 3 or 4 years old and reach peak production at 8 to 12 years. Genetic or natural dwarf trees, most of which grow to 5–6 ft. tall and produce medium-size fruit, are useful in tubs and small planting areas. Examples of dwarf peaches include 'Bonanza II', 'El Dorado', 'Honey Babe', and 'Pix Zee'. Among the best dwarf nectarines are 'Nectar Babe', 'Necta Zee', and 'Southern Belle'. Check with your local nursery for the dwarf variety best suited to your region. You can also save space by planting three or four full-size varieties in one hole: prune the new bare-root trees so that each retains just one primary branch, and point those branches outward as you plant the trees in the hole. With a few exceptions, peaches and nectarines are self-fruitful, so you don't need a pollenizer.

No room for fruit trees? Grow a genetic (natural) dwarf variety of yellow peach such as 'Honey Babe' or 'Pix Zee' in a large (at least 18-inch diameter) container. The tree can thrive and bear fruit for years without transplanting. No pollinators needed.

TOP ROW: 'Frost' peach; 'Donut' peaches. MIDDLE: Clingstone peaches. BOTTOM ROW: 'Earliblaze' nectarines; 'Harko' nectarines

P

»

PEACH AND NECTARINE: TOP PICKS TO GROW

NAME	ZONES	FRUIT	COMMENTS
PEACH			
'Arctic Supreme'	7–9, 14, 15, 18	Large. Clingstone. Red-over-cream skin; white flesh. Superb flavor. Midseason.	Among the most flavorful of all peaches.
'August Pride'	7–9, 14, 15, 18–24	Large. Freestone. Yellow skin with red blush; yellow flesh. Aromatic fruit with rich flavor. Midseason.	Low chill requirement.
'Babcock'	12, 13, 15, 16, 19–24; H1	Small to medium. Freestone. Light pink skin with red blush; little fuzz. White flesh reddens near pit. Sweet flavor with some tang. Early.	Low chill requirement. Old-time favorite.
'Baby Crawford'	7–9, 14, 15, 18	Small. Freestone. Golden orange, very fuzzy skin with slight blush; yellow flesh. Intense flavor. Midseason.	An exceptionally flavorful variety.
'Bonita'	15–24	Large. Freestone. Yellow skin with medium red blush; firm yellow flesh. Fine flavor. Midseason.	Low chill requirement.
'Champagne'	6–11, 14, 15, 18	Medium to large. Freestone. Yellow skin with light red blush; white flesh with red near the pit. Fine, sweet flavor. Midseason.	Vigorous and productive.
'Desertgold'	8, 9, 12, 13, 18–24	Medium size. Semifreestone. Yellow skin and flesh. Good quality. Very early.	Very early bloom rules it out wherever spring frosts are likely.
'Donut' ('Stark Saturn')	7–9, 13–15, 18–23	Medium size. Freestone. Shaped like a doughnut, with a sunken middle. White skin with red blush; white flesh. Mildly sweet flavor with a hint of almond. Early.	Low chill requirement. Almost evergreen in mild-winter areas.
'Double Jewel'	2, 3, 7–12, 14, 15, 18	Large. Freestone. Peach pink skin; yellow-orange flesh. Good flavor. Early.	Bears a profusion of double pink flowers late in spring.
'Earligrande'	8–24	Medium to large. Semifreestone. Yellow with red blush; yellow flesh. Excellent flavor. Early.	Fine quality. Low-chill variety for mild-winter climates.
'Elberta'	1–3, 6–11, 14	Medium to large. Freestone. Yellow skin with red blush; yellow flesh. High quality. Midseason.	Needs good amount of winter chill and high summer heat to ripen to full flavor.
'Eva's Pride'	12, 13, 18–24	Medium to large. Freestone. Yellow skin and flesh. Fine flavor. Early to midseason.	Low chill requirement.
'Fay Elberta' ('Gold Medal')	2, 3, 6–11, 14, 15, 18, 19	Medium to large. Freestone. Has more red blush on skin than 'Elberta'; yellow flesh. Midseason (ripens with 'Elberta' but keeps better).	Bears large, handsome single flowers. 'Fantastic Elberta' is a double-flowered sport; its fruit has excellent flavor.
'Flordaprince'	12, 13, 18–24; H1	Medium to large. Semifreestone, becoming freestone when fully ripe. Red-blushed yellow skin; yellow flesh. Very good quality. Very early.	Low chill requirement.
'Fortyniner'	5–9, 14–16, 18	Large. Freestone. Yellow skin with bright red blush; yellow flesh. Fine flavor. Early midseason.	Looks like its parent, 'J.H. Hale'; blooms about 1 week earlier.
'Frost'	3–9, 14, 15, 18	Medium size. Freestone. Yellow skin with slight red blush; yellow flesh. Tangy flavor. Midseason to late.	Resistant to peach leaf curl.
'Gleason's Early Elberta' ('Lemon Elberta', 'Improved Elberta')	2–11, 14, 15	Like 'Elberta' but has better color and even better flavor; ripens about 10 days later.	Late blooming and cold-hardy. Needs somewhat less heat than 'Elberta'.
'Halehaven'	1–3, 6–11, 14–16	Medium to large. Freestone. Red skin; firm yellow flesh. Juicy and flavorful. Midseason.	Flower and leaf buds are very winter-hardy. Good fresh or canned.

P

PEACH AND NECTARINE: TOP PICKS TO GROW

NAME	ZONES	FRUIT	COMMENTS
'Harken'	1–7	Large. Freestone. Yellow skin with red blush; yellow flesh. Very sweet. Midseason.	Good performer in cold climates and coastal Northwest.
'Indian Blood Cling' ('Indian Cling')	1–3, 6–11, 14–16	Medium size. Clingstone. Red skin; firm yellow flesh streaked with red. Rich flavor. Late.	Old-fashioned variety with small but devoted band of enthusiasts. Good for preserves.
'Indian Free'	7–11, 14–16	Large. Freestone. Greenish white skin with red blush; red-tinged yellow flesh, deep red at the pit. Rich and aromatic when fully ripe. Late midseason.	An old favorite with a unique flavor. Needs pollinating by any other peach except 'J.H. Hale'.
'July Elberta' ('Kim Elberta')	2, 3, 6–12, 14–16, 18, 19	Medium to large. Freestone. Yellow skin blushed red; yellow flesh. High quality. Early, 3 weeks before 'Elberta'.	Prolific bearer.
'Loring'	7–9, 14, 15, 18	Large. Freestone. Attractive yellow skin blushed red; little fuzz. Moderately juicy yellow flesh. Good quality. Midseason.	Vigorous. Showy flowers.
'Midpride'	7–9, 12–16, 18–24	Medium size. Freestone. Red-blushed yellow skin; yellow flesh. Exceptional flavor. Midseason.	Excellent variety with low chill requirement.
'Nectar'	7–11, 14–16	Medium to large. Freestone. Creamy white skin with red blush; white flesh. Excellent flavor. Early midseason.	Produces among the best white peaches.
'O'Henry'	7–10, 14–16, 18	Large. Freestone. Yellow skin with red blush; yellow flesh streaked red. Fine flavor. Midseason.	Good commercial and home-garden variety.
'Q 1-8'	3–9, 14, 15, 18	Medium size. Semifreestone. Yellow skin with red blush; white flesh. Sweet, flavorful. Early.	Resistant to peach leaf curl.
'Redhaven'	3, 5, 12, 14–16	Medium size. Freestone. Yellow skin with bright red blush; firm yellow flesh. Good flavor. Long ripening season permits numerous harvests. Early.	Colors up early, so test for ripeness. One of the best varieties. Fruit is good fresh or frozen. 'Early Redhaven' ripens 2 weeks earlier.
'Redskin'	1–3, 6–12, 14–16	Medium to large. Freestone. Yellow skin heavily blushed red; yellow flesh. Excellent quality. Midseason.	Productive tree. Fruit is good fresh, canned, or frozen.
'Reliance'	1–11	Medium to large. Freestone. Yellow skin blushed dull red; soft yellow flesh. Good flavor. Early.	Outstanding cold-hardiness.
'Rio Oso Gem'	3, 7–11, 14, 15	Medium to large. Freestone. Yellow skin with red blush; firm yellow flesh. Excellent flavor. Late midseason.	Small tree; not vigorous. Fruit is excellent fresh or frozen.
'Santa Barbara'	18–24; H1	Large. Freestone. Red-blushed yellow skin; yellow flesh. Excellent flavor; best used fresh. Midseason.	Low chill requirement. Sport of 'Ventura'.
'Snow Beauty'	7–9, 14, 15, 18	Large. Freestone. Red skin; white flesh. Sweet; exceptionally good flavor. Midseason.	Among the best flavored of white peaches.
'Strawberry Free'	7–9, 14–16, 18–20	Medium size. Freestone. Medium red blush on yellow skin; firm white flesh. Excellent flavor. Early midseason.	An old favorite among white peaches.
'Suncrest'	7–9, 14, 15, 18	Large. Freestone. Yellow skin with bright red blush; yellow flesh. Excellent flavor. Midseason.	Variety made famous in *Epitaph for a Peach: Four Seasons on My Family Farm*, by David Mas Masumoto.
'Tropi-berta'	8, 9, 14–16, 18–22; H1	Large. Freestone. Yellow skin blushed red; juicy yellow flesh. Good flavor. Late midseason.	Moderately low chill requirement.

P

»

PEACH AND NECTARINE: TOP PICKS TO GROW

NAME	ZONES	FRUIT	COMMENTS
'Tropic Snow'	12, 13, 18–23; H1	Medium size. Freestone. Red skin; white flesh. Superb flavor. Early.	Best low-chill white peach.
'Ventura'	18–23; H1	Medium size. Freestone. Very smooth yellow skin; yellow flesh. Attractive fruit with fair flavor. Midseason.	Low chill requirement. Developed especially for Southern California.
'White Lady'	2b–9, 12, 14–16	Medium to large. Freestone. Red skin; white flesh. Low-acid, high-sugar content. Midseason.	Fairly high chill requirement, but widely adapted where it gets enough cold.

NECTARINE

NAME	ZONES	FRUIT	COMMENTS
'Arctic Jay'	7–9, 14–16, 18	Large. Freestone. Deep red skin; white flesh. Excellent, rich flavor. Early to midseason.	'Arctic' series nectarines are named for white flesh, not frost-tolerance.
'Arctic Rose'	7–9, 14–16, 18	Medium size. Freestone. White to pale yellow skin with red blush; white flesh. Delicious sweet flavor. Midseason.	One of the best-tasting nectarines.
'Arctic Star'	7–9, 14, 15, 18–24	Large. Semifreestone. Bright red skin; white flesh. Very sweet, rich flavor. Early.	Low chill requirement. One of the best white nectarines for mild-winter areas.
'Double Delight'	7–9, 14–16, 18–20	Medium size. Freestone. Dark red skin; yellow flesh. Rich flavor. Midseason.	Ornamental double pink flowers. Low chill requirement.
'Flavortop'	2, 3, 6–12, 14, 15, 18	Large. Freestone. Yellow skin, heavily blushed red; yellow flesh. Good flavor. Midseason.	Vigorous, productive. Showy flowers.
'Goldmine'	7–12, 14–16, 18–22	Large. Freestone. Creamy yellow, tough skin with red blush; firm white flesh. Excellent, distinctive flavor. Late midseason.	Low chill requirement. Fruit is excellent fresh or frozen. 'Arctic Fantasy' is an improved form with even better flavor.
'Harko'	1–11, 14–16	Small to medium. Semifreestone. Yellow skin with heavy red blush; firm yellow flesh. Excellent flavor. Early.	Cold-hardy, disease-resistant variety from Canada. Large, showy pink flowers.
'Heavenly White'	7–9, 14–16, 18	Very large. Freestone. Creamy white skin heavily blushed with red; white flesh. Especially fine flavor. Midseason.	Has been called a connoisseur's delight.
'Juneglo'	3–9, 14–16, 18	Medium size. Freestone. Red skin; yellow flesh. Fine flavor. Early.	One of the most reliable varieties in the coastal Northwest.
'Le Grand'	7–9, 14–16, 18	Large. Clingstone. Bright yellow-and-red skin; yellow flesh. Delicate, sweet-tart flavor. Late.	Fruit holds well on the tree.
'Liz's Late'	7–9, 14–16, 18	Medium size. Freestone. Red-over-yellow skin; yellow flesh. Sprightly, sweet-spicy flavor. Good keeper. Late.	Unusual flavor makes this nectarine a favorite.
'Mericrest'	1–3, 10, 11, 14–16, 18	Medium size. Freestone. Bright red skin; yellow flesh. Flavorful. Midseason.	May be as cold-hardy as 'Reliance' peach. Good resistance to brown rot.
'Panamint'	7–9, 14–16, 18–24	Medium to large. Freestone. Bright red skin; yellow flesh. Very good flavor. Midseason.	Low chill requirement.
'Snow Queen'	7–9, 14–16, 18–23	Medium size. Freestone. Red skin; white flesh. Sweet and juicy. Early.	Low chill requirement.
'Sunred'	18–23	Medium size. Semifreestone. Bright red skin; yellow flesh. Good flavor. Very early.	Low chill requirement.

P

How to Grow Peaches and Nectarines

PLANTING Choose a sunny spot with protection from cold spring winds. Provide well-drained soil. (For details on preparing the soil before planting, see pages 666–669.) Dwarf varieties grow well in wine half-barrels.

FEEDING Apply 10-10-10 complete fertilizer when buds break in late March. Give young trees ½ lb. per year of age; give mature trees up to 5 lbs.

PRUNING & TRAINING Peach and nectarine trees require heavier pruning than other fruit trees because they produce fruit on year-old branches. Severe annual pruning not only renews fruiting wood, but also encourages production of fruit throughout the tree rather than at ends of sagging branches that can easily break. Genetic dwarf trees need less pruning than standard ones. Peaches and nectarines can be trained as espaliers.

Bare-root trees. When planting a bare-root tree that is an unbranched "whip," cut it back to 2–3½ ft. aboveground (the thicker the trunk, the less severe the cutting back). New branches will form below the cut. After first year's growth, select three well-placed branches for scaffold limbs.

Mature trees. On mature trees, in each dormant season cut off two-thirds of previous year's growth by removing two of every three branches formed that year; or head back each branch to one-third its length; or head back some and cut out others.

THINNING Even with good pruning, these trees form too much fruit. When fruits are 1 in. wide, remove enough fruit so that those that remain are 8–10 in. apart.

HARVESTING When peaches and nectarines are ripe, they will be fully colored and will pull easily off the tree with a gentle twist.

CHALLENGES Among the most serious diseases of peaches and nectarines are peach leaf curl and brown rot. Peach tree borers are troublesome pests.

Peach leaf curl. The fungus responsible for peach leaf curl causes emerging new leaves to thicken and pucker. Infected foliage may be tinged red, pink, yellow, or white; it usually falls in mid-summer. Severely infected trees are weakened and may stop producing.

Brown rot fungus. This disease causes flowers to wilt and decay, twigs to crack and ooze sap.

Controls. To control both diseases, practice good sanitation; get rid of diseased plant parts to keep fungus from reinfecting the tree the next year. To control these diseases as well as scale insects, spray trees thoroughly each fall after leaf drop with a mixture of liquid fungicide containing 8% metallic copper equivalent (MCE) and 1% horticultural spray oil.

Some gardeners reduce peach leaf curl by planting the trees under eaves and training them in a fan shape against a south-facing wall (dry leaves aren't susceptible to infection). Or grow resistant varieties such as 'Frost' or 'Q1-8'. Move potted genetic dwarf peaches and nectarines to a covered location in rainy weather.

Peach tree borer. This pest tends to attack trees stressed by poor growing conditions or wounds and causes defoliation, branch dieback, and possibly death. Jellylike matter exuding from the base of the tree is the first indication of the pest's presence. The insect holes will be evident at or just below ground level.

Controls. Prevention through good growing conditions is the best control; if a tree is attacked, consult your Cooperative Extension Office for the best treatment.

Peanut

Papilionaceae
ANNUAL

⚡ **ZONES 2–24**

☼ **FULL SUN**

💧 **REGULAR WATER**

Peanuts

The peanut originated in South America and bears best where summers are long and warm. It is tender to frost but worth growing even in cool regions. Plants resemble bush sweet peas (*Lathyrus*) 10–20 in. high. After the bright yellow flowers fade, a "peg" (shootlike structure) develops at each flower's base and grows down into soil; peanuts develop underground.

The four basic classes of peanuts are Virginia and Runner types, with two large seeds per pod; Spanish, with two or three small seeds per pod; and Valencia, with three to six small seeds per pod. Buy seeds (unroasted peanuts) from mail-order suppliers.

CARE

For best performance, plant in fertile, well-drained soil; sandy or other light-textured soil is ideal for penetration by pegs. In cool-summer areas, grow peanuts against a south-facing wall for maximum heat, as plants do best when soil temperature is 70°F to 80°F (21°C to 27°C). Plant as soon as soil has warmed in spring, setting seeds (with shells removed but skins intact) 1½–2 in. deep. Sow seeds of Virginia and Runner peanuts 6–8 in. apart; sow Spanish and Valencia peanuts 4–6 in. apart. Fertilize at planting time. In cool-summer areas, grow under floating row covers

to hasten growth. In 110 to 120 days after planting, foliage yellows and plants are ready to dig; loosen soil, then pull up plants. Let peanuts dry on vines in a warm, airy, shaded place for 2 to 3 weeks; then strip them from plants.

Pear, Asian

Rosaceae
DECIDUOUS FRUIT TREES

⚡ **ZONES 2–12, 14–21, EXCEPT AS NOTED**

☼ **FULL SUN**

💧 **REGULAR WATER**

'Hosui' Asian pears

These pears are descendants of two Asian species: *Pyrus pyrifolia* (*P. serotina*) and *P. ussuriensis*. Trees grow to 25–30 ft. tall and about half as wide, but they're easily kept to half that size with pruning. They are also available on a range of dwarfing and semidwarfing rootstocks. These are quite beautiful trees that would likely be grown as ornamentals even if they didn't bear fruit.

Unlike the more familiar European pears, Asian pears are generally round in shape, with a crisp, faintly gritty, firm to hard texture. Fresh Asian pears are excellent combined with other fruits and vegetables in salads. Fruit can be stored at room temperature for about 2 weeks or refrigerated for 2 to 3 months.

Asian pears need the same general culture as European pears but have a lower chilling requirement (some need as few as 400 hours) and a greater resistance to fireblight. All benefit from pollination by a second variety that flowers at the same time (consult your local nursery

P

for recommendations). European pears generally bloom too late to be reliable pollenizers for Asian pears. Asian pears should be thinned to one pear per fruiting spur and should be picked ripe. In California, harvest runs from mid-July through September; in Washington, it lasts from August through October. Following are some good choices for the West.

'Chojuro'. Large, russeted brown to orange fruit with crisp, juicy flesh and light spice flavor. Midseason.

'Hosui'. Large fruit with bronzy orange, russeted skin and outstanding flavor. Very susceptible to fireblight. Early midseason.

'Ichiban' ('Ichiban Nashi'). Medium to large, smooth, brown fruit with white flesh that has a slight butterscotch flavor. Handle with care to avoid injuring the fruit's skin. Productive; some tolerance for bacterial infection. Early.

'Kikusui'. Medium-size, flattish, yellow-green fruit with sweet, juicy flesh. Tends to drop fruit early. Fireblight-resistant. Midseason.

'Korean Giant'. Zones 1–12, 14–21. Extra-large, russeted, olive green fruit weighing up to a pound. Keeps in cool (but unrefrigerated) storage for months. Vigorous and cold-hardy. Late.

'Kosui'. Small to medium-size fruit with russeted skin and crisp, sweet, juicy flesh. Vigorous. Susceptible to bacterial infection in western Washington. Early midseason.

'Mishirasu'. Very large fruit with russeted skin and good, crisp flavor; some may weigh over a pound. Very productive. Late midseason.

'Nijisseki' ('Twentieth Century'). Small, round, yellow fruit with white, juicy, sweet, crisp flesh and excellent flavor. Stores well. Self-fruitful. Midseason.

'Seuri'. Small to medium, round fruit with orange-tinted skin and aromatic flesh. Very vigorous and productive; resists fireblight. Late midseason.

'Shinko'. Large round fruit with golden brown, russeted skin and sweet, juicy, crisp flesh. Flavor is best in hot climates. Upright growth habit; resists fireblight. Late midseason.

'Shinseiki'. Medium to large fruit with smooth, greenish yellow skin, white crisp flesh, and sweet flavor. Disease-resistant; self-fruitful. Can grow in low desert. Early midseason.

'Tsu Li'. Zones 1–12, 14–21. Elongated, yellow-green fruit; looks like a cross between a European pear and a football. Has aromatic flesh and good flavor that gets even better in storage. Vigorous, upright habit. Low chill requirement; some fireblight tolerance. Late.

'Ya Li'. Zones 1–12, 14–21. Greenish yellow, European pear–shaped fruit with crisp, mild, sweet flesh. Stores well, but fruit is easily marred. Vigorous tree. Late.

'Yoinashi'. Medium to large, brown-speckled pear with sweet, crisp flesh that has a hint of butterscotch flavor. Vigorous; resists bacterial infection. Late midseason.

Pear, European

Rosaceae
DECIDUOUS FRUIT TREES

✎ **ZONES VARY BY VARIETY**

☼ **FULL SUN**

💧 **REGULAR WATER**

» See chart on pages 485–486.

'Moonglow' pear

Pears are mostly descended from *Pyrus communis*, a European species. They are among the longest-lived fruit trees. Pyramidal in form, with strongly vertical branching, they grow 30–40 ft. tall and 15–25 ft. wide. Pears on dwarfing understocks range from one-half to three-fourths the size of standard-size trees; they make good small garden trees and even grow well in wine half-barrels. Pear trees make excellent espaliers. All types have leathery, glossy bright green leaves and bear handsome clusters of white flowers in early spring. Fruit is produced on knobby spurs that remain productive for up to 5 years.

To produce good crops, pears need winter chill: 600 hours below 45°F (7°C) is a minimum, and most do better still with 900 hours. In cold climates, their early bloom makes them prone to damage from spring frosts. Hybrids between European pears and the hardy *P. ussuriensis*, such as 'Ure', are worth trying in the coldest regions. Where winters are very mild, choose varieties needing little winter chill. Some low-chill types are Asian hybrids, crosses between European and Asian pears with fruit similar to that of European varieties. Most pears are not self-fruitful, so you'll need to plant two varieties to ensure pollination.

For ornamental relatives, see *Pyrus*.

The most trouble-free pear-growing regions are warm, dry areas of California and Oregon, where commercial orchards are located. But the trees are so lovely—and their fruit so delectable—that they're worth the extra effort elsewhere.

How to Grow European Pears

PLANTING Choose a sunny spot, and if there's a potential for late spring frosts in your garden, plant on a protected slope. These trees do best in well-drained loam, but they tolerate damp, heavy soil better than other fruit trees. Plant nursery-grown trees anytime except during extreme summer heat; bare-root stock should be planted in late winter or early spring. Space trees 8–25 ft. apart, depending on variety size.

FERTILIZING Feed with 1 lb. of 10-10-10 fertilizer per inch of trunk diameter every spring, keeping fertilizer 1 ft. away from the trunk.

HARVESTING Harvest season is July to late October, depending on variety. Pears do not ripen properly on the tree; pick them when full size but not yet ripe. The stem of a mature pear will snap free from the branch when you lift it to the horizontal. Fruit of most kinds should be stored in a cool, dark place (such as a shed, cellar, or garage); bring pears indoors to a warm room to ripen for 2 or 3 days before you plan to eat them. Exceptions are 'Anjou', 'Bosc', and 'Comice', which should be put in cold storage (32°F to 40°F/0°C to 4°C) for about a month after picking, then brought into a warm room for 2 or 3 days to ripen.

CHALLENGES Fireblight can be a serious problem for pears; in areas prone to the disease, the best strategy is to plant resistant varieties. Fireblight causes entire branches to die back quickly; as soon as you see blackened growth, cut it back to a growth bud or stem with green, healthy tissue, disinfecting pruning tools after each cut. To avoid profuse new growth, with resultant risk of fireblight, do not prune heavily in any one dormant season; also fertilize sparingly. Dormant oil sprays will control pear psylla and various other pests that may bother pear trees. Codling moth can ruin fruit; pheromone traps may be an effective control for a few trees in a home garden. Pear trees are resistant to oak root fungus.

P

PEAR, EUROPEAN: TOP PICKS TO GROW

NAME	ZONES	FRUIT	COMMENTS
'Anjou' ('d'Anjou', 'Beurre d'Anjou')	2, 3, 6–9	Medium to large fruit; may be round or have a short neck. Yellow to russeted yellow. Fine flavor. Ripens after cold storage. Late.	Upright, vigorous tree. Tie down limbs for more consistent bearing. Moderately susceptible to fireblight. 'Red d'Anjou' is a red-skinned form.
'Bartlett'	2–11, 14–18	Medium to large, with short but definite neck. Thin-skinned; yellow or slightly blushed. Very sweet and tender. Midseason.	Standard summer pear of fruit markets. Good home variety, though tree does not have the best form and is susceptible to fireblight. Generally self-fruitful but may need a pollenizer in cool California coastal areas and the Northwest; use 'Anjou', 'Bosc', 'Comice', or 'Moonglow'.
'Blake's Pride'	2–9, 14–18	Medium-size, bell-shaped fruit. Yellow to gold skin with light russeting. Fine, melting flavor. Midseason.	Excellent resistance to fireblight.
'Bosc' ('Beurre Bosc', 'Golden Russet')	2–9, 14–18	Medium to large; quite long neck, interesting and attractive in form. Heavy russeting on green or yellow skin. Fine flavor; firm, juicy flesh. Holds shape when cooked. Ripens after cold storage. Late.	Best in the Northwest and higher elevations farther south. Large, upright, vigorous tree. Needs pruning in youth. Highly susceptible to fireblight.
'Clapp's Favorite'	2–9, 14–18	Resembles 'Bartlett' but is more heavily blushed and matures 2 weeks earlier. Soft, sweet flesh. Early.	Best in the Northwest and intermountain areas. Productive, shapely tree; attractive foliage. Highly prone to fireblight. 'Bennett', popular in the Northwest, is a red-blushed strain, as is 'Red Clapp's Favorite'.
'Comice' ('Doyenne du Comice', 'Royal Riviera')	2–9, 14–18	Large to very large; roundish to pear-shaped. Thick, greenish yellow skin is russeted, sometimes blushed. Superb flavor and texture. Ripens after cold storage. Late.	Big, vigorous tree; slow to reach bearing age. Bears good crops when soil, climate, and exposure are right. Moderately susceptible to fireblight. Generally self-fruitful but does better in the Northwest with a pollenizer. 'Red Comice' is a red-skinned sport.
'Conference'	2–9, 14–18	Large, elongated fruit borne in clusters. Yellow skin. Very juicy, sweet flesh with buttery texture. Late.	Very productive. Good resistance to fireblight.
'Fan Stil'	2, 3, 7–12, 14–23	Medium-size, bell-shaped fruit. Yellow with slight red blush. Crisp, juicy; good fresh and cooked. Midseason.	Asian pear hybrid. Vigorous, upright growth. Consistently large crops. Needs little winter chill; tolerates heat. Highly resistant to fireblight.
'Flordahome'	2, 3, 7–23	Small to medium, with short pear shape. Light green fruit. Juicy flesh. Early.	Needs little winter chill. Resistant to fireblight. Pollinate with 'Hood'.
'Harrow Delight'	1b, 2–7	Resembles 'Bartlett' but is smaller. Smooth texture, very good flavor. Early.	Cold-hardy variety developed in Canada. Excellent resistance to fireblight.
'Hood'	2, 3, 7–24; H1	Large fruit with typical pear shape. Yellow-green skin. Ripens a little later than 'Flordahome'.	Vigorous tree. Needs very little winter chill. Resistant to fireblight. Pollinate with 'Flordahome'.
'Kieffer'	2, 3, 7–23	Medium to large, oval-shaped fruit. Greenish yellow skin blushed red. Gritty texture; fair flavor. Good for canning, baking. Late.	Asian pear hybrid. Low-chill variety. Good for hot or cold climates. Quite resistant to fireblight.
'Max-Red Bartlett'	2–11, 14–18	Resembles 'Bartlett' but has bright red skin and a somewhat sweeter flavor. Midseason.	Red color extends to twigs and tints leaves. Susceptible to fireblight. Bears better in the Northwest with a pollenizer; use any except 'Seckel'.
'Monterrey'	2, 3, 7–12, 14–23	Large, apple-shaped fruit. Yellow skin. Good flavor; texture not too gritty. Midseason.	Probably an Asian pear hybrid. Needs little winter chill. Very resistant to fireblight.
'Moonglow'	2, 3, 7–12, 14–23	Somewhat like 'Bartlett' in looks. Juicy, soft fruit with good flavor. Early.	Upright, vigorous tree; very heavy bearer. Highly resistant to fireblight.

P

»

PEAR, EUROPEAN: TOP PICKS TO GROW

NAME	ZONES	FRUIT	COMMENTS
'Orcas'	2–7, 14–17	Large, pear-shaped fruit with a pointier stem end than a typical pear. Yellow skin with red blush. Flavorful, melt-in-the-mouth flesh. Small core. Midseason.	Vigorous, spreading tree.
'Orient'	2–21	Large, bell-shaped fruit. Yellow skin with russeting. Firm, juicy, and somewhat sweet flesh; good for canning, baking. Late.	Asian pear hybrid. Heavy producer. Highly resistant to fireblight.
'Potomac'	2–4, 14–21	Medium-size, pear-shaped fruit. Light green skin with red blush. Flesh is buttery with fine, 'Anjou'-like flavor. Fruit keeps 8 to 10 weeks in the refrigerator. Midseason.	Tree is very productive, fireblight-resistant.
'Rescue'	2–7, 14–17	Large fruit with traditional pear shape. Yellow skin blushed red-orange. Sweet, juicy, and smooth-textured flesh. Good keeper. Midseason.	Vigorous, productive, upright tree. Northwest favorite.
'Seckel' ('Sugar')	2–11, 14–21	Very small; roundish to pear shaped. Yellow-brown skin. Granular, very sweet, aromatic flesh. A favorite for home gardens, preserving. Early midseason.	Highly productive. Fairly resistant to fireblight. Self-fruitful but bears more heavily with pollenizer (any except 'Bartlett' and its strains will do).
'Sensation Red Bartlett'	2–9, 14–18	Looks much like 'Bartlett', but skin is bright red over most of fruit. Midseason.	Medium-size tree, less vigorous than 'Bartlett'. Susceptible to fireblight.
'Summer Crisp'	A2, A3; 1–3	Small, roundish fruit. Red-blushed green skin. Crisp, mildly sweet flesh. Late.	Cold-hardy variety from Minnesota. Quite resistant to fireblight.
'Sure Crop'	2–9, 14–18	Resembles 'Bartlett' in looks and flavor. Late midseason.	Consistent annual bearer. Prolonged bloom makes it safe to grow where spring frosts come late. Fairly resistant to fireblight.
'Ure'	A2, A3; 1–3	Small, roundish fruit. Greenish yellow skin. Sweet and juicy. Good fresh or canned. Midseason.	Cold-hardy hybrid developed in Canada. Small tree, to 20 ft. tall, 12 ft. wide. Resistant to fireblight.
'Warren'	1b–9, 14–18	Medium to large fruit with teardrop shape. Pale green skin, often with a red blush. Buttery, juicy flesh with excellent flavor. Good keeper. Late.	Cold-hardy tree. Extremely resistant to fireblight.
'Winter Nelis'	2, 3, 7–9, 14–18	Small to medium, roundish fruit. Rough, dull green or yellowish skin. Not particularly attractive but has a very fine flavor. Very good keeper; fine for baking. Late.	Moderately susceptible to fireblight.

'Anjou'

'Bosc'

'Comice'

'Max-Red Bartlett'

Pecan

Juglandaceae
DECIDUOUS TREE

- ⚡ **ZONES 2 AND 3 (WARMER PARTS), 6–10, 12–14, 18–20**
- ☼ **FULL SUN**
- ◑ **REGULAR WATER**

Pecans

Native to the south-central U.S. *Carya illinoinensis* is a graceful, shapely tree to 70 ft. tall and wide; it's too large for small gardens but attractive where space is available. Leaves are divided into many leaflets, producing a fine texture that casts light shade. Inconspicuous flowers are followed by nuts enclosed in husks. Pecan trees resist oak root fungus.

Best nut production is in areas with long, hot summers (Zones 8–10, 12–14, 18–20); crops in other recommended zones are less certain but possible.

Most pecans set light crops without cross-pollination. For a good-size crop, plant a type 1 variety near a type 2 variety. The best selections include 'Burkett' (type 2), 'Mohawk' (type 2), 'Western Schley' (type 1), and 'Wichita' (type 2). Early-ripening 'Pawnee' (type 1) is the best choice for areas that normally don't have warm summer temperatures over a long enough time for pecans to ripen (Zones 6 and 7 and the warmer parts of Zones 2 and 3).

Other early-ripening varieties that may succeed in these short-season areas include 'Kanza' and 'Shoshoni' (both type 2). Note that pecans tend to be alternate bearers, with a heavy crop one year followed by a light crop the next.

How to Grow Pecans

PLANTING Pecan trees need well-drained soil loosened to a depth of 6–10 ft.; they will not grow well in saline soil. Set out bare-root trees in winter. Dig a planting hole deep enough to accommodate the long taproot; position the bud union above soil level. Firm soil around roots, then water thoroughly.

WATERING Don't let soil dry out.

FERTILIZING These trees need a lot of zinc. Spray it on three to five times each spring (more in drier climates). Young trees should be sprayed every 2 weeks from mid-April through July. If tree growth is healthy, there's no need to do more. If not, apply a complete high-nitrogen fertilizer just before leaf-out and again in May.

HARVESTING Harvest when nuts fall in autumn; you can shake or beat the branches to hasten drop. Remove husks right away. Leave the nuts in a dry, moderately warm place for several days until pecans are crisp. Store them in sealed containers or freezer bags.

CHALLENGES Prevent pecan rosette (abnormal clumps of twigs caused by zinc deficiency) by spraying zinc sulfate on expanding leaves in spring. Because pecan trees are prone to aphid infestations (and resulting sticky honeydew droppings), don't plant a tree where it will overarch a parking area or patio. Instead, plant in a place (such as near a lawn), where honeydew droppings won't be a problem.

Although there is treatment, pecan trees grow so large that you would need a professional arborist with spray gear to reach infested areas.

Pedilanthus

Euphorbiaceae
DECIDUOUS AND EVERGREEN SHRUBS

- ⚡ **ZONES VARY BY SPECIES**
- ☼ ◐ **EXPOSURE NEEDS VARY BY SPECIES**
- ◌ **LITTLE WATER, EXCEPT AS NOTED**
- ✴ **MILKY SAP CAN CAUSE STOMACH UPSET**

Pedilanthus tithymaloides smallii 'Variegatus'

All of these odd-looking plants have decorative stems, but those of *P. macrocarpus* are bare most of the year. Inconspicuous red flowers concealed in tubular or slipper-shaped red bracts. Some botanists consider *Pedilanthus* to be a part of the genus *Euphorbia*.

P. bracteatus. SLIPPER PLANT. Evergreen. Zones 12, 13, 19–24. From Mexico. Grows 6–8 ft. tall and half as wide, with upright, thick, waxy, slightly undulating stems sparsely set with oval, pointed leaves to 4 in. long. In late spring or early summer, rosy pink bracts appear near the branch tips. Full sun. No irrigation needed.

P. macrocarpus. LADY'S SLIPPER. Deciduous. Zones 12, 13, 19–24. Native to Mexico. Grows to 5 ft. tall, and 2–3 ft. wide, with small, scanty leaves that drop soon after they emerge. The fleshy, waxy, whitish, forking, half-inch-thick stems are the main feature. Bears 1-in. bracts in late spring; may repeat in summer after rainfall. Tolerates light shade, but has best form in full sun.

P. tithymaloides smallii '**Variegatus**'. DEVIL'S BACK-BONE, JACOB'S LADDER. Evergreen. Zone H2; or indoors. Caribbean native to 1–2 ft. tall,

with somewhat fleshy, zigzag-ging stems and 2–3-in., oval mid-green leaves. Has grayish stems and leaves marked with white and pink; it is fairly common as a houseplant. Under good growing conditions, may produce ½-in. bracts in summer. Partial shade. Give house-plants bright indirect light; fertilize every couple of months during warm months, and keep soil barely moist.

Pelargonium

GERANIUM
Geraniaceae
SHRUBBY PERENNIALS

- ⚡ **ZONES 8, 9, 12–24; A2, A3, 1–7, 10, 11 AS ANNUALS; OR INDOORS**
- ☼ ◐ **SOME SHADE IN HOTTEST CLIMATES**
- ◔◑ **MODERATE TO REGULAR WATER**
- ✷ **ATTRACT BIRDS**

Pelargonium × *hortorum*

The common name "geranium" has long been used for plants in this genus, but botanically speaking, it is not really accurate. True geraniums are annuals and perennials (some woody based), native mainly to the Northern Hemisphere; they typically have delicate stems and leaves, and their symmetrical flowers may be held singly or in clusters. Pelargoniums, on the other hand, are frost-tender, woody-based perennials (most of them native to South Africa) that have relatively thick, often succulent stems and leaves; their slightly asymmetrical flowers are held in clusters.

Pelargoniums perform best in areas with warm, dry days and cool nights. They can be grown outdoors year-round where winters are very mild; in these

CLOCKWISE FROM LEFT: *Pelargonium × fragrans* 'Nutmeg'; lemon-scented geranium; *P. peltatum* 'Black Magic'

P

areas, they bloom throughout warm weather. Zones 17 and 24 are ideal climates; next best are Zones 15, 16, 22, 23; possible but not as easy are Zones 8, 9, 12–14, 18–21. Elsewhere, they are summer annuals or houseplants. In cold-winter climates, move plants indoors before the first frost or take cuttings for next year.

All types do well in containers; they bloom best when somewhat pot-bound.

P. cordifolium (P. cordatum). Rounded plant to 4 ft. tall and wide, with 2½-in. heart-shaped leaves. Loose clusters of exotic-looking, reddish purple, 1-in. flowers. Good border plants.

P. × domesticum. LADY WASHINGTON PELARGONIUM, MARTHA WASHINGTON PELARGONIUM, REGAL GERANIUM. Erect or somewhat spreading, to 3 ft. high and wide. More open growing than *P. × hortorum.* Heart-shaped to kidney-shaped leaves are dark green, 2–4 in. wide, with crinkled, toothed margins. Loose, rounded clusters of large (to 3½ in.), showy flowers; colors include white and many shades of pink, red, lavender, and purple, with brilliant blotches and markings of darker colors. Can be planted in beds but tends to get rangy. First-class container plant; some well suited for use in hanging baskets. Many named varieties available.

P. × hortorum. COMMON GERANIUM, GARDEN GERANIUM. Succulent stemmed; reaches 1–2 ft. high and wide as an annual. In mild climates where they grow as perennials, older plants become woody and can top 3 ft. Round or kidney-shaped leaves are velvety, hairy, and aromatic, with edges indistinctly lobed and scalloped. Most varieties show a zone of deeper color that looks like a thick halo around the center of the leaf, though some have plain green foliage. Single or double flowers are flatter and smaller than those of *P. × domesticum*, but clusters bear many more blossoms. Varieties are sold in white and shades of pink, rose, red, orange, lavender-blue, and violet. Flowers may be solid-colored, bicolored, speckled, or splashed with contrasting colors. There are also cactus-flowered, dwarf, and other novelty varieties.

Zonal geraniums are a type of common geranium, usually propagated from cuttings. These plants are uniform, well branched, heat-resistant, and available in many colors. Look for vigorous series such as Americana, Daredevil, Eclipse, and Rocky Mountain; each comes in a wide range of colors. There are also numerous zonal novelties on the market, including ones with speckled petals and ones with single or double star-shaped flowers.

Fancy-leafed varieties have zones, borders, or splashes of brown, deep purple, gold, red, white, and green in various combinations. Some also have highly attractive flowers. A good example is the Black Velvet series, which sports purplish black leaves edged in bright green, with large single- or multicolored blooms.

P. peltatum. IVY GERANIUM. To 1–1½ ft. high, trailing to 3–5 ft. wide. Rather succulent, glossy, bright green, 2–3-in.-wide leaves have pointed lobes and look something like those of ivy (*Hedera*). Inch-wide single or double flowers in rounded clusters of 5 to 10; colors include white, pink, rose, red, and lavender. Upper petals may be blotched or striped. Many named varieties. The Freestyle series has a semitrailing habit and comes in a wide range of colors, including bicolors. 'L'Élégante' has white-edged foliage; other varieties are available with white or yellow veins in leaves. Summer Showers strain can be grown from seed, features blossoms in mixed colors (white, pink, red, lavender, and magenta).

Crosses between zonal and ivy geraniums combine the heat resistance, better branching, and heavier flowering of zonal geraniums with the glossy leaves and mounding, trailing habit of ivy geraniums. The Galleria series led the way, and the new Caliente series has developed it further; flowers of both series come primarily in the red, coral, and pink color range.

Use ivy geranium in hanging containers, window boxes, or raised beds; it also makes a good bank or groundcover (but not for erosion control). Because it does especially well with cool nights and bright days, ivy geranium is favored along the coast and in mountain gardens.

P. sidoides. Grows slowly into a dense mound 1 ft. high and wide, with silvery gray, heart-shaped leaves to 1½ in. across. Clusters of dark purple, ¾-in. flowers bloom on slender, branching, trailing stems.

P. 'Splendide'. Grows slowly to 1–1½ ft. high and wide, with spreading or stiffly trailing stems. Silvery gray, 1–1½-in.-long, oval leaves have slightly toothed edges. Distinctive blossoms, carried a few to a cluster, are 1–1¼ in. wide, have unusual coloring: the two upper petals are dark red, nearly black at the base, while the three lower ones are nearly white. Use in containers or hanging baskets.

Scented geraniums. Many aromatic species, hybrids, and selections are available. Most grow 1–3 ft. high, spreading as wide as high. Foliage scent is the main draw; clusters of small, typically white or rosy flowers are secondary in appeal. Leaves vary in shape from nearly round to finely cut and almost ferny; they range in size from minute to 4 in. across.

Common names usually refer to the fragrance of their leaves: almond geranium (*P. quercifolium*), apple geranium (*P. odoratissimum*), lime geranium (*P.* 'Nervosum'), nutmeg geranium (*P. × fragrans* 'Nutmeg'), peppermint geranium (*P. tomentosum*). There are several rose geraniums, including *P.* 'Attar of Roses', *P. capitatum*, *P.* 'Charity', *P. graveolens*, and *P.* 'Lady Plymouth'. Various types offer lemon fragrance, including *P. crispum* and *P.* 'Mabel Grey'.

CARE

Plant in any good, fast-draining soil. Amend soil with plenty of organic matter. Geraniums growing in good garden soil need little fertilizer; those in light sandy soil should receive two or three feedings during active growth. Remove faded flowers regularly to encourage new bloom. Pinch growing tips of young, small plants to force side branches.

Common pests include aphids, whiteflies, and spider mites. Geranium (tobacco) budworm may be a problem in some areas; affected flowers look tattered or fail to open at all. Prevent or limit infestation by spraying plants with *Bacillus thuringiensis* (*Bt*).

Scented geraniums make pretty additions to herb gardens and borders. Try peppermint geranium as a groundcover in mild climates. Or train it up a small trellis near your entry where it will perfume the air. Use fresh leaves of all types for flavoring jelly and iced drinks.

Pellaea
CLIFF-BRAKE
Pteridaceae
FERNS

ZONES VARY BY SPECIES

FILTERED SUNLIGHT

WATER NEEDS VARY BY SPECIES

Pellaea rotundifolia

Though these small to medium-size ferns are not striking in overall appearance, they have charmingly detailed foliage, with leaves divided into little narrow to roundish leaflets. They tolerate drier conditions than most other ferns do. All need well-drained soil.

P. andromedifolia. COFFEE FERN. Zones 7–9, 14–24. Native to dry, stony places in California, southern Oregon, and Baja California. Grows slowly to 2 ft. high and wide. Thin, wiry stalks hold finely cut gray-green to bluish green fronds. Common name refers to the small leaflets, shaped somewhat like coffee beans. Grow in bright filtered light. Use in native landscapes or rock gardens. Water regularly for the first year; needs little water thereafter.

P. atropurpurea. PURPLE STEM CLIFF-BRAKE. Zones 2–7, 14–17. Very cold-tolerant fern native from northeastern U.S. south to Guatemala. Grows 1–2 ft. high and wide, with arching fronds. Oblong to lance-shaped, bluish gray leaflets are held on purplish black midribs. Best in bright shade and alkaline soil. Use in rock gardens. Needs little water once established.

P. rotundifolia. BUTTON FERN. Zones 14–17, 19–24. From Australia, New Zealand.

Grows 1–2 ft. high, 2 ft. wide. Spreading stalks hold small, evenly spaced, rounded leaflets that are dark green and leathery. Use for contrast with finer-textured ferns or in mixed container plantings, where fronds will spill attractively over the sides. Regular water.

P. viridis. GREEN CLIFF-BRAKE. Zones 14–17, 19–24; H2. Native from Africa to India. Grows about 1 ft. high and wide, with shiny, bright green fronds. Oval to lance-shaped leaflets are held on glossy black stems. Thrives with regular water but will tolerate short periods of drought. Use as groundcover, in rock gardens, or in containers.

Peltiphyllum peltatum. See *Darmera peltata*

Pennisetum
FOUNTAIN GRASS
Poaceae
ANNUAL AND PERENNIAL GRASSES

ZONES VARY BY SPECIES

FULL SUN OR PARTIAL SHADE, EXCEPT AS NOTED

MODERATE TO REGULAR WATER, EXCEPT AS NOTED

Pennisetum orientale

Growing in lush, fountainlike mounds, these are among the most graceful of ornamental grasses. They have long, narrow leaves and bear arching stems of furry, foxtail-like flower plumes in summer, with bloom often extending into fall. Use them in containers, in perennial or shrub borders, as bank covers.

P. alopecuroides. Perennial. Zones 2b–24. From eastern Asia. To 5 ft. tall and wide. Clump of bright green foliage is

topped by pinkish plumes. Leaves turn yellow in fall, brown in winter. The following reach about 3 ft. high and wide: 'Cassian's Choice' ('Cassian'), with light brown plumes and golden, red-tinted fall foliage; 'Hameln', with white plumes; 'Moudry', with black plumes; and 'Red Head', with a more erect habit and reddish purple plumes. 'Little Bunny' is a dwarf form growing just 1½ ft. high and wide. The species and its varieties all can self-sow in moist conditions; 'Moudry' is an especially heavy self-seeder.

P. 'Fairy Tails'. Perennial in Zones 8, 9, 14–24; annual elsewhere. Hybrid of uncertain parentage. Evergreen where temperatures remain above 28°F (–2°C). Grows 3–4 ft. tall and wide, with arching, narrow, blue-green leaves. Distinctly vertical, dark wheat–colored plumes appear above them from spring to summer. Plant in full sun. Reaches full size with regular water; grows smaller (but still attractive) under drier conditions.

P. glaucum 'Purple Majesty'. PURPLE MAJESTY ORNAMENTAL MILLET. Annual. Developed from a millet species from Asia and Africa that has long been cultivated for its edible seeds. Striking plant to 6 ft. tall and 3 ft. wide, with huge, spear-shaped leaves up to 3 ft. long. Foliage is rich purple, darkest in full sun. Stiff, cylindrical, purple flower spikes up to 20 in. long appear atop foliage in midsummer. Cut bloom spikes before they mature and use them in dried arrangements, or leave them to reach maturity on the plant, where they'll attract birds. Easy to start from seed. Best in full sun with regular water.

P. macrostachyum 'Burgundy Giant'. Perennial in frost-free zones 23, 24; H1, H2; grow as annual elsewhere. Variant of a species from the East Indies. This bold, tropical-looking, very tender grass resembles a reddish purple corn plant. Grows to 4–5 ft. tall and 2 ft. across, with foot-long leaves that are broader than those of most other fountain grasses (nearly 1½ in. wide). Foliage is held on strong, upright burgundy stems. Red-purple flower plumes up to

P

1 ft. long appear on nodding stems above the foliage in mid-summer; fade to cream in fall. Needs full sun, regular water.

P. massaicum 'Red Bunny Tails'. Perennial in Zones 4–12, 14–24; annual elsewhere. Selection of an African species. Upright growth to about 2 ft. high and wide; very narrow, glossy green leaves have burgundy highlights. In spring and summer, foliage is topped by delicate, fuzzy, iridescent red flower plumes that fade to tan. Erect bloom spikes bring plant height to about 3 ft. Takes heat and drought but looks best with regular water. Good choice for meadows; tolerates coastal conditions.

P. orientale. Perennial. Zones 3–10, 14–24. From central and western Asia. Dependable grower to 2 ft. high, 2½ ft. wide, with pinkish plumes standing above a mound of green to gray-green foliage. Plumes mature to light brown; foliage turns straw-colored in winter. Seldom self-sows. Two recommended selections grow taller: 'Karley Rose', to 4 ft., has an upright form with dark green foliage and deep pink plumes. 'Tall Tails', to 6 ft. tall, 3–4 ft. wide, is more open growing, with light tan plumes; tolerates desert heat as well as coastal conditions.

P. setaceum. Perennial in Zones 8–24; H1, H2; often grown as an annual in colder climates. From tropical Africa, southwestern Asia, and the Arabian peninsula. To 5 ft. tall and wide. Forms a dense clump of medium green foliage; long plumes of coppery pink or purplish flowers are held within the clump or just above it. Dies back in winter, even in mild climates. Full sun. Can take supplemental irrigation but doesn't need any.

Thanks to heavy self-sowing, this species will threaten to crowd out native vegetation when planted near open country; it has become a rampant pest in the Hawaiian Islands. To prevent seeding, cut off flower plumes before seeds mature. The following colored-leaf forms usually do not set seed. 'Rubrum' (*P. advena* 'Rubrum'), called purple or red fountain grass, has purplish red leaves and rose-colored plumes that fade to beige. 'Eaton Canyon' ('Red Riding Hood', *P. advena* 'Eaton Canyon') is similar in color but grows just 1½–2 ft. high and wide; it is evergreen in frost-free areas. The stunning 'Fireworks' also has purplish red leaves, but with margins broadly edged in bright pink; grows to 2–3 ft. high and 1½–2 ft. wide.

P. villosum. FEATHERTOP. Perennial usually used as an annual. From Africa. Thin, cascading, medium green leaves form a mound about 3 ft. high and wide. Foliage is topped in summer by soft, feathery, creamy white plumes that look great in fresh or dried arrangements. Easy to start from seed. Self-sows readily and may become invasive in frost-free zones. Best in full sun with regular water.

Cutting the Grass— for the Vase

Fountain grasses have sturdy stems and full, fluffy blooms that are especially nice for adding interest to fresh arrangements. Cut flowering stems early in the bloom cycle—if you wait until they're fully expanded, they may shatter after just a day or two. As long as you're cutting, snip a few fresh leaves too.

Other top picks for fresh-cut grass flowers are feather reed grass (*Calamagrostis* × *acutiflora*), love grass (*Eragrostis*), natal ruby grass (*Melinis nerviglumis*), Japanese silver grass (*Miscanthus sinensis*), and switch grass (*Panicum virgatum*).

Penstemon
BEARD TONGUE
Plantaginaceae
PERENNIALS

✏ **ZONES VARY BY SPECIES**

☼ ◐ **PARTIAL SHADE IN HOTTEST CLIMATES**

◐ ◑ **LITTLE TO MODERATE WATER, EXCEPT AS NOTED**

🦋 **ATTRACT BUTTERFLIES; FLOWERS OF SOME SPECIES ATTRACT HUMMINGBIRDS**

Penstemon 'Laura'

Most of the approximately 250 species of penstemon are native to the West, ranging from Canada into Mexico. Some grow on highest mountains, some in the desert, others in forest glades, in foothills, on plains. A few are widely available, but most are sold only by specialists. Most species have narrowish, pointed leaves; those in basal foliage clump are larger, those on flower stems smaller. Narrowly bell-shaped, lipped flowers (usually ¾–1½ in. long) are most commonly seen in bright reds and blues, but they also come in shades from soft pink through salmon and peach to deep rose, lilac, dark purple, white, and, rarely, yellow.

All penstemons, but especially the wild species, need fast-draining soil. Plants are fairly short-lived (3 or 4 years). Hybrids and selections tend to be easier to grow than wild species alongside regular garden plants; wild kinds may die quickly if given too-rich soil and too much water. In dry years or with restricted water, however, plants of wild species may thrive.

P. alamosensis. Zones 3, 7–13, 18, 19. Native to southern New Mexico. Herbaceous growth to 2–3 ft. high and 1 ft. wide. Beautiful silver-gray, wavy-edged basal foliage. Coral flowers bloom in late spring for an extended period, often visited by hummingbirds.

P. ambiguus. PRAIRIE PENSTEMON, SAND PENSTEMON. Zones 2, 3, 7–15, 18–21. Native to south-central and southwestern U.S. Woody-based, shrublike growth 2–3 ft. high and wide. Grayish green, very narrow leaves. White to pink flowers come in broad (rather than tall) clusters that resemble those of phlox. Blooms from early summer to early fall. Needs heat and sandy soil to perform well. Spreads by underground stems where well adapted.

P. baccharifolius. ROCK PENSTEMON. Zones 10–13. Native to southwestern Texas. Woody-based growth to 1½ ft. high and wide. Small, broad, glossy dark green leaves have a thick, leathery feel. Coral pink flowers bloom all summer; very attractive to hummingbirds.

P. barbatus. SCARLET BUGLER. Zones 1–20; needs some winter chill for best performance. Native to mountain regions from Colorado and Utah south to Mexico. Open, somewhat sprawling habit to 3 ft. or higher, 1½ ft. wide. Bright green foliage. Long, loose spikes of red flowers over a long period, starting in late spring or mid-summer. One of the best penstemons for humid-summer areas. Look for foot-tall hybrid 'Elfin Pink', with clear pink flowers; 2½-ft. hybrid 'Rose Elf', with deep rose blooms; and 2-ft. variety 'Schooley's Yellow', with soft lemon yellow flowers.

P. cardinalis. Zones 2, 3, 7–24. Native to southern New Mexico and Texas. Leafy habit to 2½ ft. high, 2 ft. wide. Large, leathery, dark green foliage. Dark red flowers bloom all summer; very popular with hummingbirds. Long-lived, adaptable plant that thrives even in areas with humid summers.

P. centranthifolius. SCARLET BUGLER. Zones 7–23. Native to Coast Ranges of California. To 2–3 ft. high, 1½–2 ft. wide, with waxy gray leaves that vary from lance-shaped to oval. Long spikes of narrow bright red flowers in spring or early summer; attractive to hummingbirds.

LEFT COLUMN: *Penstemon pinifolius;*
P. 'Dark Towers'. MIDDLE: *P. hetero-*
phyllus 'Margarita BOP'. RIGHT
COLUMN: *P.* hybrid; *P. eatonii*

P. clutei. SUNSET PENSTE-
MON. Zones 2, 3, 7–14, 18–
21. Native to Sunset Crater in
northern Arizona. Grows to 2–
3½ ft. high and 2 ft. wide.
Toothed, luminescent blue-gray
foliage makes a nice contrast
with pink flowers that bloom
from late spring through much
of the summer, frequented by
hummingbirds. Excellent performer in the interior West. May
self-sow.

P. cobaea. WILD FOXGLOVE,
WILD SNAPDRAGON. Zones
2–11, 14–24. Native from
Nebraska through the southern
Great Plains to Texas. Herbaceous stems rise 1–2 ft. high;
plant spreads to 1 ft. wide. Foliage is bold, profuse, and dark
green. Flowers to 2 in. long, the
largest of the penstemon clan,
appear in late spring or summer
in shades of white, pink, lavender, or purple. Long-lived plant.
Regular water. Prairie Splendor
is a hybrid seed strain with
P. triflorus that includes rose
and burgundy flower colors.

P. cordifolius. See *Keckiella cordifolia.*

P. 'Dark Towers'. Zones
1–11, 14–24. Hybrid of complex parentage. Sturdy, upright
grower to 2½ ft. high and 3 ft.
wide, with glossy, deep burgundy
leaves that retain their color all
season. Soft pink blooms are
held high in summer. Tolerates
heat, cold, and high humidity.

P. davidsonii. Zones 1–7,
14, 15. Native to high mountains
of Sierra Nevada and western
Nevada, north to British Columbia. Forms a mat 4–8 in. high,
1½ ft. wide. Small dark green
leaves; violet-blue flowers in midsummer. Prefers snow cover in
winter; without it, hardy only to
about –10°F (–23°C). Regular
water.

P. digitalis. Zones 1–9, 14–
24. Native to eastern and central U.S. To 3–5 ft. tall, 2–3 ft.
wide, with long, medium green
leaves and clusters of white or
pale pink flowers in summer.
Tolerates heat and humidity.
Regular water. Popular 'Husker
Red' grows to 2½–3 ft. high
and has maroon foliage and
pinkish white flowers.

P. eatonii. FIRECRACKER
PENSTEMON. Zones 1–3, 7–13,
18–21. Native to mountains of
desert Southwest. This scarlet-
flowered species is similar to
P. centranthifolius. Grows 1–3 ft.
high and wide and has lance-
shaped, leathery green leaves,
sometimes with a whitish bloom
(but without a waxy coating).
Flowers appear on tall spikes in
spring to early summer. Adaptable and heat-tolerant.

P. grandiflorus. SHELL-
LEAF PENSTEMON, WILD SNAP-
DRAGON. Zones 1–3, 10.
Native to the Great Plains. To
3½ ft. high, 10 in. wide, with
waxy, rounded, pale gray-green
leaves. Large (to 1 ¾ in.) pink
to lavender-blue flowers in summer. 'Prairie Snow' has pure
white blooms. Prairie Jewel is a
silvery-leafed seed strain 1½–
3 ft. high, bearing flowers in colors ranging from white through
rosy pink to lavender and deep
purple. War Axe is a deeper-
colored seed strain hybridized
with a species from the south-
central U.S. The species and
its various forms are excellent
plants for Rocky Mountain and
Great Plains states.

P. heterophyllus. FOOT-
HILL PENSTEMON. Zones 7–24.
California native of variable
appearance, with glossy bluish
green foliage and crowded
spikes of narrow blossoms
ranging from reddish purple to
deep blue. Blooms in spring
and early summer; attracts
bees. 'Catherine de la Mare'
grows 1–1½ ft. high and twice
as wide, with bright purple-blue
blooms. Dependable and long-
blooming 'Margarita BOP' grows
1½–2 ft. high and 2–3 ft. wide,
with sky blue flowers that fade
to purple. *P. h. purdyi* has darker
green foliage than the species
and rosy lavender to intense
blue flowers.

P. hybrids. BORDER PEN-
STEMON, GARDEN PENSTEMON.
Perennials in Zones 6–9, 14–24;
treated as annuals elsewhere
(grow as winter annual in Zones
12, 13). All are compact, bushy,
upright plants to 2–4 ft. tall and
3 ft. wide, with narrow green
leaves. Large (to 2 in.) summer
flowers in loose spikes at stem
ends, in almost all colors but
blue and yellow. Mass these
plants in borders or group with
other summer-flowering plants.
Where they are grown as perennials, set out nursery transplants in fall for bloom in late
spring and early summer. After

P

Penstemon and Friends

Penstemons are among the most celebrated of all the wildflowers in the West. Favored for their colorful spring flowers and tough nature, they thrive in heat and poor soil—most do so on little water. Bees, butterflies, and hummingbirds love their tubular, nectar-rich blossoms. Try *Penstemon eatonii* (red-orange blooms) with grasses such as *Festuca californica*; *P. pseudospectabilis* (magenta) with blue catmint (*Nepeta × fassenii*); or *P. spectabilis* (blue) beside yellow yarrow. Other good companions: *Artemisia*, flax (*Linum*), poppies, and salvias.

the flowers fade, cut back to side growth for another round of bloom in late summer, early fall. This group of penstemons prefers regular water but is subject to root rot in wet, heavy soils.

'Alice Hindley'. Shiny foliage and pale lilac blooms with white throats.

'Apple Blossom'. Pink flowers with white throats.

'Blackbird'. Dark maroon blooms held on deep red stems.

'Evelyn'. Soft rosy pink blooms on a fine-leafed, bushy plant.

'Firebird' ('Schoenholzeri'). Scarlet flowers on a vigorous, heavy-blooming plant.

'Garnet' ('Andenken an Friedrich Hahn'). Fine-leafed plant with wine red blooms. Long-lived and floriferous.

'Hidcote Pink'. Heavy producer of coral pink flowers with a white, maroon-streaked throat.

Kissed series. These large-flowered selections have white-throated blooms with lips in bright colors: 'Cerise Kissed', 'Coral Kissed', 'Violet Kissed', 'Wine Kissed'.

'Midnight'. Vigorous, bushy plant with deep green leaves and dark bluish purple blooms.

'Sour Grapes'. The true variety has flowers in a combination of violet and metallic blue, but some plants sold under this name may have bright red-violet blooms.

P. mensarum. GRAND MESA PENSTEMON. Zones 2, 3, 10. Native to western Colorado. Herbaceous stems 2–3 ft. high and 1–1½ ft. wide. Dark green basal foliage. In spring, the plant bears the most fiercely brilliant dark blue flowers of the cultivated penstemons.

Excellent performer in mountain regions. Tolerates considerable shade and thrives with moderate watering.

P. Mexicali hybrids. Zones 1–3, 10. Bushy growth to 1½ ft. high and wide, with profuse, narrow, shiny green leaves. Blossoms of 'Pike's Peak Purple' are violet, those of 'Red Rocks' bright rose. Burgundy and pink forms are also available. Highly recommended for Rocky Mountain and Great Plains states; they rival the border penstemons for showiness of leaf and flower, yet are much hardier to cold. Bloom all summer. Do well with moderate water but tolerate regular moisture.

P. palmeri. SCENTED PENSTEMON. Zones 2, 3, 10–13. Native to mountains of desert Southwest. To 4–6 ft. tall and 2–3 ft. wide, with thick, grayish blue leaves. This is among the few scented penstemons, with flower stalks bearing fragrant light pink blossoms in early summer. Will bloom first year from seed. Thrives in hot, dry conditions. Sandy or gravelly soil is essential.

P. parryi. PARRY'S PENSTEMON. Zones 3, 10, 12, 13. Native from Arizona into Mexico. To 2–4 ft. tall and 1–3 ft. wide, with leathery gray-green leaves. Many flower stalks bear reddish pink blossoms in spring. Self-sows.

P. pinifolius. Zones 1–24. Native to southern New Mexico and Arizona. Woody-based growth to 1½ ft. high, 2 ft. wide, with short, needlelike bright green leaves crowded along stems. Red-orange summer

flowers. For rock garden, border, or small-scale groundcover. Good in dry gardens or regularly watered ones. 'Mersea Yellow', to 1 ft. by 1½ ft., has soft yellow flowers. 'Shades of Mango', about 15 in. high and wide, has orange and yellow flowers on the same plant.

P. pseudospectabilis. DESERT BEARD TONGUE. Zones 2, 3, 10, 12–21. Native to the mountains of Southern California and Arizona. Shrubby, upright plant 2–4 ft. tall, 2 ft. wide. Large bluish green leaves with bases that clasp the stems. Rosy pink to purple flowers from spring into summer. Long-lived and easy to grow.

P. richardsonii. Zones 2–10, 14–21. Native to the Pacific Northwest. Woody grower 1–1½ ft. high and wide, with toothed, blue-green foliage. Rose, pink, lavender, or white flowers bloom in late summer for an extended period. Grows well in many climates. Tolerates some shade and may self-sow.

P. rostriflorus. Zones 3, 7, 10–13, 18–24. Southwestern native. Woody-based plant 1½ ft. high and wide, with narrow, olive green foliage. Orange-red flowers bloom midsummer into fall, attracting hummingbirds. Long-lived in loose soils.

P. rupicola. ROCK PENSTEMON. Zones 2–7, 14–17. Native to the Cascades and Siskiyou Mountains. Woody-based growth to 4 in. high, 1½ ft. wide, with trailing, much-branched stems. Small, roundish blue-green leaves have finely toothed edges. Bright rose flowers bloom from late spring into summer. Beautiful in rock gardens or chinks in dry stone walls. White-flowered 'Albus' needs partial shade for best bloom.

P. spectabilis. ROYAL BEARD TONGUE. Zones 7, 14–23. Native to Southern California. To 3–4½ ft. tall and wide, with smooth green or grayish leaves that clasp the stems. Rose-colored to purplish flowers in spring, early summer.

P. strictus. ROCKY MOUNTAIN PENSTEMON. Zones 1–3, 10–13. Native from southern Wyoming to Arizona and New Mexico. To 2–3 ft. high, 2 ft. wide. Dark green leaves turn purplish in winter. Blooms in early summer, producing large

blossoms in near-violet to brilliant bluish purple. Long-lived and adaptable. Attracts beneficial insects.

P. superbus. Zones 12, 13. Native to northern Mexico. To 3–4 ft. tall and wide; gray-green leaves that blacken when they dry out. Deep rose to red flowers in spring or early summer.

P. triflorus. HILL COUNTRY PENSTEMON. Zones 3, 7–9, 10–14. Native to central Texas. Herbaceous plant 1½–2 ft. high and 1–1½ ft. wide, with rich green foliage. Pink, rose, or white flowers bloom in spring. Long-lived and adaptable, performing well in the Southwest and also in more humid areas.

Pentas lanceolata
STAR CLUSTERS
Rubiaceae
PERENNIAL OFTEN GROWN AS ANNUAL

⚹ **ZONES 23, 24; H1, H2; ANYWHERE AS ANNUAL**

☼ **FULL SUN**

🌢 **REGULAR WATER**

Pentas lanceolata

Lush-looking perennial from tropical Africa. In Hawaii, it grows as large as 6 ft. tall, 3 ft. wide; elsewhere, it reaches 2–3 ft. high and wide. Stems are topped by tight, 4-in.-wide clusters of small, star-shaped flowers in white, pink, lilac, or red. As a perennial, it provides nearly year-round color; as an annual, it blooms in summer. Good cut flowers. Green, somewhat hairy leaves are pointed ovals to 6 in. long. Where perennial, prune plant heavily each year before spring growth begins, to keep it compact and encourage flowering. Deadhead regularly for more blooms.

P

Pepper

Solanaceae
ANNUAL

✎ **ALL ZONES**

☼ **FULL SUN**

◖ **REGULAR WATER**

'Trinidad Perfume' habanero pepper

These popular vegetables, members of the genus *Capsicum*, are native to the tropical Americas. Peppers grow on attractive bushy plants ranging from less than a foot high to 4 ft. tall. Peppers are classified as sweet or hot, but breeders have blurred the distinction by developing hot bell peppers and sweet jalapeños.

Sweet peppers. These remain mild even after they ripen and change color. The group includes the big stuffing and salad peppers commonly called bell peppers. The best known is 'California Wonder', which starts green and ripens red. 'Tequila' changes from yellow to purple to red as it matures. Others start green or purple, then ripen yellow, orange, or even brown. Hybrids have been bred for early ripening, high yield, and/or disease resistance. Other sweet types include sweet cherry peppers, used for pickling; long, slender Italian frying peppers and Hungarian sweet yellow peppers, both used for cooking; and thick-walled, very sweet pimientos (sometimes called pimentos), used in salads, cooking, and canning. (Allspice, also called pimento, is not a pepper

but a spicy seasoning made from the fruits of a tree native to Jamaica.)

Hot peppers (chiles). These vary from pea-size types to narrow, 7-in.-long forms, but all are pungent, ranging from mildly hot Italian pepperoncini to nearly incandescent habanero strains like 'Caribbean Red'. Among the most popular hot peppers are jalapeños, used fresh, dried, or pickled. Others include various selections of 'Anaheim', a mildly spicy pepper from New Mexico used for making canned green chiles and the attractively strung bunches called ristras; 'Cayenne' types, usually dried, powdered, and used as a spice; and 'Hungarian Yellow Wax (Hot)' and 'Fresno Chile Grande', mostly used for pickling and cooking. Mexican cooking calls for a wide variety of hot peppers, among them 'Ancho' ('Poblano'), 'Mulato', and 'Pasilla'. Mildly spicy 'Mariachi' peppers start out green, then turn yellow and finally red.

CARE

Choose a site in full, hot sun. Warmer growing conditions result in hotter peppers; add

heat in mild-summer regions by planting in a protected place against a south-facing wall. Peppers need a long, warm growing season, so set out nursery transplants as soon as nighttime temperatures remain mostly above 55°F (13°C); space 1½–2 ft. apart. Both sweet and hot peppers do well in containers. After plants are established (but before blossoms set), give them one or two applications of a balanced liquid fertilizer. Most peppers can be picked green or purple after they have reached good size, but flavor typically becomes fuller and sweeter as fruit ripens into its mature color. Pick pimientos only when red-ripe. To harvest any kind of pepper, snip the stem with hand pruners or scissors.

Aphids, flea beetles, and whiteflies can be kept off young peppers early in the growing season with row covers. Later, use yellow sticky traps to control whiteflies. To control pepper weevils (both the larvae and adults attack fruit), destroy infested plants after harvest. Bait for slugs. (For more on pest management, see pages 726–731.)

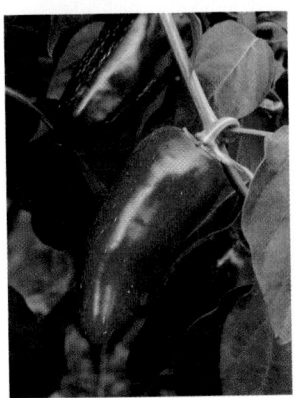

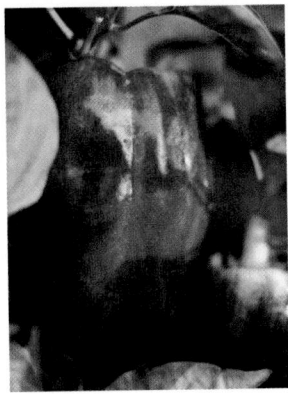

CLOCKWISE FROM TOP: 'Hungarian Yellow Wax' pepper; 'Tequila' bell pepper; jalapeño pepper

Pericallis × hybrida
(Senecio × hybridus)

FLORISTS' CINERARIA
Asteraceae
PERENNIAL USUALLY GROWN
AS AN ANNUAL

✎ **ZONES 16, 17, 22–24**

☼◖ **PARTIAL OR FULL SHADE**

◖ **REGULAR WATER**

Pericallis × hybrida

One of the showiest perennials for shade in mild climates. Grows 2 ft. high and wide, with broad clusters of 3–5-in. daisies in colors ranging from white through pink and purplish red to blue and purple, often with contrasting eyes or bands. Most common are the large-flowered dwarf kinds (12–15 in. tall) generally sold as Multiflora Nana or Hybrida Grandiflora. They bloom in late winter and early spring in mild-winter areas, spring and early summer elsewhere. Plants sold as *Cineraria stellata* (an invalid botanical name) are taller (to 2½–3 ft.), with clusters of smaller, star-shaped daisies.

CARE

Grow in loose, rich soil. Plant in fall or spring; protect plants set out in autumn from frost by choosing a location under shrubs, trees, overhang, or lath. Effective in mass plantings or combined with other shade-loving plants; excellent in containers on a lanai or patio. Even where they grow as perennials, these plants are usually discarded after bloom. Principal pests are leaf miners, spider mites, slugs, and snails.

P

Perilla frutescens

SHISO
Lamiaceae
ANNUAL

✔ **ALL ZONES**

☼ ◐ **FULL SUN OR LIGHT SHADE**

🌢 **REGULAR WATER**

Perilla frutescens crispa

Native from the Himalayas to eastern Asia. Sturdy, leafy warm-weather plant grows very quickly to 2–3 ft. high and 1 ft. wide. Broadly oval, pointed, deeply toothed leaves reach 5 in. long. The kinds most commonly seen have bronzy or purple leaves that look much like those of coleus. *P. f. crispa* has dark purple leaves with frilly edges.

Shiso makes an attractive addition to summer borders, but various parts of the plant are also edible. Use leaves as a vegetable or flavoring (they taste something like mint, something like cinnamon); fry the long, thin clusters of flower buds in tempura batter and serve as a vegetable. Extremely easy to grow; self-sows freely.

For a quick, zesty salad, toss fresh young shiso leaves with orange sections and sliced radishes. Or chop fresh leaves and sprinkle them over melons or strawberries.

Pernettya mucronata.
See *Gaultheria mucronata*

Perovskia atriplicifolia

RUSSIAN SAGE
Lamiaceae
SHRUBBY PERENNIAL

✔ **ZONES 2–24**

☼ **FULL SUN**

◐🌢 **LITTLE TO MODERATE WATER**

🦋 **ATTRACTS BUTTERFLIES, BEES**

Perovskia atriplicifolia

This popular plant is neither a sage nor from Russia. It is an airy-looking but tough plant native to Afghanistan, Pakistan, Iran, and Tibet. Many upright grayish white stems are clothed in aromatic gray-green leaves. In late spring and summer, stems are topped with widely branched sprays of small lavender-blue flowers that seem to form a soft haze above the foliage. Mature clumps may reach 3–4 ft. tall and wide; they often colonize, spreading by underground stems to send up new clumps. Can be invasive where well adapted.

Several forms are sold; many are probably hybrids. Widely grown 'Blue Spire', with deep violet blooms, is sometimes sold as *P. atriplicifolia* 'Superba'. For lighter blue flowers, grow 'Blue Mist' or 'Blue Haze'. 'Filigran' has silvery, very finely cut leaves. 'Little Spire' grows slightly over 2 ft. high and wide, with a compact habit that helps stems to stay upright.

Takes any soil as long as drainage is good. Extremely resistant to heat and drought. Performs best in warm summers. To extend the bloom

season and help prevent stems from flopping over, trim off spent blossoms. Cut nearly to the ground each spring before new growth starts.

Persea americana.
See Avocado

Persicaria

KNOTWEED
Polygonaceae
PERENNIALS

✔ **ZONES VARY BY SPECIES**

☼ ◐ **FULL SUN OR PARTIAL SHADE**

🌢 **REGULAR WATER, EXCEPT AS NOTED**

Persicaria bistorta
'Superba'

Sturdy, easy-to-grow plants with handsome leaves and showy white or pink flowers. Some kinds tend to get out of hand and need to be controlled.

P. affinis (Polygonum affine). Zones 1–9, 14–17. Himalayan native. Spreads to 1 ft. high, 2 ft. or more wide. Deep green, lance-shaped leaves can reach 4½ in. long; they turn bronze in winter. Dense, erect, 2–3-in. spikes of bright rosy red flowers bloom in summer, early fall. 'Darjeeling Red' forms 3-in.-high foliage mats, has 10-in. spikes of deep pink flowers that age to red; its foliage turns red in fall. 'Donald Lowndes' has 8-in. spikes of pale pink flowers that age to deep pink. 'Superba', usually offered as 'Dimity', has pale pink flowers and larger leaves than the species.

P. amplexicaulis (Polygonum amplexicaule). Zones 2b–9, 14–24. Himalayan native. Forms a big clump—to 4 ft. tall and wide when plants are in

flower. Blooms profusely from midsummer to fall, bearing narrow, 4-in. blossom spikes similar to those of lavender but in a wider range of colors—pink, purple, red, and white. Among the many named varieties available are 'Alba', with slender white flower spikes; 'Firetail', with fat, crimson-red spikes; 'Golden Arrow', with golden green foliage and cardinal red flowers; and 'Inverleith', a refined-looking low grower (to 1½ ft. high) with narrow foliage and crimson tapers.

P. bistorta (Polygonum bistorta). Zones 2–9, 14–24. Native to Eurasia. Makes a clump to 2½ ft. high and 3 ft. wide, with large leaves. Tight, 2–3-in. spikes of pale pink or white flowers bloom from late spring until well into summer. 'Superba' is a good pink selection.

P. capitata (Polygonum capitatum). Perennial in Zones 8, 9, 12–24; annual in colder climates. Himalayan native. Tough, trailing ground-cover 3–6 in. high; spreads indefinitely both by rooting stems and by self-seeding. Oval, 1½-in.-long leaves are bronzy dark green when new, take on pinkish overtones when mature. Stems and profuse small, round flower heads (held just above foliage) are pink. Blooms almost all year in mild climates. Best in confined spots (where it won't be able to spread) or in uncultivated areas. No irrigation needed.

P. vacciniifolia (Polygonum vacciniifolium). Zones 4–7, 15–17. Himalayan native. Prostrate plant forms a foliage mat to 3 in. high, trailing to 2 ft. or wider. Slender, branching, reddish stems are clothed in oval, ½-in.-long, shiny green leaves that turn red in fall. In late summer, 6–9-in. flower stalks bear dense, upright, fox-tail-like, 2–3-in. spikes of rose pink blossoms. Excellent as a bank cover or for draping over a boulder in a large rock garden.

P. virginiana (Polygonum virginianum, Tovara virginiana). Zones 2–9, 14–17. Native to eastern North America and eastern Asia. To 2–4 ft. tall, spreading indefinitely by creeping rhizomes. The species is rarely found in gardens. More commonly seen is 'Painter's Palette', valued for its flashy foliage: leaves are up to 10 in. long and marbled in green, pale gray-green, and ivory, with a ragged chocolate-maroon V in the center.

Persimmon

Ebenaceae
DECIDUOUS FRUIT TREES

🌡 **ZONES VARY BY SPECIES**

☼ **FULL SUN**

💧🌑 **WATER NEEDS VARY BY SPECIES**

'Fuyu' persimmon

Three kinds of persimmons are grown in the West. The native American species is a bigger, more cold-tolerant tree than the Japanese species, but the latter bears larger fruit—the kind sold in markets. The third type is a hybrid between the two. All three have inconspicuous flowers, are tolerant of many soils (as long as drainage is good), and are rarely bothered by pests or diseases.

Fruit of American, hybrid, and some Japanese persimmon varieties is astringent until soft-ripe; eat it before then, and tannins in the flesh make you pucker; eat it when the flesh is mushy and puddinglike, and the flavor is very sweet. To save the crop from birds, pick persimmons when they're fully colored (deep orange) but still firm, then bring them indoors to ripen. Nonastringent varieties are hard (like apples) when ripe, with a mildly sweet flavor; they can be eaten hard, but their flavor improves when they are allowed to soften slightly off the tree. All types can be used in cooking and baking.

Japanese or Oriental persimmon (*Diospyros kaki*). Zones 6–9, 14–16, 18–24, H1 (fruiting may be inconsistent in Hawaii—does best in dry highlands). This species grows at least 30 ft. tall and wide. It has a handsome branch pattern and is one of the best fruit trees for ornamental use; makes a good small shade tree or espalier. Leaves are light green when new, maturing to dark green, leathery ovals to 7 in. long. Foliage turns vivid yellow, orange, or red in fall (even in mild climates). After leaves drop, brilliant orange-scarlet, 3–4-in. fruits brighten the tree for weeks and persist until winter unless harvested. The tree sets fruit without pollination, though trees pollinated by another Japanese persimmon often produce tastier, more abundant crops.

'Chocolate'. Medium-size, acorn-shaped fruit. Nonastringent when unpollinated, with seedless yellow-orange flesh. Astringent until soft-ripe when pollinated, with seeded flesh that has dark streaks. Fruit from pollinated trees has best flavor.

'Fuyu'. Firm fleshed; about the size of a baseball but flattened like a tomato. Nonastringent. Favorite variety in Hawaii. 'Jiro' is very similar and often mislabeled as 'Fuyu'.

'Gosho' ('Giant Fuyu'). Very large, rounded fruit. Nonastringent. Sweet and flavorful. Widely adapted.

'Hachiya'. Big, slightly pointed fruit. Astringent. Very shapely tree for ornamental use.

'Izu'. Medium-size, round fruit borne on a tree about half the standard size. Nonastringent. Ripens early (end of summer, beginning of fall).

'Maru'. Medium-size, round fruit with shiny, orange skin and dark cinnamon-colored flesh. Nonastringent and seeded if pollinated by another variety; astringent if unpollinated. Has best flavor when seeded.

'Nishimura Wase' ('Coffee Cake'). Large, round fruit. Nonastringent when pollinated by another variety, with spicy-sweet, chocolate-colored flesh; astringent, with lighter-colored flesh, if unpollinated. Ripens early. Good choice in climates too cool to ripen 'Fuyu'. Use 'Chocolate' as a pollenizer.

'Saijo'. Elongated, dull yellow fruit. Astringent. Hardy, productive, early-ripening variety. One of the most reliable for the Pacific Northwest. Hardy.

'Tamopan'. Large, acorn-shaped fruit. Astringent.

American persimmon (*Diospyros virginiana*). Native to the eastern U.S.; grows best in Zones 3–9, 14–16, 18–23. Can grow to 15–30 ft. tall and about as wide, with attractive gray-brown bark that is fissured in a checkered pattern. Glossy green, broadly oval leaves to 6 in. long turn yellow, pink, or reddish purple in fall. Round, 1½–2-in.-wide fruit is yellow to orange (often blushed red); very astringent until soft-ripe, then very sweet. Fruit ripens in early fall after frost; some varieties do not require winter chill. Both male and female trees are usually needed to get fruit.

'Meader' is self-fruitful; its fruit is seedless if not pollinated. 'Early Golden' has more-flavorful fruit; it needs cross-pollination for best crop.

Hybrid persimmons. Zones 3–9, 14–16, 18–23. These are hybrids between American and Japanese persimmons. Two of the best are 'Russian Beauty' and 'Nikita's Gift', both developed in Russia. They are as hardy as American persimmon, with larger fruit (2–2½ in. across) that is sweet and flavorful when allowed to fully soften. Hybrids are self-fruitful.

CARE

Japanese persimmons. Let the soil dry somewhat between waterings. Too much or too little watering causes fruit drop; consistent watering prevents it. Prune trees when young to establish a good framework; thereafter, prune only to remove dead wood, shape the tree, or open up a too-dense interior. Remove any suckers that shoot up from below the graft line.

American and hybrid persimmons. These do best with regular moisture but will also perform well with moderate water. Trees usually need pruning only to remove broken or dead branches.

Petalostemon purpureum.
See *Dalea purpurea*

Petasites japonicus

JAPANESE COLTSFOOT
Asteraceae
PERENNIAL

🌡 **ZONES 2B–9, 14–17**

◐● **PARTIAL TO FULL SHADE**

💧 **AMPLE WATER**

Petasites japonicus

Native to Japan, China, Korea. This giant perennial, sometimes called fuki in the Northwest (butterbur or sweet coltsfoot elsewhere), is a dramatic choice for perpetually moist locales near ponds, streams. Creeping rhizomes give rise to big (2½ ft. wide), round leaves on edible, 3-ft.-long stalks that are used by the Japanese as a vegetable (called fuki). Short, thick spikes of small fragrant white blooms appear in early spring before the leaves emerge. Locate this plant with care; its thick rhizomes are invasive, and the plant can be difficult to eradicate. *P. j. giganteus* has leaves to 4 ft. wide on edible, 5-ft. stalks. Its selection 'Nishiki-buki', with 3–4-ft. stalks, has 2–3-ft.-wide leaves with bold white markings.

To contain the vigorous spread of Japanese coltsfoot, use the same type of root barriers you would for running bamboo. Or plant in a very large container for a dramatic—but controlled—show.

P

✕ Petchoa

Solanaceae
PERENNIAL GROWN AS ANNUAL

- 🌱 ALL ZONES
- ☼ FULL SUN OR LIGHT SHADE
- 💧 REGULAR WATER

✕ *Petchoa* SuperCal 'Terracotta'

This intergeneric hybrid was created by crossing *Petunia* with *Calibrachoa*; the resulting plants possess the best traits of each parent. Like *Calibrachoa*, they are well branched, producing many flowering stems (no pinching needed), and their spent blooms drop off cleanly and don't stick to the foliage. Like *Petunia*, they produce large flowers (2 in. across) and are easy to grow. Plants are very fast growing and withstand heat, wind, and rain better than either parent. Nearly covered in flowers from late spring until frost, they reach about 1 ft. high and 2 ft. wide, with a semi-trailing habit that makes them ideal for containers and hanging baskets. Good for planting out in beds in mild climates.

The SuperCal series includes flowers in blue, cherry red, bright rose-pink, light pink, and purple. Blooms of 'Terracotta' are yellow-orange, beautifully suffused with shades of amber and pink. 'Vanilla Blush' has soft pink flowers with a yellow throat; 'Velvet' has deep burgundy blooms, with a nearly black throat.

Plants grow best in well-drained, light soil; they will tolerate alkaline and even somewhat salty soil conditions. Best with consistent moisture but will take brief periods of drought. Weekly applications of a balanced fertilizer will keep the flowers coming.

Petrea volubilis

QUEEN'S WREATH
Verbenaceae
EVERGREEN VINE

- 🌱 ZONES 19–24; H1, H2
- ☼ FULL SUN
- 💧 REGULAR WATER
- 🦋 ATTRACTS BUTTERFLIES

Petrea volubilis

This spectacular woody vine from Mexico, Central America, and the West Indies twines to 20–40 ft. but can easily be kept smaller. Sometimes called sandpaper vine, in reference to the rough surface of its deep green, 8-in.-long leaves. Stunning floral display: dangling, foot-long clusters of star-shaped, blue-purple, 1½-in.-wide blossoms. Blue calyxes hang on after the petals drop. Main bloom period comes in winter and spring in Hawaii, late spring and summer in California; lesser displays occur at other times during warm weather. Beautiful when trained on an arbor or a pergola, along eaves, or on a high wall. Flowers are sometimes used in leis.

Grow this vine in organically enriched, moist but well-drained soil. Provide support for climbing stems. Prune and thin growth as needed in winter. Wind-resistant. Frost sensitive; may need some protection in Zones 19–22.

The bright blooms of queen's wreath fade after a few days, but the larger calyxes remain, slowly fading from blue to soft gray.

Petroselinum crispum

PARSLEY
Apiaceae
BIENNIAL GROWN AS ANNUAL

- 🌱 ZONES A1–A3; 1–24
- ☼ ◑ AFTERNOON SHADE IN HOTTEST CLIMATES
- 💧 REGULAR WATER
- 🦋 ATTRACTS BENEFICIAL INSECTS

Flat-leafed Italian parsley

From southern Europe. Parsley makes an attractive edging for the herb, flower, or vegetable garden; it's also good in window boxes and pots. Two kinds are commonly grown, both with finely cut dark green foliage: flat-leafed Italian parsley and curly-leafed French parsley. Leaves are used as a seasoning (both fresh and dried); fresh sprigs and minced leaves are classic garnishes. Flat-leafed parsley grows to 2–3 ft. high and 2 ft. wide; it is considered more flavorful than curly parsley, which grows to 6–12 in. high and wide and makes a more attractive garnish.

CARE

Parsley is best started fresh each year, from either nursery transplants or seed. Set out small plants or sow seeds in place—in spring after average last-frost date in cold-winter climates; in fall or early spring where winters are mild; in early fall in low desert. Soak seeds in warm water for 24 hours before planting. (Even after soaking, they may not come up for several weeks; according to an old story, parsley seeds must go to the devil and back before sprouting.) Thin seed-

lings to 1–1½ ft. apart for flat-leafed parsley, 6–8 in. apart for curly parsley; or space plants at these distances. Harvest sprigs from the outside of the plant so that those on the inside will keep coming.

Petunia

Solanaceae
PERENNIALS GROWN AS ANNUALS

- 🌱 ALL ZONES
- ☼ FULL SUN
- 💧 REGULAR WATER
- 🦋 ATTRACT BUTTERFLIES

Petunia

Petunias have long been among the most popular annuals, thanks to their profuse bloom, incredible color range, and relative ease of culture. Plants are bushy to spreading, with thick, broad leaves that are slightly sticky to the touch. Flowers vary from funnel-shaped single blooms to densely double, heavily ruffled ones (like carnations); bloom sizes range from 1 to 6 in. across. They come in white and every color except green—from deep jewel tones to soft pastels. Bicolors and picotees are also available, as are types that have contrasting veins on the petals and kinds with fluted or fringed edges. In most climate zones, plants bloom throughout summer until frost. In Zones 12 and 13, summer heat kills them; in these areas, grow them for winter and spring color.

Petunias have traditionally been categorized as Grandiflora (large flowers on a bouquet-shaped plant), Multiflora (more numerous, medium-size blooms on a compact, mounding plant),

P

or Milliflora (profuse small blooms on small, mounding plants). Trailing and mounding petunias were developed to grow as low as 6 in. and as wide as 6 ft. across. These categories are rarely used now, as advances in breeding have blurred the boundaries between them. New series and varieties appear each year in such numbers that no book could keep up. Check catalog descriptions and visit your local nursery to find the color, bloom size, and plant habit best suited to your purposes.

For a popular petunia relative with smaller blooms, see *Calibrachoa*. See also × *Petchoa*, an intergeneric hybrid between *Petunia* and *Calibrachoa*.

CARE

Plants thrive in rich, well-drained garden soil. Space them 8–18 in. apart, depending on plant size. After plants are established, pinch back halfway to encourage compact growth. Feed most kinds monthly with a complete liquid fertilizer; hungry trailing petunias—referred to by growers as the teenage boys of the plant world—do best when given controlled-release fertilizer at planting time in addition to weekly applications of liquid fertilizer. Near the end of the main bloom period, cut back rangy plants by half to force new growth.

In humid weather, botrytis disease can damage blossoms and foliage of most petunias. Smog damage (spotting on seedling leaves) and geranium (tobacco) budworm (flowers look tattered or fail to open) may cause problems in some areas.

Plant petunias in a hanging basket, in a wind-protected spot near an entry. You'll enjoy the vibrant blooms even more at eye level, and when you pass by, you can easily pick off fading flowers, thus encouraging more bloom.

Phacelia
Boraginaceae
ANNUALS

🗡 **ZONES 1–3, 7–24**

☼ **FULL SUN**

◌ ◌ **LITTLE TO MODERATE WATER**

🐝 **ATTRACT BENEFICIAL INSECTS**

⬧ **ALL PARTS CAN CAUSE AN ALLERGIC RASH**

Phacelia campanularia

These easy-to-grow annuals bring lovely shades of blue to the spring garden. Sow in well-drained soil in fall or earliest spring; or sow in pots and transplant while seedlings are very small. Give some water to extend bloom season. Especially showy when combined with California poppy (*Eschscholzia californica*), sticky monkeyflower (*Mimulus aurantiacus*), and other heat-loving annuals.

P. campanularia. CALIFORNIA DESERT BLUEBELLS. Native to California deserts. To 6–18 in. high and wide, with coarsely toothed gray-green leaves. Clusters of 1-in., bell-shaped deep blue spring flowers with distinctive white dots at petal bases.

P. tanacetifolia. LACY PHACELIA. From the deserts of Southern California and northern Mexico. Grows 1–4 ft. tall and 1½ ft. wide, with much-divided, ferny-looking leaves. In spring, coiled flower heads unfurl to present a multitude of blue or lavender-blue blooms up to ½ in. across. Very attractive to bees and other beneficial insects.

Phaedranthus buccinatorius. See *Distictis buccinatoria*

Phaeomeria magnifica. See *Etlingera elatior*

Phalaenopsis
MOTH ORCHID
Orchidaceae
EPIPHYTIC ORCHIDS

🗡 **ZONE H2; OR INDOORS**

☼ **FILTERED SUN; BRIGHT INDIRECT LIGHT**

⬧ **REGULAR WATER**

Phalaenopsis ungu

These tropical orchids have thick, broad, leathery leaves and no pseudobulbs. Leaves are flat, to 1 ft. long. From fall to spring, plants bear long (to 3 ft.) sprays of 3–6-in.-wide flowers in white, cream, pale yellow, or light lavender-pink; some are spotted or barred or have lips in a contrasting color. Many lovely hybrids are sold. A very popular orchid commercially. Considered beginner orchids, these are among the easiest to grow outdoors on a warm, wind-protected lanai in Hawaii, and indoors anywhere. Some smaller-flowered hybrids are promising to be even easier to grow, and to tolerate somewhat lower night temperatures.

CARE

They can be grown in a greenhouse with fairly high humidity and temperatures that average 60°F to 65°F/16°C to 18°C at night, 70°F to 85°F/21°C to 29°C during the day. Or grow them indoors near a bathroom or kitchen window with light coming through a gauze or other sheer curtain (foliage burns easily in direct sun). Give moth orchids same potting medium as cattleya (see "Meet the Orchids," page 463). During the growing and flowering season, feed weekly with a balanced liquid fertilizer diluted

to half-strength. When cutting flowers, cut back to just above one of the tiny bracts on the stem; secondary sprays may form. To promote stronger new growth, many growers prefer to cut out the entire stem after blossoms fade.

Phalaris arundinacea picta
RIBBON GRASS, GARDENER'S GARTERS
Poaceae
PERENNIAL GRASS

🗡 **ZONES A1–A3; 1–10, 14–24**

☼ ☼ **FULL SUN OR PARTIAL SHADE**

⬧ **REGULAR WATER**

Phalaris arundinacea picta

Native to North America and Eurasia. Tough, tenacious grass; forms a 2–3-ft.-high clump that spreads aggressively—and indefinitely—by underground runners. Leaves are deep green with longitudinal white stripes, turn buff-colored in autumn. Airy flower clusters are white, aging to pale brown. To keep this plant in-bounds, grow it in large containers or use same control methods as for running kinds of bamboo (see Bamboo). Less invasive selections are 'Woods Dwarf' ('Dwarf Garters'), about half as tall as the species and with brighter white striping; and 'Feesey' ('Strawberries and Cream'), to 1½–2 ft. tall, with white stripes that usually take on pink tints during cool weather.

Phaseolus caracalla. See *Vigna caracalla*

P

Philadelphus
MOCK ORANGE
Hydrangeaceae
DECIDUOUS AND EVERGREEN SHRUBS

- ✎ **ZONES VARY BY SPECIES**
- ☼ ◐ **PARTIAL SHADE IN HOTTEST CLIMATES**
- ⬤ ⬤ **MODERATE TO REGULAR WATER**
- ✻ **SINGLE-FLOWERED TYPES ATTRACT BUTTERFLIES**

Philadelphus coronarius

Prized for cream-colored or white, usually fragrant flowers that bloom in late spring or early summer. Blossoms are four petaled, typically 1–2 in. wide; they range from single to fully double. Plants are generally large and vigorous, with fountainlike form. Not fussy about soil type but must have good drainage. Prune every year just after bloom, cutting out oldest wood and surplus shoots at base. To rejuvenate, cut to the ground.

P. 'Belle Etoile'. Deciduous. Zones 2–17. This popular shrub grows 5–6 ft. tall and 8 ft. wide. Fringed, maroon-centered, single flowers to 2½ in. across are wonderfully fragrant. May be offered as a selection of P. × *lemoinei*.

P. 'Buckley's Quill'. Deciduous. Zones 3–17. Dense, compact grower to 4–5 ft. tall and wide, with clusters of fragrant, 1-in.-wide, double flowers. Petals are narrow and pointed.

P. coronarius. SWEET MOCK ORANGE. Deciduous. Zones A1–A3; 1a, 2–24. From southern Europe and the Caucasus. Strong-growing old favorite to 10–12 ft. tall and wide. Clusters of especially fragrant, 1½-in. flowers. 'Aureus', to 8 ft. tall and 5 ft. wide, has bright golden foliage that turns yellow green in summer. 'Variegatus' grows to about the same size, but its leaves are broadly and irregularly edged in white.

P. 'Glacier'. Deciduous. Zones A3; 1a, 2–17. Grows 5 ft. tall and wide, with very fragrant double blossoms to 1¼ in. wide.

P. lewisii. WILD MOCK ORANGE. Deciduous. Zones 1–10, 14–24. Native to western North America; the state flower of Idaho. Fountain-shaped, loosely branched shrub 4–10 ft. tall, typically broader than high. Satiny single flowers to 2 in. across. Tolerates some aridity. 'Goose Creek' is a double-flowered selection that reaches 8 ft. tall and wide.

P. 'Manteau d'Hermine'. Deciduous. Zones 2–17. Compact, bushy grower to just 2–3 ft. high and 4 ft. wide, with a profusion of small, heavily perfumed, double flowers to 1½ in. wide. Fine choice for smaller gardens.

P. mexicanus. EVERGREEN MOCK ORANGE. Zones 8, 9, 14–24. From Mexico. Vining shrub has long, supple stems clothed with evergreen leaves. Creamy white, 1½-in. flowers in small clusters may bloom sporadically throughout year. Can be kept to 6 ft. tall and wide as a free-standing shrub. It is best used, however, as a vine or bank cover; can climb 15–20 ft. with support.

P. microphyllus. Deciduous. Zones 1–3, 7, 10, 14–16, 18. From southwestern U.S., Mexico. To 4–5 ft. tall and wide (often smaller), with small (¾–1½ in. long) leaves. Extremely fragrant, inch-wide flowers are borne singly or in pairs. Endures some drought.

P. 'Minnesota Snowflake'. Deciduous. Zones A3; 1a, 2–17. To 6–8 ft. tall and wide, with double flowers to 2 in. across. Reputedly hardy to −30°F (−34°C). 'Miniature Snowflake' ('Dwarf Minnesota Snowflake', 'Dwarf Snowflake') grows 3–4 ft. tall and wide, with 1–1½-in. double flowers.

P. 'Natchez'. Deciduous. Zones A3; 1a, 2–17. Grows 8–10 ft. tall and wide. Very showy in bloom, when branches are covered in 2-in.-wide double flowers.

P. 'Virginal'. Deciduous. Zones A3; 1a, 2–17. To 6–8 ft. tall and wide. Fragrant double flowers are 2 in. across.

Philodendron
Araceae
EVERGREEN VINES AND SHRUBS

- ✎ **ZONES VARY BY TYPE; OR INDOORS**
- ☼ ◐ ⬤ **EXPOSURE NEEDS VARY BY TYPE; BRIGHT INDIRECT LIGHT**
- ⬤ **REGULAR WATER**

Philodendron bipinnatifidum

From tropical America. Tough, fast-growing plants favored for attractive, leathery, usually glossy leaves. In good conditions, old plants may bloom; the blossoms resemble those of calla (*Zantedeschia*), with a boatlike bract surrounding a club-shaped structure. Bracts are usually greenish, white, or reddish.

Arborescent types. Zones 8, 9, 12–24, H1, H2; or indoors. These are large, shrub-size plants with big leaves and sturdy, self-supporting trunks. As landscape plants, they do best in sun (some shade at midday in hot areas) but can take considerable shade. Use them for tropical effects or as massive silhouettes against walls or glass. Excellent in large containers; effective near swimming pools. The most widely grown is P. *bipinnatifidum* (P. *selloum*), to 6–15 ft. tall and wide, typically with a single, upright trunk that leans with age; its deeply cut leaves to 3 ft. long are held on 3-ft.-long stalks. P. *xanadu* (P. 'Xanadu') is similar but smaller and bushier, growing slowly to 3 ft. high and 5 ft. wide.

Vining and self-heading types. Zone H2; or indoors. This class includes tender plants with two different habits. Outdoors, they require partial or full shade; indoors, they thrive in bright indirect light.

Vining types do not really climb and must be tied to or leaned against a support until they eventually shape themselves to it. The support can be almost anything, but certain water-absorbent columns (sections of tree fern stem, wire and sphagnum "totem poles," slabs of bark) serve especially well, since they can be kept moist. Examples include P. *erubescens* (P. 'Hastatum'), to 10–20 ft. tall, with foot-long, arrow-shaped deep green leaves; and the commonly grown P. *scandens*, to 50 ft., with deep green, heart-shaped leaves.

Self-heading types form short, broad plants with leaves radiating out from a central point. P. 'Lynette' grows 1 ft. high, 2 ft. wide, with foot-long, bright green leaves that are strongly patterned by deeply sunken veins; good tabletop plant. P. *wendlandii* is about the same size, with compact clusters of deep green, foot-long, broadly lance-shaped leaves on short, broad stalks; indoors, this species is useful where a tough, compact foliage plant is needed.

CARE

Whether grown in containers or open ground, all philodendrons need rich, loose, well-drained soil. Feed lightly and frequently for good growth and color. Clean dust from leaves of indoor plants. Most philodendrons tend to drop their lower leaves, which results in a bare stem. Once a plant gets gangly and overgrown, the best course is often simply to discard it and replace it with a new plant. However, you can also cut the plant back to a short stub and then let it regrow. Some types send down aerial roots. Push these into soil or cut them off (removing them won't hurt the plant).

Phlebodium aureum.
See Polypodium aureum

Phlomis

Lamiaceae
PERENNIALS AND EVERGREEN SHRUBS

☀ **ZONES VARY BY SPECIES**

☼ **FULL SUN, EXCEPT AS NOTED**

◐ ◑ **LITTLE TO MODERATE WATER**

Phlomis fruticosa

Handsome Mediterranean natives grown for their upright stems set with widely spaced whorls of hooded, two-lipped flowers in yellow, purple, or lilac. The leaves are attractive too: typically gray-green and furry, they are thick and moisture conserving. Not particular about soil but must have good drainage. Need little water where summers are cool; in hot-summer regions, give them more water. Cut flowers are striking in mixed arrangements; blooming stems dry well for winter bouquets.

P. 'Edward Bowles' (P. 'Grande Verde'). Shrub. Zones 3b–24. To 3–4 ft. tall, 5–6 ft. wide. Hybrid between *P. fruticosa* and *P. russeliana*. Resembles a bulkier *P. fruticosa* with broader leaves and larger, pure yellow flowers. Often sold as *P. fruticosa* and takes the same care.

P. fruticosa. JERUSALEM SAGE. Shrub. Zones 3b–24. To 4 ft. tall and wide, with narrow, woolly gray-green leaves. Deep golden yellow, 1-in. flowers in ball-shaped whorls along upper half of stems. With watering, will produce several waves of bloom in spring and summer if cut back lightly after each flowering. In fall, cut plants back by half to keep them compact. Can tolerate light shade for part of the day. Resistant to oak root fungus.

P. italica. Shrub. Zones 5–24. Arching, suckering habit to 1–2 ft. high and a little wider. Gray-green, 2–3-in.-long leaves are covered with silvery wool. Lilac-pink flowers in 1-in. whorls from early to midsummer. To keep plant neat, remove faded flowering stems; cut out basal branches that are more than 3 years old.

P. lanata. Shrub. Zones 7–24. Dense, compact plant to 2½ ft. high, 4–6 ft. wide. Woolly, wrinkled leaves are sage green. Whorls of 1-in., deep yellow flowers bloom from spring to fall if faded stems are cut out.

P. purpurea. Shrub. Zones 7–24. Rather lax habit to 4–6 ft. tall and wide. Lance-shaped leaves are gray-green, sparsely hairy above, white and woolly beneath; new shoots are also white and woolly. Purplish pink flowers bloom mainly in late spring, but scattered blossoms appear all year long where winters are mild. After each flowering, cut plant back by one-third to keep it neat and compact.

P. russeliana. Perennial. Zones 2–24. Spreads by rhizomes to make a low clump of furry olive green foliage. Leaves are large, heart-shaped. Creates an effective weed-suppressing groundcover. Sends up 2–3-ft.-high stems bearing flowers in soft yellow fading to cream. The main bloom period comes in early summer, but some flowers are produced later as well. Flower spikes are attractive even after blossoms fade; they dry out and remain upright throughout the winter. Tolerates partial shade.

P. samia. Perennial. Zones 2–24. Similar in habit to *P. russeliana*, forming a low mat of oval, scallop-edged leaves that are medium green above and white and woolly below. Blooms throughout summer, sending up 2–3-ft.-high stems of flowers in purple or purplish pink (greenish or white in some forms).

P. tuberosa. Perennial from tuberous roots. Zones A1–A3; 1–24. Basal rosette of deep green foliage covered with fine hairs; leaves deeply toothed, arrow-shaped, to 10 in. long. Late spring into summer, sends up 3–6-ft. stems with purple or mauve blossoms along upper third. Disappears in winter.

Phlox

Polemoniaceae
PERENNIALS AND ANNUALS

☀ **ZONES VARY BY SPECIES**

☼ ☼ **FULL SUN OR LIGHT SHADE, EXCEPT AS NOTED**

● **REGULAR WATER, EXCEPT AS NOTED**

🦋 **ATTRACT BUTTERFLIES**

Phlox drummondii

Most are natives of North America; all are cherished for their showy flower clusters. With the exception of annual *P. drummondii*, the species described here are perennial. The many types show wide variation in form: tall kinds are excellent border plants, dwarf ones work well in a rock garden or edging a path. Two major problems affect phlox: red spider mites (attack almost all species) and powdery mildew (*P. paniculata* is especially susceptible).

P. bifida. SAND PHLOX. Zones 2–17. From central U.S. Forms clumps to 10 in. high and 2 ft. wide, with narrow, light green leaves. Blooms spring through early summer, bearing profuse, ½-in. lavender to white flowers with deeply notched petals. Thrives with full sun and excellent drainage; best with moderate moisture but tolerates drought well.

P. carolina 'Miss Lingard'. Zones 1–14, 18–23. Popular variety of a species native to the central and eastern U.S. Grows about 3 ft. high and half as wide, with pure white, highly fragrant blooms in early summer. Heat-tolerant and mildew-resistant. Excellent cut flowers.

P. divaricata. WILD BLUE PHLOX, WILD SWEET WILLIAM. Zones 1–17. Native to eastern North America. Grows 1 ft. high, 2 ft. wide, with creeping underground shoots. Blooms in spring, with open clusters of ¾–1½-in.-wide, somewhat fragrant blossoms; color varies from pale blue (sometimes with pinkish tones) to white. Flowers of 'Dirigo Ice' and 'May Breeze' are palest blue, while those of 'Blue Moon' are deep violet-blue. 'Montrose Tricolor' has lavender-blue blossoms; its leaves emerge pink, then age to green with white margins. *P. d. laphamii* 'Chattahoochee' has pale lavender-blue blooms with a purple eye. All are good in rock gardens or as bulb cover. Grow in good, deep soil. Light shade.

P. drummondii. ANNUAL PHLOX. Zones A2, A3; 1–24; H1. Native to Texas. To 6–18 in. high, 10–12 in. wide, with erect, leafy stems more or less covered with rather sticky hairs. Lance-shaped to oval leaves are nearly stalkless. Profuse blossoms in tight clusters at tops of stems. Comes in bright and pastel colors (all except true blue and orange), some with a contrasting eye. Tall strains (about 1½ ft. high) in mixed colors include Fordhook Finest. Plants in the heat- and drought-tolerant Intensia strain are intermediate in size (8–12 in. high) and so freely branching that they take on a rounded shape; they are available in a wide range of colors, including some with contrasting eyes or streaks, and are just right for large containers. Dwarf (6–8 in.) strains include Beauty and Globe, both with roundish flowers; and starry-blossomed Petticoat and Twinkle Star. Bloom period lasts from early summer until frost if faded flowers are removed. Plant in spring in cold-winter regions, in fall in mild climates. Grow in light, rich soil well amended with organic matter. Full sun.

P. maculata. THICK-LEAF PHLOX. Zones 1–14, 18–23. Native to eastern North America. To 3–4 ft. tall, 1½ ft. wide, with thick, narrow, pointed leaves. Early summer flowers about ¾ in. wide in 15-in.-long clusters; colors range from white (often with a colored eye) through pink shades to magenta. Shiny, mildew-resistant foliage. Varieties include 'Alpha', rose-

P

pink; 'Delta', white with pink eye; 'Natascha', pink and white bicolor in a striking pinwheel pattern; 'Omega', white with purplish pink eye; and 'Rosalinde', deep rose pink.

P. paniculata. SUMMER PHLOX. Zones 1–14, 18–21. From eastern North America. To 3–5 ft. tall, 2 ft. wide, with narrow, pointed leaves. Fragrant, 1-in. flowers in large, dome-shaped clusters appear throughout summer. Colors include white and shades of lavender, pink, rose, and red; blooms of some varieties have a contrasting eye. Mildewresistant varieties include 'David', pure white; 'Miss Marple', white with reddish pink eye; 'Eva Cullum' and 'Miss Pepper', pink with red eye; 'Miss Candy', hot pink; 'Pink Red Eye Flame', deep pink with red eye; 'Bright Eyes', rose-pink with darker eye; 'Laura', deep pinkish purple with white eye; 'Miss Violet', purple; 'Blue Paradise', deep violet-blue; and the Volcano series (white, purple, lavender, red, pink with white eye, and pink with red eye). Varieties with white-variegated leaves are available.

Summer phlox thrives in full sun, but flower color may bleach in hottest areas; performance is better in northern than in southern climates. After setting out young plants, pinch stem tips to induce branching. Mulch to keep roots cool. Divide every few years, replanting young shoots from outside of clump. Very susceptible to mildew at end of bloom season. To minimize the problem, provide good air circulation: don't crowd plants, and thin mature plants to leave only six to eight stems.

P. stolonifera. CREEPING PHLOX. Zones A2, A3; 1–17. From eastern North America. Creeping, mounding plant to 6–8 in. high, 1 ft. wide, with narrow evergreen leaves. Profuse springtime show of 1-in., lavender flowers. Varieties include 'Bruce's White', lavender-blue 'Blue Ridge', rich pink 'Home Fires', and deep lavender 'Sherwood Purple'. Light shade.

P. subulata. MOSS PINK. Zones 1–17. From eastern U.S. Forms a mat to 6 in. high and 1½ ft. or wider, with creeping stems clothed in small, needle-like evergreen to semievergreen leaves. Blooms profusely in late spring or early summer, bearing ¾-in. flowers in white and colors including pale to deep shades of pink, and lavender-blue. Plant in loose, not-too-rich soil; give moderate water. After flowering, cut back halfway. Specialists offer dozens of varieties and hybrids, such as 'Tamanonagalei' ('Candy Stripe'), which has rose-pink blossoms edged in white; it is more drought-tolerant than the average moss pink and has good fall rebloom.

Phoenix
DATE PALM
Arecaceae
PALMS

🌡 **ZONES VARY BY SPECIES**

☀ **FULL SUN, EXCEPT AS NOTED**

💧 **REGULAR WATER**

Phoenix dactylifera

These feather palms are mostly large trees, though the following list includes several small enough for home gardens. Trunks are patterned with bases of old leafstalks. Small yellowish flowers are held in large, hanging sprays. On mature female trees, blossoms are followed by clusters of dates if a male tree is nearby. Dates of *P. dactylifera* and *P. sylvestris* are used commercially; those of other species don't have as much edible flesh. Date palms hybridize freely, so buy these trees from a reliable nursery that knows the seed or plant source.

P. canariensis. CANARY ISLAND DATE PALM. Zones 8, 9, 12–24; H1, H2. Canary Island native. Hardy to 20°F (–7°C); slow to recover from hard frosts. Big, heavy-trunked plant that grows slowly to 60 ft. tall, with a great many bright green to deep green, gracefully arching fronds that form a crown to 50 ft. wide. Not for small city lots. Young plants do well in pots for many years, looking something like pineapples. Takes seacoast conditions.

P. dactylifera. DATE PALM. Zones 8, 9, 11–24; H1, H2. Leaves killed at 20°F (–7°C), but plants have survived 4°F (–16°C). Native to the Mideast. Classic palm of desert oases. Slender-trunked tree to 80 ft., with a crown 20–40 ft. wide; gray-green, waxy leaves have stiff, sharp-pointed leaflets. Sends up suckers from base; natural habit is a clump of several trunks. Bears dates of commerce; principal variety is 'Deglet Noor'. Too large and stiff for most home gardens. Does well at seaside, in desert.

P. reclinata. SENEGAL DATE PALM. Zones 9, 13–17, 21–24; H2. Damaged below 25°F (–4°C). Native to Africa. Grows to 20–30 ft. tall and wide. Produces offshoots, forming picturesque clumps with several curving trunks; if you want a single-trunked tree, remove offshoots. Fertilize for fast growth. Good seaside plant.

P. roebelenii. PYGMY DATE PALM. Zones 13, 16, 17, 22–24; H2; or indoors. Foliage browns at around 26°F (–3°C) but recovers rapidly in spring. From Laos. Small, slow-growing, single-trunked palm to 6–10 ft. tall. Fine-textured, curving leaves form a dense crown to 6–8 ft. across. Good in groves or as a potted plant. Full sun or partial shade. Indoors, provide bright indirect light.

P. rupicola. CLIFF DATE PALM. Zones 13, 16, 17, 19–24; H1, H2. Hardy to 26°F (–3°C). Native to India. As stately as *P. canariensis* but slender trunked and much smaller, reaching only 25 ft. tall and 15–20 ft. wide. Lime green foliage is soft and lush-looking; lower leaves droop gracefully. Best with some shade when young.

P. sylvestris. SILVER DATE PALM. Zones 8, 9, 12–24; H1, H2. Hardy to 22°F (–6°C).

Native to India. Beautiful single-trunked palm to 30 ft. tall, 20–25 ft. wide. Tapering trunk is wide at base, narrow at top. Dense, rounded crown of gray-green leaves. Sap is used commercially for making date sugar.

Phormium
Hemerocallidaceae
PERENNIALS

🌡 **ZONES 7–9, 14–24; H1, H2; REGROW AFTER FREEZES IN ZONES 5, 6**

☀ ◐ **FULL SUN OR PARTIAL SHADE**

◌ ◑ ● **LITTLE TO REGULAR WATER**

Phormium 'Jubilee'

From New Zealand, these dramatic plants have many sword-like evergreen leaves that grow in a fan pattern; they're good massed or used as focal points. Many variegated selections provide year-round color in perennial and shrub borders, on hillsides, in seaside plantings, near swimming pools. Cool weather intensifies foliage colors. On established plants, branched clusters of tubular flowers appear in late spring or early summer, rising to twice the height of the foliage clump in some kinds. Hummingbirds love the flowers.

Rugged *P. tenax* varieties are sturdy and fast growing. They take almost any soil, little to regular watering, hot or chilly conditions; do well at seacoast. They will take poor drainage to a point; crown rot can be a problem if they are planted too low in poorly drained soil. Rigid, upright leaves seldom sunburn. Subject to summer rot in low desert, but replacement plants set out in fall will grow quickly. Use as windbreak along coast;

A PHORMIUM SAMPLER

Upright growers such
as 8-ft.-tall *P. tenax*
'Atropurpureum' have
long, stiff leaves.

Semi-upright hybrids
including *P.* 'Maori
Maiden' have gracefully
arching foliage in a
rainbow of colors.

Arching types such as
P. 'Yellow Wave' take on
a billowing, mounding
form with maturity.

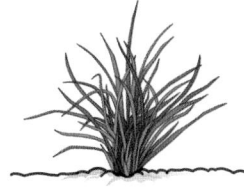

Dwarf phormiums like
'Tom Thumb' are smallest
overall and come in several
different colors.

grow in containers wherever soil doesn't freeze in winter.

More finicky than *P. tenax* are forms of *P. cookianium* and the spectacular hybrids between these two species. They require a bit more water; in hot areas, their arching leaves need afternoon shade to prevent burning.

All phormiums are harmed by temperatures below 20°F (–7°C). In cold-winter areas, you can grow smaller sorts indoors or move larger containers to shelter when deep cold threatens.

Nursery plants in containers are deceptively small; when you plant, allow enough room to accommodate a mature specimen. Cut out flower stalks when blossoms wither. As leaves age, colors fade; cut out older (outer) ones as close to base as possible to maintain best appearance. On variegated sorts, watch for reversions to solid green or bronze; remove reverted crowns down to root level before they take over the clump. Clumps can remain in place indefinitely. To increase plantings, take individual crowns from clump edges; or divide large clumps (not an easy job).

P. cookianum (P. colensoi). MOUNTAIN FLAX. Leaves arch gracefully, drooping at the tips; they grow 4–5 ft. long, 2½–3 in. wide. Mature clumps are 4–5 ft. tall, spreading to 8–10 ft. or more. 'Black Adder' grows 3–4 ft. tall and wide, with glossy, deep burgundy-black leaves. 'Flamingo' grows just 1–2 ft. high and wide, with

leaves in shades of orange, rose, light green, and yellow. *P. c. hookeri* 'Cream Delight' has leaves with a broad, creamy yellow central stripe and narrow green margins edged in dark red. *P. c. h.* 'Tricolor' has green leaves margined in cream and red; foliage is flushed with rose in cool weather.

P. hybrids. These crosses between *P. cookianum* and *P. tenax* were selected for distinctive leaf color. Leaves are 1½–2 in. wide unless otherwise noted.

'Apricot Queen'. To 3 ft. high, 5 ft. wide. Leaves are 2–3 in. wide, light yellow with green margins; blushed with apricot in cool weather.

'Bronze Baby'. To 3–5 ft. tall and wide. Leaves are deep reddish brown aging to deep bronze; narrow orange leaf edges and midrib (on underside) glow in sunlight.

'Dark Delight'. Arching habit to 4 ft. tall, 8 ft. wide. Leaves are 1–2 in. wide; very dark but vivid reddish brown with a thin orange midrib.

'Dazzler'. Slow grower to 3 ft. high, 5–6 ft. wide, with twisting, arching leaves in scarlet striped with maroon.

'Duet'. To 2–2½ ft. high and wide. Stiff, erect to slightly arching leaves to 1¾ in. wide are lime green with creamy yellow stripes at margins.

'Dusky Chief'. Dense clump to 3–5 ft. tall and wide. Wine red leaves are 2–3 in. wide and have coral edges that glow when backlit.

'Ed Carman'. Upright growth to 2–3 ft. high and wide; bronze leaves are edged with narrow bands of light pink to white.

'Firebird'. Stiffly upright, to 6 ft. tall, 3 ft. wide. Rose-red leaves have bronze-green margins.

'Golden Ray'. Upright to slightly arching grower to 4–5 ft. tall and wide. Leaves are striped in green and cream, with a red edge.

'Guardsman'. To 6–8 ft. tall and wide, with rigid, upright leaves to 3 in. wide. Bronze-maroon with bright red border.

'Jack Spratt'. To 1½ ft. high and wide, with ½-in.-wide, twisting, reddish brown leaves.

'Jester'. To 1½–2½ ft. high and wide. Arching leaves are rich pink with hints of orange, edged in lime green.

'Maori Chief' ('Rainbow Chief'). Robust, upright to 6 ft. tall and 6–8 ft. wide. Leaves to 2½ in. wide, green with rosy edges. Similar to 'Sundowner' but more refined.

'Maori Maiden' ('Rainbow Maiden'). To 3–4 ft. tall, 4–6 ft. wide. Leaves to 1¾ in. wide are salmon-pink (fading to cream) with narrow olive green stripes at edges.

'Maori Queen' ('Rainbow Queen'). To 3 ft. high, 4–5 ft. wide. Shorter, more upright, narrower-leafed version of 'Sundowner'. Stiff leaves to 2¼ in. wide are bronzy green, with broad marginal streaks of coral fading to cream.

'Maori Sunrise' ('Rainbow Sunrise'). To 3 ft. high, 5–6 ft.

wide, with stiff leaves up to 2½ in. across. Foliage is margined and striped in bronzy green; base color is pinkish orange in younger leaves, aging to cream in older ones.

'Morticia'. To 3–4 ft. tall and wide, with stiff, purple-black leaves.

'Pink Stripe' ('Pink Edge'). To 4–6 ft. tall and wide. Gray-green foliage has a purplish tinge. Each leaf has a bright pink margin that is broadest at the base.

'Platt's Black'. Somewhat arching growth to 2–3 ft. high and wide; leaves up to 1 in. wide. One of the darkest varieties, with dark burgundy to nearly black leaves. Grows best in cooler climates.

'Rainbow Warrior'. Similar to 'Maori Maiden' but with leaves in a somewhat darker salmon, fading to cream with age. Foliage turns nearly blood red in winter.

'Sea Jade'. To 4–5 ft. tall, 5–6 ft. wide, with rather stiff, upright leaves to 2½ in. wide. Maroon to bronze in center, with lime green margins and undersides.

'Sundowner'. Erect growth to 5–7 ft. tall and wide, with leaves to 3 in. wide. Olive or bronzy green foliage has stripes of pinkish red (aging to cream) at or near edges and a fine red edge; leaf undersides are grayish green.

'Sunset'. To 4–6 ft. tall and wide. Stiffly upright leaves have slightly arching tips; color is apricot to pink, striped with green.

'Surfer'. To 2–4 ft. tall and wide. Maroon-bronze leaves have grayish green undersides and a narrow, gray-green central stripe. Foliage is stiff but arching and twisting.

'Thumbelina'. Similar to 'Jack Spratt' but more upright growing and a little darker.

'Tiny Tiger' ('Aurea Nana'). A miniature, reaching barely 1 ft. high and wide. Leaves are flushed pink in cool weather. 'Tony Tiger' is a 2-ft. version.

'Tom Thumb'. Upright clump to 2–3 ft. high and wide. Green, wavy-edged, ½-in.-wide leaves have red-bronze margins.

'Yellow Wave'. To 4–5 ft. tall, 5–7 ft. wide, with 2¼-in.-wide leaves in chartreuse with lime green margins. Leaves can burn in hot sun.

P. tenax. NEW ZEALAND FLAX. Large, bold plant with bronzy green leaves to 9 ft. long and 5 in. wide; rigid and mainly upright, curving mainly (if at all) near tips. Mature clumps are about as wide as or a little wider than high. Note that bronze-leafed varieties take on a deeper color in full sun.

'Atropurpureum', 'Bronze', 'Rubrum', Purpureum Group. These names are used interchangeably in the trade for plants with purplish or brownish red foliage that grow 6–8 ft. tall and wide. Usually grown from seed and somewhat variable.

'Atropurpureum Compactum' ('Monrovia Red'). To 5 ft. tall and wide, with burgundy-bronze foliage. Uniform; propagated by tissue culture.

'Chocolate' ('Chocolate Dream'). To 4–5 ft. tall and wide, with rich brown leaves.

'Radiance'. To 5–6 ft. tall, 7 ft. wide. Green leaves have a central yellow stripe, lime green margins with a thin orange edge.

'Variegatum'. To 6–8 ft. tall and wide, with ¾-in.-wide, grayish green leaves that have creamy yellow stripes along edges.

'Wings of Gold'. Resembles 'Variegatum' but reaches just 2–3 ft. high and wide. Ideal for containers.

FOR OTHER PLANTS THAT ARE GOOD FOR NEAR POOLS, SEE PAGES 64–65.

Photinia
Rosaceae
EVERGREEN AND DECIDUOUS SHRUBS OR TREES

✏	ZONES VARY BY SPECIES
☀	FULL SUN
◐ ◑	MODERATE TO REGULAR WATER
🐦	BERRIES ATTRACT BIRDS

Photinia × fraseri

Handsome, densely foliaged plants with brightly colored new growth that matures to dark green. Good for screen and background plantings. All bear flattish clusters of small white flowers; in most types, blossoms are followed in fall by red or black berries that may last into winter. Tip-pinch plants to encourage colorful new growth. Prune to shape before spring growth begins or after bloom; don't allow new growth to get away from you and make long, bare switches. Many photinias can be converted to small trees by limbing up; or they can be trained as trees from the beginning. Evergreen species may suffer considerable damage if temperatures remain below 10°F (–12°C) for prolonged periods; they are also susceptible to a fungal leaf spot, which may cause leaves to drop in spring. All photinias are subject to fireblight; all but P. × fraseri are susceptible to powdery mildew.

P. davidiana (Stranvaesia davidiana). Evergreen shrub or small tree native to China and Vietnam. Zones 4–11, 14–17. Informal, wide-spreading plant grows at a moderate rate to 6–20 ft. tall and wide. New foliage is reddish. Some leaves turn bronze or purple in late fall and winter, a good foil for clusters of showy red berries that

form at the same time. White flowers in 4-in. clusters appear late spring to early summer. *P. d. undulata* is lower growing, forming an irregularly shaped 5-ft. shrub with wavy-edged leaves; branch tips and new foliage are bronzy red.

For best growth, give plants plenty of room and soil that is not too rich. In hot interior climates, protect from hot winds and supply adequate water.

P. × fraseri. Evergreen shrub or tree. Zones 3b (with protection), 4–24. 'Birmingham' is the usual selection sold. Moderate to fast growth to 10–15 ft. tall and wide. Leaves are bright red when new. Springtime flower clusters resemble those of *P. glabra* but are not followed by berries. Good espalier or small single-stemmed tree. Cut branches are excellent in arrangements. Resists mildew and heat, but leaf spot can be serious in the Pacific Northwest. Sometimes suffers from chlorosis in Zones 12, 13. Aphids may be a problem.

Two selections about half the size of 'Birmingham' are useful in smaller spaces: 'Indian Princess', with orange-red new growth, and 'Red Robin', with bright red new leaves and good resistance to leaf spot.

P. glabra. JAPANESE PHOTINIA. Evergreen shrub. Zones 4–9, 14–24. From Japan. Broad, dense growth to 6–10 ft. tall and wide. Leaves to 3 in. long, coppery when new; scattered leaves turn bright red through fall and winter, adding touches of color. Flowers appear in early summer in 4-in. clusters. Berries are red, aging to black. Forms with variegated foliage are available.

P. serratifolia (P. serrulata). CHINESE PHOTINIA. Evergreen shrub or tree. Zones 4–16, 18–22; can be grown in Zones 17, 23, 24, but is especially prone to mildew there. From China. Broad, dense grower; can reach 30 ft. tall and wide but is easily held to one-third that size. Stiff leaves to 8 in. long are prickly along edges. Bright copper new growth; scattered crimson leaves in fall, winter. Flower clusters to 6 in. across in late spring or early summer. Bright red berries often last until winter. 'Aculeata'

(frequently sold as 'Nova' or 'Nova Lineata') is more compact; its leaf midribs and main veins are ivory-yellow.

P. villosa. Deciduous shrub or tree. Zones 3–9, 14–17. From China, Korea, Japan. To 15 ft. tall and wide. Leaves are 1½–3 in. long; they are pale gold with rosy tints when new, green when mature, bright red or yellow in fall. Flower clusters 1–2 in. across; bright red berries.

Phygelius
CAPE FUCHSIA
Scrophulariaceae
PERENNIALS

✏	ZONES 4–9, 14–24; H1, H2
☀ ◑	FULL SUN OR LIGHT SHADE
◐	REGULAR WATER
🐦	BLOOMS ATTRACT HUMMINGBIRDS

Phygelius aequalis 'Coral Princess'

From South Africa. Showy perennials related to snapdragon (*Antirrhinum*) and penstemon, but with drooping flowers that suggest fuchsia. Plants die to the ground in cold climates, remain shrubby in milder areas. They grow 3–4 ft. tall, spreading about as wide by underground stems or rooting prostrate branches. Bloom from summer into fall, bearing tubular, curved flowers in loosely branched clusters at stem ends. To keep plants neat, cut out old flower stalks after bloom. Mulch roots in cold-winter regions.

P. aequalis. Pyramidal clusters of dusty rose flowers. 'Sani Pass' has purplish pink flowers that are creamy yellow inside. 'Trewidden Pink' bears dusty pink, yellow-throated blossoms tipped in red. 'Yellow Trumpet' has pale yellow blooms.

P. capensis. More open and sprawling than *P. aequalis*, with loose clusters of orange to red flowers.

P. × rectus. Hybrids between the previous two species. 'African Queen' has orange flowers with a yellow throat; 'Devil's Tears', scarlet with yellow throat; 'Moonraker', solid pale yellow; 'Salmon Leap' and 'Winchester Fanfare', salmon-pink with a yellow throat. 'Pink Elf' bears pink flowers on a smaller plant than the usual (2 ft. high, 3 ft. wide).

Phyllitis scolopendrium.
See *Asplenium scolopendrium*

Phyllostachys. See Bamboo

Phyla nodiflora
(Lippia repens)
LIPPIA
Verbenaceae
PERENNIAL

🌡 **ZONES 8–24; H1, H2**

☀ **FULL SUN**

◐ ◑ 💧 **LITTLE TO REGULAR WATER**

Phyla nodiflora

From many tropical and subtropical regions of the world. Ground-hugging growth and ability to endure foot traffic have established its use as a lawn substitute in some areas where a traditional lawn is impractical. Creeping stems clothed in oval, ¾-in., grayish green leaves form a mat no higher than 2 in. Rounded, ½-in. heads of tiny lavender-pink flowers appear from spring to fall. Blossoms are a magnet for bees; if this bothers you, mow plantings periodically to remove flowers. Set out plants from containers

2 ft. apart; plant rooted sprigs at 1-ft. intervals. Looks shabby in winter, but an early-spring feeding will promote fast new growth. Tolerates many soils, though performance suffers where nematodes are a problem (in the desert, for example).

Physalis alkekengi
CHINESE LANTERN PLANT
Solanaceae
PERENNIAL OFTEN GROWN AS ANNUAL

🌡 **ZONES 1–24**

☀ ◑ **FULL SUN OR LIGHT SHADE**

💧 **REGULAR WATER**

⚠ **LEAVES AND UNRIPE BERRIES ARE POISONOUS**

Physalis alkekengi

From Europe and Asia. Grown not for flowers but for the decorative, papery, 2-in. calyxes, which look like lanterns and mature to a striking orange-red in late summer and fall. Grows 1½–3 ft. high and wide, with angular branches set with large light green leaves. Small, star-shaped white flowers appear in leaf joints during summer; these are followed by inedible berries, each enclosed in a colorful inflated husk—the enlarged calyx of the flower. Dry, leafless stalks hung with these festive "lanterns" make choice winter arrangements.

Sow seeds in light soil in spring. Plant is clump forming, spreading widely by long, creeping, whitish underground stems; can become invasive. Increase established plantings by digging and dividing the roots. *P. a. franchetii* 'Zwerg' is a dwarf variety just 8 in. high; makes a good container plant.

Two other *Physalis* species produce edible fruit within papery husks. See Tomatillo (*P. ixocarpa*) and Poha, Ground Cherry (*P. peruviana*).

Physocarpus
NINEBARK
Rosaceae
DECIDUOUS SHRUBS

🌡 **ZONES VARY BY SPECIES**

☀ ◑ ● **SUN OR SHADE**

◐ 💧 **MODERATE TO REGULAR WATER**

Physocarpus opulifolius
'Diabolo'

Ninebarks are named for their peeling bark, which strips off to reveal several layers. The plants resemble spirea and are closely related to it, bearing round clusters of tiny white or pinkish flowers in spring or early summer. Prune plants as needed after bloom; rejuvenate by cutting old stems to the ground.

P. capitatus. PACIFIC NINE-BARK. Zones 2b–9, 14–19. Native to mountains of western

North America. To 5–10 ft. tall and wide, with dense clusters of white flowers. Clustered buds are as attractive as the opened blossoms.

P. monogynus. MOUNTAIN NINEBARK. Zones A1–A3; 1–3, 10. Rocky Mountain and High Plains native. To 3–5 ft. tall and wide, with pinkish to white flowers carried just a few to a cluster. Leaves turn brilliant orange and red in fall.

P. opulifolius. COMMON NINEBARK. Zones A1–A3; 1–10, 14–17. Native to eastern and central North America. To 9 ft. tall and 10 ft. wide, with clusters of white or pinkish blossoms. Varieties are more attractive than the species. 'Diabolo', to 9–12 ft. tall and wide, has intense reddish purple leaves (foliage color can tend toward dark green in very hot summers or when plant is grown in partial shade). 'Luteus' is about the same size, with leaves that are yellow when plant is grown in sunlight, yellow-green in shade. 'Center Glow' reaches 6–8 ft. tall and wide, with leaves that emerge greenish gold and mature to burgundy. Similarly sized 'Coppertina' has coppery orange foliage. Compact varieties to 4–6 ft. tall and broad include 'Dart's Gold', similar to 'Luteus' but brighter; 'Summer Wine', with dark purple leaves; 'Nanus', with small, shallowly lobed dark green leaves; 'Lady in Red', with purplish red foliage; and 'Nugget', with leaves that unfold golden yellow, gradually mature to lime green, and then turn gold again in fall.

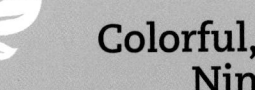

Colorful, Adaptable Ninebark

The many varieties of common ninebark offer a wide range of leaf colors, from deep purple through coppery orange and bright golden yellow. Large white or pink flower clusters are icing on the cake in spring or early summer—and they're followed by bright red bladder-shaped fruits.

If that's not enough to recommend them, consider their legendary adaptability. All ninebarks look best when grown in moist, acidic soil in full sun or partial shade, but they grow perfectly well in less-than-perfect conditions.

P

Physostegia virginiana

FALSE DRAGONHEAD,
OBEDIENT PLANT
Lamiaceae
PERENNIAL

◢ **ZONES A2, A3; 1–9, 14–24**

☼ ◑ **FULL SUN OR PARTIAL SHADE**

◐ **REGULAR WATER**

Physostegia virginiana
'Summer Snow'

From eastern and central North America. To 4 ft. tall, 3 ft. wide—or much wider, if rhizomes are allowed to spread unchecked. Slender, upright stems carry oblong, toothed, 3–5-in.-long leaves with pointed tips. In summer or early fall, each stem is topped by a 10-in.-long spike densely set with funnel-shaped, 1-in. flowers, typically in bright bluish pink. Blossoms resemble snapdragons (hence the name "false dragonhead") and will remain in place if twisted or pushed out of position (hence the name "obedient plant"). 'Bouquet Rose' reaches 3 ft. high, has rose pink flowers. Varieties growing 2 ft. tall include rose pink 'Vivid', white 'Summer Snow', and 'Variegata', with bluish pink flowers and white-edged leaves.

Attractive in borders; good cut flowers. Bloom stalks may need staking to remain upright. Cut to ground after bloom. Vigorous and notoriously invasive; to keep clumps in-bounds, divide them every 2 years in early spring.

FOR MORE ON PERENNIALS, SEE
"GROW: PERENNIALS," PAGES
686–687.

Picea

SPRUCE
Pinaceae
EVERGREEN TREES

◢ **ZONES VARY BY SPECIES**

☼ ◑ **FULL SUN OR LIGHT SHADE**

◐ ◐ **LITTLE TO MODERATE WATER, EXCEPT AS NOTED**

🐦 **ATTRACT BIRDS**

Picea glauca albertiana

Like firs (*Abies*), spruces are pyramidal trees, with branches arranged in neat tiers. Unlike firs, however, their cones hang down, and their needles are stiffer and attached to branches by small pegs that remain behind after the needles drop. Most spruces are tall timber trees, but dwarf varieties are lovely in home gardens. Plants have shallow root systems and so need a reasonably cool location. Spruces generally grow best where summers are cool or mild; most suffer in heat and humidity. *P. pungens* tolerates dry conditions better than the other species.

Spruces can be grown in containers for years as living Christmas trees and moved indoors for up to a week. In coldest climates, move potted trees to a protected location for winter.

P. abies. NORWAY SPRUCE. Zones A2, A3; 1–6, 14–17. Native to northern Europe. Fast growth to 100–150 ft. tall and 20 ft. wide. Stiff, deep green, attractive pyramid in youth; in age, branchlets droop strongly. Tolerates heat and humidity better than most spruces. Extremely hardy and wind-resistant; valued for windbreaks in cold-winter zones. The following slow growers are among the many dwarf varieties available.

'Cupressina'. Narrow, columnar growth to 20–30 ft. tall, 4–6 ft. wide, with rich green foliage. Excellent vertical accent.

'Lanham's Beehive'. To 5 ft. tall, 4 ft. wide, with a dense pyramidal shape. Needles are long and thick, with a bluish green tint.

'Little Gem'. Dense grower to 1 ft. high and wide, with short needles and flat top.

'Nidiformis'. BIRD'S NEST SPRUCE. Dense growth to 3–5 ft. tall (ultimately to 10 ft.), 4–6 ft. wide. Individual plants vary in form. Some are flat topped; in others, the semierect main branches curve outward, leaving a shallow depression at the plant's top that gives it the look of a bird's nest.

'Pendula'. Grows naturally as a groundcover about 1½ ft. high, 10 ft. wide. Looks attractive cascading downward from rocks or walls. Can be staked to desired height and grown as a short, weeping tree.

'Pusch'. Handsome, dense mound to 2 ft. high, 4 ft. wide, with profuse production of tiny cones that are red in youth, aging to brown.

P. breweriana. BREWER'S WEEPING SPRUCE. Zones 2b–7, 14–17. Native to the Siskiyou Mountains in California and Oregon. To 30–50 ft. tall and 10–12 ft. wide in gardens (larger in the wild). Stiff, upright pyramid in youth. Very striking form in maturity, with 7–8-ft.-long branchlets hanging vertically from the main branches. Needles are shiny deep green above, gray-green beneath. More tender than most spruces. Requires regular water, cool temperatures.

P. engelmannii. ENGELMANN SPRUCE. Zones A2, A3; 1–7, 10, 14–17. Native from British Columbia south to Oregon and Northern California and east to the Rockies. To 60–130 ft. tall, 20–25 ft. wide, with densely pyramidal form. Resembles blue-green forms of *P. pungens*, but needles are softer and tree is not as wide at base. Popular lawn tree in the Rocky Mountain region.

P. glauca. WHITE SPRUCE. Zones A1–A3, 1–7, 14–17, except as noted. Native to Canada and northern U.S. Cone-shaped, densely foliaged tree to 60–70 ft. tall and 10–12 ft. wide. Pendulous twigs; silver-green needles. Growth is best where winters are very cold. Many varieties offered, including the following.

'Blue Wonder'. Grows slowly into a compact, narrow cone 6 ft. tall and 2–3 ft. wide, gray-blue foliage.

'Densata'. BLACK HILLS SPRUCE. Zones A2, A3; 1–6. Slow-growing, dense pyramid can reach 20–25 ft. tall, 10–12 ft. wide in 35 years.

'Jean's Dilly'. Pyramidal tree to 4–5 ft. tall and 2–3 ft. wide, with twisted needles.

'Pendula'. Slender, formal-looking tree to an eventual 20 ft. tall and just 6 ft. wide. Pendulous branches are thickly clothed in blue-green foliage.

'Rainbow's End'. To 10 ft. tall and 4 ft. wide, with a tailored, upright, conical form and new growth in summer that is bright yellow, slowly fading to green.

P. g. albertiana 'Conica'. DWARF ALBERTA SPRUCE, DWARF WHITE SPRUCE. Zones A2, A3; 1–7, 14–17. Compact, cone-shaped, bushy shrub grows slowly, reaching 6–8 ft. tall, 4–5 ft. wide. Short, soft needles are bright grass green when new, gray-green when mature. Needs shelter from wind and strong, reflected sunlight. Popular container plant.

P. mariana. BLACK SPRUCE. Zones A1–A3; 1–7. Native to Alaska and other parts of northern North America. Forms an irregular column to 30–50 ft. tall, 6–10 ft. wide. Bluish green needles. Tolerates cold, wet soils. 'Nana' is a choice compact variety (to 3 ft. high, 4–6 ft. wide) with blue-gray foliage.

P. omorika. SERBIAN SPRUCE. Zones 2b–7, 14–17. Native to southeastern Europe. Narrow, conical, slow-growing tree to 50–60 ft. tall and just 6–10 ft. wide. Shiny, dark green needles have whitish undersides, giving a two-tone effect. Retains branches to the ground for many years. Considered by some to be the most attractive of all spruces. It is the one least likely to be seriously damaged by Cooley spruce gall adelgid. 'Nana' is a dwarf to 3–4 ft. tall and wide (possibly to 10 ft. tall), with short, closely spaced

green through all shades of blue-green to steely blue. Poor performer in Puget Sound region. Throughout its range, subject to an aphid that forms galls. Prefers dry soil.

Plants in the Glauca group (formerly listed as *P. p. glauca*) are called Colorado blue spruces; they are like the species but with bluish foliage. Among the best are the following.

'Fat Albert'. Broad, formal-looking tree to 15–20 ft. tall and 10–12 ft. wide.

'Hoopsii'. Dense, conical form with spreading branches and dependably powder blue foliage.

'Koster'. Forms a blue-gray cone, though growth habit may be irregular.

'Moerheimii'. Same blue-gray color as 'Koster', but shape is more compact and symmetrical. Needles are longer and thicker than in other selections.

'Montgomery'. Slow-growing dwarf that forms a broad, silver-blue cone to 5 ft. tall and wide.

'Pendula' ('Glauca Pendula'). WEEPING BLUE SPRUCE. This gray-blue plant with weeping branchlets can be grown as groundcover; it can also be trained to a small, weeping tree by staking at desired height when young. 'The Blues' is similar, but even more strongly weeping.

P. sitchensis. SITKA SPRUCE. Zones A2, A3; 4–6, 14–17. Native to cool, foggy areas from Alaska to California. The largest of all spruces, this is a pyramidal tree 80–160 ft. tall and 20–40 ft. wide in cultivation; plants in the wild may grow much taller. Horizontal branches hold short, flat, prickly needles that are glossy dark green above, powder blue beneath. Needs moisture in both atmosphere and soil to look its best. Subject to Cooley spruce gall. 'Tenas' ('Papoose') is a dwarf variety, eventually to 4–5 ft. tall and wide.

CARE

Check spruces for small, dull green aphids in winter; if they're present, take control measures at that time to prevent defoliation in spring. Pine needle scale (look for flat, white scale insects on needles) may encourage

sooty mold. In Rocky Mountain states, spruces may be bothered by spider mites and tussock moths. Cooley spruce gall adelgid is an aphidlike insect that attacks many spruce trees, especially in the Pacific Northwest and mountain areas. Its feeding causes green, conelike galls to form at ends of new growth. These galls gradually turn light purplish tan and then brown by autumn. Douglas fir is an alternate host for these pests, but it doesn't develop galls. Contact your local Cooperative Extension Office for control measures.

Pieris
Ericaceae
EVERGREEN SHRUBS

🖋 **ZONES VARY BY SPECIES**

◐ **FILTERED SUNLIGHT OR PARTIAL SHADE**

🌢 **REGULAR WATER**

◈ **LEAVES AND NECTAR ARE POISONOUS IF INGESTED**

Pieris japonica 'Variegata'

Elegant in foliage and form the year around, these plants make good companions for rhododendron and azalea, to which they are related. They have narrowly oval, glossy, medium to dark green leaves and bear clusters of small, urn-shaped, typically white flowers. Most plants form flower buds by autumn; these resemble strings of tiny beads in greenish pink, red, or white and provide a subtle decorative feature in winter. Flowers open from midwinter to midspring. New spring growth is often brightly colored (pink to red or bronze). Splendid in containers, in woodland and Japanese

CLOCKWISE FROM TOP: *Picea pungens* 'Globosa'; *P. abies*; *P. mariana* 'Aurea'

needles. 'Pendula Bruns', to 6–8 ft. tall and 2 ft. wide after 10 years, forms an elegant column of weeping, slightly twisting branches. 'Pimoko' forms a tight, symmetrical mound just 1½ ft. high and 2½ ft. wide, with blue-green needles.

P. orientalis. ORIENTAL SPRUCE. Zones 2b–7, 14–17. Native to Caucasus, Asia Minor. Dense, compact, cone-shaped tree with very short needles; grows slowly to 50–60 ft. tall,

20 ft. wide. Tolerates poor soils as long as they are well drained, but may suffer leaf burn in very cold, dry winds. Among the many available varieties are 'Aurea' and 'Aureospicata', with chartreuse new growth that matures to deep green; and 'Skylands', with creamy gold leaves year-round.

P. pungens. COLORADO SPRUCE. Zones A2, A3; 1–10, 14–17. Native to the Rocky Mountain region. In gardens, reaches 30–60 ft. tall and 10–20 ft. wide. Very stiff, regular, horizontal branches form a broad pyramid. Foliage of seedlings varies in color from dark

P

gardens, in entryways where year-round quality is essential.

Choose a planting location sheltered from wind, where plants will get high shade or dappled sunlight at least during the warmest afternoon hours. Where summers are cool or foggy, they can take more sun. Need acid, well-drained but moisture-retentive soil. Where water is high in salts, soil needs careful leaching. Prune by removing spent flowers. Thin older specimens by taking out whole branches; or limb them up to reveal attractive peeling bark.

P. floribunda (Andromeda floribunda). MOUNTAIN PIERIS. Zones 2–9, 14–17. Native to the southeastern U.S. Compact, rounded shrub to 6 ft. tall, 10 ft. wide. Differs from the other species—new growth is pale green, mature leaves dull dark green, 1½–3 in. long. Blossoms in upright clusters. Cold-hardy; tolerates sun, heat, and low humidity better than the others.

P. 'Forest Flame'. Zones 3b–9, 14–17. Hybrid between *P. japonica* and a form of *P. formosa forrestii*. To 6–10 ft. tall, 3–5 ft. wide. Leaves are brilliant red when new, fading to creamy pink before maturing to dark green. Blooms profusely, bearing broader, heavier flower clusters than those of *P. japonica*.

P. formosa forrestii (P. forrestii). CHINESE PIERIS. Zones 8–9, 14–17. From China. Dense grower to 10 ft. tall and 12 ft. wide. Leaves may reach 6 in. long. New growth ranges from brilliant scarlet to pale salmon-pink. Large, drooping flower clusters. Good espalier in shade.

P. japonica. LILY-OF-THE-VALLEY SHRUB, JAPANESE ANDROMEDA. Zones 2b–9, 14–17. Upright, dense, tiered growth to 9–10 ft. tall and wide. New leaves are bronzy pink to red; mature ones are glossy green. Drooping clusters of white, pink, or nearly red flowers; flower buds are often dark red.

The following, some of which are hybrids, are grown for smaller-than-usual size or unusual foliage. Flowers are white unless otherwise noted.

'Bert Chandler'. Salmon-pink new foliage ages to cream, then white; matures to pale green.

'Bisbee Dwarf'. To 1 ft. high and wide, with half-size leaves that are red when young.

'Cavatine'. To 2–3 ft. high and wide, with red new growth. Choice dwarf form.

'Compacta'. Grows to 4–5 ft. tall and wide.

'Crispa'. To 6–7 ft. tall and wide, with handsome wavy-edged leaves.

'Flaming Silver'. Excellent hybrid plant to 4–5 ft. tall and wide. Young leaves are red with pink margins, mature ones green with white edges.

'Karenoma'. Compact grower to 3–6 ft. tall and wide, with upright flower clusters.

'Little Heath'. To 2–4 ft. tall and wide, with gray-green leaves edged in creamy white.

'Mountain Fire'. Fiery red new growth.

'Prelude'. To 2–3 ft. high and wide; pink new growth.

'Pygmaea'. Tiny dwarf to 1–2 ft. high and wide, with few flowers and narrow leaves to 1 in. long.

'Sarabande'. Compact, vigorous dwarf grows to 3–4 ft. tall and wide.

'Spring Snow'. Similar to 'Karenoma'.

'Valley Fire'. Brilliant red new growth.

'Variegata'. Slow growing to 6 ft. tall and wide. Creamy white leaf edges.

These are grown principally for their flowers:

'Brouwer's Beauty'. To 5–7 ft. tall, 5 ft. wide. Deep red buds open to white flowers held on nearly horizontal stalks.

'Christmas Cheer'. Early bloomer with bicolored flowers in white and deep rose-red; flower stalks are rose-red.

'Dorothy Wyckoff'. Deep red buds open into pink flowers that age to white. Bronzy new foliage. Vigorous, compact grower.

'Purity'. To 3–4 ft. tall and wide. Late bloomer with unusually large white flowers.

'Temple Bells'. Slow grower to 3–5 ft. tall and wide. Ivory flowers.

'Valley Rose'. Light pink flowers.

'Valley Valentine'. To 5–7 ft. tall and wide. Deep red buds and flowers.

'White Cascade'. Extremely heavy show of pure white blooms.

Pimpinella anisum
ANISE
Apiaceae
ANNUAL

🌿 **ZONES 1–24; H1, H2**

☀ **FULL SUN**

💧 **REGULAR WATER**

Pimpinella anisum

Mediterranean native to 2 ft. tall, 1½ ft. wide. First growth produces a clump of bright green, roundish to heart-shaped, tooth-edged leaves. Foliage clumps send up stems set with feathery leaves; in summer, bear umbrellalike clusters of tiny white flowers at stem tips. Use fresh leaves in salads; use seeds for flavoring baked goods, confections.

Plant grows quickly in warm weather, but you'll need to allow about 4 months for a crop of seeds to grow and mature. In coldest regions, sow seeds indoors, then set out young plants when frost danger is past. In mild-winter climates, sow directly in the ground in spring for harvest in summer or early fall. Where summers are very hot, sow in fall for spring harvest. Grow in light, well-drained soil. Plants are fairly wispy and look best in groups. They are taprooted and do not transplant easily once they begin to put on size.

For a refreshing licorice-flavored tea, steep dried anise seeds in boiling water.

Pineapple
Bromeliaceae
PERENNIAL

🌿 **ZONES 24; H1, H2**

☀ **FULL SUN**

💧 **REGULAR WATER**

Pineapple

This South American native, known botanically as *Ananas comosus*, is well adapted to Hawaii, where it is a commercial crop. It can be grown in Southern California in warm, protected sites; black plastic mulch over soil increases chances of success. Plants grow 2½–5 ft. tall, 3–4 ft. wide, with a short, thick stem topped by a rosette of long, narrow dark green leaves. At bloom time, the stem lengthens and produces a head composed of small red or purple flowers, which then fuse together to form the pineapple. In ideal growing conditions, fruits reach size and heft of pineapples sold in markets. Recommended varieties include 'Del Monte Gold', 'Queen', 'Smooth Cayenne', and 'Sugarloaf'.

Pineapples take up to 2 years to begin bearing. Fruit is ready to harvest when it reaches a good size and starts to take on a yellow cast, with the bottom turning golden. After cutting the fruit from the plant, let it ripen fully at room temperature. Plants continue to produce fruit for several years.

Plants can be grown in the ground or in containers. Provide rich, well-drained soil. Start from divisions sold in nurseries; or slice off the leafy top of a market pineapple (cut about an inch below the leaf rosette) and let it dry for a couple of days.

Plant 1 ft. apart. Set divisions 3–4 in. deep; set pineapple tops 2 in. deep (base of leaf rosette should be buried). Feed every 2–3 months with a high-nitrogen fertiler.

Pineapple can also be grown indoors in a greenhouse or sunny room where temperature stays above 68°F (20°C). Root the base of a leafy pineapple top in water or in fast-draining but moisture-retentive potting mix. When roots have formed, move pineapple to 7–8-in. pot of rich soil. If you're lucky, a pineapple will form, but it will be much smaller than commercial fruit. A variety with pink, white, and olive green leaves is sometimes sold as a houseplant; it can take reduced light, since it is grown for foliage rather than fruit.

Pinus

PINE
Pinaceae
EVERGREEN TREES, RARELY SHRUBS

- ✎ **ZONES VARY BY SPECIES**
- ☀ **FULL SUN**
- ◯ **LITTLE WATER, EXCEPT AS NOTED**
- ❀ **ATTRACT BUTTERFLIES; SEEDS ATTRACT BIRDS**

Pinus nigra

Pines are the great individualists of the garden, each species differing not only in its characteristics but also in the ways it responds to wind, heat, and other growing conditions. Young trees tend to be pyramidal, while older ones are more open or round topped. Cone appearance is one identifying feature of these trees. Another is the number of needles held in a bundle: most carry their long, slender needles in groups of two, three, or five. The listings below give typical dimensions for pines in cultivation, but trees often grow much larger in the wild. Hundreds of varieties are available in different colors, forms, and growth rates; almost all are smaller than the species and thus better suited to home gardens.

P. albicaulis. WHITEBARK PINE. Zones A2, A3; 1–7, 15–17. From high mountains of Northern California and Nevada north to Canada. Grows very slowly to 20–40 ft. tall (usually much less), about half as wide. In youth, slender and symmetrical, with whitish bark; often multitrunked as it ages. Dark green, 1½–3-in.-long needles are held in groups of five. Cones to 3 in. long are roundish and purple. Licensed collectors dig plants from the wild and sell them under the name "alpine conifer." Densely foliaged pine is good for rock gardens or bonsai.

P. aristata. ROCKY MOUNTAIN BRISTLECONE PINE. Zones A2, A3; 1–11, 14–19. From high mountain areas of the West. Grows very slowly to 20–30 ft. tall, 15 ft. wide. Dense, bushy, heavy-trunked tree with ground-sweeping branches. In youth, symmetrical and narrow crowned. Dark green needles are held in groups of five and grow 1–1½ in. long. Cones to 4 in. long are dark purplish brown and bristly. Excellent container, rock garden, and bonsai plant. Protect from wind in cold climates. For a close relative sometimes offered as *P. a. longaeva*, see *P. longaeva*.

P. attenuata. KNOBCONE PINE. Zones 2–10, 14–21. Native to Oregon's northern and central Cascades, Siskiyous, and Sierra foothills in California, south to Baja California. Grows rapidly to 20–80 ft. tall, 20–25 ft. wide. Usually rounded and regular in youth, open and irregular in age. Yellow-green needles 3–5 in. long are held in groups of three. Light brown cones are 4–6 in. long. Grows well in poor soil.

P. banksiana. JACK PINE. Zones A1–A3; 1, 2. Native from the Arctic Circle to Minnesota. Slow to moderate growth to 30–50 ft. tall (often less) and 10–15 ft. wide. In youth, a symmetrical pyramid; in age, irregular and more spreading, often picturesque. Sometimes remains shrubby. Good windbreak. Olive green needles to 2 in. long are held in groups of two and are often curved or twisted. Cones are yellowish brown, 1–3 in. long. Tolerates poor soil, even sand. Popular 'Uncle Fogy' has a very irregular, weeping form.

P. brutia (P. halepensis brutia). CALABRIAN PINE. Zones 6–9, 12–24. From eastern Mediterranean, southern Russia, southern Italy. Grows fast to 30–80 ft. tall, 15–25 ft. wide. Shows rugged character even when young, with an open, irregular crown of many short, ascending branches. In maturity, the crown becomes dense and rounded. Dark green needles in groups of two reach 5–6½ in. long. Cones are oval to oblong, 3 in. long, reddish brown. Thrives in heat, wind, and poor soil.

P. bungeana. LACEBARK PINE. Zones 2–10, 14–21. From northern and central China. Grows 50–75 ft. tall, 20–35 ft. wide. Starts out pyramidal to rounded, then becomes more open, spreading, and picturesque. Often multitrunked, sometimes shrubby. Smooth, dull gray bark flakes off to reveal creamy white patches. Bright green needles in groups of three are 2–4 in. long. Cones are up to 2½ in. long and yellowish brown. Limbs are brittle, can break under heavy ice or snow load. 'Rowe Arboretum' is compact and uniform.

P. canariensis. CANARY ISLAND PINE. Zones 8, 9, 12–24. Native to Canary Islands. Grows fast to 50–80 ft. tall and 20–35 ft. wide. Gawky when young, but soon develops into a slender, graceful pyramid, after which it takes on a tiered look, then finally develops a round head. Bark is fissured, reddish brown. Needles 9–12 in. long are held in groups of three; bluish green when new, then aging to dark green. Glossy brown cones can reach 9 in. long. Resists oak root fungus.

P. cembra. SWISS STONE PINE. Zones A1–A3; 1–7, 10. Native to the mountains of central Europe. Grows extremely slowly to 50–70 ft. or taller, 20–25 ft. wide. Handsome narrow, dense pyramid in youth; becomes broad, open, and round topped in maturity. Dark green needles are 3–5 in. long, held in groups of five. Purplish blue cones are 3½ in. long. Regular water. 'Algonquin Pillar' is upright and narrow, maintaining its dense foliage all the way to the ground. 'Klein' has violet-blue cones; grows 12 ft. tall, 6 ft. wide. 'Westerstede' forms a wide, lush mass of extra-long, bluish green needles.

P. contorta. SHORE PINE, BEACH PINE. Zones A3; 4–9, 14–24; H1. Native along the Pacific Coast from Alaska to Northern California. Grows fairly quickly to 20–35 ft. tall and wide. Nursery trees are compact, pyramidal, and somewhat irregular; trees growing along the coast may be dwarfed and shaped by winds. Dark green needles are held in groups of two, reaching 1¼–2 in. long. Cones are 1–2 in. long and light yellow-brown. Good-looking tree in youth; densely foliaged. Responds well to

These noble evergreens are often seen in parks and along highways, where they're prized for their tolerance of harsh conditions, including wind, drought, and poor soils. In home gardens, pines usually look best as single specimens, with plenty of room to accommodate their mature size—although smaller types can be grouped as windbreaks or even carefully pruned into rough screens or hedges. Most develop a taproot over time, so plant them in their permanent locations when they're young.

CLOCKWISE FROM LEFT: *Pinus mugo; P. thunbergii; P. parviflora* 'Glauca'

pruning. Among the best pines for small gardens. Regular water. Picturesque 'Spaan's Dwarf' reaches 3 ft. high, 4 ft. wide, in 10 years; good choice for a container. 'Taylor's Sunburst' is broadly upright, with bright yellow new growth that matures to light yellow-green.

P. c. murrayana (P. c. latifolia). LODGEPOLE PINE, TAMARACK. Zones A1–A3; 1–7, 14–17. Native to the mountains of the western U.S. Can grow to 50–80 ft. tall, 20–25 ft. wide, but even often much smaller. Planted among other trees, lodgepole pine grows tall and slender, but in the open, the trunk can be quite thick, even though the tree remains narrow and dense. The yellow-green needles are grouped in twos, reaching 1½–3 in. long. Cones to 1½ in. long are shiny brown and oval; tend to hang onto branches for a long time. Tree needs regular water.

P. coulteri. COULTER PINE. Zones 3–10, 14–23; H1. Native to dry, rocky mountain California

slopes from Mt. Diablo and Mt. Hamilton through the Santa Lucia Range and Southern California to Baja California. Grows moderately fast to 30–80 ft. tall and 20–40 ft. wide, with shapely, open growth and wide-spreading, persistent lower branches. Can develop multiple leaders. Needles are deep green, stiff, 5–10 in. (even 14 in.) long and held in groups of three. Heavy cones are 10–14 in. long, oval, and buff-colored; they remain on the tree for a long time.

P. densiflora. JAPANESE RED PINE. Zones 2–9, 14–17; H1. Native to Japan. Grows rapidly when young, ultimately to 40–60 ft. tall (to 100 ft. tall in perfect conditions) and 40 ft. wide. Develops a broad, irregular head, even in youth; often has two trunks. Young branches have flaking, red-orange bark. Bright green needles are grouped in twos and reach 2½–5 in. long. Tawny brown cones are 2 in. long. Won't take hot, dry, or cold winds. Regular water.

'Low Glow'. Forms a dense, flat-topped mound about 3 ft. high and 4 ft. wide. Needles are bright yellowish green.

'Oculus-draconis'. DRAGON-EYE PINE. About half the size of the species. Each needle has two yellow bands, so branches appear to have concentric green and yellow bands when viewed from the tips.

'Pendula'. A dwarf form with a sprawling, weeping habit—perfect for rock gardens. Can be staked to form a weeping specimen tree.

'Umbraculifera'. TANYOSHO PINE. Grows in Zones 2–10, 14–17. It is a moderate grower to 12–20 ft. tall and 18 ft. wide. Broad, flat-topped tree with many trunks that emerge from the base; often grafted onto a short single trunk. Good for containers, rock gardens, and Asian-style gardens.

P. edulis (P. cembroides edulis). PIÑON, NUT PINE. Zones 1–11, 14–21. Native from California's desert mountains east to New Mexico and Texas, north to Wyoming. The state tree of New Mexico. Grows slowly to 10–20 ft. tall, 8–16 ft. wide. Horizontally branching tree, bushy and symmetrical in youth, spreading as it matures and developing a rounded, flat crown. Stiff, dark

green needles are usually grouped in twos, reaching ¾–1½ in. long. Light brown cones to 2 in. long produce the edible pine nuts sold in markets. This is a beautiful, dense small pine for containers and rock gardens, lending a look of age to new gardens. Water deeply but infrequently.

P. eldarica (P. brutia eldarica). AFGHAN PINE. Zones 6–9, 11–24. From southern Russia, Afghanistan, and Pakistan. Growth size, rate, habit, and both needle and cone descriptions match *P. brutia.* Among best pines for much of the desert; also thrives near Pacific Coast. Avoid planting in Southwest areas with elevations of 4,000–8,000 ft. where oaks are prevalent; fatal Comandra blister rust often kills these pines there. Christmas Blue is a blue-green strain.

P. flexilis. LIMBER PINE. Zones A1–A3; 1–11, 14–21. Native to 5,000–11,000-ft. elevations in northern Arizona, Utah, Nevada, Southern California; eastern slopes of Rockies. Grows at a slow to moderate rate to 30–55 ft. tall, 15–25 ft. wide. In youth, forms a rather straggly pyramid; in maturity, develops a thick trunk and an open, round top. Many of its limber branches may droop. At highest elevations it is dwarfed and irregular. Dark green needles to 3 in. long are held in groups of five. Buff to buff-orange cones are 3–5 in. long. Takes well to shearing; good bonsai subject. Tolerates wind and grows well on rocky slopes. 'Vanderwolf's Pyramid' has regular form, blue-green needles.

P. griffithii. See *P. wallichiana.*

P. heldreichii leucodermis (P. leucodermis). BOSNIAN PINE. Zones 2–11, 14–24. Native to the Balkans, Greece, Italy. Slow grower to 50–75 ft. tall, 15–20 ft. wide, forming a dense, erect oval or cone shape. Stiff, dark green needles to 3½ in. long are held in groups of two. Blue to bright brown cones 2–3 in. long are carried singly or in clusters of three. Young trees have pale grayish bark. Great landscape tree. Its salt-tolerance makes it especially useful both near the ocean and in colder areas where salt is used to clear the roadways in winter. Resistant to pests and diseases. Regular water.

Several dwarf forms are available. 'Irish Bell' is compact and uniform, making an upright bell shape about 8 ft. tall and wide. 'Mint Truffle' grows slowly into a teardrop shape, with densely foliaged branches all the way to the ground; reaches 12 ft. tall, 10 ft. wide. 'Emerald Arrow' has a slender, upright habit and dense, rich green foliage; grows 20 ft. tall and half as wide.

P. jeffreyi. JEFFREY PINE. Zones 2–9, 14–19; H1. Native to the mountains of California, southern Oregon, western Nevada, and Baja California. Moderate growth rate, reaching 60–120 ft. tall, 20–25 ft. wide. Pyramidal form, with straight trunk and pendulous branches; symmetrical in youth, more open with age. Blue-green needles grouped in threes are 5–8 in. long. Cones are 6–12 in. long and reddish brown. Attractive in youth, with silvery gray bark and bluish foliage. Furrows in the bark of older trees have the fragrance of vanilla, butterscotch, or oranges, depending on the tree and the sniffer. Takes much heat and drought. 'Joppi' forms a dense teardrop to about 10 ft. tall and wide.

P. lambertiana. SUGAR PINE. Zones 2–9, 15–17. Native to Sierra Nevada and California's higher Coast Ranges, high mountains of Southern California and Baja California, and north to southwestern Oregon. Grows slowly in youth, then speeds up, ultimately reaching 200 ft. tall (or taller) and 50 ft. wide. In youth, a narrow, open pyramid with spreading, rather pendulous branches; in age, usually flat topped, with a wide-spreading, open head. Dark bluish green needles 3–4 in. long are held in groups of five. Cones are light brown, 10–20 in. long, and almost cylindrical. This is the world's tallest pine. Huge cones are a hazard around play areas, patios, and parked cars—but best-ever holiday decorations. Thrives around Puget Sound.

P. leucodermis. See *P. heldreichii leucodermis.*

P. longaeva. GREAT BASIN BRISTLECONE PINE, ANCIENT PINE. Zones A2, A3; 1–11,

14–19. Native to the White Mountains of California. Grows very slowly to 30 ft. tall, 20 ft. wide, forming a dense pyramid in youth and opening up with age. Blue-green needles to 1¼ in. long are typically held in groups of five. Red cones may reach 4 in. long. These trees have been documented to have a life span of more than 4,700 years. 'Sherwood Compact' is a dense, formal-looking selection to just 3 ft. high and half as wide after 10 years.

P. monophylla. SINGLE-LEAF PIÑON. Zones 2–12, 14–21. Native to southeastern California, Arizona, Nevada, Utah, and Baja California. Grows slowly to 15–30 ft. tall and nearly as wide. Slender and symmetrical in youth, it develops a rounded crown with maturity and eventually becomes open and broad-topped, with a crooked trunk. Stiff, gray-green needles up to 2 in. long are typically carried singly, making it unique among pines. Cones are 2–3 in. long and light brown. The large seeds are edible. Young trees grow well in containers; good choice for bonsai.

P. monticola. WESTERN WHITE PINE. Zones 1–7. Native from Northern California north to British Columbia, east to Montana. Grows fast at first, then moderately to slowly, to 60 ft. tall, 20 ft. wide. Attractive, narrow, and open crowned in youth; in age, a pyramidal tree with spreading and somewhat drooping branches. Thin, soft needles to 4 in. long are blue-green, striped with white beneath; held in groups of five. Cones 5–11 in. long are light brown. Bark is purplish, weathering to a silvery color; forms plates rather than furrows. 'Pendula' has pendulous blue-green branches; it can be staked to form a weeping tree or allowed to spread as an interesting groundcover.

P. mugo. MUGO PINE, SWISS MOUNTAIN PINE. Zones A1–A3; 1–11, 14–24. From the mountains of central and southern Europe. This slow-growing, extremely variable species can reach 75 ft. tall, but smaller forms offered in nurseries and garden centers tend to be shrubby and symmetrical. Dark green needles to 3 in. long are

CLOCKWISE FROM TOP: *Pinus canariensis; P. wallichiana;* young cones of *P. longaeva* 'Sherwood Compact'

held in groups of two, crowded on the branches. Cones to 2½ in. long are tawny to dark brown. Durable and adaptable. Moderate to regular water.

Look for named varieties to ensure uniformity in size and shape. All look best if left to grow naturally; choose plants with a pleasingly rounded form rather than trying to shape them later through pruning. 'Big Tuna' is dense and upright, to 10 ft. tall and 6–8 ft. wide. 'Gnom' forms a tight globe just 2½ ft. high and wide after 10 years. The popular dwarf 'Mops' forms a dense mound to 2–3 ft. high and wide; needles take on

a golden cast in winter. 'Slowmound' is dense and slow growing to 1–2 ft. high and wide in 10 years. 'Tannenbaum' grows slowly into a dense Christmas-tree shape about 10 ft. tall and 6 ft. wide. Varieties with golden needles are available.

P. mugo mugo, dwarf mugo pine, is widely offered. It is low growing, usually topping out at 4–8 ft. tall and up to twice as wide. Excellent performer but quite variable in habit.

P

»

How to Grow Pines

DRAINAGE Well-drained soil is crucial to a pine's good health. In nature, many grow on rocky slopes or sandy barrens, where drainage is very fast. Symptoms of poor drainage or excessive moisture are yellowing needles (seen first in older growth) and generally unhealthy appearance. Most pines are quite drought-tolerant; exceptions are noted in the text.

MULCHING Pines benefit from a thick layer of mulch to protect their shallow roots. Spread 2–3 in. of organic mulch beneath trees, but keep it 6 in. away from the trunk.

PRUNING All pines can be shaped, and often improved, by some pruning. To fatten up a rangy pine or to keep a young one chubby, cut back the spires of new growth (the candles) when they begin to emerge in spring. Cutting back partway will promote bushiness and allow some overall increase in size; cutting out candles entirely will limit size without distorting the natural shape. You can remove unwanted limbs to accent a pine's branching pattern—but remember that a new one won't sprout to take its place. In time, lower limbs of most pines will die naturally; when this happens, cut them off.

CHALLENGES Pines are vulnerable to air pollution, which causes abnormal needle drop and poor growth, and may even kill trees. They are also subject to a number of diseases and pests, but healthy, well-grown plants will usually maintain their vigor with comparatively little attention. Contact your Cooperative Extension Office for advice concerning each species' adaptability to your area and any local environmental or pest problems.

P. muricata. BISHOP PINE. Zones 5, 14–17, 22–44. From northern coastal California, Santa Cruz Island, and northwestern Baja California. Rapid grower to 40–75 ft. tall, 20–40 ft. wide. Open and pyramidal form in youth, dense and rounded in middle life, and irregular in old age. Needles are dark green, 4–6 in. long, and held in groups of two. Brown, broadly oval cones are 2–3 in. long, lopsided, and held in whorls of three to five. Slower growing, denser in youth, and better mannered than *P. radiata*, another pine native to California. Tolerates salt air. First-rate windbreak tree.

P. nigra. AUSTRIAN PINE. Zones A3; 2–10, 14–21. From Europe and western Asia. Slow to moderate growth to 40–60 ft. tall and half as wide. A dense, stout, pyramidal tree with a uniform crown. Branches grow in regular whorls. In old age, this tree is broad and flat topped. Stiff, very dark green needles, 3–6½ in. long, are held in groups of two. Brown cones are 2–3½ in. long. Tree of strong character for landscape decoration or as windbreak in cold regions. Tolerates urban environments and seacoast conditions; thrives in sandy soils. Resistant to oak root fungus. Regular water. 'Arnold Sentinel', to 20–30 ft. tall and just 6–8 ft. wide, makes a fine vertical accent. 'Brepo' is dense and nearly spherical at 3 ft. high, 4 ft. wide; good choice for containers. 'Oregon Green' reaches 20 ft. tall, 15 ft. wide, with an open, sculptural form.

P. parviflora. JAPANESE WHITE PINE. Zones 2–9, 14–24. From Japan and Taiwan. Slow to moderate grower to 20–50 ft. tall and wide or larger. In youth, a dense pyramid; with age, wide spreading and flat topped. Needles are 1½–2½ in. long, bluish green, and held in groups of five. Reddish brown cones are 2–3 in. long. Widely used and popular as bonsai subject, container tree. Grows well in the Seattle area and in Northern California. 'Bergman' has thin blue-green needles and an upright habit; grows 6 ft. tall, 4 ft. wide, in 10 years. 'Glauca Brevifolia' has short blue-green needles and persistent dark cones; upright and broad, it grows to an eventual 40 ft. tall and wide. Many other blue-gray and dwarf forms are available. Regular water.

P. pinea. ITALIAN STONE PINE. Zones 8, 9, 11–24; H1. From southern Europe and Turkey. Moderate growth to 40–80 ft. tall and 40–60 ft. wide. In youth, grows as a stout, bushy globe; in middle life, develops a thick trunk topped with an "umbrella" of many branches. In maturity, tree is broad and flat topped. Stiff needles are bright green to gray-green, 5–8 in. long, and held in groups of two. Cones are 4–6 in. long and glossy chestnut brown. Excellent pine for beach gardens; also tolerates heat. Eventually too large for small gardens. This is the pine depicted in Renaissance paintings; also a source of edible seeds (pine nuts).

P. ponderosa. PONDEROSA PINE, WESTERN YELLOW PINE. Zones 1–10, 14–21; H1. Native from British Columbia to Mexico and east to Nebraska, Texas, and northeast Oklahoma. Moderate to fast grower, reaching 50–100 ft. tall and 25–30 ft. wide. In youth, straight trunked and well branched. Yellow-green to dark green needles are held in groups of three. Cones are oval, light brown to red-brown. Important lumber tree. Handsome orange-brown bark. Useful for groves and shelter belt; also good for bonsai or containers. Doesn't take desert heat and wind.

P. radiata. MONTEREY PINE. Zones 14–24; H1. From central coast of California. Very fast growth to 80–100 ft. tall, 25–35 ft. wide. Puts on 6 ft. a year when young; reaches 50 ft. in 12 years. Shapely, broad cone in youth, then drops its lower branches to develop rounded or flattish crown. Bright green needles are held in groups of two or three. Oval, light brown cones are held in clusters that persist on the branches. Often shallow rooted, subject to blowing over in wind. Even in ideal climate, suffers many pests and diseases (including pitch canker) that make it a poor risk. Try to keep established plants healthy with occasional deep watering and feeding.

P. strobus. WHITE PINE, EASTERN WHITE PINE. Zones 1–6. Slow in seedling stage, then fast to 50–80 ft. tall (or taller), 20–40 ft. wide. Forms a symmetrical pyramid, with horizontal branches in regular whorls. Becomes broad, open, and irregular with age. Fine-textured, handsome tree. Blue-green needles are soft, 3–5½ in. long, held in groups of five. Light brown cones reach 3–8 in. long. Intolerant of strong winds. Needs regular water and excellent drainage. 'Contorta' has twisted branches and needles. 'Angel Falls' and 'Pendula' have weeping, trailing branches. 'Niagara Falls' is also weeping, but with a very broad, cascading habit.

Plants in the Nana group are broad shrubs, growing slowly to 3–7 ft. tall, 6–12 ft. wide. Useful in rock gardens or containers, though plants sold under this name have been known to grow into small trees. 'Blue Shag' is a blue-needled form.

P. sylvestris. SCOTCH PINE. Zones A1–A3; 1–9, 14–21. From northern Europe, western Asia, northeastern Siberia. Grows fast at first, then moderately to 30–70 ft. (possibly to 100 ft.) tall and 25–30 ft. wide. Forms a narrow, well-branched pyramid when young. With age, becomes irregular, open, and picturesque, with drooping branches. Stiff, 1½–3 in. long, blue-green needles often turn yellow-green in winter. Cones to 2 in. long are gray to reddish brown. Popular as a Christmas tree and in gardens. Showy red bark, sparse foliage in maturity.

Female pinecones take 2 or 3 years to ripen, after which they release their (usually winged) seeds. Male pinecones are smaller, yellow, and clustered together at the shoot bases.

P

Wind-resistant. Needs regular water in hottest areas, moderate water elsewhere.

Plants in the Aurea group take on bright golden tones in winter. 'French Blue' keeps its blue color throughout the cold months. Handsome and dense 'Fastigiata' grows slowly to 20–30 ft. tall and just 4–6 ft. wide. 'Inverleith', to 40–60 ft. tall and 20–25 ft. wide, sports needles tipped in creamy white. Dwarf forms include rounded 'Beuvronensis', blue-green 'Glauca Nana', and relatively fast-growing 'Watereri'. 'Hillside Creeper' is well named; it grows to 2 ft. high and 8 ft. wide in 10 years and makes an interesting groundcover.

P. thunbergii. JAPANESE BLACK PINE. Zones 3–12, 14–21. From Japan. In the Northwest, grows fast to 100 ft. tall and 40 ft. wide; in Southern California and desert, grows slowly to moderately to 20 ft. tall and 10 ft. wide. Spreading branches form a broad, conical tree; irregular and spreading in age, often with a leaning trunk. Bright green needles are stiff, 3–4½ in. long, held in groups of two; new growth (candles) nearly white. Brown cones grow to about 3 in. long. Handsome tree that can be sheared as a Christmas tree or pruned as a cascade or giant bonsai. Regular water in hottest areas. 'Majestic Beauty' has good form and tolerates smog and salt. Dwarf 'Thunderhead' (6 ft. tall, 5 ft. wide in 10 years) has dark foliage and white candles that are eye-catching in spring.

P. wallichiana (P. griffithii). HIMALAYAN WHITE PINE. Zones A2, A3; 4–6, 15–17. From the Himalayas. Slow to moderate growth to 30–50 ft. tall, 15–30 ft. wide; much larger in the wild. Broad and conical, it often retains branches to the ground even in age. Gracefully drooping, soft-looking blue-green needles 6–8 in. long are held in groups of five. Cones are 6–10 in. long and light brown. Good form and color make this a fine choice for featured pine in a big lawn or garden. 'Nana' is dense and upright, to about 3 ft. high and wide after 10 years. 'Zebrina' has needles banded in yellow, giving the plant an overall glow.

Pistachio
Anacardiaceae
DECIDUOUS TREE

🌿 **ZONES 7–12, 14, 15, 18–21 (SEE TEXT)**

☼ **FULL SUN**

💧 **MODERATE WATER**

Pistachios

Botanically known as *Pistacia vera*, this native of southwestern and central Asia produces the pistachio nuts sold in markets; for strictly ornamental members of the genus, see *Pistacia*.

Tree grows to 25–30 ft. tall and as wide, with one or several trunks. Plants are either male or female; to get nuts, be sure to include at least one of each in your planting. 'Peters' is the most commonly grown male; 'Kerman' is the principal female (fruiting) variety. On female trees, small brownish green spring flowers are followed by heavy clusters of soft, wrinkled, reddish husks that contain the hard-shelled pistachio nuts. Take 5 to 8 years to begin bearing and many years to reach full yield. Trees tend to bear more heavily in alternate years.

Harvest the nuts in early autumn: spread a tarp beneath the tree, and then shake the tree until the nuts fall. Strip off and discard husks; dip nuts in water and dry them in the sun until the shells split (dipping in water helps the shells to split). Some people like to add flavor by boiling the husked nuts in salted water for a few minutes before drying them.

Nut production is best in Zones 8–12, where trees get just the right amount of summer heat and winter chill. Trees grow well in Zones 7, 14, 15, 18–21, but crops are unpredictable—and when they do appear, nut meats often do not properly fill shells.

When planting, avoid rough handling; budded tops are easily broken away from understock. Trees are inclined to spread and droop; stake them and train to a good framework of four or five limbs beginning 4 ft. or so aboveground. Prune to develop a central leader and strong horizontal scaffold branches. Susceptible to verticillium wilt and oak root fungus; to lessen disease risk, grow in well-drained soil and water deeply and infrequently.

Pistacia
PISTACHE
Anacardiaceae
EVERGREEN AND DECIDUOUS TREES AND SHRUBS

🌿 **ZONES VARY BY SPECIES**

☼ **FULL SUN**

💧 **WATER NEEDS VARY BY SPECIES**

Pistacia chinensis

These are ornamental species; for the plant grown for edible nuts, see Pistachio.

Glossy deep green leaves are divided into leaflets; flowers are insignificant. If male trees are nearby, female trees will bear clusters of tiny red fruits that mature to black. Verticillium wilt may strike established trees. Minimize susceptibility by planting in well-drained soil, watering deeply but infrequently. Young trees tend to be irregular in form and benefit from early training and pruning.

P. atlantica. MOUNT ATLAS PISTACHE. Semievergreen or deciduous tree. Zones 8–24. From the Mediterranean region. Slow to moderate growth to 45–60 ft. tall and wide. More regular and pyramidal than other pistaches, especially in youth. Leaves have 7 to 11 narrow leaflets to 2 in. long, rounded at tip. Nearly evergreen in mildest-winter areas of range; holds foliage into late autumn where winters are cold. Dark blue or purple fruit. Needs good drainage. Tolerates desert heat and winds. No irrigation is needed. Not widely grown as an ornamental but is much used as understock for pistachio.

P. chinensis. CHINESE PISTACHE. Deciduous tree. Zones 4–16, 17 (warmer parts), 18–23; little grown in Zones 4–7. From China. Slow to moderate growth to 30–60 ft. tall, with nearly equal spread. Foot-long leaves consist of 10 to 12 narrow leaflets. Good fall color, even in mild climates: foliage turns luminous orange to red (sometimes shades of yellow). This is the only tree to color scarlet in the desert. 'Keith Davey' and 'Pearl Street' are good male forms.

Tolerates a wide range of conditions. Accepts various watering regimes, from no water at all (this only in deep soils) to regular lawn watering (though verticillium wilt is a danger with the latter). Takes moderately alkaline soil. Resistant to oak root fungus. Reliable tree for streetside planting, lawn, patio, or garden.

P. lentiscus. MASTIC. Evergreen shrub or tree. Zones 8, 9, 12–24. From the Mediterranean region. Slow growth to 15–25 ft. tall and 20–30 ft. wide. Leaves to 4 in. long are made up of three to five pairs of leaflets. Useful as a screen plant for hot, dry locations and poor soil. Sap is the source of mastic, an aromatic resin. Little or no water (monthly soaking is best in Zones 12, 13).

P. 'Red Push'. Deciduous tree. Zones 8-24. This hybrid pistache grows fairly slowly to 25–40 ft. tall and 20–30 ft. wide, with a broad, uniformly spreading habit. The large leaves comprise 10–16 leaflets; they emerge red in spring, turn green in summer, and then color up nicely in fall, with red, orange, and yellow tones. Adapts to many different soils. Makes a good street or lawn tree. Moderate water.

P. vera. See Pistachio.

Pithecellobium flexicaule. See *Ebenopsis ebano*

Pittosporum
Pittosporaceae
EVERGREEN SHRUBS OR TREES

🗡 **ZONES VARY BY SPECIES**

☼ ☽ **FULL SUN OR PARTIAL SHADE**

◐ ● **MODERATE TO REGULAR WATER, EXCEPT AS NOTED**

Pittosporum tobira 'Wheeler's Dwarf'

These handsome plants are grown for their foliage and form, though they also bear clusters of small, bell-shaped, often sweetly fragrant flowers followed by fairly conspicuous fruits the size of large peas. All are basic, dependable shrubs or trees with pleasing outlines when allowed to branch naturally. Prune periodically to enhance form, thinning out weak branches and wayward shoots. Some make good clipped hedges. Excellent for screens, windbreaks. Susceptible to aphids and scale insects; sooty mold on leaves is a sign of infestation. Ripe fruits (usually orange) split open to reveal sticky seeds; fallen fruit can be a nuisance on lawns, paving.

P. angustifolium. See *P. phillyreoides.*

P. crassifolium. KARO. Zones 9, 14–17, 19–24. From New Zealand. Can reach 25 ft. tall and 12 ft. wide, but yearly pruning easily keeps it to 6–10 ft. tall, 6–8 ft. wide. Branches are densely clothed in 2–3-in.-long gray-green leaves with rounded ends. Tiny maroon flowers appear in late spring. Tolerates seaside conditions and some drought. 'Compactum' grows into a dense shrub 2–4 ft. tall and 4–6 ft. wide. 'Variegatum', to 8 ft. tall and wide, has leaves edged in creamy white; best with partial shade where summers are hot.

P. eugenioides. LEMON-WOOD. Zones 9, 14–17, 19–22; H1, H2. From New Zealand. To 20–40 ft. tall, 6–15 ft. wide. Often seen as a high hedge or a screen plant; unpruned, becomes a tree with a curving gray trunk. Yellow-green to medium green, wavy-edged, lance-shaped leaves to 4 in. long. Fragrant yellow flowers in spring. Set 1½ ft. apart for a hedge; force bushiness by shearing 2–6 in. from tops of plants several times each year between midwinter and early fall. 'Mini Green' grows to just 6 ft. tall, 4 ft. wide; it is densely clothed in deep emerald green foliage and makes a good low hedge or container plant. 'Platinum', 8–10 ft. tall and wide, has gray-green leaves edged in creamy white; it needs partial shade in hottest climates.

P. phillyreoides (P. angustifolium). DESERT WILLOW. Zones 8, 9, 12–24. Native to Australia. Slow grower to 20–25 ft. tall, 10–15 ft. wide. This is a slender, weeping tree with trailing branches and dark green, very narrow leaves to 3 in. long. Blooms in late winter and early spring, bearing very fragrant yellow flowers. Deep yellow fruit follows the blossoms. Good choice for narrow spaces or as a focal point near pool or patio. If drainage is poor, water infrequently but very deeply. Tolerates heat and aridity better than other pittosporums and has even naturalized in some desert areas.

P. rhombifolium. QUEENSLAND PITTOSPORUM. Zones 12–24; H1, H2. From Australia. Grows slowly to 15–35 ft. tall, 12–25 ft. wide. Rich green, glossy, nearly diamond-shaped leaves to 4 in. long. Profuse white flowers in late spring are followed by showy clusters of round, 1½-in., yellow to orange fruits that decorate the plant from fall through winter. As a small tree, well suited for lawn or patio (as long as sticky fruit won't pose a problem). Or plant several as a not-too-dense screen that needs little pruning. Resistant to oak root fungus.

P. tenuifolium. KOHUHU. Zones 9, 14–17, 19–24. From New Zealand. Fast grower to 15–25 ft. tall, 10–15 ft. wide. Similar in form to *P. eugenioides* but has darker twigs and leaf-stalks; purple flowers; shorter, more oval, deeper green leaves with less wavy edges; and greater tolerance for seacoast conditions. Leaves of 'Abbotsbury Gold' are yellow-green, with a darker green edge. 'Silver Sheen' has a somewhat more open habit than the species and smaller, silvery green leaves that sparkle in sunlight. 'Wrinkled Blue' grows 12 ft. tall and half as wide, with silvery blue leaves. 'Marjorie Channon', to 8–10 ft. tall and nearly as wide, has light green leaves bordered in creamy white. 'Purpureum' is about the same size, but with leaves that emerge green and turn bronzy purple. 'Golf Ball' is dense and compact at 3–5 ft. tall and wide; good choice for a low hedge. 'Tom Thumb' reaches just 3 ft. high and 2 ft. wide, with leaves that mature to dark bronzy purple; excellent in pots.

P. tobira. TOBIRA, JAPANESE MOCK ORANGE. Zones 8–24; H1, H2. Worth trying in Zones 4–7. From Japan. Dense, rounded growth 6–15 ft. (rarely to 30 ft.) tall and wide. You can remove lower limbs from an older plant to make a small tree, or you can hold plant to 6 ft. by careful heading back and thinning (doesn't look good sheared). Leathery, narrow, shiny dark green leaves to 5 in. long. In early spring, creamy white flowers with fragrance of orange blossoms are borne at branch tips. Very tolerant of seacoast conditions.

'Variegatum' grows 5–10 ft. tall and wide and has smaller leaves in gray-green and gray with an irregular creamy white margin. Several compact selections are available. The most common is 'Wheeler's Dwarf', to 2–3 ft. high and 4–5 ft. wide, with the same handsome leaves as *P. tobira*. It is a choice plant for foreground, low boundary, or even small-scale groundcover. 'Turner's Variegated Dwarf' is the size of 'Wheeler's Dwarf' but has foliage like that of 'Variegata'. 'Cream de Mint' grows just 2–2½ ft. high and wide and has mint green leaves with a creamy white border.

P. undulatum. VICTORIAN BOX. Zones 14 and 15 (with protection), 16, 17, 21–24; H1, H2. From Australia. Fairly fast to 15 ft., then slow to 30–40 ft. tall and wide. Makes a dense, single- or multitrunked, dome-shaped tree of great beauty. Glossy green, lance-shaped, wavy-edged leaves up to 6 in. long. Creamy white, very fragrant flowers in early spring. Plants set 5–8 ft. apart can make a thick, 10–15-ft.-tall screen with selective pruning (not shearing). Roots are strong, becoming invasive with age.

Platanus
PLANE TREE, SYCAMORE
Platanaceae
DECIDUOUS TREES

🗡 **ZONES VARY BY SPECIES**

☼ **FULL SUN**

◐ ● **MODERATE TO REGULAR WATER**

🦋 **ATTRACT BUTTERFLIES**

Platanus occidentalis

These are large trees with heavy trunks and a sculptural branch pattern. Older bark sheds in patches to reveal pale, smooth new bark beneath. Big, rough-surfaced leaves (to 10 in. across) resemble those of maple (*Acer*). Ball-shaped brown seed clusters hang on the bare branches through winter. Best in rich, deep, moist, well-drained soil. All are subject to anthracnose, which causes early leaf drop and twig dieback. Rake up and dispose of dead leaves, since fungus spores can overwinter on them. Chlorosis may be a problem in the desert. Large roots can buckle sidewalks and invade sewer lines.

P. × hispanica (P. × acerifolia). LONDON PLANE TREE. Zones 2–24. Hybrid between *P. occidentalis* and *P. orientalis*; often sold under the latter name. Grows fast to 40–80 ft. tall, with 30–40-ft. spread. Tolerates many soil types and stands up to smog, soot, dust, and reflected heat. Not the best choice for windy areas. In late spring, sheds a multitude of tiny hairs that irritate the throat when inhaled and can cause breathing difficulties for people with asthma. Susceptible to mildew. Widely planted as a street, park, or large lawn tree. Can fit smaller spaces when pollarded (a pruning technique in which the main branches are cut back to stubs every year). 'Bloodgood' is resistant to anthracnose; 'Yarwood' is mildew-resistant; 'Columbia' is resistant to both diseases. 'Morton Circle' ('Exclamation') is an upright grower to 50 ft. tall, 30 ft. wide; resists anthracnose.

P. occidentalis. AMERICAN SYCAMORE, BUTTONWOOD. Zones 1–24. Native to eastern U.S. Similar to *P. × hispanica* but with a longer leafless period. Irregular habit, contorted branches. Occasionally grows with multiple or leaning trunks. Old trees near streams sometimes reach huge size. Best in a large wild garden.

P. racemosa. CALIFORNIA SYCAMORE. Zones 4–24. Robust native of California foothills and Coast Ranges; grows near streams in the wild. Fast rate of growth to 30–80 ft. tall and 20–50 ft. wide, frequently with multiple or leaning trunks. Smooth branches are often gracefully twisted and contorted. Attractive, patchy bark in brown, gray, white. Deeply lobed leaves turn dusty brown early in autumn; in mild coastal climates, they hang on until new growth starts. Tolerates much heat and wind. With careful pruning, can be trained into picturesque multitrunked clump. For large informal or wild garden.

P. wrightii (P. racemosa wrightii). ARIZONA SYCAMORE. Zones 10–12. To 80 ft. tall, 55 ft. wide. Native along streams and canyons in mountains of southern and eastern Arizona. Resembles *P. racemosa*, but leaves are more deeply lobed and seed clusters have individual stems branching from common stalk.

Platycerium
STAGHORN FERN
Polypodiaceae
EPIPHYTIC FERNS

🌿 **ZONES VARY BY SPECIES; OR INDOORS**

◑ **PARTIAL SHADE; INDIRECT LIGHT**

💧 **REGULAR WATER**

Platycerium superbum

In the wild, these tropical natives grow on trees. In gardens, they grow best mounted on slabs of bark or tree fern stem, in hanging baskets, or attached to tree trunks. Plants have two kinds of fronds. Sterile fronds are flat, pale green, aging to tan and brown; they support the plant and accumulate organic matter to provide nutrients. Fertile fronds are forked, resembling deer antlers (hence the common name).

Good choice for a garden room, sun porch, or attached greenhouse where direct sun can be filtered by a sheer window covering. Water thoroughly but not often. Check moisture levels by pressing on the sterile brown frond base; water only when dry. Apply balanced liquid fertilizer monthly during growing season.

P. bifurcatum. COMMON STAGHORN FERN. Zones 15–17, 19–24; H2. From Australia and New Zealand. Arching or pendent gray-green fertile fronds, 3 ft. high and wide. Produces numerous offsets, which may be detached for use in propagation. This species shows much variability in form. Look for named cultivars like 'Netherlands' with distinctive grayish, upward-arching fronds.

P. superbum. GIANT STAGHORN FERN. Zones 23, 24; H2. From Australia. To 6 ft. tall, with 5 ft. spread. Broad, gray-green fertile fronds are spreading or pendent; often forked several times, resembling moose antlers. Sterile fronds are deeply lobed. Protect from frosts.

Platycladus orientalis
(Thuja orientalis)
ORIENTAL ARBORVITAE
Cupressaceae
EVERGREEN TREE

🌿 **ZONES 2–24; H1, H2**

☼ ◑ **PARTIAL SHADE IN HOTTEST CLIMATES**

💧 💧 **MODERATE TO REGULAR WATER**

Platycladus orientalis
'Aurea Nana'

Native to northern China, Manchuria, and Korea. The species grows 25 ft. tall and 15 ft. wide but is rarely grown; nurseries offer more attractive, shrubbier selections. Juvenile leaves are feathery and needlelike; mature leaves are flat and scalelike, carried in irregularly arranged sprays. Foliage is green or yellowish green, may take on bronze tones in winter. Upright cones to ¾ in. long start off gray-blue and age to brown; pleasant-smelling when crushed.

Widely used near doorways or gates, or in formal rows.

Protect plants from reflected heat of light-colored walls or pavement. In the Rocky Mountains, grows best in partial shade; shade during winter is especially helpful. Needs well-drained soil. Blight of leaves and twigs in Northwest is easily controlled by copper sprays applied in early fall and by pruning out and destroying diseased growth. Watch for spider mites.

'Aurea Nana'. DWARF GOLDEN ARBORVITAE. Golden-foliaged, compact globe. Usually 3 ft. high and 2 ft. wide but can grow as tall as 5 ft.

'Beverlyensis'. BEVERLY HILLS ARBORVITAE. Upright, globe-shaped to conical; somewhat open habit. Golden yellow branchlet tips. In time, can reach 10 ft. tall and wide; give it room. Best with regular water.

'Blue Cone'. Dense, upright, conical; good blue-green color. To 8 ft. tall, 4 ft. wide.

'Bonita' ('Bonita Upright', 'Bonita Erecta'). Rounded, full, dense cone to 3 ft. high, 2 ft. wide. Dark green with slight golden tinting at branch tips.

'Collen's Gold'. Narrow and upright, to 8 ft. tall and half as wide, with bright yellow foliage.

'Elegantissima'. Upright and conical, to 15 ft. tall, 6 ft. wide, with golden yellow foliage that turns yellow-green in summer, then takes on bronze tones in winter.

'Fruitlandii'. FRUITLAND ARBORVITAE. Compact, upright, cone-shaped, with deep green foliage.

'Minima Glauca'. DWARF BLUE ARBORVITAE. To 3–4 ft. tall and wide. Blue-green foliage.

'Raffles'. Resembles 'Aurea Nana' but is smaller, denser in growth, brighter in color.

'Westmont'. To 3 ft. high, 2 ft. wide. Green foliage has yellow tips throughout the growing season.

Oriental arborvitae is easily recognized by its upright, closely spaced branches with flat, vertical sprays of leaves that resemble intricate fans.

P

Platycodon grandiflorus

BALLOON FLOWER

Campanulaceae

PERENNIAL

🌿 **ZONES 1–10, 14–24**

☀️☼ **LIGHT SHADE IN HOTTEST CLIMATES**

💧 **REGULAR WATER**

Platycodon grandiflorus

From Siberia, northern China, and Japan. Grown for its interesting flowers, which are lovely in arrangements. The plant grows to about 2½ ft. high and 2 ft. wide. Inflated, balloonlike buds are carried on slender stalks at the ends of upright stems clad in broadly oval, light olive green leaves. Buds open to 2-in.-wide, star-shaped, blue-violet flowers with purple veins. Bloom begins in early summer and continues for 2 months or more if spent blossoms (not entire stems) are removed.

Pink, white, and double-flowered varieties are available; dwarf forms may grow just 1 ft. high. Blossoms of 1½–2-ft.-high 'Komachi' keep their balloon shape, never opening fully. 'Mariesii' is a dependable grower to 1½ ft. high, with deep violet-blue blooms.

Balloon flower dies back completely in autumn, and new growth appears quite late in spring; mark the plant's position with small stakes to avoid digging up its fleshy roots. If you do unearth a root, replace it (or the pieces) right away. Protect roots from gophers by planting in wire baskets. Grow as winter annual in Zones 12, 13.

Plectranthus

Lamiaceae

PERENNIALS AND EVERGREEN SHRUBS

🌿 **ZONES 22–24; H2; OR INDOORS**

☼ **PARTIAL SHADE, EXCEPT AS NOTED; BRIGHT INDIRECT LIGHT**

💧 **REGULAR WATER**

Plectranthus argentatus

Close relatives of coleus; native to many tropical regions of the world. Some are grown for their highly aromatic leaves, others for their striking floral displays or attractive foliage. All have square stems, opposite pairs of fleshy, tooth-edged or scalloped leaves, and whorls of tubular, two-lipped blossoms. Superb in containers, either alone or in combination with other plants.

Easy to grow. Stems take root wherever they touch the ground. Cuttings root quickly in soil or water. Remove flower spikes after they fade. Pinch all types to induce branching; discard old plants when they become leggy or too woody and start new ones.

P. amboinicus (Coleus amboinicus). CUBAN OREGANO, SPANISH THYME, INDIAN MINT. From Africa. Summer-blooming trailer to 1 ft. high, 3 ft. wide, with white, lilac-pink, or light purple flowers in 6-in. spikes. Velvety gray-green leaves are 3 in. long, with broadly toothed edges. Popular in Cuban cooking, they have a fragrance that falls midway between oregano and thyme but has a sweet note not present in either. Leaves of 'Variegatus' are bordered in cream, with the edge often tinged in bright pink; excellent flavor. 'Well Sweep Wedgwood', with extra-sweet flavor, has leaves in chartreuse

and gray-green with a dark green margin; Wedgwood blue flowers.

P. argentatus. From Australia. Erect to spreading plant to 3 ft. high, 6 ft. or wider. Densely hairy, scallop-edged, oval leaves to 7 in. long are silvery gray-green, with a light purplish flush on growing tips and stems. Pink-tinged white flowers in foot-long spikes in late summer, fall. Best in at least half-day direct sun; will take hot afternoon sun if adequately watered.

P. ciliatus. From southern Africa. Handsome, burgundy-stemmed trailer to 6–12 in. high and 3–5 ft. wide. Excellent dense groundcover. Late summer and autumn, white or purplish flowers in 8–12-in. spikes. Oval leaves to 3½ in. long, with finely toothed edges and pointed tips; leaves have deep green upper surfaces, burgundy undersides and veins. Several gold-variegated forms are offered, some with new growth flushed with red.

P. cylindraceus (P. marrubioides). VICK'S PLANT, MENTHOLATO. From Africa. Mounding growth to 1½–3 ft. high, 2–4 ft. wide. Sometimes blooms, bearing blue or lavender flowers in dense, narrow, pointed spikes 12–15 in. long (there may be a pair of shorter spikes near base). Velvety, triangular gray-green leaves 1½–3 in. long, with three to five broad teeth on each side of leaf. Foliage smells like a combination of camphor and menthol and is used medicinally in Mexico.

P. forsteri. From Australia, Fiji, New Caledonia. To 10 in. high, 3 ft. wide; stems actually grow 3 ft. high, but they arch over from weight of foliage. Tip-pinch early and regularly to keep compact. Medium green, irregularly toothed leaves to 4 in. long. White or pale mauve flowers in 6–8-in. spikes are produced intermittently throughout the year. Leaves of 'Marginatus' are irregularly edged in creamy white.

P. fruticosus. From South Africa. Upright growth to 3–5 ft. tall, 2–4 ft. wide. Lance-shaped, coarsely toothed leaves to 4 in. long are olive green above, purplish beneath. Blooms in autumn, bearing mauve-pink or bluish blossoms in very

showy clusters to 1 ft. long and half as wide.

P. madagascariensis. MINTLEAF. From southern Africa. Vigorous trailer reaches 1 ft. high; spreads 3–4 ft. wide initially, eventually much wider by rooting at leaf joints. Medium green leaves to 2 in. long are hairy, roundish, scallop edged; they smell like mint when crushed. Lavender-blue or white flower spikes in late spring, early summer. 'Variegated Mintleaf', the most commonly grown form, has irregular white leaf margins. Good groundcover to brighten shady areas.

P. oertendahlii. MOSAIC SWEDISH IVY, ROYAL CHARLIE, CANDLE PLANT. From South Africa. Easy-care specimen for hanging basket or pot; most often grown as houseplant. To 8–12 in. high, with branches trailing to 1½–2 ft. long. Roundish, irregularly toothed, velvety dark green leaves up to 2½ in. long, with purple undersides and intricate network of silver veins. In fall, whitish flowers bloom in loose, 8–12-in.-long spikes.

P. parviflorus. 'ALA 'ALA WAI NUI. From Hawaii, Australia. Occurs naturally in dry, exposed locations. Spreading, trailing plant grows to 6–8 in. or possibly higher; spreads to 3 ft. but can be easily restrained. Light green, toothed leaves are covered with short, silvery fuzz. Short spikes of pale blue flowers bloom all year. Use in hanging baskets, in a rock garden, or as small-scale groundcover.

P. verticillatus. SWEDISH IVY, CREEPING CHARLIE. From southern Africa. Typically grown in hanging basket or pot in the house or outdoors; also makes a good groundcover in a warm, protected spot. To 4–8 in. high and 4–6 ft. wide, with trailing branches. Waxy, shiny dark green, scallop-edged leaves are roundish, to 1½ in. across. White or pale purplish blossoms in 8-in. spikes bloom intermittently all year. To grow as a groundcover, plant cuttings 1–2 ft. apart for quick coverage.

FOR OTHER PLANTS THAT THRIVE WITH LESS LIGHT, SEE PAGES 68–69.

Pleioblastus. See Bamboo

Pleione
Orchidaceae
TERRESTRIAL ORCHIDS

- ✂ ZONES 5–9, 14–24; OR INDOORS
- ☼ PARTIAL SHADE; BRIGHT INDIRECT LIGHT
- ◖ REGULAR WATER DURING GROWTH AND BLOOM

Pleione forrestii

Dwarf orchids native to high mountains of India and China. Many species, all deciduous. Each pseudobulb produces one or two narrowly oval, pleated-looking leaves; leaves reach 8 in. long in the biggest species. Flowers are large (3–4 in. wide) for the size of the plant and resemble small cattleyas; they usually appear just as the leaves begin to show in early spring. Blossoms of *P. bulboco-dioides* are purple with a white lip marked with reddish spots. Those of *P. formosana* are purple, pink, or white; fringed lip has yellow center with brownish red markings. Those of *P. for-restii* are yellow; fringed lip has red markings.

Where frosts are rare and summer temperatures moderate, these orchids can be grown outdoors all year—provided they have perfect drainage, rich soil that is moist and well aerated, and some winter protection (shelter from excessive rain). Usually grown in rock gardens or in pots. For a good show, plant pseudobulbs close together. If planting in the ground, bury pseudobulbs, leaving just the tips exposed; or plant in a shallow pot and bury only the bottom quarter of each pseudobulb. Repot yearly before growth begins.

Plum
(including Prune)
Rosaceae
DECIDUOUS FRUIT TREES

- ✂ ZONES VARY BY VARIETY
- ☼ FULL SUN
- ◖ MODERATE WATER

» See chart on pages 516–518.

'Stanley' plum

Like their apricot, cherry, and peach relatives, these are stone fruits of the genus *Prunus*. For flowering plums, see page 534. For crosses involving plums, apricots, and peaches, see Plum Hybrids, page 519. Plums come in many colors—both inside and out. Skin may be yellow, red, purple, green, blue, or almost black; flesh may be yellow, red, or green.

Three categories of edible plums and prunes are grown in the West: European, Japanese, and hardy hybrids. All bloom in late winter or early spring; fruit ripens at some point from May into September, depending on variety and climate. Prunes are European plum varieties with a high sugar content that makes it possible to sun-dry the fruit without it fermenting.

European and Japanese plums. The two most widely grown groups are European (*Prunus × domestica*) and Japanese (*P. salicina*). 'Damson' plum, which is sometimes considered a separate species (*P. insititia*), is probably a type of European plum (*P. × domestica insititia*); 'Damson' interbreeds freely with other European plums.

European plums and prunes bloom later than Japanese plums and are better adapted to areas with late frosts or cool, rainy spring weather. Most of the European varieties have a moderately high chill need that excludes them from extremely mild-winter areas. Many European and Japanese varieties are self-fruitful, but others need cross-pollination to produce good crops. The accompanying chart lists proven pollenizers, but other choices also exist; consult a knowledgeable local nursery for more information.

As orchard trees, both Japanese and European plums reach 15–20 ft. tall with somewhat wider spread, but with pruning they are easily kept to 10–15 ft. high and wide. Differences in growth habit are discussed in the chart. There are no truly dwarfing rootstocks for plums, and semidwarf trees are only slightly smaller than standards.

European plums have flesh that is firmer and can be cooked or eaten fresh; prune varieties are largely used for drying or canning, but they can also be eaten fresh if you like the very sweet flavor. Japanese plums are the largest and juiciest of all, with a pleasant blend of acid and sugar; they are mainly eaten fresh.

Hardy hybrids. Where winters are severe, a third plum category dominates. This is a complex group of hardy hybrids involving Japanese plum, several species of native American wild plums, and the native Western sand cherry (*P. besseyi*). The hardy hybrids originated in Canada, the Dakotas, and Minnesota and are exceptionally tolerant of cold and wind. Pollination of hardy hybrids is difficult; ask local nurseries about effective pollenizers.

Some of the hardy hybrids are trees; others grow as bushes to about 6 ft. high and at least as broad. Those with fruit near the size and quality

How to Grow Plums

PLANTING Choose a spot with full sun where fallen fruit won't be a problem. Fertile soils are best, but these trees can grow in a wide range of soils when drainage is good.

WATERING Irrigate moderately but consistently for best fruit.

FERTILIZING Before leafout in the spring, apply ½ lb. of 10-10-10 fertilizer for each year of the tree's age, up to 6 lbs.

PRUNING & TRAINING Most Japanese plum trees are trained to a vase shape, with five or six main scaffold branches; fruiting laterals grow from these scaffolds. Where space is limited, trees can be trained in a more linear fashion (against a wall or fence, for example). Japanese varieties tend to make tremendous shoot growth, and rather severe pruning is necessary at all ages, regardless of training method. Many varieties produce excessive vertical growth; shorten these shoots to outside branchlets. Thin Japanese plums to 4–6 in. apart as soon as fruit forms, or fruit load may break branches.

European plums do not branch as freely as Japanese types, so selection of framework branches is limited; these plums are usually trained to a central leader. Mature European plums require pruning mainly to thin out annual shoot growth; otherwise, little is needed.

If you grow hardy hybrids, prune them to renew unfruitful branches (on shrubby types, remove older shoots to the ground every few years) and to keep the plant's center open.

PESTS & DISEASES In the dry-summer West, plums are subject to far fewer problems than peaches or apples. If applied at the pink-bud stage, copper-containing fungicides or synthetic fungicides such as myclobutanil will control the fungal disease brown rot. Peach tree borer is another potential pest. Consult your Cooperative Extension Office for best treatment.

P

PLUM: TOP PICKS TO GROW

NAME	ZONES	POLLINATION	FRUIT	COMMENTS
EUROPEAN VARIETIES				
'Brooks'	2–12, 14–22	Self-fruitful	Large. Yellowish red to blue skin; yellow flesh. Sweet with a little tartness. Mid-season.	Good canning variety or dried prune. Produces reliably in Pacific Northwest.
'Coe's Golden Drop'	2–12, 14–22	Any other European plum	Medium to large; oblong. Straw yellow skin, often blushed red; golden flesh. Sweet, juicy, apricot-like flavor. Late.	Intense flavor. Highly regarded in Europe.
'Damson' ('Blue Damson')	2–23	Self-fruitful	Small. Purple or blue-black skin; green flesh. Very tart. Late.	Low chill requirement. Makes fine jam and jelly. Strains of this variety are sold as 'French Damson', 'Shropshire'.
'Early Laxton'	2–12, 14–20	Any other European plum	Medium size. Pinkish orange skin; yellow flesh. Deliciously sweet flavor. Early.	Excellent for cooking. Upright, very productive tree.
'French Prune' ('Agen', 'Petite')	2, 3, 7–12, 14–22	Self-fruitful	Small. Red to purplish black skin; greenish yellow flesh. Very sweet and mild. Late.	Standard drying prune of California. Also suitable for canning.
'Green Gage' ('Reine Claude')	2–22; H1	Self-fruitful	Small to medium. Greenish yellow skin; amber flesh. Very rich, sweet flavor. Mid-season.	Very old variety; still a favorite for eating fresh, cooking, canning, jam. Selected strains are sold as 'Jefferson'.
'Imperial' ('Imperial Epineuse')	3–12, 14–18	Any other European plum	Large. Red-purple to black-purple skin; greenish yellow flesh. Fine-quality fruit with sweet, intense flavor. Late midseason.	Excellent fresh. Makes a premium dried prune or canned product.
'Italian Prune' ('Fellenburg')	2–12, 14–18	Self-fruitful	Medium size. Purplish black skin; yellow-green flesh. Sweet flavor. Late midseason.	Standard variety for prunes in the Pacific Northwest. Excellent fresh as well as for canning; dries well. 'Early Italian' ripens 2 weeks earlier.
'Mirabelle'	2–12, 14–22	Any midseason non-'Mirabelle' European plum	Small. Yellow fruit with orange to red dots on the skin; yellow flesh. Mild, sweet flavor. Ripening time varies.	A type favored in Europe for making brandy. Also good in preserves. Look for 'Geneva Mirabelle' and 'Reine de Mirabelle'.
'Opal'	A1, A2; 1–3	Self-fruitful	Small. Reddish purple skin; yellow flesh. Good, sweet flavor. Early.	Vigorous and cold-hardy.
'Reine Claude de Bavay' ('Bavay Green Gage')	2–12, 14–20	Self-fruitful	Large. Yellow skin with white dots; yellow flesh. Juicy and sweet; flavor similar to that of 'Green Gage' but better. Late.	Form of 'Green Gage' on a compact tree; good choice for smaller gardens.
'Seneca'	2–12, 14–20	Any other European plum	Very large. Red skin; yellow flesh. Deliciously sweet. Late.	Productive. One of the best for the Pacific Northwest.
'Stanley'	2–12, 14–22	Self-fruitful	Large. Purplish black skin; yellow flesh. Sweet and juicy. Midseason.	Good canning or dried prune variety. Fruit resembles a larger 'Italian Prune'.
'Sugar'	2–12, 14–22	Self-fruitful	Medium size. Dark blue skin; yellow flesh. Intensely flavored; very sweet. Early midseason.	Good fresh as well as canned; good home-drying prune. Tends to bear heavily in alternate years.
JAPANESE VARIETIES				
'Autumn Rosa'	7–12, 14–23	Self-fruitful	Medium to large. Purplish red skin; yellow flesh with red streaks. Good, sweet flavor. Very late.	Low chill requirement. Ripens over a long period; holds well on tree.
'Beauty'	2–24	Self-fruitful; yield improved with 'Santa Rosa'	Medium size. Bright red skin; amber flesh with scarlet streaks. Good, sweet flavor. Very early.	Low chill requirement. Consistent, heavy bearer. Fruit softens quickly and must be harvested promptly.

P

PLUM: TOP PICKS TO GROW

NAME	ZONES	POLLINATION	FRUIT	COMMENTS
'Burbank'	2–12, 14–20	'Beauty', 'Santa Rosa'	Large. Red skin; amber flesh. Excellent, sweet flavor. Midseason.	Hardier to cold than most Japanese plums.
'Burgundy'	7–12, 14–24	Self-fruitful	Small. Dark red skin and flesh. Excellent, rich flavor. Early to midseason.	Low chill requirement. Great fresh or canned. Fruit holds well on tree.
'Casselman'	2, 3, 7–12, 14–22	Self-fruitful	Small to medium. Purplish red skin; amber flesh (red near skin). Sweet flavor. Late.	Sport of 'Late Santa Rosa'. Ripens a few days later.
'Catalina'	7–12, 14–24	Self-fruitful	Large. Deep purple skin and flesh. Juicy and sweet. Late.	Low chill requirement. Very productive.
'El Dorado'	7–12, 14–20	'Santa Rosa', 'Catalina'	Medium to large. Dark purple, nearly black skin; amber flesh. Rich, sweet flavor. Midseason.	Low chill requirement. Fruit stays firm even when fully ripe.
'Elephant Heart'	2, 3, 7–12, 14–22	'Santa Rosa'	Very large. Dark red skin; rich red flesh. Fine flavor. Midseason to late.	Skin is tart until fruit is fully ripe. Long harvest season.
'Emerald Beaut'	7–12, 14–20	'Beauty', 'Burgundy', 'Late Santa Rosa'	Medium size. Light green skin; greenish yellow to orange flesh. Exceptional, sweet, rich flavor. Midseason to late.	Fruit holds well on the tree without losing quality.
'Friar'	2, 3, 7–12, 14–20	'Santa Rosa', 'Late Santa Rosa'	Large. Purplish black skin; amber flesh. Good, sweet flavor. Late midseason.	Fruit resists cracking; softens slowly after picking. Very vigorous, productive tree.
'Golden Nectar'	2, 3, 7–12, 14–20	Self-fruitful	Very large. Yellow skin and flesh. Excellent, sweet flavor. Small pit. Midseason.	Fruit keeps well after harvest.
'Hollywood'	2–12, 14–22	Self-fruitful	Medium size; oblong. Dark red skin; red flesh. Flavorful. Late.	Not very productive. Pink flowers and purple foliage make this double as a good ornamental.
'Howard Miracle'	7–10, 14–20	'Santa Rosa', 'Wickson'	Medium size. Yellow skin with red blush; yellow flesh. Spicy flavor reminiscent of pineapple. Midseason.	Very vigorous. Fruit more acid than that of most Japanese plums but truly distinctive in flavor.
'Kelsey'	2, 3, 7–12, 14–18; H1	Self-fruitful	Large. Green to greenish yellow skin splashed red; firm yellow flesh. Sweet but not juicy. Late midseason.	Fruit keeps well after harvest.
'Laroda'	7–12, 14–22	'Burgundy', 'Santa Rosa', 'Late Santa Rosa'	Large. Red skin; amber flesh (red near skin). Rich and juicy. Midseason.	Fruit holds well on the tree.
'Late Santa Rosa'	7–12, 14–22	Self-fruitful	Medium to large. Purplish crimson skin; amber flesh (red near skin). Sweet-tart, sprightly flavor. Late.	Ripens a month after 'Santa Rosa'.
'Mariposa' ('Improved Satsuma')	2, 3, 7–12, 14–22; H1	'Autumn Rosa', 'Beauty', 'Late Santa Rosa', 'Santa Rosa', 'Wickson'	Large. Purple-red skin; deep red flesh. Sweet. Midseason.	Good for cooking and fresh eating.
'Methley'	2–9, 12–24; H1	Self-fruitful	Medium size. Reddish purple skin; dark red flesh. Sweet and mild. Early.	Low chill requirement. Good bloom-hardiness.

»

PLUM: TOP PICKS TO GROW

NAME	ZONES	POLLINATION	FRUIT	COMMENTS
'Nubiana'	2, 3, 7–12, 14–20	Self-fruitful	Large. Deep purple-black skin; amber flesh. Sweet and firm. Midseason.	Good for fresh eating and for cooking (flesh turns red when cooked). Good keeper.
'Santa Rosa'	2, 3, 7–23	Self-fruitful	Medium to large. Purplish red skin with heavy blue bloom; yellow flesh (dark red near skin). Rich, pleasing, tart flavor. Early.	Low chill requirement. Important commercial variety for fresh eating. Good canned if skin is removed. 'Weeping Santa Rosa' has unique drooping habit, grows only 6–8 ft. tall.
'Satsuma'	2–22	'Beauty', 'Santa Rosa', 'Wickson'	Small to medium. Dull deep red skin; dark red, solid, meaty flesh. Mild, sweet flavor. Small pit. Early midseason.	Preferred for jams and jellies. Sometimes called blood plum because of red juice.
'Shiro'	2–12, 14–22	Self-fruitful	Medium to large. Yellow skin and flesh. Mild but good flavor. Early midseason.	Heavy producer. Fruit good for fresh eating and for cooking. Pretty in flower and fruit.
'Wickson'	2–12, 14–22	'Beauty', 'Santa Rosa'	Large. Greenish yellow to yellow skin, blushed with red when fruit is ripe; firm yellow flesh. Mild but fine flavor. Early midseason.	Showy fruit. Keeps well after harvest. Good for jams and jellies.

HARDY HYBRIDS

NAME	ZONES	POLLINATION	FRUIT	COMMENTS
'Opata'	A2, A3; 1–3	Check locally	Small. Purple skin; green flesh. Sweet. Late.	Cherry-plum hybrid from South Dakota. Bush form. Upper branches often freeze in coldest areas, but lower branches usually fruit well. Fruit is good fresh and for preserves.
'Pipestone'	A2, A3; 1–3	Check locally	Large. Tough red skin; yellow flesh. A little stringy but juicy and sweet. Midseason.	Vigorous Japanese-American hybrid developed in Minnesota. Tree form. Needs little heat to ripen. Very good for fresh eating and jam; good for jelly.
'Sapalta'	A2, A3; 1–3	Check locally	Small. Red-purple skin; almost black flesh. Mildly sweet. Late.	Cherry-plum hybrid developed in Canada. Bush form. Good for fresh eating, juice, canning, preserves.
'Superior'	A2, A3; 1–3	Check locally	Very large. Golden with red-blushed, lightly russeted skin; firm yellow flesh. Flavor is slightly tart near skin, dessert quality. Late midseason.	Japanese-American hybrid developed in Minnesota. Tree form. Bears at an early age and heavily. Good fresh or for jam, jelly.
'Underwood'	A2, A3; 1–3	Check locally	Medium to large. Dark red skin; amber flesh. Tender, juicy, sweet. Early.	Vigorous Japanese-American hybrid developed in Minnesota. Tree form. Good for fresh eating and jam; fair for jelly.

'Damson'

'Mirabelle'

'Santa Rosa'

'Superior'

of Japanese plums are sometimes called Japanese-American hybrids; those with smaller fruit closer in flavor to wild species are often called cherry-plum hybrids. Many hardy plums are tasty fresh, while others are better cooked or used in preserves.

Plumbago
Plumbaginaceae
EVERGREEN OR SEMIEVERGREEN SHRUBS

⚡ **ZONES VARY BY SPECIES**

☼ ☽ **FULL SUN OR LIGHT SHADE**

◐ ◑ ● **LITTLE TO REGULAR WATER**

🦋 **ATTRACT BUTTERFLIES**

Plumbago auriculata

Sprawling plants bloom over a long season, bearing clusters of blue or white flowers at branch ends. Prune these shrubs back hard in late winter to control their growth and keep them compact. For other plants called plumbago, see *Ceratostigma*.

P. auriculata (P. capensis). CAPE PLUMBAGO. Evergreen or semievergreen. Zones 8, 9, 12–24; H1, H2. Native to South Africa. Makes a mounding shrub to 6 ft. tall, 8–10 ft. wide; or, if tied to a support, grows as a vine to 12 ft. or more. Inch-wide flowers. In seedling plants, blossom color varies from white through pure light blue to sky blue; best way to get good blue color is to buy cutting-grown selections such as 'Royal Cape' or 'Imperial Blue'. *P. a. alba* has white flowers. All bloom from spring through summer—or nearly all year in warm, frost-free locations. Usually not browsed by deer. Flowers are used in leis.

Evergreen where frosts are absent or light; heavy frost can burn new growth and blacken leaves, but recovery is fast. In colder part of range, plant in spring to give plants time to become established before cold weather arrives. Not fussy about soil type but must have good drainage. Good cover for bank, fence, wall; good background and filler plant.

P. scandens. Evergreen. Zones 12, 13, 21–24; H1, H2. Native from Florida to Arizona, south to Central America. To 4 ft. or more tall and wide. Leaves are deep red when new, maturing to medium green; nearly all foliage turns red in late fall and winter. Blooms year-round (with a short break during hottest part of summer), bearing typically white (sometimes blue-tinged) flowers nearly 1 in. wide. Hard pruning both controls size and encourages the growth of colorful new foliage. Accepts most soils. Can get powdery mildew in late summer but doesn't seem to be greatly harmed by it. Attractive large-scale groundcover. 'Summer Snow' has pure white blooms.

Plumeria
FRANGIPANI, PUA MELIA
Apocynaceae
NEARLY EVERGREEN AND DECIDUOUS SHRUBS OR TREES

⚡ **ZONES VARY BY SPECIES**

☼ **FULL SUN**

◐ **MODERATE WATER**

⚠ **MILDLY TOXIC; MILKY SAP IS AN IRRITANT**

Plumeria

Handsome additions to the landscape in the warmest climates, these natives of tropical America have a spreading to round-headed form. Leathery leaves are clustered near the tips of thick, succulent branches (the branches exude caustic sap when injured). Large clusters of showy, waxy, typically fragrant, five-petaled flowers are produced at branch tips much of the year. Widely used to make leis and perfume.

In Hawaii, plumerias are easy to grow from cuttings. On the mainland, the safest method is to begin with container plants (usually sold in leaf and flower in summer). If you want to try cuttings, start with long (15–24 in.) tip sections of stem taken in early spring and allow them to callus over for a week before planting; short cuttings often succumb to rot.

Not fussy about soil type but cannot take cold, wet soils. Tolerates some salt spray and wind. Tender to frost. Beyond hardiness range, may be grown in a pot and moved indoors in winter to a bright window (for continued bloom) or to a frost-free garage or shed. Can be pruned at any time of year to maintain desired size and shape; withstands severe pruning (best done in warm season on mainland).

P. obtusa. SINGAPORE PLUMERIA, BLUNT-NOSE FRANGIPANI. Nearly evergreen. Zones 24; H2. From Cuba, Hispaniola, and Yucatán Peninsula. Fast growing to 30–35 ft. tall and 15 ft. wide. Sweet-scented, 3-in.-wide, yellow-centered white flowers spring through fall. On mainland, more difficult to grow than *P. rubra*.

P. rubra. PLUMERIA, TEMPLE TREE, NOSEGAY FRANGIPANI. Deciduous. Zones 12, 13, 19, 21–24; H1, H2. Native from Mexico to Panama. Grows at a moderate rate to 25–35 ft. tall and 15–20 ft. wide. Bloom begins in spring, often before foliage emerges, and continues for more than 6 months. Well over 100 varieties have been developed; flowers are typically 2–4½ in. wide, in colors from white through yellow, gold, and orange to shades of pink and red; fragrance varies. Dwarf and semidouble-flowered forms (rare on the mainland) are available. The following are full-size varieties with large, very fragrant single flowers.

'Aztec Gold'. Buttercup yellow shading to white at petal edges.

'Candystripe'. Vibrant pink and white blooms have bright yellow markings on upper surfaces of petals, and alternating red and white stripes on the undersides.

'Daisy Wilcox'. Extra-large blossoms in pale pink shading to white at edges.

'Dean Conklin'. Salmon with orange center.

'Guillot's Sunset'. Pink-and-white bicolor with orange center.

'Hawaiian Yellow'. Yellow with white margins. Especially sturdy plant.

'Intense Rainbow'. Yellow blossoms blending to pink.

'Kauka Wilder'. Combination of reds and yellows gives blossoms an overall rich orange color. Very sweet fragrance.

'Pink Parfait'. Large, reddish pink blooms.

'Tangerine'. Coral orange flowers.

Plum Hybrids
Rosaceae
DECIDUOUS FRUIT TREES

⚡ **ZONES VARY BY TYPE**

☼ **FULL SUN**

◐ **MODERATE WATER**

Pluots

These hybrids between plum and apricot, plum and peach, and plum and nectarine combine characteristics of their parent fruits in varying degrees. Most grow 10–20 ft. tall and wide but can be held to half that width with consistent pruning. Like their parents, they need winter chill for good fruit production. Plants are not yet widely tested, so zone listings are preliminary.

»

Aprium. Zones 3–16, 18–22. This plum-apricot hybrid will grow where apricots succeed. 'Cot-N-Candy', a self-fertile aprium, has extra-sweet, apricot-like fruit whose light-colored flesh has a plum aftertaste. 'Flavor Delight' has a similar look but is a little juicier and has a touch of plum flavor; it is partially self-fruitful, but for the best crop, pollinate it with an apricot that blooms at the same time or with 'Flavor Supreme' pluot. Fruit ripens in late spring or early summer.

Nectarine-plum hybrid (nectaplum). Zones 7–9, 14–16, 18–20. 'Spice Zee', the first nectarine-plum cross, has red skin and yellow spicy-sweet flesh redolent of both parents. Red spring leaves mature to a green-red. It is self-fruitful, late ripening, and productive.

Peach-plum hybrid. Zones 3, 7–9, 14–16, 18. 'Tri-Lite' has red skin with white flesh and a mild, classic peach flavor with a plum aftertaste. It is self-fertile and an early ripener.

Plumcot. Zones 3, 7–12, 14–16, 18–23. This was the original plum-apricot cross made by Luther Burbank. 'Flavorella' is the most promising variety, producing medium-size golden fruit with a red blush and firm, juicy, sweet-tart flesh. It has a low chill requirement and needs pollination with 'Flavorosa' plumcot or 'Floragold' or 'Gold Kist' apricot to bear fruit. 'Plum Parfait' is an older plumcot variety with pinkish orange skin, flesh marbled in crimson and amber, and a wonderfully sweet-tart, plumlike flavor; ripens in mid- to late summer. Both 'Flavorella' and 'Plum Parfait' ripen in late spring or early summer.

Pluot. Zones 3, 7–12, 14–16, 18–23. The fruit of pluot, another plum-apricot hybrid, is very sweet, closer in flavor to that of a plum. It is most likely to succeed where 'Santa Rosa' plum does. Early ripeners (late spring or early summer) include 'Flavor Supreme', with mottled green-and-maroon skin and deep red flesh; medium-to-large-fruited 'Emerald Drop', with green skin and apricot-colored flesh; and 'Splash', an ornamental edible with yellow-, orange-, or red-skinned fruit and extra-sweet yellow-orange flesh. Mid- to late-summer ripeners include 'Dapple Dandy' (often sold in markets under the name "dinosaur egg"), with mottled maroon-and-yellow skin and creamy white flesh streaked with red; 'Flavor King', with purplish red skin and flesh; and 'Flavor Queen', with greenish yellow skin and golden flesh. 'Flavor Grenade' bears elongated green fruit flushed with red; it has amber flesh. In California, it can hang on the tree until Thanksgiving. Both 'Dapple Dandy' and 'Flavor Supreme' will pollinate any other pluot; you can also use a Japanese plum that blooms at the same time.

How to Grow Plum Hybrids

SOIL Plant in fertile soil with good drainage. Mulch to maintain soil moisture.

FERTILIZING Before leaf-out in spring, sprinkle organic 5-5-5 fertilizer over the tree's root zone.

PRUNING In years when the crop is heavy, thin fruit to 8 or 9 in. apart. This keeps the heavy crop from being followed by a light crop. In winter, prune out injured, diseased, crossing, and closely parallel branches. Prune in summer to control the tree's size.

CHALLENGES All of these plum hybrids are subject to brown rot, gummosis, and peach tree borers; crosses from peaches and nectarines can also get peach leaf curl. Trees that have good sanitation (injured and diseased branches pruned out), consistent watering, periodic feeding, good soil, and plenty of sun are less likely to have problems. If diseases and insects become issues, consult your local Cooperative Extension Office for a treatment plan.

Poa
BLUEGRASS
Poaceae
PERENNIAL AND ANNUAL GRASSES

✎ **ZONES VARY BY SPECIES**

☀ **FULL SUN, EXCEPT AS NOTED**

💧 **REGULAR WATER**

Poa pratensis

Native to Europe but naturalized in North America. Of the three species described here, *P. pratensis* is the best-known cool-season lawn grass. Leaves of all have distinctive boat-prow tip.

P. annua. ANNUAL BLUE-GRASS. Annual. All zones. Cool-season weed of lawns that often furnishes much of the green in winter lawns. Bright green, soft-textured grass; it would be attractive were it not for its seed heads and propensity to die off when rain lessens in late spring. To discourage annual bluegrass in lawns, maintain a thick turf of good grasses.

P. pratensis. KENTUCKY BLUEGRASS. Perennial. Best in Zones A1–A3; 1–3; satisfactory with extra care in Zones 4–11, 14–17. Blue-green lawn grass. Many named selections are available as seed or sod; check with a local nursery for one suited to your area. Mow at 2–2½ in. (dwarf forms can be mowed lower). Use alone or in a mixture with other grasses.

P. trivialis. ROUGH-STALKED BLUEGRASS. Perennial. Zones A1–A3; 1–11, 14–17. Fine-textured bright green grass used in meadow and pasture grass mixes. Also used in lawn mixtures for shady spots—takes shade and damp soil. Can become weedy.

Podocarpus
Podocarpaceae
EVERGREEN SHRUBS OR TREES

✎ **ZONES VARY BY SPECIES**

☀ ◐ **FULL SUN OR PARTIAL SHADE**

💧 **REGULAR WATER**

Podocarpus gracilior

Versatile plants grown for their good-looking foliage and interesting form. They are adaptable to many climates and have many garden uses. Make good screens and background plants. Foliage generally resembles that of related yews (*Taxus*), but leaves of the better-known species are longer, broader, and lighter in color. If a male plant is growing nearby, female plants bear fruit after many years, producing small, fleshy fruits rather than cones. Grow well (if slowly) in most soils, but may develop chlorosis where soil is alkaline or heavy and damp.

P. elongatus. For plants sold under this name, see *P. gracilior*.

P. falcatus (Afrocarpus falcatus). Tree. Zones 8, 9, 14–24; H2. Slow-growing native of South Africa. Differs from *P. gracilior* in nativity, small botanical details. For uses, see *P. gracilior*.

P. gracilior (Afrocarpus elongatus, A. gracilior). FERN PINE. Tree, often grown as espaliered vine. Zones 8, 9, 13–24; H1, H2. From eastern Africa. Grows to 20–60 ft. tall and 10–20 ft. wide. Among the cleanest, most pest-free trees for street, lawn, patio, or garden; good as a big shrub, as a hedge, or in a container.

Method of propagation determines growth habit. If grown from seed, plants are upright even when young (and stay that way); these plants are usually sold as *P. gracilior*. In youth, they have branches set somewhat sparsely with glossy dark green leaves 2–4 in. long and ½ in. wide. With age, they produce 1–2-in., soft grayish green to bluish green leaves that are more closely spaced on the branches. Stake seedling plants until a strong trunk develops.

If grown from cuttings or grafts of a mature tree, plants have the smaller, more closely set leaves just described, but they have very limber branches and are often reluctant to make strong vertical growth. These more willowy plants, suitable for espalier or growing as vines along fences, are often sold as *P. elongatus*. Given staking and tying, *P. elongatus* types eventually become upright trees, though their foliage mass persists in drooping for some time. An exception is *P.* 'Icee Blue', which has striking blue-gray foliage and shrubby, upright growth to 25 ft. tall and wide.

P. henkelii. LONG-LEAFED YELLOWWOOD. Tree. Zones 8, 9, 14–24; H1, H2. From eastern and southern Africa. Handsome, erect tree grows slowly to 30–50 ft. tall, 15–20 ft. wide. Bears masses of drooping, shiny green leaves, pointed at both ends. Young plants have leaves 5–7 in. long; on older plants, leaves are just 1–2 in. long. Superb as a specimen plant; takes well to selective pruning (not shearing).

P. latifolius. YELLOW-WOOD. Tree. Zones 8, 9, 12 (warmest parts), 13–24; H1, H2. From eastern and southern Africa. This is the true yellow-wood, an important timber tree in Africa. Resembles *P. henkelii* in most details.

P. macrophyllus. YEW PINE. Shrub or tree. Zones 4–9, 12–24; H1, H2. Native to eastern China, Japan. Generally narrow and upright; to 15–50 ft. tall, 6–15 ft. wide. Bright green leaves 4 in. long, ½ in. wide. Good as a street or lawn tree, screen, large shrub; limber enough to espalier. Easily pruned as clipped hedge, topiary. Does well in large containers. Very heat-tolerant.

P. m. maki (P. m. 'Maki'). SHRUBBY YEW PINE. Slower growing and smaller than species—to 8–15 ft. tall, 2–4 ft. wide. Dense and upright, with leaves to 3 in. long, ¼ in. wide. A choice shrub; one of the best container plants for outdoor or indoor use.

P. nagi (Nageia nagi). Tree. Zones 8, 9, 14–24; H1, H2. From Japan, where it reaches 80–90 ft. tall. In California, more commonly seen at 15–20 ft. tall, 6–8 ft. wide. Pendulous branchlets; leathery, smooth, dark green, sharp-pointed leaves 1–3 in. long, ½–1½ in. wide. Grows upright in youth without staking; plant in groves for slender sapling effect. Makes a decorative foliage pattern against wood or masonry background. Excellent container plant.

P. nivalis. ALPINE TOTARA. Shrub. Zones 4–9, 14–17. From New Zealand. Broad, low-growing, spreading plant that eventually reaches 2–3 ft. high, 6–8 ft. wide. Branches are densely clothed with small, dark olive green needles like those of yew. Attractive as groundcover or in large rock garden.

P. totara. TOTARA. Tree. Zones 8, 9, 14–24. From New Zealand. In its native environment, this tree reaches 100 ft. tall. In California, more common size is 25–30 ft. tall and 18–25 ft. wide. Dense and rather narrow. Stiff, leathery gray-green leaves to 1 in. long, pointed at tips. General appearance like that of yew.

Podocarpus are conifers, but they produce odd-looking fruits rather than recognizable cones. If a male tree is nearby, mature female trees generate rounded or plum-shaped fruits, usually in autumn. Each holds a single seed and sits at the tip of a fleshy, swollen, bright red stalk.

Podophyllum
Berberidaceae
PERENNIALS

🌿 **ZONES VARY BY SPECIES**

◐ ● **PARTIAL OR FULL SHADE**

💧 💧 **REGULAR TO AMPLE WATER**

❖ **ALL PARTS (EXCEPT RIPE FRUIT) ARE POISONOUS IF INGESTED**

Podophyllum

These odd-looking yet striking barberry relatives grow from thick underground rhizomes that send up stalks crowned with large, umbrella-shaped, deeply lobed leaves. Shoots with a single leaf are flowerless; those with two leaves bear a single 2-in.-wide flower in mid- to late spring. Blooms are followed by juicy 2-in. berries; these are edible when fully ripe (poisonous until that stage) but can have a powerful laxative effect. Make attractive, slowly spreading deciduous groundcovers for shady areas with moist, organically enriched soil.

P. hexandrum (P. emodi, Sinopodophyllum hexandrum). Zones 4–7, 14–17. From the Himalayas and western China. To 1½–2 ft. high and wide. Dark green, brown-mottled leaves to 10 in. wide are divided into three or five lobes; each lobe is further divided. White or pink flowers are followed by bright red berries.

P. peltatum. MAY APPLE. Zones 1–7. From eastern North America. To 1–1½ ft. high, 1 ft. wide. Foliage is bronze when new; mature leaves are shiny dark green, to 1 ft. wide, divided into five to nine lobes. White flowers followed by bright yellow berries. Spreads fairly fast in its preferred rich, moist soil. Dies back completely in late summer.

Podranea ricasoliana
PINK TRUMPET VINE
Bignoniaceae
EVERGREEN VINE

🌿 **ZONES 9, 12, 13, 19–24; H1, H2**

☀ ◐ **FULL SUN OR PARTIAL SHADE**

💧 💧 **MODERATE TO REGULAR WATER**

Podranea ricasoliana

Native to South Africa. Sprawling growth to 20 ft.; to climb, it must be fastened to its support. Glossy dark green leaves make a lovely backdrop for the 2–3-in.-wide, red-veined pink flowers shaped like open trumpets. Clusters of blooms appear at tips of new growth in spring or summer (almost year-round in mild coastal areas). Grows slowly when young, then speeds up as it matures. Likes heat and good drainage. Use on posts, arbors, trellises, walls, or trunks of high-branching trees. Thin out any tangling growth in winter. Light frosts may cause leaves to drop; heavier frosts may kill the vine to the ground, but regrowth is almost certain as long as the soil doesn't freeze.

Pink trumpet vine has elegant flowers in a soft, warm pink, with red lines extending into a yellowish throat that glows when backlit.

Poha, Ground Cherry

Solanaceae
PERENNIAL

🌿 **ZONES H1, H2; ANYWHERE AS ANNUAL**

☀️ **FULL SUN**

💧 **REGULAR WATER**

Poha

From Brazil, but naturalized at higher elevations throughout Hawaiian Islands. Known botanically as *Physalis peruviana* and closely related to tomatillo (*P. ixocarpa*) and Chinese lantern plant (*P. alkekengi*). Bushy plant with heart-shaped, irregularly toothed, somewhat velvety green leaves to 2½–6 in. long. As a perennial, it can reach 6 ft. tall and 4 ft. wide (needs support); as an annual, it is more likely to grow 1½–3 ft. high and wide. Plant produces small, bell-shaped spring flowers that are whitish yellow with brown spots in the throat. After blossoms fade, the enlarged calyx forms a loose, papery, straw-colored husk around the fruit. The seedy, inch-wide yellow fruit ripens from late summer into autumn; it is smaller and sweeter than tomatillo and can be eaten fresh or used in pies and preserves.

Grow in well-drained soil in a frost-free, wind-protected site. Plant is self-fruitful, but you can help ensure pollination by gently shaking flower stems or spraying them lightly with water. No fertilizer needed. Cut back on watering when fruit is maturing. Harvest fruit when it drops to ground; remove papery husks before using. Plant often self-sows.

Polemonium

Polemoniaceae
PERENNIALS

🌿 **ZONES 1–11, 14–17, EXCEPT AS NOTED**

◐ ● **PARTIAL OR FULL SHADE**

💧 **REGULAR WATER**

Polemonium reptans
'Stairway to Heaven'

Plants form lush rosettes of finely divided, ferny foliage. Blossom stalks are typically leafy and bear clusters of bell-shaped flowers in spring or early summer. Good under trees. Need well-drained soil.

P. caeruleum. JACOB'S LADDER. Native to Europe, Asia. Fairly upright-growing plant to 1–3 ft. high, 1–1½ ft. wide. Lavender-blue, pendulous, 1-in. flowers. 'Brise d'Anjou', with each leaflet neatly outlined in white, is one of the most striking of variegated-foliage plants.

P. carneum. Native from Washington west of the Cascades to California. Sprawls to 1–1½ ft. high, 1 ft. wide. Yellowish buds open to ½–1-in. peachy pink blossoms that age to purplish blue.

P. 'Firmament'. This hybrid between *P. caeruleum* and *P. reptans* grows to 20 in. high and 1 ft. wide, with bright blue flowers. Use in borders.

P. pulcherrimum. Zones A1–A3; 1–11, 14–17; H1. Native from Alaska to California. Sprawling or erect, to 1 ft. high and wide. Crowded clusters of ¼-in. flowers in blue shades or white, often with yellow throat. Good in shaded rock gardens.

P. reptans. Native to eastern U.S. Weak-stemmed plant to 1–1½ ft. high, 1 ft. wide; light blue, ¾-in. flowers. Better known than the species is heavy-blooming 'Blue Pearl'; it grows 10 in. high, 1½ ft. wide and bears bright blue blossoms. Good choice for a shaded rock garden.

Polianthes tuberosa

TUBEROSE
Asparagaceae
PERENNIAL FROM RHIZOME

🌿 **ZONES 7–9, 14–24; H1, H2**

☀️ **FULL SUN**

💧 **REGULAR WATER DURING GROWTH AND BLOOM**

Polianthes tuberosa

Native to Mexico. Grown for the heady, powerfully sweet fragrance of its flowers. Each rhizome (actually a modified rhizome with bulblike top and tuberous roots) produces a fountain of narrow, grassy leaves about 1½ ft. high. Flower spikes rise above the leaves, bearing loose whorls of tubular, glistening white flowers in summer or early fall. Tallest tuberose (to 3½ ft.) is the form sometimes sold as 'Mexican Single'. More widely sold is double-flowered 'The Pearl', to 2½ ft. high; it is a good garden variety, but single types provide longer-lasting cut flowers.

CARE

To bloom year after year, tuberoses need a long warm season (at least 4 months) before flowering. Where this can be provided outdoors, you can plant rhizomes directly in the ground; elsewhere, start them indoors in pots and plant outside after soil warms in spring. Set rhizomes 2 in. deep and 4–6 in. apart. If soil or water is alkaline, apply acid fertilizer when growth begins. When foliage starts to yellow in fall, stop watering. Dig plants, cut off dead foliage, let rhizomes dry for 2 weeks, and store in a cool, dry place until planting time. Tuberoses can also be grown in containers and moved to protection during cold weather.

Poliomintha

Lamiaceae
EVERGREEN SHRUBS

🌿 **ZONES VARY BY SPECIES**

☀️ ◐ **EXPOSURE NEEDS VARY BY SPECIES**

💧 **REGULAR WATER**

🦅 **ATTRACT HUMMINGBIRDS**

Poliomintha maderensis

These are mint relatives with the family's typical square stems; paired opposite leaves; tubular, two-lipped flowers; and strong, often pleasant aroma. Well-grown plants reach about 3 ft. high and wide. Very tolerant of many soils.

P. incana. HOARY MINT. Zones 10–13. Native to southwestern U.S. Branching gray stems are set with narrow white leaves to ¾ in. long. Blooms profusely in summer, bearing tiny lavender-blue or white flowers in spikelike clusters up to 6 in. long. Full sun. Can survive with little or no water but looks better with regular moisture.

P. maderensis (P. longiflora). MEXICAN OREGANO, LAVENDER SPICE. Zones 8–24. Native to eastern Mexico. Habit varies from somewhat cascading to upright; reaches about 3 ft. high and wide. Leaves are shiny deep green, less than ½ in. long, with odor and flavor

P

of true oregano (*Origanum*). Long-tubed (1–1½ in.) flowers open lavender, deepen to purple, and finally fade to white; all three colors are present on the plant at once. Long bloom season, from late spring into fall. Stems are brittle, so locate away from high-traffic areas. Give light shade in hottest desert regions, full sun elsewhere.

Polygala
Polygalaceae
EVERGREEN SHRUBS

- ◪ **ZONES VARY BY SPECIES**
- ☼ ◑ **FULL SUN OR LIGHT SHADE**
- ◉ **REGULAR WATER**

Polygala fruticosa
'Petite Butterflies'

These plants are grown for colorful, asymmetrical flowers that look somewhat like sweet peas (*Lathyrus*). Grow in well-drained soil.

P. chamaebuxus. Zones 4–6. Native to Europe. To 4 in. high, 1 ft. wide; spreads slowly by underground stems. Leathery dark green leaves resemble those of boxwood (*Buxus*). Flowers combine bright yellow with creamy yellow or white, sometimes with red; spring or early summer bloom. *P. c. grandiflora* bears flowers in a combination of rosy purple and yellow. Good choice for rock gardens or containers.

P. × dalmaisiana. SWEET-PEA SHRUB. Zones 8, 9, 12–24. To 3–5 ft. high and wide; usually bare at base. Grayish green, oval to lance-shaped leaves to 1 in. long. Blooms nonstop from midsummer to fall, producing flowers in a bright, vivid purplish pink that combines well with blue shades and white.

Cut back hard in late winter to promote more compact, bushy growth. Good filler.

P. fruticosa 'Petite Butterflies'. Zones 8–9, 14–24. Native to South Africa. Dense growth to 2–3 ft. high and wide. Inch-long, rounded leaves are gray-green. Purplish pink, sweet pea–shaped blooms are about 1 in. across, with a pale pink central crest. Blooms almost year-round in mildest areas, spring to fall elsewhere. Excellent near coast. Good cut flower.

Polygonatum
SOLOMON'S SEAL
Asparagaceae
PERENNIALS

- ◪ **ZONES A1–A3; 1–9, 14–17**
- ◑ ◉ **PARTIAL OR FULL SHADE**
- ◉ **REGULAR WATER**

Polygonatum biflorum

Graceful woodland plants as lovely in leaf as they are in flower. Slowly spreading rhizomes send up arching stems clothed in bright green, broadly oval leaves arranged in nearly horizontal planes. Where leaves join stems, pairs or clusters of small, bell-shaped greenish white flowers appear in spring or early summer, hanging beneath the stems on thread-like stalks. Small blue-black berries may follow flowers. Leaves and stems turn bright yellow in autumn before plant dies to the ground.

Grow in loose, woodsy soil. Can remain in place for years; to increase your plantings, dig rhizomes from clump edges in early spring and replant. Good in containers. For the Western

native called false Solomon's seal, see *Maianthemum racemosum*.

P. biflorum. Native to eastern North America. To 1–3 ft. high, 2 ft. wide, with leaves to 4 in. long and flowers usually in pairs or threes. A form sometimes sold as *P. commutatum* or *P. canaliculatum* is much more vigorous, growing 3–7 ft. tall, 3–4 ft. wide. It has leaves to 7 in. long and flowers in groups of 2 to 10.

P. odoratum (P. japonicum, P. officinale). Native to Europe, Asia. To 1½–3½ ft. high, 2 ft. wide, with 4–6-in. leaves. Flowers are fragrant, usually borne in pairs but sometimes singly. 'Variegatum' has white-edged leaves; its stems are dark red until fully mature.

Polygonum. See *Persicaria*

Polypodium
Polypodiaceae
FERNS

- ◪ **ZONES VARY BY SPECIES**
- ◑ ◉ **PARTIAL OR FULL SHADE, EXCEPT AS NOTED**
- ◊ ◑ ◉ **WATER NEEDS VARY BY SPECIES**

Polypodium glycyrrhiza

Widespread, variable group of ferns. The ones listed here are suitable for wild gardens and in woodland. Usually grows in mosses on trees and logs. All have creeping rhizomes and shed spent fronds cleanly as new growth appears.

P. aureum (Phlebodium aureum). HARE'S FOOT FERN. Zones 15–17, 19–24; H1, H2; or indoors. From tropical America. Grows 2½ ft. high and 5 ft. wide, with showy, gracefully

arching, blue-green fronds. 'Mandaianum', sometimes called lettuce fern, has fronds with frilled and wavy edges. Regular water.

P. californicum. CALIFORNIA POLYPODY. Zones 4–9, 14–17, 22–24. Native to California and northwestern Mexico. Bright green fronds 4–12 in. long emerge in fall and stay fresh-looking until late spring or early summer, when plant goes dormant (may be nearly evergreen in coastal gardens). Spreads slowly and widely. Excellent on rocky slopes or beneath trees, as long as drainage is excellent and garden debris is not allowed to bury the rhizomes. 'Sarah Lyman' is a choice selection with finely dissected fronds and a more clumping habit. Needs moderate water during growth, little to none during summer dormancy.

P. glycyrrhiza. LICORICE FERN. Zones A3; 4–6, 14–24. Mat-forming native of coastal regions from Alaska to California. Grows 1 ft. high and spreads indefinitely. Use as groundcover in woodland or rock garden. Dark green fronds resemble those of a small sword fern (*Polystichum*). Grow in well-drained soil; mulch with leaf mold or other organic matter. Can take full sun when grown on the coast. Little to regular water.

P. scouleri. LEATHERY POLYPODY. Zones 4–6, 15–17, 24. Native along coast from British Columbia to Southern California. Slow-growing fern to 6 in. high, with indefinite spread. Thick, glossy, deep green fronds. Often found growing on trees and rocks; when grown in the ground, it tends to form a clump. Tolerates salt spray. Same culture as for *P. glycyrrhiza*.

P. vulgare. COMMON POLYPODY. Zones A2, A3; 2–9, 14–17. Native to Europe and Asia. Found in woodlands, among rocks, or on trees in areas with high rainfall. Grows 1 ft. high, with indefinite spread. Medium green fronds are held erect. Highly variable; many named forms with crested or dissected leaves are available. Thrives in acidic or alkaline soil with moderate water.

P

Polystichum
Dryopteridaceae
FERNS

⚘ **ZONES VARY BY SPECIES**

◑ ● **PARTIAL OR FULL SHADE**

💧 **REGULAR WATER**

Polystichum munitum

Hardy, symmetrical, easy-to-grow plants with evergreen fronds, except in the case of *P. braunii*. Among the most useful and widely planted ferns; combine well with other plants. Use in shady beds, along house walls, and in mixed woodland plantings. Do best in rich, well-drained soil.

P. acrostichoides. CHRISTMAS FERN. Zones 1–9, 14–24. Native to eastern North America. To 1–1½ ft. high and about 3 ft. wide. Most useful for shaded sites in cold climates, where the dark green foliage makes a fine contrast to snow or to brown dead leaves during the winter holiday season.

P. braunii. BRAUN'S HOLLY FERN. Zones 3–6, 14–17. Native to northern latitudes of America and Asia. To 1–3 ft. high and wide. New growth is silvery green, maturing to dark green. Deciduous in colder areas.

P. makinoi. MAKINO'S HOLLY FERN. Zones 3–9, 14–17, 21–24. Native to China and Japan. Grows 2 ft. high and wide, with glossy olive green fronds. Formal-looking.

P. munitum. WESTERN SWORD FERN. Zones A3; 2–9, 14–24. Native from California to Alaska and Montana, Idaho, and South Dakota. Most common fern of Western forests. To 2–4 ft. tall and wide. Leathery, lustrous dark green fronds are erect, then spreading. Each leaflet is dagger-shaped, with toothed edges and a base that looks rather like a sword hilt. Old plants may have 75 to 100 fronds. Long lasting when cut for arrangements. Established plants get by with reduced moisture.

P. neolobatum. LONG-EARED HOLLY FERN. Zones 5–7, 14–17. Native to Asia. Upright, arching growth to 2 ft. high and a bit wider, with shiny, dark green fronds that have pale green undersides. Upper leaflets closest to midrib on each frond are enlarged and a bit rounded, like little "ears."

P. polyblepharum. JAPANESE TASSEL FERN. Zones 4–9, 14–24. Native to Asia. Handsome, dense, lacy-looking plant to 2–3 ft. high and 3 ft. wide. Glossy dark green fronds. Golden, bristled unfurling fronds in spring. Sometimes sold as *P. setosum.*

P. setiferum. SOFT SHIELD FERN. Zones 4–9, 14–24. Native to southern Europe. Finely cut fronds give the effect of green lace. Many forms are sold, varying from 2–4½ ft. tall and wide. 'Congestum Cristatum' is a 6–12-in.-tall dwarf with upright gray-green fronds. Divisilobum group features named varieties with particularly lacy appearance. Plantlets form on midribs of older fronds on several types of soft shield fern; these can be detached and planted.

P. setosum. See *P. polyblepharum.*

P. tsus-simense. KOREAN ROCK FERN. Zones 4–7, 14–17. From Asia. Forms a neat, dainty clump 12–15 in. high and wide. Erect, leathery, dark green fronds are held on dark stems. Use at front of shaded borders, among rocks, in pots. Established plants can take short periods of dryness.

To rejuvenate an overgrown and untidy Western sword fern, snip off old fronds at the base in early spring, just as new ones start to unfurl.

Pomegranate
Lythraceae
DECIDUOUS SHRUB OR TREE

⚘ **ZONES 5–24 (BUT SEE TEXT); H1, H2**

☀ **FULL SUN**

💧 **REGULAR WATER**

Pomegranates

This small, showy tree from Iran and northern India has naturalized throughout the Mediterranean. It grows 15–20 ft. tall and broad, though it is often kept pruned to half that size. Showy red flowers appear at branch tips in spring and develop into roundish, 5-in.-wide fruits that ripen in fall. Self-fruitful. Resistant to oak root fungus. For ornamental pomegranate varieties, see *Punica granatum.*

Each fruit contains hundreds of sacs of seedy, sweet-tart, juicy pulp. Harvest fruit when they reach full color. Fruit left on the tree is likely to split and rot, especially if weather is rainy. Can be stored in the refrigerator for up to 7 months. To eat fresh, cut into quarters or eighths and pull rind back (starting from the ends) to expose the juicy sacs; eat them, seeds and all. To remove juice for drinking fresh or for use in jams, jellies, or sauces, cut fruit in half and ream with a juicer. Or roll fruit firmly on hard surface; then cut a hole in stem end and squeeze juice into a container.

In Zones 5, 6, and 17, where pomegranate grows and blooms but may not fruit, locate against south or west wall. Tolerates a wide variety of soils. Can take drought but produces better fruit with regular moisture.

The best-known variety is 'Wonderful', with orange-red flowers and burnished red fruit with red pulp. Other varieties are available, including the following (all have red or orange-red flowers unless noted otherwise).

'Ambrosia'. Bears huge fruit (up to three times larger than those of 'Wonderful') with pale pink skin and purple pulp.

'Angel Red'. Ripens early and produces lots of extra-juicy, red-skinned fruit with soft seeds.

'Eversweet'. Ripens very early and bears virtually seedless fruit with transparent red pulp and clear, nonstaining juice.

'Granada'. Bears pink flowers and fruit with pink pulp.

'Kashmir'. Pinkish red fruit have red seeds with intense flavor that's great for juice.

'Pink Satin'. Pinkish red fruit have light pink, soft seeds whose juice is nonstaining.

'Red Silk'. Produces medium to large red fruit with excellent sweet-tart, red pulp on a 6–8-ft. tree, ideal for containers.

'Sweet'. Bears yellow flowers and fruit with pink pulp.

'White'. Produces pink fruit with sweet, transparent pulp.

Pontederia cordata
PICKEREL WEED
Pontederiaceae
AQUATIC PERENNIAL

⚘ **ZONES 1–24; H1, H2**

☀ ◑ **FULL SUN OR LIGHT SHADE**

💧 **LOCATE IN PONDS, WATER GARDENS**

Pontederia cordata albiflora

Native to eastern North America. To 3–4 ft. tall and 2–2½ ft. wide. Long-stalked, glossy green leaves stand well above surface of water; these are heart-shaped, to 10 in. long and 6 in. wide. Blooms from late spring to fall, bearing short spikes of blue flowers at stem ends. *P. c. albiflora* has white blooms; pink-flowered forms are also available. Pink- and white-flowered forms are available. Often grown as a companion to water lilies (*Nymphaea*); plant in pots of rich soil placed in 1 ft. of water. Gives an informal garden pool the look of a wild pond. To use in natural ponds, set plants at shoreline—underwater, directly in the soil. Goes dormant in winter.

Populus

POPLAR, COTTONWOOD, ASPEN
Salicaceae
DECIDUOUS TREES

✔ ZONES VARY BY SPECIES
☀ FULL SUN
● REGULAR WATER
🦋 ATTRACT BUTTERFLIES

Populus tremuloides

Fast-growing, tough trees. Grown primarily—and especially appreciated—in interior regions with hot summers and cold winters. Don't do as well in mild-winter areas and in coastal climates where temperature fluctuation is minimal. Trees have aggressive surface roots that crowd out other plants, heave pavement, and clog sewer and drainage lines; best suited to rural areas and fringes of large properties. Most poplars will sucker if their roots are cut or disturbed. They are subject to many pests and diseases.

Despite their liabilities, some of these trees are beautiful or distinctive enough to be widely sold. Many have good fall color.

Leaves of most are roughly triangular, sometimes toothed or lobed. Pendulous catkins (denser on male trees) appear in spring before leafout. Female trees later bear masses of cottony seeds that blow about and become a nuisance; for that reason, male (seedless) varieties are the best choice and are usually offered in nurseries.

P. × acuminata. LANCE-LEAF COTTONWOOD. Zones 1–11, 14–21. Hybrid of *P. angustifolia* and another species; like *P. angustifolia*, thrives at high elevations. To 40–60 ft. tall, 35–45 ft. wide. Narrow, triangular leaves are glossy dark green above, paler dull green beneath. Yellow fall color. Seedless.

P. alba. WHITE POPLAR. Zones A3; 1–11, 14–21. Native to Europe, Asia. To 40–70 ft. tall and wide. Common name refers to woolly white leaf undersides and to light-colored young bark. A "lively" tree with leaves that move even in light breezes, showing flickering white and green highlights. Tolerates wide range of soils. Suckers profusely—an advantage if it is planted as a windbreak, otherwise a problem. 'Raket' forms a cone just 25 ft. wide. Seedless *P. a. pyramidalis*, called Bolleana poplar, forms a narrow (15 ft. wide) column and has a white or light gray trunk like that of birch (*Betula*).

P. angustifolia. NARROWLEAF POPLAR. Zones 1–11, 14–21. Native from Alberta to Mexico, primarily in Rocky Mountains; grows at elevations to 8,000 ft. To 50–60 ft. tall and 35–45 ft. wide, with finely toothed, narrow, willowlike green leaves to 5 in. long. Young bark is green.

P. balsamifera trichocarpa (P. trichocarpa). BLACK COTTONWOOD. Zones A2, A3; 1–9, 14–24. Native from Alaska to Southern California. To 30–100 ft. tall, 25–30 ft. wide. Heavy-limbed tree with furrowed dark gray bark, very brittle wood. Leaves are deep green above and distinctly silver beneath; attractive when ruffled by breezes. Good golden yellow fall color.

P. fremontii. WESTERN COTTONWOOD, FREMONT COTTONWOOD. Zones 1–12, 14–21. Native to California

and central Rockies south to Mexico. To 40–60 ft. or taller, 30 ft. wide. Glossy yellow-green, coarsely toothed, virtually triangular leaves turn bright lemon yellow in fall. Leaves persist almost all winter in Zone 12. 'Nevada' is a male variety.

P. 'Highland'. HIGHLAND POPLAR. Zones A2; 1–11, 14–21. This hybrid forms an upright oval 50 ft. tall and 30 ft. wide. Light-colored bark. Dark green leaves turn yellow in fall. Seedless. Shows fair resistance to pests and diseases.

P. nigra 'Italica'. LOMBARDY POPLAR. Zones A3; 1–11, 14–24. Male selection of a European native. Beautiful columnar tree to 40–100 ft. tall and 15–30 ft. wide, with upward-reaching branches. Bright green leaves turn golden yellow in fall. Excellent along country driveways; valuable both as windbreak and skyline decoration. Healthy and attractive in cold, dry interior climates. Suckers profusely.

P. tremula. EUROPEAN ASPEN. Zones A1–A3; 1–7. From Europe, North Africa, Asia. Similar to *P. tremuloides*, but its bark is somewhat darker and its leaves more coarsely toothed. Seedless 'Erecta', sometimes called Swedish columnar aspen, is a narrow grower with red fall color—a good substitute for Lombardy poplar (*P. nigra* 'Italica').

P. tremuloides. QUAKING ASPEN. Zones A1–A3; 1–7, 14–19. Native throughout mountains of the West, at elevations to 9,000 ft. Generally performs poorly or grows slowly in lowlands; usually short-lived in warmer climates. To 20–60 ft. tall, 15–30 ft. wide; often grows as a multitrunked tree or in a clump. Smooth, pale gray-green to whitish bark. Dainty glossy green leaves flutter with the slightest movement of air. Brilliant golden yellow fall color. Good background tree for native shrubs and wildflowers. Apt to suffer from sudden dieback or borers. 'Mountain Sentinel' is very narrow and upright at 35 ft. tall and just 8 ft. wide after 30 years. 'Prairie Gold', to 40 ft. tall and 15 ft. wide, was bred to tolerate lowland conditions and resist disease.

Portulaca

Portulacaceae
ANNUALS

✔ ALL ZONES
☀ FULL SUN
◐● MODERATE TO REGULAR WATER

Portulaca grandiflora

Low-growing, fleshy plants. One is considered a weed but can be used in cooking and salads. The others are grown for their brilliant flowers, on display from late spring until frost; generally, the blossoms open fully in bright light and close by mid-afternoon in hot weather. The various plants described here thrive in high temperatures, intense sunlight. Bright-flowered types are attractive in rock gardens, parking strips, hanging baskets, or as edgings and bank covers; they don't require deadheading to prolong bloom. Not fussy about soil.

P. grandiflora. ROSE MOSS. From South America. To 6 in. high, 1½ ft. across. Trailing, branching reddish stems are set with narrow, cylindrical, pointed leaves to 1 in. long. Inch-wide, lustrous-petaled flowers shaped like tiny roses, in white and many bright and pastel shades of red, cerise, rose-pink, orange, and yellow. Available as single colors or mixes, in single- or double-flowered strains. Afternoon Delight and Sundance strains stay open longer in the afternoon. Sunseeker strain also resists closing and has larger (2 in.), double blossoms. All self-sow, but they often fail to come true from seed.

P. oleracea. PURSLANE. Unimproved form is thought to have originated in India; it's an

P

edible weed with tiny yellow flowers and plump, oval leaves to 1¼ in. long. Warm weather and moisture encourage its growth. Control by hoeing or pulling before it goes to seed; don't let pulled plants lie about, since they can reroot or ripen seed. Stems and leaves can be added to salads, soups, sauces; improved garden strains are sold for the vegetable garden.

P. Wildfire hybrids. Sometimes offered as *P. oleracea*, or *P. grandiflora*, but is actually a strain of *P. umbraticola*. Best in hot-summer areas; popular in the Southwest. Plants grow a few inches tall and spread to 2 ft.; they have the broad leaves of *P. oleracea* but bear brightly colored, 1½-in. single flowers in red, pink, lavender, yellow, orange, peach, white, or bicolors. Each flower lasts only a day, but new ones keep the show going. Plants live over in the absence of frost.

Portulacaria afra
ELEPHANT'S FOOD
Didiereaceae
SUCCULENT SHRUB

- ✂ **ZONES 8, 9, 12–24; H1, H2**
- ☼ ◐ ● **SUN OR SHADE**
- ◌ ◐ **LITTLE TO MODERATE WATER**

Portulacaria afra

Native to South Africa. Can be grown outdoors but needs frost protection. To 12 ft. tall and nearly as wide, with thick, juicy stems and glossy green leaves. Looks a bit like jade plant (*Crassula ovata*) and is sometimes sold under the name "miniature jade plant," but it's faster growing and more loosely branched, with tapering, more

limber branches and smaller (½ in. long) leaves. In its native land, it bears clusters of tiny pink flowers, but it seldom blooms in North America.

In frost-free or nearly frostless areas, can be used as a fast-growing informal screen or unclipped hedge. Small specimens are good, easy-care potted plants and can be trained as bonsai. Forms with variegated leaves ('Tricolor', 'Variegata') are slower growing and smaller than the species.

Potato
Solanaceae
PERENNIAL TREATED AS ANNUAL

- ✂ **ALL ZONES**
- ☼ **FULL SUN**
- ● **REGULAR WATER**
- ◈ **GREEN SKIN AND RAW SHOOTS ARE POISONOUS IF INGESTED**

'Yukon Gold' potatoes

Andean native, botanically known as *Solanum tuberosum*. Though other vegetables are more common in home gardens, growing potatoes can be very satisfying: 2 lbs. of seed potatoes can yield 50 lbs. of potatoes for eating. It is an especially rewarding crop for children's gardens: digging up the potatoes is like finding buried treasure.

Grow plants from seed potatoes that you cut into 1½-in. cubes (each with at least two eyes) or from small tubers, which are planted whole and are less likely to rot in the ground. (Don't try to grow supermarket potatoes; most are treated to prevent sprouting.) Home gardeners have access to a number of varieties, including types with red, white, yellow,

How to Grow Potatoes

PLANTING Plant potatoes in loose, fertile, sandy soil amended with plenty of compost. Tubers become deformed in heavy, poorly drained soil. In cold-winter climates, plant as soon as the soil is workable in spring. In mild-winter regions, plant in early spring for a summer crop, in early fall for a winter-into-spring crop. Where frosts are not severe, potatoes can be planted in midwinter—as long as the soil isn't too wet from winter rains. Let seed potato pieces dry for a day or two before planting. Then set minitubers or potato pieces in furrows 4 in. deep and cover with 2 in. of soil. As tops grow, add more soil until you've built a ridge 4 in. above ground level. Developing tubers should always be covered with soil to keep skin from turning green (and toxic).

Another method of growing potatoes: Prepare soil so that surface is loose; then plant potato pieces or minitubers ½–2 in. deep, and water well. Mound loose soil over plants as directed above; then cover soil with a 1–1½-ft.-thick layer of straw, hay, or dead leaves. Surround the planting with chicken wire to keep loose material from blowing away. Potatoes will form on the soil surface or just beneath it, requiring little digging; you can probe through the mulch with your fingers to harvest them.

FERTILIZING At planting time, mix a complete fertilizer into the soil at least 2 in. away from seed potatoes.

WATERING Keep soil uniformly moist during growth. Water for the last time as leaves turn from yellow to brown.

HARVESTING Dig new potatoes when the plants begin to bloom; dig mature potatoes when plants die down. Dig carefully to avoid bruising or cutting the tubers. Well-matured potatoes free of defects are the best keepers; store them in a cool (40°F/4°C), dark, dry place. Where the ground doesn't freeze, late potatoes can remain in the ground until needed. Dig before warmer temperatures start them growing again.

CHALLENGES The many pests and diseases that beleaguer commercial growers are not likely to plague home gardeners. To avoid disease problems, plant certified disease-free starter potatoes or disease-resistant varieties.

russet brown, or bluish purple skins; depending on variety, flesh may be white or match the skin color of red, yellow, or blue varieties. Shapes vary from round or cylindrical to fingerlike (the latter are called fingerlings). Some varieties mature faster than others, but most reach harvesting size 2½ to 4 months after planting.

Culinary use depends greatly on whether a potato is moist or dry, and whether the starch it contains is branched (holds its shape in salads and stews) or relatively straight (allows the potato to fall apart in cooking). For baking and mashing, most people prefer a light, dry, fluffy potato like 'Butte' or 'Russet Burbank'. For velvety-textured

soups, try 'Carola', which falls apart nicely when cooked. For stews, boiling, and potato salads, choose a waxy, moist potato like 'Reddale'. For fun, make colorful fries or mashed potatoes with 'All Blue'; 'Elba', another good choice for these dishes, has traditional buff-colored skin and white flesh.

There are also potatoes for special situations. If you garden in a short-season climate, try an early all-purpose variety like 'Yukon' or 'Yukon Gold'. In wet climates or soil that tends to be damp, grow 'Nooksack'. If diseases are a problem in your area, try 'Island Sunshine' for resistance to late blight, or 'Reddale' for resistance to verticillium wilt.

The aboveground potato plant is sprawling and bushy, with much-divided dark green leaves somewhat like those of a tomato plant. Clustered inch-wide flowers may be white, pink, light red, or pale blue, depending on variety; blossoms often reflect the color of the tubers.

Potentilla

CINQUEFOIL
Rosaceae
PERENNIALS AND DECIDUOUS SHRUBS

⚡ ZONES VARY BY SPECIES

☀ ☽ PARTIAL SHADE IN HOTTEST CLIMATES

💧 💧 WATER NEEDS VARY BY TYPE

Potentilla fruticosa 'Pink Beauty'

Tough, unfussy perennials and small shrubs prized for their long season of blooms in white, cream, and soft to bright shades of pink, red, yellow, and orange. Leaves may be green, gray-green, or silvery gray. Plants are not fussy about soil; in fact, most grow best in poor to moderately fertile soil that is well drained.

PERENNIALS

These include sturdy, clumping plants for use in rock gardens or perennial borders and creeping kinds used as groundcovers. Leaves are divided fanwise into leaflets and are reminiscent of strawberry foliage. Moderate to regular water.

P. atrosanguinea. Zones 2b–9, 14–24. Sprawling, clump-forming Himalayan native to 1½ ft. high and 2 ft. wide, with furry, silver-gray leaves and deep red summer flowers to 1¼ in. across. A parent of several superior hybrids, including the excellent 'Gibson's Scarlet'.

P. nepalensis. Zones 2b–9, 14–24. Himalayan native. Forms a clump of bright green leaves to 1 ft. high and 1½ ft. wide. Summer bloomer, bearing branching clusters of ½–1-in.-wide blossoms. 'Miss Willmott' has salmon-pink flowers with a darker center. 'Ron McBeath' bears carmine blooms with distinctly heart-shaped petals. Good for borders, cut flowers. Performs well near coast.

P. neumanniana. Zones A1–A3; 1–24. European native. Dainty-looking yet tough and persistent groundcover to 4–6 in. high; spreads quickly by creeping, rooting stems. Leaves are bright green. Butter yellow, ¼-in. flowers bloom in spring and summer. 'Nana' grows just 3 in. high.

Foliage blankets the ground completely yet is permeable enough to be a good bulb cover; established plantings endure limited foot traffic. Set plants 1 ft. apart in well-drained soil. Plantings look more uniform if mowed annually before spring growth begins; in colder areas, mowing also serves to remove browned winter leaves.

P. recta 'Warrenii' (P. r. 'Macrantha'). Zones A2, A3; 1–10, 14–24. Selection of a species from Europe and Siberia. Erect clump to 2 ft. high, 1½ ft. wide, with medium green to gray-green leaves. Profuse show of bright yellow, 1-in. flowers in late spring. Tolerates a wide range of soils.

P. × tonguei. Zones 2–24. Clumping growth to 4 in. high, 1–2 ft. wide; nearly prostrate stems are set with dark green leaves. Late spring or summer blooms are ½ in. wide, apricot with a red center.

SHRUBS

The shrubby potentillas, most often sold as named forms of *P. fruticosa*, are native to northern latitudes everywhere, including the Cascades and Olympic and Rocky Mountains. They perform well in Zones A1–A3, 1–11, 14–21. Most have bright green to dark green leaves divided into three to seven leaflets; all bloom from late spring to early fall, producing cheerful, 1½–2-in.-wide blossoms.

These are fairly trouble-free plants that do best in well-drained soil with moderate water but tolerate poor soil, drought, and heat. Varieties with red- or orange-tinted blossoms should be grown in light shade; they tend to fade quickly in hot sun. After the bloom period ends, cut out some of the oldest stems from time to time to make room for new growth. Here are some of the many varieties to be found in nurseries.

'Abbotswood'. To 3 ft. high and wide. White flowers.

'Daydawn'. To 4 ft. tall and wide. Yellow flowers flushed with pink.

'Elizabeth'. Grows 3 ft. high, 3½ ft. wide, with bright yellow blooms.

'Floppy Disc'. To 2–3 ft. high, 3–4 ft. wide. Deep pink double flowers bleach to pinkish white in high heat.

'Frosty'. To 1 ft. high and 3 ft. wide. Large white flowers.

'Goldfinger'. To 3 ft. high, 4 ft. wide. Golden yellow flowers.

'Goldstar'. To 2 ft. high, 2–2½ ft. wide. Bright yellow blooms.

'Jackman's Variety'. To 3–4 ft. tall, 5 ft. wide. Bright yellow blossoms.

'Katherine Dykes'. To 3 ft. high and wide. Pale yellow flowers.

'Klondike'. Dense grower to 2 ft. high and wide. Deep yellow flowers.

'Mount Everest'. Bushy, upright plant to 4½ ft. tall and wide. Pure white blossoms.

'Pink Beauty'. To 3 ft. high and wide, with profuse clear pink blooms.

'Primrose Beauty'. To 2–3 ft. high and wide, with silvery green foliage and pale yellow flowers.

'Red Ace'. To 2 ft. high, 3–4 ft. wide. Flowers are bright red, with yellow center and yellow petal backs; they fade to solid yellow with age (fading is very rapid in hot-summer climates or under poor growing conditions).

'Sunset'. To 1½ ft. high, 3 ft. wide. Flowers are red in light shade; in hot sun, may be reddish orange, orange, or yellow.

'Sutter's Gold'. Grows to 1 ft. high, 3 ft. wide, with soft yellow blooms.

'Tangerine'. To 2½ ft. high and wide, with bright orange-yellow flowers.

Pratia

Campanulaceae
PERENNIALS

⚡ ZONES 4–9, 14–24

☀ ☽ PARTIAL SHADE IN HOTTEST CLIMATES

💧 REGULAR WATER

Pratia pedunculata 'Mini Blue'

Small, ground-hugging plants that reach just 2–3 in. high in bloom, with creeping, branching stems that root at the joints. All are useful low groundcovers where soil is reasonably rich and well drained. Small, closely set leaves and tolerance for an occasional footstep make them choice selections for use between steppingstones. They resemble baby's tears (*Soleirolia soleirolii*) but offer appealing flowers as well as attractive foliage. Set plants 8–12 in. apart; fertilize periodically. Can be invasive where well adapted.

P. angulata. Native to New Zealand. Dark green, ½-in. leaves set off small white to ice blue summer flowers like those of lobelia, with a two-lobed upper lip and a three-lobed lower lip. Small, round fruit is purplish red.

P. pedunculata (Isotoma fluviatilis, Laurentia fluviatilis). BLUE STAR CREEPER. Native to Australia. Bright green, nearly stemless, ¼-in. leaves; in late spring and summer, these form a backdrop for equally tiny, star-shaped pale blue flowers. 'Alba' has white blooms. 'County Park' has deep blue flowers.

FOR OTHER PLANTS THAT MAKE GOOD GROUNDCOVERS, SEE PAGES 60–63.

P

Primula

PRIMROSE

Primulaceae

PERENNIALS SOMETIMES GROWN
AS ANNUALS

✎ **ZONES VARY BY SPECIES OR TYPE**

☼ ◐ ● **FULL SUN IN COOLER
CLIMATES ONLY**

💧 **REGULAR WATER, EXCEPT AS NOTED**

Primula

Most primroses are native to
the Himalayas and cool regions
of Southeast Asia and Europe.
Cherished for their colorful flowers. Plants form a foliage
rosette; at bloom time, typically
circular, sometimes fragrant
flowers with five petals rise
above the leaves. Blossoms
may be borne on individual
stems, in clusters at stem
ends, or in tiered, candelabra-
like clusters along the stem.
Most primroses are spring
blooming, but some start flowering in mid- to late winter in mild
climates, and a few bloom in
early summer. Some go dormant in late fall or winter; mark
their location before they disappear. Nearly all are good plants
for the woodland garden.

Most primroses flourish in
the cool, humid Pacific Northwest; if given the right amount
of moisture and dappled shade,
they can be grown successfully
in somewhat warmer, drier
regions. Most are quite hardy;
many thrive east of the Cascades and in intermountain
regions. Where the climate is
less than favorable, they are
sometimes treated as annuals.
Some will grow indoors.

P. alpicola. MOONLIGHT
PRIMROSE. Zones 3–6, 17.
Grows 20 in. high, 1 ft. wide,
with wrinkled, medium green
leaves and clusters of sulfur yellow (sometimes white or purple),
bell-shaped blossoms in summer. Powerfully fragrant. Somewhat tender in coldest zones.

P. auricula. AURICULA.
Zones A2, A3; 1–6, 15–17, 22–
24. To 6–8 in. high and 1 ft.
wide. Evergreen. Broad, leathery
gray-green leaves, sometimes
with mealy, powdery coating
that spots and runs in rain. In
early spring, bears clustered
blooms in white, cream, yellow,
orange, pink, rose, red, purple,
blue, or brownish, with a white
or yellow eye. Usually grown in
pots for display. Many named
varieties are offered; some
have green or near-black flowers
rimmed in mealy powder or in
a contrasting color.

P. beesiana. Zones 3–6,
15–17. To 2 ft. high and wide,
with medium green leaves to
14 in. long. In mid- to late spring,
bears tiered blossoms with 2 to
8 dense whorls per stem. Color
is variable but usually reddish
purple with yellow eye. Very
deep rooted. Provide regular
water with deep soakings.

P. bulleyana. Zones 3–6,
15–17. Grows to 2 ft. high and
wide. Resembles *P. beesiana*,
but leaves have reddish midribs. Mid- to late spring production of tiered flowers with 5 to
7 whorls per stem. Blooms are
bright yellow, opening from
orange buds.

P. denticulata. DRUM-
STICK PRIMROSE. Zones A2,
A3; 1–6. To 1 ft. high and wide,
with spoon-shaped, medium
green leaves. Dense, ball-
shaped flower clusters are held
on stout stems in early spring.
Color ranges from blue-violet to
purple. Pinkish, lavender, and
white varieties are available.

P. florindae. Zones A2, A3;
3–6, 15–17. Grows 3 ft. high,
2 ft. wide, with long-stemmed
medium green leaves. Yellow,
bell-shaped, nodding flowers are
carried in clusters of up to 60.
Hybrids have red, orange, or yellow flowers. The most fragrant
primrose. Plants are late to
appear in spring and are among
the latest primroses to bloom
(late spring or summer). Provide
ample water; will even grow in
a few inches of running water or
in damp, low spot.

P. japonica. Zones A3; 2–6,
15–17. To 2½ ft. high and 1½ ft.

CLOCKWISE FROM TOP: *Primula
obconica*; *P. veris*; *P. auricula* 'Walton'

wide, with spoon-shaped, light
green leaves to 9 in. long.
Blooms in late spring or early
summer. Tiered blossoms are
purple with a yellow eye; up to
5 whorls on each stout stem.
Among the best varieties are
'Alba' (white), 'Apple Blossom'
(pale pink with a red eye), 'Miller's Crimson' (red), and 'Post-
ford White' (white with red eye).
Needs ample water; will grow
at edge of pond, even in very
shallow water

P. juliae. JULIANA PRIM-
ROSE. Zones 2–6, 14–17, 20–
23. Grows just 3–4 in. high and
10 in. wide, with rounded, bright
green leaves. Magenta, yellow-
eyed flowers are borne singly
on a long stalk in early spring.
Excellent for edging, woodland,
flower bed, or rock garden.
'Wanda' is an old-time favorite.
A white-flowered form is sometimes offered.

P. malacoides. FAIRY PRIM-
ROSE, BABY PRIMROSE. Zones
8, 9, 12–24. Grows to 8–15 in.
high and 1 ft. wide. Evergreen.
Perennial in mild-winter areas of
California and Arizona, though
often grown as annual there.
Treated only as annual, potted
plant, or houseplant elsewhere.

Soft, pale green leaves are
carried on long stalks. Tiered
blossoms appear in loose,
lacy whorls along many upright
stems in midwinter to late
spring. Blooms are white, pink,
rose, red, or lavender. Good
under high-branching trees, with
spring bulbs, in flower beds.
Tolerates light frost.

P. obconica. Zones 4–9,
14–24. Grows to to 1 ft. high
and wide. Perennial, but best
treated as annual. Soft, hairy,
roundish leaves have hairy leafstalks; these hairs (except on
Freedom and Libre strains) may
irritate skin. Produces large,
broad clusters of 1½–2-in.-wide
blooms in white, pink, salmon,
lavender, or reddish purple in
winter and spring; nearly everblooming in cool-summer areas.
Use for bedding where winters
are mild, as a houseplant in
colder regions.

P. Polyanthus group.
POLYANTHUS PRIMROSE,
ENGLISH PRIMROSE. Zones
1–24. To 8–12 in. high, 9 in.
wide, with fresh green, tongue-

P

shaped leaves that resemble romaine lettuce leaves. Evergreen in milder climates; grown as annuals in hot-summer areas. The most weather-resistant primroses. Bears large, full clusters of 1–2-in.-wide blossoms (miniature types are smaller) in winter to early or midspring. Available in almost any color; many very brilliant. Choose from the many large-flowered strains, like Crescendo and Pacific Giant, or look for novelties such as the Gold Lace group, with gold-edged, yellow-centered, deep mahogany petals; 'Penumbra', similar, with silver-edged petals; and 'Guinevere', with bronzy foliage and soft pink, yellow-eyed blooms. All are excellent for massing, with bulbs, or in containers.

P. prolifera (P. helodoxa). Zones 4–6, 15–17. To 2–3 ft. high and 2 ft. wide. Evergreen. Spoon-shaped to triangular, deep green leaves to 14 in. long. Tiered blossoms with up to 7 whorls per stem, each with 3 to 12 fragrant, light to bright yellow, inch-wide flowers, appear in late spring or summer. Ample water.

P. pulverulenta. Zones 3–6, 17. To 3 ft. high and 2 ft. wide, with deep green, wrinkled leaves to 1 ft. or longer. In late spring and summer come tiered blossoms with several to many whorls per stem. Blooms are red to red-purple, with purple eye. Flowering stems are thickly dusted with white meal. Bartley hybrids have flowers in pink and salmon range. Ample water.

P. sieboldii. Zones A2, A3; 2–7, 14–17. Grows 1 ft. high and wide, with oval, light green, deeply lobed and toothed leaves. Produces white, pink, or purple, white-eyed flowers, each 1½ in. wide, in clusters of 2 to 15 in early spring. Many named selections in deep or light colors; flowers of some have fringed petals. Leaves of all types usually die back shortly after flowering.

P. sinensis. CHINESE PRIMROSE. Indoors. To 6–8 in. high and wide. Evergreen. Soft, hairy, bright green, roundish, 2–4 in. long, with toothed, lobed edges. Hairs may irritate skin. One or more whorls per stem, each with many ½-in.-wide blossoms in white, pink, lavender, reddish,

or coral. Stellatas have star-shaped flowers. Blooms in winter. Tender. Favorite European potted plant; imported seed available from specialists. Regular water.

P. × tommasinii. Zones A3; 2a–9, 14–24. Grows to 6–12 in. high and 1½ ft. wide over time. Green leaves are tongue-shaped and up to 9 in. long. Hose-in-hose is the most common type sold; looks like one single flower emerging from the center of another. Fragrant. The You and Me series includes hose-in-hose flowers in yellow, cream, maroon, red, rose, white, purple, apricot, and blue.

P. veris. COWSLIP. Zones A3; 2–6, 15–17. To 4–10 in. high, 8 in. wide. Leaves similar to those of polyanthus primrose. Evergreen in milder climates. Clustered flowers are bright yellow, fragrant, ½–1 in. wide, produced in early spring. Lovely naturalized in wild garden or rock garden. Charming but not as sturdy as polyanthus primrose.

P. vialii (P. littoniana). Zones 4–6, 15–17. Grows 1–2 ft. high, 1 ft. wide, with oblong, irregularly toothed, hairy leaves to 8 in. long. Dense, narrow, 3–5-in.-long spikes of fragrant flowers to ½ in. wide are held on erect stems in late spring or early summer. Blooms are violet-blue, opening from red buds. Not long-lived but quite easy to grow from seed. Regular to ample water.

P. vulgaris (P. acaulis). COMMON PRIMROSE, ENGLISH PRIMROSE. Zones A3; 2–6, 14–17, 21–24. To 8 in. high, 1 ft. wide, with leaves much like those of polyanthus primrose. Evergreen in milder climates. Flowers are borne singly; vigorous garden strains often bear 2 or 3 per stem. Early spring blooms are white, yellow, red, blue, brown, bronze, or wine-colored. Single series like Danova, sweet-scented Primera, and large-flowered Supreme are ubiquitous, but doubles and rose-flowered series like Belarina and Rosanna are gaining popularity. Good in woodland gardens, as edging, and in beds and containers.

FOR OTHER PERENNIALS THAT ARE GOOD IN CONTAINERS, SEE PAGES 117–118.

Plant in organically enriched, well-drained soil, with roots mulched to keep them cool. Protect from slugs and snails. Plants form tight clumps that will need dividing when performance declines. Dig and divide overcrowded clumps right after bloom or (in mild-winter areas) in autumn.

Pritchardia

LOULU PALM
Arecaceae
PALMS

✂ **ZONES VARY BY SPECIES**

☼ **FULL SUN**

💧 **MODERATE WATER**

Pritchardia thurstonii

This complex genus includes 19 native Hawaiian species and about 25 species restricted to various other tropical Pacific islands. Erect, medium-size fan palms with straight trunk and regular form. Best in well-drained soil with moderate moisture. Plant in groups or use as specimens. Young plants tolerate shade and are good in pots, indoors or out.

P. hillebrandii. LOULU LELO. Zones 23, 24; H1, H2. Native to Hawaii. Slow growing to 20 ft. tall, 8 ft. wide. Leaves to 4 ft. long. Full sun brings out the bluish silver color of the foliage. Striking accent in the landscape during the day or under night lighting.

P. minor. Zones 17, 23, 24; H1, H2. From high-elevation Hawaii. Slow growth to 20–30 ft. tall, with attractive, deep green, rounded leaves with a silvery underside. Protect from hot sun when young.

P. pacifica. FIJI FAN PALM. Zone H2. Native to Fiji. Moderately fast growth to 30 ft. tall, 8 ft. wide. Green leaves to about 4 ft. long. Needs protection from drying winds. Moderate salt-tolerance.

P. thurstonii. THURSTON FAN PALM. Zone H2. Native to Fiji. Slow-growing, slender-trunked tree to 15–30 ft. tall and 8 ft. wide. Bright green, 5–6-ft.-long leaves. Good salt-tolerance.

Prosopis

MESQUITE
Fabaceae
EVERGREEN AND DECIDUOUS TREES OR SHRUBS

✂ **ZONES 10–13, 18–24, EXCEPT AS NOTED**

☼ **FULL SUN**

💧 **LITTLE TO MODERATE WATER**

🦋 **ATTRACT BIRDS, BUTTERFLIES**

Prosopis glandulosa

Native to deserts in the Southwest, Mexico, and South America. These are among the toughest and most useful trees for desert gardens. Mesquites may have one or many trunks; all have dark bark, a thicket of branches, and little leaflets that filter sunlight to cast airy, light shade. Small spikes of tiny greenish yellow flowers in spring and summer are followed by flat, beanlike, 2–6-in.-long pods. Flowers are a source of honey, and the pod contents are edible. Thorniness is variable; thornless varieties are available.

These plants have far-reaching roots that will travel great distances to find water (a trait that causes problems if plants tap into drainage or sewer lines). Once established, they are highly drought-tolerant but quickly adapt to regular lawn watering. In poor, rocky soil and without additional water, mesquites are shrubby; in deep soil where roots can reach groundwater, or where irrigation is generous, they grow rapidly to about 30 ft. tall, with a picturesque, spreading canopy nearly as wide. For best results, water deeply and infrequently. Little pruning is needed; prune only to cut out broken or dead limbs.

P. alba. ARGENTINE MESQUITE. Nearly evergreen. Native to South America. Vigorous and fast growing, with an erect single trunk and a dense canopy of blue-green leaves and spines. Drops some leaves throughout cold weather. Cutting-grown 'Colorado' is an erect, thornless tree with foliage slightly lighter in color than that of seedling plants.

P. chilensis. CHILEAN MESQUITE. Evergreen in mild-winter climates; deciduous in colder areas. Zones 10–13; H1, H2. Native to South America. Produces a fairly open canopy of deep green leaves. Another tree sold under this name (probably a hybrid) is deciduous, with a denser canopy.

P. glandulosa. HONEY MESQUITE, TEXAS MESQUITE. Deciduous. Native to southwestern U.S., Texas, and Mexico. Often multitrunked. Bright green leaves and drooping branchlets give this tree something of the look of California pepper tree (*Schinus molle*). Cutting-grown 'Maverick' is a superior, thornless form. The subspecies *P. g. torreyana* grows naturally westward as far as California.

P. 'Phoenix'. Semievergreen. Thornless, fast-growing hybrid grows 30–35 ft. tall and wide. Large, lush green leaves cast nice shade. Light yellow flowers in spring and summer, followed by brown seedpods.

P. pubescens. SCREW BEAN. Deciduous. Native to Arizona, Texas, and Mexico. Common name refers to the spirally twisted seedpods, which make an unusual and attractive addition to dried arrangements. Open canopy of bluish green foliage. This is a naturally shrubby plant that is often used as a barrier planting, but it can be trained as a tree.

P. velutina. ARIZONA MESQUITE. Deciduous. Native from southeastern Arizona into Mexico and West Texas. Resembles *P. glandulosa* but may be smaller and shrubbier when grown in poor, dry conditions. Common in Arizona.

Prostanthera
MINT BUSH
Lamiaceae
EVERGREEN SHRUBS

🗡 **ZONES 14–17, 19–24**

☼ **FULL SUN, EXCEPT AS NOTED**

💧 **MODERATE WATER**

Prostanthera rotundifolia

Australian natives with wonderfully fragrant foliage and an enormous profusion of small flowers, usually in shades of purplish blue or white. Although they tend to be short-lived, they grow quickly and put on a good show. Prune them carefully; avoid cutting into bare wood or doing any other hard pruning. There are many species available; look for them at specialists' nurseries or at plant sales held by botanical gardens. These plants require excellent drainage.

P. cuneata. Dense grower to 3 ft. high, 3–5 ft. wide, with shiny, dark green leaves. White flowers have throats spotted with purple; appear mainly in spring, sporadically into fall.

P. nivea induta. Upright, compact plant to 6 ft. tall, 3 ft. wide, with narrow, silvery leaves. Produces blue flowers in spring.

P. ovalifolia. Erect growth to 8–10 ft. tall, 5–8 ft. wide. Profuse purplish pink flowers in spring. Leaves are roundish to oval or lance-shaped, medium green. Takes a bit more water than the others listed here; wilts when dry but perks up quickly with irrigation. Best in light shade when grown away from the coast. 'Variegata' leaves are edged in white.

P. 'Poorinda Bride'. Upright growth to 4–6 ft. tall and wide. Narrow leaves are deep olive green. White flowers have hints of violet and are marked yellowish orange in the throat; appear late spring to summer. Best with partial shade inland. Cut back by up to one-third after bloom to maintain bushiness.

P. rotundifolia. To 6 ft. tall, 5 ft. wide, with small roundish leaves and purple-blue flowers. Selections include 'Ghost Cave', with grayish green leaves and purple flowers; 'Glen Davis', with an especially profuse showing of dark purple flowers; and 'Rosea', to only 3–4 ft., with dark green leaves and deep rose-pink flowers.

Protea
Proteaceae
EVERGREEN SHRUBS

🗡 **ZONES 16, 17, 21–24; H1**

☼ **FULL SUN**

💧 **MODERATE WATER**

Protea cynaroides

Some 150 species of spectacular flowering plants native to South Africa. Borne at branch ends, the flower heads consist of tight clusters of tubular true flowers surrounded by brightly colored bracts; the effect is that of a large, very colorful artichoke or thistle. Superb cut flowers: they hold their color for weeks and retain their shape even after fading. Leaves are leathery, often edged in red. Widely grown in Hawaii and Southern California for the cut-flower trade.

Young proteas are tender to cold; older ones of most species are hardy to 25°F to 27°F (−4°C to −3°C). Smaller species can be grown in containers. Under any conditions, plants are not long-lived. The following species are among the easiest to grow.

P. compacta. PINK PROTEA. Erect grower to 6–10 ft. tall, 4–8 ft. wide. Light green leaves. Pure rose-pink to carmine, 4-in. flower heads appear from spring to summer.

P. cynaroides. KING PROTEA. To 3–5 ft. tall and wide, with open, spreading habit. Dark green leaves. Blooms midsummer to winter or early spring; flower heads reach 1 ft. across, with pale pink to crimson bracts surrounding white true flowers. 'Mini King' is dwarf, to about 3 ft. high and wide.

P. eximia. ROSE-SPOON PROTEA. Dense and upright, to 6–8 ft. tall and 3–4 ft. wide, with silvery green foliage. Profuse bloom in winter; flower heads are rich red, to 5 in. across, with spoon-shaped bracts.

P. laurifolia. Upright grower that may reach 18 ft. tall and nearly as wide. Blue-green foliage. Blooms in winter; 4-in. flower heads with salmon-pink bracts with feathery black tips. 'Rose Mink', to 10 ft., has narrow gray-green leaves and silvery pink flowers. 'White Owl', to 8 ft., has dark green leaves and creamy white blooms.

P. neriifolia. MINK PROTEA. To 10 ft. tall, 6–8 ft. wide. Leaves are narrow, medium green. Blooms in fall and winter; pink to salmon bracts with furry black tips form heads to 5 in. long. Withstands temperatures as low as 17°F (−8°C); will grow in alkaline soil. 'Late Mink' is dense and compact at 6 ft. tall and twice as wide.

P. susannae. SUSANNA PROTEA. To about 8 ft. tall and wide, with grayish leaves. Brownish pink flower heads to 4 in. across in fall and winter. Leaves smell unpleasant; strip them from the stems when cutting flowers for arrangements.

P

P. 'Sylvia'. This hybrid between *P. eximia* and *P. susannae* grows to 6–8 ft. tall and nearly as wide, with dark gray-green leaves. Rich pink, 6-in.-long flowers appear in late fall and winter.

CARE

Proteas are not for beginners. They need perfect drainage (preferably on slopes), protection from dry winds, and good air circulation. Give regular moisture until plants are established; thereafter, water only every 2 to 4 weeks. Most need acid soil, though some accept alkaline soil. Fertilize lightly with nitrogen; avoid fertilizers containing phosphorus (plants will glut themselves, then die of the overdose). Small applications of iron can remedy chlorosis. Avoid disturbing the roots.

Prunella

SELF-HEAL
Lamiaceae
PERENNIALS

✏ ZONES 2–24

☼ ◑ FULL SUN OR LIGHT SHADE

💧 REGULAR WATER

🦋 ATTRACT BUTTERFLIES AND BENEFICIAL INSECTS

Prunella

Native to Europe. Creeping perennials that spread by runners to form low, dense foliage mats. Upright spikes of hooded flowers rise above the leaves in summer. Tough, tolerant, and deep rooted. Useful for small-scale groundcovers and can endure the occasional footstep; set 1 ft. apart. Choose the location carefully, though: these vigorous plants will overwhelm

delicate neighboring plants. After bloom, shear off spent flower spikes to keep the planting neat and to prevent seed formation.

P. grandiflora. Leaves to 4 in. long; stems to 1½ ft. high, bearing spikes of 1–1½-in. purple blossoms. Varieties include 'Blue Loveliness', 'Freelander Blue' (compact grower with violet-blue blooms over a long period), 'Pink Loveliness', 'Purple Loveliness' (lilac-purple touched with white), and 'White Loveliness'.

P. vulgaris. This is the common species. Smaller in all its parts than *P. grandiflora*, with leaves to 2 in. long, 1-ft. stems, and purple or pink flowers just ⅓ in. long.

FOR OTHER PLANTS THAT ATTRACT BUTTERFLIES, SEE PAGES 100–103.

Prunus

Rosaceae
EVERGREEN AND DECIDUOUS SHRUBS AND TREES

✏ ZONES VARY BY SPECIES

☼ FULL SUN, EXCEPT AS NOTED

💧💧 MODERATE TO REGULAR WATER, EXCEPT AS NOTED

🦋 ATTRACT BIRDS, BUTTERFLIES

» See charts on pages 532–534.

Prunus × yedoensis

Discussed here are ornamental members of the genus *Prunus*. Fruit trees belonging to this genus—collectively known as stone fruits—are described under their common names. See Almond; Apricot; Cherry; Peach and Nectarine; Plum (includes Prune); and Plum Hybrids.

Ornamental species and forms can be divided into two categories: evergreen and deciduous. Evergreen types are

used chiefly as hedges, screens, shade trees, and street trees. Deciduous flowering trees and shrubs, closely related to the fruit trees mentioned above, are valued for their winter or spring floral display as well as for attractive shape and for foliage form, texture, and sometimes even fall color. Many of these deciduous kinds offer a bonus of edible fruit.

EVERGREEN SHRUBS AND SMALL TREES

P. caroliniana. CAROLINA LAUREL CHERRY. Zones 5–24. Native from North Carolina to Texas. As an upright shrub, it branches densely from the base and can serve as a clipped hedge or tall screen to 20 ft. tall; can be sheared into formal shapes. Trained as a single-trunked tree, it typically grows to 20–30 ft. tall and 15–25 ft. wide; also looks attractive grown with multiple trunks. Plant is thickly clothed in 2–4-in.-long, smooth-edged, glossy green leaves. Small, fragrant creamy white flowers bloom in 1-in. spikes from late winter to midspring; blossoms are followed by small, inconspicuous black fruits. Flower and fruit litter can be a problem in paved areas.

Carolina laurel cherry looks best in coastal areas. Often shows salt burn and chlorosis in alkaline soils. Withstands desert heat and wind but appreciates a location protected from hottest sun in the low desert. May need moderate water in hottest climates; succeeds with little or no water elsewhere. 'Bright 'n Tight' and 'Compacta' are more densely branched than the species and reach about 8–10 ft. tall, 6–8 ft. wide.

P. ilicifolia. Zones 5–9, 12–24. The two similar forms described below are both useful as small trees, screens, or medium-size to tall clipped hedges. They often hybridize when growing near each other, producing plants with intermediate characteristics. Avoid planting near paved surfaces or parking areas, since fallen fruit causes stains. Very resistant to oak root fungus. Both need good drainage. Can take extreme drought but look best with occasional deep soakings.

P. i. ilicifolia. HOLLYLEAF CHERRY. Native to California Coast Ranges. To 10–25 ft. tall and wide. Glossy, oval to elliptical leaves to 2 in. long are light green when new, maturing to a rich deep green; they are spiny edged like holly (*Ilex*) leaves but not as prickly. Blooms at leaf-out, bearing fragrant creamy white flowers in narrow, 3–6-in.-long spikes. Round, ¾-in.-wide, dark red or reddish purple fruit is edible but has a large pit and not much flesh.

P. i. lyonii. CATALINA CHERRY. Native to California's Channel Islands. In the wild, plants can grow as trees to 45 ft. tall and over 30 ft. wide, but in gardens they're more often seen as giant shrubs to 15–20 ft. tall and wide. Leaves are similar in color and shape to those of *P. i. ilicifolia*, but they are smooth edged or very faintly toothed. Flowers identical to those of *P. i. ilicifolia*; fruit is darker red to almost black.

P. laurocerasus. ENGLISH LAUREL. Zones 4–9, 14–24, except as noted; best performance in Zones 4–6, 15–17. Native from southeastern Europe to Iran. Fast growing to 15–30 ft. tall and wide. Leathery, oblong, glossy dark green leaves are 3–7 in. long. Blooms in spring or early summer, bearing spikes of fragrant, creamy white flowers that are often hidden by the leaves. Flowers are followed by small black fruit. Seeds are spread by birds, making English laurel a weed in some parts of the West.

Needs reasonably good drainage. Looks best with regular water and occasional feeding. Needs some shade in hottest climates; can take sun or shade elsewhere. Tolerates salt spray. English laurel is often sheared but looks best when selective cuts are made back within the plant. Best used as a tall unclipped screen or trained as a tree. Smaller-growing varieties make lower, easier-to-maintain hedges.

'Castlewellan'. To 15 ft. tall and wide; leaves are densely speckled with white. Showiest in cool climates.

'Etna' ('Anbri'). Grows 6–8 ft. tall and wide. Compact growth; takes well to shearing. Coppery new leaves.

P

»»

PRUNUS—FLOWERING CHERRY: TOP PICKS TO GROW

NAME	ZONES	GROWTH HABIT, FOLIAGE	HEIGHT, SPREAD	FLOWERS, SEASON, COMMENTS
Prunus 'Accolade'	2–9, 14–17	Small tree with spreading branches, twiggy growth pattern. Very vigorous.	To 25 ft. tall and wide.	Semidouble blush pink, 1½ in. wide, in large, drooping clusters; open from rose-pink buds. Early. Hybrid between *P. sargentii* and *P.* × *subhirtella*.
P. campanulata TAIWAN FLOWERING CHERRY	6–9, 14–24	Graceful, slender, upright-growing small tree; densely branched.	To 20–25 ft. tall and wide.	Single, bell-shaped, drooping, in clusters of two to five. Striking shade of bright purplish pink. Early. Red fruit about ½ in. long. Good choice for warm-winter areas.
P. 'Dream Catcher'	4–9, 14–23	Upright, vase-shaped. Dark green leaves turn yellow-orange in fall.	To 25 ft. tall and 15 ft. wide.	Single pink. Early; about a week after parent *P.* 'Okame'. Good resistance to pests and diseases.
P. 'Hally Jolivette'	3–7, 14–20	Dense, shrubby.	Slow to 6–8 ft. high and wide; eventually reaches twice that size.	Double white blooms open from pink buds. Early; relatively long bloom, lasting several weeks. Can be used in shrub borders. Hybrid between *P.* × subhirtella and *P.* × yedoensis.
P. 'Okame'	4–9, 14–23	Upright, oval habit. Dark green, fine-textured foliage. Good yellow-orange to orange-red fall color.	To 25 ft. by 20 ft.	Single carmine-pink. Very early. Hybrid involving *P. campanulata*.
P. sargentii	2–7, 14–17	Upright, spreading branches form rounded crown. Good orange-red fall color.	To 40–60 ft. tall and wide.	Single blush pink flowers in clusters of two to four. Midseason. 'Columnaris' is narrower and more erect than species, though more vase-shaped than truly columnar.
P. s. 'Pink Flair'	2–7, 14–24	Compact; upright with narrow vase shape.	To 25 ft. tall, 15 ft. wide. Good orange-red fall color.	Single pink flowers. Midseason.
P. serrula	2–7, 14–16	Round-headed tree with narrow, willowlike leaves. Valued for its beautiful, glossy, mahogany red bark.	To 30 ft. tall and wide.	Bark more notable than small white flowers, which are almost hidden by new leaves. Midseason.
P. serrulata		Known through its many varieties. Some are listed here (may be sold by variety name only).		
P. s. 'Amanogawa'	3–7, 14–20	Columnar in youth, becoming vase-shaped with age.	To 20–25 ft. tall, 4–8 ft. wide.	Semidouble light pink with deep pink petal margins. Early midseason.
P. s. 'Kanzan' ('Kwanzan', 'Sekiyama')	3–7, 14–20	Branches stiffly upright, forming narrow, inverted cone that spreads with age.	To 30 ft. by 20 ft.	Large, double, deep rosy pink, in pendent clusters. Blossoms appear before or with red young leaves. Midseason. 'Weeping Extraordinaire' is a weeping form to 15–20 ft. high and wide.
P. s. 'Royal Burgundy'	3–7, 14–20	Habit similar to that of 'Kanzan'. Leaves are reddish purple.	Same as 'Kanzan'.	Like those of 'Kanzan', but deeper pink and with red stems.
P. s. 'Shirotae' ('Mt. Fuji')	2–7, 14–20	Strong horizontal branching. Striking yellow-orange fall foliage. Buy a tree that has not been top-pruned; that forces horizontal branching to start much too low.	To 20 ft. by 25 ft.	Semidouble. Pink in bud; white when fully open, aging to purplish pink. Early.
P. s. 'Shogetsu' ('Shimidsu Sakura')	3–7, 14–20	Spreading growth, arching branches.	To 15 ft. by 25 ft.	Semidouble and fully double pale pink, often with white center. Late.
P. s. 'Snow Fountains' ('White Fountain')	3–7, 14–20	Slightly curving trunk; weeping branches reach to ground. Sold as small tree or trunkless groundcover.	To 12–15 ft. tall and wide as tree; to 1 ft. by 10–15 ft. as groundcover.	Single white. Early.

P

PRUNUS—FLOWERING CHERRY: TOP PICKS TO GROW

NAME	ZONES	GROWTH HABIT, FOLIAGE	HEIGHT, SPREAD	FLOWERS, SEASON, COMMENTS
P. s. 'Snow Goose'	3–7, 14–20	Erect; narrow at first, eventually becoming broader.	To 20 ft. tall and wide.	Single white. Early.
P. × subhirtella 'Autumnalis'	2–7, 14–20	Loose-branching, bushy tree with flattened crown.	To 25–30 ft. tall and wide.	Double white or pinkish white. Blooms in fall as well as early spring; may also bloom during warm spells in winter. 'Autumnalis Rosea' has pink blooms.
P. × s. 'Pendula' (P. pendula 'Pendula Rosea') SINGLE WEEPING CHERRY, WEEPING HIGAN CHERRY	2–7, 14–20	Usually sold grafted at 5–6 ft. tall on upright-growing understock. Graceful branches hang down, often to ground.	To 10–12 ft. tall and wide.	Profuse show of small, pale pink single flowers. Early.
P. × s. 'Pendula Plena Rosea' ('Yae-shidare-higan') DOUBLE WEEPING CHERRY	2–7, 14–20	Same as P. × s. 'Pendula'.	Same as P. × s. 'Pendula'.	Double rose-pink. Midseason.
P. × s. 'Rosea'	2–7, 14–20	Wide spreading, horizontally branching.	To 20–25 ft. by 30 ft.	Single pink blossoms open from nearly red buds. Profuse, very early bloom. Pacific Northwest favorite.
P. × s. 'Whitcomb'	2–7, 14–20	Same as P. × s. 'Rosea'.	To 30 ft. by 35 ft.	Single; pink fading to white. Early.
P. × yedoensis YOSHINO FLOWERING CHERRY	3–7, 14–20	Horizontal branches; graceful, open pattern.	To 40 ft. by 30 ft.	Single light pink to nearly white. Early. This is the cherry planted around the Tidal Basin in Washington, D.C. Fast growing.
P. × y. 'Akebono' AKEBONO CHERRY, DAYBREAK CHERRY	3–7, 14–20	Same as P. × yedoensis.	To 25 ft. tall and wide.	Flowers pinker than those of P. × yedoensis. One of the best, most disease-free flowering cherries in the Pacific Northwest. Early.

P

FLOWERING CHERRY SAMPLER

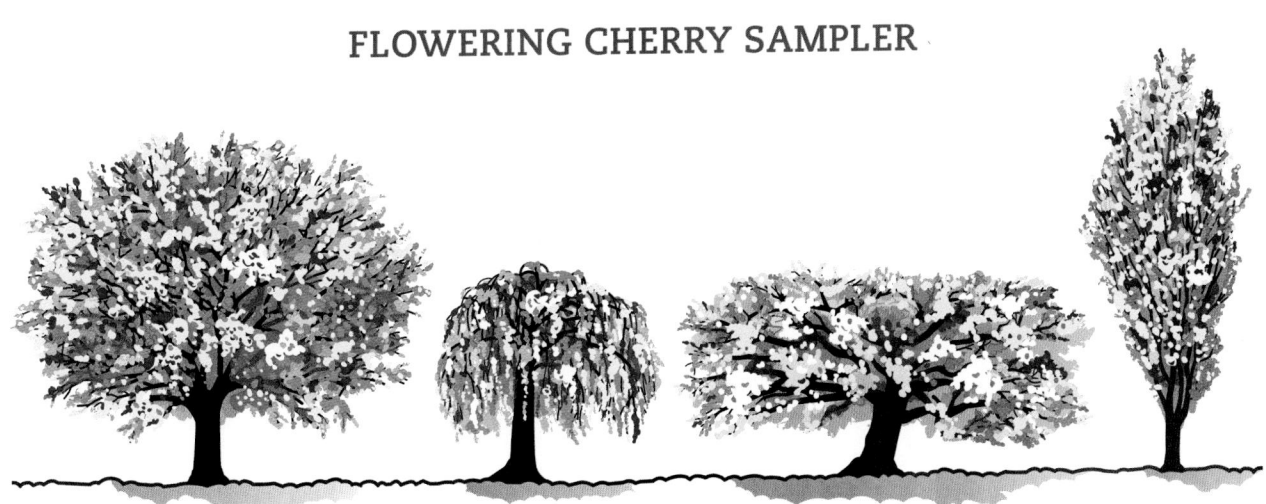

STANDARD UPRIGHTS
Use to line a driveway or arch over a perennial bed that needs partial shade. Include *Prunus serrulata* 'Kwanzan', *P. × yedoensis*, and *P. × y.* 'Akebono'.

WEEPERS
Smaller than other cherries, top out at 10–15 ft. Use singly as garden accents. *P. × subhirtella* 'Pendula'; *P. serrulata* 'Snow Fountains'.

SPREADERS
Grow wider than tall. If you need to mow under yours, prune off lowest branches as the tree grows to keep canopy higher. *P. serrulata* 'Shirotae'; *P. s.* 'Shogetsu'.

COLUMNAR TREES
Grow well in narrow spaces, or plant in rows along driveways or paths. *P. sargentii* 'Columnaris'; *P. serrulata* 'Amanogawa'.

»

PRUNUS—FLOWERING PLUM: TOP PICKS TO GROW

NAME	ZONES	GROWTH HABIT, FOLIAGE	HEIGHT, SPREAD	FLOWERS, SEASON, COMMENTS
Prunus americana WILD PLUM, GOOSE PLUM	1–3, 10	Thicket-forming shrub or small tree. Dark green foliage.	To 15–25 ft. by 10–15 ft.	Clusters of 1-in., single white flowers. Fruit yellow to red, to 1 in., sour but good for jelly. Native to Rockies. Very tough.
P. × blireana	3–22	Graceful form. New leaves reddish purple; turn greenish bronze by summer.	To 25 ft. by 20 ft.	Double, fragrant pink to rose flowers. Hybrid of P. cerasifera 'Atropurpurea' and P. mume.
P. cerasifera CHERRY PLUM, MYROBALAN	3–22	Most often used as rootstock for various stone fruits. Dark green leaves.	To 30 ft. tall and wide.	Pure white flowers. Red, 1–1¼-in.-wide fruit is sweet but bland. Self-sows freely; some seedlings bear yellow fruit. Purple- and red-leafed varieties are popular.
P. c. 'Allred'	3–22	Upright, slightly spreading. Red leaves.	To 20 ft. by 12–15 ft.	Single white flowers. Red, 1½-in., tart fruit good for preserves, jelly.
P. c. 'Crimson Pointe'	3–22	Forms a dense, narrow column. Dark red leaves.	To 25 ft. tall, just 6–8 ft. wide.	Single white flowers. Small purple fruit. Good as a single exclamation point, lining a drive, or planted close together for screening.
P. c. 'Hollywood'	3–22	Upright habit. Leaves dark green above, red beneath.	To 30–40 ft. by 25 ft.	Single light pink to white flowers. Good-quality red plums, 2–2½ in. wide. Hybrid of P. c. 'Atropurpurea' and a Japanese plum.
P. c. 'Krauter Vesuvius'	3–22	Upright, oval form. Darkest foliage (blackish purple) of any flowering plum.	To 20 ft. by 15 ft.	Single light pink flowers. Little or no fruit.
P. c. 'Mt. St. Helens'	3–22	Upright, spreading, with rounded crown. A sport of P. c. 'Newport' but more robust, with larger leaves of a richer purple color.	Faster than 'Newport', to 20 ft. tall and wide.	Same as 'Newport'.
P. c. 'Newport'	A3; 2b–22	Upright and spreading, with rounded crown. Foliage is dark purple all summer, attractively reddish in autumn.	To 20 ft. tall and wide.	Fragrant, single white to pale pink flowers. Will bear a little fruit.
P. c. 'Pissardii' ('Atropurpurea') PURPLE-LEAF PLUM	3–22	Rounded habit. Leaves are coppery red when new, later deepen to dark purple; turn red in autumn.	Fast to 25–35 ft. high and wide.	Single white flowers. Heavy crop of red, 1–1½-in. fruit.
P. c. 'Purple Pony'	3–22	Naturally semidwarf; available budded low or high. Deep purple foliage holds color throughout season.	Usually not taller than 10–12 ft. by 12 ft.	Single pale pink flowers appear with the leaves. No fruit.
P. c. 'Thundercloud'	3–22	Rounded habit. Dark coppery leaves.	To 20 ft. tall and wide.	Fragrant, single light pink to white flowers. Sometimes sets good crop of 1-in. red fruit.
P. × cistena DWARF RED-LEAF PLUM	A3; 1–22	Dainty multistemmed shrub. Can be trained as single-trunked tree; good for small patios. Intensely red-purple new leaves mature to coppery purple.	To 6–10 ft. by 6–8 ft.	Fragrant, single white flowers appear after leaf-out (unlike flowering plums above); offer striking contrast to foliage. May produce small (½ in.) blackish purple fruit.
P. × c. 'Big Cis'	A3; 1–22	Sport of P. × cistena. Dense, globular, and more vigorous than P. × cistena with larger purple leaves.	Fast to 14 ft. by 12 ft.	Same as P. × cistena.
P. 'Taihaku' GREAT WHITE CHERRY	2–7, 14–20	Vigorous, with rounded crown. Good orange fall color.	To 20–25 ft. high and wide.	Extra-large (2½ in.), pure white single blooms. Flowers appear with bronzy new leaves. Late midseason.

P

'Mount Vernon'. Very slowly forms a dense mound to about 2 ft. high and 5 ft. wide (taller in the Pacific Northwest). Though very dwarf, it has full-size leaves like those of the species. Can be used as groundcover.

'Nana'. Slow grower to 6–8 ft. tall and wide.

'Otto Luyken'. Zones 3a–9, 14–24. To 3–4 ft. tall, 5–6 ft. wide (has reportedly reached 6 ft. tall, 10 ft. wide). Leaves to 4½ in. long, exceptionally dark green. Showy in bloom.

'Rotundifolia'. Vigorous, dense, upright grower to 15 ft. tall, 12 ft. wide. Especially good for hedging.

'Schipkaensis'. SCHIPKA LAUREL. Zones 3–9, 14–17. Typically 4–6 ft. tall, 6–8 ft. wide. Narrow leaves to 4½ in. long. There is some variation in plants sold under this name.

'Zabeliana'. Zones 3–9, 14–21. To 4–6 ft. tall, 6–8 ft. wide (wider with age). Branches angle upward and outward from base. Narrow, willowlike leaves to 5 in. long. Versatile plant; good for low screen, foundation plant, bank cover (with branches pegged down), or espalier.

P. lusitanica. PORTUGAL LAUREL. Zones 4–9, 14–24. From Spain and Portugal. Densely branched shrub 10–20 ft. tall and wide; or multitrunked tree to 30 ft. tall and wide. Trained to a single trunk, it is used as a formal street tree. Narrowly oval, glossy dark green leaves to 5 in. long. Small, creamy white flowers in 5–10-in. spikes bloom in spring and early summer; these are followed by clusters of very small, bright red to dark purple fruit. Attractive background plant, screen. Slower grower than *P. laurocerasus* and more tolerant of heat, strong sunlight, wind. Little or no water. 'Variegata' has leaves with narrow, irregular white margins and fruit that ripens from red to black.

DECIDUOUS FLOWERING FRUIT TREES

Grown for their beautiful floral displays in winter and spring. Branches of all types can be cut for indoor decoration; follow proper pruning procedures when you cut, and make your selections with an eye to thinning or

CLOCKWISE FROM TOP LEFT: *Prunus serrulata* 'Kanzan'; *P.* × *subhirtella* 'Pendula'; *P. serrula* 'Shogetsu'

shaping the canopy. For longest-lasting bloom, cut branches when buds first begin to show color or when they have just opened. Place branches in a deep container of water; strip off any buds or flowers that will be below water level.

Flowering cherry. For zones, see chart. Early to midspring bloom, depending on variety. Usually blossom before leafout, but some bloom with new leaves. Some flowering cherries have especially good fall color; all are good trees to garden under. Large, sprawling kinds make good shade trees; smaller ones are indispensable in Japanese gardens. They need fast-draining, well-aerated soil; if your soil is poorly drained, plant in raised beds. Even in good growing conditions, foliage may sustain damage from insects and diseases. *P.* × *subhirtella* varieties are subject to bacterial blight. Best with moderate water. Prune to remove

awkward or crossing branches; pinch back the occasional overly ambitious shoot to force branching.

Flowering peach. Zones 3–24 (blossoms may suffer frost damage in cold climates, and leafout may be delayed in warm-winter areas). Produces blossoms about 1½ in. wide in late winter and early spring, before leafout. More widely adapted than fruiting peach but identical to it in other respects—plant size, growth habit, cultural needs, pruning requirements, and potential problems.

Some peach varieties produce both showy blossoms and good fruit; these are described under Peach and Nectarine. The following varieties have showy blooms, but fruit is either absent or worthless. In areas with late frosts, choose late bloomers; early bloomers are best in regions with hot, early springs.

'Early Double Pink'. Very early.

'Early Double Red'. Deep purplish red or rose-red. Very early. Brilliant color is beautiful but likely to clash with other pinks and reds.

'Early Double White'. Blooms with 'Early Double Pink'.

'Helen Borchers'. Semidouble, pure pink, large (2½ in.) flowers. Blooms late.

'Late Double Red'. Later than 'Early Double Red' by 3 to 4 weeks.

'Peppermint Stick'. Double flowers striped red and white; may also bear all-white and all-red flowers on the same branch. Midseason.

'Weeping Double Pink'. Smaller than other flowering peaches, with weeping branches. Requires staking to develop main stem of suitable height. Midseason.

'Weeping Double Red'. Like above; has deep rose-red flowers. Midseason.

'Weeping Double White'. White version of other weeping forms listed above. Midseason.

'White Icicle'. Double white flowers. Blooms late.

Flowering plum. For zones, see chart. Flowers appear between midwinter and mid-spring, usually before leafout. Many flowering plums feature purple foliage. If you are choosing a plum to be planted in a patio or paved area, check its

CLOCKWISE FROM TOP: *Prunus ×
blireana; P. mume; P. cerasifera*

fruiting habit. These trees are
less particular about soil than
flowering cherry or flowering
peach, but they will fail if soil
is waterlogged for prolonged
periods. Where conditions are
boggy, plant in raised beds.
Little pruning is needed. Aphids
and spider mites are possible
pests. Leaf-damaging insects
and leaf spot disease are problems in the Pacific Northwest.
(For information on pest management, see pages 726–731.)

ADDITIONAL DECIDUOUS SPECIES

The following shrubs or trees
bloom early in the season. In
some cases, blossoms are
followed by edible fruit.

P. besseyi. WESTERN SAND
CHERRY. Shrub. Zones A1–A3;
1–3, 10. Native to the Great
Plains. To 3–6 ft. tall and wide.
Good show of small white flowers in mid- to late spring, before
leafout, followed by sweet black
cherries a little more than ½ in.
across. Fruit is used for pies,
jams, and jellies. Withstands
heat, cold, wind, and drought.

P. maackii. AMUR CHOKE-
CHERRY. Tree. Zones A1–A3;
1–7, 10. Native to Manchuria
and Siberia; extremely hardy to
cold and wind. To 25–30 ft. tall
and 25 ft. wide. Main feature is
handsome, peeling, cinnamon
brown bark. Blooms after leafout in midspring, bearing small,
fragrant white flowers followed
by small black fruits.

P. mume. JAPANESE FLOW-
ERING APRICOT, JAPANESE
FLOWERING PLUM. Tree. Zones
3, 7–9, 12–22. Blooms may be
damaged by frost in coldest
areas. From China and Korea.
Picturesque, gnarled tree to
20 ft. tall and wide. Longer-
lived, tougher, more trouble-free
than other flowering fruit trees;
common names notwithstanding, it is neither a true apricot
nor a true plum. White to dark
red blossoms with a spicy
fragrance form on leafless
branches in midwinter to early
spring. Yellow to green, 1-in.
fruit is edible only if pickled.

'Beni-chidori'. Bushy and
upright, to 8 ft. tall and wide,
with dark pink flowers.

'Bonita'. Semidouble rose-red
blooms.

'Dawn'. Large, ruffled double
pink flowers.

'Matsubara Red'. Double,
deep red flowers.

'Peggy Clarke'. Double flowers in deep rose, with extremely
long stamens and red calyxes.

'Pendula'. Weeping branches
hold semidouble, rich pink
blossoms.

'Rosemary Clarke'. Double
white flowers with red calyxes.
Very early; often in bloom on
New Year's Day in California.

'W. B. Clarke'. Double pale
pink flowers; weeping form.
Effective large bonsai or container plant. Bloom and form
make it the center of attention
in a winter garden.

P. padus. EUROPEAN BIRD
CHERRY, MAYDAY TREE, MAY-
BUSH. Tree. Zones A1–A3; 1–7,
10. Native to Europe and northern Asia. Moderate growth to 15–
20 ft. tall and wide, occasionally taller. Among the first plants
to leaf out in spring. Profuse
mid- to late spring show of
small, very fragrant white flowers in slender, drooping clusters
that nearly hide foliage. Small,
dark purple fruit follows the
flowers; it is bitter but much
loved by birds. Fruit is often
used for making jelly and wine.
Branches are stiff, subject to
breakage under heavy snow
loads. Older trees tend to
sucker. 'Albertii' is a heavy
bloomer. 'Colorata' has purplish
new growth and pink flowers.
'Watereri' has extra-long flower
clusters.

P. tomentosa. NANKING
CHERRY. Shrub. Zones A1–A3;
1–3, 10. From Tibet and China.
Like *P. besseyi*, this species is
very tough and cold-hardy. To
6–8 ft. tall and 10 ft. wide, with
shiny reddish brown, peeling
bark. Leaves are dull dark green
above, woolly beneath. Small,
fragrant white flowers open from
pinkish buds before leafout in
spring; edible, ½-in.-wide, scarlet fruit follows.

P. triloba. FLOWERING
ALMOND. Tree or treelike shrub.
Zones A1–A3; 1–11, 14–20.
Native to China. Slow growth to
8–10 ft. (possibly 15 ft.) tall,
with equal spread. May be sold
as a single- or multistemmed
plant. Leaves are dark green
above, lighter green beneath.
Pink flowers to 1½ in. wide
appear on bare branches in
early spring. 'Multiplex' has
double pink flowers. A double
white form is sometimes
available.

P. virginiana. CHOKE-
CHERRY. Shrub or tree. Zones
A1–A3; 1–3, 10, except as
noted. Native to eastern North
America. To 20–30 ft. tall and
18–25 ft. wide, with suckering
habit. In late spring, very fragrant white flowers appear in
slender clusters among the
leaves; these are followed by
astringent, ½-in.-wide, dark
red to black fruit. Good autumn
foliage display; color varies
from bright red to pale yellow.
'Canada Red' has leaves that
open green, then turn red as
they mature; it is a sport of
'Schubert', which has mature
leaves in a more purplish shade.
Chokecherries are toxic to
livestock.

P. v. demissa, Western choke-
cherry (Zones 2–10, 14–24),
is native to the Pacific Coast,
Sierra Nevada, Great Basin
area, and northern Rockies. It
resembles the species in leaf,
flower, and fruit, but tolerates
more heat. Established plants
are quite drought-tolerant.

Pseudolarix amabilis
(P. kaempferi)
GOLDEN LARCH
Pinaceae
DECIDUOUS TREE

- ✒ **ZONES 2–7, 14–17**
- ☀ **FULL SUN**
- 💧 **REGULAR WATER**

Pseudolarix amabilis

Where space permits, golden larch becomes a specimen tree of great character. This Chinese native grows very slowly into a 40–70-ft. pyramid, nearly as broad as tall at the base. Foliage has a feathery look; needles are clustered in tufts except near pendulous branch ends, where they are single. Needles open light green, mature to bluish green, then turn a magnificent golden yellow very briefly in autumn before dropping. Cones and bare branches present an interesting pattern in winter. Needs shelter from cold winds. Best in deep, rich, well-drained, acid soil; performance is better in colder part of range.

The genus name *Pseudolarix* is derived from the Greek word *pseudo*, which means "false." *Larix* is the classical name for the larch, which this tree resembles. The species name *amabilis* is entirely fitting: it means "lovely."

Pseudopanax
Araliaceae
EVERGREEN SHRUBS OR TREES

- ✒ **ZONES VARY BY SPECIES**
- ☀ ◐ ● **SUN OR SHADE**
- 💧 **REGULAR WATER**

Pseudopanax lessonii 'Rangitira'

From New Zealand, these evergreen foliage plants are slow-growing aralia relatives. In *P. crassifolius* and *P. ferox*, juvenile foliage is far more interesting in shape and color than mature leaves. Flowers are inconspicuous. No special pruning needs. All make good container plants.

P. crassifolius. LANCE-WOOD. Zones 16, 17, 21–24. In time, a tree to 50 ft. tall, 15 ft. wide. Usually seen as a single-stemmed plant 3–5 ft. tall, 8–10 in. wide, with rigid, drooping, strongly toothed leaves to 3 ft. long, ½–¾ in. wide. Young leaves are dark green above and dark purple beneath, with an orange or yellow midrib on upper surface. Upright growth habit makes this a good plant for narrow areas.

P. ferox. FIERCE LANCE-WOOD. Zones 16, 17, 21–24. To 10–12 ft. tall, 3–4 ft. wide. Young plants produce strongly toothed leaves to 1–1½ ft. long and ½–1 in. wide. They are dark green to blackish green above and bronzy beneath, with brown, orange, or red midrib on upper surface. Mature leaves are unremarkable.

P. lessonii. Zones 17, 22–24. Moderate growth to 12–20 ft. tall, 6–12 ft. wide. Effective multistemmed tree in open ground. Leathery, dark green leaves are divided into three to five leaflets 2–4 in. long. 'Linearifolius' grows 6–8 ft. tall.

Pseudosasa. See Bamboo

Pseudotsuga
Pinaceae
EVERGREEN TREES

- ✒ **ZONES VARY BY SPECIES**
- ☀ ◐ **TOLERATE PARTIAL SHADE IN YOUTH**
- ◊ 💧 ● **LITTLE OR NO WATER TO REGULAR WATER**

Pseudotsuga menziesii

These big, handsome conifers include species native to the West and to Asia. Douglas fir dominates many forests from the Pacific Coast to the Rockies, and from Canada to Mexico; houses are often built among these natives. Growers have selected many smaller garden forms. The species name, which means "false hemlock," and the common names "Douglas fir" and "bigcone spruce" hint at *Pseudotsuga's* similarities with hemlock, fir, and spruce. But all are uniquely different trees.

P. japonica. JAPANESE DOUGLAS FIR. Zones 3b–9, 14–17. From southern Japan. To 45 ft. in gardens, with 1-in. needles, gray bark; purple-brown cones 3 in. long by 1 in. wide. This tree's shape is irregular but broadly conical.

P. macrocarpa. BIGCONE SPRUCE, BIGCONE DOUGLAS FIR. Zones 3–11, 14–23. Native to dry slopes of Southern California mountains, this stout-trunked tree reaches about 60 ft. tall, 30 ft. wide. It is drought-tolerant but rarely seen in gardens. It is similar to *P. menziesii*, but with cones reaching 4–7½ in. long, 2–3 in. wide; three-pronged bracts barely protrude from cones.

P. menziesii. DOUGLAS FIR. Zones A2, A3; 1–10, 14–17. In cultivation, 80–160 ft. tall, 20–30 ft. wide; in forests, regularly above 250 ft. Pyramidal young trees are branched to the ground—perfect and widely sold Christmas trees. With age, trees drop lower limbs. Needles are soft, deep green or blue-green; radiate in all directions; and are fragrant when crushed. Branch ends turn up. Pointed wine red buds form at branch tips in winter, open to apple green new growth in spring. Hanging brown, oval cones are about 3 in. long, with three-pronged bracts, each resembling the hind legs and tail of a mouse. Attracts butterflies.

Along the coast, it is fast growing and dark green. The interior (Rocky Mountain) form, *P. m. glauca*, is slower growing, blue-green, more cold-tolerant, compact, and stiffer. Dwarf, weeping, variegated, golden, fastigiate, and other garden forms are sold. All tolerate wind and all but boggy soils. Resistant to oak root fungus.

P. sinensis. Zones 4–9, 14–17. Native to China and Taiwan. Grows about 1 ft. per year to 50 ft. tall and 25 ft. wide at the base (much taller in the wild), with 1-in. needles and 2½-by-1½-in. cones. Handsome, open look. Gaussen's Douglas fir (*P. s. sinensis*, also sold as *P. gaussenii*) has chartreuse cones maturing to brown. *P. s. wilsonii* is similar, but with purple-brown cones. Long-leafed forms (2-in. needles) sold under this name are probably *P. forrestii*, a similar Chinese species with 3-in.-long, 2½-in.-wide cones.

Douglas firs are the world's second-tallest conifers, after coast redwoods (*Sequoia sempervirens*). Trees with a height of 250 feet are not uncommon, and a living specimen in Oregon has been documented at over 325 feet tall.

P

Psidium. See Guava

Psilostrophe
PAPER FLOWER
Asteraceae
PERENNIALS

▨ ZONES VARY BY SPECIES

☼ FULL SUN

◊ LITTLE OR NO WATER

🦋 ATTRACT BUTTERFLIES

Psilostrophe

The 1-in. yellow flowers on these short-lived, mounding perennials become papery and tan as they dry in place. They extend the show but eventually give plants a ragged look that is easily corrected with light shearing.

Flowers peak in spring, with repeat bloom coming after summer rains or irrigation (but regular watering reduces bloom, and poor drainage kills the plants).

P. cooperi. WHITESTEM PAPER FLOWER. Zones 7–12, 18–21. Native to 2,000–5,000-ft. elevations in the desert mountains of California, Arizona, New Mexico, Utah, and northern Mexico. Grows into a mound 12–18 in. tall and twice as wide, with whitish stems and narrow green leaves.

P. tagetina. MARIGOLD-FLOWERED PSILOSTROPHE. Zones 2b, 7–12, 18–19. Native to 4,000–7,000-ft. elevations in desert mountains of Arizona, Utah, New Mexico, Texas, and northern Mexico. Grows into a 2-ft. mound. Similar to *P. cooperi*, but with slightly larger leaves. Self-sows.

FOR MORE PLANTS THAT ATTRACT
BUTTERFLIES, SEE PAGES 100–103.

Psorothamnus spinosus
(Dalea spinosa)
SMOKE TREE
Fabaceae
DECIDUOUS TREE OR SHRUB

▨ ZONES 11–13

☼ FULL SUN

◊ LITTLE OR NO WATER

Psorothamnus spinosus

Growing 10–20 ft. tall and 10–15 ft. wide, smoke tree has small, hairy white leaves that drop in early spring, revealing a network of silvery gray, spiny branchlets that form a cloud around a few large trunks and branches. In late spring, fragrant, 1½–2-in. clusters of violet-purple, sweet pea–shaped flowers put on a good show. Cut branches (in or out of bloom) for arrangements. Easy from seed in warm weather. Native to sandy desert arroyos of Arizona, Southern California, and Baja California, smoke tree needs good drainage.

For a colorful shrub border that needs little care or water, plant smoke trees with little-leaf cordias (*Cordia parvifolia*), and add a couple of ocotillos (*Fouquieria splendens*) for vertical drama. Surround with *Verbena rigida* and a variety of colorful native penstemons.

Annual Arrangements

Statice is a top-notch cutting flower, delivering gorgeous blooms on stems just the right height for a vase. Other annuals ideal for a cutting garden are corn cockle (*Agrostemma githago*), cockscomb (*Celosia*), bachelor's button (*Centaurea cyanus*), mountain garland (*Clarkia unguiculata*), spider flower (*Cleome hasslerana*), larkspur (*Consolida ajacis*), annual coreopsis (*Coreopsis tinctoria*), sweet pea (*Lathyrus odoratus*), and love-in-a-mist (*Nigella damascena*).

Edge your cutting garden with leafy fillers for your arrangements. Among the many choices are artemisia, asparagus fern, ornamental grasses, and calla (*Zantedeschia*).

Psylliostachys suworowii
(Limonium suworowii)
STATICE
Plumbaginaceae
ANNUAL

▨ ZONES 1–24

☼ FULL SUN

◊ REGULAR WATER

Psylliostachys suworowii

Absolutely covered with slender, sinuous spikes of pink or lavender-pink blossoms in summer, this annual starts as a low, 1-ft.-wide rosette of narrow leaves to 8 in. long. Flower spikes that rise to 18 in. are useful fresh or dried in arrangements. Sow seeds in ground when danger of frost is past, or start seeds earlier indoors. Native to Iran, Afghanistan, and central Asia.

FOR MORE ON ANNUALS, SEE PAGES
674–675.

Pteridium aquilinum
BRACKEN
Polypodiaceae
FERN

▨ ZONES 1–10, 14–24

☼◐ FULL SUN OR PARTIAL SHADE

◊◖◗ LITTLE TO REGULAR WATER

✦ FRONDS ARE POISONOUS
IF INGESTED

Pteridium aquilinum

Usually colonizing open forest or disturbed areas, bracken has big, triangular fronds that rise on 2–7-ft. stalks. Found all over the world, its subspecies differ in minor details; *P. a. pubescens* is native to the West. Its coarse, much-divided fronds rise directly from deep, running rootstocks.

Bracken is fine in untamed locations, but keep it out of the garden, where deep rootstocks make it a tough, invasive weed. Fiddleheads are carcinogenic.

Pteris

BRAKE
Polypodiaceae
FERNS

🌿 ZONES VARY BY SPECIES

◐ ● PARTIAL OR FULL SHADE

◒ ● MODERATE TO REGULAR WATER

Pteris cretica

Native to the subtropics and tropics, *Pteris* includes many small evergreens that are used in dish gardens, but those that follow are large enough for landscape use.

P. cretica. CRETAN BRAKE, RIBBON FERN. Zones 17, 23, 24; H1, H2. Easy to grow. Reaches 2½ ft. high and 2 ft. wide, with thin fronds and long, narrow leaflets. Can naturalize in Southern California. Numerous varieties available, some with forked or crested fronds, others variegated. 'Albolineata' (*P. c. albolineata, P. nipponica*) has a broad white band down the center of each leaflet. 'Mayi' is like 'Albolineata' but with crested tips.

P. ensiformis 'Evergemiensis'. Zones 17, 23, 24; H1, H2. Upright 3 ft. high and slightly less wide. Fronds are divided into very narrow leaflets intricately variegated in white.

P. quadriaurita. Zone 24. Reaches 2–4 ft. tall and wide. Rather coarsely divided fronds. Not as easy to grow as other species, but worth the effort for unusual coloring of varieties 'Argyraea' (*P. argyraea*), with green fronds heavily marked white, and 'Tricolor', with fronds marked white, green, and red. Protect from frost; watch for slugs and snails.

P. tremula. AUSTRALIAN BRAKE. Zones 16, 17, 22–24.

Upright to 5 ft. tall and 3 ft. wide. Graceful fronds on slender, upright stalks. Good landscape fern, with excellent silhouette. Very fast growing.

Pterocarya stenoptera

CHINESE WINGNUT
Juglandaceae
DECIDUOUS TREE

🌿 ZONES 4–24

☀ FULL SUN

◒ ● MODERATE TO REGULAR WATER

Pterocarya stenoptera

From China. Fast to 40–90 ft. tall, 30–50 ft. wide, with heavy, wide-spreading limbs. Clearly shows its kinship to walnuts in its leaves: 8–16 in. long and divided into many finely toothed, oval leaflets.

Foot-long clusters of small, single-seeded, winged nuts hang from branches. Good looking but has only one real virtue: it succeeds well in compacted, poorly aerated soil in play yards and other high-traffic areas. Aggressive roots make it unsuitable in garden or lawn.

P. fraxinifolia, Caucasian wingnut, is similar but has slightly larger leaflets and longer nut clusters.

To landscape a large area with poor, compacted soil, keep it simple: surround a Chinese wingnut with agapanthus and red valerian (*Centranthus ruber*).

Pterostyrax

EPAULETTE TREE
Styracaceae
DECIDUOUS TREE

🌿 ZONES 3–10, 14–21

☀ ◐ FULL SUN OR PARTIAL SHADE

● REGULAR WATER

Pterostyrax hispida

Once classified with eastern American silver bell (*Halesia*), to which they are related, epaulette trees make handsome, interesting garden specimens. White flower clusters appear in late spring or early summer. Slim petals show from behind alternate leaves; plant where you can look up into them—on a bank beside a path, above a bench, in a raised bed. These are choice selections for the woodland edge or as a focal point in a large shrub border. Established trees need little pruning.

P. corymbosa. Native to Japan. Similar to *P. hispida*, but a little smaller in stature and leaf, and less widely grown. Flower clusters are slightly broader, and individual blooms are more bell-shaped with protruding stamens. Fruits are downy, not furry, and winged, not ribbed.

P. hispida. Native to Japan and China. Single- or multi-trunked tree to 20–30 ft. (possibly 40 ft.) tall and equally wide. Oval to oblong leaves are light green above, gray-green beneath. Creamy white, lightly fragrant flowers with fringed petal edges appear in drooping clusters to 9 in. long, 3 in. wide, giving bloom puffs an airy look. Pendent clusters of small, furry gray fruits hang on well into winter, are attractive on bare branches.

Ptilotus

MULLA MULLA
Amaranthaceae
ANNUALS AND PERENNIALS

🌿 ZONES 13–17, 19–24

☀ FULL SUN

◔ ◒ LITTLE TO MODERATE WATER

Ptilotus exaltatus villosus 'Platinum Wallaby'

With abundant upright flower heads shaped like feather dusters, *Ptilotus* bred for the garden are irresistible Australian natives that come in pastel colors. They grow about 18 in. high, with reddish stems that support narrow, pointed, upright leaves. Perennial kinds are often used as annuals.

P. exaltatus. Oddly, this species is divided into perennial and annual forms. Both of the following have silvery green foliage. Plants in the Joey strain are annuals that prefer acidic soil, grow to 12–15 in. high and 12 in. wide, and bear pink flowers to 4 in. long. This is a seed-grown strain, so the flower colors vary a bit. 'Platinum Wallaby' is part of a perennial subspecies, *P. e. villosus*, that naturally occurs in alkaline soil. It has blue-pink flowers that are longer (to 6 in.) and longer-lasting than those in the Joey strain, and plants can grow up to 18 in. high and wide. It is grown from tissue culture, so all plants are virtually identical.

P. nobilis 'Down Under'. Perennial. Grows 12–18 in. high and wide, with sparse green leaves and white flowers. This is an excellent filler for dry places.

FOR MORE UNTHIRSTY PLANTS, SEE PAGES 74–78.

P

Ptychosperma
Arecaceae
PALMS

✿ ZONES 23, 24; H2

☼ LIGHT SHADE

● REGULAR WATER

Ptychosperma macarthuri

Both of these garden-scale feather palms have slender, ringed trunks and well-defined crown shafts (the smooth, usually green upper trunk, formed by overlapping bases of newer leaves). Leaflets are toothed at the tips. Red fruit clusters appear in warmest frost-free climates. Grow in well-drained soil.

P. elegans. ALEXANDER PALM, SOLITAIRE PALM. From Australia. Erect, single-trunked palm to 25 ft. tall, 15 ft. wide. Leaves to 8 ft. long.

P. macarthuri. MACARTHUR PALM. Native to New Guinea. To 10–25 ft. tall, 12–15 ft. wide, with several trunks. Leaves to 6½ ft. long. Often grown in tubs.

Perennial Color in the Shade

Lungwort is one of the few perennials that reliably produce showy blooms in full shade. Others include bergenia, clivia, bleeding heart (*Dicentra*), some foxgloves (*Digitalis*), hellebores, *Mertensia, Polemonium,* Solomon's seal (*Polygonatum*), some primroses, florists' cineraria (*Pericallis* × *hybrida*), and foamflower (*Tiarella*).

For bright foliage effects, try variegated forms of caladium, coleus, *Farfugium japonicum,* Japanese forest grass (*Hakonechloa macra*), lily turf (*Liriope*), hosta, or dead nettle (*Lamium*).

Pulmonaria
LUNGWORT
Boraginaceae
PERENNIALS

✿ ZONES 1–9, 14–17

☼ ● PARTIAL OR FULL SHADE

● REGULAR WATER

Pulmonaria 'Pink Haze'

Low-growing shade lovers with quiet charm, lungworts have foliage that is, in many varieties, attractively dappled with gray or silver. (Because spotted leaves reminded Renaissance herbalists of diseased lungs, this perennial was thought to cure lung ailments—thus "lungwort.") Drooping clusters of funnel-shaped, typically blue or purplish flowers emerge in late winter or early spring, just before (or as) long-stalked leaves emerge from basal clumps. After flowering, more leaves arise. Regular watering keeps foliage ornamental through the growing season. Creeping roots make these good small-scale groundcovers or edgings for beds or woodland paths. Need moist, well-drained, organically enriched soil. Clumps may become crowded after a few years; divide them in early autumn.

P. angustifolia. COWSLIP LUNGWORT. Native to Europe. To 8–12 in. high and 1½ ft. wide, with narrowish dark green leaves and bright blue flowers that open from pink buds. *P. a. azurea* has sky blue blossoms.

P. longifolia. Native to the British Isles, western Europe. To 8–12 in. high, 18 in. wide. Slender leaves to 20 in. long are deep green spotted with silver. Blooms a little later than other species; flowers are purplish blue. *P. l. cevennensis* grows 8 in. high, 18 in. wide, with deep blue flowers that appear from late winter through late spring.

P. 'Margery Fish'. Probably a *P. saccharata* hybrid. Clumps grow 12 in. high, producing flowers that open pink and turn blue. Long, narrow green leaves are heavily spotted with silver.

P. 'Raspberry Splash'. A hybrid of *P. longifolia*. Clumps grow 12 in. high, with upright, silver-spotted dark green leaves. Produces pink flowers in profusion.

P. 'Roy Davidson'. Hybrid between *P. saccharata* and *P. longifolia*. Resembles *P. longifolia* but has slightly wider leaves and flowers that open pink before deepening to blue.

P. saccharata. BETHLEHEM SAGE. To 1½ ft. high, 2 ft. wide, with elliptical, medium green, silver-spotted leaves and blue flowers opening from pink buds. Specialists usually offer named selections, including early-blooming 'Highdown' ('Lewis Palmer'), with deep blue blossoms; old favorite 'Mrs. Moon', with large leaves and pink flowers aging from pink to blue; 'Sissinghurst White', with large white blooms; and 'Smoky Blue', with blue flowers atop deep green, white-spotted leaves.

P. 'Trevi Fountain'. Hybrid of unknown parentage. Long, silver-spotted leaves give rise to abundant cobalt blue flowers. The clump is about 1 ft. high.

FOR OTHER SHADE-LOVING PLANTS, SEE PAGES 68–69.

Pulsatilla vulgaris
(Anemone pulsatilla)
PASQUE FLOWER
Ranunculaceae
PERENNIAL

✿ ZONES 2B–6, 15–17

☼ FULL SUN

● REGULAR WATER

Pulsatilla vulgaris

This central European native starts as a foot-wide rosette of finely cut leaves covered with silky hairs; smaller leaves clothe the short flowering stems. In early spring, each stem is topped by a single cup-shaped, erect or nodding blossom with silky hairs on the outside and a mass of yellow stamens within. Colors range from white through pink shades to purple or red. The fluffy seed clusters are almost as showy as the flowers; each seed is topped by a long, twisting, feathery appendage. Plants grow from a woody root, reach 5–6 in. high in bloom, rise to about 1½ ft. high by the time seeds appear. 'Pinwheel White' and 'Alba' have white flowers; 'Rubra' and 'Red Clock' have red blooms.

Best in cool conditions with well-drained soil. May go dormant in summer.

Pasque flower is pretty at all stages. Silky, ferny foliage is followed by gold-centered blooms that develop large fluffy seed heads.

P

Pumpkin
Cucurbitaceae
ANNUAL

- **ALL ZONES**
- **FULL SUN**
- **REGULAR WATER**

'Cinderella's Carriage' pumpkin

Related to gourd and melon, the first pumpkins probably originated in South America. Most are varieties of *Cucurbita pepo*, though other squash species also have varieties called pumpkins. Fruit varies greatly in size. One of the best for a jumbo Halloween pumpkin is 'Atlantic

Giant'. 'Orange Smoothie' is smooth skinned, making it easy to decorate with paint. 'Small Sugar', a smaller pumpkin with finer-grained, sweeter flesh, is great for pies. 'Jack Be Little' and 'Wee-B-Little' are miniature (3–4 in.) types used for decoration. Novelties with white skin and orange flesh include miniature 'Baby Boo' and 8–10-in. 'Lumina'. Seeds of all are edible, but hull-less varieties like 'Trick or Treat' are easiest to eat.

Giant pumpkins aren't special varieties—just full-size pumpkins grown in a special way. As plant develops, cut off all but two main stems. After blossom set, remove all but one fruit on each stem. Along each stem's length, mound a 4-in.-wide hill of soil every 2 ft.; roots will form there.

Pumpkins are available in vining and bush types. A single vine can cover 500 sq. ft., and even bush sorts can spread over 20 sq. ft.

CARE

In most areas, sow seeds outdoors in late spring after soil has warmed; plant in rich soil. Where the growing season is

short, start plants indoors and use floating row covers early in the season. For vining pumpkins, sow five or six seeds 1 in. deep in hills 6–8 ft. apart; thin seedlings to two per hill. Plant bush pumpkins in rows spaced 3 ft. apart; plant seeds 1 in. deep in clusters of three or four, spacing clusters 2 ft. apart along the row. Thin seedlings to one or two plants per cluster.

Feed occasionally. Water regularly during rainless periods, but keep foliage dry to prevent leaf diseases. Plants suffer in high heat and humidity. In late summer, slide wooden shingles or other protection under fruit to protect it from wet soil and rot (unnecessary if soil is sandy). Depending on variety, pumpkins are ready to harvest 90 to 120 days after sowing, when shell has hardened. Pick after first frost kills the plant. Use a sharp knife or hand pruners to harvest fruit, leaving on 1–2 in. of stem. Subject to same pests and diseases as squash.

CLOCKWISE FROM LEFT: 'Green Hokkaido' pumpkin; 'Lumina' pumpkin; 'Atlantic Giant' pumpkin

Punica granatum
FLOWERING POMEGRANATE
Lythraceae
DECIDUOUS SHRUB OR TREE

- **ZONES 5–24; H1, H2**
- **FULL SUN**
- **MODERATE TO REGULAR WATER**

Punica granatum 'Nana'

Instead of thinking flavor, think color when you see these small, showy ornamentals. Native from Iran to the Himalayas, they produce single or double flowers in white to red-orange, with ruffled petals surrounding a central cluster of stamens. They either are fruitless or bear pomegranates that are more decorative than tasty. Narrow leaves are bronzy when new, maturing to glossy bright green or golden green; they turn brilliant yellow in fall except where winters are very mild. For fruiting types, see Pomegranate.

All are good landscape plants, tolerating a broad range of soils—even alkaline ones. In late dormant season, prune as needed to shape. On shrubby types, remove oldest stems occasionally to encourage strong new growth.

'Chico'. DWARF CARNATION-FLOWERED POMEGRANATE. Compact shrub to 3 ft. high and wide. Easily kept to 1½ ft. high with occasional pruning. Double orange-red flowers.

'Legrellei' ('Madame Legrelle', **'California Sunset').** To 8–10 ft. tall and wide. Creamy white double flowers heavily striped coral red.

'Nana'. DWARF POMEGRANATE. Dense grower to 2–3 ft. high, 4–5 ft. wide. Blooms when a foot tall or less. Orange-red single flowers followed by small, dry red fruit. Nearly evergreen in mild winters.

'Nochi Shibori'. To 8–10 ft. tall and wide. Double dark red flowers.

'Toyosho'. To 8–10 ft. tall and wide. Double light apricot flowers.

Purshia mexicana

CLIFFROSE

Rosaceae

EVERGREEN SHRUB

✂ **ZONES 2–3, 6–12, 14–21**

☀ **FULL SUN**

◐ ● **LITTLE TO MODERATE WATER**

🐝 **ATTRACTS HONEYBEES**

Purshia mexicana

This slow-growing, drought-tolerant evergreen shrub grows to 6 ft. tall, 4 ft. wide, with small, lobed, resinous leaves and fragrant spring flowers that look like miniature single roses. Masses of showy (but individually tiny) straw-colored, feathery fruits follow. Rugged branches have peeling bark. Native to Mexico and Arizona. *P. m. stansburiana*, native in the Great Basin, California, and Arizona, grows to 4 ft. tall, with silvery leaves and creamy yellow flowers. Tolerates clay soil.

The creamy yellow or white flowers of cliffrose have the fragrance of honey, and its ferny, dark green leaves are pleasantly aromatic.

Puschkinia scilloides

Asparagaceae

PERENNIAL FROM BULB

✂ **ZONES 1–11, 14**

☀ ◑ **FULL SUN OR LIGHT SHADE**

● **REGULAR WATER DURING GROWTH AND BLOOM**

Puschkinia scilloides

Spikes are 6 in. and loaded with star-shaped, inch-wide blossoms; they rise above *Puschkinia's* strap-shaped, bright green leaves in late winter or early spring. Flowers are pale blue with a greenish blue stripe down the center of each of their six petals. Closely related to squill (*Scilla*) and glory-of-the-snow (*Chionodoxa*), this Middle Easterner is the only species in its genus, which is named for Russian count Apollo Mussin-Pushkin, who was an avid plant collector. The plant blooms and naturalizes best where the ground freezes in winter. In the wild, it grows mostly at 6,000–12,000-ft. elevations in meadows dampened by snowmelt. The most widely sold variety is *P. s. libanotica*, which has more pointed petals that are an even paler shade of blue, with a very thin blue stripe. *P. s.* 'Alba' is a white-flowered variant.

Plants grow well in short-grass meadows, or lawns that are not mowed very often. Plant in masses from late summer into fall, setting bulbs 3 in. deep, 3 in. apart in well-drained soil. Keep soil slightly moist until foliage appears; then water regularly until leaves start to yellow in early summer. Needs very little water during summer dormant period and seldom needs dividing.

Puya berteroana

Bromeliaceae

PERENNIAL

✂ **ZONES 9, 13–17, 19–24**

☀ **FULL SUN**

◐ ● **LITTLE TO MODERATE WATER**

Puya berteroana

Growing into a spectacular evergreen foliage clump up to 10 ft. across, this Chilean native is crowded with narrow, sharp-tipped, swordlike gray-green leaves to 2 ft. long; edges are sharply spined. Develops flower stalks that resemble giant asparagus spears; they reach 4–6 ft. tall during spring bloom, when they bear massive clusters of 2-in.-wide, bell-shaped blossoms in metallic blue-green and steely turquoise, accented with vivid orange anthers. Spiky branchlet ends protrude from flower clusters. Use in large rock gardens or in big containers. Tolerates poor soil. Often mislabeled as *P. alpestris*.

The arching, narrow leaves of this bromeliad look good all year—a fine way to add textural variety to a composition of cactus and succulents. But when its huge, otherworldly flower spikes bloom, you'll want to invite friends and neighbors to see the show.

Pyracantha

FIRETHORN

Rosaceae

EVERGREEN SHRUBS

✂ **ZONES VARY BY SPECIES**

☀ **FULL SUN**

● **MODERATE WATER**

🐦 **BERRIES ATTRACT BIRDS**

Pyracantha

Most often seen as a hedge, screen, or espalier, firethorns also come in sprawling forms useful as groundcovers. Bright red or orange fruit, evergreen foliage (may be semievergreen in cold climates), and fast growth make it popular. Leaves are glossy green, generally oval or rounded at ends; all flowers and fruit on spurs emerging from last year's growth. Small, spring flowers are dull creamy white, carried in flattish clusters; they're effective thanks to their profusion. Some people find the scent unpleasant. Nearly all species have needle-like thorns—thus the common name "firethorn."

The real glory of firethorns is in their thick clusters of pea-size, orange-red berries, which light up the garden for months from late summer to midfall; some types hang on until late winter, when they're cleared out by birds, storms, or decay. Dislodge old, withered, or rotted berries with a water jet or an old broom. (This is one of the kinds of fruit that ferment on the plant, making the birds that eat it drunk.) Selections with red, orange, or yellow berries are available; buy during berry season to get what you want.

As shrubs and groundcovers, firethorns look better and produce more heavily if allowed to grow naturally. Prune to check wayward branches, but remember that hard pruning reduces fruit. For low-growing, wide-spreading types as groundcovers, set plants 4–5 ft. apart. Firethorns tolerate most soils but should not be overwatered. Subject to fireblight, scale insects, woolly aphids, red spider mites. In coastal areas of the Pacific Northwest, apple scab is sometimes a problem in early spring; it can nearly defoliate plants.

P. angustifolia 'Yukon Belle'. Zones 3–24. Variety of a Chinese native. To 8–10 ft. tall, 6–8 ft. wide. Bright orange berries.

P. coccinea. Zones 3–24. From the eastern Mediterranean. Rounded growth to 8–10 ft. tall and wide (potentially larger trained against a wall). Red-orange fruit. Best known for its varieties.

'Kasan'. To 8–10 ft. tall, 6–8 ft. wide. Long-lasting orange-red fruit.

'Lowboy'. To 2–3 ft. high, 6–8 ft. wide. Bright orange berries.

'Red Cushion'. To 3 ft. high, 4 ft. wide. Red-orange berries.

'Rutgers'. To 3 ft. high, 5 ft. wide, with orange berries. Good disease resistance.

P. crenatoserrata (P. fortuneana, P. yunnanensis). Zones 4–24. From China. Vase-shaped plant to 15 ft. tall, 10 ft. wide. Limber branches make it a good espalier subject. Pale orange to coral berries persist through winter.

'Graberi'. More erect than the species; to 10–12 ft. tall, 8–10 ft. wide. Huge clusters of dark red berries.

P. hybrids. These are plants of mixed or uncertain heritage. The group includes many of the most desirable firethorns.

'Mohave'. Zones 4–24. To 12 ft. tall and wide. Heavy producer of big orange-red berries that color late and hang on for a long time.

'Red Elf'. Zones 4–9, 12–24. Low-growing, compact plant to 2 ft. high and wide; good in containers. Bright red berries.

'Silver Lining'. Zones 4–9, 12–24. Grows to 3 ft. high and wide. Green leaves with white edges. In winter, leaves turn purple with pinkish-white edges. Few berries.

'Teton'. Zones 2b–24. Fairly upright growth to 12 ft. tall, 4–6 ft. wide. Yellow-orange berries.

P. koidzumii. Zones 4–24. From Taiwan. Loose, unruly grower to 8–12 ft. tall and wide. Best known for its varieties.

'Santa Cruz' ('Santa Cruz Prostrata'). Reaches 6 ft. tall but is easily maintained at 3 ft. or lower by pruning out erect-growing branches. Can spread as wide as 10 ft., making it a good groundcover. Red berries.

'Victory'. To 8–10 ft. tall, 6–8 ft. wide. Dark red berries color late but hang on late as well.

Pyrethrum roseum. See *Tanacetum coccineum*

Pyrostegia venusta
(P. ignea, Bignonia venusta)
FLAME VINE
Bignoniaceae
EVERGREEN VINE

📏 **ZONES 13, 16, 21–24; H1, H2**

☀ **FULL SUN**

💧 **MODERATE WATER**

🐦 **ATTRACTS BIRDS**

Pyrostegia venusta

Flame vine is as brilliant as it sounds, with branch-end clusters of tubular, 3-in., orange flowers lighting up this 20–40-ft. evergreen vine during winter; in warmest gardens, bloom starts in fall and continues into spring. Native to South America. Climbs rapidly by tendrils, twining along fences and eaves, and over pergolas and arbors, ultimately spilling off retaining walls and covering banks. Leaves consist of two or three oval, 2-in. leaflets; paired leaflets have a tendril between them rather than a third leaflet. In the mildest climates, foot-long seed capsules usually form after flowers fade.

Tolerates many soils. Revels in heat; in cooler climates, plant along a south- or west-facing wall. Prune in spring or summer, after bloom has finished.

Pyrus
ORNAMENTAL PEAR
Rosaceae
EVERGREEN AND DECIDUOUS TREES

📏 **ZONES VARY BY SPECIES**

☀ **FULL SUN**

💧 **MODERATE WATER**

Pyrus calleryana 'Jack'

Ornamental pears are grown for their profuse late-winter or early-spring show of white flowers and their lustrous leaves. Not at their best in shallow soils, they're otherwise unfussy, even growing well in heavy clay. Most are subject to fireblight. Fruiting pears are described under Pear, Asian and Pear, European.

P. betulifolia. Zones 2–9, 14–21. From northern China. To 20 ft. tall and wide, with white spring blossoms and 2–3-in. leaves that are glossy green above and downy below. 'Dancer' grows to 30 ft. tall, 20 ft. wide, with profuse white flowers appearing before foliage. Gray-green new growth shimmers like aspen leaves in light breezes.

P. calleryana. CALLERY PEAR. Deciduous tree. Zones 2b–9, 14–21. Chinese native. Needs some winter chill. To 50 ft. tall and wide, with strong horizontal branching pattern; young growth is thorny. Broadly oval, scallop-edged, leathery leaves are glossy dark green, turning rich purplish red in fall. Blooms so early that late freezes may destroy flower crop. Very small, round, inedible fruit. Some fireblight resistance.

'Aristocrat'. Essentially pyramidal, though somewhat open and rounded; to 35–40 ft. tall, 20 ft. wide. Branches curve upward to form a strong structure. Fall color ranges from yellow to red.

'Autumn Blaze'. Rounded form to 30 ft. tall, 25 ft. wide. Hardiest of the callery pears. Crimson fall color develops early.

'Bradford'. The original *P. calleryana* variety. Pyramidal to 50 ft. tall, 35 ft. wide. Strongly vertical limbs have no central leader. Very impressive for 15 to 20 years; then branches become congested, tree spreads, and tight branch crotches tend to split. Better choices are 'Aristocrat', 'Chanticleer', 'New Bradford', and 'Redspire'.

'Capital'. Columnar. To 40 ft. tall and 15 ft. wide. Coppery fall color.

'Chanticleer' ('Cleveland Select', 'Glen's Form', 'Stone Hill'). Most plants sold under this name are narrowly pyramidal in form; some are more columnar. To 40 ft. tall, 15 ft. wide. Fall color varies from orange to reddish purple.

'Jack'. Oval shape to 15 ft. tall, 10 ft. wide, with white flowers and dark green leaves that turn yellow in fall.

'New Bradford' ('Holmford'). Grows 35 ft. tall, 30 ft. wide, with glossy, dark green leaves that turn orange-red in autumn. More disease-resistant, hardier, and better branching than 'Bradford'.

'Redspire'. Pyramidal; to 35 ft. tall, 20 ft. wide. Especially large blossom clusters; yellow to red fall color.

'Trinity'. Round-headed form to 30 ft. tall and wide. Orange-red fall color.

P. 'Edgewood'. Zones 2–9, 14–21. A hybrid between *P. calleryana* and *P. betulifolia*, 'Edgewood' grows to 30 ft. tall, 25 ft. wide, with purple-tinged new growth that matures to silver-green, then flushes reddish purple in autumn.

P. fauriei 'Korean Sun' ('Westwood'). Zones 2b–9, 14–21. This selection of a Korean species is compact and rounded, growing 12 ft. tall and 15 ft. wide; can be pruned into a small tree or grown as a large shrub. Fine textured, cold hardy, and fruitless. Leaves turn orangish red to purple in fall.

P. kawakamii. EVERGREEN PEAR. Evergreen shrub or tree; partially deciduous in coldest winters. Zones 8, 9, 12–24. From Taiwan. To 15–30 ft. tall and wide, with drooping branchlets and glossy green, oval leaves with pointed tips. Masses of flowers appear in winter and early spring. Small, inedible fruit. Naturally grows as a broad, sprawling shrub, but is most often grown as a single- or multi-trunked tree. To train it this way, stake one or several stems and shorten side growth; keep tree staked until it is self-supporting. To build up framework limbs, shorten any overlong, pendent branches to upward-facing growth buds or branchlets. Can also be espaliered. An established, well-shaped tree needs little pruning—and heavily pruned plants seldom bloom. Very prone to fireblight.

P. salicifolia 'Pendula'. WEEPING WILLOW-LEAFED PEAR. Deciduous tree. Zones 2–9, 14–21; best in cold climates. Native to southeastern Europe, western Asia. Elegant specimen plant to 15 ft. tall, 12 ft. wide. Grown for silvery, willowlike foliage and beautiful weeping habit, which shows best in winter. Flowers appear as foliage emerges in early spring. Leaves are silvery white when new, turning silvery green in summer. Insignificant fruit. Very susceptible to fireblight. P. salicifolia 'Silver Ball' grows 12 ft. tall and wide, with finely textured branches that give it a compact form; fall color is yellow-orange.

P. ussuriensis. USSURIAN PEAR. Deciduous tree. Zones A1–A3; 1–3, 10. Native to Manchuria, Siberia. Another parent of Asian pear varieties. Dense, rounded tree to 15–40 ft. tall, 15–25 ft. wide. Roundish, 2–4-in., glossy bright green leaves turn red or purple in fall. Large spring flowers are followed by tiny, hard, inedible fruit. A good substitute for the similar P. calleryana in colder climates. 'Prairie Gem' grows 25 ft. tall and wide, with dark green leaves that turn golden yellow in fall.

Quamoclit pennata.
See *Ipomoea quamoclit*

Quercus

OAK
Fagaceae
DECIDUOUS AND EVERGREEN TREES AND SHRUBS

| ✎ ZONES VARY BY SPECIES |
| ☼ FULL SUN |
| ◐◑● WATER NEEDS VARY; SEE TEXT |
| ✾ ACORNS FEED A WIDE RANGE OF BIRDS AND MAMMALS |

Quercus agrifolia

The archetypal oak grows large and spreads wide, with muscular, near-horizontal lower branches that seem to defy gravity. But the group's 500 species, all native to the Northern Hemisphere, also include upright, pyramidal, and shrubby oaks; in fact, "chaparral" comes from *chaparra*—Spanish for a dwarf evergreen shrub oak. Oak leaves can be deciduous or evergreen (the latter are called live oaks); lobed, toothed, or smooth edged; but they're always arranged in an alternate pattern along stems. Some have terrific fall color. All oaks produce inconspicuous flowers followed by acorns, whose single nuts have cuplike caps covered with closely set scales. Some kinds of acorns are edible and sweet, while others are bitter and unpalatable.

Oaks come in two broad categories: white oaks have acorns that mature during the season in which they are produced, and often have leaves with rounded lobes; red and black oaks have acorns that take two seasons to mature, and often have leaves with pointed lobes. Each group can hybridize only within itself.

BEST OAKS FOR THE WEST

From among the many hundreds of oak species, here are the choices best suited to Western gardens.

Q. acutissima. SAWTOOTH OAK. Deciduous tree. Zones 2–7, 14–17. From the Himalayas, China, Korea, Japan. Moderate to fast growth to 45 ft. (ultimately 50–70 ft.) tall and wide, usually with open, spreading habit. Dark gray bark with red-brown furrows. Shiny dark green, pointed, oblong leaves have bristle-toothed, slightly wavy edges (like chestnut leaves). Foliage is yellowish when new, turns yellow to yellowish brown in fall; may hang on late into winter. Acorns are blunt cylinders to 1 in. long, enclosed for two-thirds of their length in a burlike cap. Prefers well-drained, slightly acid soil but is fairly tolerant of other soils. Good shade or lawn tree.

Q. agrifolia. COAST LIVE OAK. Evergreen tree. Zones 7–9, 14–24. Native to coastal central and Southern California. Round headed and densely foliaged; to 20–70 ft. tall, often with even greater spread. Smooth dark gray bark, deeply fissured in very old trees. Oval, convex, stiff, leathery dark green leaves are tooth edged and hollylike. Foliage is attractive all year. Conical, ¾–1½-in. acorns are enclosed for one-fourth of their length by a cap with thin, overlapping scales. Has greedy roots; drops almost all its old leaves in early spring. A worthwhile shade or street tree. Can be sheared to make a 10–12-ft. hedge. Susceptible to sudden oak death.

Q. alba. WHITE OAK. Deciduous tree. Zones A2–A3; 1–9, 14–24. Native to the eastern U.S. (and the state tree of Connecticut, Illinois, and Maryland), white oak is considered by many to be the most noble American oak. After establishment, it grows quickly to 45 ft. tall and wide (100 ft. in the wild). Bark is ash gray, checked, and scaled. Leaves emerge pink, mature to green, and turn deep red in autumn; each is 4–8½ in. long and half as wide, with five to nine deeply cut lobes. Acorn can reach 1 in. long, with a cap covering about

Transplanting an Oak

If its rootball is otherwise big and firm enough, an oak seedling up to 5–8 ft. tall seems not to suffer from having its vertical root cut. The tree may wilt or lose leaves after the root is cut, but if kept watered, it should show new growth within 4 to 6 weeks. The best time to transplant is fall or winter (or early spring, in some cold-winter areas). Oak seedlings in nursery containers should not have a spiraling taproot at the container bottom; better growers cut a seedling's taproot when moving it to a nursery container, so that the young tree will develop a branching root system.

When digging the tree's planting hole in its new location, mix some oak leaf mold or soil obtained from under an established, healthy oak into the hole to inoculate it with beneficial fungi. Large native oaks in boxes up to 7 ft. on each side are available, but for such large trees, let an experienced landscaping contractor do the planting for you.

a quarter of its length. Mildew-resistant. Can live more than 600 years.

Q. berberidifolia. SCRUB OAK. Semievergreen shrub or tree. Zones 5, 7–10, 14–24. Native to California chaparral from 300–5,000-ft. elevation. Dense growth 6–15 ft. tall and wide. Leaves variable in shape, with wavy edges; may have smooth, toothed, or spiny margins. Medium green on top, gray-green below. Oval acorns to 1 in. long enclosed by up to one-half in knobby cap with spiral pattern. Good unthirsty clipped hedge, background shrub, informal screen. Long confused with *Q. dumosa*, which is native only near the Southern California coast.

Q. bicolor. SWAMP WHITE OAK. Deciduous tree. Zones A3; 1–3. Native to eastern North America. Slow to moderate growth to 50–60 ft., rarely taller, with equal or greater spread. Bark of trunk and branches flakes off in scales. Shallowly lobed or scalloped leaves are 3–7 in. long, a little more than half as wide, shiny dark green above, silvery white beneath. Fall color is usually yellow but sometimes orange, fiery red, or purple. Oblong to egg-shaped, 1-in. acorns, one-third enclosed by rounded cap with hairy scales. Tolerates wet soil; also thrives where soil is well drained.

Q. buckleyi. TEXAS RED OAK. Deciduous tree. Zones 3b, 6–12, 18–22. Native from central Texas to northern Oklahoma. Grows 30 ft. tall and wide, often with multiple trunks. Bark can be smooth gray or black and furrowed. Green leaves grow up to 4 in. long and wide, with deep pointed lobes, turning red in fall. Egg-shaped, ½-in. acorns have a cup-shaped cap. Native to bottomlands, it does well in rich, deep soil.

Q. chrysolepis. CANYON LIVE OAK, MAUL OAK, GOLDEN-CUP OAK. Evergreen tree. Zones 3–11, 14–24. Native to foothills and desert mountains from southwestern Oregon to Baja California and east into Arizona. Handsome, round-headed or somewhat spreading tree to 20–60 ft. tall and wide. Bark is smooth and whitish when young, checked and gray with

How to Grow Oak Trees

Homeowners acquire oaks either by planting them or by inheriting trees that were present before their land was developed.

Planted oaks usually thrive with no special care, but species from summer-rainfall areas appreciate moderate to regular summer irrigation during dry spells. After the Mediterranean natives are established, they can take irrigation or leave it, and Western U.S. natives are better off with little or no extra water. It takes about two years for a small oak to become established, and up to seven years for a tree planted from a 7-ft. box.

Old native oaks from dry-summer regions must be kept dry during the warm season, since they often succumb to fungal root diseases if given routine summer watering. But don't hesitate to give all kinds of oaks monthly soakings in winter if rains fail (and do this every winter in places that get less than 20 in. of rainfall per year), applying water at the drip line.

SPECIAL TREATMENT FOR EXISTING NATIVE OAKS

Though highly prized mature oaks may look indestructible, they are easily killed by root compaction, grade changes, and overwatering. But because oaks take a decade or more to die, few gardeners connect the tree's thinning, dying canopy with the events that caused it. Here's how to prevent trouble.

1. Don't pave, excavate, or change grade level between trunk and drip line without first consulting an arborist. All those things risk smothering (or killing outright) feeder roots that only thrive in well-aerated soil close to the surface. Compaction from driving heavy equipment or vehicles over the same area puts the same roots at risk with the same effect. One arborist specializing in native oaks told us that it isn't enough to tell a contractor not to drive across the root zone: you have to

surround the protected area (everything under the tree's drip line) with rented fencing until the project is done and workers are gone.

2. When necessary, apply supplemental water over only the outer third of the root system—never over the roots closer to the trunk—to keep roots moving outward. Irrigate until soil is damp 8–12 in. deep (drip irrigation and soaker hoses make this easy). Never let water pool near the trunk. Though you should water recently planted trees weekly through summer, the most critical watering will be from March through May to support the tree's new growth.

3. To safeguard oaks, only use underplantings that require little or no summer water, and keep even these several feet from the trunk. In dry-summer parts of the West, the heavy summer watering needed to keep thirstier underplantings happy can activate oak root fungus (see "Pests & Diseases," below).

4. Old native oaks benefit from periodic grooming to remove dead wood, but don't cut thick branches without good reason. To avoid stimulating out-of-season new growth that will be susceptible to mildew and other problems, prune trees only when they're dormant. With evergreen oaks in the far West, this means pruning during the dry season—in mid- to late summer.

PESTS & DISEASES Any of a number of sucking and chewing insects and mites feed on oaks, but such creatures are usually kept in check by other insects, mites, and birds. Occasionally, though, an outbreak of some organism gets bad enough to require artificial control.

Oak moths. Oak moth caterpillars can defoliate trees and rain droppings on everything below. Severe attacks for 2 or more consecutive years can weaken or even kill a tree. However, oak moth caterpillar populations tend to

be cyclical, peaking every 7 to 10 years, then diminishing on their own. If control becomes necessary, consult an arborist or tree service; oaks are usually too large for the limited spray equipment available to home gardeners.

Galls. Most oaks produce galls of various colors, shapes, and sizes on twigs or leaf surfaces. The galls are swellings that form after insects (mostly wasps) lay eggs in the plant tissue; the larvae develop inside. Depending on the oak species and the type of insect involved, the galls may resemble apples, potatoes, mushrooms, dunce caps, or other objects. They do little harm and normally do not warrant treatment.

Fungi. Many fungi, both beneficial and pernicious, are associated with oaks. Oak root fungus (*Armillaria mellea*) occurs naturally in the roots of many oaks, but usually does not harm them unless they are under stress for other reasons. *Quercus ilex* and *Q. lobata* are especially resistant. The organism is particularly common in neighborhoods that once contained oak or walnut groves. It produces mushrooms at the base of the trunk and causes dieback in the canopy. This fungus is normally held in check in summer by drought and in winter by cool temperatures, but it grows rapidly in the warm, moist conditions caused by summer watering, especially close to the trunk—and also attacks a wide range of other plants (resistant species are mentioned throughout this book). Consult an arborist about infected trees.

Sudden oak death (*Phytophthora ramorum*). This relatively recent disease, commonly called SOD, has killed over millions of susceptible plants in coastal California and Oregon (see "Sudden Oak Death," page 547). In the species descriptions on these pages, both susceptible and apparently immune oaks are noted.

CLOCKWISE FROM TOP: *Quercus robur*; *Q. agrifolia*; *Q. lobata*

age. Oval leaves may be smooth edged or spiny; shiny medium green above, pale blue or grayish beneath, with thin felting of silvery or golden hairs on undersides when new. Oblong, sharp-tipped acorns among largest (to 2 in.) on American oaks; they are enclosed by one-third to two-thirds in a turbanlike cap covered with golden fuzz. Most widely distributed and variable of all California oaks, and most adaptable. Susceptible to sudden oak death.

Q. coccinea. SCARLET OAK. Deciduous tree. Zones 2–10, 14–24. Native to eastern U.S. Grows at moderate rate in deep, rich soil. Can reach 60–80 ft. tall, 40–60 ft. wide. Pyramidal when young, round topped in maturity. Gray-brown bark cracked into irregular plates. Bright green leaves are 3–6 in. long, with pointed, deeply cut lobes; turn scarlet where fall nights are cold. Rounded, ¾–1-in. acorns half-covered in a bowl-like cap.

Good, deep-rooted street or lawn tree.

Q. dentata. DAIMYO OAK, EMPEROR OAK. Deciduous tree. Zones 3–11, 14–24. Native to China, Japan, Korea, Mongolia, Taiwan. Growing fast to 60–75 ft. tall and wide, this oak is favored for its huge leaves. Brown bark is deeply furrowed, broken into plates. Leaves are glossy dark green on top, lighter and downy beneath, to 1 ft. long and 7 in. wide, with deep lobes; turn russet brown in fall and hang on. Rounded acorns reach ¾ in. long, caps covered with downy scales. Not long-lived. 'Carl Ferris Miller' ('C. F. Miller') grows about 30 ft. tall, 22 ft. wide. 'Pinnatifida' leaves are divided almost to the mid-rib, giving it a feathery look; grows slowly to about 15 ft.

Q. douglasii. BLUE OAK. Deciduous tree. Zones 3–11, 14–24. Native to dry foothills around California's Central Valley and interior valleys of Southern California. Low branching, wide spreading; to 30–50 ft. tall, 40–70 ft. wide. Light gray bark is shallowly checked in small squares. Shallowly lobed, oval, bluish green leaves are

1½–4 in. long, ¾–2 in. wide. Attractive fall colors: pastel pink, orange, yellow. Egg-shaped, ¾–1¼-in. acorns with sharply pointed tip and thin, flat cap. Good in dry, hot situations. Immune to sudden oak death.

Q. durata. LEATHER OAK, NUTTALL'S SCRUB OAK. Evergreen shrub. Zones 5, 7–10, 14–24. Native to northern Coast Ranges to San Luis Obispo area and to Sierra Nevada foothills, south to San Gabriel Mountains. In the wild, mostly confined to serpentine soil (a kind of nutrient-poor soil). Dense, rounded growth to 10 ft. tall and 8–12 ft. wide. Bare and somewhat leggy to 3–5 ft. aboveground, then forms open-branched tiers of foliage. Tough, oval, convex, ¾–1-in.-long leaves have smooth or prickly edges; dark green above, pale gray beneath, with a dense coating of fine, soft hairs. Acorns variable: ½–1 in. long, often almost cylindrical, half-enclosed in a warty, bowl-shaped cap.

Q. ellipsoidalis. NORTHERN PIN OAK. Deciduous tree. Zones A3; 2–3, 10. Native from south-central Canada to the northern Midwest. This close relation of pin oak is roughly strawberry-shaped, growing 55 ft. tall, 40 ft. wide, with gray fissured bark. Glossy dark green leaves grow to 6 in. long, 4½ in. wide; are toothed; turn yellow with red markings or red in autumn. Acorns are ¾ in. long, one-third covered by cap. Tolerates alkaline soils.

Q. emoryi. EMORY OAK. Evergreen tree. Zones 10–13. Native from Arizona to Texas and adjacent Mexico. Handsome

and rounded, to 50 ft. tall and 40 ft. wide. Leathery dark green, oval, sharply toothed leaves to 2–3 in. long are holly-like but flat; turn golden and drop just before new growth begins in late spring. Round-tipped, oblong, edible acorns enclosed by up to one-half in bowl-like cap. Grows well in low desert; tolerates a variety of soils. Needs periodic summer soakings.

Q. engelmannii. ENGELMANN OAK, MESA OAK, PASADENA OAK. Evergreen tree. Zones 7–9, 14–24. Native to Southern California. Spreading habit to 40–50 ft. tall, often twice as wide. Thick, leathery, dull bluish green, oval or oblong leaves; wavy surfaced or flat, usually smooth edged. Oval to cylindrical, round-tipped acorns to 1¼ in. long are half-enclosed in a warty cap. Tree grows best with monthly deep soakings in warm season, but don't keep it constantly moist. In its native area, it has the same cherished native status as the more widespread *Q. agrifolia*. Not susceptible to sudden oak death.

Q. frainetto. HUNGARIAN OAK, ITALIAN OAK. Deciduous tree. Zones 2–12, 14–21. Native to the eastern Mediterranean and south-central Europe. Majestic, fast-growing tree, ultimately to 100 ft. tall and 70 ft. wide. Dark gray, shallowly furrowed bark. Leaves to 8 in. long and 4 in. wide, deeply lobed, glossy deep green and covered with silky yellow or white hairs when new, turn yellow-brown in fall. Egg-shaped to oblong, ½–1¼-in. acorns, half-enclosed in fuzzy, bowl-shaped cap. 'Forest Green' grows 50 ft. tall, 30 ft.

 ## Training a Young Oak

Many young oaks have growth divided among so many twigs that none elongate quickly. To promote faster vertical growth, pinch off tips of small side branches, but retain as much leaf surface as possible to sustain maximum growth. Western native shrub oaks are adapted to browsing by deer and lend themselves readily to close planting and eventual shearing into handsome formal hedges. They should be used more widely for this purpose in preference to plants with higher water requirements.

wide, with beautiful, upright oval symmetry.

Q. fusiformis (Q. virginiana fusiformis). ESCARPMENT LIVE OAK, PLATEAU OAK. Briefly deciduous tree or shrub. Zones 3, 10–13. Native to the plains of central Texas, southern Oklahoma, and eastern New Mexico. To 40 ft. tall and wide, with dense crown. Rough dark brown bark has scaly ridges. Shiny, leathery leaves are oblong to elliptical; margins smooth or with a few sharp teeth, often rolled under. Foliage remains green through winter but turns yellow and drops during a 1-month spring transition. Acorns are ½–1 in. long, may have an egg shape or look like an elongated spindle; enclosed by one-third to one-half in goblet-shaped cap. Prefers well-drained alkaline soil. Easily endures heat, winter cold from Phoenix to Albuquerque; needs monthly soakings.

Q. gambellii. GAMBELL OAK, ROCKY MOUNTAIN WHITE OAK. Deciduous tree or shrub. Zones 1–3, 10. Native to Nevada, Arizona, east to Colorado and New Mexico. Slow to 15–30 ft. (rarely 50 ft.) tall, half as wide. Often forms colonies from root system. Thick, ridged trunk bark is light gray to whitish. Leaves 3–7 in. long, half as wide, with seven to nine deep lobes; dark green above, pale and densely hairy below. Foliage turns yellow, orange, or red in fall. Woolly, egg-shaped or globular, sharp-tipped acorns nearly 1 in. long, half-covered by a knobby cap. Characteristic oak of Arizona's Oak Creek Canyon and foothills south of Denver. Adaptable to wide range of soils and moisture levels; grows rapidly into a substantial tree in deep, rich soil.

Q. garryana. OREGON WHITE OAK, GARRY OAK. Deciduous tree. Zones 2a–11, 14–23. Native from British Columbia to California's Transverse Ranges. Slow to moderate growth to 40–90 ft. tall, 30–60 ft. wide, with rounded crown. Branches are often twisted; bark is gray, scaly, checked. Leathery, 3–6-in.-long, broadly oval leaves with rounded lobes. Foliage is glossy dark green above, rusty or downy beneath; turns reddish brown in

fall. Globular, edible acorns to 1¼ in. long, bulging from a small, scale-covered cap. Tree casts moderate shade and has a deep, nonaggressive root system. Immune to sudden oak death. *Q. g. breweri* is a small, very slow-growing dwarf form.

Q. ilex. HOLLY OAK, HOLM OAK. Evergreen tree. Zones 4–24. Native to the Mediterranean region. To 30–60 ft. tall and wide, with dense, rounded

head and smooth dark gray bark. Leaves vary in shape and size but are usually oval to lance-shaped, with smooth or prickly edges; rich dark green on top, covered with gray or yellow hairs beneath. Egg-shaped to nearly round, 1–1½-in. acorns are gray-brown with darker lines, half enclosed in deep cap that tapers to stem. Tolerates salt air; will grow in constant sea wind but tends to

be shrubby there. Inland, growth rate can be fairly fast but varies with soil and water conditions. Good evergreen street or lawn tree where coast live oak (*Q. agrifolia*) is difficult to maintain, though it lacks that tree's open grace. Can take hard clipping into formal shapes or hedges. Susceptible to sudden oak death.

Q. imbricaria. SHINGLE OAK, LAUREL OAK. Deciduous

Sudden Oak Death

In 1995, the previously unknown pathogen *Phytophthora ramorum* started killing tanbark oaks and coast live oaks in California's Santa Cruz and Marin counties. Still centered there, the outbreak has spread to southwest Oregon and to California's Big Sur coast. This pathogen thrives in the cool, moist evergreen forests of coastal canyons. Among potential host plants—which include bigleaf maple, camellias, rhododendrons, coast redwoods, and toyon—the most troublesome is California bay laurel (*Umbellularia californica*). When infected, it usually survives with only leaf damage but it can pass along the disease to susceptible native oaks (*Quercus agrifolia, Q. chrysolepis, Q. kelloggii,* and *Q. parvula shrevei*), which usually die within a couple of years, and tanbark oaks (*Lithocarpus densiflorus*), which usually die within a year or two.

Spores commonly spread during wet weather, traveling primarily in wind-driven rain splash and in mud on shoes and tires. But for susceptible plants to be infected, they apparently need to receive a heavy dose of spores. Rural gardens adjacent to areas populated by host plants are at much higher risk for infection than urban gardens, which are at less risk of being contaminated by the relatively small number of spores found on boots, tires, and (rarely) infected nursery plants.

Symptoms of sudden oak death often begin with oozing reddish or brownish sap from the afflicted tree's trunk and main limbs. Leaves wilt suddenly, turn dull or yellowish, curl up, and die. The pathogen is often accompanied by oak bark beetles and heartwood-boring ambrosia beetles attracted by the fermenting sap of dying trees. These

small, black native insects, each about the size of a grain of rice, previously were not considered serious pests, since they attack only obviously wounded or stressed trees. But with the sudden oak death epidemic, the beetles hasten the demise of trees that may otherwise appear to be healthy. New generations of beetles emerge in spring and early fall. Avoid pruning in spring, when the pathogen and beetles are most active.

If you live in the San Francisco Bay Area or in the coastal hills between the Big Sur coast and the southern Oregon coast and have a susceptible oak in your garden, there are two good strategies for protecting your tree:

- Remove or prune back any California bay laurel on your property that is growing within 35 ft. of your susceptible oak or tanbark oak.

- If your neighbors have lost a tree to sudden oak death, or if they are growing a California bay laurel within 35 ft. of your susceptible tree, you or an arborist can treat your tree with phosphonate (sold as Agri-Fos) to boost its defense mechanisms. The treatment must be repeated once a year, usually in fall, to provide continuous protection.

If you have an infected tree, you can cut it down after it wilts; once the leaves die, the tree will not revive. Do not transport infected wood. You can use it for firewood, but store it in a dry place, since spores can be washed off cut wood and return to the environment to infect other trees. Leaves, twigs, and small branches should also stay on-site, chipped and spread out during summer to thoroughly dry and kill the pathogen.

Q

CLOCKWISE FROM LEFT: *Quercus douglasii*; *Q. robur* acorns; *Q. palustris* leaves

tree. Zones 2–10, 14–16, 18–21. Native from the mid-Atlantic states to Nebraska. Grows about 1 ft. per year to about 50 ft. tall and 40 ft. wide (but much bigger with great age); bark is gray-brown, furrowed. Lustrous oblong or lance-shaped leaves are tinged red at opening, mature to green, then shade russet red in fall. Acorn is about ⅝ in. long, half enclosed in cap. Takes well to pruning (even hedging and screening). Does best in the colder parts of its range.

Q. kelloggii. CALIFORNIA BLACK OAK. Deciduous tree. Zones 5 (inland areas), 6, 7, 9, 14–21. Grows with conifers in upland locations from southern Oregon to Southern California. To 30–80 ft. tall and wide, with short trunk, ascending branches, and rounded crown. Dark gray, furrowed, checked bark. Handsome foliage: leaves unfold soft pink or dusty rose, mature to dark glossy green, turn yellow or yellow-orange in fall. Leaves

4–10 in. long, 2½–6 in. wide, have deep, sharply tapered lobes ending in bristly points. Oblong or almost conical, 1–1½-in. acorns are enclosed by half in bowl-shaped cap. Good moderate-size tree for spring and fall color; attractive winter trunk and branch pattern. Susceptible to sudden oak death.

Q. lobata. VALLEY OAK, CALIFORNIA WHITE OAK. Deciduous tree. Zones 3b–9, 11–24. Native to interior valleys, Sierra foothills, and Coast Ranges away from direct coastal influence. California's mightiest oak, often reaching 70 ft. or taller, with equal or greater spread. Massive trunk and limbs with thick, distinctly checked gray bark. Straight and erect during its first several decades of growth; becomes more spreading with age. Limbs are often picturesquely twisted; long, drooping outer branches sometimes sweep ground. Deeply cut, round-lobed leaves are 3–4 in. long and 2–3 in. wide; dark green above, paler beneath. Shiny, 1½–2½-in. acorns are conical, enclosed by one-third in warty, bowl-shaped cap.

Possibly the largest North American oak, this species tolerates high heat and moderate alkalinity in its native range. In deep soils where it can tap groundwater, it can grow 2½–3 ft. a year. Magnificent tree for shading a big outdoor living area, though a constant rain of debris will create a nuisance on any nearby planting areas or paved surfaces. This is the tree that gives much of California's Central Valley the look of a giant park. Immune to sudden oak death.

Q. macrocarpa. BUR OAK, MOSSYCUP OAK. Deciduous tree. Zones A2, A3; 1–11, 14–23. Native to eastern North America. Rugged-looking tree to 60–75 ft. tall and about half that wide in youth, equally wide in maturity. Flaky grayish brown bark with flattened, narrow ridges. Leaves are 8–10 in. long, broad at tip, tapered at base, with five to seven deeply cut, rounded lobes; glossy green above, whitish beneath, turning yellow and brown in autumn. Round or egg-shaped, 1–1½-in. acorns are almost completely covered by fringed, mossy-looking cap. Similar to

Q. bicolor but faster growing and more tolerant of adverse conditions.

Q. muehlenbergii. CHINQUAPIN OAK, YELLOW CHESTNUT OAK. Deciduous tree. Zones 2–12, 14–17. Native to central and eastern U.S. To 40–50 ft. tall, 50–60 ft. wide, with wide-spreading, rounded crown. Flaking whitish or gray bark. Deeply toothed, lance-shaped leaves are shiny green above, whitish and furry below. Foliage turns golden late in fall but hangs on late. Egg-shaped, edible, ½–1-in. acorns are enclosed by one-fourth to one-half in warty cap. Desirable street or shade tree for large area. Long-lived but difficult to transplant and establish. Fairly tolerant of alkaline soils.

Q. myrsinifolia. JAPANESE LIVE OAK. Evergreen tree or shrub. Zones 4–7, 14–24. Native to southern China, Japan, and Laos; almost extinct in the wild. Reaches 30–50-ft. tall in its native range, but in cultivation it usually grows as a large, round-headed shrub to 20–30 ft. high and as wide (or nearly so). Lance-shaped, glossy dark green leaves 2½–4 in. long, toothed toward tip. Purplish red new foliage. Acorns are ¾ in. long, cylindrical with abrupt point, half enclosed in unusual, shallow cap marked with seven to nine concentric rings. Not easily recognized as an oak unless seen with its acorns—unlike most of its relatives, it is wispy and graceful rather than sturdy.

Q. palustris. PIN OAK, SWAMP OAK. Deciduous tree. Zones 2–10, 14–24. Native to eastern U.S. Moderate to fairly rapid growth to 50–80 ft. tall, 30–40 ft. wide. Brownish gray bark with shallow ridges and furrows. Pyramidal in youth, with lower branches sweeping downward. If you remove those branches to gain walking space, the limbs above will simply bend into the same position—so wait to remove lower limbs until tree is mature and has formed an open, rounded top. Glossy dark green leaves are deeply cut into bristle-pointed lobes; in brisk fall weather, leaves turn yellow, red, and finally russet brown. Much dead foliage hangs on in winter.

Nearly round acorns reach ¾ in. diameter, are enclosed by about a third in saucer-shaped, fuzzy cap. Less tolerant of dry conditions than most oaks. Develops chlorosis in alkaline soils. Unlike most native Western oaks, it is a fine tree for growing in lawns.

Q. phellos. WILLOW OAK. Deciduous tree. Zones 2–4, 6–16, 18–21. Native to southeastern U.S. To 50–90 ft. tall, 30–50 ft. wide. Pyramidal in youth, spreading wider with age. Smooth gray bark. Leaves look more like those of willow (*Salix*) than those of typical oak— 2½–5 in. long, ⅓–1 in. wide, smooth edged. Foliage turns yellowish before falling; in warmer regions, dead leaves may hang on through winter. Has the most delicate foliage pattern of all the oaks. Spherical, ½-in.-wide acorns with a shallow cap enclosing only the end of the nut.

Q. polymorpha. MONTERREY OAK, MEXICAN WHITE OAK. Semievergreen tree. Zones 2, 3, 6–12, 18–21. Native from west Texas to Central America. Grows rapidly to 80 ft. tall and 60 ft. wide, its young, rather upright profile spreading in age. Scaly bark is gray-brown. Immature leaves open maroon, maturing to blue-green; to 5 in. long, half as wide, lightly toothed at the ends. Acorns 1 in. long, half covered by cap.

Q. robur. ENGLISH OAK. Deciduous tree. Zones A2, A3; 1–12, 14–21. Native to Europe. Fairly fast grower to 50–60 ft. tall, 30 ft. wide, with rather short trunk and very wide, open head. Dark green leaves have three to seven pairs of rounded lobes. Leaves hold until late fall without much color change. Acorns to 1½ in. long, varying in shape from oval to oblong, coming to an abrupt point; covered by up to one-third in velvety, bowl-shaped cap. 'Argenteamarginata' has white-edged leaves, grows slowly to 20–30 ft.; narrow in youth. 'Clemons', a hybrid with *Q. macrocarpa*, grows about 50 ft. tall, 40 ft. wide; has a little more cold tolerance than pure English oak. 'Concordia' grows about 25 ft. tall and wide, with golden foliage. 'Kindred Spirit', a hybrid between columnar English oak

and *Q. bicolor*, grows 35 ft. tall, 6 ft. wide, with good disease resistance and tolerance to wet soil and drought. 'Rosehill'— part English oak, part unknown species—grows 40 ft. tall, 20 ft. wide, with glossy green, mildew-resistant foliage. 'Skyrocket' grows about 45 ft. tall and 15 ft. wide, and holds its shape well. 'Skymaster' becomes a broad pyramid 50 ft. tall and half as wide. 'Crimson Spire', a hybrid with white oak (*Q. alba*), is another narrowly upright grower (45 ft. tall, 15 ft. wide); it has reddish fall color and good mildew resistance.

Q. r. fastigiata, upright English oak, is columnar like Lombardy poplar (*Populus nigra* 'Italica') when young, growing 50 ft. tall and 15 ft. wide, then maturing to a broad, pyramidal shape. 'Regal Prince', similar in height but slightly wider, is a cross between *Q. r. fastigiata* and an oak from the southeastern U.S.; it's adaptable and resistant to mildew.

Q. rubra. RED OAK, NORTHERN RED OAK. Deciduous tree. Zones 1–10, 14–21. Native to eastern North America. Fast growth to 60–75 ft. tall, 50 ft. wide, with spreading branches and rounded canopy. Bark becomes quite dark and fissured with age. Leaves 5–8 in. long, 4–6 in. wide, with three to seven pairs of sharp-pointed lobes. New leaves and leafstalks are red or bright yellow in spring, dark green in summer, turning dark red, ruddy brown, or orange in fall. Acorns are ¾–1 in. long, shaped like a toy top, enclosed by one-third in shallow cap; often profuse, creating litter on pavement. Needs fertile soil and regular moisture. High-branching habit and reasonably open shade make it a good tree for big lawns, parks, and broad avenues. Deep roots make it good to garden under. Known host of sudden oak death (see page 547).

Q. shumardii. SHUMARD RED OAK. Deciduous tree. Zones 2–10, 14–17. Native to eastern U.S. Similar to *Q. coccinea* but slightly less hardy. Leaves are bright yellow in spring, dark green in summer, yellow to red in autumn. Acorns to 1¼ in. long are egg-shaped, coming to an abrupt point; very

shallow cap. Tolerates a wide range of soils.

Q. suber. CORK OAK. Evergreen. Zones 5–7 (with occasional winter damage), 8–16, 18–24. Native to the western Mediterranean and North Africa. To 30–60 ft. tall and wide. Trunk and main limbs covered with handsome, thick, corky bark (the cork of commerce). Toothed, oval leaves are shiny dark green above, gray beneath. Egg-shaped acorns are ¾–1½ in. long, covered by up to one-half in bowl-shaped cap. Light-textured foliage contrasts with massive, fissured trunk. Needs good drainage. Tolerant of all but heavy, wet, or highly alkaline soils. One of the best oaks for desert. Value as street or park tree diminishes when children find out how easy it is to carve its bark.

Q. texana (Q. nuttallii). TEXAS OAK, SPANISH OAK. Deciduous tree or shrub. Zones 3, 6–12, 18–22. Native in far-western Kentucky to the Gulf Coast, east Texas to Alabama. To 35 ft. tall and as wide or wider, with trunk branching almost from the base. Bark is light brown and scaly when young, becoming dark gray, scaled, and fissured at maturity. Leaves grow to 5½ in. long, with three to seven sharply pointed, bristle-tipped lobes. Foliage is densely hairy and reddish when new, matures to yellow-green, turns bright

scarlet in fall. Egg-shaped, ¾-in. acorns with a sharp tip, one-third enclosed in reddish, densely felted cap. Similar to *Q. shumardii* and *Q. palustris*, but better adapted in warmer, milder parts of range. Takes alkaline soil. 'Charisma' (sold as *Q. nuttallii* 'Charisma') grows 60 ft. tall and 50 ft. wide, with chocolate maroon new foliage that turns green in summer, red in autumn; tolerates poorly drained soil. Takes more cold than the species (to Zone 2).

Q. tomentella. ISLAND OAK. Evergreen tree. Zones 7–9, 14–17, 19–24. Native to California's Channel Islands. To 25–40 ft. tall and wide (occasionally to 60 ft. tall in cultivation). Slightly toothed leaves are dark green above, with fine grayish or tan hairs beneath. Egg-shaped, 1–1½-in. acorns bulge from shallow, woolly cap. Endures seacoast conditions. Needs deep soaking every 2 to 3 weeks outside fog belt. Symmetrical when well grown; some consider it the handsomest of California's evergreen oaks.

Q. turbinella. DESERT SCRUB OAK, SHRUB LIVE OAK. Evergreen shrub. Zones 2–24. Native to piñon-juniper belt in desert mountains from Southern California and Baja California east to Colorado, western Texas, adjacent Mexico. To 10 ft. tall and as wide, with bushy, stiffly branched form; can be trained as a small tree. Gray,

Growing an Oak from an Acorn

Select a fallen acorn that is shiny, plump, and free of worm holes; remove cap. To protect the buried acorn from birds, squirrels, and other creatures, dig the planting hole 6 in. deep, 6 in. wide; then roll a 1½-ft.-wide length of aluminum screening into a 6-in.-diameter cylinder and insert one end of it into the hole. Refill the screen-lined hole with unamended soil. Plant the acorn sideways and cover it with 1 in. of soil (if a white root has already sprouted, point it downward). Tie screen closed at top. Or plant several acorns in one area and thin to the best seedling.

The first summer, give moderate water—just enough to keep soil moist for good root growth. After the first summer, remove the screen to allow the young oak to grow freely.

Planting Beneath Oak Trees

Western native oaks need dry summers. If you plant shade-loving bedding plants that need summer water beneath them, you'll also supply the warm, moist soil that's congenial to oak root fungus, which can enter the oak roots and kill the tree slowly over many years. The most at-risk species include coast live oak, canyon live oak, Oregon white oak, valley oak, and California black oak. Use drought-tolerant plants beneath these trees. *Arctostaphylos uva-ursi*, ceanothus (where light allows), daffodils, *Gaura lindheimeri*, *Iris douglasiana*, and *Salvia spathacea* are good choices. For more information, see pages 72–73.

smooth mature bark. Hollylike, oval, dull yellowish green leaves with sharp, spine-tipped teeth. Foliage hangs on through winter, drops in spring when replaced by new leaves. Acorns to 1¼ in. long vary in shape but often look like a toy top; they are enclosed by one-fourth to one-half in a bowl-shaped cap with short, papery scales. Tough background plant or hedge for dry, cold-winter inland areas; also does well in the temperate maritime climate of the Pacific Northwest.

Q. vacciniifolia. HUCKLE-BERRY OAK. Evergreen shrub. Zones 1–7, 14–23. Native to mountains of Northern California and southern Oregon. Grows to 2–5 ft. tall and at least twice as wide, with sprawling branches. Oblong to egg-shaped, smooth-margined leaves, pointed or round at the tip; shiny gray-green above, gray with sparse golden hairs below. Round to oval acorns to ½ in. long, with shallow cap covered in thin, hairy scales. Useful in wild gardens and as an informal hedge.

Q. velutina. NORTHERN BLACK OAK. Deciduous tree. Zones 2–12, 14–24. Native in Maine to Florida, east to Texas. Grows 50 ft. tall, 45 ft. wide, with good tolerance to a wide range of soils. Oblong, lobed, glossy dark green leaves can reach 10 in. long, have toothed lobes, develop rusty red fall color. Fringed acorn cup covers about half the nut. Furrowed, tannin-rich, blackish mature bark hides inner bark that produces bright yellow dye.

Q. virginiana. SOUTHERN LIVE OAK. Evergreen tree; partly or wholly deciduous in cold-winter regions. Zones 4–24. Native to coastal plains of southeastern U.S. Grows at a moderate to fast rate, eventually reaching 40–80 ft. tall, with a heavy-limbed crown spreading twice as wide. Long-lived; with age, bark becomes very dark and checked. Smooth-edged, narrowly oval leaves are shiny dark green above and whitish beneath. Oval acorns to 1 in. long, with sharp spine at tip; enclosed by one-fourth in bowl-shaped cap with hairy scales. Best in deep, rich, moist soil. In hot interior climates, it's the most attractive of all evergreen oaks. Best oak for lawn planting in low desert; fast-growing variety 'Heritage' is recommended for that region. For *Q. v. fusiformis*, see *Q. fusiformis*.

Q. wislizenii. INTERIOR LIVE OAK. Evergreen tree. Zones 7–9, 14–16, 18–21. Native to the Sierra foothills, eastern side of Coast Ranges, interior valleys from southern Oregon to Southern California. To 30–75 ft. tall, often broader than high, with dense, rounded canopy. Elliptical glossy green leaves have smooth or spiny edges and abruptly pointed tip. Slender, conical, sharp-pointed, ¾–1½-in. acorns are enclosed by one-fourth to one-half in a flat-scaled cap. Handsome tree for parks and big lawns. Young plants are sparse and angular, offering little hint of their ultimate beauty.

Quince, Fruiting
Rosaceae
DECIDUOUS TREE

🖋 **ZONES 2–24**

☀ **FULL SUN**

🌢🌢 **MODERATE TO REGULAR WATER**

'Pineapple' quinces

Native to western Asia, quince trees grow slowly to 10–25 ft. tall and wide, with gnarled, twisted branches that look attractive when leafless. Oval, 2–4-in. leaves are dark green above, whitish beneath; turn yellow in autumn. White or pale pink, 2-in. flowers are followed by 3–4-in., round to pear-shaped, deliciously fragrant yellow fruit. Typically too tart for fresh eating, the fruit is used for jams, jellies, or candy, or combined with other fruits in pies. Botanically, this is *Cydonia oblonga*; for the thorny shrubs grown mainly for flowers, see *Chaenomeles*.

These pear relatives need little winter chill to be productive and are self-pollinating.

'**Apple**' ('**Orange**'). This variety is an old favorite. Round fruit with tender orange-yellow flesh.

'**Aromatnaya**'. Round; sweet yellow flesh that tastes like pineapple. This variety can be thinly sliced and eaten fresh.

'**Cooke's Jumbo**'. Pear-shaped fruit with white flesh. Can be nearly twice the size of other quinces.

'**Pineapple**'. Roundish, with tender white flesh that tastes like pineapple.

'**Smyrna**'. Round to oblong fruit with white flesh; strongly aromatic.

Needs good drainage. Plant bare-root stock when available in late winter or spring, or plant container-grown stock anytime except in the hottest days of summer. Feed in late winter and early summer with 5-10-10 fertilizer; avoid high-nitrogen fertilizer, which promotes succulent growth susceptible to fireblight. Fruits on new growth; little pruning is required beyond initial shaping and periodic thinning to keep plant's center open to sunlight. Avoid deep cultivation near trunk, which can cause shallow roots to sucker.

R

Radish
Brassicaceae
ANNUAL

🖋 **ALL ZONES**

☀◑ **LIGHT SHADE IN HOTTEST CLIMATES**

🌢 **REGULAR WATER**

'Cherry Belle' radish

Colorful, crunchy, and very fast growing, radishes add zip to salads. Probably Mediterranean natives, they've been in that cuisine for 4,000 years, in China for 2,000 years, and in Japan for more than a millennium.

The most familiar radishes are short, round, red or red-and-white types like 'Cherry Belle', 'Cherriette', and 'Scarlet

White-tipped'. You can also get round radishes in white or pink; 'Easter Egg II' produces a mixture of white, pink, red, and purple. 'French Breakfast' and 'Red Flame' are sweet, long, narrow, white-tipped types known as breakfast radishes. Other long radishes such as white 'Icicle' have a more typical radish flavor, but there are also novelties like 'Misato Rose Flesh', which is green outside and pink inside. Daikon radishes are long, white radishes, with a mildly nippy to hot flavor.

CARE

Radishes need rich, evenly moist soil. Dig in well-aged manure a month before sowing; or, 10 days after planting, apply either liquid or granular fertilizer. In early spring, sow seeds ½ in. deep and 1 in. apart in rows 1–1½ ft. apart. Replant weekly until warm weather approaches (plants become bitter and go to seed when temperatures rise). In mild-winter climates, you can also sow at intervals in fall and winter. As soon as tops emerge, pull (and eat) every other plant. Radishes are best as soon as they reach full size; they become pithy and too pungent if left unharvested too long. You can pull them for the table as early as 3 weeks after sowing seeds (the slowest kinds take 2 months to reach table-ready size).

If cabbage worm or cabbage root maggot causes trouble, cover radishes with a fine mesh row cover. It lets in light and water but keeps out insects.

For a simple, elegant appetizer, start by refrigerating radishes in ice water for an hour. Then slice them thinly and top each slice with a pat of butter. Sprinkle with sea salt and serve with white wine.

Ranunculus
Ranunculaceae
PERENNIALS

⚘ **ZONES VARY BY SPECIES**

☼ ◐ ● **EXPOSURE NEEDS VARY BY SPECIES**

💧 **REGULAR WATER**

Ranunculus asiaticus

Several members of this very large genus are sold occasionally by specialty growers, but only the two listed here are common in gardens.

R. asiaticus. PERSIAN RANUNCULUS. All zones; see below. Native to Asia Minor. Tuberous-rooted plant to 2 ft. high and wide, with fresh green, almost fernlike leaves. In spring, each flowering stalk bears one to four 3–5-in.-wide, semidouble to fully double blossoms. Flowers come in white, cream, and many shades of yellow, orange, red, and pink. Popular Tecolote Giant strain is available in single colors, mixes, and picotees. Good in the ground or in pots.

Tuberous roots are hardy to 10°F (–12°C); in Zones 4–9, 12–24, plant in fall for bloom in winter, early spring. Beyond hardiness range, plant in spring as soon as ground is workable; or start roots indoors 4 to 6 weeks before the usual last-frost date. Nurseries sell tuberous roots of various sizes; all produce equally large blossoms, but bigger roots yield more flowers.

Grow in full sun, in organically enriched, well-drained soil. Set roots with prongs down, 2 in. deep and 6–8 in. apart. Water thoroughly, then withhold water until leaves emerge.

Birds are fond of ranunculus shoots; protect with netting or wire. Remove faded flowers to encourage more bloom.

When flowering tapers off and leaves start to yellow, stop watering and let foliage die back. Where tuberous roots are hardy in the ground, they can be left undisturbed—as long as soil can be kept dry during summer. However, most gardeners in the West dig plants when foliage turns yellow, cut off the tops, let roots dry for a week or two, and store them in a cool, dry place until planting time.

R. repens pleniflorus. CREEPING BUTTERCUP. Zones 1–10, 14–24. From Eurasia; naturalized in North America. Vigorous plant with thick, fibrous roots and runners that root at the joints. Forms lush, glossy green mat to 1 ft. high, 6 ft. wide; leaves are roundish, deeply cut into three toothedged, 2-in.-long leaflets. Fully double, 1-in., button-shaped bright yellow flowers are held above foliage on 1–2-ft. stems in spring. Can be invasive in constantly moist soil. Attractive deciduous groundcover for full sun to deep shade.

Raoulia australis
Asteraceae
PERENNIAL

⚘ **ZONES 2B–9, 14–24**

☼ **FULL SUN**

💧 **MODERATE WATER**

Raoulia australis

Tiny gray leaves form a very tight carpet to ½ in. high, 1 ft. wide; stems are hidden by the leaves. Inconspicuous pale yellow flowers in spring. Needs sandy soil, perfect drainage. Good in rock gardens. From New Zealand. Hybrid *R.* × 'Greenstone' grows 1 in. high, 3 ft. wide, with silvery green leaves.

Raspberry
Rosaceae
DECIDUOUS SHRUBS

⚘ **ZONES A1–A3; 1–24; BEST IN 3–6, 15–17**

☼ **FULL SUN**

💧 **REGULAR WATER**

Red raspberries

Close relatives of blackberries, raspberries are grown for their luscious fruit. Red and yellow raspberries are derived from *Rubus idaeus*, native to North America, Europe, and Asia. Black raspberries are forms of *R. occidentalis*, from eastern and central North America, while purple raspberries are hybrids of red and black kinds. Mysore raspberry, *R. niveus*, is sometimes grown in Hawaii (fruit is black, but it's cultivated like a red raspberry). But beware: it can become a troublesome weed, choking out native vegetation. For ornamental raspberries, see *Rubus*.

Raspberries grow from perennial roots that produce thorny biennial stems called canes. Generally, raspberry canes grow full size the first year, bear fruit the second. Everbearing (or fallbearing) red and yellow varieties produce two crops on the same canes—one in fall of the first year, the second in summer of the next year. Canes die after fruiting in the second year.

For raspberry fruit to reach perfection, plants need winter chill and a lingering springtime with slowly warming temperatures. In warmer zones outside best raspberry climates, satisfactory production may come from plants grown in light shade, mulched heavily to keep soil cool. See "How to Grow Raspberries," page 552.

R

»

How to Grow Raspberries

Good drainage is essential; where garden soil is heavy, plant in raised beds. Rich, slightly acid soil is ideal. Don't plant where tomatoes, potatoes, peppers, or eggplant have recently grown; they may have tainted the soil with verticillium wilt. Don't accept divisions of raspberry plants from friends: they often have diseases that reduce production. Instead, buy certified disease-free plants from nurseries.

PLANTING Set out bare-root stock during the dormant season, with the point where roots emerge from the cane buried 1–2 in. under the soil surface. Set red and yellow raspberries 2½–3 ft. apart, in rows spaced 6–10 ft. apart. Set black and purple raspberries 3–4 ft. apart, in rows spaced 8–10 ft. apart. Cut back the cane that rises from the root, leaving 6 in. to serve as a marker. Some growers have recently been selling small tissue-cultured raspberries in pots in spring and summer. Plant these at the same level as the soil in the pot, and water frequently the first summer.

Mulch all raspberry plantings to discourage weeds and keep soil moist.

WATERING & FEEDING Water need is greatest during flowering and fruiting. Feed at bloom time.

PRUNING & TRAINING Summer-bearing red and yellow varieties should produce three to five canes the first year. Tie these to a trellis or confine them in a hedgerow contained by pairs of parallel wires strung at 3 ft. and 5 ft. aboveground along either side. Dig or pull out any canes that grow more than 1 ft. away from trellis or outside hedgerow. In late dormant season, cut canes on trellis to 5–5½ ft. high, those in hedgerow to 4 ft. When growth recommences, new canes will appear all around parent plant and between

rows. After the original canes bear fruit, cut them to the ground. Then select the best 5 to 12 new canes and train these; they will bear next summer. Cut remaining new canes to the ground.

Everbearing red and yellow varieties fruit the first autumn on the top third of each cane, then again the second summer on the lower two-thirds of each cane. Cut off the upper portion of each cane after it has borne fruit; cut out the cane entirely after the second harvest. Or follow the example of growers who cut everbearing canes to the ground yearly in fall after fruiting has finished (wait until late dormant season in cold-winter regions). You'll sacrifice one of the annual crops but get an extended harvest from late summer into fall. Use a power mower in a large berry patch.

To train black and purple raspberries, in the first summer force branching by heading back new canes of black varieties to 2 ft., of purple varieties to 2½ ft. If you prefer trellising, cut black varieties to 2–2½ ft., purple ones to 2½–3 ft. In late dormant season, remove all weak or broken canes. Leave six to eight canes in a hill or spaced 6–8 in. apart in a row. Shorten the side branches to 8–10 in. for black raspberries, 12–14 in. for purple types. The side branches will bear fruit in summer. After harvest, cut to the ground all canes that have fruited and cut back all new canes as described for first summer's growth.

CHALLENGES Raspberries are susceptible to anthracnose and other fungal diseases. The best preventatives are optimal growing conditions (full sun, good air circulation, weed control) and good care.

If borers attack, prune out and destroy damaged canes below entry points, which are pinhead-size holes at or near ground level.

CLOCKWISE FROM TOP: 'Fallgold' yellow raspberries; red raspberries; black raspberries

Red and yellow raspberries are produced on erect plants with long, straight canes; they can be grown as freestanding shrubs and staked, but they are tidier and easier to manage if trained on a trellis or confined to a hedgerow. Yield is about 30 lbs. per 10-ft. row (15–20 lbs. for everbearing kinds).

Black and purple raspberries are produced on clump-forming plants with arching canes. No support is needed. Yield is about 10 lbs. per 10-ft. row.

Red and yellow varieties.
Red varieties are the most common; yellow types are mutations of red raspberries. Expected life is about 15 years.

'Anne'. Everbearing. Large, apricot gold berries with excellent, sweet flavor.

'Autumn Bliss'. Everbearing. Very large red berries with fine flavor. Resists root rot.

'Bababerry'. Everbearing. Large, firm red berries. Needs little winter chill; stands heat

well. Best in hot-summer climates.

'Boyne'. Summer-bearing. Very hardy red raspberry bred in Manitoba. Medium-size fruit. Early ripening. Subject to anthracnose.

'Canby'. Summer-bearing. Large bright red berries. Thornless.

'Caroline'. Everbearing. Large, red berries with excellent flavor and high levels of nutrients and antioxidants.

'Cascade Delight'. Summer-bearing. Long season of large red berries with great flavor. Heavy-bearing and resistant to root rot.

'Chilcotin'. Summer-bearing. Very large, firm red berries with excellent flavor. Long harvest season.

'Chilliwack'. Summer-bearing. Very large red berries with fine flavor. Somewhat resistant to root rot.

'Dinkum'. Everbearing. Medium-size, firm red fruit with good flavor.

'Fallgold'. Everbearing. Large yellow fruit with good flavor.

'Fallred'. Everbearing. Large, firm red fruit with outstanding flavor.

R

'Heritage'. Everbearing. The small red berries are tasty but a bit dry.

'Indian Summer'. Everbearing. Small crops of large, tasty red berries. Fall crop is often larger.

'Killarny'. Summer-bearing. Early harvest of firm, large berries. Very hardy.

'Kiska'. Summer-bearing. Small red berries with good flavor. Hardy; developed for Alaska.

'Latham'. Summer-bearing. Older, very hardy; for coldest regions. Mildews in humid summers. Late. Large red berries are often crumbly.

'Meeker'. Summer-bearing. Large, firm bright red berries on long, willowy branches.

'Newburgh'. Summer-bearing. Large light red berries. Late-ripening variety. Takes heavy soil fairly well.

'September'. Everbearing. Small to medium-size red berries of good flavor. Fall crop is heavier.

'Summit'. Everbearing. Large red berries with good flavor. Very productive. Resistant to root rot.

'Tulameen'. Summer-bearing. Very large, firm red berries with excellent flavor. Long harvest season. Must have well-drained soil.

'Willamette'. Summer-bearing. Large, firm dark red berries that hold color and shape well.

Black and purple varieties. Black raspberries (also called blackcap raspberries) have blue-black fruit that is firmer and seedier than that of red and yellow types, and it has a more pronounced flavor. Expected life is 4 to 8 years. Purple raspberries are crosses between black and red kinds, and while they grow more like black raspberries, the fruit shares characteristics of both. They are best cooked in pies and jams.

'Brandywine'. Large purple berries. Tart; good for jams and jellies. Ripens late.

'Cumberland'. Large black berries. Old, heavy-bearing variety.

'Jewel'. Large black berries. Vigorous, disease-resistant plant.

'Munger'. Medium-size black berries. Most popular commercial black-fruited variety.

'Royalty'. Large red berries turn purple when ripe. Sweet and fragrant fruit, vigorous plant.

Ratibida
Asteraceae
PERENNIALS

✂	**ALL ZONES**
☀	**FULL SUN**
💧	**MODERATE WATER**

Ratibida columnifera

Something like bushy black-eyed Susans (*Rudbeckia*), these branched, roughly hairy plants have deeply cut leaves and a long season of summer flowers. Use in casual, natural-looking borders with grasses and other minimum-care perennials.

R. columnifera. MEXICAN HAT. From the Great Plains. Grows to 2½ ft. high and 1 ft. wide. Flowers have wide, drooping, yellow or brownish purple rays and a tall, columnar brown cone—like a sombrero with a drooping brim. *R. c. pulcherrima* 'Red Midget' grows about 18 in. high and wide.

R. pinnata. PRAIRIE or YELLOW CONEFLOWER. Native to central North America. To 4 ft. tall, 1½ ft. wide, with long, slim yellow rays and a nearly globular brown cone.

Ratibida blooms beautifully along roadsides, so you know it's easy in almost any well-drained soil.

FOR MORE ON PALMS, SEE "MEET THE PALMS," PAGE 471.

Exotic Imports

Traveler's palm comes from Madagascar, an island nation of such great size and biodiversity, it's sometimes called "the eighth continent." Among other Madagascar natives found in this book are the striking Bismarck palm (*Bismarckia nobilis*) and two graceful feather palms (*Dypsis*). Royal poinciana (*Delonix regia*) and *Dombeya* species are spectacular flowering trees, and Madagascar jasmine vine (*Stephanotis floribunda*) is prized for its fragrant snow-white blooms. Low-growing Madagascar periwinkle (*Catharanthus roseus*) flowers reliably in even the hottest zones.

Ravenala madagascariensis
TRAVELER'S TREE, TRAVELER'S PALM
Strelitziaceae
EVERGREEN TREE

✂	**ZONES 24; H2**
☀	**FULL SUN**
💧	**REGULAR WATER**

Ravenala madagascariensis

This spectacular Madagascar native grows to 30–40 ft. tall, 25–30 ft. wide, with large, banana-like leaves held in the shape of a gigantic fan atop an unbranched trunk. Protect from strong winds, which will shred the leaves. Small plants have some shade tolerance, can be used as potted specimens. Jungle travelers can find rainwater in *Ravenala*'s flower bracts and leaf sheaths—thus the common name.

Rehmannia elata
CHINESE FOXGLOVE
Plantaginaceae
PERENNIAL

✂	**ZONES 5–10, 12–24**
☀ ☀ ●	**FULL SUN IN COOLER CLIMATES ONLY**
💧	**REGULAR WATER**

Rehmannia elata

Resembling a big foxglove (*Digitalis*), this Chinese native grows in clumps 3 ft. high, 1½–2 ft. wide. Coarse, deeply toothed leaves (evergreen in mild climates) send up stalks of tubular, 3-in. rosy purple flowers with yellow throats dotted red. There is also a fine, cream-throated white form that must be grown from cuttings or divisions. Where winters are mild, blooms from midspring well into fall; in colder climates, bloom comes in summer and fall. This perennial spreads by its roots to form colonies. Long-lasting cut flower. Easy to grow from seed, root cuttings, or divisions; give it rich soil.

R

Reinwardtia indica
(R. trigyna)
YELLOW FLAX
Linaceae
SHRUBBY PERENNIAL

🗡 **ZONES 8–10, 12–24; H1, H2**

☼ ☽ **FULL SUN OR PARTIAL SHADE**

◖ ◗ **MODERATE TO REGULAR WATER**

Reinwardtia indica

A profusion of 2-in. yellow, flax-like flowers cover this 3-ft. shrub for weeks, with new ones opening daily (and each bloom lasts just a day). In mild-winter regions, flowers appear in late fall and early winter; in colder areas, bloom comes in summer. Elliptical, evergreen leaves are deep green or grayish green, 1–3 in. long.

Native to the mountains from Pakistan to China, these thrive in fertile, well-drained soil. Pinch young plants to encourage branching, and cut back mature plants after bloom to keep them compact.

Aromatic Annuals

Mignonette's flowers are scented like raspberry and vanilla. Mass plants on either side of a path to create a fragrant corridor, or grow them in pots on a balcony to perfume the incoming breeze.

Other highly fragrant annuals (and a few perennials usually grown as annuals) include stock (*Matthiola*), some pinks and carnations (*Dianthus*), sweet pea (*Lathyrus odoratus*), flowering tobacco (*Nicotiana*), four o'clock (*Mirabilis jalapa*), sweet alyssum (*Lobularia maritima*), annual phlox (*Phlox drummondii*), and several marigolds (*Tagetes*).

Reseda odorata
MIGNONETTE
Resedaceae
ANNUAL

🗡 **ALL ZONES**

☼ ☽ **PARTIAL SHADE IN HOTTEST CLIMATES**

◗ **REGULAR WATER**

Reseda odorata

To 1½ ft. tall and wide, this rather sprawling North African plant has light green leaves and small, spicy-sweet flowers. The blossoms are greenish or white with a coppery or yellow tinge, carried in dense spikes that become loose and open with age. Flowers dry up quickly in hot weather.

Sow seeds in early spring (or in late fall or winter, in mildest climates). For longest bloom, deadhead and make successive sowings. Does best in rich soil. Plant in masses to get the full effect of the perfume. Strains with longer flower spikes and brighter colors are sold, but they are less fragrant.

Rhamnus
Rhamnaceae
EVERGREEN SHRUBS OR TREES

🗡 **ZONES VARY BY SPECIES**

☼ ☽ ● **EXPOSURE NEEDS VARY BY SPECIES**

◖ ◗ ● **WATER NEEDS VARY BY SPECIES**

🦋 **ATTRACT BIRDS, BUTTERFLIES**

Rhamnus alaternus

Form and foliage make these excel as background plantings, especially since clusters of small flowers are rather inconspicuous. Berries (typically pea size) are enjoyed by birds; volunteer seedlings may be a nuisance.

R. alaternus. ITALIAN BUCKTHORN. Evergreen shrub or small tree. Zones 4–24. Native to Mediterranean region. Fast, dense growth 10–20 ft. tall and wide. Oval, shiny bright green leaves; small black berries. Easily trained as single- or multitrunked tree. Takes well to shearing and shaping. Tolerates heat; does well with little or no water but also accepts regular watering. Full sun or partial shade. 'John Edwards' is a vigorous, fast-growing, long-lived, cutting-grown variety to 15–18 ft. tall and 6–10 ft. wide. Compact 'Variegata' ('Argenteovariegata') grows to 6–8 ft. tall and equally wide, has cream-edged foliage. If branches with plain green leaves appear, cut them out or they'll quickly take over.

R. californica. See *Frangula californica*.

R. crocea. REDBERRY. Evergreen shrub. Zones 7, 14–24. Native to Coast Ranges from Northern California into Baja California. To 2–3 ft. high, 3–6 ft. wide, with many stiff branches,

often spiny at tips. Roundish leaves frequently have finely toothed edges; glossy dark to pale green above, golden or brownish beneath. Small bright red fruit. Takes full sun or partial shade in its native territory; does best with some shade in hotter inland areas. Little water.

R. frangula. See *Frangula alnus*.

R. ilicifolia (R. crocea ilicifolia). HOLLYLEAF REDBERRY. Evergreen shrub. Zones 7–10, 14–23. Native to Coast Ranges and Sierra Nevada foothills, mountains of Southern California, Arizona, Baja California. Bulky shrub or shrubby tree to a possible 15 ft. tall, nearly as wide. Roundish, spiny-toothed leaves. Takes heat, drought; makes a good informal screen. Full sun or partial shade. No irrigation needed.

R. purshiana. See *Frangula purshiana*.

Rhaphiolepis
Rosaceae
EVERGREEN SHRUBS

🗡 **ZONES 8–10, 12–24; H1, H2; WORTH THE RISK IN ZONES 4–7**

☼ ☽ **FULL SUN OR LIGHT SHADE**

◖ ◗ ● **LITTLE TO REGULAR WATER**

Rhaphiolepis indica 'Dancer'

Glossy, leathery leaves and dense, compact growth make these especially attractive background plants and informal hedges. They produce profuse white to nearly red flowers from late fall or midwinter to late spring. Dark blue fruit follows but isn't especially showy. New growth is often bronze and reddish.

Most are low growers. The taller kinds rarely reach more

than 5–6 ft., and pruning can keep them at 3 ft. almost indefinitely. For compact plants, pinch branch tips annually after flowering. For a more open structure, let plants grow naturally and thin out branches occasionally. Plants in partial shade are less compact and produce fewer flowers than those in full sun. Good seacoast plants; tolerate salt drift. Little bothered by pests, though aphids occasionally attack them. Fireblight and a fungal leaf spot (in cool, wet weather) are possible. In hot-summer regions, plants burn in reflected heat; they need sheltering shade in low desert.

R. × delacourii. Pink-flowered hybrid of *R. indica* and *R. umbellata*. To 6 ft. tall, 8 ft. wide. Small pink flowers in upright clusters. The following have excellent disease resistance: 'Georgia Petite' grows 2½ ft. high, 3½ ft. wide, with pink buds opening to white flowers; 'Snowcap' grows 4 ft. tall and wide. Pink buds open to pale pink flowers that fade to white; foliage turns burgundy-red in winter.

R. indica. INDIAN HAWTHORN. Native to China. To 4–5 ft. tall and 5–6 ft. wide, with pointed leaves and ½-in. flowers in white tinged with pink. Species is rare in gardens, but its varieties are widespread. They differ mainly in flower color and in plant size and form; there is variation even within a variety. Flower color is especially inconsistent: in warmer climates and exposures, blossoms are usually lighter; and in general, blooms are paler in fall than in spring. In the Northwest, subject to a leaf spot fungus, which defoliates the plants. Varieties include the following.

'Ballerina'. To 2 ft. high, 4 ft. wide. Deep rosy pink flowers. Leaves take on a reddish tinge in winter.

'Clara'. To 3–5 ft. tall and wide. White flowers. Red new growth.

For best results, grow these shrubs in moderately fertile, well-drained soil in a spot sheltered from winds.

Clumping Palms

When most people think of palms, they envision tall, single-trunked trees with a tuft of big, leafy stems at the top (and perhaps a coconut or two). But several palms—including the two described on this page—don't fit that description. Instead, they grow naturally into wide, shrubby clumps.

Other clumping palms in this book are clustered fishtail palm (*Caryota mitis*); *Chamaedorea cataractarum*, *C. costaricana*, and *C. seifrizii*; cane palm (*Dypsis lutescens*); Mediterranean fan palm (*Chamaerops humilis*); and *Sabal minor*.

'Dancer'. Reaches 4 ft. tall, 5 ft. wide. Pure pink flowers.

'Eleanor Taber'. Grows 4 ft. tall, 3 ft. wide. Foliage resists leaf spot; opens reddish, turns green, then goes maroon in winter. Profuse pink flowers.

'Indian Princess'. Up to 3 ft. high, 5 ft. wide. Light pink flowers.

'Jack Evans'. To 4–5 ft. tall, 4 ft. wide. Bright pink flowers. Leaves sometimes have a purplish tinge.

'Pink Lady'. To 5–6 ft. tall and wide. Dark pink flowers.

'Springtime'. Vigorous, upright growth to 4–6 ft. tall and wide. Deep pink flowers.

R. 'Majestic Beauty'. Larger in every detail than the others. Can be trained as a single- or multitrunked tree to 25 ft. tall, 10 ft. wide; as a shrub, easily kept at 10–12 ft. tall, 6–8 ft. wide. Fragrant light pink flowers in clusters to 10 in. wide. Leaves are 4 in. long. Thought by some to be a hybrid between *Rhaphiolepis* and loquat (*Eriobotrya*).

R. umbellata (R. u. ovata, R. ovata). YEDDA HAWTHORN. Native to Japan and Korea. Vigorous to 4–6 ft. (sometimes to 10 ft.) tall and wide. Distinguished from *R. indica* by its leathery dark green, 1–3-in.-long, roundish leaves. White, about ¾-in.-wide flowers. Thick and bushy in full sun. In Northwest, less subject to leaf spot than *R. indica*. 'Minor' ('Gulf Green') is a compact, slow-growing form to 3–4 ft. tall and wide. 'Southern Moon' grows 6 ft. tall, 8 ft. wide; has exceptional disease resistance.

Rhapidophyllum hystrix

NEEDLE PALM
Arecaceae
PALM

🌿 **ZONES 4–24**

☀ ◐ ● **SUN OR SHADE**

◐ ◐ ◐ **MODERATE TO AMPLE WATER**

Rhapidophyllum hystrix

Growing in dense, suckering clumps, this coastal southeastern U.S. palm may be the hardiest in the world, taking temperatures well below 0°F (−18°C). Growing slowly to 6–8 ft. tall and wide, it does not have a distinct trunk. Smooth stems bear dramatic fans of lustrous dark green, 3-ft.-wide leaves, each deeply cut into 6 to 12 segments. "Needle palm" refers to the sharp, 4-in.-long black spines on sheaths at bases of leafstalks and on seeds. Tolerates a wide range of soils.

FOR MORE ON PALMS, SEE "MEET THE PALMS," PAGE 471.

Rhapis

LADY PALM
Arecaceae
PALMS

🌿 **ZONES VARY BY SPECIES; OR INDOORS**

☀ ● **SOME SHADE; BRIGHT INDIRECT LIGHT**

● **REGULAR WATER**

Rhapis excelsa

These choice, slow-growing Chinese fan palms form bamboo-like clumps. Foliage is deep green; trunks are covered with a net of dark, fibrous leaf sheaths. Several variegated forms exist, and fanciers are willing to pay very high prices for good examples. Good indoor plants.

R. excelsa. LADY PALM. Zones 12–17, 19–24; H1, H2. Hardy to 20°F (−7°C). To 5–12 ft. tall and wide. One of the finest houseplants. Withstands neglect and poor light but responds quickly to better light, regular watering and fertilizing.

R. humilis. RATTAN PALM, SLENDER LADY PALM. Zones 16, 17, 20–24; H1, H2. Hardy to 22°F (−6°C). To 18 ft. tall and 3 ft. wide, with tall, slender stems. Larger, longer-leafed palm than *R. excelsa*.

R. multifida. FINGER PALM. Zones 20–24; H1, H2. Hardy to 28°F (−2°C). To 6–8 ft. tall and 3 ft. wide. Looks something like a miniature *R. humilis*.

Lady palms grown indoors need regular feeding during spring and summer: apply a balanced liquid fertilizer each month.

R

Rheum

ORNAMENTAL RHUBARB

Polygonaceae

PERENNIALS

✏ **ZONES 2B–7, 14–17**

☀ ◑ **FULL SUN OR LIGHT SHADE**

💧 **AMPLE WATER**

⬥ **LEAVES ARE POISONOUS IF INGESTED**

Rheum palmatum

These are striking big-leafed plants if you have the water to sustain them. The large leaves arise directly from stout rhizomes; flowering stalks produce smaller leaves and prominent bracts that are massed in tall, branching, plumy clusters. They make a great show in late spring or early summer. Grows best in deep, organically enriched soil. For the edible plant, see Rhubarb.

R. australe (R. emodi). From the Himalayas. Grows to 4–10 ft. tall and 6–8 ft. wide. Rounded leaves to 2½ ft. across, with wavy edges and red veins. White flower plumes reach 8–12 in. long.

R. palmatum. From China and Tibet. Grows to 6–8 ft. tall and 6 ft. wide. Nearly round, 2–3-ft.-wide leaves are deeply cut into tooth-edged lobes. Red flower plumes to 2 ft. long. In variety 'Atrosanguineum', the entire plant is suffused with red. The leaves of *R. p. tanguticum* are less deeply cut than those of the species and often tinted purple; flowers may be white, pink, or red.

FOR OTHER PLANTS THAT WILL LIVE IN DAMP AREAS, SEE PAGES 79–80.

Rhodanthemum hosmariense

(Chrysanthemum hosmariense)

MOROCCAN DAISY

Asteraceae

PERENNIAL

✏ **ZONES 14–24**

☀ **FULL SUN**

◐ 💧 **LITTLE TO MODERATE WATER**

Rhodanthemum hosmariense

This native of the Atlas Mountains has been included in *Chrysanthemum*, *Leucanthemum*, and *Pyrethropsis* over the years, but botanists finally seem to agree on the name given here. Plants spread to form a bushy mass 4–12 in. high and 1–2 ft. wide. Foliage is bright silver, softly hairy, and very finely divided. Over much of the year, plants produce cheerful daisies about 2 in. across; white rays surround a large central cluster of bright yellow florets. Fine choice for a rock garden or atop a stone retaining wall; combines well with other gray-leafed plants. Grow in moderately fertile, very well-drained soil. Rarely bothered by pests or diseases, but does best with protection from excessive winter moisture.

Moroccan daisy thrives in hot, sunny spots, such as the base of a south-facing wall.

Rhododendron

(includes Azalea)

Ericaceae

EVERGREEN AND DECIDUOUS SHRUBS, RARELY TREES

✏ **FOR ZONES, SEE TEXT**

◑ **FILTERED SUNLIGHT**

💧 💧 **REGULAR TO AMPLE WATER**

🦋 **ATTRACT BUTTERFLIES**

⬥ **LEAVES ARE POISONOUS IF INGESTED**

Rhododendron augustinii

Between 800 and 900 species belong to this genus. More than 28,000 varieties, of which perhaps a few hundred are widely available in the West. Botanists have arranged species into sections and subsections; one of these sections includes the plants called azaleas.

With careful selection, gardeners in all climates—even the coldest, hottest, and driest ones—can find ways to grow certain members of this genus (in containers or as houseplants, if need be). Rhododendrons generally do best in Zones 4–6, 15–17, though there are many exceptions. Azaleas are more widely adapted, with many evergreen kinds thriving in Southern California and Hawaii, while some deciduous varieties can grow in the West's coldest climates.

KINDS OF RHODODENDRONS

Most people know rhododendrons as big, leathery-leafed shrubs with rounded clusters ("trusses") of stunning white, pink, red, or purple blossoms. But there are also dwarfs a few inches high, giants that reach 80 ft. tall in their native

Southeast Asia, and a host of species and hybrids in every intermediate size, and in a constellation of colors from white through pink, apricot, salmon, orange, red, yellow, near blue, and purple. Blossoms of some types are spotted with other colors. In other types, flowers have a blotch or flare in a different color on just the upper petal.

The following pages list named varieties by categories, to give you some idea of their adaptability to different climates and garden roles. A sampling of individual varieties is covered later.

Ironclad hybrids for coldest winters. These can take temperatures down to –25°F (–32°C): 'Catawbiense Album', 'Crete', 'Elvira', 'English Roseum', 'Hellikki', 'Henry's Red', 'Northern Starburst', 'Nova Zembla', 'PJM', 'Purple Gem', 'Purple Passion', 'Roseum Elegans', and *R. degronianum yakushimanum* and its named selections.

Northern California specials. Zones 15–17. The following three rhododendrons, called Maddenii hybrids, are too tender for Northwest gardens: 'Else Frye', 'Fragrantissimum', 'Mi Amor'. Good performers in Northern California: 'Anah Kruschke', 'Noyo Chief', 'Percy Wiseman', 'Rubicon', 'Sappho', 'Taurus'.

Vireyas for indoors and frost-free areas. The Vireya rhododendrons, from the tropics of Southeast Asia, manage nicely in frost-free and nearly frostless zones (17, 23, 24; H2). They are also fine container plants (even indoors), so they can be grown in colder zones if brought inside for the winter. They need an especially fast-draining potting mix (many species are epiphytes in the wild); a combination of equal parts peat moss, ground bark, and perlite works well. Typically, plants flower on and off throughout the year rather than in one blooming season. They bear waxy-textured flowers in exciting shades of yellow, gold, orange, vermilion, salmon, and pink, plus cream, white, and bicolors. Species, named hybrids, and unnamed seedlings are offered by some specialty growers.

R

Among the best ones you are likely to find are *R. aurigeranum* (a hybrid of *R. brookeanum* commonly listed as 'Gracile'), *R. javanicum*, *R. konori*, *R. laetum*, *R. lochae*, *R. macgregorae*, and the hybrids 'George Budgen' (orange-yellow), 'Ne Plus Ultra' (a red-flowering hybrid between *R. laetum* and *R. zoelleri*), and 'Taylori' (pink).

Widely adapted varieties. All of these are highly regarded, dependable, popular, and easy to grow just about anywhere: 'Anna Rose Whitney', 'Hallelujah', 'Loder's White', 'Mrs. G. W. Leak', 'Purple Splendour', 'Ramapo', 'The Honorable Jean Marie de Montague', 'Trude Webster'.

Low-growing species and hybrids. Although the following are rhododendrons, they have the charm and general appearance of azaleas: 'Blue Diamond', 'Sapphire', *R. impeditum*, *R. keiskei*, *R. moupinense*, and *R. pemakoense*.

Dwarfs and low growers. Distinctive foliage and bell-shaped or funnel-shaped flowers, not in typical trusses, mark these varieties: 'Ginny Gee', 'Patty Bee', 'Ramapo', and 'Snow Lady'.

RHODODENDRON HYBRIDS AND SPECIES

Listed below are some of the best rhododendrons for Western gardens; hybrids are listed first, then species. For more information on a given rhododendron, refer to the regional lists of recommended varieties compiled by the American Rhododendron Society (rhododendron.org); the lists are updated frequently as new rhododendrons are introduced and old ones drop out of production. Just as temperature listings describe cold tolerance for mature plants, the heights listed are also for mature (10-year-old) plants. Older rhododendrons may be taller; crowded or heavily shaded plants may reach the typical 10-year height at a younger age. Low plants (to 3 ft. or less) are usually slow growing and unlikely to exceed the 10-year height by much. Most

rhododendrons tend to grow about as wide as high.

Bloom time given is approximate and varies with weather and location. The bloom season starts as early as December or January (in mildest climates) and extends through August; most types are spring bloomers. In the list below, "very early" corresponds to winter; "early" to early spring; "midseason" to midspring; "late" to late spring; and "very late" to summer. All of the following plants are evergreen, unless noted.

Rhododendron Hybrids

EARLY VARIETIES (EARLY SPRING)

'Northern Starburst'. −30°F (−34°C). To 4 ft. Improved form of 'PJM' with larger flowers and bigger, thicker leaves that turn blackish purple in winter.

'PJM'. −25°F (−32°C). Dense, bushy plant to 4 ft. Exceptional purplish pink flowers; profuse bloom. Flowers when foliage still has its mahogany winter color. Takes heat and cold.

'Seaview Sunset'. −5°F (−21°C). To 3 ft. Compact

growth. Red-orange buds open light yellow with red-orange band, mature to yellow.

'Snow Lady'. 0°F (−18°C). To 2½ ft. Fuzzy light green leaves. Big show of pure white flowers.

EARLY MIDSEASON VARIETIES (EARLY TO MIDSPRING)

'Besse Howells'. −15°F (−26°C). To 3 ft. Large trusses of rosy red blooms.

'Blue Baron'. −10°F (−23°C). Grows into a 2-ft. mound, with oblong, 2-in. leaves. Flowers are light violet inside, more intense violet outside; appear in large trusses.

'Blue Diamond'. −5°F (−21°C). To 3 ft.; compact, erect. Small leaves. Small lavender-blue flowers cover plant. Takes considerable sun in Northwest.

'Crete'. −25°F (−32°C). To 4 ft. Pinkish purple buds open to light purple flowers that age to white.

'Dora Amateis'. −15°F (−26°C). To 3 ft. Compact, with small foliage; good for foreground. Profuse bloomer with green-spotted white flowers. Spicy fragrance.

'Elizabeth'. 14°F (−10°C). To 3 ft. Attractive foliage sets off

CLOCKWISE FROM TOP LEFT: *Rhododendron* 'Fragrantissimum Improved'; Vireya hybrid 'Mount Kaindi'; *R.* 'Nancy Evans'

large, bright red, waxy, trumpet-shaped flowers that are carried in clusters of three to six at branch ends and in upper leaf joints. Blooms very young. Often reblooms in early fall. Very susceptible to fertilizer burn, salts in water or soil.

'Else Frye'. 15°F (−9°C). To 4 ft. Long, limber growth makes this a natural for informal espalier. Considerable pinching is needed to achieve compact form. Intensely fragrant flowers are pink-flushed white with a gold throat.

'Fragrantissimum'. 15°F (−9°C). Loose, open, rangy growth; bright green, bristly leaves. With hard pinching in youth, a 5-ft. shrub. Easily trained as espalier or vine, reaching 10 ft. or more. Can spill over wall. Large, powerfully fragrant, funnel-shaped white flowers touched with pink. Grow as container plant in Northwest; overwinter indoors in a room that is bright but cool.

»

CLOCKWISE FROM LEFT: *Rhododendron* 'September Song'; *R. degronianum yakushimanum* 'Yaku Angel'; *R.* 'PJM'

'Ginny Gee'. –10°F (–23°C). Striking 2-ft. dwarf with small leaves, dense growth. Small pink bells are dotted inside and out with white. Profuse bloom.

'Moonstone'. –5°F (–21°C). To 3 ft. Low, compact mound with neat, small, rounded leaves. Flaring bells age from pale pink to creamy yellow. Fine facing taller rhododendrons.

'Mrs. G. W. Leak' ('Cottage Gardens Pride'). 0°F (–18°C). Strong-growing plant to 6 ft. Light pink flowers with showy reddish purple flare.

'Patty Bee'. –10°F (–23°C). To 1½ ft. Small plant, well clothed with small (1 in. wide) leaves that turn dark red in winter. Loose trusses of lemon yellow flowers cover even young plants.

'President Roosevelt'. 0°F (–18°C). To 4 ft. Dark green leaves marked with golden yellow. Tall trusses of red flowers with white centers. Named for Theodore Roosevelt.

'Purple Gem'. –25°F (–32°C). To 2 ft. Dwarf with tiny leaves that emerge bluish, take on rust tones. Blue-purple flowers.

'Ramapo'. –20°F (–29°C). Dense, spreading growth to 2 ft. in sun, taller in shade. New growth is dusty blue-green, maturing to dark green. Pinkish violet flowers cover plant. Useful rock garden or low border plant. Good choice in California.

'Rubicon'. 5°F (–15°C). To 4 ft. Well-proportioned plant. Red flowers have black freckles.

'Sapphire'. –5°F (–21°C). To 2½ ft. Twiggy, rounded, and dense, with tiny, narrow gray-green leaves. Small, azalea-like light blue flowers.

'Taurus'. –5°F (–21°C). To 6 ft. Vigorous and upright; well clothed in forest green leaves. Deep red buds open to large bright red bells with black spotting. Plants bloom only after reaching 4 to 6 years old.

'Teddy Bear'. 0°F (–18°C). To 3 ft., compact and rounded. Light purplish pink flowers age to white.

FOR OTHER PLANTS THAT WILL THRIVE WITH LESS LIGHT, SEE PAGES 68–69.

MIDSEASON VARIETIES (MIDSPRING)

'Baden Baden'. –15°F (–26°C). To 2 ft. high and 4 ft. wide. Bright red.

'Bambino'. –5°F (–21°C). To 3 ft. Peach-pink suffused with yellow and dotted with red. Large calyx gives effect of a double flower.

'Blue Peter'. –10°F (–23°C). To 4–5 ft. Broad, sprawling growth; needs regular pruning. Large trusses of lavender-blue flowers with purple blotch. Tolerates heat and sun.

'Dreamland'. –10°F (–23°C). Compact growth to 3–4 ft. tall. Leaves hold on for 3 years. Very full trusses of soft pink flowers with darker pink edges.

'Ebony Pearl'. –5°F (–21°C). To 6 ft. tall. Twisted, 3-in. leaves are maroon when new, mature to coppery green. Big mauve-pink flowers are lighter at the edges, have reddish brown spots.

'English Roseum' ('Roseum Pink'). –25°F (–32°C). Erect habit to 6 ft. Lavender-pink blooms. Tough and undemanding.

'Fastuosum Flore Pleno'. –15°F (–26°C). Open, rounded habit to 6 ft. Lavender-blue double blooms marked with gold blotch. Flower center is filled with small, lavender petal-like structures. Dependable old-timer. Tolerates heat and sun.

'Hachmann's Polaris'. –15°F (–26°C). Grows into a 3-ft. mound, with 4-in., hairy, elliptical leaves. Flowers have deep pink edges fading to very light pink at the center. Does well in sun and shade.

'Hallelujah'. –15°F (–26°C). To 4 ft. Rose-red flowers stand above thick forest green foliage. Very strong grower; fine-looking plant with or without flowers. Takes full sun.

'Henry's Red'. –25°F (–32°C). To 5 ft.; broader than tall. Dark red flowers.

'Holden'. –15°F (–26°C). To 4 ft. Compact. Rose-red flowers are marked with deeper red.

'Horizon Monarch'. 5°F (–15°C). To 6 ft. tall, spreading. Leaves are 6 in., dark green, convex. Light yellow flowers are tinged with red.

'Hotei'. 0°F (–18°C). To 3 ft. Compact plant. Canary yellow flowers backed by a prominent calyx come only when plant is 6 to 8 years old. Closest of all varieties to a deep pure yellow. Roots can rot easily; needs excellent drainage.

'Janet Blair'. –15°F (–26°C). To 5 ft.; vigorous and spreading. Large, ruffled flowers blend pastel pink, cream, white, and gold; rounded trusses. Midseason to late.

'Lemon Dream'. 0°F (–18°C). To 1 ft. Dense and spreading. Yellow flowers above oval, glossy green leaves.

'Lem's Cameo'. –5°F (–21°C). To 4–5 ft. Flowers in a blend of apricot, cream, and pink.

'Lem's Monarch' ('Pink Walloper'). –5°F (–21°C). To 6 ft. Big, heavy-branched plant with large leaves. Pink flowers, darker at the edges, bloom in huge, round trusses.

Loderi hybrids. 5°F (–15°C). Spectacular group with tall trusses of 6–7-in.-wide, very fragrant flowers in shades of pink or white. Informal, open growth to 6 ft., eventually becoming much larger and nearly treelike; too large for small garden. Slow to reach blooming age, not easy to grow; maintaining good foliage color is difficult. Best known are 'King

George', pink quickly fading to white; 'Pink Diamond', blush pink; and 'Venus', deepest pink of the group.

'Loder's White'. 0°F (−18°C). Shapely growth to 5 ft. Tall trusses of white flowers with faint yellow throat and light pink picotee edge; blooms turn pure white as they mature. Blooms freely even when young. Best white for most regions.

'Mi Amor'. 15°F (−9°C). Striking plant for mild-winter climates. Open, lanky; to 6 ft. Huge (6 in.), powerfully fragrant, bell-shaped white flowers with yellow throat are borne in clusters of three to five.

'Nancy Evans'. 5°F (−15°C). Compact growth to 3 ft., with bronzy new foliage. Orange-tinged buds open to yellow flowers; each bloom is backed by a calyx that makes it look almost double.

'Nova Zembla'. −25°F (−32°C). To 5 ft. Profuse red flowers. Takes heat.

'Noyo Chief'. 10°F (−12°C). To 5 ft. Outstanding glossy green, heavily ribbed leaves. Bright red flowers.

'Paprika Spiced'. 0°F (−18°C). To 3 ft. Flowers in a blend of yellow, pink, and orange, dotted with red. Large yellow calyx.

'Percy Wiseman'. −10°F (−23°C). To 3 ft. Compact growth. Peachy yellow flowers fade to white. Notably heat-resistant.

'Polarnacht'. −10°F (−23°C). To 3 ft. high, 6 ft. wide, with 1½-in. flat green leaves. Purplish red leaves.

'Pomegranate Splash'. 10°F (−12°C). Grows 3 ft. high, 2½ ft. wide. Flowers have purplish red reverse and edges, but tops of petals are white with a brown blotch on the top petal.

'Purple Passion'. −25°F (−32°C). To 6 ft. tall, 5 ft. wide. Dark green leaves and large, deep purple flowers.

'Rocket'. −15°F (−26°C). To 5 ft. tall, with 4-in., glossy green, veined leaves. Red-blotched, frilly pink flowers.

'Sappho'. −15°F (−26°C). To 6 ft. Easy to grow; gangly without pruning. Use at back of border. White blossoms, dark purple eye.

'Scarlet Wonder'. −15°F (−26°C). May be hardier than its rating; has survived

−45°F (−43°C) in Finland (perhaps protected by snow cover). Outstanding, compact dwarf to 2 ft. Shiny, quilted-looking foliage forms backdrop for many bright scarlet blossoms.

'Scintillation'. −15°F (−26°C). To 5 ft. Compact plant covered in lustrous dark green leaves. Rounded trusses of pastel pink flowers with deep pink markings in throat; blooms age to brownish pink.

'September Song'. 0°F (−18°C). To 4 ft.; broader than tall. Flowers shade from salmon at edges to golden orange in throat, giving trusses an overall orange look. Blooms young.

'Skookum'. −20°F (−29°C). To 4 ft. Globe-shaped red flowers on a rounded, well-proportioned plant.

'Susan'. −5°F (−21°C). To 6 ft. Handsome foliage; violet-blue flowers are held in large trusses.

'The Honorable Jean Marie de Montague'. −5°F (−21°C). To 5 ft., with attractive foliage. Brilliant scarlet flowers.

'Trude Webster'. −10°F (−23°C). To 5 ft. Strong growing, with large leaves. Huge trusses of pure pink flowers. One of the best pinks.

LATE MIDSEASON VARIETIES (MID- TO LATE SPRING)

'Anah Kruschke'. −15°F (−26°C). To 6 ft. Lavender-blue to reddish purple. Flower color not the best, but plant has good foliage, is very tolerant of heat and sun. Can be sensitive to root rot in warm, wet soils.

'Anna Rose Whitney'. −5°F (−21°C). To 6 ft., with excellent foliage. Big trusses of blossoms in rich, deep pink.

'Capistrano'. −15°F (−26°C). To 3 ft. high, 6 ft. wide. Bell-shaped yellow flowers.

'Catawbiense Album'. −25°F (−32°C). To 6 ft. Pink buds; white flowers with greenish blotch. Takes cold and heat.

'Catawbiense Boursault'. −20°F (−29°C). Like 'Catawbiense Album' but has pinkish lavender flowers. Takes cold and heat.

'Chionoides'. −15°F (−26°C). To 4 ft.; dense, compact, rounded form. White flowers with light yellow spotting. Takes sun.

'Cunningham's Blush'. −15°F (−26°C). Dependable old variety to 4 ft. Blush pink with white blotch.

CLOCKWISE FROM TOP LEFT: *Rhododendron* 'Catawbiense Album'; *R. occidentale; R.* 'Lem's Monarch'

'Cunningham's White'. −15°F (−26°C). May actually be hardier than rated; a plant in Finland has survived −45°F (−43°C). To 4 ft. An old-timer bearing white blooms with greenish yellow blotch.

'Daphnoides'. −10°F (−23°C). Grows to 3 ft. Prolific trusses of lavender-blue flowers. Well-branched, densely foliaged plant. Glossy deep green, oval leaves are convex, unusual among rhododendrons.

'Elvira'. −25°F (−32°C). Grows 2 ft. high with glossy, red-tinged leaves. Red flowers.

'Fantastica'. −5°F (−21°C). To 3 ft. Compact. Long, elliptical leaves have woolly undersides. Rose-pink flowers with white throat, green spotting on petals.

'Gomer Waterer'. −15°F (−26°C). To 5 ft. Pink buds open to white flowers with yellowish green blotch. Old-timer. Tolerates sun; endures heat and drought better than most.

'Helsinki University'. −25°F (−32°C). To 6 ft., upright. Leaves are red-tinged at opening, mature to green. Purplish pink flowers come late in the season, have wavy edges.

'Purple Splendour'. –5°F (–21°C). To 5 ft. Informal habit. Ruffled-looking deep purple blossoms with black-purple blotch. Tolerates sun.

'Roseum Elegans'. –25°F (–32°C). To 6 ft. Olive green foliage. Lilac-pink flowers. Tolerates both heat and cold.

'Vulcan'. –15°F (–26°C). To 5 ft. Bright brick red flowers. New leaves often grow past flower buds, partially hiding them.

LATE VARIETIES (LATE SPRING)

'Haaga'. –20°F (–29°C). Grows to 5 ft., upright, with 5-in. glossy green leaves. Fuchsia-pink flowers.

'Hellikki'. –25°F (–32°C). To 5 ft. Leaves narrow, 3–4 in. long. Purple flowers have wavy edges.

Rhododendron Species

R. augustinii. –5°F (–21°C). Native to western China and Tibet. Open, moderate growth to 6 ft. Bell-shaped flowers in clusters of up to six. Colors range from white to lavender-pink to blue. Early midseason. 'Barto Blue', 'Electra', 'Lackamas Blue', and 'Towercourt' are choice blue forms.

R. calostrotum keleticum. –15°F (–26°C). Native to Myanmar, Tibet, and China. Compact, spreading plant to 1 ft. high and 3 ft. wide. Leaves are tiny, smooth and dark green above, scaly brown beneath. Inch-wide, crimson-purple, saucer-shaped flowers in upright trusses of three. Fine in rock garden or as bonsai subject. Late midseason.

R. campylogynum Myrtilloides group. –10°F (–23°C). Native to Himalayas from China to India and Myanmar. Grows 1 ft. high, with small, dark green leaves with a mouse-eared look as they emerge. Nodding, plum-colored, bell-shaped flowers. Midseason.

R. degronianum yakushimanum (R. yakushimanum). –25°F (–32°C). From Japan. Forms a tight mound to 1–4 ft. tall. New growth is covered with a feltlike coat of white hairs;

older leaves are glossy dark green above, brown and felted beneath. Clear pink bells age to white. Late midseason. Selections include 'Ken Janeck', a large (to 4 ft.) form with intense pink flowers, and smaller-growing 'Yaku Angel', with pink-tinged buds opening to pure white flowers. There are also a number of hybrids that perform as well in cold climates as they do in milder ones. Among them are 'Mardi Gras', 'Yaku Sunrise', and 'Yaku Princess' (this last selection is part of a good series of hybrids, all with names including royal titles). The three hybrids just mentioned all have blooms that are white or pink-tinged white.

R. falconeri. 10°F (–12°C). Native to the Himalayas. Tree to 25 ft. tall. Leathery, 6–12-in.-long leaves with reddish, felted undersides. Clusters of creamy white to pale yellow flowers. Early midseason. Blooms when 15 to 20 years old.

R. forrestii forrestii Repens group. 5°F (–15°C). Several prostrate to very low-growing plants fall within this group, derived from a species native to China and Myanmar. Bear small clusters of tubular bright red flowers in early midseason. All are useful rock garden plants; require perfect drainage.

R. fortunei. –15°F (–26°C). From eastern China. Treelike growth to 6–10 ft. tall and about half as wide; may reach 20 ft. tall after many years. Leaves are oval and pointed, to 7 in. long, matte dark green above and lighter green below. Fragrant pink flowers 2–3 in. across are held in trusses of 6 to 12; they completely cover the plant in midseason. *R. f. discolor* (–5°F/–21°C) is a bit smaller, with a more open habit. Its late-season flowers, up to 4 in. across, are white to pink and come in trusses of 8 to 10.

R. impeditum. –15°F (–26°C). From China. Twiggy, dense dwarf to 1 ft., with tiny, closely packed leaves in light grayish green. Small lavender-blue to purple-blue flowers cover the plant in early midseason. Set 15 in. apart for dense groundcover. Takes full sun in cooler areas. Needs excellent drainage to avoid root rot.

R. keiskei. –5°F (–21°C). Native to Japan. Compact growth to 2 ft. Bears light to bright yellow flowers in clusters of three to five. Early midseason. 'Yaku Fairy' is a selected creeping form reaching just 6 in. high.

R. macrophyllum. –5°F (–21°C). COAST RHODODENDRON, WESTERN RHODODENDRON. Native near coast from Northern California to British Columbia. Rangy plant growing 4–10 ft. tall, as tall as 20 ft. in some locations. Leathery dark green leaves are 2½–6 in. long. Trusses may hold 20 flowers in pinkish purple to white, spotted with reddish brown. Late midseason.

R. moupinense. 0°F (–18°C). From China. To 1½ ft., with open, spreading habit. Small, oval leaves are deep red when new, maturing to green. White or pink flowers with red spots. Very early.

R. mucronulatum. –15°F (–26°C). From China, Mongolia, Korea, Japan. Deciduous rhododendron with open, rather thin growth to 5 ft.; makes up for bare, leggy branches with very early bloom. Small clusters of flowers, usually in bright purple. 'Cornell Pink' is a pink form.

R. pachysanthum. –5°F (–20°C). From Taiwan. Grows

30 in. high; forms a compact, dense shrub. Leaves to 4 in. long, with silvery to brown indumentum on top, tan indumentum on bottom. Flowers are white to pale pink spotted green or crimson. Early midseason.

R. pemakoense. 0°F (–18°C). From the Himalayas and China. To 1½ ft. Compact, spreading plant with small leaves. Very profuse show of pinkish purple blooms. Early. Useful in rock gardens.

R. racemosum. –5°F (–21°C). Native to China. Several forms are available, including a 6-in. dwarf; a compact, upright shrub to 2½ ft.; and a 7-footer. Small pink flowers in clusters of three to six all along stems. Early to early midseason. Easy to grow; sun-tolerant in cooler areas.

R. rex. 0°F (–18°C). Native to China. Upright growth to 6 ft. tall. Huge leaves reach 18 in. long and 6 in. wide, with gray to brown indumentum underneath. Trusses of up to 30 pink to white flowers are spotted crimson, appear in early midseason. Elegant.

R. tsariense. 0°F (–18°C). Native to Himalaya Mountains, Tibet to India. Compact growth to 2 ft. This species' white flowers, flushed pink at the base, are pretty enough, but it's grown

Compatible Companions

Rhododendrons and azaleas need moist, well-drained, acidic soil and at least a bit of shade. To keep them company in the garden, choose other plants that enjoy similar conditions—and whose roots are not so aggressive that they'll choke out the shallow roots of rhododendrons and azaleas.

Among favorite companion shrubs are camellia, winter hazel (*Corylopsis*), *Enkianthus*, *Fothergilla*, hydrangea, mountain laurel (*Kalmia latifolia*), *Leucothoe*, *Mahonia*, *Pieris*, and many viburnums.

Lots of perennials with attractive flowers fit the bill, but a few best bets are anemone, false spirea (*Astilbe*), some hellebores, hosta, toad lily (*Tricyrtis*), and trillium. Many ferns also work well in the company of azaleas and rhododendrons.

Appropriate companion trees include Japanese maple (*Acer palmatum*), katsura tree (*Cercidiphyllum japonicum*), dogwood (*Cornus*), *Franklinia alatamaha*, *Halesia*, sourwood (*Oxydendron arboreum*), Persian parrotia, *Stewartia*, and *Styrax*.

for the cinnamon-colored indumentum on the backs of the 2½-in. leaves. Early to early midseason.

R. williamsianum. –5°F (–21°C). Native to Szechuan, China. Compact, mounding growth to 3 ft. high and 3–4 ft. wide. Attractive, bronzy juvenile foliage matures to rounded, smooth green leaves about 1¾ in. across with blue-green underside. Pink, bell-shaped flowers are 2 in. wide and held on nodding stalks in trusses of two to three. Midseason.

AZALEAS

Azaleas are divided into two broad categories: evergreen and deciduous. Each category includes both hybrid groups and species.

Evergreen Azaleas

Evergreen azaleas fall into more than a dozen groups and species, though an increasing number of hybrids have such mixed parentage that they don't fit into any category. The following list includes some of the most popular groups. Except as noted, bloom season is early (see "Rhododendron Hybrids and Species," page 557, for bloom-season terms). Plants grown in greenhouses can be forced for winter bloom. Plant size tends to vary within a group, but most plants are about as wide as they are high.

Belgian Indica hybrids. Zones 14–24; H1, H2. Originally developed for greenhouse forcing, many of these excel as landscape plants where winter lows stay above 20°F (–7°C). They are profuse bloomers with lush, thick foliage and typically semidouble or double, 2–3-in. blossoms.

Brooks hybrids. Zones 8, 9, 14–24. Hardy to 20°F (–7°C). Bred in Modesto, California, for heat and drought tolerance, compact form, large flowers. Best known are white 'Madonna'; rose-colored 'My Valentine'; 'Pinkie'; and 'Red Wing'.

Encore hybrids. Zones 5–9, 14–24. These rhododendron–azalea hybrids, including about two dozen varieties, were bred to flower up to three times each year, starting in spring. They

bloom on both new and old wood. Reblooming is most successful in the warmer, more humid parts of the range; least successful in the Pacific Northwest. All variety names start with the word "Autumn," as in 'Autumn Embers', 'Autumn Ruby', 'Autumn Twist'.

Gable hybrids. Zones 4–9, 14–24. Bred to produce azaleas of Kurume type that take 0°F (–18°C) temperatures. In Zones 4–6, they may lose some leaves during winter. Bloom heavily in midseason. Frequently sold are bright pink 'Caroline Gable'; purple 'Herbert'; lavender-pink 'Karen', with its hose-in-hose bloom structure; pink 'Louise Gable', 'Pioneer', and 'Rosebud'; 'Purple Splendor'; 'Purple Splendor Compacta' (less rangy growth than 'Purple Splendor'); and white 'Rose Greeley'.

Girard hybrids. Zones 4–9, 14–24. Hardy to –5°F (–21°C) or somewhat lower. Originated from Gable crosses; all are strong performers. 'Girard Border Gem' has rose flowers that completely cover the plant; 'Girard Chiara' is ruffled pink hose-in-hose; 'Girard Rose' has deep rose flowers, foliage that tints red in fall; 'Girard Fuchsia' has reddish purple blossoms; 'Girard Hotshot', orange-red flowers and orange-red fall and winter foliage; 'Girard Roberta', 3-in., double pink flowers.

Glenn Dale hybrids. Zones 4–9, 14–24. Hardy to 0°F (–18°C). Developed primarily for hardiness, though they do drop some leaves in cold winters. Some are tall and rangy, others low and compact. Growth rate varies from slow to rapid. Some have small leaves like Kurume hybrids; others have large leaves. Familiar varieties are orange-red 'Buccaneer'; white 'Delaware Valley White', 'Everest', and 'Glacier'; and purple-pink 'Pearl Bradford'.

Gold Cup hybrids. Zones 14–24. Members of this group were originally called Mossholder-Bristow hybrids. Plants combine large flowers of Belgian Indica hybrids with vigor of Rutherfordiana hybrids. Good landscape plants where temperatures don't fall below 20°F (–7°C). Some popular varieties are

CLOCKWISE FROM TOP: *Rhododendron* 'Herbert'; *R. vaseyi*; *R.* 'Golden Lights'

'Easter Parade', pink blooms mottled in white; 'Sun Valley', white; and 'White Orchids', white with red throat.

Kaempferi hybrids. Zones 2–7. Based on *R. kaempferi*, the torch azalea, a cold-hardy plant with orange-red flowers. These are somewhat hardier (to –15°F/–26°C) than Kurume hybrids, with a taller, more open habit. Nearly leafless below 0°F (–18°C). Profuse bloom. Available choices are salmon-rose 'Fedora'; 'Holland', a late-season bloomer with large red flowers; orange-red 'John Cairns'; and red 'Johanna'.

Kurume hybrids. Zones 5–9, 14–24; H1, H2. Hardy to 5°F (–15°C). Compact, twiggy plants, densely clothed in small, glossy leaves. Small flowers are borne in incredible profusion. Plants have mounded or tiered form, look handsome even out of bloom. Widely used as houseplants. Grow well outdoors but cannot endure hot, dry summer winds. Of the many available varieties, these are most widely sold: crimson 'Hexe', bright red 'Hino-crimson', red-violet 'Sherwood Orchid', orange-red

'Sherwood Red', and pink 'Coral Bells' and 'Tradition'.

Pericat hybrids. Zones 5–9, 14–24. These were originally developed for greenhouse forcing but are as hardy as Kurume hybrids (5°F to 10°F/–15°C to –12°C) and look much the same, though flowers tend to be somewhat larger. Varieties include light pink 'Mme. Pericat', blush pink 'Sweetheart Supreme', and rose-pink 'Twenty Grand'.

Robin Hill hybrids. Zones 4–9, 14–24. Hardy to 0°F (–18°), probably lower. A large group with typically large flowers. Most are 2–4-ft. plants; some are more dwarf. Late bloom. There are so many good ones—several with "Robin Hill" in their name—that it's difficult to single out only a few. Try pink 'Betty Ann Voss'; 'Conversation Piece', pink with light center; 'Nancy of Robin Hill', pink with red blotch; red-orange 'Robin Hill Gillie'; and 'Hilda Niblett',

R

How to Grow Rhododendrons and Azaleas

EXPOSURE Though sun tolerance differs by species and variety, most fare best in filtered sunlight beneath tall trees; east and north sides of house or fence are next best. Where summers are mild or foggy, they can take more sun, but the sunnier or hotter the climate, the more protection plants will need. Too much sun causes leaf centers to bleach or burn, while too much shade results in lanky plants with sparse bloom.

SOIL & WATER Rhododendrons and azaleas need more air in the root zone than almost all other garden plants, but they also require a constant supply of moisture. Regular watering is one part of the equation, and excellent drainage is the other. If water is allowed to stand, plants can succumb to root rot, which makes them turn yellow, wilt, or collapse. Soils rich in organic matter have the desired qualities; if your soil is deficient, amend it liberally with organic material before you plant.

In clay or alkaline soil, plant in bed raised 1–2 ft. above original soil level. Mix a generous amount of organic material into the top foot of native soil; then fill bed above it with a mixture of 50 percent organic matter, 30 percent native soil, 20 percent sand. This soil mix will be well aerated but moisture retentive and will permit alkaline salts to leach through. Plant azaleas and rhododendrons with top of rootball slightly above soil level. Plants are surface rooters that benefit from a mulch such as pine needles, oak leaves, or bark or wood chips. Never cultivate around these plants.

In areas where dissolved salts accumulate, periodically leach the planting by watering heavily—enough to drain through the soil two or three times. If leaves turn yellow while veins remain green, plants have iron chlorosis; apply iron chelates to soil or spray foliage with an iron solution.

FERTILIZER Some experts dig fertilizer into the soil to get new plantings off to a good start. Feed established plants with commercial acid fertilizer well before bloom, as buds swell (in early spring, except for the earliest bloomers). Feed again when new leaves begin to grow, just as blooms are fading. Top-dress with compost in early fall.

PINCHING & PRUNING These are essential for shaping plants and encouraging thick, bushy growth.

Rhododendrons. Tip-pinch young plants to shape them and make them bushy; prune older, leggy plants to restore shape by cutting back to a side branch, leaf whorl, or cluster of latent buds. Do extensive pruning in late winter or early spring (wait until danger of frost is past in colder areas). Pruning at this time will sacrifice some flower buds, but the plant's energies will be diverted to latent growth buds, which will then be ready to push out their new growth early in the growing season. (There are several varieties that will not produce new growth from latent buds.) You can do some shaping while plants are in bloom, using cut branches in arrangements. To prevent seed formation, which can reduce next year's bloom, clip or break off spent flower trusses, taking care not to damage growth buds at base of each truss.

Azaleas. Evergreen azaleas are dense, usually shapely plants; heading back the occasional wayward branch restores symmetry. To keep bushes compact, tip-pinch frequently, starting after flowering ends and continuing until July. Prune deciduous azaleas while they are dormant and leafless (in cold climates, wait until frost danger is past). You don't have to prune azaleas as carefully as you do rhododendrons—the leaves are fairly evenly spaced along the branches, with a bud at base of each leaf, so new growth will sprout from almost anywhere you cut (in bare or leafy wood). Azaleas can even be sheared into formal hedges.

CHALLENGES If you choose the right plant for your region and your garden's conditions, you'll find rhododendrons mostly trouble-free. Still, there are problems to watch for.

Root weevils. Especially in the Pacific Northwest, root weevils are the main insect problem. Root weevil adults cause cosmetic damage by notching leaves, and their larvae can do major damage by girdling roots. A number of pesticides that range from acephate to pyrethrins can help in serious infestations, as can natural controls such as parasitic nematodes. To keep root weevils from climbing into the rhododendron's canopy at night to chew leaves, girdle the trunk with a sticky insect barrier.

Mildew. Leaf mildew has become a problem on some varieties of rhododendron. If you want to grow a variety that is susceptible, plant it in a sunny spot that gets plenty of air circulation. The best prevention, however, is to plant resistant varieties.

Sudden oak death (*Phytophthora ramorum*). Most susceptible of those we list here are *R. augustinii*, *R. catawbiense* hybrids, *R. macrophyllum*, and *R. mucronulatum*. Least susceptible are *R. keiskei* and *R. degronianum yakushimanum*, and any rhododendron with substantial indumentum (a covering of fine hairs) on the leaves. Symptoms appear as dieback along midribs of leaves, starting either at the leaf tip or at the petiole. Infected plants and the leaves and mulch beneath them should be removed and burned or sent out with the trash.

Leaf burn. Both wind and soil salts burn leaf edges; windburn shows up most often on new foliage, salt burn on older leaves. Late frosts often cause deformed leaves.

with blossoms in a combination of light pink, deep pink, and white.

Rutherfordiana hybrids. Zones 14–24. Greenhouse plants; also good in garden where temperatures don't go below 20°F (–7°C). Bushy, 2–4-ft. plants with handsome foliage. Medium-size blossoms may be single, semidouble, or double. Available varieties include 'Alaska', white with chartreuse blotch; brick red 'Dorothy Gish'; orchid-pink 'L. J. Bobbink'; and 'Red Ruffles'.

Satsuki hybrids. Zones 5–9, 14–24. Includes plants sometimes referred to as Gumpo and Macrantha azaleas. Hardy to 5°F (–15°C). Low-growing plants, some of them true dwarfs; many are pendent enough for hanging baskets. Large flowers come late. Popular varieties include orange-red 'Flame Creeper'; white 'Gumpo'; rose-pink 'Gumpo Pink'; bright pink 'Hi Gasa'; red 'Nuccio's Wild Cherry'; and 'Nuccio's Wild Moon', white with a bright purple border.

Southern Indica hybrids. Zones 8, 9, 14–24. Most take temperatures of 10°F to 20°F (–12°C to –7°C), but some are damaged even at the upper end of that range. These include varieties selected from Belgian Indica hybrids for vigor and sun tolerance, and hybrids developed by California's Monrovia Nursery, using Belgian Indica and Southern Indica azaleas. They generally grow fast into vigorous 4–6-ft. mounds, thrive in warm, dry areas. Often sold in California under the name "sun azaleas." Used for massing and as specimens—as shrubs, standards, espaliers. Popular choices include carmine-red 'Brilliant'; salmon-pink 'Duc de Rohan'; 'Fielder's White'; brilliant rose-purple 'Formosa' (also sold as 'Coccinea', 'Phoenicia', 'Vanessa'); light pink 'George Lindley Taber'; 'Iveryana', white with orchid streaks; 'Little John', a dense, rounded bush up to 6 ft. tall (despite the name) bearing burgundy foliage and a few deep red flowers; brilliant red 'Pride of Dorking'; and watermelon pink 'Southern Charm' (sometimes sold as

'Judge Solomon'). 'Imperial Princess', with single pink flowers, and 'Imperial Queen', with double pink blooms, are both hardy to 10°F (–12°C).

Vuykiana hybrids. Zones 2–7. See description of Kaempferi hybrids. Varieties sold include violet-blue 'Blue Danube', 'Vuyk's Rosy Red', and 'Vuyk's Scarlet'.

Deciduous Azaleas

Very few deciduous shrubs can equal deciduous azaleas for showiness and color range. Evergreen azaleas can't match them for blooms in the yellow, orange, and flame red range, nor for flowers with bicolor contrasts. Foliage often turns brilliant orange-red to maroon in autumn. In the list below, hybrid groups are followed by species. Plant size tends to vary within a group, but most individual plants are roughly equal in height and width. For definition of bloom-season terminology, see "Rhododendron Hybrids and Species," page 557.

'Fragrant Star'. Zones 3–9, 14–17. Hardy to –20°F (–29°C). This is a polyploid (doubled chromosome) version of 'Snowbird', which is an *R. atlanticum* × *R. canescens* hybrid; both parents are native to the eastern United States. 'Fragrant Star' has an upright growth habit to about 4 ft. high and slightly less wide, with blue foliage and larger, pure white, star-shaped flowers. Like 'Snowbird', it is extremely fragrant. Heat- and mildew-resistant.

Ghent hybrids. Zones 2b–9, 14–17. Many are hardy to –25°F (–32°C). Upright growth. Flowers are generally 1½–2¼ in. wide. Colors include shades of yellow, orange, umber, red, and pink. Midseason.

Knap Hill–Exbury hybrids. Zones 3–9, 14–17. Hardy to –20°F (–29°C). These vary from upright to spreading, 4–6 ft. tall, producing the largest flowers found on deciduous azaleas (up to 5 in. across), borne in clusters of 7 to 18. Blossoms are sometimes ruffled or fragrant, in colors ranging from white through pink and yellow to orange and red, often with contrasting blotches.

Both Knap Hill and Exbury azaleas come from the same original crosses. The first crosses were made at Knap Hill (in England); subsequent improvements were made at both Exbury (also in England) and Knap Hill. The so-called Rothschild azaleas are Exbury plants. Ilam (from New Zealand) and Arneson (from Oregon) hybrids are improvements on the original stock.

Midseason to late bloom. If you want to be sure of flower color and size, choose named varieties (this does not mean you should dismiss all seedling plants as inferior—but do select them in bloom). Some of the best named forms are pink 'Cannon's Double'; orange 'Gibraltar'; double deep pink 'Homebush'; golden tangerine 'Klondyke'; yellow-orange 'Arneson Gem'; 'Old Gold', bearing light orange-yellow blossoms flushed pink and blotched deep orange; red 'Arneson Ruby'; and 'Oxydol', white flowers with yellow markings.

Northern Lights hybrids. Zones A2, A3; 1–7. The hardiest of all deciduous azaleas, withstanding –45°F (–43°C). Developed by the University of Minnesota. To 2–4 ft., with ball-shaped trusses of fragrant sterile flowers (no need to deadhead after bloom). Late. Most widely available are 'Apricot Surprise', 'Golden Lights', 'Mandarin Lights', 'Orchid Lights', 'Rosy Lights', and 'White Lights'. Foliage can have the skunky odor of their Mollis ancestors.

Occidentale hybrids. Zones 4–7, 14–17. Hardy to –5°F (–21°C). Hybrids between *R. occidentale* and Mollis azaleas. To 8 ft. Flowers are 2½–4 in. wide, with a wide color range—from white blossoms flushed with rose and marked with yellow blotches to red blooms with orange blotch. Midseason to late. 'Irene Koster' has light rose-pink flowers with a gold flare on upper petals. 'Washington State Centennial' ('Centennial') has big, fragrant, frilly flowers in light orange-yellow marked with a large yellow flare; blossoms quickly age to white.

Viscosum hybrids. Zones 3–7. Hardy to –15°F (–26°C). Hybrids between Mollis azaleas and *R. viscosum*, an eastern U.S. native with a powerful clove perfume. Flowers have the colors of Mollis azaleas but the fragrance of *R. viscosum*. Late.

R. calendulaceum. FLAME AZALEA. Zones A3; 2b–6. Hardy to –25°F (–32°C). Native to the Appalachian Mountains from New York to Georgia. Grows fast to 5 ft. tall and 7 ft. wide, with funnel-shaped, midseason flowers ranging from yellow to orange and deep red (the colors of *Calendula* flowers, for which the species is named). Easy to grow and heavy blooming.

R. luteum (R. flavum). PONTIC AZALEA. Zones 3–7, 14–17. Hardy to –15°F (–26°C). Native to eastern Europe and Asia Minor. To 8 ft. or more. Blooms before leafout, bearing fragrant, single yellow flowers with darker blotch. Midseason.

R. occidentale. WESTERN AZALEA. Zones 4–7, 14–17, 19–24. Hardy to –5°F (–21°C). Native to mountains and foothills of California and Oregon. Erect growth to 6–10 ft. Clusters of fragrant, funnel-shaped flowers bloom after leafout. Midseason to late. Color varies from white to pinkish white with yellow blotch; some are heavily marked in carmine-rose. Superior named cutting-grown plants are scarce but available and worth looking for. 'Leonard Frisbie' is a choice variety.

R. quinquefolium (R. pentaphyllum). Zones 4–7, 14–17. Hardy to –5°F (–20°F). Native to Japan. Compact growth to 2 ft. high. Light green leaves are edged in red. White flowers appear in early midseason.

R. schlippenbachii. ROYAL AZALEA. Zones 3–7, 14–17. Hardy to –20°F (–29°C). Native to Korea and Manchuria. Densely branched shrub to 6–8 ft. Leaves in whorls of five at tips of branches. Blooms in early midseason as leaves are expanding, producing large (2–4 in.), highly fragrant, pure light pink flowers in clusters of three to six. A white form is also available. Good fall color: yellow, orange, scarlet, and crimson. Protect from full sun.

R. vaseyi. PINKSHELL AZALEA. Zones 3–7, 14–17. Hardy to –20°F (–29°C). Native to mountains of North Carolina. Upright plant with irregular, spreading form. To 10–15 ft. Blooms before leafout, bearing light pink flowers in clusters of five to eight. Midseason.

Rhodohypoxis baurii

Hypoxidaceae
PERENNIAL FROM RHIZOMELIKE STRUCTURE

🗡 **ZONES 4–7, 14–24**

☼ **FULL SUN**

💧 **REGULAR WATER DURING GROWTH AND BLOOM**

Rhodohypoxis baurii

Tufts of narrow, 2–3-in. leaves are nearly obscured by masses of inch-wide, six-petaled flowers over a long spring–summer bloom period. Blossoms range from pink shades to rosy red and white. 'Tetra Red' has especially large red flowers.

In early spring, set roots 1 in. deep and 3–5 in. apart in nonalkaline, well-drained soil; plant where winter moisture can be kept to minimum (a container, for example). Stop watering when foliage yellows in fall. Divide crowded plantings in early spring, just as growth begins. Good in rock gardens.

This little charmer is native to South African mountain meadows where summer rainfall is heavy.

Ornamental Edibles

Rhubarb is such a colorful, textural plant that it would likely be popular in gardens even if its stems weren't so delicious. Once you start growing your own edibles, you'll come to appreciate each plant's natural beauty—but some are definitely prettier than others. Consider the pleasing form of artichoke, cabbage, kale, parsley, and squash plants. And to bring color to the kitchen garden, plant scarlet runner beans, eggplant, nasturtiums, peppers, sunflowers, and colored-leaf forms of lettuce and mustard greens.

Rhodophiala bifida

Amaryllidaceae

PERENNIAL FROM BULB

- ✿ ZONES 8, 9, 12–24
- ☼ FULL SUN
- 🌢 REGULAR WATER DURING GROWTH AND BLOOM

Rhodophiala bifida

Native to the Andes Mountains of Argentina and Uruguay, this bulbous perennial puts up a few foot-long leaves and a foot-tall flower stalk that bears two to six bright red, 2-in.-long, narrow-petaled blooms in late summer, early autumn. They resemble a small amaryllis (*Hippeastrum*). Plants spread willingly and put on a fine show.

Plant drifts of bulbs in fertile, well-drained soil in fall; keep tops of bulb necks even with soil surface. Protect from slugs and snails. Water thoroughly, then keep soil barely moist until leaves emerge. Once plants sprout, increase watering, but don't let soil become soggy.

Rhoeo spathacea.

See *Tradescantia spathacea*

Rhopalostylis

Arecaceae

PALMS

- ✿ ZONES 17, 23, 24; H1, H2
- ☼ ◑ FULL SUN OR PARTIAL SHADE
- 🌢 REGULAR WATER

Rhopalostylis sapida

From the South Pacific Islands, these feather palms have long, clean trunks marked with closely spaced rings. Moderate growth rate. Best in frost-free gardens. (For more on palms, see "Meet the Palms," page 471.)

R. baueri. From Norfolk Island. To 50 ft. tall, 20 ft. wide. The beautiful curving, arching leaves grow to 6–9 ft. long.

R. sapida. NIKAU PALM, SHAVING BRUSH PALM. From New Zealand. To 30 ft. tall, 15 ft. wide. Feathery leaves 4–8 ft. long stand upright from prominent bulge at top of trunk. Good container plant where small space dictates an upright palm.

Rhubarb

Polygonaceae

PERENNIAL

- ✿ BEST IN ZONES A1–A3; 1–11; ALSO SUCCEEDS IN ZONES 14–24
- ☼ ◑ PARTIAL SHADE IN HOTTEST CLIMATES
- 🌢 REGULAR WATER
- ✦ LEAVES ARE POISONOUS IF INGESTED; USE LEAF STEMS ONLY

Rhubarb

Huge, heart-shaped, crinkled leaves are carried on rhubarb's thick, typically red-tinted stalks. These deciduous plants, which are as showy as many ornamentals, easily grow 3 ft. high and 6 ft. wide, and develop very large roots. Leafstalks have a delicious, tart flavor and are typically used like fruit in sauces and pies. Flowers are insignificant, but spikelike white (or red and white) bracts are big and showy, appear in midspring. Preferred varieties include 'Cherry' ('Crimson Cherry') and 'Mac-Donald', both with red stalks; and 'Victoria', which produces greenish stalks. Rhubarb is probably a hybrid between *Rheum rhaponticum* and *R. palmatum*, both from China. For strictly ornamental kinds, see *Rheum*.

Needs some winter chill for thick stems, good red color (if you grow a red variety). Plant divisions (containing at least one bud) 3–6 ft. apart in late winter or early spring. In Zones 10 and 11, treat as an annual, planting in fall for cool-season harvest (plants tend to rot in heat of late spring, summer). Elsewhere, delay harvest until the third season, when you can pull off leafstalks for 4 or 5 weeks in spring; older, huskier plants can take up to 8 weeks of pulling. Harvest by pulling stalks sideways and outward; don't cut, since the remaining stub would decay. Never remove all the leaves from a single plant; stop harvesting when slender leafstalks appear. After harvest, feed and water freely; cut out any blossom stalks that appear. In the mildest areas, plants won't die back completely in winter.

Rhus

SUMAC

Anacardiaceae

EVERGREEN AND DECIDUOUS SHRUBS AND TREES

- ✿ ZONES VARY BY SPECIES
- ☼ FULL SUN
- ◐ 🌢 LITTLE TO MODERATE WATER
- 🦅 RED FRUITS ATTRACT BIRDS

Rhus typhina

Of the ornamental sumacs, deciduous kinds are the most hardy to cold; they are noted for brilliant fall leaf color and, on female plants, showy clusters of (usually) red fruits. They tend to produce suckers, especially if their roots are disturbed by cultivation. All sumac species thrive in almost any soil, as long as drainage is good (soggy soils can kill them).

Poison oak and poison ivy were once members of the genus *Rhus*, but they have been reclassified as *Toxicodendron*.

R. aromatica. FRAGRANT SUMAC. Deciduous shrub. Zones 1–3, 10. Native to eastern North America. Fast-growing plant to 3–5 ft. tall, sprawling 5 ft. or wider. Three-leafleted leaves to 3 in. long are fragrant when brushed against or

CLOCKWISE FROM TOP: *Rhus integrifolia*; *R. ovata*; *R. glabra*

crushed. Foliage turns red in fall. Tiny yellowish flowers in spring; small red fruit. Coarse bank cover, groundcover for poor or dry soils. 'Gro-Low' grows 2–3 ft. high, 6–8 ft. wide.

R. copallina. SHINING SUMAC. Deciduous shrub or tree. Zones 2–9, 14–18. From eastern U.S. To 10–30 ft. tall, spreading indefinitely by suckers. Foot-long leaves are divided featherwise into 9 to 12 leaflets, each to 4 in. long; turn brilliant red in fall. Greenish, 6-in. flower spikes in summer are followed by clusters of dark red, fuzzy fruits.

R. glabra. SMOOTH SUMAC. Deciduous shrub or tree. Zones 1–10, 14–17. Native to much of North America. Upright grower to 10 ft., sometimes treelike to 20 ft. Spreads widely by suckers; in the wild, forms large patches. Looks much like *R. typhina* and has the same garden uses, but usually grows lower and does not have velvety branches. Leaves are divided into 11 to 23 tooth-edged, rather narrow, 2–5-in.-long leaflets that are deep green above, whitish beneath; scarlet autumn foliage. Inconspicuous early-

summer flowers are followed by showy clusters of scarlet fruits that remain on bare branches well into winter.

R. integrifolia. LEMONADE BERRY. Evergreen shrub. Zones 8, 9, 14–17, 19–24. Native to coastal Southern California, Channel Islands, Baja California. Generally 3–10 ft. tall and wide; rarely treelike to 30 ft. Leathery dark green leaves are oval to nearly round. White or pinkish flowers in dense clusters from midwinter to spring (sometimes from early winter into summer). Clustered small, flattish fruits are reddish and gummy, with tart pulp that can be used to flavor drinks—hence the common name.

Grows best near coast, where established plants need no irrigation. Makes a wonderful groundcover on rocky slopes exposed to salt-laden winds; one plant eventually sprawls over a wide area, even down cliffs. In less windy places, use as a tall screen or background plant. Excellent espalier against

fences and walls. Can be trimmed to make a dense formal hedge and maintained just under a foot wide. Useful in erosion control. Very susceptible to verticillium wilt.

R. lancea. AFRICAN SUMAC. Evergreen tree. Zones 8, 9, 12–24. Slow grower to 20–30 ft. tall and 20–35 ft. wide. Open, spreading habit; graceful, weeping outer branchlets. Dark green leaves are divided into three willowlike, 4–5-in.-long leaflets. Inconspicuous early-spring flowers are followed by clusters of pea-size yellow or red fruit that can make a mess on pavement. This species can be trained to a single trunk or allowed to grow as a multitrunked tree somewhat resembling olive (*Olea*). Makes a good specimen, background plant, or screen; can also be clipped into a hedge. Takes desert heat; susceptible to Texas root rot.

R. microphylla. DESERT SUMAC. Deciduous shrub. Zones 10–13. Native to southwestern U.S. and Mexico. Grows to 8 ft. (possibly 15 ft.) tall, 12 ft. wide. Leaves are divided featherwise into five to nine small (less than ½ in. long) leaflets. Clusters of little white flowers appear in spring before leafout; these are followed in early summer by tiny, hairy orange or red fruit.

R. ovata (Schmaltzia ovata). Evergreen shrub. Zones 9–12, 14–24. Typically grows to 4–10 ft. tall and wide, though it can be shorter or taller, upright or spreading. Native to the dry slopes of Arizona, Southern California, and Baja California, always away from the coast. Takes well to pruning. Glossy, leathery leaves are somewhat trough-shaped, pointed at tips. Dense clusters of white or pinkish spring flowers are followed by small, reddish, hairy fruit coated with a sugary secretion. Same landscape uses as *R. integrifolia*, but for inland areas rather than seacoast. Relatively pest-free.

R. trilobata. SQUAWBUSH, SKUNKBUSH. Deciduous shrub. Zones 1–12, 14–21. Native from Illinois westward to Texas and California, north to Washington. Similar in most details to *R. aromatica*, but most people find the scent of the bruised

leaves unpleasant. Clumping habit makes it a natural low hedge; also good for erosion control. Brilliant yellow to red fall color.

R. typhina. STAGHORN SUMAC. Deciduous shrub or tree. Zones A1–A3; 1–10, 14–17. From eastern North America. Upright to 15 ft. (sometimes 30 ft.) tall, spreading much wider by suckers. Very similar to species *R. glabra*, but the branches have a velvety coat of short brown hairs—much like antlers of a deer "in velvet." Leaves are divided into 11 to 31 toothed, 5-in.-long leaflets; foliage is deep green above, grayish beneath; turns yellow-orange to rich red in fall. Blooms in early summer, bearing 4–8-in.-long clusters of tiny greenish blossoms followed by clusters of fuzzy crimson fruits that hang on all winter, gradually turning brown. 'Laciniata' is a female selection with deeply cut leaflets; it grows 10–12 ft. tall. 'Tiger Eyes' is also dissected, but golden, growing about 6 ft. tall and wide.

Both *R. typhina* and *R. glabra* take extreme heat and cold. Big, divided leaves give tropical effect; fall show is brilliant (for best effect, plant among evergreens). Bare branches make a fine silhouette in winter; fruit is decorative. Both species colonize aggressively by root suckers—a potential problem, especially in small gardens. They grow well when confined to large containers.

R. virens. EVERGREEN SUMAC. Evergreen shrub. Zones 10–13. Native to southeastern Arizona, New Mexico, Texas, and Mexico. To 12 ft. tall and wide, with dark green leaves divided featherwise into five to nine 1½-in. leaflets. White spring and summer flowers (not showy) are followed by small, berrylike red fruit. Tolerates open shade, making it a good choice for an understory plant beneath tall trees.

Rhynchelytrum nerviglume.
See *Melinis nerviglumis*

Rhynchospermum.
See *Trachelospermum*

R

Ribes

CURRANT, GOOSEBERRY

Grossulariaceae

EVERGREEN AND DECIDUOUS SHRUBS

🌡 **ZONES VARY BY SPECIES**

☀ ◑ **FULL SUN OR PARTIAL SHADE**

◐ ◑ ● **WATER NEEDS VARY BY SPECIES**

🦋 **ATTRACT BIRDS, BUTTERFLIES**

Ribes sanguineum

Those without spines are called currants; those with spines are known as gooseberries. The following species are grown ornamentally; see Currant and Gooseberry for strictly fruiting types. Members of this genus are alternate hosts to white pine blister rust and are still banned in a few areas where white pines grow.

R. alpinum. ALPINE CURRANT. Deciduous shrub. Zones A2, A3; 1–6, 10. Native to Europe. Dense, twiggy growth to 4–5 ft. (rarely taller) and equally wide. Roundish, ½–1½-in.-wide, deep bright green leaves with toothed, lobed edges appear very early in spring. Flowers and fruit are not showy. Good hedge. 'Green Mound' and 'Green Jeans' are dwarf forms about half the size of the species. Regular water.

R. aureum (R. odoratum). GOLDEN CURRANT. Deciduous shrub. Zones A2, A3; 1–12, 14–23, except as noted. Native to inland regions of the West. Erect growth to 3–6 ft. tall and wide. Light green leaves with lobed, toothed edges. Small, bright yellow spring flowers, usually with a spicy fragrance, in 1–2½-in.-long clusters. Summer berries turn from yellow to red to black. Moderate to regular water. Rust-resistant

'Crandall' (*R. odoratum* 'Crandall') has large, shiny black fruit with the rich, sweet-tart flavor of *R. nigrum*. *R. a. gracillimum*, the more tender California form (Zones 6–10, 14–24), has unscented blooms that age to reddish orange.

R. indecorum. WHITE FLOWERING CURRANT. Deciduous shrub. Zones 7–9, 11, 14–24. Native to Coast Ranges in Southern California. To 6–9 ft. tall, 4–6 ft. wide. Thickish, scallop-edged leaves to 1½ in. long; dark green and roughly hairy above, white and fuzzy beneath. Clusters of small white flowers enclosed in pink bracts put on a good show in winter. Needs no irrigation but will tolerate garden watering.

R. malvaceum. CHAPARRAL CURRANT. Deciduous shrub. Zones 6–9, 14–24. Native to slopes in California's Coast Ranges. To 5 ft. tall and wide, with hairy, roundish dull green leaves and short clusters of fragrant pink flowers throughout fall, winter. Red fruit. Needs no irrigation, but give it moderate water if you don't want it to go dormant in summer.

R. nigrum. BLACK CURRANT. Deciduous shrub. Zones A1–A3; 1–7. Native to Europe and Asia. To 3–5 ft. tall and wide. Deep green, three-lobed leaves have an odd scent. Drooping clusters of whitish spring flowers develop into juicy, shiny black fruit with a sweet-tart flavor like that of blackberry. Regular water.

R. odoratum. See *R. aureum.*

R. sanguineum. RED FLOWERING CURRANT. Deciduous shrub. Zones A3; 4–9, 14–24. Native to Coast Ranges from California to British Columbia. To 5–12 ft. tall and wide, with maplelike, dark green leaves. In spring, produces drooping, 2–4-in.-long clusters of 10 to 30 small deep pink to red flowers. Blue-black fruit has a whitish bloom. Most commonly sold is *R. s. glutinosum* (more southerly in origin than the species); its blossoms are typically deep or pale pink, carried in clusters of 15 to 40. 'Barrie Coate', 'Elk River Red', 'King Edward VII', and 'Pulborough Scarlet' are red-flowering selections. Pink varieties include 'Brocklebankii', with

gold foliage; 'Claremont', with two-tone blossoms aging to red; 'Poky's Pink'; and 'Spring Showers', with 8-in. flower clusters. 'Album' and 'White Icicle' are good white varieties. Little to moderate water.

R. speciosum. FUCHSIA-FLOWERING GOOSEBERRY. Nearly evergreen shrub. Zones 7–9, 14–24. Native near coast, from central coast of California south to Baja California. Erect to 4–8 ft. tall, 6–10 ft. wide, with spiny, often bristly stems. Thick-textured, maplelike, 1-in. leaves are glossy dark green above, lighter beneath. Deep crimson to cherry red flowers, borne winter to spring, are drooping and fuchsia-like, with long, protruding stamens. Gummy, bristly red berries. Excellent barrier. Needs no irrigation, but moderate water keeps it nearly evergreen in summer (it can also take regular moisture). Partial shade in hottest climates.

R. viburnifolium. CATALINA PERFUME, EVERGREEN CURRANT. Evergreen shrub. Zones 5, 7–9, 14–17, 19–24. Native to Catalina Island, Baja California. To 3–6 ft. tall, spreading to 12 ft. wide. Wine red stems are arching or half trailing; they may root in moist soil. Roundish, leathery dark green leaves are fragrant after rain or when crushed (some liken the scent to pine, others to apples). Light pink to purplish flowers from midwinter into spring. Red berries. To keep plant low, cut out upright-growing stems. Needs partial shade in hottest climates. Needs no irrigation but can take moderate water. Good on banks or under native oaks where watering is undesirable.

Try red flowering currant behind a bench flanked by Western sword fern (*Polystichum munitum*), Douglas iris, hummingbird sage (*Salvia spathacea*), *Heuchera maxima*, and wild ginger (*Asarum caudatum*).

Ricinus communis

CASTOR BEAN

Euphorbiaceae

EVERGREEN SHRUB USUALLY GROWN AS ANNUAL

🌡 **ZONES 23, 24; H1, H2; ALL ZONES AS ANNUAL**

☀ **FULL SUN**

◐ ◑ **LITTLE TO MODERATE WATER**

☠ **SEEDS (OR BEANS) ARE POISONOUS IF INGESTED**

Ricinus communis 'Carmel Bright Red'

A bold-leafed plant from Africa and Asia, castor bean can provide a screen or leafy background 6–15 ft. tall and half as wide in a single season. Where winters are mild, it becomes woody and treelike. But most often it is grown as a 4–6-ft. annual shrub or container plant. Has naturalized in small parts of many climates. Don't plant it where small children play—the toxic seeds are attractive and deadly (pinch off burlike seed capsules while they are small to prevent seed formation). Foliage and seeds occasionally cause severe contact allergies as well.

Large-lobed leaves are 1–3 ft. across on vigorous young plants, smaller on older plants. Unimpressive, small white flowers are borne in clusters on foothigh stalks in summer, followed by attractive prickly husks that contain seeds. Grown commercially for castor oil extracted from seeds. Many horticultural varieties with leaves tinged in red, pink, and purple. 'Zanzibarensis' has very large green leaves.

Robinia
LOCUST
Papilionaceae
DECIDUOUS TREES OR SHRUB

🌡 **ZONES VARY BY SPECIES**

☼ **FULL SUN**

◊ 💧 **LITTLE TO MODERATE WATER**

⬧ **BARK, LEAVES, AND SEEDS ARE POISONOUS IF INGESTED**

Robinia × ambigua

These fast-growing trees are well adapted to hot, dry regions. Leaves are divided like feathers into many roundish leaflets. Clusters of white or pink, sweet pea–shaped flowers bloom from midspring to early summer, followed by beanlike pods about 4 in. long. Locust trees tolerate poor soil and can get by on little or no water, but wood is brittle, roots are aggressive, and plants often spread by suckers.

R. × ambigua. Tree. Zones 2–24. Hybrid between *R. pseudoacacia* and *R. viscosa*, a seldom-grown pink-flowering locust.

'Decaisneana'. To 40–50 ft. tall and 20 ft. wide. Flowers like those of *R. pseudoacacia*, but color is pale pink.

'Idahoensis'. IDAHO LOCUST. Tree of moderately fast growth to a shapely 40 ft. tall and 30 ft. wide. Bright magenta-rose flowers in 8-in. clusters; one of the showiest of locusts in bloom. Good flowering tree for Rocky Mountain gardens.

R. neomexicana. DESERT LOCUST. Shrub or tree. Zones 2, 3, 7–11, 14, 18–24. Native from California's desert mountains to Arizona and New Mexico. Thorny plant; usually seen as a shrub about 6 ft. high and wide but can become a 30-ft. tree. Drooping, 6-in. clusters of inch-wide pink flowers.

R. pseudoacacia. BLACK LOCUST. Tree. Zones 1–24. Native to eastern and central U.S. Fast growth to 40–75 ft. tall and 30–60 ft. wide, with rather sparse, open branching habit. Deeply furrowed brown bark. Thorny branches. Leaves divided into 7 to 19 leaflets, each 1–2 in. long. White, fragrant, ½–¾-in.-long flowers are held in dense, pendent clusters that reach 4–8 in. long.

Little valued in its native territory except as a source of honey and fence posts, it has been widely planted (and has subsequently escaped) in much of the West, including California's Gold Country. It manufactures its own fertilizer through nitrogen-fixing root nodule bacteria and can colonize the poorest soil. With some pruning and training in its early years, it can be a truly handsome flowering tree. Has been used as a street tree but is a bad choice for narrow parking strips or under power lines. Wood is extremely hard and tough; suckers are difficult to prune out where soil is not watered.

'Frisia'. To 50 ft. tall and 25 ft. wide. New growth is nearly orange; mature leaves are yellow, turning greener in summer heat. Thorns and young wood are red.

'Lace Lady' ('Twisty Baby'). Dwarf to 8–10 ft. tall and 12–15 ft. wide. Picturesquely twisted branches; few flowers.

'Pyramidalis' ('Fastigiata'). Narrow, columnar, to 50 ft. tall and 10 ft. wide.

'Tortuosa'. Slow grower to 50 ft. tall and 30 ft. wide, with twisted branches. Few flowers.

'Umbraculifera' ('Inermis'). Dense and round-headed tree, to 20 ft. tall and wide. Usually grafted 6–8 ft. tall on another locust to create a living green lollipop. Few flowers.

R. 'Purple Robe'. Tree. Zones 2–24. Hybrid of uncertain parentage often sold as *R. pseudoacacia* 'Purple Robe'. Resembles *R. × ambigua* 'Idahoensis' but has darker, purple-pink flowers, reddish bronze new growth; blooms 2 weeks earlier and over a longer period. Suckers from the rootstock spread and reseed heavily.

Rodgersia
Saxifragaceae
PERENNIALS

🌡 **ZONES 2–9, 14–17**

☼ ◑ **PARTIAL SHADE IN HOTTEST CLIMATES**

💧 **AMPLE WATER**

Rodgersia pinnata

A bold perennial for damp parts of the woodland garden, this native of China and Japan has handsome, divided leaves and clustered tiny flowers in plumes reminiscent of astilbe. Bloom comes in early to midsummer. Primary feature is foliage, which often takes on bronze tones in late summer. Plants spread by thick rhizomes, need rich soil. The species hybridize freely. Dormant in winter; provide winter mulch in cold climates.

R. aesculifolia. To 6 ft. tall, 3 ft. wide. Leaves are divided like fingers of hand into five to seven tooth-edged, 10-in. leaflets; similar to horsechestnut (*Aesculus*). White flowers.

R. pinnata. To 4 ft. tall, 2½ ft. wide. Leaves have five to nine 8-in. leaflets. Red flowers. 'Chocolate Wing' foliage is chocolate, bronze, and dark green, with red flowers; 'Fireworks' foliage has red-tinged edges, pink-red flowers; 'Superba' has bronze-tinted foliage that gives rise to bright pink flowers.

R. podophylla. To 5 ft. tall, 6 ft. wide. Coppery green leaves divided into five 10-in.-long leaflets. Creamy flowers.

R. sambucifolia. To 3 ft. high and wide. Leaves have up to 11 leaflets. Flat-topped clusters of white or pink flowers.

Romneya coulteri
MATILIJA POPPY
Papaveraceae
SHRUBBY PERENNIAL

🌡 **ZONES 4–12, 14–24; H1**

☼ **FULL SUN**

◊ 💧 **LITTLE OR NO WATER TO MODERATE WATER**

Romneya coulteri

Native to the coastal mountains and valleys of Southern California and Baja California, this spectacular 6–8-ft. perennial is covered with 9-in., yellow-centered white flowers from late spring into summer. Sends up thick stems clothed in irregularly lobed, gray-green leaves and spreads by rhizomes. Each blossom has five or six crepe-papery petals centered with a cluster of golden stamens. 'Butterfly' is a profusely branching plant with smaller flowers of rounded, overlapping petals. 'White Cloud' is exceptionally vigorous, with profuse, very large blossoms.

Use on hillsides as soil binder, in marginal areas, or in wide borders. Invasive; don't plant near less vigorous plants. Tolerates many types of soils. Withhold summer irrigation to keep growth in check. Cut nearly to ground in late fall. New shoots emerge after first rains in winter. Although easy to grow once established, the plant is very difficult to propagate. Easiest way to get more plants is to dig up rooted suckers from spreading roots. To help seeds germinate, mix them with potting soil in a foil-lined flat; burn pine needles on top of flat for 30 minutes, then water and hope for sprouting.

R

Rosa

ROSE

Rosaceae

DECIDUOUS AND EVERGREEN SHRUBS
AND VINES

✎ **ALL ZONES, EXCEPT AS NOTED**

☀ ◗ **FULL SUN OR LIGHT SHADE**

💧 **REGULAR WATER, EXCEPT AS NOTED**

Rosa 'Abraham Darby'

It might be the fragrance alone, it could be the sight of a rose arbor in full bloom, or perhaps it's just the serene grace of a single red hybrid tea rose in a vase—but sooner or later, something about roses grabs the attention of nearly every temperate-zone gardener. More than 14,000 varieties are grown, most the descendants of about 150 species. And while most are deciduous, roses can be evergreen in mild climates. Their stems, sometimes quite prickly, may be erect, arching, trailing, or scrambling. Leaves are usually divided into three, five, or seven leaflets—sometimes more—usually with toothed margins. And scent can be intense or almost nonexistent.

Many types of roses carry their blossoms in clusters, but some (notably hybrid teas) tend to bear their flowers singly, one bud per stem. Some blooms are flattish rosettes; others are cupped; hybrid tea roses have a conical shape, with high, pointed centers. The blossoms range from single (4 to 8 petals) to semidouble (9 to 16 petals), double (17 to 25 petals), full (26 to 40 petals), and very full (to 150 petals or more). Thanks to the hybridizing efforts of breeders and enthusiastic gardeners over many centuries, roses are now available in all colors except blue and black, plus color blends.

Rose bushes are natural choices for flower beds and shrub borders; some also make fine hedges or container plants. The largest are the old garden roses, the climbers, the grandifloras, and some shrub roses. Hybrid teas and floribundas generally grow with more restraint. Miniature roses are the smallest; some reach only 1 ft. high. For a little formality, consider a standard rose—a bush rose grown on a 36-in.-high, bare stem. A patio rose tree is a small standard, usually 18–24 in. high.

Groundcover roses make a low, mounding carpet of color up to 8 ft. wide. They are most often massed on a slope or an area of the garden where other knee-high shrubs might be used. They also make good container plants.

Climbing roses can be grown on vertical surfaces or freestanding supports. The most vigorous ones will cover a house roof or grow to the top of a large tree. More moderate climbers clothe arbors and tall walls. Small miniature climbers and small climbers, sometimes called pillar roses, are suitable for a pyramid or trellis. In addition to the roses that are classified as climbers, there are old garden roses and shrub roses that can climb.

CONSIDERING CLIMATE

The most reliable way to find roses that grow well in your climate is to visit municipal or private rose gardens in your region. Varieties that are performing well there are obviously good choices—and you'll see how big they grow. Climate affects the size of many roses; for example, 'Sally Holmes' in Seattle might be a 5-ft.-tall bush, but in Southern California it can be a huge rambler, with canes to 35 ft. long. David Austin roses grow with admirable reserve in England and similarly cool climates in the West, but in the warmest zones, they can grow much taller. It can also be helpful to connect with a local chapter of the American Rose Society (*ars.org*).

In mild-winter regions, some roses that are adapted to very cold climates produce few flowers. In areas with cool summers or cool nights, roses with a large number of petals tend to "ball," opening poorly or not at all. In the absence of heat, dark-colored flowers may appear muddy rather than vibrant. Also, because the overcast skies and fog common in cool-summer zones encourage foliar diseases such as mildew, rust, and black spot, varieties noted for their disease resistance grow and bloom better there.

In hot-summer areas, flowers open rapidly. Varieties with few

CLOCKWISE FROM TOP: *Rosa* 'Teasing Georgia'; *R.* 'Memorial Day'; *R.* 'Hot Cocoa'

petals (less than 25) may go from bud to fully open blossom in just a few hours on a hot day. Those with more petals take longer to open and stay attractive longer. Some colors (the golden yellow in 'Peace', for example) may fade almost to white in very hot weather, and dark reds may sunburn. During intensely hot desertlike weather, plants may almost go dormant, causing flower production to drop markedly. (To avoid

R

these problems, plant roses where they will receive afternoon shade, and away from reflected heat from light-colored surfaces.) Best flowering in hot-summer areas is in spring and autumn.

If you live in a cold-winter area, choose roses that are sufficiently cold-hardy for your region, or check out how to protect less hardy varieties in winter (see "Winter Protection for Roses," right). In Zones 1–3, hybrid teas, grandifloras, and floribundas need protection. However, the hardy hybrids (bred primarily in Canada and Iowa) can go through winter with little or no special protection. Many old roses (chiefly those that flower only in spring), as well as a number of species roses and their hybrids, also survive in Zones 1–3 with scant or no winter protection. In Alaska, the native Nootka rose is hardy enough to need no protection, as are some of the other extra-hardy species roses and their hybrids, such as the wonderfully fragrant rugosas (*R. rugosa*).

BUYING PLANTS

Mail-order catalogs and/or websites offer the widest choice of roses; they are practically the only way to shop if you are looking for lesser-known varieties. You'll also find roses for sale in local nurseries and garden centers, home improvement and hardware stores, and even some supermarkets.

Container-grown roses.
Plants in plastic or pressed-peat pots are available from retail stores from early spring through fall, year-round in mild-climate regions. The best time to shop is in mid- to late spring, when the plants are in bloom, the largest selection is available, and you have a chance to plant out your purchases before summer heat arrives. You can, however, plant container-grown roses at any time during the growing season (see "Planting," page 576).

Choose plants with strong new growth and healthy-looking leaves. A large (preferably 5 gal.) container is better than a small one; it's less likely that the roots had to be cut back severely to fit in the container when the

Winter Protection for Roses

Where winter temperatures regularly drop to 10°F (–12°C), tender roses, such as many hybrid teas, floribundas, and grandifloras, need protection. Low temperatures can kill exposed canes; repeated freezing and thawing will kill canes by rupturing their cells; and winter winds can desiccate exposed canes.

A healthy plant that is hardened off before the first hard frost withstands harsh winters better than a weak or actively growing one. Prepare plants for winter by timing your last fertilizer application of the growing season so that bushes will have stopped putting on new growth by the expected date of the first sharp frost. Leave the last crop of blooms on your plants to form hips (fruits), which will aid the ripening process by stopping growth. Keep plants well watered until the soil freezes.

After a couple of hard freezes have occurred and nighttime temperatures remain consistently below freezing, mound soil over the base of each bush to a height of 1 ft. Collect the soil from another part of the garden; do not scoop soil from around the roses, exposing their surface roots. Cut excessively long canes back to 2–4 ft. (the lower figure applies in Zones A1–A3 and 1, 2, and 3a). Use soft twine to tie the canes together to keep them from whipping around in wind.

When the mound has frozen, cover it with evergreen boughs, straw, or other fairly lightweight material that will act as insulation and keep the mound frozen. A 3–4-ft.-tall wire-mesh cylinder filled with noncompacting insulating material (such as straw, hay, oak leaves, or pine needles) may preserve much of the cane growth it encloses.

Remove the protection in spring after frost danger is past. Gradually remove the soil mounds as they thaw, working carefully to avoid breaking new growth that may have begun sprouting under the soil.

PROTECTING CLIMBERS. Mound climbing roses the same way, but protect all of their canes. Where winter lows range from 5°F to –10°F (–15°C to –23°C), insulate the canes by wrapping them in burlap stuffed with straw or a similar material. Where temperatures normally go below –10°F (–23°C), remove canes from their support, gently bend them to the ground, and cover them with soil. (A wiser plan, however, is to plant only climbers known to be hardy in such climates.)

PROTECTING STANDARDS. Standards (tree roses) may be insulated in the same manner as climbers, but they still may not survive, since the head of the tree is the most exposed. Some gardeners dig up their standards each year; pack the roots loosely in soil; and store the plants in a cool garage, basement, or shed until replanting time in spring.

A simpler technique is to grow standards in large containers and move them in fall to a cool shed or garage where temperatures won't drop below 10°F (–12°C).

PROTECTION IN ALASKA. If you are growing roses in Alaska, you'll probably agree with the rosarian in Anchorage who told us, "Roses aren't hard to grow in Alaska, just tough to keep." To overwinter tender hybrid roses, dig a trench 2 ft. deep beside the house and bury your roses in it, removing any remaining foliage first. Dig them up for replanting in mid-May. Simply mounding soil over cut-back bushes isn't enough protection.

If the roses are in pots, you can move them to a basement wall under a deck for winter and toss wood shavings over them; or take the pots into a sunroom. Some gardeners inter their roses—they dig a trench in the garden, slip in a bottomless wood box made to fit the trench, put the roses in the box, and cover them with builder's sand.

plant was potted. Avoid plants with roots protruding from the bottom of the container, as well as those showing weak growth or blackened areas of dieback on the canes. All are signs that the plant has been in the container too long and may not establish well in your garden.

Bare-root roses. During late winter and early spring, nurseries and stores may also offer bare-root roses; these are dormant plants with no soil on the roots. If you shop from mail-order nurseries, typically you'll receive bare-root plants, and the shipping may begin in fall.

It doesn't harm the roses to be dug up and transported bare-root, and although you can't see your roses in flower, bare-root plants have advantages over plants sold in containers: they are generally less expensive, and they adapt to native soil more quickly.

R

»

CLOCKWISE FROM LEFT: *Rosa*
'Dark Lady'; *R.* 'Sally Holmes';
R. 'Molineux'

Bare-root plants are graded 1, 1½, or 2, number 1 being the best. Suppliers usually offer only grade 1 plants, and they will often replace plants that fail to grow. A healthy bare-root rose has thick, green canes and a big cluster of sturdy, fibrous roots. Reject any with dried-out or squishy roots or with canes that are weak, shriveled, or beginning to leaf out.

Buy bare-root roses as soon as they appear for sale, rather than when they are marked down as bargains. Be wary of packaged bare-root roses displayed indoors on store shelves; the roots are wrapped in a moist material, but indoor warmth may cause the material to dry out. Of bare roots it is aptly said that if they dry, they die.

In milder-winter zones, you can plant bare-root roses throughout winter. In areas where the ground freezes, plant either in fall before the soil freezes (then protect plants over winter) or in early spring after the soil has thawed.

Budded or own-root roses. Many old roses, species roses and their hybrids, and virtually all miniature and shrub roses are propagated by cuttings and grown on their own roots. About 70 percent of modern roses are budded onto a standard understock—a completely different rose variety whose root system thrives in a wide range of soils and climates. There is a current trend, however, to try new varieties on their own roots and grow them that way when feasible.

Both budded and own-root roses grow well and produce fine flowers. Budded plants are often larger at the time of purchase than own-root plants, but both kinds will be equally husky within a year or two. Own-root roses do have one advantage: if the plant is killed to the ground by cold (or mowed down by accident), it will regrow from the roots as the rose you want. Regrowth from roots of a budded plant, in contrast, will be from the understock rose, whose flower won't look anything like the rose you bought. Another plus: own-root roses don't sucker.

MODERN ROSES

Most of the thousands of roses for sale are modern roses—ones introduced after 1867, the year the first hybrid tea rose was developed. For more than 100 years after that, breeders raced to produce the most perfect hybrid teas, grandifloras, and floribundas, the flowering "modern" rose bushes that form the core of many public and residential rose gardens. However, in the past few years, landscape roses, particularly the lax and leafy shrub roses, have become almost as popular.

The chart on the opposite page presents a list of excellent modern roses grouped by type and color. Refer to the information below to learn about the ancestry and growing characteristics of the different types of modern roses.

Shrub roses. Planting roses for general landscape use is not a new idea; some fine shrub roses date to the early 20th century. Today, however, rose breeders are developing new roses for use purely as flowering shrubs. The emphasis is on plants that bloom prolifically over a long season and have abundant disease-resistant foliage; some breeders are also developing plants that can survive cold winters with no special attention. Modern shrub roses need little or no pruning to remain shapely. Because they bloom almost continuously, they pair well with perennials in borders.

These shrub roses vary widely in growth habit and flower color; loose categories are listed below. Some shrub roses make tidy small climbers. For more shrub rose choices, check the section on species roses on page 575.

Hybrid musk shrub roses. These were developed in the first 30 years of the 20th century from a descendant of the musk rose (*R. moschata*). Hybrid musks are large (6–8 ft. tall) shrubs or small climbers that perform well in dappled or partial shade as well as in sun. Most are nearly everblooming, with fragrant, clustered flowers. Some hybrid musks don't flower prolifically in mild climates.

Hardy shrub roses. Canadian and Midwestern breeding programs have produced rose bushes that survive northern and Rocky Mountain winters with virtually no special protection against cold. Some resemble floribundas and grandifloras; their ancestries include hardy species roses as well as floribundas and hybrid tea roses. These have "country" names like 'Country Dancer' and 'Prairie Princess'. Others are mostly large shrubs to small climbers, bred in part from *R. rugosa*. Many of these are named for explorers: 'John Cabot' and 'William Baffin' among them.

Miscellaneous shrub roses. Many modern shrub roses are of complex or unknown ancestry and fall outside the categories listed above. Among these miscellaneous shrub roses are several very well-known ones, such as 'Home Run' and 'Knock Out'. 'Sally Holmes' grows like a climber in mild climates.

Trademarked roses. Recognizing public loyalty to brand-name products, some rose

R

MODERN ROSES

The following roses are among the best choices for Western gardens. The designation *WRHF* indicates membership in the World Rose Hall of Fame, *AARS* identifies winners of the All-America Rose Selections award, and *f* indicates roses with dependably powerful fragrance.

SHRUBS

The designation *DA* indicates David Austin roses, *h* hardy shrub roses, and *m* hybrid musk roses.

Red: Alexander Mackenzie (h), Carefree Spirit (AARS), Champlain, Darcey Bussell (DA) (f), Double Knock Out, Henry Kelsey (h), Home Run, Knock Out (AARS), Linda Campbell, Munstead Wood (DA) (f), Oso Easy Cherry Pie

Pink: Ballerina (h), Blushing Knock Out, Bonica (WRHF) (AARS), Carefree Delight (AARS), Carefree Wonder (AARS), Erfurt (f), Gertrude Jekyll (DA) (f), Harlow Carr (DA) (f), John Cabot (h), Pink Home Run, Pink Meidiland, Sunrise Sunset, Wisley 2008 (DA) (f)

Orange/warm blend: Coral Cove, Lady Elsie May, Oso Easy Honey Bun, Oso Easy Paprika, Watercolors

Yellow: Baby Love, Carefree Sunshine, Graham Thomas (WRHF) (DA), Happenstance, Lemon Splash, Molineux (DA) (f), Sunny Knock Out

White: Buff Beauty (m), Macy's Pride, Sally Holmes (shrub rose in the Northwest, climber in California), Sea Foam, Snowdrift, White Meidiland

Lavender/mauve/purple: Midnight Blue, Outta the Blue, Rhapsody in Blue (but distorted growth in heat)

GROUNDCOVERS

Red: Fire Meidiland, Red Drift, Red Flower Carpet, Red Meidiland, Red Ribbons, Scarlet Flower Carpet, Scarlet Meidiland

Pink: Appleblossom Flower Carpet, Coral Flower Carpet, Peach Drift, Pink Drift, Pink Flower Carpet, Roseberry Blanket, Sweet Drift

Orange/coral: Electric Blanket

Yellow: Happy Chappy, Sunrise Vigorosa, Yellow Flower Carpet

White: Icy Drift, White Flower Carpet, White Meidiland

CLIMBERS

Red: All Ablaze, Altissimo, Blaze Improved, Crimson Sky, Don Juan (f; needs heat to flourish), Dublin Bay, Fourth of July (AARS), Valentine's Day Cl. (miniature)

Pink: Candy Land, Cl. Cécile Brünner, Eden (Pierre de Ronsard) (WRHF), Jeanne Lajoie (miniature), New Dawn (WRHF), Nozomi, Pearly Gates, William Baffin (h)

Orange/warm blend: America (AARS) (f), Jacob's Robe, Joseph's Coat, Polka, Royal Sunset (f)

Yellow: Autumn Sunset (f), Garden Sun, Golden Showers (AARS), Royal Gold, Scent from Above (f), Sky's the Limit

White: Cl. Iceberg, White Dawn (f)

Purple: Night Owl, Purple Splash, Stormy Weather

HYBRID TEAS

Red: Firefighter (f), Ingrid Bergman, In the Mood, Lasting Love, Mister Lincoln (AARS) (f), Olympiad (AARS), Opening Night (AARS)

Pink: Aromatherapy (f), Bewitched (AARS), Falling in Love, Gemini (AARS), Grand Dame, Memorial Day (AARS) (f), New Zealand (f), Pink Promise (AARS), Secret (AARS) (f), Tiffany (AARS) (f)

Orange/warm blend: Brandy (AARS), Cary Grant, Chicago Peace, Double Delight (WRHF) (AARS) (f), Fragrant Cloud (WRHF) (f), Just Joey (WRHF) (f), Marilyn Monroe, Over the Moon, Perfect Moment (AARS), Remember Me, Rio Samba (AARS), Sunset Celebration (AARS), Sunstruck, Tahitian Sunset (AARS)

Yellow: Elina (WRHF), Mellow Yellow, Midas Touch (AARS), Peace (WRHF) (AARS), St. Patrick (AARS), Summer Love

White: Full Sail, Honor (AARS), Moonstone, Pascali (WRHF) (AARS), Sugar Moon

Lavender/mauve: Barbra Streisand (f), Fragrant Plum (f), Neptune (f), Paradise (AARS), Stainless Steel (f)

GRANDIFLORAS

Red: Cherry Parfait (AARS), Crimson Bouquet (AARS), Dick Clark (AARS), Love (AARS), Rock & Roll (f)

Pink: Fame! (AARS), Queen Elizabeth (WRHF) (AARS)

Orange/warm blend: Dream Come True (AARS), Octoberfest

Yellow: Ch-Ching (f), Gold Medal, Strike It Rich (AARS) (f)

Lavender/mauve: Fragrant Plum (f), Wild Blue Yonder (AARS)

FLORIBUNDAS

Red: Drop Dead Red, George Burns, Lavaglut (Lava Flow), Scentimental (AARS) (f), Showbiz (AARS), Topsy Turvy, Trumpeter

Pink: Betty Prior, Brilliant Pink Iceberg, Easy Does It (AARS) (f), Sexy Rexy

Orange/warm blend: Amber Queen (AARS), Betty Boop (AARS), Chihuly, Cinco de Mayo (AARS) (f), Colorific, Day Breaker (AARS), Hot Cocoa (AARS), Livin' Easy (AARS), Mardi Gras (AARS), Marmalade Skies (AARS), Playboy, Pumpkin Patch, Rainbow Sorbet (AARS)

Yellow: Easy Going, Julia Child (AARS) (f), Shockwave, Sunsprite (f), Walking on Sunshine (AARS)

White: Iceberg (WRHF), Moondance (AARS), White Licorice

Lavender/mauve: Burgundy Iceberg, Distant Drums, Ebb Tide (f), Intrigue (AARS) (f)

POLYANTHAS

Red: Wing Ding

Pink: Cécile Brünner (WRHF), China Doll, The Fairy

Orange/warm blend: Margo Koster, Perle d'Or (Yellow Cécile Brünner)

MINIATURES

Red: Gypsy Sunblaze, Red Sunblaze, Ruby Ruby, Warm & Fuzzy

Pink: Baby Boomer, Be My Baby, Coffee Bean, Cupcake, Daddy's Little Girl, Minnie Pearl, Seattle Scentsation

Orange/warm blend: All A'Twitter, Jean Kenneally, Magic Carrousel, Mandarin Sunblaze, Rainbow's End, Smoke Rings

Yellow: Hopscotch, Lemon Drop, Rise 'n' Shine (Golden Sunblaze), Sequoia Gold, Sunbeam, Texas, Tiddly Winks

White: Gourmet Popcorn, Starla

Lavender/mauve: Winsome

R

CLOCKWISE FROM TOP: *Rosa* 'Gold Medal'; *R.* 'Gentle Hermione'; *R.* 'Crimson Meidiland'

breeders have created trademarked "families" to which new varieties can be added.

The Meidiland roses from Meilland, a French firm, were the first in this category to attract significant interest. They did it with the Romantica roses, most of which are named for well-known figures in European arts and letters (such as 'Yves Piaget'); and also with the trademarked Meidiland family of roses (including 'Pink Meidiland' and 'White Meidiland'), which are mostly somewhat billowy shrubs. More recently, their Drift series ('Coral Drift', 'Peach Drift', 'Sweet Drift', and so on) continue the practice with 2-ft. plants that combine the best traits of groundcover roses and miniature roses.

The David Austin English roses are crosses of various old roses (albas, centifolias, gallicas) with modern roses. They capture the lovely old rose forms and fragrances, but they are repeat flowering and come in a range of colors only matched in today's hybrid tea roses. These roses range from low shrubs to plants determined to be climbers regardless of pruning. Many have Chaucerian or Shakespearean names, though the three most popular—'Abraham Darby', 'Graham Thomas', and 'Mary Rose'—commemorate, respectively, an English industrialist, a noted English horticulturist, and the flagship of Henry VIII's fleet.

Flower Carpet is a family of groundcover roses bred by noted German rosarian Werner Noack for easy care and a long season of prolific bloom.

Groundcover roses. These low-growing plants, around 2–2½ ft. high, spread to at least 3½ ft. wide (some reach 6 ft. or wider). Vigor, disease resistance, and a profusion of bloom from late spring until frost are the hallmarks of this category. Groundcover roses are perfect for covering slopes, creating low barriers to foot traffic on level ground, and growing in pots.

The most commonly available groundcover roses are those in the Flower Carpet series, available in red, scarlet, pink, apple blossom, coral, yellow, and white. Several of the trademarked Meidiland roses, such as 'White Meidiland', are sufficiently low growing to be used as groundcovers. 'Sea Foam', a shrub rose, makes a fine groundcover about 3 ft. high and 6 ft. wide, and some miniature roses have a pretty, sprawling habit. Several of the species roses and some of the climbing roses make good groundcovers as well.

Climbing roses. These are simply rose bushes that produce long, strong canes that will grow upright against a wall or arbor. They do not climb by twining or attachment but must be trained through or tied to their support. There are two types of modern climbing roses: large-flowered climbers and climbing sports of bush roses, such as 'Cl. Iceberg' and 'Cl. Cécile Brünner'. Large-flowered climbers generally produce the most blooms, but the climbing sports have the exquisite flowers of their famous parents.

Left to their own devices, many climbers make attractive arching shrubs or even groundcovers. For more climbers, including some very large ones, see the species roses section beginning on page 575.

Hybrid tea roses. These are the classic, aristocratic roses, with long, stylish pointed buds that spiral open to large blossoms with high centers. Typically, hybrid teas carry one blossom at the end of each flowering stem. They bloom profusely in spring, then continue to produce blossoms—either in flushes or continuously—until frosty weather. Their strong, long stems make them ideal for cutting and bringing indoors.

Hybrid tea bushes tend to have an upright, narrow, almost stiff look. They grow 2–6 ft. tall, depending on variety and climate. Group three or more together to create a generous, bushy look. Consider planting low-growing perennials beneath them or a low hedge in front of them to hide their bare ankles (bases of canes are usually sparsely foliaged). Hybrid teas need good growing conditions and more care than some other types, but for many gardeners, their spectacular blooms are worth the extra effort.

Grandiflora, floribunda, and polyantha roses. These are the workhorses of rose gardens, noted for producing large quantities of flowers all summer long. Many have hybrid tea ancestry, evident in the long stems and/or elegant shape of the flowers. Unlike the hybrid teas, however, they produce clusters of blossoms rather than a single flower at the end of each stem; this makes them excellent for providing masses of color.

Grandifloras are about the same size as full-size hybrid teas, and work well at the back of a flower bed or as barrier plants. Floribundas are smaller than hybrid teas—both in flower size and in height; use them for informal hedges, for low flower borders, or as container plants. 'Iceberg', one of the best-selling roses ever, is a floribunda.

Polyanthas produce small blossoms in large sprays; they are compact bushes, generally not much more than 2 ft. high. The first polyanthas appeared in the late 19th century. Two of the early polyanthas are now classics. 'Cécile Brünner' (the shrub dates from 1889, while the climbing form goes back to 1894) has light pink flowers of perfect hybrid tea form. 'The Fairy' (from 1932) is a groundcover rose covered with masses of 1-in. pink flowers.

Miniature roses. These are perfect replicas of hybrid teas and floribundas, but plant size is 1–1½ ft. high, with flowers and foliage in proportion. Grow outdoors in containers, window boxes, rock gardens, and flower gardens; a few also make sweet climbers. Or grow them indoors: pot in rich soil in containers at least 6 in. wide and place in a cool, bright window, or under a plant light. Miniatures are shallow rooted and need regular water and fertilizer. Mini-Floras, which are hybrids between miniatures and floribundas, are primarily known among rose exhibitors.

OLD ROSES

Strictly speaking, old roses are varieties belonging to the rose classes that existed before 1867—the year that the first hybrid tea was introduced. However, in catalogs that

Pruning Roses

Annual pruning contributes to the health, productivity, and longevity of roses. The basic objective is to promote strong growth that will bear good flowers.

1. Prune conservatively. Never chop down a vigorous 6-ft. bush to 1½-ft. stubs unless you want only a few huge blooms for exhibition. (However, in Zones A1–A3 and 1–3, where roses freeze back to their winter protection, you will remove dead wood in spring and may be left with the equivalent of a severely pruned plant.)

2. Prune at the right time. The best pruning time for most roses is at the end of the dormant season, when growth buds begin to swell. The exact time varies according to locality but is usually sometime between mid-January (in mild climates) and early April (in colder ones). Where late frosts are common, be sure not to prune too early—the resulting new growth will be vulnerable to freezes.

3. Use sharp pruners; remove the right branches. Prune out wood that is dead, wood that has no healthy growth coming from it, branches that cross through the plant's center or rub against larger canes, branches that make a bush appear lopsided, as well as any unproductive old canes that strong new ones have replaced during the past season. Removing any foliage that remains on the plant will reduce the incidence of disease later. Then cut back the previous season's growth by one-third to one-half, making cuts above outward-facing buds (except for very spreading varieties, in which some cuts to inside buds will promote more height without producing many crossing branches). The ideal result is a V-shaped bush with a relatively open center.

4. Remove suckers. If any suckers (growth produced from the understock of a budded plant) are present, completely remove them. Dig down to where the suckers grow from the understock and pull them off with a downward motion; this removes growth buds that would otherwise produce additional suckers in subsequent years. Let the wound air-dry before you replace soil around it.

Be certain you are removing a sucker rather than a new cane growing from the bud union. Suckers usually are easy to distinguish from desired canes; differences can be seen in foliage size, shape, and color, as well as in size of thorns and habit of growth. If in doubt, let the presumed sucker grow until you can establish its difference from a cane; its flowers will be noticeably different. A flowerless, climbing cane from a bush rose is almost certainly a sucker.

5. Match pruning to the roses you grow. Make your cut just above an outward-growing bud or a five-leaflet leaf.

HYBRID TEAS & GRANDIFLORAS. Prune these types according to the guidelines above.

FLORIBUNDA, POLYANTHA & SHRUB ROSES. On shrub roses, follow the guidelines above, but cut back the previous season's growth by only one-fourth to one-third, and leave as many strong new canes and stems as the plant produced. On polyanthas and floribundas, remove one-third to one-half of the previous year's foliage.

OLD ROSES & SPECIES ROSES. For kinds that bloom only once, prune after they have flowered in spring. Prune repeat-blooming types at the end of the dormant season. Most need only a light annual pruning—provided you've allowed these typically vigorous roses sufficient space. Remove any dead or weak canes; then prune the tip of each remaining cane. If the center of the plant is dense and overcrowded, completely remove a few old, woody canes. The roses in this group that produce long, arching canes (many of the hybrid

perpetuals, for example) can be pruned the same way as climbers.

CLIMBING ROSES. Leave all climbers unpruned for the first 2 or 3 years after planting, but do train the canes, even in the first season. Spread them so that they are as horizontal as possible, which will stimulate the production of flowering branches. A fan shape works best.

Prune climbing roses that bloom only in spring just after they finish flowering, removing old canes that show no signs of strong new growth. For climbers that bloom off and on in other seasons as well as in spring, prune at the same time you'd prune bush roses in your locality. Remove the oldest unproductive canes and any weak, twiggy growth; cut back the lateral branches on the remaining canes to two or three buds. Take the time to remove any remaining foliage to stimulate heavy flowering.

PILLAR ROSES. These are not quite bush roses or climbers. They produce tall, somewhat flexible canes that bloom profusely without having to be trained horizontally. Prune them according to the guidelines above.

GROUNDCOVER ROSES. Cut back the stems of low growers by about a third. To develop a more prostrate form, cut vertical stems back to the plant's main stem.

STANDARD ROSES. Standards, often called tree roses, are budded onto a tall, bare understock stem. Follow the pruning guidelines for the rose type that forms the head; pay particular attention to maintaining a symmetrical plant, pruning harder on its weak side. The 3-ft. standards are generally grandifloras, hybrid teas, or floribundas. Smaller shrub roses, floribundas, groundcover roses, and large miniatures are usually used for 2-ft. standards. Miniatures are used for 1½-ft. standards.

MINIATURE ROSES. Follow the general guidelines above, but cut back the height attained during the previous year by at least half; remove all weak and twiggy stems.

Consider cutting flowers as a form of pruning. Cut off enough stem to support the flower in a vase, but don't deprive the plant of too much foliage. Always leave a stem with at least two sets of five-leaflet leaves.

R

CLOCKWISE FROM LEFT: Rose hips; *Rosa banksiae* 'Lutea'; *R.* 'Simplicity'

specialize in old roses, you'll find some related varieties that were introduced in the 20th century. Old roses are a diverse group, popular because of their history and the beautiful fragrance many offer. Some are climbers; others are large mounding shrubs. Some are very disease-resistant, while others are prone to mildew or black spot in damp climates. Cold-hardiness varies considerably.

The old European roses that existed before 1867 are the albas, centifolias, damasks, gallicas, and moss roses; they originated from wild roses native to Europe and western Asia. Most flower only in spring. Most are hardy in Zone 2b with no protection; some albas and gallicas bloom reliably only with some winter chill.

China and tea roses originated from eastern Asia; they were taken to Europe and crossed with European roses to produce the other classes of old garden roses: Bourbons,

Portlands, hybrid perpetuals, and Noisettes. Repeat flowering is a characteristic of this group; hardiness varies, but even the hardiest—the hybrid perpetuals, Portlands, and Bourbons—are not quite as hardy as the old European roses.

Alba roses. Zones 2a–24. These were developed from *R. alba*, the white rose that symbolized the House of York in England's Wars of the Roses in the 15th century. The flowers come only in spring but generally are very fragrant. They are single to very double, white to delicate pink. The plants themselves are upright, vigorous, and long-lived, with green stems and handsome, disease-resistant gray-green leaves.

Centifolia roses. Zones 2b–24. Centifolias were developed from *R. centifolia*, the cabbage rose; these are the gorgeous roses often portrayed by Dutch painters. Plants are open growing, with prickly stems that can reach 6 ft. long, arching under the weight of the blossoms. Intensely fragrant spring flowers typically are packed with petals, often with large outer petals

that cradle a multitude of smaller petals within. Colors include white and pink shades.

Damask roses. Zones 2b–24. These descendants of *R. damascena* reach 6 ft. or more, typically with long, arching, thorny canes and light or grayish green, downy leaves. Their flowers are intensely fragrant. The summer damasks flower only in spring; forms of these are cultivated to make attar of roses (the rose oil used in the perfume industry). 'Autumn Damask' (*R. d. semperflorens*) flowers more than once a year; slender buds open to loosely double, pure pink blossoms. This is the Rose of Castile of the Spanish missions.

Gallica roses. Zones 2a–24. These are cultivated forms of *R. gallica*, the French Rose. Fragrant spring flowers run from pink through red to maroon and purple shades. Plants reach 3–4 ft. tall, with upright to arching canes bearing prickles but few thorns; leaves are dark green and often rough textured. Grown on their own roots, these plants will spread into clumps from creeping rootstocks.

Historic *R. g. officinalis*, known as the Apothecary's Rose, is presumed to be the red rose emblematic of the House of Lancaster in England's Wars of the Roses; its semi-double, cherry red flowers are held on a dense, medium-height plant. *R. g. versicolor*—generally known as 'Rosa Mundi'—has pink petals boldly striped and stippled red.

Moss roses. Zones 2b–24. Naturally occurring sports of centifolia and damask roses, these plants have mosslike, balsam-scented glands, like little hairs, on their buds and flower stems and sometimes even on their leaflets. The "moss" of centifolias is soft; that of damasks is more prickly. Flowers are white, pink, or red, and are often intensely fragrant.

China roses. Best in Zones 4–9, 12–24; H1, H2. The first two China roses to reach Europe (around 1800) were garden forms of *R. chinensis* that had been grown by the Chinese for centuries. Flowers were pink or red, under 3 in. across, and borne in small clusters on 2–4-ft. plants. 'Old Blush' ('Parsons' Pink China'), one of the original two, is still sold. 'Mutabilis' opens yellow then turns pink.

China roses were the primary source of the repeat-flowering trait in modern roses. Modern miniature roses owe their small size to *R. c. minima*.

Tea roses. These are elegant, sweetly scented, virtually ever-blooming roses that are relatively tender; they grow best in Zones 6–9, 12–24; H1, H2. Plants are long-lived, building on old wood and responding poorly to heavy pruning. Flowers are white, cream, light yellow, apricot, buff, pink, or rosy red. Though variable, many resemble hybrid teas—in fact, tea roses were crossed with hybrid perpetuals to produce the first hybrid teas.

Bourbon roses. Zones 2b–24. The original Bourbon rose was a semiclimbing hybrid between 'Old Blush', a China rose, and 'Autumn Damask'. Later came shrubs, climbers, and more semiclimbers with flowers in white, pink shades, and red, most of which were fragrant.

R

Portland roses. Zones 2b–24. Named after the first of the group, 'Duchess of Portland', these roses appeared around 1800. They were the first hybrids between China roses (mostly 'Slater's Crimson China') and old European roses (in particular, 'Autumn Damask'); sometimes they are called damask perpetuals. All are fairly short, bushy repeat bloomers with centifolia- and gallica-like flowers that are generally fragrant.

Hybrid perpetual roses. Zones 2b–24. In the 19th and early 20th centuries, hybrid perpetuals were the garden roses: big, vigorous, and hardy to about −30°F (−34°C) with minimal protection. Flowers often are large (to 6–7 in.), full, and strongly fragrant; buds usually are shorter and plumper than standard hybrid tea buds. Prune high, thin out oldest canes, and arch over remaining canes to encourage bloom in quantity. Hybrid perpetuals need more water and fertilizer than hybrid teas in order to produce their repeated bursts of bloom. Watch for rust. Colors range from white through pink shades to red and maroon.

Noisette roses. The crossing of a China rose, 'Old Blush', and the musk rose (*R. moschata*) produced the first Noisette rose, 'Champneys Pink Cluster', a fragrant, repeat-flowering shrubby climber with small pink flowers in medium-size clusters. Crossing 'Champneys Pink Cluster' with other China roses led to similar roses in white, pink shades, and red; crossed with tea roses, it yielded large-flowered, climbing tea-Noisettes. Noisettes are generally fragrant. All are best in milder climates (Zones 6–9, 12–24; H1, H2).

SPECIES ROSES AND THEIR HYBRIDS

Species roses are the original wild roses from which all other roses descend. Among the following species and their hybrids are excellent shrub roses, climbing roses, and roses that will help control erosion on slopes. Some are extremely vigorous and cold-hardy.

R. banksiae. LADY BANKS' ROSE. Evergreen climber (deciduous in cold winters). Zones 4–24; H1, H2. From China. Vigorous grower to 20 ft. or more. Aphid-resistant, practically immune to disease. Stems have few if any prickles. Large clusters of small flowers in early to late spring, depending on zone. Good for covering banks, ground, fence, or arbor. The two forms sold are 'Lutea', with scentless, double yellow flowers; and *R. b. banksiae* ('Alba Plena' or 'White Banksia'), with violet-scented, double white flowers.

R. bracteata. MACARTNEY ROSE. Evergreen climber. Zones 4–9, 12–24; H1, H2; except as noted. Native to southeastern China; naturalized in southeastern U.S. Creamy white, 2–3-in. flowers appear in spring. Without support, it trails and roots as it spreads; as a climber, it can reach 10–20 ft. Its celebrated offspring 'Mermaid' is a thorny, vigorous, tough, and disease-resistant evergreen or semievergreen climber, hardy in Zones 7–9, 12–24; H1, H2. It takes partial shade and reaches 50 ft., with profuse bloom from spring into fall; creamy yellow, single flowers are 5 in. across and lightly fragrant. Plant 'Mermaid' 8 ft. apart for quick groundcover.

R. eglanteria (R. rubiginosa). SWEET BRIAR, EGLANTINE. Deciduous shrub or climber. Zones A2, A3; 1–24. From Europe, western Asia, and North Africa; naturalized in parts of the West. Vigorous grower to 12 ft. tall, 8 ft. wide. Stems are prickly; leaves are dark green with fragrance of green apples. Single pink flowers to 2½ in. across in late spring. Red-orange hips. Good hedge, barrier, or screen (plant 3–4 ft. apart and prune annually in early spring); can be held to 3–4 ft. tall.

R. foetida. AUSTRIAN BRIER. Deciduous shrub. Zones A2, A3; 1–21. From central and western Asia. To 6 ft. tall and wide. Especially susceptible to black spot. Flowers (in mid- to late spring) are single, bright yellow, 2–3 in. across, with odd scent. This species and its well-known variety *R. f. bicolor,* commonly called Austrian Copper, are the source of orange and yellow in modern roses. *R. f. bicolor* is a 4–5-ft.-tall shrub

with brilliant coppery red petals backed with yellow. *R. f. persiana* grows 6 ft. tall, has fragrant double yellow flowers.

R. glauca (R. rubrifolia). Deciduous shrub. Zones A1–A3; 1–24. From central and southern Europe. To 6 ft. tall, 5 ft. wide. Valued for its leaves, which combine gray-green and coppery purple. Single, deep pink spring flowers have white centers, yellow anthers, and long, slender sepals; blooms are followed by ½-in. oval hips that turn red in autumn.

R. × harisonii. HARISON'S YELLOW ROSE. Deciduous shrub. Zones A2, A3; 1–24. Old rose

CLOCKWISE FROM TOP: *Rosa* 'Fourth of July'; *R.* 'Sunset Celebration'; *R.* 'Happenstance'

brought west by pioneers; still persists in California's Gold Country and around old farmhouses. To 6 ft. tall and 4 ft. wide, forming thickets of thorny stems and fine-textured foliage. Flowers (in late spring) are profuse, semidouble, bright yellow, and fragrant. Occasionally reblooms in autumn in warmer climates. Showy hips. Vigorous, disease-free, hardy to cold, and (once established) resistant to aridity.

R

»

How to Grow Roses

Plant where your roses will receive at least 6 hours of sunshine daily. If your weather is consistently cool or overcast, choose a location that's open all day to any sun that might appear. If summer heat is intense, find a spot that receives filtered sunlight during the hottest afternoon hours.

SITE Soil for roses should drain reasonably well; if the soil in your chosen spot does not, the best alternative is to plant in raised beds. Don't locate roses too close to trees or large shrubs; their roots will steal the water and nutrients intended for your roses. Choose a spot where there is good air circulation—it helps discourage foliage diseases—but avoid windy locations. High winds can wreck the flowers and increase transpiration from the leaves, making frequent watering necessary.

SPACING Generous spacing between plants aids air circulation, which reduces the incidence of mildew, black spot, and other foliage diseases. Exactly how far apart to plant depends on the growth habit of the roses and on your climate. The colder the winter and the shorter the growing season, the smaller the bushes will be. But some varieties are naturally small, others tall and massive—and those relative size differences will hold in any climate. In the coldest zones, plant the most vigorous roses 3 ft. apart; in milder climates, space vigorous sorts 6 or even 8 ft. apart.

SOIL PREP Dig it deeply, incorporating organic matter such as ground bark, peat moss, or compost to help aerate dense clay soils and improve moisture retention in sandy soils. Add a complete fertilizer to the soil and dig supplemental phosphorus and potassium into the planting holes. If you are planting new roses in a spot where existing bushes have been growing for 5 or more years, be sure to add plenty of rich organic material, as the soil is most likely quite spent.

PLANTING Plant roses from containers according to the directions on page 671.

Healthy, ready-to-plant bare-root roses should have plump, fresh-looking canes and roots. Before planting, immerse the entire plant in water for up to 2 days to be certain that all canes and roots are plumped up. Plant bare-root roses according to the directions on page 671. After planting, some gardeners mound mulch over the bud union (the knob from which the canes grow) and around the canes to conserve moisture, then gradually and carefully remove the mulch when the leaves begin to expand.

If you're planting a budded plant (whether container grown or bare-root), set the plant in the hole so that the bud union is just above or right at soil level. In Zones A1–A3 and 1–3, some gardeners set the bud union 1–2 in. beneath the soil surface for increased protection from cold, but since this usually results in fewer canes, many gardeners in these cold-winter zones keep to the standard guideline (bud union just above soil level) and give their roses plenty of winter protection.

WATERING With the exception of some old garden roses and species roses that thrive on little water once they are established, roses need watering at all times during the growing season. Inadequate water inhibits growth and bloom.

Water deeply enough to moisten the entire root system (16–18 in. deep). How often you need to water depends on the soil type and weather. Big, well-established plants need more total water than newly set plants, but you will need to water new plants more frequently until they are established.

Options Basin flooding is a simple way to water individual rose plants. If you have a drip-irrigation system, you will be able to water many plants at one time. Overhead sprinkling freshens foliage and helps remove dust; it can also wash away aphids, spider mites, and the spores of powdery mildew and other fungal leaf diseases. On the other hand, overhead sprinkling washes off sprays that were applied to control pests and diseases, and it may leave mineral deposits on foliage if water is hard. If you use an overhead sprinkler, do it early in the day to allow foliage time to dry off during daylight hours; leaves that stay wet for several hours are more likely to develop powdery mildew and other foliage diseases. Even if you irrigate in basins, give plants an occasional morning shower to clean dust off the foliage (if the rains don't do it for you).

MULCHING Each spring, spread a 2–3-in.-thick layer of fresh mulch around your roses. Mulching conserves moisture and deters weed growth. It also helps keep soil cool—a benefit in all but the coolest-summer climates.

FEEDING Nutrient needs vary depending on rose type and your soil's natural fertility. Many old roses, shrub roses, and species roses do not need regular fertilizer if growth is satisfactory. But for many repeat-flowering modern roses, regular fertilizing is needed to produce the most gratifying results.

In the mildest-winter climates (Zones 8, 9, 12–24; H1, H2), give established roses their initial feeding with a complete fertilizer in February; elsewhere, give the first feeding just as growth begins. Thereafter, time fertilizer applications to bloom periods. For roses that flower repeatedly throughout the growing season, fertilize after each blooming cycle has ended, when new growth is just beginning. For roses that bloom only in spring, one additional feeding just after flowering ends will encourage vigorous new growth and plenty of blooms next year.

Stop feeding in late summer or fall, at least 6 weeks before the first expected hard frost. In mild-winter zones experiencing virtually no subfreezing weather, you may continue fertilizing until mid-October for a crop of late-fall flowers.

Dry fertilizer, applied to the soil, is most frequently used. A variation on this type is controlled-release fertilizer; follow directions on the package for the amount and frequency of applications. Liquid fertilizers are useful in smaller gardens using basin watering. Most liquid types can also be sprayed on rose leaves, which absorb some nutrients immediately. If you are looking for an organic fertilizer for roses, try dehydrated alfalfa; it smells better than fish emulsion.

TENDING Although some roses are especially susceptible to pests and diseases, most of these plants thrive with just a little preventive care. Well-tended, healthy roses are less likely to fall prey to pest infestations or diseases. To reduce the risk of trouble, choose roses that are suitable for your climate and are notably disease-resistant; prepare the soil well; feed and water diligently (being careful about the timing of overhead watering); and prune to ensure good air circulation around the leaves.

R

CLEANUP Start each year by removing prunings, leaves, and old mulch, which may harbor overwintering insect eggs and disease spores. Then, if you think your plants need it, spray them and the soil around them to kill any remaining insect eggs and disease spores. Do this before the plants leafout; use a natural product such as dormant-season horticultural oil or lime sulfur.

INVITE BENEFICIALS Allies in the battle against rose pests include ladybugs, lacewings, beetles, flies, spiders, birds, and wasps. You can buy predators such as ladybugs at nurseries and release them in your garden; encourage them to stay awhile by setting out plants that attract them, such as dill, fennel, and yarrow. Avoid using broad-spectrum pesticides, which kill beneficial insects along with pests.

Blast insects off your roses with a jet of water as soon as you see them. For more information about pest management, see pages 726–731.

CHALLENGES Rose midges are a problem in coastal Northern California and the coastal Northwest. The almost microscopic adults lay eggs in the growing tips of rose stems; when the larvae hatch, they bore into the developing rose buds, deforming the buds and leaving blackened, withered tips. The larvae then fall to the ground and pupate, perpetuating the cycle. Snip off and bag any affected shoots as soon as you notice them, and clear and dispose of all leaf litter, weeds, and debris. Lay black plastic under the plants so that the larvae cannot pupate. If the damage continues, contact a good local nursery for advice on the best treatments; repeated soil drenches or foliar applications of systemic insecticides may be the only viable options.

Rose slugs—sawfly larvae that skeletonize rose leaves—have been a huge problem in recent years in coastal California. The most effective treatment is spinosad, a natural pesticide derived from a soil bacterium. It does not harm most beneficial insects.

Deer are the rose garden's biggest problem—literally—if they live in your neighborhood. The only perfect solution is a tall fence. But a watchful outdoor dog can be effective, as can various repellents and deer-scare devices (such as motion-activated impact sprinklers).

Powdery mildew, rust, and black spot are the most likely diseases to appear on your roses at some point. At the first sign of disease, remove affected leaves and debris. Don't wait until the damage is substantial before you spray. For more information on disease-management strategies and advice on controlling powdery mildew and rust, see pages 732–733.

Black spot is most troublesome in warm summer weather when there is humidity or rainfall to sustain and spread it. For a nontoxic control, apply a spray made from 2 tsp. of baking soda and 2 tsp. of fine-grade horticultural oil dissolved in 1 gal. of water. In years with wet springs, anticipate downy mildew; some gardeners spray a fungicide preventively in a wet spring to prevent defoliation.

For local help with pests and diseases, consider joining the American Rose Society (ars.org). Its consulting rosarians advise member gardeners on rose problems at no cost.

R. moschata. MUSK ROSE. Deciduous shrub. Zones 4–9, 12–24; H1. Probably from western Asia. Vigorous, arching plant to 10 ft. tall and wide. Densely covered with matte-finish, medium green foliage that turns butter yellow in late fall. Clustered, single ivory white flowers appear in late spring, continue through summer; scent is delicious, somewhat like honey. *R. m. plena* has double blossoms, though their effect is lessened because inner petals wither before outer ones do.

R. moyesii. SEALING WAX ROSE. Deciduous shrub. Zones 3–10, 14–21. From western China. Loose shrub to 10 ft. tall and 8 ft. wide. Spring display of single, bright red flowers to 2½ in. across, carried singly or in groups of two. In fall, large, bottle-shaped hips ripen to brilliant scarlet.

R. multiflora. Deciduous shrub. Zones 1–24. From Japan. Dense, vigorous, arching growth to 8–10 ft. tall and wide. Susceptible to mildew and spider mites. Profuse clusters of small white flowers akin in scent to honeysuckle (*Lonicera*); blooms in mid- to late spring. In fall, there follows a heavy crop of red, ¼-in. hips that are much loved by birds, and often self-sow. Useful as large hedge. Set plants 2 ft. apart for fast fill-in. Can help control erosion.

R. nutkana. NOOTKA ROSE. Deciduous shrub. Zones A1–A3; 1–11, 14–21. Native from Alaska to Northern California and eastward to the Rockies. Grows to 6 ft. tall and 4 ft. wide. Somewhat arching stems hold gray-green leaves with sharply toothed edges. Blooms in spring, bearing single, deep pink blossoms to 2½ in. wide (primarily borne singly). Showy, rosy red hips.

Many roses produce a big crop of showy hips in late summer and fall. These develop from spent flowers, so remember not to deadhead the last flush of blossoms.

R. rugosa. RAMANAS ROSE, SEA TOMATO. Deciduous shrub. Zones A1–A3; 1–24. From northern China, Siberia, Korea, and Japan. Vigorous shrub with prickly stems and wonderfully fragrant flowers. To 3–6 ft. tall and wide. Glossy bright green leaves have distinctive heavy veining that gives them a crinkled appearance. Flowers are 3–4 in. across and, in the many varieties, range from single to double and from pure white and creamy yellow through pink to deep purplish red. Blooms in spring, summer, and early fall. Bright red, tomato-shaped hips, an inch or more across.

All rugosas withstand hard freezes, wind, aridity, and salt spray. They make fine hedges. Plants grown on their own roots will make sizable, spreading colonies and help prevent erosion. Foliage remains quite free of diseases and insects, except possibly aphids. Among the most widely sold rugosas and rugosa hybrids are 'Blanc Double de Coubert', double white; 'Frau Dagmar Hartopp', single pink; 'Hansa', double purplish red; and 'Wildberry Breeze', single, clove scented, lavender-pink.

R. sericea pteracantha. Deciduous shrub. Zones 3b–11, 14–21. Native to the Himalayas from southwest China to India and Myanmar. Grows 6–12 ft. tall and wide, with ferny leaves made up of 7 to 17 leaflets. White, four-petaled flowers resemble a Maltese Cross; appear in May, followed by red, orange, or yellow hips. Huge, translucent red thorns are the show here: to 1½ in. long at the base and ½–¾ in. from stem to prickle, they give stems a wicked winged look.

R. wichurana. MEMORIAL ROSE. Evergreen or partially evergreen climber (deciduous in cold winters). Zones 3–9, 12–24; H1, H2. From Japan, Korea, and eastern China. Trailing stems grow 10–12 ft. long in one season, root in contact with moist soil. Midsummer flowers are white, to 2 in. across, held in clusters. Good groundcover, even in relatively poor soil.

Roseodendron donnell-smithii. See *Tabebuia donnell-smithii*

R

Rosmarinus officinalis

ROSEMARY

Lamiaceae

EVERGREEN SHRUB

✂ **ZONES 4–24; H1, H2**

☀ **FULL SUN**

◐ **LITTLE TO MODERATE WATER**

🐝 **FLOWERS ATTRACT HUMMING-BIRDS, BUTTERFLIES, BEES**

Rosmarinus officinalis 'Golden Rain'

Fine-leafed, aromatic, and evergreen, this Mediterranean shrub fits well in Western gardens. Its genus name means "dew of the sea," reflecting the plant's native habitat on seaside cliffs. It does as well with close ocean exposure, but thrives inland too, even with hot sun and poor alkaline soil, if given moderate water and infrequent light feeding. Habit can be stiff and erect, rounded, or prostrate and creeping. Height ranges from 1 to 8 ft. Plants are thickly clothed in narrow, resinous, aromatic leaves that are usually glossy dark green above, grayish white beneath. Small clusters of ¼–½-in. blossoms in various shades of blue (rarely pink or white) appear through winter and spring; bloom occasionally repeats in fall. Rosemary flowers are edible—add them to salads or use as a garnish—and make excellent honey. Leaves are widely used as a fresh or dry seasoning; thrown onto hot barbecue coals, they produce a heavenly fragrance.

Good drainage is essential. Too much fertilizer and water result in rank growth, subsequent woodiness. Control growth by frequent tip pinching when plants are small. Prune older plants frequently but lightly; cut to side branch or shear. If plants become woody and bare in center, cut back selected branches by half so that the plant will fill in with new growth (be sure to cut into leafy wood; plants will not regrow from bare wood). Branches root wherever they touch the ground; creeping varieties will spread indefinitely, forming extensive colonies. To get new plants, root tip cuttings or dig and replant layered branches.

Cold-hardiness depends upon selection. In general, upright varieties are hardier; prostrate ones (originally from Majorca and Corsica) are more tender, suffering damage at 20°F (−7°C) or even higher. In cold-winter areas, choose the hardiest types and shelter them from winter winds; wrap upright growers in plastic sheeting (leaving top uncovered) in late fall to prevent branches from breaking under weight of snow. Even the hardiest types can succumb to cold if they have wet feet. Beyond hardiness range, grow rosemary in pots and winter indoors on a sunny windowsill.

Use taller types as clipped or informal hedges or in dry borders with native and gray-leafed plants. Lower kinds are good ground or bank covers, useful in erosion control. Set container-grown plants or rooted cuttings 2 ft. apart for moderately quick cover. Foliage of most types has culinary uses, but flavor and fragrance vary; the best have a mildly pungent flavor and a complex aroma with sweet as well as resinous notes. Rosemary is also used in medicines, cosmetics, potpourri, and moth repellents.

Rosemary plants sold without a name are frequently seedlings, which lack the uniformity of cutting-grown, named selections. Unfortunately, variety names are often confused, and many have synonyms; but named plants are still a better bet than nameless plants.

'Albiflorus' ('Albus'). Semi-upright grower, eventually reaching 6 ft. tall and wide. White flowers veined in pale lavender. Hardy to 0°F (−18°C).

'Arp'. The hardiest rosemary, taking temperatures as low as −10°F (−23°C). Discovered in Arp, Texas. Open grower to 4 ft. tall and wide; best with frequent pruning. Dark green foliage has grayish tinge. Bright medium blue flowers.

'Barbecue'. Grows 5 ft. tall, 2–3 ft. wide, has excellent fragrance for cooking; blue flowers.

'Benenden Blue' ('Pine-Scented Rosemary'). Semi-upright plant to 3 ft. high, 4 ft. or more wide. Very narrow leaves with strong pine fragrance; light blue flowers. Bitter flavor with turpentine overtones. Tender.

Cooking with Rosemary

You can use any variety of *Rosmarinus officinalis* for cooking. But upright kinds with broader leaves contain more aromatic oil. 'Tuscan Blue' is a favorite of many chefs; its leaves are wider than average and very aromatic; flowers are dark blue. 'Blue Spires', with clear blue flowers, is good for flavoring grilled meats and roasted potatoes. 'Spice Islands', normally sold in the herb section at nurseries, is another good choice; it bears dark blue flowers. 'Barbecue' has flavorful, aromatic leaves and clear blue flowers; stiff branch clippings (scrape off lower leaves) are sometimes used as skewers for grilling kebabs.

Rosmarinus officinalis 'Barbecue'

R. o. 'Tuscan Blue'

R. o. 'Spice Islands'

'Blue Spires'. Strong vertical grower, to 5–6 ft. tall and as wide or wider with age; can be pruned for narrower form. Deep blue flowers. Superb landscape variety; makes tight-sheared hedge. Excellent for seasoning.

'Collingwood Ingram' ('Ingramii', 'Rex #4'). To 2–2½ ft. high, to 4 ft. or wider; narrower and more upright with pruning. Branches curve gracefully. Flowers in rich, bright deep blue with violet veining. Tallish bank or groundcover that provides excellent color. Not good for seasoning; flavor is too piney. Tender.

'Corsican Prostrate'. Arching, spreading, 1–1½ ft. high, with dark blue flowers. Tender.

'Golden Rain'. Also sold as Joyce DeBaggio. Bushy, upright growth to 2–3 ft. high and wide. Green leaves with irregular golden edges; variegation is most prominent in cool weather, fades in summer. Deep violet-blue flowers.

'Hill Hardy'. Compact, bushy plant grows semiupright to 5 ft. tall and wide. Stiff foliage. Light blue flowers; repeat bloom in fall. Pleasant, light fragrance. Hardy to 0°F (–18°C).

'Huntington Carpet' ('Huntington Blue'). To 1½ ft. high; spreads quickly yet maintains a dense center. Pale blue flowers. Best variety for bank or groundcover.

'Irene'. Vigorous spreader that covers 2–3 ft. or more per year, eventually mounding to 1–1½ ft. high. Deep lavender-blue flowers. One of the cold-hardiest prostrate varieties.

'Ken Taylor'. Sport of 'Collingwood Ingram'. Has the same deep blue flower color but is lower growing, with a greater tendency to trail. Tender.

'Lockwood de Forest' ('Santa Barbara', 'Lockwoodii', 'Forestii'). Resembles 'Prostratus' but mounds up to 2½ ft. or more; has lighter, brighter green foliage and bluer flowers.

'Majorca Pink'. Initially erect to 2–4 ft. tall and 1½–2 ft. wide; eventually twists into picturesque shape, flopping to 3–4 ft. wide. Lilac-pink flowers. Slightly fruity fragrance.

'Prostratus'. To 2 ft. high, with 4–8-ft. spread. Will trail down over wall or edge of raised bed to make a green curtain. Pale lavender-blue flowers come in waves from fall into spring. With age, tends to mound up and become woody and bare in center (except at seashore, where it remains lush throughout). Effective in hanging pots. Tender.

'Spice Islands'. Upright growth reaches 6–8 ft., making this a good screen or background. Large blue flowers, good fragrance. Once grown for commercial seasoning production.

'Tuscan Blue'. Vita Sackville-West's original, brought to England from Tuscany, had relatively broad (to ¼ in. wide) leaves; deep violet-blue flowers; upright habit to 6–7 ft. tall and 1½–2 ft. wide. A plant long sold as 'Tuscan Blue' in the U.S. fits this description but has light blue flowers; with age, it turns woody and bare at base.

Roystonea
ROYAL PALM
Arecaceae
PALMS

- ✎ **ZONES 24; H2**
- ☀ **FULL SUN**
- 💧 **REGULAR WATER**

Roystonea regia

Stately, symmetrical feather palms. Tall, smooth gray trunk is marked with rings and topped by a green crownshaft formed by the overlapping bases of the feathery fronds. In moist, well-drained soil, these grow at a moderate to fast rate. Good wind and salt resistance. These are useful as street trees (they look majestic in rows), to frame large buildings, and grouped with other palms. (For more on palms, see "Meet the Palms," page 471.)

R. oleracea. CABBAGE PALM, CARIBBEE ROYAL PALM. Native to the Caribbean and South America. May reach over 100 ft. tall, 35 ft. wide. Green fronds grow as long as 20 ft.; they are usually semiupright or spreading.

R. regia. ROYAL PALM, CUBAN ROYAL PALM. Native to Cuba. To 50–75 ft. tall, 30 ft. wide. Trunk is swollen at base, tapering toward top, sometimes swollen toward middle. Bright green, 10–20-ft.-long fronds arch gracefully in all directions.

Rubus
BRAMBLE
Rosaceae
DECIDUOUS AND EVERGREEN SHRUBS

- ✎ **ZONES VARY BY SPECIES**
- ☀ ◑ **FULL SUN OR LIGHT SHADE**
- 💧 **MODERATE WATER**
- 🐦 **BERRIES ATTRACT BIRDS**

Rubus rolfei 'Emerald Carpet'

Besides blackberry and raspberry (see separate entries), the brambles include many ornamental plants. Most are thornless and have perennial rather than biennial stems. Spring flowers are followed by small, edible berries. Need good drainage; spread widely by rhizomes. Plant groundcover types about 2 ft. apart.

R. arcticus 'Kenai Carpet'. NAGOONBERRY. Deciduous. Zones A1–A3; 1–3. Native to Alaska and other northern climates. Creeping groundcover plant to 6 in. high. Smooth green leaves have three to five ovate, sawtoothed leaflets; foliage turns reddish in fall. Inch-wide hot pink flowers are followed by dark red berries.

R. deliciosus. ROCKY MOUNTAIN THIMBLEBERRY, BOULDER RASPBERRY. Deciduous. Zones 1–6, 10. Native to Rocky Mountains in New Mexico, Colorado, and Wyoming. Graceful, arching plant to 3–5 ft. tall and 6 ft. wide. Bright green, lobed, nearly round leaves. White, 2–3-in.-wide flowers resemble single roses. Dark purple berries.

R. rolfei (R. pentalobus, R. calycinoides). Evergreen. Zones 4–6, 14–17. Native to mountains of Taiwan. Thickly foliaged stems spread at a moderate rate to form a dense carpet to 1 ft. high. Rounded leaves have three to five broad, ruffled-edged lobes; upper surfaces are lustrous dark green and rough textured, undersides are grayish white and felted. Small white flowers look like strawberry blossoms, are followed by salmon-colored berries. 'Emerald Carpet' has superior foliage that turns raspberry red with the onset of cool autumn nights. Plant spreads 5 ft. in 3 years; makes a durable groundcover for sun or partial shade.

Rudbeckia
Asteraceae
PERENNIALS AND BIENNIALS

- ✎ **ZONES 1–24, EXCEPT AS NOTED**
- ☀ **FULL SUN**
- 💧💧 **MODERATE TO REGULAR WATER**
- 🐦 **ATTRACT BIRDS, BUTTERFLIES, BENEFICIAL INSECTS**

Rudbeckia fulgida

These big, warm-colored daisies are stalwarts of the summer and autumn garden. Descended from wild plants native mainly to the eastern U.S., all are tough and easy to grow. Blossoms have yellow or orange rays and a raised central cone. They make good cut flowers; cutting encourages rebloom late in season. Divide perennials when they become crowded, usually every few years.

R. fulgida. Perennial. Initially to 3 ft. high, 2 ft. wide; after a few years, spreads by rhizomes to form a larger clump. Branching stems; broadly lance-shaped, 5-in.-long, hairy dark green leaves. Yellow, 2–2½-in.-wide flowers with black to brown central cone bloom in summer. Varieties are

R

more often grown than the species. 'Early Bird Gold' has an especially long bloom season, running spring to fall. *R. f. sullivantii* 'Goldsturm' bears 3-in., black-eyed yellow flowers on 2–2½-ft. stems.

R. hirta. GLORIOSA DAISY, BLACK-EYED SUSAN. Biennial or short-lived perennial; often grown as annual because it blooms the first summer from seed sown in early spring. Grown as winter annual in Zones 12, 13. To 3–4 ft. tall and 1½ ft. wide, with upright, branching habit. Stems and lance-shaped leaves to 4 in. long are rough and hairy. Daisylike, 2–4-in.-wide flowers have orange-yellow rays and a prominent purplish black cone. Attracts bees.

'Indian Summer' produces 6–9-in., single to semidouble flowers in golden yellow. 'Irish Eyes' ('Green Eyes') has 2–3-in., golden yellow flowers with a light green central cone that ages to brown. 'Prairie Sun' produces 5-in., golden yellow blooms with pale yellow tips and a light green central cone. For front of border, try lower-growing selections 'Goldilocks' (double flowers) and 'Toto', both 8–10 in. high; Becky Mix (12–15 in.); 'Tiger Eye' (16–24 in. high and wide, with unusually profuse bloom); 'Denver Daisy' (2 ft. high and 18 in. wide); and 'Cherokee Sunset' (2–2½ ft. high, with large double or semidouble blooms).

R. laciniata. Perennial. The species can reach 10 ft. tall and 4 ft. wide; it has light green, deeply lobed leaves to 4 in. long and blooms from summer to fall, bearing 2–3½-in.-wide flowers with drooping yellow rays and a green cone. More widely grown in gardens are the following two selections. 'Goldquelle', with double blooms in lemon yellow, is a less aggressive form growing to 3 ft. high and 1½ ft. wide. 'Herbstsonne' ('Autumn Sun') grows to 6 ft. tall and 2 ft. wide; bears single, 4–5-in.-wide flowers with yellow rays and a bright green cone that ages to yellow.

R. triloba. BROWN-EYED SUSAN. Perennial. Grows to 3–4 ft. tall and 18 in. wide, bearing a profusion of small yellow daisies with chocolate centers. Reseeds.

Ruellia
Acanthaceae
EVERGREEN SHRUBS AND SHRUBBY PERENNIALS

🌡 **ZONES VARY BY SPECIES**

☼ ◐ **FULL SUN OR LIGHT SHADE**

◊ ◖ ● **WATER NEEDS VARY BY SPECIES**

Ruellia brittoniana

Ruellias have opposite leaves and flaring, bell-shaped flowers with five shallow lobes. Beyond their hardiness range, they are commonly grown in greenhouses.

R. brittoniana. Shrubby perennial. Zones 8, 9, 12–24; H1, H2. Mexican native naturalized in many areas of the southern and southwestern U.S. To 3 ft. high; initially 1–1½ ft. wide, but can be invasive and should be contained (by an edging, for example). Narrow dark green leaves to 3 in. long, ¾ in. wide; 2-in.-long, lavender-blue flowers throughout warm times of year. 'Chi Chi' has soft pink blossoms. 'Katie' is a dwarf (10–12 in.), noninvasive variety. 'Blanca' (white flowers) and 'Rosa' (pink flowers) have narrow leaves, grow about 1 ft. high. Regular water.

R. californica. Shrub. Zones 12, 13. Native to Sonoran Desert of Mexico. To 2–4½ ft. tall and wide, with oval light green leaves to 1¼ in. long that drop in cold spells or after protracted dry periods. Deep purple, violet, or pink flowers to 2¼ in. long appear after spring and summer rains. Needs no irrigation but will bloom nearly all year if given little to moderate water.

R. elegans 'Ragin' Cajun'. Perennial. Zones 4–9, 11–24. The species is native from Brazil to Chile. Grows to 4 ft. tall and 8 ft. wide, and is covered with scarlet flowers from late spring through frost. Needs little to moderate water after it's established.

R. peninsularis. Shrub. Zones 12, 13, 21–24. Somewhat larger-flowered than *R. californica* but otherwise is very similar in appearance, watering needs, and performance.

Rumohra adiantiformis
(Aspidium capense)
LEATHER FERN
Dropteridaceae
FERN

🌡 **ZONES 14–17, 19–24; H1, H2**

☼ ◐ **FULL SUN OR PARTIAL SHADE**

◖ ● **MODERATE TO REGULAR WATER**

Rumohra adiantiformis

Leather fern has deep glossy green, triangular, finely cut fronds that are firm textured and last well in arrangements. Native to many tropical and subtropical areas of the Southern Hemisphere, it grows 3 ft. high and wide, spreading wider by rhizomes. Good in hanging baskets. Hardy to 24°F (−4°C).

Delicate-looking but durable, leather fern gets by with less water than other ferns, especially in the coastal fog belt, where it thrives in bright, diffused light. It's a favorite of florists everywhere.

Ruscus
BUTCHER'S BROOM
Asparagaceae
EVERGREEN SHRUBS

🌡 **ZONES 4–24; H1**

☼ ● **BEST IN SHADE, TOLERATE SOME SUN**

◊ ◖ **LITTLE TO MODERATE WATER**

Ruscus aculeatus

Flattened, leaflike branches do the work of leaves for these Old World natives, bearing tiny greenish white flowers in the centers of their upper surfaces. They are interesting in dried arrangements. If both male and female plants are present, or if you have a plant with male and female flowers, bright red (sometimes yellow), marble-size fruit follows flowers. Tolerant of dry shade, a wide variety of soils, and competition from tree roots, these are valuable groundcovers under trees. They spread widely by rhizomes. Plants are subject to chlorosis in the desert.

R. aculeatus. Native from the Mediterranean and Black seas to the British Isles and the Azores. To 1–4 ft. tall, with branched stems. Spine-tipped "leaves" are 1–3 in. long, a third as wide, leathery, dull dark green.

R. hypoglossum. Native to Italy, Czechoslovakia, and northern Turkey. To 1½ ft., with unbranched stems. "Leaves" to 4 in. long, 1½ in. wide, glossy green, not spine tipped. Spreads faster than *R. aculeatus*. Superior as a small-scale groundcover.

FOR MORE UNTHIRSTY PLANTS, SEE PAGES 74–78.

R

Russelia equisetiformis

CORAL FOUNTAIN, FIRECRACKER PLANT
Plantaginaceae
SHRUBBY PERENNIAL

↗ **ZONES 13–14, 17, 19–24; H1, H2; OR INDOORS**

☼ ◑ **SUN OR PARTIAL SHADE; BRIGHT INDIRECT LIGHT**

◌ ◑ ● **LITTLE TO REGULAR WATER**

🦋 **FLOWERS ATTRACT HUMMINGBIRDS**

Russelia equisetiformis

This Mexican native grows 5 ft. tall and wide, with trailing, almost leafless bright green stems that look good spilling from a hanging basket or over the top of a wall. Masses of tubular red flowers appear throughout spring and summer (all year in Hawaii). Tolerates drought, wet soil, salty soil. Needs regular fertilizing. Hardy to about 32°F (0°C), but comes back vigorously if cut down by frost. Easy to propagate from pencil-size stem cuttings taken in spring. 'St. Elmo's Fire' grows to 6 ft. tall and up to 8 ft. wide; it is more upright than the species, and just as floriferous and trouble-free.

Floral Fireworks

Delicate leaves and arching stems give *Russelia equi-setiformis* the look of a vibrant fireworks display. Grow it in a tall urn where its long trailing branches and nonstop show of bright coral flowers can show off best. Or, for a tropical effect in mild-winter climates, pair it with *Canna* 'Pretoria' against a backdrop of small palms.

Ruta graveolens

RUE, HERB-OF-GRACE
Rutaceae
PERENNIAL

↗ **ZONES 2–24**

☼ **FULL SUN**

◑ ● **MODERATE TO REGULAR WATER**

🦋 **ATTRACTS BUTTERFLIES**

◊ **SAP CAUSES DERMATITIS IN SOME PEOPLE**

Ruta graveolens

Growing to 2–3 ft. high and wide, with aromatic, ferny-looking blue-green leaves, this native of southeastern Europe has small, greenish yellow flowers that are followed by decorative brown seed capsules.

'Jackman's Blue' is a dense and compact plant, with a fine gray-blue color. 'Blue Mound' and 'Curly Girl' are more compact still.

CARE

Sow seeds in flats; transplant to 1 ft. apart (for information on sowing seeds, see page 670). Rue needs good garden soil; add lime to strongly acid soil. Cut back in early spring to encourage bushiness. Dry seed clusters for use in wreaths or swags.

Sabal

PALMETTO
Arecaceae
PALMS

↗ **ZONES 12–17, 19–24; H1, H2**

☼ **FULL SUN**

● **MODERATE WATER**

Sabal domingensis

Two of these slow-growing fan palms have trunks; two have either no trunk or a very short one. Tiny flowers appear among the leaves. Tolerate salt spray. All withstand 20°F (–7°C).

S. domingensis. HISPAN-IOLA PALMETTO. Native to the Caribbean. Ultimately 80 ft. or taller, 20 ft. wide, with fan-shaped, immense gray-green leaves to 9 ft. across.

S. mexicana (S. texana). OAXACA PALMETTO. Native from Texas to Guatemala. To 30–50 ft. tall, 12 ft. wide. Bright green, 3-ft. leaves. Leaf stems persist on trunk in young trees; later drop to show attractive, slender trunk.

S. minor. Native to southeastern U.S. To 3–6 ft. tall, 10 ft. wide. Green to blue-green, 6-ft. leaves. Usually trunkless but sometimes has a short trunk. Old leaves fold at base, hang down like a closed umbrella.

S. palmetto. CABBAGE PALM. From southeastern U.S. To 20 ft. tall, 10 ft. wide; much taller in its native habitat. Big (5–8 ft.) green leaves form a dense, globular head.

Sagina subulata

IRISH MOSS, SCOTCH MOSS
Caryophyllaceae
PERENNIAL

↗ **ZONES 1–11, 14–24**

☼ ◑ **FULL SUN OR PARTIAL SHADE**

● **REGULAR WATER**

Sagina subulata

Dense, green, carpeting growth makes this look like moss; but its tiny white flowers prove otherwise. Of two different prostrate plants of similar appearance, *Sagina subulata* is the more common. The other is *Minuartia verna caespitosa* (usually sold as *Arenaria verna* or *A. v. caespitosa*). Both of these European natives make dense, compact, mosslike masses of slender leaves on slender stems. But *M. verna* has tiny white flowers in few-flowered clusters, while *S. subulata* bears flowers singly and differs in other technical details. In common usage, however, green forms of the two species are called Irish moss, while the golden green form of *Sagina* (*S. s. glabrata* 'Aurea') is called Scotch moss.

Both *Sagina* and *Minuartia* are best as small-scale groundcovers. They're useful for filling gaps between pavers. In cool-summer gardens, they can seed themselves and become pests.

Unlike true mosses, these need good soil, good drainage, and occasional feeding with controlled-release fertilizer. The dark green forms take full sun in mild climates; the golden form needs partial shade. All take some foot traffic and tend to hump up in time; control humping by occasionally cutting out narrow strips, then pressing

S

or rolling lightly. Control snails, slugs, and cutworms. Cut squares from flats and set 6 in. apart for fast cover. To avoid lumpiness, plant so that soil line of squares is at or slightly below planted soil surface.

Salix

WILLOW
Salicaceae
DECIDUOUS TREES AND SHRUBS

⚡ **ZONES VARY BY SPECIES**

☼ **FULL SUN**

💧 💧 **REGULAR TO AMPLE WATER**

🦋 **ATTRACT BUTTERFLIES**

Salix alba

Classic streamside trees, willows are fast growing, weak-wooded, and short-lived. Weeping willows are best used as single trees near a stream or lake, though they can, with training, become satisfactory shade trees for a patio or terrace. They leaf out very early in spring and hold their foliage late. Shrubby willows are grown mainly for catkins (this group goes by the name "pussy willow") or colorful twigs, as screen plants, or for erosion control on stream or riverbanks. For this last purpose, locally offered native types are best. Pussy willow branches can be cut in bud and brought indoors to bloom. Willows take any soil; most even tolerate poor drainage. All have shallow, invasive roots and are difficult to garden under; don't plant near sewer lines. Most are subject to pests (tent caterpillars, aphids, borers, and spider mites).

Twig blight may be a problem in the Northwest (spray copper fungicide on new foliage); Texas root rot may cause trouble in the desert. Species hybridize readily, resulting in much confusion of names in the nursery trade.

S. alba. WHITE WILLOW. Tree. Zones A2, A3; 1–11, 14–24. From Europe and North Africa. Upright to 75–100 ft. tall, 50–100 ft. wide. Yellowish brown bark. Narrow, 1½–4-in., bright green leaves are silvery beneath, may turn golden in fall. The following forms are valued for colorful twigs.

S. a. 'Tristis' (*S. babylonica aurea*, *S.* 'Niobe'). GOLDEN WEEPING WILLOW. To 50–70 ft. tall and as wide or wider, with pendulous form. Young stems are bright yellow. Among the most attractive weeping willows.

S. a. vitellina. Upright, with brilliant yellow twigs in winter. Can grow to tree size, but cutting back gives best color display: lop to 1 ft. high yearly, just before spring growth begins. Stems may grow 8 ft. in a season. 'Britzensis' has red or orange-red winter stems.

S. babylonica. WEEPING WILLOW. Tree. Zones 3–24; H1, H2. From China. To 30–50 ft. tall and wide (or wider). Longer (3–6 in.) leaves and more pronounced weeping habit than *S. alba* 'Tristis'. Greenish or brown branchlets. 'Crispa' ('Annularis'), ringleaf or corkscrew willow, has leaves curled into rings or circles; it is somewhat narrower than the species.

S. caprea. FRENCH PUSSY WILLOW, PINK PUSSY WILLOW. Shrub or tree. Zones 2–11, 14–24. Native from Europe to northeastern Asia. Grows to 15–25 ft. tall, 12–15 ft. wide. Broad, 3–6-in.-long leaves are dark green above, gray and hairy beneath. Before leafout, male plants produce fat, woolly, pinkish gray catkins about 1 in. long. Can be kept to shrub size by cutting to ground every few years. 'Kilmarnock' ('Pendula') naturally sprawls on the ground; it is more effective grafted or staked to form a weeping tree 6–8 ft. tall, 6 ft. wide.

S. 'Golden Curls' ('Erythroflexuosa'). Shrub or tree. Zones 3–11, 14–24. Probably a hybrid between *S. alba* 'Tristis' and *S. matsudana* 'Tortuosa'. To 30 ft. tall and wide, with somewhat weeping and twisting branches. Glossy green, lance-

shaped leaves to 3 in. long turn a good golden yellow rather late in autumn; somewhat curled. Bark on new growth is bright yellow. After plant has established a framework, cut it back hard in winter to keep colorful new growth coming on. 'Scarlet Curls' has similar parentage, but young bark is scarlet.

S. gracilistyla. ROSE-GOLD PUSSY WILLOW. Shrub. Zones 3–11, 14–24. To 6–10 ft. tall, 12 ft. wide. Narrowly oval, 2–4-in.-long leaves are gray-green above, bluish green beneath. Male plants produce plump, gray, furry, 1½-in.-long catkins with numerous stamens with rose-and-gold anthers. Cut branches for arrangements to curb plant's size. Every 3 or 4 years, cut the plant back to short stubs; you'll get very vigorous shoots with large catkins. 'Melanostachys' catkins are black with red anthers.

S. integra 'Hakuro Nishiki'. DAPPLED WILLOW. Shrub. Zones 3–9, 14–17. Native to Korea and Japan. To 4–6 ft. tall and wide; somewhat weeping. Stems and leaf buds are salmon-pink; leaves are 4 in. long, ½–1¼ in. wide, light

CLOCKWISE FROM TOP: *Salix alba vitellina* 'Britzensis'; *S.* 'Golden Curls'; *S. integra* 'Hakuro Nishiki'

green mottled with white and pink. Best in partial shade.

S. matsudana (*S. babylonica pekinensis*). HANKOW WILLOW. Tree. Zones 3–11, 14–24. Upright, pyramidal growth to 40–50 ft. tall, 30–40 ft. wide. Bright green, narrow, 2–4-in.-long leaves. Can thrive on less water and saltier soil than most willows. This species and its varieties are popular in the high desert.

'Navajo'. GLOBE NAVAJO WILLOW. Large, spreading, round-topped tree to at least 40 ft. tall and 50 ft. wide.

'Snake'. Similarly contorted but grows to 40 ft. tall, 30 ft. wide, with branches that weep at the tips; attractive cinnamon brown bark.

'Tortuosa'. DRAGON-CLAW WILLOW, CORKSCREW WILLOW. Zones 3–11, 14–24. Grows to 30 ft. tall, 20 ft. wide, with branches that are twisted into upright, spiraling patterns. Valued for winter silhouette and cut branches for arrangements.

S

'Umbraculifera'. GLOBE WILLOW. To 35 ft. tall and wide. Umbrella-shaped crown with upright branches, drooping branchlets.

S. nakamurana yezo-alpina. CREEPING ALPINE WILLOW. Zones 2–6, 15–17. Native to Japan. To 2 ft. high and 10 ft. wide in 10 years; continues to spread but doesn't get taller. Heart-shaped, bright green leaves to 2 in. across are covered with silky white hairs when young, turn gold in fall. Male plants produce creamy white catkins. Interesting groundcover for rock gardens, where it seems to flow over and around stones. Needs well-drained soil that is not too high in nitrogen (add peat and fine gravel at planting time).

S. × pendulina. Zones 2–11, 14–24. Hybrid best known for two selections. 'Blanda', Wisconsin weeping willow, grows 40–50 ft. tall or taller, 70 ft. wide; it has a less strongly weeping habit than *S. babylonica*, with broader leaves in a bluer shade of green. The similar 'Fan-Giant' weeping willow is resistant to borers and twig blight.

S. purpurea. PURPLE OSIER, ALASKA BLUE WILLOW. Shrub. Zones A2, A3; 1–11. From Europe, North Africa, central and eastern Asia. To 15 ft. tall and wide, with purple branches. Narrow, 1–3-in.-long leaves are dark green above, bluish beneath. Cut shrub to ground if overgrown. 'Canyon Blue' grows fast to 5 ft. tall, 4 ft. wide, with blue-gray leaves. 'Gracilis' ('Nana'), dwarf purple osier, has slimmer branches and narrower leaves; it is usually grown as clipped hedge and kept 1–3 ft. high and wide.

S. purpurea 'Pendula', weeping arctic blue willow, is a prostrate grower usually sold as a standard grafted onto a 6- to 8-foot trunk. It's a nice weeping plant for small gardens.

Salpiglossis sinuata

PAINTED TONGUE
Solanaceae
ANNUAL

- ✎ **ZONES 1–24**
- ☼ **FULL SUN**
- 💧 **REGULAR WATER**

Salpiglossis sinuata
'Chocolate Royale'

A bit like upright petunias, these South American petunia relations grow to 2–3 ft. high and 1 ft. wide. Stems and narrowly oblong, 4-in.-long leaves are sticky. Flowers are 2–2½ in. wide; come in mahogany red, reddish orange, yellow, purple, deep blue, and pink shades, marbled and penciled with contrasting colors. 'Kew Blue' is an excellent blue with deep purple throat. Plants bloom most heavily in late spring and early summer, but in cool-summer climates they'll carry on until frost if deadheaded. Good background plant; handsome cut flower. Bolero (to 2 ft. high), Royale (12–16 in.), and Stained Glass (18 in.) are compact strains.

Sow seeds in potting mix in peat pots, several seeds to a pot, in late winter or early spring. Keep pots in a warm, protected location; thin seedlings to one per pot. When young plants are well established and frost danger is past, plant outdoors. Performs best in rich soil. Stake tall types. Tip-pinch growing plants to induce branching.

FOR INFORMATION ON PLANTING TECHNIQUES, SEE PAGE 670.

Salvia

SAGE
Lamiaceae
EVERGREEN OR DECIDUOUS SHRUBS AND PERENNIALS

- ✎ **ZONES VARY BY SPECIES**
- ☼ **FULL SUN, EXCEPT AS NOTED**
- 💧 **MODERATE TO REGULAR WATER, EXCEPT AS NOTED**
- 🐝 **FLOWERS ATTRACT BEES, BUTTERFLIES, HUMMINGBIRDS**

Salvia farinacea
'Victoria Blue'

Thought of as drought-tolerant shrubs in much of the West, this huge genus—the largest in the mint family—includes many species of shrubs and perennials that need moderate to regular water. In recent years, scores of new species and selections have appeared in Western nurseries, many tender varieties that are even being offered as annuals in cold-winter climates. All sages have square stems and whorls of two-lipped flowers, either distinctly spaced along flower stalks or so tightly crowded that they look like one dense spike; some species have branched inflorescences. Flower colors range from white and yellow through salmon and pink to scarlet and pure red, from pale lavender to true blue and darkest purple. A few sages have fragrant blossoms. Many have aromatic foliage.

Nurseries in the West offer nearly 100 species as well as dozens of selections and hybrids. Names are often confused; S. × *jamensis* varieties are often assigned to S. *greggii*; and S. *nemorosa* varieties are often interchanged with S. × *superba* and S. × *sylvestris* varieties.

S. apiana. CALIFORNIA WHITE SAGE, BEE SAGE. Evergreen shrub. Zones 7–9, 11, 13–24. From Southern California and Baja California. Coarse plant to 3–5 ft. tall and wide. Aromatic, woolly silvery gray leaves are elliptical, 3–4 in. long. In spring, lavender-tinged white flowers appear in whorls along unbranched, sometimes pinkish stems to 2 ft. long. Attractive at night; reflects moon, garden lighting. To keep neat, shear lightly after flowering. Drought-tolerant.

S. argentea. SILVER SAGE. Biennial or short-lived perennial. Zones 1–24. From southern Europe, northwestern Africa. Soft, scallop-edged, silky-haired, silvery white leaves grow 6–10 in. long, form a low foliage rosette to 2 ft. wide. In summer, many-branched, 3–4-ft. flowering stems bear 1¼-in.-long, hooded white flowers (sometimes tinged pink or yellow) with silvery calyxes. Cut to ground when flowers fade. Handsome focal point for front of border. Protect from slugs and snails. 'Hobbit's Foot' grows into a 1-ft. mound with furry basal leaves.

S. azurea grandiflora (S. pitcheri). PRAIRIE SAGE, PITCHER SAGE. Shrubby perennial. Zones 1–24. Native from Colorado and Texas east to Michigan and Georgia. Slender, vertical, usually unbranched stems to 5 ft. form a 2–3-ft.-wide clump. Plant is lax, needs support. Smooth or hairy, medium green to deep green, narrow leaves to 4 in. long. Pure azure blue flowers with white-blotched lower lip on spikes to 1 ft. long; blooms summer to frost. Not always permanent in wet winters.

S. 'Bee's Bliss'. Evergreen perennial groundcover. Zones 7–9, 14–24. Drought-tolerant hybrid between S. *leucophylla* and S. *sonomensis*. Grows 1–1½ ft. high and spreads 4–6 ft. wide, with narrow, soft-looking, gray-green leaves. Whorled spikes of lavender-blue flowers are held above the foliage from spring into summer. Good on slopes, spilling over rock wall. Little to moderate water; avoid overhead irrigation, which encourages powdery mildew.

S

»

CLOCKWISE FROM LEFT: *Salvia microphylla* 'Hot Lips'; *S. officinalis* 'Tricolor'; *S. splendens*

S. blepharophylla. EYE-LASH SAGE. Shrubby perennial. Zones 14–24. From northeastern Mexico. To 1½–2 ft. high, spreading indefinitely by creeping rhizomes. Thin, hairy, purplish stems; oval, glossy dark green leaves to 1½ in. long, edged with fine hairs resembling eyelashes. Inch-long scarlet flowers on stems that lengthen to about 1 ft. as season goes on. Blooms from spring to frost, nearly all year in mild-winter climates. If confined, makes a good groundcover in partial shade.

S. brandegeei. BRANDE-GEE SAGE, BAJA SAGE, SANTA ROSA ISLAND SAGE. Evergreen shrub. Zones 15–17, 19–24. Native to Santa Rosa Island and coastal Baja California. Sprawling plant to 4–5 ft. tall, 5–7 ft. wide. Linear, scalloped, 3–4-in.-long leaves are shiny, rough-textured dark green above, woolly white beneath. Tight, widely spaced whorls of ½-in., pale lavender, broad-lipped flowers on stems to 10 in. long; persistent violet-gray calyxes. Early-spring bloom. Shorten branches by one-third during or right after bloom. Long-lasting cut flowers. Drought-tolerant. 'Pacific Blue' has dark lavender-blue flowers.

S. buchananii. BUCHANAN SAGE. Shrubby perennial. Zones 14–24. Thought to be native to Mexico. Rounded growth to 1–2 ft. high and wide, with widely spaced, glossy dark green, oval leaves to 2 in. long. Lax, 8–12-in. stems support drooping, 2-in., brilliant magenta flowers. Blooms in summer and fall, and sporadically in other seasons in milder part of range. Sets no seed; propagate from cuttings. Handsome in pots; winter it indoors in cold climates.

S. chamaedryoides. GERMANDER SAGE. Perennial. Zones 8, 9, 12, 14–24. From eastern Mexico. Rounded plant to 1–2 ft. high, spreading 2–3 ft. or more by underground runners. Silvery, ¾-in.-long leaves; brilliant true blue, 1-in. flowers on stems to 8 in. long. Heaviest bloom comes in late spring and fall, with intermittent flowering during rest of growing season.

Deadhead to encourage rebloom. Elegant front-of-border plant. Drought-tolerant but blooms longer and better with more water.

S. chiapensis. CHIAPAS SAGE. Perennial. Zones 15, 17, 23, 24. From the cloud forests of Chiapas, Mexico. Many 1½–2-ft. stems form a relaxed clump 3–4 ft. or more wide; growth is taller and laxer in shade. Evergreen, elliptical, glossy dark green leaves up to 3 in. long. Deep hot pink, ¾-in. flowers in widely spaced whorls on stems to 1 ft. long; blooms from early summer through winter in frost-free area or greenhouse. Reseeds freely. Succeeds with moderate water but appreciates frequent wetting of leaves. Good groundcover for dryish shade; good in containers. Needs at least partial shade in hottest climates.

S. clevelandii. CLEVELAND SAGE, CALIFORNIA BLUE SAGE. Evergreen shrub. Zones 8, 9, 12–24. Hardy to 20°F (–7°C). From Southern California, northern Baja California. Rounded, arching growth to 3–5 ft. tall, 5–8 ft. wide. Wrinkled, toothed gray-green leaves to 2 in. long are elliptical or lance-shaped,

deliciously fragrant. Foliage makes a refreshing tea and is also used as a preservative in potpourri. Fragrant, inch-long, pale lavender to violet-blue flowers in widely spaced whorls along 1½–2-ft. stems. Blooms in early summer; remove faded spikes to encourage rebloom. Drought-tolerant. 'Winnifred Gilman' is more compact (3 ft. high and wide), with dark red flower stems and calyx tubes, dark violet-blue flowers. Hybrid 'Allen Chickering' grows like a typical Cleveland sage and bears abundant bright lavender-blue flowers. Hybrid 'Aromas' bears larger, darker blue flowers than the species.

S. coahuilensis. COAHUILA SAGE. Shrubby perennial. Zones 8, 9, 12–24. From the mountains of Coahuila, Mexico. To 2½ ft. high and wide. Many slender, upward-sweeping woody branches, sparsely clothed with evergreen, 1-in., linear olive green leaves. Deep violet, 1-in. flowers appear on 3–5-in. stems from early summer to frost, all year in mild-winter climates; heaviest bloom in early summer and fall. Cut back to about 8 in. from ground in late winter. Moderate water.

S. coccinea. TROPICAL SAGE. Perennial in Zones 12–24; H1, H2; usually grown as annual in all zones. From Mexico; naturalized and weedy in Hawaii. Bushy, upright; to 2–3 ft. high and 2½ ft. wide. Dark green, hairy, oval to heart-shaped leaves. In summer, slender stems to 1 ft. long carry many ¾–1-in. flowers with broad lower lip. Colors range from bright red through orange-red to pink and white, including many bicolors. Widely used as bedding plant, border filler. Stems are brittle; shelter from wind. Deadhead to encourage rebloom. If plant lives over, cut back to 4–6 in. when new spring growth begins, then fertilize. By end of second season, plant will be woody and in decline. Reseeds copiously. Good seed-grown selections include scarlet 'Lady in Red' and 'Spanish Dancer'; salmon 'Brenthurst' ('Lady in Pink'); 'Coral Nymph', near white with coral lower lip; and pure white 'Snow Nymph'.

S

S. confertiflora. Perennial. Zones 16, 17, 22–24. Native to Brazil. Upright grower to 4–6 ft. tall and wide (about twice that size in mildest climates). Lance-shaped, scalloped leaves to 8 in. long are dark green with yellowish tinge, densely hairy (especially on undersides); they have an unpleasant odor when bruised. Flowers offer a glowing color combination: flowering stems and calyx tubes are covered with red-brown velvet, and crowded ½-in. blossoms are dark orange. Blooms in fall, continuing through winter in mild areas. Stake plant; shelter from wind. Top growth may burn even in light frosts.

S. corrugata. Evergreen shrub. Zones 14–24. From high elevations of South America. Dense, upright habit, 5–6 ft. tall and almost as wide. Quilted, corrugated leaves are deep green on top, with prominent light veining and delicate, pale tan hairs beneath. From summer into fall, the plant is crowned with upright 4-in.-long spikes of tightly clustered, deep blue flowers held in dark purple calyxes. Pretty alongside roses or in shrub borders. Excellent in pots. Give weekly deep irrigation through the growing season.

S. 'Costa Rica Blue'. Evergreen shrub. Zones 15–17, 19–24. To 8 ft. tall and wide; can be kept lower by cutting back to 1 ft. in early spring. Broadly oval to heart-shaped, hairy, shiny bright green leaves to 5 in. long. Brilliant true blue, 1–1½-in. flowers on 1–1½-ft. stems. Blooms from the end of summer until frost (through spring in mildest climates). Needs support, shelter from wind and cold. 'Omaha Gold' is a sport with leaves irregularly edged in yellowish green. A violet-flowered form also exists.

S. 'Dara's Choice'. Evergreen shrub. Zones 7, 14–24. A hybrid between *S. sonomensis* and *S. mellifera*. Bushy, spreading, to 2–3 ft. high and 3–6 ft. wide, rooting where it touches the ground. Lance-shaped leaves are medium green with a grayish cast. Tight whorls of violet-blue, ½-in. spring flowers are widely spaced along many 6–12-in. stems. Good as bank cover or draped over a wall. Plant is sometimes subject to

verticillium wilt; some branches die, but plant usually survives. Best in areas with coastal influence. Drought-tolerant. Hybrid 'Mrs. Beard' has grayer foliage, lower growth (to 2 ft. high), pale lavender flowers; it is not prone to verticillium wilt.

S. darcyi. DARCY SAGE. Perennial. Zones 8, 9, 12, 14–24. From northeastern Mexico. Upright growth to 3–4 ft. tall; spreads by rhizomes to 3 ft. or more. Softly hairy, triangular light green leaves have a pleasant, fruity aroma. Widely spaced whorls of 1½-in., coral red blossoms on unbranched stems from early summer to late fall. Stems are 6–12 in. high, sometimes as high as 2 ft. They are brittle; shelter from wind. Protect from slugs and snails. Dies back to the ground in winter. Tolerates partial shade.

S. 'Dark Dancer'. Zones 8–24. Semievergreen shrub. Dies to the ground in coldest winters but comes back. Probably a hybrid of *S. muellerii* × *S. microphylla*. Grows 3 ft. high and wide, with raspberry-colored flowers over green leaves.

S. dorrii. DESERT SAGE, GREAT BASIN BLUE SAGE.

CLOCKWISE FROM TOP LEFT: *Salvia coahuilensis; S. argentea; S. splendens* 'Red Hot Sally'

Evergreen shrub. Zones 2, 3, 10–13, 18, 19. Native to high deserts from Washington and Idaho south to California and Arizona. May have a rounded habit or form a spreading mat; grows 1–3 ft. high, 2–4 ft. wide. Branches densely clothed in gray, linear or spoon-shaped leaves. Blooms in late spring; each 1–2-ft.-long stem bears three to five widely spaced whorls of light to deep blue, 1-in. flowers with deep blue bracts and calyxes. Needs sandy soil, perfect drainage. Drought-tolerant. Good in dry desert garden.

S. elegans. PINEAPPLE SAGE. Perennial. Zones 5–24. Native to southern Mexico, Guatemala. In the wild, this species is variable in habit, bloom time, leaf fragrance. The most commonly grown form, 'Scarlet Pineapple', grows upright to 3–4 ft. tall and wide, with branching, brittle stems; in part shade, growth is lush and needs support. Densely hairy, bright green leaves to 4 in. long, broadly oval with pointed tip. Foliage has a strong aroma of ripe pineapple; used in cool drinks, fruit salads. Slender, bright red flow-

ers in loose clusters of 8 to 12 are carried on 6–8-in. stems. In mild-winter areas or indoors, blooms from late fall through spring; elsewhere, it is cut off by frost. Hybrid 'Frieda Dixon' is similar but has pinkish red flowers. 'Golden Delicious' grows just 1–3 ft. high, with yellow-green foliage that makes for an eye-catching contrast with the fire-engine-red flowers; long bloom period. 'Honey Melon Sage' grows half as high as the species and spreads rapidly to form a dense groundcover; it has slightly smaller blooms and smaller, more rounded leaves that smell something like ripe honeydew melon. Blooms from early summer through fall (shear off faded flower stems two or three times a season to produce a new crop). 'Tangerine' ('Scarlet Tangerine') grows 3 ft. high and wide, has scarlet flowers.

S. farinacea. MEALYCUP SAGE, TEXAS VIOLET. Perennial in Zones 7–10, 12–24; H1, H2;

Salvias for Containers

Salvias come in all sizes (many large). But a few are just the right size for growing in containers where space is limited. Chiapas sage, with glossy green leaves and hot pink blooms, is beautiful in a pink Tuscan-style terra-cotta container. Scarlet sage (*Salvia splendens*) has vivid red blooms that can spice up a young Cape plumbago's cool blue ones. Try a potted dwarf pineapple sage (*S. elegans* 'Golden Delicious') as an accent in a sunny herb garden. Or create a hummingbird garden by mixing purple *S. leucantha*, dark blue *S. guaranitica*, and deep red-flowered *S. greggii* with red 'Firebird' penstemon and *Phygelius capensis* 'Scarlet' in a ceramic container at least 23 in. across.

usually grown as an annual in all zones. Native to southern New Mexico, Texas, and Mexico. Upright growth to 3–4 ft. tall, half as wide. Narrowly lance-shaped leaves are smooth above, woolly white below. Tall, densely packed spikes of ¾–1-in. flowers on stems 6–12 in. long, late spring to frost. Blossom color varies from deep violet-blue to white; cuplike calyxes are covered with white hairs, often have a blue or violet tinge. Many strains are sold for bedding and container use; typically have heavier bloom, better branching, more compact habit. 'Blue Frost' grows 1–2 ft. high and half as wide, with blue flowers marked with white; 'Evolution' has compact growth 20 in. high, 14 in. wide, with 9-in. purple flower spikes; 'Saga Blue' grows 10 in. high and wide, with blue flowers; 'Texas Violet' grows to 4 ft. tall, 2 ft. wide, with grape-scented deep blue flowers with white sepals.

S. greggii. AUTUMN SAGE. Evergreen or deciduous shrub. Zones 8–24. Dies to the ground in coldest winters but comes back. Native to southwest Texas and north-central Mexico. Rounded plant, branching from base; typically grows 1–4 ft. tall and wide. Slender, hairy stems are closely set with glossy green leaves that vary in shape from rounded to linear. Blooms throughout summer and fall, bearing ¼–1-in. flowers on 3–6-in. stems, in colors ranging from deep purplish red through

true red to various rose and pink shades to white. (Varieties sold as *S. greggii* with flowers in shades of orange, orange-red, or yellow actually belong with *S.* × *jamensis*.) To keep plants tidy and free blooming, prune and remove dead flower stems frequently. Before new spring growth begins, shorten and shape plants, removing dead wood. Good low hedge. Replace plants every 4 or 5 years, when they become woody and unproductive. Drought-tolerant but does best with moderate water. Full sun or partial shade (be sure to give some shade in hottest climates). A few of the best selections are pure white 'Alba'; deep red 'Furman's Red'; 'Purple Pastel'; 'Ultra Violet', with magenta-purple flowers; and hot pink 'Wild Thing'. The Heatwave series, which grows 2–3 ft. high and wide, was bred in Australia for compact growth, long flowering, and drought tolerance.

S. guaranitica (S. ambigens). ANISE-SCENTED SAGE. Perennial in Zones 8, 9, 14–24; annual in colder climates. From South America. Upright, branching plant to 4–5 ft. tall and nearly as wide. Spreads by short underground runners; roots form tubers resembling small sausages. Narrowly heart-shaped, sparsely hairy, mint green leaves to 5 in. long. Blooms from early summer to frost. Most common form bears 2-in. cobalt blue blossoms, carried several to each foot-long stem; calyxes are bright green,

turning purplish on sunny side. Needs support. Where it grows as a perennial, it gets woody by season's end—but that wood dies during winter and must be cut back to ground. Elegant container plant. Can be demolished by Mexican giant whitefly. Tolerates partial shade, especially in hottest climates. 'Argentine Skies' has light blue flowers. 'Black and Blue' bears blossoms that are deep blue with dark purplish blue calyxes.

S. 'Indigo Spires'. Shrubby perennial. Zones 8, 9, 14–24. Sprawls to 6–7 ft. by 10 ft. but easily kept to 3–4 ft. high and 2–3 ft. wide with selective pruning. Soft oval to oblong leaves have a grayish sheen above, are white and woolly beneath. Narrow, twisted spikes of closely spaced, violet-blue flowers to 3 ft. or more, from early summer to frost (almost all year in mildest climates). S. 'Mystic Spires Blue' is a dwarf form of 'Indigo Spires'; compact growth to 2–3 ft. high and wide, with gray-green leaves. Violet-blue flowers in summer. Indigo calyxes are colorful long after blossoms fall. Excellent cut flowers.

S. × jamensis. JAMÉ SAGE. Evergreen shrub. Zones 8–24. Plants sold under this name are hybrids involving *S. greggii*, *S. microphylla*, an unknown yellow-flowered species, and possibly other sages; they are found wild in Mexico. Habit varies from upright to horizontal, but plants are usually under 3 ft. high, with fairly open branching; stems often root where they touch soil. Glossy green, oval to elliptical, toothed leaves ¾–1¼ in. long. Stems 3–6 in. long bear ½–¾-in. flowers in many colors: violet, wine red, orange-red, hot pink, coral, salmon, yellow, white, and bicolors. Best in moderate climates without extreme temperature swings. Drought-tolerant but performs best with moderate water. Excellent varieties include 'Cienega de Oro' (creamy yellow flowers) and 'Sierra de San Antonio' (light peach blooms with pastel yellow lips); both grow 1½–2 ft. high, 2–3 ft. wide. 'San Isidro Moon' has an open, horizontal habit to 2 ft. high, 2–4 ft. wide; it bears two-tone flowers in peach shades. Varieties often

sold as forms of *S. greggii* include soft orange-red 'Coral' and pale yellow 'Moonlight'.

S. leucantha. MEXICAN BUSH SAGE, VELVET SAGE. Evergreen shrub. Zones 12–24; H1, H2. From central and eastern Mexico. Vigorous, upright, velvety plant to 3–4 ft. tall, 3–6 ft. or more wide; sprawls in bloom. Lance-shaped to linear leaves are dark grayish green above, whitish below. Stems to 1 ft. long bear whorls of ¾–1¼-in. white flowers with purple calyxes. Bloom period runs from fall through spring in mild-winter areas, stops with frost in colder climates. To limit plant size and renew flowering stems, cut back close to ground before spring growth begins or at end of bloom cycle; where growing season is especially long, cut back again in early to midsummer. Also limit watering to every 2 or 3 weeks and remove blossoms as soon as they fade. 'Midnight' ('Purple Velvet'), considered by many to be the best-looking form, has purple flowers and calyxes. 'Santa Barbara' has similar flowers but is a compact grower to just 2½ ft. high and 3–4 ft. wide. 'Waverly' is a hybrid that grows 5 ft. tall, with white flowers. It is hardy only to about 25°F (–4°C).

S. leucophylla. PURPLE SAGE, GRAY SAGE. Evergreen shrub. Zones 8, 9, 14–17, 19–24, except as noted. Native to Coast Ranges of Southern California. Graceful plant to 3–5 ft. tall with equal or greater width; arching branches have upturned tips, root where they touch soil. Stems and foliage thickly covered with fine white hairs. Wrinkled, oblong to lance-shaped leaves are apple green when they emerge, turn whiter as days get hotter. In spring, each 6–8-in. stem carries three to five tightly packed whorls of 1-in., pinkish purple flowers with gray calyxes. Good bank cover. Drought-tolerant. 'Point Sal Spreader' (often sold as 'Point Sal') is prostrate, 1–2½ ft. high, 10–12 ft. wide; has broader, grayer leaves than species. 'Figueroa' (Zones 7–9, 14–24), to 3–4 ft. tall and twice as wide, is especially silvery; tolerates drought, heat, cold.

S. mellifera. BLACK SAGE, HONEY SAGE. Evergreen shrub.

Zones 7–9, 14–24. Native to coastal California and Baja California. To 3–6 ft. tall, 3–5 ft. or more wide; upright to spreading. Oblong to lance-shaped, deeply veined, aromatic leaves; olive-tinged dark green above, woolly gray beneath. In late spring, bears tightly packed whorls of whitish or lavender-tinged flowers less than ½ in. long on 8–16-in.-long stems. Not spectacular-looking, but butterflies and bees love it. Good cover for dry banks. Drought-tolerant. Will stand some shade. 'Green Carpet' grows 30 in. high, 6 ft. wide, with blue flowers. 'Terra Seca' is an extra-tough variety to 2 ft. high, more than 6 ft. wide.

S. mexicana. MEXICAN SAGE. Shrubby perennial. Zones 9, 14–17, 19–24. From central Mexico. Robust, erect growth to 10 ft. or taller, 3–5 ft. wide. Leaves to 6 in. long, typically elongated oval or heart-shaped; they may be medium green and smooth above, fuzzy beneath, or gray to gray-green and densely hairy on both sides. Pleasant pine fragrance. Tightly spaced whorls of flowers on 12–20-in.-long stems; blossoms are dark blue or violet with green or reddish purple calyxes. Blooms from early fall through spring in mild-winter climates; stops with hard frost elsewhere. Protect from wind. To keep compact, remove flower stems and shape plant as blooms are fading. Tolerates some shade; good under high-branching trees. Best with moderate water; more frequent watering produces excessive, brittle growth. 'Limelight' grows 6 ft. tall, 3 ft. wide; has a striking combination of chartreuse bracts and blue flowers.

S. microphylla. Evergreen shrub. Zones 7–24. From southeastern Arizona through southern Mexico, with many local variant forms. Full sun or partial shade. Moderate water.

'Belize Form' (5 ft. tall, 8 ft. wide) is long-blooming but more tender, with bright green leaves and brilliant red flowers. 'Berzerkeley' (2 ft. high, 3–4 ft. wide) bears glowing pinkish red blossoms. 'Hot Lips' is upright, to about 1½–2 ft. high, with striking flowers that vary from fire engine red to white to red-

and-white bicolors throughout the growing season. 'San Carlos Festival' (2–3 ft. high, 4–6 ft. wide) has pink flowers.

Hybrids with *S. greggii* include vigorous 'Maraschino', 3–4 ft. tall, 6 ft. wide, with bright cherry red flowers; and purplish pink 'Plum Wine', 3–4 ft. tall and 2½–3½ ft. wide. *S. m. microphylla* (*S. grahamii*) is a tough, dense, wiry-looking plant to 3–4 ft. tall, 3–6 ft. wide. Triangular to oval, tooth-edged leaves are dark green, ½–1 in. long. Rosy red, 1-in. flowers have small, hooded upper lip, three-lobed lower lip. Blooms most heavily in late spring and fall, sporadically at other times of year. *S. m. neurepia* grows 3–5 ft. tall and wide. More open-branched plant than *S. m. microphylla*, with brilliant red, very long-blooming flowers.

S. nemorosa. Perennial. Zones 2–10, 14–24. From eastern Europe, eastward to central Asia. To 1½–3 ft. high, spreading 2–3 ft. wide by rhizomes. Forms tight foliage rosette from which rise erect, branching flower stems. Wrinkled, dull green, finely toothed leaves are oval or lance-shaped. Lower leaves are stalked, to 4 in. long; upper ones are smaller, virtually stalkless, clasping flower stem. Sprawls if not supported. Stems 3–6 in. long hold ¼–½-in. flowers in violet, purple, pink, or white, with persistent violet, purple, or green bracts. Blooms summer through fall if spent stems are removed. 'Caradonna' has violet blossoms. 'Ostfriesland' ('East Friesland') has intense violet-blue flowers. 'Rosenwein' has rose-hued blossoms. There are also several compact selections. 'Marcus' has intensely violet flowers on plants 12 in. high and 18 in. wide. Sensation series is about the same size; Sensation Rose is among the most popular, with pink flowers.

S. officinalis. GARDEN SAGE, COMMON SAGE. Shrubby perennial. Zones 2–24; H1, H2. From the Mediterranean region. Traditional culinary and medicinal sage. Grows to 1–3 ft. high and 1–2½ ft. wide; stems often root where they touch soil. Aromatic, oval to oblong, wrinkled, 2–3-in. leaves are gray-green above, white and hairy beneath.

Branching, 8–12-in. stems bear loose, spikelike clusters of ½-in. flowers in late spring, summer. Usual color is lavender-blue, but violet, red-violet, pink, and white forms exist. Delay pruning until new leaves begin to unfurl, then cut just above fresh growth; cutting into bare wood usually causes dieback. Replace plants when woody or leggy (every 3 or 4 years). Subject to root rot where drainage is less than perfect. Give afternoon shade in hottest climates.

'Aurea'. GOLDEN SAGE. Has creamy gold variegation on green leaves.

CLOCKWISE FROM TOP: *Salvia farinacea* 'Evolution'; *S. guaranitica*; *S. greggii* 'Alba'

'Berggarten' ('Mountain Garden'). Compact; to 16 in. high. Denser growth, rounder leaves, fewer flowers than species; may be longer-lived.

'Compacta' ('Nana', 'Minimus'). A half-size (or even smaller) version of the species, with narrower, closer-set leaves.

'Icterina'. Gray-green leaves with golden border. Does not bloom.

'Purpurascens' ('Red Sage'). Leaves flushed with red-violet

CLOCKWISE FROM TOP: *Salvia leucantha* 'Waverly'; *S. elegans*; *S. chamaedryoides*

when new, slowly mature to gray-green.

'Tricolor'. Gray-green leaves with irregular cream border; new foliage is flushed with purplish pink.

S. patens. GENTIAN SAGE. Perennial. Zones 9, 14–24; H1, H2. From central Mexico. Upright to 2–3 ft. or higher and 1–2 ft. wide. Spreads slowly by tuberous roots. Arrow-shaped, toothed, softly hairy leaves are bright green. Pairs of brilliant blue, 2-in. blossoms on 6–15-in.-long stems; upper lip is hooded, lower one flared and ruffled. Bloom peaks in early summer but repeats through fall if plant is fertilized and deadheaded. Best in mixed plantings. Partial shade in hottest climates. 'Cambridge Blue' has light sky blue flowers.

S. 'Purple Majesty'. Shrubby perennial. Zones 9, 14–24. To 3 ft. high, 4 ft. wide. Hybrid of *S. guaranitica*, with leaves of a yellower green; brilliant royal purple flowers with

violet-black calyxes. Blooms from summer until frost in colder climates, nearly all year in mild-winter regions (where it is evergreen).

S. regla. MOUNTAIN SAGE. Evergreen or deciduous shrub. Zones 7–10, 14–24. Native to western Texas, central Mexico. Upright stems to 4–6 ft. tall; these arch and branch out to form an almost equally wide mass. Leaves are scalloped, puckered, fan-shaped. Orange-scarlet, 1-in. flowers with flaring calyxes appear in short clusters at branch ends; calyxes persist for several weeks after flowers drop. Profuse bloom from autumn until frost (through early spring—though less profusely—in mild areas). Prune this plant (if ever) only when it is growing strongly in summer; winter-pruned plants recover slowly, may even die. Loses leaves at 28°F (–2°C). Excellent nectar source for hummingbirds. 'Huntington' has larger flowers, spreading habit (3–4 ft. tall, to 6 ft. wide); 'Royal' is an upright grower to 6–7 ft.

S. roemeriana. CEDAR SAGE. Perennial. Zones 7–24. Native to south-central Texas

and northeastern Mexico. To 1–2 ft. high and wide. Reminiscent of coral bells (*Heuchera*), with basal clump of scalloped, rounded leaves. Foliage has a cedar fragrance. Sparsely branched flowering stalks bear few-flowered whorls of scarlet, 1¼-in. blossoms on 4–8-in. stems. Deadhead to keep the brilliant show going from spring through autumn. Reseeds to form colonies. Rich soil, half-day shade. 'Hot Trumpets' grows to 10 in. high and 8 in. wide; covers itself with masses of scarlet flowers.

S. sclarea. CLARY SAGE. Biennial or short-lived perennial. Zones 2–24. Native to southern Europe, southwestern and central Asia. Foliage clump to 2–3 ft. wide. Oval to lance-shaped, 1–1½-ft.-long, toothed, dull grayish green leaves are wrinkled, unpleasant smelling when bruised. In late spring or early summer, produces much-branched 3–4-ft. flower stalks with 6–12-in. stems bearing whorls of two to six 1¼-in. flowers. Blossoms are typically lilac or lavender-blue, with arched upper lip and cream-colored lower lip; large, aromatic, purplish or lilac-pink bracts remain showy for weeks after the flowers drop. Cutting stems before seeds form sacrifices this display, but it often produces rebloom in early fall and may prolong the plant's life. (Allow some seeds to form for replacement plants.) Leaves, flowers, bracts are used to flavor wines and liqueurs; oil is used in perfume, potpourri. Little to moderate water. 'Turkestanica' is especially vigorous, with creamy white blooms and white bracts flushed deep pink on edges.

S. semiatrata. BICOLOR SAGE. Evergreen shrub. Zones 16, 17, 21–24. Native to cool, high mountains of southern Mexico. Upright growth to 3–6 ft. tall, 2–3 ft. wide, with brittle, woody stems. Wrinkled, velvety, yellowish green leaves are triangular with rounded corners. Whorls of 1–2-in. flowers on 4–6-in. stems. Dusky lavender-blue blooms, with velvety blackish violet upper lip and throat, and blotch on lower lip. Calyxes are pinkish maroon, velvety. Blooms summer through fall; some winter flowers in mildest

areas. Pinch regularly and trim lightly two or three times a year; avoid hard pruning. Protect from slugs, snails. Needs perfect drainage in winter. Give afternoon shade in hottest climates. Elegant container plant.

S. sinaloensis. SINALOA SAGE. Perennial. Zones 15–17, 20–24. From foothills of western coastal Mexico. Low, mounding, dense plant with slender, 6–12-in.-long, prostrate stems. Spreads to 1–2 ft. or more by rhizomes; stems also root where they touch soil. Good groundcover. Closely spaced, lance-shaped, finely toothed leaves to 1 in. long. Foliage is purple when new, turning green in shade; to preserve purplish color, give full sun (but not in hottest climates unless well watered). Stems 4–6 in. long bear cobalt blue, ¾-in. flowers with two small white patches on lower lip and persistent, wine-colored calyxes. Main bloom in summer; sometimes repeats in fall. Shear back near ground just as new spring growth emerges from base.

S. sonomensis. SONOMA SAGE, CREEPING SAGE. Shrubby perennial. Zones 7, 9, 14–24. Native to dry foothills of California Coast Ranges and Sierra Nevada. Mat-forming creeper grows 8–12 in. high and spreads 3–4 ft. or more, rooting where branches touch soil. Evergreen, rough, irregularly notched leaves are dull green or gray-green; they may be narrow and 3–4 in. long or much wider and shorter. Small (less than ½ in.) lavender-blue flowers rise above foliage on leafless, 6-in. stems in late spring or early summer. Needs perfect drainage, gritty soil. Drought-tolerant. Best with some high shade in hottest climates.

S. spathacea. HUMMINGBIRD SAGE, PITCHER SAGE. Perennial. Zones 7–9, 14–24. Native to low elevations of Coast Ranges in California. Hardy to 20°F (–7°C). Foliage mass to 1–2 ft. high, 3–4 ft. or more wide, spreading by rhizomes. Evergreen, scalloped, wrinkled leaves are 6–10 in. long, lance-shaped or arrow-shaped; light green above, paler and hairy beneath. Foliage has a light, fruity aroma. Flower

S

stems rise 2–3 ft. above leaves, carrying many large, ball-shaped whorls of 2-in., magenta or rosy red flowers with maroon bracts and calyxes. Bracts and calyxes remain conspicuous for weeks after flowers fade. Blooms throughout spring, with some repeat in fall. A magnet for hummingbirds. Give rich soil, partial shade. Drought-tolerant but prefers moderate water; tolerates regular garden water. 'Kawatre' has deep magenta flowers that age to orange-red; it is hardier than the species (to 10°F/–12°C).

S. splendens. SCARLET SAGE. Perennial in Zones 21–24, H2; usually grown as annual in all zones. Native to Brazil. The traditional bright scarlet bedding sage now comes in a range of colors, from vivid true red through salmon and pink to purple shades. White forms are also available. Plants vary in size from compact 1-ft. dwarfs (like the compact Vista series) to 3–4-ft. kinds. Leaves are bright green, heart-shaped. Blooms late spring or summer through fall (all year in mild-winter areas); 4–12-in. stems bear 2-in. flowers from 1-in. calyxes of same color. Can be ravaged by Mexican giant white-fly. Give afternoon shade in hottest climates.

S. × superba. Perennial. Zones 2–10, 14–24. Form generally available is 'Superba', but many plants sold under this name are seedlings or selections of S. × sylvestris or S. nemorosa. The real S. × superba forms a tight foliage clump that spreads 2–3 ft. by rhizomes and sends up erect, much-branched, 3-ft.-high flowering stems. Smooth, scallop-edged green leaves are lance-shaped; basal ones are stalked and 3–4 in. long, upper ones stalkless and smaller. At bloom time, top 6–8 in. of stems bear clusters of ½-in. violet-blue flowers with reddish purple bracts that persist long after flowers fall. (Bracts on most seedlings are green, sometimes with a purple tinge.) Blooms midsummer to fall if deadheaded. Plant will sprawl 5–6 ft. wide unless staked. 'Adora Blue' grows to 14 in. high and wide.

S. × sylvestris. Perennial. Zones 2–10, 14–24. Like its parent S. nemorosa but more compact, with stems that are less leafy. Oblong to lance-shaped, medium green, scalloped leaves are wrinkled, softly hairy. Typically unbranched or few-branched flowering stems to 6–8 in. long, set with pinkish violet, ½-in. blossoms. Blooms summer through fall if faded flowers are removed.

'Blauhügel' ('Blue Hill'). To 2 ft.; has medium blue flowers.

'Blue Queen'. Grows 18 in. high and wide.

'Mainacht' ('May Night'). Grows 2–2½ ft., bears ¾-in. indigo flowers with green bracts (purplish at base), begins blooming in midspring.

'Rosakönigen' ('Rose Queen'). Grows to 2 ft. high, with purplish pink flowers and crimson bracts.

'Schneehügel' ('Snow Hill'). Bears pure white blossoms with green bracts on a 2-ft. plant.

'Viola Klose'. Grows 18 in. high and wide; has lavender-blue flowers.

S. uliginosa. BOG SAGE, BLUE SPIKE SAGE. Perennial. Zones 6–9, 14–24. From moist lowlands in South America. Upright, dense; to 4–6 ft. tall, 3–4 ft. wide, spreading aggressively by rhizomes. Smooth green leaves are lance-shaped, toothed; they reach 3½ in. long near plant's base, decrease in size toward top. Branched inflorescence with 5–6-in. stems carries whorls of ½-in., intense sky blue flowers with white throat, wide lower lip. Blooms summer through fall. To restrain spread, give only moderate water or confine roots by planting in 15-gal. nursery can sunk in ground to rim.

S. verticillata. WHORLED CLARY. Perennial. Zones 2–10, 14–24. From central Europe and western Asia. Foliage clump to 2½ ft. wide sends up branching, 2½–3-ft.-high flower stems. Wavy-edged, medium green, softly hairy leaves to 5–6 in. long; shape varies from oval to elliptical or oblong. Basal leaves often divided into one or two pairs of smaller leaflets. Widely spaced whorls of 20 to 40 buds open to violet or lavender-blue flowers nearly ½ in. long, with purple-tinged, persistent calyxes. Blooms from early summer through fall if deadheaded. Protect from slugs, snails. 'Endless Love' grows 12 in. high, 18 in. wide, with lavender and blue-purple flowers. 'Purple Rain' is 1–2 ft. high, with profuse, showy deep purple blossoms and calyxes.

S. 'Wendy's Wish'. Evergreen shrub in Zones 20–24, H1; or annual anywhere. This spontaneous hybrid's parentage is unknown, though it bears some resemblance to S. buchananii. Grows to 4 ft. tall, 3 ft. wide, with dark green leaves and purple-red flowers emerging from pinkish brown calyxes. It is named for Wendy Smith, the Australian who found it and requested that part of the proceeds from the sale of every plant go to Make-A-Wish Foundation. Moderate to regular water.

CARE

Plant sages in an area with good air circulation to help deter mildew and other fungal diseases. Most require good drainage, especially in winter; waterlogged plants rarely make it through hard freezes. If soil is heavy, work in plenty of organic matter and apply a thick mulch of well-rotted compost. When it comes to watering, "deep" is the operative word. Most of the plants discussed here come from areas with summer rainfall; they need regular (or, in some cases, moderate) water during dry spells. Plants described as drought-tolerant require a deep soaking at least once a month during the heat of summer to retain their foliage and prolong their bloom period.

Most sages resent severe pruning except in late winter or early spring, when weather is cool and vigorous new growth is emerging from plant base. To shape during the growing season, either tip-pinch shoots or cut them back by no more than one-third (keeping most of the leaves on each stem).

Give lax varieties inconspicuous support by letting them grow through a cylinder of green-painted wire mesh. In many sages, aromatic compounds in the foliage repel pests—but this is not true for all species. Some are damaged by slugs and snails; in warm climates, others can be demolished by Mexican giant whitefly.

Aphids may be a problem. Sages are generally easy to propagate from cuttings or seeds; you can also propagate perennial kinds by dividing the roots.

Sambucus
ELDERBERRY
Adoxaceae
DECIDUOUS SHRUBS OR TREES

- ⚡ **ZONES VARY BY SPECIES**
- ☼ ◑ **FULL SUN OR LIGHT SHADE**
- 💧 **REGULAR WATER, EXCEPT AS NOTED**
- 🐦 **FLOWERS ATTRACT HUMMINGBIRDS, BUTTERFLIES; FRUIT ATTRACTS BIRDS**
- ❖ **RAW FRUIT OF SOME TYPES CAN CAUSE GASTRIC DISTRESS**

Sambucus nigra 'Aureomarginata'

Grow these large, airy deciduous shrubs for their white spring flowers and colorful summer berries. In big gardens, they make effective summer screens or windbreaks. To keep shrubby types dense, prune hard in dormant season, removing older stems and heading back last year's growth to a few inches. Overgrown plants can be cut to the ground. Types that grow into trees need early training to single or multiple trunks.

The various elder species have bright to dark green leaves and near-black, blue, or red berries. Fruit of red-berried species and of S. nigra caerulea can cause gastric upset in humans if consumed raw in large quantities. (Red-fruited forms of black- and blue-berried species are not poisonous.) Species names are presently in flux.

S. canadensis (S. nigra canadensis). AMERICAN ELDERBERRY. Zones A1–A3; 1–7, 14–17. Native to central and eastern North America. Grown mostly in cold-winter climates. Spreading, suckering shrub to 12 ft. tall and wide. Each leaf has seven 2–6-in.-long leaflets. Blooms in early summer, bearing flat, creamy white flower clusters to 10 in. wide; these are followed by tasty purple-black berries. The fruit is used for pies; both flowers and fruit are used for wine. Strictly fruiting varieties include 'Adams' and the larger-fruited (and later) 'York'; plant both for cross-pollination. 'Aurea' has golden green foliage (golden in full sun) and red berries.

S. nigra. BLACK ELDER, EUROPEAN ELDER. Shrub or tree. Zones 2–7, 14–17. Native to Europe, North Africa and Asia. Shrubby, upright growth to 20–30 ft. tall and wide. Each leaf is up to 10 in. long and divided into many oval, pointed leaflets. Scented white flowers come in flat-topped, 5–8-in.-wide clusters in late spring or early summer. Purple-black berries are less than ½ in. across; for maximum fruit production, plant two different varieties. 'Aurea', 10–20 ft. tall and broad, has yellow new growth maturing to yellow-green. 'Guincho Purple', to 15 ft. tall and 10 ft. wide, has green foliage that matures to deep purple, then turns red in fall; purple flower stems bear pink buds that open to pink-tinged white blossoms. 'Black Beauty' ('Gerda') is similar but retains its black color throughout the growing season.

Several varieties grow 6–8 ft. tall and wide: 'Aureomarginata', green leaves edged in yellow; 'Laciniata', very finely cut green

foliage; and white-fruited 'Marginata' ('Albovariegata', 'Variegata'), green leaves bordered in creamy white.

Two smaller selections (4–5 ft. tall and wide) are 'Madonna', bearing green leaves that are variegated in light green to chartreuse when young, and variegated in cream, yellow, or gray-green when mature; and 'Pulverulenta', with leaves that unfold white, then mature to green splashed and striped with white.

S. n. caerulea (S. mexicana). BLUE ELDERBERRY. Zones 2–24; H1. Shrub or tree. Native from California north to British Columbia, east to the Rockies. To 10–30 ft. tall, 8–20 ft. wide. Leaves divided into five to nine toothed, 1–6-in.-long leaflets. White or creamy white flowers in flat-topped, 2–8-in.-wide clusters in spring, summer. Clusters of blue to nearly black berries, usually covered with whitish powder, follow the flowers. Fruit is often used in jams, jellies, pies, and wine. Drought-tolerant, but it looks better (and keeps its foliage in summer) if given moderate water.

S. pubens. SCARLET ELDER. Shrub. Zones 1–6. Native to northern North America. To 12–25 ft. tall and wide. Leaves divided into five or seven 2–4-in.-long leaflets. Blooms in late spring, bearing tall (up to 5 in.), loose flower clusters; inedible bright red berries follow flowers.

S. racemosa. RED ELDERBERRY. Zones A2, A3; 1–6, except as noted. Native to northern North America, Europe, and Asia. To 8–10 ft. tall and wide. Smooth leaves to 9 in. long are divided into five or seven sharply toothed leaflets. Small, creamy white flowers in dome-shaped clusters to 2½ in. wide, late spring into summer; inedible bright red berries. Leaves of 'Sutherland Gold' are bright yellow when they unfurl, then turn to green late in the season. 'Tenuifolia' has ferny foliage, bears flowers throughout summer.

FOR OTHER PLANTS THAT ATTRACT BIRDS AND BUTTERFLIES, SEE PAGES 95–99 AND 100–103.

Sanguisorba

BURNET
Rosaceae
PERENNIALS

✎ **ZONES VARY BY SPECIES**

☀ ◐ **LIGHT SHADE IN HOTTEST CLIMATES**

💧 **REGULAR WATER**

Sanguisorba obtusa

Three of these feathery-leafed perennials are grown as ornamentals, and one as a potherb. All have dense, feathery flower spikes that resemble small bottlebrush (*Callistemon*) blossoms. Leaves are divided featherwise into toothed, oval or roundish leaflets. These plants grow from creeping rhizomes.

S. canadensis. GREAT BURNET, CANADIAN BURNET. Zones 1–6, 15–17. Native to eastern North America. Grows to 3–6 ft. tall and 3 ft. wide, with bright green foliage and 8-in. spikes of white flowers in late autumn. Dies to the ground even in mild climates.

S. menziesii. Zones 1–10, 14–21. Native to southwest China. Grows to 2 ft. high and wide, with 4-in. spikes of maroon-red flowers rising above blue-gray leaves. Earlier to bloom than other species.

S. minor. GARDEN BURNET, SALAD BURNET. Zones 1–10, 14–21. Grown as winter annual in mild-winter desert. Native to Europe, western Asia. Can reach 1½ ft. high and wide but is usually kept clipped to a few inches to maintain a fresh supply of new foliage. Leaves have a mild cucumber flavor and are used in salads, soups, and cool drinks. Can be used as an edging for border or herb garden. If not sheared too low, bears

roundish, inch-long clusters of red flowers late spring to midsummer. Self-sows prolifically if allowed to go to seed. Evergreen in mild-winter regions.

S. obtusa. Zones 2–6, 15–17. Native to Japan. Grows to 4 ft. tall and 2 ft. wide, with grayish green leaves and pink flower spikes to 4 in. tall in summer. Evergreen in mild-winter regions.

Sansevieria trifasciata

BOWSTRING HEMP, SNAKE PLANT, MOTHER-IN-LAW'S TONGUE
Asparagaceae
PERENNIAL

✎ **ZONES 13, 23, 24; H1, H2; OR INDOORS**

☀ ◐ **SOME SHADE IN HOTTEST CLIMATES; BRIGHT OR DIM LIGHT INDOORS**

💧 **MODERATE WATER**

Sansevieria trifasciata laurentii

From western tropical Africa. Grown outdoors in mildest-winter climates; houseplant anywhere. Appreciated for thick, rigidly upright, patterned leaves that grow from thick rhizomes to form 2-ft.-wide rosettes. Leaves are dark green banded with gray-green, grow 4 ft. tall, 2 in. wide. Bears erect, narrow clusters of fragrant greenish white flowers in Hawaii but seldom on mainland. *S. t. laurentii* is identical to the species but has broad, creamy yellow stripes on leaf edges. Dwarf 'Hahnii' has rosettes of 6-in.-long, broadly triangular, dark green leaves with silvery banding; rosettes pile up to make a mass 1 ft. tall and wide. Other varieties and species are

---

Elderberries have a long history of culinary use in wines, syrups, jams, and pies. Their flowers were once used in medicinal teas and astringent lotions, and their strong stems can be hollowed out to make musical pipes.

S

collectors' items; scores can be found in catalogs of succulent plants.

First common name comes from use of tough leaf fibers as bowstrings; second comes from leaf banding or mottling, which resembles some snakeskins; third probably comes from toughness of plants and pointed leaf tips. Outdoors, plants tolerate many soil types, take salt air and drought; indoors, grow in much or little light, seldom need repotting. Withstand dry air, fluctuating temperatures, and scanty, capricious watering.

Santolina
Asteraceae
EVERGREEN SHRUBS

🌿 **ZONES VARY BY SPECIES**

☀ **FULL SUN**

💧 **LITTLE OR NO WATER TO MODERATE WATER**

Santolina chamaecyparissus
'Pretty Carol'

These tough Mediterranean natives are notable for their attractive, aromatic foliage and profuse summer show of small, round, buttonlike flowers. Unpruned plants become sparse and woody in the center. Cut back yearly, before spring growth begins; either trim around the edges, haircut style, or cut the whole plant back to a few inches high. After bloom, shear off flowering shoots. Replace plants that become too woody. In coldest part of range, plants may die to the ground, but they should grow back from roots. Good as groundcovers, bank covers, edgings for walks or borders, low informal or sheared hedges. Grow in well-drained soil.

S. chamaecyparissus (S. incana). LAVENDER COTTON. Zones 2–24; H1, H2. To 2 ft. high, 3 ft. wide. Brittle, woody stems are densely clothed with rough, finely divided, whitish gray leaves. Bright yellow flower heads. Smaller versions of the species include 'Nana', to 1 ft. high, 2–3 ft. wide; and 'Pretty Carol', to 16 in. high and wide. 'Lemon Queen', to 2 ft. high and wide, has creamy yellow flowers.

S. pinnata (S. ericoides). Zones 3–24. To 2–2½ ft. high, 3 ft. wide; narrow, tooth-edged dark green leaves, cream-colored flowers. *S. p. neapolitana* is 12–15 in. high; has silvery foliage, bright yellow flowers.

S. rosmarinifolia (S. virens). Zones 3–9, 14–24. To 2 ft. high, 3 ft. wide, with narrow green leaves like those of rosemary. Leaves may have tiny teeth or none at all. Bright yellow flowers. 'Morning Mist' is similar but more compact.

Sanvitalia procumbens
CREEPING ZINNIA
Asteraceae
ANNUAL

🌿 **ZONES 1–24**

☀ **FULL SUN**

💧 **MODERATE TO REGULAR WATER**

Sanvitalia procumbens 'Sunbini'

With the look of a small-flowered, trailing zinnia, this Mexican native grows only 4–6 in. high but spreads or trails to 1½ ft. or wider. Leaves are like miniature (to 2 in. long) zinnia leaves. Flowers are nearly 1 in. wide, with bright yellow (most common)

or orange rays around a dark purple-brown center. Blooms from midsummer until frost. The Tsavo strain has single or double yellow flowers. 'Sunbini' is mounding, has yellow blooms. 'Sprite Orange' is a good orange-flowered variety.

Needs good drainage. Plant is adversely affected by transplanting, so sow seeds where plants will grow. Plant from earliest spring (in mildest-winter climates) to late spring (where soil is slow to warm up). Heat-resistant. Use as temporary filler in borders or edgings, as cover for slope or bank; or plant in hanging baskets or pots.

Sapium sebiferum.
See *Triadica sebifera*

Saponaria
Caryophyllaceae
PERENNIALS

🌿 **ZONES 1–11, 14–24, EXCEPT AS NOTED**

☀ **FULL SUN**

💧 **MODERATE TO REGULAR WATER**

Saponaria officinalis
'Rosea Plena'

Strong-growing European natives, closely related to *Lychnis* and *Silene*, just need full sun and well-draining soil to prosper. *S. officinalis* can be weedy.

S. × lempergii. GIANT-FLOWERED SOAPWORT. To 1 ft. high, 1½-ft. wide, with small green leaves, 1-in. pink flowers with rose-colored calyxes. 'Max Frei' has a profusion of pink flowers in late summer and fall.

S. ocymoides. Trailing habit to 1 ft. high, 3 ft. across. Oval dark green leaves. In spring, plants are covered with small pink flowers in loose bunches

similar to those of phlox. Useful for draping over walls and as groundcover.

S. officinalis. SOAPWORT, BOUNCING BET. To 2 ft. high, spreading by underground runners. Elliptical to ovate, dark green leaves. Loose clusters of inch-wide summer flowers in red, pink, or white. Roots crushed in water produce a detergent-like lather. This is a tough plant that has naturalized in much of the West; before herbicides, it grew along railroad rights-of-way. 'Rosea Plena', with double light pink flowers, is the common garden form. 'Rubra Plena' has crimson blooms that pale as they age.

S. pumilio. Zones 2–7, 14–17. Linear, inch-long, bright green leaves form a tight cushion to 2 ft. high and 1 ft. wide. Inch-wide, purplish pink flowers are borne singly at branch ends in spring, making a ring of blossoms around the plant's base.

Sarcococca
SWEET BOX
Buxaceae
EVERGREEN SHRUBS

🌿 **ZONES 4–9, 14–24, EXCEPT AS NOTED**

☀ **PARTIAL OR FULL SHADE**

💧 **MODERATE TO REGULAR WATER**

Sarcococca confusa

Though its small white flowers are nearly hidden among waxy evergreen leaves, *Sarcococca's* fragrance can perfume much of the winter garden. Small berry-like fruit follows. Shade tolerance gives these handsome shrubs special value under overhangs, in entryways, and beneath low-branching evergreen trees. Plants maintain

S

slow, orderly growth and polished appearance in deepest shade. They also tolerate sun in cool-summer climates if the soil is not allowed to become too dry. Best in organically enriched soil. Scale insects are the only pests.

S. confusa. Similar to *S. ruscifolia* and generally sold as such. However, *S. ruscifolia* has red fruit, while that of *S. confusa* is black.

S. hookeriana humilis (S. humilis). Zones 3–9, 14–24. Low growing, seldom more than 1½ ft. high; spreads by underground runners to 8 ft. or more. Branches are thickly set with pointed leaves. Glossy blue-black fruit. Good groundcover.

S. ruscifolia. Slow growth to 4–6 ft. tall, 3–7 ft. wide. If grown against a wall, it will form a natural espalier, with branches fanning out to create patterns. Oval to elliptical leaves are densely set on branches. Red fruit.

Sasa. See Bamboo

Satureja
Lamiaceae
ANNUALS AND PERENNIALS

✔ ZONES VARY BY SPECIES

☀ ◐ EXPOSURE NEEDS VARY BY SPECIES

💧 REGULAR WATER, EXCEPT AS NOTED

Satureja montana

The first of these low-growing, aromatic plants has long been used as a tonic, while the other two are favorite culinary herbs.

S. douglasii (Micromeria chamissonis). YERBA BUENA. Perennial. Zones 4–9, 14–24. Native from Southern California to British Columbia. Grows to

6 in. high, spreading to 3 ft. wide by slender rooting stems. Roundish, scallop-edged, 1-in. leaves have strong minty scent. Small white or lavender-tinted flowers in spring and summer. Dried leaves make a pleasant tea, which early settlers drank to treat a variety of ailments, hence the plant's common name (Spanish for "good herb"). Prefers part shade but tolerates full sun in cool-summer climates. Grows best in rich, moist soil but takes drought as well as boggy conditions.

S. hortensis. SUMMER SAVORY. Annual. All zones. From southeastern Europe. Upright to 1½ ft., with loose, open habit. Aromatic, rather narrow leaves; use fresh or dried as seasoning for meats, fish, eggs, soups, beans, and vegetables. Whorls of tiny, delicate, pinkish white to rose flowers in summer. Grow in light, well-drained, organically enriched soil. Sow seeds in place; thin to 1–1½ ft. apart. Full sun. Good potted plant.

S. montana. WINTER SAVORY. Shrubby perennial. Zones 3–11, 14–24. From southern Europe. To 15 in. high and 2 ft. wide. Stiff, narrow to roundish leaves; not as delicate in flavor as summer savory. Use leaves fresh or dried; clip at start of flowering season for drying. Blooms profusely in summer, bearing whorls of small white to lilac flowers that are attractive to bees. Use in rock garden, as dwarf clipped hedge in herb garden (space plants 1½ ft. apart). Grow in light, well-drained soil. Cut back as needed to keep compact. Full sun. Moderate water.

Yerba buena— Spanish for "good herb"—grew in such abundance around a small bayside town in California that early settlers named their hamlet after it. The settlement grew considerably and changed its name— to San Francisco.

Saxifraga
SAXIFRAGE
Saxifragaceae
PERENNIALS

✔ ZONES VARY BY SPECIES

☀ ◐ EXPOSURE NEEDS VARY BY SPECIES

💧 REGULAR WATER

Saxifraga stolonifera

These creeping groundcovers from North America and Europe need good drainage and light soil; they rot easily in soggy soil. Those listed here—all evergreen species—are shade plants. Although exacting in their requirements, forms offered by specialists are among the choicest of rock garden plants.

S. rosacea (S. decipiens). Zones 2–7, 14–17. Native to Europe. Plants grown under this name are generally known as "mossy saxifrages." Form low, compact or loose foliage cushions to 2–4 in. tall, 1 ft. wide. Glossy green leaves are neatly divided into three to five segments. In spring, wide-open flowers are borne on 2–8-in. stems. The species typically has white flowers, but numerous named forms bear blossoms in cream, pink, or red. 'Peter Pan' is a smaller hybrid, with white flowers opening from pink buds. Widely sold *S. r. sternbergii* has white flowers strongly tinged pink. Afternoon shade is best in cool-summer areas; full shade is essential where summers are hot.

S. stolonifera (S. sarmentosa). STRAWBERRY GERANIUM. Zones 2–9, 14–24; or indoors. Native to China and Japan. Creeping plant forms a rosette to 6–8 in. high and 1 ft. wide, but expands fairly rapidly,

sending out runners like strawberry. Nearly round green leaves to 4 in. across have white veins, pink undersides. Blooms from late summer to fall, bearing inch-wide white flowers in loose clusters on stems to 2 ft. high. 'Maroon Beauty' leaves have maroon markings. Good groundcover where hard freezes are infrequent. Partial or full shade.

S. umbrosa. Zones 2–7, 14–17. Native to the Pyrenees. Tongue-shaped, shiny green leaves to 1½ in. long form a foot-wide rosette only a few inches high. Blooms in spring, bearing open clusters of tiny pink flowers on wine red, 1-ft.-high stalks. *S. u. primuloides* is a dwarf form. Good groundcovers for small shady areas; effective near rocks. This species is sometimes wrongly called London pride.

S. × urbium. LONDON PRIDE. Zones 4–9. Grows 1 ft. high and 2 ft. wide (or as far as space allows). Rosettes of spoon-shaped, leathery, toothed leaves give rise to small, pale pink flowers in summer. Partial or full shade.

Scabiosa
PINCUSHION FLOWER
Caprifoliaceae
ANNUALS AND PERENNIALS

✔ ZONES VARY BY SPECIES

☀ FULL SUN, EXCEPT AS NOTED

💧 MODERATE TO REGULAR WATER

🦋 FLOWERS ATTRACT BUTTERFLIES

Scabiosa atropurpurea 'Fire King'

Resembling a pincushion full of needles, each *Scabiosa* flower has stamens that protrude well beyond the curved flower heads. Bloom begins in midsummer, continues until frost if flowers are deadheaded or cut regularly. Good in mixed or mass plantings. Excellent cut flowers.

S. atropurpurea. PINCUSHION FLOWER, MOURNING BRIDE. Annual in Zones 1–24, H1, H2; may persist as perennial where winters are mild. May also be sold as S. grandiflora. From southern Europe. To 2½–3 ft. high, 1 ft. wide. Oblong, coarsely toothed leaves. Many long, wiry stems carry flowers to 2 in. or more wide, in colors from blackish purple to salmon-pink, rose, and white. 'Black Knight' has deep maroon flowers that are almost black. Double Mixed strain reaches 3 ft. high; Dwarf Double Mixed grows to 1½ ft. high. Attracts birds.

S. caucasica. PINCUSHION FLOWER. Perennial. Zones 1–10, 14–24. From the Caucasus, Turkey, and Iran. To 1½–2½ ft. high, 1–2 ft. wide. Leaves vary from finely cut to uncut. Flowers 2½–3 in. across, in blue to bluish lavender or white, depending on variety. Needs partial shade in hottest climates. 'Fama' has branching stalks carrying 3-in. blue flowers with broad rays; 'Fama White' has white flowers. House's Hybrids contains a mixture of blue shades and white.

S. columbaria. Perennial. Zones 2–11, 14–24. Grown as winter annual in Zones 12, 13. From Europe, Africa, and Asia. To 2 ft. high and wide. Finely cut gray-green leaves. Flowers to 3 in., in lavender-blue, pink, or white; almost all year in mildest areas. 'Butterfly Blue' (deep lavender-blue) and 'Pink Mist' (bright pink) are superior selections.

S. c. ochroleuca. Biennial or short-lived perennial. Zones 4–24. From Europe and western Asia. To 2 ft. high and wide, with light yellow flowers to 2½ in. across.

S. stellata. Annual. Zones 1–24. From western Mediterranean. To 1½ ft. high, 1 ft. wide. Many heads of pale blue, 1½-in. flowers; these quickly dry to papery bronze drumsticks, useful in dried arrangements.

S. 'Vivid Violet'. Zones 2–11, 14–24. Grown as winter annual in Zones 12, 13. To 11 in. high, 18 in. wide, with violet-pink flowers from spring through frost.

Scadoxus multiflorus katherinae
(Haemanthus katherinae)
BLOOD LILY
Amaryllidacaceae
PERENNIAL FROM BULB

🌡 **ZONES 21–24; OR INDOORS**

◐ **LIGHT SHADE; BRIGHT INDIRECT LIGHT**

💧 **REGULAR WATER DURING GROWTH AND BLOOM**

Scadoxus multiflorus katherinae

This tender South African plant is closely related to amaryllis. Large (4 in. diameter) white bulb stained red (hence common name). Lance-shaped to ovate, bright green, wavy-edged leaves are 12–15 in. long. In late spring or summer, ball-shaped clusters (to 9 in. wide) of narrow-petaled, salmon-colored flowers are borne atop thick flower stems 1–2 ft. tall. Many threadlike, bright red stamens protrude from each bloom, giving clusters the look of spherical bottlebrushes.

In late winter or early spring, plant in rich, well-drained soil, keeping bulb tip even with soil surface. Can be grown in the ground in frost-free regions (set bulbs 2 ft. apart) and the clumps left undisturbed indefinitely, but it is usually grown in containers, even in those regions. Choose a pot big enough to leave 2 in. between all sides of bulb and container edges. Place planted pot in a fairly warm spot (no cooler than 55°F/13°C at night, around 70°F/21°C during the day). Water sparingly until leaves appear (in about 8 weeks); then can be brought outdoors. Water regularly and feed monthly with

liquid fertilizer. After bloom, stop feeding and gradually cut back on water; let plant dry out in a cool, protected place. Do not repot next season; either add new mix on top of original soil or tip out rootball, scrape off some soil, and replace with fresh soil.

Scaevola
Goodeniaceae
PERENNIALS AND EVERGREEN SHRUBS

🌡 **ZONES 8, 9, 14–24; H1, H2**

☀ **FULL SUN**

◐💧 **MODERATE TO REGULAR WATER**

Scaevola aemula
'New Wonder'

Notable for its fan-shaped blossoms, with all the segments on one side. Named for the Roman hero Mutius Scaevola, who burned off one of his hands to prove his bravery. Most are native to Australia, but some are beach plants from Asia, the Pacific Islands, and the Caribbean. The Australian species are evergreen in mild-winter climates and nearly everblooming as well. In colder regions, where they are often grown as annuals, they bloom from late spring until frost and are useful in hanging baskets, window boxes, and containers.

S. aemula. Perennial. From Australia. Variable. Some forms are prostrate, others upright to 2½ ft.; fleshy stems of some spread to 3 ft. wide, while those of others trail or sprawl to twice that width. Bright green, 1½–2-in.-long leaves; lavender-blue, 1½-in. flowers all along the branches. Species available mainly through its named varieties, with flowers in various shades. 'Blue Fan' and 'Blue

Ribbon' grow about 1 ft. high and slightly less wide. 'Fairy Blue' and 'Fairy White' grow about 10 in. high and 2 ft. wide, as do 'New Wonder' (blue), 'Whirlwind Blue', and 'Whirlwind White'. 'Top Pot Blue' and 'Top Pot White' grow 1 ft. high and 3–5 ft. wide, while 'Top Pot Pink' grows just 3 ft. wide.

S. albida. Perennial. From Australia. Flowers are smaller and stems less fleshy than those of S. aemula. Forms a mat 4–6 in. high, eventually spreading to 3–5 ft. across. 'Mauve Clusters' has ½-in.-wide flowers in lilac-tinged mauve. Often grown as long-lived groundcover (set plants 2 ft. apart). 'Alba' is similar, but with white flowers.

Schefflera
Araliaceae
EVERGREEN SHRUBS OR TREES

🌡 **ZONES VARY BY SPECIES; OR INDOORS**

☀◐ **SOME SHADE IN HOTTEST CLIMATES; BRIGHT INDIRECT LIGHT**

💧 **REGULAR WATER**

Schefflera arboricola
'Variegata'

Fast-growing, tropical-looking plants; long-stalked leaves are divided into leaflets that spread out like fingers of a hand. Summer flowers (showy in some species) are followed by tiny dark fruits. All need rich, moisture-retentive, well-drained soil. Love humidity but are quite tolerant of drier air. Useful near swimming pools. Good container plants for patio or lanai.

S. actinophylla (Brassaia actinophylla). QUEENSLAND UMBRELLA TREE, OCTOPUS

TREE, SCHEFFLERA. Zones 21–24; H1, H2; precariously hardy in Zones 16–20 with protection of overhang. Native to Australia. Fast growth to 20–40 ft. tall and wide. The "umbrella" of the common name comes from the foliage form: the long-stalked, glossy bright green leaves are divided into 7 to 16 large (to 1 ft. long) leaflets that radiate outward like ribs of an umbrella. Foliage grows in tiers. "Octopus" refers to showy flower heads: narrow, raylike structures to 3 ft. long, set all along their length with little blossoms, radiate from a central point. Flowers age from greenish yellow to pink to dark red. Use for striking tropical effects, for silhouette, for contrast with ferns and other foliage plants. Cut out tips occasionally to keep plant from becoming leggy. Overgrown plants can be cut back nearly to ground level; they will branch and grow back with better form. This species has become a serious pest in some lowland areas of Hawaii.

S. arboricola (Heptapleurum arboricolum). HAWAIIAN ELF SCHEFFLERA. Zones 23, 24; H1, H2. Native to Taiwan. To 20 ft. tall with equal or greater spread, but easily kept smaller with pruning. Dark green leaves are much smaller than those of *S. actinophylla*, with 3-in. leaflets that broaden toward rounded tips. If plants are set into the ground with stems at an angle, they'll continue to grow at that angle—which can give attractive multistemmed effects. Yellowish flowers are clustered in flattened, foot-wide spheres; they turn bronze with age. Overall, produces a denser, darker, less treelike effect than *S. actinophylla*.

S. elegantissima (Dizygotheca elegantissima). Zones 16, 17, 22–24; H1, H2. Native to New Caledonia. As a juvenile, it is a houseplant; when mature, it's a garden plant to 25 ft. tall and wide. Leaves are divided like fans into leaflets with notched edges. Young plants are unbranched, with narrow (1 in.), lacy-looking leaflets to 9 in. long; foliage is shiny dark green above, reddish beneath. Plant branches as it matures, and leaflets grow slightly longer, broaden to 3 in., and become

less glossy. Greenish yellow flowers in clusters to 1 ft. long.

S. pueckleri (Tupidanthus calyptratus). Zones 19–24; H1, H2. Native to southern Asia. Resembles *S. actinophylla* but is a denser plant that branches from the base. May be trained to single trunk. Leaves to nearly 2 ft. wide are divided into seven to nine stalked, glossy bright green leaflets, each to 7 in. long, 2½ in. wide. Flowers are greenish, borne on shorter, fewer "rays" than those of *S. actinophylla*.

S. taiwaniana 'Yuan Shan'. YUAN SHAN HARDY SCHEFFLERA. Zones 4–9, 14–24. Native to the high mountains of Taiwan. Grows to 15 ft. tall and wide, with beautiful, layered, tropical-looking foliage that belies its hardiness.

Schinus

PEPPER TREE
Anacardiaceae
EVERGREEN TREES

- 🌿 **ZONES VARY BY SPECIES**
- ☀️ **FULL SUN**
- 🌊 **WATER NEEDS VARY BY SPECIES**
- 🐦 **BIRDS EAT THE FRUITS**
- ◆ **FOLIAGE CAN CAUSE DERMATITIS; BERRIES OF S. TEREBINTHIFOLIUS CAN CAUSE GASTRIC DISTRESS**

Schinus molle

These medium-size evergreen trees are praised by some gardeners, heartily disliked by others. The two species discussed here differ markedly, though both tolerate many soils. *S. molle* is the most widely grown.

S. molle. CALIFORNIA PEPPER TREE. Zones 8, 9, 12–24; H1, H2. Thrives in Zone 11 but will die in severe freezes. Native

to the Peruvian Andes. Fast growth to 25–40 ft. tall and wide. Trunks of old trees are heavy and fantastically gnarled, with knots and burls that often sprout leaves or small branches. Heavy limbs support light, gracefully pendulous branchlets. Bright green leaves have many narrow leaflets to 2 in. long. Drooping, 4–6-in. clusters of tiny yellowish white summer flowers are followed by rosy berries in fall, winter. (Trees with nearly all male flowers do not bear fruit.) This tree produces copious litter, is subject to scale infestation, and has greedy surface roots that make it difficult to garden beneath. Nonetheless, it's a fine choice for shading a play area or gravel-surfaced, outdoor living space. Just plant it away from paving, sewers, or drains, and give it room to spread. Among the brightest green trees in the desert. Planted at 2-ft. intervals, a row can be pruned into a graceful, billowy hedge. Susceptible to root rots, especially Texas root rot. Little or no water to moderate water. In Hawaii, best at higher elevations.

S. terebinthifolius. BRAZILIAN PEPPER TREE. Zones 13, 14 (with shelter), 15–17, 19–24; H1, H2. Native to Brazil; naturalized in Hawaii. Moderate growth to 30 ft. tall and wide; train to single or multiple trunks. Nonpendulous growth. Has darker green, coarser glossy leaves than *S. molle*, with 5 to 13 oval leaflets; showy bright red berries in winter. Highly variable; select a tree during fruiting season, looking for the largest, showiest berries and best foliage. Dried berries are sold as pink peppercorns; eaten in quantity, they can cause gastric distress. Wood is subject to breakage, so shorten long, lanky limbs and thin canopy to let winds pass through. Prone to verticillium wilt. Attractive shade tree for patio or garden. Self-sown seedlings can be a problem. In Hawaii, where female trees are invasive, plant males only. Moderate to regular water (applied deeply).

FOR OTHER PLANTS THAT ATTRACT BIRDS, SEE PAGES 95–99.

Schizachyrium scoparium

LITTLE BLUESTEM
Poaceae
PERENNIAL GRASS

- 🌿 **ZONES 1–24**
- ☀️ **FULL SUN**
- 🌊 **MODERATE TO REGULAR WATER**

Schizachyrium scoparium 'Blaze'

An important clumping grass in North America's tall-grass prairie. Grows 2–4 ft. tall, 1–2 ft. wide, with narrow leaves that may be erect or arching. Late-summer flowers are inconspicuous but age to an attractive silvery shade. Leaf color varies from bright green to distinctly bluish in summer, from light brown to dark red in fall and winter. Types that are bluer in summer take on the deeper cold-weather colors: blue-green leaves of 'Blaze' turn a strong red in fall, while 'The Blues' has striking light blue leaves that turn burgundy-red. Needs well-drained soil. Keep mulch a few inches away from base of plant.

Little bluestem evolved in the harsh environment of the North American prairies. In gardens, be careful not to kill it with kindness. Rich, fertile soils are not to its liking, and it will flop over in any but the lightest shade.

S

Spring's Unsung Annuals

Fluttery petals and intricate markings give *Schizanthus* its nickname, "butterfly flower." For a winning combo in a container, plant pink-flowered kinds in the center of a wide bowl, with nemesias in ruby and amber hues around the rim. Use coarse, porous soil; space plants about 6 in. apart. Water just enough to keep soil moist, but not soggy.

Schizanthus pinnatus

POOR MAN'S ORCHID, BUTTERFLY FLOWER
Solanaceae
ANNUAL

- ZONES 1–9, 14–24; BEST IN ZONES 1–6, 15–17, 21–24
- FILTERED SUNLIGHT
- REGULAR WATER

Schizanthus pinnatus

A profusion of small, colorful, orchidlike flowers rise above ferny foliage on this airy, upright, 18-in.-high annual. Blossoms come in pink, rose, lilac, purple, or white, all with markings in various colors; long-lasting cut flowers. Buy potted plants or start seeds indoors a month before planting time (germination is slow). Sensitive to frost and heat. Plant in spring where summers are moderate, in fall where summers are hot and winters are normally frostless. Give well-drained, rich soil in a wind-sheltered site, or plant in a container. From Chile.

Schizocentron elegans.
See *Heterocentron elegans*

Schizophragma hydrangeoides

JAPANESE HYDRANGEA VINE
Hydrangeaceae
DECIDUOUS VINE

- ZONES 2–9, 14–17
- PARTIAL SHADE
- REGULAR WATER

Schizophragma hydrangeoides

Resembling climbing hydrangea (*Hydrangea anomala petiolaris*) and climbing by aerial rootlets to 30 ft. or more, this native of Korea and Japan is clothed in pointed, tooth-edged dark green leaves that reach 5 in. long. White summer blooms appear in flat, 8–10-in.-wide clusters. Like lacecap hydrangeas, these feature tiny fertile flowers surrounded by a ring of sterile ones—but the sterile blossoms of this plant have only a single "petal"; those of hydrangea have four. 'Moonlight' has blue-green foliage with a silvery cast. 'Roseum' is a pink-flowered variety. Use species or varieties to climb shaded walls or trees. Plant in good, well-drained soil. Prune only to remove errant growth.

Schizostylis coccinea

CRIMSON FLAG
Iridaceae
PERENNIAL FROM RHIZOME

- ZONES 5–9, 14–24; H1, H2
- FULL SUN OR LIGHT SHADE
- REGULAR TO AMPLE WATER

Schizostylis coccinea

Beloved for its autumn bloom, this South African native has upright, swordlike leaves like gladiolus, and star-shaped, 2-in.-wide flowers like watsonia. Blossoms are carried on slender, 1½–2-ft.-high stems. The species has crimson flowers; but color variants include white 'Alba', watermelon red 'Oregon Sunset', and several in pink shades ('Mrs. Hegarty', 'Sunrise', 'Viscountess Byng'). Excellent cut flowers.

In spring, set rhizomes ½–1 in. deep, 1 ft. apart in organically enriched, well-drained soil. Water generously from planting until flowering ends; then water more sparingly until growth resumes in spring. If clumps become crowded, divide them in early spring; each division should have at least five shoots. In cold-winter regions, grow in pots and protect in winter.

Fill a large pot with assorted varieties of crimson flag to showcase the grassy leaves and colorful autumn flowers, which are great for cutting.

Schlumbergera

Cactaceae
CACTI

- ZONES 16, 17, 21–24; H1, H2; OR INDOORS
- PARTIAL SHADE; BRIGHT INDIRECT LIGHT
- REGULAR WATER

Schlumbergera

Famous for profuse bloom that roughly coincides with winter holidays, these cactus live on trees in the wild. In cultivation, they need rich, porous soil—a mix of equal parts coarse sand, peat moss, and leaf mold does nicely. Feed with liquid fertilizer every 7 to 10 days during growth and bloom. The many available kinds differ principally in flower color. Leaf segments root easily, making it easy to share plants. (For more on cacti, see "Meet the Cactus Clan," page 209.)

S. × buckleyi (S. bridgesii). CHRISTMAS CACTUS. Grows to 2 ft. high and 3 ft. wide, with arching, bright green branches of flattened, scallop-edged, smooth, spineless, 1½-in. joints. Can bear hundreds of long-tubed, rosy purplish red flowers at Christmastime. To ensure bud set, give plant cool night temperatures (50°F to 55°F/10°C to 13°C) and 12 to 14 hours of darkness per day during November.

S. truncata. CRAB CACTUS, THANKSGIVING CACTUS. Native to Brazil. To 1 ft. high and 2 ft. wide. Stems consist of bright green, 1–2-in., toothed leaf joints; two large teeth tip the last joint on each branch. Short-tubed, 3-in.-long, scarlet flowers have spreading, pointed petals in fall, then again in spring. Many varieties are sold in white, pink, salmon, and orange.

S

The Other "Pines"

Common names can be confusing. Umbrella pine doesn't belong to the genus *Pinus*. It is a conifer—with needlelike leaves and small cones—but it's only distantly related to pines, and its cultural needs are quite different. Other examples include fern pine and yew pine, not pines but members of *Podocarpus*. Norfolk Island pine (*Araucaria heterophylla*) is not a pine, and neither is screw pine *Pandanus tectorius*. So while botanical names like *Sciadopitys verticillata* don't quite roll off the tongue, they are useful if you want to be precise.

Schmaltzia ovata.
See *Rhus ovata*

Schoenoplectus lacustris tabernaemontani 'Zebrinus'

ZEBRA RUSH
Cyperaceae
PERENNIAL

🌱 **ZONES 5–24**

☀️ ◐ **FULL SUN OR LIGHT SHADE**

💧 **AMPLE WATER**

Schoenoplectus lacustris tabernaemontani 'Zebrinus'

Zebra rush forms an upright, grassy clump to 2–4 ft. tall and wide. Hollow, leafless, dark green stems are banded horizontally with light yellow; striping fades late in season and in strong sun. Will grow in several inches of water. Best used at edges of pools and ponds. To increase your planting, divide clumps in spring. Native to several parts of the world.

Sciadopitys verticillata

UMBRELLA PINE
Sciadopityaceae
EVERGREEN TREE

🌱 **ZONES 4–9, 14–24**

☀️ ◐ **AFTERNOON SHADE IN HOTTEST CLIMATES**

💧 **REGULAR WATER**

Sciadopitys verticillata

In its native Japan, this tree reaches 100–120 ft. tall, but in Western gardens it is not likely to exceed 25–40 ft. tall and 25–30 ft. wide. Very slow grower. In youth, it is symmetrical, dense, and rather narrow;

Slow growing, evergreen, and easily shaped by pinching and selective pruning, the graceful umbrella pine makes a handsome container subject.

with age, it is more open, and limbs tend to droop. Small, scalelike leaves are scattered along branches and bunched at branch ends. Glossy dark green needles grow in whorls of 20 to 30 at branch and twig ends, radiating out like the spokes of an umbrella; they are flattened, firm, fleshy, 3–6 in. long. Woody, 3–5-in. cones may appear on older trees.

Choice decorative tree for open ground or containers. Plant in rich, well-drained, neutral or slightly acid soil. Watch for mites in hot, dry weather. Leave unpruned; or thin to create Oriental effect. Good for bonsai.

Scilla

SQUILL, BLUEBELL
Asparagaceae
PERENNIALS FROM BULBS

🌱 **ZONES VARY BY SPECIES**

☀️ ◐ **FULL SUN DURING BLOOM, PARTIAL SHADE AFTER**

💧 **REGULAR WATER DURING GROWTH AND BLOOM**

⬥ **ALL PARTS ARE POISONOUS IF INGESTED**

Scilla peruviana

The three hardier species are native to cold-winter regions of Europe and Asia, where they bloom with winter aconite (*Eranthis*) and snowdrop (*Galanthus*). Peruvian scilla (*S. peruviana*), a Mediterranean native, is more tender (and showy). All squills have bell-shaped or starlike flowers that come on leafless stems that rise from clumps of strap-shaped leaves.

Cold-hardy species naturalize easily and look best in small or large drifts. *S. peruviana* is most attractive in clumps along pathways, at edges of mixed plantings, and in containers.

S. bifolia. Zones 2–11, 14–21. Each 8-in. stem carries three to eight inch-wide, star-shaped flowers in turquoise-blue. White, pale purplish pink, and violet-blue varieties are available. Each bulb produces only two leaves.

S. campanulata. See *Hyacinthoides hispanica*.

S. hispanica. See *Hyacinthoides hispanica*.

S. mischtschenkoana. Zones 1–11, 14–21. Each 6-in. stem bears nodding clusters of three or four starlike flowers in pale blue with darker blue stripes.

S. non-scripta. See *Hyacinthoides non-scripta*.

S. peruviana. PERUVIAN SCILLA. Zones 14–17, 19–24. Large bulb produces numerous, rather floppy leaves; in late spring, 10–12-in. stems appear, each topped with dome-shaped cluster of 50 or more starlike flowers. Most forms have bluish purple blooms, but a white-flowered variety is sometimes sold. Bulbs are dormant for only a short time after leaves wither.

S. siberica. SIBERIAN SQUILL. Zones A2, A3; 1–7, 10. Each 3–6-in. stem bears several flowers shaped like flaring bells. Typical color is intense medium blue, but there are varieties in white, lilac-pink, and light to dark shades of violet-blue, often with darker stripes. 'Alba' is white; 'Spring Beauty' has brilliant violet-blue blooms that are larger than those of species.

CARE

Plant all types in fall, in well-drained, organically enriched soil. Set bulbs of cold-hardy species 2–3 in. deep and 4 in. apart; set those of *S. peruviana* 3–4 in. deep and 6 in. apart. Reduce watering when foliage yellows after bloom. Hardy kinds will tolerate less moisture during summer dormancy, but don't let soil dry out completely. *S. peruviana* will accept summer moisture but doesn't need any. Divide clumps (during dormancy) only when vigor and bloom quality decline.

Scirpus cernuus.
See *Isolepis cernua*

S

Scrophularia auriculata 'Variegata'

WATER BETONY, WATER FIGWORT
Scrophulariaceae
PERENNIAL

- ⚡ **ZONES 3–9, 14–24**
- ☼ ☽ **FULL SUN OR PARTIAL SHADE**
- 💧 **AMPLE WATER**

Scrophularia auriculata 'Variegata'

Though it has lent its name to a large and important plant family, the genus *Scrophularia* is relatively little known in gardens. Like other members of the figwort family, this 4-ft.-tall, 2-ft.-wide representative has more or less tubular, two-lipped flowers. Stems have flattened "wings." Wrinkled, toothed, lance-shaped green leaves are strongly marked with cream, grow 2–10 in. long. Green, ½-in.-long flowers with a purplish brown upper lip bloom from summer into early fall. From western Europe.

Water betony is a showy plant for waterside plantings or damp borders. Other pretty plants to tuck amid low boulders around garden ponds include Siberian iris, joe pye weed (*Eupatorium purpureum*), meadowsweet (*Filipendula*), and forget-me-not (*Myosotis*).

Scutellaria

SKULLCAP
Lamiaceae
PERENNIALS

- ⚡ **ZONES VARY BY SPECIES**
- ☼ ☽ **FULL SUN OR LIGHT SHADE**
- 💧 **REGULAR WATER**

Scutellaria baicalensis

These clump-forming perennials have square stems and paired leaves. Long, tubular flowers flare out into two lips, the upper one narrow and hooded, the lower one broad. Blossoms are clustered in roundish or elongated inflorescences. Easy to grow with good drainage.

S. alpina. Zones 1–9, 14–24. From southern Europe to Siberia. Sprawling, mat-forming plant to 6 in. high and 1 ft. wide, with dark green, oval leaves. Tight clusters of 1-in., purple or white flowers in late spring, early summer.

S. baicalensis. Zones 1–9, 14–24. Native to Siberia, China, and Japan. Stems first spread, then grow upright, forming a clump 1½ ft. high and wide. Narrowly ovate, medium green leaves. Dense, one-sided clusters of blue-purple, inch-long flowers in summer and fall.

S. costaricana. Zones 23, 24; H2; or indoors. From Central America. Erect plant to 3 ft. or taller, half as wide, with dark green, heavily veined, ovate to elliptical leaves to 6 in. long; showy clusters of 1½-in., orange-scarlet flowers with yellow throat. Outdoors, blooms in late spring, early summer; anytime in greenhouse or indoors.

S. resinosa. Zones 3–10, 14–24. Native from Kansas and Colorado south to Texas and Arizona. Mounding plant 6–8 in. tall and 1 ft. wide, with roundish, resinous, grayish green leaves less than ½ in. long. Elongated clusters of deep purple-blue, 1-in. flowers in late spring. Deadhead for intermittent bloom through autumn.

S. suffrutescens. TEXAS ROSE. Zones 4–12, 14–24. Native to Mexico. Grows into a dwarf mound 6–8 in. high and 12–18 in. wide, with pink, snapdragonlike flowers that bloom sporadically all summer. Tolerates drought, heat, humidity. Semievergreen.

S. 'Violet Cloud'. Zones 2–12, 14–24. This sterile hybrid grows to 6 in. high and 15 in. wide. Gray-green foliage goes perfectly with abundant violet-red flowers. Very tolerant of heat after the first year. Dies down in winter.

The Mint Clan

Skullcap belongs to the huge mint family (*Lamiaceae*), whose members are easy to grow and easily propagated by stem cuttings. Most have aromatic leaves, including such familiar herbs as mint itself (*Mentha*) and basil, hyssop, lavender, oregano, *Satureja*, shiso (*Perilla*), sage, rosemary, and thyme—but not parsley.

Many other mint cousins have small but profuse flowers in a rainbow of hues, and most attract butterflies. Besides skullcap, see *Agastache*, bee balm (*Monarda*), bluebeard (*Caryopteris*), calamint, desert lavender (*Hyptis*), *Nepeta*, *Phlomis*, pitcher sage (*Lepechinia*), Russian sage (*Perovskia*), *Salvia*, and the stunning woolly blue curls (*Trichostema lanatum*).

Seaforthia elegans.
See *Archontophoenix cunninghamiana*

Sedum

STONECROP
Crassulaceae
SUCCULENT PERENNIALS

- ⚡ **ZONES VARY BY SPECIES**
- ☼ ☽ **FULL SUN OR PARTIAL SHADE, EXCEPT AS NOTED**
- 💧 **LITTLE TO MODERATE WATER, EXCEPT AS NOTED**
- 🐝 **FLOWERS ATTRACT BEES, BUTTERFLIES, HUMMINGBIRDS**

Sedum × *rubrotinctum*

Mostly groundcover-scale succulents that grow nicely in the spaces between rocks (thus "stonecrop"), sedums are native to many parts of the world. Some are quite hardy to cold, others fairly tender; some are tiny and trailing, others much larger and upright. Fleshy leaves are evergreen unless otherwise noted, but highly variable in size, shape, and color. Typically small, star-shaped flowers, sometimes brightly colored, are borne in fairly large clusters.

Smaller sedums are useful in rock gardens, as ground- or bank covers, and in small areas where an unusual texture is needed. Some are prized by collectors of succulents, who grow them in pots, dish gardens, or miniature gardens. Larger types are good in borders or pots. Most sedums are easy to propagate by stem cuttings; even detached leaves will root and form new plants. Soft and easily crushed, they will not take foot traffic, but they are otherwise tough, low-maintenance plants.

S

»

TOP ROW: *Sedum rupestre* 'Angelina'; *S. spathulifolium* 'Cape Blanco'. SECOND ROW: *S. forsterianum* 'Oracle'. THIRD ROW: *S. spurium* 'VooDoo'; *S. telephium*. BOTTOM ROW: *S. cauticola* 'Lidakense'; *S. makinoi* 'Ogon'

S. acre. GOLDMOSS SEDUM. Zones A2, A3; 1–24. Native to Europe, North Africa, and Turkey. To 2–5 in. high, with upright branchlets rising from trailing, rooting stems. Light green leaves to ¼ in. long; clustered yellow flowers bloom in spring. Extremely hardy but can get out of bounds and become a weed. Use as groundcover (set plants 1–1½ ft. apart), between steppingstones, or in chinks of dry walls.

S. album. Zones 1–24. From Europe, Siberia, western Asia, and North Africa. Creeping plant grows to 2–6 in. high. Leaves light to medium green, sometimes red tinted. White or pinkish summer flowers. Plant 1–1½ ft. apart for groundcover. Roots from the smallest fragment; beware of planting it near choice, delicate rock garden plants.

S. anglicum. Zones 1–24. From western Europe. Low, spreading plant 2–4 in. high. Dark green leaves are tiny, to just ⅛ in. long. Pinkish or white spring flowers. For groundcover, set plants 9–12 in. apart.

S. brevifolium. Zones 8, 9, 14–24. Native to the Mediterranean region. Grows just 2–3 in. high, slowly spreading to 1 ft. wide. Gray-white, red-flushed leaves are tiny (less than ⅛ in. long), tightly packed on stems. Pinkish or white summer flowers. Needs acid soil and good drainage. Best in rock garden or with larger succulents in containers, miniature garden. Sunburns in hot, dry places.

S. cauticola. Zones 1–11, 14–24. Native to Japan. Slowly forms a mound 4–6 in. high, 1–1½ ft. wide. Blue-gray, slightly toothed leaves. Clusters of small rose-red flowers top stems in late summer or early fall. 'Coca Cola' has silvery foliage, pink flowers. Dies to ground in winter.

S. confusum. Zones 8, 9, 14–24. Native to Mexico. Spreading, branching plant grows 6–18 in. high and wide. Shiny dark green, ¾–1½-in.-long leaves tend to cluster in rosettes toward branch ends. Dense clusters of yellow flowers in spring. Makes a good groundcover but is sometimes plagued by dieback in wet soils, hot weather; it looks best during

cooler weather. Use in borders or containers, as edging, in miniature garden. A similar, smaller plant with light green leaves is the closely related S. kimnachii.

S. dasyphyllum. Zones 2–24; H1, H2. Native to the Mediterranean region. Forms a low (1½–4½ in. high) mat that spreads to 1 ft. or wider. Gray-green leaves are densely packed on stems. Blooms in summer, bearing white flowers with pink streaks. Pink-blossomed 'Riffense' has silver-gray leaves that are especially plump and succulent. Partial shade.

S. dendroideum. Zones 8, 9, 12, 14–24. Native to Mexico. Branching plant to 3 ft. tall and wide. Rounded leaves to 2 in. long are yellow-green, often bronze tinted. Deep yellow flowers in spring and summer. For the plant sometimes sold as S. d. praealtum, see S. praealtum.

S. forsterianum. Zones 2–12, 14–24. From western Europe, British Isles. To 8 in. high, 10 in. wide, with globular rosettes of blue-green needle-like leaves and yellow flowers.

S. Herbstfreude group. Zones 1–10, 14–24. Hybrids of S. telephium and S. spectabile. To 1–2 ft. high, 2 ft. wide. All make good cut flowers, die down in winter.

'Autumn Charm' ('Lajos'). White-edged leaves on 16-in. plants, light pink flowers.

'Autumn Delight' ('Beka'). Golden green leaves with darker edges on 18–24-in. plants, dusty pink flowers.

'Autumn Fire'. Green leaves and dusty pink flowers on 18–24-in. plants.

'Autumn Joy' ('Herbstfreude'). Has green leaves. Rounded clusters of blossoms are pink when they open in late summer or autumn, later age to coppery pink and finally to rust.

'Elsie's Gold'. Has golden green leaves with cream edges, shell pink flowers.

'Mini Joy'. Similar to 'Autumn Joy', but a few inches shorter and with salmon-pink flowers.

S. kamtschaticum. Zones 1–11, 14–21. Native to Korea, Japan. Variable species to 4–12 in. high and 2 ft. wide, with trailing stems set with thick, somewhat triangular, 1–1½-in., medium green leaves, toothed on the upper third. Summer flowers open yellow, age to red. Useful in colder climates as a rock garden plant or small-space groundcover (set plants 1 ft. apart). *S. k. ellacombianum* (*S. ellacombianum*) is a shorter plant (4–6 in. high) with more compact growth, unbranched stems, and brighter green leaves. *S. k. floriferum* (*S. floriferum*) is a more profuse bloomer with smaller, paler flowers; its variety 'Weihenstephaner Gold' has golden blossoms that age to orange. *S. k. kamtschaticum* 'Variegatum' has cream-edged leaves.

S. lineare. Zones 1–24. Native to China, Japan. To 4 in. high. Trailing, rooting stems to 1 ft. long are closely set with narrow, inch-long light green leaves. Profuse yellow flowers in late spring, early summer. For groundcover, set plants 1–1½ ft. apart. 'Sea Urchin' has long, narrow, light green leaves; spreads to 3 ft. wide. 'Variegatum', with white-edged leaves, is often grown in pots.

S. makinoi. Zones 5–9, 14–24. Native to Japan. Prostrate or trailing, this has small, plump leaves and yellow flowers. 'Ogon' has rounded, golden leaves; 'Limelight' has lime green leaves. 'Salsa Verde' has deep green leaves. Thrives in shady, rocky soil. Regular water.

S. 'Matrona'. Zones 1–24. To 2 ft. high and wide, with rose-edged, gray-green leaves that age to grayish brown (retaining the pink edge); large heads of pink flowers appear on red stems.

S. morganianum. DONKEY TAIL, BURRO TAIL. Zones 17, 22–24; H1, H2; with protection of lath or eaves in Zones 13–16, 18–21; or indoors. From Mexico. Produces long, trailing stems that reach 3–4 ft. in 6 to 8 years. Thick, ¾-in.-long, light gray-green leaves overlap each other along stems to form braided-looking "tails" less than 1 in. thick. Pink to deep red flowers may appear from spring to summer but are only rarely seen. Because of its long stems, this species is best grown in a hanging basket or wall pot; in mildest climates, try it spilling from top of a wall or in rock garden. Provide rich, fast-draining

soil. Protect from wind and give partial shade. Similar relatives include *S. burrito* (*S.* 'Burro'), with fatter (1 in. thick) tails composed of densely packed, ½-in. leaves; and giant donkey tail (sometimes sold as *S. orpetii*), with somewhat shorter, thicker tails.

S. oxypetalum. Zones 16, 17, 21–24. Native to Mexico. To 3 ft. tall (usually much less) and 1½ ft. wide. Even when tiny, the plant has the look of a gnarled tree. Narrow, 1–1½-in.-long, olive green leaves; dull red, aromatic summer flowers. Evergreen or semievergreen in mildest areas; deciduous elsewhere. Handsome container plant.

S. praealtum. Zones 8, 9, 12, 14–24. Native to Mexico. Similar to *S. dendroideum* (and sometimes sold as *S. d. praealtum*) but has a wider spread and is less treelike (to 5 ft. high and wide), with greener leaves and lighter yellow flowers. Blooms in spring and summer.

S. × rubrotinctum. PORK AND BEANS. Zones 8, 9, 12, 14–24; H1, H2. Thought to be native to Mexico. Sometimes sold as *S. guatemalense*. Sprawling, leaning, 6–8-in. stems are set with ¾-in. leaves that look like jelly beans; they are green with reddish brown tips, often entirely bronze-red in sun. Detach easily and root readily. Yellow spring flowers. Grow in rock garden, in pots, or as small-space groundcover (set plants 8–10 in. apart). Leaves of 'Aurora' are bright pink.

S. rupestre (S. reflexum). Zones 2–24. Native to Europe.

Sedum comes from a Latin word meaning "to sit." The plants were most likely so named because they perch on rocks, walls, or stumps. But many vigorous sedums (such as *S. acre*) spread so quickly, they might be suspected of walking.

Late Bloomers

For sturdy, long-lasting flowers from late summer through fall, it's hard to beat *Sedum spectabile* and its hybrids. The plants' flat-topped flower clusters in shades of pink, rose, and red are standouts as summer bloomers start to fade.

Even when dormant in winter, the dried flower heads add interest to the garden. Look for named forms such as 'Autumn Joy' (flowers age to coppery red and then rust as weather cools), 'Brilliant' (dark rose-red flowers'), 'Carmen' (soft pink to rose-colored blooms), and 'Meteor' (bright carmine-red). Combine these plants with other autumn performers such as *Aster × frikartii* with a fringe of Japanese forest grass (*Hakonechloa macra* 'Aureola'), and shrubby blue-green junipers behind. Or cluster them behind mounding *Festuca glauca* 'Elijah Blue' with purple smoke tree as the backdrop.

Spreading, creeping plant grows to 16 in. high, 1 ft. wide. Narrow, light blue-gray leaves to 1 in. long, closely set on stems; yellow summer flowers. Spreads freely; set plants 9–12 in. apart for groundcover. 'Angelina' is a golden-leafed form; 'Blue Spruce' has needlelike foliage reminiscent of blue spruce.

S. sediforme (S. altissimum). Zones 2–24. Mediterranean native. This spreading, creeping plant grows to 16 in. high, 1 ft. wide. Narrow, light blue-gray leaves to 1½ in. long, closely set on stems. Small greenish white to light yellow flowers in summer. Use in rock garden, for blue-green effect in pattern planting, or as small-space groundcover (set plants 1 ft. apart).

S. sieboldii. Zones 2–9, 12, 14–24. Native to Japan. Low-growing plant just 4 in. high, 8–12 in. wide, with spreading, trailing, unbranched stems to 8–9 in. long. Blue-gray leaves with red edges are carried in threes; they are nearly round, stalkless, toothed along upper half. Plant turns coppery red in fall, dies to ground in winter. Each stem bears a broad, dense, flat cluster of dusty pink flowers in autumn. Leaves of 'Variegatum' have yellowish white markings. Species and variety are beautiful in rock gardens, hanging baskets. Light shade.

S. spathulifolium. PACIFIC STONECROP. Zones 2–9, 14–24. Native from California's Coast Ranges and Sierra Nevada north to British Columbia. Spoon-shaped, ½–1-in. blue-green leaves tinged with reddish purple are packed into rosettes on short, trailing stems. Light yellow flowers bloom in spring and summer. Use it as groundcover (set plants 1–1½ ft. apart), in rock garden. Very drought-tolerant. 'Cape Blanco' is a selected form with good leaf color.

S. spectabile. Zones 1–24. Native to China and Korea. To 1½ ft. high and wide, with upright or slightly spreading stems thickly clothed in blue-green, roundish, 3-in. leaves. Dense, 6-in.-wide, dome-shaped flower clusters appear atop stems in late summer and fall; they open pink, mature to dark brown seed heads that put on a long-lasting show. Dies to ground in winter. Full sun. Regular to moderate water. Among many varieties, 'Brilliant' has deep rose-red flowers; 'Neon' has bright pink flowers.

S. spurium. Zones 1–10, 14–24. Native to the Caucasus. Low-growing plant with trailing stems and dark green or bronze-tinted leaves just an inch or so long; spreads 2 ft. or wider. In summer, pink, purple, or white flowers appear in dense clusters at ends of 4–5-in. stems.

S

»

For rock garden, pattern planting, groundcover. 'Dragon's Blood' ('Schorbuser Blut') has purplish bronze leaves, dark red blooms. Red-leafed varieties include 'Red Carpet' (with red blossoms) and 'Fuldaglut' (with rosy pink flowers). 'John Creech' has small, scalloped green leaves and pink flowers. Leaves of 'Tricolor' are variegated in green, creamy white, and pink; its flowers are pink. 'VooDoo' has reddish leaves, red flowers.

S. telephium. Zones 1–24. To 2 ft. high and 1–2 ft. wide. Native from Europe eastward to Japan. Resembles S. *spectabile* but has gray-green, somewhat narrower leaves. Long-lasting floral display begins in late summer and autumn; blossom clusters open purplish pink, age to brownish maroon. Plant dies to ground in winter. Plant in full sun (stems tend to flop in shaded sites). Regular to moderate water.

'Picolette'. To 15 in. high and 16 in. wide, with bronze-red foliage and pink flowers.

'Postman's Pride'. To 2 ft. high and wide, with small, deep purple leaves and pinkish-red flowers that mature to burgundy.

'Purple Emperor'. Grows to 18 in. high and wide, with dark purple foliage and dusty pink blooms.

'Red Cauli'. Grows 15 in. high and wide. Purple-tinted, gray-green leaves give rise to red flowers.

'Xenox'. Grows to 14 in. high and 18 in. wide, with mauve-green foliage that matures to burgundy-purple. Pink flowers.

'Yellow Xenox'. Grows 16 in. high and 20 in. wide, with dark foliage and yellow flowers.

S. tetractinum. Zones 2–9, 14–24. From China. This plant forms a 3-in.-high mat of green rosettes that spreads 1 ft. or more. Yellow flowers appear in late spring, early summer. 'Coral Reef' has rounded, rich green leaves that turn reddish bronze in fall. Moderate water at first, then little to moderate water.

S. 'Vera Jameson'. Zones 1–9, 14–24. To 8–12 in. high and about 1½ ft. wide, with spreading purple stems clothed in pinkish purple leaves. Rose-

pink flowers appear in late summer and autumn. Dies to the ground in winter.

Semiarundinaria. See Bamboo

Sempervivum
HOUSELEEK, HENS AND CHICKS
Crassulaceae
SUCCULENT PERENNIALS

🌿 **ZONES 2–24**

☼ ◐ **LIGHT SHADE IN HOTTEST CLIMATES**

◊ ◖ **LITTLE TO MODERATE WATER**

Sempervivum

Known for their tightly packed rosettes of fleshy, evergreen leaves, these spread by little offsets that cluster around parent rosette (thus "hens and chicks"). Clustered, star-shaped summer flowers in white, yellowish, pink, red, or greenish; pretty in detail but not showy. Blooming rosettes die after setting seed, but offsets (easily detached and replanted) carry on. Many species, all good in rock gardens, pots, even in pockets in boulders or pieces of porous rock. Need excellent drainage. Water only to prevent shriveling. Native to mountains of Europe; protect from full sun in hot desert regions.

S. arachnoideum. COBWEB HOUSELEEK. Gray-green rosettes of many leaves are joined by fine hairs for a cobweb-covered look. Larger rosettes (to 3 in. wide) are surrounded by host of smaller rosettes. Spreads slowly to make dense mat to 1 ft. or wider. Bright red flowers on 4–6-in. stems. 'Cebenese' has cobwebby green leaves with burgundy tips;

'Cobweb Buttons' is covered with perfect geometric web patterns.

S. hybrids. Most varieties sold fall into this category. All form crowded rosettes that vary mainly in color and leaf shape. 'Oddity' is the most widely sold, with burgundy-tipped green tubular leaves; grows 8 in. high, 12 in. wide. 'Black' has deep maroon leaves with contrasting green new growth. 'Rubikon' is red; 'Krebs' is chocolaty green.

S. tectorum. HEN AND CHICKENS. Gray-green, 2–5-in.-wide rosettes spread quickly to form clumps to 2 ft. or wider. Leaves have red-brown, bristly tips. Red or reddish blossoms are borne on stems to 2 ft. high. Colored-leaf varieties in red, purple, chartreuse, and silvery blue are available.

Senecio
Asteraceae
PERENNIALS (SOME SUCCULENT) AND EVERGREEN OR DECIDUOUS VINES

🌿 **ZONES VARY BY SPECIES**

☼ ◐ **EXPOSURE NEEDS VARY BY SPECIES**

◊ ◖ ● **WATER NEEDS VARY BY SPECIES**

Senecio cineraria

Taxonomists have shaken up this group of daisy relatives, reclassifying two of its most important members and many second-tier species as well. One plant formerly known as dusty miller, *Senecio greyi*, is now a *Brachyglottis*; florists' cineraria, S. × *hybridus*, is now *Pericallis* × *hybrida*. In addition, some succulent species have been moved here from *Kleinia*, and some former *Senecios* have been moved to *Kleinia*.

S. cineraria. DUSTY MILLER. Shrubby perennial. Zones 4–24; H1, H2. From the Mediterranean region. To 2–3 ft. high and wide, with woolly white leaves cut into blunt-tipped lobes. Blooms at almost any season in mild-winter climates, during summer in colder regions, bearing clustered heads of yellow or creamy yellow flowers. Striking in a night garden. Gets leggy unless sheared occasionally. Full sun. Provide good drainage, little to moderate water. 'Silver Dust' grows 10 in. high and wide, with deeply cut, velvety, silvery green leaves.

S. confusus (Pseudogynoxys chenopodioides). MEXICAN FLAME VINE. Evergreen or deciduous vine. Zones 13, 16–24; H1, H2; mild frost kills it to the ground, but it comes back fast from roots. Sometimes grown as a summer annual in colder climates. Native from Mexico to Honduras. Twines to 10–15 ft. in California, as much as 40 ft. in Hawaii. Light green, rather fleshy leaves to 4 in. long are broadly lance-shaped, coarsely toothed. Large clusters of ¾–1-in., startling orange-red blooms with golden centers appear at branch ends; blossoms of 'São Paulo' are a deeper orange, almost brick red. Blooms from midspring into fall, sometimes year-round in frostless areas. Provide light soil, moderate to regular water. Full sun or light shade. Use on trellis or column, let cascade over a bank or wall, or plant in a hanging basket.

S. cruentus. See S. × *hybridus*.

S. greyi. See *Brachyglottis* Dunedin Group 'Sunshine'.

S. × hybridus. FLORISTS' CINERARIA. See *Pericallis* × *hybrida*.

S. leucostachys. See S. *viravira*.

S. macroglossus. KENYA IVY, NATAL IVY, WAX VINE. Evergreen vine. Zones 12 and 13 (if given northern or eastern exposure), 22–24; H1, H2; or indoors. Native to southeastern Africa. Thin, succulent stems twine to 6½ ft. or more. Thick, waxy or rubbery, 2–3-in.-wide leaves are shaped like those of ivy (*Hedera*), with three, five, or seven shallow lobes. Tiny yellow daisies in summer. Leaves of

'Variegatum' are sharply splashed with creamy white. Little to moderate water. Can be grown as a houseplant in a sunny window; water only when soil is dry.

S. mandraliscae (Kleinia mandraliscae). Succulent shrubby perennial. Zones 12, 13, 16, 17, 21–24; H1, H2. Native to South Africa. To 1–1½ ft. high, 2 ft. wide. Cylindrical, slightly curved, striking blue-gray leaves to 6 in. long. Use as groundcover where blue-gray effect is desired. Partial shade in the desert; full sun elsewhere. Little to moderate water. Beyond hardiness range, grow in a container and provide winter protection.

S. serpens (Kleinia repens). Succulent perennial. Zones 16, 17, 21–24. From South Africa. Resembles S. mandraliscae, but it is a smaller plant (to 6 in. high and 1 ft. wide) with smaller (1¼ in.) leaves. Little to moderate water.

S. talinoides. Succulent shrubby perennial. Zones 15–17, 19–24; H1–H2. 'Jolly Gray' can grow to 1½ ft. high and 3 ft. wide, with 5-in.-long, blue-gray, fingerlike leaves that can branch at the tip. Grows like a fine-textured S. mandraliscae. 'Blue' grows to 1 ft. high and 10 in. wide, is more mounding than matting. May not be as hardy as 'Jolly Gray'. Little to moderate water.

S. viravira (S. leucostachys, S. cineraria 'Candissimus'). DUSTY MILLER. Shrubby perennial. Zones 4–24. Native to Argentina. Sprawling plant to 4 ft. tall and wide. Leaves resemble those of S. cineraria, but they are more strikingly white and are cut into much narrower, pointed segments. Creamy white summer flowers are not showy. Grown in full sun, plant is brilliantly white and densely leafy; in part shade, it is looser and more sparsely foliaged, with larger, greener leaves. Tip-pinch young plants to keep them compact. Little to moderate water.

S. vitalis. BLUE CHALK FINGERS. Zones 20–24; H1–H2. Grows to 1 ft. high and nearly as wide, with succulent, fingershaped, chalky green leaves. Little to moderate water. Full sun to partial shade. 'Serpent' is more blue.

Senna
Caesalpiniaceae
EVERGREEN AND DECIDUOUS SHRUBS OR TREES

🌡 **ZONES VARY BY SPECIES**

☀ ◐ **FULL SUN OR LIGHT SHADE, EXCEPT AS NOTED**

◔ ◖ **LITTLE TO MODERATE WATER, EXCEPT AS NOTED**

🦋 **ATTRACT BUTTERFLIES**

Senna nemophila

Previously included in *Cassia* and still often sold as such, these are grown for their lavish show of bright yellow, five-petaled flowers that look something like those of potentilla. Blossoms are followed by seedpods that may create litter; to reduce pod production, prune lightly after flowering. Rangy, rank growers should also be cut back periodically to encourage more compact growth. Good for screens, massing, background plantings. Prefer well-drained soil.

S. artemisioides (Cassia artemisioides). FEATHERY CASSIA. Evergreen shrub. Zones 8, 9, 12–16, 18–23. Native to Australia. To 3–5 ft. tall and wide, with attractive, light, airy structure. Gray leaves divided into six to eight needle-like, 1-in.-long leaflets. Bears ¾-in. flowers in clusters of five to eight in winter and spring, with bloom often continuing into summer. In the desert, plants may rest in summer, then resume flowering in fall. Heavy seed production. Very drought-tolerant but looks better with moderate to regular water.

S. corymbosa (Cassia corymbosa). FLOWERY SENNA. Evergreen shrub. Zones 12, 13, 21–24; H1, H2. Native to South America. Rangy growth to 10 ft.

tall, 10–12 ft. wide. Dark green leaves with six narrow, oblong, 1–2-in. leaflets. Rounded clusters of 1½-in. flowers, spring to fall. Self-seeding can be a problem.

S. multiglandulosa (Cassia tomentosa). WOOLLY SENNA. Evergreen shrub. Zones 13, 17, 22–24. Native to many parts of the tropics. Vigorous, rank growth to 12–15 ft. tall and wide. Upright clusters of 1½-in. flowers at branch ends in winter, early spring. Leaves are green above, white and hairy beneath, divided into 12 to 16 leaflets, each about 2½ in. long. Regular water.

S. nemophila (S. artemisiodes filifolia, Cassia eremophila). DESERT CASSIA. Evergreen shrub. Zones 12–24. Australian native similar to S. artemisioides but with green foliage and somewhat greater cold tolerance.

S. oliogophylla. OUTBACK CASSIA. Evergreen shrub. Zones 13–16, 19–20. Native to Australia. Grows to about 5 ft. tall and wide, with glossy gray-green leaves, red stems, and yellow spring flowers followed by decorative reddish brown pods. Excellent drainage required.

S. phyllodinea (S. artemisioides petiolaris, Cassia phyllodinea). SILVER LEAF CASSIA. Evergreen shrub. Zones 12–24. Native to Australia. Rapid growth to 4–6 ft. tall and wide. Silvery gray leaves are narrow, curved, 1–2 in. long. Flowers are ¾ in. wide, blooming over a long season—from winter (sometimes as early as fall) into spring.

S. splendida (Cassia splendida). GOLDEN WONDER SENNA. Evergreen shrub. Zones 12, 13, 21–24; H1, H2. Native to Brazil. Open growth to at least 9–12 ft. tall and 6–10 ft. wide; habit varies from fairly upright to horizontal. Bright green leaves with four elliptical to oblong leaflets to 3 in. long. Loose clusters of 1½-in. flowers appear at branch ends from autumn into winter. Heavy seed production. 'Golden' grows to 18 ft. tall, 15 ft. wide, with large golden-yellow blooms.

S. surattensis (Cassia surattensis). SCRAMBLED EGGS, KOLOMANA. Evergreen shrub or tree. Zones 19–24;

H1, H2. Native to tropical Asia, Polynesia, and Australia. In Hawaii, it reaches 25 ft. tall and nearly as wide, and is used as a flowering shade or street tree. In California, grows 6–8 ft. tall and wide, makes a handsome flowering shrub for a small garden. Blooms nearly year-round, producing small clusters of ¾-in. flowers at branch ends. Each green leaf has 12 to 20 roundish, 1½-in. leaflets.

S. wislizenii (Cassia wislizenii). Deciduous shrub. Zones 10–13. From southern Arizona into Texas and Mexico. Rounded habit to 5–8 ft. tall, 5–10 ft. wide, with rigid, upright branches. Bright green leaves have four to six leaflets, each to 1¼ in. long. Clusters of 1-in. flowers appear at branch ends from early summer into fall.

Sequoia sempervirens
REDWOOD, COAST REDWOOD
Cupressaceae
EVERGREEN TREE

🌡 **ZONES 4–9, 14–24**

☀ ◐ **FULL SUN OR LIGHT SHADE**

◔ ◖ **MODERATE TO REGULAR WATER**

Sequoia sempervirens

Native to Coast Ranges from southwest Oregon to California's Big Sur coast. One of the West's most famous native trees (equally renowned is its close relative *Sequoiadendron*, called giant sequoia or big tree). Coast redwood is among the tallest of the world's trees: some individuals in the wild are over 350 ft. tall. Fine landscaping tree—almost entirely pest-free and almost always fresh-looking and woodsy

S

smelling. In its native range, a young redwood tree grows 3–5 ft. a year but will reach only about 70–90 ft. tall, 15–30 ft. wide in 25 years. In less favorable areas, grows more slowly and tops out at perhaps 50 ft. Typically forms a symmetrical pyramid of soft-looking foliage. Flat, pointed, narrow, inch-long leaves are typically medium green on top, grayish beneath; they grow in one plane on both sides of stem, giving stem a featherlike look. Small (½–1½-in.), roundish brown cones. Red-brown, fibrous-barked trunk goes straight up. A trunk with nearly parallel sides indicates a healthy redwood; one with a noticeable taper means the tree is struggling. Habit is somewhat variable, but most redwoods have main branches that grow straight out from trunk and curve up at tips; slightly drooping branchlets grow from these.

The tree's natural variability has led to selection of distinct variants. 'Aptos Blue' has dense blue-green foliage on nearly horizontal branches with drooping branchlets. 'Emily Brown' is columnar, green, and very fast growing. 'Kelly's Prostrate' grows flat, at about 6 in. per year. 'Simpson's Silver' has silvery green foliage and quick-screening growth of up to 12 ft. per year.

Fine-textured 'Soquel' bears blue-tinged green foliage on horizontal branches that turn up at tips. 'Filoli' and 'Woodside' are similar if not identical to each other; both are nearly as blue as Colorado blue spruce (*Picea pungens glauca*). They have an irregular habit, with branches that tend to droop, and need careful training when young to establish good form. 'Adpressa' ('Albo-Spica'), to 3 ft. high and 6 ft. wide, is a dwarf variety for rock gardens; it has white-tipped new growth that turns solid green as summer advances.

Coast redwoods are considered the tallest trees on earth, and giant sequoias have the most massive trunks.

Grow redwood trees singly or in groves with trees spaced 7 ft. apart; can also be used for a hedge (plant 3–4 ft. apart and top at least yearly). One of the best planting locations is in or directly next to a lawn, since the tree thrives on regular moisture; in 10 to 20 years, however, it may defeat a lawn. Away from lawns, it needs occasional feeding and regular summer watering for at least the first 5 years. Where it is best adapted, an established tree gets most of the moisture it needs from fog drip. Resistant to oak root fungus. Troubles the tree encounters are mostly physiological. Inadequate moisture or a hot, dry site will make it sulk and grow slowly; too much competition from bigger trees and structures makes it lanky, thin, and open. Lack of available iron makes needles turn yellow in summer, especially on new growth; treat with iron sulfate or chelates. Remember, however, that it is normal for oldest leaves to turn from green to yellow to brown, then drop in late summer and early fall.

Sequoiadendron giganteum

GIANT SEQUOIA, BIG TREE
Cupressaceae
EVERGREEN TREE

ZONES 1–9, 14–23

FULL SUN

MODERATE WATER

Sequoiadendron giganteum

Among the world's largest living things, giant sequoias can reach a towering 325 ft. and have the most massive trunk in the world (to 30 ft. in diameter),

yet young trees (in terms of a 3,000-year life span) are neat, handsome trees for larger gardens, reaching 60–100 ft. tall, 30–50 ft. wide. Giant sequoia is closely related to coast redwood (*Sequoia*), but its mountainous native range, on the western slope of the central and southern Sierra Nevada, gives it much extra hardiness. It also grows more slowly (2–3 ft. a year) than its coastal relative and needs less water. Outside its natural habitat, this tree is subject to fungal diseases that can disfigure or kill it; it is often more successful in colder interior climates than near the coast.

Giant sequoia's dense foliage is bushier than that of coast redwood. It is a somewhat prickly tree to reach into. Branchlets are clothed with short gray-green leaves; each leaf is a pointed scale overlapping the next, like prickly cypress (*Cupressus*) foliage. Dark reddish brown, oval, 2–3-in.-long cones. Lower branches hang on for many years, so that tree form is a dense pyramid; lowest branches sometimes root where they touch the ground, forming secondary "trees" that blend into the original. Removing lower branches reveals a fissured, craggy-looking trunk covered in dark red-brown bark. In gardens, giant sequoia is primarily used as a featured tree in a large lawn (roots may surface there). Grow in good, deep, well-drained soil.

There are dozens of named varieties. 'Glaucum' has blue-green leaves. 'Pendulum' and 'Barabit's Requiem' have irregular forms and strongly weeping branches. Both grow to about 25 ft. tall; 'Pendulum' can be kept to 6 ft. wide, while 'Barabit's Requiem' grows a little wider and with a thicker trunk. 'Bultinck Yellow' has golden new growth and is slower (and ultimately smaller) than the species. 'Albospica' is a dwarf variegated form that grows 4 in. per year.

Seriphidium canum, S. tridentatum.
See *Artemisia cana, A. tridentata*

Sesleria

MOOR GRASS
Poaceae
PERENNIAL GRASSES

ZONES VARY BY SPECIES

FULL SUN TO PARTIAL SHADE

MODERATE TO REGULAR WATER

Sesleria autumnalis

These tufted evergreen to semievergreen perennial grasses are tough, long-lived, low-maintenance plants that can take considerable drought once established. Use as fillers among other ornamentals or mass as groundcovers among trees and shrubs, in meadow plantings. Both species are native to the hills and mountains of southeastern Europe.

S. autumnalis. AUTUMN MOOR GRASS. Zones 3b–10, 14–24. Spiky clumps of narrow, lime green leaves grow 8–18 in. high and wide. Attractive light tan flowers are held in elongated spikes 6–8 in. above the foliage in late summer and fall.

S. caerulea. BLUE MOOR GRASS. Zones 2b–10, 14–24. To 6–8 in. high and wide. Narrow leaves are powder blue on top, dark green beneath; their slightly twisted shape makes both colors visible. Short spike-like flowers held above the leaves in late spring emerge purplish black and lighten as they age; pretty but not showy. Best near the coast. Plant in partial shade inland.

S. 'Greenlee'. Zones 3b–10, 14–24. Probably a hybrid of *S. autumnalis* and *S. caerulea*. Grows about 1 ft. high and wide, with pretty pale purple flowers in spring and summer. Takes sun or shade, wet or dry soil.

Setcreasea pallida 'Purple Heart'. See *Tradescantia pallida* 'Purpurea'

Shallot
Alliaceae
PERENNIAL OFTEN GROWN AS ANNUAL

- ✂ **ALL ZONES**
- ☼ **FULL SUN**
- 💧 **REGULAR WATER**

Shallots

Shallots resemble onions and, like them, are in the genus *Allium*. Thought to have originated in western or central Asia. The bulb is divided into sections that grow on a common base; it is prized in cooking for its distinctive flavor, a combination of mild onion and pungent garlic. Young green shoots are also used as scallions.

Shallots are usually grown from cloves (sections of bulbs). You can purchase these from a seed company or simply buy shallots in the grocery store and separate them into cloves. Nurseries with stocks of herbs may sell growing plants.

Dutch shallots have golden brown skin and white cloves; red shallots have coppery skin, purple cloves.

In mild climates, plant shallots at least 6 weeks before average date of first fall frost to harvest green tops through winter and early spring, bulbs in late spring and summer. In cold-winter regions, plant in early spring for green shoots in summer, bulbs in autumn.

Plant cloves, pointed end up, 4–8 in. apart; cover with ½ in. of soil. From spring planting, you'll have green shoots in

about 60 days, new bulbs in 90 to 120 days. Some seed companies sell shallot seeds; plant 12 seeds per foot. Bulbs will be ready to harvest in about 100 days.

When bulbs mature, shoots yellow and die. Pull up clumps and separate the bulbs; before using them, let dry for about a month in a cool, dry place. If stored properly, shallots will keep for up to 8 months.

Shepherdia argentea
SILVER BUFFALOBERRY, SILVERBERRY
Elaeagnaceae
DECIDUOUS SHRUB

- ✂ **ZONES 1–3, 7, 10**
- ☼ **FULL SUN**
- 💧 **LITTLE TO REGULAR WATER**
- 🐦 **FRUIT ATTRACTS BIRDS**

Shepherdia argentea

This is a tough plant for harsh growing conditions, withstanding cold and wind, tolerant of most soils, and drought-resistant. Its growth habit is spreading and suckering, to 6–12 ft. tall and wide, with spine-tipped branchlets. Elongated oval leaves are silvery on both sides. Related to Russian olive (*Elaeagnus angustifolia*), another plant that readily endures difficult situations. If a male plant is nearby, females will bear small, sour bright red or orange berries that can be used for jams and jellies. Native from Canada into the intermountain areas of the West.

FOR MORE UNTHIRSTY PLANTS, SEE "PLANTS FOR WATERWISE GARDENS," PAGES 74–78.

Sida fallax
'ILIMA
Malvaceae
EVERGREEN SHRUB

- ✂ **ZONES 23, 24; H1, H2**
- ☼ **FULL SUN**
- 💧 **LITTLE WATER**

Sida fallax

Native to Hawaii; widespread in the Pacific Islands and China. There are many forms of this plant, from groundcovers to medium-size shrubs to shrubs 10 ft. high and nearly as wide. Roundish, bright green to silvery green leaves to ½ in. long. Blooms all year, producing hibiscuslike, ½–1-in. flowers in colors ranging from yellow and orange to dull red. Blossoms are used in leis. Good wind tolerance. Does best in well-drained, rocky or sandy soil. 'Ilima papa is a very low-growing form, to just 3 in. high and 2 ft. wide; it is useful as a groundcover. 'Kaneohe Gold', to 3 ft. high and wide, has double blooms in bright golden orange.

The blooms of 'ilima are popular in leis because they are sturdy and long-lasting after cutting, even without water. Other favorites for "floral jewelry" include plumeria and several jasmines, gingers, and orchids.

Sidalcea
CHECKERBLOOM
Malvaceae
PERENNIALS

- ✂ **ZONES 2–10, 14–24, EXCEPT AS NOTED**
- ☼ **FULL SUN**
- 💧 **REGULAR WATER, EXCEPT AS NOTED**

Sidalcea 'Elsie Heugh'

Grown for clusters of five-petaled flowers, these range from erect to sprawling; leaves are typically dark green, roundish to kidney-shaped, about 3 in. across.

S. candida. Native to High Plains. To 2–3 ft. high, spreading by rhizomes to 1½ ft. Unbranched stems bear bluish green leaves to 8 in. across. Crowded spikes of white, 1-in. flowers in mid- or late summer.

S. hybrids. Most garden sidalceas are hybrids between *S. candida* and *S. malviflora*. They form clumps to about 2 ft. wide and bear 1½–2-in. flowers; bloom all summer if deadheaded. Choices include 2–3-ft. 'Brilliant', with carmine-red flowers; 3-ft. 'Elsie Heugh', with fringed pale pink flowers; 2–3-ft. 'Party Girl' (deep pink); and 2–3-ft. 'Rosanna', with rose-colored flowers.

S. malviflora. CHECKERBLOOM. Zones 2–9, 14–24. Native to Oregon, California, Baja California. To 2 ft. high and wide or sprawling and spreading. Pink or purplish pink, 2-in. flowers in early spring. Attracts butterflies. Moderate water.

S. neomexicana. Zones 2, 3, 10–13, 18–24. Native from eastern Oregon to Wyoming, south to Mexico. To 3 ft. high, 1–1½ ft. wide; branched or unbranched spikes of white or pinkish, ¾-in., summer flowers.

S

Silene
Caryophyllaceae
PERENNIALS AND ANNUALS

- ✿ ZONES VARY BY SPECIES
- ☀ ◑ FULL SUN OR PARTIAL SHADE
- ◐ ◑ ● ● WATER NEEDS VARY BY SPECIES
- 🦋 FLOWERS ATTRACT BUTTERFLIES AND HUMMINGBIRDS

Silene californica

Colorful choices for front of border or rock garden. Flowers are typically single. Many species; some are erect, others cushionlike. Need well-drained soil.

S. acaulis. CUSHION PINK, MOSS CAMPION. Perennial. Zones A1–A3; 1–11, 14–16, 18–21. From the Arctic, mountains of North America, and Eurasia. Small, narrow green leaves form a mosslike mat to 2 in. high, 8 in. wide. Reddish purple, ½-in. flowers are borne singly in spring. Good for gravelly, moist but well-drained spot. Regular water.

S. californica. CALIFORNIA INDIAN PINK. Perennial. Zones 3, 6–9, 14–24. Native to foothills of California and southern Oregon. Loosely branching plant to 1 ft. high and wide. Blooms in spring, producing flaming red, 1½-in. flowers with cleft and fringed petals in clusters of few to many. Gray-green, hairy, lance-shaped to ovate leaves are somewhat sticky. Occasionally sold in seed packets. In its native range, it receives no moisture during the summer months, but it can take water then if given excellent drainage.

S. coeli-rosa (Lychnis coeli-rosa, Agrostemma coeli-rosa). VISCARIA. Annual. All zones. Mediterranean native to 1 ft. high, half as wide, with gray-green, lance-shaped to oblong leaves. Loose clusters of saucer-shaped, 1-in. flowers in blue, lavender, pink, or white, often with a contrasting eye. Long bloom period. Sow seeds in rich soil in early spring for summer bloom; in mild-winter climates, sow in fall for winter and spring bloom. Good cut flower. Regular water.

S. schafta. MOSS CAMPION. Perennial. Zones 2–9, 14–16, 18–21. From western Asia. Upright, wiry stems form a tuft 6–12 in. high and 1 ft. wide. Small tongue-shaped, bright green leaves. Profuse rosy purple, ¾-in. flowers, one or two per stalk, late summer into autumn. Moderate water.

S. uniflora (S. vulgaris maritima). Perennial. Zones 1–9, 14–24. From coastal regions of western and northern Europe. Forms a low (6 in. high, 8 in. wide) cushion of lance-shaped gray-green leaves. Abundant white, 1-in. summer flowers, each nearly enclosed by a balloonlike calyx; borne one to four per stem. Moderate water.

Simmondsia chinensis
JOJOBA, GOATNUT
Simmondsiaceae
EVERGREEN SHRUB

- ✿ ZONES 7–24
- ☀ FULL SUN
- ◐ LITTLE WATER

Simmondsia chinensis

Native to deserts of Southern California, Arizona, Mexico. Useful as informal shrub or clipped hedge, foundation planting in desert gardens. A dense plant with rigid branches; typically to 3–6 ft. tall and wide, occasionally larger. Dull gray-green leaves are leathery, narrowly egg-shaped. Inconspicuous flowers. If a male plant is present, the females bear edible, nutlike fruit ¾ in. long; flavor is like that of filbert but slightly bitter until fruit is dried or roasted. The fruit's high oil content gives the plant commercial value as a crop for marginal land, though such plantings are chancy in soil infested with verticillium wilt or Texas root rot. Young plants are rather tender; established ones will take 15°F (–9°C).

Sisyrinchium
Iridaceae
PERENNIALS

- ✿ ZONES 4–9, 14–24, EXCEPT AS NOTED
- ☀ ◑ FULL SUN OR LIGHT SHADE
- ◐ ● ● WATER NEEDS VARY BY SPECIES

Sisyrinchium 'Devon Skies'

Iris relatives with narrow leaves and small, six-segmented flowers that open in sunshine. Pretty but not showy; best suited for informal gardens or naturalizing.

S. californicum. YELLOW-EYED GRASS. From coastal areas, California to British Columbia. To 6–24 in. high, 8–10 in. wide. Dull green leaves are broader than those of *S. idahoense bellum*. Yellow flowers in late spring or early summer. Succeeds in wet or low spots. Ample water.

S. idahoense bellum (S. bellum). BLUE-EYED GRASS. Zones 2–9, 14–24. Native to coast of California and Oregon. To 4–24 in. high, 6–24 in. wide. Green or bluish green leaves. Purple to bluish purple, ½-in. flowers in spring. Several named forms and hybrids are available. Many of them, including 'Devon Skies' (4–6 in. high), are dwarf. *S. idahoense macounii* 'Album' has white flowers. Moderate to regular water.

S. striatum. Native to Chile and Argentina. Grows to 3 ft. high and 1 ft. wide, with attractive gray-green leaves. In spring, produces spikelike clusters of many ½-in. flowers in pale yellow streaked with brown; blooms well into summer if old flower clusters are removed (if you don't remove them, you may have hordes of unwanted seedlings the next year). Leaves of 'Aunt May' ('Variegatum') are striped with creamy yellow. Moderate water.

Skimmia japonica
Rutaceae
EVERGREEN SHRUB

- ✿ ZONES 4–9, 14–22
- ◑ PARTIAL SHADE
- ● REGULAR WATER

Skimmia japonica

Good-looking evergreen shrub from Japan to China. Compact, slow grower to 5 ft. tall, 6 ft. wide. Glossy rich green leaves. Blooms in spring, when pinkish to reddish buds held well above the foliage open to tiny, lightly scented white flowers (typically larger and more fragrant on males than on females). In fall and winter, female plants will bear hollylike red berries if a male plant is nearby. Plants tend to be sold simply as "male" or "female" rather than by variety name. A white-berried form is sold. *S. j. reevesiana* (often sold as *S. reevesiana*), a dwarf form to 1½–2 ft. high and 2–3 ft. wide, is self-fruitful and bears dull crimson berries.

Handsome beside shaded walks, under windows, flanking entryways, in containers. Prefers moist, highly organic, acid soil. Grows best in Zones 4–6, 17. Thrips and red spider mites are potential pests throughout its range. In the Northwest, it is prone to attack by several kinds of mites that give leaves a stippled, silvery look. Water mold is a problem in hot regions.

Smilacina racemosa.
See *Maianthemum racemosa*

Solandra maxima
CUP-OF-GOLD VINE
Solanaceae
EVERGREEN VINE

🗡 **ZONES 15–24; H2**

☼ **FULL SUN**

💧 **REGULAR WATER**

☈ **ALL PLANT PARTS ARE POISONOUS**

Solandra maxima 'Variegata'

Fast-growing, sprawling, rampant vine to 40 ft.; must be tied to its support. Native from Mexico to Venezuela and Colombia. Heavy stems bear highly polished, broadly oval, rich green leaves. Inflated-looking buds open to big (6–8 in.), leathery, bowl-shaped, five-lobed blossoms that are fragrant at night; flowers are golden yellow, with a red-brown stripe running down each lobe to flower center. Main bloom period runs from winter into early spring, but scattered flowering can occur at any time. 'Variegata' has leaves marked with white. Use on big walls and pergolas, along eaves, as bank cover. Spectacular along a fence near a swimming pool. Often sold as *S. guttata*.

CARE
Give good, well-drained soil for best growth. Cut back long, vigorous shoots to induce branching and more flowers. To make it easy to see inside the big flowers, encourage growth low on plant by tip-pinching. Can be trimmed back to make a rough hedge. Takes seacoast conditions, wind, and fog. Provide shade for roots in hottest climates; give overhead cold protection in Zones 15, 16, 18–20. Light frost blackens the leaves, but plants usually recover to produce new growth.

Solanum
Solanaceae
EVERGREEN, SEMIEVERGREEN, AND DECIDUOUS SHRUBS, VINES, PERENNIALS

🗡 **ZONES VARY BY SPECIES**

☼◑ **FULL SUN OR PARTIAL SHADE**

💧💧 **MODERATE TO REGULAR WATER, EXCEPT AS NOTED**

☈ **MANY SPECIES ARE POISONOUS IF INGESTED; MOST ARE SUSPECT**

Solanum crispum 'Glasnevin'

In addition to eggplant and potato (described under those names), *Solanum* includes a number of ornamental plants. All have small, star-shaped, five-petaled blue or white flowers with reproductive parts that form a pointed yellow structure in the blossom's center. A few of the species described here produce decorative fruit—edible in the case of *S. muricatum*, but usually poisonous (if fruit is not described as edible, you are better off not sampling it).

S. aviculare. KANGAROO APPLE. Evergreen shrub. Zones 15–17, 21–24. From Australia and New Zealand. Fast growth to 6–10 ft. tall and 5–8 ft. wide. Lance-shaped deep green leaves are smooth and deeply cut, reach 1 ft. long. Purple, 1-in.-wide flowers in spring and summer are followed by inedible scarlet fruit about 1 in. across.

S. crispum. Evergreen vine. Zones 8, 9, 12–24. From Chile and Peru. Modest (even shrubby) climber to 12 ft., with ovate to lance-shaped, soft green, often wavy-edged leaves to 5 in. long. In summer, bears 4-in. clusters of fragrant lilac-blue flowers with yellow centers. Small, inedible yellowish fruit. Must be fastened to its support; well suited to trellises, walls, posts. May lose leaves in hard frost. 'Glasnevin' has deeper blue flowers in larger clusters.

S. jasminoides. See *S. laxum.*

S. laxum (S. jasminoides). POTATO VINE. Evergreen or semievergreen vine. Zones 8, 9, 12–24; H1, H2. From Brazil. Twines rapidly to 30 ft. Purple-tinged, arrow-shaped, white, 1-in. flowers are carried on threadlike stalks in clusters of up to 12; bloom is almost continuous all year, heaviest in spring. Grown for flowers or for light overhead shade. Cut back severely at any time to prevent tangling, promote vigorous new growth. Control rampant runners that grow along ground.

S. muricatum. PEPINO. Perennial. Zones 17, 23, 24; H2. Thought to have originated in Colombia, Peru, and Chile. Grows to 2–3 ft. high, sprawling to about 4 ft. wide. Ovate to lance-shaped, bright green leaves. Clear blue flowers in spring and early summer are not especially showy; they are followed later in summer by football-shaped greenish yellow fruit with purple stripes. Fruit weighs ¼–1 lb. and tastes like a cross between melon and cucumber. Same culture as tomato. The plant is grown as much for ornament as for its edible crop. Makes a handsome choice for a hanging basket.

S. pseudocapsicum. JERUSALEM CHERRY. Evergreen shrub. Zones 23, 24; H2; annual or indoor/outdoor plant anywhere. Native to Madeira; widely naturalized in tropics and subtropics. To 3–4 ft. tall and wide (about half that size if grown as an annual). Shiny deep green, smooth, elliptical leaves. White, ½-in. summer flowers are followed in fall by a fine show of scarlet (rarely yellow), ½-in. fruits that look like cherry tomatoes but are poisonous. In mildest-winter areas, the plant bears flowers and fruit (and self-sows) year-round. More popular than taller kinds are the many dwarf strains, which grow to 1 ft. high and bear larger fruit (to 1 in. across).

S. rantonnetii. See *Lycianthes rantonnetii.*

S. seaforthianum. BRAZILIAN NIGHTSHADE. Evergreen or semievergreen vine. Zones 16, 21–24; H1, H2. Slender-stemmed plant to 15 ft.; must be fastened to its support. Oval, medium green leaves are either undivided or quite deeply cleft into three or more lobes. Clusters of violet-blue, 1-in.-wide flowers bloom in summer. Pea-size red fruits are enjoyed by birds but should not be eaten by people.

S. wendlandii. COSTA RICAN NIGHTSHADE. Deciduous vine. Zones 16, 21–24; H1, H2. To 15–20 ft., climbing by twining stems and hooked spines. Glossy green, ovate or (sometimes) lobed leaves are corrugated in texture. Foliage forms a lush backdrop for dense, domed clusters of lavender-blue, 2½-in. summer flowers. Somewhat reminiscent of bougainvillea. Let it clamber into tall trees, cover a pergola, decorate eaves of large house. Loses leaves in low temperatures, even without frost; slow to leaf out in spring.

S. xantii. Evergreen shrub. Zones 7–9, 11, 14–24. From California. Erect or sprawling to 2–3 ft. high and 3 ft. wide. Ovate green leaves to 1¾ in. long. Purple, 1-in. flowers in late winter, spring. Superior forms include 'Mountain Pride' and 'Salmon Creek'. Little or no water.

FOR MORE ON VINES, SEE "GROW: VINES," PAGES 708–709.

S

Soleirolia soleirolii
(Helxine soleirolii)
BABY'S TEARS, ANGEL'S TEARS
Urticaceae
PERENNIAL

🌿 **ZONES 4–24; H1, H2**

☀️◑ **FULL SUN OR PARTIAL SHADE**

💧💧 **REGULAR TO AMPLE WATER**

Soleirolia soleirolii

Lush mat-forming groundcover from the western Mediterranean. To 2–4 in. high, spreading indefinitely by creeping stems. Inconspicuous flowers. Stems and tiny leaves are tender, juicy, easily injured, but aggressive growth repairs damage quickly. Roots easily from pieces of stem and can become an invasive pest. Freezes to black mush in hard frosts but comes back. Cool-looking, neat underplanting for ferns or other shade-loving plants. Can be used to carpet terrariums or space under greenhouse benches. Plant 10 in. apart for small-space groundcover. With enough water, tolerates full sun in cooler climates. There is a golden green variety and one with white variegation.

Baby's tears is epecially pretty between flagstone pavers in a damp, partly shaded side-yard path. Mostly evergreen, it sends out fresh green leaves in spring.

Solenostemon scutellarioides
(Coleus × hybridus)
COLEUS
Lamiaceae
PERENNIAL USUALLY GROWN AS ANNUAL

🌿 **ZONES 24; H1, H2; ANYWHERE AS ANNUAL; OR INDOORS**

☀️◑ **SOME TYPES ARE SUN-TOLERANT**

💧 **REGULAR WATER**

Solenostemon scutellarioides
'Kong Mosaic'

Tropical plants grown for its brilliantly colored leaves. Blue flower spikes are attractive, but they spoil the plant's shape and are best pinched out in bud (pinching also encourages more vigorous leafy growth).

Seed-grown, large-leaf strains, such as Giant Exhibition and Oriental Splendor, grow 1½–2 ft. high and wide, with leaves 3–6 in. long. Plants in the Kong series have leaves up to 8 in. long. Dwarf strains such as Carefree, Fairway, and Wizard grow 8–12 in. high and wide, with leaves 1–1½ in. long. Colors include green, chartreuse, yellow, buff, salmon, orange, red, purple, and brown; a single leaf often shows many colors. The more red pigment the foliage has, the more sun-tolerant the plant tends to be. Most coleus perform best in strong indirect light or light shade, but the relatively new, cutting-grown "sun coleus" also thrive in sun; they come in a variety of leaf colors, shapes, and plant habits. The ColorBlaze series is late blooming and may not bloom at all in cool climates. Selections grow 24–36 in. high, come in a huge range of colors and leaf shapes, and can be grown in

sun or shade. Many coleus are useful for summer borders, containers, and hanging baskets.

CARE
Coleus are perennial in frost-free regions, but you'll typically get the best performance by starting new plants annually from seed or cuttings—which is easy to do. Plant in spring. Sow seeds indoors or, with frost protection, outdoors when weather is warm. Cuttings will root in water as well as other media. Started plants need warm temperatures and rich, loose, well-drained soil. Feed plants regularly with high-nitrogen fertilizer. Pinch stems often to encourage compact habit.

Solidago
GOLDENROD
Asteraceae
PERENNIALS

🌿 **ZONES 1–11, 14–23**

☀️◑ **FULL SUN OR LIGHT SHADE**

💧 **MODERATE WATER**

🦋 **FLOWERS ATTRACT BIRDS, BUTTERFLIES**

Solidago

From mid- or late summer into fall, these eastern U.S. natives enliven the garden with large, branching clusters of small bright yellow flowers. Blossoms are carried on leafy stems that rise from tough, woody, spreading rootstocks. Leaves are narrow, generally linear to lance-shaped. Goldenrods are not as widely grown as they deserve to be, largely due to the mistaken belief that their pollen causes hay fever (in fact, other plants are responsible). All are tough plants that thrive in not-too-rich

soil. Use in informal borders or naturalize in meadows.

S. hybrids. The following are among the best garden varieties.

'Crown of Rays'. To 2–3 ft. high, 1–2 ft. wide, with flattish flower clusters.

'Golden Baby'. To 2 ft. high, 1½ ft. wide; flower clusters are plumelike.

'Goldenmosa'. To 2½ ft. high, 1½ ft. wide. Very large clusters of blossoms are reminiscent of florists' mimosa (*Acacia baileyana*).

'Little Lemon'. To 10–12 in. high, 15 in. wide. Long-blooming. Great in pots.

S. rugosa 'Fireworks'. To 3–4 ft. tall and 2–3 ft. wide. Narrow streamers of flowers arch outward and downward like the vapor trails of a skyrocket.

S. sphacelata 'Golden Fleece'. To 1½ ft. high, 2 ft. wide, with many sprays of flowers. Makes a tough, fast-growing groundcover; set plants 15 in. apart for a solid mat in a year.

Sollya heterophylla
(S. fusiformis)
AUSTRALIAN BLUEBELL CREEPER
Pittosporaceae
EVERGREEN SHRUB OR VINE

🌿 **ZONES 8, 9, 14–24; H1, H2**

☀️◑ **PARTIAL SHADE IN HOTTEST CLIMATES**

💧💧 **MODERATE TO REGULAR WATER**

Sollya heterophylla
'Boddy's Choice'

Loose, spreading shrub from Australia growing to 2–3 ft. high, 4–5 ft. wide. Given support and training, climbs to 6–8 ft. Glossy green foliage has a light, delicate look. Clusters of small, bell-shaped, brilliant blue flowers bloom almost all summer. 'Alba' has white blooms; 'Rosea' bears pink flowers. Use as groundcover or bank cover, in borders, along steps, draped over low walls, in containers. Will grow under eucalyptus trees. *S. h. parviflora* (*S. parviflora*) has a more vining habit and somewhat smaller flowers in a darker blue.

CARE

Drought-tolerant but prefers some moisture. Good drainage is crucial, however; the plant will die in poorly drained soil. Prune frequently to encourage dense habit.

Sophora
Papilionaceae
EVERGREEN AND DECIDUOUS TREES AND SHRUBS

- ✔ **ZONES VARY BY SPECIES**
- ☼ ◑ **FULL SUN OR PARTIAL SHADE**
- ◑ ● **WATER NEEDS VARY BY SPECIES**
- ◆ **SEEDS OF S. SECUNDIFLORA ARE POISONOUS IF INGESTED**

Sophora secundiflora

Handsome flowering trees and shrubs with showy, drooping clusters of sweet pea–shaped blossoms. Seedpods are constricted between the seeds, giving them a bead-necklace look. Leaves divided into many leaflets. Provide good drainage.

S. arizonica. Evergreen shrub. Zones 10–13. Native to Arizona. Grows slowly to 3–10 ft. tall and wide. Dark gray-green leaves have five to nine ½–1-in.-long leaflets. Clusters of 1–1¼-in., purple to lavender flowers in spring are followed by 4–7-in.-long seedpods. Use as

an informal hedge, in borders. Takes heat. Tolerates drought but does better with moderate to regular water applied deeply during hot months.

S. japonica. See *Styphnolobium japonicum*.

S. secundiflora. MESCAL BEAN, TEXAS MOUNTAIN LAUREL. Evergreen shrub or tree. Zones 8–16, 18–24. Native to Texas, New Mexico, and northern Mexico. To 15–25 ft. tall, 10–15 ft. wide; very slow growing, especially in cool-summer regions. Naturally shrubby but can be trained into tree with short, slender trunk or multiple trunks, narrow crown, upright branches. Leaves are divided into seven to nine glossy dark green leaflets. Blooms from midwinter to early spring, bearing sweet-scented violet-blue flowers in drooping, 4–8-in. clusters reminiscent of wisteria. A white-flowered form is occasionally available. 'Silver Peso' has silvery foliage. Silvery gray or brown, woody, 1–8-in.-long seedpods open when ripe to show poisonous, bright red, ½-in. seeds. If possible, remove pods from plant before they mature. Choice small tree for street, lawn, or patio. If left untrained, makes a good large screen or background hedge. Thrives in heat and alkaline soil. Moderate water.

S. tetraptera. KOWHAI, YELLOW KOWHAI. Evergreen or deciduous shrub or tree. Zones 15–17. Native to New Zealand. Slow to 15–20 ft. tall and wide. Slender, open habit. Leaves 3–6 in. long, with 20 to 40 tiny leaflets; they are silky gray above, reddish beneath. In summer, golden yellow, 2-in.-long flowers appear in hanging clusters of four to eight. Seedpods are 2–8 in. long. Does not take low humidity. Regular water.

Sorbaria
FALSE SPIREA
Rosaceae
DECIDUOUS SHRUBS

- ✔ **ZONES VARY BY SPECIES**
- ☼ ◑ **FULL SUN OR LIGHT SHADE**
- ● **REGULAR WATER**

Sorbaria sorbifolia

Green, ferny-looking leaves are finely divided into many narrow, toothed leaflets. Bloom from mid- to late summer, producing big, plumelike clusters of tiny white or creamy flowers at branch ends. Flowers mature into brown seed clusters; cut off faded blossoms unless you like the look of brown plumes. Use in large shrub borders or at the edge of woodlands or near water; the effect is almost tropical. These shrubs spread by suckering and will cover large areas if not curbed.

S. sorbifolia. Zones A1–A3; 1–10, 14–21. Native to eastern Asia. Grows to 3–8 ft. tall, 10 ft. wide. Leaves 6–12 in. long; flower plumes to 1 ft. long.

S. tomentosa angustifolia (S. aitchisonii). Zones 3–10, 14–21. Native to Afghanistan and Pakistan. To 10 ft. tall and wide. Leaves to 1½ ft. long; flower plumes to 16 in. long.

Sorbus
MOUNTAIN ASH
Rosaceae
DECIDUOUS TREES AND SHRUBS

- ✔ **ZONES VARY BY SPECIES**
- ☼ ◑ **FULL SUN OR LIGHT SHADE**
- ◑ ● **MODERATE TO REGULAR WATER**
- 🐦 **ATTRACT BIRDS**

Sorbus americana

These natives of mountainous areas are valued for showy flowers and showier fruit. Blossoms are grouped in broad, flat clusters that are scattered over the foliage canopy in spring; they develop into hanging clusters of small, berrylike fruit that colors up in late summer or early fall. Most species have red or orange-red fruit, but white, pink, and golden forms are occasionally available. Birds feed on the fruit, but usually not until after leaves have fallen. Foliage is typically finely cut and somewhat fernlike, though some less widely planted species have undivided leaves. Some mountain ashes have good fall color; these are noted below. Plants need good, well-drained soil and some winter chill. Cankers are a problem for trees under stress. Watch for fireblight. Good small garden or street trees, though the fruit can make a mess on paved surfaces.

S. alnifolia. KOREAN MOUNTAIN ASH. Tree. Zones 1–10, 14–17. From China, Korea, and Japan. Dense growth to 40–50 ft. tall, 20–30 ft. wide. The specific name *alnifolia* refers to the leaves, which are undivided (like those of alder, *Alnus*); they are 2–4 in. long, toothed, dark green, turning yellow to orange in fall. Reddish pink to orange-red fruit.

S

»

S. americana. Tree or shrub. Zones 1–6. From eastern North America. To 10–30 ft. tall and wide. Dark green leaves with paler undersides reach 10 in. long, consist of 11 to 17 leaflets; turn yellow in fall. Orange-red fruit. This species is very hardy and tolerates damp soil, but it is not the choicest of mountain ashes. 'Red Cascade' is an attractive variety with an oval crown and compact growth to 16 ft. tall and 8 ft. wide.

S. aria. WHITEBEAM. Tree. Zones 3–10, 14–17. From Europe. Dense-crowned tree to 30–45 ft. tall, 20–30 ft. wide (probably larger in age). Undivided, 2–4-in.-long leaves are dull green above, whitish beneath. Variable fall color; the best trees turn yellow. Red or orange-red fruit. 'Lutescens' has brighter white leaf undersides.

S. aucuparia. EUROPEAN MOUNTAIN ASH. Tree. Zones A1–A3; 1–10, 14–17. Native from Europe to western Asia and Siberia; naturalized in North America. To 20–40 ft. tall (or taller), 15–25 ft. wide. Sharply rising branches form a dense, oval to round crown. Leaves are 5–9 in. long, with 9 to 15 leaflets; they are dull green above, gray-green below, turning tawny yellow to reddish in autumn. Orange-red fruit. 'Cardinal Royal' has especially large bright red berries. 'Black Hawk' and 'Fastigiata' are slightly narrower, upright forms.

S. hupehensis. Tree. Zones 2–10, 14–17. From China. To 25 ft. tall and wide, eventually much larger. Bluish green leaves to 7 in. long, with 13 to 17 leaflets; turn orange-red in fall. Pure white or pink-tinged white fruit. The form in cultivation is fireblight-resistant 'Coral Cascade', with red fruit and red fall foliage.

S. × hybrida. Tree. Zones 2–10, 14–17. Erect habit to 20–30 ft. tall and wide. Foliage is blue-green above, whitish beneath. Leaves are a little over 5½ in. long, with a large upper portion that is lobed (not divided) and one or two pairs of small leaflets at base. Red fruit.

S. reducta. Shrub. Zones 3–6, 14–17. From China. To 1–2 ft. high, 3 ft. wide, spreading by underground runners.

Dark green, 4-in.-long leaves with 9 to 15 leaflets; bronze-red fall color. Pink fruit. Good for rock garden or bonsai.

S. scopulina. WESTERN MOUNTAIN ASH. Shrub or tree. Zones A1–A3; 1–7. Native to western North America. To 3–15 ft. tall and wide, often with reddish bark. Leaves to 2½ in. long, with up to 15 deeply toothed leaflets; shiny dark green above, paler beneath. Orange-red fall color. Orange to bright red fruit.

S. × thuringiaca. Tree. Zones 3–6, 14–17. Similar to S. × hybrida but leaves are longer (to 8 in.) and fruit is smaller.

Sorghastrum nutans

INDIANGRASS
Poaceae
PERENNIAL GRASS

- 🗹 **ZONES 1–24**
- ☼ **FULL SUN**
- ◐ **LITTLE WATER ONCE ESTABLISHED**
- 🦋 **ATTRACTS BUTTERFLIES AND BIRDS**

Sorghastrum nutans

A gorgeous large, ornamental, clumping grass native to much of the United States. Blue-green foliage grows upright, 3–4 ft. tall and 1½ ft. wide, and turns golden yellow in fall. Airy flower spikes tower above the foliage beginning in midsummer; they are coppery at first, then dry to a shimmering light brown. Good in dried arrangements. Water regularly until established, then needs little. Cut back in winter. 'Cheyenne' was selected for its drought tolerance. 'Sioux Blue' has bluer foliage.

Sorrel, Garden

Polygonaceae
PERENNIAL OFTEN GROWN AS ANNUAL

- 🗹 **ZONES VARY BY TYPE; ANYWHERE AS ANNUAL**
- ☼ **FULL SUN**
- ● **REGULAR WATER**

'Blood Veined' sorrel

Two similar species are grown for their edible leaves, which can be used raw in salads or cooked in soups, sauces, and egg dishes. Flavor is like that of a sharp, sprightly spinach, but sorrel is more heat-tolerant and produces throughout the growing season.

Common sorrel is the larger plant (to 3 ft. high), with leaves to 6 in. long, many shaped like elongated arrowheads. It is native to northern climates and perennial in Zones A1–A3, 1–9, 14–17.

French sorrel is a somewhat sprawling plant to 1½ ft. high, with shorter, broader leaves and a milder, more lemony flavor than common sorrel. Native to Europe, western Asia, and North Africa, it is perennial in Zones 3–10, 14–24.

CARE

Grow sorrel in reasonably good soil. Sow seeds in early spring; thin seedlings to 8 in. apart. Or set out transplants at any time, spacing them 8 in. apart. Pick tender leaves when they are big enough to use; cut out flowering stems to encourage leaf production. Replace (or dig and divide) plants after 3 or 4 years.

FOR MORE ON VEGETABLES, SEE "GROW: VEGGIES," PAGES 698–707.

Sparaxis tricolor

HARLEQUIN FLOWER
Iridaceae
PERENNIAL FROM CORM

- 🗹 **ZONES 9, 12–24; OR DIG AND STORE**
- ☼ **FULL SUN**
- ● **REGULAR WATER DURING GROWTH AND BLOOM**

Sparaxis tricolor

These colorful spring bloomers are native to South Africa. They make a clump of sword-shaped leaves to 1 ft. high and wide. Blooms over a long period in late spring; 1–1½-ft.-high flowering stems bear loose, spikelike clusters of small, funnel-shaped blossoms to 2 in. across. Each flower has a yellow center, a dark color surrounding this, and another color—red, pink, orange, or purple—on the rest of the petals. Looks best when naturalized or grouped as an accent in a border or along a pathway. For planting and culture, see *Ixia* (to which *Sparaxis* is closely related).

This little bulb from South Africa is commonly called harlequin flower for good reason: blooms are red, orange, yellow, purple, or white with a yellow center outlined in black. They make excellent cut flowers.

Spathodea campanulata

AFRICAN TULIP TREE
Bignoniaceae
EVERGREEN TREE

- 🌓 **ZONES 21–24; H1, H2**
- ☼ **FULL SUN**
- 💧 **MODERATE WATER**

Spathodea campanulata

Very showy, fast-growing tree from tropical South Africa. Reaches 40–75 ft. tall and 20–50 ft. wide. Glossy deep green leaves to 1½ ft. long, divided featherwise into 9 to 19 oblong to ovate leaflets. Clusters of spectacular, tulip-shaped, 4-in. flowers in scarlet to blood red appear at the branch ends. In Hawaii, blossoms come throughout the year; in California, bloom is most profuse in the spring, but flowers may appear at any time. Give good drainage and a warm site. This tree grows rapidly and blooms young, but it can be devastated by frosts. Likely to attain size stated above only in truly frost-free locations.

African tulip tree has naturalized in Hawaii, becoming a rampant yet beautiful weed. The tree is especially visible on hillsides along Maui's Hana Highway, where its big, vivid orange blooms stand out against lush foliage.

Sphaeralcea

GLOBE MALLOW
Malvaceae
PERENNIALS

- 🌓 **ZONES VARY BY SPECIES**
- ☼ **FULL SUN**
- 💧 **LITTLE WATER**
- 🦋 **FLOWERS ATTRACT BUTTERFLIES**

Sphaeralcea ambigua

Grown for their attractive downy leaves and bright flowers shaped like miniature hollyhocks (*Alcea rosea*), these upright to trailing plants have a persistent woody base with softer stems above. Colorful accent plants for hot, dry locations.

S. ambigua. APRICOT MALLOW. Zones 3, 7–24. Native to Utah, Arizona, Nevada, California, and Mexico. Grows to 3–4 ft. tall, 2–3 ft. wide, with many stems covered in white or yellowish down. Broad, rounded gray-green leaves are crinkled and slightly lobed. Each stem bears many inch-wide flowers; usual color is glowing pink or orange, but white-flowered forms are occasionally available.

Blooms in summer and fall; in hot deserts, the main bloom season is spring, with a sparse showing of flowers in summer and autumn. May become partly deciduous where summers are very hot and dry. Best adapted to desert climates; cannot withstand wet winters. 'Louis Hamilton' has deep orange-red flowers. 'Papago Pink' has pink flowers.

S. munroana. Zones 1–3, 7–10, 14–24. Native to intermountain West and Rocky Mountain foothills. Grows to 3 ft. high and 1½–2 ft. wide, with upright stems and rounded, slightly lobed gray-green leaves. Bears many wands of inch-wide salmon to reddish orange flowers from midsummer to early fall. Plants sold in California under this name may be the Argentine native *S. philippiana*, which grows to 1½ ft. high and 4–5 ft. wide and has leaves that are more deeply cut than those of *S. munroana*.

CARE
Need well-drained soil. Any more than a little water causes weedy growth and rust. Cut old stems almost to ground before spring growth begins.

Sphaeropteris cooperi.
See *Cyathea cooperi*

Sphagneticola trilobata
(Wedelia trilobata)

Asteraceae
PERENNIAL

- 🌓 **ZONES 12, 13, 21–24; H1, H2**
- ☼ ◐ **FULL SUN OR LIGHT SHADE**
- 💧 **REGULAR WATER**

Sphagneticola trilobata

From Central and South America, this trailing evergreen plant grows to 1½–2 ft. high, spreading to 6 ft. or more by stems that root where they touch damp earth. Fleshy, dark glossy green leaves with a few coarse teeth or shallow lobes toward tips. Inch-wide flowers resembling tiny yellow zinnias or marigolds (*Tagetes*) bloom almost year-round.

CARE
Spreads fast; easily propagated by lifting rooted pieces or placing tip cuttings in moist soil. Best in sandy, fast-draining soils but takes heavier soils if drainage is good. If killed to ground by frost, it makes a fast comeback. Tolerates desert heat, seaside conditions. Can take lower light but blooms more sparsely in shady conditions. Good for erosion control on slopes: plant 1½ ft. apart, feed lightly. Shear close to the ground if planting mounds up or becomes stemmy.

Spinach

Chenopodiaceae, Aizoaceae, Basellaceae
ANNUALS AND PERENNIALS

- 🌓 **ZONES VARY BY TYPE**
- ☼ **FULL SUN**
- 💧 **REGULAR WATER**

True spinach

The first of the three plants described here is true spinach, which needs cool weather to succeed; the other two are warm-season vegetables used as substitutes for the real thing. All are grown for their edible leaves, used raw or cooked. All do best in rich, well-drained soil.

True spinach. This cool-season annual is from the goosefoot family (*Chenopodiaceae*) and is thought to have originated in southwestern Asia. Grows in all zones. Matures slowly during fall, winter, and spring; long days of late spring and heat of summer make it go to seed quickly. To get successive harvests, make small sowings at weekly intervals in fall or early spring. Thin established seedlings to 3–4 in. apart. When plants have reached full size (6–12 in. high; takes about 7 weeks), harvest by cutting

S

entire clump at ground level. Leaf miner is often a pest.

New Zealand spinach. A member of the ice plant family (*Aizoaceae*) from Australia and New Zealand. This succulent evergreen is a perennial in mild-winter areas (most likely to live over in Zones 15–17, 21–24; H1, H2) but goes dormant in heavy frosts. In colder climates, it can be grown as a summer annual. Sow seeds in early spring after danger of frost is past; thin established seedlings to 1–1½ ft. apart. Mature plants are spreading, 1–2 ft. high. Harvest greens by pluck-ing off top few inches of tender stems and attached leaves; a month later, new shoots will have grown up for another harvest. New Zealand spinach tolerates heat and drought but also thrives in cool, damp conditions.

Malabar spinach. This mem-ber of the *Basellaceae* family from India is a perennial vine in H1 and H2; grown as annual in Zones 3–24. It needs night tem-peratures above 58°F (14°C); it will not survive frost. There is an especially attractive red-stemmed form. Sow seeds in early summer; thin established seedlings to 1 ft. apart. When young plants are about 1 ft. high, train them on wires or a trellis. At 2 ft. high, pinch out a few inches of stem tip (har-vesting any young, tender leaves) to encourage the plants to branch and form more stems. Vine grows about 4–6 ft. tall (even taller in warm climates). As leaves reach full, succulent size, pick them individually. They are bigger and thicker than leaves of true spinach, so you'll need fewer per serving.

Malabar spinach could be called summer spinach, because it thrives during the warm season. Harvest tender young leaves for stir-fries and fresh garden salads.

Spiraea
SPIREA
Rosaceae
DECIDUOUS SHRUBS

- ✐ ZONES VARY BY SPECIES
- ☼ ☽ FULL SUN OR LIGHT SHADE
- ◗ ◖ MODERATE TO REGULAR WATER, EXCEPT AS NOTED
- ✿ FLOWERS ATTRACT BUTTERFLIES

Spiraea nipponica 'Snowmound'

There are two distinct kinds of spireas: the bridal wreath type, with clusters of white flowers cas-cading down arching branches in spring or early summer; and the shrubby type, with pink, red, or white flowers clustered at branch ends in summer to fall. Blossoms on both types are usually single.

S. × bumalda. See *S. japonica* 'Bumalda'.

S. cantoniensis 'Flore-Pleno'. DOUBLE BRIDAL WREATH. Zones 3–11, 14–23. From China and Japan. To 5–6 ft. tall, 10 ft. wide, with arch-ing branches. Double white flow-ers wreathe the leafy branches in late spring to early summer. Lance-shaped blue-green leaves; they drop late, show no fall color. Plant is nearly ever-green in mildest climates.

S. densiflora. MOUNTAIN SPIREA. Zones 1–9, 14–21. Native from central Sierra Nevada to British Columbia. To 1–3 ft. high and wide. Ovate to elliptical, dark green leaves are woolly white beneath, turn yellow in fall. In summer, branch ends bear rosy pink flowers in dense,

CLOCKWISE FROM TOP: *Spiraea japonica* 'Magic Carpet'; *S. j.* 'Little Princess'; *S. j.* 'Goldflame'

flat-topped clusters to 2 in. wide. 'Summer Song', to 2½ ft. high and wide, has bronzy new growth, bronzy fall, leaf color.

S. douglasii. WESTERN SPIREA. Zones 1–9, 14–24. Native to Coastal Ranges from Northern California to British Columbia, eastward to Rocky Mountains. Forms a clump 3–6 ft. tall and wide; suckers freely and can be invasive. Nar-rowly oblong leaves are dark green above and velvety white beneath; they turn yellowish in fall. Pale to deep purplish pink flowers in long (to 8 in.), narrow clusters at branch ends in sum-mer. Needs acid soil, regular to ample water. Useful for wild plantings near streams.

S. japonica. Zones A2, A3; 2–10, 14–21. Native to Japan, China. Upright, shrubby spirea to 4–6 ft. tall and wide, with flat, 8-in.-wide clusters of pink flowers carried above oval, sharply toothed green leaves. Best known through its selec-tions, which are typically lower than the species and bloom between summer and fall in shades of pink, red, purplish pink, and sometimes white. Some have colorful new growth.

They include plants formerly classified as hybrids of *S. × bumalda*, itself now considered merely a variety. It grows to 3 ft. high and wide with dark pink flowers and bronze-tinted new growth. Other popular varieties include 'Anthony Waterer', 3–5 ft. tall and wide with carmine-pink blossoms and reddish pur-ple new growth that matures to bright green; 'Goldflame', 2½ ft. high and wide with pink flowers and bronze new growth that matures to yellowish green then turns dark reddish orange in fall; 'Little Princess', 3 ft. high, 6 ft. wide, with rose-pink blos-soms; and 'Magic Carpet', 1½–2½ ft. high, with slightly wider, pink flowers and reddish bronze new leaves that turn chartreuse to yellow as they mature.

S. nipponica 'Snow-mound'. Zones 1–11, 14–21. From Japan. Compact, spread-ing bridal wreath spirea to 2–3 ft. high, 3–5 ft. wide. Profusion of white flowers in late spring or early summer. Ovate to round-ish, dark green leaves to 1¼ in. long; little autumn color.

S. prunifolia 'Plena'. BRIDAL WREATH SPIREA, SHOE BUTTON SPIREA. Zones A2, A3;

2–11, 14–21. From China, Taiwan. Graceful, arching branches on a suckering, clump-forming plant to 6–7 ft. tall and wide. In early to midspring, bare branches are lined with small, double white flowers resembling tiny roses. Small dark green leaves turn bright shades of red, orange, and yellow in autumn.

S. thunbergii. Zones 1–11, 14–21. From China, Japan. Showy, billowy, graceful bridal wreath species 3–6 ft. or taller, 6 ft. wide, with many slender, arching branches. Round clusters of small white flowers appear all along bare branches in early spring. Blue-green, very narrow leaves to 1½ in. long turn soft reddish brown in fall. 'Ogon' has yellowish leaves.

S. trilobata 'Swan Lake'. Zones 1–11, 14–17. Native from Siberia to northern China. Like a small version of *S. prunifolia* 'Plena'. Grows 3–4 ft. tall and wide, with a massive show of tiny white flowers in mid- to late spring. Leaves reach 1 in. long, are often three lobed. 'Fairy Queen' is more compact, seldom exceeding 3 ft. tall.

S. × vanhouttei. Zones A1–A3; 1–11, 14–21. Widely planted hybrid between *S. cantoniensis* and *S. trilobata*. The classic bridal wreath spirea. Arching branches form a fountain to about 6 ft. tall by 8 ft. or wider. Leafy branches are covered with circular, flattened clusters of white blossoms in mid- to late spring, continuing into early summer in colder regions. Dark green, diamond-shaped leaves to 1½ in. long may turn purplish in fall. 'Renaissance' resists powdery mildew and rust. 'Pink Ice' has leaves variegated white.

CARE

Spireas are tough, easy-to-grow plants; with few exceptions, they are not fussy about soil. Prune bridal wreath spireas after flowers have finished; cut to the ground wood that has produced flowers. Prune shrubby spireas in winter or earliest spring, before new growth begins; they generally need less severe pruning than bridal wreaths.

If you remove spent flower clusters, plants will produce a second (but less lavish) bloom.

Sporobolus

DROPSEED
Poaceae
PERENNIAL GRASSES

✎ **ZONES VARY BY SPECIES**

☀ **FULL SUN**

◐ **LITTLE TO MODERATE WATER**

Sporobolus heterolepis

Graceful, fine-textured, clumping grasses that are as tough as they are good-looking. Deep-rooted and drought-tolerant; excellent for massing in hot, dry areas and effective in meadow gardens, mixed borders, naturalized areas, rock gardens, even by swimming pools. Plumelike flower heads appear in summer and fall. After they fade, tiny seeds drop to the ground; hence the common name. These plants tolerate a wide range of soil conditions.

S. airoides. ALKALI SACATON. Zones 1–24. Native from South Dakota and Missouri, west to eastern Washington, south to Southern California. Foliage clump grows 3 ft. high and wide; leaves are grayish green during growing season, yellow in fall, beige in winter. At bloom time in summer or fall, showy, erect or arching flower plumes increase plant height to 5 ft.; plumes are pinkish, eventually fading to pale straw color. Extremely tough, deep-rooted plant. Good grass for alkaline conditions.

S. heterolepis. PRAIRIE DROPSEED. Zones 1–10, 14–17. Native to the Midwest, High Plains, and much of the eastern U.S. Emerald green, hairlike leaves form a billowing mass to 15 in. high and 1½ ft. wide. Foliage turns golden to orange in fall, then fades to light bronze in winter. Slender-stemmed, airy panicles of flowers rise to 3 ft. high, soaring above the foliage in late summer. Blossoms are pink to light brown and smell faintly of buttered popcorn. The seeds are highly nutritious and were ground into flour by the Plains Indians. Self-sows mildly; volunteer seedlings are seldom a problem. Plants tolerate any soil but do best when it's on the dry side.

S. wrightii. GIANT SACATON. Zones 3b, 7–16, 18–24. Native to sandy open areas and hillsides in southwestern Canada and southwestern U.S. Narrow, arching, blue-green leaves form a clump 3–4 ft. tall and wide. Feathery, golden yellow seed heads nearly double the plant's height in late summer to early fall; good in dried arrangements. Evergreen in all but the coldest climates. Quite drought-tolerant but looks best with occasional deep watering.

Sprekelia formosissima

JACOBEAN LILY, AZTEC LILY
Amaryllidaceae
PERENNIAL FROM BULB

✎ **ZONES 9, 12–24; OR DIG AND STORE**

☀ **FULL SUN**

◐ **REGULAR WATER DURING GROWTH AND BLOOM**

Sprekelia formosissima

Mexican native often sold as *Amaryllis formosissima*. Foliage looks like that of daffodil (*Narcissus*), but each 1-ft.-high stem is topped with a dark red, 6-in.-wide bloom resembling an orchid, with three erect upper segments and three drooping lower ones that are united at their bases (near the flower's center) to form a tube. Bloom comes primarily in early summer.

CARE

Where bulbs are hardy, plant them in fall, setting them 3–4 in. deep and 8 in. apart in good, well-drained soil. Look most effective in groups. Display increases if plants are left undisturbed for several years. Where winters are cold, set out bulbs in spring; lift plants in fall when foliage yellows and store in a cool, dark, dry place over winter (leave dry tops on). Or grow in pots like amaryllis (*Hippeastrum*); repot every 3 to 4 years. In mild climates, foliage may be evergreen and plant may blossom several times a year if you can give it a dry period after flowering, then resume regular watering to trigger a new growth cycle.

Squash

Cucurbitaceae
ANNUAL

✎ **ALL ZONES**

☀ **FULL SUN**

◐ **REGULAR WATER**

Summer squash

There are two general forms of squash, all derived from various species native to the Americas. Each individual squash plant has both male and female flowers, which must be pollinated by bees in order for fruit to set. The blossoms and developing fruit at the base of female flowers are eaten as delicacies.

Summer squash. Types planted for a warm-weather harvest and eaten when immature

How to Grow Squash

Bush varieties of summer squash can be planted 2–4 ft. apart in rows. They need more room if planted in circles ("hills"); allow a 4-ft. diameter for each. Vining summer or winter squash needs 5-ft. spacing in rows, 8-ft.-diameter hills. The few bush varieties of winter squash can be spaced as for bush varieties of summer squash.

WATERING & FEEDING Give all kinds of squash rich soil, periodic fertilizer. Roots need regular moisture, but leaves and stems should be kept as dry as possible to prevent leaf and fruit diseases.

HARVESTING Pick summer squash when it is small and tender. Winter squash should stay on vines until thoroughly hardened; harvest with an inch of stem and store in a cool place (about 55°F/13°C).

CHALLENGES Squash bugs cause leaves to wilt and may damage fruit. To control, destroy yellowish to brown egg clusters on undersides of leaves; trap adults with boards or burlap set in the garden at night; then collect and destroy your catch each morning. Various insecticides are also labeled for control of squash bugs.

are called summer squash. This group includes scalloped white squash (pattypan squash); yellow crookneck and straight-neck varieties; and cylindrical, green or gray zucchini or Italian squash.

Summer squash yields prodigious crops from just a few plants within 50 to 65 days after sowing, and it continues to bear for weeks. Vines are large (2½–4 ft. across at maturity) and need plenty of room; if space is limited, look for bush varieties. There are many vine and bush varieties.

Winter squash. These are grown for harvest in late summer or fall; they store well and are used for baking and for pies. Varieties come in many shapes (turban, acorn, and banana are a few), sizes, and colors; all have hard rinds and firm, close-grained, and good-tasting flesh.

Winter squash is planted and grown on vines like pumpkins; it typically needs even more space than summer squash. There are a few compact varieties, such as 'Honey Bear', a green acorn type, and 'Bonbon', a buttercup type. Most kinds of winter squash are ready to harvest 60 to 110 days after sowing. Types for storing include small kinds such as 'Table Ace' and other acorn types, butternuts, and buttercups; and the large blue Hubbard varieties and banana squash. Spaghetti squash stores as well as any other winter squash, but when you cut it open after cooking, you find that the nutty-tasting flesh is made up of long, spaghettilike strands. Winter squash doesn't grow well in high heat and humidity.

Stachys
Lamiaceae
PERENNIALS

🌱 **ZONES VARY BY SPECIES**

☼ ◑ **FULL SUN OR LIGHT SHADE**

💧 **MODERATE WATER**

Stachys byzantina

These mint-family members have the typical square stems and leaves in opposite pairs; foliage ranges from rough textured to furry. Except for *S. macrantha*, the species described

here have short-stalked or stalkless leaves. Spikelike clusters of small, usually two-lipped flowers bloom in late spring and summer; blossoms are attractive to bees.

S. albotomentosa. HIDALGO. Zones 7–10, 12–24. Native to Mexico. To 2½ ft. tall, sprawling to 5–6 ft. wide. Green, heavily veined leaves have a felty texture, elongated heart shape. They have a pleasant fragrance somewhat like lemon-lime soda. Stems and leaf undersides are covered with woolly hairs. Flowers open peach to salmon-pink, age to brick red. Sometimes listed as *S. coccinea* 'Hidalgo'.

S. byzantina (S. lanata, S. olympica). LAMB'S EARS. Zones 1–24. Native to the Caucasus and Iran. To 1½ ft. high, spreading freely by surface runners. Dense, ground-hugging rosettes of soft, thick, rather tongue-shaped, woolly white leaves. Blossom stalks 1–1½ ft. high bear small purplish flowers; many gardeners feel that these detract from the foliage and so cut off or pull out flowering stems. Continued rains can mash plants down and make them mushy, and frost can damage foliage, but recovery is strong. Attracts bees.

'Silver Carpet' does not produce flower spikes and is somewhat less vigorous than the species. 'Big Ears' ('Countess Helen von Stein') has larger leaves. Flowers of 'Cotton Boll' are like little balls of fluff spaced along the stem. 'Primrose Heron' has furry yellow leaves that mature to chartreuse, then turn gray-green.

Use all forms for contrast with dark green foliage and with different leaf shapes, such as those of strawberry or some sedums. Good edging for paths, flower beds. Excellent groundcover in high, open shade, such as under tall oaks; space plants 2 ft. apart.

S. coccinea. SCARLET HEDGE NETTLE. Zones 7–10, 12–24. Native to southern Texas, New Mexico, and Arizona. Forms a clump to 1½ ft. high and wide, with wrinkled, heavily veined, elongated oval leaves to 3 in. long. Bears short spikes of scarlet flowers.

S. macrantha (S. grandiflora). BIG BETONY. Zones 1–24. Native to the Caucasus, Turkey, and Iran. Dense foliage clump to 1 ft. high and wide, with long-stalked, heart-shaped, scallop-edged dark green leaves; they are wrinkled and roughly hairy. Showy purplish pink blossoms on 1½–2-ft.-high stems. 'Alba' has white blooms; 'Robusta' and 'Superba' offer larger flowers.

CARE

All are fairly unfussy about soil type, needing only good drainage. Green-leafed species need some shade where summers are hot. Clumps often die out in center; divide and replant outer sections.

Stachyurus praecox
Stachyuraceae
DECIDUOUS SHRUB

🌱 **BEST IN ZONES 4–6; ALSO GROWS IN ZONES 14–17**

☼ ◑ **FULL SUN OR LIGHT SHADE**

💧 **REGULAR WATER**

Stachyurus praecox 'Aurea Variegata'

Slow-growing shrub from Japan to 10 ft. tall and nearly as wide, with slender, polished-looking, chestnut brown branches. Pendulous, 3–4-in.-long flower stalks, each carrying 12 to 20 buds, hang from branches in fall and winter. In late winter, buds open into bell-shaped, pale yellow or greenish yellow flowers ⅓ in. wide. Greenish yellow, berrylike fruit follows in late summer. Bright green, toothed leaves are 3–7 in. long, tapering to sharp tip; foliage is often somewhat sparse. Rosy red and yellowish fall color is pleasant but not vivid. Grow this plant under a deciduous tree to shelter its winter buds from heavy freezes.

Stenocarpus sinuatus

FIREWHEEL TREE
Proteaceae
EVERGREEN TREE

🌿 **ZONES 16, 17, 20–24**
☼ **FULL SUN**
◗● **MODERATE TO REGULAR WATER**

Stenocarpus sinuatus

Slow-growing, densely foliaged plant from Australia to 30 ft. tall, 15 ft. wide. Shiny deep green leaves; to 1 ft. long and lobed on young plants, smaller and usually unlobed on older ones. Tubular, 2–3-in., scarlet-and-yellow flowers arranged in clusters like spokes of a wheel. Flowering usually is at its peak in early fall, but plant may bloom at any time. Blooms sometimes emerge from the bark of the trunk—an unusual sight. Plants do not bloom until established for several years.

Tender, especially when young. Does best in deep, rich, well-drained, acid soil. Prune to shape in early years. Showy flowering tree near a patio or terrace. Also good in lawn or near a swimming pool (has little leaf drop). Beautiful juvenile leaves make it an interesting indoor potted plant.

FOR OTHER TREES THAT ARE GOOD NEAR PATIOS, SEE PAGES 66–67.

Stenocereus thurberi
(Lemaireocereus thurberi)

ORGANPIPE CACTUS
Cactaceae
CACTUS

🌿 **ZONES 12–24**
☼ **FULL SUN**
◊ **LITTLE WATER**

Stenocereus thurberi

This columnar cactus is native to southern Arizona and northern Mexico. It branches from the base (also from the top, if injured) to form a clump to 12 ft. wide. Dark green or gray-green stems grow slowly to 15–20 ft. tall; each stem reaches 6 in. thick, has 12 to 19 ribs, and is covered with black spines ½–1 in. long. In old plants, the clump may contain 30 or more stems of varying heights; the arrangement is said to resemble a pipe organ. Blooms from mid- to late spring; funnel-shaped, 3-in. flowers in white with a touch of pink to reddish purple open at night. Rounded, 1½-in.-long fruits are olive green, becoming red tinged when ripe. They split open to reveal edible, sweet, bright red pulp with black seeds. Needs excellent drainage.

S. t. littoralis (*S. littoralis*), sometimes called dwarf organ-pipe cactus, is native to southern Baja California. It grows slowly to 5–10 ft. tall and may be erect or somewhat sprawling. Bright pink flowers open in the afternoon.

Stenolobium stans.
See *Tecoma stans*

Stenotaphrum secundatum

ST. AUGUSTINE GRASS
Poaceae
PERENNIAL GRASS

🌿 **ZONES 11–13, 18–24; H1, H2**
☼◖ **BEST IN SUN, TOLERATES SOME SHADE**
● **REGULAR WATER**

Stenotaphrum secundatum

This coarse-textured grass from tropical and subtropical regions spreads fast by surface runners that root at joints. Dark green leaves to ⅜ in. wide on coarse, wiry, flattened stems. Turns brown during short winter dormancy, can creep into planting beds, produces thick thatch, and must be cut with a power mower. On the plus side, it takes much traffic, has few pest problems, is fairly tolerant of salt and shade, and is easily removed from plantings (the roots are shallow). Plant from sod, plugs, or stolons. Mow to 1½–3 in. Needs somewhat less water than bluegrass (*Poa*). 'Variegatum' has pale green leaves striped with creamy white. (For more on grasses, see "Meet the Grasses," page 346.)

Try this spreading grass in a tall pot or hanging basket, where its long, leafy stems can cascade gracefully over the sides.

Stephanotis floribunda

MADAGASCAR JASMINE, FLORADORA
Apocynaceae
EVERGREEN VINE

🌿 **ZONES 23, 24; H2; OR INDOORS**
◖ **ROOTS COOL, TOPS IN FILTERED SUN; BRIGHT LIGHT**
● **REGULAR WATER**

Stephanotis floribunda

Native to Madagascar. Twines to 15–30 ft. Waxy, glossy green, oval leaves to 4 in. long. Valued for intense fragrance of its funnel-shaped, 1–2-in.-long, waxy white blossoms. Borne in open clusters, the flowers are a favorite for bridal bouquets and are also used in leis. Blooms in late winter and spring in Hawaii, from late spring through summer in Southern California. Needs warmth. Provide support; train on trellis or fence, along eaves. Thrives in moderately rich, well-drained soil. Prune lightly in late winter or early spring, cutting back stems to fit the support structure.

Excellent in a large, rounded container with an obelisk in the center to climb; before planting, put the container on a sturdy wheeled pot stand so you can move it easily. Mist regularly.

As a houseplant, it will bloom if given ample light; it is better suited to a greenhouse. Feed liberally; watch for scale and mealybugs. Give indoor plants a rest period by letting them dry out in winter. Can be brought outdoors during warm times of year. May be sold as *Marsdenia floribunda*.

Sterculia. See *Brachychiton*

S

Sternbergia lutea

Amaryllidaceae

PERENNIAL FROM BULB

🌿 **ZONES 3–10, 14–24**

☀️ **FULL SUN**

💧 **REGULAR WATER DURING GROWTH AND BLOOM**

Sternbergia lutea

Native from the western Mediterranean to central Asia. Golden yellow, 1½-in. flowers, one on each 6–9-in. stem, appear in early fall; they are chalice-shaped at first, then open out to a star. Narrow leaves emerge with or just after flowers, reach about 1 ft. long; they remain green through winter, die back in spring. Good alongside paths or in rock gardens or pockets in paved patios.

CARE

Plant bulbs in mid- to late summer, as soon as they are available. Set them 4 in. deep, 6 in. apart in well-drained soil. Where winter temperatures drop to 20°F (–7°C) or lower, protect planting area with thick layer of mulch. Divide clumps (at normal planting time) only when vigor and flower quality decline. If planting cannot be kept dry during summer dormancy, grow in pots and move to a dry spot in summer. Don't be in a hurry to repot; plant blooms better when pot-bound.

It's easy to see why these cheerful little bulbs are sometimes called autumn daffodils.

Stewartia

Theaceae

DECIDUOUS TREES OR SHRUBS

🌿 **ZONES 4–6, 14–17, 20, 21**

☀️🌤️ **FULL SUN OR PARTIAL SHADE**

💧 **REGULAR WATER**

Stewartia monadelpha

Native to Japan and Korea, these plants are slow-growing, all-season performers that show off fresh green leaves in spring, white flowers resembling single camellias in summer, and colorful foliage in fall. In winter, their pattern of bare branches is on show, as is smooth bark that flakes off in varying degrees, depending on species. All grow best in acid, organically enriched soil. Good in woodland garden and as foreground specimens against a backdrop of larger, darker-leafed trees.

S. koreana. See *S. pseudocamellia* Koreana group.

S. monadelpha. TALL STEWARTIA. Tree. To 25 ft. tall, 20 ft. wide; branches angle upward. Leaves turn brilliant red in fall. Small (to 1½ in.) flowers. Bark is rich brown when young; cinnamon-colored with age.

S. pseudocamellia. JAPANESE STEWARTIA. Tree. Pyramidal form; may reach 30–40 ft. tall, 20–25 ft. wide after many years. Leaves turn orange-red to purple in autumn. Cup-shaped, 2½-in.-wide flowers have orange anthers. Very showy bark: it flakes off to show a patchwork of green, gray, brown, rust, terra-cotta, and cream. Members of Koreana group (*S. koreana, S. pseudocamellia koreana*) have orange or orange-red fall color and 3-in.-wide flowers that open out flatter than the usual.

Stipa

FEATHER GRASS

Poaceae

PERENNIAL GRASSES

🌿 **ZONES VARY BY SPECIES**

☀️ **FULL SUN**

💧 **REGULAR WATER, EXCEPT AS NOTED**

Stipa tenuissima

These clump-forming grasses produce large, open, airy inflorescences that can add lightness and motion to the garden.

✓ **S. arundinacea.** See *Anemanthele lessoniana.*

S. gigantea. GIANT FEATHER GRASS. Zones 4–9, 14–24. From Spain, Portugal, and Morocco. Narrow, arching, evergreen leaves in a clump growing 2–3 ft. high and slightly wider. Open, airy sheaves of yellowish flowers bloom in summer, forming a broad, shimmering cloud that rises 6 ft. tall and as wide or slightly wider. Little to moderate water.

S. lessingiana. Native to Turkey, the Caucasus, Siberia, and China. Zones 1–24. Wispy clump of arching, fine-textured bright green leaves, 18–30 in. high and 20 in. wide. Open, airy sheaves of creamy flowers bloom in early summer, last into winter. Takes heat and drought but best with moderate water. Great in containers.

S. ramosissima (Austrostipa ramosissima). PILLAR OF SMOKE. Zones 14–24. From Australia. To 6–7 ft. tall and 3 ft. wide. The erect column of evergreen foliage and blossoms does somewhat resemble a pillar of smoke. Flowering is almost continuous; the airy, light tan inflorescences make up half (or a little more) of the plant's total height.

✓ **S. tenuissima (Nassella tenuissima).** MEXICAN FEATHER GRASS. Zones 2b–24. Native to Texas, New Mexico, Mexico. Among the finest textured and most billowy-looking of all ornamental grasses. To 2 ft. high and 2–3 ft. wide, with threadlike bright green leaves. In summer, produces very thin flowering stems that arch outward and downward, ending in a cloud of silvery green, 3-in. awns that age to a light straw color and remain attractive into winter. Stays green where summers are cooler. Thrives with little to regular water. Can self-sow and may become invasive; to prevent, cut plants back before seeds ripen.

FOR MORE ON GRASSES, SEE "MEET THE GRASSES," PAGE 346.

Stokesia laevis

STOKES' ASTER

Asteraceae

PERENNIAL

🌿 **ZONES 2–10, 12–24**

☀️ **FULL SUN**

💧 **REGULAR WATER**

Stokesia laevis 'Purple Rain'

Rugged, adaptable plant native to southeastern U.S. Evergreen in warmer part of range; semievergreen in cold climates. To 2 ft. high, 1½ ft. wide, with stiff, erect, much-branched stems. Smooth, firm-textured, medium green leaves, sometimes toothed at base. Leafy, curved, finely toothed bracts surround tight flower buds; in summer or early fall, these open to 3–4-in., asterlike blooms in blue, purplish blue, or white. Long-lasting cut flowers. Performs best in

S

well-drained soil. Provide winter cover of evergreen boughs in coldest regions. Good in pots. Selections include lavender 'Blue Danube' (blooms into winter in the mildest climates); white 'Silver Moon'; deep purple 'Purple Parasols'; and powder blue 'Klaus Jelitto'.

Strawberry

Rosaceae
PERENNIALS

🌱 **ZONES A1–A3; 1–9, 14–24; H1, H2; DIFFICULT IN ZONES 10–13**

☼ **FULL SUN, EXCEPT AS NOTED**

💧 **REGULAR WATER**

Strawberries

Standard market strawberries are hybrids (*Fragaria × ananassa*). Plants have toothed, roundish, medium green leaves and white flowers. They grow 6–8 in. tall, spreading by long runners to about 1 ft. across. Strawberries of one variety or another can be grown in every part of the West, though it is hard to succeed with them where soil and water salinity are very high.

June-bearing types produce one crop per year in late spring or early summer; in general, they are the highest-quality strawberries you can grow. Everbearing and day-neutral kinds have the potential to flower and set fruit over a longer season. Everbearers bear one crop in early spring and one in fall, while day-neutrals come to peak harvest in early summer and continue to produce fruit (often unevenly) through fall. The exact fruiting pattern for both types depends on variety and temperature: plants stop flowering when the thermometer rises above 85°F (29°C). Everbearers

and day-neutrals put out fewer runners than June bearers and generally have smaller fruit. The quality of day-neutral fruit is higher than that of everbearing strawberries.

JUNE-BEARING VARIETIES

'Benton'. Good crop of flavorful, somewhat soft berries. Virus-tolerant, mildew-resistant. Outstanding in the Northwest, especially in mountain and intermountain areas.

'Camarosa'. Huge, conical berries over a long season. Susceptible to mildew. Adapted to California, especially southern areas.

'Chandler'. Large, juicy berries over long period. Excellent flavor, good texture. Some resistance to leaf spot. Grows well in California, particularly Santa Barbara area and southward. Good as an annual elsewhere.

'Guardian'. Large, all-purpose fruit with good flavor. Disease-resistant. Recommended for cold-winter regions.

'Honeoye'. Large, symmetrical, bright red fruit with sweet-tart flavor. Recommended for cold-winter regions.

'Hood'. Large, conical to wedge-shaped berries for fresh eating and processing. Excellent flavor and early ripening. Resists mildew. Good in Pacific Northwest.

'Jewel'. Large, firm, bright red berries come at midseason. Best in cold winter regions.

'Puget Reliance'. Large crop of big, tasty berries; excellent flavor when processed. Vigorous plant. Tolerant of viruses. Adapted to Pacific Northwest.

'Puget Summer'. A heavy-yielding, late-season variety. Holds its fruit up off the ground, avoiding fruit rot. Susceptible to powdery mildew; disease-resistant otherwise. Excellent, sweet flavor. Best in the Pacific Northwest.

'Rainier'. Good-size berries that hold size throughout long season. Fine flavor. Vigorous plant. Fair tolerance to root rot. Best in Pacific Northwest, west of Cascades.

'Sequoia'. One of the tastiest strawberries. Bears for many months. Resistant to alkalinity, yellows, and most leaf diseases. Developed for coastal

California, but widely adapted, even to cold winters.

'Shuksan'. Soft, mealy berries. Excellent frozen; good fresh. Tolerant of alkalinity. Resistant to botrytis, viruses, red stele. Good in Pacific Northwest, east of Cascades.

'Toklat'. Large, sweet berries. Susceptible to botrytis. Well suited to Alaska.

EVERBEARING AND DAY-NEUTRAL VARIETIES

'Albion'. Day-neutral. Long, conical fruit with excellent flavor. Resists verticillium wilt and crown rot. For California.

'Fort Laramie'. Everbearing. Good yield of berries over long season. Excellent flavor. Tolerates –30°F (–34°C) without mulch. Hardy in mountain states, High Plains, milder parts of Alaska. Also good in Southern California.

'Ozark Beauty'. Everbearing. Medium-size red berries; excellent flavor in cold winter areas, just fair where winters are mild. Vigorous plant.

'Quinault'. Everbearing. Large, attractive berries are tasty, rather soft. Good producer of runners. Resists viruses and red stele. Susceptible to botrytis. Developed for the Pacific Northwest but is widely adapted. This variety is grown as an annual in Alaska.

'Seascape'. Day-neutral. Good producer of large berries. Very good for eating fresh, for jam, and for freezing. Excellent virus resistance. For California, the Pacific Northwest, Hawaii. Good choice for annual production in colder climates.

'Selva'. Day-neutral. First flush of fruit comes as late as July, but produces heavily through fall. Mild flavor develops best in warm areas; huge for everbearing variety. Gets red spider mite, leaf spotting in mild parts of Pacific Northwest, but has good resistance to red stele. Does best in California.

'Tribute'. Day-neutral. Medium-size berries with excellent flavor. Resists red stele and verticillium wilt. Prone to viruses in Pacific Northwest. Widely adapted.

Growing Strawberries as Annuals

Some home gardeners follow the example of commercial growers, who treat strawberries as annuals. Plant in summer or early fall, usually with a plastic mulch; remove runners as they develop. After harvest, tear out plants; set out new plants in another location the following year (don't replant in the same location until at least 2 years have passed). Benefits are healthier plants, fewer weeds, and bigger fruit. June-bearing 'Chandler' is especially well adapted to this system, but almost any variety can be grown this way if planted at just the right time (you may have to experiment). In Alaska, home gardeners are treating some everbearing varieties, particularly 'Quinault', as spring-planted annuals.

Varieties tend to be regionally adapted. Also consider musk strawberries: these shade-tolerant, June-bearing varieties from Italy are renowned for their intense aroma and flavor with hints of raspberry and pineapple. 'Profumata di Tortona' and 'Capron' are popular. For information on alpine strawberry, or fraise du bois, which produces tiny, delectable berries often used to edge flower and herb beds, see *Fragaria vesca*. The *Fragaria* entry also contains descriptions of ornamental strawberries.

S

»»

How to Grow Strawberries

SOIL Make sure it's well-drained and acidic (most varieties do not tolerate alkalinity).

PLANTING The season for planting usually depends on when local nurseries offer plants. In mild-winter areas, set out June bearers in late summer or fall for a crop the next spring; in colder climates, plant in early spring for harvest the following year. Set out everbearing plants in spring for summer and fall berries (in mild-winter areas, they may be available for fall planting). Plant carefully; the crown should be above soil level (a buried crown will rot), and the topmost roots should be ¼ in. beneath soil (exposed roots will dry out). Plant on flat ground if soil drains well or is high in salts, on a 5–6-in. mound if soil is heavy or drains poorly. (If soil is high in salts and drains poorly, plant in containers.) For a small harvest, grow a dozen plants in a sunny flower or vegetable garden; or put them in boxes, tubs, or hanging baskets on the patio. For a big crop of berries, set plants 14–18 in. apart, in rows 2–2½ ft. apart.

Mulch to deter weeds, conserve moisture, and keep berries clean. Hasten spring growth by planting through clear or black plastic mulch, and by covering plants with floating row covers (remove covers as soon as flowers appear). Pinch off the earliest blossoms produced in the first year to increase the plants' vigor.

WATERING & FERTILIZING Don't let plants dry out. Drip irrigation is ideal to help reduce disease problems, but overhead irrigation is satisfactory. Use a complete fertilizer for all types of strawberries. Feed June bearers twice a year—very lightly when growth begins and again, more heavily, after fruiting. Everbearing types prefer consistent light feedings. Heavy feeding of either type in spring leads to excessive plant growth, soft fruit, and fruit rot.

PINCHING & REFRESHING The majority of varieties reproduce by runners, though some make few or no offsets. Pinch off all runners to get large plants with smaller yields of big berries; let offsets grow 7–10 in. apart for heavy yields of smaller berries. When your plants have made enough offsets, pinch off additional runners.

Most June bearers benefit greatly from an annual tune-up that includes thinning and cutting back. After harvest, remove foliage with a lawn mower set high so it won't injure the plant crowns. If diseases were a problem, send leaves out with the trash. Water and fertilize to encourage new growth. This is also a good time to reduce a dense planting by removing the old "mother" plants and leaving younger, more productive "daughter" plants.

COLD WINTER CARE Strawberries need winter mulch in cold climates. Cover with a 4–6-in. layer of straw or other light, weed-free, organic material in late fall. When temperatures warm in spring, rake mulch between plants.

PESTS Plants are subject to many diseases: fruit rots (botrytis, anthracnose, and leather rot), leaf diseases (leaf spot, leaf scorch, and leaf blight), crown diseases (phytophthora), root diseases (verticillium wilt, red stele, and black root rot), and—especially in the Pacific Northwest—viruses. Root weevils, aphids, mites, slugs, and snails are among the potential pests.

To reduce problems, use certified disease-free plants; also remove diseased foliage and ripe or rotten fruit. Replace plants with new ones as they begin to decline, usually after 3 years; or, better yet, start a new bed with new plants.

'Tristar'. Day-neutral. Small to medium-size berries with excellent flavor. Bears well the first year. Resists red stele and mildew but is moderately susceptible to viruses. Widely adapted.

Strelitzia

BIRD OF PARADISE
Strelitziaceae
PERENNIALS

🗡 **ZONES VARY BY SPECIES**

☼ ◐ **LIGHT SHADE IN HOTTEST CLIMATES**

💧 **REGULAR WATER**

Strelitzia reginae

Bold evergreen plants from South Africa with long-stalked, leathery leaves and highly individual flowers. Blossoms are produced intermittently throughout year; they are long lasting on plant and as cut flowers. Both species are good for poolside plantings; they produce no litter and withstand some splashing. Hardy to about 28°F (–2°C).

S. nicolai. GIANT BIRD OF PARADISE. Zones 22–24; H1, H2; with protection in Zones 12, 13. Clumping, treelike plant to 30 ft. tall and wide. Grown mainly for its dramatic foliage (similar to that of banana plants): gray-green, 5–10-ft.-long leaves arranged fanwise on erect or curving trunks. Flowers are larger than those of *S. reginae* but not as colorful. Floral envelope is purplish gray; flower is white with dark blue "tongue." Feed young plants frequently until they reach full dramatic size; then give little or no fertilizer.

S. reginae. BIRD OF PARADISE. Zones 17, 20–24, H1, H2; under overhangs where heat can be trapped in Zones 8, 9, 13–16, 18, 19. Grown for spectacular flowers, which bear a startling resemblance to the heads of crested tropical birds. Flowers combine orange, blue, and white; are borne on long, stiff stems. Flowering is best in cooler seasons (though blooms appear year-round). Trunkless plant grows to 5–6 ft. tall and about as wide; blue-green leaves are 1½ ft. long. This species benefits greatly from frequent, heavy feeding.

Divide infrequently, since large, crowded clumps bloom best. Good in pots. Recovers slowly from frost damage.

Streptosolen jamesonii

MARMALADE BUSH
Solanaceae
EVERGREEN VINING SHRUB

🗡 **ZONES 13, 16, 17, 23, 24; H2**

☼ ◐ **PARTIAL SHADE IN HOTTEST CLIMATES**

💧 **REGULAR WATER**

Streptosolen jamesonii

Colorful vine from South America. Grows to 4–6 ft. tall and as wide; to 10–15 ft. trained against a wall, on a bank or trellis. Ribbed, oval bright green leaves to 1½ in. long. Large, loose clusters of 1-in., orange (sometimes yellow) flowers are carried at branch ends from spring to early fall (nearly all year in frost-free areas). Grow in warm spot; give fast-draining soil. Provide protection from frosts; cut back dead wood after last frost. Effective spilling over a wall, lining garden stairs, or in a hanging basket.

Strobilanthus dyeranus

PERSIAN SHIELD

Acanthaceae

TENDER SHRUB

ZONES 23, 24; H1, H2; ALSO 16, 17, 19–22 WITH PROTECTION

FULL SUN OR PARTIAL SHADE

REGULAR WATER

Strobilanthus dyeranus

Native to Burma, this beautiful foliage plant will overwinter in mostly frost-free areas but can be used as an annual almost anywhere. Grows to 4 ft. tall and 3 ft. wide; soft stems more like a perennial than a shrub. Broadly oval, pointed leaves are 6–8 in. long, somewhat puckered, dark green but richly variegated with purple and silvery blue tints. Leaf undersides are bright purple. Pale violet, tubular flowers come in summer in 1–1½-in. spikes less showy than the foliage. Needs rich soil. Becomes straggly with age; pinch regularly, replace, or start over from cuttings. May survive temperatures slightly below freezing if heavily mulched in late fall; or grow in containers and move to shelter in winter. Can be overwintered indoors in a sunny window.

Use Persian shield in beds beside silvery *Artemisia* 'Powis Castle'. Or combine it in a brown container with purple-flowered angelonias and chartreuse 'Angelina' sedum.

Styphnolobium japonicum

(Sophora japonica)

JAPANESE PAGODA TREE, CHINESE SCHOLAR TREE

Leguminosae

DECIDUOUS TREE

ZONES 2–24

FULL SUN TO PARTIAL SHADE

MODERATE WATER

Styphnolobium japonicum

Beautiful flowering tree native to China and Korea. Grows at a moderate rate to 50–70 ft. tall and about as wide. Young wood is smooth, dark gray-green; old branches and trunk gradually take on a rugged look, with rough, deeply furrowed bark. Dark green leaves are divided into leaflets. Undistinguished yellow fall color. Long (to 1 ft.), open clusters of ½-in., yellowish white flowers in summer; 2–3½-in. pods. 'Regent' is an exceptionally vigorous and uniform grower. 'Pendula', to about 10 ft. tall and wide, has long, dangling, sometimes twisted branches; it rarely blooms.

This species is one of the best trees for shading a lawn or patio, though stains from flowers and pods may be a problem on paved surfaces. Good for the Rocky Mountain area, though it is subject to damage from ice storms there. Blooms best in long, hot summers; flowers are unreliable where summers are cold and damp. Resistant to oak root fungus.

FOR OTHER TREES THAT WILL PROVIDE SHADE, SEE PAGES 91–92.

Styrax

Styracaceae

DECIDUOUS TREES AND SHRUBS

ZONES 4–9, 14–21

FULL SUN OR PARTIAL SHADE

REGULAR WATER

Styrax officinalis

These plants deserve to be better known for their subtly attractive springtime show of white, bell-shaped flowers in hanging clusters. Blossoms are fragrant (only faintly so in *S. japonicus*). Nonaggressive roots.

S. japonicus. JAPANESE SNOWDROP TREE, JAPANESE SNOWBELL. Tree. Native to eastern Asia. Grows to 30 ft. tall; often narrower than high in youth, but spreads as wide or wider than tall in maturity. Slender, graceful trunk. The branches are often strongly horizontal, giving the tree a broad, flat top. Oval, scallop-edged dark green leaves may turn a good red or yellow in fall. Small clusters of ¾-in.-wide flowers hang on short side branches; leaves angle upward from branches while flowers hang down, giving effect of parallel green and white tiers. Splendid tree to look up into; plant it in raised beds near outdoor entertaining area or on high bank above path. 'Carillon' ('Pendula') is a shrubby variety with weeping branches. 'Pink Chimes', also shrubby, is a more upright form with pink flowers. 'Snow Charm' has larger leaves and a dependably rounded form, to 20 ft. tall and wide. 'Snowcone' forms a dense, broad pyramid 25 ft. tall and 20 ft. wide.

S. obassia. FRAGRANT SNOWBELL. Tree. From eastern Asia. To 20–30 ft. tall and about two-thirds as wide. Oval to round, deep green leaves. Where frosts come very late, leaves may color yellow in fall. Flowers to 1 in. long are carried in drooping, 6–8-in. clusters at branch ends. Good against a background of evergreens, or for height and contrast above a border of rhododendrons and azaleas.

S. officinalis redivivus. CALIFORNIA SNOWDROP. Zones 6–10, 14–24; best in 14–16, 18–24. Native to dry, rocky areas of California below 3,000-ft. elevation. Upright deciduous shrub to 6–10 ft. tall and about 6 ft. wide. Rounded to oval, gray-green leaves with fuzzy undersides; turn yellow in fall. Small, waxy, fragrant white flowers with prominent yellow-tipped stamens are held in clusters at branch tips in spring. Useful in native or drought-tolerant gardens.

CARE

Provide reasonably good, well-drained, nonalkaline soil. Prune to control shape; tend to be shrubby unless lower side branches are suppressed.

S

A White Woodland

For an all-white border in a lightly shaded, wind-protected area, plant a Japanese snowdrop or fragrant snowbell tree as the centerpiece among white-blooming varieties of azalea, camellia, hydrangea, *Pieris*, rhododendron, and flowering currant (*Ribes sanguineum*). Fill in with bugbane (*Actaea*), bleeding heart (*Dicentra*), Solomon's seal (*Polygonatum*) and white varieties of astilbe, bellflower (*Campanula*), and sweet violet (*Viola odorata*).

MEET THE SUCCULENTS

Plants in this diverse group have fleshy leaves, stems, or roots that store water to help them withstand periods of drought. Most come from warm, frost-free regions of the world such as Mexico, South Africa, and Madagascar. They do not necessarily have spines, nor do they require desert conditions. In fact, many will not thrive in the summer heat of interior valleys or deserts, even in shade. Most are frost tender and can't stand prolonged wet conditions, but a few thrive in colder, rainier climates; among these are *Sempervivum* (from Europe) and many sedums.

Cactus are technically succulents, but their needlelike spines and desert growing conditions put them in a category of their own (see "Meet the Cactus Clan," page 209). For Christmas cactus, see *Schlumbergera*.

Massed Plantings

In mild-climate areas of the Southwest, succulents can serve as low-water alternatives to lawns and flower beds. Shrubby types include *Aeonium*, *Aloe*, *Bulbine*, *Cotyledon*, *Crassula*, *Portulacaria*, and *Sansevieria*.

Groundcovers

Many succulents make good groundcovers, though none withstand foot traffic. Creeping, spreading succulents such as *Sedum* and *Senecio* are useful between stepping-stones and for niches in rock gardens. Such plants, along with *Graptopetalum*, are also attractive tumbling over terraces. For succulents that produce vivid sheets of bloom and rapidly cover large banks, see "Meet the Ice Plants," page 371.

Containers

Most succulents grow well in containers. Mix sizes, shapes, and colors in pots with plenty of drainage holes. For good candidates, see *Dudleya* and *Haworthia*.

Garden Accents

Large, shapely rosettes make striking focal points. *Agave*, *Aloe*, and *Furcraea* have dramatic silhouettes. Tree succulents tend to have bulbous trunks, fat branches, and stiff, fleshy leaves; see *Aloe barberae* and *Nolina*.

Colorful Leaves or Blooms

Succulents with colorful leaves include *Aeonium arboreum* 'Zwartkop', *Cotyledon orbiculata*, *Crassula ovata*, *Dudleya brittoni*, *Echeveria agavoides* 'Lipstick', *E. elegans*, *E. secunda*, *Euphorbia tirucalli* 'Sticks on Fire', × *Graptoveria* 'Fred Ives', *Kalanchoe fedtshenkoi* 'Variegata', *K. luciae*, *Senecio mandraliscae*, and *S. serpens*. Aloe flowers ranging from reddish orange to yellow, in spires a foot tall or more, are especially showy. Other colorful choices include *Beschorneria yuccoides*, with vivid pink flower spikes; *Calandrinia grandiflora*, with airy purple flowers; and cabbagelike *Echeveria* varieties with ruffled, pastel leaves.

HOW TO GROW

EXPOSURE Sun near the coast, light shade inland. Introduce nursery-grown succulents to sunny locations gradually or their leaves may sunburn.

SOIL Fast-draining. Amend garden soil with pumice, decomposed granite, or coarse sand, or plant in fast-draining cactus mix from your nursery.

WATERING Although most succulents are drought-tolerant, prolonged periods without water may cause their leaves to lose color, shrivel, or drop. The amount of water needed depends on heat, humidity, and rainfall. Give plants just enough water to keep them plump and attractive. Occasional deep watering will help remove salts from the soil. When siting them near plants that need more water, position succulents atop small mounds of amended soil so that water drains away from the roots.

GROOMING Many succulents need little tending other than removal of spent flower stalks.

FEEDING One light feeding at the start of the growing season should be enough for most succulents. For more vigorous growth, feed several times during the growing season at half the recommended dose. Larger and later-blooming kinds, as well as container-grown plants, may also benefit from additional fertilizing.

Grow your collection! Take cuttings from stem-forming succulents and let the cut ends callus before planting. Or pick off and replant "pups" (offsets) that form around rosette-forming succulents such as *Agave*, *Aloe*, and *Sempervivum*.

Echeveria, Senecio mandraliscae

Echeveria imbricata (left), *E. subrigida* (center), and friends

CLOCKWISE FROM LEFT: *Agave stricta*, *Aloe* 'Pink Blush', *Sedum rupestre* 'Angelina', and *Echeveria*

Sutera cordata

BACOPA
Scrophulariaceae
PERENNIAL

☀ **ZONES 15–17, 21–24; H2; ANYWHERE AS ANNUAL**

☀ ☼ **AFTERNOON SHADE IN HOTTEST CLIMATES**

💧 **REGULAR WATER**

Sutera cordata

From moist regions of South Africa. Wiry-stemmed creeper with toothed leaves. Often sold as "bacopa." Blooms from late spring to frost, producing small, five-petaled, golden-throated flowers. Use in hanging baskets or as small-scale groundcover.

Original variety (sold as 'Snowflake') has ¼-in. white flowers and grows 1–2 in. high, spreading 1–2 ft. in a growing season; eventually covers 3–4 ft. in mild climates. 'Giant Snowflake' is more vigorous, reaching 6–8 in. high, 3–4 ft. wide in a season; its white flowers are ½ in. wide. 'Snowstorm' resembles 'Giant Snowflake' but blooms more profusely and has greater heat tolerance. 'Snowstorm Blue' and 'Snowstorm Pink' are also available. 'Olympic Gold' has leaves splotched with yellow but is otherwise identical to 'Snowstorm' (to which it sometimes reverts).

CARE

Needs good drainage, good air circulation; likes rich soil, regular fertilizer. Don't allow it to dry out; if it wilts, it probably won't recover. Pinch branches often to keep plant shapely. If a thick layer of dead stems builds up under foliage, remove dead material and cut plant back to leave 5–6-in.-long branches with leafy growth.

Sweet Potato

Convolvulaceae
PERENNIAL GROWN AS ANNUAL

☀ **ZONES 8–10, 12–15, 18–24; H1, H2**

☀ **FULL SUN**

💧 **REGULAR WATER**

Sweet potatoes

Not a potato, but the thickened root of a trailing tropical vine closely related to morning glory (*Ipomoea*); the scientific name is *Ipomoea batatas* (see that entry for ornamental varieties). Most varieties trail several feet, but bush and short vine varieties are also available, making it possible to grow them even in modest-size gardens.

Sweet potatoes are classified by flesh type. One has soft, sugary, yellow-orange flesh (examples are 'Centennial', 'Jewel', 'Kona-B', and bush types 'Vardaman' and 'Vineless Puerto Rico'); the other has firm, dry, whitish flesh (examples are 'Hoolehua Red', 'Waimanalo Red', 'Yellow Jersey'). Sweet yellow-orange type is incorrectly sold under the name "yam" in grocery stores.

CARE

Needs long, hot, frost-free growing season; easiest to grow in Hawaii. Requires well-drained soil (preferably sandy loam) and plenty of room. Start with certified disease-free or disease-resistant slips (rooted cuttings) from a garden center or mail-order nursery. To avoid buildup of disease organisms in the soil, don't grow sweet potatoes in the same location 2 years in a row.

Plant in late spring, when soil temperature has warmed to 70°F (21°C). (You can plant year-round in Hawaii, but spring-planted crops mature faster.) Before planting, work in a low-nitrogen fertilizer; too much nitrogen produces leafy growth at expense of roots. Set slips so that only stem tips and leaves are exposed; space 1 ft. apart, in rows 3 ft. apart. To ensure good drainage, mark off rows and ditch between them to form planting ridges. Row covers provide added heat and keep out many pests.

Harvest before first frost (110 to 120 days after planting for most varieties); if sudden frost kills tops, harvest immediately. Dig carefully to avoid cutting or bruising roots. Flavor improves in storage (starch is converted to sugar). Let roots dry in the sun until soil can be brushed off; then cure by storing 10 to 14 days in warm (about 85°F/29°C), humid place. Store in a cool, dry environment (not below 55°F/13°C).

Swiss Chard

Chenopodiaceae
BIENNIAL GROWN AS ANNUAL

☀ **ALL ZONES**

☀ **FULL SUN**

💧 **REGULAR WATER**

Swiss chard

Swiss chard, a form of beet grown for leaves and stalks instead of roots, probably originated in the Mediterranean. It is one of the easiest-to-grow vegetables for home gardens.

'Bright Lights' is especially decorative; it has leaves ranging from green to burgundy, stalks in shades of yellow, orange, pink, purple, red, and green (and in white). Red stems and red-veined green leaves of 'Rhubarb' are very decorative. Cook leaves and leafstalks separately, since stalks take longer.

CARE

Sow big, crinkly, tan seeds in spaded soil, anytime from spring to early summer. Thin seedlings to 1 ft. apart. About 2 months after sowing (plants will generally have reached 1–1½ ft. high), you can begin to cut outer leaves as needed for the table. New leaves grow up in the center of plants. Plants yield all summer and seldom bolt to seed (if one does, pull it up and throw it away or add it to the compost pile). Where winters are mild, can be grown as fall-into-spring crop. Such plantings will often bolt as the weather warms in spring, but you can often replant and extend the harvest.

Syagrus romanzoffiana
(Arecastrum romanzoffianum)

QUEEN PALM
Arecaceae
PALM

☀ **ZONES 12, 13, 15–17, 19–24; H1, H2**

☀ **FULL SUN**

💧 **REGULAR WATER**

Syagrus romanzoffiana

Brazilian native to 50 ft. tall, 20–25 ft. wide, with exceptionally straight trunk. Arching, glossy bright green, 10–15-ft.-long leaves (they break in high winds). May produce decorative orange dates. Give well-drained soil. In alkaline soils, plants yellow and slowly die. Grows quickly with fertilizer. Subject to mites; wash young plants frequently. Plants are damaged at 25°F (4°C).

Symphomyrtus. See *Eucalyptus*

S

Symphoricarpos

SNOWBERRY, CORALBERRY

Caprifoliaceae

DECIDUOUS SHRUBS

- 🌿 ZONES VARY BY SPECIES
- ☀️ ◐ ● EXPOSURE NEEDS VARY BY SPECIES
- 🌢 🌢 LITTLE TO MODERATE WATER
- 🐦 FRUIT ATTRACTS BIRDS
- ☦ INGESTING BERRIES MAY CAUSE ILLNESS

Symphoricarpos albus

Plants are upright or arching, typically 2–6 ft. tall and wide, often spreading by root suckers. They are native to North America. Most are best used as wild thicket for erosion control on steep banks. Clusters of small pink or white flowers in spring or early summer. Attractive round, berrylike fruit remains on stems after leaves drop in autumn. Cut stems look good in winter arrangements.

S. albus (S. racemosus). COMMON SNOWBERRY. Zones A3; 1–11, 14–21. Native from California to Alaska, east to Montana. Roundish, dull green leaves. Pink flowers are followed by white fruit from late summer to winter. Produces most fruit in full sun but takes shade. Not a first-rate shrub but useful for its tolerance of poor soil, lower light, general neglect.

S. × chenaultii. Zones 1–11, 14–21. Greenish white flowers, and red fruit lightly spotted with white. Can take full sun in cooler climates; needs partial or full shade in hot areas. 'Hancock' is a foot-high dwarf valued as woodland groundcover or bank cover.

S. × doorenbosii. Zones 1–11, 14–21. Dark green leaves, greenish white flowers followed by white fruit. Grows to 4–6 ft. tall and wide. 'Amethyst' (bright pink berries) and 'Magic Berry' (lilac-pink fruit) are the most common.

S. mollis. CREEPING SNOWBERRY, SPREADING SNOWBERRY. Zones 2–10, 14–24. Native to western North America. Like *S. albus* but usually less than 1½ ft. high, with earlier, sparser bloom, smaller fruit. Spreads like a groundcover, its trailing branches rooting where they touch soil. Partial shade.

S. orbiculatus (S. vulgaris). CORALBERRY, INDIAN CURRANT. Zones 1–11, 14–21. From eastern U.S. Resembles *S. albus* but bears white or sometimes pink-tinged flowers that are followed by small purplish red fruit. Fruit is bright and plentiful enough to provide a good fall-into-winter show. Full sun.

Symphytum officinale

COMFREY

Boraginaceae

PERENNIAL

- 🌿 ZONES 1–24
- ☀️ ◐ PARTIAL SHADE IN HOTTEST CLIMATES
- 🌢 REGULAR WATER
- ☦ LEAVES CAN BE HARMFUL IF INGESTED

Symphytum officinale

A deep-rooted plant from Eurasia forms a clump to 3–4 ft. tall, 2 ft. wide. Furry leaves set with stiff hairs; basal leaves 8 in. or longer, upper leaves smaller. Small (½ in. long), unshowy flowers are usually dull rose in color but sometimes white, cream, or purple. In virtually frost-free climates, plant remains leafy through winter; elsewhere, it dies to the ground in autumn.

Comfrey has a long history as a folk remedy. Leaves can be dried and brewed to make a medicinal tea, though this use is no longer recommended (the leaves have been found to contain potentially carcinogenic substances). Herb enthusiasts claim that the plant adds minerals to compost, but think hard before establishing it in your garden: it spreads freely from roots and is tough to eradicate.

Syringa

LILAC

Oleaceae

DECIDUOUS SHRUBS, RARELY TREES

- 🌿 ZONES VARY BY SPECIES
- ☀️ ◐ LIGHT SHADE IN HOTTEST CLIMATES
- 🌢 REGULAR WATER
- 🐦 FLOWERS ATTRACT BIRDS, BUTTERFLIES

Syringa vulgaris

A garden staple in cold-winter regions, cherished for big, flamboyant, fragrant flower clusters at branch tips. Best known are common lilac (*S. vulgaris*) and its many named varieties, but there are other species of great usefulness. All are medium-size to large shrubs with medium to deep green foliage and no special appeal when out of bloom. Floral show comes from number of small flowers packed into dense pyramidal to conical clusters; individual flowers are tubular, flaring into four petal-like lobes (in single types) or into a clutch of "petals" (in double kinds). Depending on climate, bloom comes from early spring (in the earliest kinds) to early summer, always after leaves have formed.

S. 'Betsy Ross'. Zones 2–12, 14–16, 18–22. Recent National Arboretum release selected for abundant white bloom, disease resistance, and good performance in mild-winter climates. Grows to 10 ft. tall by 13 ft. wide.

S. × chinensis. CHINESE LILAC. Zones A2, A3; 1–11, 14–16, 18–21. Hybrid between *S. vulgaris* and *S. × persica*. To 15 ft. tall and wide, usually much less. More graceful than *S. vulgaris*, with more finely textured foliage. Profuse, open clusters of fragrant, rosy purple flowers. Does well in mild-winter, hot-summer climates. 'Alba' has white blossoms. 'Lilac Sunday' has single, light purple blooms.

S. × hyacinthiflora. Zones A2, A3; 1–12, 14–16, 18–22. Group of hybrids between *S. vulgaris* and *S. oblata*, a Chinese species. Resemble *S. vulgaris* but they generally bloom 7 to 10 days earlier and are more heat-tolerant. Many varieties available with single or double blooms in shades of purple, magenta, pink, and white. Newer hybrids include 'Declaration', with large, reddish purple blooms, and disease-resistant 'Old Glory', with bluish purple flowers. 'Maiden's Blush' is an excellent pink flowering form.

S. 'Josée'. Zones A1–A3; 1–11, 14–16. Dwarf hybrid reaching about 6 ft. tall and 5 ft. wide. Fragrant lavender-pink blooms are produced in spring and then occasionally throughout the growing season. Hardy. 'Bloomerang Purple' is a similar rebloomer with lavender flowers.

S. × laciniata (S. × persica laciniata). Zones 3–12, 14–16, 18–22. Open-structured plant to 5–8 ft. tall and wide. Leaves divided nearly to midrib into three to nine segments; good rich green color. Many small clusters of fragrant, lilac-colored blooms.

S. meyeri 'Palibin'. Zones A2, A3; 1–9, 14–16. Dense, twiggy growth to a possible 5 ft. tall and wide; often stays at about 3 ft. Sometimes grafted high to make a standard tree with 3–4-ft. trunk. Produces 5-in. clusters of faintly fragrant flowers in purple fading to pink.

S

CLOCKWISE FROM TOP: *Syringa vulgaris* 'Olivier de Serres'; *S.* 'Josée'; *S. × hyacinthiflora* 'Angel White'

S. × persica. PERSIAN LILAC. Zones A2, A3; 2–12, 14–16, 18–22. Graceful, loose form to 6 ft. tall and wide. Fragrant, pale violet flowers appear all along arching branches.

S. × prestoniae. Zones A1–A3; 1–11, 14–16. Group of extra-hardy hybrids developed in Canada. To 12 ft. tall and wide. Flowers come on new growth at the end of the lilac season, after *S. vulgaris* has bloomed. Bulky, dense plants resemble *S. vulgaris*, but individual flowers are smaller and are not as fragrant. Many varieties available.

S. pubescens patula **'Miss Kim'.** Zones A2, A3; 1–9, 14–16. Dense, twiggy, rounded; to 8–9 ft. tall and wide. Sometimes grafted high to make a standard tree. Purple buds open to very fragrant ice blue flowers.

S. reticulata. JAPANESE TREE LILAC. Zones A2, A3; 1–12, 14–16. From Japan. To 30 ft. tall, 20 ft. wide; grow as large shrub or train as single-stemmed tree. Smooth, glossy red-brown bark. Blooms on new growth in late spring, bearing white, musky-scented flowers in clusters to 1 ft. long. Useful small shade or street tree in cold climates. 'Ivory Silk' is a compact tree to 20 ft. tall, with cream-colored flowers borne in profusion even at a young age.

S. vulgaris. COMMON LILAC. Zones A1–A3; 1–11, 14. In Zones 12–16, 18–22, the standard varieties bloom irregularly after mild winters; gradually discontinue watering near end of summer to force dormancy. From eastern Europe. Can eventually reach 20 ft. tall, with nearly equal spread. Suckers strongly; prune out suckers on grafted plants (no need to do so on own-root plants). Leaves roundish oval with pointed tips. Needs 2 to 5 years to bear flowers of full size and true color. Pinkish or bluish lavender flowers in clusters to 10 in. or longer ('Alba' has pure white flowers) in midspring. Fragrance is legendary; lilac fanciers say species and its older varieties are more fragrant than newer types. Superb cut flowers.

Varieties, often called French hybrids, number in the hundreds.

They generally flower a little later than the species and have larger clusters of single or double flowers in a wide range of colors. Singles are often as showy as doubles, sometimes more so.

Descanso hybrids, developed for mild winters, excel in Zones 18–22. Try 'Lavender Lady' (best known), 'Blue Skies' and 'Blue Boy' (both blue), 'California Rose' (single pink), 'Chiffon' (lavender), 'Forrest K. Smith' (light lavender), 'Sylvan Beauty' (rose-lavender), and 'White Angel' ('Angel White').

CARE

Most lilacs bloom best in regions with decidedly chilly winters, but some do well with only light winter chill. Give well-drained, neutral to slightly alkaline soil. If soil is strongly acid, dig lime into it before planting.

Until plants are established, just pinch back any overlong stems. Once they begin to bloom, prune yearly for best flower production. Most lilacs bloom on wood formed the previous year, so prune just after flowering ends. Remove spent blossom clusters, cutting back to a pair of leaves. For the few types that bloom on new growth, prune in late dormant season, cutting previous year's growth to varying lengths. To encourage new shoots, cut out a few of the oldest stems yearly.

Leaf miner, scale, and stem borer are the only important pests; bacterial blight, leaf spot, and downy mildew may be problems.

Most common lilacs need winter chill to deliver their best show of fragrant bloom clusters. But the low-chill Descanso hybrids, which include the richly scented 'Lavender Lady', and 'Blue Skies', thrive in mild winters.

Syzygium paniculatum
BRUSH CHERRY, AUSTRALIAN BRUSH CHERRY
Myrtaceae
EVERGREEN SHRUB OR TREE

⚐ **ZONES 16, 17, 20–24; H1, H2**

☼ ◑ **BEST IN SUN; TOLERATES SOME SHADE**

◐ ● **MODERATE TO REGULAR WATER**

Syzygium paniculatum

An Australian native with a confused botanical background. Once sold as *Eugenia myrtifolia* or *E. paniculata*, the plant most commonly sold in the West as *S. paniculatum* may actually be *S. australe*. The two plants differ slightly in leaf form, and it appears that only the botanists will be able to tell them apart.

If unclipped, brush cherry makes a single- or multitrunked tree to 30–60 ft. tall, 10–20 ft. wide, with dense foliage crown. Often sheared into formal shapes and hedges; common background or screen plant. Oblong leaves in rich glossy green, often bronze tinged; reddish bronze new growth. Small, creamy white summer flowers have conspicuous tufts of stamens that look like little brushes. Blossoms are followed by showy, edible, ¾-in., rosy purple fruit that is insipid raw but good in jellies. Several named varieties selected for good leaf color or dwarf form are sold.

CARE

Will not stand heavy frost; foliage burns at 25°F (–4°C), and even old plants may die if temperature drops much lower. Thrives in well-drained soil. Heavy root system makes it difficult to grow other plants

S

nearby. Hedges need frequent clipping to stay neat. Eugenia psyllid can cause defoliation; control is a predatory wasp that has been released throughout California but is most effective in warm weather. Frequent pruning, removing new growth, also reduces psyllid damage.

T

Tabebuia

TRUMPET TREE
Bignoniaceae
DECIDUOUS, EVERGREEN, AND
SEMIEVERGREEN TREES

🌡 **ZONES 15, 16, 20–24; H1, H2; EXCEPT AS NOTED**

☼ **FULL SUN**

🌢 **REGULAR WATER**

Tabebuia chrysotricha

S

This showy native of tropical America produces trumpet-shaped flowers borne in rounded clusters that become larger and more profuse as trees mature. Leaves are typically green; may be simple (undivided) or divided into as many as seven leaflets arranged like fingers of hand. Number of leaflets is often variable within a species. Tend to be gangly or irregular when young; benefit from training in early years. Need well-drained soil; respond well to regular fertilizing. All are useful as color accents, stand-alone flowering trees for display. Larger types

are excellent as street or park plantings; smaller species make beautiful patio trees.

T. chrysotricha (Handro-anthus chrysostricha). GOLDEN TRUMPET TREE. Briefly deciduous. Zones 13, 15, 16, 20–24; H1, H2. To 25–50 ft. tall and wide. Young twigs and leaf undersides are covered with tawny fuzz. Golden yellow flowers are 3–4 in. long, often with maroon stripes in throat. Blooms most heavily in spring, when tree loses leaves for brief period. May also bloom lightly at other times, when in leaf.

T. donnell-smithii (Roseo-dendron donnell-smithii). GOLD TREE, PRIMAVERA. Deciduous. Zones H1, H2. Upright grower to 75–100 ft. tall and 30–50 ft. wide. Bloom season is variable: spectacular clusters of yellow blossoms to 1½ in. long are commonly produced in winter or spring before leafout, but occasionally they appear later in the year.

T. heterophylla. PINK TECOMA, PINK TRUMPET TREE. Evergreen to semievergreen. Slender habit to 40 ft. tall and 20 ft. wide; sometimes grown as a large shrub. Flowers are 2–3 in. long, in colors ranging from pinkish purple through pink shades to white. Blossoms appear abundantly in spring but may also be seen occasionally throughout the rest of the year.

T. impetiginosa (Handro-anthus impetiginosus). PURPLE or PINK TRUMPET TREE. Semievergreen. Slow to 25–50 ft. tall and wide. In late winter or spring, bears 2–3-in. flowers in white to light pink and purple. Sometimes reblooms in late summer or fall. Does not bloom as a young tree.

These nonconformists greet spring by dropping their leaves. In March or April, clusters of pink or gold trumpets form a huge bouquet against the sky; a few weeks later, new leaves push out the flowers.

Tagetes

MARIGOLD
Asteraceae
ANNUALS AND PERENNIALS

🌡 **ZONES VARY BY SPECIES**

☼ **FULL SUN**

🌢 **REGULAR WATER, EXCEPT AS NOTED**

Tagetes erecta Sweet Cream

Native to Mexico, Central America. Robust, free-branching, nearly trouble-free plants ranging from 6 in. to 6 ft. tall, with flowers from pale yellow through gold to orange and brownish maroon. Finely divided, ferny, usually strongly scented leaves. Annuals will bloom early summer to frost if old flowers are picked off; in the desert, they bloom best from fall until frost. Handsome, long-lasting cut flowers; strong aroma from leaves, stems, and flowers permeates a room (some odorless varieties are available).

T. erecta. AMERICAN MARIGOLD, AFRICAN MARIGOLD. Annual. All zones. Original strains were single-flowered plants 3–4 ft. tall, 2 ft. wide. Modern strains are more varied; most have fully double flowers. Choices include Antigua (10–12 in.); Guys and Dolls, Inca, and Inca II series (12–14 in.); Lady and Perfection (16–20 in.); and Climax (2½–3 ft.). Novelty tall strains include Odorless (2½ ft.). Sweet Cream has creamy white flowers on 16-in. stems. Triploid hybrids, crosses between *T. erecta* and *T. patula,* have exceptional vigor, bear profuse 2-in. flowers over a long bloom season; they are generally shorter than other *T. erecta* strains. Examples are Zenith (12–15 in. high) and Nugget (10–12 in. high).

Avoid overhead sprinkling on taller kinds; stems will sag and even break under weight of water. To make tall types stand as firmly as possible (perhaps stoutly enough to do without staking), dig planting hole extra deep, strip any leaves off lower 1–3 in. of stem, and plant with stripped portion below soil line.

T. filifolia. IRISH LACE. Annual. All zones. Forms a mound of bright green, finely divided foliage to 6 in. high and wide; resembles an unusually fluffy, rounded fern. Used primarily as an edging plant for its foliage effect, but tiny white flowers are attractive.

T. lemmonii (T. palmeri). COPPER CANYON DAISY. Shrubby perennial. Zones 8–10, 12–24; H1. To 3–6 ft. tall and wide. Finely divided, 2–4-in.-long leaves are strongly fragrant when brushed against or rubbed— they smell like a blend of marigold, mint, and lemon. Golden orange flowers are carried at branch ends sporadically all year, peaking in winter and spring. Damaged by frost in open situations; cut back to remove damaged growth or to correct shape. Tends to be short-lived. Moderate to regular water.

T. lucida. MEXICAN MARIGOLD, MEXICAN TARRAGON. Perennial in Zones 8–10, 12–24; often grown as an annual in all zones. To 3 ft. high and wide, typically with unbranched stems. Narrow, uncut, smooth dark green leaves have strong scent and flavor of tarragon or licorice (stems and roots are similarly fragrant). Unimpressive yellow flowers, produced in fall and spring, are less than ½ in. wide. Moderate to regular water.

T. patula. FRENCH MARIGOLD. Annual. All zones. Varieties from 6 in. to 1½ ft. high and wide, in flower colors from yellow to rich maroon-brown. Blossoms may be fully double or single; many are strongly bicolored. Excellent for edging are dwarf, very double strains such as Janie (8 in.), Bonanza (10 in.), and Little Hero (10–12 in.), with 2-in. flowers in a range of colors from yellow through orange to red and brownish red. Aurora and Sophia strains have flowers that are larger (2½ in. wide) but not as double.

TOP ROW: *Tagetes patula* 'Disco Flame'; *T. p.* 'Harlequin'. MIDDLE: *T. tenuifolia* 'Paprika'. BOTTOM ROW: *T. p.* 'Queen Sophia'; *T. p.* China Cat Mix

T. tenuifolia (T. signata).
SIGNET MARIGOLD. Annual. All zones. Infrequently grown species. Flowers are small (just 1 in. wide) and single, but bloom is incredibly profuse. Finely cut foliage. Attracts beneficial insects. Gem strain offers golden yellow, lemon yellow, and tangerine orange blossoms on 10–12-in.-high plants.

CARE

Easy to grow from seed, which sprouts in a few days in warm soil; to get earlier bloom, start seeds in containers indoors or buy nursery plants. Smog will damage tender young plants, but they soon toughen up.

Tamarix

TAMARISK
Tamaricaceae
DECIDUOUS SHRUBS OR TREES

✿ ZONES VARY BY SPECIES

☀ FULL SUN

◐ ◔ LITTLE OR NO WATER TO MODERATE WATER

Tamarix parviflora

In desert regions, tamarisks have no equal in resistance to wind and aridity, and they will grow in saline soils that are toxic to other plants. They are also useful in other areas where wind, salt, and poor soil pose challenges, such as seacoast gardens. They demand only a full-sun location with good drainage. On the minus side, this same tenacious adaptability makes several of these species seriously invasive pests in the West's natural areas, especially along watercourses. Millions of dollars a year are spent removing them. Because of deep taproots, nurseries can't hold them in pots. But they are easy to grow from ½–1-in.-thick cuttings set in the soil where the plant is to grow and is kept watered until roots are established.

Tamarisks are difficult to classify, which has led to much confusion in labeling among botanists and in nurseries. Leaves are tiny, as are flowers (a hand lens is necessary to see flower details). However, you don't have to know a tamarisk's identity for pruning purposes. If it blooms only in the earlier part of spring, prune after bloom. If it starts bloom later in spring or in summer, prune just before new spring growth begins. The first two species described here can be kept shrubby by cutting back to ground yearly. If you are growing them as trees, prune only to remove dead or broken branches.

T. aphylla (T. articulata).
ATHEL TREE. Zones 7–24. Native to the eastern Mediterranean. Cuttings grow fast after planting, to 10 ft. or more in 3 years; with deep soil and some water, reach 30–50 ft. tall, 25–50 ft. wide in 15 years. True leaves are minute; the plant's evergreen appearance is due to greenish, jointed branchlets. Where soils are saline, takes on grayish look in late summer due to secretions of salt. White to pinkish, very small flowers grow in clusters at ends of branches in late summer. Tree is not as spectacular in bloom as other tamarisks. Heavily damaged at 0°F (–18°C) but recovers rapidly. Can be sheared into a hedge. Excellent windbreak. Has invasive roots; not a good choice for highly cultivated gardens.

T. chinensis. SALT CEDAR. Zones 4–24. Native to eastern Asia; naturalized in southwestern U.S. To 6–20 ft. tall, 4–10 ft. wide. Blue-green foliage. Flowers ranging from white to pink and deep purple appear mainly at branch ends. Blooms from late spring through summer. Resists heat and cold. Widely seen in desert regions but disliked there: its aggressive spreading and deep, thirsty roots displace native vegetation. Efforts are being made to remove it from many desert areas. *T. ramosissima* may be the same plant.

T

»

T. parviflora. Zones 2–24. Native to southeastern Europe. Variable habit; typically a graceful, arching large shrub to 6–15 ft. tall and wide. Profuse spring-only display of pink flowers that turn to tan, then brown. Prune to emphasize arching habit; or remove lower branches to achieve a treelike plant. An invasive pest plant in deserts, wetlands, and riparian habitats. Often sold as *T. tetrandra;* sold as *T. africana* in California.

Tanacetum
Asteraceae
PERENNIALS

- ◪ **ZONES VARY BY SPECIES**
- ☼ **FULL SUN**
- ◖◗ **MODERATE TO REGULAR WATER**

Tanacetum vulgare

Most species have finely divided leaves (often aromatic) and clusters of daisylike flower heads. Some have gray to nearly white foliage.

T. balsamita (Chrysanthemum balsamita). COSTMARY. Perennial. Zones 2–24. Native Europe to central Asia. Weedy, rhizomatous plant grown for its sweet-scented foliage (used in salads and sachets) rather than its tiny daisies. Leggy stems reach 3 ft. high; if these are cut back, the gray-green, finely scallop-margined basal leaves can make a nice edging for an herb garden. Divide clumps and reset divisions in late summer or fall.

T. coccineum (Chrysanthemum coccineum, Pyrethrum roseum). PYRETHRUM, PAINTED DAISY. Perennial. Zones A1; 1–24. Native to Iran and the Caucasus. Bushy plant

to 2–3 ft. high, 1½ ft. wide, with very finely divided bright green leaves. Bears long-stemmed single daisies in pink, red, or white in spring; if cut back, may bloom again in late summer. Also available in double- and anemone-flowered forms. Excellent for cutting, borders. Needs summer heat to perform well (except in the extreme heat of low and intermediate deserts, where it is treated as a winter annual). Sow seeds or divide clumps in spring. Double forms may not come true from sown seed, may revert to single flowers.

T. densum amani. Zones 3–24. Native to Turkey. Sometimes sold as *Chrysanthemum haradjanii.* Low-growing (6–8 in. high) plant, spreading slowly to make a mat about 1½ ft. wide. Leaves are finely cut, silvery white, featherlike in appearance. Small yellow flower heads appear a few inches above foliage in late spring. Use in rock garden, as small-scale groundcover in a bright, sunny area with good drainage. Can withstand some dry spells when established. One of the whitest-looking plants.

T. parthenium (Chrysanthemum parthenium). FEVERFEW. Perennial. Zones 2–24. Native to southern Europe and the Caucasus. Compact, leafy, aggressive, spreading by volunteer seedlings. Leaves have a strong peppery scent that some people find offensive. Attracts beneficial insects. Varieties are 1–3 ft. high. 'Golden Ball' has bright yellow flower heads and no rays; 'Silver Ball' is fully double, with only the white rays showing. In 'Aureum' (commonly sold in flats as 'Golden Feather'), chartreuse foliage is the main attraction. To propagate, divide the clumps in spring; or sow seeds in spring for bloom by midsummer.

T. ptarmiciflorum (Chrysanthemum ptarmiciflorum). DUSTY MILLER, SILVER LACE. Perennial in Zones 16, 17, 19–24; annual in Zones 1–15, 18. Canary Island native grows to 10 in. high and wide. Very finely cut, silvery white leaves. Where winter-hardy, produces white daisies on 1½-ft. stems in summer. Somewhat

drought-tolerant. (For other plants with the common name "dusty miller," see the index.)

T. vulgare. TANSY. Zones 1–24. Native to Europe. Coarse, rather weedy garden plant to 3 ft. high and 2 ft. wide, with finely divided, bright green, aromatic (some say smelly) leaves. Small, buttonlike yellow flowers appear in late summer. Thin clumps yearly to keep in bounds. This plant is no longer used medicinally, though it is still grown in herb gardens. *T. v. crispum,* fern-leaf tansy, grows to 2½ ft. high; it has finely cut foliage and is more decorative than the species. 'Isla Gold' has golden yellow foliage.

Taxodium
Taxodiaceae
DECIDUOUS AND EVERGREEN TREES

- ◪ **ZONES VARY BY SPECIES**
- ☼ **FULL SUN**
- ◌◖◗◗ **ANY AMOUNT OF WATER**

Taxodium distichum
'Cascade Falls'

Very tough, tolerant conifers of great size, with shaggy, cinnamon-colored bark and graceful sprays of short, narrow, flat, needlelike leaves. Small, roundish cones.

T. distichum. BALD CYPRESS. Deciduous. Zones 2–10, 12–24. From southeastern U.S. Can grow into 100-ft.-tall, broad-topped tree in the wild, but young and middle-aged garden trees are pyramidal to 50–70 ft. tall, 20–30 ft. wide. Feathery, delicate foliage sprays with narrow leaves in a pale, delicate, yellow-tinged green. Foliage turns orange-toned brown before dropping. Interesting winter silhouette. Takes any

soil except strongly alkaline. Tolerates extremely wet conditions (even grows in swamps) but also takes rather dry soil. Trunk is buttressed near the base. When growing in water-logged soil, develops knobby growths called knees. No particular pests or diseases bother it. Requires only corrective pruning to remove dead wood and unwanted branches. Outstanding tree for stream bank or edge of lake or pond. 'Cascade Falls' is a weeping form; grows quickly to 20 ft. tall and wide. 'Shawnee Brave' grows into a narrow pyramid just 15–20 ft. wide. 'Green Whisper' has very soft-textured, bright green foliage. 'Peve Minaret' is a dwarf to 5 ft. tall forming a compact spire with tiered branches.

T. mucronatum. MONTEZUMA CYPRESS. Evergreen in mild climates; partially or wholly deciduous in cold regions. Zones 5–9, 12–24. From Mexico. Given regular moisture, it quickly attains 40 ft. in 14 years, then grows at a more moderate rate to an eventual 75 ft. tall, 50 ft. wide. Under dry conditions, growth is uniformly slow. Extremely graceful tree with strongly weeping branches. Foliage is finer in texture, lighter in color than that of *T. distichum;* in colder part of range, it turns dull gold in autumn (color change and leaf drop both come very late). Beautiful tree for large lawns.

Bald cypress is among the few trees that can take constantly wet soil and periodic flooding. A few other members of the "wet-feet" club are red maple (*Acer rubrum*), alder (*Alnus*), river birch (*Betula nigra*), cajeput tree (*Melaleuca quinquenervia*), swamp white oak (*Quercus bicolor*), and many willows (*Salix*).

T

Taxus
YEW
Taxaceae
EVERGREEN SHRUBS OR TREES

✂ **ZONES VARY BY SPECIES**

☼ ◐ ● **SUN OR SHADE**

◖ ◗ **MODERATE TO REGULAR WATER**

◈ **FRUIT (SEEDS) AND FOLIAGE ARE
POISONOUS IF INGESTED**

Taxus baccata

Yews are conifers, but they do not bear cones. Instead, they produce fleshy, scarlet (rarely yellow), cup-shaped, single-seeded, berrylike fruit. In general, yews are darker green, more formal-looking, and more tolerant of shade and moisture than most cultivated conifers. Long-lived. Only the female plants produce berries, and many do so without male plants nearby. Excellent for hedges and screens. Yews can be moved without harm even when large, but since they grow at a slow to moderate rate, big plants are luxury items.

T. baccata. ENGLISH YEW. Tree or shrub. Zones A3; 3–9, 14–24. From Europe, North Africa, and western Asia. To 25–40 ft. or taller, 15–25 ft. wide, with broad, low crown. Needles dark green and glossy above, pale beneath; spirally arranged. Far more common than the species are garden varieties, including the following.

'Adpressa'. Usually sold as *T. brevifolia*, a name correctly belonging to the native Western yew. Dense shrub to 4–5 ft. tall, 6–8 ft. wide.

'Aurea'. Broad pyramid to 25 ft. tall, 12 ft. wide after many years. New foliage is golden yellow from spring to autumn, then turns green.

'Fastigiata' ('Stricta'). IRISH YEW. Dark green column to 15–30 ft. tall, 3–10 ft. wide. Has larger needles and more crowded, upright branches than the species. Branches tend to spread near top, especially in snowy regions or where moisture is plentiful. Branches can be tied together with wire. Plants that outgrow their space can be reduced by heading back and thinning; old wood sprouts freely. There is a form with yellowish white variegation.

'Repandens'. SPREADING ENGLISH YEW. Long, horizontal, spreading branches make 2–4-ft.-tall groundcover; extend to 8–10 ft. after many years. Useful low foundation plant. Will arch over a wall.

T. cuspidata. JAPANESE YEW. Tree or shrub. Zones A2, A3; 2–6, 14–17. In its native Japan, a tree to 50 ft. tall; in North America, usually seen as a compact, pyramidal tree to 10–25 ft., half as wide. Can be kept lower by pinching new growth. Fruits heavily. Most useful yew in cold-winter areas east of Cascades. Will succeed in shaded areas of Rocky Mountain gardens. Needles dark green above, tinged yellowish beneath; usually arranged in two rows along twigs to make a flat or V-shaped spray.

'Capitata'. Plants sold with this name are probably ordinary *T. cuspidata*.

'Nana'. Often sold as *T. brevifolia*. Grows 1–4 in. a year; can reach 3 ft. high, 6 ft. wide in 20 years. Serves as a good low barrier or foundation plant. 'Nana Aurescens' has bright yellow new growth. 'Dwarf Bright Gold' has yellow foliage and does better than most in full sun. 'Emerald Spreader' is a useful groundcover, growing to 30 in. high and 8–10 ft. wide.

T. × media. Shrubs. Zones 2–6, 14–17. Group of hybrids between *T. baccata* and *T. cuspidata*; intermediate between the two in color and texture. Of the dozens of selections available, these are among the most widely offered.

'Brownii'. Compact, rounded plant to 6–8 ft. tall and 8–10 ft. wide. Good dense hedge.

'Hatfieldii'. Broad column or pyramid. Reaches 12 ft. tall and 10 ft. wide after 20 years.

'Hicksii'. Upright-growing variety to 10–12 ft. tall, 3–4 ft. wide; grows larger with age.

CARE

Yews take many soils but do not thrive in strongly alkaline or strongly acid conditions. Do not take extreme heat, and reflected heat from a hot south or west wall will burn foliage. Even cold-hardy kinds show needle damage when exposed to dry winds, very low temperatures. Can take much shearing and pruning, since they sprout from bare wood. Subject to vine weevils, scale insects, and spider mites. During prolonged spells of hot, dry weather, hose off plants every 2 weeks.

Tecoma
Bignoniaceae
EVERGREEN SHRUBS, TREES,
AND VINES

✂ **ZONES VARY BY SPECIES**

☼ ◐ **FULL SUN OR LIGHT SHADE**

◖ **MODERATE WATER, EXCEPT
AS NOTED**

🦋 **FLOWERS ATTRACT BUTTERFLIES
AND HUMMINGBIRDS**

Tecoma stans

Various trumpet vines once lumped together as *Tecoma* now have different names. Remaining in this genus are several showy shrubs, one of which can be grown as a vine, another as a tree. All have 2-in.-long, trumpet-shaped flowers in the yellow-orange-red range and leaves divided featherwise into many leaflets. Heat-tolerant.

T. × alata (T. × smithii). ORANGE BELLS. Shrub. Zones 12, 13, 21–24. To 8 ft. tall, 4–5 ft. wide, with bright green foliage and orange flowers through-

out warm weather. Tolerates light frost; may die to ground in a hard freeze but recovers quickly in warm weather. Some consider 'Orange Jubilee' to be a selection of this plant; others identify it as a hybrid between *T. capensis* and *T. stans*.

T. capensis (Tecomaria capensis). CAPE HONEY-SUCKLE. Vine or shrub. Zones 12, 13, 20–24; H1, H2; with protection in 14, 15, 18, 19. From South Africa. If tied to a support, can scramble to 15–30 ft.; with hard pruning, makes an upright shrub 6–8 ft. tall, 4–5 ft. wide. Shiny dark green leaflets give it a fine-textured look. Brilliant orange-red flowers in compact clusters appear from fall into spring (almost all year in Hawaii). Takes wind, salt air. Use as espalier, bank cover (especially good on hot, steep slopes), barrier hedge. Little water. 'Aurea' has lighter green foliage and yellow flowers; it is somewhat less vigorous than the species. 'Buff Gold' has golden orange blossoms.

T. garrocha. ARGENTINE TECOMA. Shrub. Zones 12, 13, 21–24. From Argentina. To 5 ft. (possibly 10 ft.) tall and wide. Clusters of salmon to orange blossoms throughout warm weather. Reacts to freezes like *T. × alata*.

T. hybrids. Zones 12, 13, 21–24; H1, H2. Several new, complex hybrids, usually involving *T. stans*, which they resemble in form and foliage, are becoming available. They include 'Crimson Flare', with red flowers; 'Orange Jubilee', with scarlet-orange blooms; and 'Solar Flare', with orange flowers. They grow about 6–8 ft. tall and wide in a season if cut back or frozen; about twice that if not. 'Sierra Apricot' is more compact to 3 ft. high by 6 ft. wide and has light yellow-orange blooms.

T. ricasoliana. See *Podranea ricasoliana*.

T. stans (Stenolobium stans). YELLOW BELLS, YELLOW TRUMPET FLOWER, YELLOW ELDER. Zones 12, 13, 21–24; H1, H2; except as noted. Native from southern U.S. to Guatemala. In mildest climates, can be trained as a tree. Where frosts are common, it is usually a large shrub. Wood may die back in hard freezes, but new

T

growth comes on quickly. Can reach 25 ft. tall, 10–20 ft. wide. Large clusters of bright yellow flowers from late spring to early winter. Good for boundary planting, big shrub border, screening. Needs heat, deep soil, fairly heavy feeding. 'Gold Star' is a profuse bloomer sometimes used as an annual in cold winter areas. It grows about 3 ft. tall and wide in its first season, and may reach 8 ft. tall and wide if not cut back or frozen.

T. s. angustata. Zones 12, 13. Native from Arizona to Texas and Mexico. To 4–10 ft. tall and 3–8 ft. wide. Narrow leaflets. Blooms from midspring to late fall. Needs less water and fertilizer than the species.

CARE

Take drought but look best with periodic soakings. Tip-pinch young growth to induce branching, reduce tendency toward legginess. Cut faded flowers to prolong bloom and lessen production of seedpods. Prune to remove unwanted seedpods and wood damaged by freezes.

Tellima grandiflora

FRINGE CUPS
Saxifragaceae
PERENNIAL

☀ ZONES A3; 2–9, 14–17
◐ ● PARTIAL OR FULL SHADE
● REGULAR WATER

Tellima grandiflora

A native from central California to southern Alaska often confused with *Tiarella*. Grows to 2½ ft. high, 1½ ft. wide. Creeping rootstock sends up leafstalks to 8 in. long set with rounded

to triangular, lobed, light green, softly hairy leaves. Foliage is evergreen where winters are mild. Small, urn-shaped spring flowers with tiny fringed petals open green, age to deep red; though not showy, they're attractively arranged along tall, slender stems. Provide rich, moist soil. Choice plant to combine with ferns in a woodland garden. Spreads manageably by seed.

Ternstroemia gymnanthera

(T. japonica)
Pentaphylacaceae
EVERGREEN SHRUB

☀ ZONES 4–9, 12–24
◐ ● PARTIAL OR FULL SHADE
●● ●● REGULAR TO AMPLE WATER

Ternstroemia gymnanthera
'Variegata'

Camellia relative from China and Japan grown for its glossy, leathery foliage. May eventually reach 6–8 ft. but is usually seen as a rounded plant 3–4 ft. tall, 4–6 ft. wide. Red-stalked leaves are rounded oval to narrowly oval, bronzy red when new; color at maturity varies. In deep shade, mature foliage tends to be dark green; with some sun, it may be bronzy green to purplish red. Red tints are deeper in cold weather. Creamy yellow, ½-in. summer flowers are fragrant but not showy. Fruits (uncommon on small plants) resemble small yellow to red-orange holly berries or cherries; they split to reveal black seeds. Use as basic landscaping shrub, informal hedge, tub or poolside plant. Cut foliage keeps well.

CARE

Grow in well-drained soil. Leaves turn yellow if soil isn't acid enough; fertilize with acid plant food if necessary. Tip-pinch to encourage compact growth. Good companion for shade-loving plants. Tolerates full sun in cool-summer climates.

Tetraneuris

(Hymenoxys)
Asteraceae
PERENNIALS

☀ ZONES VARY BY SPECIES
☀ FULL SUN
◔ ● LITTLE TO MODERATE WATER

Tetraneuris acaulis

Taprooted plants with narrow, grassy, aromatic leaves that form small, evergreen foliage tufts about 8 in. high and 1 ft. wide. Blooms during warm months (nearly all year in mild-winter climates). Yellow daisies to 1½ in. wide have rays with notched edges; blossoms are usually carried singly on stems. Give well-drained soil. Cut off faded flower spikes to neaten plants and prolong bloom. Tolerant of heat, cold, drought. With some moisture, will reseed. Attractive in pots.

T. acaulis. ANGELITA DAISY. Zones 1–3, 7–14, 18–24. Native to plains from Canada to Texas. Golden yellow flowers on stems to 1 ft. high.

T. scaposa. CLUSTERED GOLDFLOWER. Zones 2, 3, 10–14, 18–24. Native from Colorado to Kansas, south to New Mexico and Texas. Leaves are sometimes lobed. Bright yellow flowers on stems to 16 in. high; rays may have red-brown veins on undersides.

Teucrium

GERMANDER
Lamiaceae
SHRUBBY PERENNIALS

☀ ZONES VARY BY SPECIES
☀ FULL SUN
● MODERATE WATER

Teucrium fruticans

Mediterranean natives with aromatic foliage and whorls of little flowers. These are tough plants that endure poor, rocky soils; they can't stand wet or poorly drained soils but will tolerate regular watering where drainage is good.

T. cossonii majoricum (T. majoricum). Zones 7–9, 14–24. Narrow, silvery gray leaves form a mound to 8 in. high, 1½ ft. wide. Virtually continuous show of small, rosy purple, honey-scented flowers in dense heads (most profuse in late spring, early summer). Good rock garden plant or small-scale groundcover. Also sold as *T. majoricum* and *T. cussonii*; a very similar plant is *T. polium pii-fontanii*.

T. fruticans. BUSH GERMANDER. Zones 4–24. Loose, silvery-stemmed plant to 4–8 ft. tall and wide (or wider). Gray-green leaves have silvery white undersides, giving the plant an overall silvery gray appearance. Blooms almost year-round, bearing lavender-blue flower spikes at branch ends. Thin and cut back before spring growth begins. 'Azureum' has deeper blue flowers than the species; 'Compactum', also with dark blue blooms, grows just 3 ft. high and wide.

T. × lucidrys (T. chamaedrys). Zones 2–24. To 1 ft. high and 2 ft. wide, with many

T

upright, woody-based stems densely clothed in toothed, dark green leaves. Red-purple or white summer flowers in loose spikes (white-flowered form is looser). Attracts bees. Use as edging, foreground, low clipped hedge, or small-scale ground-cover. Shear back once or twice a year to keep neat and force side branching. 'Prostratum' is 4–6 in. high, spreading to 3 ft. or more.

T. marum. CAT THYME. Zones 3–9, 14–24. To 1½ ft. high and wide. Upright, densely clustered stems are closely set with tiny gray-green leaves. Blooms profusely in summer, when stems are covered with many deep pink or purplish flowers in 2-in. spikes. Attracts cats.

Thalictrum
MEADOW RUE
Ranunculaceae
PERENNIALS

✂ **ZONES 2–10, 14–17**
☼ **LIGHT SHADE**
💧 **REGULAR WATER**

Thalictrum

Foliage clumps resemble those of columbine (*Aquilegia*). Plants typically bloom in late spring or summer, sending up sparsely leafed stems topped by puffs of small flowers, each consisting of four sepals and a prominent cluster of stamens. Superb for airy effect; delicate tracery of leaves and flowers is particularly effective against a dark green background. Offers a pleasing contrast to sturdier perennials. Foliage is good in arrangements.

T. aquilegiifolium. From Europe and northern Asia. Grows

to 2–3 ft. high, 1 ft. wide, with bluish green foliage. Earliest of the meadow rues to bloom: clouds of fluffy stamens (the white or greenish sepals drop off) appear for a couple of weeks in mid- to late spring. Rosy lilac is the usual color, but white and purple selections are available. If left in place, spent flowers are followed by attractive, long-lasting seed heads. Heat-tolerant.

T. delavayi (T. dipterocarpum). CHINESE MEADOW RUE. From western China. Grows to 3–4 ft. (even 6 ft.) tall, 1½–2 ft. wide, with thin, dark purple stems that need support. Green foliage. Lavender to violet sepals, yellow stamens. 'Hewitt's Double' has double lilac-colored flowers (one row of sepals, another of modified stamens that resemble petals); bloom continues for 2 months or longer.

T. flavum glaucum (T. speciosissimum). DUSTY MEADOW RUE. From Spain, Portugal, and northwest Africa. Upright growth to 3–5 ft. tall and 2 ft. wide; stems are mauve tinged in youth. Powdery blue-green leaves are divided into many leaflets. In summer, plant is topped with clouds of small, fragrant yellow flowers. Plants may need staking.

T. rochebrunianum. From Japan. To 4–6 ft. tall, 1½–2 ft. wide, with sturdy stems that don't need staking. Flowers consist of white or lavender sepals and pale yellow stamens. 'Lavender Mist', with violet sepals, is a superior selection.

CARE
Most meadow rues need some winter chill; all thrive in dappled sunlight at woodland edges, tolerate full sun in cooler climates. Protect from wind. Divide clumps every 4 or 5 years.

Delicate green leaves and full sprays of tiny lavender flowers make meadow rue a choice companion for ferns and 'Shooting Star' hydrangea.

Thevetia
Apocynaceae
EVERGREEN SHRUBS OR TREES

✂ **ZONES VARY BY SPECIES**
☼ **FULL SUN**
💧 **REGULAR WATER**
☠ **ALL PARTS ARE POISONOUS IF INGESTED**

Thevetia thevetioides

Fast-growing plants with narrow, glossy deep green leaves and clusters of showy, funnel-shaped flowers at branch ends. Thrive in heat; can take very little frost.

T. neriifolia (T. peruviana). YELLOW OLEANDER, LUCKY NUT. Zones 13, 21–24; H1, H2. From tropical America. In frost-less areas, it can be trained as a tree to 20–30 ft. tall and wide. Where frosts are light or rare, an 8-ft. (or larger) shrub; makes a good hedge, screen, or background plant. Fragrant, 2–3-in., yellow to apricot flowers bloom from early summer into fall (all year where winters are warm). Small (1 in.), squat, four-angled fruits are red at first, aging to black. Provide good drainage and wind protection. In colder part of range, mound sand 6–12 in. deep around base of stem. Dies back in freezes but recovers quickly; new growth will bloom the same year.

T. thevetioides. GIANT THEVETIA. Zones 22–24; H2; with protection in 12, 13. From Mexico. Open growth to 12 ft. or more tall and wide. Leaves are darker green than those of *T. neriifolia*; they resemble oleander (*Nerium*) leaves but are corrugated, heavily veined beneath. Large clusters of brilliant yellow, 4-in. flowers bloom

from late spring through fall. Desert heat wilts flowers in summer. Makes an attractive patio tree, but fruit (2½ in. wide, green ripening to black) can be a litter problem.

Thuja
ARBORVITAE
Cupressaceae
EVERGREEN TREES OR SHRUBS

✂ **ZONES VARY BY SPECIES**
☼◑ **PARTIAL SHADE IN HOTTEST CLIMATES**
💧💧 **MODERATE TO REGULAR WATER**

Thuja occidentalis 'Smaragd'

Neat, symmetrical plants are often trimmed into geometrical forms—globes, cones, cylinders. Juvenile foliage is feathery, with small, needlelike leaves; mature foliage is scalelike, carried in flat sprays. Foliage in better-known varieties is often yellow-green or bright golden yellow. Small cones are green or bluish green, turning to brownish. Arborvitaes will take both damp and fairly dry soils, but they grow best in well-drained soil.

T. occidentalis. AMERICAN ARBORVITAE. Zones A2, A3; 1–9, 15–17, 21–24; H1, H2. Native to eastern U.S. Upright, open growth to 30–60 ft. tall, 10–15 ft. wide, with branches that tend to turn up at ends. Bright green to yellowish green leaf sprays. Foliage often turns brown in severe cold, will scorch badly in winter in coldest, windiest Rocky Mountain gardens unless plants are shaded, watered. Needs moist air to look its best. Spider mites may cause trouble. Basic species is seldom seen, but smaller garden varieties are common. Among these, taller ones make good

T

informal or clipped screens, while lower kinds are often used along walks or walls, as hedges. The following are some good varieties among many.

'Brandon'. Fast growth to 12–15 ft. tall, 6–8 ft wide. Useful as screen.

'Degroot's Spire'. Narrow green column to 10–20 ft. tall and 4–5 ft. wide. Good narrow screen.

'Douglasii Pyramidalis'. Vigorous-growing pyramid to 15 ft. tall (or taller), 10 ft. wide.

'Fastigiata' ('Pyramidalis', 'Columnaris'). Dense, columnar growth to 25 ft. tall, 5 ft. wide. Tends to get a bit unruly as it grows larger, with branches spreading out; they can be tied together to keep plant looking neat. Set 4 ft. apart for screen. Especially valuable in damp soils and cold regions, where few other columnar choices are available.

'Golden Globe'. Dense, rounded growth to 3–5 ft. tall and wide. Bright golden foliage contrasts beautifully with deep green or blue-green evergreens.

'Hetz Midget'. Globe-shaped, with rich green foliage. Not likely to exceed 3–4 ft. tall and wide.

'Lutea' ('George Peabody'). Narrow, conical tree to 30–35 ft. tall and 10–15 ft. wide. Soft yellow new growth ages to gold; holds color through most of the season.

'Nigra'. Dense dark green cone to 20–30 ft. tall and 4–5 ft. wide.

'Rheingold' ('Improved Ell-wangeriana Aurea'). Cone-shaped, slow-growing, bright golden plant with a mixture of scale and needle foliage. Even very old plants seldom exceed 6 ft. tall and wide.

'Smaragd' ('Emerald', 'Emerald Green'). Neat, dense-growing, narrow cone to 10–15 ft. tall and 3–4 ft. wide. Holds its color throughout winter.

'Spiralis'. Fast-growing tree to 30–45 ft. tall and 10–15 ft. wide, with dark green foliage on branchlets that spiral around the branches for a full, ferny look.

'Sunkist'. Grows slowly to form a cone 4–6 ft. tall and 2–3 ft. wide, with bright golden foliage. Popular in landscapes and for bonsai.

'Woodwardii'. Widely grown dense, globe-shaped shrub with rich green color. May attain considerable size with age but stays small over a reasonably long period; to 4 ft. tall and wide in 10 years.

'Yellow Ribbon'. To 8–10 ft. tall, 2–3 ft. wide, with bright yellow foliage throughout the year.

T. orientalis. See *Platycladus orientalis*.

T. plicata. WESTERN RED CEDAR. Zones A3; 1–9, 14–24. Native from coastal Northern California northward to Alaska and inland to Montana. Plants grown from inland seed are hardy anywhere in the West; those from coastal seed are less hardy to cold. Can reach over 200 ft. tall in coastal belt of Washington, but more typical garden size is 50–100 ft. tall, 25–60 ft. wide. Slender, drooping branchlets are closely set with dark green leaf sprays. Single trees are magnificent in large lawns, but bear in mind that their lower branches spread quite broadly—and that the trees lose their characteristic beauty if these are cut off. Varieties include the following:

'Collyer's Gold'. Slow-growing, upright shrub to 4–6 ft. tall, half as wide, with dense foliage that emerges yellow and turns bright green with age.

'Green Giant'. Can grow 3–5 ft. a year, ultimately reaching 30–50 ft. tall and 10–20 ft. wide. Shear as a tall hedge or use as a tall screen.

'Spring Grove'. To 8–10 ft. tall in 5 years; ultimately to 40–60 ft. tall and 10–15 ft. wide. Can be sheared as a hedge.

'Stoneham Gold'. Dense, slow-growing dwarf to 6 ft. tall, 2 ft. wide. Orange-yellow new growth.

'Sunshine'. Bright golden foliage on a fast-growing, upright plant to 15–30 ft. tall and 10–15 ft. wide. Color develops best in full sun.

'Whipcord'. Unusual dwarf with threadlike, cascading, bright green branches. Forms a 5-ft.-tall, 4-ft.-wide mound. Turns bronze in winter.

'Zebrina'. Slow grower; same size as the species. Foliage is banded in green and golden yellow. Often sold as 'Aurea', a less commonly seen variety with green foliage tinted golden.

Thujopsis dolabrata

FALSE ARBORVITAE, DEER-HORN CEDAR, HIBA CEDAR
Cupressaceae
EVERGREEN TREE

✿ **ZONES 3B–7, 14–17**

☀ ◐ **PARTIAL SHADE IN HOTTEST CLIMATES**

◖ **MODERATE TO REGULAR WATER**

Thujopsis dolabrata

Native to Japan. Pyramidal, coniferous, often shrubby; very slow growing to 30–50 ft. tall and 10–20 ft. wide. Foliage resembles that of *Thuja*, but the sprays are coarser, glossy, branching in staghorn effect. Best where summers are cool and humid. Plant as a single tree where foliage details can be appreciated. Slow growth makes it a good container plant. 'Nana' is a dwarf variety to 3 ft. high and wide; 'Variegata' has white branch tips that tend to revert to green.

Slow-growing conifers like false arborvitae make handsome container subjects, providing an evergreen backdrop for smaller pots of flowers. Flank an entry with potted dwarf conifers, or mix conifers in a variety of shapes and colors in an all-conifer border.

Thunbergia

Acanthaceae
ANNUAL OR PERENNIAL VINE

✿ **ZONES VARY BY SPECIES**

☀ ◐ **PARTIAL SHADE IN HOTTEST CLIMATES**

◖ **REGULAR WATER**

Thunbergia alata

Tropical, typically twining plants noted for showy flowers. Some of the perennial sorts grow fast enough to bloom the first season and can be treated as annuals. Those grown as perennials are evergreen in mildest climates. In cooler part of range, tops may be killed by light frost, but roots usually stay alive to send up new stems. Provide rich, well-drained soil. Good greenhouse plants.

T. alata. BLACK-EYED SUSAN VINE. Perennial vine grown as annual anywhere; may live over in Zones 23, 24; H2. To 10 ft., with triangular, medium green leaves. Blooms all summer long; tubular flowers flare out to 1 in. wide, come in white and a variety of colors, all with purple-black throat. Start seed indoors; set plants out in good soil in a sunny spot as soon as weather warms. Display in hanging basket or window box, use as groundcover, or train on strings or low trellis. 'African Sunset' blooms in shades of red-blushed yellow, salmon, rose, copper, and terracotta; flowers open in pastel shades and deepen as they age, so each plant shows many colors at once. 'Lemon Star' ('Sunny Lemon Star') has soft yellow flowers that bloom over a long period.

T. erecta. KING'S MANTLE. Vining shrub. Zones 16, 21–24;

H1, H2. Grows to 6 ft. tall and wide. Erect, sometimes twining, with dark green, ovate to oblong leaves. Velvety dark blue flowers with orange or cream throats appear in joints of upper leaves throughout the summer and fall (for much of the year in Hawaii). 'Alba' is a white-flowered form.

T. grandiflora. SKY FLOWER. Perennial vine. Zones 16, 21–24; H1, H2. Vigorous growth to 20 ft. or more (as much as 80 ft. in Hawaii), with 8-in., heart-shaped, medium to dark green leaves. Slightly drooping clusters of tubular, flaring, sky blue flowers to 3 in. across appear through summer and into fall (throughout much of the year in Hawaii). Use on arbor, large trellis, or wire fence; casts dense shade. There is a white variety.

T. gregorii (T. gibsonii). ORANGE CLOCK VINE. Perennial vine. Zones 21–24; H1, H2; with protection in Zones 13, 16, 17; anywhere as annual. Twines to 6 ft. tall or sprawls over ground to cover a 12-ft. circle. Gray-green, triangular, tooth-edged leaves. Tubular, flaring, bright orange flowers are borne singly on 4-in. stems. Blooms nearly all year long in mildest climates, in summer where winters are cool. Set plants 3–4 ft. apart to cover a wire fence, about 6 ft. apart as groundcover. Plant it above a wall and let it cascade down; or grow in hanging basket. Showy and easy to grow.

T. mysorensis. Perennial vine. Zones 16, 21–24; H1, H2. Tall climber (15–35 ft.), with narrow, elliptical dark green leaves. Spectacular, pendent, 1–1½-ft.-long clusters of gaping flowers that are red on the outside, yellow within. Blooms much of the year, most heavily in spring. Train on pergola, arbor, or other overhead structure to permit flowers to dangle. Protect from frost.

To quickly cover an unattractive chain-link fence, plant orange clock vines every 3 to 4 feet along its length.

Thymophylla
(Dyssodia)
Asteraceae
PERENNIALS, SOME GROWN AS ANNUALS

✀ **ZONES 8–14, 18–23**

☀ **FULL SUN**

◐ **MODERATE WATER**

Thymophylla tenuiloba

These low-growing plants with little yellow daisies start easily and quickly from seed planted in flats or sown in place. Not particular about soil type but must have good drainage.

T. acerosa. PRICKLY-LEAF DOGWEED. Shrubby perennial. Native from Nevada and Utah to Texas and Mexico. Much-branched, mounding plant to 6–8 in. high, 1 ft. wide. Covers itself with daisies from late spring to fall. Sharp-pointed, needle-thin, medium green leaves. Good in beds, in cactus gardens, as edging, as informal groundcover. Especially useful for erosion control on slopes.

T. pentachaeta. GOLDEN DYSSODIA, FIVE-NEEDLE DOG-WEED. Perennial. Native from California and Nevada to southern Texas, Mexico. To 4–6 in. high and wide, with open, sparse appearance. Needlelike dark green leaves; stems are covered with fine silky hairs. Blooms most profusely in late spring, sporadically later in the year. Short-lived. Use like *T. acerosa*.

T. tenuiloba. DAHLBERG DAISY, GOLDEN FLEECE. Short-lived perennial usually grown as annual. Heat-loving plant native from Texas to Florida and Mexico. Mounding growth to 1 ft. high, 1½ ft. wide. Divided, threadlike leaves make dark green background for flowers

that look like miniature golden marguerites (*Anthemis*). Blooms from early summer to fall. Use for mass display or pockets of color. When plants become ragged with age, pull them out. In warm-winter areas, can be planted in fall for winter-to-spring bloom.

Thymus
THYME
Lamiaceae
SHRUBBY PERENNIALS

✀ **ZONES 1–24, EXCEPT AS NOTED**

☀◐ **LIGHT SHADE IN HOTTEST CLIMATES**

◐◑ **LITTLE TO MODERATE WATER**

✺ **ATTRACT BEES, BENEFICIALS**

Thymus

Diminutive Mediterranean members of the mint family with tiny, scented leaves and masses of little flowers in whorls. Well suited to an herb garden or rock garden; prostrate, mat-forming types make good small-space groundcovers. Attractive to bees. Botanical names are constantly undergoing revision and often confusing.

T. camphoratus. CAMPHOR THYME. Zones 7–9, 14–24. To 1½ ft. high and wide, with narrow gray-green leaves that smell like camphor. Blooms in late spring, early summer; flower clusters are woolly, rosy purplish bracts and tiny white flowers.

T. cherlerioides. SILVER NEEDLE THYME. Sprawling groundcover to 2 in. high and 12 in. wide. Small, silvery leaves have soft texture and can take light traffic. Spills over walls or sides of containers.

T. × citriodorus. LEMON THYME. Variable hybrid with erect or spreading growth to

6–12. high, 2 ft. wide. Lemon-scented leaves. Pale lilac flowers in summer. Leaves of 'Argenteus' are splashed with silver, those of 'Aureus' with gold. Low-growing 'Goldstream' has yellow variegated leaves. 'Lemon Frost' has white flowers on a 3–6-in.-high plant. 'Lime' has lime green foliage. 'Doone Valley', with yellow-spotted leaves, reaches only 5 in. high.

T. herba-barona. CARAWAY-SCENTED THYME. Fast growing to 2–4 in. high, 2 ft. or more wide; stems root as they spread. Forms a dense mat of wiry stems set with widely spaced ovate to lance-shaped, dark green leaves with caraway fragrance. Clusters of rose-pink flowers in midsummer.

T. lanuginosus. See *T. serpyllum*.

T. praecox arcticus. See *T. polytrichus britannicus*.

T. polytrichus britannicus (T. praecox arcticus). CREEPING THYME. Zones A2, A3; 1–24. Usually sold as *T. serpyllum*. Variable species 1–3 in. high and 6 in. to 3 ft. wide. Round leaves range from glossy green to soft gray and can be variegated or have golden highlights. Flowers come in various shades of pink and white.

There are two basic types of creeping thyme: those that grow a foot or more wide and are suited to filling large spaces, and those that grow slowly to 6–12 in. wide and are more suited to filling between pavers where foot traffic is light. The first group includes pink flowering 'Coccineum', 'Creeping Pink,' and 'Reiter'. The second group includes 1-in.-high 'Minus', nonblooming 'Elfin', 'Pink Chintz', 'White Moss', and 'Mint Thyme'.

T. pulegioides. MOTHER OF THYME, PENNSYLVANIA DUTCH TEA THYME. Fast-growing plant to 1 ft. high and wide with shiny green, oval, lemon-scented leaves. Dark purple to white flowers in summer.

T. serpyllum (T. pseudolanuginosus, T. lanuginosus). WOOLLY THYME. Zones A2, A3; 1–24. Sometimes sold as *T. praecox arcticus* 'Pseudolanuginosus'. Forms a flat to undulating mat 2–3 in. high, 3 ft. wide. Stems are densely clothed with elliptical, woolly gray leaves. Pinkish flowers appear in leaf

T

joints in midsummer. Becomes slightly rangy in winter. Use in rock crevices, between stepping-stones, spilling over a bank or a raised bed, or covering small patches of ground. 'Hall's Woolly' is a profuse bloomer.

T. vulgaris. COMMON THYME. Variable plant to 1 ft. high, 2 ft. wide, with gray-green, narrow to oval leaves. White to lilac flowers in late spring, early summer. Low edging for flower, vegetable, or herb garden. Good container plant. Use leaves fresh or dried for seasoning fish, shellfish, poultry stuffing, soups, and vegetables. 'Argenteus', called silver thyme, has leaves variegated with silver. 'Hi-Ho' has even more pronounced silver variegation and is more compact. 'Italian Oregano Thyme' has a strong oregano flavor. 'Orange Balsam' has narrow, orange-scented leaves.

CARE

Provide light, well-drained soil. Shear or cut back established plants to keep them compact. Easy to propagate from cuttings taken in early summer.

Tiarella

FOAMFLOWER, SUGAR-SCOOP
Saxifragaceae
PERENNIALS

✎ **ZONES VARY BY SPECIES**

☼ ● **PARTIAL OR FULL SHADE**

💧 **REGULAR WATER**

Tiarella 'Pink Skyrocket'

Clump-forming plants to about 1½ ft. high (in bloom) and 1½– 2 ft. wide; spread by rhizomes (and by aboveground runners, in the case of *T. cordifolia*). Leaves arise directly from rhizomes;

they are evergreen but may change color in autumn. Selections with year-round colorful foliage are becoming popular; look for new introductions in addition to those described below. Narrow, erect flower stems carry many small white or pink flowers. Useful in shady rock gardens; make pretty groundcovers but will not bear foot traffic.

T. cordifolia. FOAMFLOWER. Zones A3; 1–9, 14–24. Rapid spreader from eastern North America. Light green, lobed, 4-in. leaves show red-and-yellow fall color. Creamy white flowers on foot-high stalks. 'Oak Leaf' has deeply lobed leaves and pink flowers. 'Running Tapestry' has deeply lobed leaves with dark purple to maroon veins.

T. selections and hybrids. Zones 1–9, 14–21. Many of the choicest foamflowers are of uncertain origin. 'Cygnet' has star-shaped leaves with purple markings along the veins; its white flowers open from pink buds. In 'Mint Chocolate', deeply lobed leaves have a central zone of deep brownish purple; flowers are pinkish white. 'Neon Lights' has large, deeply cut leaves with wide, black centers and bright green edges. 'Pink Skyrocket' has large, fragrant, light pink flowers and deeply cut leaves with a small black center; leaves turn almost black in winter.

T. trifoliata unifoliata (T. unifoliata). SUGAR-SCOOP, WESTERN FOAMFLOWER. Zones A3; 1–7, 14–17. Native from Alaska to Northern California, east to the Rocky Mountains. Dark green leaves divided into three tooth-edged leaflets. Tiny white flowers on 1½-ft. stalks are followed by little fruits that look like sugar scoops.

T. wherryi (T. cordifolia collina). Zones 2–9, 14–21. From southeastern U.S. Like *T. cordifolia* but lacks aboveground runners, is slower to spread. Flower clusters are somewhat more slender, often tinged pink.

Foamflower can live for years in the same container.

Tibouchina

Melastomataceae
EVERGREEN SHRUBS

✎ **ZONES VARY BY SPECIES**

☼ ◑ **PARTIAL SHADE IN HOTTEST CLIMATES**

💧 **REGULAR WATER**

Tibouchina heteromalla

Brazilian natives with showy flowers at branch ends and broadly oval, prominently veined, velvety leaves.

T. heteromalla. SILVER LEAFED PRINCESS FLOWER. Zones 16, 17, 21–24; H1, H2. Shrub. To 4–6 ft. tall and wide. Silvery green leaves with silver undersides. Dark purple, 1– 1½-in. flowers in 1½-ft.-long clusters from early autumn into winter.

T. urvilleana (T. semidecandra). PRINCESS FLOWER. Zones 16, 17, 21–24; H1, H2; with protection in 14, 15. Fast, rather open growth to 5–18 ft. tall, 3–10 ft. wide. Branch tips, buds, new growth shaded with satiny hairs in orange and bronzy red. Green leaves, often edged red. Older leaves add spots of orange, red, or yellow, especially in winter. Brilliant royal purple, 3-in. flowers appear intermittently from late spring into winter. Prune lightly and feed after each bloom cycle. Has naturalized in Hawaii, forming thickets in wet areas. Can be used as an indoor/outdoor plant in colder climates.

CARE

Prefer slightly acid, fast-draining soil. Apply mulch to keep root zone cool. Protect from strong winds, hard frosts. Pinch young growth to induce branching; prune out damaged or badly

placed branches before new growth begins. If flower buds fail to open, check for geranium (tobacco) budworm.

Tigridia pavonia

TIGER FLOWER, MEXICAN SHELL FLOWER
Iridaceae
PERENNIAL FROM BULB

✎ **ZONES 4–24; H1; OR DIG AND STORE**

☼ ◑ **PARTIAL SHADE IN HOTTEST CLIMATES**

💧 **REGULAR WATER DURING GROWTH AND BLOOM**

Tigridia pavonia

Mexican native with flashy summertime flowers. Fans of narrow, swordlike, ribbed leaves to 1½ ft. long send up erect, 2½-ft. flower stems bearing triangular blossoms to 6 in. across. Flowers have three large outer segments in orange, red, pink, yellow, or white; the cuplike center and three small inner segments are usually boldly blotched with contrasting color. (Immaculata strain is unspotted.) Each flower lasts for only one day, but the bloom period usually lasts for several weeks.

CARE

Plant in spring, after weather warms up (night temperatures should not fall below 60°F/ 16°C). Plant in well-drained soil, setting bulbs 2–4 in. deep, 4– 8 in. apart. Stop watering after flowering is finished and when leaves turn yellow. Can be left in ground where hardy; divide every 3 or 4 years, digging in fall and waiting until spring planting time to separate bulbs and replant. Spider mites are main pest (they cause yellowish or whitish streaks on foliage); begin control when leaves are several inches long. Gophers are fond of the bulbs. Beyond hardiness range, dig bulbs after leaves yellow and store as for gladiolus; or grow in pots and protect in winter.

Tilia

LINDEN
Malvaceae
DECIDUOUS TREES

⚹ **ZONES 1–17, EXCEPT AS NOTED**
☼ **FULL SUN**
💧 **REGULAR WATER**

Tilia × flavescens 'Dropmore'

Dense trees with stately good looks and moderate growth rate. All have irregularly heart-shaped leaves and small, fragrant, yellowish white flowers in drooping clusters in late spring, early summer. Flowers develop into nutlets, each with an attached papery bract. In cold-winter areas, fall color varies from negligible to good yellow.

T. americana. AMERICAN LINDEN, BASSWOOD. Native to eastern North America. To 40–60 ft. tall, 20–25 ft. wide. Straight-trunked tree with a narrow crown. Dull dark green leaves. 'Redmond' is a pyramidal form with glossy foliage.

T. cordata. LITTLE-LEAF LINDEN. Native to Europe. Dense pyramid to 30–50 ft. tall and 15–30 ft. wide. Leaves dark green above, silvery beneath. Excellent lawn or street tree. Given room to develop its crown, it can be a fine patio shade tree (but expect bees in flowering season). Can be sheared into hedges. Very tolerant of city conditions. Selected forms include 'Corinthian', which grows into a narrow pyramid 45 ft. tall and 15 ft. wide; 'Greenspire', with an oval to pyramidal canopy; 'Olympic', which forms a broad, symmetrical pyramid; 'Shamrock', which also forms a symmetrical pyramid; and 'Summer Sprite', a slow-growing dwarf to just 20 ft. tall, 10 ft. wide.

T. × euchlora. CRIMEAN LINDEN. Hybrid derived from *T. cordata*. To 25–35 ft. (perhaps eventually to 50 ft.) tall, almost as wide. Slightly pendulous branches. Rich glossy green leaves have paler undersides. Casts more open shade than *T. cordata*.

T. × flavescens 'Glenleven' (T. cordata 'Glenleven'). A fast grower to 65 ft. tall, 40 ft. wide, with a loosely pyramidal or oval canopy.

T. mongolica 'Harvest Gold'. Upright pryramidal form to 40 ft. tall and nearly as wide. Toothed, glossy green leaves turn golden yellow in fall. Interesting flaking bark.

T. tomentosa. SILVER LINDEN. Zones 2–21. Native to Europe and western Asia. Grows to 40–50 ft. tall and 20–30 ft. wide. Leaves are light green above, silvery beneath; they turn and ripple in the slightest breeze. More tolerant of heat and drought than other species. 'Sterling' has silvery young leaves and an especially handsome winter silhouette.

CARE

Best in deep, rich, moist soil. Young trees need shaping, older ones only corrective pruning. Aphids can cause honeydew, which drips disagreeably and encourages sooty mold.

Linden tree is not just a fine shade tree. Its soft wood is prized for making everything from window blinds to drum shells. The flowers and leaves have been used for various medicinal tonics and teas.

Tillandsia

AIR PLANT
Bromeliaceae
PERENNIALS

⚹ **ZONES 22–24; OR INDOORS**
☼ ☼ ◐ **EXPOSURE NEEDS VARY BY SPECIES**
💧 ◐ **WATER NEEDS VARY BY TYPE (SEE TEXT)**

Tillandsia

Large genus of bromeliads native to Texas, Mexico, and South America. Most are epiphytes (tree dwellers) that depend on rain, fog, and dew for moisture. Plants vary greatly in size and appearance; leaves may be wide or narrow (even hairlike), twisted or curled. Flowers are often shockingly bright, sometimes fragrant, and usually quite long lasting (weeks to months). Plants of many species die after blooming but first produce offsets; over time, a single plant becomes a cluster of plants at different stages of maturity and bloom.

Usually seen mounted on plaques of wood hung on walls, or on living walls, indoors or out. In Hawaii, often clustered on tree branches. Site where air circulation is good. Types with green leaves generally need regular water and filtered light; types with gray-green to bluish foliage need less water and tolerate more sun. Drench plants every few days; if leaves curl or dry up, submerge the plant in water for several hours at a time. Once a month or so from spring to midautumn, spray with an acidic liquid fertilizer diluted to quarter-strength. Air plants need somewhat drier conditions in winter.

T. bulbosa. Thick, undulating green leaves to 4 in. long emerge from a swollen base. As the plants prepare to bloom, their central leaves redden. Red flower spike appears in late winter or early spring.

T. cyanea. Narrow, arching, bright green leaves up to 1 ft. long produce a showy flower cluster in spring or autumn: a flattened plume of deep red or pink bracts, from which violet-blue flowers emerge one or two at a time over a long season.

T. ionantha. Minute gray scales cover narrow, arching green leaves (just 1½ in. long), giving them a powdery look. Leaves turn red or coral red in spring as plant prepares to produce its central bract of bright purple, tubular flowers.

T. juncea. Fine, arching, grasslike leaves are gray-green, 10–12 in. long, and held in a rosette. In summer, erect red or pink flower stalks emerge from the center, each topped with a small purple flower.

Tipuana tipu

TIPU TREE
Fabaceae
SEMIEVERGREEN OR DECIDUOUS TREE

⚹ **ZONES 12 (WARMEST AREAS), 13–16, 18–24; H1, H2**
☼ **FULL SUN**
💧 **REGULAR WATER**

Tipuana tipu

Colorful flowering tree from South America. Grows to 25–40 ft. tall, 30–60 ft. wide (or larger). Has broad, flattened crown that is wider than high but can be pruned to make a denser, narrower, umbrella-shaped crown. Light green leaves divided into 11 to 21 oblong leaflets. Blooms from late spring to early summer, bearing clusters of apricot to yellow, sweet pea–shaped flowers; 2½-in. seedpods follow the flowers. Will not take strongly alkaline conditions but is otherwise not particular about soil. Flowers best in warm-summer areas out of immediate ocean influence. Good street tree or lawn tree. Useful as a shade tree for patio or terrace, though litter from flowers can be a slight nuisance. Hardy to 25°F (–4°C); well-ripened wood will take 18°F (–8°C) with minor damage.

Tithonia rotundifolia
(T. speciosa)
MEXICAN SUNFLOWER
Asteraceae
PERENNIAL GROWN AS ANNUAL

✎ **ALL ZONES**

☼ **FULL SUN**

🌢 **REGULAR WATER**

🦋 **FLOWERS ATTRACT BUTTERFLIES AND HUMMINGBIRDS**

Tithonia rotundifolia 'Torch'

Husky, rather coarse plant with velvety green leaves, spectacular gaudy flowers; native from Mexico to Central America. Grows rapidly to 6 ft. tall, 4 ft. wide. Blooms from summer to frost, bearing 3–4-in.-wide blossoms with orange-scarlet rays and tufted yellow centers. Use as a temporary screen. Arcadian Blend grows 2–2½ ft. high and produces gold, orange, and yellow flowers. 'Aztec Sun', to 4 ft. tall, has apricot-gold flowers. 'Fiesta del Sol', to 2½ ft. high, bears 2–3-in. orange flowers and starts blooming earlier than the others. 'Goldfinger', a bushy 4-footer with deep orange

flowers, makes a good temporary summer hedge. All have hollow stems; cut carefully for bouquets to avoid bending stalks. Sow seeds in place in spring, in well-drained, not-too-rich soil. Tolerates intense heat and some drought.

Tolmiea menziesii
PIGGYBACK PLANT
Saxifragaceae
PERENNIAL

✎ **ZONES A3; 4–9, 14–17, 20–24; OR INDOORS**

☼ 🌢 **SOME SHADE; INDIRECT LIGHT**

🌢 🌢 **REGULAR TO AMPLE WATER**

Tolmiea menziesii

Native to Coast Ranges from Northern California northward to Alaska. Chief asset is abundant production of attractive, medium green, triangular to heart-shaped, shallowly lobed leaves of variable size (up to 5 in. long), carried at that ends of leaf-stalks that also vary in length. Leaves are covered in ⅛-in.-long hairs. Tiny, rather inconspicuous reddish brown flowers top 1–2-ft.-high stems. 'Taff's Gold' has foliage irregularly mottled with chartreuse and yellow; great for brightening shady corners.

Good groundcover for shade. Spreads indefinitely by producing new plantlets at junction of leafstalk and leaf blade; plantlets root in the soil. Handsome in hanging baskets.

CARE
Start new plants anytime of the year; take leaf with plantlet and insert in moist potting mix so that base of plantlet contacts soil. As a houseplant, needs

cool temperatures, filtered light (bright light is fine if it's indirect). Mealybugs and spider mites are occasional pests.

Tomatillo
Solanaceae
ANNUAL

✎ **ALL ZONES**

☼ **FULL SUN**

🌢 **REGULAR WATER**

Tomatillos

Easy-to-grow, summer-fruiting tomato relative from Mexico known botanically as *Physalis ixocarpa*. Bushy, sprawling growth to 4 ft. tall and at least as wide. Fruit swells to fill—and eventually split—the loose, papery husk (calyx) that surrounds it. When fully ripe, fruit is yellow to purple, about 2 in. wide, and very sweet, but it is usually picked when green and tart and used in sauces and other dishes.

CARE
Sow seeds directly in fertile soil 4 to 6 weeks after last frost, when the soil has warmed; in moist, warm soil, seeds will germinate in 5 days. Thin seedlings to 10 in. apart. Or start plants indoors and set out in the garden; plant deep, as for tomatoes. Use floating row covers in short-summer areas. Tomatillos can be trained to a trellis like tomatoes but are usually left to sprawl. Once fruiting begins, cut back on water but don't let plants become stressed. Harvest fruit when walnut-size (or smaller, if it seems fully developed) and deep green. Don't remove the papery husk until you are ready to use the fruit.

Tomato
Solanaceae
PERENNIAL GROWN AS ANNUAL

✎ **ALL ZONES**

☼ **FULL SUN**

🌢 **REGULAR WATER**

'Early Girl' tomatoes

Easy to grow and prolific, tomatoes are just about the most widely grown of all garden plants, edible or otherwise. Amateur and commercial growers have varying ideas about how best to raise these Andean natives. If you've developed a successful method, continue to follow it—but if you're a novice, you may find the following information useful.

Choose varieties suited to your climate that will yield the kind of tomatoes you like on plants you can handle. Some varieties are determinate, others indeterminate. Determinate types are bushier, need little or no staking or trellising. Indeterminate ones are more vinelike, need more training, and generally bear over a longer period. (The tomato plant is really a sprawler incapable of climbing, but you'll often see it referred to as a vine.) Plant a few each of early, midseason, and late varieties for longest possible production. (Or plant in spring and again in summer where growing season is long.) Typically, six plants can supply a family of four with enough fruit to enjoy fresh and in sauce.

TOMATO VARIETIES
Following are types of tomatoes you can buy as seeds or started plants. The number of varieties is enormous and increases every year; there are choices

COLUMN ONE: 'Zapotec Pleated'; 'Tigerella'. RIGHT PHOTO: A. 'Gogoshari Striped'. B. 'Plum Lemon'. C. 'Japanese Oxheart'. D. 'Chuck's Yellow'. E. 'Texas Star'. F. 'Japanese Black Trifele'. G. 'Yellow Ruffled'. H. 'Coyote'

for every taste and every region. It's wise to consult a knowledgeable nursery, your Cooperative Extension Office, and other gardeners to find out which varieties flourish in your local climate and soil.

If certain diseases or nematodes cause trouble locally, you may be able to grow varieties that resist one or more of these problems. Keys to resistance you may see on plant labels or in catalog descriptions include V (verticillium wilt), F (fusarium wilt), FF (Race 1 and Race 2 fusarium), T (tobacco mosaic virus), N (nematodes), A (alternaria leaf spot), and L (septoria leaf spot). For example, a variety labeled VFFNT means that it resists verticillium wilt, two races of fusarium wilt, nematodes, and tobacco mosaic virus.

Recently, nurseries and mail order catalogs have begun offering grafted tomato plants. Though expensive, grafted tomatoes (like grafted fruit trees) can have increased vigor, disease resistance, and productivity over plants grown on their own roots. This can be a distinct advantage if you are growing heirloom varieties, which often lack traits that are common in hybrids. Grafted tomatoes shouldn't be planted deeply. That may cause the fruiting variety to form roots, and you'll lose the advantages of the rootstock. Handle plants carefully to avoid breaking the graft and remove suckers that grow from below the graft union.

Cool-summer tomatoes. These will ripen fruit where accumulated heat is too low for most tomatoes. Nurseries in cool-summer areas usually offer locally adapted varieties, such as 'San Francisco Fog', 'Oregon Pride', and 'Seattle Best of All'. Many early varieties, especially 'Early Girl' and 'Stupice', also do well where summers are cool. Increasingly, cool-summer varieties are also being planted in midsummer for extended fall harvest. Popular varieties for this purpose include 'Siberia', 'Glacier', 'Manitoba', 'Moscow', and 'Oregon Spring'.

Early tomatoes. These tomatoes set fruit at lower night temperatures than other tomatoes do; 'Early Girl', 'Burpee's Early Pick', and 'Quick Pick' are standards. Very short-season regions, such as Alaska and high-elevation areas, have their own very early varieties, which set fruit at surprisingly low temperatures; 'Early Tanana' and 'Subarctic Maxi' are examples.

Hawaiian tomatoes. Varieties developed especially for Hawaii resist nematodes and common diseases found there. They include 'N-5', 'N-63', 'N-65', 'Anahu', 'Healani', 'Kewalo' and 'Komohana'.

Heirloom tomatoes. Varying in size, appearance, and plant habit, these represent old varieties that have been maintained by enthusiasts in different parts of the country. Most are grown for excellent flavor. 'Brandywine' and 'Cherokee Purple' are two popular heirloom varieties.

Hybrid tomatoes. Some suppliers tout certain tomatoes as hybrids. They are usually referring to first-generation offspring of controlled parent lines, sometimes indicated by F1 after the name. These varieties are more predictable and uniform in growth and fruit quality. Some are giants like 'Beefmaster' and 'Big Beef', but hybrid paste tomatoes are also available.

Large-fruited tomatoes. These grow to full size in areas where both days and nights are warm. Fruits can weigh a pound or even more. 'Beefsteak', 'Beefmaster', and 'Big Beef' are typical. 'Burpee's Supersteak Hybrid' can produce 2-lb. fruits; 'Delicious' has borne a 7¾-lb. tomato.

Main crop or standard tomatoes. 'Celebrity', 'Big Boy', and 'Better Boy' are widely grown. 'Heatwave II' is popular in hot climates. 'Ace' and 'Pearson' are California favorites.

Novelty tomatoes. Among these are yellow and orange varieties such as 'Orange Queen', 'Mountain Gold', 'Husky Gold', and 'Lemon Boy'. 'Caro Rich' is very high in vitamin A and beta carotene. There are also tomatoes that are deep reddish brown ('Black Prince'), white ('New Snowball', 'White Beauty'), tomatoes with striped fruit ('Green Zebra', 'Tigerella'), and even one with fruit that is green when fully ripe ('Evergreen'). 'Long Keeper' will stay fresh in storage for 3 months. 'Stuffer' and 'Yellow Stuffer' yield large, nearly hollow fruits that resemble bell peppers.

Paste tomatoes. These produce huge crops of small, oval, thick-meated fruits with small seed cavities. Sometimes called plum tomatoes. Favorites for sauces and tomato paste; also good for drying. 'Roma', 'San Marzano', 'Viva Italia', and 'Italian Gold' are examples.

Small-fruited tomatoes. Fruits range from very tiny (currant size) to the size of large marbles. Shapes and colors are indicated by names: 'Red Cherry', 'Red Pear', 'Yellow Cherry', 'Yellow Pear'. Those with very small fruits include 'Gardener's Delight', 'Sun Gold', 'Supersweet 100', 'Sweet 100', and 'Sweet Million'. Grape tomatoes, such as 'Juliet',

T

How to Grow Tomatoes

WHEN TO PLANT Set out tomato plants after frost danger is past and the soil has warmed. Plant in February or early March in Zones 12, 13; in April, May, or early June in Zones 7–9, 14–24; in May or early June in Zones A1–A3, 1–6, 10, 11. In Hawaii, tomatoes can be planted year-round in most locations. To grow tomatoes from seed, sow seeds in pots of light soil mix 5 to 7 weeks before you intend to set out plants.

SEEDS OR TRANSPLANTS Cover seeds with ½ in. of fine soil; firm soil over seeds and keep surface damp. Place seed container in cold frame or sunny window—a temperature of 65°F to 70°F (18°C to 21°C) is ideal, although a range of 50°F (10°C) at night to as warm as 85°F (29°C) in the day will give acceptable results. When seedlings are 2 in. high, transplant each into a 3- or 4-in. pot; keep seedlings in sunny area until they reach planting size. When buying tomato plants, look for compact ones with sturdy stems; avoid those that are tall for the pot or have flowers or fruit.

SITE & SOIL Plant in a sunny site in well-drained soil. Tomato plants prefer neutral to slightly acid soil; add lime to very acid soil or sulfur to alkaline soil the autumn before setting out plants.

PLANTING Space plants 1½–3 ft. apart (staked or trained) to 3–4 ft. apart (untrained). Make planting holes extra deep and set in seedlings so that lowest leaves are just above soil level. Additional roots will form on buried stem and provide a stronger root system.

BEATING THE SEASONS If you live in an area where summers are cool or short (such as the Pacific Northwest, Alaska, or high-elevation regions), or if you want to get an early start, take steps to speed growth and protect tomatoes from frost. A combination of plastic mulch and floating row covers is probably most effective. Protect individual plants with paper or plastic caps known as hotcaps (some have water-filled cylinders that trap heat effectively to provide maximum protection).

TRAINING Tomato management and harvest will be most satisfying if you train plants to keep them off the ground as much as possible. Untrained plants will sprawl, and some fruit will lie on soil, where it often suffers from rot, pest damage, and discoloration. For training indeterminate varieties, the usual practice is to drive a 6-ft.-long stake (at least 1 by 1 in.) into ground a foot from each plant. Use soft ties to hold the plant to the stake as it grows.

Slightly easier in the long run—but more work at planting time—is to grow each plant in a wire cylinder made of concrete reinforcing screen (6-in. mesh). The screen is 7 ft. wide, which is just right for cylinder height. Put stakes at opposite sides of cylinder and tie cylinder firmly to them. As the vine grows, poke protruding branches back inside the cylinder.

WATERING & FERTILIZING Tomato plants need regular moisture at root level; they are deep-rooted, so water heavily each time you water. If soil is fairly rich, you won't need to fertilize. In ordinary soils, feed lightly every 2 weeks from the time first blossoms set until the end of harvest; or give a single application of controlled-release fertilizer when planting.

PESTS Whiteflies are common pests of tomato plants. Large green caterpillars with diagonal white stripes that feed upside down on leaf undersides are hornworms; handpick them. In Hawaii, wrap developing fruit clusters in paper or cloth bags to protect from melon flies. Tomatoes are subject to a long list of diseases, some common only in certain regions. Your Cooperative Extension Office is the best source of control measures for most tomato diseases. If plants are growing strongly and then suddenly wilt and die, they may have been sabotaged by gophers. If you can find no evidence of these rodents, plants probably are suffering from verticillium wilt, fusarium wilt, or both; pull out and discard plants. Diseases live over in soil, so plant in a different location every year and try varieties resistant to wilt or certain other diseases.

In Pacific Northwest, lessen chance of late blight (which spots leaves and stems, rots fruit) by avoiding overhead sprinkling. Blight declines as weather warms; destroy plant debris after harvest.

Some tomato problems—leaf roll, blossom-end rot, cracked fruit—are physiological and can usually be corrected (or prevented) by maintaining uniform soil moisture. Mulching will help conserve moisture in very hot or dry climates.

INCREASING FRUIT SET If you've done everything right and your tomatoes fail to set fruit in the spring, use hormone spray on the blossoms. Tomatoes often fail to set fruit when nighttime temperatures drop below 55°F (13°C). In chilly-night areas, select cold-tolerant varieties (especially small-fruited strains). Fruit-setting hormone often speeds up bearing in the earlier part of the season. Tomatoes can also fail to set fruit when temperatures rise above 100°F (38°C), but hormones are not effective then.

PICKING Harvest fruit when it is fully colored and juicy; keep ripe fruit picked to extend season. When frost is predicted, harvest all fruit, both green and partly ripe. Store in a dry place away from direct sunlight at 60°F to 70°F (16°C to 21°C); check often for ripening.

produce large grapelike clusters of smallish fruit. Small-fruiting types that grow on small plants suitable for pots or hanging baskets include 'Tiny Tim', 'Small Fry', and 'Patio'.

Torenia fournieri
WISHBONE FLOWER
Linderniaceae
ANNUAL

🌿 **ZONES 1–24; H1, H2**

☼ ◐ **PARTIAL SHADE IN HOTTEST CLIMATES**

💧 **REGULAR WATER**

Torenia fournieri

Compact, bushy annual from tropical Asia. Grows to 1 ft. high and wide. Blooms from summer into fall; the flowers have stamens arranged in wishbone shape. Species has pale lavender blossoms with deeper purple markings and bright yellow throats; a white-flowered form is also sold. Use as edging or in pots and window boxes. Summer Wave hybrids thrive in heat. The Moon series comes in a range of blue, purple and pink shades, as well as yellow and white, with contrasting markings. Plants sprawl nicely, grow to 6–10 in. high. Duchess strain is more compact (6–8 in. high and wide), offers blooms in four color combinations: light blue with blue throat, blue with white throat, deep blue with blue throat, and pink with white throat.

CARE

Sow seeds in pots and transplant to garden after frost danger is past; or buy nursery plants. If grown in sun, keep roots cool with a mulch.

Torreya californica

CALIFORNIA NUTMEG

Taxaceae

EVERGREEN TREE

- ZONES 4–9, 14–24
- FULL SUN OR PARTIAL SHADE
- MODERATE WATER

Torreya californica

Native to cool, shaded canyons in California mountain regions below 4,500 ft. Slow-growing conifer to 15–20 ft. tall, 12–15 ft. wide, with trunk 1–3 ft. in diameter. Wide, open pyramidal crown, domelike with age. Branches are horizontal, slender, somewhat drooping at tips. Flat sprays of rigid, sharp-pointed, flat, dark green leaves with two whitish bands underneath. Plumlike fruit is pale green with purplish markings.

Tovara virginiana.
See *Persicaria virginiana*

Trachelium caeruleum

Campanulaceae

PERENNIAL

- ZONES 7–9, 14–24; ELSEWHERE AS ANNUAL
- FULL SUN
- REGULAR WATER
- FLOWERS ATTRACT BUTTERFLIES

Trachelium caeruleum

Tough, undemanding Mediterranean native to 2½ ft. high and wide. Forms a clump of stems clothed with narrow, sharply toothed, dark green leaves. Blooms over a long summer season, when sparsely foliaged flowering stems are topped by broad, dome-shaped clusters of tiny blossoms in blue, mauve, pink, or white. Good cut flowers. If sown early, will bloom first year (and so can be treated as a summer annual in colder climates or as a winter annual in mild-winter desert).

Trachelium and Friends

Trachelium caeruleum may be short-lived, but it's worth growing for its lacy domes of tiny flowers that appear to float like soft violet blue clouds above glossy deep green leaves. The plant is especially pretty beside dark-leafed *Pennisetum glaucum* and lime green strawberry (*Fragaria vesca* 'Golden Alexandra'). Or grow it in a border with Mexican bush sage (velvety purple bloom spikes) and *Achillea* 'Anthea' (creamy white blooms), with spiky red phormiums as accents and blue catmint in front. Other good companions: purple-flowered heliotrope and silvery-white *Artemisia* 'Powis Castle'.

Trachelospermum

STAR JASMINE

Apocynaceae

EVERGREEN SHRUBS OR VINES

- ZONES VARY BY SPECIES
- LIGHT SHADE IN HOTTEST CLIMATES
- REGULAR WATER

Trachelospermum jasminoides

Groundcovers, trailers, or climbers bearing delightfully fragrant, pinwheel-shaped blossoms in spring or early summer. Among the most versatile and useful of plants.

T. asiaticum. Zones 6–24. From Japan, Korea. Like *T. jasminoides* but has smaller leaves in darker, duller green and smaller flowers in creamy yellow or yellowish white. Dense, low growth habit makes it an excellent groundcover. 'Red Top' has red new growth. 'Pink Snow' has pink new growth maturing to green marked with white.

T. jasminoides. STAR JASMINE, CONFEDERATE JASMINE, MAILE HAOLE. Zones 8–24; H1, H2. From China. Given support, a twining vine to 20–30 ft.; without support and with some tip-pinching, a spreading shrub or groundcover to 2 ft. high, 10 ft. wide. Oval leaves are glossy light green when new, mature to lustrous dark green. Profusion of white, inch-wide flowers in small clusters on short side branches. Attractive to bees. If grown as shrubby plant, it is good in raised beds or entry gardens, for edging walk or drive, as extension of lawn, spilling over walls, as groundcover under trees and shrubs. Set plants 5 ft. apart for groundcover. 'Variegatum' has leaves bordered and

blotched with white. 'Madison' is a hardy selection.

CARE

Prefer well-drained soil. For lush plants, fertilize once before spring growth begins, again after flowering. Prune back as needed to shape. Cut stems exude a milky sap.

Trachycarpus fortunei

WINDMILL PALM

Arecaceae

PALM

- ZONES 4–24
- FULL SUN OR LIGHT SHADE
- REGULAR WATER

Trachycarpus fortunei

Medium-size, very hardy fan palm (to 10°F/−12°C or lower) from China. Moderate to fast growth to 30 ft. tall, 10 ft. wide. Trunk is usually thicker at top than at bottom and is covered with dense, blackish fiber; as trunk elongates, fiber falls off its lower portion. Toothed, 1½-ft. stalks carry 3-ft.-wide leaves. May look untidy in high winds. May be sold as *Chamaerops excelsa*. Young plants can be grown indoors in bright indirect light; plant them outdoors when they become too big.

These palms bear long, dangling clusters of tiny yellow flowers that are followed (on female trees) by blue-black fruits.

T

Tradescantia

Commelinaceae

PERENNIALS

✓ ZONES 12–24; H1, H2, EXCEPT AS NOTED; OR INDOORS

☼ ◑ ● EXPOSURE NEEDS VARY BY SPECIES; BRIGHT INDIRECT LIGHT

💧 💧 💧 WATER NEEDS VARY BY SPECIES

Tradescantia pallida
'Purpurea'

Most are virtually indestructible plants with long, trailing stems. Usually seen in pots or hanging baskets, but can be used as groundcovers—though the most vigorous, rambling types are likely to be invasive. On variegated forms, pinch out growth that reverts to solid green.

T. × andersoniana. See *T. virginiana.*

T. fluminensis. WANDERING JEW. From South America. Rapid grower to 2 in. high, with indefinite spread. Succulent stems have swollen joints where dark green, oval or oblong leaves are attached. Tiny, unshowy white flowers. Easy to grow. Excellent for window boxes and dish gardens. If plants are overgrown, renovate by cutting back severely; or discard them and start new plants with fresh tip growth. Partial or full shade. Regular to ample water. Stems will live a long time in water, rooting quickly and easily. Variegated forms also available.

T. pallida 'Purpurea' (Setcreasea pallida 'Purple Heart'). PURPLE HEART, PURPLE QUEEN. From Mexico. Creeping plant to 1–1½ ft. high, 1 ft. wide; stems tend to flop. Pointed, rather narrowly oval leaves are strongly shaded with purple, particularly on undersides. Pale or deep purple flowers (not showy). Pinch back after bloom. Generally unattractive in winter. Frost may kill tops, but recovery is fast in warm weather. Use as groundcover, for bedding, or in pots. Full sun or light shade. Moderate water.

T. spathacea (Rhoeo spathacea). MOSES-IN-THE-CRADLE, MOSES-IN-THE-BOAT. From Mexico and Central America. To 2 ft. high and 1 ft. wide. Each plant has a dozen or so broad, sword-shaped, rather erect leaves that are dark green above, deep purple beneath. Small, white, three-petaled blooms are interesting rather than beautiful, crowded into boat-shaped bracts borne down among leaves. There is also a dwarf form. 'Variegata' has leaves striped in red and yellowish green. Most often used as a pot plant or in hanging baskets; grown as a groundcover and edging in Hawaii. Tough plant; takes heat, low humidity, sun or shade. Best with regular moisture but withstands inconsistent watering. Try to keep water out of leaf joints when irrigating.

T. virginiana. SPIDERWORT. Zones 1–24; H1. From eastern U.S. Clump-forming border plant to 1½ ft. high and wide. Long, grassy-looking, deep green, erect or arching leaves. Three-petaled flowers last for only a day, but buds come in large clusters and plants are seldom out of bloom in summer. May self-sow and become somewhat invasive. Divide clumps when crowded. Sun or shade. Regular to ample water. Named garden varieties come in white, blue shades, lavender, purple, and shades of pink from pale to near-red; these plants are often sold as Andersoniana group.

T. zebrina (Zebrina pendula). WANDERING JEW. Zones 24; H1, H2. From southern Mexico. Similar to *T. fluminensis* but not as hardy; bears pinkish or bluish flowers. Most widely grown are forms with colorful leaves, including 'Quadricolor', purplish green leaves with longitudinal bands of silver, pink, and red; and 'Purpusii', dark red or greenish red foliage. Attractive groundcovers for shady, frost-free sites. Partial or full shade. Provide regular water.

Tree Tomato, Tamarillo

Solanaceae

EVERGREEN OR SEMIEVERGREEN SHRUB

✓ ZONES 14–24; H1, H2

☼ ◑ FULL SUN OR PARTIAL SHADE

💧 REGULAR WATER

Tree tomatoes

Treelike Andean native known botanically as *Solanum betaceum* (*Cyphomandra betaceae*). Fast growth to 10–18 ft. tall and two-thirds as wide. Pointed oval, 4–10-in.-long leaves; small pinkish flowers in summer and fall. In winter, bears egg-shaped, 2–3-in.-long red fruit (there are also yellow varieties). Fruit has acid flavor somewhat like that of tomato—if you find it too tart, try stewing it with a little sugar.

CARE

Grow from seed like tomato. Harvest fruit when it is fully colored; pluck from tree by snapping off, leaving stem attached. Bears on new growth. In late winter, prune back branches that have fruited by one-fourth to one-third (this will prevent fruit from developing ever farther out from center of plant). Control sucking insects. Frost sensitive; give overhead protection in Zones 14, 15, 18–21. Fruiting is more reliable in warmer part of range.

Tree tomatoes are delicious in desserts and smoothies as well as on salads, pizzas, and sandwiches.

Triadica sebifera
(Sapium sebiferum)

CHINESE TALLOW TREE

Euphorbiaceae

DECIDUOUS TREE

✓ ZONES 8, 9, 12–16, 18–21; H1

☼ FULL SUN

💧 💧 MODERATE TO REGULAR WATER

⬥ MILKY SAP IS TOXIC IF INGESTED

Triadica sebifera

This tree from China and Japan grows to 30–40 ft. tall and 25–30 ft. wide, with a dense, round or conical crown. Tends toward shrubbiness, multiple trunks, and suckering but is easily trained to a single trunk. In colder areas, branch tips may freeze back in winter, but new growth will quickly cover damage. Leafs out late in spring. Foliage is dense but flutters in the slightest breeze, giving tree an airy look. Light green leaves are roundish, tapering to a slender point; with moderate autumn chill, they can turn flaming red, plum-purple, yellow-orange, or mixed colors. For good color, select a tree while it is in fall leaf. Spikes of tiny yellowish flowers at branch tips are followed in fall by clusters of small fruits with a waxy grayish white coating.

Though this tree was once considered suitable for all landscapes, it is best not to plant it if you garden near wetlands, rivers, or native plant habitats. It has become a self-seeding pest in parts of the West. Away from areas where it can do damage, it's an attractive tree for lawn, street, patio, or terrace; gives light to moderate shade. Good as a screen. Resistant to oak root fungus.

Trichostema lanatum

WOOLLY BLUE CURLS
Lamiaceae
EVERGREEN SHRUB

✄ **ZONES 14–24**

☀ **FULL SUN**

◌ **NO IRRIGATION NEEDED**

Trichostema lanatum

Native to dry, sunny slopes of California Coast Ranges. Much-branched, neat plant to 3–5 ft. tall and 4–8 ft. wide. Narrow leaves, pungently aromatic when bruised, are shiny dark green on upper surface, white and woolly beneath; leaf edges are rolled under. Flowers, in separated clusters on a long stalk, are blue with conspicuous, arching stamens. Stalks and flowers are covered with blue, pink, or whitish wool. Blooms in spring; continues throughout summer and early fall if old flower stems are cut back. Temperamental plant; needs perfect drainage.

Woolly blue curls needs perfect drainage (in nature, it grows in gravelly, serpentine soils). Standing water will kill it, as will heavy summer rains. But give it what it needs, and it will reward you with tall candles of velvety blooms and cedar-scented foliage.

Tricyrtis

TOAD LILY
Liliaceae
PERENNIALS

✄ **ZONES VARY BY SPECIES**

◑ **PARTIAL SHADE**

💧 **AMPLE WATER**

Tricyrtis 'Lightning Strike'

Woodland plants that resemble false Solomon's seal (*Maianthemum racemosum*) in foliage. Interesting, heavily spotted, inch-long flowers appear at leaf joints and in terminal clusters in late summer and autumn. They are complex in structure, somewhat orchidlike: each blossom has three petals and three sepals, with a column of decorative stamens and styles rising from the center. Need soil enriched with plenty of organic matter. Excellent companion to ferns and hostas; lovely with *Gunnera*.

T. formosana (T. stolonifera). Zones 3–9, 14–17. From Taiwan. To 2½ ft. high. Spreads by aboveground runners to form a clump 1½ ft. or wider (but is not invasive). More erect than *T. hirta*, with flowers mostly in terminal clusters. Leaves are green, mottled with deeper green; brown or maroon buds open to white to pale lilac flowers spotted with purple. 'Amethystina' blooms several weeks earlier than the species, bearing lavender-blue blossoms with a red-spotted white throat. 'Samurai' is a compact variety that blooms later into autumn and has green leaves edged with yellow.

T. hirta. Zones 2–9, 14–17. From Japan. To 3 ft. high, 2 ft. wide; it lacks runners. Arching stems bear pale green, softly hairy foliage. White to pale lilac blossoms are peppered with purple and appear in leaf joints all along the stems. 'Miyazaki' bears pink to white flowers with crimson spots; 'Miyazaki Gold' is similar but has gold-edged leaves.

Trifolium repens

WHITE CLOVER,
WHITE DUTCH CLOVER
Papilionaceae
PERENNIAL

✄ **ZONES 2–24**

☀ ◑ **FULL SUN OR PARTIAL SHADE**

💧 **REGULAR WATER**

Trifolium repens

Sometimes mixed with lawn grass or dichondra seed. Prostrate stems root freely, send up lush cover of leaves with three leaflets. Can stain clothing; white flowers attract bees. These colored-leaf varieties grow 4 in. high, spread indefinitely, and are used as groundcovers or at front of borders: 'Atropurpureum' (also sold as 'Dark Dancer') features blackish purple leaves edged with green; 'Green Ice', lime green with dark green margin; 'Purpurascens', maroon outlined in green. *T. r. minus* is one of the shamrocks. All take nitrogen from air and fix it in soil through action of bacteria on their roots.

Trifolium is a Latin derivation meaning "three-leafed." The species name *repens* means "creeping."

Trillium

WAKE ROBIN
Melanthiaceae
PERENNIALS

✄ **ZONES VARY BY SPECIES**

◑ ● **PARTIAL OR FULL SHADE**

💧 **REGULAR WATER**

Trillium ovatum

Bloom in early spring; need some winter chill. Each stem is topped with a whorl of three leaves; a single three-petaled flower appears in the center of the whorl (sometimes on a stalk, sometimes virtually stalkless). Plant in shady, woodsy site. Left undisturbed, plants will gradually increase by rhizomes. Die to the ground in mid- to late summer. In addition to the species listed below, many others are offered by specialists in native plants.

T. chloropetalum (T. sessile californicum). Zones 4–9, 14–17. Native to California. To 1–1½ ft. high and 1 ft. wide, with 6-in.-long leaves mottled in maroon. Stalkless flowers have greenish white to yellowish petals about 2½ in. long. *T. c. giganteum* has deep maroon petals.

T. erectum. PURPLE TRILLIUM. Zones 1–6. From eastern North America. To 2 ft. high and 1 ft. wide, with 7-in.-long leaves. Erect, 2–3-in. flowers are dark reddish purple, carried on stalks; they have an odd odor.

T. grandiflorum. Zones 1–6. From eastern North America. To 1½ ft. high, 1 ft. wide, with stout stems and 2½–6-in.-long leaves. Nearly stalkless flowers are nodding, to 3 in. across, white aging to rose. There are several choice double-flowered forms.

»

T

T. luteum. YELLOW TRIL-LIUM. Zones 2b–6. Native primarily to the southeastern and midsouthern U.S. Grows about 1 ft. high and wide, with 6-in.-long, medium green leaves mottled with pale green. Canary yellow flowers, with petals up to 3½ in. long, are held upright; their fragrance is lemony and sweet.

T. ovatum (T. californi-cum). Zones 2–7, 14–17. Western native. Resembles *T. grandiflorum* but has narrower petals; flowers are usually upright and are borne on stalks.

Tristania conferta.
See *Lophostemon confertus*

Tristaniopsis laurina
(Tristania laurina)
WATER GUM
Myrtaceae
EVERGREEN TREE OR SHRUB

🌿 **ZONES 15–24**

☼ **FULL SUN**

💧 **REGULAR WATER**

Tristaniopsis laurina

Slow-growing, rather formal-looking eastern Australian plant with conical, dense crown. To 10 ft. tall, 5 ft. wide at 8 years old; may eventually reach 45 ft. or taller, 30 ft. wide. Mahogany-colored bark peels off, revealing satiny white new bark beneath. Glossy green, narrow leaves. Clusters of small, faintly fragrant yellow flowers appear in late spring or early summer, borne profusely enough to put on a good show. Seedpods like those of eucalyptus but much smaller (to ¼ in. wide); they don't create a litter problem.

Excellent tall screen, boundary, and background planting. Good in large containers.

'Elegant' has broad leaves that are red when they emerge, turn green only when shaded by later growth.

CARE

Water gum is densely shrubby when young and can be kept that way with a little pinching. Can be trained as a single- or multistemmed tree; once established, trees need only light shaping.

Triteleia
Asparagaceae
PERENNIALS FROM CORMS

🌿 **ZONES 3–9, 14–24, EXCEPT AS NOTED**

☼ **FULL SUN**

○ **NO IRRIGATION NEEDED**

Triteleia ixioides

Plants of this name were formerly known as *Brodiaea*. General descriptions and culture are the same as for *Brodiaea*, which differs only in technical details. Spring and early summer bloom.

T. grandiflora (Brodiaea grandiflora). Flowering stalk to 2 ft. high; many 1¼-in.-long, blue to white trumpets.

T. hyacinthina (B. hyacin-thina, B. lactea). WHITE BRODIAEA. Zones 2–9, 14–24. Clusters of 10 to 40 papery-textured white, purple-tinged flowers with greenish veins. Flowering stalk is 9–20 in. high.

T. ixioides (B. ixioides, B. lutea). PRETTY FACE, GOLDEN BRODIAEA. Flower stalk to 2 ft.; flowers 1 in. long, golden yellow with purple-black midrib and veins.

T. laxa (B. laxa). GRASS NUT, ITHURIEL'S SPEAR. Zones 5–9, 14–24. Flower stalk to 2½ ft.; purple-blue, 1½-in. trumpets. 'Queen Fabiola' has deep violet flowers.

T. × tubergenii (B. tuber-genii). Flower stalk to 2½ ft. high; light blue flowers.

T. uniflora. See *Ipheion uniflorum*.

Tritonia crocata
Iridaceae
PERENNIALS FROM CORMS

🌿 **ZONES 9, 13–24; OR DIG AND STORE**

☼ **FULL SUN**

💧 **REGULAR WATER DURING GROWTH AND BLOOM**

Tritonia crocata

South African native related to freesia, harlequin flower (*Spar-axis*), ixia, montbretia (*Crocos-mia*). Often called flame freesia. Fans of swordlike leaves to 1 ft. long grow in early spring, followed in late spring by flower spikes holding bright orange-red flowers above the foliage. Blooms are funnel-shaped, up to 2 in. across, and long lasting in a vase. Foliage dies down after bloom, re-emerges the next spring. Good in rock gardens, borders.

T. c. miniata has bright red blooms. 'Princess Beatrix' has deep orange flowers. Others may be offered in white, yellow, and pink shades. For the plant sometimes called *T. crocos-miiflora*, see *Crocosmia × crocosmiiflora*.

CARE

Plant corms in well-drained soil, setting them 2–3 in. deep, 3 in. apart. Plant in fall where winter temperatures remain above

20°F (–7°C); wait until spring in colder areas. Corms can remain in the ground where hardy, but they are likely to rot unless planting area is kept fairly dry during summer dormancy. Divide overcrowded plantings during dormant period. Where corms cannot be protected and in colder regions, dig and store over winter or grow in pots.

Trochodendron aralioides
WHEEL TREE
Trochodendraceae
EVERGREEN TREE OR SHRUB

🌿 **ZONES 4–9, 14–24**

☼◐ **FULL SUN OR LIGHT SHADE**

💧 **REGULAR WATER**

Trochodendron aralioides

Handsome foliage plant from Japan, Korea. Grows to 30 ft. tall and 25 ft. wide, with horizontal branching pattern. Oval, 5-in.-long, glossy dark green leaves cluster near branch tips. In late spring, elongated (to 5 in.) clusters of 10 to 20 bright green flowers appear at branch ends. Each ¾-in. blossom is made up of a flat disk surrounded by stamens. Blossoms are followed by fruits consisting of small pods clustered around the disk. Prefers organically enriched soil.

Wheel tree is prized for its handsome form; shiny, dark green leaves; and distinctive, bright green flowers.

Trollius

GLOBEFLOWER

Ranunculaceae

PERENNIALS

📏 **ZONES A2, A3; 1–6**

☀️ ◑ **FULL SUN IN COOLER CLIMATES ONLY**

💧💧 **REGULAR TO AMPLE WATER**

Trollius × cultorum
'Lemon Queen'

Clumps of finely cut, shiny dark green leaves put up 2–3-ft.-high stems terminating in yellow to orange flowers typically shaped like globes or rounded cups. Excellent cut flowers.

T. chinensis (T. ledebourii). From China and Siberia. To 3 ft. high, 1½ ft. wide. Light orange-yellow, 2-in. flowers with an open bowl shape; summer bloom. 'Golden Queen' has pure orange flowers.

T. × cultorum. Group of hybrids includes 'Earliest of All' (pale orange-yellow; midspring), 'Lemon Queen' (light yellow; late spring and early summer), and 'Cheddar' (light yellow; early summer). All bear 3-in. blooms and reach 2 ft. high and 1½ ft. wide.

CARE

Deadhead to prolong bloom. Cannot take drought or heat; constantly damp area near a pond or stream is an ideal planting site. Before planting globeflowers in a regular garden bed, liberally amend the soil with organic matter and keep well watered. Divide clumps only when they thin out in the center.

FOR OTHER PLANTS THAT THRIVE IN DAMP AREAS, SEE PAGES 79–80.

Tropaeolum

NASTURTIUM

Tropaeolaceae

ANNUALS AND PERENNIALS

📏 **ZONES VARY BY SPECIES**

☀️ ◑ **EXPOSURE NEEDS VARY BY SPECIES**

💧 **REGULAR WATER**

Tropaeolum majus

Old-fashioned favorites from South America. Distinctive appearance, rapid growth, and easy culture are three of their many strong points.

T. majus. GARDEN NASTURTIUM. Annual. All zones. Two main kinds: climbing types, which trail over ground or climb to 6 ft. by coiling leafstalks; and compact, bushy, dwarf kinds to 1½ ft. high and wide (dwarf types are more widely sold). Both have round bright green leaves on long stalks. Long-spurred flowers to 2½ in. across have a refreshing fragrance, come in colors including maroon, red-brown, orange, yellow, red, and creamy white. You can get seeds of mixed colors in several strains; some single colors are also sold. Both single- and double-flowered forms are available.

All varieties make good cut flowers. Young leaves, flowers, and unripe seedpods have a peppery flavor and are frequently used in salads.

Easy to grow in most well-drained soils but does best in sandy soil. Sow in early spring; plant grows and blooms quickly, reseeds (it has naturalized in parts of Zone 17). In mild-winter, hot-summer areas, sow in fall for winter and spring bloom. Use climbing types to cover fences, banks, stumps, or rocks;

use dwarf kinds for bedding, to hide fading bulb foliage, or for quick color. Somewhat drought-tolerant. Full sun or light shade.

T. peregrinum. CANARY BIRD FLOWER. Perennial in Zones 15–24; H1, H2; annual elsewhere. Climbs to 10–15 ft. Five-lobed leaves. Frilled, fringed, ¾–1-in.-wide, canary yellow flowers with curved green spur. Sow in spring for bloom from summer until frost. Provide support such as stakes or netting; or let climb into a shrub. Light shade.

Tsuga

HEMLOCK

Pinaceae

EVERGREEN TREES

📏 **ZONES VARY BY SPECIES**

☀️ ◑ **FULL SUN OR PARTIAL SHADE, EXCEPT AS NOTED**

💧 **REGULAR WATER**

🐦 **ATTRACT BIRDS**

Tsuga heterophylla

Mostly big, shallow-rooted trees with unusually graceful appearance. Horizontal to drooping branches bear needlelike leaves that are banded with white beneath, flattened and narrowed at the base to form distinct, short stalks. Small, oval brown cones hang down from branches. Deeply furrowed bark. Need some winter chill.

T. canadensis. CANADA HEMLOCK. Zones A3; 2–7, 17. From eastern North America. Dense, pyramidal tree to 40–70 ft. or taller, half as wide. Tends to produce two or more trunks. Outer branchlets droop gracefully. Dark green needles, mostly arranged in opposite rows. Fine lawn tree, good background plant, and outstanding

clipped hedge. 'Pendula', Sargent weeping hemlock, grows slowly to 5 ft. tall and 10 ft. wide, has pendulous branches. 'Cole's Prostrate' is 1–2 ft. high and spreads to 3 ft. or more; attractive gnarled bark. 'Gentsch White', to 3–4 ft. tall and wide, has white-tipped new growth. 'Jeddeloh' spreads to 3–4 ft. tall and 4–6 ft. wide, with a bird's nest–like depression in the center. 'Moon Frost' is rounded, 3 ft. high and wide, with white new growth that blushes pink in winter. Many other dwarf, weeping, and variegated selections are sold.

T. diversifolia. NORTHERN JAPANESE HEMLOCK. Zones A2, A3; 2–7, 17. From northern Japan. Grows slowly into a pyramid 35–60 ft. tall, 25 ft. wide. Often multitrunked, with graceful, sweeping branches densely clothed in short, glossy, dark green needles ¼–½ in. long. Bark is reddish brown. Grows near the timberline in its native habitat; more tolerant of wind and frost than other hemlocks. More pest-resistant than *T. canadensis*. 'Loowit' grows 1–1½ ft. high and 2 ft. wide, with interesting bright green, blunted needles that look like grains of rice.

T. heterophylla. WESTERN HEMLOCK. Zones A2, A3; 2–7, 14–17. Native along coast from Alaska to Northern California, inland to northern Idaho and Montana. Handsome tree with narrow, pyramidal crown. Grows fairly fast to 70–130 ft. tall, 20–30 ft. wide. Somewhat drooping branchlets; fine-textured, dark green to yellowish green foliage with a fernlike quality. Needles are ¼–¾ in. long, grow in two rows. Picturesque large conifer for background, screens, hedges. 'Thorsen's Weeping' is a prostrate form that can be grown as a groundcover or staked in youth as a weeping specimen; best growth in part shade.

T. mertensiana. MOUNTAIN HEMLOCK. Zones A1–A3; 1–7, 14–17. Native to high mountains, from Alaska south through higher Sierra Nevada in California and to northern Idaho, Montana. To 50–90 ft. in the wild but is slow growing, smaller (20–30 ft. tall, half as wide) in gardens. Needles are

T

½–1 in. long, blue-green with a silvery cast; grow all around stems, giving branchlets a plump, tufty appearance. Thrives on cool slopes with highly organic soil. Least adapted to lowland, hot-summer areas. Needs partial shade in Zone 14. Somewhat resistant to hemlock woolly aphid. Good for large rock gardens, containers, bonsai. 'Elizabeth' grows at least 1 ft. high, 3 ft. wide, with soft-textured, blue-green foliage.

CARE

Do best with acid soil, summer humidity, protection from hot sun and wind. Take well to heavy pruning; make excellent clipped hedges, screens. Easily damaged by salt and drought. In the Northwest, the hemlock woolly aphid can weaken these plants, especially those grown as hedges; it affects mainly *T. heterophylla*.

Tulbaghia
Alliaceae
PERENNIALS FROM RHIZOMES

⚑ ZONES 13–24; H1, H2
☼ FULL SUN
💧 REGULAR WATER

Tulbaghia violacea

Tough, grassy plants from South Africa. Dense clumps of evergreen leaves send up slim, 1–2-ft. stems topped by clusters of small, trumpet-shaped, pinkish lavender flowers. Recover quickly from frost damage.

T. natalensis. SWEET WILD GARLIC. Narrow, shiny green leaves on a plant rarely more than 1 ft. high. Open clusters of clove-scented flowers in white and shades of pink to violet, with a greenish or yellow center.

T. simmleri (T. fragrans). Gray-green, 1-in.-wide leaves. Lightly fragrant flowers in clusters of 20 to 30 in winter or early spring. Good cut flower. 'Alba' has white blossoms.

T. violacea. SOCIETY GARLIC. Bluish green, very narrow leaves. Clusters of 8 to 20 flowers; bloom is heaviest in spring and summer. Leaves and flower stems have onion or garlic odor if cut or crushed; leaves can be used in cooking. 'Variegata' has a creamy stripe down the middle of each leaf; in 'Silver Lace', each leaf is edged in white. Leaves of 'Tricolor' have white edges with a pinkish cast that intensifies in cool weather.

CARE

Start plants from containers or divisions at any time (though early spring or early fall is best in hot-summer areas). Give well-drained, organically enriched soil. Divide clumps to increase plantings.

Tulipa
TULIP
Liliaceae
PERENNIALS FROM BULBS

⚑ ZONES 1–24, EXCEPT AS NOTED
☼☼ FULL SUN DURING BLOOM, PARTIAL SHADE AFTER IN HOT CLIMATES
💧 REGULAR WATER DURING GROWTH AND BLOOM

Tulipa Beauty of Apeldoorn

Tulips vary considerably. Some are stately and formal, others dainty and whimsical; a few look quite bizarre. Bloom comes at some time from March to May, depending on type.

Use larger tulips in colonies or masses, in company with low, spring-blooming plants. Use smaller, shorter types for close-up viewing—in rock gardens, near paths, in raised beds, or in patio insets. Tulips are superb container plants, especially unusual kinds such as Rembrandt and Parrot.

Tulips have been classified into many divisions, defined mainly by flower type. For the convenience of gardeners, we have arranged the divisions into additional groupings; the first three groupings are by bloom season, while the fourth contains species and their hybrids.

EARLY TULIPS

Single early tulips. Single flowers on 10–16-in. stems. Colors include white, yellow, salmon, pink, red, and dark purple. Most have a mild, sweet fragrance. Popular for forcing and growing indoors in pots. Because they bloom in cooler weather, flowers last longer. Not adapted to mild-winter areas.

Double early tulips. Peony-like double flowers, often measuring 4 in. across, on 6–12-in. stems. Same color range as single early tulips. Effective massed in borders. In rainy areas, mulch around plants or surround with groundcover to keep mud from splashing the short-stemmed flowers.

MIDSEASON TULIPS

Triumph tulips. Single flowers on sturdy stems to 20 in. tall. Wide range of solid colors, including red, purple, pink, white, and yellow, and bicolors.

Darwin hybrid tulips. Spectacular group with brightly colored flowers on 24–28-in. stems. Most are in scarlet-orange to red range; some have contrasting eyes or penciling. Some reach 7 in. across. Pink, yellow, and white varieties exist. When planted properly, one of the best garden performers.

LATE TULIPS

Single late tulips. Graceful plants with large, oval or egg-shaped blooms on 1½–3-ft. stems. Clear, beautiful colors: white, yellow, orange, pink, red, mauve, lilac, purple, and maroon. May have contrasting margins. Includes old Darwin and Cottage groups, as well as newer, large-flowering French or Scheepers hybrids.

Lily-flowered tulips. Graceful, lilylike flowers with recurved, pointed segments; come in white and shades of yellow, pink, red, and magenta, often with contrasting markings. Stems 20–26 in. high.

Fringed tulips. Flower edges are finely fringed. Colors include white, yellow, pink, red, and violet; fringing is often in a different color than rest of flower. Stems 16–24 in. high.

Viridiflora tulips. Flowers edged in green or colored in blends of green with other hues—white, yellow, rose, red, and buff. Stems 10–20 in. high. Good cut flowers.

Rembrandt tulips. Streaks and variegation on the original Rembrandts were caused by a transmittable virus; these infected bulbs can no longer be imported and should not be planted. Tulips now sold as Rembrandts have patterning of genetic, not viral, origin. The division now includes other variegated types and the old Bizarre and Bybloem groups.

Parrot tulips. Large, long, deeply fringed and ruffled flowers atop 16–20-in. stems are striped, feathered, and flamed in various colors, including green. They once had weak, floppy stems, but modern types are stouter.

Double late tulips. Often called peony-flowered tulips, these have very large (to 5 in. wide), long-lasting, heavy-textured double blossoms on 14–20-in. stems. Colors include orange, rose, yellow, and white.

SPECIES TULIPS

Kaufmanniana tulips. Often called waterlily tulip, *T. kaufmanniana* is a very early bloomer with 3-in., creamy yellow flowers (marked red on petal backs) with dark yellow centers; the flowers open flat in sun. Stems 6–8 in. high. Hybrids come in various colors, usually with flower centers in a contrasting color; many have mottled leaves like Greigii tulips.

CLOCKWISE FROM TOP: *Tulipa* 'Queen of Sheba'; Blue Parrot tulips; *T.* 'Apricot Parrot'

Fosteriana tulips. Early-blooming *T. fosteriana* has the largest flowers—to 8 in. wide—of any tulip. The huge red blossoms appear atop 8–10-in. stems. Hybrids include varieties with flowers in red, orange, yellow, pink, and white. The 16-in.-high 'Red Emperor' has fiery red flowers. All are good choices for perennial beds.

Greigii tulips. Midseason-blooming *T. greigii* has big (6 in.) flowers borne on 10-in. stems; leaves are heavily spotted and streaked with brown. Hybrids have flowers in white, pink, red, and orange; many feature several colors in a single blossom. Excellent in pots.

Miscellaneous tulips. A collection of species, varieties, and cultivars in which the wild species is evident. Sold mainly by bulb specialists. Most are native to western and central Asia. They tend to be simpler-looking than large hybrid tulips, with a wildflower charm. Generally best in rock gardens or wild

gardens, where plantings can remain undisturbed for many years; plant 4 in. apart. Also good in pots. Species that will persist from year to year in mild-winter areas are noted. Botanists frequently change names.

T. acuminata. Flowers have long, twisted, spidery segments of red and yellow on 1½-ft.-high stems. Late.

T. bakeri. Zones 2–24. Similar to and often listed as *T. saxatilis*. Lilac to pinkish purple flowers with a yellow base open to a wide, flat star; they are borne in clusters of three or four on stems to 6–8 in. high. 'Lilac Wonder', to 6–7 in. high, has rosy lilac flowers with a large, circular lemon yellow base. Midseason. Good in mild-winter areas.

T. batalinii. See *T. linifolia* Batalini group.

T. clusiana. LADY or CANDY TULIP. Slender flowers on 9-in. stems are rosy red outside, white inside. Blossoms of 6-in.-high *T. c. chrysantha* (*T. stellata chrysantha*) are star-shaped when fully open; they have rose-carmine outer segments (shading to buff at base), and bright yellow inner segments. *T. clusiana*

and *T. c. chrysantha* both bloom in midseason and they make good permanent tulips in mild-winter areas.

T. humilis (T. pulchella). One to three pale pink or purplish pink flowers with a yellow center atop each 4–6-in. stem. Early bloom. 'Violacea' has deep violet flowers, usually with a yellow base.

T. linifolia Batalinii group (T. batalinii). Soft yellow flowers on 6–10-in. stems. Very narrow leaves. 'Yellow Jewel' has yellow blossoms tinged with rose. Midseason.

T. praestans. Up to six orange-red flowers on each 2-ft.

stem. Midseason. 'Fusilier' is an improved selection growing 10–14 in. high. 'Unicum' is similar but has leaves edged in white.

T. pulchella. See *T. humilis*.

T. saxatilis. Zones 2–24. Fragrant, yellow-based pale lilac flowers open nearly flat, are carried one to three to each 1-ft. stem. Early bloom. Good choice in mild-winter areas.

T. stellata chrysantha. See *T. clusiana chrysantha*.

T. sylvestris. Sweetly fragrant, yellow, 2-in. flowers, one or two to each 1-ft. stem. Late. Good choice in mild-winter areas. Naturalizes freely.

How to Grow Tulips

CHILLING Nearly all hybrid tulips and most species (wild) tulips need an extended period of winter cold for best performance. In mild climates, provide the necessary chill by refrigerating bulbs for 6 weeks (not near ripening fruit) before planting; then treat the plants as annuals.

Even in cold-winter regions, there's no guarantee of consistent performance after the first year. Tulip bulbs form offsets that take a few years to reach blooming size, but as offsets mature, they draw energy from the mother bulb. The result is a decline in flowering. For this reason, most tulips are often treated as short-lived perennials in cold climates, though you can encourage repeat flowering by fertilizing with nitrogen before bloom and by letting foliage wither before removing it after bloom.

Some species tulips are exceptions to the above; they give good repeat bloom even where winters are mild.

EXPOSURE Tulips need sunshine at least while in bloom; they will lean toward the source of light if planting area is unevenly shaded. It's fine to plant under deciduous trees if the trees won't leaf out until after the bloom is finished (this is a good practice in hot-summer areas).

SOIL Rich, sandy soil is ideal, though some tulips will grow in any good, fast-draining soil. They perform poorly in soils where tulips were recently growing; choose a new site or dig out the soil to the requisite planting depth and replace it with fresh soil from elsewhere in the garden.

PLANTING Set bulbs three times as deep as they are wide (a little shallower in heavy soils). Space 4–6 in. apart, depending on the eventual size of the plant. Where temperatures regularly dip below 32°F (0°C), plant in October to November, after the soil has cooled. In warmer regions, plant in December or January.

DIVIDING If tulips do persist from year to year, they will eventually need separating. Dig and divide clumps in late summer; replant at the best time for your climate. Species tulips can be left undisturbed for many years.

PROBLEMS To protect tulips from gophers and other burrowing animals, plant in baskets made of ¼-in. wire mesh. Thwart ground squirrels and other animals that like to dig up bulbs by securing chicken wire over new plantings. Protect from slugs and snails. Aphids are another pest.

T

»

T. tarda. Zones A1–A3; 1–24. Each 3–5-in. stem has three to six upward-facing, star-like flowers with golden centers, white-tipped segments. Early.

T. turkestanica. Fragrant, creamy white flowers with yellow centers. Borne on 6–8-in.-high stems, as many as 12 per bulb.

Tupidanthus calyptratus.
See *Schefflera pueckleri*

Turnip and Rutabaga
Brassicaceae
BIENNIALS GROWN AS ANNUALS

✀ **ALL ZONES**

☼ **FULL SUN**

💧 **REGULAR WATER**

'Red Top' turnip

These Mediterranean natives are cabbage relatives and, like cabbage, belong to the genus *Brassica*. Turnips are best known for roots, though foliage is also edible (some varieties are grown for leaves only). Roots come in various colors (white, white with purple on upper part, creamy yellow) and shapes (globe, flattened globe). Rutabaga is a tasty turnip relative with large yellowish roots; its leaves are palatable only when very young. Turnip roots grow fast and should be harvested and used as soon as they are big enough to eat. Rutabaga is a late-maturing crop that stores well in the ground; its flavor improves with light frost.

Grow turnip and rutabaga in rich, loose, well-drained soil. Plant in early spring (for early summer harvest) where winters are cold or in summer (for fall harvest). Where winters are mild, plant in fall for a winter crop. Sow seeds 1 in. apart. Thin turnips to 2–6 in. apart for roots, 1–4 in. apart for greens. Thin rutabaga plants to 5–8 in. apart; each one needs ample space for root to reach full weight of 3–5 lbs. Roots of turnip and rutabaga are milder if soil is kept moist, become more pungent under drier conditions. Turnip roots are ready to harvest about 75 days after sowing, rutabaga in 90 to 120 days. Root maggot is a pest of turnip (less likely to infest rutabaga); see Cabbage for control.

Ugni molinae
(Myrtus ugni)
CHILEAN GUAVA
Myrtaceae
EVERGREEN SHRUB

✀ **ZONES 14–24**

☼ ◐ **PARTIAL SHADE IN HOTTEST CLIMATES**

💧 **REGULAR WATER**

Ugni molinae

South American native grown for foliage, flowers, and fruit. Slow to moderate growth to 3–6 ft. tall and wide. Scraggly and open in youth but has a compact, rounded form when mature. Small, oval, leathery leaves are dark green with bronze tints above, whitish beneath; edges are slightly rolled under. Rose-tinted white flowers resembling little bottle-brushes appear in late spring, early summer. These are followed by purplish or reddish, ½-in., pleasant-tasting fruit that smells like apples and can be eaten fresh or used in jams and jellies. Tidy, restrained plant for patios, terraces, near walks and paths. Give neutral to acid soil. For related plants that are grown primarily for fruit, see *Feijoa sellowiana* and Guava.

Ulmus
ELM
Ulmaceae
DECIDUOUS OR SEMIEVERGREEN TREES

✀ **ZONES VARY BY SPECIES**

☼ **FULL SUN**

💧 **REGULAR WATER**

Ulmus glabra 'Camperdownii'

Once highly prized shade trees, elms have fallen on hard times. Dutch elm disease (spread by a bark beetle) has killed millions of American elms in North America and can attack most other elm species. Many of the larger elms are appealing fare for various types of aphids, beetles, leafhoppers, and scale, making them time-consuming to care for, messy, or both. Elms have other problems not related to pests. They have aggressive, shallow root systems, so you'll have trouble growing other plants beneath them. Many produce suckers; branch crotches are often narrow, splitting easily in storms. Still, elms are widely planted, and researchers continue to devote much effort to finding disease-resistant varieties. Elms tolerate a wide range of soils. Poor yellow fall color except as noted.

U. americana. AMERICAN ELM. Deciduous. Zones 1–11, 14–21. Native to eastern North America. This majestic, arching tree once graced lawns and streets throughout its range, but it has been decimated by Dutch elm disease. Fast growth to 100 ft. or taller with nearly equal—sometimes greater—spread. Main branches upright, outer ones pendulous. Rough-surfaced, 3–6-in.-long, toothed dark green leaves; great variation in shade of yellow fall color. Leafs out very late where winters are mild. Pale green, papery seeds make a mess in spring. Disease-resistant varieties include 'Princeton' (upright, to 65 ft. tall), 'Valley Forge' (vase-shaped, to 70 ft. tall), and 'Jefferson' (vase-shaped, to 70 ft. tall).

U. glabra. SCOTCH ELM. Deciduous. Zones 2–11, 14–21. Native to Europe. Fairly upright habit to 120 ft. tall, 80 ft. wide. Sharply toothed, rough-surfaced, 3–6-in.-long leaves on very short stalks. Rarely planted now, but old trees are sometimes seen. 'Camperdownii', Camperdown elm, generally 10–20 ft. tall and wide, has weeping branches that reach to ground, making a tent of shade.

U. hybrids. Zones 2–9, 14–21. Many institutions have been carrying on breeding experiments involving various elms to produce trees resistant to Dutch elm disease. Among them, 'Accolade' has the best track record so far; it grows to 70 ft. tall and 60 ft. wide, with arching limbs and a vase shape much like that of American elm. 'Danada Charm' has a similar size and shape but is ganglier in youth. 'Frontier', just 40 ft. tall and 30 ft. wide, features reddish purple leaves in fall. 'Homestead', to 55 ft. tall and 35 ft. wide, has a symmetrical oval to pyramidal form. 'Patriot' forms a narrow vase shape to 50 ft. tall and half as wide. 'Triumph' grows 55 ft. tall, 50 ft. wide; it forms an upright oval with a strong central leader.

U. parvifolia. CHINESE ELM, CHINESE EVERGREEN ELM. Semievergreen or deciduous, according to winter temperatures and individual tree's heredity. Zones 3–24. From China, Korea, and Japan. Fast

T

growth to 40–60 ft. tall, 50–70 ft. wide; often reaches 30 ft. in 5 years. Form is extremely variable, but trees are generally spreading, with long, arching, eventually weeping branchlets. On older trees, bark of trunk sheds in patches (somewhat like bark of sycamore, *Platanus*), often creating beautiful mottling. Leathery dark green, ¾–2½-in.-long, evenly toothed leaves. Round fruit produced in fall. Patio tree, sun screen, or (with careful pruning) street tree. Rub or cut out small branches along trunk for first few years; shorten overlong branches or strongly weeping ones to strengthen scaffolding. Older trees may need thinning to lessen chance of storm damage. Subject to Texas root rot in desert but otherwise little bothered by pests or diseases.

Forms that hold their leaves are often sold as 'Sempervirens', but that is not a true variety. Two commonly offered, more or less evergreen varieties are 'Brea', with larger leaves and more upright habit than the species; and 'Drake', with smaller leaves, weeping habit. A more reliably evergreen variety is round-headed 'True Green', with small, deep green leaves. Other selections include 'Allee' ('Emer II'), vase-shaped tree to 70 ft. tall, 60 ft. wide; 'Athena Classic' ('Emer I'), moderately fast grower to 35 ft. tall, 50 ft. wide; and 'Dynasty', to 40 ft. by 40 ft., vaselike when young, later rounded. 'Everclear' has a narrow habit to 40 ft. tall and 15 ft. wide. There are also dwarf varieties commonly used for bonsai.

A note of caution: A less desirable species, *U. pumila* (Siberian elm), is sometimes sold as Chinese elm.

U. pumila. SIBERIAN ELM. Deciduous. Zones A1–A3; 1–11, 14–21; used chiefly in Zones A1–A3, 1, 2, 10, 11, where climate limits tree choices. From Russia and northern China. To 50 ft. tall, 40 ft. wide. Smooth dark green leaves are ¾–2 in. long. Resists Dutch elm disease and endures cold, heat, aridity, and poor soil—but has brittle wood and weak crotches and is not a desirable tree. Possibly useful in holding soil against erosion; fast growth also makes it suitable for windbreak or shelterbelt. Papery, winged seeds disperse seedlings over wide area.

U. wilsoniana 'Prospector'. Zones 3–9, 14–21. Fairly new variety from western China; similar in shape to *U. americana*. Likely ultimate size is 40 ft. tall, 30 ft. wide. Leaves are orange-red when new, mature to deep shiny green, turn yellow in fall. Resistant to Dutch elm disease and elm leaf beetles.

Umbellularia californica

CALIFORNIA LAUREL, CALIFORNIA BAY, OREGON MYRTLE, PEPPERWOOD
Lauraceae
EVERGREEN TREE

⚡ **ZONES 4–9, 14–24**
☀ ◑ ● **SUN OR SHADE**
◐ ◓ ◉ **LITTLE TO REGULAR WATER**

Umbellularia californica

Native to southwestern Oregon, California Coast Ranges, and lower elevations of the Sierra Nevada. In the wild, form varies. On windy hillsides near coast, it is a huge, gumdrop-shaped shrub; in forests, it's a tree to 75 ft. tall, over 100 ft. wide. In gardens, it tends to grow slowly (about 1 ft. a year) to 20–25 ft. tall and wide. Lance-shaped leaves are medium to deep yellow-green and glossy above, dull light green beneath. Leaves can be substituted for sweet bay (*Laurus nobilis*) in cooking, but they have a more pungent flavor. Clusters of tiny yellowish flowers give plant a yellowish cast in spring. Blossoms are followed by olivelike, purplish, inedible fruit.

CARE

Grows best and fastest in deep soil with regular water but tolerates many other conditions, including aridity. Will grow in deep shade and ultimately get big enough to become shade maker itself (casts very dense shade unless thinned). Though often afflicted with sooty mold resulting from aphid or scale infestation, it is nonetheless useful for screen, background planting, tall hedge. Heavy drop of yellow to tan leaves in fall.

California laurel is the main host of *Phytophthora ramorum*, the fungus that causes sudden oak death (see page 547); the tree can transmit the fungus but is not usually killed by it. In the Coast Ranges from California's Big Sur through Curry County in southern Oregon, growing California laurel within 35 ft. of any of the following plants is likely to result in their infection and death: coast live oak (*Quercus agrifolia*), canyon live oak (*Q. chrysolepis*), California black oak (*Q. kelloggii*), Shreve oak (*Q. parvula shrevei*), and tanbark oak (*Lithocarpus densiflorus*).

Uncinia rubra

RED HOOK SEDGE
Cyperaceae
PERENNIAL

⚡ **ZONES 4–6, 15–17**
☀ ◑ **FULL SUN OR PARTIAL SHADE**
● **REGULAR WATER**

Uncinia rubra

Grassy perennial from the mountains of New Zealand. Stiff, narrow, slightly arching leaves form a tuft 8–15 in. high and wide. Foliage is rich, dark

mahogany to bronze-green; lovely when backlit. Black, sharply pointed seed heads are produced in summer. Good choice for container, pond, or stream edge. Reseeds a bit, but not enough to be a problem. Does not do well in intense heat; mulch to keep roots cool.

Ungnadia speciosa

MEXICAN BUCKEYE
Sapindaceae
DECIDUOUS TREE OR LARGE SHRUB

⚡ **ZONES 10–13**
☀ ◑ **FULL SUN TO PARTIAL SHADE**
◐ **LITTLE WATER**
◆ **SEEDS ARE POISONOUS**

Ungnadia speciosa

Useful small tree for desert areas. Native to western Texas, southern New Mexico, and northeastern Mexico. Grows 15–20 ft. tall and wide with large, dark green, divided leaves that turn yellow in fall. Showy, rose-pink flowers on bare branches in spring attract butterflies; the blooms are followed by unusual, three-part seedpods containing three hard seeds. Pods hang on bare branches in winter. Naturally multitrunked but can be trained to a single trunk tree. Grows best in well-drained, alkaline soil.

This four-season showpiece has pink springtime flowers, deep green leaves that turn yellow in autumn, and showy winter seedpods.

U

Ursinia anethoides

Asteraceae
PERENNIAL USUALLY GROWN AS ANNUAL

⚸ **ALL ZONES**

☼ **FULL SUN**

◐◑ **MODERATE TO REGULAR WATER**

Ursinia anethoides
'Solar Fire'

Fast-growing, bushy plant from the Cape region of South Africa. Grows to 15 in. high and wide, with very finely divided, bright green leaves reminiscent of dill. Golden orange flowers 2 in. across have a maroon circle around a central golden eye. Flowers open during the day, close in the evening and on cloudy days. Bloom period lasts for several months, peaking in summer. Tolerant of heat and drought once established. 'Solar Fire' is an excellent variety with larger flowers.

This South African annual with orange petals and a maroon-ringed eye is a real eye-catcher. For striking contrast, try it with gentian blue *Anagallis monelli.* Or grow it singly in a container at least 12 inches wide.

Vaccinium

Ericaceae
EVERGREEN OR DECIDUOUS SHRUBS

⚸ **ZONES VARY BY SPECIES**

☼ ◑ ● **EXPOSURE NEEDS VARY BY SPECIES**

◐ ◑ ◑◑ **WATER NEEDS VARY BY SPECIES**

🦋 **BERRIES ATTRACT BIRDS, BUTTERFLIES**

Vaccinium parvifolium

Excellent ornamental shrubs. Clusters of bell-shaped flowers in spring; colorful, edible berries. Provide organically enriched, acid soil. Good for woodland gardens. For species grown largely for fruit, see Blueberry.

V. macrocarpon. CRANBERRY. Evergreen. Zones 1–6, 17. Native to northeastern U.S. and eastern Canada. To 2–6 in. high, spreading and rooting from stems to indefinite width. Narrow, dark green leaves turn coppery or purplish in winter. Tiny pinkish flowers; tart red berries in autumn. Commercial growers raise this plant in bogs—beds that can be flooded to control weeds and pests and make harvesting easier. Gardeners can use cranberry as an attractive small-scale groundcover in full sun (space plants 2 ft. apart). Provide ample water.

V. moupinense. Zones A3; 2–7, 14–17. Evergreen. Native to western China. Compact, mounded shrub to 1–2 ft. high and wide. New growth emerges bronzy red, matures to dark green, turning dark red in fall. Reddish brown flowers followed by tart, purplish black fruit.

V. ovatum. EVERGREEN HUCKLEBERRY. Zones 4–7, 14–17, 22–24. Native to Pacific coastal region, from Santa Barbara area of Southern California north to British Columbia. Erect growth to 2–3 ft. high and wide in sun, 8–10 ft. tall and broad in shade. Leathery, lustrous dark green leaves; bronzy or reddish when new. White or pinkish flowers are followed by black berries that are good in pies, jams, jellies, and syrups. Can be trimmed as a hedge or grown in containers. Cut branches are popular for arrangements. Sun or shade. Moderate to regular water.

V. parvifolium. RED HUCKLEBERRY. Deciduous. Zones A3; 2–7, 14–17. Native to Sierra Nevada, Coast Ranges from Northern California to Alaska. Slow-growing plant, eventually reaching 4–12 ft. (rarely 18 ft.) tall and 6 ft. wide. Thin green branches with spreading or cascading habit provide an intricate winter silhouette. Oval, thin-textured light green leaves. Greenish or whitish flowers are good in arrangements. Showy bright red berries can be used in jams, jellies, and pies. Partial or full shade. Regular water.

V. vitis-idaea. LINGONBERRY, COWBERRY, FOXBERRY. Evergreen. Zones 2–7, 14–17, except as noted. Native to Europe. Slow growth to 1 ft. high; spreads widely by rhizomes if grown in highly organic or thickly mulched soil. Glossy dark green leaves; new growth often tinged bright red or orange. White or pinkish flowers followed by sour red berries something like tiny cranberries; these are valued for preserves and syrups. Handsome little plant for informal edging around larger plantings; good small-scale groundcover (space plants 2–3 ft. apart). Best without potassium fertilizer. Regular to ample water. Prefers partial or full shade, but if given ample water, it will take full sun in cool-summer areas. European varieties grown for fruit production are sometimes seen.

V. v. minus. DWARF LINGONBERRY. Zones A1–A3; 1–7, 14–17. Cold-hardier form from arctic North America. Has smaller leaves (to ½ in.), is attractive in rock gardens and containers.

Valeriana officinalis

VALERIAN, GARDEN HELIOTROPE
Caprifoliaceae
PERENNIAL

⚸ **ZONES 1–24**

☼ ◑ **FULL SUN OR PARTIAL SHADE**

◐ **REGULAR WATER**

Valeriana officinalis

Hardy flowering perennial from Europe and western Asia. To 5 ft. tall in bloom, spreading to 4 ft. wide. Most of the foliage remains fairly close to ground. Light green leaves, each with 8 to 10 pairs of narrow, jagged-edged leaflets. Tall, straight flowering stems carry tiny, fragrant pink blossoms in rounded clusters at stem ends in summer; useful for cut flowers. White- and red-flowered forms exist. The strong-smelling roots are widely used in herbal preparations that are said to have sedative qualities. Roots also attract cats.

CARE

Start new plants from seed or divisions. Grow in mixed herb or flower borders, but be aware that it can become invasive; don't let it crowd other plants.

Valeriana rubra.
See *Centranthus ruber*

Vallota speciosa.
See *Cyrtanthus elatus*

Vancouveria
Berberidaceae
PERENNIALS

- ✂ ZONES VARY BY SPECIES
- ☼ PARTIAL SHADE
- ◐◑ MODERATE TO REGULAR WATER

Vancouveria hexandra

Closely related to *Epimedium* and likewise used as ground-covers in shady spots. Wiry leafstalks grow directly from creeping underground stems; leaves have numerous broad leaflets that resemble small ivy (*Hedera*) leaves. Threadlike flower stalks rise above foliage in late spring or early summer, bearing drooping clusters of small blossoms. Petals and sepals are sharply reflexed, giving flowers a windswept look. Plants spread slowly from ever-enlarging mat of roots, forming sizable patches in time.

V. chrysantha. Zones 5, 6, 14–17. Native to mountains of southwestern Oregon and extreme northwestern California. To 16 in. high, with bronzy gray-green, evergreen leaflets and yellow, ½-in. flowers.

V. hexandra. Zones 4–7, 14–17, 19–24. Native to coastal forests from Northern California to Washington. To 1 ft. high, with light green leaflets and white, ½-in. flowers. Dies back in winter.

V. planipetala (V. parvi-flora). INSIDE-OUT FLOWER. Zones 4–7, 14–17. Native to coastal areas of California and southwestern Oregon. To 2 ft. high, with light to medium green, shallowly lobed leaflets. Tiny (about ⅛ in. wide) white flowers are carried in clusters of 25 to 50. May die back in winter in colder part of range.

CARE
Set plants about 1½ ft. apart. Need cool, moist, and acid conditions.

Vauquelinia
Rosaceae
EVERGREEN SHRUBS OR TREES

- ✂ ZONES 10–13
- ☼☼ FULL SUN OR PARTIAL SHADE
- ◐◑ LITTLE TO MODERATE WATER

Vauquelinia californica

Rather open-growing plants to 20 ft. tall, 15 ft. wide, with upright, sometimes twisted branches. Somewhat reminis-cent of oleander (*Nerium*) in habit. Narrow, leathery, typically tooth-edged leaves are dark green above, grayish beneath. Small white flowers in 2–3-in. clusters decorate branch tips in spring. Blossoms are followed by woody seed capsules that last through fall and winter.

V. californica. ARIZONA ROSEWOOD. Native to southern Arizona, Baja California, and Mexico. Leaves to 4 in. long.

V. corymbosa angustifo-lia. SLIMLEAF VAUQUELINIA. Native to western Texas and northern Mexico. Has longer (6 in.), usually narrower leaves and showier flower clusters than *V. californica*. Often sold as *V. corymbosa*.

CARE
Grow as large shrubs or train as single- or multitrunked trees. Very drought-tolerant but look best with some water during the hot months.

FOR OTHER UNTHIRSTY PLANTS, SEE PAGES 74–77.

Veltheimia bracteata
Asparagaceae
PERENNIAL FROM BULB

- ✂ ZONES 13, 16–24; OR INDOORS
- ☼ PARTIAL SHADE; BRIGHT INDIRECT LIGHT
- ◐ REGULAR WATER DURING GROWTH AND BLOOM

Veltheimia bracteata

Handsome foliage is reason enough to grow this South Afri-can native. Each bulb produces a fountainlike rosette of wavy-edged, glossy green leaves to 1 ft. long, 3 in. wide. In winter or early spring, brown-mottled flower stems to about 1 ft. high are topped by elongated clus-ters of tubular, drooping, pinkish purple flowers tipped in green. Leaves turn yellow and die back in late spring; new growth resumes in fall. Most plants sold as *V. capensis* are actually *V. bracteata*; the true *V. capensis* has nonglossy blue-green leaves and green-tipped, pale pink flowers. It is also not as hardy and prefers full sun.

CARE
In frostless areas, veltheimia can be grown in the ground, but even there it is usually grown in pots. For each bulb, use a pot large enough to allow about 3 in. between all sides of bulb and container edges. Plant in fall, in fast-draining soil; set top of bulb neck just above soil sur-face. Fertilize every 2 weeks throughout growing season. Keep soil dry during summer dormancy. Can remain outdoors where temperatures stay above 25°F (−4°C); where light frosts are possible, give overhead protection.

Venidium fastuosum.
See *Arctotis fastuosa alba*

Verbascum
MULLEIN
Scrophulariaceae
BIENNIALS AND PERENNIALS

- ✂ ZONES VARY BY SPECIES
- ☼ FULL SUN
- ◐ MODERATE WATER

Verbascum hybridum
'Cotswold Queen'

Large group of rosette-forming, summer-blooming plants that send up spikes closely set with nearly flat, five-petaled, circular flowers about an inch across. Both foliage and stems are often covered in woolly hairs. Taller mulleins make striking vertical accents.

V. blattaria. MOTH MUL-LEIN. Biennial. Zones 1–11, 14–24. Native from Europe to central Asia. To 6 ft. tall, 2 ft. wide, with smooth-textured, dark green, cut or toothed leaves to 10 in. long. Yellow or creamy white flowers. There is also a pink flowering form.

V. bombyciferum 'Arctic Summer' ('Polarsommer'). Biennial. Zones 2–11, 14–24. Selection of a species native to Turkey. To 6 ft. tall, 2 ft. wide, with furry gray-green leaves to 1½ ft. long. Yellow flowers on powdery white stems.

V. chaixii. Perennial. Zones 2–11, 14–24. From Europe. To 3 ft. high and 2 ft. wide, with hairy green leaves to 6 in. long. Red-eyed, pale yellow flowers in narrow, often branching spikes. 'Album' has white flowers with purple centers. 'Sixteen Can-dles' produces abundant yellow blooms with purple eyes.

V

»

V. dumulosum. Perennial. Zones 7–9, 14–24. Dwarf to 1 ft. high and 1½ ft. wide, with velvety white leaves. Short, branching spikes of lemon yellow blossoms with purple centers. Hybrid 'Letitia' has a longer summer bloom season than the species.

V. hybridum. Zones 3–10, 14–24. Many hybrids are obtainable, either as blends or in single colors. Most must be grown from seed.

'Banana Custard'. Biennial. To 5–6 ft. tall and 2 ft. wide. Bright yellow flowers.

Benary hybrids, Cotswold hybrids. Perennials. These resemble V. phoeniceum but come in white, cream, pink, and purple. Named varieties include 'Helen Johnson' (peach pink) and 'Pink Domino' (bright pink).

'Copper Rose'. Perennial. To 4–6 ft. tall, 2 ft. wide, with buff, apricot, rose, or tan flowers. Bloom first year from seed sown in late winter, earliest spring.

'Sierra Sunset'. Perennial. Rosettes 8 in. high and 14–18 in. wide produce flower stalks 1½ ft. high that hold large blossoms in shades of melon and salmon, with rose accents.

V. olympicum. Perennial. Zones 3–10, 14–24. From Greece. To 5 ft. tall, 3 ft. wide, with soft, downy white leaves to over 2 ft. long. Bright yellow flowers; many flowering stems.

V. phoeniceum. PURPLE MULLEIN. Perennial. Zones 1–10, 14–24. To 2–4 ft. tall, 1½ ft. wide. Dark green leaves to 6 in. long are smooth on top, hairy beneath. Slender spikes of purple flowers. 'Violetta' grows 2–3 ft. high, with deep purple flowers.

CARE

Grow all in well-drained soil. Cut off spent flowers to encourage a second round of blooming. Mulleins self-sow freely—and some are downright weedy, such as the attractive roadside weed V. thapsus.

Grow these striking plants for their large leaves and spiky flowers that bees love.

Verbena
Verbenaceae
PERENNIALS, SOME GROWN AS ANNUALS

🗡 **ZONES VARY BY SPECIES**

☼ **FULL SUN**

◐ ◉ ◉ **WATER NEEDS VARY BY SPECIES**

🦋 **FLOWERS ATTRACT BUTTERFLIES**

Verbena hybrid 'Babylon Purple'

These showy perennials bear clusters of small, tubular, five-petaled flowers, usually in summer. Most are fast-growing groundcovers, good in parking strips, along driveways, on dry banks; also attractive in wall crevices and hanging baskets. Best in hot weather. Need good air circulation (to avoid mildew) and well-drained soil, especially in winter. There are many hybrid groups, which often confuses the botany.

V. bipinnatifida. Perennial. Zones 1–24. Native from western Great Plains to Mexico. To 8–16 in. high, 1½ ft. or wider. Finely divided leaves and blue flowers. Self-sows. 'Valley Lavender' is low growing, just 3–6 in. high, with bright lavender flowers over a long period. Little water.

V. bonariensis. Perennial in Zones 8–24; annual in colder climates. Native to South America; naturalized in California. Border plant to 3–6 ft. tall and 1½–3 ft. wide, with airy, branching stems carrying purple flowers. Leaves are mostly basal. Plant's see-through quality makes it suited for foreground as well as back of border. Self-sows freely. Little water.

V. gooddingii. Short-lived perennial. Zones 7–24. Native to Southwest deserts. To 1½–2 ft. high and 3–4 ft. wide, with small, deeply cut leaves. Pinkish lavender flowers at ends of short spikes. Blooms first summer from seed sown in spring. Can reseed. Little to moderate water.

V. hybrids (V. × hybrida, V. × hortensis). GARDEN VERBENA. Short-lived perennials in Zones 8–24; H1, H2; often treated as annual in all zones. Many-branched plant 6–12 in. high, 1½–3 ft. wide. Oblong, 2–4-in., bright green or gray-green leaves with toothed margins. Flowers in flat, compact clusters to 3 in. wide. Colors include white, pink, red, purple, blue, and combinations.

Older strains of hybrid verbena were seed grown, not as free blooming, and lacked resistance to powdery mildew. Newer, hardier strains include the Aztec, Superbena, Temari and Tapien series. They are usually perennials in Zones 4–9, 12–24; H1, H2; or annuals anywhere. They are low-growing plants available in a wide range of colors and, in general, are resistant to powdery mildew, free blooming, and heat-tolerant. Plants in the Babylon and Tapien series have more finely cut foliage. There is also the very popular, disease-resistant 'Homestead Purple', which is perennial in Zones 2–24 but is treated as annual anywhere. It grows a little bigger, to 1–2 ft. high and 2–3 ft. wide. 'Sissinghurst' is perennial in Zones 3–24 and grows a few inches high, 4 ft. wide, with bright red flowers. All need regular water.

V. lilacina. CEDROS ISLAND VERBENA. Perennial. Zones 12–24. Native to Baja California. To 1 ft. high, 3 ft. or wider. Light green, deeply cut leaves. Lilac-colored flowers bloom from spring to fall (nearly all year, in mildest areas). Useful groundcover for hot, dry sites. 'De La Mina' forms a 3-ft. mound, has darker purple flowers. Little to moderate water.

V. peruviana (V. chamaedrifolia). Perennial in Zones 8–24; usually treated as annual in all zones. Native to South America. Forms a flat mat that spreads rapidly by aboveground runners. Set out plants 2 ft. apart for a solid cover in one season. Neat, small, closely set

dark green leaves. Flat-topped clusters of scarlet-and-white flowers on slender stems cover foliage. Hybrids aren't as flat, spread more slowly, have slightly larger leaves and stouter stems, are available in several colors. Especially popular in Southern California and the desert. Moderate water.

V. rigida (V. venosa). Perennial in Zones 3–24; can be grown as annual (blooms in 4 months from seed). Native to South America. To 1–2 ft. high and 3–4 ft. wide. Rough, strongly toothed dark green leaves to 2–4 in. long. Lilac to purple-blue flowers in cylindrical clusters on tall, upright stems in summer and fall. Useful in low-maintenance gardens. Moderate to regular water. 'Flame', to just 4 in. high, is a cutting-grown selection with bright scarlet flowers.

V. stricta. Perennial. Zones 2–24. Native from Massachusetts to Montana, south to Mexico. Upright growth to 3 ft. high and 1½ ft. or wider. Hairy stems bear narrow to rounded, tooth-edged leaves to 4 in. long; medium green above, whitish beneath. Flower stems are also densely hairy and bear deep lavender or purple flowers. Regular water.

V. tenuisecta (V. pulchella graciliator). MOSS VERBENA. Perennial in Zones 7–9, 14–24; annual in colder climates. From South America. To 6–12 in. high and 2–5 ft. wide, with finely cut dark green leaves. Blue, purple, or violet flowers. 'Alba' is a white-flowered form. Moderate water.

Verbenas bloom best when the temperature rises. Combine them with other heat-loving perennials like yarrow (Achillea), agastache, desert marigold (Baileya multiradiata), coreopsis, blanket flower (Gaillardia), and lavender cotton (Santolina chamaecyparissus).

Veronica

SPEEDWELL

Plantaginaceae

PERENNIALS

- ✎ **ZONES VARY BY SPECIES**
- ☼ **FULL SUN, EXCEPT AS NOTED**
- ◊ ◗ ● **WATER NEEDS VARY BY SPECIES**
- 🦋 **FLOWERS ATTRACT BIRDS, BUTTERFLIES**

Veronica prostrata

Handsome plants ranging from less than an inch high to 2 ft. in height. Masses of small (¼– ½ in. wide) flowers in white, rose, pink, or pale to deep blue make an effective display. Use in borders and rock gardens. Prostrate ones are good between steppingstones and as bulb covers. Named varieties are not easily assigned to a species; authorities differ. For shrubby plants sometimes sold as *Veronica*, see *Hebe*.

V. alpina. Zones 1–7, 14– 17. From Europe, Eurasia, North America. Creeping rootstock forms low foliage rosette 4–8 in. high, 1 ft. wide. Spikelike clusters of blue flowers in spring or early summer; in warmer parts of range, often reblooms in fall. White-flowered 'Alba' grows to 10 in. high. Regular water.

V. austriaca teucrium 'Crater Lake Blue'. Zones 1–9, 14–21. Selection of a species native to Europe. To 12– 15 in. high and wide. Short spikes of intensely blue flowers in midsummer. Regular water.

V. gentianoides. GENTIAN SPEEDWELL. Zones 1–9, 14–21. From the Caucasus. Creeping rootstock forms a dense mat to 1–2 ft. high and wide. Oblong, glossy dark green leaves. In spring, foliage is topped by leafy

stems carrying 10-in. spikes of ice blue flowers with darker veining. 'Variegata' has leaves marked with white. 'Blue Streak' ('Ramona') has icy blue flowers. Regular water.

V. hybrids. The following are among the best varieties. Regular water, except as noted.

'**Blue Reflection**'. Zones 2–9, 14–21. Forms a gray-green foliage mat to 3 in. high and 1½ ft. wide, covered with blue flowers in midspring. Little to moderate water.

'**Goodness Grows**'. Zones 1–7, 14–17. To 1 ft. high and wide. Violet-blue blossoms over long bloom period—from late spring to frost, if old flowers are removed.

'**Sunny Border Blue**'. Zones A2, A3; 1–9, 14–21. Compact, clump-forming plant to 1½–2 ft. high, 1 ft. wide, with crinkled dark green leaves. Spires of dark violet-blue flowers appear in late spring or early summer; deadheading prolongs the show until frost.

'**Waterperry Blue**' ('**Water-perry**'). Zones 2–9, 14–21. Low, trailing plant to 4–6 in. high and 1½ ft. or more wide; roots as it spreads. Small, rounded, bronze-tinted leaves. Loose clusters of pale blue flowers veined in deeper blue; main bloom in spring, with sporadic flowering throughout summer and fall.

V. liwanensis. Zones 3–9, 14–24. From Turkey. Creeping groundcover to 1–2 in. high and 1½ ft. wide. In spring, the tiny, waxy deep green leaves are concealed by bright blue flowers. Foliage takes on purplish tints in hot sun. Little to regular water.

V. pectinata. Zones 1–9, 14–24. Western Mediterranean native. Forms prostrate mat of foliage to 3 in. high and 1 ft. wide; spreads by creeping stems that root at joints. Small grayish leaves have scalloped or deeply cut edges. Profuse spring or early summer show of deep blue flowers with white centers; blossoms are borne on 5–6-in. spikes among the leaves. Little to moderate water.

V. prostrata (V. rupestris). Zones 1–9, 14–24. Stems are hairy and tufted. Some are prostrate and form 1–1½-ft.-wide foliage mat; other stems grow erect to 8 in. high and are

topped by short clusters of pale blue flowers in late spring or early summer. 'Heavenly Blue' is almost entirely prostrate, with flower stems reaching 6 in. high. 'Mrs. Holt' has pale pink flowers. 'Trehane' and 'Aztec Gold' have golden yellow leaves, bright blue flowers. Little to moderate water.

V. repens. Zones 3–9, 14– 24. Mediterranean native. Flat mat to ½ in. high, 1 ft. or wider. Small, shiny green leaves clothe the prostrate stems, give plant a mossy look. Clusters of tiny lavender to white flowers appear in spring. 'Sunshine' has golden yellow foliage. Tolerates some shade. Little to moderate water.

V. spicata. Zones A2, A3; 1–9, 14–21; except as noted. From Europe, Asia. Rounded, 1½–2-ft.-wide clump sends up 2-ft.-high stems clothed in pointed oval, glossy green leaves and topped in summer with spikes of bright blue flowers. Long bloom season if faded flowers are removed. 'Glory' ('Royal Candles') grows about 1 ft. high with deep violet-blue blossoms. 'Icicle', to 15–18 in. high, has white flower spikes. 'Nana' grows only 6 in. high and

CLOCKWISE FROM TOP: *Veronica spicata* 'Red Fox'; *V. s.* 'Glory'; *V. gentianoides*

bears violet-blue blossoms. 'Red Fox' ('Rotfuchs'), to 15 in. high and wide, has deep rosy red blooms. 'Tickled Pink' is a similar size with medium pink flowers. Regular water.

V. s. incana (V. incana). SILVER SPEEDWELL. Zones A1– A3; 1–7, 14–17. Furry, silvery white foliage forms a 1–1½-ft.-wide mat. Blooms in summer, producing deep violet-blue blossoms on stems to about 1 ft. high. Little to moderate water.

V. umbrosa 'Georgia Blue'. Zones 2–9, 14–24. From country of Georgia. Forms a 6–8-in.-high mat that spreads to several feet wide; small dark green leaves turn bronze in cool weather. Profuse, white-eyed cobalt blue flowers in spring, with a few blossoms appearing throughout summer and fall. Regular water.

FOR OTHER PLANTS THAT ATTRACT BIRDS AND BUTTERFLIES, SEE PAGES 95–103.

V

Verticordia plumosa
FEATHERFLOWER
Myrtaceae
EVERGREEN SHRUB

- 🌿 **ZONES 16, 17, 22–24**
- ☼ ◐ **SUN OR PARTIAL SHADE**
- ◌ **LITTLE WATER**

Verticordia plumosa

This shrub from southwestern Australia grows to 3 ft. high and wide, with wavy branches covered in soft, needlelike foliage. From late winter into spring, produces a profusion of tiny lavender flowers at branch tips. Excellent cut flower. Requires well-drained soil; feed occasionally with low-phosphorus fertilizer. 'Pink Lace' is a compact grower to just 1½–2 ft. high and wide, with lightly fragrant, lavender-pink flowers.

At the base of featherflower plants—and some banksias and eucalypts—you may find odd swollen structures called lignotubers. These woody organs contain many dormant buds as well as nutrient reserves that allow the plant to regrow after damage, including after fires.

Viburnum
Adoxaceae
DECIDUOUS AND EVERGREEN SHRUBS OR TREES

- 🌿 **ZONES VARY BY SPECIES**
- ☼ ◐ **FULL SUN OR PARTIAL SHADE, EXCEPT AS NOTED**
- ● **REGULAR WATER, EXCEPT AS NOTED**
- 🦋 **ATTRACT BIRDS, BUTTERFLIES**

Viburnum lantana

Large, diverse group of plants with generally oval, often handsome leaves and clusters of typically white, sometimes fragrant flowers. Blossoms are usually followed by single-seeded, often brilliantly colored fruit much appreciated by birds. Many viburnums are grown for their flower display, a few for showy fruit. Many evergreen types are valuable as foliage plants. Several species (noted below) can be grown as small trees.

V. awabuki. SWEET VIBURNUM. Evergreen. Zones 15–24; at some risk of frost damage in Zones 8, 9, 14. From Asia. Often sold as *V. odoratissimum.* Shrub or small tree to 12 ft. tall, 8 ft. wide. Glossy dark green leaves. Conical, 3–6-in. clusters of fragrant flowers in spring. Pendulous clusters of red fruit that ripens to black. 'Chindo' has smaller leaves, denser habit; makes a good tall hedge or screen.

V. × bodnantense. Deciduous. Zones 4–9, 14–24. To 10 ft. (or more) tall, 6 ft. wide. Dark green leaves are deeply veined, turn dark scarlet in fall. Blooms from fall to spring, bearing loose clusters of very fragrant deep pink flowers that age to paler pink. Red fruit is not showy. Best known is 'Dawn' ('Pink Dawn'). Flower buds freeze in the coldest Northwest winters.

V. × burkwoodii. Deciduous in coldest areas, nearly evergreen elsewhere. Zones 2–12, 14–24, except as noted. To 6–12 ft. tall, 4–8 ft. wide. Glossy dark green leaves have white, hairy undersides; turn purplish red in cold weather. Dense, 4-in. clusters of pink buds open to very fragrant flowers in late winter or early spring. Blue-black fruit is not showy. Early growth is straggly, but mature plants are dense. Can be espaliered.

'Chenault' (*V. chenaultii*). Denser, more compact, slightly later blooming, more deciduous in mild climates than the species.

'Mohawk'. Zones 1–12, 14–24. To 7 ft. tall and 5 ft. wide. Red buds are showy long before they open into white flowers. Showy orange-red fall color.

V. × carlcephalum. FRAGRANT SNOWBALL. Deciduous. Zones 3–11, 14–24. To 6–10 ft. tall and wide. Dull grayish green leaves are downy beneath; turn reddish purple in autumn. Longlasting, waxy, sweetly perfumed spring flowers in dense, 4–5-in. clusters. No fruit. As showy as *V. opulus* 'Roseum' but has the bonus of fragrance.

V. carlesii. KOREAN SPICE VIBURNUM. Deciduous. Zones A3; 2–11, 14–24. From Korea, Japan. Loose, open habit to 4–8 ft. tall and wide. Leaves like those of *V. × carlcephalum*; inconsistent reddish fall color. Pink buds in 2–3-in. clusters open to sweetly fragrant white flowers in spring. Blue-black fruit is not showy. Does best with part shade in hottest months.

V. davidii. Evergreen. Zones 4–9, 14–24. From western China. Compact mound to 3–4 ft. tall and wide. Handsome, glossy dark green, deeply veined leaves. White flowers in 3-in. clusters open from dull pinkish red buds in spring; they are not showy but are followed by an arresting show of metallic turquoise-blue fruit. Grow with acid-loving plants. Partial shade. Especially good viburnum for Zones 4–6, 17.

V. dentatum. ARROWWOOD. Deciduous. Zones 1–11, 14–21. From eastern and central North America. To 6–10 ft. or taller, equally wide. Cream-colored flowers in late spring are followed by blue-black fruit. Dark green, oval to rounded, 4-in. leaves turn yellow, orange, or deep red in fall.

V. edule. HIGHBUSH CRANBERRY. Deciduous. Zones A1–A3; 1–11. Native to northern Asia and northern North America, including Alaska. Coarse-looking plant to 4–8 ft. tall, 2–4 ft. wide. Roundish dark green leaves are three lobed toward the tip, turn reddish maroon in fall. Inch-wide clusters of flowers in late spring or early summer are followed by small, musty-smelling red fruits that are tart but edible.

V. farreri (V. fragrans). Deciduous. Zones 3–9, 14–24. From northern China. Loose habit to 10 ft. tall, 8 ft. wide. Smooth, heavily veined green leaves turn soft russet red to reddish purple in fall. Fragrant white to pink flowers in 2-in. clusters on bare stems at some point between late fall and spring. Blooms survive to 20°F to 22°F (−7°C to −6°C) but freeze at lower temperatures. Bright red fruit. Prune to prevent leggy growth. 'Candidissimum' ('Album') has pure white flowers, pale yellow fruit. 'Nanum' is pink-flowered, grows to 2½ ft. high and 3 ft. wide.

V. hybrids. These spring-blooming viburnums all have complex ancestry.

'Cayuga'. Deciduous. Zones 2–11, 14–24. To 5 ft. tall and wide. Dark green, 1–3-in.-long leaves. White flowers open from pink buds.

'Chesapeake'. Semievergreen. Zones 3–11, 14–24. To 8 ft. tall, 10 ft. wide, with wavy-edged, glossy dark green leaves. Two-inch clusters of fragrant white flowers open from pink buds; dull red fruit ages to black.

'Conoy'. Evergreen. Zones 3–12, 14–24. Dense growth to 5 ft. tall and wide. Lustrous dark green, 2–2½-in. leaves are whitish beneath; take on maroon tinge in cold winters. Slightly fragrant flowers are followed by long-lasting red berries. Tolerates shearing.

'Eskimo'. Semievergreen. Zones 3–12, 14–24. Dense, compact habit to 5 ft. tall and wide. Shiny dark green leaves to 4 in. long; unscented flowers in 3–4-in., snowball-like clusters.

V. japonicum. Evergreen. Zones 5–10, 12, 14–24. From Japan. To 10–15 ft. tall, 8–12 ft. wide; can be trained as a small tree. Leathery, glossy dark green leaves. Sparse spring show of fragrant flowers in 4-in. clusters. Red fruit is likewise sparse—but very attractive. Best with some shade in hottest climates.

V. × juddii. Deciduous. Zones 2–9, 14–24. To 4–8 ft. tall, 6–10 ft. wide. More spreading and bushy than V. carlesii but similar to it in other respects, including fragrance.

V. lantana. WAYFARING TREE. Deciduous. Zones A3; 2–9, 14–17. From Europe and Asia Minor. Rounded habit to 10–20 ft. tall and wide; can be trained as a small tree. Dark green leaves turn an inconsistent purplish red in fall. Flat, 3–5-in. clusters of midspring flowers develop into yellow fruits that gradually age to red, then black; all colors are sometimes present at once. 'Mohican' is more compact (to 9 ft. tall and wide), with fruit that holds its red color longer.

V. macrocephalum (V. m. 'Sterile'). CHINESE SNOWBALL. Deciduous in coldest areas, nearly evergreen elsewhere. Zones 3–9, 14–24. This species originated in cultivation (not in the wild). Rounded habit to 12–20 ft. tall and wide. Dull green leaves, oval to oblong. Spectacular big, rounded, 6–8-in. flower clusters bloom in spring (or anytime during warm weather); they are composed of sterile flowers that start out lime green, change to white. No fruit. Can be espaliered. V. m. keteleeri, wild form from China, has sterile and fertile flowers in lacecap effect; sometimes produces fruit.

V. odoratissimum. See V. awabuki.

V. opulus. EUROPEAN CRANBERRY BUSH. Deciduous. Zones A2, A3; 1–9, 14–24. From Europe, North Africa, and central Asia. To 8–15 ft. tall and wide, with arching branches. Lobed, maplelike dark green leaves. Fall foliage color may be yellow, bright red, or reddish purple. Blooms in spring; flower heads have a lacecap look, with a 2–4-in. cluster of small fertile blossoms ringed with larger sterile blossoms. Large, showy red fruit persists from fall into winter. Takes moist to boggy soils. Control aphids.

'Aureum'. Golden yellow foliage. Give some shade to prevent sunburn.

'Compactum'. Like the species but smaller—to 4–5 ft. tall and wide.

'Nanum'. To 2 ft. high and wide. Needs no trimming as low, informal hedge. Cannot take poorly drained, wet soils. No flowers or fruit.

'Roseum' ('Sterile'). COMMON SNOWBALL. Resembles the species but has snowball-like flower clusters 2–2½ in. across, composed entirely of sterile flowers (so bears no fruit). Aphids are especially troublesome.

V. plicatum (V. tomentosum 'Sterile'). JAPANESE SNOWBALL. Deciduous. Zones 3–9, 14–24. From China and Japan. To 8–15 ft. tall and wide; horizontal branching pattern gives the plant a tiered look. Strongly veined, dull dark green leaves turn purplish red in autumn. Showy, 3-in., snowball-like clusters of sterile flowers look like those of V. opulus 'Roseum', but this plant is less bothered by aphids. Midspring bloom. No fruit. 'Popcorn' has especially heavy bloom.

V. p. tomentosum. DOUBLE-FILE VIBURNUM. Deciduous. From China and Japan. A truly beautiful viburnum. Resembles the species but has lacecap flower heads: flat, 2–4-in. clusters of small fertile flowers edged with 1–1½-in. sterile ones. Fruit is red aging to black; showy but not always profuse. 'Mariesii' grows to 6–8 ft. tall, 8–10 ft. wide; has larger sterile flowers. 'Shasta' has a very wide-spreading habit (6 ft. tall, 12 ft. wide). Varieties blooming from spring to the end of the growing season include 'Nanum Semperflorens' ('Watanabe'), 'Summer Snowflake', and 'Summer Stars'; all grow to 4–6 ft. tall and wide.

V. × pragense. PRAGUE VIBURNUM. Evergreen. Zones 3–11, 14–24. Fast-growing, rounded plant to 10 ft. tall and broad. Shiny dark green leaves. Faintly fragrant white flowers in

CLOCKWISE FROM TOP: *Viburnum sargentii* 'Onondaga'; *V. plicatum* 'Mariesii'; *V. davidii*

3–6-in. clusters open from pink buds in early spring.

V. × rhytidophylloides. Zones 3–9, 14–24. These are hybrids between V. rhytidophyllum and V. lantana. Among the best is 'Allegheny', a dense, rounded plant 6–8 ft. tall and broad; it is evergreen in most winters. Leaves resemble those of V. rhytidophyllum but are broader and less wrinkled. Flowers and fruit are also similar.

V. rhytidophyllum. LEATHERLEAF VIBURNUM. Evergreen. Zones 3–9, 14–24. Upright to 8–15 ft. tall, 6–12 ft. wide. Narrowish leaves are deep green and wrinkled above, fuzzy beneath. Yellowish white spring flowers in 4–8-in. clusters; scarlet fruit that ages to black. Leaves droop in cold weather, and plant looks tattered where cold winds blow. Tolerates deep shade. Some find this plant striking; others consider it coarse. 'Cree' is a compact variety 6–8 ft. tall and wide.

V. sargentii. Deciduous. Zones 1–9, 14–21. From northeastern Asia. Erect, rounded

V

growth to 12–15 ft. tall and wide. Lobed, somewhat maple-like leaves. Foliage is bronze-purple when new, matures to dark green by summer, may turn yellow or red in fall. Lacecap flower heads in late spring: 2–4-in. clusters of small fertile flowers edged with 1-in. sterile flowers. Bright red fruit colors up in late summer and fall, hangs on into winter. 'Onondaga', to 6 ft. tall and broad (or larger), has foliage that emerges deep maroon and maintains its purple tinge throughout summer; its flowers are pink-tinged white.

V. suspensum. SAND-ANKWA VIBURNUM. Evergreen. Zones 12–24; possible in Zones 8–10 but risky in cold winters there. From Japan. To 8–10 ft. tall and broad. Leathery leaves are glossy deep green above, paler beneath. Blooms in early spring; loose, 2–4-in. clusters of flowers have a scent that some people find objectionable. Red fruit ages to black, is not long lasting. Makes a serviceable screen or hedge. Watch for thrips, spider mites, and aphids. Little to moderate water.

V. tinus. LAURUSTINUS. Evergreen. Zones 4–10, 12–24, except as noted. Mediterranean native. To 6–12 ft. tall, half as wide. Leathery dark green, 2–3-in.-long leaves with edges slightly rolled under. Wine red new stems. Blooms from fall to spring; tight clusters of pink buds open to lightly fragrant white flowers. Bright metallic blue fruits last through summer. Dense foliage right to ground makes it good for screens, hedges, and clipped topiary shapes. Can be trained as a small tree. Susceptible to mites and prone to mildew near the ocean. Varieties include the following.

'Robustum'. ROUNDLEAF LAURUSTINUS. Leaves are coarser, rougher than those of species; flower buds are almost white. Less prone to mildew. Excellent small, narrow tree.

'Spring Bouquet' ('Compactum'). Upright to 4–6 ft. tall and wide; good for hedges. Leaves are deeper green, slightly smaller than those of the species.

'Variegatum'. Zones 4–9, 14–24. Leaves are marbled with white and pale yellow.

V. trilobum. CRANBERRY BUSH. Deciduous. Zones A1–A3; 1–11, 14–20. Native to Canada and northern U.S. To 15 ft. tall, 12 ft. wide. Leaves look much like those of *V. opulus*; they emerge reddish tinged, mature to dark green, turn yellow to red-purple in autumn. Lacecap flowers appear in mid-spring. Fruit is similar to that of *V. opulus* but is used for preserves and jellies. Less susceptible to aphid damage than *V. opulus*. 'Wentworth' has larger berries and bright red autuman foliage. 'Compactum' is a smaller form, reaching only 6 ft. tall and wide.

V. davidii needs acid soil, but the other viburnums are very soil-tolerant. Prune to prevent legginess; some evergreen species can be sheared. Aphids, thrips, spider mites, scale, and root weevils are potential pests. Keep sulfur sprays off foliage.

Vigna caracalla
(Phaseolus caracalla)
SNAIL VINE
Papilionaceae
PERENNIAL VINE SOMETIMES GROWN AS ANNUAL

☀ ZONES 12–24; H1, H2; ELSEWHERE AS ANNUAL

☀ FULL SUN

💧 REGULAR WATER

Vigna caracalla

Tropical American native that generally resembles pole bean in form and foliage. The flowers are different, though: fragrant, cream to pale purple spring and summer blossoms have lilac or purple markings, twisted keel petals that are coiled like a snail shell—odd and pretty. Twines rapidly to 10–20 ft.; makes a good summer screen or bank cover. Evergreen in frostless areas; in colder areas, cut plant to the ground if frost kills the top.

Viguiera
GOLDENEYE
Asteraceae
SHRUBBY PERENNIALS

☀ ZONES VARY BY SPECIES

☀ FULL SUN

💧 LITTLE WATER

Viguiera multiflora

These desert plants have yellow daisies that are borne singly or in loose clusters at stem ends. Cut plants back after bloom or before new growth begins to encourage bushiness and good looks. They are useful in restoring native vegetation and in stabilizing soil.

V. deltoidea (V. parishii). Zones 10–24. Native to California, Arizona, Nevada, and Mexico. Freely branching, sprawling plant to 3 ft. high and wide (possibly larger). Triangular, toothed, densely hairy, green to gray-green leaves are ½–2 in. long. Spring bloom; flowers are 1–1½ in. wide.

V. multiflora. Zones 2, 3, 10–13. Native from Montana to California and Arizona. To 1–3 ft. high and 1½ ft. wide, with hairy, lance-shaped green leaves 1–2 in. long. Spring or summer flowers to 2 in. wide; blooms first year from seed.

FOR OTHER UNTHIRSTY PLANTS, SEE PAGES 74–77.

Vinca
PERIWINKLE
Apocynaceae
PERENNIALS

☀ ZONES VARY BY SPECIES

☀ ☽ ● FULL SUN IN COOLER CLIMATES ONLY

💧 💧 LITTLE TO MODERATE WATER

Vinca minor 'Bowles'

Trailing, arching stems that root where they touch soil make these plants useful as groundcovers and bank covers. Shiny dark green, oval to oblong leaves. Lavender-blue, five-petaled, pinwheel-shaped flowers appear in leaf joints in early spring. Plant the larger species and its varieties 2–2½ ft. apart, dwarf kinds 1½ ft. apart.

V. major. Zones 5–24. The larger, more aggressive species. Flowers to 2 in. across; mounds to 1–2 ft. high. Spreads rapidly; can be extremely invasive in sheltered, forested areas. 'Variegata', probably as common as the green form, has leaves strongly edged in white.

V. minor. DWARF PERIWINKLE. Zones 1–24. Miniature version of *V. major*, with flowers to 1 in. wide and a height of just 4–6 in. More restrained, less likely to invade adjacent plantings. White-flowered and variegated forms are available.

V. rosea. See *Catharanthus roseus*.

When plantings mound up or are layered with old stems, shear or mow before new spring growth begins. Will grow in almost any soil. Vincas compete successfully with surface tree roots.

V

Viola

VIOLA, VIOLET, PANSY
Violaceae
ANNUALS AND PERENNIALS,
SOME TREATED AS ANNUALS

✎ **ZONES VARY BY SPECIES**

☀ ◐ ● **EXPOSURE NEEDS VARY BY SPECIES**

💧 **REGULAR WATER**

Viola × wittrockiana

Botanically speaking, violas, pansies, and almost all violets are perennials belonging to the genus *Viola*. However, violas and pansies are usually treated as annuals, invaluable for winter and spring bloom in mild-winter areas, for spring-through-summer color in colder climates. Typically used for mass color in borders and edgings, as covers for spring-flowering bulbs, in containers. Violets are more often used as woodland or rock garden plants. Violas and pansies take sun or partial shade; violets grow in partial or full shade (except as noted), but most are natives of deciduous forests and bloom best with at least some sun during the flowering season.

Almost all violets have two kinds of flowers: normal, conspicuous ones that rise above the foliage and may be pollinated and set seed, and short-stemmed, inconspicuous cleistogamous (Greek for "closed spouse") flowers that set copious seed without pollination and produce offspring identical to the parent. Many violets also spread by aboveground runners. Some reproduce so freely they can crowd out other small plants.

Violas and pansies have such complex ancestries that many botanists are unwilling to assign them to species, preferring to list them by variety name. However, it will avoid confusion if we retain these plants under their former names, invalid though they now may be.

V. adunca. CALIFORNIA SWEET VIOLET, WESTERN DOG VIOLET. Zones 1–9, 14–24. Native to coastal bluffs and Sierra foothills in central California, Pacific Northwest east to New England. To 3–6 in. high, spreading indefinitely by stolons and seeds. Dark green, heart-shaped leaves to 3 in. long. Half-inch or larger flowers in lavender-blue with white petal bases and conspicuous bright orange stigmas. Extremely fragrant. Blooms in spring in cold climates, fall to spring in mild-winter areas. Best with at least half-day winter sun, summer shade. Takes various soils and exposures, tolerates some drought. Can be invasive. Often sold as *V. odorata*.

V. cornuta. VIOLA, TUFTED PANSY. All zones as annuals; zones 1–10, 14–24 for kinds grown as perennials. To 6–8 in. high and 8 in. wide, with smooth, wavy-edged leaves. Purple, pansylike, slender-spurred flowers about 1½ in. across. Modern strains and varieties are complex hybrids with larger, shorter-spurred flowers; they come in solid colors (purple, blue, yellow, apricot, red, white) or with elaborate markings.

Some nurseries offer English violas—named varieties propagated by cuttings or division. These form 2-ft.-wide clumps and are reliably perennial.

V. corsica. CORSICAN VIOLET. Zones 2b–10, 14–24. From Corsica and Sardinia. Mounding perennial to 6–10 in. high and wide, with trailing foliage and many flat, violet-blue flowers marked in deep purple and white. Blooms spring into fall; tolerates extreme temperatures. Plant in well-drained soil amended with plenty of organic matter. Nice addition to the rock garden. Reseeds a bit. Full sun to partial shade.

V. hederacea. AUSTRALIAN VIOLET. Zones 7–9, 14–24. From Australia. To 1–4 in. high; eventually covers several feet, spreading by runners at slow to moderate rate. Kidney-shaped leaves. Nearly spurless, ¼–

TOP ROW: *Viola × wittrockiana* 'Angel Tiger Eye'; *V. sororia* 'Priceana'. SECOND ROW: *V.* 'Dynamite Blotch'; *V. tricolor.* THIRD ROW: *V. cornuta* 'White Jump-Up'; *V. c.* 'Skippy XL Plum-Gold'. BOTTOM ROW: *V. c.* 'Yellow Jump-Up'; *V.* 'Etain'

V

¾-in. flowers—broader than high and rather flat—in summer. They come in violet, blue, or white; commonly seen form is white with heavy blue-violet veining in throat. 'Baby Blue' has sky blue flowers. Plants go dormant at about 30°F (−1°C). Use as groundcover in light shade or (with abundant water) in sun.

V. odorata. SWEET VIOLET. Zones 1–24. The violet of song and story. To 8 in. high, 1½ ft. wide. In cool, mild climates, can spread widely by seeds and runners, possibly becoming a pest. Dark green, heart-shaped leaves with toothed margins. Fragrant, short-spurred flowers ¾ in. or wider in deep violet, bluish rose, or white. Tolerates full sun in cool-summer areas. For better spring display, remove runners and shear rank growth in late fall, then apply complete fertilizer in earliest spring.

V. sororia. DOORYARD VIOLET. Zones 1–11, 14–24. From eastern and central North America. To 4–6 in. high, 8 in. wide; does not spread by runners but self-sows freely. Leaves are somewhat heart-shaped, to 5 in. wide; vary from densely hairy to almost smooth. Good groundcover under woodland shrubs. Nearly scentless, ½–¾-in. flowers in spring to early summer are held close to leaves; colors range from red-violet to blue-violet to white. Most commonly seen are the following smooth-leafed varieties (all come true from seed): 'Albiflora', pure white with yellow in throat; 'Freckles', white liberally spotted with blue; 'Priceana' (popularly known as Confederate violet), white with blue-violet veining in throat.

V. tricolor. JOHNNY-JUMP-UP. All zones. From Europe and Asia. Spring bloomer to 6–12 in. tall and broad; spreads widely by profuse self-sowing. Oval, deeply lobed leaves. Pert, ½–¾-in., velvety purple-and-yellow or blue-and-yellow flowers are the original wild pansies. Same planting and care as pansy. Crosses with closely related small-flowered species have produced forms with flowers in violet, blue, white, yellow, lavender, mauve, apricot, orange, red—with or without markings.

V. × wittrockiana. PANSY. All zones. Erect and bushy to

6–10 in. high and 9–12 in. wide. Many strains with 2–4-in. flowers in white, blue, mahogany red, rose, yellow, apricot, and purple; also bicolors and multicolor blends. Most have dark blotches on the lower three petals; such flowers are often said to resemble faces. Shiny green leaves are oval to nearly heart-shaped, slightly lobed, 1½ in. or longer. Strains are too numerous to mention.

CARE

In cold-winter climates, set out nursery plants of pansies and violas in spring for summer bloom; in mild climates, plant in autumn for winter-to-spring (or longer) bloom. Or start from seed: in cold climates, sow in mid- to late summer and overwinter seedlings in cold frame until spring; or sow indoors in winter, plant in spring. In mild-winter areas, sow in mid- to late summer, plant out in fall. To prolong bloom, pick flowers (with some foliage) regularly and remove faded blooms before they set seed. In hot areas, plants get ragged by midsummer and should be removed.

Vitex
CHASTE TREE
Lamiaceae
DECIDUOUS AND EVERGREEN SHRUBS OR TREES

🗡 **ZONES VARY BY SPECIES**

☼ **FULL SUN**

◕ ◖ **MODERATE TO REGULAR WATER**

Vitex agnus-castus

One is a shrub or tree and the other a shrubby groundcover, but both have handsome foliage and clustered flowers. Prefer well-drained soil.

V. agnus-castus. CHASTE TREE. Deciduous shrub or small tree. Zones 4–24; H1, H2. Native from the Mediterranean region to central Asia. In warmest part of range, grows fast to make a tree to 25 ft. tall and wide, typically with multiple trunks; train high to make a good small shade tree. In colder areas, growth is slower and ultimate size is smaller—to 8–10 ft. tall and wide. Where it usually freezes to the ground in winter, it is a shrubby perennial about 3–5 ft. tall and wide.

Aromatic leaves are divided fanwise into five to seven narrow, 2–6-in.-long leaflets, grayish green above, gray beneath. No real fall color. Blooms summer to fall; small, fragrant lavender-blue flowers held in 6–12-in. spikes at branch ends and in leaf joints. They attract butterflies and hummingbirds. Varieties include 'Alba' and 'Silver Spire', with white flowers; and 'Rosea', with pink flowers. 'Shoal Creek' produces an abundance of violet-blue flowers. *V. a. latifolia* (sometimes sold as *V. macrophylla*) is a sturdy plant with large leaflets. Thrives in heat, resists oak root fungus. Good in shrub border. Cut plants treated as perennials to 1 ft. high in spring; they will bloom on new growth.

V. rotundifolia. BEACH VITEX, POHINAHINA. Evergreen shrub. Zones 13–24; H1, H2. Native to the coastal areas of Hawaii, Australia, Asia. Sprawls to 1½–4 ft. tall, 6–8 ft. wide; roots as it spreads to make a dense groundcover. Aromatic, medium green, broadly oblong to roundish leaves. Short spikes of bluish purple, ½-in. flowers (popular in leis) appear all year in warmest areas, in summer in colder part of range. Tiny bluish black fruits. Thrives at seacoast or inland.

Chaste trees offer gorgeous blue blooms late in the season. They can take drought and heat, are pest-free, and attract butterflies and honeybees.

Vitis
GRAPE
Vitaceae
DECIDUOUS VINES

🗡 **ZONES VARY BY SPECIES**

☼ ◖ **FULL SUN OR PARTIAL SHADE**

◕ ◖ **MODERATE TO REGULAR WATER**

Vitis californica 'Roger's Red'

For grapes grown for edible fruit, see Grape. The following species produce relatively tiny fruit and are grown instead for good looks. All climb by tendrils and have large, roundish, slightly lobed leaves that turn attractive colors in autumn. Prune as needed before spring growth begins.

V. californica. CALIFORNIA WILD GRAPE. Zones 4–24. From California and Oregon. To 30 ft., with 2–4-in. leaves that emerge grayish, mature to green, and turn red or yellow in autumn. 'Roger's Red' holds its gray-green leaf color all summer, turns brilliant red in fall. 'Walker Ridge', to 6–10 ft., has brilliant red and orange fall color. *V. girdiana* is a nearly identical species native to Southern California. Plants grow naturally along rivers and streams but are well adapted to periods of drought. A variety of wild animals use this plant for food and cover; bees favor the flowers.

V. coignetiae. CRIMSON GLORY VINE. Zones 3–10, 14–21. From Japan and Korea. Vigorous vine to 50 ft. tall, with foot-wide deep green leaves that turn brilliant red in fall.

V. vinifera 'Purpurea'. Zones 4–9, 14–23. To 20 ft. or more. Leaves to 6 in. across emerge downy green, mature to deep purple, turn deeper purple in autumn.

V

Walnut

Juglandaceae
DECIDUOUS TREE

🌿 **ZONES 4–9, 14–23; SOME VARIETIES IN ZONES 1–3**

☀️ **FULL SUN**

💧 **REGULAR WATER**

Walnuts

For walnut species grown mainly as landscape trees producing bonus crops of nuts, see *Juglans*. The species described here, English walnut (*J. regia*), is a widely grown orchard plant native to southeast Europe, southwest Asia; its nuts are the familiar ones sold commercially.

Species is hardy to –5°F (–21°C), but certain varieties are injured by late and early frosts. Reaches 60 ft. tall and wide; grows fast, especially when young. Trunk and heavy, horizontal or upward-angled branches have smooth gray bark; leaves have five to seven (rarely more) 3–6-in.-long leaflets. Walnut husks open in fall, dropping nuts to ground; to hasten drop, knock nuts from tree. Gather fallen nuts immediately, remove any adhering husks, and dry in single layer in airy shade until kernels are brittle (crack a nut open to test); then store. A single tree may bear as much as 100 to 150 lbs. of nuts.

In Zones 1–3, grow walnuts described as Carpathian or Hardy Persian. Varieties include 'Ambassador', 'Cascade', 'Chopaka', 'Hansen', 'Russian', and 'Somers'; these range in hardiness from –25°F (–32°C) to –35°F (–37°C). Here are best choices for other zones. In Zones 4–7, 'Chambers', 'Cooke's Giant Sweet', 'Franquette', and 'Spurgeon' bloom late enough to escape spring frosts, yield high-quality nuts. In Zones 8, 9, grow 'Carmelo', 'Chandler', 'Cooke's Giant Sweet', 'Hartley', 'Idaho', 'Payne', 'Pedro', or 'Serr'. In Zones 14–16 and warm parts of 17, try 'Carmelo', 'Chandler', 'Cooke's Giant Sweet', 'Franquette', 'Hartley', 'Payne', 'Pedro', and 'Serr'. In Zones 18–20, grow 'Payne', 'Pedro', or 'Placentia'. In Zones 21–23, 'Pedro' and 'Placentia' are best choices.

CARE

Plant English walnut as a landscape tree only on large lots. It's out of leaf a long time, messy in leaf (honeydew drip and sooty mold due to aphid infestations), and messy in fruit (husks can stain). Many people are allergic to the wind-borne pollen. Plant bare-root walnuts as soon as thay are available in winter or early spring. Choose an open planting location in full sun. In cold winter areas, grow on a slope to minimize frost damage. Most English walnuts are partially self-fruitful but bear better with a pollenizer. Grow in deep soil. Established plants survive with no supplemental moisture but need deep watering for top-quality nuts. Keep other plants beyond drip line, where feeder roots grow. Fertilize only if your tree is putting out less than 18 in. of new growth per year. Train young trees to a central leader; mature ones need pruning only to remove dead wood or correct shape. In addition to aphids, pests include scale, codling moths, and spider mites. Walnut husk fly attacks husks, causing them to turn black and adhere to shell. Husks are difficult to remove and shell is stained, but nutmeats are not damaged. In many agricultural areas, such as California's San Joaquin and Sacramento Valleys, new subdivisions are often built in old walnut groves, leaving the trees behind as landscape specimens. These tree often decline quickly due to increased watering or soil compaction.

Washingtonia

Arecaceae
PALMS

🌿 **ZONES 8, 9, 10 (WARMER PARTS), 11–24; H1, H2**

☀️ **FULL SUN**

💧 **LITTLE TO REGULAR WATER**

Washingtonia filifera

These fast-growing fan palms are too tall for most suburban gardens; they are best suited to large properties, avenues, parkways. The two species often hybridize if growing near each other. (For more on palms, see "Meet the Palms," page 471.)

W. filifera. CALIFORNIA FAN PALM. From California and Arizona. Hardy to 18°F (–8°C). To 60 ft. tall and 20 ft. wide, with a thicker trunk than *W. robusta*. Long-stalked, 3–6-ft., light green leaves stand well apart in open crown. As leaves mature, they bend down to form a "skirt" of thatch. In native stands in the desert, this species always grows near springs or other moist spots.

W. robusta. MEXICAN FAN PALM. From Mexico. Hardy to 20°F (–7°C). To 100 ft. tall and 10 ft. wide; trunk is slightly curved or bent, slimmer than that of *W. filifera*. Head of bright green foliage is more compact; leafstalks are shorter, with a red streak on the undersides.

This genus, which contains just two big, beautiful fan palms, was named in honor of the first president of the United States.

Watermelon

Cucurbitaceae
ANNUAL

🌿 **ZONES 1–24; H1, H2**

☀️ **FULL SUN**

💧 **REGULAR WATER**

Watermelon

This native of southern Africa needs a long growing season, more heat than most other melons, and more space than other vine crops—about 8 ft. by 8 ft. for each hill (circle of seed). Other than that, culture is as described under Melon. Most varieties have red flesh, but some have yellow, orange, or pink-and-yellow flesh. And though the fruit is usually large, small watermelons have also become popular in recent years; most of these "personal-size" melons weigh in at 3–6 lbs., ripening in less than 3 months. Bees pollinate watermelons, with each plant producing both male and female flowers. Seedless varieties need a seeded variety nearby to provide pollen or they won't bear fruit.

If you garden where watermelons are grown commercially (Zones 8, 9, 12–14, 18–21), choose any variety you like. If your summers are short or cool (Zones 1–7, 10, 11, 15–17, 22–24), choose a fast-maturing ("early") variety (described in catalogs and on seed packets as taking 70 to 75 days from seed to harvest). Also plant through clear plastic mulch and cover with floating row covers. In Hawaii, grow proven varieties such as 'Sugar Baby', 'Crimson Sweet', and 'Glory'. Watermelon does not become sweeter after harvest—it must be picked ripe. To check for ripeness, thump

W

the melon (it should produce a hollow "thunk"); check to see that the underside has turned from white to pale yellow; and make sure that tendrils where melon attaches to stem have darkened and withered. Cut (do not pull) melon from vine.

Watsonia

Iridaceae
PERENNIALS FROM CORMS

- ZONES 4–9, 12–24; OR DIG AND STORE DECIDUOUS TYPE
- ☼ FULL SUN
- ⬤ REGULAR WATER DURING GROWTH AND BLOOM
- 🦋 FLOWERS ATTRACT BUTTERFLIES AND HUMMINGBIRDS

Watsonia pillansii

These natives of South Africa are somewhat similar to gladiolus, but there are differences. *Watsonia's* sword-shaped, 2½-ft.-long leaves are less rigid, and it has taller, slimmer flower spikes set with smaller, more trumpet-like, fragrant blossoms.

W. borbonica (W. pyramidata). Deciduous. Blooms in late spring, bearing 2½-in. flowers in pink, rosy red, or white on 4–6-ft. stems. Hybrid forms have pink, red, or lavender blooms. Foliage dies back after bloom, reappearing in fall. Does not need regular moisture during summer dormancy but accepts it if soil is well drained.

W. pillansii (W. beatricis). Evergreen. Blooms in midsummer, with slightly branched, 3½-ft. stems bearing 3-in., bright reddish apricot flowers. Hybrids come in colors ranging from peach to nearly red. This species can take less moisture in summer after bloom is over.

CARE

Tolerates many soils but prefers good drainage. Plant in early autumn, setting corms 4 in. deep, 6 in. apart. Where hardy, corms can be left undisturbed for many years. In colder areas, you can grow *W. borbonica* as you would gladiolus: plant in spring for late spring and early summer bloom, then dig and store after foliage dies down. Because *W. pillansii* is evergreen, it cannot be dug and stored.

Wedelia hispida.
See *Zexmenia hispida*

Wedelia trilobata.
See *Sphagneticola trilobata*

Weigela

Caprifoliaceae
DECIDUOUS SHRUBS

- ZONES 1–11, 14–21
- ☼ ◐ FULL SUN OR LIGHT SHADE
- ⬤ REGULAR WATER
- 🦋 FLOWERS ATTRACT HUMMINGBIRDS

Weigela 'Variegata'

From China, Korea, and Japan, weigelas are valued for lavish springtime display of funnel-shaped, 1-in.-long flowers. They aren't attractive out of bloom, have no real fall color. Most are rather coarse-leafed and stiff, becoming rangy unless pruned. Use as background plants for flower borders, as summer screens, in mixed borders.

W. florida (W. rosea). Fast growth to 6–10 ft. tall, 9–12 ft. wide, with branches often arching to the ground. Pink to rose-red flowers. The following selections grow about 6 ft. tall

and wide: 'Bristol Snowflake', white flowers opening from pinkish buds; 'Java Red', red-tinted foliage, red buds opening to deep pink flowers; 'Pink Princess', lilac-pink flowers. 'Wine and Roses' reaches 5 ft. tall and wide, with deep purple new leaves that contrast nicely with its bright pink flowers; foliage matures to purplish green, turns blackish purple in autumn. 'Midnight Wine' reaches just 1½–2 ft. high and wide, with metallic burgundy foliage and deep pink flowers. 'My Monet' grows 1½–2 ft. high and 1½ ft. wide with pink flowers and leaves edged in white that turn pinkish in full sun.

W. hybrids. These are hybrids between *W. florida*, *W. praecox*, and other species. Here are some of the most common.

'Carnaval'. To 4–5 ft. tall and wide, with 1½-in.-wide, blush pink to vivid pink flowers that appear a little later in spring than others; reblooms in early fall. A hummingbird favorite.

'Dark Horse'. Compact growth to 3 ft. high and wide. Bronzy purple leaves with lime-colored veins and bright magenta-pink flowers make for a striking contrast. Good for low hedge or midborder shrub.

'Minuet'. Dwarf variety to 3 ft. high and 5 ft. wide. Purplish leaves. Flowers blend red, purple, and yellow.

'Variegata'. Compact growth to 4–6 ft. tall and wide, with deep rosy red flowers and creamy yellow to white leaf edges. 'Variegata Nana' is 3 ft. high and wide.

CARE

After flowering, cut back stems that have bloomed to side shoots that have not flowered; leave only one or two of these to each stem. Cut some of the oldest stems to ground. Thin new suckers to a few of the most vigorous. Another method is to cut back the entire plant about halfway just after blooms fade; do this every other year. Resulting dense new growth will provide plenty of flowers the next spring.

FOR OTHER PLANTS THAT ATTRACT BIRDS, SEE PAGES 95–99.

Westringia fruticosa

COAST ROSEMARY
Lamiaceae
EVERGREEN SHRUB

- ZONES 8, 9, 14–24
- ☼ FULL SUN
- ◐⬤ LITTLE TO MODERATE WATER

Westringia fruticosa 'Morning Light'

This evergreen shrub from Australia has spreading, rather loose growth to 3–6 ft. tall, 5–10 ft. wide. Medium green to gray-green leaves have white undersides, are slightly finer and filmier in texture than rosemary leaves. Small white flowers bloom from midwinter through spring in colder areas, all year in milder climates. Needs light, well-drained soil. Good near coast; wind-tolerant. Often sold as *W. rosmariniformis*. 'Wynyabbie Gem', possibly a hybrid, has light lavender flowers. 'Morning Light' grows 3–4 ft. tall and a little wider, has white flowers and white-edged leaves. 'Smokey' is similar but slightly more upright with an overall grayer tint.

Few mild-climate plants have the versatility of *Westringia*. Despite its delicate looks, this Australian native is really quite tough, needing little water once established.

White Sapote

Rutaceae
EVERGREEN OR DECIDUOUS TREE

🌱 **ZONES 8, 9, 14–16, 18–24; H1, H2**
☀️ **FULL SUN**
💧 **REGULAR WATER**

White sapotes

Beautiful tropical tree, botanically known as *Casimiroa edulis*. This native to Mexico withstands more cold than most avocados and does well wherever oranges are grown. May become partially deciduous in frosty or very hot weather. To 25–50 ft. tall and 25–30 ft. wide, with luxuriant glossy green leaves divided fanwise into three to seven oval, 3–5-in.-long leaflets. Heavy crop of round, 3–4-in. fruit with pale green to yellow skin and white or creamy yellow flesh with custardlike consistency and tropical flavor. California varieties include 'Lemon Gold', 'Louise', 'McDill', 'Suebelle', and 'Vernon'. 'Denzler' is grown in Hawaii.

CARE

Roots are invasive; choose planting location carefully. To keep tree lower and create a wide, umbrellalike crown, pinch out terminal bud. Needs consistent feeding. Fruit tastes best when allowed to ripen on tree, but it usually drops before reaching ripeness. Pick it when firm-ripe, at which point the flavor is mellow and sweet. (Some varieties become sweeter if left to stand at room temperature; others turn bitter.) To harvest, cut from tree, leaving a small piece of stem attached; pick carefully to avoid bruising. Eat with a spoon. Mature tree may produce several hundred pounds of fruit, far more than any one family can use. Cleanup becomes a chore, so plant where dropping fruit can be raked up or disappear into a groundcover.

Wisteria

Papilionaceae
DECIDUOUS VINES

🌱 **ZONES VARY BY SPECIES**
☀️ **FULL SUN, EXCEPT AS NOTED**
💧 **LITTLE TO MODERATE WATER**
🦋 **ATTRACT BUTTERFLIES**

Wisteria

Twining, woody vines of great size, long life, and exceptional beauty in flower. Very adaptable; can be grown as trees, shrubs, or vines. All have large, fresh green leaves divided into many leaflets; spectacular clusters of blue, white, or pinkish springtime blossoms; and velvety, pealike pods to about 6 in. long. Subdued autumn color in shades of yellow.

W. brachybotrys (W. venusta). SILKY WISTERIA. Zones 3–24. Native to Japan. Silky-haired leaves, 8–14 in. long, are divided into 9 to 13 leaflets. Very large white, long-stalked, highly fragrant flowers in 4–6-in. clusters open all at once during leafout. Older plants, especially in tree form, have remarkably profuse bloom. 'Shiro Kapitan' ('Alba') is the most commonly sold; it bears white (sometimes double) flowers with yellow markings. 'Murasaki Kapitan' ('Violacea') bears blue-violet blossoms with white markings.

W. floribunda. JAPANESE WISTERIA. Zones 2–24. From Japan. Leaves are 12–16 in. long, divided into 15 to 19 leaflets. Fragrant, 1½-ft. clusters of violet or violet-blue flowers during leafout. Clusters open gradually, starting from the base; this prolongs bloom season but makes for a less spectacular display of color than that of *W. sinensis*. Many varieties in white, pink, and shades of blue, purple, and lavender, usually marked with yellow and white.

W. sinensis. CHINESE WISTERIA. Zones 3–24. Native to China; the most common wisteria in the West. Leaves are 10–12 in. long, divided into 7 to 13 leaflets. Blooms before leafout. Clusters of violet-blue, slightly fragrant flowers are shorter (to 1 ft.) than those of *W. floribunda*—but they make quite a show, since flowers open all at once nearly all along the cluster. 'Alba' has white flowers. 'Caroline' and 'Cooke's Special' are grafted forms. 'Prolific' flowers at an early age. Plants will bloom in sun or considerable shade.

CARE

To get off to a good start, buy a cutting-grown or grafted wisteria; seedlings may not bloom for many years. If you start with grafted plants, keep suckers removed or they may take over. Wisteria is not fussy about soil, but it does need good drainage. In general, wisterias do not need fertilizer. In alkaline soil, watch for chlorosis.

Let newly planted wisteria grow to establish the framework you want, with either single or multiple trunks. Remove stems that interfere with framework; pinch back side stems and long streamers. For single-trunked specimens, rub off buds that develop on trunk; for multiple trunks, select as many vigorous stems as you wish and let them develop. If the plant has only one stem, pinch it back to encourage others to develop. Remember that the main stem will become a good-size trunk, and that weight of mature vine is considerable. Unsupported plants make a vigorous bank cover.

Tree wisterias can be bought already trained; or you can train your own. Remove all but one main stem and stake this one securely. Tie stem to stake at frequent intervals, using plastic tape to prevent girdling. When plant has reached height at which you wish head to form, pinch or prune out tip to force branching. Shorten branches to beef them up. Pinch back long streamers and rub off all buds that form below head. Replace stakes and ties as needed.

Wisterias can be trained as big shrubs or multistemmed, small, semiweeping trees; permit well-spaced branches to form the framework, shorten side branches, and nip long streamers.

Prune blooming plants every winter; cut back or thin out side shoots from main or structural stems and shorten back to two or three buds the flower-producing spurs that grow from these shoots. You'll have no trouble recognizing fat flower buds on these spurs.

In summer, cut back long streamers before they tangle up in main body of the vine; save those you want to use to extend height or length of vine and tie them to a support—eaves, wall, trellis, or arbor. If old plants grow rampantly but fail to bloom (and you have been fertilizing), withhold nitrogen fertilizers for an entire growing season (buds for the next season's bloom are started in early summer). If that fails to produce bloom the next year, you can try pruning roots in spring—after you're sure no flowers will be produced—by cutting vertically with a spade into the plant's root zone.

In the Western China province of Hubei, wisteria is called *chiao teng* (beautiful vine). In Japan, it's called *Fuji*. But by any name, this rambunctious climber with lacy foliage is an exceptional beauty in bloom, with dramatic flower clusters of blue, purple, white, or pink.

W

Woodwardia

CHAIN FERN
Blechnaceae
FERNS

- 🌡 **ZONES VARY BY SPECIES**
- ◐ ● **PARTIAL TO FULL SHADE**
- 💧 💧 **REGULAR TO AMPLE WATER**

Woodwardia fimbriata

These are medium to large, mostly evergreen ferns with arching fronds and bold texture. Common name refers to the chainlike pattern of spores beneath frond segments. Excellent as focal points or grouped on banks or near water.

W. fimbriata. GIANT CHAIN FERN. Zones 2b–9, 14–24. Native from British Columbia to Mexico. This species is among the largest of native Western ferns, topping out at 9 ft. in mild, wet coastal regions; in gardens, it typically reaches 4–5 ft. tall and 3 ft. wide. Thick, leathery, medium green fronds are upright but spreading toward the top. Foliage is twice cut but still somewhat coarse.

Use alongside a stream or brook, against a shaded wall, or in a woodland garden. Sometimes seen in desert areas where shady seeps exist. Slow to get going if dug from existing clumps; nursery plants are fast growing and vigorous, but not invasive. Withstands neglect once well established.

W. orientalis. ORIENTAL CHAIN FERN. Zones 5–9, 14–24. From the Himalayas, China, and Japan. Elegant and easy to grow. Lustrous green fronds are 3–5 ft. long and more drooping than those of *W. fimbriata*. New growth is reddish orange. Tiny wedge-shaped plantlets appear on mature fronds, giving them

a somewhat ruffled look. These can root where they touch soil; to make more plants, remove plantlets and root in damp potting mix. Likes a bit more sun than giant chain fern.

CARE

All grow best in moist, organically enriched soil with a thick layer of mulch.

Xanthocyparis nootkatensis

(Chamaecyparis nootkatensis)
ALASKA CEDAR,
NOOTKA CYPRESS
Cupressaceae
EVERGREEN TREES

- 🌡 **ZONES A2, A3; 2–6, 15–17**
- ☼ ◑ **FULL SUN OR PARTIAL SHADE**
- 💧 **REGULAR WATER**

Xanthocyparis nootkatensis 'Pendula'

Native from Alaska to California. Pyramidal tree to 80 ft. tall, 25 ft. wide at base. Tiny, scale-like, blue-green to gray-green leaves on drooping branches arranged in sprays. Is similar to but coarser than *Chamaecyparis lawsoniana* and stands greater cold, poorer soil. 'Green Arrow' is a narrow selection, reaching 35 ft. tall, only a few feet wide. 'Pendula', to 30 ft., has weeping branches.

Xanthorrhoea

GRASS TREE
Xanthorrhoeaceae
PERENNIALS

- 🌡 **ZONES 12–24**
- ☼ **FULL SUN**
- 🌢 **LITTLE OR NO WATER**

Xanthorrhoea preissii

This Australian native produces dense tufts of narrow, grasslike, 2–4-ft.-long leaves that radiate from the top of a thick, woody, nearly black, slow-growing stem. Foliage mass stays at about 3–5 ft. tall, 3 ft. wide for many years, but as stem gradually lengthens, plant height eventually increases to 12–15 ft. Sometimes blooms; white flowers are borne in a dense, narrow spike on a tall stem that increases the plant's height further. *X. preissii* and *X. quadrangulata* are similar species. Best used with yuccas or with agaves or other succulents in dry, loose, sandy soil (for information on succulents, see "Meet the Succulents," page 618).

Xerophyllum tenax

BEAR GRASS,
INDIAN BASKET GRASS
Melanthiaceae
EVERGREEN PERENNIAL

- 🌡 **ZONES 1–7, 14–17**
- ☼ ◑ **FULL SUN OR LIGHT SHADE**
- 🌢 🌢 **LITTLE TO MODERATE WATER**

Xerophyllum tenax

Native from sea level to sub-alpine areas of the western U.S. Tough, wiry, grasslike leaves grow from deep, fibrous roots to form clumps 2–3 ft. high and wide; foliage is olive green. In early summer, a tall stalk rises from the center of each clump to produce a poker-shaped inflorescence packed with small, creamy white, star-shaped blooms. Fibrous roots and leaves were used for traditional weaving.

Bear grass takes a few years to reach flowering stage and may not bloom reliably in the garden, but its attractive evergreen foliage is reason enough to grow it.

Useful Grasslike Perennials

Neither of the above plants is a grass, and they're not related to each other. But they do have in common a long history of use by native peoples. Aboriginal Australians prized the grass tree for its resin, which they used to make a strong gluelike substance, and for its flowers, which can be soaked in water to make a sweet drink. Native Americans wove the leaves of bear grass into strong, watertight baskets.

Xylosma congestum

Flacourtiaceae

EVERGREEN OR DECIDUOUS SHRUB OR TREE

🌿 **ZONES 8–24**

☼ ◐ **FULL SUN OR PARTIAL SHADE**

💧 **MODERATE WATER**

Xylosma congestum

Basic landscape foliage plant from China. Loose, spreading growth to 8–10 ft. tall and as wide or wider. Shiny yellowish green leaves are ovate with pointed tips; new growth is bronzy. Flowers are insignificant and rarely seen. Some plants are spiny. Left alone, xylosma develops an angular main stem that takes its time zigzagging upward. Meanwhile, long, graceful side branches develop; these are arching or drooping, sometimes lying on the ground. Can be trained as single or multitrunked small tree, espaliered on wall or fence, used as clipped or unclipped hedge. 'Compacta' grows slowly to half the size of species.

Hardy to 10°F (–12°C) but may lose many (or all) leaves in hard frosts. Normally sheds many old leaves when new spring growth begins; frost at that time will kill new growth. This is a useful and versatile plant, though its unattractive appearance in nursery cans (especially in winter, when stems may be nearly bare) and slow start in ground may discourage gardeners. Tolerates heat, most soils. Scale, spider mites are occasional pests. Chlorosis may be a problem.

Yucca

Asparagaceae

EVERGREEN TREES, SHRUBS, AND PERENNIALS

🌿 **ZONES VARY BY SPECIES**

☼ **FULL SUN, EXCEPT AS NOTED**

◯ 💧 **LITTLE TO MODERATE WATER, EXCEPT AS NOTED**

Yucca gloriosa 'Bright Star'

Yuccas grow over much of North America. All have tough, sword-shaped leaves and large clusters of typically white or whitish, rounded to bell-shaped flowers. Some are stemless clumps; others have trunks and reach tree size. Group yuccas with cacti or with agaves or other succulents; or grow them with softer-leafed tropical foliage plants. Taller kinds have striking silhouettes, and even stemless species provide important vertical accents when in bloom. Keep those with stiff, sharp-pointed leaves away from walks, terraces, and other well-traveled areas. (Some people clip off the sharp tips with nail clippers.)

Y. aloifolia. SPANISH BAYO-NET. Zones 7–24; H1, H2. From southern U.S., Mexico. Slow to 10 ft. by 5 ft. or larger. Single or branching trunk; sometimes sprawls for picturesque effect. Stems densely clothed in sharp-pointed dark green leaves to 2½ ft. long, 2 in. wide. Foliage of 'Variegata' is marked with yellowish white. 'Purpurea' has powdery purple leaves in full sun. White (sometimes purple-tinged) flowers to 4 in. across are carried in dense, erect clusters to 2 ft. high in late spring or summer.

Y. baccata. BANANA YUCCA, DATIL. Zones 1–3, 7, 9–14, 18–24. From southwestern U.S., Mexico. Slow to 3 ft. high, 5 ft. wide. Foliage clump may have no stem or several short, prostrate ones. Sharp-tipped, light bluish green or yellowish green leaves to 2 ft. long, 2 in. wide, with fibers along the edges. Large (2–6 in.), fleshy flowers from spring into summer are red-brown outside, white inside, carried in dense, 2-ft.-long clusters. Fleshy, edible, bananalike fruits to 6 in. long.

Y. brevifolia. JOSHUA TREE. Zones 7, 9–16, 18–23. From deserts of Southern California, Nevada, Utah, Arizona. Few-branched, slow-growing plant to 15–30 ft. by 30 ft.; both trunk and branches are heavy. Gray-green, spiny-tipped leaves to 16 in. long, 1 in. wide, clustered near branch ends. Old, dead leaves hang on. Dense, foot-long clusters of greenish white, 3-in. flowers in late winter and spring. Collected plants are sometimes sold; nursery plants are very slow to form trunks. Best in dry, well-drained soil in desert gardens. Difficult under ordinary garden conditions.

Y. elata. SOAPTREE YUCCA. Zones 7–24. From southwestern U.S., northern Mexico. Slow to 6–20 ft. tall, 8–10 ft. wide; single or branched trunk. Pale green, sharp-pointed leaves to 4 ft. long, ½ in. wide. Dead leaves hang on to form a straw-colored, shaggy "skirt" on trunk. Tall stems are topped by white, 2¼-in. flowers in spikes to 3 ft. long; blooms late spring into summer. May not bloom every year.

Y. elephantipes (Y. gigantea). GIANT YUCCA. Zones 12, 13 (protected from afternoon sun, hard frosts), 16, 17, 19–24; H1, H2. From Mexico, Central America. Fast growing (to 2 ft. per year) to an eventual 15–30 ft. by 8 ft. Usually has several trunks. Rich deep green, soft-tipped leaves to 4 ft. long and 3 in. wide. The leaves of 'Marginata' have a thin, creamy white stripe along the edge. Those of 'Variegata' are light green with wide, creamy white stripes. Striking silhouette alone or combined with other big foliage plants; looks out of proportion in smaller gardens. Tall (3–6-ft.) spikes of creamy white, 1½-in. flowers in spring. Does best in good, well-drained soil with moderate to regular water.

Y. faxoniana. EVE'S NEEDLE. Zones 12–13. Native to western Texas and northern Mexico. Grows to 15 ft. tall and 10 ft. wide, often with a branched trunk. Stiff green leaves are 3 ft. long by 2–3 in. wide, with curly threads along the edges. Dried leaves form an unattractive thatch along the trunk. Tall (3–4 ft.) spike of creamy white flowers in spring.

Y. filamentosa. ADAM'S NEEDLE. Zones 1–24. From southeastern U.S. To 2½ ft. high, 5 ft. wide; stemless. Stiff dark green leaves to 1½ ft. long, 1 in. wide, with long, loose fibers at edges. In late spring and summer, bears yellowish white, 2–3-in. flowers (lightly fragrant in evening) in narrow clusters to 4–7 ft. or taller. One of the hardiest, most widely planted yuccas in colder regions. Varieties include 'Bright Edge', with yellow-striped leaves; 'Color Guard', with leaves striped white and cream. Regular water.

Y. flaccida. Zones 1–9, 14–24. From southeastern U.S. Resembles *Y. filamentosa*, but flower clusters are somewhat shorter and leaves are less rigid, with straight fibers on edges. 'Golden Sword' has yellow-variegated foliage; 'Ivory Tower' bears outward-facing rather than drooping flowers. Give regular water.

Y. glauca. SOAPWEED. Zones 1–13. Native from New Mexico and Texas to South Dakota. To 3–4 ft. tall and wide or larger, with short or prostrate trunk. May remain in a single rosette or form clumps. Stiff leaves, 2 ft. long, 2 in. wide, grayish green edged with a hairline of white and a few thin threads. White, 2½-in. flowers on 3-ft. stalks in spring or early summer.

Y. gloriosa. SPANISH DAGGER, SOFT-TIP YUCCA. Zones 7–9, 12–24; H1, H2. True species is native to southeastern U.S. Plants sold under this

Y

name in the West are most likely a form of *Y. elephantipes* or a hybrid between that form and *Y. gloriosa*. Much like *Y. aloifolia* in appearance. To 10 ft. tall, 8 ft. wide, generally with multiple trunks—except in colder part of range, where it is usually a smaller, stemless plant. Soft-tipped leaves with good green color that blends well with lush, tropical-looking plants. 'Bright Star' has leaves with broad, bright yellow stripes along the edge. Summer bloom. Moderate to regular water; too much moisture may produce black areas on leaf margins.

Y. pallida. PALE-LEAF YUCCA. Zones 3–24. Native to north-central Texas. Trunkless, to 1–2 ft. high and 1–3 ft. wide. Light blue-green, lightly serrated leaves are 1-ft. long and 1 in. wide. Pure white flowers in spring. Good for smaller areas.

Y. recurvifolia (Y. pendula). Zones 7–10, 12–24. From southeastern U.S. To 6–10 ft. tall, 6–8 ft. wide, with single, unbranched trunk (may be lightly branched in age). Can be cut back to keep single trunked. Spreads by offsets to make large groups. Beautiful blue-gray leaves are 2–3 ft. long, 2 in. wide, sharply bent downward. Leaf tips are spined but bend to the touch; they won't cause injury. Not stiff and metallic-looking like many yuccas. White, 3-in. flowers in late spring or early summer are borne in loose, open, 3–5-ft.-tall clusters. Easy to grow under all garden conditions. Moderate to regular water.

Y. rigida. BLUE YUCCA. Zones 10 (with protection), 11–13. From Chihuahuan Desert of Mexico. To 12 ft. by 5 ft.; trunk may branch with age. Each stem is topped with a rosette of stiff, spiny-tipped, blue-green leaves to 2 ft. long, 1½ in. wide. Old leaves form tan thatch on trunk. Dense spikes of white, 2¼-in. flowers appear in spring or early summer.

Y. rostrata. Zones 7–24. Native from extreme southwestern Texas into Chihuahuan Desert of Mexico. Treelike yucca to 12 ft. by 9 ft. or larger. Notable feature is the trunk, which is covered with soft gray fuzz (fibers remaining from old leaf bases). Needle-pointed leaves

to 2 ft. long and ½ in. wide. 'Sapphire Skies' has beautiful, fine-textured, light blue leaves. Blooms in late spring, bearing 2-ft. clusters of white, 2½-in. flowers on a 2-ft. stalk. This species was once classified as *Y. thompsoniana*, which is very similar but smaller (6 ft. tall and wide) and hardier (Zones 1–3, 7–24).

Y. schidigera (Y. mohavensis). Zones 7–16, 18–24. From deserts of California, Nevada, Arizona, and Baja California. Short-stemmed plant to 3–12 ft. tall, 3 ft. wide (or wider if stem branches). Tough, sharp-tipped, medium green leaves 2–3 ft. long, 1–2½ in. wide. Purple-tinted white flowers about 1¾ in. wide, in 2-ft. clusters. Spring bloom.

Y. schottii. MOUNTAIN YUCCA. Zones 10–13. Native from Arizona and New Mexico to northern Mexico. To 6–15 ft. tall, 3–4 ft. wide, with single (rarely branching) trunk. Gray-green, sharp-tipped leaves 1½–3 ft. long, 2 in. wide. Dead leaves hang on for a long time. Clusters of white, 1½-in. flowers from spring to midsummer. Full sun or light shade.

Y. whipplei. OUR LORD'S CANDLE. Zones 2–24. From California coast, Southern California mountains, and Baja California. Dense, trunkless rosette to 3 ft. high, 6 ft. wide. Gray-green leaves are 1–2 ft. long, ¾ in. wide, with sharply toothed edges, needlelike tips; don't locate this plant where people can walk into it. Blooms in summer; 6–14-ft.-long stems carry drooping, 1–2-in., creamy white blossoms in large, branched, 3–6-ft.-long spikes. Plant dies after flowering; new plants come from seeds or offsets.

CARE

Best in well-drained soil. Most need only occasional deep soakings.

When washed, peeled, sliced, and fried, yucca roots make tasty potato-like *frites* to serve with aioli.

Z

Zamia
Zamiaceae
CYCADS

✿ ZONES 21–24; H1, H2; OR INDOORS

☼ ◐ ● EXPOSURE NEEDS VARY BY SPECIES

💧 REGULAR WATER

Zamia furfuracea

Of 100 or so species, only the following two are generally seen. Slow-growing plants. Short trunks (may be completely or partially beneath soil level) are usually marked with scars from old leaf bases. Circular crowns of leaves resembling stiff fern fronds or small palm fronds. Need organically enriched, fast-draining soil.

Z. furfuracea. CARDBOARD PALM. From southeastern coastal Mexico. To 3 ft. tall, 6 ft. wide. Stem short, sometimes subterranean. Fronds to 3 ft. long, usually much less; have as many as 12 pairs (usually fewer) of extremely stiff, leathery, dark green leaflets to 4½ in. long, 1½ in. wide. Leaflets may have a few teeth toward the tip. Best in full sun, tolerates partial or full shade.

Z. pumila (Z. integrifolia). COONTIE. From Florida, Cuba, and the West Indies. To 4 ft. tall, 6 ft. wide. Short trunk is largely below soil level. Fronds to 3 ft. long, with as many as 30 pairs of dark green leaflets to 5 in. long, 1¼ in. wide. Partial shade.

Zantedeschia
CALLA
Araceae
PERENNIALS FROM RHIZOMES

✿ ZONES 5, 6, 8, 9, 12–24; H1, H2; OR DIG AND STORE ALL BUT Z. AETHIOPICA

☼ ◐ EXPOSURE NEEDS VARY BY SPECIES

● 💧 WATER NEEDS VARY BY SPECIES

Zantedeschia 'Edge of Night'

This South African native forms clumps of long-stalked, shiny rich green, usually arrow-shaped leaves, sometimes spotted in white. Flower bract (spathe) surrounds a central spike (spadix) that is tightly covered with tiny true flowers.

Z. aethiopica. COMMON CALLA. To 2–4 ft. tall, with unspotted leaves to 1½ ft. long, 10 in. wide. In spring (sometimes continuing into summer), pure or creamy white spathes to 8 in. long appear on stems slightly taller than foliage.

Varieties include robust 'Green Goddess', with large spathes that are white at base, green toward tip; and 'Hercules', larger than species, with big spathes that open flat, curve backward. Dwarf types include 'Childsiana' (to 1 ft.).

Z. albomaculata. SPOTTED CALLA. To 2 ft. high, with bright green, white-spotted leaves 1–1½ ft. long, 10 in. wide. Creamy yellow or white spathes to 5 in. long, with red-purple blotch at base. Blooms from spring into summer.

Z. elliottiana. GOLDEN CALLA. To 2 ft. high, with bright green, white-spotted leaves to 10 in. long, 6 in. wide. Spathes to 6 in. long, greenish yellow aging to rich golden yellow.

Summer bloom. Tolerates full sun, even in hot climates.

Z. hybrids. Plants are usually about the size of *Z. rehmanii* and bloom in late spring and summer. Leaves are typically unspotted, though some selections have spots on foliage. Spathe colors include cream, buff, orange, pink shades, lavender, and purple.

Z. pentlandii. Resembles *Z. albomaculata*, but leaves are unspotted and spathes are deep golden yellow with purple throat. Summer bloom.

Z. rehmanii. RED or PINK CALLA. To 1½–2 ft., with narrow, lance-shaped, unspotted green leaves to 1 ft. long, 2½ in. wide. Pink or rosy pink spathes to 5 in. long in midspring. 'Superba' has dark pink spathes.

CARE

Common calla (*Z. aethiopica*) has different cultural needs than other callas. It is soil-tolerant and thrives in moist, even boggy, soil all year. Where summers are hot, grow in light shade; in milder climates, give full sun or light shade. Plant fall through early spring; set rhizomes 4 in. deep, 1 ft. apart. Needs year-round moisture. Dig and divide only when performance declines. Plants are evergreen to semievergreen and cannot be dug and stored over winter in cold climates. Beyond hardiness range, grow in pots and protect in winter.

The other callas described here die to the ground in fall, reappear in spring. Need regular water during growth and bloom, less during dormancy. In fall, set rhizomes 2 in. deep, 8–12 in. apart, in organically enriched, well-drained, and (ideally) slightly acid soil. Grow in full sun; in hot-summer areas, give light shade. As for *Z. aethiopica*, dig and divide when overcrowded. Beyond hardiness limits, plant in spring for summer bloom; then dig when leaves die back, store over winter in cool, dark place, replant in spring.

FOR OTHER PLANTS THAT WILL GIVE A TROPICAL LOOK TO YOUR GARDEN, SEE PAGES 119–120.

Zanthoxylum piperitum

JAPAN PEPPER, SANSHO
Rutaceae
DECIDUOUS SHRUB OR TREE

🌿 **ZONES 6–9, 14–17**

☼ **FULL SUN**

💧 **MODERATE WATER**

Zanthoxylum piperitum

Native to China, Japan, and Korea. Dense growth to 8–20 ft. tall and wide. Handsome dark green, 3–6-in.-long leaves with 11 to 23 oval, 2-in.-long leaflets; may turn yellow in autumn. Flat, ½-in.-long spines in pairs along stems. Inconspicuous green flowers. Small, aromatic red fruits ripen in fall; they have black seeds that are pulverized and used as seasoning in Japan. Peppery-tasting leaves are slightly numbing to the tongue; they too are used in Japanese cuisine.

Plants grow best in rich, well-drained soil in full sun, though they will tolerate light shade. Prune during winter dormancy to remove wayward or crossing branches.

The dried, crushed seedpods of Japan pepper (sometimes called Szechuan peppercorns) are one ingredient in Chinese five-spice powder. The others are usually star anise, cloves, cinnamon, and ground fennel seeds.

Zauschneria
(Epilobium)

CALIFORNIA FUCHSIA, HUMMINGBIRD FLOWER
Onagraceae
SHRUBBY PERENNIALS

🌿 **ZONES 2–11, 14–24, EXCEPT AS NOTED**

☼ **FULL SUN, EXCEPT AS NOTED**

💧 **LITTLE TO MODERATE WATER, EXCEPT AS NOTED**

🐦 **FLOWERS ATTRACT HUMMINGBIRDS AND BUTTERFLIES**

Zauschneria californica latifolia

Typically low, spreading plants with narrow leaves in green, gray-green, or gray. In late summer or fall, they put on a profuse show of bright orange or scarlet (sometimes white or pink), narrowly trumpet-shaped, 1–2-in.-long flowers that attract hummingbirds. Good in informal gardens, among stones, or to help stabilize banks or hillsides.

Z. californica (Epilobium canum). HUMMINGBIRD TRUMPET, CALIFORNIA FUCHSIA. Native to much of the western U.S. and northern Mexico. Upright or arching growth from 6 in. to 4 ft. tall (depending on variety), spreading as wide as 3–4 ft. There are many varieties available. All are improvements over the basic species. Flowers are orange to red and sometimes white ('Summer Snow'). 'Ghostly Red' has especially nice, silvery gray foliage.

Z. septentrionalis (Epilobium septentrionale). HUMBOLDT COUNTY FUCHSIA. Zones 5–7, 14–17, 19–24. From Northern California Coast Ranges. Mat-forming species to 6–12 in. high, 1–1½ ft. wide, with gray-green to silvery leaves. Needs afternoon shade in hottest climates.

CARE

Drought-tolerant, but look best with an occasional soaking in summer; prefer excellent drainage but adapt to heavier soils. These fast-growing plants can get a bit rangy. After their first year of growth, cut back to 1–2 in. high in late fall or winter when flowering has finished. To keep taller types bushy, lightly shear or pinch back new growth in late spring. Some species spread by invasive roots or reseeding.

Zebrina pendula.
See *Tradescantia zebrina*

Zelkova serrata

SAWLEAF ZELKOVA
Ulmaceae
DECIDUOUS TREE

🌿 **ZONES 3–21**

☼ **FULL SUN**

💧 **MODERATE TO REGULAR WATER**

Zelkova serrata

Eastern Asian relative of elm (*Ulmus*). Good shade tree; sometimes used as a substitute for American elm (*U. americana*), which is highly prone to Dutch elm disease (zelkova is also susceptible but rarely succumbs). Grows at moderate to fast rate to 60 ft. or higher, equally wide. Silhouette ranges from vase-shaped to quite spreading. Has smooth gray bark. Narrowly oval, sawtoothed leaves are similar to those of elm but rougher in texture. Fall color varies from yellow to dark red to dull reddish brown. Among vase-shaped varieties, 'Halka' is the best American elm mimic in form and foliage; 'Green Vase' has a narrower

Z

vase shape than vigorous 'Village Green'. 'City Sprite' is compact oval to about 25 ft. tall. 'Musashino' is upright to 45 ft. tall and only 15 ft. wide. 'Wireless' ('Schmidtlow') is compact, just 25 ft. tall and 35 ft. wide, and has excellent red fall color.

CARE

Takes wide range of soils. Fairly tolerant of drought, wind. You may need to train and prune young trees to establish a good framework; thin out crowded ascending branches.

Zephyranthes

ZEPHYR FLOWER, FAIRY LILY
Amaryllidaceae
PERENNIALS FROM BULBS

- ❖ ZONES VARY BY SPECIES
- ☼ ◑ FULL SUN OR PARTIAL SHADE
- ◗ REGULAR WATER DURING GROWTH AND BLOOM

Zephyranthes carinata

Clumps of foot-long, bright green, grassy leaves give rise to slender, hollow stems, each bearing a single funnel-shaped blossom with six segments. In their native Central and South America, often bloom after rains (hence another common name, rain lily). Species described here bloom in late summer and early fall. Pretty in rock gardens or foreground in borders. Excellent pot plant for patio or greenhouse.

Z. candida. Zones 4–9, 12–24; H1, H2. White, 2-in. flowers, sometimes stained pink in the throat. Evergreen in warmer part of range. Usually sold as potted plants; can be planted out at any time. 'Prairie Sunset' is a hybrid, forming a dense tuft of foliage and light apricot blooms that fade to light pink.

Z. carinata (Z. grandiflora). Zones 7–9, 12–24; H1, H2. Usually sold as *Z. grandiflora*. Extra-large flowers (to 4 in. across). Rose-pink blossoms have a lily shape in the morning, open out flat by midday, close in late afternoon.

Z. citrina. Zones 7–9, 12–24; H1, H2. Similar to *Z. candida* but has bright yellow flowers.

Z. grandiflora. See *Z. carinata.*

CARE

Plant bulbs in well-drained soil at any time (though fall planting is ideal), setting them 1–2 in. deep and 3 in. apart. In mild-winter areas with a long growing season, plants may bloom several times a year if you provide a short dry period after bloom, then resume watering to initiate another growth cycle. In other regions, give little or no water after foliage dies back. Can remain undisturbed for many years.

Zexmenia hispida

Asteraceae
SHRUBBY PERENNIAL

- ❖ ZONES 10–13
- ☼ ◑ FULL SUN OR LIGHT SHADE
- ◌ ◗ LITTLE TO MODERATE WATER

Zexmenia hispida

Native to Texas and Mexico. Compact, rounded plant to 2–3 ft. high and wide; puts on a good show of bright orange-yellow daisies from late spring into autumn. Rough-textured, somewhat sticky dark green leaves are oval to lance-shaped. In cold winters, plant can lose leaves or even die to the ground,

but it recovers quickly in spring. In light shade, it blooms less and sprawls more, making an attractive groundcover. Give well-drained soil. Some botanists have recently changed the name of this plant to *Wedelia hispida*.

Zingiber officinale

TRUE GINGER
Zingiberaceae
PERENNIAL FROM RHIZOME

- ❖ ZONES 9, 14–24; H1, H2
- ◑ PARTIAL SHADE
- ◗ ◗ REGULAR TO AMPLE WATER

Zingiber officinale

This tropical Asian plant's rhizomes are the source of the ginger root used in cooking. To 2–4 ft. tall, with indefinite spread. Narrow, glossy bright green leaves to 1 ft. long. Summer flowers are yellowish green, with purple lip marked yellow; they are only rarely seen and not especially showy. Needs heat and humidity. Grown commercially in Hawaii.

CARE

Buy roots (fresh, not dried) at the grocery store in early spring; cut into 1–2-in.-long sections, each with well-developed growth buds. Let cut ends of sections dry, then plant just below the surface of rich, moist soil (container culture is common). Water cautiously until top and root growth are active. Feed once a month. Plants are dormant in winter; rhizomes may rot in cold, wet soil. Harvest roots at any time—but allow several months after planting for them to reach some size.

Zinnia

Asteraceae
ANNUALS AND PERENNIALS

- ❖ ZONES 1–24; H1, H2; EXCEPT AS NOTED
- ☼ FULL SUN
- ◗ REGULAR WATER, EXCEPT AS NOTED
- 🦋 ATTRACT BIRDS, BUTTERFLIES

Zinnia peruviana
'Bonita Yellow'

Longtime favorites for colorful, round flowers, typically in summer and early fall. Most garden zinnias belong to *Z. elegans*.

Z. acerosa. Perennial. Zones 10–24. From southern Arizona, Texas, and Mexico. To 6–10 in. high, 2 ft. wide, with hairy, needlelike leaves. Flowers are 1½ in. wide, with relatively large, creamy white rays veined in green on underside. Blooms sporadically from spring through fall, whenever moisture is present; goes dormant during extended periods of drought.

Z. angustifolia. Annual. Compact growth to 16 in. high and wide, with very narrow leaves. Orange, inch-wide flowers; each ray has a paler stripe. Blooms in 6 weeks from seed, continues late into fall. The Classic and Star series bloom in shades of orange-yellow and white. 'Golden Eye' is much like 'Star White': both have white rays, yellow centers.

Z. elegans. Annual. From Mexico. The common garden zinnia, sold in strains ranging from less than a foot high and wide to 4 ft. tall, half as wide. Oval to lance-shaped leaves to 5 in. long; summer flowers from less than 1 in. to as much as 5–7 in. across. Forms include full double, cactus-flowered (with quilled rays), and crested

(cushionlike center surrounded by rows of broad rays); the many colors available include white, pink, salmon, rose, red, yellow, orange, lavender, and purple. Some flowers are multi-colored. 'Envy' is a novelty type with lime green flowers.

Z. grandiflora. Perennial in Zones 2–24; annual elsewhere. Native to Rocky Mountains and south into Mexico. To 4–6 in. high. Bright green leaves to 1 in. long, ⅛ in. wide. Spring-into-fall flowers are 1½ in. wide, bright yellow with orange eye. Survives with no supplemental moisture but needs regular water to bloom satisfactorily.

Z. haageana. Annual. From southeastern U.S. and Mexico. To 2 ft. high, 1 ft. wide. Narrow, 3-in. leaves. Persian Carpet (1 ft. high) and Old Mexico (16 in. high) have double blossoms in mahogany red, yellow, and orange, with all three colors usually mixed in the same flower. Long summer bloom season.

Z. marylandica. Annual. These mildew-tolerant varieties originated with a cross between *Z. angustifolia* and *Z. elegans*. They include the Profusion and Zahara series, in an ever-expanding range of colors, mostly in shades of white, red, yellow, and orange, including some bicolors. Plants grow 1–1½ ft. high and wide, with 2½-in. flower heads containing more than one row of rays.

Z. peruviana. Annual. Native from southern U.S. to Argentina. Grows to 3 ft. high and wide; leaves to 3 in. long and 1¼ in. wide. In summer, bears profuse, 1½-in. flowers in brick red or soft gold. Blossoms dry well for arrangements. It is also called Bonita zinnia or *Z. pauciflora*.

CARE

These hot-weather plants do not gain from being planted early; they merely stand still until the weather warms up. Subject to mildew in foggy places, if given overhead water, and when fall brings longer nights, more dew and shade. Sow seeds where plants are to grow (or set out nursery plants) from late spring to early summer. Give good soil, feed generously.

Ziziphus jujuba. See *Jujube*

Zoysia

Poaceae

PERENNIAL GRASSES

✎ **ZONES VARY BY SPECIES**

☼ ◑ **BEST IN SUN; TOLERATE SOME SHADE**

💧💧 **MODERATE TO REGULAR WATER**

Zoysia tenuifolia

These Asian natives tend to spread slowly and are fairly deep rooted. Dormant and straw-colored during the winter; turn green in spring. Use for lawns and groundcovers. Plant using sod, sprigs, stolons, or plugs. Mow lawns 1–2 in. high.

Z. 'Emerald'. EMERALD ZOYSIA. Zones 8, 9, 12–14, 18–24; H1, H2. Hybrid between *Z. japonica* and *Z. tenuifolia*. Makes wiry, dark green, prickly-looking turf. Dense blades are hard to cut. More frost-tolerant than other zoysias.

Z. japonica 'Meyer' ('Z-52'). MEYER ZOYSIA. Zones 8, 9, 12–14, 18–24; H1, H2. Resembles bluegrass (*Poa*). Turns brown earliest in winter, turns green latest in spring. New strains of *Z. japonica* include 'De Anza', 'El Toro', and 'Victoria'. All have increased durability and are quicker to establish. 'El Toro' is more shade-tolerant.

Z. matrella. MANILA GRASS. Zones 8, 9, 12–14, 18–24; H1, H2. Also similar to bluegrass in appearance. Holds color a little better than *Z. japonica* 'Meyer'.

Z. tenuifolia. KOREAN GRASS. Hardy in Zones 8, 9, 12–24; H1, H2. Creeping, fine textured, bumpy. Makes a beautiful grassy meadow or gives mossy Oriental effect in areas impossible to mow or water often. The farther inland, the longer the dormant season.

Z

Gardening, Start to Finish

AN UNDERSTANDING OF BASIC GARDENING PRINCIPLES will make you a better gardener. On the following pages, you'll find all you need to know about planting, tending, watering, feeding, and growing various kinds of plants, from annuals and grasses to perennials, succulents, trees, vegetables, and wildflowers—plus information on basics such as soil prep and composting; harvest tips; design ideas; and more.

SECRETS OF A HEALTHY GARDEN

Planting and caring for a garden is easy, if you follow a few general guidelines to keep it productive and healthy.

Feed the soil. A healthy garden starts with good soil. For flower and vegetable beds, till the soil between plantings and refresh it with compost. The best soil is dark, porous, and rich in humus and beneficial organisms.

Match the plants to your site. Choose plants that grow easily in your climate, site, and soil. Whether native or adapted, if the plants like the conditions in your garden, they'll thrive without heavy-handed care.

Plant for diversity. Expanses of just one sort of plant are of little interest to birds, beneficial insects, and other creatures that can help keep insect pests in check. But a diverse planting, where many different kinds of plants mingle together as in nature, encourages pollinators and beneficial species that prey on the troublemakers. Include in your garden flowers for fragrance, grasses for motion, trees for shade, nectar and seed producers to attract wildlife, and easy perennials that come back year after year and thrive with little water.

Plant disease-resistant varieties of edible plants. Seed packets and plant tags may bear code letters noting inbred resistance to certain serious problems. Tomatoes, for example, may be designated V, F, N, and/or T, indicating resistance to verticillium wilt, fusarium wilt, harmful nematodes (which cause root knots), and tobacco mosaic virus.

Rotate crops. Members of the same plant family are often susceptible to the same pests and diseases. Tomatoes, for example, are in the same family as eggplant, peppers, and potatoes. Planting these crops in different locations in your garden from one year to the next will help prevent a buildup of pest and disease organisms. Try to plan a rotation that allows at least two years between the same or related crops.

Encourage natural controls. Toads, lizards, many birds, and beneficial insects (see page 727) all prey on insect pests. Avoid chemical sprays if possible, and be aware that even sprays made from natural ingredients can harm helpful creatures as well as pests, leaving the garden vulnerable to new attack.

Keep the garden clean. Every fall, clean up garden debris, because that's where some insects and diseases overwinter or spend certain developmental stages. Rake and compost fallen leaves, along with grass clippings and spent annuals and vegetables. Cut back perennials to just above new growth.

PLAN

Imagine a less resource-dependent future. In this 21st-century backyard, the latest elements for saving water, energy, and grocery costs are in place—from unthirsty native plants to a climate-controlled, state-of-the-art irrigation system.

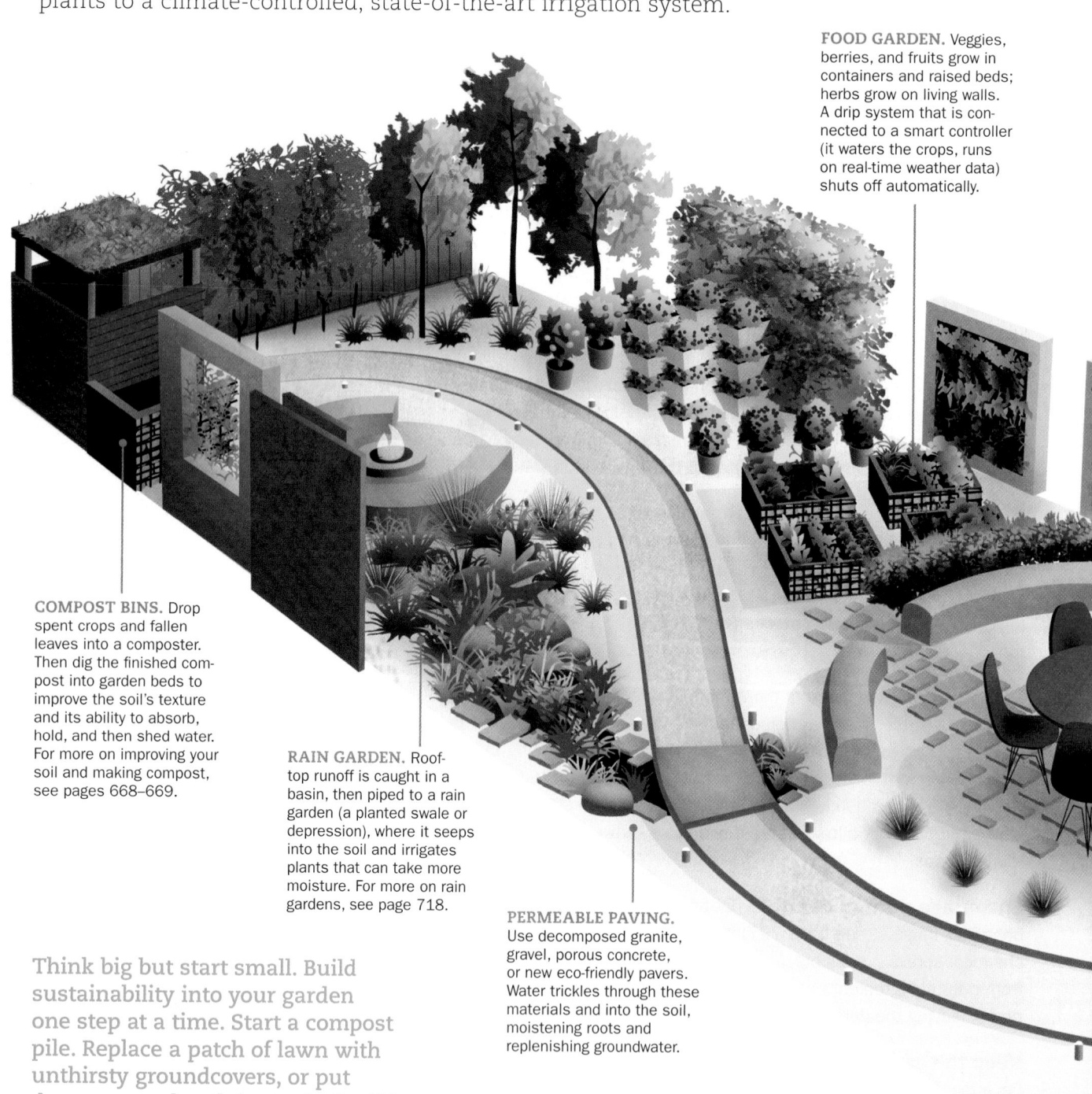

FOOD GARDEN. Veggies, berries, and fruits grow in containers and raised beds; herbs grow on living walls. A drip system that is connected to a smart controller (it waters the crops, runs on real-time weather data) shuts off automatically.

COMPOST BINS. Drop spent crops and fallen leaves into a composter. Then dig the finished compost into garden beds to improve the soil's texture and its ability to absorb, hold, and then shed water. For more on improving your soil and making compost, see pages 668–669.

RAIN GARDEN. Rooftop runoff is caught in a basin, then piped to a rain garden (a planted swale or depression), where it seeps into the soil and irrigates plants that can take more moisture. For more on rain gardens, see page 718.

PERMEABLE PAVING. Use decomposed granite, gravel, porous concrete, or new eco-friendly pavers. Water trickles through these materials and into the soil, moistening roots and replenishing groundwater.

Think big but start small. Build sustainability into your garden one step at a time. Start a compost pile. Replace a patch of lawn with unthirsty groundcovers, or put down a gravel path instead of solid concrete. Choose solar or other energy-efficient lighting.

Start with Elements That Will Help Save Reources

Straw

Hazelnut hulls

Ground bark

Decomposed granite

Shredded bark

Tumbled glass

SHADE TREES. Deciduous or evergreen trees are properly placed to shade and cool outdoor living areas from hot summer sun. Trees that are placed to shade windows on the house's south- and west-facing sides also cool the home and save energy. For details, see pages 696–697.

NATIVE PLANTS. Choose plants native to the West's dry areas; many require little water beyond the rain that nature provides. Trees, shrubs, perennials, and grasses from the world's other wet-winter, dry-summer Mediterranean climates—southern Australia, Chile, and the Mediterranean—are also good choices. For more on natives, see page 684.

1 HEALTHY SOIL. Fast draining and filled with plenty of organic matter (which earthworms love), it's essential for growing flowers, edibles, and other kinds of plants.

2 POLLINATOR PLANTS. Flowers that attract bees, butterflies, and hummingbirds are a gardener's best friends. As the pollinators feed on nectar, they move pollen from one plant to another, ensuring healthy crops of veggies, fruits, and more.

3 WATER SAVERS. The smartest gardens use water wisely. Keep water features small, recirculating. Use drip-irrigation systems and soaker hoses to apply water to plant roots, and root irrigators as needed to deep-water trees.

4 MULCH. Mulch is any material that covers soil surfaces and allows air and water through. It helps hold moisture in the soil and prevents most weed seedlings from catching hold. Take care not to pile it against plants' bases, as too much moisture can cause rot.

Organic mulch is sold by the cubic yard. Determine how many square feet you need to cover (multiply the area's length by its width); then use the guidelines below.

Kinds of Mulch

Straw. Good around vegetables and strawberries. Buy at livestock feed stores (avoid hay, which has seed heads). Apply 4–5 inches.

Hazelnut hulls. Good for general use. Most readily available around Oregon's Willamette Valley. Apply 2–3 inches.

Ground bark. An all-purpose mulch; mini size looks best. Apply 1–2 inches.

Decomposed granite (DG). Compacts quickly and doesn't blow away. Best around ornamentals. Apply 1–2 inches.

Shredded bark. Slow to decompose; has a woodsy look. Apply 2 inches.

Tumbled glass. Pricey. Used mainly to add frosty color around succulents in pots.

For more on working with mulch, see sunset.com/mulch ▶

DIG

Healthy garden soil supports plant roots and gives them access to nutrients, water, and air. It's fast draining yet moisture retentive, neither too dense nor too loose. Most roots grow in its upper layer (topsoil), which is especially biologically active—home to earthworms, fungus, and other beneficials.

In the topsoil, earthworms improve drainage and aeration as they tunnel, while their castings add nutrients. And organic matter such as ground bark and vegetable matter decomposes, creating a soft, dark substance called humus. Below the topsoil is the subsoil. Although it contains plant nutrients, it's not as hospitable to roots as the topsoil. Improving your topsoil can have the most beneficial effect on plant health. To achieve healthy soil, treat your planting beds with organic amendments (see page 668), or grow cover crops (see page 721) to add organic

material to the soil. Organic gardeners prefer natural fertilizers (see pages 720–721), which provide a more sustained release of nutrients and encourage beneficial soil-dwelling organisms.

One inhospitable type of soil is called hardpan. This impervious layer of soil is found naturally in the Southwest, where it is called caliche. Hardpan can also be created when builders spread excavated subsoil over the ground, then drive heavy equipment over it. A thin layer of topsoil may conceal hardpan, but roots cannot penetrate it, nor water drain through it. For fixes, see left box on opposite page.

Good garden soil contains about 50 percent pore spaces filled with water and air, 45 percent rock particles, and at least 5 percent organic matter.

CHECK SOIL TEXTURE

All soils contain mineral particles formed by the natural breakdown of rock (as well as varying amounts of organic matter, air, and water). The size and shape of these particles determine the soil's texture, whether clay, sandy, or loam.

SANDY (LIGHT) SOILS. Their big particles have large pore spaces between them that allow water and nutrients to drain away freely. Plants growing in them need water and feeding more often.

LOAM. It contains mineral particles of various sizes, organic matter, and enough air for healthy root growth. It drains well but doesn't dry out—or lose nutrients—too fast.

CLAY (HEAVY) SOILS. Their tiny particles pack together, helping them to hold the greatest volume of nutrients in soluble form. But they're sticky when wet, hard when dry, and slow to drain.

WHAT TO DO

- Thoroughly wet a patch of soil; let it dry out for a day.

- Pick up a handful of soil and squeeze it firmly in your fist.

  It is predominantly clay if it forms a tight ball and feels slippery.

  It's sandy if it feels gritty, doesn't hold its shape, and crumbles when you open your hand.

  It's loam if it is slightly crumbly but still holds a loose ball.

- Amend the soil as needed (see page 668).

CHECK SOIL DRAINAGE

Poor drainage causes water to remain in the pore spaces, so air—necessary to roots and beneficial soil-dwelling organisms—is unable to enter the soil. Soil texture and a low-lying location can contribute to poor drainage, as can running heavy machinery over the soil and walking on planting areas.

WHAT TO DO

- Dig a 2-foot-deep hole and fill it with water. Let it drain.

- Fill it again. If this second amount of water drains away in a few hours, the drainage is good. If it remains for 12 hours or longer, the soil drains poorly.

- Improve drainage by working organic matter into the soil. In the garden's low spots, you may need to install drainage pipes to carry away excess water, or grow plants suited to moist areas.

- If a hardpan layer is thin and close to the surface, try plowing the soil to a depth of 1 foot or more. Thick hardpan may require installation of a subsurface drainage system. Or grow plants in raised beds filled with good soil.

Areas of poorly draining soils are evident after heavy rainfall.

CHECK SOIL PH

Soil pH is a measure of how soil ranges from acid through neutral to alkaline. Soil with a pH of 7 is neutral—neither acid nor alkaline. A pH below 7 indicates acidity, while one above 7 indicates alkalinity. If the pH is extreme in either direction, key nutrients are chemically "tied up" in the soil and not available to plant roots.

Acid soil Overly acid soil typically occurs in the Northwest, along California's northern coast, and in parts of Hawaii—regions with heavy rainfall and soils high in organic matter. Most plants thrive in mildly acid soil, but highly acid soils are inhospitable.

Alkaline soil Found in regions where rainfall is light, this soil is high in calcium carbonate. Many plants grow well in moderately alkaline soil. Others, including camellias and azaleas, do not.

Salty soils Found near the seashore and in arid regions, or they can result from the overuse of fertilizers and fresh manures. Salty soil pulls water from plant roots, making it difficult for plants to take up enough moisture or nutrients. Symptoms include scorched and yellowed leaves or browned and withered leaf margins.

WHAT TO DO

- **Test the soil.** If you're not sure whether your soil is acid or alkaline, or if you suspect your soil is deficient in some nutrients, check it using a simple test kit from the nursery. For a more precise reading, have the test done at a laboratory. (Check online under soil-test labs.)

- **Adjust pH.** *Acid soil:* Raise pH by adding calcium carbonate (lime). *Alkaline soil:* Lower soil pH by adding sulfur or, over time, with compost. If your water is also alkaline, these remedies may not work. For salty soil, add organic matter and leach the soil periodically with water to wash the salts below the plants' root zones.

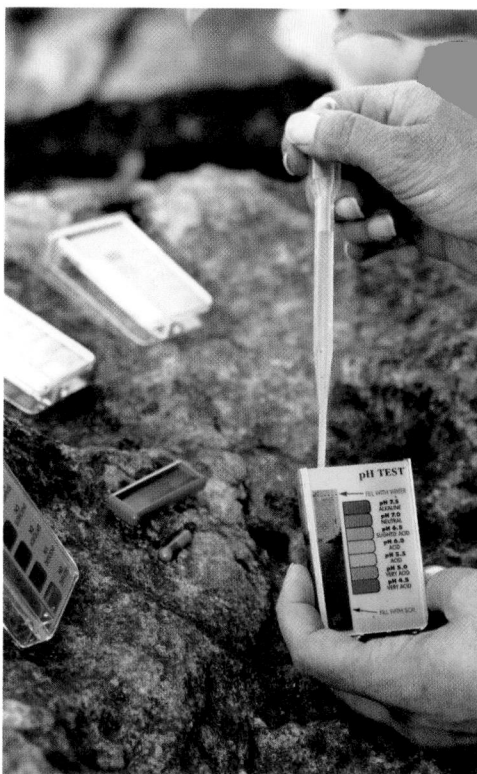

Soil test kits such as these, from a nursery, give you a general indicator of your soil pH.

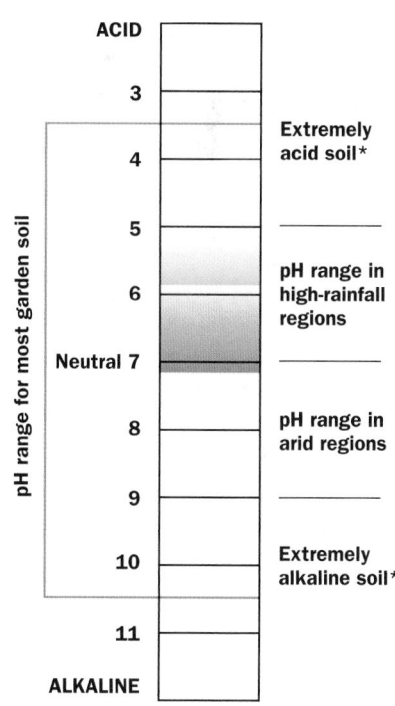

pH range preferred by acid-loving plants

pH range preferred by most garden plants

*Soils nearing extremes require professional intervention to modify pH.

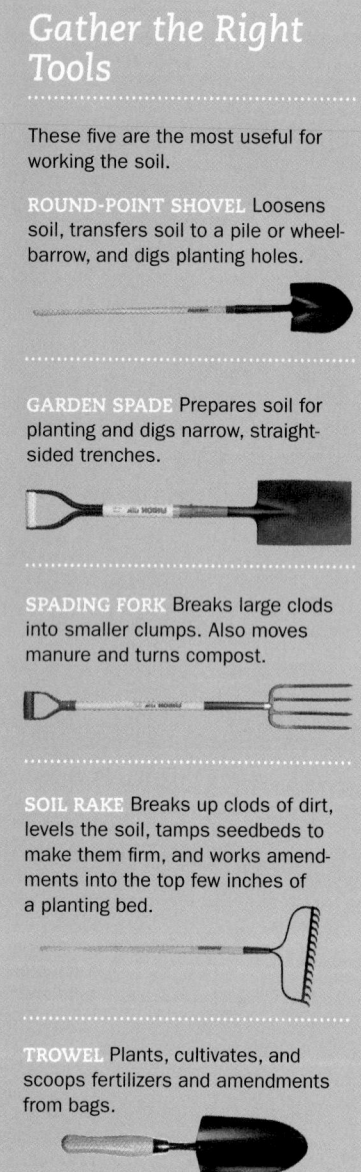

Gather the Right Tools

These five are the most useful for working the soil.

ROUND-POINT SHOVEL Loosens soil, transfers soil to a pile or wheelbarrow, and digs planting holes.

GARDEN SPADE Prepares soil for planting and digs narrow, straight-sided trenches.

SPADING FORK Breaks large clods into smaller clumps. Also moves manure and turns compost.

SOIL RAKE Breaks up clods of dirt, levels the soil, tamps seedbeds to make them firm, and works amendments into the top few inches of a planting bed.

TROWEL Plants, cultivates, and scoops fertilizers and amendments from bags.

Shovels, spades, and spading forks are available with shorter D-type handles or long handles. D-types are best for short gardeners and for digging in confined spaces; long-handled tools are better for tall gardeners.

CHOOSE A SOIL AMENDMENT

Compost Made from dried grasses, leaves, and other garden trimmings, it's easy to make, it's good for your garden, and it lightens the load at landfills.

Manure Aged or composted manures contain more plant nutrients than other amendments. But they can contain high concentrations of soluble salts, which can harm plant roots; apply them sparingly. Add about 1 pound of dry steer manure per square foot of soil surface or 1 pound of dry poultry manure for 4 to 5 square feet. Work it into the soil a month before planting to allow salts to leach below root level.

Wood products Ground bark is useful in clay soils; it helps separate fine clay particles. But it can take nitrogen from the soil as it decomposes (add nitrogen along with it for best plant growth). Some wood products, such as redwood soil conditioner, can be purchased already fortified with nitrogen; check the labels to be sure.

Sphagnum peat moss It helps acidify the soil, but there are concerns over the damage that may result from the overmining of some peat bogs. A coir fiber by-product of the coconut fiber industry is similar in texture; it's sold in bales, bricks, and discs that expand when soaked in water to make 5 to 10 quarts of fluffy material. Coir fiber won't help acidify the soil the way peat does.

WHAT TO DO

• **Buy the best type for your soil** (your nursery can help you). The amendments listed above are typically sold at nurseries in 1- or 2-cubic-foot bags, and in bulk at building suppliers. You'll need a cubic yard of organic material to cover 100 square feet of planting bed to a depth of about 3 inches.

• **Other options:** Make your own compost (see opposite page). Or grow cover crops; they're natural soil enrichers (see page 721).

Spread organic material around established plantings as a mulch.

AMEND THE SOIL

Dampen the soil thoroughly and allow it to dry for a few days before you dig. Don't try to work soil that's too wet or too dry.

Dig to a depth of about 10 inches. Break up dirt clods and remove any stones or debris as you go. In small areas, use a spading fork; for larger beds, try a rotary tiller.

Add fertilizer now as well. Spread it over the soil, using the amount indicated on the label. Then work it into the topsoil where it will have the greatest benefit.

Mix with a spading fork or tiller, incorporating the amendments evenly into the soil.

Level the bed with a rake, breaking up any remaining clods of earth.

Water well; let the improved soil settle for at least a few days before planting.

HOW TO MAKE COMPOST

Composting is a natural process that converts raw organic materials into a valuable soil conditioner. In addition to being good for your garden, composting lightens the load at the landfill, as you recycle garden and kitchen debris at home rather than consign it to the dump.

A pile of leaves, branches, and other garden trimmings will eventually decompose in a process called slow or cold composting. With hot composting—which occurs when you create optimum conditions for the organisms responsible for decay by giving them the right mixture of air, water, and carbon- and nitrogen-rich nutrients—the pile heats up quickly and delivers finished compost in just a few months.

You can make compost in a freestanding pile or use an enclosure, such as those shown below. Regardless of the methods, the fundamentals of composting are the same.

Gather and prepare ingredients.
You'll need approximately twice as much (by volume) brown matter as green matter. Brown matter (dry leaves, hay, sawdust, wood chips, woody prunings) is high in carbon. Green matter (grass clippings, fruit and vegetable scraps, coffee grounds) is high in nitrogen. Avoid badly diseased or insect-infested plants, weeds with seeds, and perennial weeds that might survive composting. Shred or chop large, rough materials into smaller pieces to speed the composting process.

Build the pile.
Put down a 4- to 8-inch layer of brown material, then add a layer of green material about 2–4 inches deep (layers of grass clippings should be only 2 inches deep). Add another layer of brown material and sprinkle the pile with water. Mix these first three layers with a spading fork. Continue adding layers, watering, and mixing.

Turn the pile.
In just a few days, the pile should heat up dramatically. In time, it will decompose on its own, but hurry things along by turning the pile to introduce more oxygen. Using a spading fork or pitchfork, restack the pile, redistributing it so that the materials originally on the outside are moved to the pile's center, where

Start your pile by mixing green and brown matter. Finished compost is dark and crumbly.

they'll be exposed to higher heat. If necessary, add water; the pile should be as moist as a wrung-out sponge. Adding an occasional shovelful of aged manure or finished compost gives the pile a dose of extra nutrients and speeds decomposition. Turn the pile weekly, if possible, until it is no longer generating internal heat and most of the materials have decomposed.

Composters

Wire cylinder.
Bend a length of wire into a cylinder about 3 or 4 feet tall and 4 feet in diameter. Secure the wire to a framework or support it with stakes. To turn the pile, lift the cylinder and move it to one side, then fork the materials back into it.

Three-bin systems.
The left bin holds new green and brown material; the center one contains partly decomposed material; the right bin holds nearly finished or finished compost. Turn the material in each bin weekly, moving decomposed material to the right.

Manufactured composters.
They include this static compost bin in which compost sits without turning. (Occasional aerating with a spading fork is helpful.) Add new materials at the top, and remove the finished compost through a door at the base.

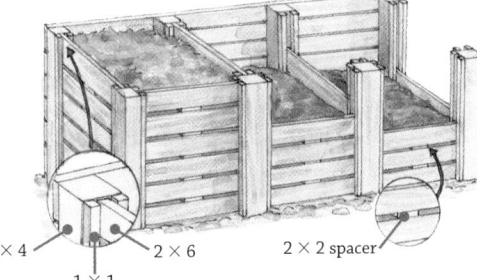

4 × 4   2 × 6   2 × 2 spacer
1 × 1

Door

PLANT

Planting techniques depend on the plant and how it is sold. Many annuals and vegetables and some perennials are sold as seedlings in small containers or flats during the growing season. Along with some groundcovers, they are also sold in plastic cell-packs, individual plastic pots, and peat pots.

SEED

Works for: Annual flowers, herbs, and vegetables; some perennials.

Look for: Fresh seeds. The packets should be dated for the current year.

Sowing

Seeds of many plants are easy to sow directly in the ground. You just scatter small ones over prepared soil, or plant larger ones atop low soil mounds or in furrows as shown in photo at right.

Others, especially for warm-season annual vegetables, get off to a better start when sown in containers and transplanted to garden beds later in the season. The information given on the seed packet will help you decide when to plant.

Sow most annual flowers and vegetables four to eight weeks before it's time to transplant them outdoors.

To start seed indoors:

1. **FILL SMALL POTS** or cell-packs to just below the rim with light, porous seed-starting mix. Moisten the mix; let drain.

2. **SOW SEEDS** following guidelines on seed packet and cover seeds with the recommended amount of mix. Moisten lightly.

3. **WHEN SEEDS GERMINATE,** move the container to a warm area with bright light. As they grow, thin out the weakest seedlings. About 10 days before planting out, "harden off" the seedlings by setting them outdoors for a few hours each day to get them acclimated.

SEEDLINGS

1. **LOOSEN ROOTS.** With your fingers, lightly separate the roots so they can grow out into the soil. If there is a pad of coiled roots at the bottom of the rootball, pull it off.

2. **PLANT.** Place each plant in its hole so the top of the rootball is even with the soil surface. Firm the soil around plant roots.

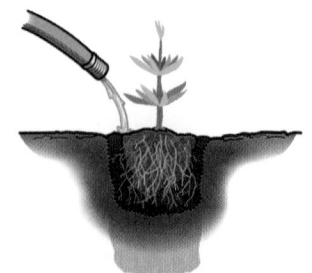

3. **WATER.** Irrigate each plant with a gentle flow that won't disturb soil or roots.

SEEDS Make furrows, following packet instructions for depth. Sow seeds evenly, spacing them as the seed packet directs. Cover with soil; water.

TRANSPLANTS Once the seedlings have developed two sets of true leaves, plant singly in pots, or in the ground.

NURSERY CONTAINERS

Works for: Most shrubs and trees; perennials, groundcovers, some annuals.

Look for: Healthy foliage and strong shoots. Avoid leggy or root-bound plants (with roots protruding above the container's soil level or growing through the drainage holes).

To remove plants from 1-gallon or larger plastic containers, tap sharply on the bottom and sides to loosen the rootball. The plant should slide out easily. With fiber or pulp pots, tear the pot away from the rootball, taking care not to damage the roots.

How to Plant

1. **DIG A PLANTING HOLE** twice as wide as the rootball and as deep, leaving a central plateau of firm soil 1 to 2 inches tall at the bottom of the hole. Roughen the hole's sides with a spading fork.

2. **SET THE PLANT IN THE HOLE,** spreading its roots over the soil plateau. The top of the rootball should be 1 to 2 inches above the surrounding soil. Backfill with the soil you dug from the hole, forming the soil around the roots with your hands.

3. **MAKE A BERM OF SOIL** to form a watering basin. Irrigate gently. Spread mulch around the plant, keeping it several inches away from the stem.

BARE ROOT

Works for: Perennial vegetables such as artichoke and asparagus; deciduous cane berries, strawberries, fruit trees, roses, and some ornamental trees.

Look for: Bare-root plants with strong stems (no leaves) and fresh-looking, well-formed roots. Avoid any with slimy roots or dry, withered ones. Bare-root plants are sold in late winter and early spring by retail nurseries and mail-order companies. They typically cost only 40 to 70 percent as much as the same varieties purchased in containers later in the year. Plant them as soon as possible after purchase—ideally, right away.

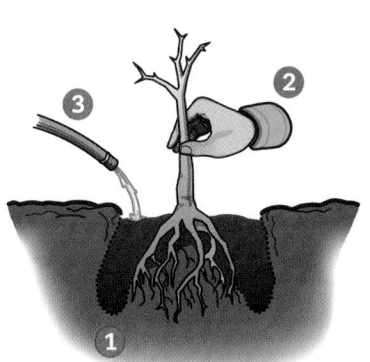

How to Plant

1. **DIG A PLANTING HOLE** that is about the same depth as the plant's roots and twice as wide as it is deep. Shape a firm cone of soil in the bottom; make it tall enough so the plant's crown will be slightly above the soil line. Roughen the hole's sides.

2. **HOLD THE PLANT IN PLACE** while you spread the plant's roots over the soil cone; then backfill the hole with more soil.

3. **WATER THE PLANT** to settle in the soil. Fill in the hole with more soil; then water. Spread mulch around the plant, keeping it several inches away from the stem or trunk.

BALLED AND BURLAPPED

Works for: Woody plants whose root systems won't survive bare-root transplanting, and field-grown evergreens such as rhododendrons, some conifers.

Look for: Healthy foliage and an even branching structure. The covering should be intact and the roots unexposed; the rootball should feel firm and moist.

Balled-and-burlapped (B-and-B) plants are dug from the field with a ball of soil around their roots; the soil ball is then wrapped in burlap or a synthetic material and tied with twine or wire. When moving the plant, support the bottom of the rootball.

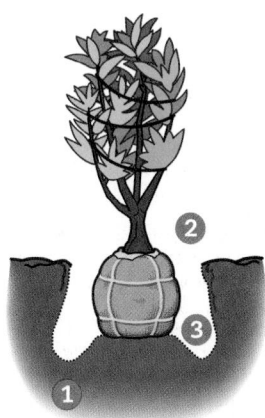

How to Plant

1. **MEASURE THE ROOTBALL** from top to bottom. Dig the planting hole a bit shallower than this distance, so that the top of the rootball will be about 2 inches above the surrounding soil.

2. **UNTIE THE COVERING.** If it's burlap, it will eventually rot, so just spread it out to uncover about half the rootball. If it's synthetic material, remove it entirely. If the plant needs staking, do it now.

3. **FILL THE HOLE WITH SOIL** to within 4 inches of the top. Water gently. Continue to fill the hole, firming the soil as you go. Form a watering basin; then water the plant.

See "How to Plant a Plant" at sunset.com/plant ▶

PLANT
Containers

Growing plants in containers lets you have a garden even when space for one is limited or nonexistent. You can use containers to turn a tiny balcony or patio into a leafy haven, to experiment with new plant combinations, or to try plants that are borderline hardy in your area.

CLOCKWISE FROM BOTTOM LEFT: *Echeveria* 'Volcano'; *Lomandra longifolia* 'Breeze'; *Aeonium haworthii*; 'Blue Elf' aloe; *Sedum acre* 'Elegans'.

CHOOSE

Container It should have at least one drainage hole to prevent root rot. Before planting, submerge terra-cotta pots in clean water and let them soak thoroughly. Scrub used containers with a solution of 1 part household bleach to 9 parts hot water. Cover the drain hole with a small piece of fine wire screen to keep soil from washing out.

Potting mix It should be fast drain-ing yet moisture retentive. Packaged pot-ting mixes that contain organic materials such as ground bark, sphagnum peat moss, and/or compost, plus mineral matter like perlite, pumice, or sand are best. Fertilizers and wetting agents may also be included. Before planting, flush the mix with water once or twice to elimi-nate excess salts.

PLANT

Fill pot partway with potting soil; press to firm, then set plants on top. For best effects, plant singly or in groups of three or five. Finish adding potting soil, firming as you go; water.

WATER

Container plants need water more often than those grown in the ground. In hot or windy weather, some may need water-ing several times a day. Test the mix with your finger: if it is dry beneath the surface, it's time to water. To moisten the entire soil mass and prevent any potentially harmful salts from accumu-lating in the mix, apply water over the entire soil surface until it flows from the pot's drainage holes.

FEED

For most plants, apply a liquid fertilizer every two weeks during the growing season, or mix controlled-release-type granules into the soil. Succulents and grasses need feeding less often.

1½ cubic feet
12" x 16"

11 quarts
9" x 10"

9¼ quarts
4" x 14"

SOIL For most plants, here's how much soil you'll need to fill common container sizes. (Soil is usually sold in quart or cubic-foot bags.)

NO SOIL Tillandsias are epiphytes (in nature they grow in trees); they need no soil to grow. These are for display in an icy white container.

MULCH Get creative with soil coverings, such as the shells in this seaside succulent planting. Or use colorful tumbled glass.

A 16-inch square pot contains blue-green *Euphorbia polychroma*; 'Rustic Orange' coleus; and pheasant's-tail grass (*Anemanthele lessoniana*); medium green *Lysimachia nummularia* and lime green *L. n.* 'Goldilocks' tumble down the sides.

Container-Plant Combos

Other popular container colors and plants we like in them:

BRONZE-CARAMEL POT. *Heuchera* 'Dolce Peach Melba' or 'Southern Comfort' (rosy caramel); *Carex* 'Toffee Twist'.

CHOCOLATE BROWN POT. 'Japanese Bishop' dahlia (bright red flowers, bronze-brown foliage); chartreuse *Heuchera* 'Lime Rickey'; 'Tequila Sunrise' coprosma; black canna (leaves are the color of milk chocolate).

LIME GREEN POT. Refreshing with *Sedum* 'Angelina' (chartreuse); basil (green and 'Dark Opal'); *Solenostemon* (especially Kong series); leaf lettuce (mix); Scotch moss.

Blue and white pots, with cooling sprays of sweet alyssum, refresh the summer garden.

Color 101

A fun way to start a container garden is to choose the pot first, in a color you like (ideally, one that pairs well with your outdoor furniture and paint colors). Then buy plants that match or contrast with it. The pot pictured suggests a beachy theme.

ACCENT. 'Sonata White' cosmos has ferny foliage and snowy white blooms all summer long. It grows about 2 feet tall; plant it in back.

TRAILER. Variegated *Helichrysum petiolare* has blue in its leaves, and stems that trail to 4 feet long; let it cascade over pot edges.

MOUND. 'Diamond Frost' euphorbia forms delicate, airy mounds of small white flowers that look like snowflakes; grows 12–18 inches tall.

Drop blooming annuals from 4-inch nursery pots into pretty ceramic containers (cachepots) for an instant tabletop arrangement.

See "How to Plant a Container" at sunset.com/plantcontainer

GROW
Annuals, Bulbs

Flowering annuals germinate, grow, flower, set seed, and die in less than a year. Bulbs have specialized roots or stem bases that store nutrients and energy for the plants' growth, and they can send up new plants year after year (depending on type). Plants in both groups are seasonal all-stars.

Poppy-flowered anemone (*Anemone coronaria*) grows from a tuber, blooms in spring.

ANNUALS

Annuals are either cool-season or warm-season growers. Some tender perennials, such as pelargonium, are grown as annuals where winters are cold. And a few hardier perennials, such as snapdragon, are grown as annuals because older plants don't perform as well as young ones.

Cool-season annuals These develop their roots and foliage in fall and early spring; they can withstand fairly heavy frosts. In cold-winter areas, plant them in very early spring, as soon as the soil can be worked. In mild-winter areas, plant in fall for winter and early-spring bloom. Or plant in late winter or very early spring for spring bloom.

Cool-season annuals include calendula, cornflower, forget-me-not, larkspur, *Nemesia strumosa*, *Phlox drummondii*, Shirley poppy, stock, sweet peas, and viola.

Warm-season annuals These grow best during the warm months between late spring and fall, and cannot withstand low temperatures. In cold-winter climates, set them out after all danger of frost has passed; in mild-winter climates, plant them in midspring. In desert regions, you can plant some warm-season annuals in early fall for winter bloom.

Warm-season annuals include calibrachoa, celosia, China aster, cosmos, globe amaranth, impatiens, lobelia, marigold, nasturtium, petunia, scabiosa, scarlet sage, spider flower (*Cleome hasslerana*), sunflower, sweet alyssum, and zinnia.

HOW TO GROW ANNUALS

Choose nursery-grown annuals that are relatively small, with healthy foliage and few flowers.

Water annuals thoroughly after planting. Thereafter, keep soil moist but not soggy. Water young plants more often in warm weather.

Feed after bloom begins in cold-winter areas. Where winters are warm and the growing season is longer, feed both after flowering starts and again in late summer.

Deadhead spent flowers to encourage more blooms and keep the plants tidy.

Fragrant sweet peas (*Lathyrus odoratus*) are spring delights. Plant in fall in mild climates.

BULBS

Bulbs are underground structures that store food for keeping the plant alive through a dormant period, ready to grow again once dormancy has ended. Some bulbs (daffodil, for example) thrive in most of the West; others have a more restricted range. Outside their preferred climate zones, grow bulbs in pots, or dig up and store them for winter. Bulbs graded "large" generally yield more flowers, but for mass planting, buy midsize specimens. Choose plump, firm bulbs that feel heavy; avoid those that are soft, squishy, or shriveled.

HOW TO GROW BULBS

Prep Work a complete fertilizer into the entire bed or mix a tablespoon of fertilizer into the bottom of individual holes; add 2 inches of compost over that.

Plant Place the bulb in the hole. For depth and spacing for specific bulbs, check the entries in the encyclopedia.

Water Irrigate bulbs while they're growing actively, from after planting until the foliage dies back.

Feed Apply a high-nitrogen fertilizer when growth starts. Leave spent foliage on the plant until it dries; then feed and water once more.

BULB-PLANTING DEPTH

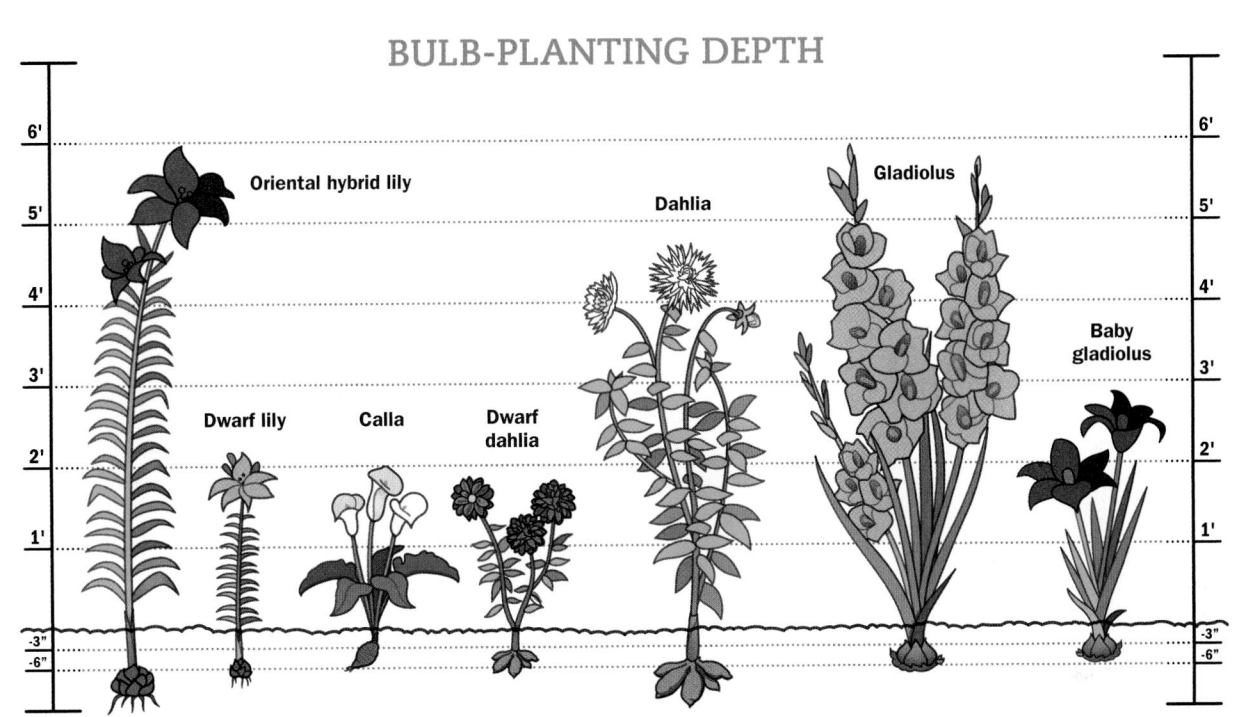

THE FIVE BULB TYPES

TRUE BULB An underground stem base containing an embryonic plant surrounded by scales. A basal plate at the bottom of the bulb holds the scales together and produces roots. Most true bulbs have a protective papery outer skin. Lilies do not, so they are more susceptible to drying and damage; handle them with care. To divide, simply separate offsets from the mother bulb.
True bulbs include *Allium*, *Hippeastrum*, hyacinth, *Ipheion*, lily, *Lycoris*, *Muscari*, *Narcissus*, tulip.

RHIZOME A thickened stem growing partially or entirely below ground. Its roots grow directly from the underside. The primary growing point is at one end of the rhizome, and additional growing points form along the sides. To divide, cut into sections that have visible growing points.
Rhizomes include *Agapanthus*, calla, *Canna*, *Dietes*, *Iris* (some), lily-of-the-valley, tuberose, and *Tulbaghia*.

TUBEROUS ROOTS Unlike the other four bulb types, these are true roots, thickened to store nutrients. Fibrous roots for the uptake of water and nutrients develop from its sides and tip. Tuberous roots grow in a cluster, with the swollen portions radiating out from a central point. The growth buds are at the bases of old stems rather than on the roots themselves. To divide, cut the root cluster apart so each division contains both roots and part of a stem base with one or more growth buds.
Tuberous roots include *Alstroemeria*, *Clivia*, *Dahlia*, *Hemerocallis*, *Liatris*, Persian ranunculus.

TUBER Swollen underground stem bases, but they lack the corm's distinct organization. There is no basal plate, so roots can grow from all sides. Instead of just one or a few growing points, a tuber has multiple growth points scattered over its surface. Some tubers, such as begonia, are perennials that increase in size each year. Others are annual. As new tubers grow, the old ones disintegrate. To divide either kind of tuber, cut it into sections, making sure each has one or more growing points.
Tubers include *Anemone* (most), *Caladium*, *Colocasia*, *Corydalis*, *Cyclamen*, tuberous begonia.

CORM A swollen underground stem base, composed of solid tissue rather than scales. Roots grow from a basal plate at the corm's bottom, and the growth point is at the top. Each corm lasts a year. As it shrinks away, a new corm and, in many species, small cormels form on top of it. To divide, separate healthy new corms and any cormels from the old corms (cormels may take as long as two to three years to reach flowering size).
Corms include *Crocosmia*, *Crocus*, *Freesia*, *Gladiolus*, *Triteleia*, *Tritonia crocata*, *Watsonia*.

GROW
Lawn Grasses

In the arid West, traditional turf grasses require more water per square foot than almost any other garden plant. As a result, some homeowners are eliminating the lawn entirely or sharply reducing its size. Perhaps most important, choose the right grass for your climate and prep the soil carefully.

In summer, lawns get hammered from play and foot traffic, coupled with heat. One solution: blend pavers with lawn as shown.

CHOOSE

Select varieties adapted to your area. The lawn will establish most quickly in spring or fall.

Cool-Season Grasses

These withstand winter cold but typically languish in hot, dry summers. Most grow best in the Northwest, in parts of the Rocky Mountains with (usually) abundant summer rainfall, and in areas with cooling marine influences. These grasses are often sold as mixes. So even if one type in the mix is not adapted to the soil or sun and shade conditions in your garden, chances are that others in the package will do well.

Bent grass (Agrostis). Fine-textured. Needs ample water, more care than other lawn grasses. Grow it in acid soil, in sun or light shade. Sold as seed, sod. Mowing height: ½–¾ inch.

Crested wheatgrass (Agropyron). Light bluish green color. Tough, drought-tolerant. Grow it in sunny areas. Adapted to Rocky Mountains and High Plains. Goes dormant in hot weather. Sold as seed. Mowing height: 2 inches.

Fine fescue (Festuca). Fine-bladed grasses that succeed in well-drained soil in shaded sites. Fairly drought-tolerant. Sometimes blended with Kentucky bluegrass or perennial ryegrass; used to overseed warm-season grasses. Sold as seed. Mowing height: 1½–2 inches.

Tall fescue (Festuca). Tough grass that tolerates heat and drought, flourishes in sun or shade. It freezes out in the coldest climates. Dwarf tall fescues are finer bladed, deeper green. Sold as seed, sod. Mowing height: 2–3 inches.

Kentucky bluegrass (Poa). Classic grass for cool regions. Needs regular water. Takes sun, light shade. Sold as seed, sod. Mowing height: 2–2½ inches.

Perennial ryegrass (Lolium). Deep green grass that does best in sun. Needs frequent watering. Used as year-round lawn in cooler regions or to overseed winter-dormant grasses. Sold as seed, sod. Mowing height: 2 inches.

Warm-Season Grasses

These thrive in hot weather and turn dormant and brown in winter. Most grow in California and the Southwest. Overseed with cool-season grasses for winter.

Bermuda grass (Cynodon). Drought-tolerant lawn for sunny areas. Sold as seed. Finer-textured hybrids do not self-sow and are less invasive. Sold as sod, sprigs, plugs. Mowing height: ½–¾ inch.

Blue grama (Bouteloua). Tolerates drought, temperature extremes, and a wide range of soils. Does best in sun. Makes a better-quality turf when blended with buffalo grass. Sold as seed. Mowing height: 2–3 inches.

Buffalo grass (Buchloe). Very drought-tolerant lawn for sun; slow growing. Best in mountain regions. Can be invasive. Sold as seed, sod, plugs. Mowing height: 3 inches.

St. Augustine grass (Stenotaphrum). Best near coast in sun, but tolerates shade. Needs regular water. Stolons can be invasive. Sold as sod, sprigs, plugs. Mowing height: 1½–3 inches.

Zoysia (Zoysia). Tolerates drought and heat, sun or shade. Sold as sod, sprigs, plugs. Mowing height: 1–2 inches.

PLANT

Before planting a lawn, till the soil to a depth of about 8 inches and spread it with a 3- to 4-inch layer of organic matter. Also apply a lawn fertilizer. Till again; then rake the area smooth, water it thoroughly, and let the soil settle for a few days.

HOW TO SEED

Seed is the cheapest way to start a lawn. Package labels list varieties included. Fall seeding is best for most grasses; in coldest climates, seed in early fall so the lawn can grow before winter.

- After preparing the area, scatter seeds. A mechanical spreader helps sow seeds evenly.
- Lightly rake seeds into the soil.
- Spread a ½-inch layer of mulch such as compost over the area. Roll with an empty roller to press seeds into soil. Water thoroughly. Keep the seedbed moist until the seeds sprout.

Plugs These are small-rooted plants used for warm-season spreading grasses such as buffalo and hybrid Bermuda. Plant them in spring, following the supplier's directions. Water often until roots take hold.

A flat of 70 plugs is enough to cover 30 square feet.

Sprigs These pieces of grass stem and root are used to plant warm-season grasses; they give faster coverage than seeds. Plant in spring, setting sprigs 2–3 inches deep at 4-inch intervals, in rows 6–12 inches apart. One end of each sprig should barely poke out of the ground.

HOW TO SOD

Sod is the most expensive way to start a lawn, but it gives instant coverage with almost no weed problems. Select varieties adapted to your area.

- After preparing the site, moisten the soil. Unroll the strips and lay them out with their ends staggered, pressing the edges together firmly.
- Use a knife to trim sod so it fits snugly around paving or plants.
- Press roots into the soil, using a roller half-filled with water. Water lawn once daily (more in hot weather) for six weeks.

WATER AND FEED

To encourage deep rooting and conserve water, irrigate established lawns as deeply and infrequently as possible. In mild climates, once or twice a week should be adequate during warm weather; in hotter regions, you'll need to water more often. Contact your local water department or Cooperative Extension Office for specific lawn watering guidelines for your area.

Irrigate in cycles Many sprinklers apply water faster than the soil can absorb it. To prevent runoff, water in cycles. Sprinkle until just before runoff or puddling occurs (typically 10 to 15 minutes), then repeat the cycle in an hour. Adjust sprinklers so they don't overshoot onto paving. To improve water penetration and reduce runoff, aerate and dethatch your lawn once a year.

Feed regularly Most lawns are heavy feeders, requiring regular applications of high-nitrogen fertilizer. In the desert, iron may also be beneficial. Give

As you mow, overlap the just-mowed row as shown. Leave some clippings on the lawn to decompose and add nutrients to the soil.

cool-season lawns two applications of fertilizer, one in spring and another in fall. Fertilize warm-season lawns several times from late spring into late summer (Bermuda grass only lightly in summer) and lightly in fall. Apply dry fertilizers using a spreader; overlap the spreader's wheel marks so swaths just touch as you pass over. Check the packages for recommended application rates. If you cut back on watering because of drought, hold back on fertilizer as well.

MOW

Cut the grass at least weekly
Never take more than a third of the blade off each time. If you do, the loss of food-producing leaf blade temporarily checks root growth. Find mowing heights on opposite page.

Use a sharp blade
A dull blade leaves the grass ragged and brown on the tips. A sharp blade cuts fast and clean, leaving the grass healthy.

TEND

To keep the lawn looking good, give it a tune-up once a year, in fall. Patch dead or damaged spots with the same type of grass as the existing lawn. In Arizona and California, overseed winter-dormant grasses such as Bermuda with ryegrass.

GROW
Ornamental Grasses

Ornamental grasses have graceful forms and varying textures that make them perfect foils for shrubs and perennials. Some multiply by spreading stolons or rhizomes (a few can self-sow and become invasive). Most have a clumping growth habit and make excellent container plants.

CONTAINER *Pennisetum massaicum* 'Red Bunny Tails' captures sunlight in its seed heads, while at its base, *Calibrachoa* bears blooms in smoldering autumn hues. Design: John Greenlee.

Tufts of Mexican feather grass nearly glow among rocks in this Santa Barbara garden; thyme grows between stacked fieldstone boulders in foreground. Design: Margie Grace, Grace Design Associates.

Festuca glauca 'Elijah Blue' and tufted hair grass (*Deschampsia cespitosa* 'Goldtau') flank a rill.

CHOOSE

Warm-season grasses are mainly deciduous; they grow from spring through summer, bloom in fall, and then go dormant, bringing beauty to the fall and winter garden with their dried leaves and flower plumes. These include most species of *Miscanthus*, *Molinia*, *Panicum*, and *Pennisetum*.

Cool-season grasses are typically evergreen, though some may die back in cold climates. They begin new growth in fall, then flower in spring and summer. *Calamagrostis*, *Deschampsia*, *Festuca*, *Helictotrichon sempervirens*, and *Sesleria* are examples.

PLANT

Plant most grasses in spring, though cool-season kinds can also be set out in fall. Before planting, work compost and a complete fertilizer into the soil. Don't bury the plants' crowns when you set them in, as this can lead to rot. Mulch around plants to keep down weeds and conserve soil moisture. Some grasses need water regularly, others rarely. Check listings in the encyclopedia for details.

If planted in well-prepared soil and mulched, most ornamental grasses can do without feeding.

GROOM

Most grasses benefit from an annual cleanup in late winter.

Warm-season grasses The foliage turns brown in fall before the plants go dormant. Cut them back to within a few inches of the ground in late winter or early spring, when new growth appears from the base. Plants will regrow quickly. If necessary, divide large clumps of grasses. Dig out the plant; then use a saw or shovel to cut the rootball into sections. Replant the divisions immediately.

Cool-season grasses Cut them back just as you see new growth emerging in spring, using pruning shears to trim dead foliage and flowering stems to within a few inches of the ground. If you have a number of large clumps, use electric hedge shears or a mechanical weed trimmer.

Evergreen grasses These won't need cutting back every year. Instead, "comb" out old growth by running your fingers through the clumps (wear gloves for grasses with sharp blades). If after a few years the grasses develop lots of unattractive or dead leaves, cut them back by two-thirds in fall or early spring to encourage fresh new growth.

FALL Faded stalks can stay through winter.

LATE WINTER After grasses are cut back, grass stems form tidy mounds.

Grow a Meadow

The term "meadow" (for the backyard) describes a casual planting of grasses and sedges mixed with flowering perennials, annuals, and small bulbs. A meadow can be as large or small as you like. It's an ideal replacement for a small lawn that serves no purpose.

Start with an evergreen ground-cover sedge such as *Carex pansa* to create the framework. Then mix in low-growing flowering perennials such as *Coreopsis* and *Gaillardia*, along with small spring-blooming bulbs such as *Ipheion uniflorum* or *Iris douglasiana*. Add taller grasses in back.

Meadows need just a few mowings per year. Set the lawn mower blade high—about 4 inches—so that you can mow over other plants without damaging their foliage. Control weeds.

SPRING, SUMMER Lush new growth takes over, followed by tawny seed heads.

GROW
Herbs

The word "herb" applies to any plant used for seasoning, medicine, or fragrance. This includes tall, willowy plants such as dill and fine-textured creepers like thyme; annuals and biennials grown for their leaves and seeds; perennials such as French tarragon; and shrubs like rosemary.

Accent the border with a potted sage. Thyme, oregano (*Origanum vulgare* 'Aureum'), sage (*Salvia officinalis* 'Icterina'), and lavender surround this one.

HERBS FOR BORDERS Mounding perennial herbs make perfect borders around a patio, where you can enjoy their fragrance. Evergreen in mild climates, they look good all year. This one, surrounding *Sunset's* outdoor kitchen, combines lavender, oregano, sage, and thyme in varying shades of green, with hits of color.

HERB BASICS

Site Choose a planting spot that receives six to eight hours of full sun each day—ideally, near the kitchen, so you can easily duck out to harvest herbs. Or grow them in large containers you can move to a sunny spot.

Soil Well-drained soil is essential. Dig in plenty of organic matter, or plant in raised beds.

Water After planting herbs from containers, water regularly until the plants are growing steadily. Thereafter, most will need only occasional irrigation. Exceptions are basil, chives, mint, and parsley, which prefer evenly moist soil.

Fertilizer Work a complete fertilizer into the soil before planting (herbs are not heavy feeders).

When perennial herbs resume growth in early spring, feed lightly with a complete fertilizer or spread compost around the base of each plant (taking care not to cover the crown).

Eight kinds of herbs grow in this tiered bed 6, 4, and 2 feet in diameter, edged with flexible aluminum bands. Parsley, thyme, and sages fill lowest level; basils pack the middle; chives are on top.

Basic Herbs

A good cook simply can't live without certain herbs. Specialists from across the West consider these essential cooking ingredients.

BASIL (*Ocimum basilicum*). Start with 'Genovese' or 'Sweet Basil'; grow six plants if you plan to make pesto. Annual. All zones.

BERGGARTEN SAGE (*Salvia officinalis* 'Berggarten'). Camphor-scented perennial; a turkey-stuffing essential. All zones.

CHIVES (*Allium schoenoprasum*). Leaves have a mild sweet onion flavor; flowers are pretty in salads. Perennial. All zones.

COMMON THYME (*Thymus vulgaris*). Leaves are sweetly pungent. Harvest before blossoms appear. Perennial. All zones.

FENNEL (*Foeniculum vulgare*). Cut green leaves taste like anise. Perennial. All zones.

FRENCH TARRAGON (*Artemisia*). Shiny narrow green leaves have a spicy anise flavor. Perennial. All zones.

MINT (*Mentha*). Spearmint (*M. spicata*), with bright green, shiny leaves, is the preferred mint for cooking. **Peppermint** (*M.* × *piperita*), with narrow, bright green leaves, is best for making tea. Roots are invasive; plant in containers. Perennial. All zones.

OREGANO. A peppery herb for tomato-based sauces and pizza. Greek oregano (*Origanum vulgare hirtum*) is good for cooking. Italian oregano (*O.* × *majoricum*) is milder. Oil in the leaves is strongest when plants are in bud but before flowers open. Perennial. All zones.

PARSLEY (*Petroselinum*). Chefs prefer Italian flat-leafed parsley (*P. crispum neapolitanum*), but curly-leafed types (*P. crispum*) are good for garnishes. Biennial grown as an annual. All zones.

ROSEMARY (*Rosmarinus officinalis*). Varieties have an intense peppery flavor and piney aroma but different habits. Complements roasted meats and potatoes. Perennial. All zones.

SWEET MARJORAM (*Origanum majorana*). Tiny gray-green leaves have a sweet floral scent and a milder flavor than Greek oregano. Perennial. Zones 4–24.

How Many Plants?

For a basic starter herb garden, use this list as a guideline, adjusting the number to reflect your preferences. If you love to cook with basil, set out six plants to start with; then add more several weeks later to extend the harvest season.

Basil: 4–6 plants	Rosemary: 1–2 plants
Chives: 3–4 plants	Sage: 1–2 plants
Cilantro: 2–3 plants	Sweet marjoram: 2–3 plants
Oregano: 2 plants	Thyme: 3–4 plants
Parsley: 1–3 plants	

See how to make pesto at sunset.com/pesto ▶

Herbs for Tea

You won't find most of these at the market, so pull out your trowel and grow your own. These herbs grow well in pots or in the ground; use them to make tea. They need fast-draining soil, full sun, and regular water until established.

ANISE HYSSOP (*Agastache foeniculum*). Try both the licorice-tasting blossoms and leaves of 'Golden Jubilee' (to 3 feet tall). Perennial. Zones A3; 1–24.

BEE BALM (*Monarda didyma*). Its mildly citrus-flavored pink, red, or pure white blossoms look spectacular in a mug or cup. Perennial. Zones A2, A3; 1–11, 14–17.

CHAMOMILE (*Matricaria recutita*). Snip the fragrant, mellow blossoms of this 2-foot-tall plant to use fresh or dried. Annual. Zones 1–24.

LAVENDER (*Lavandula angustifolia*). Although it's compact, silvery 'Thumbelina Leigh' English lavender produces plenty of blossoms for steeping. Shrub. Zones 2–24.

LEMON BALM (*Melissa officinalis*). In the same family as mint but not as invasive. Tastes like mint plus citrus. Perennial. Zones 1–24.

LEMON VERBENA (*Aloysia triphylla*). Intensely flavored and highly fragrant. Shrub. Zones 9, 10, 12–21.

NUTMEG GERANIUM (*Pelargonium × fragrans* 'Nutmeg'). Aromatic leaves taste (and smell) of nutmeg. Shrubby perennial.

TEA GARDEN This U-shaped bed allows for easy harvest. Lavender, hyssop, and nutmeg geranium grow in foreground; lemon verbena and white-flowered feverfew are at left (near potted lemon); pink-flowered bee balm is toward the fence.

Herbs on the Table

When flowering herbs such as chives are growing a few feet from your kitchen door, you can pick them minutes before you need them, then scatter the blossoms over salads or soups. (Some taste like the herbs themselves, only spicier.)

But herb foliage also makes pretty bouquets. Try basil ('Genovese' is pretty by the bunch, or mix colors, red to green), parsley, marjoram, oregano, or thyme. 'Tricolor' sage, whose leaves have a purplish tinge, pairs well with lavender-colored flowers. Chive flowers make delicate accents. Lemon verbena adds a delicious scent.

Arrange the herbs in small glasses all over the table.

▶ See how to make herb tea at sunset.com/herbtea

HERBS FOR CONTAINERS
Thai basil and cilantro fill these boat-shaped stone bowls. Other herbs that are especially pretty in containers: basil (many kinds), mint, rosemary, sage, and thyme.

Gourmet Herbs

Once you've grown and experimented with basic kitchen herbs and are familiar with their flavors, try growing herbs with more complex flavors, such as the following.

BRONZE FENNEL (*Foeniculum vulgare* 'Purpurascens'). Like green fennel, leaves have an anise taste, but foliage is bronze. Perennial. All zones.

CILANTRO (*Coriandrum sativum*). Delicate fernlike foliage has a peppery, lemony, herbal flavor ("soap-like" to non-fans) that perks up guacamole, salsa, spring rolls, and Thai dishes. Best in cool season. Annual. All zones.

GARLIC CHIVES (*Allium tuberosum*). Similar to chives, but leaves are slightly larger and they have a mild garlic flavor. Perennial. All zones.

LEMON GRASS (*Cymbopogon citratus*). The blanched white ribs (used in Thai cooking) are spicy and lemony. Perennial in Zones 12, 13, 16, 17, 23, 24; H1, H2. Elsewhere, overwinter pots indoors.

LEMON THYME (*Thymus citriodorus*). Dark green foliage has a lemon flavor. Perennial. All zones.

MEXICAN TARRAGON (*Tagetes lucida*). Narrow, dark green leaves have a sweet licorice flavor similar to tarragon. Perennial in Zones 8–10, 12–24.

SORREL, GARDEN. Tangy, lemony, bright green leaves are tasty in soups and salads. Harvest during cool weather. Perennial. All zones.

Drying Herbs

HARVEST. Snip herbs just as the first flower buds begin to open, when the oils in the leaves are most concentrated. Morning, after dew has evaporated, is the best time.

HANG THEM. For large-leafed herbs such as basil, rosemary, and sage, snip off leafy stems, tie the cut ends together with twine, and hang in a bundle upside down in a warm, dry place (away from direct sun) with good air circulation. When the leaves are crisp and crumble readily, strip them from the stems and store them whole in airtight jars.

SPREAD THEM OUT. For fine-leafed herbs such as oregano, remove leaves from stems and dry them on a clean window screen in a warm, dry place.

GROW
Native Plants

Native plants give your garden a sense of place. They harmonize with your region's landscape and bring wildlife to your garden. And because natives are naturally suited to the climate and soils in your region, they are generally self-sufficient, needing little care once established.

PLAN

You can create a backyard ecosystem that mimics your region's natural plant communities, whether desert, chaparral, oak woodland, coniferous forest, alpine tundra, valley grassland, or wetland. Or, mix natives with compatible plants. Locate natives with low water needs on the edge of your property and thirstier ones closer to the house. Or, if you have a wilderness view, use some of the plants that grow naturally around your property. Four successful plantings are pictured at right.

PLANT AND TEND

The best time to plant is fall through early spring, when cool and rainy weather allows plants to establish themselves more easily. In cold-winter climates, plant in early fall, stopping six weeks before the ground freezes.

Bringing Plants Home ❗

Travelers tempted to bring home plants or plant parts from trips abroad may not realize that the well-mannered beauty from another locale could turn into an aggressive weed at home, crowding out natives. Or that one little blossom or seedling could carry a harmful pest or disease capable of causing vast (and expensive) damage at home. Use caution. To learn more about invasives, visit the USDA's website (*invasivespecies info.gov*). See *www.aphis.usda.gov/ import_export* for details on bringing plants home.

Soil Excellent drainage is essential for many native plants. But usually, there's no need to amend the soil at planting time. Just backfill with native soil. Exception: If the native topsoil has been scraped off or the soil is compacted, replace a third of it with well-composted organic matter.

Plants Start with young container-grown plants that are not rootbound. They may not be much to look at when first planted, but they'll adapt more successfully than larger plants.

Water Irrigate thoroughly immediately after planting, then carefully and steadily for the first summer or two. After two years—assuming you have matched the plants to the conditions they need—they should do well with little or no supplemental watering. Some natives cannot tolerate any summer water (flannel bush, for example). Others adapt to regular garden water (coral bells and Western columbine are examples).

Fertilizer Western natives usually don't need fertilizing. A light mulch is beneficial, but keep it away from the plants' crowns.

Western natives and Mediterranean plants thrive in similar growing conditions. But Mediterraneans often bloom later than natives—in late spring and summer. Combine the two for a longer season of interest.

NORTHWEST WOODLAND

Before A lakeside property in Carnation, Washington. Existing tall conifers surrounded with deer and sword ferns, salal, Oregon grape, huckleberry—and invasive blackberry.

Strategy Clear away blackberry to reveal native plants. Divide and spread moss; tuck in a few more compatible plants such as rhododendron.

Accents Boulders, twiggy fences, a recirculating stream.

Northwest Natives

Two favorites are pictured. For others, see pages 81–90.

1. **WESTERN SWORD FERN** (*Polystichum munitum*). Hardy plants with evergreen fronds. Partial or full shade.

2. **WAKE ROBIN** (*Trillium ovatum*). Showy, distinctive three-petaled flowers appear in early spring. Partial to full shade.

CALIFORNIA CHAPARRAL

Before A small front-yard lawn in Santa Monica, California.

Strategy Remove the lawn and replace it with native groundcover—'Yankee Point' ceanothus, favored for its compact habit. Add *Salvia clevelandii* and compatible plants that tolerate drought and attract bees and butterflies: *Arbutus* 'Marina' and butterfly weed (*Asclepias tuberosa*).

Accents Pindo palms in terracotta pots—the only plants needing regular water.

California Natives

Two favorites are pictured. For others, see pages 81–90.

1. **PENSTEMON HETEROPHYLLUS 'MARGARITA BOP'.** Eye-catching flowers have purple throats; bloom in late spring. Sun.

2. **APRICOT MALLOW (*Sphaeralcea ambigua*).** Showy blooms in summer and fall. Sun.

SOUTHWEST DESERT

Before A desert-edge garden in Paradise Valley, Arizona, planted with oleanders and other non-natives.

Strategy Remove non-natives, and blend the garden with the natural desert by planting Palo brea trees, opuntia, spiky *Dasylirion*, and ocotillo. Add compatible Mexican natives such as Mexican honeysuckle (*Justicia spicigera*).

Accents Decomposed granite mulch, containers of rusted pipe.

Southwest Natives

Two favorites are pictured. For others, see pages 81–90.

1. **BAJA FAIRY DUSTER (*Calliandra californica*).** Red stamens attract hummingbirds. Sun.

2. **YELLOW BELLS (*Tecoma stans*).** Trumpet-shaped flowers cover this shrub late spring to early winter. Sun, partial shade.

MOUNTAIN MEADOW

Before A property on the edge of rolling grasslands and mountain meadows near Aspen, Colorado.

Strategy Plant grasses, lupines, and Shasta daisies to continue the look right up to the house. Then use trees to frame views of the wild landscape beyond.

Accents Local stone to edge the pool and complement the planting.

Mountain Natives

Two favorites are pictured. For others, see pages 81–90.

1. **ROCKY MOUNTAIN COLUMBINE (*Aquilegia coerulea*).** State flower of Colorado blooms spring to early summer. Sun, partial shade.

2. **FIRECRACKER PENSTEMON (*Penstemon eatonii*).** Fiery red blooms appear on tall spikes in spring, early summer. Sun.

GROW
Perennials

Perennials live for more than two years. Herbaceous types such as hosta die to the ground when each growing season ends, then reappear the next season. Other perennials, such as coral bells, go through winter as low tufts of leaves. Ever-green types persist almost unchanged throughout winter.

PLANT

Nurseries and garden centers sell peren-nials in containers that range from cell-packs to 1-gallon pots. Some also sell perennials bare-root during the plants' dormant period. If you'll be planting bare-root perennials within a day or two after purchase, open the bags slightly, add a little water, and hold them in a cool place.

How to Plant Perennials

1 **DIG** a hole as deep as and 1 to 2 inches wider than your plant's container.

2 **REMOVE** the plant from its pot, and if the roots are matted, gently loosen them.

3 **PLACE** the plant in its hole—the top of the rootball should be even with the soil surface. Fill in around it with soil; water thoroughly.

TEND

Water Routine watering during growth and bloom will satisfy most perennials (some prefer drier soil; others demand lots of moisture). Young plants need more frequent waterings.

Feed Give established perennials a complete fertilizer once annually in late winter or early spring.

Deadhead Clip spent flowers throughout the bloom season to keep plants tidy. Some perennials have espe-cially attractive seed heads (like echina-cea); many gardeners prefer to leave their seed heads in place through winter to provide food for seed-eating birds.
   Cut back In fall or winter. Remove old, dead, and fallen foliage, flowers, and stems.

DIVIDE

In fall, dig and divide overgrown peren-nials to stimulate fresh growth.

Cut into the soil 6–12 inches beyond the plant's perimeter with a shovel or spading fork, then dig under the roots to lift the clump out of the ground.

Tease some soil from the rootball. For fibrous-rooted perennials (daylilies), hose off as much soil as possible. Note the natural dividing points between stems and root sections.

Pull or cut apart the clump using clip-pers or a sharp-bladed shovel. Divide clumps into good-size sections.

Trim any damaged roots, stems, or leaves. Replant the divisions.

Border edging a Southern California canyon includes lavender, phormiums, santolina, and *Verbena lilacina* 'De La Mina'. Design: Marilee Kuhlman.

Use a sharp pruning saw, knife, or shovel to divide rootballs of perennials such as agapanthus.

Border Secrets

Four ways to add impact to perennial plantings.

1 LAYERS. Position plants by height, from the lowest ones in the front to the tallest ones in back. Space plants close together so their "shoulders" will touch when they are grown. Make sure to include backbone plants to give the border some structure in winter—small evergreen shrubs, perennials, grasses, or dwarf conifers, for instance.

2 COLOR ECHOES. Choose a primary color scheme, whether plum with greens, or blues and yellows. Repeat these hues throughout the border. Plant in clusters or drifts, by plant type, or by flower and foliage color. Also, choose plants that work with the colors of the house, paving, and walls.

3 ACCENTS. Use a boulder, a piece of garden art, or a shapely urn to give the border visual punch. Other dramatic accents to consider: a cluster of candle delphiniums, Oriental lilies, or tall ornamental grasses such as maiden grass; a hefty terracotta urn, a birdbath, or a small tree such as Japanese maple or smoke tree (*Cotinus*).

4 TEXTURE. Plant lacy, small-flowered perennials such as *Carex* and *Lamium maculatum* in drifts between larger-flowered plants, and as edging along the front. Creeping zinnia, curly sedge, lamb's ears, and 'Lime' thyme are other good choices.

LEFT: A Northwest border celebrates shades of green. Design: Tish Treherne.

PERENNIAL SAMPLER: FOLIAGE TO FLOWERS

EUPHORBIA. *E.* 'Ascot Rainbow' leaves have yellow edges; young foliage has a reddish blush. Flowers share these colors.

HEUCHERA. 'Electra' has cayenne red veins streaking across saffron yellow leaves; it's a pretty plant for spicing up shade.

ECHINACEA. From above, *E.* 'Flame Thrower' flowers resemble swirling skirts on a dance floor. Centers are blushed with red.

COREOPSIS. This variety's name, 'Big Bang Redshift', perfectly describes its Fourth of July explosion of color.

GROW
Succulents

Succulents have the stage presence of divas but the undemanding dispositions of support casts. They range from bold *Aeoniums* to dainty sedums no larger than rice grains. Their colorful, fleshy leaves are nearly jewel-like. On these pages are imaginative ways to use them.

SUCCULENT SECRETS

Ensure good drainage For containers, use potting soil mixes made for succulents and cactus. To improve the soil in garden beds, add compost and sharp sand or pumice.

Water carefully Too much water can kill succulents, so irrigate these plants just enough to keep leaves looking plump. Give them a thorough soaking (until water runs out the drain hole) when they need it.

Arrange them like artwork You can manipulate succulents the same way you would a group of paintings on a wall. Position the larger and most dramatic players first, then place the rest around them, playing colors and textures off one another until you're pleased with the arrangement.

Mulch your pots To give containers a finished look, cover the soil around the succulents with green moss, fine decomposed granite, or seed-size polished black stones. Or, for a more playful look, match colorful tumbled glass mulch to your plants.

Small Succulents

These are easy to grow from cuttings. Most will thrive when simply inserted into containers filled with soil an inch deep. Here are nine fresh ways to use them.

1 PARTY FAVORS. Tiny succulents, set singly in repurposed glass votives, hold place cards for an outdoor meal.

2 TABLETOP. Succulents fill a long container (with drain holes) set into the top of this table built from recycled wood. Design: Far Out Flora.

3 GREEN ROOF. Mounding sedums, knotweed, and dusty miller cover the roof of this rustic birdhouse. Design: DIG Gardens.

4 BOUQUET. String of pearls and tillandsias accent a bouquet of succulent rosettes in this bouquet. Design: Susie Nadler.

5 STARFISH CENTERPIECE. A mossy, metal-backed starfish is dotted with succulents that resemble sealife. Stems of the mounding green *Astrophytum asterias* 'Sand Dollars' and pinkish gray *Lithops* are set into floral foam. Design: Heather Lenkin.

6 WINDOW DRESSING. Tiny succulent rosettes from 2-inch nursery pots peek out from between the slats in these recycled shutters. Rootballs are secured in pockets made from 5-inch-wide strips of weedcloth, stapled horizontally to the back of each panel. Design: Baylor Chapman.

7 WALL ART. Succulent cuttings are held in place by a mesh screen behind a wood frame. *Sedum* 'Angelina' and *Sempervivums* are composed to highlight color and shape. Design: Robin Stockwell.

8 HOSTESS GIFTS. Mounds of tiny succulents and 3-inch crassulas set in moss recall frothy drinks in metallic glasses.

9 CANOE POT. *Kalanchoe thyrsifolia*, with green leaves edged in red, presides over *Sempervivum arachnoides, Senecio vitalis,* and crassulas in a canoe pot (*bauer.com*). Design: Jared Crawford/Flora Grubb Gardens.

Big Succulents: Bold Effects

Design Tips

For striking effects on living walls or tabletops, try these:

SUBTLE BACKDROP. Mass succulents with similar sizes and shapes, but choose them in contrasting colors. Here, green and silvery echeverias play off one another.

BRILLIANT ACCENTS. A ribbon of chartreuse 'Angelina' sedum separates the two types of echeveria—like a stroke of vivid color from a painter's brush. 'Pork and Beans' adds a hit of orange.

BORDER ACCENTS. Bold shapes carry the show in this Southern California border (above). Pink echeveria in the front, arranged in a running stitch fashion, echoes the much larger shape of the soft blue *Agave attenuata*, and the peachy bronze phormium. *Dymondia margaretae* edges the border. Design: Gabriela Yariv.

GALLERY. Framed like art, succulent paintings can be both fun to look at and functional. Here, a coat of mauve paint, a new fountain, and grassy plantings at the wall's base transformed a former retaining wall eyesore in Southern California. Framed succulent pictures are the final touch, turning the wall into a living gallery. Design: Brent Green.

SEABED. Imagine diving into the cool waters of a cove somewhere along the Pacific Coast, then peering through your diver's mask at the undersea life shimmering in the depths. What might you see? Perhaps a scene that looks much like the planting here, created by a Southern California succulent fanatic and snorkeler using small agaves, aloes, and ground-cover succulents. Some are easier to find than others. Design: Jeff Moore.

A coral look-alike with upright, fluted, knobby-tipped foliage appears to sway in a current.

Slender, tubular leaves make this *Dudleya* look like a convincing sea anemone.

A hybrid echeveria with frilled, reddish edges recalls a jelly-fish's undulating umbrella.

Spiny, curving leaves of *Dyckia marnier-lapostollei* give it the look of a starfish in motion.

GROW
Trees

Trees are the backbone of the garden, providing shade and year-round beauty through their foliage, flowers, fruits, bark, and branches. The difference between a tree and a large shrub is sometimes blurred, but trees are typically tall plants with one dominant trunk and a leafy crown.

CHOOSE THE RIGHT TREE

Consult local nursery personnel and look at the trees in your neighborhood to see which ones perform particularly well.

Evergreen or deciduous Deciduous trees start their growth with a burst of new leaves (and often flowers) in early spring, then remain in leaf through summer. In autumn, the foliage drops to reveal bare limbs, often changing color before it falls. The tree then goes dormant for winter.

Evergreen trees include both broad-leafed types and conifers (though there are a few deciduous conifers). Both kinds serve well as screens and windbreaks. Broad-leafed evergreens may drop some leaves, but there's always enough foliage on the branches to give the tree a well-clothed look.

Landscape function If you need shade, choose a deciduous tree with a wide canopy that blocks the sun in summer, then admits sun to the house after its leaves drop in fall. To add privacy to your home or garden, choose relatively tall, dense trees. For a specimen tree to serve as a garden focal point, search for interesting foliage or a striking display of blossoms or berries.

Appropriate Select trees that will grow well in your climate and soil, with the amount of water they'll receive naturally or that you can easily provide. Keep the tree's ultimate size in mind; an overly large one could eventually crowd structures and other plants and have to be removed.

Messy or neat Trees that produce litter from falling leaves, flowers, or fruits shouldn't be planted beside a patio, in a lawn, or near a pond or pool. They are better candidates for background areas, where the litter can remain where it falls. In regions with regular high winds or heavy annual snowfall, avoid trees with weak or brittle wood. They can be hazardous.

Longevity Some trees can be planted for future generations to enjoy, while others grow and decline quickly. Trees that are planted for screening or shade should be long-lived, but for specimen planting, shorter-lived kinds may be an excellent choice. Plant the latter only where removal will be relatively easy and won't compromise your landscape. If a flowering tree dies after 20 years, you can easily replace it.

Dogwood (*Cornus kousa*) shows off vivid red-orange leaves in fall, against a backdrop of evergreens, in a Northwest garden.

Acer saccharum 'Bonfire' shades a California house. Metal frame holds pavers off the soil, allowing the trees air, soil, and moisture. Design: Ron Lutsko.

Pine candles are showy. But to fatten up a rangy pine or to keep a young one chunky, cut candles in half before they open into needles in spring.

Inheriting a Tree

If you've just bought a house, take an inventory of the mature trees on the property. Before you start pruning, landscaping around them, or remodeling too close to them, follow the steps below to preserve their value and beauty. All too often, a mature tree is mutilated or killed by the actions of well-meaning gardeners.

Even if a tree's value seems insignificant to you, keep in mind the ambience it adds to the neighborhood. In some communities, cutting down a "heritage" tree whose girth or size exceeds certain measurements is against the law. Before you remove trees on your property, check your local ordinances.

FIND OUT WHAT KINDS OF TREES YOU HAVE. If the property's previous owner doesn't know, call an arborist. Better yet, hire an arborist certified by the International Society of Arboriculture (*isa-arbor.com*) to survey all the trees on your property. The arborist can evaluate the trees' health, their age, their present and future size, and any hazards they may pose, and can tell you whether they're structurally sound or in need of pruning.

LEARN ABOUT YOUR TREES' NEEDS. Do they need regular water during dry times? Fertilizing occasionally? Pruning every year? Do they need room to grow unencumbered? Trees such as ginkgo thrive in lawns, while the roots of magnolias tend to grow close to the soil surface, which can make a lawn difficult to grow. Native oaks cannot tolerate summer water and will do better when surrounded with a carpet of decomposed granite, perhaps accented with boulders, or a wide tapestry of native plants that thrive in dry shade.

Check the cultural information provided for each species in the encyclopedia.

Small flowering trees are good choices for compact yards. Many kinds attract butterflies and hummingbirds, or have foliage that turns from green to flaming red or orange shades in fall.

FOUR SEASONS OF TREES

To prolong the show, choose several trees that peak in different seasons, with flowers or colored foliage or both.

1. *Spring.* In the desert, yellow blooms fleck green-stemmed palo verde trees. In Pasadena and Santa Barbara, clouds of blue flowers cover the canopies of *Jacaranda mimosifolia*. In cooler climates, flowering cherry (*Prunus*) and dogwoods (*Cornus*) erupt in pink or white blooms—beautiful when underplanted with spring bulbs.

2. *Summer.* Crape myrtles pump out frothy blooms in ice cream colors in warm places such as California's Riverside and Calistoga. In the Pacific North-west, some dogwoods (*Cornus*) continue their spectacular show against a backdrop of conifers. And around the West, *Albizia julibrissin, Chilopsis linearis, Robinia × ambigua* 'Idahoensis', and *Vitex agnus-castus* are in full flower.

3. *Fall.* In the West, many deciduous trees turn brilliant colors before dropping their leaves. Chinese pistache, liquidambar, and maple foliage turns vivid orange, deep red, and burgundy—all on the same tree. *Ginkgo biloba* crowns itself with brilliant yellow leaves. Some hawthorn (*Crataegus*) trees have orange-to-yellow foliage and shiny red-orange berries at the same time; other trees, such as persimmon, also dangle plump orange fruits.

4. *Winter.* Conifers and other evergreens carry the show. But many deciduous trees, now leafless, reveal striking bark. Redtwig dogwood and paperbark maple are two. Then, in late winter, *Acacia, Erythrina*, and *Magnolia stellata* blooms usher in a new year.

When planting a tree, make sure it sits high enough for its crown—the part where the roots meet the trunk—to be just above the soil level.

PLANT

Many deciduous trees (including fruit trees) are sold bare-root during the dormant season, from late fall through early spring. Deciduous trees may also be sold balled-and-burlapped from early fall into the following spring, or in containers throughout the year. For instructions on planting balled-and-burlapped or container-grown trees, see page 671.

WHAT TO DO

- Soak roots in water for at least four hours before planting.

- Dig a hole as deep and twice as wide as the root mass; form a firm cone of soil to set the plant on.

- Backfill with soil (for extremely heavy clay or sandy soils, mix compost into the backfill), and water to settle in. Mulch around the plant to insulate roots and conserve water.

STAKE

A young tree develops a sturdier trunk if it grows unsupported and can sway with the wind. But there are times when staking is necessary: when a tree is planted in a very windy location, when the main trunk is too weak to stand upright on its own, or when the crown (the tree's top) is very large in proportion to the trunk.

WHAT TO DO

- Sink two stakes into the ground (**1**, right), one on each side of the rootball. Determine where to attach the ties. Support the trunk with two fingers, starting 3 feet above the soil surface, and move your fingers upward. Stop at the place where your support keeps the tree upright. Attach the ties 6 inches above this point.

- Use soft ties that have broad, smooth surfaces (**2**, right), such as canvas or UV-degradable fabric (available at garden centers). Allow enough slack so the trunk can move 2 inches in every direction. Do not use wire or wire-filled hose, which can girdle the bark. Remove the stakes and ties from six months to a year after planting.

TEND

Water All trees, even drought-tolerant kinds, need regular watering during the first several years after planting, until their roots have grown deep enough to carry them through dry periods. Once established, many kinds require only infrequent irrigation.

Feed Fertilize regularly for a few years after planting. By ensuring a good supply of nitrogen for the springtime growth surge, you'll encourage young trees to establish quickly. Once a tree is well settled in, though, it may grow satisfactorily with no further feeding—unless its new growth is weak, sparse, or unusually pale. In fact, fertilizing a tree that continues to put out healthy, vigorous new growth is a waste of time and fertilizer.

Position stakes perpendicular to the direction of the prevailing winds. Follow directions at left.

PRUNE

Young trees often need selective pruning of suckers or spindly lower branches to guide new growth and to establish a strong structure. On mature trees, prune to maintain shape, to open up the canopy, or to remove dead or crossing branches. Always cut back to the trunk, or to another branch.

To avoid ripping the bark, shorten the branch to a stub before cutting it off just outside the branch collar.

WHAT TO DO

- About a foot from the branch base, make a cut from the underside, approximately a third of the way through (**1**).

- About an inch farther out on the branch, cut through the top until the branch splits cleanly between the two cuts (**2**).

- Make final cut as shown; avoid cutting the branch collar (**3**).

  For more on pruning trees and shrubs, see page 746.

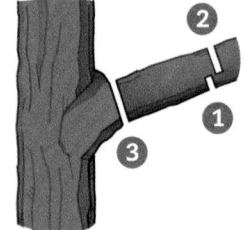

LANDSCAPING AND REMODELING AROUND TREES

The time to protect mature trees on your property from damage during a house remodel—if you decide to save them—is before construction starts. Otherwise, you could end up paying many thousands of dollars to replace trees that are injured or killed by heavy machinery or other mishaps.

When roots are compacted by heavy equipment or severed by trenching, as shown in the illustrations below, chances are you won't see the damage immediately. But injured roots are often unable to take up water, air, or nutrients, and this results in the decline and eventual death of the tree, even years later. Disease organisms or pest infestations that enter unhealed wounds can also, in time, kill the tree.

Avoid building within the root zone of a large, established tree. Allow at least 1 foot of space between the trunk and the structure for every inch of trunk diameter measured at 54 inches above soil level.

Learn where any new underground lines will go and, if possible, reroute them away from trees. If it's not possible for contractors to work outside the root zone, up to one-third of a healthy tree's roots can be removed without severely harming the tree.

If heavy equipment must be moved over the root zone, cover the area from the trunk out to the drip line with a 12-inch-thick layer of wood chips; then top the mulch with interlocking sheet-metal plates or plywood sheets to minimize soil compaction.

Make sure your contractor knows your wishes regarding your trees and will convey them to workers; the best way to do that is to spell them out in the remodeling contract.

TROUBLE SPOTS

THE CANOPY
Broken branches. Large branch stubs, left by breakage or careless pruning, seldom heal over.
Topping. Removing a tree's top to preserve the view or keep it out of the wires makes it ugly. Weak new growth follows.

THE TRUNK
Injuries. Heavy equipment can gouge the trunk, exposing the tree to disease and insect pests.

THE ROOTS
Most roots are within the top 24 inches of soil and can extend beyond the drip line. They're susceptible to damage shown below.

PROTECTIVE MEASURES

THE CANOPY
If low branches need removal to make way for heavy equipment, hire an arborist to do it. Instead of topping, cut selected branches back to lower laterals.

THE TRUNK, BRANCHES
If you need to work close to the trunk, prop hay bales against it to protect the bark. Use rope to tie thinner, flexible branches up and out of the way of trucks and machinery.

THE ROOTS
Put a fence around the tree as far outside the drip line as possible. Lay plastic tarps to keep out contaminants.

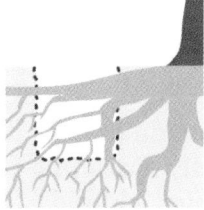

Trenching. Digging trenches for utilities too close to the trunk can seriously injure or sever tree roots.

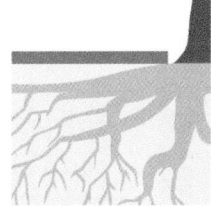

Solid paving. Nonporous paving under the canopy can prevent water and air from reaching roots.

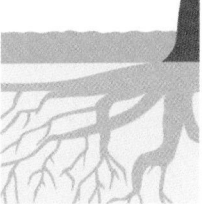

Grade change. Even 2 inches of fill dirt, if it does not have good drainage, can smother roots.

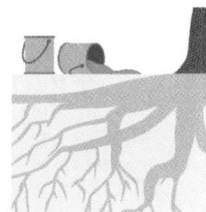

Soil contamination. Spilling wet concrete, paint, or solvents within the root zone can poison the tree.

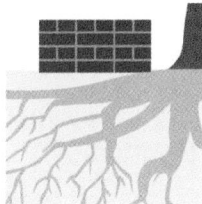

Compaction. Heavy equipment or pallets of pavers can squash a tree's shallow surface roots.

SMART TREES
FOR SHADE

Tree-shaded houses stay cooler, naturally, than unshaded houses. That's good news, considering energy is a resource that is bound to become even more expensive in the future. And cooling your house with trees—the right trees, in the right place—does save energy.

Location Is Everything

The path along which the sun travels across the sky from morning to afternoon—also from winter to summer—determines the best locations for energy-saving trees.

In midsummer, the sun shines on the east side of the house in the morning, passes over the south side of the roof near midday, then beats down on the west side in the afternoon. It is in the afternoon, when temperatures are highest, that solar radiation heats the house most and air conditioners work hardest. Consequently, the west side is the most important to shade.

As fall and winter approach, the sun is lower in the sky and shines more directly on the south side of your house. But with cooler weather, the sun becomes a benefit rather than a liability. The warmth it provides reduces heating costs, so in most cases you don't want to shade the south side of your house. There are exceptions to these rules. In hot, sunny climates (Phoenix, Palm Springs) where the weather can be very warm in spring and fall, shading the south side of the house can have some benefits. On the other hand, in cool or foggy summer climates (San Francisco, Seattle), any sunshine is a blessing, and planting shade trees may be a mistake.

Shade windows first Sun shining directly through a window heats the home quickly. Plant trees on the east, south, and west sides near windows. If possible, position them just to the side of the window so they don't block the view but still provide shade.

Don't plant too close to the house The closer you plant, the more you'll shade it. And planting trees too close could cause roots to damage the foundations. Locate small trees at least 5 feet from the foundation, larger trees at least 10 feet away.

Shade paved areas The right shade tree can turn a patio into a special garden retreat. Shade trees can also reduce heat that is stored or reflected by paved surfaces, including patios and driveways. Reflected heat can increase the temperature of your home during the day, and stored heat can slow the cooling of your house after the sun has gone down.

Shade air conditioners Keeping your air conditioner cool can reduce its workload and cut energy consumption.

Don't plant near utilities Avoid planting trees where limbs will grow into power lines or where roots may damage underground utilities. If you have questions, contact your local utility.

The ideal shade tree has a slightly sprawling canopy, grows 25 to 45 feet tall, and is deciduous—sun can shine through its leafless canopy in winter.

Palo brea trees shade this front-yard patio in Phoenix. Candelilla (a native Southwest euphorbia) dots the grid of black pea gravel, and Indian fig (*Opuntia*) punctuates the decomposed granite. Design: Christy Ten Eyck.

FOLLOW THE SUN'S PATH

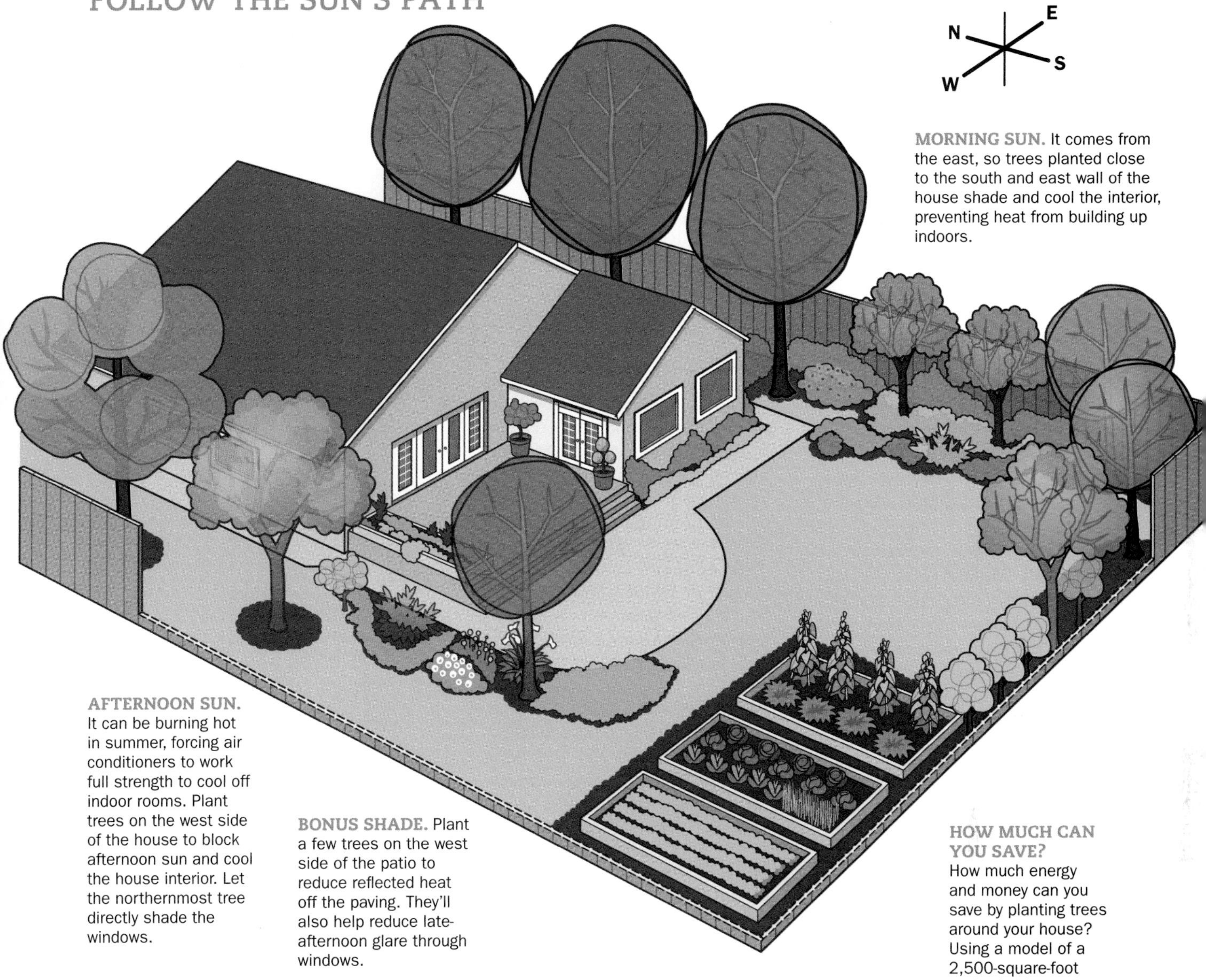

MORNING SUN. It comes from the east, so trees planted close to the south and east wall of the house shade and cool the interior, preventing heat from building up indoors.

AFTERNOON SUN. It can be burning hot in summer, forcing air conditioners to work full strength to cool off indoor rooms. Plant trees on the west side of the house to block afternoon sun and cool the house interior. Let the northernmost tree directly shade the windows.

BONUS SHADE. Plant a few trees on the west side of the patio to reduce reflected heat off the paving. They'll also help reduce late-afternoon glare through windows.

HOW MUCH CAN YOU SAVE?
How much energy and money can you save by planting trees around your house? Using a model of a 2,500-square-foot unshaded house in Sacramento, a computer program at the University of California, Davis, predicted that shading the house's east and west sides (including windows) could reduce energy use for air conditioning by as much as 40 percent annually.

Light Up Your Tree

A graceful tree always creates drama in the garden, but especially when touched with sunlight or night lighting.

The trees pictured are flecked with sunlight streaming through a custom gate of metal squares designed by artist Ned Kahn, in an Idaho garden designed by Ron Lutsko. But you can also manipulate the light on your tree to highlight its form or create unexpected silhouettes or shadows on walls.

Use stake-mounted uplights to define the tree's trunk and lower branches and leaves at night, or hedge-washing lamps with broader beams to showcase large groves of trees such as aspens, birches, melaleucas, and redwoods. (Consult a lighting designer for advice.)

GROW
Veggies

Food that's fresh and bursting with flavor: that's reason enough to grow your own vegetables. But having ripening cukes, tomatoes, and peppers right outside your kitchen door is an added bonus—no market trips needed. Just grow the crops that you and your family really enjoy.

Freshly harvested beets include 'Golden', 'Chioggia', and 'Bull's Blood'.

PLANT

If you're new to vegetable gardening, start small. An area of just 100 to 130 square feet can provide a substantial harvest. Before planting, prepare the soil to promote faster growth and a larger harvest. Follow the steps on page 668 for preparing your planting bed.

You can start vegetables by planting seeds outdoors in the garden or by setting out transplants that you have either started yourself or purchased from a nursery. For more on sowing seeds and on starting and setting out transplants, see page 670.

Exposure Vegetables grow best with at least six hours of full sun each day. Locate the garden away from trees and large shrubs that create shade and root competition; it should be protected from cold winds in spring and hot, dry winds

in summer. Steer clear of frost pockets —low-lying areas that may experience frosts later in spring and earlier in fall than other parts of the garden.

Site To make watering and other routine tasks easier, aim for a level site. If only sloping land is available, try to find a south- or southeast-facing slope to take full advantage of the sun. Lay out rows along the slope's contours to minimize water runoff and erosion.

Rows Separated by paths, rows give you access to the plants and let you easily till or hoe the soil. This layout works well for tall-growing plants like corn and for those that need support, such as tomatoes and pole beans.

Hills Grouped in a cluster but not necessarily on a mound. This method is

useful for sprawling plants such as most varieties of melons and winter squash.

Wide beds About 3 feet wide, they're fine for smaller vegetables such as beets, carrots, spinach, and lettuce. In this arrangement, you prepare a bed, then broadcast the seeds over it.

Two 'Trombetta' squash vines, planted on either side of this arching trellis, dangle their fruits.

Spuds grow up inside these 18-inch-diameter cages of galvanized wire, wrapped with bamboo screening.

'Farmer's Long' Japanese eggplant thrives in a large (16-inch diameter) terra-cotta container.

Heirlooms

Heirloom vegetables and fruits are varieties at least 60 years old, preserved for their exceptional flavor, appearance, and vigor. They haven't been genetically modified, and most have been open-pollinated by birds, insects, or wind. If you save the seeds and they don't get cross-pollinated, they will give you the same crops every year.

RATTLESNAKE SNAP BEANS
Streaked with red

'CHEROKEE CHOCOLATE'
A juicy beefsteak

'BLACK HUNGARIAN' PEPPER
Mildly hot, near black

LEMON CUCUMBER
Mild, sweet, and yellow

When to Harvest

How do you know exactly when to harvest your summer crops? Follow these tips.

BEANS. Green or snap type: nip beans off as sides of pods start to swell, but before they get stringy and lose their ability to snap.

CORN. When silk tassels start to dry, peel husk from an ear and pop a kernel with your thumbnail. If water comes out, it's immature. If it's toothpasty, the corn is past its prime. The milk of white corn is clearer, while liquid from yellow corn is yellowish.

CUCUMBERS. For eating fresh, pick standard cukes at about 8 inches long, Armenian and Japanese types up to 20 inches, and lemon cukes under 3 inches.

EGGPLANT. Shiny-skinned, immature eggplant is tender and good. Dull-skinned, mature eggplant is not.

SQUASH. Pick zucchini at 5 to 8 inches long, yellow crookneck at 4 to 7 inches, scalloped squash (pattypan) before it turns ivory white.

TOMATOES. In summer, harvest after fruit colors fully. In fall, when night temperatures drop below 55°F, pick any tomato with color to ripen indoors on a windowsill (dark green fruit will never ripen).

WATERMELONS. Look and listen for these signs of ripeness: a withered tendril where vine meets melon; creamy white belly (yellowish on seedless kinds); dull skin; hollow sound when thumped.

TEND

Water Provide a steady supply of moisture from planting until harvest. Until transplants are well established, they will need frequent watering—enough to keep the soil moist but not soggy. Rows or beds of seeds and young seedlings likewise need steady moisture, sometimes requiring a sprinkling as often as two or three times a day in hot weather. As transplants and seedlings grow and their roots reach deeper, you can water less often—but when you do, be sure to moisten the entire root zone thoroughly. To water the garden, use sprinklers, furrows, or a drip system (see pages 715–716).

Mulch An organic mulch such as straw or compost cools the soil, conserves moisture, and suppresses weed growth; it also improves soil structure as it decomposes, making the top few inches looser and more crumbly (apply when warm weather arrives). A mulch of plastic sheeting, on the other hand, helps warm the soil quickly—so it is especially useful for growing heat-loving crops such as melons and eggplant in regions with cool or short summers.

Feed For many vegetables, the fertilizer you apply when you prepare the bed at planting time will be sufficient for the entire season. However, heavy feeders, such as corn, and those requiring a long growing season, including tomatoes and some varieties of cabbage and broccoli, may need one or two follow-up feedings. Lightly scratch dry granular fertilizer into the soil, keeping it off plant foliage. Then water it in thoroughly. You can also use a water-soluble fertilizer.

Rotate crops from season to season. This prevents the buildup of diseases and insects specific to certain kinds of vegetables in any one part of the garden.

WARM-SEASON VEGETABLES

The crops listed in the chart below require both warm soil and high temperatures with little cooling at night to grow steadily and produce a harvest. They include summer crops such as peppers and tomatoes and so-called winter squashes such as acorn and hubbard that grow through summer and yield fruits that can be stored for winter consumption. For almost all of these vegetables, the fruit is the edible part. Planting times for these crops are listed by zone.

Cucumbers

Peppers

NAME	ZONES A1–A3	ZONES 1, 2	ZONE 3	ZONES 4, 5	ZONE 6	ZONE 7	ZONES 8, 9	ZONE 10
Bean (S)	Jun	May–Jun	May–Jul	May–Jul	May–Jul	Apr–Jun	Apr–Jul	Mid-Apr–May, Jul–mid-Aug
Corn (S)	Jun	May*	May	May	Apr–Jun	Apr–Jun	Mar–Jul	Apr–Jul
Cucumber (S, T)	Jun	May–Jun	Mid-Apr–Jun	May–Jun	May–Jun	Apr–Jun	Apr–Jul	Apr–mid-Jun
Eggplant (T)	Jun	May*	May	May*	May	Apr–Jun	Apr–Jun	Apr–mid-May
Melon (S, T)	Jun*	May*	May	May–mid-Jun	May	Apr–May	Apr–Jun	Apr–mid-Jun
Okra (S)	N/R	Jun (1b–2b only)	Jun	Jun*	Jun	Jun	May–Jun	Late May
Pepper (S, T)	Jun*	May*	May	May–mid-Jun	May	Apr–Jun	Apr–Jun	Apr–May
Pumpkin (S, T)	Jun	May	Mid-Apr–May	May	May	May–Jun	Apr–Jun	Apr–May
Squash, Summer (S, T)	Jun	May–Jun	Mid-Apr–May	May–Jun	May–Jun	Apr–Jul	Mar–Jul	Apr–Jul
Squash, Winter (S, T)	Jun	May	Mid-Apr–May	May	May	May–Jun	Apr–Jun	Apr–May
Sweet Potato (T)	N/R	N/R	N/R	N/R	N/R	N/R	May–Jun	May
Tomatillo (S, T)	Jun*	May*	Apr–May	May	May	Apr–Jun	Apr–Jun	Apr–May
Tomato (T)	Jun*	May*	Apr–May	May	May	Apr–Jun	Apr–Jun	Apr–May
Watermelon (S, T)	Jun*	May*	May	May–mid-Jun*	May	Apr–May	Apr–Jun	Apr–mid-Jun

S = Plant from seed. **T** = Plant from transplants. **N/R** = Not recommended. ***** = Succeeds only in warmest locations or with season extenders.

Pattypan squash

Zucchini

Cherry tomatoes

'Moon and Stars' watermelon

ZONE 11	ZONE 12	ZONE 13	ZONE 14	ZONES 15, 16	ZONE 17	ZONES 18, 19	ZONES 20, 21	ZONES 22–24	ZONES H1, H2
Mid-Mar–Apr, early Aug	Mar, mid-Jul–Aug	Feb–Mar, Aug	Apr–Jul	May–Jul	Mid-Apr–mid-Jul	Mar–Aug	Mar–Aug	Apr–Aug	All year
Mid-Mar–Apr, Jul–mid-Aug	Mid-Mar–mid-Apr, early Aug	Feb–Mar, late Aug–mid-Sep	Apr–Jul	Apr–Jul	Apr–Jul	Mar–Jul	Mar–Jul	Apr–Jul	All year
Mid-Mar–mid-Aug	Mar, Aug	Jan–mid-Apr	Apr–Jun	Apr–Jun	May–mid-Jul	Apr–Jun	Apr–Jun	Apr–Jun	All year
Apr–mid-May	Feb–Apr	Jan–Mar	May–Jun	May–Jun	May*	Apr–May	Apr–May	Apr–May	All year
Mid-Mar–mid-Jun	Mar–Apr, early Jul	Dec–Apr	Apr–Jun	May–Jun	May–Jun*	Apr–Jun	Apr–Jun	May–Jun	All year
Late May	Mar–May	Apr–May	May–Jun	Mid-May–Jun	Mid-May–Jun*	Mid-Apr–Jun	May–Jun	Jun	All year
Mid-Mar–early May	Feb (S), Mar–May (T)	Dec–Jan (S), Feb–Mar (T)	Apr–Jun	May–Jun	May–Jun*	Apr–Jun	Apr–Jun	May	All year
May–Jun	Jul	Mar–Apr, mid-Jul–mid-Aug	Apr–Jun	May–Jun	May–Jun	mid-Apr–Jun	mid-Apr–Jun	May–Jun	All year
Apr–Jul	Feb–Apr	Jan–Mar, Aug	Apr–Jul	Apr–Jul	Apr–Jul	Apr–Jul	Apr–Jun	May–Jun	All year
May–Jun	Jul	Mar–Apr, mid-Jul–mid-Aug	Apr–Jun	May–Jun	May–Jun	Apr–Jun	Apr–Jun	May–Jun	All year
N/R	Mar–May	Mar–Jun	May–Jun	Jun	N/R	May	May	May	All year
Mid-Mar–Apr	Jan–Feb (S), Mar (T)	Nov–Jan (S), Jan–mid-Mar (T)	Apr–Jul	Apr–Jun	Apr–Jun	Apr–Jun	Apr–Jun	Apr–Jun	All year
Mid-Mar–Apr	Jan–Feb, Mar (T)	Nov–Jan, Jan–mid-Mar (T)	Apr–Jul	Apr–Jun	Apr–Jun	Apr–Jun	Apr–Jun	Apr–Jun	All year
Apr–mid-Jun	Mar–Apr	Jan–Mar	Apr–Jun	May–Jun	May*	Apr–Jun	Apr–Jun	May–Jun	All year

COOL-SEASON VEGETABLES

Cool-season crops, including the ones listed in this chart, grow best at temperatures that average from 10° to 15°F (6° to 8°C) below those needed by warm-season types. Most will endure short spells of frost. Many have edible leaves or roots (lettuce, carrots); some (artichokes, cauliflower) are grown for their immature flowers. A few, such as peas, produce edible seeds. Success depends on bringing plants to maturity in cool weather; in heat, many turn bitter or bolt to seed.

'Romanesco' broccoli

Savoy cabbage

NAME	ZONES A1–A3	ZONES 1, 2	ZONE 3	ZONES 4, 5	ZONE 6	ZONE 7	ZONES 8, 9	ZONE 10
Artichoke (T)	N/R	N/R	Mar	Jan–Mar	Jan–Mar	Jan–Feb	Feb–Mar, Jul	Feb–Mar
Arugula (S, T)	Jun–Jul	Apr, late Aug	Mar–Apr, Aug	Mid-Feb–Mar, mid-Jul–Aug	Mid-Feb–Mar, mid-Jul–Aug	Mar–mid-Apr, mid-Jul–Aug	Feb–Apr, mid-Jul–Aug	Feb–Apr, Aug
Asian Greens (S, T)	Late May–Jun	Apr–May	Mar–Apr, late Aug, Sep	Mar–Apr, mid-Jul–Sep	Mar–Apr, Aug–Sep	Feb–Apr, Sep–Oct	Feb–Apr, mid-Aug–Oct	Feb–mid-Apr, Jul–Aug
Asparagus (S, T)	May	Mar–Apr	Feb–Mar	Jan–Mar	Jan–Mar	Jan–Mar	late Dec–Mar	Mar–Apr
Beet (S, T)	Late May–Jun	Apr–Jun	Mar–Jul	Mar–Aug	Mar–Jun	Feb–May, Aug–Sep	Feb–Apr, Aug–Sep	Feb–mid-Apr, Jul–mid-Aug
Broccoli (S, T)	Late May–Jun	Apr–Jun	Apr–Jul	Mar–Jun, Aug–Sep	Mar–Aug	Mar–Apr, Aug–Sep	Feb–Mar, Aug–Sep	Mid-Feb–Mar, mid-Jun–mid-Aug
Brussels Sprouts (S, T)	Late May–Jun	Apr–Jun	Apr–Jul	Mar–Jun, Aug	May–Jul	Mar–Apr, Aug	Mar–Apr, Aug	Mid-Feb–Mar, mid-Jun–mid-Aug
Cabbage (S, T)	Late May–Jun	Apr–Jun	Apr–Jul	Mar–Sep	Apr–Jun, Aug–Sep	Mar–Apr, Aug–Sep	Feb–Mar, Aug–Sep	Mid-Feb–Mar, Jun–Jul
Carrot (S)	Late May–Jun	Apr–Jun	Mar–Jul	Mar–Jun	Mar–Jul	Mar–May, Aug–Sep	Jan–Apr, Jul–Sep	Feb–Mar, Jul–Aug
Cauliflower (S, T)	Late May–Jun	Apr–May	Apr–Jul	Mar–Jun, Aug–Sep	Apr–Jul	Mar–Apr, Aug–Sep	Feb–Mar, Aug–Sep	Mid-Feb–Mar, Jun–Jul
Celery and Celeriac (T)	Late May–Jun	May–Jun	Jun–Aug	Mar–Jun, mid-Aug–Sep	Mar–Jul	May–Jul	Jun–Aug	Mar, Sep
Chicory and Radicchio (S, T)	Late May–Jun	Apr–Jun, Jul–Aug	Mar–Apr, Jul–Sep	Mar–Sep	Apr–mid-Sep	Apr–mid-Sep	Mar–Jun, late Jul–mid-Sep	Mar–Apr
Chinese Cabbage (S, T)	Late May–Jun	May, Jul	Jul	Mar–Apr, Jul	Mar–Apr, Jul	Feb–Apr, Sep–Oct	Feb–Apr, mid-Aug–Oct	late Jul–early Aug
Chives (S, T)	Jun	May–Jun	Apr–Jun	Apr–Aug	Apr–Aug	Mar–Aug	Feb–Aug	Mar–Jun
Endive and Escarole (S, T)	Jun	Mid-Apr–Jun	Apr–May	Mid-Aug–Sep	Mid-Aug–Sep	Sep	Sep–Oct	Apr
Fava Beans (S)	Late May–early Jun	Apr–May	Mar–Apr	Mar, Sep–early Nov	Mar, Sep–Oct	Sep–Oct	Sep–Oct	Apr

S = Plant from seed. **T** = Plant from transplants. **N/R** = Not recommended. **+** = Can be planted year-round in some parts of zone.

Carrots

Lacinato kale

Butterhead lettuce

Red onion

ZONE 11	ZONE 12	ZONE 13	ZONE 14	ZONES 15, 16	ZONE 17	ZONES 18, 19	ZONES 20, 21	ZONES 22–24	ZONES H1, H2
Sep–Oct	Mid-Aug–Oct	Aug–Sep	Jan–Mar, Jul	Jan–Mar	Sep–May	Jan–Feb	Jan–Feb	Jan–Feb	Jan–Feb (H2)
Feb–Mar, Aug	Sep–Mar	Sep–Feb	Feb–Apr, mid-Jul–Aug	Aug–Mar	Jul–Apr	Mid-Sep–Feb	Mid-Sep–Mar	Mid-Sep–Mar	Nov–Mar (H1)
Feb–Mar, Sep–mid-Oct	Sep–Oct	Mid-Sep–Jan	Feb–Apr, mid-Aug–Oct	Feb–May, Jul–Aug+	Jan–May, Sep–Oct	Jan–Feb, Sep–Oct	Sep–Oct, Jan–Mar	Sep–Apr	Oct–Feb
Feb–Mar	Oct–Feb	Oct–Jan	Late Dec–Mar	Jan–Mar	Jan–Mar	Jan–Apr	Jan–Apr	Jan–Apr	Jan
Feb–Mar, Sep	Sep–Mar	Mid-Sep–Feb	Feb–Apr, Aug–Sep	Feb–Aug+	Feb–Aug+	Feb–Apr, Aug–Sep	Sep–Apr	All year	All year
Feb, Sep	Sep–Nov	Sep–Dec	Feb–Apr, Aug–Sep	Feb–Apr, Aug–Sep	Feb–Apr, Aug–Sep+	Jan–Feb, Sep–Oct	Jan–Mar, Jul–Nov	Aug–Apr	Oct–Mar+
Feb, Sep	Sep–Nov	Sep–Dec	Mar–Apr, Aug	Feb–Aug	Apr–Jul	Sep–Oct	Sep–Nov	Feb–Mar, Sep–Nov	Nov–Feb (H1)
Feb, Sep	Sep–Jan	Sep–Nov	Feb–Mar, Aug–Sep	Feb–Mar, Aug–Sep	Feb–Apr, Aug–Sep+	Jan–Feb, Sep–Oct	Aug–Feb	Aug–Mar	Oct–Mar+
Feb–Mar, Aug	Sep–Feb	Aug–Jan	Feb–Mar, Jul–Sep	Feb–Mar, Jul–Sep+	Dec–Aug	Jan–Apr, Jul–Sep	Sep–Apr	Sep–Apr+	Nov–Feb+
Feb, Sep	Sep–Jan	Sep–Nov	Feb–Mar, Aug–Sep	Feb–Mar, Aug–Sep	Feb–Apr, Aug–Sep+	Sep	Jan–Feb, Jul–Oct	Jan–Feb, Jul–Aug	Oct–Jan+
Mid-Mar, Sep	Sep–Oct	Mid-Sep–mid-Oct	Jun–Aug	Feb–Apr, Jul–Sep	Feb–Aug+	Feb–Apr, Jun–Aug	Apr–Aug	Apr–Aug	Nov–Feb
Mar, late Jul–mid-Aug	Mar–Apr, late Jul–mid-Sep	Mid-Sep–Feb	Apr–Jun, late Jul–Sep	Apr–Jun, late Jul–Sep	Feb–Sep	Feb–Jun, late Jul–Sep	Feb–Jun, late Jul–mid-Oct	Feb–Jun, late Jul–mid-Oct	Nov–Feb
Late Jul–early Aug	Sep–mid-Jan	Mid-Sep–Jan	Feb–Apr, mid-Aug–Oct	Feb–May, Jul–Aug+	Jan–May, Sep–Oct	Jan–Feb, Sep–Oct	Jan–Mar, Sep–Oct	Sep–Apr	Oct–Feb
Mar–May	Feb–Apr	Sep–Feb	Apr–Jul	Apr–Jul	Apr–Aug	Mar–Aug	Feb–Aug	Feb–Aug	All year
Mar	Sep–Dec	Sep–Nov	Jul–Sep	Jul–Sep	Jul–Sep	Sep–Oct	Sep–Oct	Sep–Oct	Oct
Mar	Oct–Nov	Oct–Nov	Sep–Oct	Sep–Oct	Sep–Oct	Sep–Oct	Sep–Oct	Sep–Oct	Sep–Oct (H1)

»

COOL-SEASON VEGETABLES (continued)

NAME	ZONES A1–A3	ZONES 1, 2	ZONE 3	ZONES 4, 5	ZONE 6	ZONE 7	ZONES 8, 9	ZONE 10
Garlic (sets)	Aug–Sep	Sep–Oct	Oct–Nov	Mid-Sep–Nov	Mid-Sep–Nov	Oct–Nov	Oct–Dec	Mid-Sep–Nov
Kale (S, T)	Late May–Jun	Apr, late Jul–Aug	Mar, Aug	Mar–Apr	Apr–Jun, Aug	Mar–Apr, Aug–Sep	Feb–Mar, Aug–Sep	Mid-Feb–Mar, Jun–Jul
Kohlrabi (S, T)	Late May–Jun	Apr–May	Apr–Aug	Mar–Jun, Jul–Aug	Apr–Aug	Mar–May, Aug–Sep	Feb–Apr, Aug–Sep	Feb–mid-Apr, Jul–mid-Aug
Leek (S, T)	Late May–Jun (A2–A3)	Apr–May	May, Aug	Feb, May	Feb, May	Sep–Oct	Mid-Aug–Sep	Aug–Sep
Lettuce (S, T)	Late May–Jun	Apr–Aug	Feb–Aug	Mar–Sep	Apr–Sep	Mar–May, Aug–Sep	Feb–Mar, Aug–Sep	Feb–Mar, Aug–Sep
Mâche (S)	Jun–Aug	May–Jun	Mid-Feb–Mar, Aug	Mar–Apr, Jul–Aug	Mar–Apr, Jul–Aug	Mid-Feb–Mar, Jul–Aug	Feb–Mar, Aug–Sep	Mar–Apr, Aug–Sep
Mustard (S, T)	Late May–Jun	Apr–May	Mar–Apr, Sep	Mar–Apr, mid-Jul–Sep	Mar–Apr, Aug–Sep	Feb–Apr, Sep–Oct	Feb–Apr, mid-Aug–Oct	Feb–mid-Apr, Jul–Aug
Onion, Bulbing (S, T, and sets—small bulbs or cloves)	Late May–Jun	May–Jun	Mar	Mar–mid-Apr, mid-Aug–mid-Sep	Mar–mid-Apr, mid-Aug–mid-Sep	Feb–Apr	Jul, Oct	Mid-Jan–mid-Mar (sets), early Oct
Parsnip (S)	Jun	Jun	May–Jun	May, Jul	May, Jul	May, Sep	May, Sep	Apr–May
Pea (S)	Late May–Jun	Apr–Jun	Mar–Jun	Mar–Aug	Mar–May	Feb–Apr, Aug–Oct	Feb–Mar, Aug–Nov	Feb–mid-Apr
Potato (eyes)	Late May–Jun	May–Jun	Mar–Jun	Feb–Aug	Apr–Aug	Mar–May	Dec–Mar, Jul–Aug	Feb–Apr
Radish (S)	Late May–Jun	Apr–Jul	Mar–Sep	Mar–early Sep	Mar–Sep	Feb–Apr, Sep–Oct	Sep–Apr	Feb–Apr, Aug
Rhubarb (T)	May	Mar–Apr	Feb–Mar	Jan–Mar	Jan–Mar	Jan–Feb	Jan–Feb	Feb–Mar
Salad Blends (S, T)	Late May–Jun	Apr–Aug	Feb–Aug	Feb–Aug	Apr–Aug	Mar–May, Aug–Sep	Feb–Mar, Aug–Sep	Feb–Mar, Aug–Sep
Shallot (T)	May–Jun	May	Apr–May	Apr, Aug–Sep	Apr, Aug–Sep	Apr, Sep	Late Mar–Apr, Sep	Mar–Apr
Sorrel (S, T)	Late May–Jun	May–Jun	May	Apr–May	May	Apr–May	Apr–May	Apr–May
Spinach (S)	Late May–Jun	Apr, Jul	Feb–Mar, Sep	Feb–Mar, Aug	Feb–Mar, Aug	Feb–Apr, Sep–Oct	Sep–Jan	Mid-Jan–mid-Mar, Aug–Sep
Swiss Chard (S, T)	Late May–Jun	Mar–Jun	Feb–May	Feb–May, Jul–Aug	Apr–Jul	Mar–May, Aug–Sep	Feb–Mar, Aug	Feb–mid-Apr, Aug
Turnip and Rutabaga (S)	Late May–Jun	Apr	Mar–Apr	Mid-Jul–Aug	Mid-Jul–Aug	Feb–Mar, Jul–Aug	Feb–Mar, Jul–Aug	Mar–Apr, Aug

S = Plant from seed. **T** = Plant from transplants. **N/R** = Not recommended. **+** = Can be planted year-round in some parts of zone.

ZONE 11	ZONE 12	ZONE 13	ZONE 14	ZONES 15, 16	ZONE 17	ZONES 18, 19	ZONES 20, 21	ZONES 22–24	ZONES H1, H2
Mid-Sep–Nov	Oct–Nov	Nov	Oct–Dec	Oct–Nov	Oct–Nov	Oct–Dec	Oct–Dec	Oct–Dec	Nov
Feb, Sep	Sep–Dec	Sep–Nov	Feb–Mar, Aug–Sep	Feb–Mar, Aug–Sep	Feb–Apr, Aug–Sep+	Jan–Feb, Sep–Oct	Aug–Feb	Aug–Mar	Oct–Mar+
Feb–mid-Mar, Sep	Sep–Nov	Sep–Nov	Feb–Apr, Aug–Sep	Feb–May, Jul–Aug+	Jan, Sep–Oct	Jan, Sep–Oct	Jul–Sep	All year	All year
Sep–Oct	Sep–Dec	Mid-Sep–Nov	Mid-Aug–Sep	Mid-Aug–Sep	Mid-Aug–Sep	Mid-Sep–Oct	Sep–Oct	Sep–Oct	Oct–Nov
Feb, Sep	Sep–Feb	Oct–Dec	Feb–Mar, Aug–Sep	Feb–Apr, Aug–Sep+	Feb–Nov+	Aug, Nov–Mar	Aug–Apr	Aug–Apr	Nov–Jan
Feb–Mar, Aug–Sep	Feb–Mar, Sep	Mid-Sep–Dec	Feb–Mar, Aug–Sep	Feb–Mar, Aug–Sep	Feb–Mar, Aug–Sep	Sep–Mar	Sep–Mar	Sep–Mar	Oct–Mar
Feb–Mar, Sep–mid-Oct	Sep–mid-Jan	Mid-Sep–Jan	Feb–Apr, mid-Aug–Oct	Feb–May, Jul–Aug+	Jan–May, Sep–Oct	Jan–Feb, Sep–Oct	Sep–Oct, Jan–Mar	Sep–Apr	Oct–Feb
Mid-Sep–early Oct	Nov–Dec, Nov–Jan	Mid-Sep–mid-Jan (sets), Nov–Jan	Jul, Oct	Jan–Feb, Sep–Oct	Jan–Mar	Nov–Mar	Nov–Mar	Oct–Feb	Sep–Mar (short day), Mar–May (intermed. day)
Apr–May	Apr, Sep–Dec	Oct	May, Sep	May, Sep	May, Sep	Apr, Sep–Oct	Apr, Sep–Oct	Apr, Sep–Oct	Oct–Nov
Feb–mid-Mar, mid-Sep–mid-Oct	Feb, mid-Aug–mid-Sep	Mid-Jan–mid-Feb, Sep–Nov	Feb–Apr, Aug–Sep	Feb–Mar, Aug–Sep	Feb–Apr, Aug–Nov+	Sep–Jan	Aug, Dec–Mar	Sep–Apr	Oct–Feb+
Mid-Feb–mid-Mar	Feb–Mar	Sep–Feb	Dec–Mar, Jul–Aug	Mar–Jun, Aug	Mar–Jun, Aug	Dec–Mar, Jul–Aug	Feb–May, Jul–Aug	Feb–May, Jul–Aug	Oct–Jan
Feb–mid-Apr, mid-Sep–Oct	Sep–Apr	Sep–Mar	Sep–Apr	Jan–Apr, Aug–Dec+	All year	Sep–Apr	All year	All year	Oct–Mar+
Jan–Mar	N/R	N/R	Jan–Mar	Jan–Mar	Jan–Mar	Jan–Feb	Jan–Feb	Jan–Feb	N/R
Feb, Sep	Feb, Sep–mid-Nov	Oct–Feb	Feb–Apr, Aug–Sep	Feb–Apr, Aug–Sep+	Feb–Nov+	Mar, Oct	Sep–May	Sep–May	Nov–Jan
Mar	Late Jan–early Feb	Nov	Mar–Apr, Sep	Mar–Apr, Sep	Mar–Apr, Sep	Feb, Oct	Jan–Feb, Oct	Jan–Feb, Oct	Sep–Mar
N/R	N/R	N/R	Apr–May	Apr–May	Apr–May	Apr	Mar–Apr	Feb–Mar	Nov–Jan
Feb–Mar, mid-Sep–Oct	Mid-Sep–Jan	Oct–Jan	Aug–Feb	Sep–Apr	Feb–Apr, Jul–Sep+	Sep–Jan	Sep–Mar	Sep–Mar+	Nov–Jan+
Feb–Mar, Sep	Sep–Feb	Sep–Dec	Feb–Apr, Aug–Sep	Mar–Apr, Aug+	All year	Feb–May, Sep	Jan–May	All year	All year
Mar–Apr, Aug	Mid-Sep–Jan	Mid-Sep–Jan	Feb–Mar, Jul–Aug	Jan, Aug–Sep	Jan, Aug–Sep	Feb, Aug–Sep	Jan, Aug–Sep	Jan, mid-Jul–Sep+	Sep–Dec

Beyond Local: Homegrown Ingredients for Your Favorite Dishes

GROW A SALAD BAR. The most common salad greens grow best during the cool season. For diversity in your salad bowl, plant a mix of sweet and spicy greens, plus green onions (scallions) and radishes for bite. To ensure a steady supply, make successive sowings every two weeks or so. Baby greens are sweeter and more tender than mature leaves. **Mild:** beet greens, lettuce (butterhead, looseleaf), spinach, Swiss chard. **Spicy:** arugula, curly endive (frisée), escarole.

GROW A STIR-FRY GARDEN. Make dinner in minutes by whipping up stir-fry meals around the fresh crops from your garden. The 3-foot-square beds in this Arizona garden (pictured at right) feed a wok in an outdoor kitchen just a few feet away. Grow beans, corn, eggplant (Asian), Malabar spinach, peppers, and zucchini in summer; bok choy, broccoli raab, green onions, curly kale, mustard, snow peas, and Swiss chard for winter. Start with grilled chicken, shrimp, or tofu; season with garlic or ginger; then add the vegetables.

GROW ROOTS FOR ROASTS. Root crops such as carrots and turnips are classic side dishes for fall roasts—also for dropping into stews and casseroles. Below are five favorites. All need rich, deep soil to thrive; raised beds like the 4- by 8-foot one pictured are ideal. Line the bottom with chicken wire to keep out gophers; fill with fast-draining planting mix. Plant the crops in rows (see encyclopedia listings for spacing).

RUTABAGA. A tasty turnip relative with large yellowish roots; its leaves are palatable only when young. Roast and serve with meat, or mash with potatoes.

TURNIP. Best known for roots, which come in various colors including creamy yellow, and white with a purplish top. Foliage is also edible. Harvest and use as soon as they are big enough to eat (when flavor is sweetest). Roast and serve with meat, or mash with potatoes.

BEET. Grow for its edible roots and leafy tops, which, when young and tender, are tasty when sautéed. 'Bull's Blood' has glossy, red-bronze leaves; 'Chioggia' (sliced, the beet shows rings of red and white) and yellow-rooted varieties are also available.

PARSNIP. Related to carrot, parsnip has long, creamy white to yellowish roots that taste delicately sweet. Needs frost to develop its flavor. Roast or use in stews; or pan-roast with apples, carrots, and pork.

CARROT. Orange types are most familiar, but varieties are available with yellow, white, or purple roots. Long market kinds such as 12-inch 'Envy' need a foot of loose soil to grow well. If you can give them only a few inches, grow half-long Nantes types or miniatures like 'Short 'n Sweet'.

GROW
Vines

A vine is simply a flexible shrub that doesn't stop extending its growth. It can be used to frame entryways, and to decorate bare walls and arbors. As the vine grows, it just keeps getting taller or longer, depending on whether you train it vertically or let it ramble horizontally across the ground.

CHOOSE

Vines may be deciduous, semievergreen, evergreen, or annual. Some provide greenery alone; others bear decorative fruits or blossoms. The vine's weight at maturity and its method of attachment will determine the kind of support needed. Once you have a good idea of what you're looking for—an evergreen flowering vine for a delicate trellis, say—narrow the list to those plants appropriate to your climate zone. The list on the opposite page can get you started.

PLANT AND TEND

Most vines are sold in containers; a few deciduous kinds, such as roses and grapes, are available bare-root. See page 671 for container and bare-root planting guidelines.

Many vines grow well in ordinary soil with an annual feeding in spring and require only average amounts of water. To look their best, almost all require yearly pruning. Check the encyclopedia for information on the specific needs of each vine.

Bougainvillea blooms over an entry gate—where it's also easily viewed from the interior courtyard—in Saratoga, California.

KINDS OF VINES

   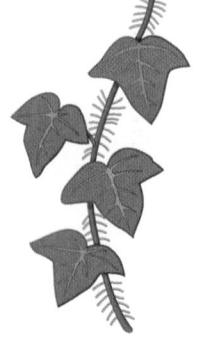 

TWINING VINES. New growth twists or spirals as it elongates, coiling around a support or even around growth on the same or nearby plants. Nearly all twiners make too tight a spiral to encircle a post, so support them with cord or wire.

VINES WITH TENDRILS. Growths along stems or at leaf tips reach out and wrap around anything within reach—a wire, another stem of the same vine, or an adjoining plant. The tendrils grow out straight until they make contact, then contract into a spiral. Supply narrow supports that they can easily grasp.

CLINGING VINES. Growths along the stems of these vines attach to flat surfaces. Some clingers have tendrils equipped at their tips with suction disks that grip the support; others have "claws" that hook into small irregularities or crevices of a flat surface. Another type of clinger has aerial rootlets along its stems that tenaciously grip all but absolutely smooth, slick surfaces. Bear in mind that all of these clinging devices—known collectively as holdfasts—can damage brick, wood, concrete, and other building materials.

VINES THAT NEED TYING. Some vines have no means of attachment. They thread their way through and over other plants, depending on this living support to hold their stems in place. A few—climbing roses, for example—have thorns on their stems, which help.

How to Use Vines

D = Deciduous; E = Evergreen;
A = Annual; P = Perennial

TRELLIS
Black-eyed Susan (*Thunbergia alata*) A, P
Bougainvillea E
Clematis D, E
Mandevilla D, E
Morning glory (*Ipomoea*) A, P
Star jasmine (*Trachelospermum*) E
Sweet peas (*Lathyrus odoratus*) A

GROUNDCOVER
Bougainvillea E
Honeysuckle (*Lonicera*) D, E
Nasturtium (*Tropaeolum*) A, P

WALL
Boston ivy (*Parthenocissus*) D
Bougainvillea E
Bower vine (*Pandorea*) E
Carolina jessamine (*Gelsemium*) E
Creeping fig (*Ficus pumila*) E
Cup-of-gold vine (*Solandra*) E
Jasmine (*Jasminum*) E
Lilac vine (*Hardenbergia*) E
Passion vine (*Passiflora*) D, E

STURDY ARBOR
Cape honeysuckle (*Tecoma*) E
Crossvine (*Bignonia*) E
Flame vine (*Pyrostegia*) E
Grape D
Kiwi D
Potato vine (*Solanum laxum*) E
Queen's wreath (*Petrea volubilis*) E
Trumpet vine (*Distictis*) E
Wisteria D

TREE (WITH TRAINING)
Bougainvillea E
Wisteria D

VINE SAMPLER: FOLIAGE, BERRIES, FLOWERS, FRUIT

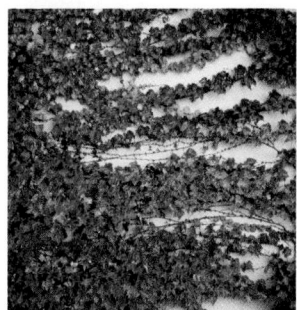

FOLIAGE. Boston ivy leaves turn vivid orange-red in fall—showy against a blank wall.

BERRIES. Grapevines are especially versatile; espalier them against a white wall, to train over a freestanding arbor.

FLOWERS. Passion vine has dramatic flowers nestled among its glossy leaves. Passion vines produce fruit too.

FRUIT. 'Hayward' kiwi stems show reddish tinge; this variety comes from New Zealand.

GROW
Wildflowers

Wildflowers provide a carefree style of gardening that is colorful and gives great bang for a dollar. You can sow a strip between your yard and the surrounding landscape. Or sprinkle wildflowers in gaps between groundcovers, or establish a flowering meadow instead of a lawn or flower beds.

Growing wildflowers is a purely regional affair, with different parts of the West offering locally adapted favorites—from lupines and poppies in California to Mexican hat in the desert to fireweed in Alaska. Specialty seed companies offer regional mixes that work well in many areas. Local native plant societies can also provide information on wildflowers suitable for your area. Plant wildflowers from seed in fall in mild-winter areas. Before sowing, check guidelines on the seed packet.

PREP

Prepare wildflower beds by tilling or digging in a 3-inch layer of rotted manure or compost; then level the soil and water. After about three weeks, hoe or pull the weeds that come up. Then you're ready to plant. Select a site that drains well and gets at least six hours of sun per day.

SCATTER SEEDS

Rake the soil lightly before sowing. Check guidelines on the seed packet. But in general, scatter seeds at the rate of 1 ounce per 300 square feet (that's 50 to 100 seeds per square foot). Rake lightly; water well. Keep the area moist (use a garden hose with a mist nozzle) until seedlings appear—usually 5 to 14 days after sowing. When seedlings are a few inches tall, taper off irrigation.

TEND

During the growing season, water when plants appear drought stressed; remove any weed seedlings as soon as they start to emerge. After plants have finished blooming, leave desirable plants to set seeds for next year.

Gather seeds by hand to save for later plantings or to fill in bare spots. In early winter, mow or cut dry stems down to 6 to 8 inches. At the same time, pull out any weeds, such as oxalis or dandelion.

Many Happy Returns

Self-sowing spring annuals make great additions to the garden, especially for forgotten corners. Some are true wildflowers; others just look like wildflowers. Sow a few one year, and they provide repeat performances year after year, almost by themselves. Fall is the perfect time to sow them. (In cold climates, wait until early spring to sow seeds.)

Keep in mind there's a fine line between a well-behaved reseeder and an aggressive pest, and the difference often depends on climate. Corn cockle, for instance, is well behaved in the West but turns up on noxious-weed lists in the Southeast.

Among our favorite reseeders—all polite here: California desert bluebells (*Phacelia campanularia*); California poppy (*Eschscholzia californica*); corn cockle (*Agrostemma githago*); desert marigold (*Baileya multiradiata*); godetia (*Clarkia amoena*); honeywort (*Cerinthe major*); larkspur (*Consolida ajacis*); love-in-a-mist (*Nigella damascena*); Shirley poppy (*Papaver rhoeas*), and sweet alyssum.

Shasta daisies (*Leucanthemum* × *superbum*) create a wildflower effect when massed or scattered among grasses.

Corn cockle (*Agrostemma githago*) has wispy but sturdy stems; for a striking combo, pair it with *Cerinthe major* 'Purpurascens'.

Drifts of deep blue lupines accent a meadow of *Elymus, Deschampsia,* and other soft grasses, in Wyoming.

Design Tips

Here are some strategies for incorporating wildflowers into the garden.

INTERSPERSE NATIVE SPECIES. Mix them in with their modern offspring. In the Northwest, this might include hybrids such as Pacific Coast irises (derived from *Iris douglasiana*).

PLANT IN DRIFTS. In the wild, plant communities are often quite minimalist, with one or two plants spreading into beautiful carpets of bloom across hills and valleys.

MIMIC A NATIVE LANDSCAPE. Use native shrubs such as coffeeberry or toyon to form the "bones" of the garden. Then fill in around them with flowering natives such as monkey flower and leopard lily.

PLANT A CUTTING GARDEN. Create an island of wildflowers in the backyard that doubles as a source of cut flowers. Choose varieties that hold up in bouquets, such as calliopsis, godetia, and Indian blanket.

FILL SMALL SPACES. Sow seeds around mailboxes or in raised beds. Or broadcast them as temporary fillers until you have time to tackle a permanent landscape.

PLANT IN POTS. No room? Fill a 24-inch-diameter bowl with potting mix, sprinkle seeds of low growers such as baby blue eyes or meadowfoam over the surface, then cover with a thin layer of potting mix. Water with a fine spray.

GARDEN-FRIENDLY WILDFLOWERS

NORTHWEST. *Lewisia tweedyi* grows wild in the mountains of central Washington. Needs perfect drainage.

CALIFORNIA. Five-spot nemophila (*Nemophila maculata*) is a California native annual that stays low (to 12 inches tall).

SOUTHWEST. Mexican hat (*Ratibida*) flowers have a raised center disk and look best in casual, natural-looking borders.

MOUNTAIN. Perennial blue flax (*Linum perenne*), a profuse bloomer, produces light blue flowers that close in shade.

GROW
A Wildlife Habitat

Times are tough—and getting tougher—for birds, butterflies, bees, and other wild creatures. As wildlands get logged, farmed, carpeted with houses and golf courses, and paved over with freeways, there's no place for the wildlife to forage or seek shelter. How can we help them to find what they need in suburbia? By creating backyard habitats.

Making your garden attractive to wildlife—including songbirds, hummingbirds, toads, lizards, frogs, and beneficial insects—is primarily a matter of providing shelter, water, and food. It's also important to avoid using chemical pesticides. Emphasize native plants, as they're familiar to the local wildlife and adapted to your climate. Also remember that a garden teeming with wildlife is not overly tidy; parts of it are left to grow naturally, providing havens for creatures of all sorts. Beginning on page 95 of the "Plant Finder" are lists of plants attractive to birds, butterflies, bees, and beneficial insects.

Hummingbird peeks out from her nest of grasses and moss in an apricot tree.

A Bee Garden

Many unpollinated flowers won't set seed or form fruit, which means no food for you. What you need are more bees—the best pollinators. (Birds, butterflies, and some other insects help too.) Lure them into your garden by planting flowers that produce lots of nectar and pollen, and both honeybees and native bee species will zoom in. Some to grow: asters, cosmos, milkweed, salvias, and sunflowers.

Native Bees

One of the biggest challenges many bees face is finding suitable nesting sites. Honeybees nest in colonies—hives usually tended by professionals. But the majority of our native bees (honeybees are a European import) are solitary, raising their young alone. Having no hive to defend, they're not aggressive and they rarely sting. While most do not produce honey, all are efficient pollinators.

About 70 percent of native bees are ground nesters. A small patch of bare earth in a sunny spot—as little as 1 square foot—is all they need. The remainder are wood nesters; they'll occupy holes in trees, or move into bee houses or nesting blocks—pieces of untreated wood drilled with a grid of small holes—that you supply (available at some nurseries, or online from suppliers such as gardeners.com).

The female bees will lay their eggs in the holes, then seal them; their offspring will emerge next spring to carry on.

For more on pollinators, see sunset.com/pollinatorpots

Elements of a Wildlife Garden

FLOWERS. Include a wide range of plants that provide nectar for butterflies, beneficial insects, and hummingbirds. Also plant species whose foliage feeds butterfly larvae. Let plants go to seed to furnish food for songbirds. Add shrubs and trees that produce berries.

TALL TREES. These provide shelter, food (seeds or fruits), and nesting places. They also protect the garden from strong winds.

HEDGEROWS. These provide food, shelter, and nesting sites for birds. Plant small trees and low to medium-tall shrubs. Include fruit-bearing types as well as kinds that feed butterfly larvae.

VINES. Flowering vines provide shelter, nesting sites, and nectar. Many also bear berries and foliage that are sources of food for both birds and butterfly larvae.

SHELTERS. Arrange rocks or place upturned flowerpots beside ponds where frogs and toads can hide from predators. Hang nesting boxes for birds; install them away from activity around feeders and face them away from prevailing weather. Put up bee houses.

WATER FEATURES. Birds are especially attracted to the splashing water of a small stream or fountain, although they relish the still water of a birdbath too. A location 10 to 20 feet away from shrubs offers a zone of safety from predators. A pond provides water for birds and a habitat for frogs and turtles (make a "beach" at one side to provide shallow water). An "island" (a large rock) in the center offers refuge for turtles and frogs.

TOP ROW (LEFT TO RIGHT): Western tiger swallowtail, newly emerged from its chrysalis (opposite, on stick), pauses before flitting into a nearby fennel patch. Dragonflies like this common green darner hang out around ponds, dining on mosquitos, ants, and flies. MIDDLE: A wildlife habitat in Prescott, Arizona, has nectar flowers for butterflies; a bubbling stream that lures birds, dragonflies, and frogs; and trees for cover. BOTTOM ROW (LEFT TO RIGHT): A bee house surrounded by plants that the bees love: sunflower, yarrow, and blue salvia (*Salvia clevelandii*). Hooded oriole splashes in a birdbath.

WATER

Most plants cannot survive long without water. A seed must absorb water before it can germinate. Roots can take up nutrients only when water is present in the soil, and water transports nutrients throughout plants. Water is also essential for photosynthesis.

In the West, most of our rainfall comes in winter, but many garden plants need irrigation in summer, during our driest months. And although each region's overall water supply remains virtually fixed, the demand for water continues to rise. In the years to come, water management will present an ever greater challenge. Here are some ways to meet that challenge.

KNOW YOUR SOIL

Examine the soil frequently, making sure it is not too wet or too dry between waterings. If necessary, add organic matter to new planting areas to improve soil texture or to hold moisture better. When determining how deeply to water, first consider your plants. Because plants with deeper roots are better able to withstand periods of drought, your goal should be to apply enough water to wet the entire root zone and to encourage deep rooting. Shallow watering leads to shallow roots and plants that are very susceptible to drought. Avoid applying so much water that it penetrates deeper than the roots actually grow.

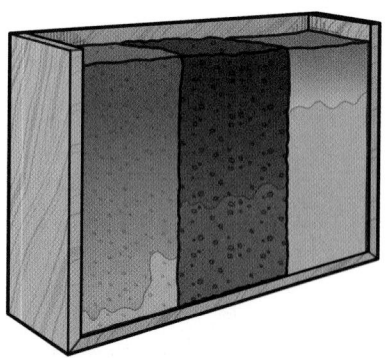

APPLIED TO SAND (left), 1 inch of water penetrates about 12 inches. Applied to loam (center), 1 inch of water reaches about 7 inches. Applied to clay (right), 1 inch of water soaks only 4–5 inches.

CHOOSE THE RIGHT PLANTS

Many beautiful shrubs, trees, and perennials—such as the golden yarrow and lavender in the photo at right—can thrive with very little water, once established. (For more choices, see pages 74–78.)

PLANT IN ZONES

Organize your landscape into "hydrozones"—groups of plants with similar water, soil, and exposure needs. Doing so makes it possible to apply water very efficiently, giving more water to thirsty plants and less to unthirsty ones. For example, separate low-water users, which thrive on rainfall alone or with minimal supplemental water (such as native plants or ones similarly adapted to drought), from high-water users (such as lawns, annual flowers, and vegetable gardens). As much as possible, maximize the amount of garden space dedicated to low-water users.

CHECK YOUR WATERING SYSTEM

Watch it run often to look for signs of leaks, malfunctions, and poor performance. Adjust sprinklers when necessary, and unclog heads as needed. Replace broken sprinklers or risers. Wet spots and a constantly running water meter are other signs of problems. Clean drip systems regularly.

In freezing climates, install a drain valve at the lowest point in each circuit. Before winter freeze, drain the system through the drain valve, and hire a professional to blow compressed air through the system to clear any remaining water if your system isn't self-draining.

Yarrow (*Achillea*), lavender, and other unthirsty plants are grouped near this garden path; all take minimal watering.

A half-inch of decomposed granite over a compacted base forms a firm, clean surface that drains well, in Rancho Mirage, California. Design: Michael Buccino.

Crave Lawn? Plant a Spot

If losing your lawn makes you nostalgic for the cooling feel of green grass underfoot, plant a lawn in a low wide bowl. Choose a sturdy container at least 14–16 inches in diameter, fill it with potting soil, press to firm it, and water to moisten. Then scatter seeds (protect from birds). Once grass is growing lustily, "mow" with hand clippers.

SHRINK THE LAWN

Most lawn grasses need enormous amounts of water to stay green and lush. Reduce your lawn's size, or—unless you need it for kids to play on—eliminate it altogether. Or give it a square, circular, or rectangular shape; such geometric lawns are easier to irrigate—without wasteful overspray on paving—than irregularly shaped lawns. If losing the lawn makes you nostalgic for a spot of green grass, grow a small patch like the one pictured above.

GO PERMEABLE

Paths and patios that are paved with gravel, decomposed granite, spaced flagstones, or porous concrete are the best choices for water-conserving gardens. They allow rainwater and irrigation to pass through them and into the soil, preventing runoff that can clog storm drains; pollute nearby lakes, streams, and coastal waters; and irrigate nearby plants. If you prefer a lusher look, plant unthirsty groundcovers between the pavers.

TAILOR YOUR IRRIGATION SYSTEM

Some irrigation systems are more efficient than others for delivering watering to certain plants. Use the following guidelines to help you decide which method is best. Local water departments will often recommend specific equipment.

Lawn

- Hose-end sprinklers with built-in timers can work well for a small lawn.
- Underground sprinklers connected to a controller (some newer ones connect to weather stations) will water more precisely.

Annuals and Perennials

- Overhead watering may cause flowers to droop or spotting on petals; certain species are more subject to disease if watered from above.
- Underground sprinklers with pop-up risers work in extensive flower beds. Risers should be tall enough that foliage doesn't block spray.
- Choose drip-emitter lines for beds with closely spaced plants, individual emitters for widely spaced plants.

Groundcovers

- Use underground sprinklers; select stationary heads for plantings more than a foot tall and low-precipitation-rate heads for groundcovers (including lawns) on a slope.
- Drip emitters are suitable for shrubby groundcovers.
- Drip mini-sprayers work well for mass plantings of small plants.

Roses

- Soaker hoses are easy to use on level ground.
- Underground sprinklers with flat-head sprayers run early in the day to keep leaves dry, preventing disease.
- Drip irrigation with emitter line works well with closely spaced bushes. Or use individual emitters for each bush.

Trees and Shrubs

- Use soil basins to direct water to roots and avoid runoff.
- Soaker hoses can handle deep-watering of established trees.
- Low-volume systems with emitters or microsprinklers are most efficient, especially on sloping ground.

Vegetables

- Hand-water in basins and furrows.
- Use soaker hoses on flat ground.
- Install a low-volume system with emitter line for closely spaced plants, individual emitters for widely spaced vegetables.

TOP: *Zinnia elegans*. BOTTOM: Mizuna 'Red Streaked' gourmet lettuce.

HOSES Use bubblers in shallow furrows to irrigate rows of vegetable or flower seedlings.

SOAKER HOSES These deliver water slowly; water seeps from the soaker along its entire length.

SPRINKLERS These apply a high volume of water over a large area, such as lawn.

WATER EFFICIENTLY

Tools for applying water range from simple handheld sprayers to hose-end sprinklers to more complex underground rigid-pipe and drip systems. The equipment appropriate for your garden depends on how often you need to water, the size of your garden, and how much gear you want to buy.

Hoses These come in lengths up to 100 feet and with standard diameters from $\frac{3}{8}$ to 1 inch. A $\frac{5}{8}$-inch size is best for all-around use. Keep in mind that as hose length increases, water pressure decreases, so the longer the hose, the larger diameter you should consider.

Portable hose-end sprinklers include stationary models that resemble salt shakers or rings; oscillating, rotating, and impulse sprinklers; and "walking" types that slowly roll through the area to be irrigated. When selecting a sprinkler, look for one with a coverage pattern that most closely matches the area to be irrigated (the shape and size of the space the sprinkler covers should be listed on the package).

Soaker hoses These long tubes made of perforated or porous plastic or rubber, with hose fittings at one or both ends, deliver water slowly, steadily. When you attach a soaker to a regular hose and turn on the system, water seeps or sprinkles from the soaker along its entire length. You can water wide beds by snaking soakers back and forth around the plants, or trees and shrubs by coiling the soaker hose over the outermost edges of the root zone. You'll probably need to leave soakers on longer than you would sprinklers. To determine timing, check water penetration with a trowel or soil sampling tube.

Sprinklers Permanent underground sprinkler systems, the traditional watering method in low-rainfall areas, offer some advantages over hose-end options. They free you from moving hoses and can be automated to operate even if you're away from home. Newer sprinklers produce less runoff and overspray, and distribute water more evenly.

You may want to hire a professional to plan and install the system, which entails much physical labor. For such a system to work properly, it must be well designed, with as few sprinklers as possible to achieve head-to-head coverage, and sprinkler heads positioned to prevent overspray onto paved areas.

Drip Irrigation

Drip or low-volume irrigation delivers water at low pressure and volume (in gallons per hour) to specific areas or individual plants. Water penetration is slow, its depth regulated by the length of time the system is on. The tubing with inline emitters, shown above, encircles a citrus. U-stakes hold the line in place.

DRIP EMITTERS These release water directly to the soil and waste virtually no water.

MINI-SPRINKLERS Available in many different styles, which vary primarily in output (gallons per hour) or in the watering pattern. Mini-sprayers and mini-sprinklers, which spray water into the air, deliver less water than ordinary sprinklers do.

CONTROLLERS Technology can help you to water more efficiently. Rain sensors override automatic controllers after significant rainfall. Newer controllers are easy to adjust seasonally and some can be connected to moisture sensors or weather stations. They can reduce waste and do a better job of watering than most gardeners can.

Putting It All Together

Nine elements of a water-conserving landscape

1. PERMEABLE PAVING. For patio surfaces, opt for paving such as gravel, flagstones, or recycled concrete pieces. You can grow unthirsty plants such as creeping thyme or snow-in-summer in spaces between.

2. RAIN-HARVESTING SYSTEM. Channel rainwater from your home's downspout into a subsurface catchment basin where it can replenish the groundwater.

3. PLANTS GROUPED BY WATER NEEDS. Place thirstier plants together and drought-resistant plants elsewhere. Then put plants that need regular water on separate irrigation systems.

4. LOW-WATER TURF. If you must have a patch of lawn, choose a native grass that's appropriate for your region. Examples: blue grama (*Bouteloua gracilis*), buffalo grass (*Buchloe dactyloides*), creeping red fescue (*Festuca rubra*), Pacific hair grass (*Deschampsia cespitosa holciformis*).

5. DRIP-IRRIGATED RAISED BEDS FOR VEGETABLES. Use drip emitter lines or soaker hoses in raised beds; they put irrigation water right where plants need it, with no runoff or waste.

6. SHADE TREES ON THE WEST SIDE OF THE HOUSE. Choose deciduous types that shade and cool the house during summer, then drop their leaves to allow in sunlight during winter. Unthirsty choices for mild climates include Chinese pistache and honey locust.

7. DROUGHT-TOLERANT GROUNDCOVER. For areas that don't get foot traffic, choose unthirsty groundcovers such as *Arctostaphylos uva-ursi*, Carmel creeper ceanothus, low-growing junipers, or creeping thyme.

8. TOUGH SHRUBS. Fill borders or spaces along fences with undemanding, low-water beauties such as chuparosa, lavender, rosemary, or smoke tree (*Cotinus coggygria*).

9. IRRIGATION CONTROLLER. Install an automatic controller to schedule irrigation times. Reset programs seasonally.

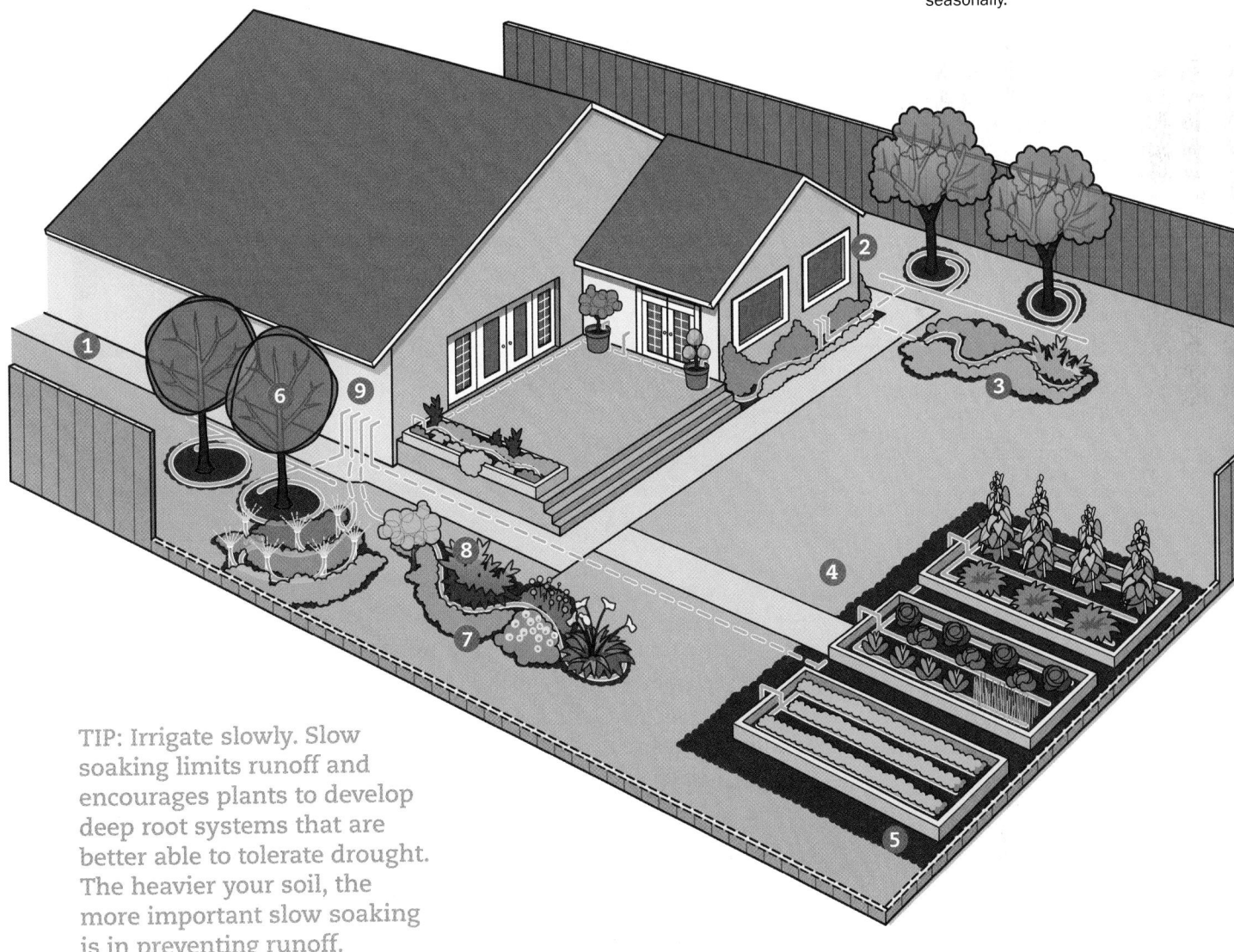

TIP: Irrigate slowly. Slow soaking limits runoff and encourages plants to develop deep root systems that are better able to tolerate drought. The heavier your soil, the more important slow soaking is in preventing runoff.

Harvest the Rain

Even in summer months, some rain usually falls in parts of the West, and roofs catch a lot of it. Channel run-off into a rain barrel, a wash, or a rain garden; then use it to water plants.

1 HANG A RAIN CHAIN. The copper chain pictured above channels rainwater from the roof into a plastic catchment basin at the base, then into the garden pictured at right.

2 PLANT A RAIN GARDEN. An infiltration basin planted with moisture lovers, this garden gets water from the rain chain via a flexible 40-inch plastic pipe that runs the length of the rock-filled channel and under a permeable path. Once in the garden, it percolates into groundwater. Design: In Harmony Sustainable Landscapes.

3 INSTALL A RAIN BARREL. Rain barrels hold about 50 to 60 gallons each—enough to irrigate houseplants or pots on the deck. The best type is made of recycled food-grade plastic (or use a recycled wine barrel like the one pictured), with an intake line, spigot, overflow attachment, screen cover to keep out leaves, and removable solid cover. Place the barrel under a downspout; to keep rainwater pure, remove the solid cover an hour or two after rainfall has washed pollen and other pollutants off the roof.

4 BUILD A WASH. In the Southwest, where monsoons come suddenly in summer, gardeners have learned to build washes that channel rainwater to swales and basins. Position them to carry rainwater from the house to the garden's low points.

HOW TO FIGHT DROUGHT

When drought comes, and with it the possibility of local bans on lawn watering or punishing hikes in water bills, what can you do? It's too late at that point to install a water-conserving landscape, but you can take steps to save the plants you have.

Wilted leaves are the first telltale sign that this *Philadelphus* tree needs a deep soaking.

Save established trees and shrubs first.
These are costly to replace and have the greatest impact on your landscape. (A lawn can be replaced with sod in an afternoon, but a 70-foot-tall redwood can take 20 years or more to replace.) Landscape trees such as ash, birch, poplar, alder, coast redwood, magnolia, and Japanese maple are often the first plants to show signs of drought stress.

Give them a deep irrigation in late spring, and they'll be far better equipped to withstand drought. Coil soaker hoses around the tree at the drip line and halfway between the drip line and the trunk, then moisten the soil around the tree to 18 to 24 inches deep. For most big trees, you'll need about 10 gallons of water per inch of trunk diameter; riparian trees need twice that amount.

Reduce lawn watering.
To stay green all summer, lawns need 1 to 2 inches of water per week. Turn on the sprinklers for about 10 minutes once a week, turn them off to let moisture soak in, then turn them on again for another few minutes. Or cut back to 1 inch of water every two weeks; under this regimen, lawns turn straw-colored and go semidormant but bounce back quickly after weather cools in fall. Also, mow high and keep the mower blades sharp. Don't overfertilize; too much nitrogen encourages thirsty new growth.

Water landscape plants near lawns.
Plants growing in or near a well-watered lawn become dependent on that irrigation. If lawn irrigation is abruptly cut off, those plants will suffer and need supplemental water.

Monitor shallow-rooted shrubs.
On azaleas, rhododendrons, and young camellias, watch for wilting or drooping of new growth. Build basins around them (make sure that water won't pool against the trunks), and give them a deep soak in April with clear water (soapy water on rhododendrons can cause leaf burn).

Runoff and Water Quality

In some areas along the Pacific Coast, runoff has caused serious pollution in coastal waters. Inland, the water quality of lakes and streams also suffers when garden runoff contains residue from chemical fertilizers and pesticides.

WHAT TO DO

- Avoid applying chemicals to your garden when rain is likely. You can easily miss your intended target, and the chemicals will wash off into storm drains.

- Avoid overwatering plants before and after you apply chemicals.

- Never dispose of lawn or garden chemicals in the storm drain or trash.

- Bag or compost yard waste so it won't clog drains.

- Use permeable paving that allows water to pass through into the soil, which acts as a filter. Impermeable surfaces simply move along rainwater or excess irrigation water to storm drains.

- Install an infiltration system. In some coastal communities, local ordinances require new building sites to include an infiltration pit or other sub-surface runoff retention system. These underground tanks or chambers are connected to downspouts. They can be installed about 5 feet beneath a driveway or lawn. Before putting in new landscaping near the coast, check local ordinances, or consult a structural engineer or geologist about installing such a system.

Most stone-fruit trees (cherries, peaches, plums) can survive some drought, but they'll produce smaller fruits and fewer flower buds next year. They'll be better off with a deep irrigation in April and again in June.

FERTILIZE

When plants are actively growing, they need a steady supply of nutrients. Many of these are present in soil, water, and air, but gardeners need to supply others. Most likely to need supplemental feeding are annual vegetables and flowers, lawns, perennials, and fruit trees.

READ THE LABEL

Macronutrients All plants need these substances in fairly large quantities. Three—carbon, oxygen, and hydrogen—are found in air and water. Plants use the others in mineral form.

Nitrogen (N) helps synthesize proteins, chlorophyll, and enzymes. Nitrogen is the nutrient most likely to be inadequate in garden soils. Too much can make plants too leafy (often at the expense of flowers and fruit) and prone to attack by sucking insects. Applied too late, it promotes new growth that's vulnerable to frost damage.

Phosphorus (P) promotes flowering and fruiting, strong root growth, and the transfer of energy within the plant. Phosphorus deficiency is rare, and an overdose can interfere with a plant's absorption of other essential elements.

Potassium (K) helps regulate the synthesis of proteins and starches that make sturdy plants. It also helps increase resistance to diseases, heat, and cold. Too much potassium interferes with the absorption of calcium and magnesium, making plants grow poorly.

Secondary nutrients Plants need these in about the same amounts as they do the macronutrients. But they're less likely to be deficient in most soils. Calcium (Ca) plays a fundamental role in cell formation and growth, and most roots require some calcium right at the growing tips. Magnesium (Mg) forms the core of the chlorophyll molecules in the cells of green leaves. Sulfur (S) acts with nitrogen in the manufacture of protoplasm for plant cells.

Dilute liquid fertilizers are ideal for small plots.

Micronutrients Also known as trace elements, micronutrients are required in very small quantities (excess amounts can be toxic). Among them are zinc (Zn) and manganese (Mn)—both thought to function as catalysts for utilizing other nutrients—and iron (Fe), essential for chlorophyll formation. Some plants, particularly vegetables such as Swiss chard, need boron (B), an element often lacking in the West's alkaline soils.

CHOOSE FERTILIZER

Simple vs. complete Complete fertilizers contain nitrogen (N), phosphorus (P), and potassium (K). Some may also include secondary and/or micronutrients. Simple fertilizers supply just one macronutrient. Most familiar are the nitrogen-only types—ammonium sulfate (21-0-0)—and phosphorus-only superphosphate (0-20-0). Incomplete fertilizers fall between simple and complete; an example is 0-10-10, providing phosphorus and potassium but no nitrogen.

General purpose Fertilizers labeled "general-purpose" or "all-purpose"

Plant Anatomy and Nutrition

Knowing the relationship between a plant's growth and its environment—water, light, soil, air, and nutrients—helps gardeners provide the best possible conditions for each plant.

1 **ROOTS** absorb water, air, and nutrients.

2 **PHLOEM** conducts nutrients down from the leaves for use or storage.

3 **XYLEM** in stems transports water and dissolved minerals up from the roots.

4 **LEAVES** use sunlight to convert carbon dioxide, water, and minerals to carbohydrates and oxygen. The process is called photosynthesis.

contain equal or nearly equal amounts of the macronutrients N, P, and K (a 10-10-10 formula, for example). They are intended to meet most plants' needs throughout the growing season.

Special purpose These formulas are designed to meet specific needs. High-nitrogen blends (such as 29-3-4), for instance, help keep lawns green and growing quickly. Higher-phosphorus mixes (6-10-4, for example) are intended to promote flowering and fruiting. Other packaged fertilizers are formulated for particular types of plants. Those designed for acid lovers such as camellias and rhododendrons are especially useful, as are fertilizers for citrus.

Inorganic (chemical) fertilizers are made from synthetic substances with precisely formulated amounts of specific nutrients, primarily nitrogen, phosphorus, and potassium. These can be formulated for fast or slow release.

Organic (natural) fertilizers are made from the remains or by-products of living or once-living organisms. Manure, fish emulsion, bonemeal, cottonseed meal, and kelp meal are all examples of organic fertilizers that can be used alone or in various combinations to produce complete fertilizers. Most release their nutrients more slowly than inorganics (but some, like blood meal, release quickly). Organics also usually have slightly lower proportions of nutrients than most inorganic fertilizers.

Signs of Nutrient Deficiencies

Your local nursery can recommend a foliar spray to solve the immediate problem and a fertilizer supplement for long-term care.

LEAF SYMPTOMS	DEFICIENCY
Yellow and smaller than normal. On some plants they may turn red or purple. Overall growth is stunted or dwarfed.	Nitrogen
Small, with edges scorched, purplish, or blue-green in color. May fall early. Overall growth is reduced and weakened. Flower and fruit production diminished. Rare.	Phosphorus
Tips and edges become yellow and scorched-looking, with brownish purple spotting underneath.	Potassium
Turn dark from the base outward and die.	Calcium
Yellow between the veins, which remain green or slightly yellow.	Iron
Leaf centers turn reddish or yellow. Dead spots appear between veins.	Magnesium
Upper leaves yellow in center, between veins, with no sign of red.	Manganese
Veins grow lighter in color than the tissue in between.	Sulfur

Natural Fertilizers from Cover Crops

Cover crops are legumes that improve garden soil. Legumes such as fava beans and vetch also add nitrogen to the soil, thanks to their association with nitrogen-fixing bacteria that "fix" nitrogen in nodules in the legume's roots. Sow cover crops in fall in prepared soil, in rows 1 foot apart and about 3 inches deep. In spring, before flowers set seed (left), cut or mow the crop down and till it into the soil. Allow a couple of days, till again. Rake smooth, and plant. When the plants decompose, the nitrogen is released back into the soil.

CHECK NPK

Every fertilizer label states the percentage by weight of the three macronutrients used in mineral form, in alphabetical order: nitrogen (N), phosphorus (P), and potassium (K). So a fertilizer labeled 10-8-6 contains 10 percent nitrogen, 8 percent phosphorus, and 6 percent potassium. The label also tells you the source of each nutrient and lists any micronutrients present.

Nitrogen may be included in a fertilizer in nitrate form. If so, it will be water soluble and fast acting, especially in cool soils, but is easily leached (requiring frequent replenishment) and can pollute surface and groundwater if used to excess. Nitrogen in the form of ammonium is from organic sources (such as blood meal) and IBDU (isobutylidene diurea, a synthetic organic fertilizer). These are released more slowly and last longer in the soil.

Phosphorus is expressed on product labels as phosphate, P_2O_5, and listed as "available phosphoric acid."

Potassium is expressed as potash, K_2O, and may be described in various ways, including "water-soluble potash."

Phosphorus and potassium do not move readily through the soil in solution and must be applied near plant roots to do the most good.

APPLY IT CORRECTLY

Dry fertilizers (powders, granules, or pellets) can be spread on the ground or dug into the soil. Controlled-release types may be beadlike granules, spikes, or tablets. Dig granules into soil at planting time or scratch them into the soil surface. Use a mallet to pound spikes into the ground; dig holes for tablets.

Liquid fertilizers are sold as crystals, granules, or liquid concentrates that you mix with water and apply with a hose or spray bottle. The spray types, known as "foliar feeds," deliver instant supplies of specific nutrients. To avoid burning leaves, follow directions on fertilizer labels.

STAKE/TRAIN

Some plants need a little help to keep from sprawling or falling over. Others—apples, for instance—make beautiful living fences when trained on horizontal trellises or as espaliers against walls. To save space, train vining edibles such as pole beans, peas, tomatoes, cucumbers, melons, and squash to grow vertically—whether in cages or up ladders or trellises.

Put up your stakes and trellises at planting time. If you try to stake plants after they have begun to sprawl, you risk disturbing the roots and breaking the stems. Train or tie the plants as they grow. Common materials for vegetable supports are wire mesh, wooden stakes and string, and bamboo, but you can also use rustic twigs, decorative metal or wooden structures, copper pipe, and bent reinforcing wire.

If you train heavy-fruited vines on slanted or vertical structures, support the fruits with netting or cloth slings.

A tall trellis topped with a colorful birdhouse supports scarlet runner beans and nasturtiums.

PERENNIALS

Not all perennials need staking. Here are types that do.

SPRAWLERS such as carnations show flowers best when stems are corralled in a support fence of twine wrapped around stakes that circle the plant.

HEAVY FLOWER HEADS—peonies or dahlias, for example, tend to flop over. Keep them upright inside a circular metal hoop from the nursery.

TALL PERENNIALS such as delphinium and foxglove need stakes close to the mature plant's height. Tie the bloom spike to the stake as it grows, using ties that won't cut the stem or stalk. Add a cork at the top for safety.

VEGETABLES

To save space and bring your crops up to eye level, grow them on arbors and trellises whenever possible.

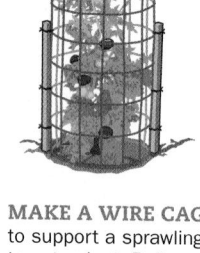

USE A WEATHERED LADDER—sink the legs into 6-inch-deep holes so it won't blow over. Wrap string, wire, or wire mesh around it to help support vining crops.

MAKE A WIRE CAGE to support a sprawling tomato plant. Roll a 6½-foot length of 5-foot-wide concrete reinforcing wire into a cylinder 24 inches in diameter.

BUILD A STURDY FRAME of wood and tilt it against a sunny garden wall for cucumbers, melons, or squash vines to climb.

STRETCH STRINGS over a wooden A-frame to provide support for climbing tendrils of beans and peas.

For how to make a tomato cage, see sunset.com/tomatocage

FRUIT TREES: INFORMAL ESPALIER

Where space is tight, train your fruit trees as an espalier;
dwarf potted varieties are good candidates for this use. Here's how.

1. CHOOSE TWO STRONG BRANCHES to form the first tie; remove all other shoots and cut back the leader to just above the bottom wire. Bend the branches at a 45° angle and secure them with soft cloth or plastic ties.

2. DURING THE FIRST GROW-ING SEASON, gradually tighten the ties so that the branches are drawn horizontally against the first wire. When the newly sprouted leader is long enough, hold it erect and tie it to the second wire.

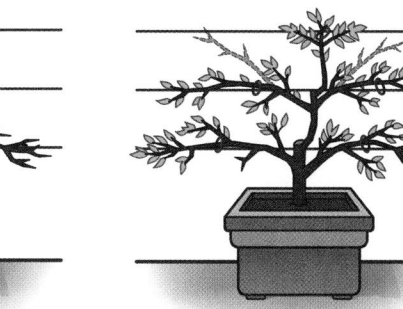

3. DURING THE DORMANT SEASON, cut back the leader to the second wire. Choose two branches for the second tier and remove competing shoots. Cut lateral growth on the lower branches back to three buds.

4. THE NEXT SEASON, gradually bring the second-tier branches into horizontal position, as you did for the first tier in step 2. Keep the leader upright and tie it to the third wire. Repeat the process for more wires, if desired. When the leader reaches the top wire, cut it back to just above the top branch.

Espaliered apple bears its fruit at easy-to-pick height in early fall.

To grow lots of fruit in a small space, train citrus, fig, or pineapple guava as informal espaliers along a fence or wall. Or try the more fanciful formal espaliers shown below; even the smallest garden can easily accommodate several. If well cared for, they look good all year, from spring bloom through fall harvest.

FORMAL ESPALIERS: LIVING GEOMETRY

Double U-shaped

Candelabra

Belgian fence

Belgian doublet

Belgian arch

Fan

PROTECT

Once you have your garden just the way you want it, watch for those curve balls that nature can send to your region. Fire, frost, hot sun, wind—even birds and squirrels can damage your garden plants, unless you take steps to protect them. For pests, diseases, and weeds, see pages 726–737.

FIRE

In wilderness plant communities such as chaparral, oak woodland, and forest, wildfires are part of the natural cycle, clearing out dead and diseased plants and helping some seeds to germinate. But your house doesn't have to sit in a forest to be vulnerable to wildfire. Wind-blown embers can fly up to a mile in front of a fire. If they land on, say, a dried-out juniper in your yard, you can be in big trouble.

That's why, if you live in a wildfire-prone part of the West, the first thing you need to do is create a fire-resistant space around your house. Think of

the first 30 feet from your house as the Garden Zone. If you're seeking maximum fire protection, areas close to your house (to 5 feet out) should emphasize hard-scaping. From there, continue paths, patios, and other hardscaping, as well as well-watered plants and fire-resistant ones such as succulents.

From 30 to 100 feet out is the Green-belt Zone, with low-growing perennials, and shrubs clustered into islands. Plant trees far enough apart—and trim them—so that flames can't spread from one to the next. The final step? Thin, mow, and rake your property so it stays fire-resistant.

Barrel cactus and agaves cluster on this San Diego slope; decomposed granite mulch surrounds them. Watered greenbelt is up top, around the house.

Fire-Resistant Zones

1. TRIM TREE BRANCHES at least 10 feet from the chimney; cut back any trees overhanging the roof.

2. IN THE GARDEN ZONE, keep grass watered and mowed to, at most, 4 inches.

5. FOR MAXIMUM SAFETY, plant sparingly within 3 to 5 feet of your house.

4. IN THE GREENBELT ZONE, don't let perennials and shrubs grow taller than 18 inches.

3. THIN AND SEPARATE TREES by two times their height. Don't plant shrubs or vines beneath them.

Fire-Resistant Plants

Low-growing herbaceous perennials are your best defense near the house; choose low-fuel-volume types such as African daisy, creeping maho-nia, ice plant (*Delosperma*), stone-crops, monkey flower, and yarrow. Fleshy succulents such as agaves, crassulas, and *Senecio mandraliscae* are other good choices. When well irrigated and pruned, these ground-covers listed below burn more slowly than wild chaparral. Deep roots help stabilize slopes.

AARON'S BEARD
(*Hypericum calycinum*)

CALIFORNIA WILD LILAC
(*Ceanothus gloriosus, Ceanothus griseus horizontalis*)

MANZANITA
(*Arctostaphylos* species)

PROSTRATE ROSEMARY
(*Rosmarinus officinalis* 'Prostratus')

SAGELEAF ROCKROSE
(*Cistus salviifolius*)

FROST

The best defense against cold damage is to choose permanent plants that are hardy in your zone. Use tender plants for summer displays, or plant them in containers and move them indoors in winter. Also, learn your garden's cold pockets.

To some extent, you can condition plants and soil for cold weather. Water and fertilize in late spring and early summer, while plants are growing the fastest. In late summer, taper off nitrogen feeding; don't stimulate new growth that won't have time to mature (harden off) before cold weather arrives. Keep soil moist through the onset of the frost season, as damp soil holds more heat than dry soil.

An early-fall or late-spring frost is more damaging than one striking when plants are semidormant or dormant. Be alert for still air, clear skies, low humidity, and, of course, low temperatures. Check weather bulletins as well. Then take steps to protect your garden's most vulnerable plants. Where ground freezes hard and temperatures drop below 0°F (−18°C), many roses and broad-leafed evergreens need protection to survive.

Glass cloches, available from mail-order seed catalogs, fit over the tops of plants, forming one-plant greenhouses that can save your crops on cold nights.

Move container plants indoors and give tender in-ground plants temporary shelter to protect them from unseasonal frosts (drape burlap over four tall stakes placed around a young citrus tree, for instance).

Buy or build a cold frame to protect tender young seedlings. Basically a wood box with a transparent lid, it acts as a passive solar energy collector and reservoir. During the day, the sun's rays heat the air and soil in the frame; at night, the heat absorbed by the soil radiates out, keeping the plants warm.

Avoid cutting back frost-damaged plants too soon after a killing frost, or you'll most likely stimulate tender new growth that will be nipped by later frosts. Wait until new growth begins in spring to remove wood that you can see is clearly dead.

HOT SUN

Too much sun can damage plants, especially seedlings or transplants that have recently undergone changes in growing conditions. Signs of damage include scorched leaves, leaf drop, blistered fruit, split bark. Plants that face south or southwest, or those that get full hot afternooon sun, are most in danger of sunburn, as are those beside heat-reflecting paving.

Protect young seedlings of flowering annuals and perennials until they establish roots in the ground. Use shade cloth or floating row covers.

Protect the bark of young trees by wrapping them with bamboo mats. Protect avocado and citrus trees that have recently been pruned from sunburn by painting the trunks or branches white.

Protect bud unions by planting grafted trees with the bud union (where the tree has been grafted onto the rootstock) facing away from afternoon sun.

Irrigate plants before a predicted heat wave arrives. On warm summer days, plants wilt because their leaves lose water faster than their roots can take it up. During the night, the plants recover—if roots have water to absorb. Water deeply so that plants can recover from an extremely hot day.

Birds

To protect fruit trees, berry bushes, and other plants from birds and squirrels, use netting or screen. Broad mesh (¾ inch) nylon or plastic netting is popular for trees, since it readily admits air, water, and sunlight. Enclose trees with netting two or three weeks before fruit ripens, tying it around the trunk beneath the lowest branches or securing it to the ground so birds can't find an opening. For ground-level crops such as strawberries, you can drape lightweight plastic netting directly over the plants or make wooden frames and drape netting over them.

WIND

Strong winds can cause severe damage in gardens. Foliage dries out, tree limbs can break, or—worse—trees with dense canopies can blow over. To protect your plants:

Stake young or newly planted trees Tie loosely, using flexible ties.

Thin dense tree canopies These can act like sails that catch the wind, causing limbs to break or the tree to blow over. (You should be able to see light through the canopy.) If necessary, call in an arborist to point out any other tree hazards on your property.

Mulch around plants This will prevent excess drying of soil. Soak the mulch before winds arrive so it won't blow away.

Water After a strong wind, irrigate trees, shrubs, and newly planted lawns.

Manage Pests

A healthy garden hosts abundant life, including insects and wildlife. Most of these share the garden without causing problems. Many are welcome visitors, performing vital functions such as pollinating plants; feeding on undesirable insects; and helping to break down plant matter, building soils and recycling nutrients. But some are pests that feed on and injure plants.

Approach pests with Integrated Pest Management (IPM), a philosophy whose primary aim is prevention. IPM uses biological, cultural, and physical controls to help avoid serious insect, disease, and other pest problems and to reduce pests' effects to tolerable levels. Chemical controls using pesticides are employed only as a last resort.

IPM begins with good cultural practices. Choose plants that are adapted to your climate and garden conditions. Buy varieties that are resistant to diseases or unpalatable to pests. Prepare planting beds well, and periodically amend the soil with organic matter to improve conditions for root growth. Water and fertilize appropriately to promote healthy plants. Check plants frequently to spot problems before they get out of hand.

1 PHYSICAL CONTROLS

Physical controls include actions that directly kill, deter, or capture pests.

Handpick to destroy snails, caterpillars, insect egg masses, and other pests that you find among the plants. Take care to leave the lady beetle larvae and other beneficial insects that are sometimes mistaken as pests.

Prune and destroy branches, canes, and other plant tissues that show evidence of actively developing pests such as borers, scales, or fire blight, and any plant diseases.

Spray plants with a strong jet of water to dislodge or kill small insects such as aphids, thrips, and spider mites.

NATURAL PESTICIDES

Natural pesticides are products whose active ingredients originate in a plant, animal, or mineral, or whose action results from a biological process. "Natural" does not mean harmless; some natural products can still harm people, pets, or plants if they are used incorrectly, and most of them will kill beneficial insects along with the pests.

When using any pesticide, read the label carefully and follow the manufacturer's directions exactly. The label will clearly state the plants and pests for which the control can be used.

Bacillus thuringiensis (Bt) is a naturally occurring bacterium. Several strains exist; each targets different kinds of insects. The most common, *Bt kurstaki*, controls leaf-feeding caterpillars.

Diatomaceous earth (DE) is a powdery substance made from the skeletons of microscopic marine organisms. It damages the protective coats of invertebrate pests such as ants, slugs, and snails, but must be kept dry to be effective. Use the horticultural product, not the one intended for swimming pool filters. Wear a mask during application.

Food-grade oils and extracts are commercial versions of homemade repellents and pesticides that gardeners have relied on for centuries. Active ingredients include citrus peels, garlic, and hot pepper. Effectiveness varies.

Horticultural oils are typically highly refined petroleum oils. Botanical oils are derived from plants, such as citrus peels or seeds of neem or soybean. Oils act on contact by smothering aphids, mites, whiteflies, scales, and other insects. Do not apply oils when plants are under drought stress and temperatures are high.

Insecticidal soap is made from potassium salts of fatty acids from plants and animals. Soaps work on contact against aphids, mealybugs, mites, scales, thrips, and whiteflies. Hard water inactivates the soap, so mix the concentrate with soft water, distilled water, or rainwater. Avoid using dish detergents.

Neem oil (Azadirachtin) is from a tropical tree (*Azadirachta indica*). Effective against aphids, beetles, caterpillars, mealybugs, mites, thrips, whiteflies, and powdery mildew.

Pyrethrins are derived from the dried flowers of *Tanacetum cinerariifolium*. Lethal to many pests. They break down quickly in sunlight; apply after sundown.

Spinosad is made from the extracts of a soil microbe, *Saccharopolyspora spinosa*. It controls caterpillars, thrips, and some beetles and sawflies. Although relatively selective, it kills some beneficial species.

Sulfur is dusted or sprayed over plants to control mites and psyllids as well as some plant diseases. Do not use in conjunction with horticultural oils or when air temperature is above 85°F (29°C).

Barriers deter pests. These may range from a high, continuous fence around an entire garden to row covers protecting a bed of plants.

Repel pests, such as aphids, thrips, and whiteflies, by planting through reflective, foil-like mulch.

Rotate the location of plants in your garden from season to season. This is particularly helpful for reducing plant diseases and root-feeding insects.

Trap to capture and monitor pests. Look during the day under pots or trap boards, and scrape any snails or slugs into a bucket of soapy water. Yellow sticky cards can capture flying insects such as whiteflies and aphids. Damp newspaper or other cover can concentrate slugs and earwigs that seek daytime shelter. Adults of some moths can be captured with pheromone traps that include as a lure the chemicals used by the female moth to attract a mate. Such traps are particularly useful in helping you know when to spray for fruit insects, such as codling moth in apples.

2 BIOLOGICAL CONTROLS

Every garden has a homegrown army of pest controls—predators, parasites, and beneficial pathogens that feed on garden pests; six garden "good guys" are profiled at right. To help increase beneficial populations, avoid using persistent pesticides and grow a diversity of plants. Many of these beneficials can be encouraged by planting flowers that provide nectar and pollen. Birds, toads, and garter snakes all prey on insects.

Spiders all feed on insects and can provide tremendous benefits in plant protection. Other insects, such as parasitic wasps and tachinid flies, lay eggs onto or inside of pests; as the larvae develop, they kill the pest.

Parasitic nematodes are microscopic roundworms that kill insects through introducing a bacterium into their body. Nematodes (which generally must be mail-ordered and applied) can help control pests that spend part of their lives in the soil, such as white grubs, root weevils, and cutworms.

BENEFICIAL INSECTS

Encourage beneficial insects by planting nectar-rich flowers (see page 106). Visit *anbp.org* for sources of beneficial insects.

Assassin bug

Damsel bug

Lacewing

Lady beetle

Assassin bugs. Slim ½–¾-inch-long insects; may be red, black, brown, or gray. They feed on a wide variety of pests.

Damsel bugs. Dull gray or brown, ½-inch-long, very slender insects with long, narrow heads. Nymphs resemble the adults but are smaller and have no wings. Both nymphs and adults feed on aphids, leafhoppers, and small worms.

Ground beetles. Shiny black, ½–1-inch-long insects. The smaller species eat other insects, caterpillars, cutworms, and grubs; some larger species prey on slugs and snails and their eggs.

Lacewings. The adults are 1-inch-long flying insects that feed only on nectar, pollen, and honeydew; but the larvae, which resemble ½-inch-long alligators, devour aphids, leafhoppers, and thrips, as well as mites. Larvae are commercially available.

Lady beetles. Adults and their larvae (which look like ¼-inch-long alligators) feed on aphids, mealybugs, and insect eggs. You can buy the aphid-eating convergent lady beetle, but these must be released repeatedly and most soon fly away. Freeing them in large numbers at night after first wetting foliage may encourage them to stay a while.

Trichogramma wasps. These very tiny parasitoid wasps attack the eggs of caterpillar pests. Commercially available species are adapted for gardens or for fruit trees. Because they are short-lived, repeated releases may be needed.

PLANT PESTS

PEST	MANAGEMENT
Ants	
Most ants don't damage plants, but some species protect sap-sucking insects—such as aphids, mealybugs, soft scales, and whiteflies—for the honeydew they produce. Sooty mold may develop from honeydew (see page 733).	Place sticky barriers around tree and shrub trunks; prune off branches that touch the ground. Insecticide baits can eliminate colonies but are deliberately slow-acting so ants will carry the insecticide to their underground colony. Which ant baits are effective varies depending on the ant species and situation. Insecticide treatments are usually short-lived.
Aphids	
Soft-bodied, rounded insects that range from pin- to match-head size. May be black, white, pink, or pale green. They cluster on new growth, sucking plant juices. Some kinds transmit viral diseases. Aphids remove sap, causing wilted, discolored, and/or stunted leaves. Sooty mold may develop from honeydew (see page 733).	Don't overfertilize or overwater; aphids thrive on succulent growth. Use floating row covers and reflective mulch to prevent infestation of small plants. Encourage beneficials. Hose aphids off with a blast of water. Spray with insecticidal soap, horticultural oil (overwintering eggs), or pyrethrins. Many synthetic pesticides are effective but usually not necessary.
Borers	
Larvae of beetles or moths; tunnel into branches, trunk, or roots of woody plants. Attracted to weakened, injured, or stressed plants, restricting water and nutrient flow, killing, deforming, or weakening branches or limbs.	Encourage healthy plant growth. Avoid wounding susceptible species. Prune out infested limbs before beetles emerge as adults. Preventive sprays of pyrethroids or carbaryl may control egg-laying adults but not borers inside plants. Imidacloprid can be effective against some types (check product label).
Caterpillars (including tobacco budworm, hornworms, cabbageworms)	
Soft-bodied crawling insects, often striped or spotted. Chew leaves or tunnel through buds and blossoms.	Handpick, especially at dusk or in early morning. Spray with *Bacillus thuringiensis* (Bt), pyrethrins, or spinosad. Synthetics, such as carbaryl and the systemic neonicotinoid clothianidin, are also effective.
Cucumber Beetles	
Oval-shaped, greenish yellow beetles with black spots or stripes. They eat all parts of cucumbers, squash, and melons. Spotted beetles also feed on roses. The beetles transmit bacterial wilt, which attacks cucumbers, and other diseases. Underground larvae may damage roots.	Handpick and destroy. Vacuum beetles from plants; dispose of bag. Use floating row cover before plants become infested. Encourage birds, soldier beetles, and tachinid flies. Apply parasitic nematodes to moist soil, spray plants with pyrethrins or appropriately labeled synthetics (e.g., pyrethroids or neonicotinoids).
Cutworms	
Dull brownish, hairless caterpillars that live in the soil and cut off stems of seedlings at ground level. Some kinds climb into plants and eat leaves.	Clear and till beds to destroy cutworms. Use protective collars or spread diatomaceous earth around stems of young seedlings. Handpick at night when the cutworms are active. Release parasitic nematodes or use *Bacillus thuringiensis* (Bt) or appropriately labeled synthetics (e.g., pyrethroids).
Earwigs	
These familiar pests aren't all bad—they also prey on aphids and other insects. They feed on tender new growth of many plants, especially flowers and vegetables.	Keep the garden clean, removing hiding places such as weedy areas and dead foliage. Trap and drown them in a low-sided can with ½ inch of tuna fish oil or vegetable oil with a drop of bacon grease. Set traps of rolled newspaper, corrugated cardboard, or hose pieces and dispose of earwigs in soapy water or sealed bags. Use pyrethroids or carbaryl bait.

PLANT PESTS

PEST		MANAGEMENT
Flea Beetles		
	Very small, shiny, oval beetles that jump like fleas. May be blue-black, brown, or bronze. Adult beetles riddle leaves with small holes. They feed on many vegetable crops and seedlings, especially cabbage and potato-family plants. Vigorous older plants usually survive.	Remove dead or damaged leaves and plants. Till the soil in fall. Plant in uninfested soil. Use floating row covers. Spray with neem. Spread diatomaceous earth. Use pyrethroids and other appropriately labeled synthetics.
Grasshoppers		
	Also called locusts. Adults are 1–2 inches long and may be brown, green, or yellow. Newly hatched nymphs resemble adults, but are wingless and smaller and feed voraciously. During their periodic outbreaks, they can cause severe damage, defoliating most plants.	Difficult. Handpick. Use floating row covers. If grasshoppers migrating in are expected or have been a problem in previous years, consider applying to uncultivated border vegetation a carbaryl bait or try the biological control *Nosema locustae*. Mobility restricts effectiveness of most insecticides.
Leaf Miners		
	A catchall term for certain moth, beetle, and fly larvae that tunnel within plant leaves, leaving a nearly transparent trail on the surface. Damage is mostly cosmetic, although yield of some crops may be reduced.	Plant vegetables under floating row covers. Remove debris, where pupae overwinter, and till the soil. Pick off and destroy infested leaves; use yellow sticky traps to catch adults. Spray with neem or spinosad to discourage adults from laying eggs; once the larvae are inside the leaves, most sprays are not effective. Systemics may be effective.
Mealybugs		
	Have an oval body with overlapping soft plates and a white, cottony covering. They move around slowly. They suck plant juices, causing stunting. Sooty mold may develop from honeydew (see page 733). In warm climates, they target a wide range of plants, but azaleas, hibiscus, and citrus trees of all kinds are prime targets.	Control ants (see page 728), which nurture mealybugs. Encourage or release beneficials. Dab pests with a cotton swab dipped in rubbing alcohol. Horticultural oils, insecticidal soap, pyrethrins, neem, and appropriately labeled synthetics are also effective.
Mites		
	Tiny spider relatives found on leaf undersides. Webbing is often present where they live. Mites suck plant juices; the damaged leaf surface is pale and stippled, and the leaves often turn brown, dry out, and die. Drought-stressed plants are prime targets.	To check plants for mites, hold a piece of white paper under the affected foliage and briskly tap it. The pepper-like pests will drop onto the paper. Don't let plants dry out. Mist foliage undersides frequently with water. Release predatory mites, which feed on the harmful mites. Spray with insecticidal soap, horticultural oil, neem, or sulfur.
Pill Bugs and Sowbugs		
	Soil-dwelling crustaceans. When disturbed, pillbugs roll up into balls about the size of a large pea; sowbugs are usually gray and don't roll up. Both pests eat decaying vegetation (which they help break down into humus), very young seedlings, the skins of melons and cucumbers, and berries.	Limit moisture and decaying matter. Water early in the day so the soil dries by evening and use drip or furrow irrigation instead of sprinklers. Use raised beds or planting boxes. Apply pyrethroids.
Root Weevils		
	Many species of long-snouted, hard-shelled insects, including the troublesome black vine weevils and (in lawns) billbugs. Adult black vine weevils feed on leaves, flowers, and bark of rhododendron, grape, and other plants; larvae consume roots. Billbugs target lawns. Larvae eat grass roots, leaving small circles of yellowish turf.	Keep planting beds free of debris, especially around plants' crowns, where adults overwinter. To help prevent billbug infestation, improve soil drainage or replace grass with plants that thrive in damp soil. Trap adult weevils in late May with sticky traps or by shaking plants in the evening and gathering fallen insects. Control larvae with parasitic nematodes.

»

PLANT PESTS (continued)

PEST	MANAGEMENT
Scales	
Classified as "armored" (hard) or soft. In spring or summer, young scales ("crawlers") emerge. Adult scale insects have a waxy, scalelike covering. As scales suck out plant juices, yellow spots appear on foliage, and leaves may drop off. If the infestation is left unchecked, the whole plant turns sickly and stunted.	Difficult to control. Encourage lady beetles and parasitic wasps that kill scales. Control ants (see page 728), which often protect soft scales. Horticultural oil and insecticidal soap will help control crawlers, as will appropriately labeled synthetics. If applied early before the problem gets bad, imidacloprid is effective against some types, but it does not control armored scales.
Snails and Slugs	
Night-feeding mollusks. Snails have shells; slugs do not. Both feast on the seedlings and leaves of many plants. They hide by day, though they may be active on gray or rainy days. Regularly search their day-hiding places and crush them or scoop them into soapy water.	Minimize garden clutter and keep organic litter and mulch back from plants during wet weather. Trap and dispose of pests. Wrap copper strip barriers around raised beds and tree trunks. Keep the copper clean. Set out shallow containers filled with beer to drown the pests. Use bait containing iron phosphate. (Baits containing metaldehyde are a hazard to pets.)
Thrips	
Tiny, elongated insects that suck plant tissue. In heavy infestations, both flowers and leaves are discolored and fail to open normally. Leaves may take on a silvery or tan cast. Greenhouse thrips feed in a group and leave small black droppings on leaves.	Use row covers or reflective mulches before plants become infested. Clip off and destroy infected plant parts. Encourage beneficials. Spray with insecticidal soap, horticultural oil, pyrethrins, spinosad, neem, or appropriately labeled synthetics, including systemics.
Whiteflies	
Adults are tiny white pests that fly up in a cloud when disturbed. The nymphs and adults suck plant juices from leaf undersides. Foliage may show yellow stippling, curl, and turn brown. Some kinds transmit plant virus diseases.	Use floating row covers and/or reflective mulch before plants are infested. For greenhouse infestations, release *Encarsia formosa*, a predatory wasp, or use sticky yellow traps. Spray leaves with strong jets of water, insecticidal soap, oils, or neem. Imidacloprid can be effective.

3 SYNTHETIC PESTICIDES

Many of the older synthetic insecticides have been removed from the market due to environmental contamination and concerns about their effects on animals and human health. They have been replaced with pesticides of natural origin (see page 726) and with new classes of synthetic pesticides, such as neonicotinoids and pyrethroids (bifenthrin, permethrin, cyfluthrin, and esfenvalerate).

While natural pesticides degrade quickly, these insecticides kill insects that contact or eat sprayed foliage for days or weeks after their application. They are more toxic to beneficial insect pollinators, predators, and parasites, and some cause problems due to contamination of surface waters.

Some synthetic pesticides applied to the soil are absorbed by roots and moved systemically throughout the plant. Pesticides formulated as baits (combined with an attractant) can be particularly selective in their effects.

Systemic insecticides that are absorbed by the plant and moved with its tissues include acephate, an organophosphate, sprayed onto nonedibles only. Neonicotinoids (such as imidacloprid) include some that can be used on edibles (check label), and are applied to soil as a granule or liquid and absorbed by roots. Some formulations can also be applied to the foliage. These systemics are mostly effective as long-lasting preventatives, applied before pests are established. To protect beneficial insects, do not apply systemics prior to or during bloom.

Storage and Disposal of Pesticides

Store pesticides where they can be locked away from children and pets and separate from food. Buy only the amount that you need, and never mix more pesticide solution than you need. Never pour pesticides down the sink, the toilet, or a storm drain, as this will pollute surface waters. The only legal way to dispose of pesticides is to take them to your local household hazardous waste facility. Only completely empty home-use pesticide containers may be disposed of in the trash. Contact your city or county public works department or your local waste disposal company for information.

ANIMAL PESTS

Most gardeners welcome some wildlife into their yards. (See page 712 for ways to attract wildlife.) Certain birds and animals, however, can cause significant damage to plants. Some of the worst trouble-makers are described here, with suggestions for control. Check with your local Cooperative Extension Office for more information. Serious problems often require professional help.

Deer. Hungry deer can eat most of a harvest in just a few hours. An 8-foot-tall fence is optimal, but a 6-foot fence may suffice if the ground slopes downhill outside the fence. Because deer cannot high-jump and broad-jump at the same time, a horizontal "outrigger" extension on the top of a fence makes it harder for deer to clear. Parallel 5-foot-tall fences 4 feet apart have the same effect. Electric fencing also works, as may motion-activated sprinklers and commercial deer repellents (but keep the latter off crops unless the label says otherwise).

Gophers and moles. Gophers feed on roots, bulbs, and occasionally foliage. They leave mounds of soil, usually with visible entry holes. Moles eat earthworms and grubs, not plants, but they often tunnel just below the surface, uprooting or damaging young plants. Their mounds have no visible entry holes. To protect individual plants from gophers or moles, line the sides and bottom of planting holes with ½-inch mesh hardware cloth, or plant in raised beds whose bottoms are lined with hardware cloth. Trap if necessary.

Rabbits. These opportunists sneak into gardens to eat young seedlings and tender shoots, as well as many vegetables. Stop them by putting a wire-mesh fence around your vegetables.

Raccoons. These bandits are most active at night and have a special taste for corn, melons, and berries. But they're opportunists, and they'll even bite into tender zucchini. Wire-mesh fences or single-strand electric fences can exclude them.

Tree squirrels. Tree squirrels feed on fruits, nuts, vegetables, tender shoots, and bark. Cover berry vines, fruits, and tomato plants with bird netting. Protect low-growing container crops with wire baskets.

Voles. They feed on vegetables, grasses, bulbs, and tubers, and gnaw on the bark of trees, just above or below ground. Voles live in shallow burrows but travel in aboveground runways hidden beneath plants. Protect the lower trunks of shrubs and young trees with hardware-cloth cylinders (bury the bottom edges so voles can't dig beneath them).

Rabbit

Raccoon

Deer

Squirrel

Gopher

Vole

Manage Diseases

The Integrated Pest Management (IPM) approach applies to diseases as well as pests. IPM aims to maintain a productive garden with minimal use of synthetic controls. The goal is to reduce diseases to tolerable levels.

All plant diseases are caused by three kinds of organisms: fungus, bacteria, and viruses. Any of the three may be responsible for leaf, stem, and flower diseases, but the vast majority of soil-borne diseases are caused by fungus. Note that often what appears to be a disease is actually a result of cultural problems, such as nutrient deficiency (or excess), sunscald, or soil compaction.

Because many diseases cannot be eradicated once their symptoms are apparent, prevention is of prime impor-tance. Choose certified and disease-free plants, and, whenever possible, plant resistant varieties. Many are noted in the entries in the encyclopedia, or con-sult your Cooperative Extension Office. "Resistant" does not mean immune; it means a plant is less likely to succumb.

If diseases do appear in your garden, immediately remove infected annuals and vegetables to keep the problem from spreading. On larger plants, includ-ing perennials, remove diseased flowers, leaves, and, if possible, branches.

1 NATURAL PRODUCTS

Natural disease controls include baking soda, which helps to control powdery mildew; biofungicides (such as *Bacillus subtilis*), copper compounds, copper soaps, garlic solutions, neem oil, potas-sium bicarbonate, and sulfur (do not use in conjunction with horticultural oil sprays or when the outdoor temperature is above 85°F/29°C). The package will clearly state the plants and diseases for which the product should be used if the substance is not subject to registration.

2 SYNTHETIC PRODUCTS

The most common synthetic fungicides include chlorothalonil and myclobutanil, both labeled for some edibles, and the systemics tebuconazole and triforine. Be sure to read all manufacturer's instruc-tions before applying any synthetic fungi-cide to your garden. Make sure the plant to be sprayed and the disease to be treated are on the label.

PLANT DISEASES

Many diseases exhibit similar symptoms. If you are unsure of a diagnosis, contact your local Cooperative Extension Office for help.

	DISEASE	PREVENTION AND CONTROL
	Anthracnose A fungal disease that affects many different plants, both edible and ornamental, but seldom kills them. Sunken, gray, or tan to dark brown spots on leaves, stems, fruit, or twigs. Leaves wither and drop. Spores that cause it are spread by rain and garden sprinkling.	Plant resistant varieties. Clip off affected plant parts and destroy them. Avoid overhead watering, mulch the soil, and provide good air circulation around plants. Keep infected plants growing vigorously. Apply copper compounds or chlorothalonil.
	Damping Off Various soil fungus that cause seeds to rot in the soil before they sprout or cause seedlings to collapse at or near the soil surface. Most common in poorly drained or too-wet soils.	Improve drainage and reduce watering. Treat seeds, potting soil, or seedlings with a biological fungicide or buy pretreated seeds. Avoid planting in too-cold soils. Use sterilized medium and containers. Provide good air circulation. Thin crowded seedlings. Discard infected seedlings and starting medium.
	Fireblight Bacterial disease that affects pome-producing mem-bers of the rose family, including apple, cotoneaster, crabapple, hawthorn, pear, pyracantha, quince, and toyon. Shoots (and sometimes entire plants) blacken, appear scorched, and die suddenly. Appears in moist weather, especially early spring. Spread by insects, splashing water.	Plant resistant varieties. Using disinfected pruners, remove and discard diseased branches, cutting 6–8 inches below blighted tissue. Spray at 3–5-day inter-vals during the bloom season with copper compounds.

PLANT DISEASES

	DISEASE	PREVENTION AND CONTROL
	Oak Root Fungus	
	A disease that destroys woody plants, especially native oaks. Symptoms may not appear until the disease is well established, then plants suddenly wilt and die. Early indicators are patches of dull or yellowed leaves and/or sparse foliage. Look for whitish fungal tissue or dark shoestring-like structures under the bark near trunk bases and for tan mushrooms.	Plant resistant species. Excavate soil from the base of the plant so it can dry out. Remove turf grass or other plants that are growing within 6–10 feet of the trunk. Water only as much as necessary. Replace infected plants. Let the soil dry out thoroughly before replanting. There are no effective chemical controls.
	Peach Leaf Curl	
	Fungal disease that affects leaves, shoots, twigs, blossoms, and fruit of peaches and nectarines. In spring, thick, puckered reddish areas appear on leaves, which turn velvety and yellowish gray in color. Leaves eventually turn yellow or brown and drop. Tree growth and fruit production may decrease. Affected shoots become thickened and distorted and often die.	Plant resistant varieties. Minimize stress with proper water and fertilizer. Prune and spray trees each autumn after the leaves have fallen, or just before bud-break in spring. Use a copper-based fungicide (some types may be combined with oil to improve coverage; check label) or chlorothalonil as a dormant spray.
	Powdery Mildew	
	Fungal disease that causes a white, powdery coating on leaves, stems, buds, and fruits. New growth and blossoms may be stunted. Most powdery mildews thrive in humid air, but the spores—unlike those of other fungus—need dry surfaces.	Plant resistant varieties. Give plants sufficient light and air circulation. Spray with jets of water early in the day. Spray with biofungicide *Bacillus subtilis*, baking soda mixtures, neem, horticultural oils, sulfur, or copper soap fungicide. Apply an antitranspirant. Several synthetic fungicides are labeled for powdery mildew.
	Root Rots and Water Molds	
	Fungal diseases active in warm soils, but can lie dormant in cool conditions. Plants wilt, and their leaves discolor, become stunted, and drop prematurely. Branches or even the entire plant may die.	Plant resistant varieties. Remove and destroy dead plants or branches. Improve drainage or plant in raised beds. Do not overwater. Also inspect roots at the nursery so you don't purchase root-rot-infected plants. There are also fungicides that will control some root-rot organisms.
	Rust	
	Various fungal diseases, many plant-specific, that cause powdery pustules to form on undersides of leaves. Upper surfaces may be spotted with yellow; eventually the whole leaf may discolor, then drop.	Plant resistant varieties. Remove and destroy infected leaves or badly infected plants. Provide good air circulation. In winter, clean up all debris. Avoid overhead watering. Spray with a garlic-based or copper soap fungicide, *Bacillus subtilis*, or an appropriately labeled synthetic fungicide.
	Sooty Mold	
	Fungus that grows on honeydew produced by sap-sucking insects. The fungus itself does not injure plants but can block sun from the leaves, which may then turn yellow and drop prematurely.	Wash or wipe the fungus from leaves. Prune to open canopy. Control honeydew-excreting insects (see page 728), such as aphids, scales, and whiteflies. Also control ants.
	Verticillium and Fusarium Wilts	
	A long-lived, soilborne fungus that plugs the water-conducting tissues in crops such as tomatoes and strawberries, and in woody plants. One side of the plant may wilt and die. Leaves, then branches, turn yellow or brown, then die. Small plants may be destroyed in one season; mature trees may survive longer.	Plant resistant varieties. Dig up and destroy infected crops, and prune out dead branches. Give deep but infrequent irrigation. Rotate crops, or grow in containers or raised beds filled with sterile soil. Soil solarization may destroy the fungus (see page 735).

Manage Weeds

Weeds are plants that grow where gardeners don't want them to grow. They rob desirable plants of water, nutrients, and sunlight; they may harbor insects and diseases. Some spread so aggressively that they jump garden fences to invade wildland. Others might be weedy in one region but well-behaved garden plants elsewhere.

Annual weeds grow shoots and leaves, flower, set seed, and die within a year. Most are summer annuals, germinating in spring or summer and dying by fall. Winter annual weeds begin growth in fall or early winter, then set seed in early spring while the weather is still cool. There are exceptions, however. Weeds such as yellow starthistle (*Centaurea solstitialis*) are winter annuals that flower in summer and set seed in late summer to fall. Biennial weeds produce a cluster or rosette of leaves in their first year of growth, and in the following year, they flower, set seed, and die.

Both annuals and biennials reproduce by seed. Most perennial weeds, which live for several years, also reproduce by seed, but weedy plants such as giant reed (*Arundo donax*) and Bermuda buttercup (*Oxalis pes-caprae*) do not produce any viable seed. Once they mature, however, they produce large deep root crowns or taproots, or structures that allow them to spread, including stolons, rhizomes, bulbs, tubers, or even creeping roots. These structures make control of perennials more difficult.

When is a plant labeled a weed? That depends. Common yarrow is an annoying weed in lawns but a useful ornamental in beds. Some asters spread so aggressively that they're thought of as weeds. Bindweed and yellow *Oxalis* are weeds wherever they grow.

1 NONCHEMICAL CONTROLS

It is rarely possible to eradicate weeds entirely, but you can substantially reduce infestations.

Hand pull or hoe. For perennial weeds that have passed the seedling stage, it's usually necessary to dig out their roots, or the weeds can resprout from fragments left behind. You'll probably need to repeat the process several times to manage perennial weeds. Don't leave pulled or hoed-out weeds on bare ground, particularly when it is moist, as they can take root again. Toss leafy annual or biennial types that do not yet have flowers or seeds into the compost pile, along with the top growth of perennial weeds (before seeding). But roots of perennials, such as dandelions, should go into the trash, as should any weeds that have set seed.

Rototill. Use this technique for annual and biennial weeds in larger areas, such as orchards and plots intended for future gardens. However, the soil must be fairly dry when using this technique and then be allowed to completely dry out to prevent plants from resprouting. This method knocks down weeds and mixes them into the soil, where they eventually decay to form humus. Perennial weeds, however, usually sprout again from the roots or crowns, and some kinds even grow more abundantly after tilling, when the vegetative reproductive structures are fragmented.

Mow. Use a rotary mower or string trimmer for seasonal annual weed control in larger areas. Both tools cut the weeds. String trimmers leave the severed tops

Pampas grass (*Cortaderia*) sends its seeds to the wind and invades wildland.

behind, while mowers grind them up as they cut them. These methods are effective for reducing weeds in fire-prone areas.

Smother. Cover weeds in areas earmarked for future planting. After mowing or cutting off the top growth, put down a layer of heavy cardboard, newspapers (at least three dozen sheets thick), or black plastic. Overlap the material so weeds can't grow through the cracks. Anchor the covering with a layer of bark chips or other organic mulch. Leave these smothering materials in place for at least a full growing season. Allow a year or more for tough or perennial weeds.

Presprout. In parts of the garden plagued by weeds, especially if you're planning to plant vegetables, perennial beds, or a new lawn there, use this method: Add needed amendments, till the soil, water it, and wait a week or two for weed seeds to germinate. When they're only a few inches high, scrape them away or hand-weed them out. Then sow or transplant your vegetables, flowers, or lawn, disturbing the soil as little as possible to avoid bringing more weed seeds to the surface.

Solarize. Use the sun to bake the soil's weed seeds as well as harmful fungus, bacteria, and some nematodes. The process (see box, far right) is carried out in summer and works best in regions that have hot, sunny weather for 4 to 8 weeks. Daytime temperatures above 80°F (27°C) are ideal. Solarization isn't effective in coastal climates with summer fog, nor does it work well in windy areas.

Apply a homemade spray.

Organic gardeners have myriad herbicide recipes that use ingredients straight from the kitchen or medicine chest. One effective formula consists of 1 tablespoon of dishwashing liquid and 1/4 cup of salt mixed with 1 quart of vinegar. You can also spray unwanted plants with isopropyl (rubbing) alcohol. A solution of 2 tablespoons per quart of water works for most weeds. For tougher ones, you may need to increase the amount of alcohol.

Regardless of the ingredients, apply the potion with a spray bottle and coat the plants thoroughly. Do the job on a hot, sunny, wind-free day, when herbicides are most effective.

Mulch. Once you've destroyed weeds, take steps to prevent their reappearance. Plant through landscape fabrics or mulch bare soil to deter weed growth.

2 NATURAL HERBICIDES

These are products whose active ingredient originate in a plant or mineral.

Corn gluten meal. Preemergence. Most often used to control weeds, especially crabgrass in lawns, but is also effective in garden beds. Also acts as a fertilizer. Relatively expensive. May take multiple applications over several years for full effectiveness.

Herbicidal soaps. Postemergence. Contact herbicides that degrade quickly. Made from selected fatty acids (as are insecticidal soaps), they kill top growth of young, actively growing weeds and are most effective on annual weeds.

Vinegar. Postemergence. Many organic-gardening catalogs sell vinegar-based herbicides, usually with soap and/or lemon juice added for extra sticking and penetrating power.

3 CHEMICAL CONTROLS

Herbicides are classified according to what stage of weed growth they affect, as well as by how they damage weeds.

Synthetic herbicides. These are manufactured compounds that do not normally occur in nature. They include preemergents, such as oryzalin, pendimethalin, and trifluralin; and postemergents like glyphosate and triclopyr, both of which are translocated systematically through the plant.

Synthetic herbicides are not recommended for food gardens. In home ornamental gardens, use them only when all other methods have failed. Beyond the potential risks they may pose to health and the environment, many of these chemicals can damage desirable plants if they drift through the air or run off in irrigation or rainwater. Some preemergence herbicides persist in the soil for long periods, injuring later plantings. And often the entire process of herbicide use—selecting a product, mixing and applying it, cleaning up—takes more effort than pulling or digging out weeds.

If you use herbicides, always make sure the product is safe for the desirable plants growing in and near the areas to be treated. Also keep in mind that you can be held responsible for any damage to neighboring properties resulting from herbicides you use.

Preemergence herbicides.

These inhibit the growth of germinating weed seeds and very young seedlings. They do not affect established plants. To be effective, they must be applied before the seeds sprout. Some preemergence products are formulated to kill germinating weeds in lawns. These may be sold

When using any herbicide, read the label directions carefully and follow them exactly. The package will clearly state the rates at which it should be applied, the weeds the product controls, as well as any other plants around which it can be safely used.

How to Solarize

CULTIVATE THE SOIL. Clear it of weeds, debris, and large clods of earth. Make a bed at least 2 feet wide, as narrower beds make it difficult to build up enough heat to have much effect.

RAKE THE BED LEVEL. Carve a small ditch around the perimeter. Soak the soil to a depth of 1 foot.

COVER WITH 1- TO 4-MIL CLEAR PLASTIC. Use UV-resistant plastic if it's available, as it won't break down during solarization. Stretch the plastic tightly so that it is in contact with the soil. Bury the edges in the perimeter ditch. An optional second layer of plastic increases heat and makes solarization more effective. Use soda cans as spacers between the two sheets.

LEAVE THE PLASTIC IN PLACE. Allow four to six weeks (eight weeks for persistent weeds) to pass, then remove it. Don't leave it down longer than eight weeks or soil structure may suffer. You can now plant. After planting, avoid cultivating more than the upper 2 inches of soil, as weed seeds at deeper levels may still be viable.

as "weeds-and-feeds." Such dual-purpose products should not be treated solely as fertilizers and reapplied whenever the lawn needs feeding. For that purpose, use a regular lawn fertilizer. Some preemergence products must be watered into the soil, while others are incorporated into it. Some may also harm seeds you sow later in the season.

Postemergence herbicides.

These act on growing weeds rather than on germinating seeds. Chemicals that are translocated like glyphosate must be absorbed by the plant through its leaves or stems; this kills the plant by interfering with specific biochemical pathways. Contact herbicides kill only the plant parts they touch—regrowth can still occur from underground reproductive parts or unsprayed buds. Some postemergence herbicides, such as glyphosate, will damage or kill any plant they touch, while others may be specific for grasses or broad-leafed plants. Use them very carefully around desirable plants; application timing is critical.

COMMON GARDEN WEEDS

	WEED	MANAGEMENT
	Annual Bluegrass (*Poa annua*)	
	Winter annual, though there are also perennial varieties. Forms a bright light green tuft of softly textured grass. Troublesome in lawns, flower borders, and winter vegetable crops.	Pull or dig when the plants are young. Appropriately labeled preemergence herbicides are effective when applied to turf in fall.
	Bermuda Grass (*Cynodon dactylon*)	
	A fine-textured, fast-growing perennial frequently planted as a lawn in warm climates. It spreads rapidly by underground stems, aboveground runners, and sometimes seed.	Use 8-inch-deep barriers to keep lawn contained. Dig up clumps in garden beds before they form sod, making sure to remove all the underground stems; any left behind can start new shoots. Soil solarization destroys seeds and shallow-growing rhizomes, but deep buried stems will survive. Ask nursery professional about herbicide options in beds and lawns.
	Blackberry (*Rubus* species)	
	Himalaya blackberry, *R. armeniacus* (*R. discolor* or *R. procera*), is the most vigorous of these perennial weeds, thriving in the mild, moist climates of Northern California, western Oregon and Washington. Plants spread by underground stems that send up new shoots. Birds enjoy the berries and scatter the seeds.	Pull young plants in spring before they develop a perennial root system. To kill established clumps, repeatedly prune back the stems as they sprout; this eventually exhausts the roots. Or mow the tops and dig out the roots. Herbicides labeled as brush killers can be effective.
	Burclover (*Medicago polymorpha*)	
	Winter annual in most areas. Low, spreading, broad-leafed weed with yellow flowers and spiny burs. Common in lawns and garden beds with nitrogen deficiency or excess phosphorus. Also troublesome in gravel paths and driveways.	Increase nitrogen fertilizing. Appropriately labeled preemergence and postemergence herbicides can be effective.
	Common Purslane (*Portulaca oleracea*)	
	A low-growing annual weed with fleshy stems and leaves and small yellow flowers. It thrives in moist conditions but can survive considerable drought. The seeds germinate in late spring.	Though common purslane is easy to pull or hoe, pieces of stem reroot readily, so be sure to remove them from the garden.
	Crabgrass (*Digitaria* species)	
	A shallow-rooted annual weed that grows in spring and summer, thriving in hot, moist areas. As the plant grows, it branches out at the base; stems can root where they touch the soil.	Crabgrass is most likely to be a problem in areas that receive frequent surface watering; infrequent deep watering of established plants can dry out the roots, killing or weakening the weed. Appropriately labeled preemergence and postemergence herbicides are effective.
	Dandelion (*Taraxacum officinale*)	
	Low-growing perennial with dark green, lobed leaves, a deep taproot, and bright yellow flowers. It reproduces both by seed and by any root fragment left in the soil.	Pull young plants before they flower, or take out the entire taproot of older plants to prevent regrowth. A healthy, vigorous lawn can outcompete this weed. Appropriately labeled preemergence and postemergence herbicides are effective in turf.

COMMON GARDEN WEEDS

WEED	MANAGEMENT
Field Bindweed (*Convolvulus arvensis*)	
Also called wild morning glory or bindweed. This perennial forms 1–4-ft.-long stems that crawl over the ground and twine over and around other plants. The trumpet-shaped flowers are white to pink.	Forms a deep, extensive root system, so hand-pulling seldom controls it—the stems break off, but the weed returns from the root. To kill it, cultivate or hoe every 6 weeks throughout the growing season. Soil solarization kills seeds but not roots. Systemic herbicides are effective.
Kikuyugrass (*Pennisetum clandestinum*)	
Perennial used as a lawn grass in some coastal areas, but has escaped cultivation to become a serious pest in lawns, ornamental beds, and even natural areas. Spreads rapidly by rhizomes and stolons, eventually forming an impenetrable mat of wiry stems. In Southern California, kikuyugrass also spreads by seed.	Contain turf with a strong barrier that extends 6–8 inches into the soil. Dig out of garden beds, removing as much of the root system as possible. Plan to repeat this process, as the grass will resprout from any rhizomes left in the soil. Spray with a postemergence herbicide that controls grassy weeds.
Mallow or Cheeseweed (*Malva* species)	
An annual in some climates, a biennial in others, sprouting in fall and setting seed the following summer. The plants grow quickly, ranging in height from a few inches to 4 feet tall.	Plants are easiest to pull when young; older plants develop a deep taproot.
Oxalis (*Oxalis corniculata*)	
An aggressive perennial that spreads quickly by seed. Small yellow flowers develop into long seed capsules that can propel seeds as far as 6 feet. Bermuda buttercup or cape oxalis (*O. pes-caprae*) is a larger relative that forms persistent bulbs but no viable seed.	Dig out small plants before—or as soon as—they flower. To manage cape oxalis, dig the whole plant in late winter, sifting through the soil to remove as many of the small bulbs as possible. Soil solarization may also help. Appropriately labeled preemergence and postemergence herbicides are effective in beds and turf.
Quackgrass (*Elymus repens repens*)	
This perennial weed can reach 3 feet tall and produces an extensive underground network of long, slender, branching, yellowish white rhizomes that can spread laterally 3–5 feet.	Because it reproduces readily from even small pieces of rhizome left in the soil, quackgrass is difficult to eliminate. Before planting, thoroughly dig the area and remove all visible pieces of rhizome. Spray postemergence herbicides labeled for grassy weeds. Spot-treat with glyphosate.
Spotted Spurge (*Euphorbia maculata*)	
This aggressive annual makes many seeds that may germinate immediately, producing several generations in one summer. Cut or broken stems exude a milky juice.	Hoe or pull out plants early in the season, before they bloom and set seed. Mulch to prevent seeds already in the soil from germinating. Spot-treat with herbicidal soap when plants are young. Appropriately labeled preemergence and postemergence herbicides are effective in beds and turf.
Yellow Nutsedge (*Cyperus esculentus*)	
This perennial weed resembles a grass, but its stems are solid and triangular in cross section. Spreads by small, roundish tubers (nutlets) at the tips of its roots as well as by seed.	Remove plants when they are still small. Older plants are mature enough to produce tubers that remain in the soil to sprout when you dig or pull the weed. Soil solarization is only partially effective. Ask nursery professional for herbicide options.

Demystifying Plant Names

Scientific (botanical) plant names can be intimidating to gardeners. So why have they been used around the world for hundreds of years? Why do we use them in this book? And why do the plants sold at nurseries so often have botanical names printed on their labels?

There's good reason: Common names for plants can be confusing or misleading. The same common name can refer to different plants in different parts of the country or the world. It can be used for two or more plants that not only look different but vary tremendously in growth habit, needs, and bloom season.

A PRECISE LANGUAGE

Botanical names are more precise than common ones. If you inquire at a nursery about a dusty miller, for example, you might be asked: "Which one?" A number of very different plants are known by that name. All are perennials with silvery foliage, but *Centaurea cineraria* has big, yellow thistlelike flowers;

Senecio cineraria has small yellow flowers; *Senecio viravira* has creamy white flowers; and *Lychnis coronaria* has magenta to crimson flowers. Likewise, "black-eyed Susan" applies to two very different plants (see below).

Similar-sounding common names may also cause confusion. "Hummingbird bush" is the Australian shrub *Grevillea thelemanniana*. "Hummingbird flower" on the other hand is the California native perennial *Zauschneria*; "hummingbird mint" is another perennial, *Agastache*.

Finally, ornamentals and weeds may bear the same common name. "Spanish broom" is either a tidy, 2-foot shrub with yellow flowers (*Genista hispanica*) or a rangy, 6- to 10-foot shrub (*Spartium junceum*) that runs wild across many parts of the West.

Iris douglasiana 'On the Edge'

WHAT'S IN A NAME?

Botanical names, if you break them down, can tell you something about the plants. The first word in a botanical name is the **genus** name. The second word is the **species** name, which is usually a descriptive word.

Many plants are named for the person who found or first described them. *Iris douglasiana*, for example, was named for Scottish horticulturist David Douglas, who collected plants in California in 1831.

Other names hold clues about a plant's physical characteristics. *Sollya heterophylla*, for example, combines *hetero* (heterogeneous or various) with *phylla* (leaves) to mean "various-size leaves." Indeed, some of the leaves of this evergreen shrub are lanceolate and others are oblong.

Some of the botanical names are so much like English words that there is no question as to their meaning. *Prostratum*, *compacta*, *deliciosa*, *fragrans*, and *pendula* all give clear clues about a plant's qualities.

Botanical names may also be inspired by where plants come from, by their texture or overall shape, or by the color of their flowers or leaves.

Listed at right are some descriptive parts of botanical names used in this book. Familiarize yourself with them and you'll know a lot about many plants as soon as you hear their name.

TWO PLANTS, BOTH BLACK-EYED SUSANS. But *Rudbeckia hirta* (left) is a perennial (named for scientist Olaus Rudbeck; hirta means "rough, hairy" as in stems, leaves). *Thunbergia alata* (right) is a twining vine grown as an annual (named for botanist Carl Peter Thunberg; alatus means "winged," as in "winged seeds").

Plant Colors

Cedrus atlantica 'Glauca Pendula'

albus—white
argenteus—silvery
aureus—golden
azureus—azure, sky blue
caeruleus—dark blue
caesius—blue-gray
candidus—pure white, shiny
canus—ashy gray, hoary
cereus—waxy
citrinus—yellow
coccineus—scarlet
concolor—one color
croceus—yellow
cruentus—bloody
discolor—two colors, separate
  colors
glaucus—covered with gray
  bloom
incanus—gray, hoary
luteus—yellow
pallidus—pale
purpureus—purple
rubens, ruber—red, ruddy
rufus—ruddy

Plant Parts

Liriodendron tulipifera

dendron—tree
flora, florum, flori, florus—flowers
phyllus, phylla—leaf or leaves

Form of Leaf
(*folius*—leaves or foliage)

Helianthus salicifolius

acerifolius—maple-like
angustifolius—narrow
aquifolius—spiny
buxifolius—boxwood-like
ilicifolius—holly-like
laurifolius—laurel-like
parvifolius—small
populifolius—poplar-like
quercifolius—oak-like
salicifolius—willow-like

Shape of Plant

Salvia elegans

adpressus—pressing against,
  hugging
altus—tall
arboreus—treelike
capitatus—headlike
compactus—compact, dense
confertus—crowded, pressed
  together
contortus—twisted
decumbens—trailing, with tips
  upright
depressus—pressed down
elegans—elegant, slender
fastigiatus—branches erect and
  close together
humifusus—ground-sprawling

humilis—low, small, humble
impressus—sunken
nanus—dwarf
pendula—hanging
procumbens—trailing
prostratus—prostrate
pumilus—dwarf, small
pusillus—puny, insignificant
repens—creeping
reptans—creeping
scandens—climbing

Plant Peculiarities

Banksia grandis

armatus—armed
augusta—majestic, notable
baccatus—berried, berrylike
barbatus—barbed or bearded
campanulatus—bell- or
  cup-shaped
ciliaris—fringed
cordatus—heart-shaped
cornutus—horned
crassus—thick, fleshy
decurrens—running down
  the stem
diversi—varying
edulis—edible
floridus—free-flowering
fruticosus—shrubby
fulgens—shiny
gracilis—slender, thin, graceful
grandis—large, showy
ifer, iferus—bearing or having;
  e.g., *stoloniferus*, having
  stolons
imperialis—showy
laciniatus—fringed or with torn
  edges
laevigatus—smooth
lobatus—lobed
longus—long
macro—large
maculatus—spotted
micro—small
mollis—soft, soft-haired
mucronatus—pointed
nutans—nodding, swaying

obtusus—blunt or flattened
officinalis—medicinal
oides—like or resembling; e.g.,
  jasminoides, like a jasmine
patens—open, spreading growth
pinnatus—like a feather
platy—broad
plenus—double, full
plumosus—feathery
praecox—early
pungens—piercing
radicans—rooting, especially
  along the stem
reticulatus—net-veined
retusus—notched at blunt apex
rugosus—wrinkled, rough
saccharatus—sweet, sugary
sagittalis—arrowlike
scabrus—rough feeling
scoparius—broomlike

Where From

Cornus canadensis

The suffix *-ensis, -us,* or *-is* (of a
place) is added to place names
to specify the habitat where the
plant was first discovered.

africanus—of Africa
alpinus—of the Alps
australis—southern
borealis—northern
campestris—of field or plains
canadensis—of Canada
canariensis—of the Canary
  Islands
capensis—of the Cape of Good
  Hope area
chilensis—of Chile
chinensis—of China
hispanicus—of Spain
hortensis—of gardens
indicus—of India
insularis—of the island
japonicus—of Japan
littoralis—of the seashore
montanus—of the mountains
riparius—of riverbanks
rivalis, rivularis—of brooks
saxatilis—inhabiting rocks

Pronunciation Guide

Scientific names are the universal language for plants, but they are pronounced differently in various parts of the world, even among English-speaking countries. Because these names come from Latin and ancient Greek, there is no obligatory pronunciation for them. But what follows is a list of the most familiar ways to say many scientific plant names.

THE SPELLING	PRONOUNCED AS IN
a	hat, hand
ay	baby
ah	hall
ai	air
e	met, bed
ee	we
i	tin
o	hot
oe	romance
u	must, burr
oo	rumor
ew	human
uh	comma

A

Abelia—uh-BEE-lee-uh
Abutilon—uh-BEW-tuh-lon
Acacia—uh-KAY-shuh
Acer—AY-sir
Achillea—a-KILL-ee-uh
Achimenes—uh-KIM-muh-neez
Aconitum—ak-oe-NYE-tuhm
Actinidia—AK-ti-NID-ee-uh
Adiantum—ad-ee-AN-tuhm
Aesculus—ES-keew-luhs
Agapanthus—ag-uh-PAN-thuhs
Agave—ah-GAH-vay
Ageratum—ad-jeh-RAY-tum
Ailanthus—uh-LAN-thuhs
Ajuga—uh-JEW-guh
Alstroemeria—
    al-struh-MEE-ree-uh
Amaryllis—am-uh-RIL-is
Anemone—uh-NEM-uh-nee
Anthurium—an-THU-ree-uhm
Aquilegia—ak-wuh-LEE-jee-uh
Arabis—AIR-uh-bis
Aralia—uh-RAY-lee-uh
Arctostaphylos—
    ark-toe-STAF-i-luhs
Arctotheca—ark-toe-THEE-kuh
Artemisia—AHR-tuh-MEE-zee-uh
Aspidistra—as-puh-DIS-truh
Astilbe—as-STIL-bee
Atriplex—AT-rip-lex

Agave bracteosa

B

Babiana—bab-ee-AN-uh
Baccharis—BAK-uh-ris
Bauhinia—bow-HIN-ee-uh
Berberis—BUR-buh-ris
Bergenia—bur-GEN-ee-uh
Betula—BET-ew-luh
Bougainvillea—
    boo-guhn-VIL-ee-uh
Buddleja—BUD-lee-uh

C

Caladium—kuh-LAY-dee-uhm
Calceolaria—
    kal-see-oe-LAIR-ee-uh
Calendula—kuh-LEN-dew-luh
Callistemon—ka-LIS-teh-muhn
Callistephus—ka-LIS-tee-fuhs
Calochortus—kal-oh-COR-tuhs
Campanula—kam-PAN-ew-luh
Carpenteria—
    CAHR-pen-TEER-ee-a
Cattleya—KAT-lee-uh
Ceanothus—see-uh-NO-thuhs
Celosia—see-LOW-see-uh
Centaurea—sen-TOR-ea
Ceratonia—sair-uh-TONE-ee-uh
Ceratostigma—
    se-RAT-o-STIG-muh
Cercidium—sir-CID-ee-uhm
Cercis—SIR-suhs
Chamaecyparis—
    kam-uh-SIP-uh-ris
Cheiranthus—kye-RAN-thuhs
Chionanthus—CHAI-o-NAN-thuhs
Chlorophytum—klor-oe-FYE-tum
Choisya—CHOY-zee-uh
Clematis—KLEM-uh-tis
Cleome—KLEE-oe-mee
Clivia—KLYE-vee-uh
Cocculus—COC-ew-lus
Colchicum—COLE-chik-uhm
Convallaria—con-va-LAIR-ee-uh
Convolvulus—
    kon-VOL-vew-luhs
Coreopsis—kor-ee-OP-suhs
Cotinus—koe-TYE-nuhs
Cotoneaster—
    ka-TOE-nee-aster
Crataegus—kruh-TEE-guhs

Crocosmia—kroe-KOZ-mee-uh
Cuphea—KEW-fee-uh
Cymbidium—sim-BID-ee-uhm
Cynoglossum—
    sin-oh-GLOS-uhm

Convolvulus sabatius

D

Daboecia—dab-EE-shee-uh
Daphne—DAFF-nee
Deutzia—DOOT-zee-uh or
    DOYT-zee-uh
Dizygotheca—
    diz-uh-GOTH-ik-uh or
    diz-uh-goe-THEE-kah
Dracaena—druh-SEE-nuh
Dryopteris—drye-OP-ter-uhs
Duchesnea—dew-KEZ-nee-uh

E

Echeveria—ek-uh-VAIR-ee-uh
Echinacea—ek-uh-NAY-see-uh
Echinops—EK-uh-nops
Echium—EK-ee-uhm
Elaeagnus—el-ee-AG-nuhs
Epidendrum—ep-uh-DEN-druhm
Epiphyllum—ep-uh-FIL-uhm
Equisetum—ek-wuh-SEE-tuhm
Eremurus—er-EM-er-us
Erica—ee-RYE-kuh (correct,
    but universally pronounced
    AIR-ik-uh)
Erigeron—ee-RIJ-uh-ron
Erythrina—air-i-THRYE-nuh

Eschscholzia—
    eh-SCHOELT-see-uh
Eucalyptus—ew-kuh-LIP-tuhs
Euonymus—ew-ON-uh-mus
Exacum—EK-suh-kuhm

F

Fatshedera—fats-HED-uh-ruh
Feijoa—fay-HOE-uh
Ficus—FYE-kuhs
Forsythia—for-SITH-ee-uh
Fragaria—fra-GAIR-ee-uh
Fraxinus—FRAK-suh-nuhs
Fuchsia—FEW-shee-uh

G

Gaillardia—gay-LAHR-dee-uh
Gazania—guh-ZAY-nee-uh
Genista—jen-NIS-tuh
Gentiana—jen-shee-AY-nah
Gerbera—GUR-bur-uh
Geum—JEE-uhm
Gleditsia—gluh-DIT-see-uh
Gomphrena—gom-FREE-nuh
Grevillea—gruh-VIL-ee-uh
Gypsophila—jip-SOF-uh-luh

Gomphrena globosa

H

Hamamelis—ham-uh-MEE-luhs
Hebe—HEE-bee
Hedera—HED-uh-ruh
Helianthemum—
    hee-lee-AN-thuh-muhm
Helianthus—hee-lee-AN-thuhs
Heliopsis—hee-lee-OP-suhs
Heliotropium—
    hee-lee-oe-TROE-pee-uhm
Hemerocallis—
    hem-uh-roe-KAL-uhs
Heteromeles—
    het-uh-ROM-e-leez
Heuchera—HEW-kuh-ruh
Hibiscus—hye-BIS-kuhs
Hippeastrum—hip-ee-AS-truhm
Hosta—HAHST-uh
Hydrangea—hye-DRAIN-jee-uh
Hymenocallis—
    hye-muh-noe-KAL-uhs
Hypericum—hye-PEER-ik-uhm

I

Iberis—IB-i-ruhs
Ilex—EYE-lex
Impatiens—im-PAY-shuns
Ipomoea—ip-oe-MEE-uh
Iresine—ir-uh-SYE-nee

J

Jacaranda—jak-uh-RAN-duh
Jasminum—jazz-MIN-num
Juniperus—joo-NIP-uh-ruhs

K

Kalanchoe—kal-an-KO-ee
Kniphofia—ni-FOE-fee-uh
Koelreuteria—
    COLE-rew-TEAR-e-uh
Kolkwitzia—koel-KWIT-zee-uh

L

Lagerstroemia—
    lay-gur-STREE-mee-uh
Lathyrus—LATH-uh-ruhs
Leptospermum—
    lep-toe-SPUR-muhm
Liatris—lie-AT-ruhs
Liriodendron—
    lear-ee-oe-DEN-druhn
Liriope—leer-EYE-oh-pee
Lobelia—loe-BEE-lee-uh
Lonicera—LAWN-NIS-uh-ruh
Lychnis—LIK-nis
Lysimachia—lye-suh-MAY-kee-uh

M

Malus—MAY-lus
Mandevilla—man-duh-VIL-uh
Matthiola—ma-thee-OE-luh

Maytenus—MAY-te-nuhs
Melaleuca—mel-uh-LOO-kuh
Metrosideros—
    MET-roe-sid-AIR-ruhs
Mimulus—MIM-ew-luhs
Musa—MEW-zuh
Myosotis—mye-oh-SO-tuhs
Myrica—MY-rick-uh

N

Nandina—nan-DEE-nuh
Narcissus—nahr-SIS-uhs
Nerine—nuh-RYE-nee
Nerium—NEE-ree-uhm
Nicotiana—ni-koe-shee-AY-nuh
Nierembergia—
    nee-rem-BURG-ee-uh
Nyssa—NIS-uh

O

Olea—O-lee-uh
Osmanthus—oz-MAN-thuhs
Osteospermum—
    os-tee-oe-SPUR-muhm
Oxalis—OK-sal-uhs
Oxydendrum—OK-see-DEN-druhm

Oxydendrum arboreum

P

Pachysandra—
    pak-ee-SAN-druh
Papaver—puh-PAY-vur
Parthenocissus—
    PAHR-thuh-noe-SIS-uhs
Pelargonium—
    pel-ahr-GOE-nee-uhm
Pennisetum—pen-uh-SEE-tuhm
Penstemon—PEN-stuh-muhn
Philadelphus—fil-uh-DEL-fuhs
Photinia—foe-TIN-ee-uh
Phyla—FYE-luh
Phyllostachys—FIL-oe-STACK-ees
Physalis—FYE-suh-luhs
Picea—pye-SEE-uh
Pieris—pee-AIR-uhs
Pinus—PYE-nuhs
Pittosporum—pit-TOS-poe-ruhm,
    pit-toe-SPOER-uhm

Platanus—PLAT-uh-nuhs
Platycladus—plat-i-CLAD-uhs
Podocarpus—poe-doe-KAR-puhs
Polianthes—pol-ee-AN-thez
Polygonatum—
    pol-ee-GON-uh-tuhm
Portulaca—por-tew-LAK-a
Potentilla—poe-ten-TIL-uh
Primula—PRIM-ew-luh
Protea—PROE-tee-uh or
    proe-TEE-uh
Pseudotsuga—soo-doe-TSOO-guh
Pyrostegia—pye-roe-STEE-jee-uh
Pyrus—PYE-ruhs

Protea neriifolia

Q

Quercus—KWER-kuhs

R

Ranunculus—ra-NUN-kew-luhs
Rhaphiolepis—raf-ee-OL-uh-pis
    or raf-ee-o-LEP-uhs
Rhoeo—REE-oe
Romneya—ROM-nee-uh
Rosmarinus—ros-muh-RYE-nuhs
Rudbeckia—rud-BECK-ee-uh

S

Salpiglossis—sal-pi-GLOS-sis
Sanvitalia—san-vi-TALE-ee-uh
Scabiosa—skay-bee-OH-suh
Schefflera—SHEF-luh-ruh
Schizanthus—ski-ZAN-thuhs
Scilla—SIL-luh
Sempervivum—
    sem-per-VYE-vuhm
Senecio—suh-NEE-shee-oe
Sequoia—suh-QUOY-uh
Solandra—soe-LAN-druh
Soleirolia—
    soe-lee-uh-ROE-lee-uh
Spiraea—spye-REE-uh
Strelitzia—stre-LIT-see-uh
Syngonium—sin-GOE-nee-uhm

Senecio mandraliscae

T

Tagetes—tuh-JEE-teez
Taxodium—taks-OE-dee-uhm
Thuja—THOO-yuh
Thymus—TYE-muhs
Tibouchina—tib-oo-SHEE-nuh
Tigridia—tye-GRID-ee-uh
Tolmiea—tol-MEE-uh
Trachelospermum—
    tra-kee-lo-SPER-muhm
Tradescantia—
    trad-es-KAN-shee-uh
Trichostema—trik-oe-STEE-mah
Tropaeolum—tro-PEE-oh-luhm
Tsuga—TSOO-guh

Trachelospermum jasminoides

V

Vaccinium—vak-SIN-ee-uhm
Vancouveria—van-koo-VEE-ree-uh
Verbascum—vur-BAS-kuhm
Verbena—ver-BEE-nuh
Vinca—VING-kuh
Vitex—VEE-teks

W–Z

Weigela—wye-JEE-luh
Xylosma—zye-LOZ-muh
Zantedeschia—
    zan-tuh-DESH-e-uh
Zephyranthes—zef-i-RAN-theez
Zoysia—ZOY-see-uh

Glossary

Gardening terms used in this book are defined here. These words have roots in botany, landscape design, soil science, the nursery business, and in generations of experienced dirt gardening.

Acid soil. A soil with pH below 7. See page 667.

Air layering. A method of propagation in which a stem in the plant's canopy is wounded, dusted with rooting hormone, encased in damp sphagnum moss, and covered with plastic wrap until roots appear in the moss. The branch is then cut free and planted.

Alkaline soil. A soil with pH above 7. See page 667.

Alternate leaves. See Opposite leaves.

Annual. A plant that completes its life cycle in one year or less.

Anther. See Flower.

Axil. The inner angle between a leaf (or other organ of a plant) and the stem from which it springs. Organs in the axil, such as flowers and buds, are called axillary.

Balled-and-burlapped (B-and-B). Field-grown woody plants sold with a ball of field soil around roots, wrapped in fabric.

Bare-root. Deciduous shrubs, trees, and perennials sold with the soil removed from the roots.

Bedding plant. Any plant suitable for massing in beds for colorful flowers or foliage. Most bedding plants are annuals or tender perennials grown as annuals.

Biennial. A plant that germinates and produces foliage during its first growing season, then blooms, sets seed, and dies during its second growing season.

Biodynamics. Views each farm or garden as a living organism, using crop rotation, manuring, tilling, and composting to improve soil and control pests, weeds, and diseases. Practitioners sow seeds by astronomical calendars and grow plants that attract beneficial insects when they're most needed. They reject artificial fertilizers or pest controls.

Blanching. Blocking light from parts of certain vegetables to keep them paler, milder in flavor, or both. It is done by tying outer leaves over the inner head or leaves, or (for asparagus) by mounding soil over emerging spears.

Bolting. Premature seed setting by flowers and vegetables.

Bonsai. Japanese for "tray planting," bonsai is growing and training dwarf plants in containers to create trees in miniature.

Bracts. Modified leaves growing below a flower or flower cluster. Bracts are usually green, but may be colorful enough to resemble flowers or petals, as in poinsettia.

Broad-leafed. Trees and shrubs with broad leaves (in contrast with the needle- or scale-like leaves of conifers). Also any nongrass weed.

Bud. A rudimentary organ or shoot. A flower bud develops into a blossom; a growth bud produces shoots or foliage. Terminal (apical) buds are produced at the end of a shoot. Lateral (axillary) buds are produced in the axils of a plant.

Budding. A method of propagation in which a bud (scion) from one plant is inserted beneath the bark of a related plant, where it grows a copy of its parent.

Bud union. The point (often swollen) at which a scion unites with the rootstock.

Bulb. A thickened underground structure from which a plant grows. See page 675.

Callus. A thick, tough layer of tissue formed where plants have been injured.

Calyx. Collectively, the sepals of a flower. See Flower.

Cambium. The layer of growing cells between the xylem and phloem.

Cane. An elongated flowering or fruiting stem (as in roses and raspberries), usually arising from the roots.

Cane pruning. A method of pruning grapevines.

Catkin. A slender, spikelike, often drooping flower cluster found in plants such as alder (*Alnus*) and willow (*Salix*).

Chill requirement. Many bulbs, perennials, and deciduous shrubs and trees need a certain number of hours below 45°F (7°C) to flower well. That number of hours is the plant's chill requirement.

Chlorosis. When a leaf looks yellower than it should (especially between leaf veins), it is often chlorotic (suffering from chlorosis). Frequently, chlorosis is caused by a plant's inability to obtain the iron it needs to produce green coloring. For one way to correct this condition, see Iron chelate.

Chlorosis

Composite head. See Inflorescence.

Compost tea. Made by soaking a compost-filled bag in a barrel of water, this liquid fertilizer is also used to make soils more bioactive, and to fight plant diseases. It can be made more potent by super-oxygenating the water.

Compound leaf. See Leaf.

Conifer. A woody plant such as juniper (*Juniperus*) or pine (*Pinus*), whose leaves are narrow and needlelike or tiny and scalelike. Most are evergreen (and often called evergreens), but a few are deciduous. All bear seeds in cones or in modified structures such as juniper berries and the berrylike cones of yew (*Taxus*).

Corm. A bulblike, swollen underground stem base composed of solid tissue. See page 675.

Corolla. Collectively, the petals of a flower.

Cover crop. Mostly cool-season annual legumes, these are usually sown in vegetable beds in fall and tilled in during spring to increase the organic content, nutrients, and tilth of the soil.

Cover crop (fava beans)

Crown. A tree's crown is its entire branch structure, including foliage. Also refers to the point at which a plant's roots and top structure join, usually at or near the soil line.

Cultivar. Shorthand for "cultivated variety." These genetically distinct plants may be of hybrid origin or selected varieties of wild plants. Cultivar names are enclosed in single quotation marks and are not italicized, as in *Lobelia erinus* 'Crystal Palace'. In general usage and throughout this book, the term "variety" refers both to cultivars and to varieties found in nature.

Deadhead. Removal of spent flowers to tidy up a plant, keep it from setting seed, and prolong bloom.

Deciduous. A woody plant that naturally sheds all of its foliage at once, usually in fall.

Defoliation. The unnatural loss of foliage, which may result from high winds, intense heat, drought, unusually early or late frosts, or severe damage caused by chemicals, insects, or diseases.

Dieback. Full or partial death of stems, beginning at the tips. Causes include inadequate moisture, nutrient deficiency, poor climate adaptation, disease, insect infestation, or mechanical injury.

Dormancy. The annual period when a plant's growth slows down. It's usually in fall and winter, but summer dormancy is common among spring-flowering bulbs and desert plants.

Double flower. See Inflorescence.

Drainage. The downward movement of water through the soil. See page 667.

Drip line. The circular area of soil around a tree directly under its outermost branch tips; rainwater tends to drip from the tree at this point.

Epiphyte. Epiphytes grow on other plants, using them for support but not nutrients. Examples include cattleya orchids and staghorn ferns (*Platycerium*). Nonparasitic, these draw nourishment from the air, rainwater, and organic debris collected on the supporting plant.

Espalier. A plant trained so its branches grow in a flat pattern against a vertical surface. See page 723.

Evergreen. Plants that never lose all their leaves at one time. See also Conifer.

Family. Every plant is classified in a family whose members share certain broad characteristics that set them apart from plants in other families. See page 122.

Fertilization. The fusion of male and female gametes

Complete Flower

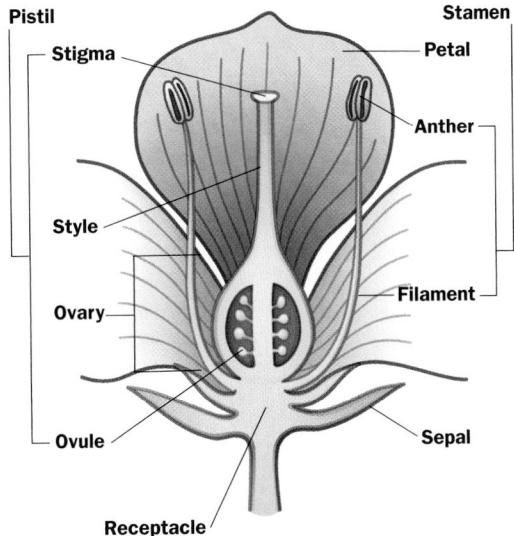

Pistil
— Stigma
Style
Ovary
Ovule
Receptacle

Stamen
Petal
Anther
Filament
Sepal

(fertile reproductive cells) following pollination.

Fertilize. To apply nutrients in the form of fertilizer to a plant. See page 720.

Flower. The part of a seed-bearing plant that contains its reproductive organs. The stamens are male parts, each consisting of a stalk-like filament and a pollen-bearing anther. The pistils are female parts, each with a basal ovary where seeds form, a stalk-like style, and a stigma that receives the pollen. The calyx (a collection of modified leaves called sepals) encloses the developing flower, folding back or dropping off as individual sepals when the blossom opens.

Forcing. Making a plant mature or flower out of season, usually in a greenhouse.

Foundation plant. Originally, a plant used to hide a house's foundation; currently, any shrub planted near house walls.

Frond. The foliage of ferns. Also applied to palm leaves or any fernlike foliage.

Fruit. The mature ovary of a plant, containing one to many seeds. Fruits may be soft and fleshy, as in the case of peaches or apples, or dry, like an acorn or dried pea pod.

Genus. See page 122.

Girdling. The removal of bark all the way around a stem, branch, or trunk, cutting off water and nutrient flow and usually killing the plant.

Grafting. Taking a section of one plant (scion) and inserting it into a branch of another plant (stock). The graft works—the two grow together as one plant—only if the cambium layers (growing cells between the bark and wood) of both scion and stock make contact. If the graft works, the scion develops foliage, flowers, and fruits like the plant it came from.

Ground layering. A method of propagation in which ground-level branches are injured, dusted with rooting hormone, and pegged to the soil below, where they root at the site of the injury. After rooting, they are cut off and planted elsewhere.

Growing season. The number of days between the average dates of the last killing frost in spring and the first killing frost in fall. Also used to describe the period of time a plant is actively growing. See pages 18–21.

Harden off. Exposing a plant grown indoors to increasing periods of time outdoors, so that when it is planted outside it makes the transition with little shock.

Hardy plant. A plant with good frost tolerance. The word does not mean tough, pest-resistant, or disease-resistant.

Heaving. Buckling and breaking of frozen soil. The process often pops plants out of the ground.

Heeling in. Temporarily storing bare-root plants until you can plant them, by burying their roots in soil or moist sawdust. You heel in fruit trees, deciduous vines, and roses before planting out to keep their roots from drying out.

Heirloom. Old plant varieties passed down, relatively unchanged, through the generations. Includes woody plants such as apples and roses, plus vegetables and flowers.

Herbaceous. A plant (usually perennial) whose fleshy (nonwoody) stems and foliage die to the ground each year and completely regrow the following season.

Hose in hose. Describes flower varieties (certain azaleas, for example) that appear to have one funnel-shaped corolla nested inside another. The outer corolla may be a calyx modified to look like a corolla.

Humus. The soft, dark, organic part of the soil formed when animal or vegetable matter decomposes to a point where it is stable. Also describes mature compost and rotted forest litter.

Hybrid. A plant parented by two species, subspecies, varieties, cultivars, strains, or any combination of the above; or, less common, between parents from different genera. Can occur naturally, but more often by controlled breeding. Hybrids are indicated with the symbol ×, as in *Buddleja* × *weyeriana*.

Hydroponics. A method of growing plants in a water-based solution rather than in soil.

Indumentum. A thick covering of hairs, especially on the undersides of certain rhododendron leaves.

Inflorescence. A group of individual flowers on a single stem. Can take many forms. A spike's flowers attach to the main stem without stalks, as in bottlebrush

Inflorescences

Spike

Umbel

Raceme

Panicle

Composite head

(*Callistemon*). In an umbel, individual flowers spring from approximately the same point, as in dill (*Anethum graveolens*). In a raceme, flowers form on individual stalks arising from the main stem, as in foxglove (*Digitalis*). The flowers of lilac (*Syringa*) emerge in panicles, which are branched racemes. A composite head refers to small, closely packed, stalkless flowers; these may include central disk flowers and outer ray flowers, as in sunflower (*Helianthus*). A single flower has one row of petals; a double flower has more than one row.

Internode. See Node.

Iron chelate (pronounced KEY-late). A chemical you add to the soil to treat plants with iron chlorosis (see Chlorosis). It is a combination of iron and a complex organic substance that makes the iron already in the soil available to plant roots.

Lath. Any overhead structure (originally a roof of spaced laths) that reduces the amount of sunlight or frost reaching the plants beneath.

Layering. A technique that encourages new roots to form on branches still attached to the parent plant. See Air layering, Ground layering.

Leaching. Deep irrigation of the soil with water to remove excess salts and other impurities from the topsoil.

Leader. The central upward-growing stem of a single-trunked tree or shrub.

Leaf. The main photosynthetic organ of most plants. A simple leaf is a single unit, whereas a compound leaf is divided into separate segments called leaflets. In a palmately compound leaf, the leaflets grow from one point at the end of a stem. In a pinnately compound (once-divided) leaf, the leaflets are arranged along a central axis; a bipinnately compound leaf is twice-divided, or twice pinnate.

Leaf burn. Damage to a whole leaf or just its margins from sunlight, chemicals (like salt or alkaline soil), strong wind, or lack of water.

Leaf Shapes

Heart-shaped

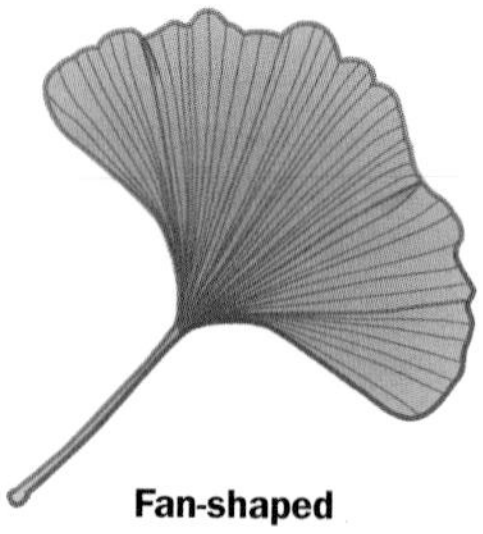

Fan-shaped

Ovate

Rounded

Shallowly lobed

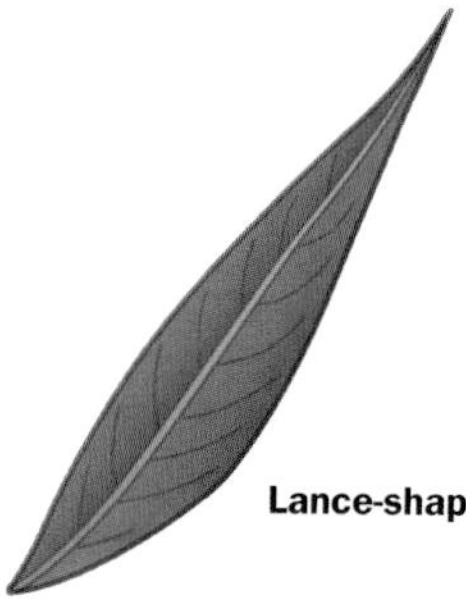

Lance-shaped

Leaf Types

Simple

Palmate

Pinnate

Bipinnate

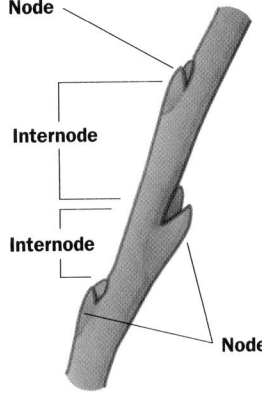

Lip

Leaflet. A division or segment of a compound leaf. See also Leaf.

Leaf mold. Decayed leaves used as an organic soil amendment.

Leaf scar. A rounded or crescent-shaped mark on a branch where a leafstalk once was attached.

Legume. A plant in the pea family (formerly *Leguminosae*, now *Papilionaceae*) whose root nodules capture nitrogen and make it available to other plants.

Lip. Flowers with unequal segments often have an upper and a lower division, each known as a lip (shown at top). Honeysuckle (*Lonicera*) is an example.

Microclimate. A small area with a slightly different climate than that of its larger surroundings. See page 22.

Mycorrhizal fungi. Naturally occurring soil organisms that

Stem Nodes

Node

Internode

Internode

Node

colonize plant roots, helping them use water and nutrients more efficiently, and suppress disease.

Naturalize. To set out plants (especially bulbs) randomly, without a precise pattern, and allow them to spread at will. Also refers to plants that become established where they are not native.

Node. The joint in a stem where a bud, branch, or leaf starts to grow. The area of stem between nodes is the internode.

Offset. A young plant that develops at or near the base of the parent plant; hen and chicks (*Echeveria*), for example. The word also refers to the increases of bulbs and corms.

Open-pollinated plants. Plants produced from natural, random pollination (in contrast with hybrids, whose pollination is carefully controlled).

Opposite leaves; alternate leaves. Describes the arrangement of leaves along a stem. Opposite leaves grow in pairs, one on each side of the same node. Alternate leaves appear one to a node, each leaf opposite the leaves growing closest to it.

Organic gardening. Usually focused on edible crops, it depends upon natural systems and hand work, not chemicals. Favored natural fertilizers include compost tea, guano, and cottonseed meal. Natural pest control marshals everything from bacteria like *Bacillus thuringiensis (Bt)* to beneficial insects and neem oil. Weed control is usually done with mulches and hoes. Organic gardening also emphasizes soil building with cover crops and compost.

Organic matter. Any material originating from a living organism—peat moss, ground bark, compost, or manure, for example—used as a soil amendment.

Ovary. See Flower, Fruit.

Panicle. See Inflorescence.

Peat moss. A water-retentive organic soil amendment that is the partially decomposed remains of mosses. It increases

soil acidity. Sphagnum peat moss is generally considered the best, and is often sold in whole pieces to line hanging baskets and do air layering.

Perennial. A nonwoody plant that lives for more than two years. See page 686.

Permaculture. A combination of the words "permanent" and "agriculture," permaculture focuses on sustainability, working with natural rhythms to produce food, fiber, and housing in environmentally healthy ways.

Petal. See Flower.

pH. A measure of alkalinity or acidity on a scale of 0 (acid) to 14 (alkaline), with 7 (pure water) as neutral. In practice, most garden soils are in the 5 to 8 range. See page 667.

Phloem. Cells that transport sugar-rich sap from the leaves throughout a plant.

Pistil. See Flower.

Pleaching. A training method in which branches are interwoven to form a hedge or arbor. Subsequent pruning maintains a neat, formal pattern.

Pollarding. A training method in which the main limbs of a young tree are drastically cut back. In each subsequent dormant season, the growth from these branch stubs is cut back to one or two buds. In time, the large, knobby branch ends support a compact, leafy dome during the growing season and a grotesque branch structure during the dormant months.

Pollenizer. A plant that provides pollen to fertilize another plant.

Pollination. The transfer of pollen from male reproductive organs to female ones, which leads to fertilization and seed production.

Pollinator. Anything that transfers pollen from one part of a flower to another or from flowers on one plant to flowers on another.

Pruners. Tool made for cutting stems and branches. Bypass pruners have two heavy, curved, scissor-like blades. Anvil pruners have a sharp top blade that cuts down onto a narrow, flat

anvil below; a permutation is the ratchet pruner, which is geared to increase cutting power with multiple cuts. For pruning, see the box on page 746.

Pseudobulb. A modified aboveground stem that serves as a storage organ. Common in orchids.

Raceme. See Inflorescence.

Rhizome. A modified, horizontally growing, underground or ground-level stem.

Rock powders (rock dusts). Pulverized mineral soil amendments that are released slowly over time, improving soil structure. They include rock phosphate (phosphorus and trace minerals), rock dust (potassium and trace minerals), greensand (iron-potassium silicate), and lime rock powder (calcium and magnesium). No rock powder contains nitrogen.

Rootbound. A container-grown plant whose roots have become matted and may encircle the inside of the pot.

Root irrigator. Like a giant hose-mounted hypodermic needle, it injects water deep into a plant's root zones.

Rootstock. The part of a budded or grafted plant that furnishes the root system and sometimes part of the branch structure (also known as an understock).

Rosette. Leaves closely set around a crown or center, usually at or close to ground level. *Aloe variegata* grows in rosettes.

Runner. See Stolon.

Scion. A shoot or bud cut from one plant to graft or bud onto the rootstock of another.

Self-seed, self-sow. When a plant sheds fertile seeds that produce seedlings.

Sepal. See Flower.

Simple leaf. See Leaf.

Single flower. See Inflorescence.

Species. See page 122.

Specimen. A large tree or shrub used singly, as a garden accent.

PRUNING

This task is especially useful for keeping plants—especially trees and shrubs—shapely. But there are other reasons that pruning makes sense: to remove branches that are badly diseased, dead, densely branched, or rubbing together; to direct growth or remove wayward branches, suckers (stems growing up from the roots), and water sprouts (upright shoots growing from the trunk and branches); to increase flowers or fruit; and to maintain safety.

   If you have to cut back a plant continually to keep it in bounds, it is probably too large for its location.

Types of Pruning

PINCHING Nipping off the terminal shoot of new growth (**A**), using your thumb and forefinger or a pair of shears, causes side shoots to grow. Pinching side shoots (**B**) causes stems to lengthen. Pinching is used primarily on annuals and perennials.

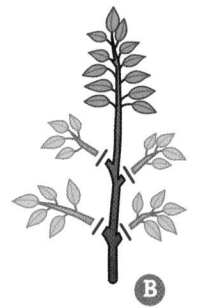

THINNING Removing entire branches, large or small, by cutting back to the main trunk or side branch (**A**), opens up a plant, enhances its natural form, and stimulates minimal regrowth (**B**).

HEADING Cutting back a branch to a bud, twig, or branch that's too small to take over the terminal role (**A**). By forcing growth of side shoots below the cut, heading produces clusters of new shoots (**B**); makes fruit trees branch at a particular point; fills holes in the crowns of mature trees; and increases bloom on flowering shrubs.

SHEARING Clipping a plant's outer foliage (**A**) creates an even surface, such as for a hedge (**B**). The plants best suited to shearing have main and lateral branches bearing closely spaced buds, so almost every cut ends up near a growing point.

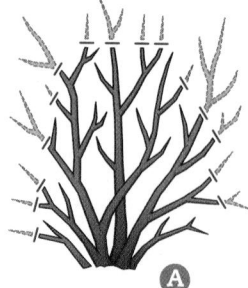

Sphagnum moss. See Peat moss.

Spike. See Inflorescence.

Spore. A simple reproductive cell. Algae, fungus, mosses, and ferns reproduce by spores.

Fern spores

Sport. A spontaneous mutation (variation)—often a branch whose leaves or flowers differ from the rest of the plant.

Spur. In fruit trees (particularly apples and cherries), a specialized short twig that bears the plant's fruit. Also refers to tubular projections from a blossom's petals or sepals. Most species of columbine (*Aquilegia*), for example, have flowers with pronounced spurs.

Spur pruning. In winter, grapevine canes that grew and fruited in the past season are pruned from a framework of permanent arms, leaving a series of spurs (short twigs, each with two buds). These buds will produce fruit in the following summer or autumn.

Stamen. See Flower.

Standard. A plant trained to a single, upright trunk topped by a rounded crown of foliage (like a lollipop). In some standards, the trunk and top are joined by grafting.

Stigma. See Flower.

Stolon. A stem (runner) that creeps and roots along the soil surface, forming new plants where it roots. Bermuda grass spreads by stolons.

Strain. Many annuals and some perennials are strains (sometimes referred to as series). An example is State

Fair zinnias. Plants in a strain are similar but vary from the norm in some respect—usually in flower color.

Stress. Any environmental factor that degrades a plant's performance or checks its growth. Inadequate water, wind, or very high or low temperatures induce stress, causing wilting, dull foliage color, and browning leaf edges.

Style. See Flower.

Subshrub. A low-growing plant with woody stems—a small shrub. Also a perennial with a woody base but soft, herbaceous stems in its upper part.

Subspecies. See page 122.

Sucker. In a grafted or budded plant, suckers grow from the rootstock rather than from the grafted or budded part of the plant. See also Water sprout.

Sustainable. A gardening style that recycles nearly everything (with composting, for example), wastes almost nothing, and can continue indefinitely with little outside resources.

Taproot. A thick central root that may penetrate deeply into the ground. In plants such as carrots, taproots are storage organs.

Tender plant. A plant with low tolerance for frost or cold. The opposite of a hardy plant.

Tendrils. Threadlike growths along the stems or at the ends of leaves on some vines. Tendrils wrap around supports, enabling the vine to climb.

Thin. Seedlings or developing fruits are thinned by removing excess plants or fruits so that the remaining ones have enough room to grow well.

Topiary. The technique of pruning and training shrubs and trees into geometric shapes (cones, spheres, pyramids) or fanciful animals or objects.

Topping. A severe form of heading that removes treetops to reduce height. It is not recommended because it sends out scores of weak new buds near cutoff points, and can shorten the tree's life.

Tree. A woody plant having an elongated stem or trunk, usually

Basic Tree Forms

Columnar

Irregular

Open

Oval

Pyramidal

Round

Spreading

Vase

with few or no branches on the lower part. See basic tree forms at right.

Truss. A typically compact cluster of flowers at the end of a stem, branch, or stalk. Many rhododendrons bear their flowers in trusses.

Tuber. A swollen underground stem with multiple growth points. See page 675.

Tuberous root. A true root, thickened to store nutrients. See page 675.

Umbel. See Inflorescence.

Underplanting. Growing one plant beneath another—a groundcover under a tree, for example.

Understock. See Rootstock.

Variegation. Striping, edging, or other markings in a color different from the primary color of a leaf or petal.

Variegated leaves of *Pittosporum tenuifolium* 'Marjorie Channon'

Variety. See page 122.

Water sprout. In trees, any strong vertical shoot growing from the main framework of trunk and branches; also called a sucker.

Whorl. Three or more leaves, branches, or flowers growing in a circle from a node on a stem or trunk.

Woody plant. One with hardened (woody) stems or trunks. An erbaceous plant, in contrast, has soft stems.

Xylem. Cells that transport water and nutrients from the roots of a plant up into its canopy.

General Index

This index covers general gardening terms and topics. For scientific and common names of plants, see the Plant Index, beginning on page 750. Italic page numbers refer to pages on which there are photographs; bold page numbers denote maps.

Plant Index

Italic page numbers refer to pages on which there are relevant photographs. The boldface page number after a scientific name—or common name, in the case of edibles—refers to the plant's encyclopedia entry. Index listings of the common names of ornamentals are followed by the scientific name; use it to find further page references to the plant.

At the end of the day,
it's your garden, to fill
with plants you love.

Low-growing ajuga, chartreuse abelia, phormiums, Japanese maple, and cape rush edge this small San Francisco garden and frame its city view. Design: Beth Mullins.

Credits

Photographs are listed sequentially either in horizontal or vertical order. For additional clarification, the following position indicators may be used: Left (L), Center (C), Right (R), Top (T), Middle (M), Bottom (B), Upper (U).

SPECIAL THANKS

We would like to express our gratitude to the following people and businesses who generously allowed us to use their photographs or to shoot at their nurseries:

Ames True Temper

Annie's Annuals & Perennials

Arterra Landscape Architects

Bailey Nurseries

Debra Lee Baldwin

Ball Horticultural Company

Janek Boniecki, Bauer Pottery Company

Burpee Seed Company

Denver Botanic Gardens

DIG Gardens

Davis Dolbak, Living Green

The Elisabeth F. Gamble Garden

Emerisa Nursery

Filoli

Nicholas Gitts, Swan Island Dahlias

Golden Nursery

Roy Hellwig, Archiphyte

The Huntington Botanical Gardens

In Harmony Sustainable Landscapes

Monrovia

Mountain Valley Growers, Inc.

Jo O'Connell, Australian Native Plants Nursery

Orchard Supply Hardware

Pacific Plug and Liner

PlantHaven, Inc.

Proven Winners

Roger Reynolds Nursery

Sage Eco Gardens & Nursery

San Marcos Growers

Skagit Gardens

Terra Nova Nurseries, Inc.

Mike Tomlinson, Dave Wilson Nursery

Tucson Botanical Gardens

PHOTOGRAPHY

AgStock Images/Bill Barksdale: 487L, 736L1; AgStock Images/ Howard Schwartz: 733L4; AgStock Images/Ed Young: 479R1, 511L, 519R; Sarl Akene (Photos Lamontagne)/Photolibrary: 237L, 498R; Leroy Alfonse/Photolibrary: 62L3; Ames True Temper: 668L1, 668L2, 668L3, 668L4; James L. Amos/ Photolibrary: 114L1; Peter Anderson/Dorling Kindersley/Getty Images: 710BL; Annie's Annuals & Perennials: 57LC, 59R4, 61R4, 64BR, 79BRC, 86L2, 98L2, 99L3, 99R3, 102L1, 102R1, 112R1, 218L, 233R, 253R, 254R, 257L, 266R, 277L, 281R, 288LC, 291LC, 294LC, 302C, 306R, 337R, 338R, 339L, 375R, 392L, 400, 415L, 452, 465C, 473R, 616R, 623R1, 644L, 660R, 711B2; Nicholas Appleby/Garden World Images: 525R; Archiphyte: 10B; Arterra Picture Library/ Alamy: 77L; Asperra Images/ Alamy: 106BRC; Caitlin Atkinson: 51L4, 53BL, 70BRC, 689BR; Quentin Bacon/StockFood

Creative/Getty Images: 636C; Bailey Nurseries: 84R, 582R2; Debra Lee Baldwin: 195L, 462R; Jan Baldwin/Photolibrary: 173R; Ball Horticultural Co.: 81BRC, 148L, 258R, 353R, 355LC, 373TR, 373RC2; Bauer Pottery: 673C; Bill Beatty/Visuals Unlimited: 728L5; Benary: 598L2; Melissa Berard/Native Sons Wholesale Nursery: 449C; Pernilla Bergdahl/GAP Photos/Getty Images: 46BRC, 738BL; Black Diamond Images: 366LC; Anthony Blake/Photolibrary: 229RC; blickwinkel/Alamy: 61L2, 112R3, 232LC, 266L, 360RC, 438R, 455L, 593L, 636R, 648R; Richard Bloom/Garden Picture Library/Getty Images: 104BLC, 509RC2, 747R; Hubertus Blume/ Photolibrary: 56L3; David Boag/ Alamy: 62L1; David Boag/Photolibrary: 62R1; Julien Boisard/ Photolibrary: 665L2; Mark Bolton/Photolibrary: 63L2, 71L1, 104BRC, 117BRC, 421R1, 466L, 621LC2, 635R; Bon Appetit/ Alamy: 707B1; Botanic Images, Inc./Garden World Images:

66BLC, 74BRC, 116L4, 239C; Marcus Botzek/Photolibrary: 727BL; Rick & Nora Bowers/ Alamy: 440L; Marion Brenner: 11, 12T, 107TR, 153R, 297LC, 307R, 404L, 491R1, 524C, 565LC2, 665L3, 681T, 692BR, 697B, 712BL; Caroline Brinkmann/ Photolibrary: 96L; Rob D. Brodman: 79BLC, 94L4, 117TR, 142RC, 145L, 159RC, 190RC, 200L, 260BR, 277LC, 357R, 368L, 425C, 458R, 461R, 467L, 472LC, 486R, 487R, 493BR, 511R, 526R, 550R, 575RC2, 592L, 606L, 615, 633L2, 633R, 665TR, 673TL, 673R, 677TR, 693TR, 698TR, 698BL, 703R, 716TL, 720T; Gene Burch: 247C; Keith Burdett/Alamy: 528R2; Burke/Triolo Productions/Botanica/Getty Images: 662; Burpee Seed Co.: 373LC, 564RC, 700L; Christopher Burrows/Alamy: 364L, 645L; Chris Burrows/ Photolibrary: 52RC3, 59R1, 60BR, 88L, 286TL, 450R, 553L, 651R1; Scott Calhoun: 168L, 297L, 370C, 408R, 460C, 594R, 711B3; Brown Cannon III: 678TR; Rob Cardillo: 89R2, 110LC1, 172L, 192L, 196LC, 199, 231LC, 251L, 277R, 278L, 290C, 304L, 318R, 323R, 324R, 325L, 326R, 366L, 374C, 379R2, 391C, 392LC, 395C, 416L, 423L, 445L, 449R, 477C, 487C, 494L, 497R, 503R, 522R, 537L, 581RC, 593R, 595R, 611L, 612R, 644R, 652L, 739L2; iStock.com/Melissa Carroll: 668TR; Nigel Cattlin/ Alamy: 276R, 483L, 733L1, 732L2; Nigel Cattlin/Visuals Unlimited: 729L7, 733L6, 733L7; Nigel Cattlin/Visuals Unlimited/ Getty Images: 729L4; David Cavagnaro: 110L3, 146, 150L, 162L, 207R, 209R, 235L, 243RC, 249RC2, 256L, 258L, 274RC, 284C, 288L, 289L, 293C, 297R, 302L, 340C, 367L, 386R1, 412, 413L1, 444C, 451L2, 459R, 552TR, 552RC2, 566R, 567L, 592C, 607C, 607R, 643L, 660L, 735L5, 736L7, 737L3, 737L4; David Cavagnaro/ Photolibrary: 610RC2; David Cavagnaro/Visuals Unlimited/ Getty Images: 120R3; Peter Chadwick/Alamy: 396C; Jess Chamberlain: 302R; Van Chaplin: 176R2; Jennifer Cheung: 10T, 15ML, 42, 93BLC, 94R4, 197, 222C, 320R, 329, 471, 585L1, 618L, 689TL, 690BR, 690BR, 706TR, 706B, 724TR; Carr Clifton/Minden Pictures/Getty

Images: 21; Rita Coates/Garden World Images: 101RC, 693BR; R. Creation/Getty Images: 238; Eric Crichton/Garden World Images: 203L; Eric Crichton/ Photolibrary: 56L1; Jeffery Cross: 699TL, 699BL, 699TC, 699BC; Cubo Images/Alamy: 331R; Claire Curran: 142LC, 147C; Robin Bachtler Cushman: 479R3, 484, 486L, 486LC, 493L1, 493BL, 541RC1, 552R2, 632RC; Sarah Cuttle/Photolibrary: 243BL; Davis Dalbok/Living Green: 9T; Darcy Daniels: 298L; Andrew Darrington/Alamy: 731R4; Francoise Davis/Garden World Images: 207L; Michael Davis/Photolibrary: 223R, 651L; Gilles Delacroix/Garden World Images: 52RC4, 99L1, 112L4, 201T, 286L2, 291R, 303L, 338L, 410LC, 427L, 433R, 500L, 608L, back cover bottom right; Marvin Dembinsky Photo Associates/Alamy: 713TR; Denver Botanic Gardens: 234RC, 349RC, 381R2; Michael DeYoung/Photolibrary: 24TR; Frédéric Didillon/ Mise au Point: 206LC, 229LC; Frédéric Didillon/Photolibrary: 223L; David Dixon/Photolibrary: 322TL; Dorling Kindersley/Getty Images: 141C, 461L; Jacqui Dracup/Garden World Images: 630L; Carole Drake/Photolibrary: 71R2, 739LC2; Laura Dunkin-Hubby: 45R1, 102L4, 127, 179C, 220L, 225R, 298R, 317R, 319R, 353L, 386RC3, 407L, 433L, 494C, 656L, 657L; Wally Eberhart/ Botanica/Getty Images: 727TR; Wally Eberhart/Visuals Unlimited: 736L6; Wally Eberhart/Visuals Unlimited/Getty Images: 683TR; Josie Elias/Life File Photo Library Ltd./Alamy: 114C1; Emerisa Nursery: 240R; Emilio Ereza/ Alamy: 385R; Roger Eritja/Alamy: 48L1; Liz Every/Garden World Images: 59L4; F1 Online/Photolibrary: 423C; Christopher Fairweather/Photolibrary: 63L4, 617R; David Fenton: 169L, 709B3; Geoff du Feu/GAP Photos/Getty Images: 369R; Bramwell Flora/Alamy: 631R; FloralImages/Alamy: 507; Florapix/Alamy: 77R, 97L2, 364R; Armin Floreth/imagebroker/ Alamy: 98R4; Flower Fotos/ Alamy: 90R1; flowerphotos/ Alamy: 370R; Nigel Forder/Alamy: 439L2; Bjorn Forsberg/Photolibrary: 78LC; fotoFlora/Alamy: 312LC2, 739RC; Paul Franklin/ Oxford Scientific/Getty Images: 468L; Dennis Frates/Alamy: 51L3; Paroli Galperti/Photolibrary: 61L3, 62R4, 76R4, 166L, 203R, 541TR; Victoria Gardner/ Photolibrary: 54L; Karl Gercens III: 607L, 643R, 659L; Lutz Gerken/Photolibrary: 728L4; Bob Gibbons/Alamy: 88RC, 113BRC, 165TR; Philippe Giraud/Photolibrary: 98R3; Nicholas Gitts/

Swan Island Dahlias: 279L1, 279L2, 279C, 279R1, 279R2, 279B; John Glover/Alamy: 176R1, 300LC, 582TR; David Goldberg: 730L4, 736L2, 736L3, 737L5; iStock.com/David T. Gomez: 384BR; Stephen Goodwin/Alamy: 518R; Thom Gourley/Flatbread Images, LLC/Alamy: 465R; John Granen: 15BR, 66TR, 109TR, 356L, 358TL, 358L2, 358LC2, 413C, 568TR, 570L, 570R2, 574R2, 575R2; Art Gray: 119TR, 119BR; Anne Green-Armytage/Photolibrary: 51L2; Harold E. Greer: 558R1, 559L1; Tatiana Gribanova/Alamy: 47BR; Dana Griffin: 542RC; Helen Guest/Alamy: 124L; Bret Gum: 44TR, 60TR, 672BR, 715 TL; Steven A. Gunther: 5, 46TR, 74TR, 75L3, 76L2, 113TR, 137R, 168R, 183RC2, 200R, 201L2, 201LC2, 201L3, 201LC3, 211R, 231L, 300R, 346R, 390L, 405L, 450C, 475L, 491C, 581L, 609LC, 619R, 620L, 676, 685TL, 685TC, 685B1, 685B2, 685B3, 685B4, 686TR, 696, 714BR, 718BR; Reinhard H/Photolibrary: 98L1; Robert Harding World Imagery/Getty Images: 651R2; Jerry Harpur/Harpur Garden Images: 46BL, 85R4, 226L, 369C; Marcus Harpur/Harpur Garden Images: 64BLC, 95BRC, 277RC, 359L, 404R, 473L2, 505TL, 515L, 582RC2, 639L, 649R2; Chris Harris/Garden World Images: 645RC; Lynne Harrison: 530L; Steffen Hauser/Photolibrary: 608R; Steffen Hauser/botanikfoto/Alamy: 58R3, 312L2, 397R, 443L, 454LC; Steffen Hauser/Garden World Images: 328L, 424L, 634, 647L; Muriel Hazan/Photolibrary: 101L; Francois De Heel/Photolibrary: 324L; William Helsel/Photolibrary: 544; Jim Henkens: 603L, 683BL; C. Andrew Henley/Dorling Kindersley/Getty Images: 648L; High Country Gardens: 401RC1; Michael J. Hipple/Photolibrary: 629L; Neil Holmes/Photolibrary: 719L, 51L1, 52LC2, 59C3, 60BLC, 63R3, 65R2, 76L1, 87RC, 89L1; Saxon Holt/Photo-Botanic: Front cover bottom #3, 89R4, 109BRC, 114L2, 116R3, 128R, 136L, 138, 151LC, 172R, 195R, 203RC, 214LC, 214RC, 234LC, 245, 257RC, 265L, 278C, 284L, 299R, 301RC, 309R, 318C, 326C, 328C, 335L, 366RC, 366R, 377, 385L, 386LC, 386RC2, 406TL, 442C, 443C, 451L3, 451R1, 454L, 457C, 458C, 472RC, 491L1, 495L, 535R, 546L2, 559L2, 578L, 597C, 623R2, 637L, 640L, 641L2, 643C, 645LC, 652L, 654L, 654R, 659C, 701RC, back cover bottom center; D. A. Horchner/Design Workshop: 14T, 81TR, 678BR, 685TR, 685B5,

710TR, 711T; Chris Howes/Wild Places Photography/Alamy: 509TR; Martin Hughes-Jones/Alamy: 66BR, 176LC2, 394L2, 440LC, 647TR, 649TR; Martin Hughes-Jones/Garden World Images: 97R1, 264L, 348R, 406LC2, 638R; D. Hurst/Alamy: 106TR; Stefan Huwiler/Photolibrary: 729L2; Anne Hyde/Photolibrary: 509R2; Stephen Ingram: 82L3, 86R1, 307L, 444L, 604LC; Andrea Innocenti/Photolibrary: 44BRC, 141L; iWebbstock/Alamy: 47BLC; Terry Jennings/Garden World Images: 561R2; Jon Jensen Photography: 91BRC, 395R, 665L1; Andrea Jones/Garden Exposures Photo Library: 49R, 65L3, 66BRC, 67R, 85L4, 107BL, 170LC1, 183R2, 212C, 274L, 285L, 292R, 313C, 326L, 407R, 422L, 424C, 426R, 445R, 446L, 468R, 498L, 541BL, 590L, 595LC, 602R, 603R, 608C, 616L, 619LC, 620C, 626R, 642C, 660RC, 725BL, 734, 741RC; Andrea Jones/Garden World Images: 290R; Andrea Jones/Photolibrary: 175LC, 372L2; Chris L. Jones/Photolibrary: 397TL, 397LC2; JTB Photo/Photolibrary: 167L; K-Pix/Alamy: 398C; Wolfgang Kaehler/Photolibrary: 80R2; Matthew Keller: 420L; Geoff Kidd/Photolibrary: 50BR, 164R; Susanne Kischnick/Alamy: 477L; Rob Klotz: 538LC; James Knight/Flickr/Getty Images: 726; Craig Knowles/Dorling Kindersley/Getty Images: 313L; Michael Krabs/Photolibrary: 739R; Ernst Kucklich: 67L, 80R1, 87R, 93BRC, 108L, 110L1, 110L4, 111BLC, 114L4, 118R1, 119BLC, 120C4, 129L1, 153L, 198C, 211LC, 240RC, 242R, 262, 263RC2, 265C, 265R, 303C, 318L, 339C, 351C, 355R, 357L, 363R, 399L, 401LC, 429L1, 429R, 431R2, 438RC, 466R, 508R1, 523C, 535L2, 536TL, 536LC2, 556R, 564R, 606RC, 631L, 692BL; Leonie Lambert/Photolibrary: 52L1; Georgianna Lane/Photolibrary: 53BLC, 58R1, 80R3, 85L3, 101R, 118C4, 558R2, 621L2; Matt Lavin/Montana State University: 603LC; Christopher Lavis-Jones/Garden World Images: Back cover main, 421, 610R2; Michel Lefèvre/Photolibrary: 624L; Hervé Lenain/Photolibrary: 372TL; Holly Lepere: 6, 678L, 709T; Chris Leschinsky: 75R1, 460L; Cristina Lichti/Alamy: 538L; Peter Lilja/Photodisc/Getty Images: 505LC2; Jenny Lilly/Garden World Images: 548R2; Jason Liske: 14BR; Mark Longley/Alamy: 113BLC; Janet Loughrey: 110L2, 293R, 597L; Diane Macdonald/Getty Images: 56L2, 76L3, 519L; Grégory Mairet/

Photolibrary: 99L4; Annie & Jean-Claude Malausa/Photolibrary: 170BL, 322L2; Allan Mandell: 358BR; Charles Mann: 167LC, 324C, 491R2, 685B6; MAP/Pierre Aversenq/Garden World Images: 742L; MAP/Arnaud Descat/Garden World Images: 107BLC, 474C, 538RC; MAP/Jacques Durand/Garden World Images: 503L; MAP/Nicole et Patrick Mioulane/Garden World Images: 196R, 244L, 256R, 521R, 540L; MAP/Nathalie Pasquel/Garden World Images: 73L2, 75L1, 372LC2, 396R, 513R, 614R; John Martin/Alamy: 394LC2; John Martin/Garden World Images: 102L2, 350C; Jennifer Martiné: 295R; Kari Marttila/Alamy: 598R4; Gunter Marx/Alamy: 97R3; Chris Mattison/Alamy: 684BR; Jim McCausland: 69R1, 83L, 84L, 86R4, 124R, 293L, 574L, 587R2, 595RC, 718BL; J. R. McCausland: 95BLC, 100BR, 408L, 469L, 614RC, 620R; Joshua McCullough/PhytoPhoto: 51R1, 63L1, 72BLC, 76R1, 90L1, 90L4, 90R2, 94L1, 101LC, 102L3, 110RC1, 114C3, 119BL, 129R, 143L, 149C, 150LC, 167R, 175L, 182R, 202R, 204L, 210R, 224RC, 225L, 236RC, 241R, 282LC, 300RC, 308R, 319RC, 327, 341R, 342L, 362R, 365L, 418L, 426L, 437R, 446R, 450L, 474R, 497C, 503C, 522L, 551R, 554LC, 556L, 590R, 603RC, 604L, 611C, 635RC, 639R, 653C, 700R, 737L2, 746R; Niall McDiarmid/Alamy: 78L, 564L; Joe McDonald/Visuals Unlimited: 731C4; Richard McDowell/Alamy: 303R, 350L; Ryan McVay/Photodisc/Getty Images: 715TR, 719R; Brent Miller: 542L; MNS Photo/Alamy: 51R3, 67LC, 384L2, 439L1, 622L; Monrovia: 215R, 216L2, 584R1, 693BL; Terrence Moore: 626RC; Mountain Valley Growers: 341C, 454RC2, 578R2; Richard Murphy Botanicals/Alamy: 307C; Daniel Nadelbach: 94R1; Susie Nadler/The Cutting Garden at Flora Grubb Gardens: 688TR; Kimberley Navabpour: Front cover bottom #2, 48L3, 52LC1, 55L4, 55R4, 58L3, 72BR, 78RC, 87L, 93TR, 93BL, 93BR, 94L2, 94R3, 100BRC, 104TR, 105R4, 118L1, 118L3, 118C1, 118R2, 118R3, 132, 133C, 140L, 145R, 152R, 159L, 159LC, 171L, 180L, 189L, 206RC, 209L, 226R, 229R, 251L, 275C, 278R, 286R, 298C, 325R, 415R, 427R, 451R3, 456L, 483R, 488R1, 499R, 541TL, 551L, 566L, 568R2, 572L2, 587TR, 592R, 611R, 640R, 641LC2, 651RC3, 651RC4, 661L1, 677BL, 680L, 680R, 701LC, 706TL, 707T, 712ML, 713TL, 715MR, 715BR, 728L2, 740R, 741R2; Jonathan

Need/Garden World Images: 56R1; iStock.com/Nancy Nehring: spine; Clive Nichols/GAP Photos/Getty Images: 328R; Clive Nichols/Photolibrary: 57L, 557L2, 647RC2, 651RC1; Marion Nickig/Photolibrary: 164C; Cora Niele/Photolibrary: 739LC1, 740L; Camille Nordgren/In Harmony Sustainable Landscapes: 718TL, 718TR; Diez O/Photolibrary: 135C; Fleur Olby/Photolibrary: 707B2; George Olson: 716BL; Pacific Plug and Liner: 105L3, 179R, 232L, 308L, 496L; Jude Parkinson-Morgan: 635L; Jerry Pavia: 45L2, 50BLC, 92R3, 97R2, 113BL, 136R, 139TR, 142R, 148C, 148R, 149R, 151L, 161L, 162R, 169LC, 182RC, 215L, 220LC, 222L, 223LC, 224L, 228, 229L, 242C, 247R1, 254L, 255L, 268L, 268RC, 269, 283R, 284R, 287L, 310R, 330L, 333C, 335C, 335R, 340L, 355L, 360L, 370L, 380TL, 380L2, 380LC2, 381R1, 386RC1, 392R, 394TR, 399R, 404C, 405RC, 409RC, 411L, 413R2, 415RC, 416LC, 420R, 431L, 436R, 437LC, 442L, 444R, 455R, 475C, 489L, 505L2, 506R, 512L, 525L, 537R, 540R, 555R, 559R, 564LC, 572TL, 579L, 579C, 587RC2, 605L, 621TL, 626LC, 632LC, 637R, 659R, 684BL, 709B4; J. Pawlak/The American Phytopathological Society: 732L1; Victoria Pearson: 8; Pam Peirce: 728L6, 729L1, 732L3, 733L2, 736L4, 737L6, 737L7; Pam Peirce/Susan A. Roth & Co.: 237RC, 475R; David E. Perry: 144L, 653L, 727BC, 729L5, 730L2, 737L4; Linda Lamb Peters: 44BR, 45L1, 45L4, 45R3, 45R4, 46BR, 47BRC, 48L2, 48R1, 48R2, 49L, 50BRC, 51R4, 52L2, 52LC3, 52RC1, 53BR, 54R, 56L4, 56R2, 56R4, 57R, 59C4, 60BRC, 61L1, 61R1, 61R2, 63L3, 63R4, 64BL, 64BRC, 65R3, 68BR, 69L2, 69R2, 69R4, 70BL, 70BLC, 71L2, 71R1, 71R4, 72BL, 73L1, 73L3, 73L4, 73R3, 73R4, 74BR, 75L4, 76L4, 76R3, 91BL, 92R2, 94L3, 95BL, 96RC, 98L3, 98L4, 99R2, 102R2, 102R4, 103LC, 103RC, 104BR, 105L4, 105C4, 105R1, 105R2, 106BL, 106BR, 107BR, 108RC, 111BRC, 112L2, 112R2, 115BL, 115BRC, 115BR, 116L1, 116L2, 116L3, 116C3, 116C4, 117BL, 117BR, 118L4, 118C3, 120L1, 121, 125L, 149L, 151RC, 165R2, 170L1, 174, 175R, 180R, 191TR, 191R2, 193L, 208L, 213R, 230R, 232R, 234R, 235R, 240LC, 241LC, 242L, 244R, 256RC, 258C, 260RC1, 261L, 267L, 267R, 268R, 280R, 286LC2, 287, 291L, 294R, 299L, 305, 310L, 313R, 316R2, 319LC, 321L, 322LC2, 334R, 337L1, 337L2, 347, 355RC, 368R, 371L, 371R, 382LC,

ILLUSTRATION